SUGGESTIONS FOR FAST, EFFECTIVE USE OF THE INDEX

1. PLEASE **READ THE FOREWORD** TO THE INDEX WHICH APPEARS IN THIS VOLUME.

2. STOP AND THINK ABOUT YOUR SUBJECT; TAKE A MOMENT TO **SELECT THE TERMS MOST DESCRIPTIVE OF YOUR RESEARCH SUBJECT.** IT HELPS TO SELECT THE PRINCIPAL SUBJECT RATHER THAN THE SECONDARY SUBJECT AND TO LOOK FOR NOUNS RATHER THAN ADJECTIVES.

3. IF YOUR SEARCH DOES NOT LEAD YOU TO THE CODE SECTION SOUGHT, OR IF YOU HAVE QUESTIONS ABOUT OR SUGGESTIONS FOR THE INDEX, PLEASE FEEL WELCOME TO **CONTACT THE INDEXERS.** THE INDEXERS MAY BE REACHED DIRECTLY BY THE FOLLOWING METHODS: **TOLL-FREE INDEX HOTLINE, 1-800-897-7922,** BETWEEN 8:00 AM AND 4:30 PM, EASTERN TIME ZONE; **FAX NUMBER, 1-434-972-7686; INTERNET E-MAIL** ADDRESSED TO **lng-cho-indexing@lexisnexis.com; POSTAGE-PAID CARDS** FOUND AT THE BACK OF THIS VOLUME.

MICHIE'S™ ANNOTATED CODE
OF THE PUBLIC GENERAL LAWS
OF MARYLAND

———

Prepared by the Editorial Staff of the Publishers

Consultants

State Department of Legislative Services

———

INDEX
A to H

2006 Replacement Volume

———

LexisNexis®

4399024

ISBN 0-8205-7303-5

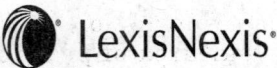

Matthew Bender & Company, Inc.

P.O. Box 7587, Charlottesville, VA 22906-7587

www.lexisnexis.com

Customer Service: 1-800-833-9844

(Pub. 43805)

Foreword to the Index

This replacement Index, contained in two volumes (A-H and I-Z), contains treatment of legislation through the 2006 Regular Session and the 2006 Special Session of the General Assembly.

Included in the General Index is treatment of the laws compiled in the Michie's™ Annotated Code of Maryland, the constitutions of Maryland and the United States and the various rules of the state courts. Statutory provisions are referred to in the index by article designation and section number. **Numbered articles (e.g., 88A §51) are found in the black volumes; the revised articles, set out in the maroon volumes, are identified by abbreviations (e.g., AG §4-311),** a complete table of abbreviations appears in the preliminary pages of this index volume. The constitutions are identified by abbreviations (e.g., MD Const Art III §1; MD Const DofR Art 40; US Const Amd IV). Rules of court and forms, which are set out in two soft-covered maroon volumes, are identified by rule number (e.g., AppRev Rule 8-101; BarAdm Rule 1; see Table of Abbreviations) and by form number (e.g., Form 22).

The index is topical, meaning the main headings represent general concepts of law or specific statutory concepts. Additionally, certain main headings may be used where the material is known by a specific legal or common term, e.g. OPEN CONTAINER LAW. Under this topical arrangement, each heading contains exhaustive treatment of the subject matter, using individual entries as well as cross references to related matters.

Below are a few general rules for use of this Index:
1) *Consult the principal and not the secondary subject.* For example, for information about motor vehicle registration, look under MOTOR VEHICLE REGISTRATION, and not under REGISTRATION.
2) *Consult related headings.* If your search for a heading or a sub-heading under a particular heading is to no avail, try a related topic. For example, if a search for "Inmates" under a particular heading proves fruitless, try looking for "Prisoners" or "Prisons and prisoners."
3) *Use cross references.* Cross references exist to direct you to the location where the subject matter you are seeking has been treated. Group section references (e.g. EN §§15-701 to 15-706) have been attached to many of our cross references as well as to many headings and sub-headings in the index. They provide the option of going directly to the statutes for the cited material, rather than delving deeper into the index.
4) *Use definitions to aid in your search.* Starting a search under the DEFINED TERMS heading presents a diverse sampling of statutory terminology which could suggest other headings to consult.

The index benefits from customer suggestions. Especially helpful are popular names or legal terms specific to your area of practice. We are grateful for your assistance in the ongoing improvement of the index. To contact the Indexing Department, you may use the following methods:
- Postage-paid cards located in the back cover of each index volume.
- Toll-free number, 1-800-897-7922, for assistance in locating material within the index, or to make comments or suggestions, or
- E-mail to lng-cho-indexing@lexisnexis.com.

For issues not directly related to the index, such as missing pages, ordering or other customer service information, you may contact Customer Service via a toll-free number, 1-800-833-9844, or by toll-free fax at 1-800-828-8341.

LexisNexis®

Table of Abbreviations

(Revised Articles)

The following abbreviations are used in the index references to the revised articles:

AG	Agriculture Article	HG	Health-General Article
BOP	Business Occupations and Professions Article	HO	Health Occupations Article
BR	Business Regulation Article	HS	Housing and Community Development Article
CA	Corporations and Associations Article	IN	Insurance Article
CJ	Courts and Judicial Proceedings Article	LE	Labor and Employment Article
CL	Commercial Law Article	NR	Natural Resources Article
CP	Criminal Procedure Article	PS	Public Safety Article
CR	Criminal Law Article	PUC	Public Utility Companies Article
COR	Correctional Services Article	RP	Real Property Article
ED	Education Article	SF	State Finance and Procurement Article
EL	Election Law Article		
EN	Environment Article	SG	State Government Article
ET	Estates and Trusts Article	SPP	State Personnel and Pensions Article
FI	Financial Institutions Article	TG	Tax-General Article
		TP	Tax-Property Article
FL	Family Law Article	TR	Transportation Article

(Court Rules)

The following abbreviations are used in the index references to the Court Rules, the text of which is set out in the softbound Maryland Rules volumes:

BarAdmRule .... Rules Governing Admission to Bar
Form; Interrogatories Form .... Appendix: Forms
CtAppIOR. .... Internal Operating Rules
ProfCondRule. .... Rules of Professional Conduct

(Maryland Rules)

Rule	Guardian Rule
CivProCir Rule	JuvRule
CivProDist Rule	PropAct Rule
Crim Rule	Receivers Rule
Evid Rule	PropSales Rule
Estates Rule	SpecPro Rule
AppRev Rule	CJA Rule
AppRevCir Rule	ADR Rule
FamLaw Rule	ChildAdv Appx

Index

A

ABANDONED MINE DRAINAGE CONTROL,
EN §§15-701 to 15-706.
Definitions, EN §15-701.
Department of the environment.
Cooperation by department with other state agencies and political subdivisions, EN §15-705.
Enforcement of subtitle.
Authority of secretary of the environment to enforce, EN §15-703.
Federal programs, EN §15-706.
Funds.
Abandoned mine drainage capital fund, EN §15-704.
Land acquisition, sale and transfer, EN §15-704.
Legislative intent, EN §15-702.
Mine reclamation and water quality restoration loan of 1970.
Use of proceeds, EN §15-704.
Rules and regulations.
Promulgation, EN §15-702.
Secretary of the environment.
Authority to implement subtitle, EN §15-702.
Enforcement of subtitle, EN §15-703.

ABANDONED MINE RECLAMATION, EN §§15-1101 to 15-1109.
Acid mine drainage abatement and treatment fund, EN §15-1103.
Administration, EN §15-1102.
Cooperative projects, EN §15-1104.
Definitions, EN §15-1101.
Development of plan, EN §15-1105.
Entry for purpose of reclamation.
Order authorizing, EN §15-1107.
Expenditures, EN §15-1106.
Federal-state reclamation fund, EN §15-1103.
Funds.
Acid mine drainage abatement and treatment fund, EN §15-1103.
Application for, EN §15-1105.
Eligibility for expenditures, EN §15-1106.
Federal-state reclamation fund, EN §15-1103.
Priorities in expenditure, EN §15-1106.
Use, EN §15-1105.
Land.
Acquisition, EN §15-1108.
Increase in market value.
Determination, EN §15-1107.
Legislative intent, EN §15-1102.
Liens, EN §15-1107.
Market value increase.
Determination, EN §15-1107.
Right of entry, EN §15-1109.
Rules and regulations, EN §15-1104.

ABANDONED MOTOR VEHICLES, TR §§25-201 to 25-210.
Definitions, TR §25-201.
Dismantler or recycler.
Disposition of vehicle, TR §25-209.
Transfer under indemnity agreement, TR §25-210.

ABANDONED MOTOR VEHICLES —Cont'd
Impoundment.
Recovery of costs of impoundment, TR §25-204.
Indemnity agreement.
Dismantler or recycler or scrap processor.
Transfer under agreement, TR §25-210.
Liability for costs of preservation and storage of vehicle, TR §25-206.1.
Restrictions on vehicle registration, TR §25-206.2.
Notice to last known registered owner, TR §§25-204, 25-205.
Parking lots.
Towing or removal from.
Subtitle inapplicable to abandoned vehicles, TR §21-10A-01.
Police.
Notice by police to last known registered owner and secured parties, TR §25-204.
Taking abandoned vehicles into custody, TR §25-203.
Preservation and storage costs, TR §25-206.1.
Restrictions on vehicle registration, TR §25-206.2.
Presumption of ownership, TR §25-202.
Prohibited, TR §25-202.
Reclamation.
Effect of failure to reclaim vehicle, TR §25-206.
Removal.
Authority of police, TR §25-203.
Costs of preservation and storage.
Liability for, TR §§25-206.1, 25-206.2.
Notice to last known registered owner and secured parties, TR §§25-204, 25-205.
Officers authorized to remove abandoned vehicle, TR §25-203.
Reclaiming vehicle.
Effect of failure to reclaim, TR §25-206.
Retention by police.
Use for public purposes, TR §25-207.
Sale, TR §25-207.
Scrapping, dismantling or destroying vehicles.
Registration.
Transfer, TR §13-505.
Scrap processor.
Disposition of vehicle, TR §25-209.
Transfer under indemnity agreement, TR §25-210.
Serial numbers.
Removed or defaced serial numbers, TR §25-207.1.
Storage costs.
Liability, TR §25-206.1.
Restrictions on vehicle registration, TR §25-206.2.
Towing.
Parking lots.
Subtitle inapplicable to abandoned vehicles, TR §21-10A-01.
Removal generally, TR §§25-203 to 25-206.2. See within this heading, "Removal."
Use for public purposes.
Retention by police, TR §25-207.
Vehicle identification numbers.
Removal or defacement, TR §25-207.1.

ABANDONED PROPERTY DISPOSITION, CL §§17-101 to 17-326.
Abandoned property office.
Establishment, CL §17-102.

1

ABANDONED PROPERTY DISPOSITION
  —Cont'd
Agreements to pay compensation, CL §17-325.
Application of title.
  Property to which title not applicable, CL §17-104.
Appropriations.
  Abandoned property office, CL §17-102.
Baggage.
  Sale of unclaimed baggage, BR §19-102.
Baltimore City.
  Liens for unpaid taxes.
    Release to facilitate transfer of vacant property
      in Baltimore City, TP §14-806.
Banking organization.
  Report by organization neither holding nor owing
    abandoned property, CL §17-310.1.
Citation.
  Short title, CL §17-326.
Claim to property or proceeds of sale.
  Consideration of claim by administrator, CL
    §17-319.
  Filing, CL §17-318.
  Hearing on claim, CL §17-319.
  Judicial review of administrator's action, CL
    §17-320.
  Payment of claim, CL §17-319.
  Price paid by administrator, CL §17-319.
Common carriers.
  Sale of freight and baggage, BR §19-102.
Compensation.
  Agreements to pay compensation, CL §17-325.
Conflict of laws.
  When property held for owner in another state
    not presumed abandoned, CL §17-309.
Construction of subtitle.
  Uniform construction, CL §17-209.
Contempt proceedings.
  Examination of records.
    Persons who have failed to report property, CL
      §17-322.
Courts.
  Intangible personal property held by court.
    When property presumed abandoned, CL
      §17-307.
Definitions, CL §17-101.
**Delivery of abandoned property to
  administrator,** CL §17-312.
  Action to enforce delivery of property, CL §17-322.
  Administrator may decline to receive certain
    property, CL §17-321.
  Custody and safekeeping of property delivered, CL
    §17-313.
  Effect of expiration of period of limitation, CL
    §17-315.
Documents under oath, CL §17-105.
Dormant accounts.
  Charges or cessation of benefits, CL §17-308.1.
Escape.
  Mental hygiene law, HG §16-303.
Exemptions from title, CL §17-104.
Federal custody.
  Actions by claimants, CL §17-203.
  Administrator.
    Agreement with federal government, CL
      §17-202.
    Duties of administrator, CL §17-201.
    Notice to administrator of claim, CL §17-206.
  Agreement with federal government, CL §17-202.
    Certification of agreement, CL §17-204.
  Consent to suit against federal government, CL
    §17-203.

ABANDONED PROPERTY DISPOSITION
  —Cont'd
Federal custody —Cont'd
  Defenses.
    Federal government defense available to state,
      CL §17-203.
  Election of claimant, CL §17-206.
  Judicial determination against claimant.
    Effect, CL §17-207.
  Notice to administrator of claim, CL §17-206.
  Report of abandoned property, CL §17-205.
Fiduciaries.
  Intangible personal property held in fiduciary
    capacity.
    When property presumed abandoned, CL
      §17-306.
Financial organization.
  Report by organization neither holding nor owing
    abandoned property, CL §17-310.1.
Fines.
  Failure to file report, perform other duties or
    deliver property to administrator, CL §17-323.
Freight.
  Sale of unclaimed freight, BR §19-102.
Funds received under article.
  Disposition, CL §17-317.
Holder.
  Compelling testimony, CL §17-322.
  Contempt proceedings.
    Failure to report property, CL §17-322.
  Delivery to administrator.
    Former holder relieved of liability after delivery,
      CL §17-313.
  Intangible personal property.
    Held or owing in ordinary course of business.
      When presumed abandoned, CL §17-308.
  Notice to apparent owner.
    Presumed abandoned property, CL §17-308.2.
  Reimbursement of former holder for payment to
    person entitled, CL §17-313.
  Reports.
    Examination of records of persons who have
      failed to report property, CL §17-322.
    Property presumed abandoned, CL §17-310.
  Wages.
    Held or owing in ordinary course of holder's
      business.
      When presumed abandoned, CL §17-308.
Inactive accounts.
  Charges or cessation of benefits, CL §17-308.1.
Insurance corporation.
  Funds held by insurance corporation.
    When property presumed abandoned, CL
      §17-302.
  Report by corporation neither holding nor owing
    abandoned property, CL §17-310.1.
Interstate cooperation.
  Agreements, CL §17-324.
  Consultation with other jurisdictions, CL §17-324.
  Enforcement, CL §17-324.
Limitation of actions.
  Effect of expiration of period of limitation, CL
    §17-315.
  Expiration not affecting state's rights, CL §17-208.
  Judicial review of administrator's action, CL
    §17-320.
Livestock.
  Sale of unclaimed livestock, BR §19-102.
Money transmission.
  Compliance with state and federal provisions
    governing, FI §12-417.

ABANDONED PROPERTY DISPOSITION
—Cont'd
Natural resources department.
Abandoned, lost or seized personal property.
Custody, return or disposition by department,
NR §1-2A-01.
Nonresidents.
When property held for owner in another state
not presumed abandoned, CL §17-309.
Notice.
Presumed abandoned property.
Apparent owners, notice by holder, CL
§17-308.2.
Oaths.
Documents under oath, CL §17-105.
Office of abandoned property, CL §17-102.
Presumed to be abandoned property.
Business organizations.
Intangible personal property held or owing in
ordinary course of business, CL §17-308.
Report by organization neither holding nor
owing abandoned property, CL §17-310.1.
Stock or sum held by, CL §17-304.
Tangible or intangible personal property.
Held by bank, CL §17-301.
Voluntary dissolution.
Personal property distributable in course of
dissolution, CL §17-305.
Court, public corporation, public authority or
public officer.
Intangible personal property held by, CL
§17-307.
Fiduciary capacity.
Intangible personal property held in fiduciary
capacity, CL §17-306.
Financial organization.
Report by organization neither holding nor
owing abandoned property, CL §17-310.1.
Tangible or intangible personal property.
Held by organization, CL §17-301.
Voluntary dissolution.
Personal property distributable in course of
dissolution, CL §17-305.
Insurance corporation.
Funds held by, CL §17-302.
Report by corporation neither holding nor owing
abandoned property, CL §17-310.1.
Limitation.
Effect of expiration of period of limitation, CL
§17-315.
Notices.
Apparent owners, notice by holder, CL
§17-308.2.
To persons who appear to be owners of
abandoned property, CL §17-311.
Officers.
Intangible personal property held by public
officer, CL §17-307.
Operation of presumption.
When presumption operates, CL §17-301.
Owners.
Notice to persons who appear to be owners of
abandoned property, CL §17-311.
Report.
Holder of property presumed abandoned, CL
§17-310.
Organization neither holding nor owing
abandoned property, CL §17-310.1.
Utility.
Funds held by utility, CL §17-303.

ABANDONED PROPERTY DISPOSITION
—Cont'd
Presumed to be abandoned property —Cont'd
Utility —Cont'd
Report by utility neither holding nor owing
abandoned property, CL §17-310.1.
Wages.
Held or owing in ordinary course of holder's
business, CL §17-308.
When presumption operates, CL §17-301.
Real property.
Land patents generally.
See LAND PATENTS.
Rules and regulations.
By administrator, CL §17-103.
Sale of abandoned property.
Auction sale, CL §17-316.
Baggage, BR §19-102.
Claim to property or proceeds of sale.
Consideration of claim by administrator, CL
§17-319.
Filing, CL §17-318.
Judicial review of administrator's action, CL
§17-320.
Freight, BR §19-102.
Immunity of state, CL §17-316.
Livestock, BR §19-102.
Notice of sale, CL §17-316.
Perishable or damaged freight, BR §19-102.
Proceeds.
Disposition, CL §17-317.
Title to property, CL §17-316.
Sentence and punishment.
Failure to file report, perform other duties or
deliver property to administrator, CL §17-323.
Sheriffs.
Guidelines for disposal of property, CJ §2-311.
Short title, CL §17-326.
Signatures.
Documents under oath.
Effect of signed statements, CL §17-105.
Special fund.
Creation by administrator, CL §17-317.
State police department.
Personal property in possession of department, PS
§2-311.
Statute of limitations. See within this heading,
"Limitation of actions."
United States.
Abandoned property in federal custody, CL
§§17-201 to 17-209. See within this heading,
"Federal custody."
Utility.
Funds held by utility.
When property presumed abandoned, CL
§17-303.
Report by utility neither holding nor owing
abandoned property, CL §17-310.1.
Wages.
Held or owing in ordinary course of holder's
business.
When presumed abandoned, CL §17-308.
Witnesses.
Compelling testimony, CL §17-322.

ABANDONING DOMESTIC ANIMAL, CR
§10-612.

ABANDONMENT.
Abandoned property disposition, CL §§17-101 to
17-326.
See ABANDONED PROPERTY DISPOSITION.

ABANDONMENT —Cont'd
Baby drop off.
Immunity from liability, CJ §5-641.
Condemnation proceeding abandonment,
PropAct Rule 12-211; RP §12-109.
Creditors.
Receivers and assignees or trustees for creditors.
Abandonment of property and records,
Receivers Rule 13-601.
Disposition of abandoned property, CL §§17-101
to 17-326.
See ABANDONED PROPERTY DISPOSITION.
Domestic animal, CR §10-612.
Eminent domain.
Condemnation proceeding abandonment, PropAct
Rule 12-211; RP §12-109.
**Franchise, right or permit by public service
company,** PUC §5-103.
Commission authorization required, PUC §5-202.
Highways.
County roads, 25 §§135 to 143.
See COUNTIES.
Sale of land no longer needed, TR §8-309.
Intestate succession.
Abandonment or failure to support minor child.
Distribution precluded, ET §3-112.
Limited liability companies.
Merger, CA §4A-704.
Mining.
Abandoned mine drainage control act, EN
§§15-701 to 15-706.
See ABANDONED MINE DRAINAGE
CONTROL.
General provisions, EN §§15-101 to 15-1109.
See MINING.
Motor vehicles, TR §§25-201 to 25-210.
See ABANDONED MOTOR VEHICLES.
Natural resources department.
Abandoned, lost or seized personal property.
Custody, return and disposition by department,
NR §1-2A-01.
Partnerships, revised act.
Merger of partnership, CA §9A-904.
Presumptions.
Disposition of abandoned property, CL §§17-101 to
17-326.
See ABANDONED PROPERTY DISPOSITION.
Railroad corridors.
Department of planning.
Acquisition and use, examining, SF §5-402.
Railroads.
Unfinished railroad not using right-of-way or
location for certain number of years, PUC
§9-307.
Real property.
Land patents generally.
See LAND PATENTS.
**Receivers and assignees or trustees for
creditors.**
Abandonment of property and records, Receivers
Rule 13-601.
Refrigerators, iceboxes or freezer cabinets.
Prohibition, penalty, CR §10-109.
Securities act.
Registration of securities.
Abandonment of registration, CA §11-508.
University of Maryland.
Lost or abandoned currency or personal property.
Disposition, ED §13-702.
Vessels and boats.
Acquiring title to abandoned vessel, NR §8-722.

ABANDONMENT —Cont'd
Vessels and boats —Cont'd
Prima facie owner of vessel, NR §8-725.1.
Prohibited, NR §8-725.1.
Seizure and removal by department, NR §8-721.
Notice to owner and secured parties, NR §8-721.
Well drilling, EN §§9-1302, 9-1309.

ABANDONMENT OF REFRIGERATOR.
Prohibition, penalty, CR §10-109.

ABATEMENT OF NUISANCES.
Fish and fisheries.
Nonnative aquatic organisms, NR §4-205.1.
**Secretary of environment or local health
officers,** EN §§10-101 to 10-305.
See NUISANCES.
**Secretary of health and mental hygiene or
local health officers,** HG §§20-310 to 20-314.
See NUISANCES.

ABATEMENT, REVIVAL AND SURVIVAL.
Arbitration and award.
Proceedings upon death of either party, CJ
§3-230.
Business trusts.
Forfeiture of right to do business.
Survival of claims and contracts, CA §12-810.
Death.
Arbitration and award.
Proceedings upon death of either party, CJ
§3-230.
Securities.
Securities act.
Civil liabilities.
Survival of cause of action, CA §11-703.
Slander.
Abatement of action, CJ §6-401.
Survival of actions, CJ §6-401.

ABATTOIRS.
Counties.
Powers of county commissioners, 25 §3.

ABDUCTION.
Child abduction, FL §§9-301 to 9-307.
Child under 16 for purposes of prostitution, CR
§11-305.
Kidnapping generally, CR §§3-501 to 3-503.
Mandatory sentence for crime of violence.
Second, third or fourth conviction, CR §14-101.

ABERDEEN.
Alcoholic beverages.
Dispensaries, 2B §15-203.
Profits and reserves.
Accounted, 2B §15-207.
Liquor control department.
Distribution of net proceeds, 2B §15-207.

ABORTIONS.
Consent, HG §20-214.
Definitions.
Viable, HG §20-209.
Immunity.
Physicians.
Good faith decision to perform abortion, HG
§20-209.
Refusal to participate or refer, HG §20-214.
Liability.
Physicians.
Good faith decision to perform abortion, HG
§20-209.
Refusal to participate or refer, HG §20-214.

ABORTIONS —Cont'd
Minors.
Disclosures to parent or guardian concerning medical treatment of minor, HG §20-102.
Notice to parent or guardian required for unmarried minors, HG §20-103.
Parental notification.
Disclosures to parent or guardian concerning medical treatment of minor, HG §20-102.
Physicians.
Good faith decision to perform abortion.
Physician not liable, HG §20-209.
Licensed physician required, HG §20-208.
Referrals.
Refusal to participate or refer, HG §20-214.
Rules and regulations, HG §20-209.
Social services.
Granting consent not condition precedent to receipt of benefits, HG §20-214.
State intervention.
Restrictions, HG §20-209.
Viability.
Definition of "viable," HG §20-209.

ABSENCES WITHOUT PAY, SPP §§9-1101, 9-1105.

ABSENTEE VOTING.
Generally, EL §§9-301 to 9-312.
See ELECTIONS.

ABSENT PERSONS.
Death.
Presumption of death, CJ §3-102.
Definitions, CJ §3-101.
Guardians.
Search for absentee, CJ §3-105.
Termination of guardianship proceedings, CJ §3-106.
Insurance.
Life insurance.
Payment to beneficiaries, CJ §3-109.
Limitation of actions.
Filing of actions, CJ §3-103.
Policy provisions.
When certain provisions invalid, CJ §3-103.
Surrender value.
Payment, CJ §3-109.
Limitation of actions.
Defendant leaving state or moving from county to county, CJ §5-205.
Insurance policies.
Filing of actions, CJ §3-103.
Presumption of death, CJ §3-102.
Property of absentee.
Distribution of property, CJ §3-110.
Proceedings for protection of property, CJ §3-104.
Reappearance of absentee.
Effect of, CJ §3-108.
Search for absentee, CJ §3-105.

ABUSE OF DRUGS.
General provisions.
See DRUG OR ALCOHOL ABUSE.

ABUSE OR NEGLECT OF ANIMAL, CR §10-604.

ABUSE OR NEGLECT OF VULNERABLE ADULTS, CR §§3-604 to 3-606.
Abuse or neglect in first degree, CR §3-604.
Abuse or neglect in second degree, CR §3-605.
Death, serious injury, sexual abuse.
Abuse or neglect in first degree, CR §3-604.

ABUSE OR NEGLECT OF VULNERABLE ADULTS —Cont'd
Definitions.
Abuse or neglect in first degree, CR §3-604.
Evidence of reputation or opinion evidence, CR §3-319.
Exploitation of vulnerable adults, CR §8-801.
Investigation, CR §3-606.

ABUSE OR NEGLECT OF VULNERABLE PERSONS.
Adults, CR §§3-604 to 3-606.
Abuse or neglect in first degree, CR §3-604.
Abuse or neglect in second degree, CR §3-605.
Death, serious injury, sexual abuse.
Abuse or neglect in first degree, CR §3-604.
Definitions.
Abuse or neglect in first degree, CR §3-604.
Evidence of reputation or opinion evidence, CR §3-319.
Exploitation of vulnerable adult, CR §8-801.
Investigation, CR §3-606.
Child abuse and neglect, FL §§5-701 to 5-714.
See CHILD ABUSE AND NEGLECT.
Domestic violence.
Generally, FL §§4-501 to 4-516.
See DOMESTIC VIOLENCE.
Local domestic violence fatality review teams, FL §§4-701 to 4-707.
See DOMESTIC VIOLENCE.
Evidence of reputation or opinion evidence, CR §3-319.

ACCELERATION OF CONSUMER LEASES.
Option to accelerate at will, CL §2A-109.

ACCEPTANCE.
Offer and acceptance.
Leases, UCC, CL §§2A-205, 2A-206.
Sale of goods, UCC, CL §2-206.
Additional terms in acceptance or confirmati[on,] CL §2-207.
Auctions, CL §2-328.
Firm offers, CL §2-205.

ACCESS CARDS.
Credit card crimes, CR §§8-201 to 8-217.
See CREDIT CARDS.

ACCESS CONTRACTS FOR INFORMAT[ION.]
Computer information transactions ge[nerally,] CL §§22-101 to 22-816.
See COMPUTER INFORMATION TRANSACTIONS.

ACCESSIONS.
Lessor's and lessee's rights.
When goods become accessions, CL §2[A-310.]
Secured transactions.
Perfection and priority of security in[terest, CL] §9-335.
Wills.
Devises and bequests, ET §4-405.

ACCESSORIES.
After the fact to a felony.
Punishment, CR §1-301.
Before the fact, CP §4-204.
Motor vehicles.
Parties to crime, TR §26-101.
Sentence and punishment.
Approver not to be admitted, C[P ...]
Venue.
Accessory after the fact to mu[rder, CP] §4-201.

ACCESSORIES —Cont'd
Venue —Cont'd
Crimes committed on Chesapeake Bay, CP §4-201.

ACCESSORY AFTER THE FACT TO A FELONY.
Sentence and punishment, CR §1-301.

ACCESSORY, SHARED AND SHELTERED HOUSING PROGRAM.
Maryland housing rehabilitation program, HS §4-926.
Units in program, HS §4-905.

ACCESS TO COURT RECORDS, CJA Rules 16-1001 to 16-1011.
See RECORDS.

ACCESS TO PUBLIC RECORDS, SG §§10-611 to 10-628.
See RECORDS.

ACCIDENT AND HEALTH INSURANCE.
Generally, IN §§12-201 to 12-210.
See HEALTH INSURANCE.
Nonprofit health service plans, IN §§14-101 to 14-140.
See NONPROFIT HEALTH SERVICE PLANS.

␣CIDENTS.
usement attractions.
␣pections and investigations, BR §3-402.
nobile insurance fund.
ral provisions, IN §§20-101 to 20-701;
␣ecPro Rules 15-801 to 15-805.
␣UTOMOBILE INSURANCE FUND.

␣f aircraft.
TR §5-1004.
§5-206.
el accidents, NR §8-724.
␣ssure vessels.
§12-909.
␣rs' licenses.
␣ccident.
␣ualification, TR §16-812.
␣ct.

␣ION.
␣erally, ␣ONGFUL ACT.
␣er, HG §4-212.
␣unavoidable accident,
␣A-310.
␣erests, CL ␣'DENTS.
to 16-605.
␣es in good
␣ccident,
P §6-228.
␣rder or felony, CP

ACCIDENTS —Cont'd
Mistake.
See MISTAKE.
Motor vehicle accidents.
Ambulance chasing, IN §§27-407, 27-408.
Automobile insurance fund.
General provisions, IN §§20-101 to 20-701;
SpecPro Rules 15-801 to 15-805.
See AUTOMOBILE INSURANCE FUND.
General provisions, TR §§20-101 to 20-113.
See MOTOR VEHICLE ACCIDENTS.
Hospital lien.
General provisions, CL §§16-601 to 16-605.
See HOSPITALS.
Insurance fraud.
Solicitation of individuals injured in accident,
IN §§27-407, 27-408.
Reports generally, TR §§20-107 to 20-113.
See MOTOR VEHICLE ACCIDENTS.
Notice.
Public service companies.
Accidents resulting in personal injury or
property damage, PUC §5-304.
Public service companies.
Notice to commission of accident resulting in
personal injury or property damage, PUC §5-304.
Railroad safety and health.
Reporting requirements, LE §5.5-121.
Reports.
Aviation, TR §5-206.
Motor vehicle accident reports generally, TR §§20-107 to 20-113.
See MOTOR VEHICLE ACCIDENTS.
Public service companies.
Notice to commission of accidents, PUC §5-304.
Vessels and boats.
Assistance, NR §8-724.
Information.
Duty to give, NR §8-724.
Injury caused by accident involving moving vessel.
Report by physicians, pharmacists, dentists or
nurses, HG §20-702.
Reports, NR §8-724.
Workers' compensation.
General provisions, LE §§9-101 to 10-320.
See WORKERS' COMPENSATION.

ACCOMMODATION PARTY.
Negotiable instruments.
Discharge, CL §3-605.
Instrument signed for accommodation, CL §3-419.

ACCOMPLICE FOR PURPOSE OF CORROBORATION.
Possession of stolen property.
Person actually stealing property not accomplice,
CR §7-104.

ACCOMPLICES.
See ACCESSORIES.

ACCORD AND SATISFACTION.
Assignments.
Secured transactions.
Inapplicability of article 9.
Accounts, chattel paper, etc., assigned to
satisfy pre-existing obligation, CL §9-109.
Negotiable instruments.
By use of instrument, CL §3-311.
Satisfaction of money judgment.
See SATISFACTION OF MONEY JUDGMENT.

ACCORD AND SATISFACTION —Cont'd
Secured transactions.
Collateral accepted in full or partial satisfaction of obligation, CL §§9-620 to 9-622.

ACCOUNTANTS.
Age requirements, BOP §2-302.
Applicability of provisions, BOP §2-102.
Applications for license, BOP §2-304.
Board of public accountancy, BOP §§2-201 to 2-211.
Fees, calculation, BR §2-106.6.
Fund, BR §2-106.5.
Sunset law, SG §8-403.
Certification of licensee or permit holder, BOP §2-206.
Citation of act.
Short title, BOP §2-701.
Continual compliance with permit requirement, BOP §2-415.
Continuing education, BOP §2-312.
Corporations.
Misrepresentation that business may provide services, BOP §2-604.
Ownership interest in unlicensed individual, BOP §2-403.
Permits.
General provisions, BOP §§2-401 to 2-416.
Registration of offices, BOP §2-501.
Resident office managed by resident stockholder, BOP §2-403.
Courts.
Special officers of court.
Appointment, CJ §2-102.
Criminal penalty for violations, BOP §2-605.
Definitions, BOP §2-101.
Accountant's document, BOP §2-502.
Out-of-state licensed accountants.
Practice certified public accountancy, BOP §2-321.
Peer review, BOP §2-4A-01.
Privileged communications, CJ §9-110.
Denial of license.
Commencement of proceedings, BOP §2-316.
Grounds, BOP §2-315.
Hearings, BOP §2-317.
Denial of permit.
Commencement of proceedings, BOP §2-411.
Grounds, BOP §2-410.
Hearings, BOP §2-412.
Limited permit, BOP §2-416.
Documents.
Ownership, BOP §2-502.
Education.
Continuing education, BOP §2-312.
Qualifications of applicants, BOP §§2-302, 2-303.
Evidence.
Privileged communications, CJ §9-110.
Examinations, BOP §§2-302, 2-305.
Partial examination credit, BOP §2-306.
Reexamination, BOP §2-307.
Waiver of requirement, BOP §2-308.
Expiration of license, BOP §2-311.
Limitation on expiration and surrender, BOP §2-318.
Reinstatement of expired licenses, BOP §2-314.
Expiration of permit, BOP §2-407.
Limitations, BOP §2-413.
Fees.
Calculation, BR §2-106.6.

ACCOUNTANTS —Cont'd
Fees —Cont'd
Certification concerning licensee or permit holder, BOP §2-206.
Disposition of money collected by board, BOP §2-209.
Deposit into state board of public accountancy fund, BR §2-106.5.
Licenses, BOP §2-309.
Examination fee, BOP §2-304.
Inactive status, BOP §2-313.
Reexamination, BOP §2-307.
Reinstatement of expired licenses, BOP §2-314.
Renewal fee, BOP §2-311.
Out-of-state licensed accountants, BOP §2-321.
Permits.
Application fee, BOP §2-404.
Renewal fee, BOP §2-407.
Fines for violations, BOP §2-605.
Inactive status, BOP §2-313.
Injunctions, BOP §2-205.
Insurance companies.
Qualified independent certified public accountants, IN §4-118.
Issuance of license, BOP §2-309.
Issuance of permit, BOP §2-405.
Licenses, BOP §§2-301 to 2-321.
Limitation on expiration and surrender of license, BOP §2-318.
Limited liability companies.
Misrepresentation that business may provide services, BOP §2-604.
Ownership interest of unlicensed individual, BOP §2-402.1.
Permanent office managed by resident member, requirement, BOP §2-402.1.
Permits generally, BOP §§2-401 to 2-416.
Registration of offices, BOP §2-501.
Limited license, BOP §2-320.
Limited permit, BOP §2-416.
List of licensees.
Board to keep, BOP §2-208.
List of permit holders.
Board to keep, BOP §2-208.
Misrepresentation as authorized practitioner, BOP §2-603.
Misrepresentation that business may provide services, BOP §2-604.
Names.
Change in name for permit holder.
Notice, BOP §2-408.
Partnership name.
Use by surviving partner, BOP §2-409.
Oaths.
Board of public accountancy.
Oath of office of members, BOP §2-202.
Licenses.
Denial, revocation or suspension or reprimand of licensee.
Administration of oaths in connection with hearings, BOP §2-317.
Permits.
Denial, revocation or suspension or reprimand of permit holder.
Administration of oaths in connection with proceedings, BOP §2-412.
Offices.
Registration, BOP §2-501.
Out-of-state licensed accountants, BOP §2-321.
Partial examination credit, BOP §2-306.

ACCOUNTANTS —Cont'd
Partnerships.
Misrepresentation that business may provide
services, BOP §2-604.
Offices.
Registration, BOP §2-501.
Ownership interest in unlicensed individual, BOP
§2-402.
Permits.
General provisions, BOP §§2-401 to 2-416.
Resident office managed by resident partner,
requirement, BOP §2-402.
Peer review, BOP §§2-4A-01 to 2-4A-06.
Approval of peer reviewers, BOP §2-4A-05.
Definitions, BOP §2-4A-01.
Disciplinary or corrective action, BOP §2-4A-06.
Duties of peer reviewers, BOP §2-4A-05.
Engagement review, BOP §2-4A-04.
Defined, BOP §2-4A-01.
Notification to board of completion of review, BOP
§2-4A-03.
Qualifications of peer reviewers, BOP §2-4A-05.
Report review, BOP §2-4A-04.
Defined, BOP §2-4A-01.
Reports of peer reviewers, BOP §2-4A-05.
Review of report by board, BOP §2-4A-06.
Requirements, BOP §§2-4A-02, 2-4A-03.
System review, BOP §2-4A-04.
Defined, BOP §2-4A-01.
Penalties.
Violations of provisions, BOP §2-605.
Permits, BOP §§2-401 to 2-416.
Applications for permits, BOP §2-404.
Qualifications of applicants, BOP §§2-402,
2-403.
Privileged communications, CJ §9-110.
Providing services without permit.
Prohibited, BOP §2-602.
Qualifications of applicants.
Licenses, BOP §§2-302, 2-303.
Permits, BOP §§2-402, 2-402.1, 2-403.
Reciprocity.
Waiver of examination requirements, BOP §2-308.
Reexamination, BOP §2-307.
Registration of offices, BOP §2-501.
Reinstatement of licenses.
Expired license, BOP §2-314.
Revoked or suspended license, BOP §2-319.
**Reinstatement of revoked or suspended
permit,** BOP §2-414.
Renewal of license, BOP §2-311.
Out-of-state licensed accountants, BOP §2-321.
Renewal of permit, BOP §2-407.
Reprimand of licensees.
Commencement of proceedings, BOP §2-316.
Grounds, BOP §2-315.
Hearings, BOP §2-317.
Reprimand of permit holder.
Commencement of proceedings, BOP §2-411.
Grounds, BOP §2-410.
Hearings, BOP §2-412.
Revocation or suspension of license, BOP
§§2-315 to 2-320.
Revocation or suspension of permit, BOP
§§2-410 to 2-414.
Right to practice, BOP §2-102.
Rules and regulations, BOP §2-207.
Termination of regulations adopted under
provisions, BOP §2-702.
Scope of license, BOP §2-310.

ACCOUNTANTS —Cont'd
Scope of permit, BOP §2-406.
Limited permit, BOP §2-416.
Scope of provisions, BOP §2-102.
Short title of act, BOP §2-701.
Surrender of license.
Suspension or revocation, BOP §2-315.
Termination of provisions, BOP §2-702.
Term of license, BOP §2-311.
Limited licenses, BOP §2-320.
Term of permit, BOP §2-407.
Limited permit, BOP §2-416.
Title of act.
Short title, BOP §2-701.
Unlicensed practice prohibited, BOP §2-601.

ACCOUNT NUMBERS.
Credit card crimes, CR §§8-201 to 8-217.
See CREDIT CARDS.
Identity fraud, CR §§8-301 to 8-305.

ACCOUNTS AND ACCOUNTING.
Accountants.
General provisions, BOP §§2-101 to 2-702.
See ACCOUNTANTS.
Admissions and amusement tax.
Administrative cost account.
Distribution of revenue to, TG §2-201.
Adoption.
Independent adoptions.
Accounting requirement, FL §5-3B-24.
Appropriations.
Supervision of recipients.
General provisions, SF §§7-401 to 7-405.
See APPROPRIATIONS.
Archives.
Publications account, SG §9-1014.
Assisted living programs.
Health care quality account for assisted living
programs, HG §19-1811.
Atlantic states marine fisheries commission.
Required, NR §4-304.
Attorneys at law.
Discipline and inactive status.
Audit of attorney's accounts and records, CJA
Rule 16-722.
Trust accounts.
General provisions, BOP §§10-301 to 10-307;
CJA Rules 16-601 to 16-612.
See ATTORNEYS AT LAW.
Auditors.
General provisions.
See AUDITORS.
Audits.
General provisions.
See AUDITS.
Uniform system of accounts, 19 §§35 to 41. See
within this heading, "Uniform system of
accounts."
Automobile insurance fund.
Special fund account, IN §20-302.
Bainbridge development corporation.
Administration of corporate funds, 83A §5-1608.
Bank deposits and collections.
General provisions, CL §§4-101 to 4-504.
See BANK DEPOSITS AND COLLECTIONS.
Campaign finance accounts.
Account books, EL §13-221.
Designation, disbursements, EL §13-220.
Charities.
Accounting required, BR §6-506.

ACCOUNTS AND ACCOUNTING —Cont'd
Charities —Cont'd
  Representatives.
    Registration before accounting, BR §6-306.
Clerks of court.
  State's attorney.
    Aid of comptroller and treasurer, 10 §38.
Clients' security fund, CJA Rule 16-811.
Commissioner of correction.
  Submission of statement of receipts and
    disbursements of division, COR §§3-206,
    3-207.
Community colleges.
  Financing.
    See COMMUNITY COLLEGES.
Comptroller, SF §6-216.
  Duty as to public accounts, MD Const Art VI §2.
  Inspection of accounts, SG §4-107.
Condominiums.
  Required accounting principles, RP §11A-128.
Consignment.
  Sale of consigned goods.
    Accounting required, CL §11-810.
Constitution of the United States.
  Receipts and expenditures of public money.
    Publication of statement and account, US Const
    Art I §9.
Corporations.
  Department.
    Fees, CA §1-203.
    Records, CA §2-111.
    Presumed proper, CA §1-402.
Counterfeiting private instrument or
  document, CR §8-601.
  Issuing counterfeited instrument or document, CR
    §8-602.
Counties.
  Special retirement or pension system.
    Method of accounting, SPP §39-102.
  State's attorney.
    Fees and expenses, 10 §39.
Credit grantor closed end credit provisions.
  Escrow account, CL §12-1026.
  Sale of repossessed property, CL §12-1021.
Credit grantor revolving credit.
  Plan connected with demand deposit account.
    Account charges enumerated, CL §12-907.
  Sale of repossessed property, CL §12-921.
Credit services businesses.
  Trust accounts, CL §§14-1908 to 14-1910.
Decedents' estates.
  Verification, Estates Rule 6-123; ET §1-102.
Draining lands.
  Board of managers, 25 §92.
Economic development corporation, 83A §5-212.
Evidence.
  Proof of accounts.
    By written record, CJ §10-101.
    Photography.
      Copies of business and public records as
      evidence act, CJ §10-102.
Executors and administrators.
  General provisions, ET §§7-301 to 7-307.
    See EXECUTORS AND ADMINISTRATORS.
Fees.
  Officers whose compensation is derived from fees,
    MD Const Art XV §1.
Fiduciaries.
  Estates including guardianships of property.
    Annual fiduciary accounts, Guardian Rule
    10-706.

ACCOUNTS AND ACCOUNTING —Cont'd
Fiduciaries —Cont'd
  Estates including guardianships of property
    —Cont'd
    Final distribution, Guardian Rule 10-710.
    Removal for cause or other sanctions.
      Final accounting and delivery of property,
      Guardian Rule 10-712.
    Report of trust clerk, Guardian Rule 10-708.
    Restricted accounts, Guardian Rule 10-705.
  Executors and administrators.
    General provisions, ET §§7-301 to 7-307.
      See EXECUTORS AND ADMINISTRATORS.
Fiscal services.
  Department of fiscal services.
    State aid cut off.
      Failure to file required financial reports, 19
      §39.
      Failure to use uniform system of financial
      reporting, 19 §38.
Fiscal year.
  Use in balancing books and accounts, SF §2-101.
Forest and park concession account, NR
  §5-212.1.
General assembly.
  House of delegates.
    Powers as grand inquest of state, MD Const Art
    III §24.
Ground rents, PropAct Rule 12-501.
Guardian and ward.
  Guardian of the person of a minor.
    Accounting not required, ET §13-703.
  Protection of property, ET §13-209.
  Veteran's guardianship, ET §13-804.
Health.
  Cost review commission.
    Accounting principles for rate determinations,
    HG §19-221.
  Uniform accounting and financial reporting
    system, HG §19-215.
Health care quality account for assisted living
  programs, HG §19-1811.
Highways.
  Gasoline and motor vehicle account.
    Highway user revenues, TR §8-402.
Home improvements.
  Salesperson failure to account for or remit
    payment, BR §8-606.
Hospitals.
  Rights of individuals, HG §19-346.
Income tax.
  Accounting period, TG §10-501.
    Change of accounting period, TG §10-504.
  Death of individual.
    Termination of taxable year, TG §10-503.
  Federal return not filed, TG §10-502.
  Withholding tax at source.
    Separate account required, TG §10-906.
Industrial development financing authority.
  Records, 83A §5-912.
Inmates in correctional facilities in division of
  correction.
  Reserve financial and spending financial accounts,
    COR §3-609.
Insurance.
  Automobile insurance fund.
    Special fund account, IN §20-302.
  Life and health insurance guaranty corporation,
    IN §9-405.
  Oversight of funds, IN §9-406.

ACCOUNTS AND ACCOUNTING —Cont'd
Insurance —Cont'd
Title insurance.
Pooling and commingling trust money
authorized, IN §22-103.
Variable life insurance and annuity contracts.
Segregated asset accounts, IN §§16-601, 16-602.
Joint tenants and tenants in common.
Accountability to co-tenant for rent received from
third party, RP §14-106.
**Life and health insurance guaranty
corporation,** IN §9-405.
Oversight of funds, IN §9-406.
Maryland correctional enterprises.
Accounting and records system, COR §3-507.
Minors.
Recoveries in tort.
Trustee not required to file accounts, ET
§13-407.
Transfers to minors.
Custodian, ET §13-319.
Money transmission.
Required records, FI §12-425.
Standard accounting and bookkeeping procedures,
FI §12-421.
Morgan State University.
Accounting system, ED §14-104.
Motorcycles.
Safety program account, TR §16-605.
Motor vehicle insurance.
Automobile insurance fund.
Special fund account, IN §20-302.
Northeast Maryland waste disposal authority,
NR §3-923.
Notoriety of crimes contracts.
Escrow account, CP §11-624.
Money for victims, CP §11-624.
Payments from, CP §11-624.
Priority of claims, CP §11-628.
Officers.
Compensation derived from fees, MD Const Art
XV §1.
Ineligibility for failure to account, SG §17-101.
Removal of ineligibility, SG §17-102.
State's attorney.
Inquiry into accounting, SG §17-104.
Personal representatives.
General provisions, ET §§7-301 to 7-307.
See EXECUTORS AND ADMINISTRATORS.
Potomac highlands airport authority.
Authority to maintain records of funds, TR
§10-103.
Premium financing companies.
Examination of books, records and accounts, IN
§23-103.
Preneed burial contracts.
Trust accounts.
Commingling money, BR §5-706.
Disbursement of money, BR §§5-708, 5-709.
Principal and income.
Separate accounting by trustee, ET §15-510.
**Prisoners in correctional facilities in division
of correction.**
Reserve financial and spending financial accounts,
COR §3-609.
Procurement.
Cost-reimbursement contracts.
Requirements as to accounting system, SF
§13-215.
Public debt.
Debt service.
Fiscal agent, SF §8-135.

ACCOUNTS AND ACCOUNTING —Cont'd
Real estate brokers.
Trust accounts, BOP §§17-501 to 17-508.
See REAL ESTATE BROKERS.
Receivers.
District Court, CivProDist Rule 3-722.
**Receivers and assignees or trustees for
creditors.**
Abandonment of property and records, Receivers
Rule 13-601.
Annual report.
Period of accounting, Receivers Rule 13-502.
Auditor's account, Receivers Rule 13-501.
Destruction or other disposition, Receivers Rule
13-601.
Open account.
Filing of claim, Receivers Rule 13-401.
Registers of wills.
State's attorney.
Aid of comptroller and treasurer, 10 §38.
Reserve accounts.
Baltimore City and counties, 24 §9-1201.
Retail credit accounts law.
General provisions, CL §§12-501 to 12-515.
See RETAIL CREDIT ACCOUNTS LAW.
Schools.
Cooperative administration of programs, ED
§4-123.
Sheriffs.
State's attorney.
Aid of comptroller and treasurer, 10 §38.
**Small business development financing
authority,** 83A §5-1011.
State's attorneys.
Public officers.
Inquiry into accounting, SG §17-104.
Services and expenses, 10 §39.
State treasurer, SF §6-217; MD Const Art VI §4.
State treasury.
Comptroller, SF §6-216.
Payments into treasury.
Comptroller, SF §6-216.
Monthly accounting, SF §6-213.
Persons, SF §6-214.
Statement of accounts, SF §6-218.
State treasurer, SF §6-217.
Units of state government, SF §6-213.
Statement of accounts, SF §6-218.
Taxation.
Correction of accounts and assessments.
Valuation, TP §2-216.
Time-sharing.
Purchase money escrow account, RP §11A-116.
Transfers to minors act.
Custodian, ET §§13-308, 13-319.
Trusts and trustees.
Commissions, ET §14-103.
Discretionary trusts, ET §14-405.
Uniform system of accounts.
Audit, 19 §40.
Counties, cities, towns and taxing districts, 19
§36.
Expenses of examination of accounts and
records, 19 §41.
Examination of books.
Rules and regulations, 19 §40.
Expenses.
Examination of accounts and records, 19 §41.
Financial reports.
Fiscal year.
Reporting, 19 §35.

ACCOUNTS AND ACCOUNTING —Cont'd
Uniform system of accounts —Cont'd
  Financial reports —Cont'd
    State aid cut off.
      Failure to file required financial reports, 19 §39.
      Failure to use uniform system of financial reporting, 19 §38.
  Fiscal year.
    Political subdivisions, 19 §35.
  Maintained by counties, cities and taxing districts, 19 §36.
  Rules and regulations.
    Establishment, 19 §40.
  State fiscal research bureau.
    State aid cut off.
      Failure to file required financial reports, 19 §39.
      Failure to use uniform system of financial reporting, 19 §38.
Veterans.
  Guardianship, ET §13-804.
Water quality financing administration.
  Financial accounting, EN §9-1617.
Watershed associations.
  Board of directors, 25 §208.
Workers' compensation.
  Injured workers' insurance fund.
    Accounts generally, LE §10-121.
    Disposition of excess money, LE §10-122.
    Insurance program.
      Uncollectible accounts, LE §10-137.
  Subsequent injury fund.
    Segregation as special indemnity fund, LE §10-215.
  Uninsured employers' fund.
    Accounts generally, LE §10-317.
    Surplus, LE §10-318.

ACCUSATION FALSELY MADE.
Extortion by, CR §3-704.

ACETONE.
Possession of destructive device, CR §§4-501 to 4-503.

ACID.
Acid deposition, NR §§3-3A-01 to 3-3A-04.
  See ACID DEPOSITION.
Maryland Transit Administration.
  Carrying or possessing in transit vehicle, TR §7-705.
Mining.
  Acid mine drainage abatement and treatment fund, EN §15-1103.

ACID DEPOSITION.
Consultation with interested parties, NR §3-3A-02.
Definitions, NR §3-3A-01.
Evaluations, NR §3-3A-02.
Interested parties.
  Consultation with, NR §3-3A-02.
Power plants.
  Siting and research program.
    Director's responsibilities, NR §3-3A-02.
Reports, NR §3-3A-04.
Research and monitoring program, NR §3-3A-03.

ACID RAIN.
Acid deposition, NR §§3-3A-01 to 3-3A-04.
  See ACID DEPOSITION.

ACKNOWLEDGMENTS, SG §§19-101 to 19-114.
Armed forces, SG §19-111.
Authentication, SG §19-109.
Banks and trust companies, FI §1-202.
Certificate, SG §19-107.
  Execution, SG §19-108.
Corporations.
  Alternative to acknowledgment, CA §1-302.
  By whom made, CA §1-303.
  Execution of articles, CA §1-301.
  Recording papers with department, CA §1-201.
Credit unions, FI §1-202.
Deeds, RP §4-204.
Electric cooperatives.
  Disqualification from taking acknowledgments prohibited, CA §5-639.
Financial institutions, FI §1-202.
Forms.
  Deeds, RP §4-204.
Generally, SG §18-106.
Illegitimate child.
  Legitimation by acknowledgment, ET §1-208.
Interpretation and construction, SG §19-113.
Laws of another state, SG §19-110.
Limited liability partnerships, revised act.
  Documents purporting to be acknowledged.
    Treatment by department, CA §9A-1002.
Limits on taking, SG §18-111.
Manner and form, SG §19-101.
Married women, SG §19-106.
Outside United States, SG §19-104.
Prior acknowledgments, SG §19-112.
Requisites, SG §19-105.
Savings and loan associations, FI §1-202.
Secured transactions.
  Filing office, CL §9-523.
    Timeliness of acknowledgment, CL §9-523.
  Perfection of security interests.
    Possession by secured party to perfect, CL §9-313.
Short title, SG §19-114.
Validation of prior acknowledgments, SG §19-301.
Within another state, SG §19-103.
Within state, SG §19-102.

ACQUIRED IMMUNE DEFICIENCY SYNDROME (AIDS).
Bawdy houses and houses of ill fame, prostitution, etc.
  Educational program for violators, HG §18-339.
Blood tests.
  Human immunodeficiency virus testing, HG §§18-336 to 18-338.3.
Boxers and kick boxers.
  Blood tests, BR §4-304.1.
Condoms.
  Sale by vending machines or other devices, HG §18-335.
Confidentiality of HIV testing records, HG §18-338.1.
Consent to HIV testing, HG §§18-336, 18-338.1.
Controlled dangerous substances.
  Education program for violators, HG §18-339.
Controlled dangerous substances violators.
  Education program on AIDS, CR §5-906.
Correctional institutions.
  Human immunodeficiency virus testing of inmates, HG §18-338.
Correctional officers.
  Notification of exposure to virus, HG §§18-213, 18-213.2.

**ACQUIRED IMMUNE DEFICIENCY
   SYNDROME (AIDS)** —Cont'd
Costs of HIV testing, HG §18-338.1.
Counseling.
   Human immunodeficiency virus testing, HG
      §18-336.
Donors of semen, blood or tissue.
   Testing of blood samples, HG §18-334.
Drugs.
   Educational program for violators of controlled
      dangerous substances act, HG §18-339.
**Educational program for violators of
   controlled dangerous substances act,** HG
   §18-339.
Emergency medical care and services.
   Notification of emergency medical technicians of
      exposure to virus, HG §§18-213, 18-213.2.
Exposure of infected persons.
   Knowingly transferring or attempting to transfer
      to another individual, HG §18-601.1.
   Notification of exposure, HG §§18-213 to 18-213.2.
Fire department.
   Notification of fire fighters or fire marshal of
      exposure to virus, HG §§18-213 to 18-213.2.
First responders.
   HIV testing, HG §18-338.3.
Health care workers.
   HIV testing, HG §18-338.3.
Human immunodeficiency virus testing, HG
   §§18-336 to 18-338.3.
Identification.
   Human immunodeficiency virus testing.
      Patient identifying numbers, HG §18-336.
Informed consent for HIV testing, HG §§18-336,
   18-338.1.
Inmates of correctional institutions.
   Human immunodeficiency virus testing, HG
      §18-338.
Insurance assistance pilot program, HG
   §§15-201 to 15-205.
   Administration, HG §15-202.
   Annual report to governor and general assembly,
      HG §15-205.
   Definitions, HG §15-201.
   Denial, restriction or termination of benefits.
      Adoption of regulations by department, HG
         §15-204.
      Adoption of rules by department, HG §15-204.
   Eligibility for enrollment, HG §15-202.
   Limitation on enrollment, HG §15-202.
   Medicare beneficiaries, HG §15-203.
   Payment of health insurance premiums under
      program.
      Adoption of regulations by department, HG
         §15-203.
   Periodic survey of recipients, HG §15-205.
Jails.
   Human immunodeficiency virus testing of
      inmates, HG §18-338.
Landlord and tenant.
   Disclosures concerning real property offered for
      lease.
      Certain matters not to constitute material fact
         or latent defect, RP §2-120.
Law enforcement personnel.
   Notification of exposure to virus, HG §§18-213,
      18-213.2.
Life insurance.
   Viatical settlement contracts, IN §§8-601 to 8-611.
   See VIATICAL SETTLEMENT CONTRACTS.

**ACQUIRED IMMUNE DEFICIENCY
   SYNDROME (AIDS)** —Cont'd
Life insurance —Cont'd
   Voiding policy because insured has had a disease
      or ailment, IN §16-216.
Misdemeanors.
   Knowingly transferring or attempting to transfer
      HIV to another individual, HG §18-601.1.
Notice.
   Donors of semen, blood or tissue.
      Positive HIV antibody test results, HG §18-334.
   Exposure to contagious disease or virus, HG
      §§18-213 to 18-213.2.
   Human immunodeficiency virus testing.
      Notification of results, HG §§18-336 to 18-338.3.
Patient identification numbers.
   HIV testing, HG §18-336.
Physician-patient privilege.
   Positive test results.
      Inmates of correctional institutions.
         Liability of health care providers, HG
            §18-338.
      Liability of hospitals or other health care
         providers for disclosure, HG §18-337.
Physicians' reports, HG §18-201.1.
Positive test results, HG §§18-336, 18-337.
   Donors of semen, blood or tissue, HG §18-334.
   Inmates of correctional institutions, HG §18-338.
Pregnant women.
   Testing, HG §18-338.2.
Prisoners.
   Human immunodeficiency virus testing, HG
      §18-338.
Privileged communications.
   Donors of semen, blood or tissue.
      Positive HIV antibody test result, HG §18-334.
   Fire fighters, emergency medical technicians,
      rescue squadmen, law enforcement officers
      and correctional officers.
      Notification of exposure to virus.
         Breach of patient confidentiality, HG §18-213.
   Human immunodeficiency virus testing.
      Boxers and kickboxers, BR §4-304.1.
      Confidentiality of records, HG §18-338.1.
      Inmates of correctional institutions, HG
         §18-338.
      Reports, HG §18-207.
         Physicians' reports, HG §18-201.1.
   Sexual or needle-sharing partners.
      Notification of positive test results.
         Physicians, hospitals or other health care
            providers not liable for breach of patient
            confidentiality, HG §18-337.
Prostitution.
   Educational program for violators, HG §18-339.
Real property.
   Disclosures concerning real property offered for
      sale or lease.
      Certain matters not to constitute material fact
         or latent defect, RP §2-120.
Reports, HG §18-207.
   Donors of semen, blood or tissue.
      Positive HIV antibody test results, HG §18-334.
   Insurance assistance pilot program.
      Annual report.
         Submission to governor and general assembly,
            HG §15-205.
   Physicians' reports, HG §18-201.1.
   Research and information program.
      Annual report, HG §18-333.

ACQUIRED IMMUNE DEFICIENCY SYNDROME (AIDS) —Cont'd
Rescue squads.
Notification of exposure to virus, HG §§18-213, 18-213.2, 18-333.
Research and information program, HG §18-333.
Sterile needle and syringe exchange.
Baltimore City, HG §§24-801 to 24-809.
See STERILE NEEDLE AND SYRINGE EXCHANGE.
Prince George's county, HG §§24-901 to 24-909.
See STERILE NEEDLE AND SYRINGE EXCHANGE.
Tests.
Human immunodeficiency virus testing, HG §§18-336 to 18-338.3.
Transferring human immunodeficiency virus to another individual.
Misdemeanors, HG §18-601.1.
Viatical settlement contracts, IN §§8-601 to 8-611.
See VIATICAL SETTLEMENT CONTRACTS.

ACTIONS.
Abatement, revival and survival.
See ABATEMENT, REVIVAL AND SURVIVAL.
Administration of courts.
Assignment of actions for trial, CJA Rule 16-202.
Advertising.
False advertising in conduct of business or trade.
Rights of parties in private litigation not affected, CL §11-707.
Affidavits.
Assignments.
In suits by assignee against obligor on sealed instruments, CL §15-402.
Agricultural cooperatives.
Power to sue and be sued, CA §5-504.
Agriculture.
Farmers permitting gleaning.
Actions against, CJ §5-404.
Air conditioning and heating contractors.
Enforcement of title, BR §9A-206.
Air quality control.
Enforcement actions, EN §2-609.
Who acquires actionable rights, EN §2-106.
Alienation of affections.
No cause of action, FL §3-103.
Aliens.
Suits against state, US Const Amd 11.
Amusements and recreation.
Proceedings for enforcement, BR §3-207.
Antitrust act.
Civil actions, CL §11-209.
Appeals.
Generally.
See APPEALS.
Appearances.
District Court, CivProDist Rule 3-131.
Arbitration and award.
Arbitration in pending court action, SpecPro Rule 15-101.
Court proceedings not provided for elsewhere, SpecPro Rule 15-101.
Assignments by assignee on obligation under seal, CL §15-402.
Assisted living facility grants.
Recovery by department of funds, HG §24-1006.
Associations.
Actions by and against unincorporated associations, CJ §6-406.

ACTIONS —Cont'd
Associations —Cont'd
Liability for judgment against unincorporated association, CJ §11-105.
Athlete agents.
Civil action by educational institution, BR §4-415.
Attachment.
Prejudgment attachment.
Circuit courts, CivProCir Rule 2-115.
District Court, CivProDist Rule 3-115.
Wages.
See ATTACHMENT.
Attorneys at law.
Appearances.
District Court, CivProDist Rule 3-131.
Automobile insurance fund.
Actions against producers, IN §§20-513, 20-514.
Bad faith.
Unjustified proceeding, Rule 1-341.
Baltimore City.
Local government tort claims act, CJ §§5-301 to 5-304.
See TORTS.
Bank deposits and collections.
Unauthorized signature or alteration, customer's duty to report, CL §4-406.
Bar exam.
See EXAMINATIONS.
Bonds, surety.
Applicability of provisions, Rule 1-401.
Approval, Rule 1-402.
Clerks of court.
Action on bond, CJ §11-203.
Constables.
Suits on bonds and remedies against.
See CONSTABLES.
Credit services businesses.
Claims against bonds, CL §14-1910.
Increase or decrease, Rule 1-402.
Proceeding against surety, Rule 1-404.
Recording, Rule 1-402.
Register of wills.
Action on bond, CJ §11-203.
State of Maryland.
Bond in name of state, Rule 1-402.
Bounding lands.
Proceedings to establish boundary lines, RP §14-111.
Boycotts.
Foreign discriminatory boycotts.
Civil actions, CL §11-109.
Breach of promise to marry, FL §3-102.
Cable television service, interference with, CR §7-303.
Cemeteries.
Sale of burial ground for another purpose, BR §5-505.
Baltimore City, BR §5-506.
Change of name.
Nature of action, SpecPro Rule 15-901.
Child access to firearm violation.
Reference to violation during trial prohibited, CR §4-104.
Child care.
Residential child care capital grant program.
Cessation of approved use of property, recovery of funds, 41 §18-706.
Priority of proceedings, 41 §18-706.
Child custody.
Uniform child custody jurisdiction and enforcement act.
Generally, FL §§9.5-101 to 9.5-318.
See CHILD CUSTODY.

ACTIONS —Cont'd

Child passenger safety technicians.
Immunity from suit for act or omission, CJ §5-640.

Cigarette sales below cost act.
Damages, CL §11-508.

Class actions.
Circuit courts, CivProCir Rule 2-231.

Code of Maryland.
Adoption of code not to affect pending actions, 1 §1.

Commencement of action.
Circuit court, CivProCir Rule 2-101.
District Court, CivProDist Rule 3-101.

Commercial code.
Enforcement of right or obligation, CL §1-106.

Commissioner of financial regulation.
Enforcement of provisions, FI §2-116.

Communications and transactional records access.
Civil actions, CJ §10-4A-08.

Condominiums.
Actions against governing body, RP §14-118.

Consignment.
Conversion.
Legal or equitable rights of owner not affected, CL §11-807.

Consolidation.
Actions in District Court and circuit court, CJ §6-104.

Constables.
Suits on bond of defaulting constable.
See CONSTABLES.

Consumer protection.
Consumer debt collection. See within this heading, "Debts."
Credit services businesses.
Actions under consumer protection act, CL §14-1914.
Damages, CL §13-408.
Defense in action for return of merchandise or for payment therefore, CL §14-1304.
Division of consumer protection.
Civil actions, CL §13-403.
Fine prints.
Civil remedies of buyers, CL §14-505.
Persons aggrieved by decision of division, CL §13-407.
Replevin action.
Waiver of right to notice and hearing in replevin action, CL §14-1303.

Continuing care contracts.
Attorney general representation of special deputy secretary, 70B §20D.
Equitable relief for subscribers, 70B §20.
Financial review committee members.
Immunity from liability, 70B §17A.
Recovery of damages by subscribers, 70B §19.
Violations of provisions by providers, 70B §18A.

Contracts.
General provisions.
See CONTRACTS.

Conversion of overhead electric or communication facilities to underground locations, PUC §§12-301 to 12-317.
See UNDERGROUND UTILITY FACILITIES.

Cooperative housing corporations.
Developers.
Implied warranty enforcement, CA §5-6B-04.
Misrepresentation of facts.
Actions to enforce liability, CA §5-6B-04.

ACTIONS —Cont'd

Corporations.
Foreign corporations.
Compliance with subtitle.
Not consent to suit, CA §7-210.
Revocation of permit for conduct connected with organized crime, CA §1-405.
When suit may be maintained by corporation, CA §7-301.
Forfeiture of charter.
Conduct in connection with organized crime, CA §1-405.
Indemnification of directors, officers, employees and agents, CA §2-418.
Proceedings by corporation.
Acting through receiver, trustee or stockholders in representative capacity, CA §1-403.
Representation in court by persons other than lawyers, BOP §10-206.
Sale of property and franchises under judicial proceedings, CA §3-302.
Sue and be sued.
Powers, CA §2-103.

Counties.
Chartered counties.
Contract actions, 25A §1A.
Commissioners, 25 §1A.
Suing or being sued with respect to county property, 25 §17.
Home rule for code counties.
Contract actions, 25B §13A.
Local government tort claims act, CJ §§5-301 to 5-304.
See TORTS.

Credit card numbers, access device numbers.
Credit card numbers printed on receipts.
Restrictions, violations, action by attorney general, CL §14-1318.
Unauthorized disclosure or use, possession, CR §8-217.

Currency transactions in trade or business.
Civil penalties.
Civil action to recover, BR §1-505.

Damages.
Remedy for injury to person or property, MD Const DofR Art 19.

Day-care centers.
Adult day care centers.
State's right of recovery.
Civil actions, HG §24-706.
Priority of proceedings, HG §24-706.

Death by wrongful act.
General provisions, CJ §§3-901 to 3-904.
See DEATH BY WRONGFUL ACT.

Debt management services.
Damages for violations, FI §12-930.

Debts.
Consumer debt collection, CL §§14-201 to 14-204.
Certain acts prohibited, CL §14-202.
Citation of subtitle, CL §14-204.
Damages.
Violator's liability, CL §14-203.
Definitions, CL §14-201.
Violator's liability for damages, CL §14-203.

Decedents' estates.
Slayer's rule.
Weight given criminal conviction, CJ §10-919.

Definitions, Rule 1-202.

Dentists.
Board of dental examiners.
Suits by and against board, HO §4-208.

ACTIONS —Cont'd
Dentists —Cont'd
Licenses.
Injunctive actions, HO §4-320.
Depositions.
Deposition taken in another action.
Use of depositions.
Circuit courts, CivProCir Rule 2-419.
General provisions.
See DEPOSITIONS.
Discovery.
General provisions.
See DISCOVERY.
Perpetuation of evidence.
Before action instituted, CivProCir Rule 2-404.
Discrimination.
Commercial discrimination.
Limitation of actions, SF §19-101.
Pending actions, effect of, SF §19-118.
Statute of limitations, SF §19-101.
Public accommodations.
Right to bring civil actions not denied, 49B §12.
Dismissal.
See DISMISSAL OF ACTIONS.
Distress for rent.
General provisions, RP §§8-301 to 8-332.
See DISTRESS FOR RENT.
Domestic violence fatality review teams.
Immunity from liability.
Local team members and persons cooperating
with, CJ §5-637.1.
Draining lands.
Public drainage associations or public watershed
associations.
Officers or directors.
Immunity from liability, 25 §60.
Drug dealer liability, CJ §§3-1601 to 3-1607.
See DRUG DEALER LIABILITY ACT.
Elections.
Local board party to judicial proceeding.
Copy of initiating pleading to state board, EL
§2-105.
Right of state board to join as party, EL §2-105.
Powers of state administrator, EL §2-103.
Elevators.
Decision to prohibit use of unsafe elevator unit.
Action to modify or vacate decision, PS
§12-814.1.
Email.
Unauthorized, false or misleading information.
Commercial electronic mail, damages, CL
§14-3003.
Employee theft.
Civil action by merchant for, CJ §3-1305.
Criminal prosecution not prerequisite, CJ
§3-1306.
Environmental actions.
Environmental standing act, NR §§1-501 to 1-508.
See ENVIRONMENTAL STANDING ACT.
Environmental covenants, EN §1-810.
Environmental service.
Remedies of bondholders and trustees, NR §3-120.
Equal credit opportunity.
Civil liability, CL §12-707.
Equipment dealer contracts.
Violations by suppliers.
Actions authorized, CL §19-303.
**Excavation or demolition near underground
facilities.**
Injunction or mandamus to prevent negligent or
unsafe excavation or demolition, PUC
§12-112.

ACTIONS —Cont'd
Executors and administrators.
General provisions.
See EXECUTORS AND ADMINISTRATORS.
Family division.
Circuit courts, CJA Rule 16-204.
Farmers permitting gleaning.
Actions against, CJ §5-404.
**Federally qualified health centers grant
program.**
Right of recovery, HG §24-1306.
Fish and fisheries.
Nonnative aquatic organisms.
Abatement of nuisance, NR §4-205.1.
Food, drugs and cosmetics.
Detainment and destruction of articles, HG
§21-253.
Immediate threat.
Actions against food posing immediate threat,
HG §21-254.
Foreclosure.
Generally, PropSales Rules 14-201 to 14-505.
See FORECLOSURES.
Protection of homeowners, RP §§7-301 to 7-321.
See FORECLOSURES.
Foreign corporations. See within this heading,
"Corporations."
Forests and parks.
Cutting and burning.
Liability to aggrieved parties, NR §5-409.
Form of action.
Circuit courts, CivProCir Rule 2-301.
Dismissal.
Action should be heard in another form, CJ
§6-104.
District Court, CivProDist Rule 3-301.
Fraternal benefit societies.
Misrepresentation by society, IN §8-468.
Gambling loss, recovery.
Competent witness to prove loss, CR §12-110.
Recovered as common debt, CR §12-110.
Gas and oil.
Petitions of interested persons, EN §14-114.
General assembly.
Civil immunity, SG §2-1801.
Gleaning.
Actions against farmers permitting gleaning, CJ
§5-404.
Grantee actions.
Applicable rules.
District Court, CivProDist Rule 3-711.
Ground rents.
Nature of action, PropAct Rule 12-501.
Health care decisions.
Actions instituted by health care providers, HG
§5-612.
Health care malpractice claims.
Commencement of action, SpecPro Rule 15-403.
Expressions of regret or apology by health care
provider.
Admissibility, CJ §10-920.
Report of claim or action by insurer, IN §4-401.
Health care worker whistleblower protection.
Civil actions for violations, HO §§1-504 to 1-506.
Heritage areas authority.
Powers, FI §13-1107.
Homebuilder registration violations, BR
§4.5-502.
Human relations commission.
Injunctions.
Power to bring civil actions for temporary
injunction, 49B §4.

ACTIONS —Cont'd
Human relations commission —Cont'd
Right to bring civil actions not denied, 49B §12.
Husband and wife.
Death by wrongful act.
General provisions.
See DEATH BY WRONGFUL ACT.
Surviving spouse.
Action to recover in right of deceased spouse.
Necessary allegations, FL §4-202.
Identity fraud.
Costs and attorneys' fees, CR §8-301.
Immigration consultants.
Violation of provisions, CL §14-3306.
Injunctions.
General provisions.
See INJUNCTIONS.
Insurance.
Acquisitions disclosure and control, IN §7-805.
Automobile insurance fund.
Actions against producers, IN §§20-513, 20-514.
Enforcement of article, IN §2-201.
Insider trading.
Recovery of profits, IN §3-119.
Insurable interest lacking.
Action to recover benefits, IN §12-201.
Malpractice action reports, IN §4-401.
Motor vehicle insurance.
Automobile insurance fund, IN §§20-513, 20-514.
Uninsured motorist coverage, IN §19-509.1.
Burden of proof, CJ §10-921.
Property and casualty insurance guaranty corporation.
Actions against insured of insolvent insurer, IN §9-309.
Reinsurance intermediaries.
Receiver authorized to bring civil action, IN §8-511.
Interpleader.
Circuit courts, CivProCir Rule 2-221.
Joint debtors.
Suits against, CJ §11-103.
Juvenile services facilities capital program.
Recovery of funds by state, 83C §4-106.
Labor and employment relations.
See LABOR AND EMPLOYMENT RELATIONS.
Land installment contracts.
Right of purchaser to enforce provisions of subtitle, RP §10-108.
Landlord and tenant.
Back rent on renewal of lease, RP §8-111.
Back rent pursuant to action by landlord or reversionary transferee, RP §8-111.1.
Breach of lease, RP §8-402.1.
Death of landlord who is life tenant.
Recovery of rent, RP §8-106.
Distress for rent.
General provisions, RP §§8-301 to 8-332.
See DISTRESS FOR RENT.
Escrow accounts.
Escrow account in wrongful detainer action, RP §8-118.1.
Escrow accounts in certain actions, RP §8-118.
Jury trial, RP §§8-601 to 8-604.
Limitation of actions, RP §8-107.
Remedies of and against transferee of reversion, RP §8-101.
Remedy upon covenants in case of merger, RP §8-102.
Tenants holding over, RP §§8-402, 8-402.2.

ACTIONS —Cont'd
Landlord and tenant —Cont'd
Wrongful detainer, RP §8-402.4.
Claimant to title of property, RP §8-404.
Law enforcement officers and personnel.
Right to sue.
Rights of officers generally, PS §3-103.
Libel and slander.
General provisions.
See LIBEL AND SLANDER.
Limitation of actions.
General provisions.
See LIMITATION OF ACTIONS.
Limited liability companies.
Derivative actions, CA §§4A-801 to 4A-804.
Foreign companies.
Compliance with title not consent to suit, CA §4A-1011.
Doing business without registration, CA §4A-1007.
Members as parties to actions, CA §4A-302.
Limited search by law enforcement officer for handgun.
Attorney general to defend if requested by officer, CR §4-206.
Lis pendens.
See LIS PENDENS.
Local government tort claims act, CJ §§5-301 to 5-304.
Lottery devices, purchasing or obtaining.
Recovery of money, CR §12-203.
Malpractice.
Health care malpractice claims.
See MALPRACTICE.
Mandamus.
See MANDAMUS.
Marriage.
Breach of promise to marry, FL §3-102.
Maryland-national capital park and planning commission.
Effect of article on criminal actions, 28 §1-102.
Local government tort claims act, CJ §§5-301 to 5-304.
See TORTS.
Maryland Transit Administration.
Administration may sue and be sued in its own name, TR §7-204.
Mechanics' liens.
Commencement of action, PropAct Rule 12-302.
Right to maintain personal action not affected, RP §9-111.
Suits to enforce or contest validity of liens, RP §9-109.
Mental hygiene law.
Community mental health facilities.
State's right of recovery, HG §24-606.
Minimum wage.
Action by employee, LE §3-427.
Judicial review and enforcement, LE §3-426.
Mining.
Strip mining.
Civil actions, EN §15-528.
Collection of forfeited bond, EN §15-514.
Minors.
Parent-child actions arising out of operation of vehicle.
Parent-child immunity and insurance provision not applicable, CJ §5-806.
Seduction or wrongful injury to minor child.
Right to sue for, FL §5-206.

ACTIONS —Cont'd

Mobile homes.
Eviction or recovery of unpaid rent, RP §8A-1601.
Rental agreements.
Enforcement by civil action, RP §8A-1501.

Mortgages and deeds of trust.
Action for possession.
Generally, RP §14-108.1.
Releases.
Enforcement of provisions, RP §7-106.

Morticians.
Injunctive relief.
Who may bring action, HO §7-316.1.

Motor clubs.
Adverse agency decision.
Judicial review, IN §§26-209, 26-308.

Motor fuel inspection.
Suit by retail dealers, BR §10-318.

Motor vehicles.
Child passenger safety technicians.
Immunity from suit for act or omission, CJ §5-640.
Consumer leasing contracts, CL §14-2005.
Insurance.
Automobile insurance fund.
Actions against producers, IN §§20-513, 20-514.
Uninsured motorist coverage, IN §19-509.1.
Burden of proof, CJ §10-921.
Manufacturers, distributors and factory branches.
Licenses.
Right of injured persons to sue, TR §15-213.
Negligence.
Cause of action preserved, TR §11-205.
Parent-child actions arising out of operation of vehicle.
Parent-child immunity and insurance provision not applicable, CJ §5-806.
Repair facilities.
Individual civil actions, CL §14-1005.
Seat belts.
Emergency vehicles.
Failure to use.
Effect in civil actions, TR §22-412.4.
Security interests.
Claims for damages against administration, TR §13-210.

Municipal corporations.
Contract actions.
Defense of sovereign immunity in action in contract, 23A §1A.
Nonliability for punitive damages, CJ §5-507.
Local government tort claims act, CJ §§5-301 to 5-304.
See TORTS.
Power to sue and be sued, 23A §1.
Taxation.
Collection.
See MUNICIPAL CORPORATIONS.

Negotiable instruments.
Inability to produce negotiable instrument.
Effect in suit on negotiable instrument, CJ §10-918.

Northeast Maryland waste disposal authority.
Power to sue and be sued, NR §3-905.

Nuisances.
Community association actions, RP §§14-123 to 14-125.1.
Controlled dangerous substances.
Property used for controlled dangerous substance offenses.
Abatement actions, RP §14-120.

ACTIONS —Cont'd

Nursing facility conversion grant program.
Recovery of funds by state, HG §24-1406.

Nursing home administrators.
Aiding and abetting unauthorized practice or misconduct, HO §9-316.1.

Occupational safety and health.
Judicial review and enforcement.
Effect of filing, LE §5-215.

Parent-child actions.
Actions arising out of operation of motor vehicle.
Not restricted by parent-child immunity or insurance provisions, CJ §5-806.

Partnerships, revised act.
Actions by and against partnership and partners, CA §9A-307.
Actions by partnership against partner or partner against partnership, CA §9A-405.

Payment device numbers printed on receipts.
Restrictions, violations, action by attorney general, CL §14-1318.

Pending actions.
Adoption of code not to affect, 1 §1.

Pharmacists and pharmacies.
Injunctions.
Unauthorized practice of pharmacy, HO §12-319.

Pleading.
See PLEADINGS.

Port administration.
Administration may sue and be sued in its own name, TR §6-204.

Prejudgment attachment.
Circuit court, CivProCir Rule 2-115.
District Court, CivProDist Rule 3-115.

Priority funding areas.
No private cause of action created, SF §5-7B-10.

Prisoner litigation, CJ §§5-1001 to 5-1007.
See PRISONER LITIGATION.

Procurement.
Collusion.
Enforcement by attorney general, SF §11-205.
Construction contracts.
Security.
Actions on security, SF §§17-108, 17-109.

Prohibited actions.
Civil defense shelters.
Damages resulting from use, CJ §5-602.
Construction industry indemnity agreements, CJ §5-401.
Defamation.
Against local government officials, CJ §5-501.
Records.
Furnishing confidential records for research purposes, CJ §5-601.

Property and casualty insurance guaranty corporation.
Actions against insured of insolvent insurer, IN §9-309.

Property taxes.
Collection of taxes.
Actions for collection of taxes generally.
See PROPERTY TAXES.
Constant yield tax rate violation by taxing authority.
Attorney general to initiate appropriate legal action, TP §2-205.

Public service commission.
Enforcement of article, PUC §2-117.
Recovery of forfeitures, PUC §2-117.
Vehicle registration, PUC §2-117.

ACTIONS —Cont'd
Public works contracts.
  Wages.
    Actions by attorney general, SF §17-223.
    Suit for wages by employees, SF §17-224.
Questions of law or fact.
  Transfer of action.
    Circuit courts, CivProCir Rule 2-327.
Radiation.
  Civil penalties, EN §8-509.
    Limitation on action to collect, EN §8-509.1.
  Final corrective orders.
    Enforcement, EN §8-506.
  Injunctions, EN §8-507.
Real estate brokers.
  Compensation for providing brokerage services.
    Prerequisites to action for, BOP §17-516.
Real property.
  Ejectment.
    See EJECTMENT.
  Partition, PropAct Rule 12-401; RP §14-107.
  Possession.
    Action for possession, RP §14-108.1.
  Quieting title, RP §14-108.
Registered returnable containers and textiles.
  Subtitle does not preclude civil action, BR
    §19-302.
Reinsurance intermediaries.
  Receiver authorized to bring civil action, IN
    §8-511.
Remedy for injury to person or property, MD
    Const DofR Art 19.
Replevin.
  Replevin bond, PropAct Rule 12-601.
Restrooms.
  Retail establishments.
    Allowing customers to use toilet facilities.
      Civil liability of retail establishments or
        employees, HG §24-210.
Retail stores.
  Restrooms.
    Allowing customers to use toilet facilities, HG
      §24-210.
Schools.
  Legal counsel in suits against teachers, agents,
    etc., ED §4-104.
Securities act.
  Exemptions.
    Burden of proof in civil proceedings, CA
      §11-604.
  Violations of title.
    Civil liability, CA §11-703.
Senior citizen activities centers.
  Capital improvement grants program.
    Civil action upon default, 70B §31.
**Service contracts and consumer products
    guaranty.**
  Exclusive remedy, CL §14-409.
  Private remedies, CL §14-407.
Shoplifting.
  Civil action by merchant, CJ §3-1305.
    Criminal prosecution not prerequisite, CJ
      §3-1306.
SLAPP suits, CJ §5-807.
Small claim actions, CJ §4-405.
  District Court, CivProDist Rule 3-701.
Social services.
  Local social services departments.
    Institution and defense for civil cases, 88A §7.
  Public assistance program.
    Death of recipient.
      Recovery from estate, 88A §77.

ACTIONS —Cont'd
Social services —Cont'd
  Public assistance program —Cont'd
    Recovery from recipient, 88A §76.
Spam.
  Civil action, CR §3-805.1.
Start-up business ventures.
  Securities commissioner.
    Civil enforcement of act, BR §14-110.
State.
  Contracts.
    General provisions.
      See CONTRACTS.
  State's attorney.
    Prosecute and defend cases in which state is
      interested, 10 §34.
  Suits against state, US Const Amd 11.
  Tort claims act, SG §§12-101 to 12-110.
    See TORTS.
State officers and employees, SG §§12-301 to
    12-318.
  See ACTIONS AGAINST STATE OFFICERS AND
    EMPLOYEES.
State personnel.
  Civil enforcement actions.
    Limitation on sovereign immunity defense, SPP
      §14-103.
  Subrogation.
    Work-related accident leave, SPP §9-705.
State treasurer.
  Failure of treasurer to give notice of inability to
    serve or unavailability, SG §5-106.
Statutes.
  Repeal or revision of statute.
    Effect on penalty or liability previously
      incurred, 1 §3.
Stay.
  Action should be heard in another form, CJ
    §6-104.
Stores.
  Restrooms.
    Allowing customers to use toilet facilities.
      Civil liability of retail establishments or
        employees, HG §24-210.
Support and maintenance.
  Criminal nonsupport and desertion.
    Effect of civil action, FL §10-209.
  Deductions from earnings.
    Violations, FL §10-129.
Surveillance by camera of private residence,
    CR §3-903.
Surveillance of individual in private place, CR
    §3-901.
  With prurient intent, CR §3-902.
Survival of actions.
  General provisions, CJ §6-401.
Surviving spouses.
  Personal action to recover in right of deceased
    spouse.
    Necessary allegations, FL §4-202.
Taxation.
  Collection of taxes.
    Actions for collection of taxes generally.
      See TAXATION.
    Attachment, TG §13-817.
    Authorized, TG §13-815.
    Certificate of tax collector, TG §13-818.
    Compromise of claim, TG §13-816.
    Initiation of action, TG §13-816.
    Multiple claims, TG §13-815.
    Priority of action, TG §13-818.

ACTIONS —Cont'd
Taxation —Cont'd
Foreclosure of rights of redemption.
General provisions.
See PROPERTY TAXES.
Jeopardy assessments.
Collection, TG §13-821.
Liens.
Unpaid tax.
Enforcement of lien by judicial proceedings, TG §13-810.
Reciprocity.
Officials of other states may bring action, TP §1-302.
Special taxing districts.
Immunity from liability, 26 §2.
Suit on collector's bond.
General provisions, TP §4-403.
Jury trial, TP §4-403.
Telecommunications services theft, CR §7-318.
Telegraph companies.
Neglecting or refusing to receive or transmit telegram, PUC §8-108.
Telegraph or telephone company lines and facilities.
Liability for damage person sustains through erection, continuance or use, PUC §8-104.
Suit for damages by owner or possessor of land after notice to remove, PUC §8-105.
Telephone solicitations.
Violations of federal telemarketing and consumer fraud and abuse prevention act and federal consumer protection act, CL §14-3202.
Third-party practice.
Circuit courts, CivProCir Rule 2-332.
Time-sharing.
Real estate commission.
Enforcement suits, RP §11A-122.
Warranties.
Suits to enforce, RP §11A-117.
Tires.
Used tire cleanup and recycling fund.
Reimbursement of costs.
Action for failure to make, EN §9-276.
Toilets.
Retail establishments.
Allowing customers to use toilet facilities.
Civil liability of retail establishments or employees, CJ §5-635; HG §24-210.
Torts.
Local government tort claims act, CJ §§5-301 to 5-304.
Remedy for injury to person or property, MD Const DofR Art 19.
Trade names.
Creditors of persons using a trade name.
Actions by, CJ §6-406.1.
Trade secrets.
Confidentiality during action.
How confidentiality preserved, CL §11-1205.
Transfer of action.
Circuit courts, CivProCir Rule 2-327.
Trial.
Date and time.
District Court, CivProDist Rule 3-102.
General provisions.
See TRIAL.
Trial by jury.
Generally.
See JURY.

ACTIONS —Cont'd
Trial of facts where they arise, MD Const DofR Art 20.
Tri-county council for western Maryland.
Immunity from suit, CJ §5-506.
Trusts and trustees.
Discretionary trusts.
Actions against trustee as fiduciary, ET §14-405.
Unemployment compensation.
Contributions.
Collection by assessment, LE §8-630.
United States.
Judicial power of United States, US Const Art III §2; Amd 11.
Universities and colleges.
Community colleges.
Board of trustees.
Defense of sovereign immunity, ED §16-107.
Usury.
No cause for action six months after payment, CL §12-111.
Venue.
General provisions.
See VENUE.
Veterinarians.
Collection of fees, CL §16-701.
Victims of crime.
Notoriety of crimes contracts.
Defendant actions barred, CP §§11-626, 11-627.
Limitations on bringing civil actions, CP §11-626.
Volunteers.
Liability, CJ §5-407.
Washington suburban sanitary district.
Collective bargaining.
Unfair labor practices, 29 §11.5-113.
Local government tort claims act, CJ §§5-301 to 5-304.
See TORTS.
Water pollution.
Additional and cumulative remedies, EN §4-403.
Collection of civil penalties.
Limitation on action, EN §9-343.1.
Cost sharing.
Action to enforce agreement, AG §8-705.
Damages.
Suits against persons liable for damage, EN §4-405.
Wetlands.
Civil action to enforce title, EN §16-502.
Whistleblower protection.
Effect on personnel actions, SPP §5-302.
Witnesses.
General provisions.
See WITNESSES.
Workers' compensation.
See WORKERS' COMPENSATION.
Wrongful death, SpecPro Rule 15-1001.
Wrongful detainer, RP §8-402.4.
Claimant to title of property, RP §8-404.
Escrow account in wrongful detainer action, RP §8-118.1.

ACTIONS AGAINST STATE OFFICERS AND EMPLOYEES, SG §§12-301 to 12-318.
Appeals.
Criminal actions.
Determinations of attorney general not subject to judicial review, SG §12-315.

**ACTIONS AGAINST STATE OFFICERS AND
    EMPLOYEES** —Cont'd
Appearance.
    Attorney general, SG §12-304.
Applicability of subtitle, SG §§12-301, 12-310.
Attorney general.
    Agreement for representation, SG §12-305.
    Appearance, SG §12-304.
    Criminal actions.
        Restrictions on representation, SG §12-313.
    Discretion in undertaking representation, SG
        §12-304.
Attorneys at law.
    Agreement for representation, SG §12-305.
    Appearance of attorney general, SG §12-304.
    Fees reimbursed, SG §12-314.
    Right to retain counsel, SG §12-304.
    Scope and effect of representation, SG §12-306.
Baltimore City board of school commissioners.
    Subtitle inapplicable, SG §12-301.
Compromise and settlement.
    Authority of attorney general to compromise or
        settle claims, SG §12-305.
Confidentiality of information, SG §12-307.
Counties.
    Subtitle inapplicable, SG §12-301.
County board of education.
    Subtitle inapplicable, SG §12-301.
County elections.
    Board of supervisors.
        Subtitle inapplicable, SG §12-301.
Liability of state, SG §12-310.
Payment by governmental unit, SG §12-310.
Payment of settlements and judgments.
    Applicability of subtitle 5, SG §12-406.
    Approval or disapproval, SG §12-501.
    Authorized, SG §12-404.
    Board of public works, SG §12-501.
        Payment authorized, SG §12-404.
        When board may not pay settlement or
            judgment, SG §12-405.
    Defenses.
        Subtitle not to affect other defenses available,
            SG §12-403.
    Exceptions to certain application requirements,
        SG §12-405.
    Findings, SG §12-402.
    Form of payment, SG §12-501.
    Immunity.
        Subtitle not to affect immunity or other defense
            available to state personnel, SG §12-403.
    Legislative findings, SG §12-402.
    Limitations on payment or settlement, SG
        §12-405.
    Scope of subtitle, SG §12-403.
    Sources of payment, SG §12-501.
    Sovereign immunity.
        Payment of settlement or judgment not to
            abrogate sovereign immunity, SG §12-403.
Privileged communications.
    Civil actions and special proceedings.
        Confidentiality of information, SG §12-307.
Public service commission.
    Subtitle inapplicable, SG §12-301.
Public works board, SG §12-501.
    Authorization of payment of settlements and
        judgments, SG §§12-404, 12-405.
    Criminal actions.
        Reimbursement authorized, SG §12-314.
Reimbursements.
    Applicants required to answer questions under
        oath, SG §12-316.

**ACTIONS AGAINST STATE OFFICERS AND
    EMPLOYEES** —Cont'd
Reimbursements —Cont'd
    By party, SG §12-309.
    By state, SG §12-310.
    Limitations on reimbursements, SG §12-315.
    Providing information on matter under
        investigation, SG §12-316.
    Subrogation of awards, SG §12-318.
Required findings, SG §12-308.
Scope and effect of representation, SG §12-306.
Scope of subtitle, SG §12-301.
Settlements.
    Authority of attorney general, SG §12-305.
    Payment of settlements and judgments. See
        within this heading, "Payment of settlements
        and judgments."
Sovereign immunity.
    Payment of settlement or judgment not to
        abrogate, SG §12-403.
Special verdict, SG §12-308.
State contractor employees.
    Violations of whistleblower protection provisions,
        SF §11-304.
        Defenses, SF §11-306.
Subrogation.
    Criminal actions.
        Subrogation of awarded money, SG §12-318.
Tort claims act, SG §§12-101 to 12-110.
    See TORTS.
Verdict.
    Special verdict, SG §12-308.
**Whistleblower protection provisions, violation
    of.**
    State contractor employees, SF §11-304.
        Defenses, SF §11-306.

ACTS OF ASSEMBLY.
Bills.
    See GENERAL ASSEMBLY.
General assembly.
    Legislation generally, SG §§2-1501 to 2-1514.
        See GENERAL ASSEMBLY.
Statutes.
    See STATUTES.

ACTS OF GOD.
Air quality control.
    Conditions not violations, EN §2-613.
Noise control.
    Conditions not violations, EN §3-408.

ACTUAL CAUSE.
Drug dealer liability act, CJ §3-1604.

ACUPUNCTURISTS, HO §§1A-101 to 1A-502.
Advertising, HO §1A-306.
Appeal of board decisions, HO §1A-311.
Application for licenses, HO §1A-303.
    Qualifications of applicants, HO §1A-302.
Board, HO §§1A-201 to 1A-206.
    Compensation, HO §1A-204.
    Creation, HO §1A-201.
    Meetings, HO §1A-204.
    Membership, HO §1A-202.
    Officers, HO §1A-203.
    Powers and duties, HO §1A-205.
    Program evaluation act.
        2004 deadline, SG §8-403.
Citation of act.
    Short title, HO §1A-501.
Continuing education.
    Requirements for license renewal, HO §1A-306.

ACUPUNCTURISTS —Cont'd
Definitions, HO §1A-101.
Dentists.
Performance of acupuncture not limited, HO §1A-102.
Direct supervision.
Non-acupuncturist may perform under, HO §1A-316.
Examination while under investigation, HO §1A-315.
Exemptions from license requirement, HO §1A-301.
Expiration of license, HO §1-306.
Reinstatement of expired license, HO §1A-307.
Funds.
Acupuncture board fund, HO §1A-206.
Grace period for license renewal, HO §1A-306.
Inactive status, HO §1A-307.
Injunctions for violations, HO §1A-314.
Issuance of license, HO §1A-304.
Licenses, HO §§1A-301 to 1A-316.
Misdemeanors.
Violations of provisions, HO §1A-403.
Misrepresentation.
Prohibited acts, HO §1A-402.
Non-acupuncturists.
Performing under direct supervision, HO §1A-316.
Notices.
Precaution.
Display of notice regarding, HO §1A-313.
Penalties.
Violations of provisions, HO §1A-403.
Physicians.
Performance of acupuncture not limited, HO §1A-102.
Practice of acupuncture.
Licenses generally, HO §§1A-301 to 1A-316.
Misrepresentations regarding authorization to practice, HO §1A-402.
Probation of licensee.
Appeals.
Administrative and judicial review, HO §1A-311.
Grounds, HO §1A-309.
Procedure, HO §1A-310.
Qualifications, HO §1A-302.
Reinstatement of expired licenses, HO §1A-307.
Reinstatement of suspended or revoked license, HO §1A-312.
Renewal of license, HO §1A-306.
Reprimand of licensee.
Appeals.
Administrative and judicial review, HO §1A-311.
Grounds, HO §1A-309.
Procedure, HO §1A-310.
Revocation or suspension of license.
Appeals.
Administrative and judicial review, HO §1A-311.
Grounds, HO §1A-309.
Procedures, HO §1A-310.
Reinstatement of suspended or revoked licenses, HO §1A-312.
Scope of license, HO §1A-305.
Scope of provisions, HO §1A-102.
Surrender of license by licensee, HO §1A-308.
Termination of provisions, HO §1A-502.
Term of license, HO §1A-306.
Title of act.
Short title, HO §1A-501.

ACUPUNCTURISTS —Cont'd
Universal precautions.
Display of notice regarding, HO §1A-313.
Unlicensed practice, HO §1A-401.
Veterinarians.
Performance of acupuncture not limited, HO §1A-102.
Practice of veterinary medicine, HO §1-211.

ADDRESSING ENVELOPES.
Unfair or deceptive trade practices.
Work-at-home advertisements, CL §13-314.

ADJOURNMENT.
Congress, US Const Art I §§5, 7; Art II §3.

ADJUDICATIVE FACTS.
Judicial notice, Evid Rule 5-201.

ADJUSTERS.
Insurance adjusters, IN §§10-401 to 10-410.
See INSURANCE.

ADJUTANT GENERAL.
Militia, PS §§13-301 to 13-306.
See MILITIA.

ADMINISTRATION OF COURTS.
Actions.
Assignment of actions for trial, CJA Rule 16-202.
Administrative judges, CJA Rule 16-101.
Disposition of records.
Approval, CJA Rule 16-818.
Applicability of rules to District Court, CJA Rule 16-501.
Asbestos cases.
Special docket, CJA Rule 16-203.
Assignment of actions for trial, CJA Rule 16-202.
Assignment of judges, CJA Rule 16-103.
Attorneys at law.
Proscribed activities, CJA Rule 16-401.
Rules of professional conduct.
Adoption, CJA Rule 16-812.
Auditors.
Code of conduct, CJA Rule 16-814.
Bail and recognizance.
Bail bond commissioner.
Appointment, CJA Rule 16-817.
Bail bondsmen.
Licensing and regulation, CJA Rule 16-817.
Baltimore City.
Assignment of judges.
Circuit administrative judge, CJA Rule 16-103.
Broadcasting in courthouses, CJA Rule 16-109.
Calendars.
Motions calendar, CJA Rule 16-201.
Chambers judge, CJA Rule 16-102.
Circuit administrative judge, CJA Rule 16-101.
Assignment of judges, CJA Rule 16-103.
Circuit court reporters, CJA Rule 16-404.
Circuit judges.
Conference of circuit judges, CJA Rule 16-108.
Clerks.
Clients' security fund.
Notice to clerk, CJA Rule 16-811.
Disposition of records.
Permanent retention, CJA Rule 16-818.
Dockets, CJA Rule 16-305.
Filing and removal of papers, CJA Rule 16-306.
Hours, CJA Rule 16-304.
Offices, CJA Rule 16-304.
Payment of money into court, CJA Rule 16-303.
District Court, CJA Rule 16-502.

ADMINISTRATION OF COURTS —Cont'd
Clerks —Cont'd
  Trust clerk.
    Designation, CJA Rule 16-403.
Clients' security fund, CJA Rule 16-811.
Code of judicial conduct, CJA Rule 16-813.
Commissioners.
  Court commissioners.
    Code of conduct, CJA Rule 16-814.
Conference of circuit judges, CJA Rule 16-108.
County administrative judge, CJA Rule 16-101.
  Assignment of judges, CJA Rule 16-103.
  Reports, CJA Rule 16-105.
Courthouses.
  Photographing, recording, broadcasting or
    televising in courthouses, CJA Rule 16-109.
Court information system, CJA Rule 16-308.
Court of appeals.
  Censure, removal or retirement of judges.
    Interested member on court of appeals or
      commission, CJA Rule 16-809.
    Review of recommendation of commission, CJA
      Rule 16-809.
  Chief judge of court of appeals.
    Administrative responsibility, CJA Rule 16-101.
    Assignment of judges, CJA Rule 16-103.
    Judicial leave.
      Supervision of rule by chief judge, CJA Rule
        16-104.
  Clients' security fund.
    Powers, CJA Rule 16-811.
Court of special appeals.
  Chief judge of court of special appeals.
    Administrative responsibility, CJA Rule 16-101.
  Information system.
    Notice to court of special appeals, CJA Rule
      16-309.
Court reporters.
  Circuit court reporters, CJA Rule 16-404.
    Videotape recording of court proceedings, CJA
      Rules 16-405, 16-406.
  District Court.
    Recording of proceedings, CJA Rule 16-504.
Criminal history record information.
  Inspection of information containing court records
    of public judicial proceedings, CJA Rule
    16-308.
  District Court, CJA Rule 16-503.
  Reporting and transmittal, CJA Rule 16-308.
    District Court, CJA Rule 16-503.
Definitions.
  Disposition of records, CJA Rule 16-818.
    District Court, CJA Rule 16-505.
  Judicial disability and sanctionable conduct, CJA
    Rule 16-803.
  Judicial leave.
    Judge, CJA Rule 16-104.
  Photographing, recording, broadcasting or
    televising in courthouses, CJA Rule 16-109.
Disposition of records, CJA Rule 16-818.
  District Court, CJA Rule 16-505.
Dockets, CJA Rule 16-305.
  Asbestos cases, CJA Rule 16-203.
  Filing and removal of papers, CJA Rule 16-306.
  Information system.
    Report of docketing and disposition of cases,
      CJA Rule 16-308.
Electronic filing of pleadings and papers, CJA
  Rule 16-804.
Examiners.
  Code of conduct, CJA Rule 16-814.

ADMINISTRATION OF COURTS —Cont'd
Filing.
  Clients' security fund.
    Report and audit, CJA Rule 16-811.
  Court reporters.
    Circuit court reporters.
      Maintenance and filing of administrative
        records, CJA Rule 16-404.
  Dockets.
    Entries in dockets, CJA Rule 16-306.
  Electronic filing of pleadings and papers, CJA
    Rule 16-307.
  Exhibits filed with pleadings, CJA Rule 16-306.
  Flat filing, CJA Rule 16-306.
  Reports to be filed, CJA Rule 16-105.
Form of interrogatories.
  Domestic relations definitions, Form 4.
  Domestic relations interrogatories, Form 5.
  General definitions, Form 2.
  General interrogatories, Form 3.
  Instructions, Form 1.
  Motor vehicle tort definitions, Form 6.
  Motor vehicle tort interrogatories, Form 7.
  Personal injury interrogatories, Form 8.
  Products liability, Interrogatories Forms 9, 10.
Funds.
  Clients' security fund, CJA Rule 16-811.
Hall of records.
  Disposition of records, CJA Rule 16-818.
Holidays.
  Sessions of court, CJA Rule 16-106.
Information system.
  Court of special appeals.
    Notice to court of special appeals, CJA Rule
      16-309.
  Criminal history record information, CJA Rule
    16-308.
    District Court, CJA Rule 16-503.
  District Court, CJA Rule 16-503.
  Notice to court of special appeals, CJA Rule
    16-309.
  Report of docketing and disposition of cases, CJA
    Rule 16-308.
Interpreters.
  Appropriations, CJ §2-511.
Interrogatories.
  Forms. See within this heading, "Form of
    interrogatories."
Judges.
  Administrative judges, CJA Rule 16-101.
  Assignment, CJA Rule 16-103.
  Chamber judge, CJA Rule 16-102.
  Circuit administration judge, CJA Rule 16-101.
  Circuit judge conference, CJA Rule 16-108.
  County administrative judge, CJA Rule 16-101.
  Court of appeals.
    Chief judge. See within this heading, "Court of
      appeals."
  Court of special appeals.
    Chief judge, CJA Rule 16-101.
  Disability of judge, CJA Rules 16-803 to 16-810.
  Disposition of records.
    Approval, CJA Rule 16-818.
  Ethics.
    Code of judicial conduct, CJA Rule 16-813.
    Judicial ethics committee, CJA Rule 16-812.1.
  Sanctionable conduct, CJA Rules 16-803 to
    16-810.
Judicial leave, CJA Rule 16-104.
Jury trial.
  Sessions, CJA Rule 16-107.

ADMINISTRATION OF COURTS —Cont'd
Leave.
Judicial leave, CJA Rule 16-104.
Maryland judicial conference, CJA Rule 16-802.
Masters.
Code of conduct, CJA Rule 16-814.
Motion day, CJA Rule 16-201.
Officers of court, attorneys, etc.
Proscribed activities, CJA Rule 16-401.
Payment of money into court, CJA Rules 16-303, 16-502.
Photographing, recording, broadcasting or televising in courthouses, CJA Rule 16-109.
Disposal if records photographed, photocopied or microphotographed, CJA Rule 16-818.
Promulgation of rules, CJA Rule 16-801.
Proscribed activities.
Attorneys, officers of court, etc., CJA Rule 16-401.
Radio.
Broadcasting in courthouses, CJA Rule 16-109.
Recording in courthouses, CJA Rule 16-109.
District Court, CJA Rule 16-504.
Records.
Circuit court reporters.
Maintenance and filing of administrative records, CJA Rule 16-404.
Disposition of records, CJA Rule 16-818.
District Court, CJA Rule 16-505.
Referees.
Code of conduct, CJA Rule 16-814.
Removal of papers.
Clerks' duties, CJA Rule 16-306.
Reporters. See within this heading, "Court reporters."
Responsibility for administration, CJA Rule 16-101.
Rules and regulations.
Promulgation of rules, CJA Rule 16-801.
Rules of professional conduct.
Adoption, CJA Rule 16-812.
Sessions.
Holidays, CJA Rule 16-106.
Judicial conference, CJA Rule 16-802.
Jury sessions, CJA Rule 16-107.
Time for convening, CJA Rule 16-106.
Tape recordings.
Photographing, recording, broadcasting or televising in courthouses, CJA Rule 16-109.
Televising in courthouses, CJA Rule 16-109.
Terms of court, CJA Rule 16-107.
Trust clerks.
Designation, CJA Rule 16-403.
Trust funds.
Clients' security fund, CJA Rule 16-811.
Videotape recording of court proceedings, CJA Rules 16-405, 16-406.

ADMINISTRATIVE HEARINGS, OFFICE OF, SG §§9-1601 to 9-1610.
Administrative law judges, SG §§9-1605 to 9-1607.

ADMINISTRATIVE INSPECTION WARRANTS.
Controlled dangerous substances.
Inspection of, areas, building, premises, CR §5-804.

ADMINISTRATIVE OFFICE OF THE COURTS.
Design of citations, CJ §13-101.
Information.
Officers of court to deliver information to director of administrative office on request, CJ §13-101.

ADMINISTRATIVE OFFICE OF THE COURTS —Cont'd
Seventh judicial circuit, CJ §13-102.
State office, CJ §13-101.

ADMINISTRATIVE PROCEDURE.
Access to public records, SG §§10-611 to 10-628.
See RECORDS.
Air quality control.
Adoption of rules and regulations.
Compliance with act, EN §2-303.
Orders.
Applicability, EN §2-605.
Appeals.
Contested cases. See within this heading, "Contested cases."
Declaratory rulings, SG §10-305.
Disposition, AppRevCir Rule 7-209.
Evidence.
Additional evidence, AppRevCir Rule 7-208.
Hearings, AppRevCir Rule 7-208.
Memoranda, AppRevCir Rule 7-207.
Petitions, AppRevCir Rule 7-202.
Time for filing, AppRevCir Rule 7-203.
Political subdivisions and instrumentalities, SG §10-121.
Record on appeal, AppRevCir Rule 7-206.
Response.
Filing, AppRevCir Rule 7-204.
Time for filing, AppRevCir Rule 7-204.
Stays.
Order of court, AppRevCir Rule 7-205.
Time for filing, AppRevCir Rule 7-203.
Appeal by other party, AppRevCir Rule 7-203.
Filing of response, AppRevCir Rule 7-204.
Applicability of provisions, AppRevCir Rule 7-202.
Asbestos.
Hearing on suspension or revocation of license, EN §6-416.
Attorney general.
Regulations.
Submission of proposed regulations, SG §10-107.
Attorneys at law.
Contested cases.
Practice before agency, SG §10-206.1.
Business.
Defined, SG §10-124.
Citation of statutory authority.
Regulations not effective unless containing citation, SG §10-106.
Committee.
Defined, SG §10-101.
Communications.
Public communications.
Written policies. See within this heading, "Written policies for public communications."
Compromise and settlement.
Contested cases.
Disposition by settlement, SG §10-210.
Conflict of laws.
Meetings, SG §10-504.
Consent.
Contested cases.
Consent orders, SG §10-210.
Construction and interpretation.
Actions with provisions applicable, AppRevCir Rule 7-201.

ADMINISTRATIVE PROCEDURE —Cont'd
Consumer credit reporting agencies.
Applicability of provisions, CL §14-1218.
Consumer loans.
Hearings.
Application of administrative procedure act, FI
§11-217.
Contested cases, SG §§10-201 to 10-226.
Administrative orders, enforcement, SG §10-222.1.
Agency.
Defined, SG §10-202.
Appeals, SG §10-222.
Court of special appeals, SG §10-223.
Political subdivisions and instrumentalities, SG
§10-204.
Applicability of subtitle, SG §10-203.
Attorneys at law.
Practice before agency, SG §10-206.1.
Claims required in contested case.
Litigation expenses for small business and
nonprofit organizations, SG §10-224.
Consent orders, SG §10-210.
Court of special appeals.
Right to appeal, SG §10-223.
Defaults.
Disposition by, SG §10-210.
Definitions, SG §10-202.
Businesses, SG §10-224.
Licenses, SG §10-226.
Delegation of hearing authority, SG §10-205.
Evidence.
Certain evidence excluded, SG §10-213.
Contents of record, SG §10-218.
Documentary evidence, SG §10-213.
Evaluation of evidence, SG §10-213.
Findings must be based on evidence of record,
SG §10-214.
Hearsay, SG §10-213.
Judicial review.
Additional evidence before agency, SG
§10-222.
Official notice of facts, SG §10-213.
Parties to offer evidence, SG §10-213.
Probative evidence, SG §10-213.
Rules of privilege applicable, SG §10-213.
Scope of evidence, SG §10-213.
Standard of proof, SG §10-217.
Exceptions, SG §10-216.
Executive orders of governor.
Suspension of provisions, SG §10-225.
Ex parte communications, SG §10-219.
Expenses.
Litigation expenses for small business and
nonprofit organizations, SG §10-224.
Final decisions and orders.
Contents, SG §10-221.
Distribution, SG §10-221.
Enforcement of administrative order, SG
§10-222.1.
Form, SG §10-221.
General exclusions, SG §10-203.
Hearings.
Delegation of hearing authority, SG §10-205.
Electronic means, holding hearings by, SG
§10-211.
Interpreters, SG §10-212.1.
Open hearings, SG §10-212.
Prehearing procedures, SG §10-206.
Telephonic hearings, SG §10-211.
Judicial review. See within this subheading,
"Appeals."

ADMINISTRATIVE PROCEDURE —Cont'd
Contested cases —Cont'd
Legislative declaration.
Purpose of provisions, SG §10-201.
Licenses.
Defined, SG §§10-202, 10-226.
Definitions, SG §10-226.
Special provisions, SG §10-226.
Maryland automobile insurance fund.
Applicability of subtitle, SG §10-203.
Notice.
Agency action, SG §10-207.
Hearing, SG §10-208.
Mailing of notice to address of licensee, SG
§10-209.
Proposed decision, SG §10-216.
Open hearings, SG §10-212.
Parties.
Political subdivisions and instrumentalities, SG
§10-204.
Pleadings.
Contents of record, SG §10-218.
Prehearing procedures, SG §10-206.
Priority funding areas.
Applicability to decisions to fund projects, SF
§5-7B-10.
Procedural regulations, SG §10-206.
Proof.
Standard of proof, SG §10-217.
Proposed decisions and orders, SG §10-220.
Notice, SG §10-216.
Purpose of provisions, SG §10-201.
Record.
Contents, SG §10-218.
Transcription of proceedings, SG §10-215.
Regulations, rulings, etc., of agency.
Binding effect, SG §10-214.
Scope of subtitle, SG §10-203.
Settlement.
Disposition by, SG §10-210.
Stipulation.
Disposition by, SG §10-210.
Suspension of provisions.
Executive order, SG §10-225.
Telephonic hearings, SG §10-211.
Transcription of proceedings, SG §10-215.
Video conferencing, SG §10-211.
Counties.
Regulations.
Subtitle inapplicable to regulations of bicounty
commissions appointed by county governing
bodies, SG §10-105.
Court of special appeals.
Contested cases.
Right to appeal, SG §10-223.
Credit services businesses.
Applicability of administrative procedure act, CL
§14-1911.
Declaratory judgments.
Appeals, SG §10-305.
Applicability of subtitle, SG §10-302.
Authority of unit to issue ruling, SG §10-305.
Effect of declaratory ruling, SG §10-305.
Finding of invalidity, SG §10-125.
Maryland automobile insurance fund.
Applicability of subtitle, SG §10-302.
Parties.
Right of political subdivisions and
instrumentalities, SG §10-303.
Petitions.
Adoption of regulations, SG §10-304.

ADMINISTRATIVE PROCEDURE —Cont'd
Declaratory judgments —Cont'd
Petitions —Cont'd
Authorized, SG §10-304.
Political subdivisions and instrumentalities.
Interested parties, SG §10-303.
Regulations.
Adoption by units, SG §10-304.
Authority to consider, SG §10-125.
Petition authorized, SG §10-125.
Scope of subtitle, SG §10-302.
Unit.
Defined, SG §10-301.
Unit as party, SG §10-125.
Defaults.
Contested cases, SG §10-210.
Definitions.
Administrative agency, AppRevCir Rule 7-201.
Businesses, SG §10-224.
Contested cases, SG §10-202.
Licenses, SG §10-226.
Meetings, SG §10-502.
Nonprofit organizations, SG §10-224.
Regulations, SG §10-101.
Regulatory review and evaluation, SG §10-130.
Unit counsel, SG §10-107.
Written policies for public communications, SG §10-801.
Dietitians.
Administrative appeals, HO §5-313.
Documents.
State documents.
See DOCUMENTS.
Emergency management.
Civil relief during emergency periods.
Administrative remedies, PS §14-206.
Environmental sanitarians.
Licenses.
Denials, reprimands, suspensions and revocations.
Hearings.
Applicability of act, EN §11-313.
Evidence.
Additional evidence, AppRevCir Rule 7-208.
Contested cases. See within this heading, "Contested cases."
Executive agencies.
Office of administrative hearings, SG §§9-1601 to 9-1610.
See EXECUTIVE DEPARTMENT.
Ex parte communications.
Contested cases, SG §10-219.
Food, drugs and cosmetics.
Compliance with act in adoption of rule or regulation, HG §21-234.
Hearings.
Application of act to hearing, HG §21-236.
Forms management, SG §§10-604 to 10-608. See within this heading, "Records."
Frozen desserts.
Denial, suspension or revocation of licenses.
Appeals.
Applicability of act, HG §21-815.
Hearings.
Application of act, HG §21-814.
Hazardous materials and substances.
Hearings.
Application of act, EN §7-261.
Immediate ban where imminent hazard exists.
Hearings in accordance with act, HG §22-504.

ADMINISTRATIVE PROCEDURE —Cont'd
Health.
Planning and development.
Appeals of decisions, HG §19-128.
Hearings.
Contested cases. See within this heading, "Contested cases."
Hospitals.
Licenses.
Appeals, HG §19-330.
Interpreters, SG §10-507.1.
Contested cases, SG §10-212.1.
Judicial notice.
Contested cases.
Official notice of facts, SG §10-213.
Judicial notice of adjudicative facts, Evid Rule 5-201.
Jurisdiction.
Contested cases.
Judicial review, SG §10-222.
Licenses.
Contested cases.
Definitions, SG §§10-202, 10-226.
Special provisions, SG §10-226.
Hospitals.
Appeals, HG §19-330.
Local government unit.
Defined, SG §10-101.
Meetings.
Administrative function.
Defined, SG §10-502.
Requirements for administrative function meeting not open to public, SG §10-503.
Advisory function.
Defined, SG §10-502.
Applicability of subtitle, SG §10-503.
Conflict of laws, SG §10-504.
Authority of court to enforce, SG §10-510.
Closed sessions.
Limitation on right of public body, SG §10-508.
Permitted, SG §10-508.
Conflict of laws, SG §10-504.
Definitions, SG §10-502.
Disruption.
Removal of individuals disrupting meeting, SG §10-507.
Enforcement of subtitle, SG §10-510.
Interpreters, SG §10-507.1.
Judicial function.
Defined, SG §10-502.
Legislative function.
Defined, SG §10-502.
Legislative policy, SG §10-502.
Meet.
Defined, SG §10-502.
Minutes.
Access to minutes, SG §10-509.
Contents, SG §10-509.
Required, SG §10-509.
Notice.
Open sessions, SG §10-506.
Open sessions.
Adjournment of open session to closed session, SG §10-508.
Attendance at open session, SG §10-507.
Board.
Chairman, SG §10-502.2.
Compensation, SG §10-502.3.
Complaints.
Filing, SG §10-502.5.
Opinions, SG §10-502.5.

ADMINISTRATIVE PROCEDURE —Cont'd
Meetings —Cont'd
Open sessions —Cont'd
Board —Cont'd
Composition, SG §10-502.2.
Creation, SG §10-502.1.
Duties, SG §10-502.4.
Meetings, SG §10-502.3.
Quorum, SG §10-502.3.
Reports, SG §10-502.4.
Staff, SG §10-502.3.
Terms of office, SG §10-502.2.
Citation of subtitle, SG §10-512.
Complaints.
Contents, SG §10-502.5.
Filing, SG §10-502.5.
Possible violations, SG §10-502.6.
Notice, SG §10-506.
Penalties.
Willful violations, SG §10-511.
Removal of individuals, SG §10-507.
Required, SG §10-505.
Short title of subtitle, SG §10-512.
State open meetings law compliance board, SG §§10-502.1 to 10-502.6.
Violation of subtitle.
Complaints, SG §§10-502.5, 10-502.6.
Willful violations.
Civil penalty, SG §10-511.
Petitions.
Authorized, SG §10-510.
Policy of state, SG §10-501.
Public body.
Defined, SG §10-502.
Quasi-judicial function.
Defined, SG §10-502.
Quasi-legislative function.
Defined, SG §10-502.
Quorum.
Defined, SG §10-502.
Scope of subtitle, SG §10-503.
Tape recordings, SG §10-509.
Videotaping, televising, etc.
Rules regarding, SG §10-507.
Memoranda, AppRevCir Rule 7-207.
Milk and milk products.
Suspension and revocation of permits.
Application of act, HG §21-419.
Motor vehicles.
Appeals from decisions of administration.
Administrative procedure act shall govern, TR §12-209.
Noise control.
Environmental noise standards.
Compliance with act in adoption of standards, EN §3-402.
Nonprofit organizations.
Litigation expenses, SG §10-224.
Notice.
Adoption of regulations, SG §10-114.
Contested cases.
Agency action, SG §10-207.
Hearing, SG §10-208.
Mailing of notice to address of licensee, SG §10-209.
Proposed decision, SG §10-216.
Hearings, SG §10-205.
Contested cases, SG §10-208.
Meetings.
Open sessions.
Notice of open session, SG §10-506.

ADMINISTRATIVE PROCEDURE —Cont'd
Notice —Cont'd
Regulations.
Procedure for publication, SG §10-112.
Proposed and emergency regulations, posting and notice, SG §10-111.2.
Office of administrative hearings.
Executive agencies, SG §§9-1601 to 9-1610.
See EXECUTIVE DEPARTMENT.
Open sessions law.
Meetings. See within this heading, "Meetings."
Orders.
Appeals.
Stay, AppRevCir Rule 7-205.
Parties.
Contested cases.
Political subdivisions and instrumentalities, SG §10-204.
Regulations.
Declaratory judgments on validity, SG §10-125.
Petitions.
Adoption of regulation, SG §10-123.
Appeals, AppRevCir Rule 7-202.
Time for filing, AppRevCir Rule 7-203.
Declaratory judgments, SG §10-125.
Enforcement of subtitle, SG §10-510.
Potomac water authority.
Application of administrative procedure act, EN §5-410.
Presumptions, Evid Rule 5-301.
Meetings.
Actions to enforce subtitle, SG §10-510.
Prince George's and Montgomery counties historic property grant program.
Act not applicable, 28 §5-307.
Priority funding areas.
Contested cases.
Applicability to decisions to fund projects, SF §5-7B-10.
Procurement.
Dispute resolution.
Applicability of administrative procedure act, SF §15-216.
Program evaluation act.
General provisions, SG §§8-401 to 8-413.
See PROGRAM EVALUATION ACT.
Proposed regulations. See within this heading, "Regulations."
Publication.
Regulations.
Procedures for publication, SG §10-112.
Publication of notices, SG §10-129.
Public communications.
Written policies. See within this heading, "Written policies for public communications."
Radiation.
Rules and regulations.
Compliance with act, EN §8-106.
Record on appeal.
Certification of costs of transcription, AppRevCir Rule 7-206.
Contents, AppRevCir Rule 7-206.
Return of agency record, AppRevCir Rule 7-210.
Statement in lieu of record, AppRevCir Rule 7-206.
Time, AppRevCir Rule 7-206.
Records.
Access to court records, CJA Rule 16-1004.
Access to public records, SG §§10-611 to 10-628.
See RECORDS.

ADMINISTRATIVE PROCEDURE —Cont'd
Records —Cont'd
Forms management.
  Approved forms.
    Use required, SG §10-607.
  Definitions, SG §10-604.
  Department.
    Defined, SG §10-604.
  Division.
    Annual report, SG §10-608.
    Defined, SG §10-604.
  Forms.
    Defined, SG §10-604.
  Independent units.
    Defined, SG §10-604.
  Officer.
    General duties, SG §10-605.
    Required, SG §10-605.
  Plans.
    Contents, SG §10-606.
    Defined, SG §10-604.
    Duties of division, SG §10-606.
    Review by division, SG §10-606.
  Racial categories.
    Identification of individuals by race, SG
      §10-606.
  Reports.
    Annual report, SG §10-608.
  Use of approved forms required, SG §10-607.
  Information which state or political subdivision
    may keep regarding persons, SG §10-602.
  Limitation on records, SG §10-602.
  Political subdivisions.
    Defined, SG §10-601.
Records management division.
See RECORDS.
Register.
Contested cases.
  Publication in register does not constitute
    notice, SG §§10-207, 10-208.
Defined, SG §10-101.
Regulations.
Action after evaluation, SG §10-124.
Adoption.
  Emergency adoptions, SG §10-111.
  Failure to adopt proposed regulation, SG
    §10-116.
  Notice, SG §10-114.
  Opposition to adoption, SG §10-111.1.
  Petitions, SG §10-123.
  Scope of part, SG §10-109.
Appeals.
  Political subdivisions and instrumentalities, SG
    §10-121.
Bicounty commissions.
  Subtitle not applicable to regulations of
    commissions appointed by county governing
    bodies, SG §10-105.
Business.
  Defined, SG §10-124.
Changes in proposed regulations, SG §10-113.
Citation of statutory authority.
  Regulation not effective unless containing, SG
    §10-106.
Comparison of texts, SG §10-115.
Declaratory judgments.
  Adoption by units, SG §10-304.
  Authority to consider, SG §10-125.
  Petition authorized, SG §10-125.
Defined, SG §10-101.

ADMINISTRATIVE PROCEDURE —Cont'd
Regulations —Cont'd
Descriptive statement.
  Units to supplement regulations, SG §10-122.
Effective date, SG §10-117.
Emergency adoptions, SG §10-111.
  Committee power over emergency or proposed
    regulations, SG §10-118.
  Effective date after emergency adoption, SG
    §10-117.
  Posting and notice, SG §10-111.2.
  Website of general assembly.
    List of proposed regulations included, SG
      §10-111.2.
Evaluation of impact, SG §10-124.
Exclusions from subtitle, SG §10-102.
Findings of court, SG §10-128.
Limited provisions.
  Scope of part, SG §10-120.
Maryland automobile insurance fund.
  Compliance with subtitle, SG §10-120.
Notices.
  Proposed and emergency regulations, posting
    and notice, SG §10-111.2.
  Publication of notice, SG §10-129.
Petitions.
  Adoption of regulation, SG §10-123.
Preliminary review.
  Action by committee, SG §10-110.
  Consultation with committee, SG §10-110.
  Generally, SG §10-110.
  Impact on children's environmental health, SG
    §10-110.
  Scope of section, SG §10-110.
Procedural regulations.
  Descriptive statement, SG §10-122.
  Required, SG §10-122.
Proposed regulations.
  Changes in proposed regulations, SG §10-113.
  Committee power over emergency or proposed
    regulations, SG §10-118.
  Failure to adopt, SG §10-116.
  Posting and notice, SG §10-111.2.
  Scope of part, SG §10-109.
  Time limit on adoption, SG §10-111.
  Withdrawal, SG §10-116.
Publication, SG §§10-112, 10-129.
Regulatory review and evaluation.
  Applicability of part, SG §10-131.
  Citation of part, SG §10-139.
  Definitions, SG §10-130.
  Disagreement with committee
    recommendations, SG §10-136.
  Resolution of disagreement, SG §10-137.
  Evaluation reports.
    Comments and recommendations of
      committee, SG §10-135.
    Copies, SG §10-135.
    Hearings, SG §10-135.
    Preparation, SG §10-135.
    Review by committee, SG §10-135.
  Executive order.
    Contents, SG §10-133.
    Deadlines, SG §10-133.
    Issuance, SG §10-133.
  Exemption from process, SG §10-132.1.
  Proposed amendments or repeals of regulations,
    SG §10-138.
  Purposes of part, SG §10-132.
  Schedule of regulations to be reviewed, SG
    §10-132.1.

ADMINISTRATIVE PROCEDURE —Cont'd
Regulations —Cont'd
Regulatory review and evaluation —Cont'd
Work plan.
Action by committee, SG §10-134.
Contents, SG §10-134.
Preparation, SG §10-134.
Reprints.
Restricted, SG §10-115.
Scope of part, SG §10-105.
Scope of subtitle, SG §10-102.
Severability of provisions, SG §10-128.
Submission of proposed text to division of state
documents, SG §10-115.
Submission to attorney general, SG §10-107.
Submission to unit counsel, SG §10-107.
Use of "African American" preferred, SG §10-108.
Withdrawal of proposed regulation, SG §10-116.
Reorganization of government, SG §§10-701 to
10-706.
See REORGANIZATION OF GOVERNMENT.
Reports.
Records management division.
Annual report, SG §10-608.
Small businesses.
Litigation expenses, SG §10-224.
State documents.
See DOCUMENTS.
State personnel.
Pay plans.
Denial of pay increases in standard pay plan,
SPP §8-107.
Stays.
Appeals.
Order of court, AppRevCir Rule 7-205.
Stipulations.
Contested cases.
Disposition by, SG §10-210.
Time.
Appeals.
Record on appeal, AppRevCir Rule 7-206.
Transcripts.
Certification of costs of transcription, AppRevCir
Rule 7-206.
Contested cases.
Transcription of proceedings, SG §10-215.
Units.
Defined, SG §10-101.
Use of "African American" preferred, SG §10-108.
Venue.
Contested cases.
Judicial review, SG §10-222.
Water pollution.
Appeals.
Application of act, EN §9-340.
Hearings on complaints, EN §9-337.
Procedures for adoption of rules.
Compliance with act, EN §9-316.
Water quality laboratories.
Appeals, EN §9-1018.
Reprimands, suspensions and revocation.
Application to hearings, EN §9-1017.
Workers' compensation act.
Compliance with act, SG §10-401.
Written policies for public communications.
Adoption.
Required, SG §10-802.
Definitions, SG §10-801.
Filing.
Required, SG §10-803.
Required, SG §10-802.

ADMINISTRATORS.
Executors and administrators.
See EXECUTORS AND ADMINISTRATORS.
Insurance.
Third party administrators, IN §§8-301 to 8-322.
See INSURANCE.

ADMIRALTY.
Federal jurisdiction, US Const Art I §8; Art III
§2.
Poultry products inspection.
Seizure and condemnation.
Proceedings to conform to admiralty, AG §4-220.
Wholesale meat act.
Condemnation and seizure of products.
Proceedings to conform to admiralty, AG §4-125.

ADMISSIONS.
Answers.
Specific admissions or denials.
Circuit courts, CivProCir Rule 2-323.
Antitrust act.
Assurance of discontinuance of prohibited act.
Not to be considered admission, CL §11-206.
Boycotts.
Foreign discriminatory boycotts.
Assurance of discontinuance of prohibited act
not considered admission, CL §11-106.
**Incompetency to stand trial, examination
made by health department.**
Admissibility of statements made by defendant,
CP §§3-105, 3-108.
Mechanics' liens.
Affidavit or verified answer.
Failure to file deemed admission, PropAct Rule
12-304.
Motions.
Mandatory motions in circuit courts.
Criminal rules, Crim Rule 4-252.
**Request for admission of facts and
genuineness of documents,** CivProCir Rule
2-424.

ADMISSIONS AND AMUSEMENT TAX.
Accounts and accounting.
Administrative cost account.
Distribution of revenue to, TG §2-201.
Additional tax, TG §4-105.
Administrative cost account.
Distribution of revenue to, TG §2-201.
Art.
Performing arts organizations.
Exemption, TG §4-104.
Assessments.
Application for revision or claim for refund, TG
§13-508.
Erroneous assessments, TG §13-509.
Associations.
Not-for-profit community associations.
Exemption, TG §4-104.
Confidentiality.
Disclosure of tax information by current and
former government personnel.
Exceptions to nondisclosure, TG §13-204.
Corporations.
Payment of tax.
Liability of corporate officers, TG §4-301.
Counties.
Authority to impose tax, TG §4-102.
Restrictions, TG §4-103.
Distribution of revenue to, TG §2-202.
Rates, TG §4-105.

ADMISSIONS AND AMUSEMENT TAX —Cont'd

Crimes and offenses.

Payment.

Willful failure to pay, TG §13-1005.

Records.

Willful failure to keep records, TG §13-1008.

Returns.

Willful failure to file return, TG §13-1001.

Willfully making false statement or misleading omission, TG §13-1003.

Definitions, TG §§1-101, 4-101.

Exemptions, TG §4-104.

Limitation of actions.

Recovery of taxes, TG §13-1102.

Limited liability companies.

Payment of tax.

Personal liability, TG §4-301.

Maryland stadium authority.

Authority to impose tax, TG §4-102.

Definition of "stadium authority," TG §4-101.

Distribution of revenue to, TG §2-202.

Refunds.

Payment from revenue attributable to authority, TG §2-203.

Misdemeanors.

Payment of tax.

Willful failure to pay, TG §13-1005.

Records.

Willful failure to keep records, TG §13-1008.

Returns.

Willful failure to file return, TG §13-1001.

Willfully making false statement or misleading omission, TG §13-1003.

Municipal corporations.

Authority to impose tax, TG §4-102.

Restrictions, TG §4-103.

Distribution of revenue to, TG §2-202.

Rates, TG §4-105.

Payment of tax, TG §4-301.

Willful failure to pay, TG §13-1005.

Performing arts organizations.

Exemption, TG §4-104.

Privileged communications.

Disclosure of tax information by current and former government personnel.

Exceptions to prohibition, TG §13-204.

Rates, TG §4-105.

Records, TG §4-202.

Assessment when records not kept, TG §13-403.

Willful failure to keep records, TG §13-1008.

Refunds.

Claim for refund, TG §13-508.

Erroneous assessments, TG §13-509.

Payment, TG §2-203.

Reports.

Change in rates or classification, TG §4-105.

Returns, TG §4-201.

Misdemeanors.

Willful failure to file return, TG §13-1001.

Willfully making false statement or misleading omission, TG §13-1003.

Wicomico county.

Tennis courts.

Exemption, TG §4-104.

ADMITTED FACTS.

Admissibility of relevant evidence, Evid Rule 5-402.

ADOPTION, FL §§5-301 to 5-415.

Accounting report, FamLaw Rule 9-110.

ADOPTION —Cont'd

Appeals, AppRev Rule 8-122.

Subsidies.

Administrative and judicial review, FL §5-411.

Attorneys at law.

Appointment of counsel, FamLaw Rule 9-106.

Disabled parties, FamLaw Rule 9-105.

Guidelines for advocacy, ChildAdv Appx.

Change of name.

Notice, FamLaw Rule 9-105.

Charging or receiving compensation.

Limitation on prosecution, CJ §5-106.

Child care facilities generally, FL §§5-506 to 5-521.

See CHILD CARE.

Child placement.

Interstate compact on the placement of children, FL §§5-601 to 5-611.

Child placement agencies.

Licenses, FL §5-507.

Children in need of assistance.

Placement for adoption, CJ §3-823.

Clerks of court.

Decree of adoption.

Reports to secretary, HG §4-211.

Compacts.

Interstate compact on adoption and medical assistance, FL §§5-4A-01 to 5-4A-08.

Interstate compact on the placement of children, FL §§5-601 to 5-611.

Compensation.

Charging or receiving.

Limitation on prosecution, CJ §5-106.

Confidentiality.

Hearings, FamLaw Rule 9-109.

Mutual consent voluntary adoption registry.

Disclosure of information contained in registry, FL §5-4C-04.

Consent, FamLaw Rule 9-102.

Local department adoptions.

Adoption after termination of parental rights.

Revocation of consent, FL §5-351.

When consent required, FL §5-350.

Withholding consent, prohibited grounds, FL §5-350.

Written consents and attachments, FL §5-351.

Adoption without prior termination of parental rights.

Required consent, FL §5-338.

Revocation of consent, FL §5-339.

Written consents and attachments, FL §5-339.

Mutual consent voluntary adoption registry, FL §§5-4C-01 to 5-4C-07. See within this heading, "Mutual consent voluntary adoption registry."

Notice to consenting persons, FamLaw Rule 9-104.

Private agency adoptions.

Revocation, FL §5-3A-35.

When required, FL §5-3A-35.

Search, contact and reunion services, FL §§5-4B-08, 5-4B-09.

Consolidation of proceedings, Juv Rule 11-501.

Criminal background investigations for employees, etc., of facilities.

Individuals requiring investigations, FL §5-561.

Decedents' estates.

Determining relationship, ET §1-207.

Decree of adoption.

Final decree, FamLaw Rule 9-111.

ADOPTION —Cont'd
Definitions, FamLaw Rule 9-101.
  Mutual consent voluntary adoption registry, FL
    §5-4C-01.
  Search, contact and reunion services, FL
    §5-4B-01.
  Subsidy act, FL §5-401.
Disability.
  Determination of disability of party, FamLaw
    Rule 9-105.
Dockets.
  Clerk to keep, FamLaw Rule 9-112.
Employment.
  Adoption leave, LE §§3-801, 3-802.
Expenses.
  Nonrecurring adoption expenses.
    Reimbursement, FL §5-410.1.
Federal aid.
  Interstate compact on adoption and medical
    assistance.
  Applications for federal aid, FL §5-4A-08.
Filing.
  Objections.
    Notice of objection, FamLaw Rule 9-107.
Foreign adoptions.
  Birth certificate, HG §4-211.
Foreign jurisdiction.
  Petition, FamLaw Rule 9-103.
Foster care.
  Adoption of child under foster care, FL §5-530.
Guardian and ward.
  Consent, FamLaw Rule 9-102.
    Notice to consenting persons, FamLaw Rule
      9-104.
  Hearings, FamLaw Rule 9-109.
  Judgment of adoption or guardianship, FamLaw
    Rule 9-111.
  Local department guardianships, FL §§5-313 to
    5-328.
  See GUARDIAN AND WARD.
  Medical history of child, FamLaw Rule 9-113.
  Notice.
    Additional notice of guardianship proceedings,
      FamLaw Rule 9-105.
  Private agency guardianship proceedings, FL
    §§5-3A-13 to 5-3A-25.
  See GUARDIAN AND WARD.
Hearings, FamLaw Rule 9-109; Juv Rule 11-501.
Income tax.
  Adoption expenses, TG §10-208.
Independent adoptions, FL §§5-3B-01 to 5-3B-32.
  Access to adoption records.
    Emergency medical information, FL §5-3B-28.
    Vital statistics and records, FL §5-3B-29.
  Accounting requirement, FL §5-3B-24.
  Appeal, right to, FL §5-3B-09.
  Applicability of subtitle, FL §5-3B-02.
  Appointment of attorney for parent and/or
    prospective adoptee, FL §5-3B-06.
  Authority to place for adoption, FL §5-3B-12.
  Consent, FL §5-3B-21.
    Nonconsensual adoption, FL §5-3B-22.
      Custody, effect, FL §5-3B-23.
  Considerations in ruling on petition, FL §5-3B-19.
  Costs and fees, FL §5-3B-08.
  Custody, effect on nonconsensual adoption, FL
    §5-3B-23.
  Definitions, FL §5-3B-01.
  Effect of order, FL §5-3B-25.
  Entry of order, FL §5-3B-20.
  Foreign orders, FL §5-3B-04.

ADOPTION —Cont'd
Independent adoptions —Cont'd
  Hearing, FL §5-3B-17.
  Investigatory powers of court, FL §5-3B-16.
  Legislative findings and purpose, FL §5-3B-03.
  Medical and dental records.
    Access for adoptive parent, FL §5-3B-30.
  Nonconsensual adoption, FL §5-3B-22.
    Custody, effect, FL §5-3B-23.
  Paternity determination, FL §5-3B-05.
  Petition.
    Invalidation of adoption, petition to, FL
      §5-3B-26.
    Notice of filing, FL §5-3B-14.
      Website for posting notices, 88A §18.
    Prerequisite for authority to place for adoption,
      FL §5-3B-12.
    Requirements generally, FL §5-3B-13.
  Post-adoption contact, agreements, FL §5-3B-07.
  Prohibition on payment or compensation for
    services, FL §5-3B-32.
  Publication of show cause order, FL §5-3B-15.
  Show cause order, FL §5-3B-15.
  Single or unmarried petitioner.
    Prohibited grounds for denial of petition, FL
      §5-3B-19.
  Time limitation for entry of order, FL §5-3B-18.
**Interstate compact on adoption and medical
    assistance,** FL §§5-4A-01 to 5-4A-08.
  Definitions, FL §5-4A-01.
  False, misleading or fraudulent claims, FL
    §5-4A-06.
  Federal law.
    Compliance with, FL §5-4A-08.
  Legislative findings, FL §5-4A-02.
  Medical assistance identification, FL §5-4A-05.
  Participation in, FL §5-4A-03.
  Purposes of provisions, FL §5-4A-02.
  Regulations, FL §5-4A-07.
  Special-needs children.
    Medical assistance identification, FL §5-4A-05.
  Terms of compact, FL §5-4A-04.
Investigations.
  Court investigation, FamLaw Rule 9-106.
  Criminal background investigations for employees,
    etc., of facilities.
    Individuals requiring investigations, FL §5-561.
Jurisdiction.
  Equity courts, FL §1-201.
  Juvenile courts.
    Termination, FL §1-201.
Juvenile causes, Juv Rule 11-501.
Limitation of actions.
  Charging or receiving compensation in, CJ §5-106.
Local department adoptions.
  Access to adoption records, FL §§5-356 to 5-360.
    Court or local department records, FL §5-357.
    Emergency medical information, FL §5-358.
    Medical and mental health history, FL §5-356.
    Vital statistics and records, FL §5-359.
  Adoption after termination of parental rights, FL
    §§5-345 to 5-353.
  Consent.
    Revocation, FL §5-351.
    When required, FL §5-350.
    Withholding consent, prohibited grounds, FL
      §5-350.
    Written consents and attachments, FL §5-351.
  Factors considered by court, FL §5-349.
  Hearing on petition, FL §5-347.
  Notice of filing of petition, FL §5-346.

ADOPTION —Cont'd
Local department adoptions —Cont'd
Adoption after termination of parental rights
—Cont'd
Order for adoption, FL §5-352.
Petition to invalidate, FL §5-353.
Petition, FL §5-345.
Time limitation for petition to invalidate, FL
§5-353.
Time limits for ruling and entry of order, FL
§5-348.
Adoption without prior termination of parental
rights, FL §§5-331 to 5-342.
Addresses of parents, clerk to keep listing, FL
§5-332.
Consent or acquiescence.
Required, FL §5-338.
Revocation, FL §5-339.
Written consents and attachments, FL §5-339.
Dismissal of contested petition, FL §5-340.
Factors considered by court, FL §5-337.
Hearing on petition, FL §5-335.
Notice of filing of petition, FL §5-333.
Order of adoption, FL §5-341.
Petition to invalidate, FL §5-342.
Petition, FL §5-331.
Show cause orders, FL §5-334.
Time limitation for petition to invalidate, FL
§5-342.
Time limits for ruling and entry of order, FL
§5-336.
Appeal, right to, FL §5-310.
Applicability of subtitle, FL §5-302.
Appointment of attorney for parent and/or child,
FL §5-307.
Costs and fees, FL §5-309.
Definitions, FL §5-301.
Foreign orders, FL §5-305.
Guardianships, FL §§5-313 to 5-328.
See GUARDIAN AND WARD.
Legislative findings and purpose, FL §5-303.
Paternity determination, FL §5-306.
Post-adoption contact, agreements, FL §5-308.
Prohibition on payment or compensation for
services, FL §5-362.
Relation to other provisions, FL §5-304.
Medical and dental records.
Access for adoptive parent.
Independent adoptions, FL §5-3B-30.
Local department adoptions, FL §5-360.
Private agency adoptions, FL §5-3A-43.
Medical history of natural parents.
Duties of persons authorized to place minor child
for adoption, FL §5-520.
Required, FamLaw Rule 9-113.
Mutual consent voluntary adoption registry,
FL §§5-4C-01 to 5-4C-07.
Affidavits.
Duty of administration upon receipt of affidavit,
FL §5-4C-07.
Information contained in, FL §5-4C-06.
Confidentiality of information, FL §5-4C-04.
Contracts.
Child placement agencies, FL §5-4C-03.
Definitions, FL §5-4C-01.
Director.
Duties, FL §5-4C-03.
Eligibility to register, FL §5-4C-05.
Information required, FL §5-4C-06.
Matches.
When match made, FL §5-4C-07.

ADOPTION —Cont'd
Mutual consent voluntary adoption registry
—Cont'd
Purpose of subtitle, FL §5-4C-02.
Who permitted to register, FL §5-4C-05.
Name changes.
Judgment of adoption, FamLaw Rule 9-111.
Notice, FamLaw Rule 9-105.
Notice.
Change of name, FamLaw Rule 9-105.
Guardianship proceedings, FamLaw Rule 9-105.
Independent adoptions.
Paternity claim, FL §5-3B-05.
Petition, notice of filing, FL §5-3B-14.
Website for posting notices, 88A §18.
Local department adoptions.
Adoption after termination of parental rights.
Notice of filing of petition, FL §5-346.
Notice of hearing, FL §5-347.
Order for adoption, FL §5-352.
Adoption without prior termination of parental
rights.
Filing of petition, FL §5-333.
Hearing on petition, FL §5-335.
Order of adoption, FL §5-341.
Paternity claim, FL §5-306.
Objections.
Filing notice of objection, FamLaw Rule 9-107.
Private agency adoptions.
Order of adoption, FL §5-3A-36.
Paternity claim, FL §5-3A-06.
Show cause order, FamLaw Rule 9-105.
Objections, FamLaw Rule 9-107.
Orders.
Show cause order, FamLaw Rule 9-105.
Penalties.
Interstate compact on adoption and medical
assistance.
False, misleading or fraudulent claims, FL
§5-4A-06.
Petition, FamLaw Rule 9-103; Juv Rule 11-501.
Guardianship, FamLaw Rule 9-103.
Independent adoptions.
Invalidation of adoption, petition to, FL
§5-3B-26.
Notice of filing, FL §5-3B-14.
Website for posting notices, 88A §18.
Prerequisite for authority to place for adoption,
FL §5-3B-12.
Requirements generally, FL §5-3B-13.
Local department adoptions.
Adoption after termination of parental rights,
FL §5-345.
Hearing on petition, FL §5-347.
Notice of filing of petition, FL §5-346.
Order for adoption.
Petition to invalidate, FL §5-353.
Adoption without prior termination of parental
rights, FL §5-331.
Dismissal of contested petition, FL §5-340.
Hearing on petition, FL §5-335.
Notice of filing of petition, FL §5-333.
Order of adoption.
Petition to invalidate, FL §5-342.
Private agency adoptions.
Hearing on petition, FL §5-3A-32.
Notice of filing, FL §5-3A-30.
Order of adoption.
Petition to invalidate, FL §5-3A-37.
Requirements generally, FL §5-3A-29.

ADOPTION —Cont'd
Post-adoption contact.
Independent adoptions.
   Agreements, FL §5-3B-07.
Local department adoptions.
   Agreements, FL §5-308.
Private agency adoptions.
   Agreements, FL §5-3A-08.
Pretermitted child and issue.
General provisions, ET §§3-301 to 3-303.
   See DECEDENTS' ESTATES.
Private agency adoptions.
Access to adoption records.
   Court and agency records, FL §5-3A-40.
   Emergency medical information, FL §5-3A-41.
   Medical and mental health history, FL
      §5-3A-39.
   Vital statistics and records, FL §5-3A-42.
Access to medical and dental records.
   Adoptive parent, FL §5-3A-43.
Appeal, right to, FL §5-3A-10.
Applicability of subtitle, FL §5-3A-02.
Appointment of attorney for parent and/or child,
   FL §5-3A-07.
Consent.
   Revocation, FL §5-3A-35.
   When required, FL §5-3A-35.
Considerations in ruling on petition, FL §5-3A-34.
Costs and fees, FL §5-3A-09.
Definitions, FL §5-3A-01.
Foreign orders, FL §5-3A-05.
Hearing on petition, FL §5-3A-32.
Legislative findings and purpose, FL §5-3A-03.
Notice of order, FL §5-3A-36.
Order of adoption, FL §5-3A-36.
   Petition to invalidate, FL §5-3A-37.
Paternity determination, FL §5-3A-06.
Petition.
   Notice of filing, FL §5-3A-30.
   Requirements generally, FL §5-3A-29.
Post-adoption contact, agreements, FL §5-3A-08.
Prohibition on payment or compensation for
   services, FL §5-3A-45.
Relation to other provisions, FL §5-3A-04.
Report prior to entry of order, FL §5-3A-31.
Time limitations for entry of order, FL §5-3A-33.
Unmarried or single petitioner.
   Prohibited grounds for denial of petition, FL
      §5-3A-34.
Real property.
Inclusion of adoptees in grants of conveyance, RP
   §2-123.
Records.
Access to birth and adoption records.
   Denial of inspection of adoption records, SG
      §10-616.
   Independent adoptions, FL §§5-3B-28, 5-3B-29.
   Local department adoptions, FL §§5-356 to
      5-360.
   Private agency adoptions, FL §§5-3A-39 to
      5-3A-43.
Clerk to keep, FamLaw Rule 9-112.
Notice of objection.
   Access to records, FamLaw Rule 9-107.
Public records.
   Denial of right to inspect adoption records, SG
      §10-616.
Sealing, FamLaw Rule 9-112.
Religion.
Preference to persons of same religious belief as
   that of child or child's parents, FL §5-520.

ADOPTION —Cont'd
Reports, FamLaw Rule 9-106.
Accounting report, FamLaw Rule 9-110.
Search, contact and reunion services.
   Confidential intermediaries, FL §5-4B-07.
      Failure to locate individual sought, FL
         §5-4B-10.
Reunion services.
Generally, FL §§5-4B-01 to 5-4B-12. See within
   this heading, "Search, contact and reunion
   services."
Rules and regulations.
Search, contact and reunion services, FL
   §5-4B-12.
Sealing records, FamLaw Rule 9-112.
Search, contact and reunion services, FL
   §§5-4B-01 to 5-4B-12.
Application to director of social services
   administration, FL §5-4B-02.
Confidential intermediaries.
   Authorization to obtain information, FL
      §5-4B-06.
   Defined, FL §5-4B-01.
   Lists, FL §5-4B-03.
      Providing to applicants, FL §5-4B-04.
   Qualifications, FL §5-4B-03.
   Reports to director, FL §5-4B-07.
      Failure to locate individual sought, FL
         §5-4B-10.
   Written agreements with, FL §5-4B-05.
Consent.
   Confidential intermediary to obtain written
      consent, FL §5-4B-04.
   Effect of lack of consent, FL §5-4B-09.
Deceased persons.
   Duties of confidential intermediary if individual
      sought is deceased, FL §5-4B-11.
   Report by confidential intermediary, FL
      §5-4B-07.
Definitions, FL §5-4B-01.
Referral of applicant to child placement agency
   that placed child for adoption, FL §5-4B-04.
Rules and regulations, FL §5-4B-12.
Siblings.
   Defined, FL §5-4B-01.
Written agreements with confidential
   intermediaries, FL §5-4B-05.
Show cause order, FamLaw Rule 9-105.
State personnel.
Sick leave use authorized, SPP §§9-501, 9-505.
Statute of limitations.
Charging or receiving compensation in adoption,
   CJ §5-106.
Subsidies, FL §§5-401 to 5-415.
Agreement, FL §5-410.
Appeals.
   Administrative and judicial review, FL §5-411.
Applications, FL §5-409.
   Annual reapplication, FL §5-410.
Appropriations.
   Funding of program, FL §5-407.
Citation of act.
   Short title, FL §5-415.
Commencement of subsidy, FL §5-410.
Definitions, FL §5-401.
Director of social services administration.
   Duties, FL §5-412.
Eligibility, FL §§5-403, 5-408.
Establishment of program, FL §5-406.
Expenses.
   Reimbursement of nonrecurring adoption
      expenses, FL §5-410.1.

ADOPTION —Cont'd
Subsidies —Cont'd
Funding of program, FL §5-407.
Local department.
Establishment of program, FL §5-406.
Purpose of provisions, FL §5-402.
Subsidy agreement, FL §5-410.
Title of act.
Short title, FL §5-415.
Taxation.
Income tax.
Adoption expenses, TG §10-208.
Temporary custody, FamLaw Rule 9-108.
Titling of case, FamLaw Rule 9-112.
Venue.
General provisions, CJ §6-203.
Vital records.
Certificates of birth.
Issuance of new certificates, HG §4-211.
Decree of adoption.
Clerks of court to send report to secretary of
health and mental hygiene, HG §4-211.
Independent adoptions.
Access to adoption records, FL §5-3B-29.
Local department adoptions.
Access to adoption records, FL §5-359.
Private agency adoptions.
Access to adoption records, FL §5-3A-42.
Wills.
Certain terms construed to include adoptees, ET
§4-414.

ADULT DEPENDENT CARE PROGRAMS.
Alcoholic beverages.
Test of potential employees, HG §19-1903.
Appeals.
Criminal history records checks.
Contesting finding of criminal conviction, HG
§19-1908.
Background checks, HG §19-1902.
Defined, HG §19-1901.
Private agency.
Defined, HG §19-1901.
Findings by, HG §19-1906.
Scope of provisions, HG §19-1912.
Confidentiality of information.
Criminal history records checks, HG §19-1907.
Controlled dangerous substances.
Test of potential employees, HG §19-1903.
Criminal history records checks, HG §19-1902.
Background investigation of employees, CJ
§5-619.
Confidentiality of information, HG §19-1907.
Contesting finding of criminal conviction, HG
§19-1908.
Defined, HG §19-1901.
Disclosure statement, HG §19-1905.
Failure to disclose conviction or pending charges,
HG §19-1909.
Fingerprint requirements, HG §19-1904.
Immunity from civil or criminal liability, HG
§19-1910.
Printed statements, HG §19-1907.
Defined, HG §19-1901.
Scope of provisions, HG §19-1912.
Submission of materials by program, HG
§19-1904.
Day-care for the elderly, HG §§14-201 to 14-206.
See DAY-CARE FOR THE ELDERLY.
Definitions, HG §19-1901.

ADULT DEPENDENT CARE PROGRAMS
—Cont'd
Eligible employees.
Alcohol or controlled dangerous substance tests,
HG §19-1903.
Background checks. See within this heading,
"Background checks."
Criminal history record checks. See within this
heading, "Criminal history records checks."
Defined, HG §19-1901.
Disclosure statement, HG §19-1905.
Failure to disclose conviction or pending charges,
HG §19-1909.
Fingerprints, HG §19-1904.
Employment references.
Disclosure of information by employer, HG
§19-1911.
Fingerprinting.
Eligible employees, HG §19-1904.
Home health agencies.
See HOME HEALTH AGENCIES.
Hospices.
See HOSPICES.
Immunity.
Criminal history records checks.
Civil or criminal liability, HG §19-1910.
Presumptions.
Employment references.
Disclosure of information by employer.
Presumption of good faith, HG §19-1911.
Residential service agencies, HG §§19-4A-01 to
19-4A-10.
See RESIDENTIAL SERVICE AGENCIES.
Scope of provisions, HG §19-1912.

ADULT EDUCATION.
Distance learning.
Maryland technology academy, ED §7-1001.
Virtual learning opportunities, ED §7-1002.
Establishment and maintenance of school.
County boards of education, ED §4-110.
Permitting full-time students to register, ED
§4-110.
External high school program, ED §7-205.1.
State aid.
Competitive grants, ED §5-218.
Virtual learning opportunities, ED §7-1002.

ADULTERATION OR MISBRANDING.
Commercial fertilizer law.
General provisions, AG §§6-201 to 6-221.
See FERTILIZERS.
Cosmetics.
See FOOD, DRUGS AND COSMETICS.
Drugs.
See FOOD, DRUGS AND COSMETICS.
Feedstuffs.
General provisions.
See FEEDSTUFFS.
Fertilizers.
Commercial fertilizers.
Generally, AG §§6-201 to 6-221.
See FERTILIZERS.
Food, drugs and cosmetics.
See FOOD, DRUGS AND COSMETICS.
Motor fuel inspection.
Adulteration and commingling of fuels prohibited,
BR §10-323.
Pesticides.
Registration and labeling law.
General provisions, AG §§5-101 to 5-114.
See PESTICIDES.

ADULTERATION OR MISBRANDING —Cont'd
Poultry products inspection.
General provisions.
See POULTRY PRODUCTS INSPECTION.
Wholesome meat act.
General provisions, AG §§4-101 to 4-131.
See WHOLESOME MEAT ACT.

ADULTERY, CR §10-501.
Divorce.
Grounds for absolute divorce, FL §7-103.
Manslaughter.
Adultery not mitigating factor, CR §2-207.

**ADULT EXTERNAL HIGH SCHOOL
   PROGRAM,** ED §7-205.1.

ADULT OFFENDERS SUPERVISION.
Amendment, COR §6-212.
Commission, COR §6-204.
Activities, COR §6-208.
Enforcement and oversight, COR §6-210.
Finance, COR §6-211.
Organization and operation, COR §6-207.
Powers and duties, COR §6-206.
Rulemaking, COR §6-209.
Conflict of laws, COR §6-215.
Construction, COR §6-214.
Definitions, COR §6-203.
Effectiveness, COR §6-212.
Eligibility of states, COR §6-212.
Purpose, COR §6-202.
Severability, COR §6-214.
Short title, COR §6-201.
State council, COR §6-205.
**Withdrawal, default, termination and judicial
   enforcement,** COR §6-213.

ADULT PROTECTIVE SERVICES.
Additional services, FL §14-104.
Arrangement for protective services, FL
   §14-307.
Confidentiality of information.
Review boards.
Records, FL §14-404.
Contracts, FL §14-203.
Definitions, FL §14-101.
Exemptions from title, FL §14-103.
Fees.
Schedule, FL §14-204.
Funding.
Additional funds, FL §14-104.
Generally, FL §14-205.
Guardians.
Contracts to act as guardian, FL §14-203.
Immunity.
Reports of abuse, etc.
Immunity from civil liability, CJ §§5-618, 5-622;
   FL §§14-302, 14-304.
Implementation of program.
Secretary of human resources, FL §14-201.
Intent of legislature, FL §14-102.
Investigations.
Agencies assisting in investigation, FL §14-303.
Completion of investigation, FL §14-303.
Duty of local department after investigation, FL
   §14-305.
Emergencies, FL §14-304.
Providing protective services, FL §14-307.
Reports of abuse, etc.
Confidentiality of persons making report, FL
   §14-308.
Contents of report, FL §14-302.

ADULT PROTECTIVE SERVICES —Cont'd
Investigations —Cont'd
Reports of abuse, etc —Cont'd
Immunity from civil liability, CJ §§5-618, 5-622;
   FL §14-309.
Mandatory reports, FL §14-302.
Scope of investigation, FL §14-303.
Scope of subtitle, FL §14-301.
Sharing information, FL §14-303.
Time of investigation, FL §14-303.
Legislative findings and intent, FL §14-102.
Providing protective services, FL §14-307.
Review boards, FL §§14-401 to 14-404.
Compensation and expense reimbursement, FL
   §14-403.
Established in each county, FL §14-401.
Guardianship review, FL §14-404.
Membership, FL §14-402.
Multicounty boards, FL §14-401.
Staff, office space, FL §14-403.
Scope of program, FL §14-202.
Scope of title, FL §14-103.
Secretary of human resources.
Implementation of program, FL §14-201.

ADULTS.
Age of majority, 1 §24.
Day-care centers.
Adult day-care centers, HG §§24-701 to 24-707.
See DAY-CARE CENTERS.
Medically handicapped adults, HG §§14-301 to
   14-304.
See DAY-CARE CENTERS.
Juvenile causes.
General provisions.
See JUVENILE CAUSES.
Schools.
Establishment and maintenance of school.
By county board of education, ED §4-110.
Permitting full-time students to register, ED
   §4-110.
Transfers to minors act.
Definition of adult, ET §13-301.
Vulnerable adults.
Abuse and neglect, CR §§3-604 to 3-606.
Exploitation of vulnerable adult, CR §8-801.
Domestic violence.
General provisions, FL §§4-501 to 4-516.
See DOMESTIC VIOLENCE.

ADULT SEXUAL DISPLAYS, CR §§11-101 to
   11-107.
See OBSCENITY AND PORNOGRAPHY.

ADVANCE DIRECTIVE REGISTRY, HG §§5-619
   to 5-626.
See HEALTH CARE DECISIONS.

ADVANCE MEDICAL DIRECTIVES, HG §§5-601
   to 5-626.
See HEALTH CARE DECISIONS.

ADVANCEMENTS.
Decedents' estates, ET §3-106.
Life insurance and annuities.
Policy loans, IN §§16-207, 16-208.
Mortgages and deeds of trust.
Priority of future advances, RP §7-102.

ADVERSE POSSESSION.
Limitation of actions.
Entry or action to recover land, CJ §5-103.
Quieting title, RP §14-108.

ADVERSE POSSESSION —Cont'd
Taxation.
   Sales, TP §14-852.

ADVERTISING.
Acupuncturists, HO §1A-306.
Adult sexual display, CR §11-105.
Air conditioning and heating contractors, BR §9A-404.
Alcoholic beverages.
   Furnishing signs, displays or other
      advertisements to retail establishments.
      Exceptions, 2B §12-104.
Appeals.
   Outdoor advertising.
      Rejection of application for permit, TR §8-720.
Aquaculture.
   Oysters and clams.
      Private oyster culture.
         Leases, NR §4-11A-06.
Attorneys at law.
   Communications to prospective clients of purpose
      for obtaining professional employment, BOP
      §§10-605.1, 10-605.2.
   Rules of professional conduct, ProfCond Rule 7.2.
Audiologists and speech-language pathologists.
   Misleading or untruthful advertisements, HO
      §2-314.2.
Bait and switch, CL §14-2903.
Baltimore City.
   Alcoholic beverages.
      Restrictions, 2B §21-105.
Banks and trust companies.
   Unauthorized representation as bank.
      Prohibited, FI §5-806.
   Unfair trade practices, FI §5-807.
Billboards.
   Outdoor advertising.
      See OUTDOOR ADVERTISING.
Blind persons.
   False representation of product, CL §14-2803.
Bond issues.
   Debt, 31 §10.
Bus shelters for bus passengers.
   Display of commercial advertising, TR §8-752.
Campaign finance entities.
   Campaign materials, EL §§13-401 to 13-403.
Cemeteries.
   Unauthorized representations, BR §5-903.
Charities.
   False or misleading material, BR §6-607.
   Promotions for charitable organizations, BR
      §6-618.
      Liability for advertising in violation of title, BR
         §6-621.
Child care.
   Family day care homes.
      Requirements, regulations to provide, FL
         §5-551.
Chiropractors.
   Rules and regulations.
      Adoption by board of chiropractic examiners,
         HO §3-401.
Commercial electronic mail.
   Unauthorized, false or misleading information, CL
      §§14-3001 to 14-3003.
Conservation easements.
   Restricting advertising, RP §2-118.
Consumer loans.
   General provisions, CL §12-304.

ADVERTISING —Cont'd
Consumer protection.
   General provisions, CL §§13-101 to 13-411.
      See CONSUMER PROTECTION.
Counties.
   Chartered counties.
      Powers of county, 25A §5.
   Compensation for removed outdoor advertising
      sign, 25 §122E.
   County commissioners.
      Powers as to, 25 §3.
Credit service businesses, CL §14-1903.1.
Debt management services, FI §12-925.
Dental plan organizations.
   False advertising, IN §14-415.
Dentists.
   Penalties for violations, HO §4-606.
   Requirements generally, HO §4-503.
Drug paraphernalia, CR §5-619.
Drugs. See within this heading, "Food, drugs and
   cosmetics."
Easements.
   Conservation easements.
      Restricting advertising, RP §2-118.
Eggs.
   Shell eggs.
      Use of terms, AG §4-303.
Elections.
   Campaign finance entities.
      Campaign materials, EL §§13-401 to 13-403.
Electrologists, HO §8-6B-23.
Email.
   Commercial electronic mail.
      Unauthorized, false or misleading information,
         CL §§14-3001 to 14-3003.
Employment agencies.
   Requirements, BR §9-304.
Expressways.
   Outdoor advertising along expressways.
      See OUTDOOR ADVERTISING.
False advertising, CL §14-2902.
   Attorney general.
      Civil action by attorney general, CL §11-705.
   Bait and switch, CL §14-2903.
   Compliance with other statutes and regulations,
      CL §11-706.
   Consumer loans, CL §12-304.
   Criminal penalty, CL §14-2902.
   Defenses.
      Compliance with other statutes and regulations,
         CL §11-706.
      Notice and opportunity to present defenses prior
         to commencement of civil action, CL
         §11-705.
   Definitions, CL §§11-701, 14-2901.
   Dental plan organizations, IN §14-415.
   Determination whether advertisement misleading,
      CL §11-704.
   Email.
      Commercial electronic mail.
         Unauthorized, false or misleading
            information, CL §§14-3001 to 14-3003.
   Fines.
      Civil penalty, CL §11-705.
   Food, drugs and cosmetics. See within this
      heading, "Food, drugs and cosmetics."
   Ground rent not stated, CL §14-2902.
   In conduct of business or trade, CL §11-703.
      Application of section to certain advertising
         media, CL §11-702.

ADVERTISING —Cont'd
False advertising —Cont'd
Insurance, IN §27-203.
Dental plan organizations, IN §14-415.
Unauthorized insurers false advertising process act, IN §§27-701 to 27-706.
Kosher food.
See KOSHER FOOD.
Misleading.
Determination whether advertisement misleading, CL §11-704.
Penalty.
Civil penalty, CL §11-705.
Prohibited.
In conduct of business or trade, CL §11-703.
Property or services not possessed or controlled by advertiser, CL §14-2902.
Repossessed, rebuilt, reconditioned or secondhand property.
Sale of unidentified property, CL §14-2902.
Rights of parties in private litigation not affected, CL §11-707.
Vessel registry omitted, CL §14-2902.
Family day care homes.
Requirements, regulations to provide, FL §5-551.
Fax machines.
Unsolicited transmissions.
Prohibited, CL §14-1313.
Finance companies.
Installment sales.
Regulations, CL §12-602.
Fireworks.
Display or discharge of fireworks, PS §10-108.
Flags.
Placing advertisement on flag, displaying flag with advertisement, CR §10-703.
Food, drugs and cosmetics.
Defined, HG §21-101.
False advertising, HG §21-247.
Liability of persons in business of disseminating advertisements, HG §21-260.
Particular representations regarding drugs and devices considered false advertisements, HG §21-248.
Kosher foods.
See KOSHER FOOD.
Misleading labeling and advertising, HG §21-102.
Surimi products.
Food service establishments.
Notice requirements, HG §21-329.
Forests and parks.
Roadside trees.
Placing on trees, fences, buildings, etc., without permission, NR §5-407.
Franchise offerings, BR §14-225.
Gas and oil.
Used oil recycling act.
Informing general public of prohibitions, EN §5-1001.
General services department.
State leasing of real property.
Need to rent building space.
Duty to advertise, SF §4-320.
Ground rent.
Advertising sale without disclosing, CL §14-2902.
Health maintenance organizations, HG §19-724.
Highways.
Outdoor advertising.
See OUTDOOR ADVERTISING.
Homebuilders, registration number, BR §4.5-503.

ADVERTISING —Cont'd
Home improvements.
False, deceptive or misleading advertising, BR §8-610.
Inducements.
Tangible items for advertising, BR §8-503.
License number requirement, BR §8-615.
Industrial and commercial areas, TR §8-728.
Fines.
Violations, TR §8-749.
Flashing or moving lights.
Federal-aid primary highways, TR §8-733.
Harford county.
Prohibited acts, 25 §122D.
Hearings.
Public hearing on rule or regulation, TR §8-705.
Information to appear on sign, TR §8-721.
Interstate highways.
Removal of sign adjacent to.
Compensation, TR §8-745.
Licenses, TR §§8-708 to 8-711.
Bonds, surety.
Nonresident licensees, TR §8-747.
Signs for which permit may not be issued, TR §8-716.
Lighting of signs.
Federal-aid primary highways, TR §8-733.
Municipal corporations.
Compensation for removed outdoor advertising sign, 25 §122E.
Nonconforming signs.
Federal-aid primary highways, TR §§8-734, 8-735.
Nonresidents.
Bond for nonresident licensees and permit holders, TR §8-747.
Penalties.
Violations, TR §8-748.
Permits, TR §§8-714 to 8-721.
Bonds, surety.
Nonresident permit holders, TR §8-747.
Removal.
Compensation for removed outdoor advertising sign.
Counties and municipalities, 25 §122E.
Rules and regulations, TR §8-705.
School bus shelter signs, TR §8-703.
Scope of subtitle, TR §8-702.
Signs existing on June 1, 1931, TR §8-722.
Traffic devices.
Erection or maintenance not prohibited, TR §8-702.
Federal-aid primary highways.
Interference with traffic devices, TR §8-733.
Violations, TR §8-748.
Insurance.
Dental plan organizations.
False advertising, IN §14-415.
False advertising, IN §27-203.
Dental plan organizations, IN §14-415.
Unauthorized insurers false advertising process act, IN §§27-701 to 27-706.
Long-term care insurance, IN §18-103.
Medicare supplement insurance, IN §§15-923 to 15-925.
Solicitations in other states, IN §3-128.
Unauthorized insurers, IN §4-204.
False advertising process act, IN §§27-701 to 27-706.
Judicial sales.
Public sale, PropSales Rule 14-303.

ADVERTISING —Cont'd

Kosher products.
See KOSHER FOOD.

Long-term care insurance, IN §18-103.

Maryland health insurance plan.
Senior prescription drug assistance program.
Outreach and promotional materials, IN
§14-515.

Massage therapists.
Prohibited acts, HO §3-5A-11.

Medicare supplement insurance, IN §§15-923 to
15-925.

Mortgages and deeds of trust.
Secondary mortgage loans.
False or misleading advertising matter, CL
§12-403.

Motor clubs.
Limitations on advertising, IN §26-401.

Motor fuel inspection.
Dispensing equipment signs, BR §10-315.
Games of chance.
Prohibition for refiners and other suppliers, BR
§10-502.

Motor vehicles.
Dealers.
Prohibited acts by licensees, TR §15-313.
Dismantlers, recyclers and scrap processors.
License requirements, TR §15-502.
License plate cover, TR §13-411.1.
Manufacturers, distributors and factory branches.
Deceptive advertising by licensees prohibited,
TR §15-210.
Signs, signals, markings or devices.
Commercial advertising prohibited, TR §21-205.

Municipal corporations.
Compensation for removed outdoor advertising
sign, 25 §122E.
Power to provide, 23A §2.

Obscenity and pornography.
Adult sexual display for advertising purposes, CR
§11-105.
Obscene matter, CR §11-205.

Optometrists.
Licenses.
False or misleading advertising as grounds for
disciplinary actions, HO §11-313.

Outdoor advertising.
See OUTDOOR ADVERTISING.

Oysters and clams.
Private oyster culture.
Leases, NR §4-11A-06.

Physicians.
Acupuncture, HO §14-504.
Medical review committee, HO §14-503.

Plumbers.
Contents of advertisements, BOP §12-504.

Publication.
See PUBLICATION.

Public debt.
Bond issues, 31 §10.

Radio and television.
Used, reconditioned, etc., television or radio sets.
Restrictions as to sale and advertisement, CL
§14-802.
Definitions, CL §14-801.
Penalties, CL §14-803.

Real estate brokers.
Advertisements on property showing cost and
capitalization of ground rent, BOP §17-606.

Real estate conservation areas.
Suspension of advertising and solicitation, BOP
§17-522.
Violation of order, BOP §17-611.

ADVERTISING —Cont'd

Registered rehabilitation practitioners, LE
§9-6A-19.

Rental-purchase agreements, CL §12-1109.
Definition of advertisement, CL §12-1101.

Respiratory care practitioners.
Misrepresentation, HO §14-5A-21.

Rules of professional conduct, ProfCond Rule
7.2.

Sales.
Installment sales, CL §12-602.

Sales tax.
Powers of political subdivisions, 24 §9-201.

Sanitary commissions.
Construction of facilities, EN §9-655.

Savings and loan associations.
Misleading advertising, FI §9-905.

**School building, improvement, supplies or
equipment costs.**
Bids, ED §5-112.

Seafood.
Surimi products, HG §21-329.

Secondary mortgage loan law.
False or misleading advertising matter, CL
§12-403.

Securities act.
Filing of sales and advertising literature, CA
§11-205.
Misleading filing, CA §11-303.

Security systems.
Statement of shorter law enforcement response
time, CL §14-1314.

Security systems technicians.
False advertising.
Grounds for disciplinary action, BOP §18-309.

Start-up business ventures.
Disclosure statement or other documents.
Reference to compliance, BR §14-124.
Use of commercial symbol, BR §14-123.

State lottery, SG §9-111.

Surimi products.
Requirements, HG §21-329.

Taxation.
Gross receipts tax.
Exemption from tax by political subdivisions, 24
§9-202.
Sale.
General provisions, TP §14-813.

Time-sharing, RP §11A-119.

**Tourist or traveler's guide for information
services.**
Regulations, BR §19-101.

Turf grass law.
Definitions of advertisements, AG §9-101.
Prohibited acts and practices, AG §9-107.

Venereal disease cure, CR §10-102.

Vessels and boats.
Registry number omitted.
False or fraudulent advertising, CL §14-2902.
Rules and regulations, NR §8-704.

Veterinarians, AG §2-313.

Watches.
Secondhand watches, CL §14-705.

Weights and measures.
Price of packaged commodity, AG §11-306.

Work-at-home advertisements, CL §13-314.

Zoning.
Expressways.
On premise outdoor signs.
Local zoning, TR §8-744.

ADVERTISING —Cont'd
Zoning —Cont'd
Outdoor advertising along federal-aid primary highways.
Local zoning regulations, TR §8-736.

ADVISERS ON INSURANCE, IN §§10-201 to 10-215.
See INSURANCE.

ADVISORY COUNCIL ON MEDICAL PRIVACY AND CONFIDENTIALITY, HG §§4-3A-01 to 4-3A-05.

AED PROGRAM, ED §13-517.
County boards of education to develop and implement programs, ED §7-425.

AERONAUTICS.
Aviation.
See AVIATION.

AFDC.
Family investment program generally, 88A §§44A to 56.
See FAMILY INVESTMENT PROGRAM.

AFFIDAVITS.
Absentee voting.
Agent's affidavit when used to pick up and deliver ballot, EL §9-307.
Actions.
Assignments.
In suits by assignee against obligor on sealed instruments, CL §15-402.
Adoption.
Mutual consent voluntary adoption registry.
Registration requirements, FL §5-4C-06.
Alcoholic beverages.
False statements.
Perjury, 2B §16-501.
Appeals.
Dismissal of appeal.
Motion to dismiss, AppRev Rule 8-603.
Injunction pending appeal.
Affidavit to accompany motion, AppRev Rule 8-425.
Motions.
Requirement that affidavit accompany or support motion, AppRev Rule 8-431.
Appropriations.
Warrants.
Issuance of warrants to institutions and corporations, SF §7-221.
Assignments.
Interest.
Paid or to be paid, CL §15-304.
Change of name.
Opposition.
Service, SpecPro Rule 15-901.
Support.
Service, SpecPro Rule 15-901.
Child custody proceedings.
Information provided as to child.
First pleadings, FL §9.5-209.
Child support.
Affidavit of support, FL §§10-1A-01 to 10-1A-03.
Clerks of court.
Photostatting and microfilming.
When instruments not readily subject to, RP §3-104.
Continuing care contracts.
Claims against impaired providers, 70B §20Q.

AFFIDAVITS —Cont'd
Corporations.
Mortgages and deeds of trust.
Consideration true and bona fide, RP §4-106.
Counterfeiting of prescription.
Authorized provider's affidavit, evidence, CR §5-705.
Credit cardholders, criminal cases or juvenile proceedings, CR §8-214.1.
Default.
Property damage.
District Court, CivProDist Rule 3-509.
Definitions, Rule 1-202.
Disqualification of judge.
District Court, CivProDist Rule 3-505.
Elections.
Absentee voting.
Agent's affidavit when used to pick up and deliver ballot, EL §9-307.
Emergency management.
Civil relief during emergency periods.
False affidavits prohibited, PS §14-218.
Executors and administrators.
Mortgages and deeds of trust.
Where mortgagee or party secured by deed of trust.
Consideration true and bona fide, RP §4-106.
Firearms.
Applications for purchases, rents or transfers, PS §5-118.
Dealers' licenses.
Applications, PS §5-107.
Forms, Rule 1-304.
Fraternal benefit societies.
Consolidations and mergers, IN §8-438.
Indian affairs commission.
Recognition process, 41 §6-910.
Insurance.
Life insurance and annuities.
Payments of proceeds without letters of administration, IN §16-110.
Liquidation, rehabilitation, etc., of insurers.
Claims against the insurer, IN §9-226.
Reciprocal insurance.
Attorney in fact, IN §3-211.
Surplus lines insurance, IN §3-307.
Judgment on affidavit.
Pleading.
District Court, CivProDist Rule 3-306.
Judicial sales.
Ratification of sale.
Purchaser's affidavit, PropSales Rule 14-305.
Kinship care relationship.
Consent to medical care for minor, HG §20-105.
Life insurance and annuities.
Payments of proceeds without letters of administration, IN §16-110.
Marriage licenses.
Parties not residents of county.
Affidavit in lieu of application, FL §2-402.
Mechanics' liens.
Affidavit or verified answer.
Failure to file deemed admission, PropAct Rule 12-304.
Mortgages and deeds of trust.
Affidavit by mortgagee or party secured by deed of trust.
Consideration true and bona fide, RP §4-106.
Forms.
Affidavit of release, RP §4-203.

AFFIDAVITS —Cont'd
Mortgages and deeds of trust —Cont'd
Purchase-money mortgage or deed of trust, RP §4-106.
Motions.
Circuit courts, CivProCir Rule 2-311.
Paternity proceedings.
Affidavit of parentage, FL §5-1028.
Pleadings.
Judgment on affidavit.
District Court, CivProDist Rule 3-306.
Postmortem examiners.
Power of medical examiner to take affidavit, HG §5-312.
Power of attorney.
Proof of nonrevocation, ET §13-602.
Prescriptions, counterfeiting.
Authorized provider's affidavit, evidence, CR §5-705.
Schools.
Admission of students in kinship care, ED §7-101.
Prince George's county.
Residency of pupils.
Affidavits of disclosure required, ED §7-102.
Searches and seizures.
Warrants.
Retention of application and affidavits, Crim Rule 4-601.
Search warrants.
In support of warrant, required, sealing, CP §1-203.
State lottery.
Assignment of prizes, information required, SG §9-122.
State's attorneys.
Accounts for services and expenses, 10 §39.
Summary judgment, CivProCir Rule 2-501.
Support and maintenance.
Child support.
Affidavit of support, FL §§10-1A-01 to 10-1A-03.
Surplus lines insurance, IN §3-307.
Taxation.
Foreclosure of right of redemption.
Unknown owner made party.
Affidavit of search, TP §14-838.
Oaths.
Oath or affirmation by affidavit, TP §1-201.
Verification that dwelling is principal residence, TP §2-218.
Traders licenses.
Display of exhibitor's affidavit, BR §17-1814.
Warrants for payment of money.
Appropriations.
Warrants for disbursement of appropriation to institution or corporation.
Issuance, SF §7-221.
Wet settlements.
Consideration and disbursement, RP §4-106.

AFFIRMATION, Evid Rule 5-603.
Definitions, 1 §9.
Oaths.
See OATHS.

AFFORDABLE HOUSING TRUST, HS §§10-101 to 10-301.
See MARYLAND AFFORDABLE HOUSING TRUST.

AFGHANISTAN CONFLICT.
Veterans' scholarships, ED §18-604.

AFRICAN AMERICAN HISTORY AND CULTURE COMMISSION, SF §§5A-201 to 5A-208.
Banneker-Douglass museum.
Operation, SF §5A-207.
Chair and vice chair, SF §5A-204.
Commission defined, SF §5A-201.
Composition, SF §5A-203.
Director, SF §5A-206.
Established, SF §5A-202.
Ethnic affairs unit, SF §§2-701, 2-702.
Historical and cultural programs division.
Units in division, SF §5A-102.
Martin Luther King, Jr. birthday.
Planning annual observation, SF §5A-207.
Meetings, SF §5A-205.
Membership, SF §5A-203.
Compensation, SF §5A-205.
Powers and duties, SF §5A-207.
Reports.
Annual report, SF §5A-207.
Revenue.
Sources, uses and audit, SF §5A-208.

AFRICAN AMERICAN MUSEUM CORPORATION, SG §§9-2601 to 9-2614.
Audits, SG §9-2610.
Board of directors, SG §9-2603.
Budget, SG §9-2609.
Citation of act, SG §9-2614.
Construction and interpretation.
Liberal construction of provisions, SG §9-2613.
Definitions, SG §9-2601.
Earnings, SG §9-2607.
Established, SG §9-2602.
Executive director, SG §9-2604.
Exemptions, SG §9-2612.
Tax exemptions, SG §9-2608.
Finances, SG §9-2610.
Investments, SG §9-2610.
Liabilities, SG §9-2611.
Officers, SG §9-2604.
Personnel, SG §9-2604.
Powers, SG §9-2605.
Preliminary museum plans, SG §9-2612.
Purpose, SG §9-2602.
Real property taxes.
Subject to, SG §9-2608.
Reports.
Annual financial report, SG §9-2610.
Annual report, SG §9-2606.
Status, SG §9-2602.
Strategic plan, SG §9-2606.
Tax exemptions, SG §9-2608.
Title of act, SG §9-2614.

AFRICAN-AMERICANS.
Health care disparities in minority populations.
Office of minority health and health disparities, HG §§20-1001 to 20-1007.
Office of minority affairs, SG §§9-301 to 9-306.
Racial minorities generally.
See RACIAL MINORITIES.
Schools.
Textbooks.
Purchase of books and other materials concerning black history, ED §7-106.
Universities and colleges.
Desegregation and equal educational opportunities.
Program development for historically black colleges and universities, ED §11-105.

AFRICAN-AMERICANS —Cont'd
Universities and colleges —Cont'd
Funding academic programs at historically black colleges and universities, ED §10-203.
University of Maryland.
Overall plan.
Development, review, etc., for historically black institutions, ED §12-106.

AFRICAN DEVELOPMENT BANK.
Investments.
Obligations issued or guaranteed by bank.
Lawful investments, ET §15-106.

AFTER-ACQUIRED PROPERTY.
Secured transactions.
Security interest in after-acquired property, CL §9-204.

AFTER-BORN CHILDREN.
Intestate succession, ET §3-107.
Statutory share of pretermitted child and issue, ET §§3-301 to 3-303.
See DECEDENTS' ESTATES.

AFTERMARKET CRASH PARTS, CL §§14-2301 to 14-2304.
Motor vehicle insurance.
Copy of warranty, IN §27-906.

AFTER-SCHOOL OPPORTUNITY FUND PROGRAM, ED §§7-1201 to 7-1207.
Administration of fund, ED §7-1204.
Advisory board, ED §7-1203.
Recommendations, ED §7-1204.
Creation, ED §7-1202.
Definitions, ED §7-1201.
Executive committee.
Duties, ED §7-1202.
Comprehensive plan, ED §7-1204.
Regulations, ED §7-1206.
Reports, ED §7-1205.
Reports.
Executive committee, ED §7-1205.
Rules and regulations.
Executive committee, ED §7-1206.
Short title of act, ED §7-1207.

AGE.
Accountants.
Licenses.
Applicants, BOP §2-302.
Adult.
Defined, 1 §24.
Alcoholic beverages.
Purchaser's age.
Citation for violations, CR §10-119.
False documentation, CR §10-115.
Jurisdiction, CR §10-120.
Misrepresentation of age, CR §10-113.
Record of documentary proof, 2B §12-109.
Retail sales, 2B §12-302.
Annuity contracts.
Misstatement of age, IN §16-405.
Assisted living programs board, SG §9-1901.
Attorneys at law.
Admission to the bar.
Qualifications of applicants, BOP §10-207.
Cemeteries.
Registration.
Qualifications, BR §5-302.
Commercial drivers' licenses, TR §16-817.
Computation generally, 1 §37.

AGE —Cont'd
Congress.
Representative in congress, US Const Art I §2.
Senator, US Const Art I §3.
Cosmetologists.
Licenses.
Qualifications of applicants, BOP §§5-304, 5-305.
Drivers' licenses. See within this heading, "Motor vehicles."
Elections.
Right to vote, US Const Amd 26.
Voters.
Requirements, MD Const Art I §1.
Equal credit opportunity, CL §§12-701 to 12-708.
See EQUAL CREDIT OPPORTUNITY.
Fish and fisheries.
Angler's license.
Exemptions, NR §4-604.
Special trout stamp.
Exemptions, NR §4-614.
General assembly.
Senators and delegates, MD Const Art III §9.
Governor, MD Const Art II §5.
Insurance.
Health insurance, IN §§15-204, 15-220.
Long-term care insurance.
Premium increases, IN §18-116.
Misstatement of age.
Annuity contracts, IN §16-405.
Group life insurance, IN §17-306.
Health insurance, IN §§15-204, 15-220.
Life insurance, IN §16-205.
Pure endowment contracts, IN §16-405.
Motor vehicle insurance.
Cancellation, nonrenewal or increase in premium based on age, IN §27-902.
Standard nonforfeiture law for life insurance.
Age at expiry for joint term life insurance policy, IN §16-301.
Interior designers.
Certificates.
Qualifications of applicants, BOP §8-302.
Judges, MD Const Art IV §2.
Retirement age, MD Const Art IV §3.
Landscape architects.
Licenses.
Qualifications of applicants, BOP §9-302.
Legal age.
Meaning of, 1 §24.
Lieutenant governor, MD Const Art II §5.
Long-term care insurance.
Increases to premiums based on age, IN §18-116.
Minors.
Meaning of, 1 §24.
Motor vehicles.
Commercial drivers' licenses, TR §16-817.
Drivers' licenses.
Learner's permit, TR §16-103.
Proof of age, TR §16-106.
Requirements, TR §16-103.
What persons shall not be licensed, TR §16-103.1.
Oysters and clams.
Licenses.
Commercial licenses.
Exemptions from fee requirement, NR §4-1004.
Population estimates, HG §4-218.
President of the United States, US Const Art II §1.

AGE —Cont'd
Private detectives.
Licenses.
Qualifications of applicants, BOP §13-302.
Pure endowment contracts.
Misstatement of age, IN §16-405.
Real estate brokers.
Licenses.
Qualifications of applicants, BOP §17-305.
Real estate salesperson license, BOP §17-303.
Schools.
Deaf and blind children, ED §8-301.
High school certificates or diplomas, ED §7-206.
Pupils.
Admission of pupils, ED §7-101.
Sheriffs, MD Const Art IV §44.
Vice-president, US Const Amd 12.
Voter registration qualifications, EL §3-102.
Wills.
Who may make a will, ET §4-101.

AGED.
Application for assistance.
False or fraudulent statements.
Punishable as perjury, 88A §62.
Written and signed, 88A §62.
Assisted living programs.
Secretary's powers, 70B §4.
Assisted living programs board, SG §9-1901.
Commission on aging, 70B §3.
Community colleges.
Waiver of tuition for senior citizens, ED §16-106.
Community home care services, 88A §§84 to 87.
See COMMUNITY HOME CARE SERVICES.
Congregate housing services.
Defined, 70B §1.
Secretary's powers, 70B §4.
Violations of provisions, 70B §4I.
Continuing care contracts, 70B §§7 to 23.
See CONTINUING CARE CONTRACTS.
Day-care for the elderly, HG §§14-201 to 14-206.
See DAY-CARE FOR THE ELDERLY.
Department of aging.
Commission on aging, 70B §3.
Established, 70B §2.
Financial review committee.
Immunity from liability, CJ §5-514.
Long-term care ombudsman program, 70B §5.
Maryland senior ride demonstration program.
Consultation with mass transportation
administration, TR §7-1004.
Nursing homes.
Delegating authority to secretary of local
department of aging, 70B §5.
Unclaimed deceased resident.
Procedure upon death, 70B §5A.
Secretary of aging.
Guardianship advisory board.
Immunity from civil liability, CJ §5-515.
Powers, 70B §4.
Senior citizen activities centers.
Capital improvement grants program, 70B §§26
to 32.
See SENIOR CITIZEN ACTIVITIES
CENTERS.
Elections.
Polling place inaccessible to elderly voters.
Alternative assigned, issuance of absentee
ballot, EL §10-102.
Family caregiver assistance program.
Grants to family caregivers.
Assistance in caring for individual with
long-term care needs, 70B §45.

AGED —Cont'd
Fish and fisheries.
Licenses.
Consolidated senior sport fishing licenses, NR
§4-216.
Forests and parks.
Admission.
Persons possessing Maryland golden age pass,
NR §5-1009.
Guardian and ward.
General provisions, ET §§13-101 to 13-222.
See GUARDIAN AND WARD.
Guardianship advisory board.
Immunity from civil liability, CJ §5-515.
Health insurance coverage for elderly care, IN
§15-801.
Income tax.
Exemptions, TG §10-211.
Subtractions from federal adjusted gross income,
TG §10-209.
Innovations in aging services program, 70B
§36.
Interagency committee on aging services.
Chairman, 70B §4B.
Duties, 70B §4C.
Established, 70B §4A.
Executive department.
Agency part of department, 70B §4A.
Membership, 70B §4B.
Powers, 70B §4C.
Reports.
Annual report to general assembly, 70B §4D.
Single points of entry program.
Availability, 70B §4F.
Established, 70B §4E.
Location of single point of entry, 70B §4F.
Personnel, 70B §4F.
Services provided, 70B §4E.
Supervision, 70B §4E.
Telephone information and referral service, 70B
§4G.
Staff, 70B §4B.
Terms, 70B §4B.
Long-term care insurance, IN §§18-101 to
18-120.
See LONG-TERM CARE INSURANCE.
Long-term care ombudsman program, 70B §5.
Maryland health insurance plan.
Senior prescription drug assistance program.
Notice of eligibility requirements, IN §14-515.
Maryland senior ride demonstration program,
TR §§7-1001 to 7-1005.
Award of grants, TR §§7-1002, 7-1003.
Consultation with department of aging, TR
§7-1004.
Definitions, TR §7-1001.
Eligibility, TR §7-1002.
Establishment, TR §7-1002.
Matching funds, TR §7-1002.
Reporting requirements, TR §7-1005.
Rulemaking authority, TR §7-1004.
Solicitation of grant applications, TR §7-1003.
Morgan State University.
Tuition.
Waiver of tuition for senior citizens, ED
§14-107.
Motor vehicle emissions inspection.
Exemptions from mandatory inspection for elderly
drivers, TR §23-206.2.
Motor vehicle insurance.
Cancellation, nonrenewal or premium increase
based on age, IN §27-902.

AGED —Cont'd
Nursing homes.
General provisions.
See HOSPITALS.
Unclaimed deceased resident.
Procedure upon death, 70B §5A.
Perjury.
False or fraudulent statements punishable as
perjury, 88A §62.
Pets in rental housing, RP §8-214.
Poisons.
Packaging for elderly or handicapped individuals,
HG §22-310.
Property taxes.
See PROPERTY TAXES.
Public assistance program.
General provisions.
See SOCIAL SERVICES.
St. Mary's College of Maryland.
Tuition.
Waiver for senior citizens, ED §14-406.
Criteria for granting waiver, ED §14-406.
School buses.
Use for transporting elderly, ED §7-803.
Secretary of aging. See within this heading,
"Department of aging."
**Security deposits by gas companies, electric
companies and telephone companies.**
Exempting dwelling units of elderly subscribers
from cash deposit requirement, PUC §5-105.
Senior citizen activities centers.
Capital improvement grants program, 70B §§26 to
32.
See SENIOR CITIZEN ACTIVITIES CENTERS.
Operating fund, 70B §§33 to 35.
Senior housing managers training program,
70B §25.
Senior ride demonstration program, TR
§§7-1001 to 7-1005.
Services system, 70B §4H.
Sheltered housing for elderly.
Area agency on aging.
Defined, 70B §1.
Interagency committee on aging services.
Defined, 70B §1.
Operation as single-family dwelling.
Civil penalties for violations, 70B §4I.
Planning and service area.
Defined, 70B §1.
State personnel management system.
Person 70 years of age or older, appointment to,
70B §4.
Transportation department.
Funding of services for elderly persons, TR
§2-103.3.
Maryland senior ride demonstration program, TR
§§7-1001 to 7-1005.
University of Maryland.
Tuition.
Waiver for senior citizens, ED §13-701.

AGENCY.
Absentee voting.
Agent used to pick up and deliver ballot, EL
§9-307.
Agriculture.
Consignees of agricultural products.
See CONSIGNMENT.
Assumed business name.
Trade names generally, CA §1-406.

AGENCY —Cont'd
Athletics.
Athlete agents, BR §§4-401 to 4-421.
See ATHLETE AGENTS.
Banks and trust companies.
Commercial banks.
Power to act as agent of depository institution
affiliate, FI §3-206.
Business trusts.
Principal office and resident agent, CA §12-203.
Collection agencies, BR §§7-101 to 7-502.
See COLLECTION AGENCIES.
Collective bargaining.
Injunctions.
Civil and criminal liability for acts of agents,
LE §4-321.
Commercial code.
Applicability of law of principal and agent, CL
§1-103.
Representative defined, CL §1-201.
Compensation.
Extra compensation to public officer, agent or
contractor, MD Const Art III §35.
Condominiums.
Resident agent, RP §11-119.
Consigned goods.
General provisions.
See CONSIGNMENT.
Corporations.
Acknowledgments.
By appointed attorney, CA §1-303.
Debt management services.
License application.
Fingerprints and background check, FI §12-909.
Deeds.
Execution by agent or attorney, RP §4-107.
Education.
Education coordinating committee.
See EDUCATION.
Elections.
Absentee voting.
Agent used to pick up and deliver ballot, EL
§9-307.
Eminent domain.
Real property acquisition policies.
See EMINENT DOMAIN.
Employment agencies, BR §§9-101 to 9-501.
See EMPLOYMENT AGENCIES.
Factors.
See FACTORS.
Fictitious business name.
Trade names generally, CA §1-406.
Fiduciaries.
General provisions, ET §§15-201 to 15-211.
See FIDUCIARIES.
Food, drugs and cosmetics.
Employees.
Imputation of act or omission, HG §21-205.
Hospitals.
Rights of individuals.
Applicant's agent, HG §19-344.
Hunting licenses and stamps.
Sale by persons in retail business as agent of
department, NR §10-302.
Income tax.
Return by person on behalf of individual, TG
§10-808.
Insurance agents and brokers.
Generally.
See INSURANCE AGENTS AND BROKERS.

AGENCY —Cont'd
Insurance agents and brokers —Cont'd
Reinsurance intermediaries, IN §§8-501 to 8-520.
See INSURANCE.
Surplus lines brokers, IN §§3-301 to 3-327.
See SURPLUS LINES INSURANCE.
Investment securities.
Effect of signature of transfer agent, CL §8-208.
Jurisdiction.
Over persons outside this state.
General provisions.
See JURISDICTION.
Limited liability companies.
Members as agent of company, CA §4A-401.
Limited liability partnerships, revised act.
Resident agent, CA §9A-1005.
Limited partnerships.
Resident agent, CA §10-104.
Lobbying.
General provisions.
See PUBLIC ETHICS.
Lottery.
State lottery.
See STATE LOTTERY.
Mining.
Foreman or superintendent agent of operator, EN §15-402.
Mortgages and deeds of trust.
Affidavit by mortgagee or party secured by deed of trust.
Consideration true and bona fide, RP §4-106.
Delivery of net proceeds, RP §4-106.
Powers.
Person taking title to property in representative or fiduciary capacity, RP §14-112.
Proceeds.
Delivery of net proceeds, RP §4-106.
Operating agreements.
Hotels and retirement communities.
Conflict between agreement and law of principal and agent, CL §23-102.
Partnerships.
Limited partnerships.
Resident agent, CA §10-104.
Partnerships, revised act.
Limited liability partnerships.
Resident agent, CA §9A-1005.
Partner agent of partnership, CA §9A-301.
Purported partner as agent, CA §9A-308.
Real estate brokers.
Securities act.
General provisions, CA §§11-401 to 11-417.
See SECURITIES.
Registration.
Broker-dealers and agents.
Securities act.
General provisions, CA §§11-401 to 11-417.
Reinsurance intermediaries, IN §§8-501 to 8-520.
See INSURANCE.
Sports agents, BR §§4-401 to 4-421.
See ATHLETE AGENTS.
State departments and agencies.
See STATE DEPARTMENTS AND AGENCIES.
Trade names.
Certificates.
Filing requirements, CA §1-406.
Trust companies.
Power to act as agent of depository institution affiliate, FI §3-206.
Universities and colleges.
Athlete agents, BR §§4-401 to 4-421.
See ATHLETE AGENTS.

AGENCY —Cont'd
Wholesale sales representatives.
Generally, LE §§3-601 to 3-607.
See LABOR AND EMPLOYMENT RELATIONS.

AGE OF MAJORITY, 1 §24.

AGGRAVATED CRUELTY TO ANIMALS, CR §10-606.
Cockfight, CR §10-608.
Dogfight.
Arranging, conducting or using dog in, CR §10-607.

AGGRAVATING CIRCUMSTANCES.
Death penalty, CR §2-303.
Evidence admissible, CR §2-303.
Jury not finding beyond a reasonable doubt.
Conclusion in writing, death sentence not imposed, CR §2-303.
Jury to consider, CR §2-303.
Whether mitigating circumstances outweighed.
Preponderance of evidence, CR §2-303.

AGGRESSIVE DRIVING, TR §21-901.2.

AGRICULTURAL AND RESOURCE-BASED INDUSTRY DEVELOPMENT CORPORATION, 41 §§13-501 to 13-515.
Agricultural land preservation foundation.
Grants to corporation, AG §2-505.
Agricultural loans, 41 §13-509.
Defined, 41 §13-501.
Annual report, 41 §13-512.
Appropriation, funding by, 41 §13-513.
Attorney general.
Legal advisor to corporation, 41 §13-506.
Audit of books and records, 41 §13-511.
Board of directors.
Chair, 41 §13-504.
Compensation, 41 §13-504.
Composition, 41 §13-504.
Established, 41 §13-504.
Expenses, 41 §13-504.
Qualifications, 41 §13-504.
Quorum, 41 §13-504.
Removal, 41 §13-504.
Terms, 41 §13-504.
Bonds.
Defined, 41 §13-501.
Refunding bonds, 41 §13-510.
Revenue bonds, 41 §13-510.
Debts, claims and obligations of corporation, 41 §13-514.
Definitions, 41 §13-501.
Established, 41 §13-503.
Executive director, 41 §13-505.
Exemption from certain laws, 41 §13-513.
Findings of general assembly, 41 §13-502.
Funding, 41 §13-513.
Interaction with other governmental units and entities, 41 §13-513.
Liberal construction of subtitle, 41 §13-515.
Powers, 41 §§13-507, 13-508.
Procurement law exemption, 41 §13-513.
Public corporation and instrumentality of state, 41 §13-503.
Public ethics act.
Applicability to corporation, board and employees, 41 §13-513.
Public information act.
Applicability to corporation, board and employees, 41 §13-513.

AGRICULTURAL AND RESOURCE-BASED INDUSTRY DEVELOPMENT CORPORATION —Cont'd
Purposes, 41 §§13-502, 13-503.
Support from governmental units, 41 §13-513.
Tax exemption, 41 §13-513.

AGRICULTURAL COOPERATIVES.
Acknowledgments.
Articles of incorporation, CA §5-505.
Actions.
Power to sue and be sued, CA §5-504.
Agricultural marketing associations.
Discrimination, etc., against producers, AG §§10-201 to 10-204.
Applicability of general corporation law, CA §5-531.
Articles of incorporation. See within this heading, "Incorporation."
Assets.
Transfer of assets, CA §5-527.
Audits.
Raw agricultural products.
Financial statement of cooperative handling, CA §5-529.
Bylaws.
Adoption, CA §5-511.
Election provisions, CA §5-514.
Kept at principal office of association, CA §5-511.
Patronage distribution, CA §5-525.
Conflicts of interest.
Directors, CA §5-516.
Consolidation or merger.
General provisions, CA §5-527.
Contracts.
Liquidated damages.
Contracts with members, CA §5-522.
Other cooperatives.
With other cooperatives for carrying on business, CA §5-524.
Power to contract, CA §5-504.
Renewal, CA §5-522.
Specific performance.
Contracts with members, CA §5-522.
Using same methods as other cooperatives, CA §5-524.
With members, CA §5-522.
Conversion.
Corporations converted into cooperatives, CA §5-507.
Corporations.
Application of general corporation law, CA §5-531.
Consumer cooperatives.
See CONSUMER COOPERATIVES.
Conversion of corporations into cooperatives, CA §5-507.
Crimes and offenses.
Violation of cooperative or general corporation law, CA §5-532.
Definitions, CA §5-501.
Directors.
Compensation, CA §5-516.
Contracting with cooperatives prohibited, CA §5-516.
Election, CA §5-513.
Districts, CA §5-514.
Management by directors, CA §5-512.
Meetings.
Calling, CA §5-519.
Number, CA §5-512.

AGRICULTURAL COOPERATIVES —Cont'd
Directors —Cont'd
Officers.
Certain officers to be directors, CA §5-517.
General provisions, CA §§5-516 to 5-518.
Qualifications, CA §5-512.
Removal.
General provisions, CA §5-518.
Residence, CA §5-512.
Term of office, CA §5-513.
Vacancies.
Filling, CA §5-515.
Discrimination.
Agricultural marketing associations, AG §§10-201 to 10-204.
Dissolution.
General provisions, CA §5-527.
Distribution.
Patronage, CA §5-525.
Districts.
Directors.
Election by districts, CA §5-514.
Elections.
Officers, CA §5-517.
Fees.
Membership fees.
Payment prior to issuance of certificate, CA §5-509.
Recording fees, CA §1-203.
Fines.
Violations, CA §5-532.
Foreign cooperatives.
Name.
Exceptions as to certain foreign cooperatives, CA §5-510.
Incorporation.
Articles of incorporation, CA §§5-505, 5-506.
Recording fees, CA §1-203.
Purpose of incorporation, CA §5-502.
Stock and stockholders.
With or without capital stock, CA §5-503.
Who may incorporate, CA §5-503.
Investments.
Power to invest, CA §5-504.
Law applicable, CA §5-531.
Management.
Directors, CA §5-512.
Market.
Marketing agencies, CA §5-524.
Meetings, CA §5-519.
Quorum, CA §5-520.
Members.
Contract with members, CA §5-522.
Defined, CA §5-501.
Fees.
Payment of membership fee, CA §5-509.
Other associations.
Membership in other association, CA §5-523.
Voting, CA §5-501.
Misdemeanors.
Violations of cooperative or general corporation law, CA §5-532.
Monopolies.
Not considered as combination in restraint of trade, CA §5-530.
Name.
Use of term "cooperative," CA §5-510.
Nonprofit basis, CA §5-526.
Notices.
Meetings, CA §5-519.
Officers, CA §§5-516 to 5-518.

AGRICULTURAL COOPERATIVES —Cont'd

Other cooperatives.
Contracts, CA §5-524.
Membership, CA §5-523.
Purchase of another cooperative, CA §5-528.

Patronage, CA §5-525.

Penalties.
Violation of cooperative or general corporation law, CA §5-532.

Powers.
Generally, CA §5-504.

Proxies.
Voting by proxy, CA §5-521.

Purchase of another business.
Payment, CA §5-528.

Quorum.
Members or stockholders, CA §5-520.

Raw agricultural products.
Audit of financial statement of cooperative handling, CA §5-529.

Recordation.
Fees, CA §1-203.

Share exchange.
General provisions, CA §5-527.

Signatures.
Articles of incorporation, CA §5-505.

Stock and stockholders, CA §5-508.
Incorporation.
With or without capital stock, CA §5-503.
Statement in articles as to stock, CA §5-505.
Subscribers.
Payment before certificate of stock issued, CA §5-509.

Trade and commerce.
Combination in restraint of trade.
Cooperative not considered as, CA §5-530.

Violations.
Penalties, CA §5-532.

Voting, CA §5-521.

AGRICULTURAL EDUCATION AND RURAL DEVELOPMENT ASSISTANCE FUND, SF §2-206.

AGRICULTURAL LAND PRESERVATION PROGRAMS.

County programs.
Certification program, department of planning, SF §5-408.

Local land preservation programs, NR §§5-9B-01 to 5-9B-06.

AGRICULTURAL PRODUCTS.

Agricultural marketing associations.
Discrimination.
General provisions, AG §§10-201 to 10-204.

Apples.
Grade law, AG §§10-801 to 10-807.
See APPLES.

Assessments. See within this heading, "Promotion of use and sale."

Cantaloupes.
General provisions, AG §§10-901 to 10-909.
See CANTALOUPES.

Consignment, CL §11-808.
Accountings of sales, AG §1-305.
Containers.
Returned containers, AG §1-303.
Security deposits, AG §1-302.
Definitions, AG §1-301.
Penalties.
Failure to provide accountings of sales, AG §1-305.

AGRICULTURAL PRODUCTS —Cont'd

Consignment —Cont'd
Penalties —Cont'd
Inapplicability of general penalties of title, AG §1-306.
Violation of duties by consignees, AG §1-304.

Conversion.
Consignment, CL §11-809.

Discrimination.
Agricultural marketing associations.
General provisions, AG §§10-201 to 10-204.

Farm products.
General provisions.
See AGRICULTURE.

Fruits and vegetables.
General provisions.
See FRUITS AND VEGETABLES.

Liens.
Consignment.
Lien not affected, CL §11-808.

Marketing associations.
Cooperative agricultural marketing associations.
Discrimination.
General provisions, AG §§10-201 to 10-204.

Presumptions.
Conversion by consignee.
Prima facie evidence, CL §11-809.

Promotion of use and sale.
Assessments.
Amount.
Publication of statement of amount received, AG §10-115.
Announcement of assessment, AG §10-108.
Bonds, surety.
Treasurer of agency, AG §10-115.
Collection, AG §10-108.
Producers of tree fruits, AG §10-112.
Suit to enforce, AG §10-114.
Use of assessments, AG §10-110.
Deductions.
By purchasers of agricultural products, AG §10-111.
By purchasers of livestock for slaughter, AG §10-113.
Defray expenses of making assessment, AG §10-116.
Refund, AG §10-114.
Right to levy, AG §10-102.
Treasurer of agency.
Bonds, surety, AG §10-115.
Tree fruits.
Collection from producers, AG §10-112.
Use, AG §10-110.
Declaration of legislative intent, AG §10-102.
Definitions, AG §10-101.
Expenses of making assessments.
Deductions to defray, AG §10-116.
Federal agricultural marketing act of 1946.
Effect of passage, AG §10-102.
Legislative intent.
Declaration, AG §10-102.
Penalties.
General provisions, AG §§12-101 to 12-104.
See AGRICULTURE.
Promotional activities.
Not deemed illegal or in restraint of trade, AG §10-103.
Referendum.
Affirmative vote.
Effect, AG §10-108.

AGRICULTURAL PRODUCTS —Cont'd
Promotion of use and sale —Cont'd
Referendum —Cont'd
Affirmative vote —Cont'd
Subsequent referendum after affirmative vote,
AG §10-109.
Application of association for certification and
approval, AG §10-104.
Ballots, AG §10-107.
Canvass of result of referendum, AG §10-107.
Certification, AG §10-104.
Management, AG §10-105.
Negative vote.
Second referendum after negative vote, AG
§10-109.
Notice, AG §10-105.
Statewide basis, AG §10-106.
Restraint of trade.
Promotional activities not deemed, AG §10-103.
Voter.
Defined, AG §10-101.
Seafood.
General provisions.
See SEAFOOD.
Trademarks, AG §§10-501 to 10-504.
See AGRICULTURE.
United States.
Promotion of use and sale.
Federal agricultural marketing act of 1946.
Effect of passage, AG §10-102.

AGRICULTURE.
Advisory boards.
Agricultural preservation advisory boards, AG
§2-504.1.
Secretary of agriculture.
Creation, AG §2-103.
Agency.
Consignees of agricultural products.
See CONSIGNMENT.
**Agricultural and resource-based industry
development corporation,** 41 §§13-501 to
13-515.
See AGRICULTURAL AND RESOURCE-BASED
INDUSTRY DEVELOPMENT
CORPORATION.
Agricultural buildings.
Building code.
Exemption from performance standards, PS
§12-508.
Agricultural commission, AG §§2-201 to 2-205.
Advisory boards.
Membership, AG §2-103.
Department of agriculture.
Unit within department, AG §§2-106, 2-202.
Agricultural land link program, AG §2-1201.
Agricultural land preservation foundation.
Board of trustees, AG §2-503.
Budget, AG §2-505.
Contracts.
Power to contract, AG §2-504.
Districts, AG §2-509.
Easements.
Application to sell easement in agricultural
land, AG §2-510.
Commercial, industrial or residential use.
Prohibited, AG §2-513.
Condemnation of land under agricultural
preservation easement, AG §2-515.
County authority to deny upon non-approval by
foundation, AG §2-513.1.

AGRICULTURE —Cont'd
Agricultural land preservation foundation
—Cont'd
Easements —Cont'd
Damages.
Eminent domain, RP §12-104.
Duration of easements.
Easement approved on or after October 1,
2004 to be held in perpetuity, AG
§2-514.1.
Grants to agricultural and resource-based
industry development corporation, AG
§2-505.
Guidelines to identify, AG §2-510.
Income tax credits.
Easements conveyed for certain purposes, TG
§10-723.
Maximum lot size restrictions, AG §2-513.
Purchases of agricultural land preservation
easements, AG §2-508.
Grant to purchase easement under certain
conditions, AG §2-510.1.
Land outside agricultural district, AG §2-509.
Release.
Conditions, AG §2-513.
Termination, AG §2-514.
Use of land for which easement purchased, AG
§2-513.
Value, AG §2-511.
Establishment, AG §2-502.
Executive director, AG §2-507.
Fund, AG §§2-505, 2-508.1.
Grants to agricultural and resource-based
industry development corporation, AG §2-505.
Intent of legislature, AG §2-501.
Legislative intent, AG §2-501.
Local programs of agricultural land preservation,
AG §2-512.
Powers.
General provisions, AG §2-504.
Procedures.
Adoption, AG §2-509.
Establishment and monitoring of agricultural
districts, AG §2-509.
Reports.
Annual report to governor and general
assembly, AG §2-506.
Rules and regulations.
Adoption, AG §§2-504, 2-509.
Sand and gravel extraction.
Pilot program determining impact, AG §2-504.
Staff, AG §2-507.
Taxation.
Property tax credits, TP §9-206.
Agricultural land preservation fund, AG §2-505.
Distribution of funds at end of fiscal year, AG
§2-508.1.
Agricultural preservation advisory boards, AG
§2-504.1.
Agricultural products.
Promotion and identification.
General provisions, AG §§10-101 to 10-909.
See AGRICULTURAL PRODUCTS.
Anne Arundel county.
Right to farm, 24 §18-101.
Any state.
Defined, AG §1-101.
Appeals.
Board of review, AG §§2-404, 2-405.
Removal of members, AG §2-403.

AGRICULTURE —Cont'd
Appeals —Cont'd
Farm products certification.
Assigned grade classifications, AG §10-605.
Apples.
General provisions.
See APPLES.
Grade law.
General provisions, AG §§10-801 to 10-807.
See APPLES.
Aquaculture.
General provisions, NR §§4-11A-01 to 4-11A-22.
See AQUACULTURE.
Assessments.
Real property tax.
Farm or agricultural use, TP §8-209.
Attorney general.
Department of agriculture.
Legal advisor and counsel, AG §2-105.
Aviation.
Dissemination of pesticides, AG §5-305.
Beekeeping industry.
General provisions, AG §§5-501 to 5-507.
See BEEKEEPING INDUSTRY.
Boards and commissions.
Advisory boards.
Agricultural preservation advisory boards, AG §2-504.1.
Creation.
Secretary of agriculture, AG §2-103.
Young farmers advisory board, AG §§2-1001 to 2-1005.
Agricultural commission, AG §§2-201 to 2-205.
Advisory board membership, AG §2-103.
Agricultural preservation advisory boards, AG §2-504.1.
Board of review, AG §§2-401 to 2-405.
Units within department, AG §2-106.
Fair board, AG §§10-301 to 10-303.
Veterinary medical examiners.
See VETERINARIANS.
Young farmers advisory board, AG §§2-1001 to 2-1005.
Bonds, surety.
Agricultural land preservation foundation.
Board of trustees, AG §2-503.
Budget.
Secretary of agriculture.
Responsibility for preparation, AG §2-103.
Building code.
Agricultural buildings.
Exemption from performance standards, PS §12-508.
Cantaloupes.
General provisions, AG §§10-901 to 10-909.
See CANTALOUPES.
Chesapeake Bay critical area and Atlantic coastal bays critical area protection programs.
Local critical area protection program.
Agricultural activities permitted, NR §8-1808.8.
Citation of article, 1 §25.
Commercial feed law.
General provisions.
See FEEDSTUFFS.
Commercial fertilizers.
General provisions, AG §§6-201 to 6-221.
See FERTILIZERS.
Commission, AG §§2-201 to 2-205.
Advisory boards.
Membership, AG §2-103.

AGRICULTURE —Cont'd
Commission —Cont'd
Department of agriculture.
Unit within department, AG §§2-106, 2-202.
Commodity quality grading fund.
Fund to comprise money collected by means of certification procedure, AG §10-604.
Compacts.
Pest control compact.
See PESTS.
Conflicts of interest.
Board of review, AG §2-404.
Contractors.
Migrant labor.
General provisions, LE §§7-101 to 7-507.
See MIGRANT LABOR.
Contracts.
Agricultural land preservation foundation.
Powers, AG §2-504.
Mediation program, AG §1-1A-03.
Cooperatives.
Agricultural marketing associations.
Discrimination.
General provisions, AG §§10-201 to 10-204.
General provisions.
See COOPERATIVES.
Correctional enterprises.
Agriculture or seafood processing services.
Open market sales, COR §3-516.
Correctional farms, COR §§11-401 to 11-407.
See CORRECTIONAL FARMS.
Counties.
Agricultural preservation advisory boards, AG §2-504.1.
Defined, AG §1-101.
Farm labor problem.
Levy to assist in solution, 25 §21.
Priority preservation areas.
Inclusion in county's comprehensive plan, AG §2-518.
County land preservation programs.
Certification program, department of planning, SF §5-408.
Criminal penalties for violations generally.
Exception to title, AG §12-104.
First offense, AG §12-101.
Rule or regulation violation, AG §12-103.
Second or subsequent offense, AG §12-102.
Crop insurance premium program, AG §2-901.
Crops.
Distress for rent.
See DISTRESS FOR RENT.
General provisions.
See CROPS.
Cultivated land.
Wanton entry, CR §6-406.
Definitions.
Drainage.
Agricultural drainage projects financed or managed by public drainage associations, AG §8-603.
Farm equipment, TR §11-120.
Farm products.
Certification, AG §10-601.
Trademarks, AG §10-501.
Motor vehicles, TR §§11-120, 11-121, 13-911.
Taxation.
Land transfer tax, TP §13-301.
Department of agriculture.
Agricultural land link program.
Duties of department, AG §2-1201.

AGRICULTURE —Cont'd
Department of agriculture —Cont'd
Agricultural land preservation foundation. See
    within this heading, "Agricultural land
    preservation foundation."
Apple commission.
    See APPLES.
Attorney general.
    Legal advisor and counsel, AG §2-105.
Board of review, AG §§2-401 to 2-405.
    Units within department, AG §2-106.
Composition, AG §2-106.
Defined, AG §1-101.
Established, AG §2-101.
Farmer disaster loan program, AG §§2-601 to
    2-605.
Head.
    Secretary of agriculture, AG §2-102.
Legal advisor.
    Attorney general, AG §2-105.
Loans.
    Farmer disaster loan program, AG §§2-601 to
        2-605.
Organic agricultural commodities.
    Certification program.
        Establishment, AG §10-1401.
        Fees, AG §10-1406.
        Powers and duties of the department, AG
            §10-1403.
    Confidentiality of information, AG §10-1407.
    Powers and duties of department, AG §10-1403.
    Promotion.
        Department may provide assistance, AG
            §10-1405.
    Regulations.
        Adoption, AG §10-1402.
Positions within department, AG §2-106.
Powers and duties.
    Exercise by secretary, AG §2-103.
    Farmer disaster loan program, AG §§2-602,
        2-604.
Reports.
    Units in department, AG §2-103.
Rules and regulations.
    Enforcement, AG §2-104.
Secretary of agriculture. See within this heading,
    "Secretary of agriculture."
Units in department.
    Appointment, AG §2-106.
    Enumeration, AG §2-106.
    Former rules and regulations.
        Transfer, AG §2-107.
    Meetings.
        Calling by secretary, AG §2-103.
    Reports, AG §2-103.
    Transfer of jurisdiction, AG §2-107.
Young farmers advisory board, AG §§2-1001 to
    2-1005.
Disasters.
Farmer disaster loan program, AG §§2-601 to
    2-605.
Discrimination.
Agricultural marketing associations.
    General provisions, AG §§10-201 to 10-204.
Distress for rent.
General provisions.
    See DISTRESS FOR RENT.
Districts, AG §2-509.
Documents of title.
Warehouse receipts.
    Storage of commodities under government bond,
        CL §7-201.

AGRICULTURE —Cont'd
Drainage of agricultural land.
Agricultural drainage projects financed or
    managed by public drainage associations, AG
    §8-603.
Cost sharing in maintenance of drainage systems,
    AG §8-602.
Powers and duties of secretary, AG §8-601.
Easements.
Agricultural land preservation foundation.
    Commercial, industrial or residential use.
        Prohibited, AG §2-513.
    County authority to deny upon non-approval by
        foundation, AG §2-513.1.
    Duration of easements.
        Easement approved on or after October 1,
            2004 to be held in perpetuity, AG
            §2-514.1.
    Guidelines to identify, AG §2-510.
    Income tax credits.
        Easements conveyed for certain purposes, TG
            §10-723.
    Maximum lot size restrictions, AG §2-513.
    Purchases of agricultural land preservation
        easements.
        Additional offers by, AG §2-508.
        Application to sell, AG §2-510.
            Notice of rejection, AG §2-510.
            Reapplication upon rejection, AG §2-510.
        Definitions, AG §2-508.
        Grant to purchase easement under certain
            conditions, AG §2-510.1.
        Maximum amount to be expended, AG §2-508.
        Purchase of easement on land outside of
            agricultural district, AG §2-509.
        Termination of easement, AG §2-514.
    Release of easements.
        Conditions, AG §2-513.
    Use of land for which easement purchased, AG
        §2-513.
Condemnation of land under agricultural
    preservation easement, AG §2-515.
Value, AG §2-511.
Eggs.
Maryland egg law.
    General provisions, AG §§4-301 to 4-312.
    See EGGS.
Eminent domain.
Condemnation of land under agricultural
    preservation easement, AG §2-515.
Employer.
Workers' compensation.
    Certificate of compliance required prior to
        issuance of license or permit, AG §1-201.
Enforcement of article, AG §2-104.
Equipment dealer contracts.
General provisions, CL §§19-101 to 19-305.
    See EQUIPMENT DEALER CONTRACTS.
Factors.
Consignees of agricultural products.
    See CONSIGNMENT.
Sale of farm products.
    See CONSIGNMENT.
Fair board, AG §§10-301 to 10-303.
Department of agriculture.
    Unit within department, AG §§2-106, 2-601 to
        2-605.
False statements for purpose of influencing
    department action, AG §2-506.
Farmers.
Cooperative demonstration work, 25 §160.

AGRICULTURE —Cont'd
Farmers —Cont'd
Definition, TR §13-911.
Farm labor contractors.
Group workers' compensation policies, IN
§§25-201 to 25-204.
Migrant labor.
General provisions, LE §§7-101 to 7-507.
See MIGRANT LABOR.
Farm machinery.
Equipment dealer contracts, CL §§19-101 to
19-305.
See EQUIPMENT DEALER CONTRACTS.
Farm products.
Agricultural products.
General provisions, AG §§10-101 to 10-909.
See AGRICULTURAL PRODUCTS.
Certification, AG §§10-601 to 10-606.
Consignees of agricultural products.
See CONSIGNMENT.
Distress for rent.
General provisions.
See DISTRESS FOR RENT.
Fruits and vegetables.
General provisions.
See FRUITS AND VEGETABLES.
Promotion of use and sale.
General provisions.
See AGRICULTURAL PRODUCTS.
Sale of farm products.
Conversion by consignee of consigned goods.
See CONSIGNMENT.
Trademarks, AG §§10-501 to 10-504.
United States.
Cooperation with United States government,
AG §10-603.
Farms.
Ponds.
See PONDS.
Small farms.
Group workers' compensation policies, IN
§§25-201 to 25-204.
Feedstuffs.
Commercial feed law.
General provisions.
See FEEDSTUFFS.
Fish farming.
Aquaculture generally, NR §§4-11A-01 to
4-11A-22.
See AQUACULTURE.
Flowers.
Multiflora rose management, AG §§9-701 to 9-705.
See MULTIFLORA ROSE MANAGEMENT.
Food.
Procurement preferences.
Percentage price preference for locally grown
foods, SF §14-407.
Forest conservation.
Applicability of subtitle.
Agricultural activities excepted, NR §5-1602.
Foundations.
Agricultural land preservation foundation. See
within this heading, "Agricultural land
preservation foundation."
Fruits and vegetables.
Distress for rent.
General provisions.
See DISTRESS FOR RENT.
Fruit growers.
Cooperatives.
See AGRICULTURAL COOPERATIVES.

AGRICULTURE —Cont'd
Fruits and vegetables —Cont'd
General provisions, AG §§10-701 to 10-708.
See FRUITS AND VEGETABLES.
Potatoes.
Seed potato inspections.
See POTATOES.
Seeds.
General provisions.
See SEEDS.
Yellows.
Inspectors.
See TREES AND TIMBER.
Funds.
Agricultural land preservation funds, AG §2-505.
Farm products.
Certification.
Money collected under subtitle deemed
commodity quality grading fund, AG
§10-604.
Gasohol.
See GASOHOL.
General assembly.
What legislature should encourage, MD Const
DofR Art 43.
Ginseng control, AG §§9-601 to 9-606.
See GINSENG.
Grain.
General provisions.
See GRAIN.
Grass.
Turf grass law.
General provisions, AG §§9-101 to 9-110.
See TURF GRASS LAW.
Greenbelt law.
Real property tax.
Assessments.
Farm or agricultural use, TP §8-209.
Gypsum.
Agricultural lime.
General provisions, AG §§6-301 to 6-311.
See LIME.
Honeybees.
General provisions, AG §§5-501 to 5-507.
See BEEKEEPING INDUSTRY.
Hunting.
Exception to license requirement.
Hunting on farmland, NR §10-301.
Farmers, reimbursement contracts with.
Planting grains, grasses and legumes, NR
§10-301.
Injunctions.
Drainage.
Agricultural drainage projects financed or
managed by public drainage associations.
Failure to obtain or comply with approved
plans, AG §8-603.
Inmates employed in agricultural work.
Queen Anne's County, COR §9-515.
**Insecticides, fungicides and various
bactericides.**
Pest control compact.
See PESTS.
Pesticides.
General provisions.
See PESTICIDES.
Inspections.
Organic agricultural commodities, AG §10-1406.
Secretary of agriculture.
Annual inspections, AG §5-302.

AGRICULTURE —Cont'd
Inspections —Cont'd
Secretary of agriculture —Cont'd
Contagious and infectious diseases.
Administrative search warrants, AG §3-105.1.
Interest.
Farm disaster loan program.
Rate of interest, AG §2-603.
Intrastate commerce.
Defined, AG §1-101.
Labor and employment relations.
Farm labor problem.
Counties.
Levy to assist in solution by county, 25 §21.
Group workers' compensation policies, IN
§§25-201 to 25-204.
Migrant labor.
General provisions, LE §§7-101 to 7-507.
See MIGRANT LABOR.
Land preservation foundation. See within this
heading, "Agricultural land preservation
foundation."
Liens.
Secured transactions.
Collateral, disposition.
Rights of secured party, CL §9-315.
Crops, CL §9-334.
Definitions, CL §9-102.
Default.
Time of default, CL §9-606.
Defined, CL §9-102.
Perfection and priority.
Buyers receiving delivery.
Interests that take priority over or take free
of agricultural lien, CL §9-317.
Choice of law governing agricultural liens, CL
§9-302.
Filed financing statement providing certain
incorrect information.
Priority of agricultural lien perfected by, CL
§9-338.
Filing, CL §9-310.
Interests that take priority over or take free
of agricultural lien, CL §9-317.
Law governing, CL §9-302.
Lessees receiving delivery.
Interests that take priority over or take free
of agricultural lien, CL §9-317.
Multiple conflicting interests in same
collateral, CL §9-322.
When perfected, CL §9-308.
Lime.
Agricultural lime.
General provisions, AG §§6-301 to 6-311.
See LIME.
Livestock.
General provisions.
See LIVESTOCK.
Loans.
Farmer disaster loan program, AG §§2-601 to
2-605.
Local land preservation programs, NR
§§5-9B-01 to 5-9B-06.
**Maryland advisory committee on historic
agricultural structure preservation,** SF
§§5A-401 to 5A-406.
Maryland agricultural land link program, AG
§2-1201.
Maryland crop insurance premium program,
AG §2-901.

AGRICULTURE —Cont'd
Mediation program, AG §§1-1A-01 to 1-1A-04.
Confidentiality of records, AG §1-1A-04.
Definitions, AG §1-1A-01.
Powers of secretary, AG §1-1A-03.
Purpose, AG §1-1A-02.
Qualifications to be established by secretary, AG
§1-1A-03.
Migrant labor.
General provisions, LE §§7-101 to 7-507.
See MIGRANT LABOR.
Misdemeanors for violations generally.
First offense, AG §12-101.
Rule or regulation violation, AG §12-103.
Mortgages and deeds of trust.
Farm disaster loan program.
Security for loans, AG §2-603.
Mosquito control.
General provisions.
See MOSQUITO CONTROL.
Motor vehicles.
Farm equipment.
Certificate of title.
Exception to requirement, TR §13-102.
Optional, TR §13-103.
Defined, TR §11-120.
Registration.
Exemption, TR §13-402.
Farmer.
Defined, TR §13-911.
Farm tractor.
Defined, TR §11-121.
Farm trailer or semitrailer.
Registration, TR §13-930.
Farm trucks.
Registration, TR §13-921.
Farm truck tractors.
Registration, TR §13-924.
Farm vehicles.
Gross weight, TR §24-109.
Lights.
Farm tractors, farm equipment and implements
of husbandry, TR §22-215.
Slow moving farm vehicles, TR §22-218.
Load limits of agricultural vehicles.
Axle load limit tolerance, TR §24-108.
Plates, TR §13-619.2.
Registration.
Exemption of nonresident congressmen, TR
§13-402.
Farm area vehicles, TR §13-935.
Farm trailer or semitrailer, TR §13-930.
Farm trucks, TR §13-921.
Farm truck tractors, TR §13-924.
Foreign harvest vehicles.
Exemption, TR §13-402.
Multiflora rose management, AG §§9-701 to
9-705.
See MULTIFLORA ROSE MANAGEMENT.
Nuisances.
Actions against agricultural operations, CJ
§5-403.
Birds.
Nuisance bird law, AG §§5-801 to 5-804.
Farm operations, exclusion from definition, HG
§20-301.
Nutrient management consultants.
General provisions, AG §§8-801 to 8-807.
See NUTRIENT MANAGEMENT
CONSULTANTS.

AGRICULTURE —Cont'd

Organic agricultural commodities, AG §§10-1401 to 10-1407.
Certification program.
Establishment, AG §10-1401.
Fees, AG §10-1406.
Powers and duties of the department, AG §10-1403.
Confidentiality of information, AG §10-1407.
Department of agriculture.
Certification program.
Establishment, AG §10-1401.
Powers and duties of the department, AG §10-1403.
Duties, AG §10-1403.
Powers, AG §10-1403.
Promotion.
Department may provide assistance, AG §10-1405.
Regulations.
Adoption, AG §10-1402.
Penalties.
Civil penalties, AG §10-1404.
Prohibited acts, AG §10-1405.
Civil penalty, AG §10-1404.
Promotion.
Department may provide assistance, AG §10-1405.
Rules and regulations.
Adoption, AG §10-1402.

Penalties.
Enclosed livestock.
Opening enclosure of another, AG §3-701.
Exception to title, AG §12-104.
Farmer disaster loan program.
False statements for purpose of influencing department action, AG §2-605.
First offense, AG §12-101.
Second or subsequent offense, AG §12-102.
Violations of rules and regulations, AG §12-103.

Pest control compact.
See PESTS.

Pesticides.
General provisions.
See PESTICIDES.

Planning.
Counties.
Agricultural land preservation programs.
Disbursements to programs, AG §2-508.1.
Priority preservation areas.
Inclusion in county's comprehensive plan, AG §2-518.
Secretary of agriculture.
Responsibilities, AG §2-103.

Plant disease control.
General provisions, AG §§5-301 to 5-314.
See PLANT DISEASE CONTROL.

Ponds.
General provisions.
See PONDS.

Potatoes.
Seed potato inspections.
General provisions, AG §§9-301 to 9-307.
See POTATOES.

Poultry.
General provisions.
See POULTRY.
Poultry products inspection.
See POULTRY PRODUCTS INSPECTION.

Procurement.
Food.
Percentage price preference for locally grown foods, SF §14-407.

AGRICULTURE —Cont'd

Property taxes.
See PROPERTY TAXES.

Quarantine.
Imposition.
Authority of secretary, AG §5-304.

Queen Anne's County.
Employment of inmates in agricultural work, COR §9-515.

Rabbits.
San Juan rabbits.
Importing or possession prohibited, AG §5-601.

Reclaimed water.
Use for irrigation of farmland, EN §9-303.1.

Records.
Authentication.
Seal of office of secretary, AG §2-103.

Reports.
Agricultural land preservation foundation.
Annual reports, AG §2-506.

Right of entry.
Farm products.
Trademarks.
Examination, AG §10-503.

Right to farm.
Anne Arundel county, 24 §18-101.

Roses.
Multiflora rose management, AG §§9-701 to 9-705.
See MULTIFLORA ROSE MANAGEMENT.

Rules and regulations.
Agricultural land preservation foundation.
Adoption, AG §§2-504, 2-509.
Establishment and monitoring of agricultural districts, AG §2-509.
Enforcement, AG §2-104.
Fair board.
Fairs and exhibits, AG §10-303.
Farm products.
Trademarks, AG §10-502.
Organic agricultural commodities.
Adoption, AG §10-1402.
Secretary of agriculture. See within this heading, "Secretary of agriculture."
Violations.
Penalties, AG §12-103.

Rural legacy program, NR §§5-9A-01 to 5-9A-09.
See RURAL LEGACY PROGRAM.

Sales.
Promotion of use and sale of farm products.
General provisions.
See AGRICULTURAL PRODUCTS.

Sales and use tax.
Exemptions.
Agricultural purposes and products, TG §11-201.

San Juan rabbits.
Importing or possession prohibited, AG §5-601.

Seafood.
General provisions.
See SEAFOOD.

Seal.
Secretary of agriculture.
Authentication of copies of records or papers, AG §2-103.

Secretary of agriculture.
Advisory boards.
Creation, AG §2-103.
Agricultural commission.
Advisory body to secretary, AG §2-202.
Agricultural land preservation foundation.
Board of trustees.
Ex officio member, AG §2-503.

AGRICULTURE —Cont'd
Secretary of agriculture —Cont'd
Appointment, AG §2-102.
  Deputy secretary, AG §2-102.
Assaults.
  Resisting performance of duties, AG §2-104.
Assistants.
  Appointment, AG §2-102.
Budget.
  Responsibility, AG §2-103.
Defined, AG §1-101.
Department. See within this heading,
  "Department of agriculture."
Deputy secretary, AG §2-102.
Drainage of agricultural land, AG §8-601.
  Cost sharing in maintenance of drainage outlet
    systems, AG §8-602.
Duties. See within this subheading, "Powers and
  duties."
Employees.
  Appointment, AG §2-102.
Enforcement of article, AG §2-104.
Governor.
  Responsibility to governor, AG §2-102.
Hazardous materials and substances.
  Rules and regulations.
    Review by secretary prior to adoption, EN
      §7-208.
Head of department, AG §2-102.
Inspections.
  Horticultural and agricultural interests.
    Annual inspections, AG §5-302.
Interference with, AG §2-104.
Mediation program, AG §1-1A-03.
Meetings of units.
  Calling by secretary, AG §2-103.
Pest control compact.
  Bylaws and amendments filed with secretary,
    AG §5-713.
  General provisions.
    See PESTS.
  Secretary designated compact administrator,
    AG §5-714.
Planning.
  Responsibilities, AG §2-103.
Powers and duties.
  Certification of farm products, AG §10-602.
  Contagious and infectious diseases.
    Prevention of spread, AG §3-105.
      Administrative search warrants, AG
        §3-105.1.
  Department.
    Exercise by secretary, AG §2-103.
    Generally, AG §2-103.
  Livestock.
    Contagious and infectious diseases, AG
      §3-101.
  Trademarks, AG §10-502.
Professional consultants.
  Appointments, AG §2-102.
Quarantine.
  Imposition, AG §5-304.
Reports.
  Units in department, AG §2-103.
Resisting performance of duties, AG §2-104.
Responsibility to governor, AG §2-102.
Right of entry.
  Plant disease control, AG §5-306.
Rules and regulations, AG §2-103.
  Cantaloupes.
    Adoption and enforcement, AG §10-902.

AGRICULTURE —Cont'd
Secretary of agriculture —Cont'd
Rules and regulations —Cont'd
  Certification of farm products, AG §10-602.
  Commercial fertilizers, AG §6-203.
  Enforcement, AG §2-104.
  Farm products.
    Certification, AG §10-602.
  Feedstuffs, AG §6-104.
  Fruits and vegetables, AG §10-702.
  Lime, AG §6-302.
  Potato seed inspection, AG §9-302.
  Turf grass law, AG §9-102.
  Violations.
    Penalties, AG §12-103.
  Weights and measures, AG §11-203.
Salaries, AG §2-102.
Seal, AG §2-103.
State merit system.
  Removal of personnel, AG §2-102.
Term of office, AG §2-102.
Sediment control.
Soil or sediment introduced, leaked, spilled, etc.,
  into waters of state.
  Persons engaged in agricultural land
    management practices, EN §4-413.
Seeds.
General provisions, AG §§9-201 to 9-214.
  See SEEDS.
Seed potato inspections.
  General provisions.
    See POTATOES.
Severn river watershed.
Riparian rights.
  Use of water not lost when land taken by
    condemnation, EN §4-311.
Sheriffs.
Enforcement of article, AG §2-104.
Soil conservation.
General provisions, AG §§8-101 to 8-603.
  See SOIL CONSERVATION.
State chemist.
See STATE CHEMIST.
State veterinarians.
See VETERINARIANS.
Taxation.
Assessments.
  Farm or agricultural land use, TP §8-209.
  Farms, MD Const DofR Art 43.
Credits.
  Property tax credits.
    Maryland agricultural land preservation
      foundation.
      Land over which easement has been
        conveyed, TP §9-206.
Exemptions.
  Farm implements, TP §7-223.
  Livestock, TP §7-224.
  Products and commodities, TP §7-219.
Land transfer tax.
  Administration of tax, TP §13-307.
  Calculation of tax, TP §13-304.
  Definitions, TP §13-301.
  Distribution of revenue, TP §13-306.
  Exemptions, TP §13-305.
  Imposition, TP §13-302.
  Liability.
    Seller to notify buyer of possible tax liability,
      TP §13-308.
  Payment, TP §13-302.

AGRICULTURE —Cont'd
Taxation —Cont'd
Land transfer tax —Cont'd
Penalty.
Seller fails to notify buyer of possible tax
liability, TP §13-308.
Rate, TP §13-303.
Valuation of improvements, TP §13-304.
Property taxes.
See PROPERTY TAXES.
Silos, TP §8-239.
Valuation of property, TP §8-209.
Tobacco.
General provisions.
See TOBACCO.
Trademarks.
Farm products, AG §§10-501 to 10-504.
Trees and timber.
General provisions.
See TREES AND TIMBER.
Plant disease control.
See PLANT DISEASE CONTROL.
Trespass.
Cultivated land, wanton entry, CR §6-406.
Turf grass law.
General provisions, AG §§9-101 to 9-110.
See TURF GRASS LAW.
Unemployment compensation.
Agricultural labor.
When covered employment, LE §8-207.
United States.
Farmers' cooperative demonstration work.
Cooperation with department of agriculture, 25
§160.
University of Maryland.
Agriculture and natural resources internship
program, ED §12-116.
Vegetables.
General provisions, AG §§10-701 to 10-708.
See FRUITS AND VEGETABLES.
Veterinarians.
See VETERINARIANS.
Washington county.
Agricultural land transfer tax, TP §§13-501 to
13-505.
See WASHINGTON COUNTY.
Water pollution.
Soil or sediment added, introduced, leaked or
spilled into waters of state.
Persons engaged in agricultural land
management practice, EN §4-413.
Water pollution control fund.
Grants related to agriculture, EN §9-350.
Water resources.
Agricultural use permits.
Waiver of notice and hearing requirements, EN
§5-506.
Farm ponds.
See PONDS.
Reservoirs, dams or waterways.
Construction or repair.
Permits.
Exceptions, EN §5-510.
Exemptions, EN §5-503.
Soil or sediment added, introduced, leaked or
spilled into waters of state.
Persons engaged in agricultural land
management practices, EN §4-413.
Weights and measures.
General provisions.
See WEIGHTS AND MEASURES.

AGRICULTURE —Cont'd
Wholesale farm machinery dealers.
Licenses.
Defined, BR §17-701.
Fees, BR §17-703.
Required, BR §17-702.
Wholesome meat act.
General provisions, AG §§4-101 to 4-131.
See WHOLESOME MEAT ACT.
Wine and grape promotion.
Council, AG §2-1103.
Definitions, AG §2-1101.
Fund, AG §2-1102.
**Winery and grape growers' advisory
commission.**
General provisions, AG §§10-1201 to 10-1206.
See ALCOHOLIC BEVERAGES.
Workers' compensation.
Covered employees and employers.
Farm workers, LE §9-210.
Issuance of license or permit to employer.
Certificate of compliance required prior to
issuance, AG §1-201.
Young farmers advisory board, AG §§2-1001 to
2-1005.

AGRITOURISM.
Building code.
Exemption for agricultural buildings used for
agritourism, PS §12-508.

AIDS.
General provisions.
See ACQUIRED IMMUNE DEFICIENCY
SYNDROME (AIDS).
Viatical settlement contracts, IN §§8-601 to
8-611.
See VIATICAL SETTLEMENT CONTRACTS.

**AID TO FAMILIES WITH DEPENDENT
CHILDREN.**
Family investment program generally, 88A
§§44A to 56.
See FAMILY INVESTMENT PROGRAM.

AIR CONDITIONERS.
Contractors.
See AIR CONDITIONING AND HEATING
CONTRACTORS.
Efficiency standards, SG §9-2006.
**Environmental sound level limits and noise
control rules and regulations,** EN §3-401.
Motor vehicles, TR §22-410.

**AIR CONDITIONING AND HEATING
CONTRACTORS.**
Advertising, BR §9A-404.
Applicability of title, BR §9A-103.
Board.
Chairman.
Appointment, BR §9A-203.
Compensation, BR §9A-204.
Composition, BR §9A-202.
Consumer members, BR §9A-202.
Creation, BR §9A-201.
Defined, BR §9A-101.
Disposition of money, BR §9A-207.
Duties, BR §9A-205.
Establishment, BR §9A-201.
Fees, BR §9A-207.
Geographical representation.
Professional members, BR §9A-202.
Injunctive powers, BR §9A-206.

AIR CONDITIONING AND HEATING CONTRACTORS —Cont'd

Board —Cont'd
Licensing. See within this heading, "Licenses."
Meetings, BR §9A-204.
Membership, BR §9A-202.
Officers.
Election, BR §9A-203.
Powers, BR §§9A-205, 9A-206.
Quorum, BR §9A-204.
Staff, BR §9A-204.
Standards code.
Adoption and enforcement, BR §9A-205.
Bonds, surety.
Licenses, BR §9A-402.
Citation of title, BR §9A-601.
Continuing education.
Inspectors, BR §9A-403.
Contracts.
Cooperative agreements.
Board authority to enter into, BR §9A-205.
County code.
Applicability, BR §9A-205.
Definitions, BR §9A-101.
Employment.
Unlicensed contractors, BR §§9A-502, 9A-503.
Providing services without license, BR §9A-501.
Fees.
Board.
Establishment, BR §9A-207.
Licenses.
Application fee, BR §9A-303.
Examination fee, BR §9A-304.
Injunctions.
Board enforcement powers, BR §9A-206.
Inspectors, BR §9A-403.
Insurance.
Licenses.
Liability insurance required, BR §9A-402.
Violation of requirement, BR §9A-505.
Proof of insurance, BR §9A-402.
Investigations.
Board.
Investigation of complaints, BR §9A-206.
Licenses.
Applications, BR §9A-303.
Fee, BR §9A-303.
New applications.
Reexamination, BR §9A-307.
Renewal of license, BR §9A-309.
Restoration, BR §9A-308.
Submission requirements, BR §9A-303.
Credit for studying or training, BR §9A-302.
Death of licensee, BR §9A-309.
Defined, BR §9A-101.
Denials.
Grounds, BR §9A-310.
Disciplinary actions.
Grounds, BR §9A-310.
Hearing.
Application of contested case provisions, BR §9A-311.
Judicial review, BR §9A-312.
Discrimination prohibited, BR §9A-506.
Display of license, BR §9A-401.
Employing unlicensed individuals prohibited, BR §9A-502.
Knowingly employing unlicensed individuals, BR §9A-503.
Examinations.
Credit for study or training, BR §9A-302.

AIR CONDITIONING AND HEATING CONTRACTORS —Cont'd

Licenses —Cont'd
Examinations —Cont'd
Failure, BR §9A-307.
Fee, BR §9A-304.
Grade notification, BR §9A-307.
Misbehavior by applicant, BR §9A-307.
Passing score, BR §9A-307.
Notification requirements, BR §9A-308.
Reciprocity.
Waiver of requirements, BR §9A-305.
Reexamination, BR §9A-307.
Subjects and method, BR §9A-304.
Testing service, BR §9A-304.
Time and place, BR §9A-304.
Waiver of requirements, BR §9A-306.
Licenses in another state, BR §9A-305.
Expiration, BR §9A-309.
Restoration, BR §9A-308.
Inactive status, BR §9A-309.
Inspectors, BR §9A-403.
Insurance requirement, BR §9A-402.
Violation, BR §9A-505.
Issuance.
Renewal of license, BR §9A-309.
Journeyman license, BR §9A-306.
Defined, BR §9A-101.
Issuance without examination, BR §9A-306.
Notification of passing examination, BR §9A-308.
Qualifications of applicants, BR §9A-302.
Journeyman restricted license.
Defined, BR §9A-101.
Notification of passing examination, BR §9A-306.
Qualifications of applicants, BR §9A-302.
Limited license, BR §9A-302.
Providing services without license, BR §9A-501.
Local licenses, BR §9A-506.
Discontinuation of requirement, BR §9A-506.
Master license.
Defined, BR §9A-101.
Notification of passing examination, BR §9A-308.
Providing services without license, BR §9A-501.
Qualifications of applicants, BR §9A-302.
Master limited license.
Notification of passing examination, BR §9A-308.
Master restricted license.
Defined, BR §9A-101.
Examinations, BR §9A-304.
Notification of passing examination, BR §9A-308.
Providing services without license, BR §9A-501.
Qualifications of applicants, BR §9A-302.
Misrepresentation, BR §9A-504.
Notice of changes required, BR §9A-401.
Proof of insurance, BR §9A-402.
Providing services without license, BR §9A-501.
Qualifications of applicants, BR §9A-302.
Reexaminations.
Applicant fee, BR §9A-307.
Misbehavior by applicant, BR §9A-307.
Renewal.
Prohibited without insurance, BR §9A-402.
Reprimands.
Grounds, BR §9A-310.
Required, BR §9A-301.

AIR CONDITIONING AND HEATING CONTRACTORS —Cont'd

Licenses —Cont'd

State license.

Required, BR §9A-506.

Term and renewal, BR §9A-309.

Transferability, BR §9A-309.

Unlicensed individuals.

Employing prohibited, BR §§9A-502, 9A-503.

Knowingly employing, BR §9A-503.

Providing services without license, BR §9A-501.

Waiver of requirements, BR §9A-305.

Misrepresentation.

Licensing, BR §9A-504.

Penalties.

Violations of provisions, BR §9A-505.

Public policy, BR §9A-102.

Purpose of title, BR §9A-102.

Scope of title, BR §9A-103.

Service contracts and consumer products guaranty.

Inapplicability of article to persons with master license, CL §14-409.

Short title, BR §9A-601.

Title of act, BR §9A-601.

AIRCRAFT.

Aviation.

See AVIATION.

AIRLINE COMPANIES.

Defined as common carrier, PUC §1-101.

AIR POLLUTION.

Acid deposition, NR §§3-3A-01 to 3-3A-04.

Air quality control.

See AIR QUALITY CONTROL.

Electric generating facilities.

Healthy air act, EN §§2-1001 to 2-1005.

Environmental policy act.

See ENVIRONMENTAL POLICY ACT.

Environmental service.

General provisions.

See ENVIRONMENTAL SERVICE.

Motor vehicles.

Alteration of air pollution control devices, TR §22-402.1.

AIRPORT AUTHORITIES.

Aviation generally.

See AVIATION.

Potomac Highlands Airport Authority.

General provisions.

See POTOMAC HIGHLANDS AIRPORT AUTHORITY.

AIRPORTS.

See AVIATION.

AIR QUALITY CONTROL.

Abatement.

Granting of extension of time to abate violation, EN §2-609.

Actions.

Enforcement of actions, EN §2-609.

Who acquires actionable rights, EN §2-106.

Acts of God.

Conditions not violations, EN §2-613.

Administrative procedure.

Adoption of rules and regulations.

Compliance with act, EN §2-303.

Orders.

Applicability, EN §2-605.

AIR QUALITY CONTROL —Cont'd

Advisory council.

Advisory role, EN §2-206.

Appointment of members, EN §2-202.

Compensation, EN §2-205.

Composition, EN §2-202.

Established, EN §2-201.

Expenses.

Reimbursement, EN §2-205.

Meetings, EN §2-205.

Membership, EN §2-202.

Officers, EN §2-203.

Recommendations, EN §2-206.

Secretary.

Appointment, EN §2-204.

Submission of rules or regulations by department, EN §2-206.

Tenure of members, EN §2-202.

Vacancies, EN §2-202.

Air pollution.

Defined, EN §2-101.

Motor vehicles.

Alteration of air pollution control devices, TR §22-402.1.

Air quality control advisory council. See within this heading, "Advisory council."

Air quality control areas.

Division of state, EN §2-302.

Standards in areas, EN §2-302.

Ambient air quality control permits, EN §2-404.

Judicial review of final decision, EN §2-404.1.

Appeals.

Permits.

Judicial review, EN §2-404.1.

Persons aggrieved by decisions of secretary, etc., EN §2-607.

Attorney general.

Cases arising under provisions.

Responsibilities as to, EN §2-614.

Attorneys at law.

Representation of persons charged, EN §2-605.

Certificates of public convenience and necessity.

Recommendations of secretary, EN §2-405.

Compromise and settlement.

Claims for civil penalties under section, EN §2-610.

Confidential information.

Secret processes or methods of manufacture or production, EN §2-605.

Contempt.

Orders.

Noncompliance with notice of hearing or subpoena issued, EN §2-605.

Corrective orders, EN §2-604.

Action after hearing, EN §2-606.

Action permitted within one year, EN §2-608.

Hearings, EN §2-604.

Service, EN §2-604.

Council. See within this heading, "Advisory council."

Crimes and offenses, EN §2-609.1.

Limitation on bringing prosecution, EN §2-610.2.

Definitions, EN §2-101.

Department of the environment.

Action permitted within one year, EN §2-608.

Emission standards, EN §2-302.

Enforcement of actions, EN §2-609.

Funds.

Authority to obtain funds, EN §2-103.

AIR QUALITY CONTROL —Cont'd
Department of the environment —Cont'd
  Jurisdiction.
    Generally, EN §2-103.
  Monitoring facilities.
    Use, EN §2-103.
  Motor vehicle mileage reduction, EN §2-303.2.
  Orders.
    Compliance with order, EN §2-608.
    Corrective orders, EN §2-604.
      Action after hearing, EN §2-606.
      Service, EN §2-604.
    Final orders, EN §2-604.
    Issuance, EN §2-602.
    Noncompliance, EN §2-605.
    Not prerequisite to other action, EN §2-602.
    Show cause orders, EN §2-603.
      Service, EN §2-603.
  Powers and duties, EN §2-103.
  Proceedings brought by department, EN §2-106.
  State agencies to consult, EN §2-304.
  Use of agency facilities and services for
    enforcement, EN §2-601.
**Electric company application for operating
  permit for generating station,** EN §2-405.
  Installation of pollution control equipment or
    changes in method of operation.
    Consolidation of procedures, EN §2-405.
    Public service commission approval, required,
      expedited review, PUC §7-206.
Emergencies.
  Air pollution emergency.
    Secretary to advise governor, EN §2-105.
  Conditions not violations, EN §2-613.
  Defined, EN §2-101.
Emission standards.
  Defined, EN §2-101.
  Duties of department, EN §2-302.
Employer-provided commuter benefits.
  Tax credits for, EN §2-901.
Environmental policy act.
  See ENVIRONMENTAL POLICY ACT.
Environmental service.
  General provisions.
    See ENVIRONMENTAL SERVICE.
Federal clean air act.
  Reports concerning, EN §2-103.1.
Fees.
  Permits and registration, EN §2-403.
Final orders.
  Action after hearing, EN §2-606.
Findings of fact.
  Determination of disregard or violation of rule or
    regulation, EN §2-106.
Fuel variances, EN §2-501.
  Duty of petitioner, EN §2-505.
  Extension, EN §2-504.
  Notice and hearing, EN §2-503.
  Petition, EN §2-502.
Funds.
  Department of the environment.
    Authority to obtain funds, EN §2-103.
  Maryland clean air fund, EN §2-107.
Gasoline dispensing systems.
  Inspection programs, EN §2-303.3.
Governor.
  Air pollution emergencies.
    Executive orders, EN §2-105.
    Secretary to advise governor, EN §2-105.
Grain drying operations.
  Rules and regulations, EN §2-301.

AIR QUALITY CONTROL —Cont'd
Hearings.
  Action after hearing, EN §2-606.
  Ambient air quality control permits.
    Issuance, EN §2-404.
  Corrective orders, EN §2-604.
  Electric company operating permit for generating
    station.
    Installation of pollution control equipment or
      changes in method of operation, EN §2-405.
  Rules and regulations.
    Adoption, EN §2-303.
  Temporary fuel variances, EN §2-503.
Incinerators for disposal of solid waste.
  Operators.
    Presence at operation.
      Required, EN §2-406.
    Qualifications, EN §2-406.
    Regulations to implement provisions of section,
      EN §2-406.
Internet.
  Ambient air monitoring data.
    Access of information via Internet, EN §2-103.2.
Judicial review.
  Right to appeal, EN §2-607.
Legislative policy, EN §2-102.
Limitation of actions.
  Permit violations.
    Criminal prosecutions and actions to collect civil
      penalty, EN §2-610.2.
Misdemeanors.
  Knowing violations of provisions, EN §2-609.1.
Monitoring facilities.
  Department of the environment.
    Contracts for use of facilities, EN §2-103.
Motor vehicles.
  Alteration of air pollution control devices, TR
    §22-402.1.
  Reduction of vehicle miles encouraged, EN
    §2-303.2.
Noncompliance.
  Penalty, EN §2-612.
Notices.
  Ambient air quality control permits.
    Intended issuance, EN §2-404.
  Electric company operating permit for generating
    station.
    Installation of pollution control equipment or
      changes in method of operation, EN §2-405.
  Rules and regulations.
    Hearing on adoption, EN §2-303.
  Temporary fuel variances.
    Hearings, EN §2-503.
Penalties.
  Attorney general.
    Duties as to recovery of penalties, EN §2-614.
  Civil penalties, EN §2-610.
    Additional civil penalties, EN §2-610.1.
    Limitation on bringing action to collected, EN
      §2-610.2.
  Compromise and settlement of claims for civil
    penalties, EN §2-610.
  Criminal penalties.
    Knowing violations of provisions, EN §2-609.1.
    Limitation on prosecution, EN §2-610.2.
  Disposition of funds collected, EN §2-612.
  Judicial enforcement, EN §2-612.
  Noncompliance penalty, EN §2-612.
  Quarterly nonpayment penalty, EN §2-612.
  Remission, EN §2-610.

AIR QUALITY CONTROL —Cont'd
Permits.
Ambient air quality control permits, EN §2-404.
Hearings, EN §2-404.
Impact analysis, EN §2-404.
Judicial review of final decision, EN §2-404.1.
Notices.
Intended issuance, EN §2-404.
Zoning and land use requirements.
Compliance with, EN §2-404.
Department may not require permit in certain cases, EN §2-402.
Electric company operating permit for generating station, EN §2-405.
Fees, EN §2-403.
Judicial review, EN §2-404.1.
Public participation in process, EN §§1-601 to 1-607.
Appeal of final determination.
Contested case hearing, EN §1-605.
Applicability of provision, EN §1-601.
Applications for departmental permits, EN §1-603.
Notice of completed applications or reasons for incompleteness, EN §1-607.
Consolidation of public meetings and hearings, EN §1-601.
Contested case hearing, EN §1-605.
Dismissal, EN §1-606.
Opportunity for, EN §1-601.
Determination, EN §1-604.
Appeal of final determination, EN §1-605.
Dismissal of request for adjudication, EN §1-606.
Informational meeting on application, EN §1-603.
Mailing notice.
Informational meetings or public hearings, EN §1-602.
Notice, publication, EN §1-602.
Applications for permits, EN §1-603.
Publication of notice, EN §§1-602, 1-603.
Request for adjudication.
Dismissal of request for adjudication, EN §1-606.
Time for submitting, EN §1-605.
Review times for licensing and permitting programs, EN §1-606.
Tentative determination, EN §1-604.
Zoning and land use requirements or conformity to county plan.
Not challenged at contested case hearing, EN §1-605.
Required generally, EN §2-401.
Person.
Defined, EN §2-101.
Petitions.
Temporary fuel variances, EN §2-502.
Political subdivisions.
Defined, EN §2-101.
Ordinances.
Adoption, EN §2-104.
Powers.
Generally, EN §2-104.
Rules and regulations.
Adoption, EN §2-104.
Requesting rules or regulations, EN §2-104.
Presumptions.
Determination of violation does not create presumption, EN §2-106.

AIR QUALITY CONTROL —Cont'd
Public service commission.
Applications for certificates of public convenience and necessity.
Recommendation of secretary, EN §2-405.
Electric company operating permit for generating station.
Installation of pollution control equipment or changes in method of operation.
Hearings conducted by commission, EN §2-405.
Registration.
Fees, EN §2-403.
Required.
Generally, EN §2-401.
When department may not require registration, EN §2-402.
Rights of persons other than in this state, EN §2-106.
Rules and regulations.
Adoption by department, EN §2-301.
Procedures for adoption, EN §2-303.
Adoption by political subdivisions, EN §2-104.
Effective date, EN §2-303.
Grain drying operations, EN §2-301.
Hearings.
Public hearing required for adoption, EN §2-303.
Incinerators for disposal of solid waste.
Operators.
Qualifications and presence at operation.
Regulations to implement provisions of section, EN §2-406.
Notice of hearing, EN §2-303.
Plan for compliance, EN §2-611.
Request by governing body, EN §2-104.
Required considerations, EN §2-301.
Volatile organic emissions control program, EN §2-303.1.
Secretary of the environment.
Secretary to advise governor, EN §2-105.
Secret processes or methods of manufacture or production.
Withholding of certain information, EN §2-605.
Service of process.
Corrective orders, EN §2-604.
Show cause orders, EN §2-603.
Show cause orders, EN §2-603.
Action permitted within one year, EN §2-608.
Small business pollution compliance loan fund.
General provisions, EN §§2-801 to 2-806.
Solid waste.
Incinerators for disposal of solid waste.
Operators, EN §2-406.
Source.
Defined, EN §2-101.
Standards.
Ambient air quality standards, EN §2-302.
Defined, EN §2-101.
Duties of department, EN §2-302.
State departments and agencies.
Consultation with department of the environment, EN §2-304.
Use of agency facilities and services for enforcement, EN §2-601.
Statute of limitations.
Permit violations.
Criminal prosecutions and actions to collect civil penalty, EN §2-610.2.
Stays.
Orders under section, EN §2-607.

AIR QUALITY CONTROL —Cont'd
Strikes.
  Conditions not violations, EN §2-613.
Variances.
  Fuel variances, EN §2-501.
    Duty of petitioner, EN §2-505.
    Extension, EN §2-504.
    Notice and hearing, EN §2-503.
    Petition, EN §2-502.
Violations.
  Civil penalty, EN §2-610.
    Additional civil penalties, EN §2-610.1.
    Limitation on action to collect, EN §2-610.2.
  Conditions not violations, EN §2-613.
  Criminal penalties.
    Knowing violations, EN §2-609.1.
    Limitation on violations, EN §2-610.2.
  Extensions of time for abatement, EN §2-609.
  Plan for compliance, EN §2-611.
Volatile organic emissions control program.
  Rules and regulations, EN §2-303.1.
Zoning.
  Ambient air quality control permits.
    Compliance with zoning and land use
      requirements, EN §2-404.

ALARM SYSTEMS.
Audible systems.
  Equipped to automatically silence, CR §9-611.
Calvert county, 25 §236D.
Defective system.
  Notice to user, use after notice, CR §9-610.
Definitions, CR §9-607.
False alarms, CR §9-608.
  Multiple alarms, CR §9-609.
Frederick county.
  Registering alarm system contractors and users,
    25 §221A.
Smoke detectors, PS §§9-101 to 9-109.
Washington county.
  Power to regulate, 25 §236E.

ALCOHOL AND DRUG COUNSELORS, HO
  §§17-101 to 17-502.
See PROFESSIONAL COUNSELORS AND
  THERAPISTS.

ALCOHOLIC BEVERAGES.
Abuse.
  See DRUG OR ALCOHOL ABUSE.
Adult dependent care programs.
  Test of potential employees, HG §19-1903.
Advertising.
  Manufacturer, wholesaler, etc.
    Furnishing signs, displays or other
      advertisements to retail establishments, 2B
      §12-104.
Affidavits.
  False statements.
    Perjury, 2B §16-501.
Age.
  Beverage server's age, 2B §§12-209.2, 12-213,
    12-219, 12-224.
  Citation for violations, CR §10-119.
  False documentation, CR §10-115.
  Jurisdiction, CR §10-120.
  Licensee's age, 2B §§10-102, 10-104.
  Misrepresentation of age, CR §10-113.
  Purchaser's age.
    Record of documentary proof, 2B §12-109.
  Retail sales, 2B §12-302.

ALCOHOLIC BEVERAGES —Cont'd
Agriculture.
  Winery and grape growers' advisory commission,
    AG §§10-1201 to 10-1206. See within this
    heading, "Winery and grape growers' advisory
    commission."
**Alcohol and tobacco tax field enforcement
  bureau,** 2B §16-407.
Alcohol awareness programs, 2B §13-101.
  Permits, 2B §2-101.
    Instructor's permits, 2B §2-101.
Allegany county.
  See ALLEGANY COUNTY.
Annapolis.
  See ANNAPOLIS.
Anne Arundel county.
  See ANNE ARUNDEL COUNTY.
Appeals.
  License commissioners.
    Appeals to court.
      Generally, 2B §16-101.
  Licenses.
    Revocation and suspension, 2B §10-403.
  Minors conviction for violations, CR §10-119.
Assignments for benefit of creditors.
  Licenses.
    Transfer of license by receiver or trustee, 2B
      §10-503.
Associations.
  Unincorporated associations.
    Fines and penalties, 2B §16-504.
    Not to receive licenses, 2B §9-101.
Athletics.
  Possession of intoxicating beverages.
    School athletic contests, ED §26-103.
Attorneys at law.
  Sales permitted without license or permit, 2B
    §1-201.
Auctions.
  Auctioneers.
    Sales permitted without license or permit, 2B
      §1-201.
  Charity wine auctions.
    Permits, 2B §2-101.
**Audiologists, hearing aid dealers and
  speech-language pathologists.**
  Providing professional services while under the
    influence of alcohol or controlled dangerous
    substances.
    Grounds for denial, reprimand, suspension or
      revocation of license, HO §2-314.
Audit.
  Liquor control boards.
    Records, 2B §15-206.
Aviation.
  Aircraft.
    Operation under influence, TR §5-1006.
  Beer, wine and liquor licenses.
    Class G, on sale, 2B §6-503.
      Repeal provisions, 2B §8-102.
  Carriers.
    Records and reports.
      Required, 2B §14-202.
    Sale.
      Exercising right to sell under lien, 2B §1-201.
  Illegal transportation.
    Confiscation and forfeiture of transportation
      equipment, 2B §1-201.
  Licenses.
    Applications.
      For airplanes, 2B §9-101.

ALCOHOLIC BEVERAGES —Cont'd
Aviation —Cont'd
  Licenses —Cont'd
    Applications —Cont'd
      Where to be filed, 2B §10-101.
    Beer, wine and liquor licenses.
      Class G, on-sale, 2B §6-503.
        Repeal provisions, 2B §8-102.
    Restrictions upon retail dealers, 2B §12-107.
    Transport planes.
      No license or permit required of transport
        planes, 2B §1-201.
Awareness programs, 2B §13-101.
  Permits, 2B §2-101.
Bailiffs.
  Enforcement of article.
    Duties, 2B §§16-401, 16-405.
Baltimore City.
  See BALTIMORE CITY.
Baltimore county.
  See BALTIMORE COUNTY.
Bar and counter sales, 2B §11-403.
Baseball stadiums.
  Harford county.
    Stadium on-sale license, limitations, 2B
      §8-213.1.
  Wicomico county.
    Beer and light wine license, 2B §8-223.
Beer.
  Adulterated or mislabeled beverage.
    Selling, 2B §22-101.
  Anne Arundel county.
    Deluxe restaurant license, 2B §8-202.1.
  Baltimore City beer festival.
    License, 2B §8-801.
  Baltimore county.
    Beer festivals, special license, 2B §8-802.
  Beverage server's age, 2B §§12-209.2, 12-213,
    12-219, 12-224.
  Brewery license, 2B §2-206.
  Brew-pub license, 2B §2-207.
  Carroll county beer tasting license, 2B §8-901.
  Cash on delivery sales.
    Manufacturer or wholesaler selling to retailers,
      2B §12-112.
  Containers.
    Deposit on returnable beer containers.
      Rules and regulations by comptroller, 2B
        §16-303.
    Detachable metal tab opening device.
      Sale prohibited, 2B §21-102.
    Keg sales.
      Registration of, 2B §21-106.
    Size of containers, 2B §21-101.
  Defined, 2B §1-102.
  Family beer.
    Defined, 2B §1-102.
  Festival license.
    Baltimore City beer festival, 2B §8-801.
    Carroll county, 2B §8-805.
    Frederick county, 2B §8-803.
    Queen Anne's county beer and wine festival, 2B
      §8-311.
    Wicomico county, 2B §8-804.
    Worcester county beer and wine festival, 2B
      §8-314.
  Franchises.
    Actions.
      Violations of subtitle, 2B §17-107.
    Alcohol content.
      Information regarding.
        Providing to wholesalers and retail dealers,
          2B §21-104.

ALCOHOLIC BEVERAGES —Cont'd
Beer —Cont'd
  Franchises —Cont'd
    Change of manufacturers.
      Obligations of successors under agreement on
        date of change of beer manufacturers, 2B
        §21-103.
    Declaration of policy, 2B §17-101.
    Deficiencies of franchisee.
      Opportunity to correct, 2B §17-104.
    Definitions, 2B §17-101.
    Delivery outside territory, 2B §17-106.
    Dual distributorships.
      Establishment prohibited, 2B §17-105.
    Information regarding alcohol content.
      Providing to wholesalers and retail dealers,
        2B §21-104.
    Manufacturer.
      Distributor's right of action, 2B §17-107.
      Orders of distributor.
        Failure or refusal to fill, 2B §17-102.
      Successor manufacturers.
        Obligations on agreements in effect on date
          of change of beer manufacturer, 2B
          §21-103.
      Unlawful inducements or threats, 2B §17-102.
    Orders of distributors.
      Failure or refusal to fill, 2B §17-102.
    Policy, 2B §17-101.
    Renewal.
      Notice of nonrenewal, 2B §17-104.
      Refusal to renew.
        Without good cause, 2B §17-103.
    Sales outside of territory, 2B §17-106.
    Successor beer manufacturers.
      Obligations under agreements in effect on
        date of change of beer manufacturers, 2B
        §21-103.
    Termination.
      Notice of intended termination, 2B §17-104.
      Without good cause, 2B §17-103.
    Unlawful inducements or threats.
      Manufacturers, 2B §17-102.
    Violations of subtitle.
      Distributor's right of action, 2B §17-107.
  Homemade beer.
    Manufacture without license, 2B §1-201.
  Improperly brewed malt beverage.
    Manufacturing and selling, 2B §22-101.
  Keg registration, 2B §21-106.
  Licenses.
    Age of licensee, 2B §§10-102, 10-104.
    Baltimore City beer festival, 2B §8-801.
    Beer and light wine licenses. See within this
      heading, "Beer and light wine licenses."
    Beer licenses. See within this heading, "Beer
      licenses."
    Beer, wine and liquor licenses. See within this
      heading, "Beer, wine and liquor licenses."
    Brewery license, 2B §2-206.
      Generally. See within this heading,
        "Manufacturers."
    Brew-pub license, 2B §2-207.
    Micro-brewery license, 2B §2-208.
    Pub-brewery license, 2B §2-207.
    Queen Anne's county beer and wine festival, 2B
      §8-311.
    Worcester county beer and wine festival, 2B
      §8-314.
  Micro-brewery license, 2B §2-208.
  Pub-brewery license, 2B §2-207.

ALCOHOLIC BEVERAGES —Cont'd

Beer —Cont'd

Queen Anne's county beer and wine festival.
    License, 2B §8-311.

Sale to retailers for cash on delivery, 2B §12-112.

Seller's age, 2B §12-302.

Taxation.
    Alcoholic beverage tax.
        See ALCOHOLIC BEVERAGE TAX.

Worcester county beer and wine festival.
    License, 2B §8-314.

Beer and light wine licenses.

Age of licensee, 2B §§10-102, 10-104.

Annapolis, 2B §5-601.

Baseball stadiums.
    Issuance to corporations or partnerships, 2B §9-101.

Class A.
    Baltimore City, 2B §4-202.
    Certain counties, 2B §§4-201, 4-202.
    Garrett county, 2B §4-203.
    Kent county, 2B §4-204.
    Off-sale, 2B §5-101.

Class A2, on-sale and off-sale licenses, 2B §4-202.
    Garrett county, 2B §4-203.

Class A, off-sale, 2B §5-101.
    Light wine, 2B §4-201.

Class B-DH, on-sale only.
    Drafthouses, 2B §8-702.

Class B-GC, on-sale.
    Golf course, 2B §16-201.

Class B, on-sale, 2B §5-201.

Class C, on-sale.
    Clubs, 2B §5-301.
    Restrictions upon retail dealers, 2B §12-107.
    Special and temporary licenses.
        Deliveries and returns before and after effective date, 2B §7-101.
        Seven days, 2B §7-101.

Class D, on-sale, 2B §5-401.

Class E, on-sale.
    Applications, 2B §10-102.
    Restrictions upon retail dealers, 2B §12-107.

Class F, on-sale.
    Applications, 2B §10-102.
    Hours and days for sale, 2B §11-201.
    Railroads, 2B §5-501.
    Restrictions upon retail dealers, 2B §12-107.

Class G, on-sale.
    Applications, 2B §10-102.
    Restrictions upon retail dealers, 2B §12-107.

Class H, on-sale only, 2B §5-202.

Clubs.
    Class C, on-sale, 2B §5-301.

Fees. See within this heading, "Licenses."

Generally. See within this heading, "Licenses."

Hotels and restaurants.
    Class B, on-sale, 2B §5-201.
    Class H, on-sale only, 2B §5-202.
    Hours and days for sale, 2B §11-302.

Hours and days for sale, 2B §11-302.

Stadiums, on-sale only, 2B §8-223.

Wholesaler, 2B §2-301.

Beer and wine tastings.

Class BWT license, on-premises.
    Baltimore City, 2B §8-403.1.

Beer licenses.

Class A, off-sale, 2B §3-101.

Class B, on-sale, 2B §3-201.

Class C, on-sale.
    Clubs, 2B §3-301.

ALCOHOLIC BEVERAGES —Cont'd

Beer licenses —Cont'd

Class C, on-sale —Cont'd
    Restrictions upon retail dealers, 2B §12-107.
    Special and temporary licenses.
        Deliveries and returns before and after effective date, 2B §7-101.
        Seven days, 2B §7-101.

Class D, on-sale, 2B §3-401.

Class E, on-sale.
    Application, 2B §10-102.
    Restrictions upon retail dealers, 2B §12-107.

Class F, on-sale.
    Application, 2B §10-102.
    Restrictions upon retail dealers, 2B §12-107.

Class G, on-sale.
    Application, 2B §10-102.
    Restrictions upon retail dealers, 2B §12-107.

Class H, on-sale only, 2B §3-202.

Clubs.
    Class C, on-sale, 2B §3-301.

Fees. See within this heading, "Licenses."

Generally. See within this heading, "Licenses."

Hotels and restaurants.
    Class B, on-sale, 2B §3-201.
    Class H, on-sale only, 2B §3-202.

Hours and days for sale, 2B §11-301.

Wholesaler, 2B §2-301.

Beer, wine and liquor licenses.

Caterers.
    Carroll county.
        Class H, 2B §6-703.

Class A-2, off-sale.
    Baltimore City, 2B §6-102.

Class A, off-sale, 2B §6-101.
    Hours and days for sale, 2B §11-303.

Class B-BB (bed and breakfast), 2B §6-201.

Class BC on-and limited off-sale.
    Hotels or restaurants and caterers, 2B §6-201.

Class B (inn), on-sale.
    Hotels and restaurants, 2B §6-201.

Class B-MB/22 micro-brewery license.
    Hotels and restaurants, 2B §6-201.

Class B, on-sale.
    Hotels and restaurants, 2B §6-201.

Class B-stadium.
    Baseball stadiums, 2B §6-201.

Class C, on-sale.
    Clubs, 2B §6-301.
    Golf courses, 2B §8-501.
    Restrictions upon retail dealers, 2B §12-107.
    Special and temporary licenses.
        Seven days, 2B §7-101.

Class D, on-sale, 2B §6-401.
    Employment of minors prohibited, 2B §12-302.
    Ocean City municipal golf course, 2B §6-401.
    Taverns, etc., 2B §6-401.

Class E, on-sale.
    Application, 2B §§9-101, 10-102.
    Restrictions upon retail dealers, 2B §12-107.
    Steamboats, 2B §6-501.

Class F, on-sale.
    Application, 2B §§9-101, 10-102.
    Hours and days for sale, 2B §11-201.
    Railroads, 2B §6-502.
    Repeal provisions, 2B §8-102.
    Restrictions upon retail dealers, 2B §12-107.

Class GC.
    Golf courses, 2B §§8-501 to 8-507.

Class G, on-sale.
    Airplanes, 2B §6-503.

ALCOHOLIC BEVERAGES —Cont'd
Beer, wine and liquor licenses —Cont'd
  Class G, on-sale —Cont'd
    Application, 2B §§9-101, 10-102.
    Repeal provisions, 2B §8-102.
    Restrictions upon retail dealers, 2B §12-107.
  Class H.
    Caterers in Carroll county, 2B §6-703.
  Class I, Worcester county, 2B §8-224.
  Clubs.
    Class C, on-sale, 2B §6-301.
  Conference center facilities, 2B §6-601.
  Fees. See within this heading, "Licenses."
  Generally. See within this heading, "Licenses."
  Golf courses, 2B §§8-501 to 8-507.
  Hours and days for sale, 2B §11-303.
  Minors.
    Employment to sell, deliver or otherwise deal
        with alcoholic beverages, 2B §12-302.
  Special licenses, 2B §6-301.
  Taverns.
    Class D, on-sale, 2B §6-401.
  Wholesaler, 2B §2-301.
Blood tests.
  Driving under the influence.
    See DRIVING UNDER THE INFLUENCE.
  Job-related alcohol testing, HG §17-214.
Boards.
  Liquor control boards. See within this heading,
      "Liquor control boards and dispensaries."
Bonds, surety.
  Liquor control department, 2B §15-201.
  Retailers.
    Required, 2B §14-101.
Bottle clubs.
  Anne Arundel county, 2B §20-101.
  Baltimore City, 2B §20-102.
  Baltimore county, 2B §20-103.
  St. Mary's county.
    Licenses, 2B §20-108.
Bowling alleys.
  More than one license for same person or
      premises.
    Exceptions as to bowling alleys, 2B §9-102.
  Wicomico county.
    Definition of "bowling alley," 2B §1-102.
Brewers.
  Licenses.
    Brewery, 2B §2-206.
    Brew-pub, 2B §2-207.
    Manufacturers generally. See within this
        heading, "Manufacturers."
    Microbreweries, 2B §2-208.
  Tied houses.
    Prohibited, 2B §12-101.
Brewery license, 2B §2-206.
Brew-pub license, 2B §2-207.
Brew-thrus. See within this heading, "Drive-thru
    purchase facilities."
Budget and management.
  License commissioners.
    County budget and fiscal policies.
      Boards subject to, 24 §8-101.
Building.
  Regulations.
    Conformance to, 2B §9-105.
Bulk sales.
  Bulk transfer permit.
    General provisions, 2B §2-101.
Calvert county.
  See CALVERT COUNTY.

ALCOHOLIC BEVERAGES —Cont'd
Candy.
  Products containing alcohol, HG §21-209.
Caroline county.
  See CAROLINE COUNTY.
Carriers.
  Planes and ships.
    Cocktail lounge in use by passengers.
      No license or permit required, 2B §1-201.
  Records and reports.
    Required, 2B §14-202.
  Sales.
    Permitted without license or permit, 2B §1-201.
Carroll county.
  See CARROLL COUNTY.
Caterer's license.
  Baltimore City, 2B §6-701.1.
  Caroline county, 2B §6-702.1.
  Frederick county, 2B §6-703.1.
  Garrett county, 2B §6-703.2.
  Statewide caterers (SCAT) license, 2B §6-701.
Cecil county.
  See CECIL COUNTY.
Chain stores.
  Licenses.
    More than one license for same person or
        premises, 2B §9-102.
Charitable organizations.
  Wine auctions.
    Charity wine auction permits, 2B §2-101.
Charles county.
  See CHARLES COUNTY.
Chiropractors.
  Providing professional services while under the
      influence of alcohol, narcotic or controlled
      dangerous substances.
  Denials, reprimands, suspensions and
      revocations of licenses, HO §3-313.
Cider.
  Home consumption.
    Manufacture without license, 2B §1-201.
Citations.
  Licenses.
    Beer, wine and liquor licenses.
      Kent county taverns, 2B §6-401.
    Violations.
      Civil citations in certain counties, 2B §16-408.
  Minors.
    Citation for violations, CR §10-119.
    Jurisdiction, CR §10-120.
    Sales to underage drinkers or intoxicated
        persons, CP §4-101.
  Open containers in motor vehicles' passenger
      areas, CR §10-126.
    Procedure, CR §10-127.
Clerks of court.
  Licenses.
    Renewal, 2B §10-301.
  Local licenses.
    Issuance.
      Baltimore City, 2B §8-203.
      Howard county, 2B §8-214.
Clubs.
  Beer and light wine licenses.
    Class C, on-sale, 2B §5-301.
  Beer licenses.
    Class C, on-sale, 2B §3-301.
  Beer, wine and liquor licenses.
    Class C, on-sale, 2B §6-301.
  Defined, 2B §1-102.

ALCOHOLIC BEVERAGES —Cont'd
Clubs —Cont'd
Hours of sale.
Beer and light wine licenses, 2B §11-302.
Beer licenses, 2B §11-301.
Beer, wine and liquor licenses, 2B §11-303.
Licenses.
Application for club, 2B §9-101.
Renewal.
Substitution of officers, 2B §10-301.
Private clubs.
Discrimination in public accommodations.
Exceptions, 49B §5.
Commercial drivers' licenses, TR §§16-205.1,
16-812, 16-813.
Commissioners.
License commissioners. See within this heading,
"License commissioners."
Comptroller.
Collection of taxes, 2B §12-113.
Confiscation of property.
Disposition of confiscated property, 2B §1-201.
Defined, 2B §1-102.
Discounts.
Regulations, 2B §12-103.
Enforcement of article, 2B §§16-401, 16-404,
16-405.
Inspections and investigations, 2B §16-405.
Hearings.
Delegation of authority to conduct hearings, 2B
§16-404.
Licenses.
Fees.
Disposition, 2B §10-204.
Nonrefundable application fee, 2B §2-402.
Issuance, 2B §10-201.
Delegation of authority to issue licenses and
permits, 2B §16-404.
Renewal, 2B §10-301.
Fee, 2B §2-402.
Revocation and suspension.
Procedure, 2B §10-403.
Powers.
Generally, 2B §16-404.
Reports.
Annual report of comptroller, 2B §14-203.
Supervision over, 2B §14-201.
Rules and regulations.
Adoption, 2B §16-301.
Deposit on returnable beer containers, 2B
§16-303.
Discrimination prohibited, 2B §12-102.
Powers as to, 2B §16-302.
Computer sales.
Out-of-state unlicensed sellers, 2B §16-506.1.
Confectioneries.
Products containing alcohol, HG §21-209.
Conference center facilities.
Beer, wine and liquor licenses, 2B §6-601.
Confiscation of property, 2B §1-201.
Searches and seizures. See within this heading,
"Searches and seizures."
Conflicts of interest.
Liquor control boards, 2B §15-208.
Constables.
Enforcement of article, 2B §16-401.
Duties, 2B §16-405.
Sales permitted without license or permit, 2B
§1-201.
Consumer.
Defined, 2B §1-102.

ALCOHOLIC BEVERAGES —Cont'd
Consumption.
Certain counties, 2B §§16-201, 16-202.
Hours and days, 2B §11-304.
Partially consumed bottle of wine.
Removal from licensed premises, 2B §12-107.1.
Public places.
Municipal regulation, 2B §19-104.
Use on licensed premises restricted, 2B §12-107.
Containers.
Beer.
Detachable metal tab opening device.
Sale prohibited, 2B §21-102.
Size of container, 2B §21-101.
Brands and labels.
Illicit alcoholic beverages, 2B §1-102.
Deposit on returnable beer containers.
Rules and regulations of comptroller, 2B
§16-303.
Detachable metal tab opening device.
Sale prohibited, 2B §21-102.
Keeping containers in violation of section, 2B
§12-113.
Kegs.
Registration of, 2B §21-106.
Unregistered kegs, CR §10-118.
Manufacturers.
Information to be filed as to containers, brands
and labels, 2B §12-103.
Penalty for violations, 2B §12-113.
Refilling container prohibited, 2B §12-113.
Tampering with contents, 2B §12-113.
Wine.
Detachable metal tab opening device.
Sale prohibited, 2B §21-102.
Contraband in place of confinement, CR §9-415.
Contracts.
Liquor control boards.
Powers, 2B §15-205.
Control of sale and distribution.
Liquor control boards.
Monopoly control, 2B §15-204.
Corporations.
Fines and penalties, 2B §16-504.
Licenses.
Application for corporation, 2B §9-101.
Renewal.
Substitution of officers, 2B §10-301.
Revocation and suspension.
Felony conviction of stockholder, 2B §10-401.
Correctional facility inmates.
Contraband in place of confinement, CR §9-415.
Counties.
Application for county license, 2B §10-103.
Commissioners.
Ex officio boards of license commissioners, 2B
§15-105.
Dispensaries.
Authorized, 2B §15-203.
License commissioners.
Appointment by county commissioners, 2B
§15-104.
Removal by county commissioners, 2B §15-110.
Taxation.
Prohibited, 2B §1-101.
Court.
Defined, 2B §1-102.
Crimes and offenses.
Adulterating or mislabeling beverage, 2B §22-101.
Advertising displays, plans, etc., 2B §12-104.

ALCOHOLIC BEVERAGES —Cont'd
Crimes and offenses —Cont'd
Beer.
Adulterating or mislabeling, 2B §22-101.
Misrepresenting coloring or poterine as malt extract or porter, 2B §22-101.
Beverage misrepresentation, 2B §22-101.
Conflicts of interest.
Liquor control boards, 2B §15-208.
Containers.
Detachable metal tab opening device, 2B §21-102.
Contraband in place of confinement, CR §9-415.
Drinking on public property, 2B §19-204.
Drunkards and mentally deficient persons.
Sales to, 2B §12-110.
Elections.
Providing voters alcoholic beverages, CR §9-203.
Sale and use on election day, 2B §11-401.
Fraud and deceit.
Tampering with or refilling containers, 2B §12-113.
Free food, 2B §12-106.
General penalty, 2B §16-503.
Handgun permit holder under the influence.
Carrying, wearing or transporting handgun, CR §4-206.
Homicide by motor vehicle or vessel while impaired or under the influence, CR §§2-501 to 2-508.
Hours and days for sale, 2B §11-304.
Sundays, 2B §11-403.
Intoxicated persons.
Sales to prohibited, 2B §12-108.
Life threatening injury by motor vehicle or vessel while impaired or under the influence, CR §§3-211, 3-212.
Malt beverages.
Improperly brewed beverages, manufacture or sale, 2B §22-101.
Minors.
Citation for violations, CR §10-119.
Jurisdiction, CR §10-120.
Misrepresentation of age, CR §10-113.
False documentation, CR §10-115.
Underage consumption.
Consumption or possession of minors on premises, 2B §12-108.
Furnishing or allowing, exceptions, CR §10-117.
Kegs, CR §10-118.
Obtaining for underage consumption, CR §10-116.
Underage possession, CR §10-114.
Possession of open container in certain places, 2B §19-302.
Worcester county.
Bringing alcohol on to, consuming on or transferring alcohol on unlicensed premises, 2B §18-104.
Criminal justice information system.
Licenses.
Criminal history check of applicants, 2B §10-103.
Criminal procedure.
Defense to prosecution.
Sale to person not of legal age, 2B §12-109.
Prosecution for selling at unlicensed premises.
Prima facie evidence of sale, 2B §16-406.
Dealers.
Nonresident dealers.
Permits, 2B §2-101.

ALCOHOLIC BEVERAGES —Cont'd
Death.
Licenses.
Death of licensee.
Effect, 2B §10-506.
Declaration of policy, 2B §1-101.
Definitions, 2B §1-102.
Beer.
Franchises, 2B §17-101.
Charity wine auctions, 2B §2-101.
Habitual drunkards.
Knowingly as to habitual drunkards, 2B §12-110.
Job-related alcohol testing, HG §17-214.
Open containers of alcoholic beverages in motor vehicles, CR §10-123.
Premises.
Defined, 2B §§12-201, 12-213.
Public property, 2B §19-201.
Wholesaler.
Delivery defined, 2B §2-301.
Winery and grape growers' advisory commission, AG §10-1201.
Deliveries.
Retail deliveries, 2B §12-301.
Dentists.
Providing professional services while under the influence of alcohol or controlled dangerous substances.
Denials, reprimands, probations, suspensions or revocations of licenses, HO §4-315.
Detoxification centers.
See DRUG OR ALCOHOL ABUSE.
Direct wine seller's permit, 2B §§7.5-101 to 7.5-110.
Discount houses.
Licenses.
More than one license for same person or premises, 2B §9-102.
Discrimination.
Public accommodations.
Premises selling alcoholic beverages.
Private clubs.
Exception, 49B §5.
Sale or distribution prohibited, 2B §12-102.
Disorderly intoxication, 2B §§19-101 to 19-104.
See DRUNKENNESS.
Distilled spirits.
Taxation. See within this heading, "Taxation."
Distilleries.
Licenses. See within this heading, "Manufacturers."
Tied houses.
Prohibited, 2B §12-101.
Warehouses.
Receipts.
Subject to provisions of subtitle, CL §18-307.
District Court.
Committing individuals for detoxification.
Authority of court, CJ §4-202.
Domicile.
Permits.
Change of domicile permit, 2B §2-101.
Dorchester county.
See DORCHESTER COUNTY.
Drafthouses.
Beer and wine licenses.
Class B-DH (on-sale only), 2B §15-101.
Licenses.
Class B-DH license, 2B §8-701.

ALCOHOLIC BEVERAGES —Cont'd
Drive-thru purchase facilities.
Licenses.
Carroll county, 2B §12-207.
Cecil county, 2B §§9-208, 10-503.
Frederick county, 2B §§9-211.1, 10-503.
Harford county, 2B §§9-213, 10-503.
Howard county, 2B §§9-214, 10-503.
St. Mary's county, 2B §§9-219, 10-503.
Transfer, 2B §10-503.
Worcester county, 2B §§9-224, 10-503.
Drugs.
Beer, wine and liquor licenses.
Class A, off-sale.
Regulations as to drugstores, 2B §6-101.
Drunkenness.
Alcoholism.
See DRUG OR ALCOHOL ABUSE.
Disorderly intoxication, 2B §§19-101 to 19-104.
See DRUNKENNESS.
General provisions.
See DRUNKENNESS.
Knowingly.
Defined, 2B §12-110.
Motor vehicles. See within this heading, "Motor vehicles."
Sales to habitual drunkards prohibited, 2B §12-110.
Sales to intoxicated persons prohibited, 2B §12-108.
Education.
Alcohol awareness programs, 2B §13-101.
Elections.
Polling places.
Use of building where owner or occupant holds ABC license, EL §10-101.
Providing voters, CR §9-203.
Sale and use prohibited on election day, 2B §11-401.
Use at polling place, EL §16-207.
Electronic means used for selling wine.
Direct wine seller's permit, 2B §§7.5-101 to 7.5-110.
Employers and employees.
Job-related alcohol testing, HG §17-214.
Enforcement of laws.
Alcohol and tobacco tax field enforcement bureau.
General provisions, 2B §16-407.
Certain counties, 2B §16-414.
Comptroller, 2B §§16-401 to 16-405.
Fines. See within this heading, "Fines."
General provisions, 2B §§16-401 to 16-414.
Inspections.
General provisions, 2B §16-405.
Peace officers.
Duties, 2B §16-405.
Witnesses.
Powers as to witnesses, 2B §16-410.
Evidence.
Beverages taken as evidence, 2B §16-405.
Confiscated property.
Destruction of evidence, 2B §1-201.
Operation of motor vehicle under influence.
Presumptions, CJ §10-307.
Sales at unlicensed premises.
Display or offer for sale of alcoholic beverages, 2B §16-405.
Witnesses.
Power to summon witnesses, 2B §16-410.
Exceptions prevail over general rule, 2B §1-103.

ALCOHOLIC BEVERAGES —Cont'd
Executors and administrators.
Death of licensee.
Effect on license, 2B §10-506.
Licenses.
Continuation of business.
Death of licensee, 2B §10-506.
Sales permitted without license or permit, 2B §1-201.
Exercise of powers authorized by article, 2B §1-101.
Family beer.
Defined, 2B §1-102.
Family breweries and wineries.
Permits, 2B §2-101.
Family wine.
Defined, 2B §1-102.
Fees.
Licenses. See within this heading, "Licenses."
Light wine licenses, 2B §4-201.
Nonrefundable application fee, 2B §2-402.
Permits, 2B §2-101.
Wholesalers' licenses, 2B §2-301.
Fines.
Associations.
Unincorporated associations, 2B §16-504.
Certain counties, 2B §§16-502, 16-507.
Corporations, 2B §16-504.
Drunkards and mentally deficient persons.
Sales to prohibited, 2B §12-110.
Election days.
Sale on, 2B §11-401.
Free food, 2B §12-106.
General penalty, 2B §16-503.
Hours of sale.
Consumption, 2B §11-304.
Illicit manufacture, 2B §16-505.
Kent county taverns, 2B §6-401.
Liquor control boards.
Financial interest of member or employee of liquor control boards, 2B §15-208.
Local penalties, 2B §16-507.
Manufacturer and wholesaler.
Having interest in retail establishment, 2B §12-104.
Partnerships, 2B §16-504.
Payable to county where offense committed, 2B §16-502.
Taverns.
Kent county.
Beer, wine and liquor licenses, 2B §6-401.
Taxation.
Evasions, 2B §16-506.
Flavoring extracts.
Manufacturers' use.
Permit, 2B §2-101.
Food and food establishments.
Free food.
Prohibited, 2B §12-106.
Food stores.
Floor space, 2B §9-108.
Forfeiture.
Confiscation of property, 2B §1-201.
Searches and seizures. See within this heading, "Searches and seizures."
Franchises.
Beer. See within this heading, "Beer."
Fraud and deceit.
False statements, 2B §16-501.
Prevention by comptroller, 2B §12-113.

ALCOHOLIC BEVERAGES —Cont'd
Frederick county.
See FREDERICK COUNTY.
Garrett county.
See GARRETT COUNTY.
General restrictions, 2B §11-403.
Golf courses.
Caroline county.
Class GC beer, wine and liquor license, 2B
§8-507.1.
Governor.
License commissioners.
Appointment by governor and senate, 2B
§15-101.
Removal by governor, 2B §15-110.
Guided tours of wineries.
Number of ounces of wine served at no charge to
persons on tour, 2B §§2-204, 2-205.
Handgun permit holder under the influence.
Carrying, wearing or transporting handgun, CR
§4-206.
Harford county.
See HARFORD COUNTY.
Home breweries, 2B §§1-201, 2-101.
Homicide by motor vehicle or vessel while
impaired or under the influence, CR
§§2-501 to 2-508.
Hotels.
Beer and light wine licenses.
Class B, on-sale, 2B §5-201.
Class H, on-sale only, 2B §5-202.
Hours and days of sale, 2B §11-302.
Beer licenses.
Class B, on-sale, 2B §3-201.
Class H, on-sale only, 2B §3-202.
Beer, wine and liquor licenses.
Class B (inn), on-sale, 2B §6-201.
Class B-MB/22 micro-brewery license.
Hotels and restaurants, 2B §6-201.
Class B, on-sale, 2B §6-201.
Defined, 2B §1-102.
Hours of sale.
Beer and light wine licenses, 2B §11-302.
Beer licenses, 2B §11-301.
Beer, wine and liquor licenses, 2B §11-303.
Hours and days for sale.
Beer and light wine licenses, 2B §11-302.
Beer licenses, 2B §11-301.
Beer, wine and liquor licenses.
Class A, off-sale, 2B §11-303.
Class F license, 2B §11-201.
Consumption, 2B §11-304.
Election days, 2B §11-401.
Liquor control boards.
Powers, 2B §15-205.
Manufacturer's license, 2B §11-101.
New Year's day, 2B §11-402.
Retail license.
General provisions, 2B §11-202.
Special licenses, 2B §11-203.
Sundays.
General restrictions, 2B §11-403.
Temporary licenses, 2B §11-203.
Wholesaler's license, 2B §11-102.
Howard county.
See HOWARD COUNTY.
Identification.
Special identification cards, TR §12-301.
Fees, TR §12-301.
Use, TR §12-301.

ALCOHOLIC BEVERAGES —Cont'd
Illicit alcoholic beverages.
Defined, 2B §1-102.
Impaired by alcohol.
Driving under the influence.
Generally.
See DRIVING UNDER THE INFLUENCE.
Import.
Defined, 2B §1-102.
Importer.
Defined, 2B §1-102.
Importing and exporting.
Definitions, 2B §1-102.
Permit, 2B §2-101.
Storage, 2B §1-201.
Indictments.
Unlawful sale of liquor or beer, 2B §16-509.
Inmates at correctional facilities.
Contraband in place of confinement, CR §9-415.
Insane persons.
Sales to prohibited, 2B §12-110.
Inspections.
Enforcement of laws.
General provisions, 2B §16-405.
Prevention of frauds, 2B §12-113.
Inspectors.
Certain counties, 2B §15-112.
Internet sales of wine.
Direct wine seller's permit, 2B §§7.5-101 to
7.5-110.
Intoxicated persons.
Sales to prohibited, 2B §12-108.
Citation, crime charged by, CP §4-101.
Job-related alcohol testing, HG §17-214.
Jurisdiction.
Minors purchasing or consuming alcohol, 2B
§12-108.
Waiver, CR §10-120.
Juvenile causes.
Citation for violation of certain alcoholic beverage
laws, CJ §3-8A-33.
Jurisdiction, CR §10-120.
Keg registration, 2B §21-106.
Kent county.
See KENT COUNTY.
Labor and industry.
Job-related alcohol testing, HG §17-214.
Landlord and tenant.
Leases.
Liquor control boards.
Powers, 2B §15-205.
Laws.
Exceptions prevail over general rule, 2B §1-103.
License commissioners.
Appeals, 2B §16-101.
Applicability of section, 2B §15-101.
Applications.
Procedure.
Generally, 2B §10-202.
Appointment.
Applicability of section, 2B §15-101.
By county commissioners, 2B §15-104.
By governor and senate, 2B §15-101.
Beer licenses.
Issuance.
Class H, on-sale only, 2B §3-202.
Budget and management.
County budget and fiscal policies.
Boards subject to, 24 §8-101.
County commissioners.
Ex officio county commissioners, 2B §15-105.

ALCOHOLIC BEVERAGES —Cont'd
License commissioners —Cont'd
Employees.
Generally, 2B §15-112.
Inspectors.
Certain counties, 2B §15-112.
General provisions, 2B §§15-112, 16-405.
Liquor control board ex officio, 2B §15-108.
Powers.
Generally, 2B §15-112.
Restriction as to number of licenses in area, 2B §§9-201, 9-203.
Procurement.
County purchasing laws.
Boards subject to, 24 §8-101.
Qualifications, 2B §15-101.
Removals.
Appointment by governor, 2B §15-110.
Boards appointed by county commissioners, 2B §15-110.
Revocation and suspension of license.
Procedure, 2B §10-403.
Rules and regulations.
Adoption, 2B §16-301.
Salaries, 2B §15-109.
Vacancies.
Filling, 2B §15-101.
License issuing authority.
Beer licenses.
Issuance.
Class A, off-sale, 2B §3-101.
Class C, on-sale, 2B §3-301.
Defined, 2B §1-102.
Licenses.
Age of licensee, 2B §§10-102, 10-104.
Airplanes.
Applications, 2B §9-101.
Where to be filed, 2B §10-101.
Alcohol awareness programs, 2B §13-101.
Appeals. See within this heading, "Appeals."
Applications.
Airplanes, 2B §9-101.
Approval by board, 2B §10-202.
Approval by comptroller, 2B §10-201.
Corporations or clubs, 2B §9-101.
County licenses.
Additional requirements, 2B §10-104.
Contents, 2B §10-103.
Exceptions, 2B §10-104.
Denial by comptroller, 2B §10-201.
Expenses.
Publication and other expenses borne by applicant, 2B §10-105.
Filing.
Where to be filed, 2B §10-101.
Investigation by comptroller, 2B §10-201.
Nonrefundable application fee, 2B §2-402.
Notice.
On premises, 2B §10-202.
Partnerships, 2B §9-101.
Refusal, 2B §10-208.
Renewal, 2B §10-301.
Special and temporary licenses, 2B §7-101.
What to contain, 2B §§10-102 to 10-104.
Classes E, F, and G, 2B §10-102.
Assignment.
Generally, 2B §10-503.
Aviation. See within this heading, "Aviation."
Beer.
Baltimore City beer festival, 2B §8-801.

ALCOHOLIC BEVERAGES —Cont'd
Licenses —Cont'd
Beer —Cont'd
Baltimore county.
Beer festivals, special license, 2B §8-802.
Beer and light wine licenses. See within this heading, "Beer and light wine licenses."
Beer licenses. See within this heading, "Beer licenses."
Beer, wine and liquor licenses. See within this heading, "Beer, wine and liquor licenses."
Brewery license, 2B §2-206.
Brew-pub license, 2B §2-207.
Carroll county beer festival, 2B §8-805.
Carroll county beer tasting license, 2B §8-901.
Frederick county beer festival, 2B §8-803.
Micro-brewery license, 2B §2-208.
Queen Anne's county beer and wine festival, 2B §8-311.
Wicomico county beer festival, 2B §8-804.
Worcester county wine and beer festival, 2B §8-314.
Beer and wine festivals.
Charles county, 2B §8-308.
Dorchester county, 2B §8-307.
Brew-pub license, 2B §2-207.
Caterer's license.
Caroline county, 2B §6-702.1.
Statewide caterers (SCAT) license, 2B §6-701.
Class B-RD license.
Prince George's county, 2B §8-1001.
Class BWT beer and wine tasting license, on-premises.
Anne Arundel county, 2B §8-402.
Baltimore City, 2B §8-403.1.
Classes.
Beer and light wine licenses. See within this heading, "Beer and light wine licenses."
Beer licenses. See within this heading, "Beer licenses."
Beer, wine and liquor licenses. See within this heading, "Beer, wine and liquor licenses."
Class WS wine sampling license, on-premises.
Anne Arundel county, 2B §8-402.
Clubs.
Applications for clubs, 2B §9-101.
Renewal.
Substitution of officers, 2B §10-301.
Comptroller. See within this heading, "Comptroller."
Conference center facilities.
Beer, wine and liquor licenses, 2B §6-601.
Conviction of offense.
Renewal.
Effect of conviction, 2B §10-301.
Corporations.
Applications for corporations, 2B §9-101.
Renewal.
Substitution of officers, 2B §10-301.
Revocation or suspension.
Felony conviction of stockholder, 2B §10-401.
Cumberland and Shenandoah Valley wine festival license, 2B §8-313.
Dealers.
Discrimination among prohibited, 2B §12-102.
Death of licensee.
Effect, 2B §10-506.
Dispensary system not applicable, 2B §9-102.
Display of license, 2B §10-505.
Disposal of stock licenses, 2B §7-101.
Disqualification of licensee, 2B §10-404.

ALCOHOLIC BEVERAGES —Cont'd
Licenses —Cont'd
Drive-thru facilities. See within this heading, "Drive-thru purchase facilities."
Duplicates.
Lost licenses, 2B §10-502.
Executors and administrators.
Continuation of business.
Death of licensee, 2B §10-506.
Expiration, 2B §10-206.
Death of licensee.
Effect, 2B §10-506.
Premises acquired for public use, 2B §10-504.
Vacation of premises, 2B §10-504.
Federal reservations.
Sales, 2B §10-507.
Fees.
Application fee, 2B §2-402.
Beer and light wine licenses.
Class A, off-sale, 2B §5-101.
Class B, on-sale, 2B §5-201.
Class C, seven days, 2B §7-101.
Class D, on-sale, 2B §5-401.
Class F, on-sale.
Railroads, 2B §5-501.
Class H, on-sale only, 2B §5-202.
Beer licenses.
Class A, off-sale, 2B §3-101.
Class B, on-sale, 2B §3-201.
Class C, on-sale.
Clubs, 2B §3-301.
Seven days, 2B §7-101.
Class H, on-sale only, 2B §3-202.
Beer, wine and liquor licenses.
Class A, off-sale, 2B §6-101.
Class C, on-sale, 2B §6-301.
Class C, seven days, 2B §7-101.
Class D, on-sale.
Taverns, etc., 2B §6-401.
Class E, on-sale.
Steamboats, 2B §6-501.
Class F, on-sale.
Railroads, 2B §6-502.
Class G, on-sale.
Airplanes, 2B §6-503.
Class H.
Caterers in Carroll county, 2B §6-703.
Disposition.
By comptroller, 2B §10-204.
Generally, 2B §10-204.
Manufacturers' licenses, 2B §2-201.
Municipal corporations.
Additional license fees and taxes by cities and towns prohibited, 2B §8-101.
Place of business in more than one county or city, 2B §10-101.
Pro rata, 2B §10-207.
Refund, 2B §10-205.
Renewal of license, 2B §2-402.
Statewide caterers (SCAT) license, 2B §6-701.
Wholesaler's license, 2B §2-301.
Food stores.
Floor space, 2B §9-108.
Forms, 2B §10-206.
Golf courses.
Caroline county.
Class GC beer, wine and liquor license, 2B §8-507.1.
Hearing.
Renewal, 2B §10-301.

ALCOHOLIC BEVERAGES —Cont'd
Licenses —Cont'd
Holder.
Defined, 2B §1-102.
Hunt Valley commercial/mixed use focal point, 2B §8-204.4.
Issuance.
By license commissioners, 2B §15-112.
Clerks of court. See within this heading, "Clerks of court."
Comptroller, 2B §10-201.
Delegation of authority to issue licenses and permits, 2B §16-404.
Date, 2B §10-206.
Procedure generally, 2B §10-202.
Refusal, 2B §10-104.
Loch Raven commercial revitalization district, 2B §8-204.7.
Loitering about place of business, 2B §12-111.
Lost licenses.
Duplicates, 2B §10-502.
Manufacturers. See within this heading, "Manufacturers."
Minors.
Issuance to minors, 2B §9-106.
Not to be employed by licensees, 2B §12-302.
More than one license for same person or premises.
Baltimore City.
Exceptions as to, 2B §9-102.
General provisions, 2B §§9-102, 9-107.
Number.
Limitation of number of licenses, 2B §§9-102, 9-107.
Numbering licenses, 2B §9-102.
Restrictions as to number, 2B §§9-201, 9-203.
Out-of-state unlicensed sellers, 2B §16-506.1.
Partnerships.
Applications, 2B §9-101.
Place of business.
Eviction of premises.
Expiration of license, 2B §10-504.
In two or more counties or cities, 2B §10-101.
Pouring license.
Washington county.
Issuance by Washington county liquor board, 2B §8-222.
Premises near churches or schools.
St. Mary's county, 2B §9-219.
Prohibited areas.
Power of license commissioners, 2B §§9-201, 9-203.
Prohibition without license or permit, 2B §1-201.
Property rights not conferred, 2B §10-501.
Protest.
Renewal, 2B §10-301.
Pub-brewery license, 2B §2-207.
Qualifications.
License holder for renewal, 2B §10-301.
Railroads. See within this heading, "Railroads."
Records.
Requirements, 2B §14-204.
Rectifying license, 2B §2-203.
Removal licenses.
Temporary removal license, 2B §7-101.
Renewal, 2B §§10-301, 10-302.
Fee, 2B §2-402.
Reopening of licensed premises, 2B §10-301.
Required, 2B §1-201.
Restrictions.
Building regulations, 2B §9-105.

ALCOHOLIC BEVERAGES —Cont'd
Licenses —Cont'd
Restrictions —Cont'd
On licensees, 2B §§12-101 to 12-303.
Renewal, 2B §10-301.
Special and temporary licenses, 2B §7-101.
Zoning law restrictions, 2B §9-103.
Retail sales.
Floor space, 2B §9-108.
Revocation or suspension.
Causes.
General provisions, 2B §10-401.
Corporations.
Felony conviction of stockholders of
corporation, 2B §10-401.
Disqualification of licensee, 2B §10-404.
Failure to keep records and reports, 2B §14-201.
General penalty, 2B §16-503.
Nudity and sexual displays on licensee's
premises, 2B §10-405.
Payment of money.
In lieu of suspension, 2B §10-402.
Procedure, 2B §10-403.
Reissuance after six months, 2B §10-404.
Renewal, 2B §10-301.
Subject to, 2B §10-501.
Vacation of premises by licensee, 2B §10-504.
Rights and duties of licensees, 2B §§10-501 to
10-506.
Special and temporary licenses, 2B §7-101.
Hours and days for sale, 2B §11-203.
Stadium on-sale license.
Harford county, 2B §8-213.1.
Stadiums, baseball, 2B §8-223.
Steamboats.
Applications, 2B §9-101.
Substitution of officers.
Renewal, 2B §10-301.
Supermarkets.
Floor space, 2B §9-108.
Suspension. See within this subheading,
"Revocation or suspension."
Temporary licenses, 2B §7-101.
Hours and days for sale, 2B §11-203.
Theaters.
Kent county.
Theater (on-sale) beer, wine and liquor
license, 2B §8-215.
Tied houses.
Prohibited, 2B §12-101.
Townson commercial revitalization district, 2B
§§8-204.3, 8-204.7.
Transfer, 2B §10-503.
Two licenses to same person prohibited, 2B
§9-102.
Wholesalers. See within this heading,
"Wholesalers."
Wicomico county wine festival, 2B §8-313.1.
Wine.
Annapolis wine festival, 2B §8-401.
Baltimore City wine festival, 2B §8-303.
Baltimore county wine festival, 2B §8-304.
Beer and light wine licenses. See within this
heading, "Beer and light wine licenses."
Beer, wine and liquor licenses. See within this
heading, "Beer, wine and liquor licenses."
Calvert county wine festival, 2B §8-305.
Garrett county, 2B §8-308.1.
Harford county wine festival, 2B §8-309.
Howard county wine festival, 2B §8-310.

ALCOHOLIC BEVERAGES —Cont'd
Licenses —Cont'd
Wine —Cont'd
Manufacturers. See within this heading,
"Manufacturers."
Montgomery county wine festival, 2B §8-310.1.
Queen Anne's county beer and wine festival, 2B
§8-311.
Somerset county.
Maryland wine festival, 2B §8-311.
Winery license, 2B §2-204.
Limited winery license, 2B §2-205.
Wine sampling licenses.
Anne Arundel county, 2B §8-402.
Baltimore City, 2B §8-403.
Howard county, 2B §8-408.
Wine tasting licenses.
Frederick county, 2B §8-406.
Howard county, 2B §8-408.1.
Queen Anne's county, 2B §8-410.1.
Somerset county, 2B §8-410.2.
Washington county, 2B §8-411.
Worcester county wine and beer festival, 2B
§8-314.
Winery license, 2B §2-204.
Limited winery license, 2B §2-205.
Workers' compensation.
Certificate of compliance with workers'
compensation act.
Required prior to issuance of license, 2B
§9-104.
Zoning.
Restrictions, 2B §9-103.
Liens.
Confiscated property.
Claim for return by lienholder, 2B §1-201.
Rights of lienholders, 2B §1-201.
Sales permitted without license or permit.
Exercising right to sell beverages under a lien,
2B §1-201.
**Life threatening injury by motor vehicle or
vessel while impaired or under the
influence,** CR §§3-211, 3-212.
Limited liability companies.
Licenses.
Applications, 2B §9-101.
Liquor control boards and dispensaries.
Applicability of subtitle.
Certain counties, 2B §15-210.
Appointment.
By governor, 2B §15-201.
Bonds, surety, 2B §15-201.
Borrowing power.
General provisions, 2B §15-202.
Compensation, 2B §15-201.
Composition, 2B §15-201.
Contracts, 2B §15-205.
Control of sale and distribution.
Monopoly control, 2B §15-204.
County commissioners ex officio members in
certain counties, 2B §15-201.
County dispensaries.
Authorized, 2B §15-203.
Certain counties, 2B §15-203.
Defined, 2B §15-201.
Employees, 2B §15-205.
Establishment, 2B §15-201.
Financial interest of member or employee of
boards.
Prohibited, 2B §15-208.

ALCOHOLIC BEVERAGES —Cont'd
Liquor control boards and dispensaries
—Cont'd
Frauds.
  Power to prevent, 2B §12-113.
Hours for opening and closing, 2B §15-205.
Lease or purchase of premises, 2B §15-205.
Loans.
  General provisions, 2B §15-202.
Meetings, 2B §15-201.
Organization, 2B §15-201.
Powers.
  Generally, 2B §15-205.
Profits and reserves.
  Generally, 2B §15-207.
Purchase of beverages, 2B §15-205.
Qualifications, 2B §15-201.
Records.
  Generally, 2B §15-206.
Reports.
  Annual report, 2B §15-206.
Restrictions as to quantity, 2B §15-205.
Rules and regulations.
  General provisions, 2B §15-205.
Sale of beverages, 2B §15-205.
  Refusal to sell, 2B §15-205.
Shipments outside of county, 2B §15-205.
Supervision.
  Chief administrative officer, 2B §15-201.
Term of office, 2B §15-201.
Vacancies.
  Filling, 2B §15-201.
Working capital, 2B §15-202.
Loans.
Liquor control boards, 2B §15-202.
Loch Raven commercial revitalization district.
Beer, wine and liquor licenses, 2B §8-204.7.
Loitering.
Licensed premises, 2B §12-111.
Lost instruments and records.
Licenses.
  Duplicates of lost licenses, 2B §10-502.
Manufacturers.
Containers, brands and labels.
  Information to be filed, 2B §12-103.
Defined, 2B §1-102.
Delivery.
  Restrictions, 2B §2-401.
Illicit alcoholic beverages.
  Defined, 2B §1-102.
Illicit manufacture.
  Fines and penalties, 2B §16-505.
Licenses.
  Additional license, 2B §2-201.
  Applicants.
    Additional licenses, 2B §2-401.
    Delivery restrictions, 2B §2-401.
    Residence qualification, 2B §2-401.
    Sale restrictions, 2B §2-401.
  Brewery license, 2B §2-206.
  Classes, 2B §2-201.
  Delivery.
    Hours and days, 2B §11-101.
  Discrimination in sale or distribution
    prohibited, 2B §12-102.
  Distillery license, 2B §2-202.
  Fees, 2B §2-201.
  Hours and days for sale, 2B §11-101.
  Micro-brewery license, 2B §2-208.
    Carroll county, 2B §9-207.
  Pub-brewery licenses, 2B §2-207.

ALCOHOLIC BEVERAGES —Cont'd
Manufacturers —Cont'd
Licenses —Cont'd
  Rectifying license, 2B §2-203.
  Required, 2B §1-201.
  Tied houses.
    Prohibited, 2B §12-101.
  Winery license, 2B §2-204.
    Limited winery license, 2B §2-205.
Out-of-state unlicensed sellers, 2B §16-506.1.
Price regulation.
  Filing schedule and proposed changes, 2B
    §12-103.
Prohibitions.
  Generally, 2B §1-201.
Records.
  Generally, 2B §14-201.
Regulations, 2B §1-201.
Reports.
  Generally, 2B §14-201.
Sales.
  Restriction, 2B §2-401.
Unlawful manufacturing.
  Apparatus, etc., designed for unlawful
    manufacture, 2B §1-201.
Winery license, 2B §2-204.
  Limited winery license, 2B §2-205.
Maryland-Washington regional district.
Zoning.
  Alcoholic beverage licenses, 28 §8-109.
Maryland wine festival.
General provisions, 2B §8-306.
Micro-brewery licenses, 2B §2-208.
Carroll county, 2B §9-207.
Militia.
Commanding officers.
  Powers to regulate or prohibit, PS §13-208.
Minors.
Age.
  Defense to prosecution for sale to person not of
    legal age, 2B §12-109.
  Misrepresentation of age, CR §10-113.
    False documentation, CR §10-115.
  Record of documentary proof of purchaser's age,
    2B §12-109.
Citation for violations, CR §10-119.
  Sales to underage drinkers, CP §4-101.
Consumption or possession by minors on
  premises.
  Prohibited, 2B §12-108.
Defense to prosecution for sale to person not of
  legal age, 2B §12-109.
Employment of minors by retail dealers.
  Regulations, 2B §12-302.
  Special provisions, 2B §12-302.
Jurisdiction, CR §10-120.
  Purchasing or consuming alcohol, 2B §12-108.
Licenses.
  Issuance to minors, 2B §9-106.
Possession and transportation.
  General provisions and prohibitions, 2B §1-201.
  In certain counties, 2B §12-108.
  Underage possession, CR §10-114.
Sales to minors.
  Prohibited, 2B §12-108.
Underage consumption.
  Furnishing or allowing, exceptions, CR §10-117.
  Kegs, CR §10-118.
  Obtaining for underage consumption, CR
    §10-116.

ALCOHOLIC BEVERAGES —Cont'd
Misdemeanors.
Containers.
Detachable metal tab opening device, 2B §21-102.
Drinking on public property, 2B §19-204.
Drunkards and mentally deficient persons.
Sales to, 2B §12-110.
Fraud and deceit.
Tampering with or refilling containers, 2B §12-113.
Free food, 2B §12-106.
General penalty, 2B §16-503.
Hours and days for sale.
Sundays, 2B §11-403.
Violations, 2B §11-304.
Intoxicated persons.
Sales to prohibited, 2B §12-108.
Minors.
Consumption or possession, 2B §12-110.
Possession of open container in certain places, 2B §19-302.
Montgomery county.
See MONTGOMERY COUNTY.
Morticians.
Providing professional services while under the influence of alcohol or controlled dangerous substances, HO §7-318.
Motor carriers.
Records and reports.
Required, 2B §14-202.
Motor vehicles.
Alcohol concentration.
Defined, TR §11-103.2.
Alcohol defined, TR §11-103.1.
Commercial drivers' licenses.
Disqualification.
Driving under the influence, TR §16-205.1.
Impoundment of vehicle, TR §27-111.
Hearings.
Disqualification on refusal to submit to chemical test, TR §16-205.1.
Operating under influence of intoxicating liquors.
Grounds for disqualification, TR §§16-812, 16-813.
Confiscation.
Transfer of illicit alcoholic beverages, 2B §1-201.
Consumption while driving on highway, TR §21-903.
Drivers' licenses.
Suspension of license on refusal to submit to chemical test, TR §16-205.1.
Suspension or revocation of licenses.
Conviction of certain offenses involving alcohol, TR §16-205.
Drunkenness.
See DRIVING UNDER THE INFLUENCE.
Homicide by motor vehicle or vessel while impaired or under the influence, CR §§2-501 to 2-508.
Life threatening injury by motor vehicle or vessel while impaired or under the influence, CR §§3-211, 3-212.
Open containers.
Possession in motor vehicles' passenger areas, CR §§10-123 to 10-127.
Possession of open containers in certain parking areas, 2B §§19-301 to 19-303.
Operation while under the influence.
See DRIVING UNDER THE INFLUENCE.

ALCOHOLIC BEVERAGES —Cont'd
Motor vehicles —Cont'd
Parking.
Drinking prohibited in certain places, 2B §19-202.
Rental of vehicles to person under influence of alcohol prohibited, TR §18-105.
Municipal corporations.
Licenses.
Additional license fees and taxes by cities and towns prohibited, 2B §8-101.
Possession and consumption in public places.
Authority to regulate, 2B §19-104.
Taxation.
Prohibited, 2B §1-101.
National family beer and wine exhibition permit, 2B §2-101.
New Year's day.
Hours and days for sale.
Exceptions, 2B §§11-304, 11-402.
Nonprofit organizations.
Fund-raising events.
Wine permits, 2B §8-401.
Nonresidents.
Dealer's permit, 2B §2-101.
Storage permit, 2B §2-101.
Notices.
Application for license.
Publication by license commissioners, 2B §10-202.
Confiscation of property.
Notification of owner of confiscated vehicle, vessel or aircraft, 2B §1-201.
Job-related alcohol and controlled dangerous substances testing.
Notice of positive test results, HG §17-214.
Licenses.
Publication of notice for application for license, 2B §10-105.
Minors' conviction of violations sent to motor vehicle administration, CR §10-119.
Nudity and sexual displays on licensee's premises.
Municipal ordinances regulating, 23A §4A.
Revocation of license, 2B §10-405.
Nurses.
Providing professional services while under the influence of alcohol or controlled dangerous substances, HO §8-316.
Nursing home administrators.
Providing professional services while under the influence of alcohol or controlled dangerous substances, HO §9-314.
Oaths.
False statements, 2B §16-501.
Occupational therapists.
Providing professional services while under the influence of alcohol or controlled dangerous substances, HO §10-315.
Open containers.
Partially consumed bottle of wine.
Removal from licensed premises permitted, 2B §12-107.1.
Possession in certain places, 2B §19-301.
Applicability of provisions, 2B §19-303.
Motor vehicles' passenger areas, CR §§10-123 to 10-127.
Applicability of provisions, CR §§10-124, 10-125.
Citation for violations, CR §10-126.
Procedure, CR §10-127.

ALCOHOLIC BEVERAGES —Cont'd
Open containers —Cont'd
  Possession in certain places —Cont'd
    Motor vehicles' passenger areas —Cont'd
      Definitions, CR §10-123.
      Drivers not subject to prosecution, CR
        §10-125.
      Penalties, 2B §19-302.
Optometrists.
  Providing professional services while under the
    influence of alcohol or controlled dangerous
    substances, HO §11-313.
Parking areas.
  Places where drinking prohibited, 2B §19-202.
Partnerships.
  Fines and penalties, 2B §16-504.
  Licenses.
    Applications, 2B §9-101.
    Renewal.
      Substitution of officers, 2B §10-301.
Penalties.
  Containers.
    Sale of containers with detachable metal tab
      opening device, 2B §21-102.
  Drinking in certain places, 2B §19-204.
  Licenses.
    Revocation or suspension.
      Payment of money in lieu of suspension, 2B
        §10-402.
  School athletic contests.
    Possession of intoxicating beverages, ED
      §26-103.
Perjury.
  Affidavits, oaths or reports, 2B §16-501.
  Application for license.
    Caroline county, 2B §10-104.
Permits.
  Alcohol awareness program permits, 2B §2-101.
  Auctions.
    Charity wine auctions, 2B §2-101.
  Bulk transfer permit.
    General provisions, 2B §2-101.
  Cancellation, 2B §2-101.
  Charity wine auctions, 2B §2-101.
  Classes.
    General provisions, 2B §2-101.
  Definition of license holder or licensee, 2B §1-102.
  Domicile permit, 2B §2-101.
  Duration, 2B §2-101.
  Family wineries and breweries.
    National family beer exhibition permit, 2B
      §2-101.
  Fees.
    General provisions, 2B §2-101.
  Fuel-alcohol permit, 2B §2-101.
  Home wineries and breweries.
    National family exhibition permit, 2B §2-101.
  Identification of vehicles, 2B §2-101.
  Import and export permits, 2B §2-101.
  Issuance, 2B §2-101.
  National family wine exhibition permit, 2B
    §2-101.
  Nonbeverage permit, 2B §2-101.
  Nonresident dealer's permit, 2B §2-101.
  Nonresident storage permit, 2B §2-101.
  Private bulk sales permit, 2B §2-101.
  Renewal.
    Procedure, 2B §2-101.
  Restriction, 2B §2-101.
  Sales.
    Bulk transfer permit, 2B §2-101.

ALCOHOLIC BEVERAGES —Cont'd
Permits —Cont'd
  Scientific purposes, 2B §2-101.
  Solicitor's permit, 2B §2-101.
  Storage.
    Individual storage permit, 2B §2-101.
    No import-export permit required for storage,
      2B §1-201.
    Nonresident storage permit, 2B §2-101.
    Public storage permit, 2B §2-101.
    Transportation permit, 2B §2-101.
  Transfers.
    Bulk transfer permit, 2B §2-101.
  Transportation, 2B §2-101.
    Individual transportation permit, 2B §2-101.
  Winery special events, 2B §2-101.
Pharmacists.
  Beer, wine and liquor licenses.
    Class A, off-sale.
      Regulations as to drugstores, 2B §6-101.
  Providing professional services while under the
    influence of alcohol or controlled dangerous
    substances, HO §12-313.
  Sale on prescription, 2B §2-101.
Physical therapists.
  Providing services while under the influence of
    alcohol or controlled dangerous substances,
    HO §13-316.
Podiatrists.
  Providing professional services while under the
    influence of alcohol or controlled dangerous
    substances, HO §16-311.
Police.
  Enforcement of article, 2B §16-401.
  Duties, 2B §16-405.
**Possession of an open container in certain
  places,** 2B §19-301.
  Applicability of provisions, 2B §19-303.
  Partially consumed bottle of wine.
    Removal from licensed premises permitted, 2B
      §12-107.1.
  Penalties, 2B §19-302.
Presumptions.
  Appeal to court from license commissioners, 2B
    §16-101.
  Motor vehicles.
    Operation while under the influence.
      Test for intoxication, CJ §10-307.
Price regulation, 2B §12-103.
Prince George's county.
  See PRINCE GEORGE'S COUNTY.
Prison inmates.
  Delivery to inmate.
    Contraband in place of confinement, CR §9-415.
Privileged communications.
  Job-related alcohol testing.
    Confidential information, HG §17-214.
Procurement.
  License commissioners.
    County purchasing laws.
      Boards subject to, 24 §8-101.
Profits and reserves.
  Liquor control boards.
    Generally, 2B §15-207.
Prohibitions.
  Generally, 2B §1-201.
Pub-brewery license, 2B §2-207.
Public property.
  Authorization of consumption.
    Adoption of standards, 2B §19-203.
  Defined, 2B §19-201.

ALCOHOLIC BEVERAGES —Cont'd
Public property —Cont'd
Drinking prohibited, 2B §19-202.
Penalty, 2B §19-204.
Pull tabs.
Sale of containers with detachable metal tab
opening device.
Penalty, 2B §21-102.
Purchases.
Only from licensees, 2B §12-107.
Queen Anne's county.
See QUEEN ANNE'S COUNTY.
Railroads.
Beer and light wine licenses.
Class F, on-sale, 2B §5-501.
Beer, wine and liquor licenses.
Class F, on-sale, 2B §6-502.
Repeal provisions, 2B §8-102.
Licenses.
Applications, 2B §9-101.
Where to be filed, 2B §10-101.
Display of license, 2B §10-505.
Harford county, 2B §§8-213, 8-407.
Hours and days for sale, 2B §11-201.
Records and reports.
Required, 2B §14-202.
Restrictions upon retail dealers, 2B §12-107.
Receivers.
Sale permitted without license or permit, 2B
§1-201.
Records.
Common carriers.
Required, 2B §14-202.
Failure to keep.
Effect, 2B §14-201.
Licenses, 2B §14-201.
Contents, 2B §14-204.
Destruction after three years, 2B §14-204.
Inspection, 2B §14-204.
Liquor control boards, 2B §15-206.
Purchaser's age.
Documentary proof, 2B §12-109.
Requirements.
Generally, 2B §14-201.
Rectifiers.
Illicit alcoholic beverages.
Defined, 2B §1-102.
License, 2B §2-203.
Tied houses.
Prohibited, 2B §12-101.
Referendum.
Prohibited as to laws of constitutional
amendments.
Relating to malt or spirituous liquors, MD
Const Art XVI §6.
Registration.
Kegs, 2B §21-106.
Unregistered kegs, CR §10-118.
Reports.
Charity wine auctions.
Permit holders to make reports, 2B §2-101.
Common carriers.
Required, 2B §14-202.
Comptroller.
Annual report of comptroller, 2B §14-203.
Distilled spirits.
Personal property tax.
Report of fair value, TP §8-112.
False statements.
Perjury, 2B §16-501.
Generally, 2B §14-201.

ALCOHOLIC BEVERAGES —Cont'd
Reports —Cont'd
Liquor control boards.
Annual report, 2B §15-206.
Local governing bodies.
Legislative enactments.
Report to department of legislative services,
2B §18-103.
Residence.
Manufacturer's license.
Residence qualification, 2B §2-401.
Restaurants.
Beer and light wine licenses.
Class B, on-sale, 2B §5-201.
Class H, on-sale only, 2B §5-202.
Beer licenses.
Class B, on-sale, 2B §3-201.
Class H, on-sale only, 2B §3-202.
Beer, wine and liquor licenses.
Class B (inn), on-sale, 2B §6-201.
Class B-MB/22 micro-brewery license.
Hotels and restaurants, 2B §6-201.
Class B, on-sale, 2B §6-201.
Defined, 2B §1-102.
Free food.
Prohibited, 2B §12-106.
Hours for sale.
Beer and light wine licenses, 2B §11-302.
Beer licenses, 2B §11-301.
Beer, wine and liquor licenses, 2B §11-303.
Retailers.
Bonds, surety.
Required, 2B §14-101.
Definitions.
Retail dealer, 2B §1-102.
Deliveries, 2B §12-301.
Floor space, 2B §9-108.
Free food.
Prohibited, 2B §12-106.
Hours and days for sale, 2B §11-202.
Minors.
Employment by retail dealers regulated, 2B
§12-302.
Purchases.
Only from licensees, 2B §12-107.
Records.
Generally, 2B §14-201.
Reports.
Generally, 2B §14-201.
Restrictions.
Generally, 2B §14-201.
Sales.
Outside sales, 2B §12-301.
Solicitations.
Outside solicitations prohibited, 2B §12-301.
Tied houses.
Prohibited, 2B §12-101.
Rules and regulations.
Adoption.
Who may adopt, 2B §16-301.
Comptroller, 2B §12-113.
Adoption, 2B §16-301.
Deposit on returnable beer containers, 2B
§16-303.
Discrimination prohibited, 2B §12-102.
Powers as to, 2B §16-302.
Inspection, marking and grading of beverages, 2B
§12-113.
License commissioners.
Adoption, 2B §16-301.

ALCOHOLIC BEVERAGES —Cont'd
Rules and regulations —Cont'd
Liquor control boards.
Powers, 2B §15-205.
St. Mary's county.
See ST. MARY'S COUNTY.
Salaries.
License commissioners, 2B §15-109.
Sales.
Age.
Beverage server's age, 2B §§12-209.2, 12-213,
12-219, 12-224.
Licensee's age, 2B §§10-102, 10-104.
Beverages.
Liquor control boards, 2B §15-205.
Carriers.
Permitted without license or permit, 2B §1-201.
Commercial code.
Implied warranty of merchantability, CL
§2-314.
Computer sales.
Out-of-state unlicensed sellers, 2B §16-506.1.
Control.
Liquor control boards.
Monopoly control, 2B §15-204.
Discounts.
Prescribing or prohibiting, 2B §12-103.
Discrimination.
Prohibited, 2B §12-102.
Disposal of stock.
Licenses, 2B §7-101.
Distribution.
Discrimination prohibited, 2B §12-102.
Election day.
Sale or use prohibited, 2B §11-401.
Federal reservations, 2B §10-507.
Food and food establishments.
Free food.
Prohibited, 2B §12-106.
Hours and days. See within this heading, "Hours
and days for sale."
Implied warranty of merchantability, CL §2-314.
Internet sales.
Out-of-state unlicensed sellers, 2B §16-506.1.
Intoxicated persons.
Sales to prohibited, 2B §12-108.
Limiting purchases or sales to producers
prohibited, 2B §12-101.
Liquor control boards.
Powers, 2B §15-205.
Manufacturers.
Restriction, 2B §2-401.
Minors. See within this heading, "Minors."
Partially consumed bottle of wine.
Removal from licensed premises, 2B §12-107.1.
Permitted.
Without license or permit, 2B §1-201.
Price regulations.
Affirmation by suppliers of wholesalers, 2B
§12-103.
Prohibitions.
Generally, 2B §1-201.
Seller's age, 2B §12-302.
Talbot county.
Power of county commissioner to regulate retail
sales, 2B §18-101.
Tied houses.
Prohibited, 2B §12-101.
Unlawful sale of liquor or beer.
Indictment, 2B §16-509.

ALCOHOLIC BEVERAGES —Cont'd
Sales —Cont'd
Unlicensed premises.
Prima facie evidence of sale, 2B §16-406.
Warranty.
Implied warranty of merchantability, CL
§2-314.
Wholesalers.
Restriction, 2B §2-401.
Samples.
Family beer and wine facility permits, 2B §2-101.
Schools.
Athletic contests.
Possession of intoxicating beverages at school
athletic contests prohibited, ED §26-103.
Drinking or possessing on school premises.
Prohibited, ED §26-103.
Health education.
Alcohol abuse program, ED §7-413.
Science.
Scientific purposes.
Permit, 2B §2-101.
Searches and seizures.
Certain counties, 2B §16-414.
Evidence.
Destruction of evidence, 2B §1-201.
Illicit alcoholic beverages.
Defined, 2B §1-102.
Sentence and punishment. See within this
heading, "Fines."
Severability of article, 2B §1-104.
Sheriffs.
Enforcement of article, 2B §16-401.
Duties, 2B §16-405.
Sales permitted without license or permit, 2B
§1-201.
Social workers.
Providing professional services while under the
influence of alcohol or controlled dangerous
substances, HO §19-311.
Solicitations.
Retailers.
Outside solicitations by retailers prohibited, 2B
§12-301.
Solicitors.
Permit, 2B §2-101.
Somerset county.
See SOMERSET COUNTY.
Sparkling wine.
Defined, 2B §1-102.
Special identification cards, TR §12-301.
Fees, TR §12-301.
Stadiums.
Beer, wine and liquor licenses.
Class B-stadium (baseball stadium), 2B §6-201.
Harford county.
Stadium on-sale license, 2B §8-213.1.
Wicomico county.
Beer and light wine license, 2B §8-223.
State's attorneys.
Enforcement of article, 2B §16-401.
Duties, 2B §16-405.
Minor's citation for violations, CR §10-119.
Open containers of alcoholic beverages in motor
vehicles' passenger areas, CR §10-127.
Storage.
Permits, 2B §1-201.
Regulation, 2B §12-105.
Warehouse receipts.
Storage under government bond, CL §7-201.

ALCOHOLIC BEVERAGES —Cont'd
Summons and process.
 Witnesses.
  Power to summons, 2B §16-410.
Sundays and holidays.
 Bar and counter sales, 2B §11-403.
 Beer, wine and liquor licenses.
  Hours and days for sale, 2B §11-303.
 Garrett county wine festival, 2B §8-308.1.
 General restrictions, 2B §11-403.
 New Year's day.
  Hours of sale, 2B §11-402.
Supermarkets.
 Floor space for sales, 2B §9-108.
 Licenses.
  More than one license for same person or premises, 2B §9-102.
Talbot county.
 General provisions.
  See TALBOT COUNTY.
Taverns.
 Age.
  Beverage server's age, 2B §§12-209.2, 12-213, 12-219, 12-224.
  Licensee's age, 2B §§10-102, 10-104.
  Seller's age, 2B §12-302.
 Beer, wine and liquor licenses.
  Class D, on-sale, 2B §6-401.
  Hours of sale, 2B §11-303.
Taxation.
 Alcohol and tobacco tax field enforcement bureau, 2B §16-407.
 Alcoholic beverage tax.
  General provisions, TG §§2-301 to 2-303, 5-101 to 5-303.
   See ALCOHOLIC BEVERAGE TAX.
 Authorized for state, 2B §1-101.
 Counties.
  Prohibited, 2B §1-101.
 Domicile permit.
  Change of domicile permit.
   Payment of taxes required, 2B §2-101.
 Evasion.
  Penalties, 2B §16-506.
 Federal reservations.
  Sales on, 2B §10-507.
 Frauds.
  Prevention, 2B §12-113.
 Municipal corporations.
  Additional license fees and taxes by cities and towns prohibited, 2B §8-101.
  Prohibited, 2B §1-101.
 Penalties.
  Evasions, 2B §16-506.
 Personal property tax on distilled spirits, TP §8-112.
 Sales.
  Permitted without license or permit.
   Purchaser a retail dealer, 2B §1-201.
 Sundays and holidays.
  Restrictions, 2B §11-403.
 Taxpayer.
  Defined, 2B §1-102.
Tests.
 Driving under the influence.
  See DRIVING UNDER THE INFLUENCE.
 Job-related alcohol and controlled dangerous substances testing, HG §17-214.
Theaters.
 Kent county.
  Theater (on-sale) beer, wine and liquor license, 2B §8-215.

ALCOHOLIC BEVERAGES —Cont'd
Tied houses.
 Prohibited, 2B §12-101.
Tours of wineries.
 Number of ounces served at no charge to persons on tour, 2B §§2-204, 2-205.
Townson commercial revitalization district.
 Beer, wine and liquor licenses, 2B §8-204.7.
Transportation.
 Confiscation of property.
  Searches and seizures. See within this heading, "Searches and seizures."
 Illicit transportation, 2B §1-201.
 Permit.
  General provisions, 2B §2-101.
Trusts and trustees.
 Sales permitted without license or permit, 2B §1-201.
Underage drinking.
 Citation, crimes charged by, CP §4-101.
 Furnishing or allowing, exceptions, CR §10-117.
 Kegs, CR §10-118.
 Obtaining for underage consumption, CR §10-116.
 Sale or furnishing to minors, possession, 2B §§1-201, 12-108.
 Underage possession, CR §10-114.
Unlawful sales.
 Election day.
  Sale or use prohibited, 2B §11-401.
 Indictment, 2B §16-509.
 Prohibitions generally, 2B §1-201.
 Tied houses.
  Prohibited, 2B §12-101.
Urinalysis.
 Job-related testing, HG §17-214.
Vessels and boats.
 Beer, wine and liquor licenses.
  Class E, on-sale.
   Steamboats, 2B §6-501.
 Carriers.
  Records and reports.
   Required, 2B §14-202.
 Homicide by motor vehicle or vessel while impaired or under the influence, CR §§2-501 to 2-508.
 Illegal transportation.
  Confiscation and forfeiture of transportation equipment, 2B §1-201.
 Licenses.
  Applications.
   Where to be filed, 2B §10-101.
 Life threatening injury by motor vehicle or vessel while impaired or under the influence, CR §§3-211, 3-212.
 Operating vessel while under the influence of alcohol or controlled dangerous substance, NR §8-738.
 Restrictions upon retail dealers, 2B §12-107.
 Steamboats.
  Licenses.
   Applications, 2B §9-101.
Walk-up facilities.
 Carroll county, 2B §12-207.
Warehouse receipts.
 Distillery warehouses.
  Subject to provisions of subtitle, CL §18-307.
 Sales permitted without license or permit, 2B §1-201.
Warehouses and warehousemen.
 Distillery warehouses.
  Subject to warehouse receipt subtitle, CL §18-307.

ALCOHOLIC BEVERAGES —Cont'd
Warehouses and warehousemen —Cont'd
Receipts.
Storage under government bond, CL §7-201.
Sales permitted without license or permit, 2B
§1-201.
Storage.
Regulation, 2B §12-105.
Warranties.
Implied warranty of merchantability, CL §2-314.
Washington county.
See WASHINGTON COUNTY.
Wholesalers.
Brands.
Information as to, 2B §12-103.
Containers.
Information as to, 2B §12-103.
Defined, 2B §1-102.
Delivery.
Defined, 2B §2-301.
Restriction, 2B §2-401.
Labels.
Information as to, 2B §12-103.
Licenses.
Additional, 2B §2-301.
Applicants.
Additional licenses, 2B §2-401.
Delivery restriction, 2B §2-401.
Residence qualification, 2B §2-401.
Sale.
Restriction, 2B §2-401.
Upon approval of application, 2B §2-301.
Classes, 2B §2-301.
Deliveries to special class C license holder, 2B
§11-102.
Delivery, 2B §2-301.
Delivery from truck or vehicle, 2B §2-301.
Draft beer on Sunday, 2B §11-102.
Sale and delivery to retail licensee, 2B §2-301.
Discrimination in sale or distribution
prohibited, 2B §12-102.
Hours and days for sale, 2B §11-102.
Limitation of number of licenses.
Exceptions, 2B §9-102.
Location.
Additional location, 2B §2-301.
Privileges, 2B §2-301.
Tied houses.
Prohibited, 2B §12-101.
Price regulation.
Proposed changes.
Filing schedule, 2B §12-103.
Records, 2B §14-201.
Reports, 2B §14-201.
Sales.
Restriction, 2B §2-401.
Wicomico county.
See WICOMICO COUNTY.
Wine.
Annapolis wine festival.
License, 2B §8-401.
Anne Arundel county.
Beer and wine tasting license, 2B §8-202.
Deluxe restaurant license, 2B §8-202.1.
Auctions.
Charity wine auctions.
Permits, 2B §2-101.
Baltimore City wine festival.
License, 2B §8-303.
Baltimore county.
Wine festival license, 2B §8-304.

ALCOHOLIC BEVERAGES —Cont'd
Wine —Cont'd
Baltimore county —Cont'd
Wine sampling permits for nonprofit
organizations, 2B §8-404.
Beverage server's age, 2B §12-302.
Calvert county wine festival.
License, 2B §8-305.
Carroll county.
Maryland wine festival, 2B §8-306.
Wine tasting licenses, 2B §8-405.
Cecil county.
Special wine festival (WF) license, 2B §8-306.1.
Charity wine auctions.
Permits, 2B §2-101.
Charles county beer and wine festival, 2B §8-308.
Class BWT beer and wine tastings license,
on-premises, 2B §8-402.
Baltimore City, 2B §8-403.1.
Containers.
Detachable metal tab opening device.
Penalty for sale, 2B §21-102.
Sale prohibited, 2B §21-102.
Defined, 2B §1-102.
Direct wine seller's permit, 2B §§7.5-101 to
7.5-110.
Alcoholic beverage tax.
Return, TG §5-201.
Brand limitations, 2B §7.5-105.
Creation, 2B §7.5-102.
Definitions, 2B §7.5-101.
Delivery to personal consumer, 2B §7.5-108.
Delivery to retail owner, 2B §7.5-107.
Entitlement of permit, 2B §7.5-104.
Fee, 2B §§2-101, 7.5-104.
Liability of wholesaler and retailer, limitation
on, 2B §7.5-109.
Limitations and restrictions, 2B §7.5-105.
Packing list, 2B §7.5-107.
Personal consumers, duties, 2B §7.5-108.
Quantity limitations, 2B §7.5-105.
Records of receipt and delivery, 2B §7.5-106.
Regulations, 2B §7.5-110.
Requirements for issuance, 2B §7.5-103.
Sales tax, payment by consumer, 2B §7.5-108.
Service charges subject to state sales tax.
Payment by personal consumer, 2B §7.5-108.
Shipping wine sold, 2B §7.5-106.
Tax return, duty to file, 2B §7.5-104.
Term, 2B §7.5-104.
Title to wine.
Wholesaler and retailer not to take, 2B
§7.5-107.
Dorchester county.
Beer and wine festival, 2B §8-307.
Wine tasting licenses, 2B §8-405.1.
Family wine.
Defined, 2B §1-102.
Fees.
Permits, 2B §2-101.
Fund-raising events by nonprofit organizations.
Wine permits, 2B §8-401.
Garrett county.
Wine tasting licenses, 2B §8-406.1.
Guided tours of wineries.
Limitation on number of ounces served to
persons on tour, 2B §§2-204, 2-205.
Harford county wine festival.
License, 2B §8-309.
Homemade wine.
Manufacture without license, 2B §1-201.

ALCOHOLIC BEVERAGES —Cont'd
Wine —Cont'd
Howard county wine festival.
  License, 2B §8-310.
Licenses.
  Annapolis wine festival, 2B §8-401.
  Baltimore City wine festival, 2B §8-303.
  Baltimore county.
    Wine festival, 2B §8-304.
  Beer and light wine licenses. See within this
    heading, "Beer and light wine licenses."
  Beer, wine and liquor licenses. See within this
    heading, "Beer, wine and liquor licenses."
  Calvert county wine festival, 2B §8-305.
  Harford county wine festival, 2B §8-309.
  Howard county wine festival, 2B §8-310.
  Licensee's requirements, 2B §§10-102, 10-104.
  Manufacturers. See within this heading,
    "Manufacturers."
  Montgomery county wine festival, 2B §8-310.1.
  Queen Anne's county beer and wine festival, 2B
    §8-311.
  Somerset county.
    Maryland wine festival, 2B §8-311.
  Winery license, 2B §2-204.
    Limited winery license, 2B §2-205.
  Wine sampling licenses.
    Anne Arundel county, 2B §8-402.
    Baltimore City, 2B §8-403.
    Howard county, 2B §8-408.
  Wine tasting.
    Wicomico county, 2B §8-412.
  Wine tasting license.
    Frederick county, 2B §8-406.
    Howard county, 2B §8-408.1.
    Queen Anne's county, 2B §8-410.1.
    Somerset county, 2B §8-410.2.
    Washington county, 2B §8-411.
  Worcester county wine and beer festival, 2B
    §8-314.
Light wine.
  Beer and light wine licenses. See within this
    heading, "Beer and light wine licenses."
  Defined, 2B §4-101.
Light wine licenses.
  Class A, off-sale, 2B §4-201.
Limited winery license, 2B §2-205.
Montgomery county wine festival, 2B §8-310.1.
Nonprofit organizations.
  Fund-raising events.
    Wine permits, 2B §8-401.
Partially consumed bottle of wine.
  Removal from licensed premises, 2B §12-107.1.
Permits.
  Fees, 2B §2-101.
Queen Anne's county beer and wine festival.
  License, 2B §8-311.
Retail establishments.
  Interest of manufacturer prohibited.
    Exceptions, 2B §12-104.
St. Mary's county.
  Wine festivals, special license, 2B §8-312.1.
Seller's age, 2B §12-302.
Somerset county.
  Maryland wine festival, 2B §8-311.
Sparkling wine.
  Defined, 2B §1-102.
Taxation.
  Alcoholic beverage tax.
    See ALCOHOLIC BEVERAGE TAX.

ALCOHOLIC BEVERAGES —Cont'd
Wine —Cont'd
Tours of wineries.
  Limitation on number of ounces served to
    persons on tours, 2B §§2-204, 2-205.
Wicomico county liquor control boards and
  dispensaries.
  Wine tasting and sampling events, 2B §15-205.
Winery license, 2B §2-204.
  Limited winery license, 2B §2-205.
Winery special event permits, 2B §2-101.
Wine sampling licenses.
  Anne Arundel county, 2B §8-402.
  Baltimore City, 2B §8-403.
  Howard county, 2B §8-408.
Worcester county wine and beer festival.
  License, 2B §8-314.
WS wine sampling license, on-premises.
  Anne Arundel county, 2B §8-402.
**Winery and grape growers' advisory
  commission.**
Appointment, AG §10-1203.
Composition, AG §10-1203.
Creation, AG §10-1202.
Definitions, AG §10-1201.
Duties, AG §10-1206.
Enology.
  Defined, AG §10-1201.
Grape grower.
  Defined, AG §10-1201.
Meetings, AG §10-1205.
Members, AG §10-1203.
  Duties, AG §10-1206.
  Expenses.
    Reimbursement for, AG §10-1205.
  Expiration of term, AG §10-1203.
  Oaths, AG §10-1203.
  Removal.
    Grounds, AG §10-1203.
  Service until appointment and qualification of
    successor, AG §10-1203.
  Staff services and support, AG §10-1205.
  Terms, AG §10-1203.
Oaths, AG §10-1203.
Officers.
  Election, AG §10-1204.
Responsibilities, AG §10-1206.
Secretary, AG §10-1201.
Staff services and support, AG §10-1205.
Vice-chairman.
  Election, AG §10-1204.
Viticulture.
  Defined, AG §10-1201.
Wine.
  Defined, AG §10-1201.
Winery.
  Defined, AG §10-1201.
Witnesses.
Power to summons, 2B §16-410.
  Minors' citation for alcoholic beverage
    violations, CR §10-119.
  Open containers of alcoholic beverages in motor
    vehicles' passenger areas, CR §10-127.
Refusal to appear.
  Powers of boards, etc., 2B §16-410.
Worcester county.
See WORCESTER COUNTY.
Workers' compensation.
Licenses.
  Certificate of compliance with workers'
    compensation act required prior to issuance
    of license to sell alcoholic beverages, 2B
    §9-104.

ALCOHOLIC BEVERAGES —Cont'd
Yacht clubs.
Beer, wine and liquor licenses.
Class C, on sale, 2B §6-301.
Zoning law restrictions, 2B §9-103.

ALCOHOLIC BEVERAGE TAX.
Administrative cost account.
Distribution of revenue to, TG §2-301.
Beer.
Defined, TG §5-101.
Rates, TG §5-105.
Burden of proof.
Presumption of taxability, TG §5-103.
Consumers.
Defined, TG §5-101.
Exemptions.
Possession for personal use, TG §5-104.
Contraband alcoholic beverages, TG §5-103.
Sale of contraband beverages and conveyances.
Distribution of proceeds, TG §2-303.
Crimes and offenses.
Evasion of tax, TG §13-1009.
Returns.
Willfully filing false return.
Perjury, TG §13-1002.
Stamps.
Counterfeiting tax stamps, TG §13-1011.
Violation of regulations, TG §13-1021.
Violations of provisions generally, TG §13-1020.
Willful possession, sale or offer to sell alcoholic
beverages on which tax not paid, TG
§13-1013.
Definitions, TG §§1-101, 5-101.
Direct wine sellers.
Return, TG §5-201.
Discrimination.
Imposition of discriminatory tax or charge by
other jurisdiction, TG §5-102.
Rate of retaliatory tax, TG §5-105.
Distilled spirits.
Defined, TG §5-101.
Rates, TG §5-105.
Enforcement of provisions.
Law enforcement officers and prosecutors, TG
§2-107.
Evasion of tax.
Penalties, TG §13-1009.
Evidence.
Payment of tax, TG §5-301.
Exemptions, TG §5-104.
General fund.
Distribution of revenue to, TG §2-301.
Imposition of tax, TG §5-102.
Law enforcement personnel.
Charging documents against law enforcement
officers, CJ §2-608.
Enforcement of law, TG §2-107.
Licenses.
Definition of "alcoholic beverage license," TG
§5-101.
Limitation of actions.
Refunds.
Filing claims for, TG §13-1104.
Manufacturers.
Defined, TG §5-101.
Payment of tax, TG §5-301.
Returns, TG §5-201.
Misdemeanors.
Counterfeiting stamps, TG §13-1011.
Evasion of tax, TG §13-1009.

ALCOHOLIC BEVERAGE TAX —Cont'd
Misdemeanors —Cont'd
Payment of tax.
Willful possession, sale, or offer to sell alcoholic
beverage on which tax not paid, TG
§13-1013.
Stamps.
Counterfeiting stamps, TG §13-1011.
Violations of provisions generally, TG §13-1020.
Violations of regulations, TG §13-1021.
Nonresidents.
Payment of tax.
Nonresident dealers, TG §5-301.
Returns.
Nonresident dealers, TG §5-201.
Payment of tax, TG §5-301.
Evidence of payment, TG §5-301.
Failure to pay.
Prohibited acts when tax not paid, TG §5-302.
Manufacturers, TG §5-301.
Misdemeanors.
Willful possession, sale, or offer to sell alcoholic
beverage on which tax not paid, TG
§13-1013.
Nonresident dealers, TG §5-301.
Stamps.
Generally. See within this heading, "Stamps."
Wholesalers, TG §5-301.
Penalties.
Criminal penalties.
Evasion of tax, TG §13-1009.
Payment of tax.
Willful possession, sale, or offer to sell
alcoholic beverage on which tax not paid,
TG §13-1013.
Returns.
Willfully filing false return.
Perjury penalty, TG §13-1002.
Rules and regulations.
Violations, TG §13-1021.
Stamps.
Counterfeiting tax stamps, TG §13-1011.
Violations of provisions generally, TG §13-1020.
Violations of regulations, TG §13-1021.
Perjury.
Willfully filing false return, TG §13-1002.
Presumptions.
Taxability, TG §5-103.
Rates, TG §5-105.
Refunds.
Claims for refunds, TG §13-901.
Time for filing claims, TG §13-1104.
Payment, TG §2-302.
Religion.
Exemptions.
Sacramental use, TG §5-104.
Retail dealers.
Defined, TG §5-101.
Returns, TG §5-201.
Crimes and offenses.
Willfully filing false return.
Perjury, TG §13-1002.
Manufacturers, TG §5-201.
Nonresident dealers, TG §5-201.
Wholesalers, TG §5-201.
Rules and regulations.
Violation of regulations.
Penalties, TG §13-1021.
Sales.
Contraband beverages and conveyances.
Distribution of proceeds of sale, TG §2-303.

ALCOHOLIC BEVERAGE TAX —Cont'd
Sales —Cont'd
  Prohibited acts.
    Sales when tax not paid, TG §5-302.
  Searches and seizures.
    Illegally manufactured distilled spirits or mash,
      TG §13-710.
    Seizure of property.
      Contraband alcoholic beverages.
        General provisions, TG §§13-834 to 13-842.
  Stamps, TG §5-303.
    Counterfeiting tax stamps.
      Penalties, TG §13-1011.
    Definition of "tax stamp," TG §5-101.
    Evidence of payment, TG §5-301.
  United States.
    Exemptions.
      Sale or use on federal reservation, TG §5-104.
  Wholesalers.
    Defined, TG §5-101.
    Payment of tax, TG §5-301.
    Returns, TG §5-201.
  Wine.
    Defined, TG §5-101.
    Rates, TG §5-105.

ALCOHOLISM.
Disorderly intoxication, 2B §§19-101 to 19-104.
    See DRUNKENNESS.
District Court.
  Treatment for alcoholism.
    Authority of court to commit individuals, CJ
      §4-202.
General provisions.
  See DRUG OR ALCOHOL ABUSE.
Health insurance.
  Private review agents.
    Review of services for treatment of alcoholism,
      IN §15-10B-03.
Minors.
  Capacity to consent to treatment, HG §20-102.
Sales of alcoholic beverages.
  Sales to inebriate prohibited, 2B §12-110.

ALDEHYDE.
Inhaling, CR §5-708.

ALE.
See ALCOHOLIC BEVERAGES.

ALIBIS.
Discovery by state.
  Criminal rules, Crim Rule 4-263.

ALIENATION OF AFFECTIONS.
Actions.
  No cause of action, FL §3-103.
Construction and interpretation.
  Liberal construction of provisions, FL §3-101.
Contracts.
  Payment or settlement of abolished or prohibited
    claims.
    Void contracts, FL §3-104.
Location of statutory provisions, CJ §5-801.

ALIENS.
Actions.
  Suits against state, US Const Amd 11.
Commercial drivers' licenses.
  Issuance to persons domiciled in foreign country,
    TR §16-817.
Congress.
  Eligibility to be representative, US Const Art I §2.
Definitions, CA §5-703.

ALIENS —Cont'd
Descent and distribution.
  Right to own and dispose of property, RP §14-101.
Executors and administrators.
  Right to letters.
    Exclusion of person not citizen of the United
      States, ET §5-105.
Heirs.
  Right to own and dispose of property, RP §14-101.
Immigration consultants, CL §§14-3301 to
    14-3306.
  See IMMIGRATION CONSULTANTS.
Machine guns.
  Presumption.
    Possession for aggressive or offensive purposes,
      CR §4-405.
Motor vehicles.
  Commercial drivers' licenses.
    Issuance to persons domiciled in foreign
      country, TR §16-817.
  Drivers' licenses.
    Exemption of nonresidents of United States, TR
      §16-102.
Naturalization, US Const Art I §8.
Personal property.
  Right to own and dispose of property, RP §14-101.
President of the United States.
  Ineligible for presidency, US Const Art II §1.
Property.
  Right to own and dispose of, RP §14-101.
Radio and television.
  Definitions, CA §5-703.
Real property.
  Right to own and dispose of property, RP §14-101.
Sales.
  Right to own and dispose of property, RP §14-101.
Suits against state, US Const Amd 11.
Unemployment compensation.
  Eligibility for benefits.
    Conditions of eligibility, LE §8-905.
  Nonimmigrant aliens, LE §8-223.
Voter registration disqualifications, EL §3-102.
Wills.
  Right to devise property, RP §14-101.
Workers' compensation.
  Death benefits.
    Nonresident alien dependent, LE §9-686.

ALIMONY.
Agreement between parties.
  Effect, FL §11-101.
Alimony pendente lite, FL §11-102.
Amount.
  Determination, FL §11-106.
  Modification, FL §11-107.
Appeals.
  Contempt of court, CJ §12-304.
Attachment, seizure and sequestration,
    FamLaw Rule 9-210.
Award.
  Agreement between parties.
    Effect, FL §11-101.
  Alimony pendente lite, FL §11-102.
  Amount.
    Determination, FL §11-106.
  Duration.
    Determination, FL §11-106.
  Grounds for divorce against parties seeking
    alimony.
    Not automatic bar, FL §11-103.

ALIMONY —Cont'd
Award —Cont'd
Nonresident defendant.
Award against, FL §11-104.
Other jurisdictions.
Award following decree by, FL §11-105.
When court may award, FL §11-101.
Circuit courts.
Family law actions, FamLaw Rules 9-201 to
9-210.
Constitution of Maryland.
Imprisonment for delinquent payment.
Not imprisonment for debt, MD Const Art III
§38.
**Contempt based on failure to pay spousal
support.**
Constructive civil contempt, SpecPro Rule 15-207.
Statute of limitations, FL §10-102.
Delinquent payments.
Imprisonment for does not constitute
imprisonment for debt, MD Const Art III §38.
Designee, FL §11-109.
Duration.
Determination, FL §11-106.
Extension of period, FL §11-107.
Termination, FL §11-108.
Enforcement.
Attachment, seizure and sequestration, FamLaw
Rule 9-210.
Imprisonment for delinquent payment not
imprisonment for debt, MD Const Art III §38.
Injunctions, FL §1-203.
Expenses.
Reasonable and necessary expenses.
Order to pay, FL §11-110.
**Grounds for divorce against party seeking
alimony.**
Not automatic bar to award, FL §11-103.
Health insurance, FL §11-111.
Hearings.
Scope of alimony hearing and determination, FL
§1-203.
Imprisonment for delinquent payment.
Not imprisonment for debt, MD Const Art III §38.
Injunctions, FL §1-203.
Insanity.
Authority of court in certain cases, FL §11-111.
Insurance.
Health insurance, FL §11-111.
Jurisdiction.
Equity courts, FL §1-201.
Nonresident defendant in civil actions involving
child support or alimony, CJ §6-103.1.
Mentally ill.
Authority of court in certain cases of insanity, FL
§11-111.
Nonresidents.
Award against nonresident defendant, FL §11-104.
Jurisdiction over nonresident defendants in civil
actions involving child support or alimony, CJ
§6-103.1.
Oral testimony required for final decree, FL
§1-203.
Orders of court.
Reasonable and necessary expenses.
Order to pay, FL §11-110.
Other jurisdictions.
Award following decree by, FL §11-105.
Procedure, FamLaw Rules 9-201 to 9-210.
Related institutions.
Considerations in determining amount and period
of award, FL §11-106.

ALIMONY —Cont'd
Related institutions —Cont'd
Spouse a resident in related institution.
When court may not award alimony, FL
§11-101.
When court may not award alimony.
Alimony pendente lite, FL §11-102.
State's attorneys.
Representation of designee, FL §11-109.
Termination, FL §11-108.
Where available, FL §11-101.

ALLEGANY COUNTY.
Agricultural land preservation foundation.
Natural gas rights owners or lessees.
Subordination of interest to foundation,
exception, AG §2-509.
Alcoholic beverages.
Beer and light wine licenses.
Class A, off-sale, 2B §5-101.
Class C.
Clubs, 2B §5-301.
Class D, on-sale, 2B §5-401.
Licenses generally. See within this subheading,
"Licenses."
Location of licensed business, 2B §9-201.
Special permits, 2B §§7-101, 9-201.
Beer licenses.
Class A, off-sale, 2B §3-101.
Class C, on-sale.
Clubs, 2B §3-301.
Class D, on-sale.
Fee, 2B §3-401.
Licenses generally. See within this subheading,
"Licenses."
Location of licensed business, 2B §9-202.
Special permits, 2B §§7-101, 9-202.
Beer, wine and liquor licenses.
Class A, off-sale, 2B §6-101.
Limitation on additional licenses, 2B §9-202.
Class B-D-T, on-sale.
Hotels and restaurants, 2B §6-201.
Class B, on-sale.
Hotels and restaurants, 2B §6-201.
Class C, on-sale.
Clubs, 2B §6-301.
Class D, on-sale, 2B §6-401.
Limitation on additional licenses, 2B §9-202.
Licenses generally. See within this subheading,
"Licenses."
Limitation on additional class A or D licenses,
2B §9-202.
Special permits, 2B §7-101.
By the drink, 2B §7-101.
Chain stores, supermarkets or discount houses.
Not to be issued licenses, 2B §9-202.
Clubs.
Determination by license commissioners, 2B
§1-102.
Licenses.
Letting privilege prohibited, 2B §12-201.
Limited number, 2B §9-202.
Consumption.
Hours and days, 2B §11-304.
Disorderly, etc., persons congregating.
Prohibited, 2B §12-201.
Display.
Violation of license, 2B §12-201.
Drinking.
Unlawful drinking.
Notices posted, 2B §12-202.

ALLEGANY COUNTY —Cont'd
Alcoholic beverages —Cont'd
Drinking —Cont'd
Unlawful drinking —Cont'd
Prohibited, 2B §12-201.
Elections.
Exercise of privileges of licensee on election day,
2B §11-401.
Enforcement of article, 2B §16-411.
Fines and forfeitures, 2B §16-502.
Consumption violations, 2B §11-304.
Violations, 2B §§12-201, 16-502, 16-507.
Gambling.
Allowing gambling prohibited, 2B §12-201.
General provisions.
See ALCOHOLIC BEVERAGES.
Hearings.
License commissioners.
Applications, 2B §10-102.
Hours and days for sale, 2B §11-501.
Consumption, 2B §11-304.
Election days, 2B §11-401.
Manufacturers' licenses, 2B §11-101.
New Year's Eve day and New Year's day, 2B
§11-402.
Inspectors.
Generally, 2B §15-112.
License commissioners.
Appointment, 2B §15-101.
Clubs.
Determination by commissioners, 2B §1-102.
Hearing.
Applications, 2B §10-202.
Inspectors.
Generally, 2B §15-112.
Qualifications, 2B §15-101.
Salaries, 2B §15-109.
Terms, 2B §15-101.
Vacancies, 2B §15-101.
Licenses.
Applications, 2B §10-104.
Notice on premises, 2B §10-202.
Processing by license commissioners, 2B
§10-202.
Beer and light wine licenses. See within this
subheading, "Beer and light wine licenses."
Beer licenses. See within this subheading, "Beer
licenses."
Beer, wine and liquor licenses. See within this
subheading, "Beer, wine and liquor
licenses."
Club license.
Letting privilege prohibited, 2B §12-201.
Limited number of licenses, 2B §9-202.
Disqualification of licensee, 2B §10-404.
Expiration.
Vacation of premises, 2B §10-504.
Fees.
Disposition, 2B §10-204.
Issuance.
Procedure, 2B §10-202.
Location of licensed business.
Restrictions, 2B §9-202.
Manufacturers.
Hours and days for sale, 2B §11-101.
Music boxes.
Limited number of licenses, 2B §9-202.
Qualifications of licensees, 2B §9-202.
Restrictions, 2B §9-202.
Revocation and suspension.
Grounds, 2B §10-401.

ALLEGANY COUNTY —Cont'd
Alcoholic beverages —Cont'd
Licenses —Cont'd
Revocation and suspension —Cont'd
Procedure, 2B §10-403.
Special and temporary permits, 2B §7-101.
Special festival license, 2B §8-301.
Transfers, 2B §10-503.
Wholesalers, 2B §2-301.
Manufacturers or wholesalers.
License, 2B §2-301.
Hours and days for sale, 2B §11-101.
Selling on credit to retailers prohibited, 2B
§12-201.
Micro-brewery license, 2B §2-208.
Minors.
Allowing to loiter about premises prohibited, 2B
§12-201.
Employment by licensees, 2B §12-201.
Limitation of actions for selling to minors, CJ
§5-106.
Nudity and sexual displays on licensed premises,
2B §10-405.
Open containers.
Possession in certain places.
Applicability of provisions, 2B §19-303.
Penalties, 2B §16-507.
Premises.
Defined, 2B §12-201.
Restaurants.
Sunday sales, 2B §11-501.
Retailers.
Selling on credit prohibited, 2B §12-201.
Sales.
Election days, 2B §11-401.
Minors.
Selling to minors.
Limitation of action, CJ §5-106.
New Year's Eve day and New Year's day, 2B
§11-402.
Prohibited to drunkards and mentally deficient
persons, 2B §12-110.
Retailers selling on credit prohibited, 2B
§12-201.
Sunday sales, 2B §11-501.
2-day Sunday sales permit, 2B §11-501.
Wholesaler's license, 2B §2-301.
Appearance fees.
Distribution, CJ §7-204.
Assessments.
Sanitary commissions.
Levy for part year, EN §9-658.
Tax sale of real property to enforce lien.
Request for, EN §9-658.
Bailiff.
Salary, CJ §2-507.
Bazaar, carnival and raffles, CR §§13-201 to
13-205.
Conducting event for benefit of qualified
organization.
Allowed, CR §13-203.
Definitions, CR §13-201.
Gaming event defined, CR §13-201.
Individual benefit prohibited, CR §13-203.
Management through organizations members, CR
§13-205.
Paper games, CR §13-302.
Prizes and gaming devices allowed, CR §13-204.
Provisions applicable to county, CR §§13-202,
13-301.
Qualified organization defined, CR §13-201.

ALLEGANY COUNTY —Cont'd
Beer and wine festivals.
Special festival license, 2B §8-301.
Bidding.
Competitive bidding, 25 §3.
Birds and game.
Spotlighting, NR §10-410.
Wildlife management areas.
Acquisition of land or water by state, NR §10-801.
Board of education. See within this heading, "Schools."
Bonds, surety.
Compliance bonds.
Competitive bidding, 25 §3.
Building code.
Adoption, 25 §3.
Chain stores.
Alcoholic beverages.
Licenses.
Prohibited, 2B §9-202.
Codes.
Plumbing, building and housing codes.
Adoption, 25 §3.
Commissioners.
Alcoholic beverages.
License commissioners. See within this heading, "Alcoholic beverages."
Plumbing and zoning permits, 25 §3.
Plumbing, building and housing codes.
Adoption, 25 §3.
Powers.
Exceptions, 25 §3.
Saturday closing of offices, 25 §5A.
Vacancy.
Filling vacancy in office, 25 §16.
Correctional facility.
Home detention program, COR §11-702.
Pretrial release program, COR §11-702.
Work release program, COR §11-702.
Courts.
Circuit court.
Judicial circuit, MD Const Art IV §19.
Number of judges, CJ §1-503.
Crimes and offenses.
Alcoholic beverages.
Unlawful display, 2B §12-201.
Unlawful drinking, 2B §12-201.
Definitions.
Study commission, 24 §12-101.
Dog licenses.
Rules and regulations, 24 §11-504.
Dog wardens, 24 §11-504.
Education.
County board of education. See within this heading, "Schools."
Schools generally. See within this heading, "Schools."
Elections.
County board of elections.
Compensation, EL §2-204.
County boards generally, EL §§2-201 to 2-303.
See ELECTIONS.
County boards of education generally, ED §2-301; EL §§8-801 to 8-806.
Election judges.
Compensation, EL §10-205.
Eminent domain.
Public roads.
Procedure, 25 §139.

ALLEGANY COUNTY —Cont'd
Fines.
Alcoholic beverages.
Violations, 2B §§12-201, 16-502, 16-507.
Fire department.
Firefighters appointed as deputy sheriffs, PS §§7-301 to 7-303.
Fish and fisheries.
Carp, NR §4-620.
Dip nets, NR §4-617.
Gigs and bait fish nets, NR §4-620.
Refuges and hatcheries.
Acquisition of land, NR §4-401.
Forest, park and wildlife rangers, NR §5-206.
Forests and parks.
Acquisition of land, NR §5-910.
Gaming events and devices.
Bazaar, carnival and raffles, CR §§13-201 to 13-205, 13-301.
Paper games, CR §13-302.
Highways.
Roads. See within this heading, "Roads."
Home detention program.
Inmates sentenced to confinement at correctional facility, COR §11-702.
Housing code.
Adoption, 25 §3.
Injury reports.
Automobile accident or lethal weapon causing injury.
Physicians, pharmacists, dentists or nurses, HG §20-701.
Licenses.
Special festival license, 2B §8-301.
Limitation of actions.
Alcoholic beverages.
Limitation of actions for sale to minors, CJ §5-106.
Marriage.
Clerk's fee for performing ceremony.
Disposition, FL §2-410.
Minors.
Alcoholic beverages.
Allowing to loiter about premises prohibited, 2B §12-201.
Employment by licensees, 2B §12-201.
Limitation of actions for selling to minors, CJ §5-106.
Misdemeanors.
Alcoholic beverages.
Unlawful display, 2B §12-201.
Unlawful drinking, 2B §12-201.
Motor vehicles.
Size and weight.
Power of county commissioners, 25 §25.
Tires.
Studs, cleats, etc.
Sale regulated, TR §22-405.2.
Use allowed during certain months, TR §22-405.2.
Municipal corporations.
Alcoholic beverages.
Enforcement of article, 2B §16-411.
Noise control.
Trapshooting, skeet shooting, etc.
Limitations on authority, EN §§3-105, 3-401.
Nuisances, EN §10-305; HG §20-313.
Obscene performances.
Prohibition, CR §11-204.
Orphans' court.
Judges.
Compensation, ET §2-108.

ALLEGANY COUNTY —Cont'd
Paper gaming, CR §13-302.
Planning and zoning.
Permits, 25 §3.
Planning commission, 66B §14.01.
Special provisions, 66B §3.02.
Plumbing.
Codes.
Adoption, 25 §3.
Permits, 25 §3.
Police.
Reciprocal agreement with municipal corporation
in county, CP §2-105.
Potomac water authority.
General provisions.
See POTOMAC WATER AUTHORITY.
Pretrial release program, COR §11-702.
Property taxes.
Manufacturing property exempt from taxation,
inapplicability, TP §7-225.
Recordation.
Plats of subdivisions.
Inapplicability of section, RP §3-108.
Restaurants.
Alcoholic beverages.
Sunday sales, 2B §11-501.
Roads.
Eminent domain.
Procedure, 25 §139.
Opening, closing or altering.
Alleys or streets less than thirty feet wide, 25
§138A.
Eminent domain.
Procedure, 25 §139.
Passing through buildings, gardens, yards or
burial grounds.
Exception as to consent of owner, 25 §144.
Sanitary commissions.
County commissions may exercise jurisdiction
over, EN §9-629.
Taxation.
Property tax.
Levy, EN §9-694.
Schools.
County board of education.
Compensation of members, ED §3-203.
Election of members, ED §3-114.
Elections, ED §3-201.
Generally, EL §§8-801 to 8-806.
Expenses, ED §3-203.
Meetings.
Annual meeting, ED §4-107.
Executive session, ED §3-204.
Nonvoting student member.
Attendance, ED §3-204.
Public, ED §3-204.
Members, ED §3-201.
Nonvoting student member, ED §3-201.
Attendance at meetings, ED §3-204.
Officers.
Elections, ED §3-202.
Persons subject to authority of board.
Ineligibility to serve as member, ED §3-114.
President, ED §3-202.
Records.
Public, ED §3-204.
Terms of office, ED §3-201.
Vacancies, ED §3-201.
Vice-president, ED §3-202.
Employee organizations.
Fees.
Contributions toward negotiation of collective
bargaining agreements, ED §6-504.

ALLEGANY COUNTY —Cont'd
Schools —Cont'd
Employee organizations —Cont'd
Negotiations between employer and employee.
Representation in Allegany county.
Fees charged for nonmember, ED §6-407.
Year-round schools.
Pilot programs, ED §7-103.
Sheriff.
Clerk-bookkeeper.
General provisions, CJ §2-309.
Deputies.
Chief deputy, CJ §2-309.
Free meals while on duty, CJ §2-309.
Expenses.
Allowance, CJ §2-309.
Firefighters appointed as deputy sheriffs, PS
§§7-301 to 7-303.
Office.
Furnishing by county, CJ §2-309.
Salary, CJ §2-309.
Second in command, CJ §2-310.
State's attorney.
Accounts for services and expenses.
County excepted from section, 10 §39.
County and assistant county investigator, 10 §40.
Generally, 10 §40.
Streets and alleys.
Roads. See within this heading, "Roads."
Study commission.
Appointment of members, 24 §12-103.
Chairman, 24 §12-103.
Composition, 24 §12-103.
Created, 24 §12-102.
Definitions, 24 §12-101.
Duties, 24 §12-105.
Established, 24 §12-102.
Establishment of salaries, 24 §12-106.
Meetings, 24 §12-104.
Number of members, 24 §12-103.
Quorum, 24 §12-104.
Recommendations, 24 §§12-103, 12-105.
Restrictions, 24 §12-106.
Subdivisions.
Plats.
Recordation.
Inapplicability of section, RP §3-108.
Sundays.
Alcoholic beverages.
Sales, 2B §11-501.
Taxation.
Hotel rental tax, 24 §§9-301 to 9-326.
See COUNTIES.
Interest.
Overdue taxes, TP §14-603.
Paper gaming, CR §13-302.
Property tax credits, TP §9-302.
Redemption.
Rate of redemption, TP §14-820.
Sale.
Exemption, TP §14-851.
Special taxing-area commissions or boards.
Annual report, 24 §9-111.
**Trapshooting, skeetshooting or other target
shooting.**
Environmental sound level limits and noise
control rules and regulations, EN §3-401.
Noise control ordinances, rules or regulations
prohibiting, EN §3-105.
Treasurer.
Salary, 25 §51.

ALLEGANY COUNTY —Cont'd
Tri-county council for western Maryland.
    See TRI-COUNTY COUNCIL FOR WESTERN
        MARYLAND.
Water and sewer authorities.
    Bond issues.
        Special provisions, EN §9-934.
Water and sewer systems.
    Liens for unpaid charges.
        Nonprofit suppliers, 78A §53.
Watersheds.
    Reports, EN §15-203.
Wine festivals.
    Special festival license, 2B §8-301.
Witnesses.
    Itinerant allowances, CJ §9-202.
    Mileage, CJ §9-202.
Work release program, COR §11-702.
Zoning.
    Permits, 25 §3.

ALLEGANY COUNTY TRANSIT AUTHORITY.
State retirement and pension system.
    Municipal participation in state employees'
        systems, SPP §§31-101 to 31-116.1.
        See STATE RETIREMENT AND PENSION
            SYSTEM.

ALLEYS.
See STREETS AND ALLEYS.

ALLIGATORS.
Dangerous animals.
    Importing, selling, or trading in, CR §10-621.

ALLOCUTION.
Sentencing.
    Capital cases, Crim Rule 4-343.
    Non-capital cases, Crim Rule 4-342.

ALTERATION OF INSTRUMENTS.
Investment securities, CL §8-206.
Negotiable instruments.
    Defined, CL §3-407.
    Liability for negligence contributing to, CL §3-406.

ALTERNATIVE DISPUTE RESOLUTION.
Administrative procedure.
    Procurement, SF §15-216.
Applicability of rules, ADR Rule 17-101; Rule
    1-101.
**Application for designation to conduct
    proceedings,** ADR Rule 17-107.
Arbitration.
    See ARBITRATION AND AWARD.
**Business and technology case management
    program.**
    Application seeking designation as mediator, ADR
        Rule 17-107.
Continuing education.
    Mediators, ADR Rule 17-104.
Counties.
    Construction contracts, 25 §1A; 25A §1A; 25B
        §13A.
Definitions, ADR Rule 17-102.
Fees.
    Schedules of fees, ADR Rule 17-108.
Health care malpractice claims, CJ §3-2A-06C.
Malpractice.
    Health care malpractice claims, CJ §3-2A-06C.
Mediation.
    Collective bargaining generally, LE §§4-101 to
        4-405.
        See COLLECTIVE BARGAINING.

ALTERNATIVE DISPUTE RESOLUTION
    —Cont'd
Mediation —Cont'd
    General provisions.
        See MEDIATION.
    Labor dispute arbitration or mediation, LE
        §§4-101 to 4-111.
        See COLLECTIVE BARGAINING.
Neutral experts.
    Qualifications and selection, ADR Rule 17-105.1.
Objection to referral, ADR Rule 17-103.
Procedure, ADR Rule 17-103.
Procurement.
    Appeals board.
        See PROCUREMENT.
    Architectural and engineering services.
        Exception to dispute resolution provisions, SF
            §15-202.
Qualifications of mediators, ADR Rule 17-104.
Qualifications of neutral experts, ADR Rule
    17-105.1.
**Qualifications of persons other than mediators
    and neutral experts,** ADR Rule 17-105.
**St. Mary's county human relations
    commission.**
    Defined, 49B §44.
    Generally, 49B §48.
**State center for alternative dispute resolution
    and violence prevention,** ED §24-401.

ALTERNATIVE FUELS.
Renewable energy credits, AG §§10-1501 to
    10-1507.
    See RENEWABLE ENERGY CREDITS.

ALZHEIMER'S DISEASE.
Assisted living programs.
    Alzheimer's special care unit or program.
        Disclosures of information by programs offering,
            HG §20-109.
Health insurance coverage, IN §15-801.
Hospitals.
    In-service education program as to, HG §19-319.1.
Long-term care insurance, IN §18-111.
Medicaid.
    Home-based and community-based services
        waiver, HG §15-131.

AMATEUR ATHLETIC ORGANIZATIONS.
Bingo.
    Frederick county, CR §13-1306.
Gaming, bazaar, carnival and raffles.
    Baltimore City, CR §§13-501 to 13-510.
    Baltimore county, CR §§13-601 to 13-607.
    Carroll county, CR §§13-901 to 13-909.
    Frederick county, CR §§13-1301 to 13-1307.
Tip jars and punch board.
    Frederick county, CR §13-1305.

AMBASSADORS AND CONSULS.
Constitutional provisions, US Const Art II §§2, 3;
    Art III §2.
Drivers' licenses, immunity, TR §§16-901 to
    16-905.

AMBULANCE CHASING.
Attorneys at law, BOP §10-604.
Insurance fraud, IN §§27-407, 27-408.

AMBULANCES.
Bingo.
    Charles county.
        Ambulance companies conducting, CR
            §§13-1109 to 13-1115.

AMBULANCES —Cont'd
Bingo —Cont'd
Frederick county.
Ambulance companies in county conducting, CR
§13-1306.
Commercial ambulance service fund, ED
§13-515.
Corporations.
Provision of fire, ambulance and rescue services
by for-profit entities, PS §7-401.
Counties.
Ambulance services.
Licenses.
Preemption of local legislation, ED §13-515.
Criminal law and procedure.
Impersonating firefighters or emergency services
personnel, PS §7-402.
Interference with or obstruction of emergency
assistance, PS §7-402.
Death in the line of duty.
Death benefits, PS §1-202.
Reward for information regarding person who
causes death, PS §1-201.
Definitions.
Ambulance services, ED §13-515.
Drivers' licenses, exemptions, TR §16-102.
Emergency vehicles.
General provisions.
See EMERGENCY VEHICLES.
Equipment and supplies.
Requirements, ED §13-515.
False alarms, CR §9-604.
False impersonations.
Impersonating firefighters or emergency services
personnel, PS §7-402.
Fees.
Licenses.
Ambulance services, ED §13-515.
For-profit entities.
Provision of fire, ambulance and rescue services
by for-profit entities, PS §7-401.
Funds.
Senator William H. Amoss fire, rescue and
ambulance fund, PS §§8-101 to 8-106.
Volunteer company assistance fund, PS §§8-201 to
8-206.
Gaming, bazaar, carnival and raffles.
Charles county.
Ambulance companies conducting, CR
§§13-1101 to 13-1115.
Good Samaritan law.
Immunity for special personnel, CJ §5-603.
Hearings.
Ambulance services.
Licenses.
Denial of applications, suspension or
revocation, ED §13-515.
**HIV testing for health care workers and first
responders,** HG §§18-336 to 18-338.3.
Inspections.
Ambulance services, ED §13-515.
Exemption from mandatory inspections, TR
§23-206.1.
Exemption stickers.
Display, TR §23-206.1.
Insurance.
Group life insurance for ambulance service
organization members, IN §17-208.
**Interference with or obstruction of emergency
assistance,** PS §7-402.

AMBULANCES —Cont'd
Licenses.
Ambulance services, ED §13-515.
Local regulation preempted, ED §13-515.
Medicaid.
Reimbursement for emergency service
transporters, HG §15-114.1.
Misdemeanors.
Ambulance services.
Licenses.
Violations of section, ED §13-515.
Motor vehicles.
Emergency vehicles.
See EMERGENCY VEHICLES.
Municipal corporations.
Ambulance services.
Licenses.
Preemption of local legislation, ED §13-515.
911 emergency telephone system, PS §§1-301 to
1-312.
See 911 EMERGENCY TELEPHONE SYSTEM.
Penalties.
Ambulance services.
Licenses.
Violations of section, ED §13-515.
Registration, TR §13-914.
Rescue squads.
General provisions.
See RESCUE SQUADS.
Reward.
Death in the line of duty.
Reward for information regarding person who
causes death, PS §1-201.
Scholarships.
Ambulance companies or squads.
Scholarships for children or spouses of public
safety employees killed in line of duty, ED
§18-601.
Tip jars and punch board.
Frederick county.
Ambulance companies in county conducting, CR
§13-1305.
University of Maryland.
Emergency medical care and services, ED
§13-515.
Vessels and boats.
Ambulance vessels.
Flashing red and yellow lights or signal devices.
Use, NR §8-727.1.
Volunteer company assistance fund, PS §§8-201
to 8-206.
Waiver.
Licenses.
Ambulance services.
Waiver of requirements, ED §13-515.

AMBULATORY CARE FACILITIES, HG
§§19-3B-01 to 19-3B-09.
See FREESTANDING AMBULATORY CARE
FACILITIES.

AMENDMENTS.
Bail and recognizance.
Pretrial release.
Orders, Crim Rule 4-216.
Baltimore City.
Charter amendments, MD Const Art XI-A §5.
Banks and trust companies.
Charters, FI §3-213.
Bill of particulars.
Circuit courts, Crim Rule 4-241.
Charging documents, Crim Rule 4-204.

AMENDMENTS —Cont'd
Code of Maryland.
Enactment of laws not amendatory of code, MD Const Art III §29.
General provisions, MD Const Art III §29.
Inconsistent amendments to same code section or subsection, 1 §17.
Reference in statute to code or other law includes amendments, 1 §21.
Condominiums.
Bylaw, declaration and plat, RP §11-124.
Plats, RP §§11-105, 11-124.
Constitution of Maryland, MD Const Art XIV §1.
See CONSTITUTION OF MARYLAND.
Constitution of the United States, US Const Amd 5.
See CONSTITUTION OF THE UNITED STATES.
Corporations.
Charter.
See CORPORATIONS.
Existing corporations be subject thereto, CA §1-102.
Counties.
Charter amendments, MD Const Art XI-A §5.
Credit unions.
Articles of incorporation.
Effective date, FI §6-320.
Mail ballot, FI §6-321.
Meetings of members, FI §6-317.
Bylaws.
Effective date, FI §6-320.
Mail ballots, FI §6-321.
Meetings of members, FI §6-317.
Procedures, FI §6-320.
Recommendation, FI §6-328.
Distress for rent.
Levy and inventory, RP §8-305.
Petition or other pleadings, RP §8-327.
Expungement of records.
Applications, petitions or answers, Crim Rule 4-506.
General assembly.
Bills.
See GENERAL ASSEMBLY.
Interpretation and construction.
Inconsistent amendments to same section or subsection, 1 §17.
Judgments.
Motion to alter or amend judgment.
District Court, CivProDist Rule 3-534.
Juvenile causes.
Juvenile petitions or pleadings, Juv Rule 11-108.
Lame duck amendment.
Congress.
Changing meeting of congress, US Const Amd 20.
Mandamus.
Amendment of pleadings, SpecPro Rule 15-701.
Mechanics' liens.
Claims, RP §9-112.
Pleadings, PropAct Rule 12-303.
Proceedings, RP §9-112.
Motions.
Circuit courts, CivProCir Rule 2-342.
District Court, CivProDist Rule 3-342.
Papers.
Circuit courts, CivProCir Rule 2-342.
District Court, CivProDist Rule 3-342.
Pleadings.
Circuit courts, CivProCir Rule 2-341.
District Court, CivProDist Rule 3-341.

AMENDMENTS —Cont'd
Pleadings —Cont'd
Juvenile causes, Juv Rule 11-108.
Mandamus, SpecPro Rule 15-701.
Mechanics' and materialmen's liens, PropAct Rule 12-303.
Post conviction procedures.
Petitions, Crim Rule 4-402.
Proposed amendments.
Religious freedom, MD Const DofR Art 36.
Savings and loan associations.
Charter amendments, FI §9-211.
Sentencing.
Release after conviction, Crim Rule 4-349.
Statutes.
Construction.
Inconsistent amendments to same section or subsection, 1 §17.
Effect of amendment on penalty or liability previously incurred, 1 §3.
Reference in statute to code or other law includes amendments, 1 §21.
Tri-county council for Western Maryland.
General development plan, 20A §3-102.
Trusts and trustees.
Real estate investment trust.
Declaration of trust, CA §8-501.

AMERICAN LEGION.
Motor vehicles.
Registration.
40-8 box car.
Exemption from registration fees, TR §13-903.

AMERICAN RED CROSS.
Assigning nurses to disaster situation in state.
Nursing license exception, HO §8-301.
General provisions.
See RED CROSS.
State personnel.
Disaster service leave, SPP §9-1102.

AMERICAN SIGN LANGUAGE.
Academic credit.
County boards of education.
Board may give credit for study of American sign language, ED §4-111.
Recognition as language system, 30 §34.

AMICUS CURIAE.
Appellate procedure, AppRev Rule 8-511.
Costs, AppRev Rule 8-607.

AMMONIUM NITRATE.
Possession of destructive device, CR §§4-501 to 4-503.

AMMUNITION.
Child's access to firearm.
Defined, CR §4-104.
Detachable magazines.
Prohibited, CR §4-305.
Militia.
Sale of superfluous armories, PS §13-217.
Minors.
Sale, rental or transfer to minors, PS §5-134.
State preemption of local regulation, CR §4-209.

AMMUNITION CLIPS.
Detachable magazines, prohibition, CR §4-305.

AMOSS, SENATOR WILLIAM H.
Senator William H. Amoss fire, rescue and ambulance fund, PS §§8-101 to 8-106.

AMPHETAMINES.
Depressant or stimulant drug, CR §5-401.
Generally, CR §§5-101 to 5-1101.
   See CONTROLLED DANGEROUS
      SUBSTANCES.
Methamphetamines.
   Importers, CR §5-614.
   Volume dealers, enhanced penalty, CR §5-612.
Schedule II, CR §5-403.

AMUSEMENTS AND RECREATION.
Abatement.
   Citations, BR §3-406.
Accidents and complaints.
   Inspections and investigations, BR §3-402.
Actions.
   Proceedings for enforcement, BR §3-207.
Administrative search warrant, BR §3-205.
Admissions and amusement tax.
   General provisions.
      See ADMISSIONS AND AMUSEMENT TAX.
Amusement devices.
   Licensing, BR §§17-401 to 17-438. See within this
      heading, "Pinball machines."
Amusement park safety.
   Advisory board.
      Program evaluation act, SG §8-403.
   Insurance.
      Counties insuring amusement rides.
         Immunity from liability, CJ §5-516.
   Liability.
      Counties.
         Insurance.
            Immunity from liability, CJ §5-516.
Appeals.
   Adverse agency action, BR §3-206.
   Adverse agency decision.
      Prohibition on use of rides, BR §3-405.
Assumption of risk, BR §3-104.
Baltimore City.
   Licensing of pinball machines.
      Municipal authority, BR §17-407.
Billiard tables.
   Licensing, BR §§17-501 to 17-505.
      See BILLIARD AND POOL TABLES.
Board.
   Chairman.
      Appointment, BR §3-305.
   Compensation, BR §3-306.
   Composition, BR §3-304.
   Consultation on regulations, BR §3-307.
   Creation, BR §3-303.
   Defined, BR §3-301.
   Established, BR §3-303.
   Meetings, BR §3-306.
   Membership, BR §3-304.
   Qualifications.
      Consumer members, BR §3-304.
   Recommendations on regulations, BR §3-308.
      Action by commissioner, BR §3-311.
      Bases for recommendation, BR §3-309.
      Delayed effective date, BR §3-312.
      Reporting requirements, BR §3-310.
   Reimbursement for expenses, BR §3-306.
   Reporting requirements, BR §3-310.
   Tenure, BR §3-304.
Bungee jumping operations, BR §3-503.
Citations.
   Contents, BR §3-406.
   Required for certain violations, BR §3-406.

AMUSEMENTS AND RECREATION —Cont'd
Commissioner.
   Administration of title, BR §3-201.
   Consultation on regulations.
      State amusement ride safety advisory board,
         BR §3-307.
   Defined, BR §3-101.
   Delegation of powers and duties, BR §3-202.
      Inspection powers, BR §3-203.
   Enforcement of title, BR §3-201.
   Judicial review of agency decision, BR §3-206.
   Powers and duties.
      Copies of regulations, BR §3-313.
      Delegation, BR §3-202.
         Inspection power, BR §3-203.
      Generally, BR §3-204.
      Inspections, BR §3-402.
      Investigations, BR §3-402.
      Safety regulations for amusement rides, BR
         §3-302.
   Recommendations on regulations.
      State amusement ride safety advisory board,
         BR §3-308.
      Action by commissioner, BR §3-311.
      Bases for recommendation, BR §3-309.
      Delayed effective date, BR §3-312.
      Reporting requirements, BR §3-310.
Community recreation.
   Program.
      Liability.
         Volunteers' immunity, CJ §5-802.
Consumer protection.
   Tickets.
      Reserved seat ticket sales.
         Seating plan showing location of seats and
            physical obstructions must be displayed,
            CL §13-310.
Counties.
   Insuring amusement rides.
      Immunity from liability, CJ §5-516.
   Licenses.
      Powers of county commissioners, 25 §3.
   Permit required for amusement park, 25 §27.
Death or serious injury.
   Penalty, BR §3-502.
   Records and reports, BR §3-404.
Definitions, BR §3-101.
   Amusement devices, BR §17-401.
      Licensing of pinball machines, BR §17-405.
   Board, BR §3-301.
   Work day, BR §3-406.
Devices.
   Amusement devices, BR §§17-401 to 17-438. See
      within this heading, "Pinball machines."
Fees.
   Copies of regulations, BR §3-313.
   Pinball machines.
      License fees, BR §17-410.
Fraud.
   False representations and statements, BR §3-501.
Garrett county.
   Licensing of amusement devices, BR §§17-432 to
      17-438.
Hearings.
   Citations.
      Hearing examiner, BR §3-406.
Immunity.
   Amusement park safety.
      Counties insuring amusement rides, CJ §5-516.
Injury.
   Records and reports.
      Serious physical injury, BR §3-404.

AMUSEMENTS AND RECREATION —Cont'd
Inspections.
Certificate of inspection.
Generally, BR §3-402.
Duty of commissioner, BR §3-402.
Operation of amusement rides, BR §3-401.
Insurance.
Amusement rides, BR §§3-401, 3-403.
Required, BR §3-401.
Requirements, BR §3-403.
Self-insurance, BR §3-403.
Operation of amusement rides, BR §3-401.
Investigations.
Duty of commissioner, BR §3-402.
Juke boxes.
Licenses.
General provisions, BR §§17-1301 to 17-1309.
See JUKE BOXES.
Harford County, BR §§17-1312 to 17-1318.
See HARFORD COUNTY.
Legislative findings, BR §3-102.
Liability.
Amusement park safety.
Counties.
Insurance.
Immunity from liability, CJ §5-516.
Licenses.
Counties.
Powers of county commissioners, 25 §3.
Pinball machines, BR §§17-401 to 17-416. See
within this heading, "Pinball machines."
Militia.
Exclusion of members from places of amusement
or recreation.
Prohibited activities, PS §13-904.
Minors.
Pinball machines.
Operation by minors prohibited, BR §17-415.
Montgomery County.
Licensing of pinball machines, BR §§17-416,
17-417.
Notices.
Citations.
Notice of penalty and hearing, BR §3-406.
New, modified or reconstructive amusement rides,
BR §3-402.
Prohibition on use of rides, BR §3-405.
Outdoor concerts.
Promoter licenses, BR §§17-1401 to 17-1407.
See OUTDOOR CONCERTS.
Penalties.
Civil penalties, BR §3-504.
False representations and statements, BR §3-501.
Pinball machines, BR §17-417.
Willful violation causing death, BR §3-502.
Pinball machines.
Applicability of title, BR §17-406.
Assignment of license, BR §17-412.
Authority of Baltimore City, BR §17-407.
Cash or tokens.
Payouts prohibited, BR §17-414.
Copies of licenses to comptroller, BR §17-402.
Display of license, BR §17-411.
Garrett county.
Licensing, BR §§17-432 to 17-438.
Issuance of license, BR §17-411.
Copies to comptroller, BR §17-402.
Keeping licensed machines lawful, BR §17-408.
Keeping machines in Montgomery County, BR
§17-416.
Penalties, BR §17-417.

AMUSEMENTS AND RECREATION —Cont'd
Pinball machines —Cont'd
Keeping unlicensed machines prohibited, BR
§17-413.
License fees, BR §17-410.
License required, BR §17-409.
Mandatory license requirement, BR §17-409.
Minors.
Operation by minors prohibited, BR §17-415.
Paying out cash or tokens prohibited, BR §17-414.
Prorated license fees, BR §17-410.
Schedule of license fees, BR §17-410.
Scope of title, BR §17-406.
Transferability of license, BR §17-412.
Unlicensed machines prohibited, BR §17-413.
Posting requirements.
Citations, BR §3-406.
Prohibition on use of rides, BR §3-405.
Prohibition on use, BR §3-405.
Promoters of outdoor musical festivals.
Licenses, BR §§17-1401 to 17-1407.
See OUTDOOR CONCERTS.
Public recreation and parks.
General provisions, 25 §§222 to 230.
See PUBLIC RECREATION AND PARKS.
Records.
Death or serious injury, BR §3-404.
Reports.
Death or serious injury, BR §3-404.
Rules and regulations.
Amusement rides.
Safety regulations for maintenance and
operation, BR §3-302.
Copies of regulations.
Duties of commissioner, BR §3-313.
Variances.
Application and grounds, BR §3-314.
Scope of title, BR §3-103.
Searches and seizure.
Administrative search warrant, BR §3-205.
State amusement ride safety advisory board.
Generally, BR §§3-301 to 3-314. See within this
heading, "Board."
Statement of purpose, BR §3-102.
Sunday blue laws.
Professional sports, BR §18-102.
Sunset law, BR §3-601.
Taxation.
Admissions and amusement tax.
General provisions, TG §§2-201 to 2-203, 4-101
to 4-301.
See ADMISSIONS AND AMUSEMENT TAX.
Termination of title, BR §3-601.
Tickets.
Reserved seat ticket sales.
Seating plan showing location of seats and
physical obstructions must be displayed, CL
§13-310.
Unfair or deceptive trade practices.
Reserved seat tickets, CL §13-310.
Variances from regulation.
Application and grounds, BR §3-314.
Washington county.
Licensing of amusement devices, 24 §11-201.
Wicomico county.
Licensing of pinball machines, BR §§17-420 to
17-429.
See WICOMICO COUNTY.
Worcester county.
Licensing of free-play machines and other
amusement devices, 24 §11-201.

AMUSEMENT TAX.
See ADMISSIONS AND AMUSEMENT TAX.

ANABOLIC STEROIDS.
Controlled dangerous substances.
Generally, CR §§5-101 to 5-1101.
See CONTROLLED DANGEROUS
SUBSTANCES.
Schedule III, CR §5-404.
Warning posted as to consequences of illegal use,
CR §5-710.

ANALINGUS.
Sexual offense in first or second degree, CR
§§3-305, 3-306, 3-311, 3-312.

ANATOMICAL GIFT ACT.
Advanced directives, HG §5-604.1.
Autopsies.
Effect of laws concerning autopsies, ET §4-508.
Blood banks.
Eligible donees, ET §4-504.
Body or part of body.
Defined, ET §4-501.
Examination of body.
Authorized, ET §4-503.
Bone marrow donations, HG §19-310.
Citation.
Short title, ET §4-512.
Competence.
Donor, ET §4-503.
Completion.
During lifetime of donor, ET §4-510.
Consent.
Document or recorded message of consent, ET
§4-503.
Hospital procedures, HG §19-310.
Corneas.
When chief medical examiner or his deputy or
assistant may provide cornea for transplant,
ET §4-509.1.
Cost of removal.
Billing estate, surviving spouse or heirs
prohibited, ET §4-504.
Death.
Time of death, ET §4-508.
Decedent's body.
Custody, ET §4-508.
Definitions, ET §4-501.
Document.
Delivery to donee, ET §4-506.
Execution.
Methods of making, ET §4-505.
Persons who may execute, ET §4-503.
Prior to July 1, 1968.
Validity of authority or instrument, ET
§4-511.
When document may be executed, ET §4-503.
Gift by document, ET §4-505.
Revocation of gift, ET §4-507.
Validity.
Executed in another state, ET §4-505.
Executed prior to July 1, 1968, ET §4-511.
Donees.
Acceptance or rejection of gift, ET §4-508.
Delivery of will or document to donee, ET §4-506.
Designation, ET §4-505.
Eligibility, ET §4-504.
Rights, ET §4-508.
Paramount, ET §4-503.
Specified donee, ET §4-504.

ANATOMICAL GIFT ACT —Cont'd
Donors.
Competence of donor, ET §4-503.
Completed during lifetime of donor, ET §4-510.
Death.
Determining time of death, ET §4-508.
Drivers' licenses.
Notation that licensee is donor, TR §§12-303,
12-303.1.
Rights of donor's next of kin, ET §4-508.
Time of death, ET §4-508.
Drivers' licenses.
Notation that licensee is donor, TR §§12-303,
12-303.1.
Federally designated organ procurement
organization.
Eligible donees, ET §4-504.
Forms.
Gift by living donor, ET §4-505.
General assembly.
Legislative policy, ET §4-502.
Hospitals.
Consent procedures, HG §19-310.
Eligible donees, ET §4-504.
Licensed hospital.
Defined, ET §4-501.
Procedure for organ donations, HG §19-310.
Procurement of organs and tissues.
Protocol for, HG §19-319.
Human organs.
Storage facilities.
Eligible donees, ET §4-504.
Liability.
Civil or criminal liability for unknowingly
violating subtitle, ET §4-508.
When chief medical examiner or deputy or
assistant may provide organ for transplant,
ET §4-509.
Corneas, ET §4-509.1.
Medical school.
Eligible donees, ET §4-504.
Methods of making, ET §§4-503, 4-505.
Minors.
Consent for minor patient's anatomical donations,
HG §19-310.
Decedent, ET §4-503.
Motor vehicles.
Drivers' licenses.
Notation that licensee is donor, TR §§12-303,
12-303.1.
Next of kin.
Defined, ET §4-501.
Nonresidents.
Validity of document of gift executed in another
state, ET §4-505.
Person.
Defined, ET §4-501.
Persons who may make, ET §4-503.
Physicians and surgeons.
Acceptance of gift by attending physician, ET
§4-505.
Defined, ET §4-501.
Designation of surgeon to carry out procedures,
ET §4-505.
Eligible donees, ET §4-504.
Purpose of subtitle, ET §4-502.
Relatives.
Authorized to make gift, ET §4-503.
Rights of donor's next of kin, ET §4-508.
Revocation of gift, ET §4-507.
Method of revocation, ET §4-507.

ANATOMICAL GIFT ACT —Cont'd
Transplants.
  Corneas.
    When chief examiner or deputy may provide, ET §4-509.1.
  Liability of medical examiner, ET §4-509.
    Corneas, ET §4-509.1.
  Provisions for the transplant of an organ, ET §4-509.
  Requirements, ET §4-509.
  When chief medical examiner or deputy or assistant may provide organ for transplant, ET §4-509.
    Corneas, ET §4-509.1.
Wills.
  Delivery of will to donee.
    To expedite procedure, ET §4-506.
  Gift by will, ET §4-505.
  Production of will, ET §4-506.
  Revocation of gift, ET §4-507.
  Validity of authority or instrument executed prior to July 1, 1968, ET §4-511.

ANATOMY BOARD.
Appointment of members, HG §5-403.
Buying, selling or transporting bodies, HG §5-408.
Claim of body, HG §5-406.
Compensation of members, HG §5-404.
Composition, HG §5-403.
Definitions, HG §5-401.
Distribution and use of dead bodies or body parts, HG §5-407.
Donated bodies.
  Embalming, HG §5-406.1.
  Exclusive control of board, HG §5-406.1.
  Notice to board of intent to donate, HG §5-406.1.
Duties, HG §5-404.1.
Embalming.
  Donated bodies, HG §5-406.1.
  Unclaimed bodies, HG §5-406.
Established, HG §5-402.
Examiners.
  Postmortem examiners.
    See POSTMORTEM EXAMINERS.
Functions, HG §5-405.
Funds, HG §5-405.
Meetings, HG §5-404.
Misdemeanors.
  Violation of subtitle, HG §5-409.
Morgues.
  Removal of dead bodies to designated morgue, HG §5-406.
Notice.
  Unclaimed bodies.
    Notice to board, HG §5-406.
Officers, HG §5-403.
Penalties.
  Violations of subtitle, HG §5-409.
Plans, proposals and projects.
  Limitations on secretary, HG §5-405.
Postmortem examiners.
  See POSTMORTEM EXAMINERS.
Powers, HG §5-404.1.
  Buying, selling or transporting of bodies, HG §5-408.
  Embalming of bodies, HG §§5-406, 5-406.1.
Public officers.
  Defined, HG §5-401.
  Violations, HG §5-409.

ANATOMY BOARD —Cont'd
Rules and regulations.
  Adoption of regulations, HG §5-404.1.
Secretary.
  Limitations, HG §5-405.
Staff, HG §5-405.
Unclaimed bodies.
  Embalming.
    Power to embalm, HG §5-406.
  Notice to board, HG §5-406.
Violations.
  Penalties, HG §5-409.

ANCIENT DOCUMENTS.
Requirement of identification or authentication, Evid Rule 5-901.

ANESTHESIOLOGISTS.
Physicians.
  Generally.
    See PHYSICIANS.

ANIMAL CONTROL.
Contraband.
  Seizure of animals deemed contraband, HG §18-222.
Counties.
  More stringent requirements by local government, HG §18-220.
Dangerous animals.
  Prohibition.
    Power of secretary, HG §18-219.
Definitions, HG §18-218.
Findings by legislature, HG §18-217.
Intergovernmental cooperation, HG §18-221.
Legislative findings and declaration, HG §18-217.
Local governments.
  More stringent requirements by, HG §18-220.
Misdemeanors.
  Violations of provisions, HG §18-222.
Municipal corporations.
  More stringent requirements by local government, HG §18-220.
Nuisances.
  Seizure of animals deemed nuisance and contraband, HG §18-222.
Penalties.
  Violations of provisions, HG §18-222.
Searches and seizures.
  Violations of provisions.
    Seizure of animals deemed nuisance and contraband, HG §18-222.

ANIMALS.
Abandoning domestic animal, CR §10-612.
Abuse or neglect of animal, CR §10-604.
Acupuncturists.
  Practice of veterinary medicine, HO §1-211.
Audiologists and speech-language pathologists.
  Practice of veterinary medicine, HO §1-211.
Birds and game.
  See BIRDS AND GAME.
Carrier pigeons.
  Injuring or trapping, CR §10-622.
Cats.
  See CATS.
Chicks.
  Selling or coloring, CR §10-614.
Cockfight, CR §10-608.
  Attending cockfight, CR §10-605.
Contagious and infectious diseases.
  Appraisals.
    Buildings or animals to be destroyed, AG §3-107.

ANIMALS —Cont'd
Crimes relating to animals, CR §§10-601 to 10-622.
Abandoning domestic animal, CR §10-612.
Abuse or neglect of animal, CR §10-604.
Aggravated cruelty, CR §10-606.
Arranging, conducting or using dog in dog fight, CR §10-607.
Cockfighting, CR §10-608.
Baltimore City.
Kennel inspections, health department to enforce, CR §10-616.
Baltimore county.
Enforcement, care of mistreated animals, CR §10-615.
Carrier pigeons, injuring or trapping, CR §10-622.
Chicks, selling or giving away, coloring, CR §10-614.
Cockfighting, CR §10-608.
Attending cockfight, CR §10-605.
Dangerous animals.
Importing into state, selling, bartering or trading, CR §10-621.
Dangerous dogs, CR §10-619.
Definitions, CR §10-601.
Dehorning, castration, taildocking and limit feeding.
Inapplicability of provisions, CR §10-603.
Disposal of unclaimed dogs or cats, CR §10-617.
Dogfight.
Arranging, conducting or using dog in dog fight, CR §10-607.
Attending, CR §10-605.
Euthanasia.
Disposal of unclaimed dogs or cats, CR §10-617.
Prohibited means of killing dogs and cats, CR §10-611.
Failure to feed or care for, CR §10-604.
Food processing, pest elimination, training and hunting.
Inapplicability of provisions, CR §10-603.
Giving unaccompanied dog or cat to shelter or pound, CR §10-613.
Humane society officers.
Arrest by, CR §10-609.
Impounded mistreated animals.
Entry to care for animal, removal, CR §10-615.
Impounded unclaimed dogs or cats.
Disposal by animal control unit, CR §10-617.
Inapplicability of provisions, CR §10-603.
Infliction of unnecessary pain or suffering, CR §10-604.
Intentional cruelty.
Protection of animals from, CR §10-602.
Kennel inspections, CR §10-616.
Killing dogs and cats, prohibited means, CR §10-611.
Normal human activities inflicting incidental pain.
Inapplicability of provisions, CR §10-603.
Overdriving or overloading, CR §10-604.
Poisoning dogs, CR §10-618.
Prizes, giving away animal as, CR §10-610.
Race horse, interference with, CR §10-620.
Removal of animal from owner.
Court order, CR §10-615.
Research.
Inapplicability of provisions, CR §10-603.
Seizure of mistreated animal, CR §10-615.
Selling puppies or kittens, CR §10-613.
Stray, when animal deemed, CR §10-615.

ANIMALS —Cont'd
Crimes relating to animals —Cont'd
Torturing, beating or killing.
Aggravated cruelty, CR §10-606.
Waiting period.
Disposal of unclaimed dog or cat, CR §10-617.
Cruelty to animals.
Crimes relating to animals generally, CR §§10-601 to 10-622.
Damages.
Injury to pet, CJ §11-110.
Dangerous animals.
Importing, selling, or trading in, CR §10-621.
Dangerous dogs, CR §10-619.
Dangerous to human health.
Prohibition on selling, purchasing, raising, keeping, HG §18-219.
Dead bodies.
Removal of carcasses from highways, TR §8-602.
Washington suburban sanitary commission.
Leaving dead animals unburied.
Prohibited, 29 §18-102.
Definitions.
Animals posing threat to poultry, livestock or human safety.
Animal defined, AG §3-115.
Pet, CJ §11-110.
Disposal of domestic animals, CR §10-617.
Dogs.
General provisions.
See DOGS.
Drugs.
Sodium pentobarbital.
Destruction of animals.
Special permit authorizing use, AG §2-305.
Elderly housing.
Pets on premises, RP §8-214.
Feedstuffs.
Commercial feed law.
See FEEDSTUFFS.
Fish.
See FISH AND FISHERIES.
Highways.
Accidents.
Duty on striking domestic animal, TR §20-106.
Livestock crossings.
Signs, TR §21-708.
Persons riding animals or driving animal-drawn vehicles.
Regulations, TR §21-104.
Removal of carcasses of animals from highways, TR §8-602.
Horses.
See HORSES.
Human safety.
Animals posing threat to.
Strict regulation, AG §3-115.
Animal defined, AG §3-115.
Impounded animals.
Mistreatment.
Entry to care for or remove, CR §10-615.
Injury to pet.
Damages, CJ §11-110.
Kennels.
Commercial boarding kennels.
Supervision of animals in care of, CL §11-905.
Inspections, CR §10-616.
Kittens or puppies.
Selling when less than eight weeks old, CR §10-613.
Lamps on animal-drawn vehicles, TR §22-216.

ANIMALS —Cont'd
Liens.
For board, etc., due, CL §16-401.
Livestock.
Animals posing threat to.
Strict regulation, AG §3-115.
General provisions.
See LIVESTOCK.
Highway crossings.
Signs, TR §21-708.
Maryland Transit Administration.
Carrying or possessing live animal on transit vehicle.
Prohibited, TR §7-705.
Meat and meat products.
See MEAT AND MEAT PRODUCTS.
Mistreated or neglected animals.
Cruelty to animals.
See CRUELTY TO ANIMALS.
Motor vehicles.
Rules of the road.
See TRAFFIC LAWS.
Pharmacists and pharmacies.
Practice of veterinary medicine, HO §1-211.
Poultry.
Animals posing threat to.
Strict regulation, AG §3-115.
General provisions.
See POULTRY.
Poultry products inspection.
See POULTRY PRODUCTS INSPECTION.
Prizes.
Giving as prizes, CR §10-610.
Rabbits.
San Juan rabbits.
Importing or possession prohibited, AG §5-601.
Rules of the road.
See TRAFFIC LAWS.
Sales.
Livestock sales.
See LIVESTOCK SALES.
San Juan rabbits.
Importing or possession prohibited, AG §5-601.
Slaughter of animals.
Meat.
See MEAT AND MEAT PRODUCTS.
Sodium pentobarbital.
Destruction of animals.
Permit authorizing use, AG §2-305.
Strays, AG §§3-601 to 3-603.
When animal deemed, CR §10-615.
Unborn young.
Sale of goods.
Definition of "goods," CL §2-105.
Veterinarians.
Generally.
See VETERINARIANS.
Supervision of animals in care of veterinarians, CL §11-905.
Turning over to animal welfare agency, CL §16-701.
Washington county.
Power to adopt animal control ordinance, 25 §236A.
Washington suburban sanitary commission.
Dead bodies.
Leaving dead animals unburied.
Prohibited, 29 §18-102.
Wildlife.
General provisions.
See BIRDS AND GAME.

ANIMALS —Cont'd
Wild or vicious animals.
Bounties.
By county commissioners, 25 §2.

ANIMAL SHELTERS.
Giving kitten or puppy unaccompanied by dam, CR §10-613.

ANNAPOLIS.
Adjutant general.
Discharge duties at seat of government, MD Const Art IX §2.
Alcoholic beverages.
Beer and light wine licenses, 2B §5-601.
Class D, on-sale.
Applicability of provisions, 2B §5-401.
Beer, wine and liquor licenses, 2B §6-202.
Hours and days of sale, 2B §11-303.
Fines, 2B §16-507.
Hours and days for sale.
Beer, wine and liquor licenses, 2B §11-303.
Fixed by mayor and council, 2B §11-502.
License commissioners.
Municipal officials ex officio, 2B §15-107.
Powers, 2B §15-112.
Licenses.
Fees.
Collection and disposition, 2B §10-204.
Fixing, 2B §8-202.
Revocation or suspension, 2B §16-507.
Micro-brewery licenses, 2B §2-208.
Minors.
Sale or delivery to prohibited, 2B §§12-202, 12-208.
Penalties.
Imposition by board of license commissioners, 2B §16-507.
Pub-brewery licenses, 2B §2-207.
Regulation of possession or consumption.
Authority of mayor and aldermen, 2B §19-103.
Wine festival.
License, 2B §8-401.
Aldermen.
Alcoholic beverages.
Authority to regulate possession or consumption on public property, 2B §19-103.
Architectural easements.
Board of public works, Maryland historical trust, SF §5A-305.
Commission on the capital city, SG §§9-401 to 9-407.
Comptroller.
Office.
Maintain office at seat of government, MD Const Art VI §1.
Court of appeals.
Meeting at, MD Const Art IV §14.
Crimes and offenses.
Alcoholic beverages.
Minors.
Sale or delivery to, 2B §12-202.
Easements.
Architectural easements.
Board of public works, Maryland historical trust, SF §5A-305.
Fire and explosive investigator.
Authority of, CP §2-208.2.
General assembly.
Meeting place, MD Const DofR Art 11.
Change place of meeting of legislature, MD Const Art II §16.

ANNAPOLIS —Cont'd
General services department.
Public buildings and grounds.
    Maintenance, operation and protection.
        Appropriation for services provided by city of
            Annapolis, SF §4-608.
Governor.
Reside at seat of government, MD Const Art II
    §21.
Housing authority, HS §§13-101 to 13-111.
Actions needing approval in open meeting, HS
    §13-108.
Annual audit, HS §13-111.
Applicability of housing authorities law, HS
    §13-102.
Budget, HS §13-110.
Commissioners.
    Defined, HS §13-101.
    Local officials, commissioners as, HS §13-105.
Conflicts of interest, HS §13-105.
Defined terms, HS §13-101.
Emergency contracts.
    Actions needing approval in open meeting, HS
        §13-108.
Established, HS §13-103.
Executive director.
    Removal, HS §13-106.
Local officials, commissioners and personnel as,
    HS §13-105.
Meetings, HS §13-107.
    Actions needing approval in open meeting, HS
        §13-108.
    Budget, HS §13-110.
    Members, HS §13-104.
Notice.
    Meetings, HS §13-107.
Personnel.
    Local officials, personnel as, HS §13-105.
Powers.
    All powers necessary and convenient, HS
        §13-103.
    Purchasing power, HS §13-109.
Reimbursements.
    Actions needing approval in open meeting, HS
        §13-108.
Removal of executive director, HS §13-106.
Terms of office, HS §13-104.
Vacancies in office, HS §13-104.
Mayor.
Alcoholic beverages.
    Authority to regulate possession or
        consumption, 2B §19-103.
Parking.
Residential parking permits, TR §21-1003.1.
Sales tax, 24 §9-602.
State house trust, SG §§9-501 to 9-506.
    See STATE HOUSE TRUST.
State treasurer.
Office.
    Maintain office at seat of government, MD
        Const Art VI §1.
Taxation.
Delinquent taxes.
    Interest penalty, TP §14-603.
Wine festival.
License, 2B §8-401.

ANNE ARUNDEL COUNTY.
Agriculture.
Right to farm, 24 §18-101.

ANNE ARUNDEL COUNTY —Cont'd
Airport.
Alcoholic beverages.
    Licenses.
        Terminal buildings, 2B §8-202.
Baltimore-Washington international Thurgood
        Marshall airport.
    Reimbursement to county for private
        development, 24 §§9-807 to 9-810.
Alcoholic beverages.
Age.
    Minimum age of waiter, waitress or bartender,
        2B §12-202.
Application.
    Made prior to June 30, 1969, 2B §8-202.
Bartenders.
    Minimum age, 2B §12-202.
Beer and light wine licenses.
    Class A, off-sale, 2B §5-101.
    Class B, on-sale.
        Hotels and restaurants, 2B §5-201.
    Class C, on-sale.
        Clubs, 2B §5-301.
        Seven days, 2B §7-101.
    Class D, on-sale, 2B §5-401.
    Class H, on-sale only.
        Fee, 2B §5-202.
        Issuance, 2B §5-202.
        Prohibited in bowling alley, billiard hall or
            drugstore, 2B §5-202.
Beer and wine festival.
    License, 2B §8-302.
Beer and wine tasting license, 2B §8-202.
Beer licenses.
    Cash on delivery or sale of beer, 2B §12-202.
    Class C, seven days, 2B §7-101.
Beer, wine and liquor licenses.
    Class A, off-sale, 2B §6-101.
    Class B, on-sale.
        Hotels and restaurants, 2B §6-201.
    Class C, on-sale.
        Clubs, 2B §6-301.
        Special and temporary licenses, 2B §7-101.
    Class D, on-sale.
        Fee, 2B §6-401.
        Limited Class D license.
            Fee, 2B §6-401.
        Window and entrance requirements, 2B
            §12-202.1.
Consumption.
    Restrictions, 2B §11-304.
Deluxe restaurant license, 2B §8-202.1.
Bottle clubs, 2B §20-101.
Buildings.
    Class D, on-sale licenses.
        Window and entrance requirements, 2B
            §12-202.1.
    Licenses extended for same building.
        Defined, 2B §9-203.
Change in classification, 2B §8-202.
    Expiration of subsection, 2B §8-202.
Churches.
    License near, 2B §9-203.
Clubs.
    Beer, wine and liquor licenses.
        Class C, on-sale, 2B §§5-301, 6-301.
Conflicts of interest.
    Direct or indirect interest in more than one
        license, 2B §9-301.
Consumption of beverage, 2B §16-201.

ANNE ARUNDEL COUNTY —Cont'd
Alcoholic beverages —Cont'd
Containers.
  Cash deposits for returnable containers, 2B
    §12-202.
Criminal history records checks.
  License applicants, 2B §10-103.
Disorderly intoxication.
  Ordinances or resolutions, 2B §19-103.
Elections.
  Exercise of privileges of licensee on election day,
    2B §11-401.
Entertainment regulated, 2B §12-202.
Fines.
  Local penalties, 2B §16-507.
  Violation of section, 2B §12-202.
General provisions.
  See ALCOHOLIC BEVERAGES.
Hotels and restaurants.
  Beer and wine licenses.
    Class H, on-sale only, 2B §5-202.
  Complex license, 2B §8-202.
  Number of licenses, 2B §9-102.
  Hours and days of sale.
    Serving food after hours, 2B §11-502.
Hours and days for sale.
  Bowling alleys, 2B §11-502.
  Election days, 2B §11-401.
  Manufacturers' licenses, 2B §11-101.
  New Year's day, 2B §11-402.
  Standard time, 2B §11-503.
  Sundays, 2B §11-403.
Inspectors.
  Bonds, surety, 2B §15-112.
  Powers, 2B §15-112.
    Issuance of citations to minors for alcoholic
      beverage violations, CR §10-119.
  Salary, 2B §15-112.
License commissioners.
  Administrator, 2B §15-112.
  Applications.
    Processing, 2B §10-202.
  Appointment, 2B §15-101.
  Attorney to board, 2B §15-112.
  Clerk, 2B §15-112.
  Enforcement of article, 2B §16-412.
  Inspection of proposed licensed premises, 2B
    §10-202.
  Inspectors.
    Bond, 2B §15-112.
  No jurisdiction in city of Annapolis, 2B §15-107.
  Political affiliations of commissioners, 2B
    §15-101.
  Powers, 2B §15-112.
  Qualifications, 2B §15-101.
  Salaries, 2B §15-109.
    Payment from license fees, 2B §10-204.
  Terms, 2B §15-101.
  Vacancies, 2B §15-101.
Licenses.
  Airport terminal buildings.
    General provisions, 2B §8-202.
  Applications.
    Exceptions as to county, 2B §10-103.
    Fees, 2B §10-104.
    Investigation, 2B §10-202.
    Notice on premises, 2B §10-202.
    Not prima facie evidence.
      Applicant is entitled to license, 2B §10-104.
    Statement as to whether applicant adjudged
      guilty of offense against laws of state or
      United States, 2B §10-103.

ANNE ARUNDEL COUNTY —Cont'd
Alcoholic beverages —Cont'd
Licenses —Cont'd
  Assignment.
    Defined, 2B §9-203.
  Beer and light wine licenses. See within this
    subheading, "Beer and light wine licenses."
  Beer and wine tasting license, 2B §8-402.
  Beer licenses. See within this subheading, "Beer
    licenses."
  Beer, wine and liquor licenses. See within this
    subheading, "Beer, wine and liquor
    licenses."
  Buildings.
    Extended for same building.
      Defined, 2B §9-203.
  Churches and schools.
    Licenses near, 2B §9-203.
  Class BWT beer and wine tastings license,
    on-premises, 2B §8-402.
  Commissioners. See within this subheading,
    "License commissioners."
  Criminal history records checks.
    License applicants, 2B §10-103.
  Death of licensee.
    Procedure, 2B §10-506.
  Fees.
    Airport terminal buildings, 2B §8-202.
    Disposition, 2B §10-204.
    Refund, 2B §10-205.
  Issuance.
    Procedure, 2B §10-202.
    Refusal.
      Reapplication, 2B §10-208.
  Local provisions, 2B §8-202.
  Manufacturers.
    Hours and days for sale, 2B §11-101.
  More than one license for same person or
    premises, 2B §9-102.
  Motel-restaurant or hotel-restaurant complex
    licenses, 2B §8-202.
    Number of licenses, 2B §9-102.
  Music, dancing and other entertainment on
    licensed premises, 2B §12-202.
  New licenses.
    Limitation.
      Expiration of subsection, 2B §8-202.
  Number.
    Restriction as to number of licenses in
      neighborhood, 2B §9-203.
  Out-of-state licensees, 2B §9-102.
  Prohibited areas, 2B §9-203.
  Race tracks, 2B §8-202.
  Renewal.
    Dormant licenses, 2B §9-203.
  Resort complex licenses, 2B §8-202.
    Number of licenses, 2B §9-102.
  Revocation and suspension.
    Grounds, 2B §10-401.
    Nudity and sexual displays on licensee's
      premises, 2B §10-405.
  Substitution of officers of corporation or club
    holding license, 2B §10-503.
  Transfer, 2B §10-503.
    Defined, 2B §9-203.
    Dormant licenses, 2B §9-203.
  Violations.
    Civil citations, 2B §16-408.
  Wine tasting.
    Beer and wine tasting license, 2B §8-402.

ANNE ARUNDEL COUNTY —Cont'd
Alcoholic beverages —Cont'd
  Licenses —Cont'd
    WS wine sampling license, on-premises, 2B §8-402.
  Manufacturers.
    Licenses.
      Hours and days for sale, 2B §11-101.
  Micro-brewery licenses, 2B §2-208.
  Minors.
    Bowling alleys, 2B §11-502.
    Citation for violations, CR §10-119.
    Employment of minors by retail dealers.
      Special provisions, 2B §12-302.
    Minimum age of waiter, waitress or bartender, 2B §12-202.
    Sales.
      At Annapolis, 2B §12-202.
      Prohibited, 2B §§12-108, 12-202.
  Music, dancing and other entertainment.
    On licensed premises, 2B §12-202.
  Nudity and sexual displays on licensee's premises.
    Revocation of license, 2B §10-405.
  Pub-brewery licenses, 2B §2-207.
  Sales.
    Beer.
      Cash on delivery or sale of beer, 2B §12-202.
      Election days, 2B §11-401.
      Minors and intoxicated persons prohibited, 2B §§12-108, 12-202.
      New Year's day, 2B §11-402.
      Standard time or daylight saving time, 2B §11-502.
  Schools.
    License near, 2B §9-203.
  Summons and process, 2B §16-410.
  Sundays.
    Hours and days for sale, 2B §§11-403, 11-502.
    Special Sunday licenses, 2B §8-202.
  Transfer of license.
    Expiration of subsection, 2B §8-202.
  Waiters and waitresses.
    Minimum age, 2B §12-202.
  Wholesalers.
    Deliveries, 2B §11-502.
  Wine tasting.
    Beer and wine tasting license, 2B §8-402.
Alleys.
  Width, 25 §145.
Appearance fees in circuit courts.
  Distribution, CJ §7-204.
Bailiff.
  Salary, CJ §2-507.
Baltimore-Washington international Thurgood Marshall airport.
  Reimbursement to county for private development.
    Authorized, 24 §9-807.
    Intent of part, 24 §9-809.
    "Private development" defined, 24 §9-810.
    User fee to be charged, 24 §9-808.
Beer and wine festival.
  License, 2B §8-302.
Beer and wine tasting.
  License, 2B §8-402.
Billiard halls.
  Beer and light wine licenses.
    Class H, on-sale only.
      Prohibited, 2B §5-202.
Bingo.
  Instant bingo included, CR §13-407.

ANNE ARUNDEL COUNTY —Cont'd
Bingo —Cont'd
  Provision applicable to counties generally, CR §§13-201 to 13-205.
  Qualified organization authorized to conduct, CR §13-407.
Birds and game.
  Spotlighting, NR §10-410.
  Trapping.
    Snare traps, NR §10-410.
    Steel jaw leghold traps, NR §10-410.
Bond issues.
  Special taxing districts, 24 §9-1301.
Borrowing money.
  Security for borrowing, 31 §2D.
Bottle clubs, 2B §20-101.
Bowling alleys.
  Beer and light wine licenses.
    Class H, on-sale only.
      Prohibited, 2B §5-202.
Cantaloupes.
  Subtitle not applicable, AG §10-909.
Casino event.
  Defined, CR §13-401.
  Prohibited in county, CR §13-404.
Chesapeake Bay critical area and Atlantic coastal bays critical area protection programs.
  Critical areas commission.
    Members on commission, NR §8-1804.
Churches.
  Alcoholic beverages.
    Licenses near, 2B §9-203.
Circuit courts. See within this heading, "Courts."
Clerks of court.
  Fees.
    Administering public money, CJ §2-213.
Clubs.
  Beer and light wine licenses.
    Class C, on-sale, 2B §5-301.
  Beer, wine and liquor licenses.
    Class C, on-sale, 2B §6-301.
Commissioners.
  Alcoholic beverages.
    License commissioners. See within this heading, "Alcoholic beverages."
  Housing authority, HS §14-103.
  Parking facilities and pedestrian malls.
    Power to levy tax for, 25 §10C.
  Powers.
    Exceptions, 25 §3.
Community college.
  Board of trustees.
    Composition, ED §16-401.
    Student member of board, ED §16-401.
Conflicts of interest.
  Alcoholic beverages.
    Direct or indirect interest in more than one license, 2B §9-301.
Conservation areas.
  Exception from section, 23A §7.
Correctional facility.
  Certified law enforcement officers.
    Custody, safekeeping and transportation of inmates, COR §11-201.
  Home detention program, COR §11-703.
  Work release, training and rehabilitation programs, COR §11-703.
Courts.
  Circuit court.
    Appearance fees.
      Distribution, CJ §7-204.

ANNE ARUNDEL COUNTY —Cont'd
Courts —Cont'd
Circuit court —Cont'd
Director of assignments.
Creation of office, CJ §2-509.
Duties, CJ §2-509.
Employees of domestic relation division
transferred to child support enforcement
administration.
Election of county or state pension system
participation, CJ §2-510.
Judges.
Number, CJ §1-503; MD Const Art IV §21.
Residence requirements, MD Const Art IV
§21.
Vacancies, MD Const Art IV §21.
Judicial circuit, MD Const Art IV §19.
Court of appeals.
Judge.
Legal residence not abandoned by residence
in county, CJ §1-204.
Court of special appeals.
Judge.
Legal residence not abandoned by residence
in county, CJ §1-204.
Director of assignments.
Employees, CJ §2-509.
Expenses, CJ §2-509.
Orphans' court.
Judges' compensation, ET §2-108.
Crabs.
Landowners.
Restrictions on catching, NR §4-811.
Crimes and offenses.
Fish and fisheries.
Restrictions in county waters, NR §4-714.
Criminal history records checks.
Prospective employees, CP §10-231.
Crofton police department, 26 §5.
Dangerous weapons.
Minors carrying, prohibited hours, CR §4-101.
Davidsonville Ruritan Foundation, Inc.
Property tax credits, TP §9-303.
Dog and kennel licenses.
Fees, 24 §11-501.
Dog tags, 24 §11-503.
Drugstores.
Beer and light wine licenses.
Class H, on-sale only.
Prohibited, 2B §5-202.
Drunkenness.
Disorderly intoxication.
Ordinances or resolutions, 2B §19-103.
Elections.
Alcoholic beverages.
Exercise of privileges of licensee on election day,
2B §11-401.
County board of elections.
Compensation, EL §2-204.
Counsel.
Compensation, EL §2-205.
County boards generally, EL §§2-201 to 2-303.
See ELECTIONS.
County boards of education generally, EL §§8-801
to 8-806.
Political fundraisers.
Paddle wheels and wheels of fortune, CR
§13-406.
Eminent domain.
Appraisals.
Right of entry, RP §12-111.

ANNE ARUNDEL COUNTY —Cont'd
Farms and farmers.
Right to farm, 24 §18-101.
Fines.
Alcoholic beverages.
Violation of hours and days for sale, 2B §11-502.
Fire and explosive investigator.
Authority of, CP §2-208.2.
Fish and fisheries.
Mobile seafood vendors generally.
See SEAFOOD.
Restrictions in county waters, NR §4-714.
Riparian rights.
Exceptions, NR §4-712.
Forfeitures.
Rent.
Failure to give receipt, RP §8-205.
Gaming, bazaar, carnival and raffles, CR
§§13-201 to 13-205, 13-401 to 13-408.
Accounting by organization, requirement, CR
§13-403.
Compensation for managing and operating
gaming device.
Prohibition, CR §13-403.
Conducting event for benefit of qualified
organization.
Allowed, CR §13-203.
Definitions, CR §§13-201, 13-401.
Gaming event defined, CR §§13-201, 13-401.
Individual benefit prohibited, CR §13-203.
Management through organization's members, CR
§13-205.
Operation of gaming devices used, CR §13-403.
Political fundraisers.
Paddle wheels or wheels of fortune, CR §13-406.
Prizes and gaming devices allowed, CR §13-204.
Provisions applicable to county, CR §§13-202,
13-301, 13-402.
Qualified member defined, CR §13-403.
Qualified organization defined, CR §13-201.
Raffles, requirements for conducting, prizes, CR
§13-405.
Unauthorized gaming event, penalty, CR §13-407.
Highways.
Riding animals on highways, TR §21-104.
Historic area zoning.
General provisions.
See ZONING.
Home detention programs, COR §11-703.
Hotels.
Alcoholic beverages.
Beer and wine licenses.
Class H, on-sale only, 2B §5-202.
Complex license, 2B §8-202.
Number, 2B §9-102.
Housing authority, HS §§14-101 to 14-103.
Applicability of housing authorities law, HS
§14-101.
Commissioners, HS §14-103.
Established, HS §14-102.
Injury reports.
Automobile accident or lethal weapon causing
injury.
Physicians, pharmacists, dentists or nurses, HG
§20-701.
Jails.
Home detention program, COR §11-703.
Rehabilitation and training of inmates at
correctional facility, COR §11-703.
Removal of convicted individual from courtroom.
Use of certified law enforcement officers, COR
§11-202.

ANNE ARUNDEL COUNTY —Cont'd
Judges.
Pensions.
  General provisions, ET §2-108.
Justices of the peace.
Alcoholic beverages.
  Violations, 2B §12-202.
Landlord and tenant.
Forfeiture of rent for failure to give receipt, RP
    §8-205.
Receipt for rent, RP §8-205.
Marriage.
Clerk's fee for performing ceremony.
  Disposition, FL §2-410.
Licenses.
  Fees, FL §2-404.
Maryland food center authority.
General provisions, 41 §§13-101 to 13-123.
  See MARYLAND FOOD CENTER
      AUTHORITY.
Maryland Ornithological Society, Inc.
Property tax credits, TP §9-303.
Metropolitan transit administration.
General provisions, TR §§7-101 to 7-707.
  See MARYLAND TRANSIT
      ADMINISTRATION.
Minors.
Alcoholic beverages.
  Bowling alleys, 2B §11-502.
  Employment by retail dealers, 2B §12-302.
  Minimum age of waiter, waitress or bartender,
      2B §12-202.
  Sales to prohibited, 2B §§12-108, 12-202.
Dangerous weapons, carrying.
  Prohibited hours, CR §4-101.
Soliciting rides, employment or business
    prohibited, TR §21-507.
Misdemeanors.
Fish and fisheries.
  Restrictions in county waters, NR §4-714.
Motor vehicles.
Parking.
  Facilities.
    Power to levy tax for, 25 §10C.
Refuse trucks.
  Load limit of axles, TR §24-108.
Weight.
  Axles.
    Load limit of axles.
      Refuse trucks, TR §24-108.
Naval Academy Alumni Association.
Property tax credits.
  Ogle Hall, TP §9-303.
Naval Academy Athletic Association.
Property tax credits, TP §9-303.
Noise control.
Trapshooting, skeet shooting, etc.
  Limitations on authority, EN §§3-105, 3-401.
**Nonprofit community civic association or
    corporation.**
Property tax credits, TP §9-303.
Northeast Maryland waste disposal authority.
Participating county, NR §3-903.
Nuisance abatement.
Community association actions, RP §14-125.1.
Obscene performances.
Prohibition, CR §11-204.
**Oil pipeline corporation acquiring property
    under power to condemn,** PUC §5-404.
Orphans' court.
Judges, ET §2-108.

ANNE ARUNDEL COUNTY —Cont'd
Orphans' court —Cont'd
Sessions, ET §2-106.
Oysters and clams.
Hydraulic clam dredge.
  Where use prohibited, NR §§4-1037, 4-1038.
Tonging.
  Patent tonging in South river in Anne Arundel
      county.
    Prohibited, NR §4-1011.
Patuxent river watershed.
General provisions.
  See PATUXENT RIVER WATERSHED.
Pedestrian malls.
Power to levy tax for, 25 §10C.
Political fundraisers.
Paddle wheels and wheels of fortune, CR §13-406.
Political parties.
Central committees.
  Election of members, EL §4-203.
  Vacancies, EL §4-202.
Port authority.
County commissioner's consent to acquisition, TR
    §6-309.
Section to prevail over other provisions, TR
    §6-309.
Taxation.
  Power to tax, TR §6-309.
Public debt.
Security for borrowing, 31 §2D.
Racing.
Alcoholic beverages.
  Race tracks.
    License fees, 2B §8-202.
Real property.
Single family residence.
  Notice pertaining to land use in contract of sale,
      RP §10-703.
Receipts.
Landlord to give tenant receipt, RP §8-205.
Recordation.
Deeds.
  Exceptions as to Anne Arundel county, RP
      §3-104.
Refuse trucks.
Load limit of axles, TR §24-108.
Rent.
Landlord to give tenant receipt, RP §8-205.
Rescue squads.
Workers' compensation.
  Volunteer fire company or rescue squad.
    Insurance coverage required, LE §9-402.
**Residential mortgage programs for certain
    counties,** HS §§4-1601 to 4-1610.
Restaurants or eating places.
Beer and wine licenses.
  Class H, on-sale only, 2B §5-202.
Beer, wine and liquor licenses.
  Deluxe restaurant license, 2B §8-202.1.
Right to farm, 24 §18-101.
Roads.
Width, 25 §145.
Sales.
Alcoholic beverages. See within this heading,
    "Alcoholic beverages."
Sales tax.
Additional taxing power, 24 §9-602.
  Disposition of revenues, 24 §9-602.
Schools.
Alcoholic beverages.
  Licenses near, 2B §9-203.

ANNE ARUNDEL COUNTY —Cont'd
Schools —Cont'd
Annual expenditure report, ED §5-106.
Capital projects for county, ED §5-305.1.
Construction funds.
Capital projects, ED §5-305.1.
Special provisions, ED §5-305.
County board of education.
Annual expenditure report, ED §5-106.
Change in boundary line of legislative district,
ED §3-110.
Composition, ED §3-110.
Elections generally, EL §§8-801 to 8-806.
Replacement of members, ED §3-110.
Student member of board, ED §3-110.
Employee organizations.
Negotiations between employer and employee.
Representation in Anne Arundel county, fees
charged for nonmember, ED §6-407.
Service fees.
Fees charged nonmembers for representation
in negotiations and grievance matters,
ED §§6-407, 6-504.
Reports.
Annual expenditure report, ED §5-106.
Year-round schools.
Pilot programs, ED §7-103.
Seafood.
Mobile seafood vendors generally.
See SEAFOOD.
Severn river watershed.
General provisions.
See SEVERN RIVER WATERSHED.
Sheriff.
Deputies, CJ §2-309.
Part-time deputies, CJ §2-309.
Employees.
Members of the county merit system, CJ §2-309.
Expenses, CJ §2-309.
Office.
Furnishing by county, CJ §2-309.
Salary, CJ §2-309.
Second in command, CJ §2-310.
Shore erosion control.
Districts.
Tax levy, 25 §167F.
Special taxing districts, 24 §9-1301.
State correctional facilities in Jessup area.
Limitation on construction, COR §10-107.
State's attorney.
Accounts for services and expenses.
County excepted from section, 10 §39.
Assistants.
Administrative assistant, 10 §40.
Deputy, 10 §40.
Duties, 10 §40.
Salaries and expenses, 10 §40.
Subdivisions.
Alleys.
Width requirements, 25 §145.
Sundays and holidays.
Alcoholic beverages.
Hours and days for sale, 2B §§11-403, 11-502.
Special Sunday licenses, 2B §8-202.
Taxation.
Deferred property tax payments, TP §10-201.
Municipal corporations.
Double taxation of municipalities, TP §6-307.
Parking facilities and pedestrian malls.
Power of commissioners to levy tax for, 25 §10C.

ANNE ARUNDEL COUNTY —Cont'd
Taxation —Cont'd
Property tax credits.
Agricultural land preservation program, TP
§9-303.
Davidsonville Ruritan Foundation, Inc., TP
§9-303.
Grants in lieu of county tax credits.
Elderly or disabled renters, TP §9-402.
Maryland Ornithological Society, Inc., TP
§9-303.
Naval Academy Alumni Association.
Ogle Hall, TP §9-303.
Naval Academy Athletic Association, TP §9-303.
Nonprofit community civic association or
corporation, TP §9-303.
Three Rivers Sportsmen, Inc., TP §9-303.
Redemption.
Rate of redemption, TP §14-820.
Sale.
Notice, TP §14-813.
Sales and use taxes.
Additional taxing power, 24 §9-602.
Special taxing districts.
Authorized, 24 §9-1301.
Transportation.
Levy of tax for public transportation services,
TR §7-801.
Three Rivers Sportsmen, Inc.
Property tax credits, TP §9-303.
Transportation.
Public transportation services.
Taxation for, TR §7-801.
**Trapshooting, skeetshooting or other target
shooting.**
Environmental sound level limits and noise
control rules and regulations, EN §3-401.
Noise control ordinances, rules or regulations
prohibiting, EN §3-105.
Treasurer.
Confinement in dwelling, building or enclosure,
FL §5-801.
Salary, 25 §51.
Use tax.
Additional taxing power.
Disposition of revenue, 24 §9-602.
Washington suburban sanitary district.
See WASHINGTON SUBURBAN SANITARY
DISTRICT.
Water.
Restrictions on use.
Ordinances and resolutions, 25 §168.
Weapons.
Target practice without landowner permission, CR
§4-108.
Wine.
Beer and wine tasting license, 2B §8-402.
Workers' compensation.
Rescue squads.
Volunteer fire company or rescue squad.
Insurance coverage required, LE §9-402.
Work release.
Inmates confined in correctional facility, COR
§11-703.
Yacht clubs.
Alcoholic beverages.
License provisions, 2B §8-202.
Zoning.
Historic area zoning.
General provisions.
See ZONING.

ANNE ARUNDEL COUNTY —Cont'd
Zoning —Cont'd
Stormwater management facility.
Prohibited in residentially zoned district, 66B
§14.10.

ANNEXATION.
Maryland-Washington regional district.
Enlargement of district in Prince George's county,
28 §7-104.
Subdivisions.
Annexation by municipalities, 28 §7-115.
Municipal corporations.
See MUNICIPAL CORPORATIONS.

ANNOYING ANOTHER.
Harassment, CR §3-803.
Misuse of telephone facilities and equipment,
CR §3-804.

ANNUITIES.
Budget and management.
State operating budget.
Budget books.
Summary of annuity bond accounts of state,
SF §7-119.
Life insurance and annuities.
See LIFE INSURANCE AND ANNUITIES.
Public debt.
Debt service.
Annuity bond fund, SF §8-132.

ANNULMENT OF MARRIAGE.
Circuit courts.
Family law actions, FamLaw Rules 9-201 to
9-210.
Clerks of court.
Reporting to secretary of health and mental
hygiene, FL §2-503.
Declaratory judgments.
Excluded from subtitle, CJ §3-409.
Equity court jurisdiction, FL §1-201.
Injunctive power of court, FL §1-203.
Lis pendens, FL §1-203.
Masters.
Referral of matters to masters, FamLaw Rule
9-208.
Oral testimony required for final decree, FL
§1-203.
Procedure, FamLaw Rules 9-201 to 9-210.
**Property disposition in divorce and
annulment,** FL §§8-201 to 8-214.
See DIVORCE.
Reports.
Clerks of court, FL §2-503.
Reports to secretary of health and mental
hygiene, FL §2-503.
Surviving spouse, ET §1-202.
Venue.
Additional venue permitted, CJ §6-202.
Vital records.
See VITAL RECORDS.
Wills.
Effect, ET §4-105.

**ANONYMOUS CONTRIBUTIONS TO
POLITICAL CAMPAIGN,** EL §13-239.
Gaming activity money, EL §13-240.

ANONYMOUS PHONE CALLS.
Misuse of telephone facilities and equipment,
CR §3-804.

ANSWERS.
Admissions.
Specific admissions or denials.
Circuit courts, CivProCir Rule 2-323.
Affirmative defenses.
Circuit courts, CivProCir Rule 2-323.
Allowed pleadings, CivProCir Rule 2-302.
Attorneys at law.
Disbarment or suspension, CJA Rule 16-754.
Catastrophic health emergency.
Proceedings to contest of isolation or quarantine.
Answer to petition, SpecPro Rule 15-1103.
Content.
Circuit courts, CivProCir Rule 2-323.
Contracts.
General denials in specified causes.
Circuit courts, CivProCir Rule 2-323.
Debts.
Denials.
General denials in specified causes.
Circuit courts, CivProCir Rule 2-323.
Defenses.
Affirmative defenses.
Circuit courts, CivProCir Rule 2-323.
Negative defenses.
Circuit courts, CivProCir Rule 2-323.
Denials.
Effect of failure to deny.
Circuit courts, CivProCir Rule 2-323.
General denials.
Circuit courts, CivProCir Rule 2-323.
Specific admissions or denials.
Circuit courts, CivProCir Rule 2-323.
Distress for rent.
To petition, RP §8-314.
Garnishment.
Circuit courts, CivProCir Rule 2-645.
District Court, CivProDist Rule 3-645.
Wages.
District Court, CivProDist Rule 3-646.
Information report, CivProCir Rule 2-323.
Jurisdiction.
Preliminary determination.
Circuit courts, CivProCir Rule 2-323.
Jury trial, demand.
Certain transfers from District Court, CivProCir
Rule 2-326.
Mechanics' liens.
Affidavit or verified answer.
Failure to file deemed admission, PropAct Rule
12-304.
Pleading.
See PLEADINGS.
Preliminary determination.
Circuit courts, CivProCir Rule 2-323.
Specific admissions or denials.
Circuit courts, CivProCir Rule 2-323.
Time for filing.
Exceptions to general rule.
Circuit courts, CivProCir Rule 2-321.
Extension of time for filing.
Automatic extension.
Circuit courts, CivProCir Rule 2-321.
General rule.
Circuit courts, CivProCir Rule 2-321.
Preliminary motions.
Automatic extension of time for filing.
Circuit courts, CivProCir Rule 2-321.
Torts.
Denials.
General denials in specified causes.
Circuit courts, CivProCir Rule 2-323.

ANTE LITEM NOTICE.
Torts.
Local government tort claims act.
Unliquidated damages actions, CJ §5-304.
Waiver of notice requirements, CJ §5-304.
Tort claims act.
Restrictions on actions.
Claim and denial required, SG §12-106.

ANTHRAX.
Catastrophic health emergency.
Disease surveillance and response program, HG
§§18-901 to 18-908.
See CATASTROPHIC HEALTH EMERGENCY.
Governor's power to proclaim, PS §§14-3A-01 to
14-3A-08.
See HEALTH EMERGENCIES.

ANTI-ARSON APPLICATIONS FOR FIRE
INSURANCE, IN §§19-301 to 19-309.

ANTICIPATORY REPUDIATION.
Leases, UCC, CL §2A-402.
Retraction, CL §2A-403.
Sales, UCC, CL §2-610.
Proof of market price, CL §2-723.
Retraction, CL §2-611.

ANTI-LAPSE STATUTE.
General provisions, ET §4-403.

ANTIQUE FIREARMS.
Defined, CR §4-201.
Use in commission of crime, CR §4-204.

ANTIQUE SLOT MACHINES.
Possession or ownership allowed, CR §12-303.

ANTITHEFT LAWS.
Motor vehicles.
General provisions, TR §§14-101 to 14-110.
See MOTOR VEHICLE THEFT.

ANTITRUST ACT.
Actions.
Civil actions.
General provisions, CL §11-209.
Judgment as evidence.
Prima facie evidence in action for damages,
CL §11-210.
Admissions.
Assurance of discontinuance of prohibited act.
Not to be considered admission, CL §11-206.
Attorney general.
Civil actions, CL §11-209.
Cooperation with federal government and with
other states, CL §11-208.
Defined, CL §11-201.
Demand production of documents for inspection,
CL §11-205.
Political subdivisions.
Duty to advise, SG §6-107.
Prosecution of violations, CL §11-207.
Boycotts.
Foreign discriminatory boycotts.
Applicability of antitrust laws, CL §11-114.
Citation.
Short title, CL §11-213.
Combinations, CL §11-204.
Commodity.
Defined, CL §11-201.
Conspiracies, CL §11-204.
Contracts.
Unlawful contracts prohibited, CL §11-204.

ANTITRUST ACT —Cont'd
Counties.
Attorney general.
Duty to advise political subdivisions, SG §6-107.
Defined, CL §11-201.
Court.
Defined, CL §11-201.
Cumulative remedies, CL §11-211.
Damages.
Actions for damages, CL §11-209.
Evidence.
Judgment as evidence, CL §11-210.
Definitions, CL §11-201.
Discontinuance of prohibited act, CL §11-206.
Evidence.
State judgment as evidence, CL §11-210.
Exemptions.
General provisions, CL §11-203.
Fines.
Violations, CL §11-212.
Foreign discriminatory boycotts.
Applicability of antitrust laws, CL §11-114.
General provisions, CL §§11-101 to 11-115.
See FOREIGN DISCRIMINATORY
BOYCOTTS.
Injunctions, CL §11-209.
Inspection of documents by attorney general,
CL §11-205.
Interpretation and construction.
General provisions, CL §11-202.
Investigations.
Violations, CL §11-207.
Judgment.
State judgment as evidence, CL §11-210.
Limitation of actions.
Civil actions, CL §11-209.
Violations, CL §11-207.
Municipal corporations.
Attorney general.
Duty to advise political subdivisions, SG §6-107.
Person.
Defined, CL §11-201.
Prohibited conduct.
General provisions, CL §11-204.
Purpose, CL §11-202.
Service.
Defined, CL §11-201.
State's attorneys.
Civil actions, CL §11-209.
Prosecution of violations, CL §11-207.
Trade or commerce.
Defined, CL §11-201.
United States.
Cooperation with federal government and with
other states, CL §11-208.
Unlawful contracts, CL §11-204.
Violations.
Misdemeanors, CL §11-212.

APARTMENTS.
Alcoholic beverages.
Possession or consumption in public places.
Municipal regulation, 2B §19-104.
Barbeque grills.
Restrictions on use, PS §9-1001.
Building codes.
Emergency power and lighting systems, PS
§12-702.
Minimum livability code, PS §12-203.
Central heating or cooling systems.
Gas company or electric company providing to
residential multiple occupancy buildings, PUC
§7-301.

APARTMENTS —Cont'd
Condominiums.
General provisions, RP §§11-101 to 11-143.
See CONDOMINIUMS.
Discrimination in housing.
General provisions, 49B §§19 to 39.
See DISCRIMINATION.
Electric or gas meters.
Submetering, PUC §7-303.
Energy allocation departments and procedures used by owners, operators or managers.
Determining amount of gas or electricity used by individual dwelling unit, PUC §7-304.
Fires and fire protection.
Evacuation procedures, PS §§9-501 to 9-506.
Gas meters or electric meters in residential multiple occupancy buildings.
Individual metering, PUC §7-301.
Submetering, PUC §7-303.
Horizontal property act.
General provisions, RP §§11-101 to 11-143.
See CONDOMINIUMS.
Landlord and tenant generally.
See LANDLORD AND TENANT.
Leases.
General provisions.
See LANDLORD AND TENANT.
Lighting.
Illumination in public buildings, guidelines, PS §12-204.
Minimum livability code, PS §12-203.
Montgomery county.
Voter information material.
Distributing or depositing, EL §1-303.
Rent.
Landlord and tenant.
See LANDLORD AND TENANT.
Sprinkler systems, PS §§9-201 to 9-206.

APIARIES.
Beekeeping industry.
General provisions, AG §§5-501 to 5-507.
See BEEKEEPING INDUSTRY.

APOLOGIES.
Malpractice.
Health care malpractice claims.
Expressions of regret or apology by health care provider, admissibility into evidence, CJ §10-920.

APPALACHIAN HOUSING FUND, HS §§11-101 to 11-106.
See MARYLAND STATE APPALACHIAN HOUSING FUND.

APPALACHIAN REGIONAL DEVELOPMENT PROGRAM.
Appalachian regional commission.
State member and alternate member to federal commission, 83A §6-702.
Housing and community development department.
Acceptance of aid, 83A §6-701.
Contracts.
Authority to enter, 83A §6-701.
Cooperation with federal government, 83A §6-701.
United States.
Cooperation with federal government, 83A §6-701.

APPALACHIAN STATES LOW-LEVEL RADIOACTIVE WASTE COMPACT.
Appeals.
Commission.
Judicial review of commission decisions, EN §7-302.
Audits.
Commission, EN §7-302.
Brokers.
Defined, EN §7-301.
Budgets.
Commission, EN §7-302.
Carriers.
Defined, EN §7-301.
Commission.
Appointment of members, EN §7-302.
Audits, EN §7-302.
Budget, EN §7-302.
Composition, EN §7-302.
Conflicts of interest.
Prohibited acts, EN §7-304.
Creation, EN §7-302.
Defined, EN §7-301.
Duties, EN §7-302.
Expenses of members.
Reimbursement, EN §7-302.
Judicial review of decisions, EN §7-302.
Meetings, EN §7-302.
Powers, EN §7-302.
Reports, EN §7-302.
Rules and regulations, EN §7-302.
Staff, EN §7-302.
Voting by members, EN §7-302.
Conflicts of interest.
Commission.
Prohibited acts, EN §7-304.
Congress.
Consent by congress, EN §7-305.
Construction and interpretation, EN §7-306.
Definitions, EN §7-301.
Disposal.
Defined, EN §7-301.
Prohibited acts, EN §7-304.
Effective date, EN §7-305.
Facilities.
Defined, EN §7-301.
Generators.
Defined, EN §7-301.
Hazardous life.
Defined, EN §7-301.
Host state.
Defined, EN §7-301.
Duties, EN §7-303.
Institutional control period.
Defined, EN §7-301.
Interpretation and construction, EN §7-306.
Low-level waste.
Defined, EN §7-301.
Management.
Defined, EN §7-301.
Notices.
Commission.
Meetings, EN §7-302.
Operators.
Defined, EN §7-301.
Party states.
Defined, EN §7-301.

APPALACHIAN STATES LOW-LEVEL RADIOACTIVE WASTE COMPACT —Cont'd
Party states —Cont'd
Eligible parties, EN §7-305.
Rights, responsibilities and obligations, EN §7-303.
Withdrawal, EN §7-305.
Prohibited acts, EN §7-304.
Region.
Defined, EN §7-301.
Reports.
Commission, EN §7-302.
Host states.
Duties, EN §7-303.
Rules and regulations.
Commission, EN §7-302.
Severability of provisions, EN §7-306.
Shallow land burial.
Defined, EN §7-301.
Transuranic waste.
Defined, EN §7-301.
Withdrawal of parties, EN §7-305.

APPALACHIAN TRAIL, NR §5-1001.

APPEALS.
Abandoned property disposition.
Claim to property or proceeds of sale.
Judicial review of administrator's action, CL §17-320.
Accountants.
Board of public accountancy.
Judicial review, BOP §2-210.
Actions against state officers and employees.
Board of public works.
Approval or disapproval of payments.
Decision of board not subject to judicial review, SG §12-501.
Criminal actions.
Determinations of attorney general not subject to judicial review, SG §12-315.
Acupuncturists.
Board decisions.
Administrative and judicial review, HO §1A-311.
Administrative procedure.
See ADMINISTRATIVE PROCEDURE.
Adoption.
Appeals from proceedings for adoption, AppRev Rule 8-122.
Independent adoptions.
Right to appeal, FL §5-3B-09.
Local department adoptions.
Right to appeal, FL §5-310.
Private agency adoptions.
Right to appeal, FL §5-3A-10.
Subsidies.
Administrative and judicial review, FL §5-411.
Adult dependent care programs.
Criminal history records checks.
Contesting finding of criminal conviction, HG §19-1908.
Advancement of cases, AppRev Rule 8-521.
Affidavits.
Dismissal of appeals.
Motion to dismiss, AppRev Rule 8-603.
Injunction pending appeal.
Affidavit to accompany motion, AppRev Rule 8-425.
Motions.
Requirement that affidavit accompany or support motion, AppRev Rule 8-431.

APPEALS —Cont'd
Agriculture.
Board of review.
Appeals to board of review, AG §2-405.
Farm products.
Certification.
Assigned grade classifications, AG §10-605.
Air conditioning and heating contractors.
Licenses.
Judicial review of board action, BR §9A-312.
Air quality control.
Permits.
Judicial review, EN §2-404.1.
Persons aggrieved by decisions of secretary, etc., EN §2-607.
Alcoholic beverages.
License commissioners.
Appeals to court, 2B §16-101.
Licenses.
Revocation and suspension, 2B §10-403.
Minors conviction for violations, CR §10-119.
Open containers.
Possession of alcoholic beverages in motor vehicles' passenger areas, CR §10-127.
Alimony.
Contempt of court, CJ §12-304.
Amicus curiae.
Briefs, AppRev Rule 8-511.
Costs, AppRev Rule 8-607.
Oral arguments, AppRev Rule 8-511.
Participation as amicus curiae, AppRev Rule 8-511.
Amusements and recreation.
Adverse agency decision, BR §3-206.
Prohibition on use of rides, BR §3-405.
Prompt hearing requirement, BR §3-206.
Annual terms of court, AppRev Rule 8-102.
Annuities.
Charitable gift annuities.
Suspension or revocation of special permit, IN §16-114.
Appalachian states low-level radioactive waste compact.
Commission.
Judicial review of commission decisions, EN §7-302.
Appearance of counsel, AppRev Rule 8-402.
Appellants.
Briefs.
Court of special appeals.
Expedited appeals, AppRev Rule 8-207.
Filing, AppRev Rule 8-502.
Court of special appeals.
Expedited appeals.
Brief of appellant, AppRev Rule 8-207.
Information reports, AppRev Rule 8-205.
Designation of parties, AppRev Rule 8-111.
Dismissal of appeals.
Costs of dismissing, AppRev Rule 8-601.
Notice of dismissal, AppRev Rule 8-601.
Stay of enforcement of judgment.
Death of appellant, AppRev Rule 8-422.
Appellees.
Briefs.
Court of special appeals.
Expedited appeals, AppRev Rule 8-207.
Dismissal of appeals.
Motion to dismiss.
Inclusion in appellee's brief, AppRev Rule 8-603.
Filing of brief, AppRev Rule 8-502.

APPEALS —Cont'd
Appellees —Cont'd
Court of special appeals.
  Expedited appeals.
    Brief of appellee, AppRev Rule 8-207.
  Information reports, AppRev Rule 8-205.
  Designation of parties, AppRev Rule 8-111.
Apples.
Stop sale orders, AG §10-802.
Applicability of title, AppRev Rule 8-101; Rule
  1-101.
Application for leave to appeal.
Court of appeals.
  Applicability of certain rules to court of appeals
    procedure, AppRev Rule 8-306.
  Methods of securing review, AppRev Rule 8-301.
  When available, AppRev Rule 8-301.
Court of special appeals, AppRev Rules 8-203,
  8-204.
Arbitration and award.
Granting of stay of arbitration, CJ §12-303.
International commercial arbitration, CJ
  §3-2B-08.
Architects.
State board of architects.
  Judicial review of board, BOP §3-210.
Assessment, AppRev Rule 8-607.
Assignment of cases.
Advancement, AppRev Rule 8-521.
Postponement of case, AppRev Rule 8-521.
Regular order, AppRev Rule 8-521.
Assisted living programs.
Civil monetary penalties, HG §19-1810.
Attachment.
Decision or motion to quash.
  Appeal to court of appeals, CJ §12-303.
Attorneys at law.
Appearance of counsel, AppRev Rule 8-402.
Oral arguments.
  Number of counsel, AppRev Rule 8-522.
**Audiologists, hearing aid dealers and
  speech-language pathologists.**
Actions of board.
  Administrative and judicial review, HO §2-316.
Automobile insurance fund.
Claims against fund, IN §§20-605, 20-607.
Rejection or cancellation of insurance, IN §20-517.
Aviation.
Administration.
  Orders, TR §5-210.
Airports.
  Zoning.
    Board of appeals, TR §5-506.
Baltimore City.
District Court, CJ §12-403.
Bankruptcy and insolvency.
Insolvency cases, CJ §12-303.
Banks and trust companies.
Savings banks.
  Termination of provisions, FI §2-401.
Barbers.
State board of barbers.
  Judicial review of board, BOP §4-208.
Bedding and upholstered furniture.
Administrative and judicial review, HG §24-429.
Birds and game.
Hunting.
  Certificate of competency and safety.
    Appeal from denial of certificate, NR
      §10-301.1.

APPEALS —Cont'd
Boilers and pressure vessels.
Civil penalties generally, PS §12-916.
Bonds, surety.
Real estate brokers.
  Appeals from commission decisions.
    Stay of suspension or revocation of license,
      BOP §17-329.
Supersedeas bond, AppRev Rule 8-423.
Boxing, sparring and wrestling.
Disciplinary actions against licensees.
  Judicial review, BR §4-312.
Briefs, AppRev Rule 8-511.
Amicus curiae, AppRev Rule 8-511.
Appellants.
  Court of special appeals.
    Expedited appeals, AppRev Rule 8-207.
  Filing, AppRev Rule 8-502.
Appellees.
  Court of special appeals.
    Expedited appeals, AppRev Rule 8-207.
  Dismissal of appeals.
    Motion to dismiss.
      Inclusion in appellee's brief, AppRev Rule
        8-603.
  Filing of brief, AppRev Rule 8-502.
Binding, AppRev Rule 8-503.
Consideration on brief.
  Directed by court of special appeals, AppRev
    Rule 8-523.
  Requests for oral argument, AppRev Rule 8-523.
  Submission on brief by party, AppRev Rule
    8-523.
Contents, AppRev Rule 8-504.
Costs.
  Indigent persons, AppRev Rule 8-505.
Court of appeals.
  Certification from court of special appeals,
    AppRev Rule 8-304.
  Consideration on brief.
    Submission on brief by party, AppRev Rule
      8-523.
Court of special appeals.
  Consideration on brief.
    Directed by court of special appeals, AppRev
      Rule 8-523.
    Submission on brief by party, AppRev Rule
      8-523.
  Expedited appeals, AppRev Rule 8-207.
  Extract of instructions or opinion in criminal
    cases.
    Contents of brief, AppRev Rule 8-504.
Covers, AppRev Rule 8-503.
Cross-appellant's brief, AppRev Rule 8-503.
Cross-appellee's brief, AppRev Rule 8-503.
Dismissal of appeals.
  Motion to dismiss, AppRev Rule 8-603.
Filing, AppRev Rule 8-502.
Form, AppRev Rule 8-503.
  Court papers generally, AppRev Rule 8-112.
  Effect of noncompliance, AppRev Rule 8-503.
Incorporation by reference, AppRev Rule 8-503.
Indigent persons, AppRev Rule 8-505.
Length, AppRev Rule 8-503.
Numbering of pages, AppRev Rule 8-503.
Record on appeal.
  Extract.
    Appendices in briefs of appellees and
      appellants, AppRev Rule 8-501.
References in briefs, AppRev Rule 8-503.
Service, AppRev Rule 8-502.

APPEALS —Cont'd
Briefs —Cont'd
Style, AppRev Rule 8-503.
Effect of noncompliance, AppRev Rule 8-503.
Tax court.
Appeals to tax court, TG §13-518.
Capital cases.
Court of appeals.
Review in court of appeals, AppRev Rule 8-306.
Catastrophic health emergency.
Contest of isolation or quarantine.
Appellate review, SpecPro Rule 15-1107.
Catastrophic health emergency disease surveillance and response program.
Secretary's quarantine directive, HG §18-906.
Cecil county.
Schools.
County board of education.
Removal of members, ED §3-4A-02.
Certification of questions of law, CJ §§12-601 to 12-613.
See CERTIFIED QUESTIONS OF LAW.
Certiorari.
See CERTIORARI.
Charitable gift annuities.
Suspension or revocation of special permit, IN §16-114.
Charles county board of community college trustees.
Decisions of board, ED §16-607.
Charter schools.
Decision on application, ED §9-104.
Chesapeake Bay critical area and Atlantic coastal bays critical area protection programs.
Authority of chairman of commission to pursue, NR §8-1812.
Child care.
Family day care homes.
Revocation of registration, FL §5-554.
Suspension or revocation of license.
Administrative review, FL §5-517.
Judicial review, FL §5-518.
Child care centers.
Administrative procedure act, FL §5-581.
Child custody proceedings.
Uniform child custody jurisdiction and enforcement act, FL §9.5-314.
Child in need of residential placement.
Decisions by state coordinating council or local coordinating councils.
Right of parent or guardian, 49D §4-103.
Child support arrearages.
Attachment and seizure of funds for arrears from financial institution, FL §10-108.3.
Consumer reporting agencies.
Contesting accuracy of information, FL §10-108.1.
Driver's license suspension or restriction, FL §10-119; TR §16-203.
Income tax refund intercept, FL §10-113.
Chiropractors.
Actions of board of chiropractic examiners.
Administrative and judicial review, HO §3-316.
Cigarette business licenses.
Disciplinary actions against licensees.
Judicial review, BR §16-213.
Circuit courts.
Appeals from final judgments, CJ §12-301.
Court of special appeals.
Review of decisions by court of appeals, CJ §12-201.
Exceptions, CJ §12-202.

APPEALS —Cont'd
Circuit courts —Cont'd
Defined, CJ §12-101.
Draining lands.
Right of appeal to circuit court, 25 §80.
Elections.
Rejection of ballots by board of canvassers.
Absentee ballots, EL §11-304.
Form of court papers, Rule 1-301.
Interlocutory orders.
Certain orders, CJ §12-303.
Peace orders, CJ §3-1506.
Probation.
Revocation of probation.
Application for leave to appeal from order revoking probation, CJ §12-302.
Right of appeal.
Exceptions, CJ §12-301.
Final judgments, CJ §12-301.
State appeals, CJ §12-302.
Clients' security fund.
Court of appeals, CJA Rule 16-811.
Collection agencies.
License disciplinary hearings.
Judicial review, BR §7-310.
Collective bargaining.
Injunctions.
Issuance or denial of temporary injunction, LE §4-318.
Computation, AppRev Rule 8-608.
Confidentiality.
Adoption proceedings, AppRev Rule 8-122.
Court of special appeals.
Information reports, AppRev Rules 8-205, 8-206.
Criminal investigations, AppRev Rule 8-123.
Guardianship appeals, AppRev Rule 8-122.
Juvenile causes.
Appeals from courts exercising juvenile jurisdiction, AppRev Rule 8-121.
Consideration of appeal on brief, AppRev Rule 8-523.
Constitutional provisions.
Review of facts tried by jury, US Const Amd 7.
Consumer loans.
Right to appeal, FI §11-218.
Contempt of court.
Alimony.
Exception as to order requiring payment of alimony, CJ §12-304.
District Court, CJ §12-402.
Right of appeal, CJ §12-304.
Continuing care contracts.
Claims against impaired providers, 70B §20Q.
Liquidation, conservation or rehabilitation orders, 70B §20K.
Violations of provisions by providers, 70B §18A.
Corporations.
Appearance of counsel.
Requirement of appearance of counsel, AppRev Rule 8-402.
Cosmetologists.
State board of cosmetologists.
Judicial review of decisions, BOP §5-209.
Costs, AppRev Rule 8-607.
Allowance.
State or state agency, CJ §7-104.
Amicus curiae.
Participation as amicus curiae, AppRev Rule 8-511.
Assessment against political subdivision.
In which case originated, CJ §7-104.

APPEALS —Cont'd
Costs —Cont'd
County commissioners.
Bridge cases, 25 §48.
Criminal procedure, CJ §7-104.
Insurance commissioner's hearing, IN §2-215.
Oral arguments, AppRev Rule 8-511.
State or state agency as party, CJ §7-104.
Counties.
Bridges between counties, 25 §§46 to 48.
Chartered counties.
Board of appeals, 25A §5.
Court of appeals.
Applicability of rules, AppRev Rule 8-101; Rule
1-101.
Application for leave to appeal.
Applicability of certain rules to court of appeals
procedure, AppRev Rule 8-306.
Methods of securing review, AppRev Rule 8-301.
When available, AppRev Rule 8-301.
Automatic review.
Death penalty, AppRev Rule 8-306; CR §2-401.
Briefs.
Certification from court of special appeals,
AppRev Rule 8-304.
Consideration on brief.
Submission on brief by party, AppRev Rule
8-523.
Capital cases reviewed by court of appeals,
AppRev Rule 8-306.
Certification of questions of law.
Decision by court of appeals, AppRev Rule
8-305.
Definition of certifying court, AppRev Rule
8-305.
Order for certification, AppRev Rule 8-305.
Proceeding in court of appeals, AppRev Rule
8-305.
Certification procedure.
Appearance of counsel, AppRev Rule 8-402.
Applicable provisions, AppRev Rule 8-301.
Court of special appeals as certifying court.
Content, AppRev Rule 8-304.
Disposition of certification, AppRev Rule
8-304.
Initiation, AppRev Rule 8-304.
Record extract and briefs, AppRev Rule 8-304.
Method of securing review, AppRev Rule 8-301.
Uniform act, CJ §§12-601 to 12-613.
See CERTIFIED QUESTIONS OF LAW.
Certiorari.
See CERTIORARI.
Death penalty.
Automatic review by court of appeals, CR
§2-401.
Direct appeals.
Capital cases, AppRev Rule 8-306.
Methods of securing review, AppRev Rule 8-301.
When available, AppRev Rule 8-301.
General provisions.
See COURT OF APPEALS.
Injunction pending appeal.
Decision of court, AppRev Rule 8-425.
Jurisdiction.
Appellate jurisdiction, CJ §12-307.
Obtaining appellate review in court of appeals.
Capital cases, AppRev Rule 8-306.
Certification from court of special appeals,
AppRev Rule 8-304.
Certification of questions of law, AppRev Rule
8-305.

APPEALS —Cont'd
Court of appeals —Cont'd
Obtaining appellate review in court of appeals
—Cont'd
Certiorari.
Procedure on petition for writ, AppRev Rule
8-303.
Time for filing petition for writ, AppRev Rule
8-302.
Method, AppRev Rule 8-301.
Reconsiderations.
Motions in court, AppRev Rule 8-605.
Record on appeal.
Capital cases.
Transcript in lieu of record extract, AppRev
Rule 8-306.
Certification from court of special appeals.
Record extract and brief, AppRev Rule 8-304.
Extract.
Capital cases.
Transcript in lieu of record extract, AppRev
Rule 8-306.
Certification from court of special appeals.
Record extract and brief, AppRev Rule
8-304.
Review of case from court of special appeals,
AppRev Rule 8-501.
Time for transmitting, AppRev Rule 8-412.
Review of cases in court of special appeals, CJ
§12-201.
Exceptions, CJ §12-202.
Scope of review.
No prior appellate decision, AppRev Rule 8-131.
Prior appellate decision, AppRev Rule 8-131.
Stay of enforcement of judgment.
Continuation of court of appeals of previously
filed security, AppRev Rule 8-422.
Court of special appeals.
Appellants.
Expedited appeals.
Brief of appellant, AppRev Rule 8-207.
Information reports, AppRev Rule 8-205.
Appellate procedure generally, AppRev Rules
8-101 to 8-611.
Appellees.
Expedited appeals.
Brief of appellee, AppRev Rule 8-207.
Information, AppRev Rule 8-205.
Applicability of rules, AppRev Rule 8-101; Rule
1-101.
Application for leave to appeal, AppRev Rule
8-204.
Striking, AppRev Rule 8-203.
Notice, AppRev Rule 8-203.
Briefs.
Consideration on brief.
Directed by court of special appeals, AppRev
Rule 8-523.
Submission on brief by party, AppRev Rule
8-523.
Expedited appeals, AppRev Rule 8-207.
Extract of instructions or opinion in criminal
cases.
Contents of brief, AppRev Rule 8-504.
Certification of question of law.
Court of special appeals to court of appeals,
AppRev Rule 8-304.
Uniform act, CJ §§12-601 to 12-613.
See CERTIFIED QUESTIONS OF LAW.
Certiorari.
See CERTIORARI.

APPEALS —Cont'd
Court of special appeals —Cont'd
En banc review.
  Notice of appeal.
    Time for filing, AppRev Rule 8-202.
Expedited appeals.
  Applicability of other rules, AppRev Rule 8-207.
  Briefs, AppRev Rule 8-207.
  Decision, AppRev Rule 8-207.
  Election, AppRev Rule 8-207.
    Withdrawal, AppRev Rule 8-207.
  Oral arguments, AppRev Rule 8-207.
  Statement of case and facts, AppRev Rule
    8-207.
Extensions of time in court of special appeals.
  Clerk may enter order, AppRev Rule 8-432.
General provisions.
  See COURT OF SPECIAL APPEALS.
Habeas corpus.
  Discharge on ground of unconstitutionality.
    Review by court of special appeals, SpecPro
      Rule 15-312.
Information reports, AppRev Rules 8-205, 8-206.
Jurisdiction, CJ §12-308.
Notice of appeal.
  Fees.
    Filing fee, AppRev Rule 8-201.
  Methods of securing review, AppRev Rule 8-201.
  Striking notice, AppRev Rule 8-203.
  Time for filing, AppRev Rule 8-202.
    Appeals by other party, AppRev Rule 8-202.
    Civil actions.
      Postjudgment motions, AppRev Rule 8-202.
    Criminal actions, AppRev Rule 8-202.
    Date of entry, AppRev Rule 8-202.
    In banc review, AppRev Rule 8-202.
    New trial motions.
      Criminal cases, AppRev Rule 8-202.
  Transmittal of record, AppRev Rule 8-201.
Obtaining review in court of special appeals.
  Expedited appeals, AppRev Rule 8-207.
  Information reports, AppRev Rule 8-205.
  Methods, AppRev Rule 8-201.
    Application for leave to appeal, AppRev Rule
      8-204.
      Striking application, AppRev Rule 8-203.
    Notice of appeal, AppRev Rule 8-201.
      Striking notice of appeal, AppRev Rule
        8-203.
      Time for filing, AppRev Rule 8-202.
  Prehearing procedure, AppRev Rule 8-206.
Opinions.
  Reporting of opinions, AppRev Rule 8-605.1.
Prehearing procedure.
  Conference, AppRev Rule 8-206.
  Initial determination by court, AppRev Rule
    8-206.
  Orders, AppRev Rule 8-206.
  Recusal of judge, AppRev Rule 8-206.
  Sanctions, AppRev Rule 8-206.
Public service commission proceedings.
  Judicial review of proceedings or orders, PUC
    §3-209.
Reconsiderations.
  Motions in court of special appeals, AppRev
    Rule 8-605.
Record on appeal.
  Application for leave to appeal.
    Record on application, AppRev Rule 8-204.
  Extract.
    Court of appeals review of case from court of
      special appeals, AppRev Rule 8-501.

APPEALS —Cont'd
Court of special appeals —Cont'd
Record on appeal —Cont'd
  Notice of appeal procedure.
    Transmittal of record, AppRev Rule 8-201.
  Time for transmitting, AppRev Rule 8-412.
  Reporting of opinions, AppRev Rule 8-605.1.
  Review of decisions by court of appeals, CJ
    §12-201.
    Exceptions, CJ §12-202.
  Scheduling conference, AppRev Rule 8-206.
  Stay of enforcement of judgment.
    Review of lower court action by court of special
      appeals, AppRev Rule 8-422.
Court papers.
Clerk of court.
  Duties, AppRev Rule 8-113.
Credit life, health and unemployment
  insurance.
Approval of forms and rates, IN §13-110.
Commissioner's orders, IN §13-117.
Criminal investigations.
Appeals from criminal investigations, AppRev
  Rule 8-123.
Criminal justice information system.
Decisions concerning inspection of or challenge to
  criminal history record information, CP
  §10-227.
  See CRIMINAL JUSTICE INFORMATION
    SYSTEM.
Criminal procedure, CJ §12-401.
Bail and recognizance.
  Termination of bond on sentencing.
    New bond on appeal, CP §5-207.
Definition of criminal case, CJ §12-101.
Jurisdiction, CJ §12-308.
Jury.
  Right to jury trial, CJ §12-401.
Post conviction procedure.
  Appeal of final order, CP §7-109.
  Effect of remedy on appeals, CP §7-107.
Probation before judgment.
  Waiver of right to appeal, CP §6-220.
Review of criminal sentences, CP §§8-101 to
  8-109.
  See SENTENCE AND PUNISHMENT.
State.
  Right of appeal by state, CJ §12-401.
Cross-appeals, AppRev Rules 8-501, 8-503.
Death penalty.
Automatic review.
  Court of appeals, CR §2-401.
Jurisdiction.
  Court of appeals has exclusive jurisdiction, CJ
    §12-307.
Defective delinquents.
Jurisdiction.
  Court of special appeals, CJ §12-308.
Definitions, CJ §12-101.
Court of appeals.
  Certification of questions of law.
    Certifying courts, AppRev Rule 8-305.
De novo, 1 §32.
Dentists.
Disciplinary proceedings.
  Administrative and judicial review, HO §4-319.
Developmental disabilities.
Decisions of secretary of health and mental
  hygiene, HG §7-407.
State residential centers.
  Release.
    Petition for release, HG §7-507.

APPEALS —Cont'd
Dietitians.
Final decisions of board, HO §5-313.
Direct appeals.
Court of appeals.
Capital cases, AppRev Rule 8-306.
Method of securing and when available, AppRev
Rule 8-301.
Discovery.
Perpetuation of evidence.
Pending appeal, CivProCir Rule 2-404.
Circuit courts, CivProCir Rule 2-404.
Discrimination.
Commercial discrimination.
Construction of policy, SF §19-105.
Final administrative decision, SF §19-113.
Dismissal of appeals.
Appellant dismissing, AppRev Rule 8-601.
Costs of dismissing, AppRev Rule 8-601.
Notice of dismissal, AppRev Rule 8-601.
Authorized dispositions, AppRev Rule 8-604.
Briefs.
Failure to file brief, AppRev Rule 8-502.
Motion to dismiss, AppRev Rule 8-603.
Court dismissal.
Grounds, AppRev Rule 8-602.
Reconsideration of dismissal.
Order entered by court, AppRev Rule 8-602.
Order entered by individual judge, AppRev
Rule 8-602.
Reinstatement on docket, AppRev Rule 8-602.
Entry of judgment.
Judgment entered after notice filed, AppRev
Rule 8-602.
Not directed under Rule 2-602, AppRev Rule
8-602.
Excluded costs, AppRev Rule 8-608.
Generally allowable costs, AppRev Rule 8-608.
Mandate.
Statement of costs contained in mandate,
AppRev Rule 8-606.
Motion to dismiss, AppRev Rule 8-603.
Notice.
Appellant dismissing, AppRev Rule 8-601.
Oral arguments.
Motion to dismiss.
Separate oral argument, AppRev Rule 8-603.
Reconsideration of dismissal.
No further reconsideration by court, AppRev
Rule 8-602.
Record on appeal.
Unnecessary correction of record.
Disallowance of costs, AppRev Rule 8-607.
Reproduction allowance, AppRev Rule 8-608.
State.
Assessment of costs against state, AppRev Rule
8-607.
Criminal appeals, AppRev Rule 8-607.
Unnecessary material.
Disallowance of costs for reproduction of
unnecessary material, AppRev Rule 8-607.
Dispositions.
Affirming judgment.
Authorized dispositions, AppRev Rule 8-604.
Partial affirmance, AppRev Rule 8-604.
Authorized dispositions, AppRev Rule 8-604.
Correctable error, AppRev Rule 8-604.
Dismissal of appeals. See within this heading,
"Dismissal of appeals."
Entry of judgment, AppRev Rule 8-604.

APPEALS —Cont'd
Dispositions —Cont'd
Modification of judgment.
Authorized dispositions, AppRev Rule 8-604.
Correctible errors, AppRev Rule 8-604.
Entry of judgment, AppRev Rule 8-604.
Partial affirmance and partial reversal or
modification or remand, AppRev Rule 8-604.
Reconsideration, AppRev Rule 8-605.
Remand.
Generally, AppRev Rule 8-604.
Vacating or reversing judgment, AppRev Rule
8-604.
Distress for rent, RP §8-332.
District Court.
Appeals from District Court.
General provisions, AppRevCir Rules 7-101 to
7-116; CJ §§12-401 to 12-404.
See APPEALS FROM DISTRICT COURT.
Divorce.
Property disposition, FL §8-213.
Docketing of appeals, AppRev Rule 8-421.
Record on appeal.
Separate appeals on same record, AppRev Rule
8-421.
Domestic violence.
Orders of court.
Protection from abuse, FL §4-507.
Dorchester county.
Schools.
County board of education.
Removal of member, ED §3-5A-02.
Shared facilities.
Appeal following denial of petition, EN §9-676.
Draining lands.
Circuit court.
Right of appeal to circuit court, 25 §80.
Classification and assessment, 25 §117.
County commissioners.
Order of review, 25 §79.
Ejectment.
When grantor remains in possession after delivery
of deed and in violation of agreement, RP
§14-109.
Election of rights and remedies.
Court of special appeals.
Expedited appeals, AppRev Rule 8-207.
Elections.
Contested elections.
Judicial review of election.
Appeal directly to court of appeals, EL
§12-203.
Petitions for nomination, ballot questions or
political party creation.
Determinations as to signatures and
satisfaction of requirements, EL §6-209.
Time for, EL §6-210.
Rejection of ballot by board of canvassers.
Absentee ballot, EL §11-304.
Electric customer choice and competition act.
Rate stabilization.
Qualified rate order, PUC §7-528.
Electricians.
Licenses.
State licenses.
Disciplinary actions.
Judicial review of board, BOP §6-318.
Electrologists.
License suspension or revocation.
Appeal of decision, HO §8-6B-21.

APPEALS —Cont'd

Elevator licenses.
Denial, refusal to renew, suspension or revocation, PS §12-838.

Emergency management.
State standby petroleum fuel set-aside program. Prime suppliers, PS §14-507.

Emergency medical care and services.
Discipline of employees.
Judicial review of final decisions, LE §§4-601 to 4-603.

Eminent domain.
Attorneys' fees, PropAct Rule 12-209; RP §12-107.
Costs, PropAct Rule 12-209; RP §12-107.
Possession of property pending appeal, RP §12-107.
Right to appeal, PropAct Rule 12-209; RP §12-107.

En banc review.
Circuit courts, CivProCir Rule 2-551.
Criminal rules, Crim Rule 4-352.

Enforcement of judgments.
Appellate court, AppRev Rule 8-611.
Trial court, AppRev Rule 8-611.

Engineers.
State board for professional engineers.
Judicial review of actions, BOP §14-210.

Environmental sanitarians.
Board of environmental sanitarians, EN §11-314.

Environmental service.
Judicial review, NR §3-128.
Public service commission.
Appeal of decision of commission, NR §3-128.

Equal employment opportunity.
Decisions, SPP §5-213.

Evidence.
Mandate as evidence of order of court, AppRev Rule 8-606.

Executors and administrators.
Commission of personal representative.
Appeal from allowance by court, ET §7-601.
Death tax generally, TG §§7-101 to 7-122.
See TAXATION.
Inheritance tax.
See INHERITANCE TAX.
Settlement of decedents' estates.
Orphans' court.
Striking of notice of appeal, Estates Rule 6-464.
Tax on commissions.
Appeals to court of special appeals, Estates Rule 6-463; TG §13-511.

Expedited appeals.
Court of special appeals, AppRev Rule 8-207.

Expungement of records.
Charges filed.
Appellate review of decision on expungement, CP §10-105.
How taken, Crim Rule 4-509.
Stay of order pending appeal, Crim Rule 4-509.

Extradition.
Denial of habeas corpus, CP §9-110.

Fees.
Court of special appeals.
Notice of appeal.
Filing fee, AppRev Rule 8-201.

Final judgment.
Defined, CJ §12-101.

Fines.
District Court.
Commitment for nonpayment of fines, CJ §12-404.

APPEALS —Cont'd

Firearms.
Applications for purchases, rents or transfers, PS §5-127.
Dealers' licenses.
Disapproval, PS §5-110.
Suspension or revocation, PS §5-116.
Handgun permits.
Informal review of secretary's actions, PS §5-311.
Review by board, PS §5-312.
Handgun roster.
Placement on roster, PS §5-405.

Fire department.
Discipline of employees.
Judicial review of final decisions, LE §§4-601 to 4-603.

Fire marshal, PS §§6-501 to 6-503.
Judicial review of commission's decision, PS §6-503.
Procedure, PS §6-502.
Right to file appeal to commission, PS §6-501.

Fire prevention commission, PS §§6-501 to 6-503.
Judicial review of commission's decision, PS §6-503.
Procedure, PS §6-502.
Right to file appeal to commission, PS §6-501.

Fires and fire protection.
Orders of compliance.
High-rise buildings, PS §9-404.

Foreign money judgments.
Stay pending appeals, CJ §10-706.

Foresters.
Licenses.
Disciplinary action.
Judicial review, BOP §7-312.

Forms.
Court papers, AppRev Rule 8-112.
Order for appeal, Form 22.

Fraternal benefit societies.
Judicial review of commissioner's decision or finding, IN §8-465.

Frozen desserts.
Denial, suspension or revocation of licenses.
Right to appeal, HG §21-815.

Gas and oil.
Coastal facilities review act.
Permit for construction of facilities.
Judicial review of action on application, EN §14-509.
Decision of department, EN §14-117.

Grain.
Licensing of grain dealers.
Suspension or revocation, AG §13-209.

Grievance procedures.
Inmates at state correctional facilities.
Judicial review of final decision of secretary, COR §10-210.
Review of administrative law judge's order by secretary, COR §10-209.
State personnel, SPP §§12-101 to 12-405.
See GRIEVANCE PROCEDURES.

Guardian and ward.
Appeals from proceedings for guardianship, AppRev Rule 8-122.
Depriving natural guardian of custody of child, CJ §12-303.
Local department guardianships.
Right to appeal, FL §5-310.

APPEALS —Cont'd
Guardian and ward —Cont'd
Private agency guardianships.
Right to appeal, FL §5-3A-10.
Habeas corpus.
Bail.
Application for leave to appeal in regard to bail,
CJ §3-707.
Handgun permits.
Informal review of secretary's actions, PS §5-311.
Review by board, PS §5-312.
Handgun roster.
Placement on roster, PS §5-405.
Hazardous materials and substances.
Final decisions of department, EN §7-264.
Persons adversely affected by rules or regulations,
HG §22-505.
Hazardous waste facility siting.
Decisions of board, EN §7-412.
Health.
Department of health and mental hygiene.
Board of review.
See HEALTH.
Health care commission.
Cost review commission.
Right to appeal, HG §19-227.
Health planning and development.
Administrative decisions, HG §19-128.
Health insurance.
Complaint process for coverage decisions, IN
§15-10D-02.
Private review agents, IN §15-10B-13.
Adverse decision, IN §15-10B-07.
Review of services for treatment of alcoholism,
drug abuse or mental illness, IN
§15-10B-03.
Health maintenance organizations.
Adjustment of capitation rates, IN §15-605.
Decisions of commissioner or orders of secretary,
HG §19-732.
Hearings.
Dismissal of appeals.
Motion to dismiss, AppRev Rule 8-603.
Motions, AppRev Rule 8-431.
Heritage areas.
Decisions of authority, FI §13-1124.
Highways.
Board of property review.
Appeal from award of board, TR §8-329.
State highway access valuation board, TR §8-310.
Homebuilder registration violations.
Administrative decision, BR §4.5-502.
Home improvements.
Licenses.
Adverse agency action, BR §8-314.
Horse racing.
State racing commission.
License disciplinary hearings, BR §11-311.
Hospitals.
Discharge or transfer of residents.
Civil damages for violations of provisions, HG
§19-345.3.
Discharge violations.
Appeal of fines imposed, HG §19-308.8.
Hazardous conditions.
Intermediate sanction, HG §§19-364, 19-367.
Licenses.
Administrative and judicial review, HG §19-330.
Human relations commission.
Denial of request for reconsideration of finding of
no probable cause, 49B §10.

APPEALS —Cont'd
Improper appeal.
Transfer of appeal improperly taken, AppRev Rule
8-132.
Income tax.
Withholding refunds due to state agency debt, TG
§13-917.
Inheritance tax.
Orphans' court.
Appeal to court of special appeals from, TG
§13-511.
Injunctions.
Granting or dissolving, CJ §12-303.
Pending appeal, AppRev Rule 8-425.
Decision.
Court of appeals, AppRev Rule 8-425.
Court of special appeals, AppRev Rule 8-425.
Factors relevant to granting of injunctive
relief, AppRev Rule 8-425.
Grounds for granting injunctive relief, AppRev
Rule 8-425.
Motions, AppRev Rule 8-425.
Refusal to dissolve, CJ §12-303.
Insurance.
Acquisitions disclosure and control act.
Actions of commissioner, IN §7-107.
Automobile insurance fund.
Claims against fund, IN §§20-605, 20-607.
Rejection or cancellation of insurance, IN
§20-517.
Commissioner's order or hearing, IN §2-215.
Credit life, health and unemployment insurance.
Approval of forms and rates, IN §13-110.
Commissioner's orders, IN §13-117.
Discrimination, IN §27-505.
Financially hazardous condition.
Regulation of entities in financially hazardous
condition, IN §9-104.
Joint insurance association.
Decisions of governing committee, IN §25-409.
Life and health insurance guaranty corporation,
IN §9-411.
Liquidation, rehabilitation, etc., of insurers, IN
§9-216.
Money judgment covered by insurance, AppRev
Rule 8-424.
Motor vehicle insurance.
Cancellation, nonrenewal, premium increase or
reduction in coverage, IN §§27-605, 27-613.
Nonprofit health service plans, IN §14-127.
Investment in or acquisition of affiliate or
subsidiary, IN §14-133.
Removal of officer or director, IN §14-116.
Property and casualty insurance guaranty
corporation.
Action or order of the commissioner, IN §9-308.
Ratemaking, IN §§11-501, 11-503.
Competitive rating, IN §11-314.
Prior approval ratemaking, IN §11-212.
Rating organization decisions, IN §11-220.
Reinsurance intermediaries.
Judicial review of commissioner's order, IN
§8-511.
Removal of officer or director, IN §14-116.
Unfair claim settlement practices, IN §27-306.
Unfair trade practices, IN §27-105.
Interior designers.
State board of certified interior designers.
Final decision in contested case, BOP §8-313.
Interlocutory orders.
Right of appeal, CJ §12-303.

APPEALS —Cont'd
Interlocutory orders —Cont'd
Scope of review, AppRev Rule 8-131.
Investigations.
Appeals from criminal investigations, AppRev
Rule 8-123.
Joinder.
Parties.
Joinder not required, AppRev Rule 8-401.
Judges.
Court of special appeals.
Prehearing procedure.
Recusal of judge who conducts prehearing
conference, AppRev Rule 8-206.
Disability and sanctionable conduct.
Review of commission's findings, CJA Rule
16-809.
Judgments and decrees.
Affirming judgment.
Authorized dispositions, AppRev Rule 8-604.
Dismissal of appeals.
Judgment entered after notice filed, AppRev
Rule 8-602.
Enforcement.
Appellate court, AppRev Rule 8-611.
Trial court, AppRev Rule 8-611.
Entry of judgment to dispose of matter, AppRev
Rule 8-604.
Final judgment.
Defined, CJ §12-101.
Foreign judgments.
Stay of enforcement, CJ §11-804.
Injunction pending appeal.
Circuit courts, CivProCir Rule 2-632.
Landlord and tenant.
Failure to pay rent.
Appeals from judgment, RP §8-401.
Holdover tenants.
Appeals from judgments, RP §8-402.
Modifying judgment.
Authorized dispositions, AppRev Rule 8-604.
Money judgment covered by insurance, AppRev
Rule 8-424.
Stay of enforcement of judgment, AppRev Rule
8-422.
Pending appeal.
Circuit courts, CivProCir Rule 2-632.
Stay pending appeal.
Circuit courts, CivProCir Rule 2-632.
District Court, CivProDist Rule 3-632.
Vacating or reversing judgment.
Authorized dispositions, AppRev Rule 8-604.
Judgments notwithstanding the verdict.
Effect of reversal on appeal.
Circuit courts, CivProCir Rule 2-532.
Jurisdiction.
Allocation of appellate jurisdiction, CJ §12-306.
Purpose of sections 12-307 and 12-308, CJ
§12-306.
Appellate jurisdiction.
Defined, CJ §12-101.
Court of appeals, CJ §12-307.
Court of special appeals, CJ §12-308.
Jury.
Administrative agencies.
Circuit courts.
Jury trial, CivProCir Rule 2-325.
Draining lands.
Circuit court.
Jury trial, 25 §80.

APPEALS —Cont'd
Juvenile causes.
Appeals from courts exercising juvenile
jurisdiction, AppRev Rule 8-121.
Montgomery county, CJ §3-8A-31.
Stay of proceedings, CJ §12-701.
Truancy reduction pilot program, CJ §3-8C-10.
Landlord and tenant.
Notice to quit.
Tenants holding over.
Liability, RP §8-402.
Repossession proceedings.
By tenant or landlord, RP §8-401.
Land patents.
Declaratory judgments, CJ §3-408.1.
Issuance of patents.
Judicial review, RP §13-410.
Law enforcement officers and personnel.
Disciplinary hearings.
Judicial review, PS §3-109.
Review by chief, PS §3-108.
**Life and health insurance guaranty
corporation,** IN §9-411.
Livestock.
Contagious and infectious diseases.
Appraisal of buildings and animals, AG §3-107.
Malpractice.
Health care malpractice claims, CJ §3-2A-06.
Managed care organizations.
Adjustment of capitation rates, IN §15-605.
Mandate, AppRev Rules 8-605, 8-606.
Maryland-Washington regional district.
Delegation of powers to municipal corporations.
Right of appeal to circuit court, 28 §8-112.4.
Zoning.
See MARYLAND-WASHINGTON REGIONAL
DISTRICT.
Medicaid.
Field verification of program participants.
Appeal of results, HG §15-108.
Mental hygiene law.
Judicial release, HG §10-805.
Private group homes.
Administrative and judicial review of secretary's
decisions, HG §10-524.
Migrant labor.
Licenses.
Judicial review of contested cases, LE §7-313.
Milk and milk products.
Suspension or revocation of permits, HG §21-419.
Mining.
Certificates or permits of competence.
Refusal to issue, EN §15-307.
Minors.
Alcoholic beverages.
Minor's conviction for violations, CR §10-119.
Depriving parent of custody of child, CJ §12-303.
Money transmission.
Licenses, FI §12-422.
Morgan State University.
Employees.
Classified employees grievance procedure, ED
§§14-302, 14-305, 14-306.
Morticians.
Disciplinary proceedings.
Administrative and judicial review, HO §7-320.
Motions, AppRev Rule 8-431.
Affidavits.
Requirement that affidavit accompany or
support motion, AppRev Rule 8-431.
Copies, AppRev Rule 8-431.

APPEALS —Cont'd
Motions —Cont'd
Dismissal of appeal, AppRev Rule 8-603.
Emergency orders, AppRev Rule 8-431.
Filing, AppRev Rule 8-431.
Forms.
  Court papers, AppRev Rule 8-112.
Hearings, AppRev Rule 8-431.
Injunction pending appeal, AppRev Rule 8-425.
Reconsideration, AppRev Rule 8-605.
Record on appeal.
  Correction of record, AppRev Rule 8-414.
Response, AppRev Rule 8-431.
Scope of review.
  Order denying motion to dismiss, AppRev Rule
    8-131.
Motor clubs.
Adverse agency action.
  Judicial review, IN §26-209.
Motor fuel inspection.
Petroleum transporters.
  Registration disciplinary hearings, BR §10-405.
Motor fuel tax.
Licenses.
  Cancellation, TG §9-332.
Motor vehicle insurance.
Automobile insurance fund.
  Claims against fund, IN §20-605.
  Rejection or cancellation of insurance, IN
    §20-517.
Motor vehicles.
Administration.
  Appeals from decisions of administration, TR
    §12-209.
Automobile insurance fund.
  Claims against fund, IN §20-607.
Certificates of title.
  Suspension or revocation, TR §13-705.
Driver license compact.
  Judicial review, TR §16-708.
Drivers' licenses.
  Suspension of license on refusal to submit to
    chemical test for intoxication, TR §16-205.1.
  Suspension or restriction for child support
    arrearages, FL §10-119; TR §16-203.
Registration.
  Suspension or revocation, TR §13-705.
Security interest.
  Claims for damages against administration.
    Judicial review of determination, TR §13-210.
Suspension of license on refusal to submit to
  chemical test for intoxication.
  Court review of suspension, TR §16-205.1.
Weight.
  Offenses involving truck weights, TR §24-114.
Municipal corporations.
Maryland-Washington regional district.
  Delegation of powers to municipal corporations.
    Right of appeal to circuit court, 28 §8-112.4.
Port wardens.
  Appeal to legislative body of municipal
    corporation, 23A §2.
Municipal infractions.
Right of appeal, CJ §12-401.
Nonprofit health service plans, IN §14-127.
Investment in or acquisition of affiliate or
  subsidiary, IN §14-133.
Removal of officer or director, IN §14-116.
Northeast Maryland waste disposal authority,
  NR §3-922.

APPEALS —Cont'd
Not criminally responsible.
Release of committed person, CP §3-118.
  Application for release, CP §3-119.
    By health department, CP §3-120.
  Revocation of conditional release for violations,
    CP §3-121.
Notice of appeal.
Court of special appeals.
  Fees.
    Filing fee, AppRev Rule 8-201.
  Methods of securing review, AppRev Rule 8-201.
  Striking notice, AppRev Rule 8-203.
    Notice of striking notice, AppRev Rule 8-203.
  Time for filing, AppRev Rule 8-202.
  Transmittal of record, AppRev Rule 8-201.
Dismissal of appeals.
  Appellant dismissing, AppRev Rule 8-601.
Public service commission proceedings.
  Appeals from order of commissioner or hearing
    examiner to full commission, PUC §3-113.
Nurse multistate licensure compact.
Limits on judicial review of other state's decisions,
  HO §8-7A-02.
Nurses.
Disciplinary proceedings.
  Administrative and judicial review, HO §8-318.
**Nursing assistant aggrieved by final decision
  of board of nursing,** HO §8-6A-11.
Nursing home administrators.
Disciplinary proceedings.
  Administrative and judicial review, HO §9-316.
Licenses.
  Denial of application, HO §9-309.
Nursing homes.
Civil money penalty, administrative appeal, HG
  §19-1406.
Medicaid.
  Liability audits and review, HG §19-14A-03.
Occupational safety and health.
Judicial review and enforcement, LE §5-215.
  Notice prohibiting use of apparatus, LE §5-210.
Occupational therapists.
Disciplinary proceedings.
  Administrative and judicial review, HO §10-317.
Opinions.
Clerk of court.
  Duties of clerk as to, AppRev Rule 8-113.
Unreported opinions.
  Citation, Rule 1-104.
  No authority, Rule 1-104.
Optometrists.
Disciplinary proceedings.
  Administrative and judicial review, HO §11-318.
Oral arguments.
Amicus curiae, AppRev Rule 8-511.
Dismissal of appeals.
  Motion to dismiss.
    Separate oral argument, AppRev Rule 8-603.
Failure to appear, AppRev Rule 8-522.
Multiple appeals in same action.
  Order of argument, AppRev Rule 8-522.
Number of counsel, AppRev Rule 8-522.
Rebuttal, AppRev Rule 8-522.
Reconsiderations.
  No oral argument on motion to reconsider,
    AppRev Rule 8-605.
Requests for oral argument, AppRev Rule 8-523.
Restrictions on oral arguments, AppRev Rule
  8-522.
Time limit, AppRev Rule 8-522.

APPEALS —Cont'd
Orders.
Court of appeals.
Certification procedure.
Certification of questions of law, AppRev Rule 8-305.
Emergency orders.
Authority of court to rule on party's motion before expiration of time for response, AppRev Rule 8-431.
Entry of order, AppRev Rule 8-432.
Forms, Form 22.
Interlocutory orders.
Right of appeal, CJ §12-303.
Scope of review, AppRev Rule 8-131.
Mandate.
Evidence of order of court, AppRev Rule 8-606.
Orphans' court.
Appeal from.
Stay of proceedings, CJ §12-701.
Circuit court or superior court, CJ §12-502.
Court of special appeals.
Jurisdiction, CJ §12-308.
Review of decisions by court of appeals, CJ §12-201.
Exceptions, CJ §12-202.
Special appeal to court, CJ §12-501.
Decision on law issues from orphans' court.
Stay of proceedings, CJ §12-701.
Jurisdiction.
Court of special appeals, CJ §12-308.
Residual parental rights and responsibilities.
Defined, CJ §3-8A-01.
Stay of proceedings.
Appeals from orphans' court, CJ §12-701.
Outdoor advertising.
Rejection of application for permit, TR §8-720.
Parole and probation.
Parole release hearing.
Review of recommendation of hearing examiner by commission, COR §7-306.
Parole revocation, COR §7-401.
Parties.
Alternative references to parties, AppRev Rule 8-111.
Appellants generally. See within this heading, "Appellants."
Appellees generally. See within this heading, "Appellees."
Formal designation.
No prior appellate decision, AppRev Rule 8-111.
Prior appellate decision, AppRev Rule 8-111.
Joinder not required, AppRev Rule 8-401.
Substitution of parties, AppRev Rule 8-401.
Paternity proceedings, FL §5-1044.
Peace orders.
Circuit court appeals, CJ §3-1506.
Modification, issuance or stay pending appeal, AppRevCir Rule 7-112.
Permits.
Joint and consolidated hearings.
Administrative and judicial review of final action, SG §11-523.
Applicant's appeal of extension of deadline, SG §11-522.
Pesticides.
Denial of registration, AG §5-107.
Pharmacists and pharmacies.
Disciplinary proceedings.
Administrative and judicial review, HO §12-316.

APPEALS —Cont'd
Pharmacists and pharmacies —Cont'd
Pharmacy permits.
Administrative and judicial review, HO §12-412.
Physical therapists.
Administrative and judicial review, HO §13-318.
Physicians.
Administrative and judicial review, HO §14-408.
Pilots.
Licenses.
Denial, revocation or suspension or reprimand of licensee.
Judicial review, BOP §11-411.
Plumbers.
Licenses.
Denial, revocation or suspension or reprimand of licensee.
Judicial review, BOP §12-314.
Podiatrists.
Administrative and judicial review, HO §16-315.
Poor.
Briefs.
Costs paid by state, AppRev Rule 8-505.
Post conviction procedure.
Appeal of final order, CP §7-109.
Application for leave to appeal, AppRev Rule 8-204.
Effect of remedy on appeals, CP §7-107.
Postmortem examiners.
Autopsies by medical examiners.
Refusal to correct findings and conclusions, HG §5-310.
Postponement of cases, AppRev Rule 8-521.
Potatoes.
Seed inspections.
Stop-sale order, AG §9-304.
Poultry products inspection.
Adulterated products.
Condemnation, AG §4-205.
Refusal or withdrawal of inspection, AG §4-212.
Precious metals and gem dealers.
License disciplinary hearings, BR §12-211.
Private detectives.
Secretary of state police.
Judicial review of decisions, BOP §13-206.
Procurement.
Architectural and engineering services.
Recommendations by selection board to board of public works, SF §13-316.
Construction contracts.
Prompt payment of subcontractors, SF §15-226.
Dispute resolution.
Appeals board.
See PROCUREMENT.
Property and casualty insurance guaranty corporation.
Action or order of the commissioner, IN §9-308.
Property taxes.
Appeal procedure, TP §§14-501 to 14-515.
See PROPERTY TAXES.
Psychologists.
Disciplinary proceedings.
Administrative and judicial review, HO §18-316.
Public assistance program.
From local unit to state department, 88A §74.
Public defender.
Briefs.
Indigent persons.
Reproduction of briefs to be filed under supervision of public defender, AppRev Rule 8-505.

APPEALS —Cont'd
Public defender —Cont'd
Denial of public defender representation.
Fees and costs of appeal paid by state, Rule
1-325.
Public ethics.
Complaints.
Decision of commission, SG §15-406.
Judicial relief available, SG §15-902.
Public safety.
Death in the line of duty, PS §1-202.
Public service commission proceedings.
Judicial review of orders and decisions of
commissions, PUC §§3-201 to 3-209.
See PUBLIC SERVICE COMMISSION.
Orders of commissioner or hearing examiner, PUC
§3-113.
Public works contracts.
Wages.
Noncompliance by public body.
Right of appeal, SF §17-223.
Quarantine.
Catastrophic health emergency disease
surveillance and response program.
Secretary's quarantine directive, HG §18-906.
Questions of law.
Uniform certification of questions of law act, CJ
§§12-601 to 12-613.
See CERTIFIED QUESTIONS OF LAW.
Radiation.
Final decisions of department.
Judicial review, EN §8-508.
Real estate appraisers and home inspectors.
Judicial review of commission decision generally,
BOP §16-218.
Real estate brokers.
Real estate commission.
Judicial review of decisions.
Contested cases, BOP §17-329.
Real estate conservation areas.
Suspension of advertising and solicitation, BOP
§17-522.
Rebuttal.
Oral arguments, AppRev Rule 8-522.
Receivers.
Answer of party appealing.
Must be filed first, CJ §12-303.
Appointment of a receiver, CJ §12-303.
Reconsideration, AppRev Rule 8-605.
Record on appeal.
Adoption proceedings.
Access to record, AppRev Rule 8-122.
Confidentiality, AppRev Rule 8-122.
Transmittal of record, AppRev Rule 8-122.
Clerk of court.
Duties, AppRev Rule 8-113.
Lower court clerk, AppRev Rule 8-413.
Contents, AppRev Rule 8-413.
Correction of record.
Authority of appellate court, AppRev Rule
8-414.
Motion.
Contents of motion, AppRev Rule 8-414.
Oral argument.
Not to be postponed to correct record, AppRev
Rule 8-414.
Order to correct record, AppRev Rule 8-414.
Unnecessary correction.
Costs withheld, AppRev Rule 8-607.
Court of appeals.
Capital cases.
Transcript in lieu of record extract, AppRev
Rule 8-306.

APPEALS —Cont'd
Record on appeal —Cont'd
Court of appeals —Cont'd
Certification from court of special appeals.
Record extract and brief, AppRev Rule 8-304.
Extract.
Review of case from court of special appeals,
AppRev Rule 8-501.
Time for transmitting, AppRev Rule 8-412.
Court of special appeals.
Application for leave to appeal.
Record on application, AppRev Rule 8-204.
Extract.
Court of appeals review of case from court of
special appeals, AppRev Rule 8-501.
Notice of appeal procedure.
Transmittal of record, AppRev Rule 8-201.
Time for transmitting, AppRev Rule 8-412.
Criminal investigations.
Access to record, AppRev Rule 8-123.
Transmittal of record, AppRev Rule 8-123.
Docketing of appeals.
Separate appeals on same record, AppRev Rule
8-421.
Extract, AppRev Rule 8-501.
Capital cases.
Transcript in lieu of record extract, AppRev
Rule 8-306.
Certification from court of special appeals,
AppRev Rule 8-304.
Form of court papers, AppRev Rule 8-112.
Form, AppRev Rule 8-413.
Guardianship proceedings.
Access to record, AppRev Rule 8-122.
Confidentiality, AppRev Rule 8-122.
Transmittal of record, AppRev Rule 8-122.
Juvenile causes, AppRev Rule 8-121.
Removal to state archives, AppRev Rule 8-113.
Request by governor.
Criminal cases, AppRev Rule 8-113.
Statement of case in lieu of entire record, AppRev
Rule 8-413.
Time for transmitting, AppRev Rule 8-412.
Transmission of mandate and record, AppRev
Rule 8-606.
When record transmitted.
Determination of when transmittal has
occurred, AppRev Rule 8-412.
Records.
Access to public records.
Corrections of public record.
Administrative and judicial review, SG
§10-625.
Reinsurance intermediaries.
Judicial review of commissioner's order, IN
§8-511.
**Release of person found not criminally
responsible,** CP §3-118.
Application for release, CP §3-119.
By health department, CP §3-120.
Revocation of conditional release for violations, CP
§3-121.
Remands, AppRev Rule 8-604.
Residential child care program administrators.
Certification.
Issuance or renewal of certificate, HO §20-308.
Disciplinary proceedings, HO §20-315.
Sales finance companies.
Licenses.
Right to appeal from decision of commissioner,
FI §11-416.

APPEALS —Cont'd
Sanitary commissions.
Service areas.
Appeal from sanitary commission, EN §9-649.
Decision of sanitary commission, EN §9-652.
Savings and loan associations.
Conversions.
Federally-chartered conversion to state chartered association.
Refusal of application to convert, FI §9-623.
Mutual association conversion to capital stock association, FI §9-609.
Corporations.
Orders of division director, FI §9-208.
Orders of division director, FI §8-403.
Scope of judicial review, FI §9-915.
Scheduling conferences, AppRev Rule 8-206.
Schools.
Charter schools.
Decision on application, ED §9-104.
Children with disabilities.
Review of placement decision, ED §8-413.
Counties.
Out-of-county living arrangements.
Education of children in.
Determinations as to funding, ED §4-122.
Expulsion of pupils.
From superintendent of schools to local boards of education, ED §7-305.
Maryland school for the blind.
Admission and dismissal of students.
Review of decisions, ED §8-307.
Superintendent of schools.
Subject to appeal to county board and state board of education, ED §4-205.
Suspension of students, ED §7-305.
Scope of review, AppRev Rule 8-131.
Securities.
Securities act.
Judicial review of orders, CA §11-704.
Security systems technicians.
Disciplinary action against licensees.
Adverse agency decision, BOP §18-311.
Registration.
Final decisions of secretary, BOP §18-3A-11.
Sediment control.
Final decisions of department.
Judicial review, EN §4-115.
Sentence and punishment.
Capital cases.
Advice of judge, Crim Rule 4-343.
De novo appeals.
Limitations on increases, CJ §12-702.
More severe sentence imposed following de novo appeal, CJ §12-702.
En banc review, Crim Rule 4-352.
Fines.
Disposition upon appeals, CJ §7-206.
Non-capital cases.
Advice to defendant, Crim Rule 4-342.
Remand for sentence.
Deduction of time already served, CJ §12-702.
Limitations on increases, CJ §12-702.
Review of criminal sentences, CP §§8-101 to 8-109.
See SENTENCE AND PUNISHMENT.
Service of process.
Briefs, AppRev Rule 8-502.
Court of special appeals.
Application for leave to appeal, AppRev Rule 8-204.

APPEALS —Cont'd
Service of process —Cont'd
Transcripts.
Filing and service, AppRev Rule 8-411.
Social services.
Public assistance program.
Appeal from local unit to state department, 88A §74.
Social workers.
Disciplinary proceedings.
Administrative and judicial review, HO §19-313.
State.
Costs.
Assessment of costs against state, AppRev Rule 8-607.
Right of state to appeal, CJ §12-302.
State lottery.
Denials of license, SG §9-112.
Statement of case in lieu of entire record, AppRev Rule 8-413.
State personnel.
Grievance procedures, SPP §§12-101 to 12-405.
See GRIEVANCE PROCEDURES.
Stationary engineers.
Disciplinary actions, BOP §6.5-316.
Stays.
Court of appeals.
Certiorari.
Petition for writ.
Stay of judgment of court of special appeals or of circuit court, AppRev Rule 8-303.
Enforcement of judgment, AppRev Rule 8-422.
Juvenile court, CJ §12-701.
Orphans' court, CJ §12-701.
Stormwater management.
Final decisions of department.
Judicial review, EN §4-214.
Supersedeas bond.
Amount, AppRev Rule 8-423.
Conditions, AppRev Rule 8-423.
Disposition of property.
Amount of bond, AppRev Rule 8-423.
Money judgment not otherwise secured.
Amount of bond, AppRev Rule 8-423.
Support and maintenance.
Driving privileges.
Suspension for child support arrearages, FL §10-119; TR §16-203.
Income tax refund intercept, FL §10-113.
Surveys and surveyors.
State board for professional land surveyors.
Judicial review of actions, BOP §15-210.
Taxation.
Appeal to tax court.
General provisions.
See TAX COURT.
Court of special appeals.
Appeals from orphans' court, TG §13-511.
Definitions, TG §13-501.
Motor fuel tax.
Licenses.
Cancellation, TG §9-332.
Orphans' court.
Appeals to court of special appeals, TG §13-511.
Property owners' bill of rights.
Rights enumerated, TP §1-402.
Taxicabs or for-hire driving services.
Denial of for-hire driver's license, PUC §10-105.
Suspension or revocation of license or imposition of civil penalty, PUC §10-110.
Terms of court, AppRev Rule 8-102.

APPEALS —Cont'd
Time.
Draining lands.
Circuit court, 25 §80.
Transcripts.
Death penalty cases.
Transcript in lieu of record extract, AppRev
Rule 8-306.
Filing, AppRev Rule 8-411.
Ordering transcript, AppRev Rule 8-411.
Time for ordering, AppRev Rule 8-411.
Service, AppRev Rule 8-411.
Transfer of appeals.
Improperly taken appeals, AppRev Rule 8-132.
Transportation department.
Board of review, TR §§2-501 to 2-506.
See TRANSPORTATION DEPARTMENT.
Human resources management system.
Employee grievance procedures, TR §2-103.4.
Trial.
En banc review.
Circuit courts, CivProCir Rule 2-551.
Truancy reduction pilot program, CJ §3-8C-10.
Unemployment compensation.
See UNEMPLOYMENT COMPENSATION.
Uniform certification of questions of law act.
Court of appeals.
Certification procedure.
Uniform act. See within this heading, "Court
of appeals."
United States courts.
Certification of questions of law from federal
courts, AppRev Rule 8-305.
Unreported opinions, Rule 1-104.
Veterinarians.
Licenses.
Suspension or revocation, AG §2-311.
Victims of crime.
Criminal injuries compensation board.
Decision of secretary, CP §11-815.
Denial of victim's rights, CP §11-103.
Notoriety of crimes contracts.
Adverse attorney general decision, CP §11-630.
Representation by victim's representative, CP
§11-103.
Volunteer company assistance fund.
Requests for money, PS §8-204.
Voter registration.
Administrative complaint by aggrieved person, EL
§3-602.
Washington suburban sanitary district.
Board of ethics.
Judicial review of adverse decisions, 29
§12-105.1.
Commission.
Pretreatment program.
Judicial review of final agency decision, 29
§18-104.3.
Water and sewer systems, EN §9-263.
Water pollution.
Administrative procedure.
Application of act, EN §9-340.
Persons aggrieved by decisions of department, EN
§9-340.
Water quality laboratories, EN §9-1018.
Watershed associations.
Right of appeal, 25 §199.
Waterworks and waste systems operators.
Disciplinary proceedings.
Administrative and judicial review, EN §12-310.

APPEALS —Cont'd
Well drillers.
Disciplinary actions.
Judicial review, EN §13-312.
Wetlands.
Judicial review of orders, EN §16-503.
Private wetlands.
Judicial appeal from decision of secretary, EN
§16-308.
Payment of court costs, EN §16-309.
Regulation or designation of person's land as
wetland, EN §16-306.
State wetlands.
Dredging or filling, EN §16-204.
Whistleblower protection, SPP §5-310.
Wholesome meat act.
Condemnation of carcasses, AG §4-108.
Workers' compensation.
See WORKERS' COMPENSATION.
Zoning.
Appeals to court.
See ZONING.
Board of appeals.
See ZONING.
Historic area zoning.
Appeal from decision of commission, 66B §8.15.
Jurisdiction.
Court of special appeals, CJ §12-308.

APPEALS FROM DISTRICT COURT.
Appearances.
Attorneys at law, AppRevCir Rule 7-107.
Applicability of rules, AppRevCir Rule 7-101;
Rule 1-101.
Attorneys at law.
Appearance of counsel, AppRevCir Rule 7-107.
**Circuit court of county in which judgment
entered.**
Where appeal taken, CJ §12-403.
Commitment for nonpayment of fine, CJ
§12-404.
Contempt cases, CJ §12-402.
Costs.
Generally, AppRevCir Rule 7-116.
Preparation of transcript, AppRevCir Rule 7-103.
State departments and agencies, AppRevCir Rule
7-116.
De novo hearings, CJ §12-401.
Application of appellate court procedure,
AppRevCir Rule 7-112.
Mode of appeal, AppRevCir Rule 7-102.
Procedure, AppRevCir Rule 7-112.
Dismissal of appeal.
By appellate court, AppRevCir Rule 7-114.
On motion, AppRevCir Rule 7-114.
**Disposition by appellate court in appeals
decided on record,** AppRevCir Rule 7-113.
Dockets.
Maintaining, AppRevCir Rule 7-110.
Record on appeal.
Contents of record, AppRevCir Rule 7-109.
Separate appeals on same record, AppRevCir Rule
7-110.
Evidence.
Applicability of rules, AppRevCir Rule 7-112.
Record on appeal.
Statement of case in lieu of entire record,
AppRevCir Rule 7-109.
Executions.
Stay of execution, AppRevCir Rule 7-111.

APPEALS FROM DISTRICT COURT —Cont'd
Fees.
Filing fees, AppRevCir Rule 7-103.
Filing.
Fees, AppRevCir Rule 7-103.
Fines.
Commitment for nonpayment, CJ §12-404.
Hearings.
De novo hearings, CJ §12-401.
Procedure, AppRevCir Rule 7-112.
Joinder, AppRevCir Rule 7-106.
Jury.
Criminal appeals.
Right to jury trial, CJ §12-401.
Memoranda.
Cases decided on record.
Filing, AppRevCir Rule 7-113.
Style and contents of memoranda, AppRevCir
Rule 7-113.
Modes of appeal, AppRevCir Rule 7-102.
Montgomery county.
Appeals from District Court sitting as juvenile
court, CJ §12-403.
Municipal infractions, CJ §12-401.
Notice of appeal.
Filing, AppRevCir Rule 7-103.
Striking by District Court, AppRevCir Rule 7-105.
Time for filing, AppRevCir Rule 7-104.
On the record, AppRevCir Rule 7-102.
Opinions, AppRevCir Rule 7-113.
Oral argument, AppRevCir Rule 7-113.
Parties.
Joinder, AppRevCir Rule 7-106.
Substitution, AppRevCir Rule 7-106.
Pleadings.
Record on appeal.
Statement of case in lieu of entire record,
AppRevCir Rule 7-109.
Record on appeal, CJ §12-401.
Contents, AppRevCir Rule 7-109.
Correction of error or omission in record,
AppRevCir Rule 7-109.
Costs.
Preparation of transcript, AppRevCir Rule
7-103.
Docket.
Entries.
Contents of record, AppRevCir Rule 7-109.
Separate appeals on same record, AppRevCir
Rule 7-110.
Error or omission in record.
Correction, AppRevCir Rule 7-109.
Evidence.
Statement of case in lieu of entire record,
AppRevCir Rule 7-109.
Heard on original papers, AppRevCir Rule 7-109.
Original papers.
Contents of record, AppRevCir Rule 7-109.
Return of record to lower court, AppRevCir Rule
7-115.
Statement of case in lieu of entire record,
AppRevCir Rule 7-109.
Time for transmitting.
Appellate court may shorten or extend time,
AppRevCir Rule 7-108.
Delay in transmitting due to mistake,
AppRevCir Rule 7-108.
Within 60 days, AppRevCir Rule 7-108.
Transcript of testimony.
Contents of record, AppRevCir Rule 7-109.
Filing, AppRevCir Rule 7-113.

APPEALS FROM DISTRICT COURT —Cont'd
Record on appeal —Cont'd
Transcript of testimony —Cont'd
Transcript instead of original papers when
lower court so orders, AppRevCir Rule
7-109.
Transmittal of record, AppRevCir Rule 7-103.
When deemed transmitted in proper time,
AppRevCir Rule 7-108.
Right to appeal.
General provisions, CJ §12-401.
Scope of review.
Review upon law and evidence, AppRevCir Rule
7-113.
Scope of rules, AppRevCir Rule 7-101.
State departments and agencies.
Costs against state agency, AppRevCir Rule
7-116.
Stays, AppRevCir Rule 7-111.
Time, CJ §12-401.
Filing.
Civil actions.
Postjudgment motions, AppRevCir Rule
7-104.
Criminal actions.
Motion for new trial, AppRevCir Rule 7-104.
Date of entry, AppRevCir Rule 7-104.
Notice of appeal, AppRevCir Rule 7-104.
Within thirty days, AppRevCir Rule 7-104.
Record on appeal.
Transmitting, AppRevCir Rule 7-108.
Transcript of testimony.
Record on appeal.
Contents of record, AppRevCir Rule 7-109.
Filing, AppRevCir Rule 7-113.
Transcript instead of original papers when
lower court so orders, AppRevCir Rule
7-109.
Trial.
De novo, CJ §12-401.
Withdrawal of appeal, AppRevCir Rule 7-112.

APPEARANCE.
Actions against state officers and employees.
Attorney general, SG §12-304.
Appeals.
Appearance of counsel, AppRev Rule 8-402.
Arrest.
Initial appearance of defendant.
Circuit court following arrest or summons, Crim
Rule 4-213.
District Court following arrest, Crim Rule
4-213.
Attorneys at law.
Appeals.
Appearance of counsel, AppRev Rule 8-402.
Circuit courts, CivProCir Rule 2-131.
Defense counsel.
Criminal cases, Crim Rule 4-214.
District Court, CivProDist Rule 3-131.
First appearance in court without counsel.
Waiver of counsel in criminal cases, Crim Rule
4-215.
Initial appearance of defendant.
District Court following arrest.
Advice of right to counsel, Crim Rule 4-213.
Sale of law practice.
Effect upon counsel of record, ProfCond Rule
1.17.
Striking appearances.
Circuit courts, CivProCir Rule 2-132.

APPEARANCE —Cont'd
Attorneys at law —Cont'd
Striking appearances —Cont'd
Defense counsel in criminal cases, Crim Rule 4-214.
District Court, CivProDist Rule 3-132.
Automatic termination of appearance.
Circuit courts, CivProCir Rule 2-132.
District Court, CivProDist Rule 3-132.
Catastrophic health emergency.
Contest of isolation or quarantine.
Appearance at hearing, SpecPro Rule 15-1104.
Charging documents.
Initial appearance of defendant.
District Court following arrest.
Advice of charges, Crim Rule 4-213.
Child custody proceedings.
Uniform child custody jurisdiction and enforcement act, FL §9.5-210.
Order to appear on filing of petition to enforce, FL §9.5-308.
Clerks.
Initial appearance of defendant.
Transfer of papers by clerk, Crim Rule 4-213.
Corporations.
Attorney requirement, CivProCir Rule 2-131; CivProDist Rule 3-131.
Exceptions to attorney requirement, BOP §10-206.
Criminal cases.
Return of summons as appearance, CP §4-203.
Criminal procedure.
Corporations.
Return of summons as appearance, CP §4-203.
Initial appearance of defendant.
Circuit court following arrest or summons, Crim Rule 4-213.
District Court following arrest or summons, Crim Rule 4-213.
Preliminary hearing, right to request, advised of, CP §4-103.
Limited liability companies.
Return of summons as appearance, CP §4-203.
Defendants.
Initial appearance of defendant, Crim Rule 4-213.
Discrimination.
Human relations commission.
Hearings, 49B §11.
Effect.
Circuit courts, CivProCir Rule 2-131.
District Court, CivProDist Rule 3-131.
Emergency management.
Failure to appear.
Emergency management service workers or persons suffering injury or damage, PS §14-208.
Entry of appearance.
Corporations.
Attorney requirement, CivProCir Rule 2-131; CivProDist Rule 3-131.
Exceptions to attorney requirement, BOP §10-206.
How entered.
Circuit courts, CivProCir Rule 2-131.
Executors and administrators.
Settlement of decedents' estates.
Attorneys at law.
Entry of appearance, Estates Rule 6-132.
Registers of wills.
Appointment of personal representative.
Presence before register not required, Estates Rule 6-131.

APPEARANCE —Cont'd
Executors and administrators —Cont'd
Settlement of decedents' estates —Cont'd
Special appearances abolished, Estates Rule 6-132.
How appearance entered.
District Court, CivProDist Rule 3-131.
Initial appearance of defendant, Crim Rule 4-213.
Preliminary hearing, right to request, advised of, CP §4-103.
Insurance.
Hearing.
Right to appear and present evidence, IN §2-213.
Juvenile causes.
Right to counsel.
Out-of-state attorney, Juv Rule 11-106.
Limited liability companies.
Criminal cases.
Return of summons as appearance, CP §4-203.
Maryland-national capital park and planning commission.
Citation issued for misdemeanor violation.
Notice to appear, promise to appear, failure to appear, 28 §2-120.1.
Motions.
Striking of attorney's appearance.
Circuit courts, CivProCir Rule 2-132.
District Court, CivProDist Rule 3-132.
Motor vehicles.
Commissioner.
Before commissioner having jurisdiction, TR §26-401.
Notice.
Striking of attorney's appearance.
Circuit courts, CivProCir Rule 2-132.
District Court, CivProDist Rule 3-132.
Parole commission hearings.
Failure to appear, COR §7-205.
Preliminary hearing.
Advised of right to request.
At initial appearance of defendant, CP §4-103.
Initial appearance of defendant, Crim Rule 4-213.
Pretrial release.
Initial appearance of defendant.
Determination of pretrial release, Crim Rule 4-213.
Proper person.
Circuit courts, CivProCir Rule 2-131.
District Court, CivProDist Rule 3-131.
Public buildings and grounds.
Watershed property.
Citation for offenses, NR §8-2003.
Security systems technicians.
Disciplinary action against licensees.
Failure or refusal to appear, BOP §18-310.
Striking of attorney's appearance.
Circuit courts, CivProCir Rule 2-132.
District Court, CivProDist Rule 3-132.
Summons and process.
Initial appearance of defendant.
Circuit court following arrest or summons, Crim Rule 4-213.
District Court following summons, Crim Rule 4-213.
Termination of appearance.
Automatic termination.
District Court, CivProDist Rule 3-132.

APPELLATE JUDICIAL CIRCUITS, MD Const Art IV §14.

APPLE CIDER.
Home consumption.
Manufacture without license, 2B §1-201.

APPLES.
Acts prohibited.
Generally, AG §10-805.
Appeals.
Stop-sale order, AG §10-802.
Citation of subtitle, AG §10-807.
Definitions.
Apple grade law, AG §10-801.
Enforcement of subtitle.
Injunction, AG §10-806.
Grades.
Standards of grades, AG §10-803.
Injunctions.
Enforcement of subtitle, AG §10-806.
Labels.
Packages, AG §10-804.
Marking and labeling packages, AG §10-804.
Packages.
Closed packages.
Defined, AG §10-801.
Sale, etc., of apples in closed containers.
Except as provided in subtitle prohibited, AG §10-805.
Information required on packages, AG §10-804.
Labeling and marking, AG §10-804.
Used packages.
Markings, AG §10-804.
Prohibited acts.
Generally, AG §10-805.
Right of entry.
Examinations, AG §10-802.
Sales.
Closed containers, AG §10-805.
Stop-sale orders.
Appeals, AG §10-802.
Issuance, AG §10-802.
Sale after issuance, AG §10-805.
Standards.
Grades, AG §10-803.
Stop-sale.
Orders, AG §10-802.
Subtitle.
Citation, AG §10-807.
Enforcement, AG §10-806.
Weights and measures.
General provisions.
See WEIGHTS AND MEASURES.

APPLIANCES.
Consumer protection.
See CONSUMER PROTECTION.
Electrical consumer products.
Unfair or deceptive trade practices, CL §13-308.
Energy start efficiency standards.
Sales and use tax exemptions, TG §11-226.
Home appliances.
Unfair or deceptive trade practices.
Bill of costs of repairing, CL §13-307.

APPORTIONMENT.
Congress, US Const Art I §§2, 3; Amds 14, 17.
General assembly.
House of delegates.
Representation, MD Const Art III §5.
Plan for legislative districting and apportionment, MD Const Art III §5.
Taxation.
Direct taxes, US Const Art I §§2, 9; Amd 16.

APPRAISALS.
Appraisers.
Decedents' estates.
General provisions, ET §§2-301 to 2-303.
See DECEDENTS' ESTATES.
Judicial sales.
Private sale.
Appraisal required, PropSales Rule 14-303.
Receivers.
Compensation and fees, Receivers Rule 13-105.
Conflicts of interest, Receivers Rule 13-303.
Employment, Receivers Rule 13-301.
Banks and trust companies.
Borrower's right to copy of appraisal made for lender, RP §14-104.1.
Commissioner of financial regulation.
Real estate appraisal policies and procedures.
Duty to develop and implement, FI §2-110.
Merger or consolidation.
Stock.
Expense of appraisal, FI §3-720.
Corporations.
Consolidation, merger and other transfers of property.
Determination of fair value for objecting stockholders.
See CORPORATIONS.
Distress for rent.
General provisions.
See DISTRESS FOR RENT.
Drug asset forfeiture.
Bond in lieu of forfeiture.
Appraisal of motor vehicle, CP §12-208.
Eminent domain.
Real estate appraisers.
Damages to or destruction of property, RP §12-111.
Right of entry.
Order to permit entry, RP §12-111.
Stakes and markers.
Obliterating, damaging or removing, RP §12-111.
Executions.
Sheriffs.
Appraisal of property at time of levy, CJ §11-504.
General services department.
Public improvements.
Duties of department as to appraisals, SF §4-406.
Highways.
Sale of land no longer needed, TR §8-309.
Housing and community development.
Assisted housing preservation.
Protected actions, right of first purchase, HS §7-205.
Insurance examinations.
Valuation of real estate, IN §2-207.
Livestock.
Contagious and infectious diseases.
Animals to be destroyed, AG §3-107.
Buildings to be destroyed, AG §3-107.
Loans.
Borrower's right to copy of appraisal made for lender, RP §14-104.1.
Mortgages and deeds of trust.
Borrower's right to copy of appraisal made for lender, RP §14-104.1.
Real estate appraisers.
Generally, BOP §§16-101 to 16-802.
See REAL ESTATE APPRAISERS AND HOME INSPECTORS.

APPRAISALS —Cont'd
Real property.
  Borrower's right to copy of appraisal made for
      lender, RP §14-104.1.
  Insurance examinations.
    Valuation of real estate, IN §2-207.
Savings and loan associations.
  Borrower's right to copy of appraisal made for
      lender, RP §14-104.1.
  Division director.
    Real estate appraisal policies and procedures.
      Duty to develop and implement, FI §8-303.

APPRENTICES.
Barbers.
  Barbershops.
    Number of apprentices allowed, BOP §4-507.
    Practice limitations, BOP §4-404.
    Supervision, BOP §§4-507, 4-509.
  Definition of "apprentice barber," BOP §4-101.
  Prohibited acts.
    Serving apprenticeship without registration,
      BOP §4-603.
  Registration, BOP §§4-401 to 4-408.
  See BARBERS.
Cosmetologists.
  Defined, BOP §5-101.
  Registration.
    Students and apprentices, BOP §§5-401 to
      5-409.
    See COSMETOLOGISTS.
Fish and fisheries.
  Tidal fish licensee's apprenticeship permit, NR
      §4-701.1.
Labor and employment relations.
  Apprenticeship standards and on-the-job training
      activities, LE §§11-401 to 11-408.
    See LABOR AND EMPLOYMENT
      RELATIONS.
Morticians.
  See MORTICIANS.
Pilots.
  See PILOTS.
Plumbers.
  See PLUMBERS AND PLUMBING.
Public works.
  Contracts.
    Wages.
      See PUBLIC WORKS.
Veterans.
  Credit for apprenticeship, LE §3-708.
Workers' compensation.
  Apprenticeship training.
    Covered employees and employers, LE §9-229.

APPROPRIATIONS.
Abandoned property office, CL §17-102.
Accounts and accounting.
  Supervision of recipients.
    General provisions, SF §§7-401 to 7-405. See
      within this heading, "Supervision of
      recipients."
Affidavits.
  Warrants.
    Issuance of warrants to institutions and
      corporations, SF §7-221.
Appropriation act.
  Defined, SF §7-201.
  State operating budget.
    General provisions.
      See BUDGET AND MANAGEMENT.
Army, US Const Art I §8.

APPROPRIATIONS —Cont'd
Arts council.
  Governor's proposed general fund appropriation,
      SF §7-325.
Atlantic states marine fisheries commission,
    NR §4-305.
Audits.
  Supervision of recipients.
    Corporation serving elderly or developmentally
      disabled.
      State funded corporations subject to audit, SF
        §7-405.
    Social organizations.
      State aid to, SF §7-402.
  Warrants.
    Audit of bills, SF §7-218.
Automobile insurance fund.
  General fund appropriations prohibited, IN
      §20-302.
Aviation.
  Local appropriations, TR §5-105.
Balances.
  Unspent balances. See within this heading,
      "Unspent balances."
Baltimore City community college.
  State appropriation.
    Defined, ED §16-502.
    Distribution of state operating fund, ED
      §16-512.
Bills. See within this heading, "General assembly."
Budget and management.
  Budget bill.
    State operating budget.
      Enumeration of required appropriations, SF
        §7-108.
      University college.
        Lump sum appropriation, SF §7-111.
  General provisions.
    See BUDGET AND MANAGEMENT.
  State operating budget, SF §§7-101 to 7-122.
    See BUDGET AND MANAGEMENT.
Capital appropriations.
  General fund capital appropriations.
    Budgeting in operating budget, SF §7-122.
Catastrophic event account, SF §7-324.
Checks.
  Disbursements and expenditures, SF §7-227.
    Additional means for transfer of funds, SF
      §7-227.1.
    Undeliverable checks fund, SF §7-229.
    Unpresented checks fund, SF §7-230.
Cigarette restitution fund, SF §7-317.
Community colleges.
  See COMMUNITY COLLEGES.
Comptroller.
  Disbursements and expenditures.
    Checks.
      Undeliverable checks fund.
        Duties of comptroller, SF §7-229.
  Warrants.
    Issuance.
      Generally. See within this heading,
        "Warrants."
Congress, US Const Art I §§7, 9.
Contracts.
  Disbursements and expenditures.
    Restrictions on contracts, SF §7-237.
  Public contracts.
    Prohibited unless authorized by appropriation,
      31 §3.

APPROPRIATIONS —Cont'd
Contracts —Cont'd
Supervision of recipients.
Health and social welfare organizations.
Accounting standards, SF §7-403.
Counties.
Draining lands, 25 §73.
Farmers' cooperative demonstration work.
Authority to make, 25 §160.
Farm labor problem, 25 §21.
Soil conservation districts, 25 §22.
Dedicated purpose account, SF §7-310.
Deficiency appropriations.
Universities and colleges.
Tuition and fees for nonresident students, ED §16-310.
Definitions, SF §7-201.
Unspent balances.
Capital expenditures, SF §7-305.
Delmarva advisory council, 32B §1-111.
Deposit insurance fund corporation.
Policy of state, FI §10-116.
Development finance division.
Workforce housing grant program.
Distribution of appropriations, HS §4-1805.
Disbursements and expenditures.
Authority.
Who authorized, SF §7-226.
Balances.
Unspent balances, SF §§7-301 to 7-308. See within this heading, "Unspent balances."
Checks, SF §7-227.
Additional means for transfer of funds, SF §7-227.1.
Undeliverable checks fund, SF §7-229.
Unpresented checks fund, SF §7-230.
Contracts.
Prohibited acts as to, SF §7-237.
Current appropriation.
Disbursement in accordance with current appropriation, SF §7-205.
Lump sum appropriation, SF §7-207.
Expenditures before schedule approved prohibited, SF §7-233.
Department of transportation.
Restrictions on, SF §7-238.
Excess of appropriation.
Administrative actions restricted, SF §7-235.
Contracts.
Prohibited acts as to, SF §7-237.
Liability, SF §7-234.
Prohibited, SF §7-234.
Initial appropriation for program, SF §7-206.
Lump sum appropriations.
Prohibited acts, SF §7-233.
Schedule, SF §7-207.
Approval.
Expenditures before schedule approved prohibited, SF §7-233.
Programs.
Amendment.
Appropriation for executive branch program, SF §7-209.
Appropriation for judicial branch program, SF §7-208.1.
Appropriations for department of transportation programs, SF §7-211.
Legislative branch, SF §7-208.
Executive branch.
Amendment of appropriation for executive branch program, SF §7-209.

APPROPRIATIONS —Cont'd
Disbursements and expenditures —Cont'd
Programs —Cont'd
Higher education.
Institutions of higher education, SF §7-212.
Judicial branch.
Amendment of appropriation for judicial branch program, SF §7-208.1.
Legislative branch.
Amendment of appropriation, SF §7-208.
Transportation department.
Amendment of appropriations for transportation department programs, SF §7-211.
Universities and colleges.
Institutions of higher education, SF §7-212.
Prohibited acts.
Administrative actions.
Restrictions, SF §7-235.
Contracts, SF §7-237.
Department of transportation, SF §7-238.
Expenditures in excess of appropriation, SF §7-234.
Administrative actions which would result in, SF §7-235.
Contracts, SF §7-237.
Lump sum appropriations, SF §7-233.
Transportation department, SF §7-238.
Receipts, SF §7-228.
Reductions.
Governor, SF §7-213.
Requirement of appropriation, SF §7-202.
Schedules.
Amendment.
Restriction on budget amendments, SF §7-210.
Staff positions.
Creation of additional permanent staff positions.
Restrictions, SF §7-236.
State treasurer.
Authority for disbursements in accordance with warrants, SF §7-226.
Transportation department.
Restrictions on, SF §7-238.
Unspent balances, SF §§7-301 to 7-308. See within this heading, "Unspent balances."
Warrants.
Generally, SF §§7-216 to 7-223. See within this heading, "Warrants."
Draining lands.
Drainage districts.
By state, 25 §121H.
Economic development corporation.
Initial appropriation, 83A §5-211.
Economic development opportunities program account, SF §7-314.
Energy overcharge restitution fund, SF §7-315.
Expenditures.
Generally. See within this heading, "Disbursements and expenditures."
Unspent balances, SF §§7-301 to 7-308. See within this heading, "Unspent balances."
Fiscal year.
Use in appropriating money, SF §2-101.
Forests and parks.
Conservancy districts.
Acceptance and custody of federal appropriations, NR §5-609.
Wildlife areas.
Limitation upon, NR §5-1204.

APPROPRIATIONS —Cont'd
Funds.
Cigarette restitution fund, SF §7-317.
State reserve fund, SF §7-309.
General assembly.
Appropriation act.
Defined, SF §7-201.
Bills.
Disapproval of items by governor, MD Const Art
II §17.
Reconsideration by legislature, MD Const Art
II §17.
How made, MD Const Art III §52.
Invalidity of part not to affect all, MD Const Art
III §52.
Restriction as to referendum, MD Const Art XVI
§2.
Supplementary appropriation bill, MD Const
Art III §52.
Disbursements and expenditures.
Program.
Amendment of appropriation for legislative
branch program, SF §7-208.
General provisions, MD Const Art III §32.
Requirements, MD Const Art III §32.
Statement of receipts and expenditures, MD Const
Art III §32.
General fund capital appropriations.
Budgeting in operating budget, SF §7-122.
General services department.
Public buildings and grounds.
Maintenance, operation and protection.
Annapolis.
Appropriation for services provided by city
of Annapolis, SF §4-608.
Governor.
Bills.
Disapproval of items by governor, MD Const Art
II §17.
Submitted to general assembly, MD Const Art
III §52.
Disbursements and expenditures.
Programs.
Amendment of appropriation for executive
branch program, SF §7-209.
Reductions, SF §7-213.
Reduction of appropriations, SF §7-213.
Heritage conservation fund.
Sources, NR §5-1505.
**Housing and community development
department.**
Workforce housing grant program.
Distribution of appropriations, HS §4-1805.
Housing authorities, HS §12-312.
Insurance.
Automobile insurance fund.
General fund appropriations prohibited, IN
§20-302.
Legal mutual liability insurance society of
Maryland.
General fund appropriations, IN §24-103.
Life and health insurance guaranty corporation.
General fund appropriations prohibited, IN
§9-405.
Medical mutual liability insurance society of
Maryland.
General fund appropriations, IN §24-203.
Property and casualty insurance guaranty
corporation.
General fund appropriations prohibited, IN
§9-304.

APPROPRIATIONS —Cont'd
Insurance —Cont'd
Small employer health reinsurance pool.
General fund appropriations prohibited, IN
§15-1220.
Labor and employment relations.
Division of labor and industry, LE §2-107.
**Legal mutual liability insurance society of
Maryland.**
General fund appropriations, IN §24-103.
**Life and health insurance guaranty
corporation.**
General fund appropriations prohibited, IN
§9-405.
Lump sum appropriations.
Disbursements and expenditures.
Prohibited acts, SF §7-233.
Schedule, SF §7-207.
Approval.
Expenditures before schedule approved
prohibited, SF §7-233.
University of Maryland.
State operating budget.
Budget bill.
Lump sum appropriation for university
college, SF §7-111.
Maryland Conservation Corps.
Federal appropriations, NR §5-218.
Maryland food center authority, 41 §13-105.
Maryland housing rehabilitation program.
Request for appropriations, information included,
HS §4-913.
Maryland public art initiative.
Establishment of program, 83A §4-6A-01.
**Medical mutual liability insurance society of
Maryland.**
General fund appropriations, IN §24-203.
Militia, PS §13-204.
Morgan State University.
Investment.
Income from investment of appropriations to
university, ED §14-105.
Mortgage originators.
Implementation of provisions, FI §11-611.
Motor vehicle insurance.
Automobile insurance fund.
General fund appropriations prohibited, IN
§20-302.
Municipal corporations.
General provisions, 23A §2.
Notice.
Unspent balances, SF §7-301.
Reversion, SF §7-308.
Nuclear compact.
Necessity for appropriation before supplementary
agreement becomes effective, 41 §16-113.
Penalties.
Disbursements and expenditures.
Contracts.
Restrictions on contracts.
Violations, SF §7-237.
Programs.
Amendment, SF §7-206.
Appropriation for executive branch program, SF
§7-209.
Department of transportation programs, SF
§7-211.
Higher education.
Appropriations for institution of higher
education program, SF §7-212.
Judicial branch program, SF §7-208.1.

APPROPRIATIONS —Cont'd
Programs —Cont'd
Amendment —Cont'd
Legislative branch, SF §7-208.
Defined, SF §7-201.
Increase or reduction in appropriation, SF §7-206.
Initial appropriation, SF §7-206.
Property and casualty insurance guaranty corporation.
General fund appropriations prohibited, IN §9-304.
Public debt.
Debt service.
Annuity bond fund, SF §8-132.
Required appropriation, 31 §3.
Public defender, 27A §13.
Public recreation and parks.
General provisions, 25 §224.
Public school construction fund, SF §7-326.
Railroad safety and health.
Cost of administration, LE §5.5-106.
Receipts.
Disbursements and expenditures, SF §7-228.
Recipients.
Supervision, SF §§7-401 to 7-405. See within this heading, "Supervision of recipients."
Records.
Supervision of recipients.
Health and social welfare organizations.
Financial records, SF §7-403.
Warrants, SF §7-223.
Reports.
Disbursements and expenditures.
Programs.
Institutions of higher education.
Governing board, SF §7-212.
Staff positions.
Creation of additional permanent staff positions, SF §7-236.
Supervision of recipients.
Providers of care.
Review of accounts, SF §7-404.
Social organizations.
State aid to, SF §7-402.
Unspent appropriations.
Pilot program for retaining, SF §7-302.
Requirements, MD Const Art III §32.
Disbursements, SF §7-202.
Rules and regulations.
Expenditures in excess of appropriation.
Restrictions on rules and regulations which would result in, SF §7-235.
Rural legacy program, NR §5-9A-09.
St. Mary's College of Maryland.
Investments.
Income from investment of appropriations, ED §14-405.
Schools.
Capital projects, ED §5-107.
Children with disabilities under the age of six.
Education and training, ED §8-411.
Failure to appropriate amount requested, ED §§5-103, 5-107.
Funds appropriated only for purpose of education, MD Const Art VIII §3.
Levy to meet appropriations, ED §5-104.
Maryland school for the blind.
Receipt and calculation of annual appropriation, ED §8-317.
School building construction aid program, ED §5-301.

APPROPRIATIONS —Cont'd
Small employer health reinsurance pool.
General fund appropriations prohibited, IN §15-1220.
Southern Maryland higher education center, ED §24-307.
Statement of receipts and expenditures, MD Const Art III §32.
State operating budget.
General provisions, SF §§7-101 to 7-122.
See BUDGET AND MANAGEMENT.
State reserve fund, SF §7-309.
Dedicated purpose account, SF §7-310.
Revenue stabilization account, SF §7-311.
State treasurer.
Disbursements and expenditures.
Authority for disbursements in accordance with warrants, SF §7-226.
Checks.
Undeliverable checks fund.
Duties of treasurer, SF §7-229.
Unpresented checks fund.
Duties of treasurer, SF §7-230.
Supervision of recipients.
Accounts and accounting.
Health and social welfare organizations.
Accounting standards, SF §7-403.
Providers of care.
Definitions, SF §7-404.
Review of accounts, SF §7-404.
Social organizations.
State aid to, SF §7-402.
Units of state government.
Accounting systems for, SF §7-401.
Recommendations of legislative auditor, SF §7-401.
Audits.
Corporations serving elderly or developmentally disabled.
State funded corporations subject to audit, SF §7-405.
Social organizations.
State aid to, SF §7-402.
Contracts.
Health and social welfare organizations.
Accounting standards, SF §7-403.
Health and social welfare organizations.
Accounting standards, SF §7-403.
Contracts.
Accounting standards, SF §7-403.
Definitions, SF §7-403.
Records.
Financial records, SF §7-403.
Legislative auditor.
Accounting systems for state units.
Recommendations, SF §7-401.
Records.
Health and social welfare organizations.
Financial records, SF §7-403.
Reports.
Providers of care.
Review of accounts, SF §7-404.
Social organizations.
State aid to, SF §7-402.
Social organizations, SF §7-402.
Transportation department.
Disbursements and expenditures.
Programs.
Amendment of appropriations for department of transportation program, SF §7-211.

APPROPRIATIONS —Cont'd
Transportation department —Cont'd
Disbursements and expenditures —Cont'd
Restrictions on department of transportation, SF §7-238.
Trees and shrubs.
Planting and care, NR §5-411.
Underground utility lines and facilities.
Local government appropriations for relocating utilities underground, PUC §4-209.
United States, US Const Art I §9.
Universities and colleges.
Deficiency appropriations.
Tuition and fees for nonresident students, ED §16-310.
Disbursements and expenditures.
Programs.
Institutions of higher education.
Reports, SF §7-212.
University of Maryland.
State operating budget.
Budget bill.
Lump sum appropriation for university college, SF §7-111.
Unspent balances.
Reversion of appropriations, SF §7-306.
University of Maryland.
State operating budget.
Budget bill.
Lump sum appropriation for university college, SF §7-111.
Unspent balances.
Amounts carried over for expenditure within unit, SF §7-302.
Capital expenditures.
Defined, SF §7-305.
Exemption from reversion, SF §7-305.
Dedicated money, SF §7-304.
Dedicated purpose account, SF §7-310.
Encumbered balances, SF §7-303.
General fund.
Reversion to, SF §§7-301 to 7-308. See within this subheading, "Reversion."
Institutions for higher education.
Reversion of appropriations, SF §7-306.
New or substantially renovated facility.
Reversion, SF §7-307.
Notice, SF §7-301.
Reversion, SF §7-308.
Scope of requirement, SF §7-301.
Pilot program for retaining unspent appropriations, SF §7-302.
Reports.
Pilot program for retaining unspent appropriations, SF §7-302.
Revenue stabilization account, SF §7-311.
Reversion.
Capital expenditures.
Exemption from reversion, SF §7-305.
Dedicated money not to revert, SF §7-304.
Encumbered balances not to revert, SF §7-303.
Generally, SF §7-302.
Institutions for higher education, SF §7-306.
New or substantially renovated facility, SF §7-307.
Notice, SF §7-308.
Requirement, SF §7-302.
State reserve fund, SF §7-309.
Universities and colleges.
Reversion of appropriations.
Institutions for higher education, SF §7-306.

APPROPRIATIONS —Cont'd
Vessels and boats.
Waterways improvement districts.
Waterways improvement fund, NR §8-707.
Volunteer company assistance fund, PS §§8-202, 8-205.
Warrants.
Abstracts.
Comptroller to keep abstract of each warrant, SF §7-223.
Advances.
Warrants for, SF §7-219.
Affidavits.
Issuance of warrants to institutions and corporations, SF §7-221.
Appropriation to be charged, SF §7-220.
Audit of bills, SF §7-218.
Bills.
Audit, SF §7-218.
Submission, SF §7-216.
Warrants for payment of, SF §7-219.
Blank warrants.
Prohibited, SF §7-219.
Charging of appropriation, SF §7-220.
Debtors.
Issuance of warrants to, SF §7-222.
Defined, SF §7-201.
Disbursements in accordance with warrants.
Authority, SF §7-226.
Excess receipts, SF §7-217.
Expenditures, SF §7-216.
Issuance, SF §7-219.
Debtors, SF §7-222.
Institutions and corporations.
Issuance of warrants to, SF §7-221.
Records, SF §7-223.
Unestimated receipts, SF §7-217.
Watershed associations.
Construction, operation, etc., of improvements.
By certain governmental divisions, 25 §210.

AQUACULTURE.
Advertising.
Oysters and clams.
Private oyster culture.
Leases, NR §4-11A-06.
Aquaculture review board and coordinating council.
Coordinating council, AG §10-1303.
Department of agriculture.
Unit within department, AG §2-106.
Review board, AG §10-1302.
Chesapeake Bay.
Defined, NR §4-11A-01.
Culture of oysters.
Private culture.
General provisions. See within this heading, "Oysters and clams."
Definitions, AG §10-1301; NR §4-11A-01.
Department of agriculture.
Aquaculture review board and coordinating council.
Unit of department, AG §2-106.
Powers and duties generally, AG §10-1301.
Department of natural resources.
Enforcement of laws, AG §10-1301.
Dredge.
Defined, NR §4-11A-01.
Fees.
Oysters and clams.
Culture of oysters.
Advertisement, NR §4-11A-06.

AQUACULTURE —Cont'd
Fees —Cont'd
Oysters and clams —Cont'd
Culture of oysters —Cont'd
Disposition, NR §4-11A-08.
Lease, NR §4-11A-06.
Privately owned artificial ponds or lakes.
Permit to establish and operate, NR §4-11A-20.
Fines.
Privately owned artificial ponds or lakes.
Operation without permit, NR §4-11A-20.
Game fish.
Breeding, propagating and selling.
Permits, NR §4-11A-21.
High schools.
Experimental oyster farming, NR §4-11A-04.
Income tax credit.
Aquaculture oyster floats.
Oysters grown under homeowner's pier, TG §10-724.
Inspections.
Aquaculture operations, NR §4-11A-02.
Lakes.
Privately owned artificial ponds or lakes.
Permit to establish and operate, NR §4-11A-20.
Regulations, NR §4-11A-20.
Leases.
Oysters and clams.
Culture of oysters.
Private culture. See within this heading, "Oysters and clams."
Legislative intent, AG §10-1301.
Licenses.
Live bait dealers.
Certain counties, NR §4-11A-19.
Oysters and clams.
Dredging.
Leased land, NR §4-11A-13.
Live bait dealers.
Licenses.
Certain counties, NR §4-11A-19.
Regulations, NR §4-11A-19.
Nonnative aquatic organisms.
Authority over, NR §4-205.1.
Oysters and clams.
Culture of oysters.
Drills.
Importing oyster drills prohibited, NR §4-11A-12.
Fees.
Disposition, NR §4-11A-08.
Kinds of oysters to be planted, NR §4-11A-12.
Private culture.
Advertisement, NR §4-11A-06.
Alteration or destruction of buoys, stakes, etc., NR §4-11A-15.
Drills.
Importation, NR §4-11A-12.
Exclusive rights, NR §4-11A-16.
Kinds of oysters permitted, NR §4-11A-12.
Leases.
Amount of land leased, NR §4-11A-05.
Application, NR §4-11A-06.
Appropriation of land without lease, NR §4-11A-15.
Area not leased, NR §4-11A-05.
Assignment, NR §4-11A-09.
Authorized, NR §4-11A-05.
Completion of lease, NR §4-11A-06.
Dredging licenses, NR §4-11A-13.
Fees, NR §4-11A-06.

AQUACULTURE —Cont'd
Oysters and clams —Cont'd
Culture of oysters —Cont'd
Private culture —Cont'd
Leases —Cont'd
Marking of leased land, NR §4-11A-10.
Power dredging, NR §4-11A-14.
Previously existing leases, NR §4-11A-05.
Protection of oysters on leased land, NR §4-11A-15.
Protest against lease, NR §4-11A-06.
Records, NR §4-11A-13.
Replanting, NR §4-11A-18.
Reports, NR §4-11A-13.
Rights of lessees, NR §4-11A-11.
Submerged lands, NR §4-11A-05.
Survey of area proposed for leasing, NR §4-11A-06.
Term, NR §4-11A-07.
Transfer, NR §4-11A-09.
Riparian owners.
Exclusive right, NR §4-11A-16.
Taking and catching.
Methods, NR §4-11A-13.
Unauthorized catching or destroying, NR §4-11A-15.
Unmarked land, NR §4-11A-10.
Wharf owner.
Exclusive right, NR §4-11A-16.
Propagation activities.
Areas for propagation research established, NR §4-11A-17.
Research.
Propagation activities, NR §4-11A-17.
Riparian or wharf owner, NR §4-11A-16.
Definitions, NR §4-11A-01.
Dredging.
Leased land.
Dredging license, NR §4-11A-13.
Power dredging, NR §4-11A-14.
Experimental oyster farming.
Public high schools, NR §4-11A-04.
Leases.
Culture of oysters.
Private culture. See within this subheading, "Culture of oysters."
Licenses.
Dredging.
Leased oyster beds, NR §4-11A-13.
Permits.
Breeding, propagating and selling of game fish, NR §4-11A-21.
Engaging in aquaculture, NR §4-11A-02.
Privately owned artificial ponds or lakes.
Establishment and operation, NR §4-11A-20.
Ponds.
Privately owned artificial ponds or lakes.
Permit to establish and operate, NR §4-11A-20.
Regulations, NR §4-11A-20.
Trespass to fish in private pond, NR §4-11A-22.
Research.
Oysters and clams.
Propagation activities.
Experimental propagation activities, NR §4-11A-17.
Rules and regulations.
Protection of wild stocks of fish, NR §4-11A-02.
Schools.
Oysters and clams.
High schools.
Experimental oyster farming, NR §4-11A-04.

AQUACULTURE —Cont'd
Tongs.
Defined, NR §4-11A-01.
Transgenic.
Defined, NR §4-11A-01.
Trespass.
Fishing in private ponds, NR §4-11A-22.
Universities and colleges.
Oysters and clams.
Culture of oysters.
Private culture.
Acquisition of submerged land for
educational and research purposes, NR
§4-11A-05.
University of Maryland.
Responsibility generally, AG §10-1301.
Wild stocks of fish.
Protection, NR §4-11A-02.

ARAB BOYCOTT.
Foreign discriminatory boycotts.
Generally, CL §§11-101 to 11-115.
See FOREIGN DISCRIMINATORY
BOYCOTTS.

ARBITRATION AND AWARD.
Actions.
Arbitration in pending court action, SpecPro Rule
15-101.
Court proceedings not provided for elsewhere,
SpecPro Rule 15-101.
Agreements. See within this heading, "Contracts."
Appeals.
Granting of stay of arbitration, CJ §12-303.
International commercial arbitration, CJ
§3-2B-08.
Applicability of subtitle.
Subtitle not retroactive, CJ §3-231.
Arbitrators.
Appointment, CJ §3-211.
Award. See within this heading, "Award of
arbitrators."
Deposition, CJ §3-218.
Determination.
Majority of arbitrators to make determination,
CJ §3-215.
Evidence.
Arbitrators not bound by technical rules of
evidence, CJ §3-214.
Expenses, CJ §3-221.
Fees, CJ §3-221.
Hearings.
Adjournment or postponement, CJ §3-213.
Determination of controversy, CJ §§3-213,
3-215.
Evidence, CJ §3-214.
Notice, CJ §3-213.
Parties.
Petition of party, CJ §3-213.
Rights of parties, CJ §3-214.
Rehearings, CJ §3-225.
Right to representation, CJ §3-216.
Time and place for hearings, CJ §3-213.
Transcript, CJ §3-220.
Oaths.
Authority to administer, CJ §3-217.
Powers.
Court appointed arbitrators, CJ §3-211.
Generally, CJ §3-212.
Subpoenas.
Authority to issue, CJ §3-217.

ARBITRATION AND AWARD —Cont'd
Attorneys at law.
Fees, CJ §3-221.
Right to be represented by attorney, CJ §3-216.
Award of arbitrators.
Applications.
Modification or correction, CJ §3-222.
Confirmation.
By court, CJ §§3-223, 3-226, 3-227.
Copies.
Delivery, CJ §3-219.
Correction, CJ §3-222.
By court, CJ §3-223.
Costs.
Award of costs, CJ §3-228.
Extension of time for parties, CJ §3-219.
Judgment.
Entry, CJ §3-228.
Modification, CJ §3-222.
By court, CJ §3-223.
Objections.
Waiver, CJ §3-219.
Rehearing before arbitrators, CJ §3-225.
Time for award, CJ §3-219.
Vacation of award.
Denial of petitions, CJ §3-226.
Grounds, CJ §3-224.
Petition, CJ §3-224.
Rehearing before arbitrators, CJ §3-225.
When award not to be vacated, CJ §3-224.
Writing required, CJ §3-219.
Baltimore City housing authority, HS §15-109.
Cemeteries.
Registration.
Complaints against registrants.
Binding arbitration, BR §5-311.
Circuit courts.
International commercial arbitration.
Jurisdiction, CJ §3-2B-04.
Citation of subtitle, CJ §3-234.
Commercial arbitration.
International commercial arbitration, CJ
§§3-2B-01 to 3-2B-09. See within this
heading, "International commercial
arbitration."
Complaints.
International commercial arbitration.
Filing, CJ §3-2B-05.
Consumer protection.
Division of consumer protection.
Arbitration of consumer disputes, CL §13-404.
Unit pricing.
Arbitration of disputes, CL §14-107.
Contempt.
Subpoenas.
Enforcement of subpoena, CJ §3-217.
Contracts.
Applicability of subtitle.
Subtitle not retroactive, CJ §3-231.
Court.
Determination of existence, CJ §3-207.
Denial of existence, CJ §3-207.
Employer and employees, CJ §3-206.
Jurisdiction.
Making up agreement confers jurisdiction, CJ
§3-202.
Validity, CJ §3-206.
Costs.
Awards, CJ §3-228.
Counties.
Bridges between counties.
Costs, 25 §45.

ARBITRATION AND AWARD —Cont'd

Courts.
Defined, CJ §3-201.
International commercial arbitration.
Intervention by courts, CJ §3-2B-07.
Jury.
Determination without jury, CJ §3-204.
Stay of proceedings, CJ §3-209.

Death.
Proceeding upon death of either party, CJ
§§3-229, 3-230.

Death taxes.
Interstate arbitration of death taxes, TG §§7-104
to 7-115.
See TAXATION.

Definitions, CJ §3-201.
Arbitration, ADR Rule 17-102.
International commercial arbitration, CJ
§3-2B-01.

Depositions.
Power of arbitrators, CJ §3-218.

Employers and employees.
Uniform arbitration act.
Inapplicable to agreements between employers
and employees, CJ §3-206.

Environmental service.
Authority of public service commission, NR
§3-128.

Executors and administrators.
Powers of personal representative, ET §7-401.

Fair distributorship act.
Dispute resolution, CL §11-1306.

Fees.
Arbitrators' expenses and fees, CJ §3-221.

Guardian.
Defined, CJ §3-201.

Health care malpractice claims.
See MALPRACTICE.

Hearings.
Arbitrators. See within this heading,
"Arbitrators."

Insane persons.
Incompetency of party, CJ §3-229.

Insurance.
Motor vehicle insurance, IN §19-514.
Uninsured motorist coverage, IN §19-509.

International commercial arbitration.
Appeals, CJ §3-2B-08.
Circuit courts.
Jurisdiction, CJ §3-2B-04.
Citation of subtitle, CJ §3-2B-09.
Complaints.
Filing, CJ §3-2B-05.
Definitions, CJ §3-2B-01.
Interpretation and construction.
Applicable laws, CJ §3-2B-03.
Construction of subtitle, CJ §3-2B-03.
Intervention by court, CJ §3-2B-07.
Jurisdiction.
Circuit courts, CJ §3-2B-04.
Jury.
Determination without jury.
Required, CJ §3-2B-07.
Purpose of subtitle, CJ §3-2B-02.
Security.
Grounds for requesting, CJ §3-2B-06.
Motion to vacate or modify order, CJ §3-2B-06.
Short title.
Title of subtitle, CJ §3-2B-09.

Interpretation and construction.
Construction of subtitle, CJ §3-232.

ARBITRATION AND AWARD —Cont'd

Interpretation and construction —Cont'd
International commercial arbitration, CJ
§3-2B-03.
Procedure subject to uniform arbitration act,
SpecPro Rule 15-101.
Subtitle not retroactive, CJ §3-231.

Judges.
Code of judicial conduct.
Judge not to act as arbitrator or mediator, CJA
Rule 16-813 Canon4.

Judgments and decrees.
Entry of judgment, CJ §3-228.

Judicial appointees.
Code of conduct for judicial appointees.
Arbitrator or mediator, service as, CJA Rule
16-814 Canon 4.

Jurisdiction.
Agreements.
Making of agreement confers jurisdiction, CJ
§3-202.
International commercial arbitration.
Circuit courts, CJ §3-2B-04.

Jury.
Determination without jury.
Required, CJ §3-204.
International commercial arbitration, CJ
§3-2B-07.

Labor and employment relations.
Collective bargaining generally, LE §§4-101 to
4-405.
See COLLECTIVE BARGAINING.
Labor dispute arbitration or mediation, LE
§§4-101 to 4-111.
See COLLECTIVE BARGAINING.

Malpractice.
Health care malpractice claims.
See MALPRACTICE.

**Montgomery County housing opportunities
commission.**
Collective bargaining, HS §16-310.
Mediators, HS §16-311.

Motor vehicle insurance, IN §19-514.
Uninsured motorist coverage, IN §19-509.

Notices.
Hearing by arbitrator, CJ §3-213.
Petitions, CJ §3-205.

Oaths.
Arbitrators.
Authority to administer, CJ §3-217.

Orders of court.
Refusal.
When order not to be refused, CJ §3-210.

Parties.
Death.
Proceedings upon death of either party, CJ
§§3-229, 3-230.
Disabilities.
Party under disability, CJ §3-229.
Incompetency of parties.
Effect, CJ §3-229.

Partnerships, revised act.
Authority of person winding up, CA §9A-803.

Personal representative.
Defined, CJ §3-201.

Petitions.
General provisions, CJ §3-205.
Initial petitions.
Venue, CJ §3-202.
Notice, CJ §3-205.
Refusal to arbitrate, CJ §3-207.

ARBITRATION AND AWARD —Cont'd
Petitions —Cont'd
  Stay of arbitration, CJ §3-208.
  Subsequent petitions.
    Venue, CJ §3-303.
Port authority.
  Baltimore City.
    Sale of property to authority, TR §6-402.
  Existing port facilities, TR §6-402.
Prince George's county community college.
  Collective bargaining impasse, ED §16-414.1.
Religion.
  Election.
    Trustees, CA §5-310.
Retroactive.
  Uniform arbitration act not retroactive, CJ §3-231.
Stay.
  Conditions, CJ §3-209.
  Petition to stay, CJ §3-208.
  Proceedings, CJ §3-209.
  When prohibited, CJ §3-210.
Subpoenas.
  Issuance.
    Authority of arbitrators, CJ §3-217.
Subtitle.
  Citation, CJ §3-234.
Summons and process.
  Subpoenas, CJ §3-217.
    Service of subpoenas, CJ §3-217.
Taxation.
  Death taxes.
    Interstate arbitration of death taxes, TG §§7-104 to 7-115.
    See TAXATION.
Transcripts.
  Proceedings, CJ §3-220.
Uniform arbitration act, CJ §§3-201 to 3-234.
  Court proceedings on awards in arbitrations not subject to Maryland uniform arbitration act, SpecPro Rule 15-101.
  Procedure to be governed by act, SpecPro Rule 15-101.
Uninsured motorist insurance coverage, IN §19-509.
Unit pricing, CL §14-107.
Vacation of award.
  Arbitrators, CJ §§3-224 to 3-226. See within this heading, "Award of arbitrators."
Venue.
  General provisions, CJ §3-203.
Waiver.
  Attorney at law.
    Right to be represented by attorney, CJ §3-216.
  Award.
    Waiver of objection, CJ §3-219.
Washington suburban sanitary district.
  Collective bargaining, 29 §11.5-108.

ARBOR DAY.
Schools.
  Appropriate exercises, ED §7-103.

ARBORISTS.
Tree experts.
  General provisions.
    See TREE EXPERTS.

ARCHAEOLOGICAL RESOURCES.
Archaeology advisory committee, SF §5A-336.
Archaeology office.
  Maryland historical trust, SF §5A-334.

ARCHAEOLOGICAL RESOURCES —Cont'd
Caves.
  Maryland historical trust, SF §5A-343.
Costs incurred in state project.
  Inclusion in budget bill for project, SF §7-114.1.
Criminal law and procedure.
  Maryland historical trust, violations, SF §5A-346.
Excavation.
  Maryland historical trust, SF §5A-342.
Hearings.
  Maryland historical trust.
    Enforcement actions, SF §5A-344.
Information about archeological sites, communication.
  Maryland historical trust, SF §5A-337.
Maryland historical trust, SF §§5A-333 to 5A-346.
  Archaeology advisory committee, SF §5A-336.
  Archaeology office.
    Duties, SF §5A-335.
  Caves, SF §5A-343.
  Costs for archaeological work, state projects, SF §5A-338.
  Enforcement actions.
    Hearings, SF §5A-344.
  Excavation, SF §5A-342.
  Information about archeological sites, communication, SF §5A-337.
  Objects and materials found on sites, SF §5A-339.
  Privately owned land, archaeological historic property on, SF §5A-345.
  Submerged archaeological historic property, SF §5A-340.
    Permits, SF §5A-341.
Maryland-Washington regional district.
  District councils.
    Power to regulate for the protection of archaeological sites, structures or districts, 28 §8-101.
Objects and materials found on sites.
  Maryland historical trust, SF §5A-339.
Permits.
  Submerged archaeological historic property, SF §5A-341.
Privately owned land, archaeological historic property on.
  Maryland historical trust, SF §5A-345.
Rural legacy program.
  Protection of archaeological areas, NR §5-9A-05.
Submerged archaeological historic property, SF §5A-340.
  Permits, SF §5A-341.

ARCHAEOLOGY ADVISORY COMMITTEE.
Maryland historical trust, SF §5A-336.

ARCHAEOLOGY OFFICE.
Maryland historical trust, SF §§5A-334, 5A-335.

ARCHITECTS.
Alteration or repair of existing building.
  When architect not required to be employed, BOP §3-103.
Appeals.
  State board of architects.
    Judicial review of board, BOP §3-210.
Arts council.
  General provisions, 83A §§4-601 to 4-609.
    See ARTS COUNCIL.
Board, BOP §§3-201 to 3-211. See within this heading, "State board of architects."

ARCHITECTS —Cont'd
Citation of act.
Short title, BOP §3-701.
Contact hours.
Defined, BOP §3-101.
Corporations.
Permits.
General provisions, BOP §§3-401 to 3-409. See
within this heading, "Permits."
Definitions, BOP §§3-101, 3-301, 3-401.
Design coordination.
Defined, BOP §3-101.
Practice by licensed architect, BOP §3-103.
Education.
Licenses.
Continuing education requirement, BOP
§3-309.1.
Qualifications of applicants, BOP §3-303.
Ethics.
Code of ethics.
Adoption by board, BOP §3-205.
Examinations.
Licenses, BOP §§3-305 to 3-306.
Fees.
Certification of permit holder, BOP §3-207.
Disposition of money collected, BOP §3-209.
Establishment of fees, BOP §3-209.
License fee defined, BOP §3-101.
Licenses.
Examination fee, BOP §3-304.
Reciprocity, BOP §3-306.
Reinstatement of expired license, BOP §3-310.
Renewal fee, BOP §3-309.
Permits, BOP §3-406.
Application fee, BOP §3-405.
Permit fee defined, BOP §3-101.
Renewal fee, BOP §3-408.
Fraud.
Licenses.
Denial, revocation or suspension or reprimand
of licensee.
Grounds, BOP §3-311.
Hearings.
Licenses.
Denial, revocation or suspension or reprimand
of licensee, BOP §3-313.
Immunity.
Personal liability beyond insurance, CJ §5-426.
Injunctions.
State board of architects.
Power to seek injunction, BOP §3-206.
Interior designers.
Provisions not to apply to licensed architects, BOP
§8-102.
Investigations.
State board of architects.
Powers, BOP §3-206.
Landscape architects, BOP §§9-101 to 9-702.
See LANDSCAPE ARCHITECTS.
Legislative declaration.
Purposes of provisions, BOP §3-102.
Licenses.
Applications, BOP §3-304.
Qualifications of applicants, BOP §3-303.
Certification of licensee, BOP §3-207.
Continuing education requirement, BOP §3-309.1.
Council defined, BOP §3-301.
Defined, BOP §3-101.
Denial.
Commencement of proceedings, BOP §3-312.
Grounds, BOP §3-311.

ARCHITECTS —Cont'd
Licenses —Cont'd
Denial —Cont'd
Hearings, BOP §3-313.
Examinations, BOP §3-305.
Testing service.
Used to administer examinations, BOP
§3-305.1.
Expiration, BOP §3-309.
Reinstatement, BOP §3-310.
Fees.
Examination fee, BOP §3-304.
Reciprocity, BOP §3-306.
Reinstatement of expired license, BOP §3-310.
Renewal fee, BOP §3-309.
Hearings.
Denial, revocation or suspension or reprimand,
BOP §3-313.
Issuance, BOP §3-307.
Notice to certain qualified applicants, BOP
§3-307.
License fee defined, BOP §3-101.
Maintenance of list of licensees, BOP §3-208.1.
Misrepresentation as authorized practitioner,
BOP §3-603.
Notice.
Examinations, BOP §3-305.
Hearings, BOP §3-313.
Issuance.
Notice to qualified applicants, BOP §3-307.
Renewal, BOP §3-309.
Qualifications of applicants, BOP §3-303.
Reciprocity, BOP §3-306.
Continuing education, BOP §3-309.1.
Reinstatement of expired license, BOP §3-310.
Renewal, BOP §3-309.
Continuing education requirement, BOP
§3-309.1.
Designation of mailing address, BOP §3-208.1.
Notice, BOP §3-309.
Reprimand of licensee.
Commencement of proceedings, BOP §3-312.
Grounds, BOP §3-311.
Hearings, BOP §3-313.
Notice of hearing, BOP §3-313.
Required, BOP §3-302.
Revocation or suspension.
Commencement of proceedings, BOP §3-312.
Grounds, BOP §3-311.
Hearings, BOP §3-313.
Notice of hearing, BOP §3-313.
Scope, BOP §3-308.
Term, BOP §3-309.
Testing service.
Used to administer examinations, BOP
§3-305.1.
Unlicensed practice.
Prohibited, BOP §3-601.
Limitation of actions.
Injuries or damages, CJ §5-108.
Malpractice, CJ §§3-2C-01, 3-2C-02.
**National council of architectural registration
boards.**
Definition of "council," BOP §3-301.
Newsletter.
Publication by board, BOP §3-208.1.
Notices.
Licenses.
Denial, revocation or suspension or reprimand
of licensee.
Hearings, BOP §3-313.

ARCHITECTS —Cont'd

Notices —Cont'd

Licenses —Cont'd

Examinations, BOP §3-305.

Issuance.

Notice to certain qualified applicants, BOP §3-307.

Renewal notice, BOP §3-309.

Permits.

Notice of changes, BOP §3-409.

Renewal notice, BOP §3-408.

Oaths.

State board of architects.

Administration of oaths in connection with investigations, BOP §3-206.

Oath of office of members, BOP §3-202.

Partnerships.

Permits.

General provisions, BOP §§3-401 to 3-409. See within this heading, "Permits."

Penalties.

Violations of provisions, BOP §3-605.

Permits.

Applications, BOP §3-405.

Qualifications of applicants, BOP §3-404.

Certification of permit holder, BOP §3-207.

Changes requiring notice to board, BOP §3-409.

Defined, BOP §3-101.

Definition of "responsible member," BOP §3-401.

Expiration, BOP §3-408.

Fees, BOP §3-406.

Application fee, BOP §3-405.

Renewal fee, BOP §3-408.

Issuance, BOP §3-406.

Misrepresentation that business may provide services, BOP §3-604.

Notice.

Changes, BOP §3-409.

Renewal, BOP §3-408.

Permit fee defined, BOP §3-101.

Practice of architecture, BOP §3-402.

Providing services without permit.

Prohibited, BOP §3-602.

Qualifications of applicants, BOP §3-404.

Renewal, BOP §3-408.

Requirement, BOP §3-403.

Scope, BOP §3-407.

Term, BOP §3-408.

Practice of architecture.

Corporations.

Authorized, BOP §3-402.

Permits.

General provisions, BOP §§3-401 to 3-409. See within this heading, "Permits."

Providing services without permit.

Prohibited, BOP §3-602.

Required, BOP §3-403.

Scope of permit, BOP §3-407.

Defined, BOP §3-101.

Licenses.

General provisions, BOP §§3-301 to 3-313. See within this heading, "Licenses."

Required, BOP §3-302.

Scope of license, BOP §3-308.

Unlicensed practice.

Prohibited, BOP §3-601.

Misrepresentation as authorized practitioner, BOP §3-603.

Misrepresentation that business may provide services, BOP §3-604.

ARCHITECTS —Cont'd

Practice of architecture —Cont'd

Partnerships.

Authorized, BOP §3-402.

Permits.

General provisions, BOP §§3-401 to 3-409. See within this heading, "Permits."

Providing services without permit.

Prohibited, BOP §3-602.

Required, BOP §3-403.

Scope of permit, BOP §3-407.

Penalties for certain violations, BOP §3-605.

Reports of violations, BOP §3-606.

Scope of provisions, BOP §3-103.

Prisons and prisoners.

Approval of design and services, COR §10-102.

Procurement of services by state, COR §10-102.

Supervisory responsibility, COR §10-104.

Professional malpractice, CJ §§3-2C-01, 3-2C-02.

Purposes of provisions, BOP §3-102.

Reciprocity.

Licenses, BOP §3-306.

Records.

State board of architects.

Proceedings, BOP §3-208.

Reports.

Violations of provisions, BOP §3-606.

Rules and regulations.

Distribution, BOP §3-208.1.

Termination of regulations adopted under provisions, BOP §3-702.

Schools.

Conformity to building regulations, ED §4-117.

County boards of education.

Power to employ, ED §4-117.

Employment of architects, ED §4-117.

Scope of provisions, BOP §3-103.

Seal required on certain documents, BOP §3-103.

Seals and sealed instruments.

Signing and sealing documents, BOP §3-501.

Short title of act, BOP §3-701.

Signatures.

Documents, BOP §3-501.

State board of architects.

Annual meeting, BOP §3-204.1.

Appeals.

Judicial review of board, BOP §3-210.

Appointment of members, BOP §3-202.

Certification of licensee or permit holder, BOP §3-207.

Chairman, BOP §3-203.

Appointment, BOP §3-203.

Code of ethics.

Adoption, BOP §3-205.

Compensation of members.

Service without compensation, BOP §3-204.

Composition, BOP §3-202.

Creation, BOP §3-201.

Definition of "board," BOP §3-101.

Duties, BOP §3-208.

Established, BOP §3-201.

Expenses of members.

Reimbursement, BOP §3-204.

Fee schedule, BOP §3-209.

Judicial review of board, BOP §3-210.

Maintenance of list of licensees, BOP §3-208.1.

Meetings, BOP §3-204.

Annual meeting, BOP §3-204.1.

Newsletter, BOP §3-208.1.

Number of members, BOP §3-202.

ARCHITECTS —Cont'd
State board of architects —Cont'd
Oaths of office, BOP §3-202.
Powers, BOP §§3-206, 3-208.
Exercised subject to authority of secretary, BOP §3-211.
Qualifications of members, BOP §3-202.
Quorum, BOP §3-204.
Record of proceedings, BOP §3-208.
Removal of members, BOP §3-202.
Secretary of licensing and regulation department.
Authority of secretary, BOP §3-211.
Staff, BOP §3-204.
Terms of members, BOP §3-202.
Vacancies, BOP §3-202.
Subpoenas.
Investigations by state board of architects, BOP §3-206.
Taxation.
Construction of architecturally compatible new structures.
Tax credits, TP §§9-204, 9-204.1.
Restoration and preservation.
Structures having architectural value.
Tax credit based upon, TP §§9-204, 9-204.1.
Termination of provisions, BOP §3-702.
Title of act.
Short title, BOP §3-701.
Website.
Publication of newsletter, BOP §3-208.1.
Witnesses.
Investigations by state board of architects.
Powers of board in connection with, BOP §3-206.

ARCHITECTURAL EASEMENTS.
Annapolis.
Board of public works, Maryland historical trust, SF §5A-305.

ARCHITECTURE.
Architects generally.
See ARCHITECTS.
Baltimore City.
Historic and landmark zoning and preservation, 66B §2.12.
Board of architectural review, SF §§4-701 to 4-704.

ARCHIVES.
Accounts and accounting.
Publications account, SG §9-1014.
Boards and commissions.
Hall of records commission.
See HALL OF RECORDS.
Definitions, SG §9-1001.
Vital records, SG §9-1015.
Disposition or destruction of records and other materials, SG §§10-637 to 10-642.
See RECORDS.
Established, SG §9-1002.
Fees.
Copies of records, SG §9-1009.
Fund, SG §9-1013.
Governor.
State archives established in office of governor, SG §9-1002.
Hall of records commission.
General provisions.
See HALL OF RECORDS.
Highway plats.
Duty to record state highway administration plats, SG §9-1011.

ARCHIVES —Cont'd
Historical records.
Duties as to, SG §9-1010.
Indexes, SG §9-1009.
Interstate agreements.
Delivery to state archives, SG §7-104.
Local records.
Custody, SG §9-1012.
Maryland manual, SG §§9-1026, 9-1027.
Plats.
Highways.
Duty to record state highway administration plats, SG §9-1011.
Preservation and use of records, SG §9-1009.
Real property.
State archivist.
Acquisition of property, SG §9-1008.
State real property records.
Duty of archives, SG §9-1011.
Reorganization of government.
Delivery of records of abolished or superseded units, SG §10-702.
Reports.
State archivist.
Annual report, SG §9-1007.
Rules and regulations.
Adoption by records management division and state archivist, SG §10-632.
Salaries.
State archivist, SG §9-1005.
Staff, SG §9-1006.
State archivist.
Acquisition and supervision of property, SG §9-1008.
Annual report, SG §9-1007.
Appointment, SG §9-1005.
Assistant state archivist, SG §9-1006.
Delegation of duty, SG §9-1011.
Hall of records commission.
See HALL OF RECORDS.
Jurisdiction, SG §9-1010.
Land patents.
Archivist to provide commissioner of land patents with space in state hall of records building, SG §9-1008.
Powers, SG §9-1007.
Preservation and use of records, SG §9-1009.
Responsibilities for records, SG §9-1009.
Salary, SG §9-1005.
Vital records.
Generally, SG §9-1015.
Websites.
Highway plats.
Posting of state highway administration plats, SG §9-1011.

ARMED CARJACKING, CR §3-405.
Mandatory sentence for crime of violence.
Second, third or fourth conviction, CR §14-101.

ARMED FORCES.
Military services.
See MILITARY SERVICES.
Standing armies.
Consent of legislature required, MD Const DofR Art 29.
Veterans.
See VETERANS.

ARMED FORCES RECRUITMENT OFFICES.
Voter registration agencies, EL §3-204.

ARMED ROBBERY.
Robbery with dangerous weapon, CR §3-403.

ARMORIES.
Militia.
See MILITIA.

ARREST.
Anne Arundel county or city of Annapolis fire and explosive investigator.
Authority to make arrests, CP §2-208.2.
Appearances.
Initial appearance of defendant.
Circuit court following arrest or summons, Crim Rule 4-213.
District Court following arrest, Crim Rule 4-213.
Arraignment.
State police department.
Confinement of arrestees, PS §2-310.
Arrest without a warrant.
Generally, CP §§2-201 to 2-210.
See WARRANTLESS ARREST.
Arson.
Fire marshal's authority.
Warrantless arrest for specified violations, CP §2-208.
Authority of police officers generally, CP §2-102.
Circuit courts.
Initial appearance of defendant, Crim Rule 4-213.
Procedure when defendant in custody.
Other offenses, Crim Rule 4-212.
Same offense, Crim Rule 4-212.
Statement of charges.
After arrest.
Filing, Crim Rule 4-211.
Before arrest.
Filing, Crim Rule 4-211.
Warrants issued in circuit court.
Failure to use, CJ §2-107.
Form and content, CJ §2-107.
Citations.
Motor vehicles.
Traffic citations. See within this heading, "Motor vehicles."
Civil arrest.
Privilege from arrest, US Const Art I §6.
Confessions.
Failure to take defendant before judicial officer after arrest.
Confession not rendered inadmissible, CJ §10-912.
Congress.
Arrest of members, US Const Art I §6.
Privilege from, US Const Art I §6.
Constitutional provisions.
Privilege from arrest, US Const Art I §6.
Correctional officers.
Power of arrest, COR §3-216.
Warrantless arrest, authority of employees, CP §2-207.
Custody of arrested person.
In another jurisdiction, CP §2-106.
Defense-related activity.
Trespassing on posted property used for.
Warrantless arrest, CP §2-210.
Destructive devices.
Warrantless arrest.
Fire marshal's authority, CP §2-208.
Domestic violence.
Protective orders.
Probable cause person in violation of order, FL §4-509.

ARREST —Cont'd
Domestic violence —Cont'd
Warrantless arrest authorized, CP §2-204.
Drug or alcohol abuse.
Intoxicated persons.
Disposition, HG §8-503.
Due process.
Required, MD Const DofR Art 24.
Educational facilities.
Pupil reportable offenses, ED §7-303.
Election judges ordering.
Authority, EL §10-303.
Protection of police officer making arrest, EL §10-304.
Escape in the second degree.
Departing custody without authorization, CR §9-405.
Extradition.
Arrest before requisition, CP §9-113.
Arrest without warrant, CP §9-114.
Authority of arresting officer, CP §9-109.
Rights of person arrested, CP §9-110.
Temporary custody of prisoner arrested, CP §9-112.
Warrant of arrest, CP §9-107.
Arrest before requisition, CP §9-113.
Authority of arresting officer under, CP §9-109.
Execution, CP §9-108.
Recall of warrant, CP §9-121.
False statement while under arrest.
Identity, address, date of birth, CR §9-502.
Federal law enforcement officers.
Immunity from suit, CJ §5-611.
Powers, CP §2-104.
United States park police officers, CP §2-104.1.
Fire marshal and assistants.
Authority, PS §6-311.
Warrantless arrest, authority, CP §2-208.
Fish and fisheries.
Endangered species of fish conservation act.
Violations of article, NR §4-2A-07.
Forests and trees.
Roadside trees.
Protection of trees by warden, NR §5-404.
Forms.
Design by district court judges, CJ §1-605.
Fresh pursuit, CP §2-301.
Authority of officers in another state to arrest in this state.
Uniform act on fresh pursuit, CP §§2-304 to 2-309.
Handguns.
Limited search, seizure and arrest, CR §4-206.
Home detention, warrantless arrest of inmates on.
Authority of persons monitoring inmates, CP §2-207.
Humane society officers, CR §10-609.
Immunity from liability and exemptions.
Police officers arresting pursuant to warrant, CP §2-103.
Interfering with arrest, CR §9-408.
Liability.
Merchants.
Civil liability of merchant for detention or arrest of person for theft, CJ §5-402.
Motion picture theater owner or lessee.
Civil liability for detention or arrest of person for commission of certain crimes, CJ §5-402.
Liquefied petroleum gas.
Person unlawfully using containers, CL §11-605.

ARREST —Cont'd
Local correctional officers.
Authority to make, COR §11-802.
Warrantless arrest authority, CP §2-207.
Mental hygiene law.
Emergency evaluation of arrested individuals, HG §10-626.
Militia.
Commanding officers.
Arrest powers, PS §13-208.
Immunity of members from arrest, PS §13-905.
Montgomery county fire and explosive investigator.
Authority to make arrests, CP §2-208.1.
Motion picture theater owner or lessee.
Detention or arrest of person for commission of certain crimes.
Civil liability, CJ §5-402.
Motor vehicles.
Authority to charge, TR §26-201.
District Court commissioners.
Appearance.
Notice to appear required in citation, TR §26-201.
Person arrested to be taken before commissioner, TR §26-202.
Release of defendant when commissioner not available, TR §26-402.
Manner of arrest, TR §26-202.
Nonresidents.
Application of subtitle, TR §26-202.
Notice to appear in court, TR §26-201.
Police.
Authority to charge, TR §26-201.
Power of arrest, TR §26-202.
Release of defendant when commissioner not available, TR §26-402.
Exception, TR §26-402.
Traffic citation.
Cancellation.
Illegal cancellation, TR §26-408.
Case to be tried only on proper charging document, TR §26-409.
Compliance.
Alternate means of compliance, TR §26-204.
Failure to comply, TR §26-204.
Disposition of penalty deposit, TR §26-405.1.
Penalty deposit, TR §26-204.
Suspension of driving privileges, TR §26-204.
Required, TR §26-204.
Contents, TR §26-201.
Disposition of citation deposited with court, TR §26-407.
Unlawfully, TR §26-407.
Issuance, TR §26-201.
Duty of officer issuing citation, TR §26-407.
Record of traffic cases.
Kept by chief administrative officer, TR §26-407.
Rules and regulations.
Distribution and disposition of forms, TR §26-407.
Signature of person charged required on citation, TR §26-203.
When citation is sufficient charging document, TR §26-409.
Natural resources.
Citations.
Failure to appear.
Issuance of warrant for arrest, NR §1-205.

ARREST —Cont'd
Parole and probation employees supervising inmates on home detention.
Warrantless arrest authority, CP §2-207.
Parole or probation violators, COR §6-106.
Paternity proceedings.
Warrant for arrest of defendant, FL §5-1014.
Peace orders.
Violation of order, CJ §3-1508.
Police.
Authority generally, CP §2-102.
Federal law enforcement officers, CJ §5-611.
Immunities from liability and exemptions, CP §2-103.
Throughout state without limitations as to jurisdiction, CP §2-103.
Warrant issued, CP §2-103.
Powers of police officers generally, CP §2-102.
Prince George's county fire investigators.
Warrantless arrest power, CP §2-209.
Privilege from arrest, US Const Art I §6.
Protective orders.
Domestic violence.
Probable cause person in violation of order, FL §4-509.
Quotas.
Arrest and citation quotas prohibited, PS §3-504.
Railroad police.
Confinement of arrestees, PS §3-413.
Resisting arrest, CR §9-408.
Schools.
Reportable offenses by pupils, ED §7-303.
Semiconscious or unconscious person.
Duty of officer before charging with crime, CP §2-107.
Shoplifting.
Civil liability of merchant for detention or arrest of person for theft, CJ §5-402.
Special police officers.
Powers, PS §3-307.
Specified crimes, warrantless arrest authorized, CP §2-203.
Domestic abuse, CP §2-204.
Fire marshal and assistants, authority, CP §2-208.
Stalking, CP §2-205.
Stalking, warrantless arrest authorized, CP §2-205.
State correctional officers.
Warrantless arrest authority, CP §2-207.
State fire marshal and assistants.
Warrantless arrest, authority, CP §2-208.
State of emergency, warrantless arrest authorized, CP §2-206.
State police.
Police powers, PS §2-412.
State police department.
Confinement of arrestees, PS §2-310.
Throughout state without limitations as to jurisdiction.
Police officers' powers, CP §2-103.
Warrantless arrest.
Extradition, CP §9-114.
Fresh pursuit, CP §2-301.
Authority of officers in another state to arrest in this state.
Uniform act on fresh pursuit, CP §§2-304 to 2-309.
Generally, CP §§2-201 to 2-210.
See WARRANTLESS ARREST.

ARREST —Cont'd
Warrants.
Circuit courts.
Failure to use, CJ §2-107.
Form and content, CJ §2-107.
Destruction.
Powers and duties of chief judge of District
Court, CJ §1-605.
Detainee entitlement to copy, COR §9-611.
District Court judges.
Authority to issue, CJ §1-609.
Destruction of warrants, CJ §1-605.
Extradition, CP §9-107.
Arrest before requisition, CP §9-113.
Authority of arresting officer under, CP §9-109.
Execution, CP §9-108.
Recall of warrant, CP §9-121.
Files and records of court pertaining to.
Access to public records, SG §10-616.
Natural resource citations.
Failure to appear, NR §1-205.
Registered returnable containers and textiles, BR
§19-305.
Witnesses.
Securing attendance from without a state.
Exemption from arrest, CJ §9-304.
Summoning witness in this state to testify in
another state, CJ §9-302.
Woodrow Wilson bridge and tunnel authority.
Police powers, TR §10-303.

ARREST WARRANTS.
Arson or burning.
Charging document, CR §6-111.
Assault.
Charging document, CR §3-206.
Bigamy.
Charging document, CR §10-502.
Breaking and entering.
Charging document, CR §6-210.
Circuit courts.
Failure to use, CJ §2-107.
Form and content, CJ §2-107.
Conspiracy.
Sufficiency of charging document, CR §1-203.
Destruction.
Powers and duties of chief judge of District Court,
CJ §1-605.
Detainee entitlement to copy, COR §9-611.
District Court judges.
Authority to issue, CJ §1-609.
Destruction of warrants, CJ §1-605.
Extradition, CP §9-107.
Arrest before requisition, CP §9-113.
Authority of arresting officer under, CP §9-109.
Execution, CP §9-108.
Recall of warrant, CP §9-121.
Federal law enforcement officers, execution,
CP §2-104.
Files and records of court pertaining to.
Access to public records, SG §10-616.
Motor vehicle theft.
Charging document, CR §7-108.
Natural resource citations.
Failure to appear, NR §1-205.
Perjury.
Charging document, CR §9-103.
Rape or sexual offense.
Charging document, CR §3-317.
Reckless endangerment.
Charging document, CR §3-206.

ARREST WARRANTS —Cont'd
Registered returnable containers and textiles,
BR §19-305.
Robbery.
Charging document, CR §3-404.
Service by police officer, CP §2-103.
Theft.
Charging document, CR §7-108.

ARREST WITHOUT A WARRANT.
Fresh pursuit, CP §2-301.
Authority of officers in another state to arrest in
this state.
Uniform act on fresh pursuit, CP §§2-304 to
2-309.
Generally, CP §§2-201 to 2-210.
See WARRANTLESS ARREST.

ARSON AND BURNING, CR §§6-101 to 6-111.
Anti-arson applications for fire insurance, IN
§§19-301 to 19-309.
Arrest without a warrant.
Fire marshal's authority, CP §2-208.
Arson in the first degree, CR §6-102.
Mandatory sentence for crime of violence.
Second, third or fourth conviction, CR §14-101.
Arson in the second degree, CR §6-103.
Attempt to burn structure or property, CR
§6-109.
Breaking and entering with intent to commit.
Burglary in the second degree, CR §6-203.
Burning trash container, CR §6-108.
Burning with intent to defraud, CR §6-106.
Charging document, CR §6-111.
Definitions, CR §6-101.
Fire marshal.
Warrantless arrest of person committing specified
violations, CP §2-208.
Insurance.
Fire insurance application act, IN §§19-301 to
19-309.
Malicious burning.
Warrantless arrest, CP §§2-203, 2-208.
**Malicious burning of personal property in the
first degree,** CR §6-104.
**Malicious burning of personal property in the
second degree,** CR §6-105.
Separate units, separate violations, CR §6-110.
Threat of arson, CR §6-107.
Warrantless arrest, CP §§2-203, 2-208.
Fire marshal's authority, CP §2-208.

ARSON IN THE FIRST DEGREE, CR §6-102.
Mandatory sentence for crime of violence.
Second, third or fourth conviction, CR §14-101.

ARSON IN THE SECOND DEGREE, CR §6-103.

ART.
Admissions and amusement tax.
Performing arts organizations.
Exemption, TG §4-104.
Commission.
Artistic property commission.
See ARTISTIC PROPERTY COMMISSION.
Consignment of works of fine art.
Art dealers.
Bailee of artist, CL §11-8A-02.
Creditors.
Bailment of property not subject to claims of
creditors, CL §11-8A-04.
Defined, CL §11-8A-01.
Artists.
Defined, CL §11-8A-01.

ART —Cont'd
Consignment of works of fine art —Cont'd
Bailment.
Art dealer as bailee of artist, CL §11-8A-02.
Period during which work of fine art remains
bailment property, CL §11-8A-03.
Property not subject to claims of art dealer's
creditors, CL §11-8A-04.
Work of fine art and proceeds of sale bailment
property, CL §11-8A-02.
Creditors.
Bailment of property not subject to claims of art
dealer's creditors, CL §11-8A-04.
Definitions, CL §11-8A-01.
On consignment.
Defined, CL §11-8A-01.
Period during which work remains bailment
property, CL §11-8A-03.
Sales.
Proceeds as bailment property, CL §11-8A-02.
Works of fine art.
Defined, CL §11-8A-01.
Constitution of Maryland.
What legislature should encourage, MD Const
DofR Art 43.
Council.
Arts council.
See ARTS COUNCIL.
Definitions.
Consignment of works of fine art, CL §11-8A-01.
Fine prints, CL §§14-501 to 14-505.
See CONSUMER PROTECTION.
Maryland public art initiative, 83A §§4-6A-01 to
4-6A-04.

ARTESIAN WATER, HG §21-336.

ARTHRITIS AND RELATED DISEASES.
Prevention and control program.
Advisory council.
Appointment, HG §13-506.
Chairman.
Appointment, HG §13-507.
Term of office, HG §13-507.
Compensation, HG §13-508.
Creation, HG §13-505.
Defined, HG §13-502.
Duties, HG §13-509.
Expenses, HG §13-508.
Meetings, HG §13-508.
Powers, HG §13-509.
Quorum, HG §13-508.
Removal of members, HG §13-506.
Staff, HG §13-508.
Terms of office, HG §13-506.
Findings by general assembly, HG §13-503.
Funding, HG §13-511.
Purpose, HG §§13-501, 13-504.
Secretary's duties, HG §13-510.
Short title, HG §13-512.
Statewide program.
Purpose to create and foster, HG §13-504.

ARTHROPODS.
State arthropodic emblem.
Baltimore checkerspot butterfly, SG §13-301.

ARTICLES OF INCORPORATION.
Banks and trust companies.
See BANKS AND TRUST COMPANIES.
Corporations.
See CORPORATIONS.

ARTICLES OF INCORPORATION —Cont'd
Credit unions.
See CREDIT UNIONS.
**Local military installation redevelopment
authorities,** 83A §5-1703.

ARTIFICIAL GAS COMPANIES.
Generally.
See GAS COMPANIES.

ARTIFICIAL INSEMINATION.
Decedents' estates.
Determining relationship, ET §1-206.
**Health insurance coverage for in vitro
fertilization,** IN §15-810.
Hospitals.
Permitting artificial insemination in hospitals, HG
§20-214.

ARTISANS.
Mechanics.
See MECHANICS.
Mechanics' liens.
See MECHANICS' LIENS.
Taxation.
Tools.
Exemptions, TP §7-229.

ARTISTIC PROPERTY COMMISSION.
Acquisitions, SG §9-1021.
Appointment of members, SG §9-1018.
Chairman, SG §9-1018.
Compensation, SG §9-1019.
Composition, SG §9-1018.
Definitions, SG §9-1016.
Duties.
Duties as to state rooms of governor's house, SG
§9-1022.
Generally, SG §9-1021.
Established, SG §9-1017.
Gifts.
Acceptance on behalf of state, SG §9-1020.
Monetary gifts.
Acceptance, SG §9-1020.
Paintings and decorative arts.
State rooms of governor's house, SG §9-1022.
Public art initiative program.
Inapplicability to artwork acquired through, SG
§9-1021.
Seeking advice, SG §9-1023.
Staff, SG §9-1019.
State rooms of governor's house, SG §9-1022.

ARTS AND ENTERTAINMENT DISTRICTS, 83A
§§4-701 to 4-703.
Definitions, 83A §4-701.
Designation, 83A §4-701.
Application for, 83A §4-702.
Regulations, 83A §4-703.
Criteria, 83A §4-702.
Regulations, 83A §4-703.
Property taxes.
Credit for buildings located in, TP §9-240.
Tax status, 83A §4-701.

ARTS COUNCIL.
Appointment.
By governor, 83A §4-604.
Appropriations.
Governor's proposed general fund appropriation,
SF §7-325.
Artistic expression.
Activities to be directed toward encouraging and
assisting artistic expression, 83A §4-603.

ARTS COUNCIL —Cont'd
Business and economic development department.
Part of department, 83A §4-604.
Chairman, 83A §4-604.
Compensation, 83A §4-604.
Composition, 83A §4-604.
Creation, 83A §4-604.
Definitions.
Meaning of "the arts," 83A §4-608.
Director, 83A §4-606.
Duties, 83A §4-606.
Employees, 83A §4-606.
Expenses, 83A §4-606.
Findings.
Legislative findings, 83A §4-601.
Freedom.
Interference with freedom of expression or arts programs, 83A §4-609.
Funding, 83A §4-609.
General assembly.
Legislative findings, 83A §4-601.
Governor.
Appointment by governor, 83A §4-604.
Proposed expenditures, 83A §4-609.
Meetings, 83A §4-605.
Policy.
Declaration of policy, 83A §4-602.
Powers, 83A §4-606.
Procurement.
Inapplicability of procurement code, SF §11-203.
Programs.
Authorized, 83A §4-607.
Subject to approval of secretary, 83A §4-607.
Public works.
Recommendations to board of public works, 83A §4-607.
Reports.
Annual report, 83A §4-607.
Secretary-treasurer, 83A §4-604.
Terms of office, 83A §4-604.
Vice-chairman, 83A §4-604.

ASBESTOS.
Accreditation.
Asbestos occupations, EN §6-417.
Administration of courts.
Special docket for asbestos cases, CJA Rule 16-203.
Administrative procedure.
Hearing on suspension or revocation of license, EN §6-416.
Asbestos occupations.
Accreditation of individuals, EN §6-417.
Defined, EN §6-401.
Business entity.
Defined, EN §6-401.
Complaints.
Grounds, EN §6-420.
Issuance, EN §6-420.
Service, EN §6-421.
Court administration.
Special docket, CJA Rule 16-203.
Definitions, EN §6-401.
Department.
Inspections.
On-site inspections, EN §6-406.
Licenses.
Power to waive license requirements in emergency, EN §6-405.

ASBESTOS —Cont'd
Department —Cont'd
Rules and regulations.
Adoption, EN §6-406.
Docket for asbestos cases.
Special docket, CJA Rule 16-203.
Emergencies.
Power of department to waive license requirements, EN §6-405.
Findings of legislature, EN §6-402.
Hearings.
Revocation and suspension of license, EN §6-416.
Housing.
Radon and asbestos abatement pilot program.
Maryland housing rehabilitation program.
Units in program, HS §4-905.
Inspections.
On-site inspections by department, EN §6-406.
Legislative policy, EN §6-402.
Licenses.
Applications, EN §6-411.
Defined, EN §6-401.
Employee knowledge and training, EN §6-410.
Facilities, EN §6-410.
Hearings.
Revocation and suspension, EN §6-416.
Notice of renewal, EN §6-413.
Qualifications for license, EN §6-410.
Records.
Required records of licensees, EN §6-414.
Renewal, EN §6-413.
Notice, EN §6-414.1.
Required, EN §6-409.
Scope of license, EN §6-412.
Suspension and revocation.
Grounds, EN §6-415.
Hearings, EN §6-416.
Term of license, EN §6-413.
Waiver in emergency.
Power of department, EN §6-405.
Maryland housing rehabilitation program.
Radon and asbestos abatement pilot program.
Units in program, HS §4-905.
Notices.
Removal or encapsulation, EN §6-414.1.
Violations, EN §§6-420, 6-421.
Occupational safety and health.
Asbestos protective clothing.
Prohibitions, LE §5-601.
Orders.
Corrective orders, EN §6-420.
Service, EN §6-421.
Penalties.
Civil penalty, EN §6-422.
Criminal penalty, EN §6-422.
Prohibited acts.
Complaints, EN §§6-420, 6-421.
Corrective orders, EN §§6-420, 6-421.
Criminal penalty, EN §6-422.
Notices requiring report concerning alleged violation, EN §§6-420, 6-421.
Penalties, EN §6-422.
Removing or encapsulating asbestos without license, EN §6-419.
Radon and asbestos abatement pilot program.
Maryland housing rehabilitation program, HS §4-930.
Units in program, HS §4-905.
Records.
Required records of licensees, EN §6-414.
Retention, EN §6-414.

ASBESTOS —Cont'd

Removal or encapsulation.

Notices, EN §6-414.1.

Signs, EN §6-414.1.

Reprimands of licensees, EN §6-415.

Rubble landfills.

Types of waste disposed in, EN §9-210.

Rules and regulations.

Adoption, EN §6-406.

Asbestos occupations.

Accreditation of individuals, EN §6-417.

Schools.

Inspections for asbestos.

Copies of inspection reports, ED §7-419.

Service of process.

Complaints, orders and notices, EN §6-421.

Signs.

Removal or encapsulation of asbestos, EN §6-414.1.

Violations.

Civil penalty, EN §6-422.

Complaints, EN §§6-420, 6-421.

Corrective orders, EN §§6-420, 6-421.

Criminal penalty, EN §6-422.

Notices, EN §§6-420, 6-421.

Removing or encapsulating asbestos without license, EN §6-419.

ASHES.

Refuse.

See GARBAGE AND REFUSE.

ASIAN AND PACIFIC ISLANDERS.

Health care disparities in minority populations.

Office of minority health and health disparities, HG §§20-1001 to 20-1007.

Minorities generally.

See MINORITIES.

ASIAN LUNAR NEW YEAR DAY.

Annual proclamation by governor, SG §13-405.

ASSAULT.

Appeals.

Jurisdiction.

Court of special appeals, CJ §12-308.

Assault by inmate, CR §3-210.

Assault in the first degree, CR §3-202.

Lesser included offense of assault in second degree.

Included in charge, CR §3-206.

Mandatory sentence for crime of violence.

Second, third or fourth conviction, CR §14-101.

Assault in the second degree, CR §3-203.

Included in charge of assault in first degree, CR §3-206.

Bill of particulars.

Charging document in general form, CR §3-206.

Charging documents, CR §3-206.

Defenses.

Judicially recognized defenses allowed, CR §3-209.

Definitions, 1 §33; CR §3-201.

Dismissal of charge, CR §3-207.

DNA database system, PS §§2-501 to 2-512.

See DNA DATABASE SYSTEM.

Escape from juvenile detention facility with assault.

Escape in the first degree, CR §9-404.

ASSAULT —Cont'd

Evidence of serious physical injury.

Expert testimony admissible, not required, CR §3-208.

Husband and wife.

Spousal assault.

Assistance to victim.

Immunity of law enforcement officers, CJ §5-610.

Immunity.

Law enforcement officers.

Spousal assault.

Assistance to victims, CJ §5-610.

Law enforcement officers.

Assault in the second degree, CR §3-203.

Spousal assault.

Assistance to victims.

Immunity, CJ §5-610.

Lesser included offense of assault in second degree.

Assault in the first degree.

Included in charge, CR §3-206.

Limitation of actions.

Actions for, CJ §5-105.

Mandatory sentence for crime of violence.

Second, third or fourth conviction, CR §14-101.

Schools.

Employees.

Assault leave, ED §6-111.

Secretary of agriculture.

Resisting secretary in performance of his duties, AG §2-104.

Spousal assault.

Law enforcement officers.

Assisting victims of spousal assault, CJ §5-610.

Spousal privilege.

Record of assertion, Crim Rule 4-632.

Taxation.

Collector, TP §14-1013.

Tax collector or bidder at tax collector's sale.

Penalties for assaulting, TG §13-1025.

Tax sale.

Assaulting bidder.

Penalties, TP §14-1014.

ASSAULT BY INMATE, CR §3-210.

ASSAULT IN THE FIRST DEGREE, CR §3-202.

Lesser included offense of assault in second degree.

Included in charge, CR §3-206.

Mandatory sentence for crime of violence.

Second, third or fourth conviction, CR §14-101.

ASSAULT IN THE SECOND DEGREE, CR §3-203.

Included in charge of assault in first degree, CR §3-206.

ASSAULT PISTOLS, CR §§4-301 to 4-306.

Defined, types and brands enumerated, CR §4-301.

Persons excepted from provisions, CR §4-302.

Punishment, CR §4-306.

Scope of subtitle, CR §4-302.

Seizure and disposal as contraband, CR §4-304.

Transporting into state, selling or purchasing, prohibition, CR §4-303.

Use in commission of crime.

Punishment, CR §4-306.

ASSAULT WEAPONS.
Regulated firearms, PS §5-101.

ASSAWOMAN BAY.
Atlantic coastal bays critical areas program.
Generally, NR §§8-1801 to 8-1817.
See CHESAPEAKE BAY CRITICAL AREA AND
ATLANTIC COASTAL BAYS CRITICAL
AREA PROTECTION PROGRAMS.

ASSEMBLY.
Firearm possessed at public demonstration, CR
§4-208.
Unlawful picketing and assembly, CR §3-904.

ASSEMBLY DISRUPTING HOME
TRANQUILITY, CR §3-904.

ASSESSMENTS.
Admissions and amusement tax.
Application for revision or claim for refund, TG
§13-508.
Erroneous assessments, TG §13-509.
Agricultural products.
Promotion of use and sale.
General provisions.
See AGRICULTURAL PRODUCTS.
Agriculture.
Real property tax.
Farm or agricultural use, TP §8-209.
Allegany county.
Sanitary commissions.
Levy for part year, EN §9-658.
Banks and trust companies.
Examinations.
Banking institutions, FI §5-203.
Condominiums.
Common expenses.
Funds for payment, RP §11-110.
Demand for payment of remaining annual
assessment, RP §11-110.
Payment.
Remaining annual assessment, RP §11-110.
Counties.
Erosion districts, 25 §165.
Credit unions.
Annual assessment of credit unions with assets of
$300,000, FI §6-712.
Dorchester county.
Uniform benefit assessments.
Bonnie Brook service area, EN §9-657.
Draining lands.
Against persons who will benefit, 25 §73.
County commissioners.
Authority to contribute or allocate funds, 25
§73.
Ditches or drains.
Already constructed, 25 §74.
Drainage districts.
By drainage commissioners, 25 §119.
Estate tax.
Federal adjustments made, TG §13-409.
Financial institution franchise tax.
Application for revision or claim for refund, TG
§13-508.
Erroneous assessments, TG §13-509.
Time for, TG §13-1101.
Generation-skipping transfer tax.
Federal adjustments made, TG §13-409.
Income tax.
Federal adjustments made, TG §13-409.
Time for, TG §13-1101.

ASSESSMENTS —Cont'd
Industry automobile insurance association, IN
§§20-401 to 20-411.
Insurance.
See INSURANCE.
Joint insurance association.
Recoupment of assessments, IN §25-405.
Kent county.
Sanitary commissions, EN §9-658.
Motor carrier tax.
Records and reports.
Inadequate or no records kept or no report filed,
TG §13-405.
Motor fuel tax.
Records.
Assessment when records not kept, TG §13-406.
Seller and buyer, TG §13-412.
Potomac water authority.
General provisions.
See POTOMAC WATER AUTHORITY.
Property and casualty insurance guaranty
corporation, IN §§9-306, 9-308.
Recoupment, IN §9-313.
Property taxes.
General provisions.
See PROPERTY TAXES.
Public service company franchise tax.
Application for revision or claim for refund, TG
§13-508.
Erroneous assessments, TG §13-509.
Real estate brokers.
Guaranty fund, BOP §17-403.
Disposition of money collected, BOP §17-402.
Sales and use tax.
Application for revision or claim for refund, TG
§13-508.
Erroneous assessments, TG §13-509.
Penalties.
Noncompliance with notice and demand for final
assessment, TG §13-709.
Records not kept or resale certificate not obtained,
TG §13-407.
Seller and buyer, TG §13-412.
Taxation.
Eminent domain.
Evidence of value of property, RP §12-105.
General provisions.
See TAXATION.
Real property.
Transfer on assessment books prior to
recording.
Buildings and improvements, RP §3-104.
Payment of taxes required, RP §3-104.
Tax rolls.
Eminent domain.
Removal of property from tax rolls, RP
§12-106.
Tobacco tax.
Application for revision or claim for refund, TG
§13-508.
Erroneous assessments, TG §13-509.
Records not kept or tax not paid, TG §13-408.
Water and sewer systems.
State to pay certain assessments, SF §2-403.
Watershed associations.
Costs of works of improvement, 25 §189.
Workers' compensation.
Self-insurers' guaranty fund, IN §25-305.

ASSIGNMENTS.
Accord and satisfaction.
Secured transactions.
Inapplicability of article 9.
Accounts, chattel paper, etc., assigned to
satisfy pre-existing obligation, CL §9-109.
Acknowledgments.
Wages.
Acknowledgment before justice of the peace
required, CL §15-302.
Requisites of assignment, CL §15-302.
Actions.
By assignee on obligation under seal, CL §15-402.
Certification of obligee, CL §15-402.
Affidavits.
Interest.
Paid or to be paid, CL §15-304.
Alcoholic beverages.
Licenses, 2B §10-503.
Assignee.
Actions.
On obligation under seal, CL §15-402.
Certification of obligee, CL §15-402.
Bankruptcy and insolvency.
Void when, CL §15-101.
Benefit of creditor.
See ASSIGNMENTS FOR BENEFIT OF
CREDITORS.
Bond issues.
Action by surety on obligation under seal, CL
§15-402.
Cigarette business licenses, BR §16-208.
Claims to nonresidents.
Depriving debtor of rights under exemptions.
General provisions, CL §§15-501 to 15-503.
Collections.
Secured transactions.
Inapplicability of article 9.
Accounts, chattel paper, etc., assigned for
collection, CL §9-109.
Contracts.
Sale of goods, CL §2-210.
Secured transactions.
Inapplicability of article 9.
Payment right assigned to one obligated to
perform under contract, CL §9-109.
**Counterfeiting private instrument or
document,** CR §8-601.
Issuing counterfeited instrument or document, CR
§8-602.
Credit.
Credit grantor closed end credit provisions.
Consumer borrowers, CL §12-1023.
Credit grantor revolving credit provisions.
Consumer borrowers, CL §12-923.
Debts.
Claims to nonresidents.
Depriving debtor of rights under exemption
laws.
General provisions, CL §§15-501 to 15-503.
Subrogation of surety, CL §15-401.
Default.
Assignee's default may release obligee, CL
§15-402.
Default, secured obligation assigned.
Secured transactions.
Rights and duties of secondary obligors, CL
§9-618.
Deposit account.
Secured transactions.
Inapplicability of article 9.
Consumer transaction assignments, CL
§9-109.

ASSIGNMENTS —Cont'd
Distress for rent.
Liability of assignee of lease, RP §§8-325, 8-329.
District Court.
Wages.
Entry upon docket, CL §15-302.
Proof of service on employer, CL §15-303.
Electric customer choice and competition act.
Rate stabilization property.
Lien or assignment, PUC §7-542.
Environmental covenants, EN §1-809.
Financing statements.
Secured party of right.
Powers assigned, CL §9-514.
Fire insurance antiarson applications.
Assignment of policy or contract, IN §19-304.
Foreclosures.
Mortgages.
Release and assignment, PropSales Rule
14-209.
Franchise by public service company.
Commission authorization required, PUC §5-202.
Frauds, statute of.
Beneficial interest in trust, RP §5-106.
General provisions, RP §5-103.
Wages.
Required to be in writing, CL §15-302.
Husband and wife.
Wages.
Requirement, CL §15-302.
Indexes.
Clerks of court, RP §3-302.
Injunctions.
Wages.
Equitable injunction against enforcement, CL
§15-305.
Insurance.
Fire insurance antiarson applications.
Assignment of policy or contract, IN §19-304.
Group life insurance.
Rights and benefits, IN §17-104.
Life and health insurance guaranty corporation.
Assignment of rights to corporation, IN §9-407.
Life insurance and annuities.
Group life insurance rights and benefits, IN
§17-104.
Viatical settlement contracts, IN §§8-601 to
8-611.
See VIATICAL SETTLEMENT CONTRACTS.
Property and casualty insurance guaranty
corporation.
Assignment of rights to corporation, IN §9-309.
Insurance policies or claims.
Secured transactions.
Inapplicability of article 9.
Transfers of policy interest or assignment of
claim, CL §9-109.
Interest.
Wages.
Usury.
Effect of, CL §12-110.
Judgments.
Circuit courts, CivProCir Rule 2-624.
District Court, CivProDist Rule 3-624.
Secured transactions.
Inapplicability of article 9.
Rights represented by judgments, CL §9-109.
Labor and employment relations.
Wage discrimination.
Action by employee.
Assignment of claims, LE §3-307.

ASSIGNMENTS —Cont'd
Landlord and tenant.
Remedies of and against transferee of reversion, RP §8-101.
Leases, UCC, CL §2A-303.
Letters of credit.
Proceeds of a letter of credit, CL §5-114.
Life and health insurance guaranty corporation.
Assignment of rights to corporation, IN §9-407.
Limited liability companies.
Assignment of interest by members, CA §4A-603.
Right of assignee to become member, CA §4A-604.
Limited partnerships.
Assignment of partnership interest, CA §10-702.
Minimum wage.
Assignment of claims, LE §3-427.
Money transmission.
Licenses.
Nonassignability and nontransferability, FI §12-410.
Mortgages and deeds of trust.
Bond taken in sale on credit, RP §14-103.
Forms.
Assignment of mortgage, RP §4-203.
Indexing.
By clerks of court, RP §3-302.
Profits.
Interests in profits, RP §3-204.
Recordation, RP §3-106.
Rent.
Interests in rents, RP §3-204.
Rights granted by assignment of mortgage, RP §2-103.
Security.
Assignment of mortgages as security, RP §7-101.
Negligence.
Assignee's negligence may release obligee, CL §15-402.
Notaries public.
Action by assignee on obligation under seal.
Certification by obligee, CL §15-402.
Wages.
Acknowledgment before notary required, CL §15-302.
Partnerships.
Limited partnerships.
Assignment of partnership interest, CA §10-702.
Perfection of security interests or agricultural liens.
Filing requirement.
Refiling not needed upon assignment of perfected interest, CL §9-310.
Profits.
Deeds of trust, RP §3-204.
Property and casualty insurance guaranty corporation.
Assignment of rights to corporation, IN §9-309.
Public assistance program.
Assistance not assignable, 88A §73.
Releases.
Choses in action.
Assignee's negligence may release obligee, CL §15-402.
Rents.
Deeds of trust, RP §3-204.
Sales.
Installment sales.
Effect on payments, CL §12-617.

ASSIGNMENTS —Cont'd
Sales —Cont'd
Installment sales —Cont'd
Payment after assignment of agreement, CL §12-611.
Seals.
Assignee of bond or obligation under seal, CL §15-402.
Certification of obligee, CL §15-402.
Service of process.
Employer.
Copies of assignments, CL §15-302.
Proof of service, CL §15-303.
Wages.
Service on employer, CL §15-302.
Proof of service, CL §15-303.
Social services.
Public assistance program.
Assistance not assignable, 88A §73.
State lottery.
Prizes, SG §9-122.
State retirement and pension system.
Permissible assignments, SPP §21-502.
Subrogation.
Suretyship, CL §15-401.
Suretyship.
Assignee suing obligee upon failure to recover from obligor, CL §15-402.
Subrogation of surety, CL §15-401.
Taxation.
Certificates of sale, TP §14-821.
Third party rights.
Secured transactions, CL §§9-401 to 9-409.
Tort claims.
Secured transactions.
Inapplicability of article 9.
Certain tort claims, CL §9-109.
Trademarks and service marks, BR §1-411.
Unemployment compensation.
Void agreements.
Assignment or pledge of benefits and rights to benefits, LE §8-106.
Usury.
Effect of assignment on usurious loan or contract, CL §12-110.
Pleading.
Usury plea not available against bona fide assignee, CL §12-112.
Validation.
Defective grants, RP §4-109.
Vendors' liens.
General provisions, RP §7-204.
Recordation, RP §3-302.
Vessels and boats.
Security interest in vessels.
Assignment of interest, NR §8-731.
Void.
Wages earned more than six months in future, CL §15-302.
Wages.
Acknowledgment.
Before notary public required, CL §15-302.
Requisites of assignment, CL §15-302.
Definitions, CL §15-301.
District Court.
Entry upon docket, CL §15-302.
Proof of service on employer, CL §15-303.
Earned more than six months in future.
Void, CL §15-302.
Future wages.
Earned more than six months in future.
Void, CL §15-302.

ASSIGNMENTS —Cont'd
Wages —Cont'd
Husband and wife.
Executing and acknowledging, CL §15-302.
Injunction.
Equitable injunction against enforcement, CL §15-305.
Interest.
Affidavit as to interest paid or to be paid, CL §15-304.
Usury.
Effect of usury, CL §12-110.
Requisites, CL §15-302.
Secured transactions.
Inapplicability of article 9.
Assignment of wage claims, CL §9-109.
Service on employer, CL §15-302.
Proof of service, CL §15-303.
Usurious loan or contract.
Effect, CL §12-110.
Writing.
Required, CL §15-302.
Water resources.
Reservoirs, dams or waterways.
Construction or repair.
Permits.
Binding of heirs, successors or assigns, EN §5-508.
Workers' compensation.
Payment of award.
Prohibition of assignment, LE §9-732.
Writing.
Wages.
Required to be in writing, CL §15-302.

ASSIGNMENTS FOR BENEFIT OF CREDITORS.
Alcoholic beverages.
Licenses.
Transfer of license by receiver or trustee, 2B §10-503.
Bankruptcy and insolvency.
General provisions.
See BANKRUPTCY AND INSOLVENCY.
Bonds, surety.
Assignee's bond, CL §15-103.
Bulk transfers.
Transfers excepted from article, CL §6-103.
Limited liability company member making.
Cessation of membership, CA §4A-606.
Parties.
Real party in interest.
Circuit courts, CivProCir Rule 2-201.
Preferences.
General provisions, CL §15-101.
Receivers and assignees or trustees for creditors, Receivers Rules 13-101 to 13-703.
See RECEIVERS.
Sales.
Bonds, surety.
Assignee's bond, CL §15-103.
Trusts and trustees.
Sales.
Prior sales made under bond with only one surety, CL §15-103.
Wages.
Preference in distribution, CL §15-102.

ASSISTANCE.
Children.
Aid to families with dependent children.
Family investment program generally, 88A §§44A to 56.
See FAMILY INVESTMENT PROGRAM.

ASSISTANCE —Cont'd
Community home care services, 88A §§84 to 87.
See COMMUNITY HOME CARE SERVICES.
Public assistance program.
General provisions.
See SOCIAL SERVICES.
Social services.
See SOCIAL SERVICES.

ASSISTANCE IN MARKING BALLOT.
Absentee voting, EL §9-308.
Choosing individual to assist, EL §10-310.
Provisional ballot voting, EL §9-406.

ASSISTED LIVING PROGRAMS, HG §§19-1801 to 19-1812.
Accreditation of health care facilities, HG §§19-2301, 19-2302.
Alzheimer's special care unit or program.
Disclosures of information by programs offering, HG §20-109.
Civil monetary penalties.
Appeals, HG §19-1810.
Misrepresenting services, HG §19-1809.
Continuing care agreements, HG §19-1806.
Continuum of care, HG §19-1803.
Criminal history records checks of employees, HG §§19-1901 to 19-1912.
See ADULT DEPENDENT CARE PROGRAMS.
Defined, HG §19-1801.
Department of health and mental hygiene.
Duties, HG §§19-1804, 19-1805.
License renewal, acceptance of reports from accredited organization, HG §19-1805.
Regulations, HG §19-1805.
Supervision and monitoring of operation, HG §19-1802.
Disclosure.
Services disclosure statement, HG §19-1808.
Emergency electrical power generator, HG §19-1812.
Emergency management plans, PS §14-110.1.
Grants to facilities, HG §§24-1001 to 24-1007.
Allocation and use of funds, HG §§24-1004, 24-1005.
Amount, HG §24-1004.
Application, HG §24-1003.
Certification of allocation, HG §24-1005.
Civil claim to recover funds, HG §24-1006.
Definitions, HG §24-1001.
Generally, HG §24-1002.
Notice of right of recovery before allocating funds, HG §24-1006.
Purposes for which grants made, HG §24-1002.
Recovery of grant, HG §24-1006.
Regulations, HG §24-1007.
Report of application, HG §24-1003.
Health care quality account for assisted living programs, HG §19-1811.
Licenses, HG §19-1804.1.
Unlicensed operation prohibited, HG §19-1809.
Managers.
Training requirements, HG §19-1807.
Misrepresenting services, HG §19-1809.
Monitoring, HG §19-1802.
Operating agreements.
Retirement communities, CL §§23-101 to 23-106.
Oversight committee on quality of care in facilities, HG §19-1409.
Powers of secretary of aging, 70B §4.
Prohibited acts, HG §19-1809.
Rules and regulations, HG §19-1805.

ASSISTED LIVING PROGRAMS —Cont'd
Services disclosure statement, HG §19-1808.
Supervision, HG §19-1802.
Training requirements.
　Managers, HG §19-1807.
Variety of services, HG §19-1803.

ASSISTED LIVING PROGRAMS BOARD, SG
　§9-1901.

ASSISTED SUICIDE, CR §§3-101 to 3-104.
Definitions, CR §3-101.
Exceptions, CR §3-103.
Family care giver.
　Exception, CR §3-103.
Generally, CR §3-102.
Palliative care, pain relief.
　Exception, CR §3-103.
Penalty, CR §3-104.
Withholding life sustaining procedures.
　Exception, CR §3-103.

ASSISTIVE ANIMALS.
**Visually handicapped or hearing impaired
　persons.**
　Rights of individuals using, 30 §33.

**ASSISTIVE TECHNOLOGY GUARANTEED
　LOAN FUND,** 41 §§14-901 to 14-914.
Administration of program, 41 §14-902.
Applications for financial assistance, 41
　§14-911.
Board of directors, 41 §§14-904, 14-905.
　Management and administration of fund, 41
　　§14-906.
　Reports, 41 §14-914.
Composition of fund, 41 §14-907.
Created, 41 §14-902.
Definitions, 41 §14-901.
Guarantee of loan or subsidy for loan interest,
　41 §§14-909, 14-912.
　Prerequisites, 41 §14-910.
　Violations by qualified borrower.
　　Powers of board upon, 41 §14-913.
Purpose of fund, 41 §14-906.
Purpose of program, 41 §14-903.
Reports.
　Board of directors, 41 §14-914.
　State Treasurer, 41 §14-908.
Reversion to general fund, 41 §14-906.
Use of fund, 41 §14-907.

ASSOCIATIONS.
Actions.
　By or against unincorporated associations, CJ
　　§6-406.
　Liability for judgment against unincorporated
　　association, CJ §11-105.
Admissions and amusement tax.
　Not-for-profit community associations.
　　Exemption, TG §4-104.
Agricultural fair associations.
　Fair board, AG §§10-301 to 10-303.
　　See AGRICULTURE.
Alcoholic beverages.
　Unincorporated associations.
　　Application for licenses, 2B §9-101.
　　Fines and penalties, 2B §16-501.
Building and loan associations.
　See BUILDING AND LOAN ASSOCIATIONS.
Community associations.
　Liability.
　　Personal liability of agents, CJ §5-406.

ASSOCIATIONS —Cont'd
Community associations —Cont'd
　Limited civil liability, SG §7-108.
Cooperatives.
　General provisions.
　　See COOPERATIVES.
Corporations.
　General provisions.
　　See CORPORATIONS.
　Unincorporated associations.
　　Indicating incorporation prohibited.
　　　Exception, CA §1-404.
　　　General provisions, CA §1-404.
　　　Penalty, CA §1-404.
Credit unions.
　General provisions.
　　See CREDIT UNIONS.
Currency transactions in trade or business, BR
　§§1-501 to 1-505.
　See CURRENCY TRANSACTIONS IN TRADE
　　OR BUSINESS.
Definitions, CJ §5-406.
Depositions.
　Designation of person to testify for organization.
　　Notice.
　　　Circuit courts, CivProCir Rule 2-412.
Draining lands, 25 §§52 to 121H.
　See DRAINING LANDS.
Fraternal benefit societies.
　General provisions, IN §§8-401 to 8-468.
　　See FRATERNAL BENEFIT SOCIETIES.
Homeowners' associations.
　General provisions, RP §§11B-101 to 11B-115.
　　See HOMEOWNERS' ASSOCIATIONS.
　Liability.
　　Personal liability of agents, CJ §5-406.
Industry automobile insurance association, IN
　§§20-401 to 20-411.
　See AUTOMOBILE INSURANCE FUND.
Insurance.
　Joint insurance association, IN §§25-401 to
　　25-410.
　　See JOINT INSURANCE ASSOCIATION.
Joint insurance association, IN §§25-401 to
　25-410.
　See JOINT INSURANCE ASSOCIATION.
Judgments and decrees.
　Liability for judgment against unincorporated
　　association, CJ §11-105.
Jurisdiction.
　Over persons outside this state.
　　General provisions.
　　　See JURISDICTION.
Money.
　Currency transactions in trade or business, BR
　　§§1-501 to 1-505.
　　See CURRENCY TRANSACTIONS IN TRADE
　　　OR BUSINESS.
Nonstock corporations.
　General provisions.
　　See CORPORATIONS.
Organizational names and insignia.
　Registration, prohibited acts, BR §§19-201 to
　　19-207.
Partnerships.
　General provisions.
　　See PARTNERSHIPS.
Public watershed associations.
　Patuxent river watershed.
　　General provisions.
　　　See PATUXENT RIVER WATERSHED.

ASSOCIATIONS —Cont'd
Real estate investment trust.
General provisions, CA §§8-101 to 8-701.
See REAL ESTATE INVESTMENT TRUST.
Receivers.
Claims.
Verification requirements, Receivers Rule
13-401.
Schedule of debtor's property and debts.
Schedule filed by corporation, association or
partnership, Receivers Rule 13-203.
Savings and loan associations.
See SAVINGS AND LOAN ASSOCIATIONS.
Service of process.
Persons to be served.
Circuit court, CivProCir Rule 2-124.
District Court, CivProDist Rule 3-124.
Teachers' associations.
General provisions, ED §6-110.
Watershed associations.
Public watershed associations, 25 §§169 to 218.
See WATERSHED ASSOCIATIONS.

ASSUMING IDENTITY OF ANOTHER.
Identity fraud, CR §§8-301 to 8-305.

ASSUMPTION OF RISK.
Amusement rides.
Ticket purchasers, BR §3-104.
Consumer protection.
Credit card issued without request.
Loss, theft or unauthorized use, CL §14-1305.
Drug dealer liability act.
Inapplicable, CJ §3-1607.

ASTHMA.
Control program, HG §§13-1701 to 13-1706.
Advisory councils.
Director may establish, HG §13-1703.
Director.
Appointment by secretary, HG §13-1703.
Duties, HG §13-1704.
Established in department, HG §13-1702.
Funded as provided in budget, HG §13-1705.
Funding for local intervention initiatives, HG
§13-1704.
Other sources of funds, HG §13-1705.
Program defined, HG §13-1701.
Rules and regulations, adoption, HG §13-1706.
Training for school personnel, HG §13-1704.
Schools.
Self-administration of asthma medication by
pupils, ED §7-421.

ASTRODON JOHNSTONI.
State dinosaur, SG §13-316.

ASYLUM.
Extradition.
No right of asylum, CP §9-126.

ATHLETE AGENTS, BR §§4-401 to 4-421.
Application for license, BR §4-404.
Civil action by educational institution, BR
§4-415.
Construction and interpretation of provisions,
BR §4-417.
Electronic signatures, federal act compliance, BR
§4-418.
Severability, BR §4-419.
Contracts.
Cancellation, BR §4-411.
Contents, BR §4-409.
Notice to athletic director, BR §4-410.

ATHLETE AGENTS —Cont'd
Contracts —Cont'd
Prohibited activities, BR §4-413.
Voiding for eligibility warning violations, BR
§4-409.
Voiding for license violation, BR §4-403.
Definitions, BR §4-401.
Electronic signatures, federal act compliance,
BR §4-418.
Eligibility warning included in contract, BR
§4-409.
Fee-splitting prohibited, BR §4-413.
Inspection of records, BR §4-412.
Licenses.
Application, BR §4-404.
Denial, BR §4-405.
Disciplinary action, BR §4-406.
Hearing, BR §4-407.
Issuance, BR §4-405.
Renewal, BR §4-405.
Suspension or revocation, BR §4-406.
Hearing, BR §4-407.
Term, BR §4-405.
Unlicensed operation, BR §4-403.
Payment of money collected, BR §4-408.
Penalties.
Civil penalties, BR §4-416.
Criminal penalties for violations, BR §4-414.
Damages to educational institution, BR §4-415.
Licenses.
Civil penalty in lieu of suspension or revocation,
BR §4-406.
Payment of money collected, BR §4-408.
Prohibited activities, BR §4-413.
Civil action by educational institution, BR §4-415.
Criminal penalties, BR §4-414.
Records retention, BR §4-412.
Rulemaking by secretary, BR §4-420.
Service of process.
Agent for service, BR §4-402.
Severability of provisions, BR §4-419.
Subpoenas.
Authority of secretary to issue, BR §4-402.
Title of act, BR §4-421.
Uniformity of construction, BR §4-417.
Unlicensed operation, BR §4-403.

ATHLETIC FACILITIES.
Steroids and human growth hormone.
Warning of consequences of illegal use, posting,
CR §5-710.

ATHLETIC FIELDS.
Reclaimed water.
Use for irrigation purposes, EN §9-303.1.

ATHLETIC ORGANIZATIONS.
Amateur athletic organizations.
Bingo.
Frederick county, CR §13-1306.
Gaming, bazaar, carnival and raffles.
Baltimore City, CR §§13-501 to 13-510.
Baltimore county, CR §§13-601 to 13-607.
Carroll county, CR §§13-901 to 13-909.
Frederick county, CR §§13-1301 to 13-1307.
Tip jars and punch board.
Frederick county, CR §13-1305.

ATHLETICS.
Agents, BR §§4-401 to 4-421.
See ATHLETE AGENTS.
Alcoholic beverages.
Possession of intoxicating beverages.
School athletic contests.
Penalties, ED §26-103.

ATHLETICS —Cont'd

Bribery of participant or person connected with contest, CR §9-204.

Acceptance of bribe by participant or person connected to contest, CR §9-205.

Clubs.

Agents.

Personal liability, CJ §5-406.

Commission.

Athletic commission.

General provisions, BR §§4-201 to 4-208.

See BOXING, SPARRING AND WRESTLING.

Possession of intoxicating beverages at school athletic contests, ED §26-103.

Drunkenness.

Possession of intoxicating beverages at school athletic contests, ED §26-103.

Interference with commercial athletic event, CR §10-203.

Maryland stadium authority, FI §§13-701 to 13-724.

See MARYLAND STADIUM AUTHORITY.

Penalties.

Alcoholic beverages.

Possession at school athletic contest, ED §26-103.

Schools.

Alcoholic beverages.

Possession of intoxicating beverages at school athletic contests, ED §26-103.

Tickets.

Reserved seat tickets sold.

Seating plan showing location of seats and physical obstructions must be displayed, CL §13-310.

Unemployment compensation.

Athletic seasons.

Between season denials, LE §8-908.

Unfair or deceptive trade practices.

Reserved seat tickets, CL §13-310.

ATHLETIC TRAINERS.

Massage therapy certification.

Exemption, HO §3-5A-05.

ATLANTIC COASTAL BAYS CRITICAL AREA PROTECTION PROGRAM.

Generally, NR §§8-1801 to 8-1817.

See CHESAPEAKE BAY CRITICAL AREA AND ATLANTIC COASTAL BAYS CRITICAL AREA PROTECTION PROGRAMS.

ATLANTIC STATES MARINE FISHERIES COMMISSION.

Accounts and accounting.

Required, NR §4-304.

Appointment.

Maryland members, NR §4-302.

Appropriations, NR §4-305.

Compact.

General provisions, NR §4-301.

Comptroller.

Duties.

Generally, NR §4-304.

Cooperation of state officials, NR §4-303.

Duties of commission, NR §4-303.

Laws of state.

Not limited, NR §4-303.

Maryland members, NR §4-302.

Natural resources department.

Membership unit of, NR §1-102.

ATLANTIC STATES MARINE FISHERIES COMMISSION —Cont'd

Powers of commission, NR §4-303.

Removal of members.

Maryland members, NR §4-302.

ATM CARDS.

Credit card crimes, CR §§8-201 to 8-217.

See CREDIT CARDS.

ATM'S, FI §§1-401 to 1-406.

See AUTOMATED TELLER MACHINES.

ATOMIC ENERGY.

Hazardous materials and substances.

General provisions.

See HAZARDOUS MATERIALS AND SUBSTANCES.

Low-level nuclear waste.

Disposal.

See RADIATION.

Facilities.

See HAZARDOUS MATERIALS AND SUBSTANCES.

Nuclear power plants.

Security officers, CR §9-706.1.

Radiation generally.

See RADIATION.

Southern interstate nuclear compact.

General provisions, 41 §§16-101 to 16-114.

See NUCLEAR COMPACT.

AT-RISK YOUTH AND FAMILIES.

Abuse.

Child abuse and neglect generally, FL §§5-701 to 5-714.

See CHILD ABUSE AND NEGLECT.

Domestic violence generally, FL §§4-501 to 4-516.

See DOMESTIC VIOLENCE.

At-risk youth prevention and diversion programs, 41 §§2-501 to 2-503.

Advisory council.

Creation, 41 §2-502.

Defined, 41 §2-501.

Public policy, 41 §2-502.

Application for funding, 41 §2-503.

Definitions, 41 §2-501.

Local management board.

Duties for prevention element of 3-year plan, 41 §2-503.

Generally, 41 §2-503.

3-year plan, defined, 41 §2-501.

Status of programs, 41 §2-503.

Children in need of assistance, CJ §§3-801 to 3-830.

See CHILDREN IN NEED OF ASSISTANCE.

Disadvantaged children.

Compensatory education programs, ED §§8-101 to 8-107.

See SCHOOLS.

Domestic violence.

Generally, FL §§4-501 to 4-516.

See DOMESTIC VIOLENCE.

Local domestic violence fatality review teams, FL §§4-701 to 4-707.

See DOMESTIC VIOLENCE.

Drug and alcohol abuse.

Generally.

See DRUG OR ALCOHOL ABUSE.

Drug or alcohol abuse.

Addiction facilities, HG §§24-601 to 24-607.

Foster care.

General provisions, FL §§5-525 to 5-547.

See FOSTER CARE.

AT-RISK YOUTH AND FAMILIES —Cont'd
Homeless individuals.
Shelter, nutrition and service program for homeless individuals, 88A §§131 to 137.
See SOCIAL SERVICES.
Juvenile residential facilities, ED §§22-301 to 22-310.
See JUVENILE RESIDENTIAL FACILITIES.
Mental health.
Community mental health facilities, HG §§24-601 to 24-607.
See MENTAL HEALTH FACILITIES.
Early childhood mental health services pilot program, HG §§10-1501 to 10-1503.
Maryland mental health crisis response system, HG §§10-1401 to 10-1405.
See MENTAL HEALTH CRISIS RESPONSE SYSTEM.
Regional institute for children and adolescents in Prince George's county, HG §§10-406, 10-406.1.
Residential boarding education programs for at-risk youth, ED §§8-701 to 8-710.
Accountability, ED §8-706.
Contract by department with operator to provide services, ED §8-704.
Definitions, ED §§8-701, 8-709.
Eligibility to participate, ED §8-703.
Funding, ED §§8-709, 8-710.
Governing board, ED §8-705.
Operation under department supervision, ED §8-702.
Operators.
Contract by department with operator to provide services, ED §8-704.
Defined, ED §8-701.
Reports, ED §8-708.
Requirements, ED §8-706.
Teachers and professional personnel.
Salaries, ED §8-707.
Runaways.
Interstate compact on juveniles, 83C §§3-101, 3-110.
Runaway youth homes.
Establishment, 83C §2-121.
Services to families with children, FL §§4-401 to 4-403.
Suicide.
Youth suicide prevention school programs, ED §§7-501 to 7-506.
See SUICIDE.
Truancy reduction pilot program, CJ §§3-8C-01 to 3-8C-10.
See TRUANCY REDUCTION PILOT PROGRAM.
Youth and teenage pregnancy.
Development of plans and objectives to resolve problems, ED §2-205.

ATTACHMENT.
Absconding debtors.
Against whom available, CJ §3-303.
Actions.
Action which attachments are available, CJ §3-304.
Prejudgment attachment.
Single action.
Circuit courts, CivProCir Rule 2-115.
Alimony.
Enforcement of alimony or support order, FamLaw Rule 9-210.

ATTACHMENT —Cont'd
Appeals.
Decision or motion to quash, CJ §12-303.
Banks and trust companies.
Adverse claim to money, etc., in hands of bank, FI §5-306.
Bills of lading.
Attachment of goods covered by a negotiable document, CL §7-602.
Body attachment.
See BODY ATTACHMENT.
Bulk transfers.
Limitation of levies, CL §6-111.
Business trusts.
Subject to attachment of property, CA §12-501.
Circuit courts, CivProCir Rule 2-115.
College savings plan of Maryland.
Seizure by attachment, execution, garnishment, etc., ED §18-1913.
Complaints.
Prejudgment attachment.
Proceedings on complaint.
District Court, CivProDist Rule 3-115.
Contracts.
Issuance of attachments, CJ §3-304.
Corporations.
Against whom available, CJ §3-303.
Creditors.
Wages.
Duties of judgment creditors, CL §15-605.
Criminal rules.
Body attachment.
Material witnesses, Crim Rule 4-267.
Debtors.
Against whom available, CJ §3-303.
Property or credits subject to attachment, CJ §3-305.
Defendants.
Prejudgment attachment.
Judgment for defendant.
Circuit courts, CivProCir Rule 2-115.
District Court, CivProDist Rule 3-115.
Definitions.
Body attachment, Rule 1-202.
Wages, CL §15-601.
Depositions.
Body attachment of material witness.
Deposition of witness in custody, Crim Rule 4-267.
District Court.
Jurisdiction, CJ §4-401.
Prejudgment attachment, CivProDist Rule 3-115.
Documents of title.
Attachment of goods covered by a negotiable document, CL §7-602.
Emergency management.
Civil relief during emergency periods, PS §14-210.
Stays, postponements or suspensions of enforcement.
Period and terms of stay, PS §14-211.
Exemptions.
Amounts of wages exempt, CL §15-601.1.
Assignment of claims to nonresidents.
Depriving debtor of rights under exemption laws.
General provisions, CL §§15-501 to 15-503.
Calculation per pay period, CL §15-601.1.
Medical insurance payments, CL §15-601.1.
Fees.
Sheriffs, CJ §7-402.

ATTACHMENT —Cont'd
Fraternal benefit societies.
Benefits exempt from attachment, IN §8-431.
Fraud.
Against whom available, CJ §3-303.
Funds transfers.
Creditor process served on receiving bank, CL §4A-502.
Garnishment.
Prejudgment attachment.
Retention of levied or garnished property.
Circuit courts, CivProCir Rule 2-115.
District Court, CivProDist Rule 3-115.
Wages, CivProCir Rule 2-646; CivProDist Rule 3-646.
Attachment of wages generally, CL §§15-601 to 15-607. See within this heading, "Wages."
Home improvements.
Actions against persons arising out of home improvement transactions, CJ §3-303.
Insurance companies.
Liquidation, rehabilitation, etc.
Attachment of assets, IN §9-220.
Issuance.
Court may issue at commencement of action or while action pending, CJ §3-302.
Judgment creditors.
Wages.
Duties of judgment creditor, CL §15-605.
Judgments.
Debts due defendant, CJ §3-301.
Jurisdiction, CJ §3-301.
Levy on debt of defendant, CJ §3-301.
Prejudgment attachment.
Circuit courts, CivProCir Rule 2-115.
District Court, CivProDist Rule 3-115.
Juvenile causes.
Writ of attachment.
Forms, Form 904-WA.
Levies.
Prejudgment attachment.
Retention of levied or garnished property.
Circuit courts, CivProCir Rule 2-115.
District Court, CivProDist Rule 3-115.
Liens.
Income tax.
Financial institution holding property subject to lien.
Notice and attachment, TG §13-812.
Prejudgment attachment.
Notice.
District Court, CivProDist Rule 3-115.
Wages.
Attachment constitutes continuing lien, CL §15-602.
Nonresidents.
Against whom available, CJ §3-303.
Notice.
Prejudgment attachment.
Lien of attachment.
District Court, CivProDist Rule 3-115.
Officers.
Wages due from or payable by state, county, municipal corporation or other political subdivision, CL §15-607.
Original process.
Action through which attachment available, CJ §3-304.
Venue, CJ §6-202.
Plaintiffs.
Prejudgment attachment.
Judgment for plaintiff.
Circuit courts, CivProCir Rule 2-115.

ATTACHMENT —Cont'd
Prejudgment attachment.
Circuit courts.
Complaint.
Proceedings on complaint, CivProCir Rule 2-115.
Dissolution of attachment.
Failure of service, CivProCir Rule 2-115.
Release of property, CivProCir Rule 2-115.
Garnishment.
Retention of garnished property, CivProCir Rule 2-115.
Issuance of writ, CivProCir Rule 2-115.
Judgment for defendant, CivProCir Rule 2-115.
Judgment for plaintiff, CivProCir Rule 2-115.
Levies.
Retention of levied property, CivProCir Rule 2-115.
Proceedings on complaint, CivProCir Rule 2-115.
Proceedings on request for writ, CivProCir Rule 2-115.
Release of property, CivProCir Rule 2-115.
Request for writ, CivProCir Rule 2-115.
Proceedings on request, CivProCir Rule 2-115.
Retention of levied or garnished property, CivProCir Rule 2-115.
Service of process.
Dissolution of attachment for lack of service, CivProCir Rule 2-115.
Single action, CivProCir Rule 2-115.
Third parties.
Claim of property by third person, CivProCir Rule 2-115.
District Court.
Complaint.
Proceedings on complaint, CivProDist Rule 3-115.
Dissolution.
Release of property or dissolution of attachment, CivProDist Rule 3-115.
Garnished property.
Retention, CivProDist Rule 3-115.
Issuance of writ, CivProDist Rule 3-115.
Judgment for defendant.
Effect, CivProDist Rule 3-115.
Judgment for plaintiff.
Effect, CivProDist Rule 3-115.
Lack of service, CivProDist Rule 3-115.
Levied or garnished property.
Retention of levied or garnished property, CivProDist Rule 3-115.
Lien of attachment.
Notice, CivProDist Rule 3-115.
Release of property, CivProDist Rule 3-115.
Request for writ, CivProDist Rule 3-115.
Proceedings on request for writ, CivProDist Rule 3-115.
Single action, CivProDist Rule 3-115.
Third parties.
Claim of property by third person, CivProDist Rule 3-115.
Secured transactions.
Security interest attachment, CL §9-203.
Financial asset.
Security interest arising in purchase or delivery of, CL §9-206.
Perfection.
Security interest perfected upon attachment, CL §9-309.

ATTACHMENT —Cont'd
Service of process.
Prejudgment attachment.
Dissolution for lack of service.
Circuit courts, CivProCir Rule 2-115.
District Court, CivProDist Rule 3-115.
Sheriffs.
Direction of writ, CJ §2-302.
Fees, CJ §7-402.
Property found only within county, CJ §2-302.
Returns.
Failure to file, CJ §2-304.
Summons and process.
Action to evade service, CJ §3-303.
Support and maintenance.
Enforcement of alimony or support order,
FamLaw Rule 9-210.
Taxation.
Actions to collect taxes, TG §13-817.
Collection.
Authorization of attachment, TP §14-867.
Income tax liens.
Financial institution holding property subject to
lien.
Notice and attachment, TG §13-812.
Third parties.
Prejudgment attachment.
Claim of property by third person.
Circuit courts, CivProCir Rule 2-115.
District Court, CivProDist Rule 3-115.
Torts.
Issuance of attachment, CJ §3-304.
Universities and colleges.
College savings plan of Maryland.
Seizure by attachment, execution, garnishment,
etc., ED §18-1913.
Wages.
Application of limitations, CL §15-602.
Creditor.
Duties of judgment creditors, CL §15-605.
Definitions, CL §15-601.
Discharge of employee because of attachment
prohibited in certain cases, CL §15-606.
Dismissal of employee, CL §15-604.
Duties of employer, CL §15-603.
Duties of judgment creditors, CL §15-605.
Employees.
Discharge because of attachment.
Prohibited in certain cases, CL §15-606.
Dismissal, CL §15-604.
Resignation, CL §15-604.
Employer.
Duties, CL §15-603.
Exemption from attachment.
Amounts of wages exempt, CL §15-601.1.
Medical insurance payments, CL §15-601.1.
Exemptions from executions.
Not applicable to wage attachments, CJ
§11-504.
Garnishment generally, CivProCir Rule 2-646;
CivProDist Rule 3-646.
Judgment creditors.
Duties, CL §15-605.
Liability of wages due from or payable by state,
county, municipal corporation or other
political subdivision, CL §15-607.
Liens.
Continuing lien, CL §15-602.
Limitations.
Waiver, CL §15-602.
Resignation or dismissal of employee, CL §15-604.

ATTACHMENT —Cont'd
Wages —Cont'd
Sovereign immunity.
Wages due from or payable by state, county,
municipal corporation or other political
subdivision.
Waiver of sovereign immunity, CL §15-607.
Waiver of limitations, CL §15-602.
Warehouse receipts.
Attachment of goods covered by a negotiable
document, CL §7-602.
Witnesses.
Refusal to appear.
Alcoholic beverage cases, 2B §16-410.
Workers' compensation.
Payment of award.
Prohibition against attachment or execution, LE
§9-732.

ATTAINDER.
Bill of attainder.
Constitutional provisions, US Const Art I §§9, 10;
Art III §3.
**No corruption of blood or forfeiture of estate
for conviction of attainder,** ET §11-109.
**No corruption of blood or forfeiture of estate
for treason or felony,** MD Const DofR Art 18.

ATTEMPTED POISONING, CR §3-213.

ATTEMPTED RAPE IN THE FIRST DEGREE,
CR §3-309.

**ATTEMPTED RAPE IN THE SECOND
DEGREE,** CR §3-310.

**ATTEMPTED SEXUAL OFFENSE IN THE
FIRST DEGREE,** CR §3-311.

**ATTEMPTED SEXUAL OFFENSE IN THE
SECOND DEGREE,** CR §3-312.

**ATTEMPT TO BURN STRUCTURE OR
PROPERTY,** CR §6-108.

ATTEMPT TO COMMIT CRIME.
Attempted poisoning, CR §3-213.
Attempt to burn structure or property, CR
§6-108.
**Punishment not to exceed maximum
punishment for crime attempted,** CR
§1-201.
Rape.
Attempted rape in the first degree, CR §3-309.
Attempted rape in the second degree, CR §3-310.
Sexual offense.
Attempted sexual offense in the first degree, CR
§3-311.
Attempted sexual offense in the second degree, CR
§3-312.

ATTENDANCE OF WITNESSES.
Failure of witness to appear, CJ §9-201.
Discharge from execution for failure to attend, CJ
§9-204.
Securing attendance from without a state, CJ
§§9-301 to 9-306.
See WITNESSES.
Summons for attendance, CJ §9-201.

ATTENDANT CARE PROGRAM.
Administration of program, 41 §18-603.
**Community attendant services and supports
program,** 41 §§6-7A-01 to 6-7A-06.
Availability of services, 41 §6-7A-03.
Consumer rights, 41 §6-7A-03.

ATTENDANT CARE PROGRAM —Cont'd
Community attendant services and supports
    program —Cont'd
  Consumer training, 41 §6-7A-03.
  Defined terms, 41 §6-7A-01.
  Development.
    Status reports, 41 §6-7A-06.
  Eligibility, 41 §6-7A-03.
  Establishment of program, 41 §6-7A-02.
  Income waivers, 41 §6-7A-02.
  Individualized support plans, 41 §6-7A-04.
  Individual service plans, 41 §6-7A-03.
  Input from eligible individuals, representatives
    and service providers, 41 §6-7A-02.
    Quality assurance, 41 §6-7A-05.
  Management and administration, 41 §6-7A-03.
  Quality assurance, 41 §6-7A-05.
  Regulations, 41 §6-7A-02.
  Status reports, 41 §6-7A-06.
Definitions, 41 §18-601.
Department of human resources.
  Administration of program, 41 §§18-603, 18-604.
  Definition of "department," 41 §18-601.
Financial assistance.
  Defined, 41 §18-601.
  Program of financial assistance, 41 §18-602.
  Requirements for recipients, 41 §18-602.
Funding, 41 §18-603.

ATTESTATION.
Deeds.
  Not required, RP §4-101.
  Power of attorney, RP §4-107.
Power of attorney.
  Deeds, RP §4-107.

ATTIC FANS.
Consumer protection.
  Firestat or fusible link in attic fan required, CL
    §13-315.

ATTORNEY GENERAL.
Acting attorney general, SG §6-110.
Actions against state officers and employees.
  Criminal actions, SG §§12-313 to 12-318.
    See ACTIONS AGAINST STATE OFFICERS
      AND EMPLOYEES.
  General provisions, SG §§12-301 to 12-318.
    See ACTIONS AGAINST STATE OFFICERS
      AND EMPLOYEES.
Additional counsel.
  Authorized by general assembly, MD Const Art V
    §3.
Administrative procedure.
  Regulations.
    Submission of proposed regulations, SG
      §10-107.
Advertising.
  False advertising in conduct of business, trade,
    etc.
    Recovery of civil penalty, CL §11-705.
Agricultural and resource-based industry
    development corporation.
  Legal advisor to corporation, 41 §13-506.
Agriculture.
  Department of agriculture.
    Legal advisor and counsel, AG §2-105.
Air quality control.
  Cases arising under provisions.
    Responsibilities as to, EN §2-614.
Amusements and recreation.
  Administrative search warrant.
    Approval by attorney general, BR §3-205.

ATTORNEY GENERAL —Cont'd
Antitrust.
  Civil actions, CL §11-209.
  Cooperation with federal government and with
    other states, CL §11-208.
  Demand production of documents for inspection,
    CL §11-205.
  Duty of attorney general to advise political
    subdivisions, SG §6-107.
  Prosecution of violations, CL §11-207.
Applicability of title, SG §6-102.
Assistants.
  Business and economic development department.
    Assignment to department, 83A §2-103.
  Consumer protection.
    Assistant in charge, CL §13-203.
  Qualifications, SG §6-105.
Baltimore City.
  Legal advisor for certain legal work, SG §6-107.
Banks and trust companies.
  Removal of director or officer for unsafe or
    unsound practices, FI §5-801.
    Report to attorney general, FI §5-802.
Boycotts.
  Foreign discriminatory boycotts.
    See FOREIGN DISCRIMINATORY
      BOYCOTTS.
Budget and management.
  Assistant attorney general.
    Assignment to department, SF §3-206.
  Legal adviser to department, SF §3-206.
Business and economic development
    department.
  Assistant attorneys general.
    Assignment to department, 83A §2-103.
  Legal advisor, 83A §2-103.
Campaign finance.
  Contributions to political campaigns during
    general assembly sessions.
    Prohibition, exceptions, EL §13-235.
Cases in which state has interest.
  Clerk of court to notify attorney general, MD
    Const Art V §6.
Cemeteries.
  Civil enforcement actions, BR §5-905.
  Perpetual care of cemeteries.
    Enforcement power, BR §5-606.
  Preneed burial contracts.
    Enforcement power, BR §5-711.
Chesapeake Bay.
  Dumping of dredged materials in bay.
    Enforcement of subtitle, EN §5-1106.
    Injunctions, EN §5-1105.
Chesapeake Bay critical area and Atlantic
    coastal bays critical area protection
    programs.
  Referral if local jurisdiction failing in duties, NR
    §8-1815.
Child custody.
  Instructional materials regarding child custody
    and visitation.
    Duties, CJ §2-206.
Child custody proceedings.
  Uniform child custody jurisdiction and
    enforcement act.
    Lawful action by, FL §9.5-315.
Child support.
  Instructional materials regarding.
    Duties, CJ §2-206.
Child support enforcement administration.
  Legal representation, FL §10-115.

ATTORNEY GENERAL —Cont'd

Citizenship.

Requirements, MD Const Art V §4.

Clerks of court.

Election.

Returns made by clerk to governor, MD Const Art V §2.

Comptroller.

Opinions in writing to, MD Const Art V §3.

Consumer protection.

Assistant attorney general.

Appointment and salary, CL §13-203.

Authority of attorney general to subpoena witnesses, etc., CL §13-405.

Division of consumer protection.

Established within office of attorney general, CL §13-201.

Unit pricing.

Enforcement, CL §14-106.

Injunctions.

Authority to seek, CL §13-406.

Mobile homes.

Enforcement of title by division of consumer protection, RP §8A-1802.

Recommendation of legislation, CL §13-203.

Unit pricing.

Enforcement, CL §14-106.

Continuing care contracts.

Representation of special deputy secretary, 70B §20D.

Contributions to political campaigns during general assembly sessions.

Prohibition, exceptions, EL §13-235.

Cooperative associations.

Agricultural products.

Discrimination, etc., against producers.

Actions to enjoin violations, AG §10-203.

Receiver of complaints, AG §10-202.

Corporations.

Forfeiture of charter.

Conduct in connection with organized crime, CA §1-405.

Institution of proceedings, CA §3-513.

Ultra vires.

In proceedings by attorney general, CA §1-403.

Counsel for officers and units, SG §6-106.

Court of appeals.

Prosecute and defend suits in, MD Const Art V §3.

Credit card number printed on receipts.

Restrictions, violations, action by, CL §14-1318.

Crime victim services.

Board.

General provisions.

See VICTIMS OF CRIME.

Currency transactions in trade or business.

Reports.

Access of office of attorney general to reports, BR §1-504.

Declaratory judgments.

Role of attorney general, CJ §3-405.

Definitions.

Office, SG §6-101.

Delegation of duties, SG §6-105.

Department of public safety and correctional services.

Legal adviser, assignment of counsel, COR §2-116.

Deputy attorney general.

Acting attorney general.

Chief deputy attorney general as, SG §6-110.

Appointment, MD Const Art V §3.

ATTORNEY GENERAL —Cont'd

Deputy attorney general —Cont'd

Assistant attorneys general. See within this heading, "Assistants."

Qualifications, SG §6-105.

Duties.

Department of disabilities, SG §9-1105.

General provisions, MD Const Art V.

Elections.

Contributions to political campaigns during general assembly sessions.

Prohibition, exceptions, EL §13-235.

Determining election, MD Const Art V §2.

Filing fee, EL §5-401.

Returns to governor, MD Const Art V §2.

Tie vote.

Determined by governor, MD Const Art V §2.

Electric companies.

Investigation of anticompetitive conduct.

Interagency cooperation, PUC §7-514.

Electronic transaction education, advocacy and mediation unit, SG §§6-201 to 6-203.

Definition of electronic transactions, SG §6-201.

Duties, SG §6-202.

Established, SG §6-202.

Regulations, SG §6-203.

Employment and social services.

Assistant attorneys general.

Assignment to department, 41 §6-103.

Counsel to department, 41 §6-103.

Legal advisor to department, 41 §6-103.

Environment.

Department.

Legal counsel, EN §1-407.

Falsifying or altering permits, licenses or certificates.

Investigation and prosecution, EN §1-302.

Water management.

Responsibility for cases arising under title, EN §4-502.

Environmental service.

Duties, NR §3-103.

Environmental trust.

Legal counsel, NR §3-206.

Fee for health care services to inmates.

Assessment to inmates in state correctional facilities, COR §2-118.

Fees.

Prohibited from receiving, MD Const Art V §3.

Flood control.

Enforcement of subtitle, EN §5-805.

Foreign discriminatory boycotts.

See FOREIGN DISCRIMINATORY BOYCOTTS.

Fraternal benefit societies.

Injunctions, IN §8-464.

Gas and oil.

Coastal facilities review act.

Violations of subtitle.

Injunctions against violations, EN §14-510.

General assembly.

Opinions in writing to, MD Const Art V §3.

General services department.

Assistant attorneys general.

Assignment to department, SF §4-205.

Legal adviser to department, SF §4-205.

Governor.

Determining election and qualification of attorney general, MD Const Art V §2.

Discharging duties of office of governor during vacancy, MD Const Art II §7.

ATTORNEY GENERAL —Cont'd
Governor —Cont'd
Election.
Tie vote.
Determining by governor, MD Const Art V §2.
Oaths.
Administering, MD Const Art V §2.
Opinions in writing to, MD Const Art V §3.
Vacancy in office of attorney general.
Filled by governor, MD Const Art V §5.
Hazardous materials and substances.
Controlled hazardous substances.
Control fund.
Actions for costs, EN §7-221.
Responsibility for cases arising under subtitle, EN §7-268.
Health.
Department of health and mental hygiene.
Counsel to department, HG §2-107.
High voltage lines.
Administrative search warrant.
Approval of attorney general, LE §6-105.
Housing and community development department.
Legal advisor, HS §2-116.
Identity theft passports, issuance, CR §8-305.
Injunctions.
Organized crime.
Actions to enjoin operation of business other than corporation, CA §1-405.
Inmates, parolees or others.
Assignment to employee with proper certification, COR §2-117.
Insurance.
Legal counsel, IN §2-201.
Liquidation, rehabilitation, etc., of insurers.
Representation of special deputy commissioners, IN §9-207.
People's insurance counsel division, SG §§6-301 to 6-308.
Insurance administration.
Legal counsel, IN §2-104.
Insurance fraud division.
Records.
Denial of access to records, SG §10-618.
Report on failure to prosecute cases, IN §2-408.
Unauthorized practice of law, BOP §§10-401 to 10-405.
See ATTORNEYS AT LAW.
Interstate agreement on detainers.
Designation as officer to carry out provisions, COR §8-415.
Investigations.
People's insurance counsel, SG §6-306.
Access to facilities and information, SG §6-307.
Juvenile justice monitoring unit, SG §§6-401 to 6-406.
Juvenile services.
Department of juvenile services.
Legal advisor, 83C §2-105.
Juvenile justice monitoring unit, SG §§6-401 to 6-406.
Labor, licensing and regulation department.
Assignment of assistants, BR §2-107.
Legal counsel to department, BR §2-107.
Legislative auditor.
Reports of criminal violations discovered during an examination, SG §2-1225.
Limited liability companies.
Foreign companies.
Doing business in violation of title.
Actions by, CA §4A-1008.

ATTORNEY GENERAL —Cont'd
Limited liability partnerships, revised act.
Foreign limited liability partnerships.
Action by attorney general to restrain violations, CA §9A-1107.
Maryland historical trust.
Legal counsel, SF §5A-317.
Mid-shore regional council.
Legal advisor to counsel, 20C §1-106.
Migrant labor.
Investigative and enforcement powers, LE §7-205.
Mining.
Strip mining.
Bond or deposit.
Forfeiture.
Suit to collect forfeited bond, EN §15-514.
Money transmission.
Enforcement of subtitle.
Prosecution of violations, FI §12-429.
Motor vehicles.
Administration.
Jury commissioners, provision of information. Enforcement, TR §12-112.1.
Display of state seal on vehicle, TR §22-404.2.
Natural resources.
Assistant attorneys general.
Assignment to department, NR §1-101.
Department.
Assistant attorneys general.
Assignment to department, NR §1-101.
Legal advisor, NR §1-101.
Nonprofit health entities.
Acquisition.
General provisions, SG §§6.5-101 to 6.5-401.
See NONPROFIT HEALTH ENTITIES.
Nonprofit health service plans.
Enforcement of unsound or unsafe practices, IN §14-116.
Notices.
Acting attorney general, SG §6-110.
Cases in which state has interest.
Clerks of courts of appeal to notify attorney general, MD Const Art V §6.
Oaths.
Administration by governor, MD Const Art V §2.
Official oath, SG §16-102.
Occupational safety and health.
Administration and enforcement.
Power of attorney general, LE §5-207.
Administrative search warrant.
Approval of attorney general, LE §5-211.
Office.
Defined, SG §6-101.
Duty of state to maintain and equip offices, SG §6-104.
Established, SG §6-104.
Office of the state prosecutor, SG §§9-1201 to 9-1213.
See OFFICE OF THE STATE PROSECUTOR.
Opinions.
In writing, MD Const Art V §3.
Publication, SG §6-108.
Payment device numbers printed on receipts.
Restrictions, violations, action by, CL §14-1318.
People's counsel.
Public service commission.
Appointment, removal, PUC §2-202.
People's insurance counsel division, SG §§6-301 to 6-308.
Administration and operation, SG §6-303.

ATTORNEY GENERAL —Cont'd
People's insurance counsel division —Cont'd
Annual assessment.
　Funding of division, SG §6-304.
Appearances before commissioner and courts.
　Rights, SG §6-307.
Appearances before federal and state tribunals or
　agencies.
　Authorization, SG §6-307.
Appointment, SG §6-302.
Budget, SG §6-303.
Defined terms, SG §6-301.
Established, SG §6-302.
Experts, authority to retain, SG §6-303.
Functions, SG §6-306.
Fund, SG §6-305.
Funding of division, SG §6-304.
Investigations, SG §6-306.
　Access to facilities and information, SG §6-307.
Legislation, recommendations, SG §6-307.
Powers, SG §6-307.
Qualifications, SG §6-302.
Rate increase proposals.
　Review, SG §6-306.
Reports.
　Annual reports, SG §6-308.
Physical therapists.
Bringing disciplinary action, HO §13-318.1.
Position created, SG §6-103.
Powers.
Additional powers, SG §6-108.
Private foundations.
Rights and powers of courts and attorney general
　not impaired, CA §5-405.
Procurement.
Collusion.
　Enforcement by attorney general, SF §11-205.
　For purpose of defrauding state.
　　Notice to office of attorney general, SF
　　　§11-205.
　　Suit by attorney general for damages, SF
　　　§11-205.
　Notice to office of attorney general, SF §11-205.
Publication.
Opinions, SG §6-108.
Public service commission.
People's counsel.
　Appointment, removal, PUC §2-202.
Public works contracts.
Wages.
　Noncompliance by public body, SF §17-223.
Qualifications, MD Const Art V §4.
Determining, MD Const Art V §2.
Special attorneys, SG §6-105.
Quo warranto.
Corporations.
　Ultra vires.
　　Asserting by attorney general, CA §1-403.
Radiation.
Enforcement of provisions, EN §8-511.
　Remedies not exclusive, EN §8-512.
Railroad safety and health.
Enforcement assistance, LE §5.5-107.
Records.
Investigations.
　Denial of access to records, SG §10-618.
Papers of office filed in offices permanently, SG
　§6-108.
Required records, SG §6-108.
Registers of wills.
Probate procedure and forms.
　Cooperation in making available to public, ET
　　§2-212.

ATTORNEY GENERAL —Cont'd
Reimbursement for expenses, SG §6-103.
Removal, MD Const Art V §1.
Reports.
Annual report, SG §6-108.
Insurance fraud division.
　Report on failure to prosecute cases, IN §2-408.
People's insurance counsel division.
　Annual reports, SG §6-308.
Residence.
Requirements, MD Const Art V §4.
Rules and regulations.
Administrative procedure act.
　Submission of proposed regulations to attorney
　　general, SG §10-107.
Rural Maryland council.
Legal advisor, 41 §15-107.
Salaries.
Annual salary, SG §6-103.
General provisions, MD Const Art V §3.
Scholarships.
Bonds, surety.
　Enforcement of obligation of bond, ED §18-109.
Schools.
Advice to state board of education, ED §2-205.
Scope of title, SG §6-102.
Securities act.
General provisions, CA §§11-101 to 11-805.
　See SECURITIES.
**Service contracts and consumer products
　guaranty.**
Injunctions against violators, CL §14-406.
　Court order, CL §14-406.
　Notice, CL §14-406.
Service of process.
Persons to be served.
　Circuit courts, CivProCir Rule 2-124.
　District Court, CivProDist Rule 3-124.
　State agencies, designation of agent for service,
　　CivProCir Rule 2-124; CivProDist Rule 3-124.
　Person other than attorney general, SG §6-109.
Soil conservation.
Committee.
　Legal services, AG §8-203.
**Special counsel for state officers and
　employees,** SG §6-105.
Staff.
Generally, SG §6-105.
State legal business.
Counsel for officers and units, SG §6-106.
Other counsel prohibited generally, SG §6-106.
Supervision.
　Duty of attorney general, SG §6-106.
State officers and employees.
Actions against, SG §§12-301 to 12-318.
　See ACTIONS AGAINST STATE OFFICERS
　　AND EMPLOYEES.
State police department.
Counsel to department, PS §2-206.
State prosecutor.
Office of the state prosecutor, SG §§9-1201 to
　9-1213.
　See OFFICE OF THE STATE PROSECUTOR.
State retirement and pension system.
Legal adviser, SPP §21-107.
State's attorneys.
General provisions, 10 §§34 to 41D.
　See STATE'S ATTORNEYS.
Support and maintenance.
Uniform interstate family support act.
　Duties of attorney general, FL §10-320.

ATTORNEY GENERAL —Cont'd
Taxation.
Collection.
Duty and actions for collection, TP §14-865.
Compromise of claim, TP §14-866.
Initiation of action, TP §14-866.
Term of office, MD Const Art V §1.
Re-eligible for office, MD Const Art V §1.
Tires.
Used tires.
State used tire cleanup and recycling fund.
Reimbursement of costs.
Action for failure to make, EN §9-276.
Tort claims act.
Attorney general to defend civil actions against
state, SG §12-108.
Transportation department.
Assistant attorneys general, TR §2-106.
Counsel to department, TR §2-106.
Legal advisor, TR §2-106.
**Tri-County Council for lower Eastern shore of
Maryland.**
Legal advisor to counsel, 20B §1-106.
Tri-County Council for Southern Maryland.
Legal advisor to council, 20 §1-105.
Tri-County Council for Western Maryland.
Legal advisor to council, 20A §1-105.
Trusts and trustees.
Administration of private foundations, charitable
trusts or split-interest trusts.
Powers of attorney general not impaired, ET
§14-307.
Turf grass law.
Prosecution of violations, AG §9-109.
Unauthorized practice of law.
Injunctions.
Action for injunction, BOP §10-406.
Investigation by attorney general, BOP §§10-401
to 10-405.
See ATTORNEYS AT LAW.
Unemployment compensation.
Legal representation.
Civil actions, LE §8-307.
Uniform interstate family support act.
Duties, FL §10-320.
United States courts.
Prosecute and defend suits in supreme court of
United States, MD Const Art V §3.
Vacancy.
Filled by governor, MD Const Art V §5.
Veterans.
Department of veterans affairs.
Legal adviser to department, SG §9-903.
Victims of crime.
Notoriety of crimes contracts.
Decisions by, CP §11-623.
Distribution of escrow account money, CP
§11-629.
Escrow account deposits, CP §11-624.
Injunctive relief, CP §11-632.
Powers of, CP §11-629.
Submission to, CP §11-622.
Water pollution.
Injunctions.
Duty of attorney general, EN §4-416.
Responsibilities, EN §§5-1302, 9-344; NR §8-2002.
Water quality financing administration.
Legal advisor, EN §9-1603.
Water resources.
Responsibilities, EN §§5-1302, 9-344; NR §8-2002.

ATTORNEY GENERAL —Cont'd
Well drillers.
Responsibility for cases, EN §§9-1311, 13-404.
Whistleblower protection.
Disclosure of protected information, SPP §5-313.
Workers' compensation.
Legal adviser to commission, LE §9-744.
Subsequent injury fund.
Legal adviser, LE §10-211.
Written opinions to governor, MD Const Art V
§3.

ATTORNEY GRIEVANCE COMMISSION.
See ATTORNEYS AT LAW.

ATTORNEY IN FACT.
General provisions.
See POWER OF ATTORNEY.

ATTORNEYS AT LAW.
Accounts and accounting.
Disbarment or suspension.
Audit of attorney's accounts and records, CJA
Rule 16-722.
Trust accounts. See within this heading, "Trust
accounts."
Actions against state officers and employees.
Agreement for representation, SG §12-305.
Appearance of attorney general, SG §12-304.
Right of officers or employees to retain counsel,
SG §12-304.
Scope and effect of representation, SG §12-306.
Administration of courts.
Proscribed activities, CJA Rule 16-401.
Rules of professional conduct.
Adoption, CJA Rule 16-812.
Administrative procedure.
Contested cases.
Practice before agency, SG §10-206.1.
Admission to the bar.
Age.
Qualifications of applicants, BOP §10-207.
Applications.
Petition, BOP §10-208.
Qualifications of applicants, BOP §10-207.
Board of law examiners.
Appointment of members, BOP §10-202.
Assistance to the board, BarAdm Rule 20.
Compensation of members, BarAdm Rule 20.
Composition, BOP §10-202.
Confidentiality of proceedings.
General policy, BarAdm Rule 19.
When disclosure authorized, BarAdm Rule 19.
Creation, BOP §10-201.
Definition of "board," BarAdm Rule 1; BOP
§10-101.
Disposition of money collected, BOP §10-203.
Established, BOP §10-201.
Examinations.
General provisions. See within this
subheading, "Examinations."
General fund.
Payment of money collected into, BOP
§10-203.
Law students.
Legal assistance by law students.
Definitions, BarAdm Rule 16.
Meetings, BarAdm Rule 20.
Multi-state examination.
Board test, BarAdmBoard Rule 5.
Out-of-state attorneys.
Examination, BarAdmBoard Rule 6.

ATTORNEYS AT LAW —Cont'd
Admission to the bar —Cont'd
Board of law examiners —Cont'd
Prescription of fees, BarAdm Rule 18.
Program evaluation date, HG §8-403.
Qualifications of members, BOP §10-202.
Quorum, BOP §10-202.
Registration of law students, BarAdm Rule 2.
Rules.
Authority to make, BarAdm Rule 20.
Secretary to board, BarAdm Rule 20.
Subpoena power of board and character
committees, BarAdm Rule 22.
Terms of members, BOP §10-202.
Vacancies, BOP §10-202.
Burden of proof.
Out-of-state attorneys, BarAdm Rule 13.
Character.
Investigation, BarAdm Rule 5.
Proof, BarAdm Rule 2.
Report, BarAdm Rule 5.
Character committees, BarAdm Rule 22.
Appointment, BarAdm Rule 17.
Compensation, BarAdm Rule 17.
Confidentiality of proceedings.
General policy, BarAdm Rule 19.
When disclosure authorized, BarAdm Rule 19.
Hearing, BarAdm Rule 5.
Court review, BarAdm Rule 5.
Terms, BarAdm Rule 17.
Construction and interpretation, BarAdm Rule 1.
Courts.
Defined, BarAdm Rule 1.
Definitions, BarAdm Rule 1; BOP §10-101.
Legal assistance by law students, BarAdm Rule
16.
Education.
Certification by law school, BarAdm Rule 6.
Law students.
Legal assistance by law students, BarAdm
Rule 16.
Registration, BarAdm Rule 2.
Pre-legal education, BarAdm Rule 3.
Qualifications of applicants, BOP §10-207.
Recognition of law schools, BarAdm Rule 4.
Required course on professionalism, BarAdm
Rule 11.
Out-of-state attorneys, BarAdm Rule 13.
Evidence.
Out-of-state attorneys.
Supporting data and exhibits, BarAdm Rule
13.
Registration of law students.
Character.
Proof of character, BarAdm Rule 2.
Examinations, BOP §10-209.
Application fees, BarAdmBoard Rule 1.
Disabled persons, accommodation,
BarAdmBoard Rule 3.
Duration, BarAdm Rule 7.
Effective date, BarAdm Rule 7.
Failure.
Taking after failure.
Deferment of retake examination, BarAdm
Rule 9.
Petition, BarAdm Rule 9.
Review procedure, BarAdm Rule 8.
Fees, BarAdm Rule 6; BOP §10-208.
Refunds, BarAdm Rule 6.
Filing late for good cause, BarAdmBoard Rule
2.

ATTORNEYS AT LAW —Cont'd
Admission to the bar —Cont'd
Examinations —Cont'd
Implementation by board, BarAdm Rule 7.
Multi-state examination.
Board test, BarAdmBoard Rule 5.
Passing grades, BarAdm Rule 7.
Notice of grades, BarAdm Rule 8; BOP §10-209.
Out-of-state attorneys, BarAdm Rule 13.
Board of law examiners, BarAdmBoard Rule
6.
Re-examinations, BarAdm Rule 13.
Report of results, BarAdm Rule 13.
Passing examination required, BOP §10-207.
Petition to take, BarAdm Rule 6.
Policy of court, BarAdm Rule 7.
Procedure to take, BarAdm Rule 4.
Publication of notice, BarAdm Rule 7.
Re-examinations, BarAdm Rule 13.
Registration of law students.
Time of taking examination, BarAdm Rule 2.
Results.
Report, BarAdm Rule 10.
Exceptions, BarAdm Rule 10.
Order of ratification, BarAdm Rule 10.
Out-of-state attorneys, BarAdm Rule 13.
Sessions, BarAdm Rule 7.
Subject matter, BarAdm Rule 7; BarAdmBoard
Rule 4; BOP §10-209.
Time and place, BarAdm Rule 7.
Registration of law students, BarAdm Rule 2.
Exceptions to requirement, BOP §10-206.
Fees.
Application fees, BarAdmBoard Rule 1.
Examination fee, BarAdm Rule 6; BOP §10-208.
Refunds, BarAdm Rule 6.
Taking after failure, BarAdm Rule 9.
No refunds, BarAdm Rule 9.
Out-of-state attorneys.
Filing fee, BarAdm Rule 13.
Prescription by board, BarAdm Rule 18.
Registration of law students.
Filing fee, BarAdm Rule 2.
Taking examinations after failure, BarAdm Rule
9.
No refunds of fee, BarAdm Rule 9.
Filing.
Defined, BarAdm Rule 1.
Out-of-state attorneys.
Petition, BarAdm Rule 13.
Registration of law students.
Fee for filing, BarAdm Rule 2.
Final order of admission, BarAdm Rule 12.
Fraud.
Revocation of admission fraudulently obtained,
BOP §10-214.
Hearings.
Character committees, BarAdm Rule 5.
Out-of-state attorneys, BarAdm Rule 13.
Ineligibility for admission.
Suspension or revocation of license, BarAdm
Rule 21.
Investigations.
Character committees, BarAdm Rule 5.
Out-of-state attorneys, BarAdm Rule 13.
Law school.
Certification by law school, BarAdm Rule 6.
Requirements for legal education, BarAdm Rule
4.
American Bar Association approval to be
required, BarAdm Rule 4.

ATTORNEYS AT LAW —Cont'd
Admission to the bar —Cont'd
Law school —Cont'd
Requirements for legal education —Cont'd
Minors, BarAdm Rule 4.
Waiver, BarAdm Rule 4.
Law students.
Legal assistance by law students.
Certification, BarAdm Rule 16.
Eligibility, BarAdm Rule 16.
Practice, BarAdm Rule 16.
Registration, BarAdm Rule 2.
Minors.
Law school.
Requirements for legal education, BarAdm
Rule 4.
Motions.
Out-of-state attorneys.
Special admission of out-of-state attorneys,
BarAdm Rule 14.
Multi-state examination.
Board of law examiners.
Board test, BarAdmBoard Rule 5.
Passing grades, BarAdm Rule 7.
Nonresidents.
Out-of-state attorneys, BarAdm Rule 13; BOP
§10-210.
Examination, BarAdmBoard Rule 6.
Special admission of out-of-state attorneys,
BarAdm Rule 14; BOP §10-215.
Special permission for out-of-state attorneys
to practice in state, BarAdm Rule 15.
Notice.
Examinations, BarAdm Rule 8; BOP §10-209.
Oath or affirmation, BOP §10-212.
Oaths defined, BarAdm Rule 1.
Order of admission, BOP §10-211.
Examinations.
Report.
Results, BarAdm Rule 10.
Final order of admission, BarAdm Rule 12.
Out-of-state attorneys, BarAdm Rule 13.
Special admission, BarAdm Rule 14.
Out-of-state attorneys, BOP §10-210.
Board of law examiners.
Examination, BarAdmBoard Rule 6.
Burden of proof, BarAdm Rule 13.
Disclosure.
Full disclosure required, BarAdm Rule 13.
Eligibility for special permission to practice in
state, BarAdm Rule 15.
Examination, BarAdm Rule 13.
Board of law examiners, BarAdmBoard Rule
6.
Re-examinations, BarAdm Rule 13.
Report of results, BarAdm Rule 13.
Exhibits, BarAdm Rule 13.
Filing.
Fees, BarAdm Rule 13.
Hearings, BarAdm Rule 13.
Ineligibility of certain applicants, BarAdm Rule
13.
Investigations, BarAdm Rule 13.
Order of admission, BarAdm Rule 13.
Petition.
Contents, BarAdm Rule 13.
Rejection, BarAdm Rule 13.
Practitioners.
Requirements, BarAdm Rule 13.
Pro hac vice, BarAdm Rule 14.

ATTORNEYS AT LAW —Cont'd
Admission to the bar —Cont'd
Out-of-state attorneys —Cont'd
Special admission, BOP §10-215.
Forms.
Motion, Form RGAB 20/M.
Order, Form RGAB 20/O.
Limitation on out-of-state attorney's practice,
BarAdm Rule 14.
Motion, BarAdm Rule 14.
Form, Form RGAB 20/M.
Order, BarAdm Rule 14.
Form, Form RGAB 20/O.
Special permission to practice in state, BarAdm
Rule 15.
Statutes and decisions relating to admission,
BarAdm Rule 15.
Supporting data, BarAdm Rule 14.
Patent lawyers.
Exception to requirements, BOP §10-206.
Petitions.
Examinations.
Petition to take scheduled examination,
BarAdm Rule 6.
Out-of-state attorneys, BarAdm Rule 14.
Taking examinations after failure, BarAdm Rule
9.
Pre-legal education, BarAdm Rule 3.
Pro bono legal services.
Reporting of services performed, CJA Rule
16-903.
Pro hac vice.
Special admission of out-of-state attorneys,
BarAdm Rule 14.
Publication.
Examinations.
Notice to be published, BarAdm Rule 8.
Qualifications of applicants, BOP §10-207.
Registration.
Law students, BarAdm Rule 2.
Application.
Content, BarAdm Rule 2.
Transmission of application, BarAdm Rule
2.
Withdrawal of application, BarAdm Rule 2.
Board of law examiners.
Authority of board, BarAdm Rule 2.
Character.
Proof, BarAdm Rule 2.
Examination.
Time of taking, BarAdm Rule 2.
Filing fee, BarAdm Rule 2.
Time, BarAdm Rule 2.
Reports.
Character committees, BarAdm Rule 5.
Examination results, BarAdm Rule 10.
Out-of-state attorneys, BarAdm Rule 13.
Procedure following report to court, BarAdm
Rule 10.
Required, BOP §10-206.
Exceptions, BOP §10-206.
Results.
Report, BOP §10-209.
Revocation of admission, BOP §10-214.
Rules and regulations, BOP §10-103.
Board of law examiners, BarAdm Rule 20.
Scope of admission, BOP §10-213.
Special admission, BOP §10-215.
State board of law examiners. See within this
subheading, "Board of law examiners."

ATTORNEYS AT LAW —Cont'd
Admission to the bar —Cont'd
Suspension or revocation of license.
Ineligibility for admission, BarAdm Rule 21.
Termination of provisions, BOP §10-218.
Time.
Examination, BarAdm Rule 7.
Registration of law students, BarAdm Rule 2.
Order of admission, BarAdm Rules 12, 13.
Registration of law students, BarAdm Rule 2.
Examination, BarAdm Rule 2.
Universities and colleges.
Pre-legal education, BarAdm Rule 3.
Waiver.
Law school.
Requirements for legal education, BarAdm
Rule 4.
Pre-legal education, BarAdm Rule 3.
Adoption.
Appointment of counsel, FamLaw Rule 9-106.
Disabled parties, FamLaw Rule 9-105.
Guidelines for advocacy, ChildAdv Appx.
Independent adoptions.
Appointment of attorney for parent and/or
prospective adoptee, FL §5-3B-06.
Local department adoptions.
Appointment of attorney for parent and/or child,
FL §5-307.
Private agency adoptions.
Appointment of attorney for parent and/or child,
FL §5-3A-07.
Show cause order.
Service.
Court appointed attorney, FamLaw Rule
9-105.
Advertising.
Communications to prospective clients for purpose
of obtaining professional employment, BOP
§§10-605.1, 10-605.2.
Rules of professional conduct, ProfCond Rule 7.2.
Affiliated attorneys.
Disbarment or suspension.
Duties, CJA Rule 16-760.
Age.
Admission to the bar.
Qualifications of applicants, BOP §10-207.
Air quality control.
Representation of persons charged, EN §2-605.
Alcoholic beverages.
Sales permitted without license or permit, 2B
§1-201.
Ambulance chasing, BOP §10-604.
Insurance fraud, IN §§27-407, 27-408.
Americans with disabilities act.
Bar examinations, accommodations,
BarAdmBoard Rule 3.
Answer.
Disbarment or suspension, CJA Rule 16-754.
Appeals.
Appearance of counsel, AppRev Rule 8-402.
Oral arguments.
Number of counsel, AppRev Rule 8-522.
Appeals from District Court.
Appearance of counsel, AppRevCir Rule 7-107.
Appearance.
Appeals.
Appearance of counsel, AppRev Rule 8-402.
Circuit courts, CivProCir Rule 2-131.
Continuance.
When continuance may be granted, CJ §6-409.

ATTORNEYS AT LAW —Cont'd
Appearance —Cont'd
Corporations.
Attorney requirement, CivProCir Rule 2-131;
CivProDist Rule 3-131.
Exceptions to attorney requirement, BOP
§10-206.
Defense counsel.
Criminal cases, Crim Rule 4-214.
District Court, CivProDist Rule 3-131.
First appearance in court without counsel.
Waiver of counsel in criminal cases, Crim Rule
4-215.
Initial appearance of defendant.
District Court following arrest.
Advice of right to counsel, Crim Rule 4-213.
Sale of practice.
Effect upon counsel of record, ProfCond Rule
1.17.
Striking appearances.
Circuit courts, CivProCir Rule 2-132.
Defense counsel in criminal cases, Crim Rule
4-214.
District Court, CivProDist Rule 3-132.
Termination.
Automatic termination, CJ §6-407.
Suspension of termination by court, CJ
§6-407.
Arbitration and award.
Fees, CJ §3-221.
Right to be represented by attorney, CJ §3-216.
Attorney-client privilege, 10 §45N.
Attorney General.
General provisions, SG §§6-101 to 6-110.
See ATTORNEY GENERAL.
Nonprofit health entities.
Acquisition, SG §§6.5-101 to 6.5-401.
See NONPROFIT HEALTH ENTITIES.
People's insurance counsel division, SG §§6-301 to
6-308.
Unauthorized practice of law.
Injunctions.
Actions for, BOP §10-406.
Investigation by attorney general, BOP
§§10-401 to 10-405. See within this
heading, "Unauthorized practice of law."
Attorney grievance commission.
Compensation, CJA Rule 16-711.
Composition, CJA Rule 16-711.
Creation and purpose, CJA Rule 16-711.
Disbarment or suspension.
Bar counsel.
Appointment, CJA Rule 16-712.
Powers and duties, CJA Rule 16-712.
Disciplinary fund.
Collection and disbursement, CJA Rule 16-714.
Enforcement of annual assessments, CJA Rule
16-714.
Payments by attorneys, CJA Rule 16-714.
Powers and duties, CJA Rule 16-711.
Quorum, CJA Rule 16-711.
Audits.
Disbarment or suspension.
Attorney's accounts and records, CJA Rule
16-722.
Legal services corporation.
Annual audits, 10 §45J.
Bar admissions. See within this heading,
"Admission to the bar."
Bar counsel.
Investigation of complaints, CJA Rule 16-731.

ATTORNEYS AT LAW —Cont'd
Bar counsel —Cont'd
  Recommendations.
    Completion of investigation, CJA Rule 16-734.
Barratry.
  Insurance fraud, IN §§27-407, 27-408.
  Presumption of compensation, BOP §10-604.
  Prohibited acts, BOP §10-604.
Board of law examiners. See within this heading,
  "Admission to the bar."
Burden of proof.
  Disbarment or suspension, CJA Rule 16-757.
Catastrophic health emergency.
  Contest of isolation or quarantine.
    Appointment of counsel, SpecPro Rule 15-1104.
Child access to firearm violation.
  Reference to violation during trial prohibited, CR
    §4-104.
Children in need of assistance.
  Guidelines for advocacy, ChildAdv Appx.
  Right to counsel, CJ §3-813.
Cigarette business licenses.
  Disciplinary actions against licensees.
    Right to counsel, BR §16-211.
Circuit courts.
  Form of court papers, Rule 1-301.
Citation of act.
  Short title, BOP §10-701.
Clerks of court.
  Disbarment or suspension.
    Audit of attorney's accounts and records, CJA
      Rule 16-722.
Clients' protection fund, CJA Rule 16-811.
  Definition of "fund," BOP §10-310.
  Distribution.
    Powers of trustees, BOP §10-312.
  Duties of trustees, BOP §10-312.
  Enforcement of claims.
    Powers of trustees, BOP §10-312.
  Establishment, BOP §10-311.
  List of those paying fees to fund, BOP §10-313.
  Powers of trustees, BOP §10-312.
  Purpose, BOP §10-311.
  Sources, BOP §10-311.
Commission.
  Attorney grievance commission. See within this
    heading, "Attorney grievance commission."
**Communications to prospective clients for
  purpose of obtaining professional
  employment,** BOP §§10-605.1, 10-605.2.
Complaints.
  Disbarment or suspension.
    Disposition of complaints, CJA Rule 16-759.
Confidentiality.
  Admissions to the bar.
    Board of law examiners and character
      committees, BarAdm Rule 19.
  Disbarment or suspension, CJA Rule 16-723.
    Audit of attorney's accounts and records, CJA
      Rule 16-722.
Conservator of client matters.
  Disbarment or suspension, CJA Rule 16-777.
Constitution of the United States.
  Right to have counsel, US Const Amd 6.
Consumer loans.
  Fees.
    Collection, CL §12-307.1.
Consumer protection.
  Legal assistance organizations.
    See CONSUMER PROTECTION.

ATTORNEYS AT LAW —Cont'd
Contempt.
  Constructive civil contempt, SpecPro Rule 15-206.
  Constructive criminal contempt, SpecPro Rule
    15-205.
Corporations.
  Acknowledgments.
    Appointed attorney, CA §1-303.
  Admission to the bar.
    Exceptions to requirement.
      House counsel, BOP §10-206.
      Officer of corporation appearing in its behalf
        in certain actions, BOP §10-206.
  Appearance.
    Attorney requirement, CivProCir Rule 2-131;
      CivProDist Rule 3-131.
    Exceptions to attorney requirement, BOP
      §10-206.
  House counsel.
    Admission to the bar.
      Exceptions to requirement, BOP §10-206.
  Representation in court by persons other than
    lawyers, BOP §10-206.
Correction.
  Practice of law by correctional employees.
    Prohibited, BOP §10-603.
Costs.
  Consumer loans.
    Attorneys' fees and court costs.
      Collection, CL §12-307.1.
  Disbarment or suspension, CJA Rule 16-761.
    Audit of attorney's accounts and records, CJA
      Rule 16-722.
County boards of elections.
  Counsel.
    Appointing or retaining, compensation, EL
      §2-205.
Credit.
  Credit grantor closed end credit provisions.
    Attorneys' fees, CL §12-1011.
  Credit grantor revolving credit provisions.
    Attorneys' fees, CL §12-911.
Criminal procedure.
  Appointment to defend accused in criminal cases,
    MD Const DofR Art 21.
    Public defender, 27A §§1 to 14.
    See PUBLIC DEFENDER.
  Counsel for accused, US Const Amd 6.
  Right of accused to counsel, MD Const DofR Art
    21.
  Sentence review.
    Right to counsel, CP §8-103.
Criminal rules.
  Defense counsel.
    Appearances, Crim Rule 4-214.
      Striking appearance, Crim Rule 4-214.
    Appointed counsel.
      Extent of duty, Crim Rule 4-214.
    Waiver of counsel.
      Discharge of counsel, Crim Rule 4-215.
      Express waiver of counsel, Crim Rule 4-215.
      Failure to obtain, Crim Rule 4-215.
      First appearance in court without counsel, Crim
        Rule 4-215.
Death row inmates.
  Execution of inmate.
    Presence of inmate's attorney, COR §3-907.
Deeds.
  Recordation.
    Certification instrument prepared by attorney.
      Required, RP §3-104.

ATTORNEYS AT LAW —Cont'd

Defense counsel.
Criminal cases, Crim Rule 4-214.
Definitions, BOP §10-101.
Clients' protection fund, BOP §10-310.
Disbarment or suspension, CJA Rule 16-701.
Lawyer counseling committees, BOP §10-502.
Legal services corporation, 10 §45C.
Trust accounts, BOP §10-301; CJA Rule 16-602.
Deposits.
Trust accounts, BOP §10-304.
Generally, CJA Rules 16-601 to 16-612. See within this heading, "Trust accounts."
Disbarment or suspension.
Activities of lawyers on disciplinary status.
Permissible activities, BOP §10-601.
Affiliated attorneys.
Duties, CJA Rule 16-760.
Amendments to pleadings, CJA Rule 16-755.
Answer, CJA Rule 16-754.
Attorney grievance commission.
Bar counsel.
Appointment, CJA Rule 16-712.
Powers and duties, CJA Rule 16-711.
Compensation, CJA Rule 16-711.
Composition, CJA Rule 16-711.
Creation and purpose, CJA Rule 16-711.
Disciplinary fund.
Collection and disbursement of disciplinary fund, CJA Rule 16-714.
Enforcement of annual assessments, CJA Rule 16-714.
Payments by attorneys, CJA Rule 16-714.
Powers and duties, CJA Rule 16-711.
Quorum, CJA Rule 16-711.
Audit of attorney's accounts and records.
Application for audit, CJA Rule 16-722.
Cost of audit, CJA Rule 16-722.
Bar counsel.
Appointment, CJA Rule 16-712.
Investigation of complaints, CJA Rule 16-731.
Powers and duties, CJA Rule 16-712.
Recommendations.
Completion of investigation, CJA Rule 16-734.
Burden of proof, CJA Rule 16-757.
Complaints, CJA Rule 16-731.
Conditional diversion agreement, CJA Rule 16-736.
Dismissal, CJA Rule 16-735.
Disposition of complaints, CJA Rule 16-759.
Reprimands, CJA Rule 16-737.
Termination, CJA Rule 16-735.
Conditional diversion agreement, CJA Rule 16-736.
Defined, CJA Rule 16-701.
Confidentiality.
Exceptions, CJA Rule 16-723.
Generally, CJA Rule 16-723.
Subpoenas, CJA Rule 16-732.
Consent to discipline or inactive status, CJA Rule 16-772.
Conservator of client matters, CJA Rule 16-777.
Costs, CJA Rule 16-761.
Definitions, CJA Rule 16-701.
Disbarment.
Defined, CJA Rule 16-701.
Discovery.
Petition for disciplinary or remedial action, CJA Rule 16-756.
Dismissal of complaints, CJA Rule 16-735.
Disposition of complaints, CJA Rule 16-759.

ATTORNEYS AT LAW —Cont'd

Disbarment or suspension —Cont'd
Duties of respondent, CJA Rule 16-760.
Employment of disbarred or suspended lawyers.
Responsibilities of firm, ProfCond Rule 5.3.
Evidence.
Perpetuation of evidence and testimony, CJA Rule 16-733.
Expedited actions, CJA Rule 16-776.
Expedited reinstatement, CJA Rule 16-781.
Hearing, CJA Rule 16-757.
Post-hearing proceedings, CJA Rule 16-758.
Inactive status.
Consent to discipline or inactive status, CJA Rule 16-772.
Order imposing discipline or inactive status, CJA Rule 16-760.
Reciprocity, CJA Rule 16-773.
Summary placement, CJA Rule 16-774.
Incapacity.
Defined, CJA Rule 16-701.
Remedies, CJA Rule 16-721.
Ineligibility for admission.
Revocation or suspension of license, BarAdm Rule 21.
Injunctions, CJA Rule 16-776.
Investigations.
Complaints, CJA Rule 16-731.
Completion, CJA Rule 16-734.
Conditional diversion agreement, CJA Rule 16-736.
Perpetuation of evidence and testimony, CJA Rule 16-733.
Reprimands, CJA Rule 16-737.
Statement of charges, CJA Rule 16-741.
Judges.
Designation of judge, order, CJA Rule 16-752.
Monitors.
Order imposing discipline or inactive status, CJA Rule 16-760.
Motion to amend order appointing judge, CJA Rule 16-752.
Office for the practice of law.
Defined, CJA Rule 16-701.
Order imposing discipline or inactive status, CJA Rule 16-760.
Peer review committee, CJA Rule 16-713.
Confidentiality of meetings, CJA Rule 16-723.
Peer review panel, CJA Rule 16-742.
Peer review process, CJA Rule 16-743.
Petition for disciplinary or remedial action, CJA Rule 16-751.
Designation of judge, order, CJA Rule 16-752.
Discovery, CJA Rule 16-756.
Service, CJA Rule 16-753.
Petition for reinstatement, CJA Rule 16-781.
Pleadings.
Amendments to pleadings, CJA Rule 16-755.
Post-hearing proceedings, CJA Rule 16-758.
Privileged communications, CJA Rule 16-723.
Pro bono legal services.
Failure to report services performed, CJA Rule 16-903.
Production of documents, CJA Rule 16-732.
Professional misconduct.
Defined, CJA Rule 16-701.
Sanctions and remedies, CJA Rule 16-721.
Reciprocity, CJA Rule 16-773.
Recommendations.
Completion of investigation, CJA Rule 16-734.

ATTORNEYS AT LAW —Cont'd
Disbarment or suspension —Cont'd
Reinstatement, CJA Rule 16-781.
Defined, CJA Rule 16-701.
Remedies.
Incapacity, CJA Rule 16-721.
Reprimands, CJA Rule 16-737.
Order imposing discipline or inactive status,
CJA Rule 16-760.
Resignation of attorney, CJA Rule 16-775.
Serious crime.
Defined, CJA Rule 16-701.
Duty of attorney charged with, CJA Rule
16-771.
Service of process and papers, CJA Rule 16-724.
Petition for disciplinary or remedial action, CJA
Rules 16-752, 16-753.
Subpoenas, CJA Rule 16-732.
Statement of charges, CJA Rule 16-741.
Attorneys charged with serious crime, CJA Rule
16-771.
Defined, CJA Rule 16-701.
Peer review panel, CJA Rule 16-742.
Service, CJA Rule 16-724.
Subpoenas, CJA Rule 16-732.
Summary placement on inactive status, CJA Rule
16-774.
Suspension.
Defined, CJA Rule 16-701.
Duties of respondent, CJA Rule 16-760.
Employment of disbarred or suspended lawyers.
Responsibilities of firm, ProfCond Rule 5.3.
Ineligibility for admission, BarAdm Rule 21.
Order imposing discipline or inactive status,
CJA Rule 16-760.
Temporary suspension.
Attorneys charged with serious crime, CJA Rule
16-771.
Termination of complaints, CJA Rule 16-735.
Transcripts.
Judicial hearings, CJA Rule 16-757.
Perpetuation of evidence and testimony, CJA
Rule 16-733.
Warnings.
Defined, CJA Rule 16-701.
Termination of complaints.
Termination accompanied by warning, CJA
Rule 16-735.
Witnesses.
Perpetuation of evidence and testimony, CJA
Rule 16-733.
Subpoenas, CJA Rule 16-732.
Discovery.
Disbarment or suspension.
Petition for disciplinary or remedial action, CJA
Rule 16-756.
Lawyer counseling committees.
Matters not discoverable, BOP §10-502.
Trial preparation.
Scope of discovery.
Circuit courts, CivProCir Rule 2-402.
Distress for rent.
Exemptions from levy, RP §8-307.
Education.
Admission to the bar. See within this heading,
"Admission to the bar."
Ejectment.
Admission to the bar.
Exceptions to requirement.
Certain persons representing tenants in
summary ejectment proceedings, BOP
§10-206.

ATTORNEYS AT LAW —Cont'd
Eminent domain.
Abandonment of condemnation proceedings.
Recovery of fees by defendant, RP §12-109.
Appeals.
Fees, PropAct Rule 12-209; RP §12-107.
Judgment for defendant.
Fees, RP §12-106.
Environmental sanitarians.
Licenses.
Denials, reprimands, suspensions and
revocations.
Right to counsel, EN §11-313.
Escrow accounts.
Attorney trust accounts. See within this heading,
"Trust accounts."
Ethics.
Rules of professional conduct.
Adoption, CJA Rule 16-812.
Evidence.
Disbarment or suspension.
Perpetuation of evidence and testimony, CJA
Rule 16-733.
Lawyer counseling committees.
Matters not discoverable or admissible, BOP
§10-502.
Unauthorized practice of law.
Investigation by attorney general.
Powers of attorney general as to, BOP
§10-404.
Rights of person under investigation, BOP
§10-403.
Execution of death row inmate.
Presence of inmate's attorney, COR §3-907.
Executions.
Lien of attorney, BOP §10-501.
Executors and administrators.
Settlement of decedents' estates.
Appearance of attorneys, Estates Rule 6-132.
Attorney may act for person, Estates Rule
6-133.
Term "person" defined, Estates Rule 6-105.
Effect of signature by attorney.
Certification by attorney with out-of-state
office, Estates Rule 6-135.
Entry of appearance, Estates Rule 6-132.
Personal representative.
Attorney may not sign documents required by
law to be filed by personal representative,
Estates Rule 6-133.
Petitions.
Certification by attorney with out-of-state
office, Estates Rule 6-135.
Requirements.
Generally, Estates Rule 6-135.
Signing of petitions and other papers.
Effect of signature by attorney, Estates
Rule 6-134.
Requirements, Estates Rules 6-134, 6-135.
Sanctions against attorney, Estates Rule
6-134.
Special appearances abolished, Estates Rule
6-132.
Withdrawal of appearance, Estates Rule 6-132.
Fees.
Admission to the bar.
Application fee, BarAdmBoard Rule 1.
Examination fee, BarAdm Rule 6; BOP §10-208.
Refunds, BarAdm Rule 6.
Retaking, BarAdm Rule 9.
No refunds, BarAdm Rule 9.

ATTORNEYS AT LAW —Cont'd
Fees —Cont'd
  Admission to the bar —Cont'd
    Law student registration, BarAdm Rule 2.
    Out-of-state attorneys.
      Filing fee, BarAdm Rule 13.
    Prescription by board, BarAdm Rule 18.
  Attorneys' fees.
    See ATTORNEYS' FEES.
  Lien of attorney, BOP §10-501.
Fiduciaries.
  Absent or unknown persons, Guardian Rule
    10-604.
  Appointment of attorney or investigator, Guardian
    Rule 10-106.
Financial institutions.
  Trust accounts. See within this heading, "Trust
    accounts."
Fraud.
  Admission to the bar.
    Revocation of admission fraudulently obtained,
      BOP §10-214.
  Legal services corporation.
    Fraudulently obtaining legal assistance, 10
      §45M.
Funds.
  Clients' protection fund, BOP §§10-310 to 10-313.
    See within this heading, "Clients' protection
    fund."
  Disbarment or suspension.
    Attorney grievance commission.
      Disciplinary fund, CJA Rule 16-714.
General assembly.
  Continuances because of legislative duties.
    Members attorneys of record in proceedings, CJ
    §6-402.
  Investigating committee.
    Counsel for persons testifying before committee,
    SG §2-1609.
  Joint committee on legislative ethics.
    Counsel to committee, SG §2-709.
Governor.
  Additional counsel.
    Governor not to employ additional counsel
      unless approved by general assembly, MD
      Const Art V §3.
Grievance commission. See within this heading,
  "Attorney grievance commission."
Guardian and ward.
  Appointment of attorney or investigator, Guardian
    Rule 10-106.
  Appointment of counsel.
    Disabled parties, FamLaw Rule 9-105.
  Local department guardianships.
    Appointment of attorney for parent and/or child,
      FL §5-307.
  Private agency guardianships.
    Appointment of attorney for parent and/or child,
      FL §5-3A-07.
  Protection of property.
    Appointment of counsel, ET §13-211.
Handicapped persons.
  Admission to the bar.
    Examinations, accommodations, BarAdmBoard
      Rule 3.
Hearing.
  Disbarment or suspension, CJA Rule 16-757.
    Post-hearing proceedings, CJA Rule 16-758.
Highways.
  Employment by commission, TR §8-204.

ATTORNEYS AT LAW —Cont'd
Home improvements.
  License disciplinary hearings, BR §8-312.
Human relations commission.
  Compensation, 49B §2.
  Employment, 49B §2.
  Hearing.
    Duty of commissions counsel, 49B §11.
  Represent commission, 49B §2.
Immunity.
  Lawyer counseling committees.
    Members, BOP §10-502; CJ §5-416.
Inactive status.
  Disbarment or suspension, CJA Rules 16-701 to
    16-781. See within this heading, "Disbarment
    or suspension."
Incapacity.
  Remedies, CJA Rule 16-721.
Injunctions.
  Disbarment or suspension, CJA Rule 16-776.
  Unauthorized practice of law.
    Action for injunction, BOP §10-406.
Insurance.
  Agents and brokers.
    Limited lines licenses, IN §10-125.
  Legal mutual liability insurance society of
    Maryland, IN §§24-101 to 24-109.
  People's insurance counsel, SG §§6-301 to 6-308.
Interest.
  Charges of attorney not considered interest, CL
    §12-105.
  Trust accounts, BOP §§10-302, 10-303.
    Interest on funds, CJA Rule 16-608.
Interior designers.
  Disciplinary proceedings.
    Right to counsel, BOP §8-312.
Interpretation and construction.
  Unauthorized practice of law.
    Additional nature of remedies, BOP §10-407.
Intervention.
  Unauthorized practice of law.
    Injunctions.
      Action for injunction, BOP §10-406.
Investigations.
  Bar admissions, BarAdm Rules 5, 13.
  Disbarment or suspension.
    Perpetuation of evidence and testimony, CJA
      Rule 16-733.
  Unauthorized practice of law, BOP §§10-401 to
    10-405. See within this heading,
    "Unauthorized practice of law."
Investments.
  Trust accounts.
    Direction of client or beneficial owner, BOP
      §10-305.
IOLTA.
  Interest on lawyer trust accounts participation,
    CJA Rule 16-608.
Judges.
  Disbarment or suspension.
    Designation of judge, order, CJA Rule 16-752.
  Practice of law prohibited.
    Code of judicial conduct, CJA Rule 16-813.
Judicial appointees.
  Code of conduct for judicial appointees.
    Practice of law, CJA Rule 16-814 Canon 4.
Juvenile causes.
  Appointment as special advocate, CJ §3-8A-32.
  Indigent persons.
    Representation of indigent persons, Juv Rule
      11-106.

ATTORNEYS AT LAW —Cont'd
Juvenile causes —Cont'd
Non-indigent cases.
Appointment of attorney to represent child, Juv
Rule 11-106.
Out-of-state attorney
Appearance of out of state attorney, Juv Rule
11-106.
Right to counsel, Juv Rule 11-106.
Waiver of representation, Juv Rule 11-106.
Land installment contracts.
Fees.
Proceedings by purchaser to enforce subtitle, RP
§10-108.
Land patents.
Filing papers, RP §13-304.
Notice to applicant, RP §13-304.
Law enforcement officers and personnel.
Police brutality allegations.
Rights of officers, PS §3-104.
Solicitation of clients by.
Prohibited, BOP §10-605.
Law firms and associations.
Affiliated attorneys.
Disbarment or suspension.
Duties, CJA Rule 16-760.
Sale of law practice, ProfCond Rule 1.17.
Law students.
Bar admission.
General provisions. See within this heading,
"Admission to the bar."
Legal assistance by law students, BarAdm Rule
16.
Registration, BarAdm Rule 2.
Lawyer-client privilege, 10 §45N.
Lawyer counseling committees.
Defined, BOP §10-502.
Evidence.
Matters not discoverable or admissible, BOP
§10-502.
Immunity of members, BOP §10-502.
Legal services corporation.
Agents.
Designated agent for service of process, 10
§45D.
Application for legal assistance.
Requirements, 10 §45L.
Appropriation in state budget, 10 §45-O.
Limitation on use of funds, 10 §45-O.
Transfer from abandoned property funds, 10
§45-O.
Attorney-client privilege, 10 §45N.
Audits.
Annual audits, 10 §45K.
Board of directors.
Defined, 10 §45C.
Members, 10 §45E.
Officers, 10 §45E.
Status of members, 10 §45E.
Term of office, 10 §45E.
Clients.
Consideration of client needs, 10 §45J.
Corporate powers and duties.
Generally, 10 §45G.
Corporation.
Defined, 10 §45C.
Declaration of purpose, 10 §45B.
Definitions, 10 §45C.
Eligible clients.
Defined, 10 §45C.
Employees, 10 §45F.

ATTORNEYS AT LAW —Cont'd
Legal services corporation —Cont'd
Established, 10 §45D.
Executive director.
Appointment, 10 §45F.
Duties.
Generally, 10 §45F.
Fraudulently obtaining legal assistance, 10 §45M.
Governor.
Defined, 10 §45C.
Grantees, 10 §45C.
Duties, 10 §45J.
Internal revenue code.
Defined, 10 §45C.
Legal assistance.
Defined, 10 §45C.
Legislative intent, 10 §45B.
Limitations.
Corporate limitations, 10 §45H.
Payment of funds to office of public defender, BOP
§10-303.
Penalties.
Fraudulently obtaining legal assistance, 10
§45M.
Powers and duties.
Corporate powers and duties generally, 10
§45G.
Principal office, 10 §45D.
Purpose of corporation generally, 10 §45D.
Service of process.
Designated agent, 10 §45D.
Short title, 10 §45A.
State departments and agencies.
Corporation not department of state, 10 §45D.
Taxation.
Exemption from taxes, 10 §45D.
Title.
Short title, 10 §45A.
Use of funds made available to grantees, 10 §45J.
Liens, BOP §10-501.
Enforcement, CivProCir Rule 2-652.
Malpractice.
Health care malpractice claims.
Attorneys' fees, CJ §3-2A-07.
Legal mutual liability insurance society of
Maryland, IN §§24-101 to 24-109.
Maryland Transit Administration.
General counsel, TR §7-209.
Minors.
Appointment of counsel for minor, FL §1-202.
Recoveries in tort.
Attorneys' fees, ET §13-406.
Special advocate appointment, CJ §3-8A-32.
Misdemeanors.
Prohibited acts generally, BOP §10-606.
Trust accounts.
Violations of provisions, BOP §10-606.
Unauthorized practice of law, BOP §10-606.
Monitors.
Disbarment or suspension.
Order imposing discipline or inactive status,
CJA Rule 16-760.
Mortgages and deeds of trust.
Application.
Attorney of borrower.
Notification to lender on application, CL
§12-120.
Borrower's attorney.
Rejection by lender for good cause, CL §12-120.
Lender's attorney.
When borrower required to pay for services, CL
§12-120.

ATTORNEYS AT LAW —Cont'd
Mortgages and deeds of trust —Cont'd
Releases.
Actions to enforce provisions.
Liability for attorneys' fees, RP §7-106.
Settlements.
Condition of settlements.
Employment of particular attorney.
Prohibited, CL §12-120.
Municipal corporations.
Municipal infractions.
Designation of attorneys to prosecute, 23A §3.
Nonresidents.
Bar admissions. See within this heading,
"Admission to the bar."
Notice.
Admission to the bar.
Examinations, BOP §10-209.
Disbarment or suspension.
Audit of attorney's accounts and records, CJA
Rule 16-722.
Trust accounts.
Approved institutions, CJA Rule 16-611.
Oaths.
Admission to the bar, BOP §10-212.
Unauthorized practice of law.
Investigation by attorney general.
Administration of oaths, BOP §10-404.
Orders.
Admission to the bar, BOP §10-211.
Orphans' court.
Judges.
Restriction on judge's practice of law, ET
§2-109.
Parole revocation hearing.
Representation of inmate, COR §7-401.
Parties.
Attorney may act for party, Rule 1-331.
Patent lawyers.
Admission to the bar.
Exception to requirements, BOP §10-206.
Paternity proceedings.
Fees.
Order for payment, FL §5-1033.
Peer review committee, CJA Rule 16-713.
Confidentiality of meetings, CJA Rule 16-723.
Peer review panel.
Disbarment or suspension, CJA Rule 16-742.
Peer review process.
Disbarment or suspension, CJA Rule 16-743.
Penalties.
Prohibited acts generally, BOP §10-606.
Trust accounts.
Violations of provisions, BOP §10-606.
Unauthorized practice of law, BOP §10-606.
People's insurance counsel, SG §§6-301 to 6-308.
Petitions.
Admission to the bar.
Examinations.
Petition to take scheduled examination,
BarAdm Rule 6.
Disbarment or suspension.
Disciplinary or remedial action, CJA Rule
16-751.
Pleadings.
Disbarment or suspension.
Amendments to pleadings, CJA Rule 16-755.
Notice of intention to defend.
Identity of attorney.
District Court, CivProDist Rule 3-307.

ATTORNEYS AT LAW —Cont'd
Poor.
Public defender.
General provisions, 27A §§1 to 14.
See PUBLIC DEFENDER.
Post conviction procedure.
Right to counsel, CP §7-108.
Practice of law.
Admission to the bar.
General provisions. See within this heading,
"Admission to the bar."
Court and correctional employees.
Practice of law prohibited, BOP §10-603.
Defined, BOP §10-101.
Judges.
Prohibited, CJ §1-203.
Code of judicial conduct, CJA Rule 16-813
Canon 4.
Office of administrative hearings.
Representation before office by person not
licensed to practice law, SG §9-1607.1.
Prohibited.
Judges, CJ §1-203.
Code of judicial conduct, CJA Rule 16-813
Canon 4.
Exceptions, CJ §1-203.
Public defender, 27A §3.
Registers of wills, ET §2-202.
Restricted.
Orphans' court judge, ET §2-109.
Sale of law practice, ProfCond Rule 1.17.
Scope of provisions, BOP §10-102.
Unauthorized practice. See within this heading,
"Unauthorized practice of law."
Presumptions.
Barratry.
Presumption of compensation, BOP §10-604.
Privileged communications.
Discipline and inactive status, CJA Rule 16-723.
Audit of attorney accounts and records, CJA
Rule 16-722.
Legal services corporation.
Attorney-client privilege, 10 §45N.
Pro bono legal services.
Reporting of services performed, CJA Rule
16-903.
Unauthorized practice of law.
Investigation by attorney general.
Confidentiality, BOP §10-402.
Pro bono legal services.
Local committees and plans, CJA Rule 16-902.
Notice of default.
Reporting of services performed, CJA Rule
16-903.
Reporting of services performed, CJA Rule 16-903.
State committee and plan, CJA Rule 16-901.
Production of documents.
Disbarment or suspension, CJA Rule 16-732.
Professional misconduct.
Sanctions and remedies, CJA Rule 16-721.
Pro se representation.
Criminal cases, Crim Rule 4-215.
Public officers and employees.
Unauthorized practice of law.
Investigation by attorney general.
Duties of public officers and staff, BOP
§10-405.
Public service commission.
Lawyers representing staff before commission.
Appointment, independent of general counsel,
PUC §2-108.

ATTORNEYS AT LAW —Cont'd
Real estate brokers.
  Prohibited acts.
    Payments of commissions to lawyers, BOP
      §17-605.
    Requiring buyer to employ particular title
      lawyer, BOP §17-607.
    Soliciting referral business from lawyers, BOP
      §17-605.
**Receivers and assignees or trustees for
    creditors.**
  Compensation and fees, Receivers Rule 13-303.
  Conflicts of interest, Receivers Rule 13-105.
  Employment, Receivers Rule 13-301.
Reciprocity.
  Disbarment or suspension, CJA Rule 16-773.
Recordation.
  Deeds.
    Certification instrument prepared by attorney.
      Required, RP §3-104.
Records.
  Disbarment or suspension.
    Audit of attorney's accounts and records, CJA
      Rule 16-722.
Registers of wills.
  Practice of law.
    Prohibited from practicing law, ET §2-202.
Reinstatement.
  Disbarment or suspension, CJA Rule 16-781.
Reprimands.
  Disbarment or suspension.
    Order imposing discipline or inactive status,
      CJA Rule 16-760.
Resignation from bar, CJA Rule 16-775.
Retail credit accounts law.
  Fees, CL §12-508.
Rules and regulations.
  Admission to the bar, BOP §10-103.
Rules of professional conduct.
  See RULES OF PROFESSIONAL CONDUCT.
Sale of law practice, ProfCond Rule 1.17.
Sales.
  Installment sales.
    Fees, CL §12-623.
Schools.
  County boards of education.
    Employment of legal counsel, ED §4-104.
    Legal counsel in suits against teachers, agents,
      etc., ED §4-104.
  Principals and teachers intervening in fights.
    Legal counsel in a suit or claim brought against,
      ED §7-307.
Scope of provisions, BOP §10-102.
Security systems technicians.
  Disciplinary action against licensees.
    Representation by legal counsel, BOP §18-310.
Sentence and punishment.
  Review of criminal sentences.
    Right to counsel, CP §8-103.
Serious crime.
  Duty of attorney charged with, CJA Rule 16-771.
Service of process and papers.
  Disbarment or suspension proceedings, CJA Rule
    16-724.
  Petition for disciplinary or remedial action, CJA
    Rules 16-752, 16-753.
  Subpoenas, CJA Rule 16-732.
  Subpoenas.
    Disbarment or suspension proceedings, CJA
      Rule 16-732.

ATTORNEYS AT LAW —Cont'd
Service of process and papers —Cont'd
  Subpoenas —Cont'd
    Service on parties represented by attorney,
      CivProDist Rule 3-510.
Short title of act, BOP §10-701.
Signatures.
  Certification by signing attorney with out-of-state
    office, Rule 1-313.
  Requirements of signing attorney, Rule 1-312.
Social services.
  Local departments.
    Fees, 88A §7.
    Institute and defend all civil cases, 88A §7.
    Representation, 88A §7.
Solicitations.
  Communications to prospective clients for purpose
    of obtaining professional employment, BOP
    §§10-605.1, 10-605.2.
  Law enforcement officials.
    Solicitation of clients by.
      Prohibited, BOP §10-605.
State's attorneys, 10 §§34 to 41; MD Const Art V
    §10.
  See STATE'S ATTORNEYS.
Subpoenas.
  Disbarment or suspension, CJA Rule 16-732.
  Service on parties represented by attorney,
    CivProDist Rule 3-510.
  State's attorneys.
    Right of person subpoenaed to counsel, 10 §39A.
  Unauthorized practice of law.
    Investigation by attorney general.
      Power of attorney general to issue, BOP
        §10-404.
Support and maintenance.
  Uniform interstate family support act.
    Employment of private counsel, FL §10-321.
Suspension. See within this heading, "Disbarment
    or suspension."
Taxation.
  Foreclosure of right of redemption.
    Reimbursement of fees to plaintiff on
      redemption, TP §14-843.
Tax court.
  Appeals to tax court.
    Representation of parties, TG §13-515.
Termination of law practice.
  Sale of practice, ProfCond Rule 1.17.
Termination of parental rights.
  Guidelines for advocacy, ChildAdv Appx.
Termination of provisions.
  Admission to the bar, BOP §10-218.
Title of act.
  Short title, BOP §10-701.
Tort claims act.
  Counsel fees, SG §12-109.
Transcripts.
  Disbarment or suspension.
    Perpetuation of evidence and testimony, CJA
      Rule 16-733.
Trust accounts.
  Applicability, CJA Rule 16-601.
  Authority to sign checks or disburse or withdraw
    funds.
    Prerequisites to, CJA Rule 16-605.
  Borrowing funds.
    Prohibited transactions, CJA Rule 16-609.
  Commingling of funds, CJA Rule 16-607.
  Compliance with rules.
    Securing, CJA Rule 16-612.

ATTORNEYS AT LAW —Cont'd
Trust accounts —Cont'd
Definitions, BOP §10-301; CJA Rule 16-602.
Deposits, BOP §10-304.
Commingling of funds, CJA Rule 16-607.
Required, CJA Rule 16-604.
Designation of account, CJA Rule 16-606.
Request of financial institution to designate,
CJA Rule 16-605.
Disciplinary action.
Violations of provisions, BOP §10-307.
Dishonored instruments.
Explanation for, CJA Rule 16-612.
Duty to maintain account, CJA Rule 16-603.
Enforcement of rules, CJA Rule 16-612.
Fiduciary accounts.
Applicability of rules, CJA Rule 16-601.
Financial institutions.
Approval of, CJA Rule 16-610.
Notice of approval, CJA Rule 16-611.
Designating account on records as attorney
trust account.
Request to, CJA Rule 16-605.
Notice of approved institutions, CJA Rule
16-611.
Remuneration for depositing funds in account.
Prohibited transactions, CJA Rule 16-609.
Written agreements.
Approval of institution by commission, CJA
Rule 16-610.
Instruments drawn payable to cash or bearer.
Prohibited transactions, CJA Rule 16-609.
Interest, CJA Rule 16-608.
Interest and noninterest bearing accounts, BOP
§10-302.
Maryland legal services corporation.
Accounts earning interest for, BOP §10-303.
Investments.
Direction of client or beneficial owner, BOP
§10-305.
Misuse of trust money, BOP §10-306.
Name of account, CJA Rule 16-606.
Notice.
Approved financial institutions, CJA Rule
16-611.
Overdrafts.
Explanation for, CJA Rule 16-612.
Places accounts maintained, CJA Rule 16-603.
Pledging funds.
Prohibited transactions, CJA Rule 16-609.
Prohibited transactions, CJA Rule 16-609.
Required deposits, CJA Rule 16-604.
Requirements, BOP §10-302.
Violations of provisions.
Disciplinary action, BOP §10-307.
Misuse of trust money, BOP §10-306.
Penalties, BOP §10-606.
Trusts and trustees.
Trust accounts. See within this heading, "Trust
accounts."
Unauthorized practice of law.
Additional nature of remedies, BOP §10-407.
Attorney general.
Injunctions.
Action for injunction, BOP §10-406.
Investigations, BOP §§10-401 to 10-405. See
within this subheading, "Investigation by
attorney general."
Injunctions.
Action for injunction, BOP §10-406.

ATTORNEYS AT LAW —Cont'd
Unauthorized practice of law —Cont'd
Intervention.
Action for injunction, BOP §10-406.
Investigation by attorney general.
Authorized, BOP §10-401.
Confidentiality, BOP §10-402.
Evidence.
Powers of attorney general as to, BOP
§10-404.
Rights of persons under investigation, BOP
§10-403.
Generally, BOP §10-401.
Oaths.
Power of attorney general to administer, BOP
§10-404.
Powers of attorney general, BOP §10-404.
Public officers and employees.
Duties, BOP §10-405.
Rights of persons under investigation, BOP
§10-403.
Subpoenas.
Power of attorney general, BOP §10-404.
Misrepresentation as authorized practitioner,
BOP §10-602.
Penalties, BOP §10-606.
Prohibited acts, BOP §10-601.
Misrepresentation as authorized practitioner,
BOP §10-602.
Penalties, BOP §10-606.
Unemployment compensation.
Legal representation.
Civil or criminal actions, LE §§8-307, 9-902.
Representation of parties, LE §8-507.
Prohibition on solicitation, LE §8-507.
University of Maryland.
Medical system.
Legal counsel for representing medical system
personnel, ED §13-308.
Upper shore regional council.
Legal counsel, 20D §1-106.
Victims of crime.
Notoriety of crimes contracts.
Payments from escrow account, CP §11-625.
Waiver.
Criminal rules, Crim Rule 4-215.
Witnesses.
Attorney-client privilege.
Person may not be compelled to testify, CJ
§9-108.
Disbarment or suspension.
Perpetuation of evidence and testimony, CJA
Rule 16-733.
Workers' compensation.
Attempt to influence choice of attorney.
Prohibited acts, LE §9-1103.
Work product.
Scope of discovery, CivProCir Rule 2-402.

ATTORNEYS' FEES.
Admission to the bar.
Examination fee, BOP §10-208.
Adoption.
Independent adoptions, FL §5-3B-08.
Local department adoptions, FL §5-309.
Private agency adoptions, FL §5-3A-09.
Appearance fees generally, CJ §7-204.
Arbitration and award, CJ §3-221.
Automobile insurance fund.
Recovery of money paid by fund, IN §20-608.

ATTORNEYS' FEES —Cont'd
Child custody proceedings.
Uniform child custody jurisdiction and
enforcement act.
Costs and expenses.
Declining jurisdiction, FL §9.5-208.
Direct expenses and costs against respondent,
FL §9.5-317.
Generally, FL §9.5-312.
Immediate physical custody of child.
Order by court of this state, FL §9.5-310.
Circuit courts.
Appearance fees.
Attorney entitled to demand and receive, CJ
§7-204.
Conflicting remedies, CL §11-1207.
Construction contracts.
Actions for prompt payment, RP §9-303.
Consumer loans.
Collection fees, CL §12-307.1.
Copyright royalties, CL §11-1405.
Credit grantor closed end credit provisions, CL
§§12-1011, 12-1028.
Credit grantor revolving credit provisions, CL
§12-911.
Discrimination.
Commercial discrimination.
Frivolous contested case proceedings, SF
§19-109.
Divorce, annulment and alimony.
Award of reasonable and necessary expenses, FL
§§7-107, 8-214.
Email.
Unauthorized, false or misleading information.
Commercial electronic mail, CL §14-3003.
Eminent domain.
Abandonment of proceedings, RP §12-109.
Appeals, PropAct Rule 12-209; RP §12-107.
Judgment for defendant, RP §12-106.
Equipment dealer contracts.
Violations by suppliers.
Civil penalties, CL §19-302.
Executors and administrators.
Settlement of decedents' estates.
Bad faith-unjustified proceedings, Estates Rule
6-141.
Commission.
Considered with commissions, Estates Rule
6-416; ET §7-602.
Debts and claims.
Payment.
Petition for attorneys' fees, Estates Rule
6-416; ET §7-602.
Generally, Estates Rule 6-416; ET §7-602.
Petition.
Filing of petitions, Estates Rule 6-416; ET
§7-602.
Foreclosure.
Action by homeowner for damages, RP §7-320.
Guardian and ward.
Local department guardianships, FL §5-309.
Private agency guardianships, FL §5-3A-09.
Health care worker whistleblower protection.
Civil actions for violations, HO §1-505.
Identity fraud.
Civil or administrative proceedings, CR §8-301.
Immigration consultants.
Violation of provisions, CL §14-3306.
Insurance.
Automobile insurance fund.
Recovery of money paid by fund, IN §20-608.

ATTORNEYS' FEES —Cont'd
Interest.
Changes not considered interest, CL §12-105.
Juvenile cases.
Compensation for appointed counsel, CJ §3-8A-20.
Labor and employment relations.
Wage discrimination.
Action by employee.
Costs recoverable, LE §3-307.
Land installment contracts.
Purchaser's action to enforce provisions, RP
§10-108.
Leases, motor vehicles, CL §§14-2005, 14-2007.
Leases, UCC.
Unconscionable lease contracts or clauses, CL
§2A-108.
Letters of credit.
Actions for remedies, CL §5-111.
Lien of attorney, BOP §10-501.
Limited liability companies.
Derivative actions by members, CA §4A-804.
Malpractice.
Health care malpractice claims, CJ §3-2A-07.
Minimum wage.
Costs recoverable, LE §3-427.
Minors.
Appointment of counsel for minor.
Imposing counsel fees against parents, FL
§1-202.
Recovery in tort, ET §13-406.
Mortgages and deeds of trust.
Lender's attorney.
When borrower to pay, CL §12-120.
Releases.
Actions to enforce provisions.
Liability for attorneys' fees, RP §7-106.
Motorized wheelchair warranty enforcement.
Violations of provisions.
Actions for damages, CL §14-2705.
Motor vehicles.
Automobile insurance fund.
Recovery of money paid by fund, IN §20-608.
Consumer leasing contracts, CL §14-2007.
Actions, CL §14-2005.
Paternity proceedings.
Order for payment, FL §5-1033.
**Receivers and assignees or trustees for
creditors,** Receivers Rule 13-303.
Retail credit accounts law, CL §12-508.
Royalties.
Copyright, CL §11-1405.
Sales.
Installment sales, CL §12-623.
**Service contracts and consumer products
guaranty.**
Actions for breach of guaranty or service contract,
CL §14-406.
Sheriffs.
Collection by sheriff, CJ §2-308.
Social service cases, 88A §7.
State contractor employees.
Whistleblower protection civil actions, SF §11-305.
Subrogation.
Health-care benefits or services paid on behalf of
injured person.
Reduction of amount payable related to
attorneys' fees incurred, CJ §11-112.
Surveillance by camera of private residence.
Civil actions for, CR §3-903.
**Surveillance of individual in private place,
civil action for,** CR §3-901.
With prurient intent, CR §3-902.

ATTORNEYS' FEES —Cont'd
Tobacco.
Escrow act compliance violations, BR §§16-507, 16-508.
Tort claims act.
Limitation on fees, SG §12-109.
Trade secrets.
Conflicting remedies, CL §11-1207.
Misappropriation.
When awarded, CL §11-1204.
Unemployment compensation.
Representation of parties.
Limitation on fees, LE §8-507.
Wheelchairs.
Motorized wheelchair warranty enforcement.
Actions for damages, CL §14-2705.
Whistleblower protection, SPP §5-311.
Workers' compensation.
Frivolous proceedings, LE §9-734.
Appeal proceedings, LE §9-749.
Liability of third parties.
Action after award or payment of compensation, LE §9-902.
Payment of award.
Lump-sum payments.
Administrative review, LE §9-731.

ATTORNEY'S LIEN, BOP §10-501.

AUCTIONS.
Alcoholic beverages.
Auctioneers.
Sales permitted without license or permit, 2B §1-201.
Charity wine auctions.
Permits, 2B §2-101.
Bedding and upholstered furniture.
Exemptions for auctioneers, HG §24-403.
Bulk transfers, CL §6-108.
Commercial code.
Bulk transfers, CL §6-108.
Credit.
Credit grantor closed end credit provisions.
Repossessed property, CL §12-1021.
Credit grantor revolving credit provisions.
Repossessed property, CL §12-921.
Distress for rent.
General provisions.
See DISTRESS FOR RENT.
Executions.
Sales.
Employment of auctioneer, CJ §11-503.
Food, drugs and cosmetics.
Fines.
Auction sale of drugs, medicine or cosmetics, HG §21-1110.
Notification of secretary required, HG §21-1110.
Order prohibiting auction sale, HG §21-1110.
General services department.
Excess and surplus property.
Disposal of property, SF §4-504.
Proceeds of auction or sale, SF §4-505.
Highways.
Sale of land no longer needed, TR §8-309.
Licenses.
Trader license.
Local licenses for auctioneers authorized, BR §17-1803.
Livestock sales generally.
See LIVESTOCK SALES.
Loans.
Public auction of goods.
Repossession of goods securing loan, CL §12-115.

AUCTIONS —Cont'd
Militia.
Commanding officers.
Powers to regulate or prohibit, PS §13-208.
Procurement.
Auction bids, SF §13-111.
Receivers.
Employment of auctioneer, Receivers Rule 13-301.
Sales.
Executions.
Employment of auctioneer, CJ §11-503.
Installment sales.
Resale, CL §12-626.
Sale of goods, CL §2-328.
Taxation.
Tax sales.
Must be at public auction, TP §14-817.
Wine.
Charity wine auctions.
Permits, 2B §2-101.

AUDIBLE ALARM SYSTEMS.
Equipped to be silenced, CR §9-611.

AUDIOLOGISTS AND SPEECH-LANGUAGE PATHOLOGISTS.
Advertising.
Misleading or untruthful advertisements.
Hearing aid dealers and audiologists, HO §2-314.2.
Alcoholic beverages.
Providing professional services while under the influence of alcohol or controlled dangerous substances.
Grounds for denials, reprimands, suspensions or revocations of license, HO §2-314.
Animals.
Practice of veterinary medicine, HO §1-211.
Appeals.
Actions of board.
Administrative and judicial review, HO §2-316.
Applicability of provisions, HO §2-102.
Assistants to licensed pathologists.
Delegation of duties, HO §2-319.
Audiologist rehabilitation committee.
Confidentiality of proceedings, records and files, HO §2-318.
Defined, HO §2-318.
Discovery.
Proceedings, records and files, HO §2-318.
Duties, HO §2-318.
Evidence.
Admissibility of proceedings, records and files, HO §2-318.
Liability.
Good faith exemption from civil liability, HO §2-318.
Scope of authority, HO §2-318.
Board of examiners.
Appointment of members, HO §2-202.
Compensation, HO §§2-202, 2-204.
Defined, HO §2-101.
Disposition of funds, HO §2-206.
Duties.
Generally, HO §2-205.
Elections, HO §2-203.
Enforcement powers of board, HO §2-312.
Established, HO §2-201.
Establishment of fees, HO §2-206.
Examination by health care provider.
Board may require in investigating allegations against licensee, HO §2-205.1.

AUDIOLOGISTS AND SPEECH-LANGUAGE PATHOLOGISTS —Cont'd

Board of examiners —Cont'd

Expenses, HO §2-206.

Fees.

Establishment, HO §2-206.

Financial interest in persons regulated by board.

Restriction on consumer member, HO §2-202.

Funds.

Disposition, HO §2-206.

Investigative powers of board, HO §2-312.

Liability.

Good faith exemption from civil liability for acts within scope of jurisdiction of board, CJ §§5-703, 5-719.

Persons giving information to board.

Immunity from civil liability, HO §2-207.

Licensing. See within this heading, "Licenses."

Meetings, HO §2-204.

Membership, HO §§2-202, 2-203.

Officer or director of professional or trade association.

Member serving as, prohibition, HO §2-202.

Officers, HO §2-203.

Powers and duties generally, HO §§2-205, 2-312.

Program evaluation act, SG §8-403.

Qualifications, HO §2-202.

Removal, HO §2-202.

Staff, HO §2-204.

State board of examiners for audiologists, hearing-aid dealers and speech-language pathologist fund, HO §2-206.

Terms, HO §2-202.

Citation of title, HO §2-501.

Continuing education, HO §2-308.

Controlled dangerous substances.

Providing professional services while under the influence of alcohol or controlled dangerous substances.

Grounds for denials, reprimands, suspensions or revocations of licenses, HO §2-314.

Deceptive trade practices.

Audiologists, HO §2-406.

Hearing aid services, HO §2-314.7.

Definitions, HO §2-101.

Audiologist rehabilitation committee, HO §2-318.

Hearing aid dealer rehabilitation committees, HO §2-318.2.

Speech-language pathologist rehabilitation committee, HO §2-318.1.

Delegation of duties, HO §2-319.

Discovery.

Audiologist rehabilitation committee.

Proceedings, records and files, HO §2-318.

Hearing aid dealer rehabilitation committees, HO §2-318.2.

Speech-language pathologist rehabilitation committee.

Proceedings, records and files, HO §2-318.1.

Door-to-door solicitations.

Hearing aid dealers, HO §2-314.6.

Evidence.

Audiologist rehabilitation committee.

Proceedings, records and files.

Admissibility, HO §2-318.

Hearing aid dealer rehabilitation committees, HO §2-318.2.

Speech-language pathologist rehabilitation committee.

Proceedings, records and files.

Admissibility, HO §2-318.1.

AUDIOLOGISTS AND SPEECH-LANGUAGE PATHOLOGISTS —Cont'd

Examinations.

Licensure, HO §§2-304, 2-305.

Medical examinations.

Board may require in investigating allegations against licensee, HO §2-205.1.

Patients.

Hearing aid dealers and audiologists, HO §2-314.1.

Fees.

Board of examiners.

Establishment, HO §2-206.

Licenses.

Applications for licenses, HO §2-303.

Issuance of licenses, HO §2-306.

Schools.

Licensing fee reimbursement program, ED §6-112.1.

Funds.

Board of examiners.

Disposition, HO §2-206.

Hearing aid dealer rehabilitation committees, HO §2-318.2.

Hearings.

Licenses, HO §2-315.

Suspension, revocation, reprimand or probation.

Generally, HO §2-314.9.

Immoral practice of audiology.

Licenses.

Grounds for suspension, revocation or reprimand, HO §2-314.

Immunity.

Audiologist rehabilitation committee.

Good faith exemption, HO §2-318.

Board of examiners.

Good faith exemption from civil liability for acts within scope of jurisdiction of board, CJ §§5-703, 5-719.

Persons giving information to board, HO §2-207.

Immunity from civil liability, HO §2-207.

Hearing aid dealer rehabilitation committees, HO §2-318.2.

Speech-language pathologist rehabilitation committee.

Good faith exemption, HO §2-318.1.

Incompetence.

Licenses.

Grounds for suspension, revocation or reprimand, HO §2-314.

Inducements.

Unlawful inducements.

Hearing aid dealers and audiologists, HO §2-314.5.

Judicial review, HO §2-316.

Liability.

Audiologist rehabilitation committee.

Good faith exemption from civil liability, HO §2-318.

Board of examiners.

Good faith exemption from civil liability for acts within scope of jurisdiction of board, CJ §§5-703, 5-719.

Persons giving information to board.

Immunity from civil liability, HO §2-207.

Hearing aid dealer rehabilitation committees, HO §2-318.2.

Speech-language pathologist rehabilitation committee.

Good faith exemption from civil liability, HO §2-318.1.

AUDIOLOGISTS AND SPEECH-LANGUAGE PATHOLOGISTS —Cont'd
Licenses.
  Addresses.
    Change, HO §2-311.
    Record of addresses, HO §2-311.
  Administrative and judicial review, HO §2-316.
  Altering licenses, HO §2-404.
  Applicants.
    Qualifications.
      Audiologists, HO §2-302.
      Hearing aid dealers, HO §2-302.1.
      Speech-language pathologists, HO §2-302.2.
  Applications.
    Fee, HO §2-303.
    Form, HO §2-303.
    Making false statements, HO §2-403.
    Renewal, HO §2-308.
  Change of address, HO §2-311.
  Defined, HO §2-101.
  Denial of licenses.
    Grounds, HO §2-314.
  Display of licenses, HO §2-311.
  Enforcement powers of board, HO §2-312.
  Exceptions to requirements, HO §2-301.
  Expired licenses.
    Reinstatement, HO §2-309.
  Fees.
    Applications for licenses, HO §2-303.
    Issuance of licenses, HO §2-306.
    Schools.
      Licensing fee reimbursement program, ED §6-112.1.
  Fraud.
    Altering licenses, HO §2-404.
    Making false statements in applications, HO §2-403.
    Misrepresentation.
      Audiologists, HO §2-402.
      Hearing aid dealers, HO §2-402.1.
      Speech-language pathologists, HO §2-402.2.
    Transferring or offering to transfer licenses, HO §2-405.
    Use of purchased or fraudulent license, HO §2-401.
  Hearings, HO §2-315.
  Immoral practice of audiology.
    Grounds for suspension, revocation or reprimand, HO §2-314.
  Incompetence.
    Grounds for suspension, revocation or reprimand, HO §2-314.
  Investigative powers of board, HO §2-312.
  Issuance, HO §2-306.
    Fee, HO §2-306.
    Limited licenses.
      Audiologists, HO §2-310.
      Hearing aid dealers, HO §2-310.1.
      Speech-language pathologists, HO §2-310.2.
    Procedure, HO §2-306.
    Renewal, HO §2-308.
  Limited licenses.
    Audiologists, HO §2-310.
    Defined, HO §2-101.
    Hearing aid dealers, HO §2-310.1.
    Speech-language pathologists, HO §2-310.2.
    Surrender.
      Conditions, HO §2-313.
      Generally, HO §2-313.
  Making false statements in applications, HO §2-403.

AUDIOLOGISTS AND SPEECH-LANGUAGE PATHOLOGISTS —Cont'd
Licenses —Cont'd
  Materially altering license, HO §2-404.
  Misrepresentation.
    Audiologists, HO §2-402.
    Hearing aid dealers, HO §2-402.1.
    Speech-language pathologists, HO §2-402.2.
  Notice.
    Renewal of licenses, HO §2-308.
  Penalties, HO §2-408.
  Practicing without license, HO §2-401.
  Qualifications of applicants.
    Audiologists, HO §2-302.
    Hearing aid dealers, HO §2-302.1.
    Speech-language pathologists, HO §2-302.2.
  Reciprocity.
    Waiver of examination requirements, HO §2-305.
  Records.
    Addresses, HO §2-311.
  Reinstatement of expired licenses, HO §2-309.
  Reinstatement of suspended or revoked licenses, HO §2-317.
  Renewal of licenses.
    Applications, HO §2-308.
    Audiologists, HO §2-310.
    Grace period, HO §2-308.
    Issuance, HO §2-308.
    Limited licenses.
      Audiologists, HO §2-310.
      Hearing aid dealers, HO §2-310.1.
      Speech-language pathologists, HO §2-310.2.
    Notice, HO §2-308.
  Reprimands.
    Grounds, HO §2-314.
  Requirements generally, HO §2-301.
    Waiver, HO §2-305.
  Revocation.
    Grounds, HO §2-314.
    Reinstatement of revoked licenses, HO §2-317.
  Scope of license.
    Audiologist, HO §2-307.
    Hearing aid dealers, HO §2-307.1.
    Speech-language pathologists, HO §2-307.2.
  Surrender.
    Conditions, HO §2-313.
    Generally, HO §2-313.
  Suspension.
    Grounds, HO §2-314.
    Reinstatement of suspended licenses, HO §2-317.
  Terms of licenses, HO §2-308.
  Transferring or offering to transfer licenses, HO §2-405.
  Use of purchased or fraudulent license, HO §2-401.
  Waiver of requirements, HO §2-305.
  When required, HO §2-301.
Limitation of activities and services, HO §2-102.
Medical examinations.
  Patients.
    Hearing aid dealers and audiologists, HO §2-314.1.
Medical records.
  Destruction, HG §4-403.
Misleading or untruthful representations regarding services.
  Hearing aid dealers and audiologists, HO §2-314.2.

AUDIOLOGISTS AND SPEECH-LANGUAGE PATHOLOGISTS —Cont'd

Names.
False names.
Hearing aid dealers, HO §2-314.4.
Notices.
Examinations, HO §2-304.
Hearings.
Mailing of notice, HO §2-317.
Licenses.
Renewal, HO §2-308.
Penalties.
License violations, HO §2-408.
Practice of audiology.
Defined, HO §2-101.
Qualifications of person or place of business.
Misrepresentation.
Hearing aid dealers, HO §2-314.3.
Receipts.
Sale of hearing aids, HO §2-314.8.
Reciprocity.
Licenses.
Reciprocal waiver of examination requirement, HO §2-305.
Records.
Destruction of patient's records, HG §4-403.
Licenses.
Addresses, HO §2-311.
Regulation of other professions, HO §2-102.
Sales.
Hearing aids.
Receipts, HO §2-314.8.
Schools.
Licensing fee reimbursement program, ED §6-112.1.
Scope of title, HO §2-102.
Sexual misconduct.
Disciplinary action, HO §1-212.
Short title, HO §2-501.
Solicitations.
Door-to-door solicitation of hearing aid sales, HO §2-314.6.
Speech-language pathologist rehabilitation committees.
Confidentiality of proceedings, records and files, HO §2-318.1.
Discovery.
Proceedings, records and files, HO §2-318.1.
Duties, HO §2-318.1.
Liability.
Good faith exemption from civil liability, HO §2-318.1.
Termination of title, HO §2-502.
Titles.
Misrepresentations of qualifications of person or place of business, HO §2-314.3.
Unfair and deceptive trade practices.
Audiologists, HO §2-406.
Hearing aid services, HO §2-314.7.
Unlawful inducements.
Hearing aid dealers and audiologists, HO §2-314.5.
Waiver.
Examination and licensure, HO §2-305.

AUDIOTAPE.
Depositions.
Generally.
Circuit courts, CivProCir Rule 2-416.
Notice.
Circuit courts, CivProCir Rule 2-412.

AUDIO-VIDEO.
Circuit courts.
Recording of proceedings, CJA Rule 16-405.
Access to recordings, CJA Rule 16-406.

AUDITORS.
Accounts.
Circuit courts, CivProCir Rule 2-543.
Administration of courts.
Code of conduct for masters, examiners, auditors, referees and District Court commissioners.
Adoption, CJA Rule 16-814.
Appointment.
Courts.
Employees of court, CJ §2-501.
Special officers, CJ §2-102.
Special auditors.
Circuit courts, CivProCir Rule 2-543.
Standing auditors.
Circuit courts, CivProCir Rule 2-543.
Code of conduct for masters, examiners, auditors, referees and District Court commissioners.
Adoption, CJA Rule 16-814.
Compensation.
Special auditors.
Circuit courts, CivProCir Rule 2-543.
Special officers of court, CJ §2-102.
Fees taxed as costs, CJ §2-102.
Standing auditors.
Circuit courts, CivProCir Rule 2-543.
Costs.
Circuit courts, CivProCir Rule 2-543.
Exceptions to account or report.
Hearing on exceptions.
Circuit courts, CivProCir Rule 2-543.
How taken.
Circuit courts, CivProCir Rule 2-543.
Transcript.
Circuit courts, CivProCir Rule 2-543.
Executors and administrators.
Employment.
Powers of personal representative, ET §7-401.
Hearings.
Exception to account or report.
Circuit courts, CivProCir Rule 2-543.
Notice.
Circuit courts, CivProCir Rule 2-543.
Record of hearing.
Circuit courts, CivProCir Rule 2-543.
Witnesses.
Attendance.
Circuit courts, CivProCir Rule 2-543.
Insurance administration, IN §2-104.
Judicial sales.
Ratification of sale.
Referral to auditor, PropSales Rule 14-305.
Mechanics' liens.
Sale under subtitle.
Referral to auditor, PropAct Rule 12-306.
Notice.
Hearings.
Circuit courts, CivProCir Rule 2-543.
Oaths.
Special officers of court, CJ §2-104.
Orders.
Referral by order.
Circuit courts, CivProCir Rule 2-543.
Powers.
Circuit courts, CivProCir Rule 2-543.

AUDITORS —Cont'd

Receivers.
Account of auditor, Receivers Rule 13-502.

Record of hearing.
Circuit courts, CivProCir Rule 2-543.

Referral by order.
Circuit courts, CivProCir Rule 2-543.

Reports.
Circuit courts, CivProCir Rule 2-543.
Time of entry of order ratifying report,
CivProCir Rule 2-543.

Special auditors.
Circuit courts, CivProCir Rule 2-543.

Standing auditors.
Circuit courts, CivProCir Rule 2-543.

Status as officer of court.
Circuit courts, CivProCir Rule 2-543.

Transcripts.
Exceptions to account or report.
Circuit courts, CivProCir Rule 2-543.

Witnesses.
Hearings.
Circuit courts, CivProCir Rule 2-543.

AUDITS.

**Accountants, state board of public
accountancy fund,** BR §2-106.5.

Accounts and accounting.
General provisions.
See ACCOUNTS AND ACCOUNTING.

**African American history and culture
commission.**
Revenue.
Sources, uses and audit, SF §5A-208.

African American museum corporation, SG
§9-2610.

**Agricultural and resource-based industry
development corporation,** 41 §13-511.

Agricultural cooperatives.
Raw agricultural products.
Financial statement of cooperative handling, CA
§5-529.

Agricultural land preservation fund, AG §2-505.

Alcoholic beverages.
Liquor control department.
Records, 2B §15-206.

Annapolis housing authority.
Annual audit, HS §13-111.

**Appalachian states low-level radioactive waste
compact.**
Commission, EN §7-302.

Appropriations.
Supervision of recipients.
Corporation serving elderly or developmentally
disabled.
State funded corporations subject to audit, SF
§7-405.
Social organizations.
State aid to, SF §7-402.
Warrants.
Audit of bills, SF §7-218.

Archives fund, SG §9-1013.

Attorneys at law.
Discipline and inactive status.
Attorney's accounts and records, CJA Rule
16-722.
Legal services corporation.
Annual audits, 10 §45K.

Automobile insurance fund, IN §20-304.

Aviation administration.
Post compliance audits, TR §5-215.1.

AUDITS —Cont'd

Bainbridge development corporation.
Corporate books and records, 83A §5-1608.

Baltimore City Community College.
Expenditures and accounts.
Requirements, ED §16-507.

Baltimore City police death relief fund, 24
§16-106.

Banks and trust companies.
Banking institutions.
Independent audits, FI §5-205.

Boxing and wrestling tax.
Inspection and preservation of records, TG §6-202.

**Canal Place preservation and development
authority,** FI §13-1010.

Charities.
Registration statements, BR §6-402.

Charter schools, ED §9-106.

Child abuse and neglect.
Centers of excellence initiative, HG §13-2206.

**Circuit court real property records
improvement fund,** CJ §13-603.

Clients' security fund, CJA Rule 16-811.

College investment plan, ED §18-19A-07.

College savings plan of Maryland, ED §18-1916.

Community health resources commission fund,
HG §19-2201.

Condominiums.
Books and records, RP §§11-116, 11A-128.
Outside audit required, RP §11-113.

Consumer cooperatives.
Annual audits, CA §5-5A-23.
Audit committee, CA §5-5A-23.

Continuing care contracts.
Appointed receivers, 70B §20I.

Contract state employees, SPP §13-205.

Counties.
Annual audit.
Expenses of examination of accounts and
records, 19 §41.
Reports, 19 §40.
Rules and regulations.
Establishment, 19 §40.
Auditor accountant.
Appointment, 25 §3.
Chartered counties.
Powers of county, 25A §5.
Expenses of examination of accounts and records,
19 §41.
Procedure, 19 §40.

Courts.
Auditor.
Special officers of court, CJ §2-102.

Credit unions.
Independent audits of members, FI §7-112.
Required by commissioner of financial regulation,
FI §6-405.
Supervisory committee.
Powers and duties, FI §6-402.
When committee fails to fulfill functions, FI
§6-405.

Debt management services.
Audits of fund, FI §12-905.
Retention of accounts and records, FI §12-922.

Dental hygienist rehabilitation committee, HO
§4-508.

Developmental disabilities.
Services co-ordination.
Funding distribution system for private
community-based services, HG §7-306.1.

AUDITS —Cont'd

Domestic violence fund for unit pilot program, FL §4-503.2.

Economic development corporation, 83A §5-212.

Electric companies.
Independent audit opinion, PUC §4-208.

Environmental service.
Annual independent audit, NR §3-126.

Executive agencies.
Office of administrative hearings, SG §9-1606.

Fiduciary estates including guardianships of property, Guardian Rule 10-706.

Fiscal compliance audits, SG §2-1221.

Gas companies.
Independent audit opinion, PUC §4-208.

General assembly.
House of delegates.
Powers as grand inquest of state, MD Const Art III §24.
Joint audit committee, SG §§2-601 to 2-605.
Office of legislative audits, SG §§2-1217 to 2-1227.
See LEGISLATIVE SERVICES DEPARTMENT.

General services department.
Procurement.
Inventory, SF §4-306.

Health.
Cost review commission.
See HEALTH.

Health and higher educational facilities authority.
Annual audit, 43C §20.

Health maintenance organizations.
Periodic audits, HG §19-710.

Homebuilder registration fund, BR §4.5-203.

Horse racing.
Licenses.
Financial disclosure by licensees, BR §11-313.

Housing authorities, HS §12-404.
Annapolis housing authority, HS §13-111.
Montgomery county.
Housing opportunities commission, HS §16-113.
Bond issues, HS §16-209.

Indian affairs commission, 41 §6-908.

Insurance.
Automobile insurance fund, IN §20-304.
Joint insurance association.
Powers and duties of commissioner, IN §25-408.
Premium finance companies, IN §23-103.
Small employer health reinsurance pool, IN §15-1222.

Joint audit committee, SG §§2-601 to 2-605.

Joint insurance association.
Powers and duties of commissioner, IN §25-408.

Legal services corporation.
Annual audits, 10 §45K.

Legislative auditor.
Automobile insurance fund, IN §20-304.
Universities and colleges.
Private donation incentive programs.
Auditor to receive copy of annual report, ED §17-303.

Legislative services department.
Office of legislative audits, SG §§2-1217 to 2-1227.
See LEGISLATIVE SERVICES DEPARTMENT.

Local military installation redevelopment authorities, 83A §5-1709.

Management and productivity council, SG §9-1806.

Maryland affordable housing trust, HS §10-110.

Maryland correctional enterprises, COR §3-510.

AUDITS —Cont'd

Maryland health care provider rate stabilization fund, IN §§19-805, 19-808.

Maryland historical trust, SF §5A-318.

Maryland-national capital park and planning commission.
Prior to annual report, 28 §2-113.

Maryland stadium authority, FI §13-719.

Maryland Transit Administration.
Post compliance audits, TR §7-211.1.

Maryland venture capital trust, 83A §5-307.

Medical mutual liability insurance society of Maryland.
Annual audits, IN §24-213.

Militia, PS §13-204.

Montgomery county.
Housing opportunities commission, HS §16-113.
Bond issues, HS §16-209.

Morgan State University.
Employees.
Classified employees grievance procedures.
Appeal to secretary of budget and management, ED §14-306.
Legislative auditor, ED §14-104.

Morticians.
Power of board to audit licensees, HO §7-205.
Subpoenas, issuance by board, HO §7-319.

Motor clubs.
Examination of books, records and accounts, IN §26-103.

Motor vehicles.
Automobile insurance fund, IN §20-304.
Compensation of dealers for incentive or reimbursement programs, TR §15-212.1.

Municipal corporations.
Annual audit.
Reports, 19 §40.
Rules and regulations.
Establishment, 19 §40.
Expenses of examination of accounts and records.
By legislative auditor, 19 §41.
Power to provide, 23A §2.
Procedure, 19 §40.

911 trust fund.
Appropriations and disbursements, PS §1-309.

Northeast Maryland waste disposal authority.
Annual audit, NR §3-923.
State audit, NR §3-923.

Nurses.
Board of nursing fund, HO §8-206.

Nursing homes.
Third party liability review for medical assistance programs, HG §§19-14A-01 to 19-14A-04.

Office of administrative hearings.
Executive agencies, SG §9-1606.

Office of legislative audits, SG §§2-1217 to 2-1227.
See LEGISLATIVE SERVICES DEPARTMENT.

Pharmacists and pharmacies.
State board of pharmacy fund, HO §12-206.

Physicians.
Board of physicians fund, HO §14-207.

Pilotage fee payments, BOP §11-508.

Police death relief fund.
Baltimore City, 24 §16-106.

Port administration.
Post compliance audits, TR §6-212.1.

Potomac highlands airport authority.
Examination of authority accounts, TR §10-103.

Premium finance companies.
Expense of examinations, IN §23-103.

AUDITS —Cont'd
Procurement.
Architectural and engineering services.
Rates of contractors, SF §13-320.
Generally, SF §15-110.
General services department.
Inventory, SF §4-306.
Public service companies providing gas or electric services.
Independent audit opinion, PUC §4-208.
Registers of wills.
Accounts and examination of vouchers, ET §2-208.
Reports.
Uniform system of accounts.
Annual audit, 19 §40.
Rules and regulations.
Establishment, 19 §40.
St. Mary's College of Maryland.
Submission to audit and examination, ED §14-407.
Schools.
Annual audit by county board of education, ED §5-109.
Charter schools, ED §9-106.
Office of legislative audits.
Local school systems.
Findings and recommendations, SG §2-1224.
Place of audit, SG §2-1222.
Procedure, SG §2-1223.
Reports, SG §2-1224.
Required and authorized audits, SG §2-1220.
Performance audits, ED §5-110.
Violation of reporting requirements, ED §5-113.
Soil conservation.
Committee.
Annual audit of accounts, AG §8-202.
Districts.
Annual audit of accounts, AG §8-303.
State lottery.
Legislative audit, SG §9-121.
State occupational and professional licensing design board's fund, BR §2-106.1.
State police department.
Departmental finances generally, PS §2-208.
State retirement and pension system.
Legislative auditor.
Duties, SPP §21-127.
Susquehanna river basin authority.
Annual independent audit, EN §5-301.
Taxation.
Returns, TG §13-301.
Universities and colleges.
College savings plan of Maryland, ED §18-1916.
Part-time students, grant program, ED §18-1404.
Private donation incentive program, ED §17-303.
Veterinarians.
State board of veterinary medical examiners fund, AG §2-303.
Washington suburban sanitary district.
Commission to organize annual audit, 29 §1-106.
Water pollution.
Oil discharge containment, control and cleanup.
Transferring oil.
Licenses.
Procedures to be established, EN §4-411.
Witness protection program.
Fund and program, CP §11-907.
Workers' compensation.
Self-insurance groups, IN §25-307.

AUDUBON NATURALIST SOCIETY.
Property tax credits, TP §9-233.

AUTHORITIES.
Airport authorities.
General provisions.
See AIRPORT AUTHORITIES.
Potomac highlands airport authority.
See POTOMAC HIGHLANDS AIRPORT AUTHORITY.
Canal Place preservation and development authority, FI §§13-1001 to 13-1031.
See CANAL PLACE PRESERVATION AND DEVELOPMENT AUTHORITY.
Chesapeake regional Olympic games authority, SG §§9-2301 to 9-2303.
Economic development assistance authority, 83A §5-1403.
Education.
Health and higher educational facilities authority, 43C §§1 to 24.
See HEALTH AND HIGHER EDUCATIONAL FACILITIES AUTHORITY.
Health.
Health and higher educational facilities authority, 43C §§1 to 24.
See HEALTH AND HIGHER EDUCATIONAL FACILITIES AUTHORITY.
Heritage areas authority, FI §§13-1103 to 13-1108.
See HERITAGE AREAS.
Housing authorities.
General provisions, HS §§12-101 to 23-101.
See HOUSING AUTHORITIES.
Industrial development financing authority, 83A §§5-901 to 5-933.
See INDUSTRIAL DEVELOPMENT FINANCING AUTHORITY.
Local military installation redevelopment authorities, 83A §§5-1701 to 5-1711.
See LOCAL MILITARY INSTALLATION REDEVELOPMENT AUTHORITIES.
Maryland food center authority, 41 §§13-101 to 13-123.
See MARYLAND FOOD CENTER AUTHORITY.
Maryland port administration.
General provisions, TR §§6-101 to 6-602.
See PORT ADMINISTRATION.
Maryland stadium authority, FI §§13-701 to 13-724.
See MARYLAND STADIUM AUTHORITY.
Maryland Transit Administration.
General provisions.
See MARYLAND TRANSIT ADMINISTRATION.
Northeast Maryland waste disposal authority.
General provisions, NR §§3-901 to 3-928.
See NORTHEAST MARYLAND WASTE DISPOSAL AUTHORITY.
Pimlico community development authority, BR §§11-1201 to 11-1205.
Potomac highlands airport authority.
General provisions.
See POTOMAC HIGHLANDS AIRPORT AUTHORITY.
Potomac water authority.
General provisions, EN §§5-401 to 5-414.
See POTOMAC WATER AUTHORITY.
Small business development financing authority, 83A §§1001 to 1049.
See SMALL BUSINESS DEVELOPMENT FINANCING AUTHORITY.
Tobacco authority.
General provisions.
See TOBACCO.

AUTHORITIES —Cont'd
Transportation authority, TR §§4-201 to 4-209.
  See TRANSPORTATION DEPARTMENT.
Washington metropolitan area transit
    authority.
  General provisions, TR §10-204.
Water and sewer authorities, EN §§9-901 to
    9-958.
  See WATER AND SEWER SYSTEMS.
Water resources.
  Potomac water authority.
    General provisions.
      See POTOMAC WATER AUTHORITY.
Woodrow Wilson bridge and tunnel authority,
    TR §§10-301 to 10-303.

AUTISM SPECTRUM DISORDERS.
Schools, screening practices.
  Pilot program to study and improve, ED §§8-601
    to 8-608.
    See SCHOOLS.

AUTO COMPANIES.
Defined as common carrier, PUC §1-101.

AUTOMATED DIALING.
Telephone solicitations by, PUC §8-204.

AUTOMATED EXTERNAL DEFIBRILLATOR
    PROGRAM, ED §13-517.
County boards of education to develop and
    implement programs, ED §7-425.

AUTOMATED TELLER MACHINES, FI §§1-401
    to 1-406.
Authorization to operate, FI §1-403.
Credit card crimes, CR §§8-201 to 8-217.
  See CREDIT CARDS.
Definitions, FI §1-401.
Exceptions to provisions, FI §1-402.
Foreign banking corporations, FI §1-405.
  State preemption of authority to enact laws
    regarding, FI §1-406.
Hours of business, FI §5-702.
Notices.
  Fees charged, FI §1-404.
  Safety precautions, FI §1-402.
Safety.
  Lightning, FI §1-402.
  Notification of customers of safety precautions, FI
    §1-402.
  Procedures for evaluating safety issues, FI §1-402.
Transactions authorized, FI §1-403.

AUTOMATIC GARAGE DOOR OPENERS.
Code grabbing devices.
  Manufacturing, selling or possessing, CR §7-301.
Deactivation tool or device.
  Possessing, using, CR §7-301.
Removal of system or device, CR §7-301.

AUTOMOBILE GRAVEYARDS.
Preventing dumping into waters of state, EN
    §§5-10A-01 to 5-10A-03.
  Criminal penalty for violations, EN §5-10A-02.
  Defined, EN §5-10A-01.
  Evidence of violation, EN §5-10A-02.
  Required, EN §5-10A-02.

AUTOMOBILE INSURANCE FUND.
Accident history reports, IN §27-216.
Account of the fund, IN §20-302.
Actions against fund.
  Applicability of rules, SpecPro Rule 15-801.
  Commencement, SpecPro Rule 15-804.

AUTOMOBILE INSURANCE FUND —Cont'd
Actions against fund —Cont'd
  Judgments.
    Consent in lieu of petition, SpecPro Rule
      15-804.
    Payment.
      District Court, SpecPro Rule 15-804.
    Venue, SpecPro Rule 15-804.
Actions against uninsured motorists.
  Commencement, SpecPro Rule 15-803.
Additional drivers.
  Effect on premiums, IN §20-508.
Add-on coverage, IN §20-504.
Administration of fund, IN §§20-201 to 20-204.
Agents and brokers.
  Producers. See within this heading, "Producers."
Appeal of rejection or cancellation of
    insurance, IN §20-517.
Appeals.
  Claims against fund, IN §§20-605, 20-607.
Applicable provisions, IN §20-201.
Appropriations from general fund prohibited,
    IN §20-302.
Audits, IN §20-304.
Binding of coverage, IN §20-509.
Board of trustees, IN §20-202.
Cancellation of coverage, IN §§20-509, 20-516.
  Appeals, IN §20-517.
  Continuation of coverage for family members, IN
    §20-519.
  Driver's license suspension or revocation, IN
    §20-518.
  Refund of unearned commissions, IN §20-512.
Certification of eligibility, IN §20-502.
Claims against fund, IN §20-505.
  Appeals, IN §20-607.
  Authorized claims, IN §20-601.
  Defense of claims, IN §20-606.
  Interest on judgments, IN §20-604.
  Limitation on amounts payable from fund, IN
    §20-602.
  Notice of intention to make claim, IN §20-603.
  Procedural requirements, IN §20-604.
  Reserves for payment, IN §20-506.
  Settlement, IN §§20-604, 20-605.
Collection of premiums, IN §20-507.
Commercial policies.
  Additional and excess coverages, IN §20-503.
  Premiums, IN §20-507.
Commission payments, IN §20-512.
  Voided policies, IN §20-502.
Composition of fund, IN §20-301.
Contents of policies, IN §20-503.
Continuation of coverage upon three years
    without violation or accident, IN §20-508.
Creation, IN §20-201.
Debts of fund not debt of state, IN §20-302.
Deductions from payments from fund, IN
    §20-602.
Defense of claims, IN §20-606.
Definitions, IN §20-101; SpecPro Rule 15-802.
  Add-on coverage, IN §20-504.
  Covered vehicle, IN §20-501.
  Net direct written premiums, IN §20-405.
  Qualified person, IN §20-601.
Disappearing driver or owner.
  Authorized claims against fund, IN §20-601.
Disclosure requirements, IN §20-503.
  Add-on coverage, IN §20-504.
Driving record.
  Effect of record on insurability, IN §20-518.

AUTOMOBILE INSURANCE FUND —Cont'd
Eligibility requirements for policyholders, IN
§20-502.
Excluded driver endorsements, IN §20-516.
Executive director, IN §20-203.
Executors and administrators.
Claims against fund.
Presentation, ET §8-104.
Expiration of policy.
Notice, IN §20-520.
Family members.
Continuation of coverage following cancellation,
IN §20-519.
Filing false notice or document, IN §20-701.
Financial management committee, IN §20-303.
Financing of premiums, IN §20-507.
Indexing of judgments, IN §20-608.
Industry automobile insurance association, IN
§§20-401 to 20-411.
Amount of assessment, IN §20-404.
Board of directors, IN §20-403.
Assessment duties, IN §20-405.
Certification of operating loss and assessment
limit, IN §20-404.
Composition, IN §20-402.
Deductions from other assessments or taxes, IN
§20-405.
Established, IN §20-401.
Exclusions from operating loss or assessment, IN
§20-404.
Identification of operating loss and assessment
limit, IN §20-404.
Industry automobile insurance fund.
Membership in association required, IN §20-402.
Money collected from association considered direct
contribution to surplus, IN §20-411.
Payment of assessment, IN §20-405.
Quarterly report and certification, IN §20-408.
Recoupment.
Statement of recoupment in premium billing, IN
§20-408.
Surcharges.
Adjustments to assessment surcharges, IN
§20-409.
Collection, IN §20-408.
Deadline for deposit of gross excess surcharge,
IN §20-410.
Election to impose surcharges, IN §20-407.
Imposition of assessment surcharges, IN
§20-406.
Nonpayment, IN §20-408.
Policyholders of fund, IN §20-406.
Zero assessment limit, IN §20-404.
Insufficiency assessment reserve fund, IN
§20-410.
Accounting of money received from fund, IN
§20-411.
Automobile insurance fund payments prohibited,
IN §20-406.
Interest on judgments, IN §20-604.
Intervention in a claim, IN §20-606.
Investments, IN §20-303.
Industry automobile insurance association, IN
§20-410.
Judgments.
Actions against fund.
Consent in lieu of petition, SpecPro Rule
15-804.
Payment, SpecPro Rule 15-804.
Actions against uninsured motorists.
Payment, SpecPro Rule 15-803.

AUTOMOBILE INSURANCE FUND —Cont'd
Lapse in coverage.
Effect on premiums, IN §20-508.
Limitation on amounts payable from fund, IN
§20-602.
Management of moneys collected, IN §20-303.
Nonrenewal of coverage.
Driver's license suspension or revocation, IN
§20-518.
Orders.
Show cause order, SpecPro Rule 15-804.
Policies, IN §§20-501 to 20-520.
Premiums, IN §§20-506 to 20-508.
Producers.
Actions against producers, IN §§20-513, 20-514.
Binding of coverage, IN §20-509.
Commission payments, IN §20-512.
Disciplinary grounds, IN §20-509.
Fiduciary duties, IN §20-510.
Recovery of money owed to fund, IN §20-515.
Surety bonds, IN §20-511.
Prohibited acts.
Add-on coverage, IN §20-504.
Collection, IN §20-408.
**Property and casualty insurance guaranty
corporation.**
Member of corporation, IN §20-201.
Purpose of fund, IN §20-301.
Record of income and expenses, IN §20-301.
Recovery of money paid by fund, IN §20-608.
Recovery of moneys owed to fund, IN §20-515.
**Refusal to issue policy to persons insured by
fund.**
Prohibited, IN §20-520.
Rejection of insurance, IN §20-516.
Appeals, IN §20-517.
Renewal of policy.
Notice, IN §20-520.
Reserves for payment of claims, IN §20-506.
Residency requirements for policyholders, IN
§20-502.
Safe driver credits.
Effect of three years without violation or accident,
IN §20-508.
Salary plan changes, IN §20-204.
Scope of rules, SpecPro Rule 15-801.
Service of process.
Commencement of action against uninsured
motorists, SpecPro Rule 15-803.
Settlement of claims, IN §§20-604, 20-605;
SpecPro Rule 15-805.
Special fund account, IN §20-302.
Spouses.
Continuation of coverage following cancellation,
IN §20-519.
Staff, IN §20-204.
Stipulations.
Actions against uninsured motorists, SpecPro
Rule 15-803.
Commencement of action against fund, IN
§20-604; SpecPro Rule 15-804.
Settlements by fund, SpecPro Rule 15-805.
Subrogation, IN §20-609.
Taxation, IN §§6-101 to 6-121.
See INSURANCE COMPANIES.
**Telephone conversations relevant to accidents
or claims.**
Recording, IN §20-505.
Trust money, IN §20-510.
Unidentified motor vehicle, owner or driver.
Authorized claims against fund, IN §20-601.

AUTOMOBILE INSURANCE FUND —Cont'd
Uninsured motorists.
  Actions against.
    Commencement, SpecPro Rule 15-803.
    Judgments.
      Payment, SpecPro Rule 15-803.
  Authorized claims against fund, IN §20-601.
  Commencement of actions against, SpecPro Rule
      15-803.
  Insurance coverage, IN §§19-509 to 19-511.
Unsatisfied claims, IN §§20-601 to 20-609.
Use of fund, IN §20-301.
Venue.
  Actions against fund, SpecPro Rule 15-804.
Workers' compensation.
  Amounts payable from fund.
    Effect of workers' compensation, IN §20-602.

AUTOMOBILES.
Automotive repair facilities, CL §§14-1001 to
    14-1009.
  See MOTOR VEHICLE REPAIR FACILITIES.
General provisions.
  See MOTOR VEHICLES.
Service stations.
  See SERVICE STATIONS.

AUTOMOTIVE CRASH PARTS ACT, CL
    §§14-2301 to 14-2304.

**AUTOMOTIVE DISMANTLER AND RECYCLER
    FACILITY.**
Preventing dumping into waters of state, EN
    §§5-10A-01 to 5-10A-03.
  Criminal penalty for violations, EN §5-10A-02.
  Defined, EN §5-10A-01.
  Evidence of violation, EN §5-10A-02.
  Required, EN §5-10A-02.

AUTOPSIES.
Anatomical gift act.
  Effect of laws concerning autopsies, ET §4-508.
General provisions.
  See POSTMORTEM EXAMINERS.
Health insurance provisions, IN §15-216.

AUTREFOIS, ACQUIT AND CONVICT.
Jeopardy, US Const Amd 5.

AVIAN INFLUENZA.
Regulation of poultry to control, AG §§3-801 to
    3-805.
  Adoption of animal health protection program, AG
    §3-803.
  Definitions, AG §3-801.
  Licensing of poultry market operators, AG §3-802.
    Refusal, suspension or revocation of license, AG
      §3-805.
  Registration of poultry, AG §3-804.

AVIATION.
Accidents.
  Collision of aircraft.
    Liability, TR §5-1004.
  Reporting, TR §5-206.
**Activities constitute public functions for
    public purposes,** TR §5-102.
Administration.
  Accidents.
    Reporting, TR §5-206.
  Airports.
    Motor vehicle parking violations.
      Citations for.
        Administration employees authorized to
          issue, TR §5-212.1.

AVIATION —Cont'd
Administration —Cont'd
  Airports —Cont'd
    Political subdivisions.
      Acquisition and operation.
        Assistance to, TR §5-215.
    State airports and facilities.
      Establishment of terms and conditions, TR
        §5-408.
      Monitoring prices and employment practices,
        TR §5-408.
      Operation and maintenance, TR §§5-404,
        5-412.
  Appeals.
    Orders of administration, TR §5-210.
  Audits.
    Post compliance audits, TR §5-215.1.
  Conflicts of interest, TR §5-217.
  Contracts.
    Law governing, TR §5-213.
  Defined, TR §5-101.
  Development of aeronautics.
    Administration to encourage, foster and assist,
      TR §5-204.
  Duties, TR §5-204.
    Enforcement of aeronautics laws, TR §§5-1101,
      5-1102.
  Established, TR §5-202.
  Executive director, TR §5-202.1.
  General supervisory powers, TR §5-204.
  Hearings.
    Joint hearings, TR §5-206.
    Notice and opportunity, TR §5-210.
  Investigations and hearings.
    Powers.
      Generally, TR §5-209.
  Licenses.
    Suspension or revocation.
      Orders denying, suspending or revoking
        license, TR §5-210.
  Orders.
    Continuation of orders, TR §5-216.
    Judicial review, TR §5-210.
    Service, TR §5-210.
  Police force.
    Charging documents against law enforcement
      officers, CJ §2-608.
  Political subdivisions.
    Cooperation with, TR §5-205.
  Powers, TR §5-204.
  Prior approval.
    Exercise of powers and duties subject to, TR
      §5-203.
  Reciprocal services, TR §5-206.
  Reports.
    Accidents, TR §5-206.
  Rules and regulations.
    Continuation, TR §5-216.
    Federal standards.
      Conformity to, TR §5-208.
    Promulgation, TR §5-208.
  Service of process.
    Orders of administration, TR §5-210.
  State airports and facilities.
    General provisions, TR §§5-404, 5-412.
  Supervision.
    General supervision of aeronautics, TR §5-204.
  Technical services of administration.
    Availability of services for planning, acquisition,
      construction, etc., of airports, TR §5-215.

AVIATION —Cont'd
Administration —Cont'd
　Transportation department.
　　Included within department, TR §2-107.
　Violations of article.
　　Exchange of information, TR §5-1101.
Administrator.
　Defined, TR §5-101.
　Management and control of administration, TR
　　§5-203.
Aeronautics.
　Defined, TR §5-101.
　Instructors.
　　Licensing, TR §§5-901 to 5-906.
Aircraft.
　Currency transactions in trade or business, BR
　　§§1-501 to 1-505.
　　See CURRENCY TRANSACTIONS IN TRADE
　　　OR BUSINESS.
　Defined, TR §5-101.
　Firearms or explosives aboard aircraft, TR
　　§5-1008.
　Landing aircraft, TR §5-1001.
　Mechanics' liens.
　　General provisions.
　　　See MECHANICS' LIENS.
　Minimum altitude of certain aircraft over sports
　　arenas in Baltimore City, TR §5-1007.
　Operation.
　　Collision.
　　　Liability, TR §5-1004.
　　Defined, TR §5-101.
　　Landing aircraft, TR §5-1001.
　　Lands and waters.
　　　Operation over lands and waters, TR §5-1001.
　　Lawfulness of operation, TR §5-1001.
　　Reckless operation, TR §5-1006.
　　　Penalty, TR §5-1006.
　　Sovereignty in space, TR §5-104.
　　Space ownership, TR §5-104.
　Sales.
　　Currency transactions in trade or business, BR
　　　§§1-501 to 1-505.
　　　See CURRENCY TRANSACTIONS IN
　　　　TRADE OR BUSINESS.
　Seaplanes.
　　Rules of water navigation, TR §5-1009.
Airports.
　Acquisition of property by political subdivision,
　　TR §5-417.
　Administration as agent of political subdivision,
　　TR §5-422.
　Bond issues, TR §5-419.
　Carriers.
　　Airports usable by air carriers, TR §5-420.
　Condemnation, TR §5-417.
　Establishment, TR §5-416.
　Federal law.
　　Prerequisites to project application, TR
　　　§5-423.
　Operation and use, TR §5-416.
　　Costs and expenses.
　　　Responsibility of political subdivision, TR
　　　　§5-418.
　State financial assistance, TR §5-421.
　Administration. See within this heading,
　　"Administration."
　Authorities.
　　General provisions.
　　　See AIRPORT AUTHORITIES.

AVIATION —Cont'd
Airports —Cont'd
　Authorities —Cont'd
　　Potomac highlands airport authority.
　　　See POTOMAC HIGHLANDS AIRPORT
　　　　AUTHORITY.
　Baltimore-Washington International Thurgood
　　Marshall Airport.
　　Citizens committee for the enhancement of
　　　communities surrounding, TR §5-414.
　　Construction of parallel transport runway, TR
　　　§5-413.
　　Noise zone.
　　　Restriction on use of residential property
　　　　purchased by state in noise zone, TR
　　　　§5-824.
　　Zoning districts, TR §5-509.
　Board of zoning appeals. See within this
　　subheading, "Zoning."
　Bond issues.
　　Political subdivisions.
　　　Issuance, TR §5-419.
　Carriers.
　　Use of airports by air carriers, TR §5-420.
　Certificates.
　　Site approval, TR §5-303.
　Commercial use airport.
　　Defined, TR §5-301.
　Compacts.
　　Potomac highlands airport authority, TR
　　　§§10-101 to 10-103.
　　　See POTOMAC HIGHLANDS AIRPORT
　　　　AUTHORITY.
　Condemnation of property.
　　By administration, TR §5-405.
　　By political subdivision, TR §5-417.
　Contracts.
　　Construction or improvement.
　　　Procedure, TR §5-213.
　Defined, TR §§5-101, 5-301.
　Discrimination.
　　State airports.
　　　Monitoring of employment practices by
　　　　administration, TR §5-408.
　Districts, establishing, TR §5-4A-01.
　Easements for future development, TR §5-4A-01.
　Electric company transmission lines near airport
　　runways, PUC §7-207.
　Facility.
　　Defined, TR §5-101.
　Federal aid.
　　General provisions, TR §5-411.
　Hearings.
　　Public hearings, TR §5-305.
　Joint operation.
　　State, municipalities and United States, TR
　　　§5-407.
　Licenses.
　　Annual renewal, TR §5-304.
　　Applicability, TR §5-302.
　　Authorization, TR §5-304.
　　Conditions of licensure, TR §5-304.
　　Definitions, TR §5-301.
　　Exemptions, TR §5-302.
　　Fees, TR §5-304.
　　Issuance, TR §5-304.
　　Prerequisites, TR §5-304.
　　Refusal, TR §5-304.
　　Registration of airports not required to be
　　　licensed, TR §5-306.
　　Required, TR §5-304.

AVIATION —Cont'd
Airports —Cont'd
Licenses —Cont'd
United States airports.
Exemptions from subtitle, TR §5-302.
Motor vehicles.
Parking regulations, TR §5-426.
Citations for violations.
Administration employees authorized to
issue, TR §5-212.1.
Noise.
Assessment of noise environment, TR §5-805.
Cumulative noise exposure.
Defined, TR §5-801.
Limits, TR §5-804.
Definitions, TR §5-801.
Noise abatement plan for impacted land use
area.
Assistance in development and
implementation of plans, TR §5-807.
Development plan, TR §5-805.
Implementation and monitoring of plans, TR
§5-806.
Political subdivisions. See within this heading,
"Political subdivisions."
Purpose of subtitle, TR §5-802.
State-owned airports.
Executive director duties, TR §5-819.
Zones.
Certification of noise zones, TR §5-806.
Defined, TR §5-801.
Noise assistance programs, TR §§5-1201 to
5-1205.
Homeowners assistance pilot program, TR
§§5-1204, 5-1205.
Legislative findings, TR §5-1202.
Voluntary land acquisition program, TR
§5-1203.
Police employees.
Charging documents against law enforcement
officers, CJ §2-608.
Political subdivisions. See within this heading,
"Political subdivisions."
Potomac highlands airport authority.
See POTOMAC HIGHLANDS AIRPORT
AUTHORITY.
Property taxes.
Exemptions.
Licensed public airport on privately owned
land, TP §7-303.
Registration.
Airports not required to be licensed under
subtitle, TR §5-306.
Roster of aircraft, TR §5-1002.
Sites.
Approval, TR §5-303.
State airports.
Acquisition of property by administration, TR
§5-405.
Condemnation.
Acquisition of property, TR §5-405.
Construction of subtitle, TR §5-402.
Definitions, TR §5-401.
Disposition of property by administration, TR
§5-406.
Employment practices.
Administration to monitor, TR §5-408.
Establishment, TR §5-404.
Establish or operate.
Defined, TR §5-401.

AVIATION —Cont'd
Airports —Cont'd
State airports —Cont'd
Executive director's duties as operator, TR
§5-819.
Financing, TR §5-404.
Noise.
Acquisition and disposition of property, TR
§5-823.
Adoption and enforcement of regulations, TR
§5-820.
Appeals, TR §5-822.
Duties of executive director, TR §5-819.
New airports, TR §5-820.
Permits, TR §5-821.
Restriction on use of residential property.
Exceptions, TR §5-824.
Variances, TR §5-822.
Operation and use privileges, TR §5-404.
Airport or facility operated by administration,
TR §5-408.
Airport or facility operated by others, TR
§5-409.
Liens, TR §5-410.
Prices.
Monitoring of prices by administration, TR
§5-408.
Property.
Acquisition by administration, TR §5-405.
Disposition of property, TR §5-406.
Terms and conditions.
Establishment by administration, TR §5-408.
Taxation.
Credits.
Property tax credits.
Residential property in airport noise zones,
TP §9-216.
Exemptions.
Licensed public airport on privately owned
land, TP §7-303.
Technical services of administration.
Availability of services for planning, acquisition,
construction, etc., of airports, TR §5-215.
Zoning.
Appeals.
Political subdivisions, TR §§5-612 to 5-615.
Board of zoning appeals, TR §5-506.
Defined, TR §5-501.
Judicial review of board decisions, TR §5-508.
Variances.
Power to grant variances, TR §5-507.
Conflicting regulations, TR §5-707.
Considerations for guidance, TR §5-503.
Definitions, TR §5-501.
Enforcement.
Political subdivisions, TR §5-617.
Penalties.
Violations of subtitle, TR §5-511.
Permits.
Administration, TR §5-506.
Political subdivisions. See within this heading,
"Political subdivisions."
Prohibited uses, TR §§5-504, 5-510.
Queen Anne's county.
Sixth election district, TR §5-106.
Regulations.
Adoption.
Administration, TR §5-502.
Political subdivisions, TR §5-607.
Conflicting regulations, TR §5-707.

AVIATION —Cont'd
Airports —Cont'd
Zoning —Cont'd
Regulations —Cont'd
Political subdivisions.
Adoption, TR §5-607.
Violation of regulations, TR §5-504.
Substantially alter.
Defined, TR §5-501.
Variances.
Administration, TR §5-507.
Air schools.
Defined, TR §5-901.
Licenses.
Authority of administration, TR §5-902.
Federal licenses, TR §5-903.
Fees, TR §5-904.
Issuance, TR §5-904.
Refusal to issue, TR §5-905.
Operating schools unlawfully, TR §5-906.
Penalties, TR §5-906.
Required, TR §5-903.
Rules and regulations.
Administration may adopt, TR §5-902.
State licenses, TR §5-903.
Suspension, revocation or refusal to issue, TR §5-905.
Air space.
Freedom of transit through air space of state, TR §5-1001.
Airways.
Freedom of transit through state air space, TR §5-1001.
Alcoholic beverages.
Aircraft.
Operation under influence, TR §5-1006.
Beer, wine and liquor licenses.
Class G, on-sale, 2B §6-503.
Repeal provisions, 2B §8-102.
Carriers.
Records and reports.
Required, 2B §14-202.
Sale.
Exercising right to sell under lien, 2B §1-201.
Illegal transportation.
Confiscation and forfeiture of transportation equipment, 2B §1-201.
Licenses.
Applications.
For airplanes, 2B §9-101.
Where to be filed, 2B §10-101.
Restrictions upon retail dealers, 2B §12-107.
Transport planes.
No license or permit required of transport planes, 2B §1-201.
Appeals.
Administration.
Orders, TR §5-210.
Zoning.
Administration.
Board of appeals, TR §5-506.
Appropriations.
Local appropriations, TR §5-105.
Authority.
Maryland airport authorities.
General provisions.
See AIRPORT AUTHORITIES.
Potomac highlands airport authority.
See POTOMAC HIGHLANDS AIRPORT AUTHORITY.

AVIATION —Cont'd
Baltimore-Washington International Thurgood Marshall Airport.
Citizens committee for the enhancement of communities surrounding, TR §5-414.
Construction of parallel transport runway, TR §5-413.
Employees.
Retirement system, TR §5-413.
International terminal name, TR §5-413.
Noise zone.
Restriction on use of residential property purchased by state in noise zone, TR §5-824.
Zoning districts, TR §5-509.
Birds and game.
Hunting.
From aircraft prohibited, NR §10-410.
Blind persons.
Rights of blind persons to public facilities, 30 §33.
Boards and commissions.
Airports.
Board of airport zoning appeals. See within this heading, "Airports."
Political subdivisions.
Board of appeals.
Noise and zoning. See within this heading, "Political subdivisions."
Cooperation with commission, TR §5-205.
Bond issues.
Airports.
Political subdivisions.
Issuance, TR §5-419.
Public debt.
General provisions, 31 §§1 to 12.
See PUBLIC DEBT.
Transportation.
Financing, TR §§3-301 to 3-310.
See COUNTIES.
Boundaries.
Sovereignty in space, TR §5-104.
Carriers.
Airports.
Use of airports by carriers, TR §5-420.
Citations.
Enforcement of aeronautics laws.
Citation to appear in court, TR §5-1104.
Commission.
Action approval, TR §5-201.1.
Appointment limitations, TR §5-201.
Budget, TR §5-201.1.
Compensation of members, TR §5-201.
Composition, TR §5-201.
Conflicts of interest, TR §5-217.
Duties, TR §5-201.
Established, TR §5-201.
Executive director, TR §5-201.1.
Expenses of commission, TR §5-201.
Meetings, TR §5-201.
Member terms, TR §5-201.
References to commission means administration, TR §5-216.
Reports, TR §5-201.2.
Compacts.
Potomac highlands airport authority, TR §§10-101 to 10-103.
See POTOMAC HIGHLANDS AIRPORT AUTHORITY.
Contracts.
Administration.
Law governing, TR §5-213.

AVIATION —Cont'd
Contracts —Cont'd
  Jurisdiction over contracts, TR §5-103.
Crimes and offenses.
  Jurisdiction, TR §5-103.
Damages.
  Collision of aircraft, TR §5-1004.
  Forced landing, TR §5-1001.
  Injuries to persons or property, TR §5-1005.
  Lien, TR §5-1005.
Deaf or hearing impaired.
  Rights of deaf or mute persons to public facilities,
    30 §33.
Definitions, TR §5-101.
  Airports, TR §§5-101, 5-301.
    Noise assistance programs, TR §5-1201.
  Air schools, TR §5-901.
  Noise.
    Airports, TR §5-801.
Development.
  By administration, TR §5-204.
Discrimination.
  Airports.
    Monitoring of employment practices in state
      airports, TR §5-408.
Drugs.
  Aircraft.
    Operation under influence, TR §5-1006.
Education.
  Air schools.
    Licensing of air schools, TR §§5-901 to 5-906.
    See within this heading, "Air schools."
Eminent domain.
  Airports.
    Administration in name of state, TR §5-405.
  State airports and facilities.
    Administration powers to condemnation of
      property, TR §5-405.
Equal employment opportunity commission.
  Employment discrimination.
    Administration to refer investigations to
      commission, TR §5-408.
Exemptions.
  Airports.
    Licenses, TR §5-302.
Federal aid.
  State airports and facilities.
    Administration as agent, TR §5-411.
Fees.
  Licenses.
    Airports, TR §5-304.
    Air schools and aeronautics instructors, TR
      §5-904.
Fines.
  Violations of article, TR §5-1105.
Forced landing.
  Liability, TR §5-1001.
Freedom.
  Right to free transit through state air space, TR
    §5-1001.
Hazards.
  Defined, TR §5-101.
Hearings.
  Administration.
    Powers.
      General provisions, TR §5-209.
  Airports.
    Approval of site, TR §5-303.
    Issuance of license, TR §5-305.
  Federal-state joint hearings, TR §5-206.
  Notice and opportunity, TR §5-210.

AVIATION —Cont'd
Human relations commission.
  Airports.
    Investigation of discriminatory employment
      practices.
      Administration to refer investigations to
        commission, TR §5-408.
Injunctions.
  Enforcement of aeronautics laws, TR §5-1103.
Insurance.
  Liability insurance, TR §5-1002.
  Life insurance liability limitations, IN §16-215.
  Transportation ticket health insurance, IN
    §15-1103.
Investigations.
  Administration.
    Powers generally, TR §5-209.
Jurisdiction.
  Contracts, TR §5-103.
  Crimes, torts and other wrongs, TR §5-103.
Lawfulness of operation.
  Generally, TR §5-1001.
  Over lands and waters, TR §5-1001.
  Sovereignty in space.
    Right to free transit through state air space, TR
      §5-1001.
Laws.
  Enforcement.
    Aeronautics laws, TR §§5-1101 to 5-1105.
Legislative policy.
  Purpose of article, TR §5-102.
Liability insurance, TR §5-1002.
Licenses.
  Airports, TR §§5-301 to 5-306. See within this
    heading, "Airports."
  Air schools, TR §§5-901 to 5-906. See within this
    heading, "Air schools."
  Alcoholic beverages, 2B §§9-101, 10-101.
  Suspension or revocation.
    Orders of administration denying, suspending
      or revoking license, TR §5-210.
Liens.
  Damages.
    Injuries to persons or property, TR §5-1005.
  Mechanics' liens.
    Aircraft.
      See MECHANICS' LIENS.
  State airport and facilities.
    Enforcement of payment of charges, etc., TR
      §5-410.
Life insurance.
  Excluded or restricted coverage, IN §16-215.
Maryland airport authorities.
  General provisions.
    See AIRPORT AUTHORITIES.
Maryland state aviation administration.
  Generally. See within this heading,
    "Administration."
Mechanics' liens.
  Creation of aircraft lien, CL §16-202.
Motor vehicles.
  Airports.
    Parking regulations, TR §5-426.
      Citations for violations.
        Administration employees authorized to
          issue, TR §5-212.1.
Navigation.
  Obstruction. See within this heading, "Obstruction
    to air navigation."
Negligence.
  Aircraft.
    Reckless operation, TR §5-1006.

AVIATION —Cont'd
Negligence —Cont'd
Injuries to person or property, TR §5-1005.
Noise.
Airports.
Abatement.
Noise abatement plan for impacted land use area, TR §5-805.
Assistance in development and implementation of plans, TR §5-807.
Implementation and monitoring of approved plans, TR §5-806.
Assessment of noise environment.
Airport operators to assess, TR §5-805.
Cumulative noise exposure.
Defined, TR §5-801.
Limits, TR §5-804.
Definitions, TR §5-801.
Noise assistance programs, TR §§5-1201 to 5-1205. See within this heading, "Airports."
Political subdivisions, TR §5-819.
Purpose of subtitle, TR §5-802.
State-owned airports. See within this heading, "Airports."
Zones.
Certification of noise zone, TR §5-806.
Defined, TR §5-801.
Political subdivisions. See within this heading, "Political subdivisions."
Zones, TR §§5-801, 5-806.
Notices.
Hearings, TR §5-210.
Obstruction to air navigation.
Adoption of regulations, TR §5-702.
Airports.
Building obstruction near airport, TR §5-703.
Conflict of regulations, TR §5-707.
Existing nonconforming uses, TR §5-706.
Height.
Maximum height variance, TR §5-704.
Legislative declaration, TR §5-701.
Markers and lights, TR §5-705.
Television or radio transmitting towers.
Pulsating high intensity white light system.
Authority of political subdivisions to cease nighttime operation of, TR §5-705.1.
Maximum height variance, TR §5-704.
Prohibited activities, TR §5-703.
Purpose of regulation, TR §5-701.
Regulation required, TR §5-701.
Television or radio transmitting towers.
Pulsating high intensity white light system.
Authority of political subdivisions to cease nighttime operation of, TR §5-705.1.
Orders of court.
Investigations and hearings, TR §5-209.
Penalties.
Airports.
Parking regulations, TR §5-427.
Exchange of information as to violations, TR §5-1101.
Violations of article, TR §5-1105.
Pesticides.
Dissemination by airplanes, AG §5-305.
Police.
Charging documents against law enforcement officers, CJ §2-608.
Police officer.
Defined, TR §5-101.
Political subdivisions.
Administration.
Cooperation with, TR §5-205.

AVIATION —Cont'd
Political subdivisions —Cont'd
Airports.
Acquisition and operation, TR §5-417.
Assistance, TR §5-215.
Administrator as agent of political subdivision, TR §5-422.
Joint operation, TR §5-407.
Operation, TR §5-418.
Zoning. See within this subheading, "Zoning."
Commission.
Cooperation with, TR §5-205.
Contracts.
Airports.
Power to contract, TR §5-422.
Noise.
Adoption of regulations by political subdivisions, TR §5-810.
Board of appeals.
Composition, TR §5-813.
Duties, TR §5-813.
Establishment, TR §5-813.
Hearing on appeal, TR §5-814.
Judicial review of board decisions, TR §5-816.
Oaths, TR §5-813.
Operation, TR §5-813.
Right of appeal to board, TR §5-814.
Stay of proceedings, TR §5-814.
Variances, TR §5-815.
Witnesses, TR §5-813.
Failure to adopt noise regulations, TR §5-811.
Permits.
Limitation on granting, TR §5-812.
Required, TR §5-812.
Plans.
Identification, TR §5-810.
Variances.
Board of appeals to grant variances, TR §5-815.
Zoning maps.
Identification on each map, TR §5-810.
Zoning.
Administration.
Appointment, TR §5-608.
Reports, TR §5-608.
Administrative agency.
Delegation of duties by political subdivision, TR §5-610.
Airports owned by and located outside of political subdivision, TR §5-609.
Applicability of subtitle, TR §5-603.
Board of appeals.
Establishment, TR §5-612.
Judicial review of decisions, TR §5-615.
Operation, TR §5-612.
Right of appeal, TR §5-613.
Variances, TR §5-614.
Condemnation.
Acquisition of property, TR §5-616.
Considerations for guidance, TR §5-606.
Declaration of purpose, TR §5-602.
Definitions, TR §5-601.
Delegation of duties, TR §5-610.
Districts.
Regulations to establish, TR §5-606.
Uniformity of regulations within districts, TR §5-606.
Enforcement, TR §5-617.
Exceptions, TR §5-603.
Joint board of political subdivisions, TR §5-605.

AVIATION —Cont'd
Political subdivisions —Cont'd
  Zoning —Cont'd
    Nonconforming structures.
      Permits, TR §5-611.
    Penalties.
      Violations, TR §5-617.
    Permits, TR §5-611.
    Property.
      Acquisition, TR §5-616.
    Rules and regulations, TR §5-604.
      Procedures for adopting and changing, TR §5-607.
    Substantially alter.
      Defined, TR §5-601.
    Variances.
      Power of board of appeals to grant, TR §5-614.
    Violations.
      Penalties, TR §5-617.
Potomac Highlands airport authority.
  See POTOMAC HIGHLANDS AIRPORT AUTHORITY.
Presumptions.
  Liability of owner or lessee of aircraft, TR §5-1005.
Property.
  Acquisition.
    Public and governmental functions, TR §5-102.
  Space.
    Ownership, TR §5-104.
Purpose of article, TR §5-102.
  Public and governmental functions, TR §5-102.
Queen Anne's county.
  Airports.
    Establishment.
      Prohibited, TR §5-106.
Reciprocity.
  Reciprocal services available to administration, TR §5-206.
Recordation.
  Notice of lien, TR §5-1005.
Registration of aircraft.
  Certificate.
    Federal certificate of competency.
      Presentation for inspection, TR §5-1003.
      Required, TR §5-1003.
Reports.
  Accident reporting.
    By administration, TR §5-206.
  Administration.
    Exchange of information as to violations, TR §5-1101.
  Airport noise assistance programs.
    Homeowners assistance pilot program, TR §5-1204.
Rules and regulations.
  Federal standards.
    Conformity to, TR §5-208.
  Motor vehicles.
    Parking at airports, TR §5-426.
      Citations for parking violations.
        Administration employees authorized to issue, TR §5-212.1.
  Promulgation.
    Administration, TR §5-208.
Runways.
  Baltimore-Washington International Thurgood Marshall Airport.
    Construction of parallel transport runway, TR §5-413.

AVIATION —Cont'd
Runways —Cont'd
  State airports.
    Noise.
      Restriction on use of residential property, TR §5-824.
Seaplanes.
  Water navigation.
    Seaplanes governed by rules of water navigation while at rest or operating in contact with water, TR §5-1009.
Service of process.
  Administration orders, TR §5-210.
Space.
  Ownership, TR §5-104.
  Right of free transit through state air space, TR §5-1001.
  Sovereignty, TR §5-104.
State.
  Airway system, TR §5-207.
  Sovereignty in space, TR §5-104.
State airports. See within this heading, "Airports."
State airway.
  Defined, TR §5-207.
State aviation administration. See within this heading, "Administration."
Structure.
  Defined, TR §5-101.
Summons and process.
  Investigations and hearings, TR §5-209.
Supervision.
  By administration, TR §5-204.
Taxation.
  Assessments.
    Airplane landing area, TP §8-302.
  Credits.
    Property tax credits.
      Airport noise zones.
        Residential property in, TP §9-216.
  Exemptions.
    Aircraft, TP §7-220.
    Licensed public airport on privately owned land, TP §7-303.
Torts.
  Jurisdiction over torts, TR §5-103.
  Liability determined by rules of law, TR §5-1004.
Transportation department.
  Boards and agencies included within department, TR §2-107.
  Officers and employees.
    Witnesses.
      Not required to testify, TR §5-211.
Trespass.
  Aircraft, TR §5-1001.
United States.
  Airports.
    Licenses.
      United States airports exempted, TR §5-302.
    Prerequisites to project application under federal law, TR §5-423.
  Air schools.
    Licenses.
      Federal license, TR §5-903.
  Contracts.
    Law governing, TR §5-213.
  State airports and facilities.
    Joint operation, TR §5-407.
Violations of article.
  Citation to appear in court, TR §5-1104.
  Exchange of information as to violations, TR §5-1101.

AVIATION —Cont'd
Violations of article —Cont'd
Penalties, TR §5-1105.
Witnesses.
Transportation department.
Officers and employees.
Not required to testify, TR §5-211.
Zoning.
Airports.
Appeals.
Political subdivisions, TR §§5-612 to 5-615.
Board of zoning appeals. See within this
heading, "Airports."
Conflicting regulations, TR §5-707.
Considerations for guidance, TR §5-503.
Definitions, TR §5-501.
Enforcement.
Political subdivisions, TR §5-617.
Penalties.
Violation of subtitle, TR §5-511.
Permits.
Administration, TR §5-505.
Political subdivisions, TR §5-611.
Prohibited uses, TR §§5-504, 5-510.
Queen Anne's county.
Sixth election district, TR §5-106.
Regulations.
Administration.
Adoption, TR §5-502.
Adoption.
Administration, TR §5-502.
Political subdivisions, TR §5-607.
Conflicting regulations, TR §5-707.
Political subdivisions.
Adoption, TR §5-607.
Violation of regulations, TR §5-504.
Substantially alter.
Defined, TR §5-501.
Variances.
Administration, TR §5-507.
Air rights.
Political subdivisions, TR §5-616.
Baltimore county.
Exemptions, TR §5-603.
Board of zoning appeals.
Airports. See within this heading, "Airports."
Political subdivisions. See within this heading,
"Political subdivisions."

AVIATION FUEL TAX.
See MOTOR FUEL TAX.

AWARDS.
Arbitration and award.
General provisions, SpecPro Rule 15-101.
Uniform arbitration act, CJ §§3-201 to 3-234.
See ARBITRATION AND AWARD.
Bridges.
Contracts by county commissioners, 25 §§38, 43.
Consumer protection.
Notification of award.
Conditioned upon purchase or submitting to
sales promotion effort, CL §13-305.
Eminent domain, PropAct Rules 12-210, 12-213.
Health care malpractice claims, SpecPro Rule
15-403.
Scholarships.
See SCHOLARSHIPS.
Schools.
Maryland performance program.
Standards improvement awards, ED §5-211.

AWARDS —Cont'd
Uniform arbitration act.
See ARBITRATION AND AWARD.
University of Maryland.
Funds provided for satisfaction of awards, ED
§13-207.

B

BABY CHICKS.
Selling or coloring, CR §10-614.

BABY DROP OFF.
Leaving newborn with responsible adult.
Immunity from liability, CJ §5-641.

BACKGROUND CHECKS.
See CRIMINAL HISTORY RECORDS CHECKS.

BACK-TO-SCHOOL CLOTHING.
Sales and use tax exemption.
Tax-free period, TG §11-228.

BACTERICIDES.
Pesticides.
General provisions.
See PESTICIDES.

BAD CHECKS, CR §§8-101 to 8-108.
**Collection of dishonored checks and other
instruments,** CL §§15-801 to 15-804.
Consumer loans.
Collection of certain fees.
Bad check fees, CL §12-307.
Costs.
Paying with bad check, CR §8-108. '
Definitions, CR §8-101.
Dishonor.
District Court jurisdiction, CJ §4-401.
Transfer of case to circuit court, CJ §4-402.
Presumption of intent, evidence of, CR §8-104.
District Court.
Costs.
Additional costs for bad checks, CJ §7-301.
Dishonor.
Jurisdiction, CJ §4-401.
Transfer of case to circuit court, CJ §4-402.
Transfer of action from District Court to circuit
court, CivProDist Rule 3-326.
False representation.
Issuing or passing not accompanied by, CR
§8-105.
Financial institution franchise tax.
Payment by dishonored checks.
Assessment of service charge, TG §13-713.
Fines.
Paying with bad check, CR §8-108.
Insufficient funds.
When drawer deemed to have, CR §8-102.
**Knowledge of insufficient funds, issuing check
with.**
Obtaining property or services, CR §8-103.
Presumption of knowledge, evidence, CR §8-104.
License fees payment by.
Suspension of license, BR §1-209.
Limitations on prosecution, CR §8-105.
Making check good after dishonor, CR §8-105.
Motor vehicles.
Service charge for presenting bad checks to
administration, TR §12-116.
No account.
Presumption, evidence of, CR §8-104.
When drawer deemed to have, CR §8-102.

BAD CHECKS —Cont'd
Obtaining property or services, CR §8-103.
Passing check with knowledge of insufficient funds, CR §8-103.
Passing check with knowledge of stop payment or dishonor, CR §8-103.
Penalties, CR §8-106.
Premium finance companies.
 Bad check fee, IN §23-308.
Presumptions, CR §8-104.
Real estate brokers.
 Dishonored checks for fees.
  Additional fee, BOP §17-521.
Refusal to pay, issuing check with intent.
 Passing to third party, CR §8-103.
Restitution, CR §8-107.
Restoration of property, CR §8-107.
Returned check charges.
 Court charges, CJ §7-208.
Sales.
 Power to transfer title, CL §2-403.
Service charge, CJ §7-208.
Stop payment, issuing check with intent to.
 Effect of intent as evidence, CR §8-104.
 Obtaining property or services, CR §8-103.
Suspension of business licenses, BR §1-209.
Theft.
 Prosecution as, CR §7-107.
Time for commencing prosecution, CR §8-105.
Value of property or services $500 or more.
 Penalty, CR §8-106.
Value of property or services less than $500.
 Penalty, CR §8-106.
Washington county.
 Fee for bad check, 25 §3.

BAD FAITH.
Actions.
 Unjustified proceeding, Rule 1-341.
Trade secrets.
 Misappropriation.
  Attorneys' fees for bad faith claim of misappropriation, CL §11-1204.
Unjustified proceeding, Rule 1-341.

BADGES.
Identification badges required for employment or visit.
 Badge defined, CR §9-701.
 Possession after employment or visit ended, CR §9-704.
 Surrender on gaining possession, CR §9-705.
 Surrender required at end of employment or visit, CR §9-704.
 Unauthorized use, CR §9-705.
Law enforcement officers and personnel.
 Impersonating a police officer, PS §3-502.
 Special police officers, PS §3-310.
Railroad police, PS §3-409.
Security guards, BOP §19-407.
 Agency equipment generally, BOP §19-507.
 Restrictions on use, BOP §19-603.
Special police officers, PS §3-310.

BAGS.
Returnable containers and textiles.
 Registration, prohibited acts, BR §§19-301 to 19-307.

BAIL AND RECOGNIZANCE.
Administration of courts.
 Bail bond commissioner.
  Appointment, CJA Rule 16-817.

BAIL AND RECOGNIZANCE —Cont'd
Administration of courts —Cont'd
 Bail bondsmen.
  Licensing and regulation, CJA Rule 16-817.
Allegany county.
 Pretrial release program, COR §11-702.
Amendments.
 Pretrial release.
  Orders, Crim Rule 4-216.
Applicability of rules, Crim Rule 4-217.
Authorization to take bail bond, Crim Rule 4-217.
Bail bond commissioner.
 Appointment, CJA Rule 16-817.
 Defined, Crim Rule 4-217.
Bail bonds. See within this heading, "Bonds."
Bail bondsmen.
 Applicability of subtitle, IN §10-302.
 Continuing education, IN §10-307.
 Defined, Crim Rule 4-217.
 Income.
  Certification, IN §10-308.
 Licenses, CJA Rule 16-817.
  Fees, IN §10-306.
  Qualifications, IN §10-305.
  Required, IN §10-304.
 Qualification of surety, Crim Rule 4-217.
 Rules and regulations, IN §10-303.
Bonds.
 Authorization to take, Crim Rule 4-217.
 Commissioner.
  Appointment of bail bond commissioner, CJA Rule 16-817.
 Condition of bail bond, Crim Rule 4-217.
 Definitions, Crim Rule 4-217.
 Discharge, Crim Rule 4-217.
 Execution, Crim Rule 4-217.
 Failure to pay bail bond judgment, IN §21-103.
 Forfeiture, Crim Rule 4-217.
 Form and contents, Crim Rule 4-217.
  Conditions of bond, Form 4-217.2.
  Declaration of trust of real estate to secure performance of bail bond, Form 4-217.1.
 Qualification of surety, Crim Rule 4-217.
 Voluntary surrender of defendant by surety, Crim Rule 4-217.
Clerks of court.
 Defined, Crim Rule 4-217.
Collateral, Crim Rule 4-217.
Commissioner.
 Bail bond commissioner.
  Appointment, CJA Rule 16-817.
 Defined, Crim Rule 4-217.
Competency to stand trial determination.
 Finding of incompetency, CP §3-106.
 Outpatient examination of defendant, CP §3-105.
Contempt.
 Right of contemnor, SpecPro Rule 15-208.
Controlled dangerous substances hearing.
 Hearsay, CR §5-809.
Definitions, Crim Rule 4-217.
 Bail bondsmen, IN §10-301.
Discharge of bond, Crim Rule 4-217.
District Court, CP §5-205.
Drug kingpins.
 Restrictions on pretrial release, CP §5-202.
Escape.
 Restrictions on pretrial release.
  Escapees, CP §5-202.
Excessive.
 Prohibited, MD Const DofR Art 25.

BAIL AND RECOGNIZANCE —Cont'd
Extradition, CP §9-115.
Bond, CP §9-116.
Discharge, recommitment, or renewal of bail, CP §9-117.
Forfeiture of bail, CP §9-118.
Forfeiture.
Appeals.
Jurisdiction.
Court of special appeals, CJ §12-308.
Bail bonds, Crim Rule 4-217.
Disposition of forfeited recognizances, CJ §7-507.
Failure to appear or testify, CJ §11-513.
Remission of forfeited recognizance, CP §1-207.
Forms.
Bail bond forms, Crim Rule 4-217.
Conditions of bond, Form 4-217.2.
Declaration of trust of real estate to secure performance of bail bond, Form 4-217.1.
Habeas corpus.
Application for leave to appeal in regard to bail, CJ §3-707.
General provisions, CJ §3-704.
Issuance of writ, SpecPro Rule 15-306.
Procedure on petition, SpecPro Rule 15-303.
Incompetency to stand trial determination.
Finding of incompetency, CP §3-106.
Outpatient examination of defendant, CP §3-105.
Interim bail.
Pretrial release, Crim Rule 4-216.
Juvenile causes.
Parents, guardians or custodians.
Forms, Form 904-R.
Review of commissioner's pretrial release order, Crim Rule 4-216.
Waiver of jurisdiction.
Juvenile petition considered charging document pending bail hearing, Juv Rule 11-113.
Life imprisonment.
Release of defendant charged with crime punishable by, CP §5-102.
Limitation of actions.
Action on bond, CJ §5-102.
Motor vehicles.
Bonds, surety.
Person taken before commissioner.
Maximum amount of bond, TR §26-403.
Guaranteed arrest bond certificate, TR §26-404.
Orders.
Pretrial release, Crim Rule 4-216.
Personal recognizance.
Forfeiture. See within this heading, "Forfeiture."
Release on, CP §5-101.
Preliminary hearing.
Discharge at preliminary hearing.
Reinstatement of bail after, CP §5-206.
Pretrial release.
Allegany county, COR §11-702.
Appearance.
Initial appearance of defendant.
Determination of pretrial release, Crim Rule 4-213.
Circuit courts.
Bail after adjournment or during recess of circuit court, CP §5-204.
Bail bonds in, CP §5-203.
Conditions, CP §5-201; Crim Rule 4-216.
Violation, CP §5-213.
Discharge at preliminary hearing.
Reinstatement of bail after, CP §5-206.
District Court, CP §5-205.

BAIL AND RECOGNIZANCE —Cont'd
Pretrial release —Cont'd
Factors relevant to conditions of release, Crim Rule 4-216.
Failure to appear in response to citation, CP §5-212.
Failure to surrender after forfeiture of bail or recognizance, CP §5-211.
Forfeiture of bail or collateral.
Failure to surrender after, CP §5-211.
Striking out, CP §5-208.
Home detention.
Conditions of pretrial release, CP §5-201.
Interim bail, Crim Rule 4-216.
Juvenile courts.
Waiver of jurisdiction.
Hearing, Crim Rule 4-222.
Order, Crim Rule 4-216.
Probable cause.
Determination, Crim Rule 4-216.
Production of defendant, CP §5-208.
Property bondsmen, CP §5-209.
Restrictions, CP §5-202.
Sentencing.
Termination of bond on sentencing, CP §5-207.
Solicitation of business by bail bondsmen or agent, CP §5-210.
Statement of conditions, Crim Rule 4-216.
Striking out forfeiture of bail or collateral, CP §5-208.
Supervision of detention pending trial, Crim Rule 4-216.
Violation of conditions, CP §5-213.
Washington county, COR §11-723.
Probable cause.
Pretrial release.
Determination, Crim Rule 4-216.
Property bondsmen, CP §5-209.
Protective orders.
Violations of orders.
Pretrial release restrictions, CP §5-202.
Recognizance.
Forfeiture. See within this heading, "Forfeiture."
Remission of forfeited recognizance, CP §1-207.
Security.
Collateral security, Crim Rule 4-217.
Sentencing.
Termination of bond on sentencing, CP §5-207.
Solicitation of business by bail bondsmen or agent, CP §5-210.
Surety insurance.
Discrimination, IN §27-502.
Failure to pay bail bond judgment, IN §21-103.
Insurers generally, IN §§21-101, 21-102.
Surety insurer, Crim Rule 4-217.
Trial.
Pretrial release.
Supervision of detention pending trial, Crim Rule 4-216.
Victims of crime.
Conditions of pretrial release.
No contact with victims, Crim Rule 4-216.
Video bail review.
Baltimore City detention center or centralized booking facility, COR §5-404.
Washington county.
Pretrial release program, COR §11-723.

BAILIFFS.
Alcoholic beverages.
Enforcement of article.
Duties, 2B §§16-401, 16-405.

BAILIFFS —Cont'd
Circuit courts, CJ §2-501.
Compensation.
Certain counties, CJ §2-507.

BAILMENT.
Consignment of works of fine art, CL §11-8A-02.
Misappropriation by bailee, CR §7-202.
Parties.
Real party in interest.
Circuit courts, CivProCir Rule 2-201.
Taxation.
Owner for taxation, TP §5-101.
Unfair or deceptive trade practices, CL §§13-301, 13-303.

BAINBRIDGE DEVELOPMENT CORPORATION, 83A §§5-1601 to 5-1609.
Accounts and accounting.
Administration of corporate funds, 83A §5-1608.
Advisory board, 83A §5-1602.
Audits.
Corporate books and records, 83A §5-1608.
Bainbridge naval training center.
Designation of offices, 83A §5-1604.
Board of directors, 83A §5-1602.
Bond issues.
Authority to issue, 83A §5-1605.
Bylaws.
Authority to adopt, 83A §5-1604.
Cecil county.
Fees and charges.
Use of earnings, 83A §5-1606.
Clerical staff, 83A §5-1603.
Conflicts of law, 83A §5-1609.
Contracts.
Authority to contract for services, 83A §5-1606.
Corporate authority, 83A §5-1604.
Corporate body, 83A §5-1602.
Corporate finances, 83A §§5-1604, 5-1605.
Corporate tax status, 83A §5-1607.
Creation, 83A §5-1602.
Definitions, 83A §5-1601.
Eminent domain.
No power to exercise, 83A §5-1604.
Executive director.
Compensation, 83A §5-1603.
Powers and duties, 83A §5-1603.
Freedom of information act.
Exempt for applicability, 83A §5-1609.
Investments.
Authority to invest corporate funds, 83A §5-1608.
Officers, 83A §5-1602.
Professional staff and consultants, 83A §5-1603.
Property taxes.
Corporate tax status, 83A §5-1607.
Public ethics law.
Exempt for applicability, 83A §5-1609.
Rate and charges.
Fees for services, 83A §5-1606.
Reports.
Annual financial reports, 83A §5-1608.
Taxation.
Corporate tax status, 83A §5-1607.

BAIT AND SWITCH, CL §14-2903.

BAKERY PRODUCTS CONTAINERS.
Containers used by distributors and retailers.
Returnable containers and textiles.
Registration, prohibited acts, BR §§19-301 to 19-307.

BALCONIES.
Barbeque grills.
Restrictions on use, PS §9-1001.

BALLAST WATER MANAGEMENT.
Dumping or throwing waste into waters of state, NR §8-726.1.

BALLOON PAYMENTS.
Closed end accounts, CL §12-505.3.
Credit grantor closed end credit provisions.
Defined, CL §12-1001.
Prohibitions, CL §12-1003.
Restrictions on installment loans, CL §12-1003.
Credit grantor revolving credit provisions.
Prohibition, CL §12-903.
Mortgages and deeds of trust, CL §12-404.
Retail credit accounts law, CL §12-505.3.
Sales finance companies, CL §12-634.
Secondary mortgage loans, CL §12-404.

BALLOT QUESTIONS, EL §§7-101 to 7-105.
Petitions.
Requirements generally, EL §§6-101 to 6-211.
See ELECTIONS.

BALLOTS.
Absentee voting, EL §§9-301 to 9-312.
See ELECTIONS.
Generally, EL §§9-201 to 9-217.
See ELECTIONS.
Provisional ballot voting, EL §§9-401 to 9-408.
See ELECTIONS.

BALTIMORE CHECKERSPOT BUTTERFLY.
Designation as state arthropodic emblem, SG §13-301.

BALTIMORE CITY.
Abandoned property.
City purchasing abandoned property, no private purchaser, TP §§14-824, 14-833, 14-835, 14-844.
Liens for unpaid taxes.
Release to facilitate transfer of vacant property in Baltimore City, TP §14-806.
Accounts.
Reserve accounts, 24 §9-1201.
Actions.
Local government tort claims act, CJ §§5-301 to 5-304.
See TORTS.
Administration of courts.
Assignment of judges.
Circuit administrative judge, CJA Rule 16-103.
Advertising.
Alcoholic beverages.
Restrictions, 2B §21-105.
Alcoholic beverages.
Adult entertainment, 2B §12-203.
Enforcing laws and regulations governing business licenses.
Board of license commissioners, 2B §12-203.1.
Baltimore City wine festival, 2B §8-303.
Bar and counter sales.
Sundays, 2B §11-403.
Beer and light wine licenses.
Class A, off-sale.
Fee, 2B §5-101.
Class B, on-sale.
Hotels and restaurants, 2B §5-201.
Class C, on-sale.
Clubs, 2B §5-301.

BALTIMORE CITY —Cont'd
Alcoholic beverages —Cont'd
Beer and light wine licenses —Cont'd
Class D, on-sale.
Fee, 2B §5-401.
Hours and days for sale, 2B §11-302.
Beer and wine (on-premises) tasting license.
Class BWT, 2B §8-403.1.
Beer festival.
Licenses, 2B §8-801.
Beer licenses.
Hours and days for sale, 2B §11-301.
Beer, wine and liquor licenses.
Churches or schools.
New licenses not to be issued in certain
legislative districts, 2B §9-204.3.
Class A-2, off-sale, 2B §6-102.
Class A, off-sale, 2B §6-101.
Class B-D-7 license, 2B §§8-203, 8-203.1.
Class B, on-sale.
Hotels and restaurants, 2B §§6-201, 9-102.
Class C, on-sale, 2B §6-301.
Class C, seven days, 2B §7-101.
Class D.
Sunday sales, 2B §11-503.
Class D, on-sale.
Taverns, 2B §6-401.
Fees.
Disposition, 2B §10-204.
Hours and days for sale, 2B §11-301.
Beer and light wine licenses, 2B §11-302.
Issuance.
New licenses not to be issued in certain areas
or districts, 2B §9-204.1.
Payment of taxes.
Prerequisite to issuance, 2B §10-202.
Procedure, 2B §10-202.
Where new license may be issued, 2B §9-204.
Licenses, 2B §8-801.
More than one license for same person or
premises, 2B §9-102.
New license.
Not to be granted premises having
nonconforming use in residential areas,
2B §9-204.2.
Not to be issued in certain districts, 2B
§9-204.1.
Out-of-state licensees, 2B §9-102.
Prohibited areas, 2B §§9-201, 9-203.
New license not to be issued in certain
districts, 2B §9-204.1.
Renewal.
Applications, 2B §10-301.
Late charge, 2B §10-301.
Payment of taxes prerequisite, 2B §10-301.
Protest.
Hearing on, 2B §10-301.
Special amusement licenses.
General provisions, 2B §§8-203, 8-203.1.
Taxation.
Payment of taxes prerequisite to renewal, 2B
§10-301.
Payment of taxes prerequisite to transfer, 2B
§10-503.
Transfer, 2B §§9-102, 10-503.
Not to be transferred in certain districts, 2B
§9-204.
Exceptions, 2B §9-204.
Payment of taxes prerequisite, 2B §10-503.
Wine festival license, 2B §8-303.
Bottle club licenses, 2B §20-102.

BALTIMORE CITY —Cont'd
Alcoholic beverages —Cont'd
Caterers, 2B §6-701.1.
Conflicts of interest.
Direct or indirect interest in more than one
license, 2B §9-301.
Elections.
Exercise of privileges of licensee on election day,
2B §11-401.
Hotels and restaurants.
Beer and light wine licenses.
Hours and days of sale, 2B §11-302.
Beer, wine and liquor licenses.
Class B, on-sale, 2B §9-102.
More than one license for same person or
premises, 2B §9-102.
Hours and days for sale, 2B §§6-401, 11-305.
Beer and light wine licenses, 2B §11-302.
Beer licenses, 2B §11-301.
Beer, wine and liquor licenses, 2B §11-303.
Election days, 2B §11-401.
New Year's day, 2B §11-402.
Consumption, 2B §11-304.
Sundays, 2B §11-503.
Wholesaler's license, 2B §11-102.
License commissioners.
Appointment, 2B §15-101.
Chairman.
Duties, 2B §15-112.
Conflicts of interest, 2B §15-112.
Duties, 2B §15-112.
Executive secretary, 2B §15-109.
Inspectors.
Powers generally, 2B §15-112.
Powers.
Generally, 2B §15-112.
Qualifications, 2B §15-101.
Rules and regulations, 2B §15-112.
Adoption, 2B §16-301.
Salaries, 2B §15-109.
Terms, 2B §15-101.
Vacancies, 2B §15-101.
Licenses.
Adult entertainment, 2B §12-203.
Enforcing laws and regulations governing,
board of license commissioners, 2B
§12-203.1.
Applications.
Exceptions, 2B §10-104.
Notice on premises, 2B §10-202.
Qualifications of applicant, 2B §10-104.
Beer and light wine licenses. See within this
subheading, "Beer and light wine licenses."
Beer festival license, 2B §8-801.
Beer, wine and liquor licenses. See within this
subheading, "Beer, wine and liquor
licenses."
Bottle clubs, 2B §20-102.
Churches or schools.
New licenses not to be issued in certain
legislative districts, 2B §9-204.3.
Commissioners. See within this subheading,
"License commissioners."
Death of licensee.
Procedure, 2B §10-506.
Light wine licenses.
Class A2, on-sale and off-sale licenses, 2B
§4-202.
Refusal to issue.
Reapplication, 2B §10-208.

BALTIMORE CITY —Cont'd
Alcoholic beverages —Cont'd
Licenses —Cont'd
Wholesalers.
Hours and days for sale, 2B §11-102.
Wine festival license, 2B §8-303.
Micro-brewery licenses, 2B §2-208.
Minors.
Employment of minors by retail dealers.
Special provisions, 2B §12-302.
Penalties.
Local penalties, 2B §16-507.
Pub-brewery licenses, 2B §2-207.
Restaurants.
Defined, 2B §1-102.
Sales.
Cash.
Beer for cash, 2B §12-112.
Election days, 2B §11-401.
New Year's day.
Hours of sale, 2B §11-402.
Summons.
Records and papers, 2B §16-410.
Taxation.
Licenses. See within this heading, "Taxation."
Transfer of licenses, 2B §9-102.
Wholesalers.
Licenses.
Hours and days for sale, 2B §11-102.
Wine festival license, 2B §8-303.
Wine sampling licenses, 2B §8-403.
Amendments.
Charter amendments, MD Const Art XI-A §5.
Amusements and recreation.
Pinball machines.
Municipal authority, BR §17-407.
Appeals.
District Court, CJ §12-403.
Generally.
See APPEALS.
Municipal court to criminal court.
See APPEALS.
Appearance fees in circuit courts.
Distribution, CJ §7-204.
Architecture.
Historic and landmark zoning and preservation,
66B §2.12.
Attorney general.
Legal advisor for certain legal work, SG §6-107.
Authorities.
Maryland Food Center Authority.
General provisions, 41 §§13-101 to 13-123.
See MARYLAND FOOD CENTER
AUTHORITY.
Bail.
Video bail review.
Centralized booking facility or detention center,
COR §5-404.
Bailiff.
Compensation, CJ §2-507.
**Baltimore Association for Retarded Citizens,
Inc.**
Property tax credits, TP §9-304.
Beer and wine (on-premises) tasting license.
Class BWT, 2B §8-403.1.
Beer festival.
License, 2B §8-801.
Billiard and pool tables.
License fees, BR §17-504.
Bingo.
Amusement or entertainment place.
Prohibition on conducting game in, CR §13-507.

BALTIMORE CITY —Cont'd
Bingo —Cont'd
Permit fees, CR §13-507.
Permit required, CR §13-507.
Prizes, CR §13-507.
Proceeds, use, CR §13-507.
Regulations, CR §13-509.
Restaurant or tavern.
Prohibition on conducting game in, CR §13-507.
Social clubs, members 60 years of age or older, CR
§13-508.
Special annual permit, CR §13-507.
Boards and commissions.
Charter board, MD Const Art XI-A §1.
Zoning.
Board of municipal and zoning appeals. See
within this heading, "Zoning."
Bond issues.
Consolidated public improvement bonds.
Sale, 31 §2C.
Interest rate exchange agreements or contracts.
Authority to enter into, 31 §34.
Parking facilities, MD Const Art XI-C §3.
Proceeds of certain bonds.
Investments, redemptions, sales, etc., 95 §22M.
Bottle clubs.
Licenses, 2B §20-102.
Business regulation and licensure.
Prohibition on local licenses, fees and taxes.
Exception to prohibition, BR §1-204.
**Cancer prevention, education, screening and
treatment program.**
Calculation of grant money distributed, HG
§13-1108.
Community health coalition.
Established, HG §13-1115.
Membership requirements applicable to city,
HG §13-1111.
Comprehensive plan for cancer prevention,
education, screening and treatment, HG
§13-1115.
Caterers.
Beer, wine and liquor licenses, 2B §6-701.1.
Cemeteries.
Sale of burial ground for another purpose, BR
§5-506.
Centralized booking facility.
Division of pretrial detention and services to
operate for City, COR §5-404.
Charter.
Adoption, MD Const Art XI-A §1.
Code of Maryland.
Rights under charter not affected by adoption,
1 §4.
Affidavits.
False signing and false affidavits, MD Const Art
XI-A §7.
Amendments, MD Const Art XI-A §5.
Amendment of article XI, MD Const Art XI-A
§6.
Board, MD Const Art XI-A §1.
Legislative bodies, MD Const Art XI-A §3.
Local laws.
Enactment, publication and interpretation, MD
Const Art XI-A §3.
General assembly not to enact.
Subjects covered by express powers, MD
Const Art XI-A §4.
Officers.
Chief executive officers, MD Const Art XI-A §3.
Petition, MD Const Art XI-A §7.

BALTIMORE CITY —Cont'd
Charter —Cont'd
Powers.
Extension, modification, etc., of such powers, MD Const Art XI-A §2.
Preparation, MD Const Art XI-A §1.
Chesapeake Bay critical area and Atlantic coastal bays critical area protection programs.
Critical areas commission.
Members on commission, NR §8-1804.
Child in need of services pilot program, CJ §3-8A-10.1.
Churches.
Alcoholic beverages.
New license not to be issued near, 2B §9-204.3.
Circuit court fees.
Clerk may not charge city unless consent given, CJ §7-202.
Circuit courts.
Asbestos cases.
Special docket, CJA Rule 16-203.
Circuit court for county includes circuit court for Baltimore City, 1 §14.
Continuing care contracts.
Jurisdiction and venue, 70B §20E.
Courts generally. See within this heading, "Courts."
Electric customer choice and competition act.
Rate stabilization.
Review by appeal of qualified rate order, PUC §7-528.
Number of judges, CJ §1-503.
Personnel merit system.
Administration of system, CJ §2-5A-04.
Affirmative action.
Supreme bench affirmative action policy applicable, CJ §2-5A-07.
Creation, CJ §2-5A-02.
Definitions, CJ §2-5A-01.
Director.
Administration of system, CJ §2-5A-04.
Appointment, CJ §2-5A-04.
Defined, CJ §2-5A-01.
Removal, CJ §2-5A-04.
Judicial personnel committee.
Composition, CJ §2-5A-03.
Positions subject to system, CJ §2-5A-06.
Purposes, CJ §2-5A-02.
Scope of system.
Positions subject to system, CJ §2-5A-06.
Status of employees, CJ §2-5A-05.
Supreme bench affirmative action policy.
Applicability, CJ §2-5A-07.
Public service commission proceedings.
Judicial review of decisions or orders, filing, PUC §3-204.
Citations.
Betting, wagering, gambling, etc.., CR §12-102.
City council.
Branches, MD Const Art XI §2.
Compensation, MD Const Art XI §2.
Composition, MD Const Art XI §2.
Contracts with city.
Interest in prohibited, MD Const Art XI §5.
Duties.
Generally, MD Const Art XI §2.
Elections.
Filing fee for candidates, EL §5-401.
General provisions, MD Const Art XI §3.
Qualification of electors, MD Const Art XI §3.

BALTIMORE CITY —Cont'd
City council —Cont'd
Emergency management.
Executive officer killed, sick or unavailable, PS §14-403.
Local governing bodies defined, PS §14-401.
Majority killed, sick or unavailable, PS §14-402.
Powers during military or warlike catastrophe, PS §14-405.
Holding other office.
Prohibited, MD Const Art XI §5.
Legislative body, MD Const Art XI-A §3.
Powers.
Generally, MD Const Art XI §2.
Industrial financing loans, MD Const Art XI-I.
Rehabilitation and improvement loans, MD Const Art XI-G.
Residential financing loans, MD Const Art XI-H.
Qualifications, MD Const Art XI §2.
Schools.
Authority to establish free school systems, ED §1-202.
Sessions, MD Const Art XI §4.
Term of office, MD Const Art XI §2.
Watershed associations, 25 §§169 to 218.
See WATERSHED ASSOCIATIONS.
City court.
See CLERKS OF COURT.
Claims.
Local government tort claims act, CJ §§5-301 to 5-304.
See TORTS.
Clerks of court.
Fees.
Administering public money, CJ §2-213.
Clubs.
Beer, wine and liquor licenses.
Class C, on-sale, 2B §6-301.
Bottle clubs.
Licenses, 2B §20-102.
Colleges.
Baltimore City Community College, ED §§16-501 to 16-513.
See BALTIMORE CITY COMMUNITY COLLEGE.
Commissioners to take depositions.
General provisions.
See DEPOSITIONS.
Comptroller.
Election.
Filing fee for candidates, EL §5-401.
Conflicts of interest.
Alcoholic beverages.
Direct or indirect interest in more than one license, 2B §9-301.
Mayor or city council in contract, MD Const Art XI §5.
Conservation areas.
Exception from section, 23A §7.
Consolidated public improvement bonds.
Sale, 31 §2C.
Constables.
General provisions.
See CONSTABLES.
Constitution of Maryland.
City council. See within this heading, "City council."
Mayor.
Contracts with city.
Interest in prohibited, MD Const Art XI §5.

BALTIMORE CITY —Cont'd
Continuing care contracts.
Jurisdiction and venue, 70B §20E.
Contracts.
Interest in by mayor or city council prohibited,
MD Const Art XI §5.
Interest rate exchange agreements or contracts.
Authority to enter into, 31 §34.
Corporations.
Industrial development corporations.
General provisions, 45A §§1 to 3.
See INDUSTRIAL DEVELOPMENT
CORPORATIONS.
Counties.
Word county to include city of Baltimore, 1 §14.
Courts.
Appeals.
Generally.
See APPEALS.
Circuit courts. See within this heading, "Circuit
courts."
Clerks of court.
General provisions.
See CLERKS OF COURT.
District Court.
Appeals, CJ §12-403.
Fees.
Appearance fees.
Distribution, CJ §7-204.
Municipal court.
General provisions. See within this heading,
"Municipal courts."
Orphans' court, ET §§2-106, 2-108.
Superior court of Baltimore City.
See SUPERIOR COURT OF BALTIMORE
CITY.
Credit.
Extension.
Regulation, MD Const Art XI §7.
Criminal court.
Appeals.
See APPEALS.
Courts generally. See within this heading,
"Courts."
Criminal procedure.
Appeals.
Municipal court to criminal court.
See APPEALS.
Damages.
Local government tort claims act, CJ §§5-301 to
5-304.
See TORTS.
Debts.
Regulation, MD Const Art XI §7.
Detention center.
See BALTIMORE CITY DETENTION CENTER.
District Court.
Appeals, CJ §12-403.
Districts.
Legislative districts. See within this heading,
"General assembly."
Downtown management districts.
Property tax exemption, TP §7-504.2.
Drug free school zone signs.
Hotline number, ED §4-124.
Dumping site surveillance systems.
Citations, procedure, CJ §7-302.
Dwellings.
Repair of dangerous defects.
Rent escrow laws, RP §8-211.

BALTIMORE CITY —Cont'd
Dwellings —Cont'd
Tax credits.
Unsold, unrented or unoccupied newly
constructed or substantially rehabilitated
dwellings, TP §9-401.
**Early childhood mental health services pilot
program,** HG §§10-1501 to 10-1503.
Elections.
Alcoholic beverages.
Exercise of privilege of licensee on election day,
2B §11-401.
Arrangement on ballots.
City offices to be voted on, EL §9-210.
Board of elections.
Absentee voting duties.
Extra compensation for performing, EL
§9-311.
Compensation, EL §2-204.
County boards generally, EL §§2-201 to 2-303.
See ELECTIONS.
Substitute members.
Compensation, EL §2-204.
Buying and selling votes.
Penalty, MD Const Art I §6.
Charter board, MD Const Art XI-A §1.
City council, MD Const Art XI §3.
Election judges.
Compensation, EL §10-205.
Filing fees for candidates, EL §3-401.
Fundraisers.
Paddle wheel and wheel of fortune, CR §13-506.
General election.
When held, EL §8-301.
Judges.
Quadrennial elections.
Exceptions, MD Const Art XVII §3.
Mayor.
Time of election, MD Const Art XI §1.
Polling places.
Private buildings.
Rent, amount, EL §10-101.
Public buildings.
Used to greatest extent feasible, EL §10-101.
Primary elections.
When held, EL §8-201.
Supervisors.
Terms.
Commencement, MD Const Art XVII §6.
Voters.
Change of residence for purpose of voting, MD
Const Art I §5.
Emergency management.
Executive officer killed, sick or unavailable, PS
§14-403.
Local governing bodies defined, PS §14-401.
Majority killed, sick or unavailable, PS §14-402.
Powers during military or warlike catastrophe, PS
§14-405.
Eminent domain.
Application of title, RP §12-101.
General provisions.
See EMINENT DOMAIN.
Relocation assistance and real property
acquisition policies.
Authority of Baltimore City in administering
project funded by federal funds, RP
§12-210.
Specific provisions, MD Const Art III §40A.

BALTIMORE CITY —Cont'd
Employees' pension system.
Service credits.
Purchase by former employees of private
vendors of child support enforcement
services in Baltimore City, SPP §23-307.4.
Employees' retirement system.
Service credits.
Purchase by former employees of private
vendors of child support enforcement
services in Baltimore City, SPP §22-305.1.
Teacher transferees, SPP §21-307.
Environmental actions.
Environmental standing act, NR §§1-501 to 1-508.
See ENVIRONMENTAL STANDING ACT.
Fire department.
Volunteer company assistance fund.
Request for money, PS §8-204.
Fire prevention commission and fire marshal,
PS §§6-401 to 6-403.
Applicability, PS §6-401.
Assistance to chief of Baltimore City fire
department, PS §6-402.
Reports, PS §6-403.
Flood control.
Requirements, EN §5-803.
Fourth legislative district.
Alcoholic beverages.
Licenses.
Not to be issued for premises near church,
school, etc., 2B §9-204.3.
Funds.
Death relief fund. See within this heading,
"Police."
Gaming.
Citations, CR §12-102.
Gaming, bazaar, carnival and raffles, CR
§§13-501 to 13-510.
Definitions, CR §13-501.
Filmed horse races, prizes, CR §13-504.
Gaming event defined, CR §13-501.
Individual benefiting financially, prohibition, CR
§13-503.
Paddle wheel or wheel of fortune.
Political fundraisers, CR §13-506.
Prizes allowed, CR §13-504.
Permit to operate required, CR §13-503.
Political fundraisers, CR §13-506.
Prizes allowed, CR §13-504.
Political fundraisers, CR §13-506.
Raffles, CR §13-505.
Provisions applicable only in city, CR §13-502.
Qualified organizations, listed, CR §13-503.
Raffle defined, CR §13-501.
Raffles, prizes, limitations, CR §13-505.
Unauthorized bazaar or raffle, CR §13-510.
Garbage and trash.
Funds.
Distribution of funds, TR §8-406.
General assembly.
Article subject to change, MD Const Art XI §9.
Charter.
Powers and restrictions, MD Const Art XI-A
§§2, 4, 6.
Control over city, MD Const Art XI §9.
Districts.
Election, MD Const Art III §2.
General services department.
Purchases through purchasing bureau, 41
§18-201.

BALTIMORE CITY —Cont'd
Governor.
Mayor.
Removal of mayor by governor, MD Const Art
XI §6.
Grand jury.
Investigations, CJ §8-417.
Reports, CJ §8-417.
State's attorney for Baltimore City.
Attendance, CJ §8-414.
Harbor.
Disposal of waste matter collected from vessels in
Baltimore Harbor area, TR §6-207.
Hawkers and peddlers.
License fees, BR §17-907.
Health department.
State police department to provide information on
child victims of violent crimes, PS §2-308.
Highways.
Baltimore Harbor tunnel.
Toll bridges and tunnels.
See TRAFFIC LAWS.
Funds.
Allocation of highway user revenues, TR §8-403.
Municipal urban area highway construction fund,
TR §8-507.
Highway user revenues.
Allocation to city, TR §8-408.
Distribution, TR §8-406.
Historic area zoning.
General provisions.
See ZONING.
Holding other office.
Mayor and councilmen not to hold other office,
etc., MD Const Art XI §5.
Home rule.
Local legislation, MD Const Art XI-A §§1 to 7. See
within this heading, "Charter."
Housing.
Repair of dangerous defects.
Rent escrow laws, RP §8-211.
Taxation.
Governmentally subsidized housing, TP §7-506.
Limited distribution housing in Baltimore City.
Exemption, TP §7-504.
Housing authority, HS §§15-101 to 15-109.
Applicability of housing authorities law, HS
§15-102.
Collective bargaining, HS §15-109.
Commissioners.
Housing employees eligible to be commissioners,
HS §15-106.
Defined terms, HS §15-101.
Employee relations, HS §15-109.
Established, HS §15-104.
Findings, HS §15-103.
Housing projects.
Approval of city board of estimates, HS §15-107.
Legislative findings, HS §15-103.
Persons of eligible income.
Number needed, HS §15-105.
Police force, HS §15-108.
Arrest without a warrant.
Generally, CP §§2-201 to 2-210.
Authority granted police officers generally, CP
§2-102.
Charging documents against law enforcement
officers, CJ §2-608.
Definitions.
Police officer, CP §2-101.
Fresh pursuit, CP §2-301.

BALTIMORE CITY —Cont'd
Housing authority —Cont'd
Police force —Cont'd
Law enforcement officers generally, PS §§3-101 to 3-603.
See LAW ENFORCEMENT OFFICERS AND PERSONNEL.
Law enforcement procedures generally, CP §§2-101 to 2-107.
See POLICE.
Police training commission, PS §§3-201 to 3-218.
See POLICE TRAINING COMMISSION.
Powers.
Granted to police officers generally, CP §2-102.
Warrantless arrest.
Generally, CP §§2-201 to 2-210.
Powers.
Generally, HS §15-105.
Howard county.
Port authority.
Article not applicable in, MD Const Art XI-D §3.
Immunity.
Local government tort claims act, CJ §§5-301 to 5-304.
See TORTS.
Improvement loans, MD Const Art XI-G.
Improvements.
Construction of works of internal improvement.
Extension of credit or debts regulated, MD Const Art XI §7.
Industrial corporations.
General provisions, 45A §§1 to 3.
See INDUSTRIAL DEVELOPMENT CORPORATIONS.
Industrial financing loans, MD Const Art XI-I.
Interpretation and construction.
Zoning powers, 66B §2.01.
Investments.
Local government investment guidelines generally, 95 §22F.
Jails.
City detention center.
See BALTIMORE CITY DETENTION CENTER.
Establishment of local correctional facility, COR §§11-102, 11-102.1.
Outside limits of municipal corporation, COR §11-102.1.
Health and welfare benefits program.
Enrollment of former jail employees, SPP §2-510.
Work release, training and rehabilitation programs, COR §11-704.
Judges.
Elections.
Exceptions as to quadrennial elections, MD Const Art XVII §3.
Pensions.
General provisions, ET §2-108.
Judgments.
Lien of money judgment.
District Court, CivProDist Rule 3-621.
Juvenile services center, 83C §2-118.1.
Fingerprinting juvenile brought to, CP §10-220.
Kennel inspections.
Enforcement, CR §10-616.
Land development and redevelopment.
Authority to acquire and dispose of property, MD Const Art XI-B §§1, 2.

BALTIMORE CITY —Cont'd
Landlord and tenant.
Repair of dangerous defects.
Rent escrow laws, RP §8-211.
Landmarks.
Zoning and preservation, 66B §2.12.
Laws.
Continued in force, MD Const Art XI §8.
Liability.
Local government tort claims act, CJ §§5-301 to 5-304.
See TORTS.
Libraries, ED §§23-302, 23-402.
Video cassette rental fee, ED §23-405.
Licenses.
Alcoholic beverages. See within this heading, "Alcoholic beverages."
Marriage.
Fees, FL §2-404.
Taxicabs.
Driver's license, PUC §10-104.
Loans.
Industrial financing loans, MD Const Art XI-I.
Rehabilitation and improvement loans, MD Const Art XI-G.
Residential financing loans, MD Const Art XI-H.
Market.
Maryland Food Center Authority.
General provisions, 41 §§13-101 to 13-123.
See MARYLAND FOOD CENTER AUTHORITY.
Marriage.
Licenses.
Fees, FL §2-404.
Mayor.
Alcoholic beverages.
Confiscation of property.
Disposition of confiscated property, 2B §1-201.
Chief executive, MD Const Art XI-A §3.
Compensation, MD Const Art XI §1.
Duties.
Generally, MD Const Art XI §1.
Elections, MD Const Art XI §1.
Filing fee for candidates, EL §5-401.
Emergency management.
Executive officer killed, sick or unavailable, PS §14-403.
Local governing bodies defined, PS §14-401.
Majority killed, sick or unavailable, PS §14-402.
Powers during military or warlike catastrophe, PS §14-405.
Holding other office.
Prohibited, MD Const Art XI §5.
Powers.
Generally, MD Const Art XI §1.
Industrial financing loans, MD Const Art XI-I.
Rehabilitation and improvement loans, MD Const Art XI-G.
Residential financing loans, MD Const Art XI-H.
Qualifications, MD Const Art XI §1.
Removal.
By governor, MD Const Art XI §6.
Term of office, MD Const Art XI §1.
Vacancy.
Election to fill, MD Const Art XI §6.
Metropolitan transit administration.
General provisions, TR §§7-701 to 7-707.
Minors.
Alcoholic beverages.
Employment by retail dealers, 2B §12-302.

BALTIMORE CITY —Cont'd
Misdemeanors.
Alcoholic beverages.
Advertising restrictions, 2B §21-105.
After hours consumption, 2B §11-305.
Motorcycles.
Off-road motorcycles.
Regulation, TR §25-102.1.
Motor vehicles.
Abandonment.
General provisions, TR §§25-201 to 25-210.
See ABANDONED MOTOR VEHICLES.
Reclamation.
Effect of failure to reclaim vehicle, TR §25-206.
Parking.
Handicapped persons.
Reservation of parking space for person confined to wheelchair, TR §21-1005.
Off-street parking. See within this heading, "Parking."
Towing.
Parking lots, TR §§21-10A-01 to 21-10A-06.
See TOWING OF MOTOR VEHICLES.
Municipal courts.
Appeals.
Generally.
See APPEALS.
District Court.
Statutory references to municipal court deemed to refer to District Court, MD Const Art IV §41-I.
Negligence.
Local government tort claims act, CJ §§5-301 to 5-304.
See TORTS.
Neighborhood preservation and stabilization demonstration project, TP §9-326.
New Year's day.
Alcoholic beverages.
Hours and days for sale, 2B §11-402.
Noise control.
Trapshooting, skeet shooting, etc.
Limitations on authority, EN §§3-105, 3-401.
Northeast Maryland waste disposal authority.
Participating member, NR §3-904.
Notices.
Schools.
Closing public schools.
Studies, ED §4-317.
Nuisance abatement.
Community association actions, RP §14-123.
Off-street parking. See within this heading, "Parking."
Oil pipeline corporation acquiring property under power to condemn, PUC §5-404.
Ordinances.
Continued in force, MD Const Art XI §8.
Orphans' court.
Judges, ET §2-108.
Sessions, ET §2-106.
Parking.
Handicapped persons.
Reservation of parking space for person confined to wheelchair, TR §21-1005.
Off-street parking.
Authority of Baltimore City to acquire and dispose of property, MD Const Art XI-C §§1, 2.
Revenue bonds for parking facilities, MD Const Art XI-C §3.

BALTIMORE CITY —Cont'd
Parking —Cont'd
Residential parking permits, TR §21-1003.1.
Parking lots.
Towing, TR §§21-10A-01 to 21-10A-06.
See TOWING OF MOTOR VEHICLES.
Physical fitness.
Advisory council, HG §§13-408, 13-409.
Pimlico community development authority, BR §§11-1201 to 11-1205.
Police.
Arrest without a warrant.
Generally, CP §§2-201 to 2-210.
See WARRANTLESS ARREST.
Authority granted police officers generally, CP §2-102.
Bribery, CR §9-201.
Charging documents against law enforcement officers, CJ §2-608.
Death relief fund, 24 §§16-101 to 16-106.
Actions.
Parties.
Board of trustees, 24 §16-105.
Administration of fund, 24 §16-104.
Annual report, 24 §16-106.
Assessments.
Payroll deduction, 24 §16-106.
Audits, 24 §16-106.
Beneficiaries, 24 §16-103.
Benefit payments, 24 §16-102.
Amount of benefit, 24 §16-103.
Not subject to process, 24 §16-103.
Board of trustees, 24 §16-105.
Administration of fund, 24 §16-104.
Investment of fund assets, 24 §16-106.
Creation, 24 §16-101.
Establishment, 24 §16-101.
Expenditures, 24 §16-106.
Investment of fund assets, 24 §16-106.
Liability.
Board of trustees liability for conduct, 24 §16-105.
Payment of benefits, 24 §§16-102, 16-103.
Payroll deductions.
Assessments, 24 §16-106.
Records.
Board of trustees, 24 §16-105.
Reports.
Annual report, 24 §16-106.
Rules and regulations.
Board of trustees, 24 §16-105.
Seals.
Adoption by board of trustees, 24 §16-105.
Definitions.
Police officer, CP §2-101.
Fresh pursuit, CP §2-301.
Funds.
Enforcement of traffic laws, TR §8-408.
Housing authority police force, HS §15-108.
Law enforcement officers generally, PS §§3-101 to 3-603.
See LAW ENFORCEMENT OFFICERS AND PERSONNEL.
Law enforcement procedures generally, CP §§2-101 to 2-107.
See POLICE.
Payroll deductions.
Death relief fund, 24 §16-106.
Police training commission, PS §§3-201 to 3-218.
See POLICE TRAINING COMMISSION.

BALTIMORE CITY —Cont'd
Police —Cont'd
Powers.
Granted to police officers generally, CP §2-102.
Retirement and pension systems.
Local fire and police pension system.
General provisions, SPP §§28-101 to 28-403.
Service of process, CJ §6-308.
Warrantless arrest.
Generally, CP §§2-201 to 2-210.
See WARRANTLESS ARREST.
Political parties.
Central committees.
Election of members, EL §4-203.
Vacancies, EL §4-202.
Port administration.
Agreements with administration.
Apportionment of duties, TR §6-407.
Continuation of certain powers, duties and prior
ordinances, TR §6-406.
Arbitration and award.
Sale of property to authority.
Referral to arbitration board, TR §6-402.
Authority to acquire and dispose of land, MD
Const Art XI-D §1.
Disposal of waste matter collected from vessels in
Baltimore Harbor area, TR §6-207.
Exercise of powers of Baltimore City not impeded,
TR §6-410.
Howard county.
Not applicable within territorial limits of
county, MD Const Art XI-D §3.
Maryland port administration.
General provisions, TR §§6-101 to 6-602.
See PORT ADMINISTRATION.
McComas street terminal.
Effect of transfer, TR §6-404.
Payments in lieu of taxes, TR §6-411.
Powers.
Additional, MD Const Art XI-D §2.
Transfer of Baltimore port facilities, TR §6-401.
Transfer of employees, TR §6-408.
Transfer of other Baltimore property, TR §6-405.
Port authority.
Transfer of specific duties and functions, TR
§6-403.
Preservation.
Historic and landmark zoning and preservation,
66B §2.12.
Primary elections.
When held, EL §8-201.
Publication.
Charter amendments, MD Const Art XI-A §5.
Local laws, MD Const Art XI-A §3.
Public debts.
Regulation, MD Const Art XI §7.
Public watershed associations.
General provisions, 25 §§169 to 218.
See WATERSHED ASSOCIATIONS.
Railroads.
Consent to pass through city, PUC §5-407.
Real estate brokers.
Discriminatory real estate practices, BOP §17-525.
Penalties, BOP §17-613.
Reports of convictions, BOP §17-614.
Solicitation of listings, BOP §17-527.
Registers of wills.
Salary, ET §2-205.
**Rehabilitation and training programs for
inmates at jail,** COR §11-704.
Rehabilitation loans, MD Const Art XI-G.

BALTIMORE CITY —Cont'd
Rent escrow laws.
Repair of dangerous defects, RP §8-211.
Reports.
Fire prevention commission and fire marshal, PS
§6-403.
Reserve accounts, 24 §9-1201.
Residential areas.
Alcoholic beverages.
New license not to be issued.
Premises having nonconforming use, 2B
§9-204.2.
Residential financing loans, MD Const Art XI-H.
Restrictions.
Additional, MD Const Art XI-D §2.
Scholarships.
See SCHOLARSHIPS.
Schools, ED §§4-301 to 4-319.
Alcoholic beverages.
New license not to be issued near, 2B §9-204.3.
Alternative learning center, ED §4-319.
Anticipation notes, ED §4-306.2.
Investment securities, ED §4-306.4.
Liberal construction of provisions, ED §4-306.6.
Purposes, ED §4-306.3.
Severability of provisions, ED §4-306.6.
Tax exemption, ED §4-306.3.
Application of article, ED §4-302.
Baltimore City Community College.
General provisions, ED §§16-501 to 16-513.
See BALTIMORE CITY COMMUNITY
COLLEGE.
Board of school commissioners, ED §3-108.1.
Bonds for cost of projects, ED §§4-306.1 to
4-306.6.
Chief academic officer, ED §4-305.
Chief executive officer, ED §4-304.
Chief financial officer, ED §4-306.
Collective bargaining agreements, ED §4-312.
Duties, ED §4-316.
Established, ED §4-303.
Feeding programs.
Subsidized and free feeding programs.
Reimbursement of board, ED §7-604.
Parent and community advisory board, ED
§4-308.
Personnel.
Appointment and compensation of public
school personnel, ED §4-103.
Suspension or dismissal.
Grounds and procedure, ED §6-202.
Personnel system, ED §4-311.
Powers, ED §§4-306.1, 4-316.
Procurement of goods and services, ED §4-310.
Reports, ED §4-313.
Research and evaluation unit, ED §4-307.
State aid.
Partnership grants, ED §5-202.
Student member.
Appointment, terms, voting, ED §3-108.1.
Bonds for costs of projects, ED §4-306.2.
Amount authorized, ED §4-306.2.
Definitive bonds, ED §4-306.2.
Payment, ED §4-306.2.
Power of board to issue, ED §4-306.1.
Procedure, ED §4-306.2.
Requirements, ED §4-306.2.
Sources of payment, separate accounts, ED
§4-306.2.
State or other political subdivision not
obligated, ED §4-306.2.

BALTIMORE CITY —Cont'd
Schools —Cont'd
  Bonds for costs of projects —Cont'd
    Trust funds, establishing, ED §4-306.2.
  City council.
    Authority to establish free school systems, ED
      §4-302.
  Closing public schools.
    Studies.
      Notice, ED §4-317.
  Collective bargaining agreements, ED §4-312.
  Construction.
    Bids.
      Provision not applicable, ED §5-112.
  Costs of projects.
    Bonds, ED §§4-306.1 to 4-306.6.
    Records, ED §4-306.1.
  Definitions, ED §4-301.
  Educational technology pilot program.
    Implementation plan.
      School systems in which implemented, ED
        §7-10A-04.
  Education reform, ED §4-309.
  Employee organizations.
    Designation of representative required, ED
      §6-505.
  Feeding programs.
    Subsidized and free feeding programs.
      Reimbursement of board of school
        commissioners, ED §7-604.
  Free school systems.
    Authority to establish, ED §1-202.
  Health program, ED §7-415.
  Health care providers, ED §§7-415, 7-416.
  Interest, payment, ED §4-306.2.
  Master plan.
    Education reform, ED §4-309.
  Negotiations between employer and employee.
    Negotiating agent.
      Designated organization to represent public
        school employees, ED §6-407.
  Parent and community advisory board, ED
    §4-308.
  Personnel.
    Negotiations between employer and employee.
      Representation in Baltimore City, ED §6-407.
    Suspension or dismissal.
      Grounds and procedure, ED §6-202.
  Police force, ED §4-318.
    Arrest without a warrant.
      Generally, CP §§2-201 to 2-210.
    Authority granted police officers generally, CP
      §2-102.
    Charging documents against law enforcement
      officers, CJ §2-608.
    Definitions.
      Police officer, CP §2-101.
    Fresh pursuit, CP §2-301.
    Law enforcement procedures generally, CP
      §§2-101 to 2-107.
      See POLICE.
    Police training commission, PS §§3-201 to
      3-218.
      See POLICE TRAINING COMMISSION.
    Powers.
      Granted to police officers generally, CP
        §2-102.
    Warrantless arrest.
      Generally, CP §§2-201 to 2-210.
  Powers of board, ED §4-306.1.

BALTIMORE CITY —Cont'd
Schools —Cont'd
  Property.
    Protection by city council, ED §4-315.
  Property acquired or constructed held in
    accordance to state law, ED §4-306.5.
  Purchases.
    Bids.
      Provisions not applicable, ED §5-112.
  Research and evaluation unit, ED §4-307.
  State aid.
    Partnership grants.
      Board of school commissioners, ED §5-202.
  Superintendent of schools.
    Provisions not applicable, ED §4-201.
  Taxation.
    Power to tax for expenses, ED §4-315.
  Walbrook senior high school.
    Health care providers, ED §7-416.
  Year-round schools.
    Pilot programs, ED §7-103.
Sentencing individual to custody of
  commissioner of correction or pretrial
  detention and services, COR §9-106.
Sheriff.
  Deputies, CJ §2-309.
    Public transportation, riding without paying
      fare, CJ §2-309.
  General provisions, CJ §2-309; MD Const Art IV
    §44.
  Second in command, CJ §2-310.
  Under-sheriff.
    Appointment, CJ §2-309.
Social services.
  Department of social services.
    Creation or continuance in city, 88A §13.
    Director.
      Appointment, 88A §13.
    Employees.
      Benefits of social security, 88A §13.
    Reimbursements to city, 88A §13.
  Local commission.
    Generally, 88A §14A.
State's attorney, MD Const Art V §7.
  Assistants, MD Const Art V §9.
  Deputies, 10 §40; MD Const Art V §9.
  Salary, MD Const Art V §9.
Streets and sidewalks.
  Fund for, TR §8-408.
  Parking.
    Off-street parking, MD Const Art XI-C §1.
      Additional powers and restrictions, MD Const
        Art XI-C §2.
Sundays and holidays.
  Alcoholic beverages.
    Hours and days for sale, 2B §11-503.
Superior court of Baltimore City.
  General provisions.
    See SUPERIOR COURT OF BALTIMORE
      CITY.
Support and maintenance.
  Criminal nonsupport and desertion.
    Special provisions for Baltimore City, FL
      §§10-212 to 10-216.
      See SUPPORT AND MAINTENANCE.
Taxation.
  Admissions and amusement tax.
    General provisions.
      See ADMISSIONS AND AMUSEMENT TAX.

BALTIMORE CITY —Cont'd
Taxation —Cont'd
Alcoholic beverages.
  Licenses.
    Payment of taxes.
      Payment prerequisite to issuance, 2B
        §10-202.
      Payment prerequisite to renewal of license,
        2B §10-301.
      Payment prerequisite to transfer, 2B
        §10-503.
Assessments.
  Date of finality.
    Decreases in assessments, TP §8-419.
  General provisions.
    See TAXATION.
Date of finality.
  Assessments.
    Decreases in assessments, TP §8-419.
Delinquent taxes.
  Penalties, TP §14-702.
Exemptions.
  Housing.
    Governmentally subsidized housing, TP
      §7-506.
    Limited distribution housing in Baltimore
      City, TP §7-504.
  Local exemptions.
    Power to change, TP §7-108.
Housing.
  Governmentally subsidized housing, TP §7-506.
  Limited distribution housing in Baltimore City.
    Exemption, TP §7-504.
Interest.
  Overdue taxes, TP §14-603.
Liens for unpaid taxes.
  Release of liens to facilitate transfer of vacant
    property in Baltimore City, TP §14-806.
Limited distribution housing in Baltimore City,
  TP §7-504.
Neighborhood preservation and stabilization
    project.
  Property tax credit in designated area for
    participation in, TP §9-326.
Property tax credits.
  Baltimore Association for Retarded Citizens,
    Inc., TP §9-304.
  Dwellings.
    Local supplement to homeowners property tax
      credit, TP §9-215.
    Repaired or reconstructed dwellings, TP
      §9-109.
    Unsold, unrented, unoccupied newly
      constructed or substantially rehabilitated
      dwellings.
      Generally, TP §9-401.
    Vacant dwellings, TP §9-304.
  Housing projects, TP §9-304.
  Newly constructed dwellings, TP §9-304.
Redemption.
  Foreclosure of right of redemption.
    Action for damages, statute of limitations, TP
      §14-845.
    Complaint, form, TP §14-835.
    Order of publication, effect, TP §14-844.
  Rate of redemption, TP §14-820.
Sales.
  Abandoned property, TP §§14-816, 14-817.
  Alley assessment charges.
    Sale of property for failure to pay, TP
      §14-849.

BALTIMORE CITY —Cont'd
Taxation —Cont'd
  Sales —Cont'd
    Auction, TP §14-817.
    Certificates of sale.
      Complaints by holders to foreclose right of
        redemption, TP §14-833.
    City purchasing abandoned property, no private
      purchaser, TP §§14-824, 14-833, 14-835,
      14-844.
    Exceptions, TP §14-808.
    Notice, TP §14-813.
  Schools.
    Power to tax for expenses, ED §4-315.
Taxicabs.
  Driver's license.
    Required course, PUC §10-104.
  Permit to operate taxi business in or from point in
    city generally, PUC §§10-202 to 10-207.
  See TAXICABS.
Telephone and telegraph companies.
  Consent of city before using surface of or ground
    beneath streets or highways, PUC §5-410.
Torts.
  Local government tort claims act, CJ §§5-301 to
    5-304.
  See TORTS.
Towing.
  Parking lots, TR §§21-10A-01 to 21-10A-06.
  See TOWING OF MOTOR VEHICLES.
**Trapshooting, skeetshooting or other target
    shooting.**
  Environmental sound level limits and noise
    control rules and regulations, EN §3-401.
  Noise control ordinances, rules or regulations
    prohibiting, EN §3-105.
Tunnels.
  Toll bridges and tunnels.
    Operation of motor vehicles.
      See TRAFFIC LAWS.
Unemployment relief.
  Industrial development corporations.
    General provisions, 45A §§1 to 3.
      See INDUSTRIAL DEVELOPMENT
        CORPORATIONS.
Universities and colleges.
  Baltimore City Community College.
    General provisions, ED §§16-501 to 16-513.
      See BALTIMORE CITY COMMUNITY
        COLLEGE.
Volunteer company assistance fund.
  Request for money by Baltimore City fire
    department, PS §8-204.
War memorial building.
  Title to building and war memorial site held
    jointly by state and city, SG §9-937.
Water and sewer systems.
  Restrictions on use of water in certain counties.
    Determination of Baltimore water engineer, 25
      §168.
    General provisions, 25 §168.
    Use of water furnished by mayor and council to
      be restricted on request, 25 §168.
Water companies.
  Powers.
    Exception, PUC §7-105.
Watershed associations, 25 §§169 to 218.
  See WATERSHED ASSOCIATIONS.
Wine festival license, 2B §8-303.
Wine sampling licenses, 2B §8-403.

BALTIMORE CITY —Cont'd
Witnesses.
  See WITNESSES.
Work release programs.
  Inmates confined to city jail, COR §11-704.
Zoning.
  Amendment.
    Generally, 66B §2.05.
  Appeals, 66B §2.09.
  Baltimore City court.
    Appeal to Baltimore City court, 66B §2.09.
  Board of municipal and zoning appeals.
    Appeals.
      From board to court, 66B §2.09.
      Hearings, 66B §2.08.
      Procedure, 66B §§2.08, 2.09.
      Stay of proceedings, 66B §2.08.
    Appointment, 66B §2.08.
    Composition, 66B §2.08.
    Decision of board, 66B §2.08.
    Functions, 66B §2.05.
    Meetings.
      Generally, 66B §2.08.
    Powers.
      Generally, 66B §2.08.
    Rules, 66B §2.08.
  City council.
    Procedure, 66B §2.04.
  Conflicts with other laws, 66B §2.11.
  Court of special appeals.
    Appeal to, 66B §2.09.
  Districts.
    Generally, 66B §2.02.
  Enforcement, 66B §2.10.
  Hearings.
    Examiners, 66B §2.06.
    Generally, 66B §2.05.
  Historic area zoning.
    General provisions.
      See ZONING.
  Landmark zoning and preservation, 66B §2.12.
  Licenses.
    Alcoholic beverages.
      Not to be issued for premises having
        nonconforming use, 2B §9-204.2.
  Modification, 66B §2.05.
  Notice, 66B §2.05.
  Planning commission.
    Functions, 66B §2.05.
  Policy statement, 66B §2.01.
  Power, 66B §2.01.
  Procedure.
    Method of procedure, 66B §2.04.
  Purposes, 66B §2.03.
  Reclassification, 66B §2.05.
  Remedies, 66B §2.10.
  Repeal.
    Generally, 66B §2.05.
  Statement of policy, 66B §2.01.
  Variance.
    Board of municipal and zoning appeals.
      Vote required to reverse official or effect
        variation, 66B §2.08.

BALTIMORE CITY COMMUNITY COLLEGE,
  ED §§16-501 to 16-513.
Appropriations.
  State appropriation.
    Defined, ED §16-502.
    Distribution of state operating fund, ED
      §16-512.

BALTIMORE CITY COMMUNITY COLLEGE
  —Cont'd
Audits.
  Expenditures and accounts.
    Legislative auditor to audit, ED §16-507.
Board of trustees.
  Appointment of members, ED §16-504.
  Budget.
    Operating budget.
      Review by board, ED §16-507.
  Chairman.
    Election, ED §16-504.
  Chief of staff.
    Appointment, ED §16-505.
  Compensation.
    Service without compensation, ED §16-504.
  Composition, ED §16-504.
  Contracts.
    Entering into, ED §16-505.
  Control and management of college, ED §16-505.
  Courses and programs.
    Adoption and change of curriculum, ED
      §16-505.
    Approval, ED §16-505.
  Credits for graduation.
    Establishing and changing requirements, ED
      §16-505.
  Defined, ED §16-502.
  Degrees for graduation.
    Establishing and changing requirements, ED
      §16-505.
  Duties, ED §16-505.
  Entrance requirements.
    Establishment, ED §16-505.
  Established, ED §16-504.
  Expenses.
    Reimbursement, ED §16-504.
  Faculty.
    Evaluation of performance, ED §16-505.
    Salaries.
      Fixing, ED §16-505.
  Former community college.
    Assumption of obligations, ED §16-511.
    Transfer of property and rights to board of
      trustees, ED §16-511.
  Gifts, ED §16-505.
  Government of college vested in board, ED
    §16-504.
  Governor.
    Appointment of members, ED §16-504.
  Grants, ED §16-505.
  Meetings, ED §16-504.
  Notes to finance projects, issuance, ED §16-302.1.
  Number of members, ED §16-504.
  Officers, ED §16-504.
  Powers, ED §16-505.
  President, ED §16-505.
  Property, ED §16-505.
  Quorum, ED §16-504.
  Recordkeeping, ED §16-505.
  Residency requirement, ED §16-504.
  Rules and regulations.
    Adoption, ED §16-505.
  Salaries.
    Fixing, ED §16-505.
  Student fees.
    Assessment, ED §16-505.
  Student member, ED §16-504.
  Terms of office, ED §16-504.
  Tuition, ED §16-505.
  Vacancies, ED §16-504.

BALTIMORE CITY COMMUNITY COLLEGE
    —Cont'd
Bond issues.
    Auxiliary facilities.
        Restrictions on use, ED §19-102.
Budget and management, ED §16-507.
Central payroll bureau.
    Payment of wages, SPP §2-402.
City of Baltimore.
    Funding by, ED §16-512.
Collective bargaining.
    Designation of representatives to participate, ED
        §16-505.
Community college of Baltimore.
    Transfer of property and rights, ED §16-511.
Community colleges generally, ED §§16-101 to
        16-418.
    See UNIVERSITIES AND COLLEGES.
Contracts.
    Procurement contracts, ED §16-511.
Control and management of college.
    Board of trustees, ED §16-505.
Courses and programs.
    Board of trustees.
        Adoption and change of curriculum, ED
            §16-505.
Created.
    Basis for creation, ED §16-501.
Credits for graduation.
    Board of trustees.
        Establishing and changing requirements, ED
            §16-505.
Definitions, ED §16-502.
Degrees for graduation.
    Board of trustees.
        Establishing and changing requirements, ED
            §16-505.
Deposits.
    Disposition of funds, ED §16-507.
Development of plan, ED §16-501.
    Time for submission, ED §16-501.
Employees.
    Independent personnel system, ED §16-510.
    Nonfaculty employees.
        Transfer from teachers' pension system, SPP
            §23-202.1.
Entrance requirements.
    Board of trustees.
        Establishment, ED §16-505.
Exemption from certain statutes.
    Statutes applicable to community colleges
        generally, ED §16-509.
Faculty.
    Board of trustees.
        Evaluation of performance, ED §16-505.
        Salaries.
            Fixing, ED §16-505.
Federal aid.
    Local educational agency.
        Classified as for federal subsidies, grants, etc.,
            ED §16-503.
Fees.
    Board of trustees.
        Fixing, ED §16-505.
    Out-of-state fee, assessment, waiver, ED §16-505.
Findings and policies of general assembly, ED
        §16-501.
Former community college.
    Assumption of obligations, ED §16-511.
    Transfer of property and rights, ED §16-511.

BALTIMORE CITY COMMUNITY COLLEGE
    —Cont'd
Gifts.
    Board of trustees.
        Powers, ED §16-505.
Governor.
    Board of trustees.
        Appointment of members, ED §16-504.
Grants.
    Board of trustees.
        Powers, ED §16-505.
    English for Speakers of Other Languages program
        (ESOL).
        Student grants, ED §16-508.
Higher education commission.
    Commission defined, ED §16-502.
    Development of plan, ED §16-501.
    Operating budget.
        Submission to commission, ED §16-507.
Institution of higher education, ED §16-503.
Local educational agency.
    College classified as, ED §16-503.
Location in Baltimore City, ED §16-503.
New community college of Baltimore.
    Transfer of property and rights, ED §16-511.
Notes to finance projects, issuance, ED
        §16-302.1.
Officers.
    Board of trustees.
        Appointment, ED §16-505.
        Election, ED §16-504.
        Salaries.
            Fixing, ED §16-505.
        Defined, ED §16-502.
Out-of-state fee, assessment, waiver, ED
        §16-505.
Police force, ED §16-513.
    Law enforcement officers generally, PS §§3-101 to
        3-603.
        See LAW ENFORCEMENT OFFICERS AND
            PERSONNEL.
    Police training commission, PS §§3-201 to 3-218.
        See POLICE TRAINING COMMISSION.
President.
    Board of trustees.
        Appointment, ED §16-505.
        Delegation of authority to, ED §16-505.
        Salaries.
            Fixing, ED §16-505.
    Budget.
        Operating budget.
            Preparation, ED §16-507.
    Delegation of authority to other officers, ED
        §16-506.
    Duties, ED §16-506.
    Officer defined as, ED §16-502.
Procurement.
    Procurement contracts, ED §16-511.
Property.
    Board of trustees, ED §16-505.
    Former community college of Baltimore.
        Transfer of property and rights, ED §16-511.
Records.
    Board of trustees.
        Keeping separate records and minutes, ED
            §16-505.
Rules and regulations.
    Board of trustees.
        Adoption, ED §16-505.
Salaries.
    Board of trustees.
        Fixing, ED §16-505.

BALTIMORE CITY COMMUNITY COLLEGE
—Cont'd
Secretary of higher education.
Secretary defined, ED §16-502.
Services, ED §16-503.
State board for community colleges.
Operating budget.
Submission to state board, ED §16-507.
State retirement and pension system.
Optional retirement program, SPP §§30-101 to
30-307.
See STATE RETIREMENT AND PENSION
SYSTEM.
**Statutes applicable to community colleges
generally.**
Exemptions from certain statutes, ED §16-509.
Teachers' pension system.
Nonfaculty employees.
Transfer from teachers' pension system, SPP
§23-202.1.
Tuition.
Board of trustees.
Fixing, ED §16-505.
Vice presidents.
Officer defined as, ED §16-502.

BALTIMORE CITY DETENTION CENTER, COR
§§5-401 to 5-406.
Assistant wardens, COR §5-403.
**Centralized booking facility for Baltimore
City,** COR §5-404.
Diminution of inmate's term of confinement,
COR §§11-501 to 11-509.
Baltimore City detention center, subtitle
applicable to, COR §11-501.
Commitment of inmate to custody of commissioner
of correction.
Forwarding of credits, COR §11-508.
Discipline rules violations, revocation of credits,
COR §11-507.
Good conduct.
Postsentence confinement, COR §11-504.
Presentence confinement, COR §11-503.
Industrial, agricultural or administrative tasks,
performance, COR §11-505.
Postsentence confinement, deductions allowed,
COR §11-502.
Postsentence, deductions allowed.
Good conduct, COR §11-504.
Presentence confinement, deductions allowed,
COR §11-502.
Good conduct, COR §11-503.
Industrial, agricultural or administrative tasks,
performance, COR §11-505.
Revocation credits, discipline rules violations,
COR §11-507.
Scope of provisions, COR §11-501.
Special programs, COR §11-506.
Transfer to another local facility.
Credits forwarded, COR §11-508.
Transfer to hospital or mental institution.
Credits not denied, COR §11-509.
Violation of rules discipline, COR §11-507.
Vocational or other educational or training
courses, COR §11-505.
Work projects or other special programs, COR
§11-506.
**Established in division of pretrial detention
and services,** COR §5-401.
Fee for health care services, inmates charged,
COR §5-405.

BALTIMORE CITY DETENTION CENTER
—Cont'd
Good conduct credit, COR §§11-503, 11-504.
Housing of inmates authorized, COR §5-401.
Juvenile inmates, medical treatment, COR
§5-406.
Medical care for inmates, COR §5-405.
Juvenile inmates, COR §5-406.
Pretrial detention facility, COR §5-401.
Pretrial release services program.
Director, COR §5-302.
Established, function, COR §5-301.
Video bail review, center to be equipped with,
COR §5-404.
Warden, COR §5-402.

**BALTIMORE CITY JUVENILE SERVICES
CENTER,** 83C §2-118.1.
Fingerprinting juvenile brought to, CP §10-220.

BALTIMORE COUNTY.
Adult entertainment.
Prohibited at places serving alcoholic beverages,
2B §12-204.
Alcoholic beverages.
Adult entertainment prohibited, 2B §12-204.
Beer and light wine licenses.
Class C, seven days, 2B §7-101.
Class D, on-sale, 2B §5-401.
Hours and days for sale, 2B §11-302.
Racing park, 2B §8-601.
Beer and wine (on-premises) testing license.
Class BWT, 2B §8-404.1.
Beer festivals, special license, 2B §8-802.
Beer licenses.
Class C, seven days, 2B §7-101.
Beer, wine and liquor licenses.
Bar and counter sales.
Sundays, 2B §11-403.
Exercising off-sale privilege on Sunday
preceding Christmas Day and Sunday
preceding New Year's Eve, 2B §11-403.
Caterers, 2B §6-702.
Class A, off-sale, 2B §6-101.
Class B, on-sale.
Hotels and restaurants, 2B §6-201.
Class C, on-sale.
Clubs, 2B §6-301.
Class C, seven days, 2B §7-101.
Class D, on-sale.
Taverns, 2B §6-401.
Unlocked entrances, 2B §12-204.
General description of site for license, 2B
§8-204.6.
Golf courses, 2B §8-508.
Hours and days for sale, 2B §11-303.
Hunt Valley commercial/mixed use focal point,
2B §§8-204.4, 8-204.7.
Loch Raven commercial revitalization district,
2B §8-204.7.
One-day class BWT beer and wine (on-premises)
tasting license, 2B §8-402.
Pikesville revitalization area or Pikesville Town
center, 2B §8-204.2.
Racing establishments, 2B §8-601.
Seven-day class BDR license, 2B §8-204.
Special theater license, 2B §8-204.1.
Townson commercial revitalization district, 2B
§8-204.7.
Transfer and conversion of class B and D
on-sale licenses, 2B §8-204.5.
Transfer to another operator, 2B §8-204.6.

BALTIMORE COUNTY —Cont'd
Alcoholic beverages —Cont'd
Beer, wine and liquor licenses —Cont'd
 Who may file application, 2B §8-204.6.
 Wine festival license, 2B §8-304.
Bottle clubs.
 Licenses, 2B §20-103.
Buildings.
 Class D, on-sale licenses.
  Unlocked entrances, 2B §12-204.
Caterers.
 Beer, wine and liquor licenses, 2B §6-702.
Conflicts of interest.
 Direct or indirect interest in more than one
  license, 2B §9-301.
Crimes and offenses.
 Bottle clubs, 2B §20-103.
Disorderly intoxication.
 Ordinances or resolutions, 2B §19-103.
Elections.
 Exercise of privileges of licensee on election
  days, 2B §11-401.
Enforcement of laws.
 Exception of sheriffs, constables and bailiffs, 2B
  §16-401.
Fines.
 Bottle clubs, 2B §20-103.
 Imposition by board of license commissioners,
  2B §16-507.
Hotels and restaurants.
 Beer, wine and liquor licenses.
  Class B, on-sale, 2B §9-102.
 More than one license for same person or
  premises, 2B §9-102.
Hours and days for sale.
 Beer and light wine licenses, 2B §11-302.
 Beer, wine and liquor licenses, 2B §11-303.
 Election days, 2B §11-401.
 Manufacturers' licenses, 2B §11-101.
 New Year's day, 2B §11-402.
  Consumption, 2B §11-304.
License commissioners.
 Appointment.
  By county executive, 2B §15-104.
 Executive secretary, 2B §15-109.
 Powers.
  Generally, 2B §15-112.
 Rules and regulations.
  Notice, 2B §16-301.
 Salaries, 2B §15-109.
 Substitute members, 2B §15-104.
License inspectors.
 Appointment, 2B §15-112.
 Salaries, 2B §15-112.
Licenses.
 Applications.
  Additional requirements, 2B §10-104.
  Exception as to Baltimore county, 2B
   §§10-103, 10-104.
  Notice on premises, 2B §10-202.
 Assignment or transfer, 2B §10-503.
 Beer and light wine licenses.
  Class A, off-sale, 2B §5-101.
  Class B, on-sale.
   Hotels and restaurants, 2B §5-201.
 Beer festivals, special license, 2B §8-802.
 Beer, wine and liquor licenses. See within this
  subheading, "Beer, wine and liquor
  licenses."
 Bottle clubs, 2B §20-103.

BALTIMORE COUNTY —Cont'd
Alcoholic beverages —Cont'd
Licenses —Cont'd
 Churches and schools.
  Measurement of distance, 2B §9-205.
  Prohibited near, 2B §9-205.
 Commissioners. See within this subheading,
  "License commissioners."
 Death of licensee.
  Procedure, 2B §10-506.
 Expiration.
  Vacation of premises, 2B §10-504.
 Fees.
  Disposition, 2B §10-204.
  Racing park, 2B §8-601.
 Inspectors.
  Appointment, 2B §15-104.
  Salaries, 2B §15-112.
 Manufacturers.
  Hours and days for sale, 2B §11-101.
 More than one license for same person or
  premises, 2B §9-102.
 One-day class BWT beer and wine (on-premises)
  tasting license, 2B §8-404.1.
 Refusal to issue.
  Reapplication, 2B §10-208.
 Renewal.
  Procedure, 2B §10-301.
  Receipt or certificate declaring no unpaid
   taxes to be presented, 2B §10-301.
 Revocation and suspension, 2B §10-403.
 Seven-day class BDR license, 2B §8-204.
 Special theater license, 2B §8-204.1.
 Suspension or revocation by board, 2B §16-507.
 Wine festival license, 2B §8-304.
 Wine sampling permits for nonprofit
  organizations, 2B §8-404.
Light wine licenses.
 Class A, off-sale, 2B §4-201.
Manufacturers.
 Licenses.
  Hours and days of sale, 2B §11-101.
Micro-brewery licenses, 2B §2-208.
Minors.
 Employment of minors by retail dealers.
  Special provisions, 2B §12-302.
 Regulations, 2B §15-112.
Open containers.
 Possession in certain places.
  Applicability of provisions, 2B §19-303.
Penalties.
 Local penalties, 2B §16-507.
Pub-brewery licenses, 2B §2-207.
Public entertainment.
 Consumption.
  Places of public entertainment, 2B §11-304.
Sales.
 Election days, 2B §11-401.
 New Year's day, 2B §11-402.
Summons.
 Records and papers, 2B §16-410.
Sunday sales, 2B §11-503.
Theaters.
 Special theater license, 2B §8-204.1.
Wine festivals.
 Licenses, 2B §8-304.
Animals mistreated, caring for.
Enforcement of provisions, CR §10-615.
Appearance fees in circuit courts.
Collection and distribution, CJ §7-204.

BALTIMORE COUNTY —Cont'd
Authorities.
Maryland Food Center Authority.
General provisions, 41 §§13-101 to 13-123.
See MARYLAND FOOD CENTER
AUTHORITY.
Aviation.
Airports.
Zoning.
Exemptions, TR §5-603.
Back River.
Pound nets or similar devices prohibited, NR
§4-715.
Bailiffs.
Alcoholic beverages.
Exception from enforcement of laws, 2B
§16-401.
Compensation, CJ §2-507.
Bear Creek bridge.
Tolls, 25 §50A.
Transfer of title to county, 25 §50A.
Beer festivals.
Special license, 2B §8-802.
Bingo, CR §13-606.
Conditions and limitation, regulations, CR
§13-606.
Gaming event provisions generally, CR §§13-601
to 13-607.
Gaming events generally, CR §§13-601 to 13-607.
License required, CR §13-606.
Qualified organizations, CR §13-606.
Bird River.
Months fishing prohibited, NR §4-715.
Birds and game.
Spotlighting, NR §10-410.
Trapping, NR §10-410.
Boundaries.
Effect of change on board of education, ED §3-109.
Business regulation and licensure.
General business licensing.
Change in place of business, BR §17-307.
Cancer prevention, education, screening and
treatment program.
Community health coalition.
Membership requirements applicable to county,
HG §13-1111.
Comprehensive plan for cancer prevention,
education, screening and treatment program.
Requirements applicable to county, HG
§13-1109.
Casino events, CR §13-604.
Conditions and limitations, CR §13-604.
Gaming event provisions generally, CR §§13-601
to 13-607.
Qualified organizations, CR §13-604.
Caterers.
Beer, wine and liquor licenses, 2B §6-702.
Cemeteries.
Real property.
Exceptions to limits on land held, BR §5-501.
Chesapeake Bay critical area and Atlantic
coastal bays critical area protection
programs.
Critical areas commission.
Members on commission, NR §8-1804.
Child in need of services pilot program, CJ
§3-8A-10.1.
Churches.
Alcoholic beverages.
Licenses.
Restriction as to nearness to church, 2B
§9-205.

BALTIMORE COUNTY —Cont'd
Circuit courts.
Appearance fees.
Collection and distribution, CJ §7-204.
Number of judges, CJ §1-503.
Clerks of court.
Fees.
Administering public money, CJ §2-213.
Clubs.
Bottle clubs.
Licenses, 2B §20-103.
Commissioners.
Pensions.
Teachers' pensions, 25 §12.
Powers.
Exceptions, 25 §3.
Community colleges.
Board of community college trustees.
Collective bargaining.
Rules and regulations, ED §16-403.
Members, ED §16-402.
Campuses, ED §16-105.
Classified employees.
Collective bargaining.
Procedures to be established by board of
trustees, ED §16-403.
Strikes.
No right to strike, ED §16-403.
Parking.
May be prohibited, TR §21-1003.
President, ED §16-105.
Procurement contracts.
Noncompetitive negotiation, ED §16-314.1.
Rules and regulations.
Classified employees.
Collective bargaining.
Board of trustees to adopt, ED §16-403.
Conflicts of interest.
Alcoholic beverages.
Direct or indirect interest in more than one
license, 2B §9-301.
Correctional facility.
Work release and home detention program, COR
§11-705.
Courts.
Circuit courts.
Judges.
Number, CJ §1-503; MD Const Art IV §21.
Residence requirements, MD Const Art IV
§21.
Vacancies, MD Const Art IV §21.
Judicial circuit, MD Const Art IV §19.
Housing court.
Statutory references to housing court deemed to
refer to District Court, MD Const Art IV
§41-I.
Crabs.
Landowners.
Restrictions on catching, NR §4-811.
Cruelty to animals.
Enforcement of provisions.
Department of health division of animal control,
CR §10-609.
Dangerous weapons.
Minors carrying, prohibited hours, CR §4-101.
Deeds.
Recordation.
Prepayment of taxes prior to transfer on
assessment books.
Exception as to, RP §3-104.

BALTIMORE COUNTY —Cont'd
Discrimination.
Civil actions for discriminatory acts, 49B §43.
District Court.
Places of sitting, CJ §1-603.
Drunkenness.
Disorderly intoxication.
Ordinances or resolutions, 2B §19-103.
Duck season.
Fishing restrictions during duck season, NR
§4-715.
Dundee Creek.
Net fishing restrictions, NR §4-715.
Elections.
Alcoholic beverages.
Exercise of privilege of licensee on election days,
2B §11-401.
County board of elections.
Compensation, EL §2-204.
Counsel.
Compensation, EL §2-205.
County boards generally, EL §§2-201 to 2-303.
See ELECTIONS.
County boards of education generally, EL §§8-801
to 8-806.
Election judges.
Compensation, EL §10-205.
Political fundraisers.
Paddle wheel or wheel of fortune, CR §13-605.
Eminent domain.
Specific provisions, MD Const Art III §40A.
Fire department.
Firefighters appointed as deputy sheriffs, PS
§§7-301 to 7-303.
Fish and fisheries.
Restrictions in certain county waters, NR §4-715.
Riparian rights.
Exceptions, NR §4-712.
Flood control.
Requirements, EN §5-803.
Gaming, bazaar, carnival and raffles, CR
§§13-201 to 13-205, 13-601 to 13-607.
Conducting event for benefit of qualified
organization.
Allowed, CR §13-203.
Definitions, CR §§13-201, 13-601.
Gaming event defined, CR §§13-201, 13-601.
Individual benefit prohibited, CR §§13-203,
13-603.
Management through organizations members, CR
§13-205.
Permit required, CR §13-603.
Political fundraisers.
Paddle wheel or wheel of fortune, CR §13-605.
Prizes and gaming devices allowed, CR §§13-204,
13-603.
Provisions applicable to county, CR §§13-202,
13-301, 13-602.
Qualified organizations, listed, CR §§13-201,
13-603.
Unauthorized event, CR §13-607.
Golf courses.
Beer, wine and liquor licenses, 2B §8-508.
Gunpowder River.
Months fishing prohibited, NR §4-715.
Jewish holiday exceptions, NR §4-715.
Handicapped persons.
Reserving parking spaces for persons confined to
wheelchair.
Approval, TR §21-1005.

BALTIMORE COUNTY —Cont'd
Hart-Miller-Pleasure Island chain.
Redeposit of spoil in island chain, EN §5-1103.
Home detention program.
Inmates sentenced to county correctional facility,
COR §11-705.
Housing court.
District Court.
Statutory references to housing court deemed to
refer to District Court, MD Const Art IV
§41-I.
Hunting.
Boats, hunting from, NR §10-605.
Anchored boat, NR §10-606.
Nongame birds and mammals.
License required, NR §10-301.
Waters, hunting while standing in, NR §10-604.
Jail.
Sheriff to operate and administer, COR §11-201.
Kennel inspections.
Enforcement, CR §10-616.
Libraries.
Video cassette rental fees, ED §23-405.
Licenses.
Alcoholic beverages. See within this heading,
"Alcoholic beverages."
Expiration.
Eviction from premises, 2B §10-504.
Marriage.
Fees, FL §2-404.
Limitation of actions.
Discrimination.
Civil actions for discriminatory acts, 49B §43.
Market.
Maryland Food Center Authority.
General provisions, 41 §§13-101 to 13-123.
See MARYLAND FOOD CENTER
AUTHORITY.
Marriage.
Clerk's fee for performing ceremony.
Disposition, FL §2-410.
Licenses.
Fees, FL §2-404.
Metro center at Owings Mills.
Beer, wine and liquor licenses.
Transfer of class B and D on-sale licenses.
Conversion to MCOM licenses, 2B §8-204.5.
Metropolitan district.
General services department.
Public improvements.
Exceptions to division.
Improvements made by district, SF §4-402.
Metropolitan transit administration.
General provisions, TR §§7-101 to 7-707.
Middle River.
Months net or seine fishing prohibited, NR §4-715.
Mining.
Surface mining.
Dewatering in karst terrain, EN §§15-812,
15-813.
Minors.
Alcoholic beverages.
Employment by retail dealers, 2B §12-302.
Dangerous weapons, carrying.
Prohibited hours, CR §4-101.
Motor vehicles.
Refuse trucks.
Load limit of axles, TR §24-108.
Size and weight.
Power of county commissioners, 25 §25.

BALTIMORE COUNTY —Cont'd
Motor vehicles —Cont'd
Weight.
  Axles.
    Load limit of axles.
      Refuse trucks, TR §24-108.
Neighborhood preservation and stabilization demonstration project, TP §9-326.
Northeast Maryland waste disposal authority.
Participating county, NR §3-903.
Nuisance abatement.
Community association actions, RP §14-125.
Oil pipeline corporation acquiring property under power to condemn, PUC §5-404.
Orphans' court.
Judges.
  Compensation, ET §2-108.
  Sessions, ET §2-106.
Parking lots.
Towing, TR §§21-10A-01 to 21-10A-06.
See TOWING OF MOTOR VEHICLES.
Pensions.
Teachers' pensions, 25 §12.
Pikesville Revitalization Area.
Beer, wine and liquor licenses, 2B §8-204.2.
Pikesville Town Center.
Beer, wine and liquor licenses, 2B §8-204.2.
Plumbers.
Provisions not to apply in, BOP §12-103.
Political fundraisers.
Paddle wheel or wheel of fortune, CR §13-605.
Political parties.
Central committees.
  Chairman, EL §4-202.
  Election of members, EL §4-203.
Democratic party central committee, EL §4-203.
Republican party central committee, EL §4-203.
Promenade and Catonsville.
Beer, wine and liquor licenses.
  Transfer of class B and D on-sale licenses.
    Conversion to PC licenses, 2B §8-204.5.
Quarry at Greenspring.
Beer, wine and liquor licenses.
  Transfer of class B and D on-sale licenses.
    Conversion to QG licenses, 2B §8-204.5.
Real estate brokers.
Solicitation of listings, BOP §17-527.
Recordation.
Deeds.
  Prepayment of taxes prior to transfer on assessment books.
    Exception as to, RP §3-104.
Refuse trucks.
Load limit of axles, TR §24-108.
Roads.
Passing through buildings, gardens, yards or burial grounds.
  Exception as to consent of owner, 25 §144.
Schools.
Alcoholic beverages.
  Licenses.
    Restriction as to nearness to school, 2B §9-205.
Buses.
  Pickup or dropoff safety procedures, ED §7-807.
  Public awareness campaign, ED §7-807.
County board of education.
  Appointment, ED §3-109.
  Boundary change.
    Effect, ED §3-109.
  Composition, ED §3-109.

BALTIMORE COUNTY —Cont'd
Schools —Cont'd
County board of education —Cont'd
  Elections generally, EL §§8-801 to 8-806.
  Legal counsel.
    Employment, ED §4-104.
  Property.
    Parking, TR §21-1003.
    Removal, ED §3-109.
  Shared space council. See within this subheading, "Shared space council."
  Student members, ED §3-109.
Employee organizations.
  Service fees, ED §6-504.
  Supervisory units, ED §6-505.
Employees.
  Public school employees.
    Defined, ED §6-401.
  Negotiations between employer and employee.
    Representation, ED §6-407.
Pensions.
  Teachers' pensions, 25 §12.
Shared space council, ED §3-109.
Teachers.
  Pensions, 25 §12.
Term of county employee members, ED §3-109.
Shared space council. See within this heading, "Schools."
Sheriff.
Alcoholic beverages.
  Exception from enforcement of law, 2B §16-401.
Captain, lieutenant and sergeant.
  Appointment, CJ §2-309.
Deputies.
  General provisions, CJ §2-309.
Employees.
  Selection, CJ §2-309.
Firefighters appointed as deputy sheriffs, PS §§7-301 to 7-303.
Jail, operation and administration, COR §11-201.
Salary, CJ §2-309.
Second in command, CJ §2-310.
Under-sheriff.
  Appointment, CJ §2-309.
State's attorney.
Accounts for services and expenses.
  County excepted from section, 10 §39.
Assistants, 10 §40.
Clerical and other assistants, 10 §40.
Deputies, 10 §40.
Statute of limitations.
Discrimination.
  Civil actions for discriminatory acts, 49B §43.
Sue Creek.
Seine or net fishing restrictions, NR §4-715.
Taxation.
Credits, TP §9-305.
  Neighborhood preservation and stabilization project.
    Participation in designated area, TP §9-326.
Deferred property tax payments, TP §10-201.
Redemption.
  Rate of redemption, TP §14-820.
Sale.
  Notice.
    Posting, TP §14-812.
Taxicabs.
Permit to operate taxicab business in or from point in county generally, PUC §§10-202 to 10-207.
See TAXICABS.

BALTIMORE COUNTY —Cont'd
Towing.
Parking lots, TR §§21-10A-01 to 21-10A-06.
See MOTOR VEHICLES.
Trader licenses.
Approval of zoning authorities, BR §17-1807.
Trapping, NR §10-410.
Treasurer.
Salary, 25 §51.
Water.
Restrictions on use, 25 §168.
Water and sewer systems.
County plans.
Exceptions to county plan, EN §9-513.
Wine.
Festival.
License, 2B §8-304.
Permits.
Wine sampling permits for nonprofit
organizations, 2B §8-404.
Workers' compensation.
Average weekly wage.
Auxiliary police officer, LE §9-602.
Volunteer fire company member, LE §9-602.
Work release program.
Inmates sentenced to county correctional facility,
COR §11-705.
Zoning.
Administrative proceeding to enforce regulations,
66B §14.02.
Civil fines and penalties.
Ordinance may include authority to impose,
66B §14.02.
Enforcement of regulations.
Administrative proceeding, 66B §14.02.
Ordinances.
Enforcement and remedies, 66B §7.01.

BALTIMORE FOOD MARKET AUTHORITY.
See MARYLAND FOOD CENTER AUTHORITY.

BALTIMORE HARBOR TUNNEL.
Traffic delay signs.
Transportation authority to erect signs, TR
§4-402.

BALTIMORE METROPOLITAN COUNCIL, 78D
§§1 to 7.
Advisory board, 78D §6.
Council, defined, 78D §1.
Creation, 78D §2.
Meetings, 78D §4.
Membership.
Admission of members, 78D §5.
Chairman, 78D §3.
Composition, 78D §3.
Duties, 78D §5.
Withdrawal of members, 78D §5.
Predecessor council.
Contracts and obligations, 78D §7.
Public policy, 78D §2.
Quorum, 78D §4.
State retirement and pension system.
Municipal participation.
Eligible governmental units, SPP §31-104.
Predecessor council.
Liabilities to system, 78D §7.

BALTIMORE ORIOLE.
Designation as state bird, SG §13-302.

**BALTIMORE REGIONAL COUNCIL OF
GOVERNMENTS.**
Metropolitan transit administration, TR §§7-101
to 7-707.
See MARYLAND TRANSIT ADMINISTRATION.
Metropolitan transit district.
General provisions.
See METROPOLITAN TRANSIT DISTRICT.

BALTIMORE ZOO.
Budget and management.
Board of public works.
Baltimore zoo lease payments to be included in
budget, SF §10-206.

BANDS.
Municipal corporations.
Municipal band.
Establishment and maintenance, 23A §2.

BANK DEPOSITS AND COLLECTIONS, CL
§§4-101 to 4-504.
Alteration of customer's account.
Customer's duty to discover and report, CL
§4-406.
Applicability of provisions, CL §4-102.
Depositary and collecting banks.
Collection of items, CL §4-201.
Variation by agreement, CL §4-103.
Bankruptcy and insolvency.
Collection of items.
Depositary and collecting banks.
Insolvency and preference, CL §4-216.
Branch offices.
Separate office of bank, CL §4-107.
Burden of proof.
Stop payment orders.
Losses resulting from violation of orders, CL
§4-403.
Charge-back, CL §4-214.
Charging account of customer.
When bank may charge, CL §4-401.
Checks.
Bad checks generally.
See BAD CHECKS.
Stale checks, CL §4-404.
Citation of article.
Short title, CL §4-101.
Collecting banks. See within this heading,
"Depositary and collecting banks."
Collection of items.
Depositary and collecting banks, CL §§4-201 to
4-216. See within this heading, "Depositary
and collecting banks."
Payor banks, CL §§4-301 to 4-303.
Commercial code's general provisions, CL
§§1-101 to 1-208.
See COMMERCIAL CODE.
Comparative negligence.
Unauthorized signature or alteration, CL §4-406.
Conflict of laws, CL §4-102.
Contracts.
Variation of article provisions by agreement, CL
§4-103.
Contributory negligence.
Unauthorized signature or alteration, CL §4-406.
Damages.
Measure of damages, CL §4-103.
Wrongful dishonor, CL §4-402.
Death of customer.
Effect, CL §4-405.

BANK DEPOSITS AND COLLECTIONS —Cont'd

Definitions, CL §§4-104, 4-105.

Agreement for electronic presentment, CL §4-110.

General commercial code definitions, CL §1-201.

Course of dealing, CL §1-205.

Reasonable time and seasonably, CL §1-204.

Usage of trade, CL §1-205.

Depositary and collecting banks.

Collection of items, CL §§4-201 to 4-216.

Agency status of collecting items, CL §4-201.

Charge-back, CL §4-214.

Credits for items.

Availability for withdrawal, CL §4-215.

Provisional status, CL §4-201.

When provisional credits become final, CL §4-215.

Death or incompetence of customer.

Effect, CL §4-405.

Debits for items.

When provisional credits become final, CL §4-215.

Generally, CL §4-201.

Holders in due course.

When bank gives value, CL §4-211.

Indorsements.

"Pay any bank," CL §4-201.

Insolvency and preference, CL §4-216.

Instructions of transferor.

Effect, CL §4-203.

"Pay any bank."

Items so indorsed, CL §4-201.

Payment of item by payor bank.

Final payment, CL §4-215.

Presentment of items.

Methods, CL §4-204.

Notice of item not payable by, through or at bank, CL §4-212.

Refunds, CL §4-214.

Responsibility required, CL §4-202.

Secondary party liability, CL §4-212.

Security interest of collecting bank, CL §4-210.

Sending items.

Methods, CL §4-204.

Settlement of items.

Medium and time of settlement, CL §4-213.

Provisional status, CL §4-201.

When provisional credits become final, CL §4-215.

Transfer of items.

Between banks, CL §4-206.

Unindorsed items.

Depositary bank holder of, CL §4-205.

When action timely, CL §4-202.

Unindorsed items.

Depositary bank holder of, CL §4-205.

Warranties.

Documents of title, CL §7-508.

Encoding and retention warranties, CL §4-209.

Presentment warranties, CL §4-208.

Transfer warranties, CL §4-207.

Documentary drafts.

Dishonor.

Duty to notify customer, CL §4-501.

Privilege of presenting bank to deal with goods, CL §4-504.

Reporting reasons for dishonor, CL §4-503.

Presentment.

Duty to send for presentment, CL §4-501.

"On arrival" drafts, CL §4-502.

Electronic presentment, CL §4-110.

BANK DEPOSITS AND COLLECTIONS —Cont'd

Good faith.

Obligation of good faith, CL §1-203.

Holders in due course.

Collection of items.

Depositary and collecting banks.

When bank gives value for purposes of holder in due course, CL §4-211.

Incapacitated persons.

Effect of incompetence of customer, CL §4-405.

Indorsements.

Items indorsed "pay any bank," CL §4-201.

Interpretation and construction.

Applicability of article, CL §4-102.

Commercial code's general provisions, CL §§1-101 to 1-208.

See COMMERCIAL CODE.

Depositary and collecting banks.

Collection of items, CL §4-201.

Variation by agreement, CL §4-103.

Letters of credit.

General provisions, CL §§5-101 to 5-118.

See LETTERS OF CREDIT.

Liability.

Depositary and collecting banks.

Liability of secondary parties, CL §4-212.

Wrongful dishonor.

Payor bank's liability to customer, CL §4-402.

Limitation of actions, CL §4-111.

Unauthorized signature or alteration.

Claims against bank, CL §4-406.

Mental illness.

Incompetency of customer.

Authority of payor or collecting bank, CL §4-405.

Negligence.

Unauthorized signature or alteration, CL §4-406.

Ordinary care.

Action constituting, CL §4-103.

Payable through or payable at bank, CL §4-106.

Payor banks.

Collection of items.

Death or incompetence of customer, CL §4-405.

Deferred posting, CL §4-301.

Dishonor of items.

Time of dishonor, CL §4-301.

Items subject to notice, stop-order, legal process or setoff, CL §4-303.

Return of items.

Late return, CL §4-302.

Method of recovery of payment, CL §4-301.

Customer relationship.

Alteration of instruments.

Customer's duty to discover and report, CL §4-406.

Charging customer's account.

When allowed, CL §4-401.

Death of customer.

Effect, CL §4-405.

Dishonor, wrongful liability to customer, CL §4-402.

Incompetency of customer.

Effect, CL §4-405.

Stale checks.

Obligation to bank to pay, CL §4-404.

Stop payment orders.

Customer's right to issue, CL §4-403.

Subrogation on improper payment.

Right of payor bank, CL §4-407.

Unauthorized signatures.

Customer's duty to discover and report, CL §4-406.

BANK DEPOSITS AND COLLECTIONS —Cont'd
Payor banks —Cont'd
Subrogation rights on improper payment, CL §4-407.
Presentment.
Documentary drafts.
Duty to send for presentment, CL §4-501.
On arrival drafts, CL §4-502.
Electronic presentment, CL §4-110.
Responsibility of presenting banks, CL §4-503.
Receipt of items.
Delay, CL §4-109.
Time, CL §4-108.
Refunds, CL §4-214.
Stale checks, CL §4-404.
Statute of limitations, CL §4-111.
Unauthorized signature or alteration.
Claims against bank, CL §4-406.
Stop payment orders, CL §§4-403, 4-407.
When items subject to stop order, CL §4-303.

BANK HOLDING COMPANIES.
Acquisitions.
Application for acquisition, FI §5-904.
Approval, FI §5-905.
Time limits, FI §5-906.
Definition of "acquire," FI §5-901.
Limitation.
Control of thirty percent or more of deposits, FI §5-905.
Notice to commissioner, FI §5-903.
Prohibited acquisitions, FI §5-903.
Applicability of provisions, FI §5-902.
Bank supervisory agencies.
Cooperation by commissioner with, FI §5-909.
Defined, FI §5-901.
Commissioner of financial regulation.
Approval of applications for acquisition, FI §5-905.
Time limits, FI §5-906.
Cooperation with other bank supervisory agencies, FI §5-909.
Definition of "commissioner," FI §5-901.
Enforcement powers, FI §5-908.
Rules and regulations, FI §5-909.
Definitions, FI §§3-314, 5-901.
Deposits.
Defined, FI §5-901.
Divestment.
Commissioner of financial regulation.
Actions for, FI §5-908.
Emergency interstate acquisitions.
General provisions, FI §§5-1101 to 5-1107.
See BANKS AND TRUST COMPANIES.
Fees.
Acquisitions.
Application for acquisition, FI §5-904.
Foreign bank holding companies.
Defined, FI §5-901.
Forms.
Applications, notices and reports, FI §5-904.
Injunctions.
Commissioner of financial regulation.
Actions for injunctive relief, FI §5-908.
Notices.
Acquisitions.
Notice to commissioner, FI §5-903.
Out-of-state bank holding companies.
Defined, FI §5-901.
Emergency interstate acquisitions, FI §§5-1101 to 5-1107.
See BANKS AND TRUST COMPANIES.

BANK HOLDING COMPANIES —Cont'd
Principal place of business.
Defined, FI §5-901.
Reports, FI §5-907.
Forms for, FI §5-904.
Rules and regulations.
Commissioner of financial regulation, FI §5-909.
Scope of provisions, FI §5-902.
Severability of provisions, FI §5-910.

BANKRUPTCY AND INSOLVENCY.
Appeals.
Insolvency cases, CJ §12-303.
Assignments for benefit of creditors.
General provisions.
See ASSIGNMENTS FOR BENEFIT OF CREDITORS.
Title.
Rights of title of assignee, CL §15-101.
Wages.
Health, welfare and pension contributions contracted in lieu of wages, CL §15-102.
Bank deposits and collections.
Collection of items by depositary and collecting banks.
Insolvency and preference, CL §4-216.
Banks and trust companies.
Accepting deposits knowing institution to be insolvent, FI §5-804.
Commercial banks.
Impairment of capital, FI §5-602.
Deposits.
Receivers, FI §5-607.
Derogatory statements.
Prohibited, FI §5-805.
Dissolution.
Voluntary dissolution on finding of solvency, FI §3-803.
Trust companies, FI §§3-804, 5-615.
Failure to make notice of deficiency.
Effect, FI §5-602.
Impairment of capital.
Sale of debt instruments, FI §3-312.
Commercial banks, FI §3-312.
Notice.
Impairment of capital.
Notice to board of directors, FI §5-602.
Receivers.
Resumption of business, FI §5-610.
Resumption of business, FI §5-610.
Bulk transfers.
Trustees in bankruptcy.
Transfers excepted from article, CL §6-103.
Carriers.
Advancement by one common carrier to another of money for freight, CL §15-102.
Commercial code.
Applicability of general principles, CL §1-103.
Insolvency proceedings defined, CL §1-201.
Insolvent defined, CL §1-201.
Congress.
Powers of congress, US Const Art I §8.
Corporations.
Dissolution.
Involuntary dissolution.
See CORPORATIONS.
Liquidation.
Partial liquidation and reorganization.
See CORPORATIONS.
Credit unions.
Impairment of capital.
Disclosure to national credit union administration, FI §6-407.

BANKRUPTCY AND INSOLVENCY —Cont'd
Credit unions —Cont'd
Notice.
Impairment of capital.
Disclosure to national credit union
administration, FI §6-407.
Declaratory judgments.
Rights of insolvent, CJ §3-408.
Deeds.
Prepayment of personal property taxes.
Inapplicable for recordation by trustees in
bankruptcy, RP §3-104.
Void if containing preference, CL §15-101.
Exceptions, CL §15-101.
Definitions.
Words used in federal bankruptcy laws, CL
§15-101.
Dental plan organizations, IN §14-417.
Deposits.
Priorities.
Unsecured claims, CL §15-102.
Discharge.
Defense, motion to dismiss, CivProCir Rule 2-322.
Fraudulent conveyances.
Void, CL §15-101.
Electric customer choice and competition act.
Rate stabilization.
Qualified rate order not effected, PUC §7-540.
Employers and employees.
Priorities.
Claims for wages and commissions of
employees, CL §15-102.
Escrow accounts.
Lender.
Funds not assets of lender, CL §12-109.2.
Executions.
Exemptions.
See EXECUTIONS.
Foreclosures.
Effect of petition, PropSales Rule 14-209.
Fraudulent conveyances.
General provisions, CL §§15-201 to 15-214.
See FRAUDULENT CONVEYANCES.
Void, CL §15-101.
Health maintenance organizations.
Insolvency plans.
Continuation of benefits to subscribers and
enrollees, HG §19-710.
Home improvements.
Guaranty fund.
Reimbursement of fund, BR §8-410.
Insolvent.
Preference.
Deed containing conveyance or lien void, CL
§15-101.
Exceptions, CL §15-101.
Insurance.
Liquidation, rehabilitation, etc., of insurers, IN
§§9-201 to 9-232.
See INSURANCE COMPANIES.
Managing general agents, IN §8-211.
Property and casualty insurance.
Insurer not to be released by bankruptcy or
insolvency of insured, IN §19-102.
Reciprocal insurers, IN §3-222.
Landlord and tenant.
Lien on crops.
Advances in certain counties, RP §8-115.
Reserved as rent, RP §8-115.
Priorities.
Three months' rent, CL §15-102.

BANKRUPTCY AND INSOLVENCY —Cont'd
Leases, UCC.
Lessee's rights to goods on lessor's insolvency, CL
§2A-522.
Liens.
Void if containing preference, CL §15-101.
Exceptions, CL §15-101.
Limitation of actions.
Claim not defeated.
Time between petition in insolvency by debtor
and dismissal of petition, CJ §5-202.
Computation of time.
Between filing and dismissal of petition, CJ
§5-202.
Limited liability company member.
Cessation of membership, CA §4A-606.
Mortgages and deeds of trust.
Void if containing preference, CL §15-101.
Exceptions, CL §15-101.
Motions.
Defense to filing, motion to dismiss, CivProCir
Rule 2-322.
Motor clubs.
Insolvency as grounds for disciplinary action, IN
§26-208.
Motor vehicles.
Registration.
Transfer by operation of law, TR §13-504.
Old aged assistance.
Continuing care contract providers, 70B §21.
Parties.
Real party in interest.
Circuit courts, CivProCir Rule 2-201.
Preferences.
General provisions, CL §15-101.
Priorities.
Carriers.
Advancement by one common carrier to another
of money for freight transportation, CL
§15-102.
Deed, conveyance or lien containing preference
void.
Exceptions, CL §15-101.
Deposits.
Unsecured claims, CL §15-102.
Employees.
Commissions, CL §15-102.
Wages, CL §15-102.
Health, welfare and pension contributions
contracted in lieu of wages, CL §15-102.
Rent.
Three months, CL §15-102.
Wages.
Health, welfare and pension contributions.
Contracted in lieu of wages, CL §15-102.
Three months' wages, CL §15-102.
Property and casualty insurance.
Insurer not to be released by bankruptcy or
insolvency of insured, IN §19-102.
Real estate brokers.
Guaranty fund.
Reimbursement of fund, BOP §17-411.
Receivers.
Title.
Rights of title, CL §15-101.
Recordation.
Deeds.
Prepayment of personal property taxes.
Inapplicable for recordation by trustees in
bankruptcy, RP §3-104.

BANKRUPTCY AND INSOLVENCY —Cont'd
Rent.
  Preferred claim, CL §15-102.
Salaries.
  Priorities.
    Claims for salaries due for three months, CL
      §15-102.
Sale of goods.
  Buyer's insolvency.
    Seller's remedies on discovery, CL §2-702.
Taxation.
  Assessments.
    Allowances for insolvency, TP §4-401.
  Collector.
    Allowances for insolvencies, removals and
      refunds, TP §4-401.
  Personal property taxes.
    Prepayment inapplicable for recordation of
      deeds by trustees in bankruptcy, RP §3-104.
  Priority of claim, CL §15-102.
Unemployment compensation.
  Contributions.
    Priorities under dissolution or distribution.
      Bankruptcy under federal law, LE §8-634.
Wages.
  Priority of three months claim, CL §15-102.
Workers' compensation.
  Insurance coverage.
    Governmental self-insurance groups, LE §9-404.
    Self-insurance by individual employer, LE
      §9-405.
    Self-insurers' guaranty fund, IN §25-305.

BANKS AND TRUST COMPANIES.
Acknowledgments.
  Articles of incorporation, FI §3-202.
  Procedure and requirements generally, FI §1-202.
Additional banking activity.
  Authorization, FI §5-504.
Address.
  Defined, FI §1-101.
Adverse claim.
  Money, etc., in hands of bank, FI §5-306.
Advertising.
  Unauthorized representation as bank.
    Prohibited, FI §5-806.
  Unfair trade practices, FI §5-807.
Affiliates.
  Defined, FI §5-401.
  Examination, FI §5-404.
  Prohibited, FI §5-403.
    Exceptions, FI §5-403.
  Scope of subtitle, FI §5-402.
Agency.
  Commercial banks.
    Power to act as agent of depository institution
      affiliate, FI §3-206.
Amendments.
  Charters, FI §3-213.
Appeals.
  Savings banks.
    Termination of provisions, FI §2-401.
**Applicability of Maryland general corporation
  law,** FI §1-201.
Appraisals.
  Borrower's right to copy of appraisal made for
    lender, RP §14-104.1.
  Merger or consolidation.
    Stock.
      Expense of appraisal, FI §3-720.

BANKS AND TRUST COMPANIES —Cont'd
Approval.
  Voting.
    Transactions affecting voting stock.
      Approval of commissioner of financial
        regulation, FI §3-314.
Articles of incorporation. See within this
  heading, "Incorporation."
Assessments.
  Examinations.
    Banking institutions, FI §5-203.
Associations.
  Savings banks. See within this heading, "Savings
    banks."
Attachment.
  Adverse claim to money, etc., in hands of bank, FI
    §5-306.
Attorney general.
  Removal of director or officer for unsafe or
    unsound practices, FI §5-801.
  Report to attorney general, FI §5-802.
Audits.
  Banking institutions.
    Independent audits, FI §5-205.
Automated teller machines, FI §§1-401 to 1-406.
  See AUTOMATED TELLER MACHINES.
Bank deposits and collections.
  Generally, CL §§4-101 to 4-504.
    See BANK DEPOSITS AND COLLECTIONS.
Bank holding companies.
  Emergency interstate acquisitions, FI §§5-1101 to
    5-1107. See within this heading, "Emergency
    interstate acquisitions."
  General provisions, FI §§5-901 to 5-910.
    See BANK HOLDING COMPANIES.
Banking activity.
  Authorization of additional banking activity, FI
    §5-504.
Banking board.
  Appointments, FI §2-202.
  Compensation, FI §2-202.
  Confidentiality of information, FI §5-209.
  Duties, FI §2-203.
  Established, FI §2-201.
  Functions and duties, FI §2-203.
  Meetings, FI §2-204.
  Membership, FI §2-202.
  Program evaluation act, SG §8-403.
  Report of director or officer by commissioner of
    financial regulation.
    Advice and consent of board, FI §§5-801, 5-802.
  Reserves, FI §3-607.
  Tenure, FI §2-202.
  Termination of provisions, FI §2-402.
  Terms, FI §2-202.
  Vacancies, FI §2-202.
Banking institutions.
  Defined, FI §§1-101, 3-101.
  Examinations. See within this heading,
    "Examinations."
Bankruptcy and insolvency.
  Accepting deposits knowing institution to be
    insolvent, FI §5-804.
  Commercial banks.
    Impairment of capital, FI §5-602.
  Deposits.
    Receivers, FI §5-607.
  Derogatory statements.
    Prohibited, FI §5-805.
  Dissolution.
    Voluntary dissolution, FI §3-803.
      Trust companies, FI §§3-804, 5-615.

BANKS AND TRUST COMPANIES —Cont'd
Bankruptcy and insolvency —Cont'd
Failure to make notice of deficiency.
Effect, FI §5-602.
Impairment of capital.
Sale of debt instruments, FI §3-312.
Notice.
Impairment of capital.
Notice to board of directors, FI §5-602.
Receivers.
Resumption of business, FI §5-610.
Resumption of business, FI §5-610.
Bank service corporations.
Approval by commissioner, FI §5-405.
Criteria, FI §5-405.
Defined, FI §5-401.
Examination, FI §5-406.
Regulation, FI §5-407.
Restrictions, FI §5-405.
Bills of exchange.
Negotiable instruments.
General provisions, CL §§3-101 to 3-605.
See NEGOTIABLE INSTRUMENTS.
Blockbusting.
Termination of provisions of certain sections in
subtitle, FI §2-401.
Board of directors.
General provisions. See within this heading,
"Directors."
Bond issues.
Debt instruments.
Issuance and sale, FI §3-312.
Books, papers and accounts.
Inspection.
Regulations, MD Const Art III §39.
Branch banking.
Applicability of provisions, FI §5-1002.
Bank supervisory agencies.
Defined, FI §5-1001.
Joint actions by bank commissioner with, FI
§5-1010.
Business days, FI §5-703.
Capital stock.
Requirements, FI §3-209.
Commissioner of financial regulation.
Approval of branch.
Considerations, FI §5-1006.
Prohibited if transactions resulting in thirty
percent or more control of deposits, FI
§5-1013.
Time limits, FI §5-1007.
Cooperation with other state or federal
regulators, FI §5-1012.
Enforcement actions, FI §5-1010.
Examinations, FI §5-1009.
Joint enforcement actions with other bank
supervisory agencies, FI §5-1010.
Supervision.
Agreements with bank supervisory agencies,
FI §5-1009.
Definitions, FI §5-1001.
De novo branch.
Defined, FI §5-1001.
Engaging in business with banks, FI §5-1008.
Establishment, FI §§3-209, 5-1003.
Approval, FI §§5-1006, 5-1007.
In another state, FI §5-1004.
Out-of-state banks, FI §5-1014.
Prerequisites, FI §5-1005.
Examinations, FI §5-1009.

BANKS AND TRUST COMPANIES —Cont'd
Branch banking —Cont'd
Fees.
Establishment of branch, FI §5-1005.
Supervisory and examination fees, FI §5-1009.
Notices.
Intention to open branch, FI §5-1005.
Off-premises customer-bank communication
terminals.
Electronic terminals, FI §12-201.
Out-of-state banks.
Defined, FI §5-1001.
Establishment of branches, FI §§5-1003, 5-1014.
Powers and rights of branches, FI §5-1008.
Reports.
Condition and income, FI §5-1011.
Savings banks, FI §4-208.
Scope of provisions, FI §5-1002.
Severability of provisions, FI §5-1015.
Surplus, FI §3-209.
Building and loan associations.
See SAVINGS AND LOAN ASSOCIATIONS.
Capital stock.
Commercial banks.
Minimum capital stock, FI §3-209.
Defined, FI §§3-101, 5-101.
Stock and stockholders. See within this heading,
"Stock and stockholders."
Cash dividends. See within this heading,
"Dividends."
Cease and desist orders.
Affirmative action requirement, FI §5-808.
Commissioner of financial regulation.
Powers and duties generally, FI §5-808.
Deposits.
Restrictions on withdrawal of money, FI §5-808.
Hearings, FI §5-808.
Order effective on service, FI §5-808.
Practices within scope of orders, FI §5-808.
Restrictions on withdrawal of money, FI §5-808.
Certificates of beneficial interest.
General provisions. See within this heading, "Debt
instruments."
**Certification of checks, drafts or money
orders,** FI §3-606.
Charges.
Service charges.
Prohibited where withdrawals restricted, FI
§5-308.
Charters.
Amendments.
Procedure, FI §§3-213, 4-210.
Defined, FI §1-101.
Check cashing services, FI §§12-101 to 12-127.
See CHECK CASHING SERVICES.
Checks.
Certification.
Prohibited when there are not sufficient funds
on deposit, FI §3-606.
Valid against bank or trust company, FI §3-606.
Generally.
See CHECKS.
Loss of checks.
Liability of banking institution, FI §5-307.
Month and year account opened to appear on
checks, FI §5-310.
Exceptions, FI §5-310.
Return of cancelled checks, FI §5-513.
Stale checks, CL §4-404.
Child support enforcement.
Attachment and seizure of funds for arrears from
financial institution, FL §§10-108.3, 10-108.4.

BANKS AND TRUST COMPANIES —Cont'd
Child support enforcement —Cont'd
Reports requested by administration, FL
§10-108.2.
Citizenship.
Incorporators, FI §3-201.
Closing of banks.
Emergency management.
Governor's powers, PS §14-307.
Collateral.
Fiduciary deposit surety bonds, FI §1-206.
Collections.
Bank deposits and collections.
General provisions, CL §§4-101 to 4-504.
See BANK DEPOSITS AND COLLECTIONS.
Commercial banks.
Acknowledgments.
Articles of incorporation, FI §3-202.
Additional banking activity or bank-related
service, FI §5-504.
Application of article, FI §3-102.
Articles of incorporation.
Amendment.
Procedure, FI §3-213.
Corporate status, FI §3-205.
Name of commercial bank, FI §3-202.
Audit of institution.
General provisions, FI §5-205.
Bankruptcy and insolvency.
Impairment of capital, FI §5-602.
Branches.
Requirements, FI §3-209.
Capital stock.
Minimum capital stock, FI §3-209.
Certificate to commence business.
Issuance by commissioner of financial
regulation, FI §3-208.
Charter amendments, FI §3-213.
Common trust fund.
Accounting for fund, FI §3-516.
Administration, FI §3-507.
Amendment of fund plan, FI §3-509.
Assets.
Investment of fund assets, FI §3-519.
Ownership, FI §3-517.
Registration of assets in name of nominee, FI
§3-518.
Transfer, FI §3-520.
Audits, FI §3-516.
Cofiduciaries, FI §3-511.
Copying of fund plan, FI §3-508.
Definitions, FI §3-501.
Distribution, FI §3-513.
Entry, FI §3-513.
Establishment, FI §3-502.
Evidence.
Participation in fund, FI §3-513.
Fees.
Management, FI §3-515.
Fiduciaries.
Designation of fiduciary account, FI §3-511.
Interest.
Limitations on, FI §3-512.
Investments.
Assets, FI §3-519.
In fund, FI §3-510.
Limitations on investments and interest, FI
§3-512.
Management.
Fees, FI §3-515.
Operation, FI §3-507.

BANKS AND TRUST COMPANIES —Cont'd
Commercial banks —Cont'd
Common trust fund —Cont'd
Optional method of administration, FI §3-507.
Participation in fund.
Evidence, FI §3-514.
Plan.
Amendment of fund plan, FI §3-509.
Copying of fund plan, FI §3-508.
Establishment and maintenance in
accordance with plan, FI §3-504.
Filing, FI §3-508.
Inspection, FI §3-508.
Optional provisions for fund plans, FI §3-506.
Required provisions for fund plans, FI §3-505.
Powers of commercial bank, FI §3-503.
Records, FI §3-517.
Special accounting, FI §3-516.
Transfer of assets from a common trust fund, FI
§3-520.
Valuation, FI §3-513.
Dates, FI §3-516.
Withdrawal, FI §3-513.
Conversion of commercial bank as national
banking association, FI §3-802.
Conversion of national banking associations as
commercial banks, FI §3-801.
Debt instruments, FI §3-312.
Definitions, FI §1-101.
Deposits.
Bankruptcy.
Pledge of security for payment of estates in
bankruptcy, FI §3-206.
Powers of commercial banks, FI §3-206.
Receipt of deposits of money, securities and
other personal property, FI §3-207.
Securities for certain deposits, FI §3-206.
Directors.
Additional directorships, FI §3-407.
Election, FI §3-405.
First directors, FI §§3-206, 3-401.
Management of companies, FI §3-401.
Meetings.
Attendance at board meetings, FI §3-408.
Number of directors, FI §3-402.
Oaths, FI §3-404.
Officers.
Election, FI §3-411.
Qualifications, FI §3-403.
Quorum, FI §§3-401, 3-410.
Terms of office, FI §3-405.
Vacancies, FI §3-409.
Dissolution.
Voluntary dissolution, FI §3-803.
Preference, FI §3-804.
Dividends.
Cash dividends.
When declared, FI §3-307.
Preferred stock, FI §3-302.
Drafts.
Acceptance, FI §§3-206, 3-604.
Certification, FI §3-606.
Emergency interstate acquisitions, FI §5-1105.
Examination.
Determination of payment of capital stock, FI
§3-212.
Existing companies.
Provisions as to, FI §3-102.
Fiduciary capacity.
Banking institutions generally. See within this
heading, "Fiduciary capacity."

BANKS AND TRUST COMPANIES —Cont'd
Commercial banks —Cont'd
Impairment of capital, FI §5-602.
Incorporation.
Additional powers of trust company, FI §3-207.
Articles of incorporation.
Amendments, FI §3-203.
Procedure, FI §3-213.
Approval, FI §3-203.
Contents, FI §3-202.
Execution, FI §3-202.
Fees for filing, FI §3-203.
Filing for record, FI §3-204.
Investigation, FI §3-203.
Recordation, FI §3-204.
Rejection, FI §3-203.
Capital payments before beginning business, FI §3-211.
Certification before beginning business, FI §3-208.
Charter amendments, FI §3-213.
Corporate status, FI §3-205.
Examination before certification, FI §3-212.
Formation in general, FI §3-201.
General powers, FI §3-206.
Additional powers of trust company, FI §3-207.
General provisions, FI §3-201.
Minimum capital requirements, FI §3-209.
Perpetual existence, FI §3-205.
Right of, FI §3-205.
Incorporators.
Citizenship, FI §3-201.
Meetings.
Quorum, FI §3-410.
Name.
Restrictions, FI §3-202.
Notices.
Plan of reorganization, FI §5-612.
Reserve requirements, FI §5-602.
Number of incorporators, FI §3-201.
Oaths.
Owner of stock before voting in election, FI §3-311.
Officers and employees.
Election of officers, FI §3-411.
Personal property.
Owning and leasing, FI §3-605.
Powers, FI §§3-206, 3-207.
Quorum, FI §3-410.
Real property, FI §§3-206, 5-503.
Reserves, FI §3-607.
Savings department.
Permitted, FI §5-301.
Stock and stockholders. See within this heading, "Stock and stockholders."
Termination of provisions, FI §2-401.
Commercial code.
General provisions, CL §§1-101 to 10-112.
See COMMERCIAL CODE.
Commissioner of financial regulation.
Additional banking activity or bank-related service.
Authorization, FI §5-504.
Affiliates.
Approval, FI §5-403.
Examination into, FI §5-404.
Appeals from decisions.
Termination of provisions, FI §2-401.
Appointment, FI §2-102.

BANKS AND TRUST COMPANIES —Cont'd
Commissioner of financial regulation —Cont'd
Bank holding companies.
See BANK HOLDING COMPANIES.
Banking activity or bank-related service.
Authorization, FI §5-504.
Branch banking.
Approval of branch.
Considerations, FI §5-1006.
Prohibited if transactions resulting in thirty percent or more control of deposits, FI §5-1013.
Time limits, FI §5-1007.
Cooperation with other state or federal regulators, FI §5-1012.
Enforcement actions, FI §5-1010.
Examinations, FI §5-1009.
Joint enforcement actions with other bank supervisory agencies, FI §5-1010.
Supervision.
Agreements with bank supervisory agencies, FI §5-1009.
Cease and desist orders.
Powers and duties generally, FI §5-808.
Compensation, FI §2-102.
Conflicts of interest.
Full-time duties of bank commissioner and deputy, FI §2-110.
Ownership of certain stock prohibited, FI §2-111.
Prohibited activities generally, FI §2-112.
Consumer complaints.
Consumer credit reporting agencies, CL §14-1217.
Credit unions.
General provisions.
See CREDIT UNIONS.
Deputy bank commissioner, FI §§2-103, 2-110.
Stock in bank.
Ownership by deputy commissioner prohibited, FI §2-111.
Director or officer.
Placing banking institution under bank commissioner, FI §5-601.
Removal by bank commissioner.
Violation of law or unsafe or unsound practices, FI §5-801.
Duties.
Generally, FI §2-110.
Employees.
Ownership of bank stock prohibited, FI §2-111.
Enforcement of provisions, FI §§2-113 to 2-116.
Equal credit opportunity.
Jurisdiction, CL §12-703.
Examination of banks.
Access to vaults and records, FI §5-201.
Affiliates, FI §5-404.
Before business starts, FI §3-212.
Certified copies of record or papers.
Fees for certified copies, FI §2-108.
Charges, FI §5-203.
Rate, FI §5-203.
Examiners.
Appointment as receiver, FI §5-605.
Information to be kept secret, FI §5-209.
Exceptions, FI §5-209.
Officers.
Examination, FI §5-202.
Procedure, FI §5-201.
Requirements.
Effect on requirements, FI §5-202.

BANKS AND TRUST COMPANIES —Cont'd
Commissioner of financial regulation —Cont'd
Examination of banks —Cont'd
Witnesses, FI §5-202.
Exercise of powers and duties of office subject to
authority of secretary of licensing and
regulation, FI §2-105.
Fees.
Certified copies of records or papers, FI §2-108.
General fund.
Payment of money to general fund, FI §2-109.
Incorporation.
Certificate to do business, FI §3-208.
Indebtedness to bank.
Bank commissioner and employees not to
become indebted to bank, FI §2-112.
Injunctions.
Bank holding companies.
Actions for injunctions, FI §5-908.
Violations of laws, rules or regulations relating
to commissioner's supervision, FI §5-809.
Insolvency.
Finding of insolvency.
Voluntary dissolution, FI §3-803.
Investigatory powers, FI §2-114.
Money transmission.
See MONEY TRANSMISSION.
Office established, FI §2-101.
Payment of money to general fund, FI §2-109.
Program evaluation act, SG §8-403.
Qualifications, FI §2-102.
Receivers.
Appointment, FI §5-605.
Additional clerks may be appointed, FI
§5-606.
Attorney at law.
Fees of council, FI §5-608.
Deposits made by receiver, FI §5-607.
Duties.
Generally, FI §5-606.
Effect of taking possession, FI §5-603.
Federal deposit insurance corporation.
Appointment as receiver for institutions in
commissioner's possession, FI §5-605.
Powers as receiver, FI §5-614.
Loans on own capital stock or purchase of same,
FI §3-304.
Notice of taking possession of institution, FI
§§5-601, 5-604.
Reorganization of bank in receivership.
Bank commissioner may permit reopening, FI
§5-610.
Consent of political subdivisions, FI §5-613.
Consideration of plan, FI §5-612.
Petition for determination of interest, FI
§5-612.
Plan proposed by board of directors.
Authority to propose plan, FI §5-611.
Substance of plan, FI §5-611.
Withdrawal of plan, FI §5-612.
Records.
Certified copies of records or papers.
Fees, FI §2-108.
Reorganizations.
When bank commissioner may take charge.
Banking institutions, FI §5-601.
Commercial banks, FI §5-602.
Report.
Governor, FI §2-107.
Violations.
Officers, etc., FI §§5-801, 5-802.

BANKS AND TRUST COMPANIES —Cont'd
Commissioner of financial regulation —Cont'd
Requirements, FI §5-201.
Reserves.
Change by, FI §3-607.
Responsibility to secretary, FI §2-102.
Rules and regulations.
Authority of commissioner, FI §2-105.1.
Savings banks.
Termination of provisions, FI §2-401.
Seal.
Filed with secretary of state, FI §2-106.
Secondary mortgage loans.
Credit provisions, CL §§12-401 to 12-415.
See MORTGAGES AND DEEDS OF TRUST.
Secretary of licensing and regulation.
Authority, FI §2-105.
Securities or negotiable loans.
Commissioners and employees not to sell, FI
§2-112.
Solvency.
Finding of solvency.
Voluntary dissolution.
Trust companies, FI §3-803.
Staff.
Employment, FI §2-104.
Stock and stockholders.
Ownership by commissioner or employees
prohibited, FI §2-111.
Stock ledger.
Duties of commissioner as to stock ledger, FI
§3-309.
Taking possession of property and business, FI
§§5-601, 5-602.
Action by commissioner.
Removal of director or officer for violations, FI
§§5-801, 5-802.
Termination of certain provisions, FI §2-401.
Term of office, FI §2-102.
Time, FI §5-201.
Violations.
Reports, FI §§5-801, 5-802.
Common trust fund.
Commercial banks. See within this heading,
"Commercial banks."
Communication terminals.
Off-premises customer-bank communication
terminals.
Electronic terminals, FI §12-201.
Compliance review documents, FI §1-205.
Comptroller.
State comptroller.
Banking board, FI §2-202.
U.S. comptroller.
Conversion of commercial bank into national
banking association, FI §3-802.
Confidential financial records.
Banking board, FI §5-209.
Definitions, FI §1-301.
Disclosure of records prohibited, FI §1-302.
Exceptions, FI §1-302.
Exemptions from subtitle, FI §1-303.
Financial exploitation, disclosure due to, FI
§1-306.
Penalties, FI §1-305.
Subpoenas, summons, warrants or court orders.
Exception to disclosure prohibition, FI §1-302.
Generally, FI §1-304.
Violations.
Penalties, FI §1-305.

BANKS AND TRUST COMPANIES —Cont'd
Conflicts of interest.
Commissioner of financial regulation.
Full-time duties of bank commissioner and
deputy, FI §2-110.
Ownership of certain stock prohibited, FI
§2-111.
Prohibited activities generally, FI §2-112.
Consolidation.
Merger, consolidation or transfer. See within this
heading, "Merger, consolidation or transfer."
Constituent bank.
Defined, FI §3-701.
Consumer credit reporting agencies.
Consumer complaints against banking institution
or credit union, CL §14-1217.
General provisions, CL §§14-1201 to 14-1218.
See CONSUMER CREDIT REPORTING
AGENCIES.
Consumer loans.
Licensing provisions.
See CONSUMER LOANS.
Continuing care contracts.
Deposit of moneys collected in delinquency
proceedings, 70B §20P.
Conversions.
Commercial bank as national banking association,
FI §3-802.
National banking associations as commercial
banks, FI §3-801.
Recordation, FI §3-801.
Copies.
Commissioner of financial regulation.
Fees for certified copies of records, FI §2-108.
Corporate takeovers.
Fiduciaries.
Successor corporate fiduciaries, ET §§15-1A-01
to 15-1A-05.
See FIDUCIARIES.
Corporations.
Applicability of Maryland general corporation law,
FI §1-201.
Articles of incorporation.
Savings banks. See within this heading,
"Savings banks."
Incorporation. See within this heading,
"Incorporation."
Loans.
Limitation on amount, FI §3-601.
Termination of provisions of sections, FI §2-401.
Unauthorized representation as bank.
Prohibited, FI §5-806.
Counties.
Bank stock taxes.
Grant to municipalities in lieu of shares tax, 25
§220.
Defined, FI §1-101.
Credit.
Extensions of credit.
State regulation, FI §1-209.
Unfair trade practices, FI §5-807.
Credit unions.
General provisions.
See CREDIT UNIONS.
Currency.
Circulating.
Termination of provisions, FI §2-401.
Debt instruments.
Commercial banks.
Sale, FI §3-312.
Defined, FI §3-101.

BANKS AND TRUST COMPANIES —Cont'd
Debt instruments —Cont'd
Issuance or sale, FI §3-312.
No stockholder liability, FI §3-312.
Priorities, FI §3-312.
Retirement, FI §3-312.
Voting rights, FI §3-312.
Debt management services, FI §§12-901 to
12-931.
See DEBT MANAGEMENT SERVICES.
Debts.
Offsets.
Defined, CL §15-702.
Prohibited, CL §15-702.
Deceptive practices.
Unfair trade practices, FI §§5-807 to 5-809. See
within this heading, "Unfair trade practices."
Definitions.
Address, FI §1-101.
Affiliates, FI §5-401.
Bank, FI §3-701.
Bank holding company, FI §§3-314, 5-901.
Banking institutions, FI §1-101.
Bank service corporations, FI §5-401.
Branch banking, FI §5-1001.
Capital stock, FI §§3-101, 5-101.
Charter, FI §1-101.
Commercial bank, FI §§1-101, 3-101, 3-501, 5-101.
Common trust funds, FI §3-501.
Compliance review documents, FI §1-205.
Confidential financial records, FI §1-301.
Constituent bank, FI §3-701.
County, FI §1-101.
Demand deposits, FI §3-607.
Emergencies, FI §5-707.
Emergency interstate acquisitions, FI §5-1101.
Examiner, FI §5-101.
Federal banking authority, FI §5-101.
Financial institution, FI §5-101.
Foreign banks, FI §§1-101, 12-201.
General provisions, FI §§1-101, 3-101, 5-101.
Holidays, FI §5-701.
Includes, FI §1-101.
Mail, FI §1-101.
Mergers, FI §3-701.
Mortgage, FI §1-101.
Multiple-party accounts, FI §1-204.
Municipal area, FI §1-101.
National banking association, FI §1-101.
Other-state bank, FI §1-101.
Person, FI §1-101.
Political subdivision, FI §1-101.
Real property, FI §1-101.
Safe-deposit companies, FI §§12-601, 12-602.
Savings banks, FI §§4-101, 5-101.
State, FI §1-101.
Stock acquisition, FI §3-314.
Successor, FI §3-701.
Time deposits, FI §3-607.
Transfer assets, FI §3-701.
Trust company, ET §§1-101, 13-101; FI §§3-101,
3-501, 5-101.
Uniform fiduciaries act, ET §15-201.
Deposit insurance fund corporation, FI
§§10-101 to 10-121.
See DEPOSIT INSURANCE FUND
CORPORATION.
Deposits.
Abandoned property disposition, CL §§17-101 to
17-326.
See ABANDONED PROPERTY DISPOSITION.

BANKS AND TRUST COMPANIES —Cont'd
Deposits —Cont'd
Adverse claim to money, etc., in hands of bank, FI §5-306.
Bank deposits and collections.
  Generally, CL §§4-101 to 4-504.
    See BANK DEPOSITS AND COLLECTIONS.
Bankruptcy.
  Pledging collateral for public funds, FI §§3-206, 4-206.
  Pledging securities for payments of estates in bankruptcy, FI §3-206.
  Receiver, FI §5-607.
Cease and desist orders.
  Restrictions on withdrawal of money, FI §5-808.
Christmas accounts.
  Minimum interest, FI §5-302.
Commercial banks. See within this heading, "Commercial banks."
Demand deposits.
  Defined, FI §3-607.
Dividends.
  Required notice to customers, FI §5-302.
Dormant accounts.
  Charges or cessation of benefits on, CL §17-308.1.
  Uniform disposition of abandoned property.
    See ABANDONED PROPERTY DISPOSITION.
Federal regulations, FI §5-302.
Fiduciaries.
  Name of fiduciary.
    Fiduciary personal account, ET §15-208.
    In name of fiduciary as such, ET §15-206.
  Principal.
    In name of principal, ET §15-207.
Inactive accounts.
  Abandoned property disposition.
    See ABANDONED PROPERTY DISPOSITION.
  Charges or cessation of benefits on, CL §17-308.1.
Insolvency.
  Knowing institution to be insolvent, FI §5-804.
Interest.
  Christmas accounts, FI §5-302.
  Recoveries in tort.
    See MINORS.
  Required notice to customers, FI §5-302.
  Short term savings accounts, FI §5-302.
Loss of check.
  Liability of banking institution, FI §5-307.
Minors.
  Generally, FI §5-305.
Notice.
  Time when funds may be withdrawn, FI §5-309.
Savings banks.
  General provisions, FI §4-206.
  Terms, FI §5-302.
  Withdrawal, FI §§4-206, 4-601.
Security.
  Certain deposits, FI §3-206.
Service charges.
  Prohibited.
    Where withdrawals restricted, FI §5-308.
Short term savings accounts.
  Minimum interest, FI §5-302.
Time deposits.
  Defined, FI §3-607.
Withdrawals restricted.
  Cease and desist orders relating to restrictions, FI §5-808.

BANKS AND TRUST COMPANIES —Cont'd
Deposits —Cont'd
Withdrawals restricted —Cont'd
  Service charges prohibited, FI §5-308.
Directors.
Additional directorships, FI §3-407.
Audit of institution.
  When required, FI §5-205.
Commercial banks. See within this heading, "Commercial banks."
Election.
  Generally, FI §§3-405, 4-402, 4-505.
Examination of banks.
  Before business starts, FI §3-212.
Impairment of capital.
  Notice by commissioner of financial regulation, FI §5-602.
Liability.
  Cash dividends.
    Liability of director to creditor, FI §3-307.
Loans.
  Restrictions on loans to directors, FI §5-512.
Management, FI §3-401.
Meetings.
  Annual meeting, FI §3-310.
  Attendance at board meetings, FI §3-408.
Multiple directorships, FI §5-511.
Notice.
  Annual meeting of stockholders, FI §3-310.
  Placing banking institution under commissioner of financial regulation, FI §5-601.
Number, FI §3-402.
Oath, FI §3-404.
Officers.
  Election, FI §3-411.
Placing banking institution under commissioner of financial regulation.
  Procedure, FI §5-601.
Powers.
  Enumeration of powers of corporation, FI §3-206.
Qualifications, FI §3-403.
Quorum, FI §§3-410, 4-509.
Removal.
  By bank commissioner.
    Approval of secretary of licensing and regulation.
      Violation of law or unsafe or unsound practices, FI §§5-801, 5-802.
Savings banks. See within this heading, "Savings banks."
Sundays and holidays.
  Action by directors, FI §5-708.
Terms of office, FI §§3-405, 4-505.
Vacancies, FI §3-409.
Dissolution.
Voluntary dissolution, FI §3-803.
  Preference for property held in fiduciary capacity, FI §3-804.
Dividends.
Cash dividends.
  Director.
    Liability to creditor, FI §3-307.
  Liability of director to creditor, FI §3-307.
  Losses charged to surplus account, FI §3-306.
  Stockholders.
    Liability of stockholder receiving, FI §3-307.
  When declared, FI §3-307.
  When prohibited, FI §§3-306, 3-307.
Preferred stock.
  Commercial banks, FI §3-302.

BANKS AND TRUST COMPANIES —Cont'd
Dividends —Cont'd
Savings accounts.
  Information concerning dividends on savings
    accounts, FI §5-302.
Savings banks.
  Cash dividends.
    When declared, FI §3-307.
Stock dividends, FI §3-308.
  Preferred stock, FI §3-302.
Dormant accounts.
See ABANDONED PROPERTY DISPOSITION.
Drafts.
Acceptance, FI §§3-206, 3-604.
  Commercial banks, FI §3-604.
  What drafts may be accepted, FI §3-604.
Certification.
  Prohibited when there are not sufficient funds
    on deposit, FI §3-606.
  Valid against commercial bank, FI §3-606.
Checks generally.
  See CHECKS.
Negotiable instruments.
  General provisions, CL §§3-101 to 3-605.
    See NEGOTIABLE INSTRUMENTS.
Return of cancelled checks, FI §5-513.
Termination of provisions, FI §2-401.
Elections.
Directors, FI §§3-405, 4-402, 4-505.
Officers, FI §3-411.
Electronic terminals.
Foreign banks.
  Defined, FI §12-201.
Emergency interstate acquisitions.
Acquisitions authorized for certain purposes, FI
  §5-1102.
Applicability of subtitle 10 restrictions, FI
  §5-1102.
Commercial banks.
  Powers of commercial bank acquired under
    subtitle, FI §5-1105.
  Restrictions on commercial bank required under
    subtitle, FI §5-1105.
Commissioner.
  Powers to consummate acquisition, FI §5-1104.
Conditions for acquisition and conversion.
  Enumeration, FI §5-1103.
Consolidations, mergers or transfer of assets
  authorized, FI §5-1102.
Definitions, FI §5-1101.
Effective period of subtitle, FI §5-1101.1.
Findings of commissioner, FI §5-1103.
Indemnification of claims, FI §5-1107.
Plan of acquisition, FI §5-1103.
  Approval, FI §5-1106.
  Notice of final action on application, FI §5-1106.
  Powers of commissioner, FI §5-1106.
Powers of commissioner to consummate
  acquisition, FI §5-1104.
Release of Maryland deposit insurance fund
  incorporation, FI §5-1107.
Repayment of indebtedness.
  Former Maryland savings-share insurance
    corporation of Maryland deposit insurance
    fund corporation, FI §5-1107.
Reports, FI §5-1103.
Requirements for merger, conversion or
  acquisition, FI §5-1103.
Scope of subtitle, FI §5-1102.
Submitting false information to commissioner, FI
  §5-1103.

BANKS AND TRUST COMPANIES —Cont'd
Emergency management.
Closing of banks.
  Governor's powers, PS §14-307.
  Emergencies defined, FI §5-707.
Employees. See within this heading, "Officers and
  employees."
Equal credit opportunity act, CL §§12-701 to
  12-708.
See EQUAL CREDIT OPPORTUNITY.
Evidence.
Stock and stockholders.
  Stock ledger.
    Presumptive evidence of fact, FI §3-309.
Stock ledger.
  Presumptive evidence of fact, FI §3-309.
Examinations.
Affiliates, FI §5-404.
Assessments, FI §5-203.
Banking institutions.
  Acceptance of federal examination, FI §5-204.
  Assessments, FI §5-203.
  Charges for regulation, FI §5-203.
  Federal examination.
    Acceptance, FI §5-204.
  Fees, FI §5-203.
  Independent audits, FI §5-205.
  Reports.
    Civil penalty for failure to make report, FI
      §5-208.
    Generally, FI §5-206.
    Special reports, FI §5-207.
  Required, FI §5-201.
  Witnesses, FI §5-202.
Bank service corporations, FI §5-406.
Branch banking, FI §5-1009.
Commissioner. See within this heading,
  "Commissioner of financial regulation."
Examiners.
Defined, FI §5-101.
Executors and administrators.
Bonds, surety.
  Not required to give when serving as personal
    representative, ET §6-102.
Fiduciaries.
  General provisions, ET §§15-201 to 15-211.
    See FIDUCIARIES.
Fiduciary capacity. See within this heading,
  "Fiduciary capacity."
Federal banking authorities.
Acceptance examination by commissioner of report
  by federal agency, FI §5-204.
Defined, FI §5-101.
Examination of banks by commissioner.
  Effect on duties, FI §5-204.
Information obtained in examinations.
  Confidentiality of information, FI §5-209.
Receiver.
  Appointment as receiver for institution in
    commissioner's possession, FI §5-605.
  Rights as receiver, FI §5-614.
Federal deposit insurance corporation.
Memberships authorized, FI §5-509.
Federal reserve system.
Information obtained in examinations.
  Commissioner may give to federal reserve
    system, FI §5-209.
Memberships authorized, FI §5-509.
Reserves.
  Requirements, FI §3-607.

BANKS AND TRUST COMPANIES —Cont'd
Fees.
  Articles of incorporation.
    Amendments, FI §§3-213, 4-210.
    Filing with commissioner.
      Commercial banks, FI §3-203.
      Savings banks, FI §4-203.
  Branch banking.
    Establishment of branch, FI §5-1005.
    Supervisory and examination fees, FI §5-1009.
  Charter amendments.
    Commercial banks, FI §3-213.
    Savings banks, FI §4-210.
  Commercial banks.
    Articles of incorporation, FI §3-203.
  Commissioner.
    Certified copy of records, FI §2-108.
  Common trust funds, FI §3-515.
  Foreign corporations.
    Offices.
      Power of commissioner to set fees for permits,
        FI §12-211.
  Incorporation, FI §§3-203, 4-203.
  Savings banks.
    Filing annual reports, CA §1-203.
      Disposition, TP §2-220.
  Trust companies.
    Articles of incorporation, FI §3-203.
Fiduciary capacity.
  Agent or custodian for fiduciary.
    Authorized to deposit securities with securities
        clearing corporation.
      Certification in writing of account to fiduciary,
        ET §15-104.
      Rules and regulations, ET §15-104.
  Authority to act as, FI §3-207.
  Defined, ET §15-201.
  Exercise of fiduciary powers by commercial banks.
    Requirements and standards, FI §3-103.
  General provisions, ET §§15-201 to 15-211.
    See FIDUCIARIES.
  Institution acting in fiduciary capacity, FI
    §§3-804, 5-615.
  Permissible holder of trust and fiduciary powers,
    ET §14-110.
  Personal account.
    Fiduciary personal account, ET §15-208.
  Powers, FI §3-207.
  Preferences.
    Acting in fiduciary capacity, FI §§3-804, 5-615.
  Successor corporate fiduciaries, ET §§15-1A-01 to
    15-1A-05.
    See FIDUCIARIES.
Fiduciary deposit surety bonds.
  Authorized collateral, FI §1-206.
Finance companies.
  Sales finance companies.
    See SALES.
Financial institution.
  Defined, FI §1-101.
Fines.
  Confidential financial records.
    Penalties for violation of subtitle, FI §1-305.
  Deposits.
    Accepting knowing institution to be insolvent,
      FI §5-804.
  Derogatory statements.
    Prohibited, FI §5-805.
  Examination of bank by commissioner.
    Disclosing information obtained in examination,
      FI §5-209.

BANKS AND TRUST COMPANIES —Cont'd
Fines —Cont'd
  False statements or entries, FI §5-803.
  Reports.
    To commissioner.
      Certain transactions affecting voting stock.
        Failure to make report, FI §5-208.
  Service charges.
    Where withdrawal restricted, FI §5-308.
  Stock and stockholders.
    Stock ledger.
      Failure of commercial bank to exhibit, FI
        §3-309.
  Unauthorized representation as bank, FI §5-806.
Foreign banks.
  Affiliated corporation.
    Defined, FI §12-201.
  Automated teller machines, FI §1-405.
  Defined, FI §1-101.
  Definitions generally, FI §12-201.
  Fees.
    Permits.
      Power of commissioner to set, FI §12-211.
  Foreign banking corporation.
    Defined, FI §12-201.
  Holding companies, FI §12-201.
  Offices.
    Permits.
      Applications, FI §12-208.
      Fees.
        Power of commissioner to set, FI §12-211.
      Issuance, FI §12-209.
      Term and renewal, FI §12-210.
    Restrictions, FI §12-207.
Fraud and deceit.
  Derogatory statements prohibited, FI §5-805.
  Records.
    False statements, FI §5-803.
  Unauthorized representation as bank prohibited,
    FI §5-806.
Funds.
  Commissioner of financial regulation.
    Payment of money collected under article into
      general fund of state, FI §2-109.
  Common trust fund.
    Taxation.
      Exemption from taxation, TP §1-204.
Funds transfers.
  General provisions, CL §§4A-101 to 4A-507.
    See FUNDS TRANSFERS.
Garnishment.
  Adverse claim to money, etc., in hands of bank, FI
    §5-306.
  Joint accounts, CJ §11-603.
  Property held in trust, CJ §11-603.
Governor.
  Banking board.
    Appointment, FI §2-202.
  Commissioner of financial regulation.
    Appointment, FI §2-102.
  Emergencies, FI §5-707.
Guaranty fund.
  Savings banks. See within this heading, "Savings
    banks."
Guardian and ward.
  Fiduciary capacity. See within this heading,
    "Fiduciary capacity."
Hearings.
  Removal of officers or directors, FI §5-801.
  Unfair trade practices.
    Cease and desist orders, FI §5-808.

BANKS AND TRUST COMPANIES —Cont'd
Holding companies.
Bank holding companies.
Emergency interstate acquisitions, FI §§5-1101
to 5-1107. See within this heading,
"Emergency interstate acquisitions."
General provisions, FI §§5-901 to 5-910.
See BANK HOLDING COMPANIES.
Holidays. See within this heading, "Sundays and
holidays."
Incorporation.
Articles of incorporation.
Acknowledgment, FI §3-202.
Amendments.
Fees for filing.
Commercial bank, FI §3-213.
Savings bank, FI §4-210.
General provisions, FI §§3-213, 4-210.
Procedure, FI §§3-213, 4-210.
Approval by commissioner, FI §§3-203, 4-203.
Contents, FI §§3-202, 4-202.
Corporate status, FI §§3-205, 4-205.
Endorsement and return of articles, FI §3-203.
Execution, FI §§3-202, 4-202.
Fees.
Generally, FI §§3-203, 4-203.
Investigations.
By commissioner, FI §§3-203, 4-203.
Recordation, FI §§3-204, 4-204.
By commissioner, FI §3-203.
Rejection by commissioner, FI §§3-203, 4-203.
Signatures, FI §§3-202, 4-202.
Capital stock.
Debt instruments included in capital structure,
FI §3-209.
Minimum capital stock of commercial bank, FI
§3-209.
Certificate to do business, FI §3-208.
Commercial banks. See within this heading,
"Commercial banks."
Incorporators.
Investigation.
By commissioner, FI §§3-203, 4-203.
Qualifications, FI §§3-201, 3-202, 4-201, 4-202.
National banking association.
Conversion into commercial bank, FI §3-801.
Number of persons required, FI §§3-201, 4-201.
Perpetual existence.
Right of, FI §§3-205, 4-205.
Powers.
Enumeration of powers of corporation, FI
§§3-206, 4-206.
Savings banks. See within this heading, "Savings
banks."
Surplus.
Required, FI §3-209.
Industrial development financing authority,
83A §§5-901 to 5-933.
See INDUSTRIAL DEVELOPMENT FINANCING
AUTHORITY.
Inhabitants.
Defined, FI §3-101.
Injunctions.
Adverse claim to money, etc., in hands of bank, FI
§5-306.
Bank holding companies.
Actions by commissioner, FI §5-908.
Laws, rules or regulations relating to
commissioner's supervision, FI §5-809.
Practices injurious to public interest, FI §5-809.
Unfair trade practices, FI §5-809.

BANKS AND TRUST COMPANIES —Cont'd
Injunctions —Cont'd
Unsafe or unsound banking practices, FI §5-809.
Insolvency. See within this heading, "Bankruptcy
and insolvency."
Inspections.
Books, papers and accounts of banks open to
inspection, MD Const Art III §39.
Stock ledger, FI §3-309.
Installment loans.
See INSTALLMENT LOANS.
Insurance.
Deposit insurance fund corporation, FI §§10-101
to 10-121.
See DEPOSIT INSURANCE FUND
CORPORATION.
Premium financing.
General provisions, IN §§23-101 to 23-506.
See PREMIUM FINANCE COMPANIES.
Interest.
Christmas accounts.
Minimum interest, FI §5-302.
Savings accounts.
Information concerning interest on savings
accounts, FI §5-302.
Savings banks.
Certificates, FI §§4-209, 4-301.
Deposits, FI §4-303.
Payable to depositors, FI §§4-302, 4-303.
Short term savings accounts, FI §5-302.
Short term savings accounts, FI §5-302.
Vacation accounts.
Minimum interest, FI §5-302.
**International bank for reconstruction and
development.**
Investments.
Obligations, ET §15-106.
Investments.
General provisions.
See INVESTMENTS.
Lawful investments, ET §15-106.
Investment securities generally, CL §§8-101 to
8-511.
See INVESTMENT SECURITIES.
Judicial sales.
Real property.
Purchase of real property at judicial sales, FI
§5-503.
Labor, licensing and regulation department.
Banking board.
Appointment, FI §2-202.
Certificate to do business, FI §3-208.
Commissioner of financial regulation.
Appointment, FI §2-102.
Authority of secretary of licensing and
regulation, FI §2-105.
Deputy, FI §2-103.
Letters of credit.
General provisions, CL §§5-101 to 5-118.
See LETTERS OF CREDIT.
Libel and slander.
Derogatory statements.
Prohibited, FI §5-805.
Limitation of actions.
Certificates of deposit.
Action to enforce obligation of depository
institution to pay, FI §1-210.
Liquidation.
Receivers.
Proceedings when reserve falls below
requirements, FI §5-602.

BANKS AND TRUST COMPANIES —Cont'd
Liquidation —Cont'd
Stock and stockholders.
Preferred stock, FI §3-302.
Voluntary dissolution.
General provisions, FI §3-803.
Preference for property held in fiduciary
capacity, FI §§3-804, 5-615.
Loans.
Borrowers.
Financial information from certain borrowers,
FI §5-506.
Capital stock.
Loans on own capital stock prohibited, FI
§3-304.
Consumer loans.
Licensing provisions.
See CONSUMER LOANS.
Corporations.
Limitation on amount, FI §3-601.
Directors.
Restrictions on loans to directors, FI §5-512.
Engaging in additional banking activity or
banking-related service, FI §5-504.
Financial information from certain borrowers, FI
§5-506.
Liability of borrowers.
Not to exceed certain percentage of surplus and
paid in capital, FI §3-601.
Officers.
Restrictions on loans to officers, FI §5-512.
Partnerships.
Limitation on, FI §3-601.
Small loans.
Credit provisions.
See SMALL LOANS.
General licensing.
See SMALL LOANS.
Stock.
Made to pay for own capital stock prohibited, FI
§3-303.
Unfair trade practices, FI §5-807.
Lost instruments and records.
Liability of banking institution for loss of check,
FI §5-307.
Mail.
Defined, FI §1-101.
Management.
Directors. See within this heading, "Directors."
Merger, consolidation or transfer.
Agreement, FI §3-703.
Filing of approved agreement, FI §3-710.
Applicability of provisions, FI §3-702.
Appraisals.
Stock.
Expense of appraisal, FI §3-720.
Approval, FI §3-703.
By commissioner, FI §3-705.
By stockholders.
Amount due is debt of successor, FI §3-721.
Appraisal of fair value, FI §3-720.
Expense of appraisal, FI §3-708.
Fair market value.
Appraisal, FI §3-720.
Dissenters offered, FI §3-718.
Right to, FI §3-719.
Notice of meeting published, FI §3-708.
Right to fair value, FI §3-719.
Submission to stockholders, FI §3-708.
Successor may offer fair value, FI §3-718.
Vote required, FI §3-708.

BANKS AND TRUST COMPANIES —Cont'd
Merger, consolidation or transfer —Cont'd
Approval —Cont'd
Disapproval by commissioner, FI §3-707.
Standards for approval by commissioner, FI
§3-706.
Stockholders, FI §3-708.
When commissioner must act, FI §3-705.
Assets.
Nonconforming assets, FI §3-712.
Transfer.
Effect, FI §3-713.
Business.
Nonconforming business, FI §3-712.
Bylaws.
Successor in merger, FI §3-711.
Certificate of merger.
Issuance, FI §3-709.
Certificates.
Recording of documents, FI §3-710.
Charter.
Successor in merger, FI §3-711.
Constituent bank.
Defined, FI §3-701.
Continuation of corporate entity, FI §3-712.
Definitions, FI §3-701.
Disapproval by commissioner, FI §3-707.
Effective date of merger, FI §3-709.
Effect of consolidation or merger, FI §3-712.
Filing merger agreement.
Publication of notice of filing, FI §3-704.
Names.
Use of old names, FI §3-712.
Nonconforming business or assets, FI §3-712.
Notices.
Public notice of filing, FI §3-704.
Other-state bank as constituent bank, FI §3-702.
Powers and duties.
Generally, FI §3-712.
Public notice of filing, FI §3-704.
Recording of documents, FI §3-710.
References to bank in writing, FI §3-712.
Rights.
Generally, FI §3-712.
Savings banks, FI §4-701.
Scope of provisions, FI §3-702.
Termination of subtitle provisions and regulations,
FI §2-401.
Transfer of assets.
Effect, FI §3-713.
Valuation of assets, FI §3-712.
Approval by stockholders, FI §3-708.
Minors.
Deposits by.
Generally, FI §5-305.
Payment of money to minor, ET §13-501.
Deposit of money.
Distributable from trust, estate or other
source, ET §13-501.
Release, ET §13-501.
Recoveries in tort.
See MINORS.
Transfers to minors, ET §§13-301 to 13-324.
See MINORS.
Money transmission, FI §§12-401 to 12-431.
See MONEY TRANSMISSION.
Mortgages and deeds of trust.
General provisions.
See MORTGAGES AND DEEDS OF TRUST.
Mortgage lender law, FI §§11-501 to 11-524.
See MORTGAGE LENDERS.

BANKS AND TRUST COMPANIES —Cont'd
Mortgages and deeds of trust —Cont'd
Mortgage originators, FI §§11-601 to 11-618.
See MORTGAGE ORIGINATORS.
Secondary mortgage loans.
Credit provisions, CL §§12-401 to 12-415.
See MORTGAGES AND DEEDS OF TRUST.
Motor vehicles.
Registration plates.
Financial institutions, TR §13-623.
Multi-party accounts, FI §1-204.
Municipal area.
Defined, FI §1-101.
Mutual holding companies. See within this
heading, "Savings banks."
Name.
Merger or consolidation.
Use of old names, FI §3-712.
Restrictions, FI §§3-202, 4-202.
National banking associations.
Conversion, FI §§3-801, 3-802.
Defined, FI §1-101.
Reorganization as commercial banks, FI §3-801.
Reorganization of commercial bank as national
banking association, FI §3-802.
Negotiable instruments.
General provisions, CL §§3-101 to 3-605.
See NEGOTIABLE INSTRUMENTS.
Termination of provisions, FI §2-401.
Notes.
General provisions. See within this heading, "Debt
instruments."
Notices.
Automated teller machines.
Fees charged, FI §1-404.
Safety precautions, FI §1-402.
Bankruptcy and insolvency.
Impairment of capital.
Notice to board of directors, FI §5-602.
Branch banking.
Intention to open branch, FI §5-1005.
Commercial banks.
Plan of reorganization, FI §5-612.
Reserve requirements, FI §5-602.
Commissioner taking possession of banking
institution, FI §5-604.
Director placing banking institution under
commissioner, FI §5-601.
Dissolutions, FI §§3-802, 4-702.
Examination before certification, FI §3-212.
Merger, consolidation or transfer, FI §3-701.
Public notice of filing, FI §3-704.
Removal of director or officer.
Violation of law or unsafe or unsound practices,
FI §§5-801, 5-802.
Reorganization plan, FI §5-612.
Reserve requirements, FI §5-602.
Stockholders' meeting, FI §3-310.
Annual meeting, FI §3-310.
Merger, consolidation or transfer, FI §3-701.
Voluntary dissolution.
Commercial banks, FI §3-803.
Savings banks, FI §4-702.
Oaths.
Directors, FI §§3-404, 4-504, 5-504.
Stockholder before voting in elections, FI §3-311.
Officers and employees.
Election of officer, FI §3-411.
Loans.
Restrictions on loans to officers or employees, FI
§5-512.

BANKS AND TRUST COMPANIES —Cont'd
Officers and employees —Cont'd
Removal by commissioner of financial regulation.
Violation of law or unsafe or unsound practices,
FI §§5-801, 5-802.
Partnerships.
Loans.
Limitation on, FI §3-601.
Penalties.
Acceptance of deposits for insolvent institutions,
FI §5-804.
Derogatory statements, FI §5-805.
False records, FI §5-803.
Removal of director or officer for unsafe or
unsound practices, FI §5-801.
Unauthorized representation as bank, FI §5-806.
Unfair trade practices, FI §5-807.
Violations, FI §5-802.
**Permissible holder of trust and fiduciary
powers,** ET §14-110.
Perpetual existence.
Right of, FI §§3-205, 4-205.
Person.
Defined, FI §1-101.
Personal property.
Owner and lessor of personal property.
Acquired for use of a customer, FI §§3-206,
3-605.
Termination of provisions, FI §2-401.
When bank or trust company may own or lease
personal property, FI §3-605.
Political subdivision.
Defined, FI §1-101.
Powers.
Additional banking activity or bank-related
service, FI §5-504.
Enumeration of powers of corporation, FI §§3-206,
4-206.
Preemptive rights of stockholders, FI §3-316.
Preferred stock.
General provisions, FI §3-302.
Presumptions.
Stock ledger.
Presumptive evidence of facts, FI §3-309.
Priorities.
Debt instruments, FI §3-312.
Fiduciary capacity.
Preferences, FI §§3-804, 5-615.
Privileged communications.
Compliance review documents, FI §1-205.
Examination of bank by commissioner.
Information to be kept secret, FI §5-209.
Property taxes.
Exempt personal property, TP §7-221.
Property used in processing deposits or loans,
TP §7-221.1.
Publication.
Dissolution.
Notice of voluntary dissolution, FI §§3-803,
4-702.
Commercial banks, FI §3-803.
Savings banks, FI §4-702.
Notice of stockholder's meeting.
Annual meeting, FI §3-310.
Merger or consolidation, FI §3-708.
Reports to commissioner, FI §§5-206, 5-208.
National banking associations' reports, FI
§5-206.1.
Public works.
Sale of stocks, etc., held by state treasurer.
Authorized, MD Const Art XII §3.

BANKS AND TRUST COMPANIES —Cont'd
Quorum, FI §§3-410, 4-509.
Real estate appraisers.
Policies and procedures governing real estate
appraisal, FI §1-208.
Real estate brokers.
Termination of certain sections, FI §2-401.
Real property.
Commercial bank, FI §§3-206, 5-503.
Conveyance to institutions and satisfaction of
debts, FI §5-503.
Defined, FI §1-101.
Judicial sale.
Purchase, FI §5-503.
Limitations on bank, FI §5-503.
Loans on real estate, FI §5-503.
Purchasing, holding or conveying.
Generally, FI §5-503.
Transaction of business.
Necessary for convenient transaction, FI §5-503.
Receivers.
Bankruptcy and insolvency.
Resumption of business, FI §5-610.
Commissioner as receiver. See within this
heading, "Commissioner of financial
regulation."
Federal banking authorities.
Appointment as receiver for institution in
commissioner's possession, FI §5-605.
Rights of, FI §5-614.
Fiduciary capacity. See within this heading,
"Fiduciary capacity."
Reorganization of bank in receivership. See within
this heading, "Commissioner of financial
regulation."
Reserves.
Proceedings when capital account impaired, FI
§5-602.
Recordation.
Articles of incorporation.
Commercial banks, FI §§3-203, 3-204.
Savings banks, FI §§4-203, 4-204.
Certificates of consolidation, merger or transfer,
FI §3-710.
Conversion, FI §3-801.
Merger agreement, FI §3-710.
Trust companies.
Articles of incorporation, FI §3-204.
Records.
Access to records, FI §5-201.
Confidential financial records. See within this
heading, "Confidential financial records."
Fraud and deceit.
False statements, FI §5-803.
Inspection.
Books, papers and accounts open to inspection,
MD Const Art III §39.
Remote locations.
Off-premises customer-bank communication
terminals.
Electronic terminals, FI §12-201.
Reorganization.
Commissioner of financial regulation.
When commissioner may take charge.
Banking institutions, FI §5-601.
Commercial banks, FI §5-602.
Receivers. See within this heading,
"Commissioner of financial regulation."
Reports.
Bank holding companies, FI §5-907.
Forms for reports, FI §5-904.

BANKS AND TRUST COMPANIES —Cont'd
Reports —Cont'd
Branch banking.
Condition and income, FI §5-1011.
Child support enforcement administration, FL
§10-108.2.
Commissioner's report to court, FI §5-609.
Emergency interstate acquisitions, FI §5-1103.
Receivers.
Report of commissioner to court, FI §5-609.
Savings banks.
Filing fees, CA §1-203.
Disposition, TP §2-220.
Taxation.
Requests for information to assist enforcement,
TG §13-804.
To commissioner, FI §5-206.
Electronic form submission, FI §5-206.
National banking associations' reports, FI
§5-206.1.
Penalty for failure to make, FI §5-208.
Regular reports, FI §5-206.
Special reports on stock, FI §§3-314, 3-315,
5-207.
Voting stock.
Contents of reports, FI §§3-314, 3-315.
Penalty for failure to make report, FI §§3-314,
3-315.
Violations of officers, FI §§5-801, 5-802.
Required business days, FI §5-703.
Reserves.
Proceeding when reserve falls below
requirements, FI §5-602.
Requirements.
Generally, FI §3-607.
Proceedings when reserve falls below
requirements, FI §5-602.
Rules and regulations, FI §3-607.
Retail credit accounts law.
Cease and desist order not to apply to, CL
§12-514.
Rules and regulations.
Affiliates, FI §5-403.
Bank holding companies, FI §5-909.
Commissioner of financial regulation, FI §2-105.1.
Reserves, FI §3-607.
Unfair trade practices, FI §5-807.
Safe-deposit boxes.
Abandoned property disposition, CL §§17-101 to
17-326.
See ABANDONED PROPERTY DISPOSITION.
Adverse claim to money, etc., in hands of bank, FI
§5-306.
Savings banks, FI §4-206.
Safe-deposit companies.
See SAFE-DEPOSIT COMPANIES.
Sales finance companies.
See SALES.
Saturdays, FI §5-706.
Savings and loan associations.
Emergency interstate acquisitions, FI §§5-1101 to
5-1107. See within this heading, "Emergency
interstate acquisitions."
General provisions.
See SAVINGS AND LOAN ASSOCIATIONS.
Savings banks.
Acting as depository of government funds, FI
§4-206.
Annual meeting of members, FI §4-402.
Appeals.
Termination of provisions, FI §2-401.

BANKS AND TRUST COMPANIES —Cont'd
Savings banks —Cont'd
  Articles of incorporation. See within this
    subheading, "Incorporation."
  Bond premiums, FI §4-303.
  Borrowing.
    Limitations on borrowing, FI §4-603.
    Procedure, FI §§4-206, 4-603.
  Branches, FI §4-208.
  Bylaws, FI §4-402.
    Permissible bylaws, FI §4-601.
  Capital stock.
    Prohibitions, FI §4-401.
  Certificate of authority, FI §4-207.
  Charter amendments, FI §4-210.
  Corporate status.
    Filing of articles of incorporation, FI §4-205.
  Defined, FI §§4-101, 5-101.
  Deposits.
    Abandoned property disposition, CL §§17-101 to
      17-326.
      See ABANDONED PROPERTY
        DISPOSITION.
    Investment, FI §4-206.
    Minors, FI §5-305.
    Pledging collateral for public funds, FI §4-206.
    Receiving, FI §4-206.
    Terms, FI §5-302.
    Withdrawal, FI §§4-206, 4-601.
  Directors.
    Attendance at board meetings, FI §4-507.
    Election, FI §4-505.
    Management of savings bank, FI §4-501.
    Meetings.
      Attendance at board meetings, FI §4-507.
    Number of directors, FI §4-502.
    Oath of directors, FI §4-504.
    Qualifications of directors, FI §4-503.
    Quorum of directors, FI §4-509.
    Terms of office, FI §4-505.
    Vacancies, FI §4-508.
  Dissolution.
    Voluntary dissolution, FI §4-702.
  Dividends.
    Cash dividends.
      When declared, FI §3-307.
  Dormant accounts.
    Charges or cessation of benefits on, CL
      §17-308.1.
    Disposition of abandoned property.
      See ABANDONED PROPERTY
        DISPOSITION.
  Fees.
    Filing annual reports, CA §1-203.
    Disposition, TP §2-220.
  Formation.
    Incorporators, FI §4-201.
  General powers, FI §4-206.
  Guaranty fund.
    Additions to fund, FI §4-301.
    Amount, FI §4-302.
    Beginning business.
      Fund payments before, FI §4-209.
    Bond premiums, FI §4-303.
    Branches.
      Abandonment, FI §4-302.
      Minimum fund, FI §4-208.
    Initial fund, FI §4-209.
      Requirements generally, FI §4-208.
    Interest on deposits, FI §4-303.
      Generally, FI §4-303.

BANKS AND TRUST COMPANIES —Cont'd
Savings banks —Cont'd
  Guaranty fund —Cont'd
    Interest on deposits —Cont'd
      Limitations, FI §4-302.
    Limitations on certificate payments, FI §4-301.
    Limitations on interest of deposits, FI §4-302.
    Limitations on reduction, FI §4-302.
    Maintenance of fund, FI §4-302.
    Minimum fund, FI §4-208.
    Payments before beginning business, FI §4-209.
    Reduction of excess, FI §4-302.
    Reduction on abandonment of branch, FI
      §4-302.
  Holding companies.
    Mutual holding companies. See within this
      subheading, "Mutual holding companies."
  Incorporation.
    Articles of incorporation, FI §4-202.
      Acknowledgments, FI §4-202.
      Amendments.
        Fees for filing, FI §4-210.
        Procedure, FI §4-210.
      Endorsement and return of articles, FI
        §4-203.
      Execution and contents, FI §4-202.
      Filing for examination and approval, FI
        §4-203.
      Filing for record, FI §4-204.
      Signatures, FI §4-202.
    Certification before beginning business, FI
      §4-207.
    Charter amendments, FI §4-210.
    Corporate status, FI §4-205.
    Formation in general, FI §4-201.
    Fund payments before beginning business, FI
      §4-209.
    General powers, FI §4-206.
    Initial guaranty fund requirements, FI §4-208.
    Perpetual existence, FI §4-205.
  Incorporators.
    Citizenship, FI §4-201.
  Individual retirement account.
    Acting as trustee under, FI §§4-206, 4-604.
  Interest.
    Certificates, FI §§4-209, 4-301.
    Deposits, FI §4-303.
    Payable to depositors, FI §§4-302, 4-303.
    Short term savings accounts, FI §5-302.
  Limitations on borrowing, FI §4-603.
  Loans.
    Borrowing procedure, FI §4-206.
  Meetings.
    Annual meeting of members, FI §4-402.
    Board of directors, FI §4-507.
  Members.
    Annual meeting, FI §4-402.
    Capital stock prohibited, FI §4-401.
  Merger or consolidation, FI §4-701.
  Mutual holding companies.
    Acquisition of assets or stock, FI §4-804.
    Applicability of federal bank holding company
      act of 1956, FI §4-805.
    Capital stock, FI §4-805.1.
    Deposits, FI §4-804.
    Records.
      Access by examiner, FI §5-210.
    Reorganization of savings bank to become
      mutual holding company, FI §4-802.
      Application for approval of reorganization, FI
        §§4-802, 4-803.

BANKS AND TRUST COMPANIES —Cont'd
Savings banks —Cont'd
  Mutual holding companies —Cont'd
    Reorganization of savings bank to become
        mutual holding company —Cont'd
      Authorized, FI §4-802.
      Disposition of stock of subsidiary savings
          bank or savings and loan association, FI
          §4-804.
      Investigation of proposed articles, FI §4-803.
      Plan of reorganization, FI §4-802.
      Powers of mutual holding company after
          reorganization, FI §4-804.
      Regulations.
        Adoption, FI §4-806.
      Retention of assets, FI §4-804.
      "Savings and loan association" defined, FI
          §4-801.
      Subject to provisions of subtitles 4, 5 and 7, FI
          §4-807.
  Mutual savings banks.
    Acting as trustee under employee benefit plan
        or individual retirement account, FI §4-604.
  Permissible holder of trust and fiduciary powers,
      ET §14-110.
  Powers generally, FI §4-206.
  Reports.
    Filing fees, CA §1-203.
      Disposition, TP §2-220.
  Retirement plan.
    Acting as trustee under employee benefit plan
        or individual retirement account, FI §4-604.
  Safe-deposit boxes, FI §4-206.
  Stock and stockholders.
    General provisions. See within this heading,
        "Stock and stockholders."
  Subsidiary savings banks.
    Annual meeting of stockholders, FI §4-402.
    Applicability of laws regulating savings banks,
        FI §4-905.
    Articles of incorporation, FI §§4-902, 4-903.
    Certificate of authority.
      Issuance or denial, FI §4-907.
    Corporations.
      When subsidiary savings banks become
          corporation, FI §4-904.
    Directors.
      Election, FI §4-505.
      Vacancies, FI §4-508.
    Dissolution, FI §4-910.
    Dividends.
      Declaration of cash dividends, FI §4-908.
    Evaluation of assets, FI §4-909.
    Examination of condition, FI §4-907.
    Incorporators, FI §4-901.
    Meetings.
      Annual meeting of stockholders, FI §4-402.
    Minimum capital requirements, FI §4-902.
    Notice of compliance, FI §4-907.
    Powers and duties.
      Generally, FI §4-905.
    Records.
      Access by examiner, FI §5-210.
    Requirements for doing business, FI §4-906.
    Right to perpetual existence, FI §4-904.
    Stock, FI §4-905.
  Termination of provisions of sections, FI §2-401.
  Trustee under federal retirement act, FI §4-206.
  Voluntary dissolution, FI §4-702.
  Withdrawal, FI §4-206.

BANKS AND TRUST COMPANIES —Cont'd
Savings department.
  Permitted, FI §5-301.
Seals.
  Commissioner.
    Filed with secretary of state, FI §2-106.
Secured transactions.
  Definition of bank, CL §9-102.
  Rights of banks.
    Control agreement.
      Refusal to enter into or disclose existence of,
          CL §9-342.
  Security interests in deposit accounts.
    Control agreements.
      Rights of banks with respect to agreements,
          CL §9-342.
    Perfection and priority.
      Law governing, CL §9-304.
      Rules of priority, CL §9-327.
    Rights and duties of banks, CL §9-341.
    Set-off or recoupment, CL §9-340.
    Transfer of funds from deposit account, CL
        §9-332.
Securities.
  Depositing securities as agent or custodian for
      fiduciaries, ET §15-104.
  Investment securities, CL §§8-101 to 8-511.
    See INVESTMENT SECURITIES.
  Own capital stock prohibited, FI §3-304.
Services.
  Additional banking activity or bank-related
      service.
    Authorization, FI §5-504.
  Bank service corporation. See within this heading,
      "Bank service corporations."
  Charges.
    Service charges.
      Prohibited where withdrawals restricted, FI
          §5-308.
  Corporation. See within this heading, "Bank
      service corporations."
Short term savings accounts.
  Minimum interest, FI §5-302.
Signatures.
  Articles of incorporation, FI §§3-202, 4-202.
Small loans.
  Consumer loans.
    See CONSUMER LOANS.
State.
  Defined, FI §1-101.
  Sale of state's interest in banking corporations,
      MD Const Art XII §3.
State banks.
  Incorporation. See within this heading,
      "Incorporation."
  Merger or consolidation. See within this heading,
      "Merger, consolidation or transfer."
State treasurer.
  Stock ownership and compensation from
      prohibited, SG §5-103.
State treasury.
  Banking services.
    Agreements, SF §6-229.
  Depositaries, SF §§6-205 to 6-210.
    See STATE TREASURY.
Stock and stockholders.
  Acquisitions.
    Defined, FI §3-314.
  Bank holding companies.
    General provisions, FI §§5-901 to 5-910.
      See BANK HOLDING COMPANIES.

BANKS AND TRUST COMPANIES —Cont'd
Stock and stockholders —Cont'd
Capital stock.
Debt instruments included in capital structures, FI §§3-209, 3-310.
Defined, FI §§3-101, 5-101.
Examination as to payment, FI §3-212.
Increase, FI §3-301.
Liability of borrowers not to exceed certain percentage of unimpaired capital stock, FI §3-601.
Minimum capital requirements, FI §§3-209, 3-310.
Minimum par value of share, FI §3-202.
Payments before beginning business, FI §3-211.
Prohibited, FI §4-401.
Requirements, FI §§3-209, 3-310.
When prohibited, FI §4-401.
Convertible stock.
Preferred stock, FI §3-302.
Dissolution.
Voluntary dissolution.
Procedure, FI §3-803.
Dividends.
Preferred stock, FI §3-302.
Stock dividends, FI §3-308.
Evidence.
Stock ledger, FI §3-309.
Examination by commissioner, FI §3-212.
Issuance.
Preferred stock, FI §3-302.
Ledger, FI §3-309.
Liability.
Cash dividends, FI §3-307.
Liquidation.
Preferred stock, FI §3-302.
Loans.
Subscriptions.
Not to be made to pay for subscription to own stock, FI §3-303.
When loans on own capital stock or purchase of same prohibited, FI §3-304.
Meetings.
Annual meeting, FI §3-310.
Merger or consolidation.
Valuation of stock, FI §3-708.
Notice.
Merger, consolidation or transfer, FI §3-708.
Notice of annual meeting of stockholders, FI §3-310.
Statement in notice as to dissenter's right to payment, FI §3-708.
Merger or consolidation.
Amount due is debt of successor, FI §3-721.
Appraisal of fair value, FI §3-720.
Approval by stockholders, FI §3-708.
Fair value.
Appraisal, FI §3-720.
Right to, FI §3-719.
Rights of dissenters, FI §3-708.
Successor may offer fair value, FI §3-718.
National banking associations.
Conversion into commercial bank, FI §3-801.
No capital stock, FI §4-401.
Oaths.
Owner of stock before voting in elections, FI §3-311.
Ownership by commissioner or employees prohibited, FI §2-111.
Own stock.
Purchase of own stock by bank prohibited, FI §3-304.

BANKS AND TRUST COMPANIES —Cont'd
Stock and stockholders —Cont'd
Par value of shares.
Minimum par value, FI §3-202.
Payment.
Before commencement of business, FI §3-211.
Personal liability of stockholders.
Diminishing, FI §§3-305, 3-308.
Preemptive rights, FI §3-316.
Preferred stock.
General provisions, FI §3-302.
Purchase of own stock by bank.
Prohibited, FI §3-304.
Reports to commissioner, FI §§3-314, 3-315.
Retirement.
Preferred stock, FI §3-302.
Stock ledger.
Commissioner.
Duties as to stock ledger, FI §3-309.
Evidence.
Presumptive evidence of facts, FI §3-309.
Inspection, FI §3-309.
Penalty for failure to exhibit, FI §3-309.
Required, FI §3-309.
Subscriptions.
Loans not to be made to pay for own stock, FI §3-303.
Original subscription, FI §3-301.
Subsidiary savings banks, FI §4-905.
Valuation of stock.
Amount due is debt of successor, FI §3-721.
Fair value.
Appraisal, FI §3-720.
Right to, FI §3-719.
Successor may offer fair value, FI §3-718.
Merger or consolidation, FI §3-708.
Voting.
Merger or consolidation, FI §3-708.
What is construed fair value, FI §3-720.
Voting.
Approval of commissioner.
Transactions affecting voting stock, FI §3-314.
General provisions, FI §§3-301, 3-302.
Oath of owner of stock before voting in elections, FI §3-311.
Proxy, FI §3-301.
Valuation of stock.
Merger or consolidation, FI §3-708.
Subsidiary savings banks. See within this heading, "Savings banks."
Successor.
Defined, FI §3-701.
Sundays and holidays.
Action by directors, FI §5-708.
Closing on Sundays, FI §5-704.
Definitions, FI §5-701.
Directors.
Action by directors, FI §5-708.
Emergencies, FI §5-707.
Federal holiday, FI §5-701.
Legal holidays, FI §5-705.
Mandatory bank holidays, FI §5-705.
Optional bank holiday, FI §§5-701, 5-705.
Required business days, FI §5-703.
Scope of subtitle, FI §5-702.
Thanksgiving day, FI §5-705.
Veterans day, FI §5-705.
Washington's birthday, FI §5-705.
Surplus.
Branches, FI §3-209.

BANKS AND TRUST COMPANIES —Cont'd
Surplus —Cont'd
Liability of borrowers not to exceed certain
    percentage of surplus, FI §3-601.
Losses, FI §3-306.
Maintenance of surplus, FI §3-306.
Minimum requirements for incorporation, FI
    §3-209.
Stock dividends.
    Not declared until surplus sufficient, FI §3-305.
    Surplus requirements, FI §3-308.
Transfer to surplus, FI §§3-305, 3-308.
Taxation.
Common trust fund.
    Exemption from taxation, TP §1-204.
Exemptions.
    Common trust fund, TP §1-204.
Information or assistance for enforcement
    purposes, TG §13-804.
Termination of certain sections.
Banking board, FI §2-402.
Commissioner, FI §2-401.
Thanksgiving day.
Closing, FI §5-705.
Transfers of assets. See within this heading,
    "Merger, consolidation or transfer."
Transfers to minors act, ET §§13-301 to 13-324.
See MINORS.
Transfer to surplus, FI §3-305.
Trust companies.
Common trust fund.
    Taxation.
        Exemption from taxation, TP §1-204.
Defined, ET §§1-101, 13-101.
Joint and several liability of trust company
    affiliates, ET §15-113.
Trusts and trustees.
Fiduciaries generally, ET §§15-201 to 15-211.
    See FIDUCIARIES.
Fiduciary capacity. See within this heading,
    "Fiduciary capacity."
General provisions.
    See TRUSTS AND TRUSTEES.
Unclaimed property.
Abandoned property disposition, CL §§17-101 to
    17-326.
    See ABANDONED PROPERTY DISPOSITION.
Unfair trade practices, FI §5-807.
Advertising, FI §5-807.
Cease and desist orders, FI §5-808.
Credit, FI §5-807.
Injunctions, FI §5-809.
Loans, FI §5-807.
Penalties, FI §5-807.
Prohibited practices, FI §5-807.
Rules and regulations, FI §5-807.
Unions.
Credit unions.
    See CREDIT UNIONS.
Vacation accounts.
Minimum interest, FI §5-302.
Verification.
Procedure and requirements generally, FI §1-202.
Veterans day.
Closing, FI §5-705.
Violations.
Penalties, FI §5-802.
Washington's birthday.
Closing, FI §5-705.
Workers' compensation.
Compliance with workers' compensation laws, FI
    §1-203.

BANNEKER-DOUGLASS MUSEUM.
**African American history and culture
    commission.**
Operation, SF §5A-207.

BAPTIST CHURCH.
Corporations.
Religious corporations generally, CA §§5-301 to
    5-313.
    See RELIGION.

BAR.
Admissions to bar.
General provisions.
    See ATTORNEYS AT LAW.
Libraries.
See LIBRARIES.

BARBEQUE.
Prince George's county.
Benefit performance by qualified organization, CR
    §§13-1901 to 13-1907.

BARBEQUE GRILLS.
Fires and fire protection.
Restrictions on use, PS §9-1001.

BARBERS.
Appeals.
State board of barbers.
    Judicial review of board, BOP §4-208.
Apprentices.
Barbershops.
    Number of apprentices allowed, BOP §4-507.
    Practice limitations, BOP §4-404.
    Supervision, BOP §§4-507, 4-509.
Definition of "apprentice barber," BOP §4-101.
Prohibited acts.
    Serving apprenticeship without registration,
        BOP §4-603.
Registration, BOP §§4-401 to 4-408. See within
    this heading, "Registration."
Barbershops.
Apprentice barbers.
    Number allowed, BOP §4-507.
    Supervision, BOP §§4-507, 4-509.
Cosmetology.
    Practice in barbershop, BOP §4-508.
Defined, BOP §4-101.
Inspections, BOP §4-512.
Permits.
    Pre-opening inspection.
        Required, BOP §4-502.
Integration with other businesses, BOP §4-508.
Journey barbers.
    Number allowed, BOP §4-507.
Licenses.
    Display of licenses, BOP §4-313.
Misrepresentation of establishment as, BOP
    §4-604.
Montgomery county.
    Restriction on days of operation, BOP §4-606.
Notices.
    Permits.
        Renewal notice, BOP §4-506.
Permits, BOP §§4-501 to 4-508. See within this
    heading, "Permits."
Practice of barbering outside barbershop or beauty
    salon, BOP §4-605.
Shampoo area.
    Separate shampoo area authorized, BOP §4-507.
Sinks, BOP §4-507.
Board, BOP §§4-201 to 4-209. See within this
    heading, "State board of barbers."

BARBERS —Cont'd
Certification concerning licensee, permit holder or registrant, BOP §4-205.
Citation of act.
Short title, BOP §4-701.
Citations for violations, BOP §4-608.
Complaints against licensees, BOP §4-314.
Barbershops, BOP §4-513.
Correction of sanitary practice violations.
Opportunity to correct, BOP §4-314.
Barbershops, BOP §4-513.
Criminal penalty, BOP §4-607.
Definitions, BOP §4-101.
Examinations.
Licenses. See within this heading, "Licenses."
Fees.
Certification concerning licensee, permit holder or registrant, BOP §4-205.
Disposition of money collected, BOP §4-207.
Licenses, BOP §4-308.
Certification concerning licensee, BOP §4-205.
Examination fee, BOP §4-303.
Journey barbers, BOP §4-308.
Renewal, BOP §4-310.
Permits.
Barbershop permits.
Application fees, BOP §4-503.
Inspections.
Pre-opening inspection, BOP §4-503.
Renewal fee, BOP §4-506.
State board of barbers.
Duty to establish fees, BOP §4-206.
Fines, BOP §4-607.
Fraud.
Licenses.
Denial, revocation or suspension, or reprimand of licensee.
Grounds, BOP §4-314.
Permits.
Denial, revocation or suspension, or reprimand of permit holder.
Grounds, BOP §4-513.
Registration.
Students and apprentice barbers.
Denial, revocation or suspension.
Grounds, BOP §4-407.
Hearings.
Licenses.
Denial, suspension or revocation, or reprimand of licensee, BOP §4-315.
Permits.
Denial, revocation or suspension, or reprimand of permit holder, BOP §4-514.
Registration.
Student and apprentice barbers.
Denial, revocation or suspension, BOP §4-408.
Inspections.
Barbershops, BOP §4-512.
Permits.
Pre-opening inspection.
Required, BOP §4-502.
Citations for violations, BOP §4-608.
Fees, BOP §§4-503, 4-512.
Schools, BOP §4-512.
Licenses.
Applications, BOP §4-303.
Barbershops.
Display of licenses, BOP §4-313.
Certification of licensee, BOP §4-205.
Defined, BOP §4-101.

BARBERS —Cont'd
Licenses —Cont'd
Denial.
Grounds, BOP §4-314.
Hearings, BOP §4-315.
Procedure, BOP §4-314.
Display, BOP §4-313.
Examinations, BOP §4-304.
Notice, BOP §4-304.
Qualifications of applicants, BOP §4-302.
Testing service.
Used to administer examinations, BOP §4-304.1.
Waiver of requirement.
Applicant licensed in another state, BOP §4-306.
Applicant licensed in foreign country, BOP §4-307.
Expiration, BOP §4-310.
Reinstatement, BOP §4-312.
Fees, BOP §4-308.
Certification of licensee, BOP §4-205.
Examination fee, BOP §4-303.
Journey barbers, BOP §4-308.
Renewal, BOP §4-310.
Hearings.
Denial, suspension or revocation, or reprimand of licensee, BOP §4-315.
Issuance, BOP §4-308.
Journey barbers.
Fees, BOP §4-308.
Notices.
Denial, revocation or suspension, or reprimand of licensee.
Hearings, BOP §4-315.
Examinations, BOP §4-304.
Issuance.
Notice to qualified applicant, BOP §4-308.
Practice of barbering.
Qualifications of applicants, BOP §4-302.
Required, BOP §4-301.
Scope of licenses, BOP §4-309.
Unlicensed practice.
Prohibited, BOP §4-601.
Practice without license.
Student in public school, BOP §4-301.2.
Student in school of barbering, BOP §4-301.1.
Qualifications of applicants.
License to practice, BOP §4-302.
Reciprocity.
Waiver of requirements, BOP §4-305.
Reinstatement of expired licenses, BOP §4-312.
Renewal, BOP §4-310.
Reprimand of licensee.
Grounds, BOP §4-314.
Hearings, BOP §4-315.
Procedure, BOP §4-314.
Revocation or suspension.
Grounds, BOP §4-314.
Hearings, BOP §4-315.
Procedure, BOP §4-314.
Substitute barber teacher license, BOP §4-314.
Scope, BOP §4-309.
Substitute barber teacher license, BOP §4-314.
Teaching.
Required, BOP §4-301.
Substitute barber teacher license, BOP §4-314.
Term, BOP §4-310.
Testing service.
Used to administer examinations, BOP §4-304.1.

BARBERS —Cont'd
Licenses —Cont'd
Waiver of requirements.
Examination requirement, BOP §§4-306, 4-307.
Reciprocity waiver, BOP §4-305.
Master barbers.
Defined, BOP §4-101.
Misdemeanors.
Violations of provisions, BOP §4-607.
Montgomery county.
Barbershops.
Restriction on days of operation, BOP §4-606.
Notices.
Barbershops.
Permits.
Renewal notice, BOP §4-506.
Licenses.
Denial, revocation or suspension, or reprimand
of licensee.
Hearings, BOP §4-315.
Examinations, BOP §4-304.
Issuance.
Notice to qualified applicant, BOP §4-308.
Permits.
Denial, revocation or suspension, or reprimand
of permit holder.
Hearings, BOP §4-514.
Registration.
Apprentice barbers.
Renewal notice, BOP §4-405.
Denial, revocation or suspension of registration.
Hearings, BOP §4-408.
Oaths.
Licenses.
Denial, revocation or suspension, or reprimand
of licensee.
Administration of oaths in connection with
proceedings, BOP §4-315.
Permits.
Denial, revocation or suspension, or reprimand
of permit holder.
Administration of oaths in connection with
proceedings, BOP §4-514.
Registration.
Students and apprentice barbers.
Denial, revocation or suspension.
Administration of oaths in connection with
proceedings, BOP §4-408.
State board of barbers.
Oath of office of members, BOP §4-202.
Penalties.
Permits.
Violations of provisions, BOP §§4-513, 4-514.
Regulations.
Violations, BOP §4-511.
Revocation or suspension of license.
Financial penalty in addition to or in lieu of,
BOP §4-314.
Violations of provisions, BOP §4-607.
Permits.
Barbershop permits.
Applications, BOP §4-503.
Issuance to applicants, BOP §4-504.
Qualifications of applicants, BOP §4-502.
Defined, BOP §4-101.
Denial, BOP §§4-513, 4-514.
Effect, BOP §4-505.
Expiration, BOP §4-506.
Reinstatement of expired permits, BOP
§4-506.1.

BARBERS —Cont'd
Permits —Cont'd
Barbershop permits —Cont'd
Fees.
Application fees, BOP §4-503.
Inspections.
Pre-opening inspection, BOP §4-503.
Renewal fee, BOP §4-506.
Inspections.
Pre-opening inspection.
Fee, BOP §4-503.
Required, BOP §4-502.
Issuance, BOP §4-504.
Notices.
Renewal notice, BOP §4-506.
Operating barbershop without permit.
Prohibited, BOP §4-602.
Qualifications of applicants, BOP §4-502.
Reinstatement of expired permits, BOP
§4-506.1.
Renewal, BOP §4-506.
Reprimand of permit holder, BOP §§4-513,
4-514.
Required, BOP §4-501.
Revocation or suspension, BOP §§4-513, 4-514.
Scope, BOP §4-505.
Separate permit for each shop, BOP §4-501.
Term, BOP §4-506.
Certification concerning permit holder, BOP
§4-205.
Integration with other business as, BOP §4-508.
Operation of barbershops, BOP §4-507.
Penalties for violations, BOP §§4-513, 4-514.
School permits.
Defined, BOP §4-101.
Denial, BOP §§4-513, 4-514.
Reprimand of permit holder, BOP §§4-513,
4-514.
Revocation or suspension, BOP §§4-513, 4-514.
Practice of barbering.
Defined, BOP §4-101.
Licenses.
Generally. See within this heading, "Licenses."
Misrepresentation of authorization to practice,
BOP §4-604.
Outside barbershop or beauty salon, BOP §4-605.
Scope of provisions, BOP §4-102.
Reciprocity.
Licenses.
Waiver of requirements, BOP §4-305.
Registration.
Applications, BOP §4-402.
Apprentice barbers, BOP §4-404.
Display of certificate, BOP §4-406.
Renewal of registration, BOP §4-405.
Required, BOP §4-401.
Serving apprenticeship without registration.
Prohibited, BOP §4-603.
Term of registration, BOP §4-405.
Certificate of registration.
Display.
Apprentice barber, BOP §4-406.
Issuance, BOP §4-403.
Denial.
Grounds, BOP §4-407.
Hearings, BOP §4-408.
Issuance of certificate, BOP §4-403.
Notices.
Apprentice barbers.
Renewal notice, BOP §4-405.

BARBERS —Cont'd
Registration —Cont'd
Notices —Cont'd
Denial, revocation or suspension of registration.
Hearings, BOP §4-408.
Required, BOP §4-401.
Revocation or suspension.
Grounds, BOP §4-407.
Hearings, BOP §4-408.
Students.
Apprentice barber registration, BOP §4-404.
Required, BOP §4-401.
Rules and regulations.
Schools, BOP §4-511.
Termination of regulations adopted under
provisions, BOP §4-702.
Sanitary practice violations.
Opportunity to correct, BOP §4-314.
Barbershops, BOP §4-513.
Schools.
Inspections, BOP §4-512.
Licenses.
Teaching licenses. See within this heading,
"Licenses."
Misrepresentation of establishment as, BOP
§4-604.
Permits. See within this heading, "Permits."
Rules and regulations, BOP §4-511.
Students.
Number of students.
Restrictions, BOP §4-511.
Practice without license, BOP §4-301.1.
Registration, BOP §§4-401, 4-404.
Teachers.
Licenses. See within this heading, "Licenses."
Misrepresentation of authorization to teach,
BOP §4-604.
Scope of provisions, BOP §4-102.
Service of citations for violations, BOP §4-608.
Service of complaints against licensees, BOP
§4-314.
Barbershops, BOP §4-513.
Short title of act, BOP §4-701.
State board of barbers.
Appeals.
Judicial review of board, BOP §4-208.
Appointment of members, BOP §4-202.
Certification concerning licensee, permit holder or
registrant, BOP §4-205.
Compensation of members, BOP §4-204.
Composition, BOP §4-202.
Creation, BOP §4-201.
Definition of "board," BOP §4-101.
Disposition of money collected, BOP §4-207.
Duties, BOP §4-206.
Established, BOP §4-201.
Expenses of members.
Reimbursement, BOP §4-204.
Fees.
Duty to establish fees, BOP §4-206.
Judicial review of decisions, BOP §4-208.
Meetings, BOP §4-204.
Oath of office of members, BOP §4-202.
Officers, BOP §4-203.
Appointment, BOP §4-203.
Powers, BOP §4-206.
Secretary of labor, licensing and regulation
department.
Exercise of powers subject to authority of,
BOP §4-209.
Program evaluation act, SG §8-403.

BARBERS —Cont'd
State board of barbers —Cont'd
Qualifications of members, BOP §4-202.
Quorum, BOP §4-204.
Removal of members, BOP §4-202.
Secretary of labor, licensing and regulation
department.
Authority of secretary, BOP §4-209.
Staff, BOP §4-204.
Terms of members, BOP §4-202.
Vacancies, BOP §4-202.
Termination of provisions, BOP §4-702.
Title of act.
Short title, BOP §4-701.
Unemployment compensation.
Certain barbers exempt from covered
employment, LE §8-206.

BARBITURATES.
See CONTROLLED DANGEROUS SUBSTANCES.

BARBITURIC ACID.
Controlled dangerous substances.
Depressant or stimulant drug for purposes of title,
CR §5-401.
Generally, CR §§5-101 to 5-1101.
See CONTROLLED DANGEROUS
SUBSTANCES.

BARLEY.
Grain.
General provisions.
See GRAIN.

BARNS.
Arson and burning, CR §§6-101 to 6-111.
Barn preservation fund, SF §5A-403.
Charles county.
Tobacco barns.
Property tax credit against certain property
formerly used solely as, TP §9-310.
Horse industry board.
Sales barns, defined, AG §2-701.
**Maryland advisory committee on historic
agricultural structure preservation,** SF
§§5A-401 to 5A-406.
Tobacco barns.
Property tax credit for property used as tobacco
barn, TP §9-212.
Charles county, TP §9-310.

BARRATRY.
Attorneys at law, BOP §10-604.
Insurance fraud, IN §§27-407, 27-408.

**BARRICADE AND HOSTAGE
COMMUNICATIONS SPECIALISTS,** CJ
§10-413.

BARS.
Strobe light warning, HG §24-206.

BASEBALL.
Alcoholic beverages.
Harford county.
Stadium on-sale license, limitations, 2B
§8-213.1.
Camden yards.
Restrictions, FI §13-715.3.
Sundays.
Regulations of sports.
See SUNDAYS AND HOLIDAYS.

BASKETS.
Returnable containers and textiles.
Registration, prohibited acts, BR §§19-301 to
19-307.

BASS.
General provisions.
See FISH AND FISHERIES.
Striped bass.
Rockfish.
See FISH AND FISHERIES.

BASTARDS.
Acknowledgment of paternity, ET §1-208.
Debts.
Imprisonment for delinquent support payment not imprisonment for debt, MD Const Art III §38.
Decedents' estates.
Determining relationship.
Illegitimate children, ET §1-208.
Inheritance from illegitimate person, ET §3-108.
Legitimation of issue.
Acknowledgment of paternity, ET §1-208.
Pretermitted child and issue.
General provisions, ET §§3-301 to 3-303.
See DECEDENTS' ESTATES.
Sentence and punishment.
Imprisonment for delinquent support payment not imprisonment for debt, MD Const Art III §38.
Support of child.
Imprisonment for delinquent support payment not imprisonment for debt, MD Const Art III §38.
Vital records.
Legitimation and paternity determination.
New birth certificates, HG §4-211.

BATTERED SPOUSES.
Definitions, CJ §10-916.
Evidence.
Admissibility of evidence, CJ §10-916.
General provisions, FL §§4-513 to 4-516.
See DOMESTIC VIOLENCE.

BATTERIES.
Disposal.
Management program, EN §6-1102.
Mechanism for returning units, EN §6-1108.
Mercuric oxide batteries, EN §§6-901, 6-902.
Notice placard, EN §6-1105.
Penalties for violations of chapter, EN §6-1114.
Removal of batteries, EN §6-1103.
Responsible entities.
Generally, EN §6-1111.
Retailer responsibility, EN §6-1108.
Unit disposal, EN §6-1106.
Unit information.
Generally, EN §6-1104.
Unit management program, EN §§6-1102, 6-1107.
Fines.
Violation of section, CL §11-902.
Fraud and deceit.
General provisions, CL §11-902.
Marks.
Removal of other marks identifying ownership prohibited, CL §11-902.
Mercuric oxide batteries.
Disposal and recycling, EN §§6-901, 6-902.
Owner.
Marks.
Removal of marks identifying ownership, CL §11-902.
Rechargeable batteries.
Cell manufacturers.
Cells generally, EN §6-1109.
Contracts with private entities, EN §6-1112.
Contracts with public entities, EN §6-1112.
Cooperative activities, EN §6-1113.

BATTERIES —Cont'd
Rechargeable batteries —Cont'd
Definitions, EN §6-1101.
Disposal of unit, EN §6-1106.
Entity liability generally, EN §§6-1112, 6-1113.
General provisions, EN §§6-1101 to 6-1114.
Institutional users.
Spent units, EN §6-1110.
Recycling.
Mercuric oxide batteries, EN §§6-901, 6-902.
Symbol, EN §6-1104.
Rental batteries, CL §11-902.

BATTERY.
Assault.
See ASSAULT.

BAY RESTORATION FUND, EN §9-1605.2.

BAZAAR.
Gaming events and devices.
Acceptance of credit to play gaming event.
Prohibition, CR §12-108.
Anne Arundel county, CR §§13-401 to 13-408.
Baltimore City, CR §§13-501 to 13-510.
Baltimore county, CR §§13-601 to 13-607.
Calvert county, CR §§13-701 to 13-709.
Carroll county, CR §§13-901 to 13-909.
Cecil county, CR §§13-1001 to 13-1005.
Charles county, CR §§13-1101 to 13-1115.
Dorchester county, CR §§13-1201 to 13-1207.
Frederick county, CR §§13-1301 to 13-1307.
Prince George's county.
Benefit performance by qualified organization, CR §§13-1901 to 13-1907.
Provisions applicable to several counties, CR §§13-101 to 13-205.
St. Mary's county, CR §§13-2111 to 13-2115.
Somerset county, CR §13-2201.
Talbot county.
Provisions applicable to county, CR §13-2301.
Generally.
See CARNIVAL.

BEACH EROSION CONTROL.
Beach erosion control district, NR §§8-1102, 8-1105.1.

BEACHES AND AMUSEMENT PARKS.
Amusement and recreation generally.
See AMUSEMENTS AND RECREATION.
Shore erosion control.
See SHORE EROSION CONTROL.

BEACH REPLENISHMENT FUND.
Ocean beach replenishment fund, NR §§8-1103, 8-1104.

BEARS.
Dangerous animals.
Importing, selling, or trading in, CR §10-621.

BEAUTY SALONS.
General provisions.
See COSMETOLOGISTS.

BEAVERS.
General provisions.
See BIRDS AND GAME.

BED AND BREAKFAST ESTABLISHMENTS.
Alcoholic beverages.
Beer, wine and liquor licenses, 2B §6-201.
Food, drugs and cosmetics, HG §21-323.1.
Hotels generally.
See HOTELS.

BED AND BREAKFAST ESTABLISHMENTS
—Cont'd
Inspections, HG §21-323.1.
Licenses, HG §21-323.1.
Sprinkler systems, PS §§9-201 to 9-206.

BEDDING AND UPHOLSTERED FURNITURE.
Administrative and judicial review, HG §24-429.
Administrative procedure act.
Applicability, HG §24-428.
Appeals.
Administrative and judicial review, HG §24-429.
Auctioneers.
Exemptions, HG §24-403.
Bedding.
Defined, HG §24-401.
Definitions, HG §24-401.
Department.
Administration and enforcement of subtitle, HG §24-402.
Inspections, HG §24-402.
Powers and duties, HG §24-402.
Disinfection.
Certificate of approval, HG §24-420.
Defined, HG §24-401.
Filling materials.
Descriptions, HG §24-423.
New filling material.
Tags, HG §24-423.
Posting certificate, HG §24-420.
Records.
Duty of licensed disinfector, HG §24-421.
Inspection by department, HG §24-421.
Requirement for applying process, HG §24-420.
Secondhand bedding, HG §24-423.
Tags.
Approval by department, HG §24-423.
Duty of disinfector to tag, HG §24-422.
Inscriptions, HG §24-424.
New filling material, HG §24-423.
Secondhand filling material, HG §24-423.
Types of tags, HG §24-423.
Disinfectors.
Defined, HG §24-401.
Evidence.
Presumptions, HG §24-417.
Filling materials.
Defined, HG §24-401.
Hearings.
Licenses, HG §24-427.
Right to hearing, HG §24-428.
Hospitals.
Selling hospital bedding, HG §24-432.
Importers.
Defined, HG §24-401.
Inspections.
Duty of department, HG §24-402.
General duty, HG §24-416.
Interfering prohibited, HG §24-416.
Object subject to inspection, HG §24-416.
Places subject to inspection, HG §24-416.
Licenses.
Applicability of section, HG §24-405.
Applications, HG §24-407.
Defined, HG §24-401.
Exceptions, HG §24-405.
Fees.
Waiver, HG §24-407.
Issuance, HG §24-408.
Manufacturers in another state, HG §24-413.

BEDDING AND UPHOLSTERED FURNITURE
—Cont'd
Licenses —Cont'd
Numbering, HG §24-408.
Optional, HG §24-406.
Renewal, HG §24-411.
Reprimands, suspensions and revocations, HG §24-427.
Required, HG §24-405.
Rules and regulations, HG §24-409.
Scope of license, HG §24-410.
Separate license for each name, HG §24-412.
Term, HG §24-411.
Wholesalers.
Optional license, HG §24-406.
Make.
Defined, HG §24-401.
Manufacturers.
Defined, HG §24-401.
Licenses.
Manufacturers in another state, HG §24-413.
Misdemeanors.
Violations of provisions, HG §24-435.
New.
Defined, HG §24-401.
Nursing homes.
Selling nursing home or hospital bedding, HG §24-432.
Penalties.
Violations, HG §24-435.
Presumptions.
Evidentiary presumption, HG §24-417.
Prohibited acts.
Sales.
General limitations on sale, HG §24-432.
Selling nursing home or hospital bedding, HG §24-432.
Tag prohibitions, HG §24-432.
Renovate.
Defined, HG §24-401.
Renovator.
Defined, HG §24-401.
Rules and regulations.
Department.
Power to make, HG §24-402.
Sales.
Definition of "sell," HG §24-401.
General limitations on sale, HG §24-432.
Secondhand bedding.
Defined, HG §24-401.
Tags, HG §24-424.
Supply dealers.
Defined, HG §24-401.
Tags.
Disinfectors.
Duty to tag, HG §24-422.
Inscriptions, HG §24-424.
Prohibitions, HG §24-432.
Secondhand bedding, HG §24-424.
Types of tags, HG §24-423.
Upholstered furniture.
Defined, HG §24-401.
Violations.
Penalties, HG §24-435.
Separate violations, HG §24-435.
Wholesalers.
Defined, HG §24-401.
Licenses.
Optional, HG §24-406.

BED LINENS.
Returnable containers and textiles.
  Registration, prohibited acts, BR §§19-301 to
      19-307.

BEDROOMS.
Surveillance of individual in private place.
  With prurient intent, CR §3-902.

BEEF.
General provisions.
  See MEAT AND MEAT PRODUCTS.

BEEKEEPING INDUSTRY.
Apiaries.
  Abandoned apiaries, AG §5-507.
  Identification of apiary on another person's
      property, AG §5-507.
  Inspections.
    Secretary of agriculture, AG §5-502.
  Quarantine.
    Diseased apiaries or colonies, AG §5-504.
Carriers.
  Refusing to deliver bee colonies without proper
      documents.
    Immunity from liability, CJ §5-415.
Colonies.
  Diseased colonies, AG §5-504.
  Movable frames required, AG §5-506.
  Shipping or transporting colonies or used
      equipment into state, AG §5-505.
Cooperatives.
  General provisions.
    See AGRICULTURAL COOPERATIVES.
Definitions, AG §5-501.
Diseased colonies.
  Destruction, AG §5-504.
  Quarantine, AG §5-504.
  Treatment, AG §5-504.
Immunity.
  Carriers refusing to deliver bee colonies.
    Lack of proper documents.
      Immunity from liability, CJ §5-415.
Inspections.
  Apiaries, AG §5-502.
Migrant labor.
  Generally, LE §§7-101 to 7-507.
    See MIGRANT LABOR.
Movable frames.
  Required, AG §5-506.
Penalties generally, AG §§12-101 to 12-104.
Promotion of industry.
  Dissemination of information, AG §5-502.
Quarantine.
  Diseased apiaries or colonies, AG §5-504.
Queen bees.
  Transportation, AG §5-505.
Records.
  Secretary of agriculture, AG §5-502.
Registration, AG §5-503.
Shipping or transporting colonies or used
    equipment into state, AG §5-505.

BEER.
Alcoholic beverages.
  General provisions, 2B §§1-101 to 22-101.
    See ALCOHOLIC BEVERAGES.
Alcoholic beverage tax.
  See ALCOHOLIC BEVERAGE TAX.
Micro-breweries.
  Retail establishments.
    Interest of manufacturer prohibited.
      Exceptions, 2B §12-104.

BEE STINGS, HG §§13-701 to 13-709.
See INSECT STING EMERGENCY TREATMENT
    PROGRAM.

BEETLES.
Endangered puritan tiger beetle.
  Incidental taking permit, NR §10-2A-05.1.

BEL AIR.
Alcoholic beverages.
  Dispensaries, 2B §15-203.
    Profits and reserves.
      Accounted, 2B §15-207.
  Liquor control department.
    Distribution of net proceeds, 2B §15-207.

BELLS.
Emergency vehicles, TR §22-218.

BENEFICIAL SOCIETIES OR ASSOCIATIONS.
Organizational names and insignia.
  Registration, prohibited acts, BR §§19-201 to
      19-207.

BENEFIT OF CLERGY.
Abolished, CR §14-103.

BENEFIT PERFORMANCES BY QUALIFIED
    ORGANIZATIONS.
Prince George's county, CR §§13-1901 to 13-1907.

BENZENE.
Possession of destructive device, CR §§4-501 to
    4-503.

BEQUESTS.
See WILLS.

BEREAVEMENT.
Hospices.
  See HOSPICES.

BERLIN.
Alcoholic beverages.
  Dispensaries.
    Profits and reserves.
      Accounting and distribution, 2B §15-207.
  Profits and reserves.
    Accounted, 2B §15-207.
Electric or gas plant.
  Disposition.
    Exceptions, 23 §183.

BETTERTON.
Alcoholic beverages.
  Profits and reserves.
    Accounted, 2B §15-207.

BETTING.
Elections.
  Wagering on elections, EL §16-902.
General provisions.
  See GAMING.
Lotteries, CR §§12-201 to 12-212.
  See LOTTERIES.
Maryland horse racing act.
  General provisions, BR §§11-101 to 11-1205.
    See HORSE RACING.
  Harness racing, BR §§11-601 to 11-636.
    See HARNESS RACING.
  Pari-mutuel betting, BR §§11-801 to 11-832.
    See PARI-MUTUEL BETTING.
  Thoroughbred racing, BR §§11-501 to 11-541.
    See THOROUGHBRED RACING.
Slot machines, CR §§12-301 to 12-307.
  See SLOT MACHINES.

BETTING —Cont'd
Statewide gaming provisions, CR §§12-101 to
12-113.
See GAMING.

BEVERAGES.
Alcoholic beverages.
See ALCOHOLIC BEVERAGES.
Sales.
Implied warranty of merchantability, CL §2-314.
Soft drinks.
General provisions.
See SOFT DRINKS.
Warranties.
Implied warranty of merchantability, CL §2-314.

BIBLE.
Schools.
Opening exercises.
Daily period of silent meditation, ED §7-104.

BICHLORIDE OF MERCURY.
Penalties.
Violations of provisions, HG §22-201.
Sales.
Restrictions on sales, HG §22-201.

**BICYCLE AND PEDESTRIAN ADVISORY
COMMITTEE,** TR §2-606.

BICYCLES.
Access.
Public institutions, TR §21-1008.
Applicability of traffic laws, TR §21-1202.
Bells.
Regulation, TR §21-1207.
Brakes.
Regulation, TR §21-1207.
Carrying articles.
Regulated, TR §21-1206.
Clinging to vehicles prohibited, TR §21-1204.
Dealers.
Copies or summaries of laws and regulations
furnished, TR §21-1212.
Definitions, TR §11-104.
Crosswalks, TR §21-101.
Public bicycle area, TR §21-101.
Earplugs.
Wearing earplugs, headsets, etc., prohibited, TR
§21-1210.
Equipment.
Regulation, TR §21-1207.
Tampering with bicycle, TR §21-1206.
Guardian and ward.
Operation of bicycles and play vehicles.
Parent knowingly permitting minor or ward to
violate provisions of subtitle, TR §21-1201.
Headsets.
Wearing earplugs, headsets, etc., prohibited, TR
§21-1210.
Hearing aids.
Wearing earplugs, headsets, etc., prohibited.
Exception to prohibition for hearing aids, TR
§21-1210.
Helmets.
Requirements, TR §21-1207.1.
Highway administration.
Assessment of needs and inventory near rail and
subway stops, TR §8-611.
Duties, TR §8-204.
Project resulting in severance or destruction of
bicycle route, TR §8-601.1.
Highways.
Pathways.
Construction of bicycle pathways, TR §8-630.

BICYCLES —Cont'd
Highways —Cont'd
Riding on roadways or highways.
Regulations, TR §21-1205.1.
Interfering with bicyclist.
Opening door of motor vehicle, TR §21-1209.
Throwing objects, TR §21-1209.
Licenses.
Motor bicycles.
Driver's license required, TR §16-101.
Lights.
Lamps on bicycles, TR §21-1207.
Minibikes.
Dealer or salesman.
Information to be given purchaser, TR §15-112.
Minors.
Operation of bicycles or play vehicles.
Parent knowingly permitting minor or ward to
violate provisions of subtitle, TR §21-1201.
Motor bicycles.
Licenses.
Driver's license required, TR §16-101.
Motor vehicles.
Opening door of motor vehicle, TR §21-1209.
Standard of care, motor vehicle operators, TR
§21-1209.
Parking.
Accommodations at public institutions, TR
§21-1008.
Parking meters.
Securing bicycles to parking meters, TR §21-1208.
Passengers on bicycles, TR §21-1203.
Pathways.
Urban highways, TR §8-630.
Persons riding bicycles.
Regulation, TR §§21-1202, 21-1203.
Public bicycle area.
Department to use funds for, TR §3-216.
Traffic laws applicable, TR §21-1202.
Public institutions.
Access and parking privileges, TR §21-1008.
Racing events, TR §21-1211.
Rail services, transporting on, TR §7-902.
Reflector.
Regulation, TR §21-1207.
Regulations.
Copies or summaries of laws and regulations
furnished, TR §21-1212.
Securing.
Fire hydrants, poles, meters, etc., TR §21-1208.
Sidewalks.
Bicycles and play vehicles on sidewalk, TR
§21-1103.
Signal.
Turning, TR §§21-604, 21-606.
Standard of care for motor vehicle operators,
TR §21-1209.
State colleges.
Access and parking, TR §21-1008.
State facilities.
Access and parking privileges, TR §21-1008.
Tampering with bicycle.
General provisions, TR §21-1206.
Toll bridges and tunnels.
Prohibited in, TR §21-1405.
Traffic laws.
Apply to persons riding bicycles, TR §21-1202.
Transportation department.
Bicycle and pedestrian access, TR §§2-601 to
2-607.
Trust fund disposition for, TR §3-216.

BICYCLES —Cont'd
Turning.
Signal, TR §§21-604, 21-606.
Wearing earplugs, headsets, etc., TR §21-1210.

BIDS AND BIDDING.
Bond issues.
Public debt.
See PUBLIC DEBT.
Environmental service.
Procurements by service, NR §3-103.
General services department.
Procurement.
Conflict of interest, SF §4-304.
Definition of "bid," SF §4-301.
Public improvements.
Duties of department as to bids, SF §4-406.
Notices.
Procurement.
Contracts.
See PROCUREMENT.
Procurement.
Auction bids, SF §13-111.
Contracts.
See PROCUREMENT.
Public debt.
General obligation debt.
State bonds.
Public sale, SF §8-123.
State units.
Sale of bonds.
County transportation revenue bonds.
Exemption, TR §3-506.
Private sale.
Rejection of all bids at public sale, SF §8-206.
Public sale.
Award of bonds to highest bidder, SF §8-206.
Simultaneous issues.
Bids for, SF §8-207.
Schools, ED §5-112.
State correctional facilities, construction, COR §10-105.

BIFURCATED TRIALS.
Death penalty, sentencing procedure, CR §2-303.
Imprisonment for life without possibility of parole, CR §2-304.

BIGAMY, CR §10-502.
Decedents' estates.
Surviving spouse.
Conviction of bigamy while married to decedent, ET §1-202.

BIG SAVAGE MOUNTAIN WILDLAND.
General provisions.
See FORESTS AND PARKS.

BILLBOARDS.
Advertising.
See ADVERTISING.
Outdoor advertising.
See OUTDOOR ADVERTISING.

BILLIARD AND POOL TABLES.
Licenses.
Commercial use.
Keeping billiard table without license, BR §17-505.
Definitions, BR §17-501.
Fees, BR §17-504.

BILLIARD AND POOL TABLES —Cont'd
Licenses —Cont'd
Mandatory license requirement, BR §17-503.
Required, BR §17-503.
Scope of title, BR §17-502.

BILL OF ATTAINDER.
Constitutional provisions, US Const Art I §§9, 10; Art III.

BILL OF COMPLAINT.
Pleading.
See PLEADINGS.

BILL OF PARTICULARS.
Amendment.
Circuit courts, Crim Rule 4-241.
Arson or burning.
General form of charging document used, CR §6-111.
Assault.
Charging document in general form, CR §3-206.
Breaking and entering.
General form of charging document used, CR §6-210.
Demand.
Circuit courts, Crim Rule 4-241.
Response.
Circuit courts, Crim Rule 4-241.
Exceptions.
Circuit courts, Crim Rule 4-241.
Gaming, CR §12-112.
Lottery violation, CR §12-211.
Rape or sexual offense.
General form of charging document used, CR §3-317.
Reckless endangerment.
Charging document in general form, CR §3-206.
Theft.
General for m of charging document used, CR §7-108.

BILL OF RIGHTS.
Constitution of Maryland.
See CONSTITUTION OF MARYLAND.
Constitution of the United States, US Const Amds 1 to Amd 10.
See CONSTITUTION OF THE UNITED STATES.
Law enforcement officers, PS §§3-101 to 3-113.

BILL PAYER SERVICES.
Definition of bill payer services, FI §12-401.
Money transmission generally, FI §§12-401 to 12-431.
See MONEY TRANSMISSION.

BILLS OF ASSEMBLY.
See GENERAL ASSEMBLY.

BILLS OF EXCHANGE.
Failure to deliver documents for merchandise, CR §7-116.
Negotiable instruments.
General provisions, CL §§3-101 to 3-605.
See NEGOTIABLE INSTRUMENTS.

BILLS OF LADING.
Attachment.
Goods covered by a negotiable document, CL §7-602.
Carriers.
Inducing carrier to issue bill when goods not received, CL §18-204.
Possession.
Negotiation of bill when goods not in carrier's possession, CL §18-203.

BILLS OF LADING —Cont'd
Consignment.
General provisions.
See CONSIGNMENT.
Damages.
Limitations of liability, CL §7-309.
Definitions, CL §18-101.
Documents of title.
General provisions, CL §§7-101 to 7-603.
See DOCUMENTS OF TITLE.
Duplicate bills.
Issuance of duplicate bill not so marked, CL §18-202.
Executions.
Lien on goods covered by a negotiable document, CL §6-111.
Fraud and deceit.
Carriers.
Inducing carrier to issue bill when goods not received, CL §18-204.
Duplicate bills.
Issuance of bills not so marked, CL §18-202.
False statement.
Issuance of bill containing, CL §18-206.
Goods not in carrier's possession.
Negotiation of bill when goods not in carrier's possession, CL §18-203.
Issuance of bill for goods not received, CL §18-201.
Inducing carrier to issue, CL §18-204.
Mortgaged goods.
Negotiation of bill for mortgaged goods, CL §18-207.
Non-negotiable bill.
Issuance when not so marked, CL §18-205.
Goods of others.
Negotiation of bill for other's goods, CL §18-207.
Injunctions.
Enjoining negotiations of document, CL §7-602.
Interpleader.
Determination of conflicting claims, CL §7-603.
Issuance.
Duplicate bills.
Issuance when not so marked, CL §18-202.
False statement.
Issuance of bill containing, CL §18-206.
Non-negotiable bill.
Issuance when not so marked, CL §18-205.
Prior to receipt of goods, CL §18-201.
Inducing carrier to issue bill, CL §18-204.
Liens.
Negotiation of bill for mortgaged goods, CL §18-207.
Limitations in bill of lading for tariff, CL §7-309.
Lost and unclaimed property.
Missing bills, CL §7-601.
Misuse of document of title, CR §8-406.
Non-negotiable bill.
Issuance when not so marked, CL §18-205.
Party receiving, accepting or taking document in trust.
Failure to fulfill terms and conditions of trust, CR §8-406.
Penalties.
Violations, CL §18-401.
Violations.
Penalties, CL §18-401.

BINGO.
Acceptance of credit to play gaming event.
Prohibition, CR §12-108.

BINGO —Cont'd
Anne Arundel county, CR §13-407.
Baltimore City, CR §§13-507 to 13-509.
Baltimore county, CR §13-606.
Calvert county, CR §§13-705 to 13-709.
Carroll county, CR §13-907, 13-908.
Cecil county, CR §§13-1001 to 13-1005.
Charles county, CR §§13-1109 to 13-1115.
Dorchester county, CR §13-1203.
Frederick county, CR §13-1306.
Gaming devices.
Defined as, CR §12-101.
Statewide gaming provisions, CR §§12-101 to 12-113.
See GAMING.
Gaming event provisions applicable to several counties, CR §§13-201 to 13-205.
Garrett county, CR §13-1405.
Harford county, CR §§13-1501 to 13-1512.
Howard county, CR §§13-1602, 13-1603.
Kent county, CR §13-1705.
Montgomery county, CR §§13-1801 to 13-1815.
Prince George's county.
Benefit performance by qualified organization, CR §§13-1901 to 13-1907.
Queen Anne's county, CR §13-2005.
St. Mary's county, CR §§13-2101 to 13-2110.
Somerset county, CR §13-2202.
Washington county, CR §§13-2401 to 13-2411.
Wicomico county, CR §§13-2501 to 13-2508.
Worcester county, CR §§13-2601 to 13-2616.

BIODIESEL.
Motor vehicles.
State fleet biodiesel fuel usage, SF §14-408.
Renewable energy credits, AG §§10-1501 to 10-1507.
See RENEWABLE ENERGY CREDITS.

BIOLOGICAL AGENTS.
Possession of destructive device, CR §§4-501 to 4-503.
Registry, HG §§17-601 to 17-605.
Biological agent defined, HG §17-601.
Confidentiality, HG §17-604.
Criminal penalty for violations, HG §17-605.
Definitions, HG §17-601.
Duties of registry, HG §17-602.
Establishment of program, HG §17-602.
Persons maintaining and possessing agents.
Reports, HG §17-603.
Regulations, HG §17-602.
Release of information, HG §17-604.
Reports.
Persons maintaining and possessing agents, HG §17-603.

BIOMASS ELECTRIC GENERATING FACILITY.
Net energy metering.
Electric companies serving eligible customer generator, PUC §7-306.

BIOTECHNOLOGY COMPANIES.
Income tax credits, TG §10-725.

BIRD FLU.
Regulation of poultry to control avian influenza, AG §§3-801 to 3-805.

BIRDS AND GAME.
Administration.
Fish and wildlife administration.
Transfer of jurisdiction to department of natural resources, NR §10-203.

BIRDS AND GAME —Cont'd
Administration —Cont'd
Secretary of natural resources.
Rulemaking authority, NR §10-601.1.
Age.
Hunting licenses.
One year gratis license, NR §10-301.1.
Agents.
Hunting licenses and stamps.
Sale by persons in retail business as agent of
department, NR §10-302.
Allegany county.
See ALLEGANY COUNTY.
Ammunition.
Regulation of use, NR §10-408.
Anne Arundel county.
Spotlighting, NR §10-410.
Trapping, NR §10-410.
Waterfowl and migratory birds.
Blinds.
Special provisions, NR §10-612.
Appeals.
Hunting.
Certificate of competency and safety.
Appeal from denial of certificate, NR
§10-301.1.
Aviation.
Hunting.
From aircraft prohibited, NR §10-410.
Bag limits.
Conformity with federal rules and regulations, NR
§10-409.
Department to regulate, NR §10-409.
Baiting.
Wetland or upland game birds.
Hunting by aid of baiting or on or over baited
area, NR §10-412.
Baltimore county.
See BALTIMORE COUNTY.
Baltimore oriole.
Designation as state bird, SG §13-302.
Beavers. See within this heading, "Fur-bearing
animals."
Black bears.
Black bear damage reimbursement fund, NR
§10-423.1.
Hunting, possessing, selling, purchasing, shipping,
carrying, transporting or exporting.
Penalties, NR §10-423.
Killing or wounding in self defense.
Penalty not applicable, NR §10-423.
Blinds.
Waterfowl. See within this heading, "Waterfowl
and migratory birds."
Bobwhite.
Raising game in captivity. See within this
heading, "Captive wildlife."
Bounties.
Prohibited.
Department prohibited to pay, NR §10-207.
Wild animals.
By county commissioners, 25 §2.
Bow and arrow.
Hunting.
Waterfowl and migratory birds, NR §10-602.
Calvert county.
See CALVERT COUNTY.
Captive wildlife.
Advisory committee, NR §10-910.
Collection of wildlife, nests or eggs.
Scientific or educational purposes.
Permits, NR §10-909.

BIRDS AND GAME —Cont'd
Captive wildlife —Cont'd
Contraband wildlife.
Nuisances.
Contraband wildlife deemed nuisance, NR
§10-911.
Coordination.
Intergovernmental coordination, NR §10-904.
Declaration.
Legislative declaration, NR §10-901.
Falcons.
Hunting with.
Permits, NR §10-907.
Native wildlife.
Permits and licenses, NR §10-902.
Findings.
Legislative findings, NR §10-901.
Game birds and mammals.
Conditions for possession and sale, NR §10-905.
Game husbandry.
Licenses, NR §10-905.
Intergovernmental coordination, NR §10-904.
Legislative findings and declaration, NR §10-901.
Licenses.
Game husbandry licenses, NR §10-905.
Native wildlife, NR §10-902.
Penalties.
Revocation or suspension, NR §10-911.
Regulated shooting grounds.
Special licenses, NR §10-906.
Revocation or suspension.
Penalties, NR §10-911.
Native wildlife.
Permits and licenses, NR §10-902.
Nonnative wildlife.
Rules and regulations.
Prohibiting or restricting importation,
exportation, etc., NR §10-903.
Nuisances.
Contraband wildlife deemed nuisance, NR
§10-911.
Penalties, NR §10-911.
Permits.
Collection of wildlife, nests or eggs.
Scientific or educational purposes, NR
§10-909.
Falcons, hawks or owls.
Hunting with, NR §10-907.
Native wildlife, NR §10-902.
Penalties.
Revocation or suspension, NR §10-911.
Regulated shooting grounds, NR §10-906.
Revocation or suspension.
Penalties, NR §10-911.
Wildlife cooperator, NR §10-908.
Records.
Game birds or mammals, NR §10-905.
Regulated shooting grounds.
General provisions, NR §10-906.
Sunday use, NR §10-906.
Rules and regulations.
Falcons, hawks or owls.
Hunting with, NR §10-907.
Native wildlife, NR §10-902.
Nonnative wildlife.
Prohibiting or restricting importation,
exportation, etc., NR §10-903.
Regulated shooting grounds.
Regulation of propagated wildlife, NR
§10-906.

BIRDS AND GAME —Cont'd
Captive wildlife —Cont'd
  Scientific or educational purposes.
    Collection of wildlife, nests or eggs.
      Permits, NR §10-909.
  Wildlife cooperator.
    Permits, NR §10-908.
Captivity.
  Raising game in captivity. See within this
    heading, "Captive wildlife."
Caroline county.
  Spotlighting, NR §10-410.
Carrier pigeons.
  Injuring or trapping, CR §10-622.
Carroll county.
  General provisions.
    See CARROLL COUNTY.
Cats.
  Killing, NR §10-413.
Cecil county.
  See CECIL COUNTY.
Charles county.
  Spotlighting, NR §10-410.
Chesapeake Bay and endangered species fund,
  NR §§1-701 to 1-706.
  See CHESAPEAKE BAY AND ENDANGERED
    SPECIES FUND.
Chukars.
  Raising game in captivity. See within this
    heading, "Captive wildlife."
Closed season.
  Game birds or mammals.
    Hunting or possession during closed season
      prohibited, NR §10-404.
    Importing during closed season, NR §10-404.
  Wildlife.
    Defined, NR §10-101.
Clothing worn by hunters or assistants, NR
  §10-418.
  Daylight fluorescent orange, NR §10-418.
Collection of wildlife, nests or eggs.
  Scientific or educational purposes.
    Permits, NR §10-909.
Commission.
  Wildlife advisory commission. See within this
    heading, "Wildlife advisory commission."
Conservation.
  Endangered species of fish conservation act.
    See FISH AND FISHERIES.
  Nongame and endangered species conservation
    act. See within this heading, "Nongame and
    endangered species conservation act."
Contraband wildlife.
  Nuisances.
    Deemed nuisance, NR §10-911.
Counties.
  Chartered counties.
    Powers as to fish and game, 25A §5.
  Defined, NR §10-101.
Coyotes.
  Open season all year, NR §10-406.
Crimes and offenses.
  Seals.
    Commercial use, NR §10-419.
  Spotlighting.
    Deer, NR §10-416.
  Violation of title, NR §10-1101.
Daylight fluorescent orange.
  Clothing worn by hunters or assistants, NR
    §10-418.

BIRDS AND GAME —Cont'd
Deer.
  Dogs.
    Hunting with, NR §10-416.
  Donation to needy.
    Revenue from sales of licenses used for, NR
      §10-308.
  Hunting.
    Automatic firearms prohibited, NR §10-416.
    Bonus deer stamp, NR §10-415.
    Bow hunting season, NR §10-415.
    Checking stations.
      Duty to report deer killed to, NR §10-415.
    Consolidated hunting license, NR §10-415.
    Deer stamp.
      Bonus antlered deer stamp.
        Fees, resident and nonresident, NR
          §10-301.
      Bonus stamps, NR §10-415.
      Consolidated hunting licenses, NR §10-414.
    Dogs.
      Hunting with, NR §10-416.
    Firearms season, NR §10-415.
    Handguns, NR §10-420.1.
    Methods.
      Prohibited methods, NR §10-416.
    Motor vehicles, accidental killing by, NR
      §10-415.
    Muzzle loader season, NR §10-415.
    Muzzle loading hunting season, NR §§10-415,
      10-420.
    Private lands, NR §10-411.
    Reporting deer killed to checking stations, NR
      §10-415.
    Seasons, NR §10-415.
      Muzzle loading hunting season, NR §10-420.
    Second deer stamp, NR §10-415.
    Spotlights.
      Use prohibited, NR §10-416.
    Waters of state, hunting deer, NR §10-415.
  Raising in captivity. See within this heading,
    "Captive wildlife."
  Restrictions on first day of firearms season for
    hunting deer, NR §10-421.
  Seasons.
    Muzzle loading hunting season, NR §10-420.
  Stamps.
    Bonus stamps, NR §10-415.
    Consolidated hunting licenses.
      Person may purchase second deer stamp, NR
        §10-414.
Definitions.
  Baiting and baited area, NR §10-412.
  Child.
    Hunting licenses, NR §10-301.
  Complimentary licenses.
    Former prisoners of war, NR §10-303.
  Exotic birds, HG §24-101.
  Feeding of wild waterfowl, NR §10-1001.
  Flighted mallard ducks, NR §10-101.
  Fur-bearing mammal, NR §10-101.
  Fur dealers, NR §10-501.
  Game birds and mammals, NR §10-101.
  Nighttime, NR §§10-101, 10-602.
  Nongame and endangered species conservation
    act, NR §10-2A-01.
  Open season, NR §10-101.
  Waterfowl processing operation, NR §10-101.
  Wildlife, NR §10-101.
  Wild waterfowl, NR §10-601.

BIRDS AND GAME —Cont'd
Dens.
  Molesting game birds or animals, NR §10-410.
Department of game and inland fish.
  Transfer of jurisdiction to department of natural
    resources, NR §10-203.
Department of natural resources.
  Department of game and inland water fish.
    Transfer of jurisdiction to department of natural
      resources, NR §10-203.
  Fish and wildlife administration.
    Transfer of jurisdiction to department of natural
      resources, NR §10-203.
  Hunting heritage protection.
    Maintenance of open lands for hunting, NR
      §10-212.
Dogs.
  Deer.
    Hunting deer, NR §10-416.
  Field trials.
    Nonresident dogs.
      Exemption from license taxes, NR §10-703.
    Permit.
      Issuance, NR §10-701.
      Required, NR §10-701.
    Shooting game birds and mammals.
      Restrictions, NR §10-702.
  Killing.
    Natural resources police officer, NR §10-413.
  Running at large, NR §10-413.
  Training, NR §10-413.
Dorchester county.
  See DORCHESTER COUNTY.
Duck blinds. See within this heading, "Waterfowl
  and migratory birds."
Ducks.
  Flighted mallard ducks.
    Defined, NR §10-101.
  Flocks of ducks.
    Infectious or contagious diseases.
      Appraisal of building, article or animal to be
        destroyed.
        Section not applicable, AG §3-107.
  Infectious or contagious disease.
    Death or quarantine and destruction.
      Appraisal of animals to be destroyed.
        When department not responsible, AG
          §3-107.
    Flocks of ducks intended to be released for
      purposes of hunting.
      Appraisal of building, article or animal to be
        destroyed.
        Section not applicable, AG §3-107.
Eggs.
  Wild and migratory birds.
    Hunting and taking prohibited, NR §10-402.
Endangered species.
  Chesapeake Bay and endangered species fund, NR
    §§1-701 to 1-706.
    See CHESAPEAKE BAY AND ENDANGERED
      SPECIES FUND.
  Endangered species of fish conservation act.
    See FISH AND FISHERIES.
  Nongame and endangered species conservation
    act. See within this heading, "Nongame and
    endangered species conservation act."
Examinations.
  Fur-bearing animals.
    Taxidermists and fur tanning license.
      Required, NR §10-512.

BIRDS AND GAME —Cont'd
Exotic birds.
  Breeding.
    Permit required, HG §24-109.
  Cleanliness of facilities, HG §24-105.
  Dead birds.
    Freezing, HG §24-107.
  Definitions, HG §24-101.
  Destruction of birds, HG §24-107.
  Diseases.
    Records relating to certain infectious diseases,
      HG §24-108.
  Distribute.
    Defined, HG §24-101.
    Permit required, HG §24-109.
  Freezing dead birds, HG §24-107.
  Handling of birds, HG §24-107.
  Importation.
    Permit required, HG §24-109.
  Inspections, HG §24-108.
  Penalties.
    Violations, HG §24-110.
  Permits.
    Defined, HG §24-101.
    Display, HG §24-104.
    Exceptions, HG §24-102.
    Importing, distributing or breeding without
      permit, HG §24-109.
    Renewal, HG §24-103.
    Required, HG §24-102.
    Separate permit for each facility, HG §24-102.
    Term, HG §24-103.
  Records.
    Infectious diseases, HG §24-108.
    Required records, HG §24-106.
  Sanitation.
    Cleanliness of facilities, HG §24-105.
  State secretary of agriculture.
    Duties, HG §24-107.
  Violations.
    Penalties, HG §24-110.
Exportation.
  Game birds and mammals, NR §10-417.
Falcons.
  Hunting with.
    Permits, NR §10-907.
Federal aid.
  Wildlife restoration.
    Assent to public law 415, NR §10-208.
Feeding.
  Waterfowl and migratory birds. See within this
    heading, "Waterfowl and migratory birds."
Fees.
  Falcons, hawks or owls.
    Hunting with.
      Permits, NR §10-907.
  Fur-bearing animals.
    Fur dealers.
      Licenses, NR §10-506.
    Taxidermist and fur tanning license, NR
      §10-512.
  Hunting licenses.
    Disposition of revenue, NR §10-304.
    Lost hunter's license, NR §10-305.
    Nonresidents, NR §10-301.
  Native wildlife.
    Possessing, importing, exporting, breeding, etc.
      Permits and licenses, NR §10-902.
  Regulated shooting grounds.
    Permits, NR §10-906.

BIRDS AND GAME —Cont'd
Fees —Cont'd
  Waterfowl and migratory birds.
    Blinds, NR §10-612.
Ferrets.
  Hunting with prohibited, NR §10-410.
Field trials. See within this heading, "Dogs."
Fines.
  Collection, NR §10-1102.
  Fur-bearing animals.
    Violations of subtitle, NR §10-513.
  General provisions, NR §10-1101.
  Rules and regulations.
    Violations, NR §10-205.
Fish.
  See FISH AND FISHERIES.
Forest game birds and mammals.
  Defined, NR §10-101.
Foxes.
  Charles county.
    Open season all year, NR §10-406.
  Damaging or destroying property.
    Hunting or trapping permitted, NR §10-406.
  Dorchester county.
    Open season all year, NR §10-406.
Funds.
  Chesapeake Bay and endangered species fund, NR
    §§1-701 to 1-706.
    See CHESAPEAKE BAY AND ENDANGERED
      SPECIES FUND.
  Nongame and endangered species conservation
    act.
    Birdwatcher's fund, NR §10-2A-06.1.
  State wildlife management and protection fund,
    NR §§10-209, 10-304.
Fur-bearing animals.
  Beaver.
    Lights.
      Use at nighttime prohibited, NR §10-504.
    Nonresidents.
      Hunting and trapping prohibited, NR
        §10-503.
    Only trapping permitted, NR §10-504.
    Open season, NR §10-406.
    Restrictions, NR §10-504.
  Certain traps prohibited near residences, NR
    §10-408.1.
  Definitions.
    Fur dealers, NR §10-501.
  Fees.
    Taxidermist and fur tanning license, NR
      §10-512.
  Fines.
    Violations, NR §10-513.
  Fur dealers.
    Defined, NR §10-501.
    Fees.
      Licenses, NR §10-506.
    Inspections.
      Right of entry, NR §10-506.
    Licenses, NR §§10-505, 10-506, 10-508.
    Penalties.
      Illegally taken furs.
        Possession, sale and transportation, NR
          §10-505.
    Records, NR §10-507.
      Inspection, NR §10-508.
    Reports, NR §10-507.
  Green pelt.
    Possession out of season.
      Prima facie evidence of violation, NR §10-505.

BIRDS AND GAME —Cont'd
Fur-bearing animals —Cont'd
  Illegally taken furs.
    Possession, sale and transportation prohibited,
      NR §10-505.
  Mink.
    Open season, NR §10-406.
  Muskrats.
    Damaging embankment or impoundment.
      Destruction, NR §10-406.
    Hunting restrictions, NR §10-504.
    Open season, NR §10-406.
  Nongame and endangered species conservation
    act.
    General provisions. See within this heading,
      "Nongame and endangered species
      conservation act."
  Nonresidents.
    Beaver and otter.
      Hunting and trapping prohibited, NR
        §10-503.
    Trapping license, NR §10-502.
  Open season, NR §10-406.
  Otter.
    Hunting restrictions, NR §10-504.
    Nonresidents.
      Hunting and trapping prohibited, NR
        §10-503.
    Open season, NR §10-406.
  Penalties.
    Illegally taken furs.
      Possession, sale and transportation, NR
        §10-505.
    Violations, NR §10-513.
  Permits.
    Trapping permits, NR §10-313.
  Seals.
    Commercial use prohibited, NR §10-419.
  Snare traps.
    Baltimore, Carroll and Harford counties, NR
      §10-410.
  Steel leghold traps in Baltimore, Montgomery and
    Prince George's counties, NR §10-410.
  Tags for out-of-state shipments.
    Composition, NR §10-509.
    Mutilation or destruction, NR §10-510.
    Receiving unmarked, untagged furs or pelts, NR
      §10-511.
  Tanners.
    Licenses.
      Generally, NR §10-512.
      Revocation.
        Possession, sale and transportation of
          illegally taken furs, NR §10-505.
    Penalties.
      Illegally taken furs.
        Possession, sale and transportation, NR
          §10-505.
    Records.
      Keeping, NR §10-512.
  Taxidermists.
    Licenses.
      Generally, NR §10-512.
      Revocation.
        Possession, sale and transportation of
          illegally taken furs, NR §10-505.
    Penalties.
      Illegally taken furs.
        Possession, sale and transportation, NR
          §10-505.

BIRDS AND GAME —Cont'd
Fur-bearing animals —Cont'd
Taxidermists —Cont'd
Records.
Keeping, NR §10-512.
Fur-bearing mammal.
Defined, NR §10-101.
Furs.
Dealers in fur. See within this heading,
"Fur-bearing animals."
Defined, NR §10-101.
Fur-bearing animals. See within this heading,
"Fur-bearing animals."
Green pelt.
Defined, NR §10-101.
Tanning.
License, NR §10-512.
Game birds and mammals.
Defined, NR §10-101.
Exportation, NR §10-417.
Game husbandry.
Possession and sale, NR §10-905.
Hunting, NR §10-404.
Importing during closed season, NR §10-404.
Open season, NR §10-405.
Possession, NR §10-404.
Purchasing, NR §10-404.
Selling, NR §10-404.
Garrett county.
See GARRETT COUNTY.
General assembly.
Nongame and endangered species conservation
act.
Legislative findings of assembly, NR §10-2A-02.
Green pelt.
Defined, NR §10-101.
Hawks.
Hunting with.
Permits, NR §10-907.
Hunting.
Aircraft.
Hunting from aircraft prohibited, NR §10-410.
Ammunition.
Regulations, NR §10-408.
Appeals.
Certificate of competency and safety.
Denial of certificate, NR §10-301.1.
Armed forces members on leave in state.
Exception to hunting license requirement, NR
§10-301.
Bag limits.
Conformity with federal rules and regulations,
NR §10-409.
Department to regulate, NR §10-409.
Beavers.
Nonresidents, NR §10-503.
Open season, NR §10-406.
Restrictions, NR §10-504.
Black bears.
Penalties, NR §10-423.
Killing or wounding in self defense.
Penalty not applicable, NR §10-423.
Black powder stamp.
Fees, residents and nonresidents, NR §10-301.
Boats, hunting from, NR §10-605.
Anchored boat, NR §10-606.
Bow and arrow.
Waterfowl and migratory birds, NR §10-602.
Bow and arrow stamp.
Fees, residents and nonresidents, NR §10-301.
Closed season, NR §§10-101, 10-404.

BIRDS AND GAME —Cont'd
Hunting —Cont'd
Clothing to be worn by hunters or assistants, NR
§10-418.
Daylight fluorescent orange, NR §10-418.
Competency in firearms and hunter safety, NR
§10-301.1.
Deer. See within this heading, "Deer."
Defined, NR §10-101.
Dens.
Molesting game birds or animals in dens, NR
§10-410.
Disabled persons.
Special permits.
Hunting from vehicles, NR §10-307.
Dogs, NR §10-416.
Field trials. See within this heading, "Dogs."
Running at large, NR §10-413.
Training, NR §10-413.
Falcons, hawks or owls.
Hunting with.
Permits, NR §10-907.
Farmers, reimbursement contracts with.
Planting grains, grasses and legumes, NR
§10-301.
Farmland.
Exception to license requirement when hunting
on, NR §10-301.
Farm livestock.
Intentionally or willfully destroying or
damaging.
Prohibited, NR §10-424.
Fees.
Licenses, NR §10-301.
Stamps, NR §10-301.
Ferrets and weasels.
Not to be used in hunting, NR §10-410.
Firearms.
Competency in firearms and hunter safety, NR
§10-301.1.
Foxhunting.
Exception to license requirement, NR §10-301.
Game birds or mammals, NR §10-404.
Guides.
Waterfowl hunting guide licenses, NR §10-309.
Highways.
Shooting on, from or across prohibited, NR
§10-410.
Hospital list.
Furnished when license issued, NR §10-301.
Hunting heritage protection.
Maintenance of open lands for hunting.
Duty of department, report to general
assembly, NR §10-212.
Interference with hunters, NR §10-422.
Internet connection, operating a gun or other
device through.
Prohibition, NR §10-426.
Licenses.
Agents.
Sale by persons in retail business as agent of
department, NR §10-302.
Application, NR §10-301.
Complimentary consolidated hunting license,
NR §10-301.1.
Complimentary licenses, NR §10-303.
Confiscation, NR §10-312.
Consent of parent.
Issuance to person under age sixteen, NR
§10-301.
Display, NR §10-306.

BIRDS AND GAME —Cont'd
Hunting —Cont'd
  Licenses —Cont'd
    Duration, NR §10-301.
    Exceptions to requirement, NR §10-301.
    Exhibition.
      Inadvertent violations, NR §10-311.
    False statements.
      Obtaining license by false statements, NR §10-310.
    Fees, NR §10-301.
      Disposition of money, NR §10-304.
      Lost hunter's license, NR §10-305.
    Gratis license, NR §10-301.1.
    Guides.
      Waterfowl hunting guide licenses, NR §10-309.
    Lost hunter's license, NR §10-305.
    Minors.
      Consent of parent.
        Issuance to person under age sixteen, NR §10-301.
      One year gratis license, NR §10-301.1.
    Nonresident hunting license, NR §10-301.
      3 day license, NR §10-301.
    One year gratis license, NR §10-301.1.
    Patron's licenses, NR §10-301.2.
    Possession, NR §10-306.
      Exhibition, NR §10-306.
    Report by sales agents, NR §10-302.
    Required to hunt, NR §10-301.
    Resident hunting license, NR §10-301.
    Revenue from sale of licenses.
      Use, NR §10-308.
    Revocation.
      Internet connection, operating a gun or other device through, NR §10-426.
    Sale by persons in retail business as agent of department, NR §10-302.
    Seller's fee, NR §10-301.
    Senior hunting license, NR §10-301.
    Snow geese.
      Nonresident hunting without license, conditions, NR §10-308.2.
    Stamps.
      Migratory waterfowl stamp, NR §10-308.1.
      Sale by persons in retail business as agent of department, NR §10-302.
    Statement signed by applicant, NR §10-301.
    Statistics on sale, NR §10-301.
    Suspension, NR §10-1108.
    Trespass upon private property, suspension, NR §10-1108.
    Types, NR §10-301.
    Use of revenue from sale of licenses, NR §10-308.
  Maryland-Washington metropolitan district property, 28 §5-113.1.
  Migratory game bird stamp.
    Fees, NR §10-301.
  Migratory wild waterfowl stamp.
    General provisions, NR §10-308.1.
  Minors.
    Licenses.
      One year gratis license, NR §10-301.1.
  Motor vehicles.
    Prohibition, NR §10-410.
    Spotlighting, NR §10-410.
  Muskrats.
    Restrictions, NR §10-504.

BIRDS AND GAME —Cont'd
Hunting —Cont'd
  Nighttime.
    Restrictions, NR §10-410.
    Wild waterfowl.
      Prohibited, NR §10-602.
  Open lands.
    Hunting heritage protection.
      Maintenance of open lands for hunting.
        Duty of department, NR §10-210.
  Open season. See within this heading, "Open season."
  Opossums, NR §10-414.
  Otters, NR §§10-406, 10-504.
  Penalties.
    Black bears, NR §10-423.
      Killing or wounding in self defense.
        Penalty not applicable, NR §10-423.
    Internet connection, operating a gun or other device through, NR §10-426.
    Licenses.
      Suspension, NR §10-1108.
  Permission.
    Required on private property, NR §10-411.
  Permits.
    Disabled persons.
      Special permit to hunt from vehicles, NR §10-307.
  Personal property.
    Intentionally or willfully destroying or damaging.
      Prohibited, NR §10-424.
  Private property.
    Permission required, NR §10-411.
  Public recreation on private and local government lands.
    General provisions, NR §§5-1101 to 5-1109.
    See RECREATIONAL TRESPASS.
  Raccoons.
    General provisions, NR §10-414.
  Real property.
    Intentionally or willfully destroying or damaging.
      Prohibited, NR §10-424.
  Regulated shooting grounds.
    Licenses.
      Special licenses, NR §10-906.
    Propagated wildlife.
      Regulations, NR §10-906.
  Reports.
    License and stamp sales agents, NR §10-302.
  Restrictions, NR §10-504.
    Restrictions on first day of firearms season for hunting deer, NR §10-421.
  Riparian shorelines.
    Licensing by riparian landowners, NR §10-607.
  Safety.
    Certificate of firearms competency and hunter safety, NR §10-301.1.
  Safety zones.
    Shooting or disturbing wildlife in safety zones prohibited, NR §10-410.
  Shooting, wounding or killing another person.
    Carelessly or negligently prohibited, NR §10-424.
    Suspension of license, NR §10-424.1.
  Snow geese.
    Nonresident hunting without license, conditions, NR §10-308.2.
  Spotlighting regulated, NR §10-410.

BIRDS AND GAME —Cont'd
Hunting —Cont'd
Stamps.
　Fees, NR §10-301.
　Migratory waterfowl stamp, NR §10-308.1.
　Sale by persons in retail business as agent of
　　department, NR §10-302.
Sundays, NR §10-410.
Trespass upon private property.
　Suspension of license, NR §10-1108.
Upland game birds.
　Baiting, NR §10-412.
Upland wildlife habitat fund, NR §10-301.
Waterfowl. See within this heading, "Waterfowl
　and migratory birds."
Waters, hunting while standing in, NR §10-604.
Weapons.
　Competency in firearms and hunter safety, NR
　　§10-301.1.
　Hunting deer with certain handguns, NR
　　§10-420.1.
　Muzzle loading hunting season, NR §10-420.
　Regulations, NR §10-408.
　Wild waterfowl.
　　Restrictions on weapons, NR §10-602.
Wetland game birds.
　Baiting, NR §10-412.
　Open seasons, NR §10-407.
Wild birds.
　Prohibited for certain wild birds, NR §10-401.
Hunting heritage protection.
Maintenance of open lands for hunting.
　Duty of department, report to general assembly,
　　NR §10-212.
Hunting on Sundays, NR §10-410.
Inspections.
Exotic birds, HG §24-108.
Fur-bearing animals.
　Fur dealers.
　　Right of entry, NR §10-506.
Waterfowl processing operations, NR §10-425.
Interstate wildlife violator compact, NR
　§§10-1201 to 10-1203.
Compact administrator, NR §10-1201.
　Compensation, NR §10-1203.
Execution, NR §10-1202.
Text, NR §10-1201.
Kent county.
See KENT COUNTY.
Liability.
Violations of provisions.
　Joint liability, NR §10-1107.
Licenses.
Captive wildlife. See within this heading, "Captive
　wildlife."
Display.
　Inadvertent violation, NR §10-311.
Feeding.
　Waterfowl and migratory birds. See within this
　　heading, "Waterfowl and migratory birds."
Fur dealers. See within this heading, "Fur-bearing
　animals."
Game husbandry licenses, NR §10-905.
Hunting licenses. See within this heading,
　"Hunting."
Native wildlife, NR §10-902.
Possession.
　Inadvertent violation of section 10-306, NR
　　§10-311.
Prisoners of war.
　Complimentary licenses, NR §10-303.

BIRDS AND GAME —Cont'd
Licenses —Cont'd
Regulated shooting grounds.
　Special licenses, NR §10-906.
Tanners, NR §10-512.
Taxidermist, NR §10-512.
Trapping license.
　Nonresidents, NR §10-502.
Veterans.
　Disabled veterans.
　　Complimentary licenses, NR §10-303.
Waterfowl and migratory birds.
　Feeding. See within this heading, "Waterfowl
　　and migratory birds."
　General provisions. See within this heading,
　　"Waterfowl and migratory birds."
Lists.
Nongame and endangered species conservation
　act. See within this heading, "Nongame and
　endangered species conservation act."
Local political subdivisions.
Statewide system of assistance.
　Secretary of natural resources to provide, NR
　　§10-202.
Migratory birds. See within this heading,
　"Waterfowl and migratory birds."
Migratory game bird.
Defined, NR §10-101.
Migratory waterfowl stamp, NR §10-308.1.
Minks. See within this heading, "Fur-bearing
　animals."
Misdemeanors.
Exotic birds.
　Violations of provisions, HG §24-110.
Hunting.
　Hunting from aircraft prohibited, NR §10-410.
Seals.
　Commercial use, NR §10-419.
Spotlighting.
　Deer, NR §10-416.
Violations of title, NR §10-1101.
Motor vehicles.
Hunting from prohibited, NR §10-410.
Lights.
　Casting artificial light from vehicle on woods,
　　wild animals, etc., NR §10-410.
Off-road vehicles.
　Pursuing wildlife prohibited, NR §10-410.
Searching without warrant, NR §10-1104.
Spotlighting, NR §10-410.
Muskrats. See within this heading, "Fur-bearing
　animals."
Native wildlife.
Possessing, importing, exporting, breeding, etc.
　Permits and licenses, NR §10-902.
Nests.
Wild and migratory birds.
　Hunting and taking prohibited, NR §10-402.
Nighttime.
Defined, NR §§10-101, 10-602.
Hunting.
　Restrictions, NR §10-410.
　Wild waterfowl.
　　Prohibited, NR §10-602.
Lights.
　Use in hunting prohibited, NR §10-410.
**Nongame and endangered species
　conservation act.**
Birdwatcher's fund, NR §10-2A-06.1.
Conservation.
　Definition of "conserve," NR §10-2A-01.

BIRDS AND GAME —Cont'd
Nongame and endangered species conservation act —Cont'd
Conservation —Cont'd
Programs for conservation, NR §10-2A-06.
Rules and regulations for conservation of species, NR §10-2A-05.
Definitions.
Natural resources, NR §10-2A-01.
Ecosystem.
Defined, NR §10-2A-01.
Endangered species.
Defined, NR §10-2A-01.
Determination of status, NR §10-2A-04.
Lists.
Changes in listings, NR §10-2A-05.
Preparation, NR §10-2A-04.
Exemptions from subtitle, NR §10-2A-08.
Forfeitures, NR §10-2A-07.
General assembly.
Legislative findings, NR §10-2A-02.
Investigations.
Secretary to investigate nongame wildlife, NR §10-2A-03.
Legislative findings, NR §10-2A-02.
Limitations on taking, possession, transporting, etc.
Rules and regulations, NR §10-2A-03.
Lists.
Changes in listings, NR §10-2A-05.
Endangered or threatened species.
Preparation of lists, NR §10-2A-04.
Nongame species.
Defined, NR §10-2A-01.
Optimum carrying capacity.
Defined, NR §10-2A-01.
Penalties.
Violations, NR §10-2A-07.
Permits.
Puritan tiger beetle.
Incidental taking permit, NR §10-2A-05.1.
Transportation under valid permit, NR §10-2A-05.
Plant.
Defined, NR §10-2A-01.
Police.
Searches and seizures, NR §10-2A-07.
Possession.
Scientific purposes, NR §10-2A-05.
Programs for conservation, NR §10-2A-06.
Puritan tiger beetle.
Incidental taking permit, NR §10-2A-05.1.
Rules and regulations.
Limitations on taking, possession, transporting, etc., NR §10-2A-03.
Short title, NR §10-2A-09.
Species.
Defined, NR §10-2A-01.
Take.
Defined, NR §10-2A-01.
Threatened species.
Defined, NR §10-2A-01.
Determination of status, NR §10-2A-04.
Lists.
Changes in listings, NR §10-2A-05.
Preparation, NR §10-2A-04.
Transportation.
Permits, NR §10-2A-05.
Prohibited.
Generally, NR §10-2A-03.
Scientific purposes, NR §10-2A-05.

BIRDS AND GAME —Cont'd
Nongame and endangered species conservation act —Cont'd
Violations.
Forfeitures, NR §10-2A-07.
Penalties for violations, NR §10-2A-07.
Searches and seizures.
Authority of law enforcement officers, NR §10-2A-07.
Nongame birds and mammals.
Defined, NR §10-101.
Nonnative wildlife.
Importation, exportation, etc.
Rules and regulations.
Prohibiting or restricting, NR §10-903.
Nonresidents.
Beaver or otter.
Trapping or hunting prohibited, NR §10-503.
Fur dealers.
License, NR §10-506.
Snow geese.
Hunting without license, conditions, NR §10-308.2.
Trapping license, NR §10-502.
Nuisance bird law, AG §§5-801 to 5-804.
See PESTS.
Nuisances.
Contraband wildlife.
Deemed nuisance, NR §10-911.
Nutria.
Management plan, NR §10-202.1.
Open lands.
Hunting heritage protection.
Maintenance of open lands for hunting.
Duty of department, NR §10-210.
Open season.
Crows, NR §10-405.
Defined, NR §10-101.
Fur-bearing mammals, NR §10-406.
Game birds and mammals, NR §10-405.
Waterfowl and migratory birds, NR §10-407.
Wetland game birds, NR §10-407.
Opossums.
Hunting.
Generally, NR §10-414.
Otters. See within this heading, "Fur-bearing animals."
Owls.
Hunting with.
Permits, NR §10-907.
Pelts. See within this heading, "Furs."
Penalties.
Black bear.
Hunting, NR §10-423.
Captive wildlife.
Licenses or permits.
Revocation or suspension, NR §10-911.
Collection, NR §10-1102.
Deer.
Hunting with spotlight, NR §10-416.
Exotic birds.
Violations of provisions, HG §24-110.
Fur-bearing animals.
Illegally taken furs.
Possession, sale and transportation, NR §10-505.
General provisions, NR §10-1101.
Hunting licenses.
Suspension of hunting licenses.
Violations of provisions of title, NR §10-1108.

BIRDS AND GAME —Cont'd
Penalties —Cont'd
Nongame and endangered species conservation
    act.
    Violations of subtitle, NR §10-2A-07.
    Restitution, NR §10-1107.
Permits.
Captive wildlife. See within this heading, "Captive
    wildlife."
Exotic birds. See within this heading, "Exotic
    birds."
Falcons, hawks or owls.
    Hunting with, NR §10-907.
Licenses. See within this heading, "Licenses."
Nongame and endangered species conservation
    act.
    Puritan tiger beetle.
        Incidental taking permit, NR §10-2A-05.1.
        Transportation under valid permit, NR
           §10-2A-05.
Regulated shooting grounds, NR §10-906.
Person.
Defined, NR §10-101.
Pests.
Nuisance bird law, AG §§5-801 to 5-804.
    See PESTS.
Pheasants.
Raising game in captivity. See within this
    heading, "Captive wildlife."
Phragmites management and control.
Wildlife habitat areas, NR §§8-2101 to 8-2107.
    See PHRAGMITES.
Poisons.
Use prohibited in killing, NR §10-410.
Ponds.
See PONDS.
Possession.
Game birds and mammals, NR §10-404.
Wild birds.
    Certain wild birds prohibited, NR §10-401.
Poultry products inspection.
Subtitle not applicable, AG §4-203.
Preserves.
Raising game in captivity. See within this
    heading, "Captive wildlife."
Wildlife management areas. See within this
    heading, "Wildlife management areas."
Prisoners of war.
Complimentary licenses, NR §10-303.
    Former prisoner of war.
        Defined, NR §10-303.
Property taxes.
Exemptions.
    Game and Fish Protective Association, property
        owned by, TP §7-306.
Protected birds.
Defined, NR §10-101.
Public recreation on private and local
    government lands.
General provisions, NR §§5-1101 to 5-1109.
    See RECREATIONAL TRESPASS.
Queen Anne's county.
See QUEEN ANNE'S COUNTY.
Raccoons and opossums.
Hunting.
    Generally, NR §10-414.
Possession.
    Closed season, NR §10-414.
Raising game in captivity, NR §§10-901 to
    10-911. See within this heading, "Captive
    wildlife."

BIRDS AND GAME —Cont'd
Records.
Exotic birds.
    Required records, HG §24-106.
Fur-bearing animals.
    Fur dealers, NR §10-507.
Taxidermists and tanners, NR §10-512.
Waterfowl processing operations, NR §10-425.
Reduction of wildlife.
Identifiable areas.
    Authority of department, NR §10-206.
Regulated shooting grounds.
Licenses.
    Special licenses, NR §10-906.
Permits, NR §10-906.
Propagated wildlife.
    Regulations, NR §10-906.
Sunday use, NR §10-906.
Reports.
Fur dealers, NR §10-507.
Hunting heritage protection.
    Maintenance of open lands for hunting.
        Department report to general assembly, NR
           §10-210.
Resident.
Defined, NR §10-101.
Restitution.
Violations of provisions of title.
    Injury, death or destruction of wildlife, NR
        §10-1107.
Right of entry.
Fur-bearing animals.
    Fur dealers.
        Inspections, NR §10-506.
Rules and regulations.
Adoption.
    Authority to adopt, NR §10-205.
Captive wildlife. See within this heading, "Captive
    wildlife."
Collection of wildlife, nests or eggs for scientific or
    educational purposes.
    Permits, NR §10-909.
Emergency situations, NR §10-205.
Falcons, hawks or owls.
    Permits, NR §10-907.
Native wildlife.
    Possessing, importing, exporting, breeding, etc.,
        NR §10-902.
Nongame and endangered species.
    Limitations, NR §10-2A-03.
Nonnative wildlife.
    Importation, exportation, etc.
        Prohibiting or restricting, NR §10-903.
Penalties.
    Violations, NR §10-205.
Petition by certain residents, NR §10-205.
Posting, NR §10-205.
Regulated shooting grounds.
    Propagated wildlife, NR §10-906.
Violations.
    General provisions, NR §10-1101.
Wildlife, NR §10-205.
Wildlife management areas, NR §10-808.
Safety zones.
Shooting or disturbing wildlife in prohibited, NR
    §10-410.
Sales.
Game birds and mammals, NR §10-404.
Wild birds.
    Prohibited, NR §10-401.

BIRDS AND GAME —Cont'd
Scientific or educational purposes.
Collection of wildlife, nests or eggs.
Permits, NR §10-909.
Seals.
Importation or possession with intent to sell dead
body, etc., of seal, NR §10-419.
Searches and seizures.
Devices, equipment or property, NR §10-1106.
Disposition of game fish or unlawful device, NR
§10-1105.
Disposition of wildlife unlawfully caught, NR
§10-1105.
Nongame and endangered species conservation
act.
Power of law enforcement officers, NR
§10-2A-07.
Search warrant, NR §10-1103.
Search without warrant.
Automobiles, NR §10-1104.
General provisions, NR §10-1104.
Seizure of wildlife unlawfully caught, NR
§10-1105.
Warrantless search, NR §10-1104.
Secretary of natural resources.
Responsibilities.
Generally, NR §10-202.
Rulemaking authority, NR §10-601.1.
Statewide system of assistance to local political
subdivisions, NR §10-202.
Shooting grounds.
Regulated shooting grounds, NR §10-906.
Skunks.
Damaging or destroying property.
Hunting or trapping permitted, NR §10-406.
Snow geese.
Nonresident hunting without license, conditions,
NR §10-308.2.
Snowmobiles.
Pursuing wildlife prohibited, NR §10-410.
Spotlighting, NR §10-410.
Deer.
Hunting with, NR §10-416.
Stamps.
Fees, NR §10-301.
Migratory wild waterfowl stamp.
General provisions, NR §10-308.1.
State bird.
Designation of Baltimore oriole as state bird, SG
§13-302.
**Statewide system of assistance to local
political subdivisions.**
Secretary of natural resources.
Secretary to provide for, NR §10-202.
Sundays and holidays.
Captive wildlife regulated shooting grounds.
Sunday use, NR §10-906.
Pen-reared game birds.
Compliance with boundary posting
requirements, NR §10-906.
Hunting on Sundays, NR §10-410.
Swans.
Population control of mute swan, NR §10-211.
Talbot county.
Waterfowl and migratory birds.
Blinds.
Stationary blind or blind site licenses, NR
§10-612.
Tanners.
Licenses, NR §10-512.

BIRDS AND GAME —Cont'd
Tanners —Cont'd
Penalties.
Illegally taken furs.
Possession, sale and transportation, NR
§10-505.
Records, NR §10-512.
Taxidermists.
Licenses, NR §10-512.
Revocation.
Illegally taken furs, NR §10-505.
Penalties.
Illegally taken furs, NR §10-505.
Records, NR §10-512.
Transportation.
Nongame and endangered species conservation
act. See within this heading, "Nongame and
endangered species conservation act."
Trapping.
Fur dealers. See within this heading, "Fur-bearing
animals."
Generally. See within this heading, "Fur-bearing
animals."
United States.
Wildlife restoration.
Assent to public law 415, NR §10-208.
Unprotected birds.
Defined, NR §10-101.
Unprotected mammals.
Defined, NR §10-101.
Upland game birds and mammals.
Defined, NR §10-101.
Hunting upland game birds.
Baiting, NR §10-412.
Upland wildlife habitat fund, NR §10-301.
Veterans.
Complimentary licenses.
Disabled veterans, NR §10-303.
Former prisoner of war, NR §10-303.
Defined, NR §10-303.
Warrants.
Search warrants.
General provisions, NR §10-1103.
Searching without warrants, NR §10-1104.
Washington county.
See WASHINGTON COUNTY.
Waterfowl and migratory birds.
Blinds.
Fees, NR §10-612.
Licenses, NR §10-612.
Fees, NR §10-612.
Locations for erecting blind sites.
Forbidden locations, NR §10-614.
Loss of blind site markers, NR §10-613.
Offshore blind sites, NR §10-609.
Public access to, NR §10-610.
Riparian shorelines.
Licensing by riparian landowners, NR
§10-607.
Site.
License, NR §10-612.
Offshore, NR §10-609.
Stationary blind.
License.
Required, NR §10-612.
Trespass and unauthorized use of licensed
stationary blinds, NR §10-615.
Body booting, NR §10-611.
Definitions, NR §§5-103, 10-101.
Eggs.
Hunting and taking prohibited, NR §10-402.

BIRDS AND GAME —Cont'd
Waterfowl and migratory birds —Cont'd
Federal law.
Hunting in violation, NR §10-403.
Feeding.
Definitions, NR §10-1001.
Federal law, NR §10-1009.
Hunting.
Prohibition, NR §10-1005.
Inapplicability of subtitle, NR §10-1007.
Legislative policy, NR §10-1002.
Licenses.
Application, NR §10-1003.
Cancellation, NR §10-1004.
Denial, NR §10-1004.
Feeding without license, NR §10-1008.
Inspection, NR §10-1006.
Location and zone, NR §10-1005.
Marking of feeding zone, NR §10-1005.
Regulation of feeding, NR §10-1005.
Without license, NR §10-1008.
Guides.
Waterfowl hunting guide licenses, NR §10-309.
Hunting.
Birds resting on land or water, NR §10-602.
Boats.
Anchored boats, NR §10-606.
Drifting boats, NR §10-605.
Federal law.
Violating federal law, NR §10-403.
First day of firearm season for hunting deer.
Restrictions on.
Hunting waterfowl from licensed gunning rig within sea duck shooting zone and gunning rig zone, NR §10-421.
Guides.
Waterfowl hunting guide licenses, NR §10-309.
Licenses.
Guides.
Waterfowl hunting guide licenses, NR §10-309.
Limitations, NR §10-603.
Limits.
Possession in excess of, NR §10-403.
Nests and eggs.
Prohibited, NR §10-402.
Nighttime, NR §10-602.
Permissible hunting, NR §10-604.
Prohibitions, NR §10-602.
Hunting on private property, NR §10-604.
Resting on land or water.
Shooting prohibited, NR §§10-602, 10-603.
Riparian shorelines.
Licensing by riparian landowners, NR §10-607.
Stamp.
Migratory wild waterfowl stamp, NR §10-308.1.
Standing in water on natural bottom, NR §10-604.
Violation of federal and state law, NR §10-403.
Waterfowl hunting guide licenses, NR §10-309.
Weapons.
Restriction, NR §10-602.
Inspections.
Waterfowl processing operations, NR §10-425.
Licenses.
Blinds, NR §10-612.
Feeding. See within this subheading, "Feeding."

BIRDS AND GAME —Cont'd
Waterfowl and migratory birds —Cont'd
Licenses —Cont'd
Maryland residents as license applicants, NR §10-608.
Required for wild waterfowl hunters, NR §10-611.
Shorelines, NR §10-607.
Waterfowl processing operations, NR §10-425.
Migratory waterfowl stamp, NR §10-308.1.
Mute swan, NR §10-211.
Nests.
Hunting prohibited, NR §10-402.
Offshore blind sites, NR §10-609.
Open seasons, NR §10-407.
Raising game in captivity. See within this heading, "Captive wildlife."
Records.
Waterfowl processing operations, NR §10-425.
Refuge.
Hunting.
Federal and state bird refuges, NR §10-403.
Sampling methods, NR §10-210.
Stamp required in addition to hunting licenses.
General provisions, NR §10-308.1.
Stationary blind.
General provisions. See within this subheading, "Blinds."
Tagging.
Waterfowl processing operations, NR §10-425.
Waterfowl processing operations.
Defined, NR §10-101.
Inspections, NR §10-425.
Licenses, NR §10-425.
Records.
Annual submission, NR §10-425.
Tagging.
Required, NR §10-425.
Wild waterfowl.
Defined, NR §10-101.
Mute swan, NR §10-211.
Sampling methods, NR §10-210.
Weapons.
Hunting. See within this heading, "Hunting."
Regulation of use, NR §10-408.
Wild waterfowl.
Restriction on weapons, NR §10-602.
Weasels.
Hunting with prohibited, NR §10-410.
Wetland game birds.
Defined, NR §10-101.
Hunting.
Baiting, NR §10-412.
Open seasons, NR §10-407.
Wetlands.
General provisions.
See WETLANDS.
Wild birds.
Defined, NR §10-101.
Eggs.
Hunting and taking, NR §10-402.
Hunting.
Prohibited for certain wild birds, NR §10-401.
Nests.
Hunting and taking, NR §10-402.
Possession.
Prohibited for certain wild birds, NR §10-401.
Sale.
Prohibited, NR §10-401.
Wildlife.
Defined, NR §10-101.

BIRDS AND GAME —Cont'd
Wildlife —Cont'd
Reduction of wildlife.
Authority of department, NR §10-206.
Wildlife advisory commission.
Composition, NR §1-102.
Continuation of membership of former
commission, NR §10-204.
Established, NR §10-204.
State boat act.
See VESSELS AND BOATS.
Terms, NR §1-102.
Wildlife cooperators.
Permits, NR §10-908.
Wildlife management areas.
Acquisition of land or water, NR §10-801.
Expenditures, NR §10-802.
Control of land or water, NR §10-802.
Deeds, NR §10-803.
Exchange of area of land or water, NR §10-803.
Expenditures.
Acquisition of land or water, NR §10-802.
Phragmites management and control, NR
§§8-2101 to 8-2107.
See PHRAGMITES.
Rules and regulations.
Adoption, NR §10-808.
Sale of area of land or water, NR §10-803.
State parks.
Use as, NR §10-803.
State wildlife refuges.
Entry on, NR §10-807.
Establishment, NR §10-805.
Leased land or water, NR §10-806.
Title of land or water, NR §10-802.
Use of land or water, NR §10-804.
Wild mammals.
Defined, NR §10-101.
Wild quadrupeds.
Defined, NR §10-101.
Wild waterfowl. See within this heading,
"Waterfowl and migratory birds."

BIRTH CERTIFICATES.
Vital records.
See VITAL RECORDS.

BIRTHS.
Certificates.
Vital records.
See VITAL RECORDS.
Hospitals.
Universal newborn hearing screening program,
HG §19-308.5.
Identification of newborns, HG §§20-401, 20-402.
Records.
Identification of newborns, HG §20-402.
Registration.
See VITAL RECORDS.
Reports.
Sentinel birth defects, HG §18-206.
Vital records.
See VITAL RECORDS.

BLACK BEARS.
Black bear damage reimbursement fund, NR
§10-423.1.
Hunting, NR §10-423.

BLACK-EYED SUSAN.
Designation as state flower, SG §13-305.

BLACKOUTS.
Duty of police officers.
Charging semiconscious or unconscious person
with crime, CP §2-107.
**Identification worn by persons suffering from
conditions causing,** CP §2-107.

BLACK POWDER HUNTING SEASON.
Deer, NR §10-420.

BLANK INDORSEMENTS.
Negotiable instruments, CL §3-205.

BLASTING.
Explosives generally, PS §§11-101 to 11-118.
See EXPLOSIONS AND EXPLOSIVES.

BLIND PERSONS.
Aviation.
Rights of blind persons to public facilities, 30 §33.
Blind industries and services of Maryland.
Application.
Blind person to operate a business, 30 §8.
Board of trustees, powers, 30 §3.
Unemployment compensation.
Eligibility for benefits.
Ability to work and availability for work, LE
§8-903.
When covered employment, LE §8-216.
Boardinghouses.
Rights of blind persons to public facilities, 30 §33.
**Board of trustees of blind industries and
services of Maryland.**
Training and employment centers. See within this
heading, "Training and employment centers."
Business.
Application to blind industries and services of
Maryland to operate a business, 30 §8.
Workers' compensation law.
Certificate of compliance, 30 §10A.
Carriers.
Rights of blind persons to public facilities, 30 §33.
Damages.
Guide dogs.
Liability of blind or visually handicapped person
for damages done by dog to premises or
facilities, 30 §33.
Definitions.
Meaning of "blind," 30 §32.
Dogs.
Guide dogs.
Blind pedestrians, TR §21-511.
Damages.
Liability of blind or visually handicapped
person for damages done to premises or
facilities by dog, 30 §33.
Right of blind person to be accompanied by
guide dog, 30 §33.
Rights of blind or visually handicapped person
not using guide dog, 30 §33.
Trainers' rights, 30 §33.
Drivers' licenses.
Public assistance for blindness.
Administration to obtain names of persons
receiving, TR §16-120.
Vision requirements, TR §16-110.1.
Bioptic telescopic lenses, TR §16-110.2.
Daylight driving only and outside mirrors each
side restricted licenses, TR §16-110.3.
Dwellings.
Tax exemption, TP §7-207.
Refund of property tax, TP §7-207.
Surviving spouse, TP §7-207.

BLIND PERSONS —Cont'd
Employers and employees.
Rights of blind or visually handicapped persons in employment, 30 §33.
Exemptions.
Dwellings.
Tax exemption, TP §7-207.
Fines.
Denial or interference with blind persons' rights, 30 §33.
Food and food establishments.
Right of blind person to public facilities, 30 §33.
Governor.
Training and employment centers.
Trustees.
Appointment by governor, 30 §5.
White cane safety day.
Proclamation by governor, 30 §33.
Guide dogs. See within this heading, "Dogs."
Hotels.
Rights of blind persons to public facilities, 30 §33.
Housing.
Damages.
Liability of blind or visually handicapped tenant for damages done by dog, 30 §33.
Guide dogs.
Blind or visually handicapped tenant not required to pay extra compensation, 30 §33.
Housing accommodations defined, 30 §33.
Rights of blind persons to public facilities, 30 §33.
Tax exemption of dwellings, TP §7-207.
Income tax.
Individuals.
Adjusted gross income.
Subtractions from federal adjusted gross income.
Blindness-related expenses, TG §10-208.
Insurance.
Discrimination in rates, premium payments or dividends, IN §27-208.
Motor carriers.
Rights of blind persons to public facilities, 30 §33.
Negligence.
Contributory negligence.
Blind or visually handicapped pedestrian not carrying white cane or using guide dog, 30 §33.
Pedestrians.
Canes.
Use of white or metal cane, TR §21-511.
Guide dogs, TR §21-511.
Right-of-way, TR §21-511.
Vehicles to come to full stop, TR §21-511.
Procurement.
Business enterprise program for the blind, SF §14-109.
Products made by the blind, CL §§14-2801 to 14-2807.
Definitions, CL §14-2801.
Effect of subtitle, CL §14-2802.
Identifying marks on products.
Generally, CL §14-2805.
Use of "blind" in name, CL §14-2804.
Penalties for violation of subtitle, CL §14-2807.
Permit requirement.
Sales of products, CL §14-2806.
Prohibited acts.
Sales of products, CL §14-2803.
Violation of subtitle.
Penalties, CL §14-2807.

BLIND PERSONS —Cont'd
Products made by the blind —Cont'd
Registration requirement.
Sales of products, CL §14-2806.
Use of "blind" in name, CL §14-2804.
Public assistance.
Application for assistance.
False or fraudulent statement, 88A §62.
Records.
Misuse of public assistance lists and records, 88A §6.
Social services.
Coordinating agency of social service and public assistance activities, 88A §3.
Public buildings and grounds.
Management of vending facilities, ED §21-304.
Rights of blind persons to public facilities, 30 §33.
Railroads.
Rights of blind persons to public facilities, 30 §33.
Schools.
Absence.
Excused by superintendent or principal, ED §8-302.
Age between six and nineteen years.
Attendance required, ED §8-301.
Definition, ED §8-301.
Examinations.
Medical examinations, ED §8-311.
Handicapped children.
General provisions.
See SCHOOLS.
Individualized education programs, ED §8-408.
Maryland School for the Blind.
General provisions.
See SCHOOLS.
Penalty.
Inducing to leave school, ED §8-311.
Person having such child under control.
Failure to comply with provisions, ED §8-311.
Rights of blind or visually handicapped persons in employment, 30 §33.
Teachers.
Certification and hiring, ED §2-205.
Streets and alleys.
Rights of blind persons to public facilities, 30 §33.
Taxation.
Exemptions.
Dwellings, TP §7-207.
Vending program for the blind, TP §§7-211, 7-235.
Income tax.
Individual gross income.
Subtractions from federal adjusted gross income.
Blindness-related expenses, TG §10-208.
Trader licenses, BR §17-1808.
Additional licenses and fees prohibited, BR §17-1803.
Applications for licenses, BR §17-1803.
Violating license provisions, BR §17-1816.
Training and employment centers.
Application of endowment fund, 30 §3.
Establishment, 30 §4.
Location, 30 §4.
Trustees, 30 §§5, 6.
Vending machines.
Management by blind persons in government buildings, ED §21-304.
Procurement.
Business enterprise program for the blind, SF §14-109.

BLIND PERSONS —Cont'd
Vending machines —Cont'd
Taxation.
Exemptions.
Vending program for the blind, TP §§7-211, 7-235.
Vessels and boats.
Rights of blind persons to public facilities, 30 §33.
White cane law.
Rights of pedestrian using a guide dog but not carrying a white cane, 30 §33.
White cane safety day.
Proclamation by governor, 30 §33.

BLINDS.
Waterfowl and migratory birds.
General provisions.
See BIRDS AND GAME.

BLOCKBUSTING.
Real estate brokers.
Prohibited acts, BOP §17-608.

BLOCK GRANTS.
Grants generally.
See GRANTS.

BLOOD BANKS.
Anatomical gift act.
General provisions, ET §§4-501 to 4-512.
See ANATOMICAL GIFT ACT.
Health insurance coverage for blood products, IN §15-803.
Liability.
Obtaining, processing, etc., blood for injection or transfusion, CJ §5-630; HG §18-402.
Medicare supplement insurance, IN §15-906.
Minors.
Donations with or without parental permission, HG §20-101.
Property taxes.
Credits.
Montgomery county, TP §9-317.
Exemptions, TP §7-302.
Public cord blood banks.
Umbilical cord blood donations, hospitals to arrange, HG §19-308.7.
Tissue banks.
General provisions, HG §§17-301 to 17-314.
See TISSUE BANKS.
Umbilical cord blood donations, hospitals to arrange, HG §19-308.7.
Warranty.
Obtaining, processing, etc., blood for injection or transfusion, CJ §5-630; HG §18-402.

BLOODBORNE PATHOGEN STANDARD.
Regulation to implement standard, notice of modification, LE §5-308.1.

BLOOD PRESSURE.
High blood pressure.
Cardiovascular disease prevention programs, HG §§13-201 to 13-206.
See HEART DISEASE AND STROKE PREVENTION PROGRAMS.

BLOOD TESTS.
Acquired immune deficiency syndrome.
Human immunodeficiency virus testing, HG §§18-336 to 18-338.3.
AIDS testing, HG §§18-336 to 18-338.3.
Altering results of drug or alcohol screening, CR §10-111.

BLOOD TESTS —Cont'd
Blood lead tests.
Case management for children with elevated levels, EN §6-304.
Reporting of results, EN §6-303.
Boxers and kick boxers.
License applicants, BR §4-304.1.
Cholesterol testing, HG §§17-501 to 17-511.
See CHOLESTEROL TESTING.
Consent.
Liability for taking blood without consent of individual, HG §20-110.
Criminal procedure.
Consent.
Liability for taking blood without consent, HG §20-110.
Driving while intoxicated.
See DRIVING UNDER THE INFLUENCE.
HIV testing, HG §§18-336 to 18-338.3.
Hospitals.
Liability for taking blood without consent, HG §20-110.
Implied consent law, TR §16-205.1.
Job-related alcohol and drug testing, HG §17-214.
Lead risk reduction in rental housing.
Availability, EN §6-829.
Disclosure of results, EN §6-847.
Notification of high blood lead, EN §6-846.
Liability.
Obtaining, processing, etc., blood for injection or transfusion, HG §18-402.
Motor vehicles.
Drunkenness.
See DRIVING UNDER THE INFLUENCE.
Paternity proceedings, FL §5-1029.
Pretrial inquiry by state's attorney, FL §5-1021.
Physicians.
Liability for taking blood without consent, HG §20-110.
Pregnancy.
Syphilis test, HG §18-307.
Syphilis.
Required blood test, HG §18-307.
Warranty.
Obtaining, processing, etc., blood for injection or transfusion, HG §18-402.

BLUE CRAB.
Crab meat generally.
See CRAB MEAT.
Crustaceans generally.
See CRABS.
State crustacean, SG §13-301.

BLUE CROSS/BLUE SHIELD PLANS.
Disclosure of medical information, IN §§4-403, 14-138.

BLUE LAWS, BR §§18-101 to 18-202.
Cambridge.
See CAMBRIDGE.
Caroline county.
See CAROLINE COUNTY.
Carroll county.
See CARROLL COUNTY.
Centreville.
See CENTREVILLE.
Definitions.
Banks and trust companies, FI §5-701.
Legal holiday, 1 §27.

BLUE LAWS —Cont'd
Dorchester county.
See DORCHESTER COUNTY.
Garrett county.
See GARRETT COUNTY.
Havre de grace.
See HAVRE DE GRACE.
Howard county.
See HOWARD COUNTY.
Hunting on Sundays, NR §10-410.
Captive wildlife regulated shooting grounds, NR §10-906.
Municipal corporations.
Acts prohibited by state law on Sabbath, MD Const Art XI-E §6.
Professional sports, BR §18-102.
Retail and wholesale establishments, BR §18-101.
Wicomico county, BR §18-202.
Scope of subtitle, BR §18-201.
Scope of subtitle, BR §18-201.
Talbot county.
See TALBOT COUNTY.
Taxation.
Legal holiday.
Defined, 24 §1-104; TP §1-303.
Time for performance of acts.
Last day falling on Saturday, Sunday or legal holiday, 24 §1-104; TP §1-303.
Worcester county.
See WORCESTER COUNTY.

BLUEPRINTS.
Inspection of public records, SG §10-618.

BLUE SKY LAW.
Savings and loan associations.
Exemption from blue sky law, FI §9-904.
Securities act.
General provisions, CA §§11-101 to 11-805.
See SECURITIES.

BOARDINGHOUSES.
Blind persons.
Rights of blind persons to public facilities, 30 §33.
Deaf or mute persons.
Rights of deaf or mute persons to public facilities, 30 §33.
Discrimination in public accommodations.
General provisions, 49B §§5 to 8A.
See DISCRIMINATION.
Hotels.
General provisions.
See HOTELS.
Liens.
Personal effects, goods or furniture of boarder or lodger, CL §16-503.

BOARDS AND COMMISSIONS.
Abolition of boards, commissions, agencies, etc.
Program evaluation act, SG §§8-401 to 8-413.
See PROGRAM EVALUATION ACT.
Reorganization of government, SG §§10-701 to 10-706.
See REORGANIZATION OF GOVERNMENT.
Accountants.
Board of public accountancy, BOP §§2-201 to 2-211.
Acupuncturists.
Board, HO §§1A-201 to 1A-206.
See ACUPUNCTURISTS.

BOARDS AND COMMISSIONS —Cont'd
Adult offender supervision interstate commission, COR §6-204.
Advisors for electronic commerce, SG §§9-2201 to 9-2204.
Advisory boards.
Agriculture.
Creation.
Secretary of agriculture, AG §2-103.
Agriculture.
Advisory boards.
Creation.
Secretary of agriculture, AG §2-103.
Young farmers advisory board, AG §§2-1001 to 2-1005.
Agricultural commission, AG §§2-201 to 2-205.
Advisory boards.
Membership, AG §2-103.
Department of agriculture.
Unit within department, AG §§2-106, 2-202.
Agricultural preservation advisory boards, AG §2-504.1.
See AGRICULTURE.
Board of agriculture.
See AGRICULTURE.
Board of review, AG §§2-401 to 2-405.
See AGRICULTURE.
Fair board, AG §§10-301 to 10-303.
Winery and grape growers' advisory commission, AG §§10-1201 to 10-1206.
See ALCOHOLIC BEVERAGES.
Young farmers advisory board, AG §§2-1001 to 2-1005.
Air conditioning and heating contractors.
General provisions, BR §§9A-201 to 9A-207.
See AIR CONDITIONING AND HEATING CONTRACTORS.
Alcoholic beverages.
Appeals.
State appeal board.
See ALCOHOLIC BEVERAGES.
License commissioners.
See ALCOHOLIC BEVERAGES.
Liquor control board.
See ALCOHOLIC BEVERAGES.
Winery and grape growers' advisory commission, AG §§10-1201 to 10-1206.
See ALCOHOLIC BEVERAGES.
Allegany county.
Salary study commissions, 24 §§12-101 to 12-106.
See ALLEGANY COUNTY.
Amusement safety advisory board.
General provisions, BR §§3-301 to 3-314.
See AMUSEMENTS AND RECREATION.
Anatomy board.
See ANATOMY BOARD.
Appalachian regional commission.
State member and alternate member to federal commission, 83A §6-702.
Appeals.
Alcoholic beverages.
State appeal board.
See ALCOHOLIC BEVERAGES.
Apple commission.
General provisions.
See APPLES.
Architects.
State board of architects, BOP §§3-201 to 3-211.
See ARCHITECTS.

BOARDS AND COMMISSIONS —Cont'd

Architecture.
General services department.
Architectural review.
Board of architectural review, SF §§4-701 to 4-704.

Artistic property commission, SG §§9-1016 to 9-1023.
See ARTISTIC PROPERTY COMMISSION.

Arts council.
General provisions, 83A §§4-601 to 4-609.
See ARTS COUNCIL.

Assisted living programs board, SG §9-1901.

Athletic commission.
General provisions, BR §§4-201 to 4-208.
See BOXING, SPARRING AND WRESTLING.

Atlantic states marine fisheries commission.
General provisions, NR §§4-301 to 4-307.
See ATLANTIC STATES MARINE FISHERIES COMMISSION.

Attorneys at law.
Admission to the bar.
Board of law examiners, BOP §§10-201 to 10-203.
See ATTORNEYS AT LAW.

Audiologists.
Board of examiners for audiologists, hearing aid dealers and speech-language pathologists.
See AUDIOLOGISTS AND SPEECH-LANGUAGE PATHOLOGISTS.

Aviation.
See AVIATION.

Banking board.
See BANKS AND TRUST COMPANIES.

Barbers.
State board of barbers, BOP §§4-201 to 4-209.
See BARBERS.

Boilers and pressure vessels.
Board of boiler rules, PS §12-904.
Board defined, PS §12-901.
Program evaluation act, SG §8-403.
Rules and regulations.
Authority to promulgate, PS §12-905.

Brain injury advisory board, HG §§13-2101 to 13-2105.

Building, savings and loan association commissioners.
General provisions.
See SAVINGS AND LOAN ASSOCIATIONS.

Business and economic development department.
Calling of meetings of boards by secretary, 83A §2-106.
Economic development commission, 83A §§1-201 to 1-204.
See BUSINESS AND ECONOMIC DEVELOPMENT DEPARTMENT.
Included within department, 83A §2-104.
Maryland advisory commission on manufacturing competitiveness, 83A §§3-801 to 3-804.
Reports to secretary, 83A §2-105.

Capital city.
Commission on the capital city, SG §§9-401 to 9-407.

Censors.
State board of censors.
See MOTION PICTURES.

Charles county.
Gaming permit review board, CR §13-1104.

Charter board.
Baltimore City.
See BALTIMORE CITY.

BOARDS AND COMMISSIONS —Cont'd

Charter board —Cont'd
Counties.
See COUNTIES.

Chesapeake Bay and coastal zone advisory commission.
Established, NR §8-201.

Chesapeake Bay commission, NR §8-301.

Chesapeake Bay critical area and Atlantic coastal bays critical area protection programs.
Critical areas commission, NR §§8-1803 to 8-1806.

Chesapeake Bay critical area commission.
See CHESAPEAKE BAY.

Chesapeake Bay trust.
Board of trustees.
See CHESAPEAKE BAY.

Children, youth and families services.
Local management boards, 49D §§2-101 to 2-105.

Chiropractors.
Board of chiropractic examiners.
See CHIROPRACTORS.

Chronic disease centers.
Advisory boards.
See HOSPITALS.

College savings plan of Maryland board, ED §§18-1904, 18-1905.

Commissioner of financial regulation.
See BANKS AND TRUST COMPANIES.

Commission on aging, 70B §3.

Commission on responsible fatherhood, 41 §§18-401 to 18-408.

Community action boards, HS §8-105.

Community reinvestment board, HS §§9-201 to 9-204.

Consumer credit.
Commissioner of consumer credit.
See CONSUMER CREDIT.

Copies.
Fees.
Commissions exempt from fees, RP §3-603.

Correctional standards, commission on, COR §§8-106 to 8-117.
See PRISONS AND PRISONERS.

Correctional training commission, COR §§8-201 to 2-210.
See CORRECTIONAL TRAINING COMMISSION.

Cosmetologists.
State board of cosmetologists, BOP §§5-201 to 5-210.
See COSMETOLOGISTS.

Counties.
County codes.
Deposited with state agencies, 25 §32A.

County boards of education.
Schools.
See SCHOOLS.

County commissioners.
General provisions, 25 §§1 to 219.
See COUNTIES.

Criminal offenses.
Board of victim services.
See VICTIMS OF CRIME.
Suspension or removal from commission, SG §8-502.

Dentists.
Board of dental examiners.
See DENTISTS.

Depositions.
Commissioners to take depositions.
See WITNESSES.

BOARDS AND COMMISSIONS —Cont'd
Disabilities.
Commission on disabilities, SG §§9-1109 to
9-1112.
Interagency disabilities board, SG §§9-1113 to
9-1115.
Discrimination.
Cases involving state agencies, 49B §7.
E-commerce, advisory board, SG §§9-2201 to
9-2204.
Economic development commission, 83A
§§1-201 to 1-204.
See BUSINESS AND ECONOMIC
DEVELOPMENT DEPARTMENT.
Elections.
Board of state canvassers, EL §11-502.
County boards of elections.
Generally, EL §§2-201 to 2-303.
See ELECTIONS.
Local boards of canvassers, EL §11-301.
State board of elections.
Generally, EL §§2-101 to 2-303.
See ELECTIONS.
Electricians.
State board of master electricians, BOP §§6-201 to
6-208.
See ELECTRICIANS.
Electrology practice committee, HO §§8-6B-05,
8-6B-06.
Elevator safety review board, PS §§12-819 to
12-842.
Emergency number systems board, PS §1-305.
Employment and social services.
Board of review.
See SOCIAL SERVICES.
Engineers.
State board for professional engineers, BOP
§§14-201 to 14-211.
See ENGINEERS.
Environmental justice commission, EN §1-701.
Environmental sanitarians.
Board of environmental sanitarians.
General provisions, EN §§11-201 to 11-207.
See ENVIRONMENTAL SANITARIANS.
Environmental service.
Board of directors, NR §3-103.
Equal pay commission, LE §3-309.
Evaluation.
Maryland program evaluation act, SG §§8-401 to
8-413.
See PROGRAM EVALUATION ACT.
Evidence.
Commissions to take testimony.
Cases pending in other states.
See WITNESSES.
Fair board, AG §§10-301 to 10-303.
Foresters.
State board of foresters, BOP §§7-201 to 7-208.
See FORESTERS.
Forests and parks.
District forestry board.
See FORESTS AND PARKS.
Gaming commission, CR §§13-2415 to 13-2419.
General services department.
Board of architectural review.
See GENERAL SERVICES DEPARTMENT.
Geological survey commission.
See MARYLAND GEOLOGICAL SURVEY.
Governor's workforce investment board, LE
§11-505.

BOARDS AND COMMISSIONS —Cont'd
Grape growers.
Winery and grape growers' advisory commission,
AG §§10-1201 to 10-1206.
See ALCOHOLIC BEVERAGES.
Guardianship advisory board.
Immunity from civil liability, CJ §5-515.
Hall of records commission, SG §§9-1001 to
9-1004.
See HALL OF RECORDS.
Handguns.
Permit review board.
See WEAPONS.
Hazardous waste facility siting board.
See HAZARDOUS WASTE FACILITY SITING.
Health.
Cost review commission, HG §§19-201 to 19-227.
See HEALTH.
Department of health and mental hygiene.
Board of review.
See HEALTH.
Maryland commission for men's health, HG
§§13-2401 to 13-2408.
See MARYLAND COMMISSION FOR MEN'S
HEALTH.
Health and human services referral board, HG
§24-1203.
Health care commission, HG §§19-101 to 19-111.
See MARYLAND HEALTH CARE COMMISSION.
Hearing aid dealers.
Board of examiners for audiologists, hearing aid
dealers and speech-language pathologists.
See AUDIOLOGISTS AND
SPEECH-LANGUAGE PATHOLOGISTS.
Herring Run public watershed association.
See HERRING RUN PUBLIC WATERSHED
ASSOCIATION.
Higher education commission.
Universities and colleges.
Higher education commission.
See UNIVERSITIES AND COLLEGES.
Highways.
Board of property review.
See HIGHWAYS.
State highway access valuation board, TR §8-310.
State roads commission.
General provisions, TR §§8-210 to 8-218.
See HIGHWAYS.
Historic district commission.
General provisions.
See ZONING.
Home improvements.
General provisions, BR §§8-201 to 8-214.
See HOME IMPROVEMENTS.
Home inspectors hearing board, BOP §16-210.1.
Horse industry board, AG §§2-701 to 2-719.
See HORSE INDUSTRY BOARD.
Hospitals.
Advisory board.
See HOSPITALS.
Chronic disease centers.
Advisory boards.
See HOSPITALS.
Housing and community development.
Community action agencies.
Community action boards, HS §8-105.
Community reinvestment fund.
Community reinvestment board, HS §§9-201 to
9-204.
Human relations commission.
General provisions, 49B §§1 to 4, 9 to 13.
See HUMAN RELATIONS COMMISSION.

BOARDS AND COMMISSIONS —Cont'd
Immunization.
Statewide advisory commission on, HG §18-214.
Indians.
Commission on Indian affairs.
Ethnic affairs unit, SF §§2-701, 2-702.
Information technology board, SF §§3-406 to 3-409.
Interior designers.
State board of certified interior designers, BOP §§8-201 to 8-208.
See INTERIOR DESIGNERS.
Joseph fund board, SF §7-327.
Judicial disabilities commission.
Appeal of decision, CJA Rule 16-809.
Confidentiality of proceedings, CJA Rule 16-810.
General provisions, CJ §§13-401 to 13-403; CJA Rule 16-804; MD Const Art IV §§4A, 4B.
See JUDICIAL DISABILITIES COMMISSION.
Proceedings before commission, CJA Rule 16-808.
Juvenile services.
State advisory board for juvenile services, 83C §§2-106 to 2-110.
Kidney diseases commission.
See KIDNEY DISEASES COMMISSION.
Landscape architects.
State board of examiners, BOP §§9-201 to 9-208.
See LANDSCAPE ARCHITECTS.
Land surveyors.
State board for professional land surveyors, BOP §§15-201 to 15-211.
See SURVEYS AND SURVEYORS.
Lead poisoning prevention commission, EN §§6-807 to 6-810.
Letterhead stationary, SG §8-503.
Library trustees board, ED §§23-401 to 23-407.
See LIBRARY TRUSTEES BOARD.
Local management boards.
Children, youth and families services, 49D §§2-101 to 2-105.
Management and productivity council, SG §§9-1801 to 9-1812.
See MANAGEMENT AND PRODUCTIVITY COUNCIL.
Maryland advisory commission on manufacturing competitiveness, 83A §§3-801 to 3-804.
Maryland commission for men's health, HG §§13-2401 to 13-2408.
See MARYLAND COMMISSION FOR MEN'S HEALTH.
Maryland geological survey.
Commission, NR §2-204.
Maryland health care commission, HG §§19-101 to 19-111.
See MARYLAND HEALTH CARE COMMISSION.
Maryland-national capital park and planning commission.
See MARYLAND-NATIONAL CAPITAL PARK AND PLANNING COMMISSION.
Maryland Transit Administration.
Public service commission.
See MARYLAND TRANSIT ADMINISTRATION.
Maryland veterans commission, SG §§9-915 to 9-919.
Maryland winery and grape growers' advisory commission, AG §§10-1201 to 10-1206.
See ALCOHOLIC BEVERAGES.
Meetings.
Failure to attend, SG §8-501.

BOARDS AND COMMISSIONS —Cont'd
Meetings —Cont'd
Regular and special meetings.
Open to public, 41 §1-205.
Men's health.
Maryland commission for men's health, HG §§13-2401 to 13-2408.
Mental hygiene law.
Citizens' advisory boards.
See MENTAL HYGIENE LAW.
Meridian line.
General provisions, 25 §§123 to 127.
See MERIDIAN LINE.
Mining.
Commission on mining laws.
General provisions.
See MINING.
Examining board.
General provisions.
See MINING.
Morticians.
Board of morticians.
See MORTICIANS.
Municipal planning and zoning commission.
General provisions.
See ZONING.
Natural resources.
Department.
Units within, NR §1-102.
Natural resources advisory commissions.
See NATURAL RESOURCES.
911 emergency telephone system.
Emergency number systems board, PS §1-305.
Nurses.
Board of nursing.
See NURSES.
Nursing home administrators.
Board of examiners of nursing home administrators.
See NURSING HOME ADMINISTRATORS.
Occupational safety and health advisory board.
General provisions, LE §§5-301 to 5-305.
See OCCUPATIONAL SAFETY AND HEALTH.
Occupational therapists.
Board of occupational therapy practice.
See OCCUPATIONAL THERAPISTS.
Ocean City convention hall commission.
General provisions.
See OCEAN CITY.
Open meetings, 41 §1-205.
Optometrists.
Board of examiners in optometry.
See OPTOMETRISTS.
Parks advisory commission.
See FORESTS AND PARKS.
Parole commission, COR §§7-201 to 7-208.
See PAROLE AND PROBATION.
Patuxent institution.
Board of review, COR §§4-205, 4-206.
Citizens advisory board, COR §4-207.
Patuxent river commission.
General provisions, SF §§5-812 to 5-816.
See PATUXENT RIVER.
Pensions.
State pension commissioner.
Office prohibited, MD Const Art III §59.
Pharmacists and pharmacies.
Board of pharmacy.
See PHARMACISTS AND PHARMACIES.

BOARDS AND COMMISSIONS —Cont'd

Physical therapists.
Board of physical therapy examiners.
See PHYSICAL THERAPISTS.

Physicians.
Board of physicians.
See PHYSICIANS.

Pilots.
State board of pilots, BOP §§11-201 to 11-208.
See PILOTS.

Planning.
Municipal planning and zoning commission, 66B §§3.01 to 3.09.
See ZONING.

Plumbers.
State board of plumbing, BOP §§12-201 to 12-210.
See PLUMBERS AND PLUMBING.

Podiatrists.
Board of podiatry examiners.
See PODIATRISTS.

Postmortem examiners commission.
See POSTMORTEM EXAMINERS.

Potomac river basin commission, EN §§5-303, 5-304.

Procurement.
Architectural and engineering services.
Selection boards.
See PROCUREMENT.
Board of public works.
See PROCUREMENT.
Dispute resolution.
Appeals board, SF §§15-201, 15-205 to 15-212.
See PROCUREMENT.

Program evaluation act, SG §§8-401 to 8-413.
See PROGRAM EVALUATION ACT.

Psychologists.
Board of examiners of psychologists.
See PSYCHOLOGISTS.

Public defender.
Board of trustees, 27A §9.

Public ethics.
State ethics commission.
See PUBLIC ETHICS.

Public service commission.
Generally, PUC §§2-101 to 5-106.
See PUBLIC SERVICE COMMISSION.

Public works.
Board of public works.
General provisions.
See PUBLIC WORKS.
Procurement.
See PROCUREMENT.
Public debt.
See PUBLIC DEBT.

Purchases.
See BUDGET AND MANAGEMENT.

Real estate appraisal hearing board, BOP §16-210.

Real estate appraisers and home inspectors.
State commission, BOP §§16-201 to 16-220.
See REAL ESTATE APPRAISERS AND HOME INSPECTORS.

Real estate commission, BOP §§17-201 to 17-214.
See REAL ESTATE BROKERS.

Recordation.
Fees.
Commissions exempt from fees, RP §3-603.

Recycling solid waste.
Newsprint recycling board, EN §9-1707.

Renewable fuels incentive board, AG §10-1503.

BOARDS AND COMMISSIONS —Cont'd

Reorganization of government, SG §§10-701 to 10-706.
See REORGANIZATION OF GOVERNMENT.

Residential child care program administrators.
State board for certification, HO §§20-201 to 20-207.

Revenues.
Board of revenue estimates.
See REVENUES.

Roads commission.
General provisions, TR §§8-210 to 8-218.
See HIGHWAYS.

Rural broadband coordination board, 41 §§21-101 to 21-103.

Rural legacy board, NR §§5-9A-03, 5-9A-04.

St. Mary's county human relations commission, 49B §§44 to 51.

Sanitarians.
Environmental sanitarians.
Board of environmental sanitarians.
General provisions, EN §§11-201 to 11-207.

Sanitary commissions.
See SANITARY COMMISSIONS.

Savings and loan associations.
Board of commissioners.
See SAVINGS AND LOAN ASSOCIATIONS.

Scenic rivers review board.
General provisions.
See WATERS OF THE STATE.

Schools.
Professional standards and teacher education board, ED §§6-701 to 6-708.
See SCHOOLS.

Sexual offender advisory board, PS §1-401.

Slavery, commission to study historical impact, SG §9-701.

Social workers.
Board of examiners.
See SOCIAL WORKERS.

Speech-language pathologists.
Board of examiners for audiologists, hearing aid dealers and speech-language pathologists.
See AUDIOLOGISTS AND SPEECH-LANGUAGE PATHOLOGISTS.

Spinal injury research, state board, HG §§13-1401 to 13-1407.
See SPINAL INJURY RESEARCH.

Sports fisheries advisory commission, NR §4-204.

State board of contract appeals.
Procurement.
Dispute resolution.
Appeals board, SF §§15-201, 15-205 to 15-212.

State board of education.
Schools.
See SCHOOLS.

State commission on the capital city, SG §§9-401 to 9-407.

State fair.
Maryland state fair board, AG §§10-301 to 10-303.

State higher education labor relations board, SPP §§3-2A-01 to 3-2A-09.

State information technology board, SF §§3-406 to 3-409.

State labor relations board, SPP §§3-201 to 3-209.

State lottery commission.
General provisions.
See STATE LOTTERY.

BOARDS AND COMMISSIONS —Cont'd
State prosecutor.
  Selection and disabilities commission, SG §9-1211.
State traumatic brain injury advisory board,
  HG §§13-2101 to 13-2105.
Statewide commission on the shortage in the
  health care workforce, HO §1-601.
Stationary, SG §8-503.
Stationary engineers.
  State board of stationary engineers, BOP
  §§6.5-201 to 6.5-208.
  See STATIONARY ENGINEERS.
Stem cell research commission.
  Maryland stem cell research program generally,
  83A §§5-2B-01 to 5-2B-13.
  See STEM CELL RESEARCH.
Sundry claims board, COR §§10-301 to 10-310.
  See PRISONS AND PRISONERS.
Sunset law.
  Maryland program evaluation act, SG §§8-401 to
  8-413.
  See PROGRAM EVALUATION ACT.
Sunshine law.
  Open meetings, 41 §1-205.
Surveys and surveyors.
  State board for professional land surveyors, BOP
  §§15-201 to 15-211.
  See SURVEYS AND SURVEYORS.
Susquehanna river basin commission, EN
  §5-301.
Teacher education board.
  Professional standards and teacher education
  board, ED §§6-701 to 6-708.
  See SCHOOLS.
Telegraph and telephone systems.
  Emergency number systems board.
  See TELECOMMUNICATIONS.
Tidal fisheries advisory commission, NR §4-204.
Tobacco authority.
  General provisions.
  See TOBACCO.
Transportation department.
  Board of review.
  See TRANSPORTATION DEPARTMENT.
  Commission.
  See TRANSPORTATION DEPARTMENT.
  Included within department, TR §2-107.
  Professional service selection board.
  See PROCUREMENT.
Uniform state laws.
  Commission on uniform state laws, SG §§9-201 to
  9-206.
  See UNIFORM LAWS.
Universities and colleges.
  Savings bond advisory board, ED §§20-101,
  20-102.
Veterans.
  Maryland veterans commission, SG §§9-915 to
  9-919.
  See VETERANS.
  Maryland veterans' home commission, SG §§9-922
  to 9-929.
  War memorial commission, SG §§9-932 to 9-937.
  See WAR MEMORIAL COMMISSION.
Veterinary medical examiners board.
  General provisions.
  See VETERINARIANS.
Victims of crime.
  Criminal injuries compensation board, CP
  §§11-801 to 11-819.
  See CRIMINAL INJURIES COMPENSATION
  BOARD.

BOARDS AND COMMISSIONS —Cont'd
Victims of crime —Cont'd
  State board of victim services, CP §§11-910 to
  11-919.
  See CRIME VICTIMS' SERVICES.
Vocational-technical education council.
  See VOCATIONAL EDUCATION.
War memorial commission, SG §§9-932 to 9-937.
  See WAR MEMORIAL COMMISSION.
Washington county.
  Salary study commissions, 24 §§12-201 to 12-205.
  See WASHINGTON COUNTY.
Washington suburban sanitary commission.
  General provisions.
  See WASHINGTON SUBURBAN SANITARY
  DISTRICT.
Water science advisory board.
  See WATER POLLUTION.
Waterworks and waste systems operators.
  Board of waterworks and waste systems
  operators.
  See WATERWORKS AND WASTE SYSTEMS
  OPERATORS.
Weapons.
  Handgun permit review board.
  See WEAPONS.
Well drillers.
  Board of well drillers.
  See WELL DRILLERS.
Wildlife advisory commission.
  See BIRDS AND GAME.
Winery and grape growers' advisory
  commission, AG §§10-1201 to 10-1206.
  See ALCOHOLIC BEVERAGES.
Witnesses.
  Commissioners to take depositions.
  General provisions.
  See DEPOSITIONS.
Women.
  Maryland commission for women, 49C §§1 to 8.
Worcester county.
  Bingo board, CR §§13-2607 to 13-2609.
Workers' compensation.
  State workers' compensation commission.
  General provisions, LE §§9-301 to 9-316.
  See WORKERS' COMPENSATION.
Workforce investment board, LE §11-505.
Young farmers advisory board, AG §§2-1001 to
  2-1005.
Zoning.
  Board of appeals, 66B §§4.07, 4.08.
  See ZONING.
  Municipal planning and zoning commission.
  General provisions.
  See ZONING.

BOATING UNDER THE INFLUENCE, NR
  §8-738.

BOAT RENTALS.
Livery vessel owners renting class A vessels,
  NR §8-712.3.

BOATS.
State boat act.
  General provisions.
  See VESSELS AND BOATS.

BOBWHITE.
See BIRDS AND GAME.

BODILY FLUID.
Ingesting.
  Causing another to ingest, CR §3-215.

BODY ARMOR.
Defined, CR §4-106.
Funds.
    Law enforcement equipment fund, PS §§4-301 to
      4-304.
    Protective body armor fund, PS §§4-101 to 4-107.
Permit to use, possess or purchase, CR §4-107.
Wearing in crime of violence or drug
    trafficking crime, CR §4-106.

BODY ATTACHMENT.
Circuit courts, CivProCir Rule 2-510.
Criminal rules, Crim Rule 4-267.
    Material witnesses, Crim Rule 4-267.
Definitions, Rule 1-202.
Depositions.
    Material witnesses.
      Deposition of witness in custody, Crim Rule
        4-267.
District Court, CivProDist Rule 3-510.
Juvenile causes.
    Forms, Form 904-WA.
Subpoenas.
    Criminal rules, Crim Rule 4-266.
    District Court, CivProDist Rule 3-510.
Witnesses.
    Material witnesses, Crim Rule 4-267.

BOILERS AND PRESSURE VESSELS, PS
    §§12-901 to 12-919.
Accidents.
    Inspections, PS §12-909.
Alterations.
    Duties of person repairing or altering, PS §12-913.
Appeals.
    Civil penalties generally, PS §12-916.
Applicability of subtitle, PS §12-903.
    Inspections, PS §12-909.
Board of boiler rules, PS §12-904.
    Board defined, PS §12-901.
    Program evaluation act, SG §8-403.
    Rules and regulations.
      Authority to promulgate, PS §12-905.
Certificates, PS §12-911.
    Certificate inspections, PS §12-909.
Citation of subtitle, PS §12-918.
Continued use of prohibited vessel.
    Civil penalty, PS §12-915.
Defined terms, PS §12-901.
Duties.
    Authorized insurers, PS §12-912.
    Owners and users, PS §12-912.
    Person repairing or altering, PS §12-913.
Exceptions, PS §12-903.
Existing boilers and vessels.
    Standards, PS §12-908.
Explosions.
    Inspections, PS §12-909.
Fees.
    Inspections, PS §12-909.
Findings, PS §12-902.
Fines.
    Civil penalties.
      Continued use of prohibited vessel, PS §12-915.
      Generally, PS §12-916.
    Criminal penalties, PS §12-917.
Hydrostatic test.
    Inspections, PS §12-909.
Inspections, PS §12-909.
    Certificates, PS §12-911.
    Chief boiler inspector, PS §12-906.
    Deputy boiler inspectors, PS §12-906.

BOILERS AND PRESSURE VESSELS —Cont'd
Inspections —Cont'd
    Model steam boilers exempt, PS §12-909.
    Prohibition on use, PS §12-914.
    Special inspectors, PS §12-907.
      Reports, PS §12-910.
Insurers.
    Duties, PS §12-912.
Legislative intent, PS §12-902.
Model steam boilers.
    Defined, PS §12-909.
    Inspectors, PS §12-909.
New boilers and vessels.
    Inspections, installation, PS §12-909.
    Standards, PS §12-908.
Notice.
    Prohibition on use, PS §12-914.
Owners.
    Duties, PS §12-912.
Penalties.
    Civil penalties, PS §12-916.
      Continued use of prohibited vessel, PS §12-915.
    Criminal penalties, PS §12-917.
Prohibited acts.
    Civil penalties, PS §12-916.
    Criminal penalties, PS §12-917.
Prohibition on use, PS §12-914.
Repairs.
    Duties of person repairing or altering, PS §12-913.
Reports.
    Duties of person repairing or altering, PS §12-913.
    Special inspectors, PS §12-910.
Right of entry.
    Inspections, PS §12-909.
Rules and regulations.
    Authority to promulgate, PS §12-905.
    Violations.
      Civil penalties generally, PS §12-916.
Scope of subtitle, PS §12-903.
Short title, PS §12-918.
Standards, PS §12-908.
Sunset provisions, PS §12-919.
Termination of subtitle, PS §12-919.
Users.
    Duties, PS §12-912.
    Prohibition on use, PS §12-914.
Violations.
    Civil penalties generally, PS §12-916.

BOMBS.
Explosives generally, PS §§11-101 to 11-118.
    See EXPLOSIONS AND EXPLOSIVES.
Possession of destructive device, CR §§4-501 to
    4-503.

BOMB SCARES.
Destructive device or toxic material.
    False statement or rumor concerning, CR §9-504.

BONA FIDE HOLDER.
Mechanics' liens.
    Effect of conveyance to, RP §9-102.

BOND ISSUES.
Advertising.
    Debt, 31 §10.
Agricultural and resource-based industry
    development corporation.
    Bond defined, 41 §13-501.
    Refunding bonds, 41 §13-510.
    Revenue bonds, 41 §13-510.
Airport authorities.
    Borrowing power.
      See AIRPORT AUTHORITIES.

BOND ISSUES —Cont'd

Allocation of private activity bond authority.
Administration, FI §13-807.
Allocation may not be carried forward, FI §13-805.
Amount of allocations, FI §13-807.
Definitions, FI §13-801.
Minority business enterprises.
Use favored, FI §13-806.
Reallocation by county, FI §13-803.
Reports, FI §13-804.
Reversion of allocations, FI §13-805.
State ceiling, FI §13-802.
Transfer of allocations, FI §13-803.
Unused balances, FI §13-805.

Anticipated debt.
Reports, SF §2-106.

Assignments.
Action by surety on obligation under seal, CL §15-402.

Aviation.
Airports.
Political subdivisions.
Issuance, TR §5-419.

Baltimore City.
Interest rate exchange agreements or contracts.
Authority to enter into, 31 §34.
Parking facilities, MD Const Art XI-C §3.
Proceeds of certain bonds.
Investments, redemptions, sales, etc., 95 §22M.

Baltimore City Community College.
Auxiliary facilities.
Restrictions on use, ED §19-102.

Baltimore City new board of school commissioners, ED §§4-306.1 to 4-306.6.

Banks and trust companies.
Debt instruments.
Issuance or sale, FI §3-312.

Bids and bidding.
Public debt.
See BIDS AND BIDDING.

Bond anticipation notes.
Public debt.
State units, SF §§8-213 to 8-221.
See PUBLIC DEBT.

Bond proceed management, 31 §31.

Canal Place Preservation and Development Authority, FI §13-1018.
Agreements to enhance marketability or provide security, FI §13-1025.
Bondholders enforcement of rights, FI §13-1023.
Definition of "bonds," FI §13-1001.
Investments.
Authorized investment, FI §13-1025.
Liability on bonds, FI §13-1023.
Payment of bonds.
Sources, FI §13-1019.
Trust agreement to secure, FI §§13-1018, 13-1021.
Refunding bonds, FI §13-1024.
Requirements of bonds, FI §13-1020.
Tax exemption, FI §13-1026.
Trust agreement, FI §13-1018.

Cecil county.
Residential mortgage loans.
Bonds to finance.
See CECIL COUNTY.

College of Southern Maryland.
Notes to finance projects, issuance, ED §16-302.1.

Community colleges.
Agreement with health and higher education facilities authority, ED §16-302.1.

BOND ISSUES —Cont'd

Community colleges —Cont'd
Issuance of notes to finance projects, ED §16-302.1.

Community development administration, HS §§4-244 to 4-253.
Financing infrastructure projects.
Local obligations.
Enabling resolution or ordinance, adoption, HS §4-232.
Pledges of faith and credit securing, HS §4-233.
Infrastructure projects, local financing, HS §§4-229 to 4-233.
Enabling resolution or ordinance.
Adoption, HS §4-232.
Contents, HS §4-231.
Issuing procedures, HS §4-230.
Local obligations, HS §4-229.
Pledges of faith and credit securing, HS §4-233.
Interest rate exchange agreements, HS §4-253.
Legal status, HS §4-250.
Lien of the pledge, HS §4-248.
Not debt of the state, HS §4-251.
Powers of administration, HS §4-244.
Authority to borrow money and issue bonds or notes, HS §4-245.
Purchase of notes or bonds, HS §4-249.
Redemption of notes or bonds, HS §4-249.
Refunding of bonds, HS §4-246.
Renewal of bonds and notes, HS §4-246.
Repayment, HS §4-248.
Tax exemption, HS §4-252.
Trust agreement to secure, HS §4-247.

Conversion of overhead electric or communication facilities to underground locations, PUC §12-317.

Corporations.
Issuing, CA §2-103.
Signatures and seals.
Facsimile on bonds, CA §2-212.

Counterfeiting private instrument or document, CR §8-601.
Issuing counterfeited instrument or document, CR §8-602.

Counties.
Charles county.
New school capacity construction bonds, 66B §14.05.
Housing and community development.
Residential mortgage programs for certain counties.
Characteristics, HS §4-1607.
New bonds, HS §4-1609.
Ordinance to issue, HS §4-1606.
Sale and payment, HS §4-1608.
Interest rate exchange agreements or contracts.
Authority to enter into, 31 §34.
Private activity bond issuance fee.
Powers, 25 §3.
Proceeds of certain bonds.
Investments, redemptions, sales, etc., 95 §22M.
Public debt.
Authorization of public bodies to issue and sell, 31 §30.
Residential mortgage program.
See MORTGAGES AND DEEDS OF TRUST.
Tax increment financing act, 41 §§14-201 to 14-214.
See TAX INCREMENT FINANCING ACT.

BOND ISSUES —Cont'd
Counties —Cont'd
Transportation bonds, TR §§3-301 to 3-310, 3-501
    to 3-519.
    See COUNTIES.
Definitions, 31 §9.
Allocation of private activity bond authority, FI
    §13-801.
Anticipated debt.
    Reports on anticipated debt, SF §2-106.
Public debt.
    See PUBLIC DEBT.
Drainage districts, 25 §§121B, 121C.
Draining lands, 25 §90.
Economic development corporation.
See ECONOMIC DEVELOPMENT
    CORPORATION.
Economic development revenue bond act, 41
    §§14-101 to 14-109.
See ECONOMIC DEVELOPMENT REVENUE
    BOND ACT.
Electric customer choice and competition act.
Rate stabilization bonds.
    Deferred expenses secured through, PUC
        §7-523.
    Defined, PUC §7-520.
    Electric bills.
        Required statements, PUC §7-541.
    Issuance of additional bonds.
        Additional order authorizing, PUC §7-534.
    New bonds.
        Additional order authorizing, status, PUC
            §7-534.
    Not debt, liability or pledge of state or other
        governmental unit, PUC §7-535.
    Notice on face of bonds.
        Not obligation of state or other governmental
            unit, PUC §7-535.
    Not obligation of state or other governmental
        unit, PUC §7-535.
    Retiring and refunding.
        Order may provide, adjustment of charges,
            PUC §7-533.
    Rights and remedies of bondholders and
        assignees.
        Orders may state and protect, PUC §7-536.
Environmental service.
General provisions, NR §§3-112 to 3-123.
    See ENVIRONMENTAL SERVICE.
Erosion.
General provisions, 25 §§161 to 167.
    See COUNTIES.
Fiduciaries.
Uniform act.
    Simplification of fiduciary security transfers.
    General provisions, ET §§15-301 to 15-311.
Frederick county.
Bond rating enhancement reserve, 25 §221B.
General assembly.
Spending affordability committee.
    Private activity bonds, SG §2-1010.
**Health and higher educational facilities
    authority.**
See HEALTH AND HIGHER EDUCATIONAL
    FACILITIES AUTHORITY.
Heritage areas, FI §§13-1115 to 13-1123.
    See HERITAGE AREAS.
Highways.
Legal investments, ET §15-106.
State highway construction bonds.
    Highway user revenues.
        Modification as to distribution and use.
            Security not affected, TR §§3-216, 8-402.

BOND ISSUES —Cont'd
Historic St. Mary's City commission, ED
    §§24-516 to 24-524.
    See HISTORIC ST. MARY'S CITY COMMISSION.
Housing and community development.
Community development administration, HS
    §§4-244 to 4-253.
Infrastructure projects, local financing, HS
    §§4-229 to 4-233.
Residential mortgage programs for certain
    counties.
    Characteristics, HS §4-1607.
    New bonds, HS §4-1609.
    Ordinance to issue, HS §4-1606.
    Sale and payment, HS §4-1608.
Housing authorities.
Montgomery county.
    Housing opportunities commission, HS §§16-201
        to 16-211.
Prince George's county, HS §17-107.
Queen Anne's county, HS §18-105.
Washington county, HS §21-106.
Industrial development corporations.
General provisions, 45A §§1 to 3.
    See INDUSTRIAL DEVELOPMENT
        CORPORATIONS.
Industrial development financing authority,
    83A §5-926.
Defined, 83A §5-901.
Interest.
General provisions, CL §§12-101 to 12-114.
    See INTEREST.
Investments.
Certain bonds to be considered investment
    securities, SF §8-302.
Lawful investments, ET §15-106.
Proceeds of certain bonds, 95 §22M.
Investment securities, CL §§8-101 to 8-511.
    See INVESTMENT SECURITIES.
Joint obligors.
General provisions.
    See DEBTORS.
Juvenile services.
Department of juvenile services.
    Bond requests for building or renovating
        facilities, 83C §2-117.
**Local military installation redevelopment
    authorities,** 83A §5-1706.
**Maryland economic development revenue
    bond act,** 41 §§14-101 to 14-109.
See ECONOMIC DEVELOPMENT REVENUE
    BOND ACT.
Maryland food center authority.
Generally.
    See MARYLAND FOOD CENTER
        AUTHORITY.
**Maryland-national capital park and planning
    commission.**
See MARYLAND-NATIONAL CAPITAL PARK
    AND PLANNING COMMISSION.
Maryland stadium authority.
See MARYLAND STADIUM AUTHORITY.
Maryland Transit Administration.
General provisions.
    See MARYLAND TRANSIT
        ADMINISTRATION.
Maryland-Washington metropolitan district.
See MARYLAND-WASHINGTON
    METROPOLITAN DISTRICT.
Montgomery county.
Housing opportunities commission, HS §§16-201
    to 16-211.

BOND ISSUES —Cont'd
Morgan State University.
See MORGAN STATE UNIVERSITY.
Mortgages and deeds of trust.
Amount.
Necessity for recitation of secured amount, RP §7-102.
Ownership.
Presumption as to ownership, RP §7-103.
Payment or cancellation.
Marking evidence of indebtedness paid or cancelled, RP §3-105.
Residential mortgage program.
See MORTGAGES AND DEEDS OF TRUST.
Motor vehicles.
Comptroller.
Payment of principal and interest, TR §12-118.
Municipal corporations.
Home rule, 23A §§31 to 39.
Infrastructure improvements.
Financing new infrastructure improvements, 23A §44A.
Infrastructure improvements.
Financing new infrastructure improvements, 23A §44A.
Public debt.
Authority of public bodies to issue and sell, 31 §30.
Tax increment financing act, 41 §§14-201 to 14-214.
See TAX INCREMENT FINANCING ACT.
Northeast Maryland waste disposal authority.
See NORTHEAST MARYLAND WASTE DISPOSAL AUTHORITY.
Parking facilities in Baltimore City, MD Const Art XI-C §3.
Penmar development corporation.
Availability of net earnings, 83A §5-1206.
Issuance, 83A §5-1206.
State or U.S. bonds.
Investments, 83A §5-1209.
Pensions.
Pension liability funding bonds, 31 §32.
Port administration.
General provisions, TR §§6-101 to 6-602.
See PORT ADMINISTRATION.
Prince George's county.
Housing authority, HS §17-107.
Private activity bond authority.
Allocation. See within this heading, "Allocation of private activity bond authority."
Private activity bond fees.
County's power to charge issuance fee, 25 §3.
Private activity bonds.
General assembly.
Spending affordability committee, SG §2-1010.
Public debt.
Definition, 31 §9.
General obligation debt.
General provisions, SF §§8-101 to 8-145.
See PUBLIC DEBT.
General provisions, 31 §§1 to 12.
See PUBLIC DEBT.
Investment securities.
Certain bonds to be considered investment securities, SF §8-302.
State units.
General provisions, SF §§8-201 to 8-221.
See PUBLIC DEBT.
Public improvements.
Issuance and term, 31 §11.

BOND ISSUES —Cont'd
Public recreation and parks.
General provisions, 25 §224.
Public service companies.
Actions for which public service commission authorization required, PUC §§5-203, 6-101.
Issuance of bonds, PUC §6-102.
Queen Anne's county.
Housing authority, HS §18-105.
Redevelopment bond act, 41 §§14-801 to 14-812.
See REDEVELOPMENT BOND ACT.
Registration.
Securities act.
General provisions, CA §§11-101 to 11-805.
See SECURITIES.
Rehypothecation of personal securities, CR §7-115.
Reports.
Allocation of private activity bond authority, FI §13-804.
Anticipated debt, SF §2-106.
Residential mortgage program.
See MORTGAGES AND DEEDS OF TRUST.
Sanitary commissions.
Advances by member counties, EN §9-697.
Defined, EN §9-601.
Determinations by sanitary commission, EN §9-685.
Enumerated, EN §9-685.
Exemption from taxation, EN §9-608.
Interest.
Computation of effective interest rate, EN §9-688.
Payment of interest from proceeds of other bonds, EN §9-695.
Limitation on total of outstanding bonds, EN §9-683.
Minimum price, EN §9-688.
Miscellaneous provisions, EN §9-697.
Multiple county districts, EN §9-696.
Payment of principal and interest, EN §9-660.
Pledge in full faith and credit of district, EN §9-682.
Prerequisites for issuance, EN §9-684.
Prior bonds ratified, EN §9-605.
Proceeds, EN §9-692.
Refunding bonds, EN §9-693.
Repayment.
Priority among sources of funds, EN §9-694.
Replacement of mutilated, destroyed or lost bonds, EN §9-691.
Required contents, EN §9-686.
Resolution by commission prerequisite for issuance, EN §9-684.
Retirement, EN §9-694.
Sales, EN §9-688.
Service areas.
Bonds unaffected, EN §9-648.
Consolidation of administrative matters.
Effect on bond obligation, EN §9-651.
Excessive bond issuance, EN §9-649.
Signing, EN §9-687.
Status of bonds, EN §9-689.
Temporary bonds and receipts.
Issuance authorized, EN §9-690.
Sanitary districts.
General provisions.
See SANITARY DISTRICTS.
Schools.
Bond issues to finance construction, ED §§5-601 to 5-604.

BOND ISSUES —Cont'd
Securities act.
General provisions, CA §§11-101 to 11-805.
See SECURITIES.
Sewerage facilities bond act, EN §§9-801 to
9-814.
See WATER AND SEWER SYSTEMS.
Special taxing districts in certain counties, 24
§9-1301.
Public hearings, 24 §9-1301.
State bonds.
See PUBLIC DEBT.
State treasurer.
General provisions.
See STATE TREASURER.
Public debt.
See STATE TREASURER.
Susquehanna river basin authority, EN §5-301.
Tax increment financing act, 41 §§14-201 to
14-214.
See TAX INCREMENT FINANCING ACT.
Transfer.
Uniform act.
Simplification of fiduciary security transfers.
General provisions, ET §§15-301 to 15-311.
Transportation.
County transportation bonds, TR §§3-301 to
3-310, 3-501 to 3-519.
See COUNTIES.
Department.
See TRANSPORTATION DEPARTMENT.
General provisions.
See TRANSPORTATION.
Special bonds and borrowings, TR §§3-601 to
3-607.
See TRANSPORTATION DEPARTMENT.
Transportation department.
Authority.
Intercounty connector, financing of, TR §4-321.
Lien of pledge of sinking fund toward payment
of bonds, TR §4-320.
Limitation on use of federal aid for repayment
of bonds, TR §4-320.
United States.
Investments.
Enumeration of political subdivisions which
may invest in, 95 §22.
Universities and colleges.
Auxiliary facilities.
See UNIVERSITIES AND COLLEGES.
Usury.
General provisions, CL §§12-101 to 12-114.
See USURY.
Vendors' liens.
Payment of notes.
General provisions, RP §7-203.
Voting systems.
Issuance by counties to pay costs, EL §9-104.
Washington county.
Housing authority, HS §21-106.
Washington suburban sanitary commission.
See WASHINGTON SUBURBAN SANITARY
DISTRICT.
Washington suburban sanitary district.
General obligation bonds and notes, 29 §§4-101 to
4-112.
Revenue bonds, 29 §§4-201 to 4-212.
Water and sewer authority.
See WATER AND SEWER SYSTEMS.
Water and sewer systems.
Authority to raise funds, EN §9-256.

BOND ISSUES —Cont'd
Water and sewer systems —Cont'd
Municipal authorities, EN §9-711.
Sewerage facilities bond act, EN §§9-801 to 9-814.
See WATER AND SEWER SYSTEMS.
Water quality financing administration.
See WATER QUALITY FINANCING
ADMINISTRATION.
Watershed associations, 25 §203.

BONDS, SURETY.
Actions.
Applicability of provisions, Rule 1-401.
Approval, Rule 1-402.
Clerks of court.
Action on bond, CJ §11-203.
Constables.
Suits on bonds and remedies against.
See CONSTABLES.
Credit services businesses.
Claims against bonds, CL §14-1910.
Increase or decrease, Rule 1-402.
Proceeding against surety, Rule 1-404.
Recording, Rule 1-402.
Register of wills.
Action on bond, CJ §11-203.
State of Maryland.
Bond in name of state, Rule 1-402.
Advertising.
Outdoor advertising.
Nonresident licensees and permit holders, TR
§8-747.
Agricultural products.
Treasurer's bond, AG §10-115.
Agriculture.
Agricultural land preservation foundation.
Board of trustees, AG §2-503.
Air conditioning and heating contractors.
Licenses, BR §9A-402.
Alcoholic beverages.
Liquor control department, 2B §15-201.
Retailers.
Required, 2B §14-101.
Animals, seizure of dangerous animals, CR
§10-621.
Appeals.
General provisions.
See APPEALS.
Supersedeas bond, AppRev Rule 8-423.
Applicability of chapter, Rule 1-401.
Approval, Rule 1-402.
Assignments.
Assignee suing obligee upon failure to recover
from obligor, CL §15-402.
Assignments for benefit of creditors.
Assignee's bond, CL §15-103.
Automobile insurance fund.
Producers, IN §20-511.
Bail and recognizance.
Definitions, Crim Rule 4-217.
General provisions.
See BAIL AND RECOGNIZANCE.
Qualification of surety, Crim Rule 4-217.
Voluntary surrender of defendant by surety, Crim
Rule 4-217.
Banks and trust companies.
Collateral.
Fiduciary deposit surety bonds, FI §1-206.
Boxing, sparring and wrestling.
Promoter license.
Surety bond required, BR §4-306.

BONDS, SURETY —Cont'd
Bridges.
Counties.
Performance bonds, 25 §38.
Cemeteries.
Perpetual care cemeteries.
Fidelity bond of trustee, BR §5-603.
Charities.
Registration of charitable representatives, BR §6-303.
Clerks of court.
Failure to give bond, CJ §2-106.
General provisions.
See CLERKS OF COURT.
Predecessor.
Completing unfinished business of predecessor.
Fees, 36 §9.
Recording, Rule 1-402.
Collection agencies.
Licenses.
Issuance of license, BR §7-304.
Collective bargaining.
Injunctions.
Temporary restraining order or temporary injunction.
Bond requirement, LE §4-316.
Commissioner of correction.
Performance bond, COR §3-217.
Comptroller, MD Const Art VI §1.
Filing, SG §4-102.
Form and conditions, SG §4-102.
Recordation, SG §4-102.
Required, SG §4-102.
Condominiums.
Corporate surety bond on new condominiums, RP §11-121.
Constables.
General provisions.
See CONSTABLES.
Consumer loans, FI §§11-206, 11-207.
Continuing care contracts.
Possession and administration of providers' assets, 70B §20M.
Contractors.
Procurement.
See PROCUREMENT.
Coroners.
Payment of premiums, 25 §33.
Stock and stockholders.
Indemnity for lost certificate, CA §2-213.
Costs.
Bond premium as costs, Rule 1-406.
Countersecurity.
Fiduciaries.
Enforcement of order to give, ET §15-110.
Counties.
Bridges.
Between counties.
Performance bond, 25 §43.
Performance bonds, 25 §38.
Chartered counties.
Contracts requiring bonds, 25A §5.
Competitive bidding and bonds, 25 §3.
Compliance bonds, 25 §3.
Official bonds.
Payment of premiums by county commissioners, 25 §33.
Performance bond.
Contracts, 25 §29.
Credit services businesses, CL §14-1908.
Actions.
Claims against bonds, CL §14-1910.

BONDS, SURETY —Cont'd
Credit services businesses —Cont'd
Aggregate liability, CL §14-1910.
Amount of bond, CL §14-1909.
Damages.
Claims against bonds, CL §14-1910.
Issuance, CL §14-1909.
Liability.
Claims against bonds, CL §14-1910.
Credit unions.
Insurance corporation.
Officers and employees, FI §7-110.
Custom home protection.
Escrow accounts.
Accounts in lieu of, RP §10-504.
Damages.
Clerk or register of wills.
Action on bond, CJ §11-203.
Credit services businesses.
Claims against bonds, CL §14-1910.
Debt management services.
Licenses, FI §§12-908, 12-914.
Decrease, Rule 1-402.
Dental plan organizations, IN §14-404.
Distress for rent.
Removal of levied goods, RP §8-310.
Affixed to property, RP §8-313.
Return of levied goods, RP §8-316.
Security for cost of sale, RP §8-321.
Stay of appeal, RP §8-332.
District Court commissioner, CJ §2-105.
Division of correction officers and employees.
Performance bond, COR §3-217.
Draining lands.
Drainage districts.
Contractor's bond, 25 §121D.
Formation of drainage districts, 25 §104.
Superintendent of construction.
Drainage districts, 25 §116.
Dwellings.
Deposits on new homes, RP §§10-301 to 10-306.
See HOUSING.
Ejectment.
Appeals.
When grantor remains in possession after delivery of deed and in violation of agreement, RP §14-109.
Elections.
Recounts, EL §12-105.
Electricians.
Licenses.
Local licenses.
Insurance.
Satisfaction of bond requirement by proof of insurance, BOP §6-604.
Emergency management.
Civil relief during emergency periods.
Stays, postponements or suspensions of enforcement.
Effect on sureties, guarantors and endorsers, PS §14-205.
Eminent domain.
Taking possession of property pending appeal, RP §12-107.
Employment agencies.
Licenses, BR §9-301.
Environmental service.
Service not required to give bonds, NR §3-124.
Treasurer, NR §3-103.
Evidence.
Parol evidence admissible, CJ §10-907.

BONDS, SURETY —Cont'd
Executions.
  Levy.
    Release of property from levy.
      Posting of bond.
        Circuit courts, CivProCir Rule 2-643.
        District Court, CivProDist Rule 3-643.
  Sheriff's bond.
    Circuit courts, CivProCir Rule 2-641.
    District Court, CivProDist Rule 3-641.
Executors and administrators.
  Additional or new security, ET §6-102.
  Copy.
    Certified copy from register, ET §6-102.
  Countersecurity, ET §6-102.
  Filed in office of register, ET §6-102.
  Form, ET §6-102.
  General provisions.
    See EXECUTORS AND ADMINISTRATORS.
  Inheritance tax.
    Liability for payment, ET §7-307.
  Opening estates.
    Personal representative's bond.
      Form, Estates Rule 6-312.
    Waiver of bond.
      Form, Estates Rule 6-312.
  Penalty.
    Amount, ET §6-102.
    Fixed by court or register, ET §6-102.
  Personal representative's bond, Estates Rule
    6-222.
  Premium.
    Payable out of estate, ET §6-102.
  Remedy.
    Failure to give new security or countersecurity,
      ET §6-102.
  Required for appointment, ET §6-101.
    When not required, ET §6-102.
    When required, ET §6-102.
  Settlement of decedents' estates.
    After-discovered property.
      Subsequent administration, Estates Rule
        6-422; ET §10-104.
  Small estates.
    Personal representative, ET §5-604.
  Special administrator, Estates Rule 6-454; ET
    §6-402.
  Surety.
    General provisions, ET §6-102.
  Trust company not required to give bond, ET
    §6-102.
  Waiver.
    When waived, ET §6-102.
Fiduciaries.
  Agreement of fiduciary and surety for deposit of
    assets, ET §15-105.
  Corporations that act as fiduciaries not liable as
    sureties, ET §15-115.
  Countersecurity.
    Attachment on order of court, ET §15-110.
    Enforcement of order to give, ET §15-110.
    Removal of fiduciary, ET §15-110.
  Executors and administrators. See within this
    heading, "Executors and administrators."
  Fiduciary estates including guardianships of
    property, Guardian Rule 10-702.
  Release from liability.
    Resignation of fiduciary does not release, ET
      §15-111.
  Resignation of fiduciary does not release from
    liability, ET §15-111.

BONDS, SURETY —Cont'd
Fiduciaries —Cont'd
  Trusts and trustees.
    See TRUSTS AND TRUSTEES.
Filing.
  Approval, Rule 1-402.
Financial institutions.
  Collateral.
    Fiduciary deposit surety bonds, FI §1-206.
Fines.
  Deposits on new homes.
    Failure of vendor to maintain surety bond or
      escrow account, RP §10-305.
Fireworks permits, PS §10-105.
Foreclosures.
  Mortgages.
    Sale, PropSales Rule 14-206.
Foresters.
  State board of foresters.
    Secretary of board, BOP §7-203.
Franchises.
  Registration.
    Escrow requirements, BR §14-217.
Fraternal benefit societies.
  Conditioned upon return of applicants' fees, IN
    §8-412.
Gas and oil.
  Drilling wells.
    Performance bonds, EN §14-111.
    Permits, EN §14-108.
  Storage.
    Prince George's county, EN §14-304.
Geothermal resources.
  Applicants for permits, EN §5-606.
Grain.
  Licensing of grain dealers.
    Bond required prior to issuance of license, AG
      §13-212.
Ground rents, PropAct Rule 12-501.
Guardian and ward.
  Guardian of the person of a minor.
    Bond not required, ET §13-703.
  Protection of property.
    General provisions, ET §13-208.
    Qualification of guardian, ET §13-206.
  Standby guardians, ET §13-908.
  Veteran's guardianship, ET §13-803.
Hazardous materials and substances.
  Transfer of hazardous materials between one
    mode of transportation and another.
    Facility permit, EN §7-111.
Health and higher educational facilities
    authority.
  Each member of authority, 43C §4.
Health club services, CL §14-12B-02.
Highways.
  Permits.
    Bond of nongovernment applicant, TR §8-646.
Home improvements.
  Commission.
    Executive director, BR §8-205.
Horse racing.
  Jockey fund.
    Board of directors, BR §11-904.
  State racing commission, BR §11-204.
Housing.
  Deposits on new homes, RP §§10-301 to 10-306.
    See HOUSING.
Incinerators, EN §9-211.
Increase, Rule 1-402.

BONDS, SURETY —Cont'd
Injunctions.
Temporary restraining orders and preliminary injunctions, SpecPro Rule 15-503.
Insurance.
Adviser's license, IN §10-206.
Agents and brokers, IN §10-111.
Title insurance, IN §10-121.
Automobile insurance fund.
Producers, IN §20-511.
Discrimination in surety insurance, IN §27-502.
Limitation of risk, IN §5-1004.
Liquidation, rehabilitation, etc., of insurers.
Commissioner as receiver, IN §9-218.
Disbursements of assets to guaranty associations, IN §9-224.
Seizure order issuance, IN §9-215.
Managing general agents, IN §8-207.
Property and casualty insurance guaranty corporation.
Obligation of the corporation as to surety bonds, IN §9-306.
Recoupment, IN §9-313.
Reciprocal insurance.
Bond of attorney in fact, IN §3-205.
Reinsurance intermediaries, IN §8-504.
Surplus line brokers, IN §3-313.
Third party administrators, IN §8-306.
Prohibited bonds, IN §8-316.
Title insurance agents and brokers, IN §10-121.
Insurance commissioner, IN §2-103.
Deputy insurance commissioner, IN §2-104.
Judgments.
Amount due on bond, CJ §11-201.
Judgment on bond, Rule 1-405.
Judicial sales.
Trustee appointed by certain instruments, PropSales Rule 14-303.
Trustee appointed by court, PropSales Rule 14-303.
Jurisdiction.
Personal jurisdiction.
Contract of surety.
Executed or performed in state, CJ §6-103.
Justices of the peace.
Premiums.
Trial magistrates, clerks, etc.
Paid by county, 25 §33.
Juvenile causes.
See JUVENILE CAUSES.
Landfills.
Required prior to permit, EN §9-211.
Land installment contracts.
Deposits on new homes, RP §§10-301 to 10-306.
See HOUSING.
Landlord and tenant.
Appeals.
Repossession proceedings, RP §8-401.
Notice to quit procedure.
Appeals, RP §8-402.
Third-party claiming title, RP §8-402.
Security bond, RP §8-203.
Levy.
Release of property from levy.
Posting of bond.
District Court, CivProDist Rule 3-643.
Liability.
Credit services businesses.
Claims against bonds, CL §14-1910.
Liens.
Commercial real estate broker's lien.
Claimant, RP §14-305.

BONDS, SURETY —Cont'd
Limitation of actions.
Action on bond.
Twelve-year period, CJ §5-102.
Public officer's bond, CJ §5-104.
Maryland-national capital park and planning commission.
Officers and employees, 28 §2-108.
Maryland state employees surety bond committee, SG §§9-1701 to 9-1707.
Maryland-Washington regional district.
Subdivision regulations, 28 §7-116.
Mechanics' liens.
Filing of pleadings, RP §9-106.
Motor vehicles, vessels and aircraft.
Repossession of property, CL §16-206.
Release of lien.
Petition to release, PropAct Rule 12-307.
Relief granted.
Sufficiency of amount and surety, PropAct Rule 12-304.
Migrant labor.
Licenses.
Security for compliance with laws, LE §7-312.
Militia.
Actions against members.
Security for court costs, PS §13-708.
Mining.
Actions.
Collection of forfeited bond, EN §15-514.
Deep mine control, EN §15-612.
Forfeiture of bond or deposit, EN §15-613.
Forfeiture.
Deposit of funds, EN §15-514.
Prospecting for coal, EN §15-518.
Strip mining.
General provisions.
See MINING.
Surface mining.
See MINING.
Minors.
Transfers to minors.
Custodians, ET §13-315.
Money transmission.
Deposit in lieu of surety bond.
Defined, FI §12-401.
Licenses, FI §12-407.
Renewal, FI §12-411.
Voluntary surrender of licenses, FI §12-422.
Surety devices, FI §12-412.
Defined, FI §12-401.
Penalties payable from, FI §12-412.
Permissible investments, FI §12-412.
Mortgages and deeds of trust.
Mortgage lenders, FI §11-508.
Sale on credit.
Requiring bond, RP §14-103.
Motions.
Relief to surety and interested persons, Rule 1-403.
Motor clubs.
Applicant for license.
Surety bond requirements, IN §26-204.
Motor fuel tax.
Licenses.
Surrender of bond, TG §9-335.
Motor vehicle insurance.
Automobile insurance fund.
Producers, IN §20-511.
Motor vehicles.
Commissioner.
Person taken before commissioner.
Maximum amount of bond, TR §26-403.

BONDS, SURETY —Cont'd
Motor vehicles —Cont'd
Dealers.
Licenses, TR §§15-103, 15-308.
Special requirements for license to deal in
new motor vehicles.
Compliance with surety bond requirements,
TR §15-305.
Drivers' schools.
Licenses, TR §§15-103, 15-705.
Proof, TR §15-706.
Driving instructors.
Licenses, TR §15-103.
Manufacturers, distributors and factory branches.
Filing and maintaining.
Rules and regulations, TR §15-205.
Liability for breach of warranty, TR §15-103.
Licenses, TR §§15-103, 15-205.
Registration without certificate of title, TR
§13-109.
Reimbursement of forfeited bond or collateral, TR
§27-104.
Salesmen.
Licenses, TR §15-103.
Title service agents.
Licenses, TR §§15-103, 15-604.
Towing.
Parking lots.
Persons undertaking towing or removal.
Required to obtain, TR §21-10A-04.
Trailers.
Fleet registration.
Prorated fee payments, TR §13-928.
Wreckers and scrap processors.
Licenses, TR §15-103.
Negotiable instruments.
Suits on, CJ §10-918.
Northeast Maryland waste disposal authority,
NR §3-903.
Outdoor advertising.
Nonresident licensees and permit holders, TR
§8-747.
Outdoor concerts.
Promoter licenses, BR §17-1405.
Paternity proceedings.
Defendant, FL §5-1014.
Orders of court.
Bond to comply with order, FL §5-1042.
Pretrial bond, FL §5-1025.
Failure of defendant to appear.
Forfeiture of bond, FL §5-1024.
Physicians.
Board of physicians.
Executive director and board chair to be
bonded, HO §14-208.
Plumbers.
Insurance.
Satisfaction of bond requirement by proof of
insurance, BOP §12-501.
Premiums.
Premium as costs, Rule 1-406.
Private detectives.
Licenses.
Applications.
Bond to be submitted, BOP §13-304.
Private home detention monitoring, BOP
§20-601.
Procurement contracts.
Bid security.
Generally, SF §§13-207, 13-208.

BONDS, SURETY —Cont'd
Procurement contracts —Cont'd
Construction contracts.
Security generally, SF §§17-101 to 17-111.
Performance or payment bonds, SF §13-216.
Property and casualty insurance guaranty
corporation.
Obligation of the corporation as to surety bonds,
IN §9-306.
Recoupment, IN §9-313.
Public debt.
Debt service.
Fiscal agent, SF §8-135.
Public safety solicitors.
Application for registration, BR §6-5A-03.
Public works contracts.
Wages.
Guarantee of performance of prevailing wage
rate clauses, SF §17-213.
Real estate brokers.
Appeals from commission decisions.
Stay of suspension or revocation of license, BOP
§17-329.
Real estate commission.
Chairman, BOP §17-203.
Executive director, BOP §17-205.
Real property.
Deposits on new homes, RP §§10-301 to 10-306.
See HOUSING.
Receivers, FI §5-605; Receivers Rule 13-107.
District Court, CivProDist Rule 3-722.
Recordation.
Clerks to record bond, Rule 1-402.
Register of wills, ET §2-204; SG §4-109.
Reinsurance intermediaries, IN §8-504.
Relief to surety and interested persons.
Motions, Rule 1-403.
Replevin.
Action on replevin bond, PropAct Rule 12-601.
Sales.
Court-ordered sales.
Requiring bond when sale on credit, RP
§14-103.
Savings and loan associations, FI §9-308.
Chairman of incorporators, FI §§9-216, 9-217.
Scholarships.
Enforcement of obligation of bond, ED §18-109.
Schools, ED §6-109.
Securities.
Registration of broker-dealers, agents, investment
advisors and investment advisor
representatives.
Bond or equivalent security, CA §11-410.
Security instead of surety, Rule 1-402.
Violations of title.
Commissioner not required to post in action
under section, CA §11-702.
Security systems technicians.
Applicants for licenses, BOP §18-303.
Fidelity bond, BOP §18-401.
Senior citizen activities centers.
Capital improvement grants program.
Temporary liens.
Releases by bond, 70B §31.
Sentence and punishment.
Deposits on new homes.
Failure of vendor to maintain escrow account or
surety bond, RP §10-305.
Service of process.
Accredited agents, CJ §6-306.

BONDS, SURETY —Cont'd
Service of process —Cont'd
Bonding company.
Accredited agents, CJ §6-306.
Sheriffs, CJ §2-105; MD Const Art IV §44.
**Small business development financing
authority.**
Surety bond guaranty program.
See SMALL BUSINESS DEVELOPMENT
FINANCING AUTHORITY.
Soil conservation.
Districts.
Supervisors.
Officers and employees, AG §8-303.
Specific performance.
Refusal to specifically enforce contract on grounds
that adequate remedy and damages available.
Party resisting specific enforcement, CJ §3-601.
Start-up business ventures.
Bond or trust account.
When required, BR §14-115.
State lottery.
Licensed agents, SG §9-114.
State of Maryland.
Bond in name of state, Rule 1-402.
State retirement and pension system.
Fiduciaries, SPP §21-210.
State's attorneys.
Payment of premiums.
By county commissioners, 25 §33.
State treasurer, MD Const Art VI §1.
Filing, SG §5-102.
Form and conditions, SG §5-102.
Renewal, SG §5-102.
Required, SG §5-102.
Subdivisions.
Deposits on new homes, RP §§10-301 to 10-306.
See HOUSING.
Supersedeas bond.
Appeals, AppRev Rule 8-423.
Support and maintenance.
Parents and adult children.
Failure to give bond, FL §13-108.
Order to give bond, FL §§13-107 to 13-109.
Surety insurance.
Discrimination, IN §27-502.
Surplus lines brokers, IN §3-313.
Survey stations.
Person authorized to enter on land, BOP §1-302.
Taxation.
Appeal bond, TP §14-514.
Attachment.
Actions for collection of taxes.
Attachment bond not required, TG §13-817.
Collector.
General provisions.
See PROPERTY TAXES.
Motor fuel tax.
Licenses.
Surrender of bond, TG §9-335.
Security for taxes.
General provisions, TG §§13-824 to 13-831.
See TAXATION.
Taxicab operators, PUC §10-207.
Time-sharing.
Definition of "bond," RP §11A-116.
Developers, RP §11A-116.
Title insurance producers, IN §10-121.
Tobacco.
Persons selling for growers, AG §7-401.

BONDS, SURETY —Cont'd
Trading stamp companies.
Amount, BR §13-104.
Claims against bond, BR §13-105.
Trusts and trustees.
Discretionary trusts, ET §14-405.
General provisions.
See TRUSTS AND TRUSTEES.
Real estate investment trust.
Requirements, CA §8-204.
Sales.
Validation.
Prior sales made under bond with only one
surety, CL §15-103.
Unemployment compensation.
Contributions.
Reimbursement payments.
Failure to file bond or make deposit, LE
§8-622.
Required security for not for profit
organizations, LE §8-618.
Universities and colleges.
See UNIVERSITIES AND COLLEGES.
Vendor and vendee.
Deposits on new homes, RP §§10-301 to 10-306.
See HOUSING.
Venue.
Corporations.
Surety on bonds, CJ §6-202.
Vessels and boats.
Manufacturers or dealers, NR §8-710.1.
Veterans.
Guardianship.
Bond of guardian, ET §13-803.
Water pollution.
Oils.
Vessels discharging or receiving oil cargo, EN
§4-407.
Watershed associations.
Official bonds, 25 §178.
Witnesses.
Holding witness until criminal proceedings.
Commitment to jail and default of bond, CJ
§9-203.
Workers' compensation.
Insurance coverage.
Governmental self-insurance groups, LE §9-404.
Self-insurance by individual employer, LE
§9-405.
Zoning.
Subdivisions.
Secure completion of improvements and
utilities, 66B §5.03.

BONE MARROW DONATIONS, HG §19-310.

BONE MASS MEASUREMENTS.
Health insurance coverage for osteoporosis, IN
§15-823.

BONG.
Drug paraphernalia, CR §5-619.

BOOK MAKING, CR §12-102.
Statewide gaming provision generally, CR
§§12-101 to 12-113.
See GAMING.

BOOKS.
Clerks of court.
Test book.
Circuit courts, CJ §2-502.
Condominiums, RP §§11-116, 11A-128.

BOOKS —Cont'd
Credit services businesses.
  Inspection of books by commissioner, CL §14-1911.
Execution.
  Exemption from execution, CJ §11-504.
General assembly.
  Purchase of books, etc., for use of general
    assembly, MD Const Art III §16.
Obscenity and pornography.
  Adult sexual displays, CR §§11-101 to 11-107.
    See OBSCENITY AND PORNOGRAPHY.
  Obscene matter generally, CR §§11-201 to 11-211.
    See OBSCENITY AND PORNOGRAPHY.
Records.
  See RECORDS.
Schools.
  Textbooks.
    See SCHOOLS.

BORROWING.
Bond issues.
  See BOND ISSUES.
Loans.
  See LOANS.
Public debt.
  See PUBLIC DEBT.

BOTTLE CLUBS.
Alcoholic beverages.
  Anne Arundel county, 2B §20-101.
  Baltimore City, 2B §20-102.
  Baltimore county, 2B §20-103.
  Cecil county, 2B §20-104.
  Charles county, 2B §20-105.
  Dorchester county, 2B §20-105.1.
  Howard county.
    Alcohol awareness program, 2B §20-106.
    Places of public entertainment generally, 2B
      §20-106.
  Montgomery county, 2B §20-107.
  St. Mary's county, 2B §§12-219, 20-107.

BOTTLED WATER, HG §21-336.1.
Analysis, HG §21-336.
Collecting, bottling or delivering drinking
  water, HG §21-336.
Containers.
  Cleaning, HG §21-334.
Contamination prevention and recalls, HG
  §21-336.
Definitions.
  Collecting, bottling or delivering drinking water,
    HG §21-336.
Inspections, HG §21-336.
Labels, HG §21-336.
Licenses.
  Collecting, bottling or delivering drinking water.
    Suspension or revocation, HG §21-336.
  Required for collecting, bottling or delivering
    drinking water, HG §21-336.
Penalties.
  Collecting, bottling or delivering drinking water.
    Violations of provisions, HG §21-336.
Registration.
  Required to sell water shipped from outside state,
    HG §21-336.
Rules and regulations, HG §21-336.
Soft drinks generally.
  See SOFT DRINKS.
Testing, HG §21-336.

BOTTLES.
Containers.
  See CONTAINERS.

BOULEVARD RULE.
Entering or crossing through highways, TR
  §§21-401 to 21-404.1.

BOUNDARIES.
Aviation.
  Sovereignty in space, TR §5-104.
Baltimore City, 1 §12.
Baltimore county.
  Effect on composition of county board of
    education, ED §3-109.
Condominiums.
  Presumptions, RP §11-125.
Counties.
  See COUNTIES.
Crimes and offenses.
  State boundary monuments.
    Violations of subtitle, NR §2-407.
Environmental service.
  Region boundaries, NR §3-106.
Fish and fisheries.
  Tidal and nontidal waters.
    Authority to establish, NR §4-205.
Forests and parks.
  Wildland areas.
    Adjustment, NR §5-1209.
Heritage areas.
  Recognized areas, FI §13-1110.
Jails.
  Establishment of local correctional facility.
    Outside limits of municipal boundary, COR
      §11-102.1.
Maryland-Washington metropolitan district.
  Generally, 28 §3-102.
  Jesup Blair park.
    Survey and recording of boundaries, 28 §5-106.
  Lower Montgomery county metropolitan district.
    1963 addition, 28 §3-106.
    1965 addition, 28 §3-107.
  Rockville.
    Excluded from district, 28 §3-104.
  Upper Montgomery county metropolitan district,
    28 §3-103.
Maryland-Washington regional district, 28
  §7-103.
Mechanics' liens.
  Commencement of construction.
    Designation, PropAct Rule 12-308.
Mid-shore regional council, 20C §1-102.
Misdemeanors.
  State boundary monuments.
    Violations of subtitle, NR §2-407.
Municipal corporations.
  Annexation, 23A §19.
  Home rule.
    Registration.
      Annexation, 23A §19.
  Parish boundaries, CA §5-335.
  Registration, 23A §19.
Northeast Maryland waste disposal authority.
  Waste disposal region, NR §3-903.
Proceedings to establish boundary lines, RP
  §14-111.
Protestant Episcopal Church.
  Parish boundaries, CA §5-335.
Schools.
  School near line of two counties, ED §4-121.
Soil conservation.
  District boundaries, AG §8-301.
State boundary monuments.
  Adjacent states.
    Joint property of states, NR §2-401.

BOUNDARIES —Cont'd
State boundary monuments —Cont'd
Destruction prohibited, NR §2-404.
Enforcement of subtitle, NR §2-405.
Examination.
  Maryland geological survey, NR §2-402.
Exception to subtitle, NR §2-406.
Fines.
  Violation of subtitle, NR §2-407.
Forest and park wardens.
  Enforcement of subtitle, NR §2-405.
Maryland geological survey.
  Authority, NR §2-402.
Mason and Dixon monument, NR §2-406.
Natural resources police officers.
  Enforcement of subtitle, NR §2-405.
Ownership.
  Joint ownership, NR §2-401.
Possession of monument prohibited, NR §2-404.
Replacement and repair, NR §2-402.
Right of entry.
  Maryland geological survey, NR §2-403.
Violations.
  Fines, NR §2-407.
Tri-county council for lower eastern shore of
    Maryland, 20B §1-102.
Tri-county council for southern Maryland.
  Tri-county area, 20 §1-101.
Tri-county council for western Maryland.
  Tri-county area, 20A §1-101.
Waters of the state.
  Wild and scenic rivers.
    Youghiogheny river.
      Scenic corridor, NR §8-408.
Wetlands.
  Private wetlands, EN §16-301.
Youghiogheny river.
  Scenic corridor, NR §8-408.
Zoning.
  See ZONING.

BOUNTIES.
Birds and game.
  Counties.
    Powers, 25 §2.
  Wildlife prohibited, NR §10-207.
Counties.
  Powers as to, 25 §2.
Crows.
  Counties, 25 §2.
Foxes.
  Killing.
    Counties, 25 §2.
Hawks.
  Killing.
    Counties, 25 §2.
Minks.
  Killing.
    Counties, 25 §2.
Owls.
  Killing.
    Counties, 25 §2.
Reward.
  Counties.
    Powers as to, 25 §2.
Wildcats.
  Killing.
    Counties, 25 §2.

BOW AND ARROW.
Fish and fisheries.
  Carp.
    Shooting carp, NR §4-620.

BOW AND ARROW —Cont'd
Waterfowl and migratory birds, hunting, NR
    §10-602.

BOWIE KNIFE.
Carrying concealed or with intent to injure,
    CR §4-101.
Minor carrying, hours prohibited, CR §4-101.

BOWIE STATE UNIVERSITY.
Payments from state relative to private
    donations, ED §17-302.
Police force.
  General provisions.
    See UNIVERSITIES AND COLLEGES.
State center for alternative dispute resolution
    and violence prevention, ED §24-401.

BOWLING ALLEYS.
Alcoholic beverages.
  Harford county, 2B §9-213.
  More than one license for same person or
      premises.
    Exceptions as to bowling alleys, 2B §9-102.
  Wicomico county.
    Definition of "bowling alley," 2B §1-102.
Sundays and holidays.
  Regulations.
    See SUNDAYS AND HOLIDAYS.

BOWLING MACHINES.
Licensing of amusement devices, BR §§17-401 to
    17-438.

BOXES.
Returnable containers and textiles.
  Registration, prohibited acts, BR §§19-301 to
      19-307.

BOXING AND WRESTLING TAX.
Administrative cost account.
  Distribution of tax revenue, TG §2-401.
Amateur contests.
  Exemption, TG §6-103.
Athletic commission.
  Definition of "commission," TG §6-101.
Audits.
  Inspection and preservation of records, TG §6-202.
Broadcast right.
  Charge for sale of.
    Imposition of tax on, TG §6-102.
Correction of erroneous assessment, TG
    §13-509.
Crimes and offenses.
  Payment.
    Willful failure to make, TG §13-1005.
  Records.
    Willful failure to keep records, TG §13-1008.
  Returns.
    Willful failure to file return, TG §13-1001.
    Willful false statement or misleading omission,
        TG §13-1003.
  Violations of provisions generally, TG §13-1020.
Definitions, TG §§1-101, 6-101.
Distributions, TG §§2-401, 2-402.
  General fund, TG §2-402.
Evasion of tax.
  License forfeiture, TG §13-712.
Exemptions, TG §6-103.
Failure of promoter to pay.
  Suspension or revocation of license, BR §4-310.
General fund.
  Distribution of tax revenue, TG §2-401.
Imposition of tax, TG §6-102.

BOXING AND WRESTLING TAX —Cont'd
Misdemeanors.
  Payment of tax.
    Willful failure to pay, TG §13-1005.
  Records.
    Willful failure to keep records, TG §13-1008.
  Returns.
    Willful failure to file return, TG §13-1001.
    Willful false statement or misleading omission,
      TG §13-1003.
  Violations of provisions, TG §13-1020.
Payment of tax, TG §6-301.
  Willful failure to pay, TG §13-1005.
Penalties.
  Criminal penalties.
    Payment of tax.
      Willful failure to pay, TG §13-1005.
    Records.
      Willful failure to keep, TG §13-1008.
    Returns.
      Willful failure to file return, TG §13-1001.
      Willful false statement or misleading
        omission, TG §13-1003.
    Violations of provisions, TG §13-1020.
Perjury.
  Willful failure to file return, TG §13-1001.
Rates, TG §6-104.
Records.
  Inspection and preservation, TG §6-202.
  Willful failure to keep records, TG §13-1008.
Returns.
  Contents, TG §6-201.
  Crimes and offenses.
    Willful failure to file return, TG §13-1001.
    Willful false statement or misleading omission,
      TG §13-1003.
  Required, TG §6-201.
Revision of assessment or refund, TG §13-508.
**Suspension or revocation of promoter's
  license.**
  Failure to pay, BR §4-310.
Telecast.
  Charge to view.
    Imposition of tax on, TG §6-102.
    Rate of tax on, TG §6-104.
  Defined, TG §6-101.
Universities and colleges.
  Exemptions, TG §6-103.

BOXING, SPARRING AND WRESTLING.
Amateur boxing.
  Headgear, BR §4-302.
Athletic commission.
  Authority of secretary, BR §4-207.
  Boxing and wrestling tax.
    See BOXING AND WRESTLING TAX.
  Chairman.
    Election, BR §4-203.
  Compensation, BR §4-204.
  Composition, BR §4-202.
  Creation, BR §4-201.
  Defined as "commission," BR §4-101.
  Disposition of money, BR §4-206.
  Establishment, BR §4-201.
  Injunctive relief, BR §4-323.
  Licenses.
    Generally. See within this heading, "Licenses."
  Meetings, BR §4-204.
  Membership, BR §4-202.
  Powers and duties, BR §4-205.
    Authority of secretary, BR §4-207.

BOXING, SPARRING AND WRESTLING
  —Cont'd
Athletic commission —Cont'd
  Powers and duties —Cont'd
    Contests authorization, BR §4-313.
    License issuance, BR §4-307.
  Program evaluation act, SG §8-403.
  Quorum, BR §4-204.
  Rulemaking authority, BR §4-205.
  Staff and office, BR §4-204.
  Tenure, BR §4-202.
    Chairman, BR §4-203.
  Termination of certain provisions, BR §4-208.
Authorized contests, BR §4-313.
  Boxing contests, BR §4-315.
  Fake contests prohibited, BR §4-316.
  Unlicensed participant.
    Contest participation prohibited, BR §4-320.
Blood tests.
  License requirement, BR §4-304.1.
Bribery.
  Accepting money or gifts for favors, BR §4-321.
Building or other structure.
  Ventilation and safety, BR §4-319.
Commission. See within this heading, "Athletic
  commission."
Controlled dangerous substances.
  Urine tests to detect.
    Required by each boxer or kick boxer in contest,
      BR §4-315.
Counties.
  Permit required for arena, 25 §27.
Definitions, BR §4-101.
  License, BR §4-301.
Fake boxing or wrestling contest.
  Suspension or revocation of promoter's license, BR
    §4-310.
Fake contests.
  Prohibition, BR §4-316.
Gifts.
  Accepting money or gifts for favors, BR §4-321.
Headgear for amateur boxing, BR §4-302.
Injunctions, BR §4-323.
Licenses.
  Acting in contest.
    Required, BR §4-303.
  Applications.
    Blood tests, BR §4-304.1.
    Contents, BR §4-305.
    Generally, BR §4-305.
    Neurological examination, BR §4-304.
    Surety bond requirements, BR §4-306.
  Boxer license.
    Scope of license, BR §4-308.
  Boxing and wrestling tax.
    Failure of promoter to pay.
      Suspension or revocation of license, BR
        §4-310.
  Defined, BR §4-301.
  Denials.
    Grounds, BR §4-310.
  Disciplinary actions.
    Grounds, BR §4-310.
    Hearings, BR §4-311.
      Application of contested case provisions, BR
        §4-311.
      Failure to appear, BR §4-311.
    Judicial review, BR §4-312.
  Expiration of license, BR §4-309.
  Fake boxing or wrestling contest.
    Suspension or revocation of promoter's license,
      BR §4-310.

BOXING, SPARRING AND WRESTLING
—Cont'd
Licenses —Cont'd
Fees, BR §4-305.
Issuance, BR §4-307.
Judge license.
Scope of license, BR §4-308.
Kick boxer license.
Scope of license, BR §4-308.
Manager license.
Scope of license, BR §4-308.
Matchmaker license.
Scope of license, BR §4-308.
Neurological examination.
Applicant for license not fit based on.
Denial of license to boxing or kick boxing
applicant, BR §4-310.
Participating in contest.
Required, BR §4-303.
Penalties.
Disciplinary actions, BR §4-310.
Promoter license.
Scope of license, BR §4-308.
Referee license.
Scope of license, BR §4-308.
Reprimands.
Grounds, BR §4-310.
Required, BR §4-303.
Scope of license, BR §4-308.
Second license.
Scope of license, BR §4-308.
Surety bond.
Required for promoter license, BR §4-306.
Suspension or revocation.
Grounds, BR §4-310.
Term of license, BR §4-309.
Unlicensed participants.
Contest participation prohibited, BR §4-320.
Urine test.
Mandatory grounds for suspending or revoking
boxing license, BR §4-310.
Wrestler license.
Scope of license, BR §4-308.
Neurological examination, BR §4-314.
Applicant for license not fit based on.
Denial of license to boxing or kick boxing
applicant, BR §4-310.
License requirement, BR §4-304.
Required, BR §§4-304, 4-314.
Number of rounds.
Boxing contests, BR §4-315.
Penalties.
License disciplinary actions, BR §4-310.
Violations of provisions, BR §4-322.
Physically fit participants.
Boxing contests, BR §4-315.
Scope of subtitle, BR §4-302.
Seat prices.
Publication, BR §4-317.
Space requirements.
Publication of seat prices, BR §4-317.
Taxation.
Boxing and wrestling tax.
General provisions, TG §§2-401, 6-101 to 6-104,
13-1020.
See BOXING AND WRESTLING TAX.
Ticket scalping, BR §4-318.
Urine test required.
Boxing contests, BR §4-315.
Mandatory grounds for suspending or revoking
license, BR §4-310.

BOXING, SPARRING AND WRESTLING
—Cont'd
Weight of gloves.
Boxing contests, BR §4-315.

BOYCOTTS.
Foreign discriminatory boycotts, CL §§11-101 to
11-115.
See FOREIGN DISCRIMINATORY BOYCOTTS.
Insurance unfair trade practices, IN §27-206.

BOYS' AND GIRLS' CLUB WORK.
Counties.
Farmers' cooperative demonstration work, 25
§160.

BOY SCOUTS.
Forests and parks.
Free admission to state parks, NR §5-1008.
Taxation.
Exemptions, TP §7-233.

BRAIN DEATH.
Health care decisions.
Advance directive registry, HG §§5-619 to 5-626.
General provisions, HG §§5-601 to 5-618.
See HEALTH CARE DECISIONS.

BRAIN INJURY ADVISORY BOARD, HG
§§13-2101 to 13-2105.
Chair, HG §13-2104.
Compensation, HG §13-2104.
Definition of advisory board, HG §13-2101.
Established, HG §13-2102.
Meetings, HG §13-2104.
Members, HG §13-2103.
Terms, HG §13-2104.
Powers and duties, HG §13-2105.
Vacancies, HG §13-2104.

BRAKE LIGHTS, TR §22-206.
Lighted as prescribed, TR §22-201.1.
Lights generally.
See MOTOR VEHICLE EQUIPMENT.
Signal lamps and devices, TR §22-219.

BRAKES, TR §§22-301 to 22-305.

BRANCH BANKING, FI §§5-1001 to 5-1015.
See BANKS AND TRUST COMPANIES.

BRANT.
Waterfowl.
See BIRDS AND GAME.

BREACH OF LEASE, RP §8-402.1.

BREACH OF PROMISE TO MARRY.
Actions.
Corroboration required, FL §3-102.
Location of statutory provisions, CJ §5-801.
No cause of action unless individual pregnant, FL
§3-102.
Prohibited actions.
General provisions.
See ACTIONS.
Construction and interpretation.
Liberal construction of provisions, FL §3-101.
Contracts.
Payment or settlement of abolished or prohibited
claims.
Void, FL §3-104.

BREACH OF THE PEACE.
General provisions.
See DISTURBANCE OF THE PEACE.

BREAKFAST PROGRAM, ED §§7-701 to 7-704.

BREAKING AND ENTERING, CR §§6-201 to 6-210.
Burglary in the first degree, CR §6-202.
Burglary with explosives or destructive device, CR §6-207.
Burglary in the second degree, CR §6-203.
Burglary in the third degree, CR §6-204.
Burglary in the fourth degree, CR §6-205.
Charging document, CR §6-210.
Definitions, CR §6-201.
Motor vehicle, CR §6-206.
Research facility, CR §6-208.
Separate units, separate violations, CR §6-209.

BREAST CANCER.
Alternative methods of treatment, HG §20-113.
  Department of health and mental hygiene.
    Duties, HG §20-113.
  Exceptions to provisions, HG §20-113.
  Physicians.
    Duty to educate patient, HG §20-113.
    Violations by, HG §20-113.
Diethylstilbestrol exposure.
  Public information campaign and screening program, HG §18-303.
Health insurance.
  Mastectomy coverage, IN §15-832.
  Prosthesis coverage, IN §15-834.
Hospitals.
  Educational materials, HG §19-348.
Mammography testing, HG §20-115.
  Insurance coverage, IN §15-814.
  Low-income underinsured or uninsured women, HG §20-116.
  Medicare supplement insurance, IN §15-907.
Mastectomies, HG §20-116.
  Health insurance coverage, IN §15-832.
    Prosthesis coverage, IN §15-834.
    Reconstructive breast surgery, IN §15-815.
Program, HG §20-116.
Reconstructive breast surgery.
  Health insurance coverage, IN §15-815.

BREASTFEEDING.
Rights of mother, HG §20-801.

BREAST IMPLANTS.
Action for damages.
  Statute of limitations, CJ §5-116.
Duty of physicians to inform as to risks, advantages, etc., HG §20-114.
Health insurance.
  Coverage information, IN §15-105.
  Effect of implants on coverage, IN §15-504.

BREATH TEST.
Motor vehicles.
  Driving while under influence of alcohol or drugs, TR §16-205.2.
    Chemical tests generally.
      See DRIVING UNDER THE INFLUENCE.

BREWERY LICENSE, 2B §2-206.

BREW-PUB LICENSE, 2B §2-207.

BREW-THRU.
Frederick county, 2B §9-211.1.
Generally.
  See DRIVE-THRU PURCHASE FACILITIES.
Harford county, 2B §9-213.
Howard county, 2B §9-214.
Transfer of licenses, 2B §10-503.

BRIBERY, CR §§9-201 to 9-205.
Acceptance of bribe by juror, CR §9-202.

BRIBERY —Cont'd
Acceptance of bribe by person participating in athletic contest, CR §9-205.
Alcoholic beverages provided voters on election day, CR §9-203.
Athletic contest participants, CR §9-204.
Competency of witness.
  Bribery of participants in athletic contest.
    Person violating provisions, CR §9-204.
  Bribery of public employee, employee demanding or receiving bribe.
    Person violating provisions, CR §9-201.
Constitutional provisions, US Const Art II §4.
Contracts.
  Procurement.
    Debarment of contractors, SF §§16-101 to 16-312.
    See PROCUREMENT.
Demanding or receiving bribe.
  Public employee, CR §9-201.
Evidence.
  Compelling testimony in such cases, MD Const Art III §50.
Fines.
  Legislature to provide penalty, MD Const Art III §50.
General assembly.
  Member or officer, MD Const Art III §50.
Immunity from prosecution.
  Bribery of participants in athletic contest.
    Person violating provisions compelled to testify, CR §9-204.
  Bribery of public employee, employee demanding or receiving bribe.
    Compelling person violating provisions to testify, CR §9-201.
Investigations.
  State prosecutor.
    See STATE PROSECUTOR.
Judges.
  Legislature to provide for penalty and punishment, MD Const Art III §50.
Juror, CR §9-202.
Medicaid fraud, CR §8-511.
Officers.
  Disfranchised and disqualified from holding any office of trust or profit, MD Const Art III §50.
Penalties.
  Legislature to provide for, MD Const Art III §50.
Procurement.
  Contractors.
    Debarment, SF §§16-101 to 16-312.
    See PROCUREMENT.
  Unlawful conduct, SF §13-211.
Public employee, CR §9-201.
Sentence and punishment.
  Legislature to provide punishment for bribery, MD Const Art III §50.
State police department.
  Compensation other than salary prohibited, PS §2-408.
State prosecutor.
  See STATE PROSECUTOR.
Statute of limitations on prosecution.
  Bribery of juror, acceptance by juror, CR §9-202.
  Bribery of participants in athletic contest, CR §9-204.
  Bribery of public employee, employee demanding or receiving bribe, CR §9-201.
Voter, CR §9-203.
  Influencing voter's decision by use of, EL §16-201.

BRIBERY —Cont'd
Witnesses.
Compelling testimony in certain cases, MD Const Art III §50.
Exemption from trial and punishment, MD Const Art III §50.

BRICKS.
Throwing object at vehicle, CR §6-302.

BRIDGE AND CANAL COMPANIES.
Contracts.
Erection of bridges or construction of canals, 23 §141.
Counties.
Erection of bridges or construction of canals.
Consent of county commissioners required, 23 §140.
Report of corporations to county commissioners, 23 §142.
Eminent domain.
Condemnation in event of failure to agree or disability to contract, 23 §141.
Real property.
Agreement of corporation with owners of real property, 23 §141.
Recordation.
Erection of bridges or construction of canals.
Resolution of county commissioners authorizing construction recorded, 23 §140.
Reports.
Erection of bridges or construction of canals.
Corporation's report to county commissioners, 23 §142.
Waters of the state.
Erection of bridge on navigable river, 23 §143.

BRIDGES.
Arson and burning, CR §§6-101 to 6-111.
Awards.
Contracts by county commissioners, 25 §§38, 43.
Bear Creek bridge.
Baltimore county.
Tolls, 25 §50A.
Transfer of title to county, 25 §50A.
Bonds, surety.
Counties.
Performance bonds, 25 §38.
Bungee jumping, BR §3-503.
Chesapeake Bay toll bridge.
General provisions.
See HIGHWAYS.
Choptank river bridge.
See CHOPTANK RIVER.
Closing.
By state highway administration, TR §24-205.
Companies.
Bridge and canal companies, 23 §§140 to 143.
See BRIDGE AND CANAL COMPANIES.
Counties.
Chartered counties.
Powers of county, 25A §5.
County commissioners to have control of county bridges, 25 §1.
Dorchester county.
Construction or repair, 25 §37B.
Draining lands.
Cost of construction, 25 §99.
Littering.
Refuse on bridges prohibited, TR §21-1111.
Mechanics' liens.
Attachment of lien, RP §9-102.

BRIDGES —Cont'd
Militia.
Free passage over roads, bridges and ferries while traveling to and from duties, PS §13-212.
Motor vehicles.
Closing of bridges, TR §24-205.
Damages caused by low clearance.
Owner of bridge or overpass not liable for, TR §24-104.
Speed.
Establishment of maximum safe speed, TR §21-806.
Stopping, standing or parking on, TR §21-1003.
Names.
Advisory committee on naming state facilities, roads and bridges, SG §2-10A-09.
Senator Frederick C. Malkus, Jr., bridge, TR §8-649.
Notices.
Application to county commissioners.
Building or repair of bridge, 25 §35.
Examiner's notice of acceptance of intercounty bridge, 25 §44.
Signs.
Weight and speed of vehicles passing over bridges, TR §24-206.
Speed.
Vehicles passing over bridges.
Authority to regulate, TR §24-206.
Signs, TR §24-206.
Toll bridges and tunnels.
Bear Creek bridge, 25 §50A.
Chesapeake Bay toll bridge.
General provisions.
See HIGHWAYS.
Militia.
Free passage over roads, bridges and ferries while traveling to and from duties, PS §13-212.
Operation of motor vehicles on, TR §§21-1401 to 21-1414.
Toll bridge company defined as common carrier, PUC §1-101.
Watershed associations.
Constructing and maintaining, 25 §§215, 216.
Weight of vehicles passing over bridges.
Authority to regulate, TR §24-206.
Signs, TR §24-206.
Woodrow Wilson bridge and tunnel compact, TR §§10-301 to 10-303.

BRIEFS.
Appeals.
General provisions.
See APPEALS.
General assembly.
Continuance to prepare, CJ §6-402.

BRITISH COMMON LAW AND STATUTES.
Applicability, MD Const DofR Art 5.
Certain British statutes no longer in force in Maryland, RP §14-115.

BROADBAND COMMUNICATIONS.
Highways.
Rights-of-way.
Infrastructure installation by nonprofit telecommunications services, TR §8-654.
Rural broadband assistance fund, 83A §§5-1901, 5-1902.
Rural broadband coordination board, 41 §§21-101 to 21-103.

BROADCAST DEFAMATION.
Statements made by candidates for public
    office, CJ §§3-503, 3-504.

BROADCASTING IN COURTHOUSES, CJA Rule
    16-109.
Criminal proceedings.
    Prohibition, exception, violation contempt, CP
        §1-201.

BROADENED OWNERSHIP ACT, 83A §2-106.

BROKERS.
Insurance agents and brokers.
    See INSURANCE AGENTS AND BROKERS.
Poultry products inspection.
    Broker.
        Defined, AG §4-201.
Real estate brokers, BOP §§17-101 to 17-702.
    See REAL ESTATE BROKERS.
Securities.
    Registration.
        Broker-dealers and agents.
            General provisions, CA §§11-401 to 11-417.
Wholesome meat act.
    Meat broker.
        Defined, AG §4-101.

BROKERS' LIENS.
Secured transactions, CL §9-206.

BROMINATED FLAME RETARDANTS.
OctaBDE and pentaBDE.
    Manufacturing, processing, selling or distributing
        product containing, EN §§6-1201 to 6-1205.
    Civil penalty, EN §6-1204.
    Definitions, EN §6-1201.
    Enforcement of prohibition, EN §6-1203.
    Fines, EN §6-1204.
    Injunction to enforce prohibition, EN §§6-1203,
        6-1204.
    Original equipment replacement service parts.
        Inapplicability of prohibition, EN §6-1202.
    Prohibited, EN §6-1202.
    Recyclables, inapplicability of prohibition, EN
        §6-1202.
    Regulations, adoption, EN §6-1205.

BROTHELS.
Prostitution.
    See PROSTITUTION.

BROTHERS AND SISTERS.
General provisions.
    See RELATIVES.

BROWNFIELDS REDEVELOPMENT.
Economic development assistance fund.
    Brownfields revitalization incentive program, 83A
        §5-1408.
    Uses of fund for, 83A §5-1405.

**BROWNFIELDS REVITALIZATION
    INCENTIVE PROGRAM.**
Property taxes.
    Abatement on property designated as Brownfields
        site, TP §14-902.
    Financial incentives for qualified Brownfields
        sites, TP §9-229.
        Insurance companies, IN §6-116.
Voluntary cleanup program, EN §7-507.

BRUTALITY.
Police brutality.
    Investigations and interrogations.
        Rights of officers, PS §3-104.

BUDGET AND MANAGEMENT.
Agriculture.
    Agricultural commission, AG §2-204.
    Secretary of agriculture.
        Responsibility, AG §2-103.
Alcoholic beverages.
    License commissioners.
        County budget and fiscal policies.
            Boards subject to, 24 §8-101.
Amendment of budget.
    Restriction on, SF §7-210.
Annuities.
    State operating budget.
        Budget books.
            Summary of annuity bond accounts of state,
                SF §7-119.
Appalachian states low-level radioactive waste
    compact.
    Commission, EN §7-302.
Attorney general.
    Assistant attorney general.
        Assignment to department, SF §3-206.
        Legal adviser to department, SF §3-206.
Balanced budget.
    Required, MD Const Art III §52.
Bill, MD Const Art III §52.
Bond and revenue bills, submission by
    Governor, SF §7-106.
Budget analyst, SF §3-203.
Budget bill.
    State operating budget, SF §§7-108 to 7-114.1. See
        within this heading, "State operating budget."
Budget books.
    State operating budget, SF §§7-115 to 7-121. See
        within this heading, "State operating budget."
Bureau of purchasing.
    General services department.
        See GENERAL SERVICES DEPARTMENT.
Business and economic development
    department.
    Division of tourism and promotion.
        Consolidated publications account, 83A §4-105.
    Responsibility of secretary for budget, 83A §2-105.
Capital appropriation.
    Budgeting in operating budget.
        General fund capital appropriations, SF §7-122.
Central collection unit, SF §3-301.
    Central collection fund, SF §3-306.
    Debt collection, SF §3-302.
        Costs, SF §3-304.
        Delinquent accounts, SF §3-302.
        Disposition of funds, SF §3-305.
        Exceptions, SF §3-302.
        Rules and regulations, SF §3-303.
    Disposition of funds collected, SF §3-305.
    Duties, SF §3-302.
    Employees, SF §3-301.
    Established, SF §3-301.
    Insurance companies.
        Retaliatory tax, collection, IN §6-305.
    Powers, SF §3-304.
    Rules and regulations.
        Debt collection, SF §3-303.
Child support reinvestment fund.
    Expenditures.
        Budget procedure, FL §10-106.1.
Cigarette restitution fund.
    Budget bill to included funding for funded
        programs, SF §7-114.
    Budget books to contain expenditure overview, SF
        §7-121.

BUDGET AND MANAGEMENT —Cont'd
Circuit courts.
County budget and fiscal policies.
Circuit courts subject to, 24 §8-101.
Clerks of court.
Annual budget submitted by clerks, CJ §2-504.1.
Collections.
Central collection unit, SF §§3-301 to 3-306. See
within this heading, "Central collection unit."
Community college of Baltimore.
Operating budget, ED §16-507.
Computers.
Telecommunication and computer network, SF
§3-705.
Condominiums.
Council of unit owners.
Annual proposed budget.
See CONDOMINIUMS.
Counties.
Accrual method.
Authorized, 24 §1-103.
Entities subject to county budget and fiscal
policies, 24 §8-101.
Definitions, SF §3-101.
State operating budget, SF §7-101.
Budget bill.
Transportation department, SF §7-110.
Telecommunications, SF §3-701.
Department.
Budget analyst.
Appointment by secretary, SF §3-203.
Duties, SF §3-203.
Qualifications, SF §3-203.
Budget of department.
Responsibility of secretary, SF §3-204.
Central collection unit, SF §§3-301 to 3-306. See
within this heading, "Central collection unit."
Citizens' advisory units, SF §3-204.
Counsel to department, SF §3-206.
Defined, SF §3-101.
Established, SF §3-201.
Funds.
Volunteer company assistance fund, PS §§8-201
to 8-206.
Legal counsel to department, SF §3-206.
Secretary. See within this heading, "Secretary."
Units to report to secretary, EN §1-404.
Director. See within this heading, "Secretary."
Environment.
Secretary.
Responsibilities, EN §1-404.
Establishment of department, SF §3-201.
Fiscal planning.
Natural resources.
Secretary.
Responsibility for, NR §1-103.
General assembly.
Bills.
Bond and revenue bills, submission by
Governor, SF §7-106.
Extension of session of general assembly for
passage, MD Const Art III §52.
Inquiries to secretary from general assembly, SF
§3-205.
State operating budget.
Budget bill.
General provisions, SF §§7-108 to 7-114.1.
Budget books.
Distribution of copies to general assembly
members, SF §7-115.

BUDGET AND MANAGEMENT —Cont'd
General fund capital appropriations.
Budgeting in operating budget, SF §7-122.
General services department.
Secretary.
Responsibility for budgets of units of
department, SF §4-204.
Governor.
Bills, MD Const Art III §52.
Bond and revenue bills, submission to General
Assembly, SF §7-106.
Health.
Secretary of health and mental hygiene.
General authority and duties of secretary, HG
§2-104.
Special supplemental food program for women,
infants and children.
Funds included in annual budget, HG §18-108.
Healthy air act.
Electric generating facilities.
Emissions budgets, EN §2-1002.
Historic St. Mary's City commission, ED
§24-511.
Housing authorities, HS §12-404.
Montgomery county.
Housing opportunities commission, HS §16-111.
Information processing.
Executive branch of state government generally,
SF §§3-401 to 3-413.
See INFORMATION TECHNOLOGY.
Information technology board, SF §§3-406 to
3-409.
Judges.
Salaries.
Budget treatment, CJ §1-704.
Judgments.
Sovereign immunity.
Actions in contract.
Budget request to satisfy judgments, SG
§12-203.
Kidney diseases.
Annual budget request, HG §13-316.
Labor, licensing and regulation department.
General authority of secretary, BR §2-104.
Management and productivity council, SG
§9-1806.
Managing for results.
Definitions, SF §3-1001.
Review by secretary, SF §3-1003.
State comprehensive plan.
Review and update of contents, SF §3-1002.
Strategic plan.
Inclusion in budget books, SF §7-121.
Submission by agency, SF §3-1002.
Maryland correctional enterprises.
Budget included in department of public safety
and correctional services' budget, COR §3-507.
**Maryland-national capital park and planning
commission.**
See MARYLAND-NATIONAL CAPITAL PARK
AND PLANNING COMMISSION.
Montgomery county.
Housing opportunities commission, HS §16-111.
Motor fuel tax.
State operating budget.
Budget bill.
Fuel tax revenues, SF §7-113.
Motor vehicles.
Purchase, lease or rental, SF §3-502.
Exceptions to provisions, SF §3-501.

BUDGET AND MANAGEMENT —Cont'd
Motor vehicles —Cont'd
Reassignment of state-owned motor vehicles.
Power of secretary, SF §3-503.
Report to general assembly by secretary, SF §3-503.
Rules and regulations, SF §3-503.
Municipal corporations.
Accrual method.
Authorized, 24 §1-103.
Nuclear compact.
Submission of budgets, 41 §16-111.
Oaths.
Secretary.
Oath of office, SF §3-202.
Postmortem examiners.
State budget to include appropriation for carrying subtitle, HG §5-305.
Potomac water authority.
Preparation of budget, EN §5-414.
Procedure.
How made, MD Const Art III §52.
Procurement.
Information processing.
Equipment and services.
Review and approval of procurement, SF §3-405.
Resource sharing, SF §3-405.
Proposed budget.
State operating budget. See within this heading, "State operating budget."
Public debt.
General obligation debt.
General provisions, SF §§8-108 to 8-112.
See PUBLIC DEBT.
Management program.
Consolidated loan budget, SF §8-114.
Public works, board of.
Baltimore zoo lease payments to be included in budget, SF §10-206.
Purchasing.
General provisions. See within this heading, "Secretary."
Reports.
Motor vehicles.
Purchase, lease or rental.
Report to general assembly by secretary, SF §3-503.
Rules and regulations.
Central collection unit.
Debt collection, SF §3-303.
Motor vehicles.
Purchase, lease or rental, SF §3-503.
Secretary.
Adoption, EN §1-404; SF §3-204.
Central collection unit.
Debt collection, SF §3-303.
Salaries.
Judges.
Budget treatment, CJ §1-704.
Secretary of agriculture, AG §2-102.
Deputy secretary, AG §2-102.
State operating budget.
Budget bill.
Appropriations to pay.
Use of salary plan, SF §7-108.
Conformity with statutes, SF §7-112.
Executive pay plan, SF §7-109.
Nonclassified positions.
Statement, SF §7-109.

BUDGET AND MANAGEMENT —Cont'd
Schools.
Amount requested, ED §5-103.
Annual school budget.
Prepared and transmitted to governor by state board of education, ED §2-205.
Prepared by county board of education, ED §5-101.
Categories, ED §5-101.
Transfers within and between major categories, ED §5-105.
Copies, ED §5-102.
Deficits, ED §5-114.
Expenditure of nonlocal funds received after adoption of budget, ED §5-105.
Fiscal status report, ED §5-109.
Forms.
By state board of education, ED §2-205.
Maryland school for the blind.
Detailed account of operating and administrative budget for school.
Budget submitted by governor to general assembly to include, ED §8-318.
Overruns of budget, ED §5-105.
Preparation by state superintendent, ED §4-205.
Public broadcasting commission, ED §24-204.
Reductions, ED §5-102.
Semi-annual fiscal status report, ED §5-111.
Submission to governing body of county, ED §5-102.
Superintendent of schools.
Prepare annual budget, ED §4-205.
Violation of reporting requirements, ED §5-113.
Seal.
Secretary, SF §3-204.
Secretary.
Advisory boards and councils, EN §1-404.
Appointment, SF §3-202.
Budget analyst.
Appointment, SF §3-203.
Budget of department.
Responsibility of secretary, SF §3-204.
Citizens' advisory units.
Creation, SF §3-204.
Defined, SF §3-101.
Deputy secretary, SF §3-203.
Duties, SF §3-204.
General assembly.
Inquiries from general assembly, SF §3-205.
Head of department, SF §3-202.
Information processing.
Delegation of secretary's duties, SF §3-413.
Equipment and services.
Procurement.
Approval, SF §3-405.
Inquiries from general assembly, SF §3-205.
Motor vehicles.
Purchase, lease or rental.
Approval, SF §3-502.
Reassignment of state-owned motor vehicles, SF §3-503.
Regulations, SF §3-503.
Report to general assembly, SF §3-503.
Oath of office, SF §3-202.
Planning, EN §1-404.
Purchases.
Contracts and purchases.
Powers of house of delegates as grand inquest of state, MD Const Art III §24.
General services department.
See GENERAL SERVICES DEPARTMENT.

BUDGET AND MANAGEMENT —Cont'd
Secretary —Cont'd
Qualifications, SF §3-202.
Rules and regulations.
Adoption, EN §1-404; SF §3-204.
Debt collection, SF §3-303.
Salary, SF §3-202.
Seal, SF §3-204.
Staff, SF §3-203.
State operating budget.
Defined, SF §7-101.
Proposed budget.
Preparation, SF §7-104.
Revenue estimates, SF §7-103.
Studies, SF §7-103.
Transfer of functions, staff or funds, EN §1-404.
Units of department to report to secretary, EN §1-405.
Secretary of agriculture.
Responsibility for office, AG §2-103.
Salaries, AG §2-102.
Deputy secretary, AG §2-102.
Sheriffs.
County budget and fiscal policies.
Sheriffs' offices subject to, 24 §8-101.
Social services.
Administration.
Director to submit budget to secretary, 88A §2.
Southern Maryland higher education center, ED §24-306.
Sovereign immunity.
Actions in contract.
Budget request to satisfy judgments, SG §12-203.
State operating budget.
Annuity bond accounts.
Budget books to contain summary of annuity bond accounts, SF §7-119.
Budget bill.
Appropriations.
Enumeration of required appropriations, SF §7-108.
University college.
Lump sum appropriation, SF §7-111.
Cigarette restitution fund, funded programs, SF §7-114.
Motor vehicle fuel tax.
Revenues, SF §7-113.
Motor vehicle licensing.
Revenues, SF §7-113.
Salaries.
Appropriations to pay.
Use of salary plan, SF §7-108.
Conformity with statutes, SF §7-112.
Executive pay plan, SF §7-109.
Nonclassified positions.
Statement, SF §7-109.
Statutes.
Conformity with statutes, SF §7-112.
Supporting documents.
Budget books, SF §§7-115 to 7-121. See within this subheading, "Budget books."
University college.
Lump sum appropriation, SF §7-111.
Transportation department, SF §7-110.
University college.
Appropriations.
Lump sum appropriation, SF §7-111.
Budget books.
Annuity bond accounts, SF §7-119.

BUDGET AND MANAGEMENT —Cont'd
State operating budget —Cont'd
Budget books —Cont'd
Cigarette restitution fund, funded programs.
Expenditure overview, SF §7-121.
Contents.
Annuity bond accounts, SF §7-119.
Estimated revenues.
Statement of estimated revenues, SF §7-117.
Federal reimbursement, SF §7-120.
Operating expenses of state units, SF §7-121.
Spending affordability committee recommendations, SF §7-116.
Statement of estimated revenues, SF §7-117.
Tax exemptions.
Statement and recommendations as to effect on revenues, SF §7-118.
Distribution, SF §7-115.
Estimated revenues.
Statement of estimated revenues, SF §7-117.
Expenses of state units.
Operating expenses.
Information to be included, SF §7-121.
Federal reimbursement.
Information to be included, SF §7-120.
General assembly.
Distribution of copies to members, SF §7-115.
Managing for results strategic agency plan to be included, SF §7-121.
Operating expenses of state units.
Information to be included, SF §7-121.
Spending affordability committee recommendations, SF §7-116.
Tax exemptions.
Effect on revenues.
Statement and recommendations, SF §7-118.
Capital appropriation.
General fund capital appropriations, SF §7-122.
Capital improvements.
Proposed budget.
Inclusion in draft of proposed budget, SF §7-104.
Cigarette restitution fund, funded programs.
Appropriations in budget bill, SF §7-114.
Expenditure overview in budget books, SF §7-121.
Definitions, SF §7-101.
Budget bill.
Transportation department, SF §7-110.
Detail.
Requirements, SF §7-105.
General fund capital appropriations, SF §7-122.
Legislative intent, SF §7-102.
Proposed budget.
Capital improvements.
Inclusion in draft, SF §7-104.
Defined, SF §7-101.
Form, SF §7-105.
Preparation, SF §7-104.
Legislative intent, SF §7-102.
Submission.
Legislative intent, SF §7-102.
Secretary.
Defined, SF §7-101.
Proposed budget.
Preparation, SF §7-104.
Revenue estimates, SF §7-103.
Studies, SF §7-103.
Studies, SF §7-103.

BUDGET AND MANAGEMENT —Cont'd
State operating budget —Cont'd
Supporting documents.
  Budget books, SF §§7-115 to 7-121. See within
    this subheading, "Budget books."
  University college.
    Lump sum appropriation, SF §7-111.
State personnel.
  Health and welfare benefits program, SPP §2-504.
  Pay plans subject to budget, SPP §8-101.
State prosecutor, SG §9-1208.
State retirement and pension system.
  Board of trustees' annual budget submission to
    governor, SPP §21-109.
State's attorneys.
  County budget and fiscal policies.
    State's attorneys offices subject to, 24 §8-101.
Taxation.
  State operating budget.
    Budget books.
      Tax exemptions.
        Statement and recommendations as to
          effect on revenues, SF §7-118.
Telecommunications.
  Agreements for use of state equipment, SF §3-702.
  Applicability of provisions, SF §3-703.
  Definitions, SF §3-701.
  Duties, SF §3-702.
  System standard, SF §3-704.
  Telecommunication and computer network, SF
    §3-705.
Transportation department.
  Secretary of transportation.
    Duties of secretary as to budgets, TR §2-103.
Tri-County Council for Southern Maryland, 20
  §2-403.
United States.
  State operating budget.
    Budget books.
      Federal reimbursement.
        Information to be included, SF §7-120.
Universities and colleges.
  Annual operating budget request, ED §11-105.
University of Maryland.
  State operating budget.
    Budget bill.
      Appropriations.
        Lump sum appropriation for university
          college, SF §7-111.
Workers' compensation commission.
  Advisory committee on commission budget, LE
    §9-317.
  Tentative budget.
    Preparation, review, recommendations of
      advisory committee, LE §9-318.

BUFFERS.
**Chesapeake Bay critical area and Atlantic
  coastal bays critical area protection
  programs.**
  Commercial timber harvest.
    Buffer management plan, NR §8-1808.7.
  Community pier in buffer, NR §8-1808.5.
  Perennial and intermittent streams.
    Local jurisdiction adopting provisions, NR
      §8-1808.9.
  Planned unit developments.
    Alternative buffer provision, NR §8-1813.1.

BUILDERS.
Contractors generally.
  See CONTRACTORS.

BUILDERS —Cont'd
Homebuilder registration, BR §§4.5-101 to
  4.5-701.
  See HOMEBUILDER REGISTRATION.

BUILDING AND LOAN ASSOCIATIONS.
General provisions.
  See SAVINGS AND LOAN ASSOCIATIONS.

BUILDING CODES, PS §§12-101 to 12-1007.
Accessibility code, PS §12-202.
Additions.
  Building rehabilitation code generally, PS
    §§12-1001 to 12-1007.
  Defined, PS §12-1001.
Administrative search warrants, PS §12-101.
Adoption of performance standards, PS
  §12-503.
Agricultural buildings.
  Exemption from standards when building used for
    agritourism, PS §12-508.
Amendments to performance standards.
  Local codes, PS §12-504.
Applicability of performance standards, PS
  §12-503.
Boilers and pressure vessels, PS §§12-901 to
  12-919.
  See BOILERS AND PRESSURE VESSELS.
Building rehabilitation code, PS §§12-1001 to
  12-1007.
Central automated database, PS §12-506.
Change of occupancy.
  Building rehabilitation code generally, PS
    §§12-1001 to 12-1007.
  Defined, PS §12-1001.
Community development administration.
  Plan approval process, HS §4-213.
Conflict of laws.
  Effect of subtitle, PS §12-502.
  Local codes.
    Amendments to performance standards, PS
      §12-504.
  Rehabilitation code.
    Effect of subtitle on other laws, PS §12-1002.
Conflict resolution.
  Department's powers and duties, PS §12-507.
Construction.
  Model performance code for building construction,
    PS §12-201.
Cooperative housing corporations.
  Full force and effect, CA §5-6B-19.
Defined terms, PS §12-501.
  Electrical code, PS §12-601.
  Elevator safety, PS §12-801.
  Industrialized buildings and manufactured homes,
    PS §12-301.
  Rehabilitation code, PS §12-1001.
  Safety glazing, PS §12-401.
Department.
  Defined, PS §12-501.
  Industrialized buildings and manufactured homes.
    Defined, PS §12-301.
    Duties, PS §12-304.
    Enforcement authority, PS §12-312.
  Powers and duties, PS §12-507.
Effect of subtitle, PS §12-502.
Electrical code, PS §§12-601 to 12-607.
  Applicability, PS §12-602.
  Authorized electrical inspection agencies, PS
    §12-605.
  Defined, PS §12-601.

BUILDING CODES —Cont'd
Electrical code —Cont'd
Certification of installation, PS §12-604.
Authorized electrical inspection agencies, PS §12-605.
Conforming electrical installations, PS §12-603.
Defined terms, PS §12-601.
Electrical installations.
Certification of installation, PS §12-604.
Conforming, PS §12-603.
Defined, PS §12-601.
Homeowner installations, PS §12-606.
Homeowners.
Installations by homeowners, PS §12-606.
Inspections.
Authorized electrical inspection agencies, PS §12-605.
Fire marshal, duties, PS §12-605.
Penalties, PS §12-607.
Prohibited acts, PS §12-607.
Scope of subtitle, PS §12-602.
Violations, PS §12-607.
Elevator safety, PS §§12-801 to 12-842.
See ELEVATORS.
Emergency power and lighting systems, PS §12-702.
Energy conservation building standards, PUC §§7-401 to 7-408.
See ENERGY CONSERVATION BUILDING STANDARDS.
Enforcement.
Effect of subtitle, PS §12-502.
Industrialized buildings and manufactured homes, PS §12-312.
Department's duties, PS §12-304.
Local laws, PS §12-505.
Exit signs.
Buildings with three or more floors, PS §12-701.
Fees.
Implementation and enforcement of performance standards, PS §12-505.
Industrialized buildings and manufactured homes.
Department's duties, PS §12-304.
General services department.
Enforcement of state building code, SF §4-402.
Generators.
Emergency power and lighting systems, PS §12-702.
Glass.
Safety glazing, PS §§12-401 to 12-407.
Industrialized buildings and manufactured homes, PS §§12-301 to 12-313.
Authorized testers, PS §12-307.
Certification, PS §12-306.
Denial, PS §12-310.
Forfeiture, PS §12-310.
Issuance, PS §12-310.
Modification, PS §12-310.
Procedure, PS §12-308.
Defined terms, PS §12-301.
Department.
Defined, PS §12-301.
Duties, PS §12-304.
Enforcement authority, PS §12-312.
Enforcement, PS §12-312.
Department's duties, PS §12-304.
Evaluation and testing, PS §12-307.
Fees.
Department's duties, PS §12-304.
Insignias, PS §12-306.
Effect, PS §12-309.

BUILDING CODES —Cont'd
Industrialized buildings and manufactured homes —Cont'd
Insignias —Cont'd
Forfeiture, PS §12-310.
Required, PS §12-309.
Inspections, PS §12-311.
Legislative findings, PS §12-302.
Local laws.
Powers reserved to local governments, PS §12-303.
New building materials and methods.
Standards for buildings, PS §12-305.
Pamphlets.
Regulations, PS §12-305.
Penalties, PS §12-313.
Prohibited acts, PS §12-313.
Purpose, PS §12-302.
Regulations.
Standards for buildings, PS §12-305.
Standards for buildings, PS §12-305.
Certification procedure, PS §12-308.
Evaluation and testing, PS §12-307.
Violations, PS §12-313.
Inspections.
Electrical code.
Authorized electrical inspection agencies, PS §12-605.
Fire marshal, duties, PS §12-605.
Industrialized buildings and manufactured homes, PS §12-311.
Inspectors.
Administrative search warrants, PS §12-101.
International building code.
Defined, PS §12-501.
Modifications, PS §12-503.
Notice to local jurisdictions.
Department's powers and duties, PS §12-507.
Lighting.
Illumination in public buildings, guidelines, PS §12-204.
Local codes.
Amendments to performance standards, PS §12-504.
Effect of subtitle, PS §12-502.
Implementation and enforcement of performance standards, PS §12-505.
Industrialized buildings and manufactured homes.
Powers reserved to local governments, PS §12-303.
Minimum livability code, PS §12-203.
Rehabilitation code.
Meetings regarding complex projects, PS §12-1005.
Safety glazing.
Effect on local laws, PS §12-402.
Manufactured homes.
Industrialized buildings and manufactured homes, PS §§12-301 to 12-313.
Maryland accessibility code, PS §12-202.
Maryland building rehabilitation code, PS §§12-1001 to 12-1007.
Maryland building rehabilitation code advisory council, PS §12-1003.
Meetings.
Rehabilitation code.
Complex projects, PS §12-1005.
Minimum livability code, PS §12-203.
Model performance code for building construction, PS §12-201.

BUILDING CODES —Cont'd
Notice.
Modifications to international building code.
Notice to local jurisdictions, PS §12-507.
Safety glazing.
Additional requirements, adoption, PS §12-403.
Hazardous location determinations, PS §12-404.
Penalties.
Electrical code, PS §12-607.
Industrialized buildings and manufactured homes,
PS §12-313.
Safety glazing, PS §12-407.
Performance standards, PS §§12-501 to 12-508.
Permit fees, 25 §10D-1.
Prohibited acts.
Electrical code, PS §12-607.
Industrialized buildings and manufactured homes,
PS §12-313.
Safety glazing, PS §12-407.
Regulations.
Industrialized buildings and manufactured homes.
Standards for buildings, PS §12-305.
Rehabilitation code, PS §§12-1001 to 12-1007.
Adoption, PS §12-1004.
Advisory council, PS §12-1003.
Amendments, PS §12-1007.
Applicability, PS §12-1004.
Changes to other codes.
Conforming, PS §12-1006.
Complex projects, PS §12-1005.
Conflict of laws.
Effect of subtitle on other laws, PS §12-1002.
Conforming to changes in other codes, PS
§12-1006.
Amendments, PS §12-1007.
Defined terms, PS §12-1001.
Effect of subtitle on other laws, PS §12-1002.
Meetings.
Complex projects, PS §12-1005.
Minimum requirements, PS §12-1005.
Purpose, PS §12-1004.
Rules and regulations.
Conforming to changes in other codes, PS
§12-1006.
Renovations.
Building rehabilitation code generally, PS
§§12-1001 to 12-1007.
Defined, PS §12-1001.
Repairs.
Building rehabilitation code generally, PS
§§12-1001 to 12-1007.
Defined, PS §12-1001.
Rules and regulations.
Rehabilitation code.
Conforming to changes in other codes, PS
§12-1006.
Safety glazing, PS §§12-401 to 12-407.
Additional requirements, adoption, PS §12-403.
Defined terms, PS §12-401.
Effect on local laws, PS §12-402.
Employer liability.
Sale of material other than safety glazing
material, PS §12-406.
Hazardous locations.
Defined, PS §12-401.
Determination, PS §12-404.
Sale of material other than safety glazing
material, PS §12-406.
Labels, PS §12-405.
Local laws, effect, PS §12-402.

BUILDING CODES —Cont'd
Safety glazing —Cont'd
Notice.
Additional requirements, adoption, PS §12-403.
Hazardous location determinations, PS §12-404.
Penalties, PS §12-407.
Prohibited acts, PS §12-407.
Respondeat superior.
Sale of material other than safety glazing
material, PS §12-406.
Sale of material other than safety glazing
material, PS §12-406.
Scope of subtitle, PS §12-402.
Violations, PS §12-407.
Search warrants.
Administrative search warrants, PS §12-101.
Standards for buildings.
Building performance standards, PS §§12-501 to
12-508.
Industrialized buildings and manufactured homes,
PS §12-305.
Evaluation and testing, PS §12-307.
State boards and commissions.
Effect of subtitle, PS §12-502.
Statewide building and housing codes, PS
§§12-201 to 12-204.
Structural iron or steel.
Beams or girders with studs or reinforcing shear
connectors, PS §12-704.
Temporary fastening devices.
Use of "clip-type" connectors prohibited, PS
§12-703.
Violations.
Electrical code, PS §12-607.
Industrialized buildings and manufactured homes,
PS §12-313.
Safety glazing, PS §12-407.
Windows.
Safety glazing, PS §§12-401 to 12-407.
Zoning.
Effect of subtitle, PS §12-502.

**BUILDING REHABILITATION CODE
ADVISORY COUNCIL,** PS §12-1003.

BUILDINGS.
Abatement orders.
Fire marshal, PS §6-318.
Failure to comply with order, PS §6-320.
Service of process, PS §6-319.
Alcoholic beverages.
Regulations.
Conformance to, 2B §9-105.
Arson and burning, CR §§6-101 to 6-111.
Automatic fire extinguishing system.
High rise buildings, PS §§9-401 to 9-404.
Specified buildings, PS §9-503.
Boxing, sparring and wrestling.
Ventilation and safety structures, BR §4-319.
Burglary and related crimes, CR §§6-201 to
6-210.
See BURGLARY.
Condominiums, RP §§11-101 to 11-143.
See CONDOMINIUMS.
Construction.
Building codes generally, PS §§12-101 to 12-1007.
See BUILDING CODES.
**Construction apprenticeship assistance
program,** LE §11-601.
Cooperative housing corporations.
Building codes.
Full force and effect, CA §5-6B-19.

BUILDINGS —Cont'd
Counties.
Chartered counties.
Building ordinances, 25A §5.
County codes.
Building code, 25 §3.
Erection of buildings.
Powers of county commissioners, 25 §11A.
Permits.
Building permit fees and fees payable after approval of property plans in St. Mary's county, 25 §10D-1.
Furnished supervisors of assessments, TP §5-103.
Energy conservation building standards, PUC §§7-401 to 7-408.
See ENERGY CONSERVATION BUILDING STANDARDS.
Energy conservation in buildings.
Public works.
See PUBLIC WORKS.
Fire hazards.
Abatement orders, PS §6-318.
Failure to comply with order, PS §6-320.
Service of process, PS §6-319.
Additional remedies, PS §6-321.
Maintenance of fire hazard prohibited, PS §6-317.
Fire marshal.
Abatement orders, PS §6-318.
Failure to comply with order, PS §6-320.
Service of process, PS §6-319.
Inspections, PS §6-307.
Fires and fire protection.
Evacuation procedures, PS §§9-501 to 9-506.
High-rise buildings, PS §§9-401 to 9-404.
Fireworks plants.
Building construction, PS §10-205.
Building location, PS §10-204.
Safety standards, PS §10-207.
Gambling.
Keeping building for gaming device, CR §12-105.
Keeping, owning, renting or managing for purposes of gambling, CR §12-104.
General services department.
Building code.
Enforcement of state building code, SF §4-403.
Energy.
Generally, SF §§4-801 to 4-808.
See GENERAL SERVICES DEPARTMENT.
Public buildings and grounds.
Architectural review.
Board of architectural review, SF §§4-701 to 4-704.
Energy.
Generally, SF §§4-801 to 4-808.
Maintenance, operation and protection, SF §§4-601 to 4-608.
See GENERAL SERVICES DEPARTMENT.
High-rise buildings.
Fires and fire protection, PS §§9-401 to 9-404.
Home improvement law.
General provisions, BR §§8-101 to 8-702.
See HOME IMPROVEMENTS.
Horizontal property act, RP §§11-101 to 11-143.
See CONDOMINIUMS.
Horse racing.
Approval required for improvements, BR §11-318.
Income tax.
Green buildings credits, TG §10-722.
Injunctions.
Fire marshal.
Abatement orders, PS §6-318.
Failure to comply with order, PS §6-320.

BUILDINGS —Cont'd
Injunctions —Cont'd
Fire marshal —Cont'd
Abatement orders —Cont'd
Service of process, PS §6-319.
Inspections.
Fire marshal, PS §6-307.
Livestock.
Contagious and infectious diseases.
Destroying buildings.
Appraisals, AG §3-107.
Maryland-Washington metropolitan district.
House numbers.
Renumbering, 28 §5-117.
Maryland-Washington regional district.
See MARYLAND-WASHINGTON REGIONAL DISTRICT.
Mechanics' liens.
General provisions.
See MECHANICS' LIENS.
Mobile homes.
See MOBILE HOMES.
Municipal corporations.
Permits.
Furnished supervisors of assessments, TP §5-103.
Grading and building permits.
Power to issue, EN §4-103.
Regulations, 23A §2.
New home warranties, RP §§10-601 to 10-610.
See WARRANTY.
Permits.
Consolidated permit procedures.
General provisions.
See PERMITS.
Counties. See within this heading, "Counties."
Grading and building permits.
Power of counties and municipalities to issue, EN §4-103.
Water and sewer systems.
County plans, EN §9-512.
Procurement.
Lease of real property.
General provisions, SF §§4-318 to 4-321, 12-204, 12-205, 13-105.
See PROCUREMENT.
Property taxes.
Tax credits.
High performance buildings, TP §9-242.
Public buildings and grounds.
General services department.
Architectural review.
Board of architectural review, SF §§4-701 to 4-704.
Energy.
Generally, SF §§4-801 to 4-808.
Maintenance, operation and protection, SF §§4-601 to 4-608.
See GENERAL SERVICES DEPARTMENT.
Public works.
Energy conservation in buildings.
See PUBLIC WORKS.
Records, access to.
Inspection of public records, SG §10-618.
Safety.
Building codes generally, PS §§12-101 to 12-1007.
See BUILDING CODES.
Schools.
See SCHOOLS.
Setback line restrictions.
Limitation of actions, CJ §5-114.

BUILDINGS —Cont'd
Streets and alleys.
Mapped streets.
General provisions.
See ZONING.
Task force on green building, SF §5-9A-01.
Trespass, CR §§6-401 to 6-410.
Warranties.
New home warranties, RP §§10-601 to 10-610.
See WARRANTY.
Zoning and planning.
See ZONING.

BULKHEADS.
Wetlands.
Construction of bulkheads, EN §16-105.
Private wetlands.
Routine maintenance and repair of bulkheads.
Exemption of landowners from local permit
requirements, EN §16-305.
Lawful, EN §16-304.
State wetlands.
Routine maintenance and repair of bulkheads.
Exemption of landowners from local permit
requirements, EN §16-203.

BULK SALES.
Alcoholic beverages.
Bulk transfer permit.
General provisions, 2B §2-101.
Business opportunity sales act, BR §§14-101 to
14-129.
See START-UP BUSINESS VENTURES.
Commercial code, CL §§6-101 to 6-111.
See BULK TRANSFERS.
Sales and use tax.
Notice of bulk transfer, TG §11-505.
Failure to give notice, TG §13-802.
Unlawful transfers, TG §13-802.

BULK TRANSFERS, CL §§6-101 to 6-111.
Applicability of article.
Enterprises and transfers subject to article, CL
§6-102.
Transfers excepted from article, CL §6-103.
Assignments for the benefit of creditors.
Transfers excepted, CL §6-103.
Auctions and auctioneers, CL §6-108.
Citation of article.
Short title, CL §6-101.
Commercial code's general provisions, CL
§§1-101 to 1-208.
See COMMERCIAL CODE.
Debtors and creditors.
Lists, CL §6-104.
Notice to creditors, CL §§6-105, 6-107.
Protected creditors, CL §6-109.
Definitions, CL §6-102.
Auctioneer, CL §6-108.
Enterprises.
Applicability of article, CL §6-102.
Equipment, CL §6-102.
Executors and administrators.
Transfers excepted, CL §6-103.
Exemptions, CL §6-103.
Fiduciaries.
Transfers exceeded, CL §6-103.
Interpretation and construction.
Commercial code's general provisions, CL §§1-101
to 1-208.
See COMMERCIAL CODE.

BULK TRANSFERS —Cont'd
Interpretation and construction —Cont'd
Enterprises and transfers subject to article, CL
§6-102.
Transfers excepted from article, CL §6-103.
Levies, CL §6-111.
Limitation of actions, CL §6-111.
New business enterprises.
Transfer to new enterprise organized to take over
and continue business.
Excepted from article, CL §6-103.
Public notice, CL §6-106.
Notice to creditors, CL §§6-105, 6-107.
Schedule of property, CL §6-104.
Statute of limitations, CL §6-111.
Subsequent transfers, CL §6-110.
Title of article.
Short title, CL §6-101.

BULLETPROOF BODY ARMOR.
Defined, CR §4-106.
Funds.
Law enforcement equipment fund, PS §§4-301 to
4-304.
Protective body armor fund, PS §§4-101 to 4-107.
Permit to use, possess or purchase, CR §4-107.
**Wearing in crime of violence or drug
trafficking crime,** CR §4-106.

BULLIES.
Schools.
Reporting harassment or intimidation incidents
against students, ED §7-424.

BUMPERS, TR §§22-105, 22-416.

BUNGEE JUMPING.
Operations prohibited, BR §3-503.

BUOYS, LIGHTS AND WATER MARKERS.
Waters of the state.
Interference with prohibited, NR §4-511.
Placement of buoys, mooring buoys, etc., NR
§8-704.

BURDEN OF PROOF.
Alcoholic beverage tax.
Presumption of taxability, TG §5-103.
Attorneys at law.
Disbarment or suspension, CJA Rule 16-757.
Bank deposits and collections.
Loss resulting from stop payment order, CL
§4-403.
Bar admissions.
Out-of-state attorneys, BarAdm Rule 13.
Charities.
Injunctions.
Acting as charitable representative, BR §6-307.
Soliciting after registration, BR §6-406.
Commercial code.
Burden of establishing defined, CL §1-201.
Definitions, CL §1-201.
Option to accelerate at will.
Establishing lack of good faith, CL §1-208.
**Construction of water system or sewage
disposal system for public use.**
Public interest, PUC §5-204.
Continuing care contracts.
Discharge of appointed receivers, 70B §20I.
Controlled dangerous substance.
Establishing exemption, proviso or exception, CR
§5-807.
Credit.
Credit grantor closed end credit provisions.
False or misleading financing statements, CL
§12-1023.1.

BURDEN OF PROOF —Cont'd
Credit —Cont'd
Credit grantor revolving credit provisions.
    False or misleading financing statement, CL
        §12-923.1.
Credit services businesses.
Proceedings involving subtitle, CL §14-1907.
Death by wrongful act.
Slayer's rule.
    Weight given criminal conviction, CJ §10-919.
Discrimination.
Commercial discrimination.
    Discrimination and retaliation complaints, SF
        §19-107.
    Initial findings and recommendations, SF
        §19-108.
Explosives, PS §11-118.
Food, drugs and cosmetics.
Defenses to charges, HG §21-260.
Guardianships.
Local department guardianships.
    Nonconsensual guardianship in best interests of
        child, FL §5-323.
Health care decisions, HG §5-609.
Health care malpractice claims.
Award, SpecPro Rule 15-403.
Health insurance.
Complaint process for adverse decisions or
    grievances.
    Review of complaint by commissioner, IN
        §15-10A-03.
Heritage areas.
Decisions of authority, appeals, FI §13-1124.
Insanity defense.
Establishing eligibility of committed to person to
    be released, CP §3-114.
Establishing not criminally responsible, CP
    §3-110.
Insurance.
Discrimination in underwriting, IN §27-501.
Motor vehicle insurance.
    Cancellation, nonrenewal, premium increase or
        reduction in coverage, IN §27-613.
Nonprofit health service plans.
    Unfair and discriminatory trade practices, IN
        §14-136.
Ratemaking.
    Determining degree of competition in market,
        IN §11-308.
Surety insurance discrimination hearings, IN
    §27-502.
Juvenile cases.
Competency or incompetency to proceed.
    Competency hearings, CJ §3-8A-17.4.
Leases, UCC.
Default of lessor.
    Burden of establishing default after acceptance
        of goods, CL §2A-516.
Minors.
Citation for alcoholic beverage violations, CR
    §10-119.
Motor vehicles.
Drivers' licenses.
    Suspension, revocation or refusal of licenses.
        Driving while privilege is suspended, refused
            or revoked.
            Administration has burden of proof, TR
                §13-705.1.
Negotiable instruments.
Incomplete instrument, CL §3-115.

BURDEN OF PROOF —Cont'd
Nonprofit health service plans.
Unfair and discriminatory trade practices, IN
    §14-136.
**Not criminally responsible by reason of
    insanity.**
Eligibility of committed to person to be released,
    CP §3-110.
Establishing, preponderance of evidence, CP
    §3-110.
**Open containers of alcoholic beverages in
    motor vehicles' passenger areas.**
Procedure, CR §10-127.
Paternity proceedings, FL §5-1027.
Pharmacists and pharmacies.
Injunction against unauthorized practice of
    pharmacy.
    Proof of damages, HO §12-319.
Physicians.
Disciplinary actions, standards of proof, HO
    §14-405.
Presumptions.
See PRESUMPTIONS.
Public service commission proceedings, PUC
    §3-112.
Sales and use tax.
Exemptions, TG §11-103.
Secured transactions.
Purchase-money security interest.
    Non-consumer goods, CL §9-103.
Securities.
Securities act.
    Exemptions, CA §11-604.
Support enforcement actions.
Contempt, SpecPro Rule 15-207.
Tobacco tax.
Exemptions, TG §12-103.
Unemployment compensation.
Aliens.
    Eligibility for benefits.
        Standard of proof, LE §8-905.
Victims of crime.
Crime victims' compensation.
    Restitution hearing, CP §11-615.
HIV testing of charged person, CP §11-110.
Workers' compensation.
Conduct of appeal proceedings, LE §9-745.

BUREAUS.
Control surveys and maps.
Coordinate system.
    See SURVEYS AND SURVEYORS.
Generally.
See BOARDS AND COMMISSIONS.
Mining.
General provisions, EN §§15-201 to 15-205.
See MINING.

BURGLAR ALARMS.
Audible systems.
Equipped to automatically silence, CR §9-611.
Defective system.
Notice to user, use after notice, CR §9-610.
Definitions, CR §9-607.
False alarms, CR §9-608.
Multiple alarms, CR §9-609.

BURGLAR'S TOOLS.
Defined, CR §6-201.
Possession, CR §6-205.
Breaking and entering motor vehicle, CR §6-206.

BURGLARY, CR §§6-201 to 6-210.
Being in or on dwelling, storehouse.
  Burglary in fourth degree, CR §6-205.
Breaking and entering with intent to commit theft, violence or arson.
  Burglary in second degree, CR §6-202.
Breaking and entering with intent to steal firearm.
  Burglary in second degree, CR §6-202.
Burglar's tools possession, CR §6-205.
  Breaking and entering motor vehicle, CR §6-206.
Burglary with explosives or destructive device, CR §6-207.
Charging document, CR §6-210.
Definitions, CR §6-201.
Dwelling.
  Breaking and entering.
    Burglary in the first degree, CR §6-202.
    Burglary in the third degree, CR §6-204.
    Burglary in the fourth degree, CR §6-205.
Firearm.
  Breaking and entering with intent to steal.
    Burglary in the second degree, CR §6-202.
Lesser included offenses, CR §6-210.
Motor vehicle, breaking and entering, CR §6-206.
Research facility, breaking and entering, CR §6-208.
Separate units, separate violations, CR §6-209.
Storehouse.
  Burglary in second degree, CR §6-202.
  Burglary in the fourth degree, CR §6-205.
Theft, crime of violence or arson.
  Breaking and entering with intent to commit.
    Burglary in second degree, CR §6-202.
Vaults, safes or other secure depositories.
  Burglary with explosives or destructive device, CR §6-207.
Wiretapping and electronic surveillance.
  Breaking and entering to place or remove equipment, CJ §10-412.
Yard or garden belonging to dwelling.
  Being in or on.
    Burglary in fourth degree, CR §6-205.

BURGLARY IN THE FIRST DEGREE, CR §6-202.

BURGLARY IN THE SECOND DEGREE, CR §6-203.

BURGLARY IN THE THIRD DEGREE, CR §6-204.

BURGLARY IN THE FOURTH DEGREE, CR §6-205.

BURIAL AND REMOVAL OF DEAD BODIES.
Disinterment and reinterment.
  Permits, HG §4-215.
Funeral expenses.
  General provisions.
    See FUNERALS.
Funeral processions.
  See FUNERALS.
Inmates at state correctional facilities.
  Indigent inmates, burial expenses, unclaimed bodies, COR §9-604.
Institutions.
  Duties, HG §4-216.
Insurance.
  Burial insurance, IN §27-218.
    Business subject to provisions concerning life insurers, IN §16-115.

BURIAL AND REMOVAL OF DEAD BODIES —Cont'd
Insurance —Cont'd
  Preneed burial contracts not insurance, BR §5-702.
Livestock.
  Animals dying with infectious disease, AG §3-109.
Nursing homes.
  Unclaimed deceased resident.
    Director to set guidelines for funeral and burial arrangements, 70B §5A.
Permits.
  Authority throughout state, HG §4-215.
  Burial-transit permit.
    Exemption from requirement to be under direction of licensed mortician or funeral director, HO §7-312.
    Required, HG §4-215.
  Cemetery.
    Defined, HG §4-215.
  Disinterment and reinterment, HG §4-215.
  Duty of person in charge of cemetery, HG §4-215.
  Generally, HG §4-215.
  Transportation of body.
    Burial-transit permit required, HG §4-226.
Removal of human remains or funerary objects.
  Ascertaining cause of death.
    Removal of human remains, CR §10-402.
  Authorization to relocate human remains, procedure, CR §10-402.
  Definitions, CR §10-401.
  Determining whether erroneously interred.
    Removal of human remains, CR §10-402.
  Notice of intent to relocate human remains, CR §10-402.
  Reburial.
    Removal of human remains, CR §10-402.
  Reinterment of removed human remains, CR §10-402.
  Selling unlawfully removed human remains or funerary objects, CR §10-403.
  Statute of limitation on prosecution.
    Unauthorized removal of human remains, CR §10-402.
  Unauthorized removal of human remains, CR §10-402.

BURIAL CONTRACTS.
Preneed burial contracts generally, BR §§5-701 to 5-712.
  See CEMETERIES.

BURIAL GROUNDS OR SITES.
Access, RP §14-121.
Complaints.
  Sale for other purposes.
    Contents of complaint, PropSales Rule 14-401.
    How commenced, PropSales Rule 14-401.
County maintenance and preservation, RP §14-122.
Definitions, RP §§14-121, 14-122.
Eminent domain.
  Acquisition of cemetery, PropAct Rule 12-204.
Liability.
  Owner of land, RP §14-121.
Municipal corporations.
  Maintenance and preservation, RP §14-122.
Municipal maintenance and preservation, RP §14-122.
Notice.
  Sale for other purposes.
    Order of publication, PropSales Rule 14-401.

BURIAL GROUNDS OR SITES —Cont'd

Orders.
Sale for other purposes.
Order of publication, PropSales Rule 14-401.
Proceedings after order, PropSales Rule 14-401.

Posting.
Sale for other purposes.
Order of publication, PropSales Rule 14-401.

Publication.
Sale for other purposes.
Order of publication, PropSales Rule 14-401.
Proceedings after order, PropSales Rule 14-401.

Removal of human remains or funerary objects.
Ascertaining cause of death.
Removal of human remains, CR §10-402.
Authorization to relocate human remains, procedure, CR §10-402.
Definitions, CR §10-401.
Determining whether erroneously interred.
Removal of human remains, CR §10-402.
Notice of intent to relocate human remains, CR §10-402.
Reburial.
Removal of human remains, CR §10-402.
Reinterment of removed human remains, CR §10-402.
Selling unlawfully removed human remains or funerary objects, CR §10-403.
Statute of limitation on prosecution.
Unauthorized removal of human remains, CR §10-402.
Unauthorized removal of human remains, CR §10-402.

Sale for other purposes.
Complaint.
Contents of complaint, PropSales Rule 14-401.
How commenced, PropSales Rule 14-401.
Order of publication.
Generally, PropSales Rule 14-401.
Proceedings after order of publication, PropSales Rule 14-401.
Posting, PropSales Rule 14-401.
Venue, PropSales Rule 14-401.

Venue.
Sale for other purposes, PropSales Rule 14-401.

BURNING, CR §§6-101 to 6-111.

Arson in the first degree, CR §6-102.

Arson in the second degree, CR §6-103.

Attempt to burn structure or property, CR §6-109.

Burning trash container, CR §6-108.

Burning with intent to defraud, CR §6-106.

Charging document, CR §6-111.

Definitions, CR §6-101.

Flag, CR §10-704.

Malicious burning of personal property in the first degree, CR §6-104.

Malicious burning of personal property in the second degree, CR §6-105.

Separate units, separate violations, CR §6-110.

Threat of arson, CR §6-107.

BURNING FLAG, CR §10-704.

BURNING TRASH CONTAINER, CR §6-108.

BURNING WITH INTENT TO DEFRAUD, CR §6-106.

BUSES.

Bus company defined as common carrier, PUC §1-101.

Counties.
Grants to local bus systems, TR §10-207.

Definitions, TR §11-105.
Grants to local bus systems, TR §10-207.

Drivers.
Motor carriers.
See MOTOR CARRIERS.

Drivers' licenses.
Class C and D licenses, TR §16-104.

Identification.
Required, TR §22-404.3.
Exceptions, TR §22-404.3.

Inspections.
Titling and registration, TR §23-107.

Maximum length limits, TR §24-104.1.

Motor carriers.
General provisions.
See MOTOR CARRIERS.

Municipal corporations.
Taxation.
Special taxing districts.
Creation to finance bus system, 23A §44.

New bus services.
Grants to local bus systems, TR §10-207.

Open containers.
Alcoholic beverages.
Possession in motor vehicles' passenger areas, CR §§10-123 to 10-127.

Protectors or flaps behind rear wheels, TR §22-413.

Registration.
Fees.
Passenger buses, TR §13-933.
Inspections.
Titling and registration, TR §23-107.

School buses.
See SCHOOLS.

Shelters for bus passengers, TR §§8-750 to 8-752.
Definitions, TR §8-750.
Local agreements to construct, operate and maintain, TR §8-752.
Transit administration authorized to establish, TR §8-751.

Smoking on buses, PUC §9-206.

Washington metropolitan area transit authority.
General provisions, TR §10-204.

BUSINESS AND ECONOMIC DEVELOPMENT CORPORATION.

Maryland technology development corporation, 83A §§5-2A-01 to 5-2A-09.

Technology development corporation, 83A §§5-2A-01 to 5-2A-09.

BUSINESS AND ECONOMIC DEVELOPMENT DEPARTMENT.

Advisory councils, boards and committees, 83A §2-104.

Arts council, 83A §§4-601 to 4-609.
See ARTS COUNCIL.

Attorney general.
Assistant attorneys general.
Assignment to department, 83A §2-103.
Counsel to department, 83A §2-103.
Legal advisor, 83A §2-103.

Bainbridge development department.
General provisions, 83A §§5-1601 to 5-1609.
See BAINBRIDGE DEVELOPMENT CORPORATION.

BUSINESS AND ECONOMIC DEVELOPMENT DEPARTMENT —Cont'd
Boards and commissions.
Calling of meetings of boards by secretary, 83A §2-105.
Economic development commission, 83A §§1-201 to 1-204. See within this heading, "Economic development commission."
Included within department, 83A §2-104.
Report to secretary, 83A §2-105.
Budget and management.
Consolidated publications account, 83A §4-105.
Responsibility of secretary for budgets, 83A §2-105.
Business development and resources.
Coordination of programs, 83A §3-601.
Maryland advisory commission on manufacturing competitiveness, 83A §§3-801 to 3-804.
Objectives of department, 83A §3-101.
Office of international business, 83A §§3-301, 3-302.
Generally, 83A §3-301.
Reports, 83A §3-302.
Community reinvestment fund.
Powers, HS §9-307.
Composition.
Boards and commissions included within department, 83A §2-104.
Created, 83A §2-101.
Data used from other state agencies, 83A §3-203.
Definitions, 83A §1-101.
Maryland economic adjustment fund, 83A §6-501.
Division of tourism and promotion.
Consolidated publications account, 83A §4-105.
Deputy director, 83A §4-104.
Director, 83A §§4-102, 4-104.
Duties.
Generally, 83A §4-103.
Employees, 83A §4-104.
Establishment, 83A §4-101.
Powers.
Generally, 83A §4-103.
Dredged material disposal alternatives program, 83A §§6-801, 6-802.
Duties, 83A §3-201.
Economic development and financial assistance programs.
Administration of programs and funds, 83A §5-102.
Consideration in providing financial assistance, 83A §5-105.
Economic development assistance fund, 83A §§5-1401 to 5-1412.
Economic development corporation, 83A §§5-201 to 5-217.
See ECONOMIC DEVELOPMENT CORPORATION.
Enterprise fund, 83A §§5-501 to 5-503.
Enterprise zones, 83A §§5-401 to 5-405.
See ENTERPRISE ZONES.
Enumerated, 83A §5-102.
Focus area or enterprise zone.
Location of project in, consideration, 83A §5-105.
Maryland venture capital trust, 83A §§5-301 to 5-309.
See MARYLAND VENTURE CAPITAL TRUST.
Purpose, 83A §5-101.
Small business investment companies.
Specialized small business investment companies.
Investment, 83A §5-104.

BUSINESS AND ECONOMIC DEVELOPMENT DEPARTMENT —Cont'd
Economic development and financial assistance programs —Cont'd
Transfer of funds, 83A §5-103.
Economic development assistance fund, 83A §§5-1401 to 5-1412.
Economic development commission.
Composition, 83A §1-203.
Definition of "commission," 83A §1-101.
Duties, 83A §1-202.
Established, 83A §1-201.
Ethics.
Applicability of public ethics law, 83A §1-203.
Executive committee, 83A §1-202.
Membership, 83A §1-203.
Personnel and pensions article.
Applicability of provisions to personnel of commission, 83A §1-201.
Purpose, 83A §1-202.
Reports.
Annual report, 83A §1-204.
Staff, 83A §1-202.
Strategic plan, 83A §1-202.
Economic development corporation, 83A §§5-201 to 5-217.
See ECONOMIC DEVELOPMENT CORPORATION.
Economic development opportunities program account, SF §7-314.
Enterprise fund.
Accounting, 83A §5-503.
Composition, 83A §5-502.
Definition of "fund," 83A §5-501.
Equity investment financing, 83A §5-501.
Established, 83A §5-502.
Repayment of grants, 83A §5-501.
Uses, 83A §5-503.
Enterprise zones, 83A §§5-401 to 5-405.
See ENTERPRISE ZONES.
Film office.
Creation, 83A §4-401.
Duties, 83A §4-403.
Coordination with, 83A §4-404.
Gifts.
Acceptance and expenditure, 83A §4-402.
Local government agencies.
Coordination with, 83A §4-404.
Powers, 83A §§4-402, 4-403.
Job creation tax credit, 83A §§5-1101 to 5-1103.
See JOB CREATION TAX CREDIT.
Loans.
Liability for loans, CJ §5-521.
Maryland economic adjustment fund.
General provisions, 83A §§6-501 to 6-512. See within this heading, "Maryland economic adjustment fund."
Lower eastern shore tourism center advisory committee, 83A §4-301.
Maryland advisory commission on manufacturing competitiveness, 83A §§3-801 to 3-804.
Maryland economic adjustment fund.
Application.
Eligibility for loan, 83A §6-507.
False statement or report, 83A §6-511.
Form and contents, 83A §6-508.
Committee.
Defined, 83A §6-501.
Establishment, 83A §6-504.
Scope of authority, 83A §6-504.

BUSINESS AND ECONOMIC DEVELOPMENT DEPARTMENT —Cont'd
Maryland economic adjustment fund —Cont'd
Composition, 83A §6-504.
Creation, 83A §6-502.
Definitions, 83A §6-501.
Delegation of underwriting, closing, etc., 83A §6-503.
Eligibility for loans, 83A §6-507.
Establishment, 83A §6-502.
Foreclosure, 83A §6-509.
Funding, 83A §6-503.
Loan documents.
    Contents, 83A §6-509.
    False statement or report, 83A §6-511.
    Terms and conditions, 83A §6-509.
Loans to designated areas, 83A §6-504.
Loan violations.
    Remedies, 83A §6-510.
Maximum loan, 83A §6-509.
Placement of money received, 83A §6-505.
Priority of making loans, 83A §6-506.
Purpose, 83A §6-503.
Reporting requirements, 83A §6-506.
Rulemaking authority, 83A §6-512.
Use of funds, 83A §6-506.
Use of proceeds, 83A §6-509.
Maryland economic development commission, 83A §§1-201 to 1-204. See within this heading, "Economic development commission."
Maryland economic development corporation, 83A §§5-201 to 5-217.
See ECONOMIC DEVELOPMENT CORPORATION.
Maryland food center authority, 41 §§13-101 to 13-123.
See MARYLAND FOOD CENTER AUTHORITY.
Maryland lower eastern shore tourism center advisory committee, 83A §4-301.
Maryland venture capital trust.
General provisions, 83A §§5-301 to 5-309.
    See MARYLAND VENTURE CAPITAL TRUST.
Military installations.
Contact for issues relating to realignment and closure, 83A §5-106.
Mobile homes.
General provisions.
    See MOBILE HOMES.
Motion picture and television development office.
Creation, 83A §4-401.
Duties, 83A §4-403.
    Coordination with, 83A §4-404.
Gifts.
    Acceptance and expenditure, 83A §4-402.
Local government agencies.
    Coordination with, 83A §4-404.
Powers, 83A §§4-402, 4-403.
One Maryland economic development tax credits.
Generally, 83A §5-1501.
Partnership for workforce quality.
Advisory board, 83A §3-702.
Definitions, 83A §3-701.
Eligibility criteria, 83A §3-703.
Established, 83A §3-701.
Fund, 83A §3-702.1.
    Use, 83A §3-703.
Purpose, 83A §3-701.
Reports, 83A §3-704.
Secretary, 83A §3-703.

BUSINESS AND ECONOMIC DEVELOPMENT DEPARTMENT —Cont'd
Partnership for workforce quality —Cont'd
Training assistance, 83A §3-703.
Powers, 83A §3-201.
Regional technology councils.
Support, 83A §3-202.
Reports.
Boards.
    Reports to secretary, 83A §2-105.
Economic.
    Annual report, 83A §1-204.
Maryland economic adjustment fund.
    False statement or report, 83A §6-511.
    State treasurer process report, 83A §6-506.
Office of international business, 83A §3-302.
Partnership for workforce quality.
    Annual report by secretary, 83A §3-704.
Rules and regulations.
Maryland economic adjustment fund.
    Regulatory authority, 83A §6-512.
One Maryland economic development tax credits, 83A §5-1501.
Promulgation by secretary, 83A §2-105.
Seal.
Secretary's seal, 83A §2-105.
Secretary.
Appointment.
    By governor, 83A §2-101.
Assistants, 83A §2-101.
Boards and commissions.
    Calling of meetings, 83A §2-105.
    Reports to secretary, 83A §2-105.
Budgets.
    Responsibility for, 83A §2-105.
Consultants, 83A §2-101.
Defined, 83A §1-101.
Deputy secretary.
    Appointment, 83A §2-101.
    Duties, 83A §2-102.
Duties, 83A §2-101.
Employees.
    Appointment, 83A §1-202.
    Removal of appointee, 83A §2-101.
        Approval by governor, 83A §2-105.
Head of department, 83A §2-101.
Investment authorization.
    Specialized small business investment companies, 83A §5-104.
Partnership for workforce quality.
    Direction of program, 83A §3-703.
    Eligibility criteria.
        Establishing, 83A §3-703.
    Powers and duties as to, 83A §3-703.
    Reports.
        Annual report, 83A §3-704.
Plans, proposals and projects.
    Duties as to, 83A §2-105.
Rules and regulations.
    One Maryland economic development tax credits, 83A §5-1501.
    Promulgation, 83A §2-105.
Salary, 83A §2-101.
Seal.
    Purpose, 83A §2-105.
Specialized small business investment companies.
Investment authorized, 83A §5-104.
Support for regional technology councils, 83A §3-202.

BUSINESS AND ECONOMIC DEVELOPMENT DEPARTMENT —Cont'd

Tourism development board.
Defined, 83A §4-201.
Duties, 83A §§4-206, 4-207.
Established, 83A §4-203.
Executive director, 83A §4-205.
Facilities and equipment, 83A §4-205.
Fund, 83A §4-208.
Meetings, 83A §4-204.
Members, 83A §4-203.
Powers, 83A §4-206.
Reports, 83A §4-203.
Staff, 83A §4-205.
Statement of policy, 83A §4-202.
Vacancies, 83A §4-203.

Urban enterprise zones, 83A §§5-401 to 5-405.
See ENTERPRISE ZONES.

Use of data from other state agencies, 83A §3-203.

BUSINESS ENTERPRISE PROGRAM FOR THE BLIND, SF §14-109.

BUSINESS OPPORTUNITY SALES, BR §§14-101 to 14-129.
See START-UP BUSINESS VENTURES.

BUSINESS PARTNERSHIPS PROGRAM.
Promotion of economic interests, ED §15-107.

BUSINESS RECORDS.
Business license records.
Access to court records, CJA Rule 16-1004.

Evidence.
Photographic copies of business records as evidence, CJ §10-102.

Interrogatories.
Interrogatories to parties.
Option to produce business records, CivProCir Rule 2-421.
District Court, CivProDist Rule 3-421.

Preservation of private business records, BR §§1-301 to 1-307.
"Business" defined, BR §1-301.
Destruction of business records.
When authorized, BR §1-304.
Effect of act, BR §1-303.
Reproductions, BR §1-305.
Scope of act, BR §1-302.
Short title, BR §1-307.
Uniformity of interpretation, BR §1-306.

BUSINESS REGULATION AND LICENSURE.
Accountants, BOP §§2-101 to 2-702.
See ACCOUNTANTS.

Air conditioning and heating contractors.
General provisions, BR §§9A-101 to 9A-602.
See AIR CONDITIONING AND HEATING CONTRACTORS.

Amusement devices.
Garrett county, BR §§17-432 to 17-438.
General provisions, BR §§17-401 to 17-438.
See AMUSEMENTS AND RECREATION.
Wicomico county, BR §§17-420 to 17-429.
See WICOMICO COUNTY.

Applicability of title.
General business licensing, BR §17-102.

Architects, BOP §§3-101 to 3-702.
See ARCHITECTS.

Assumed business name.
Trade names generally, CA §1-406.

Athlete agents.
General provisions, BR §§4-401 to 4-421.
See ATHLETE AGENTS.

BUSINESS REGULATION AND LICENSURE —Cont'd

Attorneys at law, BOP §§10-101 to 10-701.
See ATTORNEYS AT LAW.

Baltimore City.
Prohibition on local licenses, fees and taxes.
Exception to prohibition, BR §1-204.

Barbers, BOP §§4-101 to 4-702.
See BARBERS.

Billiard tables.
General provisions, BR §§17-501 to 17-505.
See BILLIARD AND POOL TABLES.

Business opportunity sales act, BR §§14-101 to 14-129.
See START-UP BUSINESS VENTURES.

Cemeteries.
General provisions, BR §§5-101 to 5-1002.
See CEMETERIES.

Certified interior designers, BOP §§8-101 to 8-602.
See INTERIOR DESIGNERS.

Charitable organizations and representatives.
General provisions, BR §§6-101 to 6-701.
See CHARITIES.

Cigarette business licenses.
General provisions, BR §§16-101 to 16-401.
See CIGARETTE BUSINESS LICENSES.

Citation of article, 1 §25.

Collection agencies.
General provisions, BR §§7-101 to 7-502.
See COLLECTION AGENCIES.

Comptroller.
Blank licenses.
Preparation and delivery, BR §17-203.
Copies of licenses and applications.
Submission requirements, BR §17-205.
Delegation of powers, BR §17-202.
Distribution of money, BR §17-206.
Enforcement of title, BR §17-202.
Enforcement powers, BR §17-202.
Initiation of prosecution, BR §17-2104.
Investigative powers, BR §17-202.
List of licenses issued.
Required, BR §17-204.
Powers and duties, BR §17-202.
Rulemaking authority, BR §17-202.
Submission requirements.
Copies of licenses and applications, BR §17-205.

Concerts.
Outdoor concert promoters, BR §§17-1401 to 17-1407.
See OUTDOOR CONCERTS.

Conflict of laws.
Local licenses, fees and taxes.
Effect of public local law, BR §1-204.

Construction licenses, BR §§17-601 to 17-603.

Cooling system contractors.
General provisions, BR §§9A-101 to 9A-602.
See AIR CONDITIONING AND HEATING CONTRACTORS.

Corporations.
General provisions.
See CORPORATIONS.

Cosmetologists, BOP §§5-101 to 5-702.
See COSMETOLOGISTS.

Currency transactions in trade or business, BR §§1-501 to 1-505.
See CURRENCY TRANSACTIONS IN TRADE OR BUSINESS.

Definitions, BOP §1-101; BR §1-101.
General business licensing, BR §17-101.
License, BR §§17-201, 17-301, 17-2101.

BUSINESS REGULATION AND LICENSURE
—Cont'd
Detectives.
  Private detectives, BOP §§13-101 to 13-801.
    See PRIVATE DETECTIVES.
Dry cleaners, BR §§17-1101 to 17-1103.
Electricians, BOP §§6-101 to 6-702.
  See ELECTRICIANS.
Emergency management.
  Governor's powers.
    Closing of businesses, PS §14-307.
Employment agencies, BR §§9-101 to 9-501.
  See EMPLOYMENT AGENCIES.
Engineers.
  Generally, BOP §§14-101 to 14-602.
    See ENGINEERS.
  Stationary engineers, BOP §§6.5-101 to 6.5-502.
    See STATIONARY ENGINEERS.
Evidence.
  Witness refusal to give evidence, BR §1-203.
Fees.
  Dishonor of instrument paying fee.
    Suspension of license, BR §1-209.
  Late fees.
    Failure to get license in timely manner, BR
      §1-206.
  Local licenses, fees and taxes.
    Prohibition, BR §1-204.
  Proration of certain license fees, BR §1-208.
Fictitious names generally.
  Trade names generally, CA §1-406.
Foresters, BOP §§7-101 to 7-602.
  See FORESTERS.
Franchises.
  General provisions, BR §§14-201 to 14-233.
    See FRANCHISES.
Garages, BR §§17-801 to 17-803.
Gas fitters, BR §§17-1501 to 17-1504.
General business licensing.
  Applicability of title, BR §17-102.
  Applications for licenses, BR §17-302.
    Receipt or certificate for taxes required, BR
      §17-302.
  Blank licenses, BR §17-203.
  Change in place of business, BR §17-307.
  Comptroller list of licenses issued, BR §17-204.
  Contents of application, BR §17-302.
  Death of licensee, BR §17-308.
  Definitions, BR §17-101.
  Display of license, BR §17-306.
    Failure to display, BR §17-2103.
  Doing business without license, BR §17-2102.
  Expiration of license, BR §17-305.
  Failure to display license, BR §17-2103.
  Failure to get license in timely manner, BR
    §17-303.
  Initiation of prosecution, BR §17-2104.
  Issuance of license, BR §17-304.
  Levy and certification by county or municipal
    corporation required.
    Distribution of money, BR §17-206.
  "License" defined, BR §§17-201, 17-301.
  License fees, BR §17-303.
Harness racing.
  General provisions, BR §§11-601 to 11-636.
    See HARNESS RACING.
Heating contractors.
  General provisions, BR §§9A-101 to 9A-602.
    See AIR CONDITIONING AND HEATING
      CONTRACTORS.

BUSINESS REGULATION AND LICENSURE
—Cont'd
Home improvements.
  General provisions, BR §§8-101 to 8-702.
    See HOME IMPROVEMENTS.
Home inspectors.
  Generally, BOP §§16-101 to 16-802.
    See REAL ESTATE APPRAISERS AND HOME
      INSPECTORS.
Horse racing.
  General provisions, BR §§11-101 to 11-1205.
    See HORSE RACING.
  Harness racing, BR §§11-601 to 11-636.
    See HARNESS RACING.
  Pari-mutuel betting, BR §§11-801 to 11-832.
    See PARI-MUTUEL BETTING.
  Thoroughbred racing, BR §§11-501 to 11-541.
    See THOROUGHBRED RACING.
Hotels.
  Loss of property generally, BR §§15-101 to 15-107.
    See HOTELS.
Interior designers, BOP §§8-101 to 8-602.
  See INTERIOR DESIGNERS.
Juke boxes.
  General provisions, BR §§17-1301 to 17-1309.
    See JUKE BOXES.
  Harford county, BR §§17-1312 to 17-1318.
    See HARFORD COUNTY.
Junk dealers.
  Calvert county, BR §§17-1015 to 17-1024.
    See CALVERT COUNTY.
  General provisions, BR §§17-1001 to 17-1013.
    See JUNK DEALERS.
Kick boxing.
  General provisions, BR §§4-301 to 4-323.
    See BOXING, SPARRING AND WRESTLING.
Labor, licensing and regulation department.
  See LABOR, LICENSING AND REGULATION
    DEPARTMENT.
Landscape architects, BOP §§9-101 to 9-702.
  See LANDSCAPE ARCHITECTS.
Land surveyors, BOP §§15-101 to 15-702.
  See SURVEYS AND SURVEYORS.
Laundries, BR §§17-1101 to 17-1103.
Limited liability companies.
  See LIMITED LIABILITY COMPANIES.
Lists of licensees, BR §1-207.
Local licenses, fees and taxes, BOP §1-203.
  Dishonor of fee paid.
    Suspension of licensure upon, BOP §1-208.
  Late fees, BOP §1-206.
  Notice of dishonor of fee paid, BOP §1-208.
  Notice requirements, BOP §1-205.
  Payment of taxes and unemployment insurance
    contributions, BOP §1-204.
    Renewal of license or permit, BR §1-210.
  Prohibition, BR §1-204.
  Proration of certain license fees, BOP §1-207.
    Renewal of license or permit, BR §1-210.
Miscellaneous state business licenses.
  General provisions, BR §§17-101 to 17-308. See
    within this heading, "General business
    licensing."
  Penalty for violations.
    General penalty, BR §17-2106.
  Posting of licenses, BR §17-306.
  Prima facie evidence of sale, BR §17-2105.
  Prorating license fees, BR §17-303.
  Scope of title, BR §17-102.
  Submission requirements.
    Copies of licenses and applications, BR §17-205.

BUSINESS REGULATION AND LICENSURE
    —Cont'd
Miscellaneous state business licenses —Cont'd
    Term of license, BR §17-305.
        Doing business without license, BR §17-2102.
Motor fuel inspection.
    General provisions, BR §§10-101 to 10-502.
        See MOTOR FUEL INSPECTION.
Multilevel distribution companies.
    General provisions, BR §§14-301 to 14-305.
        See MULTILEVEL DISTRIBUTION
            COMPANIES.
Oaths, BOP §1-201.
    Document requirements, BR §1-201.
    False swearing, BR §1-202.
    Witnesses.
        Refusal to be sworn, BR §1-203.
Pari-mutuel betting.
    General provisions, BR §§11-801 to 11-832.
        See PARI-MUTUEL BETTING.
Pawnbrokers.
    General provisions, BR §§12-101 to 12-601.
        See PRECIOUS METALS AND GEM
            DEALERS.
Peddlers.
    Calvert county, BR §§17-915 to 17-922.
        See CALVERT COUNTY.
    General provisions, BR §§17-901 to 17-913.
        See HAWKERS AND PEDDLERS.
Penalties.
    Fees.
        Failure to get license in timely manner, BR
            §1-206.
Perjury.
    Oaths generally, BOP §1-201.
Pilots, BOP §§11-101 to 11-802.
    See PILOTS.
Pinball machines.
    Garrett county, BR §§17-432 to 17-438.
    General provisions, BR §§17-401 to 17-438.
        See AMUSEMENTS AND RECREATION.
    Wicomico county, BR §§17-420 to 17-429.
        See WICOMICO COUNTY.
Plumbers.
    General provisions, BOP §§12-101 to 12-702.
        See PLUMBERS AND PLUMBING.
    Plumbers and gas fitters, BR §§17-1501 to
        17-1504.
Pool rooms.
    General provisions, BR §§17-501 to 17-505.
        See BILLIARD AND POOL TABLES.
Prince George's county.
    Prohibition on local licenses, fees and taxes.
        Exception to prohibition, BR §1-204.
Private detectives, BOP §§13-101 to 13-801.
    See PRIVATE DETECTIVES.
Private home detention monitoring, BOP
    §§20-101 to 20-701.
    See PRIVATE HOME DETENTION
        MONITORING.
Professional engineers, BOP §§14-101 to 14-602.
    See ENGINEERS.
Professional land surveyors, BOP §§15-101 to
    15-702.
    See SURVEYS AND SURVEYORS.
Real estate appraisers.
    Generally, BOP §§16-101 to 16-802.
        See REAL ESTATE APPRAISERS AND HOME
            INSPECTORS.
Real estate brokers, BOP §§17-101 to 17-702.
    See REAL ESTATE BROKERS.

BUSINESS REGULATION AND LICENSURE
    —Cont'd
Real estate investment trusts.
    See REAL ESTATE INVESTMENT TRUST.
Refrigeration contractors.
    General provisions, BR §§9A-101 to 9A-602.
        See AIR CONDITIONING AND HEATING
            CONTRACTORS.
Restaurants, BR §§17-1601 to 17-1604.
Scope of title.
    General business licensing, BR §17-102.
Scrap metal processors.
    Calvert county, BR §§17-1015 to 17-1024.
        See CALVERT COUNTY.
    General provisions, BR §§17-1001 to 17-1013.
        See JUNK DEALERS.
Secondhand precious metal objects dealers.
    General provisions, BR §§12-101 to 12-601.
        See PRECIOUS METALS AND GEM
            DEALERS.
Security guards, BOP §§19-101 to 19-701.
    See SECURITY GUARDS.
Security systems technicians, BOP §§18-101 to
    18-701.
    See SECURITY SYSTEMS TECHNICIANS.
Soda fountains, BR §§17-1701 to 17-1703.
Start-up business ventures.
    General provisions, BR §§14-101 to 14-129.
        See START-UP BUSINESS VENTURES.
Stationary engineers, BOP §§6.5-101 to 6.5-502.
    See STATIONARY ENGINEERS.
Storage warehouses, BR §§17-1201 to 17-1204.
Subpoenas.
    Failure to comply with subpoena, BR §1-203.
Sunday blue laws, BR §§18-101, 18-102.
    Wicomico county, BR §§18-201, 18-202.
Surveys and surveyors.
    Land surveyors, BOP §§15-101 to 15-702.
        See SURVEYS AND SURVEYORS.
Taxation.
    Local licenses, fees and taxes, BOP §1-203.
        Payment of taxes and unemployment insurance
            contributions, BOP §1-204.
            Renewal of license or permit, BR §1-210.
        Renewal of license or permit, BR §1-210.
Thoroughbred racing.
    General provisions, BR §§11-501 to 11-541.
        See THOROUGHBRED RACING.
Trademarks and service marks.
    General provisions, BR §§1-401 to 1-415.
        See TRADEMARKS AND SERVICE MARKS.
Trade names.
    See TRADE NAMES.
Traders.
    General provisions, BR §§17-1801 to 17-1816.
        See TRADERS.
Trade secrets.
    Uniform trade secrets act, CL §§11-1201 to
        11-1209.
        See TRADE SECRETS.
Trading stamp companies.
    General provisions, BR §§13-101 to 13-110.
        See TRADING STAMP COMPANIES.
Trading stamp issuers.
    General provisions, BR §§17-2001 to 17-2003.
        See TRADING STAMP COMPANIES.
Transient vendors.
    General provisions, BR §§17-20A-01 to 17-20A-06.
        See TRANSIENT VENDORS.
**Uniform preservation of private business
    records act,** BR §§1-301 to 1-307.
    See BUSINESS RECORDS.

BUSINESS REGULATION AND LICENSURE
—Cont'd
Vending machines.
General provisions, BR §§17-1901 to 17-1907.
See VENDING MACHINES.
Ventilation contractors.
General provisions, BR §§9A-101 to 9A-602.
See AIR CONDITIONING AND HEATING
CONTRACTORS.
Wholesale farm machinery dealers, BR §§17-701
to 17-703.
Worcester county.
Prohibition on local licenses, fees and taxes.
Exception to prohibition, BR §1-204.
Workers' compensation.
Compliance with workers' compensation laws, BR
§1-204.
Payment of taxes and unemployment insurance
contributions, BOP §1-204.
Renewal of license or permit, BR §1-210.
Wrestling.
General provisions, BR §§4-301 to 4-323.
See BOXING, SPARRING AND WRESTLING.

BUSINESS TRUSTS, CA §§12-101 to 12-810.
Actions, CA §12-501.
Agent for service of process, CA §12-203.
**Attachment and execution, property subject
to,** CA §12-501.
Authorized business transactions, CA §12-201.
Beneficial interest, CA §12-303.
Beneficial owners.
Contributions, CA §12-301.
Death or incapacity, effect on existence of trust,
CA §12-202.
Governing instrument, binding effect, CA §12-207.
Indemnification, CA §12-304.
Information available to owner, CA §12-305.
Interest of owner, CA §12-303.
Liability limitation, CA §12-302.
Obligations, CA §12-301.
Penalties for failure to contribute, CA §12-302.
Usury defenses, CA §12-302.
Certificate of trust, CA §12-204.
Copy available to owner, CA §12-305.
Filing and recordation, CA §12-205.
Change of address of office or agent, CA
§12-203.
Claims against trust.
Capacity to sue and be sued, CA §12-501.
Dissolution and winding up, CA §12-202.
Survival after forfeiture of right to do business,
CA §12-810.
Survival of merger, CA §12-610.
Confidential information, CA §12-305.
Conflict of laws, law governing, CA §12-102.
Definitions, CA §12-101.
Dissolution, CA §12-202.
Excluded business operations, CA §12-201.
Fees, CA §12-701.
Filing of annual report, CA §1-203.
Forfeiture of right to do business, CA §§12-801
to 12-810.
Correction of mistaken proclamation, CA §12-803.
Grounds, CA §12-801.
Notice and cure, CA §12-802.
Other laws applicable, CA §12-804.
Reinstatement.
Application, CA §12-805.
Certificate, CA §12-806.

BUSINESS TRUSTS —Cont'd
Forfeiture of right to do business —Cont'd
Reinstatement —Cont'd
Evidentiary effect of acceptance of certificate,
CA §12-808.
Requirements to be fulfilled, CA §12-807.
Survival of contracts or claims after forfeiture, CA
§12-810.
Transactions after forfeiture, penalties, CA
§12-809.
Formation and powers, CA §§12-201 to 12-208.
Governing instrument, CA §12-207.
Liability limitations of trustee as part of
instrument, CA §12-402.
Merger or consolidation, CA §12-607.
Governing law, CA §12-102.
Limited liability companies.
Merger with or into limited liability company
generally, CA §§4A-701 to 4A-710.
See LIMITED LIABILITY COMPANIES.
Merger or consolidation.
Articles of merger or consolidation.
Contents, CA §12-605.
Filing, CA §12-604.
Authorization, CA §12-601.
Certificates of merger, CA §12-608.
Consummation of merger, effect, CA §12-610.
Effective date, CA §12-606.
Exchange of securities, CA §12-603.
Governing instrument provisions, CA §12-607.
Property certificates, CA §12-609.
Votes to approve, CA §12-602.
Name, CA §12-206.
Offices, CA §12-203.
Perpetual existence, CA §12-202.
Property certificates.
Merger or consolidation, CA §12-609.
Real estate investment trusts.
See REAL ESTATE INVESTMENT TRUST.
Records, CA §12-305.
Report, failure to file, CA §12-801.
Seizure of assets, limitations, CA §12-501.
Separate legal entity, CA §12-103.
Effect of merger, CA §12-610.
Shares in trust.
Effect of merger generally, CA §12-610.
Exchange upon merger or consolidation, CA
§12-603.
Provisions contained in articles of merger or
consolidation, CA §12-605.
Short title of provisions, CA §12-104.
Signatures on certificate, CA §12-205.
Successors to trust.
Approval of merger or consolidation, CA §12-602.
Effect of merger, CA §12-610.
Taxation.
Classification for tax purposes, CA §12-102.
Income tax exemption, CA §12-102.
List of trusts not paying taxes, CA §12-801.
Trustees.
Examination of information, CA §12-305.
Indemnification, CA §12-403.
Liability limitations, CA §§12-401, 12-402.
Management of trust, CA §12-401.
Personal liability, CA §12-402.
Supervision of trust, CA §12-208.
Unemployment insurance.
Failure to obtain, CA §12-801.
Voting.
Approval of merger or consolidation, CA §12-602.

BUSINESS TRUSTS —Cont'd
Voting —Cont'd
Rights granted by governing instrument, CA §12-207.
Winding up, CA §12-202.

BUTANE.
Inhaling, CR §5-708.
Possession of destructive device, CR §§4-501 to 4-503.

BUTTER.
Weights and measures.
Sale, AG §11-311.

BUTTERFLIES.
Baltimore checkerspot butterfly.
State arthropodic emblem, SG §13-301.

BUTYL NITRATE.
Inhaling, CR §5-708.

BUY AMERICAN STEEL ACT, SF §§17-301 to 17-306.

BYLAWS.
Acknowledgments.
Credit unions, FI §6-306.
Agricultural cooperatives.
Adoption, CA §5-511.
Election provisions, CA §5-514.
Kept at principal office of association, CA §5-511.
Patronage distribution, CA §5-525.
Children, youth and families services.
Residential child care operators, 49D §6-101.
Condominiums.
Administration of condominium, RP §11-104.
Amendments, RP §§11-104, 11-124.
Corrective amendments, RP §11-103.1.
Contents, RP §11-104.
Interpretation and construction, RP §11-124.
Purchaser.
Furnishing by vendor, RP §11-126.
Recordation.
With declaration, RP §11-104.
Required particulars, RP §11-104.
Consumer cooperatives.
Adoption, CA §§5-5A-11, 5-5A-21.
Amendment, CA §§5-5A-11, 5-5A-21.
Contents, CA §5-5A-07.
Election provisions, CA §5-5A-14.
Repeal, CA §5-5A-21.
Corporations.
General provisions.
See CORPORATIONS.
Counties.
Regional council of governments, 25 §26A.
Credit unions.
Amendment of bylaws.
Effective date, FI §6-320.
Mail ballot, FI §6-321.
Meetings, FI §6-317.
Procedure, FI §6-320.
Recommendation, FI §6-328.
Credit union insurance corporation.
Adoption by board, FI §7-111.
Filing for examination and approval, FI §6-307.
Filing for record, FI §6-308.
Loans.
Bylaws determine purpose and terms of loan, FI §6-601.
Environmental service.
Adoption, NR §3-104.

BYLAWS —Cont'd
Mining.
Interstate mining compact.
Commission, EN §15-902.
Political parties.
Adoption, EL §4-204.
Conflict with provisions, EL §4-101.
Forming new party, EL §4-102.
Protestant Episcopal Church, CA §5-334.
Easton Diocese, CA §5-338.
Residential child care operators, 49D §6-101.
Savings and loan associations.
Contents, FI §9-204.
Filing.
Division director may require filing, FI §9-213.
Savings banks, FI §4-402.
Tobacco authority.
Adoption of bylaws, AG §7-203.
United Methodist Church, CA §5-325.
Washington suburban sanitary district.
Collective bargaining.
Constitution and bylaws of employee organization, 29 §11.5-105.

C

CABLE OPERATED RAILROADS.
Power to condemn, PUC §5-409.

CABLE TELEVISION COMPANIES.
Consumer protection.
Waivers of consumer liability not considered insurance, IN §1-203.1.
Counties.
Franchise for community antenna television systems, 25 §3C.
Decoders, use, CR §7-303.
Fraud, receiving programing, CR §7-303.
Interference with service, CR §7-303.
Municipal corporations.
Franchises' powers, 23A §2.
Obstructing or delaying programing, CR §7-303.
Receiving services without payment, CR §7-303.
Telecommunications theft, CR §§7-313 to 7-318.
Unauthorized transfer or recording or sounds or images, CR §§7-306 to 7-310.

CADMIUM.
Toxics in packaging, EN §§9-1901 to 9-1907.
See TOXICS IN PACKAGING.

CAIMANS.
Dangerous animals.
Importing, selling, or trading in, CR §10-621.

CAKES.
Food, drug and cosmetic act.
See FOOD, DRUGS AND COSMETICS.

CALICO CAT.
State cat, SG §13-317.

CALIFORNIA EMISSIONS PROGRAM.
See AIR QUALITY CONTROL.

CALL BEFORE DIGGING.
Excavation or demolition near underground facilities, PUC §§12-101 to 12-113.
See UNDERGROUND UTILITY FACILITIES.

CALLER IDENTIFICATION.
Telephone solicitation.
Caller identification blocking, PUC §8-205.

CALLIGRAPHY.
Consignment of works of fine art generally, CL §§11-8A-01 to 11-8A-04.
See ART.

CALVERT COUNTY.
Alarm systems, 25 §236D.
Alcoholic beverages.
Beer and light wine licenses.
Class A, off-sale, 2B §5-101.
Class B, on-sale, 2B §5-201.
Beer licenses.
Class A, off-sale, 2B §3-101.
Class B, on-sale, 2B §3-201.
Class C, on-sale, 2B §3-301.
Class D, on-sale, 2B §3-401.
Beer, wine and liquor licenses.
Class A, off-sale, 2B §6-101.
Class B, on-sale, 2B §6-201.
Class C, on-sale, 2B §6-301.
Class C, seven days, 2B §7-101.
Class D, on-sale, 2B §6-401.
Wine festival license, 2B §8-305.
Elections.
Exercise of privileges of licensee on election day, 2B §11-401.
Hours and days for sale.
Election days, 2B §11-401.
General requirements, 2B §11-505.
Manufacturer's license, 2B §11-101.
New Year's day, 2B §11-402.
Inspectors.
Appointment, 2B §15-112.
License commissioners.
Appointment, 2B §15-101.
Expenses, 2B §15-109.
Inspection of premises once every three months, 2B §16-402.
Inspectors, 2B §15-112.
Personnel, 2B §15-112.
Qualifications, 2B §15-101.
Salaries, 2B §15-109.
Terms, 2B §15-101.
Vacancies, 2B §15-101.
Licenses.
Applications.
Notice or sign posted on premises, 2B §10-202.
Commissioners. See within this subheading, "License commissioners."
Corporations, 2B §9-101.
Expiration, 2B §10-206.
Fees.
Disposition, 2B §10-204.
Refund, 2B §10-205.
Limitation, 2B §9-102.
Manufacturers.
Hours and days for sale, 2B §11-101.
More than one license for same person or premises, 2B §9-102.
Renewal.
Time limits on renewal applicants, 2B §10-301.
Revocation and suspension.
Nudity and sexual displays on licensee's premises, 2B §10-405.
Transfer, 2B §10-503.
Wine festival license, 2B §8-305.
Light wine licenses.
Class A, off-sale, 2B §4-201.

CALVERT COUNTY —Cont'd
Alcoholic beverages —Cont'd
Manufacturers.
Licenses.
Hours and days for sale, 2B §11-101.
Micro-brewery license, 2B §2-208.
Minors.
Purchase, consumption or possession prohibited, 2B §12-108.
North Beach and Chesapeake Beach.
Hours and days for sale, 2B §11-505.
Nudity and sexual displays on licensee's premises.
Revocation of license, 2B §10-405.
Open containers.
Possession in certain places.
Applicability of provisions, 2B §19-303.
Pub-brewery licenses, 2B §2-207.
Regulation of retail sale.
Powers of commissioners, 25 §3.
Sales.
Election days, 2B §11-401.
New Year's Day, 2B §11-402.
Sales to minors and intoxicated persons prohibited, 2B §12-108.
Wine festivals.
Licenses, 2B §8-305.
Appearance fees in circuit courts.
Distribution, CJ §7-204.
Aquaculture.
Right of riparian or wharf owners to cultivate shellfish, NR §4-11A-16.
Bailiff.
Compensation, CJ §2-507.
Bingo, CR §§13-705 to 13-709.
Classes of licenses issued, CR §13-705.
Fees for licenses, CR §13-705.
Instant bingo considered bingo, CR §13-705.
License required, CR §13-705.
Limitations on issuing license, CR §13-705.
Organizations exempt from license requirement, CR §13-706.
Prizes allowed, CR §13-707.
Public liability insurance required, CR §13-705.
Regulations, adoption, CR §13-709.
Resident agent, designation, CR §13-705.
Revocation of license, CR §13-708.
Sunday bingo, limitation on license, CR §13-705.
Birds and game.
Spotlighting, NR §10-410.
Building code.
Agricultural buildings.
Exemption for buildings used for agritourism, PS §12-508.
Provision for, 25 §3.
Building excise taxes, 25 §9G.
Chesapeake Bay critical area and Atlantic coastal bays critical area protection programs.
Critical areas commission.
Members on commission, NR §8-1804.
Growth allocation, location in resource conservation area, NR §8-1808.1.
Circuit courts.
Appearance fees.
Distribution, CJ §7-204.
Number of judges, CJ §1-503.
Citations.
Erosion and sediment control.
Violations, 25 §10K.
Clubs.
Alcoholic beverages.
Beer, wine and liquor licenses.
Class C, on-sale, 2B §6-301.

CALVERT COUNTY —Cont'd
Clubs —Cont'd
Alcoholic beverages —Cont'd
Hours of sale, 2B §11-505.
Commissioners.
Alcoholic beverages.
License commissioner. See within this heading,
"Alcoholic beverages."
Building excise taxes.
Power to fix and impose, 25 §9G.
Erosion and sediment control.
Providing for, 25 §10K.
Libraries.
Authority to borrow for capital construction
costs, 25 §235.
Real property.
Power to acquire, etc., real or personal property,
25 §9B.
Storm water management districts.
Actions by commissioner at final hearing, 25
§155B.
Community colleges.
Parking, TR §21-1003.
**Community services alternative sentencing
program,** COR §11-706.
Conservation areas.
Exception from section, 23A §7.
Consumer affairs.
Tri-county council for southern Maryland.
See TRI-COUNTY COUNCIL FOR SOUTHERN
MARYLAND.
Contracts.
Competitive bidding, 25 §3.
Correctional facility.
Community services alternative sentencing
program, COR §11-706.
Substance abuse treatment program,
reimbursement, COR §11-706.
Work release program, COR §11-706.
County board of elections.
Compensation, EL §2-204.
County boards generally, EL §§2-201 to 2-303.
See ELECTIONS.
Substitute members.
Compensation, EL §2-204.
Courts.
Circuit courts.
Judicial circuit, MD Const Art IV §19.
Number of judges, CJ §1-503.
Crabs.
Restrictions on catching by landowners, NR
§4-811.
Detention center.
Correctional officers.
Lie-detector test, LE §3-702.
Development.
Tri-county council for southern Maryland.
See TRI-COUNTY COUNCIL FOR SOUTHERN
MARYLAND.
Distress for rent.
Lien on crops, RP §8-115.
Dog licenses, 24 §11-501.
Administration and enforcement of provisions, 24
§11-504.
Dogs running at large, 24 §11-510.
Dog tags, 24 §11-503.
Dog warden and pound, 24 §11-504.
Donation of interest in realty.
Powers of county commissioners, 25 §11A.
Dumps.
Screening or fencing, 25 §122C.

CALVERT COUNTY —Cont'd
Election judges.
Compensation, EL §10-205.
Electrical code.
Provision for, 25 §3.
Eminent domain.
Powers of commissioners, 25 §9B.
Erosion and sediment control, 25 §10K.
Fines.
Alcoholic beverages.
Minors.
Purchase, consumption or possession by
minor prohibited, 2B §12-108.
Erosion and sediment control.
Violations, 25 §10K.
Screening or fencing junk yards.
Violation, 25 §122C.
Fines and forfeited recognizances.
Disposition, CJ §7-507.
Fire department.
Volunteer fire departments.
Length of service awards, PS §7-208.
Property tax credits, TP §9-306.
Fish and fisheries.
Riparian rights, NR §4-712.
Floating homes.
Regulation, 25 §234A.
Gaming, bazaar, carnival and raffles, CR
§§13-201 to 13-205, 13-701 to 13-709.
Bingo, CR §§13-705 to 13-709.
Conducting event for benefit of qualified
organization.
Allowed, CR §13-203.
Definitions, CR §§13-201, 13-701.
Gambling permit review committee, CR §13-704.
Gaming event defined, CR §§13-201, 13-701.
Individual benefit prohibited, CR §13-203.
Management through organizations members, CR
§13-205.
Permit required for gaming event, CR §13-703.
Prizes and gaming devices allowed, CR §13-204.
Provisions applicable to county, CR §§13-202,
13-301, 13-702.
Qualified organization defined, CR §13-201.
Qualified organizations to conduct, listed, CR
§13-703.
Hawkers and peddlers.
Licensing, BR §§17-915 to 17-922. See within this
heading, "Peddlers."
Hearings.
Real property.
Sales at public or private sale, 25 §11A.
Storm water management districts, 25 §155B.
Hotels and restaurants.
Beer and light wine licenses.
Class B, on-sale, 2B §§5-201, 5-202.
Beer licenses.
Class B, on-sale, 2B §3-201.
Beer, wine and liquor licenses.
Class B, on-sale, 2B §6-201.
Housing code.
Provision for, 25 §3.
Internal improvements.
Extension of state credit.
Limitation, MD Const Art III §34.
Judges.
Pensions.
General provisions, ET §2-108.
Junk dealer licensing, BR §§17-1015 to 17-1024.
Applicability of title, BR §17-1016.
Applications, BR §17-1018.

CALVERT COUNTY —Cont'd
Junk dealer licensing —Cont'd
Calvert county junk dealer or scrap metal
processor license.
Defined, BR §17-1015.
Change of address.
Notification requirements, BR §17-1020.
Expiration of license, BR §17-1019.
Fees, BR §17-1018.
Mandatory license requirement, BR §17-1017.
Motor vehicle registration number.
Change in information, BR §17-1020.
Penalty for violations, BR §17-1024.
Purchases from minors prohibited, BR §17-1023.
Reporting requirements, BR §17-1022.
Required, BR §17-1017.
Scope of title, BR §17-1016.
Stolen property liability, BR §17-1021.
Term of license, BR §17-1019.
Junkyards.
Screening or fencing.
Requirements, 25 §122C.
Landlord and tenant.
Lien on crops.
Advances, RP §8-115.
Share reserved as rent, RP §8-115.
Libraries.
Authority of county commissioners to borrow for
capital construction costs, 25 §235.
Licenses.
Alcoholic beverages. See within this heading,
"Alcoholic beverages."
Junk dealers, BR §§17-1015 to 17-1024. See
within this heading, "Junk dealer licensing."
Marriage licenses.
Fees, FL §2-404.
Peddlers, BR §§17-915 to 17-922. See within this
heading, "Peddlers."
Liens.
Power to provide for lien upon real property for
certain charges, 25 §9E.
Loans.
Tri-county council for southern Maryland.
Review of applications for loans, 20 §3-103.
Maritime museum.
Power of commissioners to convey, etc., certain
property for public maritime museum, 25
§9B.
Marriage licenses.
Fees, FL §2-404.
Merit system.
Application, 25 §3.
Minors.
Alcoholic beverages.
Purchase, consumption or possession by minor,
2B §12-108.
Unattended children.
Confinement in dwelling, building or enclosure,
FL §5-801.
Mortgages and deeds of trust.
Interest payable after sale, RP §7-105.
Motor vehicles.
Private roadway in residential subdivision.
Enforcement of vehicle laws by police, TR
§11-205.
Motor vehicle size and weight.
Power of county commissioners, 25 §25.
Noise control.
Trapshooting, skeet shooting, etc.
Limitations on authority, EN §§3-105, 3-401.

CALVERT COUNTY —Cont'd
Notice.
Erosion and sediment control.
Notice of noncompliance, 25 §10K.
Real property.
Sales at public or private sale, 25 §11A.
Storm water management districts, 25 §155B.
Orphans' court.
Compensation of judge, ET §2-108.
Oysters and clams.
Handscraping of oysters, NR §4-1008.1.
Right of riparian or wharf owners to cultivate
shellfish, NR §4-11A-16.
Palm readers, fortune-tellers and soothsayers.
License requirements, 24 §11-403.
Patuxent river watershed.
General provisions.
See PATUXENT RIVER WATERSHED.
Peddlers.
Acting as magazine seller without license, BR
§17-922.
Acting as peddler without license, BR §17-921.
Applicability of title, BR §17-916.
Definitions, BR §17-915.
Display of tag, BR §17-920.
Fees, BR §17-918.
Issuance of metal tag, BR §17-919.
Mandatory license requirement, BR §17-917.
Posting of tag, BR §17-920.
Scope of title, BR §17-916.
Permits.
Erosion and sediment control, 25 §10K.
Personal property.
Purchase or lease.
Powers, 25 §9D.
Planning.
Tri-county council for southern Maryland.
See TRI-COUNTY COUNCIL FOR SOUTHERN
MARYLAND.
Plumbing code.
Provision for, 25 §3.
Political parties.
Central committees.
Election of members, EL §4-203.
Port administration.
Jurisdiction.
Consent to territorial jurisdiction, TR §6-103.
Private activity bonds.
Power to charge fee for issuance, 25 §3.
Property tax credits, TP §9-306.
Property tax reimbursement, 24 §9-1103.
Real property.
Acquisition, etc., of real or leasehold property.
Powers of commissioners, 25 §9B.
Conveyance to other political subdivision for
public purpose, 25 §9B.
Liens.
Power to provide liens upon real property for
certain charges, 25 §9E.
Recordation.
Plats of subdivisions.
Combining multiple subdivision lots, RP §3-108.
**Residential mortgage programs for certain
counties, HS §§4-1601 to 4-1610.**
Road construction districts, 25 §155A.
Schools.
County board of education.
Composition, ED §3-301.
Election, ED §3-114.
Generally, EL §§8-801 to 8-806.
Expenses, ED §4-107.

CALVERT COUNTY —Cont'd
Schools —Cont'd
County board of education —Cont'd
Health insurance.
Elected members, ED §3-303.
Meetings, ED §3-304.
Persons subject to authority of board.
Ineligibility to serve as member, ED §3-114.
President, ED §3-303.
Qualifications, ED §3-301.
Removal of members, ED §3-302.
Term of office, ED §3-301.
Vacancies, ED §3-301.
Vice-president, ED §3-303.
Holidays, ED §7-103.
Year-round schools.
Pilot programs, ED §7-103.
Sediment control.
Erosion and sediment control in Calvert county, 25 §10K.
Sheriff.
Deputies, CJ §2-309.
Pension, CJ §2-309.
Plan for sheriff's department, 25 §3.
Surviving spouse, CJ §2-309.
Salary, CJ §2-309.
Second in command, CJ §2-310.
State's attorney.
Accounts for services and expenses.
County excepted from section, 10 §39.
Assistant attorneys, 10 §40.
Deputy state's attorney, 10 §40.
Erosion and sediment control.
Prosecution of violations, 25 §10K.
Expenses, 10 §40.
Storm water management districts, 25 §155B.
Subdivisions.
Plats.
Combining multiple subdivision lots, RP §3-108.
Substance abuse treatment program at county treatment facility.
Reimbursement by individual sentenced to participate, COR §11-706.
Sundays and holidays.
Alcoholic beverages.
Hours and days for sale, 2B §11-505.
Taxation.
Building excise taxes, 25 §9G.
Credits.
Property tax credits, TP §9-306.
Delinquent taxes.
Interest penalty, TP §14-603.
Penalties, TP §§14-603, 14-702.
Exemptions.
Personal property.
Commercial, manufacturing or professional businesses, TP §7-510.
Private activity bonds.
Fee for issuance, 25 §3.
Hotel rental tax, 24 §§9-301 to 9-326.
See COUNTIES.
Municipal corporations.
Sale by municipal collector after notice to county collector.
Special provisions, TP §14-809.
Redemption.
Rate of redemption, TP §14-820.
Sales.
Municipal collector.
Sale after notice to county collector.
Special provisions, TP §14-809.

CALVERT COUNTY —Cont'd
Taxation —Cont'd
Sales —Cont'd
Special provisions, TP §14-808.
Transportation services, public, TR §7-801.
Tax exempt private activity bonds.
Power to charge fee for issuance, 25 §3.
Transportation services tax, TR §7-801.
Trapshooting, skeetshooting or other target shooting.
Environmental sound level limits and noise control rules and regulations, EN §3-401.
Noise control ordinances, rules or regulations prohibiting, EN §3-105.
Treasurer, 25 §51.
Trial notice.
Erosion and sediment control, 25 §10K.
Tri-county council for southern Maryland.
See TRI-COUNTY COUNCIL FOR SOUTHERN MARYLAND.
Volunteer fire departments.
Length of service awards, PS §7-208.
Property tax credits, TP §9-306.
Wine festivals.
Licenses, 2B §8-305.
Work release program for individual sentenced to correctional facility, COR §11-706.
Zoning.
Stormwater management facility.
Prohibited in residentially zoned district, 66B §14.11.

CALVERT STATION.
See BALTIMORE CITY.

CAMBRIDGE.
Port administration, TR §6-205.
Funding to address vulnerability concerns.
Reporting on funding, TR §6-210.
Taxation.
Interest.
Overdue taxes, TP §14-603.

CAMDEN YARDS.
Development, FI §13-708.1.
Dome restriction, FI §13-715.3.
Professional baseball games restrictions, FI §13-715.3.

CAMERAS.
Surveillance of individual in private place, CR §3-901.
With prurient intent, CR §3-902.
Surveillance of private residence, CR §3-903.
Traffic control devices, TR §21-202.1.

CAMPAIGN FINANCE, EL §§13-101 to 13-605.
Account books.
Treasurers' duties to keep, requirements, preservation, EL §13-221.
Advertising by campaign finance entity.
Campaign materials, EL §§13-401 to 13-403.
Anonymous contributions, EL §13-239.
Gaming activity money, EL §13-240.
Applicability of title, EL §13-101.
Campaign finance activity, EL §13-201.
Campaign accounts, EL §13-220.
Campaign finance contribution receipts, EL §13-222.
Campaign finance reports.
Assumption of office prohibited.
Failure to file, EL §13-333.
Content requirements, EL §13-304.

CAMPAIGN FINANCE —Cont'd
Campaign finance reports —Cont'd
Continuing requirement for candidates, EL §13-304.
Contribution receipt information included in, EL §13-222.
Copies as evidence, EL §13-341.
Deadline for filing.
Final report, EL §13-310.
Generally, EL §13-309.
Timeliness of filing, EL §13-322.
Duplicate, local board filing in, EL §13-317.
Electronic filing, EL §13-324.
Evidence, copies as, EL §13-341.
Exceptions to filing requirements, EL §13-305.
Failure to file, EL §13-327.
Assumption of office prohibited, EL §13-333.
Collections unit, forwarding to, EL §13-335.
Criminal penalty, EL §13-335.
Disqualification as candidate or as treasurer, EL §13-332.
Forfeiture of salary, EL §13-334.
Late filing fee, EL §13-331.
Administrative waiver, EL §13-337.
Distributions, EL §13-340.
List of entities failing to file, EL §13-328.
Overdue reports, acceptance, EL §13-331.
Prosecution, referral for, EL §13-335.
Relief from sanctions, EL §13-337.
Show cause notice, EL §13-335.
Failure to provide required information, EL §13-327.
List of violators, EL §13-328.
False or misleading statements, EL §13-601.
Filing schedule, EL §13-309.
Final report.
Payment of obligations and disposal of assets prior to filing, EL §13-311.
Required, time for filing, EL §13-310.
First report.
Reporting period, EL §13-312.
Forfeiture of salary.
Failure to file, EL §13-334.
Forms, state board to prescribe, EL §13-320.
Late filing fee, EL §13-331.
Administrative waiver, EL §13-337.
Distributions, EL §13-340.
Limited fund raising activity by personal treasurer.
Exception to required filing, EL §13-305.
List of entities failing to file, EL §13-328.
Location for filing, EL §13-316.
Mandatory nature of provisions, EL §13-336.
Notice of overdue reports.
Local board to provide state board, EL §13-328.
Notice of requirement to file.
Boards of elections to give, EL §13-321.
Out-of-state finance entities.
Applicability of subtitle to, EL §13-301.
Overdue reports, acceptance, EL §13-331.
Separate record kept of overdue reports, EL §13-341.
Payment of obligations and disposal of assets.
Prior to filing final report, EL §13-311.
Preservation by board, EL §13-341.
Public access, EL §13-341.
Electronically filed reports, EL §13-324.
Receipt provided for hand delivered reports, EL §13-323.
Reporting periods, EL §13-312.

CAMPAIGN FINANCE —Cont'd
Campaign finance reports —Cont'd
Requirement to file, EL §13-304.
Exceptions, EL §13-305.
Notice of requirement to file.
Boards of elections to give, EL §13-321.
Retention by boards, EL §13-341.
Show cause notice.
Failure to file, EL §13-335.
State archives, transfer to, EL §13-341.
State board, when filed with, EL §13-316.
Subsequent reports.
Reporting periods, EL §13-312.
Subtreasurers report attached to, EL §13-219.
Timeliness of filing, EL §13-322.
Campaign managers.
Appointment by individual, EL §13-212.
Campaign materials, EL §§13-401 to 13-403.
Advertising or press agency used.
Rates charged by newspaper or periodical, EL §13-402.
Advertising rates charged by newspapers or periodical, EL §13-402.
Authority line, EL §13-401.
Copies retained by finance entity, EL §13-403.
Legislative newsletters, EL §§13-406 to 13-409.
Material not authorized by candidate.
Statement required, EL §13-401.
Candidates ineligible to be officers, EL §13-215.
Checks.
Contributions.
Attributable to election cycle in which issued, EL §13-232.
Disbursement to be by, EL §13-220.
Money contributions in excess of $100.
Check required, EL §13-226.
Civil penalties for violations, EL §13-604.
Claim for payment of money due, EL §13-246.
Consent of candidate.
Loan to candidates finance entity, EL §13-230.
Contribution receipts, EL §13-222.
Contributions.
Aggregate contributions, limitations.
Contributions other than transfers, EL §13-226.
Anonymous contributions, EL §13-239.
Gaming activity money, EL §13-240.
Attributable to election cycle in which received, EL §13-232.
Checks.
Attributable to election cycle in which issued, EL §13-232.
Corporations, subsidiaries or affiliated corporations.
Considered as one contributor, EL §13-226.
Credit cards, restrictions, EL §13-226.
Disclosures by persons doing public business, EL §§14-101 to 14-108.
Applicability, EL §14-102.
Attributable contributions, EL §14-105.
Time of attribution, EL §14-106.
Attribution of contribution to candidate, EL §14-103.
Business entities, subsidiaries, officers, directors and partners.
Attributable contributions, EL §14-105.
Contribution finance entity.
Attribution of contribution to candidate, EL §14-103.
Criminal penalty for violations, EL §14-107.
Definitions, EL §14-101.

CAMPAIGN FINANCE —Cont'd
Contributions —Cont'd
Disclosures by persons doing public business
—Cont'd
Derivative liability of officer or partner, EL
§14-107.
Employees, agents or other persons affiliated
with business entity.
Attributable contributions, EL §14-105.
Initial statement of contribution.
Filed at time of contract signing, EL §14-104.
Liberal construction of provisions, EL §14-108.
Not-for-profit organizations.
Attributable contributions, EL §14-105.
Semi-annual statement of contribution, EL
§14-104.
Statement of contribution, EL §14-104.
Time of attribution, EL §14-106.
During general assembly sessions.
Prohibition, exceptions, EL §13-235.
Employee payroll deductions, EL §13-241.
Collection by employer, EL §13-242.
Collection by membership entities, EL §13-243.
Expenditures prohibited, EL §13-245.
Gaming activity money, EL §13-240.
Inducing or procuring vote, EL §13-602.
In name other than person's name, EL §13-602.
Loans to finance entity, EL §13-230.
Making, EL §13-225.
Money in excess of $100.
Check required, EL §13-226.
Multiple candidates or entities, limit on, EL
§13-226.
Party central committee.
Aggregate in-kind contributions, restrictions,
EL §13-226.
Personal funds of candidates or spouses, EL
§13-231.
Public campaign financing, EL §§15-101 to 15-111.
Receipt before depositing, EL §13-222.
Signing other's name without authority, EL
§13-602.
State funded entities.
Prohibited from making, EL §13-236.
To other than finance entity, EL §13-602.
Transfer, limitations, EL §13-227.
Political action committee to candidate, EL
§13-228.
Prohibited if intended to conceal source, EL
§13-229.
Uncharged interest on loan, EL §13-230.
Volunteerism not affected, EL §13-233.
Voting or refraining from voting in consideration,
EL §13-602.
When deemed received, EL §13-232.
Control of contributions and expenses, EL
§13-218.
**Corporations, subsidiaries or affiliated
corporations.**
Contributions by.
Considered as one contributor, EL §13-226.
Credit cards.
Contributions by, restrictions, EL §13-226.
Criminal penalties, EL §§13-601 to 13-603.
Designation of campaign accounts, EL §13-220.
Disbursement of campaign assets, EL §13-218.
By check, EL §13-220.
Surplus funds, EL §13-247.
Disclosures by persons doing public business.
Contributions to candidates, EL §§14-101 to
14-108.

CAMPAIGN FINANCE —Cont'd
Eligibility to be responsible officer, EL §13-215.
Employee payroll deductions.
Contributions, EL §13-241.
Collection by employer, EL §13-242.
Collection by membership entities, EL §13-243.
Endorsements.
Receiving money for prohibited, EL §13-245.
Enforcement actions.
Termination of finance entity, EL §13-313.
Expenditures prohibited, EL §13-245.
False or misleading statements, EL §13-601.
Federal law, activity governed by.
Inapplicability of title, EL §13-101.
Gaming activity money.
Anonymous contributions, EL §13-240.
Garnishment of salary.
Failure to file finance report, EL §13-334.
General assembly sessions.
Contributions during, prohibition, exceptions, EL
§13-235.
Howard county.
Contributions to county executive, county council
member or candidate for offices.
Applicability of state government article, part
VII, EL §13-503.
Independent expenditures by individuals, EL
§13-102.
Inducing or procuring vote, EL §13-602.
Injunctions, violations, EL §13-605.
Interest.
Contributions.
Uncharged interest on loan, EL §13-230.
**Joint and several liability of responsible
officers of finance entity,** EL §13-214.
Legal expenses for contested results.
Volunteering to pay, EL §13-233.
Legislative newsletters, EL §§13-406 to 13-409.
Campaign account of campaign finance entity.
Payment from, EL §13-408.
Definitions, EL §13-406.
Late filing fee for overdue campaign finance
report, EL §13-409.
Paid for with public funds, prohibition, EL
§13-408.
Personal funds of incumbent.
Payment from, EL §13-408.
Use of funds appropriated in state budget not
restricted, EL §13-407.
Loans to finance entity, EL §13-230.
Personal funds of candidates or spouses, EL
§13-231.
Lobbyists.
Subject to finance activity limitations of state
government article, EL §13-210.
Money due, claim for, EL §13-246.
Montgomery county.
Contributions to county executive, county council
member or candidate for offices.
Applicability of state government article, part
V, EL §13-502.
Notice to finance entity.
Service on responsible officers, EL §13-214.
Party central committee.
Aggregate in-kind contributions, restrictions, EL
§13-226.
Disbursement of assets by treasurer.
Authority and direction of chairman required,
EL §13-218.
Incurring liability on behalf of committee.
Authority and direction of chairman required,
EL §13-218.

CAMPAIGN FINANCE —Cont'd
Party central committee —Cont'd
Subtreasurers.
  Appointment by treasurer of committee, EL §13-211.
Payment of obligations and disposal of assets.
Prior to filing final report, EL §13-311.
Payroll deductions.
Contributions, EL §§13-241 to 13-243.
Personal funds of candidates or spouses, EL §13-231.
Petty cash fund, EL §13-220.
Political committee.
Appointment of chairman and treasurer.
  Required to establish, EL §13-207.
Campaign finance entity, EL §13-202.
Establishment of finance entity by candidate required, EL §§13-201, 13-207.
  How established, EL §13-207.
Limitation on contributions by transfer, EL §13-228.
Name, EL §13-208.
Purpose, statement, EL §13-208.
Reporting requirements.
  Compliance by finance entity required, EL §13-203.
Required to conduct finance activity, EL §§13-201, 13-207.
Resignation of chairman or treasurer, EL §13-207.
Statement of organization, EL §13-208.
Termination of finance entity, EL §13-313.
Vacancy in office of chairman or treasurer, EL §13-207.
Prince George's county.
Contributions to county executive, county council member or candidate for offices.
  Applicability of state government article, part IV, EL §13-501.
Prohibited acts generally, EL §13-602.
Civil penalty, EL §13-604.
Criminal penalty, EL §13-603.
Injunction, EL §13-605.
Public campaign financing, EL §§15-101 to 15-111.
Administration of title by state board, EL §15-109.
Balance in fund to remain, EL §15-108.
Criminal penalty for violations, EL §15-110.
Definitions, EL §15-102.
Distribution of public contributions, EL §15-103.
  To eligible gubernatorial ticket, EL §15-106.
Eligible gubernatorial ticket.
  Defined, EL §15-102.
  Distribution of public contributions to, EL §15-106.
  Expenditure limitations, EL §15-105.
  Qualification to receive public contribution, EL §15-104.
  Repayment of unspent contributions, EL §15-107.
  Unspent contributions, use, EL §15-107.
  Use of public contributions, EL §15-107.
Expenditure limitations.
  Eligible gubernatorial ticket accepting public contribution, EL §15-105.
Fair campaign financing fund, EL §15-103.
  Balance in fund to remain, EL §15-108.
Public financing act.
  Short title, EL §15-111.
Purpose of provision, EL §15-101.
Qualification to receive public contribution.
  Eligible gubernatorial ticket, EL §15-104.

CAMPAIGN FINANCE —Cont'd
Public campaign financing —Cont'd
Regulations adopted by state board, EL §15-109.
Repayment of unspent contributions.
  Eligible gubernatorial ticket, EL §15-107.
Tax add-on system.
  Contributions to fund, filing personal state income tax return, EL §15-103.
Unspent contributions, use.
  Eligible gubernatorial ticket, EL §15-107.
Use of public contributions.
  Eligible gubernatorial ticket, EL §15-107.
Public contracts.
Disclosures by persons doing public business.
  Contributions to candidates, EL §§14-101 to 14-108.
Qualifications to be responsible officer, EL §13-215.
Receipt before depositing contribution, EL §13-222.
Records of finance entity.
Preservation, EL §13-221.
Responsibility of officers of finance entity, EL §13-214.
Samples of forms.
State board to provide to local boards, EL §13-103.
Service on responsible officers.
Notice to finance entity, EL §13-214.
Signing other's name without authority, EL §13-602.
Slates.
Two or more candidates with separate finance entities.
  Forming, joining, notice of joining, EL §13-209.
Spin or chance, money received from.
Contribution without naming source, EL §13-240.
State funded entities.
Contributions to finance entity.
  Prohibited from making, EL §13-236.
Summary of law.
State board to prepare, providing candidates copy, EL §13-103.
Surplus funds, distribution, EL §13-247.
Termination of finance entity, EL §13-313.
Time.
Campaign finance reports.
  Deadlines and reporting periods, EL §§13-309 to 13-313.
Transfers.
Restrictions on contributions by, EL §13-227.
  Political action committee to candidate, EL §13-228.
  Prohibited if intended to conceal source, EL §13-229.
Treasurers.
Account books.
  Duty to keep, requirements, preservation, EL §13-221.
Claim for payment of money due.
  Presentation to, EL §13-246.
Control of contributions and expenses, EL §13-218.
Disbursement of campaign assets, EL §13-218.
Disqualification.
  Failure to file finance report, EL §13-332.
Failure to file finance report.
  Disqualification, EL §13-332.
Personal treasurer.
  Campaign finance entity, EL §13-202.
  Establishment of finance entity by candidate required, EL §13-201.

CAMPAIGN FINANCE —Cont'd
Treasurers —Cont'd
Personal treasurer —Cont'd
Reporting requirements.
Compliance by finance entity required, EL
§13-203.
Required to conduct finance activity, EL
§13-201.
Termination of finance entity, EL §13-313.
Subtreasurers.
Appointment by finance entity, EL §13-211.
Duties, EL §13-219.
Report attached to campaign finance report, EL
§13-219.
**Two or more candidates with separate finance
entities.**
Slates.
Forming, joining, notice of joining, EL §13-209.
University of Maryland.
Campaign fund-raising by members of board of
regents.
Restrictions, ED §12-115.
**Volunteerism not affected by part on
contributions,** EL §13-233.
**Voting or refraining from voting in
consideration of thing of value,** EL §13-602.
Walk-around services.
Defined, receiving money for prohibited, EL
§13-245.
Workplace publications, prohibitions, EL
§13-602.

CAMPAIGN MANAGERS.
Appointment by individual, EL §13-212.

CAMPAIGN MATERIALS, EL §§13-401 to 13-403.
Advertising or press agency used.
Rates charged by newspaper or periodical, EL
§13-402.
**Advertising rates charged by newspapers or
periodical,** EL §13-402.
Authority line, EL §13-401.
Copies retain by finance entity, EL §13-403.
Legislative newsletters, EL §§13-406 to 13-409.
Campaign account of campaign finance entity.
Payment from, EL §13-408.
Definitions, EL §13-406.
Late filing fee for overdue campaign finance
report, EL §13-409.
Paid for with public funds, prohibition, EL
§13-408.
Personal funds of incumbent.
Payment from, EL §13-408.
Use of funds appropriated in state budget not
restricted, EL §13-407.
Material not authorized by candidate.
Statement required, EL §13-401.

CAMP FIRE GIRLS.
Forests and parks.
Free admission to state parks, NR §5-1008.

CAMPS.
Blanket health insurance.
Eligible organizations, IN §15-305.
**Criminal background investigations for
employees, etc., of facilities.**
Caring for and supervising children, FL §§5-560 to
5-568.
See CHILD CARE.
Unemployment compensation.
Student employment at camps.
When not covered employment, LE §8-220.

CAMPS —Cont'd
Youth camps, HG §§14-401 to 14-411.
See YOUTH CAMPS.

CAMPUS POLICE.
Sex offender registration.
Notice, registrant commencing or terminating
enrollment, CP §11-710.

CANADA.
Securities.
Securities act.
Exempt securities, CA §11-601.

**CANAL PLACE HISTORIC PRESERVATION
DISTRICT.**
Certified heritage area, FI §13-1111.
Heritage areas generally, FI §§13-1101 to
13-1124.
See HERITAGE AREAS.

**CANAL PLACE PRESERVATION AND
DEVELOPMENT AUTHORITY,** FI §§13-1001
to 13-1031.
Audits, FI §13-1010.
Bond issues, FI §13-1018.
Agreements to enhance marketability or provide
security, FI §13-1025.
Bondholders enforcement of rights, FI §13-1023.
Definition of "bonds," FI §13-1001.
Investments.
Authorized investment, FI §13-1025.
Liability on bonds, FI §13-1023.
Payment of bonds.
Sources, FI §13-1019.
Trust agreement to secure, FI §§13-1018,
13-1021.
Pledge of revenue as security, FI §13-1022.
Refunding bonds, FI §13-1024.
Requirements of bonds, FI §13-1020.
Tax exemption, FI §13-1026.
Trust agreement, FI §§13-1018, 13-1021.
Chairman, FI §13-1005.
Citation of act.
Short title, FI §13-1031.
Composition, FI §13-1005.
Cumberland.
Failure of city to implement provisions.
Effect, FI §13-1030.
Ordinance.
Adoption by city as prerequisite to
expenditures, FI §13-1014.
Proposed activities affecting property within park
corridor.
Submission by city to authority, FI §13-1015.
Definitions, FI §13-1001.
Duties, FI §13-1010.
Eminent domain.
Acquisition of property interests, FI §13-1009.
Established, FI §13-1004.
Executive director, FI §13-1007.
Expenditures.
Prerequisites, FI §13-1014.
Expenses of members.
Reimbursement, FI §13-1006.
Failure to implement provisions.
Effect, FI §13-1030.
Financial assistance, FI §13-1028.
Findings of legislature, FI §13-1002.
Funds.
Financing fund, FI §13-1017.
Intergovernmental cooperation, FI §13-1029.
Interpretation and construction, FI §13-1003.

CANAL PLACE PRESERVATION AND
** DEVELOPMENT AUTHORITY** —Cont'd
Investments.
   Authorized investments, FI §13-1025.
Legislative declaration, FI §13-1002.
Management plan.
   Adoption as prerequisite to expenditures, FI
      §13-1014.
   Approval or disapproval by Maryland historical
      trust, FI §13-1013.
   Contents, FI §13-1011.
   Duty to develop, FI §§13-1010, 13-1011.
   Public hearing, FI §13-1012.
Management plan task force, FI §13-1016.
Maryland historical trust.
   Management plan.
      Approval or disapproval, FI §13-1013.
Meetings, FI §13-1006.
   Executive director.
      Attendance, FI §13-1007.
Motor vehicles.
   Parking regulations, FI §13-1008.1.
Notice.
   Management plan.
      Public hearing on, FI §13-1012.
Park corridor.
   Defined, FI §13-1001.
   Proposed activities affecting property within.
      Submission by city of Cumberland to authority,
         FI §13-1015.
Parking regulations, FI §13-1008.1.
Powers, FI §13-1008.
Property.
   Acquisition of interests in property, FI §13-1009.
   Powers of authority, FI §13-1008.
Quorum, FI §13-1006.
Removal of members, FI §13-1005.
Status, FI §13-1004.
Taxation.
   Exemption, FI §13-1027.
   Bonds, FI §13-1026.
Terms of members, FI §13-1005.
Title of act.
   Short title, FI §13-1031.

CANALS.
Companies.
   Bridge and canal companies, 23 §§140 to 143.
   See BRIDGE AND CANAL COMPANIES.
Counties.
   Restriction on aid to construction of canals, MD
      Const Art III §54.
Railroads.
   Crossings, PUC §9-304.

CANCELLATION.
Funds transfers.
   Payment orders, CL §4A-211.
      Security procedure verifying communication
         canceling, CL §4A-201.
      Time of receipt of order canceling, CL §4A-106.
Negotiable instruments.
   Discharge by cancellation, CL §3-604.

CANCER.
Amygdaline, HG §§18-302, 18-304.
Breast cancer.
   Alternative methods of treatment, HG §20-113.
   Diethylstilbestrol exposure.
      Public information campaign and screening
         program, HG §18-303.

CANCER —Cont'd
Breast cancer —Cont'd
   Health insurance.
      Mastectomy coverage, IN §15-832.
      Prosthesis coverage, IN §15-834.
   Health insurance coverage.
      Mammograms, IN §15-814.
      Reconstructive breast surgery, IN §15-815.
   Hospitals.
      Educational materials, HG §19-348.
   Mammography testing, HG §20-115.
      Health insurance, required coverage, IN
         §15-814.
      Low-income underinsured or uninsured women,
         HG §20-116.
   Medicare supplement insurance, IN §15-907.
Cancer control agencies in other states.
   Release of information to, EN §1-405.
Cancer prevention, education, screening and
   treatment program, HG §§13-1101 to 13-1119.
Cervical cancer.
   Diethylstilbestrol exposure.
      Public information campaign and screening
         program, HG §18-303.
   Hospitals.
      Pap smears, required services, HG §19-348.
Checkoffs.
   Income tax contribution.
      Maryland cancer fund, HG §20-117.
Colorectal cancer screening.
   Health insurance coverage, IN §15-837.
Definitions.
   Cancer report, HG §18-204.
Diethylstilbestrol exposure.
   Public information campaign and screening
      program, HG §18-303.
Environment, secretary.
   Information about certain cancers, EN §1-405.
Funds.
   Maryland cancer fund.
      Income tax checkoff, HG §20-117.
Hospitals.
   Breast cancer and cervical cancer.
      Required services, HG §19-348.
Income tax checkoff.
   Maryland cancer fund, HG §20-117.
Life insurance.
   Viatical settlement contracts, IN §§8-601 to 8-611.
      See VIATICAL SETTLEMENT CONTRACTS.
   Voiding policy because insured has had a disease
      or ailment, IN §16-216.
Maryland cancer fund.
   Income tax checkoff, HG §20-117.
Mastectomies.
   Health insurance coverage, IN §15-832.
      Prosthesis coverage, IN §15-834.
      Reconstructive breast surgery, IN §15-815.
Nonresidents.
   Information provided to cancer control agencies in
      other states, HG §18-203.
Oral cancer.
   Oral health program to prevent and detect, HG
      §§18-801 to 18-803.
      Educational programs, HG §18-802.
      Report by secretary, HG §18-803.
      Secretary to establish and promote, HG
         §18-801.
Patient-identification information.
   Release to cancer control agencies in other states,
      EN §1-405.

CANCER —Cont'd
Penalties.
Treatment of cancer.
Violations of provisions, HG §18-304.
Prostate cancer.
Insurance coverage for diagnosis and treatment, IN §15-825.
Reports.
Diethylstilbestrol exposure.
Annual report to General Assembly, HG §18-303.
Required cancer reports, HG §18-204.
Secretary of health and mental hygiene.
General responsibilities of secretary for disease prevention, HG §18-104.
Testicular cancer.
Diethylstilbestrol exposure.
Public information campaign and screening program, HG §18-303.
Tobacco related diseases.
Cancer prevention, education, screening and treatment program, HG §§13-1101 to 13-1119.
Treatment of cancer.
Amygdaline.
Use authorized, HG §18-302.
Penalties for violation of provisions, HG §18-304.
Breast cancer.
Alternative methods of treatment, HG §20-113.
Dispensing drugs, medicines and devices, HG §18-301.
Misrepresentations, HG §18-301.
Penalties for violation of provisions, HG §18-304.
Vaginal cancer.
Diethylstilbestrol exposure.
Public information campaign and screening program, HG §18-303.

CANCER PREVENTION, EDUCATION, SCREENING AND TREATMENT PROGRAM, HG §§13-1101 to 13-1119.
Administrative component, HG §13-1119.
Defined, HG §13-1101.
Baltimore City.
Calculation of grant money distributed, HG §13-1108.
Community health coalition.
Established, HG §13-1115.
Membership requirements applicable to city, HG §13-1111.
Comprehensive plan for cancer prevention, education, screening and treatment, HG §13-1115.
Baltimore county.
Community health coalition.
Membership requirements applicable to county, HG §13-1111.
Comprehensive plan for cancer prevention, education, screening and treatment program.
Requirements applicable to county, HG §13-1109.
Baseline cancer study, HG §13-1103.
Defined, HG §13-1101.
Biennial cancer study, HG §§13-1103, 13-1104.
Budget bill to include appropriations for funding, SF §7-114.
Budget requirements, HG §13-1102.
Community health coalition, HG §13-1111.
Baltimore City, HG §13-1115.
Established before applying for grant, HG §13-1109.

CANCER PREVENTION, EDUCATION, SCREENING AND TREATMENT PROGRAM —Cont'd
Components of program set out, HG §13-1102.
Comprehensive plan for cancer prevention, education, screening and treatment.
Baltimore City, HG §13-1115.
Defined, HG §13-1101.
Developed before applying for grant, requirements, HG §13-1109.
Review, HG §13-1113.
Definitions, HG §13-1101.
Established, HG §13-1102.
Expenditure overview, budget books to contain, SF §7-121.
Funded from cigarette restitution fund, HG §13-1102.
Goals for counties, establishment, HG §13-1108.
Identification of targeted cancers, initiation of program, HG §13-1102.
Inventory of number of publicly funded screening programs.
Developed before distribution of grants, HG §§13-1105, 13-1112.
Johns Hopkins institutions.
Collaboration with community health coalition, HG §13-1114.
Defined, HG §13-1101.
Statewide academic health center cancer research grant, HG §13-1116.
Statewide academic health center network grant, HG §13-1118.
Statewide academic health center public health grants, HG §13-1115.
Statewide academic health center tobacco related diseases grant, HG §13-1117.
Local public health cancer grants.
Application, HG §13-1109.
Joint application, HG §13-1110.
Defined, HG §13-1101.
Distribution, HG §13-1108.
Inventory of number of publicly funded screening programs.
Developed before distribution of grants, HG §13-1105.
Inventory of publicly funded programs before receiving grant, HG §13-1112.
Regions, joint application, amount distributed, HG §13-1110.
Requirements before applying, HG §13-1109.
Spending base-year funding required for distribution, HG §13-1112.
Use to supplement base-year funding prohibited, HG §13-1112.
Local public health component, HG §13-1107.
Defined, HG §13-1101.
Montgomery county.
Community health coalition.
Membership requirements applicable to county, HG §13-1111.
Comprehensive plan for cancer prevention, education, screening and treatment program.
Requirements applicable to county, HG §13-1109.
Prince George's county.
Community health coalition.
Membership requirements applicable to county, HG §13-1111.
Comprehensive plan for cancer prevention, education, screening and treatment program.
Requirements applicable to county, HG §13-1109.

CANCER PREVENTION, EDUCATION, SCREENING AND TREATMENT PROGRAM —Cont'd
Purpose, HG §13-1102.
Regulations, adoption, HG §13-1102.
Report by department, HG §13-1102.
Reversion of unspent allocated money, HG §13-1102.
Statewide academic health center cancer research grant, HG §13-1116.
Defined, HG §13-1101.
Statewide academic health center component, HG §13-1114.
Defined, HG §13-1101.
Statewide academic health center network grant, HG §13-1118.
Defined, HG §13-1118.
Statewide academic health center public health grants, HG §13-1115.
Defined, HG §13-1101.
Statewide academic health center tobacco related diseases grant, HG §13-1117.
Defined, HG §13-1101.
Tobacco-related diseases defined, HG §13-1101.
Statewide anti-cancer initiatives, HG §13-1106.
Statewide public health component, HG §13-1106.
Defined, HG §13-1101.
Surveillance and evaluation component, HG §13-1103.
Defined, HG §13-1101.
University of Maryland medical group.
Collaboration with community health coalition, HG §13-1114.
Defined, HG §13-1101.
Statewide academic health center cancer research grant, HG §13-1116.
Statewide academic health center network grant, HG §13-1118.
Statewide academic health center public health grants, HG §13-1115.
Statewide academic health center tobacco related diseases grant, HG §13-1117.

C. & F.
Sale of goods, UCC, CL §§2-320, 2-321.

CANDIDATES FOR PUBLIC OR PARTY OFFICE.
Generally, EL §§5-101 to 5-1303.
See ELECTIONS.

CANDY.
Adulteration.
Rules and regulations, HG §21-209.
Alcoholic beverages.
Confectionery products containing alcohol, HG §21-209.
Food, drug and cosmetic act.
See FOOD, DRUGS AND COSMETICS.

CANTALOUPES.
Anne Arundel county.
Subtitle not applicable, AG §10-909.
Certificates.
Inspection certificates, AG §10-905.
Closed containers.
Defined, AG §10-901.
Labeling, AG §10-904.
Standard grades, AG §10-904.
Grades.
Standard grades.
Closed containers, AG §10-904.

CANTALOUPES —Cont'd
Immature cantaloupes.
Sale.
Not in closed containers, AG §10-906.
Inspections.
Certificates of inspection, AG §10-905.
General provisions, AG §10-903.
Right of entry, AG §10-903.
Sale of uninspected cantaloupes, AG §10-905.
Labels.
Closed containers, AG §10-904.
Mature cantaloupes.
Defined, AG §10-901.
Migrant labor.
General provisions, LE §§7-101 to 7-507.
See MIGRANT LABOR.
Penalties generally, AG §§12-101 to 12-104.
Prosecution.
State's attorney, AG §10-908.
Violations.
Persons not party to and without knowledge of wrong, AG §10-907.
Right of entry.
Inspection, AG §10-903.
Rules and regulations.
Adoption and enforcement, AG §10-902.
Sale.
Immature cantaloupes.
Not in closed containers, AG §10-906.
Uninspected cantaloupes, AG §10-905.
Secretary of agriculture.
Rules and regulations.
Adoption and enforcement, AG §10-902.
Standard grades.
Closed containers, AG §10-904.
State's attorney.
Prosecutions, AG §10-908.
Violations.
Nonliable persons.
Not party to and without knowledge of wrong, AG §10-907.

CANVASS.
Generally, EL §§11-101 to 11-605.
See ELECTIONS.

CAPACITY TO SUE OR BE SUED.
Parties.
Circuit courts, CivProCir Rule 2-202.
District Court, CivProDist Rule 3-202.
Pleadings.
Circuit courts, CivProCir Rule 2-304.

CAPITAL CITY.
Commission on the capital city, SG §§9-401 to 9-407.
Chairman, SG §9-404.
Definition of "commission," SG §9-401.
Established, SG §9-402.
Funds, SG §9-407.
Meetings, SG §9-405.
Members, SG §9-403.
Powers and duties, SG §9-406.

CAPITAL DEBT MANAGEMENT PROGRAM.
Capital debt affordability committee.
General obligation debt, SF §§8-108 to 8-112.
See PUBLIC DEBT.

CAPITAL PROGRAM, SF §§3-601 to 3-609.
See PLANNING.

CAPITAL PUNISHMENT.
See DEATH PENALTY.

CAP ON DAMAGES.
Health care malpractice claims.
Noneconomic damages, limitation, CJ §3-2A-09.
Noneconomic damages in personal injury
action, CJ §11-108.

CAPPING.
Attorneys at law, BOP §10-604.

CARCINOGENIC FIRE RETARDANTS.
Flammable substances, HG §22-404.

CAR COMPANIES.
Defined as common carrier, PUC §1-101.

CARD GAMES.
Carroll county.
Prohibition, CR §13-906.
Howard county.
Prohibited, CR §§13-1603, 13-1604.
Queen Anne's county, CR §§13-2001 to 13-2006.
St. Mary's county, CR §§13-2111 to 13-2115.

CARDIAC ARREST.
Automated external defibrillator program, ED
§13-517.
County boards of education to develop and
implement programs, ED §7-425.

CARDIAC CONDITION.
Identification bracelet, tag or card.
Persons with condition wearing, CP §2-107.

CARDIAC RESCUE TECHNICIANS.
Performance of specified medical procedures,
ED §13-516.

CARDIOPULMONARY RESUSCITATION.
Family day care homes.
Current certification.
Regulations to provide, FL §5-551.

CARDIOVASCULAR DISEASE PREVENTION
PROGRAMS, HG §§13-201 to 13-206.
See HEART DISEASE AND STROKE
PREVENTION PROGRAMS.

CARD PARTIES.
Prince George's county.
Benefit performance by qualified organization, CR
§§13-1901 to 13-1907.

CAREER AND TECHNOLOGY EDUCATION.
Community colleges.
Use of land, buildings, etc., in connection with
education, ED §16-103.
County advisory councils, ED §21-101.
Definitions, ED §21-201.
Eyes.
Protective eye devices.
Career and technology classrooms or
laboratories, ED §7-407.
Federal aid.
Acceptance, ED §21-202.
Funds.
Maintenance and use of funds received under act,
ED §21-202.
Goals, ED §21-203.
Librarians.
Salaries.
General provisions, ED §6-302.
Purpose of programs, ED §21-203.
Schools.
Development of plans and objectives to assess
status and needs, ED §2-205.
State treasurer.
Custodian of funds, ED §21-202.

CAREER AND TECHNOLOGY EDUCATION
—Cont'd
Teachers.
Salaries.
General provisions, ED §6-302.

CAREGIVERS.
Attendant care program.
Community attendant services and supports
program, 41 §§6-7A-01 to 6-7A-06.
Generally, 41 §§18-601 to 18-604.
See ATTENDANT CARE PROGRAM.
Maryland caregivers support coordinating
council, 88A §129A.

CARGO.
Wrongful disposal, CR §8-405.

CARJACKING, CR §3-405.
Armed carjacking, CR §3-405.
Intention not to permanently deprive owner.
Not defense, CR §3-405.
Mandatory sentence for crime of violence.
Second, third or fourth conviction, CR §14-101.

CARNAL KNOWLEDGE.
Rape.
See RAPE.

CARNIVAL.
Amusements and recreation.
General provisions, BR §§3-101 to 3-601.
See AMUSEMENTS AND RECREATION.
Gaming events and gaming devices.
Acceptance of credit to play gaming event.
Prohibition, CR §12-108.
Anne Arundel county, CR §§13-401 to 13-408.
Baltimore City, CR §§13-501 to 13-510.
Baltimore county, CR §§13-601 to 13-607.
Calvert county, CR §§13-701 to 13-709.
Carroll county, CR §§13-901 to 13-909.
Cecil county, CR §§13-1001 to 13-1005.
Charles county, CR §§13-1101 to 13-1115.
Dorchester county, CR §§13-1201 to 13-1207.
Frederick county, CR §§13-1301 to 13-1307.
Prince George's county.
Benefit performance by qualified organization,
CR §§13-1901 to 13-1907.
Provisions applicable to several counties, CR
§§13-101 to 13-205.
St. Mary's county, CR §§13-2111 to 13-2115.
Somerset county, CR §13-2201.
Talbot county.
Provisions applicable to county, CR §13-2301.

CAROLINE COUNTY.
Alcoholic beverages.
Bar and counter sales.
Sundays, 2B §11-403.
Beer and light wine licenses.
Annual license fee, 2B §5-201.
Class A, off-sale, 2B §5-101.
Class B, on-sale, 2B §5-401.
Class H, on-sale only, 2B §5-202.
Hours and days of sale, 2B §§11-302, 11-403,
11-506.
Beer and wine (on-premises) tasting license.
Class BWTS, 2B §8-404.2.
Beer licenses.
Class A, off-sale, 2B §3-101.
Class B, on-sale, 2B §3-201.
Class C, on-sale, 2B §3-301.
Class D, on-sale, 2B §3-401.
Hours and days of sale, 2B §§11-301, 11-506.

CAROLINE COUNTY —Cont'd
Alcoholic beverages —Cont'd
Beer, wine and liquor licenses.
  Bar and counter sales.
    Sundays, 2B §11-403.
  Caterer's license, 2B §6-702.1.
  Class A, off-sale, 2B §6-101.
  Class B, on-sale, 2B §6-401.
  Class C, on-sale, 2B §6-301.
  Hours and days of sale, 2B §§11-303, 11-403,
    11-506.
Clubs.
  Beer licenses.
    Class C, on-sale, 2B §3-301.
  Beer, wine and liquor licenses.
    Class C, on-sale, 2B §6-301.
Disorderly intoxication.
  Ordinances or resolutions, 2B §19-103.
Elections.
  Exercise of privileges of licensee on election day,
    2B §11-401.
Gambling.
  Persons under age 18 engaging in games of
    chance or skill, 2B §12-206.
Golf courses.
  Class GC beer, wine and liquor license, 2B
    §8-507.1.
Hotels and restaurants.
  Beer and wine licenses.
    Class H, on-sale only, 2B §5-202.
  Beer licenses.
    Class B, on-sale, 2B §3-201.
  Beer, wine and liquor licenses.
    Class B, on-sale, 2B §6-201.
Hours and days for sale.
  Bar and counter sales, 2B §11-403.
  Beer license, 2B §11-301.
  Beer, wine and liquor licenses, 2B §§11-303,
    11-403, 11-506.
  Election days, 2B §11-401.
  General provisions, 2B §11-506.
  New Year's day, 2B §11-402.
  Sundays, 2B §11-403.
  Wholesaler's license, 2B §11-102.
Inspectors.
  County codes administrator is inspector, 2B
    §15-112.
  Duties, 2B §15-112.
  Salaries, 2B §15-112.
License commissioners.
  Appointment.
    By governor, 2B §15-101.
  Expenses, 2B §15-109.
  Inspection of applicant and premises, 2B
    §10-202.
  Liquor control board constitutes board of license
    commissioners, 2B §15-101.
  Salaries, 2B §15-109.
  Substitute member, 2B §15-101.
  Terms of office, 2B §15-101.
  Vacancies, 2B §15-101.
Licenses.
  Application, 2B §9-102.
    Exceptions, 2B §10-104.
  Commissioners. See within this subheading,
    "License commissioners."
  Death of licensee.
    Procedure, 2B §10-506.
  Expiration, 2B §10-206.
  Fees.
    Collection and disposition, 2B §10-204.

CAROLINE COUNTY —Cont'd
Alcoholic beverages —Cont'd
Licenses —Cont'd
  Fees —Cont'd
    Refund, 2B §10-206.
  Issuance.
    Date, 2B §10-206.
    Procedure, 2B §10-202.
    Refusal to issue.
      Reapplication, 2B §10-208.
  Refusal.
    Reapplication, 2B §10-208.
  Regulations of purchases, 2B §15-204.
  Revocation and suspension.
    Nudity and sexual displays on licensee's
      premises, 2B §10-405.
  Special licenses, 2B §7-101.
  Wholesalers.
    Hours and days for sale, 2B §11-102.
Liquor control board.
  Applicability of subtitle, 2B §15-210.
  Appointment.
    Generally, 2B §15-201.
  Books and records.
    Audit, 2B §15-206.
  Compensation, 2B §15-201.
  Control of purchases by licensees, 2B §15-204.
  County dispensaries.
    Regulations of purchases, 2B §15-204.
  Members constitute board of license
    commissioners, 2B §15-101.
  Qualifications, 2B §15-201.
  Records and reports.
    Audit, 2B §15-206.
  Term of office, 2B §15-201.
Minors.
  Possession prohibited, 2B §12-108.
  Selling or furnishing, 2B §12-108.
Nudity and sexual displays on licensee's premises.
  Revocation of license, 2B §10-405.
One-day class BWTS beer and wine (on-premises)
  tasting license, 2B §8-404.2.
Open containers.
  Possession in certain places, 2B §19-303.
Sales.
  Beer for cash, 2B §12-112.
  Election days, 2B §11-401.
  New Year's day, 2B §11-402.
Taverns.
  Beer, wine and liquor licenses.
    Class D, on sale, 2B §6-401.
Amusement parks.
  Permits required, 25 §27.
Appearance fees in circuit courts.
  Distribution, CJ §7-204.
Bailiff.
  Compensation, CJ §2-507.
Birds and game.
  Spotlighting, NR §10-410.
Boxing and wrestling arenas.
  Permits required, 25 §27.
Building code.
  Provision for, 25 §3.
Caterers.
  Beer, wine and liquor licenses, 2B §6-702.1.
**Chesapeake Bay critical area and Atlantic
  coastal bays critical area protection
  programs.**
  Critical areas commission.
    Members on commission, NR §8-1804.

CAROLINE COUNTY —Cont'd

Chesapeake Bay critical area and Atlantic coastal bays critical area protection programs —Cont'd

Growth allocation, location in resource conservation area, NR §8-1808.1.

Circuit court.

Appearance fees.

Distribution, CJ §7-204.

Number of judges, CJ §1-503.

Codes.

Building, electrical and plumbing codes.

Adoption, 25 §3.

Commissioners.

Alcoholic beverages.

License commissioners. See within this heading, "Alcoholic beverages."

Powers.

Enumerated, 25 §3.

Community Civic League, Inc.

Day care center facility.

Property tax credits, TP §9-307.

County board of elections.

Compensation, EL §2-204.

Confirmation of member by house of delegates, EL §2-201.

County boards generally, EL §§2-201 to 2-303.

See ELECTIONS.

Court crier.

Compensation, CJ §2-507.

Courts.

Circuit court.

Appearance fees, CJ §7-204.

Judicial circuit, MD Const Art IV §19.

Number of judges, CJ §1-503.

Dance halls.

Permits required, 25 §27.

Dangerous weapons.

Minors carrying, prohibited hours, CR §4-101.

Dog and kennel licenses, 24 §11-501.

Dog licenses.

Rules and regulations, 24 §11-504.

Dog wardens and pounds, 24 §11-504.

Drunkenness.

Disorderly intoxication.

Ordinances or resolutions, 2B §19-103.

Eastern Shore Threshermen and Collectors Association, Inc.

Property tax credits, TP §9-307.

Fire department.

Firefighters appointed as deputy sheriffs, PS §§7-301 to 7-303.

Fish and fisheries.

Restrictions in county waters, NR §4-716.

Riparian rights, NR §4-712.

Gambling.

Alcoholic beverages.

Class A beer, wine or liquor licenses.

Persons under age 18 engaging in games of chance or skill, 2B §12-206.

Gaming, bazaar, carnival and raffles, CR §§13-201 to 13-205.

Conducting event for benefit of qualified organization.

Allowed, CR §13-203.

Definitions, CR §13-201.

Gaming event defined, CR §13-201.

Individual benefit prohibited, CR §13-203.

Management through organizations members, CR §13-205.

Prizes and gaming devices allowed, CR §13-204.

CAROLINE COUNTY —Cont'd

Gaming, bazaar, carnival and raffles —Cont'd

Provisions applicable to county, CR §§13-202, 13-301, 13-801.

Qualified organization defined, CR §13-201.

Golf courses.

Class GC beer, wine and liquor license, 2B §8-507.1.

Habitat for Humanity, Incorporated.

Property tax credit, TP §9-307.

Hotels and restaurants.

Alcoholic beverages. See within this heading, "Alcoholic beverages."

Housing code.

Provision for, 25 §3.

Investigations.

Funds for special investigations, 25 §3.

Jail.

Employment of inmate as alternative to confinement.

Payment by inmate for restitution and food, lodging and clothing, COR §11-707.

Licenses.

Alcoholic beverages. See within this heading, "Alcoholic beverages."

Marshyhope Rod and Gun Club, Inc.

Property tax credits, TP §9-307.

Maryland Ornithological Society, Inc.

Property tax credits, TP §9-307.

Minors.

Alcoholic beverages.

Class A beer, wine or liquor licenses.

Persons under age 18 engaging in games of chance or skill, 2B §12-206.

Possession prohibited, 2B §12-108.

Dangerous weapons, carrying.

Prohibited hours, CR §4-101.

Mortgages and deeds of trust.

Interest.

Payable after sale, RP §7-105.

Orphans' court.

Compensation of judge, ET §2-108.

Permits.

Dance halls and other places of amusement, tourist camps, etc., 25 §27.

Personal property.

Purchase or lease of.

Power of Caroline county, 25 §9D.

Plumbing code.

Provision for, 25 §3.

Recordation.

Plats of subdivision.

Copies of certain plats, RP §3-108.

Schools.

County board of education.

Expenses, ED §4-107.

Health program, ED §7-415.

Health care providers, ED §7-417.

Holidays, ED §7-103.

Sheriff.

Deputies, appointment, CJ §2-309.

Firefighters appointed as deputy sheriffs, PS §§7-301 to 7-303.

Salary, CJ §2-309.

Second in command, CJ §2-310.

Slot machines.

Ownership and operation by eligible organization, CR §12-304.

State's attorney, 10 §40.

Subdivisions.

Plats.

Recordation.

Copies of certain plats, RP §3-108.

CAROLINE COUNTY —Cont'd
Sundays and holidays.
Alcoholic beverages.
    Sales on New Year's day, 2B §11-402.
Taxation.
Assessments.
    Date of finality.
        Decreases in assessments after date, TP
           §8-419.
Credits.
    Property tax credits, TP §9-307.
Delinquent taxes.
    Interest penalty, TP §14-603.
Exemptions.
    Personal property.
        Commercial, manufacturing or professional
           businesses, TP §7-510.
Redemption.
    Rate of redemption, TP §14-820.
Sales.
    Expenses of sales.
        Auctioneer's fee, TP §14-813.
Tourist camps.
Permits required, 25 §27.
Treasurer.
Draining lands.
    Fees.
        Payment into general fund, 25 §89.
Generally, 25 §51.
Weapons.
Target practice without landowner permission, CR
    §4-108.
Witnesses.
Mileage, CJ §9-202.
**Work release program for inmates confinement
    county jail.**
Employment of inmate as alternative to
    confinement.
    Payment by inmate for restitution and food,
        lodging and clothing, COR §11-707.

CARP.
Fish and fisheries.
See FISH AND FISHERIES.

CARRIER PIGEONS.
Injuring or trapping, CR §10-622.

CARRIERS.
Alcoholic beverages.
Planes and ships.
    Cocktail lounge in use by passengers.
        No license or permit required, 2B §1-201.
Records and reports.
    Required, 2B §14-202.
Sales.
    Permitted without license or permit, 2B §1-201.
Annual reports by public service companies,
    PUC §§6-201 to 6-210.
Aviation.
Charter permits.
    See AVIATION.
Bankruptcy and insolvency.
Advancement by one common carrier to another of
    money for freight, CL §15-102.
Bills of lading.
Inducing carrier to issue bill when goods not
    received, CL §18-204.
Possession.
    Negotiation of bill when goods not in carrier's
        possession, CL §18-203.

CARRIERS —Cont'd
Blind persons.
Rights of blind persons to public facilities, 30 §33.
Classification of common carrier companies,
    PUC §6-202.
Commercial drivers' licenses.
General provisions.
    See COMMERCIAL DRIVERS' LICENSES.
Common carriers.
Compensation for transporting passengers over
    same line and in same direction, PUC §9-102.
Defined, PUC §1-101.
Inflammable liquids and products.
    See INFLAMMABLE LIQUIDS AND
        PRODUCTS.
Interchange and transfer of passengers between
    lines and lines of other common carriers, PUC
    §9-101.
Railroads.
    Generally, PUC §§9-301 to 9-403.
        See RAILROADS.
Safety violations, penalty, PUC §13-202.
Vital records.
    See VITAL RECORDS.
Compacts.
Transit regulation compact.
    General provisions, TR §§10-201 to 10-207.
**Compensation for common carrier for
    transporting passengers over same line
    and in same direction,** PUC §9-102.
Contract carriers.
Inflammable liquids and products.
    See INFLAMMABLE LIQUIDS AND
        PRODUCTS.
Criminal procedure.
Venue.
    Crimes committed on common carriers, CP
        §4-201.
Damages.
Limitation of liability.
    Carrier issuing bill of lading, CL §7-309.
Deaf or mute persons.
Rights of deaf or mute persons to public facilities,
    30 §33.
Drivers' licenses.
Commercial drivers' licenses.
    See COMMERCIAL DRIVERS' LICENSES.
Evidence.
Food, drugs and cosmetics.
    Use of evidence against carrier prohibited, HG
        §21-250.
Food, drugs and cosmetics.
Evidence.
    Use of evidence against carrier prohibited, HG
        §21-250.
Records.
    Inspection of records, HG §21-250.
Freight.
Sale of unclaimed freight, BR §19-102.
Household goods movers act.
Enforcing carrier's lien during intrastate move,
    CL §§14-3101 to 14-3104.
Inflammable liquids and products.
See INFLAMMABLE LIQUIDS AND
    PRODUCTS.
Inspections.
Records.
    Food, drugs and cosmetics.
        Inspection of records, HG §21-250.
Insurance.
Agents and brokers.
    Limited lines licenses, IN §10-122.

CARRIERS —Cont'd
Insurance —Cont'd
Blanket health insurance.
Eligible persons and organizations, IN §15-305.
Transportation ticket health insurance, IN §15-1103.
Interchange and transfer of passengers between lines and lines of other common carriers, PUC §9-101.
Intrastate moves.
Enforcing carrier's lien during intrastate move, CL §§14-3101 to 14-3104.
Liabilities.
Contractual limitation of liability.
Carrier issuing bill of lading, CL §7-309.
Liens, CL §7-307.
Enforcement, CL §7-308.
Maryland Transit Administration.
General provisions.
See MARYLAND TRANSIT ADMINISTRATION.
Metropolitan transit authority.
General provisions.
See METROPOLITAN TRANSIT DISTRICT.
Mile tickets, commission ordering to issue, PUC §5-102.
Negligence.
Contractual limitation of liability.
Bill of lading, CL §7-309.
Duty of carrier.
Carrier issuing bill of lading, CL §7-309.
Notices.
Sales.
Unclaimed freight, BR §19-102.
Permits for motor carriers, PUC §§9-201 to 9-204.
Poultry products inspection.
Liability of carrier, AG §4-227.
Procedure before public service commission.
Generally, PUC §§3-101 to 3-114.
See PUBLIC SERVICE COMMISSION.
Public service commission.
Generally, PUC §§2-101 to 5-106.
See PUBLIC SERVICE COMMISSION.
Railroads.
Generally, PUC §§9-301 to 9-403.
See RAILROADS.
Rate regulation and proceedings.
Generally, PUC §§4-101 to 4-503.
See PUBLIC SERVICE COMMISSION.
Through routes and joint rates, commission orders, PUC §5-102.
Records.
Food, drugs and cosmetics.
Inspection of records, HG §21-250.
Safety violations by common carriers, penalty, PUC §13-202.
Sale of unclaimed freight, BR §19-102.
Taxation.
Motor carrier tax, TG §§2-1001, 2-1002, 9-201 to 9-222.
See MOTOR CARRIER TAX.
Through routes and joint rates, commission orders, PUC §5-102.
Transit regulation compact, TR §§10-201 to 10-207.
Venue.
Crimes committed on common carriers, CP §4-201.
Washington metropolitan area transit authority.
General provisions, TR §10-204.

CARRIER'S LIEN.
Household goods movers.
Enforcing during intrastate move.
Prohibition, CL §14-3102.
Definitions, CL §14-3101.
Unfair or deceptive trade practice, penalty, CL §14-3103.
Short title, CL §14-3104.

CARRIER TRANSFER TICKETS.
Selling or giving to unauthorized person, CR §8-903.

CARROLL COUNTY.
Alcoholic beverages.
Bar and counter sales.
Sundays, 2B §11-403.
Beer and light wine licenses.
Class A, off-sale, 2B §5-101.
Class B, on-sale, 2B §5-201.
Class C, on-sale, 2B §5-301.
Class C, seven days, 2B §7-101.
Class D, on-sale, 2B §5-401.
Beer licenses.
Class A, off-sale, 2B §3-101.
Class B, on-sale, 2B §3-201.
Class C, on-sale, 2B §3-301.
Class C, seven days, 2B §7-101.
Class D, on-sale, 2B §3-401.
Festival license, 2B §8-805.
Beer tasting license, 2B §8-901.
Beer, wine and liquor licenses.
Class A, off-sale, 2B §6-101.
Class B, on-sale, 2B §6-201.
Class C (golf course) beer, wine and liquor (on-sale) license, 2B §8-501.
Class C, on-sale.
Special and temporary licenses, 2B §7-101.
Class C, seven days, 2B §7-101.
Class H, 2B §6-703.
Club licenses, 2B §6-301.
Fire department.
Class C licenses, 2B §7-101.
Criminal history records checks.
License applicants, 2B §10-103.
Election days, 2B §11-401.
Fines and forfeitures, 2B §16-502.
Local penalties, 2B §16-507.
Hours and days for sale, 2B §11-507.
Election days, 2B §11-401.
Manufacturer's license, 2B §11-101.
New Year's day, 2B §11-402.
License commissioners.
Appeals.
General provisions, 2B §16-101.
Appointment.
By county commissioners, 2B §15-104.
Exemption from hearing requirement, 2B §10-202.
Salaries, 2B §15-109.
Substitute member.
Appointment, 2B §15-104.
Licenses.
Applications.
Exceptions, 2B §10-104.
Beer festival license, 2B §8-805.
Commissioners. See within this subheading, "License commissioners."
Criminal history records checks.
License applicants, 2B §10-103.
Death of licensee.
Procedure, 2B §10-506.

CARROLL COUNTY —Cont'd
Alcoholic beverages —Cont'd
Licenses —Cont'd
Fees.
Beer, wine and liquor licenses.
Class C, seven days, 2B §7-101.
Disposition, 2B §10-204.
Transfer or assignment of license, 2B §10-503.
Issuance, 2B §10-202.
Manufacturers.
Hours and days for sale, 2B §11-101.
Maryland wine festival.
Special license, 2B §8-306.
Micro-brewery licenses, 2B §9-207.
Renewal.
Late fees, 2B §10-301.
Residency requirement, 2B §10-103.
Revocation and suspension.
Nudity and sexual displays on licensee's
premises, 2B §10-405.
Transfer or assignment of license, 2B §10-503.
Wine tasting licenses, 2B §8-405.
Light wine licenses.
Class A, off-sale, 2B §4-201.
Manufacturers.
Licenses.
Hours and days for sale, 2B §11-101.
Maryland wine festival, 2B §8-306.
Micro-brewery licenses, 2B §2-208.
Minors.
Employment of minors by retail dealers.
Special provisions, 2B §12-302.
Sales to minors prohibited, 2B §12-108.
Nudity and sexual displays on licensee's premises.
Revocation of license, 2B §10-405.
Open containers.
Possession in certain places.
Applicability of provisions, 2B §19-303.
Sales.
Drunkards and mentally deficient persons.
Sales to prohibited, 2B §12-110.
Minors and intoxicated persons.
Sales to prohibited, 2B §12-108.
New Year's day, 2B §11-402.
Special wine festival (WF) license, 2B §8-306.1.
Summons.
Records and papers, 2B §16-410.
Sundays.
Bar and counter sales, 2B §11-403.
Amusement parks.
Permits required, 25 §27.
Appearance fees in circuit courts.
Distribution, CJ §7-204.
Bailiff.
Compensation, CJ §2-507.
Beer tasting license, 2B §8-901.
Bingo, CR §§13-907, 13-908.
Limitations on conducting, CR §13-907.
Permit required, CR §13-907.
Prizes, CR §13-908.
Birds and game.
Spotlighting, NR §10-410.
Trapping.
Snare traps, NR §10-410.
Boxing and wrestling arenas.
Permits required, 25 §27.
Bridges.
Power to regulate construction and use, 25 §10B.
Cemeteries.
Requirements, RP §14-119.

CARROLL COUNTY —Cont'd
Circuit courts.
Appearance fees.
Distribution, CJ §7-204.
Number of judges, CJ §1-503.
Commissioners.
Development impact fees.
Power to fix, impose and collect, 25 §9F.
Roads and bridges.
Powers as to, 25 §10B.
School board property no longer needed.
Power of commissioners to negotiate for sale, 25
§11A.
Surplus supplies, equipment or other personal
property.
Disposal by commissioners, methods, 25 §11A.
Courts.
Circuit courts.
Judicial circuit, MD Const Art IV §19.
Number of judges, CJ §1-503.
Criminal history records checks.
Current or prospective employees, CP §10-232.
Dance halls.
Permits required, 25 §27.
Deeds.
Straw deeds.
Recordation, RP §3-104.
Detention center.
Home detention program, COR §11-708.
Work release program and rehabilitation
activities, COR §11-708.
Development impact fees.
Commissioners.
Power to fix, impose and collect, 25 §9F.
Dog and kennel licenses, 24 §11-501.
Dog licenses.
Rules and regulations, 24 §11-504.
Dog wardens, 24 §11-504.
Domestic animals.
Regulation, 24 §11-511.
Drive-thru facilities.
Alcoholic beverages, 2B §12-207.
Elections.
Alcoholic beverages.
Days of elections, 2B §11-401.
County board of elections.
County boards generally, EL §§2-201 to 2-303.
See ELECTIONS.
Erosion prevention works.
Annual benefit assessment, 25 §165.
Fines.
Alcoholic beverages.
Violations, 2B §§16-502, 16-507.
Disposition, CJ §7-507.
Fire department.
Firefighters appointed as deputy sheriffs, PS
§§7-301 to 7-303.
Fish and fisheries.
Bush-bobs or bank poles, NR §4-617.
Certain lines or nets regulated, NR §4-620.
Forfeitures.
Disposition, CJ §7-507.
Gaming, bazaar, carnival and raffles, CR
§§13-201 to 13-205, 13-901 to 13-909.
Billiard games.
Prizes allowed, CR §13-905.
Card games, dice games, roulette or casino night.
Prohibition on conducting, CR §13-906.
Conducting event for benefit of qualified
organization.
Allowed, CR §13-203.

CARROLL COUNTY —Cont'd
Gaming, bazaar, carnival and raffles —Cont'd
Definitions, CR §§13-201, 13-901.
Gaming event defined, CR §§13-201, 13-901.
Individual benefit prohibited, CR §13-203.
Limitations on conducting gaming event, CR §13-903.
Management through organizations members, CR §13-205.
Paddle wheel or wheel of fortune.
Prizes allowed, CR §13-905.
Permit required to conduct gaming event, CR §13-903.
Prizes and gaming devices allowed, CR §§13-204, 13-906.
Provisions applicable to county, CR §§13-202, 13-301, 13-902.
Qualified organizations to conduct, listed, CR §§13-201, 13-903.
Raffles generally, CR §13-904.
Unauthorized gaming event, penalty, CR §13-909.
Golf courses.
Beer, wine and liquor licenses.
Class C (golf course) beer, wine and liquor (on-sale) license, 2B §8-501.
Historic area zoning.
General provisions.
See ZONING.
Historic districts.
Property tax credits, TP §9-308.
Hotels and restaurants.
Beer and light wine licenses.
Class B, on-sale, 2B §5-201.
Beer and wine and liquor licenses.
Class B, on-sale, 2B §6-201.
Beer licenses.
Class B, on sale, 2B §3-201.
Inmates confined in detention center, employment, COR §9-516.
Jaycees.
Property tax credits, TP §9-308.
Licenses.
Alcoholic beverages. See within this heading, "Alcoholic beverages."
Maryland food center authority.
General provisions, 41 §§13-101 to 13-123.
See MARYLAND FOOD CENTER AUTHORITY.
Maryland wine festival, 2B §8-306.
Mining.
Surface mining.
Dewatering in karst terrain, EN §§15-812, 15-813.
Minors.
Alcoholic beverages.
Employment of minors regulated, 2B §12-302.
Sales to minors prohibited, 2B §12-108.
Monocacy river.
Speed limit on certain areas, NR §8-725.6.
Motor vehicles.
Size and weight.
Power of county commissioners, 25 §25.
Tires.
Studs, cleats, etc.
Use allowed during certain months, TR §22-405.2.
Nonprofit community or civic improvement association or corporation.
Property tax credits, TP §9-308.
Northeast Maryland waste disposal authority.
Participating county, NR §3-903.

CARROLL COUNTY —Cont'd
Oil pipeline corporation acquiring property under power to condemn, PUC §5-404.
Orphans' court.
Judges.
Compensation, ET §2-108.
Permits.
Dance halls and other places of amusement, tourist camps, etc., 25 §27.
Planning and zoning commission.
Abatement of violation of zoning ordinance.
Assessment of costs, 66B §14.03.
Alternate member designated from planning commission, 66B §14.03.
Member of board of county commissioners appointed to commission, 66B §14.03.
Planning commission.
Special provisions, 66B §3.02.
Political parties.
Central committees.
Election of members, EL §4-203.
Real property.
Purchase, sale or transfer, 25 §5D.
Sale.
Private sale.
Public sale fails to yield reasonable price, 25 §11A.
School property no longer needed.
Power of commissioners to negotiate for sale, 25 §11A.
Recordation.
Rights of way.
Recordation of plats, RP §3-109.1.
Straw deeds.
Exceptions as to Carroll county, RP §3-104.
Rights of way.
Recordation of plats, RP §3-109.1.
Roads.
Power to regulate construction, use, etc., 25 §10B.
Sales.
Alcoholic beverages. See within this heading, "Alcoholic beverages."
Schools.
County board of education.
Chairman, ED §3-402.
Compensation, ED §3-403.
Compensation, ED §3-403.
Composition, ED §3-401.
Election of members, ED §§3-114, 3-401.
Executive sessions, ED §3-404.
Meetings, ED §3-404.
Members, ED §3-401.
Membership, ED §3-401.
Persons subject to authority of board.
Ineligibility to serve as member, ED §3-114.
Qualifications, ED §3-401.
Records.
Public records, ED §3-404.
Removal of members, ED §3-401.
Term of office, ED §3-401.
Vacancies, ED §3-401.
Sheriff.
Firefighters appointed as deputy sheriffs, PS §§7-301 to 7-303.
General provisions, CJ §2-309.
Second in command, CJ §2-310.
State's attorney, 10 §40.
Sundays and holidays.
Alcoholic beverages.
Hours and days for sale, 2B §11-507.
Sales on New Year's day, 2B §11-402.

CARROLL COUNTY —Cont'd
Surplus supplies, equipment or other personal property.
Disposal by commissioners, methods, 25 §11A.
Sykesville Little League, Inc.
Property tax credits, TP §9-308.
Taxation.
Credits.
Property tax credits, TP §9-308.
Hotel rental tax, 24 §§9-301 to 9-326.
Redemption.
Rate of redemption, TP §14-820.
Refund of taxes.
Applications for, TP §14-905.
Sale.
Deductions from collections, TP §14-810.
Expenses of sale.
Auctioneer's fee, TP §14-813.
Transportation.
Levy of tax for public transportation services, TR §7-801.
Tobacco product sales, 24 §§15-101 to 15-104.
Tourist camps.
Permits required, 25 §27.
Transient or temporary vendors.
Licenses, 24 §11-301.
Transportation.
Taxation for, TR §7-801.
Trapping.
Snare traps, NR §10-410.
Treasurer.
Salary, 25 §51.
Water and sewer systems.
County plans.
Exceptions to county plan, EN §9-513.
On-site and small community waste water disposal fund, EN §9-1105.
Wine.
Maryland wine festival, 2B §8-306.
Special wine festival (WF) license, 2B §8-306.1.
Wine tasting licenses, 2B §8-405.
Work by inmates confined in detention center, COR §9-516.
Workforce investment act.
Contracts for training of workers, funding, LE §11-504.
Zoning.
General provisions.
See ZONING.
Historic area zoning.
General provisions.
See ZONING.
Subdivision.
Lots.
Sale or transfer in approved subdivisions, 66B §5.05.

CARRYING CONCEALED WEAPON.
Dangerous weapons, CR §4-101.
Warrantless arrest, CP §2-203.

CARRYING, WEARING OR TRANSPORTING HANDGUN.
Prohibition, exceptions, CR §4-203.

CARS.
Motor vehicles generally.
See MOTOR VEHICLES.
Railroads.
See RAILROADS.

CASA PROGRAM.
Children in need of assistance, CJ §3-830.

CASA PROGRAM —Cont'd
Juvenile causes, CJ §3-8A-32.

CASE RECORDS.
Inmates sentenced to jurisdiction of division of correction, COR §§3-601 to 3-609.
Admissibility in evidence, COR §3-605.
Another state, providing record to, COR §3-606.
Character of offense committed by inmate, COR §3-601.
Conduct, effort and progress, COR §3-601.
Disclosure prohibited, exceptions, conditions, COR §3-602.
Division to assemble promptly, COR §3-601.
Exchange of information with division of parole and probation, COR §3-608.
Makeup of record, COR §3-601.
Parole commission, providing record to, COR §3-603.
Police officer of county or municipal corporation, providing, COR §3-607.
Reimbursement by state for cost of providing record, COR §3-604.

CASHIER'S CHECKS.
Negotiable instruments generally, CL §§3-101 to 3-605.
See NEGOTIABLE INSTRUMENTS.

CASINO EVENTS.
Anne Arundel county.
Prohibited in county, CR §13-404.
Baltimore county, CR §13-604.
Carroll county.
Prohibition, CR §13-906.
Prince George's county.
Defined, prohibited, penalty, CR §13-1912.

CASSETTE PLAYERS.
Maryland Transit Administration.
Playing music on transit vehicles or facility, TR §7-705.

CASUALTY INSURANCE.
Fire insurance antiarson applications, IN §§19-301 to 19-309.
See FIRE INSURANCE.
Generally, IN §§19-101 to 19-706.
See PROPERTY AND CASUALTY INSURANCE.
Guaranty corporation, IN §§9-301 to 9-316.
See PROPERTY AND CASUALTY INSURANCE GUARANTY CORPORATION.
Holocaust victims insurance act, IN §§28-101 to 28-110.
See HOLOCAUST VICTIMS INSURANCE.
Homeowner's insurance policies, IN §§19-201 to 19-207.
Insurance pools, IN §§19-601 to 19-603.
Lead hazard coverage for rental property, IN §§19-701 to 19-706.
Motor vehicle insurance.
See MOTOR VEHICLE INSURANCE.
Workers' compensation insurance, IN §§19-402 to 19-406.
Ratemaking, IN §§11-329, 11-330.

CATALYTIC CONVERTERS.
Alteration of air pollution control device, TR §§22-402.1, 22-402.2.

CATASTROPHIC EVENT ACCOUNT, SF §7-324.

CATASTROPHIC HEALTH EMERGENCY.
Construction, SpecPro Rule 15-1101.
Definitions, SpecPro Rule 15-1102.

CATASTROPHIC HEALTH EMERGENCY
—Cont'd

Disease surveillance and response program, HG §§18-901 to 18-908.

Appeals of secretary's quarantine directive, HG §18-906.

Authority of secretary, HG §18-902.

Enforcement, HG §18-905.

Contingency plans.

Development and implementation, HG §18-903.

Definitions, HG §18-901.

Enforcement authority of secretary, HG §18-905.

Health facilities.

Contingency plans, development and implementation, HG §18-903.

Immunity.

Providers acting in good faith in accordance with program, HG §18-907.

Investigation and prevention of exposure.

Authority of secretary, HG §18-902.

Licensing, certifying or credentialing practitioners.

Development of process, HG §18-903.

Noncompliance with order, directive or regulation, HG §18-907.

Noncompliance with order, directive or regulation, HG §18-907.

Orders issued by secretary.

Enforcement authority, HG §18-905.

Protocols and plans to assist practitioners.

Publication by secretary, HG §18-903.

Quarantine.

Directive issued by secretary, hearings, discharge from employment prohibited, HG §18-906.

Report by secretary, HG §18-908.

Reporting or disclosing information.

Methods, limitation on use, confidentiality, HG §18-904.

Proceedings to contest isolation or quarantine.

Answer to petition, SpecPro Rule 15-1103.

Appearance at hearing, SpecPro Rule 15-1104.

Appellate review, SpecPro Rule 15-1107.

Appointment of counsel, SpecPro Rule 15-1104.

Conduct of hearing, SpecPro Rule 15-1104.

Consolidation of actions, claims and issues, SpecPro Rule 15-1104.

Decision and order, SpecPro Rule 15-1105.

Initiation of proceedings, SpecPro Rule 15-1103.

Motion to continue order, SpecPro Rule 15-1106.

Notice, SpecPro Rule 15-1103.

Petition for relief, SpecPro Rule 15-1103.

Stay of an order, SpecPro Rule 15-1105.

Time for hearing, SpecPro Rule 15-1104.

Venue of proceedings, SpecPro Rule 15-1103.

CATASTROPHIC HEALTH INSURANCE POLICIES, IN §15-1101.

CATERERS.
Alcoholic beverages.

Statewide caterers (SCAT) license, 2B §6-701.

Baltimore City.

Beer, wine and liquor licenses, 2B §6-701.1.

Baltimore county.

Beer, wine and liquor licenses, 2B §6-702.

Caroline county.

Beer, wine and liquor licenses, 2B §6-702.1.

Carroll county.

Beer, wine and liquor licenses, 2B §6-201.

Frederick county.

Beer, wine and liquor licenses, 2B §6-703.1.

CATERERS —Cont'd
Garrett county.

Beer, wine and liquor licenses, 2B §6-703.2.

Harford county.

Beer, wine and liquor licenses, 2B §§6-704, 9-213.

Kent county.

Beer, wine and liquor licenses, 2B §6-705.

Montgomery county.

Beer, wine and liquor licenses, 2B §§6-706, 6-706.1.

Prince George's county.

Beer, wine and liquor licenses, 2B §6-201.

Queen Anne's county.

Beer, wine and liquor licenses, 2B §6-707.

St. Mary's county.

Beer, wine and liquor licenses, 2B §6-708.

Volunteer fire company.

Beer, wine and liquor licenses.

Exclusive lease with volunteer fire companies, 2B §6-704.

Wicomico county.

Beer, wine and liquor licenses, 2B §§6-709, 9-102.

Worcester county.

Beer, wine and liquor licenses, 2B §6-710.

CATHOLIC CHURCH.
See ROMAN CATHOLIC CHURCH.

CATS.
Abandoning domestic animal, CR §10-612.

Killing.

Prohibited means, CR §10-611.

Right to kill.

Hunting game birds and animals, NR §10-413.

Kittens.

Selling less than eight week old puppy, CR §10-613.

Motor vehicles.

Standing or parked vehicle.

Cats left in, TR §21-1004.1.

Rules and regulations, 24 §11-504.

State cat.

Calico cat designated as, SG §13-317.

Strays.

When animal deemed, CR §10-615.

Vaccinations.

Required vaccination, HG §18-318.

Responsibilities of veterinarian, HG §18-319.

CATTLE.
Livestock.

General provisions.

See LIVESTOCK.

Stray domestic animals, AG §§3-601 to 3-603.

CAUSTIC OR CORROSIVE SUBSTANCES.
Poisons.

See POISONS.

CAVEATS.
Probate of will.

See WILLS.

CAVES.
Archaeological resources.

Maryland historical trust, SF §5A-343.

See ARCHAEOLOGICAL RESOURCES.

Cave life.

Defined, NR §5-1401.

Disturbing, NR §5-1404.

Collecting permits, NR §5-1404.

Commercial cave.

Defined, NR §5-1401.

CAVES —Cont'd
Crimes and offenses.
Disturbing cave life, NR §5-1404.
Exploration permits, NR §5-1405.
Prohibited uses, NR §5-1402.
Speleothems.
Sale, NR §5-1403.
Definitions, NR §5-1401.
Disturbing cave life, NR §5-1404.
Gate.
Defined, NR §5-1401.
Immunity.
Owners.
Liability, CJ §5-804.
Liability.
Owner, CJ §5-804.
Immunity from liability, NR §5-1406.
Maryland historical trust.
Archaeological resources.
See ARCHAEOLOGICAL RESOURCES.
Misdemeanors.
Disturbing cave life, NR §5-1404.
Exploration permits, NR §5-1405.
Prohibited uses, NR §5-1402.
Speleothems.
Sale, NR §5-1403.
Owner.
Defined, NR §5-1401.
Liability, CJ §5-804; NR §5-1406.
Permits.
Scientific exploration, NR §§5-1404, 5-1405.
Person or persons.
Defined, NR §5-1401.
Prohibited uses, NR §5-1402.
Science.
Collecting permits, NR §5-1404.
Exploration permits, NR §5-1405.
Sinkhole.
Defined, NR §5-1401.
Speleogen.
Defined, NR §5-1401.
Speleothems.
Defined, NR §5-1401.
Sale, NR §5-1403.
Use of caves.
Prohibited uses, NR §5-1402.

CDS.
Unauthorized recording of sounds or images,
CR §§7-306 to 7-310.

CEASE AND DESIST ORDERS.
Banks and trust companies, FI §5-808.
Charities.
Secretary of state.
Issuance, BR §6-205.
Check cashing services.
Violations, FI §12-121.
Commissioner of consumer credit, FI §11-215.
Commissioner of financial regulation, FI §2-115.
Consumer credit.
Denial of credit complaints, CL §14-1706.
Consumer protection division, CL §13-403.
Credit.
Credit grantor closed end credit provisions, CL §12-1016.
Credit grantor revolving credit provisions, CL §12-916.
Equal credit opportunity, CL §12-703.
Retail credit accounts law, CL §12-514.
Credit unions, FI §§6-905, 6-906.
Unsafe or unsound practices, FI §6-907.

CEASE AND DESIST ORDERS —Cont'd
Credit unions —Cont'd
Violations of provisions, FI §6-908.
Debt management services.
Enforcement of provisions generally, FI §12-928.
Discrimination, 49B §11.
Electric customer choice and competition act,
PUC §7-507.
Franchises, BR §14-210.
Health club services, CL §14-12B-08.
Insurance commissioner.
Sale of securities, IN §3-127.
Insurance companies, IN §4-114.
Dental plan organizations, IN §14-416.
Failure to renew certificate of authority, IN §4-112.
Impairment notification or contribution, IN §9-231.
Unfair trade practice, IN §§27-103, 27-105.
Unauthorized insurers false advertising process act, IN §27-705.
Migrant labor licenses, LE §7-311.
Judicial review, LE §7-313.
Mining.
Open-pit mining, EN §15-508.
Mortgage lenders, FI §11-516.
Disciplinary actions, FI §11-517.
Hearings, FI §11-518.
Mortgage originators.
Violations, FI §11-615.
Nursing home administrators.
Unauthorized practice as, HO §9-316.1.
Public service commission, PUC §13-208.
Securities.
Summary cease and desist orders, CA §11-701.1.
Start-up business ventures, BR §14-110.
Time shares.
Real estate commissioner, RP §11A-122.
Washington suburban sanitary district.
Board of ethics.
Power to issue, 29 §12-106.

CEASE FIRE COUNCIL, PS §§5-501 to 5-504.
Council defined, PS §5-501.
Duties, PS §5-503.
Established, PS §5-502.
Grants, PS §5-504.
Members, PS §5-502.
Powers, PS §5-503.
Purpose, PS §5-503.

CECIL COUNTY.
Air pollution.
Power of commissioners to control, 25 §11B.
Alcoholic beverages.
Beer and light wine licenses.
Class A, off-sale, 2B §5-101.
Class B, on-sale, 2B §5-201.
Class C, on-sale, 2B §5-301.
Class D, on-sale, 2B §5-401.
Special and temporary licenses, 2B §7-101.
Beer licenses.
Class A, off-sale, 2B §3-101.
Class B, on-sale, 2B §3-201.
Class C, on-sale, 2B §3-301.
Class E, on-sale, 2B §3-401.
Special and temporary licenses, 2B §7-101.
Beer, wine and liquor licenses.
Class A, off-sale, 2B §6-101.
Class B, on-sale, 2B §6-201.
Class C, on-sale, 2B §6-301.
Class D, on-sale, 2B §6-401.

CECIL COUNTY —Cont'd
Alcoholic beverages —Cont'd
Beer, wine and liquor licenses —Cont'd
Special and temporary licenses, 2B §7-101.
Bottle clubs.
Licenses, 2B §20-104.
Clubs.
Licenses, 2B §8-208.
Criminal history records checks.
License applicants, 2B §10-103.
Disorderly intoxication.
Ordinances or resolutions, 2B §19-103.
Drive-thru purchase facilities.
Licenses.
Transfer, 2B §10-503.
Elections.
Exercise of privileges of licensee on election day,
2B §11-401.
Fines and forfeitures, 2B §16-502.
Consuming alcohol in an unlicensed building,
2B §20-104.
Golf courses, 2B §8-501.1.
Hotels.
Average daily receipts not applicable to licenses,
2B §1-102.
Hours and days for sale, 2B §11-508.
Election days, 2B §11-401.
Manufacturer's license, 2B §11-101.
New Year's Eve day and New Year's day, 2B
§11-402.
Inspectors.
Employment.
By board, 2B §15-112.
General provisions, 2B §15-112.
License commissioners.
Appointment.
By county commissioners, 2B §15-104.
Chairman.
Designated, 2B §15-104.
County commissioners as ex officio license
commissioners, 2B §15-105.
Expenses, 2B §15-109.
Issuance of licenses, 2B §15-112.
Meetings.
Generally, 2B §15-104.
Qualifications, 2B §15-104.
Salaries, 2B §15-109.
Term of office, 2B §15-104.
Licenses.
Application.
Criminal records of applicants, 2B §10-103.
Different class or type of license, 2B §8-208.
Bottle clubs, 2B §20-104.
Clubs and organizations, 2B §8-208.
Consumption in unlicensed buildings, 2B
§20-104.
Corporations, 2B §9-101.
Criminal history records checks.
License applicants, 2B §10-103.
Different class or type of license.
Application, 2B §8-208.
Drive-thru purchase facilities, 2B §9-208.
Transfer of license, 2B §10-503.
Fees, 2B §8-208.
Issuance.
Board of license commissioners, 2B §15-112.
Limited liability companies, 2B §9-101.
Manufacturers.
Hours and days for sale, 2B §11-101.
Motel-restaurant or hotel-restaurant complex,
2B §20-104.

CECIL COUNTY —Cont'd
Alcoholic beverages —Cont'd
Licenses —Cont'd
Null and void licenses.
When declared null and void, 2B §10-504.
Number of licenses restricted, 2B §8-208.
Revocation or suspension.
General provisions, 2B §8-208.
Nudity and sexual displays on licensee's
premises, 2B §10-405.
Special licenses, 2B §7-101.
Special wine festival (WF) license, 2B §8-306.1.
Transfer of license, 2B §10-503.
Fees, 2B §8-208.
Premises destroyed by fire, 2B §8-208.
Liquor control board agents.
Out of state agents.
Registration, 2B §16-409.
Penalty for violations, 2B §16-409.
Manufacturers.
Licenses.
Hours and days for sale, 2B §11-101.
Minors.
Employment of minors by retail dealers, 2B
§12-302.
Possession by prohibited, 2B §12-108.
Nudity and sexual displays on licensee's premises.
Revocation of license, 2B §10-405.
Open containers.
Possession in certain places.
Applicability of provisions, 2B §19-303.
Out of state control board agents.
Registration, 2B §16-409.
Penalty for violation, 2B §16-409.
Penalties.
Local penalties, 2B §16-507.
Restaurants.
Average daily receipts not applicable to licenses,
2B §1-102.
Defined, 2B §11-508.
Sales.
Beer for cash, 2B §12-112.
Election days, 2B §11-401.
New Year's Eve Day and New Year's Day, 2B
§11-402.
Sunday sales.
General restrictions, 2B §11-508.
Sundays.
General restrictions, 2B §11-403.
Unlicensed buildings, 2B §20-104.
Yacht clubs.
Licenses, 2B §8-208.
Amusement parks.
Permits required, 25 §27.
Appearance fees in circuit courts.
Distribution, CJ §7-204.
Attachment.
Sheriff's fees, CJ §7-402.
Bailiff.
Compensation, CJ §2-507.
Bainbridge development corporation.
Fees and charges.
Use of earnings, 83A §5-1606.
Birds and game.
Hunting.
Snare traps, NR §10-410.
Spotlighting, NR §10-410.
Susquehanna Flats.
General provisions.
See BIRDS AND GAME.

CECIL COUNTY —Cont'd
Bond issues.
  Residential mortgage loans, 25 §11D.
Boxing and wrestling arenas.
  Permits required, 25 §27.
Bridges.
  Construction, 25 §37A.
Building code.
  Adoption, amendment and enforcement.
    Powers of commissioners, 25 §10.
Chesapeake Bay critical area and Atlantic coastal bays critical area protection programs.
  Critical areas commission.
    Members on commission, NR §8-1804.
  Growth allocation, location in resource
    conservation area, NR §8-1808.1.
Circuit courts.
  Appearance fees.
    Distribution, CJ §7-204.
  Number of judges, CJ §1-503.
Clerks of court.
  Recordation.
    Plats of subdivisions, RP §3-108.
Clubs.
  Alcoholic beverages.
    Bottle clubs.
      Licenses, 2B §20-104.
    Licenses, 2B §8-208.
Commissioners.
  Alcoholic beverage license commissioners. See
    within this heading, "Alcoholic beverages."
  Building code.
    Power to adopt, amend and enforce, 25 §10.
  Powers.
    Additional powers, 25 §8.
    Control of air and water pollution and
      industrial wastes, 25 §11B.
    Exceptions, 25 §3.
Community adult rehabilitation center.
  Director, appointment and removal.
    Sheriff to appoint and remove, COR §11-313.
  Placement of state correctional system inmates in
    center, COR §11-316.
Corporations.
  Alcoholic beverages.
    Licenses, 2B §9-101.
Correctional facility.
  Home detention program, COR §11-709.
Court crier.
  Compensation, CJ §2-507.
Courts.
  Circuit court.
    Judge.
      Number, CJ §1-503.
      Two judges may reside in county at one time,
        MD Const Art IV §21.
    Judicial circuit, MD Const Art IV §19.
Crimes and offenses.
  Alcoholic beverages.
    Registration of outer state agents, 2B §16-409.
  Dog regulations, 24 §11-504.
  Fish and fisheries.
    Restrictions in county waters, NR §4-720.
Dance halls.
  Permits required, 25 §27.
Dangerous weapons.
  Minors carrying, prohibited hours, CR §4-101.
Deeds.
  Straw deeds.
    Recordation, RP §3-104.

CECIL COUNTY —Cont'd
Dog and kennel licenses, 24 §11-501.
Dog regulations, 24 §11-504.
Dogs running at large.
  Females in heat, 24 §11-512.
Drive-thru purchase facilities.
  Alcoholic beverages.
    Licenses.
      Transfer, 2B §10-503.
Drunkenness.
  Disorderly intoxication.
    Ordinances or resolutions, 2B §19-103.
Ejectment papers.
  Sheriff's fees, CJ §7-402.
Elections.
  Alcoholic beverages.
    Exercise of privileges of licensee on election day,
      2B §11-401.
  County board of education generally, EL §§8-801
    to 8-806.
  County board of elections.
    County boards generally, EL §§2-201 to 2-303.
    See ELECTIONS.
  Supervisors.
    Quadrennial elections.
      Exceptions as to, MD Const Art XVII §7.
Eminent domain.
  Specific provisions, MD Const Art III §40A.
Executions.
  Sheriff's fees, CJ §7-402.
Fair Hill.
  Taxation.
    Valuation of property, TP §8-303.
Fines.
  Alcoholic beverages.
    Violations, 2B §16-502.
  Disposition, CJ §7-507.
Fire department.
  Firefighters appointed as deputy sheriffs, PS
    §§7-301 to 7-303.
  Volunteer fire departments.
    Length of service awards, PS §7-209.
Fish and fisheries.
  Restrictions in county waters, NR §§4-717, 4-720.
    Elk Neck state park, NR §4-717.
Forfeitures.
  Disposition, CJ §7-507.
Friends of the Library of Cecil County, Maryland, Inc.
  Property tax credits, TP §9-309.
Gaming, bazaar, bingo, carnival, raffles, CR
    §§13-1001 to 13-1005.
  Bingo includes instant bingo, CR §13-1001.
  Definitions, CR §13-1001.
  Gaming event defined, CR §13-1001.
  Managed personally by members of organization,
    CR §13-1005.
  Prizes or money, awarding, CR §13-1004.
  Provision applicable only in county, CR §13-1002.
  Qualified organization conducting, requirements,
    limitations, CR §13-1003.
  Qualified organizations, listed, CR §13-1001.
Golf courses.
  Alcoholic beverages, 2B §8-501.1.
Hearings.
  Real property.
    Transfers by commissioners, 25 §8.
Highways.
  Bridge or road construction or repair, 25 §37A.
Historic area zoning.
  General provisions.
    See ZONING.

CECIL COUNTY —Cont'd
Home detention programs, COR §11-709.
Hotels and restaurants.
  Beer and light wine licenses.
    Class B, on-sale, 2B §5-201.
  Beer licenses.
    Class B, on-sale, 2B §3-201.
  Beer, wine and liquor licenses.
    Class B, on-sale, 2B §6-201.
Industrial wastes.
  Power of commissioners, 25 §11B.
John F. Kennedy memorial highway.
  Elimination of ramp tolls, TR §4-312.1.
Limited liability companies.
  Alcoholic beverages.
    Licenses, 2B §9-101.
Marriage.
  Fee for performing ceremony.
    Judge's and clerk's fee, disposition, FL §2-410.
  Licenses.
    Application.
      Both parties to appear together before clerk,
        FL §2-402.
    Fees, FL §2-404.
Minors.
  Alcoholic beverages.
    Employment of minors by retail dealers, 2B
      §12-302.
    Possession by prohibited, 2B §12-108.
  Dangerous weapons, carrying.
    Prohibited hours, CR §4-101.
Misdemeanors.
  Alcoholic beverages.
    Registration of out-of-state agents, 2B §16-409.
  Dog regulations, 24 §11-504.
  Fish and fisheries.
    Restrictions in county waters, NR §4-720.
Mortgages and deeds of trust.
  Interest.
    Payable after sale, RP §7-105.
  Residential mortgage loans, 25 §11D.
Motor vehicles.
  Size and weight.
    Power of county commissioners, 25 §25.
Nuisances, EN §10-305; HG §20-313.
**Oil pipeline corporation acquiring property
  under power to condemn,** PUC §5-404.
Orphans' court.
  Judges.
    Compensation, ET §2-108.
Pedestrians.
  Soliciting rides, employment or business, TR
    §21-507.
Permits.
  Dance halls and other places of amusement,
    tourist camps, etc., 25 §27.
Planning and zoning, director, 66B §14.04.
Planning commission, 66B §14.04.
Real property.
  Additional powers of commissioners, 25 §8.
  Hearings.
    Transfers by commissioners, 25 §8.
  Transfers by commissioners.
    Hearings, 25 §8.
Recordation.
  Straw deeds, RP §3-104.
Residential mortgage loans, 25 §11D.
Schools.
  County board of education.
    Annual school budget.
      Information regarding school-based
        noninstructional personnel, ED §5-101.

CECIL COUNTY —Cont'd
Schools —Cont'd
  County board of education —Cont'd
    Compensation and reimbursement, ED
      §3-4A-04.
    Election generally, ED §3-114; EL §§8-801 to
      8-806.
    Expenses, ED §4-107.
    Meetings, ED §3-4A-03.
    Members, ED §3-4A-01.
    Qualifications, ED §3-4A-01.
    Removal of members, ED §3-4A-02.
    Terms, ED §3-4A-01.
Service of process.
  Sheriff's fees, CJ §7-402.
Sheriff.
  Deputies.
    Appointment, CJ §2-309.
  Fees, CJ §7-402.
  Firefighters appointed as deputy sheriffs, PS
    §§7-301 to 7-303.
  General provisions, CJ §2-309.
  Second in command, CJ §2-310.
  Volunteer deputy.
    Workers' compensation.
      Average weekly wage, LE §9-602.
      Covered employees and employers, LE §9-233.
Slot machines.
  Ownership and operation by eligible organization,
    CR §12-304.
Social services.
  Local social services departments.
    Attorneys to represent, 88A §7.
State's attorney, 10 §40.
Subdivisions.
  Plats.
    Recording by clerks of court, RP §3-108.
Sundays and holidays.
  Alcoholic beverages.
    Hours and days of sale, 2B §§11-403, 11-508.
Susquehanna Flats.
  General provisions.
    See BIRDS AND GAME.
Taxation.
  Assessments.
    Fair Hill.
      Property used for raising funds for Union
        Hospital of Cecil county, TP §8-303.
  Credits.
    Property tax credits.
      Friends of the Library of Cecil County,
        Maryland, Inc., TP §9-309.
      Society for the Preservation of Maryland
        Antiquities, Inc., TP §9-309.
  Electricity facilities.
    Agreement for negotiated payment in lieu of
      taxes, TP §7-512.
  Exemptions.
    Electricity facilities.
      Agreement for negotiated payment in lieu of
        taxes, TP §7-512.
    Personal property.
      Commercial, manufacturing or professional
        businesses, TP §7-510.
  Hotel rental tax, 24 §§9-301 to 9-326.
    See COUNTIES.
  Redemption.
    Rate of redemption, TP §14-820.
  Residential mortgage loans.
    Bonds to finance.
      Exemption from taxation, 25 §11D.

CECIL COUNTY —Cont'd
Taxation —Cont'd
Sales.
Deductions from collections, TP §14-810.
Expenses of sales.
Auctioneer's fees, TP §14-813.
Society for the Preservation of Maryland
Antiquities, Inc.
Property tax credits, TP §9-309.
Tourist camps.
Permits required, 25 §27.
Trader licenses.
Approval of zoning authorities, BR §17-1807.
Trapping.
Snare traps, NR §10-410.
Treasurer.
Salary, 25 §51.
Volunteer fire departments.
Firefighters appointed as deputy sheriffs, PS
§§7-301 to 7-303.
Firefighters in municipal corporation located in
county.
Property tax credit on residences owned by, TP
§9-309.
Length of service awards, PS §7-209.
Water pollution.
Power of commissioners, 25 §11B.
Workers' compensation.
Volunteer deputy sheriff.
Average weekly wage, LE §9-602.
Covered employees and employers, LE §9-233.
Yacht clubs.
Alcoholic beverages.
Licenses, 2B §8-208.
Zoning.
Board of appeals, 66B §14.04.
Director of planning and zoning, 66B §14.04.
Historic area zoning.
General provisions.
See ZONING.

CEILING FAN LIGHT KITS.
Efficiency standards, SG §9-2006.

CELL PHONES.
911 emergency telephone system, PS §§1-301 to
1-312.
See 911 EMERGENCY TELEPHONE SYSTEM.
Traffic laws.
Minors, use of wireless communications device
while driving, TR §21-1124.

CEMETERIES.
Advertising.
Unauthorized representations, BR §5-903.
Baltimore City.
Sale of burial ground for another purpose, BR
§5-506.
Baltimore county.
Real property.
Exceptions to limits on land held, BR §5-501.
Burial contracts, BR §§5-701 to 5-712. See within
this heading, "Pre-need burial contracts."
Burial goods.
Contracts for sale.
Disclosures required, BR §5-801.
Defined, BR §5-101.
Engaging in operation of burial goods business,
BR §5-401.
Registration of persons providing.
Generally, BR §§5-301 to 5-312. See within this
heading, "Registration."

CEMETERIES —Cont'd
Burial grounds.
Access and maintenance, RP §§14-121, 14-122.
Generally.
See BURIAL GROUNDS OR SITES.
Burial lots and crypts, BR §5-503.
Certificate of ownership, BR §5-504.
Cemetery corporations.
Perpetual care.
Corporate violations, BR §5-608.
Citation of act, BR §5-1001.
Civil penalties, BR §5-905.
Corporations.
Engaging in operation of cemetery or burial goods
business, BR §5-401.
Permits, BR §§5-402 to 5-404.
Counties.
Roads.
Consent of owner to pass through required, 25
§144.
Criminal penalties, BR §§5-802, 5-904.
Definitions, BR §5-101; RP §14-119.
Perpetual care of cemeteries.
Developed land area, BR §5-602.
Preneed burial contracts, BR §5-701.
Seller's account, BR §5-707.
Disclosures required, BR §5-801.
Druid Hill park.
Burial or funeral procession prohibited, BR
§5-802.
Eminent domain.
Acquisition of cemetery, PropAct Rule 12-204.
Dead bodies.
Allowance for removal, RP §12-112.
Grave markers or monuments.
Allowance for removal, RP §12-112.
Enforcement of provisions, BR §5-905.
Engaging in the operation of a cemetery, BR
§5-401.
Defined, BR §5-101.
Registration generally, BR §§5-301 to 5-312. See
within this heading, "Registration."
Exemptions from provisions, BR §5-102.
Fines.
Civil penalties, BR §5-905.
Foliage, destroying, CR §10-404.
Frederick county.
Real property.
Exceptions to limits on land held, BR §5-501.
Funerary objects, destroying, CR §10-404.
Hate crime.
Damaging property of religious entity, CR
§10-302.
Highways.
Roads through.
Consent of owner required to pass through, 25
§144.
Indecent or disorderly conduct in, CR §10-404.
Injunctions.
Civil enforcement actions by attorney general, BR
§5-905.
Lots.
Burial lots or crypts, BR §5-503.
Certificate of ownership, BR §5-504.
Municipal corporations.
Regulations, 23A §2.
Office of cemetery oversight, BR §§5-201 to
5-206.
Advisory council on cemetery operations, BR
§5-201.
Cemetery oversight fund, BR §5-205.

CEMETERIES —Cont'd
Office of cemetery oversight —Cont'd
Director, BR §5-202.
Duties, BR §§5-202, 5-204.
Full time devotion to duties, BR §5-202.
Powers, BR §5-204.
Staff, BR §5-203.
Established, BR §5-201.
Immunity of persons participating in activities of office, BR §5-206; CJ §5-720.
Program evaluation act, SG §8-403.
Staff.
Employment by director, BR §5-203.
Partnerships.
Engaging in operation of cemetery or burial goods business, BR §5-401.
Permits, BR §§5-402 to 5-404.
Permits, BR §§5-402 to 5-404.
Denial, BR §5-310.
Display, BR §5-309.
Prohibited acts without permit, BR §5-902.
Renewal, BR §5-307.
Suspension or revocation, BR §5-310.
Perpetual care of cemeteries.
Below-ground earth-covered chambers.
Scope of subtitle, BR §5-601.
Burial rights.
Records required, BR §5-605.
Corporate violations, BR §5-608.
Definitions.
Developed land area, BR §5-602.
Deposit from sales.
Trust fund required, BR §5-602.
Enforcement of subtitle, BR §5-606.
Examination of records, BR §5-605.
Excluded cemeteries.
Scope of subtitle, BR §5-601.
Fidelity bond.
Trustees, BR §5-603.
Irrevocability of trust agreement, BR §5-604.
Perpetuities.
Rule not applicable, ET §11-102.
Prohibited acts, BR §5-607.
Penalty, BR §5-608.
Recordkeeping requirements, BR §5-605.
Reporting requirements, BR §5-605.
Sales of burial rights.
Records required, BR §5-605.
Scope of subtitle, BR §5-601.
State as to whether cemetery perpetual care or not.
Required on all documents, BR §5-602.
Trust agreements.
Effect on preexisting agreements, BR §5-601.
Required, BR §5-604.
Trustees.
Appointment, BR §5-603.
Prohibited activities, BR §5-603.
Trust fund.
Report on deposits, BR §5-605.
Underfunding, correction, BR §5-605.
Trust fund required, BR §5-602.
Perpetuities.
Perpetual care.
Rule not applicable, ET §11-102.
Pre-need burial contracts, BR §§5-701 to 5-712.
Cancellation.
Disbursement of money, BR §5-709.
Caskets or casket vaults.
Contract termination, BR §5-709.
Dating, BR §5-704.

CEMETERIES —Cont'd
Pre-need burial contracts —Cont'd
Definitions, BR §5-701.
Delivery of goods, BR §5-704.
Duplicate original, BR §5-704.
Enforcement of subtitle, BR §5-711.
Exclusions from subtitle, BR §5-702.
Execution, BR §5-704.
Form, BR §5-704.
Interest, BR §5-704.
Performance of services, BR §5-704.
Cemetery not required, BR §5-702.
Prohibited acts, BR §5-712.
Recordkeeping requirements, BR §5-710.
Reporting requirements, BR §5-710.
Scope of subtitle, BR §5-702.
Applicability to certain contracts, BR §5-703.
Termination.
Disbursement of money, BR §5-709.
Trust requirements, BR §5-705.
Administration of trust accounts, BR §5-707.
Disbursement of money, BR §5-708.
Contract termination, BR §5-709.
Establishment of trust accounts, BR §5-706.
Waiver void, BR §5-704.
Price lists to be provided, BR §5-801.
Prince George's county.
Real property.
Exceptions to limits on land held, BR §5-501.
Prohibited acts, BR §§5-901 to 5-905.
Qualifications for permit, BR §5-403.
Qualifications for registration, BR §5-302.
Real property.
Limit on land held, BR §5-501.
Recordation.
Carroll county.
Required documents, RP §14-119.
Registration, BR §§5-301 to 5-312.
Application, BR §5-303.
Changes, BR §5-308.
Financial statement, BR §5-304.
Authority of registrants, BR §5-306.
Complaints against registrants.
Proceedings on, BR §5-311.
Denial, BR §5-310.
Display, BR §5-309.
Effect, BR §5-306.
Expiration, BR §5-307.
Financial stability.
Requirement, BR §5-302.
Statement demonstrating, BR §5-304.
Hearings, BR §5-312.
Complaint procedures, BR §5-311.
Issuance, BR §5-305.
Penalties.
Civil penalty in lieu of suspension or revocation, BR §5-310.
Qualifications, BR §5-302.
Renewal, BR §5-307.
Required, BR §5-301.
Suspension or revocation, BR §5-310.
Transfer prohibited, BR §5-305.
Unregistered acts, BR §5-901.
Religious, nonprofit cemeteries.
Exemption from provisions, BR §5-102.
Statement filing, BR §5-405.
Removal of human remains or funerary objects from burial site.
Ascertaining cause of death.
Removal of human remains, CR §10-402.

CEMETERIES —Cont'd
Removal of human remains or funerary objects from burial site —Cont'd
Authorization to relocate human remains, CR §10-402.
Definitions, CR §10-401.
Destruction of funerary objects, CR §10-404.
Medical or scientific examination.
Removal of human remains, CR §10-402.
Notice of intent to relocate human remains, CR §10-402.
Reburial.
Removal of human remains, CR §10-402.
Reinterment of removed human remains, CR §10-402.
Selling unlawfully removed human remains or funerary objects, CR §10-403.
Unauthorized removal of human remains, CR §10-402.
Roads.
Public thoroughfares in cemeteries, BR §5-502.
Rules and regulations.
Municipal corporations, 23A §2.
Sale of burial grounds.
Action for sale for another purpose, BR §5-505.
Baltimore City, BR §5-506.
Sale for other purposes, PropSales Rule 14-401.
Sanitary commissions.
Burial of water and sewer lines in cemetery land, EN §9-668.
Condemnation, EN §9-668.
State-owned cemeteries, SF §10-309.
Taxation.
Credits.
Dwelling on cemetery property, TP §9-202.
Exemptions.
Property owned by cemetery or mausoleum, TP §7-201.
Property owned by individuals or religious groups, TP §7-201.
Termination of provisions, BR §5-1002.
Thoroughfares.
Public thoroughfares in cemeteries, BR §5-502.
Title of act, BR §5-1001.
Veterans.
State veterans' cemeteries, SG §9-906.
Registry of graves, SG §9-907.
Veterans' memorials and monuments program, SG §9-908.

CEMETERY OVERSIGHT FUND, BR §5-205.

CENSUS.
Constitutional provisions, US Const Art I §§2, 9.
Schools.
Handicapped children.
By county boards of education, ED §4-113.
School census.
By county board of health, ED §4-113.

CENTER FOR ENVIRONMENTAL SCIENCE, NR §§3-401 to 3-403.
Academic rank and faculty status.
Assignment to director and qualified personnel staff, NR §3-402.
Board of regents of University system of Maryland.
Supervision, direction and control of center, NR §3-402.
Collection of research samples, NR §3-403.
Designation, NR §3-401.
Duties, NR §3-403.

CENTER FOR ENVIRONMENTAL SCIENCE —Cont'd
Functions, NR §3-403.
Research and education program, NR §3-403.

CENTER FOR THE STUDY OF THE HEALTH EFFECTS OF FIRE, HG §§18-701 to 18-711.

CENTER STAGE THEATER.
Designation as state theater, SG §13-309.

CENTRAL COLLECTION UNIT, SF §§3-301 to 3-306.
Central collection fund, SF §3-306.
Debt collection, SF §3-302.
Costs, SF §3-304.
Delinquent accounts, SF §3-302.
Disposition of funds, SF §3-305.
Exceptions, SF §3-302.
Rules and regulations, SF §3-303.
Disposition of funds collected, SF §3-305.
Duties, SF §3-302.
Employees, SF §3-301.
Established, SF §3-301.
Insurance companies.
Retaliatory tax, collection, IN §6-305.
Powers, SF §3-304.
Rules and regulations.
Debt collection, SF §3-303.

CENTREVILLE.
Electric or gas plant.
Disposition.
Exceptions, 23 §183.

CERTIFICATES.
Agency.
Requirements generally, CA §1-406.
Agriculture.
Farm products.
General provisions, AG §§10-601 to 10-606.
See AGRICULTURE.
Assumed business name.
Trade names generally, CA §1-406.
Boats.
Certificate of title.
State boat act.
See VESSELS AND BOATS.
Candidates for public or political office.
Certificate of election.
Issued after primary, EL §5-705.
Certificate of nomination, EL §5-705.
Certificates of candidacy, EL §§5-301 to 5-304.
Certificates of withdrawal, EL §§5-501 to 5-504.
Declination of nomination, EL §5-801.
Driver education program.
See DRIVER EDUCATION PROGRAM.
Elections.
Certificate of election.
Issued after primary, EL §5-705.
Certificate of nomination, EL §5-705.
Certificates of candidacy, EL §§5-301 to 5-304.
Certificates of withdrawal, EL §§5-501 to 5-504.
Declination of nomination, EL §5-801.
Farm products certification, AG §§10-601 to 10-606.
Fictitious business name.
Trade names generally, CA §1-406.
Insect sting emergency treatment program, HG §§13-701 to 13-709.
See INSECT STING EMERGENCY TREATMENT PROGRAM.

CERTIFICATES —Cont'd
Life and health insurance guaranty corporation.
Certificate of contribution for assessment, IN §9-409.
Marriage.
See MARRIAGE.
Motor vehicles.
See MOTOR VEHICLE TITLING.
Names.
Fictitious names, CA §1-406.
Trade names.
Requirements generally, CA §1-406.
Questions of law.
Uniform certification of questions of law act.
See CERTIFIED QUESTIONS OF LAW.
Tobacco.
See TOBACCO.
Trade names.
Requirements generally, CA §1-406.
Wholesome meat act.
False statements, AG §4-123.
Forged, counterfeit, etc., AG §4-123.
Official certificate.
Defined, AG §4-101.

CERTIFICATES OF CANDIDACY, EL §§5-301 to 5-304.
Withdrawal, EL §§5-501 to 5-504.

CERTIFICATES OF DEPOSIT.
Bank deposits and collections.
General provisions, CL §§4-101 to 4-504.
See BANK DEPOSITS AND COLLECTIONS.
Limitation of actions.
Action to enforce obligation of depository institution to pay, FI §1-210.
Negotiable instruments generally, CL §§3-101 to 3-605.
See NEGOTIABLE INSTRUMENTS.

CERTIFICATES OF TITLE.
Boats.
See VESSELS AND BOATS.
Motor vehicles.
See MOTOR VEHICLE TITLING.

CERTIFIED ADULT RESIDENTIAL ENVIRONMENT PROGRAM, 88A §§138 to 143.
See SOCIAL SERVICES.

CERTIFIED CHECKS.
Checks.
See CHECKS.
Negotiable instruments generally, CL §§3-101 to 3-605.
See NEGOTIABLE INSTRUMENTS.

CERTIFIED COPIES.
See COPIES.

CERTIFIED INTERIOR DESIGNERS, BOP §§8-101 to 8-602.
See INTERIOR DESIGNERS.

CERTIFIED MAIL.
Defined, Rule 1-202.
Insurance companies.
Liquidation, rehabilitation, etc.
Notice concerning disbursement of assets to guaranty associations, IN §9-224.
Mail generally.
See MAIL.

CERTIFIED NURSING ASSISTANTS, HO §§8-6A-01 to 8-6A-16.
See NURSING ASSISTANTS.

CERTIFIED PUBLIC ACCOUNTANTS.
See PUBLIC ACCOUNTANTS.

CERTIFIED QUESTIONS OF LAW, CJ §§12-601 to 12-613.
Citation of subtitle, CJ §12-613.
Costs, CJ §12-610.
Court of appeals.
Appellate jurisdiction, CJ §12-307.
Notification to certifying court, CJ §12-607.
Opinion, CJ §12-609.
Power to answer, CJ §12-603.
Power to certify, CJ §12-602.
Power to reformulate question, CJ §12-604.
Procedure, AppRev Rules 8-304, 8-305.
Record.
Power to require certifying court to deliver, CJ §12-605.
Court of special appeals.
Power to certify, CJ §12-602.
Definitions, CJ §12-601.
Interpretation and construction.
Severability of provisions, CJ §12-611.
Uniformity of application and construction, CJ §12-612.
Notices, CJ §12-607.
Opinion.
Court of appeals, CJ §12-609.
Orders of court.
Certification order, CJ §12-605.
Contents, CJ §12-606.
Procedures.
Appearance of counsel, AppRev Rule 8-402.
Applicable provisions, AppRev Rule 8-301.
Applicable rules, CJ §12-608.
Certification of questions of law, AppRev Rule 8-305.
Court of appeals, AppRev Rules 8-304, 8-305.
Court of special appeals of certifying court, AppRev Rule 8-304.
Method of securing review, AppRev Rule 8-301.
Records.
Delivery of record by certifying court.
Court of appeals may require, CJ §12-605.
Reformulation of question.
Power of court of appeals, CJ §12-604.
Rules of procedure.
Applicability, CJ §12-608.
Title of act.
Short title, CJ §12-613.

CERTIORARI.
Circuit courts, AppRevCir Rule 7-301.
Allocation of appellate jurisdiction, CJ §12-306.
Review of decisions.
Securing uniformity of decisions, CJ §12-305.
Court of appeals.
Allocation of appellate jurisdiction, CJ §12-306.
Method of securing review, AppRev Rule 8-301.
Petition for writ.
Form of court papers, AppRev Rule 8-112.
Procedure, AppRev Rule 8-303.
Time for filing, AppRev Rule 8-302.
Review by court of appeals generally. See within this heading, "Review by court of appeals."
Review of cases in court of special appeals, CJ §§12-201, 12-203.
Exceptions, CJ §12-202.

CERTIORARI —Cont'd
Court of appeals —Cont'd
Securing uniformity of decisions, CJ §12-305.
Court of special appeals.
Action by court of appeals, CJ §12-203.
Review of case by court of appeals, CJ §§12-201, 12-203.
Exceptions, CJ §12-202.
Petitions.
Court of appeals, AppRev Rules 8-302, 8-303.
Review by court of appeals.
Court of special appeals.
Review by court of appeals, CJ §12-203.
Review in court of special appeals, CJ §§12-201, 12-202.
Method of securing review, AppRev Rule 8-301.
Petition.
Procedure on petition, AppRev Rule 8-303.
Time for filing, AppRev Rule 8-302.
Securing uniformity of decisions.
Circuit courts.
Review of decisions, CJ §12-305.

CERVICAL CANCER.
Diethylstilbestrol exposure.
Public information campaign and screening program, HG §18-303.
Hospitals.
Pap smears, required services, HG §19-348.

CESSATION OF OPERATION OF CORRECTIONAL FACILITY.
Life-threatening or health-endangering conditions, COR §8-115.
Violation of minimum mandatory condition, COR §8-114.

CHAIN STORES.
Alcoholic beverages.
Allegany county.
Prohibited, 2B §9-202.
More than one license for same person or premises, 2B §9-102.
Prince George's county.
Restrictions on off-sale privileges, 2B §9-217.
Licenses.
Fees, BR §17-1809.
Required, BR §17-1805.
Trader licenses generally, BR §§17-1801 to 17-1816.
See TRADERS.

CHALLENGES.
Juries.
See JURY.
Preemptory challenges.
See JURY.

CHANCE BOOK.
Cecil county.
Awarding prizes at gaming events, CR §13-1004.
Gaming devices.
Defined as, CR §12-101.
Statewide gaming provisions, CR §§12-101 to 12-113.
See GAMING.
Gaming event provisions applicable to several counties, CR §§13-201 to 13-205.
Howard county, CR §13-1603.
Kent county, CR §§13-1701 to 13-1706.
Queen Anne's county, CR §§13-2001 to 13-2006.
St. Mary's county, CR §§13-2111 to 13-2115.
Wicomico county, CR §§13-2501 to 13-2508.

CHANCE BOOK —Cont'd
Worcester county, CR §§13-2619 to 13-2628.

CHANCROID.
Venereal disease cures or remedies.
Advertising cure.
Prohibition, penalty, CR §10-102.
Defined, CR §10-101.
Prescription requirements, CR §10-103.
Selling or dispensing remedies.
Prohibition, penalties, CR §10-103.

CHANGE OF NAME, SpecPro Rule 15-901.
Adoption.
Judgment of adoption, FamLaw Rule 9-111.
Notice, FamLaw Rule 9-105.
Birth certificates.
Amendment to reflect, HG §4-214.
Commercial drivers' licenses, TR §16-810.
Divorce.
Restoration of former name, FL §7-105.
Domestic violence.
Address confidentiality program.
Notification by program participant, FL §4-524.
Failure to notify as grounds for cancellation of participation, FL §4-525.
Drivers' licenses, TR §16-106.
Not to be done by special or local laws, MD Const Art III §33.
Nurses.
Notice to board, HO §8-312.
Secured transactions.
Financing statement.
Effect of change of name, CL §9-507.
Sex offender registration.
Notice of legal name change, CP §§11-705, 11-710.
Vital records.
Amendment to certificate of birth to reflect, HG §4-214.

CHARACTER EVIDENCE.
Generally, Evid Rule 5-404.
Methods of proving character, Evid Rule 5-405.
Not admissible to prove conduct, Evid Rule 5-404.
Witnesses.
Evidence of character of witness, Evid Rule 5-608.

CHARGE-BACK.
Bank deposits and collections, CL §4-214.

CHARGING DOCUMENTS.
Appearances.
Initial appearance of defendant.
District Court following arrest.
Advice of charges, Crim Rule 4-213.
Arson or burning, CR §6-111.
Assault, CR §3-206.
Bigamy, CR §10-502.
Bill of particulars.
Arson or burning.
General form of charging document used, CR §6-111.
Assault.
Charging document in general form, CR §3-206.
Breaking and entering.
General form of charging document used, CR §6-210.
Gaming, CR §12-112.
Lottery violation, CR §12-211.
Rape or sexual offense.
General form of charging document used, CR §3-317.

CHARGING DOCUMENTS —Cont'd
Bill of particulars —Cont'd
  Reckless endangerment.
    Charging document in general form, CR §3-206.
  Theft.
    General form of charging document used, CR
        §7-108.
Breaking and entering, CR §6-210.
Burglary, CR §6-210.
Circuit courts.
  Motions in circuit courts in criminal cases, Crim
      Rule 4-252.
  Use, Crim Rule 4-201.
Citation, charging by, CP §4-101.
Citations.
  Content, Crim Rule 4-202.
  Defined, Crim Rule 4-102.
  Docket in place of citation, Crim Rule 4-201.
  Municipal infractions, 23A §3.
Conspiracy.
  Sufficiency, CR §1-203.
Content.
  Requirements.
    General requirements, Crim Rule 4-202.
Criminal information, CP §4-102.
Criminal rules.
  Defined, Crim Rule 4-102.
Definitions, CP §1-101; Crim Rule 4-102.
District Court.
  Use, Crim Rule 4-201.
Dockets.
  Citations.
    Docket in place of citation, Crim Rule 4-201.
False instruments, using, CP §4-108.
**Felony and misdemeanor counts in same
    document,** CP §4-104.
Gaming, CR §12-112.
**Homicide by motor vehicle or vessel while
    impaired or under the influence,** CR §2-507.
Instruments in writing, printing or figures, CP
    §4-108.
Joinder.
  Multiple offenses, Crim Rule 4-203.
Juvenile causes.
  Waiver of jurisdiction.
    Juvenile petition considered charging document
        pending bail hearing, Juv Rule 11-113.
Juvenile courts.
  Waiver of jurisdiction.
    Filing of charging document, Crim Rule 4-222.
**Life threatening injury by motor vehicle or
    vessel while impaired or under the
    influence,** CR §3-212.
Lottery violation, CR §12-211.
Manslaughter.
  By vehicle or vessel, CR §2-209.
  Sufficiency, CR §2-208.
**Merging common law misdemeanor into
    statutory felony.**
  Prohibition, CP §4-104.
Money, describing, CP §4-106.
Motions.
  Mandatory motions in circuit courts.
    Criminal rules, Crim Rule 4-252.
Motor vehicle theft, CR §7-108.
Murder.
  Sufficiency, CR §2-208.
**Naming two or more persons with like
    interest,** CP §4-105.
Offenses.
  Joinder.
    Multiple offenses, Crim Rule 4-203.

CHARGING DOCUMENTS —Cont'd
Ordinance violations, CP §4-107.
Owners or possessors of property.
  Laying ownership or possession in named person
      and another or others, CP §4-105.
**Partners, joint tenants, heirs, tenants in
    common or trustees.**
  Naming one and speaking of named person and
      another or others, CP §4-105.
Perjury, CR §9-103.
Rape or sexual offense, CR §3-317.
Reckless endangerment, CR §3-206.
Registered returnable containers and textiles,
    BR §19-306.
Requirements.
  Content.
    General requirements, Crim Rule 4-202.
  Use, Crim Rule 4-201.
Robbery, CR §3-404.
Sealing charging document, Crim Rule 4-201.
Signatures, Crim Rule 4-202.
Statement of charges.
  Defined, Crim Rule 4-102.
Theft, CR §7-108.
Unnatural or perverted sexual practice, CR
    §3-322.
Use.
  Requirements, Crim Rule 4-201.

CHARITABLE CORPORATIONS.
**Disposition of property by court on
    dissolution,** CA §5-209.

CHARITABLE IMMUNITY.
Agents.
  Personal liability of agents, CJ §5-406.
Physicians and volunteers.
  Immunity from civil liability, CJ §5-606.
Property and casualty insurance.
  Insured may not assert defense, IN §19-103.

CHARITABLE ORGANIZATIONS, BR §§6-101 to
    6-701.
See CHARITIES.

CHARITABLE TRUSTS.
**Administration of private foundations,
    charitable trusts or split-interest trusts.**
  Applications of sections 14-303, 14-305.
    Judicial determination of application, ET
        §14-306.
  Attorney general.
    Rights and powers not impaired, ET §14-307.
  Courts.
    Rights and powers not impaired, ET §14-307.
  Distributions, ET §14-305.
    Judicial determination of application to trusts,
        ET §14-306.
  Internal revenue code.
    Amendment of instrument to conform to code,
        ET §14-304.
      Judicial determination of application to trust,
          ET §14-306.
  Investments.
    Prohibited investments, ET §14-303.
  Prohibited acts.
    General provisions, ET §14-303.
  Retention of excess business holdings, ET §14-303.
  Self-dealing, ET §14-303.
  Taxable expenditures, ET §14-303.
Distributions, ET §14-305.
Enforcement.
  Generally, ET §14-301.

CHARITABLE TRUSTS —Cont'd
Enforcement —Cont'd
Impossibility or impracticability of enforcement, ET §14-302.
Illegal.
Becoming illegal, ET §14-302.
Investments.
Prohibited acts in administration of private foundations, charitable trusts and split-interest trusts, ET §14-303.
Perpetuities.
Rule not applicable, ET §11-102.
Private foundations.
Administration. See within this heading, "Administration of private foundations, charitable trusts or split-interest trusts."
Split-interest trusts.
Administration. See within this heading, "Administration of private foundations, charitable trusts or split-interest trusts."
Uniform charitable trusts administration act, ET §14-302.

CHARITIES.
Accounts and accounting.
Accounting required, BR §6-506.
Representatives.
Registration before accounting, BR §6-306.
Advertising.
False or misleading material, BR §6-607.
Promotions for charitable organizations, BR §6-618.
Liability for solicitations violating title, BR §6-621.
Agents.
Personal liability.
Conditions prohibiting imposition of personal damages, CJ §5-406.
Liability in cases of malice or gross negligence, CJ §5-406.
Limitation on recovery, CJ §5-406.
Section inapplicable to suits proving willful violation of registration provisions, CJ §5-406.
Alcoholic beverages.
Beer licenses.
St. Mary's county, 2B §7-101.
Wine auctions.
Charity wine auction permits, 2B §2-101.
Annuity agreements with donors, IN §16-114.
Audits.
Registration statements, BR §6-402.
Benefit performances.
Prince George's county, CR §§13-1901 to 13-1907.
Bingo.
Anne Arundel county, CR §13-407.
Baltimore City, CR §§13-507 to 13-509.
Baltimore county, CR §13-606.
Benefit performances.
Prince George's county, CR §§13-1901 to 13-1907.
Calvert county, CR §§13-705 to 13-709.
Exemption from license requirement, CR §13-706.
Carroll county, CR §§13-907, 13-908.
Cecil county, CR §§13-1001 to 13-1005.
Charles county, CR §§13-1109 to 13-1115.
Dorchester county, CR §§13-1203 to 13-1205.
Frederick county, CR §13-1306.
Harford county, CR §§13-1501 to 13-1512.
Howard county, CR §§13-1602, 13-1603.

CHARITIES —Cont'd
Bingo —Cont'd
Kent county, CR §13-1705.
Montgomery county, CR §§13-1801 to 13-1815.
Queen Anne's county, CR §13-2005.
St. Mary's county, CR §§13-2101 to 13-2110.
Somerset county, CR §13-2202.
Wicomico county, CR §§13-2501 to 13-2508.
Worcester county, CR §§13-2601 to 13-2616.
Casino.
Baltimore county, CR §13-604.
Charitable representatives. See within this heading, "Representatives."
Charitable solicitations. See within this heading, "Solicitations."
Charitable trusts.
Administration.
See TRUSTS AND TRUSTEES.
Citation of title, BR §6-701.
Conflicts of interest.
Directors, officers, etc.
Restrictions on voting, BR §6-415.
Containers for deposits of money.
Requirements, BR §6-620.
Contracts.
Contents of agreement between charitable organization and fund-raising counsel, BR §6-615.
Contents of agreement between charitable organizations and professional solicitors, BR §6-616.
Secretary of state.
Reciprocal agreements, BR §6-206.
Solicitation agreements, BR §6-501.
Soliciting after cancellation of contract, BR §6-612.
Unregistered charitable organization, BR §6-603.
Contributions.
Application.
Substantially inconsistent with solicitation, BR §6-606.
Charitable contribution.
Defined, BR §6-101.
Fund-raising counsel.
Compensation dependent on number or value of contributions, BR §6-605.
Defined, BR §6-101.
Corporations.
Charitable corporations.
See CORPORATIONS.
Nonstock corporations.
Assets subject to charitable or other restrictions, CA §5-702.
Restrictions on property holdings, CA §5-701.
Credit cards.
Acceptance for payment of contributions, BR §6-414.
Crimes and offenses.
Grossly negligent violations, BR §§6-614, 6-619.
Willful violations, BR §§6-613, 6-619.
Criminal prosecutions.
Inadmissibility of information obtained during investigation by secretary, BR §6-205.
Cy pres.
Doctrine recognized, ET §14-302.
Definitions, BR §6-101.
Foreign charitable organization or representative, BR §6-202.
Health care services, CJ §5-606.
Compensation, CJ §5-606.
Physician, CJ §5-606.

CHARITIES —Cont'd
Definitions —Cont'd
Health care services —Cont'd
Suit, CJ §5-606.
Volunteer, CJ §5-606.
Member, BR §6-102.
Program, BR §6-201.
Volunteers' liability provisions, CJ §5-407.
Wine auctions.
Defined for purposes of, 2B §2-101.
Disclosure statement.
Conspicuous display, BR §6-411.
Defined, BR §6-101.
Grossly negligent violations, BR §6-614.
Criminal penalty, BR §6-619.
Required, BR §6-411.
Willful violations, BR §6-613.
Criminal penalty, BR §6-619.
Executors and administrators.
Satisfaction of charitable pledges of decedent, ET
§7-401.
Exemptions from act, BR §6-102.
Requirement of exempt person, BR §6-405.
Fees.
Registration.
Noncompliance with title by applicant.
Notice and fee, BR §6-404.
Registration of charitable representatives.
Single fees, BR §6-302.
Schedule of annual fees, BR §6-407.
Financial records.
Recordkeeping requirements, BR §6-412.
Financial statement.
Contents, BR §6-410.
Grossly negligent violations, BR §6-614.
Criminal penalty, BR §6-619.
Requests for, BR §6-410.
Willful violations, BR §6-613.
Criminal penalty, BR §6-619.
Fraternal benefit societies.
Creation and operation of charitable institutions,
IN §8-437.
Fraud and deceit.
Misrepresentation generally, BR §§6-607 to 6-611.
See within this heading, "Misrepresentation."
Fund-raising notice.
Exempt person requirements, BR §6-405.
Gaming, bazaar, carnival and raffles.
Anne Arundel county, CR §§13-401 to 13-408.
Baltimore City, CR §§13-501 to 13-510.
Calvert county, CR §§13-701 to 13-704.
Carroll county, CR §§13-901 to 13-909.
Cecil county, CR §§13-1001 to 13-1005.
Charles county, CR §§13-1101 to 13-1115.
Frederick county, CR §§13-1301 to 13-1307.
Harford county.
Raffles generally, CR §§13-1501 to 13-1512.
Kent county.
Raffles and other gaming devices generally, CR
§§13-1701 to 13-1706.
Local gaming events generally, CR §§13-201 to
13-205.
Montgomery county.
Raffles generally, CR §§13-1801 to 13-1815.
Prince George's county, CR §§13-1901 to 13-1912.
Queen Anne's county.
Raffles and other gaming devices, CR §§13-2001
to 13-2006.
Raffles generally, CR §12-106.
St. Mary's county, CR §§13-2111 to 13-2115.
Wicomico county, CR §§13-2501 to 13-2508.

CHARITIES —Cont'd
Health care services.
Physicians and volunteers.
Liability, CJ §5-606.
Immunity.
Agents.
Personal liability of agents, CJ §5-406.
Physicians and volunteers.
Immunity from civil liability, CJ §5-606.
Property and casualty insurance.
Insured may not assert defense of charitable
immunity, IN §19-103.
Income tax.
Trusts.
Administration of private foundations,
charitable trusts or split-interest trusts.
See TRUSTS AND TRUSTEES.
Injunctions.
Acting as charitable representative, BR §6-307.
Registration.
Soliciting after registration, BR §6-406.
Secretary of state.
Injunctive remedies, BR §6-205.
Insurance.
Blanket health insurance.
Eligible organizations, IN §15-305.
Immunity of charitable institution.
Liability insured may not claim defense, IN
§19-103.
Pooling to purchase casualty or property
insurance, IN §19-601.
Investigations.
Secretary of state.
Power to investigate alleged violations, BR
§6-205.
IRS Form 990.
Exempt person requirements, BR §6-405.
Liability.
Health care services.
Physicians and volunteers, CJ §5-606.
Personal liability of agents, CJ §5-406.
Misrepresentation.
Charitable organizations, BR §6-610.
Deceptive acts prohibited, BR §6-608.
Marks or printed matter, BR §6-609.
Sponsorship or endorsement, BR §6-611.
Use of proceeds, BR §6-610.
**Noncompliance with title by applicant for
registration.**
Notice and fee, BR §6-404.
Nonprofit health entities.
Acquisition.
Charitable entities, SG §6.5-306.
General provisions, SG §§6.5-101 to 6.5-401.
See NONPROFIT HEALTH ENTITIES.
Rights and powers of court and attorney general
with respect to charities.
Provisions not to impair, SG §6.5-104.
Notices.
Exempt person requirements.
Fund-raising notice, BR §6-405.
Registration.
Noncompliance with title by applicant, BR
§6-404.
Solicitations.
Fund-raising notice, BR §6-502.
Organization.
Charitable organization.
Defined, BR §6-101.
Perpetuities.
Transfer from charitable corporation on
contingency.
Rule not applicable, ET §11-102.

CHARITIES —Cont'd
Perpetuities —Cont'd
Trust for charitable purposes.
Rule not applicable, ET §11-102.
Physicians.
Liability.
Immunity of physicians and volunteers
providing health care services, CJ §5-606.
Prize awards.
Disclosure requirements, BR §6-503.
Public containers.
Requirements, BR §6-620.
Public safety solicitors, BR §§6-5A-01 to 6-5A-11.
Action on application, BR §6-5A-04.
Applicant requirements, BR §6-5A-02.
Bond, surety, BR §6-5A-03.
Expiration of registration, BR §6-5A-05.
False statements, BR §6-5A-09.
Information contained in solicitations, BR
§6-5A-06.
Negligence, BR §6-5A-09.
Prerequisites to solicitation, BR §6-5A-07.
Prohibitions on solicitations, BR §6-5A-08.
Registration required, BR §6-5A-01.
Unregistered solicitations, BR §6-5A-10.
Violations, penalties, BR §6-5A-11.
Records.
Financial records.
Availability, BR §6-412.
Grossly negligent violations, BR §6-614.
Criminal penalty, BR §6-619.
Willful violations, BR §6-613.
Criminal penalty, BR §6-619.
Public records.
Recordkeeping requirements, BR §6-203.
Solicitations, BR §6-507.
Refunds to donors, BR §6-205.
Registration.
Affiliates, branches and chapters.
Required, BR §6-401.
Agreement with unregistered charitable
organization, BR §6-603.
Approval of application, BR §6-404.
Charitable representatives, BR §§6-301 to 6-307.
See within this heading, "Representatives."
Misuse of registration, BR §6-604.
Noncompliance with title by applicant.
Notice and fee, BR §6-404.
Registration statements.
Auditing, BR §6-402.
Contents, BR §6-402.
Duty of officers, BR §6-403.
Form, BR §6-402.
Grossly negligent violations, BR §6-614.
Criminal penalty, BR §6-619.
Submission requirement, BR §6-402.
Exemption, BR §6-413.
Willful violations, BR §6-613.
Criminal penalty, BR §6-619.
Required, BR §6-401.
Reports.
Annual report.
Duty of officers, BR §6-409.
Grossly negligent violations, BR §6-614.
Submission deadline, BR §6-408.
Submission requirement, BR §6-408.
Exemption, BR §6-413.
Willful violations, BR §6-613.
Fee for failure to file, BR §6-407.
Representatives.
Acting without registration, BR §6-601.
Use of services of unregistered representative,
BR §6-602.

CHARITIES —Cont'd
Representatives —Cont'd
Charitable representative.
Defined, BR §6-101.
Compensation dependent on number or value of
contributions, BR §6-605.
Defined, BR §6-101.
Fund-raising activities.
Compensation dependent on number or value of
contributions, BR §6-605.
Misuse of registration, BR §6-604.
Registration.
Acting as representative after application for
registration, BR §6-307.
Acting without registration, BR §6-601.
Applications, BR §6-302.
Fees.
Single fees, BR §6-302.
Irrevocable letters of credit, BR §6-303.
Notice of noncompliance, BR §6-304.
Surety bond, BR §6-303.
Expiration, BR §6-305.
Grace period for associate solicitor, BR §6-301.
Issuance, BR §6-304.
Misuse of registration, BR §6-604.
New registration.
Accounting requirements, BR §6-306.
Required, BR §6-301.
Term of registration, BR §6-305.
Solicitation without authorization, BR §6-617.
Unregistered representative.
Use of services, BR §6-602.
Restitution.
Grossly negligent violations, BR §§6-614, 6-619.
Restraining orders, BR §6-205.
Rules and regulations.
Secretary of state.
Rules promulgation, BR §6-204.
Scope of act, BR §6-102.
Secretary of state.
Action against alleged violators, BR §6-205.
Cease and desist orders.
Issuance, BR §6-205.
Charitable giving information program.
Establishment, BR §6-201.
Materials available to the public, BR §6-201.
Disposition of money, BR §6-207.
Foreign charitable organizations or
representatives.
Service of process, BR §6-202.
Fund-raising notice.
Submission requirements, BR §6-502.
Injunctive powers, BR §6-205.
Investigative powers, BR §6-205.
Reciprocal agreements, BR §6-206.
Recordkeeping requirements, BR §6-203.
Rules promulgation, BR §6-204.
Service on foreign charitable organizations or
representatives, BR §6-202.
Solicitations.
Ending of soliciting.
Submission requirements, BR §6-417.
Service of process.
Foreign charitable organizations or
representatives.
Secretary of state as agent, BR §6-202.
Settlement agreements with violators, BR
§6-205.
Short title, BR §6-701.

CHARITIES —Cont'd
Social services.
State agencies engaged in charitable or welfare activities.
Charges against by state administration, 88A §3.
Solicitations.
Accounting required, BR §6-506.
Agreements, BR §6-501.
Application of charitable contribution, BR §6-606.
Charitable corporations.
See CORPORATIONS.
Charitable solicitation defined, BR §6-101.
Without authorization, BR §6-617.
Contents of text used, BR §6-501.
Contract cancellation.
Soliciting after cancellation, BR §6-612.
Controls over fund-raising activities, BR §6-416.
Criminal offenses.
Statute of limitations, CJ §5-106.
Deposit requirements, BR §6-505.
Disclosures when awarding prizes.
Required, BR §6-503.
Donor requests, BR §6-416.
Information, BR §6-416.
Ending of solicitation.
Submission requirements, BR §6-417.
Failure to comply with requirements, BR §6-509.
Fiduciaries.
Directors, officers, partners, etc., BR §6-508.
Fund-raising notice.
Contents, BR §6-502.
Misrepresentation prohibited, BR §6-416.
Noncompliance with requirements, BR §6-509.
Offenses, prosecution for.
Statute of limitations, CJ §5-106.
Prize awards.
Required disclosures, BR §6-503.
Public safety solicitors, BR §§6-5A-01 to 6-5A-11.
Recordkeeping requirements, BR §6-507.
Restrictions on soliciting and spending money, BR §6-416.
Telephone solicitation.
Receipt required, BR §6-504.
Subpoenas.
Examinations or investigations by secretary, BR §6-205.
Taxation.
Property transferred to nonprofit organization, TP §7-202.
Real and personal property, TP §7-202.
Tip jars and punch board.
Frederick county, CR §13-1305.
Washington county.
Tip jars generally, CR §§13-2414 to 13-2439.
Title of act, BR §6-701.
Tortuous conduct.
Grossly negligent violations, BR §§6-614, 6-619.
Trusts and trustees.
Charitable trusts.
Administration of private foundations, charitable trusts or split-interest trusts, ET §§14-303 to 14-307.
See TRUSTS AND TRUSTEES.
Distributions, ET §14-305.
Enforcement.
Beneficiaries as an indefinite class, ET §14-301.
Definition of charitable purposes, ET §14-301.
Generally, ET §14-301.

CHARITIES —Cont'd
Trusts and trustees —Cont'd
Charitable trusts —Cont'd
Enforcement —Cont'd
Impossible or impracticable of enforcement, ET §14-302.
Power of court, ET §14-301.
Illegal.
Becoming illegal, ET §14-302.
Perpetuities.
Rule not applicable, ET §11-102.
Uniform charitable trusts administration act, ET §14-302.
Unemployment compensation.
Charitable organizations.
When covered employment, LE §8-208.
Volunteers.
Definitions, CJ §5-407.
Liability, CJ §5-407.
Immunity of volunteers providing health care services, CJ §5-606.
Voting rights.
Restrictions on voting, BR §6-415.
Wills.
Legacy for charitable uses, ET §4-409.
Formation of corporation to take, ET §4-409.
Wine auctions.
Permits, 2B §2-101.
Workers' compensation.
Worker for aid or sustenance.
Covered employees and employers, LE §9-235.

CHARLES COUNTY.
Agricultural preservation districts.
Agricultural land located in.
Property tax credits, TP §9-310.
Alcoholic beverages.
Beer and light wine licenses.
Class D, on-sale, 2B §5-401.
Class H, on-sale only, 2B §5-202.
Limitation on number, 2B §9-209.
Beer and wine festival, 2B §8-308.
Beer licenses.
Class D, on-sale, 2B §3-401.
Religious and charitable organizations, ten days, 2B §7-101.
Limitations on number, 2B §9-209.
Beer, wine and liquor licenses.
Applicability of transferability, 2B §9-209.
Bottle clubs, 2B §20-105.
Class A, off-sale, 2B §6-101.
Class BLX, on-sale.
Hotels and restaurants, 2B §6-201.
Luxury-type restaurant, 2B §9-102.
Class B, on-sale, 2B §6-201.
Class C, on-sale, 2B §6-201.
Class D, on-sale, 2B §6-401.
Bottle clubs, 2B §20-105.
Criminal history records checks.
License applicants, 2B §10-103.
Elections.
Exercise of privileges of licensee on election day, 2B §11-401.
Entertainment.
Consumption.
Places of public entertainment, 2B §11-304.
"Go cup" prohibited, 2B §12-209.1.
Hours and days for sale, 2B §11-509.
Election days, 2B §11-401.
New Year's day, 2B §11-402.

CHARLES COUNTY —Cont'd
Alcoholic beverages —Cont'd
License commissioners.
  Appeals.
    General provisions, 2B §16-101.
  Appointment, 2B §15-104.
  Clerk, 2B §15-109.
  Counsel.
    Salaries, 2B §15-109.
  Investigations of applications and violations.
    Limitation on funds, 2B §15-112.
  Meetings, 2B §15-104.
  Notice of application.
    Publication of notice, 2B §10-202.
  Quorum, 2B §15-104.
  Salaries, 2B §15-109.
  Secretary.
    Compensation, 2B §15-112.
  Term of office, 2B §15-104.
Licenses.
  Administrative renewal, 2B §10-506.
  Applications, 2B §10-104.
    Investigation of applicant, place of business
      and patrons, 2B §10-202.
    Police records of applicants, 2B §10-103.
  Assignment or transfer, 2B §10-503.
  Commissioners. See within this subheading,
    "License commissioners."
  Corporations, 2B §9-101.
  Criminal history records checks.
    License applicants, 2B §10-103.
  Death of licensee.
    Procedure, 2B §10-506.
  Disciplinary action against licensees, 2B §9-209.
  Fees.
    Disposition, 2B §10-204.
  Golf courses, 2B §8-502.
  Issuance.
    Limitations on number, 2B §9-209.
    Procedure, 2B §10-202.
    Refusal, 2B §10-208.
  Limitations on number of licenses, 2B §9-209.
  Limited liability companies, 2B §9-101.
  Manufacturers.
    Hours and days for sale, 2B §11-101.
  Place of business.
    Restrictions on licensee, 2B §12-209.
  Premises close to churches or schools, 2B
    §9-209.
  Premises under construction, 2B §9-209.
  Renewal.
    Procedure, 2B §10-301.
  Revocation and suspension.
    Nudity and sexual displays on licensee's
      premises, 2B §10-405.
  Transferability, 2B §9-209.
Liquor control board.
  Terms of office, 2B §15-201.
Manufacturers.
  Licenses.
    Hours and days for sale, 2B §11-101.
Micro-brewery licenses, 2B §2-208.
Minors.
  Age of persons serving alcoholic beverages in
    county, 2B §12-209.2.
  Possession by prohibited, 2B §12-108.
Nudity and sexual displays on licensee's premises.
  Revocation of license, 2B §10-405.
Open containers.
  Possession in certain places.
    Applicability of provisions, 2B §19-303.

CHARLES COUNTY —Cont'd
Alcoholic beverages —Cont'd
Penalties.
  Local penalties, 2B §16-507.
Premises under construction or close to churches
    or schools.
  Issuance of licenses, 2B §9-209.
Pub-brewery licenses, 2B §2-207.
Public entertainment.
  Consumption.
    Places of public entertainment, 2B §11-304.
Public property.
  Regulation of consumption on public property in
    county, 25 §3.
Sales.
  Beer for cash, 2B §12-112.
  Election days, 2B §11-401.
  New Year's day, 2B §11-402.
  Prohibited to drunkards and mentally deficient
    persons, 2B §12-110.
  Restrictions, 2B §12-209.
Seasonal operation of premises.
  Authorized closings, 2B §10-504.
Serving.
  Age of persons serving alcoholic beverages in
    county, 2B §12-209.2.
Sundays.
  Applicability of restrictions, 2B §11-403.
Amusement parks.
Permits required, 25 §27.
Appearance fees in circuit courts.
Distribution, CJ §7-204.
Aquaculture.
Oysters and clams.
  Private oyster culture.
    Leases.
      Restrictions, NR §4-11A-05.
      Special provisions for termination, NR
        §4-11A-07.
Bailiff.
Compensation, CJ §2-507.
Barbeque grills.
Restrictions on use, PS §9-1001.
Beer and wine festival, 2B §8-308.
Bingo.
Conducting generally, CR §13-1109.
Donations to fair board, permitted, CR §13-1112.
Generally prohibited, CR §13-1105.
Management, CR §13-1110.
Prizes, CR §13-1109.
Proceeds, use, limitations, CR §13-1111.
Time limits on conducting, CR §13-1109.
Violations, criminal penalty, CR §13-1113.
Bond issues.
New school capacity construction bonds, 66B
  §14.05.
Special taxing districts, 24 §9-1301.
Bottle clubs.
Alcoholic beverages, 2B §20-105.
Boxing and wrestling arenas.
Permits required, 25 §27.
Building code.
Adoption, amendment and enforcement.
  Powers of county commissioners, 25 §10E.
Agricultural buildings.
  Exemption for buildings used for agritourism,
    PS §12-508.
**Chesapeake Bay critical area and Atlantic
  coastal bays critical area protection
  programs.**
Critical areas commission.
  Members on commission, NR §8-1804.

CHARLES COUNTY —Cont'd
Chesapeake Bay critical area and Atlantic coastal bays critical area protection programs —Cont'd
Growth allocation, location in resource conservation area, NR §8-1808.1.
Circuit courts.
Appearance fees.
Distribution, CJ §7-204.
Number of judges, CJ §1-503.
Clerks of court.
Fees.
Administering public money, CJ §2-213.
Codes.
Building, electrical and plumbing codes.
Adoption, 25 §3.
Commissioners.
Alcoholic beverage license commissioners. See within this heading, "Alcoholic beverages."
Building code.
Power to adopt, amend and enforce, 25 §10E.
Powers.
Exceptions, 25 §3.
Real property.
Power to acquire, etc., real or leasehold property, 25 §9A.
Transfer or sale of real property no longer needed, 25 §11A.
Community college.
Board of community college trustees.
Appeals of board decisions, ED §16-607.
Hearing examiners.
Appointment, ED §16-607.
Hearings.
Considerations by board, ED §16-607.
College of southern Maryland.
General provisions, ED §§16-601 to 16-610.
See COLLEGE OF SOUTHERN MARYLAND.
Legislative declaration as to Charles county community college, ED §16-601.
Renaming of Charles county community college, ED §16-603.
Hearing examiners, ED §16-607.
Hearings.
Considerations by board of trustees, ED §16-607.
Parking.
May be prohibited, TR §21-1003.
Consumer affairs.
Tri-county council for southern Maryland.
See TRI-COUNTY COUNCIL FOR SOUTHERN MARYLAND.
County work and contracts.
Competitive bidding and bonds.
Special provisions, 25 §3.
Court reporters.
Contributions by employers to pension system, SPP §21-307.
Courts.
Circuit courts.
Judicial circuit, MD Const Art IV §19.
Number of judges, CJ §1-503.
Crabs.
Landowners.
Restrictions on catching, NR §4-811.
Crimes and offenses.
Alcoholic beverages.
Obstructed windows and doors, 2B §12-209.
Dogs running at large, 24 §11-504.

CHARLES COUNTY —Cont'd
Dance halls.
Permits required, 25 §27.
Deeds.
Straw deeds.
Recordation, RP §3-104.
Development.
Additional public facilities required by development.
Charles county to be compensated by landowner, 66B §5.08.
New school capacity financing mechanism, 66B §14.05.
Tri-county council for southern Maryland.
See TRI-COUNTY COUNCIL FOR SOUTHERN MARYLAND.
Distress for rent.
Lien on crops, RP §8-115.
Dog licenses.
Fees, 24 §11-501.
Rules and regulations, 24 §11-504.
Elections.
County board of elections.
County boards generally, EL §§2-201 to 2-303.
See ELECTIONS.
County boards of education generally, EL §§8-801 to 8-806.
Polling places.
Use of private firehouses, halls or other buildings, EL §10-101.
Eminent domain.
Powers of commissioners, 25 §9A.
Fines.
Alcoholic beverages.
Hours and days for sale violated, 2B §11-509.
Possession by prohibited, 2B §12-108.
Disposition, CJ §7-507.
Junkyards.
Failure to screen or fence, 25 §122B.
Fire department.
Volunteer fire or rescue company.
Length of service awards, PS §7-210.
Workers' compensation.
Covered employees and employers, LE §9-234.
Fires and fire prevention.
Barbeque grills.
Restrictions on use, PS §9-1001.
Fish and fisheries.
Restrictions in county waters, NR §4-718.
Riparian rights.
Exceptions, NR §4-712.
Turtles.
Snapping turtles.
Restrictions, NR §4-738.
Floating homes.
Regulation, 25 §234A.
Forfeited recognizances.
Disposition, CJ §7-507.
Funds.
Navigable waters.
Powers of commissioners, 25 §3.
Gaming, bazaar, carnival and raffles, CR §§13-1101 to 13-1115.
Authority of county commissioners, CR §13-1103.
Conducted only by fundraising organization, CR §13-1106.
Conduct of gaming event generally, CR §13-1108.
Definitions, CR §13-1101.
Donations to fair board, permitted, CR §13-1112.
Fundraising organizations listed, CR §13-1101.
Gaming device defined, CR §13-1101.

CHARLES COUNTY —Cont'd
Gaming, bazaar, carnival and raffles —Cont'd
Gaming event defined, CR §13-1101.
Gaming permit.
Contents, CR §13-1107.
Defined, CR §13-1101.
Required, application, CR §13-1106.
Violations, disqualification, CR §13-1114.
Gaming permit review board, CR §13-1104.
Generally prohibited, CR §13-1105.
Hour limitation on event, CR §13-1108.
Management of event, CR §13-1110.
Management of gaming device, CR §13-1108.
Minors, participation prohibited, CR §13-1108.
Number of events conducted each quarter, CR §13-1108.
Proceeds, use, limitations, CR §13-1111.
Provisions applicable to county only, CR §13-1102.
Records, required, access, CR §13-1108.
Regulations on amusements and entertainment's.
Commissioners' authority not restricted, CR §13-1115.
Report by organization conducting, CR §13-1108.
Violations, criminal penalty, CR §13-1113.
Golf courses.
Alcoholic beverage licenses, 2B §8-502.
Greater Waldorf Jaycees, Inc.
Property tax credits, TP §9-310.
Hearings.
Real property.
Transfer or sale of real property no longer needed, 25 §11A.
Highways.
Grading, paving and repairing of roads and sidewalks, 25 §3.
Riding animals or driving animal-drawn vehicles.
Regulations, TR §21-104.
Historic area zoning.
General provisions.
See ZONING.
Housing.
Affordable housing for families of limited income.
Transfer of real property no longer needed, 25 §11A.
Fair share school construction excise tax on new residential dwellings, 66B §14.05.
Hunting.
Spotlighting, NR §10-410.
Injury reports.
Automobile accident or lethal weapon causing injury.
Physicians, pharmacists, dentists or nurses, HG §20-701.
Internal improvements.
Extension of state credit.
Limitation, MD Const Art III §34.
Judges.
Former judges.
Recall for temporary assignment.
Maximum period of assignment, CJ §1-302.
Pensions.
General provisions, ET §2-108.
Junkyards.
Screening or fencing, 25 §122B.
Landlord and tenant.
Lien on crops.
Advances, RP §8-115.
Share reserved as rent, RP §8-115.
Libraries.
Board of library trustees.
Terms of members, ED §23-403.

CHARLES COUNTY —Cont'd
Libraries —Cont'd
Video cassette rental fees, ED §23-405.
Licenses.
Alcoholic beverages. See within this heading, "Alcoholic beverages."
Limited liability companies.
Alcoholic beverages.
Licenses, 2B §9-101.
Loans.
Tri-county council for southern Maryland.
Review of applications for loans, 20 §3-103.
Massage therapists.
Practice in Charles county, HO §3-5A-14.
Prohibited acts, HO §3-5A-11.
Minors.
Alcoholic beverages.
Possession prohibited, 2B §12-108.
Serving alcoholic beverages in county, 2B §12-209.2.
Misdemeanors.
Alcoholic beverages.
Obstructed windows and doors, 2B §12-209.
Dogs running at large, 24 §11-504.
Mobile homes.
Occupancy tax, 24 §9-402.
Mortgages and deeds of trust.
Interest.
Payable after sale, RP §7-105.
Motor vehicles.
Graveyards.
Screening or fencing junkyards required, 25 §122B.
Junkyards.
Screening or fencing, 25 §122B.
New or expanding businesses in county.
Property tax credit, TP §9-310.
Noise control.
Trapshooting, skeet shooting, etc.
Limitations on authority, EN §§3-105, 3-401.
Nonprofit community or civic improvement association or corporation.
Property tax credits, TP §9-310.
Notices.
Fair share school construction excise tax on new residential dwellings, 66B §14.05.
Real property.
Transfer or sale of real property no longer needed, 25 §11A.
Obscene performances.
Prohibition, CR §11-204.
Orphans' court.
Judges.
Compensation, ET §2-108.
Sessions.
Place, ET §2-106.
Time, ET §2-106.
Oysters and clams.
Hydraulic clam dredge.
Where use prohibited, NR §4-1038.
Private oyster culture.
Leases.
Restrictions, NR §4-11A-05.
Special provisions for termination, NR §4-11A-07.
Taking or catching.
Prohibited during open season for migratory wild waterfowl, NR §4-1006.
Parking.
Towing or removal ordinances, TR §21-1009.

CHARLES COUNTY —Cont'd
Patuxent river watershed.
General provisions.
See PATUXENT RIVER WATERSHED.
Pedestrians.
Soliciting rides, employment or business, TR §§21-313, 21-507.
Permits.
Dance halls and other places of amusement, tourist camps, etc., 25 §27.
Personal property.
Purchase or lease of.
Powers, 25 §9D.
Planning.
Tri-county council for southern Maryland.
See TRI-COUNTY COUNCIL FOR SOUTHERN MARYLAND.
Planning commission, 66B §14.05.
Property tax exemption.
Reserved property, TP §7-241.
Special provisions, 66B §3.02.
Port administration.
Jurisdiction.
Consent to territorial jurisdiction, TR §6-103.
Property taxes.
Fair share school construction excise tax on new residential dwellings, 66B §14.05.
Reserved property by planning commission, exemption, TP §7-241.
Publication.
Alcoholic beverages.
License commissioners.
Publication of notice of application, 2B §10-202.
Real property.
Acquire or dispose of.
Powers of commissioners, 25 §9A.
Fair share school construction excise tax on new residential dwellings, 66B §14.05.
Sale.
Powers of commissioners, 25 §5E.
Transfer or sale of real property no longer needed, 25 §11A.
Recordation.
Deeds.
Straw deeds.
Exception as to, RP §3-104.
Plats of subdivisions.
Exception for certain conveyances, RP §3-108.
Tax.
Prepayment of personal property taxes, RP §3-104.
Rehabilitated business real property.
Property tax credits, TP §9-310.
Retirement funds.
Employees who retire before origination of retirement system, 25 §3.
Roads, restricted access to trucks.
Board of county commissioners selecting, 25 §25.
Rural legacy program.
Property tax credits, TP §9-310.
Schools.
Additional school sites required by development.
Compensation of county by landowner, 66B §5.08.
County board of education.
Chairman, ED §3-502.
Salary and expenses, ED §3-503.
Compensation and expenses, ED §§3-503, 4-107.
Election generally, EL §§8-801 to 8-806.
Election of members, ED §3-114.

CHARLES COUNTY —Cont'd
Schools —Cont'd
County board of education —Cont'd
Meetings, ED §3-504.
Members, ED §3-501.
Persons subject to authority of board.
Ineligibility to serve as member, ED §3-114.
Property.
Parking, TR §21-1003.
Records.
Public records, ED §3-504.
Vice chairman, ED §3-502.
Salary and expenses, ED §3-503.
Employees.
Public school employees, defined, ED §6-401.
Negotiations between employer and employee.
Representation in Charles county.
Fees charged for nonmembers, ED §§6-407, 6-504.
New school capacity financing mechanism, 66B §14.05.
Real property.
Sale or donation of property no longer needed, 25 §11A.
Sheriff.
Deputies, CJ §2-309.
General provisions, CJ §2-309.
Pension plan for department, 25 §3.
Second in command, CJ §2-310.
Smoking.
Tobacco smoking in retail stores.
Limitation on local legislation, HG §24-505.
Southern Maryland Youth Organization, Inc.
Property tax credits, TP §9-310.
Special taxing districts, 24 §9-1301.
State's attorney, 10 §40.
Subdivisions.
Additional school sites required by development.
Charles county to be compensated by landowner, 66B §5.08.
Fair share school construction excise tax on new residential dwellings, 66B §14.05.
Plats.
Exception for certain conveyances, RP §3-108.
Public facilities.
Additional public facilities required by development.
Charles county to be compensated by landowner, 66B §5.08.
Sundays and holidays.
Alcoholic beverages.
Applicability of restrictions, 2B §11-403.
Sales on New Year's day, 2B §11-402.
Taxation.
Credits.
Property tax credits, TP §9-310.
Deferred property tax payments, TP §10-204.4.
Fair share school construction excise tax on new residential dwellings, 66B §14.05.
Hotel rental tax, 24 §§9-301 to 9-326.
See COUNTIES.
Mobile home occupancy tax, 24 §9-402.
Receipt.
Exhibition required.
Transfer of alcoholic beverage license, 2B §10-503.
Recordation.
Exemptions from recordation tax.
Rental transfer exemption, TP §12-114.
Targeted businesses exemption, TP §12-115.

CHARLES COUNTY —Cont'd
Taxation —Cont'd
Redemption.
Rate of redemption, TP §14-820.
Special taxing districts.
Authorized, 24 §9-1301.
Tobacco barns.
Property tax credit against certain property
formerly used solely as, TP §9-310.
Tourist camps.
Permits required, 25 §27.
**Trapshooting, skeetshooting or other target
shooting.**
Environmental sound level limits and noise
control rules and regulations, EN §3-401.
Noise control ordinances, rules or regulations
prohibiting, EN §3-105.
Treasurer.
General provisions, 25 §51.
Tri-county council for southern Maryland.
See TRI-COUNTY COUNCIL FOR SOUTHERN
MARYLAND.
Trucks, tractors or trailers.
Through traffic restricted on certain roads, power
of county commissioners to select, 25 §25.
Volunteer fire departments.
Length of service awards, PS §7-210.
Workers' compensation.
Covered employees and employers, LE §9-234.
Watershed associations.
Rights of way and easements, 25 §200A.
Waters of the state.
Fund to make navigable waters, 25 §3.
Wine festival, 2B §8-308.
Workers' compensation.
Fires and fire prevention.
Covered employees and employers.
Volunteer fire or rescue company, LE §9-234.
Zoning.
Board of appeals, 66B §14.05.
Historic area zoning.
General provisions.
See ZONING.
Junkyards.
Screening or fencing, 25 §122B.
Subdivision.
Lots.
Sale or transfer in approved subdivisions, 66B
§5.05.
Surface, mining, asphalt plant, concrete plant,
sand and gravel mining.
Special exception, 66B §14.05.

CHARLES H. HICKEY, JR. SCHOOL.
Citizen's advisory committee, 83C §2-119.1.
Educational program development, ED §22-308.
Responsibility for, ED §22-303.

**CHARLES MCC. MATHIAS, JR. NATIONAL
STUDY CENTER FOR TRAUMA AND
EMERGENCY MEDICAL SYSTEMS,** ED
§13-513.

**CHARLES W. RILEY FIRE AND EMERGENCY
MEDICAL SERVICES TUITION
REIMBURSEMENT PROGRAM,** ED §18-603.

CHARTER FOR HIGHER EDUCATION, ED
§§10-101 to 10-213.
See UNIVERSITIES AND COLLEGES.

CHARTERS.
Aviation.
Charter permits.
See AVIATION.

CHARTERS —Cont'd
Baltimore City, MD Const Art XI-A §§1 to 7.
See BALTIMORE CITY.
Corporations.
See CORPORATIONS.
Counties.
See COUNTIES.

CHARTER SCHOOLS, ED §§9-101 to 9-110.
See SCHOOLS.

CHASTITY.
Rape or sexual offense prosecution.
Reputation or opinion as to victim's chastity, CR
§3-319.
Specific instances of victim's prior sexual conduct,
CR §3-319.

CHATTELS.
Personal property.
See PERSONAL PROPERTY.

CHATTELS REAL.
Ground rent.
See GROUND RENT.
Leases.
See LANDLORD AND TENANT.
Life estates.
See LIFE ESTATES.
Remainders.
See REMAINDERS, REVERSIONS AND
EXECUTORY INTERESTS.

CHECK CASHING SERVICES, FI §§12-101 to
12-127.
Accounts, recordkeeping, FI §12-114.
Cease and desist order upon violations, FI
§12-121.
Change of place of business, FI §12-113.
Criminal violations.
Penalties, FI §12-125.
Report of, FI §12-124.
Damages to third party, FI §12-127.
Definitions, FI §12-101.
Disciplinary actions.
Grounds, FI §12-122.
Hearing, FI §12-123.
**Endorsements required on payment of
instrument,** FI §12-116.
Exemptions from provisions, FI §§12-102,
12-103.
Fee ceilings, FI §12-120.
Fee schedule, posting, FI §12-118.
Fines, civil penalties, FI §12-126.
Fingerprinting of licensees, FI §12-107.
Identification required to pay on instrument,
FI §12-119.
Inspection of records, FI §12-115.
Licenses.
Application, FI §12-108.
Authority under license, FI §12-110.
Commissioner approval or denial of application,
FI §12-109.
Display, FI §12-112.
Fingerprints, FI §12-107.
Grounds for revocation or suspension, FI §12-122.
Information on license, FI §12-110.
Nontransferable, FI §12-112.
Qualifications, FI §12-106.
Renewal, FI §12-111.
Required, FI §12-105.
Money laundering, compliance with laws, FI
§12-117.

CHECK CASHING SERVICES —Cont'd
Recordkeeping, FI §12-114.
Regulations, FI §12-104.
Third party actions under title, FI §12-127.

CHECKOFFS.
Income tax contribution.
Chesapeake Bay and endangered species fund, TG
§2-110.
Checkoff system defined, NR §1-701.
Maryland cancer fund, HG §20-117; TG §2-112.

CHECKS.
Appropriations.
Disbursements and expenditures, SF §§7-227,
7-227.1, 7-229, 7-230.
See APPROPRIATIONS.
Bad checks, CR §§8-101 to 8-108.
See BAD CHECKS.
Banks and trust companies.
Certification.
Prohibited when there are not sufficient funds
on deposit, FI §3-606.
Valid against bank or trust company, FI §3-606.
Loss of checks.
Liability of banking institutions, FI §5-307.
Month and year account opened to appear on
checks, FI §5-310.
Exceptions, FI §5-310.
Return of cancelled checks, FI §5-513.
Board of public works.
Experimental check cashing program.
Authority to establish, 78A §55.
Campaign finance.
Contributions.
Attributable to election cycle in which issued,
EL §13-232.
Disbursement by, EL §13-220.
Money contributions in excess of $100.
Check required, EL §13-226.
Cashier's checks.
Defined as negotiable instruments, CL §3-104.
Effect of obligation for which taken, CL §3-310.
Liability to pay, CL §3-411.
Lost, destroyed or stolen, CL §3-312.
Obligation of issuer, CL §3-412.
Certified checks.
Acceptance, CL §3-409.
Defined, CL §3-409.
Lost, destroyed or stolen, CL §3-312.
Obligation for which taken, CL §3-310.
Refusal to pay, CL §3-411.
**Collection of dishonored checks and other
instruments,** CL §§15-801 to 15-804.
Commercial code.
Negotiable instruments generally, CL §§3-101 to
3-605.
See NEGOTIABLE INSTRUMENTS.
Consumer loans.
Collection of certain fees.
Bad check fees, CL §12-307.
Consumer protection.
Discharge checks.
Return to buyer or borrower, CL §14-1312.
Costs.
Bad checks.
Paying costs with bad check, CR §8-108.
Credit cards.
General provisions.
See CREDIT CARDS.
Use of credit card information.
Payments by check, CL §13-318.

CHECKS —Cont'd
Credit unions.
Selling and cashing checks, FI §6-312.
Disbursements and expenditures.
Appropriations, SF §§7-227, 7-227.1, 7-229, 7-230.
See APPROPRIATIONS.
Dishonored checks, collection, CL §§15-801 to
15-804.
Experimental check cashing program.
Board of public works.
Authority to establish, 78A §55.
Fiduciaries.
Drawn by and payable to fiduciary, ET §15-205.
Drawn by fiduciary to third person, ET §15-204.
Financial institution franchise tax.
Payment by dishonored checks.
Assessment of service charge, TG §13-713.
Fines.
Bad checks.
Paying fines with bad check, CR §8-108.
Forgery.
Bank customer's duty to discover and report, CL
§4-406.
Minors.
Recoveries in tort.
Appointment of trustee by issuance of check, ET
§13-403.
Deposit or investment of check, ET §13-404.
Guardian.
Payment by check to, ET §13-403.
Money transmission.
General provisions, FI §§12-401 to 12-431.
See MONEY TRANSMISSION.
Motor vehicles.
Service charge for presenting bad checks to
administration, TR §12-116.
Negotiable instruments generally, CL §§3-101 to
3-605.
See NEGOTIABLE INSTRUMENTS.
Real estate brokers.
Dishonored checks.
Additional fee, BOP §17-521.
Returned check charges.
Court charges, CJ §7-208.
Sale of goods, UCC.
Payment by check, CL §2-511.
Sales.
Bad checks.
Power to transfer title, CL §2-403.
Savings and loan associations.
Month and year account opened to appear on
checks, FI §9-412.1.
Stale checks.
Payment.
Bank not obligated to pay, CL §4-404.
State treasury.
Appropriations.
Disbursements and expenditures, SF §§7-227,
7-227.1, 7-229, 7-230.
See APPROPRIATIONS.
Stop payment.
Bank's right to subrogation on improper payment,
CL §4-407.
Customer's right, CL §4-403.
Issuing or passing check with knowledge.
Bad checks, CR §§8-101 to 8-108.
Teller's checks.
Defined as negotiable instrument, CL §3-104.
Effect of obligation for which taken, CL §3-310.
Lost, destroyed or stolen, CL §3-312.
Refusal to pay, CL §3-411.

CHECKS —Cont'd
Travelers' checks.
Defined as negotiable instrument, CL §3-104.
Truncated checking accounts.
Return of checks, FI §5-513.
Unemployment compensation.
Unemployment insurance fund.
Checks for benefits and refunds, LE §8-406.
Washington county.
Bad check fee, 25 §3.
Worthless checks.
See BAD CHECKS.

CHELTENHAM YOUTH FACILITY.
Juvenile facilities.
Bond request for building or renovating facilities, 83C §2-117.
Librarians employed in certain institutions.
Salaries generally, ED §6-302.

CHEMICAL MACE.
Wearing or carrying with intent to injure, CR §4-101.

CHEMICALS.
Acid deposition, NR §§3-3A-01 to 3-3A-04.
See ACID DEPOSITION.

CHEMICAL WARFARE MATERIALS.
General provisions, EN §§7-239.1 to 7-239.4.
See HAZARDOUS MATERIALS AND SUBSTANCES.

CHEMIST.
Controlled dangerous substances, CJ §§10-1001 to 10-1004.
See CONTROLLED DANGEROUS SUBSTANCES.
State chemist.
See STATE CHEMIST.

CHESAPEAKE AUDUBON SOCIETY, INC.
Property tax credits.
Dorchester county, TP §9-311.
Talbot county, TP §9-322.

CHESAPEAKE BAY.
Aquaculture.
Defined, NR §4-11A-01.
Attorney general.
Dumping of dredged materials in bay, EN §§5-1104, 5-1106.
Big Blackwater River.
Public access to Chesapeake Bay and tributaries.
Condemnation and eminent domain, NR §8-204.
Boats.
State boat act.
See VESSELS AND BOATS.
Bridge.
Toll bridge.
General provisions.
See TRAFFIC LAWS.
Charter boat permit, NR §4-210.2.
Chlorine.
Discharge into Chesapeake Bay or tributaries, EN §9-329.2.
Commercial timber harvesting.
Forest conservation.
Applicability of subtitle, NR §5-1602.
Commission, NR §8-301.
Chesapeake Bay and coastal zone advisory commission.
Established, NR §8-201.
Critical area commission. See within this heading, "Critical area protection program."

CHESAPEAKE BAY —Cont'd
Commission —Cont'd
Oysters and clams.
General provisions.
See OYSTERS AND CLAMS.
State boat act.
See VESSELS AND BOATS.
Condemnation.
Public access to Chesapeake Bay and tributaries.
Big Blackwater River and Little Blackwater River, NR §8-204.
Contracts.
Green Shores program, NR §5-430.
Counties.
Critical area protection program.
Local jurisdictions. See within this heading, "Critical area protection program."
Cox creek citizens oversight committee, EN §5-1102.1.
Crimes and offenses.
Dumping of dredged materials, EN §5-1107.
Criminal procedure.
Venue.
Crimes committed on bay, CP §4-201.
Critical area protection program.
Commercial timber harvesting.
Forest conservation.
Applicability of subtitle, NR §5-1602.
Definitions, NR §§8-1802, 8-1808.5.
Forest conservation.
Applicability of subtitle.
Exception to commercial logging and timber harvesting conducted under program, NR §5-1602.
Extension of critical area forest protection measures in lieu of requirements, NR §5-1602.
Generally, NR §§8-1801 to 8-1817.
See CHESAPEAKE BAY CRITICAL AREA AND ATLANTIC COASTAL BAYS CRITICAL AREA PROTECTION PROGRAMS.
Private wetlands.
Modification of maps.
Amendment not deemed to alter boundaries of area, EN §16-303.
Program development.
Approval and adoption of program.
Public hearing, NR §§8-1809, 8-1810.
Trees.
Forest conservation.
Applicability of subtitle, NR §5-1602.
Definitions.
Dumping of dredged materials, EN §5-1101.
Department of natural resources.
Chesapeake Bay and coastal zone advisory commission.
Established, NR §8-201.
Intergovernmental agreements.
Preserve resources of Chesapeake Bay, NR §8-203.
Powers, duties and responsibilities.
Generally, NR §§8-202, 8-204.
Public access to Chesapeake Bay and tributaries.
Powers and duties.
Generally, NR §8-204.
Dredging.
Dumping of dredged materials in bay or tributaries. See within this heading, "Dumping of dredged materials."
Submerged aquatic vegetation zones, NR §4-1006.1.

CHESAPEAKE BAY —Cont'd
Drilling wells.
Gas and oil.
Prohibited in Chesapeake Bay or tributaries, EN §14-107.
Dumping of dredged materials, EN §§5-1101 to 5-1107.
Cox creek citizens oversight committee, EN §5-1102.1.
Definitions, EN §5-1101.
Enforcement.
Attorney general to enforce provisions of subtitle, EN §5-1106.
Evaluating and monitoring dumping, EN §4-414.
Executive committee, EN §5-1104.2.
General assembly.
Legislative declaration, EN §5-1101.
Injunctions.
Attorney general may seek injunction, EN §5-1105.
Kent island citizens oversight committee, EN §5-1104.1.
Penalties.
Violations of subtitle, EN §5-1107.
Planning.
Executive committee, EN §5-1104.2.
Prohibited, EN §5-1102.
Redeposit of spoil in Hart-Miller-Pleasure Island chain, EN §5-1103.
Hart-Miller-Pleasure Island citizens oversight committee, EN §5-1104.
Sewage sludge.
Defined, EN §5-1101.
Dumping prohibited, EN §5-1102.
Violations.
Penalty for violations of subtitle, EN §5-1107.
Dumping or throwing waste into waters of state, NR §8-726.1.
Eminent domain.
Public access to Chesapeake Bay and tributaries.
Big Blackwater River and Little Blackwater River, NR §8-204.
Excavated material from bay.
Dumping prohibited, EN §5-1102.
Fertilizers.
Commercial fertilizers.
Signs required at retail outlets advising customers as to effects of overuse, AG §6-210.1.
Fish and fisheries.
General provisions.
See FISH AND FISHERIES.
Forest conservation.
Applicability of subtitle, NR §5-1602.
Funds.
Chesapeake Bay and endangered species fund, NR §§1-701 to 1-706.
See CHESAPEAKE BAY AND ENDANGERED SPECIES FUND.
Gas and oil.
Drilling wells.
Prohibited in Chesapeake Bay or tributaries, EN §14-107.
General assembly.
Dumping of dredged materials in bay or tributaries.
Legislative declaration, EN §5-1101.
Green Shores program.
Contracts.
Authority to enter, NR §5-430.
Declaration of legislature, NR §5-428.

CHESAPEAKE BAY —Cont'd
Green Shores program —Cont'd
Establishment, NR §5-429.
Legislative findings, NR §5-428.
Priorities, NR §5-430.
Regulations.
Adoption, NR §5-430.
Scope, NR §5-429.
Hart-Miller-Pleasure Island chain.
Redeposit of spoil, EN §5-1103.
Citizens oversight committee, EN §5-1104.
Injunctions.
Dumping of dredged materials in bay or tributaries.
Attorney general to seek injunction, EN §5-1105.
Little Blackwater River.
Public access to Chesapeake Bay and tributaries.
Condemnation and eminent domain, NR §8-204.
Minerals.
See MINING.
Misdemeanors.
Dumping of dredged materials, EN §5-1107.
Municipal corporations.
Critical area protection program.
Local jurisdictions. See within this heading, "Critical area protection program."
Oysters and clams.
General provisions.
See OYSTERS AND CLAMS.
Pilots.
Waste disposal in Chesapeake Bay.
Regulations, BOP §11-601.
Protection program.
Critical area protection program, NR §§8-1801 to 8-1817. See within this heading, "Critical area protection program."
Public access to Chesapeake Bay and tributaries, NR §8-204.
Rules and regulations.
Green Shores program, NR §5-430.
SAV protection zone.
Submerged aquatic vegetation zones, NR §4-1006.1.
Sewage sludge.
Defined, EN §5-1101.
Dumping prohibited, EN §5-1102.
Shells.
Oyster shell purchase program, NR §4-1019.2.
Return of oyster shells to Chesapeake Bay.
Program, NR §4-1019.1.
Shore erosion control.
General provisions.
See SHORE EROSION CONTROL.
Submerged aquatic vegetation zones, NR §4-1006.1.
Susquehanna Flats.
General provisions.
See BIRDS AND GAME.
Throwing waste into waters of state, NR §8-726.1.
Trees and timber.
Critical area protection program.
Forest conservation generally, NR §5-1602.
Trust.
Accounting, NR §8-1908.
Board of trustees.
Chairman, NR §8-1904.
Composition, NR §8-1903.
Expenses, NR §8-1904.
Meetings, NR §8-1904.

CHESAPEAKE BAY —Cont'd

Trust —Cont'd

Body corporate, NR §8-1902.

Citizen involvement or corporate sponsorship
projects.

Application of funds, NR §8-1907.

Development criteria, NR §8-1906.

Political activities not to be considered, NR
§8-1906.

Deposits, NR §8-1908.

Duties.

Generally, NR §8-1905.

Established, NR §8-1901.

Exemption from certain code provisions, NR
§8-1909.

Investments, NR §8-1908.

Powers and duties.

Generally, NR §8-1905.

Purposes, NR §§8-1901, 8-1902.

Venue.

Crimes committed on Chesapeake Bay, CP §4-201.

Waste.

Throwing waste into waters of state, NR §8-726.1.

Water pollution.

Chlorine.

Discharge into Chesapeake Bay or tributaries,
EN §9-329.2.

Monitoring program, EN §9-321.

Wells.

Gas and oil.

Drilling prohibited in Chesapeake Bay or
tributaries, EN §14-107.

Wetlands.

General provisions, EN §§16-101 to 16-503.

See WETLANDS.

**CHESAPEAKE BAY AND ENDANGERED
SPECIES FUND.**

Administration, NR §1-702.

Advice and recommendations.

Use of funds.

Solicitation, NR §1-705.

Conservation.

Promotion.

Use of funds, NR §1-705.

Credits to fund, NR §1-702.

Definitions, NR §1-701.

Distributions, NR §1-703.

Established, NR §1-702.

Expenditures.

Supplemental, NR §1-702.

General assembly.

Annual report to, NR §1-706.

Grants, NR §1-704.

Habitat protection.

Use of fund, NR §1-705.

Income tax.

Checkoff system, TG §2-110.

Defined, NR §1-701.

**Nonprofit organizations, community
associations, etc.**

Grants to, NR §1-704.

Promotional account.

Distributions to, NR §1-703.

Purposes, NR §1-702.

Reports.

Annual report to general assembly, NR §1-706.

Schools.

Grants to, NR §1-704.

Uses, NR §§1-702, 1-705.

CHESAPEAKE BAY COMMISSION.

State retirement and pension system.

Municipal participation in state employees'
systems, SPP §§31-101 to 31-116.1.

See STATE RETIREMENT AND PENSION
SYSTEM.

**CHESAPEAKE BAY CRITICAL AREA AND
ATLANTIC COASTAL BAYS CRITICAL
AREA PROTECTION PROGRAMS,** NR
§§8-1801 to 8-1817.

**Administrative, judicial or other original
proceeding or appeal.**

Authority of chairman of commission, NR §8-1812.

Adverse impact.

Applicants who minimize, NR §8-1808.6.

Agricultural activities permitted.

Local critical area protection program, NR
§8-1808.8.

Amendments to program, NR §8-1809.

Anne Arundel county.

Critical areas commission.

Members on commission, NR §8-1804.

Appeals.

Authority of chairman of commission to pursue,
NR §8-1812.

Approval and adoption of program, NR §8-1809.

Programs adopted by commission, NR §8-1810.

Approval of projects, NR §8-1811.

Local agency projects, NR §8-1814.

Atlantic coastal bays.

Area designated as critical area, NR §8-1807.

Initial planning area, NR §8-1807.

Local critical area protection program, NR
§8-1808.8.

Attorney general.

Referral if local jurisdiction failing in duties, NR
§8-1815.

Baltimore City.

Critical areas commission.

Members on commission, NR §8-1804.

Baltimore county.

Critical areas commission.

Members on commission, NR §8-1804.

Buffers.

Commercial timber harvest.

Buffer management plan, NR §8-1808.7.

Community pier in buffer, NR §8-1808.5.

Perennial and intermittent streams.

Local jurisdiction adopting provisions, NR
§8-1808.9.

Planned unit developments.

Alternative buffer provision, NR §8-1813.1.

Calculation of 1-in-20 density of development,
NR §8-1808.1.

Calvert county.

Critical areas commission.

Members on commission, NR §8-1804.

Growth allocation, location in resource
conservation area, NR §8-1808.1.

Caroline county.

Critical areas commission.

Members on commission, NR §8-1804.

Growth allocation, location in resource
conservation area, NR §8-1808.1.

Cecil county.

Critical areas commission.

Members on commission, NR §8-1804.

Growth allocation, location in resource
conservation area, NR §8-1808.1.

**CHESAPEAKE BAY CRITICAL AREA AND
    ATLANTIC COASTAL BAYS CRITICAL
    AREA PROTECTION PROGRAMS** —Cont'd
Charles county.
    Critical areas commission.
        Members on commission, NR §8-1804.
    Growth allocation, location in resource
        conservation area, NR §8-1808.1.
Chesapeake Bay.
    Area designated as critical area, NR §8-1807.
    Environmental impact study.
        Exploratory drilling under critical area, NR
            §8-1817.
    Initial planning area, NR §8-1807.
**Combining amendments and refinements for
    approval,** NR §8-1809.
Commercial timber harvest.
    Buffer management plan, NR §8-1808.7.
Community pier in buffer, NR §8-1808.5.
Credits.
    Applicants who minimize adverse impact, NR
        §8-1808.6.
Criminal prosecution or civil suit.
    Violators subject, NR §8-1815.
**Criteria for program development and
    approval.**
    Regulations to be adopted, NR §8-1808.
Critical areas, NR §8-1807.
    Local program, NR §8-1808.8.
Critical areas commission.
    Created, NR §8-1803.
    Initiation or intervention in proceedings or
        appeals.
        Authority of chairman, NR §8-1812.
    Members, compensation, terms, vacancies and
        quorum, NR §8-1804.
        Atlantic coastal bays watershed residents, NR
            §8-1806.
    Powers, NR §8-1806.
    Programs adopted by, NR §8-1810.
    Report, NR §8-1816.
Cutting and clearing trees.
    Violations, sanctions and remedies, NR §8-1815.1.
Deficiency in adopted program, NR §8-1809.
Definitions, NR §8-1802.
    Intrafamily transfers, NR §8-1808.2.
    Pier.
        Community pier in buffer, NR §8-1808.5.
        Prince George's county.
            Construction, building permits, NR §8-1808.4.
        Single family dwellings, NR §8-1813.1.
Development and implementation.
    Local jurisdiction responsibility, NR §8-1808.
Dorchester county.
    Critical areas commission.
        Members on commission, NR §8-1804.
    Growth allocation, location in resource
        conservation area, NR §8-1808.1.
**Drilling under Chesapeake critical area
    critical area.**
    Environmental impact study, NR §8-1817.
Elements of program, NR §8-1808.
Enforcement, NR §8-1815.
Environmental impact study.
    Exploratory drilling under Chesapeake Bay
        critical area, NR §8-1817.
Equitable remedies.
    Local jurisdiction failing in duties, NR §8-1815.
**Exclusion of area from critical area
    designation.**
    Local jurisdictions, NR §8-1807.

**CHESAPEAKE BAY CRITICAL AREA AND
    ATLANTIC COASTAL BAYS CRITICAL
    AREA PROTECTION PROGRAMS** —Cont'd
Failure of local jurisdiction to adopt program.
    Adoption by commission, NR §8-1810.
Findings of general assembly, NR §8-1801.
Forest conservation act.
    Local critical area protection program replaces
        requirements,' NR §8-1808.8.
Goals of program, NR §8-1808.
Growth allocation.
    Resource conservation areas, NR §8-1808.1.
Harford county.
    Critical areas commission.
        Members on commission, NR §8-1804.
Hearing on adoption of program, NR §8-1809.
Hearing on amendments and refinements, NR
    §8-1809.
Hearing on proposed program, NR §8-1809.
Hearings on criteria for plan development.
    Location, NR §8-1808.
Heritage conservation fund, NR §§5-1501 to
    5-1506.
    See HERITAGE CONSERVATION FUND.
Impervious surface limitation, NR §8-1808.3.
Initial land classification, NR §8-1808.
Initial planning area, NR §8-1807.
Intent to development program.
    Statement by local jurisdiction, NR §8-1809.
Intervention.
    Administrative, judicial or other original
        proceeding or appeal.
        Authority of chairman of commission, NR
            §8-1812.
Intrafamily transfers, NR §8-1808.2.
Kent county.
    Critical areas commission.
        Members on commission, NR §8-1804.
    Growth allocation, location in resource
        conservation area, NR §8-1808.1.
Local agency projects.
    Approval, NR §8-1814.
Local critical area protection program, NR
    §8-1808.8.
**Maryland-national capital park and planning
    commission.**
    Obligations imposed by subtitle.
        When shared with Maryland-national capital
            park and planning commission, NR
            §8-1802.
**New intensely developed or limited
    development areas.**
    Guidelines for locating, NR §8-1808.1.
Notice.
    Projects requiring notice to commission, NR
        §8-1811.
Ocean City.
    Critical areas commission.
        Mayor as member, NR §8-1804.
Oil and gas production or exploration.
    Chesapeake Bay critical area, NR §8-1817.
Perennial and intermittent streams.
    Buffers.
        Local jurisdiction adopting provisions, NR
            §8-1808.9.
Piers.
    Community pier in buffer, NR §8-1808.5.
    Prince George's county.
        Construction, building permits, NR §8-1808.4.
Planned unit developments, NR §8-1813.1.

CHESAPEAKE BAY CRITICAL AREA AND ATLANTIC COASTAL BAYS CRITICAL AREA PROTECTION PROGRAMS —Cont'd

Prince George's county.
Critical areas commission.
Members on commission, NR §8-1804.
Obligations imposed by subtitle.
When shared with Maryland-national capital park and planning commission, NR §8-1802.
Piers.
Construction, building permits, NR §8-1808.4.
Prior project approval, NR §8-1813.
Program development.
Local jurisdiction responsibility, NR §8-1808.
Project approval, NR §8-1811.
Local agency projects, NR §8-1814.
Prior project approval, NR §8-1813.
Proposed program.
Preparation by local jurisdiction, NR §8-1809.
Public policy, declaration, NR §8-1801.
Purpose in enacting subtitle, NR §8-1801.
Queen Anne's county.
Critical areas commission.
Members on commission, NR §8-1804.
Growth allocation, location in resource conservation area, NR §8-1808.1.
Refinements to program, NR §8-1809.
Report by commission, NR §8-1816.
Resource conservation areas.
Growth allocation, NR §8-1808.1.
Restraining violations, actions, NR §8-1815.
St. Mary's county.
Critical areas commission.
Members on commission, NR §8-1804.
Growth allocation, location in resource conservation area, NR §8-1808.1.
Sanctions or remedies.
Local jurisdiction failing in duties, NR §8-1815.
Tree clearing or cutting, NR §8-1815.1.
Secretary's authority under title 1 of article.
Limitations, NR §8-1803.
Single family dwellings, NR §8-1813.1.
Somerset county.
Growth allocation, location in resource conservation area, NR §8-1808.1.
Statement of intent to adopt program.
Local jurisdiction, NR §8-1809.
Stromwater runoff.
Impervious surface limitation, NR §8-1808.3.
Subdivisions.
Single family dwellings, NR §8-1813.1.
Talbot county.
Critical areas commission.
Members on commission, NR §8-1804.
Growth allocation, location in resource conservation area, NR §8-1808.1.
Timber harvest.
Buffer management plan, NR §8-1808.7.
Tree clearing or cutting.
Violations, sanctions and remedies, NR §8-1815.1.
Variance to local jurisdiction's program, NR §8-1808.
Impervious surface limitation, NR §8-1808.3.
Wicomico county.
Critical areas commission.
Members on commission, NR §8-1804.
Growth allocation, location in resource conservation area, NR §8-1808.1.
Worcester county.
Critical areas commission.
Members on commission, NR §8-1804.

CHESAPEAKE BAY CRITICAL AREA AND ATLANTIC COASTAL BAYS CRITICAL AREA PROTECTION PROGRAMS —Cont'd

Worcester county —Cont'd
Growth allocation, location in resource conservation area, NR §8-1808.1.

CHESAPEAKE BAY FOUNDATION, INC.
Taxation.
Exemption of property, TP §7-203.

CHESAPEAKE BAY RETRIEVER.
Designation as state dog, SG §13-303.

CHESAPEAKE COLLEGE.
Board of trustees, ED §16-406.
Expenses, ED §16-305.
Governor.
Board of trustees.
Appointment of members, ED §16-406.

CHESAPEAKE REGIONAL OLYMPIC GAMES AUTHORITY, SG §§9-2301 to 9-2303.
Compact, SG §9-2303.
Execution, SG §9-2302.
Definitions, SG §9-2301.

CHICKENS.
Avian influenza, regulation to control, AG §§3-801 to 3-805.
Feedstuffs.
Additives to reduce phosphorus in poultry waste.
Inclusion in contact feed fed to chickens, AG §6-107.1.
Poultry products inspection.
General provisions.
See POULTRY PRODUCTS INSPECTION.

CHICKS.
Selling or coloring, CR §10-614.

CHILD ABDUCTION.
Custody and visitation, FL §§9-301 to 9-307.

CHILD ABUSE AND NEGLECT.
Abuse.
Defined, FL §5-701.
Applicability of provisions, FL §5-703.
Birthing care centers and hospitals, disclosures to, 88A §6.
Centers of excellence.
Definitions, HG §13-2201.
Establishment of initiative, HG §13-2202.
Expert panel, HG §13-2205.
Faculty duties, HG §13-2203.
Funding of initiative, HG §13-2206.
Information sharing, HG §13-2204.
Purposes, HG §13-2202.
Training of panel, HG §13-2205.
Central registry, FL §5-714.
Availability of information, FL §5-714.
Maintenance, FL §5-714.
Source of information, FL §5-714.
Child abuse prevention awareness week, FL §5-1104.
Child custody.
Evidence of abuse against certain individuals, FL §9-101.1.
Protection of child and victim, FL §9-101.1.
Visitation.
Denial on basis of likely abuse or neglect.
Determination by court, FL §9-101.
Specific finding required, FL §9-101.
Children's trust fund, HG §13-2207.

CHILD ABUSE AND NEGLECT —Cont'd

Child welfare accountability.

General provisions, FL §§5-1301 to 5-1311.

See CHILD WELFARE ACCOUNTABILITY.

Community grant program.

Award of grants.

Authority of governor, FL §5-1101.

Criteria for judging proposals, FL §5-1104.

Procedures.

Department of health and mental hygiene, FL §5-1103.

Department of human resources, FL §5-1102.

Reports, FL §5-1104.

Competitive basis of award, FL §5-1101.

Department of health and mental hygiene.

Grant award procedures, FL §5-1103.

Department of human resources.

Grant award procedures, FL §5-1102.

Funding, FL §5-1101.

Confidentiality of information.

Developmentally or mentally disabled, FL §5-714.

Reports and records, FL §5-707.

State council on child abuse and neglect.

Disclosures regarding child protection cases, FL §5-7A-07.

Crime of child abuse or sexual abuse of minor, CR §3-601.

Mandatory sentence for crime of violence, CR §14-101.

Definitions, FL §5-701.

Drug and alcohol abuse prevention awareness week, FL §5-1104.

Drug treatment.

Intervention by human resources department, FL §5-706.3.

Educator or social worker.

Defined, FL §5-701.

Reports.

Required to report, FL §5-704.

Emergency medical treatment, FL §5-712.

Evidence.

Custody or visitation proceedings.

Evidence of abuse against certain individuals, FL §9-101.1.

Reputation or opinion evidence for sexual abuse, CR §3-319.

Expungement of reports and records, FL §5-707.

Faith healing.

Nonmedical religious remedial care and treatment recognized by state law.

Abuse and neglect not to include, FL §5-701.

Family day care homes, FL §5-556.

Family members.

Defined, FL §5-701.

Female genital mutilation, HG §§20-601 to 20-603.

Health practitioners.

Defined, FL §5-701.

Reports.

Required to report, FL §5-704.

Household members.

Defined, FL §5-701.

Human service workers.

Reports, FL §5-704.

Immunity.

Examination and treatment of abused or neglected children by physicians, CJ §5-621; FL §5-712.

Person making report, CJ §5-620; FL §5-708.

CHILD ABUSE AND NEGLECT —Cont'd

Indicated abuse or neglect.

Conference, FL §5-706.1.

Definition of "indicated," FL §5-701.

Hearing, FL §5-706.1.

Notice of finding, FL §5-706.1.

Integration of child welfare and substance abuse services, FL §§5-1201 to 5-1209.

See CHILD WELFARE AND SUBSTANCE ABUSE SERVICES, INTEGRATION.

Intervention by human resources department, FL §5-706.3.

Investigations, FL §5-706.

Access to child's medical record, FL §5-711.

Law enforcement agencies.

Defined, FL §5-701.

Family day care homes.

State police to assist, FL §5-556.

Legislative policy, FL §5-702.

Liability.

Examination and treatment of abused or neglected child by physician.

Immunity from civil liability, CJ §5-621; FL §5-712.

Immunity of persons making report, CJ §5-620; FL §5-708.

Local departments.

Actions, FL §5-710.

Defined, FL §5-701.

Medical examinations.

Examination and treatment of abused or neglected children by physicians, FL §5-712.

Temporary removal of child from home without court approval, FL §5-709.

Medical records.

Access to child's medical record, FL §5-711.

Monitoring of household after child's return, FL §5-713.

Neglect.

Defined, FL §5-701.

Notice.

Abuse occurring out of state.

Notice to local department, FL §5-705.1.

Family day care homes.

Notice of report, FL §5-556.

Indicated or unsubstantiated abuse or neglect.

Finding of, FL §5-706.1.

Reports by other persons.

Notification of other agencies, FL §5-705.

Out-of-state, abuse occurring.

Investigations, FL §5-706.

Reports, FL §5-705.1.

Physicians.

Examination and treatment of abused or neglected children, FL §5-712.

Immunity, CJ §5-621; FL §5-712.

Police officers.

Defined, FL §5-701.

Family day care homes.

State police to assist law enforcement agencies, FL §5-556.

Reports.

Required to report, FL §5-704.

Temporary removal of child from home without court approval.

Police officer to accompany representative, FL §5-709.

Privileged communications.

Family day care homes.

Multidisciplinary teams, FL §5-556.

CHILD ABUSE AND NEGLECT —Cont'd
Privileged communications —Cont'd
Reports and records made in accordance with
subtitle, FL §5-707.
Purposes of subtitle, FL §5-702.
Records.
Expungement of reports and records, FL §5-707.
Medical records.
Access to child's medical record, FL §5-711.
Registry.
Central registry, FL §5-714.
Religion.
Nonmedical religious remedial care and treatment
recognized by state law.
Abuse and neglect not to include, FL §5-701.
Removal of child from home.
Supervision and monitoring of household after
child's return, FL §5-713.
Temporary removal without court approval, FL
§5-709.
Reports, FL §5-704.
Birthing care centers and hospitals, disclosures to,
88A §6.
Confidentiality, FL §5-707.
Contents, FL §5-704.
Reports by other persons, FL §5-705.
Cooperation among departments and agencies, FL
§5-704.
Defined, FL §5-701.
Disclosures authorized, 88A §6A.
Expungement, FL §5-707.
Family day care homes.
Notice of report, FL §5-556.
Form.
Reports by other persons, FL §5-705.
Generally, FL §5-704.
Immunity of person making report, CJ §5-620; FL
§5-708.
Investigations, FL §5-706.
Misuse of public assistance records and lists, 88A
§6.
Notification of other agencies.
Reports by other persons, FL §5-705.
Oral and written reports, FL §5-704.
Other persons, FL §5-705.
Out-of-state, abuse occurring, FL §5-705.1.
Investigations, FL §5-706.
State council on child abuse and neglect.
Annual reports, FL §5-7A-09.
Right of entry.
Temporary removal of child from home without
court approval, FL §5-709.
Scope of subtitle, FL §5-703.
Sexual abuse.
Defined, FL §5-701.
Evidence of reputation or opinion evidence, CR
§3-319.
Limitation of actions, CJ §5-117.
Sexual abuse of minor, CR §3-602.
Social services administration.
Continuing child welfare services beyond
eighteenth birthday, 88A §3.
Coordinating agency of social service and public
assistance activities, 88A §3.
Intervention by department of human resources,
FL §5-706.3.
Supervision over child care institutions, 88A §3.
State council on child abuse and neglect, FL
§§5-7A-01 to 5-7A-09.
Chairperson, FL §5-7A-03.
Committees, FL §5-7A-05.

CHILD ABUSE AND NEGLECT —Cont'd
State council on child abuse and neglect
—Cont'd
Disclosures regarding child protection cases, FL
§5-7A-07.
Duties, FL §5-7A-06.
Established, FL §5-7A-01.
Intergovernmental relations, FL §5-7A-08.
Meetings, FL §5-7A-04.
Members, FL §5-7A-02.
Expenses, FL §5-7A-04.
Reports.
Annual reports, FL §5-7A-09.
Staff, FL §5-7A-04.
State police.
Family day care homes.
Assistance to local law enforcement agencies,
FL §5-556.
State's attorneys.
Actions by state attorney's office, FL §5-710.
Definition of local state's attorney, FL §5-701.
Investigations.
Assistance, FL §5-706.
**Supervision and monitoring of household after
child's return,** FL §5-713.
Extension of monitoring period, FL §5-713.
Time.
Expungement of reports and records, FL §5-707.
Unsubstantiated abuse or neglect.
Conference, FL §5-706.1.
Definition of "unsubstantiated," FL §5-701.
Hearing, FL §5-706.1.
Notice of finding, FL §5-706.1.
Visitation.
Denial of custody.
Likely abuse or neglect, FL §9-101.
Evidence of abuse against certain individuals, FL
§9-101.1.
Witnesses.
Husband and wife.
Criminal procedure.
Not compelled to testify against spouse.
Exception as to abuse of child under 18, CJ
§9-106.

**CHILD ABUSE PREVENTION AWARENESS
WEEK,** FL §5-1104.

CHILDBIRTH.
Discrimination in employment, 49B §17.
Drive thru deliveries, IN §15-812.
Fetal alcohol syndrome.
Public awareness campaign, HG §18-309.
Gonococcal ophthalmia neonatorum, HG
§18-308.
Health insurance, IN §§15-811 to 15-813.
Information on home visits, IN §15-817.
In vitro fertilization, IN §15-810.
Marital status of woman, IN §15-506.
Health maintenance organizations.
Hospitalization benefits for newborns, HG
§19-703.
Hereditary and congenital disorders programs.
General provisions, HG §§13-101 to 13-110.
See HEREDITARY AND CONGENITAL
DISORDERS PROGRAMS.
Maternity leave.
Employment requirements, 49B §17.
Reports.
Gonococcal ophthalmia neonatorum.
Physician's report, HG §18-308.

CHILD CARE.

Adoption.
Foster care, FL §5-525.1.

Agents, officers and representatives of corporations.
Authority, interfering with or obstructing, FL §5-503.

Appeals.
Family day care homes.
Revocation of registration, FL §5-554.
Suspension or revocation of license.
Administrative review, FL §5-517.
Judicial review, FL §5-518.

Child abuse and neglect.
Family day care homes, FL §5-556.

Child care facilities.
Child care centers, FL §§5-570 to 5-589.
See CHILD CARE CENTERS.
Child care homes.
Criminal background investigations for employees, etc., of facilities.
Facilities requiring investigation, FL §5-561.
Licenses, FL §5-508.
Child care institutions.
Criminal background investigations for employees, etc., of facilities.
Facilities requiring investigation, FL §5-561.
Licenses, FL §5-509.
Volunteers at facilities.
Criminal background investigations for employees, etc., of facilities, FL §5-561.

Child care providers.
Defined, FL §5-501.

Child welfare services, FL §5-524.

Confidentiality of information.
State citizens review board for children.
Prohibited acts by members and staff, FL §5-539.3.

Construction and interpretation.
Family day care homes.
Registration, FL §5-558.
Foster care review boards, FL §5-547.

Corporations for care and protection of minor children.
Agents, officers and representatives.
Authority, interfering with or obstructing, FL §5-503.

Criminal background investigations for employees, etc., of facilities.
Appeals.
Contested findings, FL §5-565.
Application by employee, FL §5-562.
Applications by individuals requiring investigations, FL §5-562.
Confidentiality of information, FL §5-564.
Contested findings, FL §5-565.
Costs of investigations.
Payment, FL §5-561.
Definitions, FL §5-560.
Duties of department, FL §5-564.
Facilities requiring investigation, FL §5-561.
Failure to disclose prior conviction or existence of pending charge, FL §5-566.
Fees, FL §5-561.
Payment, FL §5-561.
Fingerprints.
Information accompanying application, FL §5-562.
Waiver of requirement, FL §5-562.
Immunities.
Civil or criminal liability, CJ §5-619; FL §5-567.

CHILD CARE —Cont'd

Criminal background investigations for employees, etc., of facilities —Cont'd
Individuals requiring investigations, FL §5-561.
Applications by, FL §5-562.
Information accompanying application, FL §5-562.
Offenses requiring disclosure, FL §5-563.
Printed statements, FL §5-562.
Information contained in, FL §5-564.
Prior criminal offenses.
Disclosure statement mailed to employer, FL §5-563.
Offenses requiring disclosure, FL §5-563.
Required, FL §5-561.
Secretary.
Duties, FL §5-568.
Volunteers at facilities, FL §5-561.
Investigation may be required, FL §5-561.
Volunteers at local departments of social services, FL §5-561.

Definitions, FL §5-501.
Criminal background investigations for employees, etc., of facilities, FL §5-560.
Early childhood development advisory council, FL §5-590.
Family day care homes.
Condominiums, RP §11-111.1.
Homeowners' associations, RP §11B-111.1.
Residential child care capital grant program, 41 §18-701.

Direct incentive grants.
Child care quality incentive grant program, FL §§5-594 to 5-594.8.

Early childhood development advisory council, FL §§5-590 to 5-593.
Advise and counsel to child care administration.
Duties, FL §5-593.
Compensation, FL §5-592.
Composition, FL §5-592.
Created, FL §5-591.
Definitions, FL §5-590.
Duties, FL §5-592.
Established, FL §5-591.
Expenses, FL §5-592.
Issues and problems relating to child care.
Review, FL §5-593.
Meetings, FL §5-592.
Regulations.
Review of proposed regulations by state agencies, FL §5-593.
Vacancies, FL §5-592.

Economic development assistance fund.
Child care special loans, 83A §5-1409.

Economic development student assistance grants program.
Child care provider grant program, ED §18-705.

Employees of facilities.
Criminal background investigations for employees, etc., of facilities, FL §§5-560 to 5-568. See within this heading, "Criminal background investigations for employees, etc., of facilities."

Family day care.
Defined, FL §5-501.

Family day care homes.
Advertisements, FL §5-552.
Regulations, FL §5-551.
Appeals.
Revocation of registration, FL §5-554.
Child abuse.
Notice of report, FL §5-556.

CHILD CARE —Cont'd
Family day care homes —Cont'd
Child care centers generally, FL §§5-570 to 5-589.
  See CHILD CARE CENTERS.
Condominiums, RP §11-111.1.
Confidentiality of information.
  Child abuse.
    Shared information, FL §5-556.
Covenants restricting, RP §2-121.
CPR training.
  Current certification.
    Regulations to provide, FL §5-551.
Criminal background investigations for employees,
    etc., of facilities.
  Facilities requiring investigation, FL §5-561.
Defined, RP §2-121.
Family day care provider direct grant fund, FL
    §§5-559.1 to 5-559.8.
First aid training.
  Current certification.
    Regulations to provide, FL §5-551.
Group size, FL §5-553.
Homeowners' associations, RP §11B-111.1.
Informational pamphlet, FL §5-555.
Inspections.
  Announced and unannounced.
    Regulations to provide for, FL §5-551.
Insurance.
  Liability insurance, IN §§19-106, 19-202,
    19-203.
Law enforcement agencies.
  State police to assist, FL §5-556.
Misdemeanors.
  Direct grant fund.
    Violations of subtitle, FL §5-559.7.
Multidisciplinary team, FL §5-556.
Notice.
  Child abuse.
    Notice of report, FL §5-556.
  Condominiums.
    Notice of operation, RP §11-111.1.
  Homeowners' associations.
    Notice of opening home, RP §11B-111.1.
Penalties.
  Violations of part.
    Civil penalty, FL §5-557.1.
Property tax exemption.
  Property used in family day care home, TP
    §7-227.
Registration.
  Construction and interpretation, FL §5-558.
  Definitions, FL §5-550.
  Group size, FL §5-553.
  Injunctions.
    Unregistered operation, FL §5-554.
  Legislative intent, FL §5-550.1.
  Purpose, FL §5-550.1.
  Regulations, FL §5-551.
  Required, FL §5-552.
    Exceptions, FL §5-552.
  Revocation, FL §5-554.
    Appeal, FL §5-554.
  Unregistered family day care homes.
    Amnesty for unregistered family day care
      providers, FL §5-552.1.
    Defined, FL §5-501.
    Search warrants, FL §5-554.1.
  Violations of provisions.
    Penalty, FL §5-557.
Reports.
  Child abuse.
    Notice of report, FL §5-556.

CHILD CARE —Cont'd
Family day care homes —Cont'd
  Reports —Cont'd
    Notice, FL §5-556.
  Searches and seizures.
    Unregistered family day care homes.
      Search warrants, FL §5-554.1.
  State police.
    Assistance to local law enforcement agencies,
      FL §5-556.
  Taxation.
    Property tax credits, TP §9-214.
  Unregistered family day care homes.
    Amnesty for unregistered family day care
      providers, FL §5-552.1.
    Defined, FL §5-501.
    Search warrants, FL §5-554.1.
  Violations of part.
    Civil penalty, FL §5-557.1.
    Service of citation, FL §5-552.
Family day care provider direct grant fund, FL
    §§5-559.1 to 5-559.8.
  Administration, FL §5-559.1.
  Applications.
    Contents, FL §5-559.5.
    Form, FL §5-559.5.
  Appropriations, FL §5-559.3.
  Approval of grants, FL §5-559.2.
  Creation, FL §5-559.1.
  Limitations, FL §5-559.4.
  Maximum grant amounts, FL §5-559.4.
  Priorities, FL §5-559.6.
  Promulgation of rules, FL §5-559.8.
  Purpose of grants, FL §5-559.2.
  Qualifications, FL §5-559.4.
  Rules, FL §5-559.8.
  Terms and conditions, FL §5-559.6.
  Use of grant funds, FL §5-559.3.
Fees.
  Criminal background investigations for employees,
    etc., of facilities, FL §5-561.
Financial institution franchise tax.
  Credits, TG §8-216.
Fingerprinting.
  Criminal background investigations for employees,
    etc., of facilities.
    Complete set of legible fingerprints.
      Information accompanying application, FL
        §5-562.
    Waiver of requirement, FL §5-562.
Foster care.
  Administrative review, FL §5-525.
  Adoption, FL §5-525.1.
    Support by department, FL §5-530.
  Criminal background investigations for employees,
    etc., of facilities.
    Foster care family homes or group facilities.
      Facilities requiring investigation, FL §5-561.
  Defined, FL §5-501.
  Duties of local department, FL §5-525.
  Foster care family homes.
    Criminal background investigations for
      employees, etc., of facilities.
      Facilities requiring investigation, FL §5-561.
  Funeral expenses.
    Payment, FL §5-531.
  Group homes and institutions.
    Criminal background investigations for
      employees, etc., of facilities.
      Facilities requiring investigation, FL §5-561.
    Provision of services through, FL §5-526.

CHILD CARE —Cont'd
Foster care —Cont'd
Hearings.
Contesting of placement with adoptive family,
FL §5-525.
Insurance.
Liability insurance, FL §5-529.
Medical costs.
Reimbursement, FL §5-528.
Out-of-home placement, FL §5-525.
Defined, FL §5-501.
Establishment of program, FL §5-525.
Local boards of review for minor children in
out-of-home placement, FL §§5-540 to
5-545.
Permanency plan.
Considerations in developing, FL §5-525.
Preparation, notice and amendment of, FL
§5-525.
Rates, FL §5-527.
Reimbursement for loss to foster parents, FL
§5-529.
Reimbursement for medical costs, FL §5-528.
Review boards. See within this heading, "Foster
care review boards."
Rights of foster parents, FL §5-504.
Rules and regulations, FL §5-532.
Adoption, FL §5-525.
Sibling placement and visitation rights, FL
§5-525.2.
Visitation.
Sibling visitation rights, FL §5-525.2.
Voluntary placement agreement.
Custody of child with developmental disability
or mental illness, FL §5-525.
Foster care review boards.
Construction and interpretation, FL §5-547.
Cooperation by agencies, FL §5-546.
Local boards.
Chairman.
Election, FL §5-542.
Term of office, FL §5-542.
Compensation.
Prohibited, FL §5-543.
Composition, FL §5-541.
Confidentiality of information, FL §5-543.
Defined, FL §5-501.
Duties, FL §5-545.
Established, FL §5-540.
Goals, FL §5-544.
Multicounty local boards.
Composition, FL §5-541.
Establishment, FL §5-540.
Powers, FL §5-545.
Qualifications of members, FL §5-541.
Recommendations.
Power to recommend, FL §5-545.
Terms of members, FL §5-541.
Vacancies, FL §5-541.
Funerals.
Foster care.
Payment of funeral expenses, FL §5-531.
Grants.
Child care provider grant program, ED §18-705.
Child care quality incentive grant program, FL
§§5-594 to 5-594.8.
Group homes and institutions.
Foster care.
Provision of services through, FL §5-526.
Hearings.
Foster care.
Contest of placement with adoptive family, FL
§5-525.

CHILD CARE —Cont'd
Immunity.
Criminal background investigations for employees,
etc., of facilities.
Persons immune, CJ §5-619; FL §5-567.
Family day care homes.
Unregistered family day care providers.
Amnesty for.
Local or state enforcement authorities, FL
§5-552.1.
Income tax.
Credits, TG §§10-704.7, 10-716.
Injunctions.
Family day care homes.
Unregistered operation, FL §5-554.
Unlicensed facilities, FL §5-519.
Inspections.
Family day care homes.
Unregistered family day care homes.
Administrative search warrants, FL §5-554.1.
Insurance.
Family day care homes.
Condominiums.
Liability insurance, RP §11-111.1.
Homeowners' associations.
Liability insurance, RP §11B-111.1.
Foster care.
Liability insurance, FL §5-529.
Investigations.
Criminal background investigations for employees,
etc., of facilities, FL §§5-560 to 5-568. See
within this heading, "Criminal background
investigations for employees, etc., of
facilities."
Licenses.
Powers of administration, FL §5-519.
Kinship care program, FL §5-534.
Admission of students in kinship care, ED §7-101.
Consent to medical care for minor, HG §20-105.
Education funding for child in informal kinship
care relationship, ED §4-122.1.
Law enforcement agencies.
Family day care homes.
Child abuse.
State police to assist, FL §5-556.
Lead poisoning screen, FL §5-556.1.
Legislative declaration, FL §5-502.
Licensing of child care facilities, FL §5-506.
Licenses.
Applications, FL §5-510.
Action required on application, FL §5-513.
Child care homes, FL §5-508.
Child care institutions, 83C §2-124; FL §5-509.
Exceptions, 83C §2-124.
Only one license required, 83C §2-125.
Child placement agencies, FL §5-507.
Defined, FL §5-501.
Duration, FL §5-514.
Duties of licensees, FL §5-520.
Hearings.
Suspension or revocation of license, FL §5-516.
Injunctions.
Unlicensed activities, FL §5-519.
Investigations.
Powers of administration, FL §5-519.
Legislative intent, FL §5-506.
Multiple licenses not required, FL §5-506.
Reciprocity, FL §5-512.
Regulations, FL §5-506.
Residential educational facility, FL §5-509.1.

CHILD CARE —Cont'd
Licenses —Cont'd
Suspension or revocation, FL §5-515.
Appeals.
Administrative review, FL §5-517.
Judicial review, FL §5-518.
Hearing, FL §5-516.
Investigations, FL §5-519.
Term of license, FL §5-514.
Violations of provisions.
Penalty, FL §5-521.
Workers' compensation law.
Compliance required for issuance, FL §5-511.
Misdemeanors.
Family day care homes.
Registration.
Violations of provisions, FL §5-557.
Licenses.
Violations of provisions, FL §5-521.
Unattended children.
Confinement in dwelling, building or enclosure, FL §5-801.
Notice.
Family day care homes.
Child abuse and neglect.
Notice of report, FL §5-556.
Condominiums.
Notice of opening home, RP §11-111.1.
Homeowners' associations.
Notice of opening home, RP §11B-111.1.
Out-of-home placement.
Administration to establish program, FL §5-525.
Children placed in program, FL §5-525.
Evaluation of success of services of children in.
Cooperation in determining cost of developing and implementing, FL §5-506.
Permanency plan, FL §5-525.
Short-term placement, FL §5-525.
Voluntary placement agreement, FL §5-525.
Penalties.
Family day care homes.
Registration.
Violations of provisions, FL §5-557.
Violations of part.
Civil penalty, FL §5-557.1.
Licenses.
Violations of provisions, FL §5-521.
Police.
Family day care homes.
Child abuse.
State police to assist law enforcement agencies, FL §5-556.
Policy of state, FL §5-502.
Privileged communications.
Family day care homes.
Child abuse.
Multidisciplinary teams.
Confidentiality of shared information, FL §5-556.
Public service company franchise tax.
Credits, TG §8-413.
Quality incentive grant program, FL §§5-594 to 5-594.8.
Reciprocity.
Licensing of child care facilities, FL §5-512.
Religion.
Religious affiliation to be taken into account, FL §5-520.
Reports.
Family day care homes.
Child abuse.
Notice of report, FL §5-556.

CHILD CARE —Cont'd
Residential child care capital grant program, 41 §§18-701 to 18-707.
Acquisition of existing buildings authorized, 41 §18-702.
Application for grants.
Contents, 41 §18-703.
Eligibility, 41 §18-703.
Appropriations.
Use of state funds, 41 §18-704.
Board of public works.
Project plans, reporting approval of, 41 §18-703.
State funds, allocation by board, 41 §18-705.
Conversion of public building authorized, 41 §18-702.
Definitions, 41 §18-701.
Establishment, 41 §18-702.
Executive director.
Defined, 41 §18-701.
Project plans, approval of, 41 §18-703.
Office.
Defined, 41 §18-701.
Rulemaking authority, 41 §18-707.
Project plans.
Application for grants, 41 §18-703.
Purchase of capital equipment authorized facilities, 41 §18-702.
Recovery of funds.
Cessation of approved use of property, 41 §18-706.
Notice of right of recovery, 41 §18-706.
Renovation of current child care facilities, 41 §18-702.
Rulemaking authority, 41 §§18-705, 18-707.
Use of state funds.
Allocations by board of public works, 41 §18-705.
Approved purpose criteria, 41 §18-704.
Certification and payment, 41 §18-705.
Eligible projects, 41 §18-704.
Prohibited uses, 41 §18-704.
Terms and conditions, 41 §18-704.
Use of recovered funds, 41 §18-706.
Residential child care program administrators, HO §§20-101 to 20-502.
See RESIDENTIAL CHILD CARE PROGRAM ADMINISTRATORS.
Residential educational facility.
Defined, FL §5-501.
Licensing to operate, FL §5-509.1.
Residential facility for children.
Defined, FL §5-533.
Health care services provided by, FL §5-533.
School enrollment, duties of facility, ED §7-309.
Rights of foster parents, FL §5-504.
Rules and regulations.
Early childhood development advisory council.
Regulations proposed by state agencies.
Review, FL §5-593.
Family day care homes.
Condominiums.
Regulation of operation, RP §11-111.1.
Homeowners' associations.
Regulation of operation, RP §11B-111.1.
Registration, FL §5-551.
Foster care, FL §5-532.
Kinship care program, FL §5-534.
Licensing of child care facilities, FL §5-506.
Schools.
Residential child care programs.
School enrollment, duties of facility, ED §7-309.

CHILD CARE —Cont'd
Searches and seizures.
　Family day care homes.
　　Unregistered family day care homes.
　　　Search warrants, FL §5-554.1.
Sex offender registrant.
　Entry onto day care property prohibited, CP
　　§11-722.
State citizens review board for children.
　Appointment of members, FL §5-536.
　Chairman.
　　Election, FL §5-537.
　　Term of office, FL §5-537.
　Citizens review panels, FL §5-539.2.
　Composition, FL §5-536.
　Defined, FL §5-501.
　Duties, FL §5-539.
　Established, FL §5-535.
　Expenses of members.
　　Reimbursement, FL §5-538.
　Meetings, FL §5-538.
　Powers, FL §5-539.
　Prohibited acts by members and staff, FL
　　§5-539.3.
　Responsibilities, FL §5-539.1.
　Staff, FL §5-538.
　Terms of members, FL §5-536.
　Vacancies, FL §5-536.
State police.
　Family day care homes.
　　Child abuse.
　　　Assistance to local law enforcement agencies,
　　　　FL §5-556.
Unattended children.
　Confinement in dwelling, building or enclosure,
　　FL §5-801.
Violations of provisions.
　Penalty, FL §5-521.
　Suspension or revocation of license, FL §5-515.
Volunteers.
　Criminal background investigations.
　　Investigations may be required, FL §5-561.
Workers' compensation.
　Licensing of child care facilities.
　　Compliance required for issuance, FL §5-511.

CHILD CARE CENTERS.
Administrative procedures.
　Review under administrative procedures act, FL
　　§5-581.
Appeals.
　Administrative procedure act, FL §5-581.
Child abuse.
　Clearance, FL §5-580.3.
　Multidisciplinary teams, FL §5-584.
　Reports, FL §5-584.
**Criminal background investigations for
　employees, etc., of facilities.**
　Facilities requiring investigations, FL §5-561.
Definitions, FL §5-570.
　State-occupied buildings, FL §5-586.
Drinking water suppliers.
　Notices to, requirements, EN §9-410.
Employees.
　Child abuse and neglect clearance, FL §5-580.3.
　Criminal background investigations for employees,
　　etc., of facilities.
　　Facilities requiring investigation, FL §5-561.
Findings, FL §5-571.
Injunctions.
　Licenses.
　　Operating center without license or letter of
　　　compliance, FL §5-580.

CHILD CARE CENTERS —Cont'd
Inspections.
　Announced and unannounced inspections, FL
　　§5-578.
　Unlicensed child care centers.
　　Administrative search warrants, FL §5-580.1.
Investigations.
　Criminal background investigations for employees,
　　etc., of facilities.
　　Facilities requiring investigation, FL §5-561.
**Judith P. Hoyer early child care and education
　enhancement program,** ED §5-217.
Jurisdiction.
　State supersession and preemption of subordinate
　　jurisdiction, FL §5-585.
Lead poisoning screen, FL §5-580.2.
　State-occupied buildings, FL §5-589.1.
Legislative findings, FL §5-571.
Licenses.
　Applicability of provisions, FL §5-574.
　Applications for licenses.
　　Contents, FL §5-575.
　　Generally, FL §5-575.
　Denials, FL §5-580.
　Exceptions, FL §5-574.
　Injunctions.
　　Operating center without license or letter of
　　　compliance, FL §5-580.
　Issuance of license, FL §5-576.
　Prohibited acts, FL §5-582.
　Renewal of license, FL §5-578.
　Required, FL §5-574.
　Scope of license, FL §5-577.
　　Changes, FL §5-577.
　State supersession and preemption of subordinate
　　jurisdictions, FL §5-585.
　Suspension or revocation, FL §5-580.
　　Emergency suspensions, FL §5-580.
　Term of licenses, FL §5-578.
　Transferability, FL §5-579.
　Unlicensed child care centers.
　　Search warrants, FL §5-580.1.
Local codes, FL §5-572.
Misdemeanors.
　Violations of subtitle, FL §5-583.
Notices.
　Employees, child abuse and neglect convictions,
　　FL §5-580.3.
　State-occupied buildings.
　　Notice of availability of space, FL §5-587.
Penalties.
　Violations.
　　Civil penalties, FL §5-583.1.
　　　Maximum penalty, FL §5-583.1.
　　　Separate violations, FL §5-583.1.
Prohibited acts, FL §5-582.
Purpose of subtitle, FL §5-571.
Religion.
　Compliance with rules and regulations.
　　Programs operated by tax exempt religious
　　　organizations, FL §5-574.
Rules and regulations.
　Compliance with rules and regulations.
　　Programs operated by tax exempt religious
　　　organizations, FL §5-574.
　　Programs operated in school buildings, FL
　　　§5-574.
　Contents of rules and regulations, FL §5-573.
　Generally, FL §5-573.
　Violations.
　　Civil penalty, FL §5-583.1.

CHILD CARE CENTERS —Cont'd
Schools.
Programs operated in school buildings.
Compliance with rules and regulations, FL
§5-574.
Scope of subtitle, FL §5-572.
Searches and seizures.
Unlicensed child care centers, FL §5-580.1.
State-occupied buildings.
Authority to establish child care centers in, FL
§5-587.
Closure, FL §5-588.
Cooperation by state departments, FL §5-588.
Definitions, FL §5-586.
Employees.
Periodic assessment of needs, FL §5-588.
Survey of employees for child care needs, FL
§5-587.
Lead poisoning screens, FL §5-589.1.
Notice.
Availability of space, FL §5-587.
Pilot program, FL §5-589.
Survey of employees for child care needs, FL
§5-587.
Unlicensed child care centers.
Search warrants, FL §5-580.1.
Violations of subtitle.
Civil penalties, FL §5-583.1.
Misdemeanors, FL §5-583.
Water suppliers.
Notices to, requirements, EN §9-410.

**CHILD CARE QUALITY INCENTIVE GRANT
PROGRAM,** FL §§5-594 to 5-594.8.
Administration of grants.
Power of department to contract for, FL §5-594.1.
Application for grant, FL §5-594.5.
Award, requirements, FL §5-594.4.
Creation, FL §5-594.1.
Definitions, FL §5-594.
Eligibility to receive, FL §5-594.3.
False statements or reports, FL §5-594.7.
Grant funds, FL §5-594.3.
Incentive to improve quality of care.
Award as, FL §5-594.2.
Limitations as to centers and homes eligible,
FL §5-594.3.
Priorities for distribution.
Department may set, FL §5-594.6.
Prohibited acts, criminal penalty, FL §5-594.7.
Purposes and use of program, FL §5-594.3.
Regulations, FL §5-594.8.
Terms and conditions.
Department may set, FL §5-594.6.

CHILD CUSTODY.
Abduction of child.
Child under twelve.
Clear and present danger to child, FL §9-306.
Misdemeanor.
Prohibited acts in state, FL §9-307.
Prohibited acts in state, FL §9-304.
Prohibited acts outside of state, FL §9-305.
Felony, FL §9-307.
Clear and present danger to child, FL §9-306.
Conflict as to lawful custodian, FL §9-303.
Defenses.
Clear and present danger to child, FL §9-306.
Definitions, FL §9-301.
Jurisdiction over custody and visitation.
Child removed from state, FL §9-303.
Penalties, FL §9-307.

CHILD CUSTODY —Cont'd
Abduction of child —Cont'd
Petitions.
Clear and present danger to child, FL §9-306.
Prohibited acts.
In this state, FL §9-304.
Outside of this state, FL §9-305.
Adoption.
Independent adoptions.
Nonconsensual adoption.
Effect of custody, FL §5-3B-23.
Affidavits.
Information provided as to child.
Affidavit attached to first pleadings, FL
§9.5-209.
Attorney general.
Instructional materials regarding child custody
and visitation.
Duties, CJ §2-206.
Awarding custody to parent.
If parents live apart, FL §5-203.
Change in custody.
Hearings.
Petition by child to change custody.
Hearing required, FL §9-103.
Petition by child, FL §9-103.
Change of residence.
Notification prior to relocation of child, FL §9-106.
Child abuse and neglect.
Denial of custody or visitation on basis of likely
abuse or neglect, FL §9-101.
Evidence of abuse against certain individuals, FL
§9-101.1.
Protection of child and victim, FL §9-101.1.
Children in need of assistance.
Custody order, CJ §3-819.
Granting custody and guardianship, CJ §3-819.2.
Taking child into custody, CJ §3-814.
Circuit courts.
Family law actions, FamLaw Rules 9-201 to
9-210.
Classes.
Educational seminars required, FamLaw Rule
9-204.
Conflict of laws.
Lawful custodian.
Conflict as to, FL §9-303.
Crimes and offenses.
Abduction of child.
Generally, FL §§9-301 to 9-307. See within this
heading, "Abduction of child."
Custodial interference.
Abduction of child.
Generally, FL §§9-301 to 9-307. See within this
heading, "Abduction of child."
Defenses.
Abduction of child.
Clear and present danger to child, FL §9-306.
Relocation of child.
Violation of notification requirement, FL §9-106.
Definitions, FL §9-301.
Uniform child custody jurisdiction and
enforcement act, FL §§9.5-101, 9.5-301.
Record, FL §9.5-109.
Denial of custody.
Likely abuse or neglect, FL §9-101.
Murder.
Parent convicted of murder of certain persons,
FL §9-101.2.
Divorce, FamLaw Rule 9-202.

CHILD CUSTODY —Cont'd

Educational seminars required, FamLaw Rule 9-204.

Evidence.
Child abuse and neglect.
Evidence of abuse against certain individuals, FL §9-101.1.
Uniform child custody jurisdiction and enforcement act.
Testimony of witness located in another state. Obtaining, CL §9.5-110.

Felonies.
Abduction of child.
Child under twelve.
Prohibited acts outside state, FL §9-307.
Prohibited acts, FL §9-307.

Food stamps.
Controlled substance felony.
Custodial parent with prior conviction, 88A §65A.

Foreign custody determinations.
Uniform child custody jurisdiction and enforcement act.
Generally, FL §§9.5-101 to 9.5-318. See within this heading, "Uniform child custody jurisdiction and enforcement act."

Grandparents.
Visitation.
Petition by grandparents, FL §9-102.

Hearings.
Change of custody.
Petition by child to change custody.
Hearing required, FL §9-103.

Inmate at correctional facility giving birth to child.
Care and custody of child by father, COR §9-601.

Instructional materials regarding child custody and visitation.
Provision to public, CJ §2-206.

Interstate enforcement of custody determinations.
Uniform child custody jurisdiction and enforcement act.
Generally, FL §§9.5-101 to 9.5-318. See within this heading, "Uniform child custody jurisdiction and enforcement act."

Jurisdiction.
Equity court jurisdiction, FL §1-201.
Removal of child from state.
Equity court jurisdiction over custody and visitation, FL §9-302.
Uniform child custody jurisdiction and enforcement act.
Generally. See within this heading, "Uniform child custody jurisdiction and enforcement act."

Lawful custodian.
Conflict as to, FL §9-303.
Defined, FL §9-301.

Mediation of disputes, FamLaw Rule 9-205.
Qualifications of mediators.
Additional qualifications for child access disputes, ADR Rule 17-104.
Training programs for mediators, ADR Rule 17-106.

Medical, dental and educational records.
Access to by noncustodial parent, FL §9-104.

Misdemeanors.
Abduction of child.
Child under twelve.
Prohibited acts in state, FL §9-307.

CHILD CUSTODY —Cont'd

Misdemeanors —Cont'd
Prohibited acts, FL §9-307.

Murder.
Parent convicted of murder of certain persons, FL §9-101.2.

Neglected children.
Denial of custody or visitation based on likely abuse or neglect, FL §9-101.

Notice.
Relocation of child, FL §9-106.
Uniform child custody jurisdiction and enforcement act.
Petition to enforce and order to appear.
Service, FL §9.5-308.

Parent and child.
Abduction of child. See within this heading, "Abduction of child."

Parents living apart.
Court may award custody, FL §5-203.

Paternity proceedings.
Orders relating to custody of child, FL §5-1035.

Penalties.
Prohibited acts, FL §9-307.

Petitions.
Abduction of child.
Clear and present danger to child, FL §9-306.
Change in custody.
Petition by child, FL §9-103.
Clear and present danger to child, FL §9-306.
Grandparents.
Visitation, FL §9-102.
Uniform child custody jurisdiction and enforcement act.
Enforcement of out-of-state determinations, FL §9.5-308.
Visitation.
Grandparents, FL §9-102.

Pleading.
Information provided as to child in first pleadings, FL §9.5-209.

Procedure generally, FamLaw Rules 9-201 to 9-210.

Prohibited acts.
Clear and present danger to child, FL §9-306.
In this state, FL §9-304.
Outside of this state, FL §9-305.
Penalties, FL §9-307.

Records.
Medical, dental and educational records.
Access by noncustodial parent, FL §9-104.

Relocation of child.
Notification prior to, FL §9-106.

Removal of child from state.
Clear and present danger to child, FL §9-306.
Conflict as to lawful custodian, FL §9-303.
Definitions, FL §9-301.
Jurisdiction of equity courts, FL §9-302.
Jurisdiction over custody and visitation, FL §9-302.
Prohibited acts, FL §9-305.
Penalties, FL §9-307.

Uniform child custody jurisdiction and enforcement act, FL §§9.5-101 to 9.5-318.
Abandonment of child.
Temporary emergency jurisdiction, FL §9.5-204.
Administrative matters.
Communications between courts allowed, FL §9.5-109.
Appeal from final order, FL §9.5-314.

CHILD CUSTODY —Cont'd
Uniform child custody jurisdiction and enforcement act —Cont'd

Appearance before court, FL §9.5-210.
Order to appear, FL §9.5-308.
Attorney general.
Lawful action by, FL §9.5-315.
Audiovisual testimony.
Witnesses located in another state, FL §9.5-110.
Binding effect of custody determinations, FL §9.5-105.
Citation of title, FL §9.5-318.
Civil litigation based on acts unrelated to proceedings.
Immunity from personal jurisdiction not extended to, FL §9.5-108.
Communications between courts allowed, FL §9.5-109.
Modification proceeding pending in another state, FL §9.5-307.
Temporary emergency jurisdiction.
Request to court of this state to make determination, FL §9.5-204.
Conclusiveness of determinations, FL §9.5-105.
Concurrent custody determination.
Temporary emergency jurisdiction, effect, FL §9.5-204.
Costs and expenses, FL §9.5-312.
Appearance before court, FL §9.5-210.
Declining jurisdiction, FL §9.5-208.
Direct expenses and costs against respondent, FL §9.5-317.
Immediate physical custody of child.
Order by court of this state, FL §9.5-310.
Requests to another state, FL §9.5-111.
Declining jurisdiction, FL §9.5-208.
Divorce or other proceeding, determination incidental to, FL §9.5-207.
Defense of immunity based on husband-wife relationship.
Prohibition against invoking, FL §9.5-310.
Definitions, FL §§9.5-101, 9.5-301.
Record, FL §9.5-109.
Depositions.
Witnesses located in another state, FL §9.5-110.
Divorce or other proceeding.
Determination incidental to, FL §9.5-207.
Documentary evidence transmitted from another state by electronic means, FL §9.5-110.
Electronic testimony.
Witnesses located in another state, FL §9.5-110.
Emergency medical treatment for child, FL §9.5-102.
Exclusive continuing jurisdiction, FL §9.5-202.
Foreign countries.
Applicability of title to proceedings, recognition of determinations, FL §9.5-104.
Full faith and credit, order issued by another state, FL §9.5-313.
Grounds for jurisdiction, FL §9.5-201.
Temporary emergency jurisdiction, FL §9.5-204.
Hague convention.
Enforcement of orders made under, FL §9.5-302.
Immediate physical custody of child.
Issuance of warrant to take, FL §9.5-311.
Order by court of this state, FL §9.5-310.
Immunity of party from personal jurisdiction, FL §9.5-108.
Inconvenient forum, FL §9.5-207.
Indian children.
Applicability of title to proceedings pertaining to, FL §9.5-103.

CHILD CUSTODY —Cont'd
Uniform child custody jurisdiction and enforcement act —Cont'd

Indian children —Cont'd
Recognition and enforcement of determinations by tribe, FL §9.5-103.
Information provided as to child.
First pleadings or attached affidavit, FL §9.5-209.
Inquiry before proceeding.
Pending proceedings in another state, FL §9.5-206.
Intervention.
Right to intervene, FL §9.5-205.
Joinder of parties, FL §9.5-205.
Jurisdiction, FL §9.5-201.
Declining jurisdiction, FL §9.5-208.
Exclusive continuing jurisdiction, FL §9.5-202.
Inconvenient forum, FL §9.5-207.
Modification of out-of-state determination, FL §9.5-203.
Jurisdictional questions, FL §9.5-106.
Law enforcement officers.
Lawful action by, FL §9.5-316.
Mistreatment or abuse of child, sibling or parent.
Temporary emergency jurisdiction, FL §9.5-204.
Modification of out-of-state determinations, FL §9.5-203.
Court without exclusive continuing jurisdiction, FL §9.5-202.
Pending proceedings in another state, FL §9.5-206.
Registered determinations, FL §9.5-306.
Modification proceeding pending in another state, FL §9.5-307.
Notice.
Manner of giving, publication allowed, proof of service, FL §9.5-107.
Required before determination made, FL §9.5-205.
Pending proceedings in another state, FL §9.5-206.
Modification proceeding, FL §9.5-307.
Personal jurisdiction over party or child.
Not necessary or sufficient to make determination, FL §9.5-201.
Petition for enforcement of out-of-state determination, FL §9.5-308.
Physical custody of child.
Issuance of warrant to take immediate custody, FL §9.5-311.
Order by court of this state, FL §9.5-310.
Physical presence of party or child.
Not necessary or sufficient to make determination, FL §9.5-201.
Preservation of records, FL §9.5-111.
Priority of jurisdictional questions, FL §9.5-106.
Privileged communication between spouses.
Prohibition against invoking privilege in proceedings, FL §9.5-310.
Recognition and enforcement of out-of-state determinations, FL §9.5-303.
Full faith and credit to order issued by another state, FL §9.5-313.
Registered determinations, FL §9.5-306.
Temporary orders when court of this state without jurisdiction, FL §9.5-304.
Record of communications between courts.
Record defined, required to be made, FL §9.5-109.

CHILD CUSTODY —Cont'd
Uniform child custody jurisdiction and enforcement act —Cont'd
Registration of out-of-state determinations.
Documents required, contest of validity, FL §9.5-305.
Recognition and enforcement, FL §9.5-306.
Requests to another state, FL §9.5-111.
Scope of title.
Emergency medical treatment for child.
Inapplicability of title, FL §9.5-102.
Foreign countries.
Applicability of title to proceedings, recognition of determinations, FL §9.5-104.
Indian children.
Applicability of title to proceedings pertaining to, FL §9.5-103.
Sealing of information provided as to child, FL §9.5-209.
Service of process.
Notice required for exercise of jurisdiction.
Manner of giving, publication allowed, proof of service, FL §9.5-107.
Person subject to personal jurisdiction or present in state.
Not immune from service, FL §9.5-108.
Petition to enforce and order to appear, FL §9.5-308.
Short title, FL §9.5-318.
Spousal privilege.
Prohibition against invoking in proceedings, FL §9.5-310.
Stay of proceedings.
Appeal from final order, FL §9.5-314.
Inconvenient forum, FL §9.5-207.
Information as to child not provided in first pleadings, FL §9.5-209.
Telephone testimony.
Witnesses located in another state, FL §9.5-110.
Temporary emergency jurisdiction, FL §9.5-204.
Temporary orders.
Issuance when court of this state without jurisdiction, FL §9.5-304.
Unjustifiable conduct.
Declining jurisdiction, FL §9.5-208.
Warrant to take immediate custody, FL §9.5-311.
When court has jurisdiction, FL §9.5-201.
Witnesses located in another state.
Obtaining testimony, FL §9.5-110.
Visitation.
See CHILD VISITATION.

CHILD FATALITY REVIEW TEAMS, HG §§5-701 to 5-709.
Confidentiality of information.
Discovery.
Information, documents and records not subject to, HG §5-709.
Public meetings.
Prohibited disclosures, HG §5-708.
Records, HG §5-709.
State team.
Prohibited disclosures, HG §5-704.
Discovery.
Information, documents and records not subject to discovery, HG §5-709.
Local teams.
County-wide teams, HG §5-705.
Defined, HG §5-701.
Duties, HG §5-706.

CHILD FATALITY REVIEW TEAMS —Cont'd
Local teams —Cont'd
Information to be provided to, HG §5-707.
Meetings, HG §5-708.
Purpose, HG §5-706.
Medical examiners.
Definitions, HG §5-701.
Unexpected death of child.
Notification of child fatality review team, HG §5-309.
Meetings.
Closed meetings, HG §5-709.
Penalties.
Public meetings.
Prohibited disclosures, HG §5-708.
State team.
Prohibited disclosures.
Civil penalty, HG §5-704.
State team, HG §5-702.
Defined, HG §5-701.
Disclosure of information, HG §5-704.
Duties, HG §5-704.
Meetings, HG §§5-703, 5-708.
Membership, HG §5-703.
Purpose, HG §5-704.
Subpoenas.
Information, documents, and records not subject to subpoena, HG §5-709.
Unexpected child death.
Defined, HG §5-701.
Medical examiner to notify team, HG §5-309.
Witnesses.
Requesting at meetings, HG §5-708.
Testimony by members, persons attending meetings, and persons presenting information to team, HG §5-709.

CHILD IN NEED OF ASSISTANCE.
Generally.
See CHILDREN IN NEED OF ASSISTANCE.

CHILD IN NEED OF RESIDENTIAL PLACEMENT.
Children, youth and families services.
Generally, 49D §§1-101 to 7-106.
See CHILDREN, YOUTH AND FAMILIES SERVICES.

CHILD IN NEED OF SERVICES PILOT PROGRAM, CJ §3-8A-10.1.

CHILD KIDNAPPING, CR §3-503.

CHILD LABOR.
Administration.
Powers and duties of commissioner.
Delegation of powers and duties, LE §3-104.
Duties generally, LE §3-102.
Interference with performance of duties, LE §3-216.
Investigations, LE §3-103.
Miscellaneous powers, LE §3-204.
Crimes and offenses.
Interference with performance of duties of commissioner, LE §3-216.
Prohibited employment, LE §3-216.
Definitions.
Minor, LE §3-201.
Interpretation and construction.
Scope of subtitle, LE §3-203.
Statement of policy, LE §3-202.
Sunset provision, LE §3-706.
Work hours.
Restricted employment during certain hours.
Scope of section, LE §3-212.

CHILD LABOR —Cont'd
Minors under 14 years of age.
Employment prohibited, LE §3-209.
Misdemeanors.
Interference with performance of duties of
commissioner, LE §3-216.
Prohibited employment, LE §3-216.
Notices.
Posting notice of subtitle, LE §3-214.
Penalties.
Interference with performance of duties of
commissioner, LE §3-216.
Prohibited employment, LE §3-216.
Permits.
Special permits.
Generally, LE §§3-205 to 3-208. See within this
heading, "Special permits."
Work permits.
Generally, LE §§3-205 to 3-208. See within this
heading, "Work permits."
Prohibited employment, LE §3-213.
Minors under 14 years of age, LE §3-209.
Minors under 16 years of age, LE §3-213.
Penalties, LE §3-216.
Special permits.
Application, LE §3-207.
Contents, LE §3-207.
Issuance, LE §3-207.
Authority to issue, LE §3-207.
Required, LE §3-205.
Revocation, LE §3-215.
Scope of, LE §3-208.
Sunset provision, LE §3-706.
Work hours.
Exceptions to restrictions, LE §3-210.
Minors under 16 years of age, LE §3-211.
Generally, LE §3-210.
Minors under 16 years of age.
Exception to restrictions, LE §3-211.
Generally, LE §3-211.
Restricted employment during certain hours, LE
§3-212.
Restrictions, LE §3-210.
Employment during certain hours, LE §3-212.
Minors under 16 years of age, LE §3-211.
Work permits.
Issuance, LE §3-206.
Validation of application, LE §3-206.
Permit restrictions, LE §3-206.
Proof of age, LE §3-206.
Required, LE §3-205.
Revocation, LE §3-215.
School superintendents.
County superintendents.
Powers as to issuance of work permits, ED
§4-205.
Scope of, LE §3-208.
Validation of application, LE §3-206.

CHILD PASSENGER SAFETY TECHNICIANS.
Immunity from suit for act or omission, CJ
§5-640.

CHILD PLACEMENT.
Agencies.
Licenses, FL §5-507.
Child care facilities generally, FL §§5-506 to
5-521.
See CHILD CARE.
Construction and interpretation.
Interstate compact on the placement of children.
Liberal construction, FL §5-611.

CHILD PLACEMENT —Cont'd
Definitions.
Interstate compact on the placement of children,
FL §§5-601, 5-603.
Delinquent children.
Interstate compact on the placement of children.
Placement, FL §5-607.
Foster care.
Sibling placement and visitation rights, FL
§5-525.2.
**Interstate compact on the placement of
children.**
Agreements for services, FL §5-606.
Applicability of compact.
Exceptions, FL §5-609.
Construction and interpretation.
Liberal construction of provisions, FL §5-611.
Definitions, FL §§5-601, 5-603.
Delinquent children.
Placement, FL §5-607.
Entry into compact, FL §5-601.
General coordinator of activities.
Powers, FL §5-608.
Joinder by other jurisdiction, FL §5-610.
Jurisdiction.
Courts, FL §5-601.
Sending agency.
Retention of jurisdiction over child, FL
§5-606.
Notice.
Intention to send child into state, FL §5-604.
Private charitable agencies.
Authority, FL §5-606.
Purpose, FL §5-602.
Sending agency.
Defined, FL §5-603.
Jurisdiction over child.
Retention by sending agency, FL §5-606.
Sending child into state.
Procedure, FL §5-604.
Severability of provisions, FL §5-611.
Violations of compact.
Penalties, FL §5-605.
Withdrawal from compact, FL §5-610.
Jurisdiction.
Interstate compact on the placement of children.
Court, FL §5-601.
Sending agency.
Retention of jurisdiction over child, FL
§5-606.
Kinship care program, FL §5-534.
Admission of students in kinship care, ED §7-101.
Education funding for child in informal kinship
care relationship, ED §4-122.1.
Notice.
Interstate compact on the placement of children.
Sending child into state, FL §5-604.
Out-of-home placement.
Administration to establish program, FL §5-525.
Children placed in program, FL §5-525.
Evaluation of success of services of children in.
Cooperation in determining cost of developing
and implementing, FL §5-506.
Permanency plan, FL §5-525.
Short-term placement, FL §5-525.
Voluntary placement agreement, FL §5-525.
Penalties.
Interstate compact on the placement of children.
Violations of compact, FL §5-605.
Sibling placement and visitation rights, FL
§5-525.2.

CHILD PLACEMENT —Cont'd
Visitation.
Sibling visitation rights, FL §5-525.2.
Voluntary placement hearings.
Children in need of assistance.
Closed hearing, CJ §3-810.
Conduct of hearing, CJ §3-819.1.
Defined, CJ §3-801.
Jurisdiction, CJ §§3-803, 3-804.
Masters, appointment, CJ §3-807.
Petition, CJ §3-811.
Venue, CJ §3-805.

CHILD PORNOGRAPHY, CR §11-207.
County libraries.
Minors accessing obscene materials through
library by Internet, world wide web, etc.
Policies to prevent, implementation required,
ED §23-506.1.
Internet, CR §11-207.
Obscene materials or material constituting child
pornography.
Minors accessing through county libraries,
prevention, ED §23-506.1.
Removal of child pornography from Internet, CR
§11-208.1.
Pornography generally.
See OBSCENITY AND PORNOGRAPHY.

CHILDREN.
Abduction.
See ABDUCTION.
Adoption.
See ADOPTION.
After-born child.
Intestate succession, ET §3-107.
Statutory share of pretermitted child issue, ET
§§3-301 to 3-303.
See DECEDENTS' ESTATES.
Aid to families with dependent children.
Family investment program generally, 88A §§44A
to 56.
See FAMILY INVESTMENT PROGRAM.
Child abuse and neglect.
General provisions, FL §§5-701 to 5-714.
See CHILD ABUSE AND NEGLECT.
Child care centers, FL §§5-570 to 5-589.
See CHILD CARE CENTERS.
Child care quality incentive grant program, FL
§§5-594 to 5-594.8.
Child custody.
See CHILD CUSTODY.
Child in need of residential placement, 49D
§§1-101 to 7-106.
See CHILDREN, YOUTH AND FAMILIES
SERVICES.
Child labor.
Employment of minors generally, LE §§3-201 to
3-216.
See CHILD LABOR.
Child placement.
General provisions.
See CHILD PLACEMENT.
**Children's environmental health and
protection advisory council,** HG §§13-1501
to 13-1506.
See CHILDREN'S ENVIRONMENTAL HEALTH
AND PROTECTION ADVISORY COUNCIL.
Children's health care program, HG §§15-301 to
15-304.
Child support.
Enforcement administration.
See CHILD SUPPORT ENFORCEMENT
ADMINISTRATION.

CHILDREN —Cont'd
Child support —Cont'd
General provisions.
See SUPPORT AND MAINTENANCE.
Child visitation.
See CHILD VISITATION.
Child with intensive needs, 49D §§1-101 to
7-106.
See CHILDREN, YOUTH AND FAMILIES
SERVICES.
Definitions, ET §§1-101, 1-205 to 1-208.
Child to include illegitimate child, 1 §16.
Descent and distribution.
Determining relationship.
General provisions, ET §§1-201 to 1-210.
See DECEDENTS' ESTATES.
Environmental health.
Children's environmental health and protection
advisory council, HG §§13-1501 to 13-1506.
See CHILDREN'S ENVIRONMENTAL
HEALTH AND PROTECTION ADVISORY
COUNCIL.
Family investment program, 88A §§44A to 56.
See FAMILY INVESTMENT PROGRAM.
Fingerprinting.
Voluntary fingerprinting programs, FL §9-403.
General provisions.
See MINORS.
Handicapped persons.
Services to handicapped children.
See HANDICAPPED PERSONS.
Health insurance.
See HEALTH INSURANCE.
Hearing impaired infants, HG §§13-601 to
13-605.
See DEAF AND HEARING IMPAIRED.
Housing discrimination, 49B §22.
Juvenile causes, Juv Rules 11-101 to 11-122.
See JUVENILE CAUSES.
Labor.
Child labor, LE §§3-201 to 3-216.
See CHILD LABOR.
Life insurance and annuities.
Payment of proceeds to minor without
appointment of legal guardian, IN §16-110.
Minors.
General provisions.
See MINORS.
Neglected children.
General provisions, FL §§5-701 to 5-714.
See CHILD ABUSE AND NEGLECT.
Newborn infant identification, HG §§20-401,
20-402.
Office for children and youth.
Generally.
See MINORS.
Maryland school-based health policy advisory
council, ED §§7-4A-01 to 7-4A-05.
See MARYLAND SCHOOL-BASED HEALTH
POLICY ADVISORY COUNCIL.
Optometrists, therapeutic.
Treatment of children under a certain age, HO
§11-404.2.
**Uniform child custody jurisdiction and
enforcement act,** FL §§9.5-101 to 9.5-318.
See CHILD CUSTODY.

CHILDREN IN NEED OF ASSISTANCE.
Adoption.
Placement for, CJ §3-823.

CHILDREN IN NEED OF ASSISTANCE —Cont'd
Applicability of provisions to certain other proceedings, CJ §3-8A-04.
At-risk youth prevention and diversion programs, 41 §§2-501 to 2-503.
Attorneys at law.
Guidelines for advocacy, ChildAdv Appx.
Right to counsel, CJ §3-813.
CASA program, CJ §3-830.
Chronic abuse, child subject to.
Waiver of reunification efforts, CJ §3-812.
Commitment.
Facility for the developmentally disabled, CJ §3-819.
Limitations on place of, CJ §3-825.
Psychiatric facility, CJ §3-819.
Confidentiality of records, CJ §3-827.
Construction of provisions, CJ §3-802.
Contributing to certain conditions of child, CJ §3-828.
Correctional facilities.
Limitations on place of commitment, CJ §3-825.
County superintendent or supervisor of pupil personnel.
Notice that child found to be in need of assistance, CJ §3-819.
Court-appointed special advocate program, CJ §3-830.
Crime of violence, conviction.
Waiver of reunification efforts, CJ §3-812.
Custody.
Custody order, CJ §3-819.
Granting custody and guardianship, CJ §3-819.2.
Taking child into custody, CJ §3-814.
Defined, CJ §§3-8A-01, 3-801.
Disposition hearing, CJ §3-819.
Findings required in hearings, CJ §3-816.1.
Voluntary placement hearing, CJ §3-819.1.
Emergency medical or psychiatric treatment, CJ §3-824.
Evidence.
Report of study of child, CJ §3-816.
Rules of evidence, CJ §3-817.
Examination of child, CJ §3-816.
Exclusion of general public from proceedings, CJ §3-810.
Files.
Separate file for each case, CJ §3-810.
Guardians.
Granting custody and guardianship, CJ §3-819.2.
Rights of guardian, CJ §3-819.
Venue of action for guardianship, CJ §6-203.
Hearings.
Adjudication hearing, CJ §3-817.
Disposition hearing, CJ §3-819.
Findings required in hearings, CJ §3-816.1.
Masters, CJ §3-807.
Permanency plan for out-of-home placement, CJ §3-823.
Removal of child from court ordered placement, CJ §3-820.
Voluntary placement hearing, CJ §3-819.1.
Judges.
Appointment of masters, CJ §3-807.
Assignment and rotation of judges, CJ §3-806.
Jurisdiction, CJ §3-803.
Retention or termination of jurisdiction, CJ §3-804.
Local juvenile court committees, CJ §3-829.
Masters, CJ §3-807.

CHILDREN IN NEED OF ASSISTANCE —Cont'd
Orders.
Controlling conduct of person before court, CJ §3-821.
Custody order, CJ §3-819.
Juvenile court order treated in same manner as circuit court order, CJ §3-808.
Permitted dispositions, CJ §3-819.
Voluntary placement, CJ §3-819.1.
Parents.
Address and identity, CJ §3-822.
Support of child.
Liability of parents, CJ §3-819.
Permanent placement of child, CJ §3-812.
Findings required in hearings, CJ §3-816.1.
Permanency plan for out-of-home placement, CJ §3-823.
Petitions, CJ §3-809.
Allegations, CJ §3-811.
Contributing to certain conditions of child.
Petition alleging violations, CJ §3-828.
Rules governing, CJ §3-810.
Where filed, CJ §3-805.
Placement.
Adoption.
Placement for, CJ §3-823.
Child alleged to be in need of assistance, CJ §3-815.
Findings required in hearings, CJ §3-816.1.
Permanency plan for out-of-home placement, CJ §3-823.
Permitted dispositions, CJ §3-819.
Removal of child from court ordered placement, CJ §3-820.
Voluntary placement.
Closed hearing, CJ §3-810.
Conduct of hearing, CJ §3-819.1.
Defined, CJ §3-801.
Jurisdiction, CJ §§3-803, 3-804.
Masters, appointment, CJ §3-807.
Petition, CJ §3-811.
Venue, CJ §3-805.
Presumptions.
Child not receiving ordinary and proper care and attention, CJ §3-818.
Progress reports, CJ §3-826.
Psychiatric treatment.
Emergency psychiatric treatment, CJ §3-824.
Purpose of provisions, CJ §3-802.
Reunification of child with natural parent or guardian.
Reasonable efforts, CJ §3-812.
Sexual abuse.
Waiver of reunification efforts, CJ §3-812.
Shelter care, CJ §3-815.
Study of child, CJ §3-816.
Substance abuse testing of parents, local department request, FL §5-1203.
Support of child.
Enforcement powers of court, CJ §3-822.
Liability of parents, CJ §3-819.
Torture.
Waiver of reunification efforts, CJ §3-812.
Trial by court without jury, CJ §3-808.
Venue, CJ §3-805.
Waiver of reunification efforts, CJ §3-812.

CHILDREN'S CABINET.
Children, youth and families services.
Generally, 49D §§1-101 to 7-106.
See CHILDREN, YOUTH AND FAMILIES SERVICES.

CHILDREN'S CABINET FUND.
Children, youth and families services, 49D §§5-101 to 5-104.

CHILDREN'S ENVIRONMENTAL HEALTH AND PROTECTION ADVISORY COUNCIL, HG §§13-1501 to 13-1506.
Analysis of current state structure, HG §13-1505.
Definitions, HG §13-1501.
Duties, HG §13-1506.
Educational programs, creation, HG §13-1506.
Environmental hazards defined, HG §13-1501.
Established, HG §13-1503.
Expenses, reimbursement, HG §13-1505.
Findings of general assembly, HG §13-1502.
Meetings, quorum, HG §13-1505.
Members, terms, HG §13-1504.
Regulations impacting environmental hazards affecting children's health.
Preliminary review by council, SG §10-110.
Report, HG §13-1506.
Rules and regulations, review, recommendations, comment, HG §13-1506.
Staffing, HG §13-1505.

CHILDREN'S HEALTH PROGRAM, HG §§15-301 to 15-304.
Administration of program, HG §15-301.
Applications.
Review, monitoring and disapproval, HG §15-302.
Comprehensive medical care and other health services.
Program to provide, HG §15-301.
Created, HG §15-301.
Definitions, HG §15-301.
Directory or other listing, HG §15-301.
Eligible participants, HG §15-301.
Employer-sponsored health benefit plan, HG §15-301.1.
Expedited eligibility, HG §15-303.
Managed care organizations.
Enrollment of recipients, HG §15-303.
Outreach for program, mechanisms, HG §15-304.
Premium plan, HG §15-301.1.
Purposes, HG §15-301.
School-based outreach program, HG §15-304.
Termination of coverage, HG §15-302.

CHILDREN'S TRUST FUND, HG §13-2207.

CHILDREN WITH SPECIAL NEEDS.
Children, youth and families services generally, 49D §§1-101 to 7-106.
See CHILDREN, YOUTH AND FAMILIES SERVICES.
Handicapped persons generally.
See HANDICAPPED PERSONS.
Schools.
Handicapped children.
See SCHOOLS.
Services to, 49D §§4-101 to 4-103.
Medical assistance.
Program for crippled children, HG §15-125.
Sign language.
Academic credit, ED §4-111.

CHILDREN, YOUTH AND FAMILIES SERVICES, 49D §§1-101 to 7-106.
Child in need of out-of-state placement.
Defined, 49D §1-101.
Child in need of residential placement.
Defined, 49D §1-101.

CHILDREN, YOUTH AND FAMILIES SERVICES —Cont'd
Children's cabinet.
Local management boards.
Regulations concerning, adoption, 49D §2-104.
Children's cabinet fund, 49D §§5-101 to 5-104.
Application for money from fund.
Local management boards, 49D §5-103.
Community partnership agreements.
Development by local management boards, 49D §5-103.
Composition, reversion, 49D §5-101.
Disbursement and use of money, 49D §5-103.
Established, 49D §5-101.
Expenditures to counties, 49D §5-102.
Fiscal agent.
State department of education, 49D §5-104.
Children with special needs, 49D §§4-101 to 4-103.
Local coordinating councils.
Establishment, members, terms, chair, duties, 49D §4-102.
State coordinating council.
Duties as to, 49D §4-101.
Multiple unit information system.
Establishment by state coordinating council, 49D §4-101.
Parents and guardians and child's attorney.
Participation and notification, 49D §4-103.
State coordinating council.
Established, members, chair, duties, 49D §4-101.
Child with intensive needs.
Defined, 49D §1-101.
Community partnership agreements.
Development by local management boards, 49D §5-103.
Contracts.
Residential child care programs, 49D §§7-101 to 7-106.
Definitions, 49D §1-101.
Contracts for residential child care programs, 49D §7-101.
Operators of residential child care programs, 49D §6-101.
Disclosure of information and records to public agencies, 49D §§3-101 to 3-106.
Confidentiality of disclosed information and records, 49D §3-106.
Consent required.
Person in interest, 49D §§3-104, 3-105.
Exchange of information by agencies serving children, youth and families.
Purpose and intent, 49D §3-102.
Identity of recipient of services.
Protection, 49D §3-104.
Information specifically identified.
Disclosure limited to, 49D §3-104.
Legislative intent, 49D §3-102.
Limitation on disclosures, 49D §3-104.
Office for children.
Disclosure to office required, 49D §3-103.
Person in interest defined, 49D §3-101.
Purpose, 49D §3-102.
Required disclosures, 49D §3-103.
Limitation, 49D §3-104.
Scope of disclosure, 49D §3-104.
Legislative purpose, 49D §1-102.
Local coordinating council.
Defined, 49D §1-101.

CHILDREN, YOUTH AND FAMILIES SERVICES —Cont'd

Local coordinating council —Cont'd

Establishment. members, terms, chair, duties, 49D §4-102.

State coordinating council.

Duties as to, 49D §4-101.

Local management boards, 49D §§2-101 to 2-105.

Children's cabinet fund.

Application for money from fund, disbursement, use, 49D §5-103.

Community partnership agreements.

Development, 49D §5-103.

Composition, 49D §2-102.

Defined, 49D §1-101.

Designation of entities by counties, 49D §2-101.

Duties, 49D §2-103.

Establishment and maintenance by counties.

Purpose, 49D §2-101.

Required, 49D §2-101.

Regulations concerning.

Children's cabinet to adopt, 49D §2-104.

Report by state association of local management boards, 49D §2-105.

Operators of residential child care programs, 49D §§6-101, 6-102.

Policy of state, 49D §1-102.

Public agencies.

Defined, 49D §1-101.

Disclosure of information and records to, 49D §§3-101 to 3-106.

Residential child care programs.

Contracts, 49D §§7-101 to 7-106.

Definitions, 49D §7-101.

Generally, 49D §7-104.

Legislative intent, 49D §7-102.

Quality of child care provided.

Legislative intent, 49D §7-102.

Regulations, adoption, 49D §7-106.

Requirements, 49D §7-104.

Sample provided by single point of entry, 49D §7-105.

Statements required, 49D §7-104.

Operators, 49D §§6-101, 6-102.

Board of directors.

Requirements, 49D §6-101.

Business plan.

Requirement, 49D §6-101.

Bylaws.

Requirements, 49D §6-101.

Definitions, 49D §6-101.

Denial of license, grounds, 49D §6-101.

Documentation required, 49D §6-101.

Experience in field of human services.

Documentation required, 49D §6-101.

License required, 49D §6-102.

Operating without license, criminal penalty, 49D §6-102.

Prior licensing reports.

Documentation required, 49D §6-101.

Quality assurance plan.

Documentation required, 49D §6-101.

Requirements, 49D §6-101.

Structure requirements, 49D §6-101.

Unannounced inspections, 49D §6-101.

Waiver from requirements, regulations, adoption, 49D §6-101.

State resource plan, 49D §7-103.

Residential placement.

Decisions by councils.

Appeal, right of parent or guardian, 49D §4-103.

CHILDREN, YOUTH AND FAMILIES SERVICES —Cont'd

Residential placement —Cont'd

Decisions by councils —Cont'd

Notification to parent or guardian and child's attorney, 49D §4-103.

Defined, 49D §1-101.

Local coordinating councils.

Duties, review, 49D §4-102.

Meeting of councils discussing.

Attendance by parent or guardian, 49D §4-103.

Notification to parent or guardian and child's attorney, 49D §4-103.

Plans of care for placements.

Development and implementation by local councils, 49D §4-102.

State coordinating council.

Established, members, chair, duties, 49D §4-101.

State coordinating council for children.

Defined, 49D §1-101.

State resource plan.

Residential child care programs, 49D §7-103.

CHILD RESISTANT PACKAGING OF DANGEROUS HOUSEHOLD SUBSTANCES.

General provisions, HG §§22-301 to 22-312.

See POISONS.

CHILD'S ACCESS TO FIREARM, CR §4-104.

CHILD SAFETY SEATS, TR §22-412.2.

Immunity of child safety seat technicians from suit, CJ §5-640.

CHILD SEXUAL PREDATORS.

Registration of sex offenders, CP §§11-701 to 11-726.

See SEX OFFENDER REGISTRATION.

CHILD SUPPORT.

See SUPPORT AND MAINTENANCE.

CHILD SUPPORT ENFORCEMENT ADMINISTRATION.

Appeals.

Attachment and seizure of funds for arrears from financial institution, FL §10-108.3.

Consumer reporting agencies.

Information regarding arrears.

Contesting accuracy of information, FL §10-108.1.

Income tax refund intercept, FL §10-113.

Approval for child support services.

Duties, FL §10-109.

Attachment and seizure of funds for arrears.

From financial institution, FL §§10-108.3, 10-108.4.

Attorney general.

Legal representation, FL §10-115.

Best interests of child.

Responsibility to promote and serve, FL §10-118.

Child support reinvestment fund, FL §10-106.1.

Clerks of circuit courts.

Delegation of responsibilities for support enforcement to, FL §10-114.

Support enforcement services provided by, FL §10-114.

Collection and disbursement of support payments.

State disbursement unit, FL §10-108.7.

Commission on responsible fatherhood, 41 §§18-401 to 18-408.

Compromise and settlement.

Arrearages.

Power to settle, FL §10-112.

CHILD SUPPORT ENFORCEMENT
   ADMINISTRATION —Cont'd
Consumer reporting agencies.
   Defined, FL §10-108.1.
   Information regarding arrears.
      Supplying to, FL §10-108.1.
Cooperative agreements.
   Powers as to, FL §10-111.
Coordination of statewide program.
   Duties of administration, FL §10-108.
Deductions from support payments.
   Fees charged to defray cost of enforcement
      services, FL §10-110.
Duties, FL §10-108.
   Approval for child support services, FL §10-109.
   Secretary of human resources, FL §10-114.
Established, FL §10-106.
Establishment of state disbursement unit, FL
   §10-108.7.
Fees.
   Charged to defray costs of enforcement services.
      Deduction from support payments prohibited,
         FL §10-110.
   Collection of fees, FL §10-110.
Financial institutions.
   Attachment and seizure of funds for arrears from
      institution, FL §§10-108.3, 10-108.4.
   Defined, FL §10-108.2.
   Reports to administration, FL §10-108.2.
Income taxes.
   Powers of administration.
      Income tax refund intercept, FL §10-113.
Interception of state payments to obligor, FL
   §§10-113.1, 10-113.2.
Investigations.
   Income tax refund intercept, FL §10-113.
   Interception of state payments to obligor, FL
      §10-113.2.
Issuance of subpoena duces tecum, FL
   §10-108.6.
Legal representation, FL §10-115.
Local support enforcement offices.
   Best interests of child.
      Responsibility to promote and serve, FL
         §10-118.
   Enforcement by, FL §10-116.
   Transfer of support enforcement by, FL §10-117.
Lotteries.
   Certification to state lottery agency, FL §10-113.1.
Notice.
   Attachment and seizure of funds for arrears from
      financial institution, FL §10-108.3.
   Consumer reporting agencies.
      Information regarding arrears.
         Proposed supplying of information to, FL
            §10-108.1.
   Payment through support enforcement agency, FL
      §10-108.7.
Paternity proceedings.
   Administration as complainant, FL §5-1011.
   Definition of "administration," FL §5-1001.
Payment through support enforcement agency,
   FL §10-108.7.
Powers.
   Collection of fees, FL §10-110.
   Cooperative agreement, FL §10-111.
   Income tax refund intercept, FL §10-113.
   Settlement of arrearage, FL §10-112.
Presumptions.
   Compromise and settlement.
      Best interest of state presumed, FL §10-112.

CHILD SUPPORT ENFORCEMENT
   ADMINISTRATION —Cont'd
Reports.
   Financial institutions, FL §10-108.2.
Secretary of human resources.
   Authority, FL §10-107.
   Duties, FL §10-114.
State disbursement unit, FL §10-108.7.
State's attorneys.
   Legal representation, FL §10-115.
Subpoena duces tecum, FL §10-108.6.

CHILD SUPPORT ENFORCEMENT
   PRIVATIZATION PILOT PROGRAM, FL
   §§10-119.1, 10-119.2.

CHILD SUPPORT GUIDELINES, FL §§12-201 to
   12-204.

CHILD SUPPORT LIENS, FL §§10-140 to 10-144.

CHILD SUPPORT REINVESTMENT FUND, FL
   §10-106.1.

CHILD VISITATION.
Attorney general.
   Duties concerning instructional materials
      regarding, CJ §2-206.
Child abuse and neglect.
   Denial of custody.
      Likely abuse or neglect, FL §9-101.
   Evidence of abuse against certain individuals, FL
      §9-101.1.
Denial.
   Likely abuse or neglect, FL §9-101.
Educational seminars required, FamLaw Rule
   9-204.
Evidence.
   Child abuse and neglect.
      Evidence of abuse against certain individuals,
         FL §9-101.1.
Foster care.
   Sibling visitation rights, FL §5-525.2.
Grandparents.
   Petitions, FL §9-102.
Instructional materials regarding.
   Provision to public, CJ §2-206.
Interference with visitation, FL §9-105.
Jurisdiction.
   Equity court jurisdiction, FL §1-201.
   Removal of child from state.
      Equity court jurisdiction, FL §9-302.
Mediation of visitation disputes, FamLaw Rule
   9-205.
   Mediators.
      Qualifications, ADR Rule 17-104.
      Training programs, ADR Rule 17-106.
Murder.
   Parent convicted of murder of certain persons.
      Supervised visitation, FL §9-101.2.
Paternity proceedings.
   Orders relating to visitation privileges, FL
      §5-1035.
Petitions.
   Grandparents, FL §9-102.
Removal of child from state.
   Equity court jurisdiction, FL §9-302.
Unjustifiable denial, FL §9-105.

CHILD WELFARE ACCOUNTABILITY, FL
   §§5-1301 to 5-1311.
Caseload ratios, FL §5-1310.

CHILD WELFARE ACCOUNTABILITY —Cont'd
Commitment of children.
  Health, mental health, education and well-being
    of committed children.
    Measurement of effectiveness of efforts, FL
      §5-1306.
Definitions, FL §5-1301.
Effectiveness of efforts, measurement.
  Addressing child abuse and neglect, FL §5-1303.
  Health, mental health, education and well-being
    of committed children, FL §5-1306.
  Permanency and stability of living conditions, FL
    §5-1305.
  Protection of children removed from homes from
    abuse and neglect, FL §5-1304.
  Use of measures, FL §5-1307.
Local departments.
  Defined, FL §5-1301.
  Self-assessments, FL §5-1309.
Outcome measurement system, FL §5-1302.
  Measurement of effectiveness of efforts, FL
    §§5-1303 to 5-1307.
  Quality assessment, FL §5-1308.
Quality assessment, FL §5-1308.
Regulations.
  Outcome measurement system, FL §5-1302.
**Removal of children from homes from abuse
    and neglect.**
  Efforts to protect.
    Measurement of effectiveness, FL §5-1304.
Self-assessments by local departments, FL
    §5-1309.
Training, FL §5-1311.

**CHILD WELFARE AND SUBSTANCE ABUSE
    SERVICES, INTEGRATION,** FL §§5-1201 to
    5-1209.
Child in need of assistance proceedings.
  Substance abuse testing of parents, local
    department request, FL §5-1203.
Definitions, FL §5-1201.
**Excess hospital beds to locate new substance
    abuse treatment programs.**
  Exploring use, FL §5-1205.
Funds included in budget, FL §5-1204.
**Integration of child welfare and substance
    abuse treatment act,** FL §5-1209.
**Memorandum of understanding on department
    responsibilities,** FL §5-1207.
Regulations, adoption, FL §5-1208.
**Report by departments on compliance with
    provisions,** FL §5-1206.
Report submitted by department.
  Statewide protocol, FL §5-1202.
Statewide protocol, FL §5-1202.

CHILD WELFARE TRAINING ACADEMY, FL
    §5-1311.

CHILD WELLNESS SERVICES.
Health insurance coverage, IN §15-817.

CHILD WITH INTENSIVE NEEDS.
Children, youth and families services.
  Generally, 49D §§1-101 to 7-106.
    See CHILDREN, YOUTH AND FAMILIES
      SERVICES.

CHIMNEY FIRES.
Fire marshal's report, PS §6-313.

CHINCOTEAGUE BAY.
Atlantic coastal bays critical areas program.
  Generally, NR §§8-1801 to 8-1817.
    See CHESAPEAKE BAY CRITICAL AREA AND
      ATLANTIC COASTAL BAYS CRITICAL
      AREA PROTECTION PROGRAMS.
Lands formed by channel excavation, EN
    §§16-401 to 16-403.
  Construction of subtitle, EN §16-401.
  Patent restriction, EN §16-402.
  Title to land, EN §16-402.
  Use, EN §16-402.
    Conservation purposes, EN §16-403.
    Hunting and fishing, EN §16-403.

CHIROPRACTORS.
Administrative review, HO §3-316.
Advertising.
  Rules and regulations.
    Adoption by board of chiropractic examiners,
      HO §3-401.
  Trade names, HO §3-407.
Alcoholic beverages.
  Providing professional services while under the
    influence.
    Denials, reprimands, suspensions or revocations
      of licenses, HO §3-313.
Appeals.
  Actions of board of chiropractic examiners.
    Administrative and judicial review, HO §3-316.
Applicability of provisions, HO §3-102.
Assistants, HO §3-404.
Board of chiropractic examiners.
  Administrative and judicial review, HO §3-316.
  Advertising and solicitation.
    Adoption of rules and regulations by board, HO
      §3-401.
  Compensation of members, HO §3-204.
  Composition, HO §3-202.
  Consumer member, HO §3-202.
  Defined, HO §3-101.
  Elections, HO §3-203.
  Established, HO §3-201.
  Expenses.
    Reimbursement, HO §3-204.
  Fees.
    Establishment, HO §3-206.
  Funds.
    Disposition, HO §3-206.
  Liability.
    Good faith exemption from civil liability for acts
      within scope of jurisdiction of board, CJ
      §5-704.
    Immunity of persons giving information to
      board, HO §3-207.
  Licenses. See within this heading, "Licenses."
  Meetings, HO §3-204.
  Membership, HO §3-202.
  Miscellaneous powers and duties, HO §3-205.
  Oaths, HO §3-202.
  Officers, HO §3-203.
  Powers and duties.
    Generally, HO §3-205.
  Program evaluation act, SG §8-403.
  Quorum, HO §3-204.
  Removal of members, HO §3-202.
  Schools of chiropractic.
    Approval of board, HO §3-402.

CHIROPRACTORS —Cont'd
Board of chiropractic examiners —Cont'd
  Secretary-treasurer, HO §3-203.
  Staff, HO §3-204.
  State board of chiropractic examiners fund, HO
    §3-206.
  Tenure, HO §3-202.
  Vacancies, HO §3-202.
Chiropractor rehabilitation committees, HO
  §3-406.
Citation of title, HO §3-601.
Contempt.
  Licenses.
    Hearings, HO §3-315.
Controlled dangerous substances.
  Providing professional services while under the
    influence.
    Denials, reprimands, suspensions or revocations
      of licenses, HO §3-313.
Definitions, HO §3-101.
  Chiropractor rehabilitation committee, HO §3-406.
Discovery.
  Chiropractor rehabilitation committees.
    Proceedings, records and files, HO §3-406.
Education.
  Board approval of schools of chiropractic, HO
    §3-402.
Evidence.
  Chiropractor rehabilitation committees.
    Admissibility of proceedings, records and files,
      HO §3-406.
Examinations.
  Required examination performance, HO §3-304.
  Waiver of examination requirement, HO §3-305.
Fees.
  Board of chiropractic examiners.
    Establishment, HO §3-206.
  Licenses.
    Applications for licenses, HO §3-303.
    Establishment, HO §3-206.
    Issuance of licenses, HO §3-306.
  Review of fees or charges for service of another
    licensed chiropractor.
    Liability, HO §3-405.
Funds.
  Board of chiropractic examiners.
    Disposition, HO §3-206.
Hearings.
  Licenses, HO §3-315.
Immoral practice of chiropractic.
  Licenses.
    Grounds for denial, reprimand, revocation or
      suspension of license, HO §3-313.
Immunity.
  Board of chiropractic examiners.
    Good faith exemption from civil liability for acts
      within scope of jurisdiction of board, CJ
      §5-704.
    Persons giving information to board, HO §3-207.
  Chiropractor rehabilitation committees, HO
    §3-406.
  Reviewing fees or charges for service of another
    licensed chiropractor, CJ §5-636.
Inactive status.
  Licenses, HO §3-311.
    Reactivation, HO §3-311.
Injunctions against, HO §3-316.1.
Insurance coverage for services, IN §15-705.
Insurance fraud.
  Licenses.
    Grounds for denial, reprimand, revocation or
      suspension, HO §3-313.

CHIROPRACTORS —Cont'd
Judicial review, HO §3-316.
Liability.
  Board of chiropractic examiners.
    Good faith exemption from civil liability for acts
      within scope of jurisdiction of board, CJ
      §5-704.
    Immunity of persons giving information to
      board, HO §3-207.
  Chiropractor rehabilitation committees.
    Good faith exemption from civil liability, HO
      §3-406.
  Reviewing fees or charges for service of another
    licensed chiropractor, HO §3-405.
Licenses.
  Administrative and judicial review, HO §3-316.
  Appeals.
    Administrative and judicial review, HO §3-316.
  Applicants.
    Qualifications, HO §3-302.
  Applications for licenses, HO §3-303.
  Authority of license, HO §3-307.
  Certificate.
    Execution, HO §3-307.
  Contents of licenses, HO §3-306.
  Defined, HO §3-101.
  Denials.
    Grounds, HO §3-313.
  Diplomas.
    Prohibited transfer, HO §3-503.
  Execution of certificate, HO §3-307.
  Expired licenses.
    Reinstatement.
      Requirements, HO §§3-309, 3-310.
  Fees.
    Applications for licenses, HO §3-303.
    Establishment, HO §3-206.
    Issuance of licenses, HO §3-306.
  Fraud.
    Misrepresentation, HO §3-502.
    Transfers of diplomas or licenses, HO §3-503.
  Hearings, HO §3-315.
  Immoral practice of chiropractic.
    Grounds for denial, reprimand, revocation or
      suspension of license, HO §3-313.
  Inactive status, HO §3-311.
  Issuance of licenses, HO §3-306.
    Authority of board, HO §3-301.
  Kinds of licenses, HO §3-301.
  Misrepresentation, HO §3-502.
  Notice.
    Renewal notice, HO §3-308.
  Penalties, HO §3-506.
  Practice of physical therapy.
    Permitted, HO §3-301.
    Representations by certain licensees, HO
      §3-403.
  Practicing without license, HO §3-501.
  Qualifications of applicants, HO §3-302.
  Reinstatement.
    Requirements for reinstatement of expired
      license, HO §§3-309, 3-310.
  Renewal of licenses.
    Generally, HO §3-308.
  Representations by certain licensees, HO §3-403.
  Reprimands.
    Grounds, HO §3-313.
  Requirements generally, HO §3-301.
  Revocations.
    Grounds, HO §3-313.

CHIROPRACTORS —Cont'd
Licenses —Cont'd
  Rules and regulations.
    Grounds for denial, reprimand, revocation or
      suspension, HO §3-313.
    Scope of license, HO §3-307.
    Surrender.
      Generally, HO §3-312.
    Suspensions.
      Grounds, HO §3-313.
      Penalty instead of suspension, HO §3-314.
    Transfer of diploma or license.
      When prohibited, HO §3-503.
Medical records.
  Personal medical records generally, HG §§4-401 to
    4-403.
    See MEDICAL RECORDS.
Notices.
  Examinations, HO §3-304.
  Licenses.
    Renewal notice, HO §3-308.
Oaths.
  Licensing hearing, HO §3-315.
Occupational therapists.
  See OCCUPATIONAL THERAPISTS.
Penalties.
  Licenses.
    Penalty instead of suspension or revocation, HO
      §3-314.
    Violations, HO §3-506.
Physical therapists.
  See PHYSICAL THERAPISTS.
Practice chiropractic.
  Defined, HO §3-101.
Practice physical therapy.
  Defined, HO §3-101.
Records.
  Personal medical records generally, HG §§4-401 to
    4-403.
    See MEDICAL RECORDS.
Rules and regulations.
  Advertising and solicitation.
    Adoption by board, HO §3-401.
  Licenses.
    Denials, reprimands, suspensions or
      revocations.
      Violation of rules and regulations, HO §3-313.
Schools.
  Board approval of school of chiropractic, HO
    §3-402.
Scope of title, HO §3-102.
Sexual misconduct.
  Disciplinary action, HO §1-212.
Short title, HO §3-601.
Solicitations.
  Rules and regulations.
    Adoption by board of chiropractic examiners,
      HO §3-401.
Subpoenas.
  Licensing hearings, HO §3-315.
Termination of title, HO §3-602.
Title.
  Scope of title, HO §3-102.
  Short title, HO §3-601.
  Termination, HO §3-602.
Trade name use, HO §3-407.
Waiver.
  Examination and licensure requirements, HO
    §3-305.

CHLAMYDIA SCREENING TESTS.
Health insurance.
  Required coverage, IN §15-829.

CHLORINATED HYDROCARBON.
Inhaling, CR §5-708.

CHLORINE.
Water pollution.
  Chlorine systems, EN §§9-329 to 9-329.2.
    See WATER POLLUTION.

CHLORINE GAS.
Possession of destructive device, CR §§4-501 to
  4-503.

CHOICE OF LAW.
Conflict of laws generally.
  See CONFLICT OF LAWS.

CHOLERA.
General provisions.
  See CONTAGIOUS DISEASES.

CHOLESTEROL TESTING.
Certification of personnel not required, HG
  §17-504.
Definitions, HG §17-501.
Fees.
  Permits.
    Applications, HG §17-506.
    Renewal.
      Waiver of renewal fees for local and county
        health departments, HG §17-508.
    Waiver for local and county health departments,
      HG §17-506.
Hearings.
  Permits.
    Denial, suspension or revocation, HG §17-509.
Misdemeanors.
  Violations of provisions, HG §17-511.
Notices.
  Permits.
    Denial, suspension or revocation, HG §17-509.
Penalties.
  Violations of subtitle, HG §17-511.
Permits.
  Applications, HG §17-506.
    Renewal, HG §17-508.
  Defined, HG §17-501.
  Denial, HG §17-509.
  Fees.
    Applications, HG §17-506.
    Renewal.
      Waiver of renewal fees for local and county
        health departments, HG §17-508.
    Waiver for local and county health departments,
      HG §17-506.
  Hearings.
    Denial, suspension or revocation, HG §17-509.
  Issuance and contents, HG §17-507.
  Nontransferability, HG §17-510.
  Notice.
    Denial, suspension or revocation, HG §17-509.
    Renewal, HG §17-508.
  Qualifications, HG §17-505.
  Renewal, HG §17-508.
  Required, HG §17-502.
    Waiver of requirements, HG §17-503.
  Suspension or revocation, HG §17-509.
  Term of permit, HG §17-508.
  Testing without permit, HG §17-510.
  Waiver of requirement, HG §17-503.
Personnel.
  Certification not required, HG §17-504.
Plans.
  Submission, HG §17-503.

CHOLESTEROL TESTING —Cont'd

Rules and regulations.
Implementation of subtitle, HG §17-504.

Submission of plans, HG §17-503.

Violations of subtitle.
Misdemeanors, HG §17-511.

Waiver.
Permit fees.
Renewal.
Waiver for local and county health
departments, HG §17-508.
Waiver for local or county health departments,
HG §17-506.
Permit requirement, HG §17-503.

CHOPTANK RIVER.

Fish and fisheries.
Restriction in waters, NR §4-729.

Senator Frederick C. Malkus, Jr. bridge, TR
§8-649.

CHRISTIAN SCIENCE NURSES.

Generally.
See NURSES.

CHRISTIAN SCIENTISTS.

Motor vehicle insurance.
Primary coverage.
Christian Science care, IN §19-502.

CHRISTMAS DAY.

Defined, 1 §27.

Legal holiday, 1 §27.

Schools.
Legal holiday, ED §7-103.

CHRISTMAS TREES AND SHRUBS.

Bills of sale.
Contents, NR §5-412.
Production required, NR §5-414.
Required unless transported by owner of land, NR
§5-412.

Investigation of transportation, NR §5-414.

Owner of land.
Bill of sale required unless transported by, NR
§5-412.
Identification.
Ownership identification, NR §5-414.
When identification of owner of land to
accompany shipment, NR §5-413.

CHRONIC DISEASE CENTERS, HG §§19-501 to
19-513.
See HOSPITALS.

CHURCHES.

Annuity agreements with donors, IN §16-114.

Church buses.
Railroad grade crossings.
Stopping required, TR §21-703.

Episcopal Church.
Corporations.
See PROTESTANT EPISCOPAL CHURCH.

General provisions.
See RELIGION.

Hate crime.
Damaging property of religious entity, CR
§10-302.

Methodist Church.
Corporations.
See UNITED METHODIST CHURCH.

Presbyterian Church.
Corporations.
See UNITED PRESBYTERIAN CHURCH.

CHURCHES —Cont'd

Protestant Episcopal Church.
Corporations.
See PROTESTANT EPISCOPAL CHURCH.

Roman Catholic Church.
Corporations.
See ROMAN CATHOLIC CHURCH.

United Methodist Church.
Corporations.
See UNITED METHODIST CHURCH.

United Presbyterian Church.
Corporations.
See UNITED PRESBYTERIAN CHURCH.

CIDER.

Home consumption.
Manufacture without license, 2B §1-201.

C.I.F.

Sale of goods, UCC, CL §§2-320, 2-321.

CIGARETTE BUSINESS LICENSES, BR
§§16-101 to 16-401.

Applications.
County retail sales, BR §16-302.
Generally, BR §16-204.
Qualifications of applicants, BR §16-203.
Renewal of license, BR §16-207.

Assignment, BR §16-208.

**Compromise in lieu of suspension or
revocation of license.**
Petition prior to suspension or revocation, BR
§16-212.

Comptroller.
Common carrier records, BR §16-217.
Delegation of powers and duties under title, BR
§16-102.
Distribution of license fees, BR §16-216.
Issuance of licenses, BR §16-205.
License transfer by, BR §16-208.
Sealing vending machines.
Removal by comptroller, BR §16-220.

Computer network orders, BR §16-223.

County retail sales, BR §§16-301 to 16-309.
Applications for licenses, BR §16-302.
Disciplinary actions against licensees.
Grounds, BR §16-306.
Hearings, BR §16-307.
Display of license, BR §16-305.
Issuance of license, BR §16-303.
License required, BR §16-301.
Selling cigarettes without license, BR §16-308.
Penalty, BR §16-309.
Term of license, BR §16-304.

Definitions, BR §§16-101, 16-201.

Delegation of powers and duties.
Comptroller, BR §16-102.

Denials.
Grounds, BR §16-210.
County retail sales, BR §16-306.

Disciplinary actions against licensees.
Change of license status, BR §16-212.
Comptroller.
Hearings.
Administration of oaths, BR §16-211.
County retail sales, BR §16-306.
Grounds, BR §16-210.
County retail sales, BR §16-307.
Hearings.
Application of contested case provisions, BR
§16-211.
Judicial review, BR §16-213.

CIGARETTE BUSINESS LICENSES —Cont'd
Disciplinary actions against licensees —Cont'd
  Limitation on applications, BR §16-204.
  Notice requirements, BR §16-212.
  Period of suspension, BR §16-212.
  Right to counsel, BR §16-211.
Display requirements, BR §16-209.
Distribution of license fees, BR §16-216.
Doing business without license, BR §16-214.
  County retail sales, BR §16-308.
  Penalty, BR §16-309.
Electronic network orders, BR §16-223.
Exception to license requirement, BR §16-202.
Importing or shipping.
  Restrictions, BR §16-222.
Intended use of license fees, BR §16-216.
Issuance, BR §16-205.
  County retail sales, BR §16-303.
  Renewal of license, BR §16-207.
**Mail order, computer network orders,
  telephonic orders or order by other
  electronic network,** BR §16-223.
Mandatory, BR §16-202.
  County retail sales, BR §16-301.
Manufacturers.
  Scope of license, BR §16-206.
Multiple licenses, BR §16-202.
Penalties.
  Violating comptroller regulations, BR §16-401.
Posting requirements, BR §16-209.
Records.
  Common carriers, BR §16-217.
  Retention and examination, BR §16-218.
  Transporter records, BR §16-219.
Renewal of license, BR §16-207.
Reprimands.
  Grounds, BR §16-210.
    County retail sales, BR §16-306.
Required, BR §16-202.
  County retail sales, BR §16-301.
Restrictions on shipping, importing, or selling,
  BR §16-222.
Retailers.
  Scope of license, BR §16-206.
Revocation of license.
  Period, notice of action, offer of compromise, BR
    §16-212.
Sales.
  Restrictions, BR §16-222.
Scope of licenses, BR §16-206.
Sealing vending machines, BR §16-220.
  Removing or tampering prohibited, BR §16-221.
    Removal by comptroller authorized, BR §16-220.
Storage warehouses.
  Scope of license, BR §16-206.
Subwholesalers.
  Scope of license, BR §16-206.
Surrender of license, BR §16-208.
Suspension of license.
  Period, notice of action, offer of compromise, BR
    §16-212.
Telephonic orders, BR §16-223.
Term of license, BR §16-207.
  County retail sales, BR §16-304.
Transferability, BR §16-208.
Unstamped cigarettes.
  Accepting delivery prohibited, BR §16-215.
  Defined, BR §16-201.
  Duty to inspect, BR §16-215.
Vending machine label requirements, BR
  §16-209.

CIGARETTE BUSINESS LICENSES —Cont'd
Vending machine operators.
  Business licenses generally, BR §§17-1901 to
    17-1907.
    See VENDING MACHINES.
  Defined, BR §16-201.
  Qualifications of applicants, BR §16-203.
  Scope of licenses, BR §16-206.
Voluntary surrender of license, BR §16-208.
Wholesalers, BR §16-202.
  Scope of licenses, BR §16-206.

CIGARETTE RESTITUTION FUND, SF §7-317.
Funded programs.
  Budget bill to include appropriations for funding,
    SF §7-114.
  Cancer prevention, education, screening and
    treatment program, HG §§13-1101 to 13-1119.
    See CANCER PREVENTION, EDUCATION,
      SCREENING AND TREATMENT
      PROGRAM.
  Expenditure overview, budget books to contain, SF
    §7-121.
  Tobacco use prevention and cessation program,
    HG §§13-1001 to 13-1015.
    See TOBACCO USE PREVENTION AND
      CESSATION PROGRAM.

CIGARETTE SALES BELOW COST ACT.
See CIGARS AND CIGARETTES.

**CIGARETTE SALES, LESS THAN 20 PER
  PACKAGE,** CL §§11-5A-01 to 11-5A-03.

CIGARS AND CIGARETTES.
**Cancer prevention, education, screening and
  treatment program,** HG §§13-1101 to 13-1119.
  See CANCER PREVENTION, EDUCATION,
    SCREENING AND TREATMENT
    PROGRAM.
Cigarette sales below cost act.
  Administration, CL §11-507.
  Application of general unfair sales act, CL
    §11-509.
  Cash and carry basis.
    Markup on sales at wholesale on cash and carry
      basis, CL §11-503.
  Citation.
    Short title, CL §11-510.
  Clearance sales.
    Exceptions, CL §11-502.
  Combination sales and concessions, CL §11-505.
  Cost.
    Basic cost of cigarettes.
      Calculating basic cost, CL §11-502.
      Defined, CL §11-501.
    Evidence bearing on cost, CL §11-506.
    Replacement cost.
      Defined, CL §11-501.
    Special cost provisions, CL §11-503.
  Damages.
    Action for, CL §11-508.
  Definitions, CL §11-501.
  Discounts.
    Retailer or vending machine operator receiving
      wholesalers' discounts, CL §11-503.
  Enforcement, CL §11-507.
  Evidence.
    Prima facie evidence of intent, CL §11-506.
  Exceptions, CL §11-502.
  Injunctions.
    Retailer or wholesaler enjoined, CL §11-508.

CIGARS AND CIGARETTES —Cont'd
Cigarette sales below cost act —Cont'd
  Intent.
    Prima facie evidence of intent, CL §11-506.
  Licenses.
    Suspension or revocation, CL §11-508.
  Liquidation sales.
    Exceptions, CL §11-502.
  Person.
    Defined, CL §11-501.
  Remedies, CL §11-508.
  Retailer.
    Cost.
      Defined, CL §11-501.
    Defined, CL §11-501.
    Receiving wholesalers' discounts, CL §11-503.
    Sale of cigarettes at retail.
      Defined, CL §11-501.
  Sale at less than cost.
    General provisions, CL §11-504.
  Seller.
    At both retail and wholesale, CL §11-503.
  Vending machine operators.
    Defined, CL §11-501.
    Discounts.
      Receiving wholesalers' discounts, CL §11-503.
    Sales by wholesalers to vending machine
      operators, CL §11-503.
  Wholesaler.
    Cost.
      Defined, CL §11-501.
    Defined, CL §11-501.
    Sale of cigarettes at wholesale.
      Defined, CL §11-501.
    Sales by wholesalers to other wholesalers, CL
      §11-503.
    Subwholesaler.
      Defined, CL §11-501.
Clove cigarettes.
  Sale prohibited, penalty, CR §10-106.
Computer network orders.
  Direct sales and shipping, BR §16-223.
Damages.
  Cigarette sales below cost act.
    Action for, CL §11-508.
Definitions.
  Cigarette sales below cost act, CL §11-501.
Electronic network orders.
  Direct sales and shipping, BR §16-223.
Evidence.
  Cigarette sales below cost act.
    Prima facie evidence of intent, CL §11-506.
Injunctions.
  Cigarette sales below cost act.
    Retailer or wholesaler enjoined, CL §11-508.
Licenses.
  Cigarette business licenses, BR §§16-101 to
    16-401.
    See CIGARETTE BUSINESS LICENSES.
  Cigarette sales below cost act.
    Suspension or revocation, CL §11-508.
  Traders.
    Revocation, CL §11-508.
    Suspension, CL §11-508.
Mail order, computer network orders,
  telephonic orders or orders by other
  electronic network.
  Direct sales and shipping, BR §16-223.
Minors.
  Possession by minor.
    Acting as agent of employer.
      Inapplicability, CR §10-108.

CIGARS AND CIGARETTES —Cont'd
Minors —Cont'd
  Possession by minor —Cont'd
    Citation issued to minor, CR §10-108.
    Prohibition, CR §10-108.
  Sales to minors.
    Coupons contained in newspaper, magazine or
      other publication.
        Inapplicability of prohibition, CR §10-107.
    Defense.
      Examination of purchaser's driver's license or
        other identification, CR §10-107.
    Each violation separate, CR §10-107.
    Prohibited, CR §10-107.
Presumptions.
  Cigarette sales below cost act.
    Prima facie evidence of intent, CL §11-506.
Sales.
  Less than 20 cigarettes per package, CL
    §§11-5A-01 to 11-5A-03.
    Definitions, CL §11-5A-01.
    Enforcement, CL §11-5A-03.
    Prohibitions, CL §11-5A-02.
  Mail order, computer network orders, telephonic
    orders or orders by other electronic network.
    Direct sales and shipping, BR §16-223.
  Sales below cost. See within this heading,
    "Cigarette sales below cost act."
Smoking in certain public places.
  General provisions.
    See SMOKING.
Taxation.
  Tobacco tax.
    General provisions, TG §§2-1601 to 2-1603,
      12-101 to 12-306.
    See TOBACCO TAX.
Telephonic orders.
  Direct sales and shipping, BR §16-223.
Tobacco.
  Collection of taxes.
    Constitution of Maryland, TG §§2-1601 to
      2-1603, 12-101 to 12-306.
    See TOBACCO TAX.
  General provisions.
    See TOBACCO.
Tobacco use prevention and cessation
  program, HG §§13-1001 to 13-1015.
  See TOBACCO USE PREVENTION AND
    CESSATION PROGRAM.
Vending machines.
  Cigarette sales below cost act.
    Vending machine operators.
      Defined, CL §11-501.
      Discounts.
        Receiving wholesalers' discounts, CL
          §11-503.
      Sales by wholesalers to vending machine
        operators, CL §11-503.
  Licenses.
    See VENDING MACHINES.
  Sale of tobacco products through vending
    machine, BR §§16-3A-01 to 16-3A-03.

CINEMA.
See MOTION PICTURES.

CIRCUIT COURT MASTERS.
Standing masters of the circuit courts, CJ
  §2-501.

CIRCUIT COURTS.
Administration of courts, CJA Rules 16-101 to
  16-824.
  See ADMINISTRATION OF COURTS.

CIRCUIT COURTS —Cont'd

Appeals.
Court of special appeals.
  Review of decisions by court of appeals, CJ §12-201.
    Exceptions, CJ §12-202.
Defined, CJ §12-101.
Elections.
  Rejection of ballots by board of canvassers.
    Absentee ballots, EL §11-304.
Form of court papers, Rule 1-301.
General provisions.
  See APPEALS.
Insurance commissioner's orders or hearings, IN §2-215.
Interlocutory orders.
  Certain orders, CJ §12-303.
  Peace orders, CJ §3-1506.
Probation.
  Revocation of probation.
    Application for leave to appeal from order revoking probation, CJ §12-302.
Right of appeal.
  Exceptions, CJ §12-301.
  Final judgments, CJ §12-301.
  State appeals, CJ §12-302.

Appearances.
Fees, CJ §7-204.
Initial appearance of defendant.
  Criminal cases, Crim Rule 4-213.

Applicability of rules, Rule 1-101.

Arbitration.
International commercial arbitration.
  Jurisdiction, CJ §3-2B-04.
Uniform arbitration act.
  See ARBITRATION AND AWARD.

Arrest.
See ARREST.

Arrest warrants issued in circuit court.
Failure to use, CJ §2-107.
Form and content, CJ §2-107.

Assignment commissioners.
General provisions, CJ §2-501.

Attorneys at law.
Form of court papers, Rule 1-301.

Attorneys' fees.
Appearance fees.
  Attorney entitled to demand and receive, CJ §7-204.

Audio recording of proceedings, CJA Rule 16-504.

Auditors.
General provisions, CJ §2-501.

Authority, MD Const Art IV §20.

Bad check actions.
Transfer of action from district court, CivProDist Rule 3-326.

Bail and recognizance.
Pretrial release.
  Bail after adjournment or during recess of circuit court, CP §5-204.
  Bail bonds in circuit courts, CP §5-203.

Bailiffs.
General provisions, CJ §2-501.
Salaries, CJ §2-507.

Baltimore City.
Courts.
  See BALTIMORE CITY.
Number of judges, CJ §1-503.
Personnel merit system, CJ §§2-5A-01 to 2-5A-07.
  See BALTIMORE CITY.

CIRCUIT COURTS —Cont'd

Bill of particulars.
Criminal rules, Crim Rule 4-241.

Board of property review.
Appointment of members, TR §8-327.

Boxing, sparring and wrestling.
Injunctive relief, BR §4-323.

Budget and management.
County budget and fiscal policies.
  Circuit courts subject to, 24 §8-101.

Certiorari, AppRevCir Rule 7-301.
Review of decisions.
  Securing uniformity of decisions, CJ §12-305.

Charging documents.
Motions in circuit courts in criminal cases, Crim Rule 4-252.
Use, Crim Rule 4-201.

Civil procedure, CivProCir Rules 2-101 to 2-652.
See CIVIL PROCEDURE.

Clerks of court.
Audits, CJA Rule 16-302.
Budget.
  Submission, CJA Rule 16-302.
Child support enforcement administration.
  Delegation of responsibilities for support enforcement to, FL §10-114.
    Services provided by clerks, FL §10-114.
Divorce.
  Record of divorce decrees, FL §7-106.
Emergency management.
  Compulsory work during state of war.
    Registration for work, duties, PS §14-903.
Operations in offices, CJA Rule 16-302.
Personnel, CJA Rule 16-301.
Procurement, CJA Rule 16-302.
Rental space, CJ §1-504.
Voter registration.
  Report of convicted persons and name changes, EL §3-504.

Commission on judicial disabilities.
Generally, CJ §§13-401 to 13-403.
Rules regarding, CJA Rule 16-804; MD Const Art IV §§4A, 4B.
  Appeal of decision, CJA Rule 16-809.
  Confidentiality of proceedings, CJA Rule 16-810.
  Proceedings before commission, CJA Rule 16-808.

Common law.
Highest common-law court of records, CJ §1-501.

Contempt.
Fines.
  Disposition of fines, CJ §7-207.
Generally, SpecPro Rules 15-201 to 15-208.
  See CONTEMPT.

Corporations.
Appearances in civil matters.
  Attorney requirement, CivProCir Rule 2-131.
  Exceptions to attorney requirement, BOP §10-206.

Costs.
Bad checks.
  Service charge, CJ §7-208.
Criminal cases.
  Additional costs imposed, CJ §7-409.
  Criminal injuries compensation.
    Waiver of costs, CJ §7-405.
Fees. See within this heading, "Fees."
Removal of case, CJ §7-205.

Counties.
Appeals.
  By citizens to county commissioners in bridge cases, 25 §§46 to 48.

CIRCUIT COURTS —Cont'd

Counties —Cont'd

Circuit court for county includes circuit court for Baltimore City, 1 §14.

Court administrators.

General provisions, CJ §2-501.

Court criers, CJ §2-501.

Court en banc, MD Const Art IV §22.

Right of appeal, CJ §12-302.

Courts of record, MD Const Art IV §1.

Crime victims' compensation.

Restitution judgment.

Recording and indexing, CP §11-609.

Criminal rules.

See CRIMINAL RULES.

Definitions, CJ §1-101.

Real property records improvement fund, CJ §13-601.

Depositions.

Criminal rules, Crim Rule 4-261.

Docket.

Asbestos cases, CJA Rule 16-203.

Paternity docket, FL §5-1047.

Domestic violence.

Transfer of actions from circuit court to District Court, CivProCir Rule 2-327.

Transfer of actions from District Court to circuit court, CivProDist Rule 3-326.

Elections.

Contested elections.

Judicial review of election, EL §§12-201 to 12-204.

Rejection of ballot by board of canvassers.

Absentee ballot, appeal, EL §11-304.

Employees.

General provisions, CJ §2-501.

Equity.

Highest equity court of records, CJ §1-501.

Examiners.

General provisions, CJ §2-501.

Executors and administrators.

Settlement of decedents' estates.

Contested issues of fact.

Transmitting issues to circuit court, Estates Rule 6-434.

Orphans' court, Estates Rule 6-463.

Striking of notice of appeal, Estates Rule 6-464.

Family division.

Established, CJA Rule 16-204.

Family law actions, FamLaw Rules 9-201 to 9-210.

Attachment, seizure and sequestration.

Enforcement of alimony or support orders, FamLaw Rule 9-210.

Child support guidelines, FamLaw Rule 9-206.

Educational seminars for child custody, support or visitation actions, FamLaw Rule 9-204.

Financial statements, form, FamLaw Rule 9-203.

Joint statement of marital and nonmarital property, FamLaw Rule 9-207.

Masters.

Referral of divorce and annulment matters, FamLaw Rule 9-208.

Mediation of child custody and visitation disputes, FamLaw Rule 9-205.

Pleadings, FamLaw Rule 9-202.

Scope of rules, FamLaw Rule 9-201.

Testimony.

Required, divorce, annulment or alimony, FamLaw Rule 9-209.

CIRCUIT COURTS —Cont'd

Fees.

Appearance fees, CJ §7-204.

Distribution in certain counties, CJ §7-204.

Collection by clerks, CJ §7-202.

Criminal proceedings.

Prohibition on charging fees or costs in certain criminal proceedings, CJ §7-203.

Determination by state court administrator, CJ §7-202.

Officials exempt from fees, CJ §7-202.

Other services, CJ §7-202.

Parties aggrieved by fee, CJ §7-202.

Payment.

Required, CJ §7-201.

Reasonableness determination.

Request by party feeling aggrieved by fee permitted, CJ §7-202.

Uniformity, CJ §7-202.

Waiver, CJ §7-201.

Fines.

Appeals to circuit court.

Disposition upon appeal, CJ §7-206.

Contempt.

Disposition of fines, CJ §7-207.

First judicial circuit.

Election of judges, MD Const Art IV §3.

Grand jury.

Stenographers. See within this heading, "Stenographers."

Grievances by inmates state correctional facilities.

Judicial review of final decision of secretary, COR §10-210.

Guardian and ward.

Jurisdiction, ET §13-105.

Minors without proper care or guardianship.

See JUVENILE CAUSES.

Habeas corpus.

General provisions, CJ §§3-701 to 3-707.

See HABEAS CORPUS.

Held in each county, MD Const Art IV §20.

Indigency.

Waiver of fees, CJ §7-201.

Insurance commissioner's orders or hearings.

Appeal to circuit courts, IN §2-215.

Interpreters.

Appropriations, CJ §2-511.

Judges.

Assignment of judges.

By chief judge of court of appeals, MD Const Art IV §18.

Associate judges, MD Const Art IV §21.

Salaries.

Diminishing during term of office prohibited, MD Const Art IV §24.

Chief judge, MD Const Art IV §21.

Salary.

Diminishing during term of office prohibited, MD Const Art IV §24.

Clerks of court.

Vacancies.

Filled by judge, MD Const Art IV §25.

Commission on judicial disabilities, CJA Rule 16-804; MD Const Art IV §§4A, 4B.

Appeal of decision, CJA Rule 16-809.

Confidentiality of proceedings, CJA Rule 16-810.

Generally, CJ §§13-401 to 13-403.

Proceedings before commission, CJA Rule 16-808.

CIRCUIT COURTS —Cont'd
Judges —Cont'd
Decisions, MD Const Art IV §23.
  Rendered within two months of argument or
    submission, MD Const Art IV §23.
Elections, MD Const Art IV §21.
  Exceptions as to quadrennial elections, MD
    Const Art XVII §3.
  General provisions, MD Const Art IV §3.
  Quadrennial elections.
    Exceptions, MD Const Art XVII §3.
Eligibility, MD Const Art IV §21.
Expenses.
  Reimbursable expenses, CJ §1-706.
General assembly.
  Eligibility of members of general assembly for
    judgeship, MD Const Art IV §21.
Law clerks.
  Employment by each judge, CJ §2-512.
Number, CJ §1-503.
Quorum, MD Const Art IV §21.
Reports.
  Circuit court to chief judge, MD Const Art IV
    §18.
  Periodic reports to chief judge of court of
    appeals, MD Const Art IV §18.
Residence requirements, MD Const Art IV §21.
Salaries.
  Diminishing during term of office prohibited,
    MD Const Art IV §24.
Terms of court, MD Const Art IV §21.
Vacancies.
  Filling by chief judge of court of appeals, MD
    Const Art IV §18.
Judgments.
Decisions rendered within two months of
    argument or submission, MD Const Art IV
    §23.
Judicial circuits.
Composition, MD Const Art IV §19.
First judicial circuit.
  Election of judges, MD Const Art IV §3.
Second judicial circuit.
  Election of judges, MD Const Art IV §3.
Seventh judicial circuit, CJ §2-501.
  Administrative office, CJ §13-102.
State divided into judicial circuits, MD Const Art
  IV §19.
Juries.
Demand for jury trial.
  Transmittal of record from District Court to
    circuit court upon timely demand for jury
    trial, CivProDist Rule 3-325.
General provisions, CJ §§2-501, 8-101 to 8-507.
  See JURY.
Jurisdiction.
Bad check actions.
  Transfer of action to circuit court, CivProDist
    Rule 3-326.
Disabled persons, ET §13-105.
General provisions, CJ §1-501.
Misdemeanor offenses, CJ §1-502.
Juvenile causes.
General provisions.
  See JUVENILE CAUSES.
Law clerks.
Employment by each judge, CJ §2-512.
General provisions, CJ §2-501.
Librarians.
General provisions, CJ §2-501.
Local rules, Rule 1-102.

CIRCUIT COURTS —Cont'd
Masters.
General provisions, CJ §2-501.
Messengers.
General provisions, CJ §2-501.
Motions.
Generally.
  Criminal rules, Crim Rule 4-252.
Motor vehicles.
Administration.
  Appeals from decisions to circuit court, TR
    §12-209.
  Subpoena power.
    Enforcement, TR §12-108.
Security interest.
  Claims for damages against administration.
    Judicial review of administration's
      determination, TR §13-210.
Orders of court.
Interlocutory orders.
  Right of appeal, CJ §12-303.
Parole revocation, judicial review, COR §7-401.
Peace orders.
Appeals, CJ §3-1506.
Personnel.
Authorized, CJ §2-501.
Baltimore City.
  Merit system, CJ §§2-5A-01 to 2-5A-07.
    See BALTIMORE CITY.
Compensation, CJ §2-501.
Duties.
  Generally, CJ §2-501.
Pleas.
Time, Crim Rule 4-242.
Powers, MD Const Art IV §20.
Procedure.
Civil procedure in circuit courts, CivProCir Rules
  2-101 to 2-652.
  See CIVIL PROCEDURE.
Procurement.
County purchasing laws.
  Circuit courts subject to, 24 §8-101.
Public service commission orders or decisions.
Judicial review generally, PUC §§3-201 to 3-209.
  See PUBLIC SERVICE COMMISSION.
Quorum.
General provisions, MD Const Art IV §21.
Railroad crossings.
Streams or canals.
  Application to circuit court for approval, PUC
    §9-304.
Railroad safety and health.
Injunctive relief, LE §5.5-120.
Real property records improvement fund.
Audit, CJ §13-603.
Definitions, CJ §13-601.
Generally, CJ §§13-602, 13-603.
Investments, CJ §13-602.
  Interest from.
    Annual report, CJ §13-605.
Oversight committee, CJ §13-602.
Recordable instruments.
  Defined, CJ §13-601.
  Surcharge, CJ §13-604.
Reports.
  Annual report by state treasurer, CJ §13-605.
Rules, CJ §13-606.
Surcharge for recordable instruments, CJ §13-604.
Termination of subtitle, CJ §13-607.
Recording of proceedings, CJA Rule 16-504.

CIRCUIT COURTS —Cont'd
Records.
Real property records improvement fund, CJ
§§13-601 to 13-607. See within this heading,
"Real property records improvement fund."
Test book, CJ §2-502.
Removal of cases.
Costs, CJ §7-205.
Reporters.
General provisions, CJ §2-501.
Grand jury.
See GRAND JURY.
Salaries.
Bailiff, CJ §2-507.
Court criers, CJ §2-507.
Judge's salary not to be diminished, MD Const
Art IV §24.
Seals, MD Const Art IV §1.
Second judicial circuit.
Election of judges, MD Const Art IV §3.
Secretaries.
General provisions, CJ §2-501.
Sentencing of individuals.
Generally, COR §§9-101 to 9-202.
See SENTENCE AND PUNISHMENT.
Seventh judicial circuit.
Administrative office, CJ §13-102.
Court administrator, CJ §13-102.
Employees.
General provisions, CJ §2-501.
Reporters.
General provisions, CJ §2-501.
Stenographers.
General provisions, CJ §2-501.
Pensions.
Court stenographers of second judicial circuit,
CJ §2-501.
Terms of court.
General provisions, MD Const Art IV §21.
Videotape recording of proceedings, CJA Rule
16-504.
Appellate review, AppRev Rule 8-415.
Wetlands.
Judicial review of orders, EN §16-503.
Private wetlands.
Regulation or designation of person's land as
wetland.
Judicial review of administrative appeals.
Appeal to circuit courts, EN §16-306.
Zoning.
Appeals.
Decision of circuit court, 66B §4.08.

CIRCUITS.
Definitions, Rule 1-202.

CIRCUSES.
See THEATERS AND SHOWS.

CITATION OF RULES, Rule 1-103.

CITATIONS.
Airports.
Parking regulations, TR §5-212.1.
Alcoholic beverage violations.
Beer, wine and liquor licenses.
Kent county taverns, 2B §6-401.
Citation issued for violation.
Sales to underaged drinkers and intoxicated
persons, CP §4-101.
Drinking or possessing on school premises, ED
§26-103.

CITATIONS —Cont'd
Alcoholic beverage violations —Cont'd
Licenses.
Violations.
Civil citations in certain counties, 2B §16-408.
Minors, CR §10-119.
Jurisdiction, CR §10-120.
Open containers in motor vehicles' passenger
areas, CR §10-126.
Procedure, CR §10-127.
Amusements and recreation.
Required for certain violations, BR §3-406.
Baltimore City.
Betting, wagering, gambling, etc., CR §12-102.
Calvert county.
Erosion and sediment control.
Violations, 25 §10K.
Campaign finance violations.
Civil citation, EL §13-604.
Charging by, CP §4-101.
Charging documents.
See CHARGING DOCUMENTS.
Defined, CP §4-101.
Disturbing the peace or disorderly conduct.
Police authorize to issue for, CP §4-101.
False alarms.
Multiple false alarms by alarm system user.
Issuance of civil citation, CR §9-608.
Fire hazard, maintaining.
Fire marshal authorized to issue, CP §4-101.
Fire marshal issuing, CP §4-101.
Fireworks, discharging without permit.
Fire marshal authorized to issue, CP §4-101.
Gaming.
Baltimore City, CR §12-102.
General assembly.
Investigating committee.
Subpoenas.
Contempt citation, SG §2-1608.
Malicious destruction of property.
Police authorize to issue for, CP §4-101.
**Maryland-national capital park and planning
commission.**
Misdemeanor violations.
Issuance by park police, failure to appear, 28
§2-120.1.
Maryland Transit Administration.
Police powers, TR §7-207.
Vehicles, articles and equipment improperly
placed or abandoned on administration
property, TR §7-707.
Minor possessing tobacco product, CR §10-108.
Mobile seafood vendors.
Traffic citations, TR §24-304.
Motor vehicles.
Overtaking and passing school vehicle, TR
§§21-706, 21-706.1.
Stopping, standing or parking on private property,
TR §21-1004.
Traffic citations.
Cancellation.
Illegal cancellation, TR §26-408.
Case to be tried only on proper charging
document, TR §26-409.
Compliance.
Alternate means of compliance, TR §26-204.
Failure to comply, TR §26-204.
Disposition of penalty deposit, TR
§26-405.1.
Penalty deposit, TR §26-204.

CITATIONS —Cont'd
Motor vehicles —Cont'd
Traffic citations —Cont'd
Compliance —Cont'd
Failure to comply —Cont'd
Suspension of driving privileges, TR §26-204.
Contents, TR §26-201.
Disposition.
Citation deposited with court, TR §26-407.
Rules and regulations, TR §26-407.
Unlawfully, TR §26-407.
Issuance, TR §26-201.
Duty of officer issuing citation, TR §26-407.
Mobile seafood vendors, TR §24-304.
Noncompliance with traffic citation issued under federal law, TR §26-206.
Signature of person charged required on citation, TR §26-203.
Uniform forms, CJ §1-605.
When citation is sufficient charging document, TR §26-409.
Municipal corporations.
Municipal infractions, 23A §3.
Occupational safety and health.
Abatement requirements.
Order of commissioner, LE §5-214.
Assessment of fine, LE §§5-809 to 5-811.
Collection, LE §5-811.
Considerations, LE §5-810.
Maximum amount, LE §5-810.
Required for serious violation, LE §5-809.
Commissioner's action, LE §5-214.
De minimis violations, LE §5-212.
Enforcement of citation, LE §5-213.
Hearings, LE §5-214.
Inspections.
Notice of violation from employee, LE §5-208.
Issuance of citation, LE §5-212.
Limitations period, LE §5-212.
Period for correction of violation, LE §5-213.
Place of hearing, LE §5-214.
Posting of citation, LE §5-212.
Police officer issuing, CP §4-101.
Public buildings and grounds.
Watershed property.
Offenses committed on, NR §8-2003.
Quotas.
Arrest and citation quotas prohibited, PS §3-504.
Repair facility records.
Recordkeeping violations, TR §§13-113.1 to 15-116.
Theft.
Misdemeanor theft, police authorize to issue for, CP §4-101.
Tobacco sales.
Carroll county and Garrett county, 24 §15-103.
Uniform statewide form.
District Court to prescribe, CP §3-101.
United States park police officers.
Authority to issue, CP §§2-104.1, 4-101.
Washington county.
Animal control violations, 25 §236A.
Health officers.
Authority to issue for health code violation, 25 §236F.

CITIES.
Municipal corporations.
General provisions.
See MUNICIPAL CORPORATIONS.

CITIZENS ADVISORY BOARD.
Patuxent institution, COR §4-207.

CITIZENS' ADVISORY COMMITTEES FOR STATE CORRECTIONAL FACILITIES, COR §§10-401 to 10-407.
See PRISONS AND PRISONERS.

CITIZENSHIP.
Attorney general.
Requirements, MD Const Art V §4.
Banks and trust companies.
Commercial banks, FI §3-201.
Savings and loan associations, FI §9-202.
Savings banks, FI §4-201.
Constitution of the United States, US Const Art IV §2; Amd 14.
General assembly.
Senators and delegates, MD Const Art III §9.
Governor.
Requirements, MD Const Art II §5.
Judges, MD Const Art IV §2.
Rights and immunities of citizens, US Const Amd 14.
Savings and loan associations.
Control by noncitizen, FI §9-216.
Social services.
Citizenship promotion program, 88A §145.
Voter registration qualifications, EL §3-102.

CIVIC ORGANIZATIONS.
Benefit performances.
Prince George's county, CR §§13-1901 to 13-1907.
Bingo.
Benefit performances.
Prince George's county, CR §§13-1901 to 13-1907.
Calvert county, CR §§13-705 to 13-709.
Exemption from license requirement, CR §13-706.
Carroll county, CR §§13-907, 13-908.
Cecil county, CR §§13-1001 to 13-1005.
Charles county, CR §§13-1109 to 13-1115.
Frederick county, CR §13-1306.
St. Mary's county, CR §§13-2101 to 13-2110.
Blanket health insurance.
Eligible organizations, IN §15-305.
Casino.
Baltimore county, CR §13-604.
Gaming, bazaar, carnival and raffles.
Anne Arundel county, CR §§13-401 to 13-408.
Baltimore City, CR §§13-501 to 13-510.
Baltimore county, CR §§13-601 to 13-607.
Calvert county, CR §§13-701 to 13-704.
Carroll county, CR §§13-901 to 13-909.
Cecil county, CR §§13-1001 to 13-1005.
Charles county, CR §§13-1101 to 13-1115.
Frederick county, CR §§13-1301 to 13-1307.
Kent county.
Raffles and other gaming devices, CR §§13-1701 to 13-1706.
Local gaming events generally, CR §§13-201 to 13-205.
Prince George's county, CR §§13-1901 to 13-1912.
Queen Anne's county.
Raffles and other gaming devices, CR §§13-2001 to 13-2006.
Raffles generally, statewide provisions, CR §12-106.
St. Mary's county, CR §§13-2111 to 13-2115.
Worcester county, CR §§13-2619 to 13-2628.

CIVIC ORGANIZATIONS —Cont'd
Tip jars and punch board.
Frederick county, CR §13-1305.
Washington county.
Tip jars generally, CR §§13-2414 to 13-2439.

CIVIL AIR PATROL.
Motor vehicles.
Excise tax on certificates of title.
Exemptions, TR §13-810.
Registration.
Exemption from registration fees, TR §13-903.

CIVIL CASES.
Actions.
See ACTIONS.
Pleading.
See PLEADINGS.

CIVIL CITATION.
False alarms.
Multiple false alarms by alarm system user, CR §9-608.

CIVIL DEFENSE.
Emergency management.
See EMERGENCY MANAGEMENT.

CIVIL INFRACTIONS.
Home rule for code counties, 25B §13C.
Jurisdiction, CJ §4-401.

CIVIL LIABILITY.
Damages.
See DAMAGES.

CIVIL PROCEDURE.
Actions.
Class actions.
Circuit courts, CivProCir Rule 2-231.
Commencement of action.
Circuit court, CivProCir Rule 2-101.
District Court, CivProDist Rule 3-101.
Form of action.
District Court, CivProDist Rule 3-301.
Process.
Requirements preliminary to summons.
District Court, CivProDist Rule 3-111.
Questions of law or fact.
Transfer of action.
Circuit courts, CivProCir Rule 2-327.
Transfer of action.
Circuit courts, CivProCir Rule 2-327.
Appearances.
Circuit courts, CivProCir Rule 2-131.
Corporations.
Attorney requirement, CivProCir Rule 2-131; CivProDist Rule 3-131.
Exceptions to attorney requirement, BOP §10-206.
District Court, CivProDist Rule 3-131.
Striking of attorney's appearance.
Circuit courts, CivProCir Rule 2-132.
District Court, CivProDist Rule 3-132.
Attachment.
Prejudgment attachment.
Circuit courts, CivProCir Rule 2-115.
District Court, CivProDist Rule 3-115.
Attorneys at law.
Appearances.
Circuit courts, CivProCir Rule 2-131.
District Court, CivProDist Rule 3-131.
Striking of attorney's appearance.
Circuit courts, CivProCir Rule 2-132.

CIVIL PROCEDURE —Cont'd
Attorneys at law —Cont'd
District Court, CivProDist Rule 3-132.
Liens.
Enforcement, CivProCir Rule 2-652.
Auditors.
Circuit courts, CivProCir Rule 2-543.
Circuit courts.
Actions.
Class actions, CivProCir Rule 2-231.
Commencement of action, CivProCir Rule 2-101.
Form of action.
One form of action, CivProCir Rule 2-301.
Questions of law or fact.
Transfer of action, CivProCir Rule 2-327.
Transfer of action, CivProCir Rule 2-327.
Appearances, CivProCir Rule 2-131.
Attorneys at law.
Striking of attorney's appearance, CivProCir Rule 2-132.
Attachment.
Prejudgment attachment, CivProCir Rule 2-115.
Attorneys at law.
Appearances, CivProCir Rule 2-131.
Striking of attorney's appearance, CivProCir Rule 2-132.
Auditors, CivProCir Rule 2-543.
Class actions, CivProCir Rule 2-231.
Confessed judgments, CivProCir Rule 2-611.
Consent judgments, CivProCir Rule 2-612.
Continuances, CivProCir Rule 2-508.
Counterclaim, CivProCir Rule 2-331.
Cross-claims, CivProCir Rule 2-331.
Default judgments, CivProCir Rule 2-613.
Depositions.
See DEPOSITIONS.
Discovery.
Depositions.
See DEPOSITIONS.
General provisions, CivProCir Rules 2-401 to 2-434.
See DISCOVERY.
Interrogatories.
See INTERROGATORIES.
En banc review, CivProCir Rule 2-551.
Examiners, CivProCir Rule 2-542.
Executions.
See EXECUTIONS.
Form of action.
One form of action, CivProCir Rule 2-301.
Garnishment, CivProCir Rule 2-645.
Wages, CivProCir Rule 2-646.
Instructions to the jury, CivProCir Rule 2-520.
Interpleader, CivProCir Rule 2-221.
Interrogatories.
See INTERROGATORIES.
Intervention.
Parties, CivProCir Rule 2-214.
Judges.
Disability of judge, CivProCir Rule 2-536.
Judgments and decrees.
General provisions, CivProCir Rules 2-601 to 2-652.
See JUDGMENTS AND DECREES.
Motion to alter or amend.
Court decisions, CivProCir Rule 2-534.
Revisory power, CivProCir Rule 2-535.
Jury trial.
Certain transfers from District Court, CivProCir Rule 2-326.
Demand for jury trial, CivProCir Rule 2-325.

CIVIL PROCEDURE —Cont'd
Circuit courts —Cont'd
Masters, CivProCir Rule 2-541.
Motions.
See MOTIONS.
New trial.
Motion for new trial, CivProCir Rule 2-533.
Parties.
Capacity, CivProCir Rule 2-202.
Class actions, CivProCir Rule 2-231.
Intervention, CivProCir Rule 2-214.
Joinder.
Permissive joinder, CivProCir Rule 2-212.
Required joinder, CivProCir Rule 2-211.
Misjoinder, CivProCir Rule 2-213.
Nonjoinder, CivProCir Rule 2-213.
Real party in interest, CivProCir Rule 2-201.
Substitution of parties, CivProCir Rule 2-241.
Pleadings.
Allowable pleadings, CivProCir Rule 2-302.
Amendment, CivProCir Rule 2-341.
Answers.
Generally, CivProCir Rule 2-323.
Time for filing, CivProCir Rule 2-321.
Capacity, CivProCir Rule 2-304.
Claims for relief, CivProCir Rule 2-305.
Conditions precedent, CivProCir Rule 2-304.
Counterclaims and cross-claims, CivProCir Rule 2-331.
Defenses.
Preservation of certain defenses, CivProCir Rule 2-324.
Form of action.
One form of action, CivProCir Rule 2-301.
Form of pleadings, CivProCir Rule 2-303.
Jury trial, CivProCir Rule 2-325.
Parties.
Capacity, CivProCir Rule 2-304.
Place, CivProCir Rule 2-304.
Time, CivProCir Rule 2-304.
Process.
Content, CivProCir Rule 2-114.
Real party in interest, CivProCir Rule 2-201.
Service of process.
By whom served, CivProCir Rule 2-123.
In personam service, CivProCir Rule 2-121.
In rem or quasi in rem, CivProCir Rule 2-122.
Persons to be served, CivProCir Rule 2-124.
Return, CivProCir Rule 2-126.
Sundays and holidays, CivProCir Rule 2-125.
Subpoenas, CivProCir Rule 2-510.
Substitution of parties, CivProCir Rule 2-241.
Summary judgment, CivProCir Rule 2-501.
Summons.
Content, CivProCir Rule 2-114.
Duration, dormancy and renewal, CivProCir Rule 2-113.
Issuance, CivProCir Rule 2-112.
Requirements preliminary to summons, CivProCir Rule 2-111.
Third-party practice, CivProCir Rule 2-332.
Transfer of action, CivProCir Rule 2-327.
Trial.
General provisions.
See TRIAL.
Claims for relief.
Circuit courts, CivProCir Rule 2-305.
Commencement of actions.
Circuit courts, CivProCir Rule 2-101.
Computer generated evidence, CivProCir Rule 2-504.3.

CIVIL PROCEDURE —Cont'd
Confessed judgments.
Circuit courts, CivProCir Rule 2-611.
Consent judgments.
Circuit courts, CivProCir Rule 2-612.
Contempt.
General provisions, SpecPro Rules 15-201 to 15-208.
See CONTEMPT.
Continuances.
Circuit courts, CivProCir Rule 2-508.
District Court, CivProDist Rule 3-508.
Corporations.
Appearances.
Attorney requirement, CivProCir Rule 2-131; CivProDist Rule 3-131.
Exceptions to attorney requirement, BOP §10-206.
Counterclaims.
Circuit courts, CivProCir Rule 2-331.
Cross-claims.
Circuit courts, CivProCir Rule 2-331.
Default judgments.
Circuit courts, CivProCir Rule 2-613.
Defenses.
Preservation of certain defenses.
Circuit courts, CivProCir Rule 2-324.
Depositions.
See DEPOSITIONS.
Detinue.
General provisions.
See DETINUE.
Discovery.
Depositions.
See DEPOSITIONS.
General provisions.
See DISCOVERY.
Interrogatories.
See INTERROGATORIES.
District Court.
Actions.
Commencement of action, CivProDist Rule 3-101.
Form of action, CivProDist Rule 3-301.
Process.
Requirements preliminary to summons, CivProDist Rule 3-111.
Appearances, CivProDist Rule 3-131.
Attachment.
Prejudgment attachment, CivProDist Rule 3-115.
Attorneys at law.
Appearances, CivProDist Rule 3-131.
Continuances, CivProDist Rule 3-508.
Discovery, CivProDist Rules 3-401 to 3-431.
See DISCOVERY.
Execution, CivProDist Rules 3-641, 3-642.
Garnishment, CivProDist Rules 3-645, 3-646.
Interpleader, CivProDist Rule 3-221.
Interrogatories, CivProDist Rule 3-421.
Intervention, CivProDist Rule 3-214.
Joinder.
General provisions.
See JOINDER.
Judgments and decrees.
Attachment before judgment, CivProDist Rule 3-115.
General provisions, CivProDist Rules 3-601 to 3-649.
See JUDGMENTS AND DECREES.

CIVIL PROCEDURE —Cont'd
District Court —Cont'd
Judgments and decrees —Cont'd
Prejudgment attachment, CivProDist Rule 3-115.
Jury trial.
Certain transfers from District Court, CivProCir Rule 2-326.
Liens.
Judgment liens, CivProDist Rule 3-621.
Motions.
General provisions.
See MOTIONS.
Parties, CivProDist Rules 3-201 to 3-241.
See PARTIES.
Pleading, CivProDist Rules 3-301 to 3-342.
See PLEADINGS.
Pretrial conference, CivProDist Rule 3-504.
Service of process, CivProDist Rules 3-121 to 3-126.
See SERVICE OF PROCESS.
Small claim actions, CivProDist Rule 3-701.
Subpoenas, CivProDist Rule 3-510.
Substitution of parties, CivProDist Rule 3-241.
Summons.
Content, CivProDist Rule 3-114.
Duration, dormancy and renewal, CivProDist Rule 3-113.
Issuance of summons, CivProDist Rule 3-112.
Requirements preliminary to summons, CivProDist Rule 3-111.
Third-party practice, CivProDist Rule 3-332.
Trial, CivProDist Rule 3-533.
Date and time, CivProDist Rule 3-102.
General provisions, CivProDist Rules 3-503 to 3-536.
See TRIAL.
En banc review.
Circuit courts, CivProCir Rule 2-551.
Examiners.
Circuit courts, CivProCir Rule 2-542.
Executions.
Circuit courts.
See EXECUTIONS.
District Court, CivProDist Rules 3-641, 3-642.
General provisions.
See EXECUTIONS.
Garnishment.
Circuit courts, CivProCir Rule 2-645.
Wages, CivProCir Rule 2-646.
District Court, CivProDist Rules 3-645, 3-646.
Holocaust victim insurance.
Applicability of rules, IN §28-104.
Information report.
Defendant's report, CivProCir Rule 2-323.
Requirements preliminary to summons, CivProCir Rule 2-111.
Injunctions.
Ancillary relief in aid of enforcement of judgments, CivProCir Rule 2-651.
Enforcement of judgment prohibiting or mandating action, CivProCir Rule 2-648; CivProDist Rule 3-648.
Stay.
Injunctions pending appeal, CivProCir Rule 2-632; CivProDist Rule 3-632.
Instructions to the jury.
Circuit courts, CivProCir Rule 2-520.
Interpleader.
Circuit courts, CivProCir Rule 2-221.
District Court, CivProDist Rule 3-221.

CIVIL PROCEDURE —Cont'd
Interrogatories.
See INTERROGATORIES.
Intervention.
Circuit courts, CivProCir Rule 2-214.
District Court, CivProDist Rule 3-214.
Joinder.
General provisions.
See JOINDER.
Judges.
Disability of judge.
Circuit courts, CivProCir Rule 2-536.
Judgment notwithstanding the verdict,
CivProCir Rule 2-532.
Judgments and decrees.
Attachment.
District Court, CivProDist Rule 3-115.
Prejudgment attachment.
Circuit courts, CivProCir Rule 2-115.
Circuit courts.
General provisions, CivProCir Rules 2-601 to 2-652.
See JUDGMENTS AND DECREES.
District Court.
General provisions, CivProDist Rules 3-601 to 3-649.
See JUDGMENTS AND DECREES.
Motion to alter or amend.
Court decisions.
Circuit courts, CivProCir Rule 2-534.
District Court, CivProDist Rule 3-534.
Exhibits, CivProCir Rule 2-311.
Hearings, CivProCir Rule 2-311; CivProDist Rule 3-311.
Revisory power.
Circuit courts, CivProCir Rule 2-535.
District Court, CivProDist Rule 3-535.
Jury trial.
Demand for jury trial.
Circuit courts, CivProCir Rule 2-325.
District Court.
Certain transfers from District Court, CivProCir Rule 2-326.
Liens.
Attorneys' liens.
Enforcement, CivProCir Rule 2-652.
Judgment liens.
Circuit courts, CivProCir Rule 2-621.
District Court, CivProCir Rule 2-621; CivProDist Rule 3-621.
Masters.
Circuit courts, CivProCir Rule 2-541.
Motions.
See MOTIONS.
New trial.
Motion for new trial.
Circuit courts, CivProCir Rule 2-533.
District Court, CivProDist Rule 3-533.
Parties.
Capacity.
Circuit courts, CivProCir Rule 2-202.
Class actions.
Circuit courts, CivProCir Rule 2-231.
District Court, CivProDist Rules 3-201 to 3-241.
See PARTIES.
Individual not in being.
Appointment of attorney, CivProCir Rule 2-203.
Intervention.
Circuit courts, CivProCir Rule 2-214.
Joinder.
Permissive joinder.
Circuit courts, CivProCir Rule 2-212.

CIVIL PROCEDURE —Cont'd
Parties —Cont'd
Joinder —Cont'd
Required joinder.
Circuit courts, CivProCir Rule 2-211.
Misjoinder.
Circuit courts, CivProCir Rule 2-213.
Nonjoinder.
Circuit courts, CivProCir Rule 2-213.
Real party in interest.
Circuit courts, CivProCir Rule 2-201.
Substitution of parties.
Circuit courts, CivProCir Rule 2-241.
Pleading.
Actions.
One form of action, CivProCir Rule 2-301.
Allowable pleadings.
Circuit courts, CivProCir Rule 2-302.
Amendment.
Circuit courts, CivProCir Rule 2-341.
Answers.
Generally.
Circuit courts, CivProCir Rule 2-323.
Time for filing.
Circuit courts, CivProCir Rule 2-321.
Capacity.
Circuit courts, CivProCir Rule 2-304.
Claims for relief.
Circuit courts, CivProCir Rule 2-305.
Conditions precedent.
Circuit courts, CivProCir Rule 2-304.
Counterclaims and cross-claims.
Circuit courts, CivProCir Rule 2-331.
Defenses.
Preservation of certain defenses.
Circuit courts, CivProCir Rule 2-324.
District Court, CivProDist Rules 3-301 to 3-342.
See PLEADINGS.
Form of pleadings.
Circuit courts, CivProCir Rule 2-303.
Jury trial.
Circuit courts, CivProCir Rule 2-325.
Parties.
Capacity.
Circuit courts, CivProCir Rule 2-304.
Time and place.
Circuit courts, CivProCir Rule 2-304.
Pretrial conference.
Circuit courts, CivProCir Rule 2-504.2.
District Court, CivProDist Rule 3-504.
Scheduling conference.
When required, CivProCir Rule 2-504.1.
Scheduling order, CivProCir Rule 2-504.
Process.
Circuit court.
Content, CivProCir Rule 2-114.
Content.
Circuit court, CivProCir Rule 2-114.
Summons. See within this heading, "Summons."
Real party in interest.
Circuit courts, CivProCir Rule 2-201.
Replevin.
General provisions, PropAct Rule 12-601.
Scheduling conferences and orders.
Circuit court, CivProCir Rules 2-504, 2-504.1.
Service of process.
By whom served.
Circuit courts, CivProCir Rule 2-123;
CivProDist Rule 3-123.
Content.
Circuit courts, CivProCir Rule 2-114.

CIVIL PROCEDURE —Cont'd
Service of process —Cont'd
In personam service.
Circuit courts, CivProCir Rule 2-121.
District Court, CivProDist Rule 3-121.
In rem or quasi in rem.
Circuit courts, CivProCir Rule 2-122.
Persons to be served.
Circuit courts, CivProCir Rule 2-124.
District Court, CivProDist Rule 3-124.
Return.
Circuit courts, CivProCir Rule 2-126.
District Court, CivProDist Rule 3-126.
Sundays and holidays.
Circuit courts, CivProCir Rule 2-125.
District Court, CivProDist Rule 3-125.
Sheriffs.
Summons.
Requirements preliminary to summons.
Circuit courts, CivProCir Rule 2-111.
Small claim actions.
District Court, CivProDist Rule 3-701.
Subpoenas.
Circuit courts, CivProCir Rule 2-510.
District Court, CivProDist Rule 3-510.
Substitution of parties.
Circuit courts, CivProCir Rule 2-241.
District Court, CivProDist Rule 3-241.
Summary judgment.
Circuit courts, CivProCir Rule 2-501.
Summons.
Content.
Circuit courts, CivProCir Rule 2-114.
District Court, CivProDist Rule 3-114.
Copies to be furnished.
Circuit courts, CivProCir Rule 2-111.
District Court, CivProDist Rule 3-111.
Delivery to another county.
Circuit courts, CivProCir Rule 2-112.
District Court, CivProDist Rule 3-112.
Duration, dormancy and renewal of summons.
Circuit courts, CivProCir Rule 2-113.
District Court, CivProDist Rule 3-113.
Issuance.
Circuit courts, CivProCir Rule 2-112.
District Court, CivProDist Rule 3-112.
Requirements preliminary to summons, CivProCir Rule 2-111.
District Court, CivProDist Rule 3-111.
Sheriffs.
Instructions for sheriff.
Circuit courts, CivProCir Rule 2-111.
District Court, CivProDist Rule 3-111.
Sundays and holidays.
Service of process.
Circuit courts, CivProCir Rule 2-125.
District Court, CivProDist Rule 3-125.
Third-party practice.
Circuit courts, CivProCir Rule 2-332.
District Court, CivProDist Rule 3-332.
Trial.
General provisions.
See TRIAL.

CIVIL RIGHTS.
Discrimination generally.
See DISCRIMINATION.
Discrimination in employment, 49B §§14 to 18.
See LABOR AND EMPLOYMENT RELATIONS.
Discrimination in housing.
See DISCRIMINATION.

CIVIL RIGHTS —Cont'd
Discrimination in public accommodations.
  See DISCRIMINATION.
Emergency management.
  Civil relief during emergency periods.
    Attempts to delay enforcement, PS §14-206.
Equal credit opportunity, CL §§12-701 to 12-708.
  See EQUAL CREDIT OPPORTUNITY.
Holocaust victims insurance act, IN §§28-101 to
  28-110.
  See HOLOCAUST VICTIMS INSURANCE.
Human relations commission.
  See HUMAN RELATIONS COMMISSION.
Voter registration qualifications, EL §3-102.

CIVIL SERVICE.
Alcohol abuse.
  State substance abuse policy, SPP §2-306.
Contract employees.
  Generally, SPP §§13-101 to 13-405.
  See CONTRACT STATE EMPLOYEES.
Department of personnel.
  Generally, SPP §§4-103 to 4-401.
    See PERSONNEL DEPARTMENT.
Drug abuse.
  State substance abuse policy, SPP §2-306.
Equal employment opportunity.
  Generally, SPP §§5-201 to 5-215.
  See EQUAL EMPLOYMENT OPPORTUNITY.
Grievance procedures.
  Generally, SPP §§12-101 to 12-405.
  See GRIEVANCE PROCEDURES.
State personnel.
  General provisions, SPP §§1-101 to 15-201.
  See STATE PERSONNEL.
Substance abuse policy of state, SPP §2-306.
Whistleblower protection.
  Executive branch, SPP §§5-301 to 5-313.
  See WHISTLEBLOWER PROTECTION.
  Generally, SPP §§2-305, 5-301 to 5-313.
  See WHISTLEBLOWER PROTECTION.

CIVIL WAR STATE BATTLEFIELD.
South Mountain battlefield, NR §5-1801.

CLAIMS.
Abandoned property disposition, CL §§17-101 to
  17-326.
  See ABANDONED PROPERTY DISPOSITION.
Absentee.
  Reappearance of absentee.
    Barring of claims, CJ §3-108.
Accounts and accounting.
  Evidence.
    General provisions.
      See EVIDENCE.
Automobile insurance fund, IN §20-505.
  Reserves for payment of claims, IN §20-506.
Baltimore City.
  Local government tort claims act, CJ §§5-301 to
    5-304.
  See TORTS.
Business trusts.
  Claims against trust, winding up, CA §12-202.
Circuit courts, CivProCir Rule 2-305.
Clients' security fund.
  Disposition, CJA Rule 16-811.
Continuing care contracts.
  Impaired providers, claims against, 70B §20Q.
Counties.
  Against counties.
    See COUNTIES.

CLAIMS —Cont'd
Credit life, health and unemployment
  insurance, IN §13-113.
Criminal injuries compensation board, CP
  §§11-801 to 11-819.
  See CRIMINAL INJURIES COMPENSATION
    BOARD.
District Court, CivProDist Rule 3-305.
  Pleadings.
    Maryland district rules, CJ §6-403.
  Small claims.
    No formal pleadings, CJ §6-403.
Documents of title.
  Conflicting claims.
    Interpleader, CL §7-603.
Evidence.
  Proof of accounts.
    Photography.
      Copies of business and public records as
        evidence act, CJ §10-102.
    Written record, CJ §10-101.
Health care malpractice claims, SpecPro Rules
  15-401 to 15-403.
  See MALPRACTICE.
Health maintenance organizations.
  Rehabilitation or liquidation of health
    maintenance organizations, HG §19-706.1.
Insurance.
  Automobile insurance fund, IN §20-505.
    Reserves for payment of claims, IN §20-506.
  Credit life, health and unemployment insurance,
    IN §13-113.
  Liquidation, rehabilitation, etc., of insurers, IN
    §§9-226 to 9-228.
  Malpractice claim reporting, IN §4-401.
  Unfair claim settlement practices, IN §§27-301 to
    27-306.
Judgments.
  Judgment on claim and counterclaim.
    Circuit courts, CivProCir Rule 2-615.
    District Court, CivProDist Rule 3-615.
  Multiple claims.
    Circuit courts, CivProCir Rule 2-602.
    District Court, CivProDist Rule 3-602.
  Stay.
    Circuit courts, CivProCir Rule 2-632.
    District Court, CivProDist Rule 3-632.
Levy.
  Release of property from levy.
    Third person claim.
      Circuit courts, CivProCir Rule 2-643.
      District Court, CivProDist Rule 3-643.
Malpractice.
  Health care malpractice claims.
    See MALPRACTICE.
Maryland tort claims act, SG §§12-101 to 12-110.
  See TORTS.
Motions.
  Defense of failure to state claim for relief not
    waived.
    Circuit courts, CivProCir Rule 2-324.
  Preliminary motions.
    Permissive motions.
      Circuit courts, CivProCir Rule 2-322.
Motor vehicles.
  Automobile insurance fund, IN §20-505.
    Reserves for payment of claims, IN §20-506.
Municipal corporations.
  Claims against.
    See MUNICIPAL CORPORATIONS.

CLAIMS —Cont'd
Pleadings.
Circuit courts, CivProCir Rule 2-305.
Defense of failure to state claim not waived.
Circuit courts, CivProCir Rule 2-324.
Proof.
Accounts for money, goods or labor.
General provisions.
See EVIDENCE.
Real estate brokers.
Guaranty fund.
Claims against fund, BOP §§17-404 to 17-412.
See REAL ESTATE BROKERS.
Receivers, assignees or trustees for creditors.
Exceptions, Receivers Rule 13-402.
Filing.
Day of finality for filing.
Cost of restating account, Receivers Rule 13-401.
Instrument lost or destroyed, Receivers Rule 13-401.
Manner.
Proof, Receivers Rule 13-401.
Late claims, Receivers Rule 13-401.
Notice, Receivers Rule 13-401.
Open account, Receivers Rule 13-401.
Verification.
Requirements, Receivers Rule 13-401.
Withdrawal of instrument, Receivers Rule 13-401.
Sheriffs.
Debts not to be purchased by, SG §17-107.
State.
By and against state.
See STATE.
Claims of state.
See STATE.
Tort claims act, SG §§12-101 to 12-110.
See TORTS.
Third parties.
Defendant's claim against third party.
Circuit courts, CivProCir Rule 2-332.
District Court, CivProDist Rule 3-332.
Plaintiff's claim against third party.
Circuit courts, CivProCir Rule 2-332.
District Court, CivProDist Rule 3-332.
Response by third party.
Circuit courts, CivProCir Rule 2-332.
District Court, CivProDist Rule 3-332.
Time for filing.
Circuit courts, CivProCir Rule 2-332.
District Court, CivProDist Rule 3-332.
Trial.
Voluntary dismissal.
Circuit courts, CivProCir Rule 2-506.
Effect on claim.
District Court, CivProDist Rule 3-506.

CLAMS.
General provisions.
See OYSTERS AND CLAMS.

CLASS ACTIONS.
Breast implants.
Action for damages.
Statute of limitations, CJ §5-116.
Circuit courts, CivProCir Rule 2-231.
District Court.
Civil jurisdiction.
Separate claims of the proposed members of the class may be aggregated to meet the minimum amount in controversy requirements, CJ §4-402.

CLASSIFICATION OF INMATES.
Standards for correctional facilities generally, COR §§8-101 to 8-117.
See PRISONS AND PRISONERS.

CLASSIFIED SERVICE.
Assisting another to violate subtitle, SPP §15-108.
Community services administration.
Employees subject to, 41 §6-203.
Counties.
Establishment for officers and employees, 25 §3.
Power of commissioners.
Exception of certain counties, 25 §3.
Deception by applicant, SPP §15-104.
Dorchester county.
Special provisions, 25 §3.
Garrett county.
Special provisions, 25 §3.
Maryland-national capital park and planning commission.
See MARYLAND-NATIONAL CAPITAL PARK AND PLANNING COMMISSION.
Maryland venture capital trust.
Exemption from merit system provisions, 83A §5-308.
Motor vehicles.
Department.
Employees, TR §12-104.
Municipal corporations.
Power to establish and maintain, 23A §2.
Notice.
See NOTICE.
Public broadcasting commission.
Membership of employees in classified service, ED §24-204.
Queen Anne's county.
Special provisions, 25 §3.
Reorganization of government.
Disposition of employees of abolished or superseded units, SG §10-703.
Secretary of agriculture.
Removal of personnel, AG §2-102.
University of Maryland.
Montebello employee transfer to classified service position, ED §13-404.
Whistleblower protection.
State employees, SPP §§2-305, 5-301 to 5-313.
See WHISTLEBLOWER PROTECTION.

CLAW MACHINES.
Licensing of amusement devices, BR §§17-401 to 17-438.

CLEANERS, DYERS AND PRESSERS.
Mechanics' liens.
Lien for work done, CL §16-302.

CLEAN-FUEL VEHICLE PROPERTY.
Income tax.
Credits, TG §10-704.2.

CLEANING AGENTS.
Applicability of subtitle, EN §9-1502.
Defined, EN §9-1501.
Enforcement of subtitle, EN §9-1504.
Penalties.
Violation of provisions, EN §9-1505.
Phosphorus.
Prohibited amounts of phosphorus, EN §9-1503.
Reports, EN §9-1504.
Rules and regulations.
Adoption, EN §9-1504.

CLEANING AGENTS —Cont'd
Violations of provisions.
Penalties, EN §9-1505.

CLEARING CORPORATIONS.
Investment securities.
Effectiveness of rules, CL §8-111.

CLEFT LIP OR PALATE.
Health insurance coverage, IN §15-818.

CLERGY.
Benefit of clergy abolished, CR §14-103.
Generally.
See RELIGION.

CLERKS OF COURT.
Access to court records.
Duty of clerk, CJA Rule 16-1010.
Accounts and accounting.
State's attorney.
Aid of comptroller and treasurer, 10 §38.
Administration of courts.
Clients' security fund.
Notice to clerk, CJA Rule 16-811.
Disposition of records.
Permanent retention, CJA Rule 16-818.
Dockets, CJA Rule 16-305.
Filing and removal of papers, CJA Rule 16-306.
Hours, CJA Rule 16-304.
Offices, CJA Rule 16-304.
Payment of money into court, CJA Rule 16-303.
District Court, CJA Rule 16-502.
Trust clerk.
Designation, CJA Rule 16-403.
Adoption.
Decree of adoption.
Report.
Sent to secretary of health and mental
hygiene, HG §4-211.
Reports to secretary, HG §4-211.
Affidavits.
Photostatting and microfilming.
When instruments not readily subject to, RP
§3-104.
Alcoholic beverages.
Local licenses.
Issuance.
Baltimore City, 2B §8-203.
Annulment of marriage.
Reports, FL §2-503.
Appearances.
Initial appearance of defendant.
Transfer of papers by clerk, Crim Rule 4-213.
Attorney general.
Election.
Returns made by clerk to governor, MD Const
Art V §2.
Bail and recognizance.
Defined, Crim Rule 4-217.
Baltimore City.
Courts.
General provisions.
See BALTIMORE CITY.
Birds and game.
Funds.
State wildlife management and protection fund.
Transmission of funds.
Money received for hunting licenses and
stamps, NR §10-209.
Waterfowl and migratory birds.
Stationary blind or blind site.
Licenses.
Issuance, NR §10-612.

CLERKS OF COURT —Cont'd
Bonds, surety.
Action on bond.
Damages, CJ §11-203.
Amount.
Increase or decrease.
State comptroller, CJ §2-105.
Prescribed by state comptroller, CJ §2-105.
Damages.
Action on bond, CJ §11-203.
Duration, CJ §2-105.
Failure to give bond, CJ §2-106.
Predecessor.
Completing unfinished business of predecessor.
Fees, 36 §9.
Premiums.
Payment, CJ §2-105.
Recordation, CJ §2-105; Rule 1-402.
Required.
Before acting as clerk, CJ §2-105.
Surety.
Approval by judge, CJ §2-105.
Books and papers.
Records. See within this heading, "Records."
Test book.
Circuit courts, CJ §2-502.
Budgets.
Annual budget submitted by clerks, CJ §2-504.1.
Certificate of qualification of officer.
When clerk to give, CJ §2-212.
Chattel records.
Financing records. See within this heading,
"Records."
Child support enforcement administration.
Delegation of responsibilities for support
enforcement to clerks, FL §10-114.
Circuit courts.
Audits, CJA Rule 16-302.
Budget.
Submission, CJA Rule 16-302.
Business trusts, filing certificate of merger, CA
§12-608.
Child support enforcement administration.
Delegation of responsibilities for support
enforcement to, FL §10-114.
Generally, MD Const Art IV §§25, 26.
Masters.
Referral of cases, CivProCir Rule 2-541.
Operations in offices, CJA Rule 16-302.
Personnel, CJA Rule 16-301.
Procurement, CJA Rule 16-302.
Civil commissions.
Delivery, CJ §2-211.
Tax on officer's commission, CJ §2-212.
Clients' security fund.
Notice to clerk, CJA Rule 16-811.
Commissions of office.
Form, MD Const Art IV §13.
Issuance by governor, MD Const Art IV §12.
Copies.
Plats of subdivisions.
Disposition of copies, RP §3-304.
Corporations.
Charter or other paper.
Recordation, CA §1-202.
Costs.
General provisions.
See COSTS.
Counties.
Ordinances.
Filed with, 25 §4.

CLERKS OF COURT —Cont'd
Counties —Cont'd
Recordation.
   Chartered counties, 25A §5.
   Indexing, 25 §3.
   Ordinances, 25 §4.
   Provisions for, 25 §3.
Court of appeals.
See COURT OF APPEALS.
Court of special appeals.
See COURT OF SPECIAL APPEALS.
Deeds.
Recordation.
   Endorsement on instrument of time of receipt
     by clerk, RP §3-301.
Defalcation.
Revenue officers detaining and neglecting to pay
   money due, CR §7-114.
Definitions, CA §1-101; Rule 1-202.
Deputy clerks.
Appointment, MD Const Art IV §26.
Minimum work week, CJ §2-506.
Removal, MD Const Art IV §26.
District Court.
Assistant chief clerks, CJ §§2-601, 2-602.
Chief administrative clerk, CJ §2-601; MD Const
   Art IV §41F.
   Appointment, CJ §§1-605, 2-602.
   Terms of employment, CJ §2-602.
Chief clerk.
   Appointment, CJ §§1-605, 2-602.
   General provisions, MD Const Art IV §41F.
   Office, CJ §1-606.
   Terms of employment, CJ §2-602.
Deputies, MD Const Art IV §41F.
Duties, CJ §2-603.
In each county, MD Const Art IV §41F.
Divorce.
Record of divorce decrees, FL §7-106.
Reports, FL §2-503.
Docket.
Hospital lien docket, CL §16-605.
   Fees of clerk, CL §16-605.
Documents.
Records. See within this heading, "Records."
Dorchester county.
Recording and indexing.
   Ordinances, resolutions and regulations, 25 §4.
Duties.
Generally, CJ §2-201.
Record books, RP §3-301.
Elections.
Certification of election returns to governor, MD
   Const Art IV §11.
Circuit court, MD Const Art IV §25.
Contested elections, MD Const Art IV §12.
   Decided by house of delegates, MD Const Art IV
     §12.
Eminent domain.
Board of property review.
   Certification to board.
     Duty of clerk, PropAct Rule 12-213.
Employees.
Generally, CJ §2-505.
Minimum work week, CJ §2-506.
Environmental service.
Liens.
   Created in favor of service.
     Recording and indexing, NR §3-125.
Executors and administrators.
Right to letters.
   Exclusion, ET §5-105.

CLERKS OF COURT —Cont'd
Fees.
Administering public money, CJ §2-213.
Certificate of qualification of officer, CJ §2-212.
Circuit court, CJ §7-202.
   Criminal proceedings.
     Prohibition from charging fees or costs in
       certain criminal proceedings, CJ §7-203.
Collection.
   By sheriffs.
     See SHERIFFS.
Court of appeals, CJ §7-102.
Court of special appeals, CJ §7-102.
Examination of judgment debtor, CJ §7-401.
Federal liens, RP §3-404.
Hospital lien docket, CL §16-605.
Instruments not typed or printed.
   Triple charges, RP §3-104.
Legislature to provide system of fees and charges,
   MD Const Art III §45.
Photostatting.
   Triple charges when, RP §3-104.
Recordation.
   Commissions exempt from fees, RP §3-603.
   Counties exempt from fees, RP §3-603.
   Schedule, RP §3-601.
Signature.
   Failure to type or print name above or below
     signatures, RP §3-104.
Stenographic fees, CJ §7-401.
Successor.
   Completing unfinished business of predecessor,
     36 §9.
Supplementary proceedings, CJ §7-401.
Unfinished business on retirement.
   How clerks to complete unfinished business and
     fees therefore, 36 §9.
   Time allowed to complete, 36 §8.
Fiduciaries.
Trust clerks.
   See FIDUCIARIES.
Financing records. See within this heading,
   "Records."
Fish and fisheries.
Licenses.
   Anglers, NR §4-604.
   Chesapeake Bay sport fishing, NR §4-745.
   Live bait dealers, NR §4-11A-19.
Forms.
Recordation.
   Typed or printed, RP §3-104.
Hazardous materials and substances.
Judicial review of rules or regulations.
   Duties of clerk, HG §22-505.
Homeowners associations.
Depository.
   Duties, RP §11B-113.
Hours clerk's offices open, CJA Rule 16-304.
Indexes.
Assignments.
   Mortgages and deeds of trust, RP §3-302.
Changing of system.
   Authority, CJ §2-202.
Deeds, RP §3-302.
Federal lien index, RP §3-403.
   Fee for indexing, RP §3-404.
Financing records, RP §3-301.
Hospital lien docket, CL §16-605.
Land records, RP §§3-301, 3-302.
Microfilming.
   Deeds, mortgages, releases or leases.
     Requested by state archivist, RP §3-303.

CLERKS OF COURT —Cont'd
Indexes —Cont'd
Mortgages and deeds of trust, RP §3-302.
  Assignments and leases, RP §3-302.
Ordinances of county, 25 §4.
Powers of appointment.
  Release, ET §11-108.
Property identifiers, RP §3-302.
Provided by county commissioners, 25 §3.
System.
  Authority to change, CJ §2-202.
Vendors' liens, RP §3-302.
Judgments.
Costs.
  Assessment by clerk.
    Circuit courts, CivProCir Rule 2-603.
Judicial sales.
Recording papers upon payment of costs, RP
  §14-103.
Juvenile causes.
Duties of clerk, Juv Rule 11-104.
Landlord and tenant.
Rent escrow accounts.
  Authority to hold rent in escrow, RP §8-118.
Land patents.
Committee of clerks, RP 13-203.
Land records, RP §§3-301, 3-302.
Licenses.
Account of licenses, CJ §2-210.
Blank licenses.
  Application for, CJ §2-208.
  Renewal, 2B §10-301.
Liens.
Federal liens.
  United States. See within this heading, "United
    States."
Hospital lien docket, CL §16-605.
Limited liability companies.
Certificates of merger.
  Duties, CA §4A-706.
Filing of documents.
  Duties of clerk, CA §4A-207.
Limited partnerships.
Certificates.
  Duties of clerk receiving partnership certificate,
    CA §10-206.
Marriage.
Authority to perform marriage ceremony, FL
  §2-406.
  Fee for performing, FL §2-410.
Foreign marriage record book.
  Duties as to, FL §2-502.
Marriage license book, FL §2-501.
  Duties as to, FL §2-501.
Marriage record book.
  Foreign marriage record book, FL §2-502.
Reporting to secretary of health and mental
  hygiene, FL §2-503.
Masters.
Circuit courts.
  Referral of cases, CivProCir Rule 2-541.
Mechanics' liens.
Filing of claims, RP §9-105.
Hospital lien docket, CL §16-605.
Microfilming. See within this heading,
  "Photography."
Military affairs.
Copies of records for former armed forces
  members, CJ §7-406.
Military discharge papers.
  Recording, CJ §2-207.

CLERKS OF COURT —Cont'd
Minimum work week, CJ §2-506.
Mortgages and deeds of trust.
Endorsement on instrument of time of receipt by
  clerk, RP §3-301.
Indexes.
  Assignments and releases, RP §3-302.
  Dating changes or corrections, RP §3-302.
Releases, RP §3-105.
Motor vehicle traffic and criminal cases.
Uniform procedures for reporting.
  Establishment in conjunction with motor vehicle
    administration, CJ §2-201.
Name.
Recordation.
  Names typed or printed above or below
    signatures, RP §3-104.
Notice.
Orders, Rule 1-324.
Oaths.
Report of officers who have taken oaths, CJ
  §2-212.
Office.
Days open, CJ §2-204.
Equipment, CJ §2-202.
Hours, CJ §2-204.
Officers.
Qualification.
  Officers may qualify before clerk, MD Const Art
    I §10.
Orders.
Notice, Rule 1-324.
Ordinances of county.
Recordation, 25 §4.
Papers.
Books and papers.
  Circuit courts, CJ §2-502.
Records. See within this heading, "Records."
Partnerships.
Certificates.
  Filing certificates with department, CA §10-206.
Limited partnerships.
  Certificates.
    Duties of clerk receiving partnership
      certificate, CA §10-206.
Paternity.
Decree of paternity.
  Report sent to secretary of health and mental
    hygiene, HG §4-211.
Reports of adjudication of paternity, HG §4-211.
Personal property.
Financing records.
  Duties of clerk, RP §3-301.
Photography.
Affidavit.
  When instrument not readily subject to
    Photostatting or microfilming, RP §3-104.
Microfilming.
  Index to records of deeds, etc., RP §3-303.
  Land records.
    Duty of clerk, RP §3-301.
  Records of deeds, mortgages, etc., RP §3-303.
Recordation.
  Requirements as to printing, paper and typing,
    RP §3-104.
Plats.
Subdivisions.
  Recordation. See within this heading,
    "Recordation."
Pleadings.
Destruction of certain pleadings, papers and files.
  Procedure, CJ §2-205.

CLERKS OF COURT —Cont'd
Pleadings —Cont'd
Service of process.
Nonoriginal pleadings.
Requests to clerk.
Exceptions, Rule 1-321.
Pleas.
Pleas to other offenses.
Forwarding court clerk, Crim Rule 4-244.
Sentencing court clerk, Crim Rule 4-244.
Powers of appointment.
Release.
Recordation, ET §11-108.
Printing.
Signature on instruments.
Names to be typed or printed above or below
signatures, RP §3-104.
Public defender.
Recording of lien against defendant's property,
27A §7.
Fees paid by public defender, 27A §7.
Queen Anne's county.
Subdivisions.
Recordation of plats.
Distribution and maintenance after recording,
RP §3-108.1.
Real property.
Land records.
Duties of clerk, RP §3-301.
Indexes, RP §§3-301, 3-302.
**Receivers and assignees or trustees for
creditors.**
Dividends.
Disposition of unclaimed money or dividends,
Receivers Rule 13-503.
Recordation.
Charges.
Instruments not conforming to requirements,
RP §3-104.
Corporations.
Charter or other paper, CA §1-202.
Cost.
No duty to record until costs paid, CJ §2-201.
Endorsement on instrument of time of receipt by
clerk, RP §3-301.
Federal lien registration act.
Certification necessary for recording federal
liens, RP §3-402.
Fees, RP §3-601.
Commissions exempt from fees, RP §3-603.
Counties exempt from fees, RP §3-603.
Financing records, RP §3-301.
Forms.
Typed or printed forms, RP §3-104.
Intake sheet.
Requirements, RP §3-104.
Land records, RP §3-301.
Microfilming, RP §3-301.
Records of deeds, mortgages, etc., RP §3-303.
Military discharge papers, CJ §2-207.
Mortgages and deeds of trust.
Assignments, RP §3-106.
Paper.
Requirements, RP §3-104.
Photostatting.
Requirements, RP §3-104.
Plats of subdivisions.
Copies.
Disposition, RP §3-304.
Furnished to clerk, RP §3-304.
Fees, RP §3-304.

CLERKS OF COURT —Cont'd
Recordation —Cont'd
Plats of subdivisions —Cont'd
General provisions, RP §3-108.
Prerequisites to recording, RP §3-104.
Refusal of deed or document, RP §3-101.
Revised uniform tax lien registration act. See
within this heading, "United States."
Signatures on instruments.
Fees.
Extra fee for failure to type or print name
above or below signatures, RP §3-104.
Time of receipt.
Endorsement on instrument by clerk, RP
§3-301.
Vendors' liens.
Duties of clerk, RP §3-107.
Records.
Access to court records.
Duty of clerk, CJA Rule 16-1010.
Bond book.
Circuit courts, CJ §2-502.
Copies to state archivist, RP §3-303.
Destruction of certain pleadings, papers and files.
Procedure, CJ §2-205.
Divorce records, FL §7-106.
Financing records.
Duties of clerk, RP §3-301.
Indexing. See within this heading, "Indexes."
Inspection.
Public inspection, CJ §2-203.
Land records. See within this heading, "Real
property."
Microfilming.
Deeds, mortgages, releases or leases, RP §3-303.
Duties of clerk, RP §3-301.
Index to records of deeds, etc., RP §3-303.
Military discharge papers, CJ §2-207.
Registers of wills.
Acting as clerks of court, ET §2-208.
Defined, ET §2-201.
Regulations, MD Const Art IV §10.
Releases.
Mortgages and deeds of trust. See within this
heading, "Mortgages and deeds of trust."
Powers of appointment.
Recordation, ET §11-108.
Reports.
Officers who have taken oaths.
Report to secretary of state, CJ §2-212.
Salaries.
Circuit court.
General provisions, CJ §2-504.
Employees of clerk.
Circuit court, CJ §2-505.
Service of process.
Pleadings.
Nonoriginal pleadings.
Request to clerk.
Exception, Rule 1-321.
Severn river watershed.
Liens.
Recording and indexing, EN §4-312.
Signatures.
On instruments.
Names to be typed or printed above or below
signatures, RP §3-104.
State's attorneys.
Elections.
Certification and delivery of returns to judges,
MD Const Art V §8.

CLERKS OF COURT —Cont'd
Subdivisions.
Plats of subdivisions.
Recordation. See within this heading,
"Recordation."
Subpoenas.
Trial or hearing.
Preparation by clerk.
Criminal rules, Crim Rule 4-265.
Successor.
Completing unfinished business of predecessor.
Fees, 36 §9.
Superior court of Baltimore City.
See SUPERIOR COURT OF BALTIMORE CITY.
Support and maintenance.
Child support.
Delegation of responsibility for support
enforcement to circuit court clerks, FL
§10-114.
Tax court.
See TAX COURT.
Terms of court.
End of term.
How clerks to complete unfinished business and
fees therefore, 36 §9.
Six months allowed to complete unfinished
business of office, 36 §8.
Terms of office.
Circuit court, MD Const Art IV §25.
Time.
Endorsement on instrument of time of receipt by
clerk, RP §3-301.
Trusts and trustees.
Not to serve as trustee, ET §14-104.
United States.
Federal liens.
Certificates and notices affecting lien.
Filing.
Fees, RP §3-404.
Place of filing, RP §3-401.
Certification necessary for recording, RP §3-402.
Citation of uniform act, RP §3-405.
Fees.
Billing district directors of internal revenue,
RP §3-404.
Filing notices, RP §3-404.
Filing.
Certificates and notices.
Place of filing, RP §3-401.
Fees.
Notice of lien, RP §3-404.
Indexes.
Fees, RP §3-404.
Billing district directors of internal revenue,
RP §3-404.
Internal revenue.
Billing district directors of internal revenue
for fees, RP §3-404.
Interpretation of uniform act, RP §3-405.
Notices.
Filing.
Fees, RP §3-404.
Place of filing, RP §3-401.
Recordation.
Certification necessary, RP §3-402.
Vacancy.
Filling by judge, MD Const Art IV §25.
Vendors' liens.
Indexes, RP §3-302.
Recording.
Duties of clerk, RP §3-107.

CLERKS OF COURT —Cont'd
Worcester county.
Recording and indexing.
Ordinances, resolutions and regulations, 25 §4.
Workers' compensation.
Certificate of compliance with workers'
compensation act, CJ §2-209.

CLIENTS' PROTECTION FUND, BOP §§10-310
to 10-313.
See ATTORNEYS AT LAW.

CLIENTS' SECURITY FUND, BOP §§10-310 to
10-313; CJA Rule 16-811.

CLIFTON T. PERKINS HOSPITAL CENTER.
Security attendants.
Correctional officers' retirement system.
General provisions, SPP §§25-101 to 25-404.
See CORRECTIONAL OFFICERS'
RETIREMENT SYSTEM.

**CLINICAL ALCOHOL AND DRUG
COUNSELORS.**
Licensing, HO §§17-3A-01 to 17-3A-13.
See PROFESSIONAL COUNSELORS AND
THERAPISTS.

**CLINICAL MARRIAGE AND FAMILY
THERAPISTS.**
Licensing, HO §§17-3A-01 to 17-3A-13.
See PROFESSIONAL COUNSELORS AND
THERAPISTS.

CLINICAL PROFESSIONAL COUNSELORS.
Licensing, HO §§17-3A-01 to 17-3A-13.
See PROFESSIONAL COUNSELORS AND
THERAPISTS.

CLINICS.
**Interference with access to or egress from
medical facility,** CR §10-204.
Rabies.
Antirabies clinics, HG §18-315.
Smoking in health clinics, HG §24-205.

CLIPS USED TO HOLD AMMUNITION.
Detachable magazines, prohibition, CR §4-305.

CLOCKS.
Watches.
Secondhand watches, CL §§14-701 to 14-706.
See WATCHES.

CLONING.
Human cloning.
Defined, 83A §5-2B-01.
Prohibited, criminal penalty, 83A §5-2B-13.
State-funded stem cell research.
Prohibited by person conducting, 83A §5-2B-02.
Human subject research.
Generally, HG §§13-2001 to 13-2004.

CLOSE CORPORATIONS, CA §§4-101 to 4-603.
See CORPORATIONS.

CLOSED-END CREDIT PROVISIONS.
Credit grantor closed end credit provisions, CL
§§12-1001 to 12-1029.
See CREDIT.

CLOSED HEARINGS.
**Parole release hearings, formal action of
commission,** COR §7-304.
Rape or sexual offense prosecutions.
Reputation for chastity, prior sexual conduct, CR
§3-319.

CLOSING CORRECTIONAL FACILITY.
Violation of minimum mandatory condition,
  COR §8-114.

CLOSING COSTS.
Attorney fees of lender, CL §12-120.
Deed recordation tax, TP §§12-103 to 12-105.
Eminent domain.
  Relocation assistance, RP §12-202.
    Park and planning commission, 28 §5-105.1.
Misdemeanors, CL §12-122.
Notice by lenders, CL §12-119.
Transfer taxes, TP §§13-101 to 13-410.
  See PROPERTY TAXES.

CLOSING OF BUSINESSES.
Emergency management.
  Governor's powers, PS §14-307.

CLOSING OUT SALES, CL §§11-1101 to 11-1106.
See DISTRESS SALES.

CLOTHES WASHERS.
Commercial washers.
  Efficiency standards, SG §9-2006.

CLOUD SEEDING.
Powers of certain counties as to weather
    modification, 25 §3.

CLOVE CIGARETTES.
Sale prohibited, penalty, CR §10-106.

CLUBS.
Alcoholic beverages.
  Application for club license, 2B §9-101.
    Renewal.
      Substitution of officers, 2B §10-301.
    Beer and light wine licenses.
      Class C, on-sale, 2B §5-301.
    Beer licenses.
      Class C, on-sale, 2B §3-301.
    Beer, wine and liquor licenses.
      Class C, on-sale, 2B §6-301.
    Hours of sale.
      Beer and light wine licenses, 2B §11-302.
      Beer licenses, 2B §11-301.
      Beer, wine and liquor licenses, 2B §11-303.
Associations.
  See ASSOCIATIONS.
Barbeque grills.
  Restrictions on use, PS §9-1001.
Country clubs.
  Taxation.
    Assessments.
      Agreements, TP §8-213.
      Discrimination, TP §8-214.
        Determination of discrimination and
            consent agreements, TP §8-215.
      Qualifications of clubs, TP §8-212.
    Calculation, TP §8-216.
    Deferred taxes, TP §8-216.
    Forms, TP §8-218.
    Lien for taxes, TP §8-216.
    Partial sale of property, TP §8-216.
    Regulations, TP §8-218.
    Transfer of agreements, TP §8-217.
Definitions.
  Alcoholic beverages, 2B §1-102.
Fraternal benefit societies, IN §§8-401 to 8-468.
  See FRATERNAL BENEFIT SOCIETIES.
Motor vehicles.
  Bail.
    Guaranteed arrest bond certificate by
        automobile club, TR §26-404.

CLUBS —Cont'd
Taxation.
  Country clubs.
    Assessments.
      Agreements, TP §8-213.
      Discrimination, TP §8-214.
        Determination of discrimination and
            consent agreements, TP §8-215.
      Qualifications of clubs, TP §8-212.
    Calculation of taxes, TP §8-216.
    Deferred taxes, TP §8-216.
    Forms, TP §8-218.
    Lien for taxes, TP §8-216.
    Partial sale of property, TP §8-216.
    Regulations, TP §8-218.
    Transfer of agreements, TP §8-217.

CLUSTER DEVELOPMENT.
Ordinances providing for or requiring
    encouraged, 66B §10.01.

COAL.
Income tax.
  Credits.
    Purchase of Maryland-mined coal, TG
        §10-704.1.
Mining.
  General provisions, EN §§15-101 to 15-1109.
  See MINING.
Procurement.
  Preferences, SF §14-404.

COAL POLLUTION.
Electric generating facilities.
  Healthy air act, EN §§2-1001 to 2-1005.
Property tax exemptions.
  Certified coal pollution control facility, TP §7-239.

COAL TAX.
Counties, 24 §§9-501 to 9-509.
  See COUNTIES.

COAL WASTE DISPOSAL POWER PROJECT.
Property taxes.
  Exemptions, TP §7-239.

COASTAL FACILITIES REVIEW.
Gas and oil, EN §§14-501 to 14-511.
  See GAS AND OIL.

COASTING TRADE VESSELS.
See VESSELS AND BOATS.

COBBLERS.
Mechanics' liens.
  Shoe repairs.
    Lien for repairing, CL §16-302.

COBRA BENEFITS.
Continued coverage of health insurance, IN
    §15-409.

COCAINE.
Controlled dangerous substances.
  Generally, CR §§5-101 to 5-1101.
    See CONTROLLED DANGEROUS
        SUBSTANCES.
Importers, CR §5-614.
Schedule II, CR §5-403.
Volume dealers, enhanced penalty, CR §5-612.

COCA LEAF.
Controlled dangerous substances.
  Generally, CR §§5-101 to 5-1101.
    See CONTROLLED DANGEROUS
        SUBSTANCES.
Schedule II, CR §5-403.

COCA LEAF —Cont'd
Defined, CR §5-101.

COCKFIGHT, CR §10-608.
Attending cockfight, CR §10-605.

C.O.D.
Buyer not entitled to inspect goods, CL §2-513.

CODEINE.
Controlled dangerous substances.
Generally, CR §§5-101 to 5-1101.
See CONTROLLED DANGEROUS
SUBSTANCES.
Dispensing.
Prescription required, exception, CR §5-503.
Possession, penalty, CR §5-503.
Schedule I, CR §5-402.
Schedule II, CR §5-403.
Schedule III, CR §5-404.
Schedule V, CR §5-406.

CODE OF JUDICIAL CONDUCT, CJA Rule
16-813.
See JUDGES.

CODE OF MARYLAND.
Adoption of code.
Not to affect vested rights, contracts, pending
suits and prosecutions, 1 §1.
Prosecution for offenses previously committed, 1
§2.
Rights under charter or grant from state, 1 §4.
Amendments.
Enactment of laws not amendatory of code, MD
Const Art III §29.
General provisions, MD Const Art III §29.
Inconsistent amendments to same code section or
subsection, 1 §17.
Reference in statute to code or other law includes
amendments, 1 §21.
Captions or headlines.
Sections and subsections.
Construction, 1 §18.
Citation.
Revised articles, 1 §25.
Contracts.
Adoption of code not to affect, 1 §1.
Criminal procedure.
Adoption of code not to affect pending
prosecutions, 1 §1.
Prosecution for offenses committed previous to
adoption of code, 1 §2.
Definitions, Rule 1-202.
Evidence.
Public general law, CJ §10-201.
References to the public general laws, 1 §2A.
Replacement volumes, CJ §10-201.
General assembly.
Amendments.
Inconsistent amendments to same code section
or subsection, 1 §17.
Grant.
Rights under charter or grant from state, 1 §4.
Indictments and informations.
Prosecution for offenses committed prior to
adoption of code, 1 §2.
Interpretation and construction.
Captions or headlines of code sections and
subsections, 1 §18.
Judgments and decrees.
Adoption of code not to affect, 1 §1.
Misdemeanors.
Adoption.
Not to affect prosecution, 1 §1.

CODE OF MARYLAND —Cont'd
Misdemeanors —Cont'd
Prosecution for offenses committed prior to
adoption of code, 1 §2.
References to the public general laws, 1 §2A.
Replacement volumes.
Evidence, CJ §10-201.
Revised articles.
Citation, 1 §25.
Severability.
Provisions of statutes severable, 1 §23.
Validity.
Severability of provisions of statutes, 1 §23.

CODE OF MARYLAND REGULATIONS.
General provisions, SG §§7-201 to 7-222.
See DOCUMENTS.

CODES.
Counties.
Copies deposited with state agencies, 25 §32A.
Home rule for code counties.
General provisions.
See COUNTIES.
Plumbing, building and housing codes.
In certain counties, 25 §3.
Municipal corporations.
Annual publication of code of ordinances.
Required, 23A §17D.
Deposit with department of legislative services,
23A §9A.
Home rule.
Charter.
Codification of amendments, 23A §18.
Rules and regulations.
Code of regulations.
Evidence.
Judicial notice, CJ §10-203.
State documents, SG §§7-201 to 7-222.
See DOCUMENTS.

CODICILS.
Counterfeiting private instrument or
document.
Issuing counterfeited instrument or document, CR
§8-602.
Embezzle, steal, destroy, impair or alter, CR
§8-701.

CODIS.
DNA database system, PS §§2-501 to 2-512.
See DNA DATABASE SYSTEM.

COERCION.
Athlete agents.
Prohibited activities, BR §4-413.
Contributions or donations, CR §3-707.
Duress.
General provisions.
See DURESS.
Extortion and other threats, CR §§3-701 to
3-708.
Grievance procedures.
Right to bring grievance free of coercion, SPP
§12-103.
Transportation department employees, TR
§2-103.4.
Insurance.
Sale of insurance, IN §27-214.
Unfair trade practices, IN §27-206.
Physician assistants.
Coercion to enter delegation agreement with
physician, HO §15-302.

COIN-OPERATED MACHINES.
Console machines.
See CONSOLE MACHINES.
Pinball machines.
See PINBALL MACHINES.
Slot machines, CR §§12-301 to 12-307.
See SLOT MACHINES.
Vending machines.
General provisions.
See VENDING MACHINES.
Licenses, BR §§17-1901 to 17-1907.
See VENDING MACHINES.

COIN PAY TELEPHONES.
Placing calls to operator without requiring insertion of coins, PUC §8-302.

COINS.
Counterfeiting and issuing tokens, CR §8-612.
Money.
General provisions.
See MONEY.
Sales and use tax.
Precious metal bullion or coins.
Exemption, TG §11-214.1.

COINSURANCE PAYMENTS FOR HEALTH CARE SERVICES, IN §15-118.
Child birth, IN §15-812.
Diabetes treatment, IN §15-822.
HMO, HG §19-706.
Mental illness, emotional disorder and drug and alcohol abuse treatment, IN §15-802.

COLLATERAL.
Sales.
Installment sales.
Statement as to collateral, CL §12-606.
Securities.
State treasurer.
Loans of securities, SF §2-603.
State treasurer.
Securities.
Loans of securities, SF §2-603.
State treasury, SF §§6-202, 6-209, 6-210.
See STATE TREASURY.

COLLATERAL SOURCE RULE.
Motor vehicle insurance, IN §19-513.
Personal injury protection coverage, IN §19-507.
Workers' compensation.
Claims, LE §9-736.
Permanent total disability, LE §9-635.

COLLECTION AGENCIES.
Board.
Commissioner.
Chairman of board, BR §7-203.
Defined, BR §7-101.
Ex officio member of board, BR §7-202.
Composition, BR §7-202.
Consumer members, BR §7-202.
Creation, BR §7-201.
Defined, BR §7-101.
Disposition of money, BR §7-206.
Enforcement powers, BR §7-205.
Establishment, BR §7-201.
Expense reimbursement, BR §7-204.
Injunctive powers, BR §7-205.
Meetings, BR §7-204.
Membership, BR §7-202.
Program evaluation act, SG §8-403.
Removal, BR §7-202.
Staff, BR §7-204.

COLLECTION AGENCIES —Cont'd
Bonds, surety.
Licenses.
Issuance of license, BR §7-304.
Citation of title, BR §7-501.
Conflict of laws.
Title effect on other laws, BR §7-103.
Definitions, BR §§7-101, 7-102.
Exclusions from provisions, BR §7-102.
Fees.
License applications.
Nonrefundable fee, BR §7-302.
Local license fees prohibited, BR §7-104.
Injunctions.
Board enforcement powers, BR §7-205.
Licenses.
Action against licensees.
Local or state action prohibited, BR §7-103.
Applications.
Approval.
Time limit, BR §7-303.
Denial.
Grounds, BR §7-303.
Generally, BR §7-302.
Nonrefundable fee, BR §7-302.
Oath required, BR §7-302.
Places of business.
Separate application and fee, BR §7-302.
Defined, BR §7-101.
Disciplinary actions.
Effect of revocation or suspension, BR §7-311.
Enforcement of board orders, BR §7-309.
Grounds, BR §7-308.
Hearings.
Application of contested case provisions, BR §7-309.
Judicial review, BR §7-310.
Right to hearing, BR §7-309.
Doing business without license.
Prohibited, BR §7-401.
Exceptions to requirement, BR §7-301.
Expiration, BR §7-306.
Issuance, BR §7-304.
Local license prohibited, BR §7-104.
Multiple licenses authorized, BR §7-305.
Effect of disciplinary action, BR §7-308.
Renewal, BR §7-302.
Reprimands.
Grounds, BR §7-308.
Required, BR §7-301.
Scope of license, BR §7-305.
Surety bond prerequisite to issuance, BR §7-304.
Surrender.
Effect, BR §7-307.
Term, BR §7-306.
Notices.
Licenses.
Issuance of license, BR §7-304.
Short title, BR §7-501.
Sunset law, BR §7-502.
Title of act, BR §7-501.

COLLECTIONS.
Bank deposits and collections.
Commercial code, CL §§4-101 to 4-504.
See BANK DEPOSITS AND COLLECTIONS.
Budget and management.
Central collection unit, SF §§3-301 to 3-306.
See BUDGET AND MANAGEMENT.
State.
Budget and management.
Central collection unit, SF §§3-301 to 3-306.
See BUDGET AND MANAGEMENT.

COLLECTIVE BARGAINING.
Agents.
Injunctions.
Civil and criminal liability for acts of agents,
LE §4-321.
Appeals.
Injunctions.
Issuance or denial of temporary injunction, LE
§4-318.
Arbitration.
Labor dispute arbitration or mediation, LE
§§4-101 to 4-111. See within this heading,
"Labor dispute arbitration or mediation."
Baltimore City housing authority, HS §15-109.
Baltimore City schools.
New board of school commissioners, ED §4-312.
Bonds, surety.
Injunctions.
Temporary restraining order or temporary
injunction.
Bond requirement, LE §4-316.
Choice of bargaining representative.
Administration of subtitle, LE §4-202.
Consent elections, LE §§4-206 to 4-217. See
within this heading, "Consent elections."
Decertification, LE §4-220.
Definitions, LE §4-201.
Rulemaking authority, LE §4-203.
Sunset provision, LE §4-405.
Community colleges.
Prince George's county public employment
relations, ED §16-414.1.
Consent elections, LE §§4-206 to 4-217.
Agreement.
Contents, LE §4-209.
Generally, LE §4-209.
Certification.
Generally, LE §4-217.
Challenged ballots.
Defined, LE §4-206.
Duties of mediation service, LE §4-212.
Report on investigations, LE §4-214.
Disposition after report, LE §4-217.
Exception to report, LE §4-215.
Consideration of exception, LE §4-216.
Definitions, LE §4-206.
Maryland-national capital park and planning
commission, 28 §5-114.1.
Employees, 28 §2-112.1.
Objection to consent election.
Generally, LE §4-213.
Investigations, LE §4-213.
Report on investigations, LE §4-214.
Disposition after report, LE §4-217.
Exception to report, LE §4-215.
Consideration of exception, LE §4-216.
Petitions.
Defined, LE §4-206.
Form, LE §4-207.
Notice requirement, LE §4-207.
Objection, LE §4-207.
No objection.
Effect, LE §4-208.
Period for objecting to petition, LE §4-207.
Procedure for consent election.
Generally, LE §4-210.
Tally of ballots, LE §4-211.
Conspiracy.
Trade dispute agreements.
Conduct not conspiracy, LE §4-404.

COLLECTIVE BARGAINING —Cont'd
Contempt.
Injunctions.
Constructive criminal contempt, LE §4-322.
Contracts.
Consent elections.
Agreement for consent election, LE §4-209.
Trade dispute agreements.
Conduct not conspiracy, LE §4-404.
Yellow Dog contract act.
General provisions, LE §§4-301 to 4-322. See
within this heading, "Injunctions."
Crimes and offenses.
Conspiracy.
Trade dispute agreements.
Conduct not conspiracy, LE §4-404.
Injunctions.
Constructive criminal contempt, LE §4-322.
Payment of union dues or employee benefits, LE
§4-401.
Refusal to leave property, LE §4-402.
Strikebreakers.
Recruitment and employment restricted, LE
§4-403.
Criminal procedure.
Injunctions.
Constructive criminal contempt.
Recusal of judge, LE §4-322.
Decertification.
Generally, LE §4-220.
Definitions.
Choice of bargaining representative, LE §4-201.
Consent elections, LE §4-206.
Injunctions, LE §4-301.
Promise, LE §4-304.
Labor dispute arbitration or mediation, LE
§4-101.
Maryland-national capital park and planning
commission, 28 §§2-112.1, 5-114.1.
Emergency medical services personnel, LE
§§4-501 to 4-505. See within this heading,
"Public safety officers."
Employee benefits.
Payment of, LE §4-401.
Evidence.
Injunctions.
Temporary restraining orders.
Opportunity to show cause, LE §4-315.
Fines.
Injunctions.
Constructive criminal contempt, LE §4-322.
Firefighters, LE §§4-501 to 4-505. See within this
heading, "Public safety officers."
Forms.
Consent elections.
Petition for consent election, LE §4-207.
Hearings.
Consent elections.
Report on investigations.
Consideration of exception to report, LE
§4-216.
Interpreters.
Proceedings before administrative or executive
board, LE §3-707.
Immunity.
Injunctions.
Civil and criminal liability, LE §4-321.
Injunctions, LE §§4-301 to 4-322.
Acts protected from injunctive relief.
Generally, LE §4-307.

COLLECTIVE BARGAINING —Cont'd
Injunctions —Cont'd
Civil and criminal liability.
Liability for acts of agents, members or officers,
LE §4-321.
Construction of subtitle, LE §4-303.
Constructive criminal contempt.
Generally, LE §4-322.
Definitions, LE §4-301.
Promise, LE §4-304.
Legislative findings and policy, LE §4-302.
Promises restricting association, LE §4-304.
Protected acts from injunctive relief, LE §4-307.
Restrictions on injunctive relief.
Acts prohibited from injunctive relief, LE
§4-307.
Appeals to court of special appeals.
Issuance or denial of temporary injunction,
LE §4-318.
Bond requirements, LE §4-316.
Construction of part, LE §4-312.
Effect of relief, LE §4-317.
Failure of plaintiff to fulfill obligations, LE
§4-313.
Findings required, LE §4-317.
Labor dispute cases, LE §4-310.
Legislative findings and policy, LE §4-311.
Permanent injunctions, LE §4-314.
Scope of relief, LE §4-317.
Temporary injunctions, LE §4-314.
Bond requirement, LE §4-316.
Temporary restraining orders, LE §4-315.
Bond requirement, LE §4-316.
Temporary and permanent injunctions, LE §4-314.
Bond requirement for temporary injunction, LE
§4-316.
Findings required, LE §4-317.
Scope and effect of relief, LE §4-317.
Temporary restraining orders, LE §4-315.
Bond requirement, LE §4-316.
Interpretation and construction.
Choice of bargaining representative.
Administration of subtitle, LE §4-202.
Injunctions.
Restrictions on injunctive relief.
Construction of part, LE §4-312.
Legislative findings and policy, LE §4-311.
Labor dispute arbitration or mediation.
Administration of subtitle, LE §4-103.
Scope of applicability, LE §4-108.
Scope of subtitle, LE §4-102.
Public safety officers, LE §4-505.
Sunset provision.
Choice of bargaining representative, LE §4-405.
Labor dispute arbitration or mediation, LE
§4-405.
Investigations.
Certification, LE §4-220.
Consent elections.
Objection to consent election, LE §4-213.
Disposition after report on investigation, LE
§4-217.
Exception to report on investigations, LE
§4-215.
Consideration of exception, LE §4-216.
Report on investigations, LE §4-214.
Labor dispute arbitration or mediation, LE
§§4-101 to 4-111.
Administration of subtitle, LE §4-103.
Applicability of subtitle, LE §4-108.

COLLECTIVE BARGAINING —Cont'd
Labor dispute arbitration or mediation
—Cont'd
Collective bargaining agreements.
Reporting requirements, LE §4-111.
Termination, LE §4-111.
Confidentiality of information, LE §4-107.
Decision and award.
Finality and binding effect, LE §4-109.
Definitions, LE §4-101.
Designation as bargaining representative.
Reporting requirements, LE §4-110.
Determination of dispute, LE §4-109.
Failure of arbitration or mediation, LE §4-108.
Information storage, LE §4-107.
Mediation service and boards.
"Board" defined, LE §4-101.
Chief mediator.
Defined, LE §2-104.
Duties, LE §4-104.
Formation of board, LE §4-105.
"Mediation service" defined, LE §4-101.
Powers, LE §4-106.
Recordkeeping requirements, LE §4-107.
Reporting requirements.
Collective bargaining agreements, LE §4-111.
Designation as bargaining representative, LE
§4-110.
Restrictions on injunctive relief, LE §4-310.
Scope of subtitle, LE §4-102.
Sunset provision, LE §4-405.
**Maryland-national capital park and planning
commission,** 28 §§2-112.1, 5-114.1.
Mediation.
Labor dispute arbitration or mediation, LE
§§4-101 to 4-111. See within this heading,
"Labor dispute arbitration or mediation."
Misdemeanors.
Payment of union dues or employee benefits, LE
§4-401.
Refusal to leave property, LE §4-402.
Strikebreakers.
Recruitment and employment restricted, LE
§4-403.
**Montgomery County housing opportunities
commission,** HS §§16-301 to 16-319.
Notices.
Consent elections.
Petition for consent election, LE §4-207.
Ordinances.
Public safety officers.
Authority to enact, LE §4-502.
Paramedics, LE §§4-501 to 4-505. See within this
heading, "Public safety officers."
Parties.
Injunctions.
Failure of plaintiff to fulfill obligations, LE
§4-313.
Penalties.
Injunctions.
Constructive criminal contempt, LE §4-322.
Payment of union dues or employee benefits, LE
§4-401.
Refusal to leave property, LE §4-402.
Strikebreakers.
Recruitment and employment restricted, LE
§4-403.
Prince George's county.
Board of community college trustees.
Public employment relations, ED §16-414.1.

COLLECTIVE BARGAINING —Cont'd
Prince George's county —Cont'd
Sheriff.
Civilian employees, CJ §2-309.
Privileged communications.
Labor dispute arbitration or mediation, LE §4-107.
Public safety officers, LE §§4-501 to 4-505.
Applicability, LE §4-505.
Definitions, LE §4-501.
Discipline of firefighters and emergency medical personnel.
Judicial review.
Election to exercise rights under collective bargaining agreement, LE §4-603.
Interpretation and construction, LE §4-505.
Local laws or ordinances.
Authority to enact, LE §4-502.
Memorandum of understanding.
Binding effect, LE §4-504.
Ratification and approval, LE §4-504.
Terms and conditions of employment, LE §4-503.
Terms and conditions of employment.
Memorandum of understanding, LE §4-503.
Refusal to leave property.
Generally, LE §4-402.
Reports.
Labor dispute arbitration or mediation.
Reporting requirements.
Collective bargaining agreements.
Termination, LE §4-111.
Designation as bargaining representative, LE §4-110.
Rules and regulations.
Choice of bargaining representative.
Rulemaking authority, LE §4-203.
Service of process.
Consent elections.
Report on investigations.
Exception to report, LE §4-215.
State personnel, SPP §§3-101 to 3-602.
See STATE PERSONNEL.
Strikebreakers.
Recruitment and employment restricted, LE §4-403.
Subpoenas.
Labor dispute arbitration or mediation.
Mediation service and boards.
Enforcement of subpoena, LE §4-106.
Trade dispute agreements.
Conduct not conspiracy, LE §4-404.
Union dues.
Payment of, LE §4-401.
Washington suburban sanitary district, 29 §§11.5-101 to 11.5-114.
See WASHINGTON SUBURBAN SANITARY DISTRICT.
Yellow Dog contract act.
General provisions, LE §§4-301 to 4-322. See within this heading, "Injunctions."

COLLECTORS.
General assembly.
Failure to account for public money.
Disqualification, MD Const Art III §12.

COLLEGE INVESTMENT PLAN, ED §§18-19A-01 to 18-19A-07.
See UNIVERSITIES AND COLLEGES.

COLLEGE OF SOUTHERN MARYLAND, ED §§16-601 to 16-610.
Board of trustees.
Hearing examiner.
Appointment, ED §16-607.
Hearings, ED §16-607.
Meetings, ED §16-605.
Members, ED §16-604.
Notes to finance projects, issuance, ED §16-302.1.
Officers, ED §16-605.
Powers, ED §16-606.
Bond issues.
Notes to finance projects, issuance, ED §16-302.1.
Charles county community college.
Legislative declaration as to, ED §16-601.
Renamed, ED §16-603.
Definitions, ED §16-602.
Established, ED §16-601.
Immunity.
Defense of sovereign immunity.
Applicability of provisions, ED §16-609.
Notes to finance projects, issuance, ED §16-302.1.
Operational cost, ED §16-603.
President.
Appointment by board of trustees, ED §16-606.
Responsibilities, ED §16-608.
Reports, ED §16-610.
Status, ED §16-603.
Tuition waivers.
Applicability of provisions, ED §16-609.

COLLEGE PREPARATION INTERVENTION PROGRAM, ED §§11-701 to 11-705.
Activities, ED §11-703.
Budget, ED §11-705.
Established, ED §11-701.
Purpose, ED §11-702.
Reports.
Annual report to governor, ED §11-704.

COLLEGES.
General provisions.
See UNIVERSITIES AND COLLEGES.

COLLEGE SAVINGS PLAN OF MARYLAND.
Board, ED §§18-1904, 18-1905.
Generally, ED §§18-1901 to 18-1916.
See UNIVERSITIES AND COLLEGES.

COLLISION COVERAGE FOR MOTOR VEHICLES, IN §19-512.

COLLUSION.
Procurement, SF §11-205.

COLOR CODE FOR MARKING LOCATION OF UNDERGROUND FACILITIES.
Excavation or demolition near, PUC §12-110.

COLUMBUS DAY.
Defined, 1 §27.
Legal holiday, 1 §27.
Schools.
Appropriate exercises, ED §7-103.

COMBUSTIBLES.
Explosions and explosives.
See EXPLOSIONS AND EXPLOSIVES.
Fire inspection.
See FIRES AND FIRE PROTECTION.
Flammable materials and liquids.
See INFLAMMABLE LIQUIDS AND PRODUCTS.

COMBUSTIBLES —Cont'd
Inflammable liquids and products.
See INFLAMMABLE LIQUIDS AND
PRODUCTS.

COMIC BOOKS.
Obscenity.
See OBSCENITY AND PORNOGRAPHY.

COMITY.
Reciprocity.
See RECIPROCITY.

COMMANDER-IN-CHIEF.
Militia.
Consent of legislature to command in person, MD
Const Art II §8.
President of the United States, US Const Art II
§2.

COMMEMORATIVE DAYS.
Asian lunar new year day, SG §13-405.
John Hanson's birthday, SG §13-401.
Law day, SG §13-402.
Poetry day, SG §13-403.

COMMEMORATIVE MONTHS.
Women's history month, SG §13-501.

COMMENTATORS.
Rate regulation and proceedings generally,
PUC §§4-101 to 4-503.
See PUBLIC SERVICE COMMISSION.

COMMERCE.
Antitrust act.
General provisions, CL §§11-201 to 11-213.
See ANTITRUST ACT.
**Business and economic development
department.**
See BUSINESS AND ECONOMIC
DEVELOPMENT DEPARTMENT.
Business opportunities.
General provisions, BR §§14-101 to 14-129.
See START-UP BUSINESS VENTURES.
Currency transactions in trade or business, BR
§§1-501 to 1-505.
See CURRENCY TRANSACTIONS IN TRADE
OR BUSINESS.
Debt adjusting.
Collection agencies, BR §§7-101 to 7-502.
See COLLECTION AGENCIES.
Insurance unfair trade practices.
See INSURANCE.
**Maryland advisory commission on
manufacturing competitiveness,** 83A
§§3-801 to 3-804.
Trade generally.
See TRADE AND COMMERCE.
Trade secrets.
Uniform trade secrets act, CL §§11-1201 to
11-1209.
See TRADE SECRETS.

COMMERCIAL BANKS.
See BANKS AND TRUST COMPANIES.

COMMERCIAL CODE, CL §§1-101 to 10-112.
Bank deposits and collections, CL §§4-101 to
4-504.
Alteration of customer's account.
Customer's duty to discover and report, CL
§4-406.
Applicability of article, CL §4-102.
Depositary and collecting banks.
Collection of items, CL §4-201.

COMMERCIAL CODE —Cont'd
Bank deposits and collections —Cont'd
Applicability of article —Cont'd
Variation by agreement, CL §4-103.
Bankruptcy and insolvency.
Collection of items.
Depositary and collecting banks.
Insolvency and preference, CL §4-216.
Branch offices.
Separate offices of bank, CL §4-107.
Burden of proof.
Stop payment orders.
Losses resulting from violations of orders, CL
§4-403.
Charge-backs, CL §4-214.
Charging customer's account.
When allowed, CL §4-401.
Checks.
Stale checks, CL §4-404.
Citation of article.
Short title, CL §4-101.
Collecting banks. See within this subheading,
"Depositary and collecting banks."
Collection of items.
Depositary and collecting banks. See within this
subheading, "Depositary and collecting
banks."
Comparative negligence.
Unauthorized signature or alteration, CL
§4-406.
Conflict of laws, CL §4-102.
Contracts.
Variation of article provisions by agreement, CL
§4-103.
Contributory negligence.
Unauthorized signature or alteration, CL
§4-406.
Damages.
Measure of damages, CL §4-103.
Death of customer.
Effect, CL §4-405.
Definitions, CL §§4-104, 4-105.
Agreement for electronic presentment, CL
§4-110.
Course of dealing, CL §4-205.
General commercial code definitions, CL §1-201.
Course of dealing, CL §1-205.
Reasonable time and seasonably, CL §1-204.
Usage of trade, CL §1-205.
Usage of trade, CL §1-205.
Delays, CL §4-108.
Depositary and collecting banks.
Collection of items, CL §§4-201 to 4-216.
Agency status of collecting banks, CL §4-201.
Charge-backs, CL §4-214.
Credits for items.
Availability for withdrawal, CL §4-215.
Provisional status, CL §4-201.
When provisional credits become final, CL
§4-215.
Death or incompetence of customer.
Effect, CL §4-405.
Debits for items.
When provisional credits become final, CL
§4-215.
Holders in due course.
When bank gives value, CL §4-211.
Indorsements.
"Pay any bank," CL §4-201.
Insolvency and preference, CL §4-216.

COMMERCIAL CODE —Cont'd
Bank deposits and collections —Cont'd
  Depositary and collecting banks —Cont'd
    Collection of items —Cont'd
      Instructions of transferor.
        Effect, CL §4-203.
      Liability of secondary parties, CL §4-212.
      "Pay any bank."
        Items so indorsed, CL §4-201.
      Payment of item by payor bank.
        Final payment, CL §4-215.
      Presentment of items.
        By notice of item not payable by, through or
          at bank, CL §4-212.
        Methods, CL §4-204.
      Refunds, CL §4-214.
      Responsibility required, CL §4-202.
      Security interest of collecting bank.
        Items accompanying documents and
          proceeds, CL §4-210.
      Sending items.
        Methods, CL §4-204.
      Settlement of items.
        Medium and time of settlement, CL §4-213.
        Provisional status, CL §4-201.
        When provisional credits become final, CL
          §4-215.
      Transfer of items, CL §4-206.
      Unindorsed items.
        Depositary bank holder of, CL §4-205.
      When action timely, CL §4-202.
    Defined, CL §4-105.
    Unindorsed items.
      Depositary bank holder of, CL §4-205.
    Warranties.
      Encoding and retention warranties, CL
        §4-209.
      Presentment warranties, CL §4-208.
      Transfer warranties, CL §4-207.
  Dishonor and notice of dishonor.
    Wrongful dishonor.
      Liability of payor bank to customer, CL
        §4-402.
  Documentary drafts.
    Dishonor, CL §4-503.
      Duty to notify customer, CL §4-501.
      Privilege of presenting bank to deal with
        goods, CL §4-504.
        Security interests for expenses, CL §4-504.
    Presentment.
      Duty to send for presentment, CL §4-501.
      "On arrival" drafts, CL §4-502.
      Responsibility of presenting bank, CL §4-503.
  Electronic presentment, CL §4-110.
  Funds transfers.
    Generally, CL §§4A-101 to 4A-507. See within
      this heading, "Funds transfers."
  Good faith.
    Obligation of good faith, CL §1-203.
  Holders in due course.
    When bank gives value for purposes of holder in
      due course, CL §4-211.
  Incapacitated persons.
    Effect of incompetence of customer, CL §4-405.
  Indorsements.
    Item indorsed "pay any bank," CL §4-201.
    Missing indorsements.
      Supplying, CL §4-205.
  Interpretation and construction.
    Applicability of article, CL §4-102.

COMMERCIAL CODE —Cont'd
Bank deposits and collections —Cont'd
  Interpretation and construction —Cont'd
    Commercial code's general provisions, CL
      §§1-101 to 1-208. See within this heading,
      "General provisions."
    Variation by agreement, CL §4-103.
  Liability.
    Collection of items.
      Liability of secondary parties, CL §4-212.
    Wrongful dishonor.
      Bank's liability to customer, CL §4-402.
  Limitation of actions, CL §4-111.
  Negligence.
    Unauthorized signature or alteration, CL
      §4-406.
  Ordinary care.
    Action constituting, CL §4-103.
  Payable through or payable at bank, CL §4-106.
  Payor banks.
    Collection of items.
      Death or incompetence of customer, CL
        §4-405.
      Deferred posting, CL §4-301.
      Dishonor of items.
        Generally. See within this heading,
          "Negotiable instruments."
        Time of dishonor, CL §4-301.
      Items subject to notice, stop-order, legal
        process or setoff, CL §4-303.
      Return of items.
        Late returns, CL §4-302.
        Method of recovery of payment, CL §4-301.
    Customer relationship.
      Alteration of instruments.
        Customer's duty to discover and report, CL
          §4-406.
      Charging customer's account.
        When allowed, CL §4-401.
      Death of customer, CL §4-405.
      Incompetency of customer, CL §4-405.
      Stale checks.
        Obligation of bank to pay, CL §4-404.
      Stop payment orders.
        Customer's right to issue, CL §4-403.
      Subrogation on improper payment.
        Right of payor bank, CL §4-407.
      Unauthorized signatures.
        Customer's duty to discover and report, CL
          §4-406.
      Wrongful dishonor.
        Liability to customer, CL §4-402.
    Defined, CL §4-105.
    Subrogation rights on improper payment, CL
      §4-407.
  Receipt of items.
    Time, CL §4-108.
  Refunds, CL §4-214.
  Separate offices of bank, CL §4-107.
  Setoffs.
    Items subject to setoff, CL §4-303.
  Signatures.
    Unauthorized signature of customer.
      Duty of customer to discover and report, CL
        §4-406.
  Stale checks, CL §4-404.
  Statute of limitations, CL §4-111.
  Stop-orders.
    Collection of items.
      Payor banks, CL §4-303.
    Customer's right to stop payment, CL §4-403.

COMMERCIAL CODE —Cont'd
Bank deposits and collections —Cont'd
Stop-orders —Cont'd
Payor bank's right to subrogation on improper
payment, CL §4-407.
Subrogation.
Payor bank's right on improper payment, CL
§4-407.
Time.
Dishonor and notice of dishonor.
Time of dishonor, CL §§4-109, 4-301.
Receipt of items, CL §4-108.
Title of article.
Short title, CL §4-101.
Warranties.
Documents of title, CL §7-508.
Wrongful dishonor.
Bank's liability to customer, CL §4-402.
Bulk transfers, CL §§6-101 to 6-111.
Applicability of article.
Enterprises and transfers subject to article, CL
§6-102.
Transfers excepted from article, CL §6-103.
Auction sales, CL §6-108.
Citation of article.
Short title, CL §6-101.
Creditors.
Lists, CL §6-104.
Notice to creditors, CL §§6-105, 6-107.
Protected creditors, CL §6-109.
Definitions.
Auctioneer, CL §6-108.
Enterprises.
Applicability of article, CL §6-102.
Equipment, CL §6-102.
Exemptions, CL §6-103.
Interpretation and construction.
Commercial code's general provisions, CL
§§1-101 to 1-208. See within this heading,
"General provisions."
Enterprises and transfers subject to article, CL
§6-102.
Transfers excepted from article, CL §6-103.
Levies, CL §6-111.
Limitation of actions, CL §6-111.
New business enterprises.
Transfer to new enterprise organized to take
over and continue business.
Excepted from article, CL §6-103.
Public notice, CL §6-106.
Notice to creditors, CL §§6-105, 6-107.
Schedule of property, CL §6-104.
Statute of limitations, CL §6-111.
Subsequent transfers, CL §6-110.
Title of article.
Short title, CL §6-101.
Documents of title, CL §§7-101 to 7-603.
Agriculture.
Warehouse receipts.
Storage of commodities under government
bond, CL §7-201.
Alcoholic beverages.
Warehouse receipts.
Storage under government bond, CL §7-201.
Alteration.
Bills of lading, CL §7-306.
Warehouse receipts, CL §7-208.
Attachment of goods.
Goods covered by negotiable document, CL
§7-602.

COMMERCIAL CODE —Cont'd
Documents of title —Cont'd
Bailments.
Law not modified or repealed, CL §7-103.
Bills of lading.
Altered bills, CL §7-306.
Care owing from carrier, CL §7-309.
Consignments.
Reconsignment, CL §7-303.
Contractual limitation of carrier's liability, CL
§7-309.
Delivery of goods, CL §7-303.
Description of goods.
Liability for misdescription, CL §7-301.
"Said to contain," CL §7-301.
"Shipper's weight, load and count," CL §7-301.
Destination bills, CL §7-305.
Diversion of goods, CL §7-303.
Generally, CL §§7-301 to 7-309.
Handling of goods.
Improper handling, CL §7-301.
Instructions.
Change, CL §7-303.
Liability.
Contractual limitation of carrier's liability, CL
§7-309.
Nonreceipt or misdescription of goods, CL
§7-301.
Lien of carrier, CL §7-307.
Enforcement, CL §7-308.
Naming person to be notified of arrival of goods.
Negotiability not limited, CL §7-501.
Negotiability, CL §7-104.
Negotiation.
Generally, CL §§7-501 to 7-509. See within
this subheading, "Negotiation and
transfer."
Overseas shipments, CL §2-323.
Receipt of goods.
Liability for nonreceipt, CL §7-301.
Sale of goods.
Enforcement of carrier's lien, CL §7-308.
Set of parts.
Tangible bill issued in, CL §7-304.
Third-party documents.
Prima facie evidence, CL §1-202.
Through bills and similar documents, CL
§7-302.
Transfer.
Generally, CL §§7-501 to 7-509. See within
this subheading, "Negotiation and
transfer."
Certain laws not repealed, CL §10-104.
Citation of article.
Short title, CL §7-101.
Claims.
Conflicting claims.
Interpleader, CL §7-603.
Commercial code's general provisions, CL §§1-101
to 1-208. See within this heading, "General
provisions."
Consignor and consignee.
Bills of lading.
Reconsignment, CL §7-303.
Construction and interpretation.
Certain laws not repealed, CL §10-104.
Relationship of article to treaty, statute, tariff,
classification or regulation, CL §7-103.
Contracts.
Bills of lading.
Limitation of carrier's liability, CL §7-309.

COMMERCIAL CODE —Cont'd
Documents of title —Cont'd
Contracts —Cont'd
Sale, lease or conditions of letter of credit.
Document adequate to fulfill obligations, CL §7-509.
Warehouse receipts.
Limitation of warehouse's liability, CL §7-204.
Crops.
Warehouse receipts.
Storage under government bond, CL §7-201.
Definitions, CL §7-102.
General commercial code definitions, CL §1-201.
Course of dealing, CL §1-205.
Reasonable time and seasonably, CL §1-204.
Usage of trade, CL §1-205.
Index of definitions, CL §7-102.
Delivery of goods.
Bills of lading, CL §7-303.
Excuses, CL §7-403.
Good faith delivery by bailee.
No liability, CL §7-404.
Negotiation and transfer.
Seller's stoppage of delivery.
Rights acquired in absence of due negotiation, CL §7-504.
Obligation of bailee, CL §7-403.
Description of goods.
Bills of lading.
Liability for misdescription, CL §7-301.
"Said to contain," CL §7-301.
"Shipper's weight, load and count," CL §7-301.
Misdescription, liability, CL §7-203.
Diversion of goods.
Bills of lading, CL §7-303.
Negotiation and transfer.
Rights acquired in absence of due negotiation.
Effect of diversion, CL §7-504.
Duplicates, CL §7-402.
Electronic documents of title.
Control, CL §7-106.
Negotiable documents.
Rules applicable, CL §7-501.
Substitute for tangible document, CL §7-105.
Tangible document issued as substitute for electronic document, CL §7-105.
Electronic signatures in global and national commerce act.
Title modifies, limits and supersedes, CL §7-103.
Forms.
Warehouse receipts, CL §7-202.
Fungible goods.
Warehouse receipts, CL §7-207.
Good faith.
Obligation of good faith, CL §1-203.
Guaranty.
Indorser of tangible document not guarantor for other parties, CL §7-505.
Handling of goods.
Bills of lading.
Improper handling, CL §7-301.
Household goods.
Warehouse's lien, CL §7-209.
Indorsement of nonnegotiable document, CL §7-501.
Indorsement of tangible document.
Delivery without indorsement, right to compel indorsement, CL §7-506.
Indorser not guarantor for other parties, CL §7-505.

COMMERCIAL CODE —Cont'd
Documents of title —Cont'd
Irregularities in issue or conduct of issuer, CL §7-401.
Laws not repealed, CL §10-104.
Liability.
Carrier's liability.
Contractual limitation of carrier's liability, CL §7-309.
Description of goods.
Liability for misdescription, CL §7-301.
Receipt of goods.
Liability for nonreceipt, CL §7-301.
Good faith delivery by bailee.
No liability, CL §7-404.
Nonreceipt or misdescription of goods, CL §7-203.
Warehouse's liability.
Contractual limitation of liability, CL §7-204.
Liens.
Carrier's lien, CL §7-307.
Enforcement, CL §7-308.
Warehouse lien, CL §§7-209, 7-210.
Lost instruments and records, CL §7-601.
Missing documents, CL §7-601.
Negotiability, CL §7-104.
Negotiation and transfer, CL §§7-501 to 7-509.
Delivery of goods.
Seller's stoppage of delivery.
Rights acquired in absence of due negotiation, CL §7-504.
Diversion of goods.
Rights acquired in absence of due negotiation.
Effect of diversion, CL §7-504.
Indorsement of tangible document.
Delivery without indorsement, right to compel indorsement, CL §7-506.
Indorser of tangible document not guarantor for other parties, CL §7-505.
Rights acquired.
Absence of due negotiation, CL §7-504.
Rights acquired by due negotiation, CL §7-502.
Rules applicable to negotiable documents, CL §7-501.
Title to goods.
Defeated in certain cases, CL §7-503.
Warranties, CL §7-507.
Collecting bank's warranties as to documents, CL §7-508.
Overissues, CL §7-402.
Receipt of goods.
Bills of lading.
Liability for nonreceipt, CL §7-301.
Nonreceipt, liability, CL §7-203.
Secured transactions.
Priority of security interests, CL §9-331.
Security interest.
Warehouse receipts.
Warehouse reserving against bailor, CL §7-209.
Separation of goods.
Warehouse receipts, CL §7-207.
Title of article.
Short title, CL §7-101.
Transfer.
Generally, CL §§7-501 to 7-509. See within this subheading, "Negotiation and transfer."
United States treaty or statute.
Relationship of article, CL §7-103.
Warehouse receipts.
Altered receipts, CL §7-208.

COMMERCIAL CODE —Cont'd
Documents of title —Cont'd
  Warehouse receipts —Cont'd
    Contractual limitation of liability, CL §7-204.
    Duty of care, CL §7-204.
    Forms, CL §7-202.
    Fungible goods, CL §7-207.
    Generally, CL §§7-202 to 7-210.
    Government bond.
      Storage under, CL §7-201.
    Household goods.
      Warehouse's lien, CL §7-209.
    Liability.
      Contractual limitation of liability, CL §7-204.
    Lien of warehouse, CL §7-209.
      Enforcement, CL §7-210.
    Removal of goods from warehouse.
      Warehouse requiring, CL §7-206.
    Sale of goods by warehouse, CL §7-206.
      Enforcement of warehouse lien, CL §7-210.
    Security interest.
      Warehouse reserving against bailor, CL §7-209.
    Separation of goods, CL §7-207.
    Termination of storage by warehouse, CL §7-206.
    Terms.
      Essential terms, CL §7-202.
      Optional terms, CL §7-202.
    Title defeated in certain cases, CL §7-205.
    Transfer.
      Generally, CL §§7-501 to 7-509. See within this subheading, "Negotiation and transfer."
    Who may issue, CL §7-201.
  Warranties.
    Negotiation and transfer, CL §7-507.
      Collecting bank's warranties as to documents, CL §7-508.
Funds transfers, CL §§4A-101 to 4A-507.
  Account of customer.
    Debit of account.
      Preclusion of objection, CL §4A-505.
  Account of sender.
    Order in which items may be charged to account, CL §4A-504.
    Order of withdrawals from account, CL §4A-504.
  Applicability of article, CL §4A-102.
  Bank deposits and collections, CL §§4-101 to 4-504. See within this heading, "Bank deposits and collections."
  Citation of article.
    Short title, CL §4A-101.
  Commercial code's general provisions, CL §§1-101 to 1-208. See within this heading, "General provisions."
  Conflict of laws, CL §4A-507.
    Federal electronic fund transfer act of 1978, CL §4A-107.
    Federal reserve regulations and operating circulars, CL §4A-107.
  Creditor process served on receiving bank, CL §4A-502.
  Definitions, CL §§4A-103 to 4A-105.
    Creditor process, CL §4A-502.
    Execution and execution date, CL §4A-301.
    Funds-transfer system rule, CL §4A-501.
    Payment date, CL §4A-401.
    Security procedure, CL §4A-201.

COMMERCIAL CODE —Cont'd
Funds transfers —Cont'd
  Discharge of underlying obligation.
    Payment of payment order by originator to beneficiary, CL §4A-406.
  Federal electronic fund transfer act of 1978.
    Applicability of article, CL §4A-108.
  Federal reserve regulations and operating circulars.
    Effect on article, CL §4A-107.
  Funds-transfer system rule, CL §4A-501.
  Injunctions, CL §4A-503.
  Instructions.
    Payment orders.
      Instruction to make more than one payment to a beneficiary.
        Effect as separate payment order with respect to each payment, CL §4A-103.
  Payment orders.
    Acceptance, CL §4A-209.
    Amendment, CL §4A-211.
    Authorized orders, CL §4A-202.
    Beneficiary bank's description.
      Misdescription, CL §4A-208.
    Beneficiary's description.
      Misdescription, CL §4A-207.
    Cancellation, CL §4A-211.
    Charging to account, CL §4A-504.
    Defined, CL §4A-103.
    Erroneous orders, CL §4A-205.
    Execution, CL §4A-301.
      Erroneous execution, CL §4A-303.
        Duty of sender to report, CL §4A-304.
      Failure to execute payment order.
        Liability, CL §4A-305.
      Improper execution.
        Liability, CL §4A-305.
      Late execution.
        Liability, CL §4A-305.
      Obligations of receiving bank, CL §4A-302.
    Execution date, CL §4A-301.
    Interest, CL §4A-506.
    Intermediary bank's description.
      Misdescription, CL §4A-208.
    Issuance.
      When sent, CL §4A-103.
    Payment.
      Obligation of beneficiary's bank to pay, CL §4A-404.
      Obligation of sender to pay receiving bank, CL §4A-402.
      Payment by beneficiary's bank to beneficiary, CL §4A-405.
      Payment by originator to beneficiary, CL §4A-406.
      Payment by sender to receiving bank, CL §4A-403.
    Payment date, CL §4A-401.
    Refund of payment, CL §4A-204.
      Unauthorized orders, CL §4A-204.
    Rejection, CL §4A-210.
      Liability and duty of receiving bank, CL §4A-212.
    Security procedure, CL §4A-201.
    Time received, CL §4A-106.
    Transmission, CL §4A-206.
    Unauthorized orders.
      Duty of customer to report, CL §4A-204.
      Verified orders, CL §4A-202.
      Unenforceability of certain orders, CL §4A-203.

COMMERCIAL CODE —Cont'd
Funds transfers —Cont'd
Restraining orders, CL §4A-503.
Security procedure, CL §4A-201.
Setoff by beneficiary's bank, CL §4A-502.
Short title, CL §4A-101.
Variation of article by agreement, CL §4A-501.
General provisions.
Acceleration at will.
Options, CL §1-208.
Acceptance under reservation of rights, CL §1-207.
Agreements.
Variation of code, CL §1-102.
Applicable law.
Parties' power to choose, CL §1-105.
Supplementary general principles of law, CL §1-103.
Captions of sections.
Construction, CL §1-109.
Citation of title.
Short title, CL §1-101.
Claims under code.
Waiver of renunciation of claim after breach, CL §1-107.
Construction and interpretation.
Course of dealing, CL §1-205.
General rules of construction, CL §1-102.
Implicit repeal.
Construction against, CL §1-104.
Parties' power to choose applicable law, CL §1-105.
Reasonable time, CL §1-204.
Remedies to be liberally administered, CL §1-106.
Seasonably, CL §1-204.
Definitions, CL §1-201.
Course of dealing, CL §1-205.
Seasonably, CL §1-204.
Usage of trade, CL §1-205.
Evidence.
Third-party documents.
Prima facie evidence, CL §1-202.
Good faith obligations, CL §1-203.
Legislative intent, CL §1-104.
Option to accelerate at will, CL §1-208.
Performance under reservation of rights, CL §1-207.
Purposes of code, CL §1-102.
Remedies to be liberally administered, CL §1-106.
Renunciation of claims or rights after breach, CL §1-107.
Section captions, CL §1-109.
Severability of provisions, CL §1-108.
Supplementary general principles of law.
Applicable, CL §1-103.
Territorial application of act, CL §1-105.
Time, CL §1-204.
Usage of trade, CL §1-205.
Severability of provisions, CL §1-108.
Short title, CL §1-101.
Statute of frauds.
Personal property not otherwise covered, CL §1-206.
Transitional provisions, CL §§10-101 to 10-112.
See within this heading, "Transitional provisions."
Variation of code by agreement, CL §1-102.
Waiver of claims or rights after breach, CL §1-107.
Investment securities, CL §§8-101 to 8-511.
Acquisition of security or interest therein, CL §8-104.

COMMERCIAL CODE —Cont'd
Investment securities —Cont'd
Adverse claims.
Notice, CL §8-105.
Persons not liable to adverse claimant, CL §8-115.
Securities entitlements.
Assertion of adverse claim against entitlement holder, CL §8-502.
Alteration of security certificate, CL §8-206.
Choice of law, CL §8-110.
Citation of article.
Short title, CL §8-101.
Clearing corporation rules.
Effectiveness, CL §8-111.
Commercial code's general provisions, CL §§1-101 to 1-208. See within this heading, "General provisions."
Completion of security certificate, CL §8-206.
Control, CL §8-106.
Creditor's legal process, CL §8-112.
Defenses.
Issuer's defenses.
Generally, CL §8-202.
Notice of defense, CL §§8-202, 8-203.
Definitions, CL §8-102.
General commercial code definitions, CL §1-201.
Course of dealing, CL §1-205.
Reasonable time and seasonably, CL §1-204.
Usage of trade, CL §1-205.
Delivery, CL §8-301.
Generally. See within this subheading, "Transfer."
Destroyed security certificates.
Notification to issuer, CL §8-406.
Replacement, CL §8-405.
Entitlement orders.
Defined, CL §8-102.
Effectiveness, CL §8-107.
Evidence.
Rules concerning certificated securities, CL §8-114.
Exchangeability of securities, CL §4-407.
Financial assets.
Acquisition of financial asset or interest therein, CL §8-104.
Defined, CL §8-102.
Rules for determining status as, CL §8-103.
Frauds, statute of.
Inapplicability, CL §8-113.
Good faith.
Obligation of good faith, CL §1-203.
Indorsements, CL §8-304.
Defined, CL §8-102.
Effectiveness, CL §8-107.
Guaranteeing signature, indorsement or instruction.
Effect, CL §8-306.
Registration of securities.
Assurance that indorsements are effective, CL §8-402.
Duty of issuer to register transfer, CL §8-401.
Instructions, CL §8-305.
Assurance that instructions are effective, CL §8-402.
Defined, CL §8-102.
Effectiveness, CL §8-107.
Guaranteeing signature, indorsement or instruction.
Effect, CL §8-306.

COMMERCIAL CODE —Cont'd
Investment securities —Cont'd
  Issuers.
    Defenses.
      Generally, CL §8-202.
      Notice of defense, CL §§8-202, 8-203.
    Defined, CL §8-201.
    Liens, CL §8-209.
    Registration.
      Transfer of security.
        Duty of issuer, CL §8-401.
    Responsibility, CL §8-202.
    Rights with respect to registered owners, CL §8-207.
    Transfer restrictions.
      Effect, CL §8-204.
  Issues.
    Overissues.
      Defined, CL §8-210.
      Effect, CL §8-210.
  Liens.
    Issuer's lien, CL §8-209.
  Lost security certificates.
    Notification of issuer, CL §8-406.
    Replacement, CL §8-405.
  Notice.
    Adverse claims, CL §8-105.
    Defects or defenses, CL §§8-202, 8-203.
    Lost, destroyed or wrongfully taken security certificate.
      Obligation to notify issuer, CL §8-406.
  Overissues.
    Defined, CL §8-210.
    Effect, CL §8-210.
  Purchasers.
    Delivery to, CL §8-301.
    Protected purchaser, CL §8-303.
    Requisites for registration of transfer.
      Right of purchaser to, CL §8-307.
    Rights acquired, CL §8-302.
      Protected purchaser, CL §8-303.
  Registration.
    Assurance that indorsements are effective, CL §8-402.
    Authenticating trustee's duty, CL §8-407.
    Demand that issuer not register transfer, CL §8-403.
    Issuers.
      Rights with respect to registered owners, CL §8-207.
    Registrar's duty, CL §8-407.
    Replacement of lost, destroyed or wrongfully taken security certificates, CL §8-405.
    Requisites for registration of transfer.
      Purchaser's right to, CL §8-307.
    Signature of registrar.
      Effect, CL §8-208.
    Transfer.
      Duty of issuer to register transfer, CL §8-401.
      Duty of transfer agent, CL §8-407.
    Wrongful registration, CL §8-404.
  Secured transactions.
    Priority of security interests, CL §9-331.
    Security entitlements.
      Priority among security interest and entitlement holders, CL §8-511.
  Securities intermediaries.
    Adverse claims.
      Not liable to adverse claimant, CL §8-115.
    Defined, CL §8-102.
    Purchaser for value, CL §8-116.

COMMERCIAL CODE —Cont'd
Investment securities —Cont'd
  Security entitlements.
    Adverse claims.
      Assertion against entitlement holder, CL §8-502.
    Defined, CL §8-102.
    Priority among security interest and entitlement holders, CL §8-511.
    Purchaser of security entitlement from entitlement holder.
      Rights, CL §8-510.
    Securities account.
      Defined, CL §8-501.
    Securities intermediary.
      Acquisition from, CL §8-501.
      Change of entitlement holder's position to other form of security holding.
        Duty, CL §8-508.
      Compliance with entitlement order.
        Duty, CL §8-507.
      Duties, CL §§8-504 to 8-509.
      Exercise of rights as directed by entitlement holder.
        Duty, CL §8-506.
      Financial asset held by.
        Duty to maintain, CL §8-504.
        Property interest of entitlement holder in, CL §8-503.
      Manner of performance of duties, CL §8-509.
      Payments and distributions.
        Duty with respect to, CL §8-505.
      Specification of duties by other statute or regulation, CL §8-509.
    Security interest.
      Priority among security interest and entitlement holders, CL §8-511.
  Signatures.
    Authenticating trustee's, registrar's or transfer agent's signature.
      Effect, CL §8-208.
    Guaranteeing signature.
      Effect, CL §8-306.
    Unauthorized signature on security certificate.
      Effect, CL §8-205.
  Statute of frauds.
    Inapplicable, CL §8-113.
  Title of article.
    Short title, CL §8-101.
  Transfer.
    Agent's duties as to registration, CL §8-407.
    Agent's signature.
      Effect, CL §8-208.
    Issuer's restrictions.
      Effect, CL §8-204.
    Registration.
      Duty of issuer to register transfer, CL §8-401.
      Duty of transfer agent, CL §8-407.
  Trusts and trustees.
    Authenticating trustee.
      Registration of securities.
        Duties, CL §8-407.
      Signature.
        Effect, CL §8-208.
  Warranties.
    Direct holding, CL §8-108.
    Effect of signature of authenticating trustee, registrar or transfer agent, CL §8-208.
    Guaranteeing signature, endorsement or instruction.
      Effect, CL §8-306.

COMMERCIAL CODE —Cont'd
Investment securities —Cont'd
  Warranties —Cont'd
    Indirect holding, CL §8-109.
  Wrongfully taken security certificates.
    Notification to issuer, CL §8-406.
    Replacement, CL §8-405.
  Wrongful registration, CL §8-404.
Leases.
  Acceptance of goods, CL §2A-515.
    Accessions.
      Lessor's and lessee's rights when goods
        become accessions, CL §2A-310.
    Burden of establishing default after acceptance,
      CL §2A-516.
    Damages.
      Lessor's damages for nonacceptance, CL
        §2A-528.
    Effect, CL §2A-516.
    Nonconforming goods or delivery of goods, CL
      §2A-509.
    Notice of default, CL §2A-516.
    Rejection of goods. See within this subheading,
      "Shipment and delivery."
    Revocation of acceptance, CL §2A-517.
      Damages, CL §2A-519.
      Justifiable revocation, CL §2A-517.
        Lessee's rights and remedies, CL §2A-508.
      Wrongful revocation, CL §2A-523.
  Accessions.
    Defined, CL §§2A-103, 2A-310.
    Lessor's and lessee's rights.
      When goods become accessions, CL §2A-310.
  Alienability of interest.
    Lessor's residual interest in goods, CL §2A-303.
    Party's interest under lease contract, CL
      §2A-303.
  Animals.
    Unborn young.
      Definition of "goods," CL §2A-103.
      Identification, CL §2A-217.
  Anticipatory repudiation, CL §2A-402.
    Retraction, CL §2A-403.
  Applicability of article.
    Certificates of title.
      Territorial application of article to goods
        covered by certificates, CL §2A-105.
    Leases subject to other statutes, CL §2A-104.
    Scope, CL §2A-102.
  Assignments, CL §2A-303.
  Attorneys' fees.
    Unconscionable lease contracts or clauses, CL
      §2A-108.
  Cancellation.
    Defined, CL §2A-103.
    Effect on rights and remedies, CL §2A-505.
    Lessor's remedies, CL §2A-523.
  Casualty to identified goods, CL §2A-221.
  Citation of article, CL §2A-101.
  Claims.
    Limitation of actions, CL §2A-506.
    Notice of claim to person answerable over, CL
      §2A-516.
    Rent.
      Action by lessor, CL §2A-529.
    Third parties.
      Standing to sue for injury to goods, CL
        §2A-531.
    Waiver or renunciation, CL §2A-107.
  Commercial code's general provisions, CL §§1-101
    to 1-208. See within this heading, "General
    provisions."

COMMERCIAL CODE —Cont'd
Leases —Cont'd
  Conflict of laws.
    Leases subject to other statutes, CL §2A-104.
    Limitation on power of parties to choose
      applicable law and judicial forum, CL
      §2A-106.
  Construction of lease agreements.
    Course of performance, CL §2A-207.
    Practical construction, CL §2A-207.
  Consumer leases.
    Choice of judicial forum, CL §2A-106.
    Defined, CL §2A-103.
    Option to accelerate at will, CL §2A-109.
    Unconscionability, CL §2A-108.
  Cover by lessor, CL §2A-518.
  Creditors' special rights, CL §2A-308.
  Damages.
    Acceptance of goods.
      Nonacceptance.
        Lessor's damages, CL §2A-528.
    Consequential damages, CL §2A-520.
    Cover by lessor.
      Effect, CL §2A-518.
    Incidental damages, CL §2A-520.
      Lessor's damages, CL §2A-530.
    Lessee's incidental and consequential damages.
      Generally, CL §2A-520.
    Lessor's damages.
      Generally, CL §2A-523.
      Incidental damages, CL §2A-530.
      Nonacceptance or repudiation by lessee, CL
        §2A-528.
      Residual interest, CL §2A-532.
    Liquidation, CL §2A-504.
    Nondelivery of goods, CL §2A-519.
    Rejection of goods, CL §2A-519.
    Repudiation by lessee.
      Lessor's damages, CL §2A-528.
    Repudiation by lessor, CL §2A-519.
    Revocation of acceptance of goods, CL §2A-519.
    Warranties.
      Breach of warranty, CL §§2A-508, 2A-519.
  Default.
    Anticipatory repudiation, CL §§2A-402, 2A-403.
    Cover.
      Right of lessor, CL §2A-518.
    Installment lease contracts.
      Lessee's rights and remedies, CL §2A-508.
      Rejection and default, CL §2A-510.
    Limitation of actions, CL §2A-506.
    Modification or impairment, CL §2A-503.
    Notice, CL §§2A-502, 2A-516.
    Procedure generally, CL §2A-501.
    Replevin of goods, CL §§2A-508, 2A-521.
    Rights and remedies.
      Default by lessee.
        Disposal of goods by lessor, CL §§2A-523,
          2A-524, 2A-527.
        Identification of goods to lease contract, CL
          §2A-524.
        Possession of goods, CL §§2A-523, 2A-525.
        Rent action by lessor, CL §2A-529.
      Default by lessor.
        Cover, CL §2A-518.
        Lessee's rights and remedies generally, CL
          §2A-508.
        Nonconforming goods or delivery of goods,
          CL §§2A-509, 2A-510.
        Replevy of goods, CL §§2A-508, 2A-521.
        Specific performance, CL §§2A-508, 2A-521.

COMMERCIAL CODE —Cont'd
Leases —Cont'd
Default —Cont'd
Rights and remedies —Cont'd
Default by lessor —Cont'd
Substitute goods, CL §2A-518.
Waiver or renunciation of rights after default, CL §2A-107.
Risk of loss.
Effect of default on risk, CL §2A-220.
Defenses.
Unconscionability, CL §2A-108.
Definitions, CL §2A-103.
Accessions, CL §2A-310.
Fixtures, CL §§2A-103, 2A-309.
Index of definitions, CL §2A-103.
Delegation of performance, CL §2A-303.
Delivery of goods.
Generally. See within this subheading, "Shipment and delivery."
Disposal of goods.
Lessor's rights and remedies, CL §§2A-523, 2A-524, 2A-527.
Documents of title.
Document adequate to fulfill obligations of contract, CL §7-509.
Enforcement of lease contract, CL §2A-301.
Evidence.
Extrinsic evidence, CL §2A-202.
Excused performance, CL §2A-405.
Procedure on excused performance, CL §2A-406.
Express warranties.
Generally, CL §2A-210.
Third-party beneficiaries, CL §2A-216.
Extrinsic evidence, CL §2A-202.
Finance leases.
Defined, CL §2A-103.
Irrevocable promises, CL §2A-407.
Lessee under finance lease as beneficiary of supply contract, CL §2A-209.
Losses.
Casualty to identified goods, CL §2A-221.
Risk of loss, CL §2A-219.
Supply contracts.
Lessee under finance lease as beneficiary, CL §2A-209.
Warranties.
Implied warranty of fitness for particular purpose, CL §2A-213.
Implied warranty of merchantability, CL §2A-212.
Warranty against infringement, CL §2A-211.
Firm offers, CL §2A-205.
Fitness for particular purpose.
Implied warranties, CL §2A-213.
Fixtures.
Defined, CL §§2A-103, 2A-309.
Lessor's and lessee's rights.
When goods become fixtures, CL §2A-309.
Formation.
Firm offers, CL §2A-205.
Generally, CL §2A-204.
Offer and acceptance.
Firm offers, CL §2A-205.
Generally, CL §2A-206.
Fraud.
Effect on rights and remedies, CL §2A-505.
Identification of goods, CL §2A-217.
Casualty to identified goods, CL §2A-221.
Insurable interest in existing goods.
Vesting in lessee, CL §2A-218.

COMMERCIAL CODE —Cont'd
Leases —Cont'd
Identification of goods —Cont'd
Lessor's right to identify goods upon lessee's default, CL §2A-524.
Implied warranties.
Fitness for particular purpose, CL §2A-213.
Merchantability, CL §2A-212.
Third-party beneficiaries, CL §2A-216.
Infringement.
Warranty against, CL §2A-211.
Insecurity.
Adequate assurance of performance, CL §2A-401.
Insolvency of lessor.
Lessee's rights to goods, CL §2A-522.
Installment lease contracts.
Default.
Lessee's rights and remedies, CL §2A-508.
Rejection and default, CL §2A-510.
Defined, CL §2A-103.
Insurance, CL §2A-218.
Interference with goods.
Warranty against interference, CL §2A-211.
Liens.
Defined, CL §2A-103.
Priority of certain liens arising by operation of law, CL §2A-306.
Priority of liens arising by attachment or levy on, security interest in and other claims to goods, CL §2A-307.
Limitation of actions.
Action for default, CL §2A-506.
Losses.
Casualty to identified goods, CL §2A-221.
Risk of loss, CL §2A-219.
Effect of default, CL §2A-220.
Market rent.
Proof, CL §2A-507.
Merchantability.
Implied warranties, CL §2A-212.
Merchant lessees.
Defined, CL §2A-103.
Rightfully rejected goods.
Duties, CL §2A-511.
Modification, CL §2A-208.
Notice.
Default, CL §§2A-502, 2A-516.
Objections to goods.
Waiver of lessee's objections, CL §2A-514.
Offer and acceptance.
Firm offers, CL §2A-205.
Generally, CL §2A-206.
Parol evidence, CL §2A-202.
Payment or performance.
Course of performance.
Construction of lease agreements, CL §2A-207.
Delegation of performance, CL §2A-303.
Excused performance, CL §2A-405.
Procedure on excused performance, CL §2A-406.
Insecurity.
Adequate assurance of performance, CL §2A-401.
Option to accelerate at will, CL §2A-109.
Repudiation. See within this subheading, "Repudiation."
Substituted performance, CL §2A-404.
Possession of goods, CL §2A-302.
Lessor's rights and remedies, CL §§2A-523, 2A-525.

COMMERCIAL CODE —Cont'd
Leases —Cont'd
Priorities.
  Liens.
    Certain liens arising by operation of law, CL
      §2A-306.
    Liens arising by attachment or levy on,
      security interest in and other claims to
      goods, CL §2A-307.
  Subordination of priority, CL §2A-311.
Promises.
  Irrevocable promises, CL §2A-407.
Rejection of goods. See within this subheading,
  "Shipment and delivery."
Remedies. See within this subheading, "Rights
  and remedies."
Rent.
  Action by lessor for rent, CL §2A-529.
  Proof of market rent, CL §2A-507.
Replevy of goods, CL §§2A-508, 2A-521.
Repudiation.
  Anticipatory repudiation, CL §2A-402.
    Retraction, CL §2A-403.
  Damages.
    Lessee's damages, CL §2A-519.
    Lessor's damages, CL §2A-528.
  Insecurity.
    Failure to provide adequate assurance of
      performance, CL §2A-401.
  Lessee's rights and remedies.
    Damages for repudiation, CL §2A-519.
  Lessor's remedies, CL §2A-523.
Rescission, CL §2A-208.
  Effect on rights and remedies, CL §2A-505.
Rights and remedies.
  Cancellation, termination, rescission or fraud.
    Effect on rights and remedies, CL §2A-505.
  Default by lessee.
    Disposal of goods by lessor, CL §§2A-523,
      2A-524, 2A-527.
    Identification of goods to lease contract, CL
      §2A-524.
    Lessor's remedies generally, CL §2A-523.
      Residual interest, CL §2A-532.
    Possession of goods, CL §§2A-523, 2A-525.
    Rent.
      Action by lessor, CL §2A-529.
    Stoppage of delivery of goods, CL §§2A-523,
      2A-526.
  Default by lessor.
    Lessee's rights and remedies generally, CL
      §2A-508.
    Nonconforming goods or delivery of goods, CL
      §§2A-509, 2A-510.
    Replevin of goods, CL §2A-508.
    Specific performance, CL §2A-508.
  Installment lease contracts.
    Lessee's rights and remedies, CL §2A-508.
    Modification or impairment, CL §2A-503.
Risk of loss, CL §2A-219.
  Effect of default, CL §2A-220.
Sales.
  Sale of goods by lessee, CL §2A-305.
Scope of article, CL §2A-102.
Seals.
  Inoperative to render lease a sealed instrument,
    CL §2A-203.
Secured transactions.
  Security interests arising under provisions, CL
    §9-110.

COMMERCIAL CODE —Cont'd
Leases —Cont'd
Shipment and delivery.
  Acceptance of goods, CL §2A-515.
    Accessions.
      Lessor's and lessee's rights when goods
        become accessions, CL §2A-310.
    Burden of establishing default after
      acceptance, CL §2A-516.
    Damages.
      Lessor's damages for nonacceptance, CL
        §2A-528.
    Effect, CL §2A-516.
    Nonconforming goods or delivery, CL §2A-509.
    Notice of default, CL §2A-516.
    Revocation of acceptance, CL §2A-517.
      Damages, CL §2A-519.
      Justifiable revocation, CL §§2A-508,
        2A-517.
      Wrongful revocation, CL §2A-523.
  Casualty to identified goods, CL §2A-221.
  Failure to deliver goods.
    Lessee's rights and remedies, CL §2A-508.
  Identification of goods, CL §2A-217.
  Improper tender or delivery.
    Burden of establishing default after
      acceptance of goods, CL §2A-516.
    Cure by lessor, CL §2A-513.
    Lessee's rights.
      Installment lease contracts, CL §2A-510.
    Notice of default after acceptance of goods, CL
      §2A-516.
    Objection by lessee.
      Waiver, CL §2A-514.
  Notice of default.
    Accepted goods, CL §2A-516.
  Rejection of goods.
    Accepted goods.
      Rejection precluded, CL §2A-516.
    Cure by lessor, CL §2A-513.
    Damages, CL §2A-519.
    Installment lease contracts, CL §2A-510.
    Replacement of rejected goods.
      Cure by lessor, CL §2A-513.
    Rightfully rejected goods, CL §2A-509.
      Lessee's duties generally, CL §2A-512.
      Lessee's rights and remedies, CL §2A-508.
      Merchant lessee's duties, CL §2A-511.
    Wrongfully rejected goods.
      Lessor's remedies, CL §2A-523.
  Revocation of acceptance of goods, CL §2A-517.
    Damages, CL §2A-519.
    Justifiable revocation, CL §2A-517.
      Lessee's rights and remedies, CL §2A-508.
    Wrongful revocation, CL §2A-523.
  Stoppage of delivery.
    Failure of agreed means or manner of
      payment, CL §2A-404.
    Lessor's remedies, CL §§2A-523, 2A-526.
  Subsequent lease of goods by lessor, CL
    §2A-304.
  Withholding delivery.
    Failure of agreed means or manner of
      payment, CL §2A-404.
Special rights of creditors, CL §2A-308.
Specific performance, CL §§2A-208, 2A-521.
Statute of frauds, CL §2A-201.
Sublease by lessee, CL §2A-305.
Subsequent lease of goods by lessor, CL §2A-304.
Substituted performance, CL §2A-404.

COMMERCIAL CODE —Cont'd
Leases —Cont'd
Substitute goods, CL §2A-518.
Cover by lessor, CL §2A-518.
Supply contracts.
Beneficiaries.
Lessee under finance lease, CL §2A-209.
Defined, CL §2A-103.
Termination.
Effect on rights and remedies, CL §2A-505.
Third parties.
Standing to sue for injury to goods, CL §2A-531.
Warranties.
Third-party beneficiaries, CL §2A-216.
Title of article.
Short title, CL §2A-101.
Title to goods, CL §2A-302.
Infringement.
Warranty against, CL §2A-211.
Unconscionability, CL §2A-108.
Waiver.
Claims, rights after default or breach of
warranty, CL §2A-107.
Generally, CL §2A-208.
Objections by lessee to goods, CL §2A-514.
Warranties.
Breach of warranty.
Damages, CL §§2A-508, 2A-519.
Notice of claim or litigation answerable over,
CL §2A-516.
Waiver or renunciation of rights after breach,
CL §2A-107.
Cumulation and conflict, CL §2A-215.
Damages.
Breach of warranty, CL §§2A-508, 2A-519.
Exclusion, CL §2A-214.
Limitation of exclusion, CL §2A-214.1.
Express warranties.
Generally, CL §2A-210.
Third-party beneficiaries, CL §2A-216.
Fitness for particular purpose.
Implied warranties, CL §2A-213.
Implied warranties.
Fitness for particular purpose, CL §2A-213.
Merchantability, CL §2A-212.
Third-party beneficiaries, CL §2A-216.
Infringement.
Warranty against, CL §2A-211.
Interference with goods.
Warranty against, CL §2A-211.
Merchantability.
Implied warranties, CL §2A-212.
Modification, CL §2A-214.
Limitation of modification, CL §2A-214.1.
Third-party beneficiaries, CL §2A-216.
Letters of credit, CL §§5-101 to 5-118.
Adviser, CL §5-107.
Amendment, CL §5-106.
Applicant.
Subrogation, CL §5-117.
Attorneys' fees.
Actions for remedies, CL §5-111.
Beneficiaries.
Secured transactions.
Superior rights of beneficiary or nominated
person under letter, CL §9-109.
Cancellation, CL §5-106.
Choice of law and forum, CL §5-116.
Citation of article.
Short title, CL §5-101.

COMMERCIAL CODE —Cont'd
Letters of credit —Cont'd
Commercial code's general provision, CL §§1-101
to 1-208. See within this heading, "General
provisions."
Confirmer, CL §5-107.
Consideration, CL §5-105.
Contracts.
Sale of goods, CL §2-325.
Damages, CL §5-111.
Definitions, CL §5-102.
General commercial code definitions, CL §1-201.
Reasonable time and seasonably, CL §1-204.
Index of definitions, CL §5-102.
Proceeds of a letter of credit, CL §5-114.
Dishonor.
Wrongful dishonor.
Remedies, CL §5-111.
Documents of title.
Document adequate to fulfill obligations of
contract, CL §7-509.
Duration, CL §5-106.
Forgery, CL §5-109.
Formal requirements, CL §5-104.
Fraud, CL §5-109.
Good faith.
Obligation of good faith, CL §1-203.
Issuance, CL §5-106.
Issuer.
Rights and obligations, CL §5-108.
Security interest of, CL §5-118.
Subrogation, CL §5-117.
Wrongful dishonor or repudiation of obligation.
Remedies, CL §5-111.
Limitation of actions, CL §5-115.
Nominated person, CL §5-107.
Secured transactions.
Superior rights of beneficiary or nominated
person under letter, CL §9-109.
Security interest of, CL §5-118.
Subrogation, CL §5-117.
Proceeds of a letter of credit.
Assignment, CL §5-114.
Defined, CL §5-114.
Remedies, CL §5-111.
Sale of goods.
Contracts, CL §2-325.
Scope of article, CL §5-103.
Secured transactions.
Applicability of article 9.
Superior rights of beneficiary or nominated
person under letter, CL §9-109.
Security interest of issuer or nominated person,
CL §5-118.
Signatures, CL §5-104.
Statute of limitations, CL §5-115.
Subrogation.
Issuer, applicant and nominated person, CL
§5-117.
Title of article.
Short title, CL §5-101.
Transfer, CL §5-112.
Operation of law, CL §5-113.
Warranties, CL §5-110.
Wrongful dishonor.
Remedies, CL §5-111.
Negotiable instruments, CL §§3-101 to 3-605.
Acceptance.
Defined, CL §3-409.
Acceptance by mistake.
Liability, CL §3-418.

COMMERCIAL CODE —Cont'd
Negotiable instruments —Cont'd
Acceptor.
    Defined, CL §3-103.
    Liability, CL §3-116.
    Obligation of acceptor.
        Liability, CL §3-413.
Accommodation party.
    Discharge of accommodation party, CL §3-605.
    Instruments signed for accommodation.
        Liability, CL §3-419.
Accord and satisfaction.
    By use of instrument, CL §3-311.
Actions.
    Notice of right to defend action, CL §3-119.
Agreements affecting instrument, CL §3-117.
Alteration of instrument.
    Defined, CL §3-407.
    Negligence contributing to, CL §3-406.
Antedated instruments, CL §3-113.
Applicability of article, CL §3-102.
"As originally drawn" defined, CL §3-413.
Breach of fiduciary duty.
    Notice, CL §3-307.
Burden of proof.
    Incomplete instrument, CL §3-115.
Cancellation.
    Discharge by cancellation, CL §3-604.
Cashier's check.
    Defined as negotiable instrument, CL §3-104.
    Effect of obligation for which taken, CL §3-310.
    Lost, destroyed or stolen, CL §3-312.
    Obligation of issuer.
        Liability, CL §3-412.
    Refusal to pay.
        Liability, CL §3-411.
Certificate of deposit.
    Defined as negotiable instrument, CL §3-104.
Certified check.
    Acceptance.
        Liability, CL §3-409.
    Defined, CL §3-409.
    Effect on obligation for which taken, CL §3-310.
    Lost, destroyed or stolen, CL §3-312.
    Refusal to pay.
        Liability, CL §3-411.
Check.
    Defined, CL §§3-104, 3-312.
    Dishonor.
        Rules governing, CL §3-502.
    Effect on obligation for which taken, CL §3-310.
Citation of title, CL §3-101.
Claimant.
    Defined, CL §3-312.
Claims in recoupment, CL §3-305.
Claims to an instrument, CL §3-306.
Comparative negligence.
    Forged signature or alteration of instrument,
        CL §3-406.
Conflict of laws, CL §3-102.
Consideration.
    Defined, CL §3-303.
Contradictory terms of instrument, CL §3-114.
Contribution, CL §3-116.
Contributory negligence.
    Forged signature or alteration of instrument,
        CL §3-406.
Conversion of instrument.
    Liability, CL §3-420.
Date of instrument, CL §3-113.

COMMERCIAL CODE —Cont'd
Negotiable instruments —Cont'd
Declaration of loss.
    Defined, CL §3-312.
Defenses in recoupment, CL §3-305.
Definitions, CL §3-103.
Destroyed instrument, CL §3-309.
Discharge and payment.
    Accommodation parties, CL §3-605.
    Cancellation, CL §3-604.
    Effect of discharge, CL §3-601.
    Indorsers, CL §3-605.
    Renunciation, CL §3-604.
    Stolen instrument, CL §3-602.
    Tender of payment, CL §3-603.
    When payable, CL §3-602.
    Wrongful possession of instrument, CL §3-602.
Dishonor.
    Certificate of dishonor, CL §3-505.
    Evidence of, CL §3-505.
    Form, CL §3-503.
        Evidence of dishonor, CL §3-505.
    Notice, CL §3-503.
        Excused presentment, CL §3-504.
        How given, CL §3-503.
    Presentment, CL §3-501.
    Presumption of, CL §3-505.
    Protest.
        Defined, CL §3-505.
    Special provisions, CL §3-502.
Draft.
    Acceptance of draft.
        Liability, CL §3-409.
    Acceptance of varying draft.
        Liability, CL §3-410.
    Defined as negotiable instrument, CL §3-104.
    Dishonor.
        Rules governing, CL §3-502.
    Unaccepted draft.
        Drawee liability, CL §3-408.
Drawee.
    Defined, CL §3-103.
Drawer.
    Defined, CL §3-103.
    Liability, CL §3-116.
    Obligation of drawer.
        Liability, CL §3-414.
Employee.
    Defined, CL §3-405.
    Fraudulent indorsement.
        Employer's responsibility for, CL §3-405.
Evidence.
    Parol evidence, CL §3-117.
Evidence of dishonor, CL §3-505.
Excused presentment.
    Notice of dishonor, CL §3-504.
Fictitious payees.
    Liability, CL §3-404.
Fiduciaries.
    Breach of duty, CL §3-307.
Foreign money.
    Instrument payable in, CL §3-107.
Good faith.
    Defined, CL §3-103.
Holder in due course.
    Defined, CL §3-302.
    Proof of signatures and status, CL §3-308.
    Signatures and status.
        Proof of, CL §3-308.
    Special provisions, CL §3-302.

COMMERCIAL CODE —Cont'd
Negotiable instruments —Cont'd
Identification of person to whom instrument
    payable, CL §3-110.
Impostors.
    Liability, CL §3-404.
Incomplete instrument.
    Defined, CL §3-115.
Index of definitions, CL §3-103.
Indorsement.
    Anomalous indorsement, CL §3-205.
    Blank indorsement, CL §3-205.
    Defined, CL §3-204.
    Employee.
        Fraudulent indorsement.
            Employer's responsibility for, CL §3-405.
    Restrictive indorsement, CL §3-206.
    Special indorsement, CL §3-205.
    Without recourse.
        Obligation of indorser, CL §3-415.
Indorser.
    Discharge of indorsers, CL §3-605.
    Joint and several liability, CL §3-116.
    Liability, CL §3-415.
Interest.
    Instrument not payable with interest, CL
        §3-112.
    Interest-bearing instrument.
        Date interest payable, CL §3-112.
Issue.
    Defined, CL §3-105.
Issuer.
    Defined, CL §3-105.
    Liability, CL §3-412.
Joint and several liability, CL §3-116.
Liability of parties, CL §§3-401 to 3-420.
Limitation of actions, CL §3-118.
Lost instrument, CL §3-309.
Maker.
    Defined, CL §3-103.
    Liability, CL §3-116.
Negligence.
    Forged signature or alteration of instrument,
        CL §3-406.
Negotiable instrument defined, CL §3-104.
Negotiation.
    Defined, CL §3-201.
    Rescission, CL §3-202.
    Transfer of instruments, CL §3-201.
        Rights acquired by transfer, CL §3-203.
Note.
    Defined as negotiable instrument, CL §3-104.
    Dishonor.
        Rules governing, CL §3-502.
    Effect on obligation for which taken, CL §3-310.
    Obligation of issuer.
        Liability, CL §3-412.
Notice.
    Breach of fiduciary duty, CL §3-307.
    Third party written notice.
        Right to defend action, CL §3-119.
Notice of dishonor, CL §3-503.
    Excused presentment, CL §3-504.
    Form, CL §3-503.
        Evidence of dishonor, CL §3-505.
Obligated bank.
    Defined, CL §§3-312, 3-411.
    Wrongful refusal to pay negotiable instrument.
        Liability, CL §3-411.
Order.
    Defined, CL §3-103.

COMMERCIAL CODE —Cont'd
Negotiable instruments —Cont'd
Order —Cont'd
    Payable at a definite time.
        Defined, CL §3-108.
    Payable on demand.
        Defined, CL §3-108.
    Payable to bearer.
        Defined, CL §3-109.
    Payable to order.
        Defined, CL §3-109.
    Unconditional order.
        Defined, CL §3-106.
Ordinary care.
    Defined, CL §3-103.
Overdue instrument, CL §3-304.
Party.
    Defined, CL §3-103.
Payment by mistake.
    Liability, CL §3-418.
Person entitled to enforce.
    Defined, CL §3-301.
Place of payment, CL §3-111.
Postdated instruments, CL §3-113.
Presentment.
    Defined, CL §3-501.
    Excused presentment, CL §3-504.
        Notice of dishonor, CL §3-504.
    Rules governing, CL §3-501.
    Warranties, CL §3-417.
Presumption of dishonor, CL §3-505.
Promise.
    Defined, CL §3-103.
    Payable at a definite time.
        Defined, CL §3-108.
    Payable on demand.
        Defined, CL §3-108.
    Payable to bearer.
        Defined, CL §3-109.
    Payable to order.
        Defined, CL §3-109.
    Unconditional promise.
        Defined, CL §3-106.
Protest.
    Defined, CL §3-505.
Prove.
    Defined, CL §3-103.
Reacquisition of instrument, CL §3-207.
Recoupment.
    Defense and claims in recoupment, CL §3-305.
Refusal to pay, CL §3-411.
Remitter.
    Defined, CL §3-103.
Renunciation.
    Discharge by renunciation, CL §3-604.
Represented person.
    Defined, CL §3-307.
Scope of article, CL §3-102.
Secured transactions.
    Priority of security interests, CL §9-331.
Short title, CL §3-101.
Signature.
    By representative.
        Liability, CL §3-402.
    Forged signature.
        Negligence contributing to, CL §3-406.
    Liability, CL §3-401.
    Unauthorized signature.
        Liability, CL §3-403.
Statute of limitations, CL §3-118.
Stolen instrument, CL §3-309.

COMMERCIAL CODE —Cont'd
Negotiable instruments —Cont'd
  Teller's check.
    Defined as negotiable instrument, CL §3-104.
    Effect of obligation for which taken, CL §3-310.
    Lost, destroyed or stolen, CL §3-312.
    Refusal to pay.
      Liability, CL §3-411.
  Tender of payment, CL §3-603.
  Third parties.
    Notice of right to defend action, CL §3-119.
  Title of article, CL §3-101.
  Transfer of instrument.
    Bank deposits and collections.
      Collection by depositary and collecting banks.
        Transfer of warranties, CL §4-207.
    Negotiation, CL §3-201.
    Reacquisition, CL §3-207.
    Rights acquired, CL §3-203.
    Value and consideration, CL §3-303.
    Warranties, CL §3-416.
  Traveler's check.
    Defined as negotiable instrument, CL §3-104.
  Unauthorized signature.
    Liability, CL §3-403.
  Warranties.
    Presentment warranties, CL §3-417.
    Transfer warranties, CL §3-416.
Sale of goods, CL §§2-101 to 2-725.
  Acceptance of goods.
    Breach in regard to accepted goods.
      Buyer's damages, CL §2-714.
    Effect of acceptance, CL §2-607.
    Nonacceptance.
      Seller's damages, CL §2-708.
    Obligation of buyer, CL §2-301.
    Rejection of goods. See within this subheading,
      "Rejection of goods."
    Revocation in whole or in part, CL §§2-607,
      2-608.
    Buyer's remedies.
      Enumerated, CL §2-711.
    Seller's remedies.
      Enumerated, CL §2-703.
    What constitutes, CL §2-606.
  Action for price.
    Seller's remedies, CL §2-709.
  Affirmations.
    Express warranties, CL §2-313.
  Antecedent breach.
    Effect of cancellation or rescission on claims, CL
      §2-720.
  Anticipatory repudiation, CL §2-610.
    Proof of market price, CL §2-723.
    Retraction, CL §2-611.
  Approval.
    Sale on approval, CL §§2-326, 2-327.
  Assignment of rights, CL §2-210.
  Assortment of goods.
    Buyer's option, CL §2-311.
  Assurance of performance.
    Right to adequate assurance, CL §2-609.
  Auction sales, CL §2-328.
  Bailee, possession in.
    Tender of delivery without moving goods, CL
      §2-503.
  Breach of obligation.
    Antecedent breach.
      Effect of cancellation or rescission on claims,
        CL §2-720.

COMMERCIAL CODE —Cont'd
Sale of goods —Cont'd
  Breach of obligation —Cont'd
    Damages. See within this subheading,
      "Damages."
    Installment contracts, CL §2-612.
    Limitation of actions, CL §2-725.
    Notice requirements, CL §2-607.
  Burden of proof.
    Breaches with respect to accepted goods, CL
      §2-607.
  Cancellation of contract.
    Buyer's remedies, CL §2-711.
    Seller's remedies, CL §2-703.
  C. & F. terms, CL §§2-320, 2-321.
  Casualty to identified goods, CL §2-613.
  C.I.F. terms, CL §§2-320, 2-321.
  Citation of article, CL §2-101.
  Collateral contracts.
    Remedies for breach unimpaired, CL §2-701.
  Commercial code's general provisions, CL §§1-101
    to 1-208. See within this heading, "General
    provisions."
  Consignment sales, CL §2-326.
  Cooperation respecting performance, CL §2-311.
  Course of dealing.
    Implied warranties, CL §2-314.
  Cover.
    Buyer's procurement of substitute goods, CL
      §2-712.
  Credit.
    Confirmed credit, CL §2-325.
    Letters of credit, CL §2-325.
  Creditors' rights and remedies.
    Sale on approval and sale or return
      transactions, CL §2-326.
    Sold goods.
      Rights of seller's creditors, CL §2-402.
  Cure.
    Improper tender or delivery of goods.
      Seller's right to cure, CL §2-508.
  Damages.
    Acceptance of goods.
      Buyer's damages for breach in regard to
        accepted goods, CL §2-714.
    Antecedent breach.
      Effect of cancellation or rescission on claims,
        CL §2-720.
    Consequential damages.
      Buyer's consequential damages, CL §2-715.
    Contractual limitations, CL §2-719.
    Cover by buyer.
      Right to recover, CL §2-712.
    Deduction from price, CL §2-717.
    Delivery of goods.
      Buyer's damages for nondelivery, CL §2-713.
    Incidental damages.
      Buyer's incidental damages, CL §2-715.
      Recovery by person in position of seller, CL
        §2-707.
      Seller's incidental damages, CL §2-710.
    Limitation, CL §2-718.
    Liquidation, CL §2-718.
    Nonacceptance of goods.
      Seller's damages, CL §2-708.
    Repudiation by seller.
      Buyer's damages, CL §2-713.
    Repudiation of buyer.
      Seller's damages, CL §2-708.
    Resale of goods by seller, CL §§2-703, 2-706.
    Warranty breaches, CL §2-714.

COMMERCIAL CODE —Cont'd
Sale of goods —Cont'd
Definitions.
    Agreement, CL §2-106.
    Banker's credit, CL §2-325.
    Between merchants, CL §2-104.
    Buyer, CL §2-103.
    Cancellation, CL §2-106.
    Commercial unit, CL §2-105.
    Confirmed credit, CL §2-325.
    Conforming to contract, CL §2-106.
    Contract, CL §2-106.
    Contract for sale, CL §2-106.
    Cover, CL §2-712.
    Entrusting, CL §2-403.
    Financing agency, CL §2-104.
    Future goods, CL §2-105.
    General commercial code definitions, CL §1-201.
      Course of dealing, CL §1-205.
      Reasonable time and seasonably, CL §1-204.
      Usage of trade, CL §1-205.
    Good faith, CL §2-103.
    Goods, CL §2-105.
    Identification, CL §2-501.
    Index of definitions, CL §2-103.
    Installment contract, CL §2-612.
    Letter of credit, CL §2-325.
    Lot, CL §2-105.
    Merchant, CL §2-104.
    Overseas, CL §2-323.
    Person in position of seller, CL §2-707.
    Present sale, CL §2-106.
    Receipt, CL §2-103.
    Sale, CL §2-106.
    Sale on approval, CL §2-326.
    Sale or return, CL §2-326.
    Seller, CL §2-103.
    Termination, CL §2-106.
Delegation of performance, CL §2-210.
Delivery of goods. See within this subheading,
    "Shipment and delivery."
Description of goods.
    Express warranties by description, CL §2-313.
Detinue.
    Right of buyer, CL §2-716.
Disputed goods.
    Preservation of evidence, CL §2-515.
Documents against which draft is drawn.
    When deliverable, CL §2-514.
Documents of title.
    Document adequate to fulfill obligations of
      contract, CL §7-509.
Entrusters and entrustees, CL §2-403.
Evidence.
    Breaches with respect to accepted goods, CL
      §2-607.
    Disputed goods.
      Preserving evidence, CL §2-515.
    Price.
      Admissibility of market quotations, CL
        §2-724.
      Proof of market price, CL §2-723.
Excludable security and other transactions, CL
    §2-102.
Exclusive dealings, CL §2-306.
Executory portion of contract.
    Waiver, CL §2-209.
Extrinsic evidence, CL §2-202.
Failure of buyer to pay.
    Seller's remedies.
      Action for price, CL §2-709.

COMMERCIAL CODE —Cont'd
Sale of goods —Cont'd
Finality of written expression, CL §2-202.
Financing agencies.
    Shipment of goods.
      Drafts paid or purchased by agency.
        Rights of agency, CL §2-506.
Firm offers, CL §2-205.
Fitness for particular purpose.
    Implied warranties, CL §2-315.
      Exclusion or modification, CL §§2-316,
        2-316.1.
Formation of contract.
    Generally, CL §2-204.
    Offer and acceptance, CL §2-206.
      Auctions, CL §2-328.
      Firm offers, CL §2-205.
Fraud.
    Remedies for fraud, CL §2-721.
Good faith.
    Obligation of good faith, CL §1-203.
Good faith purchasers, CL §2-403.
Goods severed from realty, CL §2-107.
Identification of goods, CL §2-501.
    Casualty to identified goods, CL §2-613.
    Seller's right notwithstanding breach of
      contract, CL §2-704.
Improper tender or delivery.
    Buyer's right on improper delivery, CL §2-601.
Infringement of enjoyment of goods.
    Warranty against infringement, CL §2-312.
Insolvency of buyer.
    Remedies of seller on discovery, CL §2-702.
Insolvency of seller.
    Buyer's right to goods, CL §2-502.
Inspection of goods.
    Buyer's right, CL §2-513.
    Inspection after arrival of goods but before
      payment is due, CL §2-310.
    Payment by buyer before inspection, CL §2-512.
Installment contracts, CL §2-612.
Insurable interest in goods, CL §2-501.
Interpretation and construction.
    Cancellation.
      Effect of term on claims for antecedent
        breach, CL §2-720.
    Course of performance, CL §2-208.
    Delivery of goods.
      Absence of specified place for delivery, CL
        §2-308.
      Time for delivery.
        Absence of specified time, CL §2-309.
    Open price terms, CL §2-305.
    Practical construction, CL §2-208.
    Rescission.
      Effect of term on claims for antecedent
        breach, CL §2-720.
    Risks.
      Allocation or division, CL §2-303.
    Shipment of goods.
      Time for shipment.
        Absence of specified time, CL §2-309.
    Letters of credit, CL §2-325.
    Contracts for sale of goods, CL §2-325.
Merchantability of goods.
    Implied warranties, CL §2-314.
      Exclusion or modification, CL §§2-316,
        2-316.1.
Minerals.
    Applicability of chapter, CL §2-107.
Modification of contract, CL §2-209.

COMMERCIAL CODE —Cont'd
Sale of goods —Cont'd
Notice, CL §2-607.
  Breach of obligations, CL §2-607.
  Termination of contract, CL §2-309.
Obligations of parties.
  Generally, CL §2-301.
Offer and acceptance, CL §2-206.
  Auctions, CL §2-328.
  Firm offers, CL §2-205.
Oil and gas.
  Applicability of chapter, CL §2-107.
Open price terms, CL §2-305.
Options respecting performance, CL §2-311.
Output contracts, CL §2-306.
Overseas shipments.
  Bill of lading, CL §2-323.
Parol evidence, CL §2-202.
Payment.
  Accepted goods, CL §2-607.
  Before inspection, CL §2-512.
  By check, CL §2-511.
  Confirmed credit, CL §2-325.
  Credit.
    Running of credit, CL §2-310.
  Failure of buyer to pay.
    Person in position of seller.
      Recovery of incidental damages, CL §2-707.
    Seller's remedies.
      Action for price, CL §2-709.
      Enumerated, CL §2-703.
      Incidental damages, CL §2-710.
  Letters of credit, CL §2-325.
  Obligation of buyer, CL §2-301.
  On arrival of goods, CL §2-321.
  Open time for payment, CL §2-310.
  Price payable in money, goods, realty, etc., CL §2-304.
  Tender by buyer, CL §2-511.
  When due, CL §2-310.
Performance.
  Assurance.
    Right to adequate assurance of performance, CL §2-609.
  Cooperation, CL §2-311.
  Course of performance.
    Interpretation of agreement, CL §2-208.
  Delegation, CL §2-210.
  Generally, CL §§2-501 to 2-515.
  Options, CL §2-311.
  Substituted performance, CL §2-614.
  Suspension until adequate assurance of performance, CL §2-609.
Price.
  Action for price.
    Seller's remedies, CL §§2-703, 2-709.
  Deduction of damages, CL §2-717.
  Failure of buyer to pay.
    Person in position of seller.
      Recovery of incidental damages, CL §2-707.
    Seller's remedies.
      Action for price, CL §2-703.
      Incidental damages, CL §2-710.
  Net landed weights, CL §2-321.
  Open price terms, CL §2-305.
  Payable in money, goods, realty, etc., CL §2-304.
  Payment. See within this subheading, "Payment."
  Proof of market price, CL §2-723.
    Admissibility of market quotations, CL §2-724.

COMMERCIAL CODE —Cont'd
Sale of goods —Cont'd
Promises.
  Express warranties, CL §2-313.
Reclamation of goods.
  Seller's remedies on discovery of buyer's insolvency, CL §2-702.
Rejection of goods.
  Acceptance of goods. See within this subheading, "Acceptance of goods."
  Rightful rejection.
    Buyer's options as to salvage of rightfully rejected goods, CL §2-604.
    Buyer's remedies.
      Enumerated, CL §2-711.
    Effect, CL §2-602.
    Manner, CL §2-602.
    Merchant buyer's duties as to rightfully rejected goods, CL §2-603.
    Waiver of buyer's objections by failure to particularize, CL §2-605.
  Wrongful rejection.
    Seller's remedies.
      Enumerated, CL §2-703.
Remedies.
  Buyer's remedies.
    Acceptance of goods.
      Breach in regard to accepted goods, CL §2-714.
    Collateral contracts.
      Remedies for breach unimpaired, CL §2-701.
    Consequential damages, CL §2-715.
    Cover, CL §2-712.
    Detinue, CL §2-716.
    Fraud, CL §2-721.
    Incidental damages, CL §2-715.
    Modification or limitation by contract, CL §2-719.
    Nondelivery of goods, CL §2-713.
    Options and cooperation respecting performance.
      Additional remedies, CL §2-311.
    Repudiation of contract by seller, CL §2-713.
    Restitution, CL §2-718.
    Specific performance, CL §2-716.
  Person in position of seller, CL §2-707.
  Seller's remedies.
    Action for price, CL §2-709.
    Buyer's insolvency, CL §2-702.
    Collateral contracts.
      Remedies for breach unimpaired, CL §2-701.
    Delivery of goods.
      Stoppage in transit or otherwise, CL §2-705.
    Fraud, CL §2-721.
    Generally, CL §2-703.
    Identification of goods.
      Seller's right notwithstanding breach of contract, CL §2-704.
    Modification or limitation by contract, CL §2-719.
    Nonacceptance of goods by buyer, CL §2-708.
    Options and cooperation respecting performance.
      Additional remedies, CL §2-311.
    Repudiation of contract by buyer, CL §2-708.
    Resale of goods, CL §2-706.
    Salvaging unfinished goods, CL §2-704.

COMMERCIAL CODE —Cont'd
Sale of goods —Cont'd
Repudiation.
    Anticipatory repudiation, CL §§2-610, 2-611.
        Proof of market price, CL §2-723.
    Buyer's damages, CL §2-713.
    Buyer's repudiation of contract.
        Enumeration of seller's remedies, CL §2-703.
        Seller's damages, CL §2-708.
    Seller's repudiation of contract.
        Buyer's remedies.
            Enumerated, CL §2-711.
Requirements contracts, CL §2-306.
Resale of goods.
    Remedy of person in position of seller, CL §2-707.
    Seller's remedies, CL §2-706.
Rescission of contract, CL §2-209.
Restitution.
    Buyer's remedies, CL §2-718.
Return of goods.
    Sale or return transactions, CL §§2-326, 2-327.
Risk of loss.
    Absence of breach, CL §2-509.
    Casualty to identified goods, CL §2-613.
    Effect of breach, CL §2-510.
Sale on approval transactions, CL §§2-326, 2-327.
Sale or return transactions, CL §§2-326, 2-327.
Salvaging unfinished goods.
    Right of seller, CL §2-704.
Samples of goods.
    Express warranties by samples, CL §2-313.
Scope of chapter, CL §2-102.
Seals.
    Inoperability, CL §2-203.
Shipment and delivery.
    Acceptance of goods. See within this subheading, "Acceptance of goods."
    C. & F. terms.
        Bill of lading required in overseas shipments, CL §2-323.
    Casualty to identified goods, CL §2-613.
    C.I.F. terms.
        Bill of lading required in overseas shipments, CL §2-323.
    Condition.
        Delivery on, CL §2-507.
    Cure by seller of improper tender or delivery, CL §2-508.
    Delay in delivery.
        Excuse by failure of presupposed conditions, CL §§2-615, 2-616.
    Ex-ship delivery, CL §2-322.
    F.A.S. terms, CL §2-319.
    Financing agency's rights.
        Drafts paid or purchased by agency, CL §2-506.
    F.O.B. terms, CL §2-319.
        Bill of lading required in overseas shipments, CL §2-323.
    Improper tender or delivery.
        Cover by buyer, CL §2-712.
        Cure by seller, CL §2-508.
        Damages of buyer for nondelivery, CL §2-713.
        Excuse by failure of presupposed conditions, CL §§2-615, 2-616.
    Inspection of goods, CL §§2-512, 2-513.
    Net landed weights, CL §2-321.
    No arrival, no sale terms, CL §2-324.
        Casualty to identified goods, CL §2-613.

COMMERCIAL CODE —Cont'd
Sale of goods —Cont'd
Shipment and delivery —Cont'd
    Obligation of seller to transfer and deliver goods, CL §2-301.
    Overseas shipments, CL §2-323.
    Payment on arrival, CL §2-321.
    Place for delivery.
        Absence of specified place, CL §2-308.
    Refusal of delivery.
        Buyer's remedies.
            Enumerated, CL §2-711.
        Seller's remedies on discovery of buyer's insolvency, CL §2-702.
    Rejection of goods. See within this subheading, "Rejection of goods."
    Reservation.
        Authority to ship under reservation, CL §2-310.
    Risk of loss.
        Absence of breach, CL §2-509.
        Effect of breach, CL §2-510.
    Sale on approval transactions, CL §§2-326, 2-327.
    Sale or return transactions, CL §§2-326, 2-327.
    Seller's option.
        Specifications or arrangements relating to shipment, CL §2-311.
    Shipment by seller, CL §2-504.
        Under reservation, CL §2-505.
    Single lot or several lots, CL §2-307.
    Stoppage of goods in transit or otherwise.
        Remedy of person in position of seller, CL §2-707.
        Remedy of seller, CL §§2-703, 2-704.
    Substituted performance, CL §2-614.
    Tender of delivery.
        Buyer's rights on improper delivery, CL §2-601.
        Cover by buyer where tender improper, CL §2-712.
        Cure by seller of improper tender, CL §2-508.
        Effect of seller's tender, CL §2-507.
        Excuse by failure of presupposed conditions, CL §§2-615, 2-616.
        Manner of seller's tender, CL §2-503.
    Time for shipment or delivery.
        Absence of specified time, CL §2-309.
    Warranty of condition on arrival, CL §2-321.
    Withholding delivery.
        Seller's remedies, CL §2-703.
Specific performance.
    Right of buyer, CL §2-716.
Statute of limitations, CL §2-725.
Substituted performance, CL §2-614.
Termination of contract.
    Contracts of indefinite duration, CL §2-309.
    Definition of "termination," CL §2-106.
    Notice of termination, CL §2-309.
Third-party actions.
    Who can sue third parties for injury to goods, CL §2-722.
Third-party beneficiaries.
    Warranties, CL §2-318.
Timber.
    Applicability of chapter, CL §2-107.
Title of article.
    Short title, CL §2-101.
Title to goods.
    Passing of title, CL §2-401.
    Power to transfer title, CL §2-403.

COMMERCIAL CODE —Cont'd
Sale of goods —Cont'd
  Title to goods —Cont'd
    Reservation for security, CL §2-401.
    Warranty of title, CL §2-312.
  Transfer of goods.
    Requisites, CL §2-105.
  Unconscionability, CL §2-302.
  Unfinished goods.
    Seller's right to salvage, CL §2-704.
  Usage of trade.
    Implied warranties, CL §2-314.
  Waiver of executory portion of contract, CL
      §2-209.
  Warranties.
    Damages for breach, CL §2-714.
    Express warranties, CL §2-313.
      Cumulation and conflict, CL §2-317.
      Exclusions.
        Generally, CL §§2-316, 2-316.1.
      Modification.
        Generally, CL §§2-316, 2-316.1.
      Third-party beneficiaries, CL §2-318.
    Implied warranties.
      Course of dealing or usage of trade, CL
          §2-314.
      Cumulation and conflict, CL §2-317.
      Exclusions.
        Generally, CL §§2-316, 2-316.1.
      Fitness for particular purpose, CL §2-315.
        Exclusion or modification, CL §§2-316,
            2-316.1.
      Merchantability.
        Exclusion or modification, CL §§2-316,
            2-316.1.
      Modification.
        Generally, CL §§2-316, 2-316.1.
      Third-party beneficiaries, CL §2-318.
    Infringement of enjoyment of goods.
      Warranty of title and against infringement,
          CL §2-312.
    Merchantability, CL §2-314.
    Shipment and delivery of goods.
      Warranty of condition on arrival, CL §2-321.
    Third-party beneficiaries, CL §2-318.
    Title.
      Warranty of title and against infringement,
          CL §2-312.
Sales.
  Buyer's remedies.
    Security interest.
      Rejected goods.
        Applicability of article 9, CL §9-110.
  Secured transactions.
    Buyer's security interest in rejected goods.
      Applicability of article 9, CL §9-110.
    Reservation of title.
      Applicability of article 9, CL §9-110.
    Security interests arising under provisions, CL
        §9-110.
  Title.
    Reservation for security.
      Applicability of article 9, CL §9-110.
Secured transactions, CL §§9-101 to 9-710.
  Accessions.
    Perfection and priority of security interest in,
        CL §9-335.
  Accounting.
    Defined, CL §9-102.
    Request for.
      Charge for response, CL §9-210.

COMMERCIAL CODE —Cont'd
Secured transactions —Cont'd
  Accounting —Cont'd
    Request for —Cont'd
      Damages for noncompliance, CL §9-625.
      Defined, CL §9-210.
      Duty to respond to, CL §9-210.
      Limitation of security interest for
          noncompliance, CL §9-625.
      List of collateral, CL §9-210.
      No interest claimed, CL §9-210.
  After-acquired property.
    Security interest in, CL §9-204.
    When after-acquired property clause not
        effective, CL §9-204.
  Agricultural liens.
    Default.
      Time of default, CL §9-606.
    Defined, CL §9-102.
    Perfection and priority.
      Filed financing statement providing certain
          incorrect information.
        Priority of agricultural lien perfected by, CL
            §9-338.
      Filing, CL §9-310.
      Interests that take priority over or take free
          of agricultural lien, CL §9-317.
      Law governing, CL §9-302.
      Multiple conflicting interests in same
          collateral.
        Other UCC provisions governing, CL
            §9-322.
      Proceeds and supporting obligations, time
          of perfection, CL §9-322.
      Rules governing priority, CL §9-322.
      When perfected, CL §9-308.
  Applicability of provisions, CL §§9-109, 9-110.
    Articles 2 and 2A security interests, CL §9-110.
    Conflict of laws, CL §9-109.
    Exclusions from article, CL §9-109.
    General scope, CL §9-109.
    Letters of credit.
      Beneficiaries and nominated persons rights
          superior, CL §9-109.
    Secured interest in obligation secured outside of
        article 9, CL §9-109.
  Assignments.
    Applicability of article 9.
      Certain assignments not covered by
          provisions, CL §9-109.
  Attachment of security interest, CL §9-203.
    Financial asset.
      Security interest arising in purchase or
          delivery of, CL §9-206.
    Perfection.
      Security interests perfected upon attachment,
          CL §9-309.
  Bank deposits and collections.
    Depositary and collecting banks.
      Collection of items.
        Security interests of collecting banks, CL
            §4-207.
    Documentary drafts.
      Dishonor.
        Privilege of presenting bank to deal with
            goods, CL §4-504.
  Banks.
    Control agreement.
      Refusal to enter into or disclose existence of,
          CL §9-342.
    Defined, CL §9-102.

COMMERCIAL CODE —Cont'd
Secured transactions —Cont'd
Banks —Cont'd
Rights of banks.
Deposit accounts, CL §§9-340, 9-341.
Chattel paper.
Perfection of security interests in, CL §9-312.
Purchaser of chattel paper or instrument.
Priority, CL §9-330.
Choice of law.
Debtor's location.
Applicability of section limited, CL §9-307.
Continuation of location, CL §9-307.
Foreign air carriers, CL §9-307.
General rules, CL §9-307.
Limitation, CL §9-307.
Place of business.
Defined, CL §9-307.
Registered organizations, CL §9-307.
Investment property, CL §9-305.
Commodity intermediary jurisdiction
determinations, CL §9-305.
Exceptions to general rule, CL §9-305.
Perfection and priority.
Agricultural liens, CL §9-302.
Certificates of title covering goods, CL §9-303.
Deposit accounts, CL §9-304.
Letter-of-credit rights, CL §9-306.
Security interests, CL §9-301.
Citation of provisions, CL §9-101.
Collateral.
Control of collateral.
Rights and duties of secured party having, CL
§§9-207, 9-208.
Default.
Acceptance in full or partial satisfaction of
obligation, CL §§9-620 to 9-622.
Disposition after default, CL §§9-610 to 9-617.
Redemption, CL §9-623.
Waiver of right, CL §9-624.
Title transfers, legal or record, CL §9-619.
Description, CL §9-108.
Disposition.
Permissible, CL §9-205.
Possession requirement not relaxed, CL
§9-205.
Rights of secured party on, CL §9-315.
List of collateral.
Request regarding, CL §9-210.
Limitation of security interest for
noncompliance, CL §9-625.
Possession of collateral.
Rights and duties of secured party having, CL
§9-207.
Secured party in possession or control.
Buyers of accounts, paper, notes, etc., CL
§9-207.
Care, duty of, CL §9-207.
Deposit account, electronic chattel paper,
investment property or letter-of-credit
right as collateral, CL §9-208.
Discharge of account debtor, CL §9-209.
Expenses to preserve collateral, CL §9-207.
Preservation of collateral, CL §9-207.
Proceeds from collateral, CL §9-207.
Risk of loss, CL §9-207.
Security interest in collateral, CL §9-207.
Title immaterial, CL §9-202.
Transferred collateral.
Priority of security interests in, CL §9-325.

COMMERCIAL CODE —Cont'd
Secured transactions —Cont'd
Collateral —Cont'd
Use.
Permissible, CL §9-205.
Possession requirement not relaxed, CL
§9-205.
Commercial code's general provisions, CL §§1-101
to 1-208. See within this heading, "General
provisions."
Commingled goods.
Priority of security interests, CL §9-336.
Compliance with article. See within this
subheading, "Remedies for noncompliance
with article."
Crops.
Priority of security interests in, CL §9-334.
Production-money crops.
Defined, CL §9-102.
Production-money obligation.
Defined, CL §9-102.
Production of crops.
Defined, CL §9-102.
Debtor.
Defined, CL §9-102.
Location, CL §9-307.
Default.
Acceptance of collateral in full or partial
satisfaction of obligation.
Conditions to acceptance, CL §9-620.
Consent of debtor, CL §9-620.
Consumer goods, mandatory disposition, CL
§9-620.
Waiver of mandatory disposition, CL
§9-624.
Noncompliance with provisions.
Effect, CL §9-622.
Notification of objection, CL §9-620.
Notification of proposal.
Partial satisfaction, secondary obligors to be
notified, CL §9-621.
Partial satisfaction, CL §9-620.
Purported acceptance, CL §9-620.
Agricultural lien.
Time of default, CL §9-606.
Assembly of collateral for convenience of
secured party, CL §9-609.
Assignments, transfers or subrogations.
Effect, CL §9-618.
Rights and duties of secondary obligors, CL
§9-618.
Collateral.
Acceptance in full or partial satisfaction of
obligation, CL §§9-620 to 9-622.
Disposition after default, CL §§9-610 to 9-617.
Redemption, CL §9-623.
Waiver of right, CL §9-624.
Title transfers, legal or record, CL §9-619.
Collection and enforcement by secured party,
CL §9-607.
Application of proceeds, CL §9-608.
Commercial reasonableness, CL §9-607.
Determination of commercial
reasonableness, CL §9-627.
Deficiency, responsibility for, CL §9-608.
Damage actions when surplus or deficiency
an issue, CL §9-626.
Duty to secured party not affected by section,
CL §9-607.
Expenses, CL §9-607.

COMMERCIAL CODE —Cont'd
Secured transactions —Cont'd
  Default —Cont'd
    Collection and enforcement by secured party
      —Cont'd
      Nonjudicial enforcement of mortgage, CL
        §9-607.
      Surplus, application, CL §9-608.
        Certain sales, CL §9-608.
        Damage actions when surplus or deficiency
          an issue, CL §9-626.
    Disposition of collateral after, CL §9-610.
      Commercially reasonable disposition, CL
        §9-610.
        Determination of commercial
          reasonableness, CL §9-627.
      Compulsory disposition, CL §9-620.
        Waiver of mandatory disposition, CL
          §9-624.
      Notification before, CL §9-611.
        Consumer goods transactions, contents and
          form, CL §9-614.
        Timeliness, CL §9-612.
        Waiver, CL §9-624.
      Perishable collateral exception to notification
        requirement, CL §9-611.
      Proceeds, CL §9-615.
      Purchase by secured party, CL §9-610.
      Recognized market exception to notification
        requirement, CL §9-611.
      Surplus or deficiency, CL §9-615.
        Damage actions when surplus or deficiency
          an issue, CL §9-626.
        Explanation of calculation, CL §9-616.
        Explanation of calculation, limitation of
          liability, CL §9-628.
        Explanation of calculation, required
          information, CL §9-616.
        Explanation of calculation, substantial
          compliance, CL §9-616.
        Sales of rights to payment, CL §9-615.
      Transferee's rights, CL §9-617.
      Warranties on disposition, CL §9-610.
        Disclaimer, CL §9-610.
  Fixtures.
    Procedure if security agreement covers, CL
      §9-604.
    Removal, CL §9-604.
  Judicial enforcement, CL §9-601.
  Nonjudicial enforcement of mortgage, CL
    §9-607.
  Real property.
    Procedure if security agreement covers, CL
      §9-604.
  Rendering equipment unusable, CL §9-609.
    Breach of the peace not sanctioned, CL
      §9-609.
    Process, CL §9-609.
  Repossession, CL §9-609.
    Breach of the peace not sanctioned, CL
      §9-609.
    Process, CL §9-609.
  Rights after default, CL §9-601.
    Agreement on standards concerning, CL
      §9-603.
    Consignors or buyers of accounts, etc., CL
      §9-601.
    Debtors' rights and obligations, CL §9-601.
    Execution sales, CL §9-601.
    Lien of levy after judgment, CL §9-601.
    Waiver and variance, CL §9-602.

COMMERCIAL CODE —Cont'd
Secured transactions —Cont'd
  Default —Cont'd
    Secondary obligor.
      Rights and duties, CL §9-618.
    Secured party in possession of collateral, CL
      §9-601.
    Unknown debtor or secondary obligor, CL
      §9-605.
    Waiver of certain rights, CL §9-624.
  Definitions.
    Article 9 definitions, CL §9-102.
    Commingled goods, priority of security
      interests, CL §9-336.
    Explanation of calculation.
      Disposition of collateral after default, surplus
        or deficiency, CL §9-616.
    General commercial code definitions, CL §1-201.
      Course of dealing, CL §1-205.
      Reasonable time and seasonably, CL §1-204.
      Usage of trade, CL §1-205.
    General provisions article definitions.
      Applicability, CL §9-102.
    Licensee of general intangible, priority of
      security interests, CL §9-321.
    Non-article 9 definitions, CL §9-102.
    Notification date.
      Disposition of collateral after default,
        notification before, CL §9-611.
    Place of business, debtor's location for choice of
      law issues, CL §9-307.
    Possessory liens, priority of security interests,
      CL §9-333.
    Purchase money security interests, CL §9-103.
    Request for accounting, CL §9-210.
    Transfer statement defined, title transfers upon
      default, CL §9-619.
    Value, third parties, CL §9-403.
  Deposit account.
    Bank's rights and duties with respect to, CL
      §9-341.
      Setoff or recoupment against deposit account,
        CL §9-340.
    Control, CL §9-104.
    Defined, CL §9-102.
    Inapplicability of article 9.
      Consumer transaction assignments, CL
        §9-109.
    Perfection and priority of security interest in,
      CL §9-312.
      Law governing, CL §9-304.
      Perfection by control, CL §9-314.
      Priority of security interests, CL §9-327.
      Transfer of funds from deposit account.
        Transferee takes funds free of security
          interest, CL §9-332.
  Description of property, CL §9-108.
    Type, description by, CL §9-108.
  Duties of secured party.
    Control or possession of collateral.
      Secured party having, CL §§9-207, 9-208.
  Effective date of provisions, CL §9-701.
    Action taken before.
      Effectiveness, CL §9-705.
    Amendment of information in pre-effective-date
      financing statement, CL §9-707.
    Pre-effective date proceedings, CL §9-702.
    Pre-effective date transactions, CL §9-702.
    Security interest not perfected before effective
      date, CL §9-704.
      Priority, CL §9-703.

COMMERCIAL CODE —Cont'd
Secured transactions —Cont'd
Effective date of provisions —Cont'd
Security interest perfected before effective date,
CL §9-703.
Electronic chattel paper.
Control, CL §9-105.
Perfection by control, CL §9-314.
Defined, CL §9-102.
Perfection and priority of security interests in.
Perfection by control, CL §9-314.
Enforceability of security interest.
Commodities contracts carried in commodities
accounts, CL §9-203.
Conditions for enforceability, CL §9-203.
Lien securing right to payment.
Attachment of security interest in the
security interest, CL §9-203.
Proceeds, right to, CL §9-203.
Securities accounts, CL §9-203.
Security agreement of another binding person,
CL §9-203.
Supporting obligations for collateral.
Attachment of interest in supporting
obligations, CL §9-203.
UCC provisions from other articles overriding
enforceability, CL §9-203.
Filing office, CL §9-501.
Acknowledgments.
Filing of other records, CL §9-523.
Filing of written record, CL §9-523.
Timeliness, CL §9-523.
Communication of requested information, CL
§9-523.
Fee, CL §9-525.
Medium, CL §9-523.
Timeliness, CL §9-523.
Destruction of records, CL §9-522.
Duties, CL §§9-519, 9-520, 9-522, 9-523.
Generally, CL §9-519.
Fees, CL §9-525.
Initial statements or records, CL §9-525.
Number of names immaterial, CL §9-525.
Record of mortgage as financing statement,
CL §9-525.
Response to information request, CL §9-525.
File numbers, CL §9-519.
Indexing.
Assignments.
Real property-related assignments, CL
§9-519.
Financing statements, CL §9-519.
Real property-related financing statements,
CL §9-519.
Information from, CL §9-523.
Fee, CL §9-525.
Maintenance of records, CL §9-522.
Name of debtor.
Removal, CL §9-519.
Refusal to accept record, CL §9-520.
Amend form.
Prohibition on refusal when in proper form,
CL §9-521.
Communication regarding, CL §9-520.
Effectiveness of certain refused records, CL
§9-520.
Initial financing statement form.
Prohibition on refusal when in proper form,
CL §9-521.
Multiple debtors, separate applications, CL
§9-520.

COMMERCIAL CODE —Cont'd
Secured transactions —Cont'd
Filing office —Cont'd
Retrieval and association of records, CL §9-519.
Timeliness of performance, CL §9-519.
Transmitting utilities, CL §9-501.
Filing-office rules, CL §9-526.
Harmonization of rules, CL §9-526.
Financial asset.
Priority of certain interests in, CL §9-331.
Purchase or delivery of.
Security interest arising in, CL §9-206.
Financing statement.
Amendment, CL §9-512.
Collateral added, CL §9-512.
Debtor added, CL §9-512.
Deleting secured party of record, CL §9-511.
Extension of period of effectiveness not
accomplished by, CL §9-512.
Form, CL §9-521.
Multiple secured parties of record, CL §9-509.
Naming secured party of record, CL §9-511.
Persons entitled to file, CL §9-509.
Prohibited amendments, CL §9-512.
Collateral.
Indication of collateral, CL §9-504.
Consignors, lessors, and other bailors.
Filing financing statement permitted, CL
§9-505.
Effect, CL §9-505.
Contents, CL §9-502.
Continuation statement.
Effect of filing, CL §9-515.
Time for filing, CL §9-515.
Transitional provisions, CL §§9-705, 9-708.
Correction statements, CL §9-518.
Debtor information.
Name of debtor, CL §9-503.
Change of name, CL §9-507.
Trade names, CL §9-503.
Representative capacity not required, CL
§9-503.
Disposition of collateral, CL §9-507.
Duration of effectiveness.
Five year period, CL §9-515.
Manufactured home transactions, CL §9-515.
Public finance transactions, CL §9-515.
Record of mortgage as financing statement,
CL §9-515.
Transmitting utilities, CL §9-515.
Errors and omissions.
Correction statement, CL §9-518.
Effect, CL §9-518.
Sufficiency, CL §9-518.
Effect.
Indexing errors, CL §9-517.
Minor errors and omissions, CL §9-506.
Name of debtor, CL §9-506.
Not seriously misleading statement, CL
§9-506.
Seriously misleading statement, CL §9-506.
Events with impact on effectiveness, CL §9-507.
Filing.
Amendments, CL §9-512.
Form, CL §9-521.
Multiple secured parties of record, CL
§9-509.
Persons entitled to file, CL §9-509.
Authorization by debtor.
Collateral acquisition, CL §9-509.
Security agreement, CL §9-509.

COMMERCIAL CODE —Cont'd
Secured transactions —Cont'd
Financing statement —Cont'd
Filing —Cont'd
Continuation statement, CL §9-510.
Amendment to continue financing
statement, CL §9-512.
Transitional provisions, CL §9-708.
Effectiveness of filed record, CL §9-510.
Initial financing statement.
Transitional provisions, CL §9-708.
When filing suffices to continue
effectiveness of financing statement, CL
§9-706.
Permissive filing.
Consignors, lessors and other bailors, CL
§9-505.
Persons authorized to file record.
Effectiveness of filed record, CL §9-510.
Persons entitled to file record, CL §9-509.
Amendments, CL §9-509.
Pre-effective date filing, CL §9-705.
Prior to attachment or security agreement,
CL §9-502.
Refusal to accept record for filing, CL §9-516.
When effective as filed record, CL §9-516.
Termination statements, CL §9-513.
What constitutes, CL §9-516.
Form, CL §9-521.
Indexing errors, CL §9-517.
Correction statements, CL §9-518.
Information becoming seriously misleading, CL
§9-507.
Lapse, CL §9-515.
Mortgage record as statement, CL §9-502.
Name of debtor and secured party.
Errors and omissions, CL §9-506.
Pre-effective date statement with post-effective
date continuation statement, CL §9-705.
Real property-related statements, CL §9-502.
Secured party of record, CL §9-511.
Assignment of powers of, CL §9-514.
Deletion by amendment, CL §9-511.
Naming by amendment, CL §9-511.
Subsequent or new debtor.
Effectiveness of statement naming original
debtor, CL §9-508.
Effect of CL §9-507, CL §9-508.
Seriously misleading statement as result, CL
§9-508.
Termination statement.
Amendment to terminate statement, CL
§9-512.
Collateral other than consumer goods, CL
§9-513.
Consumer goods, CL §9-513.
Effect of filing, CL §9-513.
Transitional provisions.
Initial statement in lieu of continuation
statement, CL §9-706.
Transmitting utility.
Transitional provisions, CL §9-705.
Financing statements.
Transitional filing, CL §10-109.
Fixtures.
Priority of security interests in, CL §9-334.
Future advances.
Priority of security interests, CL §9-323.
Security interest in, CL §9-204.
Good faith.
Obligation of good faith, CL §1-203.

COMMERCIAL CODE —Cont'd
Secured transactions —Cont'd
Grandfather clause, CL §9-702.
Identification and proof of assignment, CL §9-406.
Investment property.
Control, CL §9-106.
Defined, CL §9-102.
Description of property, CL §9-108.
Perfection and priority of security interests in,
CL §9-312.
Law governing, CL §9-305.
Perfection by control, CL §9-314.
Priority of security interests, CL §9-328.
Temporary perfection, CL §9-312.
Investment securities.
Security entitlements.
Priority among security interest and
entitlement holders, CL §8-511.
Leases.
Restrictions on security interest in leasehold
interest or in lessor's residual interest, CL
§9-407.
Leases, UCC.
Rejected goods, buyer's security interest.
Applicability of article 9, CL §9-110.
Letter-of-credit right.
Assignment.
Restrictions on assignment ineffective, CL
§9-409.
Exceptions, CL §9-409.
Control, CL §9-107.
Defined, CL §9-102.
Perfection and priority of security interests in,
CL §9-312.
Law governing, CL §9-306.
Perfection by control, CL §9-314.
Priority of security interests, CL §9-329.
Noncompliance with article. See within this
subheading, "Remedies for noncompliance
with article."
Perfected security interest.
Continuity of perfection, CL §10-110.
Effective date on which security interest
deemed perfected, CL §10-108.
Filing.
Financing statements. See within this
subheading, "Financing statements."
On January 1, 1981, CL §10-107.
Perfection of security interests.
Attachment.
Security interests perfected upon attachment,
CL §9-309.
Chattel paper, CL §9-312.
Commodity accounts, CL §9-308.
Continuity of perfection, CL §9-308.
Change in governing law, CL §9-316.
Bank's, issuer's, nominated person's,
intermediary's jurisdiction changes, CL
§9-316.
Certificates of title, CL §9-316.
Perfection or imperfection under law of new
jurisdiction, CL §9-316.
Possessory security interest in collateral
moved to new jurisdiction, CL §9-316.
Control, perfection by.
Duration of perfection by control, CL §9-314.
Investment property, CL §9-314.
Security interests perfectible by control, CL
§9-314.
Delivery to secured party to perfect, CL §9-313.
Duration of perfection by delivery, CL §9-313.

COMMERCIAL CODE —Cont'd
Secured transactions —Cont'd
Perfection of security interests —Cont'd
  Deposit accounts, CL §9-312.
    Perfection by control, CL §9-314.
  Effective date of provisions.
    Security interest not perfected before, CL
      §9-704.
      Priority, CL §9-703.
    Security interest perfected before, CL §9-703.
  Filing.
    Assigned perfected interests need not be
      refiled, CL §9-310.
    Instruments.
      Permissive filing, CL §9-312.
    Laws, treaties, etc., making filing
      unnecessary or ineffective, CL §9-311.
    Permissive filing, CL §9-312.
    When filing not required, CL §9-310.
    When required, CL §9-310.
  Instruments, CL §9-312.
  Investment property, CL §9-312.
    Perfection by control, CL §9-314.
    Temporary perfection, CL §9-312.
  Law governing, CL §9-301.
    Agricultural liens, CL §9-302.
    Deposit accounts, CL §9-304.
    Goods covered by certificate of title, CL
      §9-303.
    Investment property, CL §9-305.
    Letter-of-credit rights, CL §9-306.
  Letter-of-credit rights, CL §9-312.
    Law governing, CL §9-306.
    Perfection by control, CL §9-314.
  Lien securing right to payment, CL §9-308.
  Money, CL §9-312.
  Negotiable documents governing goods, CL
    §9-312.
  Nonnegotiable documents governing goods, CL
    §9-312.
  Possession by secured party to perfect, CL
    §9-313.
    Certificate of title covering goods, CL §9-313.
    Collateral in possession of person other than
      debtor.
      Acknowledgments, CL §9-313.
    Collateral possessed by person other than
      debtor, CL §9-313.
    Delivery by secured party to third party, CL
      §9-313.
  Pre-effective date actions to perfect, CL §9-705.
  Proceeds, CL §9-315.
    Duration of perfection, CL §9-315.
  Securities account, CL §9-308.
  Supporting obligations, CL §9-308.
  Temporary perfection.
    Availability of goods or documents to debtor,
      CL §9-312.
    Delivery to debtor, CL §9-312.
    Expiration, CL §9-312.
    New value, CL §9-312.
  Treaties.
    Security interest in property subject to
      certain treaties, CL §9-311.
  When perfected, CL §9-308.
Priorities.
  Determination of questions of priorities, CL
    §10-111.
Priority of security interests.
  Accessions, CL §9-335.
    Certificates of title, CL §9-335.

COMMERCIAL CODE —Cont'd
Secured transactions —Cont'd
Priority of security interests —Cont'd
  Accessions —Cont'd
    Creation and continuation of interest in
      accession, CL §9-335.
    Perfection of interest in accession, CL §9-335.
    Removal of accession, CL §9-335.
  Agricultural liens.
    Buyers receiving delivery.
      Interests that take priority over or take free
        of, CL §9-317.
    Filed financing statement providing certain
      incorrect information.
      Agricultural lien perfected by, CL §9-338.
    Interests that take priority over or take free
      of, CL §9-317.
    Law governing, CL §9-302.
    Lessees receiving delivery.
      Interests that take priority over or take free
        of, CL §9-317.
    Multiple conflicting interests in same
      collateral, CL §9-322.
  Buyer of goods, CL §9-320.
    Consumer goods buyers, CL §9-320.
      Filing, effectiveness, CL §9-320.
    Ordinary course of business, CL §9-320.
      Wellhead or minehead, buyers at, CL
        §9-320.
    Possessory security interests, CL §9-320.
  Buyers receiving delivery.
    Interests that take priority over or take free
      of, CL §9-317.
  Certificate of title.
    Security interest in goods covered by, CL
      §9-337.
  Chattel paper or instrument purchasers'
    priorities, CL §9-330.
  Commingled goods.
    Definition of commingled goods, CL §9-336.
    Transformation of interest in goods to interest
      in product or mass, CL §9-336.
  Consignees.
    Rights and title with respect to creditors and
      purchasers, CL §9-319.
      Conflict of laws, CL §9-319.
  Crops.
    Security interest in, CL §9-334.
  Deposit account, CL §9-327.
    Transfer of funds from, CL §9-332.
  Filed financing statement providing certain
    incorrect information.
    Security interest perfected by, CL §9-338.
  Financial asset.
    Priority of certain interests in, CL §9-331.
  Fixtures, CL §9-334.
  Future advances, CL §9-323.
  General intangibles, accounts, electronic chattel
    paper, or investment property.
    Buyers or licensees of certain collateral.
      Interests that take priority over or take free
        of, CL §9-317.
  Investment property, CL §9-328.
  Law governing, CL §9-301.
    Agricultural liens, CL §9-302.
    Deposit accounts, CL §9-304.
    Goods covered by certificate of title, CL
      §9-303.
    Investment property, CL §9-305.
    Letter-of-credit rights, CL §9-306.

COMMERCIAL CODE —Cont'd
Secured transactions —Cont'd
  Priority of security interests —Cont'd
    Lessee of goods in ordinary course of business,
      CL §9-321.
    Lessees receiving delivery.
      Interests that take priority over or take free
        of, CL §9-317.
    Letter-of-credit right, CL §9-329.
      Law governing, CL §9-306.
    Licensee of general intangible, CL §9-321.
      Defined, CL §9-321.
    Liens arising by operation of law.
      Possessory liens, CL §9-333.
        Defined, CL §9-333.
    Money transfers.
      Transferee takes money free of security
        interest, CL §9-332.
    Multiple conflicting interests in same collateral,
      CL §9-322.
    Negotiable instrument holders, negotiable
      documents of title holders or security
      purchasers.
      Filing under article 9 not considered notice,
        CL §9-331.
      Operation of other articles of UCC, CL
        §9-331.
    Subordination.
      Priority subject to, CL §9-339.
    Transition provisions.
      Attachment, CL §9-709.
      Governing provisions, CL §9-709.
  Proceeds.
    Rights of secured party in, CL §9-315.
  Purchase money security interests, CL §9-103.
    Application of payments.
      Non-consumer goods, CL §9-103.
    Consignments.
      Security interests in consignor's inventory, CL
        §9-103.
    Definitions, CL §9-103.
    Goods.
      Security interests in goods, CL §9-103.
    Non-consumer goods.
      Application of payments, CL §9-103.
      Burden of proof, CL §9-103.
      Inferences as to consumer goods from rules
        governing non-consumer goods not to be
        drawn, CL §9-103.
      Maintenance of status as purchase money
        security interest, CL §9-103.
    Priority, CL §9-324.
    Software.
      Security interests in software, CL §9-103.
  Remedies for noncompliance with article.
    Commercial reasonableness, CL §9-627.
    Damages, CL §9-625.
      Limitation of liability, CL §9-628.
        General rules, CL §9-626.
        Nonconsumer transactions, CL §9-626.
    Injunctions, CL §9-625.
      Limitation of liability, CL §9-628.
    Limitation of liability of secured party, CL
      §9-628.
    Limitation of security interest.
      Requests for accounting, collateral, etc., CL
        §9-625.
  Sale of goods, UCC.
    Buyer's security interest in rejected goods.
      Applicability of article 9, CL §9-110.

COMMERCIAL CODE —Cont'd
Secured transactions —Cont'd
  Sale of goods, UCC —Cont'd
    Reservation of title.
      Applicability of article 9, CL §9-110.
    Savings clause, CL §9-702.
    Scope of provisions, CL §§9-109, 9-110.
    Security agreement.
      Effectiveness, CL §9-201.
      Enforceability of security interest.
        Security agreement of another binding
          person, CL §9-203.
    Statement of account.
      Request regarding, CL §9-210.
        Damages for noncompliance, CL §9-625.
    Third parties.
      Alienability of debtor's rights.
        Agreements against transfer do not prevent
          transfer, CL §9-401.
        Governing law, CL §9-401.
      Assignments.
        Agreement not to assert defenses against
          assignee, CL §9-403.
        Claims and defenses against assignee, taking
          subject to, CL §9-404.
        Discharge of account debtor, CL §9-406.
        Leases.
          Material impairment, security interest not
            considered, CL §9-407.
          Restrictions on assignments, CL §9-407.
        Modification of assigned contract.
          Effect, CL §9-405.
          Governing law for individuals indebted for
            certain purposes, CL §9-405.
          Health care insurance receivable,
            inapplicability, CL §9-405.
        Notes and general intangibles.
          Conflicting laws, CL §9-408.
          Legal restrictions on assignments, CL
            §9-408.
          Restrictions on assignments, CL §9-408.
        Notice to debtor of assignment, CL §9-406.
        Restrictions on certain assignments, CL
          §9-406.
        Rights acquired by assignee, CL §9-404.
      Contract of debtor.
        Secured party not obligated on, CL §9-402.
      Torts of debtor.
        Secured party not obligated on, CL §9-402.
    Transitional provisions.
      Effective date, CL §§10-101, 11-101.
      Filing, CL §§11-104, 11-105.
        Required refilings, CL §11-106.
      General rule for transition, CL §11-103.
      Presumption that rule of law continues
        unchanged, CL §11-108.
      Priorities, CL §11-107.
Transitional provisions, CL §§10-101 to 10-112.
  Applicability of act.
    Effective date, CL §10-101.
  Applicability of section 10-102.
    Continuation of, CL §10-106.
  Declaratory nature of provisions, CL §10-112.
  Effective date.
    Questions of priorities.
      Determination of, CL §10-111.
  General repealer, CL §10-103.
  Perfected security interest.
    Continuation of, CL §10-110.
  Priorities.
    Determination of questions of priorities.
      Effective date, CL §10-111.

COMMERCIAL CODE —Cont'd
Transitional provisions —Cont'd
Provisions deemed declaratory, CL §10-112.
Repeals.
General repealer, CL §10-103.
Laws not repealed, CL §10-104.
Provisions for transition, CL §10-102.
Specific repealer, CL §10-102.
Secured transactions.
Effective date, CL §10-101.
Effective date on which security interest
deemed perfected, CL §10-108.
Filing statement.
Transitional filing, CL §10-109.
Validity of transactions entered after February
1, 1964, and before January 1, 1981, CL
§10-107.
Simplification of fiduciary security transfers.
Uniform act not repealed, CL §10-104.

COMMERCIAL DISCRIMINATION, SF §§19-101
to 19-120.
See DISCRIMINATION.

COMMERCIAL DRIVERS' LICENSES, TR
§§16-801 to 16-820.
Address.
Change of address.
Applications, TR §16-810.
Age requirements, TR §16-817.
Alcoholic beverages, TR §§16-205.1, 16-812,
16-813.
Aliens.
Issuance.
Persons domiciled in foreign countries, TR
§16-817.
Applications, TR §16-810.
Fees, TR §16-818.
Citation of subtitle.
Short title, TR §16-801.
Classification, TR §16-815.
Driving vehicles not authorized by license, TR
§16-815.
Identified clearly as to specific class, TR §16-811.
Construction of subtitle, TR §16-802.
Contents, TR §16-811.
Controlled dangerous substances.
Disqualification from driving commercial motor
vehicles, TR §16-812.
Licensing of persons convicted of drug crimes, 41
§§1-501 to 1-507.
See CONTROLLED DANGEROUS
SUBSTANCES.
Conversion to commercial drivers' licenses.
Fees, TR §16-818.
Convictions.
Notice of.
Required disclosures, TR §16-805.
Corrected licenses.
Fees, TR §16-818.
Obtaining, TR §16-114.1.
Definitions, TR §§11-109, 16-803.
Disclosures.
Required disclosures, TR §16-805.
Disqualification, TR §§16-208.1, 16-812.
Defined, TR §11-111.1.
Drug crime convictions.
Licensing persons convicted of, 41 §§1-501 to
1-507.
See CONTROLLED DANGEROUS
SUBSTANCES.

COMMERCIAL DRIVERS' LICENSES —Cont'd
Disqualification —Cont'd
Ineligibility to drive commercial motor vehicles,
TR §16-808.
Notice, TR §16-805.
Nonresidents.
Notifying licensing authority of state, TR
§16-812.
Operating vehicle under influence of intoxicating
liquors, TR §16-205.1.
Driving records.
Driving record information obtained from national
driver register, TR §16-811.
Retention, TR §16-819.
Driving under influence of drugs.
Disqualification, TR §16-812.
Drunkenness, TR §§16-205.1, 16-312.
Duplicate licenses.
Fees, TR §16-818.
Eligibility for licenses, TR §§16-807, 16-809.
Employers.
Duties, TR §16-806.
Violation of provisions, civil penalties, TR
§27-101.1.
Surcharge, TR §27-101.2.
Information to be supplied prospective employers,
TR §16-805.
Unauthorized drivers.
Allowing to drive commercial motor vehicles.
Prohibited, TR §16-806.
Violation of provisions, civil penalties, TR
§27-101.1.
Surcharge, TR §27-101.2.
Endorsements.
Additional endorsements.
When required, TR §16-815.
Examinations.
Fees, TR §16-818.
Issuance upon passing, TR §16-811.
Knowledge and skill tests, TR §16-807.
Fees, TR §16-818.
Issuance upon paying, TR §16-811.
Fraud.
Obtaining license by misrepresentation, TR
§16-813.1.
Hazardous materials.
Disqualification.
Offenses occurring while transporting, TR
§16-812.
Identifying numbers.
Assigned each license, TR §16-811.
**Ineligibility to drive commercial motor
vehicles.**
Persons ineligible, TR §§16-807, 16-808.
Instructional permits, TR §§16-807, 16-815.
Fees, TR §16-818.
Issuance, TR §§16-811, 16-817.
Knowledge and skill tests, TR §16-807.
Minors, TR §16-817.
Misrepresentation.
Obtaining license, TR §16-813.1.
Multiple violations.
Disqualification.
Duration, TR §16-812.
Name.
Change of name.
Applications, TR §16-810.
New residents.
Applications, TR §16-810.
Noncommercial licenses.
Disqualification.
Issuance to individual disqualified, TR §16-812.

COMMERCIAL DRIVERS' LICENSES —Cont'd
Nonresidents.
Conviction of violations of state law or local
ordinances.
Notification to licensing authority of state, TR
§16-814.
Issuance.
Ineligible persons, TR §16-817.
Notice.
Convictions.
Required disclosures, TR §16-805.
Issuance, TR §16-811.
Nonresidents.
Conviction of violations of state law or local
ordinances.
Notification to licensing authority of state, TR
§16-814.
Suspension, revocation, cancellation or
disqualification, TR §16-805.
Nonresidents' commercial drivers' privileges.
Notifying licensing authority of state, TR
§16-812.
Number of licenses, TR §16-804.
Out-of-service orders.
Conviction for violation.
Civil penalties, TR §27-101.1.
Surcharge, TR §27-101.2.
Disqualification for violations, TR §16-812.
Duties of employers, TR §16-806.
Perjury.
Applications.
Certification of truth of statements under
penalty of perjury, TR §16-810.
Permits.
Instructional permits, TR §§16-807, 16-815.
Fees, TR §16-818.
Purposes of subtitle, TR §16-802.
Railroad crossings.
Disqualification for violations, TR §16-812.
Reckless driving.
Disqualification for serious traffic offenses, TR
§16-812.
Records.
Driving records.
Retention, TR §16-819.
Suspension, revocation, cancellation or
disqualification.
Records to reflect action taken, TR §16-812.
Regulations, TR §16-820.
Reissuance.
Termination of disqualification, TR §16-812.
Renewal.
Fees, TR §16-818.
Required, TR §16-807.
School vehicles.
Prerequisites for operating, TR §16-816.
Serious traffic violations.
Disqualification, TR §16-812.
Short title, TR §16-801.
Signatures.
Applications, TR §16-810.
Speeding violations.
Disqualification for serious traffic violations, TR
§16-812.
Surrender of license.
Disqualification, TR §16-812.
**Suspension, revocation or cancellation of
licenses.**
Drug crimes.
Licensing persons convicted of offenses, 41
§§1-501 to 1-507.
See CONTROLLED DANGEROUS
SUBSTANCES.

COMMERCIAL DRIVERS' LICENSES —Cont'd
**Suspension, revocation or cancellation of
licenses** —Cont'd
Ineligibility to drive commercial motor vehicles,
TR §16-808.
Nonresidents.
Notifying licensing authority of state, TR
§16-812.
Notice, TR §16-805.
Nonresidents.
Notifying licensing authority of state, TR
§16-812.
Providing information incomplete or incorrect.
Cancellation, TR §16-812.
Records to reflect action taken, TR §16-812.
Tests.
Knowledge and skill tests, TR §16-807.
Title of subtitle.
Short title, TR §16-801.
Unauthorized drivers.
Employers allowing to drive commercial motor
vehicles.
Prohibited, TR §16-806.
Violation of provisions, civil penalties, TR
§27-101.1.
Surcharge, TR §27-101.2.

COMMERCIAL ELECTRONIC MAIL.
Unauthorized, false or misleading information,
CL §§14-3001 to 14-3003.

COMMERCIAL FEED LAW.
General provisions.
See FEEDSTUFFS.

COMMERCIAL FERTILIZER LAW.
General provisions, AG §§6-201 to 6-221.
See FERTILIZERS.

COMMERCIAL FISHING.
General provisions.
See FISH AND FISHERIES.

COMMERCIAL LEASES.
Gas meters or electric meters.
Submetering, PUC §7-303.

**COMMERCIAL NONDISCRIMINATION
POLICY.**
Citation of title and regulations, SF §19-120.
General provisions, SF §§19-101 to 19-120.
See DISCRIMINATION.

COMMERCIAL PAPER.
Negotiable instruments, CL §§3-101 to 3-605.
See NEGOTIABLE INSTRUMENTS.

COMMERCIAL REDEVELOPMENT.
Industrial and commercial redevelopment.
See INDUSTRIAL AND COMMERCIAL
REDEVELOPMENT.

**COMMERCIAL VEHICLE INFORMATION
SYSTEMS AND NETWORK.**
Cloned CVISN transponders, TR §25-112.
Penalties, TR §27-112.

**COMMINGLED GOODS IN SECURED
TRANSACTIONS.**
Priority of security interests.
Provisions effective July 1, 2001, CL §9-336.

COMMISSIONER OF CORRECTION, COR
§§3-101 to 3-222.
See CORRECTION, DIVISION OF.

COMMISSIONER OF FINANCIAL REGULATION.
Banks and trust companies.
See BANKS AND TRUST COMPANIES.
Credit unions.
See CREDIT UNIONS.
Examinations.
Expense reimbursements, FI §11-101.
Secondary mortgage loans.
Credit provisions, CL §§12-401 to 12-415.
See MORTGAGES AND DEEDS OF TRUST.

COMMISSIONERS.
Administration of courts.
Court commissioners.
Code of conduct for masters, examiners, auditors, referees and District Court commissioners.
Adoption, CJA Rule 16-814.
Bonds, surety, CJ §2-105.
County commissioners.
See COUNTIES.
District Court.
Appointment, CJ §1-605.
General provisions, CJ §2-607.
Multicounty district.
Performance of duties in multicounty districts, CJ §2-607.
Partition, PropAct Rule 12-401.
Report.
Exceptions, PropAct Rule 12-401.
Service, PropAct Rule 12-401.

COMMISSION MERCHANTS.
Agents.
See AGENCY.
Factors.
See FACTORS.

COMMISSION OF ELECTION.
Issuance by governor, EL §11-602.

COMMISSION ON CORRECTIONAL STANDARDS, COR §§8-106 to 8-117.
See PRISONS AND PRISONERS.

COMMISSIONS.
Commissions of office.
Generally.
See PUBLIC OFFICERS AND EMPLOYEES.
Natural resources.
Police force, NR §1-203.
General provisions.
See BOARDS AND COMMISSIONS.

COMMITMENT.
Drug or alcohol abuse.
See DRUG OR ALCOHOL ABUSE.
Juvenile causes.
General provisions.
See JUVENILE CAUSES.
Local correctional facilities.
See JAILS.
Mentally ill.
See MENTAL HEALTH FACILITIES.
Sentence and punishment.
See SENTENCE AND PUNISHMENT.
State correctional facilities.
See PRISONS AND PRISONERS.

COMMITTEE OR TRUSTEE.
Fiduciaries.
Successor corporate fiduciaries, ET §§15-1A-01 to 15-1A-05.
See FIDUCIARIES.

COMMITTEE OR TRUSTEE —Cont'd
Guardian and ward.
General provisions.
See GUARDIAN AND WARD.
Investments.
General provisions.
See INVESTMENTS.
Protection of property.
See GUARDIAN AND WARD.

COMMON CARRIERS.
Annual reports by public service companies, PUC §§6-201 to 6-210.
Carriers generally.
See CARRIERS.
Classification of companies, PUC §6-202.
Compensation for transporting passengers over same line and in same direction, PUC §9-102.
Costs and expenses of public service commission, payment, PUC §2-110.
Defined, PUC §1-101.
Discrimination against other common carriers in transferring, receiving or forwarding passengers, PUC §9-101.
Interchange of passengers between lines and lines of other common carriers, PUC §9-101.
Mile tickets.
Power of public service commission to order carrier to issue, PUC §5-102.
Permits for motor carriers, PUC §§9-201 to 9-204.
Procedure before public service commission.
Generally, PUC §§3-101 to 3-114.
See PUBLIC SERVICE COMMISSION.
Public service commission.
Generally, PUC §§2-101 to 5-106.
See PUBLIC SERVICE COMMISSION.
Railroads.
Generally, PUC §§9-301 to 9-403.
See RAILROADS.
Rate regulation and proceedings.
Just and reasonable rate defined, PUC §4-101.
Operating ratio, PUC §4-302.
Tariff schedules, PUC §9-103.
Through routes and joint rates, commission orders, PUC §5-102.
Safety violations, penalties, PUC §13-202.
Tariff schedules, PUC §9-103.
Through routes and joint rates.
Powers of commission to order, PUC §5-102.
Transfer of passengers between lines and lines of other common carriers, PUC §9-101.
Use of tracks or terminal facilities by other common carriers.
Common carrier not required to allow, PUC §9-101.

COMMON LAW.
Applicability, MD Const DofR Art 5.
Circuit courts.
Highest common-law court of records, CJ §1-501.
Constitutional provisions.
Suits at common law, US Const Amd 7.
Construction and interpretation.
Effect on common law, Rule 1-201.
Executors and administrators.
Settlement of decedents' estates.
Rules of construction, Estates Rule 6-104.
Judicial notice.
Uniform judicial notice of foreign laws.
General provisions.
See JUDICIAL NOTICE.

COMMON LAW —Cont'd
Trusts and trustees.
Real estate investment trust.
Law as to not limited, CA §8-103.

COMMUNICABLE DISEASES.
See CONTAGIOUS DISEASES.

COMMUNICATION DEVICES.
Law enforcement officers and personnel.
Law enforcement equipment fund, PS §§4-301 to 4-304.
State police department.
Use of communications system by other law enforcement agencies, PS §2-304.
Telecommunications generally.
See TELECOMMUNICATIONS.
Two-way radio frequency.
Interference with emergency communication, CR §9-601.

COMMUNICATIONS AND TRANSACTIONAL RECORDS ACCESS.
Actions.
Civil actions, CJ §10-4A-08.
Alteration of authorized access, CJ §10-4A-02.
Backup copies of communications, CJ §10-4A-05.
Damages, CJ §10-4A-08.
Definitions, CJ §10-4A-01.
Disclosure of information.
Costs.
Reimbursement of costs, CJ §10-4A-07.
Investigative or law enforcement officers.
By electronic or wire communications service, CJ §10-4A-04.
By remote computing service, CJ §10-4A-04.
Reimbursement of costs, CJ §10-4A-07.
Divulging contents of communications, CJ §10-4A-03.
Limitation of actions, CJ §10-4A-08.
Notice.
Delay in giving notices, CJ §10-4A-06.
Preventing authorized access, CJ §10-4A-02.

COMMUNISTS.
See SEDITION AND SUBVERSIVE ACTIVITIES.

COMMUNITY ACTION AGENCIES.
Housing and community development, HS §§8-101 to 8-109.

COMMUNITY ADULT REHABILITATION CENTERS, COR §§11-301 to 11-320.
Acquisition, construction and renovation costs, COR §11-309.
Acquisition of sites and facilities, COR §11-307.
Advisory board, COR §11-312.
Agreement between state and counties as to start-up costs, COR §11-308.
Assistant director.
Appointment and removal, COR §11-313.
Capacity, COR §11-307.
Cecil County.
Director, appointment and removal, sheriff, COR §11-313.
Placement of state correctional system inmates in center, COR §11-316.
Certification of need, COR §11-306.
Community advisory board, COR §11-312.
Community use of facilities at center, COR §11-315.
Confidentiality of personal information about inmate, COR §11-320.

COMMUNITY ADULT REHABILITATION CENTERS —Cont'd
Contract for operation of center by nonpublic person, COR §11-311.
Contracts by counties, COR §11-314.
Conversion of work release programs into centers, COR §11-304.
Costs.
Acquisition, construction and renovation costs, COR §11-309.
Operation, COR §11-310.
Start-up, COR §11-308.
County operation of center, COR §11-311.
Charter county, COR §11-313.
Noncharter county, COR §11-313.
Criteria and guidelines for state standards, COR §11-305.
Definitions, COR §11-301.
Director.
Appointment and removal, COR §11-313.
Earnings of inmates, collection and disposition, COR §11-319.
Establishment, COR §11-307.
Evaluation and determination of need, COR §11-306.
Federal funds, operation costs, COR §11-310.
Leave for inmates, COR §11-319.
Legislative findings, COR §11-303.
Local correctional system inmates, placement in centers, COR §11-317.
Maximum capacity, COR §11-307.
Minimum state standards, COR §11-305.
Operation, COR §11-311.
Operation costs, COR §11-310.
Personal information about inmate, released by center director, COR §11-320.
Placement of individuals sentenced to or detained in state correctional system, COR §§11-316, 11-317.
Powers of counties to carry out subtitle, COR §11-314.
Programs, COR §11-315.
Purposes, COR §11-303.
Regional center, director and assistant director, COR §11-313.
Regional center, operation by, COR §11-311.
Regional centers, center to include, COR §11-302.
Release of inmate, recommendation of center director, COR §11-317.
Release of personal information of inmate, COR §11-320.
Revocation of participation, COR §§11-317, 11-318.
Scope of title, COR §11-304.
Selection of site, COR §11-307.
Standards, COR §11-305.
Start-up costs, COR §11-308.
State correctional system inmates, placement of individuals, COR §11-316.
State operation of center, COR §11-311.
Director and assistant director, COR §11-313.
State share of costs.
Acquisition, construction in renovation costs, COR §11-309.
Start-up costs, COR §11-308.
State subsidy.
Operation cost, COR §11-310.
Terms and conditions, established by center director, COR §11-318.
Use of facilities by community, COR §11-315.

COMMUNITY ADULT REHABILITATION CENTERS —Cont'd
Work release programs, conversion into centers, COR §11-304.

COMMUNITY ASSOCIATIONS.
Agents.
  Personal liability, CJ §5-406.
Insurance.
  Pooling to purchase casualty or property insurance, IN §19-601.
Limited civil liability, SG §7-108.
Nuisance actions by associations, RP §§14-123 to 14-125.1.
Personal property tax credit, TP §9-238.

COMMUNITY COLLEGES.
Acceptance of gifts by board of trustees, ED §16-103.
Accounts and accounting.
  Audits, ED §16-315.
  Financing. See within this heading, "Financing."
Actions.
  Local government tort claims act, CJ §§5-301 to 5-304.
  See TORTS.
Anne Arundel county.
  Composition of board of trustees, ED §16-401.
  Student member of board of trustees, ED §16-401.
Annual grant factor.
  Defined, ED §16-305.
Appropriations.
  Current expenses, ED §16-203.
  Power to appropriate and borrow funds, ED §16-304.
  Receipt by board of trustees, ED §16-103.
  Required appropriations, ED §16-304.
  Reserve fund for maintenance and repair, ED §16-304.
  Transfer of appropriations, ED §16-304.
Assets.
  Disposition, ED §16-103.
Authority to establish and maintain, ED §16-103.
Baccalaureate degree programs.
  Proposals to offer, ED §16-108.
Baltimore City community college, ED §§16-501 to 16-513.
  See BALTIMORE CITY COMMUNITY COLLEGE.
Bids, ED §16-311.
Board of trustees.
  Actions.
    Defense of sovereign immunity, ED §16-107.
  Anne Arundel county.
    Composition, ED §16-401.
    Student member of board, ED §16-401.
  Assets.
    Disposition, ED §16-103.
  Baccalaureate degree programs.
    Proposals to offer, ED §16-108.
  Baltimore county, ED §16-402.
  Borrowing authority, ED §16-302.
  Budget, ED §16-301.
  Capital budget, ED §16-301.
  Capital improvement program, ED §16-301.
  Chairman, ED §16-102.
  Chesapeake college, ED §16-406.
  Composition, ED §16-101.
  Comprehensive liability insurance, ED §16-107.
  Control.
    General control, ED §16-103.

COMMUNITY COLLEGES —Cont'd
Board of trustees —Cont'd
  Defenses.
    Sovereign immunity, ED §16-107.
  Defined, ED §16-202.
  Established, ED §16-101.
  Frederick county, ED §16-407.
  Funds.
    Receipt of funds, ED §16-103.
  Harford county, ED §16-408.
  Howard county, ED §16-410.
  Immunity.
    Defense of sovereign immunity, ED §16-107.
  Insurance.
    Comprehensive liability insurance, ED §16-107.
  Lease-purchase agreements.
    Term extension, ED §16-302.
    Validation, ED §16-303.
  Meetings, ED §16-102.
  Montgomery county, ED §16-411.
    Multi-year financing agreements.
      Right of cancellation, ED §16-302.
  Name, ED §16-103.
  Notes to finance project, issuance.
    Agreement with health and higher education facilities authority, ED §16-302.1.
  Officers, ED §16-102.
  Powers, ED §16-103.
  Prince George's county, ED §16-414.
  Records, ED §16-103.
  Rules and regulations, ED §16-103.
  Seal.
    Adoption of corporate seal, ED §16-103.
  Sovereign immunity.
    Defense, ED §16-107.
  Suits.
    Power to sue and be sued, ED §16-103.
  Term, ED §16-101.
  Vacancies, ED §16-101.
  Washington county, ED §16-419.
Bond issues.
  Agreement with health and higher education facilities authority, ED §16-302.1.
Budgets, ED §16-301.
  Contents of operating budget, ED §16-301.
  Preparation by board, ED §16-301.
  Review and approval, ED §16-315.
  Submission of annual budget request, ED §16-307.
  Submissions to state agencies, ED §16-301.
  Wor-Wic community college.
    Assent of supporting counties, ED §16-418.
Cecil community college.
  Apportionment of expenses, ED §16-305.
  State's share, ED §16-305.
Charter for higher education.
  Duties, ED §10-210.
  Expenses.
    Apportionment of expenses, ED §16-305.
    State's share, ED §16-305.
Chesapeake college.
  Board of trustees, ED §16-406.
  Expenses, ED §16-305.
Claims.
  Local government tort claims act, CJ §§5-301 to 5-304.
  See TORTS.
Collective bargaining.
  Classified employees of Baltimore county community colleges, ED §16-403.
  Prince George's county public employment relations, ED §16-414.1.

COMMUNITY COLLEGES —Cont'd
College investment plan, ED §§18-19A-01 to 18-19A-07.
See UNIVERSITIES AND COLLEGES.
College savings plan of Maryland, ED §§18-1901 to 18-1916.
See UNIVERSITIES AND COLLEGES.
Community college transfer scholarship program, ED §§18-2501 to 18-2507.
Computer-based instructional technology.
Procurement, ED §16-318.
Contracts, ED §16-311.
Contributions.
State contributions with respect to voluntary contributions by eligible donors, ED §16-317.
County aid.
Computation, ED §16-305.
County share.
Basis for annual total state appropriation, ED §16-305.
Defined, ED §16-305.
Curriculum.
Determined by state board, ED §16-103.
Definitions, ED §16-202.
Contributions, ED §16-317.
Distinguished scholar program, ED §18-1106.
Employees.
Collective bargaining.
Classified employees of Baltimore county community colleges, ED §16-403.
Prince George's county, ED §16-414.1.
Enrollment of employees without payment of tuition, ED §16-106.
Sick pay, ED §16-316.
English for Speakers of Other Languages (ESOL).
Student grants, ED §16-305.
Entrance requirements.
Determined by state board, ED §16-103.
Facilities of board of education.
Use by board of trustees, ED §16-103.
Federal government.
Power of board to make agreements, ED §16-103.
Fees.
Outside state, county or region, ED §16-310.
Payment by credit card, ED §15-102.
Student fees.
Charged by board of trustees, ED §16-103.
Outside state, county or region, ED §16-310.
Students enrolled in statewide or regional program, ED §16-310.
Waiver of out-of-state, out-of-county or out-of-region fee, ED §16-310.
Financing.
Borrowing authority, ED §16-302.
Budgets.
Submission of annual budget request, ED §16-307.
County share, ED §16-305.
Payment, ED §16-309.
General provisions, ED §§16-203 to 16-315.
Lease-purchase agreements.
Term extension, ED §16-302.
Validation, ED §16-303.
Payment of county's share, ED §16-305.
Proportion of current expenses paid by state, county and students, ED §§16-203, 16-305.
Definitions, ED §16-305.
Senator John A. Cade funding formula, ED §16-305.

COMMUNITY COLLEGES —Cont'd
Financing —Cont'd
State's share.
Amount, ED §16-305.
Basis for annual total state appropriation, ED §16-307.
Payment, ED §16-308.
Student share.
Amount, ED §16-305.
Fines.
Trespass on grounds, ED §26-102.
Frederick county.
Board of trustees, ED §16-407.
Garrett community college.
State's share.
Apportionment of expenses, ED §16-305.
Handicapped students.
Supplemental services and support for students with disabilities, ED §16-319.
Harford county.
Board of trustees, ED §16-408.
Merger with educational foundation, ED §16-409.
Hazing, CR §3-607.
Higher education commission.
Powers and duties.
Generally, ED §11-105.
HOPE for nontraditional students.
Community college transfer scholarship program, ED §§18-2501 to 18-2507.
Immunity.
Local government tort claims act, CJ §§5-301 to 5-304.
See TORTS.
Inspections.
General services department, SF §4-409.
Investments.
Local investment guidelines generally, 95 §22F.
Labor and employment relations.
Division of employment and training.
Coordination with community colleges, LE §11-104.
Liability.
Local government tort claims act, CJ §§5-301 to 5-304.
See TORTS.
Maintenance of effort law, ED §16-305.
Montgomery county.
See MONTGOMERY COUNTY.
Motor vehicles.
Operation on property.
Applicability of rules of the road, TR §21-101.1.
Negligence.
Local government tort claims act, CJ §§5-301 to 5-304.
See TORTS.
Notes to finance project, issuance.
Agreement with health and higher education facilities authority, ED §16-302.1.
Per pupil grant amount.
Defined, ED §16-305.
President.
Appointment.
By board of trustees, ED §§16-103, 16-104.
Prince George's county.
See PRINCE GEORGE'S COUNTY.
Property.
Acquisition and disposition by board of trustees, ED §16-103.
Public employment relations.
Prince George's county, ED §16-414.1.

COMMUNITY COLLEGES —Cont'd
Regional community colleges.
Applicability of subtitle provisions, ED §16-201.
Authority to establish, ED §16-202.
Board of trustees.
Chesapeake college, ED §16-406.
New board.
Appointment by governor, ED §16-202.
Notes to finance projects, issuance, ED
§16-302.1.
Chesapeake college.
Board of trustees, ED §16-406.
Fees.
Students enrolled in statewide or regional
programs, ED §16-310.
Students from outside state, county or region,
ED §16-310.
Financing.
General provisions, ED §§16-203 to 16-315.
Funds, ED §16-304.
Inspections.
General services department, SF §4-409.
Notes to finance projects, issuance, ED §16-302.1.
Retirement contributions, ED §16-306.
Rules and regulations.
By board, ED §16-103.
Salaries.
Fixed by board of trustees, ED §16-103.
Sick pay for employees, ED §16-316.
Scholarships.
Graduate and professional scholarship program,
ED §18-2601.
Secondary education.
Use of land, buildings, etc., ED §16-103.
Sick pay for employees, ED §16-316.
Small community colleges.
Defined, ED §16-305.
State aid, ED §16-305.
State aid.
Amount, ED §§16-305, 16-307.
Basis for annual total state appropriation, ED
§16-307.
Computation, ED §16-305.
Defined, ED §16-305.
Garrett community college.
Apportionment of expenses, ED §16-305.
Payment, ED §16-308.
Retirement contributions, ED §16-306.
Small community colleges, ED §16-305.
State board.
Approval for establishment of community colleges,
ED §16-103.
Curriculum.
Approval by board, ED §16-103.
Entrance requirements.
Determination, ED §16-103.
Immunity.
Raising defense of sovereign immunity, CJ
§5-519.
Sovereign immunity.
Raising of defense, CJ §5-519.
State retirement and pension system.
Optional retirement program, SPP §§30-101 to
30-307.
See STATE RETIREMENT AND PENSION
SYSTEM.
Student share.
Amount, ED §16-305.
Supplemental funding escalator.
Defined, ED §16-305.

COMMUNITY COLLEGES —Cont'd
Tenure of teachers.
Board of trustees to fix, ED §16-103.
Torts.
Local government tort claims act, CJ §§5-301 to
5-304.
See TORTS.
Transfer to four year institution.
Community college transfer scholarship program,
ED §§18-2501 to 18-2507.
Trespass.
Upon grounds.
Penalty, ED §26-102.
Tuition.
College investment plan, ED §§18-19A-01 to
18-19A-07.
See UNIVERSITIES AND COLLEGES.
College savings plan of Maryland, ED §§18-1901
to 18-1916.
See UNIVERSITIES AND COLLEGES.
Enrollment of persons over sixty or retired and
disabled without payment of tuition, ED
§16-106.
Payment by credit card, ED §15-102.
Students from outside state, county or region, ED
§16-310.
Waiver, ED §16-106.
Vocational education.
Use of land, buildings, etc., in connection with,
ED §16-103.
Voter registration agencies.
Designation of, EL §3-204.
Waiver of out-of-state fee, ED §16-310.
Wor-Wic community college.
Budget.
Assent of supporting counties, ED §16-418.

**COMMUNITY COLLEGE TRANSFER
SCHOLARSHIP PROGRAM,** ED §§18-2501 to
18-2507.
**Amount awarded, use, retention of
scholarship,** ED §18-2504.
Established, ED §18-2501.
Funding, ED §18-2507.
List of individual receiving award.
Sent general assembly members, ED §18-2505.
Publication of availability, ED §18-2506.
Qualifications, ED §18-2503.
Use at four year public or private institution,
ED §18-2502.

COMMUNITY DEVELOPMENT.
Fines.
False statements or reports, HS §4-255.
Housing and community development, HS
§§1-101 to 11-106.
See HOUSING AND COMMUNITY
DEVELOPMENT.

**COMMUNITY DEVELOPMENT
ADMINISTRATION,** HS §§4-201 to 4-255.
Bond issues, HS §§4-244 to 4-253.
Infrastructure projects, local financing, HS
§§4-229 to 4-233.
Enabling resolution or ordinance.
Adoption, HS §4-232.
Contents, HS §4-231.
Issuing procedures, HS §4-230.
Local obligations, HS §4-229.
Pledges of faith and credit securing, HS §4-233.
Interest rate exchange agreements, HS §4-253.
Legal status, HS §4-250.

**COMMUNITY DEVELOPMENT
    ADMINISTRATION** —Cont'd
Bond issues —Cont'd
Lien of the pledge, HS §4-248.
Not debt of the state, HS §4-251.
Powers of administration, HS §4-244.
    Authority to borrow money and issue bonds or
        notes, HS §4-245.
Purchase of notes or bonds, HS §4-249.
Redemption of notes or bonds, HS §4-249.
Refunding of bonds, HS §4-246.
Renewal of bonds and notes, HS §4-246.
Repayment, HS §4-248.
Tax exemption, HS §4-252.
Trust agreement to secure, HS §4-247.
Building codes.
Plan approval process, HS §4-213.
Criminal law and procedure.
False statements or reports, HS §4-255.
Defined terms, HS §4-201.
Development finance division.
Units in division, HS §4-103.
Director, HS §4-207.
Duties and powers, HS §§4-211 to 4-215.
Duties generally, HS §4-211.
Financing community development projects, HS
    §4-226.
Mortgages purchases and loans, HS §4-237.
Elderly rental housing program.
Powers and duties of department, HS §4-404.
Eminent domain, HS §4-214.
Energy conservation projects, HS §4-218.
Financing, HS §4-227.
Establishment, HS §4-204.
False statements or reports, HS §4-255.
Families of limited income.
Community development projects.
    Housing and facilities requirements, exception,
        HS §4-217.
Determination, HS §4-212.
Financing, HS §§4-225 to 4-241.
Energy conservation projects, HS §4-227.
Infrastructure projects, HS §4-228.
    Local obligations, HS §4-229.
        Enabling resolution or ordinance.
            Adoption, HS §4-232.
            Contents, HS §4-231.
        Issuing procedures, HS §4-230.
        Pledges of faith and credit securing, HS
            §4-233.
Liens.
    Powers of administration, HS §4-226.
Mortgage lenders.
    Certificate, HS §4-240.
    Limitations, HS §4-236.
    Loans to eligible, HS §4-239.
Mortgage loans.
    Assignment and assumption, residential, HS
        §4-241.
    Commitment to purchase, HS §4-238.
    Guarantee by GNMA, HS §4-234.
    Purchases and mortgage loans.
        Powers of administration, HS §4-237.
    Requirement of mortgage, HS §4-225.
    Reverse equity mortgage loans and other
        mortgage loans, HS §4-235.
Powers of administration, HS §4-226.
Procedures generally, HS §4-225.
Recipients, HS §4-225.
Reverse equity mortgage loans, HS §4-235.
Solar energy projects, HS §4-227.

**COMMUNITY DEVELOPMENT
    ADMINISTRATION** —Cont'd
Financing —Cont'd
Sources of money, HS §4-225.
Findings of general assembly, HS §4-202.
Grants.
Limitation on grants, HS §4-206.
Home improvement projects, HS §4-219.
**Housing and community development
    department.**
Governmental units of department, HS §2-201.
Housing finance review committee, HS §4-208.
Income tax.
Bond issues.
    Tax exempt status, HS §4-252.
Infrastructure projects, HS §4-220.
Financing, HS §4-228.
    Local obligations, HS §4-229.
        Enabling resolution or ordinance.
            Adoption, HS §4-232.
            Contents, HS §4-231.
        Issuing procedures, HS §4-230.
        Pledges of faith and credit securing, HS
            §4-233.
Lease of property.
Community development projects.
    Plan approval process, HS §4-213.
Liens.
Powers of administration, HS §4-226.
Live near your work program, HS §§4-215,
    4-217.
Loans.
Powers of administration.
    Authority to borrow money and issue bonds or
        notes, HS §4-245.
Local approval.
Plan approval process, HS §4-213.
Mortgages and deeds of trust.
Financing community development projects.
    Mortgage lenders.
        Certificate, HS §4-240.
        Limitations, HS §4-236.
        Loans to eligible, HS §4-239.
    Mortgage loans.
        Assignment and assumption, residential, HS
            §4-241.
        Commitment to purchase, HS §4-238.
        Guarantee by GNMA, HS §4-234.
        Purchases and mortgage loans.
            Powers of administration, HS §4-237.
        Requirement of mortgage, HS §4-225.
        Reverse equity mortgage loans and other
            mortgage loans, HS §4-235.
        Reverse equity mortgage loans, HS §4-235.
Plan approval process, HS §4-213.
Powers and duties, HS §§4-211 to 4-215.
Borrowing money and issuing bonds or notes, HS
    §4-245.
Financing community development projects, HS
    §4-226.
Mortgages purchases and loans, HS §4-237.
Projects, HS §§4-217 to 4-222.
Community development projects generally, HS
    §4-217.
Energy conservation projects, HS §4-218.
Home improvement projects, HS §4-219.
Housing and facilities requirements, HS §4-217.
Infrastructure projects, HS §4-220.
Plan approval process.
    Sale or lease of project property, HS §4-213.
Public purpose projects, HS §4-221.

COMMUNITY DEVELOPMENT ADMINISTRATION —Cont'd
Projects —Cont'd
Solar energy projects, HS §4-222.
Public purpose projects, HS §4-221.
Purpose, HS §4-205.
Findings of general assembly, HS §4-202.
Sale of property.
Community development projects.
Plan approval process, HS §4-213.
Solar energy projects, HS §4-222.
Financing, HS §4-227.
Staff, HS §4-207.
Taxation.
Bond issues.
Exemptions, HS §4-252.
Teachers.
Homeownership program for teachers, HS §4-203.
Weatherization program.
Duties generally, HS §4-211.
Zoning.
Plan approval process, HS §4-213.

COMMUNITY ENERGY LOAN PROGRAM, SG §§9-2101 to 9-2109.
Applications, SG §9-2105.
Contracts with third parties, SG §9-2108.
Definitions, SG §9-2101.
Established, SG §9-2102.
Fund, SG §9-2107.
Maryland energy administration generally, SG §§9-2001 to 9-2007, 9-2104.
Prohibited acts, SG §9-2109.
Purpose, SG §9-2103.
Terms and conditions, SG §9-2106.

COMMUNITY FORESTRY, NR §§5-424 to 5-427.
See URBAN AND COMMUNITY FORESTRY.

COMMUNITY FOUNDATIONS.
Charitable gift annuities, IN §16-114.

COMMUNITY HEALTH RESOURCES COMMISSION.
Fund, HG §19-2201.
Health maintenance organizations.
Reimbursement, HG §19-712.7.

COMMUNITY HOME CARE SERVICES.
Administration of services, 88A §84.
Community services.
Defined, 88A §85.
Declaration of policy, 88A §84.
Department of employment and social services.
Duties, 88A §86.
Responsibility for administration of system of services, 88A §84.
Department of health and mental hygiene and department of aging.
Duties, 88A §86.
Elderly persons.
Defined, 88A §85.
Employment of elderly persons to perform services, 88A §87.
Legislative intent, 88A §84.

COMMUNITY MENTAL HEALTH FACILITIES, HG §§24-601 to 24-607.
See MENTAL HEALTH FACILITIES.

COMMUNITY MENTAL HEALTH SERVICES.
Community programs, HG §10-903.
Comprehensive plan.
Community-based services, HG §10-207.

COMMUNITY MENTAL HEALTH SERVICES —Cont'd
Funds.
Transition funding option, HG §10-902.1.
Use of funds, HG §10-902.
Health officers.
Responsibilities, HG §10-904.
Intercounty programs, HG §10-903.
Providers.
Reimbursement for approved services, HG §16-201.2.
Residential mental health programs for children and adolescents.
Definitions.
Private therapeutic group home, HG §10-920.
Director.
Duties, HG §10-921.
Evaluation of private therapeutic group homes, HG §10-926.
Plan, HG §10-925.
Funding.
State funding, HG §16-304.
Individual treatment plans, HG §10-924.
Placement of child or adolescent in private therapeutic group home, HG §10-923.
Private therapeutic group homes.
Defined, HG §10-920.
Evaluation, HG §10-926.
Individual treatment plans, HG §10-924.
Placement of child or adolescent in, HG §10-923.
Rules and regulations, HG §10-922.
Individual treatment plans, HG §10-924.
Secretary.
Rules and regulations, HG §10-922.
Rules and regulations.
Adoption by secretary, HG §10-901.
Salaries.
Certain employees of programs, HG §10-905.
Secretary.
Duties, HG §10-901.

COMMUNITY NOTIFICATION OF SEX OFFENDERS, CP §§11-709 to 11-712, 11-718.
See SEX OFFENDER REGISTRATION.

COMMUNITY OR OTHER MERITORIOUS PROGRAM PARTICIPATION.
Leave of inmate from confinement.
Inmates sentenced to jurisdiction of division of correction, COR §3-810.

COMMUNITY RECREATION.
Volunteer program, CJ §5-802.

COMMUNITY REHABILITATION PROGRAMS, ED §§21-401 to 21-404.
Contracts.
Division may contract for furnishing of programs and services, ED §21-404.
Definitions, ED §21-401.
Inspections, ED §21-403.
Listing, ED §21-403.
Rules and regulations, ED §21-402.
Supervision of program, ED §21-402.

COMMUNITY REINVESTMENT FUND, HS §§9-101 to 9-501.
Administration, HS §9-204.
Community reinvestment board, HS §§9-201 to 9-204.
Established, HS §9-201.
Meetings, HS §9-203.

COMMUNITY REINVESTMENT FUND —Cont'd
Community reinvestment board —Cont'd
Membership, HS §9-202.
Operation, powers and duties, HS §9-204.
Conflict of laws.
Application of other laws, HS §9-304.
Defined terms, HS §9-101.
Department of housing and community development.
Duties of department, HS §9-306.
Powers of department, HS §9-307.
Established, HS §9-301.
Exemptions, HS §9-302.
Findings, HS §9-102.
Household income limits.
Reinvestment assistance, HS §9-401.
Loan committee, HS §9-204.
Organization, HS §9-303.
Purpose of fund, HS §9-301.
Records, HS §9-204.
Reinvestment assistance, HS §§9-401 to 9-404.
Applications for assistance, HS §9-403.
Community reinvestment projects, requirements, HS §9-402.
Household income limits, HS §9-401.
Methods of providing, HS §9-404.
Short title, HS §9-501.
Standards and guidelines, HS §9-204.
Status of fund, HS §9-302.
Use of fund money, HS §9-305.

COMMUNITY RESIDENTIAL SERVICES PROGRAMS.
Receivership.
General provisions, HG §§19-333 to 19-339.
See HOSPITALS.

COMMUNITY RIGHT-TO-KNOW.
Hazardous materials and substances, EN §§6-501 to 6-504.
Collection of required information from owners or operators.
Community right-to-know fund.
Establish, use, EN §7-604.
Definitions, EN §7-601.
Exception from paying annual fee, EN §7-604.
False information submitted, prohibition, EN §7-603.
Fee for facilities required to report, EN §7-604.
Information required to be provided, EN §7-602.
Regulations, EN §7-602.
Repository for information.
Department to serve as, EN §7-602.
Violations, enforcement and penalties, EN §7-605.
Community right-to-know fund, EN §§7-601 to 7-605.
Public access to information on hazardous or toxic chemicals.
Duties of department, EN §6-503.
"Hazardous or toxic chemical" defined, EN §6-501.
Notice of request for information, EN §6-503.
Persons allowed access, EN §6-503.
Purpose of subtitle, EN §6-502.
Rules and regulations, EN §6-504.

COMMUNITY SERVICE PROGRAMS, COR §§8-701 to 8-711.
Administration of program, COR §8-706.
Administrator's report, COR §8-709.
Authority of court to order, COR §8-703.

COMMUNITY SERVICE PROGRAMS —Cont'd
Compensation for work required, COR §8-704.
Consent to assignment required, COR §8-704.
County may establish, COR §8-702.
County report to administering agency, COR §8-709.
Crime of violence conviction, defendant not eligible, COR §8-704.
Definitions, COR §8-701.
Department of juvenile services, administration of juvenile program, COR §8-706.
Monitoring program, COR §8-707.
Division of parole and probation, administration of adult program, COR §8-706.
Monitor of program, COR §8-707.
Dorchester County.
Person sentenced to confinement in department of corrections, COR §11-711.
Establishment, COR §8-702.
Information to be provided by participating agencies, COR §8-705.
Kent County, COR §11-716.
Local correctional facilities.
Calvert County, COR §11-706.
Monitoring program, COR §8-707.
Payments by county, COR §8-708.
Other meritorious programs, COR §3-810.
Participation by institutions, associations and agencies, COR §8-705.
Payments by county, COR §8-708.
Prince George's County.
Rubbish cleanup on private property.
Request by owner for assignment of community service worker, COR §8-711.
Responsibility of participating agency, COR §8-710.
Restitution by participant, COR §8-710.
Rubbish cleanup in Prince George's County.
Request by owner of private property.
Assignment of community service worker, COR §8-711.
Unsuitability of community service worker, report by participating agency, COR §8-710.
Wicomico county, authorized program, COR §11-724.

COMMUNITY SERVICES ADMINISTRATION.
Acceptance of federal or private aid and assistance, 41 §6-204.
Contracts, 41 §6-203.
Creation, 41 §6-201.
Department of human resources.
Part of department, 41 §6-202.
Duties, 41 §6-203.
Energy assistance program act.
Office of home energy programs, 41 §6-404.
Executive director, 41 §6-202.
Deputy director, 41 §6-202.
Federal aid.
Acceptance, 41 §6-204.
Federal programs.
Administration, 41 §6-203.
Information.
Collection and dissemination, 41 §6-203.
Merit system.
Employee subject to, 41 §6-203.
Office of community services.
References construed to mean community services administration, 41 §6-201.

COMMUNITY SERVICES ADMINISTRATION
—Cont'd
Office of economic opportunity.
References construed to mean community services administration, 41 §6-201.
Personnel, 41 §6-203.
Purposes, 41 §6-201.

COMMUNITY SERVICES REIMBURSEMENT RATE COMMISSION, HG §§13-801 to 13-810.
Chairmen, HG §13-804.
Compensation of members, HG §13-805.
Creation, HG §13-802.
Definitions, HG §13-801.
Development duties, HG §13-806.
Duties, HG §13-806.
Findings and recommendations, HG §13-810.
Functions, HG §13-802.
Meetings, HG §13-805.
Members, HG §13-803.
Powers, HG §13-807.
Reimbursement to community service providers, HG §7-307.
Reports, HG §13-809.
Response to recommendations, HG §13-810.
Secretary of health and mental hygiene.
Authority over commission, HG §13-808.
Staff, HG §13-805.
Vice-chairman, HG §13-804.

COMMUNITY SERVICES TRUST FUND, HG §§24-1101 to 24-1105.
Accounting, HG §24-1103.
Accounts.
Structure of fund, HG §24-1104.
Defined terms, HG §24-1101.
Established, HG §24-1102.
Investments, HG §24-1103.
Nature of fund, HG §24-1103.
Purpose, HG §24-1102.
Structure, HG §24-1104.
Transfers from fund, HG §24-1105.
Uses, HG §24-1105.

COMMUTATION OF SENTENCE.
Conditional commutation of sentence.
Defined, COR §7-101.
Death sentence, power of governor, COR §7-601.
Defined, COR §7-101.
Power of governor, COR §7-601.
Pregnant inmate, COR §9-601.
Restitution, COR §7-701.
Victim, notice, impact statement, COR §7-805.
Written executive order to evidence, COR §7-601.

COMMUTER BENEFITS.
Air quality control.
Employer-provided commuter benefits.
Tax credits, EN §2-901.
Financial institution franchise tax.
Credits, TG §8-221.
Income tax.
Credits, TG §10-715.
Insurance companies.
Premium taxes, credit for costs, IN §6-120.
Taxation.
Employer-provided commuter benefits.
Tax credits, EN §2-901.
Insurance company premium tax credits, IN §6-120.

COMPACTS.
Adoption.
Interstate compact on adoption and medical assistance, FL §§5-4A-01 to 5-4A-08.
Interstate compact on the placement of children, FL §§5-601 to 5-611.
See CHILD PLACEMENT.
Adult offender supervision, COR §§6-201 to 6-215.
See ADULT OFFENDERS SUPERVISION.
Appalachian states low-level radioactive waste compact, EN §§7-301 to 7-306.
See APPALACHIAN STATES LOW-LEVEL RADIOACTIVE WASTE COMPACT.
Atlantic states marine fisheries commission.
General provisions.
See ATLANTIC STATES MARINE FISHERIES COMMISSION.
Chesapeake regional Olympic games authority, SG §9-2303.
Execution of compact, SG §9-2302.
Child placement.
Interstate compact on the placement of children, FL §§5-601 to 5-611.
See CHILD PLACEMENT.
Constitutional provisions.
Between state and foreign power, US Const Art I §10.
Between the states, US Const Art I §10.
Corrections.
Interstate corrections compact, COR §§8-601 to 8-611.
See PRISONS AND PRISONERS.
Detainers.
Interstate agreement on detainers, COR §§8-401 to 8-417.
See INTERSTATE AGREEMENT ON DETAINERS.
Driver license compact.
General provisions, TR §§16-701 to 16-708.
See DRIVER LICENSE COMPACT.
Education.
Compact for education, ED §§25-101 to 25-104.
See SCHOOLS.
Interstate agreement on qualification of educational personnel, ED §§6-601 to 6-604.
See SCHOOLS.
Southern regional education compact, ED §§25-201 to 25-205.
See SCHOOLS.
Emergency management.
Emergency management assistance compact, PS §§14-701, 14-702.
Interstate emergency management and civil defense compact, PS §§14-601 to 14-605.
Maryland emergency management assistance compact, PS §§14-801 to 14-803.
Forests and parks.
Middle Atlantic interstate forest fire protection compact.
General provisions, NR §5-801.
Hazardous materials and substances.
Appalachian states low-level radioactive waste compact, EN §§7-301 to 7-306.
See APPALACHIAN STATES LOW-LEVEL RADIOACTIVE WASTE COMPACT.
Horse racing.
National racing compact, BR §§11-1301 to 11-1312.
See NATIONAL RACING COMPACT.

COMPACTS —Cont'd
Insects.
    Pest control compacts.
        See PESTS.
Insurance.
    Interstate insurance product regulation compact,
        IN §§29-101, 29-102.
**Interstate emergency management and civil
    defense compact,** PS §§14-601 to 14-605.
Interstate mining compact.
    General provisions, EN §§15-901, 15-902.
Interstate oil and gas compact.
    General provisions, EN §§14-401 to 14-404.
        See GAS AND OIL.
Jennings Randolph lake project compact, NR
    §8-4A-01.
Juveniles.
    Interstate compact on juveniles.
        See JUVENILES, COMPACT ON.
Libraries, ED §§25-301 to 25-303.
    See LIBRARY COMPACT.
Low-level nuclear waste.
    See RADIATION.
Low-level radioactive waste.
    Appalachian states low-level radioactive waste
        compact, EN §§7-301 to 7-306.
        See APPALACHIAN STATES LOW-LEVEL
            RADIOACTIVE WASTE COMPACT.
Mental health.
    Interstate compact on mental health.
        See MENTAL HEALTH COMPACT.
Mining.
    Interstate mining compact.
        See MINING.
Minors.
    Interstate compact on the placement of children.
        General provisions.
            See CHILD PLACEMENT.
    Juvenile services.
        Interstate compact on juveniles.
            See JUVENILES, COMPACT ON.
Motor vehicles.
    Driver license compact, TR §§16-701 to 16-708.
        See DRIVER LICENSE COMPACT.
    Potomac river bridges towing compact, TR
        §25-301.
**National crime prevention and privacy
    compact,** CP §§10-237 to 10-250.
        See NATIONAL CRIME PREVENTION AND
            PRIVACY COMPACT.
Northeast interstate dairy compact, AG §§2-801
    to 2-805.
Nuclear compact.
    Southern interstate nuclear compact.
        General provisions, 41 §§16-101 to 16-114.
            See NUCLEAR COMPACT.
Nurse multistate licensure compact, HO
    §§8-7A-01 to 8-7A-05.
Oil and gas.
    Interstate oil and gas compact.
        General provisions.
            See GAS AND OIL.
Pest control compact.
    See PESTS.
Potomac river basin compact, EN §§5-301 to
    5-304.
Potomac river compact of 1958.
    Powers of Potomac river fisheries commission, NR
        §4-307.
    Regulations.
        Recording, NR §4-306.

COMPACTS —Cont'd
Potomac river compact of 1958 —Cont'd
    Terms, NR §4-306.
Radioactive waste.
    Appalachian states low-level radioactive waste
        compact, EN §§7-301 to 7-306.
        See APPALACHIAN STATES LOW-LEVEL
            RADIOACTIVE WASTE COMPACT.
Secretary of state.
    Delivery of copies to office of secretary, SG §7-104.
Southern interstate nuclear compact, 41
    §§16-101 to 16-114.
    See NUCLEAR COMPACT.
States.
    Compacts between the states or with foreign
        powers, US Const Art I §10.
Susquehanna river basin compact, EN §5-301.
**Washington metropolitan area transit
    authority.**
    General provisions, TR §10-204.
**Washington metropolitan area transit
    authority compact.**
    General provisions, TR §§10-201 to 10-207.
        See WASHINGTON METROPOLITAN AREA
            TRANSIT AUTHORITY COMPACT.
Waste.
    Radioactive waste.
        Appalachian states low-level radioactive waste
            compact, EN §§7-301 to 7-306.
            See APPALACHIAN STATES LOW-LEVEL
                RADIOACTIVE WASTE COMPACT.
Water resources.
    Potomac river basin compact, EN §§5-301 to
        5-304.
    Susquehanna river basin compact, EN §5-301.
Wildlife.
    Interstate wildlife violator compact, NR §§10-1201
        to 10-1203.
Woodrow Wilson bridge and tunnel compact,
    TR §§10-301 to 10-303.

COMPANIONSHIP, LOSS OF.
Drug dealer liability act.
    Noneconomic damages, CJ §3-1606.
Noneconomic damages, limitation on, CJ
    §11-108.

COMPARATIVE NEGLIGENCE.
Bank deposits and collections.
    Unauthorized signature or alteration.
        Customer's duty to report, CL §4-406.
Negotiable instruments.
    Forged or altered instrument, CL §§3-405, 3-406.

**COMPASSIONATE LEAVE FROM
    CONFINEMENT.**
Dorchester County department of corrections,
    COR §11-711.
**Inmates sentenced to jurisdiction of division
    of correction,** COR §3-808.

COMPENSATION.
Fees.
    General provisions.
        See FEES.
Salaries.
    See SALARIES.
Unemployment compensation.
    General provisions, LE §§8-101 to 8-1608.
        See UNEMPLOYMENT COMPENSATION.
Workers' compensation.
    General provisions, LE §§9-101 to 10-320.
        See WORKERS' COMPENSATION.

COMPENSATION —Cont'd
Wrongful death.
Death by wrongful act.
General provisions.
See DEATH BY WRONGFUL ACT.

COMPETENCY.
General rule, Evid Rule 5-601.
Judges, Evid Rule 5-605.
Jurors, Evid Rule 5-606.
Juvenile cases.
Competency or incompetency to proceed, CJ
§§3-8A-17.1 to 3-8A-17.12.
Testators, ET §4-101.
Witnesses.
See WITNESSES.

COMPETENCY TO STAND TRIAL, CP §§3-101
to 3-108.
See INCOMPETENCY TO STAND TRIAL.

COMPETENCY TO TESTIFY.
Witnesses.
Competency.
See WITNESSES.

COMPETITION.
Antitrust act.
General provisions, CL §§11-201 to 11-213.
See SALES.
Electric customer choice and competition act.
Generally, PUC §§7-501 to 7-517.
See ELECTRIC CUSTOMER CHOICE AND
COMPETITION ACT.
Rate stabilization, PUC §§7-520 to 7-549.
See ELECTRIC CUSTOMER CHOICE AND
COMPETITION ACT.
Freestanding ambulatory care facilities.
Joint ventures allowed, HG §19-3B-06.
**Maryland advisory commission on
manufacturing competitiveness,** 83A
§§3-801 to 3-804.

COMPLAINANT.
Parties.
See PARTIES.

COMPLAINTS.
Administration of courts.
Conference of circuit judges, CJA Rule 16-108.
Allowed pleadings, CivProCir Rule 2-302.
District Court, CivProDist Rule 3-302.
Apartment residents.
Electric and gas submetering.
Occupant complaints, PUC §7-303.
Arbitration and award.
International commercial arbitration.
Filing of complaints, CJ §3-2B-05.
Attachment.
Prejudgment attachment.
Proceedings on complaint.
Circuit courts, CivProCir Rule 2-115.
District Court, CivProDist Rule 3-115.
Attorneys at law.
Disbarment or suspension.
Disposition of complaints, CJA Rule 16-759.
Burial grounds.
Sale for other purposes.
Contents of complaint, PropSales Rule 14-401.
How commenced, PropSales Rule 14-401.
Divorce.
Pleadings, FamLaw Rule 9-202.
Eminent domain, PropAct Rule 12-205.

COMPLAINTS —Cont'd
General assembly.
Conflicts of interest, SG §15-515.
Human relations commission.
General provisions, 49B §§5 to 13.
See HUMAN RELATIONS COMMISSION.
Insurance adviser misconduct, IN §10-212.
Judicial disabilities and sanctionable conduct,
CJA Rule 16-805.
Confidentiality, CJA Rule 16-810.
Disposition without proceedings on charges, CJA
Rule 16-807.
Further investigation, CJA Rule 16-806.
Juvenile causes, Juv Rule 11-102.
Definitions, Juv Rule 11-101.
Landlord and tenant.
Distress for rent.
See DISTRESS FOR RENT.
Limited liability companies.
Derivative actions by members, CA §4A-803.
Mandamus.
Commencement of action, SpecPro Rule 15-701.
Montgomery county.
Preparation of complaints.
Immunity from liability of certain officials, CJ
§5-503.
Public ethics.
Conflicts of interest.
General assembly, SG §15-515.
Public service commission proceedings, PUC
§3-102.
Sufficiency of service, PUC §3-103.
Simulation of document to induce payment, CR
§8-522.
Tax sales.
Foreclosure of right of redemption, PropSales Rule
14-502.
Wetlands.
Violations.
Service, EN §16-503.

COMPOST.
Composting.
Defined, EN §9-1701.
**Composting by consumers or farmers for
personal purposes.**
Scope of part not intended to regulate or interfere,
EN §9-1721.
Defined, EN §9-1701.
Public lands.
Consideration and preference to use of compost in
maintenance activity, EN §9-1722.
Recycling solid waste generally.
See RECYCLING SOLID WASTE.
Yard waste composting activities, EN §9-1723.

COMPREHENSIVE HEALTH PLANNING.
Secretary.
Powers, HG §2-108.

**COMPREHENSIVE PHYSICAL
REHABILITATION FACILITIES.**
Accreditation, HG §19-1204.
Health care facilities.
Specialized rehabilitation programs.
Requirement for providing, HG §19-1207.
Accreditation of health care facilities, HG
§§19-2301, 19-2302.
Compliance with provisions.
Required, HG §19-1202.
Definitions, HG §19-1201.

COMPREHENSIVE PHYSICAL
REHABILITATION FACILITIES —Cont'd
Health care facilities.
Accreditation.
Specialized rehabilitation programs.
Requirement for providing, HG §19-1207.
Defined, HG §19-1201.
Provision of comprehensive physical
rehabilitation, HG §19-1207.
Specialized rehabilitation programs.
Provision by health care facilities, HG §19-1207.
Inspections, HG §19-1205.
Licenses, HG §19-1203.
Revocation, HG §19-1206.
Misdemeanors.
Violations of provisions, HG §19-1208.
Penalties.
Violations of provisions, HG §19-1208.
Requirements, HG §19-1204.
Specialized rehabilitation programs.
Compliance with provisions as prerequisite to
providing, HG §19-1202.
Defined, HG §19-1201.
Health care facilities.
Provision by health care facilities, HG §19-1207.
Violations of provisions.
Penalties, HG §19-1208.

COMPREHENSIVE PLANS.
Charter counties, 66B §1.03.

COMPROMISE.
Actions against state officers and employees.
Authority of attorney general to compromise or
settle claims, SG §12-305.
Administrative procedure.
Contested cases.
Disposition by settlement, SG §10-210.
Air quality control.
Claims for civil penalties under section, EN
§2-610.
Automobile insurance fund, SpecPro Rule
15-805.
Claims against fund, IN §§20-604, 20-605.
Bank deposits and collections.
Collection of items by depository and collecting
banks.
Settlement of items.
Medium and time of settlement, CL §4-213.
Provisional status, CL §4-201.
When provisional credits become final, CL
§4-215.
Charities.
Settlement agreements with violators, BR §6-205.
Child support enforcement administration.
Arrearages.
Power to settle, FL §10-112.
Cigarette business licenses.
Offer of compromise in lieu of suspension or
revocation of license.
Petition prior to suspension or revocation, BR
§16-212.
Class actions.
Circuit courts, CivProCir Rule 2-231.
Commercial code.
Written waiver of claim or right after breach, CL
§1-107.
Comptroller.
Claims of state, SF §6-219.
Contribution among joint tortfeasors.
Effect of settlement, CJ §3-1402.
Evidence, Evid Rule 5-408.

COMPROMISE —Cont'd
Executors and administrators.
Powers of personal representative, ET §7-401.
Fiduciary estates including guardianships of
property, Guardian Rule 10-703.
Health care malpractice claims.
Offer of judgment, CJ §3-2A-06C.
Settlement conference.
Alternative dispute resolution, CJ §3-2A-06C.
Insurance.
Automobile insurance fund.
Claims against fund, IN §§20-604, 20-605.
Credit life, health and unemployment insurance,
IN §13-113.
Property and casualty insurance guaranty
corporation.
Receiver, liquidator or successor of insolvent
insurer bound by settlements, IN §9-309.
Reinsurance managers' settlement of claims, IN
§8-515.
Third party claim for bodily injury.
Notice of settlement payment, IN §4-117.
Unfair claim settlement practices, IN §§27-301 to
27-306.
Foreign risk retention groups, IN §25-103.
Uninsured motorist coverage.
Settlement procedures, IN §19-511.
Viatical settlement contracts, IN §§8-601 to 8-611.
See VIATICAL SETTLEMENT CONTRACTS.
Joint tortfeasors.
Contribution among joint tortfeasors.
Effect of settlement, CJ §3-1402.
Malpractice.
Health care malpractice claims.
Offer of judgment, CJ §3-2A-08A.
Settlement conference.
Alternative dispute resolution, CJ §3-2A-06C.
Motor vehicle insurance.
Automobile insurance fund.
Claims against fund, IN §§20-604, 20-605.
Motor vehicles.
Consumer leasing contracts.
Informal settlement procedure, CL §14-2005.
Uninsured motorist coverage.
Settlement procedures, IN §19-511.
Warranty.
Automotive warranty enforcement act.
Informal dispute settlement procedure, CL
§14-1502.
Noise control.
Civil penalties.
Claims for penalty, EN §3-406.
Personal injuries.
Release or settlement of claim by injured
individual, CJ §5-401.1.
Preneed burial contracts.
Administration of trust accounts, BR §5-707.
Receivers.
Compromise or settlement of claims, Receivers
Rule 13-403.
Service contracts and consumer products
guaranty.
Informal dispute settlement procedures.
Voluntary establishment by guarantors or
providers, CL §14-406.
State treasury.
Claims of state, SF §6-219.
Structured settlements.
Transfer of payment rights, CJ §§5-1101 to
5-1105.
Application for transfer authorization, filing,
serving, CJ §5-1103.

COMPROMISE —Cont'd
Structured settlements —Cont'd
Transfer of payment rights —Cont'd
Basis for ordering transfer, CJ §5-1102.
Definitions, CJ §5-1101.
Jurisdiction over application for transfer, CJ §5-1103.
No liability for payment pursuant to authorized transfer, CJ §5-1104.
Notice of proposed transfer, filing, serving, CJ §5-1103.
Order of court required to authorize, CJ §5-1102.
Structured settlement defined, CJ §5-1101.
Transfer in contravention of law prohibited, CJ §5-1105.
Waiver of provision prohibited, CJ §5-1105.
Taxation.
Actions to collect taxes.
Compromise of claim, TG §13-816.
Death taxes.
Interstate compromise of death taxes, TG §§7-118 to 7-122.
See TAXATION.
Tort claims act.
Settlement of claims, SG §12-107.
Unemployment compensation.
Administration of claims.
Recovery of benefits.
Benefit recovery under governmental offset agreement, LE §8-809.
Contributions.
Enforcement and collection, LE §8-635.
University of Maryland.
Montebello center.
Settlements or judgments against state officer or employee, ED §13-404.
Workers' compensation.
Claim settlement.
Approval and contents, LE §9-722.
Generally, LE §9-722.
Injured workers' insurance fund.
Insurance program.
Payment of premiums, LE §10-133.
Settlement of claims, LE §10-138.
Offset against other benefits, LE §9-610.
Permanent partial disability awards, LE §9-610.1.
Uninsured employers.
Assessment on awards and settlements.
Generally, LE §9-1007.
Compromise of judgment, LE §9-1013.
Settlement by covered employee or dependents, LE §9-1014.

COMP TIME.
State personnel.
Holiday work, SPP §9-205.

COMPTROLLER.
Abandoned property disposition.
Administrator, CL §§17-101 to 17-326.
See ABANDONED PROPERTY DISPOSITION.
Accounts and accounting, SF §6-216.
Duty as to public accounts, MD Const Art VI §2.
Inspection of accounts, SG §4-107.
Manner of expressing accounts, SG §4-111.
Uniform accounts.
Uniform system of accounts, 19 §§35 to 41.
See ACCOUNTS AND ACCOUNTING.
Acting comptroller, SG §4-105.

COMPTROLLER —Cont'd
Admissions and amusement tax.
General provisions.
See ADMISSIONS AND AMUSEMENT TAX.
Alcoholic beverages.
Collection of taxes, 2B §12-113.
Confiscation of property.
Disposition of confiscated property, 2B §1-201.
Discounts.
Regulations, 2B §12-103.
Enforcement of article, 2B §§16-401, 16-404, 16-405.
Inspections and investigations, 2B §16-405.
Hearings.
Delegation of authority to conduct hearings, 2B §16-404.
Licenses.
Fees.
Disposition, 2B §10-204.
Nonrefundable application fee, 2B §2-402.
Issuance, 2B §10-201.
Delegation of authority to issue licenses and permits, 2B §16-404.
Renewal, 2B §10-301.
Fee, 2B §2-402.
Revocation and suspension.
Procedure, 2B §10-403.
Powers, 2B §16-404.
Reports.
Annual report of comptroller, 2B §14-203.
Supervision over, 2B §14-201.
Rules and regulations.
Adoption, 2B §16-301.
Deposit on returnable beer containers, 2B §16-303.
Discrimination prohibited, 2B §12-102.
Powers as to, 2B §16-302.
Appropriations.
Disbursements and expenditures.
Checks.
Undeliverable checks fund.
Duties of comptroller, SF §7-229.
Atlantic states marine fisheries commission.
Duties.
Generally, NR §4-304.
Attorney general.
Written opinions to, MD Const Art V §3.
Authority over units.
Effect on staff, SG §4-106.
Generally, SG §4-106.
Banks and trust companies.
Banking board.
Ex officio member, FI §2-202.
Reorganization of commercial bank as national banking association, FI §3-802.
State comptroller.
Banking board.
Ex officio member, FI §2-202.
U.S. comptroller.
Conversion of commercial bank into national banking associations, FI §3-802.
Blank licenses, SG §4-110.
Bond issues.
Countersigning, MD Const Art VI §3.
Bonds, surety, MD Const Art VI §1.
Filing, SG §4-102.
Form and conditions, SG §4-102.
Recordation, SG §4-102.
Required, SG §4-102.
Books and papers.
Records. See within this heading, "Records."

COMPTROLLER —Cont'd
Campaign finance.
Contributions to political campaigns during
general assembly sessions.
Prohibition, exceptions, EL §13-235.
Chief deputy comptroller, SG §4-104.
Acting comptroller, SG §4-105.
Child support enforcement administration.
Interception of state payments to obligor, FL
§§10-113.1, 10-113.2.
Cigarette sales, less than 20 per package, CL
§§11-5A-01 to 11-5A-03.
Compensation, MD Const Art VI §1.
Compromise and settlement.
Claims of state, SF §6-219.
**Contributions to political campaigns during
general assembly sessions.**
Prohibition, exceptions, EL §13-235.
Corporations.
Forfeiture of charter.
Nonpayment of taxes.
Duties of comptroller, CA §3-503.
Counterfeiting stamp, CR §8-608.
Counties.
Transportation bonds.
Withholding by comptroller upon failure of
county to levy tax, TR §3-308.
Court of appeals.
Acting comptrollers.
Court of appeals to have exclusive original
jurisdiction, SG §4-105.
Creation of position, SG §4-101.
Debts.
Certification of debts to state agencies and
withholding of income tax refunds.
Interception of refund for support and
maintenance payments, FL §10-113.
Decedents' estates.
Appraisers.
Appointment and remuneration subject to
approval of comptroller, ET §2-301.
Defined, TG §1-101.
Deputy comptroller, SG §4-104.
Chief deputy comptroller, SG §4-104.
Duties.
Generally, MD Const Art VI §2.
Elections, MD Const Art VI §1.
Contributions to political campaigns during
general assembly sessions.
Prohibition, exceptions, EL §13-235.
Examination.
By governor, MD Const Art II §18.
Fees.
Officers whose compensation is derived from fees.
Report showing officers who complied with
section, MD Const Art XV §1.
Property liens.
Recording and indexing of property liens arising
under certain taxes.
Exemption from fees, RP §3-603.
Field enforcement division.
Law enforcement officers generally, PS §§3-101 to
3-603.
See LAW ENFORCEMENT OFFICERS AND
PERSONNEL.
Finance department.
Supervise fiscal affairs of state, MD Const Art VI
§2.
General assembly.
Inspection of records or accounts by members, SG
§4-107.

COMPTROLLER —Cont'd
Governor.
Discharging duties of office of governor during
vacancy, MD Const Art II §7.
Examination by governor, MD Const Art II §18.
Inspection of records, SG §4-107.
Removal.
Hearing of charges, MD Const Art VI §6.
Hall of records commission.
Member of commission, SG §9-1003.
Income tax.
Certification of debt and withholding of income
tax refunds.
Interception of refund for support and
maintenance payments, FL §10-113.
Property liens.
Fees.
Recording and indexing of property liens
arising under income tax law.
Exemption from fees, RP §3-603.
Withholding refunds due to state government
debts, TG §§13-912 to 13-922.
Industrial development financing authority.
State comptroller ex officio member, 83A §5-905.
Inspections.
Authority of governor or members of general
assembly to inspect records, SG §4-107.
Investigative services unit.
Arrest without a warrant.
Generally, CP §§2-201 to 2-210.
See WARRANTLESS ARREST.
Authority granted police officers generally, CP
§2-102.
Definitions.
Police officer, CP §2-101.
Fresh pursuit, CP §2-301.
Law enforcement procedures generally, CP
§§2-101 to 2-107.
See POLICE.
Powers.
Granted to police officers generally, CP §2-102.
Warrantless arrest.
Generally, CP §§2-201 to 2-210.
See WARRANTLESS ARREST.
Licenses.
Blank licenses, SG §4-110.
Liens.
Fees.
Property liens.
Recording and indexing of property liens
arising under certain taxes.
Exemption from fees, RP §3-603.
Manner of expressing accounts, SG §4-111.
Maryland food center authority.
Ex officio member, 41 §13-103.
Term of office, 41 §13-103.
Motor fuel inspection.
Administration and enforcement generally, BR
§§10-101 to 10-502.
See MOTOR FUEL INSPECTION.
Motor vehicles.
Display of state seal on vehicle, TR §22-404.2.
Reimbursement of forfeited bond or collateral, TR
§27-104.
Revenues.
Disposition by comptroller, TR §12-118.
Remitted to comptroller, TR §12-118.
Notice.
Inability to serve or unavailability, SG §4-105.
Oaths, MD Const Art VI §1.
Official oath, SG §16-102.

COMPTROLLER —Cont'd
Oaths —Cont'd
When to qualify, MD Const Art VI §5.
Office, MD Const Art VI §1.
Position, SG §4-101.
Powers.
Generally, MD Const Art VI §2.
Public debts.
Duties as to, MD Const Art VI §2.
Public works.
Member of board of public works, MD Const Art XII §1.
Qualification.
When to qualify, MD Const Art VI §5.
Recordation.
Fees.
Property liens.
Recording and indexing of property liens arising under certain taxes.
Exemption from fees, RP §3-603.
Records.
Inspection of records, SG §4-107.
Payments into treasury, SF §6-215.
Settlement of claims, SF §6-219.
Warrants for disbursements of appropriations, SF §7-223.
Refunds.
Certification of debts to state agencies and withholding of income tax refunds.
Interception of refund for support and maintenance payments, FL §10-113.
Register of wills.
Bonds, surety, SG §4-109.
Compensation, SG §4-108.
Number, SG §4-108.
Removal.
Procedure, MD Const Art VI §6.
Reports.
Annual report, MD Const Art VI §2.
Fiscal operations of state, SF §2-102.
Fees.
Officers whose compensation is derived from fees, MD Const Art XV §1.
Statement of receipts and expenditures, SF §2-103.
Salaries.
Annual salary, SG §4-103.
General provisions, MD Const Art VI §1.
Sales tax.
Property liens.
Fees.
Recording and indexing of property liens arising under sales and use tax laws.
Exemption from fees, RP §3-603.
Schools.
Payments, ED §5-212.
Comptroller to draw warrant for amount due, ED §5-212.
Withholding or suspending payment of funds, ED §5-213.
Small business development financing authority.
State comptroller ex officio member, 83A §5-1004.
Staff.
Authority over units.
Effect on staff, SG §4-106.
Authority to employ staff, SG §4-104.
Duties, SG §4-104.
Statement of receipts and expenditures, SF §2-103.

COMPTROLLER —Cont'd
State's attorneys.
Assisting and adjusting accounts, 10 §38.
Bond of state's attorney.
Deposit with comptroller, 10 §35.
State treasurer.
Accounts.
Inspection by comptroller, MD Const Art VI §4.
Taxation.
Administration of laws, TG §2-102.
Certification of assessments.
Submission by supervisor to comptroller, TP §8-421.
Collection of taxes.
Constitution of Maryland, MD Const Art VI §2.
Duties, TG §2-109; TP §1-304.
Defined, TG §1-101.
Distribution of tax revenue.
Duties, TG §2-109.
Examination of records.
Collector of state taxes, TP §4-301.
Failure to take action required by comptroller.
Penalties, TG §13-1022.
Rules and regulations, TG §2-103.
Term of office, MD Const Art VI §1.
Use tax.
General provisions.
See USE TAX.
Property liens arising under sales and use tax laws.
Exemption from fees, RP §3-603.
Vacancy.
Filling, MD Const Art VI §1.
Warrants for payment of money.
Drawn by comptroller, MD Const Art VI §3.
Duties as to, MD Const Art VI §2.

COMPULSIVE GAMBLING, HG §§19-801 to 19-804.
See GAMING.

COMPULSORY SCHOOL ATTENDANCE, ED §§7-301, 7-302.
Deaf and blind children.
Inducing absence, ED §8-311.

COMPUTATION OF AGE, 1 §37.

COMPUTATION OF TIME.
Elections.
Performing any act, EL §1-301.
Generally, 1 §36; Rule 1-203.
Limitation of actions.
General provisions, CJ §§5-201 to 5-205.
See LIMITATION OF ACTIONS.

COMPUTER ACCESS CODE.
Unauthorized possession or distribution, CR §7-302.

COMPUTER DISCS.
Unauthorized recording of sounds or images, CR §§7-306 to 7-310.

COMPUTER INFORMATION TRANSACTIONS, CL §§22-101 to 22-816.
Acceptance, CL §22-203.
Conditionally, CL §22-205.
Electronic agents, CL §22-206.
Varying terms, CL §22-204.
Acceptance of copy, CL §22-609.
Effect, CL §22-610.
Accommodation contract.
Financier does become licensee, CL §22-508.

COMPUTER INFORMATION TRANSACTIONS
—Cont'd

Accommodation contract —Cont'd
Financier does not become licensee, CL §22-507.
Acquisition of rights.
Transfer by licensee, CL §22-506.
Adequate assurance of performance, CL §22-708.
Adopting terms of records, CL §22-208.
Mass-market license, CL §22-209.
Agents, electronic, CL §22-107.
Offer and acceptance, CL §22-206.
Anticipatory repudiation, CL §22-709.
Assent, CL §22-112.
Authentication, CL §22-108.
Determining attribution, CL §22-213.
Breach of contract, CL §22-701.
Cure, CL §22-703.
Performance generally, CL §22-601.
Waiver of remedy, CL §22-702.
Cancellation.
Enforcement of financing arrangements, CL §22-510.
Remedies, CL §22-802.
Choice of law, CL §22-109.
Contractual choice of forum, CL §22-110.
Commercial practice, CL §22-113.
Commercial reasonableness of attribution procedure, CL §22-212.
Completing performance, CL §22-604.
Remedies, CL §22-812.
Conduct.
Terms of contract, CL §22-210.
Construction and interpretation, CL §§22-106, 22-301 to 22-309.
Practical construction, CL §22-302.
Consumer defenses, CL §22-214.
Continuing contractual terms, CL §22-304.
Continuing use.
Remedies, CL §22-813.
Contract formation generally, CL §22-202.
Contractual modification of remedies, CL §22-803.
Contract with previous vested grant of rights.
Copy, CL §22-705.
Conveyance of ownership, CL §22-501.
Copy.
Acceptance, CL §22-609.
Effect of, CL §22-610.
Contract with previous vested grant of rights, CL §22-705.
Delivery, CL §22-606.
Duties upon rightful refusal, CL §22-706.
Inspection, CL §22-608.
Performance related to delivery, CL §22-607.
Refusal of defective tender, CL §22-704.
Revocation of acceptance, CL §22-707.
Correction and support contracts.
Special types of contracts, CL §22-612.
Culmination and conflict of warranties, CL §22-408.
Cumulative remedies, CL §22-801.
Cure of breach of contract, CL §22-703.
Damages.
Generally, CL §22-807.
Licensee's damages, CL §22-809.
Licensor's damages, CL §22-808.
Recoupment, CL §22-810.
Defective copies.
Refusal of defective tender, CL §22-704.
Definitions, CL §22-102.

COMPUTER INFORMATION TRANSACTIONS
—Cont'd

Delivery of copy, CL §22-606.
Determining attribution, CL §22-213.
Disclaimer or modification of warranty, CL §22-406.
Discontinuing access.
Remedies, CL §22-814.
Duration of contract, CL §22-308.
Effectiveness of releases, CL §22-207.
Effect of acknowledgment, CL §22-215.
Efficacy of attribution procedure, CL §22-212.
Electronic error, CL §22-214.
Electronic regulation of performance, CL §22-605.
Electronic self-help, CL §22-816.
Enabling use, CL §22-602.
Enforcement of financing arrangements, CL §22-510.
Enforcement of termination, CL §22-618.
Evidence.
Parole or extrinsic, CL §22-301.
Exclusions, CL §22-103.
Express warranty, CL §22-402.
Failure of presupposed conditions, CL §22-615.
Federal law, CL §22-105.
Financing.
Arrangements, CL §§22-509 to 22-511.
Financier does not become licensee, CL §22-507.
Licenses, CL §22-508.
Formal requirements, CL §22-201.
Formation and terms, CL §§22-201 to 22-216.
Fraud.
Remedies, CL §22-806.
General provisions, CL §§22-101 to 22-114.
Governing law, CL §22-109.
Contractual choice of forum, CL §22-110.
Grants, CL §22-307.
Idea or information submission, CL §22-216.
Immediately completed performance, CL §22-604.
Implied warranty, CL §22-403.
Informational content, CL §22-404.
Purpose of licensee, CL §22-405.
Information submission, CL §22-216.
Inspection of copy, CL §22-608.
Internet-type transactions.
Pretransaction disclosures, CL §22-211.
Interpretation and construction, CL §§22-106, 22-301 to 22-309.
Practical construction, CL §22-302.
Irrevocable obligations.
Enforcement of financing arrangements, CL §22-509.
Legal recognition, CL §22-107.
Licensee's damages, CL §22-809.
License grants, CL §22-307.
Modification of computer program, CL §22-307.
Licensor's damages, CL §22-808.
Limitation of actions, CL §22-805.
Limitations on electronic self-help, CL §22-816.
Liquidated damages.
Remedies, CL §22-804.
Loss.
Risk of loss of copy, CL §22-614.
Manifesting assent, CL §22-112.
Mass-market license, CL §22-209.
Material breach of contract, CL §22-701.
Measurement of damages, CL §22-807.
Merchantability of computer program, CL §22-403.

COMPUTER INFORMATION TRANSACTIONS
—Cont'd
Mixed transactions, CL §22-104.
Modification, CL §22-303.
Modification of computer program, CL §22-407.
Modification of warranty, CL §22-406.
Noninterference and noninfringement.
  Warranties, CL §22-401.
Offer and acceptance, CL §22-203.
  Conditionally, CL §22-205.
  Electronic agents, CL §22-206.
  Varying terms, CL §22-204.
Opting in or out, CL §22-104.
Ownership, CL §22-501.
  Duration of contract, CL §22-308.
  Title to copy, CL §22-502.
Performance, CL §22-601.
  Adequate assurance of, CL §22-708.
  Anticipatory repudiation, CL §22-709.
    Retraction of, CL §22-710.
  By delegate, CL §22-505.
  Related to delivery of copy, CL §22-607.
  Right to possession and prevent use, CL §22-815.
  To satisfaction, CL §22-309.
  Under open terms, CL §22-306.
Practical construction, CL §22-302.
Presupposed conditions, failure of, CL §22-615.
Pretransaction disclosures, CL §22-211.
Proof and effect of authentication, CL §22-108.
Public policy, CL §22-105.
Publishers, dealers, and end users.
  Special types of contracts, CL §22-613.
Regulation of performance.
  Electronic regulation, CL §22-605.
Releases, CL §22-207.
Remedies.
  Cancellation, CL §22-802.
  Completing performance, CL §22-812.
  Continuing use, CL §22-813.
  Contractual modification, CL §22-803.
  Discontinuing access, CL §22-814.
  Fraud, CL §22-806.
  Generally, CL §22-801.
  Limitation of actions, CL §22-805.
  Liquidated damages, CL §22-804.
  Specific performance, CL §22-811.
Requirements, CL §22-201.
Rescission, CL §22-303.
Retraction of anticipatory repudiation, CL §22-709.
Revocation of acceptance of copy, CL §22-707.
Rightful refusal of copy, CL §22-706.
Rights of licensor.
  Financing arrangements, CL §22-511.
Right to possession and prevent use, CL §22-815.
Risk of loss of copy, CL §22-614.
Rules governing access contracts.
  Special types of contracts, CL §22-611.
Rules governing transfer of interest, CL §22-503.
  Effect of transfer, CL §22-504.
Rules of construction, CL §22-106.
Rules pertaining to enabling use, CL §22-602.
Satisfaction, CL §22-309.
Scope, CL §22-103.
Short title, CL §22-101.
Special types of contracts.
  Access contracts, CL §22-611.
  Correction and support contracts, CL §22-612.
  Publishers, dealers, and end users, CL §22-613.

COMPUTER INFORMATION TRANSACTIONS
—Cont'd
Subcontracts, CL §22-505.
Submission of information to satisfaction of party, CL §22-603.
Supplemental principles, CL §22-114.
Survival of obligations.
  Termination, CL §22-616.
Termination, CL §22-616.
  Enforcement, CL §22-618.
  Notice of termination, CL §22-617.
Terms.
  Conduct, CL §22-210.
  Continuing contractual terms, CL §22-304.
  Generally, CL §§22-201 to 22-216.
  Open terms, CL §22-306.
  Supplemental principles, CL §22-114.
  To be specified, CL §22-305.
  Unconscionable contracts or terms, CL §22-111.
Terms of records, CL §22-208.
  Mass-market license, CL §22-209.
Third-party beneficiaries of warranties, CL §22-409.
Title, CL §§22-101, 22-502.
Transfer of contractual interest, CL §22-503.
  Effect, CL §22-504.
    Transfer by licensee, CL §22-506.
  Transfer by licensee, CL §22-506.
Unconscionable contracts or terms, CL §22-111.
Unsatisfactory submission of information, CL §22-603.
Validity.
  Terms to be specified, CL §22-305.
Variation by agreement, CL §22-113.
Waiver of remedy for breach of contract, CL §22-702.
Warranties, CL §§22-401 to 22-409.
  Culmination and conflict, CL §22-408.
  Disclaimer or modification, CL §22-406.
  Express warranty, CL §22-402.
  Implied warranty, CL §22-403.
    Informational content, CL §22-404.
    Purpose of licensee, CL §22-405.
  Noninterference and noninfringement, CL §22-401.
  Third-party beneficiaries, CL §22-409.
When electronic message effective, CL §22-215.

COMPUTER MANUFACTURERS.
Name of manufacturer.
  Computer required to be labeled with, EN §9-1727.
Recycling, refurbishing or reuse.
  Takeback program.
    Defined, EN §9-1701.
    Registration to include, EN §9-1728.
Registration, EN §§9-1727 to 9-1730.
  Annual submission and update, EN §9-1728.
  Content requirements, EN §9-1728.
  Effective date of requirement, EN §9-1727.
  Enforcement, violations, penalties, EN §9-1730.
  Fee, EN §9-1728.
  Regulations, adoption, EN §9-1729.
  Required, EN §9-1727.
  Review by department, EN §9-1728.
  Scope of provisions, EN §9-1727.
Takeback program.
  Defined, EN §9-1701.
  Implementation by manufacturer.
    Registration to include, EN §9-1728.

COMPUTER NETWORK.
Unauthorized access, CR §7-302.

COMPUTERS.
Access code.
Unauthorized possession or distribution, CR §7-302.
Budget and management department.
Telecommunication and computer network, SF §3-705.
Building codes.
Central automated database, PS §12-506.
Child pornography, CR §11-207.
Removal of child pornography from Internet, CR §11-208.1.
Documents.
Charitable giving information program.
Data available to the public, BR §6-201.
State documents.
Data bases, SG §7-206.2.
Electronic transactions generally, CL §§21-101 to 21-120.
See ELECTRONIC TRANSACTIONS.
Information transactions generally, CL §§22-101 to 22-816.
See COMPUTER INFORMATION TRANSACTIONS.
Manufacturers.
Registration, EN §§9-1701, 9-1727 to 9-1730.
Personal jurisdiction.
Causes arising from conduct in state or tortious injury outside state.
Applicability of provision to computer information, CJ §6-103.
Procurement.
Streamlined process for information technology services, SF §§13-401, 13-402.
Property taxes.
Exemptions.
Computer software and related documentation, TP §7-238.
Tax credits.
Business personal property that is computer software, TP §9-227.
Business that provides computers to employees for home use, TP §9-241.
Recycling, refurbishing or reuse.
Takeback program by manufacturers.
Defined, EN §9-1701.
Registration to include information on, EN §9-1728.
Registration.
Manufacturers, EN §§9-1727 to 9-1730.
Sales and use tax.
Exemptions.
Computer programs, TG §11-225.
Schools.
Distance learning.
Maryland technology academy, ED §7-1001.
Virtual learning opportunities, ED §7-1002.
Technology for education, ED §§7-901 to 7-910.
State police department.
Use of computer system by other law enforcement agencies, PS §2-304.
Takeback program by manufacturers.
Defined, EN §9-1701.
Recycling, refurbishing or reuse.
Registration to include information on, EN §9-1728.
Theft of services available only for compensation, CR §7-104.

COMPUTERS —Cont'd
Unauthorized access to computers, CR §7-302.
Limitation of actions, CJ §5-106.

COMPUTER SERVICES.
Unauthorized access, CR §7-302.

COMPUTER SOFTWARE PROGRAMS.
Local governments.
Authority to sell, lease or license programs to the public, 24 §17-101.
Personal jurisdiction.
Causes arising from conduct in state or tortious injury outside state.
Applicability of provision to computer programs, CJ §6-103.

CONCEALED WEAPONS.
Carrying, wearing or transporting.
Dangerous weapon, CR §4-101.
Handgun, CR §4-203.
Warrantless arrest, CP §2-203.

CONCERTS.
Outdoor concerts.
Promoter licenses, BR §§17-1401 to 17-1407.
See OUTDOOR CONCERTS.
Prince George's county.
Benefit performance by qualified organization, CR §§13-1901 to 13-1907.

CONCURRENT SENTENCES, COR §9-202.
Burglary with explosives or destructive device, CR §6-207.
Burning with intent to defraud, CR §6-106.
Child abuse or sexual abuse of minor, CR §§3-601, 3-602.
Contraband in place of confinement, CR §9-417.
Destructive device violations, CR §4-503.
Disarming law enforcement officer, CR §4-103.
Exploitation of vulnerable adult.
Separate sentence, concurrent or consecutive sentence, CR §8-801.
Identity fraud.
Separate sentence, consecutive or concurrent sentence, CR §8-301.
Rape.
Continuing course of conduct against child, CR §3-315.
Sexual offense.
Continuing course of conduct against child, CR §3-315.
Stalking, CR §3-802.

CONDEMNATION.
Chesapeake Bay.
Public access to Chesapeake Bay and tributaries.
Big Blackwater River and Little Blackwater River, NR §8-204.
Eminent domain.
General provisions, PropAct Rules 12-201 to 12-213; RP §§12-101 to 12-212.
See EMINENT DOMAIN.
Highways.
Acquisition of real property.
General provisions, TR §§8-301 to 8-339.
See HIGHWAYS.
Quick-take act.
See HIGHWAYS.
Local boards of elections.
Report of condemned buildings to local board for voter registration purposes, EL §3-504.
Outdoor advertising.
Removal of preexisting, nonconforming signs, TR §8-743.

CONDOMINIUMS.
Accounts and accounting.
  Required accounting principles, RP §11-128.
Actions against governing body.
  Actual damages, RP §14-118.
Additional and supplemental to other
    provisions, RP §11-141.
Additions.
  Improvements, alterations or additions by unit
    owner, RP §11-115.
Advertising for political candidates, RP
    §11-111.2.
Agency.
  Resident agent, RP §11-119.
Alcoholic beverages.
  Possession or consumption in public places.
    Municipal regulation, 2B §19-104.
Alterations.
  By unit owner, RP §11-115.
Amendments.
  Bylaws, RP §§11-104, 11-124.
  Plats, RP §§11-105, 11-124.
Applicability of title, RP §11-142.
Assessments.
  Common expenses.
    Payment, RP §11-110.
Audits.
  Books and records, RP §11A-128.
  Outside audit required, RP §11-116.
Board of directors.
  Closed meetings, RP §§11-109.1, 11A-128.
  Defined, RP §11-101.
  Meetings.
    Closed meetings, RP §§11-109.1, 11A-128.
Bonds, surety.
  Corporate surety bond on new condominiums, RP
    §11-121.
Books.
  Required to be kept, RP §11-116.
Boundaries.
  Presumptions, RP §11-125.
Budgets.
  Council of unit owners.
    Annual proposed budget, RP §11-109.2.
Buildings.
  Regulations.
    General provisions, RP §11-122.
Bylaws.
  Amendments, RP §§11-104, 11-124.
    Corrective amendments, RP §11-103.1.
  Contents, RP §11-104.
  Govern administration of buildings, RP §11-104.
  Indexing.
    Establishment of condominium regime, RP
      §11-102.
  Interpretation and construction, RP §11-124.
  Purchaser.
    Furnishing by vendor, RP §11-126.
  Recordation.
    Establishment of condominium regime, RP
      §11-102.
    With declaration, RP §11-104.
  Required particulars, RP §11-104.
Campaign literature.
  Montgomery county.
    Distributing or depositing, EL §1-303.
Candidate signs, RP §11-111.2.
Citation of act, RP §11-143.
Common elements.
  Conveyance.
    Limited common elements, RP §11-108.

CONDOMINIUMS —Cont'd
Common elements —Cont'd
  General common elements.
    Defined, RP §11-101.
  Liability.
    Injuries, RP §11-118.
  Limited common elements.
    Conveyance by deed, RP §11-108.
    Defined, RP §11-101.
  Maintenance.
    Responsibility for maintenance, repair and
      replacement, RP §11-108.1.
  Meetings in, RP §11-108.
  Percentage interest, RP §11-107.
  Responsibility for maintenance, repair and
    replacement, RP §11-108.1.
  Use, RP §11-108.
Complaints.
  Dispute settlement mechanism, RP §11-113.
Consumer protection, RP §11-130.
Contracts.
  Contract liens, RP §§14-201 to 14-206.
    See LIENS.
  Sale of unit subsequent to initial sale, RP §11-126.
  Termination.
    Authority of council of unit owners, RP §11-133.
    Purchaser's right to rescind contract, RP
      §11-126.
Conversion of residential rental facility to
    condominium.
  Notice.
    Failure of landlord or owner to give notice
      defense to action for possession, RP
      §11-102.1.
  Tenant's right to purchase property occupied as
    residence, RP §11-136.
  Tenant's right to purchase property occupied as
    residence, RP §11-136.
Cooperative housing corporations.
  See COOPERATIVE HOUSING
    CORPORATIONS.
Council of unit owners.
  Actions against governing body.
    Actual damages, RP §14-118.
  Budget.
    Annual proposed budget.
      Adoption, RP §11-109.2.
  Common elements.
    Responsibility for maintenance, repair and
      replacement, RP §11-108.1.
  Composition, RP §11-109.
  Contracts.
    Termination.
      Authority, RP §11-133.
  Damages.
    Actions against governing body.
      Actual damages, RP §14-118.
  Defined, RP §11-101.
  Department of assessments and taxation.
    Registration, RP §11-119.
  Easements.
    Approval, RP §11-125.
  Immunity.
    Directors or officers, RP §14-118.
  Incorporation, RP §11-109.
  Insurance policies.
    Council to maintain and make available for
      inspection, RP §11-114.
  Leases.
    Termination.
      Authority, RP §11-133.

CONDOMINIUMS —Cont'd
Council of unit owners —Cont'd
Liability.
Directors or officers, CJ §5-406.
Immunity, RP §14-118.
Meetings, RP §11-109.
Notice of meetings, RP §11-109.
Electronic transmission, RP §11-139.1.
Powers.
Delegation, RP §11-109.
Property.
Unit owner's interest, RP §11-109.
Quorum, RP §11-109.
Responsibility for maintenance, repair and
replacement of common elements, RP
§11-108.1.
Right of entry.
Repairs, RP §11-125.
Roster.
Maintenance, RP §11-109.
Voting, RP §11-109.
Electronic transmission of votes or proxies, RP
§11-143.
Damages.
Actions against governing body.
Actual damages, RP §14-118.
Eminent domain.
Priority of distribution, RP §11-112.
Declaration.
Amendments, RP §11-103.
Corrective amendments, RP §11-103.1.
Rules of construction, RP §11-124.
Contents, RP §11-103.
Corrections.
Petitions in equity to correct declaration, RP
§11-103.
Establishment of condominium regime.
Indexing declaration, RP §11-102.
Recordation, RP §11-102.
Interpretation and construction, RP §11-124.
Purchaser.
Furnishing by vendor, RP §11-126.
Recordation.
Amendments.
Expanding condominiums, RP §11-120.
References to plats, RP §11-103.
Reformation.
Order of reformation, RP §11-103.
Required particulars, RP §11-103.
Definitions.
Actions against governing body.
Governing body, RP §14-118.
Family day care homes, RP §11-111.1.
General provisions, RP §11-101.
Termination of leases, RP §11-102.2.
Unit lease by designated household, RP §11-137.
Deposits.
Escrow deposits on new condominiums, RP
§11-121.
Sale of units, RP §11-121.
Developer.
Defined, RP §11-101.
Expanding condominium.
Origination of right, RP §11-120.
Sales.
Provisions requiring employment.
Deemed void, RP §11-134.
Section not applicable to condominium
occupied and used solely for
nonresidential purposes, RP §11-134.

CONDOMINIUMS —Cont'd
Developer —Cont'd
Statements.
Construction progress statements.
Filing, RP §11-127.
Disclosures.
Requirements.
Applicability of provisions, RP §11-126.
General provisions, RP §11-126.
Dispute settlement mechanism, RP §11-113.
**Distribution of written information or
materials,** RP §11-111.3.
Documents.
Delivery to council of unit owners by developer,
RP §11-132.
Easements.
General provisions, RP §11-125.
Electronic transmission.
Defined, RP §11-101.
Notices, RP §11-139.1.
Votes or proxies, RP §11-143.
Emergencies.
Rental housing emergency.
Local laws and regulations, RP §11-140.
Eminent domain.
Award.
Allocation, RP §11-112.
Encroachment.
General provisions, RP §11-125.
Equity.
Declaration.
Amendments or corrections.
Petition of council of unit owners to circuit
court in equity, RP §11-103.
Escrow.
Deposits on new condominiums, RP §11-121.
Existing condominiums.
Applicability of title, RP §11-128.
Expanding.
Conditions, RP §11-120.
Expenses.
Common expenses.
Assessments.
Payment of expenses, RP §11-110.
Defined, RP §11-101.
Percentage interest, RP §11-107.
Unit owner's rights, RP §11-109.
Moving expenses.
Defined, RP §11-101.
Landlord and tenant.
Payment of moving expenses.
Tenant's right to purchase property
occupied as residence, RP §11-136.
Family day care homes, RP §11-111.1.
Foreign condominium units sold in state, RP
§11-129.
Fraud and deceit.
Disclosure requirements, RP §11-126.
Homeowners' associations.
General provisions, RP §§11B-101 to 11B-115.
See HOMEOWNERS' ASSOCIATIONS.
Housing.
Rental housing emergency, RP §11-140.
Housing agencies.
Defined, RP §11-101.
Immunity.
Actions against governing body.
Directors or officers, RP §14-118.
Improvements.
By unit owner, RP §11-115.

CONDOMINIUMS —Cont'd
Indexing declaration, bylaws and plats.
Establishment of condominium regime, RP §11-102.
Inspections.
Books and records, RP §11-126.
Insurance policies.
Council of unit owners to maintain and make available for inspection, RP §11-114.
Instruments affecting title.
Recordation, RP §11-102.
Insurance.
Required coverage, RP §11-114.
Interest.
Percentage interest.
Changes, RP §11-107.
Common elements, RP §11-107.
Common expenses and profits, RP §11-107.
Defined, RP §11-101.
Eminent domain.
Adjustment following taking, RP §11-112.
Unit owner's rights as holder, RP §11-109.
Interpretation and construction.
Declaration, bylaws and plats, RP §11-124.
Title additional and supplemental, RP §11-141.
Landlord and tenant.
Payment of moving expenses.
Tenant's right to purchase property occupied as residence, RP §11-136.
Leasehold estate subjected to condominium regime.
Limitation, conditions, RP §11-102.
Leases.
Termination, RP §§11-102.2, 11-133.
Notice, RP §11-102.2.
Unit lease by designated household, RP §11-137.
Liability.
Actions against governing body.
Directors or officers.
Immunity from liability, RP §14-118.
Unit owner.
Injuries, RP §11-118.
Liens.
Assessments.
Payment of common expenses.
Constitutes lien, RP §11-110.
Contract liens, RP §§14-201 to 14-206.
See LIENS.
Mechanics' and materialmen's liens, RP §11-118.
Limitation of actions.
Seller's liability for nondisclosure, RP §11-126.
Warranty, RP §11-131.
Lists of names and addresses of officers, directors, etc., RP §11-119.
Local governments.
Right of first refusal to purchase rental facility, RP §11-138.
Right of first refusal to purchase units, RP §11-139.
Mechanics' liens.
General provisions, RP §11-118.
Montgomery county.
Voter information material.
Distributing or depositing, EL §1-303.
Mortgagee.
Defined, RP §11-101.
Moving expenses.
Defined, RP §11-101.
Landlord and tenant.
Payment of moving expenses.
Tenant's right to purchase property occupied as residence, RP §11-136.

CONDOMINIUMS —Cont'd
Notices.
Conversion to condominiums.
Failure of landlord or owner to give notice defense to action for possession, RP §11-102.1.
Council of unit owners.
Meetings, RP §11-109.
Electronic transmission of notice, RP §11-139.1.
Electronic transmission, RP §11-139.1.
Leases.
Termination, RP §11-102.2.
Right of tenant to purchase, RP §11-136.
Rules and regulations.
Adoption.
Notice to owners, RP §11-111.
Sales.
Holders of subordinate interest, RP §7-105.
Occupants.
Defined, RP §11-101.
Plats.
Amendment, RP §§11-105, 11-124.
Corrective amendments, RP §11-103.1.
Certification, RP §11-105.
Contents, RP §11-105.
Declaration.
References to plats, RP §11-103.
Indexing.
Establishment of condominium regime, RP §11-102.
Interpretation and construction, RP §11-124.
Recordation.
Amendments.
Expanding condominiums, RP §11-120.
Establishment of condominium regime, RP §11-102.
To be filed for records, RP §11-105.
Required particulars, RP §11-105.
Surveyor's certificate.
Attachment to plat required, RP §11-105.
Political candidate signs, RP §11-111.2.
Presumptions.
Boundaries, RP §11-125.
Priorities.
Eminent domain.
Distribution of award, RP §11-112.
Profits.
Common profits.
Defined, RP §11-101.
Disposition, RP §11-110.
Percentage interest, RP §11-107.
Unit owner's rights, RP §11-109.
Property.
Defined, RP §11-101.
Status of units, RP §11-106.
Property lying in two counties.
Establishment of condominium regime, RP §11-102.
Public offering statements.
Disclosure requirements, RP §11-126.
Filing of current public offering information, RP §11-127.
Reconstruction.
Eminent domain.
Following taking, RP §11-112.
Recordation.
Bylaws.
Recorded with declaration, RP §11-104.
Declaration.
Amendments.
Expanding condominiums, RP §11-120.

CONDOMINIUMS —Cont'd
Recordation —Cont'd
Establishment of condominium regime, RP §11-102.
Instruments affecting title, RP §11-102.
Plats, RP §11-105.
Amendments.
Expanding condominiums, RP §11-120.
Records.
Audits, RP §§11-116, 11A-128.
Reformation of declaration.
Order of reformation, RP §11-103.
Regime.
Establishment of condominium regime, RP §11-102.
Units. See within this heading, "Units."
Registration, RP §11-127.
Council of unit owners to register with department of assessments and taxation, RP §11-119.
Fees, RP §11-119.
Registration with secretary of state required, RP §11-127.
Termination of leases.
Violation of notice requirement.
Denial or revocation of registration for violation, RP §11-102.2.
Rental facilities.
Defined, RP §§11-101, 11-138.
Local government's right to purchase, RP §11-138.
Repairs.
Council of unit owners.
Right of entry, RP §11-125.
Encroachment as result to authorize repair, RP §11-125.
Responsibility for maintenance, repair and replacement, RP §11-108.1.
Resale of unit, RP §11-135.
Resident agents.
Service of process, RP §11-119.
Right of entry.
Council of unit owners.
Repairs, RP §11-125.
Right of first refusal.
Local government's right of first refusal to purchase rental facility, RP §11-138.
Local government's right of first refusal to purchase units, RP §11-139.
Tenant's rights.
Purchase of property occupied as residence, RP §11-136.
Right of tenant to purchase, RP §11-136.
Rules and regulations, RP §11-111.
Conflict in provisions, RP §11-124.
Exceptions to provisions, RP §11-111.
Family day care homes, RP §11-111.1.
Sanctions for rule violations.
Procedure prior to imposition, RP §11-113.
Sales.
Contracts.
Purchaser's right to rescind, RP §11-126.
Deposits.
Purchases of new units, RP §11-121.
Employment of developer or vendor.
Provisions requiring deemed void, RP §11-134.
Section not applicable to condominium occupied and used solely for nonresidential purposes, RP §11-134.
Foreign condominium units sold in state, RP §11-129.

CONDOMINIUMS —Cont'd
Sales —Cont'd
Notice.
Holders of subordinate interest, RP §7-105.
Resale of unit, RP §11-135.
Sale of unit subsequent to initial sale, RP §11-126.
Waiver of purchaser's right, RP §11-126.
Secretary of state.
Copies of local provisions forwarded to secretary, RP §11-130.
Duties of secretary, RP §11-128.
File of local legislation affecting condominium.
Duty of secretary to establish, RP §11-128.
Registration with secretary required, RP §11-127.
Service of process.
Resident agent, RP §11-119.
Severability of provisions, RP §11-124.
Short title of act, RP §11-143.
Statements.
Developers.
Construction progress statements.
Filing, RP §11-127.
Surveys and surveyors.
Surveyor's certificate, RP §11-105.
Taxation.
Assessment of condominium property, TP §8-207.
Termination of condominiums, RP §11-123.
Time-sharing.
General provisions, RP §§11A-101 to 11A-129.
See TIME-SHARING.
Title.
Short title of act, RP §11-143.
Units.
Common elements. See within this heading, "Common elements."
Consolidation, RP §11-107.
Defined, RP §11-101.
Description.
Sufficiency, RP §11-106.
Designation.
Plats, RP §11-105.
Foreign condominium units sold in state, RP §11-129.
Grant of part of unit, RP §11-107.
Leased by designated household, RP §11-137.
Maintenance.
Responsibility for maintenance, repair and replacement, RP §11-108.1.
Owners.
Council. See within this heading, "Council of unit owners."
Defined, RP §11-101.
Liabilities.
Injuries in connection with common elements, RP §11-118.
Roster.
Maintenance, RP §11-109.
Real property.
Status, RP §11-106.
Repair.
Responsibility for maintenance, repair and replacement, RP §11-108.1.
Replacement.
Responsibility for maintenance, repair and replacement, RP §11-108.1.
Resale, RP §11-135.
Sale.
Deposits.
Purchasers, RP §11-121.
Resale, RP §11-135.
Status, RP §11-106.

CONDOMINIUMS —Cont'd
Units —Cont'd
Subdividing, RP §11-107.
Voter information material.
Montgomery county.
Distributing or depositing, EL §1-303.
Warranty, RP §11-131.
Limitation of actions, RP §11-131.
Zoning.
General provisions, RP §11-120.

CONDOMS.
Sales.
Vending machines or other devices, HG §18-335.
Vending machine sales.
Nonlatex condoms sold from, CR §10-104.
Sales at schools, CR §10-105.

CONFECTIONERY PRODUCTS.
Adulteration.
Rules and regulations, HG §21-209.
Alcoholic beverages.
Confectionery products containing alcohol, HG §21-209.

CONFERENCE CENTERS.
Alcoholic beverages.
Beer, wine and liquor licenses, 2B §6-601.

CONFERENCES PRIOR TO TRIAL OR HEARING.
Circuit courts, CivProCir Rules 2-504.1, 2-504.2.
Court of special appeals, AppRev Rule 8-206.
District Court, CivProDist Rule 3-504.

CONFESSION OF JUDGMENT.
Circuit courts, CivProCir Rule 2-611.
Consumer loans.
Prohibited, CL §12-311.
District Court, CivProDist Rule 3-611.
Judgments and decrees generally.
See JUDGMENTS AND DECREES.
Unfair or deceptive trade practices, CL §13-301.

CONFESSIONS.
Arrests.
Failure to take defendant before judicial officer after arrest.
Confession not rendered inadmissible, CJ §10-912.
Judgments.
Confession of judgment.
See JUDGMENTS AND DECREES.
Maryland district rules.
Effect of failure to comply strictly with Maryland district rules, CJ §10-912.
Motions.
Mandatory motions in circuit courts.
Criminal rules, Crim Rule 4-252.
Treason, US Const Art III §3.

CONFIDENTIAL COMMUNICATION OR INFORMATION.
General provisions.
See PRIVILEGED AND CONFIDENTIAL COMMUNICATIONS AND INFORMATION.

CONFINEMENT.
Commitment.
See COMMITMENT.
Local correctional facilities.
See JAILS.
Mentally ill.
Admissions.
See MENTALLY ILL.

CONFINEMENT —Cont'd
State correctional facilities.
See PRISONS AND PRISONERS.

CONFISCATION.
Fines.
See FINES.
Seizures.
See SEARCHES AND SEIZURES.
Sheriffs.
Guidelines for disposal of property, CJ §2-311.

CONFLICT OF LAWS.
Abandoned property disposition.
When property held for owner in another state not presumed abandoned, CL §17-309.
Administrative procedure.
Meetings, SG §10-504.
Adult offender supervision, COR §6-215.
Bainbridge development corporation, 83A §5-1609.
Bank deposits and collections, CL §4-102.
Building codes.
Effect of subtitle, PS §12-502.
Local codes.
Amendments to performance standards, PS §12-504.
Rehabilitation code.
Effect of subtitle on other laws, PS §12-1002.
Business regulation and licensure.
Local licenses, fees and taxes.
Effect of public local law, BR §1-204.
Penalties.
Effect of general penalty provision, BR §17-2106.
Business trusts.
Applicable governing law, CA §12-102.
Child custody.
Lawful custodian.
Conflict as to, FL §9-303.
Collection agencies.
Title effect on other laws, BR §7-103.
Commercial code.
Parties' power to choose applicable law, CL §1-105.
Territorial application of chapter, CL §1-105.
Community reinvestment fund.
Application of other laws, HS §9-304.
Corporations.
Foreign corporations.
Consolidation, merger and other transfers of property, CA §3-117.
Counties.
Code counties.
Public local law, MD Const Art XI-F §10.
Conflict between general and local laws.
Public local laws shall prevail, 1 §13.
Public local law.
Section 3 conveys supplementary authority, 25 §6.
Credit unions.
Share guaranty corporations.
Insurance article of code.
Not applicable, FI §7-222.
Death by wrongful act.
General provisions, CJ §3-903.
Dentists.
Dental review bodies and peer review activities.
Law governing recoveries, HO §4-502.
Firearms.
Preemption by state, PS §5-104.
Sale, rental or transfer, PS §5-134.

CONFLICT OF LAWS —Cont'd
Fire prevention commission.
Regulations, PS §6-206.
Fires and fire protection.
Evacuation procedures.
Effect on other fire safety laws, PS §9-501.
Sprinkler systems.
More stringent local laws, PS §9-202.
Fast response residential systems, PS §9-301.
Franchises.
Act in addition to other law, BR §14-204.
Funds transfers, CL §4A-507.
Federal electronic fund transfer act of 1978, CL §4A-107.
Federal reserve regulations and operating circulars, CL §4A-107.
Health insurance.
Prohibited provisions in policy or contract, IN §12-209.
Hearing aid sales act.
Remedies in addition to other law, CL §14-2502.
Holocaust victim insurance.
Compliance, effect on other laws, IN §28-108.
Horse racing.
Contrary local laws invalid, BR §11-102.
Hot pursuit.
Natural resources police force.
Pursuit of offenders across Maryland-Virginia water boundary, NR §1-210.
Housing and community development.
Assisted housing preservation.
Effect of title, HS §7-106.
Community reinvestment fund.
Application of other laws, HS §9-304.
Housing authorities, HS §12-107.
Life and health insurance and annuities.
Prohibited provisions in policy or contract, IN §12-209.
Insurance.
Holocaust victim insurance.
Compliance, effect on other laws, IN §28-108.
Nonprofit health service plans.
Investment in or acquisition of affiliate or subsidiary, IN §14-133.
Investment securities, CL §8-110.
Parties' power to choose applicable law, CL §1-105.
Law enforcement officers' bill of rights, PS §3-102.
Leases, UCC.
Leases subject to other statutes, CL §2A-104.
Limitation on power of parties to choose applicable law and judicial forum, CL §2A-106.
Letters of credit.
Choice of law and forum, CL §5-116.
Life insurance and annuities.
Prohibited provisions in policy or contract, IN §12-209.
Limited liability companies.
Foreign companies.
Doing business as assent to state laws, CA §4A-1010.
Governing law, CA §4A-1001.
Law governing merger, CA §4A-1012.
Local laws.
Public local laws shall prevail, 1 §13.
Medicaid.
Subrogation claims, HG §15-120.
Mining.
Strip mining.
Civil actions, EN §15-528.

CONFLICT OF LAWS —Cont'd
Municipal corporations.
Conflict between general and local laws.
Public local laws shall prevail, 1 §13.
State law, MD Const Art XI-E §6.
Negotiable instruments, CL §3-102.
Nonprofit health service plans.
Investment in or acquisition of affiliate or subsidiary, IN §14-133.
Nurse multistate licensure compact, HO §8-7A-03.
Partnerships, revised act.
Law governing internal relations, CA §9A-106.
Paternity proceedings.
Inconsistent statutes or rules, FL §5-1007.
Permits.
Consolidated procedures for development permits.
Conflicts with federal requirements, SG §11-104.
Physicians.
Medical review bodies and professional peer review activities.
Law governing recoveries, HO §4-502.
Police.
Hot pursuit.
Natural resources police force.
Pursuit of offenders across Maryland-Virginia water boundary, NR §1-210.
Police training commission.
Local laws, PS §3-218.
Political parties.
Provisions conflicting with constitution and bylaws, EL §4-101.
Procurement.
Inconsistent provisions, SF §11-201.
Minority business participation.
Federal requirements, SF §14-302.
Public ethics.
Most stringent provisions prevail, SG §15-105.
Radiation.
State preemption of local regulations, EN §8-107.
Secured transactions.
Applicability of article, CL §9-109.
Investment property, CL §9-305.
Commodity intermediary jurisdiction determinations, CL §9-305.
Exceptions to general rule, CL §9-305.
Perfection and priority.
Agricultural liens, CL §9-302.
Certificates of title covering goods, CL §9-303.
Consignees.
When other law governs priority, CL §9-319.
Debtor's location, CL §9-307.
Deposit accounts, CL §9-304.
Letter-of-credit rights, CL §9-306.
Operation of other articles of UCC, CL §9-331.
Security interests, CL §9-301.
Security agreement, CL §9-201.
Third party assignments.
Agreements not to assert defenses against assignees, CL §9-403.
Alienability of debtor's rights.
Governing law, CL §9-401.
Notes, general intangibles and health care insurance receivables.
Restrictions on assignments, CL §9-408.
Notice to debtor of assignment, CL §9-406.
Smoke detectors.
New residential construction.
More stringent local laws, PS §9-103.

CONFLICT OF LAWS —Cont'd

Sprinkler systems.
More stringent local laws, PS §9-202.
Fast response residential systems, PS §9-301.

Time-sharing, RP §11A-126.

Trade secrets.
Remedies in conflict with subtitle, CL §11-1207.

Transient vendors.
Effect on other laws, BR §17-20A-06.

Universities and colleges.
Interstate and regional cooperation programs.
Provisions inconsistent with reciprocal
interstate agreements, ED §11-105.

Workers' compensation.
Temporary total disability.
Effect on other laws, LE §9-619.

Zoning, 66B §7.03.

CONFLICTS OF INTEREST.

Agricultural cooperatives.
Directors, CA §5-516.

Agriculture.
Board of review, AG §2-404.

Air conditioning and heating contractors.
Inspectors.
Financial interest restricted, BR §9A-403.

Alcoholic beverages.
Anne Arundel county.
Direct or indirect interest in more than one
license, 2B §9-301.
Baltimore City.
Direct or indirect interest in more than one
license, 2B §9-301.
Baltimore county.
Direct or indirect interest in more than one
license, 2B §9-301.
Howard county.
Direct or indirect interest in more than one
license, 2B §9-301.
Liquor control department, 2B §15-208.
Worcester county.
Direct or indirect interest in more than one
license, 2B §9-301.

Anne Arundel county.
Alcoholic beverages.
Direct or indirect interest in more than one
license, 2B §9-301.

**Appalachian states low-level radioactive waste
compact.**
Commission.
Prohibited acts, EN §7-304.

Attorneys at law.
Rules of professional conduct.
See RULES OF PROFESSIONAL CONDUCT.

Aviation commission, TR §5-217.

Baltimore City.
Alcoholic beverages.
Direct or indirect interest in more than one
license, 2B §9-301.
Mayor or city council in contract, MD Const Art
XI §5.

Baltimore county.
Alcoholic beverages.
Direct or indirect interest in more than one
license, 2B §9-301.

Board of review, Patuxent institution, COR
§4-206.

Charitable organizations.
Officers, directors, partners, trustees.
Restrictions on voting, BR §6-415.

CONFLICTS OF INTEREST —Cont'd

Commissioner of financial regulation.
Full-time duties of commissioner and deputy, FI
§2-110.
Ownership of certain stock prohibited, FI §2-111.
Prohibited activities generally, FI §2-112.

Corporations.
Interested director transactions, CA §2-419.

Counties.
Claims against county.
County commissioners not to acquire claims
against county, 25 §31.
Contracts.
County commissioners not to be interested in
contracts, 25 §30.
County commissioners, 25 §3.
Officers and employees, 25 §3.
Penalty for violations, 25 §32.

Deposit insurance fund corporation.
Fund director, FI §10-108.

Depositions.
Officers before whom depositions taken.
Circuit courts, CivProCir Rule 2-414.

Electricians.
Electrical inspectors, BOP §6-313.

Ethics.
Public ethics act.
General provisions.
See PUBLIC ETHICS.

Financial interest.
Financial disclosure requirements of public
officers.
See PUBLIC OFFICERS AND EMPLOYEES.

General assembly.
Joint committee on legislative ethics, SG §§2-701
to 2-709.
Public ethics.
See PUBLIC ETHICS.

General services department.
Procurement, SF §4-304.

Health.
Secretary of health and mental hygiene.
Personnel at grade 18 and above.
Conflict of interest prohibited, HG §2-103.

**Health and higher educational facilities
authority,** 43C §4.

Heritage areas authority, FI §13-1104.

Highways.
Commissioners and employees not to be interested
in contracts, TR §8-217.
State roads commission.
Not to be interested in contracts, TR §8-217.

Horse racing.
Licenses.
Financial disclosure by licensees, BR §§11-313,
11-315.
State racing commission, BR §11-206.

Hospitals.
Pharmaceutical suppliers.
Penalty for violation, HG §19-357.

Housing authorities.
Annapolis, HS §13-105.
Interest of commissioner or employee in housing
projects, etc., HS §12-310.

Howard county.
Alcoholic beverages.
Direct or indirect interest in more than one
license, 2B §9-301.

Industrial development financing authority.
Members of authority, 83A §5-909.

Insurance administration, IN §2-107.

CONFLICTS OF INTEREST —Cont'd
Investigations.
State prosecutor.
See STATE PROSECUTOR.
Judges.
Financial disclosure statements, CJA Rule 16-815.
Judicial appointees, CJA Rule 16-816.
Judicial appointees.
Code of conduct for judicial appointees.
Financial activities, CJA Rule 16-814 Canon 4.
Juvenile services.
Advisory board members, 83C §2-109.
Kent county.
Alcoholic beverages.
Board of license commissioners, 2B §15-106.
Law enforcement officers and personnel.
Rights of officers generally, PS §3-103.
Limitation of actions, CJ §5-106.
Maryland economic adjustment fund.
Committee members, 83A §6-504.
Maryland-national capital park and planning commission.
Generally, 28 §2-115.
Maryland Transit Administration.
General provisions, TR §7-211.
Mining.
Director of bureau of mines, EN §15-202.
Strip mining.
Civil actions, EN §15-528.
State employees not to have financial interest, EN §15-527.
Pilots, BOP §11-603.
Plumbers.
Plumbing inspectors, BOP §12-503.
Port administration.
Interest in contracts prohibited, TR §6-212.
Port commission.
Interest in contracts prohibited, TR §6-212.
Procurement.
Affidavit by bidder disclosing actual or potential conflicts, SF §13-212.
Architectural and engineering services.
General selection board, SF §13-302.
Transportation selection board, SF §13-303.
General services department, SF §4-304.
Prosecution.
State prosecutor.
See STATE PROSECUTOR.
Public ethics act.
See PUBLIC ETHICS.
Public officers and employees.
State government, SG §§15-501 to 15-523.
See PUBLIC ETHICS.
Public service commissioners, general counsel, people's counsel and officers and employees of public service commission.
Ethics generally, PUC §§2-301 to 2-310.
See PUBLIC SERVICE COMMISSION.
Receivers and assignees or trustees for creditors.
Disclosure.
Generally, Receivers Rule 13-105.
Rules of professional conduct.
Former client, ProfCond Rule 1.9.
General rule, ProfCond Rule 1.7.
Prohibited transactions, ProfCond Rule 1.8.
Savings and loan associations.
Director, officer and controlling person, FI §9-307.
Division.
Director, FI §8-307.
Staff, FI §8-307.

CONFLICTS OF INTEREST —Cont'd
Small business development financing authority.
Members of authority, 83A §5-1008.
Stem cell research program.
Peer review committee members, 83A §5-2B-06.
Treasurer.
Generally, SG §5-103.
Unemployment compensation.
Board of appeals.
Conduct of hearings, LE §8-506.
University of Maryland.
Medical system.
Officials or employees of university not barred from becoming directors or officials of corporation, ED §13-305.
Washington suburban sanitary commission, 29 §§12-101 to 12-106.
See WASHINGTON SUBURBAN SANITARY DISTRICT.
Witnesses.
Disqualification to testify because of interest.
Removal, CJ §9-101.
Woodrow Wilson bridge and tunnel authority, TR §10-303.
Worcester county.
Alcoholic beverages.
Direct or indirect interest in more than one license, 2B §9-301.
Workers' compensation.
Uninsured employers' fund.
Legal adviser, LE §10-310.

CONFRONTATION OF WITNESSES, MD Const DofR Art 21; US Const Amd 6.
Veterinarians.
Revocation or suspension of license, AG §2-311.

CONFUSION.
Exclusion of relevant evidence on grounds of confusion, Evid Rule 5-403.

CONGENITAL DISORDERS.
Hereditary and congenital disorders programs, HG §§13-101 to 13-110.
See HEREDITARY AND CONGENITAL DISORDERS PROGRAMS.

CONGRESS.
Absent members, US Const Art I §5.
Adjournment, US Const Art I §§5, 7; Art II §3.
Admiralty, US Const Art I §8.
Amendments to the constitution, US Const Amd 5.
Appalachian states low-level radioactive waste compact.
Consent by congress, EN §7-305.
Apportionment.
Representatives, US Const Art I §2; Amd 14 §2.
Appropriations, US Const Art I §9.
Approval by president of order, resolution or vote, US Const Art I §7.
Army and navy.
Powers of congress, US Const Art I §8.
Arrest.
Arrest of members, US Const Art I §6.
Privilege from, US Const Art I §6.
Bankruptcy and insolvency.
Powers of congress, US Const Art I §8.
Borrowing money, US Const Art I §8.
Changing meeting of congress, US Const Amd 20.
Commerce, US Const Art I §§8, 9.

CONGRESS —Cont'd

Compensation of members, US Const Art I §6; Amd 27.

Consists of senate and house of representatives, US Const Art I §1.

Copyright, US Const Art I §8.

Counterfeiting.
  Powers of congress, US Const Art I §8.

Courts.
  Power to constitute tribunals inferior to supreme court, US Const Art I §8.

Debate, US Const Art I §6.

Debts.
  Powers of congress, US Const Art I §8.

Declaration of war, US Const Art I §8.

Defense.
  Powers of congress, US Const Art I §8.

District of Columbia, US Const Art I §8.

Duties and imposts.
  Powers of congress, US Const Art I §8.

Elections.
  Certificate of results issued to member.
    Effect, EL §11-604.
  Filing fee.
    Senator or representative, EL §5-401.
  Governor's determination of votes cast and proclamation of results, EL §11-601.
  House of representatives, US Const Art I §§2, 4.
    Congressional districts.
      First congressional district, EL §8-702.
      Second congressional district, EL §8-703.
      Third congressional district, EL §8-704.
      Fourth congressional district, EL §8-705.
      Fifth congressional district, EL §8-706.
      Sixth congressional district, EL §8-707.
      Seventh congressional district, EL §8-707.
      Eighth congressional district, EL §8-709.
      Eight districts, state divided into, EL §8-701.
      References to districts, wards, precincts, etc., EL §8-701.
  Judge of elections, returns and qualifications of members, US Const Art I §5.
  President, US Const Art II §1; Amds 12, 20.
  Vacancy for representative.
    Special election to fill, EL §8-710.
      Nomination by petition, filing petition, EL §5-703.
      Withdrawal of candidacy, EL §§5-502, 5-503.
      Special primary, EL §§8-710, 8-711.
  Vacancy in nomination after primary election, EL §5-1003.
  Payment of poll tax not required, US Const Amd 24.
  President, US Const Art II §1; Amds 12, 20.
  Proclamation by governor of names of members of congress elected.
    Judge of elections, returns, qualifications of members, US Const Art I §5.
  Senate, US Const Art I §4; Amd 17.
    Vacancy in office.
      Appointment by governor of eligible individual, EL §8-602.
      Special primary and special general election, EL §8-602.
    When election held, EL §8-601.
  Vacancy in nomination after primary election, EL §5-1003.
  Vice-president, US Const Art II §1; Amds 12, 20.

Excises.
  Powers of congress, US Const Art I §8.

CONGRESS —Cont'd

Foreign commerce, US Const Art I §8.

Freedom of speech.
  Members of congress, US Const Art I §6.

General assembly.
  Persons holding office under United States not eligible as senators or delegates, MD Const Art III §10.
  Exceptions, MD Const Art III §10.

Holding other office, US Const Art I §6.
  Members of general assembly not eligible, MD Const Art III §10.
  Exceptions, MD Const Art III §10.

House of representatives, US Const Art I §2.
  Absent members, US Const Art I §5.
  Adjournment, US Const Art I §§5, 7; Art II §3.
  Apportionment of representatives, US Const Art I §2; Amd 14 §2.
  Arrest of members, US Const Art I §6.
  Compensation of members, US Const Art I §6; Amd 27.
  Congressional districts.
    First congressional district, EL §8-702.
    Second congressional district, EL §8-703.
    Third congressional district, EL §8-704.
    Fourth congressional district, EL §8-705.
    Fifth congressional district, EL §8-706.
    Sixth congressional district, EL §8-707.
    Seventh congressional district, EL §8-708.
    Eighth congressional district, EL §8-709.
    Eight districts, state divided into, EL §8-701.
    References to districts, wards, precincts, etc., EL §8-701.
  Debate, US Const Art I §6.
  Elections.
    Filing fee, EL §5-401.
    Vacancy for representative.
      Special election to fill, EL §8-710.
        Nomination by petition, filing petition, EL §5-703.
        Withdrawal of candidacy, EL §§5-502, 5-503.
      Special primary, EL §§8-710, 8-711.
  Expulsion of member, US Const Art I §5.
  Freedom of speech, US Const Art I §6.
  Holding other office, US Const Art I §6.
  Impeachment, US Const Art I §2.
  Journals, US Const Art I §§5, 7.
  Libel and slander.
    Privilege of members, US Const Art I §6.
  Oath, US Const Art VI; Amd 14.
  Officers, US Const Art I §2.
  Presidential elector.
    Representative ineligible, US Const Art II §1.
  Punishment of members, US Const Art I §5.
  Qualifications.
    Electors, US Const Art I §2.
    Members, US Const Art I §2.
    Judge of qualifications, US Const Art I §5.
  Quorum, US Const Art I §5; Amd 12.
  Revenue bills, US Const Art I §7.
  Rules of procedure, US Const Art I §5.
  Speaker, US Const Art I §2.
  Term, US Const Art I §2.
  Vacancies in office, US Const Art I §2.
  Vice-president of the United States.
    Vacancy in office.
      Confirmation on nomination of president, US Const Amd 25 §2.

Insurrections, US Const Art I §8.

CONGRESS —Cont'd
International law.
  Power to punish offenses against, US Const Art I
    §8.
Interstate commerce, US Const Art I §§8, 9.
Invasions, US Const Art I §8.
Legislative powers vested in, US Const Art I §1.
Letters of marque and reprisal, US Const Art I
    §8.
Libel and slander.
  Privilege of members of congress, US Const Art I
    §6.
Messages to congress, US Const Art II §3.
Militia.
  Powers of congress, US Const Art I §8.
Money.
  Powers of congress, US Const Art I §8.
Naturalization, US Const Art I §8.
Navy.
  Powers of congress, US Const Art I §8.
Oaths.
  Oath of office, US Const Art VI.
Patents, US Const Art I §8.
Piracy.
  Powers of congress, US Const Art I §8.
Post offices and post roads, US Const Art I §8.
Powers of congress, US Const Art I §8.
  Limitations on powers, US Const Art I §9.
President of the United States.
  Declaration of president's disability.
    Determination of issue, US Const Amd 25 §4.
      By two-thirds vote of both houses, US Const
        Amd 25 §4.
Qualifications of members of congress, US
    Const Art I §§2, 3, 5.
Quorum, US Const Art I §5.
Rules of procedure, US Const Art I §5.
Senate.
  Absent members, US Const Art I §5.
  Adjournment, US Const Art I §§5, 7; Art II §3.
  Arrest of members, US Const Art I §6.
  Compensation of members, US Const Art I §6;
    Amd 27.
  Debate, US Const Art I §§4, 6.
  Elections.
    Filing fee, EL §5-401.
    Vacancy in nomination after primary election,
      EL §5-1003.
    Vacancy in office.
      Appointment by governor of eligible
        individual, EL §8-602.
      Special primary and special general election,
        EL §8-602.
    When election held, EL §8-601.
  Equal suffrage in senate, US Const Art V.
  Expulsion of member, US Const Art I §5.
  Freedom of speech, US Const Art I §6.
  Holding other office, US Const Art I §6.
  Impeachment, US Const Art I §3.
  Journals, US Const Art I §§5, 7.
  Libel and slander.
    Privilege of members, US Const Art I §6.
  Number of senators from each state, US Const Art
    I §3; Amd 17.
  Oath, US Const Art VI; Amd 14.
  Officers, US Const Art I §3.
  President.
    Pro tempore, US Const Art I §3.
  Presidential elector.
    Senator ineligible, US Const Art II §1.
  Punishment of members, US Const Art I §5.

CONGRESS —Cont'd
Senate —Cont'd
  Qualifications.
    Members, US Const Art I §3.
      Judge of qualifications, US Const Art I §5.
    Qualifications of electors, US Const Amd 17.
  Quorum, US Const Art I §5.
  Revenue bills, US Const Art I §7.
  Rules of procedure, US Const Art I §5.
  Term, US Const Art I §3; Amd 17.
  Vacancy in office.
    Appointment by governor of eligible individual,
      EL §8-602.
    Special primary and special general election, EL
      §8-602.
  Vice-president of the United States.
    Vacancy in office.
      Confirmation of nomination of president, US
        Const Amd 25 §2.
Sessions, US Const Art I §4; Amd 20 §2.
  Special sessions, US Const Art II §3.
Taxation.
  Powers of congress, US Const Art I §8.
Territories, US Const Art IV §3.
War.
  Articles of war, US Const Art I §8.
  Declaration of war, US Const Art I §8.
Weights and measures, US Const Art I §8.
Welfare.
  Power of congress to provide for general welfare,
    US Const Art I §8.

CONGRESSIONAL DISTRICTS.
First congressional district, EL §8-702.
Second congressional district, EL §8-703.
Third congressional district, EL §8-704.
Fourth congressional district, EL §8-705.
Fifth congressional district, EL §8-706.
Sixth congressional district, EL §8-707.
Seventh congressional district, EL §8-708.
Eighth congressional district, EL §8-709.
Eight districts, state divided into, EL §8-701.
References to districts, wards, precincts, etc.,
    EL §8-701.

CONNECTIONS.
Sanitary commissions.
  See SANITARY COMMISSIONS.
Water and sewer systems.
  See WATER AND SEWER SYSTEMS.

CONSANGUINITY.
Judges.
  In what cases judge disqualified, MD Const Art IV
    §7.

CONSECUTIVE SENTENCES.
Assault by inmate, CR §3-210.
Burglary with explosives or destructive
    device, CR §6-207.
Burning with intent to defraud, CR §6-106.
Carjacking, CR §3-405.
Child abuse or sexual abuse of minor, CR
    §§3-601, 3-602.
Commencement, COR §9-202.
Contraband in place of confinement, CR §9-417.
Destructive device violations, CR §4-503.
Disarming law enforcement officer, CR §4-103.
Escape, CR §9-407.
Exploitation of vulnerable adult.
  Separate sentence, concurrent or consecutive
    sentence, CR §8-801.

CONSECUTIVE SENTENCES —Cont'd
Identity fraud.
Separate sentence, consecutive or concurrent sentence, CR §8-301.
Inmates committing crimes.
Blood, seminal fluid, urine or feces of inmate.
Causing correctional employee to come in contact with, CR §3-205.
Rape.
Continuing course of conduct against child, CR §3-315.
Sexual offenses, COR §9-201.
Continuing course of conduct against child, CR §3-315.
Stalking, CR §3-802.

CONSENT.
Abortion.
Not condition precedent to receipt of public benefits, HG §20-214.
Refusal to consent.
Not grounds for loss of privileges, immunities, etc., HG §20-214.
Acquired immune deficiency syndrome (AIDS).
Human immunodeficiency virus testing.
Informed consent, HG §18-338.1.
Written informed consent.
Required, HG §18-336.
Administrative procedure.
Consent orders in contested cases, SG §10-210.
Adoption.
Independent adoptions, FL §5-3B-21.
Nonconsensual adoption, FL §5-3B-22.
Custody, effect, FL §5-3B-23.
Local department adoptions.
Adoption after termination of parental rights.
Revocation of consent, FL §5-351.
When consent required, FL §5-350.
Withholding consent.
Prohibited grounds, FL §5-350.
Written consents and attachments, FL §5-351.
Adoption without prior termination of parental rights.
Required consent, FL §5-338.
Revocation of consent, FL §5-339.
Written consents and attachments, FL §5-339.
Mutual consent voluntary adoption registry, FL §§5-4C-01 to 5-4C-07.
Private agency adoptions.
Revocation, FL §5-3A-35.
When required, FL §5-3A-35.
Search, contact and reunion services, FL §§5-4B-08, 5-4B-09.
Anatomical donations, HG §19-310.
Automobile insurance fund.
Commencement of action against fund, IN §20-604.
Blood tests.
Liability for taking blood without consent of individual, HG §20-110.
Children, youth and facilities services.
Disclosure of information and records to public agencies serving, 49D §§3-104, 3-105.
Corporations.
Consent to informal actions by stockholders, CA §2-505.
Dead bodies.
Postmortem examinations, HG §5-501.
Diesel vehicle emissions control program.
Implied consent to testing, TR §23-403.

CONSENT —Cont'd
Environmental covenants.
Amending or terminating, requirements, EN §1-809.
Executors and administrators.
Closing estates.
Personal representative's acceptance and consent.
Form, Estates Rule 6-342.
Settlement of decedents' estates.
Waiver, Estates Rule 6-126.
Small estates.
Personal representative.
Consent to appointment of personal representative.
Form, Estates Rule 6-203.
Guardian and ward.
Local department guardianships.
Requirements for written consents, FL §5-321.
When required, FL §5-320.
Private agency guardianships.
Failed conditional consent, FL §5-3A-24.
Revocation, FL §5-3A-19.
When required, FL §5-3A-18.
Written consents, contents, FL §5-3A-19.
Health care generally, HG §§20-101 to 20-117.
Hospitals.
Written consent to discharge or transfer, HG §19-345.2.
Violations by facility or resident's agent, HG §19-345.3.
Human immunodeficiency virus.
Blood tests.
Form for consent document, HG §18-336.
Informed consent, HG §18-338.1.
Refusal, HG §18-336.
Substitute consent, HG §18-336.
Written informed consent.
Required, HG §18-336.
Implied consent law, TR §16-205.1.
Limited liability companies.
Consent by members on decisions concerning affairs of company, CA §4A-403.
Unanimous consent of members, CA §4A-404.
Acts requiring, CA §4A-401.
Marriage.
Minors.
When consent of parents required, FL §2-301.
Penalties for violations, FL §2-302.
Receipt of consent, FL §2-405.
Minors.
Anatomical donations, HG §19-310.
Blood donation.
Donating with or without consent of parent, HG §20-101.
Kinship care, relative providing.
Consent to health care for minor, HG §20-105.
Marriage, FL §§2-301, 2-302.
Medical or surgical care or services, HG §20-102.
Mental or emotional disorders.
Capacity to consent, HG §20-104.
Motor carriers.
Inspections, TR §25-111.
Motor vehicles.
Implied consent to chemical test, TR §16-205.1.
Nolle prosequi with requirement of drug or alcohol treatment, CP §6-229.
Pandering.
Parent or guardian may not consent, CR §11-303.
Partnerships, revised act.
Becoming partner.
Consent of all partners, CA §9A-401.

CONSENT —Cont'd
Postmortem examiners.
Consent for postmortem examination, HG §5-501.
Sterilization.
Not condition precedent to receipt of public
benefits, HG §20-214.
Refusal to consent.
Not grounds for loss of privileges, immunities,
etc., HG §20-214.
**Stet with requirement of drug or alcohol
treatment,** CP §6-229.

CONSENT JUDGMENTS.
Circuit courts, CivProCir Rule 2-612.
District Court, CivProDist Rule 3-612.

CONSERVATION.
Buildings.
Energy conservation in buildings.
Public works.
See PUBLIC WORKS.
Conservation areas.
Defined, 23A §7.
Deep Creek Lake.
Recreation and land use plan, NR §5-215.1.
Districts.
Forest conservancy districts.
General provisions, NR §§5-601 to 5-610.
See FORESTS AND PARKS.
Easements.
See EASEMENTS.
Energy conservation in buildings.
Public works.
See PUBLIC WORKS.
Environmental policy act.
See ENVIRONMENTAL POLICY ACT.
Forest conservation, NR §§5-1601 to 5-1613.
See FORESTS AND PARKS.
Funds.
Heritage conservation fund, NR §§5-1501 to
5-1506.
See HERITAGE CONSERVATION FUND.
Heritage conservation fund, NR §§5-1501 to
5-1506.
See HERITAGE CONSERVATION FUND.
Land trust grant fund.
General provisions, NR §§3-2A-01 to 3-2A-14.
See LAND TRUST GRANT FUND.
Maryland Conservation Corps, NR §5-218.
Municipal corporations.
Conservation areas.
General provisions, 23A §7.
Patuxent river watershed.
Sediment and waste control.
General provisions.
See PATUXENT RIVER WATERSHED.
Restrictions on land.
Easements, covenants, restrictions or conditions.
Incorporeal property interest created.
Easement in gross, RP §2-118.
Release by dominant owner, RP §2-118.
Rural legacy program, NR §§5-9A-01 to 5-9A-09.
See RURAL LEGACY PROGRAM.
Soil conservation.
General provisions, AG §§8-101 to 8-603.
See SOIL CONSERVATION.
Taxation.
Conservation lands.
Property tax credits, TP §9-220.
Water.
Public water systems, EN §§5-5B-01 to 5-5B-05.

CONSERVATION —Cont'd
Watershed associations, 25 §§169 to 218.
See WATERSHED ASSOCIATIONS.

CONSERVATION CORPS, NR §5-218.

CONSERVATION OF ENERGY.
**Electric companies to include in long-range
service plans,** PUC §2-118.
Energy conservation building standards, PUC
§§7-401 to 7-408.
See ENERGY CONSERVATION BUILDING
STANDARDS.
**Gas company and electric company to promote
energy efficiency,** PUC §7-211.
Property taxes.
Tax credits.
High performance buildings, TP §9-242.
Report by public service commission, PUC
§2-122.

CONSERVATORS.
Attorneys at law.
Conservator of client matters.
Disbarment or suspension, CJA Rule 16-777.
Custodian.
Transfers to minors act, ET §§13-301 to 13-324.
See MINORS.
Fiduciaries.
General provisions, ET §§15-201 to 15-211.
See FIDUCIARIES.
Successor corporate fiduciaries, ET §§15-1A-01 to
15-1A-05.
See FIDUCIARIES.
Insurance companies.
Liquidation, rehabilitation, reorganization and
conservation, IN §§9-201 to 9-232.
See INSURANCE COMPANIES.
Investments.
General provisions.
See INVESTMENTS.
Minors.
Transfers to minors.
Definition of conservator, ET §13-301.
Irrevocable transfers, ET §13-306.
Savings and loan associations.
See SAVINGS AND LOAN ASSOCIATIONS.
Securities.
Securities act.
Persons engaging in violations.
Appointment of conservator for defendants or
defendant's assets, CA §11-702.

CONSIDERATION.
Athlete agents.
Agency contract.
Prohibition, BR §4-411.
Contracts.
General provisions.
See CONTRACTS.
Fraternal benefit societies.
Prohibited consideration for insurance, IN §8-467.
Fraudulent conveyances.
General provisions, CL §§15-201 to 15-214.
See FRAUDULENT CONVEYANCES.
**Health insurance policies to state
consideration,** IN §15-201.
Letters of credit, CL §5-105.
Mortgages and deeds of trust, RP §4-106.

CONSIGNMENT.
Actions.
Legal or equitable rights of owner not affected, CL
§11-807.

CONSIGNMENT —Cont'd
Agricultural products.
Accountings of sales, AG §1-305.
Consignee's right and title, CL §11-808.
Containers.
Returned containers, AG §1-303.
Security deposits, AG §1-302.
Conversion, CL §11-809.
Definitions, AG §1-301.
Disposal without consent, CL §11-808.
Lien.
Not affected, CL §11-808.
Penalties.
Failure to provide accountings of sales, AG §1-305.
Inapplicability of general penalties of title, AG §1-306.
Violation of duties by consignees, AG §1-304.
Presumptions.
Conversion by consignee, CL §11-809.
Art.
Works of fine art, CL §§11-8A-01 to 11-8A-04.
See ART.
Consignee.
Agricultural products.
Right and title, CL §11-808.
Contracts.
Between consignee and third person, CL §11-804.
Conversion.
Penalty, CL §11-809.
Presumption, CL §11-809.
Debt.
Due purchaser or pledgee, CL §11-806.
Definitions, CL §11-801.
Deposit, CL §11-805.
Legal and equitable rights of owner.
Not affected against consignee, CL §11-807.
Lien.
When authorized, CL §11-802.
Notice of status, CL §11-805.
Owner of goods.
Holding possessory document, CL §11-803.
Pledge, CL §11-805.
Possessory document.
Consignee holding considered owner of goods, CL §11-803.
Contracts.
Between consignee and third person, CL §11-804.
Conversion.
Consignee.
Penalties, CL §11-809.
Debt.
Consignee.
Due purchaser or pledgee, CL §11-806.
Deposit.
Consignee, CL §11-805.
Container deposits.
Agricultural products, AG §1-302.
Evidence.
Conversion by consignee, CL §11-809.
Prima facie evidence, CL §11-809.
Goods.
Defined, CL §11-801.
Owner.
Consignee holding possessory document, CL §11-803.
Lien.
Agricultural products.
Not affected, CL §11-808.

CONSIGNMENT —Cont'd
Lien —Cont'd
Consignee's lien.
When authorized, CL §11-802.
Notice.
Status of consignee, CL §11-805.
Owner.
Legal and equitable rights.
Against consignee not affected, CL §11-807.
Penalties.
Agricultural products.
Failure to provide accountings of sales, AG §1-305.
Inapplicability of general penalties of title, AG §1-306.
Violation of duties by consignees, AG §1-304.
Conversion of consigned goods, CL §11-809.
Person.
Defined, CL §11-801.
Pledge.
Consignee, CL §11-805.
Debt of consignee due pledgee, CL §11-806.
Possessory document.
Consignee holding.
Considered owner of goods, CL §11-803.
Defined, CL §11-801.
Presumptions.
Conversion by consignee, CL §11-809.
Sale of consigned goods.
Accounting required, CL §11-810.
Taxation.
Owner for taxation, TP §5-101.
Title.
Agricultural products.
Consignee, CL §11-808.
Transporters of consigned goods.
Purchasing from, prohibition, liability, CL §14-1317.

CONSIGNOR AND CONSIGNEE.
Consignment generally.
See CONSIGNMENT.

CONSOLE MACHINES.
Pinball machines.
See PINBALL MACHINES.

CONSOLIDATED SENIOR SPORT FISHING LICENSES, NR §4-216.

CONSOLIDATION.
Adoption proceedings, Juv Rule 11-501.
Agricultural cooperatives.
Consolidation or merger.
Generally, CA §5-527.
Banks and trust companies.
Merger, consolidation or transfer.
See BANKS AND TRUST COMPANIES.
Catastrophic health emergency.
Contest of isolation or quarantine.
Consolidation of actions, claims and issues, SpecPro Rule 15-1104.
Circuit courts.
Civil cases, CivProCir Rule 2-503.
Criminal cases.
Joinder of offenses and defendants, Crim Rule 4-203.
Joint trials, Crim Rule 4-253.
Juvenile cases.
Multiple petitions, Juv Rule 11-110.
Preliminary motions.
Consolidation of defenses in motion, CivProCir Rule 2-322.

CONSOLIDATION —Cont'd
Close corporations, CA §4-601.
Condominium units, RP §11-107.
Consumer cooperatives, CA §5-5A-24.
Cooperative housing corporations, CA §5-6B-18.
Corporations.
  Close corporations, CA §4-601.
  Foreign corporations.
    See CORPORATIONS.
  General provisions.
    See CORPORATIONS.
  Nonstock corporations, CA §§5-207, 5-702.
District Court.
  Civil cases, CivProDist Rule 3-503.
  Criminal cases.
    Joinder of offenses and defendants, Crim Rule 4-203.
    Joint trials, Crim Rule 4-253.
  Juvenile cases.
    Multiple petitions, Juv Rule 11-110.
Foreign corporations.
  See CORPORATIONS.
Fraternal benefit societies, IN §§8-438, 8-439.
Grievance procedures, SPP §12-404.
Guardianship proceedings, Juv Rule 11-501.
Health cost review commission.
  Incentives, HG §19-222.
Health maintenance organizations, HG §§19-711, 19-711.3.
Hospitals.
  Health planning and development, HG §19-129.
Insurance companies.
  Mutual insurers, IN §3-123.
  Reciprocal insurance, IN §3-221.
  Stock insurers, IN §3-122.
Limited liability companies.
  Merger.
    See LIMITED LIABILITY COMPANIES.
Limited partnerships, CA §§3-101, 3-102.
Nonstock corporations, CA §§5-207, 5-702.
Partnerships.
  Limited partnerships, CA §§3-101, 3-102.
Public utilities.
  Electric company.
    Application for operating permit for generating station.
      Consolidation of procedures, EN §2-405.
Sanitary commissions.
  Bond issues.
    Service areas.
      Consolidation of administrative matters, EN §9-651.
Schools.
  Power of county boards of education, ED §4-120.
Unemployment compensation.
  Board of appeals.
    Consolidation of claims, LE §8-506.

CONSOLIDATION OF CASES.
Circuit court.
  Civil cases, CivProCir Rule 2-503.
  Criminal cases.
    Joinder of offenses and defendants, Crim Rule 4-203.
    Joint trials, Crim Rule 4-253.
  Juvenile cases.
    Multiple petitions, Juv Rule 11-110.
District Court, CivProDist Rule 3-503.
  Civil cases, CivProDist Rule 3-503.
  Criminal cases.
    Joinder of offenses and defendants, Crim Rule 4-203.

CONSOLIDATION OF CASES —Cont'd
District Court —Cont'd
  Criminal cases —Cont'd
    Joint trials, Crim Rule 4-253.
  Juvenile cases.
    Multiple petitions, Juv Rule 11-110.

CONSORTIUM, LOSS OF.
Drug dealer liability act.
  Noneconomic damages, CJ §3-1606.

CONSPIRACY.
Antitrust act, CL §11-204.
Charging document.
  Sufficiency, CR §1-203.
Collective bargaining.
  Trade dispute agreements.
    Conduct not conspiracy, LE §4-404.
Drug kingpin, CR §5-613.
Limitation of actions.
  Actions for, CJ §5-106.
Motor vehicles.
  Parties to crime, TR §26-101.
Procurement.
  Falsification, concealment, etc., of material facts in connection with contracts, SF §11-205.1.
Punishment not to exceed punishment for crime conspired to commit, CR §1-202.
Sentence and punishment.
  Approver not to be admitted, CP §6-228.
State retirement and pension system.
  Fiduciaries, SPP §21-209.

CONSTABLES.
Alcoholic beverages.
  Enforcement of article, 2B §16-401.
    Duties, 2B §16-405.
  Sales permitted without license or permit, 2B §1-201.
Compensation.
  See SALARIES.
Debts.
  Not to be purchased by, SG §17-107.
District Court.
  Appointment, MD Const Art IV §41F.
  General provisions.
    See DISTRICT COURT.
Executions.
  Sales.
    General provisions.
      See EXECUTIONS.
    Seizure and sale of property, CJ §11-501.
Fees.
  Accounts and returns.
    Exception, MD Const Art XV §1.
Sales.
  Executions.
    General provisions.
      See EXECUTIONS.

CONSTITUTIONAL CONVENTIONS.
Calling.
  Ballot questions generally, EL §§7-101 to 7-105.
Holding.
  Automatic qualification of ballot question, EL §7-102.

CONSTITUTION OF MARYLAND.
Accounts and accounting.
  State treasurer, MD Const Art VI §4.
Actions.
  Remedy for injury to person or property, MD Const DofR Art 19.

CONSTITUTION OF MARYLAND —Cont'd

Actions —Cont'd
Trial of facts where they arise, MD Const DofR Art 20.

Adjutant general of militia. See within this heading, "Militia."

Agriculture.
Taxation.
Assessment of farm or agricultural land, MD Const DofR Art 43.

Alcoholic beverages.
Referendum.
Prohibited as to laws of constitutional amendments.
Relating to malt or spirituous liquors, MD Const Art XVI §6.

Amendments.
Constitutional conventions, MD Const Art XIV §2.
Elections.
Ballot questions generally, EL §§7-101 to 7-105.
Submission to voters, MD Const Art XIV §1.
Expiration.
Provisions of limited duration, MD Const Art XVIII.
Governor.
Proclamation, MD Const Art XIV §1.
Proposal in general assembly, MD Const Art XIV §1.
Proposed amendments.
Agents.
Compensation.
Extra compensation, MD Const Art III §35.
Anne Arundel county.
Courts.
Judges of circuit court, MD Const Art IV §21.
Eminent domain.
Specific provisions, MD Const Art III §40A.
Attorney at law.
Additional counsel.
Governor not to employ unless authorized by legislature, MD Const Art V §3.
Attorney general, MD Const Art V §3.
Baltimore City.
City counsel.
Compensation may be increased or diminished during term of office, MD Const Art III §35.
Eminent domain.
Specific provisions, MD Const Art III §40A.
Industrial financing loans.
Powers general assembly may grant, MD Const Art XI-I.
Mayor.
Compensation may be increased or diminished during term of office, MD Const Art III §35.
Off-street parking.
Additional powers, MD Const Art XI-C §3.
Rehabilitation and improvement loans.
General provisions, MD Const Art XI-G.
Residential financing loans.
Generally, MD Const Art XI-H.
Baltimore county.
Courts.
Judges of circuit court, MD Const Art IV §21.
Eminent domain.
Specific provisions, MD Const Art III §40A.
Cecil county.
Eminent domain.
Specific provisions, MD Const Art III §40A.

CONSTITUTION OF MARYLAND —Cont'd

Amendments —Cont'd
Proposed amendments —Cont'd
Circuit courts.
Judges.
Effective date of amendments, MD Const Art IV §21A.
Generally, MD Const Art IV §21.
Quorum, MD Const Art IV §21.
Terms of court, MD Const Art IV §21.
Clerks of court.
Appointment and removal, MD Const Art IV §26.
Elections.
Certification of election returns to governor, MD Const Art IV §11.
Rules of court.
Office and business governed by, MD Const Art IV §10.
Commissions.
Governor's salary commission, MD Const Art II §21A.
Recommendations to general assembly, MD Const Art II §21A.
Comptroller.
Removal.
Procedure, MD Const Art VI §6.
Vacancy.
Filling, MD Const Art VI §1.
Contractors.
Compensation.
Extra compensation, MD Const Art III §35.
Counties.
Boundaries.
Changing, MD Const Art XIII §§1, 2.
New counties.
Formation, MD Const Art XIII §§1, 2.
Officers.
Removal or suspension from office, MD Const Art XV §2.
Court of appeals.
Circuits.
Appellate judicial circuits, MD Const Art IV §14.
Composition, MD Const Art IV §14.
Judges.
Tenure, MD Const Art IV §18B.
Credit.
Restrictions on extension, MD Const Art III §34.
Crimes and offenses.
Officers.
Removal or suspension from office, MD Const Art XV §2.
Debtors.
Protection.
Laws to be passed to protect debtors, MD Const Art III §44.
Debts.
Authorization.
Requirements, MD Const Art III §34.
District Court.
Jurisdiction, MD Const Art IV §41A.
Elections.
Absentee voters, MD Const Art I §3.
Commissions.
Issuance by governor, MD Const Art IV §11.
Judges, MD Const Art IV §3.
Eminent domain.
Specific provisions for Baltimore City and Anne Arundel, Baltimore, Cecil and Montgomery counties, MD Const Art III §40A.

CONSTITUTION OF MARYLAND —Cont'd
Amendments —Cont'd
Proposed amendments —Cont'd
Executions.
Laws to be passed protecting property from execution, MD Const Art III §44.
General assembly.
Appointments, MD Const Art XV §5.
Counties.
Formation and change of boundaries, MD Const Art XIII §§1, 2.
Credit.
Restrictions on extension, MD Const Art III §34.
Executions.
Laws to be passed protecting property from execution, MD Const Art III §44.
Holding other office.
Congressmen or persons holding civil or military office in United States, MD Const Art III §10.
Judges.
Eligibility of members to be judges, MD Const Art IV §21.
Loans.
Restrictions, MD Const Art III §34.
Replacement of absent officers, MD Const Art XV §5.
Governor.
Compensation, MD Const Art II §21.
Judges.
Filling of vacancies, MD Const Art IV §5.
Not to employ additional counsel unless authorized by legislature, MD Const Art V §3.
Residence, MD Const Art II §21.
Salary, MD Const Art II §§21, 21A.
Judges.
Circuit courts, MD Const Art IV §21.
Commissions of office.
Issuance by governor, MD Const Art IV §11.
Court of appeals.
Elections, MD Const Art IV §14.
Tenure, MD Const Art IV §18B.
Effective date of amendments, MD Const Art IV §21A.
Elections, MD Const Art IV §3.
Certification of returns to governor, MD Const Art IV §11.
Holding other office.
Prohibited, MD Const DofR Art 33.
Retirement, MD Const Art IV §3.
Term of office, MD Const Art IV §3.
Vacancies.
Filling of vacancy, MD Const Art IV §5A.
Lieutenant governor.
Salary, MD Const Art II §§1A, 21A.
Loans.
Restrictions, MD Const Art III §34.
Montgomery county.
Courts.
Judges of circuit court, MD Const Art IV §21.
Eminent domain.
Specific provisions, MD Const Art III §40A.
Municipal corporations.
Officers.
Removal or suspension from office, MD Const Art XV §2.
Officers.
Compensation.
Extra compensation, MD Const Art III §35.

CONSTITUTION OF MARYLAND —Cont'd
Amendments —Cont'd
Proposed amendments —Cont'd
Officers —Cont'd
Compensation —Cont'd
Increasing or diminishing during term of office, MD Const Art III §35.
Crimes and offenses.
Suspension or removal from office, MD Const Art XV §2.
Holding more than one office.
Prohibited, exceptions, MD Const DofR Art 35.
Parking.
Off-street parking.
Additional powers of Baltimore City, MD Const Art XI-C §3.
Prince George's county.
Courts.
Judges of circuit court, MD Const Art IV §21.
Provisions for election of council, MD Const Art XI-A §3A.
Public officers.
Compensation.
Extra compensation, MD Const Art III §35.
Increasing or diminishing during term of office, MD Const Art III §35.
Quorum.
Circuit courts, MD Const Art IV §21.
Referendum.
Petitions.
Effect if signed by more than one half of required number, MD Const Art XVI §3.
Form, MD Const Art XVI §4.
Number of signors, MD Const Art XVI §3.
Verification of signatures, MD Const Art XVI §4.
Registers of wills.
Elections.
Certification of returns to governor, MD Const Art IV §11.
Residence requirements, MD Const Art IV §21.
Salaries.
Governor, MD Const Art II §§21, 21A.
Lieutenant governor, MD Const Art II §§1A, 21A.
State's attorneys.
Duties, MD Const Art V §9.
State treasurer.
Removal.
Procedure, MD Const Art VI §6.
Vacancy.
Filling, MD Const Art VI §1.
Vacancies in office.
Appointments by general assembly, MD Const Art XV §5.
Wicomico county.
Eminent domain.
Specific provisions, MD Const Art III §40A.
Provisions of limited duration, MD Const Art XIV §1A.
Expiration, MD Const Art XVIII.
Publication, MD Const Art XIV §1.
Annapolis.
Adjutant general.
Discharge duties at seat of government, MD Const Art IX §2.
Comptroller.
Office.
Maintain office at seat of government, MD Const Art VI §1.

CONSTITUTION OF MARYLAND —Cont'd
Annapolis —Cont'd
Court of appeals.
Meeting at, MD Const Art IV §14.
General assembly.
Meeting place, MD Const DofR Art 11.
Change place of meeting of legislature, MD
Const Art II §16.
Governor.
Reside at, MD Const Art II §21.
State treasurer.
Office.
Maintain office at seat of government, MD
Const Art VI §1.
Appellate judicial circuits. See within this
heading, "Court of appeals."
Applicability.
In war as well as peace, MD Const DofR Art 44.
Apportionment.
Legislative districting and apportionment, MD
Const Art III §5.
Appropriations.
Bills. See within this heading, "General assembly."
Requirements, MD Const Art III §32.
Statement of receipts and expenditures, MD Const
Art III §32.
Armies.
Standing armies.
Consent of legislature required, MD Const DofR
Art 29.
Arrest.
Due process.
Required, MD Const DofR Art 24.
Art.
What legislature should encourage, MD Const
DofR Art 43.
Assistance, MD Const Art V §9.
Attainder.
No law to attain for treason or felony, MD Const
DofR Art 18.
Attorney at law.
Criminal prosecution.
Right of accused to counsel, MD Const DofR Art
21.
Attorney general.
Additional counsel.
Authorized by general assembly, MD Const Art
V §3.
Cases in which state has interest.
Clerk of court of appeals to notify attorney
general, MD Const Art V §6.
Comptroller.
Opinions in writing to, MD Const Art V §3.
Duties.
Generally, MD Const Art V §3.
Elections, MD Const Art V §1.
Determining election, MD Const Art V §2.
Returns to governor, MD Const Art V §2.
Tie vote.
Determined by governor, MD Const Art V §2.
Fees.
Prohibited from receiving, MD Const Art V §3.
General assembly.
Opinions in writing to, MD Const Art V §3.
Governor.
Opinions in writing to, MD Const Art V §3.
Oath.
Administration by governor, MD Const Art V
§2.
Opinions.
In writing, MD Const Art V §3.

CONSTITUTION OF MARYLAND —Cont'd
Attorney general —Cont'd
Powers.
Generally, MD Const Art V §3.
Qualifications, MD Const Art V §4.
Determining, MD Const Art V §2.
Removal, MD Const Art V §1.
Salary.
General provisions, MD Const Art V §3.
State's attorneys.
Aid to, MD Const Art V §3.
Opinions in writing to, MD Const Art V §3.
Removal of state's attorneys.
Recommended by attorney general, MD Const
Art V §7.
Term of office, MD Const Art V §1.
Vacancy.
Filled by governor, MD Const Art V §5.
Bail and recognizance.
Excessive.
Prohibited, MD Const DofR Art 25.
Baltimore City.
Charter.
Adoption, MD Const Art XI-A §1.
Affidavits.
False signing and false affidavits, MD Const
Art XI-A §7.
Amendments, MD Const Art XI-A §5.
Amendment of article XI, MD Const Art XI-A
§6.
Board, MD Const Art XI-A §1.
Legislative bodies, MD Const Art XI-A §3.
Local laws.
Enactment, publication and interpretation,
MD Const Art XI-A §3.
General assembly not to enact.
Subjects covered by express powers, MD
Const Art XI-A §4.
Officers.
Chief executive officers, MD Const Art XI-A
§3.
Petition, MD Const Art XI-A §7.
Powers.
Extension, modification, etc., of such powers,
MD Const Art XI-A §2.
General assembly to provide grant of express
powers, MD Const Art XI-A §2.
Preparation, MD Const Art XI-A §1.
City council.
Branches.
First branch, MD Const Art XI §2.
Second branch, MD Const Art XI §2.
Compensation, MD Const Art XI §2.
Composition, MD Const Art XI §2.
Contracts with city.
Interest in prohibited, MD Const Art XI §5.
Duties.
Generally, MD Const Art XI §2.
Elections.
General provisions, MD Const Art XI §3.
Qualification of electors, MD Const Art XI §3.
Holding other office.
Prohibited, MD Const Art XI §5.
Powers.
Generally, MD Const Art XI §2.
Qualifications, MD Const Art XI §2.
Sessions.
Regular session, MD Const Art XI §4.
Special sessions, MD Const Art XI §4.
Term of office, MD Const Art XI §2.

CONSTITUTION OF MARYLAND —Cont'd
Baltimore City —Cont'd
Courts.
 Superior court of Baltimore City.
  See SUPERIOR COURT OF BALTIMORE
   CITY.
 Supreme bench.
  Judges.
   Exceptions as to quadrennial elections, MD
    Const Art XVII §3.
Credit.
 Extension.
  Regulation, MD Const Art XI §7.
Debts.
 Regulation, MD Const Art XI §7.
Elections.
 Supervisors.
  Terms.
   Commencement, MD Const Art XVII §6.
Eminent domain.
 Specific provisions, MD Const Art III §40A.
General assembly.
 Article subject to change, MD Const Art XI §9.
 Control over city, MD Const Art XI §9.
General provisions.
 See BALTIMORE CITY.
Improvements.
 Construction of works of internal improvement.
  Extension of credit or debts regulated, MD
   Const Art XI §7.
Industrial financing loans, MD Const Art XI-I.
Land development and redevelopment.
 Authority to acquire and dispose of property,
  MD Const Art XI-B §1.
 Eminent domain.
  Powers, MD Const Art XI-B §1.
 Powers.
  Additional, MD Const Art XI-B §2.
 Restrictions.
  Additional, MD Const Art XI-B §2.
Laws.
 Continued in force, MD Const Art XI §8.
Mayor.
 Compensation, MD Const Art XI §1.
 Contracts with city.
  Interest in prohibited, MD Const Art XI §5.
 Duties.
  Generally, MD Const Art XI §1.
  Election, MD Const Art XI §1.
 Holding other office.
  Prohibited, MD Const Art XI §5.
 Powers.
  Generally, MD Const Art XI §1.
 Qualifications, MD Const Art XI §1.
 Removal.
  By governor, MD Const Art XI §6.
  Grounds, MD Const Art XI §6.
 Term of office, MD Const Art XI §1.
  Ineligible for two successive terms, MD Const
   Art XI §1.
 Vacancy.
  Election to fill, MD Const Art XI §6.
Ordinances.
 Continued in force, MD Const Art XI §8.
Parking.
 Off-street parking.
  Authority to Baltimore City to acquire and
   dispose of property, MD Const Art XI-C
   §1.
  Powers.
   Additional, MD Const Art XI-C §2.

CONSTITUTION OF MARYLAND —Cont'd
Baltimore City —Cont'd
Parking —Cont'd
 Off-street parking —Cont'd
  Restrictions.
   Additional, MD Const Art XI-C §2.
  Revenue bonds for parking facilities, MD
   Const Art XI-C §3.
Port authority.
 Authority to acquire and dispose of land, MD
  Const Art XI-D §1.
 Howard county.
  Not applicable within territorial limits of
   county, MD Const Art XI-D §3.
 Powers.
  Additional, MD Const Art XI-D §2.
 Restrictions.
  Additional, MD Const Art XI-D §2.
Rehabilitation and improvement loans.
 General provisions, MD Const Art XI-G.
Residential financing loans.
 General provisions, MD Const Art XI-H.
Sheriffs.
 General provisions, MD Const Art IV §44.
State's attorney, MD Const Art V §9.
Streets and sidewalks.
 Parking.
  Off-street parking, MD Const Art XI-C §1.
  Additional powers and restrictions, MD
   Const Art XI-C §2.
  Revenue bonds for facilities, MD Const Art
   XI-C §3.
Baltimore county.
 Eminent domain.
  Specific provisions, MD Const Art III §40A.
Banks and trust companies.
 Books, papers and accounts.
  Inspection.
   Regulations, MD Const Art III §39.
Bastards.
 Support of child.
  Imprisonment for delinquent payment not
   imprisonment for debt, MD Const Art III
   §38.
Bill of rights, MD Const Arts I to XIV.
 Enumeration of rights not to be construed to
  impair or deny those retained by the people,
  MD Const DofR Art 45.
Boards and commissions.
 Pensions.
  State pension commissioner.
   Office prohibited, MD Const Art III §59.
Bonds, surety.
 Comptroller, MD Const Art VI §1.
 Sheriffs, MD Const Art IV §44.
 State's attorneys, MD Const Art V §12.
 State treasurer, MD Const Art VI §1.
Bribery.
 Evidence.
  Compelling testimony, MD Const Art III §50.
 Penalty.
  Legislature to provide penalty, MD Const Art
   III §50.
Budget.
 Balanced budget.
  Required, MD Const Art III §52.
 Bill, MD Const Art III §52.
Cecil county.
 Eminent domain.
  Specific provisions, MD Const Art III §40A.

CONSTITUTION OF MARYLAND —Cont'd
Charters.
Baltimore City. See within this heading, "Baltimore City."
Counties. See within this heading, "Counties."
Municipal corporations, MD Const Art XI-E §§1 to 6. See within this heading, "Municipal corporations."
Circuit courts.
Authority, MD Const Art IV §20.
Clerks.
General provisions, MD Const Art IV §§25, 26.
Court en banc.
Procedure, MD Const Art IV §22.
Court of record, MD Const Art IV §1.
First judicial circuit.
Election of judges, MD Const Art IV §3.
Held in each county, MD Const Art IV §20.
Judges.
Associate judges, MD Const Art IV §21.
Salaries.
Diminishing during term of office prohibited, MD Const Art IV §24.
Chief judge, MD Const Art IV §21.
Salary.
Diminishing during term of office prohibited, MD Const Art IV §24.
Decisions, MD Const Art IV §23.
Elections, MD Const Art IV §21.
Exceptions as to quadrennial elections, MD Const Art XVII §3.
First and second judicial circuits, MD Const Art IV §3.
Eligibility, MD Const Art IV §21.
Reports from circuit court to chief judge, MD Const Art IV §18.
Residence requirements, MD Const Art IV §21.
Salaries.
Diminishing during term of office prohibited, MD Const Art IV §24.
Term of office, MD Const Art IV §21.
Terms of court, MD Const Art IV §21.
Judgments.
Decisions rendered within two months of argument or submission, MD Const Art IV §23.
Judicial circuits.
Composition, MD Const Art IV §19.
State divided into judicial circuits, MD Const Art IV §19.
Jurisdiction, MD Const Art IV §20.
Power, MD Const Art IV §20.
Second judicial circuit.
Election of judges, MD Const Art IV §3.
Clerks of court.
Circuit court, MD Const Art IV §§25, 26.
Commissions of office.
Form, MD Const Art IV §13.
Issuance by governor, MD Const Art IV §12.
Deputy clerks, MD Const Art IV §26.
Duties, MD Const Art IV §10.
Elections.
Certification of election returns to governor, MD Const Art IV §11.
Circuit court, MD Const Art IV §25.
Contested elections, MD Const Art IV §12.
Fees, MD Const Art IV §10.
Legislature to provide system of fees and charges, MD Const Art III §45.
Regulations, MD Const Art IV §10.

CONSTITUTION OF MARYLAND —Cont'd
Clerks of court —Cont'd
Rules of court.
Office and business governed by, MD Const Art IV §10.
Term of office.
Circuit court, MD Const Art IV §25.
Vacancy.
Filling by judge, MD Const Art IV §25.
Common law.
Applicability, MD Const DofR Art 5.
Comptroller.
Bond issues.
Countersigning, MD Const Art VI §3.
Bond, surety, MD Const Art VI §1.
Compensation, MD Const Art VI §1.
Duties.
Generally, MD Const Art VI §2.
Election, MD Const Art VI §1.
Examination.
By governor, MD Const Art II §18.
Oath, MD Const Art VI §1.
Office, MD Const Art VI §1.
Powers.
Generally, MD Const Art VI §2.
Qualifying.
When to qualify, MD Const Art VI §5.
Removal.
Grounds, MD Const Art VI §6.
Procedure, MD Const Art VI §6.
State treasurer.
Inspection by comptroller, MD Const Art VI §4.
Term of office, MD Const Art VI §1.
Vacancy.
Filling, MD Const Art VI §1.
Warrants for payment of money.
Drawn by comptroller, MD Const Art VI §3.
Conventions.
Constitutional conventions, MD Const Art XIV §2.
Ballot questions generally, EL §§7-101 to 7-105.
Holding.
Automatic qualification of ballot question, EL §7-102.
Convicts.
Parole, MD Const Art III §60.
Corporations.
Foreign corporations.
Taxation of revenues, MD Const Art III §58.
General assembly.
Regulations, MD Const Art III §48.
Counties.
Boundaries.
Changing, MD Const Art XIII §§1, 2.
Charter.
Adoption, MD Const Art XI-A §1.
Alternate procedure, MD Const Art XI-A §1A.
Affidavits.
False signing and false affidavits, MD Const Art XI-A §7.
Amendments, MD Const Art XI-A §5.
Board.
Composition, MD Const Art XI-A §1.
Election, MD Const Art XI-A §1.
Petition.
For charter, MD Const Art XI-A §1.
County commissioners.
Power to prescribe number, compensation, powers and duties, MD Const Art XI-A §6.
Election of county councils.
Charter providing method, MD Const Art XI-A §3A.

CONSTITUTION OF MARYLAND —Cont'd
Counties —Cont'd
  Charter —Cont'd
    Legislative bodies, MD Const Art XI-A §3.
    Local laws.
      Enactment, publication and interpretation,
        MD Const Art XI-A §3.
      General assembly not to enact.
        Subjects covered by express powers, MD
          Const Art XI-A §4.
    Officers.
      Chief executive officers, MD Const Art XI-A
        §3.
    Petition, MD Const Art XI-A §7.
    Powers.
      Extension, modification, etc., MD Const Art
        XI-A §2.
      General assembly not to enact on subjects
        covered by, MD Const Art XI-A §4.
      General assembly to provide grant of express
        powers, MD Const Art XI-A §2.
    Preparation, MD Const Art XI-A §1.
    Signature.
      False signing, MD Const Art XI-A §7.
  Code counties.
    Charter.
      Submission to voters, MD Const Art XI-F §2.
    Classification, MD Const Art XI-F §5.
    Conflict of laws.
      Generally, MD Const Art XI-F §10.
    Creation.
      Procedure for becoming, MD Const Art XI-F
        §2.
    Debt.
      Limitation of indebtedness, MD Const Art
        XI-F §8.
    Defined, MD Const Art XI-F §1.
    Elections.
      Charter, MD Const Art XI-F §2.
      Procedure for becoming code county, MD
        Const Art XI-F §2.
    Fees.
      Restrictions on levy, MD Const Art XI-F §9.
    Home rule.
      General provisions, MD Const Art XI-F §§1 to
        10.
    Licenses.
      Restrictions on levy, MD Const Art XI-F §9.
    Public local law.
      Conflict of laws, MD Const Art XI-F §10.
      Defined, MD Const Art XI-F §1.
      Enactment, amendment or repeal, MD Const
        Art XI-F §3.
        By resolution of commissioners, MD Const
          Art XI-F §6.
      Limiting tax rate and indebtedness, MD
        Const Art XI-F §8.
      Power of general assembly to enact, MD
        Const Art XI-F §4.
      Subject to referendum, MD Const Art XI-F §7.
    Referendum.
      Public local law subject to referendum, MD
        Const Art XI-F §7.
    Taxation.
      Limiting tax rate, MD Const Art XI-F §8.
      Restrictions on levy, MD Const Art XI-F §9.
  Commissioners.
    Amendment of article XI, MD Const Art XI-A
      §6.
    Chartered counties.
      Power to prescribe number, compensation,
        powers and duties, MD Const Art XI-A
        §6.

CONSTITUTION OF MARYLAND —Cont'd
Counties —Cont'd
  Commissioners —Cont'd
    Compensation.
      Powers, MD Const Art XI-A §6.
      Prescribed by law, MD Const Art VII §2.
    Duties.
      General provisions, MD Const Art VII §2; Art
        XI-A §6.
    Election, MD Const Art VII §1.
      Continuation of existing method, MD Const
        Art XVIII.
      Number, MD Const Art VII §2.
    Powers.
      Generally, MD Const Art VII §2.
  Council.
    Charter may provide method of election, MD
      Const Art XI-A §3A.
  County seats.
    Changing, MD Const Art XIII §§1, 2.
  Debts.
    Restrictions on, MD Const Art III §54.
  Elections.
    Board of supervisors.
      Terms.
        Commencement, MD Const Art XVII §6.
    Council.
      Charter may provide method of election, MD
        Const Art XI-A §3A.
  Lines.
    Changing, MD Const Art XIII §1.
  New counties.
    Formation, MD Const Art XIII §1.
    General assembly to pass necessary laws, MD
      Const Art XIII §2.
    Organization, MD Const Art XIII §1.
  Officers and employees.
    Definition of officers, MD Const Art XVII §1.
    Elections.
      When elections for county officers held, MD
        Const Art XVII §2.
    Removal or suspension from office.
      Elected officials convicted of crimes, MD
        Const Art XV §2.
    Terms.
      Appointed by county commissioners, MD
        Const Art XVII §5.
      Elected by voters, MD Const Art XVII §3.
  Slum clearance.
    Authority granted to counties, MD Const Art III
      §61.
Court of appeals.
  Circuits, MD Const Art IV §14.
  Clerk of court.
    Appointment, MD Const Art IV §17.
    Notify attorney general of cases in which state
      has interest, MD Const Art V §6.
    Term of office, MD Const Art IV §17.
  Composition, MD Const Art IV §14.
  Court of record, MD Const Art IV §1.
  Decisions.
    Concurrence of a majority, MD Const Art IV
      §14.
    Judgment final, MD Const Art IV §15.
    Opinions in writing filed within three months
      after argument or submission, MD Const
      Art IV §15.
  Intermediate courts of appeal.
    Court of special appeals.
      See COURT OF SPECIAL APPEALS.
    Creation, MD Const Art IV §14A.

CONSTITUTION OF MARYLAND —Cont'd
Court of appeals —Cont'd
Intermediate courts of appeal —Cont'd
Decisions.
Judgment final, MD Const Art IV §15.
Written opinion filed within three months after argument or submission, MD Const Art IV §15.
Judges.
Chief judge of court of appeals.
Administrative head of system, MD Const Art IV §18.
Disqualification.
When judge heard cause below, MD Const Art IV §15.
Elections.
Exceptions as to quadrennial elections, MD Const Art XVII §3.
Eligibility of members of general assembly, MD Const Art IV §14B.
Generally. See within this heading, "Judges."
Reports.
Judicial work to chief judge of court of appeals, MD Const Art IV §18.
Terms of appointment, MD Const Art XVIII.
Vacancies.
Filled by chief judge of court of appeals, MD Const Art IV §18.
Judgments and decrees.
Final, MD Const Art IV §15.
Jurisdiction.
Prescribed by general assembly, MD Const Art IV §14A.
Powers.
Provided by general assembly, MD Const Art IV §1.
Reports.
Publication, MD Const Art IV §16.
Judges.
Chief judge, MD Const Art IV §14.
Administrative head of judicial system, MD Const Art IV §18.
Assignment of judges, MD Const Art IV §18.
Designation by governor, MD Const Art IV §14.
Duties.
Generally, MD Const Art IV §18.
Substitute when absent, MD Const Art IV §18.
Disqualification.
When judge heard cause below, MD Const Art IV §15.
Elections, MD Const Art IV §14.
Exceptions as to quadrennial elections, MD Const Art XVII §3.
Eligibility.
Member of general assembly, MD Const Art IV §21.
Generally, MD Const Art IV §§2 to 9. See within this heading, "Judges."
Number, MD Const Art IV §14.
Residence, MD Const Art IV §14.
Rules and regulations.
Prosecution of appeals, MD Const Art IV §18.
Regulation of practice, MD Const Art IV §18.
Salary, MD Const Art IV §14.
Term of office, MD Const Art IV §14; Art XVIII.
Vacancies.
Filling of vacancies by chief judge, MD Const Art IV §18.

CONSTITUTION OF MARYLAND —Cont'd
Court of appeals —Cont'd
Judgments and decrees.
Final, MD Const Art IV §15.
Jurisdiction, MD Const Art IV §14.
Laws.
Recorded with, MD Const Art III §30.
Powers.
Vested in, MD Const Art IV §1.
Quorum, MD Const Art IV §14.
Recordation.
Laws recorded with, MD Const Art III §30.
Reports.
Publication, MD Const Art IV §16.
Rules and regulations.
General provisions, MD Const Art IV §18.
Sessions, MD Const Art IV §14.
Statutes.
Laws to be recorded with court, MD Const Art III §30.
Courts.
Administrative head of judiciary department.
Chief judge, MD Const Art IV §18.
Commission on judicial disabilities, MD Const Art IV §§4A, 4B.
See JUDICIAL DISABILITIES COMMISSION.
Court of appeals, MD Const Art IV §§14 to 18. See within this heading, "Court of appeals."
Courts of record, MD Const Art IV §1.
District Court, MD Const Art IV §§41A to 41-I.
See DISTRICT COURT.
Enumeration, MD Const Art IV §1.
Existing at time of adoption of constitution, MD Const Art IV §1A.
Judges. See within this heading, "Judges."
Officers.
Compensation.
Fixed by general assembly, MD Const Art IV §9.
Orphans' court, MD Const Art IV §§40, 41. See within this heading, "Orphans' court."
Powers.
Judicial power vested in enumerated courts, MD Const Art IV §1.
Separation, MD Const DofR Art 8.
Seals, MD Const Art IV §1.
Creation of new constitution.
Ballot questions generally, EL §§7-101 to 7-105.
Crimes and offenses.
Attainder of treason or felony.
Prohibited, MD Const DofR Art 18.
Officers.
Removal or suspension from office.
Elected officials convicted of crimes, MD Const Art XV §2.
Crime victims rights, MD Const DofR Art 47.
Criminal procedure.
Accused.
Counsel.
Right to representation, MD Const DofR Art 21.
Indictment.
Copy of indictment, MD Const DofR Art 21.
Jury.
Impartial and unanimous jury, MD Const DofR Art 21.
Rights, MD Const DofR Art 21.
Self-incrimination.
Prohibited, MD Const DofR Art 22.
Witnesses.
Confrontation of witnesses, MD Const DofR Art 21.

CONSTITUTION OF MARYLAND —Cont'd
Criminal procedure —Cont'd
Corruption of blood.
Prohibited, MD Const DofR Art 27.
Evidence.
Sustaining conviction.
Question for court, MD Const DofR Art 23.
Forfeiture of estate.
Prohibited, MD Const DofR Art 27.
Jury.
Impartial and unanimous, MD Const DofR Art 21.
Judges of law and fact, MD Const DofR Art 23.
Witnesses.
Confrontation of witnesses, MD Const DofR Art 21.
Damages.
Remedy for injury to person or property, MD Const DofR Art 19.
Debtors.
Protection.
Laws to be passed to protect debtors, MD Const Art III §44.
Debts.
Imprisonment for debt.
Prohibited, MD Const Art III §38.
Declaratory judgments.
Attorney general as party, CJ §3-405.
Definitions.
Officers, MD Const Art XVII §1.
Departments.
Judiciary department. See within this heading, "Courts."
Treasury department.
Comptroller. See within this heading, "Comptroller."
State treasurer. See within this heading, "State treasurer."
Depositories.
Bonds, surety.
Security approved by governor, MD Const Art VI §3.
Deputies, MD Const Art V §9.
Desertion and nonsupport.
Imprisonment for nonsupport.
Not imprisonment for debt, MD Const Art III §38.
Discrimination.
Sex discrimination.
Equality of rights not abridged because of sex, MD Const DofR Art 46.
District Court.
General provisions, MD Const Art IV §§41A to 41-I.
See DISTRICT COURT.
Divorce.
Alimony.
Imprisonment for delinquent payment.
Not imprisonment for debt, MD Const Art III §38.
Due process.
Requirements, MD Const DofR Art 24.
Education, MD Const Art VIII §§1 to 3. See within this heading, "Schools."
Elections.
Absentee voters, MD Const Art I §3.
Amendments.
Submission to voters, MD Const Art XIV §1.
Ballots.
Joint listing of names of candidates for governor and lieutenant governor, MD Const Art II §1B.

CONSTITUTION OF MARYLAND —Cont'd
Elections —Cont'd
Ballots —Cont'd
Required, MD Const Art I §1.
Bribery.
Buying and selling votes, MD Const Art I §6.
Commissions.
Issuance by governor, MD Const Art IV §§11 to 13.
Constitutional amendments, MD Const Art XIV §1.
Contested elections.
Legislature to make provisions for, MD Const Art I §8.
County councils.
Charter providing method, MD Const Art XI-A §3A.
Date.
Time for holding general elections, MD Const Art XV §7.
Districts, MD Const Art I §1.
Fines.
Buying and selling votes, MD Const Art I §6.
Illegal voting, MD Const Art I §5.
Franchise, MD Const Art I §§1 to 12.
Free and frequent, MD Const DofR Art 7.
General assembly.
General provisions. See within this heading, "General assembly."
Regulation of elections.
Power of legislature to regulate, MD Const Art III §49.
General elections.
Time for holding, MD Const Art XV §7.
Governor.
Designating candidate for lieutenant governor, MD Const Art II §1B.
Joint listing of names of candidates for governor and lieutenant governor on ballot, MD Const Art II §1B.
Manner of holding, MD Const Art II §2.
Place of holding, MD Const Art II §2.
Questions relating to election decided by house of delegates, MD Const Art II §4.
Result.
Ascertainment, MD Const Art II §2.
Returns, MD Const Art II §2.
Tied elections.
New election ordered by governor, MD Const Art XVII §8.
Resolution, MD Const Art II §4.
Time of holding, MD Const Art II §2.
Lieutenant governor. See within this heading, "Lieutenant governor."
Oaths.
Officers.
Refusal to take, MD Const Art I §11.
Violations, MD Const Art I §11.
Preservation of purity.
Laws to be passed for, MD Const Art I §7.
Quadrennial elections.
Board of supervisors.
Terms.
Commencement, MD Const Art XVII §6.
Exceptions to provisions, MD Const Art XVII §7.
Provisions inconsistent with article.
Repealed or abrogated, MD Const Art XVII §9.
Purpose of article, MD Const Art XVII §1.

CONSTITUTION OF MARYLAND —Cont'd
Elections —Cont'd
  Quadrennial elections —Cont'd
    State and county officers, MD Const Art XVII
      §3.
      Appointed by governor and county
        commissioners.
        Terms, MD Const Art XVII §5.
      Definition of officers, MD Const Art XVII §1.
      Exceptions, MD Const Art XVII §3.
      Terms.
        Elected by voters, MD Const Art XVII §3.
        When elections to be held, MD Const Art
          XVII §2.
  Referendum, MD Const Art XVI §§1 to 6. See
    within this heading, "Referendum."
  Registration.
    Officers.
      Persons not registered voters ineligible to
        serve in elective office, MD Const Art I
        §12.
      Uniform system to be provided, MD Const Art I
        §2.
  Right of suffrage, MD Const DofR Art 7.
  State's attorneys, MD Const Art V §§7, 8.
    Determining election, MD Const Art V §8.
  Tied elections.
    New election ordered by governor.
      Execution, MD Const Art XVII §8.
  Voters.
    Absent voters, MD Const Art I §3.
    Age, MD Const Art I §1.
    Buying and selling votes, MD Const Art I §6.
      Penalty, MD Const Art I §6.
    Convicts, MD Const Art I §4.
    Insane persons, MD Const Art I §4.
    Qualifications, MD Const Art I §1.
      Governor's election, MD Const Art II §2.
    Removal.
      Effect, MD Const Art I §1.
    Residence.
      Change of residence for purpose of voting, MD
        Const Art I §5.
    Requirements, MD Const Art I §1.
  Voting.
    Buying and selling votes.
      Penalty, MD Const Art I §6.
    Illegal voting, MD Const Art I §5.
    More than one district, MD Const Art I §5.
    Registration required, MD Const Art I §2.
Eminent domain.
  Baltimore City.
    Land development and redevelopment, MD
      Const Art XI-B §1.
  Baltimore City and Baltimore, Cecil, Harford and
    Montgomery counties.
    Specific provisions, MD Const Art III §40A.
  Highways.
    Generally.
      See HIGHWAYS.
    Regulations, MD Const Art III §40B.
  Prince George's county.
    Water, sewerage and drainage systems of the
      Washington suburban sanitary commission,
      MD Const Art III §40C.
  Regulations, MD Const Art III §40.
  State road commission.
    Highways generally.
      See HIGHWAYS.
England.
  Common law and statutes applicable, MD Const
    DofR Art 5.

CONSTITUTION OF MARYLAND —Cont'd
Equality of rights.
  Women.
    Equality not abridged because of sex, MD Const
      DofR Art 46.
Evidence.
  Criminal procedure.
    Sustaining conviction.
      Question for jury, MD Const DofR Art 23.
Executions.
  Laws to be passed protecting property from
    execution, MD Const Art III §44.
  Expenses, MD Const Art V §9.
Executive department, MD Const Art II §§1 to
  24. See within this heading, "Governor."
Exemptions.
  Executions.
    Protecting property from execution.
      Expenses, MD Const Art V §9.
      Laws to be passed, MD Const Art III §44.
Ex post facto laws.
  Prohibited, MD Const DofR Art 17.
Federal aid.
  General assembly.
    Power to receive grants from United States,
      administer and distribute same, MD Const
      Art III §46.
Fees.
  Officers whose compensation is derived from fees.
    Accounts, MD Const Art XV §1.
    Disposition of excess fees, MD Const Art XV §1.
    Returns, MD Const Art XV §1.
Felony.
  No law to attaint for treason or felony, MD Const
    DofR Art 18.
Fines.
  Excessive fines prohibited, MD Const DofR Art 25.
Forfeitures.
  Criminal procedure.
    Corruption of blood or forfeiture of estate.
      Prohibited, MD Const DofR Art 27.
Forms, MD Const Art IV §13.
Freedom.
  Press and speech, MD Const DofR Art 40.
  Religion.
    Religious freedom, MD Const DofR Art 36.
  Speech, debate and proceedings in legislature, MD
    Const DofR Art 10.
Genders.
  Equality of rights not abridged because of sex,
    MD Const DofR Art 46.
General assembly.
  Adjournment.
    Consent of both houses required, MD Const Art
      III §25.
  Annapolis.
    Meeting place, MD Const DofR Art 11.
  Apportionment.
    Legislative districting and apportionment, MD
      Const Art III §5.
  Appropriations, MD Const Art III §32.
    Bills.
      General provisions. See within this
        subheading, "Bills."
  Baltimore City.
    Article subject to change, MD Const Art XI §9.
    Control over city, MD Const Art XI §9.
  Banks and trust companies.
    Books, papers and accounts.
      Inspection, MD Const Art III §39.

CONSTITUTION OF MARYLAND —Cont'd
General assembly —Cont'd
Bills.
  Amendment, MD Const Art III §27.
  Appropriations, MD Const Art III §§32, 52.
    Contingent fund, MD Const Art III §32.
    Disapproval of items in bills by governor, MD
        Const Art II §17.
    Invalidity of part not to affect all, MD Const
        Art III §52.
    Made how, MD Const Art III §52.
    Procedure generally, MD Const Art III §52.
    Restriction as to referendum, MD Const Art
        XVI §2.
    Statement of receipts and expenditures, MD
        Const Art III §32.
    Supplementary appropriation bill, MD Const
        Art III §52.
  Approval or disapproval by governor, MD Const
      Art II §17.
    Passage without approval, MD Const Art II
        §17.
  Budget bill.
    Balanced budget required, MD Const Art III
        §52.
    General provisions, MD Const Art III §52.
  Certified, MD Const Art III §30.
  Consent calendar, MD Const Art III §27.
    Passage of bills, MD Const Art III §28.
  Effective date, MD Const Art III §31; Art XVI
      §2.
  Embrace but one subject, MD Const Art III §29.
  Emergency law, MD Const Art XVI §2.
  Governor.
    Presented to governor for approval, MD Const
        Art III §30.
    Signing.
      Procedure, MD Const Art III §30.
  Introduction.
    Limit on time of introduction, MD Const Art
        III §27.
    When and where originated, MD Const Art III
        §27.
  Local laws.
    Enumeration of cases prohibited, MD Const
        Art III §33.
    General provisions, MD Const Art III §33.
  Origination.
    When and where, MD Const Art III §27.
  Passage.
    Final vote, MD Const Art III §28.
    Majority required, MD Const Art III §28.
  Publication, MD Const Art III §30.
    Statement of receipts and expenditures, MD
        Const Art III §32.
  Reading.
    Three readings, MD Const Art III §27.
  Recordation.
    Court of appeals, MD Const Art III §30.
  Revival, MD Const Art III §29.
  Special laws.
    Enumeration of cases prohibited, MD Const
        Art III §33.
    Prohibited when, MD Const Art III §33.
  Style, MD Const Art III §29.
  Titles, MD Const Art III §29.
  Vetoed, MD Const Art II §17.
    Power of governor, MD Const Art II §17.
    Reconsideration by legislature, MD Const Art
        II §17.

CONSTITUTION OF MARYLAND —Cont'd
General assembly —Cont'd
Bills —Cont'd
  Veto power of governor.
    Item veto, MD Const Art III §52.
  Yeas and nays.
    Recorded, MD Const Art III §28.
Books.
  Purchase of books for use of general assembly,
      MD Const Art III §16.
Branches.
  Consist of two branches, MD Const Art III §1.
Bribery.
  Compelling testimony in such cases.
    Legislature to provide for, MD Const Art III
        §50.
  Sentence and punishment, MD Const Art III
      §50.
Budget.
  Balanced budget.
    Required, MD Const Art III §52.
Clerks of court.
  Fees and charges.
    Provision of system for fees and charges, MD
        Const Art III §45.
Code of Maryland.
  Amendments, MD Const Art III §29.
    Enactment of laws not amendatory of code,
        MD Const Art III §29.
Collectors.
  Failure to account for public money.
    Disqualification, MD Const Art III §12.
Comptroller.
  Report of comptroller to legislature, MD Const
      Art VI §2.
Consent calendar, MD Const Art III §27.
  Passage of bills, MD Const Art III §28.
  Reading, MD Const Art III §27.
Corporations.
  Charter.
    Powers over, MD Const Art III §48.
  Foreign corporations.
    Taxation of revenues, MD Const Art III §58.
  Regulations, MD Const Art III §48.
Counties.
  Debts.
    Authorized by act of general assembly, MD
        Const Art III §54.
    Restrictions on, MD Const Art III §54.
  Formation, MD Const Art XIII §§1, 2.
  Internal improvements.
    Restrictions on, MD Const Art III §54.
Courts.
  Officers.
    Compensation, MD Const Art IV §9.
Credit.
  Restrictions on extension of state credit, MD
      Const Art III §34.
Debate.
  Freedom of speech, MD Const DofR Art 10.
  Not liable for words spoken in debate, MD
      Const Art III §18.
Debts.
  Imprisonment for debt prohibited, MD Const
      Art III §38.
  Restrictions on loans and extension of credit,
      MD Const Art III §34.
Districts.
  Requirements, MD Const Art III §4.
Doors kept open, MD Const Art III §21.

CONSTITUTION OF MARYLAND —Cont'd
General assembly —Cont'd
  Elections.
    Contested elections.
      Legislature to make provisions for, MD Const
        Art I §8.
    Each house judge of elections of its members,
      MD Const Art III §19.
    House of delegates, MD Const Art III §6.
    Preservation of purity of elections, MD Const
      Art I §7.
    Regulation by legislature, MD Const Art III §49.
    Senate, MD Const Art III §6.
    Time, MD Const Art III §7.
  Eminent domain.
    Highways.
      Regulations, MD Const Art III §40B.
    Regulations, MD Const Art III §40.
  Encouragement.
    What legislature should encourage, MD Const
      DofR Art 43.
  Executions.
    Laws to be passed protecting property from
      execution, MD Const Art III §44.
  Federal aid.
    Power to receive grants from United States,
      administer and distribute same, MD Const
      Art III §46.
  Fees.
    Consent of legislature required for levy, MD
      Const DofR Art 14.
  Governor.
    Approval or disapproval of bills, MD Const Art
      II §17.
    Pardons.
      Report to general assembly, MD Const Art II
        §20.
    Vacancy in legislature.
      Filling by governor, MD Const Art III §13.
    Vacancy in office.
      Filling by general assembly, MD Const Art II
        §6.
  Habeas corpus.
    Suspension.
      Legislature not to suspend writ, MD Const
        Art III §55.
  Highways.
    Eminent domain.
      Regulations, MD Const Art III §40B.
  Holding other office, MD Const Art III §11.
    Congressmen or persons holding any civil or
      military office in the United States
      prohibited, MD Const Art III §10.
    Exceptions, MD Const Art III §10.
  Home rule.
    Powers and restrictions, MD Const Art XI-A
      §§2, 4, 6.
  House of delegates.
    Accounts.
      Failure to account for public money, MD
        Const Art III §12.
    Adjournment.
      Consent of both houses required, MD Const
        Art III §25.
    Age, MD Const Art III §9.
    Clerk.
      Chief clerk.
        Bill signed in presence of, MD Const Art III
          §30.
    Committees.
      Committee of the whole.
        Doors kept open, MD Const Art III §21.

CONSTITUTION OF MARYLAND —Cont'd
General assembly —Cont'd
  House of delegates —Cont'd
    Committees —Cont'd
      Joint standing committee of senate and
        house, MD Const Art III §24.
    Compensation, MD Const Art III §15.
    Debate.
      Not liable for words spoken in debate, MD
        Const Art III §18.
    Districts, MD Const Art III §3.
      Requirements, MD Const Art III §4.
    Doors kept open, MD Const Art III §21.
    Elections, MD Const Art III §6.
      Districts, MD Const Art III §§3, 4.
        Subdivision of districts, MD Const Art III
          §3.
      Each house judge of elections, MD Const Art
        III §19.
      Governor.
        Deciding question of election, MD Const Art
          II §4.
      Time of holding, MD Const Art III §7.
    Established, MD Const Art III §1.
    Expulsion and punishment of members, MD
      Const Art III §19.
    Grand inquest of state.
      Powers of house, MD Const Art III §24.
    Holding other office.
      Civil office in state prohibited, MD Const Art
        III §11.
      United States office prohibited, MD Const Art
        III §10.
      Exceptions, MD Const Art III §10.
    Impeachments.
      Power in house of delegates, MD Const Art III
        §26.
    Journals, MD Const Art III §22.
    Liability.
      Not liable for words spoken in debate, MD
        Const Art III §18.
    Mileage, MD Const Art III §15.
    Number of members, MD Const Art III §2.
    Office created during own term.
      Not eligible, MD Const Art III §17.
    Officers.
      Appointment of own officers, MD Const Art
        III §19.
    Punishment and expulsion of members, MD
      Const Art III §19.
    Qualifications, MD Const Art III §9.
      Each house judge of qualifications, MD Const
        Art III §19.
    Quorum, MD Const Art III §20.
      Powers of smaller number than quorum, MD
        Const Art III §20.
    Residence, MD Const Art III §9.
    Rules and regulations.
      Making, MD Const Art III §19.
    Sentence and punishment, MD Const Art III
      §23.
      Imprisonment.
        Limitation on, MD Const Art III §23.
    Speaker.
      Bill signed in presence of, MD Const Art III
        §30.
      Compensation, MD Const Art III §15.
      Discharge duties of governor during vacancy,
        MD Const Art II §7.
      Governor.
        Open election returns for governor, MD
          Const Art II §§2, 3.

CONSTITUTION OF MARYLAND —Cont'd
General assembly —Cont'd
House of delegates —Cont'd
Terms of office, MD Const Art III §6.
Vacancy.
Filling by governor, MD Const Art III §13.
Husband and wife.
Property of wife protected from debts of
husband, MD Const Art III §43.
Impeachments.
General procedure, MD Const Art III §26.
Interest.
Legal rate of interest, MD Const Art III §57.
Intermediate courts of appeal.
Judges.
Eligibility of members of general assembly,
MD Const Art IV §14B.
Investigations.
Powers of house of delegates as grand inquest of
state, MD Const Art III §24.
Journals.
General provisions, MD Const Art III §22.
Veto passage entered in, MD Const Art II §17.
Votes entered in, MD Const Art II §17.
Judges.
Eligibility of members to be judge, MD Const
Art IV §21.
Removal, MD Const Art IV §4.
Retirement, MD Const Art IV §3.
Laws.
Suspension, MD Const DofR Art 9.
Local laws.
Not to enact local laws on subjects covered by
express powers, MD Const Art XI-A §4.
Prohibited when, MD Const Art III §33.
Lotteries.
Grants, MD Const Art III §36.
Meetings.
Annapolis.
Place of meeting, MD Const DofR Art 11.
Convened by secretary of state to fill vacancy in
office of governor, MD Const Art II §7.
Convening by governor, MD Const Art II §16.
Convening frequently, MD Const DofR Art 12.
Duration of sessions, MD Const Art III §15.
Extended session.
Passage of budget bill, MD Const Art III §52.
Extraordinary sessions.
Upon petition of members, MD Const Art III
§14.
Special sessions.
Budget amendment not to affect, MD Const
Art III §52.
Duration of sessions, MD Const Art III §15.
Proclamation for special session, MD Const
Art III §14.
Time of meeting, MD Const Art III §14.
Mileage, MD Const Art III §15.
Military service.
Aiding or compensating members of armed
forces in time of war, MD Const Art III §34.
Militia.
Consent to governor to command in person, MD
Const Art II §8.
Provision for, MD Const Art IX §§1, 2.
Mortgages and deeds of trust.
Taxation, MD Const Art III §51.
Officers.
Compensation.
Extra compensation to public officers, MD
Const Art III §35.

CONSTITUTION OF MARYLAND —Cont'd
General assembly —Cont'd
Officers —Cont'd
Compensation —Cont'd
Income tax.
Not exempted from income tax, MD Const
Art III §35A.
Increasing or diminishing during term of
office prohibited, MD Const Art III §35.
Imprisonment.
Limit on, MD Const Art III §23.
Replacement of vacancies, MD Const Art XV §5.
Pardons.
Governor's pardons reported to assembly, MD
Const Art II §20.
Parole.
Convicts, MD Const Art III §60.
Pensions.
General pension system prohibited, MD Const
Art III §59.
Port development.
Baltimore City, MD Const Art XI-D §§1, 2.
Powers.
Legislature may pass laws for carrying into
execution powers vested by constitution,
MD Const Art III §56.
Separation of powers, MD Const DofR Art 8.
Proceedings.
Not to be impeached in any court, MD Const
DofR Art 10.
Publication.
Statement of receipts and expenditures, MD
Const Art III §32.
Qualifications.
Disqualification.
Failure to account for public money, MD
Const Art III §12.
Receivers.
Failure to account for public money.
Disqualification, MD Const Art III §12.
Recommendations to general assembly.
By governor, MD Const Art II §19.
Referendum.
Soldiers' bonus, MD Const Art III §34.
Registers of wills.
Fees and charges.
Provision for system, MD Const Art III §45.
Resolutions.
Passage, MD Const Art III §28.
Right to petition for redress of grievances, MD
Const DofR Art 13.
Salaries.
Compensation and allowances of members, MD
Const Art III §15.
Compensation commission, MD Const Art III
§15.
Seal.
Great seal affixed thereto, MD Const Art III
§30.
Secretary of state.
Convening general assembly to fill vacancy in
office of governor, MD Const Art II §7.
Records inspected by general assembly, MD
Const Art II §23.
Senate.
Accounts.
Failure to account for public money, MD
Const Art III §12.
Adjournment.
Consent of both houses required, MD Const
Art III §25.

CONSTITUTION OF MARYLAND —Cont'd
General assembly —Cont'd
  Senate —Cont'd
    Age, MD Const Art III §9.
    Budget bill sent to, MD Const Art III §52.
    Committees.
      Committee of the whole.
        Doors kept open, MD Const Art III §21.
      Joint standing committee of senate and
        house, MD Const Art III §24.
    Compensation, MD Const Art III §15.
    Convening by governor, MD Const Art II §16.
    Debate.
      Not liable for words spoken in debate, MD
        Const Art III §18.
    Districts, MD Const Art III §3.
      Requirements, MD Const Art III §4.
    Doors kept open, MD Const Art III §21.
    Elections, MD Const Art III §6.
      Districts, MD Const Art III §§3, 4.
      Each house to be judge of elections, MD Const
        Art III §19.
      Time of holding, MD Const Art III §7.
    Established, MD Const Art III §1.
    Holding other office.
      Civil offices under state prohibited, MD Const
        Art III §11.
      Failure to account for public money, MD
        Const Art III §12.
      United States office prohibited, MD Const Art
        III §10.
        Exceptions, MD Const Art III §10.
    Impeachment.
      Tried by, MD Const Art III §26.
    Journals, MD Const Art III §22.
    Liability.
      Not liable for words spoken in debate, MD
        Const Art III §18.
    Mileage, MD Const Art III §15.
    Number of members, MD Const Art III §2.
    Office created during own term.
      Not eligible, MD Const Art III §17.
    Officers.
      Appointment of own officers, MD Const Art
        III §19.
    President.
      Bill signed in presence of, MD Const Art III
        §30.
      Budget bill sent to, MD Const Art III §52.
      Compensation, MD Const Art III §15.
      Discharge duties of governor during vacancy
        in office, MD Const Art II §7.
    Punishment and expulsion of members, MD
      Const Art III §19.
    Qualifications, MD Const Art III §§9 to 12.
      Each house to be judge of qualifications, MD
        Const Art III §19.
    Quorum, MD Const Art III §20.
      Powers of smaller number than quorum, MD
        Const Art III §20.
    Residence, MD Const Art III §9.
    Rules and regulations.
      Making own rules, MD Const Art III §19.
    Secretary.
      Bill signed in presence of, MD Const Art III
        §30.
    Sentence and punishment, MD Const Art III
      §23.
      Imprisonment.
        Limitation on, MD Const Art III §23.
    Terms of office, MD Const Art III §6.

CONSTITUTION OF MARYLAND —Cont'd
General assembly —Cont'd
  Senate —Cont'd
    Vacancy in office.
      Filling by governor, MD Const Art III §13.
    Sentence and punishment.
      Indeterminate sentences, MD Const Art III §60.
      Senate, MD Const Art III §23.
      Suspension, MD Const Art III §60.
    Soldiers' bonus.
      Referendum, MD Const Art III §34.
    Special laws.
      Prohibited when, MD Const Art III §33.
    State pension commissioner.
      Office prohibited, MD Const Art III §59.
    State treasurer.
      Selection of treasurer by legislature, MD Const
        Art VI §1.
    Styled general assembly of Maryland, MD Const
      Art III §1.
    Taxation.
      Consent of legislature required for levy, MD
        Const DofR Art 14.
      Mortgages and deeds of trust.
        Taxed where, MD Const Art III §51.
      Personal property.
        Where taxed, MD Const Art III §51.
    Trustees of public, MD Const DofR Art 6.
    United States.
      Power to receive grants from United States,
        administer and distribute same, MD Const
        Art III §46.
      Senators and delegates.
        Holding federal office prohibited, MD Const
          Art III §10.
        Exceptions, MD Const Art III §10.
    Vacancies.
      Filling by governor, MD Const Art III §13.
      Replacement of officers, MD Const Art XV §5.
    Yeas and nays.
      Recorded, MD Const Art III §28.
God.
  Belief in existence of God, MD Const DofR Arts
    36, 37.
Government.
  Compact theory of government, MD Const DofR
    Art 1.
  Exclusive right of people to regulate, MD Const
    DofR Art 4.
  Origin, MD Const DofR Art 1.
  Powers of the people, MD Const DofR Art 4.
  Reformation.
    Establishment of new government, MD Const
      DofR Art 6.
  Right to alter, MD Const DofR Arts 1, 6.
Governor.
  Acting governor, MD Const Art II §6.
  Age, MD Const Art II §5.
  Appointment by.
    Officers, MD Const Art II §10.
      Between primary election and inauguration of
        next governor, MD Const Art II §10A.
      Defined, MD Const Art XVII §1.
  Recess of senate, MD Const Art II §11.
  Rejection by senate or person nominated by
    governor.
    Effect, MD Const Art II §12.
  Secretary of state, MD Const Art II §22.
  Terms of such officers, MD Const Art II §13.
  Vacancies.
    During session of senate, MD Const Art II
      §14.

CONSTITUTION OF MARYLAND —Cont'd
Governor —Cont'd
  Appointment by —Cont'd
    Vacancies —Cont'd
      Power of governor to fill, MD Const Art II §11.
    When civil officers to be nominated to senate, MD Const Art II §13.
  Apportionment.
    Plan for legislative districting and apportionment, MD Const Art III §5.
  Appropriations.
    Bills.
      Disapproval of items by governor, MD Const Art II §17.
      Submitted to general assembly, MD Const Art III §52.
  Attorney general.
    Election.
      Determining election and qualification by governor, MD Const Art V §2.
    Tie vote.
      Determining, MD Const Art V §2.
    Oaths.
      Administration, MD Const Art V §2.
    Vacancy in office of attorney general.
      Filling by governor, MD Const Art V §5.
  Budget.
    Duties as to budget bill, MD Const Art III §52.
  Commander-in-chief.
    Land and naval forces of state, MD Const Art II §8.
  Compensation, MD Const Art II §21.
  Comptroller.
    Examination, MD Const Art II §18.
  Disability.
    Procedure for filling office, MD Const Art II §6.
  Elections.
    Designating candidate for lieutenant governor, MD Const Art II §1B.
    Joint listing of names of candidates for governor and lieutenant governor on ballot, MD Const Art II §1B.
    Manner of holding, MD Const Art II §2.
    Qualifications of voters, MD Const Art II §2.
    Questions relating to elections determined by house of delegates, MD Const Art II §4.
    Results.
      Ascertaining, MD Const Art II §3.
    Returns, MD Const Art II §2.
    Tie election.
      How decided, MD Const Art II §4.
  Executive department.
    Reorganization, MD Const Art II §24.
  Executive power vested in, MD Const Art II §1.
  Fines.
    Remission, MD Const Art II §20.
  Funds.
    Contingent fund, MD Const Art III §32.
      Report to general assembly, MD Const Art III §32.
  General assembly.
    Bills.
      Appropriation bills.
        Disapproval of items on bills by governor, MD Const Art II §17.
      Approval or disapproval by governor, MD Const Art II §17.
      Presented to governor for approval and signing, MD Const Art III §30.
    Convene legislature on extraordinary occasions, MD Const Art II §16.
    Proclamation for special session, MD Const Art III §14.

CONSTITUTION OF MARYLAND —Cont'd
Governor —Cont'd
  General assembly —Cont'd
    House of delegates.
      Speaker.
        Opening election returns for governor, MD Const Art II §3.
    Meetings.
      Change of place for meeting of legislature, MD Const Art II §16.
      Proclamation convening extraordinary session, MD Const Art III §14.
    Recommendations to assembly by governor, MD Const Art II §19.
    Vacancy in legislature.
      Filling by governor, MD Const Art III §13.
  Impeachment.
    Power of legislature, MD Const Art II §7.
  Judges.
    Commissions of office.
      Issuance, MD Const Art IV §11.
    Removal, MD Const Art IV §4.
    Retirement, MD Const Art IV §3.
    Vacancies.
      Appointment to fill vacancy, MD Const Art IV §5.
  Laws.
    Enforcement, MD Const Art II §9.
  Lieutenant governor, MD Const Art II §§1A to 4.
    See within this heading, "Lieutenant governor."
  Military service.
    Commander-in-chief.
      Land and naval forces of state, MD Const Art II §8.
  Militia.
    Commander-in-chief, MD Const Art II §8.
  Officers.
    Appointment, MD Const Art II §10.
      Between primary election and inauguration of next governor, MD Const Art II §10A.
    Nominations to senate, MD Const Art II §13.
    Qualifying before, MD Const Art I §10.
    Removal, MD Const Art II §15.
    Suspension, MD Const Art II §15.
    Vacancies.
      Approval of state senate, MD Const Art II §11.
      Declared for officers whose compensation is from fees.
        Failure to file reports, MD Const Art XV §1.
      Filling by governor, MD Const Art II §11.
  Order of succession, MD Const Art II §7.
  Orphans' court.
    Judges.
      Vacancy.
        Filled by governor, MD Const Art IV §40.
  Pardons, MD Const Art II §20.
  Powers.
    Separation, MD Const DofR Art 8.
  Proclamations.
    Constitutional amendments, MD Const Art XIV §1.
    Extension of session of general assembly for passage of budget bill, MD Const Art III §52.
    Extraordinary session of general assembly.
      Upon petition of members, MD Const Art III §14.
    Special session of general assembly, MD Const Art III §14.

CONSTITUTION OF MARYLAND —Cont'd
Governor —Cont'd
Qualifications, MD Const Art II §5.
  Eligibility determined by house of delegates, MD Const Art II §4.
  Time for qualifying for office, MD Const Art II §3.
Referendum.
  Election.
    Proclamation of result, MD Const Art XVI §5.
  Proclamation of results, MD Const Art XVI §5.
Residence, MD Const Art II §21.
  Requirements, MD Const Art II §5.
Salary, MD Const Art II §21.
Secretary of state.
  Clerical duties, MD Const Art II §23.
State treasurer.
  Examination, MD Const Art II §18.
Succession to office.
  Ineligible to succeed self after two terms, MD Const Art II §1.
Term of office, MD Const Art II §1.
  Commencement, MD Const Art II §1.
  Ineligible to succeed self after two terms, MD Const Art II §1.
  Number of successive terms, MD Const Art II §1.
Vacancy in office of governor.
  Approval of state senate.
    Effect of rejection, MD Const Art II §12.
  Disability, MD Const Art II §6.
  During session of senate, MD Const Art II §14.
  Filling.
    By general assembly, MD Const Art II §§6, 7.
  General assembly to fill.
    During recess of general assembly, MD Const Art II §7.
  Officers.
    Approval of governor's appointment by state senate, MD Const Art II §11.
  Vacancy not provided for in constitution, MD Const Art II §7.
Veto.
  Item veto, MD Const Art III §52.
  Power of veto, MD Const Art II §17.
Grants.
Form of grants, MD Const Art IV §13.
Habeas corpus.
Discharge for unconstitutionality of law, CJ §3-706.
Review by court of special appeals, SpecPro Rule 15-312.
Suspension.
  Legislature not to suspend writ, MD Const Art III §55.
Harford county.
Eminent domain.
  Specific provisions, MD Const Art III §40A.
Highways.
Eminent domain.
  Regulations, MD Const Art III §40B.
Holding more than one office of profit, MD Const DofR Art 35.
Home rule.
Baltimore City.
  Charter, MD Const Art XI-A §§1 to 7. See within this heading, "Baltimore City."
Code counties, MD Const Art XI-F §§1 to 10. See within this heading, "Counties."
Counties.
  Charter, MD Const Art XI-A §§1 to 7. See within this heading, "Counties."

CONSTITUTION OF MARYLAND —Cont'd
Home rule —Cont'd
  Counties —Cont'd
    Code counties, MD Const Art XI-F §§1 to 10. See within this heading, "Counties."
  Municipal corporations, MD Const Art XI-E §§1 to 6. See within this heading, "Municipal corporations."
House of delegates. See within this heading, "General assembly."
Housing authorities.
Slum clearance.
  Authority granted to municipal corporations and counties, MD Const Art III §61.
Husband and wife.
Property.
  Wife's property.
    Protected from debts of husband, MD Const Art III §43.
Impeachment.
Governor or lieutenant governor.
  Powers of legislature, MD Const Art II §7.
Indictments and informations.
Conclusion of indictment, MD Const Art IV §13.
Copy of indictment to accused, MD Const DofR Art 21.
Interest.
Legal rate, MD Const Art III §57.
Interpretation and construction.
Construction of words and phrases.
  Used in creating public offices, MD Const Art I §10.
Judges.
Age, MD Const Art IV §2.
  Retirement age, MD Const Art IV §3.
Assignment of judges.
  By chief judge of court of appeals, MD Const Art IV §18.
  Former judges, MD Const Art IV §3A.
Circuit courts. See within this heading, "Circuit courts."
Commission on judicial disabilities, MD Const Art IV §§4A, 4B.
  See JUDICIAL DISABILITIES COMMISSION.
Commissions of office.
  Issued by governor, MD Const Art IV §11.
Conservators of the peace, MD Const Art IV §6.
Court of appeals. See within this heading, "Court of appeals."
Disqualifications.
  In what cases judges disqualified, MD Const Art IV §7.
Elections, MD Const Art IV §3.
  Certification of returns to governor, MD Const Art IV §11.
  Commissions of office.
    Issuance, MD Const Art IV §11.
  Contested elections.
    How decided, MD Const Art IV §11.
    Procedure, MD Const Art IV §12.
  Tie vote.
    Determining election, MD Const Art V §8.
  Who elected, MD Const Art IV §11.
Expenses.
  Investigation and report by judge, MD Const Art IV §9.
Fees or prerequisites.
  Receiving prohibited, MD Const Art IV §6; DofR Art 33.
Holding other office.
  Prohibited, MD Const DofR Art 33.
    Exceptions, MD Const DofR Art 33.

CONSTITUTION OF MARYLAND —Cont'd
Judges —Cont'd
  Judicial disabilities commission, MD Const Art IV §§4A, 4B.
    See JUDICIAL DISABILITIES COMMISSION.
  Oaths.
    Administering oath to state's attorney, MD Const Art V §8.
  Officers of court.
    Appointment, MD Const Art IV §9.
    Compensation.
      Fixed by general assembly, MD Const Art IV §9.
  Orphans' court, MD Const Art IV §40.
  Qualifications, MD Const Art IV §2.
  Removal.
    By general assembly, MD Const Art IV §4.
    By governor, MD Const Art IV §4.
    General provisions, MD Const DofR Art 33.
  Removal of causes, MD Const Art IV §8.
  Residence, MD Const Art IV §2.
  Retirement.
    Age, MD Const Art IV §§3, 3B.
    General provisions, MD Const Art IV §3.
    Temporary assignment of former judges, MD Const Art IV §3A.
  Term of office, MD Const Art XVII §4.
    Commencement, MD Const Art XVII §4.
    Court of appeals, MD Const Art XVIII.
  Vacancies, MD Const Art IV §5.
Judiciary department, MD Const Art IV §§1 to 45. See within this heading, "Courts."
Jury.
  Civil procedure.
    Trial by jury.
      Sums over $10,000, MD Const DofR Art 23.
  Criminal procedure.
    Judges of law and fact, MD Const DofR Art 23.
  Impartial jury, MD Const DofR Art 21.
  Judges of law and fact.
    Criminal procedure, MD Const DofR Art 23.
  Not incompetent if believe in God, MD Const DofR Art 36.
  Trial by jury.
    Application, MD Const DofR Art 5.
    Civil cases.
      Sums over $10,000, MD Const DofR Art 23.
      Right of trial in civil proceedings, MD Const DofR Art 23.
  Unanimous verdict, MD Const DofR Art 21.
Justices of the peace.
  Official character.
    Authentication, MD Const Art IV §1.
  Powers.
    Vested in, MD Const Art IV §1.
  Process.
    Authentication, MD Const Art IV §1.
Laws.
  Ex post facto laws.
    Prohibited, MD Const DofR Art 17.
  Martial law.
    Restrictions, MD Const DofR Art 32.
  Pass laws for carrying into execution powers vested by constitution, MD Const Art III §56.
  Sanguinary laws.
    Avoided, MD Const DofR Art 16.
  Suspension, MD Const DofR Art 9.
Legislative department. See within this heading, "General assembly."
Lieutenant governor.
  Acting governor, MD Const Art II §6.

CONSTITUTION OF MARYLAND —Cont'd
Lieutenant governor —Cont'd
  Age, MD Const Art II §5.
  Disability.
    Procedure for filling office, MD Const Art II §6.
  Duties, MD Const Art II §1A.
  Elections.
    Candidate for governor to designate candidate for lieutenant governor, MD Const Art II §1B.
    Manner of holding, MD Const Art II §2.
    Qualifications of voters, MD Const Art II §2.
    Questions relating to elections determined by house of delegates, MD Const Art II §4.
    Results.
      Ascertaining, MD Const Art II §3.
    Returns, MD Const Art II §2.
    Tie election.
      How decided, MD Const Art II §4.
  Eligibility, MD Const Art II §1A.
  Impeachment.
    Powers of legislature, MD Const Art II §7.
  Office created, MD Const Art II §1A.
  Qualifications, MD Const Art II §§1A, 5.
    Eligibility determined by house of delegates, MD Const Art II §4.
    Time for qualifying for office, MD Const Art II §3.
  Salary, MD Const Art II §1A.
  Vacancy in office, MD Const Art II §6.
Local laws.
  Charters.
    Baltimore City, MD Const Art XI-A §§1 to 7. See within this heading, "Baltimore City."
    Counties, MD Const Art XI-A §§1 to 7. See within this heading, "Counties."
    Municipal corporations, MD Const Art XI-E §§1 to 6. See within this heading, "Municipal corporations."
Lord Baltimore.
  Property derived under charter, MD Const DofR Art 5.
Lotteries.
  Grants, MD Const Art III §36.
Manufacturers.
  What legislature should encourage, MD Const DofR Art 43.
Married women.
  Property.
    Protection from debts of husband, MD Const Art III §43.
Martial law.
  Restrictions, MD Const DofR Art 32.
Maryland equal rights for women law.
  Equality of rights not abridged because of sex, MD Const DofR Art 46.
Military services.
  Armies.
    Standing armies.
      Consent of legislature required, MD Const DofR Art 29.
  Martial law.
    Restrictions, MD Const DofR Art 32.
  Militia. See within this heading, "Militia."
  Pensions.
    General pension system prohibited, MD Const Art III §59.
  Power subordinate to civil power, MD Const DofR Art 30.
  Soldiers.
    Quartering, MD Const DofR Art 31.

CONSTITUTION OF MARYLAND —Cont'd
Militia.
Adjutant general, MD Const Art IX §2.
Disciplining, MD Const Art IX §1.
Equipping, MD Const Art IX §1.
Organization, MD Const Art IX §1.
Proper defense, MD Const DofR Art 28.
Monopolies.
Prohibited, MD Const DofR Art 41.
Montgomery county.
Eminent domain.
Specific provisions, MD Const Art III §40A.
Municipal corporations.
Alcoholic beverages.
Acts prohibited by state law, MD Const Art
XI-E §6.
Charters.
Adoption.
Procedure, MD Const Art XI-E §4.
Amendment.
Procedure, MD Const Art XI-E §4.
Classes of municipal corporations, MD Const
Art XI-E §2.
Debts.
Limitations, MD Const Art XI-E §5.
Franchises.
Authorization, MD Const Art XI-E §5.
Home rule, MD Const Art XI-E §3.
Effect of and limitations upon home rule
charters, MD Const Art XI-E §6.
Licenses.
Authorization, MD Const Art XI-E §5.
Power and authority, MD Const Art XI-E §3.
Repeal.
Procedure, MD Const Art XI-E §4.
Special charters generally prohibited, MD Const
Art XI-E §1.
Taxation.
Authorization, MD Const Art XI-E §5.
Classes, MD Const Art XI-E §2.
Home rule.
Charters.
Effect of and limitations upon, MD Const Art
XI-E §6.
Power and authority, MD Const Art XI-E §3.
Local laws, MD Const Art XI-E §1.
Officers.
Removal or suspension from office.
Elected officials convicted of crimes, MD
Const Art XV §2.
Slum clearance.
Authority granted to municipal corporations,
MD Const Art III §61.
New constitution.
Ballot questions generally, EL §§7-101 to 7-105.
Newspapers.
Freedom of press and speech, MD Const DofR Art
40.
Nobility.
No title of nobility or hereditary honors to be
granted, MD Const DofR Art 42.
Notaries public.
Appointment, MD Const Art IV §45.
Holding more than one office.
Office of notary not within meaning of article,
MD Const DofR Art 35.
Powers, MD Const Art IV §45.
Oaths.
Administration.
Manner of administering, MD Const DofR Art
39.

CONSTITUTION OF MARYLAND —Cont'd
Oaths —Cont'd
Attorney general.
Administration by governor, MD Const Art V
§2.
Comptroller, MD Const Art VI §1.
Counties.
Officers qualifying out of county.
Recording oath, MD Const Art I §10.
Official oath, MD Const Art I §9.
Refusal to take oath, MD Const Art I §11.
Violation of oath, MD Const Art I §11.
Religious test prohibited, MD Const DofR Art 37.
Retrospective oaths.
Prohibited, MD Const DofR Art 17.
State's attorneys, MD Const Art V §8.
State treasurer, MD Const Art VI §1.
Officers.
Appointed officers.
Nominations to senate, MD Const Art II §13.
Term of office, MD Const Art II §13; Art XVII
§5.
Commissions for public office.
Form, MD Const Art IV §13.
Compensation.
Derived from fees, MD Const Art XV §1.
Construction of certain words and phrases.
Used in creating office, MD Const Art I §10.
County officers.
General provisions. See within this heading,
"Counties."
Defined, MD Const Art XVII §1.
Elections.
When elections for state and county officers to
be held, MD Const Art XVII §2.
Fees.
Compensation derived from fees, MD Const Art
XV §1.
Disposition of excess fees, MD Const Art XV §1.
Return of officers.
Compensation derived from fees, MD Const
Art XV §1.
Form.
Oath of office, MD Const Art I §9.
Gifts, MD Const DofR Art 35.
Nominations to senate, MD Const Art II §13.
Oaths.
Official oath, MD Const Art I §9.
Refusal to take, MD Const Art I §11.
Violation, MD Const Art I §11.
Organizations.
Members of certain organizations ineligible to
hold office, MD Const Art XV §3.
Qualifications.
Disqualification.
Buying and selling votes, MD Const Art I §6.
Qualifying, MD Const Art I §10.
Outside of county of residence.
Recording of oath, MD Const Art I §10.
Registration to vote.
Persons not registered voters ineligible to serve
in elective office, MD Const Art I §12.
Replacement.
Temporary replacement of officers unavailable
for duty, MD Const Art XV §5.
Rotation of executive offices, MD Const DofR Art
34.
Subversive organizations.
Members ineligible to hold office or positions of
profit or trust, MD Const Art XV §3.

CONSTITUTION OF MARYLAND —Cont'd

Officers —Cont'd

Suspension and removal.

Elected officials convicted of crimes, MD Const Art XV §2.

Temporary replacement.

Officer unavailable to perform duties, MD Const Art XV §5.

Terms.

Appointed by governor and county commissioners, MD Const Art XVII §5.

Commencement, MD Const Art II §13; Art XVII §4.

Elected by voters, MD Const Art XVII §3.

Trustees of public, MD Const DofR Art 6.

Women.

Competent to hold office, MD Const Art I §10.

Orphans' court.

Court of record, MD Const Art IV §1.

Harford county, MD Const Art IV §20.

Judges, MD Const Art IV §40.

Montgomery county, MD Const Art IV §20.

Powers.

Vested in, MD Const Art IV §1.

Parole and probation.

Parole of convicts, MD Const Art III §60.

Paupers.

Taxation.

Assessment prohibited, MD Const DofR Art 15.

Penalties.

Excessive.

Prohibited, MD Const DofR Art 25.

Pensions.

State pension commissioner.

Office prohibited, MD Const Art III §59.

System.

General pension system prohibited, MD Const Art III §59.

People.

Reservation of rights of people, MD Const DofR Art 45.

Police.

Exclusive right of people, MD Const DofR Art 4.

Poll tax.

Prohibited, MD Const DofR Art 15.

Poor.

Taxation.

Assessment prohibited, MD Const DofR Art 15.

Port development.

Baltimore City.

Port authority. See within this heading, "Baltimore City."

Prisoners.

Parole of convicts, MD Const Art III §60.

Proposed amendments. See within this heading, "Amendments."

Provide for procedures.

Judicial disabilities commission.

Referendum.

See REFERENDUM.

Provisions of limited duration, MD Const Art XIV §1A.

Publication.

Amendment to constitution, MD Const Art XIV §1.

Public debts.

County debt.

Restrictions on, MD Const Art III §54.

Municipal corporations.

Limitations, MD Const Art XI-E §5.

CONSTITUTION OF MARYLAND —Cont'd

Public works.

Board.

Borrowing money.

Anticipation of taxes, MD Const Art III §34.

Composition, MD Const Art XII §1.

Duties, MD Const Art XII §2.

Established, MD Const Art XII §1.

Journal.

Keeping, MD Const Art XII §1.

Powers, MD Const Art XII §§1, 2.

Public improvements and banking corporations.

Sale of state's interest in works, MD Const Art XII §3.

Salaries.

Members serve without additional salary, MD Const Art XII §2.

Sale of state's interest.

Public improvements and banking corporations, MD Const Art XII §3.

Sessions, MD Const Art XII §1.

Quadrennial elections. See within this heading, "Elections."

Referendum.

Additional legislation, MD Const Art XVI §1.

Alcoholic beverages.

Laws.

Relating to malt or spirituous liquors not to be referred, MD Const Art XVI §6.

Appropriation bills.

Restriction as to referendum, MD Const Art XVI §2.

Article self-executing, MD Const Art XVI §1.

Effective date of law, MD Const Art XVI §2.

Elections.

Ballots, MD Const Art XVI §5.

Results.

Proclamation of results, MD Const Art XVI §5.

Text of measures furnished voters, MD Const Art XVI §5.

Governor.

Proclamation of results, MD Const Art XVI §5.

Petitions.

Filing.

Effect, MD Const Art XVI §2.

Form, MD Const Art XVI §4.

Signers.

Effect if signed by more than one half of number required, MD Const Art XVI §3.

Number of signers, MD Const Art XVI §3.

Verification of signatures, MD Const Art XVI §4.

Submitted by petition, MD Const Art XVI §1.

Power.

Reservation of power of referendum in people, MD Const Art XVI §1.

Prohibited.

Laws.

Relating to malt or spirituous liquors not to be referred, MD Const Art XVI §6.

Self-executing.

Article self-executing, MD Const Art XVI §1.

Registers of wills.

Duties.

Generally, MD Const Art IV §41.

Elections.

Certification of returns to governor, MD Const Art IV §11.

Contested elections.

How decided, MD Const Art IV §12.

CONSTITUTION OF MARYLAND —Cont'd
Registers of wills —Cont'd
Elections —Cont'd
General provisions, MD Const Art IV §11.
Fees.
Legislature to provide system of fees and charges, MD Const Art III §45.
Qualifications, MD Const Art IV §41.
Removal, MD Const Art IV §41.
Term of office, MD Const Art IV §41.
Vacancy.
Filled by judges of orphans' court, MD Const Art IV §41.
Religion.
Establishment of religion.
Provisions not to constitute, MD Const DofR Art 36.
Freedom.
Religious freedom, MD Const DofR Arts 36, 37.
Oath of office.
Religious test prohibited, MD Const DofR Art 37.
Removal of causes.
General provisions, MD Const Art IV §8.
Repeal.
Provisions inconsistent with article repealed, MD Const Art XVII §9.
Reserved powers of states and people, MD Const DofR Art 3.
Restrictions.
Retrospective restrictions.
Prohibited, MD Const DofR Art 17.
Salaries.
Governor, MD Const Art II §21.
Schools.
Continuance.
System enforced at adoption of constitution, MD Const Art VIII §2.
Establishment.
General assembly to establish system of free public schools, MD Const Art VIII §1.
Free public schools.
General assembly to establish system of free public schools, MD Const Art VIII §1.
Funds.
School fund, MD Const Art VIII §3.
Local boards of education.
Elections.
Exceptions as to quadrennial elections, MD Const Art XVII §7.
What legislature should encourage, MD Const DofR Art 43.
Science.
What legislature should encourage, MD Const DofR Art 43.
Searches and seizures.
Due process.
Required, MD Const DofR Art 24.
Requirements, MD Const DofR Art 26.
Secretary of state.
Appointment.
By governor, MD Const Art II §22.
Duties.
General provisions, MD Const Art II §23.
Salary.
Fixed by general assembly, MD Const Art II §22.
Term of office, MD Const Art II §22.
Senate. See within this heading, "General assembly."

CONSTITUTION OF MARYLAND —Cont'd
Sentence and punishment.
Corruption of blood or forfeiture of estate.
Prohibited, MD Const DofR Art 27.
Cruel and unusual punishment, MD Const DofR Arts 16, 25.
Excessive.
Prohibited, MD Const DofR Art 25.
Ex post facto laws.
Prohibited, MD Const DofR Art 17.
Indeterminate sentences.
General provisions, MD Const Art III §60.
Parole of convicts, MD Const Art III §60.
Suspension of sentence.
General provisions, MD Const Art III §60.
Separation of powers, MD Const DofR Art 8.
Sex discrimination.
Equality of rights not abridged because of sex, MD Const DofR Art 46.
Sheriffs, MD Const Art IV §44.
Speech.
Freedom of press and speech, MD Const DofR Art 40.
State.
Powers.
Reserved powers of state and people, MD Const DofR Art 3.
Separation of powers, MD Const DofR Art 8.
Sovereignty of the state, MD Const DofR Art 4.
State pension commissioner.
Office prohibited, MD Const Art III §59.
State's attorneys.
Assistants.
General provisions, MD Const Art V §9.
Bonds, surety, MD Const Art V §12.
Collection of revenue.
In name of state, MD Const Art V §12.
Compensation, MD Const Art V §9.
Deputies.
General provisions, MD Const Art V §9.
Duties, MD Const Art V §9.
Elections.
Determining, MD Const Art V §8.
Tie vote.
Determining, MD Const Art V §8.
Time of election, MD Const Art V §7.
Expenses.
General provisions, MD Const Art V §9.
Fees.
Prohibited, MD Const Art V §9.
Oath, MD Const Art V §8.
One in each county, MD Const Art V §7.
Qualifications, MD Const Art V §10.
Determining, MD Const Art V §8.
Removal.
Recommendation of attorney general, MD Const Art V §7.
Term of office, MD Const Art V §7.
Vacancy.
Filling.
By judge or judges, MD Const Art V §11.
State treasurer.
Accounts.
Inspection by comptroller, MD Const Art VI §4.
Publishing abstracts and submitting copies to legislature, MD Const Art VI §4.
Rendering to comptroller, MD Const Art VI §4.
Appointment, MD Const Art VI §1.
Bond issues.
Signing, MD Const Art VI §3.
Bond, surety, MD Const Art VI §1.

CONSTITUTION OF MARYLAND —Cont'd
State treasurer —Cont'd
 Compensation, MD Const Art VI §1.
 Depositories.
  Duties as to, MD Const Art VI §3.
 Deputies.
  Duties, MD Const Art VI §3.
 Duties, MD Const Art VI §3.
 Examination.
  By governor, MD Const Art II §18.
 Oath, MD Const Art VI §1.
 Office, MD Const Art VI §1.
 Powers, MD Const Art VI §3.
 Qualifying.
  When to qualify, MD Const Art VI §5.
 Receipts, MD Const Art VI §3.
 Removal.
  Procedure, MD Const Art VI §6.
 Term of office, MD Const Art VI §1.
 Vacancy.
  Filling, MD Const Art VI §1.
Statutes.
 Effective date, MD Const Art XVI §2.
 Emergency law, MD Const Art XVI §2.
 English statutes.
  Applicable, MD Const DofR Art 5.
 Powers vested by constitution.
  Legislature may pass laws for carrying into
   execution, MD Const Art III §56.
 Referendum, MD Const Art XVI §§1 to 6. See
  within this heading, "Referendum."
Summons and process.
 Due process.
  Required, MD Const DofR Art 24.
 Form, MD Const Art IV §13.
Superior court of Baltimore City.
 General provisions, MD Const Art IV §11.
Supreme law of the land, MD Const DofR Art 2.
Suspension of laws, MD Const DofR Art 9.
Taxation.
 Assessments.
  Farm or agricultural land, MD Const DofR Art
   43.
  Paupers not to be assessed, MD Const DofR Art
   15.
 Corporations.
  Foreign.
   Revenues, MD Const Art III §58.
 Levy.
  Consent of legislature required, MD Const DofR
   Art 14.
 Municipal corporations.
  General provisions, MD Const Art XI-E §5.
 Personal property.
  Where taxed, MD Const Art III §51.
 Poll taxes prohibited, MD Const DofR Art 15.
 Uniformity.
  Required, MD Const DofR Art 15.
Torts.
 Remedy for injury to person or property, MD
  Const DofR Art 19.
Treason.
 Attainder.
  No law to attaint for treason or felony, MD
   Const DofR Art 18.
Treasury.
 Comptroller. See within this heading,
  "Comptroller."
 Department.
  Finance department.
   See FINANCE DEPARTMENT.

CONSTITUTION OF MARYLAND —Cont'd
Treasury —Cont'd
 State treasurer. See within this heading, "State
  treasurer."
Treaties.
 Supreme law of land, MD Const DofR Art 2.
Trial.
 Facts where they arise, MD Const DofR Art 20.
 Jury trial, MD Const DofR Art 5.
  In civil cases for sums over $5,000, MD Const
   DofR Art 23.
 Speedy trial, MD Const DofR Art 21.
United States.
 Laws and treaties.
  Supreme law of land, MD Const DofR Art 2.
 State of Maryland.
  Power to receive grants from United States,
   administer and distribute same, MD Const
   Art III §46.
Vacancies in office.
 Replacements by general assembly, MD Const Art
  XV §5.
Venue.
 Trial of facts where they arise, MD Const DofR
  Art 20.
Verdict.
 Unanimous verdict, MD Const DofR Art 21.
War.
 Applicability in war as well as in peace, MD Const
  DofR Art 44.
Warrants.
 Requirements.
  Searches and seizures, MD Const DofR Art 26.
Witnesses.
 Competency.
  Not incompetent if believe in God, MD Const
   DofR Art 36.
 Self-incrimination.
  Prohibited, MD Const DofR Art 22.
Women.
 Equality of rights not abridged because of sex,
  MD Const DofR Art 46.
 Officers.
  Construction of words and phrases.
   Used in creating public offices, MD Const Art
    I §10.
Writs.
 Form, MD Const Art IV §13.

CONSTITUTION OF THE UNITED STATES.
Absence.
 Congress.
  Members of congress, US Const Art I §5.
 Vice-president.
  Senate to choose president pro tem, US Const
   Art I §3.
Accounts and accounting.
 Receipts and expenditures of public money.
  Publication of statement and account, US Const
   Art I §9.
Accused persons.
 Rights of the accused, US Const Art III §2; Amds
  5, 6.
Actions to which United States a party, US
 Const Art III §2.
Adjournment of congress, US Const Art I §§5, 7;
 Art II §3.
Admiralty, US Const Art I §8.
 Jurisdiction of courts, US Const Art III §2.
Age.
 Congress.
  Representative in congress, US Const Art I §2.

CONSTITUTION OF THE UNITED STATES
—Cont'd
Age —Cont'd
Congress —Cont'd
Senator, US Const Art I §3.
Elections.
Right to vote not to be abridged on account of age, US Const Amd 26.
Voting by persons 18 years of age, US Const Amd 26.
President of the United States, US Const Art II §1.
Vice-president, US Const Amd 12.
Alcoholic beverages, US Const Amds 18, 21.
Aliens.
Congress.
Eligibility to be representative, US Const Art I §2.
Naturalization, US Const Art I §8.
Presidency.
Ineligibility for presidency, US Const Art II §1.
Suits against state, US Const Amd 11.
Ambassadors and consuls, US Const Art II §§2, 3; Art III §2.
Amendments, US Const Amd 5.
Bail, US Const Amd 8.
Congress.
Sessions, US Const Amd 20 §2.
Terms of office, US Const Amd 20 §1.
Time of convening, US Const Amd 20 §2.
Criminal law, US Const Amds 5, 6.
Due process of law, US Const Amds 5, 14.
Effect of enumeration of rights, US Const Amd 9.
Election of senators, US Const Amd 17.
Eminent domain, US Const Amd 5.
Freedom of religion, speech and press, US Const Amd 1.
Guarantees in criminal cases, US Const Amds 5, 6.
House of representatives.
Terms of representatives, US Const Amd 20 §1.
Income tax, US Const Amd 16.
Intoxicating liquors, US Const Amds 18, 21.
Lame duck amendment, US Const Amd 20.
Manner of making amendments, US Const Amd 5.
President.
Death, US Const Amd 20.
Election, US Const Amds 12, 20.
Failure to qualify, US Const Amd 20.
Succession upon death, resignation or removal of president, US Const Amd 25.
Terms of office, US Const Amds 20, 22.
Limitation on terms, US Const Amd 22.
Prohibition, US Const Amds 18, 21.
Proposal and ratification of amendments, US Const Amd 5.
Punishments, US Const Amd 8.
Quartering soldiers in houses, US Const Amd 3.
Ratification of amendment, US Const Amd 5.
Repeal of the 18th amendment, US Const Amd 21.
Reservation of powers to state, US Const Amd 10.
Restriction of judicial power, US Const Amd 11.
Rights and immunities of citizens, US Const Amd 14.
Right to bear arms, US Const Amd 2.
Right to vote, US Const Amd 15.
Searches and seizures, US Const Amd 4.
Self-incrimination, US Const Amd 5.
Senate.
Election of senators, US Const Amd 17.
Terms of senators, US Const Amd 20 §1.

CONSTITUTION OF THE UNITED STATES
—Cont'd
Amendments —Cont'd
Slavery, US Const Amd 13.
Suits against state, US Const Amd 11.
Terms of office, US Const Amd 20 §1.
Limitation on terms of president, US Const Amd 22.
Trial by jury, US Const Amds 6, 7.
Vice-president.
Death, US Const Amd 20.
Election, US Const Amds 12, 20.
Failure to qualify, US Const Amd 20.
Terms of office, US Const Amd 20 §1.
Woman suffrage, US Const Amd 19.
Appeals.
Review of facts tried by jury, US Const Amd 7.
Applicability.
In war as well as in peace, MD Const DofR Art 44.
Apportionment.
Congress, US Const Amds 14, 17.
Taxes.
Direct taxes, US Const Art I §§2, 9; Amd 16.
Appropriations, US Const Art I §9.
Army, US Const Art I §8.
Revenue bills, US Const Art I §7.
Approval of laws by president, US Const Art I §7.
Arms.
Right to bear, US Const Amd 2.
Army and navy, US Const Art I §8.
Commander-in-chief, US Const Art II §2.
Arrest.
Privilege from arrest, US Const Art I §6.
Assembly.
Right of, US Const Amd 1.
Attainder, US Const Art III §3.
Bill of attainder, US Const Art I §§9, 10.
Attorney and client.
Right to have counsel, US Const Amd 6.
Authors.
Protection of rights, US Const Art I §8.
Autrefois, acquit or convict, US Const Amd 5.
Bail and recognizance.
Excessive bail, US Const Amd 8.
Bankruptcy.
Powers of congress, US Const Art I §8.
Bill of attainder, US Const Art I §§9, 10.
Bill of rights, US Const Amds 1 to Amd 10.
Bills of credit, US Const Art I §10.
Bribery, US Const Art II §4.
Capitation tax, US Const Art I §9.
Census, US Const Art I §§2, 9.
Citizenship.
Privileges and immunities, US Const Art IV §2; Amd 14.
Civil war amendments, US Const Amds 13 to Amd 15.
Commerce, US Const Art I §§8, 9.
Common law.
Suits at, US Const Amd 7.
Compacts.
Between state and foreign power, US Const Art I §10.
Between the states, US Const Art I §10.
Congress, US Const Art I §1.
Absent members, US Const Art I §5.
Adjournment, US Const Art I §§5, 7; Art II §3.
Admiralty, US Const Art I §8.

CONSTITUTION OF THE UNITED STATES
—Cont'd

Congress —Cont'd

Amendments to the constitution, US Const Amd 5.

Apportionment of representatives, US Const Art I §2; Amd 14 §2.

Appropriations, US Const Art I §9.

Approval by president of order, resolution or vote, US Const Art I §7.

Army and navy.
Powers of congress, US Const Art I §8.

Arrest, US Const Art I §6.

Bankruptcy.
Powers of congress, US Const Art I §8.

Borrowing money, US Const Art I §8.

Commerce, US Const Art I §§8, 9.

Compensation of members, US Const Art I §6; Amd 27.

Consists of senate and house of representatives, US Const Art I §1.

Copyright, US Const Art I §8.

Counterfeiting.
Powers of congress, US Const Art I §8.

Courts.
Power to constitute tribunals inferior to supreme court, US Const Art I §8.

Debate, US Const Art I §6.

Debt.
Powers of congress, US Const Art I §8.

Declaration of war, US Const Art I §8.

Defense.
Powers of congress, US Const Art I §8.

District of Columbia, US Const Art I §8.

Duties and imposts.
Powers of congress, US Const Art I §8.

Elections, US Const Art I §§2, 4, 5; Amd 17.

Excises.
Powers of congress, US Const Art I §8.

Foreign commerce, US Const Art I §8.

Freedom of speech.
Members of congress, US Const Art I §6.

Holding other office, US Const Art I §6.

House of representatives, US Const Art I §§1, 2.
Absent members, US Const Art I §5.
Adjournment, US Const Art I §§5, 7; Art II §3.
Apportionment of representatives, US Const Art I §2; Amd 14 §2.
Arrest of members, US Const Art I §6.
Compensation of members, US Const Art I §6; Amd 27.
Debate, US Const Art I §6.
Elections. See within this heading, "Elections."
Expulsion of member, US Const Art I §5.
Freedom of speech, US Const Art I §6.
Holding other office, US Const Art I §6.
Impeachment, US Const Art I §2.
Journal, US Const Art I §§5, 7.
Libel and slander.
Privilege of members, US Const Art I §6.
Oath, US Const Art VI; Amd 14.
Officers, US Const Art I §2.
Presidential elector.
Representative ineligible, US Const Art II §1.
Punishment of members, US Const Art I §5.
Qualifications.
Electors, US Const Art I §2.
Members, US Const Art I §2.
Judge of qualifications, US Const Art I §5.
Quorum, US Const Art I §5.
Revenue bills, US Const Art I §7.

CONSTITUTION OF THE UNITED STATES
—Cont'd

Congress —Cont'd

House of representatives —Cont'd
Rules of procedure, US Const Art I §5.
Speaker, US Const Art I §2.
Term, US Const Art I §2.
Vacancies, US Const Art I §2.
Vice-president.
Vacancy in office.
Confirmation of nomination of president, US Const Amd 25 §2.

Insurrections, US Const Art I §8.

International law.
Power to punish offenses against, US Const Art I §8.

Interstate commerce, US Const Art I §§8, 9.

Invasions, US Const Art I §8.

Journals, US Const Art I §§5, 7.

Legislative powers vested in, US Const Art I §1.

Letters of marque and reprisal, US Const Art I §8.

Libel and slander.
Privilege of members of congress, US Const Art I §6.

Messages to congress, US Const Art II §3.

Militia.
Powers of congress, US Const Art I §8.

Money.
Powers of congress, US Const Art I §8.

Naturalization, US Const Art I §8.

Navy.
Powers of congress, US Const Art I §8.

Oath, US Const Art VI; Amd 14.

Patents, US Const Art I §8.

Piracy.
Powers of congress, US Const Art I §8.

Post offices and post roads, US Const Art I §8.

Powers of congress, US Const Art I §8.
Limitations on powers, US Const Art I §9.

President of the United States.
Declaration of president's disability.
Determination of issue, US Const Amd 25 §4.
By two-thirds vote of both houses, US Const Amd 25 §4.

Qualifications of members of congress, US Const Art I §§2, 3, 5.

Quorum, US Const Art I §5.

Rules of procedure, US Const Art I §5.

Senate.
Absent members, US Const Art I §5.
Adjournment, US Const Art I §§5, 7; Art II §3.
Arrest of members, US Const Art I §6.
Compensation of members, US Const Art I §6; Amd 27.
Debate, US Const Art I §6.
Elections. See within this heading, "Elections."
Equal suffrage in senate, US Const Art V.
Expulsion of member, US Const Art I §5.
Freedom of speech, US Const Art I §6.
Holding other office, US Const Art I §6.
Impeachment, US Const Art I §3.
Journal, US Const Art I §§5, 7.
Libel and slander.
Privilege of members, US Const Art I §6.
Number of senators from each state, US Const Art I §3; Amd 17.
Oath, US Const Art VI; Amd 14.
Officers, US Const Art I §3.
President, US Const Art I §3.
Pro tempore, US Const Art I §3.

CONSTITUTION OF THE UNITED STATES
—Cont'd
Congress —Cont'd
Senate —Cont'd
Presidential elector.
Senator ineligible, US Const Art II §1.
Punishment of members, US Const Art I §5.
Qualifications.
Members, US Const Art I §3.
Judge of qualifications, US Const Art I §5.
Qualifications of electors, US Const Amd 17.
Quorum, US Const Art I §5.
Revenue bills, US Const Art I §7.
Rules of procedure, US Const Art I §5.
Term, US Const Art I §3; Amd 17.
Vacancies, US Const Amd 17.
Vice-president of the United States.
Vacancy in office.
Confirmation of nomination of president, US Const Amd 25 §2.
Sessions, US Const Art I §4; Amd 20 §2.
Special sessions, US Const Art II §3.
Taxation.
Powers of congress, US Const Art I §8.
Territories, US Const Art IV §3.
Vice-president.
Vacancy in office.
Nomination by president, US Const Amd 25 §2.
Confirmation by majority of both houses of congress, US Const Amd 25 §2.
War.
Articles of war, US Const Art I §8.
Declaration of war, US Const Art I §8.
Weights and measures, US Const Art I §8.
Welfare.
Power of congress to provide for general welfare, US Const Art I §8.
Construction.
Effect of enumeration of rights, US Const Amd 9.
Consuls, US Const Art II §§2, 3; Art III §2.
Contracts.
Impairment of obligations of contracts, US Const Art I §10.
Conventions, US Const Arts V, VII.
Copyright, US Const Art I §8.
Corruption of blood.
Attainder of treason not to work, US Const Art III §3.
Counsel for defense, US Const Amd 6.
Counterfeiting, US Const Art I §8.
Courts.
Congress.
Power to constitute tribunals inferior to supreme court, US Const Art I §8.
Inferior courts, US Const Art III §1.
Judges.
Compensation, US Const Art III §1.
Oath, US Const Art VI; Amd 14.
Tenure, US Const Art III §1.
Jurisdiction, US Const Art III §2; Amd 11.
Restriction of judicial power, US Const Amd 11.
Criminal law.
Accused persons.
Rights of, US Const Art III §2; Amds 5, 6.
Constitutional provisions, US Const Amd 8.
Cruel and unusual punishment, US Const Amd 8.
Excessive bail, US Const Amd 8.
Extradition, US Const Art IV §2.
Fugitives from justice, US Const Art IV §2.

CONSTITUTION OF THE UNITED STATES
—Cont'd
Criminal law —Cont'd
Guarantees in criminal cases, US Const Amds 5, 6.
Public trial, US Const Amd 6.
Right of trial by jury, US Const Art III §2; Amd 6.
Rights of the accused, US Const Art III §2; Amds 5, 6.
Self-incrimination, US Const Amd 5.
Speedy trial, US Const Amd 6.
Cruel and unusual punishment, US Const Amd 8.
Customs.
Congress.
Power to lay and collect, US Const Art I §8.
Exportations from any state.
Duties not to be laid on, US Const Art I §9.
Importation of persons, US Const Art I §9.
State may not impose without consent of congress, US Const Art I §10.
Death.
President and vice president of the United States.
Duty of congress, US Const Art II §1; Amd 25.
President elect.
Provision in case of, US Const Amd 20.
Debts.
Aid of rebellion, US Const Amd 14.
Debts and engagements contracted before adoption, US Const Art VI.
Not to be questioned, US Const Amd 14.
Powers of congress, US Const Art I §8.
Declaration of rights, US Const Amds 1 to Amd 10.
Declaratory judgments.
Attorney general to be notified of suit challenging constitutionality of statute, CJ §3-405.
Defense.
Powers of congress, US Const Art I §8.
District of Columbia, US Const Art I §8.
Electors for president and vice president, US Const Amd 23.
Double jeopardy, US Const Amd 5.
Due process of law, US Const Amds 5, 14.
Duties and imposts.
Powers of congress, US Const Art I §8.
States, US Const Art I §§9, 10.
Tonnage, US Const Art I §10.
Elections.
Age.
Right to vote not to be abridged on account of age, US Const Amd 26.
Voting by persons 18 years of age, US Const Amd 26.
District of Columbia.
Electors for president and vice president, US Const Amd 23.
House of representatives, US Const Art I §2.
Election of members, US Const Art I §2.
Judge of elections, returns and qualifications of members, US Const Art I §5.
President, US Const Art II §1; Amd 12.
Qualifications of electors, US Const Art I §2.
Time, places and manner of holding, US Const Art I §4.
President, US Const Art II §1; Amds 12, 20.
Race, US Const Amd 15.
Senate, US Const Amd 17.
Judge of elections, returns and qualifications of members, US Const Art I §5.
Qualifications of electors, US Const Amd 17.

CONSTITUTION OF THE UNITED STATES
—Cont'd

Elections —Cont'd

Senate —Cont'd

Time, places and manner of holding, US Const Art I §4.

Vice-president, US Const Art II §1; Amd 12.

Suffrage, US Const Amds 15, 19.

Vice-president, US Const Art II §1; Amds 10, 12, 20.

Electors.

District of Columbia, US Const Amd 23.

Presidential electors, US Const Art II §1; Amd 12.

Qualifications, US Const Art II §1; Amds 14, 15, 17.

Eminent domain, US Const Amd 5.

Emoluments, US Const Art I §9.

Equal protection of the laws, US Const Amd 14.

Equity.

Judicial power to extend to cases in, US Const Art III §2.

Excessive bail, US Const Amd 8.

Excessive fines, US Const Amd 8.

Excises.

Powers of congress, US Const Art I §8.

Execution of laws, US Const Art II §3.

Executive department, US Const Art II §§1 to 4.

See within this heading, "President."

Expenditures.

Necessity for appropriation, US Const Art I §9.

Publication of statement, US Const Art I §9.

Exports, US Const Art I §§9, 10.

Ex post facto laws, US Const Art I §§9, 10.

Extradition, US Const Art IV §2.

Fines.

Excessive fines, US Const Amd 8.

Foreign presents, US Const Art I §9.

Former jeopardy, US Const Amd 5.

Freedom of conscience, US Const Amd 1.

Freedom of speech, US Const Amd 1.

Members of congress, US Const Art I §6.

Freedom of the press, US Const Amd 1.

Fugitives, US Const Art IV §2.

Full faith and credit clause, US Const Art IV §1.

General provisions, US Const Art VI.

Gifts.

Foreign presents to United States officials, US Const Art I §9.

Grand jury.

Presentments by, US Const Amd 5.

Habeas corpus, US Const Art I §9.

Discharge for unconstitutionality of law, CJ §3-706.

Review by court of special appeals, SpecPro Rule 15-312.

House of representatives, US Const Art I §§1, 2.

See within this heading, "Congress."

Immigration, US Const Art I §9.

Immunities, US Const Art IV §2; Amd 14.

Impairment of obligations of contracts, US Const Art I §10.

Impeachment, US Const Art I §§2, 3; Art II §4; Art III §2.

Imports and exports, US Const Art I §§9, 10.

Income tax, US Const Amd 16.

Indians.

Apportionment of representatives, US Const Art I §2; Amd 14 §2.

Indictments, informations and presentments, US Const Amd 5.

Insurrection, US Const Art I §8; Amd 14.

CONSTITUTION OF THE UNITED STATES
—Cont'd

International law.

Power of congress to punish offenses against, US Const Art I §8.

Interstate commerce, US Const Art I §§8, 9.

Intoxicating liquors.

Prohibition, US Const Amds 18, 21.

Repeal of the 18th amendment, US Const Amd 21.

Invasion, US Const Art I §§8 to 10; Art IV §4.

Involuntary servitude, US Const Amd 13.

Jeopardy.

Double jeopardy, US Const Amd 5.

Journals.

Congress, US Const Art I §§5, 7.

Judges.

Compensation, US Const Art III §1.

Oath, US Const Art VI; Amd 14.

Tenure, US Const Art III §1.

Judgments.

Full faith and credit clause, US Const Art IV §1.

Proof, US Const Art IV §1.

Judiciary, US Const Art I §8; Art III §§1 to 3. See within this heading, "Courts."

Jurisdiction of the United States courts, US Const Art III §2; Amd 11.

Jury.

Jury of vicinage, US Const Amd 6.

Right of trial by jury, US Const Art III §2; Amds 6, 7.

Lame duck amendment, US Const Amd 20.

Legal tender, US Const Art I §10.

Letters of marque and reprisal, US Const Art I §§8, 10.

Libel and slander.

Congress.

Privilege of members of congress, US Const Art I §6.

Limitations on powers of states, US Const Art I §10.

Liquors, US Const Amds 18, 21.

Messages to congress, US Const Art II §3.

Militia.

Quartering soldiers, US Const Amd 3.

Ministers.

Jurisdiction of cases affecting, US Const Art III §2.

Receiving, US Const Art II §3.

Money, US Const Art I §§8, 10.

Coinage, US Const Art I §§8, 10.

Counterfeiting, US Const Art I §8.

Powers of congress, US Const Art I §8.

Naturalization, US Const Art I §8.

Navy, US Const Art I §8.

New states, US Const Art IV §3.

Nonresidents.

Jurisdiction of suits against state, US Const Amd 11.

Oaths.

Affirmation, US Const Art II §1; Art VI; Amd 4.

Congress, US Const Art VI; Amd 14.

Governor, US Const Art VI; Amd 14.

Lieutenant governor, US Const Art VI; Amd 14.

House of representatives, US Const Art VI; Amd 14.

Judges, US Const Art VI; Amd 14.

Lieutenant governor, US Const Art VI; Amd 14.

President, US Const Art II §1; Amd 14.

Public officers, US Const Art VI; Amd 14.

Senate, US Const Art VI; Amd 14.

Vice-president, US Const Art VI; Amd 14.

CONSTITUTION OF THE UNITED STATES
—Cont'd

Pardons, US Const Art II §2.

Patents.
Piracy, US Const Art I §8.

Payments.
Legal tender, US Const Art I §10.

Petition.
Right of, US Const Amd 1.

Poll tax.
Failure to pay poll tax or other tax.
Denial or abridgement of right to vote.
Prohibited, US Const Amd 24.

Post offices, US Const Art I §8.

Post roads, US Const Art I §8.

Powers of congress, US Const Art I §8.

Powers reserved to states and people, US Const Amd 10.

President.
Age, US Const Art II §1.
Ambassadors and consuls, US Const Art II §§2, 3.
Appointment of officers, etc., US Const Art II §2.
Approval of laws by president, US Const Art I §7.
Approval of order, resolution or vote of congress, US Const Art I §7.
Bribery, US Const Art II §4.
Commander-in-chief, US Const Art II §2.
Compensation, US Const Art II §1.
Congress.
Adjourning congress, US Const Art II §3.
Convening congress, US Const Art II §3.
Messages to congress, US Const Art II §3.
Special sessions of congress, US Const Art II §3.
Death, US Const Art II §1; Amd 20 §3.
Succession upon death, US Const Amd 25 §1.
Disability, US Const Art II §1.
Declaration by president.
Inability to perform duties, US Const Amd 25 §3.
Declaration by vice-president and other officers, US Const Amd 25 §4.
Determination of issue by congress, US Const Amd 25 §4.
Duties, US Const Art II §3.
Declaration by president of inability to perform duties, US Const Amd 25 §3.
Transmittal to senate and house of representatives, US Const Amd 25 §3.
Election, US Const Art II §1; Amds 12, 20, 22, 23.
Electors, US Const Art II §1; Amds 12, 20, 22, 23.
District of Columbia, US Const Amd 23.
Eligibility, US Const Art II §1.
Execution of laws, US Const Art II §3.
Executive power, US Const Art II §1.
Failure to qualify, US Const Amd 20.
Impeachment, US Const Art I §3; Art II §4.
Inability, US Const Art II §1.
Limitation on terms, US Const Amd 22.
Message to congress, US Const Art II §3.
Ministers.
Receiving, US Const Art II §3.
Oath, US Const Art II §1; Art VI; Amd 14.
Opinions from principal officers in executive departments, US Const Art II §2.
Pardons, US Const Art II §2.
Powers of president, US Const Art II §§2, 3.
Presidential electors, US Const Art II §1; Amd 12.
Public officers.
Commissions, US Const Art II §3.
Qualifications, US Const Art II §1.

CONSTITUTION OF THE UNITED STATES
—Cont'd

President —Cont'd
Removal, US Const Art II §§1, 4.
Succession upon removal, US Const Amd 25 §1.
Resignation, US Const Art II §1.
Succession upon resignation, US Const Amd 25 §1.
Signing of bills, US Const Art I §7.
Statutes.
Approval of laws by president, US Const Art I §7.
Veto, US Const Art I §7.
Succession to office, US Const Art II §1; Amd 20.
Upon death, resignation or removal of president, US Const Amd 25 §1.
Supreme court.
Appointment of justices, US Const Art II §2.
Terms of office, US Const Art II §1; Amds 20, 22.
Limitation on terms, US Const Amd 22.
Time of taking office, US Const Amd 20.
Treason, US Const Art II §4.
Treaties, US Const Art II §2.
Vacancies in office, US Const Art II §1; Amd 20.
During senate recess, US Const Art II §2.
Veto, US Const Art I §7.
Vice-president, US Const Art I §3.
When vice-president acts, US Const Art II §1; Amd 20.

Press.
Freedom of the press, US Const Amd 1.

Privileges.
Privileged from arrest, US Const Art I §6.
Privileges of citizens of the states, US Const Art IV §2; Amd 14.

Prohibition, US Const Amds 18, 21.

Protection and aid of states, US Const Art IV §4.

Public debt, US Const Art I §8; Amd 14.

Public officers.
Appointment, US Const Art II §2.
Senate recess, US Const Art II §2.
Bribery, US Const Art II §4.
Commissions, US Const Art II §3.
Disqualification, US Const Art I §6; Amd 14.
Emoluments, US Const Art I §9.
Foreign office or title, US Const Art I §9.
Holding more than one office, US Const Art I §6.
Impeachment, US Const Art II §4.
Ineligibility of members of congress, US Const Art I §6.
Oath, US Const Art VI; Amd 14.
Presents from foreign states, US Const Art I §9.
Presidential electors.
Eligibility, US Const Art II §1.
Religious tests, US Const Art VI.
Removal, US Const Art II §4.
Treason, US Const Art II §4.
Vacancies during senate recess, US Const Art II §2.

Public trial, US Const Amd 6.

Punishment.
Cruel and unusual punishment, US Const Amd 8.

Quartering soldiers in houses, US Const Amd 3.

Quorum, US Const Art I §5; Amd 12.

Ratification, US Const Art VII.

Records.
Full faith and credit clause, US Const Art IV §1.
Proof, US Const Art IV §1.

Redress of grievances.
Right to petition for, US Const Amd 1.

Religious test, US Const Art VI.

CONSTITUTION OF THE UNITED STATES
—Cont'd

Republican form of government, US Const Art IV §4.

Reservation of rights of the people, US Const Amd 9.

Revenue bills, US Const Art I §7.

Right of assembly, US Const Amd 1.

Right of trial by jury, US Const Art III §2; Amds 6, 7.

Rights and immunities of citizens, US Const Art IV §2; Amds 1 to Amd 10, 14.

Right to bear arms, US Const Amd 2.

Right to counsel, US Const Amd 6.

Right to petition for a redress of grievances, US Const Amd 1.

Searches and seizures, US Const Amd 4.

Self-incrimination, US Const Amd 5.

Senate, US Const Art I §§1, 3; Amd 17. See within this heading, "Congress."

Sentence and punishment, US Const Amd 8.

Sessions of congress, US Const Art I §4.
  Special sessions, US Const Art II §3.

Slavery, US Const Amds 13 to Amd 15.

Soldiers.
  Quartering prohibited, US Const Amd 3.

Speech.
  Freedom of speech, US Const Amd 1.

Speedy trial, US Const Amd 6.

States.
  Admission of new states, US Const Art IV §3.
  Apportionment of representatives, US Const Art I §2; Amd 14 §2.
  Bill of attainder, US Const Art I §10.
  Bills of credit, US Const Art I §10.
  Commerce, US Const Art I §§8, 9.
  Compacts between the states or with foreign powers, US Const Art I §10.
  Contracts.
    Impairing obligations of contracts, US Const Art I §10.
  Controversies between citizens of different states, US Const Art III §2.
  Controversies between states, US Const Art III §2.
  Duties and imposts, US Const Art I §10.
  Equal suffrage in senate, US Const Art V.
  Exports, US Const Art I §§9, 10.
  Ex post facto laws, US Const Art I §10.
  Full faith and credit clause, US Const Art IV §1.
  Gold and silver coin tender in payment of debts, US Const Art I §10.
  Impairing obligations of contracts, US Const Art I §10.
  Imports and exports, US Const Art I §10.
  Invasion.
    Protection against, US Const Art IV §4.
  Legal tender, US Const Art I §10.
  Letters of marque and reprisal, US Const Art I §10.
  Limitations on powers of states, US Const Art I §10.
  Money.
    Coining money, US Const Art I §10.
  New states, US Const Art IV §3.
  Powers reserved to states, US Const Art I §10; Amd 10.
  Protection and aid of states, US Const Art IV §4.
  Republican form of government guaranteed, US Const Art IV §4.

CONSTITUTION OF THE UNITED STATES
—Cont'd

States —Cont'd
  Reservation of powers to states, US Const Amd 10.
  Right to coin money, US Const Art I §10.
  Suits against state, US Const Amd 11.
  Tender in payment of debts, US Const Art I §10.
  Tonnage, US Const Art I §10.
  Treaties, US Const Art I §10.
  Troops or ships of war in time of peace, US Const Art I §10.
  War, US Const Art I §10.

Statutes.
  Approval of laws by president, US Const Art I §7.
  Ex post facto laws, US Const Art I §§9, 10.
  Full faith and credit clause, US Const Art IV §1.
  Limitations on legislation, US Const Art I §9.
  Proof, US Const Art IV §1.
  Revenue bills, US Const Art I §7.
  Supreme law of the land, US Const Art VI.
  Veto, US Const Art I §7.

Suits against state, US Const Amd 11.

Suits against United States, US Const Art III §2.

Supreme court.
  Chief justice presides in impeachment of president, US Const Art I §3.
  Jurisdiction, US Const Art III §2.
  Justices.
    Appointment, US Const Art II §2.
    Compensation, US Const Art III §1.
    Oath, US Const Art VI; Amd 14.
    Tenure, US Const Art III §1.

Supreme law of the land, US Const Art VI.

Taxation.
  Apportionment of direct taxes, US Const Art I §§2, 9; Amd 16.
  Capitation tax, US Const Art I §9.
  Direct taxes.
    Apportionment, US Const Art I §§2, 9; Amd 16.
  Excises.
    Powers of congress, US Const Art I §8.
  Exports, US Const Art I §§9, 10.
  Income tax, US Const Amd 16.
  Limitations on powers of states, US Const Art I §10.
  Powers of congress, US Const Art I §8.
  Revenue bills, US Const Art I §7.

Tender, US Const Art I §10.

Territories, US Const Art IV §3.

Time when constitution effective, US Const Art VII.

Titles of nobility, US Const Art I §§9, 10.

Tonnage, US Const Art I §10.

Treason, US Const Art I §6; Art II §4; Art III §3.
  Supreme law of the land, US Const Art VI.

Treaties, US Const Art I §10; Art II §2; Art III §3.

Trial.
  Public trial, US Const Amd 6.
  Right of trial by jury, US Const Art III §2; Amds 6, 8.
  Speedy trial, US Const Amd 6.

Venue, US Const Art III §2; Amd 6.

Vessels and shipping.
  Bound to and from one state not to be obliged to clear, etc., in another, US Const Art I §9.

Veto, US Const Art I §7.

Vice-president.
  Bribery, US Const Art II §4.
  Death, US Const Art II §1; Amds 20, 25.
  Election, US Const Art II §1; Amds 12, 20, 22, 23.

CONSTITUTION OF THE UNITED STATES
—Cont'd
Vice-president —Cont'd
Electors.
District of Columbia, US Const Amd 23.
Failure to qualify, US Const Amd 20.
Impeachment, US Const Art II §4.
Oath, US Const Art VI; Amd 14.
Presidential electors, US Const Art II §1; Amd 12.
President of senate, US Const Art I §3.
Qualifications, US Const Amd 12.
Removal, US Const Art II §4.
Succession to office of president, US Const Art II §1; Amds 20, 25.
Upon death, resignation or removal of president, US Const Amd 25 §1.
Terms of office, US Const Art II §1; Amd 20 §1.
Treason, US Const Art II §4.
Vacancy in office, US Const Art II §1; Amds 20, 25.
War.
Articles of war, US Const Art I §8.
Declaration by congress, US Const Art I §8.
Grand jury.
Presentment as dispensable in certain cases, US Const Amd 5.
Quartering of soldiers in times of war, US Const Amd 3.
State engaging in, US Const Art I §10.
Treason.
In levying against the United States, US Const Art III §3.
Warrants.
Searches and seizures.
Conditions for issuance, US Const Amd 4.
Weights and measures, US Const Art I §8.
Welfare.
General welfare.
Powers of congress, US Const Art I §8.
Witnesses.
Confrontation with witnesses, US Const Amd 6.
Process to obtain, US Const Amd 6.
Self-incrimination, US Const Amd 5.
Treason.
Number in treason cases, US Const Art III §3.
Woman suffrage, US Const Amd 19.

CONSTRUCTION LAW.
Building codes generally, PS §§12-101 to 12-1007.
See BUILDING CODES.
Construction apprenticeship assistance program, LE §11-601.
Contracts.
Attorneys' fees.
Actions for prompt payment, RP §9-303.
Contractor.
Defined, RP §9-301.
Costs.
Actions for prompt payment, RP §9-303.
Counties.
Disputes in construction contracts.
Resolution, 25 §1A; 25A §1A; 25B §13A.
Definitions, RP §9-301.
Exemptions, RP §9-304.
Interest.
Remedies for default of prompt payment, RP §9-303.
Owner.
Defined, RP §9-301.

CONSTRUCTION LAW —Cont'd
Contracts —Cont'd
Prompt payment, RP §9-302.
Remedies for default, RP §9-303.
Subcontractor.
Defined, RP §9-301.
Undisputed amount.
Defined, RP §9-301.
Correctional facilities.
Construction of state correctional facilities, COR §§10-101 to 10-107.
See PRISONS AND PRISONERS.
Counties.
Disputes in construction contracts.
Resolution.
Chartered counties, 25A §1A.
County commissioners.
Resolution of disputes in counties governed by county commissioners, 25 §1A.
Home rule for code counties, 25B §13A.
Definitions.
Construction contracts, RP §9-301.
Energy conservation standards, PUC §§7-401 to 7-408.
See ENERGY CONSERVATION BUILDING STANDARDS.
Equipment dealer contracts.
General provisions, CL §§19-101 to 19-305.
See EQUIPMENT DEALER CONTRACTS.
Excavation or demolition near underground facilities.
Generally, PUC §§12-101 to 12-113.
See UNDERGROUND UTILITY FACILITIES.
Montgomery county, PUC §§12-201 to 12-203.
Fire marshal.
Plan review.
Fees, PS §6-308.
Licenses.
See LICENSES.
Procurement.
See PROCUREMENT.
Schools.
See SCHOOLS.
Sediment control, EN §§4-105, 4-106.
Trust relationships in construction industry, RP §§9-201 to 9-204.
See TRUSTS AND TRUSTEES.
Water and sewer systems.
Lateral system construction costs.
Defined, SF §2-401.
State to pay, SF §2-402.

CONSTRUCTIVE CONTEMPT, SpecPro Rules 15-205 to 15-207.
Defined, SpecPro Rule 15-202.

CONSTRUCTIVE EVICTION, RP §§2-117, 8-208.2.

CONSULAR OFFICER.
See AMBASSADORS AND CONSULS.

CONSUMER COOPERATIVES.
Applicability of general corporation law, CA §5-5A-29.
Applicability of subtitle, CA §§5-5A-01, 5-5A-26.
Articles of incorporation.
Amendments, CA §5-5A-21.
Contents, CA §5-5A-07.
Assets.
Transfer of assets, CA §5-5A-24.
Audits.
Annual audit, CA §5-5A-23.

CONSUMER COOPERATIVES —Cont'd
Bylaws.
  Adoption, CA §§5-5A-11, 5-5A-21.
  Amendment, CA §§5-5A-11, 5-5A-21.
  Contents, CA §5-5A-07.
  Election provisions, CA §5-5A-14.
  Repeal, CA §5-5A-21.
Citation of subtitle, CA §5-5A-30.
Consolidation or merger.
  General provisions, CA §5-5A-24.
Conversion.
  Corporations converted into cooperatives, CA §5-5A-09.
Cooperatives generally.
  See COOPERATIVES.
Corporations.
  Applicability of general corporation law, CA §5-5A-29.
  Conversion of corporations into cooperatives, CA §5-5A-09.
  Generally.
    See CORPORATIONS.
Definitions, CA §5-5A-02.
Directors.
  Compensation, CA §5-5A-17.
  Election, CA §§5-5A-13, 5-5A-14.
  Management by directors, CA §5-5A-12.
  Number, CA §5-5A-12.
  Officers.
    Certain officers to be directors, CA §5-5A-15.
  Original directors, CA §5-5A-13.
  Qualifications, CA §5-5A-12.
  Removal.
    General provisions, CA §5-5A-16.
  Residents, CA §5-5A-12.
  Term of office, CA §5-5A-13.
Dissolution.
  General provisions, CA §5-5A-24.
Districts.
  Directors.
    Election by district, CA §5-5A-14.
Division.
  Articles of division and articles of incorporation, CA §5-5A-25.
  Plan of division, CA §5-5A-25.
Evidence.
  Membership interest, CA §5-5A-05.
Incorporation.
  Articles of incorporation.
    Amendments, CA §5-5A-21.
    Contents, CA §5-5A-07.
  Authority, CA §5-5A-03.
  Formation, CA §5-5A-05.
  Number required for incorporation, CA §5-5A-04.
  Stock and stockholders.
    With or without capital stock, CA §5-5A-05.
  Who may incorporate, CA §5-5A-04.
Law applicable, CA §5-5A-29.
Management.
  Directors, CA §5-5A-12.
Meetings.
  Annual meeting.
    Required, CA §5-5A-19.
  Notice of meetings, CA §5-5A-19.
  Quorum, CA §5-5A-19.
  Special meetings, CA §5-5A-19.
Membership.
  Eligibility for membership, CA §5-5A-18.
Membership interest.
  Evidence, CA §5-5A-05.
  Not security, CA §5-5A-28.

CONSUMER COOPERATIVES —Cont'd
Monopolies.
  Not considered as combination in restraint of trade, CA §5-5A-27.
Name.
  Use of word "cooperative" in conducting business, CA §5-5A-10.
Net savings.
  Apportionment, CA §5-5A-22.
    Allocation as savings returns, CA §5-5A-22.
  Deferral of payment or variable distribution, CA §5-5A-22.
  Use to lower fees, CA §5-5A-22.
Notices.
  Meetings, CA §5-5A-19.
Officers.
  Compensation, CA §5-5A-17.
  Directors.
    Certain officers to be directors, CA §5-5A-15.
  Enumeration, CA §5-5A-15.
  General provisions, CA §5-5A-15.
  Removal, CA §5-5A-16.
Organization of corporation into cooperative, CA §5-507.
Permissible business activities, CA §5-5A-03.
Powers.
  Generally, CA §5-5A-06.
Quorum.
  Membership or delegates, CA §5-5A-19.
Reports.
  Annual report, CA §5-5A-23.
Short title of subtitle, CA §5-5A-30.
Stock and stockholders.
  Classes of ownership, CA §5-5A-08.
  Evidence of membership capital not security, CA §5-5A-28.
  Incorporation.
    With or without capital stock, CA §5-5A-05.
  Nonvoting capital stock, CA §5-5A-08.
  Restrictions on ownership, CA §5-5A-08.
  Sale of stock.
    General provisions, CA §5-5A-08.
  Stock conversion, CA §5-5A-08.
  Termination of nonstock voting membership, CA §5-5A-08.
Trade and commerce.
  Combination and restraint of trade.
    Cooperative not considered as, CA §5-5A-27.
Voting.
  By mail, CA §5-5A-20.
  One vote.
    Each member entitled to one vote, CA §5-5A-20.
  Only members entitled to vote, CA §5-5A-20.

CONSUMER CREDIT.
Commissioner.
  Consumer loans.
    See CONSUMER LOANS.
  Program evaluation act, SG §8-403.
Consumer loans.
  See CONSUMER LOANS.
Credit agreements.
  Enforceability, CJ §5-408.
Credit cards.
  General provisions.
    See CREDIT CARDS.
Credit grantor closed end credit provisions, CL §§12-1001 to 12-1029.
  See CREDIT.
Credit grantor revolving credit provisions, CL §§12-901 to 12-921.
  See CREDIT.

CONSUMER CREDIT —Cont'd
Definitions.
Credit agreements, CJ §5-408.
Examination expenses, FI §11-101.
Frauds, statute of.
Credit agreements.
Enforceability, CJ §5-408.
Health club services, CL §§14-12B-01 to
14-12B-08.
See HEALTH CLUB SERVICES.
Mortgages and deeds of trust.
Mortgage lender law, FI §§11-501 to 11-524.
See MORTGAGE LENDERS.
Mortgage originators, FI §§11-601 to 11-618.
See MORTGAGE ORIGINATORS.
Rental-purchase agreements, CL §§12-1101 to
12-1112.
See RENTAL-PURCHASE AGREEMENTS.
Reporting agencies, CL §§14-1201 to 14-1218.
See CONSUMER CREDIT REPORTING
AGENCIES.
Sales finance companies.
See SALES.
Small loans.
See SMALL LOANS.

CONSUMER CREDIT REPORTING AGENCIES.
Accuracy of information.
Disputed accuracy.
Frivolous or irrelevant disputes, CL §14-1208.
Procedures in cases of disputed accuracy, CL
§14-1208.
Procedures to assure, CL §14-1205.
Administrative procedure act.
Applicability, CL §14-1218.
Civil liability.
Failure to comply with subtitle, CL §14-1213.
Clerk of courts.
Enforcement of subtitle, CL §14-1218.
Complaints.
Consumer complaints, CL §14-1217.
Compliance with subtitle.
Willful failure to comply with subtitle.
Civil liability, CL §14-1213.
Consumer reports.
Accuracy of information.
Procedures to assure, CL §14-1205.
Defined, CL §14-1201.
Investigative reports.
Defined, CL §14-1201.
Disclosure, CL §14-1204.
Unauthorized disclosure by officers and
employees, CL §14-1216.
Restrictions on subsequent use of adverse
information, CL §14-1211.
Permissible purposes, CL §14-1202.
Reporting obsolete information prohibited, CL
§14-1203.
Restrictions on sale or transfer, CL §14-1202.
Contempt.
Failure to comply with orders of court, CL
§14-1218.
Credits.
Denial.
Duty of user of consumer report to notify
consumer, CL §14-1212.
Credit services businesses.
Defined, CL §14-1901.
Damages.
Willful failure to comply with subtitle, CL
§14-1213.

CONSUMER CREDIT REPORTING AGENCIES
—Cont'd
Definitions, CL §14-1201.
Credit services businesses, CL §14-1901.
Disclosures.
Files. See within this heading, "Files."
Investigative consumer reports. See within this
heading, "Investigative consumer reports."
Disputed accuracy of information.
Frivolous or irrelevant disputes, CL §14-1208.
Procedure in cases of disputed accuracy, CL
§14-1208.
Enforcement of subtitle, CL §14-1218.
Fees.
Files.
Furnishing copy to consumer, CL §14-1206.
Files.
Conditions of disclosure of consumer's file, CL
§14-1207.
Copies furnished to consumer on request, CL
§14-1206.
Defined, CL §14-1201.
Disclosure of consumer's file.
Charge for disclosures, CL §14-1209.
Conditions of disclosure, CL §14-1207.
Copy to be furnished consumer, CL §14-1206.
Unauthorized disclosure, CL §14-1216.
Fraud and deceit.
Obtaining information under false pretenses, CL
§14-1215.
**Identifying information to governmental
agency,** CL §14-1205.
Inspections.
Books, records, etc.
Consumer complaints, CL §14-1217.
Insurance.
Denial.
Duty of users of consumer reports to notify
consumer, CL §14-1212.
Investigative consumer reports.
Defined, CL §14-1201.
Disclosure, CL §14-1204.
Unauthorized disclosure by officers and
employees, CL §14-1216.
Restrictions on subsequent use of adverse
information, CL §14-1211.
Limitations of actions.
Violations of subtitle, CL §14-1214.
Motor vehicle insurance.
Cancellations, nonrenewals or premium increases,
IN §27-613.
Negligence.
Failure to comply with subtitle.
Civil liability, CL §14-1213.
Notices.
Consumer credit reporting agencies.
Public record information.
Notice of report for employment purposes, CL
§14-1210.
User of consumer reports.
Duty to notify consumer in certain situations,
CL §14-1212.
Obsolete information.
Reporting.
Compliance procedures, CL §14-1203.
Officers or employees.
Unauthorized disclosures, CL §14-1216.
Public records.
Notice of report of records for employment
purposes, CL §14-1210.

CONSUMER CREDIT REPORTING AGENCIES
—Cont'd
Records.
Inspection.
Consumer complaints, CL §14-1217.
Rules and regulations.
Enforcement of subtitle, CL §14-1218.
Sources of information.
Deletion.
Copy of file furnished to consumer, CL
§14-1206.

CONSUMER LEASES.
Commercial code leases.
General provisions, CL §§2A-101 to 2A-532.
See LEASES, UCC.

CONSUMER LOANS.
Administrative procedure.
Hearings.
Application of administrative procedure act, FI
§11-217.
Advertising.
General provisions, CL §12-304.
Amount of loan, CL §12-303.
Appeals.
Right to appeal, FI §11-218.
Application of subtitle, CL §12-303.
Attorneys at law.
Fees.
Collection, CL §12-307.1.
Bonds, surety, FI §§11-206, 11-207.
Books.
To be kept by licensee, FI §11-213.
Cease and desist orders.
Commissioner of consumer credit, FI §11-215.
Checks.
Bad checks.
Collection of certain fees.
Bad check fees, CL §12-307.
Citation of subtitle, CL §12-317.
Collateral.
Profit or advantage considered charge, CL
§12-310.
Exceptions, CL §12-310.
Collection agencies, BR §§7-101 to 7-502.
See COLLECTION AGENCIES.
Commissioner.
Advertising.
Supervision of licensees, CL §12-304.
Defined, CL §12-301.
Confidential financial records.
See BANKS AND TRUST COMPANIES.
Construction of subtitle, FI §11-221.
Defenses.
Lender.
Borrower against seller, CL §12-309.
Subject to certain defenses, CL §12-309.
Definitions.
Credit provisions, CL §12-301.
Licensing provisions, FI §11-201.
Discrimination.
Prohibited, CL §12-305.
Enabling borrower to buy goods or services.
Determination of knowing participation in sale,
CL §12-309.
Extent of lender's liability, CL §12-309.
False advertising, CL §12-304.
Fees.
Applications for licenses, FI §11-206.
Collection, CL §12-307.
Attorneys' fees, CL §12-307.1.

CONSUMER LOANS —Cont'd
Fees —Cont'd
Excess fees, CL §12-313.
License, FI §11-206.
Financing statements.
Applicable provisions, CL §12-308.
Hearings, FI §11-217.
Application of administrative procedure act, FI
§11-217.
Right to hearing, FI §11-217.
Insurance, CL §12-312.
Interest.
Balance unpaid after original maturity date, CL
§12-306.
Computation, CL §12-306.
Excess interest, CL §12-313.
General provisions.
See INTEREST.
Loans at greater than authorized rate.
Prohibited, CL §12-314.
Maximum rate, CL §12-306.
Loans at greater than authorized rate, CL
§12-314.
Refinanced loan, CL §12-306.
Interpretation and construction, CL §12-315.
Interpretation of subtitle, FI §11-221.
Investigations.
Commissioner of consumer credit.
General provisions, FI §11-214.
Judgments and decrees.
Confession of judgment, CL §12-311.
Judicial review.
Right to appeal, FI §11-218.
Lender.
Defined, CL §12-301.
Duties.
General provisions, CL §12-308.
Extent of liability, CL §12-309.
Subrogation, CL §12-309.
Licenses.
Additional licenses, FI §11-208.
Appeals.
Right to appeal, FI §11-218.
Applicants.
Qualifications, FI §11-205.
Application.
Fees, FI §11-206.
Generally, FI §11-206.
Investigation, FI §11-207.
Contents, FI §11-208.
Denial, FI §11-207.
Display, FI §11-210.
Expiration, FI §11-209.
Fees, FI §11-206.
Interpretation and construction of subtitle, FI
§11-221.
Issuance, FI §11-207.
Qualifications of applicants, FI §11-205.
Renewal, FI §11-209.
Required, FI §11-204.
Consumer loans credit provisions, CL §12-302.
Penalty, FI §11-222.
Sale of loan account to unlicensed person, FI
§11-219.
Scope of licenses, FI §11-208.
Scope of subtitle, FI §11-202.
Short titles, FI §11-223.
Suspensions and revocations.
Grounds, FI §11-216.
Term, FI §11-209.

CONSUMER LOANS —Cont'd
Licenses —Cont'd
Transferability.
License not transferable, FI §11-210.
Loan.
Defined, CL §12-301.
Loan accounts.
Sale to unlicensed person, FI §11-219.
Maximum term, CL §12-306.
Mortgages and deeds of trust.
Mortgage lender law, FI §§11-501 to 11-524.
See MORTGAGE LENDERS.
Mortgage originators, FI §§11-601 to 11-618.
See MORTGAGE ORIGINATORS.
Name of business.
General provisions, FI §11-204.
Offsets.
Defined, CL §15-701.
Prohibited, CL §15-702.
Orders.
Cease and desist orders.
Commissioner of consumer credit, FI §11-215.
Payment.
Prepayment, CL §12-308.
Receipt, CL §12-308.
Penalties.
Violations.
Consumer loans credit provisions, CL §12-316.
Consumer loans licensing provisions, FI §11-222.
Reliance upon written opinions, CL §12-316.1.
Person.
Defined, CL §12-301.
Place of business.
Change of place of business, FI §11-211.
General provisions, FI §11-204.
Posting license, FI §11-210.
Scope of license, FI §11-208.
Pretended purchase of property or services.
Considered loan, CL §12-303.
Receipt.
Payments, CL §12-308.
Records.
Books and records to be kept by licensee, FI §11-213.
Rental-purchase agreements, CL §§12-1101 to 12-1112.
See RENTAL-PURCHASE AGREEMENTS.
Reports.
Criminal violations, FI §11-220.
Rules and regulations.
Commissioner of consumer credit may adopt, FI §11-203.
Sales.
Determination of knowing participation in sale, CL §12-309.
Scope of subtitle, FI §11-202.
Security.
Certain security not allowed, CL §12-311.
Return, CL §12-308.
Short titles, FI §11-223.
Small loans.
General provisions.
See SMALL LOANS.
Statement to borrower, CL §12-308.
Subrogation.
Lender, CL §12-309.
Term.
Maximum term, CL §12-306.
Unenforceable loans.
Loans sold to unlicensed persons, FI §11-219.

CONSUMER LOANS —Cont'd
Usury.
Excess interest, CL §12-313.
Loans at greater than authorized rate of interest, CL §12-314.
Violations.
Cease and desist orders, FI §11-217.
Penalties.
Consumer loans credit provisions, CL §12-316.
Consumer loans licensing provisions, FI §11-222.
Reliance upon written opinions, CL §12-316.1.
Reporting of criminal violations, FI §11-220.
Wages.
Assignment.
Certain security for loan not allowed, CL §12-311.
Considered loan, CL §12-303.
Defined, CL §12-301.
Purchase.
Considered loan, CL §12-303.

CONSUMER PROTECTION.
Actions.
Credit services businesses.
Actions under consumer protection act, CL §14-1914.
Damages, CL §13-408.
Defense in action for return of merchandise or for payment therefore, CL §14-1304.
Division of consumer protection.
Civil actions, CL §13-403.
Fine prints.
Violation of subtitle.
Civil remedies of buyers, CL §14-505.
Persons aggrieved by decision of division, CL §13-407.
Replevin action.
Waiver of right to notice and hearing in replevin action, CL §14-1303.
Administration of subtitle, CL §13-201.
Advertising.
Advertisement.
Defined, CL §13-101.
Kosher food.
See KOSHER FOOD.
Work-at-home advertisements, CL §13-314.
Amounts paid by the debtor.
Defined, CL §14-1302.
Amusements and recreation.
Tickets.
Reserved seat tickets sold.
Seating plan showing location of seats and physical obstructions must be displayed, CL §13-310.
Antitrust act, CL §§11-201 to 11-213.
See ANTITRUST ACT.
Appliances.
Definitions, CL §13-307.
Labels.
Electrical consumer products, CL §13-308.
Extension cords, CL §13-309.
Service contracts, CL §14-1306.
Applicability of title, CL §13-104.
Consumer contracts, CL §13-101.1.
Kosher food, CL §14-906.
Arbitration of disputes.
General provisions, CL §13-404.
Unit pricing, CL §14-107.
Assumption of risk.
Credit card issued without request.
Loss, theft or unauthorized use, CL §14-1305.

CONSUMER PROTECTION —Cont'd

Athletics.

Tickets.

Reserved seat tickets sold.

Seating plan showing location of seats and physical obstructions must be displayed, CL §13-310.

Attic fans.

Firestat or fusible link in attic fan required, CL §13-315.

Attorney general.

Assistant attorney general.

Appointment and salary, CL §13-203.

Authority of attorney general to subpoena witnesses, etc., CL §13-405.

Division of consumer protection. See within this heading, "Division."

Legal assistance organizations, CL §13-206.

Mobile homes.

Enforcement of title by division of consumer protection, RP §8A-1802.

Recommendation of legislation, CL §13-203.

Unit pricing.

Enforcement, CL §14-106.

Attorneys at law.

Legal assistance organizations, CL §13-206.

Automotive warranty enforcement act, CL §§14-1501 to 14-1504.

See MOTOR VEHICLE WARRANTIES.

Awards.

Notification of award.

Conditioned upon purchase or submitting to sales promotion effort.

Disclosures relating to sale, lease or rental of real property, CL §13-305.

Certificate.

Gift certificate.

When gift or other inducement not available to customer, CL §13-306.

Checks.

Discharge check.

Return to buyer or borrower, CL §14-1312.

Citation of title, CL §13-501.

Civil penalties, CL §13-410.

Collections.

Consumer debt collection. See within this heading, "Debts."

Conciliation of complaints, CL §13-402.

Condominiums, RP §11-130.

Secretary of state.

Copies of local provisions forwarded to secretary, RP §11-130.

Consumer.

Credit, debts, goods and services.

Defined, CL §13-101.

Defined, CL §13-101.

Consumer credit reporting agencies, CL §§14-1201 to 14-1218.

See CONSUMER CREDIT REPORTING AGENCIES.

Consumer loans.

See CONSUMER LOANS.

Contracts.

Appliance service contracts, CL §14-1306.

Applicability of title to consumer contracts, CL §13-101.1.

Credit services businesses.

Contracts with consumers.

Breach of contract, CL §14-1907.

Cancellation.

Notice, CL §14-1906.

CONSUMER PROTECTION —Cont'd

Contracts —Cont'd

Credit services businesses —Cont'd

Contracts with consumers —Cont'd

Requirements, CL §14-1906.

Void contracts, CL §14-1907.

Late fees, CL §14-1315.

Preservation of consumers' claims and defenses, CL §14-1302.

Exceptions to application of section, CL §14-1302.

Service contracts.

Not prerequisite to sale of merchandise, CL §13-311.

Cooperative housing corporations, CA §5-6B-12.

Costs.

Actions under title, CL §13-409.

Council, CL §13-202.

Counties.

Adoption of more stringent provisions, CL §13-103.

Credit.

Credit card or card of identification.

Assumption of risk of loss, theft or unauthorized use, CL §14-1305.

Service of subpoena on issuer.

Certification of compliance with FI §1-304, CL §13-312.

Credit grantor closed end credit provisions, CL §§12-1001 to 12-1029.

See CREDIT.

Credit grantor revolving credit provisions, CL §§12-901 to 12-921.

See CREDIT.

Denial.

Complaints, CL §14-1706.

Cease and desist orders, CL §14-1706.

Hearings, CL §14-1706.

Investigations, CL §14-1706.

Definitions, CL §14-1701.

Federal consumer protection act.

Effect of compliance with, CL §14-1705.

Notice of action upon application for credit, CL §14-1702.

Statement upon adverse action or denial.

Contents, CL §14-1703.

Required, CL §14-1702.

Specific reasons for adverse action, CL §14-1704.

Retail credit accounts law, CL §§12-501 to 12-515.

See RETAIL CREDIT ACCOUNTS LAW.

Credit cards.

See CREDIT CARDS.

Credit services businesses.

General provisions, CL §§14-1901 to 14-1916.

See CREDIT.

Criminal penalties, CL §13-411.

Damages.

Action for damages, CL §13-408.

Fine prints.

Violations of subtitle, CL §14-505.

Debt adjusting.

Business of prohibited, exceptions, CL §14-1316.

Debts.

Consumer debt collection.

Certain acts prohibited, CL §14-201.

Citation of subtitle, CL §14-204.

Damages.

Violator's liability for damages, CL §14-203.

Definitions, CL §14-201.

CONSUMER PROTECTION —Cont'd
Deceptive trade practices. See within this
heading, "Unfair or deceptive trade practices."
Defenses.
Return of merchandise or payment therefore, CL
§14-1304.
Definitions.
Appliances, CL §13-307.
Consumer debt collection, CL §14-201.
Contracts.
Preservation of consumers' claims and defenses
in consumer credit contracts, CL §14-1302.
Credit.
Denial, CL §14-1701.
Credit services businesses, CL §14-1901.
Extended warranties, CL §14-1311.
Late fees, CL §14-1315.
Layaway sales, CL §14-1101.
Legal assistance organizations, CL §13-206.
Merchandise delivery, CL §14-1801.
Mortgage servicers, CL §13-316.
Repair company, CL §13-307.
Unit pricing, CL §14-101.
Video movie sales and rentals, CL §14-1601.
Warranties.
Extended warranties, CL §14-1311.
Division.
Arbitration of consumer disputes, CL §13-404.
Cease and desist orders, CL §13-403.
Issuance without hearing, CL §13-403.
Stipulation of conditions, CL §13-402.
Civil actions, CL §13-403.
Complaints.
Conciliation, CL §13-402.
Investigation by division, CL §13-401.
Council.
Established within division, CL §13-202.
Credit services businesses.
Power of division to bring proceedings against,
CL §14-1914.
Defined, CL §13-101.
Duties.
Generally, CL §13-204.
Established, CL §13-201.
Generally, CL §13-204.
Hearings.
Public hearings to determine violations, CL
§13-403.
Housing and community development.
Assisted housing preservation, enforcement, HS
§7-403.
Legal assistance organizations.
Subject to powers and duties of division, CL
§13-206.
Orders.
Action by person aggrieved by decision of
division, CL §13-407.
Cease and desist orders, CL §13-403.
Persons aggrieved by decision of division.
Institution of legal proceedings, CL §13-407.
Powers.
Generally, CL §13-204.
Rules and regulations. See within this heading,
"Rules and regulations."
Door-to-door sales, CL §§14-301 to 14-306.
See HOME SOLICITATION SALES.
Door-to-door solicitations act, CL §§14-2601 to
14-2603.
Education.
Funds.
Education of public and study of consumer
problems, CL §13-203.

CONSUMER PROTECTION —Cont'd
Electricity.
Appliance service contracts, CL §14-1306.
Extension cords.
Labeling, CL §13-309.
Labeling electrical consumer product with symbol
of testing laboratory.
Enforcement, CL §13-308.
Penalties for violation, CL §13-308.
Required, CL §13-308.
Ladders.
Capable of conducting electricity, CL §14-1307.
Email.
Unauthorized, false or misleading information.
Commercial electronic mail, CL §§14-3001 to
14-3003.
Enforcement.
Action for damages, CL §13-408.
By all agencies of state, CL §13-103.
Injunctions, CL §13-406.
Summons and process, CL §13-405.
Equal credit opportunity, CL §§12-701 to 12-708.
See EQUAL CREDIT OPPORTUNITY.
Exemptions from title, CL §13-104.
Extended warranties, CL §14-1311.
False and fraudulent advertising, CL §§14-2901
to 14-2903.
Fine print.
Application of subtitle, CL §14-502.
Artists.
Defined, CL §14-501.
Catalog.
Disclosures required, CL §14-503.
Damages.
Violations of subtitle, CL §14-505.
Definitions, CL §14-501.
Disclosures.
Reproductions excepted, CL §§14-503, 14-504.
Required informational details, CL §14-504.
Exemptions of subtitle, CL §14-502.
Invoice.
Disclosures required, CL §§14-503, 14-504.
Limitation of actions.
Civil remedies of buyers, CL §14-505.
Person.
Defined, CL §14-501.
Plate.
Defined, CL §14-501.
Print.
Defined, CL §14-501.
Remedies.
Civil remedies of buyers, CL §14-505.
Signed print.
Defined, CL §14-501.
Violations of subtitle.
Civil remedies of buyers, CL §14-505.
Fines.
General penalty, CL §13-411.
Fireplaces.
Sale, distribution or installation of, CL §14-1309.
Fire resistant insulating material, CL §13-313.
Freestanding fireplaces, CL §14-1309.
Funds.
Education of public and study of consumer
problems, CL §13-203.
Gas companies.
Suppliers and supply, PUC §§7-601 to 7-607.
General assembly.
Legislative findings, CL §13-102.
Gift cards.
Terms and conditions, CL §14-1320.

CONSUMER PROTECTION —Cont'd
Gift certificates.
Terms and conditions, CL §14-1319.
Gifts.
Certificate when gift or other inducement not available to customer, CL §13-306.
Unconditional gift.
Unsolicited sending of merchandise, CL §14-1304.
Health club services, CL §§14-12B-01 to 14-12B-08.
See HEALTH CLUB SERVICES.
Health education and advocacy unit.
Creation, CL §13-4A-01.
Duties, CL §13-4A-02.
Funds.
Administration and operation of unit, CL §13-4A-03.
Reports, CL §13-4A-04.
Hearings.
Adoption of rules and regulations, CL §13-205.
Public hearings to determine violations, CL §13-403.
Waiver of right to hearings in replevin action, CL §14-1303.
Homebuilder registration, BR §§4.5-101 to 4.5-701.
See HOMEBUILDER REGISTRATION.
Home solicitation sales, CL §§14-301 to 14-306.
See HOME SOLICITATION SALES.
Household goods movers.
Enforcing carrier's lien during intrastate move, CL §§14-3101 to 14-3104.
Immigration consultants, CL §§14-3301 to 14-3306.
See IMMIGRATION CONSULTANTS.
Implied warranties.
Fitness for particular use, CL §2-315.
Merchantability and trade usage, CL §2-314.
Injunctions.
Enforcement of article, CL §13-406.
Sending of bill statements.
After receipt of unconditional gift, CL §14-1304.
Installment sales, CL §§12-601 to 12-636.
See SALES.
Insurance.
Consumer education and advocacy program, IN §§2-301 to 2-305.
Mortgage servicers.
Payment of insurance premiums, CL §13-316.
Unfair trade practices.
See INSURANCE.
Intent of title, CL §13-103.
Internet sales contracts.
Merchant contact information, CL §14-1321.
Interpretation and construction.
Title liberally construed, CL §13-105.
Investigations.
Of consumer complaints, CL §13-401.
Powers of division of consumer protection, CL §13-204.
Investigators and clerical staff.
Employment, CL §13-203.
Kerosene-fired heaters.
Manufacturer's warning label, CL §14-1310.
Use of unvented portable heaters in dwelling units, CL §14-1310.
Labels.
Electricity.
Electrical consumer products, CL §13-308.
Extension cords, CL §13-309.

CONSUMER PROTECTION —Cont'd
Ladders.
Electricity.
Capable of conducting electricity, CL §14-1307.
Late fees, CL §14-1315.
Layaway sales.
Agreement.
Cancellation before default, CL §14-1106.
Contents, CL §14-1103.
Layaway agreement to be in writing and signed, CL §14-1102.
Buyer.
Default by, CL §14-1106.
Defined, CL §14-1101.
Remedies, CL §14-1109.
Cancellation of agreement before default, CL §14-1106.
Cash price.
Defined, CL §14-1101.
Citation of act, CL §14-1110.
C.O.D. transaction.
Defined, CL §14-1101.
Consumer goods.
Defined, CL §14-1101.
Contents of agreement, CL §14-1103.
Default by buyer, CL §14-1106.
Cancellation of agreement before default, CL §14-1106.
Rights and remedies of seller upon default under special order transaction, CL §14-1107.
Definitions, CL §14-1101.
Down payment.
Defined, CL §14-1101.
Duties of seller, CL §14-1104.
Increasing price, CL §14-1105.
Layaway agreement.
Defined, CL §14-1101.
Layaway price.
Defined, CL §14-1101.
Noncompliance by seller, CL §14-1109.
Penalties.
Noncompliance or violation by seller, CL §14-1109.
Price.
Increasing or reducing, CL §14-1105.
Reducing price, CL §14-1105.
Retail installment sales act.
Inapplicable, CL §14-1108.
Retail sale.
Defined, CL §14-1101.
Seller.
Defined, CL §14-1101.
Duties, CL §14-1104.
Noncompliance or violation by seller, CL §14-1109.
Rights and remedies of seller upon default under special order transaction, CL §14-1107.
Signing provision.
Layaway agreement to be in writing and signed, CL §14-1102.
Special order transaction.
Defined, CL §14-1101.
Rights and remedies of seller upon default under, CL §14-1107.
Violations.
Noncompliance or violation by seller, CL §14-1109.
Writing requirement.
Layaway agreement to be in writing, CL §14-1102.

CONSUMER PROTECTION —Cont'd
Leases.
Motor vehicles.
Consumer leasing contracts, CL §§14-2001 to
14-2010.
See MOTOR VEHICLES.
Legal assistance organizations, CL §13-206.
Legislative findings, CL §13-102.
Lemon law.
Automotive warranty enforcement act, CL
§§14-1501 to 14-1504.
See MOTOR VEHICLE WARRANTIES.
Limitation of actions.
Fine prints.
Civil remedies of buyers, CL §14-505.
Loans.
Compliance with section 14-1302, CL §12-117.
Small loans.
Credit provisions.
See SMALL LOANS.
Mail.
Unsolicited sending of merchandise, CL §14-1304.
Merchandise.
Defined, CL §§13-101, 14-1301.
Merchandise credit.
Estimated delivery date.
Defined, CL §14-1801.
Merchandise delivery.
Actions.
Attorneys' fees, CL §14-1805.
Attorneys at law.
Actions.
Fees, CL §14-1805.
Deceptive trade practices, CL §14-1804.
Definitions, CL §14-1801.
Estimated delivery date.
Factors bearing on, CL §14-1802.
Information provided consumer by dealer, CL
§14-1802.
Noncompliance by dealer.
Remedies of consumer, CL §14-1803.
Request for refund or credit, CL §14-1803.
Information provided consumer by dealer, CL
§14-1802.
Other remedies not limited, CL §14-1806.
Unfair trade practices, CL §14-1804.
Merchant.
Defined, CL §13-101.
Mortgages and deeds of trust.
Mortgage lender law, FI §§11-501 to 11-524.
See MORTGAGE LENDERS.
Mortgage originators, FI §§11-601 to 11-618.
See MORTGAGE ORIGINATORS.
Mortgage servicers, CL §13-316.
Motion pictures.
Tickets.
Reserved seat tickets sold.
Seating plan showing location of seats and
physical obstructions must be displayed,
CL §13-310.
Video movie sales and rentals, CL §§14-1601 to
14-1603.
See VIDEO MOVIE SALES AND RENTALS.
Motorized wheelchairs.
Warranties, CL §§14-2701 to 14-2706.
See MOTORIZED WHEELCHAIR
WARRANTIES.
Motor vehicles.
Consumer leasing contracts, CL §§14-2001 to
14-2010.
See MOTOR VEHICLES.

CONSUMER PROTECTION —Cont'd
Motor vehicles —Cont'd
Warranty.
Automotive warranty enforcement act, CL
§§14-1501 to 14-1504.
See MOTOR VEHICLE WARRANTIES.
Municipal corporations.
Adoption of more stringent provisions, CL
§13-103.
New home warranties.
Unfair and deceptive trade practices, RP §10-608.
Notice.
Mortgage servicers.
Notice to mortgagor after acquisition of
mortgage servicing, CL §13-316.
Termination of membership in organization.
By certified mail.
Return receipt requested, CL §14-1304.
Waiver of right to notice in replevin action, CL
§14-1303.
Orders.
Cease and desist orders.
Issuance without hearing, CL §13-403.
Penalties.
Civil penalty, CL §13-410.
Criminal penalties, CL §13-411.
Layaway sales.
Noncompliance or violations by seller, CL
§14-1109.
Mortgage servicers.
Noncompliance with statutory provisions, CL
§13-316.
Person.
Defined, CL §§13-101, 14-1301.
Photography.
Processing instructions required on certain
photographic film, CL §14-1308.
**Preservation of consumers' claims and
defenses.**
Exceptions to application of section, CL §14-1302.
Prizes.
Notification of prize.
Conditioned upon purchase or submitting to
sales promotion effort.
Disclosures relating to sale, lease or rental of
real property, CL §13-305.
Purpose, CL §13-102.
Reciprocity.
Reciprocal agreements with other states, CL
§13-204.
Referral sales.
Unfair or deceptive trade practice, CL §13-304.
Rental-purchase agreements, CL §§12-1101 to
12-1112.
See RENTAL-PURCHASE AGREEMENTS.
Repair company.
Bills, CL §13-307.
Replevin.
Waiver of right to notice and hearing in replevin
action, CL §14-1303.
Retail credit accounts law, CL §§12-501 to
12-515.
See RETAIL CREDIT ACCOUNTS LAW.
Rules and regulations.
Challenge of rule by consumer group or trade
association, CL §13-205.
Division of consumer protection.
Power to promulgate rules and standards, CL
§13-204.
Procedure for adoption of rules and regulations,
CL §13-205.

CONSUMER PROTECTION —Cont'd
Rules and regulations —Cont'd
Division of consumer protection —Cont'd
Public hearings to determine violations, CL §13-403.
Under direction of attorney general, CL §14-105.
Sales.
Defined, CL §§13-101, 14-1301.
Installment sales, CL §§12-601 to 12-636.
See SALES.
Layaway sales. See within this heading, "Layaway sales."
Sales finance companies.
See SALES.
Secured transactions.
Security agreements.
Effect of consumer protection and other laws, CL §9-201.
Sentence and punishment.
General penalty, CL §13-411.
Service.
Defined, CL §§13-101, 14-1301.
Service contracts and consumer products guaranty act, CL §§14-401 to 14-410.
See SERVICE CONTRACTS AND CONSUMER PRODUCTS GUARANTY.
Small loans.
See SMALL LOANS.
Stoves.
Sale, distribution or installation of, CL §14-1309.
Summons and process.
Attorney general.
Subpoena power, CL §13-405.
Taxation.
Mortgage servicers.
Payments of tax, CL §13-316.
Telephone consumer protection act, CL §§14-3201, 14-3202.
Telephone solicitations.
Federal telemarketing and consumer fraud and abuse prevention act and federal telephone consumer protection act.
Remedies, CL §14-3202.
Separate violations, CL §14-3202.
Unfair or deceptive trade practice, CL §14-3202.
Violations prohibited, CL §14-3201.
Generally, CL §§14-2201 to 14-2205.
Violations as unfair or deceptive trade practices, CL §13-301.
Termination of membership in organization.
Notice by certified mail, CL §14-1304.
Unordered merchandise sent after, CL §14-1304.
Theaters and shows.
Tickets.
Reserved seat tickets sold.
Seating plan showing location of seats and physical obstructions must be displayed, CL §13-310.
Time-sharing, RP §§11A-101 to 11A-129.
See TIME-SHARING.
Toll-free telephone number.
Mortgage servicers to provide, CL §13-316.
Trade practices.
Unfair or deceptive trade practices. See within this heading, "Unfair or deceptive trade practices."
Tri-county council for southern Maryland.
See TRI-COUNTY COUNCIL FOR SOUTHERN MARYLAND.

CONSUMER PROTECTION —Cont'd
Unfair or deceptive trade practices.
Automotive crash parts act, CL §§14-2301 to 14-2304.
Automotive repair facilities, CL §§14-1001 to 14-1009.
Automotive warranty enforcement act, CL §§14-1501 to 14-1504.
Civil penalty, CL §13-410.
Complaints by consumers, CL §13-401.
Conciliation, CL §13-402.
Consumer motor vehicle leasing contracts, CL §§14-2001 to 14-2010.
Contracts.
Preservation of consumers' claims and defenses in consumer credit contracts, CL §14-1302.
Credit services businesses.
Violations of provisions of subtitle, CL §14-1914.
Criminal penalties, CL §13-411.
Damages.
Unnecessary, CL §13-302.
Debt collection, CL §§14-201 to 14-204.
Deception or damage unnecessary, CL §13-302.
Defined, CL §13-101.
Door-to-door sales, CL §§14-301 to 14-306.
See HOME SOLICITATION SALES.
Enumerated, CL §13-301.
Exemptions, CL §13-104.
Investigations by division, CL §13-401.
Kosher products, CL §§14-901 to 14-907.
See KOSHER FOOD.
Layaway sales, CL §§14-1101 to 14-1110. See within this heading, "Layaway sales."
Motorized wheelchair warranty enforcement.
Violations to constitute, CL §14-2705.
Motor vehicles.
Consumer leasing contracts.
Violations of subtitle, CL §14-2007.
Warranty.
Automotive warranty enforcement act.
Violations, CL §14-1504.
Prohibited practices, CL §13-303.
Referral sales techniques, plans, etc., CL §13-304.
Rental motor vehicles.
Collision damage waivers, CL §14-2101.
Telephone solicitations.
General provisions, CL §§14-2201 to 14-2205.
Unit pricing, CL §§14-101 to 14-107. See within this heading, "Unit pricing."
Unit pricing.
Arbitration of disputes, CL §14-107.
Compliance, CL §14-106.
Consumer commodity.
Defined, CL §14-101.
Definitions, CL §14-101.
Disclosure.
Extent, CL §14-103.
Manner of disclosure, CL §14-104.
Required, CL §14-103.
Disputes.
Arbitration, CL §14-107.
Division.
Defined, CL §14-101.
Exemption, CL §14-102.
Grant of exemption, CL §14-105.
Information.
Price information required, CL §14-103.
Manner of disclosure, CL §14-104.
Person.
Defined, CL §14-101.
Rules and regulations, CL §14-105.

CONSUMER PROTECTION —Cont'd
Unordered goods.
Sent after termination of membership in
organization, CL §14-1304.
Unsolicited sending of merchandise.
Offer to sell which includes, CL §14-1304.
Video movie sales and rentals, CL §§14-1601 to
14-1603.
See VIDEO MOVIE SALES AND RENTALS.
Waiver.
Right to notice at hearing in replevin action, CL
§14-1303.
Warranties.
Automotive warranty enforcement act, CL
§§14-1501 to 14-1504.
Extended warranties, CL §14-1311.
Implied warranties.
Fitness for particular use, CL §2-315.
Merchantability and trade usage, CL §2-314.
Motorized wheelchairs, CL §§14-2701 to 14-2706.
See MOTORIZED WHEELCHAIR
WARRANTIES.
New home warranties, RP §§10-601 to 10-610.
Unfair and deceptive trade practices, RP
§10-608.
Waterproofing, CL §§14-12A-01 to 14-12A-04.
See WATERPROOFING.

CONTACT LENSES.
Plano and Zero powered lenses.
Selling and dispensing, HG §24-301.1.
Replacement prescriptions.
Optometrists, HO §11-404.4.
Physicians, HO §14-507.
Selling or dispensing contact lenses without valid
and unexpired prescription.
Optometrists, HO §11-504.
Physicians, HO §14-607.

CONTAGIOUS DISEASES.
AIDS.
See ACQUIRED IMMUNE DEFICIENCY
SYNDROME (AIDS).
Animal control.
General provisions, HG §§18-217 to 18-222.
See ANIMAL CONTROL.
Avian influenza, regulation to control, AG
§§3-801 to 3-805.
Catastrophic health emergency.
Disease surveillance and response program, HG
§§18-901 to 18-908.
See CATASTROPHIC HEALTH EMERGENCY.
Governor's power to proclaim, PS §§14-3A-01 to
14-3A-08.
See HEALTH EMERGENCIES.
Confidentiality of information.
Reports.
Institution's report, HG §18-202.
Physicians' reports, HG §18-201.
AIDS reports, HG §18-201.1.
Control of diseases.
Animal control.
General provisions, HG §§18-217 to 18-222.
See ANIMAL CONTROL.
Disinfecting.
Expenses, HG §18-210.
Generally, HG §18-210.
Health officers.
Duties.
Generally, HG §18-208.
Records required, HG §18-212.

CONTAGIOUS DISEASES —Cont'd
Control of diseases —Cont'd
Moving infected individuals, HG §18-211.
Refusal to move infected individual, HG
§18-216.
Notice.
School boards, HG §18-209.
Records.
Health officer's records, HG §18-212.
School boards.
Notice to boards, HG §18-209.
Correctional officers.
Exposure to contagious disease.
Notification, HG §18-213.
Notification of exposure to contagious disease, HG
§18-213.
Counties.
Prevention of introduction into county, 25 §3.
Definitions, HG §§18-213, 18-213.1.
Diphtheria.
Medical and law enforcement personnel.
Notification of exposure, HG §§18-213 to
18-213.2.
Disinfection.
Control of diseases, HG §18-210.
Emergency medical technicians.
Notification of exposure to contagious disease, HG
§18-213.
Exposure of infected individuals.
Human immunodeficiency virus.
Individual knowingly transferring or attempting
to transfer virus to another individual, HG
§18-601.1.
Penalties for violations of provisions, HG
§§18-601, 18-602.
Individuals with human immunodeficiency
virus, HG §18-601.1.
Prohibited acts, HG §§18-601, 18-602.
Individuals with human immunodeficiency
virus, HG §18-601.1.
Fire fighters.
Notification of exposure to contagious disease, HG
§18-213.
**Food establishment employee with
communicable diseases,** HG §21-328.
Health officers.
Control of diseases.
General duties, HG §18-208.
Records.
Required records, HG §18-212.
Hemorrhagic fevers.
Medical and law enforcement personnel.
Notification of exposure, HG §§18-213 to
18-213.2.
Hepatitis.
Medical and law enforcement personnel.
Notification of exposure to, HG §§18-213 to
18-213.2.
HIV.
General provisions.
See HUMAN IMMUNODEFICIENCY VIRUS.
Hospitals.
Institution reports, HG §18-202.
Human immunodeficiency virus.
General provisions.
See HUMAN IMMUNODEFICIENCY VIRUS.
Immunization.
See IMMUNIZATION.
Institution reports, HG §18-202.
Investigation by secretary.
Suspected disease endangering public health, HG
§18-102.

CONTAGIOUS DISEASES —Cont'd
Laboratory examination reports, HG §18-205.
Law enforcement personnel.
  Notification of exposure to contagious diseases,
    HG §18-213.
Life insurance.
  Prohibited policy provisions, IN §16-216.
Livestock.
  Avian influenza, regulation to control, AG §§3-801
    to 3-805.
  General provisions, AG §§3-101 to 3-117.
    See LIVESTOCK.
  Tuberculin or mallein.
    General provisions.
      See LIVESTOCK.
Meningitis.
  College or university student residing in
    on-campus housing.
    Vaccination, HG §18-102.
  Fire fighters, emergency medical technicians,
    rescue squadmen, law enforcement officers
    and correctional officers.
    Notification of exposure to, HG §18-213.
Misdemeanors.
  Human immunodeficiency virus.
    Individual knowingly transferring or attempting
      to transfer virus to another individual, HG
      §18-601.1.
Mononucleosis.
  Fire fighters, emergency medical technicians,
    rescue squadmen, law enforcement officers
    and correctional officers.
    Notification of exposure to, HG §18-213.
Municipal corporations.
  Powers as to, 23A §2.
Notices, HG §18-213.2.
  Exposure to contagious diseases.
    Fire fighters, emergency medical technicians,
      rescue squadmen, law enforcement officers
      and correctional officers, HG §18-213.
    Fire fighters, emergency medical technicians,
      rescue squadmen, law enforcement officers
      and correctional officers.
      Exposure to contagious diseases, HG §18-213.
  School boards to be notified, HG §18-209.
Penalties.
  Exposure of infected individuals, HG §§18-601,
    18-602.
    Individuals with human immunodeficiency
      virus, HG §18-601.1.
  Moving infected individuals.
    Refusal to move infected individual, HG
      §18-216.
  Reports.
    Institution's reports, HG §18-215.
    Physicians' reports.
      Failure to submit, HG §18-215.
  Rules and regulations.
    Violations of rules and regulations, HG §18-604.
Physicians.
  Reports required by physicians, HG §18-201.
    AIDS reports, HG §18-201.1.
Plague.
  Medical and law enforcement personnel.
    Notification of exposure, HG §§18-213 to
      18-213.2.
Poultry.
  Avian influenza, regulation to control, AG §§3-801
    to 3-805.
  General provisions, AG §§3-101 to 3-117.
    See LIVESTOCK.

CONTAGIOUS DISEASES —Cont'd
Privileged communications.
  Fire fighters, emergency medical technicians,
    rescue squadmen, law enforcement officers
    and correctional officers.
    Notification of exposure to contagious diseases.
      Breach of patient confidentiality, HG §18-213.
Quarantine.
  Vessels and boats, authority of governor, HG
    §18-212.1.
Rabies.
  Medical and law enforcement personnel.
    Notification of exposure, HG §§18-213 to
      18-213.2.
Records.
  Health officer records, HG §18-212.
Reports.
  Institution's reports, HG §18-202.
    Penalty for violation of provisions, HG §18-215.
  Laboratory examination reports, HG §18-205.
  Physicians' reports, HG §18-201.
    AIDS reports, HG §18-201.1.
    Penalty for failure to submit, HG §18-215.
Rescue squadmen.
  Notification of exposure to contagious disease, HG
    §18-213.
Rules and regulations.
  Violations of rules and regulations.
    Penalty, HG §18-604.
Schools.
  Notice to school boards, HG §18-209.
Secretary of health and mental hygiene.
  General responsibilities of secretary for disease
    prevention, HG §§18-102, 18-103.
Sexually transmitted diseases.
  Chlamydia screening tests.
    Health insurance, required coverage, IN
      §15-829.
  Consent by minor to treatment, HG §20-102.
Subpoenas.
  Reports.
    Institution's report.
      When subject to subpoena, HG §18-202.
Tuberculosis.
  See TUBERCULOSIS.
Vaccination.
  See VACCINATION.
Venereal diseases.
  Chlamydia screening tests.
    Health insurance, required coverage, IN
      §15-829.
  Consent by minor to treatment, HG §20-102.
  Cures or remedies.
    Advertising cure.
      Prohibition, penalty, CR §10-102.
    Defined, CR §10-101.
    Prescription requirements, CR §10-103.
    Selling or dispensing remedies.
      Prohibition, penalties, CR §10-103.
Vessels and boats.
  Quarantine, authority of governor, HG §18-212.1.

CONTAINERS.
Apples.
  Packages.
    See APPLES.
Beer kegs.
  Sales of.
    Registration, 2B §21-106.
    Unregistered kegs, CR §10-118.

CONTAINERS —Cont'd
Bottled water.
Cleaning, HG §21-334.
Burning trash container, CR §6-108.
Cantaloupes.
Closed containers.
Defined, AG §10-901.
Labeling, AG §10-904.
Standard grades, AG §10-904.
Consignment of agricultural products.
Returned containers, AG §1-303.
Security deposits, AG §1-302.
Crab meat.
Labeling, HG §21-339.
Crimes and offenses.
Toxics in packaging, EN §9-1906.
Definitions.
Toxics in packaging, EN §9-1901.
Detachable metal tab opening devices.
Sale, 2B §21-102.
Injunctions.
Toxics in packaging, EN §§9-1905, 9-1906.
Kegs of beer.
Sales.
Registration of, 2B §21-106.
Unregistered kegs, CR §10-118.
Liquefied petroleum gas.
Unlawful use, CL §§11-601 to 11-606.
See LIQUEFIED PETROLEUM GAS.
Misdemeanors.
Plastic containers.
Labels.
Violations of requirements for sale of certain
plastic containers, EN §9-1710.
Toxics in packaging, EN §9-1906.
Motor fuel inspection.
Delivery of gasoline and special fuel in same
container, BR §10-319.
Open containers.
Alcoholic beverages.
Possession in motor vehicles' passenger areas,
CR §§10-123 to 10-127.
Penalties.
Detachable metal tab opening devices, 2B
§21-102.
Plastic containers.
Labels.
Violations of requirements for sale of certain
plastic containers, EN §9-1710.
Plastic containers.
Definitions, EN §9-1710.
Labels.
Requirements for sale of certain plastic
containers, EN §9-1710.
Penalties.
Labels.
Violations of requirements for sale of certain
plastic containers, EN §9-1710.
Pull tabs.
Sale, 2B §21-102.
Recycling solid waste.
Beverage container deposits.
County recycling plans, EN §9-1703.
Plastic containers.
Labels.
Requirements for sale of certain plastic
containers, EN §9-1710.
Returnable containers and textiles.
Registration, prohibited acts, BR §§19-301 to
19-307.

CONTAINERS —Cont'd
Rigid plastic containers or bottles.
Sale prohibited without required label, EN
§9-1710.
Rules and regulations.
Plastic containers.
Labels.
Requirements for sale of certain plastic
containers, EN §9-1710.
Toxics in packaging, EN §9-1907.
Soft drinks.
Cleaning of containers, HG §21-334.
Sale of containers with detachable metal tab
opening devices, HG §21-335.
Toxics in packaging.
Applicability of subtitle, EN §9-1903.
Conditional exemptions, EN §9-1904.
Certification, EN §9-1905.
Criminal penalties, EN §9-1906.
Definitions, EN §9-1901.
Enforcement of provisions, EN §9-1905.
Injunctions, EN §§9-1905, 9-1906.
Penalties, EN §9-1906.
Prohibited acts, EN §9-1902.
Regulations, EN §9-1907.
Wholesome meat act.
General provisions, AG §§4-101 to 4-131.
See WHOLESOME MEAT ACT.

CONTAMINATED FOOD.
See FOOD, DRUGS AND COSMETICS.

CONTAMINATION OF WATER SUPPLY, CR
§3-214.
Noncollegiate educational institutions.
Notices required, ED §2-206.
Notice to family day care homes, FL §5-551.
Public schools.
Notices required, ED §7-422.

CONTEMPT.
Abandoned property disposition.
Examination of records.
Persons who have failed to report property, CL
§17-322.
Adjudication of contempt.
Not barred to obtain relief in same proceedings,
CJ §1-202.
Air quality control.
Orders.
Hearings.
Subpoenas.
Noncompliance with notice of health or
subpoena issued, EN §2-605.
Appeals.
Alimony.
Exception as to order requiring payment of
alimony, CJ §12-304.
District Court, CJ §12-402.
Right of appeal, CJ §12-304.
Arbitration and award.
Subpoenas.
Enforcement of subpoena, CJ §3-217.
Attorneys at law.
Clients' security fund.
Decertification orders.
Defiance of order, CJA Rule 16-811.
Bail and recognizance.
Right of contemnor, SpecPro Rule 15-208.
Broadcasting criminal proceeding, CP §1-201.
Chiropractors.
Licenses.
Hearings, HO §3-315.

CONTEMPT —Cont'd
Circuit courts.
  Fines.
    Disposition of fines, CJ §7-207.
Civil contempt.
  Applicability of rule, SpecPro Rule 15-201.
  Constructive civil contempt, SpecPro Rule 15-206.
Clients' security fund.
  Defiance of decertification orders, CJA Rule
    16-811.
Collective bargaining.
  Constructive criminal contempt, LE §4-322.
Commissioner of financial regulation.
  Failure to obey subpoenas from, FI §2-114.
Constructive contempt, SpecPro Rules 15-205 to
    15-207.
  Defined, SpecPro Rule 15-202.
Consumer credit reporting agencies.
  Failure to comply with orders of court, CL
    §14-1218.
Credit services businesses.
  Failure to comply with court order, CL §14-1911.
Criminal contempt.
  Applicability of rule, SpecPro Rule 15-201.
  Constructive criminal contempt, SpecPro Rule
    15-205.
Definitions, SpecPro Rule 15-202.
Dentists.
  Licenses.
    Subpoenas.
      Enforcement by contempt, HO §4-318.
Desertion and nonsupport.
  Failure to obey order of court.
    Constructive civil contempt, SpecPro Rule
      15-207.
    Contempt proceedings for failure to pay child or
      spousal support, CJ §5-111.
Dietitians.
  Board of dietetic practice.
    Enforcement of subpoenas, etc., HO §5-312.
Direct contempt, SpecPro Rules 15-203, 15-204.
  Defined, SpecPro Rule 15-202.
District Court.
  Appeals, CJ §12-402.
Divorce.
  Deeds, agreements and settlements between
    spouses.
    Powers of courts to enforce provisions by, FL
      §8-105.
Domestic violence.
  Protective order violations, FL §4-508.
Drinking water.
  Failure to obey orders of department in connection
    with, EN §9-415.
**Enforcement of judgment prohibiting or
    mandating action.**
  District Court, CivProDist Rule 3-648.
Environmental sanitarians.
  Licenses.
    Denials, reprimands, suspensions and
      revocations.
      Hearings, EN §11-313.
Equity.
  Fines.
    Disposition of fines for contempt of court of
      equity, CJ §7-207.
Executors and administrators.
  Settlement of decedents' estates.
    Orphans' court.
      Enforcement, Estates Rule 6-113; ET §2-103.

CONTEMPT —Cont'd
Fines.
  Disposition of fines, CJ §7-207.
Gas and oil.
  Subpoenas.
    Enforcement of subpoena, EN §14-115.
General assembly.
  Investigating committee, SG §2-1608.
  Joint committee on administrative, executive and
    legislative review.
    Subpoenas.
      Contempt to enforce, SG §2-507.
  Joint committee on the management of public
    funds.
    Subpoenas.
      Enforcement by contempt, SG §2-807.
  Legislative policy committee.
    Subpoenas.
      Enforcement, SG §2-408.
  Standing committees.
    Subpoenas.
      Enforcement by contempt, SG §2-1104.
Hazardous materials and substances.
  Complaints.
    Hearings on complaint.
      Enforcement of subpoenas, EN §7-261.
Hearings.
  Constructive contempt, SpecPro Rule 15-207.
Human relations commission.
  Hearings.
    Subpoenas.
      Enforcement by contempt, 49B §11.
Husband and wife.
  Deeds, agreements and settlements between
    spouses.
    Powers of courts to enforce provisions by, FL
      §8-105.
Judges.
  Constructive contempt.
    Hearing.
      Disqualification of judge, SpecPro Rule
        15-207.
Judgments and decrees.
  Modification.
    Adjudication of contempt not barred to obtain
      relief in same proceedings, CJ §1-202.
Judicial disabilities commission.
  Enforcement of subpoenas or court orders, CJ
    §13-402.
Juvenile causes.
  Hearings.
    Controlling conduct of person before court, Juv
      Rule 11-110.
Limitation of actions.
  Support and maintenance.
    Statute of limitations for contempt proceedings,
      FL §10-102.
Masters.
  Time of entry of order.
    Circuit courts, CivProCir Rule 2-541.
Minors.
  Citation for alcoholic beverage violations, CR
    §10-119.
Morticians.
  Licenses.
    Hearings, HO §7-318.
Nursing home administrators.
  Licenses.
    Hearings.
      Reprimand, suspension or revocation, HO
        §9-315.

CONTEMPT —Cont'd

Occupational therapists.
Licenses.
Hearings, HO §10-316.

Open containers.
Possession of alcoholic beverages in motor
vehicles' passenger areas, CR §10-127.

Orders of court.
Modification.
Adjudication of contempt not barred to obtain
relief in same proceedings, CJ §1-202.

Paternity proceedings.
Pretrial inquiry by state's attorney.
Failure to appear or obey, FL §5-1019.
Support orders.
Sanctions for, FL §5-1041.

Pharmacists and pharmacies.
Licenses.
Hearings, HO §12-315.

Physical therapists.
Licenses.
Hearings, HO §13-316.

Physicians.
Board.
Power of board, HO §14-206.

Podiatrists.
Licenses.
Hearings, HO §16-313.

Poultry products inspection.
Jurisdiction of courts, AG §4-225.

Power of court, CJ §1-202.

Protective order violations, FL §4-508.

Public service commission proceedings.
Witnesses failure to comply with order, PUC
§3-110.

Radiation.
Hearings on violations.
Failure to obey orders of court, EN §8-505.

Railroad safety and health.
Commissioner's issuance of subpoena.
Noncompliance, LE §5.5-104.

Receivers.
Schedule of debtor's property and debts.
Failure to file schedule or disclose information.
Punishment by contempt, Receivers Rule
13-203.

**Recording or broadcasting criminal
proceedings,** CP §1-201.

Residential child care program administrators.
Disciplinary proceedings.
Investigations.
Disobedience of subpoena, HO §20-314.

Savings and loan associations.
Board of commissioners.
Orders and hearings.
Subpoenas.
Enforcement, FI §8-403.

Searches and seizures.
Warrants, Crim Rule 4-601.

Securities.
Securities act.
Subpoenas.
Enforcement of subpoenas, CA §11-701.

Sediment control.
Enforcement of subtitle.
Witnesses.
Failure to obey subpoena or order, EN §4-112.

Sheriffs.
Service of process.
Return.
Failure to file.
Citation for contempt, CJ §2-304.

CONTEMPT —Cont'd

Social workers.
Licenses.
Hearings, HO §19-312.

Subpoenas.
Criminal rules, Crim Rule 4-266.

Summary imposition of sanctions, SpecPro Rule
15-203.

**Sundry claims board, failure to comply with
board subpoena,** COR §10-306.

Support and maintenance.
Constructive civil contempt, SpecPro Rule 15-207.
Criminal nonsupport and desertion.
Baltimore City.
Witnesses.
Sanctions for failure to appear or to obey
summons or to testify, FL §10-213.
Limitation of actions, FL §10-102.
Parents and adult children.
Witnesses.
Pretrial inquiry.
Sanctions for failure to appear or to obey
summons or to testify, FL §13-104.
Withholding earnings, FL §10-138.

Taxation.
Death taxes.
Interstate arbitration of death taxes.
Subpoenas of board of arbitrators.
Failure to obey, TG §7-106.
Tax court.
Appeals to tax court.
Noncompliance with directives of court, TG
§13-522.

Tax court.
Appeals to tax court.
Noncompliance with directives of court, TG
§13-522.

Tobacco.
Authority.
Subpoenas.
Enforcement of subpoenas, AG §7-206.

Vessels and boats.
Disobedience of subpoenas, NR §8-716.2.

Water pollution.
Complaints.
Subpoenas.
Enforcement of subpoenas, EN §9-337.

Witnesses.
Immunity for compulsory testimony.
District Court, CivProDist Rule 3-508.
Refusal to comply with order to testify, CJ
§9-123.

Yellow Dog contracts.
Constructive criminal contempt, LE §4-322.

CONTESTED ELECTIONS.

Judicial review of election, EL §§12-201 to
12-204.

Recounts, EL §§12-101 to 12-107.
See ELECTIONS.

CONTESTED WILLS.

**Penalizing interested person for institution of
proceedings,** ET §4-413.

CONTESTS.

Lotteries.
General provisions.
See LOTTERIES.

CONTINGENT FEES.

Procurement.
Contract clause as to.
Required clause, SF §13-223.

CONTINGENT FEES —Cont'd
Procurement —Cont'd
Prohibited, SF §13-223.
Real estate appraisers.
Specialized appraisal services, BOP §16-402.

CONTINGENT INTEREST.
Decedents' estates.
See DECEDENTS' ESTATES.
Remainders.
See REMAINDERS, REVERSIONS AND
EXECUTORY INTERESTS.

CONTINUANCE.
Absent witnesses.
Circuit courts, CivProCir Rule 2-508.
Circuit courts, CivProCir Rule 2-508.
Costs.
Circuit courts, CivProCir Rule 2-508.
District Court, CivProDist Rule 3-508.
Discovery not completed.
Circuit courts, CivProCir Rule 2-508.
District Court, CivProDist Rule 3-508.
District Court, CivProDist Rule 3-508.
Emergency management.
Effect on sureties, guarantors and endorsers, PS
§14-205.
Failure to appear.
Emergency management service workers or
persons suffering injury or damage, PS
§14-208.
Juvenile petitions or pleadings.
Amended pleadings or petitions, Juv Rule 11-108.
Legislative privilege, CJ §6-402.
Circuit courts, CivProCir Rule 2-508.
District Court, CivProDist Rule 3-508.

CONTINUING CARE COMMUNITIES.
**Exemption from certificate of need
requirement.**
Admission of subscriber to comprehensive care
nursing bed, HG §19-124.
Loss, HG §19-123.
Operating agreements.
Retirement communities, CL §§23-101 to 23-106.

CONTINUING CARE CONTRACTS.
Actions.
Damages.
Actions by subscribers for recovery of damages,
70B §19.
Equitable relief.
Action by subscriber for, 70B §20.
Violations of provisions by providers, 70B §18A.
Advertising.
Dissemination of prohibited advertising or
information.
Penalty, 70B §18.
Assisted living program services, HG §19-1806.
Applicability of other provisions, 70B §23.
Defined, 70B §7.
Disclosure statement, 70B §11C.
Extensive or modified contracts, 70B §14A.
Required provisions of agreement, 70B §13.
Cancellation of agreement.
Election by subscriber to terminate, notice, 70B
§15A.
Refund, 70B §14.
Entrance fee, 70B §15A.
When automatically cancelled, 70B §14.
Certificates of registration.
Providers. See within this heading, "Providers."
Certified financial statement defined, 70B §7.

CONTINUING CARE CONTRACTS —Cont'd
Claims, 70B §20Q.
Contingent and unliquidated claims, 70B §20S.
Preferred claims, 70B §20R.
Secured claims.
Defined, 70B §7.
Priority of claims, 70B §§20R, 20S.
Special deposit claims.
Defined, 70B §7.
Subscribers' claims in providers' bankruptcy, 70B
§21.
Conflict of laws.
Applicability of other provisions, 70B §23.
Continuing care agreement defined, 70B §7.
Continuing care defined, 70B §7.
Contractual entrance fee refund, 70B §15A.
Defined, 70B §7.
Conversion of facility, 70B §11F.
Costs.
Secretary or deputy secretary, 70B §20C.
Creditor.
Defined, 70B §7.
Damages.
Actions by subscribers for recovery of damages,
70B §19.
Subscribers injured by violations, 70B §14.
Definitions, 70B §§7, 22A.
Deposits, collection and refunding, 70B §§10, 11.
Disclosure statement, 70B §11C.
Facility ownership, sale or transfer, 70B §11D.
Feasibility studies, 70B §10.
Meetings.
Annual meeting, 70B §11A.
Net operating expenses defined, 70B §11B.
Operating reserves, 70B §11B.
Receivership, 70B §21.
Reserves.
Operating reserves, 70B §11B.
Sale of facility ownership, 70B §11D.
Sale or transfer of assets, 70B §11E.
Statement.
Disclosure statement, 70B §11C.
Transfer of assets, 70B §11E.
Transfer of facility ownership, 70B §11D.
Delinquency proceedings.
Commencement of proceedings, 70B §20F.
Notice of commencement, 70B §20J.
Defined, 70B §7.
Deposit of moneys collected, 70B §20P.
Jurisdiction and venue, 70B §20E.
Liens, garnishments and executions prohibited
during proceedings, 70B §§20N, 20O.
Liquidating, rehabilitating or conserving
providers, 70B §§20A, 20G.
Appeals, 70B §20K.
Claims against impaired providers, 70B §§20Q,
20R, 20S.
Offsets, 70B §20T.
Possession and administration of assets, 70B
§20M.
Scope of orders, 70B §20H.
Powers of secretary.
Avoidance of liens, 70B §20O.
Department of aging.
Duties, 70B §8.
Inspection and investigation of facilities, 70B §17.
Deposit defined, 70B §7.
**Discharge of subscriber prior to expiration of
agreement,** 70B §15.
Disclosure statement, 70B §11C.

CONTINUING CARE CONTRACTS —Cont'd
Entrance fee.
Charges for medical and nursing and other health related services, 70B §7A.
Defined, 70B §7.
Refunds, 70B §15A.
Equity.
Action for equitable relief, 70B §20.
Expansion defined, 70B §7.
Extensive contract.
Defined, 70B §7.
Services, 70B §14A.
Facilities.
Conversion of facility, 70B §11F.
Defined, 70B §7.
Inspection and investigation, 70B §17.
Financial difficulty defined, 70B §7.
Financial review committee, 70B §17A.
Appointment of receivers for providers, 70B §20.
General assets.
Defined, 70B §7.
Governing body.
Defined, 70B §7.
Providers, 70B §11A.
Grievance procedures.
Internal grievance procedures, 70B §11G.
Health related benefits defined, 70B §7.
Injunctions.
Actions by subscribers for equitable relief, 70B §20.
Inspections.
Facilities, 70B §17.
Investigations.
Facilities, 70B §17.
Liens, garnishments and executions prohibited during delinquency proceedings against providers, 70B §§20N, 20O.
Loans.
Receivers, 70B §20L.
Making available either medical and nursing or other health related services.
Defined, 70B §7.
Entrance fees, 70B §7A.
Materials disclosed under public information act.
Availability to provider's subscribers, 70B §11A.
Meeting open to provider's subscribers, 70B §11A.
Modified contract.
Defined, 70B §7.
Services, 70B §14A.
Office defined, 70B §7.
Orders of court.
Delinquency proceedings, commencement of, 70B §20F.
Liquidation, conservation or rehabilitation of providers, 70B §20G.
Appeals, 70B §20K.
Claims against impaired providers, 70B §§20Q, 20R, 20S.
Offsets, 70B §20T.
Possession and administration of assets, 70B §20M.
Scope of orders, 70B §20H.
Penalties.
Violations of provisions, 70B §18.
Providers, 70B §§18A, 20G.
Person defined, 70B §7.
Processing fee defined, 70B §7.
Prohibited acts, 70B §18.

CONTINUING CARE CONTRACTS —Cont'd
Providers.
Additional requirements, 70B §10.
Annual meeting, 70B §11A.
Appointment of receivers, 70B §§20, 20I.
Assets, sale or transfer, 70B §11E.
Appointed receivers, 70B §20I.
Avoidance of transfers, 70B §20O.
Transfer, defined, 70B §7.
Bankruptcy, 70B §21.
Certificates of registration.
Applications, 70B §11.
Existing providers, 70B §9.
Maintenance or operation of facility without certificate.
Penalty, 70B §18.
Preliminary certificate, 70B §10.
Renewal certificate, 70B §§11, 17A.
Required, 70B §9.
Sale or transfer of assets, 70B §11E.
Suspension or revocation, 70B §22.
Claims against impaired providers, 70B §20Q.
Contingent and unliquidated claims, 70B §20S.
Preferred claims, 70B §20R.
Continuing care at home.
Agreements, 70B §22A.
Court costs, 70B §20C.
Delinquency proceedings, 70B §20A.
Commencement of proceedings, 70B §§20F, 20J.
Deposit of moneys collected, 70B §20P.
Jurisdiction and venue, 70B §20E.
Liens, garnishments and executions prohibited during proceedings, 70B §§20N, 20O.
Offsets, 70B §20T.
Powers of secretary, 70B §§20D, 20O.
Facilities, 70B §§7, 17.
Financial condition, 70B §17A.
Governing body, 70B §11A.
Internal grievance procedures, 70B §11G.
Liquidation, conservation or rehabilitation orders, 70B §20G.
Appeals, 70B §20K.
Claims against impaired providers, 70B §§20Q, 20R, 20S.
Offsets, 70B §20T.
Possession and administration of assets, 70B §20M.
Scope of orders, 70B §20H.
Net operating expenses, 70B §11B.
Penalties for violations of provisions, 70B §18A.
Liquidation, conservation or rehabilitation orders, 70B §20G.
Removal of records or assets from state, 70B §12.
Select committee to meet with facility residents.
Appointment, provider without governing body, 70B §11A.
Provisions of agreements.
Required provisions, 70B §13.
Existing agreements not affected, 70B §13.
Receivers.
Action by subscriber for appointment of receiver, 70B §20.
Appointed receivers, 70B §20I.
Defined, 70B §§7, 20I.
Immunity from liability, 70B §20B.
Liquidation, conservation or rehabilitation orders, 70B §20G.
Appeals, 70B §20K.
Claims against impaired providers, 70B §§20Q, 20R, 20S.
Offsets, 70B §20T.

CONTINUING CARE CONTRACTS —Cont'd
Receivers —Cont'd
Liquidation, conservation or rehabilitation orders —Cont'd
Possession and administration of assets, 70B §20M.
Scope of orders, 70B §20H.
Loans, 70B §20L.
Powers of secretary in delinquency proceedings, 70B §20D.
Avoidance of liens, 70B §20O.
Subscribers' claims in providers' bankruptcy, 70B §21.
Records.
Defined, 70B §7.
Providers.
Removal from state, 70B §12.
Regulations.
Department of aging, 70B §8.
Renovation defined, 70B §7.
Rescission of agreement, 70B §14.
Refund, 70B §14.
Entrance fee, 70B §15A.
Select committee to meet with facility residents.
Appointment, provider without governing body, 70B §11A.
Subscribers.
Bankruptcy of providers, 70B §21.
Claims against impaired providers, 70B §§20Q, 20R, 20S.
Damages.
Actions for recovery of damages, 70B §19.
Defined, 70B §7.
Discharge of subscriber prior to expiration of agreement, 70B §15.
Equitable relief.
Action for, 70B §20.
Rescission of agreement, 70B §14.
Entrance fee refunds, 70B §15A.
Waiver of certain provisions prohibited, 70B §16.
Surcharge defined, 70B §7.
Termination of agreement by subscriber.
Election, notice, 70B §15A.
Violations of provisions.
Damages.
Actions for recovery of damages, 70B §19.
Penalties, 70B §18.
Providers, 70B §§18A, 20G.
Waiver of provisions.
Waiver of certain provisions prohibited, 70B §16.
Withdrawal of application, 70B §14.
Written agreement.
Defined, 70B §7.

CONTINUING EDUCATION.
Accountants, BOP §2-312.
Acupuncturists.
Requirements for license renewal, HO §1A-306.
Air conditioning and heating contractors.
Inspectors, BR §9A-403.
Alternative dispute resolution.
Mediation, ADR Rule 17-104.
Architects.
Licenses, BOP §3-309.1.
Audiologists and speech-language pathologists, HO §2-308.
Bail bondsmen, IN §10-307.
Cosmetologists.
Teachers, BOP §5-311.
Dental hygienists, HO §4-205.

CONTINUING EDUCATION —Cont'd
Dentists, HO §4-205.
Dietitians, HO §5-308.
Electrologists, HO §8-6B-14.
Elevators.
Licenses, PS §12-833.
Insurance agents and brokers, IN §10-116.
Interior designers' certificates, BOP §8-308.
Requirement for renewal, BOP §8-307.
Mediation, ADR Rule 17-104.
Mining.
Fire-boss, EN §15-312.
First-class mine foreman, EN §15-312.
Mortgage lenders.
License renewal, FI §11-511.1.
Nursing home administrators, HO §9-311.
Renewal of licenses, HO §9-311.
Nutrient management consultants, AG §8-803.3.
Optometrists, HO §11-309.
Certification of attendance, HO §11-309.
Failure to certify attendance, HO §11-309.
Pharmacists and pharmacies, HO §12-309.
Registered pharmacy technicians, HO §12-6B-07.
Physical therapists.
Requirements for license renewal.
Board may establish, HO §§13-303, 13-311.
Physician assistants.
Certificates, HO §15-307.
Physicians, HO §14-316.
Podiatrists, HO §16-307.
Polysomnographic technologists, HO §13-5C-14.
Psychologists, HO §18-309.
Radiation oncology/therapy, medical radiation, and nuclear medicine technologists, HO §14-5B-12.
Real estate appraisers.
Certification of appraisers.
Renewal of certificate, BOP §16-511.
Renewal of appraiser's license, BOP §16-309.
Real estate brokers, BOP §17-315.
Residential child care program administrators.
Certification.
Renewal of certificate, HO §20-310.
Social workers, HO §19-308.
Licenses, HO §19-308.
Well drillers, EN §13-308.

CONTRABAND.
Assault pistols.
Seizure, disposal, CR §4-304.
Correctional facilities.
Contraband defined, COR §8-801.
Holding personal property of inmate, COR §10-801.
To effect escape.
Concealing or depositing in or about correctional facility, COR §8-803.
Delivery to inmate, COR §8-803.
Possession with intent to deliver to inmate, COR §8-803.
Receipt by inmate, COR §8-803.
Drug asset forfeiture.
Photographing of contraband money, CP §12-202.
Gambling forfeitures.
Money presumed contraband, CP §13-102.
Deposit and investment of seized money, CP §13-104.
Photographing the money, CP §13-103.
Prima facie evidence, CP §13-107.
Recording the sum quantity of each denomination, CP §13-103.

CONTRABAND —Cont'd
Jails, prisons or places of confinement, CR §§9-410 to 9-417.
Alcoholic beverages.
Delivery or possession, CR §9-415.
Concealing in place of confinement.
Escape, CR §9-412.
Weapons, CR §9-414.
Controlled dangerous substances.
Delivery or possession, CR §9-416.
Definitions, CR §9-410.
Delivery to person in confinement, CR §9-412.
Alcoholic beverages, CR §9-415.
Controlled dangerous substances, CR §9-416.
For escape purposes, CR §9-412.
Weapons, CR §9-414.
Escape.
Delivery for purposes of, concealing in place of confinement, receiving, CR §9-412.
Possession with intent to deliver, CR §9-412.
Alcoholic beverages, CR §9-415.
Controlled dangerous substances, CR §9-416.
Weapons, CR §9-414.
Prescription.
Inapplicability to drug or substance possessed under, CR §9-411.
Receipt by person in confinement.
Escape, CR §9-412.
Weapons, CR §9-414.
Separate sentence, concurrent or consecutive sentences, CR §9-417.
Weapons.
Delivery, concealing, receiving, CR §9-414.
Tobacco manufacturers.
Escrow act compliance.
Violations, seizure of contraband, BR §16-507.

CONTRACEPTIVES.
Condoms.
Sale of condoms by vending machines or other devices, HG §18-335.
Minors.
Capacity to consent to treatment or advice about contraception, HG §20-102.
Vending machine sales.
Nonlatex condoms sold from, CR §10-104.
Sales at schools, CR §10-105.

CONTRACT CARRIERS.
Carriers generally.
See CARRIERS.

CONTRACT LIENS, RP §§14-201 to 14-206.

CONTRACTORS.
Bonds, surety.
Counties.
Commissioner to require bond of, 25 §29.
Procurement.
See PROCUREMENT.
Building codes generally, PS §§12-101 to 12-1007.
See BUILDING CODES.
Construction licenses, BR §§17-601 to 17-603.
Definitions, BR §17-601.
Fees, BR §17-603.
Required, BR §17-602.
Cooling system contractors.
Air conditioning and heating contractors, BR §§9A-101 to 9A-602.
See AIR CONDITIONING AND HEATING CONTRACTORS.

CONTRACTORS —Cont'd
Counties.
Bonds, surety.
Commissioner to require bond of, 25 §29.
Custom home protection.
General provisions, RP §§10-501 to 10-509.
See CUSTOM HOME PROTECTION.
Defense contractors.
Maryland economic adjustment fund, 83A §§6-501 to 6-512.
See BUSINESS AND ECONOMIC DEVELOPMENT DEPARTMENT.
Defined, RP §9-101.
Discrimination.
State contracts.
Commercial discrimination, SF §§19-101 to 19-120.
See DISCRIMINATION.
Farm labor contractors.
Group workers' compensation policies, IN §§25-201 to 25-204.
Migrant labor.
General provisions, LE §§7-101 to 7-507.
See MIGRANT LABOR.
General assembly.
Compensation to contractors, MD Const Art III §35.
Heating contractors.
Air conditioning and heating contractors, BR §§9A-101 to 9A-602.
See AIR CONDITIONING AND HEATING CONTRACTORS.
Homebuilder registration, BR §§4.5-101 to 4.5-701.
See HOMEBUILDER REGISTRATION.
Home improvements.
General provisions, BR §§8-101 to 8-702.
See HOME IMPROVEMENTS.
Limitation of actions.
Injuries or damages, CJ §5-108.
Mechanics' liens.
Defined, PropAct Rule 12-301.
Notices.
Subcontractors.
Notice to owner by subcontractor, RP §9-104.
Prohibited waiver provisions in executory contracts, RP §9-113.
Releases from material suppliers and subcontractors, RP §9-114.
Right of owner on receipt of notice from subcontractor, RP §9-104.
Right of owner to retain amounts due subcontractor giving notice, RP §9-104.
Subcontractors.
Conditioning payment to subcontractor on payment to contractor.
Prohibited provisions in executory contracts, RP §9-113.
Waiver.
Prohibited waiver provisions in executory contracts, RP §9-113.
Migrant labor.
General provisions, LE §§7-101 to 7-507.
See MIGRANT LABOR.
New home warranties, RP §§10-601 to 10-610.
See WARRANTY.
Procurement.
See PROCUREMENT.
Refrigeration contractors.
Air conditioning and heating contractors, BR §§9A-101 to 9A-602.
See AIR CONDITIONING AND HEATING CONTRACTORS.

CONTRACTORS —Cont'd
Shore erosion control.
Projects.
Payment of contractors, NR §8-1005.
State contracts.
Discrimination.
Commercial discrimination, SF §§19-101 to
19-120.
See DISCRIMINATION.
Subcontractors.
Workers' compensation.
Covered employees and employers.
Owner operator of class F tractor, LE §9-218.
Work in confined places.
Notice to commissioner by subcontractors, LE
§5-602.
Taxation.
Withholding payment to nonresident contractors.
Pending verification of tax clearance certificate,
TG §13-803.
Trust relationships in construction industry,
RP §§9-201 to 9-204.
See TRUSTS AND TRUSTEES.
Unemployment compensation.
Foreign contractors as new employers.
Contributions.
Rate for new employing units, LE §8-609.
Independent contractors.
When not covered employment, LE §8-205.
Ventilation contractors.
Air conditioning and heating contractors, BR
§§9A-101 to 9A-602.
See AIR CONDITIONING AND HEATING
CONTRACTORS.
Waiver.
Mechanics' liens.
Prohibited waiver provisions in executory
contracts, RP §9-113.
Warranties.
New home warranties, RP §§10-601 to 10-610.
See WARRANTY.
Waterproofing, CL §§14-12A-01 to 14-12A-04.
See WATERPROOFING.
Workers' compensation.
Covered employees and employers.
Owner operator of class F tractor, LE §9-218.
Liability for compensation.
Compensation from subcontractor, LE §9-508.

CONTRACTS.
Adoption.
Post-adoption contact agreements.
Independent adoptions, FL §5-3B-07.
Local department adoptions, FL §5-308.
Private agency adoptions, FL §5-3A-08.
Agricultural cooperatives. See within this
heading, "Cooperatives."
Agricultural mediation program, AG §1-1A-03.
Air conditioning and heating contractors.
Cooperative agreements.
Board authority to enter into, BR §9A-205.
Alcoholic beverages.
Liquor control board.
Powers, 2B §15-205.
Alienation of affections.
Payment or settlement of abolished or prohibited
claims.
Void contracts, FL §3-104.
Allegany county.
Competitive bidding and bonds, 25 §3.

CONTRACTS —Cont'd
Answers.
General denials in specified causes.
Circuit courts, CivProCir Rule 2-323.
Antitrust act.
Unlawful contracts prohibited, CL §11-204.
Appropriations.
Disbursements and expenditures.
Restrictions on contracts, SF §7-237.
Public contracts.
Prohibited unless authorized by appropriation,
31 §3.
Supervision of recipients.
Health and social welfare organizations.
Accounting standards, SF §7-403.
Arbitration.
Uniform arbitration act, CJ §§3-201 to 3-234.
See ARBITRATION AND AWARD.
Architectural and engineering services.
Generally.
See PROCUREMENT.
General using authorities.
See PROCUREMENT.
Transportation agencies.
See PROCUREMENT.
Assignments.
Secured transactions.
Inapplicability of article 9.
Payment right assigned to one obligated to
perform under contract, CL §9-109.
At-risk youth.
Residential boarding education programs for
at-risk youth.
Contract by department with operator to
provide services, ED §8-704.
Attachment.
Issuance of attachment, CJ §3-304.
Aviation.
Administration.
Law governing, TR §5-213.
Airports.
Construction and improvement.
Procedure, TR §5-213.
Jurisdiction over contracts, TR §5-103.
Bainbridge development corporation.
Authority to contract for services, 83A §5-1606.
Baltimore City.
Interest in by mayor or city council prohibited,
MD Const Art XI §5.
Interest rate exchange agreements or contracts.
Authority to enter into, 31 §34.
Baltimore City Community College.
Procurement contracts, ED §16-511.
Bank deposits and collections.
Variation of article provisions by agreement, CL
§4-103.
Bids and bidding.
Procurement.
General provisions.
See PROCUREMENT.
Board of contract appeals.
Procurement.
Dispute resolution.
Appeals board, SF §§15-201, 15-205 to 15-212.
Boards and commissions.
Architectural and engineering services.
General professional services selection board.
See PROCUREMENT.
Transportation professional services selection
board.
See PROCUREMENT.

CONTRACTS —Cont'd

Boycotts.

Foreign discriminatory boycotts.

Voiding of contract provisions, CL §11-112.

Breach of contract.

Emergency management.

Civil relief during emergency periods.

Fines or penalties for nonperformance, PS §14-209.

Installment contracts, PS §14-213.

Insurance companies.

Order of rehabilitation does not constitute anticipatory breach by insurer, IN §9-212.

Jurisdiction over persons outside this state.

General provisions.

See JURISDICTION.

Limitation of action, CJ §5-101.

Liquidation, rehabilitation, etc., of insurers.

Seizure order not to constitute anticipatory breach of contract, IN §9-215.

Service contracts and consumer products guaranty.

Actions for breach of guaranty or service contract, CL §14-406.

Breach of promise to marry.

Payment or settlement or abolished or prohibited claims.

Void, FL §3-104.

Bribery.

Procurement.

Debarment of contractors, SF §§16-101 to 16-312.

See PROCUREMENT.

Bridge and canal companies.

Erection of bridges or construction of canals, 23 §141.

Business opportunities.

General provisions, BR §§14-101 to 14-129.

See START-UP BUSINESS VENTURES.

Business trusts.

Forfeiture of right to do business.

Survival of claims and contracts, CA §12-810.

Calvert county.

Competitive bidding, 25 §3.

Cemeteries.

Perpetual care of cemeteries, BR §5-604.

Preneed burial contracts.

General provisions, BR §§5-701 to 5-712.

See CEMETERIES.

Charities.

Content of agreement between charitable organization and fund-raising counsel, BR §6-615.

Contents of agreement between charitable organization and professional solicitors, BR §6-616.

Secretary of state.

Reciprocal agreements, BR §6-206.

Solicitation agreements, BR §6-501.

Soliciting after cancellation of contract, BR §6-612.

Unregistered charitable organization, BR §6-603.

Charles county.

Competitive bidding and bonds, 25 §3.

Chesapeake Bay.

Green Shores program, NR §5-430.

Children, youth and families services.

Residential child care programs, 49D §§7-101 to 7-106.

Code of Maryland.

Adoption of code not to affect, 1 §1.

CONTRACTS —Cont'd

Collective bargaining.

Consent elections.

Agreement for consent election, LE §4-209.

Trade dispute agreements.

Conduct not conspiracy, LE §4-404.

Yellow Dog contract act, LE §§4-301 to 4-322.

See COLLECTIVE BARGAINING.

Commercial code.

Agreement.

Defined, CL §1-201.

Capacity to contract.

Applicability of general principles, CL §1-103.

Exception as to age, CL §1-103.

Construction.

Conspicuous, CL §1-201.

Course of dealing, CL §1-205.

Usage of trade, CL §1-205.

Defined, CL §1-201.

Obligation of good faith, CL §1-203.

Power to choose applicable law, CL §1-105.

Secured transactions.

General provisions, CL §§9-101 to 9-710.

See SECURED TRANSACTIONS.

Term.

Defined, CL §1-201.

Time.

Fixing reasonable time, CL §1-204.

Variation from code by agreement, CL §1-102.

Community energy loan program.

Contracts with third parties, SG §9-2108.

Community programs.

Receivership, HG §19-337.

Community rehabilitation programs.

Division may contract for furnishing of programs and services, ED §21-404.

Community services administration.

Generally, 41 §6-203.

Computer information transactions generally, CL §§22-101 to 22-816.

See COMPUTER INFORMATION TRANSACTIONS.

Condominiums.

Contract liens, RP §§14-201 to 14-206.

See LIENS.

Sale of unit subsequent to initial sale, RP §11-126.

Termination.

Authority of council of unit owners, RP §11-123.

Purchaser's right to rescind contract, RP §11-126.

Consignment.

Consignee.

Between consignee and third person, CL §11-804.

General provisions.

See CONSIGNMENT.

Constitutional provisions.

Impairment of obligations of contracts, US Const Art I §10.

Construction.

Attorneys' fees.

Actions for prompt payment, RP §9-303.

Contractor.

Defined, RP §9-301.

Costs.

Actions for prompt payment, RP §9-303.

Counties.

Disputes in construction contracts.

Resolution, 25 §1A; 25A §1A; 25B §13A.

Definitions, RP §9-301.

Exemptions, RP §9-304.

CONTRACTS —Cont'd
Construction —Cont'd
Interest.
Remedies for default of prompt payment, RP §9-303.
Owner.
Defined, RP §9-301.
Prompt payment, RP §9-302.
Remedies for default, RP §9-303.
Subcontractor.
Defined, RP §9-301.
Undisputed amount.
Defined, RP §9-301.
Construction industry indemnity agreements.
Prohibited actions, CJ §5-401.
Consumer protection.
See CONSUMER PROTECTION.
Continuing care contracts.
See CONTINUING CARE CONTRACTS.
Contractors.
General provisions.
See CONTRACTORS.
Contract state employees.
Service contracts, SPP §§13-401 to 13-405.
Cooperative housing corporations.
Contract for initial sale of cooperative interest.
Public offering statements.
Prerequisite to enforcement, CA §5-6B-02.
Cooperatives.
Agricultural cooperatives.
Liquidation damages.
Contracts with members, CA §5-522.
Other cooperatives.
With other cooperatives for carrying on business, CA §5-524.
Power to contract, CA §5-504.
Renewal, CA §5-522.
Using same methods as other cooperatives, CA §5-524.
With members, CA §5-522.
Directors.
Transaction or contract between director and corporation, CA §2-419.
Copyright royalties, CL §11-1402.
Corporations.
Close corporation, CA §4-401.
Directors.
Contract or transaction between corporation and director, CA §2-419.
Foreign corporations.
Failure to comply with subtitle 2 does not affect contracts, CA §7-305.
Powers, CA §2-103.
Stockholders.
Consolidation, merger and other transfers of property.
Alteration of contract rights before subtitle applies, CA §3-202.
Ultra vires.
Defense of ultra vires, CA §1-403.
Counties.
General provisions.
See COUNTIES.
Court of appeals.
Reports.
By reporter, CJ §13-204.
Credit services businesses.
Consumer contracts.
Breaches, CL §14-1907.
Requirements, CL §14-1906.
Void contracts, CL §14-1907.

CONTRACTS —Cont'd
Credit unions.
Share guaranty corporations.
Participating credit unions.
Contracts with participating credit unions, FI §7-214.
Crime laboratories.
DNA database system, PS §2-502.
Custom home contracts.
Between custom home builders and buyers.
Contents.
Requirements, RP §10-505.
Disclosures, RP §10-506.
Required, RP §10-505.
Defined, RP §10-501.
Debt management services agreement, FI §§12-916, 12-918.
Decedents' estates.
Waiver of rights in decedent's estate, ET §3-205.
Declaratory judgments.
Construction or validity, CJ §3-406.
Before or after breach, CJ §3-407.
Defenses.
Bonds, surety.
Performance bond, 25 §29.
Bridges.
Between counties, 25 §43.
Building and repairing, 25 §§37 to 39.
Chartered counties.
Powers of county, 25A §5.
Competitive bidding and bonds.
General provisions, 25 §3.
County commissioners.
Interest in contracts prohibited, 25 §30.
Erosion districts, 25 §164.
Made by county commissioners, 25 §§29 to 32.
Not authorized by appropriation prohibited, 31 §3.
Purchasing contracts, 25 §3.
Requirements of contracts for work to be done, 25 §29.
Roads.
Right of way, 25 §138.
Taking over private roads in certain counties, 25 §155.
Unconscionability.
Sale of goods, CL §2-302.
Definitions.
Construction contracts, RP §9-301.
Discrimination.
State contracts.
Commercial discrimination, SF §§19-101 to 19-120.
See DISCRIMINATION.
District Court.
Jurisdiction, CJ §4-401.
Division of correction officers or employees.
Prohibited from entering into contract with inmate, COR §3-218.
Documents.
State documents.
Contract Weekly.
See DOCUMENTS.
Printing contracts, SG §7-211.
Documents of title.
Bills of lading.
Limitation of carrier's liability, CL §7-309.
Warehouse receipts.
Limitation of warehouse's liability, CL §7-204.
Door-to-door solicitations act, CL §§14-2601 to 14-2603.

CONTRACTS —Cont'd
Drug or alcohol abuse.
Facilities and services.
Authority of administration to enter contracts, HG §8-402.
Economic development revenue bonds.
Applicability and prerequisites for contract as security, 41 §14-108.
Electronic transactions generally, CL §§21-101 to 21-120.
See ELECTRONIC TRANSACTIONS.
Emergency management.
Civil relief during emergency periods.
Fines or penalties for nonperformance, PS §14-209.
Installment contracts, PS §14-213.
Employment agencies.
Required language, BR §9-305.
Employment contracts.
Limitation of actions, CJ §5-101.
Environmental service.
Federal, state and municipal governments, NR §3-104.
Generally, NR §3-104.
Mandatory agreements to provide requested service, NR §3-107.
Municipality.
Contract with municipality in district, NR §3-106.
Waste collection services.
Management and operation, NR §3-107.
Water supply, wastewater purification and solid waste disposal.
Review of contract, NR §3-108.
Environmental trust.
General provisions, NR §3-208.
Evidence.
Sales contracts.
Parol and extrinsic evidence, CL §2-202.
Executors and administrators.
Liability.
Contracts made during the administration, ET §8-109.
Perform decedent's contracts.
Powers of personal representative, ET §7-401.
Executory contracts.
Statute of frauds, CJ §5-901.
Fiduciaries.
Power to perform, ET §15-102.
Fish and fisheries.
Department of natural resources.
Research or scientific investigation, NR §4-205.
Foreclosures.
Foreclosure consulting contract, RP §7-306.
Land installment contract, PropSales Rule 14-203.
Fraud.
Interparty agreements, CL §20-103.
Frauds, statute of.
Executory contracts.
Requirements, RP §5-104.
Gasoline.
Marketing agreements, CL §§11-301 to 11-308.
See GASOLINE.
General services department.
Architectural and engineering services.
See PROCUREMENT.
Land acquisition division.
Review and approval of contracts for acquisition of land, SF §4-415.
Printing for state, SF §4-305.

CONTRACTS —Cont'd
Harford county.
Competitive bidding and bonds.
General provisions, 25 §3.
Health cost review commission, HG §19-207.
Notification of certain contracts, HG §19-217.
Health maintenance organizations.
Administrative service provider contracts, HG §§19-712, 19-713.2.
Plan requirements, HG §19-713.2.
Amendments, HG §19-713.
Filing, HG §19-713.
Hold harmless clause, HG §19-710.
Nonduplication or coordination of coverage provisions, HG §19-713.1.
Rehabilitation or liquidation.
Authority of commissioner as rehabilitator or liquidator, HG §19-706.1.
Standards of quality and care, HG §19-710.
Subrogation provision, HG §19-713.1.
Terms of contracts, HG §19-710.
Hearing aid sales.
Cancellation of purchase, CL §14-2503.
Deceptive trade practices, CL §14-2504.
Hearing impaired.
Infants.
Program.
Contracts for administration of program.
Powers of secretary, HG §13-604.
Heritage areas authority.
Powers generally, FI §13-1107.
Higher education investment contracts.
Inspection, SG §10-616.
Highways.
Commissioners and employees not to be interested in contracts, TR §8-217.
Homebuilder registration.
Enforceability, unregistered builder, BR §4.5-605.
Home improvement contracts.
Abandonment of or failure of performance, BR §8-605.
Contents, BR §8-501.
Debt limitation, BR §8-609.
Defined, BR §8-101.
Deposit limited, BR §8-617.
Doing business with unlicensed person, BR §8-612.
Form, BR §8-501.
Fraud, BR §8-608.
Gifts as inducements, BR §8-503.
Misrepresentation, BR §8-607.
Payment before signing contract, BR §8-617.
Waiver of title provisions prohibited, BR §8-103.
Homeowners' associations.
Lots.
Sale of lots.
See HOMEOWNERS' ASSOCIATIONS.
Home solicitation sales, CL §§14-301 to 14-306.
See HOME SOLICITATION SALES.
Horse racing.
Approval required, BR §11-318.
Mile thoroughbred racing.
Transfer or sale of Preakness Stakes, BR §11-520.
Pari-mutuel betting.
Betting on out-of-state races, BR §11-804.
Satellite simulcast betting, BR §11-825.
Hospitals.
Community programs.
Receivership, HG §19-337.

CONTRACTS —Cont'd
Hospitals —Cont'd
Comprehensive care facilities.
Contracts for admission, HG §19-308.3.
Extended care facilities.
Contracts for admission, HG §19-308.3.
Nursing facilities.
Receivership, HG §19-337.
Rights of individuals.
Contracts for admission, HG §19-344.
Hotels, motels and retirement communities.
Operating agreements, CL §§23-101 to 23-106.
Husband and wife.
Liability.
Husband not liable for wife's contracts, FL §4-301.
Immigration consultants.
Contracting requirements, CL §14-3304.
Indemnity agreements.
Construction industries.
Prohibited actions, CJ §5-401.
Installment sales.
General provisions, CL §§12-601 to 12-636.
See SALES.
Insurance.
Legal mutual liability insurance society of Maryland.
Terms of license insurer contract, IN §24-105.
Licensing services, IN §2-104.
Life insurance policies, IN §§12-201 to 12-210, 16-201 to 16-217.
Managing general agents.
Contract with insurer, IN §§8-208, 8-212.
Medical mutual liability insurance society of Maryland.
Terms of licensed insurer contract, IN §24-205.
Premium finance companies.
Cancellation of insurance contract under power of attorney, IN §§23-401 to 23-406.
See PREMIUM FINANCE COMPANIES.
Rehabilitation of insurer.
Order of rehabilitation not anticipatory breach of contract by insurer, IN §9-212.
Reinsurance managers.
Contract with reinsurers, IN §8-515.
Unfair trade practices.
Contracts as inducement to insurer, IN §27-207.
Variable life insurance and annuity contracts, IN §§16-601 to 16-603.
Insurance companies.
Liquidation, rehabilitation, etc.
Financial contracts and netting agreements, IN §9-229.1.
Seizure order not to constitute anticipatory breach of contract, IN §9-215.
Standard valuation law, IN §§5-301 to 5-312.
See LIFE INSURANCE AND ANNUITIES.
Interest.
General provisions, CL §§12-101 to 12-114.
See INTEREST.
Interparty agreements, CL §§20-101 to 20-106.
Authorized, CL §20-101.
Discharge.
Merger of obligation and right, CL §20-102.
Fraudulent transactions, CL §20-103.
Interpretation, CL §20-105.
Merger of obligation and right.
Discharge of contract, CL §20-102.
Retroactivity of title, CL §20-104.
Title of act, CL §20-106.

CONTRACTS —Cont'd
Joint debtors.
Contract actions against, CJ §11-103.
Joint obligors.
General provisions.
See DEBTORS.
Judgments and decrees.
Penalties.
Amount due on contract with penalty, CJ §11-201.
Jurisdiction.
Personal jurisdiction.
Contracting to supply goods, foods, services or products in this state, CJ §6-103.
Kent county.
Competitive bidding and bonds, 25 §3.
Labor and employment relations.
Wage payment and collection.
Reciprocal agreements, LE §3-506.
Wholesale sales representatives.
Termination of contract.
Payment of commission, LE §3-604.
Void waivers, LE §3-603.
Yellow Dog contract act, LE §§4-301 to 4-322.
See COLLECTIVE BARGAINING.
Land.
Installment contracts, RP §§10-101 to 10-108.
See LAND INSTALLMENT CONTRACTS.
Under seal.
Twelve-year period, CJ §5-102.
Legal mutual liability insurance society of Maryland.
Terms of licensed insurer contract, IN §24-105.
Liens.
Contract liens, RP §§14-201 to 14-206.
See LIENS.
Life insurance and annuities.
Variable contracts, IN §§16-601 to 16-603.
Viatical settlement contracts, IN §§8-601 to 8-611.
See VIATICAL SETTLEMENT CONTRACTS.
Life insurance policies, IN §§12-201 to 12-210, 16-201 to 16-217.
Limitation of actions.
Employment contracts, CJ §5-101.
Sale of goods.
Breach of contract, CL §2-725.
Limitations by agreements may be reduced to less than one year, CL §2-725.
Sovereign immunity.
Limitation on claims under subtitle, SG §12-202.
Limited liability companies.
Foreign companies.
Doing business without registration.
Validity of contract not impaired, CA §4A-1007.
Liability of members to third persons, CA §4A-301.
Limited liability partnerships, revised act.
Foreign limited liability partnerships.
Doing business without registration, CA §9A-1106.
Liability of partners, CA §9A-306.
Local military installation redevelopment authorities.
Contracting for services, 83A §5-1707.
Marketing agreements.
Gasoline, CL §§11-301 to 11-308.
See GASOLINE.
Marriage.
Breach of promise to marry.
Prohibited actions, FL §3-102.

CONTRACTS —Cont'd

Maryland economic adjustment fund.
Enforceability of agreements entered into by committee, 83A §6-504.

Maryland food center authority.
Power to contract, 41 §§13-103, 13-105.

Maryland-national capital park and planning commission.
Acquiring park lands in district, 28 §4-105.
Continued, 28 §1-102.
Payment of commission obligations, 28 §§2-201 to 2-204.
See MARYLAND-NATIONAL CAPITAL PARK AND PLANNING COMMISSION.

Maryland stadium authority.
Acquisition or construction of facility or facility site.
Approval of contracts, FI §13-709.

Maryland Transit Administration, TR §7-204.
Conflicts of interest.
Voids contract, TR §7-211.
Labor contracts, TR §7-601.
Collective bargaining agreements.
Administration to enter into, TR §7-601.
Cost of living adjustments.
Limitations, TR §7-601.
Definitions, TR §7-601.
Liability, TR §7-702.
Providing transit facilities and services, TR §7-501.

Maryland-Washington metropolitan district.
Park land.
Acquisition of park lands in district, 28 §4-105.

Mechanics' liens.
Defined, PropAct Rule 12-301.
For what debts lien attaches, RP §9-102.
Prohibited waiver provisions in executory contracts, RP §9-113.

Medicaid.
Care contracts, HG §15-103.
Department of human resources, HG §15-104.

Migrant labor.
Void agreements.
Agreement to waive or modify right, LE §7-103.

Minimum wage.
Employment contracts.
Void agreements.
Agreement to work for less than the wage required, LE §3-405.

Minors.
Age of majority for capacity to contract, CL §1-103.

Money transmission.
Authorized delegates, FI §12-413.

Morticians.
Additional statements, HO §7-404.
Preneed contracts.
Definitions, HO §§7-101, 7-404.
Requirements generally, HO §7-405.
Violations, HO §7-504.
Statement of initial agreement, HO §7-404.

Mosquito control.
Political subdivisions, AG §5-404.

Motor clubs.
Service contracts, IN §26-402.

Motorcycles.
Safety program.
Award of contracts, TR §16-605.

Motor fuel inspection.
Exchange agreements.
Approval required, BR §10-306.

CONTRACTS —Cont'd

Motor fuel inspection —Cont'd
Retail service station dealers.
Contract between producer or refiner and station dealer.
Prohibited provisions, BR §10-311.1.
Contractual relationship with suppliers, BR §10-313.
Terminal agreements.
Approval required, BR §10-306.
Waiver of comptroller approval, BR §10-306.

Motor vehicles.
Dealers.
Mechanical repair contracts, TR §15-311.2.
Sales.
Contents of vehicles sales contract, TR §§15-311, 15-410.

Municipal corporations.
Actions.
Nonliability for punitive damages, CJ §5-507.
Not authorized by appropriation prohibited, 31 §3.
Privately owned residential communities.
Residential street service agreements, 23A §50.
Who may contract, 23A §51.

New home warranties.
General provisions, RP §§10-601 to 10-610.
See WARRANTY.

Northeast Maryland waste disposal authority.
Powers of authority generally, NR §3-905.
Purchases.
Award of contracts for purchases, NR §3-921.
Subdivision and authority, NR §3-915.
Subdivision and Maryland environmental service, NR §3-919.

Nuclear compact.
Supplementary agreements, 41 §16-107.

Nursing facilities.
Receivership, HG §19-337.

Operating agreements.
Hotels, motels and retirement communities, CL §§23-101 to 23-106.

Parol evidence.
Sales contracts, CL §2-202.

Partnerships, revised act.
Partner's liability, CA §9A-306.

Patuxent river watershed.
Agreements between secretary and counties, NR §8-1316.
General provisions, NR §8-1311.

Pesticides.
Applicators.
Information to be supplied to customer upon entering into contract for pest control, AG §5-208.
Issuance by secretary, AG §5-202.

Pharmacists.
Therapy management contracts, HO §§12-6A-01 to 12-6A-10.

Physicians.
Therapy management contracts, HO §§12-6A-01 to 12-6A-10.

Port administration.
Employees and agents.
Interest in contracts prohibited, TR §6-212.
Existing contracts unaffected, TR §6-404.
Powers.
Generally, TR §6-208.

Potomac highlands airport authority.
Power of authority to enter contracts, TR §10-103.

Potomac water authority.
Bloomington dam project.
Contracts relative to, EN §5-406.

CONTRACTS —Cont'd
Potomac water authority —Cont'd
Contracts with federal government, EN §5-406.
District of Columbia, EN §5-408.
Federal government, EN §5-406.
Individual liability on contracts, EN §5-407.
Premium finance companies.
Cancellation of insurance contract pursuant to
power of attorney, IN §§23-401 to 23-406.
See PREMIUM FINANCE COMPANIES.
Preneed burial contracts.
General provisions, BR §§5-701 to 5-712.
See CEMETERIES.
Printing.
General services department.
Printing for state, SF §4-305.
Privately owned residential communities.
Municipal corporations, 23A §§50, 51.
Procurement.
See PROCUREMENT.
Public debt.
Contract to spend general obligation loan
proceeds.
Approval by board of public works, SF §8-301.
Public ethics.
Conflicts of interest.
Participation in procurement contracts, SG
§15-508.
Generally.
See PUBLIC ETHICS.
Public works.
General provisions.
See PUBLIC WORKS.
Purchases.
See BUDGET AND MANAGEMENT.
Real estate brokers.
Buyer's right of selection.
Notice of.
Contracts to include, BOP §17-524.
Taxation.
Notice concerning taxes.
Contracts to include, BOP §17-523.
When broker entitled to commission, RP §14-105.
Real property.
Applicability of article, RP §§15-102, 15-103.
Deposits on new homes, RP §§10-301 to 10-306.
See HOUSING.
Installment contracts, RP §§10-101 to 10-108.
See LAND INSTALLMENT CONTRACTS.
Lease option agreements.
Defined, RP §8-202.
Statements required, RP §8-202.
Modifications.
Contractual modifications, RP §1-104.
Recordation.
Contracts for grant of property or any
subordination agreement, RP §3-102.
Limitation on enforcement of recorded contract,
RP §10-401.
Limitation on notice of recorded option, RP
§10-402.
Sale of realty.
Development impact fees, RP §14-117.
Disclosure requirements, RP §14-117.
Prince George's county.
Development impact fees.
Imposition, RP §14-117.
Sales.
See REAL PROPERTY.
Recordation.
Limitation on enforcement of recorded land
contract, RP §10-401.

CONTRACTS —Cont'd
Recordation —Cont'd
Options to purchase real property.
Limitation on recorded notice, RP §10-402.
Real property. See within this heading, "Real
property."
Reinsurance managers.
Contracts with reinsurers, IN §8-515.
Releases.
Interparty agreements. See within this heading,
"Interparty agreements."
Rental-purchase agreements, CL §§12-1101 to
12-1112.
See RENTAL-PURCHASE AGREEMENTS.
Reorganization of government.
Abolished or superseded units, SG §10-706.
Residence.
Preferences.
Political subdivisions and certain entities to
grant resident business preference, 24
§8-102.
Residential child care programs, 49D §§7-101 to
7-106.
Rights of way.
Public roads.
With owners for right of way, 25 §138.
St. Mary's county.
Competitive bidding and bonds, 25 §3.
Sale of goods.
Commercial code, CL §§2-101 to 2-725.
See SALE OF GOODS, UCC.
Secured transactions.
General provisions, CL §§9-101 to 9-710.
See SECURED TRANSACTIONS.
Security interests arising under provisions, CL
§9-110.
Sales.
Time-sharing. See within this heading,
"Time-sharing."
Sanitary commissions.
Buying and selling services, EN §9-635.
Construction contracts, EN §9-636.
Additional terms of contract, EN §9-655.
Advertising solicitation of bids, EN §9-655.
Schools.
Approval.
By county superintendent of schools, ED §4-205.
Construction of buildings.
Approval of state superintendent of schools, ED
§2-303.
Provisions of section not applicable, ED
§2-303.
Technology for education.
Development of educational applications using
advanced technology, ED §7-909.
Visual and auditory aids.
By state superintendent of schools, ED §2-303.
Seals and sealed instruments.
Sales contracts.
Seals inoperative, CL §2-203.
Securities.
Securities act.
Effect of making or performing contract with
knowledge of facts, CA §11-703.
Investment advisory contracts.
Required provisions, CA §11-302.
State treasurer.
Loans of securities, SF §2-603.
Service contracts.
Contract state employees, SPP §§13-401 to 13-405.

CONTRACTS —Cont'd

Service contracts —Cont'd

Extension of appliance service contract, CL §14-1306.

Generally, CL §§14-401 to 14-410.

See SERVICE CONTRACTS AND CONSUMER PRODUCTS GUARANTY.

Not prerequisite to sale of merchandise, CL §13-311.

Procurement.

See PROCUREMENT.

Unfair or deceptive trade practices, CL §13-311.

Shore erosion control.

Awarding construction contracts, NR §8-1005.

Social services.

Department of human resources.

Medical assistance, HG §15-104.

Solid waste disposal facilities.

Charter counties, NR §3-9A-01.

Not deemed debt or gift of county, NR §3-9A-01.

Somerset county.

Competitive bidding and bonds, 25 §3.

Sovereign immunity.

Defense barred, SG §12-201.

Exclusions under subtitle, SG §12-201.

Legislative or judicial branches.

Applicability to contracts of, SG §12-204.

Limitation of actions, SG §12-202.

Specific performance.

General provisions.

See SPECIFIC PERFORMANCE.

Refusal to specifically enforce contract on grounds that adequate remedy in damages available, CJ §3-601.

State board of contract appeals.

Procurement.

Dispute resolution.

Appeals board, SF §§15-201, 15-205 to 15-212.

State contracts.

Discrimination.

Commercial discrimination, SF §§19-101 to 19-120.

See DISCRIMINATION.

State retirement and pension system.

Annuity contracts.

Application for contract required, SPP §30-307.

Defined, SPP §30-101.

Ownership, SPP §30-206.

Review required, SPP §30-208.

Fiduciary responsibilities.

Exculpatory agreements, SPP §21-208.

Social security benefits.

Agreement authorized, SPP §36-102.

Statute of limitations.

Employment contracts, CJ §5-101.

Sale of goods.

Breach of contract, CL §2-725.

Limitations by agreements may be reduced to less than one year, CL §2-725.

Sovereign immunity.

Limitation on claims under subtitle, SG §12-202.

Subdivisions.

Prince George's county.

Notice in contract of sale, RP §10-701.

Talbot county.

Competitive bidding and bonds, 25 §3.

Telegraph and telephone companies.

Telephone solicitations.

Enforcement of contract, CL §14-2203.

CONTRACTS —Cont'd

Therapy management contracts, HO §§12-6A-01 to 12-6A-10.

Time-sharing.

Sales contract, RP §11A-118.

Cancellation, RP §11A-114.

Information in contract, RP §11A-118.

Resale, RP §11A-115.

Vacation club membership, CL §14-2402.

Defined, RP §11A-101.

Information to be included, RP §11A-118.

Unconscionable contract or clause.

Remedies, RP §11A-125.

Vacation club membership, CL §14-2402.

Transportation department.

Bidding.

Waiver of requirements for competitive bidding, TR §2-109.

Responsibility of secretary, TR §2-103.

Waterborne marine fire protection, TR §2-110.

Unconscionability.

Sale of goods, CL §2-302.

Unemployment compensation.

Reciprocal arrangements.

Generally, LE §§8-701 to 8-705.

See UNEMPLOYMENT COMPENSATION.

Void agreements.

Agreement to commute, release or waive a right to benefits, LE §8-106.

United States.

Powers of counties and municipalities.

Authorized to enter into contracts for any works of improvement, 24 §6-202.

University of Maryland.

Medical system.

Annual contract, ED §13-306.

Variable life insurance and annuity contracts, IN §§16-601 to 16-603.

Viatical settlement contracts, IN §§8-601 to 8-611.

See VIATICAL SETTLEMENT CONTRACTS.

Victims of crime.

Notoriety of crimes contracts, CP §§11-621 to 11-633.

See NOTORIETY OF CRIMES CONTRACTS.

Video movie sales and rentals.

Membership contracts in video clubs, CL §14-1602.1.

Waiver.

Sale of goods.

Waiver of executory portion of contract, CL §2-209.

Warranty.

New home warranties.

General provisions, RP §§10-601 to 10-610.

See WARRANTY.

Washington suburban sanitary district.

Authority of public agencies, EN §9-1103.

Collective bargaining.

Outsourcing of work, 29 §11.5-110.

Payment of commission obligations, 29 §§1-301 to 1-304.

See WASHINGTON SUBURBAN SANITARY DISTRICT.

Water resources.

Federally constructed reservoirs.

Repayment of water-supply costs, EN §5-702.

Weights and measures.

Construed, AG §11-301.

Worcester county.

Competitive bidding and bonds, 25 §3.

CONTRACTS —Cont'd

Workers' compensation.
Agreements for waiver of rights, LE §9-104.
Insurance coverage.
Restrictions on agreements, LE §9-408.
Self-insurance agreement, IN §§25-301, 25-303, 25-306.
Yellow Dog contract act, LE §§4-301 to 4-322.
See COLLECTIVE BARGAINING.

CONTRACT STATE EMPLOYEES, SPP §§13-101 to 13-405.
Audits, SPP §13-205.
Certification, SPP §13-202.
Continuing certification, SPP §13-204.
Compliance with guidelines, SPP §13-203.
Construction of subtitle, SPP §13-201.
Continuing certification, SPP §13-204.
Transfer of contractual employees to budgeted positions, SPP §13-303.
Contractual employee.
Defined, SPP §1-101.
Definitions.
Contractual employee, SPP §1-101.
Service contracts, SPP §13-401.
Discrimination.
Recruitment and selection, SPP §13-203.
Guidelines.
Recruitment and selection, SPP §13-203.
Period of certification, SPP §13-202.
Recruitment and selection, SPP §13-203.
Scope of subtitle, SPP §13-201.
Service contracts, SPP §§13-401 to 13-405.
Approval, SPP §13-403.
Certifications by department, SPP §13-404.
Consideration of alternatives, SPP §13-405.
Cost comparison, SPP §13-405.
Definitions, SPP §13-401.
Exceptions to approval, SPP §13-403.
Exempt contracts, SPP §13-404.
Information by unit, SPP §13-405.
Nonexempt contracts, SPP §13-404.
Plan of assistance, SPP §13-405.
Public policy, SPP §13-402.
State policy, SPP §13-402.
Transfer of contractual employees to budgeted positions, SPP §§13-301 to 13-305.
Authorization, SPP §13-302.
Construction of subtitle, SPP §13-301.
Continuing certification, SPP §13-303.
Effect of subtitle, SPP §13-305.
Qualifications for transfer, SPP §13-302.
Rights on transfer, SPP §13-304.
Scope of subtitle, SPP §13-301.
Whistleblower protection.
Civil actions, SF §11-304.
Defenses, SF §11-306.
Damages and relief, SF §11-305.
Definitions, SF §11-301.
Reprisals against employees prohibited, SF §11-303.
Written notice to employees, SF §11-302.

CONTRIBUTING TO THE DELINQUENCY OF A MINOR.
Juvenile causes.
See JUVENILE CAUSES.

CONTRIBUTION AMONG JOINT TORTFEASORS, CJ §§3-1401 to 3-1409.
Citation of act, CJ §3-1408.

CONTRIBUTION AMONG JOINT TORTFEASORS —Cont'd
Construction and interpretation.
Severability of provisions, CJ §3-1409.
Uniformity of interpretation, CJ §3-1407.
Definitions, CJ §3-1401.
Discharge of liability or payment of share, CJ §3-1402.
Indemnity.
Rights of indemnity not impaired, CJ §3-1406.
Judgment against one tortfeasor.
Effect, CJ §3-1403.
Release.
Effect on injured person's claim, CJ §3-1404.
Effect on right of contribution, CJ §3-1405.
Right of contribution, CJ §3-1402.
Release.
Effect on right, CJ §3-1405.
Settlement.
Effect, CJ §3-1402.
Severability of provisions, CJ §3-1409.
Title of act, CJ §3-1408.

CONTRIBUTION AND EXONERATION.
Corporate director's liability for unlawful distributions, CA §2-312.
Corporations.
Director's liability for unlawful distributions.
Entitlement to contribution.
Limitation of action enforcing, CA §2-312.
Executors and administrators.
Exoneration of personal representatives for certain payments, ET §7-101.
Order in which assets appropriated.
Adjustments and contributions in other interests in remaining assets, ET §9-103.
Hazardous materials and substances.
Controlled hazardous substances.
Control fund.
Uniform contribution among tortfeasors act.
Applicability, EN §7-221.
Heirs.
Right of contribution against other heirs, ET §10-102.
Joint tortfeasors, CJ §§3-1401 to 3-1409.
See CONTRIBUTION AMONG JOINT TORTFEASORS.
Judgments.
Judgment of contribution or recovery over.
Circuit courts, CivProCir Rule 2-614.
District Court, CivProDist Rule 3-614.
Landlord and tenant.
Exculpatory clause.
Void in agreement between landlord and tenant, RP §8-105.
Legatees.
Right of contribution against other legatees, ET §10-102.
Wills.
When legatee entitled to exoneration, ET §4-406.
Limitation of actions.
Corporate director's liability for unlawful distributions, CA §2-312.

CONTRIBUTIONS AND EXPENSES OF ELECTION CAMPAIGN.
Disclosures by persons doing public business, EL §§14-101 to 14-108.
See CAMPAIGN FINANCE.
Generally, EL §§13-101 to 13-605.
See CAMPAIGN FINANCE.

CONTRIBUTIONS TO ASSOCIATIONS OR ORGANIZATIONS.
Coercing or intimidating another to contribute or donate, CR §3-707.

CONTRIBUTIONS TO CHARITABLE FUNDRAISING.
Fraudulent fundraising.
 Campaigns to benefit police, fire departments or public safety officers, CR §8-520.

CONTRIBUTORY NEGLIGENCE.
Bank deposits and collections.
 Unauthorized signature or alteration, customer's duty to report, CL §4-406.
Blind persons.
 Failure to carry cane or use guide dog, 30 §33.
Child's having access to firearm violation.
 Not evidence of contributory negligence, CR §4-104.
Criminal injuries compensation board.
 Effect upon awards on claims, CP §11-810.
Deaf or mute persons.
 Failure to use guide dog, 30 §33.
Drug dealer liability act.
 Inapplicable, CJ §3-1607.
Motor vehicles.
 Seatbelt or restraining devices.
  Failure to use in emergency vehicles, TR §22-412.4.

CONTROLLED DANGEROUS SUBSTANCE ANALOGUE.
Defined, CR §5-402.
Schedule I, CR §5-402.

CONTROLLED DANGEROUS SUBSTANCES, CR §§5-101 to 5-1101.
Acquired immune deficiency syndrome (AIDS).
 Educational program for violators, HG §18-339.
Administering.
 Drug induced conduct.
  Administering controlled dangerous substance without person knowledge, CR §5-624.
 Without prescription or order form, CR §5-601.
Administrative inspection warrants.
 Inspection of, areas, building, premises, CR §5-804.
Adult dependent care programs.
 Test of potential employees, HG §19-1903.
AIDS education program.
 Convicted person may be required to complete, CR §5-906.
Anabolic steroids.
 Controlled dangerous substances.
  Warning posted as to consequences of illegal use, CR §5-710.
Arrests.
 Warrantless arrest, CP §2-203.
Audiologists, hearing aid dealers and speech-language pathologists.
 Providing professional services while under the influence of alcohol or controlled dangerous substances.
  Grounds for denial, reprimand, suspension or revocation of license, HO §2-314.
Authorized providers.
 Registration, CR §§5-301 to 5-310.
 Unauthorized acts, CR §5-902.
Bail hearing.
 Hearsay, CR §5-809.
Boxing, sparring and wrestling.
 Urine tests to detect.
  Required by each boxer or kick boxer in contest, BR §4-315.

CONTROLLED DANGEROUS SUBSTANCES —Cont'd
Burden of proof.
 Establishing exemption, proviso or exception, CR §5-807.
Chain of custody.
 Statement establishing, CJ §10-1004.
Chemical tests, CJ §10-1001.
 Altering results of drug or alcohol screening, CR §10-111.
 Job-related alcohol and drug testing, HG §17-214.
 Reports.
  Availability to defense counsel, CJ §10-1003.
Chemist.
 Chain of physical custody or control, CJ §10-1002.
 Presence at criminal proceeding, CJ §10-1003.
 Reports of chemist, CJ §10-1001.
  Availability to defense counsel, CJ §10-1003.
Chiropractors.
 Providing professional services while under the influence.
  Denials, reprimands, suspensions and revocations of licenses, HO §3-313.
Commercial drivers' licenses.
 Disqualification of license, TR §16-812.
Contraband in place of confinement, CR §9-416.
Controlled paraphernalia, CR §5-620.
 Defined, CR §5-101.
Conviction of license holders.
 Report of conviction to licensing authority.
  Relationship between license and conviction, CR §5-810.
Correctional facility inmates.
 Good conduct credit for inmate serving sentence for violation.
  Calculating credit, COR §3-704.
Counterfeit substances.
 Possessing, manufacturing or distributing, CR §§5-604, 5-607.
Crimes, CR §§5-601 to 5-628, 5-808.
 Administering.
  Without prescription or order form, CR §5-601.
 AIDS education program.
  Convicted person may be required to complete, CR §5-906.
 Controlled paraphernalia, CR §5-620.
 Convictions.
  Reporting to licensing agency, Crim Rule 4-340.
 Counterfeiting or altering prescription.
  Issuing, passing, making or possession, CR §§5-606, 5-607.
  Obtaining controlled substance, CR §5-601.
 Counterfeit substance.
  Distributing, manufacturing or possessing, CR §§5-604, 5-607.
 Dispensing prescription drug without prescription or label, CR §5-701.
 Distributing, CR §§5-602, 5-607 to 5-609.
  Counterfeit substance, CR §§5-604, 5-607.
  Drug kingpins, CR §5-613.
  Equipment to produce controlled substances, CR §§5-603, 5-607.
  Faked controlled substances, CR §5-617.
  Firearm possessed, used, worn, carried or transported.
   Separate offense, enhanced sentence, forfeiture, CR §5-621.
  Minors used to distribute, CR §5-628.
  Registrants, unauthorized, CR §5-902.
  Schools, distributing near, CR §5-627.
  Unlawful distribution by registrants, CR §5-904.

CONTROLLED DANGEROUS SUBSTANCES
—Cont'd
Crimes —Cont'd
Distributing —Cont'd
Volume dealers, enhanced penalty, CR §5-612.
Drug induced conduct.
Administering controlled dangerous substance
without person knowledge, CR §5-624.
Drug kingpins, CR §5-613.
Drug paraphernalia, CR §5-619.
Authorized providers, prohibited acts, CR
§5-902.
Controlled paraphernalia, CR §5-620.
Immunity for public officials and employees
engaged in enforcement or prosecution, CR
§5-808.
Equipment to produce controlled substances.
Manufacturing, possessing or distributing, CR
§§5-603, 5-607 to 5-609.
Establishing exemption, proviso or exception.
Burden of proof, CR §5-807.
Faked controlled substances.
Distributing, CR §5-617.
Falsely assuming title of authorized provider or
dispenser.
Obtaining controlled substance, CR §5-601.
False name or address.
Obtaining controlled substance, CR §5-601.
False prescription.
Issuing, passing, making or possession, CR
§5-606.
False registration by manufacturer, distributor, or
dispenser, CR §5-903.
Felony offenses, CR §5-901.
Distribution, manufacture, possession, CR
§§5-607 to 5-609.
Financial transactions involving proceeds of drug
crime, CR §5-623.
Firearm possessed, used, worn, carried or
transported.
Separate offense, enhanced sentence, forfeiture,
CR §5-621.
Firearm possession by person convicted of drug
crime, CR §5-622.
Fraud, deceit, misrepresentation.
Obtaining controlled substance, CR §5-601.
Hearsay.
Admissibility at bail or sentencing hearing, CR
§5-809.
Immunity from criminal liability.
Officers and employees engaged in enforcement
or prosecution, CR §5-808.
Importers, CR §5-614.
Information communicated to physician not
privileged.
Attempting to obtain by fraud or other
subterfuge, CR §5-601.
Inhaling listed substances, CR §5-708.
Distribution of inhalant and instructions on
inhaling, CR §5-709.
Inspection of registrants premises.
Refusal of entry, CR §5-902.
Investigations by law enforcement officers, CR
§5-802.
Investigations by state police, CR §5-801.
Payment for information as to violations, CR
§5-803.
Keeping common nuisance, CR §§5-605, 5-607 to
5-609.
Keeping place for users or for selling.
Registrants, CR §5-902.

CONTROLLED DANGEROUS SUBSTANCES
—Cont'd
Crimes —Cont'd
License holders.
Report of conviction to licensing authority,
relationship between license and conviction,
CR §5-810.
Mandatory minimum sentence.
Repeat offenders, distribution, manufacture,
possession, CR §§5-607 to 5-609.
Manufacturing, CR §§5-602, 5-607 to 5-609.
Counterfeit substance, CR §§5-604, 5-607.
Drug kingpins, CR §5-613.
Equipment to produce controlled substances, CR
§§5-603, 5-607 to 5-609.
Firearm possessed, used, worn, carried or
transported.
Separate offense, enhanced sentence,
forfeiture, CR §5-621.
Minors used to distribute, CR §5-628.
Registrants, unauthorized, CR §5-902.
Schools, manufacturing near, CR §5-627.
Volume dealers, enhanced penalty, CR §5-612.
Minors used to distribute, deliver or manufacture,
CR §5-628.
Noncontrolled substance believing it to be
controlled substance.
Possessing or purchasing, CR §5-618.
Obtaining by fraud, misrepresentation or
subterfuge, CR §5-601.
Payment for information as to violations, CR
§5-803.
Penalties.
Additional penalties, CR §5-907.
Restitution, CR §5-610.
Possessing.
Counterfeit substance, CR §§5-604, 5-607 to
5-609.
Drug kingpins, CR §5-613.
Equipment to produce controlled substances, CR
§§5-603, 5-607.
Firearm possessed, used, worn, carried or
transported.
Separate offense, enhanced sentence,
forfeiture, CR §5-621.
Noncontrolled substance believing it to be
controlled substance, CR §5-618.
Registrants, unauthorized, CR §5-902.
Schools, possessing near, CR §5-627.
Volume dealers, enhanced penalty, CR §5-612.
With intent to distribute, manufacture or
dispense, CR §§5-602, 5-607.
Without prescription or order form, CR §5-601.
Presenting false or counterfeit prescription.
Obtaining controlled substance, CR §5-601.
Records and information.
Failure to keep, CR §5-902.
Repeat offenders.
Distribution, manufacture, possession, CR
§§5-607 to 5-609.
Punishment, CR §5-905.
Restitution, CR §5-610.
Sale of drug different from that offered, CR
§5-702.
Schedule I or II hallucinogenic substances.
Punishment, repeat offenders, mandatory
minimum, CR §5-609.
Schedule I or II narcotic drugs.
Distribution, manufacture, possession.
Punishment, repeat offenders, mandatory
minimum, CR §5-608.

CONTROLLED DANGEROUS SUBSTANCES
—Cont'd
Crimes —Cont'd
Schools.
Manufacturing, distributing, dispensing or
possessing near school, CR §5-627.
Second, third or fourth time offenders.
Distribution, manufacture, possession, CR
§§5-607 to 5-609.
Symbol required, removal, altering, CR §5-902.
Unsolicited mailing, CR §5-703.
Volume dealers, enhanced penalty, CR §5-612.
Criminal procedure.
Chemical tests, CJ §§10-1001 to 10-1004.
Custody.
Chain of physical custody or control.
Statements signed by successive officers or
persons having custody, CJ §10-1002.
**Dealers liability for death caused by use of
controlled dangerous substances,** CJ
§§3-1601 to 3-1607.
See DRUG DEALER LIABILITY ACT.
Definitions, CR §5-101.
Job-related controlled dangerous substances
testing, HG §17-214.
Licenses.
Persons convicted of controlled dangerous
substance offenses, 41 §1-501.
Nuisances.
Property used for controlled dangerous
substance offenses.
Abatement of nuisance action, RP §14-120.
Deliver defined, CR §5-101.
Dentists.
Providing professional services while under the
influence of alcohol or controlled dangerous
substances.
Denials, reprimands, probations, suspensions
and revocations of licenses, HO §4-315.
Department of health and mental hygiene.
Powers and responsibilities, CR §§5-201 to 5-204.
Dispensers.
Inspection of registrants premises, CR §5-305.
Prescriptions, CR §§5-501 to 5-505.
Recordkeeping requirements registrants, CR
§5-306.
Registration and inspection of premises, CR
§§5-301 to 5-310.
Distributing, CR §§5-602, 5-607 to 5-609.
Counterfeit substances, CR §§5-604, 5-607.
Distribute defined, CR §5-101.
Drug kingpins, CR §5-613.
Equipment to produce controlled substances, CR
§§5-603, 5-607.
Faked controlled substances, CR §5-617.
Firearm possessed, used, worn, carried or
transported.
Separate offense, enhanced sentence, forfeiture,
CR §5-621.
Minors used, CR §5-628.
Registrants.
Unauthorized distribution, CR §5-902.
Schools, distributing near, CR §5-627.
Unlawful distribution by registrants, CR §5-904.
Volume dealers, enhanced penalty, CR §5-612.
Distributors.
Inspection of registrants premises, CR §5-305.
Order form.
Distributing schedule I and II substances, CR
§5-303.

CONTROLLED DANGEROUS SUBSTANCES
—Cont'd
Distributors —Cont'd
Recordkeeping requirements registrants, CR
§5-306.
Registration and inspection of premises, CR
§§5-301 to 5-310.
Drug abuse.
General provisions.
See DRUG OR ALCOHOL ABUSE.
Drug asset forfeiture, CP §§12-101 to 12-505.
See DRUG ASSET FORFEITURE.
Drug free school zones.
Signs.
Board may designate areas and adopt
regulations, ED §4-124.
Drug induced conduct.
Administering controlled dangerous substance
without person knowledge, CR §5-624.
Drug kingpins, CR §5-613.
Conspiracy to manufacture, distribute, dispense or
transport into state, CR §5-613.
Defined, CR §5-613.
Enhanced penalty allowed, CR §5-613.
Merger of conviction with other crimes,
prohibition, CR §5-613.
Probation, prohibition, CR §5-613.
Prosecution for other crime allowed, CR §5-613.
Drug or alcohol abuse.
Neighborhood crime, drug and alcohol abuse
prevention and education programs, CR
§5-1001.
Maryland drug and alcohol grants program
fund, CR §5-1002.
Drug paraphernalia, CR §5-619.
Advertising, CR §5-619.
Authorized providers, prohibited acts, CR §5-902.
Defined, CR §5-101.
Delivery or sale, CR §5-619.
Factors considered to determine, CR §5-619.
Immunity for public officials and employees
engaged in enforcement or prosecution of
laws, CR §5-808.
Innocence of owner.
Not dispositive of finding intention or design,
CR §5-619.
Use or possession with intent to use, CR §5-619.
Drug trafficking, CR §§5-602, 5-607 to 5-609.
Counterfeit substances, CR §§5-604, 5-607.
Drug kingpins, CR §5-613.
Faked controlled substances, CR §5-617.
Firearm possessed, used, worn, carried or
transported.
Separate offense, enhanced sentence, forfeiture,
CR §5-621.
Minors used, CR §5-628.
Schools.
Manufacturing, distributing, dispensing or
possessing near, CR §5-627.
Employers and employees.
Job-related controlled dangerous substances
testing, HG §17-214.
Enforcement of title, CR §5-201.
Equipment to produce controlled substances.
Counterfeit substances, CR §§5-604, 5-607.
Manufacturing, possessing or distributing, CR
§§5-603, 5-607 to 5-609.
Eradication of plants.
Power of department, CR §5-201.
Establishing exemption, proviso or exception.
Burden of proof, CR §5-807.

CONTROLLED DANGEROUS SUBSTANCES
—Cont'd
Evidence.
Applicability of rules.
Procedure required after sentencing, Crim Rule 4-340.
Chain of custody.
Statement establishing chain, CJ §10-1004.
Chemical tests.
Reports, CJ §10-1001.
Nuisances.
Property used for controlled dangerous substance offenses.
Abatement actions.
Admissible evidence, RP §14-120.
Reports.
Availability to defense counsel, CJ §10-1003.
Exchange of information between government officials.
Department may arrange for, CR §5-201.
Exemptions from title, CR §5-103.
Faked controlled substances.
Distributing, CR §5-617.
Fees relating to registration and control of manufacture, distribution and dispensing.
Department may charge, CR §5-204.
Financial transactions involving proceeds of drug crime, CR §5-623.
Firearm possessed, used, worn, carried or transported.
Separate offense, enhanced sentence, forfeiture, CR §5-621.
Firearm possession by person convicted of drug crime, CR §5-622.
Forfeitures.
Firearms, CR §5-621.
Generalized unit to collect and file statistics.
Department may establish, CR §5-201.
Good conduct credit for inmate serving sentence for violations.
Calculating credit, COR §3-704.
Handgun permit holder under the influence.
Carrying, wearing or transporting handgun, CR §4-206.
Hearsay.
Admissibility at bail or sentencing hearing, CR §5-809.
Homicide by motor vehicle or vessel while impaired or under the influence, CR §§2-501 to 2-508.
Human immunodeficiency virus.
Educational program for violators, HG §18-339.
Immunity from criminal liability.
Public officials and employees engaged in enforcement or prosecution, CR §5-808.
Impaired by drugs.
Driving under the influence.
Generally.
See DRIVING UNDER THE INFLUENCE.
Informants.
Payment for information as to violations, CR §5-803.
Inhaling listed substances, CR §5-708.
Distribution of inhalant and instructions on inhaling, CR §5-709.
Injunctions restraining violations, CR §5-806.
Inmates at correctional facilities.
Good conduct credit for inmate serving sentence for violation.
Calculating credit, COR §3-704.

CONTROLLED DANGEROUS SUBSTANCES
—Cont'd
Inspection of registrants premises, CR §§5-305, 5-805.
Administrative inspection warrants, CR §5-804.
Investigations by law enforcement officers, CR §5-802.
Investigations by state police, CR §5-801.
Payment for information as to violations, CR §5-803.
Job-related controlled dangerous substances testing, HG §17-214.
Keeping common nuisance, CR §§5-605, 5-607.
Labor and industry.
Job-related alcohol and drug testing, HG §17-214.
Law enforcement officers.
Immunity from criminal liability.
Officers and employees engaged in enforcement or prosecution, CR §5-808.
Investigations by, CR §5-802.
Legislative findings, CR §5-102.
License holders.
Persons convicted of drug crimes.
Commercial drivers' licenses, 41 §1-506.
Definitions, 41 §1-501.
Determining whether defendant holds license, Crim Rule 4-340.
Disclosure of convictions, 41 §1-502.
Issuance of license, 41 §1-502.
Probation.
Conditions, 41 §1-504.
Imposition, 41 §1-503.
Violations, 41 §1-504.
Procedures, 41 §1-505.
Rules and regulations, 41 §1-507.
Suspension or revocation.
Completion of contracts, 41 §1-501.
Considerations, 41 §1-505.
Imposition, 41 §1-503.
Report of conviction to licensing authority.
Relationship between license and conviction, CR §5-810.
Life threatening injury by motor vehicle or vessel while impaired or under the influence, CR §§3-211, 3-212.
Mailing.
Unsolicited mailing, CR §5-703.
Manufacturing, CR §§5-602, 5-607 to 5-609.
Counterfeit substances, CR §§5-604, 5-607.
Drug kingpins, CR §5-613.
Equipment to produce controlled substances, CR §§5-603, 5-607 to 5-609.
Firearm possessed, used, worn, carried or transported.
Separate offense, enhanced sentence, forfeiture, CR §5-621.
Inspection of registrants premises, CR §5-305.
Manufacture defined, CR §5-101.
Minors used, CR §5-628.
Recordkeeping requirements registrants, CR §5-306.
Registrants.
Unauthorized distribution, CR §5-902.
Registration and inspection of premises, CR §§5-301 to 5-310.
Schools, manufacturing near, CR §5-627.
Marijuana.
Defined, CR §5-101.
Importers, CR §5-614.
Volume dealers, enhanced penalty, CR §5-612.

CONTROLLED DANGEROUS SUBSTANCES
—Cont'd

Methadone.
Dispensing by authorized provider, CR §5-502.

Minors used to distribute, deliver or manufacture, CR §5-628.

Morticians.
Chain of custody.
Statement of mortician establishing chain, CJ §10-1004.
Providing professional services while under the influence of alcohol or controlled dangerous substances, HO §7-318.

Motor vehicles.
Commercial drivers' licenses.
Driving under influence of.
Grounds for disqualification, TR §16-812.
Persons convicted of offenses, 41 §§1-501 to 1-507. See within this heading, "License holders."
Driving under the influence, TR §21-902.
Lesser included offenses, TR §26-405.
Homicide by motor vehicle or vessel while impaired or under the influence, CR §§2-501 to 2-508.
Life threatening injury by motor vehicle or vessel while impaired or under the influence, CR §§3-211, 3-212.

Noncontrolled substance believing it to be controlled substance.
Possessing or purchasing, CR §5-618.

Notices.
Job-related controlled dangerous substances testing.
Notification of positive test results, HG §17-214.
Nuisances.
Property used for controlled dangerous substance offenses, RP §14-120.

Nuisances.
Abatement of nuisances.
Property used for controlled dangerous substance offenses, RP §14-120.
Keeping common nuisance, CR §§5-605, 5-607.

Nurses.
Providing professional services while under the influence of alcohol or controlled dangerous substances, HO §8-316.

Nursing home administrators.
Providing professional services while under the influence of alcohol or controlled dangerous substances, HO §9-314.

Obtaining.
Fraud, misrepresentation or other subterfuge, CR §5-601.

Occupational therapists.
Providing professional services while under the influence of alcohol or controlled dangerous substances, HO §10-315.

Optometrists.
Providing professional services while under the influence of alcohol or controlled dangerous substances, HO §11-313.

Order form.
Distributing schedule I and II substances in accordance with, CR §5-303.

Payment for information as to violations, CR §5-803.

Penalties.
Additional penalties, CR §5-907.

Pharmacists and pharmacies.
Providing professional services while under the influence of alcohol or controlled dangerous substances, HO §12-313.

CONTROLLED DANGEROUS SUBSTANCES
—Cont'd

Physical therapists.
Providing professional services while under the influence of alcohol or controlled dangerous substances, HO §13-316.

Physician assistants.
Authority to prescribe, HO §15-302.2.
List of PA's with authority to board of pharmacy, HO §15-302.3.

Podiatrists.
Providing professional services while under the influence of alcohol or controlled dangerous substances, HO §16-311.

Possessing.
Counterfeit substances, CR §§5-604, 5-607.
Drug kingpins, CR §5-613.
Equipment to produce controlled substances, CR §§5-603, 5-607 to 5-609.
Firearm possessed, used, worn, carried or transported.
Separate offense, enhanced sentence, forfeiture, CR §5-621.
Noncontrolled substance believing it to be controlled substance, CR §5-618.
Opium, CR §5-503.
Possess defined, CR §5-101.
Registrants.
Unauthorized distribution, CR §5-902.
Schools, possessing near, CR §5-627.
With intent to distribute, manufacture or dispense, CR §§5-602, 5-607 to 5-609.
Without prescription or order form, CR §5-601.

Precursors to immediate precursors.
Control, CR §5-202.

Prescriptions and prescription drugs.
Codeine, CR §5-503.
Counterfeiting or altering prescription.
Evidence, affidavit of by authorized provider, CR §5-705.
Issuing, passing, making or possession, CR §5-606.
Dispense defined, CR §5-101.
Dispensing prescription drug without prescription or label, CR §5-701.
False prescriptions.
Issuing, passing, making or possession, CR §5-606.
Generally.
See PRESCRIPTIONS AND PRESCRIPTION DRUGS.
Inspection of registered dispensers premises, CR §5-305.
Methadone.
Dispensing by authorized provider, CR §5-502.
Opium, CR §5-503.
Possessing or administering without prescription, CR §5-601.
Prescription drug defined, CR §5-101.
Registration of dispensers and inspection of premises, CR §§5-301 to 5-310.
Regulations.
Adoption by department of health and mental hygiene, CR §5-704.
Sale of drug different from that offered, CR §5-702.
Sales of prescription drugs.
Inapplicability of title, CR §5-103.
Schedule II substances.
Required, exceptions, records inventories, refills, CR §5-501.

CONTROLLED DANGEROUS SUBSTANCES
—Cont'd
Prescriptions and prescription drugs —Cont'd
Schedule IV.
Dispensing, prescriptions, refills, CR §5-504.
Schedule V.
Dispensing for medical purposes.
Limited to, labels on containers, CR §5-505.
Unauthorized prescribing, CR §5-902.
Unsolicited mailing, CR §5-703.
Presumption as to registration.
Registration of manufactures, distributors or
dispensers.
Absence of proof person registrant, CR §5-807.
Prison inmates.
Contraband in place of confinement.
Delivery to, CR §9-416.
Good conduct credit for inmate serving sentence
for violation.
Calculating credit, COR §3-704.
Privileged communications.
Job-related controlled dangerous substances
testing.
Confidential information, HG §17-214.
Produce.
Defined, CR §5-101.
Professional or business license holders.
Report of conviction to licensing authority.
Relationship between license and conviction, CR
§5-810.
Purpose of article, CR §5-102.
Real property.
Nuisances.
Property used for controlled dangerous
substance offenses.
Abatement actions, RP §14-120.
Recordkeeping requirements registrants, CR
§5-306.
**Registration of manufacturers, distributors
and dispensers,** CR §§5-301 to 5-310.
Authority of persons registered, CR §5-301.
Manufacturers and distributors, CR §5-303.
Authorized providers, CR §5-304.
Each location, separate registration, CR §5-301.
Exceptions to registration requirement, CR
§5-301.
False registration, CR §5-903.
Inconsistent with public interest.
Manufacturers and distributors, CR §5-303.
Inspection of registrants premises, CR §§5-305,
5-805.
Administrative inspection warrants, CR §5-804.
Refusal of entry, penalty, CR §5-902.
Keeping a place resorted to by users or for selling
substances, CR §5-902.
Manufacturers and distributors, CR §5-303.
Presumption as to registration.
Absence of proof person registrant, CR §5-807.
Recordkeeping requirements registrants, CR
§5-306.
Regulations, department to adopt, CR §5-301.
Renewal.
Limitation on renewal term, CR §5-302.
Required, CR §5-301.
Suspension, revocation or denial.
Drug enforcement agency, notice to, CR §5-310.
Forfeiture of substances, CR §5-309.
Grounds, CR §5-307.
Limiting suspension to particular substance, CR
§5-307.
Notice and hearing, CR §5-308.

CONTROLLED DANGEROUS SUBSTANCES
—Cont'd
**Registration of manufacturers, distributors
and dispensers** —Cont'd
Suspension, revocation or denial —Cont'd
Sealing substance owned or possessed by
registrant, CR §5-309.
Term of registration, CR §5-302.
Unauthorized manufacture, distribution or
possession, CR §5-902.
Unlawful distribution, CR §5-904.
Waiver of requirement by department, CR §5-301.
Regulation to implement title.
Department may adopt, CR §5-203.
Reports.
Chemical tests, CJ §10-1001.
Availability to defense counsel, CJ §10-1003.
Sale of drug different from that offered, CR
§5-702.
Sales tax.
Imposition of tax, 24 §9-601.
Schedules, CR §§5-401 to 5-406.
Adding substances.
Factors considered, findings and orders,
objection to inclusion, CR §5-202.
Schedule II, required factors, CR §5-403.
Schedule IV, required factors, CR §5-405.
Schedule V, required factors, CR §5-406.
Control of substances listed.
Department's powers, CR §5-202.
Schedule I, CR §5-402.
Defined, CR §5-101.
Order form, distributing in accordance with, CR
§5-303.
Schedule II, CR §5-403.
Adding substances, CR §5-403.
Defined, CR §5-101.
Order form, distributing in accordance with, CR
§5-303.
Prescriptions.
Required, exceptions, records inventories,
refills, CR §5-501.
Schedule III, CR §5-404.
Defined, CR §5-101.
Schedule IV, CR §5-405.
Adding substances, CR §5-405.
Defined, CR §5-101.
Dispensing, prescriptions, refills, CR §5-504.
Schedule V, CR §5-406.
Adding substances, CR §5-406.
Defined, CR §5-101.
Dispensing for medical purposes.
Limited to, labels on containers, CR §5-505.
Updating and publication, CR §5-202.
Schools.
Drug free school zones.
Signs.
Board may designate areas and adopt
regulations, ED §4-124.
Manufacturing, distributing, dispensing or
possessing near school, CR §5-627.
Sentence and punishment.
Determination of whether defendant holds a
license, Crim Rule 4-340.
Good conduct credit for inmate serving sentence
for violation.
Calculating credit, COR §3-704.
Prior convictions.
Determination, Crim Rule 4-340.
Sentencing hearing.
Hearsay, CR §5-809.

CONTROLLED DANGEROUS SUBSTANCES —Cont'd

Short title.
Maryland controlled dangerous substances act, CR §5-1101.

Social workers.
Providing professional services while under the influence of alcohol or controlled dangerous substances, HO §19-311.

State police investigations, CR §5-801.
Payment for information as to violations, CR §5-803.

Sterile needle and syringe exchange.
Baltimore City, HG §§24-801 to 24-809.
See STERILE NEEDLE AND SYRINGE EXCHANGE.
Prince George's county, HG §§24-901 to 24-909.
See STERILE NEEDLE AND SYRINGE EXCHANGE.

Tests.
Chemical tests.
Reports, CJ §10-1001.
Availability to defense counsel, CJ §10-1003.
Job-related alcohol and controlled dangerous substances testing, HG §17-214.

Training programs on law enforcement.
Department may coordinate and cooperate in, CR §5-201.

Trial.
Chemist or analyst.
Presence at criminal proceedings, CJ §10-1003.

Unsolicited mailing, CR §5-703.

Use tax.
Accepted sales, 24 §9-601.
Imposition of tax, 24 §9-601.

Vessels and boats.
Homicide by motor vehicle or vessel while impaired or under the influence, CR §§2-501 to 2-508.
Life threatening injury by motor vehicle or vessel while impaired or under the influence, CR §§3-211, 3-212.

Volume dealers, enhanced penalty, CR §5-612.

Warrantless arrest, CP §2-203.

Warrants.
Administrative inspection warrants.
Inspection of, areas, building, premises, CR §5-804.

CONTROLLED HAZARDOUS SUBSTANCES.

General provisions.
See HAZARDOUS MATERIALS AND SUBSTANCES.

CONTROLLED PARAPHERNALIA.

Evidence of unlawful intent, CR §5-620.
Prohibition, CR §5-620.

CONTROLLED POISONS.

General provisions.
See POISONS.

CONVALESCENT OR CARE HOMES.

Hospitals.
See HOSPITALS.

Nursing homes.
Administrators.
See NURSING HOME ADMINISTRATORS.
General provisions.
See HOSPITALS.

CONVENTION CENTER FACILITIES.

Baltimore convention center financing fund, FI §13-716.

CONVENTION CENTER FACILITIES —Cont'd

Defined, FI §13-701.
Montgomery county conference center financing fund, FI §13-717.1.
Ocean City convention center financing fund, FI §13-717.

CONVENTIONS.

Constitutional conventions, MD Const Art XIV §2; US Const Art V.
Ballot questions generally, EL §§7-101 to 7-105.
Holding.
Automatic qualification of ballot question, EL §7-102.

National presidential nomination conventions.
Delegates and alternates.
Selection and certification by political parties, EL §8-501.

Ocean City convention hall.
General provisions, 41 §§14-701, 14-702.
See OCEAN CITY.

Trader licenses, BR §§17-1801 to 17-1816.
See TRADERS.

CONVERSIONS.

Appeals.
General provisions.
See CONSIGNMENT.

Banks and trust companies.
See BANKS AND TRUST COMPANIES.

Credit unions.
See CREDIT UNIONS.

Embezzlement.
See EMBEZZLEMENT.

Factors.
General provisions.
See CONSIGNMENT.

Food donated under federal program, CR §8-505.

Fraudulent conversion of leased or rented goods, CR §8-407.

Insurance companies.
Nonprofit health service plans, IN §14-130.
Stock and mutual insurers, IN §§3-120 to 3-121.1.

Larceny.
See LARCENY.

Medicaid fraud.
Converting benefit or payment intended for another, CR §8-510.

National banking associations, FI §§3-801, 3-802.

Negotiable instruments, CL §3-420.

Nonprofit health service plans, IN §14-130.

Partnership assets.
Fraudulent conversion, CR §8-401.

Savings and loan associations.
See SAVINGS AND LOAN ASSOCIATIONS.

Workers' compensation.
Injured workers' insurance fund.
Accounts' excess money, LE §10-122.
Special indemnity fund.
Conversion of investments, LE §10-217.
Uninsured employers' fund.
Accounts surplus, LE §10-318.

CONVEYANCES.

Business opportunities.
General provisions, BR §§14-101 to 14-129.
See START-UP BUSINESS VENTURES.

Deeds.
General provisions.
See DEEDS.

CONVEYANCES —Cont'd
Deeds of trust.
  See MORTGAGES AND DEEDS OF TRUST.
Easements.
  Generally.
    See EASEMENTS.
Foreclosures.
  Mortgages.
    Sale, PropSales Rule 14-206.
Forms.
  General provisions.
    See FORMS.
Fraudulent conveyances.
  Bulk transfers generally, CL §§6-101 to 6-111.
    See BULK TRANSFERS.
  General provisions, CL §§15-201 to 15-214.
    See FRAUDULENT CONVEYANCES.
Grants.
  General provisions.
    See GRANTS.
Ground rents.
  Order of conveyances, PropAct Rule 12-501.
Horizontal property act.
  See CONDOMINIUMS.
Insurance companies.
  Liquidation, rehabilitation, etc.
    Voidable transfers, IN §9-221.
Land installment contracts, RP §§10-101 to
  10-108.
  See LAND INSTALLMENT CONTRACTS.
Land patents.
  General provisions.
    See LAND PATENTS.
Land trust grant fund.
  Sale or transfer of property of land trust, NR
  §3-2A-08.
Leases.
  General provisions.
    See LANDLORD AND TENANT.
Lottery being engaged in.
  Void conveyance, CR §12-209.
Maryland railroad companies.
  Signature of president of company required, PUC
  §9-303.
Minors.
  Married minors, ET §13-503.
  Veterans.
    Disability of infancy removed for veterans, etc.,
    and their wives, ET §13-503.
Mortgages and deeds of trust.
  General provisions.
    See MORTGAGES AND DEEDS OF TRUST.
Partnerships.
  General provisions.
    See PARTNERSHIPS.
Public works.
  Board.
    Lands owned by state due to their relationship
    to state waters.
      Conditions to conveyance of title, SF §10-402.
      Scope of provisions, SF §10-401.
Railroad companies organized under laws of
  state.
  Signature of president required, PUC §9-303.
Receivers.
  District Court, CivProDist Rule 3-722.
Recordation.
  General provisions.
    See RECORDATION.
Releases.
  General provisions.
    See RELEASES.

CONVEYANCES —Cont'd
Releases —Cont'd
  Mortgages and deeds of trust.
    See MORTGAGES AND DEEDS OF TRUST.
Southern Maryland higher education center.
  Real property, ED §24-308.
Uniform laws.
  Uniform fraudulent conveyance act.
    General provisions, CL §§15-201 to 15-214.
    See FRAUDULENT CONVEYANCES.
Vendors' liens.
  See VENDORS' LIENS.
Warranty.
  General provisions.
    See WARRANTY.
Water and sewer systems.
  Authorities.
    Conveyance of project by authority to
    municipality, EN §9-953.
Waters of the state.
  Public works board.
    Lands owned by state due to their relationship
    to state waters.
      Conveyance of title, SF §§10-401, 10-402.

CONVICTIONS.
Impeachment by evidence of conviction of
  crime, Evid Rule 5-609.
Motor vehicles.
  Driver license compact.
    See DRIVER LICENSE COMPACT.
Persons erroneously convicted, sentenced or
  confined.
  Payment of grant, SF §10-501.
Post conviction procedure, Crim Rules 4-401 to
  4-408.
  Generally.
    See POST CONVICTION PROCEDURE.
Sentence and punishment.
  See SENTENCE AND PUNISHMENT.

CONVICTS.
Escape.
  See ESCAPE.
Habeas corpus.
  General provisions.
    See HABEAS CORPUS.
Local correctional facilities.
  See JAILS.
Parole.
  See PAROLE AND PROBATION.
State correctional facilities.
  See PRISONS AND PRISONERS.
Voter registration disqualifications, EL §3-102.
  Report of voter status from clerk of court, EL
  §3-504.

COOLING SYSTEM CONTRACTORS.
Air conditioning and heating contractors, BR
  §§9A-101 to 9A-602.
  See AIR CONDITIONING AND HEATING
    CONTRACTORS.

COOPERATIVE HOUSING CORPORATIONS.
Actions.
  Actions against governing body.
    Actual damages, RP §14-118.
  Developers.
    Implied warranty, CA §5-6B-04.
    Misrepresentation of facts.
      Actions to enforce liability, CA §5-6B-03.
Applicability of provisions.
  Applicability of sections 5-6B-02 through 5-6B-04
    and 5-6B-06 through 5-6B-12, CA §5-6B-20.

COOPERATIVE HOUSING CORPORATIONS —Cont'd

Applicability of provisions —Cont'd
Cooperative interests.
Applicability of commercial law article, CA §5-6B-17.
Corporation law.
Applicability of general corporation law, CA §5-6B-15.
Statewide effect, CA §5-6B-19.
Subtitle applicable to all cooperative housing corporations, CA §5-6B-20.

Articles of incorporation.
Articles filed with department of assessments and taxation, CA §5-6B-20.

Building codes.
Full force and effect, CA §5-6B-19.

Candidate signs.
Prohibition or restriction of display of, CA §5-6B-18.2.

Certificates.
Membership certificates.
Defined, CA §5-6B-01.

Commercial law.
Cooperative interests.
Applicability of Title 8, CA §5-6B-13.
Applicability of Title 9, CA §5-6B-17.

Consumer protection, CA §5-6B-12.

Cooperative interest.
Commercial law article.
Applicability of Title 8, CA §5-6B-13.
Applicability of Title 9, CA §5-6B-17.
Contract for initial sale, CA §5-6B-02.
Defined, CA §5-6B-01.
Interests of secured party, CA §5-6B-17.
Maryland security law.
Not security under, CA §5-6B-13.
Personal property.
Deemed personal property, CA §5-6B-16.
Possessory interest.
Evidenced by proprietary lease not severed from cooperative interest, CA §5-6B-16.
Sales.
Deposits made held in escrow, CA §5-6B-11.
Securities.
Not security under Maryland security law, CA §5-6B-13.
Transfers.
Deemed personal property, CA §5-6B-16.

Cooperative project.
Defined, CA §5-6B-01.

Corporation law.
Applicability of general corporation law, CA §5-6B-15.

Counties.
Local governments. See within this heading, "Local governments."

Damages.
Actions against governing body.
Actual damages, RP §14-118.

Definitions, CA §5-6B-01.
Actions against governing body.
Governing body, RP §14-118.
Consumer protection.
Consumer, CA §5-6B-12.
Lease extension for designated households, CA §5-6B-07.

Deposits.
Sales of cooperative interests held in escrow, CA §5-6B-11.

COOPERATIVE HOUSING CORPORATIONS —Cont'd

Developer.
Actions.
Limitation of action, CA §5-6B-04.
Defined, CA §5-6B-01.
Failure of developer to comply with requirements.
Initial purchaser may rescind, CA §5-6B-03.
Applicability to units used and occupied for nonresidential purposes.
Section inapplicable, CA §5-6B-03.
Waiver of rights.
Rights of initial purchasers may not be waived, CA §5-6B-03.
Misrepresentation of facts.
Liability, CA §5-6B-03.
Actions to enforce, CA §5-6B-03.

Effect of act.
Statewide effect, CA §5-6B-19.

Electronic notice of meetings and other member information, CA §5-6B-18.3.

Electronic transmission of votes, CA §5-6B-18.4.

Enforcement.
Consumer protection.
Violations, CA §5-6B-12.

Escrow.
Sales of cooperative interests.
Deposits held in escrow, CA §5-6B-11.

Forms.
Residential rental facility.
Facility acquired or owned by cooperative housing corporation.
Notice to tenants, CA §5-6B-05.

Governing body, RP §14-118.

Immunity.
Actions against governing body.
Directors or officers, RP §14-118.

Implied warranties, CA §5-6B-04.

Leases, CA §5-6B-07.
Proprietary lease.
Defined, CA §5-6B-01.

Liability.
Actions against governing body.
Directors or officers.
Immunity, RP §14-118.
Agents, CJ §5-406.
Developers.
Misrepresentation of facts, CA §5-6B-03.
Actions to enforce, CA §5-6B-03.

Limitation of actions.
Implied warranties.
Suit for enforcement, CA §5-6B-04.

Local governments.
Laws and ordinances.
Consumer protection.
Adoption, CA §5-6B-12.
Copies forwarded to secretary of state, CA §5-6B-12.
First right of purchase, CA §§5-6B-08, 5-6B-09.
Imposing unfair burden.
Preempted, CA §5-6B-19.
Rental housing emergencies, CA §5-6B-10.
Same terms and conditions initially offered, CA §5-6B-09.
Waiver.
Local government may waive right to purchase, CA §5-6B-08.

Maryland securities law.
Cooperative interests not security under, CA §5-6B-13.

COOPERATIVE HOUSING CORPORATIONS
—Cont'd
Membership certificates.
Affidavit of title in.
Holder or transferee takes title free and clear of
all claims and rights, CA §5-6B-06.
Local governments.
First right of purchase.
Affidavit in membership certificate.
Grantee takes title free and clear of claims
and rights, CA §5-6B-09.
Mergers or consolidations.
Circumventing subtitle.
Mergers or consolidations undertaken for
purpose of circumventing subtitle.
Prohibited, CA §5-6B-18.
Misrepresentation of facts.
Developers.
Liability, CA §5-6B-03.
Month to month tenancy.
Residential rental facility.
Facility acquired or owned by cooperative
housing corporation.
Conversion to month to month tenancy, CA
§5-6B-05.
Municipal corporations.
Local governments. See within this heading,
"Local governments."
No-impact home-based businesses.
Defined, CA §5-6B-01.
Fees, CA §5-6B-18.1.
Prohibition on use of residential unit as, CA
§5-6B-18.1.
Prohibition or restriction of commercial or
business activity in general.
Establishment and operation not construed to
be prohibited by, CA §5-6B-18.1.
Nonresidential purposes.
Units used and occupied for.
Applicability of section, CA §5-6B-03.
Contract for initial sale of cooperative interest.
Public offering statements.
Applicability of section, CA §5-6B-02.
Notice.
Meetings and other member information, CA
§5-6B-18.3.
Rescission rights.
Contract for initial sale.
Notice of rescission rights.
Prerequisite to enforcement, CA §5-6B-02.
Residential rental facility.
Facility acquired or owned by cooperative
housing corporation.
Lease extension for designated households.
Delivery of additional documents with
notice, CA §5-6B-07.
Notice to tenants, CA §5-6B-05.
When notice given, CA §5-6B-20.
Warranties.
Implied warranties.
Notice of defects, CA §5-6B-04.
Option to purchase.
Residential rental facilities, CA §5-6B-06.
Personal property.
Cooperative interests.
Deemed personal property, CA §5-6B-16.
**Possessory interest evidenced by proprietary
lease.**
Cooperative interest.
Not severed from, CA §5-6B-16.

COOPERATIVE HOUSING CORPORATIONS
—Cont'd
Public offering statements.
Amendments, supplements or modifications, CA
§5-6B-03.
Contents, CA §5-6B-02.
Initial sales, CA §5-6B-02.
Summaries, CA §5-6B-02.
Purchaser.
Initial purchaser.
Defined, CA §5-6B-01.
Records, examination and copying by public,
CA §5-6B-18.5.
Rental housing emergencies, CA §5-6B-10.
Rescission of contract.
Applicability to units used and occupied for
nonresidential purposes.
Section inapplicable, CA §5-6B-03.
Failure of developer to comply with requirements,
CA §5-6B-03.
Notice of rescission rights.
Prerequisite to enforcement, CA §5-6B-02.
Waiver.
Attempted waiver void, CA §5-6B-03.
Rights of initial purchaser may not be waived,
CA §5-6B-03.
When initial purchaser may rescind, CA §5-6B-03.
Residential rental facilities.
Acquired or owned by cooperative housing
corporation.
Lease extension for designated households, CA
§5-6B-07.
Local governments.
First right of purchase. See within this
heading, "Local governments."
Notice to tenants.
Failure of landlord or owner to give notice,
CA §5-6B-05.
When notice given, CA §5-6B-20.
Option to purchase, CA §5-6B-06.
Vacation of premises by tenants, CA §5-6B-05.
Notice to tenants.
Delivery of additional documents with
notice concerning lease extension for
designated households, CA §5-6B-07.
Defined, CA §5-6B-01.
Resolution to confirm status, CA §5-6B-20.
Restraints of trade.
Economic activity not deemed conspiracy or
combination in restraint of trade, CA
§5-6B-14.
Sales.
Escrow.
Deposits held in escrow, CA §5-6B-11.
Initial sale.
Defined, CA §5-6B-01.
Public offering statements, CA §5-6B-02.
Security interests.
Cooperative interests.
Not security under Maryland securities law, CA
§5-6B-13.
Perfection.
Membership certificates.
Financial statement.
Filing, CA §5-6B-17.
Possession of, CA §5-6B-17.
Security interests attached prior to July 1,
1986, CA §5-6B-20.
Standards.
Consumer protection.
Minimum standards.
Provided, CA §5-6B-12.

COOPERATIVE HOUSING CORPORATIONS —Cont'd

Status.
Articles of incorporation reflecting status, CA §5-6B-20.
Resolution to confirm status, CA §5-6B-20.

Taxation.
Assessments.
Valuation.
Real property owned by cooperative housing corporation, TP §8-106.

Transfers.
Cooperative interest.
Transferred by notation on books and records and the execution and delivery to transferee, CA §5-6B-16.

Unit.
Defined, CA §5-6B-01.

Votes.
Assignment of votes.
Each unit to have one vote, CA §5-6B-18.
E-mail transmission of votes or proxies, CA §5-6B-18.4.

Waiver.
Attempted waiver void, CA §5-6B-03.
Local governments.
First right of purchase.
Local government may waive rights, CA §5-6B-08.
Residential rental facilities.
Facility acquired or owned by cooperative housing corporations.
Tenants may not waive rights, CA §5-6B-05.
Rights of initial purchasers may not be waived, CA §5-6B-03.

Warranties, CA §5-6B-04.

Zoning codes.
Full force and effect, CA §5-6B-19.

COOPERATIVES.

Agricultural cooperatives.
Agricultural marketing associations.
See AGRICULTURAL COOPERATIVES.
General provisions, CA §§5-501 to 5-532.
See AGRICULTURAL COOPERATIVES.

Consumer cooperatives.
See CONSUMER COOPERATIVES.

Contracts.
Directors.
Transaction or contract between director and corporation, CA §2-419.

Corporations.
Consumer cooperatives.
See CONSUMER COOPERATIVES.
Cooperative housing corporations.
See COOPERATIVE HOUSING CORPORATIONS.

Credit unions.
General provisions.
See CREDIT UNIONS.

Electric cooperatives.
General provisions, CA §§5-601 to 5-642.
See ELECTRIC COOPERATIVES.
Governing law, PUC §7-104.

Foreign cooperatives.
Name.
Exceptions as to certain foreign cooperatives, CA §5-5A-10.

Housing.
Cooperative housing corporations.
See COOPERATIVE HOUSING CORPORATIONS.

COOPERATIVES —Cont'd

Name.
Use of term "cooperative," CA §5-5A-10.

Stores.
Mining company.
Operation of any but cooperative stores prohibited, 23 §235.

Transportation cooperatives, CA §5-6A-01.

COORDINATE SYSTEM, RP §§14-401 to 14-407.

Applicability of provisions.
Exceptions, RP §14-402.

Definition of "Maryland coordinate system," RP §14-401.

Designation that survey based on Maryland coordinate system, RP §14-403.

National geodetic survey.
Adoption of standards of, RP §14-405.
Conformance with, RP §14-404.

Non-exclusive nature of system, RP §14-407.

Plane rectangular coordinates, RP §14-404.

Scope of provisions.
Exceptions, RP §14-402.

Standards, RP §14-405.

Triangulation stations, RP §14-406.

Use for land description.
Designation on land description, RP §14-403.
System not exclusive, RP §14-407.

COPARTNERS.

General provisions.
See PARTNERSHIPS.

COPIES.

Banks and trust companies.
Commissioner of financial regulation.
Certified copies of records, FI §2-108.

Boards and commissions.
Fees.
Commissions exempt from fees, RP §3-603.

Certified copies.
Fees, RP §3-602.
Commissioners exempt from fees, RP §3-603.
Counties exempt from fees, RP §3-603.
Public records, CJ §10-204.

Clerks of court.
Plats of subdivisions.
Disposition of copies, RP §3-304.

Corporations.
Articles or certificate of incorporation.
Evidence of existence of corporation, CA §1-206.

Counties.
Fees.
Counties exempt from fees, RP §3-603.
Home rule for code counties.
Compilation of public local law, 25B §12.
Maps.
Certified copies as evidence, 75 §84.

Depositions.
Furnishing copies.
Circuit courts, CivProCir Rule 2-415.

Duplicate copies.
Fees exemptions, RP §3-603.

Evidence, CJ §10-204.

Expungement of records.
Applications.
No charges filed, Crim Rule 4-503.
Petitions.
Charges filed, Crim Rule 4-504.

Fees.
Certified copies, RP §3-602.
Exemption from fees, RP §3-603.

COPIES —Cont'd
Fees —Cont'd
Reproduced copies, RP §3-602.
Exemption from fees, RP §3-603.
Health insurance.
Request for copy of application when policy
reinstated or renewed, IN §12-206.
Insurance.
Health insurance.
Request for copy of application when policy
reinstated or renewed, IN §12-206.
Life insurance and annuities.
Request for copy of application when policy
reinstated or renewed, IN §12-206.
Reports of examinations, IN §2-209.
Insurance commissioner.
Regulations adopted, IN §2-109.
Insurance companies.
Certificates of authority, IN §2-111.
Land installment contracts.
Purchaser to give receipt for copy, RP §10-102.
Vendor to give copy to purchaser, RP §10-102.
Life insurance and annuities.
Request for copy of application when policy
reinstated or renewed, IN §12-206.
Maps.
Certified copies.
County maps, 75 §84.
Medical records.
Costs, HG §4-304.
Request for copies, HG §4-304.
Motor vehicles.
Security interests.
Duplicate of security interest filing, TR §13-202.
Post conviction procedures.
Copy of order and statement of court, Crim Rule
4-407.
Records.
Access to court records, CJA Rule 16-1003.
Access to public records, SG §10-620.
Certified copies of public records, CJ §10-204.
Registers of wills.
Fees, ET §2-206.
Subdivisions.
Plats of subdivisions.
Disposition of copies, RP §3-304.
Summons and process.
Requirements preliminary to summons.
District Court, CivProDist Rule 3-111.
Vital records.
See VITAL RECORDS.

COPPIN STATE UNIVERSITY.
**Payments from state relative to private
donations,** ED §17-302.

COPYRIGHTS.
Authors.
Protection of rights, US Const Art I §8.
Constitutional provisions, US Const Art I §8.
Court of appeals.
Reports, CJ §13-203.
Royalties, CL §§11-1401 to 11-1405.
Applicability of provisions, CL §11-1404.
Area.
Defined, CL §11-1401.
Attorneys' fees, CL §11-1405.
Contract for payment, CL §11-1402.
Copyright owner.
Defined, CL §11-1401.
Damages, CL §11-1405.
Definitions, CL §11-1401.

COPYRIGHTS —Cont'd
Royalties —Cont'd
Disclosures, CL §11-1403.
Generally, CL §11-1402.
Performing rights societies.
Applicability of subtitle, CL §11-1404.
Defined, CL §11-1401.
Proprietor.
Defined, CL §11-1401.
Royalty or royalties.
Defined, CL §11-1401.
Unfair or deceptive acts, CL §11-1403.

CORAM NOBIS.
Writs of error coram nobis.
District Court judges.
Authority to issue, CJ §1-609.

CORD.
Weights and measures.
Defined, AG §11-101.

CORD BLOOD BANKS.
**Umbilical cord blood donations, hospitals to
arrange,** HG §19-308.7.

CORN.
Grain.
General provisions.
See GRAIN.

CORN MEAL.
Weights and measures.
Sale, AG §11-313.

CORONERS.
Morticians.
See MORTICIANS.
Postmortem examiners.
See POSTMORTEM EXAMINERS.

CORPORAL PUNISHMENT.
Schools, ED §7-306.

CORPORATE TAKEOVERS.
Fiduciaries.
Successor corporate fiduciaries, ET §§15-1A-01 to
15-1A-05.
See FIDUCIARIES.

CORPORATIONS.
Abandoned property disposition, CL §§17-101 to
17-326.
See ABANDONED PROPERTY DISPOSITION.
Accountants.
Misrepresentation that business may provide
services, BOP §2-604.
Offices.
Registration, BOP §2-501.
Permits.
General provisions, BOP §§2-401 to 2-416.
See ACCOUNTANTS.
Accounts and accounting.
Department.
Fees, CA §1-203.
Records, CA §2-111.
Presumed proper, CA §1-402.
Acknowledgments.
Alternative to acknowledgment, CA §1-302.
Articles of incorporation, CA §2-102.
By whom made, CA §1-303.
Certificate of incorporation, CA §2-102.
Charter.
Articles of amendment, CA §1-301.
Articles of incorporation, CA §2-102.
Restatement, CA §1-301.

CORPORATIONS —Cont'd
Acknowledgments —Cont'd
Consolidation, merger and other transfers of
property, CA §1-301.
Recording papers with department, CA §1-201.
Acquisition of another corporation.
Issuance of stock, CA §2-303.
Actions.
By or in right of corporation.
Indemnification of directors, officers, employees
and agents, CA §2-418.
Foreign corporations.
Compliance with subtitle.
Not consent to suit, CA §7-210.
Revocation of permit for conduct connected with
organized crime, CA §1-405.
When suit may be maintained by foreign
corporations, CA §7-301.
Forfeiture of charter.
Conduct in connection with organized crime, CA
§1-405.
Indemnification of directors, officers, employees
and agents, CA §2-418.
Proceedings by corporation.
Acting through receiver, trustee or stockholders
in representative capacity, CA §1-403.
Representation in court by persons other than
lawyers, BOP §10-206.
Sale of property and franchises under judicial
proceedings.
General provisions, CA §3-302.
Sue and be sued.
Powers, CA §2-103.
Address.
Defined, CA §1-101.
Admissions and amusement tax.
Payment of tax.
Liability of corporate officers, TG §4-301.
Affidavits.
Mortgages and deeds of trust.
Consideration true and bona fide, RP §4-106.
African American museum corporation, SG
§§9-2601 to 9-2614.
See AFRICAN AMERICAN MUSEUM
CORPORATION.
Agency.
Acknowledgments.
By appointed attorney, CA §1-303.
Agents.
Foreign corporations.
See FOREIGN CORPORATIONS.
Generally. See within this heading, "Officers and
agents."
**Agricultural and resource-based industry
development corporation,** 41 §§13-501 to
13-515.
See AGRICULTURAL AND RESOURCE-BASED
INDUSTRY DEVELOPMENT
CORPORATION.
Alcoholic beverages.
Fines and penalties, 2B §16-504.
Licenses.
Application for corporation, 2B §9-101.
Renewal.
Substitution of officers, 2B §10-301.
Revocation and suspension.
Felony conviction of stockholder, 2B §10-401.
Ambulances.
Provision of fire, ambulance and rescue services
by for-profit entities, PS §7-401.

CORPORATIONS —Cont'd
Amendments.
Charters. See within this heading, "Charters."
Existing corporations be subject thereto, CA
§1-102.
Transfer of assets. See within this heading,
"Consolidation, merger and other transfers of
property."
Appeals.
Appearance of counsel.
Requirement of appearance of counsel, AppRev
Rule 8-402.
Appearance.
Appeals.
Requirement of appearance of counsel, AppRev
Rule 8-402.
Attorney requirement, CivProCir Rule 2-131;
CivProDist Rule 3-131.
Exceptions to attorney requirement, BOP
§10-206.
Criminal cases.
Return of summons as appearance, CP §4-203.
Applicability of article, CA §1-102.
Appraisals.
Consolidation, merger and other transfers of
property.
Proceedings by objecting stockholders. See
within this heading, "Stock and
stockholders."
Architects.
Permits.
General provisions, BOP §§3-401 to 3-409.
See ARCHITECTS.
Articles of incorporation. See within this
heading, "Charters."
Articles of transfer.
Defined, CA §1-101.
Assets.
Defined, CA §1-101.
Transfer of assets. See within this heading,
"Consolidation, merger and other transfers of
property."
Associations.
Directors and officers.
Standard of care required of directors, CA
§2-405.1.
Unincorporated associations, CA §1-404.
Assumed business name.
Trade names generally, CA §1-406.
Attachment.
Against whom available, CJ §3-303.
Attorney general.
Forfeiture of charter.
Conduct in connection with organized crime, CA
§1-405.
Institution of proceedings, CA §3-513.
Ultra vires.
In proceedings by attorney general, CA §1-403.
Attorneys at law.
Acknowledgments.
Appointed attorney, CA §1-303.
Admission to the bar.
Exceptions to requirement.
House counsel, BOP §10-206.
Officer of corporation appearing in its behalf
in certain actions, BOP §10-206.
Appearances in civil matters, CivProCir Rule
2-131; CivProDist Rule 3-131.
Exception to attorney requirement, BOP §10-206.
House counsel.
Admission to the bar.
Exceptions to requirement, BOP §10-206.

CORPORATIONS —Cont'd
Attorneys at law —Cont'd
Legal services corporation, 10 §§45A to 45O.
See ATTORNEYS AT LAW.
Representation in court by persons other than
lawyers, BOP §10-206.
Audits.
Fund for costs, CA §1-203.3.
Aviation.
Potomac highlands airport authority.
Authority constitutes public corporation, TR
§10-103.
Bainbridge development department.
General provisions, 83A §§5-1601 to 5-1609.
See BAINBRIDGE DEVELOPMENT
CORPORATION.
Bankruptcy and insolvency, CA §3-301.
Banks and trust companies.
See BANKS AND TRUST COMPANIES.
Bank service corporations.
See BANKS AND TRUST COMPANIES.
Benevolent corporations.
Property.
Restrictions on holdings, CA §5-701.
Bond issues.
Issuing, CA §2-103.
Securities act.
General provisions, CA §§11-101 to 11-805.
See SECURITIES.
Signatures and seals.
Facsimile on bonds, CA §2-212.
Bonds, surety.
Stock and stockholders.
Indemnity for lost certificate, CA §2-213.
Venue.
Surety on bonds, CJ §6-202.
Bonus tax.
Payment.
Acceptance of records of filing by department.
Conclusive evidence of payment, CA §1-206.
Bridges, 23 §§140 to 143.
See BRIDGE AND CANAL COMPANIES.
Bulk transfers.
Exception of sales on dissolution or
reorganization, CL §6-103.
Business combinations.
Real estate investment trust.
Power to enter into business combinations, CA
§8-301.
Special voting requirements, CA §§3-601, 3-603.
Applicability of subtitle to Maryland
corporations only, CA §3-604.
Definitions, CA §§3-601, 3-603.
Exemptions, CA §3-603.
Generally, CA §3-602.
Title of act, CA §3-605.
Trusts and trustees.
Real estate investment trust.
Power to enter into business combination, CA
§8-301.
Business opportunities.
General provisions, BR §§14-101 to 14-129.
See START-UP BUSINESS VENTURES.
Business regulation and licensure.
General penalty.
Application to corporations, BR §17-2106.
Business trusts.
Classified as for tax purposes, CA §12-102.
Generally, CA §§12-101 to 12-810.
See BUSINESS TRUSTS.

CORPORATIONS —Cont'd
Bylaws.
Classification of directors, CA §2-110.
Contents, CA §2-110.
Corrections.
Certificate of correction. See within this
heading, "Certificate of correction."
Directors.
Classification of directors, CA §2-110.
Power to adopt, CA §2-109.
Specifying number of directors, CA §2-402.
Keeping of bylaws, CA §2-110.
Power to make and alter, CA §2-103.
Provisions of articles of incorporation included in,
CA §2-104.
Special meeting of stockholders.
Calling, CA §2-502.
Stockholder meetings.
Remote communications, CA §2-502.1.
Subsequent bylaws.
Adoption by stockholders, CA §2-109.
Campaign finance.
Contributions by corporations, subsidiaries or
affiliated corporations.
Considered as one contributor, EL §13-226.
Canals.
Bridge and canal companies, 23 §§140 to 143.
See BRIDGE AND CANAL COMPANIES.
Capital.
Stock.
Capital stock and stockholders. See within this
heading, "Stock and stockholders."
Catholic church.
See ROMAN CATHOLIC CHURCH.
Cecil county.
Alcoholic beverages.
Licenses, 2B §9-101.
Cemeteries.
Engaging in operation of cemetery or burial goods
business, BR §5-401.
Permits, BR §§5-402 to 5-404.
Certificate of correction.
Contents.
Acknowledgments.
Consolidation, merger and other transfers of
property.
Articles of share exchange, CA §1-301.
Fees.
Recording, filing and other fees, CA §1-203.
Generally, CA §1-207.
Certificate of notice.
Generally, CA §1-207.1.
Charitable corporations.
Disposition of property by court on dissolution, CA
§5-209.
Nonstock corporations.
Assets subject to charitable or other
restrictions, CA §5-702.
Property.
Restrictions on holdings, CA §5-701.
Transfers from charitable corporations on
contingency.
Rule against perpetuities not applicable, ET
§11-102.
Charters.
Adoption of code of Maryland.
Rights under charter or grant from state, 1 §4.
Amendments.
Abandonment of proposed amendments, CA
§2-612.

CORPORATIONS —Cont'd
Charters —Cont'd
Amendments —Cont'd
Articles of amendment, CA §§1-203, 1-301.
Acknowledging, CA §1-301.
Effect, CA §2-611.
Effective date of articles, CA §2-610.1.
Execution, CA §2-610.
Fees, CA §1-203.
Filing, CA §2-610.
Reduction of stated capital, CA §2-306.
Signing, CA §1-301.
Verification under oath, CA §1-301.
Witnessing, CA §1-301.
Contents, CA §2-609.
Generally, CA §2-607.
When increases authorized stock of
corporation, CA §2-607.
Department.
Action of, CA §2-611.
Directors.
Voting on amendments, CA §2-604.
No stock outstanding or subscribed for, CA
§2-603.
Execution of articles, CA §2-610.
Filing of articles.
Department of assessments and taxation, CA
§2-610.
No stock outstanding or subscribed for, CA
§2-603.
Generally, CA §2-601.
Multiple amendments, CA §2-606.
Name.
Change of name, CA §2-605.
Deletion of name of county or city, CA §2-605.
No stock outstanding or subscribed for, CA
§2-603.
Notice to stockholders, CA §2-604.
Power to amend charter, CA §2-602.
Procedure.
General provisions, CA §2-604.
No stock outstanding or subscribed for, CA
§2-603.
Proposed amendments.
Abandonment, CA §2-612.
Purpose of amendment, CA §2-602.
Restatement.
Acknowledging, CA §1-301.
Amendments to charter included in
restatement, CA §2-609.
Approval by stockholders, CA §2-609.
Compliance with section required, CA §1-301.
Contents, CA §§2-608, 2-609.
Effective date of articles, CA §2-610.1.
Effect of articles, CA §2-611.
Evidence, CA §2-611.
Execution of articles, CA §2-610.
Filing of articles, CA §2-610.
Generally, CA §2-601.
Signing, CA §1-301.
Verification under oath, CA §1-301.
Witnessing, CA §1-301.
Reverse stock splits, CA §2-309.
Stockholders.
Objecting stockholders.
Remedies, CA §2-602.
Voting on amendment, CA §2-604.
Voting on amendment, CA §2-604.
Articles of incorporation.
Acknowledgments, CA §2-102.

CORPORATIONS —Cont'd
Charters —Cont'd
Articles of incorporation —Cont'd
Certificate of correction. See within this
heading, "Certificate of correction."
Contents, CA §2-104.
Fees, CA §1-203.
Filing, CA §2-102.
Provisions included in bylaws, CA §2-104.
Signing, CA §2-102.
Articles supplementary.
Acquisition of own.
Reduction of number of authorized shares
effective upon filing, CA §2-310.
Business combinations.
Special voting requirements, CA §3-603.
Classification or reclassification of unissued
stock by board, CA §2-208.
Fees, CA §1-203.
Body corporate.
Conclusive evidence of formation of corporation,
CA §1-206.
Close corporation.
Reference to close corporation status, CA
§4-202.
Removal from charter, CA §4-203.
Statement of election.
Contained in charter, CA §4-201.
Control shares.
Voting rights.
Applicability of charter provisions, CA §3-702.
Corporate existence.
Expiration by charter provisions, CA §3-519.
Correction.
Certificate of correction. See within this
heading, "Certificate of correction."
Defined, CA §1-101.
Directors.
Forfeiture of charter, CA §§3-514, 3-515.
Liability.
Corporate limitations on director liability, CA
§2-405.2.
Number.
Specifying number of directors, CA §2-402.
Special meeting of stockholders.
Calling, CA §2-502.
Document.
Defined, CA §1-101.
Effective date, CA §1-206.
Evidence.
Conclusive evidence of formation of corporation,
CA §§1-206, 2-102.
Restatement, CA §2-611.
Revival.
Evidentiary effect of acceptance of articles,
CA §3-510.
Expenses.
Organization, reorganization and financing, CA
§2-305.
Expiration of corporate existence by charter
provisions, CA §3-519.
Extension of existence, CA §3-501.
Articles of extension, CA §3-502.
Effect, CA §3-512.
Procedure, CA §3-501.
Fees.
General provisions, CA §1-203.
Foreign corporations.
General provisions.
See FOREIGN CORPORATIONS.

CORPORATIONS —Cont'd

Charters —Cont'd

Forfeiture.

Appointment of receiver, CA §3-516.

Attorney general.

Authorization to institute proceedings, CA §3-513.

Conduct connected with organized crime, CA §1-405.

Distributions to stockholders on forfeiture.

When number of outstanding shares known, CA §3-517.

When number of outstanding shares unknown, CA §3-518.

Failure to file report, CA §3-503.

Misuse, abuse or nonuse of powers and franchises, CA §3-513.

Nonpayment of taxes or failure to file report, CA §3-503.

Correction of mistakes, CA §3-505.

Effect of compliance, CA §3-504.

Other remedies not affected, CA §3-506.

Revival.

Procedure, CA §3-507.

Powers of directors on forfeiture, CA §3-515.

Procedure, CA §3-513.

Prohibition against doing business after forfeiture, CA §§3-514, 3-515.

Receiver.

Appointment on forfeiture, CA §3-516.

Ultra vires.

Proceedings by attorney general, CA §1-403.

General assembly.

Powers to regulate, MD Const Art III §48.

Modification.

Subject to, CA §1-102.

Nonstock corporations, CA §5-202.

Forfeiture of charter, CA §5-208.

Powers.

Limitation, CA §2-103.

Principal office. See within this heading, "Office."

Recording and filing with department, CA §§1-201, 1-205.

Effect of acceptance, CA §§1-206, 2-102.

Endorsement, CA §1-202.

Facsimile devices.

Documents filed for record by means of, CA §1-201.

Payment of fees required, CA §1-201.

Refusal to accept for record.

Unless the originals or certified copies delivered, CA §1-205.

Reorganization.

Expenses, CA §2-305.

Repeal.

Subject to, CA §1-102.

Restatement, CA §2-608.

Acknowledging, CA §1-301.

Amendments to charter included in restatement, CA §2-609.

Approval by stockholders, CA §2-609.

Contents, CA §§2-608, 2-609.

Effect of articles, CA §2-611.

Execution of articles, CA §2-610.

Filing of articles, CA §2-610.

Generally, CA §2-601.

Signing, CA §1-301.

Verification under oath, CA §1-301.

Witnessing, CA §1-301.

Revival.

Article of revival.

Acceptance.

Conditions, CA §3-509.

CORPORATIONS —Cont'd

Charters —Cont'd

Revival —Cont'd

Article of revival —Cont'd

Acceptance —Cont'd

Evidentiary effect, CA §3-510.

Contents, CA §3-508.

Execution, CA §3-507.

Taxes.

Payment, condition or acceptance, CA §3-509.

Effect, CA §3-512.

Power to revive, CA §3-501.

Procedure, CA §§3-507, 3-508.

Stockholders meeting after revival, CA §3-511.

Special meeting of stockholders.

Calling, CA §2-502.

Stock and stockholders.

Capital stock and stockholders. See within this heading, "Stock and stockholders."

Control shares.

Voting rights.

Applicability of charter provisions, CA §3-702.

Supplementary articles. See within this subheading, "Articles supplementary."

Child care or protection on minors, corporations form for.

Authority of agents, officers and representatives, FL §5-503.

Interfering with or obstructing, FL §5-503.

Child labor.

General provisions, LE §§3-201 to 3-216.

See CHILD LABOR.

Churches.

Protestant Episcopal Church.

See PROTESTANT EPISCOPAL CHURCH.

Religious corporations.

General provisions.

See RELIGION.

Roman Catholic Church.

See ROMAN CATHOLIC CHURCH.

United Methodist Church.

See UNITED METHODIST CHURCH.

United Presbyterian Church.

See UNITED PRESBYTERIAN CHURCH.

Clerks of court.

Charter or other paper.

Recordation, CA §1-202.

Defined, CA §1-101.

Close corporations.

Charter.

References to close corporation status, CA §4-202.

Removal from charter, CA §4-203.

Statement of election.

Contained in charter, CA §4-201.

Consolidation, merger and other transfers of property.

General provisions, CA §4-601.

Definitions, CA §4-101.

Transfer of stock, CA §4-503.

Directors.

At least one director required initially, CA §4-301.

Election to have no board.

Cessation of director's status, CA §4-302.

Effect, CA §4-303.

Time of election, CA §4-302.

Number, CA §4-301.

CORPORATIONS —Cont'd
Close corporations —Cont'd
Dissolution.
  Involuntary dissolution.
    Petition.
      Avoidance of dissolution by purchase of
        stock, CA §4-603.
      Right of stockholder to petition for
        dissolution, CA §4-602.
    Procedure, CA §4-602.
    Stockholder's right to require, CA §4-602.
Documents.
  Execution by officer in more than one capacity,
    CA §4-102.
Elections.
  Statement of election, CA §4-201.
Inspection.
  Stockholder's right of inspection, CA §4-403.
Oaths.
  Statement of affairs.
    Verified under oath, CA §4-404.
Officers and employees.
  Execution of documents in more than one
    capacity, CA §4-102.
Reference to close corporation status.
  Removal from charter, CA §4-203.
  Required on certain documents, CA §4-202.
Sale, lease, exchange or transfer of assets.
  General provisions, CA §4-601.
Statement of affairs.
  Filing, CA §4-404.
    Duty to prepare and file, CA §4-404.
    Verification, CA §4-404.
  Stockholder's right to request, CA §4-404.
Stock and stockholders.
  Agreements.
    Stockholders' agreements, CA §4-401.
      Amendment, CA §4-401.
    Unanimous stockholder agreement.
      Defined, CA §4-101.
  Certificates.
    Reference on certificates, CA §4-202.
  Convertible stock.
    Prohibited, CA §5-502.
  Dissolution.
    Avoidance of dissolution by purchase of stock,
      CA §4-603.
    Right of stockholder to petition for
      involuntary dissolution, CA §4-602.
  Inspection.
    Right of inspection, CA §4-403.
  Issuance.
    Restrictions on issuance, CA §4-501.
  Meetings.
    Annual meeting of stockholders, CA §4-402.
  Sale.
    Restrictions on sale, CA §4-501.
  Transfer of stock.
    Meaning of transfer, CA §4-503.
    Restrictions.
      Enumeration, CA §4-503.
  Voting.
    Denial or restriction of voting rights, CA
      §4-504.
    Issuance of voting securities other than stock,
      CA §4-502.
    Unanimous stockholder vote, CA §4-504.
Close-end investment companies.
Defined, CA §2-112.
Submissions to stockholders required, CA §2-112.

CORPORATIONS —Cont'd
Commercial code.
  Creditor rights under commercial law article, CA
    §3-115.
Committees.
  Forming standing committees, CA §2-411.
Comptroller.
  Forfeiture of charter.
    Nonpayment of taxes.
      Duties of comptroller, CA §3-503.
Condemnation.
  General provisions, RP §§12-101 to 12-212.
    See EMINENT DOMAIN.
Conflict of laws.
  Foreign corporations.
    Consolidation, merger and other transfers of
      property, CA §3-117.
Conflicts of interest.
  Interested director transactions, CA §2-419.
Consent to actions by stockholders.
  Methods of delivery, CA §2-505.
**Consolidation, merger and other transfers of
  property.**
  Abandonment of proposed consolidation, etc., CA
    §3-108.
  Acknowledgments, CA §1-301.
  Agent.
    Resident agent.
      Notice of change of address.
        Recording fee, CA §1-203.
  Amendments.
    Adoption pursuant to articles of merger, CA
      §2-601.
  Articles of consolidation.
    Contents, CA §3-109.
    Execution, CA §3-110.
    Fees.
      Recording, CA §1-203.
    Filing, CA §3-107.
    Signing and acknowledging, CA §1-301.
    Verification under oath, CA §1-301.
    Witnessed, CA §1-301.
  Articles of merger.
    Amendments.
      Adopted pursuant to articles of merger, CA
        §2-601.
    Contents, CA §3-109.
    Execution, CA §3-110.
    Fees.
      Recording, CA §1-203.
    Filing, CA §3-107.
    Signing and acknowledging, CA §1-301.
    Subsidiary corporation.
      How articles become effective, CA §3-106.
    Verification under oath, CA §1-301.
    Witnessing, CA §1-301.
  Articles of sale, lease, exchange or transfer.
    Contents, CA §3-109.
    Execution, CA §3-110.
    Filing, CA §3-107.
    Not required.
      Transfers in ordinary course of business.
        Mortgages and share exchanges, CA §3-104.
    Signing and acknowledging, CA §1-301.
    Verification under oath, CA §1-301.
    Witnessing, CA §1-301.
  Assets.
    Transfer assets.
      Defined, CA §1-101.
  Business trust.
    Defined, CA §3-101.

CORPORATIONS —Cont'd
Consolidation, merger and other transfers of property —Cont'd
Bylaws.
   Successor corporation, CA §3-114.
Certificate of consolidation, etc., CA §3-111.
   Counties.
      For each county in which property owned by corporation located, CA §3-111.
   Recordation, CA §3-111.
Certificate of resulting corporation filed with department, CA §3-113.
Cessation of shares to be converted or exchanged, CA §3-114.
Close corporations, CA §4-601.
Confirmatory instruments.
   Consolidation or merger, CA §3-114.
   Sale, lease, exchange or transfer, CA §3-115.
Consideration for stock, CA §3-103.
Consummation of share exchange.
   Effect, CA §3-114.1.
Control shares.
   Voting rights, CA §§3-701 to 3-710. See within this heading, "Stock and stockholders."
Correction of documents.
   Certificate of correction. See within this heading, "Certificate of correction."
Creditors.
   Commercial code.
      Rights under commercial law article, CA §3-115.
Deeds.
   Transferred without deed, CA §3-115.
   Validation of certain deeds, RP §14-113.
Definitions, CA §3-101.
Directors.
   Indemnification, CA §2-418.
   Resolution of board of directors, CA §3-105.
Domestic limited liability company.
   Defined, CA §3-101.
Domestic limited partnerships.
   Defined, CA §3-101.
   General rule, CA §3-102.
Domestic partnerships.
   Defined, CA §3-101.
   General rule, CA §3-102.
Effective.
   When consolidation, etc., effective, CA §3-113.
Effect of consolidation or merger, CA §3-114.
   Devise or bequest to the corporation, CA §3-114.
Effect of sale, lease, exchange or transfer of property, CA §3-115.
Exemption from repeal or modification of charter.
   Waiver, CA §3-116.
Fees.
   Recording and filing fees, CA §1-203.
Filing of articles, CA §3-107.
   Fees, CA §1-203.
Foreign business trust.
   Defined, CA §3-101.
Foreign corporations.
   Approval of articles by foreign corporations, CA §3-106.
   Defined, CA §3-101.
   Effect, CA §3-102.
   General provisions, CA §3-117.
   Ownership of land in state.
      Statement of certain actions filed with department, CA §7-206.
Statement of certain actions filed with department, CA §7-206.

CORPORATIONS —Cont'd
Consolidation, merger and other transfers of property —Cont'd
Foreign corporations —Cont'd
   Time articles effective, CA §3-113.
Foreign limited liability company.
   Defined, CA §3-101.
Foreign limited partnerships.
   Defined, CA §3-101.
   General rule, CA §3-102.
Foreign partnerships.
   Defined, CA §3-101.
   General rule, CA §3-102.
Indemnification of directors, officers, employees and agents, CA §2-418.
Interest in land.
   Defined, CA §3-101.
Limitation of actions.
   Proceedings to set aside deeds, RP §14-113.
Limitations not affected, CA §3-102.
Limited liability company.
   Defined, CA §3-101.
   Merger into, CA §3-102.
Nonstock corporations, CA §5-207.
   Assets subject to charitable or other restrictions, CA §5-702.
Officers and agents.
   Indemnification, CA §2-418.
Partnerships.
   Defined, CA §3-101.
   General rule, CA §3-102.
Powers, CA §3-102.
Procedure, CA §3-105.
Property certificate for each county where entity owns interest in land, CA §3-112.
Recordation.
   Tax, TP §12-106.
      Calculation, TP §12-106.
Restrictions not affected, CA §3-102.
Rights of objecting stockholders. See within this subheading, "Stock and stockholders."
Rights, privileges and franchises.
   Devise or bequest to either of the corporations, CA §3-114.
   Effect of consolidation or merger, CA §3-114.
   Sale, lease, exchange or transfer of property, CA §3-115.
Sale of property or franchise under court order, CA §3-302.
Separate corporation created, CA §3-114.
Share exchange.
   Abandonment of proposed share exchange, CA §3-108.
   Articles of share exchange.
      Execution, CA §1-301.
      Not required, CA §3-104.
      Recording fees, CA §1-203.
   Cessation of shares to be converted or exchanged, CA §3-114.
   Close corporations, CA §4-601.
   Consummation.
      Effect of consummation of share exchange, CA §3-114.1.
   Contents of articles, CA §3-109.
   Defined, CA §1-101.
   Execution of articles, CA §3-110.
   Filing articles, CA §3-107.
   Recording fee for articles of share exchange, CA §1-203.
   Stockholders.
      Authorization or consent not required, CA §3-104.

CORPORATIONS —Cont'd
Consolidation, merger and other transfers of property —Cont'd
Stock and stockholders.
  Alteration of contract rights before subtitle applies, CA §3-202.
  Appraisals.
    Appointment of appraisers, CA §3-210.
    Cost of proceedings, CA §3-211.
    Petition for appraisal, CA §3-208.
    Reports of appraisers, CA §3-210.
      Consideration by court, CA §3-211.
    Submission of certificates when notation of pendency of appraisal, CA §3-209.
  Approval of stockholders, CA §3-105.
  Authorization or consent not required.
    Mortgages, CA §3-104.
    Share exchanges, CA §3-104.
    Transfers in ordinary course of business, CA §3-104.
  Consideration for stock, CA §3-103.
  Control shares, CA §§3-701 to 3-710. See within this heading, "Stock and stockholders."
  Issuance of stock, CA §2-303.
  Judgment.
    Effect of judgment, CA §3-211.
  Merger of subsidiary corporation.
    Rights of minority stockholders, CA §3-106.
  Notice of stockholders' meeting, CA §3-105.
  Objecting stockholders.
    Consolidation of suits, CA §3-208.
    Dividend.
      Effect of demand on dividend, CA §3-204.
      Restoration of dividend and other rights, CA §3-206.
      Withdrawal of demand, CA §3-205.
    Fair value of shares, CA §3-202.
      Appraisals, CA §3-210.
      Procedure to obtain, CA §3-203.
    Joinder of objectors, CA §3-208.
    Notice of offer, CA §3-207.
    Offer to stockholders, CA §3-207.
    Petition for appraisal, CA §3-208.
    Procedure to obtain fair value, CA §3-203.
    Restoration of status as stockholder, CA §3-206.
    Right to fair value of stock, CA §3-202.
      Exceptions, CA §3-202.
      Procedure to obtain, CA §3-203.
    Successor.
      Defined, CA §3-201.
      Rights of successor with respect to stock, CA §3-213.
    Surrender of stock.
      Successor entitled to, CA §3-212.
    Value of stock.
      Appraisal of fair value, CA §3-210.
      Basis of fair value, CA §3-202.
      Right to fair value, CA §3-202.
    Withdrawal of demand.
      No withdrawal without consent of successor, CA §3-205.
  Procedure to obtain fair value, CA §3-203.
  Reduction of capital stock not necessary, CA §3-213.
  Subsidiary corporation.
    Procedure for merger, CA §3-106.
    Rights of minority stockholders, CA §3-106.
Subsidiary corporation.
  Merger of subsidiary corporation, CA §3-106.
    Procedure, CA §3-106.

CORPORATIONS —Cont'd
Consolidation, merger and other transfers of property —Cont'd
Successor.
  Defined, CA §1-101.
    Extraordinary actions, CA §3-201.
  Liability, CA §3-114.
  Powers.
    Generally, CA §3-114.
Taxation.
  Certificate for each county in which property located, CA §3-112.
  Exemption.
    Waiver, CA §3-116.
  Recordation tax.
    Applicability, TP §12-106.
    Calculation, TP §12-105.
Transfer assets.
  Defined, CA §1-101.
Validation of certain deeds, RP §14-113.
Consumer cooperatives.
See CONSUMER COOPERATIVES.
Contracts.
Close corporation, CA §4-401.
Directors.
  Contract or transaction between corporation and director, CA §2-419.
Foreign corporations.
  Failure to comply with subtitle 2 does not affect contracts, CA §7-305.
Powers, CA §2-103.
Stockholders.
  Consolidation, merger and other transfers of property.
    Alteration of contract rights before subtitle applies, CA §3-202.
Ultra vires.
  Defense of ultra vires, CA §1-403.
Contribution and exoneration.
Director's liability for unlawful distributions.
  Entitlement to contribution, CA §2-312.
  Limitation of action enforcing, CA §2-312.
Contributions.
Power to make, CA §2-103.
Control shares.
Voting rights of certain control shares, CA §§3-701 to 3-710. See within this heading, "Stock and stockholders."
Conveyances.
Taxation.
  Property transfer tax.
    Applicability to corporate conveyances, TP §13-206.
    County transfer tax, TP §13-405.
Cooperative housing corporations.
See COOPERATIVE HOUSING CORPORATIONS.
Cooperatives.
Agricultural cooperatives.
  See AGRICULTURAL COOPERATIVES.
Consumer cooperatives.
  See CONSUMER COOPERATIVES.
General provisions.
  See COOPERATIVES.
Copies.
Articles or certificate of incorporation.
  Evidence of existence of corporation, CA §1-206.
Corporate existence.
Expiration by charter provisions, CA §3-519.
Corporate take-over law.
See SECURITIES.

CORPORATIONS —Cont'd
Costs.
Consolidation, merger and other transfers of property.
Proceedings by objecting stockholders, CA §3-211.
Counties.
County commissioners declared to be corporation, 25 §1.
Defined, CA §1-101.
Creditors.
Sale, lease, exchange or transfer.
Commercial code.
Rights under commercial law article, CA §3-115.
Rights not impaired by, CA §3-115.
Credit unions.
General provisions.
See CREDIT UNIONS.
Insurance corporation.
See CREDIT UNIONS.
Crimes and offenses.
Directors.
Doing business after forfeiture, CA §3-514.
Prohibited acts, CA §2-216.
Foreign corporations.
Doing business without qualifying or registering, CA §7-302.
Forfeiture of charter, etc.
Conduct in connection with organized crime, CA §1-405.
Officers and agents.
Doing business after forfeiture, CA §3-514.
Prohibited acts, CA §2-216.
Stock and stockholders.
Prohibited acts, CA §2-216.
Criminal procedure.
Appearance.
Return of summons as appearance, CP §4-203.
Indemnification of directors, officers, employees and agents, CA §2-418.
Summons, CP §4-203.
Currency transactions in trade or business, BR §§1-501 to 1-505.
See CURRENCY TRANSACTIONS IN TRADE OR BUSINESS.
Death.
Nonstock corporations.
When membership reduced by death, CA §5-205.
Debt management services.
License application, FI §12-909.
Debts or obligations.
Consolidation or merger.
Liability of new corporation, CA §3-114.
Sale, lease, exchange or transfer.
Assumption, CA §3-115.
Deeds.
Acknowledgments, CA §1-303.
By whom made, CA §1-303.
Seal not required, RP §4-101.
Transfer without, CA §3-115.
Validation.
Certain deeds granting all or substantially all of property of corporations, RP §14-113.
Definitions, CA §1-101.
Business combinations.
Special voting requirements, CA §§3-601, 3-603.
Close corporation, CA §4-101.
Transfer of stock, CA §4-503.

CORPORATIONS —Cont'd
Definitions —Cont'd
Control shares.
Voting rights of certain control shares, CA §3-701.
Directors and officers, CA §2-418.
Distributions, CA §2-301.
Facsimile devices, CA §1-201.
Foreign corporations, CA §1-101.
Organized crime, CA §1-405.
Person to include corporation, 1 §15.
Special voting requirements.
Business combinations, CA §§3-601, 3-603.
Unsolicited takeovers of corporations and real estate investment trusts, CA §3-801.
Departments.
Defined, CA §1-101.
Fees.
Schedule, CA §1-203.
Foreign corporations.
Index of agents and officers, CA §7-209.
Merger and consolidation.
Certificates of successor to be filed with department, CA §3-117.
Department to prepare and file certificate of consolidation or merger, CA §3-117.
Forfeiture of charter.
Nonpayment of taxes or failure to file report.
Duty of department, CA §3-503.
Proclamation, CA §3-503.
Correction of mistakes, CA §3-505.
Notice, CA §3-504.
Publication, CA §3-504.
Fund for costs of reviewing, processing, and auditing documents, CA §1-203.3.
Instruments required to be filed with department.
Signature, CA §1-301.
Recording and filing.
Endorsement.
By department and clerk of court, CA §1-202.
Fees.
Payment of fees required, CA §1-201.
Papers not in conformity with law not to be recorded, CA §1-201.
Statement that papers have been received, CA §1-202.
Service of process.
Fees.
Acceptance of service of process or notice upon department, CA §1-203.
Deposit insurance fund corporation, FI §§10-101 to 10-121.
See DEPOSIT INSURANCE FUND CORPORATION.
Depositions.
Designation of person to testify for organization.
Notice.
Circuit courts, CivProCir Rule 2-412.
Directors.
Amendments.
Voting on amendments, CA §2-604.
No stock outstanding or subscribed for, CA §2-603.
Associations.
Standard of care required of directors, CA §2-405.1.
Bylaws.
Classification of directors, CA §2-110.
Number of directors, CA §2-402.
Power to make, CA §2-109.

CORPORATIONS —Cont'd
Directors —Cont'd
Chairman of board.
Signing certificates of stock, CA §2-212.
Charter.
Forfeiture of charter, CA §§3-514, 3-515.
Liability of directors.
Corporate limitations, CA §2-405.2.
Number of directors, CA §2-402.
Classes, CA §2-104.
Bylaws, CA §2-110.
Close corporations. See within this heading,
"Close corporations."
Committees, CA §2-411.
Conflicts of interest.
Interested director transactions, CA §2-419.
Consolidation, merger and other transfers of
property.
Resolution of board, CA §3-105.
Contracts.
Between corporation and director, CA §2-419.
Contribution.
Entitlement where liable for unlawful
distribution, CA §2-312.
Deadlocks.
Grounds for involuntary dissolution, CA §3-413.
Defense of action or suit.
Indemnification for expense, CA §2-418.
Definitions, CA §§1-101, 2-418.
Dissent of director to action of board, CA §2-410.
Effect, CA §2-410.
Dissolution.
Voluntary dissolution.
Powers, CA §3-410.
Resolution of directors.
No stock outstanding or subscribed for, CA
§3-402.
Duties.
Limitations of duty, CA §2-405.1.
Standards for performance, CA §2-405.1.
Election, CA §2-404.
Holding over, CA §2-405.
Failure to elect director.
Holding over of old directors, CA §2-405.
Forfeiture of charter.
Powers of directors on forfeiture, CA §3-515.
Presumed to know of forfeiture, CA §3-514.
Holding over.
Generally, CA §2-405.
Immunity.
Standards for performance of duties.
Persons performing duties in accordance with
standards, CA §2-405.1.
Indemnification, CA §2-418.
Informal action, CA §2-408.
Initial directors, CA §2-404.
Investment companies.
Director deemed independent and disinterested,
CA §2-405.3.
Liability.
Charter provisions, CJ §5-418.
Corporate limitations on director liability, CA
§2-405.2; CJ §5-417.
Criminal penalty for unauthorized issuance of
stock, CA §2-216.
Dissent of director to action of board, CA
§2-410.
Dissolution of corporation, CA §3-419.
Distributions, CA §2-312.
Indemnification, CA §2-418.

CORPORATIONS —Cont'd
Directors —Cont'd
Liability —Cont'd
Standards for performance of duties, CA
§2-405.1.
Limitation of actions.
Proceedings to enforce liability of director or
contribution, CA §2-312.
Loan guarantee or assistance to director, CA
§2-416.
Management, CA §2-401.
Meetings.
Action of majority.
Generally, CA §2-408.
Conference telephone, etc., CA §2-409.
General provisions, CA §2-409.
Minutes, CA §2-111.
Form, CA §2-111.
Keeping, CA §2-111.
Notice of meetings, CA §2-409.
Service of notice, CA §1-401.
Waiver of notice, CA §2-409.
Organization, CA §2-109.
Place of meeting, CA §2-409.
Quorum, CA §2-408.
Remote communications, CA §2-409.
Votes per director, CA §2-408.
Merger of subsidiary corporation.
Record of board, CA §3-106.
Minutes, CA §2-111.
Nonstock corporations, CA §§5-202, 5-204.
Number.
Bylaws, CA §2-402.
General provisions, CA §2-402.
Provided in charter, CA §2-402.
Required number, CA §2-402.
Penalty.
Unauthorized issuance of stock, CA §2-216.
Powers, CA §2-401.
Presumption of satisfaction of standards for
performance of duties, CA §2-405.1.
Prohibited acts, CA §2-216.
Prudent man rule.
Standard of care required of directors, CA
§2-405.1.
Qualifications, CA §2-403.
Record date.
Fixing, CA §2-511.
Limitations, CA §2-511.
Reduction of stated capital.
Procedure, CA §2-306.
Removal.
Limitations on removal without cause, CA
§2-406.
Procedure, CA §2-406.
Reorganization.
Ratification by directors not required, CA
§3-301.
Revival or extension of charter, CA §3-501.
Standards for performance of duties, CA §2-405.1.
Stock and stockholders.
Prohibited acts, CA §2-216.
Subsidiary corporation.
By resolution of board of directors, CA §3-106.
Term of office, CA §§2-104, 2-404.
Bylaws, CA §2-110.
Filling of vacancy, CA §2-407.
Transactions.
Between corporation and director, CA §2-419.
Unsolicited takeovers of corporations and real
estate investment trusts.
Corporation that elects to be subject to
provisions, CA §§3-801 to 3-805.

CORPORATIONS —Cont'd
Directors —Cont'd
Vacancies.
General provisions, CA §2-407.
Dissolution.
Abandoned property disposition, CL §§17-101 to 17-326.
See ABANDONED PROPERTY DISPOSITION.
Bulk transfers.
Exception from article of sales on dissolution, CL §6-103.
Foreign corporations.
Statement of certain actions filed with department, CA §7-206.
Involuntary dissolution.
Assets and liabilities.
Powers of receiver, CA §3-418.
Close corporation, CA §4-602.
Deadlocks.
Grounds for filing petition, CA §3-413.
Effect of dissolution, CA §3-419.
Fraudulent preferences.
Payments and transfers.
Power of receivers, CA §3-418.
Illegal, oppressive or fraudulent acts.
Grounds for filing petition, CA §3-413.
Liabilities of stockholders, directors or officers, CA §3-419.
Order.
Certification of order to department, CA §3-417.
Notice to tax authorities that entry of order requested, CA §3-417.
Petition to court.
By stockholder or creditor, CA §3-413.
Grounds for filing petition, CA §3-413.
Receivers.
Appointment, CA §§3-414, 3-415.
Insolvent corporations, CA §3-415.
Officers, directors or stockholders as receiver, CA §3-416.
Temporary receivers appointed, CA §3-414.
Stockholders.
Who may file petition, CA §3-413.
Trustees.
Appointment, CA §3-414.
Temporary trustees appointed, CA §3-414.
Receivers.
Appointment, CA §§3-414, 3-415.
Insolvent corporations, CA §3-415.
Who may be appointed, CA §3-416.
Assets and liabilities.
Powers of receiver, CA §3-418.
Officers, directors or stockholders as receivers, CA §3-416.
Powers, CA §§3-414, 3-418.
Sale under mortgage or deed of trust, CA §3-418.
Stockholders.
Defenses pleaded, CA §3-419.
Liability, CA §3-419.
Suits.
Defenses by stockholder, CA §3-419.
Taxation.
Notice to tax authorities that entry of order requested, CA §3-417.
Nonstock corporations, CA §§5-208, 5-702.
Disposition of charitable or religious corporation's property by court, CA §5-209.
Receivers.
Involuntary dissolution. See within this subheading, "Involuntary dissolution."

CORPORATIONS —Cont'd
Dissolution —Cont'd
Receivers —Cont'd
Voluntary dissolution. See within this subheading, "Voluntary dissolution."
Taxation.
Advance payment of personal property taxes.
By corporation filing articles of dissolution, TP §10-206.
Requirement as to payment of taxes, CA §3-407.
Trusts and trustees. See within this heading, "Trusts and trustees."
Unemployment insurance.
Payments required, CA §3-407.
Voluntary dissolution.
Abandonment of dissolution proceedings, CA §3-405.
Approval.
No stock outstanding or subscribed for, CA §3-402.
Stock outstanding or subscribed for, CA §3-403.
Articles of dissolution.
Contents, CA §3-406.
Execution, CA §3-406.
Fee for recording, CA §1-203.
Taxes.
Requirements as to payment of taxes, CA §3-407.
Time for filing, CA §3-407.
Authority of corporation, CA §3-401.
Continuance of existence of corporation for certain purposes, CA §3-408.
Directors.
Authorization from court, CA §3-411.
Powers of directors, CA §3-410.
Distributions to stockholders upon dissolution, CA §3-412.
Effective date, CA §3-408.
Final distribution, CA §3-412.
Liabilities of stockholders, directors or officers, CA §3-419.
Notices.
Abandonment of proceedings, CA §3-405.
Creditors, CA §3-404.
Abandonment of proceedings, CA §3-405.
Employees, CA §3-404.
Stockholders, CA §3-403.
Stockholders to prove interest, CA §3-412.
Procedure.
No stock outstanding or subscribed for, CA §3-402.
Pro rata shares.
Distribution, CA §3-412.
Receivers.
Appointment, CA §3-411.
Directors become trustees of assets until appointment of receiver, CA §3-410.
Discharge, CA §3-412.
Revocation of dissolution proceedings, CA §3-405.
Stockholders.
Defenses pleaded, CA §3-419.
Distribution to stockholders, CA §3-412.
Liability, CA §3-419.
Notice to stockholders to prove interest, CA §3-412.
Suits.
Defenses by stockholder, CA §3-419.
Taxation.
Requirement as to payment of taxes, CA §3-407.

CORPORATIONS —Cont'd
Dissolution —Cont'd
Voluntary dissolution —Cont'd
Unclaimed assets, CA §3-412.
Unemployment insurance.
Payments required, CA §3-407.
Distress for rent.
Corporate tenant ceasing to exist, RP §8-328.
Distributions.
Amount and terms of distribution.
Delegation of power to determine, CA §2-309.
Authorized, CA §2-309.
Defined, CA §2-301.
Determination of whether distribution permitted,
CA §2-311.
Liabilities of directors, CA §2-312.
Measuring effect of distribution, CA §2-311.
Restrictions, CA §2-311.
Status of indebtedness to stockholder, CA §2-311.
Dividends.
Consolidation, merger and other transfers of
property.
Rights of objecting stockholders, CA §3-204.
Restoration of dividend and other rights, CA
§3-206.
Withdrawal of demand for dividend, CA
§3-205.
Successors' rights, CA §3-213.
Stock dividends, CA §2-309.
Issuance, CA §§2-203, 2-309.
Documents.
Acknowledgments, CA §1-303.
By whom made, CA §1-303.
Expedited processing of documents, CA §1-203.2.
Fees, CA §1-203.
Electric cooperatives.
Conversion of corporation to cooperative, CA
§5-630.
General provisions, CA §§5-601 to 5-642.
See ELECTRIC COOPERATIVES.
Electronic transmissions.
Defined, CA §1-101.
Notice of stockholders' meetings, CA §2-504.
Email.
Electronic transmissions defined, CA §1-101.
Notice of stockholders' meetings, CA §2-504.
Eminent domain.
General provisions, RP §§12-101 to 12-212.
See EMINENT DOMAIN.
Employees.
Employee stock ownership plans.
Broadened ownership act, 83A §2-106.
Loan guarantee or assistance to an employee, CA
§2-416.
Engineers.
Licenses.
Exceptions to requirement.
Practice by corporate officers and employees,
BOP §14-302.
Practice through corporation, BOP §14-401.
Environmental service.
Creation of private corporations, NR §3-104.
Exercise of general corporate powers, NR §3-104.
Perpetual corporate existence, NR §3-104.
Episcopal Church.
See PROTESTANT EPISCOPAL CHURCH.
Equity.
Assets subject to charitable or other restrictions.
Decree as to dissolution, merger, consolidation
or transfer of assets, CA §5-702.

CORPORATIONS —Cont'd
Evidence.
Charter.
Acceptance of record.
Conclusive evidence of formation of
corporation, CA §§1-206, 2-102.
Restatement, CA §2-611.
Revival.
Evidentiary effect of acceptance of article, CA
§3-510.
Fees and taxes.
Acceptance of charter for record.
Conclusive evidence of payment of fees and
taxes, CA §1-206.
Formation of corporation.
Conclusive evidence of formation, CA §§1-206,
2-102.
Incorporation.
Conclusive evidence of formation of corporation,
CA §§1-206, 2-102.
Copy of articles or certificate of incorporation as
evidence of existence of corporation, CA
§1-206.
Existence of corporation.
Copy of articles of certificates of incorporation
as evidence, CA §1-206.
Formation of corporation.
Conclusive evidence, CA §1-206.
Payment of fees and taxes.
Conclusive evidence, CA §1-206.
Executors and administrators.
Powers of personal representative, ET §7-401.
Existence.
Effect of article on existing corporations, CA
§1-102.
Expiration of corporate existence by charter
provisions, CA §3-519.
Extension. See within this heading, "Charters."
Perpetual existence, CA §2-103.
Facsimile devices.
Documents filed for record by means of, CA
§1-201.
Family farms, cessation.
Filing charter amendments, CA §1-209.
Fees.
Amount, CA §1-203.
Certificate of correction, CA §1-203.
Department.
Payment to, CA §1-201.
Disposition, TP §2-220.
Documents, CA §1-203.
Expedited processing, CA §1-203.2.
General provisions, CA §1-203.
Organization and capitalization fees, CA §1-204.
Payment.
Acceptance for recording and filing by
department.
Conclusive evidence, CA §1-206.
Conclusive evidence of payment of fees and
taxes, CA §1-206.
Organization and capitalization fees, CA §1-204.
Required before department will record papers,
CA §1-201.
Recording and filing with department of
assessments and taxation.
Disposition, TP §2-220.
Schedule, CA §1-203.
Service of process.
Fee for acceptance, CA §1-203.

CORPORATIONS —Cont'd
Felonies.
Alcoholic beverages.
Licenses.
Revocation and suspension.
Felony conviction of stockholder, 2B
§10-401.
Fictitious business name.
Trade names generally, CA §1-406.
Fiduciaries, ET §§15-1A-01 to 15-1A-05.
General provisions.
See FIDUCIARIES.
Incorporation.
Powers of fiduciaries, ET §15-102.
Investments by corporate fiduciary.
Lawful investments, ET §15-106.
Liability of corporations that act as fiduciaries.
Not liable as sureties, ET §15-115.
Liability of holder of stock in fiduciary capacity,
CA §2-215.
Stock subscriptions.
Powers of fiduciaries, ET §15-102.
Voting of shares by certain holders, CA §2-508.
Financial statements.
Presumed proper, CA §1-402.
Fines.
Directors.
Indemnification, CA §2-418.
Unauthorized issuance of stock, CA §2-216.
Foreign corporations.
Doing business without qualifying or
registering, CA §7-302.
Forfeiture of charter.
Prohibition against doing business after
forfeiture, CA §3-514.
Officers and agents.
Indemnification, CA §2-418.
Unauthorized issuance of stock, CA §2-216.
Unincorporated organizations not to indicate
incorporation, CA §1-404.
Firearms.
Applications for purchases, rents or transfers, PS
§5-118.
Dealers' licenses.
Applications, PS §5-107.
Fire departments.
Provision of fire, ambulance and rescue services
by for-profit entities, PS §7-401.
Volunteer fire companies.
Recording.
Exemption, CA §1-203.1.
Foreign banks.
See BANKS AND TRUST COMPANIES.
Foreign corporations.
See FOREIGN CORPORATIONS.
Forfeiture of charters. See within this heading,
"Charters."
Formation. See within this heading,
"Incorporation."
Forms.
Fees, CA §1-203.
Foundations.
Private foundations.
General provisions.
See PRIVATE FOUNDATIONS.
Franchise registration and disclosure law, BR
§§14-201 to 14-233.
See FRANCHISES.
Franchises.
Municipal corporations, 23A §2.

CORPORATIONS —Cont'd
Franchises —Cont'd
Taxation.
Franchise tax.
See TAXATION.
Fraternal benefit societies.
General provisions, IN §§8-401 to 8-468.
See FRATERNAL BENEFIT SOCIETIES.
Fraud and deceit.
Sale or disposition of stock for services at less
than par, CA §2-216.
Fraudulent conveyances.
Involuntary dissolution.
Fraudulent preferences, payments and
transfers, CA §3-418.
Fraudulent misrepresentation.
Officers or agents, CR §8-402.
Fund for costs of reviews and audits, CA
§1-203.3.
General assembly.
Regulations, MD Const Art III §48.
Taxation.
Foreign corporations, MD Const Art III §58.
General corporation law.
Citation, CA §1-103.
Gifts.
Power to make, CA §2-103.
Health maintenance organizations.
General provisions.
See HEALTH MAINTENANCE
ORGANIZATIONS.
Homestead associations.
See SAVINGS AND LOAN ASSOCIATIONS.
Housing.
Cooperative housing corporations.
See COOPERATIVE HOUSING
CORPORATIONS.
Immunity.
Directors.
Liability, CJ §5-417.
Standards for performance of duties.
Persons performing duties in accordance with
standards, CA §2-405.1.
Income tax.
See INCOME TAX.
Incorporation.
Application of other statutes, CA §2-101.
Charters. See within this heading, "Charters."
Evidence.
Conclusive evidence of formation of corporation,
CA §§1-206, 2-102.
Copy of articles or certificate of incorporation as
evidence of existence of corporation, CA
§1-206.
Existence of corporation.
Copy of articles or certificate of incorporation
as evidence, CA §1-206.
Formation of corporation.
Conclusive evidence, CA §§1-206, 2-102.
Purposes for which corporation may be formed,
CA §2-101.
Who may form, CA §2-102.
Indemnity.
Indemnification of directors, officers, employees
and agents, CA §2-418.
Indexes.
Foreign corporations.
Resident agents and principal offices, CA
§7-209.
Industrial development corporations.
General provisions, 45A §§1 to 3.
See INDUSTRIAL DEVELOPMENT
CORPORATIONS.

CORPORATIONS —Cont'd

Injunctions.

Organized crime, CA §1-405.

Ultra vires.

In proceedings by stockholders or attorney general, CA §1-403.

Inspections.

Close corporation.

Stockholder's right of inspection, CA §4-403.

Right of stockholders. See within this heading, "Stock and stockholders."

Instruments required to be filed with department.

Signature, CA §1-301.

Insurance.

Acquisitions disclosure and control act, IN §§7-101 to 7-807.

See INSURANCE ACQUISITIONS DISCLOSURE AND CONTROL.

Advisers.

Conducting business as corporation, IN §10-210.

Agents and brokers.

Conducting business as business entity, IN §10-114.

Licenses.

Applications, IN §10-111.

Qualifications, IN §10-106.

Requirement, IN §10-103.

Suspension, revocation, etc., IN §10-126.

Title insurance, IN §10-121.

Credit unions.

Insurance corporation.

See CREDIT UNIONS.

General provisions.

See INSURANCE COMPANIES.

Indemnification of directors, officers, employees and agents, CA §2-418.

Life and health insurance guaranty corporation, IN §§9-401 to 9-419.

See LIFE AND HEALTH INSURANCE GUARANTY CORPORATION.

Premium finance companies, IN §§23-101 to 23-506.

See PREMIUM FINANCE COMPANIES.

Property and casualty insurance guaranty corporation, IN §§9-301 to 9-316.

See PROPERTY AND CASUALTY INSURANCE GUARANTY CORPORATION.

Interest.

Commercial and corporate loans.

When legal rate may be exceeded, CL §12-103.

Judgments and decrees.

Proceedings by objecting stockholders.

Judgment includes interest, CA §3-211.

Interpretation and construction.

General provisions, CA §1-102.

Investment securities, CL §§8-101 to 8-511.

See INVESTMENT SECURITIES.

Involuntary dissolutions. See within this heading, "Dissolution."

Joint tenants and tenants in common.

Voting of shares, CA §2-508.

Judgments and decrees.

Forfeiture of charter, CA §3-513.

Indemnification of directors, officers, employees and agents, CA §2-418.

Involuntary dissolution.

Certification of order to department, CA §3-417.

Proceedings by objecting stockholders, CA §3-211.

Interest included in judgment, CA §3-211.

CORPORATIONS —Cont'd

Judicial sales.

Property and franchises sold under judicial proceedings, CA §3-302.

Jurisdiction.

Over persons outside this state.

General provisions.

See JURISDICTION.

Labor and industry.

Industrial development corporations.

General provisions, 45A §§1 to 3.

See INDUSTRIAL DEVELOPMENT CORPORATIONS.

Landscape architects.

Permits.

General provisions, BOP §§9-401 to 9-409.

See LANDSCAPE ARCHITECTS.

Laws.

Foreign corporations.

Assent to state laws, CA §7-105.

Leases.

Consolidation. See within this heading, "Consolidation, merger and other transfers of property."

Ledger for stocks.

Form, CA §2-209.

Legal services corporation, 10 §§45A to 45O.

See ATTORNEYS AT LAW.

Liability.

Directors and officers.

Charter provisions, CJ §5-418.

Defenses, CA §2-405.1.

Dissent of director to action of board, CA §2-410.

Indemnification, CA §2-418.

Limitations, CJ §5-417.

Workers' compensation.

Assessments, LE §§9-1005, 9-1007.

Payments, LE §9-1003.

Liens.

Consolidation or merger.

Liability of new corporation, CA §3-114.

Libraries.

Cooperative library corporation, ED §23-206.

Liens.

Consolidation or merger.

Liability of new corporation, CA §3-114.

Life and health insurance guaranty corporation, IN §§9-401 to 9-419.

Limitation of actions.

Director's liability for unlawful contributions, CA §2-312.

Director's liability for unlawful distributions.

Contribution, CA §2-312.

Foreign corporations.

Denial of defense of limitations, CJ §5-204.

Setting aside deeds.

Granting of all or substantially all of property of corporations, RP §14-113.

Limited liability companies.

See LIMITED LIABILITY COMPANIES.

Limited partnerships.

Consolidation, merger and other transfers of property.

Defined, CA §3-101.

General rule, CA §3-102.

Liquidation.

Dissolution. See within this heading, "Dissolution."

Insolvency, CA §3-301.

Partial liquidation and reorganization, CA §3-301.

CORPORATIONS —Cont'd
Loan associations.
Savings and loan associations.
See SAVINGS AND LOAN ASSOCIATIONS.
Loans.
Banks.
Limitation on amounts loaned by banks, FI §3-601.
Directors, officers or employees, FI §3-315.
Loan guarantee or assistance to officer or employee, CA §2-416.
Lost instruments and records.
Stock and stockholders.
Certificates of stock, CA §2-213.
Mail.
Defined, CA §1-101.
Notice of stockholders' meetings, CA §2-504.
Maryland African American museum corporation, SG §§9-2601 to 9-2614.
See AFRICAN AMERICAN MUSEUM CORPORATION.
Maryland general corporation law.
Citation, CA §1-103.
Meetings.
Directors. See within this heading, "Directors."
Nonstock corporations. See within this heading, "Nonstock corporations."
Stockholders. See within this heading, "Stock and stockholders."
Merger. See within this heading, "Consolidation, merger and other transfers of property."
Methodist Church.
See UNITED METHODIST CHURCH.
Mining.
Strip mining.
Liability of officers or agents for corporate violations, EN §15-522.
Minors.
Child labor.
General provisions, LE §§3-201 to 3-216.
See CHILD LABOR.
Minutes.
Directors, CA §2-111.
Stock and stockholders, CA §2-111.
Misdemeanors.
Directors.
Doing business after forfeiture, CA §3-514.
Prohibited acts, CA §2-216.
Foreign corporations.
Doing business without qualifying or registering, CA §7-302.
Name.
Improper use of corporate indication, CA §1-404.
Officers and agents.
Doing business after forfeiture, CA §3-514.
Prohibited acts, CA §2-216.
Stock and stockholders.
Prohibited acts, CA §2-216.
Mistake.
Forfeiture of charter.
Nonpayment of taxes or failure to file report.
Proclamation to correct mistake, CA §3-505.
Effect, CA §3-505.
Money.
Currency transactions in trade or business, BR §§1-501 to 1-505.
See CURRENCY TRANSACTIONS IN TRADE OR BUSINESS.
Mortgages and deeds of trust.
Acknowledgments.
By whom made, CA §1-303.

CORPORATIONS —Cont'd
Mortgages and deeds of trust —Cont'd
Consideration true and bona fide.
Affidavit by president or other officer, RP §4-106.
Delivery of net proceeds, RP §4-106.
Doing business in this state by foreign corporations.
Foreclosing mortgages, etc., CA §7-104.
Involuntary dissolution.
Property decreed to be sold under mortgage or deed of trust, CA §3-418.
Power to execute, CA §2-103.
Sale of property and franchises under, CA §3-302.
Motor vehicles.
Certificates of title.
Exemptions from registration, TR §13-810.
Dealers.
Licenses, TR §15-303.
Salesmen.
Licenses issued only to individuals, TR §15-403.
Municipal area.
Defined, CA §1-101.
Municipal corporations.
General provisions, 23 §§181 to 183; 23A §§1 to 44A.
See MUNICIPAL CORPORATIONS.
Name.
Change.
Amendment of charter, CA §2-605.
Power to change, CA §2-602.
Entity names generally, CA §§1-501 to 1-508.
Fictitious names.
Trade names generally, CA §1-406.
Foreign corporations, CA §2-106.
Registration of names, CA §7-101.
Foreign entities generally, CA §1-506.
Indication of incorporation, CA §1-404.
Recordation of name, CA §2-106.
Registered name.
Fee for filing, CA §1-203.
Reservation of corporate name.
Fee for filing, CA §1-203.
Fee for recording, CA §1-203.
Trade names.
Certificates.
Filing requirements generally, CA §1-406.
Nonresidents.
Merger of subsidiary corporation.
Action by a corporation of another state, CA §3-106.
Nonstock corporations.
Application of Maryland general corporation law, CA §5-201.
Charitable corporation.
Disposition of property by court on dissolution, CA §5-209.
Charter.
Forfeiture of charter, CA §5-208.
Provisions, CA §5-202.
Consolidation, merger or other transfers of property.
Assets subject to charitable or other restrictions, CA §5-702.
General provisions, CA §5-207.
Directors.
Classification, CA §5-202.
When members of corporation, CA §5-204.
Dissolution.
Assets subject to charitable or other restrictions, CA §5-702.

CORPORATIONS —Cont'd
Nonstock corporations —Cont'd
  Dissolution —Cont'd
    Disposition of charitable or religious
        corporation's property by court, CA §5-209.
    General provisions, CA §5-208.
    Procedure, CA §5-208.
    Subject to charitable or other restrictions, CA
        §5-702.
  Industrial development corporations.
    General provisions, 45A §§1 to 3.
      See INDUSTRIAL DEVELOPMENT
          CORPORATIONS.
  Life and health insurance guaranty corporation,
      IN §§9-401 to 9-419.
    See LIFE AND HEALTH INSURANCE
        GUARANTY CORPORATION.
  Meetings.
    Notice of meeting.
      Manner of giving, CA §5-202.
    Organization meeting.
      Calling, CA §5-203.
    Quorum.
      Absence of quorum, CA §5-206.
    Voting.
      Provisions, CA §5-202.
      Proxy or mail, CA §5-202.
  Members.
    Absence of quorum, CA §5-206.
    Classification, CA §5-202.
    Death, CA §5-205.
    Reduction of membership below majority.
      Power of remaining members, CA §5-205.
    Resignation, CA §5-205.
    Vacancies, CA §5-205.
    Voting.
      By proxy or mail, CA §5-202.
    When members of governing board constitute
        members, CA §5-204.
  Merger, CA §5-207.
    Assets subject to charitable or other
        restrictions, CA §5-702.
  Property holdings.
    Restrictions on, CA §5-701.
  Religious corporations.
    Disposition of property by court on dissolution,
        CA §5-209.
    Generally, CA §§5-301 to 5-313.
      See RELIGION.
Notices.
  Call for subscription to capital stock, CA §2-202.
  Certificate of notice, CA §1-207.1.
  Change of address, CA §2-108.
  Charter.
    Amendments, CA §2-604.
  Consolidation, merger and other transfers of
      property.
    Abandonment of proposed consolidation, etc.,
        CA §3-108.
    Notice of offer to objecting stockholders, CA
        §3-207.
    Proceedings by objecting stockholders, CA
        §3-203.
    Stockholders' meeting, CA §3-105.
    Subsidiary corporation merged.
      Stockholders of subsidiary notified, CA
          §3-106.
  Control shares.
    Special meetings, CA §3-706.
  Corporate charter forfeited.
    Nonpayment of taxes and failure to file report,
        CA §3-504.

CORPORATIONS —Cont'd
Notices —Cont'd
  Directors' meeting, CA §2-409.
    Waiver of notice, CA §2-409.
  Dissolution.
    Involuntary dissolution.
      Tax authorities notified that entry of order
          requested, CA §3-417.
      Notice to stockholders to prove interest, CA
          §3-412.
    Voluntary dissolution.
      Abandonment of proceedings, CA §3-405.
      Creditors, CA §3-404.
      Employees, CA §3-404.
      Stockholders, CA §3-403.
  Meetings.
    Control shares.
      Special meetings, CA §3-706.
    Nonstock corporations.
      Manner of giving notice, CA §5-202.
    Single notice to shared addresses, CA §2-504.1.
    Stockholders' meetings, CA §2-504.
    Waiver of notice, CA §2-504.
  Merger of subsidiary corporation.
    Stockholders of subsidiary notified, CA §3-106.
  Nonstock corporations.
    Meetings, CA §5-202.
  Recording fees, CA §1-203.
  Reduction of stated capital, CA §2-306.
  Reverse stock splits, CA §2-309.
  Service, CA §1-401.
Oaths.
  Close corporations.
    Statement of affairs.
      Verified under oath, CA §4-404.
  Verification.
    Alternative, CA §1-302.
    Generally, CA §1-301.
Office.
  Principal office.
    Change, CA §2-108.
      Notice to commission, CA §2-108.
        Fee, CA §1-203.
    Defined, CA §1-101.
    Designation, CA §2-108.
    Required, CA §2-108.
    Stock ledger maintained at office, CA §2-209.
Officers and agents.
  Acknowledgments.
    By whom made, CA §1-303.
  Appointment of agent.
    Powers, CA §2-103.
  Close corporation.
    Execution of documents in more than one
        capacity, CA §4-102.
  Defense of action or suit.
    Indemnification for expense, CA §2-418.
  Definitions, CA §2-418.
  Dues.
    Generally, CA §2-414.
  Election.
    Generally, CA §2-413.
    Power, CA §2-103.
  Enumeration of required officers, CA §2-412.
  Fines. See within this heading, "Fines."
  Foreign corporations.
    Agents.
      See FOREIGN CORPORATIONS.
  Forfeiture of charter.
    Presumption of forfeiture, CA §3-514.
  Fraudulent misrepresentation, CR §8-402.

CORPORATIONS —Cont'd
Officers and agents —Cont'd
Holding more than one office, CA §2-415.
Indemnification.
  Assertion of indemnity, CA §2-418.
  General provisions, CA §2-418.
  Hearing and decree, CA §2-418.
Liability.
  Charter provisions, CJ §5-418.
  Criminal penalty for unauthorized use of stock,
    CA §2-216.
  Dissolution of corporation, CA §3-419.
  Indemnification, CA §2-418.
  Workers' compensation.
    Assessments, LE §§9-1005, 9-1007.
    Payments, LE §9-1003.
Loans, guarantees or assistance to officer or
  employee, CA §2-416.
Notice.
  Service of notice, CA §1-401.
Permitted officers, CA §2-412.
Powers, CA §2-414.
Prohibited acts, CA §2-216.
Registered agent.
  Designation.
    Written consent to be obtained, CA §1-208.
  Removal.
    General provisions, CA §2-413.
Required officers, CA §2-412.
Resident agent.
  Address.
    Change, CA §2-108.
  Defined, CA §1-101.
  Designation, CA §2-108.
  Foreign corporations.
    See FOREIGN CORPORATIONS.
  Name.
    Change of name or address, CA §2-108.
  Notice.
    Change of name or address.
      Recording fee, CA §1-203.
    Service, CA §1-401.
  Required, CA §2-108.
  Resignation, CA §2-108.
    Fee not required, CA §1-208.
  Service of process, CA §1-401.
Signatures, CA §2-212.
Statement of affairs, CA §2-313.
  Presumed proper, CA §1-402.
Term of office, CA §2-413.
Vacancy.
  Filling, CA §2-413.
Open-ended companies.
Stock and stockholders.
  Increase or decrease in aggregate number of
    shares or in the number of shares in any
    class of stock.
    Articles supplementary, CA §2-208.1.
    Charter provisions, CA §2-105.
  Redemption of shares of stock from
    stockholders, CA §2-310.1.
Options.
Stock options.
  Warrants or options relating to rights to
    subscribe, CA §2-204.
Organization.
Meeting of directors, CA §2-109.
Organization and capitalization fees, CA §1-204.
Organized crime.
Fines. See within this heading, "Fines."

CORPORATIONS —Cont'd
Organized crime —Cont'd
Forfeiture of charter, revocation of permit, etc.,
  CA §1-405.
Parties.
Capacity.
  Circuit courts, CivProCir Rule 2-202.
Partnerships.
Limited partnerships.
  Consolidation, merger and other transfers of
    property.
    Defined, CA §3-101.
    General rule, CA §3-102.
Penalties.
Fines. See within this heading, "Fines."
Foreign corporations.
  Failure to pay late filing penalties.
    Forfeiture of rights to intrastate business, CA
      §7-304.
  Forfeiture of charter, CA §3-513.
Person.
Defined, CA §1-101; SG §1-101.
Include corporation, 1 §15.
Petitions.
Consolidation, merger and other transfers of
  property.
  Proceedings by objecting stockholders, CA
    §3-208.
Forfeiture of charter.
  Attorney general may institute proceedings by
    filing petition, CA §3-513.
  Involuntary dissolution, CA §3-413.
Pleading.
Stockholders.
  Dissolution of corporation.
    Stockholder may plead defenses, CA §3-419.
Pleas.
Guilty pleas or nolo contendere.
  Method of pleading, Crim Rule 4-242.
Pledge.
Liability of pledgee or other holder of stock as
  security, CA §2-215.
Stock and stockholders.
  Voting pledged shares, CA §2-508.
Post office.
Address.
  Defined, CA §1-101.
Mail.
  Defined, CA §1-101.
Potomac highlands airport authority.
Authority constitutes public corporation, TR
  §10-103.
Power of attorney.
Acknowledgments.
  By appointed attorney, CA §1-303.
Powers.
Consolidation, merger and other transfers of
  property, CA §3-102.
Enumeration, CA §2-103.
  Not necessary to set forth in charter, CA §2-103.
Presbyterian Church.
See UNITED PRESBYTERIAN CHURCH.
Presumptions.
Evidence of formation of corporation, CA §§1-206,
  2-102.
Officers and directors.
  Forfeiture of charter.
    Persons presumed to know of forfeiture, CA
      §3-514.
  Satisfaction of standard for performance of
    duties, CA §2-405.1.

CORPORATIONS —Cont'd
Principal and income.
  Receipts received from corporate entity, ET §15-508.
Principal office. See within this heading, "Office."
Private foundations.
  General provisions.
    See PRIVATE FOUNDATIONS.
Proclamation.
  Corporate charter forfeited.
    Nonpayment of taxes or failure to file report, CA §3-503.
      Notice, CA §3-504.
      Publication, CA §3-504.
Professional service corporations.
  General provisions.
    See PROFESSIONAL SERVICE CORPORATIONS.
Property.
  Charitable or benevolent corporations.
    Restrictions on holdings, CA §5-701.
  Nonstock corporations.
    Restrictions on property holdings, CA §5-701.
  Power to purchase and sell, CA §2-103.
  Sale of property and franchises under judicial proceedings.
    General provisions, CA §3-302.
Property and casualty insurance guaranty corporation, IN §§9-301 to 9-316.
  See PROPERTY AND CASUALTY INSURANCE GUARANTY CORPORATION.
Protestant Episcopal Church.
  See PROTESTANT EPISCOPAL CHURCH.
Proxies.
  Nonstock corporations, CA §5-202.
  Voting of stockholders. See within this heading, "Stock and stockholders."
Prudent man rule.
  Directors.
    Standard of care required of directors, CA §2-405.1.
Quorum.
  Directors, CA §2-408.
  Nonstock corporations, CA §5-202.
  Stockholders, CA §2-506.
Quo warranto.
  Ultra vires.
    Attorney general.
      Asserting by attorney general, CA §1-403.
Radio and television.
  Restrictions on transferability of stock of radio stations, CA §5-703.
Real estate brokers.
  Associate real estate brokers.
    Professional service corporations.
      Formation by associate brokers, BOP §17-512.
        Effect of limitation on interest in business, BOP §17-511.
  Practice through corporations, BOP §17-321.
  Prohibited acts.
    Violations by corporations, BOP §17-612.
      Penalties, BOP §17-613.
  Real estate salespersons.
    Professional service corporations.
      Formation by salespersons, BOP §17-512.
        Effect of limitation on interest in business, BOP §17-511.
Real estate investment trust.
  General provisions, CA §§8-101 to 8-701.
  See TRUSTS AND TRUSTEES.

CORPORATIONS —Cont'd
Real property.
  General provisions. See within this heading, "Property."
Receivers.
  Claims.
    Verification requirements, Receivers Rule 13-401.
  Dissolution.
    Discharge, CA §3-412.
    Involuntary dissolution.
      Appointment, CA §§3-414 to 3-416.
        Insolvent corporations, CA §3-415.
      Assets and liabilities.
        Powers of receiver, CA §3-418.
      Officers, directors or stockholders as receivers, CA §3-416.
      Powers, CA §§3-414, 3-418.
    Voluntary dissolution.
      Appointment, CA §3-411.
      Directors become trustees of assets until appointment of receiver, CA §3-410.
      Discharge, CA §3-412.
  Forfeiture.
    Appointment of receiver on forfeiture, CA §3-516.
  Reorganization.
    Action by, CA §3-301.
  Schedule of debtor's property and debts.
    Schedule filed by corporation, Receivers Rule 13-203.
  Ultra vires.
    Proceedings by corporation acting through receiver, CA §1-403.
Recordation.
  Acknowledgments, CA §1-201.
  Certificate of consolidation, etc., CA §3-111.
  Certificate of correction, CA §1-207.
  Certificate of notice, CA §1-207.1.
  Charter and other papers, CA §1-201.
  Consolidation, merger and other transfers of property.
    Certificate, CA §3-111.
  Department.
    Papers not recorded with department, CA §1-205.
  Facsimile devices.
    Documents filed for record by means of facsimile devices, CA §1-201.
  Fees, CA §1-203.
    Exemption of volunteer fire companies and rescue squads, CA §1-203.1.
  Religious corporations.
    Articles of incorporation, CA §5-304.
    Plan of operation, CA §5-303.
  Resident agent or office.
    Designating or changing name or address of resident agent or office, CA §1-202.
Records.
  Accounts and minutes, CA §2-111.
    Keeping, CA §2-111.
    Presumed proper, CA §1-402.
  Capital account.
    General provisions, CA §2-302.
  Statement of affairs, CA §2-313.
  Stock ledger, CA §2-209.
Registration.
  Foreign corporations.
    General provisions.
      See FOREIGN CORPORATIONS.
  Name. See within this heading, "Name."

CORPORATIONS —Cont'd
Religious corporations.
Disposition of property by court on dissolution, CA §5-209.
General provisions.
See RELIGION.
Nonstock corporations.
Assets subject to charitable or other restrictions, CA §5-702.
Protestant Episcopal Church.
See PROTESTANT EPISCOPAL CHURCH.
Roman Catholic Church.
See ROMAN CATHOLIC CHURCH.
United Methodist Church.
See UNITED METHODIST CHURCH.
United Presbyterian Church.
See UNITED PRESBYTERIAN CHURCH.
Reorganization.
Action by trustee or receiver, CA §3-301.
Bulk transfers.
Exception of sales on reorganization from article, CL §6-103.
Charter papers.
Required to be filed with department, CA §3-301.
Reports.
Consolidation, merger and other transfers of property.
Proceedings by objecting stockholders.
Reports of appraisers, CA §3-210.
Corporate charter forfeited.
Failure to file report, CA §3-504.
Failure to file annual report with department.
Forfeiture of charter, CA §3-503.
Filing fees, CA §1-203.
Disposition, TP §2-220.
Foreign corporations.
Failure to pay late filing penalties.
Forfeiture of rights to do intrastate business, CA §7-304.
Public corporations.
Financial reports, 24 §2-101.
Rescue squads.
Provision of fire, ambulance and rescue services by for-profit entities, PS §7-401.
Recordation.
Exemption, CA §1-203.1.
Resident agent.
Defined, CA §1-101.
General provisions. See within this heading, "Officers and agents."
Revival of charter.
Articles of revival.
Fee for recording, CA §1-203.
Extension of existence. See within this heading, "Charters."
Roman Catholic Church.
See ROMAN CATHOLIC CHURCH.
Rules and regulations.
Powers of general assembly, MD Const Art III §48.
Rules of court.
Forfeiture of charter.
Conduct in connection with organized crime.
Applicability of rules, CA §1-405.
Safe-deposit companies.
Liability.
Limitation of liability, FI §12-604.
Sales.
Close corporations, CA §4-601.

CORPORATIONS —Cont'd
Sales —Cont'd
Consolidation, merger and other transfers of property. See within this heading, "Consolidation, merger and other transfers of property."
Property and franchises under judicial sales or mortgages and deeds of trust, CA §3-302.
Sales and use tax.
Personal liability for tax.
Corporate buyer or vendor, TG §11-601.
Savings and loan associations.
See SAVINGS AND LOAN ASSOCIATIONS.
Seals.
Corporate seal, CA §2-103.
Deeds.
Not required for deed, RP §4-101.
Facsimile signatures and seals on certificates, CA §2-212.
Placing word "seal" next to signature, CA §1-304.
Stock certificates, CA §2-212.
Securities.
Convertible securities. See within this heading, "Stock and stockholders."
General provisions, CA §§11-101 to 11-805.
See SECURITIES.
Securities clearing corporations.
Fiduciary authorized to deposit securities with, ET §15-104.
Stock and stockholders. See within this heading, "Stock and stockholders."
Service of process.
Agent.
Resident agent, CA §1-401.
Criminal cases.
Summons, CP §4-203.
Fees.
Acceptance of service or notice, CA §1-203.
Service on department, CA §1-203.
Foreign corporations.
Resident agent, CA §1-401.
Notice, CA §1-401.
Persons to be served.
Circuit courts, CivProCir Rule 2-124.
District Court, CivProDist Rule 3-124.
Resident agent, CA §1-401.
Share exchange. See within this heading, "Consolidation, merger and other transfers of property."
Short title.
Maryland general corporation law, CA §1-103.
Signatures.
Facsimile signatures and seals on certificates, CA §2-212.
Instruments required to be filed with department, CA §1-301.
Stock and stockholders.
Certificates, CA §2-212.
Facsimile signatures and seals on certificates, CA §2-212.
Special voting requirements.
Business combinations, CA §§3-601, 3-603.
Applicability of subtitle to Maryland corporations only, CA §3-604.
Definitions, CA §§3-601, 3-603.
Exemptions, CA §3-603.
Generally, CA §3-602.
Statement of affairs.
Generally, CA §2-313.
Presumed proper, CA §1-402.

CORPORATIONS —Cont'd
Statute of limitations.
Director's liability for unlawful distributions, CA §2-312.
  Contribution, CA §2-312.
Stock and stockholders.
Account.
  Capital account, CA §2-302.
Acquisition of another corporation.
  Issuance of stock, CA §2-303.
Acquisitions.
  Control shares, CA §§3-701 to 3-710. See within this subheading, "Control shares."
Adjourned meeting of stockholders, CA §2-511.
Alcoholic beverages.
  Licenses.
    Revocation and suspension.
      Felony conviction of stockholder, 2B §10-401.
Amendments.
  Voting on amendments, CA §2-604.
Assignees.
  Liability, CA §2-215.
Banks and trust companies.
  See BANKS AND TRUST COMPANIES.
Business combinations generally, CA §§3-601 to 3-603. See within this heading, "Business combinations."
Bylaws.
  Adoption of subsequent bylaws, CA §2-109.
  Powers as to, CA §2-109.
Capital.
  Charter provisions relating to capital stock, CA §2-105.
    Terms of capital stock, CA §2-105.
      Terms dependent upon facts ascertainable outside charter, CA §2-105.
  Stated capital.
    Defined, CA §1-101.
    Determination of amount, CA §2-303.
    Par value of stock, CA §2-303.
    Records, CA §2-302.
    Stock without par value, CA §2-303.
  Surplus.
    Application, CA §§2-303, 2-304, 2-308.
    Determination of amount, CA §2-303.
    When surplus deemed capital surplus, CA §2-308.
Certificates.
  Close corporation.
    Reference on certificates, CA §4-202.
  Contents, CA §2-211.
  Designations, preferences and limitations.
    Statement, CA §2-211.
  Each stockholder entitled to certificate, CA §2-210.
    Issuance of certain shares without certificates, CA §2-210.
  Form, CA §2-211.
  Fractional shares or scrip, CA §2-214.
  Issuance.
    Fractional shares or scrip, CA §2-214.
    Issuance of certain shares without certificates, CA §2-210.
    Not to issue before payment, CA §2-210.
  Limitations, CA §2-211.
  Lost certificates.
    Procedure, CA §2-213.
  Payment.
    Required before issuance of certificates, CA §2-210.

CORPORATIONS —Cont'd
Stock and stockholders —Cont'd
Certificates —Cont'd
  Preference, CA §2-211.
  Representation of stock held, CA §2-211.
  Restrictions, CA §2-211.
    Statement as to relative rights and restrictions, CA §2-211.
    Alternative statement, CA §2-211.
  Seals, CA §2-212.
  Signatures, CA §2-212.
    Facsimile signatures, CA §2-212.
  Statement.
    Statement as to relative rights and restrictions, CA §2-211.
    Alternative statement, CA §2-211.
  Transfer.
    Restrictions on certificate, CA §2-211.
Certification that stock is held for person other than stockholder, CA §2-514.
Charter provisions, CA §2-105.
  Control shares.
    Applicability of charter provisions, CA §3-702.
  Supplementary articles when shares classified or reclassified, CA §2-208.
Classification or reclassification of stock.
  Articles supplementary to charter to be filed, CA §2-208.
  Debts, liabilities and obligations of particular class of stock.
    Enforcement, CA §2-208.2.
Close corporations. See within this heading, "Close corporations."
Closed-end investment companies.
  Required submissions to stockholders, CA §2-112.
Consolidation, merger and other transfers of property.
  Alteration of contract rights before subtitle applies, CA §3-202.
  Appraisals.
    Appointment of appraisers, CA §3-210.
    Consolidation of suits, CA §3-208.
    Cost of proceedings, CA §3-211.
    Joinder of objectors, CA §3-208.
    Petition for appraisal, CA §3-208.
    Procedure on report of appraisers, CA §3-210.
    Reports of appraisers, CA §3-210.
      Consideration by court, CA §3-211.
    Submission of certificates for notation of pendency of appraisal, CA §3-209.
  Approval, CA §3-105.
  Authorization or consent of stockholders.
    Transfers in ordinary courses of business, mortgages and share exchanges, CA §3-104.
  Consideration for stock, CA §3-103.
  Control shares, CA §§3-701 to 3-710. See within this subheading, "Control shares."
  Issuance of stock, CA §2-303.
  Judgment.
    Effect of, CA §3-211.
  Merger of subsidiary corporation.
    Rights of minority stockholders, CA §3-106.
  Notice of meeting, CA §3-105.
  Objecting stockholders.
    Consolidation of suits, CA §3-208.
    Control shares.
      Status as objecting stockholders, CA §3-708.
    Dividend.
      Effect of demand on dividend, CA §3-204.

CORPORATIONS —Cont'd
Stock and stockholders —Cont'd
Consolidation, merger and other transfers of
    property —Cont'd
  Objecting stockholders —Cont'd
    Dividend —Cont'd
      Restoration of dividend and other rights,
        CA §3-206.
      Withdrawal of demand, CA §3-205.
    Fair value of shares, CA §3-202.
      Appraisals, CA §3-210.
      Procedure to obtain, CA §3-203.
    Joinder of objectors, CA §3-208.
    Notice of offer, CA §3-207.
    Offer to stockholders, CA §3-207.
    Petition for appraisal, CA §3-208.
    Procedure to obtain fair value, CA §3-203.
    Restoration of status as stockholder, CA
      §3-206.
    Right to fair value of stock, CA §3-202.
      Exceptions, CA §3-202.
      Procedure to obtain, CA §3-203.
    Successor.
      Defined, CA §3-201.
      Shares acquired have status of unissued
        stock, CA §3-213.
    Surrender of stock.
      Successor entitled to, CA §3-212.
    Value of stock.
      Appraisal of fair value, CA §3-210.
      Basis of fair value, CA §3-202.
      Right to fair value, CA §3-202.
    Withdrawal of demand.
      No withdrawal without consent of
        successor, CA §3-205.
  Petition to court to determine fair value.
    Consolidation of proceedings, CA §3-208.
    Joinder of objectors, CA §3-208.
    Right to petition, CA §3-208.
    Submission of certificates for notation of
      pendency of appraisal, CA §3-209.
    Time, CA §3-208.
  Procedure to obtain fair value, CA §3-203.
    Costs, CA §3-211.
  Reduction of capital stock not necessary, CA
    §3-213.
  Sale of property or franchise under court order,
    CA §3-302.
  Subsidiary corporation.
    Procedure for merger, CA §3-106.
    Rights of minority stockholders, CA §3-106.
  Successor.
    Defined, CA §3-201.
Contracts.
  Consolidation, merger and other transfers of
    property.
    Alteration of contract rights before subtitle
      applies, CA §3-202.
Control shares.
  Acquiring personal statements.
    Contents, CA §3-703.
    Redemption rights, CA §3-707.
  Applicability of subtitle, CA §3-702.
  Applicability of subtitle to Maryland
    corporations only, CA §3-709.
  Beneficial owners, CA §3-702.
  Charters.
    Voting rights.
      Applicability of provisions, CA §3-702.
  Definitions, CA §3-701.

CORPORATIONS —Cont'd
Stock and stockholders —Cont'd
Control shares —Cont'd
  Fair value.
    Redemption rights, CA §3-707.
  Meetings.
    Special meetings, CA §3-704.
      Calls, CA §3-705.
      Notice, CA §3-706.
  Notice.
    Meetings, CA §3-706.
    Objecting stockholders.
      Notice of entitlement to rights of, CA
        §3-708.
  Objecting stockholders.
    Status, CA §3-708.
  Redemption rights, CA §3-707.
  Special meetings.
    Calls, CA §3-705.
    Delay at request of acquiring persons, CA
      §3-704.
    In absence of request, CA §3-704.
    Notice, CA §3-706.
    Request by acquiring person, CA §3-704.
    Request by acquiring person in absence of
      request, CA §3-704.
      Delay at request, CA §3-704.
    Time for, CA §3-704.
  Title of act, CA §3-710.
  Voting rights.
    Acquisition of shares, CA §3-702.
    Applicability of subtitle, CA §3-702.
    Approval by stockholders, CA §3-702.
    Charter provisions.
      Applicability, CA §3-702.
    Objecting stockholders.
      Status as, CA §3-708.
    Redemption rights, CA §3-707.
    Special meetings, CA §3-704.
      Calls, CA §3-705.
      Notice, CA §3-706.
Convertible securities.
  Deemed fully paid and nonassignable, CA
    §2-206.
  Defined, CA §1-101.
  Issuance, CA §2-201.
Debts, liabilities and obligations of particular
  class of stock.
  Enforcement, CA §2-208.2.
Directors.
  Election by stockholders.
    Manner of voting, CA §2-404.
    Plurality vote, CA §2-404.
  Prohibited acts, CA §2-216.
  Removal, CA §2-406.
Distributions. See within this heading,
  "Distributions."
Dividends. See within this heading, "Dividends."
Employee stock ownership plans.
  Broadened Ownership Act, 83A §2-106.
Expenses.
  Organization, reorganization and financing, CA
    §2-305.
Felonies.
  Alcoholic beverage licenses.
    Revocation and suspension.
      Felony conviction of stockholder, 2B
        §10-401.
Fiduciaries.
  Liability of holder of stock in fiduciary capacity,
    CA §2-215.

CORPORATIONS —Cont'd
Stock and stockholders —Cont'd
Fiduciaries —Cont'd
Voting of shares, CA §2-508.
Forfeiture of charter.
Distributions to stockholders on forfeiture.
When number of outstanding shares known,
CA §3-517.
When number of outstanding shares
unknown, CA §3-518.
Fractional shares.
Issuance, CA §2-214.
Holding stock for person other than stockholder.
Certification, CA §2-514.
Charter provisions, CA §2-205.
Increase or decrease of number of shares or par
value, CA §2-602.
Informal action, CA §2-505.
Inspection right of stockholder.
Close corporation, CA §4-403.
During usual business hours, CA §§2-512,
2-513.
Five percent of capital stock, CA §2-513.
Holders of certificates of voting trust, CA
§2-512.
What may be inspected, CA §2-512.
Investment company.
Shares held in fiduciary capacity for benefit of
other class of shares, CA §2-310.2.
Investment securities, CL §§8-101 to 8-511.
See INVESTMENT SECURITIES.
Issuance of stock.
Acquisition of another corporation, CA §2-303.
Authorization.
Effect, CA §2-201.
Committees, CA §2-411.
Convertible securities, CA §§2-201, 2-204.
Exceptions, CA §2-203.
Fractional shares or scrip, CA §2-214.
Future labor, services or payment, CA §2-206.
Issuance of certain shares without certificates,
CA §2-210.
Merger or consolidation, CA §2-303.
Nonassessable, CA §2-203.
Outstanding shares.
Effect of outstanding shares entitled to vote,
CA §2-204.
Par value, CA §2-203.
Payment after issuance, CA §2-206.
Not to issue before payment.
Exception, CA §2-210.
Price.
Provisions as to, CA §2-203.
Requisites, CA §2-204.
Right to issue, CA §2-201.
Statement as to stock issued, CA §2-512.
Unauthorized issuance of stock, CA §2-216.
Joint owners.
Voting jointly by two or more persons, CA
§2-508.
Ledger for stocks.
Contents, CA §2-209.
Location, CA §2-209.
Liability of subscribers or stockholders, CA
§2-215.
Debts, liabilities and obligations of particular
class of stock.
Enforcement, CA §2-208.2.
Dissolution of corporation, CA §3-419.
Surplus deemed capital surplus, CA §2-308.
Who may collect, CA §2-215.

CORPORATIONS —Cont'd
Stock and stockholders —Cont'd
Meetings.
Adjourned meeting of stockholders, CA §2-511.
Annual meetings, CA §2-501.
Calls.
Control shares.
Special meetings, CA §3-705.
Close corporation, CA §4-402.
Consent to actions by writing or e-mail, CA
§2-505.
Control shares.
Special meetings, CA §3-704.
Calls, CA §3-705.
Notice, CA §3-706.
Dissolution.
Voluntary dissolution, CA §3-403.
Informal action, CA §2-505.
Minutes, CA §2-111.
Notice.
Control shares.
Special meetings, CA §3-706.
Generally, CA §2-504.
Service, CA §1-401.
Single notice to shared addresses, CA
§2-504.1.
Waiver, CA §2-504.
Place, CA §2-503.
Quorum of stockholders, CA §2-506.
Remote communications, CA §2-502.1.
Place for meetings, CA §2-503.
Revival of charter.
Stockholders meeting.
After revival, CA §3-511.
Special meetings.
Calling, CA §2-502.
Control shares, CA §3-704.
Calls, CA §3-705.
Notice, CA §3-706.
General provisions, CA §2-502.
Notice, CA §2-504.
Control shares, CA §3-706.
Unsolicited takeovers of corporations and real
estate investment trusts, CA §3-805.
Statement of affairs, CA §2-313.
Presumed proper, CA §1-402.
Stockholder proposals, CA §2-504.
Teleconference communications, CA §2-502.1.
Time.
Annual meetings, CA §2-501.
Control shares.
Special meetings, CA §3-704.
Where held, CA §2-503.
Minutes, CA §2-111.
Nonassessable.
Securities deemed full paid and nonassessable,
CA §2-206.
Stock having par value may be issued, CA
§2-203.
Notice.
Consolidation, merger and other transfers of
property.
Objecting stockholders.
Notice of offer, CA §3-207.
Control shares.
Special meetings, CA §3-706.
Open-ended companies.
Increase or decrease in aggregate number of
shares or in the number of shares in any
class of stock.
Articles supplementary, CA §2-208.1.

CORPORATIONS —Cont'd
Stock and stockholders —Cont'd
Open-ended companies —Cont'd
Increase or decrease in aggregate number of
shares or in the number of shares in any
class of stock —Cont'd
Charter provisions, CA §2-105.
Redemption of shares of stock from
stockholders, CA §2-310.1.
Outstanding shares.
Effect of outstanding shares entitled to vote, CA
§2-204.
Owned by corporation.
Acquisition.
Articles supplementary.
Reduction of number of authorized shares
effective upon filing, CA §2-310.
Authority, CA §2-310.
Open-end investment companies, CA §2-310.1.
Reduction of number of authorized shares, CA
§2-310.
Status of shares, CA §2-310.
Reduction of stated capital, CA §2-306.
Voting, CA §2-509.
Par value.
Determination of amount of stated capital and
capital surplus, CA §2-303.
Issuing stock with par value with stock without
par value, CA §2-302.
Stock having par value may be issued as full
paid and nonassessable, CA §2-203.
Payment for stock, CA §2-206.
Certificates.
Payment required before issuance of
certificates, CA §2-210.
Property, labor or other services, CA §2-206.
Pledge.
Liability of pledgee or other holder of stock as
security, CA §2-215.
Powers.
Enumeration of powers of corporations, CA
§2-103.
Preemptive rights of stockholders, CA §2-205.
Banks and trust companies, FI §3-316.
Defined in charter, CA §2-105.
Denied in charter, CA §2-105.
Limited in charter, CA §2-105.
Waiver, CA §2-205.
Price.
Provisions as to, CA §2-203.
Proxies. See within this subheading, "Voting."
Radio and television stations.
Restrictions on transferability, CA §5-703.
Record date.
Fixing, CA §2-511.
Records, CA §2-111.
Presumed proper, CA §1-402.
Redemption.
Control shares.
Rights, CA §3-707.
Registration of stock.
Securities act, CA §§11-101 to 11-805.
See SECURITIES.
Reorganization.
Ratification not required, CA §3-301.
Restrictions on transferability.
Charter provisions providing, CA §2-105.
Reverse stock splits, CA §2-309.
Revival or extension of charter.
Approval, CA §3-501.

CORPORATIONS —Cont'd
Stock and stockholders —Cont'd
Scrip.
Issuance, CA §2-214.
Securities.
Convertible securities.
Deemed full paid and nonassessable, CA
§2-206.
Defined, CA §1-101.
Issuance, CA §2-201.
Deemed full paid and nonassessable, CA §2-206.
General provisions, CA §§11-101 to 11-805.
See SECURITIES.
Statement as to stock or securities issued, CA
§2-512.
Share exchange.
Defined, CA §1-101.
Splits, CA §2-309.
Stated capital.
Defined, CA §1-101.
Determination of amount, CA §2-303.
Generally, CA §2-303.
Reduction.
Procedure, CA §2-306.
Surplus deemed capital surplus, CA §2-308.
When stock issued without par value, CA
§2-302.
Stockholder rights plan, CA §2-201.
Defined, CA §1-101.
Stockholders.
Defined, CA §1-101.
Subscription for shares.
Call.
Uniform as to shares of same class, CA
§2-202.
Liability of subscribers, CA §2-215.
Notice, CA §2-202.
Payment.
Time, CA §2-202.
Revocability, CA §2-202.
Warrants or options relating to rights to
subscribe, CA §2-204.
Successor.
Defined, CA §1-101.
Supplementary articles when shares classified or
reclassified, CA §2-208.
Surplus.
Application of capital surplus, CA §§2-303,
2-304, 2-308.
Transfer of stock.
Close corporation, CA §4-503.
Closing transfer books.
Fixing time, CA §2-511.
Fiduciaries.
Uniform act for simplification of fiduciary
security transfers, ET §§15-301 to 15-311.
Radio stations.
Restrictions on transferability of stock of
radio stations, CA §5-703.
Record date.
Fixing, CA §2-511.
Restrictions on certificate, CA §2-211.
Transferees.
Liability, CA §2-215.
Trust.
Voting trust, CA §2-510.
Ultra vires.
Representative suit against officers or
corporations, CA §1-403.
Validation.
Certain deeds granting all or substantially all of
property, RP §14-113.

CORPORATIONS —Cont'd
Stock and stockholders —Cont'd
Value.
  Appraisal.
    Objecting stockholders to merger or
      consolidation, CA §3-210.
  Consolidation, merger and other transfers of
    property.
    Right to fair value, CA §3-202.
  Fixed by directors or set out in charter, CA
    §2-203.
Voting.
  Belonging to another, CA §2-508.
  Charter.
    Effect of charter requirements for greater or
      smaller proportion, CA §2-104.
    Revival or extension of charter, CA §3-501.
  Consent to actions by writing or e-mail, CA
    §2-505.
  Control shares.
    Voting rights of certain control shares, CA
      §§3-701 to 3-710. See within this
      subheading, "Control shares."
  Cumulative voting, CA §2-104.
  Each share entitled to one vote, CA §2-507.
  Effect of outstanding shares, CA §2-204.
  Fiduciaries, CA §2-508.
    Shares held by fiduciaries, CA §2-508.
  How shares voted, CA §2-507.
  Informal action, CA §2-505.
  Joint owners.
    Shares held jointly by two or more persons,
      CA §2-508.
  Majority vote, CA §2-506.
    Effect of charter requirements for greater or
      smaller proportion, CA §2-104.
  Notice.
    Waiver of notice, CA §2-504.
  Owned by corporation, CA §2-509.
  Pledged shares, CA §2-508.
    Fiduciaries, CA §2-508.
    Generally, CA §2-507.
  Proxies, CA §2-507.
    Duration, CA §2-507.
    Manner of voting, CA §2-507.
    Nonstock corporations, CA §5-202.
    Quorum, CA §2-506.
    Revocability, CA §2-507.
    Validity, CA §2-507.
  Reduction of stated capital, CA §2-306.
  Trust.
    Voting trust, CA §2-510.
      Rights of holders of certificates to inspect,
        CA §2-512.
  Two or more classes of stock.
    Entitled to vote separately, CA §2-506.
  Voting trust, CA §2-510.
    Rights of holders of certificates to inspect, CA
      §2-512.
  What shares voted, CA §2-507.
  Voting trusts, CA §2-510.
Warrants.
  Rights to subscribe, CA §2-204.
Subsidiary corporations.
Consolidation, merger and other transfers of
  property.
  Merger of subsidiary.
    Procedure, CA §3-106.
Summons and process.
Criminal cases, CP §4-203.

CORPORATIONS —Cont'd
Supplementary articles.
Charters. See within this heading, "Charters."
Surveys and surveyors.
Permits.
  General provisions, BOP §§15-401 to 15-406.
  See SURVEYS AND SURVEYORS.
Takeovers.
Fiduciaries.
  Successor corporate fiduciaries, ET §§15-1A-01
    to 15-1A-05.
  See FIDUCIARIES.
Unsolicited takeovers, CA §§3-801 to 3-805. See
  within this heading, "Unsolicited takeovers of
  corporations and real estate investment
  trusts."
Taxation.
Acceptance of record or filing by department.
  Conclusive evidence of payment, CA §1-206.
Admissions and amusement tax.
  Payment of tax.
    Liability of corporate officers, TG §4-301.
Assets.
  Sale or transfer of assets.
    Applicability of tax, TP §12-106.
    Calculation, TP §12-105.
  Transfer of corporate assets.
    Collection of county property tax, TP §13-404.
Bonus tax, CA §1-206.
Consolidation, merger and other transfers of
  property.
  Certificate for each county in which property
    located, CA §3-112.
  Recordation tax.
    Applicability, TP §12-106.
    Calculation, TP §12-105.
  Waiver of exemption, CA §3-116.
Department of assessments and taxation. See
  within this heading, "Departments."
Dissolution.
  Filing articles of dissolution.
    Advance payment of personal property taxes,
      TP §10-206.
  Involuntary dissolution.
    Certification of order to department, CA
      §3-417.
  Voluntary dissolution.
    Requirements as to payment of taxes, CA
      §3-407.
Excise tax on vessels and boats.
  Personal liability, NR §8-716.1.
Exemptions.
  Waiver on consolidation, merger and other
    transfers of property, CA §3-116.
Expiration of corporate existence by charter
  provisions.
  Payment of taxes, CA §3-519.
Foreign corporation.
  Failure to file annual tax report.
    Effect, CA §7-304.
Forfeiture of charter for nonpayment of taxes.
  Correction of mistakes.
    Proclamation, CA §3-505.
  Other remedies not affected, CA §3-507.
  Proclamation of department.
    Duties of officers in regard to proclamation,
      CA §3-504.
    When made, CA §3-504.
Franchise tax.
  General provisions.
    See TAXATION.

CORPORATIONS —Cont'd
Taxation —Cont'd
General provisions.
 See TAXATION.
Income tax.
 See INCOME TAX.
Payment.
 Conclusive evidence of payment of fees and
  taxes, CA §1-205.
Property transfer tax.
 Applicability of tax to corporate conveyances,
  TP §13-206.
 County transfer tax, TP §13-405.
Reports.
 Annual report to be filed with department.
  Required, TP §11-101.
Revival of charter.
 Acceptance of articles of revival as evidence of
  payment of taxes, CA §3-510.
 Payment conditions on acceptance of articles of
  revival, CA §3-509.
Tax court.
Appeals to tax court.
 Representation of corporations.
  Corporate officers, TG §13-515.
Telegraph and telephone companies.
Formation as corporation, PUC §8-102.
Trade names.
Certificates.
 Filing requirements generally, CA §1-406.
Transfer of property. See within this heading,
 "Consolidation, merger and other transfers of
 property."
Transportation cooperatives, CA §5-6A-01.
Trusts and trustees.
Business combinations.
 Real estate investment trust.
  Power to enter into business combination, CA
   §8-301.
Dissolution.
 Involuntary dissolution.
  Appointment, CA §3-414.
  Powers of trustees, CA §3-414.
 Voluntary dissolution.
  Powers of directors, CA §3-410.
Reorganization.
 Action by trustee, CA §3-301.
Termination of certain trusts without order of
 court.
 Corporate fiduciaries, ET §14-107.
Ultra vires.
 Proceedings by corporation acting through
  trustee, CA §1-403.
Voting trust, CA §2-510.
 Right of holders of certificates to inspection of
  corporate documents, CA §2-512.
Ultra vires.
Attorney general.
 Proceedings through, CA §1-403.
Defense of, CA §1-403.
Proceedings by corporation.
 Acting through receiver, trustee or stockholders
  in representative capacity, CA §1-403.
Unemployment compensation.
Contributions.
 Priorities under dissolution or distribution.
  Dissolution of corporation, LE §8-634.
  Forfeiture of corporate charter, LE §8-634.
Insurance payments.
 Delinquency list.
  Duty of secretary of economic and
   employment development, CA §3-503.

CORPORATIONS —Cont'd
Unemployment compensation —Cont'd
Insurance payments —Cont'd
 Failure to pay.
  Correction of record errors, CA §3-505.
  Expiration of corporate existence by charter
   provisions, CA §3-519.
  Notice of proclamation.
   Reinstatement of corporate charter after
    payment of delinquent contribution, CA
    §3-504.
  Revival of corporate charter.
   Acceptance of article of revival as evidence
    of payment, CA §3-510.
   Payment conditions on acceptance of
    articles of revival, CA §3-509.
   Procedure, CA §3-507.
  Other remedies not affected, CA §3-506.
  Required, CA §3-407.
Unincorporated associations.
See ASSOCIATIONS.
United Methodist Church.
See UNITED METHODIST CHURCH.
United Presbyterian Church.
See UNITED PRESBYTERIAN CHURCH.
**Unsolicited takeovers of corporations and real
 estate investment trusts,** CA §§3-801 to
 3-805.
Applicability of provisions, CA §3-802.
Definitions, CA §3-801.
Directors of corporation that elects to be subject to
 provisions.
 Classes of directors, CA §3-803.
 Number, CA §3-804.
 Removal, CA §3-804.
 Requirements as to, CA §3-802.
 Terms of office, CA §3-803.
 Vacancies, CA §3-804.
Meetings of stockholders.
 Special meetings, CA §3-805.
Usury.
Defense of usury, CL §12-103.
Validation.
Certain deeds granting all or substantially all of
 property, RP §14-113.
Venue.
Bonds, surety.
 Surety on bonds, CJ §6-202.
Forfeiture of charter.
 Conduct in connection with organized crime, CA
  §1-405.
Office.
 Where no principal office in state, CJ §6-202.
Verification.
Alternative to verification, CA §1-302.
Vessels and boats.
Personal liability for excise taxes and penalties,
 NR §8-716.1.
Voluntary dissolution. See within this heading,
 "Dissolution."
Volunteer fire companies.
Recordation.
 Exemption, CA §1-203.1.
Voting trusts.
Stockholders, CA §2-510.
Waiver.
Notice.
 General provisions, CA §2-504.
Wills.
Legacy for charitable uses.
 Formation of corporation to take, ET §4-409.

CORPORATIONS —Cont'd
Workers' compensation.
Covered employees and employers.
Corporate officers.
Generally, LE §9-206.

CORRECTIONAL ADMINISTRATOR.
Defined, COR §8-201.
Leave of absence for probationary appointee during training, COR §8-209.
Probationary appointment, COR §8-209.
Qualifications for probationary or permanent appointment, COR §8-209.
Training.
Municipal or county governments' rights, powers, duties or responsibilities not limited, COR §8-210.
Probationary appointees, COR §8-209.

CORRECTIONAL ENTERPRISES.
Maryland correctional enterprises, COR §§3-501 to 3-528.
See MARYLAND CORRECTIONAL ENTERPRISES.

CORRECTIONAL FACILITIES.
Another state operating facility in state, COR §10-601.
Baltimore City detention center, COR §§5-401 to 5-406.
Case records.
Inmates in custody of division of correction, COR §§3-601 to 3-609.
See CORRECTION, DIVISION OF.
Citizens' advisory committees for state correctional facilities, COR §§10-401 to 10-407.
See PRISONS AND PRISONERS.
Commission on correctional standards, COR §§8-106 to 8-117.
See PRISONS AND PRISONERS.
Community adult rehabilitation centers, COR §§11-301 to 11-320.
See COMMUNITY ADULT REHABILITATION CENTERS.
Community service programs, COR §§8-701 to 8-711.
See COMMUNITY SERVICE PROGRAMS.
Construction of state correctional facilities, COR §§10-101 to 10-107.
See PRISONS AND PRISONERS.
Contraband in correctional facility.
Holding personal property of inmate, COR §10-801.
Correctional farms, COR §§11-401 to 11-407.
See CORRECTIONAL FARMS.
Correctional mutual aid agreements, COR §§2-401 to 2-406.
See CORRECTIONAL MUTUAL AID AGREEMENTS.
Correctional training commission, COR §§8-201 to 2-210.
See CORRECTIONAL TRAINING COMMISSION.
Crimes committed at correctional facilities, COR §§8-801 to 8-803.
See PRISONS AND PRISONERS.
Death penalty.
Procedures for carrying out death penalty generally, COR §§3-901 to 3-909.
See DEATH PENALTY.
Defined, COR §1-101.

CORRECTIONAL FACILITIES —Cont'd
Department of public safety and correctional services.
Generally, COR §§2-101 to 2-201.
See PUBLIC SAFETY AND CORRECTIONAL SERVICES DEPARTMENT.
Detainers.
Interstate agreement on detainers, COR §§8-401 to 8-417.
See INTERSTATE AGREEMENT ON DETAINERS.
Intrastate detainers, COR §§8-501 to 8-503.
Diminution credits.
Inmates committed to custody of commissioner of correction, COR §§3-701 to 3-711.
See DIMINUTION OF INMATE'S TERM OF CONFINEMENT.
Inmates imprisoned at local correctional facilities, COR §§11-501 to 11-509.
See DIMINUTION OF INMATE'S TERM OF CONFINEMENT.
Division of correction, COR §§3-101 to 3-222.
See CORRECTION, DIVISION OF.
Division of parole and probation, COR §§6-101 to 6-116.
See PAROLE AND PROBATION.
Division of pretrial detention and services, COR §§5-101 to 5-203.
Grievances.
Inmate grievance office, COR §§10-201 to 10-210.
See PRISONS AND PRISONERS.
Home detention program.
Inmates in custody of commissioner of correction, COR §§3-401 to 3-415.
See HOME DETENTION PROGRAM.
Inmates sentenced to jurisdiction of division of correction.
Generally.
See PRISONS AND PRISONERS.
Inmate welfare funds, COR §§10-501 to 10-504.
Inmate work force, COR §§9-501 to 9-520.
See PRISONS AND PRISONERS.
Internal investigative unit, COR §10-701.
Interstate corrections compact, COR §§8-601 to 8-611.
See PRISONS AND PRISONERS.
Law-enforcement and correctional training fund, COR §§8-301 to 8-305.
Local correctional facilities.
Correctional farms, COR §§11-401 to 11-407.
See CORRECTIONAL FARMS.
Defined, COR §1-101.
Diminution credits, COR §§11-501 to 11-509.
See DIMINUTION OF INMATE'S TERM OF CONFINEMENT.
Employment of inmate as alternative to confinement, COR §§11-601 to 11-607.
See JAILS.
Generally, COR §§11-101 to 11-204.
See JAILS.
Individual county provisions, COR §§11-701 to 11-726.
See JAILS.
Mandatory supervision, COR §§7-501 to 7-506.
See PAROLE AND PROBATION.
Maryland correctional enterprises, COR §§3-501 to 3-528.
See MARYLAND CORRECTIONAL ENTERPRISES.
Mutual aid agreements, COR §§2-401 to 2-406.
See CORRECTIONAL MUTUAL AID AGREEMENTS.

CORRECTIONAL FACILITIES —Cont'd
Offender employment coordination, COR §§2-301 to 2-307.
 See OFFENDER EMPLOYMENT COORDINATION.
Parole commission, COR §§7-201 to 7-208.
 See PAROLE AND PROBATION.
Parole, release on mandatory supervision generally, COR §§7-101 to 7-805.
 See PAROLE AND PROBATION.
Patuxent institution, COR §§4-101 to 4-401.
 See PATUXENT INSTITUTION.
Permanent partial or permanent total disability while working for wage.
 Sundry claims board, COR §§10-301 to 10-310.
 See PRISONS AND PRISONERS.
Personal property of inmate.
 Holding period, COR §10-801.
Prerelease unit for women, COR §§3-301 to 3-305.
Pretrial release services program, COR §§5-301, 5-302.
Prohibited acts at correctional facilities, COR §§8-801 to 8-803.
 See PRISONS AND PRISONERS.
Road work by inmates, COR §§9-501 to 9-520.
 See PRISONS AND PRISONERS.
Sentencing to correctional facility, COR §§9-101 to 9-202.
 See SENTENCE AND PUNISHMENT.
Standards for correctional services, COR §§8-101 to 8-117.
 See PRISONS AND PRISONERS.
State correctional facilities.
 Defined, COR §1-101.
Transfer of inmates.
 Generally, COR §§9-301 to 9-308.
 See PRISONS AND PRISONERS.
Wardens at correctional facilities in division of correction, COR §§3-210 to 3-213.
Work release program.
 Inmate sentenced to the jurisdiction of division of correction, COR §§3-801 to 3-807.
 See PRISONS AND PRISONERS.
 Local correctional facilities.
  Employment of inmate as alternative to confinement, COR §§11-601 to 11-607.
  See JAILS.

CORRECTIONAL FARMS, COR §§11-401 to 11-407.
Acquisition of property, COR §11-404.
Acreage for each crop, governing body to determine, COR §11-405.
Budget of proposed expenditures, county to compare, COR §11-404.
Compensation to inmate for work, COR §11-407.
Control of governing body of county, COR §11-405.
Crops to be planted and grown, governing body to determine, COR §11-405.
Establishment, COR §11-403.
Frederick, Garrett, Harford, Howard, Washington and Worcester counties.
 Subtitle not applicable, COR §11-402.
Governing body defined, COR §11-401.
Operation, COR §11-405.
Payment of inmate, COR §11-407.
Purchase of property, COR §11-404.
Transfer of inmate to correctional farm, COR §11-406.

CORRECTIONAL FARMS —Cont'd
Use of proceeds, COR §11-405.
Work as directed, duty of inmate, COR §11-406.

CORRECTIONAL INDUSTRIES.
Maryland correctional enterprises, COR §§3-501 to 3-528.
 See MARYLAND CORRECTIONAL ENTERPRISES.

CORRECTIONAL MUTUAL AID AGREEMENTS, COR §§2-401 to 2-406.
Construction and interpretation, COR §2-402.
Definitions, COR §2-401.
Entering or renewing agreement, COR §2-403.
Expenditures, COR §2-406.
Indemnification, COR §2-403.
Liberal construction, COR §2-402.
Training requirements, COR §2-404.
Waiver of certain claims, COR §2-403.
Workers' compensation.
 Services considered in course of employment and in line of duty, COR §2-405.

CORRECTIONAL OFFICERS.
Arrest without a warrant, authority, CP §2-207.
Correctional training commission, COR §§8-201 to 2-210.
 See CORRECTIONAL TRAINING COMMISSION.
Death in the line of duty.
 Death benefits, PS §1-202.
 Killed in line of duty.
  Scholarships to children or spouses, ED §18-601.
Defined, COR §8-201.
Designation by commissioner, power of arrest, qualifications, COR §3-216.
Health and welfare benefits program.
 Enrollment and participation, SPP §2-507.
Heart attack.
 Death benefits.
  Death as result of personal injury in performance of duties.
  Presumption, PS §1-202.
Killed in line of duty.
 Scholarships to children or spouses, ED §18-601.
Leave of absence for probationary appointee during training, COR §8-209.
Notification of exposure to contagious disease, HG §18-213.
Probationary appointment, COR §8-209.
Qualifications for probationary or permanent appointment, COR §8-209.
Retirement system, SPP §§25-101 to 25-404.
Scholarships to children or spouses.
 Public safety employee killed in line of duty, ED §18-601.
Stroke.
 Death benefits.
  Death as result of personal injury in performance of duties.
  Presumption, PS §1-202.
Training.
 Municipal or county governments' rights, powers, duties or responsibilities not limited, COR §8-210.
 Probationary appointees, COR §8-209.
Warrantless arrest, authority, CP §2-207.

CORRECTIONAL OFFICERS' RETIREMENT SYSTEM, SPP §§25-101 to 25-404.
Benefits, SPP §§25-401 to 25-404.
 Death benefits, SPP §§29-201 to 29-207.

CORRECTIONAL OFFICERS' RETIREMENT SYSTEM —Cont'd
Benefits —Cont'd
Deferred vested benefits, SPP §§29-301 to 29-305.
Disability benefits generally, SPP §§29-101 to 29-118.
   See STATE RETIREMENT AND PENSION SYSTEM.
Early service retirement, SPP §25-401.1.
Normal service retirement, SPP §25-401.
Other benefits, SPP §25-404.
Re-employment after retirement, SPP §25-403.
Retirement after termination of membership, SPP §25-402.
Contributions.
Accumulated contributions, SPP §§29-501, 29-502.
Employer contributions, SPP §21-306.2.
   Transfer from employees' pension or employees' retirement system, SPP §25-206.
Cost-of-living adjustments.
General provisions, SPP §§29-401 to 29-427.
   See STATE RETIREMENT AND PENSION SYSTEM.
Unlimited adjustment, SPP §§29-410 to 29-413.
Death benefits, SPP §§29-201 to 29-207.
Election of allowance by surviving spouse, SPP §29-205.
Special death benefit, SPP §29-204.1.
Deferred vested benefits, SPP §§29-301 to 29-305.
Vested allowances for members, SPP §29-302.
Disability benefits.
General provisions, SPP §§29-101 to 29-118.
   See STATE RETIREMENT AND PENSION SYSTEM.
Promotion from system and not-transfer of service credit to employees' pension system, SPP §§29-105, 29-108, 29-110.
Early service retirement, SPP §25-401.1.
Employer contributions, SPP §21-306.2.
Transfer from employees' pension or employees' retirement system, SPP §25-206.
Legislative policy, SPP §25-102.
Local governmental unit participation in system, SPP §§31-2B-01 to 31-2B-05.
Approval of participation as though local system not in operation, SPP §31-2B-03.
Credit for local employment, SPP §31-2B-04.
Definitions, SPP §31-2B-01.
Eligible governmental units, SPP §31-2B-02.
Transition to state plan, SPP §31-2B-05.
Withdrawal from participation, SPP §31-302.
Membership, SPP §§25-201 to 25-205.
Applicability, SPP §25-201.
Condition of employment, SPP §25-202.
Contributions by members, SPP §§25-203, 25-205.
Exceptions to applicability, SPP §25-201.
Interest on member contributions, SPP §25-203.
Optional membership for certain local officers, SPP §25-202.
Retirement after termination of membership, SPP §25-402.
Termination of membership, SPP §25-205.
Transfer from employees' pension or employees' retirement system, SPP §25-203.1.
   Employer contributions, SPP §25-206.
Military service credits, SPP §§38-101 to 38-105.
Public policy, SPP §25-102.
Re-employment after retirement, SPP §25-403.
Scope of title, SPP §25-101.
Service credits, SPP §§25-301 to 25-307.
Creditable service, SPP §25-307.

CORRECTIONAL OFFICERS' RETIREMENT SYSTEM —Cont'd
Service credits —Cont'd
Eligibility, SPP §25-301.
Eligibility service.
   Purchases, SPP §§25-305, 25-307.
   Redeposit of accumulated contributions, SPP §25-304.
   Types, SPP §25-303.
Military service credits, SPP §§38-101 to 38-105.
Purchase of service credits, SPP §§25-306, 25-307.
   Full cost, SPP §25-306.
   Separation of member from employment, SPP §25-304.1.
Redeposit of accumulated contributions, SPP §25-304.
Rules for computation, SPP §25-302.
Transfer, SPP §25-306.1.
Types of eligibility service, SPP §25-303.
Social security benefits, SPP §§36-101, 36-102.
Transfer of service credit, SPP §25-306.1.
Transfers between retirement or pension systems, SPP §§37-101 to 37-206.
From employees' pension or employees' retirement system, SPP §25-203.1.
   Transfer of employer contributions, SPP §25-206.

CORRECTIONAL SERVICES.
Another state operating facility in state, COR §10-601.
Baltimore City detention center, COR §§5-401 to 5-406.
Case records.
Inmates in custody of division of correction, COR §§3-601 to 3-609.
   See CORRECTION, DIVISION OF.
Citizens' advisory committees for state correctional facilities, COR §§10-401 to 10-407.
See PRISONS AND PRISONERS.
Commission on correctional standards, COR §§8-106 to 8-117.
See PRISONS AND PRISONERS.
Community adult rehabilitation centers, COR §§11-301 to 11-320.
See COMMUNITY ADULT REHABILITATION CENTERS.
Community service programs, COR §§8-701 to 8-711.
See COMMUNITY SERVICE PROGRAMS.
Construction of state correctional facilities, COR §§10-101 to 10-107.
See PRISONS AND PRISONERS.
Correctional farms, COR §§11-401 to 11-407.
See CORRECTIONAL FARMS.
Correctional training commission, COR §§8-201 to 2-210.
See CORRECTIONAL TRAINING COMMISSION.
Crimes committed at correctional facilities, COR §§8-801 to 8-803.
See PRISONS AND PRISONERS.
Death penalty.
Procedures for carrying out death penalty generally, COR §§3-901 to 3-909.
See DEATH PENALTY.
Definitions, COR §1-101.
Department of public safety and correctional services.
Generally, COR §§2-101 to 2-201.
   See PUBLIC SAFETY AND CORRECTIONAL SERVICES DEPARTMENT.

CORRECTIONAL SERVICES —Cont'd
Detainers.
Interstate agreement on detainers, COR §§8-401 to 8-417.
See INTERSTATE AGREEMENT ON DETAINERS.
Intrastate detainers, COR §§8-501 to 8-503.
Diminution credits.
Inmates committed to custody of commissioner of correction, COR §§3-701 to 3-711.
See DIMINUTION OF INMATE'S TERM OF CONFINEMENT.
Inmates imprisoned at local correctional facilities, COR §§11-501 to 11-509.
See DIMINUTION OF INMATE'S TERM OF CONFINEMENT.
Division of correction, COR §§3-101 to 3-222.
See CORRECTION, DIVISION OF.
Division of parole and probation, COR §§6-101 to 6-116.
See PAROLE AND PROBATION.
Division of pretrial detention and services, COR §§5-101 to 5-203.
Grievances.
Inmate grievance office, COR §§10-201 to 10-210.
See PRISONS AND PRISONERS.
Home detention program.
Inmates in custody of commissioner of correction, COR §§3-401 to 3-415.
See HOME DETENTION PROGRAM.
Individual counties, COR §§11-701 to 11-726.
See JAILS.
Inmates sentenced to jurisdiction of division of correction.
Generally.
See PRISONS AND PRISONERS.
Inmate welfare funds, COR §§10-501 to 10-504.
Inmate work force, COR §§9-501 to 9-520.
See PRISONS AND PRISONERS.
Internal investigative unit, COR §10-701.
Interstate corrections compact, COR §§8-601 to 8-611.
See PRISONS AND PRISONERS.
Law-enforcement and correctional training fund, COR §§8-301 to 8-305.
Local correctional facilities.
Generally, COR §§11-101 to 11-204.
See JAILS.
Individual county provisions, COR §§11-701 to 11-726.
See JAILS.
State reimbursement, COR §§9-401 to 9-405.
Mandatory supervision, COR §§7-501 to 7-506.
See PAROLE AND PROBATION.
Maryland correctional enterprises, COR §§3-501 to 3-528.
See MARYLAND CORRECTIONAL ENTERPRISES.
Parole commission, COR §§7-201 to 7-208.
See PAROLE AND PROBATION.
Parole, release on mandatory supervision generally, COR §§7-101 to 7-805.
See PAROLE AND PROBATION.
Patuxent institution, COR §§4-101 to 4-401.
See PATUXENT INSTITUTION.
Permanent partial or permanent total disability while working for wage.
Sundry claims board, COR §§10-301 to 10-310.
See PRISONS AND PRISONERS.
Prerelease unit for women, COR §§3-301 to 3-305.

CORRECTIONAL SERVICES —Cont'd
Pretrial release services program, COR §§5-301, 5-302.
Prohibited acts at correctional facilities, COR §§8-801 to 8-803.
See PRISONS AND PRISONERS.
Road work by inmates, COR §§9-501 to 9-520.
See PRISONS AND PRISONERS.
Sentencing to correctional facility, COR §§9-101 to 9-202.
See SENTENCE AND PUNISHMENT.
Standards for correctional services, COR §§8-101 to 8-117.
See PRISONS AND PRISONERS.
State reimbursement of local correctional facilities, COR §§9-401 to 9-405.
Transfer of inmates.
Generally, COR §§9-301 to 9-308.
See PRISONS AND PRISONERS.
Work release program.
Inmate sentenced to the jurisdiction of division of correction, COR §§3-801 to 3-807.
See PRISONS AND PRISONERS.
Local correctional facilities.
Employment of inmate as alternative to confinement, COR §§11-601 to 11-607.
See JAILS.

CORRECTIONAL STANDARDS, COMMISSION ON, COR §§8-106 to 8-117.
See PRISONS AND PRISONERS.

CORRECTIONAL SUPERVISOR.
Defined, COR §8-201.
Leave of absence for probationary appointee during training, COR §8-209.
Probationary appointment, COR §8-209.
Qualifications for probationary or permanent appointment, COR §8-209.
Training.
Municipal or county governments' rights, powers, duties or responsibilities not limited, COR §8-210.
Probationary appointees, COR §8-209.

CORRECTIONAL TRAINING COMMISSION, COR §§8-201 to 2-210.
Chairperson, COR §8-205.
Compensation and expenses, COR §8-207.
Correctional officers, appointment as members, COR §8-204.
Correctional training schools, powers and duties, COR §8-208.
Definitions, COR §8-201.
Deputy director, COR §8-206.
Designation of representative to act at meetings, COR §8-204.
Established in department of public safety and correctional services, COR §8-203.
Executive director, COR §8-206.
Legislative findings, COR §8-202.
Meetings, quorum, COR §8-207.
Membership, COR §8-204.
Minutes of meetings and other records, duty to maintain, COR §8-207.
Powers and duties, COR §8-208.
Staff, COR §8-206.
Vice chairperson, COR §8-205.

CORRECTIONAL TRAINING SCHOOLS.
Powers of correctional training commission, COR §8-208.

CORRECTION, DIVISION OF, COR §§3-101 to 3-222.

Acquisition of property, COR §3-219.

Acting commissioner, deputy commissioner, COR §3-209.

Annual accounting by commissioner to secretary, COR §§3-206, 3-207.

Annual report for each correctional facility.
Commissioner to submit to secretary and governor, COR §3-207.

Appointing officer for other officers and employees in division.
Commissioner appointing officer, COR §3-215.

Appointment of commissioner, COR §3-202.

Appointment of deputy by commissioner, COR §3-208.

Appointment of officers and employees, COR §3-215.

Assignment of inmate to appropriate treatment, training or employment, COR §3-601.

Assistant wardens.
Appointment by commissioner, qualifications, term, duties, COR §3-213.

Background data of inmate, recording for identification purposes, COR §3-601.

Bills or accounts against unit in division, approval, COR §3-220.

Case records of inmates sentenced to jurisdiction of division, COR §§3-601 to 3-609.
Admissibility in evidence, COR §3-605.
Another state, providing record to, COR §3-606.
Character of offense committed by inmate, COR §3-601.
Conduct, effort and progress, COR §3-601.
Disclosure prohibited, exceptions, conditions, COR §3-602.
Division to assemble promptly, COR §3-601.
Exchange of information with division of parole and probation, COR §3-608.
Makeup of record, COR §3-601.
Parole commission, providing record to, COR §3-603.
Police officer of county or municipal corporation, providing, COR §3-607.
Reimbursement by state for cost of providing record, COR §3-604.

Classification of inmates on basis of information assembled in case record, COR §3-601.

Commissioner of division defined, COR §1-101.

Community adult rehabilitation centers, COR §§11-301 to 11-320.
See COMMUNITY ADULT REHABILITATION CENTERS.

Compensation for commissioner provided in state budget, COR §3-202.

Compensation for officers and employees, COR §3-215.
Salaries generally, ED §6-302.

Contract with inmate.
Officer or employee prohibited from accepting, COR §3-218.

Correctional officers.
Designation by commissioner, power of arrest, qualifications, COR §3-216.

County not billed for expenses of inmates sentenced to jurisdiction of division, COR §3-222.

CORRECTION, DIVISION OF —Cont'd

Death penalty.
Procedures for carrying out death penalty generally, COR §§3-901 to 3-909.
See DEATH PENALTY.

Definitions, COR §§1-101, 3-101.

Deputy commissioner.
Appointment, status, qualifications, COR §3-208.
Powers and duties, COR §3-209.

Devise or bequest from inmate.
Officer or employee prohibited from accepting, COR §3-218.

Diminution credits.
Inmates committed to custody of commissioner of correction, COR §§3-701 to 3-711.
See DIMINUTION OF INMATE'S TERM OF CONFINEMENT.

Discipline and conduct of inmates.
Required regulations by commissioner, COR §3-205.

Duties, discipline and conduct of officers and employees.
Regulations by commissioner, COR §3-205.

Established, COR §3-201.

Examination of persons under oath, power of commissioner, COR §3-204.

Expenses relating to inmates sentenced to jurisdiction of division.
County not billed or to pay, COR §3-222.

Failure to appear before commissioner, misdemeanor, COR §3-204.

False swearing under oath before commissioner.
Perjury, COR §3-204.

Federal grants and loans, COR §3-221.

Financial affairs of each unit in division, control, COR §3-220.

Fingerprinting inmate for identification purposes, COR §3-601.

Gift or reward from inmate.
Officer or employee prohibited from accepting, COR §3-218.

Head of division, commissioner, COR §3-203.

Home detention program.
Inmates in custody of commissioner of correction, COR §§3-401 to 3-415.
See HOME DETENTION PROGRAM.

Inmates sentenced to jurisdiction of division.
Generally.
See PRISONS AND PRISONERS.

Leave of inmate from confinement.
Work release program.
Inmate sentenced to jurisdiction of division of correction, COR §§3-801 to 3-807.
See WORK RELEASE PROGRAMS.

List of inmates whose sentences expire.
Providing police of county or municipal corporation from which inmate committed, COR §3-607.

Maryland correctional enterprises, COR §§3-501 to 3-528.
See MARYLAND CORRECTIONAL ENTERPRISES.

Oaths, power of commissioner to administer, COR §3-204.

Oath taken by commissioner prior to entering office, COR §3-202.

Offender employment coordination, COR §§2-301 to 2-307.
See OFFENDER EMPLOYMENT COORDINATION.

CORRECTION, DIVISION OF —Cont'd
Optional regulations by commissioner, COR §3-205.
Patuxent institution, COR §§4-101 to 4-401.
See PATUXENT INSTITUTION.
Perjury.
False swearing under oath before commissioner, COR §3-204.
Photograph of inmate for identification purposes, COR §3-601.
Physical, mental and educational examination of inmate after sentencing, COR §3-601.
Prerelease unit for women, COR §§3-301 to 3-305.
Processing inmates sentenced to jurisdiction of division, COR §3-601.
Punishments for violations of discipline by inmates.
Required regulations by commissioner, COR §3-205.
Qualifications of commissioner, COR §3-202.
Receipts and disbursements of division.
Statement submitted to secretary, COR §§3-206, 3-207.
Referral of inmate to Patuxent institution.
Authority of commissioner, COR §4-301.
Refusal to testify in subpoenaed by commissioner, misdemeanor, COR §3-204.
Regulations for operation and maintenance of units in division.
Adoption by commissioner, COR §3-205.
Removal of officers and employees, COR §3-215.
Responsibility of commissioner to secretary and governor, COR §3-203.
Sale or otherwise conveying property, COR §3-219.
Sentencing to correctional facility, COR §§9-101 to 9-202.
See SENTENCE AND PUNISHMENT.
Service of commissioner at pleasure of secretary, COR §3-202.
Statement of receipts and disbursements.
Commissioner to submit the secretary, COR §§3-206, 3-207.
State reimbursement of local correctional facilities, COR §§9-401 to 9-405.
Status in state personnel management system.
Officers and employees, COR §3-215.
Subpoenas, power of commissioner to issue, COR §3-204.
Surety bond for commissioner and officers and employees, COR §3-217.
Title to property previously acquired by former department of correction, COR §3-219.
Transfer of inmates.
Generally, COR §§9-301 to 9-308.
See PRISONS AND PRISONERS.
Trustee of state, holding property as, COR §3-219.
Wardens and administrators for each correctional facility in division.
Appointing officer for officers and other employees of facility, COR §3-215.
Appointment by commissioner, qualifications, term, COR §3-210.
Assistant wardens.
Appointment by commissioner, qualifications, term, duties, COR §3-213.
Compensation, COR §3-215.
Dwellings for wardens, COR §3-215.

CORRECTION, DIVISION OF —Cont'd
Wardens and administrators for each correctional facility in division —Cont'd
Powers and duties, COR §3-211.
Report and statement on affairs of correctional facility, COR §3-212.
Retake warrant for apprehension and return of escapee.
Issuance, copy the state's attorney, COR §3-214.
Work release program.
Inmate sentenced to the jurisdiction of division of correction, COR §§3-801 to 3-807.
See WORK RELEASE PROGRAMS.

CORROBORATION OF TESTIMONY.
Possession of stolen property.
Person actually stealing property not accomplice for purposes of, CR §7-104.

CORRUPTION.
Jurors, CR §9-305.
Obstruction of justice, CR §9-306.

COSMETICS.
Food, drugs and cosmetics.
General provisions, HG §§21-101 to 21-1215.
See FOOD, DRUGS AND COSMETICS.

COSMETOLOGISTS.
Appeals.
State board of cosmetologists.
Judicial review of decisions, BOP §5-209.
Apprentices.
Complaints against, BOP §5-407.
Defined, BOP §5-101.
Registration.
Students and apprentices, BOP §§5-401 to 5-409. See within this heading, "Registration."
Sanitary practice violations, correcting, BOP §5-407.
Beauty salons.
Defined, BOP §5-101.
Inspections, BOP §5-520.
Citations for violations, BOP §5-610.
Limited practice beauty salons.
Permits, BOP §§5-501, 5-504, 5-505.
Misrepresentation of establishment as beauty salon.
Prohibited, BOP §5-604.
Permits, BOP §§5-501 to 5-506. See within this heading, "Permits."
Residential purposes.
Use for, BOP §5-606.
Sale of methyl methacrylate liquid monomer in salon prohibited, HG §24-303.
Board, BOP §§5-201 to 5-210. See within this heading, "State board of cosmetologists."
Certification concerning licensee, permit holder or registrant, BOP §5-206.
Citation of act.
Short title, BOP §5-701.
Citations for violations, BOP §5-610.
Complaints against, BOP §5-314.
Apprentices, BOP §5-407.
Beauty salons, BOP §5-522.
Continuing education.
Teachers, BOP §5-311.
Correction of sanitary practice violations.
Opportunity to correct, BOP §5-314.
Apprentices, BOP §5-407.
Beauty salons, BOP §5-522.
Criminal penalties, BOP §5-609.

COSMETOLOGISTS —Cont'd
Definitions, BOP §5-101.
Diseases.
  Infectious or contagious diseases.
    Careless or negligent practice, BOP §5-607.
      Penalties, BOP §5-609.
    Restrictions on certain personnel, BOP §5-607.
Exceptions to provisions, BOP §5-102.
Fees.
  Certification of licensee, permit holder or
    registrant, BOP §5-206.
  Disposition of money collected, BOP §5-208.
  Licenses, BOP §5-309.
    Examination fees, BOP §5-306.
    Renewal fees, BOP §5-311.
  Permits.
    Beauty salon permits.
      Application fee, BOP §5-503.
      Renewal fee, BOP §5-506.
  Registration.
    Students and apprentices.
      Application fee, BOP §5-402.
      Renewal fee, BOP §5-405.
  State board of cosmetologist.
    Duty to establish fees, BOP §5-205.
Fines, BOP §5-609.
Fraud.
  Licenses.
    Denial, revocation or suspension of license or
      reprimand of licensee.
        Grounds, BOP §5-314.
Hearings.
  Licenses.
    Denial, revocation or suspension, or reprimand
      of licensee, BOP §5-315.
  Permits.
    Denial, revocation or suspension, or reprimand
      of permittee, BOP §5-523.
  Registration.
    Students and apprentices.
      Denial, revocation or suspension, or
        reprimand of registrant, BOP §5-408.
Inspections.
  Beauty salons, BOP §5-520.
    Citations for violations, BOP §5-610.
  Methyl methacrylate liquid monomer.
    Violations, BOP §5-608.1.
  Schools, BOP §5-520.
Lasers.
  Use or possession in beauty salons.
    Board may prohibit or restrict, BOP §5-608.2.
Licenses.
  Age.
    Qualifications of applicants.
      License to practice, BOP §5-304.
      Limited license, BOP §5-305.
  Applications, BOP §5-306.
  Certification concerning licensee, BOP §5-206.
  Cosmetologist aides.
    Applications, BOP §5-306.
  Defined, BOP §5-101.
  Denial.
    Grounds, BOP §5-314.
    Hearings, BOP §5-315.
    Procedure, BOP §5-314.
  Display, BOP §5-313.
  Examinations, BOP §5-307.
    Testing service.
      Used to administer examinations, BOP
        §5-307.1.

COSMETOLOGISTS —Cont'd
Licenses —Cont'd
  Examinations —Cont'd
    Waiver of examination requirement, BOP
      §5-308.
  Expiration, BOP §5-311.
    Reinstatement of expired licenses, BOP §5-312.
  Fees, BOP §5-309.
    Examination fees, BOP §5-306.
    Renewal fees, BOP §5-311.
  Issuance, BOP §5-309.
  Limited licenses, BOP §5-301.
    Defined, BOP §5-101.
    Display.
      Limited license to provide demonstrating
        services, BOP §5-313.
    Qualifications of applicants, BOP §5-305.
  Notices.
    Examinations, BOP §5-307.
    Issuance.
      Notice to qualified applicants, BOP §5-309.
    Renewal notice, BOP §5-311.
  Qualifications of applicants.
    License to practice, BOP §5-304.
    Limited licenses, BOP §5-305.
    Senior cosmetologist, BOP §5-304.
  Reinstatement of expired licenses, BOP §5-312.
  Reinstatement of suspended or revoked license,
    BOP §5-316.
  Renewal, BOP §5-311.
  Reprimand of licensees.
    Grounds, BOP §5-314.
    Hearings, BOP §5-315.
    Procedure, BOP §5-314.
    Required, BOP §5-301.
  Revocation or suspension.
    Grounds, BOP §5-314.
    Hearings, BOP §5-315.
    Penalty in lieu of, BOP §5-314.
    Procedure, BOP §5-314.
    Reinstatement, BOP §5-316.
  Scope, BOP §5-310.
  Senior cosmetologist.
    Qualifications of applicants, BOP §5-304.
  Teachers.
    Continuing education, BOP §5-311.
    Required, BOP §5-301.
    Scope of licenses, BOP §5-310.
  Term, BOP §5-311.
  Testing service.
    Used to administer examinations, BOP
      §5-307.1.
  Unlicensed practice.
    Prohibited, BOP §5-601.
  Waiver of examination requirement, BOP §5-308.
Methyl methacrylate liquid monomer.
  Use or possession prohibited, BOP §5-608.1.
Misdemeanors.
  Methyl methacrylate liquid monomer.
    Use or possession, BOP §5-608.1.
  Violations of provisions, BOP §5-609.
Monetary penalties, BOP §5-609.
Negligence.
  Diseases.
    Infectious or contagious diseases.
      Careless or negligent practice, BOP §5-607.
        Penalties, BOP §5-609.
Notices.
  Licenses.
    Examinations, BOP §5-307.

COSMETOLOGISTS —Cont'd
Notices —Cont'd
  Licenses —Cont'd
    Issuance.
      Notice to qualified applicants, BOP §5-309.
    Renewal notice, BOP §5-311.
  Permits.
    Beauty salon permits.
      Renewal notice, BOP §5-506.
    Denial, revocation or suspension, or reprimand
      of permittee.
      Hearings, BOP §5-523.
  Registration.
    Students and apprentices.
      Denial, revocation or suspension, or
        reprimand of registrant.
        Hearing, BOP §5-408.
      Renewal notice, BOP §5-405.
Oaths.
  State board of cosmetologists.
    Administration of oaths, BOP §5-207.
    Oath of office of members, BOP §5-202.
Penalties.
  Licenses.
    Revocation or suspension.
      Penalty in lieu of, BOP §5-314.
  Methyl methacrylate liquid monomer.
    Use or possession, BOP §5-608.1.
  Permits.
    Revocation or suspension.
      Penalty in lieu of, BOP §5-522.
  Registration.
    Students and apprentices.
      Revocation or suspension.
        Penalty in lieu of, BOP §5-407.
  Schools.
    Regulations for operation in sanitary manner.
      Violations, BOP §5-509.
  Violations of provisions, BOP §5-609.
Permits.
  Beauty salon permits.
    Applicants.
      Qualifications of applicants, BOP §5-502.
    Applications, BOP §5-503.
      Qualifications of applicants, BOP §5-502.
    Defined, BOP §5-101.
    Display, BOP §5-521.
    Expiration.
      Reinstatement of expired permits, BOP
        §5-506.1.
      Staggered expirations, BOP §5-506.
    Fees.
      Application fee, BOP §5-503.
      Renewal fee, BOP §5-506.
    Issuance, BOP §5-504.
    Limited practice beauty salons, BOP §5-501.
      Issuance of permits, BOP §5-504.
      Scope of permit, BOP §5-505.
    Notices.
      Renewal notice, BOP §5-506.
    Operating without permit.
      Prohibited, BOP §5-602.
    Reinstatement of expired permits, BOP
      §5-506.1.
    Renewal, BOP §5-506.
    Required, BOP §5-501.
    Scope of permit, BOP §5-505.
    Separate permit for each beauty salon, BOP
      §5-501.
    Term of permit, BOP §5-506.

COSMETOLOGISTS —Cont'd
Permits —Cont'd
  Certification concerning permit holder, BOP
    §5-206.
  Denial.
    Grounds, BOP §5-522.
    Hearings, BOP §5-523.
    Procedure, BOP §5-522.
  Display, BOP §5-521.
  Reinstatement of suspended or revoked permit,
    BOP §5-524.
  Reprimand of permittee.
    Grounds, BOP §5-522.
    Hearings, BOP §5-523.
    Procedure, BOP §5-522.
  Revocation or suspension.
    Grounds, BOP §5-522.
    Hearings, BOP §5-523.
    Penalty in lieu of, BOP §5-522.
    Procedure, BOP §5-522.
    Reinstatement, BOP §5-524.
  School permits.
    Defined, BOP §5-101.
    Display, BOP §5-521.
Practice of cosmetology.
  Defined, BOP §5-101.
  Licenses.
    Generally, BOP §§5-301 to 5-316. See within
      this heading, "Licenses."
  Locations.
    Allowed only in specified places, BOP §5-605.
    Exceptions, BOP §5-605.
  Misrepresentation as authorized practitioner.
    Prohibited, BOP §5-604.
  Students, BOP §§5-302, 5-608.
    Public school students, BOP §5-303.
  Unlicensed practice.
    Prohibited, BOP §5-601.
Records.
  State board of cosmetologists, BOP §5-207.
Registration.
  Certification concerning registrant, BOP §5-206.
  Students and apprentices, BOP §5-401.
    Applications, BOP §5-402.
    Certificate of registration, BOP §5-403.
      Display, BOP §5-406.
    Denial.
      Grounds, BOP §5-407.
      Hearings, BOP §5-408.
      Procedure, BOP §5-407.
    Display of certificates, BOP §5-406.
    Effect of registration, BOP §5-404.
    Expiration of registration, BOP §5-405.
    Failure to register.
      Prohibited, BOP §5-603.
    Fees.
      Application fee, BOP §5-402.
      Renewal fee, BOP §5-405.
    Issuance of certificate, BOP §5-403.
    Limited practice apprentice.
      Term of registration, BOP §5-405.
    Reinstatement of suspended or revoked
      registration, BOP §5-409.
    Renewal of registration, BOP §5-405.
      Notice, BOP §5-405.
    Reprimand of registrant.
      Grounds, BOP §5-407.
      Hearings, BOP §5-408.
      Notice of hearing, BOP §5-408.
      Procedure, BOP §5-407.
    Required, BOP §§5-401, 5-603.

COSMETOLOGISTS —Cont'd
Registration —Cont'd
Students and apprentices —Cont'd
Revocation or suspension.
Grounds, BOP §5-407.
Hearings, BOP §5-408.
Notice of hearing, BOP §5-408.
Penalty in lieu of, BOP §5-407.
Procedure, BOP §5-407.
Reinstatement, BOP §5-409.
Scope of registration, BOP §5-404.
Term of registration, BOP §5-405.
Rules and regulations.
Schools.
Operation in sanitary manner, BOP §5-509.
State board of cosmetologists, BOP §5-205.
Termination of regulations adopted under
provisions, BOP §5-702.
Salons. See within this heading, "Beauty salons."
Sanitary practice violations.
Opportunity to correct, BOP §5-314.
Apprentices, BOP §5-407.
Beauty salons, BOP §5-522.
Sanitation.
Schools.
Regulations for operation in sanitary manner,
BOP §5-509.
Schools.
Definition of "cosmetology school," BOP §5-101.
Inspections, BOP §5-520.
Regulations for operation in sanitary manner.
Adoption, BOP §5-509.
Penalty for violations, BOP §5-509.
Procedure for imposition, BOP §5-509.
Students.
Practice by, BOP §§5-301, 5-608.
Public school students, BOP §5-303.
Registration, BOP §§5-401 to 5-409. See within
this heading, "Registration."
Teachers.
Licenses. See within this heading, "Licenses."
Scope of provisions, BOP §5-102.
**Secretary of labor, licensing and regulation
department.**
State board of cosmetologists.
Authority of secretary, BOP §5-210.
Service of citations for violations, BOP §5-610.
Service of complaints against, BOP §5-314.
Short title of act, BOP §5-701.
State board of cosmetologists.
Appeals.
Judicial review of decisions, BOP §5-209.
Appointment of members, BOP §5-202.
Bylaws, BOP §5-205.
Chairman, BOP §5-203.
Election, BOP §5-203.
Compensation of members, BOP §5-204.
Composition, BOP §5-202.
Creation, BOP §5-201.
Definition of "board," BOP §5-101.
Disposition of money collected, BOP §5-208.
Duties, BOP §5-207.
Established, BOP §5-201.
Executive director, BOP §5-204.
Expenses of members.
Reimbursement, BOP §5-204.
Fees.
Duty to establish fees, BOP §5-205.
Judicial review of decisions, BOP §5-209.
Meetings, BOP §5-204.
Number of members, BOP §5-202.

COSMETOLOGISTS —Cont'd
State board of cosmetologists —Cont'd
Oaths.
Administration of oaths, BOP §5-207.
Oath of office of members, BOP §5-202.
Office, BOP §5-204.
Program evaluation act, SG §8-403.
Qualifications of members, BOP §5-202.
Quorum, BOP §5-204.
Records, BOP §5-207.
Removal of members, BOP §5-202.
Rules and regulations, BOP §5-205.
Secretary of labor, licensing and regulation
department.
Authority of secretary, BOP §5-210.
Staff, BOP §5-204.
Terms of members, BOP §5-202.
Vacancies, BOP §5-202.
Subpoenas.
Licenses.
Denial, revocation or suspension of license or
reprimand of licensee, BOP §5-315.
Permits.
Denial, revocation or suspension of permit or
reprimand of permittee, BOP §5-523.
Registration.
Students and apprentices.
Denial, revocation or suspension of
registration or reprimand of registrant,
BOP §5-408.
Termination of provisions, BOP §5-702.
Title of act.
Short title, BOP §5-701.
Unemployment compensation.
Certain cosmetologists exempt from covered
employment, LE §8-206.

COSTS.
Acupuncturists.
Disciplinary proceedings, HO §1A-311.
Adoption.
Independent adoptions, FL §5-3B-08.
Local department adoptions, FL §5-309.
Private agency adoptions, FL §5-3A-09.
Amicus curiae, AppRev Rule 8-607.
Appeals generally.
See APPEALS.
Attorneys at law.
Disbarment or suspension, CJA Rule 16-761.
Discipline and inactive status.
Audit of attorney's accounts and records, CJA
Rule 16-722.
Fees.
See ATTORNEYS' FEES.
Auditors.
Circuit courts, CivProCir Rule 2-543.
Automobile insurance fund.
Recovery of money paid by fund, IN §20-608.
Bad checks. See within this heading, "Checks."
Bonds, surety.
Bond premium as costs, Rule 1-406.
Bounding lands.
Fees of engineers, surveyors or other experts, RP
§14-111.
Certified questions of law, CJ §12-610.
Checks.
Bad checks.
Paying costs with bad check, CR §8-108.
Service charges for bad checks, CJ §7-208.
Circuit courts, CJ §7-208.
District Court, CJ §7-301.

COSTS —Cont'd
Child custody proceedings.
Uniform child custody jurisdiction and
enforcement act.
Appearance before court, FL §9.5-210.
Costs and expenses.
Declining jurisdiction, FL §9.5-208.
Requests to another state, FL §9.5-111.
Direct expenses and costs against respondent,
FL §9.5-317.
Generally, FL §9.5-312.
Immediate physical custody of child.
Order by court of this state, FL §9.5-310.
Chiropractors.
Licensing hearing.
Cost of court reporter, HO §3-315.
Circuit courts.
See CIRCUIT COURTS.
Clerks of court.
Recordation.
No duty to record until costs paid, CJ §2-201.
Consignment of agricultural products.
Failure to provide accountings of sales, AG
§1-305.
Violation of duties by consignees, AG §1-304.
Construction contracts.
Actions for prompt payment, RP §9-303.
Consumer protection.
In actions under title, CL §13-409.
Continuances.
Circuit courts, CivProCir Rule 2-508.
District Court, CivProDist Rule 3-508.
Corporations.
Consolidation, merger and other transfers of
property.
Proceedings by objecting stockholders, CA
§3-211.
Counties.
Bridge cases, 25 §48.
Courts.
Employees of court, CJ §2-501.
Courts-martial.
Militia, PS §13-805.
Credit.
Credit grantor closed end credit provisions.
Court and other collection costs, CL §12-1011.
Credit grantor revolving credit provisions.
Court or other collection costs, CL §12-911.
Criminal injuries compensation.
Additional cost to be imposed in criminal cases,
CJ §7-405.
Waiver of costs, CJ §7-405.
Criminal procedure.
Addition costs imposed on defendant, CJ §7-409.
Collection of unpaid costs, CJ §7-505.
Criminal injuries compensation.
Additional cost to be imposed in criminal cases,
CJ §7-405.
Waiver of costs, CJ §7-405.
Imprisonment for failure to pay costs prohibited,
CJ §7-505.
Liability of person found guilty for costs of
prosecution, CJ §7-502.
Waiver of right to trial and payment of fine or
penalty.
Addition costs, CJ §7-409.
Criminal proceedings.
Nolle prosequi, payment by applicant, CP §1-208.
Criminal rules.
Trial, Crim Rule 4-353.

COSTS —Cont'd
Declaratory judgments.
Award of costs, CJ §3-410.
Developmental disabilities.
See DEVELOPMENTAL DISABILITIES.
Discrimination.
Commercial discrimination.
Contested case hearings, SF §19-109.
Distress for rent.
Items included, RP §8-322.
Removing goods for sale, RP §8-319.
Restitution of possession of premises, RP §8-324.
Security for cost of sale, RP §8-321.
Time of payment, RP §8-322.
District Court.
Bad checks.
Additional costs, CJ §7-301.
Service charge, CJ §7-208.
Civil cases, CJ §7-301.
Collection, CJ §7-302.
Criminal cases, CJ §7-301.
Additional costs imposed on defendant, CJ
§7-409.
Criminal injuries compensation fund.
Payment into, CJ §7-301.
Waiver, CJ §7-405.
Disposition, CJ §7-302.
Indigent persons.
Waiver of prepayment in cases of indigency, CJ
§7-301.
Law enforcement and correctional training fund.
Payments into, CJ §7-301.
Maintenance, operation and administration costs,
CJ §1-608.
Schedule, CJ §7-301.
State helicopter replacement fund.
Surcharge for in traffic cases, CJ §7-301.
Traffic cases, CJ §7-301.
Victim and witness protection and relocation
program.
Payment into, CJ §7-301.
Volunteer company assistance fund.
Surcharge for in traffic cases, CJ §7-301.
Waiver of prepayment in cases of indigency, CJ
§7-301.
Domestic violence.
Petition for relief from abuse.
Waiver or deferral of cost of petition, FL §4-504.
Draining lands.
Amendment of petition, 25 §78.
Ejectment.
Warrant of resurvey.
Deposit of costs, PropAct Rule 12-101.
Election recount, EL §12-107.
Eminent domain.
Abandonment.
Recovery of expenses, PropAct Rule 12-211.
Recovery of fees by defendant, RP §12-109.
Appeals, PropAct Rule 12-209.
Land in more than one county, PropAct Rule
12-212.
On appeal, RP §12-107.
Payment, PropAct Rule 12-210.
Effect, RP §12-108.
When property deemed to have been taken, RP
§12-102.
Trial court, RP §12-106.
Equity.
Court-ordered sales.
Payment of costs, RP §14-103.

COSTS —Cont'd
Examiners.
Circuit courts, CivProCir Rule 2-542.
Executions.
By state's attorney, 10 §36.
Sales.
Publication of notice of sale.
Defendant liable for costs, CJ §11-502.
Executors and administrators.
Expenses of estate litigation, ET §7-603.
Order of payment when assets insufficient, ET §8-105.
Foreclosures.
Protection of homeowners.
Violation of provisions, RP §7-319.
Ground rents, PropAct Rule 12-501.
Actions to recover, RP §8-402.3.
Guardian and ward.
Local department guardianships, FL §5-309.
Private agency guardianships, FL §5-3A-09.
Identity fraud.
Civil or administrative proceedings, CR §8-301.
Insurance.
Appeal from commissioner's order or hearing, IN §2-215.
Life and health insurance guaranty corporation.
Examination of member insurer, IN §9-412.
Liquidation, rehabilitation, etc., of insurers, IN §9-206.
Nonprofit health service plans.
Fraudulent health insurance claims, IN §14-105.
Risk based capital standards for insurers.
Regulatory action level event.
Costs relating to actuaries, investment experts or other consultants, IN §4-306.
Judgments.
Allowance and allocation.
Circuit courts, CivProCir Rule 2-603.
District Court, CivProDist Rule 3-603.
Assessment.
Circuit courts, CivProCir Rule 2-603.
District Court, CivProDist Rule 3-603.
Domestic relations cases.
Waiver, CivProCir Rule 2-603.
Joint liability.
Circuit courts, CivProCir Rule 2-603.
District Court, CivProDist Rule 3-603.
Satisfaction of money judgments.
Circuit courts, CivProCir Rule 2-626.
District Court, CivProDist Rule 3-626.
Judicial sales.
Payment, RP §14-103.
Jury trial.
Criminal rules, Crim Rule 4-353.
Special costs in first, second and fourth judicial circuits, CivProCir Rule 2-509.
Labor and employment relations.
Commissioner of labor and industry.
Payment not to be required in certain actions, CJ §7-403.
Wage discrimination.
Action by employee, LE §3-307.
Land installment contracts.
Enforcement of subtitle by purchaser, RP §10-108.
Landlord and tenant.
Ground rent actions.
Costs and expenses recoverable, RP §8-402.3.
Land patents.
Schedule of costs.
Adoption, RP §13-205.

COSTS —Cont'd
Land patents —Cont'd
Surveyors.
Expenses of surveyors, RP §13-312.
Life and health insurance guaranty corporation.
Examination of member insurer, IN §9-412.
Limited liability companies.
Derivative actions by members.
Expenses generally, CA §4A-804.
Malpractice.
Health care malpractice claims, CJ §§3-2A-05, 3-2A-06.
Action maintained in bad faith, CJ §3-2A-07.
Arbitration.
Assessment of costs, CJ §3-2A-05.
Rejection of assessment, CJ §3-2A-06.
Masters.
Circuit courts, CivProCir Rule 2-541.
Medical records.
Copying costs, HG §4-304.
Mental hygiene law.
Court ordered examinations, HG §16-302.
Meridian line.
Carrying out provisions of section 123, 25 §127.
Militia.
Actions against members.
Security for court costs, PS §13-708.
Courts-martial, PS §13-805.
Minimum wage.
Action by employee, LE §3-427.
Morgan State University.
Employees.
Classified employees grievance procedures, ED §14-307.
Mortgages and deeds of trust.
Releases.
Actions to enforce provisions.
Liability for costs and expenses in bringing action, RP §7-106.
Motorized wheelchair warranty enforcement.
Violations of provisions.
Actions for damages, CL §14-2705.
New trial.
District Court, CivProDist Rule 3-533.
Motion for new trial.
Circuit courts, CivProCir Rule 2-533.
Nolle prosequi, payment by applicant, CP §1-208.
Nonprofit health service plans.
Fraudulent health insurance claims, IN §14-105.
Nuisances.
Abatement.
Controlled dangerous substances.
Property used for controlled dangerous substance offenses, RP §14-120.
Open containers of alcoholic beverages in motor vehicles' passenger areas, CR §10-126.
Paternity proceedings, FL §5-1036.
Podiatrists.
Disciplinary proceedings, HO §16-313.
Postmortem examiners.
Autopsies by medical examiners.
Contested case hearings, HG §5-310.
Poultry products inspection.
Payment of cost of inspection, AG §4-207.
Seizure and condemnation of products, AG §4-220.
Procurement.
Architectural and engineering services.
Appeal of recommendations, SF §13-316.

COSTS —Cont'd
Procurement —Cont'd
Construction contracts.
  Security.
    Actions on security, SF §17-109.
  Dispute resolution.
    Appeals to appeals board, SF §15-221.1.
    Cost incurred by contractor, SF §15-221.2.
Recordation.
Clerks of court.
  No duty to record until costs paid, CJ §2-201.
Court-ordered sales, RP §14-103.
Fees, RP §3-601.
  Exemptions, RP §3-603.
Financing statement filing fee, RP §3-601.
Page.
  Defined, RP §3-601.
Records.
Personal records.
  Unlawful disclosure, SG §10-626.
Risk based capital standards for insurers.
Regulatory action level event.
  Costs related to actuaries, investment experts
    or other consultants, IN §4-306.
Sales.
Court-ordered sales.
  Payment of costs, RP §14-103.
Satisfaction of money judgments.
Circuit courts, CivProCir Rule 2-626.
District Court, CivProDist Rule 3-626.
Sentence and punishment, Crim Rule 4-353.
Service charges for bad check, CJ §§7-208,
7-301.
**Service contracts and consumer products
  guaranty.**
Actions for breach of guaranty or service contract,
  CL §14-406.
Service of process.
Private process servers, CJ §7-404.
Social workers.
Disciplinary actions against, HO §19-312.
State.
Appeals by state.
  Jurisdiction to pay appeal costs, CJ §12-302.
State contractor employees.
Whistleblower protection civil actions, SF §11-305.
State police department.
Communications systems.
  Use by other law enforcement agencies, PS
    §2-304.
Computer systems.
  Use by other law enforcement agencies, PS
    §2-304.
Departmental finances generally, PS §2-208.
Expenses, reimbursement, PS §2-406.
Local division.
  Reimbursement to department, PS §2-602.
Survey stations.
Damage to property, reimbursement proceedings,
  BOP §1-303.
Taxation.
Foreclosure of right of redemption.
  Plaintiff entitled to reimbursement, TP §14-843.
Tires.
Used tires.
  State used tire cleanup and recycling fund.
    Reimbursement and recovery of costs, EN
      §9-276.
Tobacco.
Escrow act compliance violations, BR §§16-507,
  16-508.

COSTS —Cont'd
Tobacco sales.
Carroll county and Garrett county.
  Judicial proceedings generally, 24 §15-104.
Trial.
Continuances.
  Circuit courts, CivProCir Rule 2-508.
  District Court, CivProDist Rule 3-508.
Criminal rules, Crim Rule 4-353.
Voluntary dismissal.
  Circuit courts, CivProCir Rule 2-506.
  District Court, CivProDist Rule 3-506.
Victims of crime.
District Court.
  Payment into criminal injuries compensation
    fund and victim and witness protection and
    relocation program, CJ §7-301.
Washington county.
Animal control violations, proceedings, 25 §236A.
Washington suburban sanitary district.
Collective bargaining.
  Unfair labor practices hearings, 29 §11.5-113.
Water pollution control.
Cost sharing, AG §§8-701 to 8-705.
  See WATER POLLUTION.
Water quality financing administration.
Security for court costs, EN §9-1616.
Watershed associations.
Award, 25 §197.
Wholesome meat act.
Payment of cost of inspection, AG §4-110.
Workers' compensation.
Court costs and allowance for witnesses, LE
  §9-746.
Zoning.
Appeals.
  Not allowed against board of appeals, 66B
    §4.08.

COST SHARING.
Water pollution control, AG §§8-701 to 8-705.
See WATER POLLUTION.

COUNSEL.
Attorneys at law.
See ATTORNEYS AT LAW.

COUNSELORS.
Insurance coverage for services, IN §15-704.
Professional counselors and therapists, HO
  §§17-101 to 17-502.
See PROFESSIONAL COUNSELORS AND
  THERAPISTS.

COUNTERCLAIMS.
Allowed pleadings, CivProCir Rule 2-302.
District Court, CivProDist Rule 3-302.
Cross-claims.
See CROSS-CLAIMS.
Electric customer choice and competition act.
Rate stabilization.
  Assignee's or pledgee's interests in rate
    stabilization property, not subject to, PUC
    §7-540.
Executors and administrators.
Deduction of counterclaim, ET §8-113.
Filing.
Time for filing.
  Circuit courts, CivProCir Rule 2-331.
  District Court, CivProDist Rule 3-331.
Joinder, CivProCir Rule 2-331.
District Court, CivProDist Rule 3-331.

COUNTERCLAIMS —Cont'd
Judgments.
Judgment on claim and counterclaim.
Circuit courts, CivProCir Rule 2-615.
District Court, CivProDist Rule 3-615.
Multiple claims.
Circuit courts, CivProCir Rule 2-602.
District Court, CivProDist Rule 3-602.
Jurisdiction.
Exceeding jurisdictional amount.
District Court, CivProDist Rule 3-331.
Parties.
Circuit courts, CivProCir Rule 2-331.
District Court, CivProDist Rule 3-331.
Pleadings.
Allowed pleadings.
Circuit courts, CivProCir Rule 2-302.
District Court, CivProDist Rule 3-302.
Exceeding jurisdiction amount.
District Court, CivProDist Rule 3-331.
Filing.
Time for filing.
Circuit courts, CivProCir Rule 2-331.
Joinder of additional parties.
Circuit courts, CivProCir Rule 2-331.
District Court, CivProDist Rule 3-331.
Time for filing.
Circuit courts, CivProCir Rule 2-331.
District Court, CivProDist Rule 3-331.
Trial.
Time of trial.
Circuit courts, CivProCir Rule 2-331.
District Court, CivProDist Rule 3-331.
Secured transactions.
Banks.
Security interests in deposit accounts, CL
§9-340.
Small claim actions.
District Court, CivProDist Rule 3-701.
Time.
Circuit courts, CivProCir Rule 2-331.
District Court, CivProDist Rule 3-331.
Tort claims act.
Certain restrictions inapplicable to claims
asserted by cross-claim or counterclaim, SG
§12-106.
Trial.
Time of trial.
Circuit courts, CivProCir Rule 2-331.
District Court, CivProDist Rule 3-331.
Voluntary dismissal.
Circuit courts, CivProCir Rule 2-506.
District Court, CivProDist Rule 3-506.
Effect on counterclaim.
District Court, CivProDist Rule 3-506.

**COUNTERFEIT CONTROLLED DANGEROUS
SUBSTANCES,** CR §§5-604, 5-607.

COUNTERFEITING AND FORGERY, CR
§§8-601 to 8-613.
Charging documents.
Crimes involving instruments, CP §4-108.
Commercial code.
Unauthorized signature includes forgery, CL
§1-201.
Constitutional provisions, US Const Art I §8.
Controlled dangerous substances.
Counterfeit substance, CR §§5-604, 5-607.
Counterfeit defined, CR §1-101.
Credit cards, CR §8-205.
Machinery, plates or contrivance to reproduce.
Possessing, CR §8-208.

COUNTERFEITING AND FORGERY —Cont'd
Credit cards —Cont'd
Obtaining property by counterfeiting card, CR
§8-206.
Receiving property by counterfeit card, CR §8-209.
**Environmental permits, licenses or
certificates.**
Falsifying or altering, EN §1-302.
False pretenses and false statements.
See FALSE PRETENSES AND FALSE
STATEMENTS.
Fraud and deceit generally.
See FRAUD.
Intent to defraud.
Proving, CR §1-401.
Investment securities.
Unauthorized signature, CL §8-205.
Letters of credit, CL §5-109.
Medicaid fraud.
General provisions.
See MEDICAID.
Mining.
Certificates.
Forged or counterfeit certificates prohibited, EN
§15-309.
Money.
Possessing or issuing counterfeit United States
Currency, CR §8-604.1.
Intent to defraud, CR §8-604.
Motor vehicles.
Altered or forged documents and plates, TR
§14-110.
Orders for money or goods, CR §8-609.
Pari-mutuel betting tickets, CR §8-905.
**Prescriptions for controlled dangerous
substances,** CR §§5-601, 8-610.
Evidence, affidavit by authorized provider, CR
§5-705.
Issuing, passing, making or possession, CR
§§5-606, 5-607.
Private instruments and documents, CR §8-601.
Issuing counterfeit instruments and documents,
CR §8-602.
Public documents, CR §8-605.
Making false entries, altering destroying, removal,
concealing or accessing, CR §8-606.
Public seal, CR §8-607.
Slugs, manufacturing, CR §8-613.
Stamp of comptroller, CR §8-608.
Taxation.
Washington county.
Agricultural land transfer tax, TP §13-505.
Title to motor vehicle.
Possessing counterfeit title, CR §8-603.
Tokens, CR §8-612.
Trademarks, CR §8-611.
Universities and colleges.
Transcripts, diplomas or grade reports, ED
§26-301.
Vending machines.
Unlawful operation by use of slug or counterfeited
or foreign currency, CR §8-613.
Venue.
Private instruments and documents, CR §8-601.

COUNTERSIGNATURES.
Negotiable instruments.
Unconditional promise or order.
Requiring as condition to payment
countersignature, CL §3-106.

COUNTIES.

Abattoirs.
Powers of county commissioners, 25 §3.

Accounts.
Reserve accounts, 24 §9-1201.
State's attorney.
Fees and expenses, 10 §39.
Uniform system of accounts.
Required, 19 §§35 to 41.
See ACCOUNTS AND ACCOUNTING.

Actions.
Against state officers and employees.
Subtitle inapplicable, SG §12-301.
Commissioners.
Contract actions, 25 §1A.
Suing or being sued with respect to county property, 25 §17.
Contract actions, 25A §1A.
Home rule for code counties, 25B §13A.
Tort actions.
Sovereign immunity, 25A §5.

Administrative procedure.
Regulations.
Subtitle inapplicable to regulations of bicounty commissions appointed by county governing bodies, SG §10-105.

Admissions and amusement tax.
Authority to impose tax, TG §4-102.
Restrictions, TG §4-103.
Distribution of revenue to, TG §2-202.
Rates, TG §4-105.

Advertising.
Chartered counties.
Powers of county, 25A §5.
Compensation for removed outdoor advertising sign, 25 §122E.
County commissioners.
Powers as to, 25 §3.
Publication. See within this heading, "Publication."

Agricultural land preservation programs.
Certification program, department of planning, SF §5-408.

Agriculture.
Agricultural preservation advisory boards, AG §2-504.1.
Farmers' cooperative demonstration work, 25 §160.
Farm labor problem.
Levy to assist in solution, 25 §21.

Airports.
See AVIATION.

Alcoholic beverages.
Dispensaries.
Authorized, 2B §15-203.
License commissioners.
Appointment, 2B §15-104.
County commissioners as ex officio license commissioners, 2B §15-105.
Removals by county commissioners, 2B §15-110.
Taxation.
Prohibited, 2B §1-101.

Allegany county.
See ALLEGANY COUNTY.

Ambulance service.
Local regulation preempted, ED §13-515.

Amendments.
Charter amendments, MD Const Art XI-A §5.

Amusements and recreation.
Licenses.
Powers of county commissioners, 25 §3.

COUNTIES —Cont'd

Amusements and recreation —Cont'd
Permit required for amusement park, 25 §27.
Recreational facilities.
Power of county commissioners to provide, 25 §14.

Animal control.
More stringent requirements by local government, HG §18-220.

Anne Arundel county.
See ANNE ARUNDEL COUNTY.

Annexation.
Municipal corporations.
Petition for referendum by county governing body, 23A §19.

Appeals.
Appeal tax courts.
General provisions.
See TAXATION.
Bridges between counties, 25 §§46 to 48.
Chartered counties.
Board of appeals, 25A §5.
Taxation.
Refunds, 24 §9-712.

Appropriations.
Draining lands, 25 §73.
Farmers' cooperative demonstration work.
Authority to make, 25 §160.
Farm labor problem, 25 §21.
Soil conservation districts, 25 §22.

Arbitration and award.
Bridges between counties.
Costs, 25 §45.

Arts and entertainment districts, 83A §§4-701 to 4-703.

Assessments.
Erosion districts, 25 §165.
Taxation. See within this heading, "Taxation."

Assistance.
To other political subdivisions, 25 §219.

Audit.
Annual audit, 19 §40.
Expenses of examination of accounts and records, 19 §41.
Auditor accountant.
Appointment, 25 §3.
Chartered counties.
Powers of county, 25A §5.
Expenses of examination of accounts and records, 19 §41.
Procedure, 19 §40.
Rules and regulations.
Establishment, 19 §40.

Aviation.
Airports.
Acquisition and operation, TR §5-417.
Potomac highlands airport authority.
See POTOMAC HIGHLANDS AIRPORT AUTHORITY.

Bailiffs.
Compensation, CJ §2-507.

Baltimore City.
Word "county" to include city of Baltimore, 1 §14.

Baltimore County.
See BALTIMORE COUNTY.

Banks and trust companies.
Bank stock taxes.
Grant to municipalities in lieu of shares tax, 25 §220.

Bidding.
Competitive bidding, 25 §3.

COUNTIES —Cont'd
Birds, game and inland water fish.
Chartered counties.
Powers as to fish and game, 25A §5.
Boards and commissions.
Chartered counties.
Board of appeals, 25A §5.
Charter board. See within this heading,
"Charter."
County codes.
Deposited with state agencies, 25 §32A.
Physical fitness.
County commission.
See PHYSICAL FITNESS.
Planning commission.
General provisions, 66B §§3.01 to 3.09.
See ZONING.
Boards of education.
Election, EL §§8-801 to 8-806.
General provisions.
See SCHOOLS.
Bond issues.
Chartered counties.
Powers as to bonds or evidences of
indebtedness, 25A §5.
Consolidated public improvement bonds.
Sale, 31 §2C.
County transportation bonds. See within this
heading, "Transportation bonds."
Erosion prevention works, 25 §§163, 166.
Housing and community development.
Residential mortgage programs for certain
counties.
Characteristics, HS §4-1607.
New bonds, HS §4-1609.
Ordinance to issue, HS §4-1606.
Sale and payment, HS §4-1608.
Interest rate exchange agreements or contracts.
Authority to enter into, 31 §34.
Private activity bond issuance fee.
Powers, 25 §3.
Proceeds of certain bonds.
Investments, redemptions, sales, etc., 95 §22M.
Public debt.
Authorization of public bodies to issue and sell,
31 §30.
General provisions, 31 §§1 to 12.
See PUBLIC DEBT.
Residential mortgage programs.
See MORTGAGES AND DEEDS OF TRUST.
Restrictions on county debts, MD Const Art III
§54.
Tax increment financing act, 41 §§14-201 to
14-214.
See TAX INCREMENT FINANCING ACT.
Transportation bonds. See within this heading,
"Transportation bonds."
Voting systems.
Issuance to pay costs, EL §9-104.
Bonds, surety.
Bridges.
Performance bonds, 25 §38.
Bridges between counties, 25 §43.
Chartered counties.
Contracts requiring bonds, 25A §5.
Compliance bonds, 25 §3.
Official bonds.
Payment of premiums by county commissioners,
25 §33.
Performance bond.
Contracts, 25 §29.

COUNTIES —Cont'd
Bonds, surety —Cont'd
Taxation.
Hotel rental tax.
County treasurer, 24 §9-317.
Boundaries.
As established at adoption of code of Maryland, 1
§12.
Ballot questions generally, EL §§7-101 to 7-105.
Changing, MD Const Art XIII §§1, 2.
Maps.
Admissible as evidence, 75 §83.
Certified copies, 75 §84.
Venue.
Crimes committed on or near boundary lines of
counties, CP §4-201.
Bounties.
Powers as to, 25 §2.
Boxing, sparring and wrestling.
Permit required for arena, 25 §27.
Boys' and girls' club work.
Farmers' cooperative demonstration work, 25
§160.
Bridge and canal companies.
Erection of bridges or construction of canals.
Consent of county commissioners required, 23
§140.
Report of corporations to county commissioners,
23 §142.
Bridges.
Between counties.
Advertising for sealed proposals, 25 §42.
Appeal by objecting citizens, 25 §46.
Costs on appeal, 25 §48.
Procedure, 25 §47.
Right of appeal, 25 §46.
Contracts, 25 §43.
Costs.
Appeal, 25 §48.
Levy for, 25 §44.
Payment, 25 §44.
Proportion, 25 §41.
Levy for proportion, 25 §44.
Examiners.
Appointment, 25 §40.
Arbitration when examiners do not agree, 25
§45.
Authority, 25 §44.
Costs.
Apportionment, 25 §41.
Determining expediency of building or
repairing, 25 §41.
Notice to commissioners of acceptance, 25
§44.
Number, 25 §40.
Petition for, 25 §40.
Plan, 25 §41.
Qualification, 25 §40.
Report to commissioners, 25 §41.
Building and repair.
Application to commissioners, 25 §34.
Notice.
Same as for opening roads, 25 §35.
Cecil county, 25 §37A.
Commissioners, 25 §26.
Contracts.
Advertising, 25 §37.
Award of contract, 25 §38.
Bonds, surety.
Performance bond, 25 §38.
Payment on completion, 25 §39.

COUNTIES —Cont'd
Bridges —Cont'd
Building and repair —Cont'd
Contracts —Cont'd
Required, 25 §37.
Sealed proposals, 25 §37.
Advertising for sealed proposals, 25 §42.
Opening proposals, 25 §38.
Costs.
Levy to cover, 25 §36.
Payment on completion, 25 §39.
Power of county commissioners, 25 §26.
Chartered counties.
Powers of county, 25A §5.
County commissioners to have control of county bridges, 25 §1.
Draining lands.
Improvements crossing highway at intersection of highway with watercourse, 25 §99.
Navigable rivers.
Building across prohibited, 25 §49.
Repair.
Application to commissioners, 25 §34.
Notice.
Same notice as for opening roads, 25 §35.
Budget and management.
Accrual method.
Authorized, 24 §1-103.
Entities subject to county budget and fiscal policies, 24 §8-101.
Buildings.
Chartered counties.
Building ordinances, 25A §5.
County codes.
Building code, 25 §3.
Energy conservation building standards, PUC §§7-401 to 7-408.
See ENERGY CONSERVATION BUILDING STANDARDS.
Erection of buildings.
Powers of county commissioners, 25 §11A.
Permits.
Furnished supervisor of assessments, TP §5-103.
Grading and building permits.
Power to issue, EN §4-103.
Buses.
Grants to local bus systems.
Authorized, TR §10-207.
Bus shelters for bus passengers.
Local agreements to construct, operate and maintain, TR §8-752.
Bylaws.
Regional council of governments, 25 §26A.
Cable television companies.
Franchise for community antenna television systems, 25 §3C.
Calvert county.
See CALVERT COUNTY.
Canals.
Restriction on aid to construction of canals, MD Const Art III §54.
Cardiovascular disease prevention programs.
Guidelines for programs, HG §13-206.
Career and technology education.
County advisory councils, ED §21-101.
Caroline county.
See CAROLINE COUNTY.
Carroll county.
See CARROLL COUNTY.

COUNTIES —Cont'd
Cecil county.
See CECIL COUNTY.
Cemeteries.
Maintenance and preservation, RP §14-122.
Roads.
Consent of owner to pass through required, 25 §144.
Charges collected by county.
Payment by credit or debit card, 24 §9-1401.
Charles county.
See CHARLES COUNTY.
Charter.
Actions.
Contract actions, 25A §1A.
Not liable for punitive damages, CJ §5-509.
Adoption, MD Const Art XI-A §1.
Agencies to be notified of adoption of charter, 25A §3B.
Alternate procedure, MD Const Art XI-A §1A.
Authority to adopt, 25A §1.
Effect of adoption, 25A §1.
Adoption of code of Maryland.
Rights under charter or grant from state, 1 §4.
Advertising.
Powers of county, 25A §5.
Affidavits.
False signing and false affidavits, MD Const Art XI-A §7.
Amendment of article XI, MD Const Art XI-A §6.
Amendment of charter, MD Const Art XI-A §5.
Procedure, 25A §5.
Appeals.
County board of appeals, 25A §5.
Article.
Severability, 25A §6.
Board.
Composition, MD Const Art XI-A §1.
Election, MD Const Art XI-A §1.
Petition.
For charter, MD Const Art XI-A §1.
Bond issues.
Powers of county, 25A §5.
Bonds, surety.
Contract bonds, 25A §5.
Bridges.
Powers of county, 25A §5.
Buildings.
Regulations, 25A §5.
Claims against county.
Provide for proof of claims, 25A §5.
Compilation of laws enacted, 25A §7.
Comprehensive plans for charter counties, 66B §1.03.
Construction contracts.
Resolution of disputes, 25A §1A.
Contracts.
Actions on contract, 25A §1A.
Not liable for punitive damages, CJ §5-509.
General provisions, 25A §5.
Council.
Commission to establish compensation, 25A §5.
Councilmen to reside in specified districts.
Charter may require, 25A §3.
Election of members, 25A §§2, 3.
Councilmen to reside in specified districts.
Charter may require, 25A §3.
Legislative body, MD Const Art XI-A §3.
Specified districts.
Councilmen to reside in.
Charter may require, 25A §3.

COUNTIES —Cont'd
Charter —Cont'd
County commissioners.
  Power to prescribe number, compensation,
    powers and duties, MD Const Art XI-A §6.
Courthouses, 25A §5.
Credit.
  Protection of county credit, 25A §5.
Damages.
  Punitive damages.
    Not liable in contract actions, CJ §5-509.
Drainage.
  Powers of county, 25A §5.
Easements.
  Public utilities granted easement without
    advertisement, 25A §5.
Elections.
  Ballot questions generally, EL §§7-101 to 7-105.
  Council members, 25A §§2, 3.
  Districts and precincts, 25A §5.
  Powers of county, 25A §5.
  Referendum.
    Reservation in charter of power of
      referendum, 25A §8.
Erosion.
  Soil erosion and preservation of natural
    topography, 25A §5.
Express powers act, 25A §§1 to 8.
  Enumeration of powers, 25A §5.
  Grant of powers, 25A §4.
Fences.
  Powers of county, 25A §5.
Fines.
  Enforcement of local legislation, 25A §5.
Fish and game.
  Powers of county, 25A §5.
Health.
  Powers of county, 25A §5.
Hospitals.
  Establishment, 25A §5.
Immunity from liability.
  Contract actions, 25A §1A.
Indexes.
  Provision for, 25A §5.
Institutions.
  County institutions, 25A §5.
Land use, 66B §§1.00 to 1.03.
Laws.
  Compilation of laws enacted, 25A §7.
Legislative bodies, MD Const Art XI-A §3.
Limitation of actions.
  Contract actions, 25A §1A.
Livestock.
  Powers of county, 25A §5.
Local laws.
  Enactment, publication and interpretation, MD
    Const Art XI-A §3.
  General assembly not to enact.
    Subjects covered by express powers, MD
      Const Art XI-A §4.
  Publication, 25A §7.
Nuisances.
  Powers of county, 25A §5.
Officers and employees.
  Audits, 25A §5.
  Chief executive officers, MD Const Art XI-A §3.
  Generally as to county officers, 25A §5.
Ordinances.
  Local legislation, 25A §5.
Parks and recreation, 25A §5.

COUNTIES —Cont'd
Charter —Cont'd
Petition.
  Defined, MD Const Art XI-A §7.
Planning and zoning, 25A §5.
Powers.
  Displacement or limitation of competition, 25A
    §5A.
  Enumeration of express powers, 25A §5.
  Extension, modification, etc., MD Const Art
    XI-A §2.
  General assembly not to enact on subjects
    covered by, MD Const Art XI-A §4.
  General assembly to provide grant of express
    powers, MD Const Art XI-A §2.
  General provisions, 25A §1.
  Grant of powers generally, 25A §4.
Preparation, MD Const Art XI-A §1.
Printing.
  Powers of county, 25A §5.
Property.
  Powers as to county property, 25A §5.
Public transportation.
  Power of chartered counties to displace or limit
    competition, 25A §5A.
Purchases.
  Through state purchasing bureau, 25A §5.
Records.
  Provision for, 25A §5.
Referendum.
  Reservation in charter of power of referendum,
    25A §8.
Rejection.
  Agencies to be notified of rejection of charter,
    25A §3B.
Sovereign immunity.
  Contract actions, 25A §1A.
  Tort actions, 25A §5.
Streets and highways.
  Powers of county, 25A §5.
Taxation.
  Assessments, levy and collection of taxes, 25A
    §5.
Water and sewer systems.
  Power of chartered counties to displace or limit
    competition, 25A §5A.
Watershed projects.
  Federally assisted watershed projects.
    Powers, 25A §5.
Zoning.
  Comprehensive plans for charter counties, 66B
    §1.03.
  Historic and landmark zoning and preservation,
    25A §5.
Chesapeake Bay.
Critical area protection program.
  Local jurisdictions.
    See CHESAPEAKE BAY.
Children, youth and families services.
Local management boards, 49D §§2-101 to 2-105.
Circuit court fees.
Clerk may not charge county unless consent
  given, CJ §7-202.
Circuit courts.
Appeals.
  By citizens to county commissioners in bridge
    cases, 25 §§46 to 48.
Citizen's nursing home boards, 25 §254.
Claims against county.
Chartered counties.
  Proof of claim, 25A §5.

COUNTIES —Cont'd
Claims against county —Cont'd
  Claimant.
    Must produce voucher, 25 §23.
  Commissioners not to acquire, 25 §31.
    Penalty for violation, 25 §32.
  Contract actions, 25A §1A.
    Home rule for code counties, 25B §13A.
  Local government tort claims act, CJ §§5-301 to
    5-304.
    See TORTS.
  Payment.
    Commissioners not to pay except by legal
      voucher, 25 §23.
  Proof.
    Power of commissioners, 25 §3.
  Sovereign immunity.
    Court actions, 25A §5.
  Voucher.
    Claimant must produce, 25 §23.
Classification.
  Code counties, MD Const Art XI-F §5.
Clerks of court.
  Recordation.
    Chartered counties, 25A §5.
    Indexing, 25 §3.
    Ordinances, 25 §4.
Coal tax.
  Code counties, 24 §§9-501 to 9-509.
    Authorization, 24 §9-501.
    County treasurer, 24 §9-508.
    Deposit of tax revenue, 24 §9-504.
    Exemptions, 24 §9-503.
    Interest.
      Late payment, 24 §9-509.
    Liens, 24 §9-505.
    Municipal corporation share, 24 §9-506.
    Penalties.
      Late payment, 24 §9-509.
    Rate, 24 §9-502.
  County treasurer.
    Regulations.
      Issuance, 24 §9-508.
Code counties.
  Coal tax, 24 §§9-501 to 9-509.
    Authorization, 24 §9-501.
    County treasurer.
      Adoption of regulations, 24 §9-508.
    Deposit of tax revenue, 24 §9-504.
    Exemptions, 24 §9-503.
    Interest.
      Late payment, 24 §9-509.
    Liens, 24 §9-505.
    Municipal corporation share, 24 §9-506.
    Penalties.
      Late payment, 24 §9-509.
    Rate, 24 §9-502.
  Home rule, 25B §§1 to 22; MD Const Art XI-F §§1
    to 10. See within this heading, "Home rule for
    code counties."
Codes.
  Chartered counties.
    Compilation of laws enacted, 25A §7.
  Copies deposited with state agencies, 25 §32A.
  Plumbing, building and housing codes.
    In certain counties, 25 §3.
Commercial district management authority.
  Authority to establish, 25 §3; 25A §5.
Commissioners.
  Actions.
    Contract actions.
      Immunity from liability, 25 §1A.

COUNTIES —Cont'd
Commissioners —Cont'd
  Actions —Cont'd
    Contract actions —Cont'd
      Not liable for punitive damages, CJ §5-508.
    Suing or being sued with respect to county
      property, 25 §17.
  Alcoholic beverages.
    Confiscation of property.
      Disposition of confiscated property, 2B §1-201.
    License commissioners.
      Appointment of license commissioners, 2B
        §15-104.
      Ex officio license commissioners, 2B §15-105.
      Removals, 2B §15-110.
  Amendment of article XI, MD Const Art XI-A §6.
  Appointments.
    Officers and agents appointed by commissioners,
      25 §1.
  Bonds, surety.
    Payment of premiums, 25 §33.
    Road and bridge engineers, 25 §1.
  Bridge and canal companies.
    Consent to erection or construction of bridges
      and canals, 23 §140.
    Report of corporation to county commissioners,
      23 §142.
  Bridges.
    Building and repair, 25 §26.
      General provisions. See within this heading,
        "Bridges."
    Powers as to, 25 §1.
  Buildings.
    Erection of buildings, 25 §11A.
  Chartered counties.
    Chief executive officers, MD Const Art XI-A §3.
    Power to prescribe number, compensation,
      powers and duties, MD Const Art XI-A §6.
  Claims against county.
    Prohibited from acquiring, 25 §31.
      Penalty, 25 §32.
  Clerk.
    Appointment, 25 §1.
    Drainage file, 25 §75.
    Meridian line.
      Fees, 25 §125.
      Recording variations, 25 §124.
  Compensation.
    Powers, MD Const Art XI-A §6.
    Prescribed by law, MD Const Art VII §2.
  Conflicts of interest, 25 §3.
  Construction contracts.
    Resolution of disputes, 25 §1A.
  Contracts.
    Actions, 25 §1A.
    Interest in prohibited, 25 §30.
    Not liable for punitive damages, CJ §5-508.
    Penalty for violation, 25 §32.
    Requirements of contracts for work to be done,
      25 §29.
  Corporations.
    Declared to be a corporation, 25 §1.
  Drainage associations.
    Establishment, 25 §52.
  Draining lands.
    Authority to contribute or allocate funds, 25
      §73.
    General provisions, 25 §§52 to 121H.
      See DRAINING LANDS.
  Duties, MD Const Art VII §2; Art XI-A §6.

COUNTIES —Cont'd
Commissioners —Cont'd
Election, MD Const Art VII §2.
  Continuation of existing method, MD Const Art
      XVIII.
  Emergency management.
    Executive officer killed, sick or unavailable, PS
        §14-403.
    Local governing bodies defined, PS §14-401.
    Majority killed, sick or unavailable, PS §14-402.
    Powers during military or warlike catastrophe,
        PS §14-405.
  Eminent domain.
    Power of eminent domain, 25 §11A.
  Erosion districts, 25 §§161 to 167. See within this
      heading, "Erosion."
  Executive sessions.
    Regulations, 25 §5.
  Expenditures.
    County expenditures, 25 §20.
  Farm labor problem.
    Taxation.
      Levy to assist in solution, 25 §21.
  Home rule for code counties, 25B §§1 to 22; MD
      Const Art XI. See within this heading, "Home
      rule for code counties."
  Immunity.
    Contract actions, 25 §1A.
  Investments.
    Regulations, 95 §22.
  Junkyards.
    Rules and regulations for control, etc., of
        junkyards, 25 §122A.
  Liability.
    Contract actions, 25 §1A.
  Limitation of actions.
    Contract actions, 25 §1A.
      Washington county, 25 §5C.
    Public meetings, 25 §5.
    Quarterly meetings, 25 §19.
  Motor vehicles.
    Restriction of right to use highways, TR
        §24-204.
  Number, MD Const Art VII §2.
    Fixed by code of local laws, 25 §18.
  Oath of office, 25 §19.
  Ordinances.
    Adoption.
      Meetings to be public, 25 §5.
  Pensions.
    Teachers' pensions, 25 §12.
  Permits.
    Dance halls and other amusements, tourist
        camps, etc., 25 §27.
  Powers.
    Bounties, 25 §2.
    Community antenna television systems.
      Franchise, 25 §3C.
    Displacement or limitation of competition, 25
        §3D.
    Enumerated, 25 §3.
    Fire hydrants, 25 §2.
    Generally, 25 §1.
    Parking, 25 §2.
    Purchases.
      Through state purchasing bureau, 25 §3A.
    Regulation of sale of alcoholic beverages in
        Talbot county, 2B §18-101.
    Roads, 25 §2.
    Section 3 conveys supplementary authority, 25
        §6.

COUNTIES —Cont'd
Commissioners —Cont'd
  Powers —Cont'd
    Streets and sidewalks, 25 §2.
    Trailer camps, 25 §2.
  Property, acquisition or sale, 25 §11A.
  Qualifications.
    Time for qualifying, 25 §19.
  Records.
    Provisions for, 25 §3.
  Recreational facilities.
    How to provide, 25 §14.
  Refuse and garbage disposal facilities.
    Powers of commissioners, 25 §14A.
  Roads.
    Powers as to, 25 §1.
  Salary, 25 §1.
  Schools.
    Power to receive in trust.
      Gifts, 25 §158.
  Shore erosion control districts, 25 §§167A to 167F.
      See SHORE EROSION CONTROL.
  Soil conservation districts.
    Levy for cooperation, 25 §22.
  Sovereign immunity.
    Contract actions.
      Counties governed by county commissioners.
        Defense of sovereign immunity, 25 §1A.
  Taxation.
    Levy and collection, 25 §20.
    Tax sale.
      Purchase by commissioners, TP §14-824.
        Payment of other tax claims, TP §14-826.
        Right to sell, TP §14-825.
  Vacancy.
    Filling vacancy, 25 §16.
  Watershed associations, 25 §§169 to 218.
      See WATERSHED ASSOCIATIONS.
Community action agencies.
  Housing and community development, HS §§8-101
      to 8-109.
Community forestry, NR §§5-424 to 5-427.
  See URBAN AND COMMUNITY FORESTRY.
Community service programs, COR §§8-701 to
      8-711.
  See COMMUNITY SERVICE PROGRAMS.
Community services.
  Powers of county commissioners, 25 §3.
Comprehensive plans.
  Charter counties, 66B §1.03.
Comptroller.
  Right to succeed himself in office, 25 §51A.
Conflict of laws.
  Code counties.
    Public local law, MD Const Art XI-F §10.
  Conflict between general and local laws.
    Public local laws shall prevail, 1 §13.
  Public local law.
    Section 3 conveys supplementary authority, 25
        §6.
Conflicts of interest.
  Claims against county.
    County commissioners not to acquire claims
        against county, 25 §31.
  Contracts.
    County commissioners not to be interested in
        contracts, 25 §30.
  County commissioners, 25 §3.
  Officers and employees, 25 §3.
  Penalty for violations, 25 §32.

COUNTIES —Cont'd
Conservation areas.
General provisions, 23A §7.
Consolidated public improvement bonds.
Sale, 31 §2C.
Construction.
Disputes in construction contracts.
Resolution.
Chartered counties, 25A §1A.
County commissioners, 25 §1A.
Home rule for code counties, 25B §13A.
Contagious diseases.
Prevention of introduction into county, 25 §3.
Contractors.
Bonds, surety.
Commissioner to require bond of, 25 §29.
Contracts.
Actions.
Chartered counties.
Not liable for punitive damages, CJ §5-509.
Code counties.
Not liable for punitive damages, CJ §5-510.
Counties governed by county commissioners.
Defense of sovereign immunity, 25 §1A.
Immunity from liability, 25 §1A.
Nonliability for punitive damages, CJ §5-508.
Bonds, surety.
Performance bond, 25 §29.
Bridges.
Between counties, 25 §43.
Building and repair, 25 §§37 to 39, 42.
Chartered counties.
Contract actions.
Nonliability for punitive damages, CJ §5-509.
Powers of county, 25A §5.
Commissioners. See within this heading,
"Commissioners."
Competitive bidding and bonds.
General provisions, 25 §3.
Construction contracts.
Dispute resolution, 25 §1A; 25A §1A; 25B §13A.
County commissioners. See within this heading,
"Commissioners."
Erosion districts, 25 §164.
Home rule for code counties.
Actions, 25B §13A.
Interest in by county commissioners prohibited.
Penalty for violation, 25 §32.
Interest rate exchange agreements or contracts.
Authority to enter into, 31 §34.
Made by county commissioners, 25 §§29 to 32.
Not authorized by appropriation prohibited, 31 §3.
Purchasing contracts, 25 §3.
Requirements of contracts for work to be done, 25
§29.
Roads.
Right of way, 25 §138.
Taking over private roads in certain counties,
25 §155.
Cooperative activities.
County commissioners.
Powers.
Generally, 25 §3.
Cooperative housing corporations.
Consumer protection, CA §5-6B-12.
First right of purchase.
Deeds containing affidavits that provisions of
section fulfilled, CA §5-6B-08.
Local law or ordinance, CA §5-6B-08.
Same terms and conditions initially offered, CA
§5-6B-09.

COUNTIES —Cont'd
Cooperative housing corporations —Cont'd
First right of purchase —Cont'd
Waiver.
County may waive right to purchase, CA
§5-6B-08.
Local laws or ordinances.
Consumer protection, CA §5-6B-12.
First right of purchase, CA §5-6B-08.
Same terms and conditions initially offered,
CA §5-6B-09.
Imposing unfair burden.
Preempted, CA §5-6B-19.
Rental housing emergencies.
Action to protect from displacement, CA
§5-6B-10.
Rental housing emergencies, CA §5-6B-10.
Copies.
Chartered counties.
Compilation of laws enacted.
Distribution, 25A §7.
Fees.
Counties exempt from fees, RP §3-603.
Home rule for code counties.
Compilation of public local law, 25B §12.
Maps.
Certified copies as evidence, 75 §84.
Corporations.
County commissioners declared to be corporation,
25 §1.
Industrial development corporations.
General provisions, 45A §§1 to 3.
See INDUSTRIAL DEVELOPMENT
CORPORATIONS.
Correctional facilities.
Chartered counties, establishment, 25A §5.
Correctional farms, COR §§11-401 to 11-407.
See CORRECTIONAL FARMS.
Employment of inmate as alternative to
confinement, COR §§11-601 to 11-607.
See JAILS.
Expenses of inmates sentenced to jurisdiction of
division of correction.
County not billed or to pay, COR §3-222.
Generally, COR §§11-101 to 11-204.
See JAILS.
Individual county provisions, COR §§11-701 to
11-726.
See JAILS.
Local correctional facilities.
Defined, COR §1-101.
State reimbursement, COR §§9-401 to 9-405.
Correctional farms, COR §§11-401 to 11-407.
See CORRECTIONAL FARMS.
Correctional officers' retirement system.
Local governmental unit participation in system,
SPP §§31-2B-01 to 31-2B-05.
Costs.
Bridge cases, 25 §48.
Council.
Compensation.
Commission to establish, 25A §5.
Election.
Charter may provide method, MD Const Art
XI-A §3A.
Emergency management.
Executive officer killed, sick or unavailable, PS
§14-403.
Local governing bodies defined, PS §14-401.
Majority killed, sick or unavailable, PS §14-402.

COUNTIES —Cont'd
Council —Cont'd
Emergency management —Cont'd
Powers during military or warlike catastrophe, PS §14-405.
Executive sessions.
Regulations, 25 §5.
Legislative body, MD Const Art XI-A §3.
Meetings.
Public meetings required, 25 §5.
Metropolitan Washington council of governments.
State aid, 25 §26A.
Ordinances.
Adoption.
Meetings to be public, 25 §5.
Regional council of governments, 25 §26A.
County seats.
Changing, MD Const Art XIII §§1, 2.
Courthouses.
Chartered counties.
Powers of county, 25A §5.
Courts.
Bridges between two counties.
Petition for, 25 §40.
Provisions for, 25 §20.
Credit.
Chartered counties.
Protection of county credit, 25A §5.
Credit cards.
Payment of governmental charges by, 24 §9-1401.
Crimes and offenses.
Officers and employees.
Political activities of employees, 24 §13-106.
Suspension and removal of elected officials convicted of crimes, MD Const Art XV §2.
Criminal justice coordinating councils.
Local drug and alcohol abuse councils, designation, HG §8-1001.
Curfew.
Juvenile, 25B §13C-1.
Damages.
Local government tort claims act, CJ §§5-301 to 5-304.
Roads.
Opening or altering roads, 25 §§146 to 149.
Dance halls.
Permits required, 25 §27.
Death sentence, detention of inmate under.
Expenses not billed or paid by county, COR §3-901.
Debit cards.
Payment of governmental charges by, 24 §9-1401.
Debts.
Code counties.
Limitation, MD Const Art XI-F §8.
Home rule.
Code counties. See within this heading, "Home rule for code counties."
Restrictions on, MD Const Art III §54.
Schools.
Reimbursement of state for debt service, ED §5-308.
Declaratory judgments.
Parties to proceeding, CJ §3-405.
Defenses.
Contract actions.
Defense of sovereign immunity.
Chartered counties, 25A §1A.
Home rule for code county, 25B §13A.
Definitions, Rule 1-202.
Buses.
Grants to local bus systems, TR §10-207.

COUNTIES —Cont'd
Definitions —Cont'd
Code county, MD Const Art XI-F §1.
County roads, TR §8-101.
County transportation bonds, TR §3-301.
Generally, FL §1-101; SF §1-101; SG §1-101.
Home rule for code counties, 25B §1.
Hotel rental tax, 24 §9-301.
Include city of Baltimore, 1 §14.
Political activities of employees.
Local entity, 24 §13-101.
Political subdivisions, 24 §1-101.
Public local law, MD Const Art XI-F §1.
Taxation.
Hotel rental tax, 24 §9-301.
Departments.
Creation, change or abolition.
Powers of county commissioners, 25 §3.
Deposits.
Deposit of unexpended or surplus money without security, 95 §22O.
Development.
Tax increment financing act.
Financing development of industrial, commercial or residential areas generally, 41 §§14-201 to 14-214.
See TAX INCREMENT FINANCING ACT.
Developmental disabilities.
Family support services program.
Grants.
Amount of grant to county, HG §7-703.
Group homes.
Public group homes.
Acquisition of site.
Notice required prior to acquisition, HG §7-606.
Discharge of firearms.
Regulation allowed, CR §4-209.
District Court.
General provisions.
See DISTRICT COURT.
Districts.
Electric lighting districts, 25 §2B.
Erosion.
Separate taxing districts, 25 §§161 to 167. See within this heading, "Erosion."
Shore erosion control districts, 25 §§167A to 167F.
See SHORE EROSION CONTROL.
Division of correction expenses for inmates under jurisdiction.
County not billed or to pay, COR §3-222.
Dorchester county.
See DORCHESTER COUNTY.
Draining lands.
Chartered counties.
Powers of county, 25A §5.
General provisions, 25 §§52 to 121H.
See DRAINING LANDS.
Drains.
Chartered counties.
Storm drainage.
Powers of county, 25A §5.
Roads, 25 §138.
Drug or alcohol abuse.
Local drug and alcohol abuse councils, HG §8-1001.
Drunkenness.
Ordinances or resolutions prohibited, 2B §19-101.
Excepted counties, 2B §19-103.
Dumps.
Regulation of public or private dumps, 25 §122A.

COUNTIES —Cont'd
Easements.
Chartered counties.
Public utilities.
Granted without advertisement, 25A §5.
Elections.
Ballot questions generally, EL §§7-101 to 7-105.
Board of supervisors.
Terms.
Commencement, MD Const Art XVII §6.
Boards of elections.
Powers and duties generally, EL §§2-201 to
2-303.
See ELECTIONS.
Charter board, MD Const Art XI-A §1.
Chartered counties. See within this heading,
"Charter."
Code counties.
Procedure for becoming code county, MD Const
Art XI-F §2.
Commissioners, MD Const Art VII §1.
Continuation of existing method, MD Const Art
XVIII.
Council.
Charter may provide method, MD Const Art
XI-A §3A.
Officers.
When elections for county officers held, MD
Const Art XVII §2.
Political parties.
County central committees, EL §4-202.
Election of members, EL §4-203.
Voter registration, EL §§3-101 to 3-602.
See VOTER REGISTRATION.
Voters.
Registered voter.
Defined, 25B §1.
Electric companies.
Conversion of overhead electric or communication
facilities to underground locations, PUC
§§12-301 to 12-317.
See UNDERGROUND UTILITY FACILITIES.
Selling and furnishing electric power, laying of
power lines, PUC §7-103.
Electricity.
County codes.
Electrical code, 25 §3.
Districts.
Electric lighting districts, 25 §2B.
Electrical code.
Powers of county commissioners, 25 §3.
Emergency management.
Local governing bodies.
Defined, PS §14-401.
Executive officer killed, sick or unavailable, PS
§14-403.
Majority killed, sick or unavailable, PS §14-402.
Powers during military or warlike catastrophe,
PS §14-405.
Local organizations for emergency management,
PS §14-109.
Riots.
Liability of county or municipality for damages,
PS §§14-1001 to 14-1004.
Emergency telephone systems.
See 911 EMERGENCY TELEPHONE SYSTEM.
Eminent domain.
Acquisition of property for public purposes, 25
§11A.
Applicable provisions, RP §12-101.
Erosion districts, 25 §162.

COUNTIES —Cont'd
Eminent domain —Cont'd
Roads, 25 §138.
Employees. See within this heading, "Officers and
employees."
Energy conservation building standards, PUC
§§7-401 to 7-408.
See ENERGY CONSERVATION BUILDING
STANDARDS.
Engineers.
County engineer.
Provisions for, 25 §3.
Environmental actions.
Environmental standing act, NR §§1-501 to 1-508.
See ENVIRONMENTAL STANDING ACT.
Erosion.
Acquisition of lands, 25 §162.
Benefit charges, 25 §165.
Bonds, notes or certificates of indebtedness, 25
§163.
Levy of taxes to pay for interest and principal,
25 §166.
Chartered counties.
Powers as to soil erosion, 25A §5.
Condemnation, 25 §162.
Contracts.
Letting of contracts, 25 §164.
County commissioners.
District council, 25 §162.
Duties as to records, deposits, etc., 25 §167.
Deposits, 25 §167.
Districts.
Shore erosion control districts, 25 §§167A to
167F.
See SHORE EROSION CONTROL.
Erosion prevention works.
Construction, 25 §163.
Letting of contracts, 25 §164.
Plans.
Hearings.
By county commissioners, 25 §164.
Expenses.
Levy of taxes to pay, 25 §166.
Financing.
Alternative method of financing erosion control
works on countywide basis, 25 §163A.
Hearings on plans.
By county commissioners, 25 §164.
Shore erosion control.
General provisions.
See SHORE EROSION CONTROL.
Taxing and assessment districts.
Acquisition of lands, 25 §162.
Creation of certain subdivisions as separate
taxing districts, 25 §161.
District council.
Condemnation, 25 §162.
Records, deposits, etc., 25 §167.
Tax levy, 25 §166.
Ethics.
Public ethics.
See PUBLIC ETHICS.
Evidence.
Maps.
Boundaries, 75 §83.
Certified copies, 75 §84.
Ordinances, 25 §4.
**Excavation or demolition near underground
facilities.**
Marking or re-marking fees, PUC §12-111.

COUNTIES —Cont'd
Expenditures.
County expenditures, 25 §20.
Expenses.
Annual publication, 24 §2-103.
Treasurers, 25 §51.
Express powers act.
Chartered counties, 25A §§1 to 8. See within this
heading, "Charter."
Farmers, 25 §160.
Farm labor problem.
Taxation.
Levy for, 25 §21.
Federal aid.
Acceptance of federal aid, 25 §3.
Housing.
Participation in federal lower-income housing
assistance programs, 24 §6-203.
Notices.
Instructional and research aid, 24 §6-301.
Regulations, 24 §6-301.
Powers to participate in federal projects.
Enumeration of powers, 24 §6-201.
Regional council of governments, 25 §26A.
Watershed projects.
Federally assisted watershed projects.
Powers of counties, 25 §3.
Fees.
Code counties.
Restriction on levy, MD Const Art XI-F §9.
Housing and community development.
Residential mortgage programs for certain
counties.
Fees from borrowers, HS §4-1605.
Payment by credit or debit card, 24 §9-1401.
Private activity bond issuance fee.
Powers, 25 §3.
Fences.
Chartered counties.
Powers of county, 25A §5.
Fertilizers.
Manufacturers.
Regulation, 25 §3.
Financial reports, 24 §2-101.
Time for filing, 19 §37.
Fines.
Chartered counties.
Compilation of laws enacted.
Noncompliance, 25A §7.
County commissioners.
Acquiring claims against county or interest in
contracts, 25 §32.
Home rule for code counties.
Failure to comply with compilation and
publication of laws, 25B §12.
Motor vehicles.
Size and weight.
Violation, 25 §25.
Permits.
Dance halls and other amusements, tourist
camps, etc.
Failure to obtain permits, 25 §27.
Road signs or fingerboards.
Injuring or destroying, 25 §154.
Rules and regulations.
Violation, 25 §2.
Signboards on roads.
Injuring or destroying, 25 §154.
Firearms.
State preemption of regulation, CR §4-209.

COUNTIES —Cont'd
Fire marshal.
Plan review.
County and municipal fire prevention codes, PS
§9-702.
Fires and fire protection.
Assistance to other political subdivisions, 25 §219.
Authority to adopt fire prevention codes, PS
§9-701.
Fire hydrants.
Powers as to, 25 §2.
Inspections by local fire departments, PS §§9-801
to 9-805.
Plan review, PS §9-702.
Powers of county commissioners, 25 §3.
Retirement and pension system.
General provisions, SPP §§28-101 to 28-403.
See LOCAL FIRE AND POLICE PENSION
SYSTEM.
Volunteer fire departments.
Guarantee of loans to, 25 §3.
Powers of county commissioners, 25 §3.
Fiscal year, 24 §1-102.
General provisions, 19 §35.
Fish and fisheries.
Chartered counties.
Powers of county, 25A §5.
Foreclosure sales.
Noticed and disclosure requirements, RP §14-126.
Forest conservation programs.
Local programs, NR §5-1603.
Forests and parks.
Planning.
Assistance of secretary, NR §5-210.
Urban and community forestry, NR §§5-424 to
5-427.
See URBAN AND COMMUNITY FORESTRY.
For-hire driving services.
Power to adopt reasonable traffic regulations,
PUC §10-102.
Franchises.
Chartered counties, 25A §5.
Power to displace or limit competition, 25A §5A.
Code counties.
Power to displace or limit competition, 25B
§13B.
Powers of county commissioners, 25 §§3, 3D.
Frederick county.
See FREDERICK COUNTY.
Freestanding medical facilities.
Rules and regulations.
Adoption, HG §19-3A-04.
Funds.
State funds.
Acceptance of state funds, 25 §3.
Funeral expenses.
Provided for paupers, 25 §20.
Garbage and trash.
Chartered counties.
Powers as to waste disposal, 25A §5.
Collection and disposal.
Disposal facilities.
Powers of county commissioners, 25 §14A.
Household hazardous waste.
Definitions, EN §9-1801.
Feasibility study, EN §9-1802.
Assistance by secretary, EN §9-1803.
Powers of county commissioners, 25 §3.
Household hazardous waste.
Collection and acceptance from residents.
Definitions, EN §9-1801.

COUNTIES —Cont'd
Garbage and trash —Cont'd
Household hazardous waste —Cont'd
Collection and acceptance from residents
—Cont'd
Feasibility study, EN §9-1802.
Assistance by secretary, EN §9-1803.
Municipal corporations.
Contracts with county for disposal of refuse.
Power of county commissioners, 25 §14A.
Powers of county commissioners, 25 §3.
Garrett county.
See GARRETT COUNTY.
Gas and oil.
Coastal facilities review act.
Permits for construction of facilities.
County action prerequisite to processing
application for permit, EN §14-506.
Gas companies.
Selling or furnishing gas to county, laying pipes
under roadways, PUC §7-102.
General assembly.
Charter.
Powers and restrictions, MD Const Art XI-A
§§2, 4, 6.
Code counties.
Power to elect public local laws effecting code
county, MD Const Art XI-F §4.
Home rule for code counties.
Limitations on property tax rate and
indebtedness.
Authority of general assembly, 25B §22.
Subsidizing members in maintenance of space,
services or equipment prohibited, SG §2-102.
General services department.
Public improvements.
Exceptions to provisions.
Improvements made by counties or units
thereof, SF §4-402.
Purchases.
Purchases through purchasing bureau, 41
§18-201.
Chartered counties, 25A §5.
Powers of commissioners, 25 §3A.
Governor.
Commissioners.
Filling vacancy in office of county
commissioners, 25 §16.
Grading and building permits.
Power to issue, EN §4-103.
Grants.
Local bus systems, TR §10-207.
Harford county.
See HARFORD COUNTY.
Hawkers and peddlers.
Licenses.
Powers of county commissioners, 25 §3.
Health.
Assistance to other political subdivisions, 25 §219.
Chartered counties.
Board of health.
Powers of county, 25A §5.
County boards of health.
See HEALTH.
Officers.
See HEALTH.
Provisions provided by county commissioners, 25
§3.
Health maintenance organizations.
Limited benefits for low income individuals, HG
§19-703.

COUNTIES —Cont'd
Hearings.
Adoption of code form of home rule.
Public hearings by board of county
commissioners, 25B §5.
Erosion prevention works.
By county commissioners, 25 §164.
Home rule for code counties.
Resort taxes, 25B §13H.
Hotel rental tax.
Required in certain counties, 24 §9-303.
Ordinances or resolutions, 25 §3.
Highways.
Administration.
Report of expenditures allocated for each
county, TR §8-412.
Allocation of highway user revenues, TR §§8-403,
8-404.
Bond issues. See within this heading,
"Transportation bonds."
Chartered counties.
Powers of county, 25A §5.
Convict road force. See within this heading,
"Roads."
County highway construction fund.
Transfer to and from construction fund, TR
§8-507.
County roads, 25 §§135 to 155A. See within this
heading, "Roads."
County transportation bonds. See within this
heading, "Transportation bonds."
Federal aid.
Power to comply with federal acts, TR §8-503.
Power to raise funds, TR §8-504.
Grants to local bus systems, TR §10-207.
Highway user revenues.
See HIGHWAYS.
Land clearing of trees and other woody plants.
Cutting and clearing restrictions, reforestation,
NR §5-103.
Levy.
Relief from county levy, TR §8-406.
Municipal corporations.
Payment of cost of highway projects within
municipalities, 25 §2A.
Reports by counties, TR §8-636.
State highways.
Administration generally responsible only for
state highways, TR §8-633.
State roads commission.
Engineering advice to counties, TR §8-635.
Transfer of jurisdiction to state, TR §8-303.
Utility sleeves.
General provisions, TR §8-608.
Historic area zoning.
General provisions.
See ZONING.
Home demonstration work.
Farmers' cooperative demonstration work, 25
§160.
Home improvement law.
General provisions, BR §§8-101 to 8-702.
See HOME IMPROVEMENTS.
Home rule for code counties.
Actions.
Contract actions, 25B §13A.
Nonliability for punitive damages, CJ §5-510.
Adoption of code form of home rule.
Authority, 25B §3.
Hearings, 25B §5.
Notice of intent, 25B §4.

COUNTIES —Cont'd
Home rule for code counties —Cont'd
Adoption of code form of home rule —Cont'd
Referendum, 25B §7.
Resolution, 25B §6.
Return to prior form of government, 25B §7A.
Bond issues.
Additional revenue, 25B §19.
Authority to issue, 25B §14.
Covenants not affected by subsequent statutes, 25B §19.
General provisions, 25B §15.
Investment into sinking fund, 25B §18.
Issuance, 25B §14.
Limitations on authority to issue, 25B §16.
Payment by tax levy, 25B §19.
Pledge of county faith and credit, 25B §19.
Proceeds of bonds, 25B §18.
Public local law authorizing, 25B §15.
Resolution of county commissioners, 25B §15.
Solely from revenues of revenue-producing project, 25B §20.
Terms not impaired by a previously issued bond, 25B §21.
Central Maryland.
Counties comprising, 25B §2.
Charter.
Submission to voters, MD Const Art XI-F §2.
Civil infractions.
Declaring certain violations as civil infractions, 25B §13C.
Classification of code counties, 25B §2; MD Const Art XI-F §5.
Compilation and publication of laws.
Generally, 25B §12.
Conflict of laws.
Generally, MD Const Art XI-F §10.
Construction contracts.
Resolution of disputes, 25B §13A.
Contract actions, 25B §13A.
Punitive damages, CJ §5-510.
Creation, MD Const Art XI-F §2.
Curfew, juvenile, 25B §13C-1.
Debt.
Borrowing money.
Authority, 25B §14.
Exemption from taxation, 25B §17.
Limitation of indebtedness, 25B §19; MD Const Art XI-F §8.
Authority of general assembly to limit, 25B §22.
Negotiable, 25B §17.
Definitions, MD Const Art XI-F §1.
Department of public facilities and services.
Establishment, 25B §13E.
Development excise tax, 25B §13F.
Agricultural land preservation, 25B §13G.
Development impact fees, 25B §13D.
Eastern shore.
Counties comprising, 25B §2.
Elections.
Charter, MD Const Art XI-F §2.
Registered voter.
Defined, 25B §1.
Fees.
Restrictions on levy, MD Const Art XI-F §9.
Four classes of code counties, 25B §2.
General provisions, MD Const Art XI-F §§1 to 10.
Immunity.
Contract actions, 25B §13A.
Punitive damages, CJ §5-510.

COUNTIES —Cont'd
Home rule for code counties —Cont'd
Juvenile curfew, 25B §13C-1.
Legislative procedure, 25B §10.
Licenses.
Restrictions on levy, MD Const Art XI-F §9.
Limitation of actions.
Contract actions, 25B §13A.
Limitations, 25B §1.
Meetings.
Public meetings, 25B §10.
Powers.
Displacement or limitation of competition, 25B §13B.
Generally, 25B §13.
Public local law.
Amendment, MD Const Art XI-F §3.
Applicability of subtitle to enactment, 25B §8.
Compilation.
Furnished annually, 25B §12.
Conflict of laws, MD Const Art XI-F §10.
Copies.
Distributions, 25B §12.
Defined, 25B §1.
Effective date, 25B §10.
Enactment, 25B §10; MD Const Art XI-F §3.
By resolution of commissioners, MD Const Art XI-F §6.
Journal.
Board of county commissioners, 25B §11.
Legislative sessions.
Board of county commissioners, 25B §9.
Limiting tax rate and indebtedness, MD Const Art XI-F §8.
Meetings.
Public meetings, 25B §10.
Power of general assembly to enact, MD Const Art XI-F §4.
Procedure.
Passing bills, 25B §10.
Proposed laws, 25B §10.
Publication, 25B §§10, 12.
Referendum, 25B §10.
General provisions, 25B §10.
Information to department of legislative reference, 25B §12.
Subject to referendum, MD Const Art XI-F §7.
Repeal, MD Const Art XI-F §3.
State department of legislative reference.
Duties, 25B §12.
Title, 25B §10.
Voting.
Requirements, 25B §10.
Public transportation.
Power to displace or limit competition, 25B §13B.
Resort tax, 25B §13H.
Return to prior form of government, 25B §7A.
Schools.
Development excise tax, 25B §13F.
Southern Maryland.
Counties comprising, 25B §2.
Sovereign immunity.
Contract actions, 25B §13A.
Status.
Code county rule status, 25B §1.
Taxation.
Limiting tax rate, MD Const Art XI-F §8.
Property tax rates.
Authority of general assembly to limit, 25B §22.

COUNTIES —Cont'd
Home rule for code counties —Cont'd
Taxation —Cont'd
Restrictions on levy, MD Const Art XI-F §9.
Water and sewer systems.
Agreements with local communities, 25B
§13E-1.
Department of public facilities and services, 25B
§13E.
Power to displace or limit competition, 25B
§13B.
Western Maryland.
Counties comprising, 25B §2.
Horse racing.
Special fund.
Failure to submit timely reports, BR §11-405.
Hospitals.
Authority to establish hospital or reception center,
25 §252.
Chartered counties.
Establishment, 25A §5.
Hotel rental tax. See within this heading,
"Taxation."
Household hazardous waste.
Collection and acceptance from residents of
counties.
Definitions, EN §9-1801.
Feasibility study, EN §9-1802.
Assistance by secretary, EN §9-1803.
Housing and community development.
Community action agencies, HS §§8-101 to 8-109.
Residential mortgage programs for certain
counties, HS §§4-1601 to 4-1610.
Bond issues.
Characteristics, HS §4-1607.
New bonds, HS §4-1609.
Ordinance to issue, HS §4-1606.
Sale and payment, HS §4-1608.
Defined terms, HS §4-1601.
Fees from borrowers, HS §4-1605.
Findings, HS §4-1602.
Goals, HS §4-1603.
Legislative findings, HS §4-1602.
Nature of program, HS §4-1610.
Power of county to borrow money, HS §4-1604.
Purposes, HS §4-1603.
Source of funds, HS §4-1604.
Types of transactions, HS §4-1610.
Howard county.
See HOWARD COUNTY.
Immunity.
Chartered counties.
Contract actions.
Immunity from liability, 25A §1A.
Commissioners.
Contract actions.
Counties governed by county commissioners.
Immunity from liability, 25 §1A.
Home rule for code counties.
Contract actions.
Immunity from liability, 25B §13A.
Local government tort claims act, CJ §§5-301 to
5-304.
See TORTS.
Officers and employees.
Acting outside territorial limit, CJ §5-612.
Sending police officers beyond county or municipal
boundaries, CP §2-105.
Improvements.
Restriction on construction of other work of
internal improvement, MD Const Art III §54.

COUNTIES —Cont'd
Income tax.
County income tax, TG §10-103.
Computation, TG §10-604.
Credits.
Effect on computation, TG §10-706.
Defined, TG §10-101.
Rate, TG §§10-106, 10-106.1.
Disparities in local income tax revenues.
Grants to counties to offset, 24 §9-1101.
Distribution of revenue from income tax on
individuals, TG §§2-608, 2-610.
Property tax credits to offset, TP §9-221.
Reimbursement for tax exemptions, 24 §9-1102.
Calvert County, 24 §9-1103.
Indexes.
Chartered counties.
Powers of county, 25A §5.
Compilation of laws enacted.
Chartered counties.
Duty of state department of legislative
services, 25A §7.
Home rule for code counties.
Compilation of laws.
State department of legislative services to
index, 25B §12.
Power of county commissioners to provide for, 25
§3.
Provisions as to clerk of court, register of wills
and county commissioners, 25 §3.
Industrial and commercial redevelopment.
Chartered counties.
Powers of county, 25A §5.
Projects.
Use of federal or state financial assistance, 25
§3.
Tax increment financing act, 41 §§14-201 to
14-214.
See TAX INCREMENT FINANCING ACT.
Industrial development corporations.
General provisions, 45A §§1 to 3.
See INDUSTRIAL DEVELOPMENT
CORPORATIONS.
Inspections.
Bridges built by contracts, 25 §39.
Insurance.
Group insurance.
Officers and employees, 25 §3.
Pooling to purchase property or casualty
insurance, 25 §3; IN §§19-602, 19-603.
**Insurance agents, brokers, etc., certificates of
authority.**
Local certificates prohibited, IN §1-205.
Interest.
Erosion districts.
Bonds, notes and certificates of indebtedness, 25
§§163, 166.
Hotel rental tax.
Delinquent payments, 24 §9-321.
Interpretation and construction.
Power of county commissioners.
Section 3 conveys supplementary authority, 25
§6.
Investments.
Deposit of unexpended or surplus money without
security, 95 §220.
Home rule for code counties.
Sinking funds and proceeds of funds, 25B §18.
Investment companies or trusts, 95 §22N.
Local government investment guidelines, 95 §22F.
Local government investment pool, 95 §22G.

COUNTIES —Cont'd
Jails.
Chartered counties.
Establishment, 25A §5.
Correctional farms, COR §§11-401 to 11-407.
See CORRECTIONAL FARMS.
Employment of inmate as alternative to
confinement, COR §§11-601 to 11-607.
See JAILS.
Individual county provisions, COR §§11-701 to
11-726.
See JAILS.
Local correctional facilities generally, COR
§§11-101 to 11-204.
See JAILS.
Local correctional facility defined, COR §1-101.
State reimbursement, COR §§9-401 to 9-405.
Junk dealers.
Yards.
Regulation of junkyards in counties, 25 §122A.
Juries.
Compensation for jurors, 25 §20.
Jurisdiction.
Navigation.
County lying on navigable river, 75 §81.
Juvenile curfew, 25B §13C-1.
Land development.
Chartered counties.
Powers of counties, 25A §5.
Residential purposes.
Conditional acceptance of land development, 25
§3.
Landings.
Establishment.
Application, 25 §157.
Authority to establish public landings, 25 §156.
Lead risk reduction in rental housing.
Regulation of landlords, 24 §§19-101 to 19-104.
Legislative services.
Chartered counties.
Compilation of laws enacted.
Duties of state department of legislative
services, 25A §7.
Department to be notified of adoption or
rejection of charter, 25A §3B.
Copies of county codes deposited with department,
25 §32A.
Home rule for code counties.
Compilation and publication of laws, 25B §12.
State departments.
Home rule for code counties.
Compilation and publication of laws, 25B §12.
Liability.
Contract actions, 25A §1A.
Home rule for code counties.
Defense of sovereign immunity, 25B §13A.
Local government tort claims act, CJ §§5-301 to
5-304.
See TORTS.
Libraries.
See LIBRARIES, COUNTY.
Licenses.
Code counties.
Restriction on levy, MD Const Art XI-F §9.
Hawkers and peddlers.
Powers of county commissioners, 25 §3.
Insurance agents, brokers, etc.
Local certificates of authority prohibited, IN
§1-205.
Powers of county commissioners, 25 §3.
Trailers and tourist courts, 25 §3.

COUNTIES —Cont'd
Licenses —Cont'd
Workers' compensation act.
Certificate of compliance.
Required prior to issuance of license, 24
§1-106; 25 §231.
Liens.
Benefit charges.
Erosion districts, 25 §165.
Hotel rental tax, 24 §9-325.
Limitation of actions.
Chartered counties.
Contract actions.
Claims against counties, 25A §1A.
Home rule for code counties.
Contract actions, 25B §13A.
Lines. See within this heading, "Boundaries."
Livestock.
Chartered counties.
Powers of county, 25A §5.
Local correctional facilities.
Chartered counties, establishment, 25A §5.
Correctional farms, COR §§11-401 to 11-407.
See CORRECTIONAL FARMS.
Defined, COR §1-101.
Employment of inmate as alternative to
confinement, COR §§11-601 to 11-607.
See JAILS.
Generally, COR §§11-101 to 11-204.
See JAILS.
Individual county provisions, COR §§11-701 to
11-726.
See JAILS.
State reimbursement, COR §§9-401 to 9-405.
Local government tort claims act, CJ §§5-301 to
5-304.
See TORTS.
Local land preservation programs, NR
§§5-9B-01 to 5-9B-06.
Local laws.
Home rule for code counties. See within this
heading, "Home rule for code counties."
Landlord and tenant.
Repair of dangerous defects.
Rent escrow, RP §8-211.
Local management boards.
Children, youth and families services, 49D
§§2-101 to 2-105.
Manufacturers.
County commissioners.
Approval of location of certain manufacturing
establishments, 25 §3.
Maps.
Certified copies, 75 §84.
Maryland Transit Administration.
Financing.
Participation by counties, TR §7-306.
Mental health facilities.
County advisory committees.
See MENTAL HEALTH FACILITIES.
Mental hygiene law.
Private group homes.
Application for license.
Notice to be given to county where the private
group home is to be located, HG §10-520.
Meridian line.
General provisions, 25 §§123 to 127.
See MERIDIAN LINE.
Merit system.
Establishment for officers and employees, 25 §3.

COUNTIES —Cont'd

Misdemeanors.
Political activities of employees, 24 §13-106.

Montgomery county.
See MONTGOMERY COUNTY.

Mosquito control, AG §5-404.

Motorcycles.
Off-road motorcycles.
State and local regulation, TR §25-102.1.

Motor vehicles.
Operation on property owned or under control of counties.
Applicability of rules of the road, TR §21-101.1.
Parking.
Powers as to county commissioners, 25 §2.
Violations, TR §26-301.
Powers of local authorities, TR §25-102.
Limitation, TR §25-101.1.
Size and weight, 25 §25.
Wrongful towing, impounding or storage.
Reimbursement of owner of vehicle, TR §26-306.

Municipal corporations.
Annexation.
Petition for referendum by county governing body, 23A §19.
Assistance to other political subdivisions, 23A §8C.
Grant in lieu of shares tax, 25 §220.
Highway projects.
Payment of cost, 25 §2A.
Legislation.
Administration or enforcement of municipal legislation, 23A §2B.

Mutual aid agreements.
National capital region mutual aid agreements, PS §§14-8A-01 to 14-8A-03.
Reciprocal agreements by counties and municipal corporations.
Providing police officers, CP §2-105.

National capital region mutual aid agreements, PS §§14-8A-01 to 14-8A-03.

Negligence.
Local government tort claims act, CJ §§5-301 to 5-304.
See TORTS.

New counties.
Ballot questions generally, EL §§7-101 to 7-105.
Formation, MD Const Art XIII §1.
General assembly to pass necessary laws, MD Const Art XIII §2.

911 emergency telephone system, PS §§1-301 to 1-312.
See 911 EMERGENCY TELEPHONE SYSTEM.

Noise control ordinances, rules or regulations.
Power of political subdivisions, EN §3-105.

Notices.
Adoption of code form of home rule.
Notice of intent, 25B §4.
Bridges.
Building and repair.
Application for building and repair to commissioners, 25 §35.
County roads.
Meeting of examiners for public roads, 25 §141.
Credit or debit card used to pay governmental charges, 24 §9-1401.
Federal aid, 24 §6-301.
Home rule for code counties.
Resort taxes, 25B §13H.
Petition to open or close roads, 25 §136.

COUNTIES —Cont'd

Nuisances.
Chartered counties.
Powers of county, 25A §5.
Permits.
Place of establishment for which permit not obtained, 25 §27.
Prevention and removal.
By county commissioners, 25 §3.

Nursing homes.
Citizens' nursing home boards, 25 §254.

Oaths.
County commissioners.
Official oath, 25 §19.
County roads.
Examiners, 25 §140.
Documents under oath, 24 §1-105.

Ocean beach replenishment fund.
Plans.
Financing plans submitted by, NR §8-1103.
Projects.
Failure of county to raise or pay percentage of costs, NR §8-1103.

Officers and employees.
Appointment.
By county commissioners, 25 §§1, 3.
Audit of accounts, 25 §3.
Bonds, surety.
Payment of premiums by county commissioners, 25 §33.
Bribery, CR §9-201.
Chartered counties.
Chief executive officers, MD Const Art XI-A §3.
Powers of county as to county officers, 25A §5.
Compensation.
Fixed by commissioners, 25 §3.
Conflicts of interest, 25 §3.
Definition of officers, MD Const Art XVII §1.
Elections.
When elections for county officers held, MD Const Art XVII §2.
Ethics.
See PUBLIC ETHICS.
Extortion by officer or employee, CR §3-702.
General provisions.
See PUBLIC OFFICERS AND EMPLOYEES.
Immunity.
Acting outside territorial limit, CJ §5-612.
Inducing another to give up compensation, CR §3-703.
Insurance.
Group insurance, 25 §3.
Merit system.
Establishment, 25 §3.
Political activities of employees.
Constitutional rights, 24 §13-102.
Effect of title, 24 §13-104.
"Local entity" defined, 24 §13-101.
Penalties, 24 §13-106.
Public policy, 24 §13-102.
Restrictions on political activities, 24 §13-105.
Rights of employees.
Generally, 24 §13-103.
Promotions.
Points or credits, 24 §1-107.
Public ethics.
See PUBLIC ETHICS.
Removal.
Elected officials convicted of crimes, MD Const Art XV §2.
Power of commissioners, 25 §3.

COUNTIES —Cont'd
Officers and employees —Cont'd
  Residency requirement, 24 §§1-107, 1-108.
  Retirement system.
    Establishment, 25 §3.
  Social security number on identification cards, 24
    §1-109.
  Suspension.
    Elected officials convicted of crimes, MD Const
      Art XV §2.
  Terms.
    Appointed by county commissioners, MD Const
      Art XVII §5.
    Elected by voters, MD Const Art XVII §3.
  Threats against, CR §3-708.
  Veterans.
    Reemployment rights of returning veterans, 24
      §10-101.
Ordinances.
  Adoption, 25 §3.
    Meetings to be public, 25 §5.
  Advertising, 25 §3.
  Chartered counties.
    Enactment, publication and interpretation of
      local laws, MD Const Art XI-A §3.
    Local legislation, 25A §5.
  County codes.
    Copies deposited with state agencies, 25 §32A.
  Effective when, 25 §4.
  Evidence.
    Admissibility, 25 §4.
  Filed with clerk of court, 25 §4.
  Hearings, 25 §3.
  Indexing, 25 §4.
  Printing and publishing, 25 §3.
  Recordation, 25 §4.
Packing and slaughterhouses.
  Powers of county commissioners, 25 §3.
Parking.
  Powers as to, 25 §2.
Parks and recreation.
  Authority to establish and conduct program, 25
    §222.
  Chartered counties.
    Powers of county, 25A §5.
  Powers of county commissioners, 25 §3.
  Recreational facilities.
    Power of commissioners to provide, 25 §14.
Patuxent river watershed.
  General provisions.
    See PATUXENT RIVER WATERSHED.
Paupers. See within this heading, "Poor."
Penalties.
  Civil penalties.
    Considerations in setting amount, 24 §14-101.
  Hotel rental tax.
    Failure to pay, 24 §9-322.
Pensions.
  Establishment of officers and employees, 25 §3.
  Governing principles for local pension systems,
    SPP §40-101.
  Reports.
    Annual report of pension system, 24 §2-102.
  Special retirement or pension system, SPP
    §§39-101 to 39-104. See within this heading,
    "Special retirement or pension system."
  Teachers.
    Additional allowance, 25 §12.
Permits.
  Building permits, 25 §3.
    Furnished supervisor of assessments, TP
      §5-103.

COUNTIES —Cont'd
Permits —Cont'd
  Dance halls and other amusements, tourist
    camps, etc., 25 §27.
  Workers' compensation.
    Certificate of compliance with workers'
      compensation act.
      Required prior to issuance, 25 §231.
Petitions.
  Bridges between two counties.
    Petition for building or repairing, 25 §40.
Physical fitness.
  County commission.
    See PHYSICAL FITNESS.
Pipelines.
  Gas company laying pipes under roadways or
    other public ways, PUC §7-102.
Planning and zoning.
  Chartered counties.
    Powers of county, 25A §5.
  Comprehensive plans.
    Charter counties, 66B §1.03.
Plats.
  County roads.
    Location when examiners are in favor, 25 §142.
Plumbers.
  County codes, 25 §3.
  Enforcement of plumbing codes, BOP §12-206.
Police.
  Appointment.
    By county commissioners, 25 §3.
  Arrest without a warrant.
    Generally, CP §§2-201 to 2-210.
    See WARRANTLESS ARREST.
  Authority granted police officers generally, CP
    §2-102.
  Charging documents against law enforcement
    officers, CJ §2-608.
  Compensation, 25 §3.
  Definitions.
    Police officer, CP §2-101.
  Duties.
    Generally, 25 §3.
  Fresh pursuit, CP §2-301.
  Immunity.
    Acting outside territorial limit, CJ §5-612.
  Law enforcement procedures generally, CP
    §§2-101 to 2-107.
    See POLICE.
  Mutual aid agreements.
    Reciprocal agreements by counties and
      municipal corporations, CP §2-105.
  Powers.
    Granted to police officers generally, CP §2-102.
  Retirement and pension systems.
    General provisions, SPP §§28-101 to 28-403.
      See LOCAL FIRE AND POLICE PENSION
      SYSTEM.
  Sending police officers beyond county or municipal
    boundaries, CP §2-105.
  Supervision.
    Commissioners in charge, 25 §3.
  Warrantless arrest.
    Generally, CP §§2-201 to 2-210.
    See WARRANTLESS ARREST.
Political activities of employees, 24 §§13-101 to
    13-106. See within this heading, "Officers and
    employees."
Political parties.
  County central committees, EL §4-202.
    Election of members, EL §4-203.

COUNTIES —Cont'd
Poor.
Funeral expenses.
Provided for paupers, 25 §20.
Health maintenance organizations.
Limited benefits through county programs, HG §19-703.
Trustees of the poor.
Appointment, 25 §1.
Levy for outpensions allowed, 25 §20.
Population estimates, HG §4-218.
Port administration.
Planning and development regulations.
Compliance by administration, TR §6-305.
Potomac highlands airport authority.
See POTOMAC HIGHLANDS AIRPORT AUTHORITY.
Power lines.
Electric companies laying, PUC §7-103.
Powers.
Chartered counties.
Express powers act, 25A §§1 to 8. See within this heading, "Charter."
Code counties.
Displacement or limitation of competition, 25B §13B.
Generally, 25B §13.
Commissioners. See within this heading, "Commissioners."
Express powers, 25 §§1 to 11C-1.
Chartered counties, 25A §§1 to 8.
Interpretation.
Section 3 conveys supplementary authority, 25 §6.
Printing.
Chartered counties.
Powers of county, 25A §5.
Power of commissioners as to printing and publishing, 25 §3.
Priority funding areas.
Designating priority funding areas, SF §5-7B-03.
Prisoners.
Compensation for boarding and keeping prisoners, 25 §3.
Convict road force. See within this heading, "Roads."
Private activity bond issuance fee.
Powers, 25 §3.
Procurement.
Entities subject to county budget and fiscal policies and purchasing laws, 24 §8-101.
Property.
Acquisition of property for public purpose, 25 §11A.
Assistance to other political subdivisions, 25 §219.
Chartered counties.
Powers of county, 25A §5.
Sale.
Property no longer needed, 25 §11A.
Publication.
Adoption of code form of home rule.
Notice of intent, 25B §4.
Bridges.
Notice for bids to erect, 25 §§37, 42.
Bridges between counties.
Advertising for sealed proposals, 25 §42.
Charter amendments, MD Const Art XI-A §5.
Chartered counties.
Publication of laws, 25A §7.
Code counties.
Compilation and publication of laws, 25B §12.

COUNTIES —Cont'd
Publication —Cont'd
Expenses.
Annual publication of county expenses, 24 §2-103.
Home rule for code counties.
Compilation and publication of laws, 25B §12.
Proposed law, 25B §10.
Ordinances.
Power of commissioners, 25 §3.
Power of commissioners, 25 §3.
Roads.
Notice of opening, altering or closing roads, 25 §136.
Sale of property no longer needed, 25 §11A.
Public debt.
Bond anticipation notes, 31 §12.
Bond issues.
Authority to issue, 31 §30.
Public ethics.
See PUBLIC ETHICS.
Public local law.
Home rule for code counties, 25B §§1 to 22; MD Const Art XI. See within this heading, "Home rule for code counties."
Landlord and tenant.
Rent escrow law, RP §8-211.
Public recreation and parks.
Authority to establish and conduct program, 25 §222.
Chartered counties.
Powers.
Authority to exercise, 25A §5.
Powers.
Authority to exercise, 25A §5.
County commissioners, 25 §3.
Recreational facilities, 25 §14.
Public transportation.
Charter.
Power of chartered counties to displace or limit competition, 25A §5A.
Code counties.
Power to displace or limit competition, 25B §13B.
Power of county commissioners to displace or limit competition, 25 §3D.
Public utilities.
Chartered counties.
Easements granted without advertisement, 25A §5.
Purchases and supplies.
Bidding.
Competitive bidding, 25 §3.
Bonds, surety.
Compliance bond, 25 §3.
Through state purchasing bureau.
Chartered counties, 25A §5.
Powers of commissioners, 25 §3A.
Radium pilot grant program.
County participation, HS §4-1304.
Railroads.
Restriction on aid to construction of railroads, MD Const Art III §54.
Safety devices for crossing, PUC §9-311.
Reciprocal agreements.
Mutual aid, providing police officers, CP §2-105.
Recordation.
Bridge and canal companies.
Authorizing construction of bridges and canals.
Resolution of county commissioners recorded, 23 §140.

COUNTIES —Cont'd

Recordation —Cont'd

Chartered counties.

Powers of county, 25A §5.

Fees.

Counties exempt from fees, RP §3-603.

Place of recording, RP §3-103.

Power to provide for, 25 §3.

Real estate.

Transfer on county records before recording, RP §3-104.

Roads.

Plat of opening or altering, 25 §138.

Taxes. See within this heading, "Taxation."

Records.

Chartered counties.

Powers of county, 25A §5.

Documents under oath, 24 §1-105.

Indexing.

Power of county commissioners, 25 §3.

Power of county commissioners to provide for, 25 §3.

Recycling solid waste.

Newsprint recycling by newspapers.

Limitations on counties, EN §9-1707.

Recycling plans, EN §9-1703.

Reduction in volume of waste, EN §9-1703.

Reports, EN §9-1705.

Requests for funds, EN §9-1702.

Solid waste stream.

Inability to achieve reduction of, EN §9-1704.

Referendum.

Adoption of code form of home rule, 25B §7.

Certification or reporting results, EL §11-605.

Charter.

Reservation in charter of power of referendum, 25A §8.

Statement as to referendum, 25A §7.

Code counties.

Public local laws, MD Const Art XI-F §7.

Home rule for code counties.

Compilation and publication of laws, 25B §12.

Public local law, 25B §10.

Refuse. See within this heading, "Garbage and trash."

Regional council of governments. See within this heading, "Council."

Registers of wills.

Recording.

Chartered counties, 25A §5.

Indexing.

Provision for, 25 §3.

Removal of cases.

Costs.

See COSTS.

Rent escrow laws.

Repair of dangerous defects, RP §8-211.

Reports.

Annual audit, 19 §40.

Bridges between counties.

Building and repair.

Examiners, 25 §41.

County roads.

Examiners.

Examiners in favor, 25 §142.

Examiners opposing, 25 §143.

Financial reports, 24 §2-101.

Time for filing, 19 §37.

Pension systems.

Annual reports, 24 §2-102.

COUNTIES —Cont'd

Reports —Cont'd

Regional council of governments.

Annual report, 25 §26A.

Reserve accounts, 24 §9-1201.

Residential child care programs.

Children, youth and families services.

Generally, 49D §§1-101 to 7-106.

See CHILDREN, YOUTH AND FAMILIES SERVICES.

Contracts, 49D §§7-101 to 7-106.

Requirements, 49D §§6-101, 6-102.

Residential mortgage programs for certain counties, HS §§4-1601 to 4-1610.

Resort taxes.

Home rule for code counties, 25B §13H.

Restaurants.

Defined, 2B §1-102.

Retirement.

Establishment for officers and employees, 25 §3.

Special retirement or pension system, SPP §§39-101 to 39-104. See within this heading, "Special retirement or pension system."

Riots.

Liability of county or municipality for damages, PS §§14-1001 to 14-1004.

Conditions of liability, PS §14-1002.

Generally, PS §14-1001.

Limitation of actions, PS §14-1003.

Notice and ability to prevent damage, effect, PS §14-1002.

Pleadings, PS §14-1004.

Reasonable diligence, effect, PS §14-1002.

Roads.

Buildings, gardens or yards.

Consent of owner to pass through required, 25 §144.

Cemeteries.

Consent of owner required, 25 §144.

Chartered counties.

Powers of county, 25A §5.

Closing.

Action by county commissioners on own initiative, 25 §136.

Examiners.

Appointment, 25 §138.

Determination at meeting on premises, 25 §141.

Official oath, 25 §140.

Report.

Location when examiners are in favor, 25 §142.

When examiners oppose, 25 §143.

Frederick county.

Roads presumed closed, 25 §137A.

Petition to county commissioners, 25 §135.

Counter petitions, 25 §137.

Notice, 25 §136.

Power of commissioners, 25 §25.

Construction and supervision.

By county commissioners, 25 §1.

Contracts.

Right of way, 25 §138.

Taking over private roads in certain counties, 25 §155.

Correctional facility inmates.

Road work by inmates at correctional facilities, COR §§9-501 to 9-520.

See PRISONS AND PRISONERS.

County commissioners.

Powers as to, 25 §1.

COUNTIES —Cont'd
Roads —Cont'd
Definition, TR §8-101.
Eminent domain.
Powers generally, 25 §138.
Engineers.
Duties and powers.
Defining, 25 §3.
Establishing office of county roads engineer, 25
§3.
Grading.
General provisions, 25 §3.
Highways. See within this heading, "Highways."
Inmates at correctional facilities.
Road work, COR §§9-501 to 9-520.
See PRISONS AND PRISONERS.
Municipal corporations.
Unincorporated towns and villages.
Applicability of road provisions to streets,
lanes and alleys, 25 §15.
Opening or altering.
Action by county commissioners on own
initiative, 25 §136.
Cemeteries.
Consent of owner required, 25 §144.
Condemnation, 25 §138.
Costs.
Liability of signer of petition, 25 §149.
County commissioners.
Action on return of examiners, 25 §150.
Damages.
Ascertainment, 25 §146.
By whom paid, 25 §147.
Liability of signer of petition, 25 §149.
Payment.
By whom paid, 25 §147.
To whom paid, 25 §148.
Drains, 25 §138.
Examiners.
Action of commissioners on return, 25 §150.
Appointment, 25 §138.
Compensation, 25 §151.
Damages.
Ascertainment, 25 §146.
Determination at meeting on premises, 25
§141.
Location, 25 §142.
Official oath, 25 §140.
Report.
Opposition by examiners, 25 §143.
When examiners are in favor, 25 §142.
When examiners oppose, 25 §143.
Location, 25 §142.
Passing through buildings, gardens, yards or
burial grounds.
Consent of owner required, 25 §144.
Petition to county commissioners, 25 §135.
Counter petitions, 25 §137.
Liability of signer for damages or costs, 25
§149.
Notice, 25 §136.
Plat, 25 §138.
Power of commissioners, 25 §25.
Right of way.
Contract with owner, 25 §138.
Taxation.
Levy of taxes when road opened or altered, 25
§152.
Width.
Requirements, 25 §145.

COUNTIES —Cont'd
Roads —Cont'd
Paving.
General provisions, 25 §3.
Powers as to, 25 §2.
Prisoners working on roads, COR §§9-501 to
9-520.
See PRISONS AND PRISONERS.
Public roads.
Open to public, 25 §145.
Repairing.
General provisions, 25 §3.
Signs or fingerboards.
Erection, 25 §153.
Form, 25 §153.
Injuring or destroying, 25 §154.
Supervisors.
Appointed by county commissioners, 25 §1.
Unincorporated towns and villages.
Applicability of road provisions to streets, lanes
and alleys, 25 §15.
Width.
Requirements, 25 §145.
Rules and regulations.
Printing and publishing, 24 §3-101; 25 §3.
Rural legacy program, NR §§5-9A-01 to 5-9A-09.
See RURAL LEGACY PROGRAM.
St. Mary's county.
See ST. MARY'S COUNTY.
Salaries.
Treasurers, 25 §51.
Sales.
Property no longer needed, 25 §11A.
Sales and use tax.
Exemptions.
Sale to political subdivision, TG §11-220.
Imposition of tax by political subdivisions.
Limitation, TG §11-102.
Powers of political subdivisions as to sales tax, 24
§9-201.
Sanitary districts.
Deputy state health officers.
See HEALTH.
Saturday.
Board of county commissioners.
Saturday closing of offices.
Authority to direct closing, 25 §5A.
Schools.
See SCHOOLS.
Secretary of state.
Chartered counties.
Secretary to be notified of adoption or rejection
of charter, 25A §3B.
Service of process, designation of agent for.
Local entities, 24 §1-110.
Circuit court, CivProCir Rule 2-124.
District Court, CivProDist Rule 3-124.
Sewage disposal rates.
Interjurisdictional sewage disposal rates.
Public service commission to set rates for
service.
One jurisdiction supplies within taxable limits
of another jurisdiction, PUC §4-304.
Sewers.
Water and sewer system plans.
See WATER AND SEWER SYSTEMS.
Sheriffs.
Compensation, CJ §2-309.
Deputies.
Compensation, CJ §2-309.
Fees, CJ §7-402.

COUNTIES —Cont'd
Sheriffs —Cont'd
General provisions.
See SHERIFFS.
Office.
Furnishing by county, CJ §2-309.
Pension plans.
Powers of commissioners, 25 §3.
Second in command, CJ §2-310.
Shore erosion control.
Ocean beach replenishment fund.
Plans.
Financing plans submitted by, NR §8-1103.
Projects.
Failure of county to raise or pay percentage of
costs, NR §8-1103.
Sidewalks.
Powers as to, 25 §§2, 3.
Signs.
Road signs and fingerboards.
Erection and form, 25 §153.
Injuring or destroying, 25 §154.
Sinking fund.
Investments.
General provisions, 31 §§6, 7.
See SINKING FUND.
Slum clearance.
Authority granted to counties, MD Const Art III
§61.
Soap.
Manufacturers.
Regulations, 25 §3.
Social services.
County social services boards.
See SOCIAL SERVICES.
Software programs.
Authority to sell, lease or license to the public, 24
§17-101.
Soil conservation.
Districts.
Levy for cooperation with districts, 25 §22.
Solid waste disposal facilities.
Chartered counties.
Contracts by charter counties for solid waste
disposal facilities, NR §3-9A-01.
Sovereign immunity.
Chartered counties.
Contract actions.
Defense of sovereign immunity, 25A §1A.
Home rule for code counties.
Contract actions.
Defense of sovereign immunity, 25B §13A.
Special retirement or pension system.
Accounting system, SPP §39-102.
Assets.
Distribution following termination of system,
SPP §39-104.
Benefits, SPP §39-102.
Creation or amendment by means other than
ordinance, SPP §39-103.
Immediate payment after separation, SPP
§39-102.
Payment following termination of system, SPP
§39-104.
Termination.
Creation or amendment by means other than
ordinance, SPP §39-103.
Contributions, SPP §39-102.
Creation.
Ordinance required, SPP §39-102.
Defined, SPP §39-101.

COUNTIES —Cont'd
Special retirement or pension system —Cont'd
Distribution of assets and benefits following
termination of system, SPP §39-104.
Modification of system.
Benefits created or amended by means other
than ordinance, SPP §39-103.
Ordinance to create system, SPP §39-102.
Rate certification.
Contributions, SPP §39-102.
Requirements for creation, SPP §39-102.
Service credits.
Unused sick leave, SPP §39-102.
Sick leave.
Creditable service, SPP §39-102.
Termination of system.
Benefits created or amended by means other
than ordinance, SPP §39-103.
Distribution of assets and benefits, SPP
§39-104.
Trustees.
Member of system as trustee, SPP §39-102.
Method of selection, SPP §39-102.
State aid.
Cooperative activities.
Acceptance of state funds, 25 §3.
State archives.
Notification of adoption or rejection of charter,
25A §3B.
State law library.
Chartered counties.
State library to be notified of adoption or
rejection of charter, 25A §3B.
County codes.
Copies deposited with state agencies, 25 §32A.
State police department.
Local division, PS §§2-601 to 2-604.
Agreements with local governments, PS §2-602.
Stormwater management.
Fees.
Adoption of fee system, EN §4-204.
Implementation of management program, EN
§4-202.
Management plan.
Review and approval, EN §4-204.
Streets and alleys.
Chartered counties.
Powers of county, 25A §5.
Correctional facility inmates.
Road work by inmates at correctional facilities,
COR §§9-501 to 9-520.
See PRISONS AND PRISONERS.
Inmates at correctional facilities, COR §§9-501 to
9-520.
See PRISONS AND PRISONERS.
Meridian line, 25 §§123 to 127.
See MERIDIAN LINE.
Prisoners working on roads, COR §§9-501 to
9-520.
See PRISONS AND PRISONERS.
Substitute surveyor.
See SURVEYS AND SURVEYORS.
Unincorporated towns and villages.
Applicability of road provisions to streets, lanes
and alleys, 25 §15.
Substance abuse advisory councils.
Local drug and alcohol abuse councils,
designation, HG §8-1001.
Susquehanna Flats.
General provisions.
See BIRDS AND GAME.

COUNTIES —Cont'd
Talbot county.
  See TALBOT COUNTY.
Taxation.
  Admissions and amusement tax. See within this
      heading, "Admissions and amusement tax."
  Advance payment, TP §10-205.
    Interest, TP §14-607.
  Appeals.
    Refunds, 24 §9-712.
  Assessments.
    Supervisors.
      Building permits furnished supervisors, TP
        §5-103.
  Building and repair of bridges.
    Levy to cover costs, 25 §36.
  Building excise tax.
    Dorchester county, 24 §9-1002.
    Talbot county, 24 §9-1001.
  Chartered counties.
    Assessments, levy and collection of taxes.
      Powers of county, 25A §5.
  Coal tax.
    Code counties, 24 §§9-501 to 9-509. See within
      this heading, "Code counties."
  Code counties.
    Authorization to levy any type of tax, MD Const
      Art XI-F §9.
    Coal tax, 24 §§9-501 to 9-509. See within this
      heading, "Code counties."
    Enactment of local laws limiting tax rate, MD
      Const Art XI-F §6.
    Home rule. See within this subheading, "Home
      rule for code counties."
  Collection, 25 §3.
    Actions for collection, 24 §9-704.
      Attachment, 24 §9-706.
      By county attorney.
        Duty to initiate action, TP §14-866.
      Compromise of claim, 24 §9-705; TP §14-866.
      County attorney, TP §14-865.
      Evidence.
        Certificate of collector, 24 §9-707; TP
          §14-869.
      Initiation, 24 §9-705.
      Naming of plaintiff, TP §14-868.
      Priority of actions, 24 §9-707.
    Generally, 25 §3.
    Limitation of actions, 24 §9-723.
    Powers of commissioners, 25 §20.
  Collector.
    Appointment, TP §4-101.
    By county commissioners, 25 §1.
    General provisions.
      See PROPERTY TAXES.
  Credit or debit card used to pay taxes, 24 §9-1401.
  Definitions, TG §1-101.
    Hotel rental tax, 24 §9-301.
  Delinquent taxes.
    Penalties, TP §14-702.
  Disclosure of tax information, 24 §9-702.
    Penalties, 24 §9-721.
  Districts.
    Electric lighting districts, 25 §2B.
  Erosion.
    Districts, 25 §§161 to 167. See within this
      heading, "Erosion."
  Failure to provide information.
    Penalties, 24 §9-716.
      Willful failure, 24 §9-717.

COUNTIES —Cont'd
Taxation —Cont'd
  Farm labor problem.
    Levy for, 25 §21.
  Grants in lieu of tax credits.
    Elderly or disabled renters in certain counties,
      TP §9-402.
  Harford county.
    Development impact fee, school construction
      financing, 24 §9-10A-01.
  Hearings.
    Hotel rental tax.
      Required in certain counties, 24 §9-303.
  Home rule for code counties.
    Bond issues.
      Exemptions, 25B §17.
    Levy to pay bonds, 25B §19.
    Limitations on property tax rates, 25B §22.
    Resort taxes, 25B §13H.
  Hotel rental tax.
    Administration, 24 §9-314.
    Authorization to impose, 24 §9-303.
      Limitations in Cecil county, 24 §9-303.
    Bonds, surety.
      County treasurer, 24 §9-317.
    Calvert county.
      Exemptions, 24 §9-305.
    Carroll county.
      Exemptions, 24 §9-305.
    Cecil county.
      Limitations in, 24 §9-303.
    Certain classes of hotels, 24 §9-305.
    Collection, 24 §9-309.
      Distraint, 24 §9-324.
      Judicial proceedings, 24 §9-323.
    Definitions, 24 §9-301.
    Discounts, 24 §9-311.
    Distribution, 24 §9-318.
    Exemptions.
      Certain classes of hotels, 24 §9-305.
    Frederick county.
      Exemptions, 24 §9-305.
    Hearings.
      Required in certain counties, 24 §9-303.
    Interest.
      Delinquent payments, 24 §9-321.
    Liens, 24 §9-325.
    Limitations on distribution, 24 §9-318.
    Local exemptions.
      Certain real property exempt from local
        taxation.
        Treated as taxable in computing state aid
          payments, TP §7-107.
      Power to reduce percent of assessment, TP
        §7-108.
    Payment.
      Failure to pay.
        Interest, 24 §9-321.
      Payment to county, 24 §9-311.
      Payment to hotel, 24 §9-308.
      Penalties.
        Failure to pay, 24 §9-322.
    Penalties.
      Failure to pay, 24 §9-322.
    Rates, 24 §9-304.
      Limitation, 24 §9-304.
    Reports, 24 §9-319.
    Return.
      Form, 24 §9-310.
      Required, 24 §9-310.
    Rules and regulations, 24 §9-315.

COUNTIES —Cont'd
Taxation —Cont'd
Hotel rental tax —Cont'd
St. Mary's county.
Exemptions, 24 §9-305.
Scope of subtitle, 24 §9-302.
Security for tax, 24 §9-326.
State assistance, 24 §9-316.
Time for distribution, 24 §9-318.
Washington county.
Exemptions, 24 §9-305.
Western Maryland class.
Reports, 24 §9-319.
Income tax. See within this heading, "Income tax."
Industrial development corporations.
General provisions, 45A §§1 to 3.
See INDUSTRIAL DEVELOPMENT
CORPORATIONS.
Insurance companies, agents, brokers, etc.
Local taxes prohibited, IN §1-205.
Interest.
Advance payment of taxes, TP §14-607.
Hotel rental tax.
Delinquent payments, 24 §9-321.
Overdue taxes, TP §§14-603, 14-604.
Levy.
Farm labor problem, 25 §21.
General provisions, TP §6-202.
Industrial development corporations.
Payment of bonds and interest, 45A §2.
Municipal corporations.
Municipalities performing services in lieu of
county services, TP §§6-305, 6-306.
Paupers.
Pensions, 25 §20.
Powers of commissioners, 25 §20.
Roads.
Opening or altering, 25 §152.
Taxable year, TP §6-204.
Teachers' pensions, 25 §12.
Liens.
Hotel rental tax, 24 §9-325.
Limitation of actions.
Time for collection, 24 §9-723.
Municipal corporations.
Municipalities performing services in lieu of
county services, TP §§6-305, 6-306.
Setoffs, TP §§6-305, 6-306.
Payment.
Deferred payment.
Liens, TP §14-804.
Hotel rental tax. See within this subheading,
"Hotel rental tax."
Prepayment authorized.
Advance payment, TP §10-205.
Interest, TP §14-607.
Penalties.
Hotel rental tax.
Failure to pay, 24 §9-322.
Pensions.
Outpensions for commissioners or trustees of
the poor, 25 §20.
Property transfer tax.
See PROPERTY TAXES.
Public officers and employees.
Negligent failure to perform duties, 24 §9-719.
Willful failure to perform duties, 24 §9-720.
Public property.
Exemptions, TP §7-210.
Interest in public property, TP §7-211.

COUNTIES —Cont'd
Taxation —Cont'd
Rates.
Hotel rental tax, 24 §9-304.
No additional law necessary for special rate, TP
§6-304.
Setting of county property tax rate, TP §6-302.
Real property.
Certain real property exempt from local
taxation.
Treated as taxable in computing state aid
payments, TP §7-107.
Credit by reason of income, TP §9-104.
Local supplement to homeowners property tax
credit program, TP §§9-215, 9-215.1.
Recordation tax.
Effect of failure to use uniform system of
financial reporting, 19 §38.
Paid to political subdivisions, 19 §38.
Payment of recordation taxes to.
Discontinuance, 19 §39.
Refund of taxes.
Appeals, 24 §9-712.
Claimants, 24 §9-710.
Criteria, TP §14-905.
Determination on claim, 24 §9-712.
Form of claim, 24 §9-711.
Limitation, TP §14-905.
Payment, 24 §9-713.
Personal property tax.
Interest, TP §14-608.
Time for filing claims, 24 §§9-711, 9-724.
Resort taxes.
Home rule for code counties, 25B §13H.
Roads.
Opening or altering.
Levy of tax, 25 §152.
Sales.
Assaulting of bidder, 24 §9-718.
Liability of judicial officer making sale, 24
§9-701.
Priority of unpaid claims, 24 §9-701.
Property may be bought by and sold, TP
§§14-824, 14-825.
Payment of other tax claims, TP §14-826.
Sales and use tax.
Exemption of sale to political subdivision, TG
§11-220.
Imposition of tax by political subdivision.
Limitation, TG §11-102.
Powers of political subdivisions as to sales tax,
24 §9-201.
Special county and municipal taxes.
General provisions, 24 §§9-101 to 9-113.
See TAXATION.
Tax collector.
Assaulting, 24 §9-718.
Tax credits.
Open spaces or open areas, TP §9-208.
Tax increment financing act, 41 §§14-201 to
14-214.
See TAX INCREMENT FINANCING ACT.
Tobacco tax.
Imposition of tax.
Limitation, TG §12-102.
Trailer parks or mobile home courts or parks, 24
§9-401.
Transportation bonds.
Exemption, TR §3-509.
Taxicabs.
Cruising along public streets, power to restrict or
prohibit, PUC §10-102.

COUNTIES —Cont'd
Taxicabs —Cont'd
Power to designate taxicab stands, PUC §10-102.
Power to license taxicab drivers, PUC §10-103.
Tax increment financing act, 41 §§14-201 to
14-214.
See TAX INCREMENT FINANCING ACT.
Teachers' retirement system.
Additional allowance by counties, 25 §12.
Telegraph and telephone companies.
Emergency telephone systems.
See TELECOMMUNICATIONS.
Television.
Community antenna television systems.
Franchise, 25 §3C.
Tobacco tax.
Imposition of tax.
Limitation, TG §12-102.
Toll facilities.
Construction.
Prohibited without consent of majority of
governments of affected counties, 25 §236.
Torts.
Local government tort claims act, CJ §§5-301 to
5-304.
See TORTS.
Trailer and tourist courts.
License and regulation.
County commissioners, 25 §3.
Permits.
Required for tourist camps and cabins, 25 §27.
Trailer camps.
Powers as to, 25 §2.
Transportation bonds.
Agreements between department and county, TR
§3-307.
Alternative bonds, TR §§3-501 to 3-519.
Agreements between department and counties,
TR §3-517.
Agreements to participate, TR §3-518.
Authorization, TR §3-503.
Resolution, TR §3-504.
Bond anticipation notes, TR §3-508.
Borrowing of proceeds, TR §3-518.
County participation, TR §3-514.
Bonds as obligations, TR §3-513.
Requirements, TR §3-516.
Definitions, TR §3-501.
Department debt, TR §3-513.
Designation, TR §3-503.
Distinguished, TR §3-503.
Execution, TR §3-504.
Interim certificates, TR §3-507.
Investment securities, TR §3-505.
Issuance.
Amount, TR §3-515.
Consent requirements, TR §3-511.
Revenue refunding bonds, TR §3-519.
Payments, TR §§3-512, 3-518.
Purpose, TR §3-502.
Revenue refunding bonds.
Issuance, TR §3-519.
Revenues of state and department.
Provision for payment of bonds, TR §3-512.
State debt, TR §3-513.
State finance and procurement exemption, TR
§3-506.
Taxation exemption, TR §3-509.
Temporary bonds, TR §3-507.
Transportation trust fund.
Provisions for payment of bonds, TR §3-512.

COUNTIES —Cont'd
Transportation bonds —Cont'd
Alternative bonds —Cont'd
Trust agreements.
Authorization, TR §3-510.
Amount.
Determination of amount, TR §3-305.
Maximum amount, TR §§3-305, 3-306.
Authorized, TR §3-303.
Comptroller.
Extraordinary withholding, TR §3-308.
Debts.
Bonds are departmental debt, TR §3-309.
Debt service limitation, TR §3-306.
Definitions, TR §3-301.
Designation, TR §3-303.
Highway user revenues.
Defined, TR §3-301.
Issuance.
Limitations on issuance, TR §3-306.
Notice.
Participation of counties, TR §3-304.
Participation of counties, TR §3-304.
Payment, TR §3-310.
Government obligation.
Defined, TR §3-310.
Transfer of government obligations from
transportation trust fund to state treasurer,
or bank or trust company, TR §3-310.
Purposes of subtitle, TR §3-302.
Sinking fund.
Sufficient to pay debt service, TR §3-104.
Tax.
Failure to levy.
Withholding by comptroller, TR §3-308.
Transportation, paratransit grants, TR §2-103.5.
**Trapshooting, skeetshooting or other target
shooting.**
Noise control ordinances, rules or regulations
prohibiting.
Power of political subdivision restricted, EN
§3-105.
Treasurer.
Bonds, surety.
Hotel rental tax, 24 §9-317.
Premiums.
Payment, 25 §33.
Draining lands.
Compensation, 25 §89.
Disbursement of taxes, 25 §89.
Report and distribution of taxes, 25 §90.
Right to succeed himself in office, 25 §51A.
Salary, 25 §51.
Watershed associations.
Payments of funds received from sale of bonds,
25 §203.
Report of collection of taxes for payment of
bonds, 25 §203.
Taxation.
Duties of county treasurer, 25 §205.
Trees and timber.
Urban and community forestry, NR §§5-424 to
5-427.
See URBAN AND COMMUNITY FORESTRY.
Trust gifts.
Commissioners to have power to receive, 25 §158.
State's attorneys.
Duty to see that trust carried into effect, 25
§159.
Underground utility lines and facilities.
Appropriation for relocating utilities underground,
PUC §4-209.

COUNTIES —Cont'd
Unemployment relief.
Taxation.
Industrial development corporations.
General provisions, 45A §§1 to 3.
Special county and municipal taxes.
General provisions, 24 §§9-101 to 9-113.
United States.
Cooperation with department of agriculture of the
United States.
Farmers' cooperative demonstration work, 25
§160.
Federal aid.
Notices.
Instructional and research aid, 24 §6-301.
Power to participate in federal projects.
Authorized to enter into agreements or
contracts, 24 §6-202.
Enumeration of powers, 24 §6-201.
Validation of prior acts or contracts, 24 §6-201.
Urban and community forestry, NR §§5-424 to
5-427.
See URBAN AND COMMUNITY FORESTRY.
Validation.
Participation in federal projects.
Prior acts or contracts, 24 §6-201.
Veterans.
Reemployment rights of returning veterans, 24
§10-101.
Voter registration, EL §§3-101 to 3-602.
See VOTER REGISTRATION.
Washington county.
See WASHINGTON COUNTY.
Washington suburban sanitary commission.
Highways and streets.
Relocation, etc., of facilities.
Costs.
Reimbursement of commission by counties,
29 §10-106.
Waste.
Garbage and trash. See within this heading,
"Garbage and trash."
Household hazardous waste.
Collection and acceptance from residents.
Definitions, EN §9-1801.
Feasibility study, EN §9-1802.
Assistance by secretary, EN §9-1803.
Water and sewer systems.
Assistance by secretary, EN §9-207.
Assistance to other political subdivisions, 25 §219.
Charter.
Power of chartered counties to displace or limit
competition, 25A §5A.
Code counties.
Agreements with local communities, 25B
§13E-1.
Department of public facilities and services, 25B
§13E.
Power to displace or limit competition, 25B
§13B.
County water and sewerage plans, EN §§9-501 to
9-521.
See WATER AND SEWER SYSTEMS.
Health officers.
Duties generally, EN §9-102.
Interjurisdictional water rates.
Public service commission to set rates for water.
One jurisdiction supplies within another, PUC
§4-305.
Power of county commissioners to displace or limit
competition, 25 §3D.

COUNTIES —Cont'd
Water and sewer systems —Cont'd
Restrictions on use of water in certain counties
authorized, 25 §168.
Secretary to advise counties that may tend to
pollute, EN §9-205.
Soil percolator tests.
Privatization programs.
Established in, EN §9-1104.
Water pollution.
Secretary to advise counties tending to pollute,
EN §9-205.
Watershed associations.
Federally assisted watershed projects.
Powers of counties, 25 §3.
General provisions, 25 §§169 to 218.
See WATERSHED ASSOCIATIONS.
Patuxent river watershed.
General provisions.
See PATUXENT RIVER WATERSHED.
Watershed projects.
Chartered counties.
Powers, 25A §5.
Federally assisted watershed projects.
Powers, 25 §3.
Waters of the state.
Boundaries.
Maps as evidence, 75 §83.
Federally assisted watershed projects.
Powers of counties, 25 §3.
Jurisdiction.
County lying on navigable river, 75 §81.
Effect of boundaries of state, 75 §82.
Watershed projects.
Chartered county powers, 25A §5.
Weather modification.
Powers of certain counties as to, 25 §3.
Weeds.
Noxious weeds.
Agreement between secretary and county for
control or eradication, AG §9-403.
Weights and measures.
Sealers.
General provisions.
See WEIGHTS AND MEASURES.
Welfare.
Tax authorized for general welfare.
Special county and municipal taxes.
General provisions, 24 §§9-101 to 9-113.
Well drillers.
Powers of units of state, EN §13-401.
Requirements by political subdivisions.
Prohibited, EN §13-402.
Well permit fees.
Collection, EN §9-1305.
Wharves.
Acquiring land for public wharf, 25 §138.
Wicomico county.
Generally.
See WICOMICO COUNTY.
Witnesses.
Compensation of state witnesses, 25 §20.
Workers' compensation.
Certificate of compliance with workers'
compensation act.
Required prior to issuance of licenses or
permits, 24 §1-106; 25 §231.
Covered employees and employers.
Official of political subdivision, LE §9-217.
Volunteers, LE §9-231.

COUNTIES —Cont'd
Year.
Fiscal year, 19 §35.
Zoning and planning.
Chartered counties.
Historic and landmark zoning and preservation,
25A §5.
Comprehensive plans.
Charter counties, 66B §1.03.
General provisions.
See ZONING.
Historic area zoning.
General provisions.
See ZONING.

COUNTING VOTES.
Canvass generally, EL §§11-101 to 11-605.
See ELECTIONS.

COUNTRY CLUBS.
General provisions.
See CLUBS.

COUNTY BOARDS OF EDUCATION.
Generally.
See SCHOOLS.

COUNTY BOARDS OF ELECTIONS.
Election, EL §§8-801 to 8-806.
Powers and duties generally, EL §§2-201 to
2-303.
See ELECTIONS.
Voter registration, EL §§3-101 to 3-602.
See VOTER REGISTRATION.

COUPONS.
Counterfeiting and issuing tokens, CR §8-612.
Tobacco sales to minors.
Inapplicability of prohibition.
Coupons in newspapers or magazines, CR
§10-17.

COURSE OF DEALING.
Sale of goods, UCC.
Implied warranties, CL §2-314.

**COURT-APPOINTED SPECIAL ADVOCATE
PROGRAM (CASA).**
Children in need of assistance, CJ §3-830.
Juvenile causes, CJ §3-8A-32.

COURT OF APPEALS.
Administration of courts.
General provisions, CJA Rules 16-101 to 16-824.
See ADMINISTRATION OF COURTS.
Administrative office of the courts.
Information.
Officers of court to deliver information to
director of administrative office on request,
CJ §13-101.
Pro bono legal services.
Reporting of services performed, CJA Rule
16-903.
Seventh judicial circuit, CJ §13-102.
State office, CJ §13-101.
Appeal of decision, CJA Rule 16-809.
Appellate jurisdiction, CJ §12-307.
Appellate procedure.
General provisions, AppRev Rules 8-101 to 8-611.
See APPEALS.
Attorney general.
Prosecute and defend suits in, MD Const Art V §3.
Certified questions of law.
General provisions, CJ §§12-601 to 12-613.
See CERTIFIED QUESTIONS OF LAW.

COURT OF APPEALS —Cont'd
Certiorari.
Allocation of appellate jurisdiction, CJ §12-306.
Petition for writ.
Procedure on petition, AppRev Rule 8-303.
Review of cases in court of special appeals, CJ
§12-201.
Exceptions, CJ §12-202.
Securing uniformity of decisions, CJ §12-305.
Chief judge. See within this heading, "Judges."
Circuits.
Appellate judicial circuits, MD Const Art IV §14.
Clerks.
Law clerks, CJ §2-402.
Clerks of court.
Appointment, CJ §2-401.
Compensation, CJ §2-403.
Duties.
Generally, CJ §2-401.
Employees, CJ §2-401.
Fees, CJ §7-102.
Notify attorney general of cases in which state
has interest, MD Const Art V §6.
Oaths, SG §16-102.
Term of office, CJ §2-401.
Composition, MD Const Art IV §14.
Comptroller.
Acting comptrollers.
Court of appeals to have exclusive original
jurisdiction, SG §4-105.
Copyrights.
Reports, CJ §13-203.
Costs.
Defined, CJ §7-101.
State or state agency.
Party, CJ §7-104.
Court of special appeals.
General provisions.
See COURT OF SPECIAL APPEALS.
Courts of record, MD Const Art IV §1.
Death penalty.
Automatic review by court of appeals, CR §2-401.
Rules governing proceedings.
Adoption, CR §2-305.
Decisions.
Concurrence of a majority, MD Const Art IV §14.
Judgment final, MD Const Art IV §15.
Opinions.
In writing filed within three months after
argument or submission, MD Const Art IV
§15.
Documents.
Submission of copies by clerk, SG §7-213.
Elections.
Contested elections.
Judicial review of election.
Appeal directly to court of appeals, EL
§12-203.
Electric customer choice and competition act.
Rate stabilization.
Review by appeal of qualified rate order, PUC
§7-528.
Employees.
Compensation, CJ §2-403.
General provisions, CJ §2-402.
Established.
Highest court of state, CJ §1-301.
Fees, CJ §7-102.
Habeas corpus.
General provisions, CJ §§3-701 to 3-707.
See HABEAS CORPUS.

COURT OF APPEALS —Cont'd
Hall of records commission.
Chief judge member, SG §9-1003.
Highest court of state, CJ §1-301.
Intermediate courts of appeal.
Clerk.
Notify attorney general of cases in which state
has interest, MD Const Art V §6.
Court of special appeals.
See COURT OF SPECIAL APPEALS.
Creation, MD Const Art IV §14A.
Decisions.
Judgment final, MD Const Art IV §15.
Written opinion filed within three months after
argument or submission, MD Const Art IV
§15.
Judges.
Chief judge of court of appeals.
Administrative head of system, MD Const Art
IV §18.
Disqualification.
When judge heard cause below, MD Const Art
IV §15.
Elections.
Exceptions as to quadrennial elections, MD
Const Art XVII §3.
Eligibility of members of general assembly, MD
Const Art IV §14B.
Generally.
See JUDGES.
Reports.
Judicial work and business to chief judge of
court of appeals, MD Const Art IV §18.
Vacancies.
Filled by chief judge of court of appeals, MD
Const Art IV §18.
Judgments and decrees.
Final, MD Const Art IV §15.
Jurisdiction.
Prescribed by general assembly, MD Const Art
IV §14A.
Powers.
Provided by general assembly, MD Const Art IV
§1.
Reports.
Publication, MD Const Art IV §16.
Judges.
Chief judge.
Administrative head of the judicial system, MD
Const Art IV §18.
Designation by governor, MD Const Art IV §14.
Powers, MD Const Art IV §18.
Commission on judicial disabilities, CJ §§13-401
to 13-403; CJA Rule 16-804; MD Const Art IV
§§4A, 4B.
Appeal of decision, CJA Rule 16-809.
Confidentiality of proceedings, CJA Rule 16-810.
Proceedings before commission, CJA Rule
16-808.
Disqualification.
When judge heard cause below, MD Const Art
IV §15.
Elections, MD Const Art IV §14.
Exceptions as to quadrennial elections, MD
Const Art XVII §3.
Notice to state board of name of judge to be
placed on ballot, EL §5-301.
Eligibility.
Member of general assembly, MD Const Art IV
§21.

COURT OF APPEALS —Cont'd
Judges —Cont'd
Former judges.
Defined, CJ §1-302.
Recall for temporary assignment, CJ §1-302.
Generally, MD Const Art IV §§2 to 9.
See JUDGES.
Hall of records commission.
Member of commission, SG §9-1003.
Number, MD Const Art IV §14.
Removal.
Judicial disabilities commission, MD Const Art
IV §§4A, 4B.
See JUDICIAL DISABILITIES
COMMISSION.
Residence.
Abandonment.
Legal residence not abandoned by residing in
Anne Arundel county, CJ §1-204.
Retirement.
Judicial disabilities commission, MD Const Art
IV §§4A, 4B.
See JUDICIAL DISABILITIES
COMMISSION.
Rules and regulations.
Regulation of practice, MD Const Art IV §18.
Salary, MD Const Art IV §14.
Term of office, MD Const Art IV §14.
Vacancies.
Filling of vacancies by chief judge, MD Const
Art IV §18.
Judgments and decrees.
Final, MD Const Art IV §15.
Judicial disabilities commission, CJ §§13-401 to
13-403; CJA Rule 16-804; MD Const Art IV
§§4A, 4B.
Confidentiality of proceedings, CJA Rule 16-810.
Jurisdiction, MD Const Art IV §14.
Allocation of jurisdiction between appellate courts.
See APPEALS.
Jury.
General provisions, CJ §§8-101 to 8-507.
See JURY.
Law clerks, CJ §2-402.
Laws.
Recorded with, MD Const Art III §30.
Letterhead stationery.
Telephone number on letterhead stationery, CJ
§1-102.
Mandamus.
See MANDAMUS.
Oaths.
Judges.
Official oaths, SG §16-102.
Peace orders.
Rules and forms, CJ §3-1509.
Powers.
Vested in, MD Const Art IV §1.
Pro bono legal services.
Attorneys at law.
Local committees and plans, CJA Rule 16-902.
Reporting on services performed, CJA Rule
16-903.
State committee and plan, CJA Rule 16-901.
Proceedings before commission, CJA Rule
16-808.
Publication.
Reports, MD Const Art IV §16.
Pro bono legal services, CJA Rule 16-901.
Questions of law.
Uniform certification of questions of law act.
See CERTIFIED QUESTIONS OF LAW.

COURT OF APPEALS —Cont'd
Quorum, MD Const Art IV §14.
Recordation.
　Laws recorded in office, MD Const Art III §30.
Reporter.
　Appointment, CJ §13-201.
　Clerical assistance, CJ §13-203.
　Compensation, CJ §13-202.
　Contracts.
　　For reports, CJ §13-204.
　Copies of reports, CJ §13-203.
　Duties.
　　Generally, CJ §13-203.
　Establishment of office, CJ §13-201.
　Expenses, CJ §13-203.
　Office established, CJ §13-201.
　Publication of reports, CJ §13-203.
　Term of office, CJ §13-201.
Reports.
　Contracts.
　　By reporter, CJ §13-204.
　Copies.
　　Delivered by clerk to reporter, CJ §13-203.
　Copyrights, CJ §13-203.
　Court of special appeals.
　　See COURT OF SPECIAL APPEALS.
　Distribution, CJ §13-203.
　Interest on lawyer trust accounts participation,
　　CJA Rule 16-608.
　Pro bono legal services.
　　Attorneys at law, CJA Rule 16-901.
　Publication, MD Const Art IV §16.
Review by court of appeals.
　Appellate procedure generally, AppRev Rules
　　8-101 to 8-611.
　See APPEALS.
Rules and regulations.
　Amendment.
　　Disruptive behavior, CtAppIOR 6.
　　Extended coverage.
　　　Coverage at public hearing, CtAppIOR 8.
　　　Nature and extent, CtAppIOR 7.
　　　Open meetings, CtAppIOR 9.
　　　Standards of conduct and technology,
　　　　CtAppIOR 10.
　　Open doors for meeting rooms, CtAppIOR 4.
　　Open meetings, CtAppIOR 1.
　　Opportunity for comment, CtAppIOR 2.
　　Personal conduct at proceedings, CtAppIOR 5.
　　Record of proceedings, CtAppIOR 3.
　Committee on rules.
　　Appointment, CJ §13-301.
　　Assistants.
　　　Employment, CJ §13-302.
　　　Expenses.
　　　　Payment, CJ §13-303.
　　　Salaries, CJ §13-302.
　　　　Payment, CJ §13-303.
　　Compensation, CJ §13-301.
　　Expenses, CJ §13-301.
　General provisions, MD Const Art IV §18.
　Power to prescribe, CJ §1-201.
　Rule-making power of court of appeals, MD Const
　　Art IV §18.
Salaries.
　Judges, MD Const Art IV §14.
Seals, MD Const Art IV §1.
Sessions, MD Const Art IV §14.
Sheriffs.
　Attendance of services directed, CJ §2-404.

COURT OF APPEALS —Cont'd
Special appeals.
　General provisions.
　　See COURT OF SPECIAL APPEALS.
State reporter. See within this heading,
　　"Reporter."
Stenographers.
　Employment, CJ §2-402.
Treasurer.
　Inability or unavailability of treasurer.
　　Original jurisdiction of court, SG §5-106.
Zoning.
　Appeals to, 66B §4.08.

COURT OF SPECIAL APPEALS.
Administration of courts, CJA Rules 16-101 to
　　16-824.
　See ADMINISTRATION OF COURTS.
Administrative procedure.
　Contested cases.
　　Right to appeal, SG §10-223.
Appeals.
　Appellate jurisdiction, CJ §12-308.
　Certiorari.
　　Review of cases by court of appeals, CJ §12-203.
Appellate procedure generally, AppRev Rules
　　8-101 to 8-611.
　See APPEALS.
Certification of questions of law.
　General provisions, CJ §§12-601 to 12-613.
　　See CERTIFIED QUESTIONS OF LAW.
Certiorari.
　Allocation of appellate jurisdiction, CJ §12-306.
　Review of case by court of appeals, CJ §12-203.
　Review of case in court of special appeals.
　　Exceptions, CJ §12-202.
Clerks of court.
　Appointment, CJ §2-401.
　Compensation, CJ §2-403.
　Duties.
　　Generally, CJ §2-401.
　Fees, CJ §7-102.
　Law clerk.
　　Appointment, CJ §2-402.
　Oaths, SG §16-102.
　Term of office, CJ §2-401.
Composition, CJ §1-402.
Costs.
　Defined, CJ §7-101.
　State or state agency.
　　Party, CJ §7-104.
Courts of record, MD Const Art IV §1.
Employees.
　Appointment, CJ §2-402.
　Compensation, CJ §2-403.
Established, CJ §1-401.
Fees.
　State court administrator to determine amount,
　　CJ §7-102.
Habeas corpus.
　Discharge on ground of unconstitutionality.
　　Review by court of special appeals, SpecPro
　　　Rule 15-312.
　General provisions, CJ §§3-701 to 3-707.
　　See HABEAS CORPUS.
Hearings.
　In banc, CJ §1-403.
Intermediate courts of appeal, CJ §1-401.
　See COURT OF APPEALS.
Judges.
　Appointment, CJ §1-402.

COURT OF SPECIAL APPEALS —Cont'd
Judges —Cont'd
Chief judge.
Designation, CJ §1-402.
Elections.
Notice to state board of name of judge to placed on ballot, EL §5-301.
Number, CJ §§1-402, 1-403.
Removal, CJ §1-402.
Residence.
Abandonment.
Not abandoned by residing in Anne Arundel county, CJ §1-204.
Requirements, CJ §1-402.
Retirement, CJ §1-402.
Selection, CJ §1-402.
Terms of office, CJ §1-402.
Jurisdiction.
Allocation of jurisdiction between appellate courts. See APPEALS.
Law clerks.
Appointment, CJ §2-402.
Mandamus.
See MANDAMUS.
Opinions.
Reporting of opinions, AppRev Rule 8-605.1.
Panels.
General provisions, CJ §1-403.
Public service commission proceedings.
Judicial review of proceedings or orders, PUC §3-209.
Quorum.
Panels, CJ §1-403.
Reporting of opinions, AppRev Rule 8-605.1.
Rules of procedure.
Power of judges of court of appeals to make, MD Const Art IV §18.
Sessions.
General provisions, CJ §1-403.
Sheriffs.
Attendance or services directed, CJ §2-404.
Stenographers.
Appointment, CJ §2-402.
Veterinarians.
Suspension or revocation of license, AG §2-311.
Wetlands.
Private wetlands.
Judicial appeal from decision of secretary.
Appeal to court of special appeals, EN §16-308.
Regulation or designation of person's land as wetland.
Judicial review of administrative appeal.
Appeal to court of special appeals, EN §16-306.
Zoning.
Appeals to, 66B §4.08.

COURT REPORTERS.
Administration of courts.
See ADMINISTRATION OF COURTS.

COURTS.
Abandoned property disposition.
Intangible personal property held by court, CL §17-307.
Accountants.
Special officers of court.
Appointment, CJ §2-102.
Administration of courts, CJA Rules 16-101 to 16-824.
See ADMINISTRATION OF COURTS.

COURTS —Cont'd
Administrative head of judiciary department.
Chief judge, MD Const Art IV §18.
Administrative office, CJ §13-101.
Design of citations, CJ §13-101.
Information.
Officers of court to deliver information to director of administrative office on request, CJ §13-101.
Seventh judicial circuit, CJ §13-102.
Anne Arundel county.
See ANNE ARUNDEL COUNTY.
Answers generally.
See ANSWERS.
Appeals.
Generally.
See APPEALS.
Appeals from District Court.
See APPEALS FROM DISTRICT COURT.
Appearance generally.
See APPEARANCE.
Arbitration and award.
Uniform arbitration act.
General provisions, CJ §§3-201 to 3-234.
See ARBITRATION AND AWARD.
Attachment.
General provisions, CJ §§3-301 to 3-305.
See ATTACHMENT.
Auditors.
Special officers of court, CJ §2-102.
Bar admissions generally.
See ATTORNEYS AT LAW.
Body attachment.
See BODY ATTACHMENT.
Bonds, surety.
Officers of court, CJ §2-105.
Broadcasting trials, CJA Rule 16-109.
Certified questions of law.
Uniform certification of questions of law act.
See CERTIFIED QUESTIONS OF LAW.
Circuit courts.
See CIRCUIT COURTS.
Civil procedure generally.
See CIVIL PROCEDURE.
Commissioner.
Bonds, surety, CJ §2-105.
Commission on judicial disabilities, CJ §§13-401 to 13-403; CJA Rule 16-804; MD Const Art IV §§4A, 4B.
Appeal of decision, CJA Rule 16-809.
Confidentiality of proceedings, CJA Rule 16-810.
Proceedings before commission, CJA Rule 16-808.
Constitutional provisions.
United States.
See CONSTITUTION OF THE UNITED STATES.
Constitution of Maryland.
Courts of record, MD Const Art IV §1.
District Court, MD Const Art IV §§41A to 41-I.
See DISTRICT COURT.
Enumeration, MD Const Art IV §1.
Existing at time of adoption of constitution, MD Const Art IV §1A.
Powers.
Judicial power vested in enumerated courts, MD Const Art IV §1.
Seals, MD Const Art IV §1.
Contempt.
General provisions.
See CONTEMPT.

COURTS —Cont'd

Costs.
Employees of court, CJ §2-501.

Counsel.
Assistant counsel.
Special officers of court, CJ §2-102.

Counties.
Bridges between two counties.
Petition for, 25 §40.
Provisions for, 25 §20.

Court of appeals.
See COURT OF APPEALS.

Court of special appeals.
See COURT OF SPECIAL APPEALS.

Courts of record, MD Const Art IV §1.

Criminal rules.
See CRIMINAL RULES.

Defamation.
General provisions, CJ §§3-501 to 3-504.
See LIBEL AND SLANDER.

Definitions, CJ §1-101; Rule 1-202.
Officers of court, CJ §2-101.

Depositions.
General provisions.
See DEPOSITIONS.

Detinue generally.
See DETINUE.

Discovery generally.
See DISCOVERY.

Dismissal generally.
See DISMISSAL OF ACTIONS.

District Court.
General provisions.
See DISTRICT COURT.

Equity.
Appeals.
See EQUITY.

Examiners.
See EXAMINERS.

Executions.
General provisions, CJ §§11-501 to 11-513.
See EXECUTIONS.

Executors and administrators.
Petition by representative for permission to act,
ET §7-402.
Powers of personal representative.
Approval when, ET §7-401.

Expungement of records.
Defined, Crim Rule 4-502.
Notice to defendant of right to file for, CP §6-232.

Fees.
General provisions.
See CLERKS OF COURT.

Filing.
See FILING.

Foreign.
Uniform judicial notice foreign law act.
General provisions.
See JUDICIAL NOTICE.

Habeas corpus.
General provisions, CJ §§3-701 to 3-707.
See HABEAS CORPUS.

Handicapped persons.
Need for accommodation notification, Rule 1-332.

Health care malpractice claims.
Declaration, SpecPro Rule 15-403.

Interpleader.
See INTERPLEADER.

Interrogatories generally.
See INTERROGATORIES.

COURTS —Cont'd

Joinder.
See JOINDER.

Judgments and decrees.
General provisions, CJ §§11-701 to 11-703.
See JUDGMENTS AND DECREES.
Revisory power of courts, CJ §6-408.

Judicial notice.
Adjudicative facts, Evid Rule 5-201.
Uniform judicial notice foreign law act.
General provisions.
See JUDICIAL NOTICE.

Judiciary department.
Interpreters for circuit courts.
Appropriations, CJ §2-511.
State law library.
Part of judiciary department, CJ §13-501.

Jurisdiction.
General provisions.
See JURISDICTION.

Jury.
General provisions, CJ §§8-101 to 8-507.
See JURY.

Juvenile causes.
General provisions, CJ §§3-8A-01 to 3-8A-34.
See JUVENILE CAUSES.

Juvenile services.
Juvenile courts.
Service to, 83C §2-126.
System to provide court staff, 83C §2-128.

Letterhead stationery.
Telephone number on stationery, CJ §1-102.

Limitation of actions.
General provisions.
See LIMITATION OF ACTIONS.

Mandamus.
See MANDAMUS.

Mental hygiene law.
Cost of court ordered examinations, HG §16-302.

Mental retardation.
Costs of court ordered examinations, HG §16-406.

Militia.
Courts-martial, PS §§13-801 to 13-814.

Motions generally.
See MOTIONS.

Motor vehicles.
Conflict with courts article, TR §26-412.
Records to be kept by administration, TR §16-117.

New trial generally.
See NEW TRIAL.

Officers of court.
Bonds, surety, CJ §2-105.
Failure of clerk to give bond, CJ §2-106.
Compensation.
Fixed by general assembly, MD Const Art IV §9.
Definitions, CJ §2-101.
Failure to qualify for office, CJ §2-106.
Oaths, CJ §2-104.
Refusal or neglect to take, CJ §2-106.
Responsibility for duties, CJ §2-103.
Special officers.
Enumeration, CJ §2-102.
Oaths, CJ §2-104.
Successor officers.
Responsibility for uncompleted duties, CJ
§2-103.

Orders of court.
General provisions.
See ORDERS OF COURT.

Orphans' court.
See ORPHANS' COURT.

COURTS —Cont'd

Papers.

Filing, Rule 1-322.

Form of court papers, Rule 1-301.

Service of process, Rule 1-321.

Proof of service, Rule 1-323.

Signatures, Rule 1-311.

People's court.

Statutory references to people's court deemed to refer to District Court, MD Const Art IV §41-I.

Powers.

Judicial power vested in enumerated courts, MD Const Art IV §1.

Separation, MD Const DofR Art 8.

Private foundations.

Rights and powers of courts and attorney general not impaired, CA §5-405.

Probate court.

General provisions, ET §§2-101 to 2-109.

See ORPHANS' COURT.

Questions of law.

Uniform certification of questions of law act.

See CERTIFIED QUESTIONS OF LAW.

Receivers and assignees or trustees for creditors.

Defined, Receivers Rule 13-101.

Recording or broadcasting trial, CJA Rule 16-109.

Reporters.

Circuit courts.

See CIRCUIT COURTS.

Court of appeals.

See COURT OF APPEALS.

Rules of court.

General provisions.

See RULES OF COURT.

Salaries.

Judges.

General provisions, CJ §§1-701 to 1-708.

See JUDGES.

Officers of court.

Special officers, CJ §2-102.

Seals.

Administrative office, CJ §13-101.

Provided for, MD Const Art IV §1.

Seventh judicial circuit.

Administrative office.

Administrator.

Appointment, CJ §13-102.

Sheriffs.

General provisions.

See SHERIFFS.

Stenographers.

Fees, CJ §7-401.

Surveyors.

Special officers of court, CJ §2-102.

Tax court.

General provisions, TG §§3-101 to 3-113.

Property taxes, TP §§2-206, 14-512 to 14-514.

See TAX COURT.

Telephone number on letterhead stationery, CJ §1-102.

Time-sharing.

Managing entity.

Court appointment, RP §11A-109.

Uniform certification of questions of law act.

General provisions.

See CERTIFIED QUESTIONS OF LAW.

United States courts.

Constitutional provisions.

See UNITED STATES COURTS.

COURTS —Cont'd

Venue.

General provisions, CJ §§6-201 to 6-203.

See VENUE.

Witnesses.

General provisions.

See WITNESSES.

COURTS-MARTIAL.

Militia, PS §§13-801 to 13-814.

COVENANTS.

Deeds.

Deed poll.

Effect of acceptance of deed by grantee, RP §4-102.

Encumbrance.

Effect of covenant that grantor has not encumbered land, RP §2-110.

Effect of general covenant against encumbrances, RP §2-111.

Further assurances.

Effect of covenant, RP §2-112.

Family day care homes.

Covenants restricting, RP §2-121.

Forms.

Addition of covenant, RP §4-201.

General warranty.

Effect, RP §2-105.

Implied covenant or warranty of title or possession, RP §2-115.

Meaning of term "the said covenant," RP §2-104.

Quiet enjoyment.

Effect of covenant, RP §2-109.

Right to grant.

Effect of covenant, RP §2-108.

Seisin.

Effect of covenant, RP §2-107.

Special warranty.

Effect, RP §2-106.

Definitions.

Family day care home, RP §2-121.

Meaning of term "the said covenant," RP §2-104.

Environmental covenants.

Uniform environmental covenants act, EN §§1-801 to 1-815.

See ENVIRONMENTAL COVENANTS.

Family day care homes.

Covenants restricting, RP §2-121.

Good faith and fair dealing.

Operating agreements.

Hotels and retirement communities.

Implied covenant, CL §23-105.

Homeowners' associations.

Recorded covenants and restrictions.

Defined, RP §11B-101.

Housing and community development.

Assisted housing preservation, protected actions.

Covenants as to use of property, HS §7-208.

Implied covenants.

Of title or possession, RP §2-115.

Interpretation and construction.

Deeds.

Encumbrance.

Effect of covenant that grantor has not encumbered land, RP §2-110.

Effect of general covenant against encumbrances, RP §2-111.

Further assurance.

Effect of covenant, RP §2-112.

General warranty.

Effect, RP §2-105.

COVENANTS —Cont'd
Interpretation and construction —Cont'd
Deeds —Cont'd
Quiet enjoyment.
Effect of covenant, RP §2-109.
Seisin.
Effect of covenant, RP §2-107.
Special warranty.
Effect, RP §2-106.
Judgments and decrees.
Amount due on covenant, CJ §11-201.
Landlord and tenant.
Quiet enjoyment, RP §8-204.
Remedy upon covenants in case of merger, RP §8-102.
Renewal of lease.
Effect of covenant for perpetual renewal, RP §8-109.
Judgment for, RP §8-108.
Surrendering premises in good repair.
Effect of covenant, RP §8-113.
Leases.
Implied covenants, RP §2-115.
Renewal of leases.
Effect of covenant for perpetual renewal, RP §8-109.
Merger.
Leases.
Remedy upon covenants in case of merger, RP §8-102.
Mortgages and deeds of trust.
Incorporation by reference, RP §7-108.
Operating agreements.
Hotels and retirement communities.
Enforceable duties and obligations created by express covenant, CL §23-103.
Good faith and fair dealing.
Implied covenant, CL §23-105.
Solar collection panels.
Restrictions on installation, RP §2-119.

COVER.
Sales under UCC.
Buyer's procurement of substitute goods, CL §2-712.

COVERED LOADS LAW, TR §24-106.1.
Liability for violations, TR §24-106.3.

COVERTURE.
Husband and wife.
See HUSBAND AND WIFE.

COWS.
Livestock.
See LIVESTOCK.

COX CREEK CITIZENS OVERSIGHT COMMITTEE, EN §5-1102.1.

COYOTES.
Hunting.
Open season all year, NR §10-406.

C.P.A.
See PUBLIC ACCOUNTANTS.

CPR.
Family day care homes.
Current certification.
Regulations to provide, FL §5-551.

CRAB MEAT.
Compliance with standards, HG §21-340.
Containers.
Information required on containers, HG §21-339.

CRAB MEAT —Cont'd
Definitions.
Repacked crab meat, HG §21-339.
Frozen crab meat.
Storage above certain temperatures prohibited, HG §21-342.
Labeling, HG §21-339.
Markings on containers, HG §21-339.
Misrepresentations.
Unfit crab meat, HG §21-341.
Repacked crab meat.
Repacking crab meat prohibited, HG §21-339.
Sales.
Unfit crab meat, HG §21-341.
Seizure and condemnation of certain crab meat, HG §21-343.
Shellfish.
Generally.
See SHELLFISH.
Storage.
Above certain temperatures.
Prohibited, HG §21-342.
Temperatures.
Processed crabs to be maintained at certain temperatures, HG §21-350.
Unfit crab meat.
Sale or possession, HG §21-341.
Seizure and condemnation, HG §21-343.

CRABS.
Applicability of subtitle, NR §4-802.
Bank traps.
Harvesting crabs in St. Mary's County by, NR §4-815.
Buckram crabs.
Defined, NR §4-801.
Regulations, NR §4-809.
Channel pounds.
Harvesting crabs in St. Mary's County by, NR §4-815.
Chinese mitten crabs.
Nonnative crab restrictions, NR §4-816.
Closed seasons.
Hard crabs, NR §4-808.
Crab meat.
See CRAB MEAT.
Crab pots.
Harvesting crabs with crab pots in Somerset county, NR §4-813.
Limitation on number, NR §4-814.
Number of authorized licenses, NR §4-814.
Use in Chesapeake Bay waters in Dorchester and Somerset counties, NR §4-812.
Definitions, NR §4-801.
Dorchester county.
Use of crab pots in Chesapeake Bay waters, NR §4-812.
Fat crabs.
Regulations, NR §4-809.
Female crabs.
Regulations, NR §4-809.
Restrictions, NR §4-810.
Fines.
Collection of fines, NR §4-1202.
Violation of title, NR §4-1201.
Green crabs.
Defined, NR §4-801.
Nonnative crab restrictions, NR §4-816.
Regulations, NR §4-809.
Hard crabs.
Closed seasons, NR §4-808.

CRABS —Cont'd
Hard crabs —Cont'd
Limits on catch, NR §4-809.
Regulations, NR §4-809.
Imported crabs.
Exemptions, NR §4-809.
Japanese shore crabs.
Nonnative crab restrictions, NR §4-816.
Landing.
Crabs caught in Worcester county, NR §4-802.1.
Landowners.
Restrictions on catching.
Certain counties, NR §4-811.
Licenses.
Commercial crabbing license, NR §4-804.
Restrictions to certain days, NR §§4-701, 4-803.
Declaration of day off, NR §4-804.
Noncommercial crabbing license, NR §4-804.
Packers, NR §4-807.
Required.
Packers, NR §4-807.
Suspension or revocation.
Violation of title, NR §4-1207.
Tidal fish license, NR §4-701.
Maryland blue crab.
State crustacean, SG §13-301.
Meat.
See CRAB MEAT.
Nonnative crab restrictions, NR §4-816.
Packers.
Licenses, NR §4-807.
Peeler crabs.
Bycatch.
Limits on catch or possession, NR §4-809.
Defined, NR §4-801.
Limits on catch or possession, NR §4-809.
Rules and regulations.
Commercial licenses.
Restrictions to certain days, NR §4-804.
Female crabs, NR §4-810.
St. Mary's County harvesting with bank trap or channel pound, NR §4-815.
Sales.
Possession or marketing of shellfish caught in compliance with regulations of Potomac river fisheries commission, NR §4-102.
Scope of subtitle, NR §4-802.
Searches and seizures.
Illegally caught, sold, etc., crabs, NR §4-1205.
Unlawful devices, equipment, etc., NR §4-1206.
Warrantless search, NR §4-1204.
Warrants, NR §4-1203.
Smith Island.
Tyler creek.
Use of crab pots in Chesapeake Bay waters, NR §4-812.
Soft crabs.
Regulations, NR §4-809.
Somerset county.
Harvesting crabs with crab pots, NR §4-813.
Use of crab pots in Chesapeake Bay waters, NR §4-812.
State crustacean.
Maryland blue crab, SG §13-301.
Tyler creek on Smith Island.
Use of crab pots in Chesapeake Bay waters, NR §4-812.
Worcester county.
Catching or possessing certain kinds, NR §4-809.
Landing of crabs caught in waters of Worcester county, NR §4-802.1.

CRABS —Cont'd
Worcester county —Cont'd
Landowners.
Restrictions on catching, NR §4-811.
CRACK COCAINE.
Volume dealers, enhanced penalty, CR §5-612.
CRAMMING.
Telephone slamming, PUC §§8-401 to 8-409.
See TELEPHONE SLAMMING.
CRAPS.
Gaming.
See GAMING.
Playing game prohibited, CR §12-103.
CRASH PARTS, CL §§14-2301 to 14-2304.
CREATION OF NEW JOBS.
Job creation tax credit, 83A §§5-1101 to 5-1103.
See JOB CREATION TAX CREDIT.
CREDIT.
Accounts and accounting.
Credit grantor closed end credit provisions.
Escrow account, CL §12-1026.
Sale of repossessed property, CL §12-1021.
Credit grantor revolving credit provisions.
Plan connected with demand deposit account.
Account charges enumerated, CL §12-907.
Sale of repossessed property, CL §12-921.
Credit services businesses.
Trust accounts.
Aggregate liability.
Claims against accounts, CL §14-1910.
Amount, CL §14-1909.
Claims against, CL §14-1910.
Damages.
Claims against accounts, CL §14-1910.
Establishment, CL §14-1908.
Liability.
Claims against accounts, CL §14-1910.
Requirements, CL §14-1909.
Advertising.
Credit service businesses, CL §14-1903.1.
Assignments.
Credit grantor closed end credit provisions.
Consumer borrowers, CL §12-1023.
Credit grantor revolving credit provisions.
Consumer borrowers, CL §12-923.
Attorneys at law.
Credit grantor closed end credit provisions.
Attorneys' fees, CL §12-1011.
Credit grantor revolving credit provisions.
Attorneys' fees, CL §12-911.
Auctions.
Credit grantor closed end credit provisions.
Repossessed property, CL §12-1021.
Credit grantor revolving credit provisions.
Repossessed property, CL §12-921.
Balloon payments.
Credit grantor closed end credit provisions.
Balloon payments prohibited, CL §12-1003.
Credit grantor revolving credit provisions.
Balloon payments prohibited, CL §12-903.
Extension of time for payment, CL §12-1003.
Bills of credit.
Constitutional provisions, US Const Art I §10.
Bonds, surety.
Credit services businesses.
Actions.
Claims against surety bonds, CL §14-1910.

CREDIT —Cont'd
Bonds, surety —Cont'd
  Credit services businesses —Cont'd
    Aggregate liability.
      Claims against bonds, CL §14-1910.
    Amount, CL §14-1909.
    Damages.
      Claims against bonds, CL §14-1910.
    Establishment, CL §14-1908.
    Issuance, CL §14-1909.
    Liability.
      Claims against bonds, CL §14-1910.
Business opportunities.
  General provisions, BR §§14-101 to 14-129.
  See START-UP BUSINESS VENTURES.
Closed end credit provisions, CL §§12-1001 to
  12-1029. See within this heading, "Credit
  grantor closed end credit provisions."
Consumer credit reporting agencies, CL
  §§14-1201 to 14-1218.
  See CONSUMER CREDIT REPORTING
    AGENCIES.
Consumer loans.
  General provisions.
    See CONSUMER LOANS.
Consumer protection.
  Denial of credit, CL §§14-1701 to 14-1706.
    See CONSUMER PROTECTION.
  General provisions.
    See CONSUMER PROTECTION.
Costs.
  Credit grantor closed end credit provisions.
    Court and other collection costs, CL §12-1011.
  Credit grantor revolving credit provisions.
    Court or other collection costs, CL §12-911.
Counties.
  Chartered counties.
    Protection of county credit, 25A §5.
Credit assurance division.
  Housing and community development department,
    HS §§3-101 to 3-208.
  Governmental units of department, HS §2-201.
Credit cards.
  General provisions.
    See CREDIT CARDS.
Credit grantor closed end credit provisions.
  Accounts and accounting.
    Escrow account, CL §12-1026.
    Sale of repossessed property, CL §12-1021.
  Applicability of other laws, CL §12-1013.
  Attorneys at law.
    Attorneys' fees, CL §§12-1011, 12-1028.
  Attorneys' fees, CL §12-1028.
  Authorized extensions of credit, CL §12-1002.
  Balloon payments.
    Defined, CL §12-1001.
    Restrictions, CL §12-1003.
  Borrowers.
    Defined, CL §12-1001.
  Cease and desist orders.
    Issuance by commissioner, CL §12-1016.
  Charges.
    Additional charges, CL §12-1005.
    Attorneys' fees, CL §12-1011.
    Authorized, CL §12-1002.
    Defaults or delinquencies, CL §12-1008.
    Deferral charges, CL §12-1006.
    Finance charges.
      Applicability of other laws, CL §12-1013.
    Insurance premiums, CL §12-1006.
    Permitted charges, CL §12-1012.

CREDIT —Cont'd
Credit grantor closed end credit provisions
  —Cont'd
  Charges —Cont'd
    Points.
      When permitted, CL §12-1005.
    Prepayment charges.
      When prohibited, CL §12-1009.
    Service charges.
      Applicability of other laws, CL §12-1013.
  Civil penalties, CL §12-1018.
  Closed end credit.
    Defined, CL §12-1001.
  Commissioner of financial regulation.
    Complaints.
      Scope of jurisdiction, CL §12-1016.
    Licenses.
      Issuance, CL §12-1015.
  Complaints.
    Cease and desist orders, CL §12-1016.
    Investigations, CL §12-1016.
    Notice to credit grantor against whom
      complaint filed, CL §12-1016.
  Consumer borrowers.
    "Borrow" defined, CL §12-1022.
    Defined, CL §12-1001.
    Insurance, CL §12-1007.
    Obligations of credit grantor, CL §12-1024.
    Prepayment, CL §12-1009.
    Written receipt requirement, CL §12-1023.
  Contracts.
    Mechanical repair contracts.
      Defined, CL §12-1001.
  Costs.
    Court and other collection costs, CL §12-1011.
    Permitted transactions and charges, CL
      §12-1012.
  Credit grantor.
    Defined, CL §12-1001.
    Failure to comply with provisions of subtitle.
      Limitations on credit grantor's liability, CL
      §12-1020.
    Financing statements, CL §12-1013.
    Mechanical repair contracts.
      Costs included in loan amount, CL §12-1012.
    Option to make loan, CL §12-1013.1.
      Delivery of evidence of loan, CL §12-1013.2.
  Criminal penalties, CL §12-1017.
  Damages.
    Treble damages, CL §12-1018.
  Debt cancellation agreement.
    Defined, CL §12-1001.
  Defaults.
    Charges, CL §12-1008.
  Definitions, CL §12-1001.
    Prepayment of charges, CL §12-1009.
  Delinquencies.
    Charges, CL §12-1008.
  Disclosure.
    Applicability of certain disclosure requirements,
      CL §12-1014.
  Discounts.
    Applicability of other laws, CL §12-1013.
  Escrow account.
    Defined, CL §12-1026.
    Interest, CL §12-1026.
    Severability of funds, CL §12-1026.
  Extensions of credit.
    Authorized, CL §12-1002.
  Federal truth in lending act.
    Applicability of disclosure requirements, CL
      §12-1014.

CREDIT —Cont'd
Credit grantor closed end credit provisions
—Cont'd
Fees, CL §12-1028.
Additional fees and charges, CL §12-1005.
Applicability of other laws, CL §12-1013.
Attorneys' fees, CL §12-1011.
Finance charges.
Charges for default or delinquency.
Charges not considered finance charges, CL §12-1008.
Financial institutions article.
Applicability of provisions, CL §12-1015.
Financing agreement evidencing secured loan.
Agreement or other evidence of loan, CL §12-1023.
"Financing agreement" defined, CL §12-1022.
Frequency of interest and charges, CL §12-1025.
Obtaining loan to acquire interest in commercial enterprise, CL §12-1023.1.
Prohibitions, CL §12-1023.
Requirements, CL §12-1022.
Requirements upon loan repayment, CL §12-1024.
Written statement of interest and charges, CL §12-1025.
Financing statements, CL §12-1013.
Consumer borrowers, CL §§12-1022 to 12-1025.
Fines.
Applicability of other laws, CL §12-1013.
Installment loans.
Balloon payments.
Restrictions on balloon payments, CL §12-1003.
Defined, CL §12-1001.
Insurance.
Binders, CL §12-1007.1.
Consumer borrowers, CL §12-1007.
Premiums, CL §12-1006.
Not considered interest, CL §12-1007.
Property insurance in excess of replacement value, CL §12-1007.
Refund of unearned insurance premiums paid by borrower, CL §12-1009.
When insurance required, CL §12-1007.
Interest.
Authorized, CL §§12-1002, 12-1003.
Calculation of interest, CL §12-1003.
Charges for default or delinquency.
Charges not considered interest, CL §12-1008.
Consumer borrowers.
Written statement requirement, CL §12-1025.
Insurance article applicable, CL §12-1007.
Insurance premiums.
Not considered interest, CL §12-1007.
Rate of interest.
Applicability of other laws, CL §12-1013.
Refund of unearned portion of precomputed interest charged, CL §12-1009.
Variation in periodic percentage rate, CL §12-1004.
Investigations.
Complaints, CL §12-1016.
Lender's inspection fee, CL §12-1027.
Liability.
Limitation on credit grantor's liability, CL §12-1020.
Licenses.
Issuance by commissioner of financial regulation, CL §12-1015.
Limitation of actions, CL §12-1019.

CREDIT —Cont'd
Credit grantor closed end credit provisions
—Cont'd
Loans.
Balloon payment.
Defined, CL §12-1001.
Restrictions, CL §12-1003.
Defaults or delinquencies.
Charges, CL §12-1008.
Deferral of scheduled payments, CL §12-1006.
Defined, CL §12-1001.
Entire outstanding unpaid amount of loan.
Calculated, CL §12-1010.
Extending or deferring portions of payment under loan, CL §12-1012.
Installment loan.
Defined, CL §12-1001.
Option to make loan, CL §12-1013.1.
Permitting prepayment or refinancing of loans, CL §12-1012.
Refinancing, CL §12-1010.
Mechanical repair contracts.
Defined, CL §12-1001.
Disclosures required to include in loan amount, CL §12-1012.
Motor vehicles.
Original manufacturer's warranty.
Conditions under which sold, CL §12-1012.
Misdemeanors.
Criminal penalties, CL §12-1017.
Notice.
Complaints.
Notice to credit grantor against whom complaint filed, CL §12-1016.
Repossession, CL §12-1021.
Option to make loan, CL §12-1013.1.
Delivery of evidence of loan, CL §12-1013.2.
Payment.
Deferral of scheduled payment, CL §12-1006.
Extending or deferring payments, CL §12-1012.
Prepayment, CL §12-1009.
Penalties.
Civil penalties, CL §12-1018.
Criminal penalties, CL §12-1017.
Periodic percentage rate.
Authorized, CL §12-1004.
Limitations, CL §12-1004.
Permitted transactions and charges, CL §12-1012.
Points.
Applicability of other laws, CL §12-1013.
When permitted, CL §12-1005.
Prepayment charges, CL §12-1009.
When prohibited, CL §12-1009.
Refinancing, CL §12-1010.
Remaining loan balance.
Defined, CL §12-1001.
Repossession.
Accounts and accounting.
Sale of repossessed property, CL §12-1021.
Auctions.
Public auction of repossessed property, CL §12-1021.
Authorized, CL §12-1021.
Notice.
Right to redeem, CL §12-1021.
Sales, CL §12-1021.
Redemption of repossessed property, CL §12-1021.
Retention of property by credit grantor, CL §12-1021.

CREDIT —Cont'd
Credit grantor closed end credit provisions
—Cont'd
Repossession —Cont'd
Sales.
Authorized, CL §12-1021.
Disposition of proceeds, CL §12-1021.
Notice of sale, CL §12-1021.
Service of notice, CL §12-1021.
Violation of criminal law not authorized, CL
§12-1021.
Right to require consumer to tender payment of
entire balance due, CL §12-1021.
Security.
Credit grantor may take security as collateral,
CL §12-1002.
Severability of provisions, CL §12-1014.
Violations.
Civil penalties, CL §12-1018.
Criminal penalties, CL §12-1017.
Limitation of actions for violations, CL
§12-1019.
Credit grantor revolving credit provisions.
Accounts and accounting.
Sale of repossessed property, CL §12-921.
Acquisition of certain obligations by credit
grantor.
Authorized extensions of credit, CL §12-902.
Agreement.
Amendment of plan agreement, CL §12-912.
Applicability of other laws, CL §12-913.
Attorneys' fees, CL §12-911.
Balloon payments.
Prohibited, CL §12-903.
Billing.
Determination of billing payment, CL §12-903.
Borrowers.
Defined, CL §12-901.
Cease and desist orders, CL §12-916.
Finality, CL §12-916.
Charges.
Account charges.
Enumeration, CL §12-907.
Additional charges, CL §12-905.
Applicability of other laws limiting charges, CL
§12-913.
Customary charges, CL §12-907.
Defaults, CL §12-910.
Deferral of scheduled payments, CL §12-908.
Inclusion of charges in outstanding unpaid
indebtedness, CL §12-907.
Insurance premiums not considered interest or
finance charges, CL §12-909.
Commissioner of financial regulation.
Licenses.
Issuance, CL §12-915.
Scope of jurisdiction, CL §12-916.
Complaining party.
Defined, CL §12-916.
Complaints.
Cease and desist orders, CL §12-916.
Commissioner of financial regulation.
Scope of jurisdiction, CL §12-916.
Investigation of written complaint, CL §12-916.
Notice, CL §12-916.
Procedure, CL §12-916.
Consumer borrowers.
"Borrower" defined, CL §12-922.
Defined, CL §12-901.
Financing agreements.
Agreements governing revolving credit plans,
CL §12-923.

CREDIT —Cont'd
Credit grantor revolving credit provisions
—Cont'd
Consumer borrowers —Cont'd
Financing agreements —Cont'd
Assignment of account, CL §12-923.
Defined, CL §12-922.
Prohibited provisions, CL §12-923.
Reliance on statement, CL §12-923.1.
Requirements, CL §12-922.
Use to acquire interest in commercial
enterprise, CL §12-923.1.
Financing statements.
False or misleading statement, CL §12-923.1.
Plan established, CL §12-905.
Release of lien securing extension of credit, CL
§12-924.
Written receipt requirement, CL §12-923.
Costs.
Court or other collection costs, CL §12-911.
Credit devices.
Defined, CL §12-901.
Credit grantors.
Acquisition of certain obligations by credit
grantor, CL §12-902.
Amendment of plan agreement.
Notice, CL §12-912.
Civil penalties.
Collection permitted, CL §12-918.
Defined, CL §12-901.
Financing statement, CL §12-913.
Liability.
Limitation on liability, CL §12-920.
Notice.
Amendment of plan agreement, CL §12-912.
Notice to credit grantor against whom
complaint filed, CL §12-916.
Credit plan.
Secured open-end credit plan, CL §12-905.
Unsecured open-end credit plan, CL §12-905.
Criminal penalties, CL §12-917.
Damages.
Treble damages, CL §12-918.
Defaults.
Charges, CL §12-910.
Deferral of scheduled payments, CL §12-908.
Charges, CL §12-908.
Definitions, CL §12-901.
Delinquencies.
Charges, CL §12-910.
Demand deposit account.
Plan connected with, CL §12-907.
Disclosure requirements, CL §12-914.
Discounts.
Applicability of other laws limiting discounts,
CL §12-913.
Fees.
Additional fees, CL §12-905.
Finance charges, CL §12-903.
Certain additional charges not considered
finance charges, CL §12-905.
Charges for default or delinquency.
Charges not considered finance charges, CL
§12-910.
Limitations on imposition, CL §12-903.
Financial institutions article.
Applicability of provisions, CL §12-915.
Financing statements.
Consumer borrowers, CL §§12-922 to 12-924.
Credit grantors, CL §12-913.

CREDIT —Cont'd
Credit grantor revolving credit provisions
  —Cont'd
Insurance.
  Binders, CL §12-909.1.
  Insurance article applicable, CL §12-909.
  Premiums not considered interest or finance
    charges, CL §12-909.
  Purchase of insurance optional, CL §12-909.
Interest.
  Applicability of other laws limiting rate or
    amount of interest, CL §12-913.
  Calculation, CL §12-903.
  Certain additional charges not considered
    interest, CL §12-905.
  Charges, CL §12-903.
  Charges for default or delinquency.
    Charges not considered interest or finance
      charges, CL §12-910.
  Insurance premiums not considered interest, CL
    §12-909.
  Limitations on imposition, CL §12-903.
  Variation in periodic percentage rate, CL
    §12-904.
Liability.
  Limitation on credit grantor's liability, CL
    §12-920.
Licenses.
  Issuance by commissioner of financial
    regulation, CL §12-915.
  Unlicensed home improvement contractors, CL
    §12-915.
Liens.
  Limitations on plan secured by lien on
    residential real property, CL §12-902.
Limitation of actions, CL §12-919.
Loans.
  Defined, CL §12-901.
  Plan authorizing both loans and purchases, CL
    §12-906.
Misdemeanors.
  Criminal penalties, CL §12-917.
Nonconsumer borrower.
  Defined, CL §12-901.
Notice.
  Amendment of plan agreement, CL §12-912.
    Credit grantors, CL §12-912.
    Effective date of amendment, CL §12-912.
  Complaints, CL §12-916.
  Credit grantors.
    Amendment of plan agreement, CL §12-912.
  Repossession, CL §12-921.
  Sale of repossessed goods, CL §12-921.
Option to offer plan, CL §12-914.
Outstanding unpaid indebtedness.
  Amendment of plan agreement, CL §12-912.
    Effective date of amendment, CL §12-912.
  Defined, CL §12-901.
Payments.
  Decrease in required amount of scheduled
    payments, CL §12-912.
Penalties.
  Civil penalties, CL §12-917.
  Criminal penalties, CL §12-917.
  Treble damages, CL §12-918.
Periodic percentage rate.
  Limitation, CL §12-904.
  Variations, CL §12-904.
Plan.
  Amendment of plan agreement, CL §12-912.
    Effective date of amendment, CL §12-912.

CREDIT —Cont'd
Credit grantor revolving credit provisions
  —Cont'd
Plan —Cont'd
  Applicability of other subtitles, CL §12-913.1.
  Decrease in required amount of scheduled
    payments.
    Amendment of plan agreement, CL §12-912.
      Effective date of amendment, CL §12-912.
  Delivery of plan agreement, CL §12-913.2.
  Demand deposit account, CL §12-907.
  Election of applicable laws, CL §12-913.1.
  Establishment of plan for consumer borrower,
    CL §12-905.
  Limitations on plan secured by lien on
    residential real property, CL §12-902.
  Loans and purchases authorized, CL §12-906.
  Multiple borrowers, CL §12-913.2.
  Option to offer plan, CL §12-914.
  Proof of delivery, CL §12-913.2.
  Time requirements, CL §12-913.2.
  Written election, CL §12-913.1.
Points.
  Applicability of other laws limiting points, CL
    §12-913.
Purchases.
  Defined, CL §12-901.
Repossession.
  Accounts and accounting.
    Sale of repossessed property, CL §12-921.
  Auctions.
    Public auction of property repossessed, CL
      §12-921.
  Authorized, CL §12-921.
  Disposition of proceeds, CL §12-921.
  Notice.
    Intent to repossess, CL §12-921.
    Sale of repossessed goods, CL §12-921.
  Private or public sale of repossessed property,
    CL §12-921.
  Redemption of repossessed property, CL
    §12-921.
  Retention of property by credit grantor, CL
    §12-921.
  Sale of property repossessed, CL §12-921.
  Service of notice, CL §12-921.
  Violation of criminal law not authorized, CL
    §12-921.
Residential real property.
  Limitations on plans secured by lien on
    residential real property, CL §12-902.
Revolving credit plan.
  Defined, CL §12-901.
Secured open-end credit plan, CL §12-905.
Service of process.
  Notice to repossess, CL §12-921.
Severability of provisions, CL §12-914.
Unauthorized extensions of credit, CL §12-902.
Unsecured open-end credit plan, CL §12-905.
Violations.
  Civil penalties, CL §12-918.
  Criminal penalties, CL §12-917.
  Limitation of actions, CL §12-919.
  Treble damages, CL §12-918.
Credit services businesses.
Accounts and accounting.
  Trust accounts.
    Aggregate liability.
      Claims against accounts, CL §14-1910.
    Amount, CL §14-1909.
    Claims against, CL §14-1910.

CREDIT —Cont'd
Credit services businesses —Cont'd
Accounts and accounting —Cont'd
Trust accounts —Cont'd
Damages.
Claims against accounts, CL §14-1910.
Establishment, CL §14-1908.
Liability.
Claims against accounts, CL §14-1910.
Requirements, CL §14-1909.
Actions.
Consumer protection act, CL §14-1914.
Administrative procedure.
Applicability of administrative procedure act,
CL §14-1911.
Advertising, CL §14-1903.1.
Applicability of subtitle, CL §14-1903.
Bonds, surety.
Actions.
Claims against surety bonds, CL §14-1910.
Aggregate liability.
Claims against bonds, CL §14-1910.
Amount, CL §14-1909.
Damages.
Claims against bonds, CL §14-1910.
Establishment, CL §14-1908.
Issuance, CL §14-1909.
Liability.
Claims against bonds, CL §14-1910.
Books.
Inspection, CL §14-1911.
Burden of proof.
Proceedings involving subtitle, CL §14-1907.
Citation of subtitle.
Short title, CL §14-1916.
Commissioner, CL §14-1901.
Defined, CL §14-1901.
Inspection of books and records, CL §14-1911.
Orders.
Failure to comply, CL §14-1911.
Finality, CL §14-1911.
Powers, CL §14-1911.
Complaints.
Filing, CL §14-1911.
Notice, CL §14-1911.
Compliance with requirements.
Noncompliance, CL §14-1912.
Consumer.
Defined, CL §14-1901.
Consumer protection division.
Power to bring proceedings, CL §14-1914.
Consumer report.
Defined, CL §14-1901.
Consumer reporting agency.
Defined, CL §14-1901.
Contempt.
Failure to comply with court order, CL
§14-1911.
Contracts with consumers.
Breach of contract, CL §14-1907.
Cancellation notice.
Form, CL §14-1906.
Requirements, CL §14-1906.
Void contracts, CL §14-1907.
Definitions, CL §14-1901.
Duties, CL §14-1902.
Information statement.
Duty to provide, CL §14-1904.
Extension of credit, CL §14-1901.
Defined, CL §14-1901.

CREDIT —Cont'd
Credit services businesses —Cont'd
File.
Defined, CL §14-1901.
Fines, CL §14-1915.
Forms.
Cancellation of contract with consumer.
Notice, CL §14-1906.
Hearings.
Investigation of businesses, CL §14-1911.
Notice, CL §14-1911.
Information statement.
Additional requirements of licensees, CL
§14-1905.
Contents, CL §14-1905.
Duty to provide, CL §14-1904.
Enumeration of contents, CL §14-1905.
Filing, CL §14-1904.
Inspection.
Books and records, CL §14-1911.
Investigations.
Power of commissioner to investigate
businesses, CL §14-1911.
Investigative consumer report, CL §14-1901.
Licenses.
Exemptions, CL §14-1903.
Information statement.
Additional requirements of licensees, CL
§14-1905.
Issuance, CL §14-1903.
Required, CL §14-1903.
Limitation of actions, CL §14-1913.
Misdemeanors, CL §14-1915.
Misrepresentation.
Material and willful misrepresentation.
Limitation of actions.
Enforcement of liability, CL §14-1913.
Negligent noncompliance with requirements, CL
§14-1912.
Notice.
Cancellation of contract with consumer, CL
§14-1906.
Complaints, CL §14-1911.
Hearings, CL §14-1911.
Orders of commissioner.
Failure to comply, CL §14-1911.
Finality, CL §14-1911.
Orders of court.
Failure to comply, CL §14-1911.
Penalties, CL §14-1915.
Person.
Defined, CL §14-1901.
Prohibitions, CL §14-1902.
Records.
Inspection, CL §14-1911.
Requirements.
Failure to comply, CL §14-1912.
Sentence and punishment, CL §14-1915.
Title of subtitle.
Short title, CL §14-1916.
Trusts and trustees.
Amount, CL §14-1909.
Requirements, CL §14-1909.
Trust accounts.
Aggregate liability, CL §14-1910.
Claims against, CL §14-1910.
Damages.
Claims against accounts, CL §14-1910.
Establishment, CL §14-1908.
Liability.
Claims against accounts, CL §14-1910.

CREDIT —Cont'd
Credit services businesses —Cont'd
Unfair or deceptive trade practices.
Violations of provisions of subtitle, CL §14-1914.
Waiver.
Provisions of subtitle, CL §14-1907.
Willful noncompliance with requirements, CL §14-1912.
Damages.
Credit grantor closed end credit provisions.
Consumer borrowers, CL §12-1022.
Treble damages, CL §12-1018.
Credit grantor revolving credit provisions.
Consumer borrowers, CL §12-922.
Treble damages for violations, CL §12-918.
Debt management services, FI §§12-901 to 12-931.
See DEBT MANAGEMENT SERVICES.
Definitions.
Credit grantor closed end credit provisions, CL §12-1001.
Consumer borrowers, CL §12-1022.
Credit grantor revolving credit provisions, CL §12-901.
Consumer borrowers, CL §12-922.
Credit services businesses, CL §14-1901.
Denial of credit.
Consumer protection, CL §§14-1701 to 14-1706.
See CONSUMER PROTECTION.
Discounts.
Credit grantor closed end credit provisions.
Applicability of other laws, CL §12-1013.
Credit grantor revolving credit provisions.
Applicability of other laws limiting discounts, CL §12-913.
Equal credit opportunity act, CL §§12-701 to 12-708.
See EQUAL CREDIT OPPORTUNITY.
Extension of credit.
State regulation, FI §1-209.
Unfair or deceptive trade practices, CL §§13-301, 13-303.
Federal truth in lending act.
Credit grantor closed end credit provisions.
Applicability of disclosure requirements, CL §12-1014.
Finance charges.
Credit grantor revolving credit provisions. See within this heading, "Credit grantor revolving credit provisions."
Financial institutions.
Credit grantor closed end credit provisions.
Applicability of certain provisions of financial institutions article, CL §12-1015.
General provisions, CL §§12-1001 to 12-1029. See within this heading, "Credit grantor closed end credit provisions."
Credit grantor revolving credit provisions.
Applicability of financial institutions article, CL §12-915.
General provisions, CL §§12-901 to 12-924. See within this heading, "Credit grantor revolving credit provisions."
Fraud.
Credit grantor closed end credit provisions.
False or misleading financing statements, CL §12-1023.1.
Credit grantor revolving credit provisions.
False or misleading financing statement, CL §12-923.1.

CREDIT —Cont'd
General assembly.
Restrictions on extension of state credit, MD Const Art III §34.
Housing and community development department.
Credit assurance division, HS §§3-101 to 3-208.
Governmental units of department, HS §2-201.
Insurance.
Credit grantor closed end credit provisions.
Binders, CL §12-1007.1.
Insurance article applicable, CL §12-1007.
Premiums not considered interest, CL §12-1007.
Property insurance in excess of replacement value, CL §12-1007.
Refund of unearned insurance premiums paid by borrower, CL §12-1009.
When insurance required, CL §12-1007.
Credit grantor revolving credit provisions.
Binders, CL §12-909.1.
Insurance article applicable, CL §12-909.
Plan for consumer borrower, CL §12-909.
Premiums not considered interest or finance charges, CL §12-909.
Provisions concerning other than consumer borrower not altered, CL §12-909.
Interest.
Credit grantor closed end credit provisions. See within this heading, "Credit grantor closed end credit provisions."
Credit grantor revolving credit provisions. See within this heading, "Credit grantor revolving credit provisions."
Investigations.
Credit grantor closed end credit provisions.
Investigation of written complaint, CL §12-1016.
Credit grantor revolving credit provisions.
Investigation of written complaint, CL §12-916.
Credit services businesses.
Power of commissioner to investigate businesses, CL §14-1911.
Letters of credit.
Commercial code, CL §§5-101 to 5-118.
See COMMERCIAL CODE.
Liability.
Credit grantor closed end credit provisions.
False or misleading financing statements, CL §12-1023.1.
Limitations on credit grantor's liability, CL §12-1020.
Credit grantor revolving credit provisions.
False or misleading financing statement, CL §12-923.1.
Limitation on credit grantor's liability, CL §12-920.
Licenses.
Credit grantor closed end credit provisions.
Issuance by commissioner of financial regulation, CL §12-1015.
Unlicensed home improvement contractors, CL §12-915.
Credit grantor revolving credit provisions.
Issuance by commissioner of financial regulation, CL §12-915.
Unlicensed home improvement contractors, CL §12-915.
Credit services businesses, CL §14-1903.
Information statement.
Additional requirements of licensees, CL §14-1905.

CREDIT —Cont'd
Liens.
Credit grantor revolving credit provisions.
Consumer borrowers, CL §12-924.
Limitations on plans secured by lien on
residential real property, CL §12-902.
Limitation of actions.
Credit grantor closed end credit provisions.
Actions for violations of subtitle, CL §12-1019.
Credit grantor revolving credit provisions.
Actions for violations of subtitle, CL §12-919.
Credit services businesses, CL §14-1913.
Misdemeanors.
Credit grantor closed end credit provisions.
Criminal penalties for violations, CL §12-1017.
Credit grantor revolving credit provisions.
Criminal penalties for violations, CL §12-917.
Credit services businesses, CL §14-1915.
Mortgages and deeds of trust.
Mortgage lender law, FI §§11-501 to 11-524.
See MORTGAGE LENDERS.
Mortgage originators, FI §§11-601 to 11-618.
See MORTGAGE ORIGINATORS.
Motor vehicle insurance.
Cancellations, nonrenewals or premium increases,
IN §27-613.
Notice.
Credit grantor closed end credit provisions.
Complaints.
Notice to credit grantor against whom
complaint filed, CL §12-1016.
Consumer borrowers.
Notice of assignment, CL §12-1023.
Repossession, CL §12-1021.
Credit grantor revolving credit provisions.
Amendment of plan agreement, CL §12-912.
Effective date of amendment, CL §12-912.
Complaints, CL §12-916.
Repossession, CL §12-921.
Sale of repossessed property, CL §12-921.
Credit services businesses.
Cancellation of contract with consumer, CL
§14-1906.
Complaints, CL §14-1911.
Hearings, CL §14-1911.
Penalties.
Credit grantor closed end credit provisions.
Civil penalties, CL §12-1018.
Criminal penalties, CL §12-1017.
Credit grantor revolving credit provisions.
Collection of civil penalties, CL §12-918.
Criminal penalties for violations, CL §12-917.
Credit services businesses, CL §14-1915.
Points.
Credit grantor closed end credit provisions.
Applicability of other laws, CL §12-1013.
When permitted, CL §12-1005.
Credit grantor revolving credit provisions.
Applicability of other laws limiting points, CL
§12-913.
Property taxes.
See PROPERTY TAXES.
Real property.
Credit grantor revolving credit provisions.
Liens on residential real property.
Limitations on plans secured by lien, CL
§12-902.
Receivers.
Receivers and assignees or trustees for creditors,
Receivers Rules 13-101 to 13-703.
See RECEIVERS.

CREDIT —Cont'd
Recordation.
Credit grantor revolving credit provisions.
Consumer borrowers.
Release of lien securing extension of credit,
CL §12-924.
Releases.
Credit grantor revolving credit provisions.
Consumer borrowers, CL §12-924.
Rental-purchase agreements, CL §§12-1101 to
12-1112.
See RENTAL-PURCHASE AGREEMENTS.
Repossession.
Credit grantor closed end credit provisions, CL
§12-1021.
Credit grantor revolving credit provisions, CL
§12-921.
Retail credit accounts law.
General provisions, CL §§12-501 to 12-515.
See RETAIL CREDIT ACCOUNTS LAW.
Revolving credit.
Credit grantor revolving credit provisions, CL
§§12-901 to 12-924. See within this heading,
"Credit grantor revolving credit provisions."
Service of process.
Credit grantor closed end credit provisions.
Repossession.
Service of notice, CL §12-1021.
Credit grantor revolving credit provisions.
Notice to repossess, CL §12-921.
State regulation of extensions of credit, FI
§1-209.
Taxation.
See TAXATION.
Telegraph and telephone companies.
Telephone solicitations.
Credit services.
Application of subtitle to solicitations offering,
CL §14-2202.
Violations involving solicitation offering.
Violation of Maryland credit services
business act, CL §14-2205.
Trusts and trustees.
Credit services businesses.
Amount, CL §14-1909.
Requirements, CL §14-1909.
Trust accounts.
Aggregate liability, CL §14-1910.
Claims against, CL §14-1910.
Damages.
Claims against accounts, CL §14-1910.
Establishment, CL §14-1908.
Liability.
Claims against accounts, CL §14-1910.
Receivers and assignees or trustees for creditors,
Receivers Rules 13-101 to 13-703.
See RECEIVERS.
Unfair or deceptive trade practices.
Extension of consumer credit, CL §§13-301,
13-303.

CREDIT ASSURANCE DIVISION, HS §§3-101 to
3-208.
Administration authority, HS §3-104.
Division defined, HS §3-101.
Elements, HS §3-103.
Established, HS §3-102.
**Housing and community development
department.**
Governmental units of department, HS §2-201.

CREDIT ASSURANCE DIVISION —Cont'd
Maryland housing fund, HS §§3-201 to 3-208.
  Administration of fund, HS §3-203.
  Composition, HS §3-203.
  Construction and interpretation, HS §3-208.
  Defined terms, HS §3-201.
  Established, HS §3-203.
  Findings, HS §3-202.
  Insurance, guarantees or other credit
    enhancements.
    Effect, HS §3-204.
    Eligibility, HS §3-206.
  Powers of department, HS §3-205.
  Purpose, HS §3-203.
  Regulations.
    Authority to adopt, HS §3-207.
    Reports, HS §3-207.
Reports.
  Maryland housing fund, HS §3-207.

CREDIT CARDS, CR §§8-201 to 8-217.
Address.
  Use of consumer identification information, CL
    §13-317.
**Affidavits of cardholders, use in criminal cases
  or juvenile proceedings,** CR §8-214.1.
Aggregation of value.
  Determining penalty, CR §8-202.
Buying or selling, CR §8-204.
Campaign finance.
  Contributions by, restrictions, EL §13-226.
Charities.
  Acceptance for payment of contributions, BR
    §6-414.
Checks.
  Use of credit card information.
    Payments by check, CL §13-318.
**Construed not to preclude other provision of
  criminal law,** CR §8-202.
Consumer identification information.
  Use in connection with credit card payments, CL
    §13-317.
Consumer protection.
  Assumption of risk of loss, theft or unauthorized
    use, CL §14-1305.
  Service of subpoena on issuer.
    Certification of compliance with FI §1-304, CL
      §13-312.
Counterfeiting, CR §8-205.
  Honoring counterfeited card, CR §8-207.
  Machinery, plates or contrivance designed to
    reproduce.
    Possessing, CR §8-208.
  Receiving property by counterfeit card, CR §8-209.
  Use of counterfeited card, CR §8-206.
County taxes, fees or other charges.
  Payment by credit card, 24 §9-1401.
Credit reporting disclosures.
  Requirements, CR §8-214.
Defenses.
  Prohibited defenses to credit card crimes, CR
    §8-211.
Definitions, CR §8-201.
**Disclosure of card numbers or access device
  numbers.**
  Marketing purposes.
    Disclosure against holder's direction, CR §8-214.
    Nondisclosure option, notification requirement,
      CR §8-214.
  Prohibition, CR §8-214.

CREDIT CARDS —Cont'd
Electronic printed receipts.
  Restrictions on printing numbers, CL §14-1318.
False representation.
  False statement as to identity in order to procure,
    CR §8-203.
  Issue, CR §8-207.
  Obtaining property by credit card, CR §8-206.
Fraud.
  Falsely making or embossing, CR §8-205.
  False representation by issuer, CR §8-207.
  Honoring counterfeited or stolen card, CR §8-207.
  Obtaining property with procured by
    misrepresentation, CR §8-206.
  Procuring issuance, CR §8-203.
  Receiving property by stolen, counterfeit or
    misrepresented card, CR §8-209.
Hospitals.
  Acceptance as payment for bills, 25 §253.
Identity fraud, CR §§8-301 to 8-305.
  False statement to procure, CR §8-203.
Incomplete card.
  Possessing with intent to complete without
    consent, CR §8-208.
John F. Kennedy memorial highway.
  Service facilities on highway.
    Acceptance of credit cards, TR §4-404.
Lesser included offenses.
  Credit card crimes not to be considered lesser
    included crimes unless charged, CR §8-211.
Lost or misdelivered card.
  Receiving, CR §8-204.
**Machinery, plates or contrivance designed to
  reproduce.**
  Possessing, CR §8-208.
Marketing purposes.
  Nondisclosure option, notification required, CR
    §8-214.
  Using number against holder's direction, CR
    §8-214.
**Municipal corporation taxes, fees or other
  charges.**
  Payment by credit card, 24 §9-1401.
No call provision.
  Nondisclosure of card numbers for marketing
    purposes.
    Notification of option required, CR §8-214.
**Numbers, payment device numbers or
  signature,** CR §§8-213 to 8-217.
  Civil penalty, injunction, CR §8-217.
  Credit reporting disclosure, requirements, CR
    §8-214.
  Criminal penalty, CR §8-216.
  Definitions, CR §8-213.
  Marketing against holder's direction, CR §8-214.
  Nondisclosure option, notification required, CR
    §8-214.
  Telephone credit cards.
    Publishing number or code, CR §8-210.
  Unauthorized use or disclosure, CR §8-214.
**Obtaining property by counterfeiting, theft or
  misrepresentation,** CR §8-206.
One violation.
  Course of conduct considered, CR §8-202.
Receiving lost or misdelivered card, CR §8-204.
**Receiving property by stolen, counterfeit or
  misrepresented card,** CR §8-209.
Receiving stolen card, CR §8-204.
Restrictions on printing numbers.
  Electronic printed receipts, CL §14-1318.

CREDIT CARDS —Cont'd

Retail credit accounts law.
Discount to consumer paying cash in lieu of using credit card, CL §12-509.

Signature by other than cardholder, CR §8-205.

Subpoenas.
Service on issuer.
Notice to credit cardholder, CL §13-312.

Telephone credit cards.
Number or code.
Publishing, CR §8-210.

Telephone numbers.
Use of consumer identification information, CL §13-317.

Theft, CR §8-204.
Assumption of risk of theft, CL §14-1305.
Honoring stolen card, CR §8-207.
Obtaining property with stolen card, CR §8-206.
Receiving property by stolen card, CR §8-209.

Universities and colleges.
Payments by credit card, ED §15-102.

Use of stolen or counterfeit card, CR §8-206.

CREDIT COUNSELING.

Debt management services, FI §§12-901 to 12-931.
See DEBT MANAGEMENT SERVICES.

CREDIT GRANTOR CLOSED END CREDIT PROVISIONS, CL §§12-1001 to 12-1029.
See CREDIT.

CREDIT GRANTOR REVOLVING CREDIT PROVISIONS, CL §§12-901 to 12-924.
See CREDIT.

CREDIT LIFE, HEALTH AND UNEMPLOYMENT INSURANCE, IN §§13-101 to 13-117.

Amounts of insurance, IN §13-106.

Applicability of title, IN §13-103.

Claims, IN §13-113.

Commencement of coverage, IN §13-107.

Competition not prohibited or discouraged, IN §13-102.

Consent requirement, IN §27-901.

Construction and interpretation, IN §13-102.

Definitions, IN §13-101.
Premium rates, IN §13-111.

Delivery of policy or certificate, IN §§13-104, 13-109.

Enforcement of title, IN §13-117.

Finance charge computation considerations, IN §27-901.

Forms.
Approval by commissioner, IN §13-110.

Forms of insurance, IN §13-105.

Fronting agreements, IN §13-116.

Group certificates, IN §13-108.
Delivery, IN §13-109.

Husband and wife, IN §13-115.

Legislative policy, IN §13-102.

License, certificate, etc., suspension or revocation, IN §13-117.

Loss ratio for case, IN §13-111.

Maximum commissions and policyholder benefits, IN §13-110.

Maximum premium, IN §13-111.

Option of debtor to provide insurance, IN §13-114.

Penalties, IN §13-117.

Periodic indemnity amounts, IN §13-106.

CREDIT LIFE, HEALTH AND UNEMPLOYMENT INSURANCE —Cont'd

Policies, IN §13-108.
Delivery, IN §§13-104, 13-109.
Issuance, IN §13-104.

Prima facie rates, IN §13-111.

Prohibited payments for insurance, IN §13-111.

Purpose of title, IN §13-102.

Rates, IN §13-111.
Approval by commissioner, IN §13-110.

Refunds, IN §13-112.
Termination of insurance before scheduled maturity date of indebtedness, IN §13-107.

Regulations, IN §13-117.

Settlement or adjustment of claims, IN §13-113.

Term of insurance, IN §13-107.

CREDITORS.

Art.
Consignment of works of fine art.
Bailment of property not subject to claims of art dealer's creditors, CL §11-8A-04.

Art dealers.
Bailment of property not subject to works of art dealer's creditors, CL §11-8A-04.

Bankruptcy and insolvency.
General provisions.
See BANKRUPTCY AND INSOLVENCY.

Commercial code.
Defined, CL §1-201.

Constables.
Suits on bond of defaulting constable.
See CONSTABLES.

Corporations.
Sale, lease, exchange or transfer.
Commercial code.
Rights under commercial law article, CA §3-115.
Rights not impaired by, CA §3-115.

Debt management services, FI §§12-901 to 12-931.
See DEBT MANAGEMENT SERVICES.

Decedents' estates.
Death of legatee prior to testator.
Creditor of deceased legatee has no interest in property, ET §4-403.
Debts and claims.
General provisions, ET §§8-101 to 8-115.
See EXECUTORS AND ADMINISTRATORS.

Deeds.
Effective date of deed, RP §3-201.

Executors and administrators.
Debts and claims.
See EXECUTORS AND ADMINISTRATORS.
Distribution to creditors.
Meeting, Estates Rule 6-441; ET §8-109.
Proposal for distribution, Estates Rule 6-442.
General provisions.
See EXECUTORS AND ADMINISTRATORS.
Liability of heir or legatee to creditor, ET §10-102.
Limitation of actions.
Effect of death, ET §8-102.
Meeting for distribution, Estates Rule 6-441; ET §8-109.
Notice.
Proposed payment to personal representative or attorney, Estates Rule 6-414; ET §7-502.
Notice upon appointment, Estates Rule 6-401; ET §7-103.1.
Opening estates.
Petition for probate.
Notice of appointment, Estates Rule 6-311.

CREDITORS —Cont'd
Executors and administrators —Cont'd
Order of right to letters, ET §5-104.
Proposal for distribution, Estates Rule 6-442.
Settlement of decedents' estates.
Meeting for distribution, Estates Rule 6-441; ET §8-109.
Fraudulent conveyances.
General provisions, CL §§15-201 to 15-214.
See FRAUDULENT CONVEYANCES.
Insurance companies.
Liquidation, rehabilitation, etc.
Transfers made to give creditor a preference, IN §9-221.
Judgments and decrees.
Deeds.
Recordation.
Prepayment of personal property taxes not required, RP §3-104.
Life and health insurance guaranty corporation.
Corporation as creditor of impaired insurer, IN §9-414.
Life insurance and annuities.
Group policies covering debtors, IN §17-206.
Statement to insured debtors, IN §17-103.
Proceeds exempt from creditors, IN §16-111.
Limited liability company members.
Rights of creditors of members, CA §4A-607.
Limited partnerships.
Rights of creditors, CA §10-705.
Status of partner as creditor upon distributions, CA §10-606.
Partnerships.
Limited partnerships.
Rights of creditors, CA §10-705.
Status of partner as creditor upon distributions, CA §10-606.
Partner's interest subject to charging order.
Circuit court, CivProCir Rule 2-649.
District Court, CivProDist Rule 3-649.
Removal of personal property.
Intent to defraud secured party, CR §8-403.
Sales.
Bonds, surety.
Requiring when sale made on credit, RP §14-103.
Wills.
Death of legatee prior to testator.
Effect, ET §4-403.

CREDIT REPORTS.
Credit card number or payment device number contained in report.
Requirements, CR §8-214.

CREDIT SERVICES BUSINESSES.
General provisions, CL §§14-1901 to 14-1916.
See CREDIT.

CREDITS ON TERMS OF CONFINEMENT.
Diminution credits.
Inmates committed to custody of commissioner of correction, COR §§3-701 to 3-711.
See DIMINUTION OF INMATE'S TERM OF CONFINEMENT.
Inmates imprisoned at local correction facilities, COR §§11-501 to 11-509.
See DIMINUTION OF INMATE'S TERM OF CONFINEMENT.

CREDIT UNIONS.
Accounts.
Interest bearing or share accounts, FI §6-501.

CREDIT UNIONS —Cont'd
Accounts —Cont'd
Share guaranty corporations.
Share and deposit accounts.
Insuring, FI §7-204.
Acknowledgments.
Articles of incorporation, FI §6-305.
Bylaws, FI §6-306.
Powers authorized by federal law, FI §6-313.
Procedure and requirements generally, FI §1-202.
Requirements and procedure, FI §1-202.
Allowance for loan and lease loss, FI §6-704.
Amendments.
Articles of incorporation.
Effective date, FI §6-320.
Mail ballot, FI §6-321.
Meetings of members, FI §6-317.
Procedures, FI §6-320.
Bylaws.
Effective date, FI §6-320.
Mail ballot, FI §6-321.
Meetings of members, FI §6-317.
Procedures, FI §6-320.
Recommendation, FI §6-328.
Articles of incorporation. See within this heading, "Incorporation."
Assessments.
Credit unions with assets of $300,000.
Annual assessment, FI §6-712.
Assets.
Facilities, FI §6-707.
Audits.
Independent audits of members, FI §7-112.
Meetings, FI §6-402.
Required by commissioner, FI §6-405.
Supervisory committee.
Powers and duties, FI §6-402.
When committee fails to fulfill functions, FI §6-405.
Banking laws.
Sections not applicable, FI §6-201.
Bankruptcy and insolvency.
Dissolution.
Voluntary dissolution, FI §6-804.
Notice.
Disclosure to national credit union administration, FI §6-407.
Banks and trust companies.
See BANKS AND TRUST COMPANIES.
Bonds, surety.
Credit union insurance corporation.
Officers and employees, FI §7-110.
Books and papers.
Maintaining, FI §6-715.
Borrowing.
Power to borrow, FI §6-708.
Branches, FI §6-807.
Out-of-state credit unions, FI §6-808.
Bylaws, FI §6-203.
Amendment of bylaws.
Mail ballot, FI §6-321.
Meetings, FI §6-317.
Procedure, FI §6-320.
Recommendation, FI §6-328.
Credit union insurance corporation.
Adoption by board, FI §7-111.
Directors emeritus, FI §6-327.
Filing for examination and approval, FI §6-307.
Filing for record, FI §6-308.
Loans.
Bylaws determine purpose and terms of loan, FI §6-601.

CREDIT UNIONS —Cont'd
Bylaws —Cont'd
Preparation, FI §6-306.
Capital, FI §6-314.
Capital composition, FI §6-314.
Cease and desist orders, FI §6-906.
Changing membership type, FI §6-304.
Closed end loans.
Applicable law, FI §6-601.
Commissioner of financial regulation.
Books and records, FI §6-715.
Cooperative and information sharing agreements,
FI §6-407.
Corrective action, FI §6-905.
Credit union insurance corporation.
Bylaws.
Approval by commissioner, FI §7-111.
Exchange of information, FI §7-113.
Rules and regulations.
Approval by commissioner, FI §7-111.
Supervision by commissioner, FI §7-104.
Examinations, FI §6-403.
Reports to commissioner, FI §6-404.
Incorporation, FI §6-307.
Indebtedness to credit unions.
Commissioner and employees not to become
indebted, FI §2-112.
Insurance, FI §6-713.
Liabilities of another credit union.
Purchase or assumption, FI §6-806.
Marketing, FI §6-714.
Requiring audit by certified public accountant, FI
§6-405.
Securities and negotiable loans.
Commissioner and employees not to sell, FI
§2-112.
Service organization, FI §6-706.
Share guaranty corporations.
Exchanges of information, FI §7-213.
Notice to commissioner.
Liquidation and receivership, FI §7-218.
Termination of participation, FI §7-219.
When required, FI §7-215.
Rulemaking to implement provisions, FI §7-224.
Supervision, FI §6-202.
Committees.
Credit committee, FI §6-602.
Appointment, FI §6-602.
Approval of loans, FI §6-603.
Bylaws, FI §6-306.
Loan officers, FI §6-603.
Meetings, FI §6-603.
Suspension of members, FI §6-332.
Vacancies, FI §§6-328, 6-502.
Supervisory committee.
Appointment, FI §6-401.
Audits.
When committee fails to fulfill functions, FI
§6-405.
Bylaws, FI §6-306.
Duties, FI §6-402.
Examination of accounts.
Commissioner to examine upon request of
committee, FI §6-403.
Number, FI §6-401.
Powers and duties, FI §6-402.
Qualifications, FI §6-401.
Reports, FI §6-404.
Required, FI §6-401.
Tenure, FI §6-401.
Vacancies, FI §§6-328, 6-401.

CREDIT UNIONS —Cont'd
Common bond membership fields, FI §6-303.
Compensation.
Officials, FI §6-331.
Confidentiality of information.
Confidential financial records generally.
See BANKS AND TRUST COMPANIES.
Disclosure of credit union information, FI §6-909.
Construction of provisions, FI §6-205.
Consumer credit reporting agencies.
Consumer complaint against credit union, CL
§14-1217.
General provisions, CL §§14-1201 to 14-1218.
See CONSUMER CREDIT REPORTING
AGENCIES.
Conversions.
Savings and loan associations.
Mutual association conversion to credit union,
FI §§9-1101 to 9-1109.
See SAVINGS AND LOAN ASSOCIATIONS.
State credit union into federal union, FI §6-801.
Corporate status, FI §6-206.
Credit committee. See within this heading,
"Committees."
Credit union insurance corporations. See
within this heading, "Insurance corporation."
Definitions, FI §§1-101, 6-101, 6-301.
Compensation, FI §6-331.
Credit union insurance corporation, FI §7-101.
Examiners, FI §6-403.
Immediate family relative, FI §6-302.
Insurance corporation.
Dissolution, FI §7-120.
Purchase of obligations and loans, FI §6-609.
Share guaranty corporations, FI §7-201.
Deposits.
Bylaws, FI §6-306.
Permitted deposits and investments, FI §6-705.
Directors.
Compensation, FI §6-331.
Dividends, FI §§6-306, 6-328.
Declared by board of directors, FI §6-502.
Duties, FI §6-328.
Elections.
Procedures, FI §6-329.
Emeritus, FI §6-327.
Insurance corporation. See within this heading,
"Insurance corporation."
Investments, FI §6-328.
Management of credit union, FI §6-324.
Meetings, FI §§6-306, 6-328.
Membership meetings, FI §6-317.
Number, FI §6-325.
Oaths, FI §6-325.
Qualifications, FI §6-325.
Resignation or removal.
Vacancies, FI §6-326.
Suspension, FI §6-332.
Tenure, FI §6-325.
Vacancies, FI §§6-326, 6-328.
Disclosure of credit union information, FI
§6-909.
Dissolution, FI §6-306.
Voluntary dissolution, FI §6-804.
Dividends.
Directors, FI §§6-306, 6-328.
General provisions, FI §6-502.
Duties of officials, FI §6-333.
Elections.
Directors, FI §6-329.
Officers, FI §6-330.

CREDIT UNIONS —Cont'd
Examinations, FI §6-403.
  Commissioner of financial regulation.
    Reports to commissioner, FI §6-404.
  Disclosure to national credit union administration,
    FI §6-407.
  Independent audits, FI §6-405.
  Reports to commissioner, FI §6-404.
  Share guaranty corporations, FI §7-210.
    Exchanges of information, FI §7-213.
    Expenses, FI §7-211.
  Supervisory committee.
    Generally, FI §6-401.
    Powers and duties, FI §6-402.
  Unsafe or unauthorized practices, FI §6-406.
    Action by board and members, FI §6-406.
Exercise of powers, FI §6-204.
Expulsion of members, FI §6-319.
Facilities, FI §6-707.
Federal credit union.
  Conversion of state credit union into federal credit
    union, FI §6-801.
Federal law.
  Powers authorized by federal law, FI §6-313.
Federal provisions, FI §6-702.
Fees.
  Capital, FI §6-314.
  Filing annual report, CA §1-203.
    Disposition, TP §2-220.
  Filing articles of incorporation and bylaws, FI
    §6-307.
  Loans, FI §6-601.
  Organization and capitalization fees, CA §1-204.
  Share guaranty corporations.
    Certificates of authority.
      Application fee, FI §7-206.
Fidelity bonds.
  Board of directors to set amount, FI §6-328.
Fiscal year, FI §6-710.
Fraud and deceit.
  Unauthorized use of word "credit union," FI
    §6-901.
Funds, FI §6-306.
  Reserve fund, FI §§6-306, 6-703.
    Composition, FI §6-703.
    Transfers to, FI §6-703.
Government guarantees.
  Loans, FI §6-608.
Group life insurance for members, IN §17-207.
Guaranty corporations.
  Share guaranty corporations, FI §§7-201 to 7-224.
Hours of operation, FI §6-711.
Improper loans, FI §6-904.
Incorporation.
  Articles of incorporation.
    Acknowledgments, FI §6-305.
    Amendments.
      Effective date, FI §6-320.
      Mail ballot, FI §6-321.
      Meetings, FI §6-317.
      Procedures, FI §6-320.
    Application, FI §6-309.
    Approval, FI §6-307.
    Contents, FI §6-305.
    Endorsement, FI §6-307.
    Execution, FI §6-305.
    Filing, FI §6-309.
    Filing for examination, FI §6-307.
    Filing for record, FI §6-308.
    Preparation, FI §6-305.
    Signatures, FI §6-305.

CREDIT UNIONS —Cont'd
Incorporation —Cont'd
  Corporate status, FI §6-206.
  Incorporators.
    Generally, FI §6-301.
Insurance.
  Disclosure to national credit union administration,
    FI §6-407.
  Group life insurance for members, IN §17-207.
  Members, FI §6-713.
  Premium financing.
    General provisions, IN §§23-101 to 23-506.
      See PREMIUM FINANCE COMPANIES.
  Share insurance.
    Insurance required, FI §6-701.
    Share guaranty corporations, FI §§7-201 to
      7-224.
Insurance corporation.
  Accumulation of earnings, FI §7-114.
  Application of state insurance laws, FI §7-115.
  Applications for membership, FI §7-106.
    End of authority to accept, FI §7-118.
  Audits.
    Independent audits of members, FI §7-112.
  Bonds, surety.
    Employers and employees, FI §7-110.
  Buying and selling property, FI §7-104.
  Bylaws.
    Approval by commissioner, FI §7-111.
    Directors.
      Adoption, FI §7-111.
  Commissioner of financial regulation, FI §7-111.
    Bylaws.
      Approval by commissioner, FI §7-111.
    Cooperation and exchange of information, FI
      §7-113.
    Rules and regulations.
      Approval by commissioner, FI §7-111.
    Supervision by commissioner, FI §7-104.
  Composition, FI §7-107.
  Definitions, FI §7-101.
  Dissolution, FI §7-120.
  Deposit accounts.
    Insurance, FI §7-105.
  Directors.
    Bylaws.
      Adoption, FI §7-111.
    Compensation, FI §7-109.
    Composition, FI §7-109.
    Election, FI §§7-108, 7-109.
    Officers, FI §7-110.
    Qualifications, FI §7-109.
    Quorum, FI §7-109.
    Rules and regulations.
      Adoption, FI §7-111.
    Staff, FI §7-110.
    Tenure, FI §7-109.
    Vacancies, FI §7-109.
  Dissolution.
    Generally, FI §7-120.
    Phase out and dissolution, FI §§7-118 to 7-121.
  Earnings.
    Accumulation, FI §7-114.
  Enumeration of powers, FI §7-104.
  Establishment, FI §7-102.
  Exchange of information.
    Commissioner and representatives of
      corporations, FI §7-113.
  Exemptions from taxation, FI §7-116.
  Faith or credit of state.
    Not pledged, FI §7-117.

CREDIT UNIONS —Cont'd
Insurance corporation —Cont'd
  Financial assistance, FI §7-104.
  General corporate powers, FI §7-104.
  Governor, FI §7-109.
  Insurance of share and deposit accounts, FI
    §7-105.
    Application of state insurance laws, FI §7-115.
  Investments, FI §7-104.
  Membership, FI §7-102.
    Applications for membership, FI §7-106.
    Duties, FI §7-107.
    Foreign credit unions, FI §7-113.
    Independent audits of members, FI §7-112.
    Qualifications, FI §7-107.
    Term, FI §7-107.
    Termination, FI §7-107.
    Voting by members, FI §7-108.
  National organizations.
    Membership in, FI §7-104.
  Not deemed department, unit, agency or
    instrumentality of state, FI §7-102.
  Officers, FI §7-110.
  Perpetual existence, FI §7-104.
  Phase out and dissolution, FI §§7-118 to 7-121.
    Applications for membership.
      End of authority to accept, FI §7-118.
    Articles of dissolution, FI §7-120.
    Assets.
      Defined, FI §7-120.
      Transfer, FI §7-120.
      Transferee corporation, FI §7-120.
    Compliance with provisions.
      Information provided to assure, FI §7-121.
    Dissolution generally, FI §7-120.
    Information required for commissioner to
      determine compliance with provisions, FI
      §7-121.
    Primary share guaranty insurance.
      Requirements, FI §7-119.
    Winding up, FI §7-120.
  Powers.
    Enumeration, FI §7-104.
  Purposes of corporation, FI §7-103.
  Quorum, FI §7-109.
  Rules and regulations.
    Directors.
      Adoption, FI §7-111.
  Share accounts.
    Insurance, FI §7-105.
  Share guaranty corporations, FI §§7-201 to 7-224.
  Stabilization and liquidation of credit unions, FI
    §7-104.
  Taxation.
    Exemptions from taxation, FI §7-116.
  Voting by members, FI §7-108.
Interest.
  Loans, FI §6-601.
    Mortgages, FI §6-606.
    Participation with other institutions, FI §6-607.
  Members overruling board of directors, FI §6-317.
  Termination of provisions of certain sections in
    subtitle, FI §2-401.
Investments.
  Credit union insurance corporation, FI §7-104.
  Directors, FI §6-328.
  Permitted deposits and investments, FI §6-705.
Laws.
  Provisions of general banking law not applicable,
    FI §6-201.

CREDIT UNIONS —Cont'd
Leases.
  Losses, allowance, FI §6-704.
Liabilities of another credit union.
  Purchase or assumption, FI §6-806.
Liens.
  Loans, FI §6-314.
Life insurance and annuities.
  Group life policies for members, IN §17-207.
Liquidation.
  Share guaranty corporations.
    Liquidation and receivership, FI §7-218.
  Voluntary receivership, FI §6-805.
Loan officers, FI §6-603.
Loans.
  Closed end loans.
    Applicable law, FI §6-601.
  Directors and officers, FI §6-328.
  Government guarantees, FI §6-608.
  Improper loans, FI §6-904.
  Interest.
    Mortgages, FI §6-606.
    Rates, FI §6-507.
  Liens, FI §6-314.
  Loan officers, FI §6-603.
  Losses, FI §6-704.
  Maximum of loans to single members, FI §6-604.
  Mortgages and deeds of trust.
    General provisions, FI §6-606.
  Officials, FI §6-610.
  Participation with other institutions, FI §6-603.
  Power to make, FI §6-601.
  Prohibited loans, FI §6-611.
  Purchase of obligations and loans, FI §6-609.
  Real property.
    Mortgages, FI §6-606.
  Reserve fund, FI §6-703.
  Revolving credit plans.
    Applicable law, FI §6-601.
  Security.
    Required security, FI §6-605.
    What constitutes, FI §6-605.
  Termination of provisions of certain section in
    subtitle, FI §2-401.
  Total of loan to single member, FI §6-604.
Mail ballots.
  Voting by members, FI §6-318.
    Conversion of foreign credit union into state
      credit union, FI §6-802.
    Conversion of state credit union into federal
      credit union, FI §6-801.
    Voluntary receivership, FI §6-805.
Management of credit union, FI §6-324.
Marketing, FI §6-714.
Maryland credit union insurance corporation.
  See within this heading, "Insurance
  corporation."
Meetings.
  Amendments.
    Articles of incorporation.
      Procedures, FI §6-320.
    Bylaws, FI §6-317.
      Effective date, FI §6-320.
      Mail ballot, FI §6-321.
      Procedure, FI §6-320.
  Annual meetings, FI §§6-306, 6-317.
  Audits, FI §6-402.
  Bylaws.
    Amendments, FI §§6-317, 6-320.
      Mail ballot, FI §6-321.

CREDIT UNIONS —Cont'd
Meetings —Cont'd
Elections.
Directors, FI §6-317.
Mail ballot, FI §6-329.
Notice, FI §6-317.
Special meetings, FI §6-317.
Unsafe and unauthorized activities, FI §6-406.
Voting, FI §6-317.
Membership.
Bylaws, FI §6-306.
Changing membership type, FI §6-304.
Common bond membership fields, FI §6-303.
Directors may appoint officer, FI §6-328.
Expulsion of members.
Authority of board, FI §6-319.
Notice of expulsion policy, FI §6-319.
Reconsideration of expulsion, FI §6-319.
Insurance, FI §6-713.
Insurance corporation. See within this heading, "Insurance corporation."
Officer.
Directors may appoint, FI §6-328.
What constitutes, FI §6-302.
Withdrawal from membership, FI §6-319.
Merger, FI §6-803.
Mortgages and deeds of trust.
Defined, FI §1-101.
General provisions, FI §6-606.
Loans on mortgages, FI §6-606.
Mortgage lender law, FI §§11-501 to 11-524.
See MORTGAGE LENDERS.
Mortgage originators, FI §§11-601 to 11-618.
See MORTGAGE ORIGINATORS.
Termination of provisions of certain sections in subtitle, FI §2-401.
Name.
Proposed credit union, FI §§6-305, 6-306.
Unauthorized use of credit union.
Prohibited, FI §6-901.
Notices.
Accounts, FI §6-501.
Amendment of articles of incorporation, FI §6-320.
Amendment of bylaws, FI §6-320.
Conversion of foreign credit union into state credit union, FI §6-802.
Conversion of state credit union into federal credit union, FI §6-801.
Liquidation.
Voluntary receivership, FI §6-805.
Meetings, FI §6-317.
Oaths.
Directors, FI §6-325.
Officers, FI §6-330.
Officers and employees.
Bonds, surety, FI §6-328.
Bylaws, FI §6-306.
Compensation, FI §§6-328, 6-331.
Education, FI §6-204.
Elections, FI §6-330.
Executive officers.
Enumeration, FI §6-330.
General provisions, FI §6-330.
Loans, FI §6-610.
Operations.
Officer in charge of, FI §6-330.
Suspension, FI §6-332.
Operational hours, FI §6-711.
Organizations.
Defined, FI §6-301.
Out-of-state credit unions, FI §6-808.

CREDIT UNIONS —Cont'd
Penalties.
Corrective action, FI §6-905.
Disclosure of credit union information, FI §6-909.
False statements or records, FI §6-903.
Making, circulating, or sending, FI §6-902.
Improper loans, FI §6-904.
Violations, FI §6-908.
Place of business.
Change, FI §6-709.
Location of place of business, FI §6-305.
Powers.
Authorized by federal law, FI §6-313.
Borrowing powers, FI §6-708.
Generally, FI §§6-204, 6-312.
Termination of provisions of certain sections in subtitle, FI §2-401.
Prohibited loans, FI §6-611.
Property taxes.
Exempt personal property, TP §7-221.
Proxies.
No shareholder may vote by proxy, FI §6-317.
Quorum, FI §6-306.
Real property.
Loans on mortgages, FI §6-606.
Receivers.
Share guaranty corporations.
Liquidation and receivership, FI §7-218.
Voluntary receivership, FI §6-805.
Records.
Confidential financial records.
See BANKS AND TRUST COMPANIES.
Maintaining, FI §6-715.
Reports.
Additional reports, FI §6-404.
Annual report to commissioner, FI §6-404.
Failure to report.
Fine, FI §6-404.
Fees for filing annual reports, CA §1-203.
Disposition, TP §2-220.
Form of report, FI §6-404.
Furnishing copies to national credit union administration, FI §6-407.
Reserve fund, FI §6-306.
Share guaranty corporations.
Annual report, FI §7-212.
Interim reports, FI §7-212.
Supervisory committee.
Recommendations, charges and findings, FI §6-402.
Revolving credit plans.
Applicable law, FI §6-601.
Sales and use tax.
Exempt organizations, TG §11-204.
Savings and loan associations.
Conversions.
Mutual association conversion to credit union, FI §§9-1101 to 9-1109.
See SAVINGS AND LOAN ASSOCIATIONS.
Secretary.
Suspension, FI §6-332.
Service organization, FI §6-706.
Share guaranty corporations, FI §§7-201 to 7-224.
Applicability of provisions, FI §7-202.
Assessments, FI §7-211.
Certificates of authority.
Applications, FI §7-206.
Approval, FI §7-207.
Denial, FI §7-208.
Eligibility, FI §7-205.

CREDIT UNIONS —Cont'd
Share guaranty corporations —Cont'd
Certificates of authority —Cont'd
Fees.
Application fee, FI §7-206.
Issuance, FI §7-207.
Names.
Limitations on similarly named entities, FI
§7-205.
Qualifications, FI §7-205.
Required, FI §7-203.
Revocation, FI §7-209.
Submissions with application, FI §7-206.
Suspension, FI §7-209.
Transferability, FI §7-203.
Definitions, FI §7-201.
Deposit accounts.
Insuring, FI §7-204.
Enforcement of provisions, FI §7-209.
Examinations, FI §7-210.
Exchanges of information, FI §7-213.
Expenses, FI §7-211.
Exchanges of information, FI §7-213.
Fines.
Enforcement of provisions, FI §7-209.
Violations of subtitle, FI §7-220.
Funds.
Guaranty fund, FI §7-216.
Guaranty fund, FI §7-216.
Insurance article of code.
Not applicable, FI §7-222.
Insurance corporation.
Applicability of provisions, FI §7-202.
Investigations, FI §7-210.
Certificates of authority.
Applications, FI §7-207.
Expenses, FI §7-211.
Liquidation, FI §7-218.
Losses.
Guaranty loss reserves, FI §7-217.
Misdemeanor for violations, FI §7-220.
Nonprofit share guaranty corporations.
Tax exemptions, FI §7-223.
Notice and hearing.
Denial of certificate of authority, FI §7-208.
Enforcement of provisions, FI §7-209.
Notice to commissioner.
Liquidation and receivership, FI §7-218.
Termination of participation, FI §7-219.
When required, FI §7-215.
Participating credit unions.
Contracts with participating credit unions, FI
§7-214.
Defined, FI §7-201.
State liability for funds, FI §7-221.
Termination of participation, FI §7-219.
Phase out and dissolution of insurance
corporation.
Primary share guaranty insurance.
Requirements, FI §7-119.
Receivership, FI §7-218.
Reinsurance, FI §7-204.
Reports.
Annual report, FI §7-212.
Interim reports, FI §7-212.
Reserves.
Guaranty losses, FI §7-217.
Rulemaking to implement provisions, FI §7-224.
Share accounts.
Insuring, FI §7-204.
State liability for funds, FI §7-221.

CREDIT UNIONS —Cont'd
Share guaranty corporations —Cont'd
Subpoenas.
Examinations and investigations, FI §7-210.
Summons.
Examinations and investigations, FI §7-210.
Termination of participation, FI §7-219.
Shares.
Bylaws, FI §6-306.
Directors, FI §6-328.
Insurance.
Required, FI §6-701.
Share guaranty corporations, FI §§7-201 to
7-224.
Lien on shares, FI §6-314.
Month and year account opened to appear on
share drafts, FI §6-503.
Par value, FI §6-305.
Withdrawals, FI §6-809.
Signatures.
Articles of incorporation, FI §6-305.
State branches, FI §6-807.
Out-of-state credit unions, FI §6-808.
State credit union.
Conversion into federal credit union, FI §6-801.
Foreign credit union.
Conversion, FI §6-802.
**Supervision by commissioner of financial
regulation,** FI §6-202.
Supervisory committee. See within this heading,
"Committees."
Taxation.
Exemption from, FI §6-203.
Share guaranty corporations.
Nonprofit share guaranty corporations, FI
§7-223.
Title.
Short title, FI §6-206.
Treasurer.
Suspension, FI §6-332.
Unsafe and unauthorized activities.
Calling of special meeting, FI §6-406.
Unsafe or unsound practices.
Cease and desist orders, FI §6-906.
Removal of officers, directors or committee
members, FI §6-907.
Reports, FI §6-907.
Warnings, FI §6-907.
Untrue statements.
Making, circulating, or sending, FI §6-902.
Violations.
Penalties, FI §6-908.
Winding up.
Voluntary dissolution, FI §6-804.
Withdrawal of members, FI §6-809.

CREMATION.
Caskets.
Use of casket not required, HG §5-505.
Dead bodies.
Required identification and authorization, HG
§5-502.
Definitions, HG §5-508.
Disposition of bodies.
Authorized agents.
Crematory operator's reliance on
representations, HG §5-511.
Need not be personal representative, HG
§5-512.
Crematory operators.
Reliance on authorized agents' representations,
HG §5-511.

CREMATION —Cont'd
Disposition of bodies —Cont'd
Disposing of one's own body.
  Written formalities, HG §5-509.
Documents negating cremation, HG §5-512.
Failure to agree on disposition, HG §5-510.
Identification tag for body, HO §7-411.
Missing persons.
Unidentified human remains, PS §3-603.
Morticians.
Casket requirements, HO §7-505.
Requirements generally, HO §7-406.
Penalties.
Violations of subtitle, HG §5-507.
Time interval, HG §5-503.
Transporting body to crematory, HG §5-504.

CRIERS.
Compensation.
Certain counties, CJ §2-507.
Fees.
Collection by sheriff.
  See SHERIFFS.

CRIME LABORATORIES.
Contracts.
DNA database system, PS §2-502.
DNA database system, PS §§2-501 to 2-512.
See DNA DATABASE SYSTEM.
Firearms.
Handgun identification requirements, PS §5-131.
Handguns.
Identification requirements, PS §5-131.
Proficiency testing.
DNA database system, PS §2-507.
Records.
DNA database system.
  Record retention, PS §2-502.

CRIMES AND OFFENSES.
Generally.
See CRIMINAL LAW AND PROCEDURE.

CRIMES AT CORRECTIONAL FACILITIES,
COR §§8-801 to 8-803.
See PRISONS AND PRISONERS.

CRIMES OF VIOLENCE.
Firearms.
Dealers' licenses.
  Suspension or revocation, PS §5-114.
Restrictions on possession, PS §5-133.
Restrictions on sale, rental or transfer, PS §5-134.
Good conduct credit, inmate's term of confinement including sentence for crime of violence.
Calculating credit, COR §3-704.
Parole eligibility, COR §7-301.
Violent crime defined, COR §7-101.
Voter registration.
Disqualification, second or subsequent conviction, EL §3-102.

CRIME VICTIMS.
Compensation of victims.
Criminal injuries compensation board, CP §§11-801 to 11-819.
  See CRIMINAL INJURIES COMPENSATION BOARD.
Restitution and other payments, CP §§11-601 to 11-633.
  See CRIME VICTIMS' COMPENSATION.
General provisions, CP §§11-101 to 11-1005.
See VICTIMS OF CRIME.

CRIME VICTIMS —Cont'd
Influencing or intimidating, CR §§9-301 to 9-306.
Megan's law.
Community notification, CP §§11-709 to 11-712, 11-718.
  See SEX OFFENDER REGISTRATION.
Registration of sex offenders, CP §§11-701 to 11-726.
  See SEX OFFENDER REGISTRATION.
Notoriety of crimes contracts, CP §§11-621 to 11-633.
See NOTORIETY OF CRIMES CONTRACTS.
Registration and community registration of sex offenders, CP §§11-701 to 11-726.
See SEX OFFENDER REGISTRATION.
Services for victims and witnesses, CP §§11-901 to 11-1005.
See CRIME VICTIMS' SERVICES.

CRIME VICTIMS' COMPENSATION, CP §§11-601 to 11-633.
Construction of subtitle, CP §11-619.
Criminal injuries compensation board, CP §§11-801 to 11-819.
See CRIMINAL INJURIES COMPENSATION BOARD.
Criteria for denial, CP §11-605.
Definitions, CP §11-601.
Earnings withholding orders, CP §11-617.
Failure to make restitution, CP §11-607.
Graffiti, acts of, CP §11-603.
Monetary limitation, CP §11-604.
Overdue restitution.
Payment or compromise and settlement, CP §11-616.
Victims' consent required, CP §11-616.
Parents, rights of, CP §11-604.
Payers of restitution, CP §11-604.
Payment of restitution, CP §11-606.
Persons who may act for victim, CP §11-602.
Priority of payments, CP §11-606.
Earnings withholding orders, CP §11-617.
Profits from crime, CP §§11-621 to 11-633.
See NOTORIETY OF CRIMES CONTRACTS.
Restitution hearings.
Proof of injuries and damages, CP §11-615.
Restitution judgments.
Compliance as requirement or condition, CP §11-607.
Conditions for judgment, CP §11-603.
Judgment as lien, CP §11-609.
Recording and indexing, CP §11-608.
  Assessment of costs, CP §11-611.
  Circuit court, CP §11-609.
  District Court, CP §11-610.
Stay of execution of sentence, CP §11-613.
Termination of judgment or probation, CP §11-612.
Right to restitution, CP §11-603.
Notification of victim, CP §11-614.
Scope of court's authority, CP §11-619.
State lottery interception, CP §11-618.

CRIME VICTIMS' SERVICES, CP §§11-901 to 11-1005.
Definitions.
Help and treatment for victims, CP §11-1001.
Sexual assault, CP §11-922.
State board of victim services, CP §11-910.
Victim and witness protection and relocation program, CP §11-901.

CRIME VICTIMS' SERVICES —Cont'd
Help and treatment for victims, CP §§11-922 to 11-1005.
  Cost of health services, CP §11-1005.
  Definitions, CP §11-1001.
  Effect of provisions, CP §11-1004.
  Guidelines for treatment of victims of crime, CP §11-1002.
  Guidelines for victims of delinquent act, CP §11-1003.
  Sexual assault victims, CP §§11-922 to 11-925.
  Victim and responsible relative.
    Cost of health services, CP §11-1005.
Sexual assault victims, CP §§11-922 to 11-925.
  Grant program, CP §11-923.
  Health care services, CP §11-925.
  Sexual assault, defined, CP §11-922.
  Transporting alleged victim, CP §11-924.
State board of victim services, CP §§11-910 to 11-919.
  Compensation, CP §11-913.
  Definitions, CP §11-910.
  Duties, CP §11-914.
  Establishment, CP §11-911.
  Grant program, CP §11-919.
  Membership, CP §11-912.
  Quorum, CP §11-913.
  State victims of crime fund, CP §§11-916 to 11-918.
    Audits, CP §11-918.
    Establishment, CP §11-916.
    Status, CP §11-917.
  Tenure of members, CP §11-912.
  Victim services coordinator, CP §11-915.
Victim and witness protection and relocation program, CP §§11-901 to 11-907.
  Administration, CP §11-903.
  Audits.
    Fund and program, CP §11-907.
  Definitions, CP §11-901.
  Establishment, CP §11-902.
  Federal matching funds, CP §11-904.
  Fund.
    Audits, CP §11-907.
    Defined, CP §11-901.
    Establishment, CP §11-905.
    Legislative audits, CP §11-907.
    Special continuing, nonlapsing status, CP §11-906.
    Status, CP §11-906.
  Matching federal funds, CP §11-904.
  Public policy, CP §11-904.
Victim services coordinator.
  Appointment, CP §11-915.

CRIMINAL BACKGROUND CHECKS.
See CRIMINAL HISTORY RECORDS CHECKS.

CRIMINAL DEFAMATION.
Common law crime repealed, CR §9-507.

CRIMINAL HISTORY RECORDS CHECKS, CP §§10-231 to 10-250.
Adult dependent care programs, HG §§19-1901 to 19-1912.
  See ADULT DEPENDENT CARE PROGRAMS.
Alcoholic beverage licenses.
  County licenses, 2B §10-103.
Anne Arundel county.
  Prospective employees, CP §10-231.
Carroll county.
  Current or prospective employees, CP §10-232.

CRIMINAL HISTORY RECORDS CHECKS —Cont'd
Child care.
  Appeals of contested findings, FL §5-565.
  Applications by employees, FL §5-562.
  Confidentiality of information, FL §5-564.
  Costs of investigation, FL §5-561.
  Definitions, FL §5-560.
  Duties of department, FL §5-564.
  Failure to disclose prior conviction or existence of pending charge, FL §5-566.
  Fingerprints, FL §5-562.
  Immunity from civil or criminal liability, CJ §5-619; FL §5-567.
  Offenses requiring disclosure, FL §5-563.
  Secretary, duties, FL §5-568.
  Volunteers at facilities, FL §5-561.
Debt management services.
  License application, FI §12-909.
Electrologists.
  License applicants, HO §§8-6B-08, 8-6B-09.
  Renewal of license, HO §8-6B-14.
Explosions and explosives.
  Licenses and permits, PS §11-106.
Firearms.
  Applications for purchases, rents or transfers.
    Multiple purchases within thirty days, PS §5-129.
  Dealers' licenses, PS §5-108.
Fire marshal.
  Firefighters, rescue squad members and paramedics, PS §6-306.
Handgun permits, PS §5-305.
Horse racing.
  Compact committee.
    Powers and duties, BR §11-1307.
  Individuals subjected to, BR §11-312.
  Prospective buyers of licensees, BR §11-316.
Howard county.
  Prospective employees, CP §10-233.
Montgomery county.
  Taxicab licensees, CP §10-234.
Mortgage originators.
  License applicants, FI §11-606.
National crime prevention and privacy compact, CP §§10-237 to 10-250.
  See NATIONAL CRIME PREVENTION AND PRIVACY COMPACT.
Nurses.
  License applicants, HO §§8-302 to 8-304.
  Renewal of license, HO §8-312.
Nursing assistants.
  Applicants for certification, HO §8-6A-05.
  Renewal of certification, HO §8-6A-08.
Nursing referral service agencies, HG §19-4B-03.
Paramedics, PS §6-306.
Pharmacists.
  Registered pharmacy technicians.
    Applicants for registration, HO §12-6B-02.
Precious metals and gem dealers.
  License applications, BR §12-204.
  Secretary may require check of licensee, BR §12-207.
Prince George's county.
  Prospective employees, CP §10-236.
Private detectives.
  Applicants for licenses, BOP §13-304.
  Renewal of certification, BOP §13-404.1.
Private home detention monitoring, BOP §§20-304 to 20-306.

CRIMINAL HISTORY RECORDS CHECKS —Cont'd

Rescue squad members, PS §6-306.

Residential child care program administrators.

Certification.

Applicants, HO §20-302.

Security guards.

Security guard agencies, BOP §19-304.

Security systems technicians.

Registration, BOP §18-3A-04.

Minors in apprenticeship program.

Not required to meet criminal background check or fingerprint requirement, BOP §18-3A-03.

Renewal, BOP §18-3A-07.

Renewal of license, BOP §18-307.

Taxicab license applicants, PUC §10-104.

Washington county.

Prospective employees, CP §10-235.

CRIMINAL INFORMATION.

Charging by, CP §4-102.

False instruments, using, CP §4-108.

Felony and misdemeanor counts in same document, CP §4-104.

Instruments in writing, printing or figures, CP §4-108.

Merging common law misdemeanor into statutory felony.

Prohibition, CP §4-104.

Money, describing, CP §4-106.

Naming two or more persons with like interest, CP §4-105.

Ordinance violations, CP §4-107.

Owners or possessors of property.

Laying ownership or possession in named person and another or others, CP §4-105.

Partners, joint tenants, heirs, tenants in common or trustees.

Naming one and speaking of named person and another or others, CP §4-105.

CRIMINAL INJURIES COMPENSATION.

Costs.

Additional cost to be imposed in criminal cases, CJ §7-405.

CRIMINAL INJURIES COMPENSATION BOARD, CP §§11-801 to 11-819.

Claims for award.

Amount award, CP §11-811.

Conditions for awards on claims, CP §11-810.

Contributory conduct, CP §11-810.

Debt collection activities stayed by claim, CP §11-809.

Decisions on claims, CP §11-814.

Eligibility, CP §11-808.

Emergency awards pending final decision, CP §11-813.

False claims, CP §11-818.

Filing of claim.

Place of filing, CP §11-809.

Time for filing, CP §11-809.

Who may file claim, CP §11-808.

Finality of secretary's actions, CP §11-814.

Multiyear awards, CP §11-812.

Required reductions, CP §11-811.

Secretary review of board decision, CP §11-814.

Serious financial hardship, CP §11-810.

Terminated awards, CP §11-812.

Composition, CP §11-804.

CRIMINAL INJURIES COMPENSATION BOARD —Cont'd

Confidentiality of information.

Confidential records and reports, CP §11-806.

Criminal incident report, CP §11-807.

Debt collection activities stayed by claim for award, CP §11-809.

Definitions, CP §11-801.

Emergency awards pending final decision, CP §11-813.

Execution or attachment of award, CP §11-816.

False claims, CP §11-818.

Fund, CP §11-819.

Hiring employees, CP §11-805.

Lump sum payments, CP §11-816.

Minimum allowable claim, CP §11-810.

Payment of award, CP §11-816.

Amount of award, CP §11-811.

Criteria for denial, CP §11-810.

Lump sum payments, CP §11-816.

Powers and duties, CP §11-805.

Public policy statement, CP §11-802.

Records of proceedings, CP §11-806.

Rulemaking authority, CP §11-805.

Secretary.

Delegation of duties, CP §11-803.

Finality of actions, CP §11-814.

Judicial review of decision, CP §11-815.

Review of board decision, CP §11-814.

Subrogation of award, CP §11-817.

Tenure of service, CP §11-804.

Termination of award, CP §11-812.

CRIMINAL INJURIES COMPENSATION FUND, CP §11-819.

Alcoholic beverages.

Minors to pay costs.

Conviction of violations, CR §10-119.

CRIMINAL INVESTIGATIONS.

Appeals from criminal investigations, AppRev Rule 8-123.

Currency transactions in trade or business, BR §§1-501 to 1-505.

See CURRENCY TRANSACTIONS IN TRADE OR BUSINESS.

CRIMINAL JUSTICE INFORMATION SYSTEM, CP §§10-201 to 10-228.

Advisory board.

Duties, CP §10-210.

Established, CP §10-207.

Meetings, CP §10-209.

Members, CP §§10-208, 10-209.

Quorum, CP §10-209.

Staff, CP §10-209.

Alcoholic beverages.

Licenses.

Criminal history check of applicants, 2B §10-103.

Central repository.

Administration, CP §10-213.

Agreements with criminal justice units, CP §10-217.

Challenge of criminal history record information, CP §10-223.

Appeal from decision concerning, CP §10-227.

Correction of information, CP §10-224.

Information recorded before July 1, 1976, CP §10-225.

Information relevant to pending criminal proceeding, CP §10-226.

CRIMINAL JUSTICE INFORMATION SYSTEM
—Cont'd
Central repository —Cont'd
Challenge of criminal history record information
—Cont'd
Prohibited acts concerning, CP §10-228.
Defined, CP §10-201.
Dissemination of criminal history information, CP
§§10-219, 10-220.
Establishment, CP §10-213.
Fingerprinting, CP §10-216.
Inspection of criminal history record information,
CP §10-222.
Appeal from decision concerning, CP §10-227.
Information recorded before July 1, 1976, CP
§10-225.
Information relevant to pending criminal
proceeding, CP §10-226.
Prohibited acts concerning, CP §10-228.
Reporting data to, CP §10-214.
Reportable events, CP §10-215.
Rules and regulations, CP §10-221.
Appeal of decisions concerning inspection of or
challenge to criminal history record
information, CP §10-227.
Sharing criminal history record information.
Procedures for, CP §10-218.
**Challenge of criminal history record
information,** CP §10-223.
Appeal from decision concerning, CP §10-227.
Correction of information, CP §10-224.
Information recorded before July 1, 1976, CP
§10-225.
Information relevant to pending criminal
proceeding, CP §10-226.
Prohibited acts concerning, CP §10-228.
Competency to stand trial determination.
Notified of commitment orders or releases
authorized, CP §3-106.
Notified of dismissal of charges, CP §3-107.
Compliance with provisions required, CP
§10-204.
Definitions, CP §§10-201, 10-216.
Dissemination of information.
Children, CP §10-220.
Child charged as adult, CP §10-219.
Compliance with provisions required, CP §10-204.
Generally, CP §10-219.
Findings of legislature, CP §10-202.
Fingerprinting, CP §10-216.
Juvenile brought to Baltimore City juvenile
services center, CP §10-220.
Incompetency to stand trial determination.
Notified of commitment orders or releases
authorized, CP §3-106.
Notified of dismissal of charges, CP §3-107.
**Inspection of criminal history record
information,** CP §10-222.
Appeal from decision concerning, CP §10-227.
Information recorded before July 1, 1976, CP
§10-225.
Information relevant to pending criminal
proceeding, CP §10-226.
Prohibited acts concerning, CP §10-228.
Legislative findings, CP §10-202.
Not criminally responsible determination.
Notification of committed person's escape, CP
§3-113.
Notification of persons ordered committed, CP
§3-112.
Release of committed person, CP §3-118.

CRIMINAL JUSTICE INFORMATION SYSTEM
—Cont'd
Purpose of provisions, CP §10-203.
Reporting data to central repository, CP
§10-214.
Reportable event, CP §10-215.
Rules and regulations, CP §10-221.
Appeal of decisions concerning inspection of or
challenge to criminal history record
information, CP §10-227.
Sharing criminal history record information.
Procedures for, CP §10-218.

CRIMINAL LAW AND PROCEDURE.
Abandoned property disposition.
Mental hygiene law, HG §16-303.
Abuse or neglect of animal, CR §10-604.
Abuse or neglect of vulnerable adults, CR
§§3-604 to 3-606.
Abuse or neglect in first degree, CR §3-604.
Abuse or neglect in second degree, CR §3-605.
Death, serious injury, sexual abuse.
Abuse or neglect in first degree, CR §3-604.
Definitions.
Abuse or neglect in first degree, CR §3-604.
Exploitation of vulnerable adult, CR §8-801.
Investigation, CR §3-606.
Academic papers.
Sales, ED §26-201.
Accessory after the fact to a felony.
Sentence and punishment, CR §1-301.
Accessory before the fact, CP §4-204.
Accused.
Counsel.
Right to representation, MD Const DofR Art 21.
Defense.
Appointment of counsel, MD Const DofR Art 21.
Indictment.
Copy of indictment, MD Const DofR Art 21.
Jury.
Impartial and unanimous jury, MD Const DofR
Art 21.
Rights, MD Const DofR Art 21; US Const Art III.
Self-incrimination.
Prohibited, MD Const DofR Art 22.
Speedy trial.
Right to, MD Const DofR Art 21.
Federal right, US Const Amd 6.
Trial date, Crim Rule 4-271.
Witnesses.
Confrontation with witnesses, MD Const DofR
Art 21.
Actions against state officers and employees,
SG §§12-313 to 12-318.
See ACTIONS AGAINST STATE OFFICERS AND
EMPLOYEES.
Admissions and amusement tax.
See ADMISSIONS AND AMUSEMENT TAX.
Adoption.
Independent adoptions.
Payment or compensation for services, FL
§5-3B-32.
Local department adoptions.
Payment or compensation for services, FL
§5-362.
Private agency adoptions.
Payment or compensation for services, FL
§5-3A-45.
Adult dependent care programs.
Criminal history records checks.
Failure to disclose conviction or pending
charges, HG §19-1909.

CRIMINAL LAW AND PROCEDURE —Cont'd
Adultery, CR §10-501.
Advertising.
  False advertising and related crimes.
    Bait and switch advertising, CL §14-2903.
    Definitions, CL §14-2901.
    False and fraudulent advertising, CL §14-2902.
Agricultural cooperatives.
  Violation of cooperative or general corporation
    law, CA §5-532.
Agriculture violations generally, AG §§12-101 to
  12-104.
Air conditioning and heating contractors.
  Violation of act, BR §9A-505.
Aircraft.
  Firearms or explosives aboard, TR §5-1008.
  Minimum altitude over sporting arenas, TR
    §5-1007.
Airport parking violations, TR §5-427.
Airport zoning violations, TR §§5-511, 5-617.
Air quality control, EN §2-609.1.
  Limitation on bringing prosecution, EN §2-610.2.
Air schools.
  Licensing violations, TR §5-906.
Alarm systems.
  Audible systems.
    Equipped to automatically silence, CR §9-611.
  Defective system.
    Notice to user, use after notice, CR §9-610.
  Definitions, CR §9-607.
  False alarms, CR §9-608.
    Multiple alarms, CR §9-609.
Alcoholic beverages.
  Defense to prosecution.
    Sale to person not of legal age, 2B §12-109.
  Prosecution for selling at unlicensed premises.
    Prima facie evidence of sale, 2B §16-406.
    See ALCOHOLIC BEVERAGES.
Alcoholic beverage tax.
  See ALCOHOLIC BEVERAGE TAX.
Ambulance chasing, IN §27-408.
Ambulances, ED §13-515.
  Impersonating firefighters or emergency services
    personnel, PS §7-402.
  Interference with or obstruction of emergency
    assistance, PS §7-402.
  Recyclable materials, ED §13-703.
Amphetamines.
  Methamphetamines.
    Importers, CR §5-614.
Amusements and recreation.
  Bungee jumping operations, BR §3-503.
  False representations and statements, BR §3-501.
  Garrett county.
    Licensing of amusement devices, BR §17-438.
  Militia.
    Exclusion of members from places of
      amusement or recreation, PS §13-904.
  Pinball machines, BR §17-417.
    Wicomico County, BR §17-429.
  Willful violation causing death, BR §3-502.
Anatomy board.
  Violations of provisions, HG §5-409.
Animal control.
  Violations of provisions, HG §18-222.
Animals, CR §§10-601 to 10-621.
  Abandoning domestic animal, CR §10-612.
  Abuse or neglect of animal, CR §10-604.
  Aggravated cruelty, CR §10-606.
    Arranging, conducting or using dog in dog fight,
      CR §10-607.

CRIMINAL LAW AND PROCEDURE —Cont'd
Animals —Cont'd
  Aggravated cruelty —Cont'd
    Cockfighting, CR §10-608.
  Baltimore City.
    Kennel inspections, health department to
      enforce, CR §10-616.
  Baltimore county.
    Enforcement, care of mistreated animals, CR
      §10-615.
  Carrier pigeons, injuring or trapping, CR §10-622.
  Chicks, selling or giving away, coloring, CR
    §10-614.
  Cockfighting, CR §10-608.
    Attending cockfight, CR §10-605.
  Dangerous animals.
    Importing into state, selling, bartering or
      trading, CR §10-621.
  Dangerous dogs, CR §10-619.
  Definitions, CR §10-601.
  Dehorning, castration, taildocking and limit
    feeding.
    Inapplicability of provisions, CR §10-603.
  Disposal of unclaimed dogs or cats, CR §10-617.
  Dogfight.
    Arranging, conducting or using dog in dog fight,
      CR §10-607.
    Attending, CR §10-605.
  Euthanasia.
    Disposal of unclaimed dogs or cats, CR §10-617.
    Prohibited means of killing dogs and cats, CR
      §10-611.
  Failure to feed or care for, CR §10-604.
  Food processing, pest elimination, training and
    hunting.
    Inapplicability of provisions, CR §10-603.
  Giving unaccompanied dog or cat to shelter or
    pound, CR §10-613.
  Humane society officers.
    Arrest by, CR §10-609.
  Impounded mistreated animals.
    Entry to care for animal, removal, CR §10-615.
  Impounded unclaimed dogs or cats.
    Disposal by animal control unit, CR §10-617.
  Inapplicability of provision, CR §10-603.
  Infliction of unnecessary pain or suffering, CR
    §10-604.
  Intentional cruelty.
    Protection of animals from, CR §10-602.
  Kennel inspections, CR §10-616.
  Killing dogs and cats, prohibited means, CR
    §10-611.
  Normal human activities inflicting incidental
    pain.
    Inapplicability of provisions, CR §10-603.
  Overdriving or overloading, CR §10-604.
  Poisoning dogs, CR §10-618.
  Prizes, giving away animal as, CR §10-610.
  Race horse, interference with, CR §10-620.
  Removal of animal from owner.
    Court order, CR §10-615.
  Research.
    Inapplicability of provisions, CR §10-603.
  Seizure of mistreated animal, CR §10-615.
  Selling puppies or kittens, CR §10-613.
  Stray, when animal deemed, CR §10-615.
  Torturing, beating or killing.
    Aggravated cruelty, CR §10-606.
  Waiting period.
    Disposal of unclaimed dog or cat, CR §10-617.

CRIMINAL LAW AND PROCEDURE —Cont'd
Antique firearm.
  Defined, CR §4-201.
  Use in commission of crime, CR §4-204.
Antitrust violations, CL §11-212.
Appeals, CJ §12-401.
  Bail and recognizance.
    Termination of bond on sentencing.
      New bond on appeal, CP §5-207.
  Baltimore City.
    Municipal court to criminal court.
      See APPEALS.
  Court of special appeals.
    Jurisdiction, CJ §12-308.
  Definition of criminal case, CJ §12-101.
  Investigations.
    Appeals from criminal investigations, AppRev
      Rule 8-123.
  Jurisdiction.
    Court of special appeals, CJ §12-308.
  Jury.
    Right to jury trial, CJ §12-401.
  Post conviction procedure.
    Appeal of final order, CP §7-109.
    Effect of remedy on appeals, CP §7-107.
      See POST CONVICTION PROCEDURE.
  Probation before judgment.
    Waiver of right to appeal, CP §6-220.
  Review of criminal sentences, CP §§8-101 to
    8-109.
    See SENTENCE AND PUNISHMENT.
Appearance.
  Corporations and limited liability companies.
    Return of summons as appearance, CP §4-203.
Archaeological resources.
  Maryland historical trust, violations, SF §5A-346.
**Architectural and engineering services act
    violations,** SF §13-322.
Architectural license violations generally, BOP
    §3-605.
Arrest.
  General provisions.
    See ARREST.
Arrest warrants.
  See ARREST WARRANTS.
Arrest without a warrant.
  Generally, CP §§2-201 to 2-210.
    See WARRANTLESS ARREST.
Arson and burning, CR §§6-101 to 6-111.
  Arson in the first degree, CR §6-102.
  Arson in the second degree, CR §6-103.
  Attempt to burn structure or property, CR §6-109.
  Burning trash container, CR §6-108.
  Burning with intent to defraud, CR §6-106.
  Charging document, CR §6-111.
  Definitions, CR §6-101.
  Malicious burning of personal property in the first
    degree, CR §6-104.
  Malicious burning of personal property in the
    second degree, CR §6-105.
  Separate units, separate violations, CR §6-110.
  Threat of arson, CR §6-107.
Assault.
  Assault by inmate, CR §3-210.
  Assault in the first degree, CR §3-202.
    Lesser included offense of assault in second
      degree.
      Included in charge, CR §3-206.
  Assault in the second degree, CR §3-203.
    Included in charge of assault in first degree, CR
      §3-206.

CRIMINAL LAW AND PROCEDURE —Cont'd
Assault —Cont'd
  Bill of particulars.
    Charging document in general form, CR §3-206.
  Charging documents, CR §3-206.
  Defenses.
    Judicially recognized defenses allowed, CR
      §3-209.
  Definitions, 1 §33; CR §3-201.
  Dismissal of charge, CR §3-207.
  Escape from juvenile detention facility with
    assault.
    Escape in the first degree, CR §9-404.
  Evidence of serious physical injury.
    Expert testimony admissible, not required, CR
      §3-208.
  Law enforcement officers.
    Assault in the second degree, CR §3-203.
  Lesser included offense of assault in second
    degree.
    Included in charge of assault in first degree, CR
      §3-206.
Assault pistols, CR §§4-301 to 4-306.
  Defined, types and brands enumerated, CR
    §4-301.
  Persons excepted from provisions, CR §4-302.
  Punishment, CR §4-306.
  Scope of subtitle, CR §4-302.
  Seizure and disposal as contraband, CR §4-304.
  Transporting into state, selling or purchasing,
    prohibition, CR §4-303.
  Use in commission of crime.
    Punishment, CR §4-306.
Assembly disrupting home tranquility, CR
    §3-904.
Assisted living programs.
  Unlicensed operation, HG §19-1809.
Assisted suicide, CR §§3-101 to 3-104.
  Definitions, CR §3-101.
  Exceptions, CR §3-103.
  Family care giver.
    Exception, CR §3-103.
  Generally, CR §3-102.
  Palliative care, pain relief.
    Exception, CR §3-103.
  Penalty, CR §3-104.
  Withholding life sustaining procedures.
    Exception, CR §3-103.
Athlete agents.
  Contract inducement, BR §4-414.
Athletic contests.
  Possession of intoxicating beverages at school
    events, ED §26-103.
Athletic events.
  Interference with commercial athletic event, CR
    §10-203.
Attachment.
  Discharge of employee, CL §15-606.
Attainder.
  No corruption of blood or forfeiture of estate.
    For treason or felony, MD Const DofR Art 18.
Attainder of treason or felony.
  Prohibited, MD Const DofR Art 18.
Attempt to commit crime.
  Attempted poisoning, CR §3-213.
  Attempted rape in the first degree, CR §3-309.
  Attempted rape in the second degree, CR §3-310.
  Attempted sexual offense in the first degree, CR
    §3-311.
  Attempted sexual offense in the second degree, CR
    §3-312.

CRIMINAL LAW AND PROCEDURE —Cont'd

Attempt to commit crime —Cont'd

Attempt to burn structure or property, CR §6-108.

Punishment not to exceed maximum punishment for crime attempted, CR §1-201.

Attorney at law.

Appointment to defend accused, MD Const DofR Art 21.

Public defender, 27A §§1 to 14.

See PUBLIC DEFENDER.

Counsel for accused, US Const Amd 6.

Sentence review.

Right to counsel, CP §8-103.

Authorized communication interception.

Interference, CJ §10-414.

Automated dialing, telephone solicitation, PUC §8-204.

Automobile insurance fund.

Filing false notice or document, IN §20-701.

Aviation administration.

Conflicts of interest, TR §5-217.

Aviation commission.

Conflicts of interest, TR §5-217.

Aviation provision violations, TR §5-1105.

Bad checks, CR §§8-101 to 8-108.

Costs.

Paying costs with bad checks, CR §8-108.

Definitions, CR §8-101.

Dishonor.

Presumption of intent, evidence of, CR §8-104.

False representation.

Issuing or passing not accompanied by, CR §8-105.

Fines.

Paying fines with bad checks, CR §8-108.

Insufficient funds.

When drawer deemed to have, CR §8-102.

Knowledge of insufficient funds, issuing check with.

Obtaining property or services, CR §8-103.

Presumption of knowledge, evidence, CR §8-104.

Limitations on prosecution, CR §8-105.

Making check good after dishonor, CR §8-105.

No account.

Presumption, evidence of, CR §8-104.

When drawer deemed to have, CR §8-102.

Obtaining property or services, CR §8-103.

Passing check with knowledge of insufficient funds, CR §8-103.

Passing check with knowledge of stop payment or dishonor, CR §8-103.

Penalties, CR §8-106.

Presumptions, CR §8-104.

Prosecution as theft, CR §7-107.

Refusal to pay, issuing check with intent.

Passing to third party, CR §8-103.

Restitution, CR §8-107.

Restoration of property, CR §8-107.

Stop payment, issuing check with intent to.

Effect of intent as evidence, CR §8-104.

Obtaining property or services, CR §8-103.

Theft.

Prosecution as, CR §7-107.

Time for commencing prosecution, CR §8-105.

Value of property or services $500 or more.

Penalty, CR §8-106.

Value of property or services less than $500.

Penalty, CR §8-106.

Bail and recognizance.

Failure to appear in response to citation, CP §5-212.

CRIMINAL LAW AND PROCEDURE —Cont'd

Bail and recognizance —Cont'd

Failure to surrender after forfeiture of bail or recognizance, CP §5-211.

Restrictions on pretrial release.

Escapees, CP §5-202.

Solicitation of business by bail bondsmen or agent, CP §5-210.

Bailee, misappropriation, CR §7-202.

Bait and switch advertising, CL §14-2903.

Banks and trust companies.

Confidential financial records.

Violations, FI §1-305.

Deposits.

Accepting deposits knowing institution to be insolvent, FI §5-804.

Derogatory statements, FI §5-805.

Emergency interstate acquisitions.

Submitting false information to commissioner, FI §5-1103.

Examination of banks.

Interference with, FI §5-202.

Violation of confidentiality, FI §5-209.

False records, FI §5-803.

Mergers, consolidation or transfer.

Submitting false information to commissioner, FI §3-703.

Unauthorized representation as bank, FI §5-806.

Unfair trade practices, FI §5-807.

Violations of provisions, FI §5-802.

Barber shop violations generally, BOP §4-607.

Batteries.

Rental electric storage batteries, CL §11-902.

Battery.

General provisions.

See ASSAULT.

Benefit of clergy abolished, CR §14-103.

Beyond county lines, process issued, CP §1-205.

Bigamy, CR §10-502.

Billiard and pool tables.

Commercial use of billiard table.

Unlicensed operation, BR §17-505.

Prizes for billiard games.

Carroll County, CR §13-905.1.

Bill of particulars.

Arson or burning.

General form of charging document used, CR §6-111.

Assault.

Charging document in general form, CR §3-206.

Breaking and entering.

General form of charging document used, CR §6-210.

Gaming, CR §12-112.

Rape or sexual offense.

General form of charging document used, CR §3-317.

Reckless endangerment.

Charging document in general form, CR §3-206.

Theft.

General for m of charging document used, CR §7-108.

Bills of lading, CL §18-401.

Bingo.

Acceptance of credit to play gaming event.

Prohibition, CR §12-108.

Anne Arundel county, CR §13-407.

Baltimore City, CR §§13-507 to 13-509.

Baltimore county, CR §13-606.

Calvert county, CR §§13-705 to 13-709.

Carroll county, CR §§13-907, 13-908.

CRIMINAL LAW AND PROCEDURE —Cont'd
Bingo —Cont'd
　Cecil county, CR §§13-1001 to 13-1005.
　Charles county, CR §§13-1109 to 13-1115.
　Dorchester county, CR §13-1203.
　Frederick county, CR §13-1306.
　Gaming devices.
　　Defined as, CR §12-101.
　　Statewide gaming provisions, CR §§12-101 to
　　　12-113.
　　See GAMING.
　Gaming event provisions applicable to several
　　counties, CR §§13-201 to 13-205.
　Harford county, CR §§13-1501 to 13-1512.
　Howard county, CR §§13-1602, 13-1603.
　Kent county, CR §13-1705.
　Montgomery county, CR §§13-1801 to 13-1815.
　Prince George's county.
　　Benefit performance by qualified organization,
　　　CR §§13-1901 to 13-1907.
　Queen Anne's county, CR §13-2005.
　St. Mary's county, CR §§13-2101 to 13-2110.
　Somerset county, CR §13-2202.
　Washington county, CR §§13-2401 to 13-2411.
　Wicomico county, CR §§13-2501 to 13-2508.
　Worcester county, CR §§13-2601 to 13-2616.
Biological agents registry violation, HG
　§17-605.
Birds and game.
　Hunting from aircraft prohibited, NR §10-410.
　Seals.
　　Commercial use, NR §10-419.
　Spotlighting.
　　Deer, NR §10-416.
　Violation of title, NR §10-1101.
Blind persons.
　Products made by the blind, CL §14-2807.
　Rights of blind or visually handicapped persons,
　　30 §33.
Blood tests.
　Consent.
　　Liability for taking blood without consent, HG
　　　§20-110.
Bodily fluid.
　Ingesting.
　　Causing another to ingest, CR §3-215.
Boilers and pressure vessels.
　Criminal penalties, PS §12-917.
Boundaries.
　State boundary monuments.
　　Violations of subtitle, NR §2-407.
Boxing and wrestling tax.
　Payment.
　　Willful failure to make, TG §13-1005.
　Records.
　　Willful failure to keep records, TG §13-1008.
　Returns.
　　Willful failure to file return, TG §13-1001.
　　Willful false statement or misleading omission,
　　　TG §13-1003.
　Violations of provisions generally, TG §13-1020.
Boxing, sparring and wrestling.
　Bribery, BR §4-321.
　Ticket scalping, BR §4-318.
　Violations of provisions, BR §4-322.
Boycotts.
　Foreign discriminatory boycotts, CL §11-107.
Bribery, CR §§9-201 to 9-205.
　Acceptance of bribe by juror, CR §9-202.
　Acceptance of bribe by person participating in
　　athletic contest, CR §9-205.

CRIMINAL LAW AND PROCEDURE —Cont'd
Bribery —Cont'd
　Alcoholic beverages provided voters on election
　　day, CR §9-203.
　Athletic contest participants, CR §9-204.
　Boxing, sparring and wrestling, BR §4-321.
　Competency of witness.
　　Bribery of participants in athletic contest.
　　　Person violating provisions, CR §9-204.
　　Bribery of public employee, employee
　　　demanding or receiving bribe.
　　　Person violating provisions, CR §9-201.
　Demanding or receiving bribe.
　　Public employee, CR §9-201.
　Immunity from prosecution.
　　Bribery of participants in athletic contest.
　　　Person violating provisions compelled to
　　　　testify, CR §9-204.
　　Bribery of public employee, employee
　　　demanding or receiving bribe.
　　　Compelling person violating provisions to
　　　　testify, CR §9-201.
　Juror, CR §9-202.
　Medicaid fraud, CR §8-511.
　Public employee, CR §9-201.
　Statute of limitations on prosecution.
　　Bribery of juror, acceptance by juror, CR §9-202.
　　Bribery of participants in athletic contest, CR
　　　§9-204.
　　Bribery of public employee, employee
　　　demanding or receiving bribe, CR §9-201.
　Voter, CR §9-203.
Broadcasting criminal trials.
　See TRIAL.
Brutality.
　Investigations and interrogations.
　　Rights of officers, PS §3-104.
Builders.
　Energy conservation building standards.
　　Failure to submit certification or statement of
　　　waiver, false certification or statement,
　　　PUC §7-407.
Building codes.
　Electrical code violations, PS §12-607.
　Industrialized buildings and manufactured homes.
　　Knowing and willful violations, PS §12-313.
　Safety glazing violations, PS §12-407.
　Structural iron or steel.
　　Beams or girders with studs or reinforcing
　　　shear connectors, PS §12-704.
Bulletproof body armor.
　Defined, CR §4-106.
　Permit to use, possess or purchase, CR §4-107.
　Wearing in crime of violence or drug trafficking
　　crime.
　　Prohibition, CR §4-106.
Bungee jumping operations, BR §3-503.
Burglar's tools.
　Possession, CR §6-205.
　　Breaking and entering motor vehicle, CR
　　　§6-206.
Burglary and related crimes, CR §§6-201 to
　6-210.
　Burglary in the first degree, CR §6-202.
　Burglary in the second degree, CR §6-203.
　Burglary in the third degree, CR §6-204.
　Burglary in the fourth degree, CR §6-205.
　Burglary with explosives or destructive device, CR
　　§6-207.
　Charging document, CR §6-210.
　Definitions, CR §6-201.

CRIMINAL LAW AND PROCEDURE —Cont'd

Burglary and related crimes —Cont'd

Motor vehicle, breaking and entering, CR §6-206.

Research facility, breaking and entering, CR §6-208.

Separate units, separate violations, CR §6-209.

Burial contracts.

Failure to deposit money, BR §5-712.

Burial sites.

Removal of human remains from burial sites.

Ascertaining cause of death.

Removal of human remains, CR §10-402.

Authorization to relocate human remains, procedure, CR §10-402.

Definitions, CR §10-401.

Determining whether erroneously interred.

Removal of human remains, CR §10-402.

Notice of intent to relocate human remains, CR §10-402.

Reburial.

Removal of human remains, CR §10-402.

Reinterment of removed human remains, CR §10-402.

Selling unlawfully removed human remains or funerary objects, CR §10-403.

Statute of limitation on prosecution.

Unauthorized removal of human remains, CR §10-402.

Unauthorized removal of human remains, CR §10-402.

Burning, CR §§6-101 to 6-111.

Arson in the first degree, CR §6-102.

Arson in the second degree, CR §6-103.

Attempt to burn structure or property, CR §6-109.

Burning trash container, CR §6-108.

Burning with intent to defraud, CR §6-106.

Charging document, CR §6-111.

Definitions, CR §6-101.

Malicious burning of personal property in the first degree, CR §6-104.

Malicious burning of personal property in the second degree, CR §6-105.

Separate units, separate violations, CR §6-110.

Threat of arson, CR §6-107.

Buses.

Fare citations.

Failure to appear, TR §7-704.1.

Business and economic development department.

Maryland economic adjustment fund.

False statement or report, 83A §6-511.

Business regulation and licensure.

Blank licenses, BR §17-203.

General penalty provision, BR §17-2106.

Initiation of prosecution, BR §17-2104.

Prima facie evidence of sale, BR §17-2105.

Business trusts.

Transacting business after forfeiture of right to do so, CA §12-809.

Cable television companies.

Interference with service, CR §7-303.

Caller identification blocking by telephone solicitors, PUC §8-205.

Camera surveillance of private residence, CR §3-903.

Campaign finance.

Contributions by persons doing public business.

Disclosure violations, EL §14-107.

Generally, EL §§13-602, 13-603.

Public campaign financing, EL §15-110.

CRIMINAL LAW AND PROCEDURE —Cont'd

Campaign finance —Cont'd

Reports.

Failure to file.

Referral for prosecution, penalty, EL §13-335.

False or misleading statements, EL §13-601.

Cancer.

Treatment of cancer.

Violations of provision, HG §18-304.

Candy or cakes.

Adulteration or misbranding of food.

See FOOD, DRUGS AND COSMETICS.

Cargo of vessel.

Wrongful disposal, CR §8-405.

Carjacking, CR §3-405.

Intent not to permanently deprive owner not defense, CR §3-405.

Carrier pigeons.

Injuring or trapping, CR §10-622.

Carriers.

Venue.

Crimes committed on common carriers, CP §4-201.

Carrier transfer tickets.

Selling or giving to unauthorized person, CR §8-903.

Cats.

Killing by prohibited means, CR §10-611.

Caves.

Disturbing cave life, NR §5-1404.

Exploration permits, NR §5-1405.

Prohibited uses, NR §5-1402.

Speleothems.

Sale, NR §5-1403.

Cemeteries, BR §5-904.

Burial contracts.

Failure to deposit money, BR §5-712.

Druid Hill park.

Burial or funeral procession prohibited, BR §5-802.

Indecent conduct, destruction of funerary objects or foliage, CR §10-404.

Perpetual care of cemeteries.

Corporate violations, BR §5-608.

Charging documents.

Arson or burning, CR §6-111.

Assault, CR §3-206.

Bigamy, CR §10-502.

Bill of particulars.

Gaming, CR §12-112.

Breaking and entering, CR §6-210.

Burglary, CR §6-210.

Citation, charging by, CP §4-101.

Conspiracy.

Sufficiency, CR §1-203.

Criminal information, CP §4-102.

Defined, CP §1-101.

False instruments, using, CP §4-108.

Felony and misdemeanor counts in same document, CP §4-104.

Homicide by motor vehicle or vessel while impaired or under the influence, CR §2-507.

Instruments in writing, printing or figures, CP §4-108.

Life threatening injury by motor vehicle or vessel while impaired or under the influence, CR §3-212.

Manslaughter, CR §2-208.

Manslaughter by vehicle or vessel, CR §2-209.

Merging common law misdemeanor into statutory felony.

Prohibition, CP §4-104.

CRIMINAL LAW AND PROCEDURE —Cont'd
Charging documents —Cont'd
Money, describing, CP §4-106.
Motor vehicle theft, CR §7-108.
Murder, CR §2-208.
Naming two or more persons with like interest,
CP §4-105.
Ordinance violations, CP §4-107.
Owners or possessors of property.
Laying ownership or possession in named
person and another or others, CP §4-105.
Partners, joint tenants, heirs, tenants in common
or trustees.
Naming one and speaking of named person and
another or others, CP §4-105.
Perjury, CR §9-103.
Rape or sexual offense, CR §3-317.
Reckless endangerment, CR §3-206.
Registered returnable containers and textiles, BR
§19-306.
Robbery, CR §3-404.
Theft, CR §7-108.
Unnatural or perverted sexual practice, CR
§3-322.
Charities.
Criminal prosecutions.
Inadmissibility of information obtained during
investigation by secretary, BR §6-205.
Grossly negligent violations, BR §§6-614, 6-619.
Willful violations, BR §§6-613, 6-619.
Checks.
Bad checks, CR §§8-101 to 8-108.
Prosecution as theft, CR §7-107.
Chemical mace.
Wearing or carrying with intent to injure, CR
§4-101.
Chesapeake Bay.
Dumping of dredged materials, EN §5-1107.
Venue.
Crimes committed on bay, CP §4-201.
Chicks.
Selling or coloring, CR §10-614.
Child abuse, CR §3-601.
Mandatory sentence for crime of violence, CR
§14-101.
Childbirth.
Gonococcal ophthalmia neonatorum.
Violations of provision, HG §18-308.
Child care.
Family day care homes.
Direct grant fund.
Violations of provisions, FL §5-559.7.
Registration.
Violations of provisions, FL §5-557.
Licenses.
Violations of provisions, FL §5-521.
Unattended children.
Confinement in dwelling, building or enclosure,
FL §5-801.
Violations of provisions, FL §5-583.
**Child care and protection, corporations
formed for.**
Interfering with or obstructing agents, officers or
representatives, FL §5-503.
Child care quality incentive grant program.
False statements or reports, FL §5-594.7.
Child fatality review teams.
Prohibited disclosures, HG §§5-708, 5-709.
Child kidnapping, CR §3-503.
Imprisonment for life without possibility of parole.
Rape or sexual offense conviction in same
proceeding, CR §3-503.

CRIMINAL LAW AND PROCEDURE —Cont'd
Child labor.
Interference with performance of duties of
commissioner, LE §3-216.
Prohibited employment, LE §3-216.
Children in need of assistance.
Contributing to certain conditions of child, CJ
§3-828.
Children, youth and families.
Residential child care program operators.
Operating without license, 49D §6-102.
Child's access to firearm, CR §4-104.
Chiropractors.
Title violations.
Generally, HO §§3-506, 13-407.
Cholesterol testing.
Violations of provisions, HG §17-511.
Cigarette business licenses.
Doing business without license, BR §16-214.
Sealing vending machines, BR §16-221.
Violating comptroller regulations, BR §16-401.
Cigarettes and tobacco products.
Licensing violations, BR §16-309.
Circuit courts.
General provisions.
See CIRCUIT COURTS.
Citation of article, 1 §25.
Charging by, CP §4-101.
Charging document defined, CP §1-101.
Citations.
Traffic citations.
See MOTOR VEHICLES.
Clergy, sentencing for crime.
Benefit of clergy abolished, CR §14-103.
**Clinical alcohol and drug abuse counselors,
clinical marriage and family therapists
and clinical professional counselors,** HO
§17-3A-11.
Clove cigarettes.
Sale prohibited, penalty, CR §10-106.
Cocaine.
Importers, CR §5-614.
Volume dealers, enhanced penalty, CR §5-612.
Cockfight, CR §10-608.
Attending cockfight, CR §10-605.
Codeine.
Possession, penalty, CR §5-503.
Code of Maryland.
Adoption of code not to affect pending
prosecutions, 1 §1.
Prosecution for offenses committed previous to
adoption of code, 1 §2.
**Coercing or intimidating another to contribute
or donate,** CR §3-707.
Collection agencies.
Doing business without license, BR §7-401.
Collective bargaining.
Conspiracy.
Trade dispute agreements.
Conduct not conspiracy, LE §4-404.
Constructive criminal contempt, LE §4-322.
Injunctions.
Constructive criminal contempt, LE §4-322.
Recusal of judge, LE §4-322.
Payment of union dues or employee benefits, LE
§4-401.
Refusal to leave property, LE §4-402.
Strikebreakers.
Recruitment and employment restricted, LE
§4-403.

CRIMINAL LAW AND PROCEDURE —Cont'd
College activities.
Willful disturbance, ED §26-101.
College grounds.
Trespassing, ED §26-102.
College transcripts, diplomas or grade reports.
Forging or counterfeiting, ED §26-301.
Committed person found not criminally responsible, CP §3-113.
Communications interception.
Manufacturing interception devices, CJ §10-403.
Violations, CJ §10-402.
Community development administration.
False statements or reports, HS §4-255.
Community energy loan program, SG §9-2109.
Computer access code.
Unauthorized possession or distribution, CR §7-302.
Computers.
Unauthorized access, CR §7-302.
Condoms or contraceptives sold by vending machines.
Nonlatex condoms sold, CR §10-104.
Sales at schools, CR §10-105.
Confessions.
Failure to comply strictly with rules, CJ §10-912.
Consecutive sentence, CR §9-407.
Consignment.
Sale of consigned goods.
Failure to account, CL §11-810.
Conspiracy.
Antitrust act, CL §11-204.
Charging document.
Sufficiency, CR §1-203.
Collective bargaining.
Trade dispute agreements.
Conduct not conspiracy, LE §4-404.
Drug kingpin, CR §5-613.
Limitation of actions.
Actions for, CJ §5-106.
Motor vehicles.
Parties to crime, TR §26-101.
Procurement.
Falsification, concealment, etc., of material facts in connection with contracts, SF §11-205.1.
Punishment not to exceed punishment for crime conspired to commit, CR §1-202.
Sentence and punishment.
Approver not to be admitted, CP §6-228.
State retirement and pension system.
Fiduciaries, SPP §21-209.
Constitution of the United States.
Criminal law.
See CONSTITUTION OF THE UNITED STATES.
Consumer loans, CL §12-316.
Violations of licensing provisions, FI §11-222.
Contact lenses.
Plano and Zero powered lenses.
Dispensing or selling, HG §24-301.1.
Contagious diseases.
Exposure of other individuals by infected individual, HG §18-601.
Human immunodeficiency virus, HG §18-601.1.
Institution reports.
Violation of requirements, HG §18-215.
Laboratory examination reports.
Violations of requirements, HG §18-215.
Moving infected individuals.
Refusal to move, HG §18-216.

CRIMINAL LAW AND PROCEDURE —Cont'd
Contagious diseases —Cont'd
Rules and regulations.
Violations, HG §18-604.
Containers.
Toxics in packaging.
Criminal penalties, EN §9-1906.
Contaminating water supply or food or drink, CR §3-214.
Contraband.
Jails, prisons or other places of confinement, CR §§9-410 to 9-417.
Alcoholic beverages.
Delivery or possession, CR §9-415.
Concealing in place of confinement.
Escape, CR §9-412.
Weapons, CR §9-414.
Controlled dangerous substances.
Delivery or possession, CR §9-416.
Definitions, CR §9-410.
Delivery to person in confinement, CR §9-412.
Alcoholic beverages, CR §9-415.
Controlled dangerous substances, CR §9-416.
For escape purposes, CR §9-412.
Weapons, CR §9-414.
Escape.
Delivery for purposes of, concealing in place of confinement, receiving, CR §9-412.
Possession with intent to deliver, CR §9-412.
Alcoholic beverages, CR §9-415.
Controlled dangerous substances, CR §9-416.
Weapons, CR §9-414.
Prescription.
Inapplicability to drug or substance possessed under, CR §9-411.
Receipt by person in confinement.
Escape, CR §9-412.
Weapons, CR §9-414.
Separate sentence, concurrent or consecutive sentences, CR §9-417.
Weapons.
Delivery, concealing, receiving, CR §9-414.
Contraband in correctional facility to effect escape, COR §8-803; CR §9-413.
Controlled dangerous substances, CP §§12-101 to 12-505.
Administering.
Without prescription or order form, CR §5-601.
AIDS education program.
Convicted person may be required to complete, CR §5-906.
Burden of proof.
Establishing exemption, proviso or exception, CR §5-807.
Chemical tests.
Altering results of drug or alcohol screening, CR §10-111.
Chain of physical custody or control, CJ §10-1002.
Reports, CJ §10-1001.
Availability to defense counsel, CJ §10-1003.
Controlled paraphernalia, CR §5-620.
Counterfeiting or altering prescription.
Obtaining controlled substance, CR §5-601.
Passing, issuing, making or possessing, CR §§5-606 to 5-609.
Definitions, general provisions, CR §§5-101 to 5-103.
Department of health and mental hygiene.
Powers and responsibilities, CR §§5-201 to 5-204.

CRIMINAL LAW AND PROCEDURE —Cont'd
Controlled dangerous substances —Cont'd
Repeat offenders.
Punishment, CR §5-905.
Restitution, CR §5-610.
Sale of drug different from that offered, CR §5-702.
Schedule I or II hallucinogenic substances.
Punishment, repeat offenders, mandatory minimum, CR §5-609.
Schedule I or II narcotic drugs.
Distribution, manufacture, possession.
Punishment, repeat offenders, mandatory minimum, CR §5-608.
Schedules, CR §§5-401 to 5-406.
Schools.
Manufacturing, distributing, dispensing or possessing near, CR §5-627.
Symbol required, removal, altering, CR §5-902.
Unsolicited mailing, CR §5-703.
Volume dealers, enhanced penalty, CR §5-612.
Controlled paraphernalia, CR §5-620.
Defined, CR §5-101.
Conversion by consignee, CL §11-809.
Convict-made goods.
Importation and sale of convict-made goods, CL §11-903.
Corporations.
Appearance.
Return of summons as appearance, CP §4-203.
Directors.
Doing business after forfeiture, CA §3-514.
Prohibited acts, CA §2-216.
Foreign corporations.
Doing business without qualifying or registering, CA §7-302.
Forfeiture of charter, etc.
Conduct in connection with organized crime, CA §1-405.
Indemnification of directors, officers, employees and agents, CA §2-418.
Officers and agents.
Doing business after forfeiture, CA §3-514.
Misrepresentation with intent to defraud, CR §8-402.
Prohibited acts, CA §2-216.
Stock and stockholders.
Prohibited acts, CA §2-216.
Summons, CP §4-203.
Correctional facilities.
Crimes committed at correctional facilities, COR §§8-801 to 8-803.
See PRISONS AND PRISONERS.
Corroboration of testimony.
Possession of stolen property.
Person actually stealing property not accomplice for purposes of, CR §7-104.
Corruption of blood.
Prohibited, MD Const DofR Art 27.
Costs.
Additional costs imposed on defendant, CJ §7-409.
Collection of unpaid costs, CJ §7-505.
Criminal injuries compensation.
Additional cost to be imposed in criminal cases, CJ §7-405.
Waiver, CJ §7-405.
Imprisonment for failure to pay costs prohibited, CJ §7-505.
Liability of person found guilty for costs of prosecution, CJ §7-502.
Nolle prosequi, payment by applicant, CP §1-208.

CRIMINAL LAW AND PROCEDURE —Cont'd
Costs —Cont'd
Waiver of right to trial and payment of fine or penalty.
Addition costs, CJ §7-409.
Counterfeiting and forgery, CR §§8-601 to 8-613.
Controlled dangerous substances.
Counterfeit substance, CR §§5-604, 5-607.
Counterfeit defined, CR §1-101.
Credit cards, CR §8-205.
Machinery, plates or contrivance to reproduce.
Possessing, CR §8-208.
Obtaining property by counterfeiting card, CR §8-206.
Receiving property by counterfeit card, CR §8-209.
Intent to defraud.
Proving, CR §1-401.
Money.
Possessing or issuing counterfeit United States Currency, CR §8-604.1.
Intent to defraud, CR §8-604.
Orders for money or goods, CR §8-609.
Pari-mutuel betting tickets.
Counterfeit or altered betting tickets, CR §8-905.
Prescriptions for controlled dangerous substances, CR §§5-601; 8-610.
Evidence, affidavit by authorized provider, CR §5-705.
Issuing, passing, making or possession, CR §§5-606, 5-607.
Private instruments and documents, CR §8-601.
Issuing counterfeit instruments and documents, CR §8-602.
Public documents, CR §8-605.
Making false entries, altering destroying, removal, concealing or accessing, CR §8-606.
Public seal, CR §8-607.
Slugs, manufacturing, CR §8-613.
Stamp of comptroller, CR §8-608.
Title to motor vehicle.
Possessing counterfeit title, CR §8-603.
Tokens, CR §8-612.
Trademarks, CR §8-611.
Vending machines.
Unlawful operation by use of slug or counterfeited or foreign currency, CR §8-613.
Court of special appeals.
General provisions.
See COURT OF SPECIAL APPEALS.
Crack cocaine.
Volume dealers, enhanced penalty, CR §5-612.
Craps.
Playing game prohibited, CR §12-103.
Credit.
Affidavits of cardholders, use, CR §8-214.1.
Credit grantor closed end credit provisions, CL §12-1017.
Credit grantor revolving credit provisions, CL §12-917.
Credit services businesses, CL §14-1915.
Credit cards, CR §§8-201 to 8-217.
Aggregation of value.
Determining penalty, CR §8-202.
Buying or selling, CR §8-204.
Construed not to preclude other provision of criminal law, CR §8-202.

CRIMINAL LAW AND PROCEDURE —Cont'd
Credit cards —Cont'd
  Counterfeiting, CR §8-205.
    Honoring counterfeited card, CR §8-207.
    Machinery, plates or contrivance designed to
      reproduce.
      Possessing, CR §8-208.
    Receiving property by counterfeit card, CR
      §8-209.
    Use of counterfeited card, CR §8-206.
  Credit reporting disclosures.
    Requirements, CR §8-214.
  Definitions, CR §8-201.
  Disclosure of card numbers or access device
    numbers.
    Marketing purposes.
      Disclosure against holder's direction, CR
        §8-214.
      Nondisclosure option, notification
        requirement, CR §8-214.
      Prohibition, CR §8-214.
  False representation.
    Issue, CR §8-207.
    Obtaining property by credit card, CR §8-206.
  False statement as to identity in order to procure,
    CR §8-203.
  Fraud.
    Falsely making or embossing, CR §8-205.
    False representation by issuer, CR §8-207.
    Honoring counterfeited or stolen card, CR
      §8-207.
    Obtaining property with procured by
      misrepresentation, CR §8-206.
    Procuring issuance, CR §8-203.
    Receiving property by stolen, counterfeit or
      misrepresented card, CR §8-209.
  Identity.
    False statement to procure, CR §8-203.
  Incomplete card.
    Possessing with intent to complete without
      consent, CR §8-208.
  Lost or misdelivered card.
    Receiving, CR §8-204.
  Machinery, plates or contrivance designed to
    reproduce.
    Possessing, CR §8-208.
  Marketing purposes.
    Nondisclosure option, notification required, CR
      §8-214.
    Using number against holder's direction, CR
      §8-214.
  No call provision.
    Nondisclosure of card numbers for marketing
      purposes.
      Notification of option required, CR §8-214.
  Numbers, payment device numbers or signature,
    CR §§8-213 to 8-217.
    Civil penalty, injunction, CR §8-217.
    Credit reporting disclosure, requirements, CR
      §8-214.
    Criminal penalty, CR §8-216.
    Definitions, CR §8-213.
    Marketing against holder's direction, CR §8-214.
    Nondisclosure option, notification required, CR
      §8-214.
    Telephone credit cards.
      Publishing number or code, CR §8-210.

CRIMINAL LAW AND PROCEDURE —Cont'd
Credit cards —Cont'd
  Numbers, payment device numbers or signature.
    —Cont'd
    Unauthorized use or disclosure, CR §8-214.
  Obtaining property by counterfeiting, theft or
    misrepresentation, CR §8-206.
  One violation.
    Course of conduct considered, CR §8-202.
  Protection of payment device numbers, CL
    §14-404.
  Receiving lost or misdelivered card, CR §8-204.
  Receiving property by stolen, counterfeit or
    misrepresented card, CR §8-209.
  Receiving stolen card, CR §8-204.
  Signature by other than cardholder, CR §8-205.
  Telephone credit cards.
    Number or code.
      Publishing, CR §8-210.
  Theft, CR §8-204.
    Honoring stolen card, CR §8-207.
    Obtaining property with stolen card, CR §8-206.
    Receiving property by stolen card, CR §8-209.
  Unauthorized access to computers.
    Statute of limitations, CJ §5-106.
  Use of stolen or counterfeit card, CR §8-206.
Credit unions.
  Disclosure of credit union information, FI §6-909.
  Share guaranty corporations.
    Violations of subtitle, FI §7-220.
  Unauthorized use of words "credit union," FI
    §6-901.
  Untrue statements.
    Making, circulating, or sending, FI §6-902.
  Violations of provisions, FI §6-908.
Cremation.
  Violations of provisions, HG §5-507.
Crime against nature.
  General provisions.
    See SEXUAL OFFENSE.
Crime of violence.
  Mandatory sentence for crime of violence.
    Second, third or fourth conviction, CR §14-101.
Crime statistics.
  State police department, PS §2-307.
Criminal defamation.
  Common law crime repealed, CR §9-507.
Criminal history records checks, CP §§10-231 to
  10-250.
Criminal information.
  Charging by, CP §4-102.
  False instruments, using, CP §4-108.
  Felony and misdemeanor counts in same
    document, CP §4-104.
  Instruments in writing, printing or figures, CP
    §4-108.
  Merging common law misdemeanor into statutory
    felony.
    Prohibition, CP §4-104.
  Money, describing, CP §4-106.
  Naming two or more persons with like interest,
    CP §4-105.
  Ordinance violations, CP §4-107.
  Owners or possessors of property.
    Laying ownership or possession in named
      person and another or others, CP §4-105.

CRIMINAL LAW AND PROCEDURE —Cont'd
Criminal information —Cont'd
 Partners, joint tenants, heirs, tenants in common
  or trustees.
  Naming one and speaking of named person and
   another or others, CP §4-105.
Criminal justice information system, CP
  §§10-201 to 10-228.
 See CRIMINAL JUSTICE INFORMATION
  SYSTEM.
 Prohibited acts concerning inspection of or
  challenge to criminal history record
  information, CP §10-228.
 See CRIMINAL JUSTICE INFORMATION
  SYSTEM.
Cruelty to animals.
 Crimes relating to animals generally, CR §§10-601
  to 10-622.
Custody of arrested person in another
 jurisdiction.
 Peace officer appointed in jurisdiction person
  arrested, CP §2-106.
Custom home protection, RP §10-507.
Dams.
 Fish ladders.
  Violations of section, NR §4-502.
Dangerous animals.
 Importing, selling, or trading in, CR §10-621.
Dangerous dogs, CR §10-619.
Dangerous weapons.
 Armed carjacking, CR §3-405.
 Carrying concealed or with intent to injure, CR
  §4-101.
 Defined, CR §4-101.
 Minor carrying weapon, hours prohibited.
  Counties applicable, CR §4-101.
 Minor possessing pepper mace, prohibition, CR
  §4-101.
 Robbery with dangerous weapon, CR §3-403.
 Wearing concealed or with intent to injure, CR
  §4-101.
Day of rest for employees.
 Retail and wholesale establishments, LE §3-704.
Deadly weapons on school property, CR §4-102.
Deaf or hearing impaired defendants.
 Interpreters, court appointment, compensation
  and expenses, CP §1-202.
  Incompetency or not criminally responsible
   proceedings, CP §3-103.
Death penalty.
 Age limitation for imposing, CR §2-202.
 Aggravating circumstances, CR §2-303.
  Evidence admissible, CR §2-303.
  Jury to consider, CR §2-303.
  Whether mitigating circumstances outweighed.
   Preponderance of evidence, CR §2-303.
 Argument for or against.
  Presentation by state and defendant, CR
   §2-303.
 Certification of proceedings to court where
  charging document filed, CR §2-303.
 Court.
  Findings, determination in writing, CR §2-303.
  When proceedings conducted before, CR §2-303.
 Definitions, CR §2-303.
 Determination by court of jury, CR §2-303.
 Docket entries by clerk of court in which charging
  document filed, CR §2-303.
 Evidence, CR §2-303.
 Failure of state to notify of intent to seek, CR
  §2-301.

CRIMINAL LAW AND PROCEDURE —Cont'd
Death penalty —Cont'd
 Findings by court or jury, CR §2-303.
 Imposition by court, CR §2-303.
 Intravenous injection.
  Method of imposing, CR §2-303.
 Jury.
  Alternate jurors, appointment, CR §2-303.
  Findings, determination in writing, CR §2-303.
  Unable to agree within reasonable time, CR
   §2-303.
  When proceedings conducted before, CR §2-303.
 Jury instructions, CR §2-303.
 Lethal injection.
  Method of imposing, CR §2-303.
 Limitations on imposing, CR §2-202.
 Mentally retarded.
  Defined, sentence not imposed, CR §2-202.
 Method of imposing, CR §2-303.
 Mitigating circumstances, CR §2-303.
  Evidence admissible, CR §2-303.
  Jury to consider, CR §2-303.
  Whether mitigating circumstances outweighed
   by aggravating circumstances.
   Preponderance of evidence, CR §2-303.
 Notice to defendant of state's intention to seek,
  CR §2-301.
  Required for imposition, CR §2-202.
 Presentence investigative reports.
  Evidence admissible, CR §2-303.
 Prior criminal convictions.
  Evidence admissible, CR §2-303.
 Punishment for murder in first degree, CR §2-201.
 Requirements for imposition, CR §2-202.
 Sentencing procedure, CR §2-303.
 Under age of 18 years at time of murder.
  Sentence not imposed, CR §2-202.
 Withdrawal of intent to seek.
  Notice, CR §2-301.
Debtors.
 Removal of personal property.
  Intent to defraud secured party or judgment
   creditor, CR §8-403.
Defalcation, CR §7-114.
Defendant.
 Presence of defendant.
  See PRESENCE OF DEFENDANT.
Defendant to have copy of process, CP §1-206.
Defense related activity.
 Acting with intent to hinder, CR §§9-701 to 9-703.
Defenses.
 Arson in the first degree.
  Person owns property not defense, CR §6-102.
 Arson in the second degree.
  Person owns property not defense, CR §6-103.
 Assault.
  Judicially recognized defenses allowed, CR
   §3-209.
 Carjacking.
  Intent not to permanently deprive owner not
   defense, CR §3-405.
 Counterfeiting prescription.
  Payment or offer to pay for drug not defense,
   CR §8-610.
 Escape.
  Intoxication not defense, CR §9-406.
 Faked controlled substances.
  Distributing.
   Belief that substance was controlled
    substance not defense, CR §5-617.

CRIMINAL LAW AND PROCEDURE —Cont'd
Defenses —Cont'd
Hazing.
Implied or express consent not defense, CR §3-607.
Homicide by motor vehicle or vessel while impaired by controlled dangerous substance.
Entitlement to use substance, CR §2-506.
Homicide by motor vehicle or vessel while impaired by drugs.
Entitlement to use drugs, CR §2-505.
Intoxication not defense.
Escape, CR §9-406.
Noncontrolled substance believing it to be controlled substance.
Possessing or purchasing.
Belief substance controlled substance not defense, CR §5-618.
Not criminally responsible, CP §§3-109 to 3-123.
See NOT CRIMINALLY RESPONSIBLE.
Possession of stolen property.
Defenses not allowed, CR §7-104.
Pyramid promotional schemes.
Prohibited defenses, CR §8-404.
Rape or sexual offense.
Spousal defense, CR §3-318.
Reckless endangerment.
Judicially recognized defenses allowed, CR §3-209.
Surveillance by camera of private residence.
Defendant's ownership of private residence.
Not defenses, CR §3-903.
Good faith reliance on court order, CR §3-903.
Theft.
Good faith or honest belief, CR §7-110.
Interest in property, not defense, CR §7-110.
Property illegally obtained by victim, not defense, CR §7-110.
Spouse's property, CR §7-110.
Tobacco sales to minors.
Examination of purchaser's driver's license or other identification, CR §10-107.
Unauthorized removal of property.
Intention to hold or keep property for personal use, not defense, CR §7-203.
Unlawful subleasing of motor vehicle.
Defenses not allowed, CR §8-408.
Visual surveillance of individual in private place.
Defendant owner of premises where private place located.
Not defense, CR §3-901.
Definitions, CP §§1-101, 2-101; CR §1-101.
Dental hygienists.
Unauthorized practice, HO §4-606.
Dentists, HO §4-606.
Departing from custody without authorization.
Escape in the second degree, CR §9-405.
Deposit insurance fund corporation.
Submitting false information, FI §10-119.
Destruction of property.
Malicious destruction, CR §6-301.
Malicious destruction of property.
Throwing object at vehicle, CR §6-302.
Destructive devices, CR §§4-501 to 4-503.
Definitions, CR §4-501.
Exceptions to subtitle, CR §4-502.
False statement or rumor, CR §9-504.
Manufacture or possession prohibited, CR §4-503.
Representation of device.
Manufacturing, possessing or transporting, CR §9-505.

CRIMINAL LAW AND PROCEDURE —Cont'd
Destructive devices —Cont'd
Restitution ordered for violation, CR §4-503.
Scope of subtitle, CR §4-502.
Detachable magazines.
Prohibited, CR §4-305.
Detainers.
Interstate agreement on detainers, COR §§8-401 to 8-417.
See INTERSTATE AGREEMENT ON DETAINERS.
Intrastate detainers, COR §§8-501 to 8-503.
Developmental disabilities.
Compensation.
Receiving unauthorized compensation, HG §7-1104.
Licenses.
Applications.
False statements, HG §7-910.
Nonbudgeted funds.
Accepting, HG §7-1104.
Providing services unlawfully, HG §7-1101.
Rights of individuals.
Interference with, HG §7-1102.
Dietitians.
Title violations.
Generally, HO §5-403.
Disarming a law enforcement officer, CR §4-103.
Discharge of firearm from motor vehicle.
Reckless endangerment, CR §3-204.
Discrimination in public accommodations.
Violations of article.
Aiding or abetting violations, 49B §12A.
Dismissal of charges.
Defendant incompetent to stand trial, CP §3-107.
Disorderly conduct, CR §10-201.
In cemeteries, CR §10-404.
Disorderly house.
Keeping, CR §10-202.
District Court.
General provisions, CJ §§4-301 to 4-304.
See DISTRICT COURT.
Insane persons.
Authority of court as to competency or sanity of criminal defendants, CJ §4-202.
Service of process, CJ §2-605.
Disturbing the peace, CR §10-201.
DNA database system.
Generally, PS §§2-501 to 2-512.
See DNA DATABASE SYSTEM.
Prohibited acts, PS §2-512.
DNA profiles.
Evidence.
Admissibility, CJ §10-915.
New trial, Crim Rule 4-331.
Postconviction review, CP §8-201.
Preservation of scientific identification evidence, time period, CP §8-201.
DNA technology fund, 41 §4-301.
DNA testing.
Post-conviction procedure, Crim Rule 4-401.
Documents of title, CL §18-401.
Documents of title, misuse, CR §8-406.
Dogfights.
Arranging, conducting or using dog in, CR §10-607.
Attending, CR §10-605.
Dogs.
Killing by prohibited means, CR §10-611.
Violation of dog regulation, 24 §11-509.

CRIMINAL LAW AND PROCEDURE —Cont'd
Domestic violence.
Address confidentiality program.
Applications to participate.
False attestation or information, FL §4-523.
Obtaining actual address or telephone number,
FL §4-529.
Local domestic violence fatality review teams.
Confidential information, FL §4-707.
Meetings, FL §4-706.
Violations of orders, FL §4-509.
**Down payment and settlement expense loan
program.**
False statements or reports, HS §4-309.
Drug induced conduct.
Administering controlled dangerous substance
without person knowledge, CR §5-624.
Drug kingpins, CR §5-613.
Conspiracy to manufacture, distribute, dispense or
transport into state, CR §5-613.
Defined, CR §5-613.
Enhanced penalty allowed, CR §5-613.
Merger of conviction with other crimes,
prohibition, CR §5-613.
Probation, prohibition, CR §5-613.
Prosecution for other crime allowed, CR §5-613.
Drug or alcohol abuse.
Adjudication as drug or alcohol abuser or
dependent.
Unlawful or improper adjudication, HG §8-701.
Commitment of defendants convicted of crimes.
See DRUG OR ALCOHOL ABUSE.
Commitment of defendants for evaluation, HG
§8-506.
Commitment of defendants for treatment, HG
§8-507.
Evaluation of criminal defendants before or
during trial, HG §8-505.
Treatment programs.
Neighborhood crime, drug and alcohol abuse
prevention and education programs, CR
§5-1001.
Maryland drug and alcohol grants program
fund, CR §5-1002.
Operation in violation of provisions, HG §8-702.
Violations of provisions, HG §8-404.
Drug paraphernalia, CR §5-619.
Advertising, CR §5-619.
Authorized providers, prohibited acts, CR §5-902.
Controlled paraphernalia, CR §5-620.
Defined, CR §5-101.
Defined, CR §5-101.
Delivery or sale, CR §5-619.
Factors considered to determine, CR §5-619.
Immunity for public officials and employees
engaged in enforcement or prosecution of
laws, CR §5-808.
Innocence of owner.
Not dispositive of finding intention or design,
CR §5-619.
Use or possession with intent to use, CR §5-619.
Drugs.
Controlled dangerous substances.
Definitions, CR §5-101.
Generally, CR §§5-101 to 5-1101.
See CONTROLLED DANGEROUS
SUBSTANCES.
Drug trafficking, CR §§5-602, 5-607 to 5-609.
Counterfeit substances, CR §§5-604, 5-607.
Drug kingpins, CR §5-613.
Faked controlled substances, CR §5-617.

CRIMINAL LAW AND PROCEDURE —Cont'd
Drug trafficking.—Cont'd
Firearm possessed, used, worn, carried or
transported.
Separate offense, enhanced sentence, forfeiture,
CR §5-621.
Minors used, CR §5-628.
Schools.
Manufacturing, distributing, dispensing or
possessing near, CR §5-627.
Drunkenness.
Disorderly intoxication, 2B §19-102.
Ducklings.
Selling or coloring, CR §10-614.
Dumping site surveillance systems, CR §10-112.
Dyed diesel fuel.
Operation of vehicle containing fuel in tanks, BR
§10-323.2.
Sale or delivery from retail pump, BR §10-323.2.
Eavesdropping equipment violations, CJ
§10-412.
Elections.
Absentee voting, EL §9-312.
Adding or deleting votes, EL §16-304.
Alcoholic beverage use at polling place, EL
§16-207.
Ballots and balloting offenses, EL §16-206.
Campaign finance generally, EL §§13-602, 13-603.
Contributions by persons doing public business.
Disclosure violations, EL §14-107.
Public campaign financing, EL §15-110.
Campaign finance reports.
Failure to file.
Referral for prosecution, penalty, EL §13-335.
False or misleading statements, EL §13-601.
Canvassing.
Certification or statement of results.
False reports, EL §16-601.
Certificates of candidacy or nomination, EL
§16-901.
Corrupt or fraudulent acts in performance of
official duties, EL §16-301.
Defacing or removing election records, EL
§16-701.
Disobeying lawful command of election official, EL
§16-203.
Disturbing the peace, EL §16-204.
Election officials, individuals attired or equipped
as prohibited, EL §16-903.
Violations, penalty, EL §16-1002.
False oath or affirmation, EL §16-501.
General penalty provision, EL §16-1001.
Interfering with election officials, EL §16-205.
Neglect of official duties, EL §16-301.
Operation of polling place, EL §16-303.
Petitions, offenses relating to, EL §16-401.
Provisional ballot voting, EL §9-408.
Public campaign financing, EL §15-110.
Removal of equipment or supplies placed in
polling place, EL §16-803.
Tampering with election records, EL §16-302.
Voter registration, EL §16-601.
Copy of voter registration list used for
commercial solicitation, EL §3-506.
Voting equipment.
Concealing, damaging, destroying or removing
from official's custody, EL §16-801.
Tampering with or attempting to damage, EL
§16-802.
Voting offenses, EL §16-201.
Person convicted of infamous crime, EL §16-202.

CRIMINAL LAW AND PROCEDURE —Cont'd
Elections —Cont'd
Voting systems.
Tampering with electronic system, EL §16-804.
Wagering on elections, EL §16-902.
Electric companies.
Energy conservation building standards.
Knowingly providing service in violation of provisions, PUC §7-407.
Electric company materials, equipment or facilities.
Interfering with or tampering with, CR §6-303.
Electrologists.
Violations of subtitle, HO §8-6B-27.
Electronic mail.
Misuse, CR §3-805.
Spam, CR §3-805.1.
Electronic security systems.
Code grabbing devices.
Manufacturing, selling or possessing, CR §7-301.
Deactivation tool or device.
Possessing, using, CR §7-301.
Devices shielding merchandise from system detection.
Possessing, CR §7-301.
Removal of system or device, CR §7-301.
Elevator licenses.
Violations, PS §12-840.
Embezzlement, CR §7-113.
Intent to defraud.
Proving, CR §1-401.
Wills, codicils, deeds, land patents, writs of estate, CR §§8-701, 8-702.
Emergency communications.
Interference with, CR §9-601.
Prerecorded emergency message.
Transmitting, CR §9-603.
Emergency management.
Civil relief during emergency periods, PS §14-218.
Compulsory work during state of war.
Failure to register for work, PS §14-907.
Failure to work, PS §14-908.
Governor's orders, violations, PS §14-309.
Maryland emergency management agency (MEMA), PS §14-114.
State standby petroleum fuel set-aside program violations, PS §14-511.
Emergency medical care and services.
Impersonating firefighters or emergency services personnel, PS §7-402.
Interference with or obstruction of emergency assistance, PS §7-402.
Unlicensed or not certified persons providing emergency medical services, ED §13-516.
Employee discharges.
Attachment of wages, CL §15-606.
Employment agencies.
Licenses.
Doing business without license, BR §9-401.
Energy conservation buildings standards.
Electric company knowingly providing service in violation for provisions, PUC §7-407.
Failure to submit certification or statement of waiver, false certification or statement, PUC §7-407.
Energy efficiency and economic development loan program.
False statements, SG §9-20A-09.
Engineering license violations, BOP §14-508.

CRIMINAL LAW AND PROCEDURE —Cont'd
Environment.
Asbestos licensing violations, EN §6-422.
Cleaning agent violations, EN §9-1505.
Controlled hazardous substance violations generally, EN §7-265.
Drinking water violations, EN §9-413.
Falsifying or altering permits, licenses or certificates, EN §1-302.
Hazardous waste.
False statements in required documents, EN §7-267.
Offenses generally, EN §7-265.
Health officer abatement notice violations, EN §10-301.
Industrial operator.
Certification violations, EN §12-504.
Interference with state inspections, EN §1-404.
Judicial abatement order violations, EN §10-302.
Lead based paint violations, EN §6-302.
Mercuric oxide battery violations, EN §6-902.
Municipal failure to enforce subtitle, EN §4-215.
Municipal regulation violations, EN §9-717.
Nuisance abatement generally, EN §§10-304, 10-305.
Occupational disease violations, EN §6-701.
Oil discharges, EN §4-411.
Oil vessel bond violations, EN §4-407.
Permit violations generally, EN §2-609.1.
Limitation on bringing prosecution, EN §2-610.2.
Plastic container labeling violations, EN §9-1710.
Pollution offenses generally, EN §4-501.
Radiation licensing violations, EN §8-509.
Limitation on prosecution, EN §8-509.1.
Recycling violations generally, EN §9-1906.
Sanitary waste violations, EN §9-699.
Sediment control violations, EN §4-116.
Septic tank violations in Garrett county, EN §9-1101.
Summary abatement interference, EN §10-303.
Treatment works violations, EN §9-343.
Limitation on prosecution, EN §9-343.1.
Vessels discharging oil, EN §4-418.
Water pollution violations generally, EN §4-417.
Limitation on prosecution, EN §9-343.1.
Water quality laboratory violations, EN §9-1026.
Watershed sediment and waste control violations, EN §4-314.
Well drillers license violations, EN §13-505.
Well drilling violations, EN §9-1311.
Environmental service.
Violations of subtitle, NR §3-129.
Escape.
Abandoned property disposition.
Mental hygiene law, HG §16-303.
Bail and recognizance.
Restrictions on pretrial release.
Escapees, CP §5-202.
Committed person found not criminally responsible, CP §3-113.
Consecutive sentence, CR §9-407.
Contraband in correctional facility to effect escape, COR §8-803; CR §9-413.
Departing from custody without authorization.
Escape in the second degree, CR §9-405.
Escape in the first degree, CR §9-404.
Escape in the second degree, CR §9-405.
Expenses incurred in returning person, CR §9-407.
Harboring escaped inmate, CR §9-403.

CRIMINAL LAW AND PROCEDURE —Cont'd

Escape —Cont'd

Home detention.

Escape in the second degree, CR §9-405.

Inmates in correctional facilities in division of corrections.

Violation of restriction on movement constitutes, COR §3-409.

Local correctional facility.

Violation of restriction on movement, COR §11-726.

Interstate agreement on detainers.

After execution of request for final disposition, request void, COR §8-405.

Temporary custody, COR §§8-407, 8-413.

Intoxication not defense.

Voluntary intoxication, CR §9-406.

Juvenile detention facility.

Departing from custody without authorization.

Escape in second degree, CR §9-405.

With assault.

Escape in first degree, CR §9-404.

Leave of inmate from confinement.

Local correctional facility.

Violation of restriction on movement, COR §11-726.

Prerelease unit for women, COR §3-305.

Local correctional facilities.

Leave, work release or home detention order.

Violation of restriction on movement, COR §11-726.

Retake warrants, issuance by managing official or designee, COR §11-803.

Mental hygiene law.

Disposition of property on escape of individual, HG §16-303.

Natural resources police force.

Pursuit of offenders across Maryland-Virginia water boundary, NR §1-210.

Order to report to place of confinement.

Failure to obey.

Escape in the second degree, CR §9-405.

Patuxent institution.

Parole, work release program or leave of absence program.

Return to division of correction, COR §4-306.

Restriction of movement conditions.

Violation as escape in second degree, CR §9-405.

Retake warrant for apprehension and return of escapee from correctional facility.

Issuance by warden, copy to state's attorney, COR §3-214.

Sheriff or police officer to execute on receipt, COR §3-214.

Notice to division of correction on arrest, COR §3-214.

Retake warrants.

Managing official of local correctional facility, issuance, COR §11-803.

Sentencing, CR §9-407.

Sex offender registration.

Notification escape and recapture, CP §11-712.

Sick inmates temporarily removed from correctional facility, COR §9-602.

Suspension of sentence prohibited, CR §9-407.

Victims of crime.

Notification escape and recapture, CP §11-508.

Work release programs.

Local correctional facility.

Violation of restriction on movement, COR §11-726.

CRIMINAL LAW AND PROCEDURE —Cont'd

Escape in the first degree, CR §9-404.

Escape in the second degree, CR §9-405.

Evidence.

Bad checks.

Issuing or passing, CR §8-104.

Battered spouse syndrome.

Admissibility of evidence, CJ §10-916.

Cable television service, interference with.

Prima facie evidence of intent, CR §7-303.

Charities, criminal prosecutions.

Inadmissibility of information obtained during investigation by secretary, BR §6-205.

Child pornography, CR §11-207.

Controlled dangerous substances bail or sentencing hearing.

Hearsay, CR §5-809.

Controlled substances near schools.

Map as evidence, CR §5-627.

Counterfeiting of prescriptions.

Affidavit of authorized provider, CR §5-705.

Counterfeit mark, CR §8-611.

DNA profiles.

Admissibility, CJ §10-915.

New trial, Crim Rule 4-331.

Postconviction review, CP §8-201.

Preservation of scientific identification evidence, time period, CP §8-201.

DNA testing.

Post-conviction procedure, Crim Rule 4-401.

Electric company materials, equipment or facilities.

Interfering with or tampering with, CR §6-303.

Gas company material, equipment or facilities.

Interference with, CR §6-304.

Hearsay exception.

Unavailability of declarant of statement.

Statement by declarant offered against defendant, CJ §10-901.

Identification evidence.

Preservation of scientific identification evidence, time period, CP §8-201.

Insufficient evidence.

Motion for judgment of acquittal on grounds of, CP §6-104.

Junkyards and related facilities.

Dumping into waters of state, EN §5-10A-03.

Machine guns, possession.

Presence in room, boat or vehicle, CR §4-402.

Prescriptions, counterfeiting.

Affidavit of authorized provider, CR §5-705.

Preservation of evidence.

Scientific identification evidence, CP §8-201.

Rape or sexual offense.

Reputation or opinion as to victim's chastity, CR §3-319.

Specific instances of victim's prior sexual conduct, CR §3-319.

Rape shield law, CR §3-319.

Registered returnable containers and textiles.

Possession, BR §19-307.

Robbery.

Proof of intent to withhold property of another, CR §3-401.

Scientific identification evidence.

Preservation, time period, CP §8-201.

Serious physical injury.

Assault or reckless endangerment.

Expert testimony admissible, not required, CR §3-208.

CRIMINAL LAW AND PROCEDURE —Cont'd
Evidence —Cont'd
　Sustaining conviction.
　　Question for court, MD Const DofR Art 23.
　Theft.
　　Proof of theft generally, CR §7-109.
　Unavailability of declarant of statement.
　　Statement by declarant offered against
　　　defendant, CJ §10-901.
　Wiretapping.
　　General provisions.
　　　See WIRETAPPING.
Exemptions.
　Assignment of claims to nonresidents, CL §15-503.
Expenses incurred in returning person, CR
　§9-407.
Explosions and explosives.
　Aircraft, TR §5-1008.
　Expungement of criminal records, CP §§10-108,
　　10-109.
Explosive, incendiary or toxic material.
　Destructive devices, CR §§4-501 to 4-503.
　　Definitions, CR §4-501.
　　Exceptions to subtitle, CR §4-502.
　　False statement or rumor, CR §9-504.
　　Manufacture or possession prohibited, CR
　　　§4-503.
　　Representation of destructive device.
　　　Manufacturing, possessing or transporting,
　　　　CR §9-505.
　　Restitution ordered for violation, CR §4-503.
　　Scope of subtitle, CR §4-502.
　Firearms, explosives for use in, PS §11-115.
　Forfeiture of vehicle for violations, CP §13-301.
　License or other violations, PS §11-114.
　　Additional penalties, PS §11-116.
　　Merger of convictions, PS §11-117.
Expungement of records, CP §§10-101 to 10-109.
　See EXPUNGEMENT OF RECORDS.
Extortion, CR §§3-701 to 3-707.
　Contributions or donations.
　　Coercing or intimidating another to make, CR
　　　§3-707.
　False accusation, CR §3-704.
　Generally, CR §3-701.
　Property of five hundred dollars or more.
　　Extortion by local or state government officer or
　　　employee, CR §3-702.
　　Penalty, CR §3-701.
　Property of less than five hundred dollars.
　　Extortion by local or state government officer or
　　　employee, CR §3-702.
　　Penalty, CR §3-701.
　State or local officer or employee, CR
　　§3-702.
　　Inducing another to give up compensation, CR
　　　§3-703.
　Statute of limitation on prosecution, CR §3-701.
　　By state or local government officer or
　　　employee, CR §3-702.
　　Inducing another to give up compensation, CR
　　　§3-703.
　Verbal threat, CR §3-705.
　Wages, hours or working conditions.
　　Provisions inapplicable to employees seeking to
　　　obtain, CR §3-701.
　Written threat, CR §3-706.
Extradition.
　Criminal extradition act, CP §§9-101 to 9-128.
　General provisions, US Const Art IV §2.

CRIMINAL LAW AND PROCEDURE —Cont'd
Extradition —Cont'd
　Noncompliance with delivery procedures, CP
　　§9-111.
**Failure to appear before commissioner of
　correction,** COR §3-204.
Failure to deliver documents for merchandise,
　CR §7-116.
False alarms, CR §9-604.
　Activation of alarm system.
　　Defective system, notice to user, use after
　　　notice, CR §9-610.
　　Definitions, CR §9-607.
　　Nonemergency activation of signal, CR §9-608.
False impersonation.
　See FALSE IMPERSONATIONS.
False or fraudulent advertising, CL §14-2902.
False pretenses and false statements.
　Common law criminal defamation.
　　Repealed, CR §9-507.
　Controlled dangerous substances.
　　Obtaining, CR §5-601.
　Credit card crimes.
　　False statements as to identity to procure, CR
　　　§8-203.
　　Generally, CR §§8-201 to 8-217.
　　　See CREDIT CARDS.
　　Obtaining property by counterfeiting, theft or
　　　misrepresentation, CR §8-206.
　False statement or report as to crime or hazard,
　　CR §9-503.
　False statement or rumor as to destructive device
　　or toxic material, CR §9-504.
　False statement, report or complaint to law
　　enforcement officer, CR §9-501.
　　When person under arrest, CR §9-502.
　Intent to defraud.
　　Proving, CR §1-401.
　Maryland higher education commission fund
　　application.
　　False or concealed material fact, CR §9-506.
　Theft.
　　Generally, CR §§7-101 to 7-110.
　　See THEFT.
Federal law enforcement officers, powers, CP
　§2-104.
Female genital mutilation, HG §§20-601 to
　20-603.
Fentanyl analogue.
　Importers, CR §5-614.
Fetus.
　Murder or manslaughter of viable fetus, CR
　　§2-103.
Financial institution franchise tax.
　Returns.
　　Willful failure to file, TG §13-1001.
　　Willfully filing false return, TG §13-1002.
Fines.
　General provisions.
　　See FINES.
　Remission, CP §1-207.
Firearms.
　Aboard aircraft, TR §5-1008.
　Antique firearm.
　　Defined, CR §4-201.
　　Use in commission of crime, CR §4-204.
　Applications for purchases, rents or transfers.
　　Multiple purchases within thirty days, PS
　　　§5-129.
　Assault pistols.
　　Defined, prohibition, seizure, CR §§4-301 to
　　　4-306.

CRIMINAL LAW AND PROCEDURE —Cont'd

Firearms —Cont'd

Assault with firearm.

   Assault in first degree, CR §3-202.

Breaking and entering with intent to steal.

   Burglary in the second degree, CR §6-203.

Child's access to firearm, CR §4-104.

Contraband in place of confinement, CR §9-414.

Detachable magazines.

   Prohibited, CR §4-305.

Disarming a law enforcement officer, CR §4-103.

Discharge.

   From motor vehicle.

      Reckless endangerment, CR §3-204.

   Local regulation allowed, CR §4-209.

Drug crimes.

   Firearm possessed, used, worn, carried or
transported.

      Separate offense, enhanced sentence,
forfeiture, CR §5-621.

   Possession by person convicted of, CR §5-622.

Handguns.

   Generally, CR §§4-201 to 4-209.

   Manufacture or sale of guns not on roster, PS
§5-406.

Knowing participation in violation of subtitle, PS
§5-143.

Machine guns.

   Uniform act, CR §§4-401 to 4-407.

Possession at public demonstration, CR §4-208.

Possession of short-barreled rifles or shotguns, PS
§5-203.

Reckless endangerment.

   Discharge from motor vehicle, CR §3-204.

Restrictions on possession, PS §5-133.

Restrictions on sale, rental or transfer, PS §5-134.

Rifles.

   Defined, CR §4-201.

   Possession by person with mental disorder, PS
§5-205.

   Short-barreled rifle.

      Defined, CR §4-201.

Short-barreled rifle.

   Defined, CR §4-201.

Short-barreled shotgun.

   Defined, CR §4-201.

Shotgun.

   Defined, CR §4-201.

   Possession by person with mental disorder, PS
§5-205.

   Short-barreled shotgun.

      Defined, CR §4-201.

State preemption of local regulation, CR §4-209.

Straw purchases.

   Knowing participation in, PS §5-141.

Fire insurance.

Disclosure of fire loss investigation reports.

   Violations, PS §9-606.

Fire marshal.

Impersonation of fire marshal or employee, PS
§6-602.

Interference with or obstruction of emergency
assistance, PS §6-602.

Interference with or obstruction of investigations,
PS §6-602.

Fireplaces.

Stoves and freestanding fireplaces, CL §14-1309.

Fires and fire protection.

Evacuation procedure violations, PS §9-506.

Impersonating firefighters or emergency services
personnel, PS §7-402.

CRIMINAL LAW AND PROCEDURE —Cont'd

Fires and fire protection —Cont'd

Inspections by local fire departments.

   Hindering, obstructing or refusing to allow
inspection, PS §9-805.

Interference with or obstruction of emergency
assistance, PS §§6-602, 7-402.

Smoke detectors.

   Violations, PS §9-109.

Sprinkler systems.

   Fire sprinkler contractor licensing violations, PS
§9-905.

   Violations, PS §9-206.

Fireworks.

Possession, sale or permit violations, PS §10-111.

Sparklers, PS §10-112.

   Registration of distributors and wholesalers, PS
§10-113.

Fireworks plants, PS §10-210.

Fish and fisheries.

Dams.

   Fish ladders.

      Violations of section, NR §4-502.

Dynamite.

   Use in streams, NR §4-503.

Electronic and electrical devices, NR §4-509.

Interference with lawful taking of fish, NR
§4-506.1.

Nets and seines.

   Pound or stake nets, NR §4-711.

   Vessels and boats passing through nets, NR
§4-508.

Nonnative aquatic organisms, NR §4-205.1.

Nontidal waters.

   Violation of rules and regulations affecting fish
in, NR §4-602.

Prohibitions and restrictions on method of fishing,
NR §4-710.

Restrictions in county waters, NR §4-714.

Rockfish.

   Purchase, sale or transportation, NR §4-731.

Violation of title, NR §4-1201.

Flags.

Uniform flag law, CR §§10-701 to 10-706.

   Construed to carry out general purpose, CR
§10-705.

   Display of flag with word, figure, mark, picture,
design or advertisement, CR §10-703.

   Flag defined, CR §10-701.

   Mutilating, defacing, destroying, burning or
trampling flag, CR §10-704.

   Placing word, figure, mark, picture, design or
advertisement on flag, CR §10-703.

   Scope of law, CR §10-702.

   Selling, manufacturing or possessing
merchandise marked with flag, CR §10-703.

   Short title, CR §10-706.

Food donations under federal programs.

Unauthorized disposition or conversion, CR
§8-505.

Food, drugs and cosmetics.

Generally, HG §§21-201 to 21-263.

See FOOD, DRUGS AND COSMETICS.

Food or drink.

Contaminating, CR §3-214.

Foreclosure.

Protection of homeowners.

   Violation of provisions, RP §7-321.

Forest and parks.

Fires.

   Maliciously setting fires, NR §5-704.

CRIMINAL LAW AND PROCEDURE —Cont'd
Forest and parks —Cont'd
Forestry license violations, BOP §7-506.
Railroads.
 Engines to be provided with appliances to prevent fires, NR §5-711.
Violations of title, NR §5-1301.
Forfeitures.
Cable television service, interference with.
 Devices used, CR §7-303.
Drug asset forfeiture, CR §§12-101 to 12-505.
 See DRUG ASSET FORFEITURE.
Drug trafficking crimes.
 Firearms, CR §5-621.
Gambling forfeitures, CP §§13-101 to 13-109.
 See GAMBLING FORFEITURES.
Interference with emergency communication.
 Two way radio and related equipment used in violation, CR §9-601.
Recorded devices.
 Unauthorized recording of sounds or images, CR §7-309.
Remission, CP §1-207.
 See FORFEITURES.
Telecommunications services theft.
 Unlawful devices, CR §7-316.
Forgery.
Counterfeiting and forgery generally, CR §§8-601 to 8-613.
Fortune-telling.
Calvert county, 24 §11-403.
Franchises.
Criminal proceedings authorized, BR §14-211.
Fraud or deceit, BR §14-229.
 Applications, notices or reports, BR §14-231.
 Prospectus offering or amendment, BR §14-230.
Privilege against self-incrimination, BR §14-213.
Registration.
 Amendments to registration.
  Failure to notify of material change, BR §14-232.
 Offer or sale of franchise without registration, BR §14-228.
Fraternal benefit societies.
Misrepresentations, IN §8-468.
Fraternal society insignia or name.
Unauthorized use, BR §19-207.
Fraud.
Bait and switch advertising, CL §14-1903.
False or fraudulent advertising, CL §14-1902.
Generally.
 See FRAUD.
Horse racing.
 Racing horse under false name, CR §8-904.
Housing assistance fraud, CR §8-523.
Insurance fraud, IN §27-408.
Intent to defraud.
 Proving, CR §1-401.
Pari-mutuel betting tickets.
 Counterfeit or altered betting tickets, CR §8-905.
Freestanding ambulatory care facilities.
Violation of subtitle, HG §19-3B-09.
Freestanding medical facilities.
Violation of provisions, HG §19-3A-05.
Fresh pursuit, CP §2-301.
Authority of officers in another state to arrest in this state.
 Uniform act on fresh pursuit, CP §§2-304 to 2-309.

CRIMINAL LAW AND PROCEDURE —Cont'd
Fundraising for police, fire departments or public safety officers.
Fraudulent conduct, CR §8-520.
Funerals, obstruction of entry or exit or of procession, CR §10-205.
Gambling forfeitures, CP §§13-101 to 13-109.
 See GAMBLING FORFEITURES.
Gaming and gambling, CR §§12-101 to 12-113.
Betting, wagering or gambling prohibited, CR §12-102.
Bill of particulars.
 Charging document, CR §12-111.
Book or pool.
 Making or selling prohibited, CR §12-102.
Certain games prohibited, CR §12-103.
Charging document, CR §12-111.
Charitable organization.
 Raffles, CR §12-106.
Craps, playing prohibited, CR §12-103.
Definitions, CR §12-101.
Fixing horse race results, CR §12-109.
Gaming device.
 Conducting or keeping on or over the waters of the state, CR §12-105.
 Defined, CR §12-101.
 Keeping, dealing, managing or having interest in, CR §12-104.
Law enforcement officer's duty.
 Suspicion that gaming device kept unlawfully, CR §12-111.
Recovery of money lost.
 Common debt, competent witness as to loss, CR §12-110.
Gaming events.
 Accepting credit to allow person to play, CR §12-108.
 Defined, CR §12-101.
 Local provisions.
  Anne Arundel county, CR §§13-401 to 13-408.
  Baltimore City, CR §§13-501 to 13-510.
  Baltimore county, CR §§13-601 to 13-607.
  Calvert county, CR §§13-701 to 13-709.
  Carroll county, CR §§13-901 to 13-909.
  Cecil county, CR §§13-1001 to 13-1005.
  Charles county, CR §§13-1101 to 13-1115.
  Dorchester county, CR §§13-1201 to 13-1207.
  Frederick county, CR §§13-1301 to 13-1307.
  Garrett county, CR §§13-1401 to 13-1406.
  Harford county, CR §§13-1501 to 13-1512.
  Howard county, CR §§13-1601 to 13-1604.
  Kent county, CR §§13-1701 to 13-1706.
  Montgomery county, CR §§13-1801 to 13-1815.
  Prince George's county, CR §§13-1901 to 13-1912.
  Provision applicable to several counties, CR §§13-201 to 13-205.
  Queen Anne's county, CR §§13-2001 to 13-2006.
  St. Mary's county, CR §§13-2101 to 13-2115.
  Scope of provisions, CR §13-101.
  Somerset county, CR §§13-2201, 13-2202.
  Talbot county, CR §13-2301.
  Washington county, CR §§13-2401 to 13-2438.
  Wicomico county, CR §§13-2501 to 13-2508.
  Worcester county, CR §§13-2601 to 13-2628.
Horse racing.
 Fixing results, CR §12-109.
 Interference with race horse, CR §10-620.
 Racing horse under false name, CR §8-904.

CRIMINAL LAW AND PROCEDURE —Cont'd
Gaming and gambling —Cont'd
Keeping place for purposes of betting, wagering or gambling, CR §§12-102, 12-104.
  For gaming device, CR §12-105.
Law enforcement officer's duty.
  Suspicion that gaming device kept unlawfully, CR §12-111.
Liberal construction of provisions, CR §12-111.
Little joker, playing prohibited, CR §12-103.
Lotteries, CR §§12-201 to 12-212.
Pari-mutuel betting.
  Games, contests or jai alai, prohibition, CR §12-107.
Pari-mutuel betting tickets.
  Counterfeit or altered betting tickets, CR §8-905.
Political committee or candidate.
  Raffles, CR §12-106.
Prearrangement or predetermination of horse race results, CR §12-109.
Raffles, CR §12-106.
Receiving or becoming depository of money, CR §12-102.
Recovery of money lost.
  Common debt, competent witness as to loss, CR §12-110.
Slot machines, CR §§12-301 to 12-307.
Thimbles, playing prohibited, CR §12-103.
Tokens, use allowed, CR §12-108.
Gang offenses, CR §§9-801 to 9-803.
Gas and oil.
Multiple violations of provisions and subtitle, EN §14-120.
Storage.
  Prince George's county, EN §14-308.
Used oil recycling act.
  Violations, EN §5-1001.
General assembly.
Debate.
  Members not liable for criminal prosecution for words spoken in debate, MD Const Art III §18.
Electrical voting machines.
  Use by nonmembers, SG §2-1701.
Interfering or disrupting activities of, SG §2-1702.
Investigating committee hearings, SG §2-1609.
Gift enterprise.
Barter, sale or trade, CR §12-212.
Gold.
Merchandise made of gold, CL §14-608.
Grain.
Dealer licensing violations, AG §13-214.
Grocery carts.
Theft, CR §7-201.
Ground rent.
Advertising sale without disclosing, CL §14-2902.
Group home financing program.
False statements or reports, HS §4-612.
Guardian and ward.
Local department guardianships.
  Payment or compensation for services, FL §5-362.
Private agency guardianships.
  Payment or compensation for services, FL §5-3A-45.
Guns.
Weapons.
  See WEAPONS.
Habeas corpus.
General provisions, CJ §§3-701 to 3-707.
  See HABEAS CORPUS.

CRIMINAL LAW AND PROCEDURE —Cont'd
Handgun permits.
Carrying, wearing or transporting handgun while under the influence, PS §5-314.
Disqualification, PS §5-306.
Failure to return revoked permit, PS §5-313.
Handguns, CR §§4-201 to 4-209.
Assault pistols.
  Defined, prohibition, seizure, CR §§4-301 to 4-306.
Child's access to firearm, CR §4-104.
Definitions, CR §4-201.
Disarming law enforcement officer, CR §4-103.
Discharge.
  Local regulation, CR §4-209.
Forfeitures, CP §§13-201 to 13-206.
Legislative findings, CR §4-202.
Limited search, seizure and arrest, CR §4-206.
Manufacture or sale of guns not on roster, PS §5-406.
Probation on conviction.
  Limitation, CR §4-205.
Public demonstration.
  Possession at, CR §4-208.
Reduction of mandatory minimum sentence by court.
  Limitation, CR §4-205.
School property.
  Carrying or possessing on, CR §4-102.
State preemption of regulation, CR §4-209.
Suspension of mandatory minimum sentence by court.
  Limitation, CR §4-205.
Use in commission of crime, CR §4-204.
Wearing, carrying or transporting.
  Prohibition, penalty, sentencing, CR §4-203.
Handicapped students, ED §8-311.
Harassment, CR §3-803.
Misuse of electronic mail, CR §3-805.
Misuse of laser pointer, CR §3-806.
Misuse of telephone facilities and equipment, CR §3-804.
Unlawful picketing and assembly, CR §3-904.
Harboring.
Escaped inmate, CR §9-403.
Fugitive, CR §9-402.
Hate crimes, CR §§10-301 to 10-308.
Damage to property because of race, color, religious beliefs, national origin or sexual orientation, CR §10-304.
  Associated building, damage to, CR §10-305.
  Religious entity, damaging property of, CR §10-302.
First amendment rights protected, CR §10-308.
Harassment because of race, color, religious beliefs, national origin or sexual orientation, CR §10-304.
Penalty, CR §10-306.
Prosecution for other crimes not precluded, CR §10-307.
Religious belief.
  Obstructing exercise of religious belief, CR §10-303.
Religious entity.
  Damaging property of, CR §10-302.
Sexual orientation.
  Defined, CR §10-301.
Statistics.
  State police department, PS §2-307.
Hawkers and peddlers.
Acting as peddler without license, BR §17-911.

CRIMINAL LAW AND PROCEDURE —Cont'd
Hawkers and peddlers —Cont'd
Calvert County.
Acting without license, BR §§17-921, 17-922.
Sale of produce in municipal corporation, BR §17-912.
Hazardous materials and substances.
Toxics in packaging, EN §9-1906.
Hazing, CR §3-607.
Health.
ImmuNet program.
Confidentiality violations, HG §18-109.
Misdemeanors.
See HEALTH.
Records.
Confidential records.
Violations of provisions, HG §4-103.
Secretary of health and mental hygiene.
Right of entry.
Violations of provisions, HG §2-104.
Health care decisions.
Advance directive.
Willful destruction, etc., HG §5-610.
Health insurance.
Private review agents, IN §§15-10B-12, 15-10B-17.
Health occupations.
Audiology practice without license, HO §2-408.
Hearing aid devices.
Impairment of usage, CL §14-25A-01.
Hearsay exception.
Unavailability of declarant of statement.
Statement by declarant offered against defendant, CJ §10-901.
Higher education commission fund application.
False or concealed material fact, CR §9-506.
High voltage lines.
Violations of title, LE §6-110.
Highway land.
Removal of material, TR §8-647.
Highways.
Closure or restricted access to certain properties.
Violation of order, TR §8-627.
Construction provision violations, TR §8-749.
Junkyards.
Provision violations, TR §8-812.
Maintenance provision violations, TR §8-749.
Railroad grade crossings or separations.
Administration orders.
Compliance failures, TR §8-643.
Sign removal, damage or defacement, TR §8-605.
Historical and cultural museum assistance program.
False statements or reports, SF §5A-359.
Hit and run, TR §27-101.
Serious bodily harm, TR §27-113.
Home detention.
Escape in the second degree, CR §9-405.
Inmates in correctional facilities in division of corrections.
Violation of restriction on movement constitutes, COR §3-409.
Local correctional facility.
Violation of condition, COR §11-726.
Allegany county, CJ §11-702.
Violation of restriction on movement, COR §11-726.
Home improvements.
False proof of completion, BR §8-602.
Licenses.
Acting without license, BR §8-601.

CRIMINAL LAW AND PROCEDURE —Cont'd
Home improvements —Cont'd
Violations of act.
General criminal penalty, BR §8-623.
Home solicitation sales.
Unlawful practices, CL §14-305.
Homicide.
By vehicle or vessel while impaired or under the influence. See within this heading, "Homicide by vehicle or vessel while impaired or under the influence."
Definitions, CR §2-101.
Fetus.
Murder or manslaughter of viable fetus, CR §2-103.
Manslaughter.
By vehicle or vessel, CR §2-209.
Indictment, sufficiency, CR §2-209.
Vehicle defined, CR §2-209.
Vessel defined, CR §2-101.
Indictment, sufficiency, CR §2-208.
By vehicle or vessel, CR §2-209.
Punishment, CR §2-207.
Spousal adultery not mitigating factor, CR §2-207.
Murder in the first degree, CR §2-201.
Attempt to commit.
Punishment, CR §2-205.
Death sentence, CR §§2-201, 2-202.
Automatic review by court of appeals, CR §2-401.
Notice of intent to seek or withdrawal of intent.
Filing with clerk of court of appeals, CR §2-301.
Procedure, CR §2-303.
Rules governing sentencing proceedings, adoption, CR §2-305.
Indictment, sufficiency, CR §2-208.
Life imprisonment, CR §2-201.
Life imprisonment without possibility of parole, CR §§2-201, 2-203.
Defined, CR §2-101.
Procedure, CR §2-304.
Rules governing sentencing proceedings, adoption, CR §2-305.
Verdict.
Jury to state degree of murder found, CR §2-302.
Murder in the second degree, CR §2-204.
Attempt.
Punishment, CR §2-206.
Indictment, sufficiency, CR §2-208.
Verdict.
Jury to state degree of murder found, CR §2-302.
Year and day rule.
Rule eliminated in homicide prosecutions, CR §2-102.
Homicide by vehicle or vessel while impaired or under the influence.
Alcohol concentration measurement, determining, CR §2-502.
Indictment, information or charging document, sufficiency, CR §2-507.
Notice of conviction to motor vehicle administration, CR §2-508.
Presumptions and evidentiary rules, CR §2-502.
Under the influence of alcohol or under the influence of alcohol per se, CR §2-503.
Under the influence of alcohol per se defined, CR §2-501.

CRIMINAL LAW AND PROCEDURE —Cont'd
Homicide by vehicle or vessel while impaired or under the influence —Cont'd
While impaired by alcohol, CR §2-504.
While impaired by controlled dangerous substance, CR §2-506.
Entitlement to use of controlled dangerous substance, exception, CR §2-506.
While impaired by drugs, CR §2-505.
Entitlement to use of drugs, defense, CR §2-505.
Horse industry board.
Violations of provisions, AG §2-718.
Horse races.
Licenses.
Holding race meet without license, BR §11-1001.
Horse racing.
Fixing results, CR §12-109.
Interference with race horse, CR §10-620.
Racing horse under false name, CR §8-904.
Hospitals.
Misdemeanors.
See HOSPITALS.
House of prostitution, CR §11-306.
Housing and community development.
Neighborhood business development program.
False statement or reports, HS §6-311.
Housing assistance fraud, CR §8-523.
Human cloning, 83A §5-2B-13.
Human remains.
Removal of human remains from burial sites.
Ascertaining cause of death.
Removal of human remains, CR §10-402.
Authorization to relocate human remains, procedure, CR §10-402.
Definitions, CR §10-401.
Determining whether erroneously interred.
Removal of human remains, CR §10-402.
Notice of intent to relocate human remains, CR §10-402.
Reburial.
Removal of human remains, CR §10-402.
Reinterment of removed human remains, CR §10-402.
Selling unlawfully removed human remains or funerary objects, CR §10-403.
Statute of limitation on prosecution.
Unauthorized removal of human remains, CR §10-402.
Unauthorized removal of human remains, CR §10-402.
Identification badges or cards.
Badges or cards required for employment or visit.
Badge defined, CR §9-701.
Possession after employment or visit ended, CR §9-704.
Surrender on gaining possession, CR §9-705.
Surrender required at end of employment or visit, CR §9-704.
Unauthorized use, CR §9-705.
Blank or incorrect cards.
Selling or issuing, offering to sell or issue, CR §8-302.
Identification worn by person suffering semiconscious or unconscious periods.
Falsification of identification, CP §2-107.
Identity fraud, CR §§8-301 to 8-305.
Illness causing blackouts, semiconsciousness or unconsciousness.
Misrepresentation of illness, CP §2-107.
Immigration consultants, CL §14-3306.

CRIMINAL LAW AND PROCEDURE —Cont'd
ImmuNet program.
Confidentiality violations, HG §18-109.
Immunity of witnesses compelled to testify.
Bribery of public employee.
Person violating provisions compelled to testify, CR §8-201.
Impersonating a police officer, PS §3-502.
Imprisonment for life without possibility of parole.
Child kidnapping.
Rape or sexual offense conviction in same proceeding, CR §3-503.
Defined, CR §2-101.
Jury.
Determination by, CR §2-304.
Findings, CR §2-304.
Unable to agree within reasonable time, CR §2-304.
Punishment for murder in first degree, CR §2-201.
Rape in the first degree.
Child victim under age of 16 years, CR §3-303.
Rules governing sentencing proceedings.
Adoption by court of appeals, CR §2-305.
Sentencing procedure, CR §2-304.
Sexual offense in the first degree.
Child victim under age of 16 years, CR §3-305.
Incest, CR §3-323.
Marriage.
Performance of ceremony between individuals within prohibited degrees.
Prohibited, FL §2-406.
Void marriages, FL §2-202.
Income tax.
See INCOME TAX.
Incompetency to stand trial, CP §§3-101 to 3-108.
See INCOMPETENCY TO STAND TRIAL.
Indecency.
General provisions.
See OBSCENITY AND PORNOGRAPHY.
Indecent exposure.
Punishment, CR §11-107.
Indian affairs commission.
False statements or representations, 41 §6-912.
Indictments and informations.
Charging by criminal information, CP §4-102.
Charging document defined, CP §1-101.
False instruments, using, CP §4-108.
Felony and misdemeanor counts in same document, CP §4-104.
Instruments in writing, printing or figures, CP §4-108.
Merging common law misdemeanor into statutory felony.
Prohibition, CP §4-104.
Money, describing, CP §4-106.
Naming two or more persons with like interest, CP §4-105.
Ordinance violations, CP §4-107.
Owners or possessors of property.
Laying ownership or possession in named person and another or others, CP §4-105.
Partners, joint tenants, heirs, tenants in common or trustees.
Naming one and speaking of named person and another or others, CP §4-105.
Registered returnable containers and textiles, BR §19-306.
Inducing another to give up compensation.
State or local officer inducing by force, intimidation or threat, CR §3-703.

CRIMINAL LAW AND PROCEDURE —Cont'd
Industrial development financing.
False statements or reports, 83A §5-931.
Inhaling listed substances, CR §5-708.
Distribution of inhalant and instructions on
inhaling, CR §5-709.
Insane persons.
Defense of not criminally responsible by reason of
insanity, Crim Rule 4-314.
District Court.
Authority of court as to competency or sanity of
criminal defendants, CJ §4-202.
Pleas.
Not criminally responsible by reason of insanity.
Permitted pleas, Crim Rule 4-242.
Insanity defense.
Not criminally responsible, CP §§3-109 to 3-123.
See NOT CRIMINALLY RESPONSIBLE.
Installment loans.
Violations of licensing provisions, FI §11-304.
Installment sales, CL §12-636.
Insufficient evidence.
Motion for judgment of acquittal on grounds of,
CP §6-104.
Insurance.
Agents and brokers, IN §10-131.
Medical professional liability insurance.
Exclusive appointment agreements
prohibited, IN §10-133.
Title insurance agents and brokers, IN §10-132.
Automobile insurance fund.
Filing false notice or document, IN §20-701.
Examinations, investigations or hearings.
Failure to appear, testify, produce evidence or
give answer, IN §2-203.
General criminal penalty, IN §1-301.
Liquidation, rehabilitation, etc., of insurers.
Contributing to impairment, IN §9-231.
Obstruction, interference or failure to cooperate
with commissioner, IN §9-230.
Receipt of premium after insolvency, IN §9-232.
Nonprofit health service plans, IN §14-140.
Premium finance companies, IN §23-506.
Surplus lines insurance.
Delivery of false binder or cover note, IN
§3-326.
Workers' compensation insurance.
Approval of policy forms, IN §19-402.
Setting premium rates, IN §19-403.
Insurance acquisitions disclosure and control,
IN §7-807.
Domestic insurer or insurance holding company.
Failure to file statement or making
unauthorized acquisition, IN §7-309.
Registration of insurers.
Holding company systems.
Failure to file statement, IN §7-607.
Intent to defraud, proving intent, CR §1-401.
Interfering with arrest, CR §9-408.
Interior designer license violations generally,
BOP §8-502.
Internet solicitation.
Sexual solicitation of minor.
Generally, CR §3-324.
Interpreters for criminal proceedings.
Court appointment to help defendant,
compensation and expenses, CP §1-202.
Incompetency or not criminally responsible
proceedings, CP §3-103.
Interrogations.
Conduct, PS §3-104.

CRIMINAL LAW AND PROCEDURE —Cont'd
Interrogations —Cont'd
Law enforcement officers and personnel.
Rights of officers, PS §3-104.
Interstate agreement on detainers.
After execution of request for final disposition,
request void, COR §8-405.
Temporary custody, COR §§8-407, 8-413.
Intoxication not defense.
Voluntary intoxication, CR §9-406.
Invasion of privacy.
Crimes against privacy, CR §§3-901 to 3-907.
Camera surveillance, CR §3-903.
Divulging or failing to deliver private
communications, CR §3-906.
Opening letter without permission, CR §3-905.
Unlawful picketing and assembly, CR §3-904.
Video tape distributor publishing information,
CR §3-907.
Visual surveillance, CR §3-901.
With prurient intent, CR §3-902.
Investigations.
Appeals from criminal investigations, AppRev
Rule 8-123.
Judicial notice of adjudicative facts, Evid Rule
5-201.
Juke boxes.
Keeping without license, BR §17-1309.
Harford county, BR §17-1318.
Junk dealers.
Failure to submit report, BR §17-1022.
General penalty, BR §17-1024.
Historic markers or plaques, BR §17-1012.
Licenses, BR §17-1013.
Purchases from minors, BR §17-1023.
Junkyards and related facilities.
Dumping into waters of state, EN §5-10A-02.
Definitions, EN §5-10A-01.
Evidence of violation, EN §5-10A-03.
Jury.
Appeals.
Right to jury trial, CJ §12-401.
Array, CJ §8-421.
Capital cases.
Disqualification by trial judge, CJ §8-404.
Peremptory challenges, CJ §8-420.
Challenges, CJ §8-409.
Peremptory challenges, CJ §8-420.
Employers.
Prohibited acts, CJ §§8-501, 8-502.
Failure to appear for jury service, CJ §8-504.
Failure to complete jury service, CJ §8-505.
Failure to return completed juror qualification
form, CJ §8-503.
Generally.
See JURY.
Grand jury.
Secrecy violations, CJ §8-507.
Impartial and unanimous, MD Const DofR Art 21.
Instructions to jury.
See JURY.
Intimidating or corrupting juror, CR §9-305.
Judge of law and fact, MD Const DofR Art 23.
Juror qualification form.
Failure to return completed form, CJ §8-503.
Material misrepresentation, CJ §8-506.
Right to trial by jury, CP §6-101; US Const Art III
§2; Amds 6, 7.
Role of jury.
Judge of law and fact, CP §6-102.

CRIMINAL LAW AND PROCEDURE —Cont'd
Jury —Cont'd
　Verdict.
　　See VERDICT.
Justices of the peace.
　Trial magistrates.
　　Post conviction procedure.
　　　See POST CONVICTION PROCEDURE.
Juvenile causes.
　Evidence.
　　Certain information inadmissible in subsequent
　　　criminal proceedings, CJ §3-8A-12.
　　Effect of proceedings under subtitle, CJ
　　　§3-8A-23.
　Jurisdiction.
　　Waiver.
　　　Prosecution barred in absence of waiver, CJ
　　　　§3-8A-07.
　Transfer of criminal cases to juvenile court, CP
　　§4-202.
　　At sentencing, CP §4-202.2.
　　Cases involving detained child, CP §4-202.1.
　　Expungement of criminal charge transferred to
　　　juvenile court, CP §10-106.
　　Procedure and form, Juv Rule 11-601.
　Waiver of jurisdiction.
　　Prosecution barred in absence of waiver, CJ
　　　§3-8A-07.
Juvenile curfew, 25B §13C-1.
Juvenile detention facility.
　Escape.
　　Departing from custody without authorization.
　　　Escape in second degree, CR §9-405.
　　With assault.
　　　Escape in first degree, CR §9-404.
Keys.
　State-owned keys, theft or duplication, CR §7-204.
Kidnapping, CR §§3-501 to 3-503.
　Child kidnapping, CR §3-503.
　Generally, CR §3-502.
　Home or usual place of abode.
　　Defined, CR §3-501.
　Parent carrying minor in or out of state.
　　Not kidnapping, CR §3-502.
Kittens.
　Selling less than eight week old puppy, CR
　　§10-613.
Knives and switchblades.
　Weapons.
　　See WEAPONS.
Kosher food.
　False or misleading representations, CL §14-901.
Labor and employment relations.
　See LABOR AND EMPLOYMENT RELATIONS.
Laboratories.
　Medical laboratories.
　　Violations of provisions, HG §17-216.
Landscape architect violations generally, BOP
　§9-605.
Land surveyor license violations, BOP §15-610.
Land trust grant fund.
　Violation of provisions, NR §3-2A-12.
Laser pointer.
　Misuse of laser pointer, CR §3-806.
Law enforcement officers and personnel.
　Criminal activity.
　　Statute of limitations for administrative
　　　charges, waiver, PS §3-106.
　Impersonating a police officer, PS §3-502.
　Special police officers.
　　Acting or employing without commission, PS
　　　§3-315.

CRIMINAL LAW AND PROCEDURE —Cont'd
**Lead hazard reduction grant and loan
　programs.**
　False statements or reports, HS §4-712.
Leased or rented goods.
　Fraudulent conversion, CR §8-407.
Leave of inmate from confinement.
　Local correctional facility.
　　Violation of condition, COR §11-726.
　　Violation of restriction on movement, COR
　　　§11-726.
　Prerelease unit for women, COR §3-305.
Leaving scene of accident.
　Serious bodily harm, TR §27-113.
Letters.
　Opening letter without permission, CR §3-905.
Libraries.
　Theft or mutilation of books or other property, ED
　　§23-408.
Lie-detector tests, LE §3-702.
**Life imprisonment without possibility of
　parole.**
　Child kidnapping.
　　Rape or sexual offense conviction in same
　　　proceeding, CR §3-503.
　Defined, CR §2-101.
　Punishment for murder in first degree, CR §2-201.
　Rape in the first degree.
　　Child victim under age of 16 years, CR §3-303.
　Rules governing sentencing proceedings.
　　Adoption by court of appeals, CR §2-305.
　Sentencing procedure, CR §2-304.
　Sexual offense in the first degree.
　　Child victim under age of 16 years, CR §3-305.
**Life threatening injury by motor vehicle or
　vessel while impaired or under the
　influence,** CR §3-211.
　Alcohol concentration.
　　Determining, presumptions, evidentiary rules,
　　　CR §3-211.
　Charging documents, CR §3-212.
　Definitions, CR §3-211.
　Impaired by alcohol, CR §3-211.
　Impaired by controlled dangerous substance, CR
　　§3-211.
　Impaired by drugs, CR §3-211.
　Under the influence of alcohol or alcohol per se,
　　CR §3-211.
Limited liability companies.
　Appearance.
　　Return of summons as appearance, CP §4-203.
　Foreign companies.
　　Doing business without registration, CA
　　　§4A-1007.
Limited liability partnerships, revised act.
　Forfeiture of right to do business.
　　Transacting business after forfeiture, CA
　　　§9A-1015.
Limited partnerships.
　Foreign limited partnerships.
　　Doing business without registering, CA §10-907.
　Forfeiture of right to do business, CA §10-217.
Liquefied natural gas facilities, PUC §11-101.
Liquefied petroleum gas.
　Issuance of warrant, CL §11-606.
　Presumptive evidence of unlawful use, CL
　　§11-604.
　Return of property unlawfully seized, CL §11-605.
　Unlawful use of containers, CL §§11-603, 11-606.
Litter control law, CR §10-110.

CRIMINAL LAW AND PROCEDURE —Cont'd

Little joker.
Playing game prohibited, CR §12-103.

Livestock.
Certificate or paper showing livestock purebred.
Seller not providing purchaser, CR §8-901.

Local correctional facilities.
Leave, work release or home detention order.
Violation of restriction on movement, COR §11-726.
Retake warrants, issuance by managing official or designee, COR §11-803.

Long arm jurisdiction.
Process issued across county lines, CP §1-205.

Lotteries, CR §§12-210 to 12-212.
Agreement to repay if ticket drawn, CR §12-207.
Authorized lotteries.
Applicability of provisions, CR §12-202.
Bill of particulars.
Charging document, CR §12-211.
Book, list, slip or record, possession, CR §12-205.
Charging document, CR §12-211.
Civil recovery.
Person giving money to obtain lottery device, CR §12-203.
Conveyance or transfer occurring during lottery.
Void, CR §12-209.
Enhanced sentence.
Repeat offenders, CR §12-210.
Gift enterprise.
Barter, sale or trade, CR §12-212.
Holding lottery, prohibition, CR §12-203.
Insuring against drawing of lottery ticket, CR §12-207.
Liberal construction of provision, CR §12-208.
Lottery device.
Allowing place to be used for purpose of selling or bartering, CR §12-204.
Defined, CR §12-201.
Keeping place for purposes of selling or bartering, CR §12-204.
Possession or bringing into state, CR §12-205.
Selling for lottery draw, prohibition, CR §12-203.
Prizes available.
Publishing, CR §12-206.
Publishing account of lottery, CR §12-206.
Repeat offenders.
Enhanced sentenced, CR §12-210.
Sentencing of repeat offenders, CR §12-210.
State lottery.
Inapplicability of provision, CR §12-202.

LSD.
Importers, CR §5-614.
Volume dealers, enhanced penalty, CR §5-612.

Mace.
Wearing or carrying with intent to injure, CR §4-101.

Machine guns, CR §§4-401 to 4-407.
Confiscation or destruction of seized machine gun, CR §4-402.
Definitions, CR §4-401.
Evidence of possession.
Presence in room, boat or vehicle, CR §4-402.
Exceptions to possession prohibition, CR §4-402.
Fee for registering, CR §4-403.
Possession, CR §4-402.
Presumption of aggressive or offensive purposes, CR §4-405.
Public record exception.
Registration data, CR §4-403.

CRIMINAL LAW AND PROCEDURE —Cont'd

Machine guns —Cont'd
Registration by person acquiring machine gun, CR §4-403.
Registration of machine guns manufactured or handled by manufacturer, CR §4-403.
Search warrants to seize illegally possessed machine gun, CR §4-402.
Statute of limitations for prosecutions.
Use for aggressive or offensive purposes, CR §4-405.
Uniformity of interpretation and construction of subtitle, CR §4-406.
Uniform machine gun act.
Short title, CR §4-407.
Use for aggressive or offensive purposes, CR §4-405.
Use in commission of crime, CR §4-404.

Mail.
Opening letter without permission, CR §3-905.

Malfeasance, misfeasance or nonfeasance.
See MALFEASANCE, MISFEASANCE OR NONFEASANCE.

Malicious destruction of property, CR §6-301.
Aggregation of damages, CR §6-301.
Damage of at least $500.
Penalty, CR §6-301.
Damage of less than $500.
Penalty, CR §6-301.
Restitution.
Graffiti, CR §6-301.
Throwing object at vehicle, CR §6-302.
Value of damages, CR §6-301.

Mandatory sentence for crime of violence.
Second, third or fourth conviction, CR §14-101.

Manslaughter.
By vehicle or vessel, CR §2-209.
Indictment, sufficiency, CR §2-209.
Vehicle defined, CR §2-209.
Vessel defined, CR §2-101.
Charging document, sufficiency, CR §2-208.
Manslaughter by vehicle or vessel, CR §2-209.
Fetus.
Murder or manslaughter of viable fetus, CR §2-103.
Punishment, CR §2-207.
Spousal adultery not mitigating factor, CR §2-207.
Year and day rule.
Rule eliminated in homicide prosecutions, CR §2-102.

Marijuana.
Controlled paraphernalia, CR §5-620.
Defined, CR §5-101.
Drug paraphernalia, CR §5-619.
Importers, unlawful amounts, smaller amounts, CR §5-614.
Schedule I, CR §5-402.
Volume dealers, enhanced penalty, CR §5-612.

Marriage.
Certificates.
Disposition.
Violations of provisions, FL §2-409.
Incest, FL §2-202.
Licenses.
Issuance.
Prohibited acts by clerks, FL §2-405.
Marriage without license, FL §2-401.
Minors.
Restrictions on marriages of certain minors.
Violations, FL §2-302.

CRIMINAL LAW AND PROCEDURE —Cont'd
Marriage —Cont'd
Performance of ceremony.
Prohibited acts, FL §2-406.
Records and reports.
Violations of provisions by clerks, FL §2-503.
Solicitation, FL §2-408.
Maryland economic adjustment fund.
False statement or report, 83A §6-511.
Maryland historical trust.
Archaeological property, violations, SF §5A-346.
Historical and cultural museum assistance
program.
False statements or reports, SF §5A-359.
Maryland home financing program.
False statements or reports, HS §4-816.
Maryland housing rehabilitation program.
False statements or reports, HS §4-933.
**Maryland-national capital park and planning
commission.**
Citation issued for misdemeanor violation.
Notice to appear, promise to appear, failure to
appear, 28 §2-120.1.
Conflicts of interest, 28 §2-115.
Effect of article on legal actions, 28 §1-102.
Right of entry.
Restraint or hindrance, 28 §2-116.
Violations of provisions, 28 §2-120.
Maryland stem cell research program.
Human cloning prohibited, 83A §5-2B-13.
Unused material provided by persons being
treated for infertility.
For profit transactions, solicitation for valuable
consideration.
Prohibition, penalty, 83A §5-2B-12.
Maryland-Washington metropolitan district.
Commission in fractions, 28 §5-113.
Street names and house numbers.
Changing.
Violations of rules and regulations, 28 §5-117.
Maryland-Washington regional district.
Building permits.
Issuance in violation of provisions, 28 §8-120.
Roads.
Unauthorized grading, 28 §7-113.
Zoning.
Licenses.
Issuance of invalid licenses, 28 §8-109.
Massage therapists, HO §3-5A-11.
Mass transit.
Fare citations.
Failure to appear, TR §7-704.1.
Provision violations, TR §7-705.
Medicaid fraud, CR §§8-508 to 8-517.
Benefit card, unauthorized possession, CR §8-515.
Business entity violation, fine, CR §8-516.
Civil penalty, CR §8-517.
Conversion of benefit or payment by state health
plan, CR §8-510.
Criminal penalties, CR §8-516.
Death resulting from violation, penalty, CR
§8-516.
Definitions, CR §8-508.
Defrauding state health plan, CR §8-509.
False statement to aid qualifications to receive
reimbursement, CR §8-513.
Kickback or bribe in connection with state health
plan, CR §8-511.
Obtaining benefit by fraud, CR §8-514.
Rebate, fee or charge for referral, CR §8-512.
Restitution, CR §8-517.

CRIMINAL LAW AND PROCEDURE —Cont'd
Medicaid fraud —Cont'd
Serious injury resulting from violation, penalty,
CR §8-516.
Value of money, goods or services $500 or more,
penalty, CR §8-516.
Medical records.
Personal medical records.
Concealment of records, HG §4-401.
Violations of provisions, HG §4-309.
Megan's law.
Community notification, CP §§11-709 to 11-712,
11-718.
See SEX OFFENDER REGISTRATION.
Registration of sex offenders, CP §§11-701 to
11-726.
See SEX OFFENDER REGISTRATION.
Mental hygiene law.
Disposition of property on escape of individual,
HG §16-303.
Facility operators without licenses, HG §10-1001.
Interfering with rights of patients, HG §10-1003.
Making false applications or certificates, HG
§10-1002.
Records.
Failure to comply with provisions, HG §10-1004.
Mentally defective or mentally incapacitated.
Rape in second degree.
Victim mentally defective or incapacitated, CR
§3-304.
Sexual offense in the second degree.
Victim mentally defective or incapacitated, CR
§3-306.
Sexual offense in the third degree.
Victim mentally defective or incapacitated, CR
§3-307.
Mentally ill.
Incompetency to stand trial, CP §§3-101 to 3-108.
See INCOMPETENCY TO STAND TRIAL.
Insane persons. See within this heading, "Insane
persons."
Not criminally responsible, CP §§3-109 to 3-123.
See NOT CRIMINALLY RESPONSIBLE.
Mercuric oxide batteries.
Disposal and recycling.
Violations, EN §6-902.
Merger of offenses.
Common law misdemeanor into statutory felony.
Prohibition, CP §4-104.
Methamphetamines.
Importers, CR §5-614.
Methaqualone.
Importers, CR §5-614.
Methyl alcohol.
Putting in medicine, CR §8-902.
Metrorail and metrobus.
Fare citations.
Failure to appear, TR §7-704.1.
Mass transit violations, TR §7-705.
Migrant labor.
Prohibited acts, LE §7-507.
Military organization insignia or name.
Unauthorized use, BR §19-207.
Militia.
Exclusion of members from places of amusement
or recreation, PS §13-904.
Misapplication or conversion of property, PS
§13-903.
Sale, purchase or improper use of property, PS
§13-902.
Unlawful wearing of uniform, PS §13-901.

CRIMINAL LAW AND PROCEDURE —Cont'd
Milk and milk products.
Fluid dairy products violations, AG §11-414.
Minimum wage.
Prohibited acts, LE §3-428.
Mining.
Conflicts of interest in strip mining.
State employees not to have financial interest,
EN §15-527.
Deep mine control, EN §15-618.
Strip mining.
Operation without license, EN §15-520.
Surface mining.
Failure to obtain license, EN §15-807.
Failure to obtain permit, EN §15-808.
Violation of title, EN §15-1001.
Minority business participation violations, SF
§14-308.
Minors.
Abduction of child under 16 for purposes of
prostitution, CR §11-305.
Access to firearm, CR §4-104.
Alcoholic beverages.
Citation for violations, CR §10-119.
Jurisdiction, CR §10-120.
Misrepresentation of age, CR §10-113.
False documentation, CR §10-115.
Underage consumption.
Furnishing or allowing, exceptions, CR
§10-117.
Kegs, CR §10-118.
Obtaining for underage consumption, CR
§10-116.
Underage possession, CR §10-114.
Child abuse, CR §3-601.
Controlled dangerous substance crimes.
Use of minor manufacture, distribute or deliver,
CR §5-628.
Dangerous weapons.
Carrying or wearing after prohibited hours, CR
§4-101.
Juvenile curfew, 25B §13C-1.
Kidnapping.
Child kidnapping, CR §3-503.
Marriage, FL §2-302.
Murder in first degree.
Death sentence.
Not imposed on persons under 18 years at
time of murder, CR §2-202.
Obscenity and pornography.
Adult sexual displays.
Allowing minor to remain on premises where
activity displayed, CR §11-104.
Bookstores and entertainment venues in
certain counties, CR §11-104.1.
Exhibiting to minor, CR §11-103.
Selling or offering to, CR §11-102.
Child pornography, CR §11-207.
Removal of child pornography from Internet,
CR §11-208.1.
Hiring minor for prohibited acts, CR §11-209.
Sale or distribution of obscene matter, CR
§11-203.
Visual representation of child under 16 engaged
in certain acts.
Possession, CR §11-208.
Parent carrying child in or out of state.
Not kidnapping, CR §3-502.
Pepper mace.
Possessing prohibited, CR §4-101.

CRIMINAL LAW AND PROCEDURE —Cont'd
Minors —Cont'd
Rape in first degree.
Child victim under 16 years of age.
Continuing course of conduct against child,
CR §3-315.
Life imprisonment, CR §§3-303, 3-313.
Rape in second degree, CR §3-304.
Continuing course of conduct against child, CR
§3-315.
Life imprisonment, CR §3-313.
Sale of minor, CR §3-603.
Sexual conduct between juvenile services
employee and confined child, CR §3-314.
Sexual offense in the first degree.
Child victim under age of 16 years.
Continuing course of conduct against child,
CR §3-315.
Life imprisonment, CR §§3-305, 3-313.
Sexual offense in the second degree.
Victim under 14 years of age, CR §3-306.
Continuing course of conduct against child,
CR §3-315.
Life imprisonment, CR §3-313.
Sexual offense in the third degree, CR §3-307.
Continuing course of conduct against child, CR
§3-315.
Sexual offense in the fourth degree, CR §3-308.
Sexual solicitation of minor, CR §3-324.
Tobacco products.
Possession by minor.
Acting as agent of employer.
Inapplicability, CR §10-108.
Citation issued to minor, CR §10-108.
Prohibition, CR §10-108.
Sales to minors.
Coupons contained in newspaper, magazine or
other publication.
Inapplicability of prohibition, CR §10-107.
Defense.
Examination of purchaser's driver's license
or other identification, CR §10-107.
Each violation separate, CR §10-107.
Prohibited, CR §10-107.
Witnesses.
Testimony by child in criminal case, CJ §9-103.
Misdemeanor prosecutions.
Statute of limitations, CJ §5-106.
Misuse of telephone facilities and equipment,
CR §3-804.
Mobile seafood vendors, TR §24-304.
Money transmission.
Knowing and willful violation of subtitle, FI
§12-430.
**Monitoring or recording telephone
conversation.**
State personnel, CR §9-602.
Morphine.
Importers, CR §5-614.
Volume dealers, enhanced penalty, CR §5-612.
Mortgages and deeds of trust.
Mortgage lenders.
Misappropriation or conversion, FI §11-523.
Willful violations of provisions, FI §11-523.
Mortgage originators.
Willful violations of provisions, FI §11-617.
Secondary mortgage loans, CL §12-414.
Morticians.
Title violations generally, HO §7-508.
Unauthorized practice of mortuary science.
Injunction no bar to criminal prosecution, HO
§7-316.1.

CRIMINAL LAW AND PROCEDURE —Cont'd

Motions.
Insufficient evidence.
Motion for judgment of acquittal on grounds of, CP §6-104.
New trial, CP §6-105.

Motor carrier tax.
Violations of provisions, TG §13-1020.

Motor clubs.
Representatives.
Acting without registration, IN §§26-501, 26-502.
Unlicensed motor clubs, IN §§26-501, 26-502.

Motor fuel inspection.
Refueling service for disabled drivers, BR §10-320.
Violation of provisions, BR §10-324.
Petroleum transporters, BR §10-411.

Motor fuel tax, TG §§13-1029 to 13-1031.
See MOTOR FUEL TAX.

Motor vehicles.
Accessories, TR §26-101.
Antitheft laws, TR §§14-101 to 14-110.
See MOTOR VEHICLE THEFT.
Automobile insurance fund.
Filing false notice or document, IN §20-701.
Disabled drivers.
Parking permit violations, TR §13-616.1.
Temporary parking permits, TR §13-616.2.
Refueling service by retail dealer, BR §10-320.
Special registration plate violations, TR §13-616.
Driver's license exemptions.
Provision violations, TR §16-102.
Driving under the influence.
See DRIVING UNDER THE INFLUENCE.
Excise tax.
Payment failures, TR §13-809.
Hit and run, TR §27-101.
Homicide by vehicle while impaired or under the influence, CR §§2-501 to 2-508.
Life threatening injury by motor vehicle while impaired or under the influence, CR §3-211.
Mobile seafood vendors.
Provision violations, TR §24-304.
Owning or controlling vehicles.
Offenses by persons owning or controlling, TR §26-102.
Parties to crime, TR §26-101.
Preventive maintenance program.
Provision violations, TR §23-305.
Registration violations, TR §13-402.
Vehicles of nonresidents, TR §13-402.1.
School vehicle regulations.
Violations, TR §25-110.
Theft, CR §7-105.
Owner's affidavit, CR §7-105.1.
Traffic citations.
See MOTOR VEHICLES.

Multilevel distribution companies.
Violations of provisions, BR §14-305.

Municipal corporations.
Officers and employees.
Removal of elected officials convicted of crimes, MD Const Art XV §2.

Murder.
Charging document, sufficiency, CR §2-208.
Fetus.
Murder or manslaughter of viable fetus, CR §2-103.
Murder in the first degree.
Death sentence, CR §§2-201, 2-202.
Automatic review by court of appeals, CR §2-401.

CRIMINAL LAW AND PROCEDURE —Cont'd

Murder —Cont'd
Murder in the first degree —Cont'd
Death sentence —Cont'd
Notice of intent to seek or withdrawal of intent.
Filing with clerk of court of appeals, CR §2-301.
Procedure, CR §2-303.
Rules governing sentencing proceedings, adoption, CR §2-305.
Indictment, sufficiency, CR §2-208.
Life imprisonment without possibility of parole, CR §§2-201, 2-203.
Defined, CR §2-101.
Procedure, CR §2-304.
Rules governing sentencing proceedings, adoption, CR §2-305.
Verdict.
Jury to state degree of murder found, CR §2-302.
Murder in the second degree.
Indictment, sufficiency, CR §2-208.
Verdict.
Jury to state degree of murder found, CR §2-302.
Verdict.
Jury to state degree found, CR §2-302.
Year and day rule.
Rule eliminated in homicide prosecutions, CR §2-102.

Museums.
Historical and cultural museum assistance program.
False statements or reports, SF §5A-359.

National crime prevention and privacy compact, CP §§10-237 to 10-250.
See NATIONAL CRIME PREVENTION AND PRIVACY COMPACT.

Natural resources.
Police force.
Violations of subtitle, NR §1-209.

Natural resources police force.
Pursuit of offenders across Maryland-Virginia water boundary, NR §1-210.

Neighborhood revitalization division.
Neighborhood business development program.
False statement or reports, HS §6-311.

Newspaper theft, CR §7-106.

New trial.
Motion for, CP §6-105.
Victim or victim's representative.
Rights in connection with hearing on motion, CP §6-106.

Nolle prosequi.
Costs, payment by applicant, CP §1-208.
Defined, CP §1-101.
Drug or alcohol treatment requirement attached, CP §6-229.

Nolo contendere.
Defined, CP §1-101.

Nonprofit health service plans, IN §14-140.

Not criminally responsible, CP §§3-109 to 3-123.
See NOT CRIMINALLY RESPONSIBLE.

Nudity and sexual displays.
Violation of municipal ordinances regulating, 23A §4A.

Nuisances.
Secretary of environment or local health officers.
Abatement order, failure to obey, EN §10-302.

CRIMINAL LAW AND PROCEDURE —Cont'd
Nuisances —Cont'd
Secretary of environment or local health officers
—Cont'd
Interference with secretary or representative,
EN §10-303.
Notice of abatement, violation, EN §10-301.
Rules and regulations, violation, EN §10-304.
Secretary of health and mental hygiene or local
health officers.
Interference or refusal to allow abatement, HG
§20-311.
Notice of abatement, violating, HG §§20-309,
20-310.
Rules or regulations, violating, HG §20-312.
Nurses.
Title violations.
Generally, HO §8-710.
Nursing home administrators.
Title violations.
Generally, HO §9-407.
Nursing referral service agencies.
Operation without license, HG §19-4B-05.
Obscenity and pornography.
Acceptance of obscene matter.
Required as condition of sale, allocation or
consignment, CR §11-206.
Adult sexual displays, CR §§11-101 to 11-107.
Advertising, displaying for purposes of, CR
§11-105.
Definitions, CR §11-101.
Minors.
Allowing minor to remain on premises where
activity displayed, CR §11-104.
Bookstores and entertainment venues in
certain counties, CR §11-104.1.
Exhibiting to minor, CR §11-103.
Selling or offering to, CR §11-102.
Presumption as operator of premises, CR
§11-106.
Advertising obscene matter, CR §11-205.
Anne Arundel county.
Obscene performances, prohibition, CR §11-204.
Bona fide scientific, educational, governmental,
artistic, news or other justification.
Exemption from provisions, CR §11-210.
Bringing or sending obscene matter into state, CR
§11-202.
Charles county.
Obscene performances, prohibition, CR §11-204.
Child pornography, CR §11-207.
Removal of child pornography from Internet, CR
§11-208.1.
Condition of sale, allocation or consignment.
Acceptance of obscene matter, CR §11-206.
Court ordering destruction of obscene matter, CR
§11-211.
Definitions, CR §11-201.
Destruction of obscene matter under court order,
CR §11-211.
Distributing obscene matter in state, CR §11-202.
To minors, CR §11-203.
Exemptions from provisions, CR §11-210.
Howard county.
Obscene performances, prohibition, CR §11-204.
Indecent exposure.
Punishment, CR §11-107.
Injunctions.
Distributing, exhibiting, importing or publishing
obscene matter, CR §11-202.

CRIMINAL LAW AND PROCEDURE —Cont'd
Obscenity and pornography —Cont'd
Minors.
Adult sexual displays.
Allowing minor to remain on premises where
activity displayed, CR §11-104.
Bookstores and entertainment venues in
certain counties, CR §11-104.1.
Exhibiting to minor, CR §11-103.
Selling or offering to, CR §11-102.
Child pornography, CR §11-207.
Removal of child pornography from Internet,
CR §11-208.1.
Hiring minor for prohibited acts, CR §11-209.
Sale or distribution of obscene matter, CR
§11-203.
Visual representation of child under 16 engaged
in certain acts.
Possession, CR §11-208.
Obscene performances, prohibition.
Certain counties, CR §11-204.
Possessing obscene matter with intent to
distribute, CR §11-202.
Sale or distribution of obscene matter, CR
§11-202.
To minors, CR §11-203.
Seizure and destruction of obscene matter, CR
§11-202.
Somerset county.
Obscene performances, prohibition, CR §11-204.
Surrender of obscene matter, CR §11-202.
Wicomico county.
Obscene performances, prohibition, CR §11-204.
Worcester county.
Obscene performances, prohibition, CR §11-204.
Obstruction of justice, CR §9-306.
Occupational safety and health.
Administrative search warrant.
Generally, LE §5-211.
Advance notice of inspections.
Prohibition, LE §5-805.
False representations and statements.
Prohibition, LE §5-804.
Willful violation causing death.
Criminal fine and imprisonment, LE §5-806.
Occupational therapists.
Title violations.
Generally, HO §10-407.
Office of legislative audits, SG §2-1227.
Opening letter without permission, CR §3-905.
Opium.
Importers, CR §5-614.
Possession, CR §5-503.
Volume dealers, enhanced penalty, CR §5-612.
Optometrists.
Title violations.
Generally, HO §11-505.
Order to report to place of confinement.
Failure to obey.
Escape in the second degree, CR §9-405.
Organizational insignia or name.
Unauthorized use, BR §19-207.
Organized crime.
Defined, CA §1-405.
Injunction against operation of business, CA
§1-405.
Outdoor concerts.
Acting as promoter without license, BR §17-1407.
Oysters and clams.
Nonnative oysters.
Introduction into waters of state.
Violation of requirements, NR §4-1008.

CRIMINAL LAW AND PROCEDURE —Cont'd

Paddle wheel.

Anne Arundel county.

Gaming events generally, CR §§13-401 to 13-408.

Political fundraisers, CR §13-406.

Baltimore City.

Gaming events generally, CR §§13-501 to 13-510.

Political fundraisers, CR §13-506.

Baltimore county.

Gaming events generally, CR §§13-601 to 13-607.

Political fundraisers, CR §13-605.

Carroll county.

Gaming events generally, CR §§13-901 to 13-909.

Prizes allowed, CR §13-905.

Cecil county.

Awarding prizes at gaming event, CR §13-1004.

Gaming events generally, CR §§13-1001 to 13-1005.

Frederick county.

Gaming provisions generally, CR §§13-1301 to 13-1307.

Gaming devices.

Defined as, CR §12-101.

Statewide gaming provisions, CR §§12-101 to 12-113.

See GAMING.

Gaming event provisions applicable to several counties, CR §§13-201 to 13-205.

Harford county.

Gaming generally, CR §§13-1501 to 13-1512.

Howard county, CR §13-1603.

Kent county.

Gaming generally, CR §§13-1701 to 13-1706.

Queen Anne's county.

Gaming generally, CR §§13-2001 to 13-2006.

St. Mary's county.

Gaming generally, CR §§13-2111 to 13-2115.

Wicomico county.

Gaming generally, CR §§13-2501 to 13-2508.

Worcester county.

Gaming generally, CR §§13-2619 to 13-2628.

Paint.

Antifouling paints, AG §5-906.

Pandering, CR §11-303.

Pari-mutuel betting.

Contests, events, jai-alai, CR §12-107.

Pari-mutuel betting tickets.

Counterfeit or altered betting tickets, CR §8-905.

Parking authorities.

Violations of rules and regulations, 41 §14-308.

Parking in Prince George's county.

Commercial vehicles, TR §21-1010.

Parole commission hearings.

Failure to appear or testify, false statements, COR §7-205.

Partnership assets.

Fraudulent conversion, CR §8-401.

Partnership rental housing program.

False statements or reports, HS §4-1209.

Partnerships.

Limited partnerships.

Foreign limited partnerships.

Doing business without registering, CA §10-907.

Patriotic organization insignia or name.

Unauthorized use, BR §19-207.

CRIMINAL LAW AND PROCEDURE —Cont'd

Patuxent institution.

Parole, work release program or leave of absence program.

Return to division of correction, COR §4-306.

Peace orders, CJ §§3-1501 to 3-1509.

See PEACE ORDERS.

Peeping toms.

Visual surveillance of individual in private place, CR §3-901.

With prurient intent, CR §3-902.

Pepper mace.

Minors possessing, prohibition, CR §4-101.

Wearing or carrying with intent to injure, CR §4-101.

Perjury, CR §9-101.

Adoption.

Interstate compact on adoption and medical assistance.

False, misleading or fraudulent claims, FL §5-4A-06.

Aged, assistance for.

False or fraudulent statements punishable as perjury, 88A §62.

Alcoholic beverages.

Affidavits, oaths or reports, 2B §16-501.

Application for license.

Caroline county, 2B §10-104.

Alcoholic beverage tax.

Willfully filing false return, TG §13-1002.

Boxing and wrestling tax.

Willful failure to file return, TG §13-1001.

Business occupations and professions.

Oaths generally, BOP §1-201.

Business regulation and licensure.

False swearing, BR §1-202.

Campaign finance reports or other filings.

False or misleading statements, EL §13-601.

Charging document, CR §§9-101, 9-103.

Commercial drivers' licenses.

Applications, TR §16-810.

Commissioner of division of correction.

False swearing before commissioner, COR §3-204.

Contradictory statements.

Proving either statement false without specifying which one, CR §9-101.

Elections.

False oath or affirmation, EL §16-501.

Environment.

Verification of documents.

Declaration made under penalty of perjury, EN §1-201.

Financial institution franchise tax.

Willfully filing false return, TG §13-1002.

General assembly.

Legislative policy committee.

False swearing by witness before committee, SG §2-408.

Standing committees.

False swearing before standing committee, SG §2-1104.

Health.

Verification of documents, HG §1-201.

Health occupations.

Verification of documents, HO §1-201.

Income tax.

Willfully filing false return, TG §13-1002.

Insurance.

Competitive rating, IN §11-343.

CRIMINAL LAW AND PROCEDURE —Cont'd
Perjury —Cont'd
  Insurance —Cont'd
    Investigations, examinations or hearings, IN
      §2-203.
    Nonprofit health service plans, IN §14-140.
  Landfills.
    Documents under oath.
      Effect of signed statement, EN §9-228.1.
  Land patents.
    False verification or oaths, RP §13-105.
  Marriage.
    False statements to obtain license or marriage
      ceremony, FL §2-407.
  Minors.
    False or fraudulent statements in application,
      88A §62.
  Mortgage lenders.
    License applications.
      False statements, FI §11-507.
  Nonprofit health service plans, IN §14-140.
  Procurement.
    Dispute resolution.
      False statements to appeals board, SF
        §15-212.
  Social services.
    False or fraudulent statements in applications
      for assistance, 88A §62.
  Statute of limitations, CR §9-101.
  Subornation of perjury, CR §9-102.
  Subornation of perjury, CR §9-102.
  Vessels and boats.
    Individual testifying not exempt from
      prosecution and punishment, NR §8-716.2.
  Water and sewer systems.
    Documents under oath.
      Effect of signed statement, EN §9-228.1.
  Witnesses.
    Perjurer prohibited from testifying, CJ §9-104.
  Workers' compensation.
    Claims procedure, LE §9-716.
Perverted sexual practices.
  General provisions.
    See SEXUAL OFFENSE.
Pesticides.
  Applicators, AG §5-211.
Pharmacists.
  Title violations.
    Generally, HO §12-707.
Phencyclidine.
  Importers, CR §5-614.
  Volume dealers, enhanced penalty, CR §5-612.
Photographing court proceedings.
  Prohibition, exception, violation contempt, CP
    §1-201.
Physicians.
  Title violations.
    Generally, HO §14-606.
Picketing and assembly.
  Unlawful picketing and assembly, CR §3-904.
Pimping.
  Receiving earnings from prostitution, CR §11-304.
Plastic containers.
  Sale without required label, EN §9-1710.
Pleas.
  Nolo contendere.
    Defined, CP §1-101.
  Not criminally responsible, CP §§3-109 to 3-123.
    See NOT CRIMINALLY RESPONSIBLE.
Plumbing violations generally, BOP §12-607.

CRIMINAL LAW AND PROCEDURE —Cont'd
Podiatrists.
  Title violations.
    Generally, HO §16-505.
Poisoning, attempt, CR §3-213.
Poisoning dog, CR §10-618.
Police.
  Authority, CP §2-102.
  Defined, CP §2-101.
  Disarming law enforcement officer, CR §4-103.
  Law enforcement procedures and arrest process.
    Generally, CP §§2-101 to 2-107.
    See POLICE.
Police brutality.
  Investigations and interrogations.
    Rights of officers, PS §3-104.
Political parties, EL §4-205.
Polysomnographic technologists.
  Title violations, HO §13-5C-23.
Ponzi schemes, CR §8-404.
Port administration.
  Conflicts of interest, TR §6-212.
  Provision violations, TR §6-602.
  Violation of regulations, TR §6-211.
Possessing stolen property, CR §7-104.
Post conviction procedure.
  General provisions, CP §§7-101 to 7-301.
    See POST CONVICTION PROCEDURE.
Posted property.
  Trespass, CR §6-402.
Potomac river.
  Recreational use.
    Violations of regulations, NR §1-604.
Poultry products inspection.
  Failure to obey subpoena, AG §4-228.
  False records, accounts and documents, AG
    §4-228.
  Proceedings to be in name of state, AG §4-225.
  Violations of provisions, AG §4-226.
Precious metals and gem dealers.
  Violations of act, BR §12-502.
Preliminary hearings.
  See PRELIMINARY HEARINGS.
Premium finance companies, IN §23-506.
Prescriptions and prescription drugs.
  Codeine, CR §5-503.
  Counterfeiting or altering, CR §5-601.
    Evidence, affidavit of by authorized provider,
      CR §5-705.
    Passing, issuing, making or possessing, CR
      §§5-606, 5-607.
  Defined, CR §5-101.
  Dispense defined, CR §5-101.
  Dispensing prescription drug without prescription
    or label, CR §5-701.
  Falsely assuming title of authorized provider or
    dispenser, CR §§5-601, 5-701.
  False name or address, CR §§5-601, 5-701.
  False prescription.
    Passing, possessing, CR §5-606.
  Fraud, deceit, misrepresentation, CR §§5-601,
    5-701.
  Methadone.
    Dispensing by authorized provider, CR §5-502.
  Possessing or administering without prescription,
    CR §§5-601, 5-701.
  Sale of drug different from that offered, CR
    §5-702.
  Unsolicited mailing, CR §5-703.
Presence of defendant.
  See PRESENCE OF DEFENDANT.

CRIMINAL LAW AND PROCEDURE —Cont'd
Presumptions.
Adult sexual displays.
Operator of premises, CR §11-106.
Bad checks.
Issuing or passing, CR §8-104.
Prosecution as theft, CR §7-107.
Controlled dangerous substances.
Registration of manufactures, distributors or dispensers.
Absence of proof person registrant, CR §5-807.
Litter control law.
Responsibility, CR §10-110.
Lottery.
Allowing place to be used for selling or bartering lottery devices.
Person deemed allowing, CR §12-204.
Machine gun possessed for aggressive or offensive purpose, CR §4-405.
Obscenity and pornography.
Adult sexual displays.
Operator of premises, CR §11-106.
Theft, CR §7-110.
Prince George's county.
General provisions.
See PRINCE GEORGE'S COUNTY.
Prisons and prisoners, COR §§8-801 to 8-803.
Alcoholic beverages.
Defined, COR §8-801.
Assault by inmate, CR §3-210.
Blood, seminal fluid, urine or feces.
Causing correctional employee to come in contact with, CR §3-205.
Contraband in correctional facilities.
Concealing or depositing in or about correctional facility to effect escape, COR §8-803.
Defined, COR §8-801.
Delivery by individual to inmate to effect escape, COR §8-803.
Possession with intent to deliver to inmate to effect escape, COR §8-803.
Receipt by inmate to effect escape, COR §8-803.
Contraband in places of confinement, CR §§9-410 to 9-417.
Alcoholic beverages.
Delivery or possession, CR §9-415.
Concealing in place of confinement.
Escape, CR §9-412.
Weapons, CR §9-414.
Controlled dangerous substances.
Delivery or possession, CR §9-416.
Definitions, CR §9-410.
Delivery to person in confinement, CR §9-412.
Alcoholic beverages, CR §9-415.
Controlled dangerous substances, CR §9-416.
For escape purposes, CR §9-412.
Weapons, CR §9-414.
Escape.
Delivery for purposes of, concealing in place of confinement, receiving, CR §9-412.
Possession with intent to deliver, CR §9-412.
Alcoholic beverages, CR §9-415.
Controlled dangerous substances, CR §9-416.
Weapons, CR §9-414.
Prescription.
Inapplicability to drug or substance possessed under, CR §9-411.
Receipt by person in confinement.
Escape, CR §9-412.

CRIMINAL LAW AND PROCEDURE —Cont'd
Prisons and prisoners —Cont'd
Contraband in places of confinement —Cont'd
Receipt by person in confinement —Cont'd
Weapons, CR §9-414.
Separate sentence, concurrent or consecutive sentences, CR §9-417.
Weapons.
Delivery, concealing, receiving, CR §9-414.
Controlled dangerous substances.
Defined, COR §8-801.
Convict-made goods.
Importation and sale prohibited, CL §11-903.
Definitions, COR §8-801.
Escape in the first degree, CR §9-404.
Escape in the second degree, CR §9-405.
Indecent exposure by inmate.
In presence of officer or authorized personnel, COR §8-803.
Sexual conduct between correctional employee and inmate, CR §3-314.
Weapons.
Defined, COR §8-801.
Delivery to inmate by individual, COR §8-802.
Possession by individual with intent to deliver to inmate, COR §8-802.
Receipt by inmate, COR §8-802.
Work release program.
Extended work release program.
Violation of terms and conditions, COR §3-807.
Failure to return, COR §3-803.
Privacy.
Crimes against privacy, CR §§3-901 to 3-907.
Camera surveillance, CR §3-903.
Divulging or failing to deliver private communications, CR §3-906.
Opening letter without permission, CR §3-905.
Unlawful picketing and assembly, CR §3-904.
Video tape distributor publishing information, CR §3-907.
Visual surveillance, CR §3-901.
With prurient intent, CR §3-902.
Private communication.
Divulging or failing to deliver, CR §3-906.
Private detective license violations, BOP §13-707.
Private home detention monitoring, BOP §20-701.
Procurement.
Falsification, concealment, etc., of material facts in connection with contracts, SF §11-205.1.
Professional counselors and therapists.
Graduate counselors and marriage and family therapists.
Violation of requirements for practicing as, HO §17-3A-02.1.
Title violations.
Generally, HO §17-402.
Property and casualty insurance.
Disclosure of fire loss investigation reports.
Violations, PS §9-606.
Property taxes.
General provisions, TP §§14-1001 to 14-1017.
See PROPERTY TAXES.
Prostitution.
Abducting child under 16 for purposes of, CR §11-305.
Definitions, CR §11-301.
House of prostitution, CR §11-306.
Pandering, CR §11-303.

CRIMINAL LAW AND PROCEDURE —Cont'd
Prostitution —Cont'd
  Prosecution and sentence for violating other laws,
    CR §11-302.
  Receiving earnings of prostitute, CR §11-304.
Psychologists.
  Title violations.
    Generally, HO §18-404.
Public accountancy violations generally, BOP
    §2-605.
Public assistance fraud, CR §§8-501 to 8-505.
  Application for assistance.
    Fraudulent statement or signature, CR §8-504.
  Change in household or financial condition.
    Failure to disclose.
      Fraud defined as, CR §8-501.
  Criminal penalty, CR §8-503.
    Fraudulent application, CR §8-504.
    Unauthorized disposition of donated food, CR
      §8-505.
  Donated food.
    Unauthorized disposition or conversion, CR
      §8-505.
  False statement or false representation.
    Fraud defined as, CR §8-501.
  Fraud defined, CR §8-501.
  Inapplicability of part, CR §8-502.
  Medicaid fraud, CR §§8-508 to 8-517.
    Benefit card, unauthorized possession, CR
      §8-515.
    Business entity violation, fine, CR §8-516.
    Civil penalty, CR §8-517.
    Conversion of benefit or payment by state
      health plan, CR §8-510.
    Criminal penalties, CR §8-516.
    Death resulting from violation, penalty, CR
      §8-516.
    Definitions, CR §8-508.
    Defrauding state health plan, CR §8-509.
    False statement to aid qualifications to receive
      reimbursement, CR §8-513.
    Kickback or bribe in connection with state
      health plan, CR §8-511.
    Obtaining benefit by fraud, CR §8-514.
    Rebate, fee or charge for referral, CR §8-512.
    Restitution, CR §8-517.
    Serious injury resulting from violation, penalty,
      CR §8-516.
    Value of money, goods or services $500 or more,
      penalty, CR §8-516.
  Prohibited, CR §8-503.
  Recitation, CR §8-503.
Public defender representation.
  Obtaining by fraud, CR §8-521.
Public ethics.
  Violations of title.
    Criminal penalties, SG §15-903.
Public officers and employees.
  Bribery, CR §9-201.
    Demanding or receiving bribe, CR §9-202.
  Extortion by state or local officers and employees,
    CR §3-702.
  Inducing another to give up compensation, CR
    §3-703.
  Monitoring or recording telephone conversation.
    State personnel, CR §9-602.
  Threats against, CR §3-708.
Public records.
  False statements and other crimes, CR §8-606.
Public service commission.
  Rule, order, etc., violations, PUC §13-101.

CRIMINAL LAW AND PROCEDURE —Cont'd
Public utility interference.
  Electrical equipment, CR §6-303.
  Gas equipment, CR §6-304.
  Water equipment, CR §6-305.
Punchboard.
  Frederick county.
    Generally, CR §13-1305.
Punishment.
  Cruel and unusual punishment, US Const Amd 8.
Puppies.
  Selling less than eight week old puppy, CR
    §10-613.
Pyramid promotional schemes, CR §8-404.
Rabies.
  Reports of possible rabies case.
    Failure or refusal to comply with provision, HG
      §18-316.
Radiation licensing violations, EN §8-509.
  Limitation on prosecution, EN §8-509.1.
**Radiation oncology/therapy, medical radiation,
    and nuclear medicine technologists.**
  Penalties for violations, HO §14-5B-19.
Radio.
  Broadcasting criminal proceeding.
    Prohibition, exception, violation contempt, CP
      §1-201.
Radio and television.
  Used, reconditioned, etc., sets, CL §14-803.
Raffles.
  Acceptance of credit to play gaming event.
    Prohibition, CR §12-108.
  Anne Arundel county, CR §§13-401 to 13-408.
  Baltimore City, CR §§13-501 to 13-510.
  Baltimore county, CR §§13-601 to 13-607.
  Carroll county, CR §§13-901 to 13-909.
    Definitions, chance books, prizes, CR §13-904.
  Cecil county, CR §§13-1001 to 13-1005.
  Charitable organizations, CR §12-106.
  Charles county, CR §§13-1101 to 13-1115.
  Dorchester county, CR §§13-1201 to 13-1207.
  Frederick county, CR §§13-1301 to 13-1307.
  Gaming events generally.
    Provisions applicable to several counties, CR
      §§13-101 to 13-205.
  Generally, statewide provisions, CR §12-106.
  Harford county, CR §§13-1501 to 13-1512.
  Kent county, CR §§13-1701 to 13-1706.
  Local provisions.
    Gaming events generally, CR §§13-101 to
      13-205.
  Montgomery county, CR §§13-1801 to 13-1815.
  Political committee or candidate for public office,
    CR §12-106.
  Prince George's county, CR §§13-1908 to 13-1911.
  Queen Anne's county, CR §§13-2001 to 13-2006.
  St. Mary's county, CR §§13-2111 to 13-2115.
  Somerset county, CR §13-2201.
  Talbot county.
    Provisions applicable to county, CR §13-2301.
  Wicomico county, CR §§13-2501 to 13-2508.
  Worcester county, CR §§13-2619 to 13-2628.
Railroads.
  Crimes involving.
    Arson and burning.
      Railroad cars, CR §§6-101 to 6-111.
    Breaking or damaging, CR §6-502.
    Definitions, CR §§6-501, 6-503.
    False train signal, CR §6-504.
    Interference with, CR §6-502.
    Railroad vehicle defined, CR §6-501.

CRIMINAL LAW AND PROCEDURE —Cont'd
Railroads —Cont'd
Crimes involving —Cont'd
Shooting or throwing object at, CR §6-505.
Unauthorized access to railroad vehicle, CR §6-503.
Unauthorized buying or selling of tickets access to railroad vehicle, CR §6-506.
Safety and health.
Prohibited acts, LE §5.5-122.
Rape.
Charging documents, CR §3-317.
Definitions, CR §3-301.
Imprisonment for life without possibility of parole.
Rape in the first degree.
Child victim under age of 16 years, CR §3-303.
Instructions judge may not use, CR §3-320.
Phrases describing element of common law rape.
Construction, CR §3-302.
Prior sexual conduct or chastity.
Evidence, CR §3-319.
Rape in the first degree, CR §3-303.
Attempted rape in the first degree, CR §3-309.
Continuing course of conduct against child, CR §3-315.
Life imprisonment, CR §§3-303, 3-313.
Rape in the second degree, CR §3-304.
Attempted rape in the second degree, CR §3-310.
Continuing course of conduct against child, CR §3-315.
Life imprisonment, CR §3-313.
Spousal defense, CR §3-318.
Venue.
Victim transported with intent to commit, CR §3-316.
Rape shield law, CR §3-319.
Real estate appraisers and home inspectors, BOP §16-706.
Real estate brokerage violations, BOP §17-613.
Real estate sales.
Builder surety bond violations, RP §11A-116.
New home deposits.
Surety bond violations, RP §10-305.
New home warranty misrepresentation, RP §10-609.
Public offering statement violations, RP §11A-112.
Real property.
Consideration for settlement of real estate transactions.
Payment or receipt, RP §14-127.
Deeds of trust.
Release fee violations, RP §7-106.
Interference with surveyor's markers, RP §12-111.
Reentry after eviction, RP §14-114.
Survey marker interference, RP §14-111.
Receiving stolen property.
Credit cards, CR §8-204.
Property obtained by stolen, counterfeit or misrepresented card, CR §8-209.
Reckless endangerment, CR §3-204.
Bill of particulars.
Charging document in general form, CR §3-206.
Charging documents, CR §3-206.
Defenses.
Judicially recognized defenses allowed, CR §3-209.
Evidence of serious physical injury.
Expert testimony admissible, not required, CR §3-208.

CRIMINAL LAW AND PROCEDURE —Cont'd
Reckless endangerment —Cont'd
Inmate's blood, seminal fluid, urine or feces.
Causing correctional employee to come in contact with, CR §3-205.
Recording or broadcasting criminal proceeding.
Prohibition, exception, violation contempt, CP §1-201.
Recording or broadcasting criminal trials.
See TRIAL.
Recording sounds or images without consent, CR §§7-306 to 7-310.
Records.
Access to public records.
Prohibited acts, SG §10-627.
Criminal justice information system, CP §§10-201 to 10-228.
See CRIMINAL JUSTICE INFORMATION SYSTEM.
Criminal records.
See RECORDS.
Criminal records generally.
See RECORDS.
Expungement of criminal records, CP §§10-101 to 10-109.
See EXPUNGEMENT OF RECORDS.
Refrigerators, iceboxes or freezer cabinets.
Abandonment, CR §10-109.
Registered organizational insignia or name.
Unauthorized use, BR §19-207.
Registered returnable containers and textiles.
Charging documents, BR §19-306.
Possession, evidence of, BR §19-307.
Prohibited acts, BR §19-304.
Search warrants, arrest warrants, BR §19-305.
Theft prosecution not precluded by subtitle, BR §19-302.
Registers of wills.
Acceptance of fees and gifts, ET §2-203.
Surety bond requirements, ET §2-204.
Rehypothecation of personal securities, CR §7-115.
Remission of fines and forfeitures, CP §1-207.
Removal of case from one county to another.
Defendant detained in correctional facility.
Presence of defendant in court to which case removed required for transfer, COR §9-301.
Removal of causes.
General provisions, MD Const Art IV §8.
Rental housing production program.
False statements or reports, HS §4-1511.
Rental vehicles.
Failure to return rental vehicle, CR §7-205.
Repossessed, reconditioner, rebuilt or secondhand property sales.
Failure to identify property, CL §14-2902.
Rescue squads.
Impersonating firefighters or emergency services personnel, PS §7-402.
Interference with or obstruction of emergency assistance, PS §7-402.
Residential child care program administrators, HO §20-405.
Residential child care program operators.
Operating without license, 49D §6-102.
Resisting arrest, CR §9-408.
Respiratory care practitioners, HO §14-5A-23.
Restitution.
Controlled dangerous substances, CR §5-610.
Destructive device violations, CR §4-503.

CRIMINAL LAW AND PROCEDURE —Cont'd
Restitution —Cont'd
False statement or rumor concerning destructive device or toxic material, CR §9-504.
Graffiti, CR §6-301.
Identity fraud, CR §8-301.
Leased or rented goods.
Fraudulent conversion, CR §8-407.
Public assistance fraud, CR §8-503.
Telecommunications services theft, CR §7-316.
Victims.
Restitution and other payments, CP §§11-601 to 11-633.
See CRIME VICTIMS' COMPENSATION.
Retail and wholesale establishments.
Day of rest violations, LE §3-704.
Sunday blue laws, BR §18-101.
Retail credit accounts, CL §12-515.
Retail installment sales, CL §12-636.
Retail-purchase agreements, CL §12-1110.
Retake warrants.
Issuance by warden, copy to state's attorney, COR §3-214.
Managing official of local correctional facility, issuance, COR §11-803.
Sheriff or police officer to execute on receipt, COR §3-214.
Notice to division of correction on arrest, COR §3-214.
Review of criminal sentences, CP §§8-101 to 8-109.
See SENTENCE AND PUNISHMENT.
Rifles.
Defined, CR §4-201.
Possession by person with mental disorder, PS §5-205.
Short-barreled rifle.
Defined, CR §4-201.
Rights of the accused, MD Const DofR Art 21; US Const Art III.
Counsel.
Right to representation, MD Const DofR Art 21.
Defense.
Appointment of counsel, MD Const DofR Art 21.
Indictment.
Copy of indictment, MD Const DofR Art 21.
Jury.
Impartial and unanimous jury, MD Const DofR Art 21.
Self-incrimination.
Prohibited, MD Const DofR Art 22.
Speedy trial.
Right to, MD Const DofR Art 21.
Federal right, US Const Amd 6.
Trial date, Crim Rule 4-271.
Witnesses.
Confrontation with witnesses, MD Const DofR Art 21.
Robbery, CR §§3-401 to 3-405.
Carjacking, CR §3-405.
Charging documents, CR §3-404.
Definitions, CR §3-401.
Generally, CR §3-402.
Proof of intent to withhold property of another, CR §3-401.
Robbery with dangerous weapon, CR §3-403.
Rules, criminal.
See CRIMINAL RULES.
Rules of the road.
See TRAFFIC LAWS.

CRIMINAL LAW AND PROCEDURE —Cont'd
Sabbath day violations.
Retail and wholesale establishments, LE §3-704.
Sabotage, CR §§9-701 to 9-708.
Acting with intent to hinder defense related activity.
Defective workmanship, CR §9-703.
Defense related activity defined, CR §9-701.
Injury to or interference with property, CR §9-702.
Conviction for violation of other laws, CR §9-708.
Definitions, CR §9-701.
Identification badges or cards at certain facilities.
Badge or card defined, CR §9-701.
Possession after employment or visit, CR §9-704.
Surrender after gaining possession, CR §9-705.
Surrender at end of employment or visit, CR §9-704.
Unauthorized use, CR §9-706.
Labor right not affected, CR §9-707.
St. Mary's county.
Open meetings act.
Repeated violations, 24 §4-211.
Violations, 24 §4-212.
Sale of minor, CR §3-603.
Sales and use tax.
See SALES AND USE TAX.
Sales finance companies.
Violations of licensing provisions, FI §11-419.
Savings and loan associations.
Conflicts of interest.
Director, officer or controlling person, FI §9-307.
Net worth certificates.
Violations of provisions, FI §9-224.
Prohibition on service as officer or director, FI §9-911.
Shares and shareholders.
Acquisition of shares of stock.
Violations of prohibitions, FI §9-216.
Violations of provisions, FI §§9-102, 9-913.
Withdrawing funds from failing institution, FI §9-914.
School activities.
Willful disturbance, ED §26-101.
School attendance.
Violations, ED §7-301.
School census information.
Withholding, ED §4-113.
School employees.
Nonpublic schools.
Convictions of certain crimes, ED §2-206.1.
School papers.
Sales, ED §26-201.
School premises.
Alcoholic beverages.
Drinking or possessing intoxicating beverages on school premises, ED §26-103.
Disturbing activities, ED §26-101.
Gangs.
Criminal gang offenses, CR §9-803.
Molesting or threatening students prohibited, ED §26-101.
Trespass on, ED §26-102.
Vehicle violations, TR §25-110.
School property.
Deadly weapons on, CR §4-102.
School records.
Arrest of pupils for reportable offenses.
Reporting, ED §7-303.

CRIMINAL LAW AND PROCEDURE —Cont'd
School records —Cont'd
Failure to file before private school ends
operations, ED §2-304.
School suspensions or expulsions.
Violations, ED §7-305.
Seafood vendors, mobile.
Provision violations, TR §24-304.
Search warrants.
See SEARCH WARRANTS.
Secondary mortgage loans, CL §12-414.
Secondhand watch dealers, CL §14-706.
Securities.
Securities act.
Exemptions.
Burden of proof in criminal proceedings, CA
§11-604.
Limitation of actions.
Returning indictments or informations, CA
§11-705.
Securities act.
General provisions, CA §§11-101 to 11-805.
See SECURITIES.
Security guards, BOP §19-607.
Security systems technicians.
Criminal penalties, BOP §18-504.
False statements in applications, BOP §18-503.
Misrepresentation, BOP §18-502.
Unlicensed businesses, BOP §18-501.
Sellers.
Removal of personal property.
Intent to defraud buyer, CR §8-403.
Semiconscious or unconscious person.
Duty of officer before charging with crime, CP
§2-107.
Sentencing on conviction of crime.
Generally.
See SENTENCE AND PUNISHMENT.
Serial numbers.
Altering, sale of good with altered number,
possession, CR §§6-306, 6-307.
Serious physical injury.
Assault or reckless endangerment.
Expert testimony admissible, not required, CR
§3-208.
Service of process.
Across county lines, CP §1-205.
Copy of process given defendant after service, CP
§1-206.
Summons of corporation or limited liability
company, CP §4-203.
Trial date, Crim Rule 4-271.
Severn river.
Vessels and boats.
Speed limit violations, NR §8-725.3.
Sex offender registration.
Notification escape and recapture, CP §11-712.
Sexual abuse of a minor, CR §3-602.
Limitation of actions, CJ §5-117.
Sexual abuse of a vulnerable adult, CR §§3-604,
3-606.
**Sexual conduct between correctional or
juvenile services employee and inmate or
confined child,** CR §3-314.
Sexual crimes.
Child abuse.
Sexual abuse of minor, CR §3-602.
Definitions, CR §3-301.
Incest, CR §3-323.
Indecent exposure, CR §11-107.
Pandering, CR §11-303.

CRIMINAL LAW AND PROCEDURE —Cont'd
Sexual crimes —Cont'd
Pimping.
Receiving earnings from prostitution, CR
§11-304.
Prostitution and related crimes, CR §§11-301 to
11-306.
Rape.
Charging documents, CR §3-317.
Imprisonment for life without possibility of
parole.
Rape in the first degree.
Child victim under age of 16 years, CR
§3-303.
Phrases describing element of common law
rape.
Construction, CR §3-302.
Prior sexual conduct or chastity.
Evidence, CR §3-319.
Rape in the first degree, CR §3-303.
Attempted rape in the first degree, CR
§3-309.
Continuing course of conduct against child,
CR §3-315.
Life imprisonment, CR §§3-303, 3-313.
Rape in the second degree, CR §3-304.
Attempted rape in the second degree, CR
§3-310.
Continuing course of conduct against child,
CR §3-315.
Life imprisonment, CR §3-313.
Spousal defense, CR §3-318.
Sexual abuse of minor, CR §3-602.
Sexual abuse of vulnerable adult, CR §§3-604,
3-606.
Sexual conduct between correctional or juvenile
services employee and inmate or confined
child, CR §3-314.
Sexual offense.
Charging documents, CR §3-317.
Drug induced conduct.
Sexual offense in the third degree.
Administering controlled dangerous
substance without person's knowledge,
CR §5-624.
Prior sexual conduct or chastity.
Evidence, CR §3-319.
Sexual offense in the first degree, CR §3-305.
Attempted sexual offense in the first degree,
CR §3-311.
Continuing course of conduct against child,
CR §3-315.
Life imprisonment, CR §3-313.
Sexual offense in the second degree, CR §3-306.
Attempted sexual offense in the second
degree, CR §3-312.
Continuing course of conduct against child,
CR §3-315.
Life imprisonment, CR §3-313.
Sexual offense in the third degree, CR §3-307.
Continuing course of conduct against child,
CR §3-315.
Drug induced conduct.
Administering controlled dangerous
substance without person's knowledge,
CR §5-624.
Sexual offense in the fourth degree, CR §3-308.
Spousal defense, CR §3-318.
Sexual solicitation of minor, CR §3-324.
Unnatural or perverted sexual practice, CR
§3-322.

CRIMINAL LAW AND PROCEDURE —Cont'd
Sexual offense.
Charging documents, CR §3-317.
Drug induced conduct.
Sexual offense in the third degree.
Administering controlled dangerous substance without person's knowledge, CR §5-624.
Instructions judge may not use, CR §3-320.
Prior sexual conduct or chastity.
Evidence, CR §3-319.
Sexual offense in the first degree, CR §3-305.
Attempted sexual offense in the first degree, CR §3-311.
Continuing course of conduct against child, CR §3-315.
Life imprisonment, CR §3-313.
Sexual offense in the second degree, CR §3-306.
Attempted sexual offense in the second degree, CR §3-312.
Continuing course of conduct against child, CR §3-315.
Life imprisonment, CR §3-313.
Sexual offense in the third degree, CR §3-307.
Continuing course of conduct against child, CR §3-315.
Drug induced conduct.
Administering controlled dangerous substance without person's knowledge, CR §5-624.
Sexual offense in the fourth degree, CR §3-308.
Spousal defense, CR §3-318.
Venue.
Victim transported with intent to commit, CR §3-316.
Sexual solicitation of minor, CR §3-324.
Shooting knife.
Transfer, prohibition, CR §4-105.
Shotguns.
Defined, CR §4-201.
Possession by person with mental disorder, PS §5-205.
Short-barreled shotgun.
Defined, CR §4-201.
Sick inmates temporarily removed from correctional facility, COR §9-602.
Silver.
Merchandise made of silver, CL §14-608.
Simulation of document to induce payment, CR §8-522.
Slot machines, CR §§12-301 to 12-307.
Antique slot machine.
Possession or ownership, CR §12-303.
Change of location of allowed machines, CR §12-307.
Defined, CR §12-301.
Antique slot machine, CR §12-303.
Distributing machines to persons allowed to purchase, CR §12-305.
Possessing, keeping or operating.
Antique slot machine, defense, CR §12-303.
Eligible organizations in specified counties, CR §12-304.
Prohibition, CR §12-302.
Registration and storage of machines previously allowed, CR §12-306.
Selling machines to persons allowed to purchase, CR §12-305.
Slugs.
Counterfeiting and issuing tokens, CR §8-612.
Depositing in vending machines.
Theft, CR §7-104.
Deception defined to include, CR §7-101.

CRIMINAL LAW AND PROCEDURE —Cont'd
Slugs —Cont'd
Depositing in vending machines —Cont'd
Theft —Cont'd
Slug defined, CR §7-101.
Manufacture, sell or give away, CR §8-613.
Small business development financing authority.
Guaranty fund.
False statements or reports to authority, 83A §5-1031.
Surety bond program.
False statements in applications, 83A §5-1040.
Smoke detectors.
Violations, PS §9-109.
Social workers.
Title violations.
Generally, HO §19-407.
Sodomy.
Punishment, CR §3-321.
Spam, CR §3-805.1.
Special police officers.
Acting or employing without commission, PS §3-315.
Speedy trial.
Constitutional provisions, MD Const DofR Arts 19, 21; US Const Amd 6.
Sprinkler systems.
Fire sprinkler contractor licensing violations, PS §9-905.
Violations, PS §9-206.
Stalking, CR §3-802.
Start-up business ventures.
Fraud and deceit, BR §14-127.
Privilege against self-incrimination, BR §14-112.
Violations of act, BR §14-128.
State buildings and grounds.
Violations by public, SF §4-607.
State employees.
Assisting another to violate subtitle, SPP §15-108.
Construction contract violations, SF §7-237.
Contracts.
Conflict of interest violations, SF §4-304.
Deception by applicant, SPP §15-104.
Falsifying examination grade, result or standing, SPP §15-103.
Giving special information to affect rating, SPP §15-105.
Impersonating another in examination, SPP §15-101.
Interference with examination rights of others, SPP §15-102.
Penalty for violations, SPP §15-201.
Threats or coercion, SPP §15-107.
Use of influence to secure appointment, SPP §15-106.
State finance and procurement violations, SF §2-305.
State lottery.
Unlawful sale of tickets or shares, SG §9-124.
State police department.
Crime statistics, PS §2-307.
State retirement and pension system.
Fiduciaries, SPP §21-209.
State's attorneys.
Post conviction procedure.
See POST CONVICTION PROCEDURE.
Stationary engineers.
Penalties for violations, BOP §6.5-404.
Statistics.
State police department, PS §2-307.

CRIMINAL LAW AND PROCEDURE —Cont'd
Statute of limitations on prosecutions.
Abduction of child under 16 for purposes of
    prostitution, CR §11-305.
Bribery.
    Jurors, acceptance of bribe, CR §9-202.
    Participants in athletic contest, CR §9-204.
    Public employee, CR §9-201.
Burning with intent to defraud, CR §6-106.
Counterfeiting public seals, CR §8-607.
Counterfeit mark, CR §8-611.
Defalcation by revenue officer, CR §7-114.
Documents of title, misuse, CR §8-406.
Embezzlement, CR §7-113.
Extortion, CR §3-701.
    By state or local officer or employee.
        Inducing another to give up compensation, CR
            §3-703.
    Extortion by state or local government officer or
        employee, CR §3-702.
Failure to deliver documents for merchandise, CR
    §7-116.
Fraudulent conversion of partnership assets, CR
    §8-401.
Fraudulent misrepresentation by corporate
    officers and agents, CR §8-402.
Identity fraud, CR §8-301.
Machine gun used for aggression purposes,
    prosecutions, CR §4-405.
Pandering, CR §11-303.
Perjury, CR §9-101.
    Subornation of perjury, CR §9-101.
Receiving earnings from prostitution, CR §11-304.
Rehypothecation of personal securities, CR §7-115.
Removal of human remains from burial site, CR
    §10-402.
Sale of minor.
    Prosecution for, CR §3-603.
Subornation of perjury, CR §9-101.
Theft of services or property prosecutions, CR
    §7-104.
Wills.
    Embezzle, steal, destroy, impair or alter, CR
        §§8-701, 8-702.
Wills, codicils, deeds, land patents, writs of estate.
    Embezzle, steal, destroy, impair, alter, CR
        §§8-701, 8-702.
Statutes.
Repeal or revision of statute.
    Effect on penalty or liability previously
        incurred, 1 §3.
Stem cell research.
Human cloning prohibited, 83A §5-2B-13.
Unused material provided by persons being
    treated for infertility.
    For profit transactions, solicitation for valuable
        consideration.
        Prohibition, penalty, 83A §5-2B-12.
Stet.
Drug or alcohol treatment requirement attached,
    CP §6-229.
Stoves and freestanding fireplaces, CL
    §14-1309.
Students.
Handicapped children, ED §8-311.
Hazing, CR §3-607.
Molesting or threatening, ED §26-101.
Subleasing motor vehicle, CR §8-408.
Subornation of perjury, CR §9-102.
Suicide.
Assisted suicide, CR §§3-101 to 3-104.
    Definitions, CR §3-101.

CRIMINAL LAW AND PROCEDURE —Cont'd
Suicide —Cont'd
Assisted suicide —Cont'd
    Exceptions, CR §3-103.
    Family care giver.
        Exception, CR §3-103.
    Generally, CR §3-102.
    Palliative care, pain relief.
        Exception, CR §3-103.
    Penalty, CR §3-104.
    Withholding life sustaining procedures.
        Exception, CR §3-103.
Summons and process.
General provisions.
    See SUMMONS AND PROCESS.
Sunday.
Sabbath breaking.
    See SUNDAYS AND HOLIDAYS.
Sunday blue laws.
Retail and wholesale establishments, BR §18-101.
Support and maintenance.
Criminal nonsupport and desertion, FL §§10-201,
    10-203.
Desertion of minor child, FL §10-219.
Surplus lines insurance.
Delivery of false binder or cover note, IN §3-326.
Surveillance.
Activities by officers from other states, PS §3-503.
Camera surveillance of private residence, CR
    §3-903.
Visual surveillance of individual in private place.
    With prurient intent, CR §3-902.
Survey stations, BOP §1-304.
Switchblade knives.
Weapons.
    General provisions.
        See WEAPONS.
Switchblades.
Transfer, prohibition, CR §4-105.
Taxation.
Admissions and amusement tax.
    See ADMISSIONS AND AMUSEMENT TAX.
Alcoholic beverage tax.
    See ALCOHOLIC BEVERAGE TAX.
Assaulting tax collector or bidder at auction, 24
    §9-718.
Failure to provide information, 24 §§9-716, 9-717.
General provisions, TG §§13-1001 to 13-1031.
    See TAXATION.
Income tax.
    See INCOME TAX.
Motor fuel tax.
    See MOTOR FUEL TAX.
Public officers and employees.
    Negligent or willful failure to perform duties, 24
        §§9-719, 9-720.
Sales and use tax.
    See SALES AND USE TAX.
Tobacco tax.
    See TOBACCO TAX.
Unlawful disclosure of tax information, 24 §9-721.
Tear gas device.
Wearing or carrying with intent to injure, CR
    §4-101.
Telecommunications services.
Caller identification blocking, PUC §8-205.
Telephone records, obtaining without
    authorization, CR §7-304.
Unlawful telecommunications device, access
    device or access code, CR §§7-313 to 7-318.
    Actual damages, computing, CR §7-318.

CRIMINAL LAW AND PROCEDURE —Cont'd
Telecommunications services —Cont'd
Unlawful telecommunications device, access
 device or access code —Cont'd
Civil action and remedies, CR §7-318.
Defense prohibited.
 Some acts occurred out of state, CR §7-317.
Definitions, CR §7-313.
Forfeiture, CR §7-316.
Impounding of devices, CR §7-318.
Inapplicability of part, CR §7-314.
Injunction, CR §7-318.
Location of violation, CR §7-317.
Modification or destruction.
 Part of civil remedy, CR §7-318.
Penalties, CR §7-316.
Possession, use, manufacture, distribute, sell,
 prohibition, CR §7-315.
Profits of violator, actual damages, CR §7-318.
Restitution, CR §7-316.
Telegraph companies.
Private communication.
 Divulging or failing to deliver, CR §3-906.
Telephone companies.
Private communication.
 Divulging or failing to deliver, CR §3-906.
Telephone records, obtaining without
 authorization, CR §7-304.
Telephone credit cards.
Number or code.
 Publishing, CR §8-210.
Telephone facilities and equipment.
Misuse, CR §3-804.
Telephone solicitation.
Automated dialing, PUC §8-204.
Caller identification blocking, PUC §8-205.
Sexual solicitation of minor.
 Generally, CR §3-324.
Television.
Broadcasting criminal proceeding.
 Prohibition, exception, violation contempt, CP
 §1-201.
Term papers.
Sale of academic papers, ED §26-201.
Terrorism.
Defense related activity.
 Acting with intent to hinder, CR §§9-701 to
 9-703.
Identification badges and cards, CR §§9-704 to
 9-706.
Sabotage, CR §§9-701 to 9-708.
Theft, CR §§7-101 to 7-110.
Aggregation of value, CR §7-103.
Bad checks prosecuted as theft, CR §7-107.
 Obtaining property or services by issuing or
 passing, CR §§8-101 to 8-108.
Bailee, misappropriation, CR §7-202.
Bill of particulars.
 Charging document in general form, CR §7-108.
Breaking and entering with intent to commit.
 Burglary in second degree, CR §6-203.
Cable television companies.
 Interference with service, CR §7-303.
Charging documents, CR §7-108.
Computers, network, services. program.
 Unauthorized access, CR §7-302.
Credit card crimes, CR §§8-201 to 8-217.
Crimes included in conduct described as theft, CR
 §7-102.
Deception.
 Services of another.
 Obtaining services available only for
 compensation, CR §7-104.

CRIMINAL LAW AND PROCEDURE —Cont'd
Theft —Cont'd
Deception —Cont'd
 Unauthorized control over property, CR §7-104.
Defalcation, CR §7-114.
Defenses allowed in prosecution, CR §7-110.
Defenses prohibited in prosecution, CR §7-110.
Definitions, CR §7-101.
 Knowingly, CR §7-102.
 Value, CR §7-103.
Determination of value, CR §7-103.
Electronic security systems.
 Code grabbing devices.
 Manufacturing, selling or possessing, CR
 §7-301.
 Deactivation tool or device.
 Possessing, using, CR §7-301.
 Devices shielding merchandise from system
 detection.
 Possessing, CR §7-301.
 Removal of system or device, CR §7-301.
Embezzlement, CR §7-113.
Evidence to prove theft, CR §7-109.
Failure to deliver documents for merchandise, CR
 §7-116.
General provisions, CR §7-104.
Good faith claim of right.
 Defense allowed, CR §7-110.
Grocery carts, CR §7-201.
Honest belief.
 Defense allowed, CR §7-110.
Illegally obtained property.
 Not defense, CR §7-110.
Intent to defraud.
 Proving, CR §1-401.
Interest in property.
 Not defense, CR §7-110.
Joint or common owner.
 No superior right of possession, CR §7-110.
Knowing conduct defined, CR §7-102.
Lesser included crime of robbery, CR §3-404.
Lost, mislaid or delivered by mistake property.
 Obtaining control over, CR §7-104.
Motor vehicle theft, CR §7-105.
 Charging documents, CR §7-108.
 Owner's affidavit, CR §7-105.1.
Newspaper theft, CR §7-106.
One crime, course of conduct considered, CR
 §7-103.
Possessing stolen property, CR §7-104.
Presumptions, CR §7-110.
Proof of theft, CR §7-109.
Property or service.
 Determination of value, CR §7-103.
Rehypothecation of personal securities, CR §7-115.
Rental vehicles.
 Failure to return rental vehicle, CR §7-205.
Right of possession.
 Determining superior right, CR §7-110.
Robbery, CR §§3-401 to 3-405.
 Lesser included crime of robbery, CR §3-404.
Security interest holder.
 Right not superior to person in lawful
 possession, CR §7-110.
Services of another.
 Obtaining services available only for
 compensation, CR §7-104.
Spouse's property.
 Defense allowed, CR §7-110.
State-owned keys, theft or duplication, CR §7-204.
Statute of limitations on prosecutions, CR §7-104.

CRIMINAL LAW AND PROCEDURE —Cont'd
Theft —Cont'd
Telecommunications services.
  Unlawful telecommunications device, access
      device or access code, CR §§7-313 to 7-318.
  Trade secret.
    Defendant rightfully knew or secret available
        from other source, CR §7-110.
    Determination of value, CR §7-103.
  Unauthorized control over property, CR §7-104.
  Unauthorized removal of property, CR §7-203.
  Unauthorized transfer or recording or sounds or
      images, CR §§7-306 to 7-310.
  Value deemed less than $500.
    Value cannot be determined, CR §7-103.
  Value defined, CR §7-103.
  Value of property or services $500 or more.
    Penalty, CR §7-104.
  Value of property or services less than $500.
    Penalty, CR §7-104.
  Wills, codicils, deeds, land patents, writs of estate,
      CR §§8-701, 8-702.
  Written instrument.
    Determination of value, CR §7-103.
Thimbles.
  Playing game prohibited, CR §12-103.
Threats.
  Against state or local officers and employees, CR
      §3-708.
  Extortion, CR §§3-701 to 3-707.
    By false accusation, CR §3-704.
    By state or local government officer or
        employee, CR §3-702.
      Inducing another to give up compensation, CR
          §3-703.
    By verbal threat, CR §3-705.
    By written threat, CR §3-706.
    Contributions or donations.
      Coercing or intimidating another to make, CR
          §3-707.
    Generally, CR §3-701.
    Property of five hundred dollars or more.
      Extortion by local or state government officer
          or employee, CR §3-702.
      Penalty, CR §3-701.
    Property of less than five hundred dollars.
      Extortion by local or state government officer
          or employee, CR §3-702.
      Penalty, CR §3-701.
    Statute of limitation on prosecution, CR §3-701.
      By state or local government officer or
          employee, CR §3-702.
      Inducing another to give up compensation, CR
          §3-703.
    Wages, hours or working conditions.
      Provisions inapplicable to employees seeking
          to obtain, CR §3-701.
  Inducing another to give up compensation.
    State or local officer inducing by force,
        intimidation or threat, CR §3-703.
  Stalking, CR §3-802.
Throwing object at vehicle, CR §6-302.
Ticket scalping.
  Boxing, sparring and wrestling, BR §4-318.
Tip jar.
  Frederick county, CR §§13-1301 to 13-1307.
    Generally, CR §13-1305.
  Washington county, CR §§13-2414 to 13-2439.
Tissue banks.
  Violations of provisions, HG §17-314.

CRIMINAL LAW AND PROCEDURE —Cont'd
Tobacco growing.
  Interference by tenant, RP §8-116.
Tobacco products.
  Escrow act compliance.
    Violations, BR §16-507.
  Minors.
    Possession by minor.
      Acting as agent of employer.
        Inapplicability, CR §10-108.
      Citation issued to minor, CR §10-108.
      Prohibition, CR §10-108.
    Sales to minors.
      Coupons contained in newspaper, magazine or
          other publication.
        Inapplicability of prohibition, CR §10-107.
      Defense.
        Examination of purchaser's driver's license
            or other identification, CR §10-107.
      Each violation separate, CR §10-107.
      Prohibited, CR §10-107.
Tobacco tax.
  See TOBACCO TAX.
Tokens.
  Counterfeiting and issuing, CR §8-612.
**Tourist or travelers' guide or information
    services,** BR §19-101.
Toxic material.
  False statement or rumor, CR §9-504.
Toxics in packaging.
  Criminal penalties, EN §9-1906.
Trademarks and service marks.
  Counterfeiting trademark, CR §8-611.
Trade names.
  Filing false certificates, CA §1-406.
  Fraudulent use or imitation of trade names, BR
      §1-415.
Traders.
  Visually handicapped applicants.
    Violating license provisions, BR §17-1816.
Trade secrets.
  Uniform trade secrets act, CL §§11-1201 to
      11-1209.
  See TRADE SECRETS.
Trading stamp companies.
  Violations of provisions, BR §13-110.
Traffic citations.
  See MOTOR VEHICLES.
Traffic laws.
  See TRAFFIC LAWS.
**Transfer of defendant on removal of case from
    one county to another.**
  Presence of defendant in court to which case
      removed required, COR §9-301.
Transient vendors.
  Conducting business without displaying license,
      BR §17-20A-05.
Trespass, CR §§6-401 to 6-410.
  Definitions, CR §6-401.
  General provisions.
    See TRESPASS.
  Invading privacy of occupants.
    Entry of property for purposes of, CR §6-408.
  Off-road vehicle on public property, CR §6-405.
  Posted property, CR §6-402.
  Racetrack stable area, CR §6-407.
  Railroads.
    Unauthorized access to railroad vehicle, CR
        §6-503.
  Refusal to leave.
    Public building or grounds, CR §6-409.

CRIMINAL LAW AND PROCEDURE —Cont'd
Trespass —Cont'd
Vehicle on private property, CR §6-404.
Wanton entry on cultivated land, CR §6-406.
Wanton trespass on private property, CR §6-403.
Wanton trespass on property of government
    house, CR §6-410.
Trial.
Date, CP §6-103.
    Setting of date, CP §6-103.
Date in circuit court.
    Criminal rules, Crim Rule 4-271.
District Court.
    Beginning of trial in District Court, Crim Rule
        4-301.
Exhibits, Crim Rule 4-322.
Incompetency to stand trial, CP §§3-101 to 3-108.
    See INCOMPETENCY TO STAND TRIAL.
Interstate agreement on detainers.
    Time for trial after arrival of prisoner in
        receiving state, COR §8-406.
    Time for trial after prisoner delivered to
        prosecuting officer and appropriate court,
        COR §8-405.
    Tolling of time periods when prisoner unable to
        stand trial, COR §8-408.
Intrastate detainers.
    Time for trial after inmate's request for final
        disposition, COR §8-502.
        Dismissal of indictment for failure to bring to
            trial, COR §8-503.
Jury. See within this heading, "Jury."
Jury trial, Crim Rule 4-253.
New trial.
    Motion for, CP §6-105; Crim Rule 4-331.
    Victim or victim's representative.
        Rights in connection with hearing on motion,
            CP §6-106.
Objections.
    Method of making, Crim Rule 4-323.
Prejudicial joinder, Crim Rule 4-253.
Public trial, US Const Amd 6.
Recording or broadcasting criminal proceeding.
    Prohibition, exception, violation contempt, CP
        §1-201.
Recording or broadcasting criminal trials.
    See TRIAL.
Removal in circuit courts, Crim Rule 4-254.
Right to trial by jury, US Const Art III §2; Amds
    6, 7.
Setting date for trial.
    Trial date, Crim Rule 4-271.
Speedy trial.
    Right to, MD Const DofR Arts 19, 21; US Const
        Amd 6.
Tuberculosis.
Violations of provisions, HG §18-325.
Unauthorized removal of property, CR §7-203.
**Unauthorized transfer or recording of sounds
    or images,** CR §§7-306 to 7-310.
Definitions, CR §7-308.
Delivery of recorded article or device without
    consent, CR §7-308.
Forfeiture and destruction of recorded article, CR
    §7-310.
Inapplicability of part, CR §7-306.
Penalty, CR §7-309.
Private litigation not effected, CR §7-307.
Transfer of sound or images without consent and
    credit, CR §7-308.

CRIMINAL LAW AND PROCEDURE —Cont'd
**Unauthorized transfer or recording of sounds
    or images** —Cont'd
Transfer without consent of sound recordings, CR
    §7-308.
Unemployment compensation.
Criminal penalties, LE §8-1305.
    Contributions.
        Transfers for purpose of lowering contribution
            rates, LE §8-614.
Unfair or deceptive trade practices, CL §13-301.
Electrical consumer products, CL §13-308.
Electrical extension cords, CL §13-309.
Fire resistant insulating material, CL §13-313.
Penalty for violations, CL §13-301.
Uniform laws.
Criminal extradition act, CP §§9-101 to 9-128.
    See EXTRADITION.
Post conviction procedure, CP §§7-101 to 7-301.
    See POST CONVICTION PROCEDURE.
Securing attendance of witnesses from without a
    state.
    General provisions.
        See WITNESSES.
Unit pricing, CL §13-411.
Universities and colleges.
Disturbing activities at colleges, ED §26-101.
Molesting or threatening students, etc., ED
    §26-101.
Sale of academic papers, ED §26-201.
Trespassing on school grounds, ED §26-102.
Unlawful picketing and assembly, CR §3-904.
Unnatural or perverted sexual practice, CR
    §3-322.
Charging documents, CR §3-322.
Usury, CL §§12-114, 12-122.
Vandalism.
Malicious destruction of property, CR §6-301.
Vending machines.
Condoms or contraceptives sold by.
    Nonlatex condoms, CR §10-104.
    Sales at schools, CR §10-105.
Removing or tampering with seal, BR §17-1907.
Selling without license, BR §17-1906.
Unlawful operation, CR §8-613.
Venereal disease cures or remedies.
Advertising cure.
    Prohibition, penalty, CR §10-102.
Defined, CR §10-101.
Prescription requirements, CR §10-103.
Selling or dispensing remedies.
    Prohibition, penalties, CR §10-103.
Venue, CP §4-201.
Accessory before the fact, CP §4-204.
Computers, unauthorized access prosecution, CR
    §7-302.
False statement or rumor concerning destructive
    device or toxic material, CR §9-504.
Pandering, CR §11-303.
Rape or sexual offense.
    Victim transported with intent to commit, CR
        §3-316.
Simulation of document to induce payment, CR
    §8-522.
Telecommunications services theft.
    Location of violation, CR §7-317.
Vessels and boats.
Abandonment, NR §8-725.1.
Advertising omitting registry number, CL
    §14-2902.
Antifouling paints, AG §5-906.

CRIMINAL LAW AND PROCEDURE —Cont'd
Vessels and boats —Cont'd
Cargo, wrongful disposal, CR §8-405.
Concealed number, name or home port
 designation.
 Operating vessel with, NR §8-713.1.
Emergency vessels.
 Violation of section of operators, NR §8-727.1.
Enforcement of subtitle.
 Violations of section, NR §8-727.
Excise tax.
 Collection and remittance, NR §8-716.1.
 Failure to pay, NR §8-739.
Homicide by vessel while impaired or under the
 influence, CR §§2-501 to 2-508.
Intoxicated or under the influence of drugs, NR
 §8-738.
Life threatening injury by vessel while impaired
 or under the influence, CR §3-211.
Monocacy river, speed limit, exceeding, NR
 §8-725.6.
Operating in reckless or dangerous manner, NR
 §8-738.1.
Operation of vessels.
 Boating safety violations, NR §8-712.2.
Pilots license violations generally, BOP §11-706.
Seneca creek, speed limit, exceeding, NR §8-725.5.
Severn river.
 Speed limit violations, NR §8-725.3.
Ship-to-shore communication device.
 Failure to possess on vessels carrying certain
 number of passengers, NR §8-740.1.
Throwing waste into waters of state, NR §8-726.1.
Tidal waters.
 Noise level for vessels operating in, NR
 §8-725.4.
Unnumbered vessel, NR §8-739.
Veterans' organization insignia or name.
Unauthorized use, BR §19-207.
Victim and witness protection and relocation
 program, 10 §41D.
Victims.
Criminal injuries compensation board, CP
 §§11-801 to 11-819.
 See CRIMINAL INJURIES COMPENSATION
 BOARD.
General provisions, CP §§11-101 to 11-1005.
 See VICTIMS OF CRIME.
Influencing or intimidating, CR §§9-301 to 9-306.
 Absence from proceeding, inducing, CR §9-302.
 Avoidance of summons or subpoena, inducing,
 CR §9-302.
 Contempt power.
 Enforcement of order to stop or prevent, CR
 §9-304.
 Court order to stop or prevent, CR §9-304.
 Definitions, CR §9-301.
 False testimony, inducing, CR §9-302.
 Pretrial release, conditions imposed, CR §9-304.
 Retaliation for giving testimony or reporting
 crime, CR §9-303.
Notification escape and recapture, CP §11-508.
Notoriety of crimes contracts, CP §§11-621 to
 11-633.
 See NOTORIETY OF CRIMES CONTRACTS.
Registration of sex offenders, CP §§11-701 to
 11-726.
 See SEX OFFENDER REGISTRATION.
Restitution and other payments, CP §§11-601 to
 11-633.
 See CRIME VICTIMS' COMPENSATION.

CRIMINAL LAW AND PROCEDURE —Cont'd
Victims —Cont'd
Services for victims and witnesses, CP §§11-901 to
 11-1005.
 See CRIME VICTIMS' SERVICES.
Video movie sales and rentals, CL §14-1603.
Video tape distributors.
Unlawful publishing of information, CR §3-907.
Visual surveillance of individual in private
 place, CR §3-901.
With prurient intent, CR §3-902.
Vital records, HG §4-227.
Voter registration, EL §16-601.
Copy of voter registration list used for commercial
 solicitation, EL §3-506.
Vulnerable adults.
Abuse or neglect, CR §§3-604 to 3-606.
Exploitation of vulnerable adults, CR §8-801.
Wage payment and collection.
Prohibited acts, LE §3-508.
Warehouse receipts, CL §18-401.
Warehouses and warehousemen.
Storage warehouses.
 Buyer's purchase of insurance, BR §17-1204.
Warrantless arrest.
Generally, CP §§2-201 to 2-210.
 See WARRANTLESS ARREST.
Washington county.
Animal control violations, 25 §236A.
Health code violation.
 Criminal prosecution of civil violation, 25 §236F.
 Persons authorized to prosecute, 25 §236F.
Washington suburban sanitary district.
Rules violations, 29 §§18-104.1, 18-104.2.
Violations generally, 29 §18-104.
Watches.
Secondhand dealers, CL §14-706.
Water and sewer systems, EN §9-268.1.
Water company equipment.
Interference with, CR §6-305.
Water pollution violations, EN §9-343.
Limitation on prosecution, EN §9-343.1.
Water resources.
Appropriation or use permits.
 Violations of chapter, EN §5-514.
Penalties, EN §5-1301; NR §8-2001.
Waters of the state.
Dumping or throwing waste into waters of state,
 NR §8-726.1.
Water supply.
Contaminating, CR §3-214.
Water treatment works violations, EN §9-343.
Limitation on prosecution, EN §9-343.1.
Weapons.
Antique firearm.
 Defined, CR §4-201.
 Use in commission of crime, CR §4-204.
Assault pistols.
 Defined, prohibition, seizure, CR §§4-301 to
 4-306.
Assault with firearm.
 Assault in first degree, CR §3-202.
Breaking and entering with intent to steal
 firearm.
 Burglary in the second degree, CR §6-203.
Bulletproof body armor.
 Defined, CR §4-106.
 Permit to use, possess or purchase, CR §4-107.
 Wearing in crime of violence or drug trafficking
 crime.
 Prohibition, CR §4-106.

CRIMINAL LAW AND PROCEDURE —Cont'd
Weapons —Cont'd
Child's access to firearm, CR §4-104.
Contraband in place of confinement, CR §9-414.
Dangerous weapons.
  Armed carjacking, CR §3-405.
  Carrying concealed or with intent to injure, CR §4-101.
  Defined, CR §4-101.
  Minor carrying weapon, hours prohibited.
    Counties applicable, CR §4-101.
  Minor possessing pepper mace, prohibition, CR §4-101.
  Robbery with dangerous weapon, CR §3-403.
  Wearing concealed or with intent to injure, CR §4-101.
Destructive devices, CR §§4-501 to 4-503.
  Definitions, CR §4-501.
  Exceptions to subtitle, CR §4-502.
  Manufacture or possession prohibited, CR §4-503.
  Restitution ordered for violation, CR §4-503.
  Scope of subtitle, CR §4-502.
Detachable magazines.
  Prohibited, CR §4-305.
Disarming a law enforcement officer, CR §4-103.
Discharge of firearm.
  From motor vehicle.
    Reckless endangerment, CR §3-204.
    Local regulation allowed, CR §4-209.
Drug crimes, firearm possession by person convicted of, CR §5-622.
Drug trafficking offenses.
  Firearm possessed, used, worn, carried or transported.
    Separate offense, enhanced sentence, forfeiture, CR §5-621.
Handguns.
  Generally, CR §§4-201 to 4-209.
Machine guns.
  Uniform act, CR §§4-401 to 4-407.
Possession of firearm at public demonstration, CR §4-208.
Reckless endangerment.
  Discharge of firearm from motor vehicle, CR §3-204.
Rifles.
  Defined, CR §4-201.
  Short-barreled rifle.
    Defined, CR §4-201.
School property.
  Deadly weapons on, CR §4-102.
Short-barreled rifle.
  Defined, CR §4-201.
Short-barreled shotgun.
  Defined, CR §4-201.
Shotgun.
  Defined, CR §4-201.
State preemption of local regulation, CR §4-209.
Target practice without landowner permission, CR §4-108.
Weights and measures, AG §11-208.1.
  Impersonation of officer, AG §11-208.
Welfare fraud, CR §§8-501 to 8-505.
  Application for assistance.
    Fraudulent statement or signature, CR §8-504.
  Change in household or financial condition.
    Failure to disclose.
      Fraud defined as, CR §8-501.
  Criminal penalty, CR §8-503.
    Fraudulent application, CR §8-504.

CRIMINAL LAW AND PROCEDURE —Cont'd
Welfare fraud —Cont'd
  Criminal penalty —Cont'd
    Unauthorized disposition of donated food, CR §8-505.
  Donated food.
    Unauthorized disposition or conversion, CR §8-505.
  False statement or false representation.
    Fraud defined as, CR §8-501.
  Fraud defined, CR §8-501.
  Inapplicability of part, CR §8-502.
  Medicaid fraud, CR §§8-508 to 8-517.
    Benefit card, unauthorized possession, CR §8-515.
    Business entity violation, fine, CR §8-516.
    Civil penalty, CR §8-517.
    Conversion of benefit or payment by state health plan, CR §8-510.
    Criminal penalties, CR §8-516.
    Death resulting from violation, penalty, CR §8-516.
    Definitions, CR §8-508.
    Defrauding state health plan, CR §8-509.
    False statement to aid qualifications to receive reimbursement, CR §8-513.
    Kickback or bribe in connection with state health plan, CR §8-511.
    Obtaining benefit by fraud, CR §8-514.
    Rebate, fee or charge for referral, CR §8-512.
    Restitution, CR §8-517.
    Serious injury resulting from violation, penalty, CR §8-516.
    Value of money, goods or services $500 or more, penalty, CR §8-516.
  Prohibited, CR §8-503.
  Restitution, CR §8-503.
Wetlands.
  Nontidal wetlands.
    Penalties, EN §5-911.
Wheel of fortune.
  Anne Arundel county.
    Gaming events generally, CR §§13-401 to 13-408.
    Political fundraisers, CR §13-406.
  Baltimore City.
    Gaming events generally, CR §§13-501 to 13-510.
    Political fundraisers, CR §13-506.
    Prizes allowed, CR §13-504.
  Baltimore county.
    Gaming events generally, CR §§13-601 to 13-607.
    Political fundraisers, CR §13-605.
  Carroll county.
    Gaming events generally, CR §§13-901 to 13-909.
    Prizes allowed, CR §13-905.
  Cecil county.
    Awarding prizes at gaming events, CR §13-1004.
    Gaming events generally, CR §§13-1001 to 13-1005.
  Frederick county.
    Gaming provisions generally, CR §§13-1301 to 13-1307.
  Gaming devices.
    Defined as, CR §12-101.
    Statewide gaming provisions, CR §§12-101 to 12-113.
    See GAMING.

CRIMINAL LAW AND PROCEDURE —Cont'd
Wheel of fortune —Cont'd
Gaming event provisions applicable to several
counties, CR §§13-201 to 13-205.
Howard county, CR §13-1603.
Kent county, CR §§13-1701 to 13-1706.
Queen Anne's county, CR §§13-2001 to 13-2006.
St. Mary's county, CR §§13-2111 to 13-2115.
Wicomico county, CR §§13-2501 to 13-2508.
Worcester county, CR §§13-2619 to 13-2628.
Wholesome meat act.
Prohibited acts violations, AG §4-130.
**Wills, codicils, deeds, land patents, writs of
estate.**
Embezzle, steal, destroy, impair, alter, CR
§§8-701, 8-702.
Wiretapping.
General provisions.
See WIRETAPPING.
Interception of communications.
Unlawful acts, CJ §10-402.
Witnesses.
Accused.
Confrontation of accused by witnesses, MD
Const DofR Art 21.
Neglect or refusal to testify.
No presumption against him, CJ §9-107.
Proof of crime committed by another, CJ
§10-904.
Bonds, surety, CJ §9-203.
Bribery of public employees.
Immunity of witness compelled to testify, CR
§9-201.
Person violating provisions competent witness,
CR §9-201.
Competency of witness.
Bribery of public employees, person violating,
CR §9-201.
Confrontation of accused by witnesses, MD Const
DofR Art 21; US Const Amd 6.
Conviction of infamous crime.
Proof, CJ §10-905.
Failure to testify not admissible in civil actions,
CJ §10-903.
Holding state witness, CJ §9-203.
Husband and wife.
Not compelled to testify against spouse, CJ
§10-906.
Exceptions, CJ §9-106.
Immunity of witness compelled to testify.
Bribery of public employees, CR §9-201.
Influencing or intimidating, CR §§9-301 to 9-306.
Absence from proceeding, inducing, CR §9-302.
Avoidance of summons or subpoena, inducing,
CR §9-302.
Contempt power.
Enforcement of order to stop or prevent, CR
§9-304.
Court order to stop or prevent, CR §9-304.
Definitions, CR §9-301.
False testimony, inducing, CR §9-302.
Pretrial release, conditions imposed, CR §9-304.
Retaliation for giving testimony or reporting
crime, CR §9-303.
Oath.
Examine witnesses for and against accused on
oath, MD Const DofR Art 21.
Perjury, CR §9-101.
Charging document, CR §9-103.
Contradictory statements.
Proving either statement false without
specifying which one, CR §9-101.

CRIMINAL LAW AND PROCEDURE —Cont'd
Witnesses —Cont'd
Perjury —Cont'd
Statute of limitations, CR §9-101.
Subornation of perjury, CR §9-102.
Protection and relocation program, 10 §41D.
Securing attendance of witnesses from outside
state.
Uniform law.
See WITNESSES.
Self-incrimination.
Prohibited, MD Const DofR Art 22; US Const
Amd 5.
Woodrow Wilson bridge and tunnel compact.
Provision violations, TR §10-303.
Workers' compensation.
See WORKERS' COMPENSATION.
Work release programs.
Extended work release program.
Violation of terms and conditions, COR §3-807.
Failure to return, COR §3-803.
Local correctional facility.
Violation of condition, COR §11-726.
Violation of restriction on movement, COR
§11-726.
Worthless checks.
Bad checks, CR §§8-101 to 8-108.
Year and day rule.
Murder, manslaughter and unlawful homicide
prosecutions.
Rule eliminated, CR §2-102.

CRIMINAL RULES.
Acquittal.
Advice of expungement, Crim Rule 4-329.
Motion for judgment of acquittal, Crim Rule
4-324.
Amendments, Crim Rule 4-204.
Appeals.
En banc review, Crim Rule 4-352.
Appearances, Crim Rule 4-213.
Applicability of rules, Crim Rule 4-101; Rule
1-101.
Arrest.
Procedure when defendant in custody.
Other offenses, Crim Rule 4-212.
Same offense, Crim Rule 4-212.
Statement of charges, Crim Rule 4-211.
Attachment.
Body attachment.
Material witnesses, Crim Rule 4-267.
Attorneys at law.
Defense counsel, Crim Rule 4-214.
Waiver of counsel, Crim Rule 4-215.
Bill of particulars.
Circuit courts, Crim Rule 4-241.
Body attachment of material witness, Crim
Rule 4-267.
Capital cases.
Sentencing.
Generally, Crim Rule 4-342.
Charging documents.
Defined, Crim Rule 4-102.
General provisions.
See CHARGING DOCUMENTS.
Circuit courts.
Applicability of rules, Rule 1-101.
Bill of particulars, Crim Rule 4-241.
Discovery, Crim Rule 4-263.
Motions, Crim Rule 4-252.
Removal in circuit courts, Crim Rule 4-254.

CRIMINAL RULES —Cont'd
Circuit courts —Cont'd
Subpoena for tangible evidence before trial, Crim Rule 4-264.
Trial date, Crim Rule 4-271.
Warrants.
Issuance, Crim Rule 4-212.
Citations.
Charging documents generally.
See CHARGING DOCUMENTS.
Defined, Crim Rule 4-102.
Filing, Crim Rule 4-211.
Service, Crim Rule 4-212.
Clerical mistakes.
Correction, Crim Rule 4-621.
Construction and interpretation.
Applicability, Crim Rule 4-101; Rule 1-101.
Costs, Crim Rule 4-353.
Defendants.
Defined, Crim Rule 4-102.
Joinder.
Circuit courts, Crim Rule 4-203.
Presence of defendants, Crim Rule 4-231.
Definitions.
Charging documents, Crim Rule 4-102.
Depositions, Crim Rule 4-261.
Discovery.
Circuit courts, Crim Rule 4-263.
District Court, Crim Rule 4-262.
District Court.
Applicability of rules, Rule 1-101.
Motions, Crim Rule 4-251.
Reassignment in District Court, Crim Rule 4-254.
Trial.
Beginning of trial in District Court, Crim Rule 4-301.
Date.
Change in District Court, Crim Rule 4-271.
Video conferencing, Crim Rule 4-231.
Warrants.
Issuance, Crim Rule 4-212.
DNA evidence.
New trial, Crim Rule 4-331.
Post-conviction procedure, Crim Rule 4-401.
Evidence.
Applicability of rules of evidence.
Issuance, service and execution of summons or warrant, Crim Rule 4-212.
Preliminary hearing in District Court, Crim Rule 4-221.
Pre-trial release, Crim Rule 4-216.
Suppression of evidence.
Motions in circuit court in criminal cases, Crim Rule 4-252.
Expungement of records, Crim Rules 4-501 to 4-512.
See EXPUNGEMENT OF RECORDS.
Filing, Crim Rule 4-211.
Guilty pleas.
Method of pleading, Crim Rule 4-242.
Pleas generally.
See PLEAS.
Pleas to other offenses, Crim Rule 4-244.
Requirements for court to accept, Crim Rule 4-242.
Subsequent offenders.
Disclosure of notice of additional or mandatory penalties, Crim Rule 4-245.
Habitual offenders.
Subsequent offenders, Crim Rule 4-245.

CRIMINAL RULES —Cont'd
Immunity.
Compelling testimony or documents on condition of immunity, Crim Rule 4-631.
Indictments.
Charging documents generally.
See CHARGING DOCUMENTS.
Defined, Crim Rule 4-102.
Filing, Crim Rule 4-211.
Informations.
Charging documents generally.
See CHARGING DOCUMENTS.
Defined, Crim Rule 4-102.
Filing, Crim Rule 4-211.
Insanity defense.
Appeals.
Guilty plea entered with plea of not criminally responsible.
Appeals on issue of criminal responsibility, Crim Rule 4-314.
Defense of not criminally responsible.
Plea.
Permitted plea, Crim Rule 4-242.
Guilty plea entered with plea of not criminally responsible.
Trial on issue of criminal responsibility, Crim Rule 4-314.
Motion.
Bifurcation of trial, Crim Rule 4-314.
Plea of not criminally responsible by reason of insanity.
Permitted pleas, Crim Rule 4-242.
Trial, Crim Rule 4-314.
Instructions to jury, Crim Rule 4-325.
Interception of wire or oral communications, Crim Rule 4-611.
Investigations.
Applicability, Crim Rule 4-641.
Court records.
Secrecy, Crim Rule 4-642.
Enforcement of subpoenas, Crim Rule 4-643.
File.
Maintenance, Crim Rule 4-644.
Grand jury.
Subpoenas to appear before grand jury, Crim Rule 4-643.
Hearings.
Secrecy, Crim Rule 4-642.
Motion for disclosure.
Secrecy, Crim Rule 4-642.
Orders.
Protective orders, Crim Rule 4-643.
Secrecy, Crim Rule 4-642.
Subpoenas, Crim Rule 4-643.
Record of subpoena, Crim Rule 4-644.
Joinder.
Multiple defendants, Crim Rule 4-203.
Judges.
Disability of judge, Crim Rule 4-361.
Judgments.
Enforcement of money judgment, Crim Rule 4-354.
Judicial officers.
Defined, Crim Rule 4-102.
Jury trial.
Challenges.
Array, Crim Rule 4-312.
Peremptory challenges, Crim Rule 4-313.
Communications, Crim Rule 4-326.
Demand for jury trial, Crim Rule 4-301.
Exhibits, Crim Rule 4-322.

CRIMINAL RULES —Cont'd
Jury trial —Cont'd
Instructions to jury, Crim Rule 4-325.
Juror's notes, Crim Rule 4-326.
Number of jurors, Crim Rule 4-311.
Objections.
Method of making, Crim Rule 4-323.
Peremptory challenges, Crim Rule 4-313.
Review of evidence, Crim Rule 4-326.
Right preserved, Crim Rule 4-311.
Selection, Crim Rule 4-312.
Separation of jury, Crim Rule 4-311.
Verdicts, Crim Rule 4-327.
Waiver.
Circuit courts, Crim Rule 4-246.
Juvenile courts.
Jurisdiction.
Waiver, Crim Rule 4-222.
Mistake.
Correction of clerical mistakes, Crim Rule 4-621.
Motions.
Circuit court motions, Crim Rule 4-252.
District Court motions, Crim Rule 4-251.
New trial, Crim Rule 4-331.
New trial.
Motions for new trial, Crim Rule 4-331.
Nolle prosequi, Crim Rule 4-247.
Nolo contendere.
See PLEAS.
Not guilty pleas.
Permitted pleas, Crim Rules 4-242, 4-243.
Offenses.
Defined, Crim Rule 4-102.
Peace officers.
Defined, Crim Rule 4-102.
Petty offenses.
Defined, Crim Rule 4-102.
Plea bargains, Crim Rule 4-243.
Pleadings.
Pleas.
See PLEAS.
Pleas.
See PLEAS.
Post conviction procedure, Crim Rules 4-401 to
4-408.
See POST CONVICTION PROCEDURE.
Preliminary hearings.
District Court, Crim Rule 4-221.
Initial appearance of defendant.
Advice of preliminary hearing, Crim Rule 4-213.
Presence of defendants, Crim Rule 4-231.
Depositions, Crim Rule 4-261.
Pretrial procedures.
Charging documents.
See CHARGING DOCUMENTS.
Pretrial release.
Appearances.
Initial appearance of defendant.
Determination of pretrial release, Crim Rule
4-213.
Bail bonds, Crim Rule 4-217.
General provisions, Crim Rule 4-216.
Probation, Crim Rule 4-346.
General provisions.
See PROBATION.
Prosecution.
Motions in circuit courts in criminal cases.
Effect of determination of certain motions, Crim
Rule 4-252.
Recidivism.
Subsequent offenders, Crim Rule 4-245.

CRIMINAL RULES —Cont'd
Records.
Expungement of records, Crim Rules 4-501 to
4-512.
See EXPUNGEMENT OF RECORDS.
Removal in circuit courts, Crim Rule 4-254.
Returns.
Service of summons in warrant, Crim Rule 4-212.
Search warrants, Crim Rule 4-601.
Mandatory motions in circuit courts, Crim Rule
4-252.
Sentence and punishment.
General provisions.
See SENTENCE AND PUNISHMENT.
Service of process, Crim Rule 4-212.
Statement of charges.
After arrest.
Filing, Crim Rule 4-211.
Before arrest.
Filing, Crim Rule 4-211.
Charging documents generally.
See CHARGING DOCUMENTS.
Defined, Crim Rule 4-102.
State's attorneys.
Defined, Crim Rule 4-102.
General provisions.
See STATE'S ATTORNEYS.
Stay of execution of sentence, Crim Rule 4-348.
Stet.
Disposition of case by stet, Crim Rule 4-248.
Effect of stet, Crim Rule 4-248.
Expungement of records.
Petition for expungement of records.
Form, Form 4-504.2.
Subpoenas.
Evidence.
Tangible evidence before trial in circuit court,
Crim Rule 4-264.
Generally, Crim Rule 4-266.
Investigations, Crim Rule 4-643.
Record of subpoena, Crim Rule 4-644.
Trial or hearing, Crim Rule 4-265.
Subsequent offenders, Crim Rule 4-245.
Summons.
Issuance, Crim Rule 4-212.
Service, Crim Rule 4-212.
Trial.
Bifurcation of trial.
Defense of not criminally responsible by reason
of insanity, Crim Rule 4-314.
Date in circuit court, Crim Rule 4-271.
Date in District Court.
Change of trial date, Crim Rule 4-271.
Defense of not criminally responsible by reason of
insanity.
Bifurcation of trial.
Plea of not guilty and not criminally
responsible entered by defendant, Crim
Rule 4-314.
Criminal responsibility.
Trial of issue of, Crim Rule 4-314.
Guilty plea and not criminally responsible.
Entered by defendant.
Trial of issue of criminal responsibility,
Crim Rule 4-314.
Not guilty plea and plea of not criminally
responsible.
Entered by defendant.
Bifurcation of trial, Crim Rule 4-314.
District Court.
Beginning of trial in District Court, Crim Rule
4-301.

CRIMINAL RULES —Cont'd
Trial —Cont'd
Exhibits, Crim Rule 4-322.
Insanity defense.
Defense of not criminally responsible by reason
of insanity, Crim Rule 4-314.
Joint trial, Crim Rule 4-253.
New trial.
Motions for new trial, Crim Rule 4-331.
Objections.
Method of making, Crim Rule 4-323.
Prejudicial joinder, Crim Rule 4-253.
Removal in circuit courts, Crim Rule 4-254.
Verdicts.
Court verdict, Crim Rule 4-328.
Defined, Crim Rule 4-102.
Jury trial, Crim Rule 4-327.
Video conferencing.
District Court, Crim Rule 4-231.
Waiver.
Attorneys at law.
Waiver of counsel, Crim Rule 4-215.
Jury trial.
Circuit courts, Crim Rule 4-246.
Warrants.
Defined, Crim Rule 4-102.
Execution.
Defendant not in custody, Crim Rule 4-212.
Issuance, Crim Rule 4-212.
Procedure when defendant in custody.
Other offenses, Crim Rule 4-212.
Search warrants, Crim Rule 4-601.
Service.
Return of service, Crim Rule 4-212.
Witnesses.
Body attachment of material witness, Crim Rule
4-267.

CRIPPLED CHILDREN.
See HANDICAPPED PERSONS.

CRISFIELD.
Alcoholic beverages.
Enforcement of article, 2B §16-414.
Profits and reserves.
Accounted, 2B §15-207.
Hospitals.
Alice Byrd Tawes Nursing Home.
Construction, 25 §255.

CROCODILES.
Dangerous animals.
Importing, selling, or trading in, CR §10-621.

CROFTON POLICE DEPARTMENT, 26 §5.
Arrest without a warrant.
Generally, CP §§2-201 to 2-210.
See WARRANTLESS ARREST.
Authority granted police officers generally, CP
§2-102.
Definitions.
Police officer, CP §2-101.
Fresh pursuit, CP §2-301.
Law enforcement officers generally, PS §§3-101
to 3-603.
See LAW ENFORCEMENT OFFICERS AND
PERSONNEL.
Law enforcement procedures generally, CP
§§2-101 to 2-107.
See POLICE.
Police training commission, PS §§3-201 to 3-218.
See POLICE TRAINING COMMISSION.

CROFTON POLICE DEPARTMENT —Cont'd
Powers.
Granted to police officers generally, CP §2-102.
Warrantless arrest.
Generally, CP §§2-201 to 2-210.
See WARRANTLESS ARREST.

CROP INSURANCE PREMIUM PROGRAM, AG
§2-901.

CROPS.
Contracts.
Sale of goods.
Definition of "goods," CL §2-105.
Distress for rent.
General provisions.
See DISTRESS FOR RENT.
Lien on crops, RP §8-115.
Documents of title.
Warehouse receipts.
Storage under government bond, CL §7-201.
Landlord and tenant.
Reserved as rent, RP §8-115.
Mortgages and deeds of trust.
Annual crops not to pass with mortgage, RP
§7-105.
Effect.
See MORTGAGES AND DEEDS OF TRUST.
Foreclosure.
Effect of foreclosure on annual crops, RP §7-105.
Secured transactions.
Priority of security interests in, CL §9-334.
Production-money crops.
Defined, CL §9-102.
Production-money obligation.
Defined, CL §9-102.
Production of crops.
Defined, CL §9-102.
Warehouse receipts.
Storage under government bond, CL §7-201.

CROSS-CLAIMS.
Allowed pleadings, CivProCir Rule 2-302.
District Court, CivProDist Rule 3-302.
Filing.
Time for filing.
Circuit courts, CivProCir Rule 2-331.
District Court, CivProDist Rule 3-331.
Joinder.
Circuit courts, CivProCir Rule 2-331.
District Court, CivProDist Rule 3-331.
Judgments.
Multiple claims.
Circuit courts, CivProCir Rule 2-602.
District Court, CivProDist Rule 3-602.
Jurisdiction.
Exceeding jurisdictional amount.
District Court, CivProDist Rule 3-331.
Parties.
Circuit courts, CivProCir Rule 2-331.
District Court, CivProDist Rule 3-331.
Joinder of additional parties.
Circuit courts, CivProCir Rule 2-331.
District Court, CivProDist Rule 3-331.
Pleadings.
Against co-parties.
Circuit courts, CivProCir Rule 2-331.
District Court, CivProDist Rule 3-331.
Allowed pleadings, CivProDist Rule 3-302.
District Court, CivProDist Rule 3-302.
Filing.
Time for filing.
Circuit courts, CivProCir Rule 2-331.

CROSS-CLAIMS —Cont'd
Pleadings —Cont'd
Filing —Cont'd
Time for filing —Cont'd
District Court, CivProDist Rule 3-331.
Joinder of additional parties.
Circuit courts, CivProCir Rule 2-331.
District Court, CivProDist Rule 3-331.
Jurisdiction.
Exceeding jurisdictional amount.
District Court, CivProDist Rule 3-331.
Parties.
Joinder of additional parties.
Circuit courts, CivProCir Rule 2-331.
Time for filing.
Circuit courts, CivProCir Rule 2-331.
District Court, CivProDist Rule 3-331.
Trial.
Time of trial.
District Court, CivProDist Rule 3-331.
Small claim actions.
District Court, CivProDist Rule 3-701.
Tort claims act.
Certain restrictions inapplicable to claims
asserted by cross-claim, SG §12-106.
Trial.
Time.
District Court, CivProDist Rule 3-331.
Voluntary dismissal.
Circuit courts, CivProCir Rule 2-506.
District Court, CivProDist Rule 3-506.

CROSS-EXAMINATION, SCOPE, Evid Rule
5-611.

CROSSINGS.
Highways.
See HIGHWAYS.
Railroad crossings.
General provisions, TR §§8-639 to 8-643.
See RAILROADS.

CROWNSVILLE STATE HOSPITAL.
Mental health facilities.
See MENTAL HEALTH FACILITIES.

CROWS.
Bounties.
Counties, 25 §2.

CRUELTY TO ANIMALS.
Cats.
Motor vehicles.
Pets left in standing or parked vehicles, TR
§21-1004.1.
Crimes relating to animals generally, CR
§§10-601 to 10-622.
See ANIMALS.
Dogs.
Motor vehicles.
Pets left in standing or parked vehicles, TR
§21-1004.1.
Pets.
Motor vehicles.
Left in standing or parked vehicles, TR
§21-1004.1.
Poultry.
Sale, coloring, etc., of baby chickens, ducklings,
etc.
Person defined, CL §11-901.
Veterinarians.
Immunity for good faith reports, AG §2-304.

CRUSTACEANS.
Crab meat.
See CRAB MEAT.

CRUSTACEANS —Cont'd
Crabs generally.
See CRABS.
Lobsters, NR §4-901.
State crustacean.
Maryland blue crab, SG §13-301.

CULLING OYSTERS, NR §§4-1015, 4-1015.1.

CULTIVATED LAND.
Wanton entry, CR §6-406.

CULTURAL COMPETENCY PILOT PROGRAM,
HG §20-1201.

CULTURAL EVENTS.
Unfair or deceptive trade practices.
Reserved seat tickets, CL §13-310.

CUMBERLAND.
Canal place preservation and development
authority.
Failure of city to implement provisions.
Effect, FI §13-1030.
Ordinance.
Adoption by city as prerequisite to
expenditures, FI §13-1014.

CUMBERLAND CITY.
Taxicabs.
Permit to operate taxicab business in or from
point in city generally, PUC §§10-202 to
10-207.
See TAXICABS.

CUNNILINGUS.
Sexual offense in first or second degree, CR
§§3-305, 3-306, 3-311, 3-312.

CURATIVE ACTS.
Validation.
See VALIDATION.

CURATORS.
Fiduciaries.
General provisions, ET §§15-201 to 15-211.
See FIDUCIARIES.
Jurisdiction.
Over persons outside this state.
General provisions.
See JURISDICTION.

CURFEW.
Juvenile curfew, 25B §13C-1.
Municipal corporations.
Regulations, 23A §2.

CURRENCY.
General provisions.
See MONEY.

CURRENCY TRANSACTIONS.
General provisions, FI §§12-801 to 12-806.
See FINANCIAL INSTITUTIONS.

CURRENCY TRANSACTIONS IN TRADE OR
BUSINESS, BR §§1-501 to 1-505.
Actions.
Civil penalties.
Civil action to recover, BR §1-505.
Attorney general.
Reports.
Access of office of attorney general to reports,
BR §1-504.
Criminal investigations or proceedings.
Purposes of subchapter, BR §1-501.
Criminal justice agencies.
Access to reports, BR §1-504.

CURRENCY TRANSACTIONS IN TRADE OR BUSINESS —Cont'd
Currency.
Defined, BR §1-502.
Definitions, BR §1-502.
Department of labor, licensing and regulation.
Department defined, BR §1-502.
Secretary.
Adoption of regulations, BR §1-503.
Civil penalties.
Assessments, BR §1-505.
Defined, BR §1-502.
Department of public safety and correctional services.
Access to reports, BR §1-504.
Penalties, BR §1-505.
Persons engaged in trade or business.
Defined, BR §1-502.
Purposes of subtitle, BR §1-501.
Records.
Access to required records, BR §1-504.
Required records of currency transactions, BR §1-503.
Reports.
Access to reports, BR §1-504.
Required, BR §1-503.
Rules and regulations.
Adoption, BR §1-503.
Violations of subtitle.
Civil penalties, BR §1-505.

CURSING.
General provisions.
See OBSCENITY AND PORNOGRAPHY.

CURTESY.
Abolished, ET §3-202.
Surviving spouse.
Elective share.
General provisions, ET §§3-203 to 3-208.
See DECEDENTS' ESTATES.
Share, ET §3-102.

CUSTODIAL INTERFERENCE.
Abduction of child.
General provisions, FL §§9-301 to 9-307.
See CHILD CUSTODY.

CUSTODIAN.
Descent and distribution.
Appointment for distribution to minor, ET §9-109.
Juvenile causes.
Defined, CJ §3-8A-01.
Minors.
Appointment, ET §9-109.
Transfers to minors act, ET §§13-301 to 13-324.
See MINORS.
Taxation.
Owner for taxation, TP §5-101.
Transfers to minors act, ET §§13-301 to 13-324.
See MINORS.

CUSTODY.
Child custody.
See CHILD CUSTODY.
Child visitation.
See CHILD VISITATION.
Controlled dangerous substances.
Chain of physical custody or control.
Statements signed by successive officers or persons having custody, CJ §10-1002.
Juvenile causes.
See JUVENILE CAUSES.

CUSTOM HOME BUILDERS.
Homebuilder registration, BR §§4.5-101 to 4.5-701.
See HOMEBUILDER REGISTRATION.

CUSTOM HOME PROTECTION.
Bonds, surety.
Escrow accounts.
Accounts in lieu of, RP §10-504.
Builders.
Custom home builders.
Certification by builder.
Inclusion in custom home contract.
Required, RP §10-506.
Contracts required, RP §10-505.
Defined, RP §10-501.
Escrow accounts, RP §10-504.
Notice.
Inclusion in custom home contract required, RP §10-506.
Trusts.
Failure to pay lawful claims of person furnishing labor or material.
Presumption of appropriation in violation of trust, RP §10-503.
Payments received held in trust, RP §10-502.
Buyers.
Defined, RP §10-501.
Citation of subtitle, RP §10-509.
Contracts.
Custom home contracts.
Contents.
Requirements, RP §10-505.
Disclosures.
Buyer's risk under mechanics' lien laws, RP §10-506.
Certification by builder, RP §10-506.
Escrow account requirement notice, RP §10-506.
Required, RP §10-505.
Defined, RP §10-501.
Custom home.
Defined, RP §10-501.
Custom home builders. See within this heading, "Builders."
Definitions, RP §10-501.
Deposits.
Defined, RP §10-501.
Disclosures.
Contracts between custom home builders and buyers, RP §10-506.
Draw schedules.
Defined, RP §10-501.
Escrow.
Accounts in lieu of, RP §10-504.
Notice.
Inclusion in custom home contracts, RP §10-506.
Injunctions.
Violations of provisions, RP §10-507.
Labor or materials.
Custom home builders.
Failure to pay lawful claims of any person furnishing.
Presumption of appropriation in violation of trust, RP §10-503.
Mechanics' lien laws.
Buyer's risk under.
Disclosure required, RP §10-506.
Notice.
Escrow account requirement notice.
Inclusion in custom home contracts.
Required, RP §10-506.

CUSTOM HOME PROTECTION —Cont'd
Penalties.
Violations of provisions, RP §10-507.
Presumptions.
Custom home builders.
Failure to pay lawful claims of any person
furnishing labor or material.
Presumption of appropriation in violation of
trust, RP §10-503.
Title.
Citation of subtitle, RP §10-509.
Trusts.
Custom home builders.
Failure to pay lawful claims of any person
furnishing labor or material.
Presumption of appropriation in violation of
trust, RP §10-503.
Payments received held in trust, RP §10-502.
Unfair or deceptive trade practices.
Conduct constituting, RP §10-507.
Violations of provisions, RP §10-507.

CVISN TRANSPONDERS.
Cloned CVISN transponders, TR §25-112.
Penalties, TR §27-112.

CY PRES.
Charities.
Doctrine recognized, ET §14-302.
Investment of institutional funds.
Doctrine not limited by section, ET §15-407.

D

DAIRIES.
General provisions.
See MILK AND MILK PRODUCTS.

DAIRY PRODUCTS CONTAINERS.
Containers used by distributors and retailers.
Returnable containers and textiles.
Registration, prohibited acts, BR §§19-301 to
19-307.

DAMAGES.
Actions.
Remedy for injury to person or property, MD
Const DofR Art 19.
Alienation of affection.
Prohibited actions.
General provisions.
See ACTIONS.
Animals.
Injury to pet, CJ §11-110.
Antitrust act.
Action for damages, CL §11-209.
Evidence.
Judgment as evidence, CL §11-210.
Athlete agents.
Civil action by educational institution, BR §4-415.
Aviation.
Collision of aircraft, TR §5-1004.
Forced landing, TR §5-1001.
Injuries to persons or property, TR §5-1005.
Lien for damages, TR §5-1005.
Baltimore City.
Local government tort claims act, CJ §§5-301 to
5-304.
See TORTS.
Bank deposits and collections.
Measure of damages, CL §4-103.
Wrongful dishonor, CL §4-402.

DAMAGES —Cont'd
Bills of lading.
Limitations of liability in bill of lading, CL §7-309.
Blind persons.
Guide dogs.
Liability of blind or visually handicapped person
for damages done by dog to premises or
facilities, 30 §33.
Bonds, surety.
Clerk or register of wills.
Action on bond, CJ §11-203.
Credit services businesses.
Claims against bonds.
Liability for damages, CL §14-1910.
Bounding lands.
Penalty for damage or removal of markers, RP
§14-111.
Cable television service, interference with, CR
§7-303.
Cap.
Health care malpractice claims.
Noneconomic damages, limitation, CJ §3-2A-09.
Noneconomic damages in personal injury action,
CJ §11-108.
Caps on damages.
Motor vehicles.
Claims against administration, TR §13-210.
Carriers.
Limitation of liability.
Carrier issuing bill of lading, CL §7-309.
Charities.
Solicitations.
Failure to comply with requirements, BR
§6-509.
Check cashing services.
Third parties injured by, FI §12-127.
Checks.
Dishonored checks.
Collection of dishonored checks and other
instruments.
Time for seeking after dishonor, when
prohibited, CL §15-802.
Child access to firearm violation.
Recovery not diminished by violation, CR §4-104.
Cigars and cigarettes.
Cigarette sales below cost act.
Action for damages, CL §11-508.
Clerks of court.
Action on bond, CJ §11-203.
Commercial code.
When consequential, special or penal damages
recoverable, CL §1-106.
**Communications and transactional records
access,** CJ §10-4A-08.
Comparative negligence.
Bank deposits and collections.
Unauthorized signature or alteration,
customer's duty to report, CL §4-406.
Computer information transactions.
Generally, CL §22-807.
Licensee's damages, CL §22-809.
Licensor's damages, CL §22-808.
Recoupment, CL §22-810.
Condominiums.
Actions against governing body.
Actual damages, RP §14-118.
Conflicting remedies, CL §11-1207.
Consequential damages.
Funds transfers.
Failure of beneficiary's bank to pay, CL
§4A-404.

DAMAGES —Cont'd
Consequential damages —Cont'd
Funds transfers —Cont'd
Late or improper execution or failure to execute
payment orders, CL §4A-305.
Letters of credit.
Wrongful dishonor.
Incidental but not consequential damages, CL
§5-111.
Consumer credit reporting agencies.
Failure to comply with subtitle, CL §14-1213.
Consumer protection.
Action for damages, CL §13-408.
Fine prints.
Violations of subtitle, CL §14-505.
Unfair or deceptive trade practices.
Damages unnecessary, CL §13-302.
Continuing care contracts.
Action by subscribers for recovery of damages,
70B §19.
Contributory fault.
Bank deposits and collections.
Unauthorized signature or alteration,
customer's duty to report, CL §4-406.
Cooperative housing corporations.
Actions against governing body.
Actual damages, RP §14-118.
Copyright royalties, CL §11-1405.
Counties.
Local government tort claims act, CJ §§5-301 to
5-304.
See TORTS.
Roads.
Opening or altering roads, 25 §§146 to 149.
Credit.
Credit grantor closed end credit provisions.
Consumer borrowers, CL §12-1022.
Treble damages, CL §12-1018.
Credit grantor revolving credit provisions.
Consumer borrowers, CL §12-922.
Treble damages for violations, CL §12-918.
Credit card numbers, access device numbers.
Unauthorized disclosure or use, possession, CR
§8-217.
Deaf or mute persons.
Guide dogs.
Liability of deaf or mute person for damages
done by dog to premises or facilities, 30
§33.
Death by wrongful act.
General provisions.
See DEATH BY WRONGFUL ACT.
Discrimination.
Commercial discrimination.
Frivolous contested case proceedings, SF
§19-109.
Dishonored checks.
Collection of dishonored checks and other
instruments.
Time for seeking after dishonor, when
prohibited, CL §15-802.
Distress for rent.
Rights of third party when goods sold under
distress, RP §8-323.
Dogs.
Guide dogs.
Liability for damages done by dog to premises
or facilities, 30 §33.
Vicious dogs.
Payment of damages for claims, 24 §11-507.

DAMAGES —Cont'd
Draining lands.
Consideration of damage by board of viewers, 25
§72.
Ditches across land of another, 25 §97.
Payment from first funds available, 25 §91.
Drug dealer liability, CJ §§3-1601 to 3-1607.
See DRUG DEALER LIABILITY ACT.
Email.
Unauthorized, false or misleading information.
Commercial electronic mail, CL §14-3003.
Eminent domain.
General provisions, PropAct Rule 12-208; RP
§§12-101 to 12-212.
See EMINENT DOMAIN.
Equal credit opportunity.
Civil liability, CL §12-707.
Equipment dealer contracts.
Violations by suppliers.
Civil penalties, CL §19-302.
Evidence.
Punitive damages for personal injuries.
Evidence of defendant's financial means, CJ
§10-913.
Fish and fisheries.
Nonnative aquatic organisms.
Abatement of nuisance, NR §4-205.1.
Foreclosure.
Action by homeowner for damages, RP §7-320.
Forests and parks.
Cutting and burning.
Liability to aggrieved parties, NR §5-409.
Railroads.
Maintenance of safety strips.
Compliance not to bar recovery of damages,
NR §5-712.
Foster parents.
Reimbursement for damages, 83C §2-131.
Franchises.
Civil liability, BR §14-227.
Gasoline.
Marketing agreements.
Wrongful termination or cancellation, CL
§11-307.
Hazardous waste facility siting.
Liability of subdivisions, EN §7-413.
Health care malpractice claims.
Noneconomic damages, limitation, CJ §3-2A-09.
Highways.
County roads.
Assessments for opening or altering public
roads, 25 §§146 to 149.
Motor vehicles.
Liability for damage to highway or structure,
TR §24-208.
Homeowners' associations.
Actions against governing body.
Actual damages, RP §14-118.
Sale of lots.
Information to be supplied by vendor.
Untrue statements or omissions by vendor.
Liability for damages, RP §11B-109.
Home solicitation sales.
Violations of subtitle.
Liability for damages, CL §14-304.
Immigration consultants.
Violation of provisions, CL §14-3306.
Immunization.
Child immunizations.
Damages arising from properly authorized
immunization, HG §18-4A-05.

DAMAGES —Cont'd
Injunctions.
Adequate remedy at law, SpecPro Rule 15-502.
Waste after injunction, RP §14-102.
Insurance.
Joint insurance association.
Limits of liability, IN §25-405.
Joint insurance association.
Limits of liability, IN §25-405.
Joint tenants and tenants in common.
Waste, RP §14-102.
Judgments and decrees.
See JUDGMENTS AND DECREES.
Jurisdiction.
Over persons outside this state.
General provisions.
See JURISDICTION.
Jury.
Personal injuries.
Noneconomic damages.
Limitation on.
Jury trials, CJ §11-108.
Labor and employment relations.
Wholesale sales representatives.
Action by sales representative.
Treble damages, LE §3-605.
Landlord and tenant.
Failure to provide tenant with possession.
Consequential damages, RP §8-204.
Duty of landlord to mitigate damages, RP
§8-207.
Military personnel.
Receipt of permanent or temporary transfer
orders.
Liability of personnel, RP §8-212.1.
Mitigation of damages.
Breach of lease, RP §8-207.
Failure to provide tenant with possession, RP
§8-207.
Prohibited provisions in lease agreement.
Recovery of damages by tenant, RP §8-208.
Tenant holding over, RP §8-402.
Tenant's failure or refusal to take possession at
beginning of term.
Mitigation of damages by landlord, RP §8-207.
Termination of occupancy before end of term.
Duty of aggrieved party to mitigate damages,
RP §8-207.
Law enforcement personnel.
Local government tort claims act.
Act or omission giving rise to judgment for
punitive damages.
Indemnification prohibited, CJ §5-303.
Letters of credit, CL §5-111.
Life estates.
Waste, RP §14-102.
Malpractice.
Health care malpractice claims.
Noneconomic damages, limitation, CJ §3-2A-09.
Mandamus, SpecPro Rule 15-701.
Marriage.
Breach of promise to marry.
Prohibited actions.
General provisions.
See ACTIONS.
Medical records.
Destruction of records.
Liability for actual damages, HG §4-403.
Disclosure, HG §4-309.
Mental hygiene law.
Violations, HG §10-1002.

DAMAGES —Cont'd
Mining.
Measure of damages for abstracting minerals from
plaintiff's land, CJ §11-202.
Strip mining.
Open-pit mining.
Right of entry.
Damages by agents, employees or
contractors of department, EN §15-515.
Minors.
Recoveries in tort, ET §§13-401 to 13-407.
See MINORS.
Montgomery county.
Alcoholic beverages.
Liquor control department.
Immunity from suits for damages, CJ §5-504.
Mortgages and deeds of trust.
Waste, RP §14-102.
Morticians.
Injunctive relief.
Proof of actual damages, HO §7-316.1.
Motorized wheelchair warranty enforcement.
Violations of provisions, CL §14-2705.
Motor vehicles.
Automotive warranty enforcement act.
Violations, CL §14-1504.
Highways.
Liability for damage to highway or structure,
TR §24-208.
Manufacturers, distributors and factory branches.
Licenses.
Violations of subtitle.
Right of injured persons to sue for damages,
TR §15-213.
Security interests.
Claims for damages against administration, TR
§13-210.
Towing.
Parking lots.
Persons undertaking towing or removal.
Violations of subtitle, TR §21-10A-06.
Municipal corporations.
Actions in contracts.
Liability for punitive damages.
Immunity, 23A §1A.
Noneconomic damages.
Health care malpractice claims.
Limitation, CJ §3-2A-09.
Personal injury actions.
Limitation on, CJ §11-108.
Personal injuries, CJ §11-109.
Noneconomic damages.
Limitation on, CJ §11-108.
Punitive damages.
Evidence of defendant's financial means, CJ
§10-913.
Pets.
Injury to, CJ §11-110.
Pharmacists and pharmacies.
Injunction against unauthorized practice of
pharmacy, HO §12-319.
Port administration.
Right of entry to make surveys and examinations.
Damages resulting from entry, TR §6-306.
Prisoner litigation.
Compensatory or punitive damages, CJ §5-1006.
Prisons and prisoners.
Payment to individuals convicted, sentenced, and
confined in error, SF §10-501.
Procurement.
Collusion.
Liability for damages, SF §11-205.

DAMAGES —Cont'd
Public works contracts.
Wages.
Payroll records.
Noncompliance with requirements, SF
§17-220.
Violations of provisions, SF §17-222.
Punitive damages.
Charitable solicitations.
Failure to comply with requirements, BR
§6-509.
Counties.
Commissioners.
Contract actions.
Not liable for punitive damages, CJ §5-508.
Municipal corporations.
Contract actions.
Not liable for punitive damages, CJ §5-507.
Personal injuries.
Evidence of defendant's financial means, CJ
§10-913.
Prisoner litigation, CJ §5-1006.
Tort claims act.
Local government tort claims act.
No liability for punitive damages, CJ §5-303.
Waiver of immunity.
Immunity not waived for punitive damages,
SG §12-104.
Trade secrets.
When punitive damages allowed, CL §11-1203.
Railroads.
Change in location or grade of road, PUC §5-406.
Crossings.
Disposition between highway administration
and railroads, TR §8-641.
Draining lands.
Improvement crossing railroad right of way, 25
§100.
Forests and parks.
Maintenance of safety strips.
Compliance not to bar recovery of damages,
NR §5-712.
Using or occupying road, street, alley or other
public way.
Responsibility for damages to private property,
PUC §5-407.
Records.
Access to public records.
Liability for damages, SG §10-623.
Registers of wills.
Action on bond, CJ §11-203.
Remedy for injury to person or property, MD
Const DofR Art 19.
Rental-purchase agreements.
Penalties.
Violations of subchapter, CL §12-1110.
Sale of goods, UCC.
Acceptance of goods.
Buyer's damages for breach in regard to, CL
§2-714.
Antecedent breach.
Effect of cancellation or rescission on claims, CL
§2-720.
Consequential damages.
Buyers, CL §2-715.
Contractual limitations, CL §2-719.
Cover by buyer, CL §2-712.
Deduction from price, CL §2-717.
Delivery of goods.
Buyer's damages for nondelivery, CL §2-713.

DAMAGES —Cont'd
Sale of goods, UCC —Cont'd
Incidental damages.
Buyers, CL §2-715.
Recovery by person in position of seller, CL
§2-707.
Sellers, CL §2-710.
Limitation, CL §2-718.
Liquidation, CL §2-718.
Nonacceptance of goods.
Sellers, CL §2-708.
Repudiation by sellers.
Buyers' remedies, CL §2-713.
Repudiation of buyer.
Seller's damages, CL §2-708.
Resale of goods by seller, CL §§2-703, 2-706.
Warranty breaches, CL §2-714.
Schools.
Principals and teachers intervening in fights.
Compensation for injury and time lost from
duties, ED §7-307.
Use of property for other than school purposes.
Liability for damages, ED §7-110.
Secured transactions.
Remedies for noncompliance with article, CL
§9-625.
Consumer goods transactions.
Statutory damages, CL §9-625.
Limitation of liability, CL §9-628.
Statutory damages.
Consumer goods transactions, CL §9-625.
Generally, CL §9-625.
Requests for accounting, collateral, etc., CL
§9-625.
Surplus or deficiency an issue.
Applicable rules, CL §9-626.
Deficiency eliminated or reduced, CL §9-625.
Nonconsumer transactions, CL §9-626.
Securities.
Securities act.
Violations of title.
Civil liability, CA §11-703.
Sediment control.
Liability for damages, EN §4-116.
Shoplifting generally, CJ §§3-1301 to 3-1308.
See SHOPLIFTING.
Specific performance.
Refusal to specifically enforce contract on grounds
that adequate remedy and damages available,
CJ §3-601.
Start-up business ventures.
Remedy for violation, BR §14-126.
State.
Tort claims act.
Generally, SG §§12-101 to 12-110.
See TORTS.
Stray domestic animals.
Valuation and notice of damages, AG §3-603.
Support and maintenance.
Earnings.
Withholding.
Deductions from earnings.
Violations, FL §10-129.
Surveillance by camera of private residence,
CR §3-903.
Surveillance of individual in private place, CR
§3-901.
With prurient intent, CR §3-902.
Survey stations.
Agreement on damages, BOP §1-302.

DAMAGES —Cont'd
Tax sales.
Foreclosure of right of redemption.
Action for damages, TP §14-845.
Telecommunications services theft, CR §7-318.
Telegraph or telephone company lines and facilities.
Liability for damage person sustains through erection, continuance or use, PUC §8-104.
Suit by owner or possessor of land after notice to remove, PUC §8-105.
Tenants.
Waste, RP §14-102.
Time-sharing.
Violations of provisions, RP §11A-125.
Tort claims act.
Local government tort claims act.
Limitation on liability, CJ §5-303.
Punitive damages.
Indemnification for judgment for punitive damages, CJ §5-303.
Prohibition on liability, CJ §5-303.
Waiver of immunity.
Immunity not waived for punitive damages, SG §12-104.
Trademarks and service marks.
Infringement, BR §1-414.
Trade secrets.
Misappropriation, CL §11-1203.
Treble damages.
Check cashing services, FI §12-127.
Foreclosure.
Action by homeowner for damages, RP §7-320.
Immigration consultants, CL §14-3306.
Wholesale sales representatives.
Action by sales representative, LE §3-605.
Universities and colleges.
Trespass upon grounds.
Penalty, ED §26-102.
Visual surveillance of individual in private place, CR §3-901.
With prurient intent, CR §3-902.
Volunteers.
Liability, CJ §5-407.
Washington suburban sanitary district.
Water and sewer systems.
Damage caused by sanitary sewer backup, 29 §18-106.
Waste.
After injunction, RP §14-102.
General provisions, RP §14-102.
Water pollution.
Aquatic resources.
Investigation of damage, EN §4-405.
Defined, EN §4-401.
Oils.
Liability for damages caused by spillage, EN §4-409.
Persons responsible for discharge, EN §4-419.
Suits against persons liable for damage, EN §4-405.
Watershed associations.
Eminent domain, 25 §201.
Examination by watershed viewers, 25 §188.
Preference, 25 §207.
Wills.
Custodian of will.
Liability for failure or refusal to deliver will, ET §4-202.
Register of wills.
Action on bond, CJ §11-203.

DAMS.
Agriculture.
Construction or repair permits.
Exceptions, EN §5-510.
Exemptions, EN §5-503.
Appropriation or use permits, EN §§5-501 to 5-514.
Application and construction of subtitle, EN §5-512.
Applications.
Procedures, EN §5-506.
Compliance, EN §5-508.
Conditions, EN §5-507.
Recording required, EN §5-508.
Grant or denial, EN §5-507.
Hearings.
Permit applications, EN §5-506.
Materials to accompany applications, EN §5-505.
Misdemeanors.
Violations of chapter, EN §5-514.
Notices.
Permit applications, EN §5-506.
Periodic review, EN §5-511.
Policy of state, EN §5-501.
Power plants.
Application for certificates of public convenience and necessity, EN §5-502.
Required, EN §5-502.
Time limits, EN §5-510.
Water supply emergencies.
Priority of uses, EN §5-502.
Aquatic habitat below dam.
Maintenance, NR §4-513.
Bloomington dam project.
Potomac water authority.
Contracts with federal government, EN §5-406.
Construction or repair permits.
Application and construction of subtitle, EN §5-512.
Applications.
Procedure, EN §5-506.
Compliance, EN §5-508.
Conditions, EN §5-507.
Recording required, EN §5-508.
Grant or denial, EN §5-507.
Hearings.
Permit applications, EN §5-506.
Materials to accompany applications, EN §5-505.
Notices.
Permit applications, EN §5-506.
Required, EN §5-503.
Time limits, EN §5-510.
Crimes and offenses.
Fish ladders.
Violations of section, NR §4-502.
Demolition of residential structures.
Construction or repair permits.
Exemptions, EN §5-503.
Fish.
Ladders.
Required, NR §4-502.
Obstructions to passage of fish, NR §4-501.
Flood control, EN §§5-701 to 5-809.
See FLOOD CONTROL.
Hearings.
Permit applications, EN §5-506.
Injunctions.
Fish ladders.
Enforcement of section, NR §4-502.
Jones Falls.
Flood plan management, EN §5-503.

DAMS —Cont'd
Misdemeanors.
Appropriation or use permits.
Violations of chapter, EN §5-514.
Fish ladders.
Violations of section, NR §4-502.
Notices.
Department of the environment.
Repair or removal, EN §5-509.
Fish ladders.
Violations of section, NR §4-502.
Permit applications, EN §5-506.
Power plants.
Appropriation or use permits.
Application for certificates of public convenience
and necessity, EN §5-502.
Repair or removal.
Required by department of the environment, EN
§5-509.
Water pollution.
Maintenance of water quality and aquatic habitat
below dam, NR §4-513.
Water resources.
Appropriation or use permits, EN §§5-501 to
5-514. See within this heading,
"Appropriation or use permits."
Watersheds.
Jurisdiction.
Safety and flood control, EN §5-503.
Water supply emergencies.
Appropriation or use permits.
Priority of uses, EN §5-502.
Wild and scenic rivers.
Construction, operation or maintenance of dams,
NR §8-406.

DANCE HALLS.
Permits.
Certain counties, 25 §27.

DANCES.
Prince George's county.
Benefit performance by qualified organization, CR
§§13-1901 to 13-1907.

DANGEROUS ANIMALS.
Dogs, CR §10-619.
Importing, selling, or trading in, CR §10-621.

DANGEROUS HOUSEHOLD SUBSTANCES.
Child resistant packaging.
General provisions, HG §§22-301 to 22-312.
See POISONS.

DANGEROUS WEAPONS.
Armed carjacking, CR §3-405.
Carrying concealed or with intent to injure,
CR §4-101.
Defined, CR §4-101.
Firearms generally.
See FIREARMS.
Minor carrying weapon, hours prohibited.
Counties applicable, CR §4-101.
Minor possessing pepper mace, prohibition, CR
§4-101.
Robbery with dangerous weapon, CR §3-403.
Transfer of switchblade or shooting knife.
Prohibition, CR §4-105.
Weapons generally.
See WEAPONS.
Wearing concealed or with intent to injure, CR
§4-101.

DATABASES.
Agriculture department.
Agricultural land link program, AG §2-1201.

DATABASES —Cont'd
Building codes.
Central automated database, PS §12-506.
Veterans.
Veterans' database.
Department of veterans affairs to develop and
maintain, SG §9-943.

DATA PROCESSING.
Compilation of data.
Requirement of identification or authentication,
Evid Rule 5-901.
Documents.
Charitable giving information program.
Data available to the public, BR §6-201.
State documents.
Data bases, SG §7-206.2.
Sales and use tax.
Exemptions.
Custom computer software service, TG §11-219.
Unauthorized access to computers, CR §7-302.
Statute of limitations, CJ §5-106.

DATE OF FINALITY.
See PROPERTY TAXES.

DATE RAPE.
**Administering controlled dangerous substance
without persons knowledge,** CR §5-624.

DAY-CARE CENTERS.
Actions.
Adult day care centers.
State's right of recovery.
Civil actions, HG §24-706.
Adult day care centers, HG §§24-701 to 24-707.
Criminal history records checks of employees, HG
§§19-1901 to 19-1912.
Definitions, HG §24-701.
Grants.
Allocation and use of state funds.
Certification of allocations, HG §24-704.
Compliance with subtitle, HG §24-705.
Generally, HG §24-704.
Prohibited uses, HG §24-704.
Terms and conditions, HG §24-704.
Application.
Approval and recommendation, HG §24-703.
Authorization, HG §24-702.
Uses, HG §24-702.
Regulations generally, HG §24-707.
State's right of recovery of facility, HG §24-706.
Aged persons.
Day-care, HG §§14-201 to 14-206.
See DAY-CARE FOR THE ELDERLY.
Child care centers, FL §§5-570 to 5-589.
See CHILD CARE CENTERS.
Definitions.
Adult day care centers, HG §24-701.
Deposits.
Adult day care centers.
State's right of recovery.
Deposit of funds recovered, HG §24-706.
Elderly persons.
Day-care for the elderly, HG §§14-201 to 14-206.
See DAY-CARE FOR THE ELDERLY.
Grants.
Adult day care centers, HG §§24-702 to 24-705.
See within this heading, "Adult day care
centers."
Judgments and decrees.
Adult day care centers.
State's right of recovery.
Finding of no default or payment of judgment,
HG §24-706.

DAY-CARE CENTERS —Cont'd
Judgments and decrees —Cont'd
Adult day care centers —Cont'd
State's right of recovery —Cont'd
Judgment for state, HG §24-706.
Liens.
Adult day care centers.
State's right of recovery.
Temporary lien, HG §24-706.
Medically handicapped adults.
Applicability of subtitle, HG §14-303.
Cooperation between departments, HG §14-304.
Definitions, HG §14-301.
Department of health and mental hygiene.
Purchase of services, HG §14-304.
Responsibilities.
General responsibilities, HG §14-304.
Department of human resources.
Cooperation between departments, HG §14-304.
Intent of legislature, HG §14-302.
Legislative intent, HG §14-302.
Medical assistance.
Reimbursement authorized, HG §15-111.
Purposes of subtitle, HG §14-302.
Scope of subtitle, HG §14-303.
Statement of purpose, HG §14-302.
Notice.
Adult day care centers.
State's right of recovery.
Record notice, HG §24-706.
Poor.
Medical assistance.
Reimbursement authorized, HG §15-111.
Public works.
Facilities capital programs.
Adult day care centers, HG §§24-701 to 24-707.
See within this heading, "Adult day care centers."
Rules and regulations.
Adult day care centers.
Department adoption of regulations for implementation of subtitle provisions, HG §24-707.
Sex offender registration.
Entry onto day care property prohibited, CP §11-722.
Taxation.
Credits.
Property tax credits for day care providers, TP §9-213.
Property tax credits for family day care homes, TP §9-214.
Property tax credits for group day care centers, TP §9-214.
Waiver.
Adult day care centers.
State's right of recovery, HG §24-706.

DAY-CARE FOR THE ELDERLY.
Applicability of subtitle, HG §14-203.
Definitions, HG §14-201.
Department of aging.
Plans, rules and regulations.
Submission to department of aging, HG §14-206.
Department of health and mental hygiene.
Funds.
Use of appropriated funds, HG §14-205.
General responsibility, HG §14-204.
Responsibilities.
General responsibilities, HG §14-204.

DAY-CARE FOR THE ELDERLY —Cont'd
Funds.
Use of appropriated funds, HG §14-205.
Legislative intent, HG §14-202.
Plans, HG §14-206.
Poor.
Medical assistance.
Reimbursement authorized, HG §15-111.
Purposes of subtitle, HG §14-202.
Rules and regulations.
Adoption of rules and regulations, HG §14-206.
Scope of subtitle, HG §14-203.
Standards, HG §14-206.

DEADBEAT PARENTS.
Child support enforcement administration, FL §§10-106 to 10-118.
Clerks of court.
Delegation of responsibility for support enforcement to clerks, FL §10-114.
Desertion of minor child, FL §§10-203, 10-219.
Drivers' license suspension, FL §10-119; TR §16-203.
Failure to pay child support, CJ §5-111.
Imprisonment for delinquent support payment not imprisonment for debt, MD Const Art III §38.
Income withholding, FL §§10-121 to 10-138.
Occupational license suspension.
Support and maintenance, FL §10-119.3.
Privatization of enforcement pilot program, FL §§10-119.1, 10-119.2.
Unemployment compensation.
Deduction from benefits for support obligations, LE §§8-803, 8-807.
Uniform interstate family support act, FL §§10-301 to 10-359.
See SUPPORT AND MAINTENANCE.

DEAD BODIES.
Anatomical gift act.
General provisions, ET §§4-501 to 4-512.
See ANATOMICAL GIFT ACT.
Anatomy board.
See ANATOMY BOARD.
Animals.
Removal of carcasses from highways, TR §8-602.
Boards and commissions.
Anatomy board.
See ANATOMY BOARD.
Body.
Defined, HG §5-101.
Body parts.
Distribution and use, HG §5-407.
Burial sites.
Removal of human remains, CR §§10-401 to 10-404.
Buying, selling or transporting, HG §5-408.
Caskets.
Cremation.
Casket not required, HG §5-505.
Claim of body, HG §5-406.
Consent.
Postmortem examinations, HG §5-501.
Control after 72 hours, HG §5-406.
Cremation.
Caskets.
Use of casket not required, HG §5-505.
Definitions, HG §5-508.
Disposition generally, HG §§5-509 to 5-512.
Crematory operators.
Reliance on authorized agents of deceased, HG §5-511.

DEAD BODIES —Cont'd
Cremation —Cont'd
Disposition generally —Cont'd
Disposing of one's own body.
Written formalities, HG §5-509.
Documents negating cremation, HG §5-512.
Failure to agree on disposition, HG §5-510.
Identification tag required, HO §7-411.
Penalty for violation, HG §5-507.
Required identification and authorization, HG §5-502.
Time interval, HG §5-503.
Transporting to crematory, HG §5-504.
Definitions.
Cremation, HG §5-508.
Disposition of body.
Decisions made by individual or family members, HO §7-410.
Wills.
Right to dispose of body by will, HG §5-408.1.
Dissection.
Burial-transit permit required, HG §4-226.
Distribution and use.
Anatomy board to distribute, HG §5-407.
Donated bodies.
Embalming, HG §5-406.1.
Exclusive control of board, HG §5-406.1.
Notice to board, HG §5-406.1.
Removal to designated morgue, HG §5-406.1.
Eminent domain.
Allowance for removal, RP §12-112.
Funeral directors and embalmers.
See MORTICIANS.
Guardian and ward.
Consent for postmortem examination, HG §5-501.
Health officers.
Control of body by health officer, HG §5-506.
Husband and wife.
Consent for postmortem examination, HG §5-501.
Identification tag, HO §7-411.
Inmates at state correctional facility.
Unclaimed body of indigent inmate, disposition, COR §9-604.
Maryland historical trust.
Unlawfully sold human remains or funerary objects.
Appropriation and disposition, CR §10-403.
Medical schools.
Distribution and use of dead bodies or body parts, HG §5-407.
Minors.
Consent for postmortem examinations, HG §5-501.
Morgues.
Removal to designated morgue, HG §5-406.
Postmortem examiners.
See POSTMORTEM EXAMINERS.
Pre-need burial contracts.
Decisions concerning disposition of body, HO §7-410.
Removal of human remains from burial sites, CR §§10-401 to 10-404.
Ascertaining cause of death.
Removal of human remains, CR §10-402.
Authorization to relocate human remains, procedure, CR §10-402.
Definitions, CR §10-401.
Determining whether erroneously interred.
Removal of human remains, CR §10-402.
Notice of intent to relocate human remains, CR §10-402.

DEAD BODIES —Cont'd
Removal of human remains from burial sites —Cont'd
Reburial.
Removal of human remains, CR §10-402.
Reinterment of removed human remains, CR §10-402.
Selling unlawfully removed human remains or funerary objects, CR §10-403.
Statute of limitation on prosecution.
Unauthorized removal of human remains, CR §10-402.
Unauthorized removal of human remains, CR §10-402.
Transportation.
Permit required, HG §4-226.
Wills.
Disposition of body by will, HG §5-408.1.

DEADLY AGENTS.
Catastrophic health emergency.
Governor's power to proclaim, PS §§14-3A-01 to 14-3A-08.
See HEALTH EMERGENCIES.

DEADLY WEAPONS.
Firearms generally.
See FIREARMS.
School property, CR §4-102.
Weapons generally.
See WEAPONS.

DEAD MAN'S STATUTE, CJ §9-116.

DEAF AND HEARING IMPAIRED.
Advisory council for the deaf and hard of hearing, SG §§9-2404 to 9-2406.
American sign language.
Academic credit.
County boards of education may give credit for study of American sign language, ED §4-111.
Recognition as language system, 30 §34.
Blind persons.
See BLIND PERSONS.
Contracts.
Infant program.
Administration of program, HG §13-604.
Criminal proceedings.
Interpreters.
Court appointment to help defendant, compensation and expenses, CP §1-202.
Incompetency or not criminally responsible proceedings, CP §3-103.
Cultural minority, 30 §34.
Damages.
Guide dogs.
Liability of deaf and hearing impaired persons for damages done by dog to premises or facilities, 30 §33.
Definitions, HG §10-908.
Hearing impaired infants, HG §13-601.
Meaning of deaf, mute and blind, 30 §31.
Office of the deaf and hard of hearing, SG §9-2401.
Dogs.
Guide dogs, 30 §33.
Employers and employees.
Rights of deaf and hearing impaired persons in employment, 30 §33.
Fines.
Denial or interference with deaf and hearing impaired person's rights, 30 §33.

DEAF AND HEARING IMPAIRED —Cont'd
Food and food establishments.
Right of deaf and hearing impaired person to
public facilities, 30 §33.
Guide dogs, 30 §33.
Hotels.
Rights of deaf and hearing impaired persons to
public facilities, 30 §33.
Housing.
Damages.
Liability of deaf and hearing impaired tenant
for damages done by dog, 30 §33.
Rights of deaf and hearing impaired persons to
public facilities, 30 §33.
Identification as cultural minority, 30 §34.
Infants program, HG §§13-601 to 13-605.
Advisory council, HG §13-603.
Based on model system, HG §13-602.
Contracts for administration of program, HG
§13-604.
Definitions, HG §13-601.
Establishment, HG §13-602.
Guidelines for operations, HG §13-603.
Health insurance.
Screening, required child wellness coverage, IN
§15-817.
Results of universal hearing screening, HG
§13-605.
Secretary.
Powers and duties, HG §13-604.
Interpreters.
Parties and witnesses.
Certain persons in civil proceedings may have
interpreters, CJ §9-114.
Minorities.
Identification as cultural minority, 30 §34.
Minors.
Infants program, HG §§13-601 to 13-605. See
within this heading, "Infants program."
Newborn hearing screening.
Health insurance.
Required child wellness coverage, IN §15-817.
Schools. See within this heading, "Schools."
Motor carriers.
Rights of deaf and hearing impaired persons to
public facilities, 30 §33.
Motor vehicles.
Pedestrians.
Right-of-way, TR §21-511.
Stopping.
Vehicles to come to full stop, TR §21-511.
Negligence.
Contributory negligence.
Deaf and hearing impaired pedestrian not
carrying cane or using guide dog, 30 §33.
Newborn hearing screening.
Health insurance.
Required child wellness coverage, IN §15-817.
Not modified or altered by section, 30 §33.
Occupational deafness.
Workers' compensation, LE §§9-649 to 9-652.
See WORKERS' COMPENSATION.
Office of the deaf and hard of hearing, SG
§§9-2401 to 9-2407.
Advisory council for the deaf and hard of hearing,
SG §§9-2404 to 9-2406.
Duties, SG §9-2406.
Members, SG §§9-2404, 9-2405.
Definitions, SG §9-2401.
Director, SG §9-2402.
Reports, SG §9-2407.

DEAF AND HEARING IMPAIRED —Cont'd
Office of the deaf and hard of hearing —Cont'd
Duties, SG §§9-2402, 9-2403.
Established, SG §9-2402.
Programs.
Advisory committee, HG §10-910.
Appropriations, HG §10-913.
Definitions, HG §10-908.
Infants. See within this heading, "Infants
program."
Location, HG §10-909.
Required, HG §10-909.
Secretary.
Duties, HG §10-911.
Staff.
Professionals and paraprofessionals, HG
§10-912.
Public buildings and grounds.
Rights of deaf and hearing impaired persons to
public facilities, 30 §33.
Railroads.
Rights of deaf and hearing impaired persons to
public facilities, 30 §33.
**Rights of deaf and hearing impaired persons
to public facilities,** 30 §33.
Scholarships.
Teachers of persons with impaired hearing.
Preparation of teachers, ED §18-701.
Schools.
Absence.
Excused by superintendent or principal, ED
§8-302.
Age between six and nineteen years, ED §8-301.
Attend school for deaf, ED §8-302.
Definition, ED §8-301.
Examinations.
Medical examinations, ED §8-311.
Handicapped children.
General provisions, ED §§8-401 to 8-417.
See SCHOOLS.
Maryland School for the Deaf.
General provisions.
See SCHOOLS.
Penalty.
Inducing to leave school, ED §8-311.
Person who has child under control.
Failure to comply with provisions, ED §8-311.
Rights of deaf and hearing impaired persons in
employment, 30 §33.
Sign language.
Academic credit.
County boards of education.
Board may give credit for study of American
sign language, ED §4-111.
Recognition as language system, 30 §34.
Streets and alleys.
Rights of deaf and hearing impaired persons to
public facilities, 30 §33.
Telegraph and telephone companies.
Facilities for the handicapped.
Teletypewriters.
Requirements, SF §2-507.
Vessels and boats.
Rights of deaf and hearing impaired persons to
public facilities, 30 §33.

DEALERS, MOTOR VEHICLES, TR §§15-301 to
15-315.
See MOTOR VEHICLE DEALERS.

DEATH.
Absence of person.
Presumption of evidence of death.
General provisions, CJ §§3-101 to 3-110.
See ABSENT PERSONS.
Absence of respiratory and cardiac function,
HG §5-202.
Alcoholic beverages.
Licenses.
Death of licensee.
Effect, 2B §10-506.
Amusement attractions.
Records and reports regarding death, BR §3-404.
Willful violation causing death, BR §3-502.
Anatomical gift act.
Time of death, ET §4-508.
Anatomy board.
See ANATOMY BOARD.
Arbitration and award.
Proceeding upon death of either party, CJ
§§3-229, 3-230.
Autopsies.
Medical examiners.
General provisions, HG §5-310.
Bank deposits and collections.
Effect, CL §4-405.
Boards and commissions.
Anatomy board.
See ANATOMY BOARD.
Postmortem examiners commission.
See POSTMORTEM EXAMINERS.
Brain death.
Health care decisions.
Advance directive registry, HG §§5-619 to
5-626.
General provisions, HG §§5-601 to 5-618.
See HEALTH CARE DECISIONS.
Capital punishment.
See DEATH PENALTY.
Cause of death.
Medical examiners.
When cause of death established by medical
examiner, HG §5-310.
Certificates.
Vital records.
See VITAL RECORDS.
Corporations.
Nonstock corporations.
When membership reduced by death, CA
§5-205.
Cremation.
See CREMATION.
Dangerous animals, owner.
Arrangements for transfer of custody, CR §10-621.
Death by wrongful act.
General provisions, SpecPro Rule 15-1001.
Death penalty.
See DEATH PENALTY.
Death with dignity.
Advance directive registry, HG §§5-619 to 5-626.
Health care decisions, HG §§5-601 to 5-618.
See HEALTH CARE DECISIONS.
Deeds.
Effect of use of terms "die without issue" etc., RP
§2-113.
Definitions.
Absence of respiratory and cardiac function, HG
§5-202.
Body, HG §5-101.
Purpose of definition, HG §5-201.
Scope of subtitle, HG §5-201.

DEATH —Cont'd
Descent and distribution.
Absence as evidence of death and absentee
property act.
See ABSENT PERSONS.
Determination of death, HG §5-202.
Developmental disabilities.
Individuals in service or program, HG §7-207.
Mortality and quality review committee, HG
§§5-801 to 5-810.
See DEVELOPMENTAL DISABILITIES.
Distress for rent.
Effect of death of tenant, RP §8-328.
Recovery of rent on death of landlord who is life
tenant, RP §8-106.
Domestic violence.
Local domestic violence fatality review teams, FL
§§4-701 to 4-707.
See DOMESTIC VIOLENCE.
Equipment dealer contracts.
Death of dealer.
Repurchase of inventory, CL §§19-201, 19-202.
Evidence.
Absence as evidence of death and absentee
property act.
See ABSENT PERSONS.
Executors and administrators.
Creditors' claims.
Effect of death, ET §8-102.
Effect, ET §6-304.
Personal representative or guardian of deceased
or disabled personal representative.
Duties, ET §6-304.
Termination.
See EXECUTORS AND ADMINISTRATORS.
Federal finding of presumed death.
Admissibility as evidence, CJ §10-208.
Signature and authority, CJ §10-210.
Fetal death.
Vital records.
See VITAL RECORDS.
Fire department.
Autopsies of fire fighters, HG §5-310.
Funeral directors and embalmers.
General provisions.
See MORTICIANS.
Guardian and ward.
Protection of property.
Effect of death of guardian, ET §13-220.
Health insurance.
Addition of children after death of spouse, IN
§15-404.
Autopsy of insured, IN §15-216.
Continuation coverage for surviving spouses and
dependent children, IN §§15-407, 15-410.
Conversion right of surviving spouse, IN §15-414.
Payment of claim upon death of insured, IN
§15-215.
Hospices.
See HOSPICES.
Income tax.
Taxable year of individual.
Termination on date of death, TG §10-503.
Landlord and tenant.
Payment of rent on death of landlord who is life
tenant, RP §8-106.
Legal death.
When individual considered medically and legally
dead, HG §5-202.
Licenses.
Licensee.
Alcoholic beverage licensee.
Effect of death, 2B §10-506.

DEATH —Cont'd
Life estates.
  Payment of rent on death of landlord who is life
    tenant, RP §8-106.
  Provisions.
    See HEALTH CARE DECISIONS.
Life insurance and annuities.
  See LIFE INSURANCE AND ANNUITIES.
Limited liability company member.
  Cessation of membership, CA §4A-606.
Living wills.
  Health care decisions, HG §§5-601 to 5-618.
    See HEALTH CARE DECISIONS.
Local domestic violence fatality review teams,
  FL §§4-701 to 4-707.
    See DOMESTIC VIOLENCE.
Medical records.
  Destruction of patient's records.
    Procedure upon death of health care provider,
      HG §4-403.
Mental hygiene law.
  Disposition of property on death of individual, HG
    §16-303.
  Patients.
    Reporting requirements, HG §10-714.
Mental retardation.
  Disposition of property on death of mentally
    retarded individual, HG §16-407.
Military services.
  Financial institution franchise tax.
    Abatement of tax, TG §13-908.
Motor vehicle dealers.
  Operation of dealership, TR §15-211.1.
Natural death.
  Advance directive registry, HG §§5-619 to 5-626.
  Health care decisions, HG §§5-601 to 5-618.
    See HEALTH CARE DECISIONS.
Negligence.
  Death by wrongful act.
    General provisions.
      See DEATH BY WRONGFUL ACT.
Nursing homes.
  Unclaimed deceased resident.
    Procedure upon death, 70B §5A.
Occupational safety and health.
  Willful violation causing death.
    Criminal fine and imprisonment, LE §5-806.
Postmortem examiners.
  See POSTMORTEM EXAMINERS.
Power of attorney.
  Not revoked without actual knowledge of death,
    ET §13-602.
  Uncertainty as to whether principal is dead or
    alive.
    When power of attorney not affected by
      disability of principal, ET §13-601.
**President and vice-president of the United
  States.**
  Duty of congress, US Const Art II §1.
  President-elect.
    Provision in case of, US Const Amd 20.
Presumptions.
  Absence as evidence of death and absentee
    property act.
    See ABSENT PERSONS.
Real estate brokers.
  Licenses.
    Continuation of business, BOP §17-319.
Records.
  Vital records.
    See VITAL RECORDS.

DEATH —Cont'd
Simultaneous death act.
  Application.
    No sufficient evidence of survivorship, CJ
      §10-801.
    Not applicable if decedent provides otherwise,
      CJ §10-805.
  Beneficiaries of another's property, CJ §10-802.
  Citation.
    Short title, CJ §10-807.
  Deeds or wills.
    Decedent provides otherwise.
      Subtitle not applicable if decedent provides
        otherwise, CJ §10-805.
  Insurance.
    Decedent provides otherwise.
      Subtitle does not apply if decedent provides
        otherwise, CJ §10-805.
    Policies, CJ §10-804.
  Interpretation.
    Uniform interpretation, CJ §10-806.
  Joint tenants, CJ §10-803.
  Survivorship.
    No sufficient evidence of survivorship, CJ
      §10-801.
  Tenants by entirety, CJ §10-803.
  Trust and trustees.
    Subtitle does not apply if decedent provides
      otherwise, CJ §10-805.
Uniform determination of death act, HG §5-202.
Viatical settlement contracts, IN §§8-601 to
  8-611.
    See VIATICAL SETTLEMENT CONTRACTS.
Vice-president, US Const Art II §1.
Vital records.
  See VITAL RECORDS.
Voter registration.
  Report of deceased persons, EL §3-504.
**When individual considered medically and
  legally dead,** HG §5-202.
Wills.
  Living wills.
    Health care decisions, HG §§5-601 to 5-618.
      See HEALTH CARE DECISIONS.
Wrongful death.
  General provisions.
    See DEATH BY WRONGFUL ACT.

DEATH BY WRONGFUL ACT, SpecPro Rule
  15-1001.
Action for wrongful death.
  Beneficiaries, CJ §3-904.
  Distribution for amount of recovery, CJ §3-904.
  Liability notwithstanding death, CJ §3-902.
  Limitation of actions, CJ §3-904.
  One action, CJ §3-904.
  Verdict, CJ §3-904.
Act occurs outside of state.
  Law applicable, CJ §3-903.
  Rules of pleading and procedure, CJ §3-903.
Child.
  Defined, CJ §3-901.
Conflict of laws.
  General provisions, CJ §3-903.
Damages.
  Death of spouse, minor child or parent of minor
    child, CJ §3-904.
  Death of unmarried child who is not minor, CJ
    §3-904.
  Distribution, CJ §3-904.

DEATH BY WRONGFUL ACT —Cont'd
Decedents' estates.
  Slayer's rule.
    Weight given criminal conviction, CJ §10-919.
Definitions, CJ §3-901.
Drug dealer liability.
  Death caused by use of controlled dangerous
    substances, CJ §§3-1601 to 3-1607.
    See DRUG DEALER LIABILITY ACT.
Executors and administrators.
  Funeral expenses.
    Limitation on recovery, ET §7-401.
  Plaintiff's death.
    Limitation of actions, CJ §3-904.
Funeral expenses.
  Petition and order for funeral expenses.
    Form, Estates Rule 6-415.
Husband and wife.
  Damages.
    Death of spouse, CJ §3-904.
Liability.
  Notwithstanding death, CJ §3-902.
Limitation of actions.
  General provisions, CJ §3-904.
  Occupational diseases, CJ §5-113.
Minors.
  Child of unmarried parents.
    Judicial determination of father, CJ §3-904.
  Damages, CJ §3-904.
  Definition of "parent," CJ §3-901.
  Negligence.
    Parent's or custodian's negligence.
      Not imputed to infant, CJ §10-910.
Noneconomic damages, limitation on, CJ
    §11-108.
Occupational disease.
  Death caused by.
    Limitation of actions, CJ §3-904.
Person.
  Defined, CJ §3-901.
Slayer's rule.
  Weight given criminal conviction, CJ §10-919.
Statute of limitations, CJ §§3-904, 5-113.
Unmarried children.
  Death of unmarried child who is not minor, CJ
    §3-904.
Verdict.
  Action for wrongful death, CJ §3-904.
Vessels and boats.
  Liability notwithstanding death, CJ §3-902.
Wrongful act.
  Defined, CJ §3-901.

**DEATH CAUSED BY USE OF CONTROLLED
  DANGEROUS SUBSTANCES.**
Drug dealer liability, CJ §§3-1601 to 3-1607.
  See DRUG DEALER LIABILITY ACT.

DEATH PENALTY.
Advice of the judge, Crim Rule 4-343.
Age limitation for imposing, CR §2-202.
Aggravating circumstances, CR §2-303.
  Evidence admissible, CR §2-303.
  Jury to consider, CR §2-303.
  Whether mitigating circumstances outweighed.
    Preponderance of evidence, CR §2-303.
Allocution, Crim Rule 4-343.
Appeals.
  Advice of judge, Crim Rule 4-343.
  Court of appeals has exclusive jurisdiction, CJ
    §12-307.
  Review in court of appeals, AppRev Rule 8-306.

DEATH PENALTY —Cont'd
Applicability of provisions, Crim Rule 4-343.
Argument for or against.
  Presentation by state and defendant, CR §2-303.
Automatic review by court of appeals, CR
    §2-401.
Burial of inmate after execution, COR §3-909.
**Certificate prepared by commissioner of
  correction,** COR §3-908.
**Certification of proceedings to court where
  charging document filed,** CR §2-303.
Clergy member may be present at execution,
  COR §3-907.
Commutation or change into confinement.
  Power of governor, COR §7-601.
**Counsel for inmate may be present at
  execution,** COR §3-907.
Court.
  Findings, determination in writing, CR §2-303.
  When proceedings conducted before, CR §2-303.
Custody of individual sentenced to death, COR
    §3-901.
  Reprieve or stay of warrant, COR §3-903.
Definitions, CR §2-303.
Determination by court or jury, CR §2-303.
Disclosures by state's attorney, Crim Rule 4-343.
Disposition of body after execution, COR
    §3-909.
**Docket entries by clerk of court in which
  charging document filed,** CR §2-303.
Evidence, CR §2-303.
Execution warrant, COR §3-902.
**Expenses of division relating to detention of
  inmate under sentence.**
  County not to be billed or pay, COR §3-901.
Failure of state to notify of intent to seek, CR
    §2-301.
Findings by court or jury, CR §2-303.
Forms.
  Written findings and determinations, Crim Rule
    4-343.
  Deletions from form, Crim Rule 4-343.
Governor's stay of warrant of execution, COR
    §3-902.
Imposition by court, CR §2-303.
Incompetent inmates not to be executed, COR
    §3-904.
Intravenous injection.
  Method of imposing, CR §2-303.
**Judge of sentencing court to cause individual
  to be taken into custody,** COR §3-901.
Judges, Crim Rule 4-343.
Jurisdiction.
  Court of appeals has exclusive appellate
    jurisdiction, CJ §12-307.
Jury.
  Alternate jurors, appointment, CR §2-303.
  Disqualification by trial judge in capital cases, CJ
    §8-404.
  Findings, determination in writing, CR §2-303.
  Peremptory challenges in capital or life cases, CJ
    §8-420.
  Unable to agree within reasonable time, CR
    §2-303.
  When proceedings conducted before, CR §2-303.
Jury instructions, CR §2-303.
Lethal injection.
  Administration of injection not practice of
    medicine, COR §3-905.
  Commissioner of correction, duties, COR §3-906.

DEATH PENALTY —Cont'd
Lethal injection —Cont'd
  Individuals performing injection, qualifications,
    COR §3-906.
  Method of imposing, COR §3-905; CR §2-303.
  Pharmacist or pharmaceutical supplier may
    dispense drugs without prescription, COR
    §3-905.
  Supervision by commissioner of correction, COR
    §3-906.
Limitations on imposing, CR §2-202.
Mentally retarded.
  Defined, sentence not imposed, CR §2-202.
Method of imposing, CR §2-303.
Mitigating circumstances, CR §2-303.
  Evidence admissible, CR §2-303.
  Jury to consider, CR §2-303.
  Whether mitigating circumstances outweighed by
    aggravating circumstances.
    Preponderance of evidence, CR §2-303.
Notice to defendant of state's intention to seek,
  CR §2-301.
  Required for imposition, CR §2-202.
Post conviction procedure.
  Proceedings after death sentences, CP §§7-201 to
    7-204.
Pregnant inmates, revocation of warrant of
  execution.
  Medical evidence showing inmate pregnant, COR
    §3-902.
Presentence investigative reports.
  Evidence admissible, CR §2-303.
  Required, COR §6-112.
Prior criminal convictions.
  Evidence admissible, CR §2-303.
Punishment for murder in first degree, CR
  §2-201.
Removal in circuit courts, Crim Rule 4-254.
Report of judge, Crim Rule 4-343.
Reprieve granted to inmate under sentence of
  death.
  Notice, retention in custody, COR §3-903.
Requirements for imposition, CR §2-202.
Return of inmate's body after execution to
  relative, COR §3-909.
Review of death sentence, CP §8-108.
Rules governing sentencing proceedings.
  Adoption by court of appeals, CR §2-305.
Sentencing procedure, CR §2-303.
Sheriff.
  Custody of individual sentenced to death, duties,
    COR §3-901.
Statutory sentencing procedure, Crim Rule
  4-343.
Stay of warrant of execution, COR §3-902; CP
  §7-202.
  Notice to inmate, retention in custody, COR
    §3-903.
Time when sentence of death executed.
  Commissioner of correction to set time within
    period designated within warrant, COR
    §3-902.
Under age of 18 years at time of murder.
  Sentence not imposed, CR §2-202.
Victims of crime.
  Sentencing and disposition hearings.
    Right of victim to address court, CP §11-403.
    Right of victim to address jury, CP §11-404.
Warrant of execution, COR §3-902.
Withdrawal of intent to seek.
  Notice, CR §2-301.

DEATH PENALTY —Cont'd
Witnesses to execution, COR §3-907.
Written findings and determinations, Crim Rule
  4-343.

DEATH TAXES.
Definitions, TG §7-101.
Estate tax.
  Federal estate tax.
    See FEDERAL ESTATE TAX.
General provisions, TG §§7-101 to 7-122.
  See TAXATION.
Generation-skipping transfer tax, TG §§2-901,
  2-902, 7-401 to 7-406.
  See GENERATION-SKIPPING TRANSFER TAX.
Inheritance tax, TG §§2-701, 2-702, 7-201 to
  7-234.
  See INHERITANCE TAX.
Interstate arbitration of death taxes, TG
  §§7-104 to 7-115.
  See TAXATION.
Interstate compromise of death taxes, TG
  §§7-118 to 7-122.
  See TAXATION.

DEATH WITH DIGNITY.
Health care decisions.
  See HEALTH CARE DECISIONS.

DEBIT CARDS.
Credit card crimes, CR §§8-201 to 8-217.
  See CREDIT CARDS.
Governmental charges by counties on
  municipal corporations.
  Payment by debit cards, 24 §9-1401.

DEBT ADJUSTING.
Business of prohibited, exceptions, CL §14-1316.
Collection agencies, BR §§7-101 to 7-502.
  See COLLECTION AGENCIES.

DEBT COUNSELING.
Credit services businesses generally, CL
  §§14-1901 to 14-1916.
  See CREDIT.

DEBT MANAGEMENT SERVICES, FI §§12-901
  to 12-931.
Accounting to consumer, FI §12-919.
Advertising, FI §12-925.
Agreement for services, FI §12-918.
  Contents, FI §12-916.
Applicability of provisions, FI §12-902.
Audits.
  Fund, FI §12-905.
  Licensee books and records, FI §12-922.
Change of licensee information, FI §12-915.
Citation of provisions, FI §12-931.
Civil actions, FI §12-930.
Confidentiality of records, FI §12-922.
Definitions, FI §12-901.
Dishonored payments, FI §12-918.
Enforcement of provisions generally, FI
  §12-928.
Examination of licensee, FI §12-924.
Exemptions from provisions, FI §12-902.
Extension of credit.
  Prohibited activities, FI §12-920.
Fees, FI §12-904.
  Additional fees, FI §12-918.
Fines.
  Enforcement of provisions generally, FI §12-928.
  Reports, failure to file, FI §12-921.
  Specific penalty for violations, FI §12-929.

DEBT MANAGEMENT SERVICES —Cont'd
Fund, FI §12-905.
Information provided to consumer, FI §12-918.
Information sharing agreements, FI §12-903.
Investigation of complaints, FI §12-923.
Licenses.
    Application, FI §12-908.
    Bond requirement, FI §§12-908, 12-914.
    Change of licensee information, FI §12-915.
    Contents, FI §12-911.
    Disciplinary action, FI §12-926.
      Hearings, FI §12-927.
    Display, FI §12-911.
    Expiration, FI §12-912.
    Fingerprints and background check, FI §12-909.
    Investigation of application, FI §12-910.
    Issuance, FI §12-910.
    Net worth requirements, FI §12-907.
    Prerequisites to providing services, FI §12-916.
    Qualifications, FI §12-907.
    Renewal, FI §12-912.
    Requirement, FI §12-906.
    Surrender, FI §12-913.
    Time for decision, FI §12-910.
    Waiver of surety bond, FI §12-914.
Net worth requirements, FI §12-907.
Notice.
    Change of licensee information, FI §12-915.
    Website posting for complaints and questions, FI §12-911.
Penalties.
    Enforcement of provisions generally, FI §12-928.
    Reports, failure to file, FI §12-921.
    Suspension or revocation of license, FI §12-926.
      Hearings, FI §12-927.
Prerequisites to providing services, FI §12-916.
Prohibited activities, FI §12-920.
Record-keeping, FI §12-922.
Reports, FI §12-921.
    Examination of licensee, FI §12-924.
Rescission of agreement, FI §12-918.
Rulemaking authority, FI §12-903.
Title of provisions, FI §12-931.
Trust accounts.
    Accounting to consumer, FI §12-919.
    Requirements, FI §12-917.
    Retention of accounts and records, FI §12-922.
Unlicensed operation, FI §12-906.
Voluntary contributions from consumers, FI §12-918.

DEBTORS.
Absconding debtors.
    Venue.
      Additional venue permitted, CJ §6-202.
Bulk transfers.
    Lists, CL §6-104.
    Notice to creditors, CL §§6-105, 6-107.
    Protected creditors, CL §6-109.
Collection agencies, BR §§7-101 to 7-502.
    See COLLECTION AGENCIES.
Contracts.
    Sale of goods.
      Creditors' rights and remedies.
        Sale on approval and sale or return transactions, CL §2-326.
        Sold goods.
          Rights of seller's creditors, CL §2-402.
Debt management services, FI §§12-901 to 12-931.
    See DEBT MANAGEMENT SERVICES.

DEBTORS —Cont'd
Insurance.
    Credit life, health and unemployment insurance, IN §§13-101 to 13-117.
      See CREDIT LIFE, HEALTH AND UNEMPLOYMENT INSURANCE.
    Group life insurance on debtors, IN §17-206.
    Statement to insured debtors, IN §17-103.
Investment securities.
    Creditor's legal process, CL §8-112.
Minors.
    Payment or delivery of money or chattels to minor.
      Method of payment, ET §13-501.
      Not responsible for proper application, ET §13-501.
      Release, ET §13-501.
Protection.
    Laws to be passed to protect debtors, MD Const Art III §44.
Receivers and assignees or trustees for creditors, Receivers Rules 13-101 to 13-703.
    See RECEIVERS.
Removal of personal property.
    Intent to defraud secured party, CR §8-403.

DEBTS.
Actions.
    Assignment of claims to nonresidents.
      Purpose of depriving debtor of rights under exemption laws.
        Recovery, CL §15-501.
    Consumer debt collection.
      Certain acts prohibited, CL §14-202.
      Citation of subtitle, CL §14-204.
      Collector.
        Defined, CL §14-201.
      Consumer transaction.
        Defined, CL §14-201.
      Damages.
        Violator's liability, CL §14-203.
      Person.
        Defined, CL §14-201.
      Violator's liability for damages, CL §14-203.
Adjusting.
    Collection agencies, BR §§7-101 to 7-502.
    See COLLECTION AGENCIES.
Answers.
    Denials.
      General denials in specified causes.
        Circuit courts, CivProCir Rule 2-323.
Assignments.
    Claims to nonresidents.
      Depriving debtor of rights under exemption laws.
      General provisions, CL §§15-501 to 15-503.
Attachment, CJ §§3-301 to 3-305.
    See ATTACHMENT.
Bastards.
    Imprisonment for delinquent support payment not imprisonment for debt, MD Const Art III §38.
Collection.
    Certain acts prohibited, CL §14-202.
      Consumer transaction.
        Defined, CL §14-201.
      Damages.
        Violator's liability for damages, CL §14-203.
    Consumer debt collection.
      General provisions. See within this heading, "Actions."
    Definitions, CL §14-201.

DEBTS —Cont'd
Collection —Cont'd
Offsets.
Defined, CL §15-701.
Prohibited, CL §15-702.
Collection agencies, BR §§7-101 to 7-502.
See COLLECTION AGENCIES.
Congress.
Powers of congress, US Const Art I §8.
Consignment.
Consignee.
Due purchaser or pledgee, CL §11-806.
Constables.
Not to be purchased by, SG §17-107.
Constitutional provisions.
See CONSTITUTION OF THE UNITED STATES.
Consumer debt collection. See within this
heading, "Actions."
Consumer debt defined, CL §15-701.
Debt management services, FI §§12-901 to
12-931.
See DEBT MANAGEMENT SERVICES.
Decedents' estates.
Rule for claim.
See EXECUTORS AND ADMINISTRATORS.
Desertion and nonsupport.
Imprisonment for nonsupport not imprisonment
for debt, MD Const Art III §38.
Fiduciaries.
Compromise.
Power to compromise debt, ET §15-102.
Foreign debts.
Method of proof, CJ §10-601.
Money judgment recognition.
General provisions, CJ §§10-701 to 10-709.
See FOREIGN MONEY JUDGMENTS.
Proof of foreign debts and other instruments.
General provisions.
See EVIDENCE.
Gambling loss.
Recovery as common debt, CR §12-110.
Imprisonment for debt.
Prohibited, MD Const Art III §38.
Interest.
General provisions, CL §§12-101 to 12-114.
See INTEREST.
Life insurance and annuities.
Proceeds exempt from creditors, IN §16-111.
Limited liability companies.
Merger.
Successor liable for debts and obligations, CA
§4A-709.
Maryland affordable housing trust.
Debts and liabilities of trust, status, HS §10-107.
Maryland venture capital trust.
Trust debts not considered state debts, 83A
§5-309.
Mechanics' liens.
For what debts lien attaches, RP §9-102.
Priorities, RP §9-108.
Municipal corporations.
See MUNICIPAL CORPORATIONS.
Offsets.
Defined, CL §15-701.
Prohibited, CL §15-702.
Potomac highlands airport authority.
Power of authority to incur debts, TR §10-103.
Taxation.
Exemption of authority obligations, TR §10-103.
Potomac water authority.
Creating debt or obligation, EN §5-407.

DEBTS —Cont'd
Principal and income.
Allocation of receipts on obligation, ET §15-513.
Public debt.
General provisions, SF §§8-101 to 8-302.
See PUBLIC DEBT.
Public officers and employees.
Purchased by sheriffs, constables or collectors of
taxes, SG §17-107.
Schools.
Reimbursement of state for debt service, ED
§5-308.
Secured transactions.
General provisions governing secured debt, CL
§§9-101 to 9-710.
See SECURED TRANSACTIONS.
Sheriffs.
Not to be purchased by, SG §17-107.
State.
Collection of debts due state.
Budget and management.
Central collection unit, SF §§3-301 to 3-306.
Public debt.
General provisions, SF §§8-101 to 8-302.
See PUBLIC DEBT.
Taxation.
Certification of debt and withholding of income
tax refunds.
Interception of refund for support and
maintenance payments, FL §10-113.
Unpaid tax as personal debt, TG §13-102.
Usury.
General provisions, CL §§12-101 to 12-114.
See USURY.

DECEDENTS' ESTATES.
Accounts and accounting.
Verification, Estates Rule 6-123; ET §1-102.
Administrative probate.
Defined, ET §1-101.
Adoption.
Determining relationship, ET §1-207.
Inclusion of adoptees in instruments of
conveyance, RP §2-123.
Advancements.
General provisions, ET §3-106.
After-born child.
Intestate succession, ET §3-107.
After-discovered property.
Small estates, Estates Rule 6-212; ET §5-605.
Appraisers.
Appointment.
By register, ET §2-301.
Delivery of appraisal, ET §2-303.
Duties.
Generally, ET §2-303.
Fees.
Subject to review by court, ET §2-301.
Form of appraisal, ET §2-303.
General appraisers.
Designation, ET §2-302.
Performance.
Expeditious performance of duties, ET §2-303.
Standing appraisers.
Appointment.
By register, ET §2-301.
Verification of appraisal, ET §2-303.
Who makes appraisal, ET §2-301.
Artificial insemination.
Determining relationship, ET §1-206.

DECEDENTS' ESTATES —Cont'd

Attainder.
Conviction of attainder not to work forfeiture of estate, ET §11-109.

Bigamy.
Surviving spouse.
Conviction of bigamy while married to decedent, ET §1-202.

Business regulation and licensure.
General business licensing.
Death of licensee, BR §17-308.

Casualty.
Effect on right to estate, ET §11-109.

Children. See within this heading, "Minors."

Closing estates.
General provisions, ET §§10-101 to 10-105.
See EXECUTORS AND ADMINISTRATORS.

Comptroller.
Appraisers.
Appointment and remuneration subject to approval of comptroller, ET §2-301.

Contracts.
Waiver of rights in decedent's estate, ET §3-205.

Court.
Probate court.
General provisions, ET §§2-101 to 2-109.
See ORPHANS' COURT.

Creditors.
Death of legatee prior to testator.
Creditor of deceased legatee has no interest in property, ET §4-403.
Debts and claims.
General provisions, ET §§8-101 to 8-115.
See EXECUTORS AND ADMINISTRATORS.

Curtesy.
Abolished, ET §3-202.

Debts and claims.
General provisions, ET §§8-101 to 8-115.
See EXECUTORS AND ADMINISTRATORS.

Declaration of rights and legal relations, CJ §3-408.

Definitions, ET §1-101.
Decedent to include testator and intestate, 1 §6.

Determining relationship.
Application of rules, ET §1-201.
Children.
Adoption, ET §1-207.
Artificial insemination, ET §1-206.
General provisions, ET §1-205.
Illegitimate, ET §1-208.
Legitimate, ET §1-206.
Marriage of parents, ET §1-206.
Degrees of relationship.
Civil law.
Reckoned according to civil law, ET §1-203.
Half blood.
Relative of half blood, ET §1-204.
Issue.
Defined, ET §1-209.
General provisions, ET §1-209.
Person related to decedent through two lines, ET §3-109.
Per stirpes.
Division of shares.
Issue of parent, grandparent or great-grandparent of decedent, ET §1-210.
Issue of the decedent, ET §1-210.
Wills, ET §1-210.1.
Representation.
Intestate succession, ET §1-210.

DECEDENTS' ESTATES —Cont'd

Determining relationship —Cont'd
Surviving spouse, ET §1-202.

Disability.
Notice to disabled person, ET §1-103.
Surviving spouse under disability.
Right of election, ET §3-204.

Disclaimer.
Uniform disclaimer of property interests act, ET §§9-201 to 9-216.
See DESCENT AND DISTRIBUTION.

Distribution.
Intestate succession. See within this heading, "Intestate succession."

Divorce.
Waiver of rights in decedent's estate, ET §3-205.

Documents.
Verification, Estates Rule 6-123; ET §1-102.

Dower.
Abolished, ET §3-202.

Election of rights and remedies.
Surviving spouse. See within this heading, "Surviving spouse."

Environmental law.
Defined, ET §1-101.

Escheat, ET §3-105.

Executors and administrators.
General provisions, ET §§6-101 to 7-604.
See EXECUTORS AND ADMINISTRATORS.
Modified administration generally, ET §§5-701 to 5-710.
Personal representative.
Defined, ET §1-101.
Special administrator.
Defined, ET §1-101.

Exploitation of vulnerable adult.
Disqualification from receiving property or benefiting from the estate, CR §8-801.

Family allowance.
Amount, ET §3-201.

Federal estate tax.
Distribution in kind, using federal estate tax values, ET §11-107.

Fees.
Appraisers, ET §2-301.
Registers of wills, ET §2-206.

Forms.
Election of surviving spouse, ET §3-207.
Surviving spouse.
Elective share.
Extension of time for making election, Estates Rule 6-411.
Form of election, Estates Rule 6-411.
Verification, Estates Rule 6-123; ET §1-102.

Fraud against the estate.
Embezzle, steal, destroy, impair alter.
Wills, codicils or writs of administration, CR §§8-701, 8-702.

Heirs.
Defined, ET §1-101.
Determining relationship. See within this heading, "Determining relationship."
Intestate succession.
Certain heirs not surviving decedent for 30 days, ET §3-110.

Husband and wife.
Surviving spouse. See within this heading, "Surviving spouse."

Illegitimate children.
Determining relationship, ET §1-208.
Inheritance from illegitimate person, ET §3-108.

DECEDENTS' ESTATES —Cont'd

Indexes.

Deed for distribution in kind.

Indexed in grantor index, ET §9-105.

Inheritance tax.

General provisions.

See INHERITANCE TAX.

Inmate's estate, liability for damages and expenses, COR §9-605.

Insane persons.

Surviving spouse.

Right of election personal, ET §3-204.

Interested persons.

Defined, ET §1-101.

Distribution by court, ET §9-112.

Meeting of interested persons.

Notice of meeting, ET §9-112.

Procedure when interested person not known, ET §9-112.

Notice of matters filed in proceeding.

Account, ET §7-501.

Probate court.

Rights of interested person, ET §2-102.

Proposed payment to personal representative or attorney, Estates Rule 6-414; ET §7-502.

Interpretation and construction.

Liberal construction, ET §1-105.

Intestate succession.

Abandonment or failure to support minor child.

Distribution precluded, ET §3-112.

Advancement.

General provisions, ET §3-106.

After-born child, ET §3-107.

Crimes.

Prohibition of distribution upon commission of certain crimes or acts, ET §3-111.

Disclaimer.

Uniform disclaimer of property interests act, ET §§9-201 to 9-216.

See DESCENT AND DISTRIBUTION.

Distribution.

Net intestate estate.

Order of distribution, ET §3-101.

No surviving blood relative, ET §3-104.

No surviving issue, ET §3-104.

Escheat, ET §3-105.

Heirs not surviving decedent for 30 days.

General provisions, ET §3-110.

Illegitimate person.

Inheritance from, ET §3-108.

Issue.

No surviving issue.

Distribution when there is no surviving issue, ET §3-104.

Surviving issue.

Division among, ET §3-103.

Net estate.

Calculation of share of surviving spouse, ET §3-102.

Order of distribution, ET §3-101.

Per stirpes.

Representation, ET §1-210.

Relationship.

Person related to decedent through two lines, ET §3-109.

Renunciation.

Uniform disclaimer of property interests act, ET §§9-201 to 9-216.

See DESCENT AND DISTRIBUTION.

Surviving spouse.

Share, ET §3-102.

DECEDENTS' ESTATES —Cont'd

Inventory.

Verification, Estates Rule 6-123; ET §1-102.

Issue.

Defined, ET §§1-101, 1-209.

Determining relationship, ET §1-209.

No surviving issue.

Distribution when there is no surviving issue, ET §3-104.

Pretermitted issue.

Share.

Amount of share, ET §3-302.

Payment, ET §3-303.

When child entitled to share, ET §3-301.

Surviving issue.

Division among, ET §3-103.

Law.

Applicability, ET §12-102.

Effective date, ET §12-101.

Prior laws, ET §12-103.

Legacy.

Defined, ET §1-101.

Legatee.

Defined, ET §1-101.

Wills.

See WILLS.

Letters.

Defined, ET §1-101.

Letters of administration.

General provisions.

See EXECUTORS AND ADMINISTRATORS.

Probate of will.

See WILLS.

Life insurance and annuities.

Payment of proceeds without letters of administration, IN §16-110.

Viatical settlement contracts, IN §§8-601 to 8-611.

See VIATICAL SETTLEMENT CONTRACTS.

Limitation of actions.

Closing estates.

Claims against heirs and legatees, ET §10-103.

Proceedings against personal representative, ET §10-103.

Mail.

Restricted delivery mail.

Notice sent by mail, ET §1-103.

Minors.

Children defined, ET §1-101.

Determining relationship. See within this heading, "Determining relationship."

Family allowance, ET §3-201.

Illegitimate children.

Determining relationship, ET §1-208.

Intestate succession.

Abandonment or failure to support minor child.

Distribution precluded, ET §3-112.

After-born child, ET §3-107.

Illegitimate children.

Inheritance from illegitimate person, ET §3-108.

Issue. See within this heading, "Issue."

Notice to minor, ET §1-103.

Payment or delivery of money or chattels to minor.

Absence of guardian.

Court order for deposit of funds, ET §13-502.

Funds under court jurisdiction, ET §13-502.

Deposit of money.

Distributable from trust, estate or other source, ET §13-502.

DECEDENTS' ESTATES —Cont'd
Minors —Cont'd
Surviving spouse.
Right of election personal, ET §3-204.
Modified administration, ET §§5-701 to 5-710.
Applicability of other provisions, ET §5-710.
Closing of estate, ET §5-709.
Consent of residuary legatees, ET §5-702.
Notice of consent, ET §5-706.
Date of appointment.
Defined, ET §5-701.
Election for, ET §5-702.
Contents, ET §5-705.
Proceedings after filing, ET §5-704.
Extension of time periods.
Prohibited, ET §5-703.
Reports.
Final report, ET §5-707.
Acknowledgment that verified final report
shall be filed.
Election for modified administration to
include, ET §5-705.
Time for filing, extension, ET §5-703.
Revocation, ET §5-708.
Trustees, limitations, ET §5-702.
Morticians.
Licenses.
Personal representative of deceased mortician's
estate, HO §7-308.1.
Net estate.
Calculation of share of surviving spouse, ET
§3-102.
Defined, ET §1-101.
Distribution.
Order of distribution of net intestate estate, ET
§3-101.
Nonresidents.
Claims against nonresident decedents, ET §5-503.
Foreign personal representatives.
See EXECUTORS AND ADMINISTRATORS.
Nontestamentary transfers, ET §1-401.
Notices, Estates Rule 6-401; ET §§1-103, 7-103.1.
Perpetuities.
Rule against perpetuities.
Limitations on application, ET §11-103.
Preservation of rule, ET §11-102.
Personal property, ET §1-301.
Personal representative.
General provisions, ET §§6-101 to 7-604.
See EXECUTORS AND ADMINISTRATORS.
Modified administration generally, ET §§5-701 to
5-710.
Posthumous child.
After-born child, ET §3-107.
Predeceased.
Certain heirs not surviving decedent for 30 days,
ET §3-110.
Presumptions.
Rebuttable, ET §1-105.
Pretermitted children.
After-born child.
General provisions, ET §3-107.
Share.
Amount of share, ET §3-302.
Payment, ET §3-303.
When child entitled to share, ET §3-301.
Principal and income, uniform act, ET §§15-501
to 15-530.
See PRINCIPAL AND INCOME.
Prior laws, ET §12-103.

DECEDENTS' ESTATES —Cont'd
Prisoners.
Liability for damages and expenses from estate of
prisoner, COR §9-605.
Surviving spouse.
Right of election personal, ET §3-204.
Probate.
Judicial probate.
Defined, ET §1-101.
Probate court.
General provisions.
See ORPHANS' COURT.
Property.
All property subject to article, ET §1-301.
Defined, ET §1-101.
Devolution at death, ET §1-301.
Foreign personal representatives.
Order directing transfer of title to real property,
ET §5-506.
Personal property.
Title determination, ET §1-301.
Provisions of law.
Applicability, ET §12-102.
Effective date, ET §12-101.
Purpose of law, ET §1-105.
Real property. See within this heading, "Property."
Registers of wills.
Defined, ET §§1-101, 2-201.
General provisions, ET §§2-201 to 2-212.
See REGISTERS OF WILLS.
Relationship.
Determining relationship. See within this
heading, "Determining relationship."
**Remainders, reversions and executory
interests.**
Contingent remainders.
Indestructibility, ET §11-101.
Trustee.
Not necessary to appoint trustees, ET
§11-101.
Renunciation.
Uniform disclaimer of property interests act, ET
§§9-201 to 9-216.
See DESCENT AND DISTRIBUTION.
Representation.
Defined, ET §§1-101, 1-210.
Per stirpes, ET §1-210.
Rules of court.
Applicability, Estates Rule 6-101; Rule 1-101.
Form of court papers, Estates Rule 6-121.
Maryland rules.
Defined, ET §1-101.
Schools.
Escheat.
Payment to board of education in county, ET
§3-105.
Secured transactions.
Financing statements.
Name of debtor and secured party, CL §9-503.
Securities.
Transfer-on-death registration, ET §§16-101 to
16-112.
See SECURITIES.
Sequestration.
Right of legatee to sequestration, ET §3-208.
Service of process.
Notices, ET §1-103.
Small estates.
General provisions, ET §§5-601 to 5-607.
See EXECUTORS AND ADMINISTRATORS.

DECEDENTS' ESTATES —Cont'd
Suicide.
Effect on right to estate, ET §11-109.
Surviving spouse.
Bigamy, ET §1-202.
Determining relationship. See within this
    heading, "Determining relationship."
Disability.
    Right of election, ET §3-204.
Divorce.
    In another state, ET §1-202.
    Marriage to third party, ET §1-202.
    Valid divorce, ET §1-202.
Elective share.
    Adjustment of applicable share, ET §3-203.
    Contribution to payment, ET §3-208.
    Fee for filing by register of wills, ET §2-206.
    Form of election, ET §3-207.
    Limitation, ET §3-203.
        Time limitation for making election, ET
            §3-206.
            Form for extension of time for making
                election, Estates Rule 6-411.
    Personal.
        Right of election personal to surviving spouse,
            ET §3-204.
    Right of spouse, ET §3-203.
    Waiver.
        Rights in decedent's estate, ET §3-205.
    Will.
        Effect of election upon will, ET §3-208.
        Withdrawal, ET §3-206.
Family allowance, ET §3-201.
Gift qualifying for estate tax marital deduction,
    ET §11-106.
Intestate succession.
    Share, ET §3-102.
Marriage to third party, ET §1-202.
Minors.
    Right of election, ET §3-204.
Right of election personal, ET §3-204.
Share, ET §3-102.
Statutory share.
    Form of election, Estates Rule 6-411.
    Limitation, Estates Rule 6-411; ET §3-203.
        Time limitation for making election, Estates
            Rule 6-411; ET §3-206.
    Withdrawal, Estates Rule 6-411; ET §3-206.
Taxation.
Death taxes.
    General provisions, TG §§7-101 to 7-122.
    See TAXATION.
    Generation-skipping transfer tax, TG §§2-901,
        2-902, 7-401 to 7-406.
        See GENERATION-SKIPPING TRANSFER
            TAX.
    Inheritance tax, TG §§2-701, 2-702, 7-201 to
        7-234.
        See INHERITANCE TAX.
Excise tax.
    Deed for distribution in kind.
        Exemption from excise tax, ET §9-105.
Gift to surviving spouse, qualifying for estate tax
    marital deduction, ET §11-106.
Title to property.
Personal property, ET §1-301.
Torts.
Death of legatee prior to testator.
    Creditors of deceased legatee have no interest
        in property, ET §4-403.

DECEDENTS' ESTATES —Cont'd
Trust companies.
Defined, ET §1-101.
Trusts and trustees.
Applicability of certain provisions of estates of
    decedents law to trusts, ET §14-102.
Testamentary trustee.
    Renunciation by, ET §9-102.
Unemployment compensation.
Contributions.
    Priorities under dissolution or distribution.
        Estate of deceased employer, LE §8-634.
Uniform disclaimer of property interests act.
Descent and distribution.
    See DESCENT AND DISTRIBUTION.
Verification.
Appraisal.
    Upon completion, ET §2-303.
Documents, Estates Rule 6-123; ET §1-102.
Form, Estates Rule 6-123; ET §1-102.
Requirement, Estates Rule 6-123; ET §1-102.
Waiver.
Notice, ET §1-103.
Rights in decedent's estate, ET §3-205.
Wills.
Defined, ET §1-101.
General provisions, ET §§4-101 to 4-512.
    See WILLS.

DECEIT.
Counterfeiting and forgery, CR §§8-601 to 8-613.
Credit card crimes, CR §§8-201 to 8-217.
    See CREDIT CARDS.
Fraud generally.
    See FRAUD.
Theft.
Generally, CR §§7-101 to 7-110.
    See THEFT.

DECEPTIVE TRADE PRACTICES.
Banks and trust companies.
General provisions, FI §§5-807 to 5-809.
    See BANKS AND TRUST COMPANIES.
Cigarettes.
Cigarette sales below cost act.
    General provisions, CL §§11-501 to 11-510.
        See CIGARS AND CIGARETTES.
Custom home protection.
Unfair or deceptive trade practices, RP §10-507.
Foreign discriminatory boycotts.
See FOREIGN DISCRIMINATORY BOYCOTTS.
General provisions, CL §§13-301 to 13-315.
    See CONSUMER PROTECTION.
Health club services, CL §14-12B-08.
Housing.
Deposits on new homes, RP §10-305.
Insurance.
See INSURANCE.
New home warranties, RP §10-608.
Telephone solicitations.
Federal telemarketing and consumer fraud and
    abuse prevention act and federal consumer
    protection act.
    Violations prohibited, CL §14-3201.
        Deceptive trade practice, remedies, separate
            violations, CL §14-3202.
Generally, CL §§14-2201 to 14-2205.
    See TELECOMMUNICATIONS.
Violations as unfair or deceptive trade practices,
    CL §13-301.
Viatical settlement contracts.
Disciplinary action against registrants, IN §8-608.

DECEPTIVE TRADE PRACTICES —Cont'd
Viatical settlement contracts —Cont'd
Misappropriation of funds or benefits, IN §27-403.
Reporting insurance fraud, IN §§27-802 to 27-805.
Waterproofing.
General provisions, CL §§14-12A-01 to 14-12A-04.
See WATERPROOFING.

DECLARATIONS.
Pleading.
General provisions.
See PLEADINGS.

DECLARATORY JUDGMENTS.
Administrative procedure.
See ADMINISTRATIVE PROCEDURE.
Affirmative or negative form or effect, CJ
§3-411.
Annulment of marriage.
Excluded from subtitle, CJ §3-409.
Appeals.
Jurisdiction.
Court of special appeals, CJ §12-308.
Attorney general.
Role of attorney general, CJ §3-405.
Bankruptcy and insolvency.
Rights of insolvent, CJ §3-408.
Citation.
Short title, CJ §3-415.
Constitutional law.
Attorney general as party, CJ §3-405.
Contracts.
Construction or validity, CJ §3-406.
Before or after breach, CJ §3-407.
Costs.
Award of costs, CJ §3-410.
Counties.
Parties to proceeding, CJ §3-405.
Decedents' estates.
Declaration of rights and legal relations, CJ
§3-408.
Deeds.
Construction or validity, CJ §3-406.
Definitions.
Person, CJ §3-401.
Discretion of court, CJ §3-409.
Divorce.
Excluded from subtitle, CJ §3-409.
Environmental standing act, NR §1-503.
Final judgment or decree.
Form and effect, CJ §3-411.
Franchises.
Construction, CJ §3-406.
Hearings.
Advancing on court calendar, CJ §3-409.
Interpretation and construction.
Construction of instruments and rights.
Powers, CJ §3-406.
Purpose of subtitle, CJ §3-402.
Remedial provisions, CJ §3-402.
Rights construed.
Enumeration not exclusive, CJ §3-403.
Uniformity of interpretation, CJ §3-414.
Jurisdiction.
Appeals.
Court of special appeals, CJ §12-308.
General provisions, CJ §3-403.
Jury.
Trial by jury, CJ §3-404.
Land patents.
Generally, CJ §3-408.1.

DECLARATORY JUDGMENTS —Cont'd
Municipal corporations.
Parties to proceeding, CJ §3-405.
Natural resources.
Environmental standing act, NR §1-503.
Negative form or effect, CJ §3-411.
Ordinances.
Construction or validity, CJ §3-406.
Parties.
General provisions, CJ §3-405.
Persons.
Defined, CJ §3-401.
Petitions.
Supplementary relief, CJ §3-412.
Relief.
Discretionary relief, CJ §3-409.
Supplementary relief, CJ §3-412.
Rights construed.
Discretionary relief, CJ §3-409.
Enumeration not exclusive, CJ §3-403.
Rights of persons regarding decedents' estates,
CJ §3-408.
Rules and regulations.
Construction or validity, CJ §3-406.
Securities.
Securities act.
Violations of title.
Persons engaging in violations, CA §11-702.
Severability of subtitle, CJ §3-413.
Short title, CJ §3-415.
Show cause order, CJ §3-412.
Start-up business ventures.
Securities commissioner, BR §14-110.
Statutes.
Construction or validity, CJ §3-406.
Supplementary relief, CJ §3-412.
Uniformity of interpretation, CJ §3-414.
Victims of crime.
Notoriety of crimes contracts.
Priority of claims, CP §11-628.
Wills.
Construction or validity, CJ §3-406.
Rights of devisees, legatees, heirs, etc., CJ §3-408.

DECREES.
Adoption.
See ADOPTION.
Change of name, SpecPro Rule 15-901.
Divorce.
See DIVORCE.
Fiduciaries.
See FIDUCIARIES.
Foreclosures.
Assent to a decree.
Defined, PropSales Rule 14-201.
Mortgages.
Person authorized to sell under assent to a
decree, PropSales Rule 14-207.
Who may institute action, PropSales Rule
14-202.
Injunctions generally.
See INJUNCTIONS.
Judgments and decrees.
See JUDGMENTS AND DECREES.
Judicial sales.
When court may decree, PropSales Rule 14-302.
Legal disabilities.
See LEGAL DISABILITIES.
Mechanics' and materialmen's liens.
Enforcement of lien, PropAct Rule 12-305.

DECREES —Cont'd
Orders generally.
See ORDERS OF COURT.

DEDUCTIONS.
Income tax, TG §§10-217 to 10-223.
See INCOME TAX.

DEEDS.
Abolished.
Shelley's case, ET §11-104.
Acknowledgments.
Effective date of deed, RP §3-201.
Power of attorney, RP §4-107.
Presumption of validity, RP §4-103.
Required, RP §4-101.
Validation of defective grants, RP §4-109.
Agency.
Execution by agent or attorney, RP §4-107.
Attestation.
Not required, RP §4-101.
Power of attorney, RP §4-107.
Attorneys at law.
Recordation.
Certification instrument prepared by attorney.
Required, RP §3-104.
Bankruptcy and insolvency.
Prepayment of personal property taxes.
Inapplicable for recordation by trustees in bankruptcy, RP §3-104.
Void if containing preference, CL §15-101.
Exceptions, CL §15-101.
Bargain and sell.
Construed to pass whole interest, RP §2-101.
Birds and game.
Wildlife management areas.
Sale or exchange of land or water, NR §10-803.
Clerks of court.
Recordation.
Endorsement on instrument of time of receipt by clerk, RP §3-301.
Contents.
Sufficiency, RP §4-101.
Corporations.
Acknowledgments, CA §1-303.
Seal not required, RP §4-101.
Transfer without, CA §3-115.
Validation.
Certain deeds granting all or substantially all of property of corporations, RP §14-113.
Counterfeiting private instrument or document, CR §8-601.
Issuing counterfeited instrument or document, CR §8-602.
Covenants.
Deed poll.
Effect of acceptance of deed by grantee, RP §4-102.
Encumbrance.
Effect of covenant that grantor has not encumbered land, RP §2-110.
Effect of general covenant against encumbrances, RP §2-111.
Further assurances.
Effect of covenant, RP §2-112.
Family day care homes.
Covenants restricting, RP §2-121.
Forms.
Addition of covenant, RP §4-201.
General warranty.
Effect, RP §2-105.

DEEDS —Cont'd
Covenants —Cont'd
Implied covenant or warranty of title or possession, RP §2-115.
Meaning of term "the said covenant," RP §2-104.
Quiet enjoyment.
Effect of covenant, RP §2-109.
Right to grant.
Effect of covenant, RP §2-108.
Seisin.
Effect of covenant, RP §2-107.
Special warranty.
Effect, RP §2-106.
Creditors.
Effective date of deed, RP §3-201.
Date.
Takes effect between parties from its effective date, RP §3-201.
Death.
Effect of use of terms "die without issue" etc., RP §2-113.
Simultaneous death act.
Subtitle does not apply if decedent provides otherwise, CJ §10-805.
Declaratory judgments.
Construction or validity, CJ §3-406.
Defective grants.
Validation, RP §4-109.
Definitions, RP §1-101.
Bargain and sell.
Construed to pass whole interest, RP §2-101.
Covenant.
Meaning of term "the said covenant," RP §2-104.
Grants.
Construed to pass whole interest, RP §2-101.
Descent and distribution.
Distribution in kind.
Evidence of title, ET §9-105.
Description.
Requirements, RP §4-101.
Easements.
General provisions.
See EASEMENTS.
Effective date, RP §3-201.
Embezzle, steal, destroy, impair or alter, CR §8-701.
Encumbrance.
Effect of covenant that grantor has not encumbered land, RP §2-110.
Effect of general covenant against encumbrances, RP §2-111.
Further assurances.
Effect of covenant, RP §2-112.
Estate tail.
Tenant of estate tail may grant in fee simple, RP §2-102.
Execution.
By agent or attorney.
Description in deed and manner of signing, RP §4-107.
Personal representatives.
Execution and delivery of evidence of title, ET §9-105.
Presumption of validity, RP §4-103.
Recordation.
Protection of purchaser against unrecorded interest, RP §14-103.
Requirements, RP §4-101.
Trustee to execute.
Appointment by court, CJ §11-111.

DEEDS —Cont'd
Execution —Cont'd
Validation of defective grants, RP §4-109.
Executors and administrators.
Execution and delivery of evidence of title, ET §9-105.
Indexing, ET §9-105.
Personal representative's deed.
Forms, RP §4-202.
Recordation.
Payment of costs of recordation, ET §9-105.
Taxation.
Exemption from excise taxes, ET §9-105.
Fee simple.
Form of deed, RP §4-202.
Limitation on rights of entry or reverter.
General provisions, RP §§6-101 to 6-105.
See REMAINDERS, REVERSIONS AND EXECUTORY INTERESTS.
Tenant of estate tail may grant in fee simple, RP §2-102.
Words of inheritance not necessary to create fee simple estate, RP §4-105.
Fee tail.
Tenant of estate tail may grant in fee simple, RP §2-102.
Forms.
Assignment.
Mortgage, RP §4-203.
Covenants.
Limitations and restrictions.
Conditions, RP §4-201.
Deed of trust.
Secure debts or for other purposes, RP §4-202.
Executors and administrators.
Personal representative's deed, RP §4-202.
Fee simple interest in real estate, RP §4-202.
Landlord and tenant.
Lease, RP §4-202.
Life estate, RP §4-202.
Mortgage of real estate, RP §4-202.
Partition.
Commissioner's deed, RP §4-202.
Release.
Affidavit, RP §4-203.
Mortgage or deed of trust, RP §4-203.
Sheriff's or other officer's deed, RP §4-202.
Sufficient for purpose intended, RP §4-201.
Trustee's deed under a decree, RP §4-202.
General warranty.
Effect, RP §2-105.
Grant.
Construed to pass whole interest, RP §2-101.
Grantee.
Covenants and reservations.
Binding on in deed poll, RP §4-102.
Possession under an unrecorded deed, RP §3-202.
Grantor.
Signed only by grantor.
Covenants and reservations.
Binding on by grantee, RP §4-102.
Highways.
Acquisition of property to protect highways, TR §8-313.
Husband and wife.
Entireties.
Granting of property held by the entireties, RP §4-108.
Minors.
Conveyances of certain property by married minors, ET §13-503.

DEEDS —Cont'd
Indenting.
Not required, RP §4-104.
Indexes.
Clerks of court, RP §3-302.
Decedents' estates.
Distribution in kind, ET §9-105.
Personal representatives.
Evidence of title, ET §9-105.
Inheritance.
Words of inheritance unnecessary, RP §4-105.
Interest passed.
Construction of words, RP §2-101.
Interpretation and construction.
Encumbrance.
Effect of covenant that grantor has not encumbered land, RP §2-110.
Further assurance.
Effect of covenant, RP §2-112.
General warranty.
Effect, RP §2-105.
Grant or bargain and sell.
Construed to pass whole interest, RP §2-101.
Issue.
Effect of use of terms "die without issue" etc., RP §2-113.
Power of person taking title to property in representative or fiduciary capacity, RP §14-112.
Quiet enjoyment.
Effect of covenant, RP §2-109.
Seisin.
Effect of covenant, RP §2-107.
Special warranty.
Effect, RP §2-106.
Issue.
Effect of use of terms "die without issue" etc., RP §2-113.
Joint tenants and tenants in common.
Abolition of straw deeds in certain cases, RP §4-108.
Creation of joint tenancies, RP §2-117.
Entireties.
Granting of property held by the entireties, RP §4-108.
Judgments and decrees.
Judgment creditor's deed.
Recordation.
Prepayment of personal property taxes not required, RP §3-104.
Judicial sales.
Recordation.
Protection of purchaser against unrecorded interest, RP §14-103.
Land installment contracts, RP §§10-101 to 10-108.
See LAND INSTALLMENT CONTRACTS.
Liens.
Recordation.
Prepayment of personal property taxes not required, RP §3-104.
Life estates.
Form of deed, RP §4-202.
Limitation of actions.
Setting aside deeds granting all or substantially all of property of corporations, RP §14-113.
Shelley's case.
Abolished, ET §11-104.
Validation of defective grants, RP §4-109.
Livery of seisin.
Not required, RP §4-104.

DEEDS —Cont'd
Married persons.
  Minors.
    Conveyances of certain property by married
      minors, ET §13-503.
Maryland railroad companies.
  Signature of president of company required, PUC
    §9-303.
Military services.
  Minors.
    Disability of infancy removed in certain
      instances, ET §13-503.
Minors.
  Married persons.
    Conveyances of certain property by married
      minors, ET §13-503.
  Military services and veterans.
    Disability of infancy removed in certain
      instances, ET §13-503.
  Veterans.
    Disability of infancy removed in certain
      instances, ET §13-503.
Mortgages and deeds of trust.
  General provisions.
    See MORTGAGES AND DEEDS OF TRUST.
Notices.
  Constructive notice.
    Possession under an unrecorded deed, RP
      §3-202.
Order of court to execute deed.
  Appointment of trustee, CJ §11-111.
Partition.
  Commissioner's deed to make partition of land.
    Forms, RP §4-202.
  Effect, RP §14-107.
  Execution, RP §14-107.
Poll.
  Deed poll.
    General provisions, RP §4-102.
Power of attorney, RP §4-107.
Presumptions.
  Validity, RP §4-103.
Priorities.
  First recorded deed, RP §3-203.
Quiet enjoyment.
  Effect of covenant, RP §2-109.
**Railroad companies organized under laws of
    state.**
  Signature of president required, PUC §9-303.
Receivers.
  Recordation.
    Prepayment of personal property taxes not
      required, RP §3-104.
Recordation.
  Attorneys at law.
    Certification instrument prepared by attorney.
      Required, RP §3-104.
  Court-ordered sales.
    Protection of purchaser against unrecorded
      interest, RP §14-103.
  Delivery by mail, RP §3-110.
  Estates for more than seven years.
    Exceptions, RP §3-101.
  Interest in rents or profits.
    Deed transferring an interest, RP §3-204.
  Personal representatives.
    Evidence of title.
      Payment of costs of recordation, ET §9-105.
  Place of recording, RP §3-103.
  Possession by grantee.
    Unrecorded deed, RP §3-202.

DEEDS —Cont'd
Recordation —Cont'd
  Power of attorney, RP §4-107.
    Revocation, RP §4-107.
  Priority.
    First recorded deed, RP §3-203.
  Required, RP §3-101.
  Straw deeds.
    Exception in certain counties, RP §3-104.
  Tax.
    Calculation.
      Property partly in state, TP §12-105.
    Prepayment of personal property taxes
      inapplicable to mortgagees, lien creditors,
      etc., RP §3-104.
    Rates, TP §12-103.
    Statement of actual consideration paid, TP
      §12-104.
  Time.
    Endorsement on instrument of time of receipt
      by clerk, RP §3-301.
  Transfer on assessment books or county records,
    RP §3-104.
  Unrecorded deed.
    Possession by grantee, RP §3-202.
  Where recorded, RP §3-103.
Religion.
  Corporations.
    Property held by trustee prior to incorporation,
      CA §5-305.
**Remainders, reversions and executory
    interests.**
  Tenant of estate tail may grant in fee simple, RP
    §2-102.
Requirements.
  Sufficiency for a good deed, RP §4-101.
Reservations.
  Deed poll.
    Effect of acceptance of deed by grantee, RP
      §4-102.
Residential leases.
  Sufficiency, RP §4-103.
Restrictions.
  Forms, RP §4-201.
Right to grant.
  Effect of covenant, RP §2-108.
Seals.
  Defective.
    Validation, RP §4-109.
  Not required, RP §4-101.
Seisin.
  Effect of covenant of seisin, RP §2-107.
Shelley's case.
  Abolished, ET §11-104.
Sheriffs.
  Form of sheriff's or other officer's deed, RP §4-202.
Signatures.
  Agent or attorney.
    Power of attorney, RP §4-107.
Special warranty.
  Effect, RP §2-106.
Straw deeds.
  Abolition in certain cases, RP §4-108.
Subdivisions.
  Validation.
    Conveyance of land in unapproved subdivision,
      RP §4-110.
Subsequent deed.
  Effect, RP §3-203.
Sufficiency.
  What deeds sufficient, RP §4-101.

DEEDS —Cont'd
Taxation.
Collector.
Execution of tax deed when copy of judgment served on him, TP §14-847.
Division of cost of recordation taxes, RP §14-104.
Excise taxes.
Exemption of personal representatives, ET §9-105.
Recordation tax.
Property partly in state, TP §12-105.
Rate, TP §12-103.
Statement of consideration paid, TP §12-104.
Tax sale.
Delivery, TP §14-818.
Subsequent taxes must be paid before delivery, TP §14-831.
Tenants.
Entireties.
Conveyances of certain property by married minors, ET §13-503.
Granting of property held by the entireties, RP §4-108.
Terms.
Issue.
Effect of use of terms "die without issue" etc., RP §2-113.
Time.
Effective date of deed, RP §3-201.
Endorsement on instrument of time of receipt by clerk, RP §3-301.
Takes effect between parties from its date, RP §3-201.
Trustee to execute deed.
Appointment by court, CJ §11-111.
Trusts and trustees.
Deed under decree.
Forms, RP §4-202.
United Methodist Church.
Absence of trust clause in deeds, CA §5-327.
United States.
Acquisition of land, SG §14-103.
Validation.
Corporations.
Granting of all or substantially all of property of corporations, RP §14-113.
Defective grants.
General provisions, RP §4-109.
Limitation of actions.
Action to validate defective grants, RP §4-109.
Not to be validated by special act, MD Const Art III §33.
Subdivisions.
Unapproved subdivisions.
Conveyance of land, RP §4-110.
Veterans.
Minors.
Disability of infancy removed in certain instances, ET §13-503.
Rights as to, ET §13-503.
Warranty.
Breach of warranty, RP §10-204.
Encumbrance.
Effect of covenant that grantor has done no act to encumber, RP §2-110.
Effect of general covenant against encumbrances, RP §2-111.
Expiration of warranty, RP §10-204.
Express warranty.
Exclusion or modification, RP §10-202.
Expiration, RP §10-204.

DEEDS —Cont'd
Warranty —Cont'd
Further assurances.
Effect of covenant, RP §2-112.
General warranty.
Effect of general warranty, RP §2-105.
Grant to intermediate purchaser to evade liability, RP §10-205.
Implied covenant of title or possession, RP §2-115.
Implied warranties.
Exclusion or modification, RP §10-203.
Fitness for particular purpose, RP §10-203.
Grantors or lessors, RP §2-115.
Reliance on seller's skill and judgment, RP §10-203.
What warranties are implied, RP §10-203.
Interpretation and construction.
Express warranty, RP §10-202.
Intervening grant.
Effect where made to evade liability, RP §10-205.
Liability.
Grant to intermediate purchaser to evade liability, RP §10-205.
Limitation of actions, RP §10-204.
Quiet enjoyment, RP §2-109.
Right to grant, RP §2-108.
Seisin.
Effect of covenant of seisin, RP §2-107.
Special warranty.
Effect of special warranty, RP §2-106.

DEEDS OF TRUST.
Mortgages and deeds of trust.
General provisions.
See MORTGAGES AND DEEDS OF TRUST.

DEEP CREEK LAKE.
Fees, NR §5-215.
Fish and fisheries.
Police.
Effect of section, NR §4-625.
Wharf, pier or dock.
Permission of department required, NR §4-625.
Permits.
Fees, NR §5-215.
Policy and review board, NR §5-216.
Recreation and land use plan, NR §5-215.1.
Recreation maintenance and management fund, NR §5-215.

DEEPWATER PORTS.
Siting, NR §§3-601 to 3-605.
See HARBORS.

DEER.
General provisions.
See BIRDS AND GAME.

DEFALCATION, CR §7-114.

DEFAMATION.
Criminal defamation.
Common law crime repealed, CR §9-507.
Generally.
See LIBEL AND SLANDER.

DEFAULT.
Administrative procedure.
Contested cases.
Disposition by, SG §10-210.
Assignments.
Assignee's default may release obligee, CL §15-402.

DEFAULT —Cont'd

Land installment contracts.

Effect of compliance on or before date designated in notice to terminate, RP §10-106.

Notice to purchaser, RP §10-106.

Officers.

One person appointed or elected is in default, SG §17-104.

Senior citizen activities centers.

Capital improvement grants program, 70B §31.

DEFAULT JUDGMENTS.

Automobile insurance fund.

Authority of fund to defend claims, IN §20-606.

Circuit courts, CivProCir Rule 2-613.

District Court, CivProDist Rule 3-509.

Divorce, annulment and alimony, CivProCir Rule 2-613.

Insurance.

Property and casualty insurance guaranty corporation, IN §9-315.

Insurance companies.

Liquidation, rehabilitation, etc.

Claims against the insurer.

Judgments as evidence of liability or damages, IN §9-228.

Land installment contracts.

Disclosure as to liability, RP §10-103.

Life and health insurance guaranty corporation, IN §9-418.

Parties.

Pleadings.

Service of pleadings.

Nonoriginal pleadings, Rule 1-321.

Possession.

Action for possession, RP §14-108.1.

Property and casualty insurance guaranty corporation, IN §9-315.

Purchase money mortgage, RP §10-105.

Real property.

Action for possession, RP §14-108.1.

Trial upon default.

District Court, CivProDist Rule 3-509.

DEFENDANTS.

Appearances.

Initial appearance of defendant, Crim Rule 4-213.

Attachment.

Prejudgment attachment.

Judgment for defendant.

Circuit courts, CivProCir Rule 2-115.

District Court, CivProDist Rule 3-115.

Criminal rules.

Defined, Crim Rule 4-102.

Presence of defendants, Crim Rule 4-231.

Definitions.

Criminal rules, Crim Rule 4-102.

Depositions.

Presence of defendant.

Criminal rules, Crim Rule 4-261.

Discovery.

Matters not subject to discovery by defendant.

Criminal rules, Crim Rule 4-263.

Property of defendant.

Disclosure upon request.

Criminal rules, Crim Rule 4-263.

Statements of codefendants.

Disclosure upon request.

Criminal rules, Crim Rule 4-263.

Statements of the defendant.

Disclosure upon request.

Criminal rules, Crim Rule 4-263.

DEFENDANTS —Cont'd

Joinder.

Charging documents, Crim Rule 4-203.

Circuit courts, Crim Rule 4-203.

Depositions.

Criminal rules, Crim Rule 4-261.

Parties.

General provisions.

See PARTIES.

Limitation of actions.

See LIMITATION OF ACTIONS.

Pleas.

Pleas to other offenses.

Request of defendant, Crim Rule 4-244.

DEFENDERS' DAY.

Defined, 1 §27.

Legal holiday, 1 §27.

DEFENSE RELATED ACTIVITY.

Acting with intent to hinder, CR §§9-701 to 9-703.

DEFENSES.

Answers.

Affirmative defenses.

Circuit courts, CivProCir Rule 2-323.

Negative defenses.

Circuit courts, CivProCir Rule 2-323.

Arson in the first degree.

Person owns property not defense, CR §6-102.

Arson in the second degree.

Person owns property not defense, CR §6-103.

Assault.

Judicially recognized defenses allowed, CR §3-209.

Carjacking.

Intent not to permanently deprive owner not defense, CR §3-405.

Charities.

Property and casualty insurance.

Insurer may not assert defense of charitable immunity, IN §19-103.

Solicitations.

Failure to comply with requirements, BR §6-509.

Child custody.

Abduction of child.

Clear and present danger to child, FL §9-306.

Relocation of child.

Violation of notification requirement, FL §9-106.

Civil procedure.

Preservation of certain defenses.

Circuit courts, CivProCir Rule 2-324.

Comparative negligence.

Bank deposits and collections.

Unauthorized signature or alteration, customer's duty to report, CL §4-406.

Contempt.

Support enforcement actions, SpecPro Rule 15-207.

Contracts.

Unconscionability.

Sale of goods, CL §2-302.

Contributory fault.

Bank deposits and collections.

Unauthorized signature or alteration, customer's duty to report, CL §4-406.

Counterfeiting prescription.

Payment or offer to pay for drug not defense, CR §8-610.

DEFENSES —Cont'd
Counties.
  Commissioners.
    Contract actions.
      Counties governed by county commissioners.
        Defense of sovereign immunity, 25 §1A.
  Home rule for code county.
    Contract actions.
      Defense of sovereign immunity, 25B §13A.
Credit cards.
  Prohibited defenses to credit card crimes, CR §8-211.
Detinue, PropAct Rule 12-602.
Dishonored checks and other instruments.
  Collection, CL §15-802.
Electric customer choice and competition act.
  Rate stabilization.
    Assignee's or pledgee's interests in rate stabilization property.
      Not subject to, PUC §7-540.
Escape.
  Intoxication not defense, CR §9-406.
Faked controlled substances.
  Distributing.
    Belief that substance was controlled substance not defense, CR §5-617.
Food, drugs and cosmetics.
  Lack of direct dealing and overcharge actions, HG §21-1114.
  Violations generally, HG §21-260.
Hazing.
  Implied or express consent not defense, CR §3-607.
Health care worker whistleblower protection, HO §1-506.
Homicide by motor vehicle or vessel while impaired by controlled dangerous substance.
  Entitlement to use substance, CR §2-506.
Homicide by motor vehicle or vessel while impaired by drugs.
  Entitlement to use drugs, CR §2-505.
Insanity defense.
  Not criminally responsible, CP §§3-109 to 3-123.
  See NOT CRIMINALLY RESPONSIBLE.
Insurance companies.
  Waiver of defense by insurers, IN §12-105.
Intoxication not defense.
  Escape, CR §9-406.
Investment securities.
  Notice of defenses, CL §§8-202, 8-203.
Labor and employment relations.
  Wage discrimination.
    Action by employee, LE §3-307.
Leases, UCC.
  Unconscionability, CL §2A-108.
Minimum wage.
  Action by employee, LE §3-427.
Motions.
  Consolidation of defenses in motion.
    Circuit courts, CivProCir Rule 2-322.
  Motion to dismiss.
    Circuit courts.
      Defenses which may be made by motion to dismiss, CivProCir Rule 2-322.
  Preservation of certain defenses.
    Circuit courts, CivProCir Rule 2-324.
Negotiable instruments.
  Defenses to recoupment, CL §3-305.
  Rescission of negotiation, CL §3-202.

DEFENSES —Cont'd
Noncontrolled substance believing it to be controlled substance.
  Possessing or purchasing.
    Belief substance controlled substance not defense, CR §5-618.
Not criminally responsible, CP §§3-109 to 3-123.
  See NOT CRIMINALLY RESPONSIBLE.
Pleadings.
  Answers, CivProCir Rule 2-323.
  Form of pleadings.
    Circuit courts, CivProCir Rule 2-303.
  Preservation of certain defenses.
    Circuit courts, CivProCir Rule 2-324.
Possession of stolen property.
  Defenses not allowed, CR §7-104.
Pyramid promotional schemes.
  Prohibited defenses, CR §8-404.
Rape or sexual offense.
  Spousal defense, CR §3-318.
Reckless endangerment.
  Judicially recognized defenses allowed, CR §3-209.
Securities.
  Investment securities, CL §§8-202, 8-203.
  Securities act.
    Crimes and offenses, CA §11-705.
Service contracts and consumer products guaranty.
  Available to guarantor and provider, CL §14-405.
Setback line restrictions, CJ §5-114.
Support and maintenance.
  Withholding earnings.
    Subsequent payment not defense, FL §10-133.
Surveillance by camera of private residence.
  Defendant's ownership of private residence.
    Not defenses, CR §3-903.
  Good faith reliance on court order, CR §3-903.
Tax sales.
  Defense of invalidity, PropSales Rule 14-505.
Theft.
  Good faith or honest belief, CR §7-110.
  Interest in property, not defense, CR §7-110.
  Property illegally obtained by victim, not defense, CR §7-110.
  Spouse's property, CR §7-110.
Tobacco sales to minors.
  Examination of purchaser's driver's license or other identification, CR §10-107.
Torts.
  Local government tort claims act.
    Availability of defenses to government, CJ §5-303.
    Government to provide legal defense to employees, CJ §5-302.
    Waiver.
      Certain defenses not waived, CJ §5-303.
Unauthorized removal of property.
  Intention to hold or keep property for personal use, not defense, CR §7-203.
Universities and colleges.
  Community colleges.
    Board of trustees.
      Defense of sovereign immunity, ED §16-107.
Unlawful subleasing of motor vehicle.
  Defenses not allowed, CR §8-408.
Viatical settlement contracts.
  Statements required in contracts and applications.
    Absence of statement not defense, IN §8-611.
Visual surveillance of individual in private place.
  Defendant owner of premises where private place located.
    Not defense, CR §3-901.

DEFENSES —Cont'd
Workers' compensation.
Hearings.
Defenses not available to insurer, LE §9-723.

DEFINED TERMS.
Abandon.
Well drilling, EN §9-1301.
Abandoned.
Deep mine control, EN §15-601.
Uniform child custody jurisdiction and
enforcement act, FL §9.5-101.
Vehicles abandoned in garages, TR §25-208.
Abandoned apiary.
Honeybees, AG §5-501.
Abandoned land.
Land patents, RP §13-101.
Abandoned property, CL §17-101.
Abandoned vehicle, TR §25-201.
Abandoned vessel.
Boats and boating, NR §8-721.
Abatement.
Lead paint, EN §6-1001.
Absentee.
Absent persons.
Courts, CJ §3-101.
Absentee ballot, EL §1-101.
Abuse.
Abuse or neglect of vulnerable adult, CR §3-604.
Adult protective services, FL §14-101.
Child abuse, CR §3-601.
Child abuse and neglect, FL §5-701.
Children in need of assistance, CJ §3-801.
Child welfare accountability, FL §5-1301.
Domestic violence, FL §4-501.
Health care rights, HG §7-1005.
Health program integrity and recovery activities,
HG §2-501.
Hospital residents, HG §19-347.
Insurance discrimination, IN §27-504.
Local domestic violence fatality review teams, FL
§4-701.
Rights of mentally ill, HG §10-705.
Abuse of funds.
Hospital residents property, HG §19-346.
Abutting lot.
Water and sewer projects, EN §9-950.
Academic facility.
Higher education.
Bond authority, ED §19-101.
Academic fees.
Higher education.
Auxiliary and academic facilities bond
authority, ED §19-101.
Academic paper.
Sale of, ED §26-201.
Academic year.
Universities and colleges.
Tuition increases, ED §15-106.5.
Accelerated mortgage payment service.
Money transmission, FI §12-401.
Accept.
Qualifications of educational personnel, ED
§6-604.
Acceptable collateral.
Investments of life insurers, IN §5-511.
Acceptable release rate.
Antifouling paints, AG §5-901.
Acceptance.
Funds transfers, CL §4A-209.
Negotiable instruments, CL §§3-103, 3-409.

DEFINED TERMS —Cont'd
Acceptance —Cont'd
Sale of goods, CL §2-606.
Acceptance of goods.
Sales, UCC, CL §2-606.
Acceptance of position by client.
Employment agencies, BR §9-305.
Acceptor.
Negotiable instruments, CL §3-103.
Return of checks.
Consumer protection, CL §14-1312.
Access.
Public records, CR §8-606.
Unauthorized access to computers, CR §7-302.
Access area.
Automated teller machines, FI §1-401.
Access contract.
Computer information transactions, CL §22-102.
Access device.
Automated teller machines, FI §1-401.
Accession.
Secured transactions, CL §9-102.
Access material.
Computer information transactions, CL §22-102.
Accidental personal injury.
Workers' compensation, LE §9-101.
Accident history report.
Motor vehicle insurance, IN §27-216.
Accommodated party.
Negotiable instruments, CL §§3-103, 3-419.
Accommodation party.
Negotiable instruments, CL §§3-103, 3-419.
Account.
Appropriations, SF §7-310.
Bank deposits and collections, CL §4-104.
Catastrophic events, SF §7-324.
Credit life, health and unemployment insurance,
IN §13-111.
Economic development opportunities program, SF
§7-314.
Financial institutions, FI §1-204.
Income tax liens, TG §13-812.
Internet sales contracts, CL §14-1321.
Life and health insurance guaranty corporation,
IN §9-401.
Property and casualty insurance guaranty
corporation, IN §9-301.
Retail credit accounts, CL §12-501.
Revenue stabilization account, SF §7-311.
Sales and use tax, TG §13-804.
Secured transactions, CL §9-102.
Account agreement.
Financial institutions, FI §§1-204, 1-210.
Accountant's document, BOP §2-502.
Account debtor.
Secured transactions, CL §9-102.
Account holder.
College savings plan of Maryland, ED §18-1901.
Account holder of interest.
Income tax liens, TG §13-812.
Tax enforcement, TG §13-804.
Accounting.
Secured transactions, CL §9-102.
Accounting period.
Principal and income act, ET §15-501.
Accreditation.
Judith P. Hoyer early child care and education
enhancement program, ED §5-217.
Accreditation organization.
Health care facilities, HG §19-2301.

DEFINED TERMS —Cont'd

Accredited hospital.
Hospitals, HG §19-301.

Accredited representative.
Labor relations.
Mass transit, TR §7-601.

Accredited residential treatment center, HG §19-301.

Accrediting agency.
Judith P. Hoyer early child care and education enhancement program, ED §5-217.

Accrediting organization.
Physicians, HO §14-501.

Accumulated contributions.
Legislative pension plan, SG Title 2 Subtitle 3 (note).
Pensions, SPP §20-101.

Acid.
Acid rain, NR §3-3A-01.

Acid deposition precursor.
Acid rain, NR §3-3A-01.

ACOTE.
Occupational therapists, HO §10-101.

Acquire.
Bank holding companies, FI §5-901.
Savings and loan associations.
Emergency interstate acquisitions, FI §5-1101.
Initial capitalization, FI §9-216.
Interstate acquisitions, FI §9-1001.

Acquiring person.
Corporations, CA §3-701.
Unsolicited takeovers of corporations and real estate investment trusts, CA §3-801.

Acquisition.
Industrial development financing, 83A §5-901.
Nonprofit health entities, SG §6.5-101.

Action.
Commercial code, CL §1-201.
Lead poisoning, EN §6-826.
Uniform commercial code, CL §1-201.

Active enforcement.
Voluntary cleanup program, EN §7-501.

Active ingredient.
Pesticide registration and labeling, AG §5-101.

Actively used.
Property tax.
Farm or agricultural use land, TP §8-209.

Active member.
Employees' and teachers' pension systems, SPP §23-221.
Homestead property tax credit, TP §9-105.

Activities of daily living.
Viatical settlement contracts, IN §8-601.

Activity and use limitation.
Environmental covenants, EN §1-801.

Actual address.
Domestic violence.
Address confidentiality program, FL §4-519.

Actual administrative costs.
Taxation of counties, 24 §9-318.

Actual harm deficiency.
Nursing homes, HG §19-1401.

Actual income.
Child support guidelines, FL §12-201.

Actual loss.
Home improvement, BR §8-401.

Actual malice.
Local government tort claims act, CJ §5-301.

Actuarial method.
Closed end credit, CL §12-1009.

DEFINED TERMS —Cont'd

Actuarial method —Cont'd
Prepayment of outstanding unpaid indebtedness, CL §12-126.

Actuary.
Reinsurance intermediaries, IN §8-520.

Acupuncture, HO §1A-101.

Acute unemployment.
Industrial development, 45A §3.

Adaptive reuse.
Land use, 66B §1.00.

Addition.
Building rehabilitation code, PS §12-1001.

Additional charge.
911 emergency telephone system, PS §1-301.

Additional contributions.
Pensions, SPP §20-101.

Additional education appropriation.
Schools, guaranteed tax base grants, ED §5-210.

Additional education effort.
Schools, guaranteed tax base grants, ED §5-210.

Additional optional coverage.
Homeowner's insurance policies, IN §19-201.

Add-on contract.
Retail installment sales, CL §12-618.

Add-on coverage.
Automobile insurance fund, IN §20-504.

Address.
Corporations, CA §1-101.
Financial institutions, FI §1-101.

Address of record.
Judicial disability and sanctionable conduct, CJA Rule 16-803.

Adjacent coastal state.
Deepwater port siting, NR §3-602.

Adjacent county.
State personnel.
Credits in selection tests, SPP §7-207.

Adjacent district.
State personnel.
Credits in selection tests, SPP §7-207.

Adjacent state.
Purchases of rifles and shotguns, PS §5-204.

Adjudication hearing.
Children in need of assistance, CJ §3-801.

Adjudicatory hearing.
Juvenile causes, CJ §3-8A-01.

Adjunct claims documentation.
Health maintenance organizations.
Payments to providers not under contract, HG §19-710.1.

Adjusted actual income.
Child support guidelines, FL §12-201.

Adjusted annual income.
Maryland home financing program, HS §4-801.

Adjusted assessed valuation of real property.
County public libraries, ED §23-501.
State police.
Protection fund, 41 §4-403.

Adjusted basic child support obligation.
Child support guidelines, FL §12-201.

Adjusted capitalized cost.
Motor vehicle leasing contracts, CL §14-2001.

Adjusted RBC report.
Risk based capital standards for insurers, IN §4-301.

Adjuster.
Vehicle damage, IN §10-501.

Administer.
Controlled dangerous substances, CR §5-101.

DEFINED TERMS —Cont'd

Administration.
Adoption subsidy act, FL §5-401.
Aviation, TR §5-101.
Child abuse and neglect, FL §5-701.
Child care, FL §5-501.
Developmental disabilities, HG §7-101.
Highways, TR §8-101.
Maryland transit administration, TR §7-101.
Motor vehicles, TR §11-102.
Mutual consent voluntary adoption registry, FL
§5-4C-01.
Paternity proceedings, FL §5-1001.
Ports, TR §6-101.
State standby petroleum fuel set-aside program,
PS §14-501.
Water quality financing, EN §9-1601.
Water resources, EN §5-101.
Administration funds.
Motor vehicles, TR §15-101.
Administrative component.
Cancer prevention, education, screening and
treatment program, HG §13-1101.
Tobacco use prevention and cessation program,
HG §13-1001.
Administrative function.
Governmental procedures, meetings, SG §10-502.
Administrative law judge.
Commercial discrimination, SF §19-103.
Disabled student placement, ED §8-413.
Administrative probable cause.
Administrative inspection warrants, CR §5-804.
Administrative record.
Access to court records, CJA Rule 16-1001.
Administrative remedy.
Prisoner litigation, CJ §5-1001.
Administrative service provider contracts, HG
§19-713.2.
Health maintenance organizations, HG
§§19-713.2, 19-713.3.
Administrator.
Alcohol and drug abuse, HG §8-101.
Anne Arundel county correctional facility, COR
§11-703.
Aviation, TR §5-101.
Counties and municipal corporations, 24 §1-107.
Highways, TR §8-101.
Insurance, IN §8-301.
Maryland health insurance plan, IN §14-501.
Maryland transit administration, TR §7-101.
Motor vehicles, TR §11-103.
Natural resources, NR §1-404.
Service by local detention center employees, CJ
§6-310.
Workers' compensation, IN §25-301.
Work release and home detention programs,
Baltimore County, COR §11-705.
Admission.
Developmental disabilities, HG §7-101.
Mental hygiene, HG §10-101.
Admissions and amusement tax, TG §1-101.
Admissions at amusement charged.
Taxation, TG §4-101.
Admission to the bar.
Lawyers, BOP §10-101.
Adoptee.
Mutual consent voluntary adoption registry, FL
§5-4C-01.
Adopting authority.
Administrative procedure.
Regulations, SG §10-130.

DEFINED TERMS —Cont'd

Adoption assistance state.
Interstate compact on adoption and medical
assistance, FL §5-4A-01.
Adoptive parent.
Children generally, FL §5-101.
Adult.
Adult offender supervision, COR §6-203.
Discretionary trusts, ET §14-401.
Juvenile causes, CJ §3-8A-01.
Rules of interpretation, 1 §24.
UTMA, ET §13-301.
Adult day care center, HG §24-701.
Adult dependent care programs, HG §19-1901.
Adult entertainment.
Alcoholic beverage licenses, 2B §12-204.
Alcoholic beverages, 2B §12-203.
Adulterated.
Commercial feed, AG §6-101.
Commercial fertilizers, AG §6-201.
Pesticide registration and labeling, AG §5-101.
Wholesome meat act, AG §4-101.
Adulterated poultry products inspection act,
AG §4-201.
Adult stem cell.
Maryland stem cell research program, 83A
§5-2B-01.
Advance directive.
Advance directive registry, HG §5-619.
Drivers' licenses, organ donation, TR §12-303.1.
Health care decisions, HG §5-601.
Adverse action.
Denial of credit, CL §14-1701.
Adverse benefit determination.
Health insurance, disability and adverse benefit
determination, IN §15-1010.
Adverse claim.
Investment securities, CL §§8-102, 8-301.
Adverse decision.
Health insurance.
Complaint process, IN §15-10A-01.
Private review agents, IN §15-10B-01.
Adverse event.
Residential treatment centers, HG §19-305.
Adverse report.
Accountants.
Peer review, BOP §2-4A-01.
Adverse result.
Evidence, CJ §10-4A.06.
Advertise.
Distress sales, CL §11-1101.
False advertising and related crimes, CL
§14-2901.
Real estate brokers and sales persons, BOP
§17-527.2.
Advertise falsely, CL §11-701.
Advertisement.
Consumer protection, CL §13-101.
Food and drugs, HG §21-101.
Franchises, BR §14-201.
Interstate insurance product regulation compact,
IN §29-101.
Real estate brokers and sales persons, BOP
§17-527.2.
Rental-purchase agreements, CL §12-1101.
Seeds, AG §9-201.
Advertising.
Long-term care insurance, IN §18-103.
Waterproofing.
Consumer protection, CL §14-12A-01.

DEFINED TERMS —Cont'd
Advertising purposes.
  Adult sexual displays, CR §11-101.
Advice.
  Patient care, HG §19-370.
Adviser.
  Insurance, IN §10-201.
  Letters of credit, CL §5-102.
Advisory body.
  Public ethics, SG §15-102.
Advisory committee.
  Horse racing, BR §11-529.
  Maryland correctional enterprises, COR §3-501.
  Patient care, HG §19-370.
  Registration of rehabilitation practitioners, LE
    §9-6A-01.
Advisory council.
  Arthritis, HG §13-502.
  Heart disease, HG §13-201.
  Prevailing wage rates, SF §17-203.
  William Donald Schaefer scholarship program, ED
    §18-2701.
Advisory function.
  Governmental meetings, SG §10-502.
Advisory organization.
  Insurance rates, IN §11-101.
Aerial survey.
  SAV protection zone, NR §4-1006.1.
Aeronautics.
  Aviation, TR §5-101.
Affected area.
  Deep mine control, EN §15-601.
Affected employee.
  Unemployment insurance.
    Work sharing, LE §8-1201.
Affected facility.
  Healthy air act, EN §2-1001.
Affected land.
  Surface mining, EN §15-801.
Affected property.
  Lead hazard insurance for rental property, IN
    §19-701.
  Lead poisoning, EN §6-801.
  Lead risk reduction in rental housing, regulation
    of landlords, 24 §19-101.
Affected unit.
  Unemployment insurance.
    Work sharing, LE §8-1201.
Affidavit.
  Community associations, SG §7-108.
  Elections.
    Petitions, EL §6-101.
Affiliate.
  Banking institutions, FI §5-401.
  Branch banking, FI §5-1001.
  Corporations, CA §3-601.
  Electric customer choice and competition act, PUC
    §7-501.
  Fiduciaries, ET §15-106.
  Homeowner's insurance, geographic distribution of
    premiums, IN §11-321.
  Insurance acquisitions disclosure and control, IN
    §7-101.
  Motor vehicle insurance, IN §11-321.
  Nonprofit health service plans, IN §14-133.
  Nursing homes, HG §19-333.
  Property and casualty insurance guaranty
    corporation, IN §9-310.1.
  Property taxes.
    Job creation, TP §9-230.
  Purchase money mortgages, RP §7-109.

DEFINED TERMS —Cont'd
Affiliate —Cont'd
  Real estate brokers, BOP §17-101.
  Savings and loan associations.
    Board of commissioners and division, FI §8-101.
  Unsolicited takeovers of corporations and real
    estate investment trusts, CA §3-801.
Affiliated corporation.
  Foreign banks, FI §12-201.
Affiliated person.
  Corporations, CA §3-601.
Affiliated political action committee.
  Elections, EL §13-241.
Affiliation period.
  Health insurance, IN §§15-1301, 15-1401.
  Health insurance portability, IN §15-1301.
Affirmation.
  Rules of interpretation, 1 §9.
Afforestation, NR §5-1601.
After-care.
  Mental health compact, HG §11-103.
Aftercare services.
  Rights of mentally ill, HG §10-809.
Aftermarket crash parts.
  Automotive, CL §14-2301.
Afternoon.
  Bank deposits and collections, CL §4-104.
After-school opportunity programs, ED §7-1201.
Aged.
  Long-term care insurance, IN §§18-101 to 18-120.
    See LONG-TERM CARE INSURANCE.
Agency.
  Children, youth and family services.
    Contracts for residential child care programs,
      49D §7-101.
  Contested cases, SG §10-202.
  Managing for results, SF §3-1001.
  Residential child care program administrators,
    HO §20-101.
Agency contract.
  Athlete agents, BR §4-401.
Agency equipment.
  Private detectives, BOP §13-607.
  Security guards, BOP §19-507.
Agency head.
  Administrative procedures.
    Contested cases, SG §10-202.
Agency on aging.
  State retirement and pension system, SPP
    §31-101.
Agency-provider model.
  Community attendant services and supports
    program, 41 §6-7A-01.
Agency relationship.
  Real estate brokers, BOP §17-528.
Agent.
  Bail and recognizance, CP §5-210.
  Community service providers, CJ §5-805.
  Controlled dangerous substances, CR §5-101.
  Health care decisions, HG §5-601.
  Junk dealer licenses, BR §17-1001.
  Securities, CA §11-101.
Agent license.
  Junk dealer licenses, BR §17-1005.
Agent of a charitable organization, CJ §5-404.
Agent of an association or organization.
  Personal liability, CJ §5-406.
Age of majority.
  Rules of interpretation, 1 §24.
Aggravated misconduct.
  Unemployment insurance, LE §8-1002.1.

DEFINED TERMS —Cont'd

Aggregate amount.
Unauthorized access to computers, CR §7-302.

Aggregate attachment point.
Health insurance, stop-loss policies, IN §15-129.

Aggregate expenditures for police protection.
State police, 41 §4-403.

Aggregate incident data.
Mortality and quality review committee, HG §5-801.

Aggregate par value of capital stock.
Corporations, CA §1-204.

Aggregate state funding for the LEP formula.
Grants for limited-English proficiency education, ED §5-208.

Aggregate state funding for the special education formula.
Special education grants, ED §5-209.

Aggregate state funding level for the compensatory education formula.
Schools, compensatory education grants, ED §5-207.

Aggrieved party.
Commercial code, CL §1-201.
Computer information transactions, CL §22-102.
Health care planning and development, HG §19-128.
Uniform commercial code, CL §1-201.

Aggrieved person.
Evidence, CJ §10-401.
Heritage areas, FI §13-1124.
Housing discrimination, 49B §20.

Agreement.
Beer franchise fair dealing act, 2B §17-101.
Commercial code, CL §1-201.
Computer information transactions, CL §22-102.
Distributorships, CL §11-1301.
Electronic transactions, CL §21-101.
Interstate agreement on detainers, COR §8-401.
Labor relations.
    Community colleges, ED §16-412.
Maryland medical professional liability insurance rate stabilization fund, IN §19-104.1.
Prince George's county public employment relations, ED §16-414.1.
Retail installment sales, CL §12-601.
Sale of goods, CL §2-106.
Sales finance companies, FI §11-401.
Sales, UCC, CL §2-106.
Streamlined sales and use tax agreement, TG §11-106.
Uniform commercial code, CL §1-201.

Agreement for electronic presentment.
Bank deposits and collections, CL §§4-104, 4-110.

Agricultural activity.
Forest conservation, NR §5-1601.
Nontidal wetlands, EN §5-901.

Agricultural and resource areas.
Forest conservation, NR §5-1601.

Agricultural building.
Building codes, PS §12-508.

Agricultural commodity.
Agricultural commodity promotion, AG §10-101.

Agricultural cooperative.
Corporations, CA §5-501.

Agricultural drainage project.
Agricultural land drainage, AG §8-603.

Agricultural land.
Property tax.
    Preservation foundation, TP §9-206.

DEFINED TERMS —Cont'd

Agricultural land —Cont'd
Transfer taxes, TP §13-301.
    Washington county, TP §13-501.

Agricultural land transfer tax, TP §13-301.

Agricultural land unit.
Property tax, TP §8-209.

Agricultural lien.
Secured transactions, CL §9-102.

Agricultural loan.
Agricultural and resource-based industry development corporation, 41 §13-501.

Agricultural mediation.
Agricultural mediation program, AG §1-1A-01.

Agricultural operation.
Farm labor contractors, LE §7-101.

Agricultural preservation land.
Frederick county.
    Property tax credits, TP §9-312.

Agricultural seed, AG §9-201.

Agricultural work.
Farm labor contractors, LE §7-101.
Unemployment insurance, LE §8-207.

Agriculture.
Agricultural and resource-based industry development corporation, 41 §13-501.
Rural Maryland prosperity investment fund, SF §2-207.

Aide.
Occupational therapists, HO §10-101.

Air conditioning equipment.
Motor vehicles, TR §22-410.

Aircraft, TR §5-101.
Liens on, CL §16-201.

Air navigation facility, TR §5-101.

Air pollution, EN §2-101.

Airport, TR §5-101.
Airport noise assistance programs, TR §5-1201.
Airport zoning, TR §5-601.
Noise zone regulations, TR §5-801.

Airport district.
Development easements, TR §5-4A-01.

Airport facility, TR §5-101.
Transportation, TR §3-101.

Airport hazard, TR §5-101.

Air school, TR §5-901.

Alarm system, CR §9-607.

Alarm system contractor, CR §9-607.
Calvert county, 25 §236D.
Frederick county, 25 §221A.
Washington county, 25 §236E.

Alarm user.
Alarm systems, CR §9-607.
Calvert county, 25 §236D.
Frederick county, 25 §221A.
Washington county, 25 §236E.

Alcohol.
Motor vehicles, TR §11-103.1.

Alcohol abuse, HG §8-101.
Discrimination by health insurers, HG §19-703.1; IN §15-802.

Alcohol abuse and drug abuse treatment program, HG §8-403.
Inmate programs, HG §8-6A-01.

Alcohol and drug counseling, HO §17-101.

Alcohol and drug counselor training, HO §17-302.3.

Alcohol awareness program, 2B §13-101.

Alcohol concentration.
Motor vehicles, TR §11-103.2.
State substance abuse policy, SPP §2-306.

DEFINED TERMS —Cont'd

Alcohol dependence.
 Alcohol and drug abuse, HG §8-101.
Alcoholic beverage, 2B §1-102.
 Contraband at place of confinement, CR §9-410.
 Correctional facilities, COR §8-801.
 Drinking while driving, TR §21-903.
 Open containers of alcoholic beverages in motor
  vehicles, CR §10-123.
Alcoholic beverage license.
 Taxation, TG §5-101.
Alcoholic beverage tax, TG §§1-101, 5-101.
Alcohol misuse, HG §8-101.
**Alcohol or controlled dangerous substance
  testing.**
 Medical laboratories, HG §17-214.
Alien insurer, IN §1-101.
Aliens.
 Transferability of stock.
  Radio stations, CA §5-703.
All county costs.
 Charles county, 66B §14.05.
Alley.
 Traffic laws, TR §21-101.
Allotted purchases.
 Agricultural land preservation foundation, AG
  §2-508.
Allowable costs.
 Income tax, TG §10-722.
Allowance.
 Healthy air act, EN §2-1001.
 Legislative pension plan, SG Title 2 Subtitle 3
  (note).
 Pensions, SPP §20-101.
Alteration.
 Negotiable instruments, CL §§3-103, 3-407.
Alternate supervising physician.
 Physician assistants, HO §15-101.
Alternative accreditation.
 Maryland youth camp, HG §14-401.
**Alternative dispute resolution, ADR Rule
  17-102.**
 Health care malpractice, alternative dispute
  resolution, CJ §3-2A-06C.
 St. Mary's county human relations commission,
  49B §44.
Alternative living unit.
 Developmental disabilities, HG §7-101.
**Alternative teaching opportunity program, ED
  §6-120.**
Alzheimer's disease.
 Long-term care insurance, IN §18-101.
Ambient air monitoring data.
 Access via Internet, EN §2-103.2.
Ambulance, ED §13-515.
Ambulance service, ED §13-515.
Ambulatory surgical facilities, HG §19-3B-01.
 Health insurance, provider panels, IN §15-112.
 Health planning, HG §19-114.
 Medical care data collection, HG §19-132.
Amendment.
 Sanitary commissions, EN §9-614.
American aircraft.
 Unemployment insurance.
  Location of employment, LE §8-202.
American employer.
 Unemployment insurance.
  Location of employment, LE §8-202.
American steel product.
 Steel procurement, SF §17-301.

DEFINED TERMS —Cont'd

Ammunition.
 Bulletproof body armor, CR §4-106.
 Child's access to firearm, CR §4-104.
 Hunting deer, NR §10-416.
Amortizable basis.
 Taxation, TG §10-207.
Amounts paid by the debtor.
 Consumer credit contracts, CL §14-1302.
Amusement attraction, BR §3-101.
Amusement device.
 Garrett county licenses, BR §17-432.
 Political subdivisions, 24 §11-202.
Amusement owner, BR §3-101.
Amusement park, BR §3-101.
Amusement ride, BR §3-101.
Ancillary state.
 Insurer liquidation, rehabilitation, etc., IN §9-201.
Angling.
 Fish and fisheries, NR §4-601.
Animal.
 Animal control, HG §18-218.
 Crimes relating to animals, CR §10-601.
 Livestock and poultry, AG §3-115.
 Metropolitan district property.
  Hunting on, 28 §5-113.1.
Animal control officer, 25 §236A.
Animal food manufacturer.
 Poultry products inspection act, AG §4-201.
 Wholesome meat act, AG §4-101.
Animal waste technology project.
 Economic development assistance fund, 83A
  §5-1401.
Annapolis authority.
 Annapolis housing authority, HS §13-101.
**Anne Arundel county or city of Annapolis fire
  and explosive investigator, CP §2-208.2.**
Announcement date.
 Business combinations.
  Corporations, CA §3-603.
Annual charge.
 Homeowners' associations, RP §11B-113.4.
Annual contract.
 University of Maryland medical system, ED
  §13-301.
Annual day-night (average) sound level.
 Airport noise assistance programs, TR §5-1201.
Annual gross revenue.
 Debt management services, FI §12-901.
Annual income.
 Condominium conversions, RP §11-102.1.
 Condominiums, RP §11-137.
 Cooperative housing corporation, CA §§5-6B-05,
  5-6B-07.
Annual operating costs.
 Water and sewerage systems, SF §2-401.
Annual payroll.
 Unemployment insurance.
  Contributions, LE §8-606.
Annual per pupil foundation amount.
 Educational financing.
  State assistance, ED §5-202.
Annual program.
 Forests and parks.
  Open space program, NR §5-901.
Annuities.
 Insurance, IN §1-101.
 Pensions, SPP §20-101.
Annuity contract.
 Insurance, IN §1-101.

DEFINED TERMS —Cont'd
Annuity contract —Cont'd
State retirement and pension system, SPP §30-101.
Annuity reserve.
Pensions, SPP §20-101.
Anomalous indorsement.
Negotiable instruments, CL §§3-103, 3-205.
ANSI standard.
Building codes, safety glazing, PS §12-401.
Antiarson application.
Fire insurance, IN §19-301.
Antibiotic drug.
Food and drugs, HG §21-218.
Antidote.
Pesticide registration and labeling, AG §5-101.
Antifouling paint, AG §5-901.
Antique firearm, CR §4-201; PS §5-101.
Antique slot machine, CR §12-303.
Any state.
Education, ED §1-101.
Financial institutions, FI §1-101.
Transportation, TR §1-101.
Apartment house.
Energy allocation equipment, PUC §7-304.
Gas or electric meters, PUC §7-303.
Submetering, PUC §7-303.
Apartment unit.
Hospitals, HG §19-301.
Apiary, AG §5-501.
Apparatus.
Occupational safety and health, LE §5-210.
Appeal.
Health insurance.
Complaint process for coverage decisions, IN §15-10D-01.
Appeal decision.
Health insurance.
Complaint process for coverage decisions, IN §15-10D-01.
Appeals board.
Procurement, SF §15-201.
Appellate court, CJ §2-101.
Appeals, CJ §12-101.
Appellate jurisdiction, CJ §12-101.
Appendix plat.
Real property, RP §3-108.1.
Appliance.
Extension of service contract, CL §14-1306.
Honeybees, AG §5-501.
Appliances, fixtures and items of equipment.
New home warranties, RP §10-601.
Applicable contributions.
Disclosures by persons doing public business, EL §14-101.
Lobbying, SG §15-715.
Applicable energy efficiency standards.
Income tax credits, TG §10-722.
Applicable poverty income level.
Income tax, TG §10-709.
Applicable recipient.
Lobbying, SG §15-715.
Applicants.
Access to public records, SG §10-611.
AIDS insurance, HG §15-201.
Development permits, SG §11-101.
Equal credit opportunity, CL §12-701.
Industrial development financing authority, 83A §5-927.
Insurance cancellation or nonrenewal, IN §27-604.
Letters of credit, CL §5-102.

DEFINED TERMS —Cont'd
Applicants —Cont'd
Long-term care insurance, IN §18-101.
Medicare supplement insurance, IN §15-901.
Nurses, HO §8-208.
Public assistance programs, 88A §64.
Statewide nutrition assistance program, 88A §130A.
Trademarks, BR §1-401.
Voluntary cleanup program, EN §7-501.
Application.
Community legacy program, HS §6-201.
Deepwater port siting, NR §3-602.
Expungement of records, Crim Rule 4-502.
Local land preservation programs, NR §5-9B-01.
Pesticide applicators, AG §5-201.
Rural legacy program, NR §5-9A-02.
Application service provider.
E-commerce, advisory board, SG §9-2201.
Appointed official.
Employees' and teachers' pension systems, SPP §23-404.
Employees' and teachers' retirement systems, SPP §22-404.
Appointed receiver.
Liquidation, rehabilitation, etc., of insurers, IN §9-213.
Appointing authority.
State personnel, SPP §1-101.
Appointment.
Insurance agents, IN §1-101.
Appraisal.
Eminent domain, RP §12-201.
Professional counselors and therapists, HO §17-101.
Real estate appraisers, BOP §16-101.
Appraisal report.
Real estate appraisers, BOP §16-101.
Appraiser.
Vehicle damage, IN §10-501.
Apprentice.
Morticians, HO §7-101.
Public works contracts, SF §17-201.
Apprentice barber, BOP §4-101.
Apprentice natural gas fitter, BOP §12-101.
Apprentice plumber, BOP §12-101.
Apprenticeship permit.
Fish and fisheries, NR §4-101.
Apprentice sponsor.
Morticians, HO §7-101.
Approach.
Toll facilities, TR §21-1401.
Appropriate authority in the receiving state.
Interstate placement of children, FL §5-601.
Appropriate county governing body.
Water resources, EN §5-101.
Appropriate county official.
Property tax.
Supervisors of assessments, TP §2-105.
Appropriate court.
Interstate agreement on detainers, COR §8-401.
Appropriate official.
Property tax.
Correction of assessments, TP §8-419.
Appropriate person.
Investment securities, CL §§8-102, 8-107.
Appropriate public authorities.
Interstate placement of children, FL §5-601.
Appropriation act.
See APPROPRIATIONS.

DEFINED TERMS —Cont'd

Approval.
Environmental enforcement, EN §2-609.1.
Approved alcohol and drug supervisor, HO §17-301.
Approved correctional training school.
Correctional training commission, COR §8-201.
Approved employer.
State retirement and pension system, SPP §21-313.
Approved facility.
Scrap tire disposal, EN §9-228.
Approved foreign trade zone.
Taxation, TG §8-201.
Approved medication technician training program, HO §8-6A-01.
Approved nursing assistant training program, HO §8-6A-01.
Approved practice.
Woodland incentives program, NR §5-301.
Approved project.
Neighborhood and community assistance program, HS §6-401.
Approved school of osteopathy.
Physicians, HO §14-312.
Approved seed.
Seeds, AG §9-201.
Approved service provider.
Ignition interlock system, TR §16-404.1.
Approved sod.
Turf grass, AG §9-101.
Approved standards.
Standards for correctional facilities, COR §8-101.
Approved work sharing plan.
Unemployment insurance, LE §8-1201.
Appurtenances.
Historic area zoning, 66B §8.01.
Aquaculture, AG §10-1301; NR §4-11A-01.
Aquaculture oyster floats.
Income tax credit, TG §10-724.
Aquaculture project.
Economic development assistance fund, 83A §5-1401.
Aquatic organism.
Natural resources, NR §4-205.1.
Arbitral tribunal.
International commercial arbitration, CJ §3-2B-01.
Arbitration, ADR Rule 17-102.
Labor relations.
Community colleges, ED §16-412.
Prince George's county public employment relations, ED §16-414.1.
Arbitration panel.
Health care malpractice, CJ §3-2A-01.
Archaeology office.
Maryland historical trust, archaeological property, SF §5A-333.
Architect, BOP §3-101.
Architectural services.
Procurement, SF §11-101.
Archives, SG §9-1001.
Area.
Copyrights royalties, CL §11-1401.
Enterprise zones, 83A §5-401.
Mid-shore regional council, 20C §1-101.
Southern Maryland tri-county council, 20 §1-102.
Tri-county council for lower Eastern shore of Maryland, 20B §1-101.
Upper shore regional council, 20D §1-101.
Western Maryland tri-county council, 20A §1-102.

DEFINED TERMS —Cont'd

Area agency on aging, 70B §1.
Area franchise, BR §14-201.
Area of critical shortage.
McAuliffe teacher education award, ED §18-703.
Service retirement benefits, SPP §§21-307, 22-406, 23-407.
Area of geographic shortage.
McAuliffe teacher education award, ED §18-703.
Area of nontidal inundation.
Flood control and watershed management, EN §5-801.
Area of operation.
Housing authorities, HS §12-101.
Area of shortage.
Health occupations, HO §1-204.
Area of tidal inundation.
Flood control and watershed management, EN §5-801.
Areas under Nazi influence.
Holocaust victim insurance, IN §28-101.
Armed forces.
Copies of records for former armed forces members, CJ §7-406.
Arrestee.
Driving under the influence, TR §21-902.1.
Art dealer.
Consignment of works of fine art, CL §11-8A-01.
Article.
Driver license compact, TR §16-701.
Mental health, HG §11-101.
Articles of amendment.
Water and sewer authorities, EN §9-908.
Articles of consolidation.
Recordation taxes, TP §12-101.
Transfer taxes, TP §13-101.
Articles of incorporation.
Cooperative housing corporation, CA §5-6B-01.
Articles of merger.
Recordation taxes, TP §12-101.
Transfer taxes, TP §13-101.
Articles of organization.
Limited liability companies, CA §4A-101.
Articles of transfer.
Corporations, CA §1-101.
Recordation taxes, TP §12-101.
Transfer taxes, TP §13-101.
Artisan.
Liens by, CL §16-301.
Artist.
Consignment of works of fine art, CL §11-8A-01.
Consumer protection.
Fine print, CL §14-501.
Artistic work.
Arts and entertainment districts, 83A §4-701.
Arts and entertainment district.
Economic development assistance fund, 83A §5-1401.
Arts and entertainment enterprise.
Arts and entertainment districts, 83A §4-701.
Economic development assistance fund, 83A §5-1401.
Arts and entertainment project.
Economic development assistance fund, 83A §5-1401.
Asbestos material, EN §6-401.
Asbestos occupation, EN §6-401.
As-extracted collateral.
Secured transactions, CL §9-102.
ASHRAE.
Illumination in public buildings, guidelines, PS §12-204.

DEFINED TERMS —Cont'd

ASP.
E-commerce, advisory board, SG §9-2201.
Assault, 1 §33; CR §3-201.
Assault pistol, CR §4-301.
Assault weapons.
Firearms, PS §5-101.
Assess.
Property tax, TP §1-101.
Assessed valuation of real property.
Community colleges.
State and county aid, ED §16-305.
Educational financing.
State assistance, ED §5-202.
Assessed value of personal property.
Educational financing.
State assistance, ED §5-202.
Assessment.
Insurance regulation assessment, IN §2-501.
Property tax, TP §1-101.
Assessment roll.
Property tax, TP §1-101.
Asset-backed security.
Investments of life insurers, IN §5-511.
Principal and income, ET §15-522.
Assets.
Corporations, CA §1-101.
Credit union insurance corporation, dissolution,
FI §7-120.
Debt collection.
Fraudulent conveyances, CL §15-201.
Nonprofit health service plans, IN §14-117.
Property tax.
Elderly or disabled renters, TP §9-102.
Homeowner's credit, TP §9-104.
Assets attributable to covered policies.
Life and health insurance guaranty corporation,
IN §9-414.
Assignation.
Prostitution and related crimes, CR §11-301.
Assignee.
Electric customer choice and competition act, PUC
§7-501.
Electric customer competition and choice act.
Rate stabilization, PUC §7-520.
Assignment.
Assignment of wages, CL §15-301.
Fiduciary security transfers, ET §15-301.
State standby petroleum fuel set-aside program,
PS §14-501.
Assignment of local license.
Electricians, BOP §6-101.
Assistance.
Public assistance programs, 88A §64.
Assistance at public expense.
Social services administration.
Reading of statement of conduct constituting
fraud, 88A §16.
Assisted family housing.
Montgomery county housing opportunities
commission, HS §16-110.
Assisted household.
Assisted housing preservation, HS §7-101.
Assisted living facility.
Grants, HG §24-1001.
Assisted living program, HG §19-1801.
Continuing care contracts, 70B §7.
Assisted living services.
Medicaid, HG §15-132.
Assisted project.
Assisted housing preservation, HS §7-101.

DEFINED TERMS —Cont'd

Assisted unit.
Assisted housing preservation, HS §7-101.
Assistive technology, 41 §14-901.
Associate.
Corporations, CA §§3-601, 3-703.
Unsolicited takeovers of corporations and real
estate investment trusts, CA §3-801.
Associated development and carrying costs.
Economic development assistance fund, 83A
§5-1401.
Associated funerary object.
Crimes relating to human remains, CR §10-401.
Maryland historical trust, archaeological property,
SF §5A-333.
Associate real estate broker, BOP §17-101.
Associate solicitor.
Charitable organizations, BR §6-101.
Association.
Health insurance portability, IN §15-1301.
Volunteer company assistance fund, PS §8-201.
Association member.
Automobile insurance fund, IN §20-101.
Joint insurance association, IN §25-401.
Association or organization.
Automobile insurance fund, IN §20-101.
Charitable organization volunteer personal
liability, CJ §5-407.
Financial institutions.
Deposit insurance, FI §10-101.
Health insurance portability, IN §§15-1301,
15-1401.
Liquidation, rehabilitation, etc., of insurers, IN
§9-224.
Personal liability, CJ §5-406.
Time-sharing, RP §11A-101.
Assumed ending date.
Insurance companies.
Standard valuation law, IN §5-307.
Assumed real property tax.
Elderly or disabled renters, TP §9-102.
Athlete agent, BR §4-401.
Athletic club.
Personal liability, CJ §5-406.
Athletic director.
Athlete agents, BR §4-401.
Athletic official.
Community recreation program.
Personal liability, CJ §5-802.
Atlantic coastal bays.
Chesapeake Bay critical area and Atlantic coastal
bays critical area protection programs, NR
§8-1802.
Atlantic coastal bays critical area.
Chesapeake Bay critical area and Atlantic coastal
bays critical area protection programs, NR
§8-1802.
At-risk parent.
Integration of child welfare and substance abuse
treatment act, FL §5-1201.
At-risk youth.
Residential boarding education programs for
at-risk youth, ED §8-701.
Attached.
Rental electric storage batteries, CL §11-902.
Attendant services and supports.
Community attendant services and supports
program, 41 §6-7A-01.
Attending physician.
Health care decisions, HG §5-601.
Standby guardians, ET §13-901.

DEFINED TERMS —Cont'd

Attending provider.
  Health insurance, IN §15-812.
  Private review agents.
    Maternity and newborn care, IN §15-10B-09.
Attorney General.
  Antitrust, CL §11-201.
  Foreign discriminatory boycotts, CL §11-102.
  National crime prevention and privacy compact,
    CP §10-239.
Attorneys.
  Discipline of attorneys, CJA Rule 16-701.
  Insurance agents and brokers, IN §10-125.
Attorneys at law, BOP §10-101.
Attorney trust account, BOP §10-301.
Attrition procedure.
  Computer information transactions, CL §22-102.
At will.
  Commercial code, CL §1-208.
Auctioneer.
  Bulk transfers, CL §6-108.
Audible alarm system, CR §9-611.
Audiologist, HO §2-101.
Audiologists rehabilitation committee, HO
  §2-318.
Audio or visual programming.
  Computer information transactions, CL §22-103.
Auger mining, EN §15-501.
Aural transfer.
  Evidence, CJ §10-401.
Auricular detoxification.
  Acupuncture, HO §1A-101.
Authenticate.
  Computer information transactions, CL §22-102.
  Secured transactions, CL §9-102.
Authority.
  Health and educational facilities, 43C §3.
  Heritage areas authority, FI §13-1101.
  Housing authorities, HS §12-101.
  Local military installation redevelopment
    authorities, 83A §5-1701.
  Property tax exemptions.
    Housing authority property, TP §7-215.
  Revenue facilities, TR §4-101.
  Sewerage systems, EN §9-205.
  Tobacco, AG §7-101.
  Water and sewer authorities, EN §9-901.
Authority affiliate.
  Maryland stadium authority, FI §13-701.
Authority staff.
  Small business development financing authority,
    83A §5-1001.
Authorization.
  Fish and fisheries, NR §4-101.
Authorized account.
  Funds transfers, CL §4A-105.
Authorized candidate campaign committee, EL
  §1-101.
Authorized county.
  Hotel rental tax, 24 §9-301.
Authorized delegate.
  Money transmission, FI §12-401.
Authorized electrical inspection agency.
  Electrical code, PS §12-601.
Authorized employment.
  Child care provider grant program, ED §18-705.
Authorized facility.
  Automated external defibrillator program, ED
    §13-517.
Authorized insurer, IN §1-101.
  Workers' compensation, LE §9-401.

DEFINED TERMS —Cont'd

Authorized officer.
  State finance, SF §2-301.
Authorized official.
  Marriage, FL §2-101.
Authorized person.
  Limited liability companies, CA §4A-101.
  Survey stations, BOP §1-301.
Authorized prescriber.
  Food, drugs and cosmetics, HG §21-1113.
  Health insurance, IN §§15-805, 15-824.
  Health insurance, prescription drug coverage, IN
    §15-831.
  Health insurance smoking cessation treatment
    coverage, IN §15-841.
  Pharmacists and pharmacies, HO §12-101.
Authorized provider.
  Controlled dangerous substances, CR §5-101.
Authorized representative.
  Maryland emergency management assistance
    compact, PS §14-801.
Authorized use, disclosure or receipt.
  Credit card number protection, CR §8-213.
Authorized user.
  Handgun safety devices, PS §5-132.
  ImmuNet program, HG §18-109.
Automated external defibrillator (AED), ED
  §13-517.
Automated teller machine, FI §1-401.
Automated transaction.
  Computer information transactions, CL §22-102.
  Electronic transactions, CL §21-101.
Automatic restraint.
  Computer information transactions, CL §22-605.
Automobile.
  Electric or hybrid motor vehicles, TR §13-815.
  Length and loads, TR §24-104.1.
Automobile graveyard, EN §5-10A-01; TR §8-801.
Automotive dismantler and recycler, TR
  §15-501.
Automotive dismantler and recycler facility,
  EN §5-10A-01; TR §8-801.
Automotive repair facility.
  Consumer protection, CL §14-1001.
  Motor vehicle repair facilities, TR §15-113.1.
Auxiliary facilities fees.
  Higher education.
    Bond authority, ED §19-101.
Auxiliary facility.
  Higher education.
    Bond authority, ED §19-101.
Average final compensation.
  Pensions, SPP §20-101.
Average gross income.
  Property tax.
    Farm or agricultural use land, TP §8-209.
Average handle.
  Horse racing, BR §11-601.
Aviation fuel.
  Taxation, TG §8-101.
Aviation gasoline.
  Taxation, TG §8-101.
Avigation easement.
  Airport noise assistance programs, TR §5-1201.
Award.
  Maryland affordable housing trust, HS §10-101.
  State personnel.
    Satisfaction of awards, SPP §14-201.
Background checks.
  Adult dependent care programs, HG §19-1901.
  Nursing referral service agencies, HG §19-4B-01.

DEFINED TERMS —Cont'd
Background level.
  Voluntary cleanup program, EN §7-501.
Backplant.
  Insurance companies.
    Admitted assets, IN §5-104.
Baggage.
  Sale of unclaimed baggage, BR §19-102.
Bail bond, IN §10-301.
Bail bondsman, CP §5-210; IN §10-301.
Bailee.
  Documents of title, CL §7-102.
Baited area.
  Hunting game birds, NR §10-412.
Baiting.
  Hunting game birds, NR §10-412.
Balloon payment.
  Closed end credit, CL §12-1001.
Ballot, EL §1-101.
Ballot face, EL §1-101.
Ballot issue committee, EL §1-101.
Ballot style, EL §1-101.
Baltimore authority.
  Baltimore City housing authority, HS §15-101.
Baltimore authority police officer.
  Housing authorities, HS §15-108.
Baltimore City school police officer, ED §4-318.
Baltimore City school system.
  Alternative learning center, ED §4-319.
Baltimore convention center site.
  Stadium authority, FI §13-701.
Baltimore county tributary spoil.
  Chesapeake Bay and tributaries, EN §5-1101.
  Hart-Miller-Pleasure Island chain, NR §5-1202.2.
Baltimore Harbor.
  Chesapeake Bay and tributaries, EN §5-1101.
  Hart-Miller-Pleasure Island chain, NR §5-1202.2.
Baltimore housing authority entity.
  Housing authorities, tax-exempt status, HS
    §12-104.
Bank.
  Consolidations, mergers and transfers of assets,
    FI §3-701.
  Fiduciaries, ET §15-1A-01.
  Funds transfers, CL §4A-105.
  Hospital residents property, HG §19-346.
  Secured transactions, CL §9-102.
  Uniform commercial code, CL §1-201.
  Uniform fiduciaries act, ET §15-201.
Banker's credit.
  Sales, UCC, CL §2-325.
Bank holding company, FI §§3-314, 5-901.
  Fiduciaries, ET §15-1A-01.
  Foreign banks, FI §12-201.
Banking day.
  Bank deposits and collections, CL §4-104.
Banking institution, FI §1-101.
  State treasury, SF §6-201.
Banking organization.
  Abandoned property, CL §17-101.
Bank or trust company.
  Property tax exemption.
    Property used in processing deposits or loans,
      TP §7-221.1.
Bankrupt.
  Limited liability companies, CA §4A-101.
Bank service corporation, FI §5-401.
Bank supervisory agency.
  Bank holding companies, FI §5-901.
  Branch banking, FI §5-1001.

DEFINED TERMS —Cont'd
Bar.
  Lawyers, BOP §10-101.
Barbeque grills.
  Restrictions on use, PS §9-1001.
Barber, BOP §4-101.
Barbershop, BOP §4-101.
Barbershop permit, BOP §4-101.
Bar or bar area.
  Smoking restrictions, LE §5-314.
  Tobacco smoking, LE §2-106.
Barrel.
  Oil spills, EN §4-411.
Base building.
  Income tax credits, TG §10-722.
Base hospital rate.
  Cost review commission, HG §19-219.
Baseline cancer study.
  Cancer prevention, education, screening and
    treatment program, HG §13-1101.
Baseline tobacco study.
  Tobacco use prevention and cessation program,
    HG §13-1001.
Basement waterproofing.
  Consumer protection, CL §14-12A-01.
Base period.
  Unemployment insurance, LE §8-101.
Base period employer.
  Unemployment insurance, LE §8-101.
Base period wages.
  Unemployment insurance.
    Contributions, LE §8-606.
Base year.
  Community colleges.
    Contributions, ED §16-317.
  Higher education.
    Private donation incentive program, ED
      §17-301.
  Property tax.
    Enterprise zones, TP §9-103.
Base year assessment.
  Property tax.
    Enterprise zones, TP §9-103.
Basic allowance.
  Pensions, SPP §20-101.
Basic child support obligation.
  Child support guidelines, FL §12-201.
Basic cost.
  Handicapped children.
    Shared cost of education, ED §8-415.
Basic cost of cigarettes.
  Cigarettes sales below cost, CL §11-501.
Basic main facility.
  Sewerage systems, EN §9-207.
Basin.
  Susquehanna river basin compact, EN §5-301.
Battered spouse syndrome.
  Evidence, CJ §10-916.
Battery.
  Rental electric storage batteries, CL §11-902.
Bay restoration fund.
  Water quality financing, EN §9-1601.
Bayside mixed use district.
  Chesapeake Bay critical area and Atlantic coastal
    bays critical area protection programs.
    Single family dwellings, NR §8-1813.1.
Bearer.
  Uniform commercial code, CL §1-201.
Bearer form.
  Investment securities, CL §8-102.

DEFINED TERMS —Cont'd

Beauty salon.
Cosmetologists, BOP §5-101.

Beauty salon permit.
Cosmetologists, BOP §5-101.

Bed and breakfast establishments.
Food, drugs and cosmetics, HG §21-323.1.

Bedding, HG §24-401.

Bee, AG §5-501.

Bee equipment, AG §5-501.

Beer, 2B §1-102.
Taxation, TG §5-101.

Beer distributor.
Beer franchise fair dealing act, 2B §17-101.

Beer manufacturer.
Beer franchise fair dealing act, 2B §17-101.

Behavioral health care services.
Health insurance coverage, IN §15-127.

Behavior intervention plan.
Student behavior intervention, ED §7-1101.

Below cost.
Motor fuel, BR §10-301.

Beneficial interest.
Health occupations, HO §1-301.

Beneficial owner.
Attorney trust accounts, BOP §10-301.
Business trusts, CA §12-101.
Corporations, CA §3-601.
Real estate brokers.
Trust accounts, BOP §17-501.
Title insurance, IN §22-103.
Unsolicited takeovers of corporations and real estate investment trusts, CA §3-801.

Beneficial ownership.
Horse racing, BR §11-301.
Procurement, SF §13-221.
Savings and loan associations.
Initial capitalization, FI §9-216.

Beneficiary.
Discretionary trusts, ET §14-401.
Donation of conservation easement by trustee, ET §14-111.
Fiduciaries, ET §15-1A-01.
Financial institutions, FI §1-204.
Funds transfers, CL §4A-103.
Legislative pension plan, SG Title 2 Subtitle 3 (note).
Letters of credit, CL §5-102.
Pensions, SPP §20-101.
Pre-need contracts, HO §7-405.
Principal and income act, ET §15-501.
Trusts, ET §§14-106, 14-107.

Beneficiary designation.
Disclaimer of property interests, ET §9-201.

Beneficiary form.
Transfer-on-death security registration, ET §16-101.

Beneficiary's bank.
Funds transfers, CL §4A-103.

Benefit contract.
Fraternal benefit societies, IN §8-401.

Benefited property.
Shore erosion control, NR §8-1001.

Benefit member.
Fraternal benefit societies, IN §8-401.

Benefit package.
HMOS, HG §19-701.

Benefit performance.
Prince George's county, CR §13-1901.

Benefit plan.
UTMA, ET §13-301.

DEFINED TERMS —Cont'd

Benefits.
Unemployment insurance, LE §8-101.

Benefit year.
Unemployment insurance, LE §8-101.

Best interest.
Disabled persons, ET §13-711.
Health care decisions, HG §5-601.

Best management practice.
Nontidal wetlands, EN §5-901.
Water pollution control, AG §8-701.

Between merchants.
Sales, UCC, CL §2-104.

Bi-county unit.
Litter control law, CR §10-110.

Bicycle, TR §11-104.
Driving on sidewalk, TR §21-1103.

Bicycle and pedestrian priority area, TR §8-101.

Bicycle path, TR §21-101.

Bicycle way, TR §21-101.

Bid.
Procurement, SF §§4-301, 11-101.

Biennial.
Mammography testing, HG §20-116.

Bike lane, TR §21-101.

Bill.
Legislation.
Preparation, introduction and consideration, SG §2-1501.
Return on final passage, SG §2-1508.

Billiard table.
Business licenses, BR §17-501.

Billiard table license, BR §17-501.

Billing error.
Retail credit accounts, CL §12-511.

Bill of lading, CL §18-101.
Uniform commercial code, CL §1-201.

Bill payer service.
Money transmission, FI §12-401.

Binder.
Closed end credit, CL §12-1007.1.
Interest in usury, CL §12-123.
Revolving credit, CL §12-909.1.

Bingo.
Harford county, CR §13-1501.

Biodiesel.
Renewable energy credits, AG §10-1501.

Biological agent.
Registry program, HG §17-601.

Biological evidence.
Post conviction review, CP §8-201.

Biological nutrient removal.
Water quality financing, EN §9-1601.

Biological product.
Livestock and poultry, AG §3-201.

Biomass.
Gas and electric companies, PUC §7-306.

Bioptic telescopic lenses.
Drivers' licenses, TR §16-110.2.

Biotechnology company.
Income tax credits, TG §10-725.

Birdwatcher, NR §10-2A-06.1.

Birdwatching, NR §10-2A-06.1.

Birth.
Vital statistics, HG §4-201.

Blanket encumbrance.
Cooperative housing corporation, CA §5-6B-01.

Blanket health insurance, IN §15-301.

Blank indorsement.
Negotiable instruments, CL §§3-103, 3-205.

DEFINED TERMS —Cont'd

Blend.
Motor fuel tax, TG §9-301.

Blind.
Products made by blind persons, CL §14-2801.

Blind child.
Education, ED §8-301.

Blind individual.
Property tax exemptions.
Dwelling house, TP §7-207.

Blind person.
Business enterprise program for the blind, SF §14-109.

Block grant.
State finance, SF §2-202.

Boarding stable.
Horse industry board, AG §2-701.

Board, lodging or other advantage.
Wages.
Computation, LE §3-418.

Board of canvassers, EL §11-101.

Board of county commissioners.
Queen Anne's county housing authority, HS §18-101.
Washington county housing authority, HS §21-101.

Board of directors.
Condominiums, RP §11-101.

Board of education district.
Montgomery county board of education, ED §3-901.

Board of review.
Patuxent institution, COR §4-101.

Board of trustees.
Pensions, SPP §20-101.

Boat.
Liens on, CL §16-201.
Waterfowl hunting, NR §10-601.

Boat trailer, TR §11-104.1.

Bobtailer.
Milk products, HG §21-401.

Bodily fluid.
Altering results of drug or alcohol screening, CR §10-111.
Criminal law and procedure, CR §3-215.

Bodily fluid adulterant.
Altering results of drug or alcohol screening, CR §10-111.

Body.
Anatomical gift act, ET §4-501.
Death, HG §5-101.
Vital statistics, HG §4-201.

Body fluids.
Contagious disease or virus, HG §18-213.2.
Disease reports, HG §18-213.1.
Health care providers, HG §18-338.1.
HIV testing, CP §11-109.
HIV testing for health care workers and first responders, HG §18-338.3.

Body mass index.
Health insurance coverage for treatment of morbid obesity, IN §15-839.

Body shop.
Automotive crash parts, CL §14-2301.

Boiler.
Boilers and pressure vessels, PS §12-901.

Boilers and pressure vessels, PS §12-901.

Bona fide association.
Health insurance portability, IN §§15-1301, 15-1401.

DEFINED TERMS —Cont'd

Bona fide intrafamily transfer.
Chesapeake Bay critical area and Atlantic coastal bays critical area protection programs, NR §8-1808.2.

Bond resolution.
Water quality financing, EN §9-1601.

Bonds.
Agricultural and resource-based industry development corporation, 41 §13-501.
Allocation of private activity bond authority, FI §13-801.
Bainbridge development corporation, 83A §5-1601.
Baltimore City schools, ED §4-301.
Canal place preservation and development authority, FI §13-1001.
County transportation bonds, TR §3-301.
Economic development corporation, 83A §5-201.
Environmental service, NR §3-101.
Health and educational facilities, 43C §3.
Heritage areas, FI §13-1101.
Higher education.
Auxiliary and academic facilities, ED §19-101.
Auxiliary and academic facilities bond authority, ED §19-103.
Housing authorities, HS §12-101.
Industrial development financing, 83A §5-901.
Interest rate exchange agreements or contracts, 31 §34.
Local military installation redevelopment authorities, 83A §5-1701.
Municipal corporations, 23A §44A.
Northeast Maryland waste disposal authority, NR §3-904.
Penmar development corporations, 83A §5-1201.
Public schools financing, 31 §34.
Sanitary commissions, EN §9-601.
Senior citizen activities centers capital improvement grants, 70B §26.
Special taxes authorized in certain counties, 24 §9-1301.
Special taxing districts, 24 §9-1301.
State debt, SF §8-201.
State finance, SF §2-106.
Time-sharing, RP §11A-116.
Transportation, TR §3-103.
Water and sewer authorities, EN §9-901.
Water quality financing, EN §9-1601.

Bonds of prior issues.
Transportation, TR §3-101.

Bone mass measurement.
Health insurance, IN §15-823.

Bonus points.
Minority business enterprise program.
County public libraries, ED §23-402.
Prince George's Community College, ED §16-312.
Prince George's county board of education, ED §4-125.

Born.
Newborn infants, HG §20-401.

Borrower.
Closed end credit, CL §12-1001.
Financing agreements, CL §12-1022.
Energy efficiency and economic development loan program, SG §9-20A-01.
Financing agreements, CL §12-125.
Interest in usury, CL §12-101.
Loans.
Finder's fees, CL §12-801.
Mortgage lending, FI §11-501.

DEFINED TERMS —Cont'd
Borrower —Cont'd
Mortgage originator, FI §11-601.
Mortgage releases, RP §3-105.1.
Revolving credit, CL §12-901.
Financing agreements, CL §12-922.
Water quality financing, EN §9-1601.
Borrow pit.
Surface mining, EN §15-801.
Bottle club.
Anne Arundle county, 2B §20-101.
Baltimore City alcoholic beverage licenses, 2B §20-102.
Baltimore county alcoholic beverage licenses, 2B §20-103.
Cecil county.
Alcoholic beverage licenses, 2B §20-104.
Charles county.
Alcoholic beverage licenses, 2B §20-105.
Dorchester county.
Alcoholic beverage licenses, 2B §20-105.1.
Montgomery county alcoholic beverage license, 2B §20-107.
St. Mary's county.
Alcoholic beverage licenses, 2B §§20-108, 20-109.
Boxing, BR §4-101.
Boxing and wrestling tax, TG §1-101.
Boxing or wrestling contest.
Taxation, TG §6-101.
Box lacrosse and indoor soccer club.
Class C, on-sale beer, wine and liquor license in Harford county, 2B §6-301.
Braille.
Blind children, ED §8-408.
Individualized education programs to insure ability to communicate effectively, ED §8-408.
Branch.
Banks, FI §5-1001.
Credit unions, FI §6-101.
Uniform commercial code, CL §1-201.
Brand.
Commercial feed, AG §6-101.
Commercial fertilizers, AG §6-201.
Turf grass, AG §9-101.
Brand family.
Tobacco, escrow act compliance, BR §16-501.
Brand name.
Pharmacists and pharmacies, HO §12-504.
Break.
Burglary, CR §6-201.
Breakage.
Horse racing, BR §11-101.
Break in service.
Employees' and teachers' pension systems, SPP §23-303.
Law enforcement officers' pension system, SPP §26-303.
Breakout ticket.
Gaming, Montgomery county, CR §13-1801.
Breeder seed, AG §9-201.
Breeder sod.
Turf grass, AG §9-101.
Bridge.
Toll facilities, TR §21-1401.
Broadcast right.
Boxing tax, TG §6-101.
Broker.
Commercial real estate broker's lien, RP §14-301.
Investment securities, CL §§8-102, 8-303.
Plant disease control, AG §5-301.

DEFINED TERMS —Cont'd
Broker —Cont'd
Radioactive waste, EN §7-301.
Real estate brokers, BOP §17-528.
UTMA, ET §13-301.
Brokerage agreement.
Real estate brokers, BOP §17-528.
Brokerage relationship.
Real estate brokers, BOP §17-528.
Broker-dealer.
Securities, CA §11-101.
Broker's lien.
Commercial real estate broker's lien, RP §14-301.
Brownfields revitalization incentive program.
Economic development assistance fund, 83A §5-1401.
Brownfields site.
Economic development assistance fund, 83A §5-1401.
B.T.U. energy conservation building standards, PUC §7-401.
Buckram crab, NR §4-801.
Budget and management, SF §3-101.
State operating budget, SF §7-101.
Budget bill.
Transportation department, SF §7-110.
Buffer.
Chesapeake Bay critical area and Atlantic coastal bays critical area protection programs.
Community pier in buffer, NR §8-1808.5.
Builder.
Energy conservation building standards, PUC §7-401.
New home warranties, RP §10-601.
Building.
Building codes, PS §12-501.
Energy, SF §4-801.
Energy conservation building standards, PUC §7-401.
Mechanics' liens, RP §9-101.
Building code.
Homebuilder registration, BR §4.5-602.
Home improvement, BR §8-505.
Building inspection official.
Professional architects immunity, CJ §5-426.
Professional engineers immunity, CJ §5-425.
Building permit.
Setback line restrictions.
Limitation of actions, CJ §5-114.
Sewerage systems, EN §9-512.
Bulk fertilizer.
Commercial fertilizers, AG §6-201.
Bulk milk hauler/sampler, HG §21-401.
Bulk transfer, CL §6-102.
Bulk vending machine.
Sales and use tax, TG §11-201.1.
Bulletproof body armor, CR §4-106.
Bungee jump, BR §3-503.
Bungee jumping operation, BR §3-503.
Burden of establishing.
Commercial code, CL §1-201.
Computer information transactions, CL §22-102.
Uniform commercial code, CL §1-201.
Bureau.
Regional tourism bureau, 20A §4-101.
Revenues, SF §6-101.
Burglar's tool, CR §6-201.
Burial goods, BR §5-101.
Burial goods business, BR §5-101.
Burial insurance, IN §1-101.

DEFINED TERMS —Cont'd
Burial site, RP §§14-121, 14-122.
Crimes relating to human remains, CR §10-401.
Burial space.
Preneed burial contract, BR §5-701.
Burning ban.
Forest fire prevention, NR §5-720.
Bus, TR §11-105.
Open containers of alcoholic beverages in motor vehicles, CR §10-123.
Business.
Administrative procedures.
Evaluation of regulatory impact, SG §10-124.
Litigation expenses, SG §10-224.
Eminent domain, RP §12-201.
Evidence, CJ §10-101.
Partnerships, CA §9A-101.
Procurement, SF §16-101.
Real estate brokers.
Limitation on interest in business by associate brokers and salespersons, BOP §17-511.
Savings and loan associations.
Incorporation, FI §9-210.
Business and economic development services.
Procurement, unsolicited proposals, SF §13-107.1.
Business arrangement.
Consumer credit contracts, CL §14-1302.
Business association.
Abandoned property, CL §17-101.
Business combination.
Corporations, CA §3-601.
Business day.
Door-to-door sales, CL §14-301.
Health club services, CL §14-12B-01.
Business district.
Traffic laws, TR §21-101.
Business entity.
Aid to families with dependent children.
Tax credits for wages and child care expenses for qualified employment opportunity employees, 88A §54.
Asbestos removal, EN §6-401.
Commercial discrimination, SF §19-103.
Disclosures by persons doing public business, EL §14-101.
Enterprise zones, 83A §5-401.
Family investment program, 88A §54.
Insurance, IN §10-401.
Insurance producers, IN §10-101.
Investments of life insurers, IN §5-511.
Maryland historical trust, rehabilitation tax credits, SF §5A-303.
Micro-breweries, 2B §12-104.
Neighborhood and community assistance program, HS §6-401.
Pilot program for long term employment of qualified ex-felons, LE §11-701.
Property tax.
Enterprise zones, TP §9-103.
Job creation, TP §9-230.
Public ethics, SG §15-102.
Rehabilitation services, ED §21-309.
Tax credits, TG §10-702.
Tax credits for employer-provided commuter benefits, EN §2-901.
Business league.
Charitable organization volunteer personal liability, CJ §5-407.
Business license record.
Access to court records, CJA Rule 16-1001.

DEFINED TERMS —Cont'd
Business opportunity.
Business regulation, BR §14-101.
Business record, BR §1-301.
Business relationship.
Foreign discriminatory boycotts, CL §11-102.
Business trust, CA §12-101.
Corporations, CA §3-101.
Limited liability companies, CA §4A-101.
Limited partnerships.
Merger, CA §10-208.
Real estate investment trusts, CA §8-501.1.
Bus passenger shelter, TR §8-750.
Buy boat.
Oysters and clams, NR §4-1001.
Buyer.
Business opportunities, BR §14-101.
Custom home protection, RP §10-501.
Layaway sales, CL §14-1101.
Pre-need burial contracts, BR §5-701; HO §7-405.
Retail credit accounts, CL §12-501.
Retail installment sales, CL §12-601.
Sales finance companies, FI §11-401.
Sales tax, TG §11-101.
Sales, UCC, CL §2-103.
Buyer in the ordinary course of business.
Uniform commercial code, CL §1-201.
Buyer's agent.
Real estate brokers, BOP §17-530.
Buyer's guide, IN §18-106.
Buyer's mixture.
Commercial fertilizers, AG §6-201.
Bylaws.
Adult offender supervision, COR §6-203.
Cooperative housing corporation, CA §5-6B-01.
Interstate insurance product regulation compact, IN §29-101.
Cable television company.
Interference with cable television service, CR §7-303.
Cable television service.
Interference with cable television service, CR §7-303.
Calendar quarter.
Unemployment insurance, LE §8-101.
Calibrate.
Fluid dairy products, AG §11-401.
Calvert county junk dealer or scrap metal processor license.
Business licenses, BR §17-1015.
Camden Yards.
Stadium authority, FI §13-701.
Campaign finance entity.
Elections, EL §1-101.
Campaign finance report.
Elections, EL §1-101.
Campaign manager, EL §1-101.
Campaign material.
Elections, EL §1-101.
Camper.
Maryland youth camp, HG §14-401.
Camping shelter.
Mobile home and trailer park taxes, 24 §9-401.
Camping trailer, TR §11-106.
Campuses.
University system of Maryland, ED §12-101.
Cancel.
Distributorships, CL §11-1301.
Driver's license, TR §11-107.
Cancellation.
Computer information transactions, CL §22-102.

DEFINED TERMS —Cont'd

Cancellation —Cont'd

Sales, UCC, CL §§2-106, 2-720.

Cancer report.

Disease prevention, HG §18-204.

Cancer research.

Maryland cancer fund income tax checkoff, HG §20-117.

C. & F.

Sales, UCC, CL §2-320.

Candidate.

Disclosures by persons doing public business, EL §14-101.

Elections, EL §1-101.

Gaming, CR §12-101.

Candidate sign.

Condominiums, RP §11-111.2.

Cooperative housing corporations, CA §5-6B-18.2.

Homeowners' associations, RP §11B-111.2.

Candlefoot power.

Automated teller machines, FI §1-401.

Canvass.

Elections, EL §11-101.

Capable of use as human food.

Poultry products inspection act, AG §4-201.

Wholesome meat act, AG §4-101.

Capital appreciation bond.

State debt, SF §8-101.

Capital asset.

Board of public works, SF §10-306.

Capital contribution.

Limited liability companies, CA §4A-101.

Capital equipment.

Public debt.

Capital leases, SF §8-402.

Senior citizen activities centers capital improvement grants, 70B §26.

Capital expenditure.

Department of transportation, SF §7-110.

State finance, SF §7-305.

Capital expense.

County public libraries, ED §23-501.

Capital interest.

Limited liability companies, CA §4A-101.

Capital investment.

Alcoholic beverages, 2B §§8-202.1, 8-204.

Capitalized cost.

Motor vehicle leasing contracts, CL §14-2001.

Capitalized cost reduction.

Motor vehicle leasing contracts, CL §14-2001.

Capital lease.

Capital projects, SF §3-602.

Higher education.

Auxiliary and academic facilities bond authority, ED §19-101.

Public debt, SF §8-402.

Capital project.

County library capital project grant program, ED §23-510.

Transportation, TR §2-103.1.

Capital renewal.

Forests and parks.

Open space program, NR §5-901.

Capital requirement.

Successor corporate fiduciaries, ET §15-1A-01.

Capital stock.

Banking institutions, FI §5-101.

Commercial banks, FI §3-101.

Conversion of national banking association into commercial bank, FI §3-801.

Savings and loan associations, FI §9-101.

DEFINED TERMS —Cont'd

Capital stock association.

Savings and loan associations, FI §9-101.

Carcass.

Wholesome meat act, AG §4-101.

Cardholder.

Credit card crimes, CR §8-201.

Cardiac rescue technician (CRT), ED §13-516.

Health occupations, HO §14-303.

Caregiver.

Abuse or neglect of vulnerable adult, CR §3-604.

Local department guardianships and adoptions, FL §5-301.

Care program.

Adult residential environment program, 88A §138.

Care providers.

Nursing referral service agencies, HG §19-4B-01.

Cargo.

Port administration drug-free workplace, TR §6-102.1.

Cargo handling facilities.

Ports, TR §6-308.

Carnival, BR §3-101.

Carrier.

Communication of information by health care provider, IN §15-116.

Compensation of health care practitioners, IN §15-113.

Consignment of farm products, AG §1-301.

Dental plans, IN §15-114.

Disclosures required in enrollment sales materials, IN §15-121.

Documents of title, CL §7-102.

Emerging medical and surgical treatments, IN §15-123.

Health care regulatory fund, IN §2-112.2.

Health insurance, IN §§15-405, 15-606.

Behavioral health care services, IN §15-127.

Complaint process for adverse decisions or grievances, IN §15-10A-01.

Complaint process for coverage decisions, IN §15-10D-01.

Credentialing of providers, IN §15-112.1.

Portability, IN §§15-1301, 15-1401.

Provider panels, IN §15-112.

Referrals to specialists, IN §15-830.

Reimbursement for preauthorized care, IN §15-1009.

Restrictions on transferring contracts, IN §15-125.

Transfer of provider's contract, IN §15-124.

Health insurance portability, IN §15-1301.

Health maintenance organizations, HG §19-710.2.

Insurance unfair trade practices, IN §27-221.

Long-term care insurance, IN §18-101.

Managed care organizations, IN §15-115.

Maryland health insurance plan, IN §14-501.

Medicare supplement insurance, IN §15-901.

Notice of renewal, IN §15-122.

Provider panels, IN §15-112.

Provider participation in managed care organizations, IN §15-115.

Radioactive waste, EN §7-301.

Retroactive denial of reimbursements, IN §15-1008.

Small employer health insurance, IN §15-1201.

Carrier's lien.

Household goods movers enforcing, CL §14-3101.

Case.

Credit life, health and unemployment insurance, IN §13-111.

DEFINED TERMS —Cont'd

Case management.
Mental health records, HG §4-307.
Case management services.
Medicaid, HG §15-132.
Case record.
Access to court records, CJA Rule 16-1001.
Cash equivalent.
Investments of life insurers, IN §5-511.
Cashier's check.
Negotiable instruments, CL §§3-103, 3-104.
Cash in lieu of parking program.
Tax credits for employer-provided commuter benefits, EN §2-901.
Cash price.
Layaway sales, CL §14-1101.
Rental-purchase agreements, CL §12-1101.
Retail installment sales, CL §12-601.
Cash proceeds.
Secured transactions, CL §9-102.
Cash sale price.
Retail credit accounts, CL §12-501.
Casino event.
Anne Arundel county, CR §13-401.
Casino night.
Prince George's county, CR §13-1912.
Casualty insurance, IN §1-101.
Catastrophic health emergency, SpecPro Rule 15-1102.
Catastrophic health emergency disease surveillance and response program, HG §18-901.
Governor's health emergency powers, PS §14-3A-01.
Catastrophic illness or injury.
State personnel, SPP §9-601.
Catch.
Fish and fisheries, NR §4-101.
Caterer.
Alcoholic beverages, 2B §§6-703, 6-704.
Cave, NR §5-1401.
Maryland historical trust, archaeological property, SF §5A-333.
Cave life, NR §5-1401.
Ceding insurer.
Insurance companies.
Reinsurance, IN §5-901.
Ceiling fan.
Maryland efficiency standards act, SG §9-2006.
Ceiling fan light kit.
Maryland efficiency standards act, SG §9-2006.
Cell.
Rechargeable batteries, EN §6-1101.
Cell manufacturer.
Rechargeable batteries, EN §6-1101.
Cemetery, BR §5-101.
Burial permits, HG §4-215.
Cemeteries in Carroll County, RP §14-119.
Center.
Baltimore City alternative learning center, ED §4-319.
Chronic disease centers, HG §19-501.
Emergency medical services.
University of Maryland, ED §13-501.
Health effects of fire, HG §18-701.
Mammography testing, HG §20-115.
Maryland food center, 41 §13-104.
Psychiatric research center, HG §10-417.
University system of Maryland, ED §12-101.
Centerline.
Highways, TR §8-732.

DEFINED TERMS —Cont'd

Center of excellence.
Child abuse and neglect centers of excellence, HG §13-2201.
Centers of excellence faculty.
Child abuse and neglect centers of excellence, HG §13-2201.
Central collection unit.
Crime victims' restitution, CP §11-601.
Income tax refunds, TG §13-912.
Central financial, real estate, or insurance services.
Job creation tax credit, 83A §5-1101.
One Maryland economic development tax credits, 83A §5-1501.
Central Maryland.
Code counties, 25B §2.
Central nervous system tumor.
Cancer reports, HG §18-204.
Central registry.
Child abuse and neglect, FL §5-701.
Central repository.
Criminal history record checks, CP §§10-235, 10-236.
Criminal justice information system, CP §10-201.
Expungement of criminal records, CP §10-101.
Expungement of records, Crim Rule 4-502.
Firearms dealers' licenses, PS §5-108.
Handgun permits, PS §5-305.
Horse racing, BR §11-101.
Nursing referral service agencies, HG §19-4B-01.
Pawnbrokers, BR §12-204.
Private detectives, BOP §13-101.
Security guards, BOP §19-101.
Certificate.
Automated external defibrillator program, ED §13-517.
Boats and boating, NR §8-701.
Boilers and pressure vessels, PS §12-901.
Certified interior designers, BOP §8-101.
Elevator safety, PS §12-801.
Farm products certification, AG §10-601.
Fraternal benefit societies, IN §8-401.
Hazardous waste facilities, EN §7-401.
Health maintenance organizations.
Medical directors, IN §15-10C-01.
Insect sting emergency treatment program, HG §13-702.
Limited partnerships, CA §10-101.
Long-term care insurance, IN §18-101.
Maryland youth camp, HG §14-401.
Massage therapists, HO §3-5A-01.
Medicare supplement insurance, IN §15-901.
Nursing assistants, HO §8-6A-01.
Physician assistants, HO §15-101.
Private review agents, IN §15-10B-01.
Professional counselors therapists, HO §17-101.
Radiation oncology/therapy, medical radiation, and nuclear medicine technologists, HO §14-5B-01.
Real estate appraisers, BOP §16-101.
Residential child care program administrators, HO §20-101.
Waterworks operators, EN §12-101.
Certificated security.
Investment securities, CL §8-102.
Certificate fee.
Certified interior designers, BOP §8-101.
Certificate form.
Medicare supplement insurance, IN §15-901.

DEFINED TERMS —Cont'd
Certificate inspection.
  Boilers and pressure vessels, PS §12-901.
Certificate of authority.
  Insurers, IN §1-101.
Certificate of deposit.
  Financial institutions, FI §1-210.
  Negotiable instruments, CL §§3-103, 3-104.
Certificate of guarantee.
  Insurance, IN §1-203.
Certificate of need.
  Health planning, HG §19-114.
Certificate of origin.
  Boats and boating, NR §8-718.
  Motor vehicles, TR §13-101.
Certificate of qualification.
  Insurance managing general agents, IN §8-201.
Certificate of reservation.
  Land patents, RP §13-101.
Certificate of title.
  Secured transactions, CL §9-102.
Certificates of insurance, IN §18-107.
Certification.
  Medical laboratories, HG §17-214.
  Procurement.
    Minority business participation, SF §14-301.
  Water quality laboratories, EN §9-1001.
Certification agency.
  Procurement.
    Minority business participation, SF §14-301.
Certification card.
  Private detectives, BOP §13-101.
  Security guards, BOP §19-101.
Certified.
  Social workers, HO §19-101.
Certified agency.
  Agricultural commodity promotion, AG §10-101.
Certified applicator.
  Pesticide applicators, AG §5-201.
Certified appraisal report.
  Real estate appraisers, BOP §16-101.
Certified associate counselor-alcohol and drug,
  HO §17-101.
Certified check.
  Negotiable instruments, CL §§3-103, 3-409.
Certified coal pollution control facility.
  Property taxes, TP §7-239.
Certified financial statement.
  Continuing care contracts, 70B §7.
Certified heritage area, FI §13-1101.
  Maryland historical trust, rehabilitation tax
    credits, SF §5A-303.
Certified heritage structure.
  Maryland historical trust, rehabilitation tax
    credits, SF §5A-303.
Certified individual massage therapist, HO
  §3-5A-01.
Certified industrial operator.
  Waterworks operators, EN §12-101.
Certified industry dairy farm inspector, HG
  §21-401.
Certified institution.
  Nursing home administrators, HO §9-307.
Certified interior design services, BOP §8-101.
Certified Irish potato.
  Potato seed inspection, AG §9-301.
Certified local government.
  Taxation, TG §10-207.
Certified mail.
  Rules of interpretation, 1 §20.

DEFINED TERMS —Cont'd
Certified mail —Cont'd
  Settlement of decedents' estates, Estates Rule
    6-105.
Certified medical radiation technologist, HO
  §14-5B-01.
Certified medication technician, HO §8-6A-01.
Certified medicine aide, HO §8-6A-01.
Certified minority business enterprise.
  Procurement, SF §14-301.
Certified nondepreciable historic structure.
  Taxation, TG §10-207.
Certified nuclear medicine technologist, HO
  §14-5B-01.
Certified nurse practitioner.
  Health insurance, IN §15-703.
  Medical assistance, HG §15-103.
Certified nursing assistant, HO §8-6A-01.
Certified nutrient management consultant.
  Soil conservation districts, AG §8-801.
Certified nutrition specialist, HO §5-101.
Certified or abridged copy.
  Archives, SG §9-1015.
Certified professional counselor, HO §17-101.
**Certified professional counselor-alcohol and
  drug,** HO §17-101.
**Certified professional counselor-marriage and
  family therapist,** HO §17-101.
Certified program administrators.
  Children, youth and family services.
    Contracts for residential child care programs,
      49D §7-101.
  Residential child care program administrators,
    HO §20-101.
Certified propane gas fitter.
  Plumbers, BOP §12-101.
Certified real estate appraiser, BOP §16-101.
Certified rehabilitation.
  Maryland historical trust, rehabilitation tax
    credits, SF §5A-303.
Certified seed, AG §9-201.
Certified sod.
  Turf grass, AG §9-101.
Certified superintendent.
  Waterworks operators, EN §12-101.
**Certified supervised counselor-alcohol and
  drug,** HO §17-101.
Certifying court.
  Certification of questions of law to the court of
    appeals, AppRev Rule 8-305.
Chain of custody.
  Evidence, CJ §10-1002.
Chain store license.
  Business licenses, BR §17-1801.
Challenged ballot.
  Labor relations.
    Consent elections, LE §4-206.
Challenge grants.
  School improvement research project, ED §5-204.
Champion tree.
  Forest conservation, NR §5-1601.
Change.
  Property tax.
    Medical condition of residents, TP §8-233.
Change in condition.
  Nursing homes, notice of change in condition of
    resident, HG §19-1415.
  Residential treatment centers, HG §19-305.
Change in fund basis.
  Insurance companies.
    Standard valuation law, IN §5-306.

DEFINED TERMS —Cont'd
Change in occupancy.
  Lead poisoning, EN §6-801.
Change in status.
  Health insurance, IN §§15-408, 15-409.
  Involuntarily terminated employees, IN §15-409.
Change of occupancy.
  Building rehabilitation code, PS §12-1001.
Change order.
  Procurement, SF §13-201.
Change the use, purpose or function.
  Executive branch of government, SG §8-306.
Charge.
  Public recreation on private and local government
    lands, NR §5-1101.
Chargeable person.
  Health care collections, HG §16-101.
Charged.
  Victims of crime, CP §11-107.
Charges.
  Judicial disability and sanctionable conduct, CJA
    Rule 16-803.
Charging document, CP §1-101.
  Law enforcement officers, CJ §2-608.
Charitable contribution.
  Charitable organizations, BR §6-101.
Charitable organization, BR §6-101.
  Alcoholic beverages, 2B §2-101.
  Gleaning.
    Limitation of actions, CJ §5-404.
  Personal liability, CJ §5-406.
  Volunteer personal liability, CJ §5-407.
  Volunteers and physicians, CJ §5-606.
Charitable representative.
  Charitable organizations, BR §6-101.
Charitable trusts, ET §14-305.
Charter.
  Corporations, CA §1-101.
  Financial institutions, FI §1-101.
  Unsolicited takeovers of corporations and real
    estate investment trusts, CA §3-801.
Charter document.
  Corporations, CA §1-101.
Chattel paper.
  Secured transactions, CL §9-102.
Check.
  Bad checks, CR §8-101.
  Negotiable instruments, CL §§3-103, 3-104, 3-312.
  Return of checks to customers, FI §5-513.
Chemical warfare material.
  Controlled hazardous substances, EN §7-239.1.
Chesapeake Bay.
  Aquaculture, NR §4-11A-01.
  Oysters and clams, NR §§4-1001, 4-1101.
Chesapeake Bay critical area.
  Chesapeake Bay critical area and Atlantic coastal
    bays critical area protection programs, NR
    §8-1802.
Chief.
  Law enforcement officers' bill of rights, PS §3-101.
  Revenues, SF §6-101.
Chief elected official.
  Housing authorities, HS §12-101.
Chief election official.
  Petitions, EL §6-101.
Chief executive.
  Local government investment guidelines, 95 §22F.
Chief executive officer.
  Baltimore City schools, ED §4-301.
  Counties and municipal corporations, 24 §1-108.
  Drug asset forfeiture, CP §12-101.

DEFINED TERMS —Cont'd
Chief executive officer —Cont'd
  Liquidation, rehabilitation, etc., of insurers, IN
    §9-231.
Chief of police.
  State property, SF §4-606.
Child.
  Child abuse and neglect, FL §5-701.
  Child care centers, FL §5-570.
  Child fidelity review teams, HG §5-701.
  Child flotation devices, NR §8-743.
  Children in need of assistance, CJ §3-801.
  Child's access to firearm, CR §4-104.
  Child welfare accountability, FL §5-1301.
  Crime victims' restitution, CP §11-601.
  Death benefits, public safety officers and
    personnel, PS §1-202.
  Death benefits, survivors of state employees, SPP
    §10-404.
  Divorce, FL §8-201.
  Handicapped children.
    Education, ED §8-412.
  Hunting licenses, NR §10-301.
  Interstate compact on juveniles, 83C §3-104.
  Interstate placement of children, FL §5-603.
  Juvenile causes, CJ §3-8A-01.
  Lead poisoning, EN §6-801.
  Local department guardianships and adoptions,
    FL §5-301.
  Private agency adoptions and guardianships, FL
    §5-3A-01.
  Sexual offenses, HG §15-127.
  Transfer of cases involving detained child, CP
    §4-202.1.
  Uniform child custody jurisdiction and
    enforcement act, FL §9.5-101.
  Uniform interstate family support act, FL
    §10-301.
  Workers' compensation, LE §9-101.
  Wrongful death, CJ §3-901.
Child advocacy center.
  Child abuse and neglect centers of excellence, HG
    §13-2201.
Child care administration, FL §5-590.
Child care center.
  Child care quality incentive grant program, FL
    §5-594.
  Family law, FL §5-570.
  Lead hazard reduction grant and loan programs,
    HS §4-701.
  Student financial assistance, ED §18-705.
Child care facility.
  Economic development assistance fund, 83A
    §5-1401.
Child care provider.
  Child care quality incentive grant program, FL
    §5-594.
  Domestic violence, FL §4-501.
  Student financial assistance, ED §18-705.
Child care special loan.
  Economic development assistance fund, 83A
    §5-1401.
Child custody determination.
  Uniform child custody jurisdiction and
    enforcement act, FL §9.5-101.
Child custody proceeding.
  Uniform child custody jurisdiction and
    enforcement act, FL §9.5-101.
Child in an out-of-county living arrangement.
  Educational funding, ED §4-122.

DEFINED TERMS —Cont'd

Child in need of assistance, CJ §§3-8A-01, 3-801.
　Family law, FL §1-101.
Child in need of out-of-state placement.
　Children, youth and families services, 49D §1-101.
Child in need of residential placement.
　Children, youth and families services, 49D §1-101.
Child in need of supervision, CJ §3-8A-01.
Child in state-supervised care.
　Education of children in state-supervised care, ED
　　§8-501.
Child passenger safety technicians, CJ §5-640.
Child placement agency.
　Children generally, FL §5-101.
Child pornography.
　Internet, CR §11-208.1.
Child resistant packaging, HG §22-301.
Child respondent.
　Victims of crime, CP §11-101.
Child safety seat.
　Child passenger safety technicians, CJ §5-640.
　Motor vehicles, TR §22-412.2.
Child sexual offender.
　Sex offender registration, CP §11-701.
Child support.
　Unemployment compensation, LE §8-101.
　Unemployment insurance, LE §8-807.
Child support enforcement administration.
　Drivers' licenses, TR §16-203.
Child support enforcement unit.
　Unemployment compensation, LE §8-101.
　Unemployment insurance, LE §8-807.
Child support order.
　Affidavit of support, FL §10-1A-01.
　Uniform interstate family support act, FL
　　§10-301.
Child welfare personnel.
　Integration of child welfare and substance abuse
　　treatment act, FL §5-1201.
Child wellness services.
　Health insurance, IN §15-817.
Child who is blind or visually impaired.
　Individualized education programs to insure
　　ability to communicate effectively, ED §8-408.
Child with a disability.
　Education, ED §8-401.
Child with intensive needs.
　Children, youth and families services, 49D §1-101.
Chiropractor, HO §3-101.
Chiropractor rehabilitation committee, HO
　§3-406.
Chlamydia screening tests.
　Health insurance, IN §15-829.
Cholesterol testing, HG §17-501.
Christian Science nurse, HO §8-102.
Chronically ill.
　Viatical settlement contracts, IN §8-601.
Church.
　Alcoholic beverages, 2B §9-223.
　Religious corporations, CA §5-301.
Church plan.
　Health insurance portability, IN §§15-1301,
　　15-1401.
C.I.F.
　Sales, UCC, CL §2-320.
Cigarette restitution fund.
　Tobacco use prevention and cessation program,
　　HG §13-1001.
Cigarettes.
　Cigarette licenses, BR §16-101.
　Medicaid subrogation claims, HG §15-120.

DEFINED TERMS —Cont'd

Cigarettes —Cont'd
　Sales below cost, CL §11-501.
　Tobacco, escrow act compliance, BR §16-501.
　Tobacco tax, TG §12-101.
CINA case.
　Family law, FL §1-101.
Circuit.
　Discipline of attorneys, CJA Rule 16-701.
Circuit court, CJ §1-101.
　Appeals, CJ §12-101.
Circulator.
　Elections.
　　Petitions, EL §6-101.
Circumventional information.
　Security systems technicians, BOP §18-101.
Citation, CP §4-101.
　Interstate wildlife violator compact, NR §10-1201.
　Juvenile causes, CJ §3-8A-01.
　Law enforcement officers, CJ §2-608.
Civic league or organization.
　Charitable organization volunteer personal
　　liability, CJ §5-407.
　Personal liability, CJ §5-406.
Civil action.
　Physicians, HO §14-101.
　Prisoner litigation, CJ §5-1001.
Civil child support warrants.
　State police department, interagency law
　　enforcement system, PS §2-305.
Civil defense volunteer.
　Workers' compensation, LE §9-232.1.
Civilian classification.
　State police department, PS §2-101.
Civilian employee.
　State police department, PS §2-101.
Civil infraction.
　Code counties, 25B §13C.
Civil penalty.
　Political subdivisions, 24 §14-101.
Civil protective orders.
　State police department, interagency law
　　enforcement system, PS §2-305.
Claimant.
　Commercial real estate broker's lien, RP §14-301.
　Criminal injuries compensation fund, CP §11-801.
　Landlord and tenant, RP §8-404.
　Land patents for abandoned land, RP §13-107.
　Negotiable instruments, CL §3-312.
　Unemployment insurance, LE §8-101.
Claim information.
　Unemployment compensation, LE §8-811.
Claims.
　Fiduciary security transfers, ET §15-301.
　Health program integrity and recovery activities,
　　HG §2-501.
　Insurance fraud, IN §27-401.
　Professional malpractice, CJ §3-2C-01.
　Revenues, SF §6-219.
　Savings and loan associations, FI §9-101.
Class.
　State personnel, SPP §1-101.
Class A vessel, NR §8-712.3.
Classification of abode.
　Estates and trusts, ET §13-101.
Class I milk.
　Northeast interstate dairy compact, AG §2-801.
Class of business.
　Credit life, health and unemployment insurance,
　　IN §13-111.

DEFINED TERMS —Cont'd
Classroom instructor.
Driver education, TR §16-501.
Clean-burning fuel.
Property tax exemptions.
Refueling equipment, TP §7-236.
Cleaning agent, EN §9-1501.
Cleanup.
Oil cleanups, EN §4-701.
Water pollution, EN §4-401.
Clearing corporation.
Investment securities, CL §8-102.
Clearing house.
Bank deposits and collections, CL §4-104.
Clear value.
Inheritance tax, TG §7-204.
Clerical error.
Voter registration, EL §3-601.1.
Clerk.
County clerks, BR §1-101.
Marriage, FL §2-101.
Settlement of decedents' estates, Estates Rule
6-105.
Clerk of the court.
Corporations, CA §1-101.
Liens on aircraft, boats, mobile homes and motor
vehicles, CL §16-201.
Client.
Employment agencies, BR §9-101.
Homeless women.
Shelter, 88A §125.
Immigration consultants, CL §14-3301.
Privileged communications.
Psychiatric-mental health nursing specialist, CJ
§9-109.1.
Real estate brokers, BOP §§17-528, 17-532.
Clinical breast examination.
Breast cancer program, HG §20-116.
Clinical social worker.
Mental hygiene admissions, HG §10-601.
Clock hour.
Business occupations and professions, BOP
§1-101.
Cloned CVISN transponder, TR §25-112.
Close corporation, CA §4-101.
Closed container.
Cantaloupes, AG §10-901.
Closed end account.
Retail credit accounts, CL §12-501.
Closed end credit, CL §12-1001.
Closed-end investment company, CA §2-112.
Closed package.
Apple grades, AG §10-801.
Closed season.
Fish and fisheries, NR §4-101.
Wildlife, NR §10-101.
Close economic association.
Public ethics, SG §15-511.
Closure costs.
Closed or delicensed hospitals, 43C §16A.
Club.
Alcoholic beverages, 2B §1-102.
Charitable organization volunteer personal
liability, CJ §5-407.
CMS.
Medicare supplement insurance, IN §15-901.
Coalbed methane.
Natural resources, EN §14-102.
Coal products.
Procurement, SF §§14-404, 14-407.

DEFINED TERMS —Cont'd
Coal waste disposal power project.
Property taxes, TP §7-239.
Coastal area.
Gas and oil.
Coastal facilities review, EN §14-501.
Coastal environment.
Deepwater port siting, NR §3-602.
Coca leaf.
Controlled dangerous substances, CR §5-101.
Code.
Allocation of private activity bond authority, FI
§13-801.
Health insurance, retroactive denial of
reimbursement, IN §15-1008.
Medical care data collection, HG §19-133.
Settlement of decedents' estates, Estates Rule
6-105.
State debt, SF §8-131.1.
Transportation, TR §3-103.
Code authority.
Housing authorities, HS §12-101.
Code county.
Home rule, 25B §1.
Property tax.
Tax sales, TP §14-810.
Code grabbing devices, CR §7-301.
Code home rule status, 25B §1.
Code official.
Architects, BOP §§3-101, 3-208.1.
Engineers, BOP §14-208.1.
Interior designers, BOP §8-206.1.
Landscape architects, BOP §9-206.1.
Coding guidelines.
Health insurance, retroactive denial of
reimbursement, IN §15-1008.
CODIS.
DNA database system, PS §2-501.
C.O.D. transaction.
Layaway sales, CL §14-1101.
Coerce.
Criminal gang offenses, CR §9-801.
Motor vehicle dealers, TR §15-207.
Cogeneration.
Industrial development financing, 83A §5-901.
Cohabitant.
Domestic violence, FL §4-501.
Insurance discrimination, IN §27-504.
Coin-operated game.
Amusement devices, 24 §11-202.
Collateral.
Interstate wildlife violator compact, NR §10-1201.
Secured transactions, CL §9-102.
State treasury, SF §6-201.
Collateral costs.
Motorized wheelchair warranty enforcement, CL
§14-2701.
Collateral security.
Bail bondsmen, IN §10-301.
Retail installment sales, CL §12-601.
Sales finance companies, FI §11-401.
Collecting bank.
Bank deposits and collections, CL §§4-104, 4-105.
Collection agency, BR §§6-101, 7-101.
Collective bargaining.
Community colleges, ED §16-412.
Prince George's county public employment
relations, ED §16-414.1.
State personnel, SPP §3-101.
Collector.
Consumer debt collection, CL §14-201.

DEFINED TERMS —Cont'd
Collector —Cont'd
Property tax, TP §1-101.
Collision damage waiver.
Rental motor vehicles, CL §14-2101.
Colony.
Honeybees, AG §5-501.
Color additive.
Food and drugs, HG §21-101.
Poultry products inspection act, AG §4-201.
Wholesome meat act, AG §4-101.
Combination.
Motor vehicles, TR §11-108.
Combined adjusted actual income.
Child support guidelines, FL §12-201.
Combined income.
Property tax.
Elderly or disabled renters, TP §9-102.
Homeowners credit, TP §9-104.
Combustible material.
Inspections by local fire departments, PS §9-801.
Commanding officer.
Firefighters appointed as deputy sheriffs, PS §7-301.
Commencement.
Uniform child custody jurisdiction and enforcement act, FL §9.5-101.
Commencement of the case.
Debt collection, CL §15-101.
Commerce.
Commercial driver's licenses, TR §16-803.
Commercial activities.
Banks, FI §5-1001.
Commercial advertising sign.
Bus passenger shelter program, TR §8-750.
Commercial and industrial uses.
Forest conservation, NR §5-1601.
Commercial athletic event.
Interference with commercial athletic event, CR §10-203.
Commercial bank, FI §1-101.
Commercial boat yard.
Antifouling paints, AG §5-901.
Commercial building.
Community development administration, HS §4-201.
Industrial development financing, 83A §5-901.
Commercial cave, NR §5-1401.
Commercial clothes washer.
Maryland efficiency standards act, SG §9-2006.
Commercial customer.
Commercial discrimination, SF §19-103.
Commercial discrimination.
Public contracts, SF §19-103.
Commercial driver's license, TR §11-109.
Commercial electronic mail.
Unauthorized, false or misleading information, CL §14-3001.
Commercial electronic mail message.
Spam, CR §3-805.1.
Commercial energy audit.
Community development administration, HS §4-201.
Commercial goods.
Distributorships, CL §11-1301.
Commercial insurance.
Cancellation or nonrenewal of insurance, IN §27-601.
Commercial lease.
Commercial real estate broker's lien, RP §14-301.

DEFINED TERMS —Cont'd
Commercial leasing brokerage agreement.
Commercial real estate broker's lien, RP §14-301.
Commercial leasing commission.
Commercial real estate broker's lien, RP §14-301.
Commercial loan.
Banking institutions.
Loans to directors, officers or employees, FI §5-512.
Closed end credit, CL §12-1001.
Interest in usury, CL §12-101.
Revolving credit, CL §12-901.
Commercial logging or timber harvesting operations.
Forest conservation, NR §5-1601.
Commercial mobile radio service (CMRS).
911 emergency telephone system, PS §1-301.
Commercial mobile radio service provider.
911 emergency telephone system, PS §1-301.
Commercial motor vehicle, TR §16-812.
Commercial drivers' licenses, TR §16-803.
Parking in Prince George's county.
Parking of commercial vehicles, TR §21-1010.
Taxation, TG §9-201.
Vehicle theft prevention council and fund, PS §2-701.
Commercial or industrial area.
Outdoor advertising, TR §8-725.
Commercial paper.
Commercial banks.
Maximum liabilities of person, FI §3-601.
Commercial property.
Commercial real estate broker's lien, RP §14-301.
Commercial real estate.
Nonresident commercial real estate brokers, BOP §17-536.
Commercial refrigeration cabinet.
Maryland efficiency standards act, SG §9-2006.
Commercial rehabilitation.
Maryland historical trust, rehabilitation tax credits, SF §5A-303.
Commercial rental.
Submetering, PUC §7-303.
Commercial rental unit.
Gas or electric meters, PUC §7-303.
Commercial solicitation.
Fax transmissions, CL §14-1313.
Commercial tenant.
Commercial real estate broker's lien, RP §14-301.
Commercial tort claim.
Secured transactions, CL §9-102.
Commercial unit.
Sales, UCC, CL §2-105.
Commercial use airport.
Aviation, TR §5-301.
Development easements, TR §5-4A-01.
Commingled goods.
Secured transactions, priority of security interests, CL §9-336.
Commission.
Highways, TR §8-101.
Land patents, RP §13-101.
Ports, TR §6-101.
Time-sharing, RP §11A-101.
Transportation, TR §2-201.
Wholesale sales representatives.
Compensation, LE §3-601.
Commissioned rank.
State police department, PS §2-101.
Commissioner.
Adult offender supervision, COR §6-203.

DEFINED TERMS —Cont'd

Commissioner —Cont'd
Domestic violence, FL §4-501.
Land patents, RP §13-101.
Public works contracts, SF §17-201.
Securities, CA §11-101.
Southern Maryland tri-county council, 20 §1-102.
Western Maryland tri-county council, 20A §1-102.
Commissioner of correction, COR §1-101.
Commissioning.
Income tax credits, TG §10-722.
Commission marketing order.
Northeast interstate dairy compact, AG §2-801.
Commission record.
Judicial disability and sanctionable conduct, CJA
Rule 16-803.
Commission selling agency.
Tobacco, AG §7-101.
Commit.
Children in need of assistance, CJ §3-801.
Juvenile causes, CJ §3-8A-01.
Commitment.
Closed end credit, CL §12-1022.
Financing agreements, CL §12-125.
Revolving credit, CL §12-922.
Commitment unit.
Release from confinement, CP §11-508.
Committed person.
Not criminally responsible, CP §3-101.
Committee.
Fiduciaries, ET §15-101.
Procurement, SF §§14-104, 14-106.
Commodity.
Antitrust, CL §11-201.
Commodity account.
Secured transactions, CL §9-102.
Commodity contract.
Insurance companies, liquidation and
rehabilitation, IN §9-229.1.
Secured transactions, CL §9-102.
Commodity customer.
Secured transactions, CL §9-102.
Commodity in bulk.
Weights and measures, AG §11-101.
Commodity in packaged form.
Weights and measures, AG §11-101.
Commodity intermediary.
Secured transactions, CL §9-102.
Common areas.
Homeowners association, RP §11B-101.
Common carrier, PUC §1-101.
Common elements.
Condominiums, RP §11-101.
Time-sharing, RP §11A-101.
Common expenses.
Time-sharing, RP §11A-101.
Common expenses and common profits.
Condominiums, RP §11-101.
Common interest community.
Environmental covenants, EN §1-801.
Common nuisance.
Controlled dangerous substances, CR §§5-605,
5-607.
Common ownership.
Collection agencies, BR §7-102.
Common source information company.
Real estate brokers, BOP §17-528.
Common stock.
Corporations, CA §3-601.
Common trust fund.
Commercial banks, FI §3-501.

DEFINED TERMS —Cont'd

Communicate.
Investment securities, CL §8-102.
Secured transactions, CL §9-102.
Communications common carrier.
Evidence, CJ §10-401.
Communication service.
Conversion of overhead electric or communication
facilities to underground locations, PUC
§12-301.
Community.
Indian affairs commission, 41 §6-901.
Community action agencies, HS §8-101.
Community assistance.
Housing and community development, HS §1-101.
Community association, CJ §5-406.
Nuisance actions, RP §§14-120, 14-123 to
14-125.1.
Personal property tax credit, TP §9-238.
Community attendant services and supports,
41 §6-7A-01.
Community-based program.
Developmental disabilities, mental health, child
welfare and juvenile services workforce
tuition assistance program, ED §18-2101.
Community benefit.
Nonprofit hospitals, HG §19-303.
Community care organization.
Medicaid, community choice programs, HG
§15-141.
Community choice program.
Medicaid, community choice programs, HG
§15-141.
Community college.
Local government investment guidelines, 95 §22F.
Powers and duties of higher education
commission, ED §11-105.
State and county aid, ED §16-305.
Community detention.
Juvenile causes, CJ §3-8A-01.
Community developmental disabilities services
provider, HG §16-201.2.
Community development financial institution.
Community legacy program, HS §6-201.
Community development organization.
Community legacy program, HS §6-201.
Community development project.
Community development administration, HS
§4-201.
Community direct service worker.
Developmental disabilities, HG §7-307.
Community foundation.
Charitable gift annuities, IN §16-114.
Community health coalition.
Tobacco use prevention and cessation program,
HG §13-1001.
Community legacy agreement.
Community legacy program, HS §6-201.
Community legacy area.
Community legacy program, HS §6-201.
Community legacy plan.
Community legacy program, HS §6-201.
Community legacy project.
Community legacy program, HS §6-201.
Community mental health services provider,
HG §16-201.2.
Community naturally served.
University of Maryland medical system, ED
§13-301.
Community needs assessment.
Nonprofit hospitals, HG §19-303.

DEFINED TERMS —Cont'd

Community pier.
Chesapeake Bay critical area and Atlantic coastal bays critical area protection programs. Community pier in buffer, NR §8-1808.5.

Community provider.
Developmental disabilities, HG §7-307.

Community recreation program.
Volunteer liability, CJ §5-802.

Community rehabilitation program, ED §21-401.

Community reinvestment assistance.
Community reinvestment fund, HS §9-101.

Community reinvestment project.
Community reinvestment fund, HS §9-101.

Community services.
Home care, 88A §85.

Community sewerage system, EN §9-501.

Community supported living arrangements services.
Developmental disabilities, HG §7-709.

Community water supply system, EN §9-501.

Community water system, EN §9-401.

Commutation of sentence, COR §7-101.

Compact.
Maryland emergency management assistance compact, PS §14-801.

Compact administrator.
Adult offender supervision, COR §6-203.

Compact committee.
National racing compact, BR §11-1301.

Compacting state.
Adult offender supervision, COR §6-203.
Interstate insurance product regulation compact, IN §29-101.

Compact license.
National racing compact, BR §11-1301.

Compact officer.
National crime prevention and privacy compact, CP §10-239.

Compact over-order price.
Northeast interstate dairy compact, AG §2-801.

Company.
Franchise taxes, TG §8-101.
Public utility companies, PUC §1-101.

Company headquarters.
Job creation tax credit, 83A §5-1101.
One Maryland economic development tax credits, 83A §5-1501.

Comparable replacement dwelling.
Eminent domain, RP §12-201.

Comparison of benefit levels, IN §18-106.

Compensation.
Charitable organization volunteer, CJ §5-407.
Community recreation programs.
Personal liability, CJ §5-802.
Credit unions, FI §6-331.
Medicare supplement insurance, IN §15-922.
Personal liability of agents of certain associations or organizations, CJ §5-406.
Public ethics, SG §15-102.
Pyramid promotional schemes, CR §8-404.
Sovereign immunity.
County boards of education, CJ §5-518.
Volunteers.
Charitable health care services, CJ §5-606.
Volunteer sports program physicians.
Civil liability, CJ §5-607.
Workers' compensation, LE §9-101.

Compensation arrangement.
Health occupations, HO §1-301.

DEFINED TERMS —Cont'd

Compensation ratio.
Nontidal wetlands, EN §5-901.

Compensatory education enrollment count.
Schools, compensatory education grants, ED §5-207.

Compensatory education per pupil amount.
Schools, compensatory education grants, ED §5-207.

Competency hearing.
Juvenile cases, CJ §3-8A-01.

Competent individual.
Health care decisions, HG §5-601.

Competitive market.
Insurance rate making, IN §11-301.

Competitive transition charge.
Electric customer choice and competition act, PUC §7-501.

Compilation.
Accountants.
Peer review, BOP §2-4A-01.

Complainant.
Housing discrimination, 49B §20.
Judicial disability and sanctionable conduct, CJA Rule 16-803.

Complaining party.
Closed end credit, CL §12-1016.
Credit grantor revolving credit, CL §12-916.
Revolving credit, CL §12-916.

Complaint.
Health insurance, IN §15-10A-01.
Complaint process for coverage decisions, IN §15-10D-01.
Judicial disability and sanctionable conduct, CJA Rule 16-803.
Paternity proceedings, FL §5-1001.

Completed.
Deep mine control, EN §15-601.

Completed operations liability.
Risk retention groups, IN §25-101.

Completed vehicle, TR §13-113.2.

Compliance.
Interstate wildlife violator compact, NR §10-1201.

Compliance plan.
Year 2000 litigation, CJ §5-527.

Compliance review committee.
Financial institutions, FI §1-205.

Compliance review documents.
Financial institutions, FI §1-205.

Compost.
Recycling, EN §9-1701.

Composting.
Recycling, EN §9-1701.

Compounding.
Pharmacists and pharmacies, HO §12-101.

Comprehensive physical rehabilitation services, HG §19-1201.

Comprehensive plan for cancer prevention, education, screening and treatment.
Cancer prevention, education, screening and treatment program, HG §13-1101.

Comprehensive plan for tobacco use prevention and cessation.
Tobacco use prevention and cessation program, HG §13-1001.

Comprehensive rehabilitation facility, HG §19-1201.

Comprehensive services.
University of Maryland medical system, ED §13-301.

DEFINED TERMS —Cont'd
Comprehensive standard health benefit plan.
  Medical care data collection, HG §19-132.
Comptroller.
  Public campaign financing, EL §15-102.
  State officials, BR §1-101.
  Taxation, TG §1-101.
  Tobacco, escrow act compliance, BR §16-501.
Compulsive gambler.
  HMO's, HG §19-801.
Compulsory process.
  Medical records.
    Disclosure.
      Investigations, HG §4-306.
Computation date.
  Unemployment insurance.
    Contributions, LE §8-606.
Computer.
  Computer information transactions, CL §22-102.
  Recycling, EN §9-1701.
  Unauthorized access to computers, CR §7-302.
Computer-based instructional technology.
  Community colleges, ED §16-318.
  Morgan State University, ED §14-109.
  University of Maryland system, ED §12-101.
Computer-based technology.
  Technology for education, ED §7-901.
Computer control language.
  Unauthorized access to computers, CR §7-302.
Computer database.
  Unauthorized access to computers, CR §7-302.
Computer generated evidence, CivProCir Rule
  2-504.3.
Computer information.
  Computer information transactions, CL §22-102.
  Personal jurisdiction, long-arm statute, CJ §6-103.
Computer information transaction.
  Computer information transactions, CL §22-102.
Computer network.
  Unauthorized access to computers, CR §7-302.
Computer program.
  Computer information transactions, CL §22-102.
  Electronic transactions, CL §21-101.
  Personal jurisdiction, long-arm statute, CJ §6-103.
  Unauthorized access to computers, CR §7-302.
Computer services.
  Unauthorized access to computers, CR §7-302.
Computer software.
  Property taxes, TP §7-238.
  Unauthorized access to computers, CR §7-302.
Computer software program, 24 §17-101.
Computer system.
  Unauthorized access to computers, CR §7-302.
Computer takeback program, EN §9-1701.
Concealment.
  Harboring and escape, CR §9-401.
Conciliation.
  Housing discrimination, 49B §20.
Concurrent review.
  Nursing homes, HG §19-1401.
Condemned for repair.
  Weights and measures, AG §11-207.
Conditional commutation of sentence, COR
  §7-101.
Conditional diversion agreement.
  Discipline of attorneys, CJA Rule 16-701.
Conditional pardon, COR §7-101.
Conditions of confinement.
  Prisoner litigation, CJ §5-1001.
Conditions of well-being.
  General assembly.
    Joint committee on children, youth and families,
      SG §2-10A-06.

DEFINED TERMS —Cont'd
Condominium.
  Real property, RP §11-101.
Confidential employee.
  Labor relations.
    Community colleges, ED §16-412.
  Labor unions.
    School personnel, ED §6-501.
  Prince George's county public employment
    relations, ED §16-414.1.
  Washington suburban sanitary district, 29
    §11.5-101.
Confidential information.
  Real estate brokers, BOP §17-528.
Confidential intermediary.
  Adoption search, contact and reunion services, FL
    §5-4B-01.
Confidential record, EN §1-501.
  Health, HG §4-101.
  Juvenile services, 83C §2-115.
Confined space.
  Occupational safety and health, LE §5-602.
Confirmation notice.
  Elections, EL §3-502.
Confirmed credit.
  Sales, UCC, CL §2-325.
Confirmer.
  Letters of credit, CL §5-102.
Conforming.
  Sale of goods, CL §2-106.
Conforming to contract.
  Sales, UCC, CL §2-106.
Congenital disorder.
  Health care, HG §13-101.
Congenital or genetic birth defect.
  Health insurance.
    Required benefits, IN §15-835.
Congregate housing services.
  Aging, 70B §1.
Consent.
  Limited partnerships, CA §10-101.
Consent election.
  Labor relations.
    Choice of bargaining representative, LE §4-201.
Consequential damages.
  Computer information transactions, CL §22-102.
Conservation and management measures.
  Fishery management plans, NR §4-215.
Conservation area.
  Municipal corporations, 23A §7.
Conservation easement.
  Natural resources, NR §1-404.
Conservation land.
  Property tax, TP §9-220.
Conservation property.
  Property tax, TP §§8-209.1, 9-107.
Conservation tillage equipment.
  Income tax, TG §10-208.
  Taxation, TG §10-207.
Conservator.
  Discretionary trusts, ET §14-401.
  UTMA, ET §13-301.
Conserve.
  Fish and fisheries.
    Endangered species, NR §4-2A-01.
  Nongame and endangered species, NR §10-2A-01.
Consideration.
  Negotiable instruments, CL §§3-103, 3-303.
  Pyramid promotional schemes, CR §8-404.
  Real estate settlements, RP §14-127.

DEFINED TERMS —Cont'd

Consignee, CL §11-801.
  Consignment of farm products, AG §1-301.
  Documents of title, CL §7-102.
  Secured transactions, CL §9-102.
Consignment.
  Secured transactions, CL §9-102.
Consignor.
  Documents of title, CL §7-102.
  Secured transactions, CL §9-102.
Console machine license.
  Business licenses, BR §17-405.
Consolidated hearing.
  Development permits, SG §11-501.
Consolidated transportation program.
  Transportation, TR §1-101.
Consortium.
  E-commerce, advisory board, SG §9-2201.
Conspicuous.
  Bills of lading and warehouse receipts, CL
    §18-101.
  Commercial code, CL §1-201.
  Computer information transactions, CL §22-102.
  Uniform commercial code, CL §1-201.
Constituent bank.
  Consolidations, mergers and transfers of assets,
    FI §3-701.
Constituent institutions.
  University system of Maryland, ED §12-101.
Constituent service.
  General assembly members.
    Immunity, CJ §5-525.
Constitutional officer.
  State retirement and pension system, SPP
    §29-305.
Constructing agency.
  Reforestation, NR §5-103.
Construction.
  Gas and oil.
    Coastal facilities review, EN §14-501.
  Geothermal resources, EN §5-601.
  Health and educational facilities, 43C §3.
  Procurement, SF §11-101.
  Public works contracts, SF §17-201.
  Water management, EN §4-105.
Construction activity.
  Reforestation, NR §5-103.
Construction license.
  Business licenses, BR §17-601.
Construction or improvement.
  Bond issues to finance school construction, ED
    §5-602.
  County library capital project grant program, ED
    §23-510.
Construction permit application.
  Building rehabilitation code, PS §12-1001.
Construction phase.
  Long range highway programs, TR §8-610.
  Transportation, TR §2-103.1.
Construction related services.
  Procurement, SF §11-101.
Consultation fee.
  Debt management services, FI §12-901.
Consumer.
  Alcoholic beverages, 2B §1-102.
  Alcoholic beverage tax, TG §5-101.
  Automotive warranty enforcement, CL §14-1501.
  Community attendant services and supports
    program, 41 §6-7A-01.
  Computer information transactions, CL §22-102.
  Condominiums, RP §11-130.

DEFINED TERMS —Cont'd

Consumer —Cont'd
  Consumer credit reporting agencies, CL §14-1201.
  Consumer protection, CL §13-101.
  Cooperative housing corporation, CA §5-6B-12.
  Credit contracts, CL §14-1302.
  Credit services businesses, CL §14-1901.
  Debt management services, FI §12-901.
  Door-to-door solicitation, CL §14-2601.
  Egg law, AG §4-301.
  Electric customer choice and competition act, PUC
    §7-501.
  Homebuilder registration, BR §4.5-101.
  Household goods movers enforcing carrier's lien,
    CL §14-3101.
  Merchandise delivery, CL §14-1801.
  Motorized wheelchair warranty enforcement, CL
    §14-2701.
  Natural gas supplier licensing and consumer
    protection, PUC §7-601.
  Rental-purchase agreements, CL §12-1101.
  Secondhand watches, CL §14-701.
  Seeds, AG §9-201.
  Southern Maryland tri-county council, 20 §1-102.
  Telephone solicitation, CL §14-2201.
  Tobacco tax exemptions, TG §12-104.
Consumer borrower.
  Closed end credit, CL §12-1001.
  Revolving credit, CL §12-901.
Consumer claim.
  Collection agencies, BR §7-101.
Consumer commodity.
  Food and drugs, HG §21-101.
  Unit pricing, CL §14-101.
Consumer contract.
  Computer information transactions, CL §22-102.
  Late fees, CL §14-1315.
Consumer cooperative, CA §5-5A-02.
Consumer credit contracts, CL §14-1302.
Consumer credit, debts, goods, realty and
  services.
  Closed end credit, CL §12-1021.
  Consumer protection, CL §13-101.
  Debt collection.
    Offsets, CL §15-701.
  Door-to-door sales, CL §14-301.
  Extended warranties, CL §14-1311.
  Layaway sales, CL §14-1101.
  Retail installment sales, CL §12-601.
  Revolving credit, CL §12-921.
  Southern Maryland tri-county council, 20 §1-102.
  Telephone solicitation, CL §14-2201.
Consumer debtor.
  Secured transactions, CL §9-102.
Consumer education program.
  Debt management services, FI §12-901.
Consumer goods.
  Internet sales contracts, CL §14-1321.
  Secured transactions, CL §9-102.
Consumer-goods transaction.
  Secured transactions, CL §9-102.
Consumer lease.
  Commercial code, CL §2A-103.
Consumer leasing act.
  Motor vehicle leasing contracts, CL §14-2001.
Consumer loan.
  Banking institutions.
    Loans to directors, officers or employees, FI
      §5-512.
Consumer member.
  Business occupations and professions, BOP
    §1-101.

DEFINED TERMS —Cont'd
Consumer member —Cont'd
Regulatory units, BR §1-101.
Consumer obligor.
Secured transactions, CL §9-102.
Consumer price index.
State retirement and pension system, SPP §29-401.
Consumer product.
Service contracts and consumer products guaranty, CL §14-401.
Consumer report.
Consumer credit reporting agencies, CL §14-1201.
Credit services businesses, CL §14-1901.
Consumer reporting agency.
Consumer credit, CL §14-1201.
Credit services businesses, CL §14-1901.
Support, FL §10-108.1.
Consumer safety costs.
Community services reimbursement rate commission, HG §13-801.
Consumer services.
Door-to-door sales, CL §14-301.
Internet sales contracts, CL §14-1321.
Consumer transaction.
Consumer credit contracts, CL §14-1303.
Consumer debt collection, CL §14-201.
Secured transactions, CL §9-102.
Consummation.
Rental-purchase agreements, CL §12-1101.
Contact.
Athlete agents, BR §4-401.
Contact exposure, HG §18-213.2.
Disease reports, HG §18-213.1.
Contact hour.
Architects, BOP §3-101.
Contact person.
Pesticide application in schools, AG §5-208.1.
Contagious disease or virus, HG §18-213.2.
Body fluids, HG §18-213.2.
Disease reports, HG §§18-213, 18-213.1.
Container.
Liquefied petroleum gas containers, CL §11-601.
Recycling, EN §9-1710.
Container package.
Poultry products inspection act, AG §4-201.
Contaminant.
Drinking water, EN §9-401.
Contamination.
Voluntary cleanup program, EN §7-501.
Contents.
Evidence, CJ §10-401.
Contest.
Boxing, BR §4-101.
Elections, EL §1-101.
Contested case.
Administrative procedures, SG §10-202.
Contested case hearing, EN §1-101.
Contiguous.
Surface mining, EN §15-801.
Continuation statement.
Secured transactions, CL §9-102.
Continuing care.
Continuing care contracts, 70B §7.
Continuing care agreement, 70B §7.
Continuing care at home.
Continuing care contracts, 70B §22A.
Continuing care facility.
Prince George's county housing authority, HS §17-101.
Continuing political committee, EL §1-101.

DEFINED TERMS —Cont'd
Contraband.
Contraband at place of confinement, CR §9-410.
Contraband in correctional facilities, COR §8-801.
Property of prisoners, COR §10-801.
Contraband alcoholic beverage.
Taxation, TG §13-834.
Contraband motor fuel.
Taxation, TG §13-834.
Contraband tobacco products.
Taxation, TG §13-834.
Contract.
Commercial discrimination, SF §19-103.
Computer information transactions, CL §22-102.
Consumer credit contracts, CL §14-1302.
Contract liens, RP §14-201.
Disclosures by persons doing public business, EL §14-101.
Electronic transactions, CL §21-101.
Equipment dealer contracts, CL §19-101.
Health insurance, IN §15-121.
Transfer of provider's contract, IN §15-124.
Transfer restrictions, IN §15-125.
Late fees, CL §14-1315.
Mechanics' liens, RP §9-101.
Procurement, SF §16-101.
Sales, UCC, CL §2-106.
Subrogation provision, HG §19-713.1.
Uniform commercial code, CL §1-201.
Contract claim.
Procurement, SF §15-215.
Contract fee.
Computer information transactions, CL §22-102.
Contract feed.
Commercial feed, AG §6-101.
Contract feeder.
Commercial feed, AG §6-101.
Contract for sale.
Sales, UCC, CL §2-106.
Contracting party.
Sanitary commissions, EN §9-635.
Contracting provider.
Health maintenance organizations, HG §§19-713.2, 19-713.3.
Contracting unit.
Maryland correctional enterprises, COR §3-501.
Contract modification.
Procurement, SF §13-201.
Contractor.
Excavation or demolition near underground facilities, PUC §12-101.
Heating and air conditioning, BR §9A-101.
Home improvement, BR §8-101.
Insurance, IN §1-203.
Mechanics' liens, RP §9-101.
Contract purchaser.
Homebuilder registration, BR §4.5-101.
Contract term.
Small business surety bond program, 83A §5-1032.
Contractual employees.
State personnel, SPP §13-101.
Contractual entrance fee refund.
Continuing care contracts, 70B §7.
Contractual obligation.
Life and health insurance guaranty corporation, IN §9-401.
Contractual right.
Insurance companies, liquidation and rehabilitation, IN §9-229.1.

DEFINED TERMS —Cont'd

Contractual use term.
Computer information transactions, CL §22-102.
Contract weekly online.
Procurement, SF §13-101.
Contribution.
Community colleges, ED §16-317.
Disclosures by persons doing public business, EL §14-101.
Elections, EL §1-101.
Limited partnerships, CA §10-101.
Unemployment insurance, LE §8-101.
Contributor.
College investment plan, ED §18-19A-01.
Contributory system.
State retirement and pension system, SPP §37-101.
Control.
Automated teller machines, FI §1-401.
Foreign discriminatory boycotts, CL §11-102.
Insurance, IN §8-101.
Insurance acquisitions disclosure and control, IN §7-101.
Investment securities, CL §§8-102, 8-106.
Money transmission, FI §12-401.
Nonprofit health service plans, IN §14-133.
Reporting requirements for public service companies, PUC §6-201.
Savings and loan associations.
Board of commissioners and division, FI §8-101.
Initial capitalization, FI §9-216.
Interstate acquisitions, FI §9-1001.
Unsolicited takeovers of corporations and real estate investment trusts, CA §3-801.
Control, controlling and controlled by, under common control with.
Corporations, CA §3-601.
Controlled access highway, TR §8-101.
Traffic laws, TR §21-101.
Controlled by.
Insurance acquisitions disclosure and control, IN §7-101.
Controlled conditions.
Seeds, AG §9-201.
Controlled dangerous substance, CR §5-101.
Altering results of drug or alcohol screening, CR §10-111.
Contraband at place of confinement, CR §9-410.
Controlled dangerous substance in correctional facilities, COR §8-801.
Food, drugs and cosmetics, HG §21-1113.
Medical laboratories, HG §17-214.
Nuisance actions, RP §14-120.
Physician assistants, HO §15-101.
Controlled dangerous substance analogue, CR §5-402.
Controlled dangerous substances law.
Drug asset forfeiture, CP §12-101.
Controlled hazardous substance, EN §7-201.
Controlled hazardous substance facility, EN §7-201.
Controlled hazardous substance hauler, EN §7-201.
Controlled hazardous substance vehicle, EN §7-201.
Controlled hazardous substance vehicle driver, EN §7-201.
Controlled insurer, IN §8-101.
Controlled or owned.
Child pornography.
Internet, CR §11-208.1.

DEFINED TERMS —Cont'd

Controlled outlet.
Gasohol and gasoline products marketing, CL §11-301.
Controlled paraphernalia, CR §5-101.
Controlling.
Insurance acquisitions disclosure and control, IN §7-101.
Controlling insurance producer, IN §8-101.
Controlling person.
Reinsurance intermediaries, IN §8-507.
Savings and loan associations.
Board of commissioners and division, FI §8-101.
Controlling stockholder.
Procurement, SF §16-101.
Control share acquisition, CA §3-701.
Control shares, CA §3-701.
Convenience person.
Financial institutions, FI §1-204.
Convention Center facilities.
County resort taxes, 25B §13H.
Stadium authority, FI §13-701.
Conversion.
Continuing care contracts, 70B §7.
Conversion of overhead electric or communication facilities to underground locations, PUC §12-301.
Cooperative housing corporation, CA §5-6B-01.
Conversion building.
Time-sharing, RP §11A-101.
Convert.
Conversion of overhead electric or communication facilities to underground locations, PUC §12-301.
Converted funds.
Medicaid, HG §15-122.2.
Convertible securities.
Corporations, CA §1-101.
Converting institution.
Conversion of national banking association into commercial bank, FI §3-801.
Conveyance.
Debt collection.
Fraudulent conveyances, CL §15-201.
Motor fuel, BR §10-101.
Taxation, TG §13-834.
Convicted.
Drug asset forfeiture, CP §12-101.
Health care fraud, HG §15-123.
Pharmacists and pharmacies, HO §12-313.
Procurement, SF §16-101.
Conviction.
Adult dependent care programs, HG §19-1901.
Alcoholic beverages, 2B §10-401.
Child care facilities, FL §5-560.
Commercial driver's licenses, TR §16-803.
Driver license compact, TR §16-703.
Interstate wildlife violator compact, NR §10-1201.
Motor vehicles, TR §11-110.
Co-offer.
Lead poisoning, EN §6-826.
Cooling system.
Heating and air conditioning, BR §9A-101.
Cooperating agent.
Real estate brokers, BOP §17-530.
Cooperative.
Corporations, CA §5-5A-02.
Electric cooperatives, CA §5-601.
Fluid dairy products, AG §11-401.
Cooperative basis.
Consumer cooperatives, CA §5-5A-02.

DEFINED TERMS —Cont'd

Cooperative group.
Health insurance, IN §15-827.
Cooperative housing corporation, CA §5-6B-01.
Cooperative interest.
Cooperative housing corporation, CA §5-6B-01.
Cooperative living project.
Family investment program, 88A §44A.
Cooperative project.
Cooperative housing corporation, CA §5-6B-01.
Cooperator.
Nuisance bird law, AG §5-801.
Coordinate.
Real property, RP §3-108.
Copy.
Computer information transactions, CL §22-102.
Copyright owner.
Copyright royalties, CL §11-1401.
Cord.
Weights and measures, AG §11-101.
Cord blood sampling.
Newborn infants, HG §20-401.
Core service agency.
Children, youth and families services, 49D §1-101.
Mental health, HG §10-1201.
Mental health crisis response system, HG §10-1401.
Mental health records, HG §4-307.
Corporate document.
Sanitary commissions, EN §9-617.
Corporate fiduciary.
Trusts, ET §15-1A-01.
Corporation, CA §§1-204, 2-418, 3-601.
Agricultural and resource-based industry development corporation, 41 §13-501.
Children, youth and families services.
Operators of residential child care programs, 49D §6-101.
Criminal process, CP §4-203.
Fiduciary security transfers, ET §15-301.
Income tax, TG §2-601.
Limited partnerships.
Merger, CA §10-208.
Maryland stem cell research program, 83A §5-2B-01.
Morticians, HO §7-101.
Property and casualty insurance guaranty corporation, IN §9-301.
Property tax, TP §1-101.
Unsolicited takeovers of corporations and real estate investment trusts, CA §3-801.
Corporation income tax, TG §10-101.
Correctional administrator, COR §8-201.
Correctional employee.
Inmate diseases, HG §18-338.
Correctional facility, COR §1-101.
Criminal law, CR §1-101.
Criminal procedure, CP §1-101.
Death penalty, sentencing procedure, CR §2-303.
Physician assistants, HO §15-101.
Correctional institution, HG §18-213.2.
Disease reports, HG §18-213.
Inmate diseases, HG §18-338.
Interstate agreement on detainers, COR §8-401.
Correctional officer, COR §8-201; HG §18-213.2.
Death benefits, public safety officers and personnel, PS §1-202.
Disease reports, HG §18-213.
Correctional officers' retirement system, SPP §20-101.
Correctional supervisor, COR §8-201.

DEFINED TERMS —Cont'd

Correctional unit.
Correctional mutual aid agreements, COR §2-401.
Correctional training commission, COR §8-201.
Corrective order.
Risk based capital standards for insurers, IN §4-301.
Cosmetic.
Food and drugs, HG §21-101.
Cosmetologist, BOP §5-101.
Cost of care.
Health care collections, HG §16-101.
Cost of developments or projects.
Maryland food center, 41 §13-104.
Cost of land.
Alcoholic beverages, 2B §§8-202.1, 8-204.
Cost of providing a system product.
Automated mapping-geographic information systems, SG §10-901.
Cost of providing a system service.
Automated mapping-geographic information systems, SG §10-901.
Cost of the building shell.
Alcoholic beverages, 2B §§8-202.1, 8-204.
Cost of the loan.
Secondary mortgage loan, CL §12-407.
Cost per pupil.
Residential boarding education programs for at-risk youth, ED §8-709.
Cost-reimbursement contract.
Procurement, SF §13-201.
Costs.
Abandoned mine drainage control, EN §15-701.
Appeals, CJ §7-101.
Bainbridge development corporation, 83A §5-1601.
Baltimore City schools, ED §4-301.
Criminal prosecutions, CJ §7-501.
Economic development corporation, 83A §5-201.
Environmental service, NR §3-101.
Health and educational facilities, 43C §3.
Higher education.
Auxiliary and academic facilities bond authority, ED §19-101.
Infrastructure improvements.
Municipal corporations, 23A §44A.
Issuance of notes by community colleges, ED §16-302.1.
Local bus systems grants, TR §10-207.
Local military installation redevelopment authorities, 83A §5-1701.
Northeast Maryland waste disposal authority, NR §3-904.
Penmar development corporations, 83A §5-1201.
Revenue facilities, TR §4-101.
Sanitary commissions, EN §9-601.
Senior citizen activities centers capital improvement grants, 70B §26.
Special taxes authorized in certain counties, 24 §9-1301.
Special taxing districts, 24 §9-1301.
Susquehanna river basin compact, EN §5-301.
Water and sewer authorities, EN §9-901.
Woodrow Wilson bridge and tunnel compact, TR §10-303.
Cost-share assistance.
Woodland incentives program, NR §5-301.
Cost to the retailer.
Sales below cost, CL §11-401.
Cigarettes, CL §11-501.
Cost to the wholesaler.
Sales below cost, CL §11-401.
Cigarettes, CL §11-501.

DEFINED TERMS —Cont'd

Council.
Local military installation redevelopment authorities, 83A §5-1701.
Maryland youth camp, HG §14-401.
National crime prevention and privacy compact, CP §10-239.
Procurement, SF §12-105.
Public works contracts, SF §17-201.
Wine and grape promotion fund and council, AG §2-1101.

Council of unit owners.
Condominiums, RP §11-101.

Counseling.
Professional counselors and therapists, HO §17-101.

Counterfeit, CR §1-101.

Counterfeit drug.
Food and drugs, HG §21-201.

Counterfeit mark.
Trademark counterfeiting, CR §8-611.

Counterfeit marking tool.
Drug trademarks, HG §21-258.

Counterfeit substance.
Controlled dangerous substances, CR §§5-604, 5-607.

Counter-marketing and media component.
Tobacco use prevention and cessation program, HG §13-1001.

Counterparty exposure amount.
Investments of life insurers, IN §5-511.

Counting center.
Elections, EL §11-101.

Country club.
Class C, on-sale beer, wine and liquor license in Harford county, 2B §6-301.

Country inn.
Alcoholic beverages.
   Hotels and restaurants, 2B §6-101.

County.
Abandoned property, CL §17-101.
Agricultural land preservation foundation, AG §2-508.
Agriculture, AG §1-101.
Allocation of private activity bond authority, FI §13-801.
Antitrust, CL §11-201.
Assignment of wages, CL §15-301.
Business occupations and professions, BOP §1-101.
Community energy loan program, SG §9-2101.
Corporations, CA §1-101.
Correctional services, COR §1-101.
County health boards, HG §3-101.
Criminal law, CR §1-101.
Criminal procedure, CP §1-101.
Economic development assistance authority, 83A §5-1401.
Education, ED §1-101.
Elections, EL §1-101.
Enterprise zones, 83A §5-401.
Environmental service, NR §3-101.
Family law, FL §1-101.
Financial institutions, FI §1-101.
Fish and fisheries, NR §4-101.
Forests and parks, NR §5-101.
Highway user revenues, TR §8-401.
Housing and community development, HS §1-101.
Housing authorities, HS §12-101.
Industrial development, 45A §3.
Industrial development financing, 83A §5-901.

DEFINED TERMS —Cont'd

County —Cont'd
Insurance, IN §1-101.
Interest rate exchange agreements or contracts, 31 §34.
Juvenile services, 83C §1-101.
Labor and employment, LE §1-101.
Liens on personal property, CL §16-101.
Municipal corporations, 23A §2B.
Natural resources, EN §14-102.
Northeast Maryland waste disposal authority, NR §3-904.
Pensions, SPP §20-101.
Political subdivisions, 24 §1-101.
Procurement, SF §11-101.
Property tax, TP §1-101.
   Elderly or disabled renters, TP §9-402.
Public assistance programs, 88A §64.
Public safety, PS §1-101.
Public schools financing, 31 §34.
Public utility companies, PUC §1-101.
Public watershed associations, 25 §169.
Retail installment sales, CL §12-601.
Shore erosion control districts, 25 §167E.
Special retirement or pension system, SPP §39-101.
State government, SG §1-101.
State personnel, SPP §1-101.
State retirement and pension system, SPP §37-101.
Taxation, TG §1-101.
Tobacco use prevention and cessation program, HG §13-1001.
Transportation, TR §2-103.3.
Water and water resources, NR §8-101.
Water resources, EN §5-101.
Wetlands and riparian rights, EN §16-101.
Wildlife, NR §10-101.

County advisory council.
Physical fitness, HG §13-401.

County agricultural land transfer tax, TP §13-501.

County attorney.
Ballot questions, EL §7-103.

County board.
Education, ED §1-101.

County board employee.
Sovereign immunity, CJ §5-518.

County board member.
Sovereign immunity, CJ §5-518.

County board of community college trustees, ED §16-202.

County commissioners.
College of southern Maryland, ED §16-602.
Public watershed associations, 25 §169.
Shore erosion control districts, 25 §167E.

County governing body.
Incorporation of municipal corporation, 23A §20.

County grant for national certification.
Teachers, ED §6-306.

County health, HG §1-101.

County income tax, TG §§2-601, 10-101.

County liaison.
Incorporation of municipal corporation, 23A §20.

County library.
County library capital project grant program, ED §23-510.

County license.
Cigarette licenses, BR §16-101.

County plan.
911 emergency telephone system, PS §1-301.

DEFINED TERMS —Cont'd
County plan —Cont'd
Sewerage systems, EN §9-501.
County police.
Alcoholic beverages, 2B §10-103.
County property tax, TP §1-101.
County registrar.
Vital statistics, HG §4-201.
County road, TR §8-101.
County roads authority.
Inmate work force, COR §9-501.
County share.
Community colleges.
State and county aid, ED §16-305.
County superintendent.
Education, ED §1-101.
County transfer tax, TP §13-401.
County waters.
Oysters and clams, NR §§4-1001, 4-1101.
Course of conduct.
Stalking and harassment, CR §3-801.
Course of dealing.
Commercial code, CL §1-205.
Computer information transactions, CL §22-102.
Course of performance.
Computer information transactions, CL §22-102.
Court, CJ §§1-101, 2-101.
Access to court records, CJA Rule 16-1001.
Alcoholic beverages, 2B §1-102.
Antitrust, CL §11-201.
Assignment of wages, CL §15-301.
Children in need of assistance, CJ §3-801.
Civil relief during emergency periods, PS §14-201.
Computer information transactions, CL §22-102.
Death taxes, TG §7-101.
Discretionary trusts, ET §14-401.
Domestic violence, FL §4-501.
Emergency mental health evaluations, HG §10-620.
Estates and trusts, ET §2-101.
Expungement of records, Crim Rule 4-502.
Highways, TR §8-301.
Incompetency and criminal responsibility, CP §3-101.
Interstate wildlife violator compact, NR §10-1201.
Juvenile causes, CJ §3-8A-01.
Juvenile services.
Interstate compact on juveniles, 83C §3-103.
Landlord and tenant, RP §8-301.
Lawyers, BOP §10-101.
Limited liability companies, CA §4A-101.
Local correctional facilities, individual county provisions, COR §11-701.
Peace orders, CJ §3-1501.
Uniform child custody jurisdiction and enforcement act, FL §9.5-101.
URESA, FL §10-301.
Courtesy card.
Morticians, HO §7-101.
Court of competent jurisdiction.
Pen registers and trap and trace devices, CJ §10-4B-01.
Court records.
Access to court records, CJA Rule 16-1001.
Expungement of criminal records, CP §10-101.
Expungement of records, Crim Rule 4-502.
Cover.
Sales, UCC, CL §2-712.
Coverage decision.
Health insurance.
Complaint process for coverage decisions, IN §15-10D-01.

DEFINED TERMS —Cont'd
Covered claim.
Property and casualty insurance guaranty corporation, IN §9-301.
Covered county.
Residential mortgage programs for certain counties, HS §4-1601.
Covered employee.
Workers' compensation, LE §9-101.
Covered employment.
Unemployment insurance, LE §8-101.
Covered individual.
State retirement and pension system, SPP §30-210.1.
Covered loan.
Closed end credit, insurance, CL §12-1007.
Consumer loans, insurance, CL §12-312.
Homeowner equity protection, CL §§12-124.1, 12-311, 12-312, 12-409.1, 12-1007, 12-1029.
Homeowner's ability to repay loan, CL §12-127.
Secondary mortgage loans, CL §§12-409.1, 12-410.
Covered multifamily dwelling.
Housing discrimination, 49B §20.
Covered policy.
Life and health insurance guaranty corporation, IN §9-401.
Covered service.
Health maintenance organizations, HG §19-701.
Covered vehicle.
Automobile insurance fund, IN §20-501.
Crab, NR §4-801.
Crab meat.
Food establishments, HG §21-301.
Crab meat plant, HG §21-301.
Crack and crevice treatment.
Pesticide application in schools, AG §5-208.1.
Crash parts.
Automotive, CL §14-2301.
Credentialing.
Judith P. Hoyer early child care and education enhancement program, ED §5-217.
Credentialing intermediaries.
Health insurance, credentialing of providers, IN §15-112.1.
Credit.
Equal credit opportunity, CL §12-701.
Creditable coverage.
Health insurance portability, IN §§15-1301, 15-1401.
Maryland health insurance plan, IN §14-501.
Creditable service.
Health insurance portability, IN §15-1301.
Legislative pension plan, SG Title 2 Subtitle 3 (note).
Pensions, SPP §20-101.
Health and welfare benefits, SPP §2-508.
Credit agreements.
Enforceability, CJ §5-408.
Credit allowance year.
Income tax, TG §10-722.
Credit balance.
Retail credit accounts, CL §12-506.1.
Credit card.
Credit card crimes, CR §8-201.
Credit card issuer.
Consumer credit contract, CL §14-1302.
Credit card use.
Gasohol and gasoline products marketing, CL §11-301.
Credit device.
Revolving credit, CL §12-901.

DEFINED TERMS —Cont'd
Credit enhancement.
  Maryland housing fund, HS §3-201.
Credit enhancer.
  Viatical settlement contracts, IN §8-601.
Credit grantor.
  Closed end credit, CL §12-1001.
  Denial of credit, CL §14-1701.
  Revolving credit, CL §12-901.
Credit health insurance, IN §13-101.
  Closed end credit, insurance, CL §12-1007.
  Consumer loans, CL §12-312.
  Secondary mortgage loans, CL §12-410.
Credit instrument.
  Transportation, TR §3-104.
Credit instrument provider.
  Transportation, TR §3-104.
Credit involuntary unemployment benefit
    insurance, IN §13-101.
  Closed end credit, insurance, CL §12-1007.
  Consumer loans, CL §12-312.
  Secondary mortgage loans, CL §12-410.
Credit life insurance, IN §13-101.
  Closed end credit, insurance, CL §12-1007.
  Consumer loans, CL §12-312.
  Homeowner equity protection, CL §§12-124.1,
    12-312, 12-409.1, 12-1007.
  Secondary mortgage loans, CL §§12-409.1, 12-410.
Credit life or disability insurance, IN §27-901.
Creditor.
  Consumer credit contracts, CL §14-1302.
  Continuing care contracts, 70B §7.
  Credit life, health and unemployment insurance,
    IN §13-101.
  Debt collection.
    Fraudulent conveyances, CL §15-201.
  Equal credit opportunity, CL §12-701.
  Insurer liquidation, rehabilitation, etc., IN §9-201.
  Uniform commercial code, CL §1-201.
Creditor process.
  Funds transfers, CL §4A-502.
Credit services.
  Telephone solicitation, CL §14-2201.
Credit services business, CL §14-1901.
Credit union, FI §6-101.
  Credit unions, share guaranty corporations, FI
    §7-201.
  Insurance corporation, FI §7-101.
Credit union service organization.
  Credit unions, FI §6-101.
Credit union share guaranty corporation, FI
    §7-201.
  Credit unions, FI §6-101.
Credit year.
  Job creation tax credit, 83A §5-1101.
Cremation, HG §5-508.
Crematory, HG §5-508.
Crew leader.
  Unemployment insurance.
    Agricultural labor, LE §8-207.
Crew member.
  Fish and fisheries, NR §4-101.
Crime.
  Additional cost in criminal cases, CJ §7-409.
  Crime victims' restitution, CP §11-601.
  Crime victims' services, CP §11-910.
  Criminal injuries compensation fund, CP §11-801.
  Fines and forfeitures, CJ §7-501.
Crime assessment.
  State aid for police protection, 41 §4-403.

DEFINED TERMS —Cont'd
Crime laboratory.
  DNA database system, PS §2-501.
Crime of violence, CP §1-101.
  Bulletproof body armor, CR §4-106.
  Burglary, CR §6-201.
  Children generally, FL §5-101.
  Children in need of assistance, CJ §3-812.
  Community service programs, COR §8-701.
  Criminal law, CR §2-303.
  Firearms, PS §5-101.
  Local correctional facilities, individual county
    provisions, COR §11-701.
  Mandatory sentences, CR §14-101.
  Parole and probation, COR §6-101.
  Uniform machine gun act, CR §4-401.
Criminal action.
  Appeals, CJ §12-101.
Criminal case.
  Appeals, CJ §12-101.
  District Court, CJ §4-101.
Criminal gang, CR §9-801.
  Arrest of pupils for reportable offenses, ED
    §7-303.
Criminal history record information.
  Criminal justice information system, CP §10-201.
Criminal history records.
  National crime prevention and privacy compact,
    CP §10-239.
Criminal history records check.
  Adult dependent care programs, HG §19-1901.
Criminal history records repository.
  National crime prevention and privacy compact,
    CP §10-239.
Criminal justice.
  National crime prevention and privacy compact,
    CP §10-239.
Criminal justice agency.
  National crime prevention and privacy compact,
    CP §10-239.
Criminal justice information system, CP
    §10-201.
Criminal justice services.
  National crime prevention and privacy compact,
    CP §10-239.
Criminal justice unit.
  Criminal justice information system, CP §10-201.
Criminal offense.
  Expungement of driving records, TR §16-117.1.
Crisis response system.
  Mental health crisis response system, HG
    §10-1401.
Criterion offense.
  National crime prevention and privacy compact,
    CP §10-239.
Criterion-reference test.
  Public schools, ED §7-204.
Critical area.
  Chesapeake Bay critical area and Atlantic coastal
    bays critical area protection programs, NR
    §8-1802.
Critical habitat area, NR §5-1601.
Critical habitat for endangered species, NR
    §5-1601.
Critical information technology system or
    product.
  Year 2000 litigation, CJ §5-527.
Crossover, TR §21-101.
Cross-training.
  Integration of child welfare and substance abuse
    treatment act, FL §5-1201.

DEFINED TERMS —Cont'd

Crosswalk, TR §21-101.

Cruelty.
Crimes relating to animals, CR §10-601.

Cultural affiliation.
Burial sites, RP §14-121.

Cultural competency, HG §20-1201.

Cumulative noise exposure.
Airport noise assistance programs, TR §5-1201.
Aviation noise zones, TR §5-801.

Curfew hours.
Juvenile curfew, 25B §13C-1.

Currency.
Corporations, BR §1-502.
Transaction reporting, FI §12-802.

Current expenses.
Maryland food center, 41 §13-104.

Current market.
Property tax.
Homeowners credit, TP §9-104.

Current model.
Equipment dealer contracts, CL §19-101.

Current net price.
Equipment dealer contracts, CL §19-101.

Current prepaid contract obligations.
College savings plan of Maryland, ED §18-1901.

Custodial confinement.
Probation after judgment, CP §6-225.
Probation before judgment, CP §6-220.
Suspension of sentence, CP §6-219.

Custodial parent.
Pubic assistance program, 88A §65A.

Custodial property.
UTMA, ET §13-301.

Custodian.
Access to court records, CJA Rule 16-1001.
Access to public records, SG §10-611.
Children in need of assistance, CJ §3-801.
Health care rights, HG §7-1103.
Juvenile causes, CJ §3-8A-01.
Prisoner litigation, CJ §5-1001.
Service of subpoena for public records, CJ §6-410.
UTMA, ET §13-301.

Custodian of records.
Housing authorities, HS §12-101.

Custody.
Children in need of assistance, CJ §3-801.

Customer.
Automated teller machines, FI §§1-206, 1-401.
Bank deposits and collections, CL §4-104.
Funds transfers, CL §4A-105.
Natural gas supplier licensing and consumer
protection, PUC §7-601.
911 emergency telephone system, PS §1-301.
Pesticide applicators, AG §5-201.
Renewable energy credits, PUC §7-704.
Retail establishment liability, CJ §5-635.
Telephone records, obtaining without
authorization, CR §7-304.

Customer choice.
Electric customer choice and competition act, PUC
§7-501.

Customer-formula feed.
Commercial feed, AG §6-101.

Custom home, RP §10-501.

Custom home contract, RP §10-501.

Custom-mix.
Commercial fertilizers, AG §6-201.

Cutting operation.
Pine tree reforestation, NR §5-501.

CVISN, TR §25-112.

DEFINED TERMS —Cont'd

CVISN transponder, TR §25-112.

Cyclodiene termiticide.
Pesticide applicators, AG §5-210.5.

Dairy farm.
Milk products, HG §21-401.

Damaged property.
Property tax.
Reductions in payment, TP §10-304.

Damages.
Contract liens, RP §14-201.
Water pollution, EN §4-401.

Dangerous contaminant.
Drinking water, EN §9-405.

Dangerous dog, CR §10-619.

Data-based areas.
School improvement research project, ED §5-204.
School performance program standards
improvement awards, ED §5-211.

Date data.
Year 2000 litigation, CJ §5-527.

Date of adoption.
Health insurance, IN §15-401.

Date of appointment.
Modified administration of estate, ET §5-701.

Date of employment.
Unemployment compensation, LE §8-626.1.

Date of finality.
Property tax, TP §1-101.

Date of issuance.
Transient or temporary vendors licenses, 24
§§11-301, 11-302.

Date of the filing of the petition.
Debt collection, CL §15-101.

Day.
Employee grievance procedures.
University of Maryland, ED §13-201.
Maryland youth camp, HG §14-401.
State personnel, SPP §1-201.

Day camp.
Maryland youth camp, HG §14-401.

Day care center for adults.
Mentally handicapped adults, HG §14-301.

Day care center for the elderly, HG §14-201.

Day care provider.
Child care, FL §5-501.
Family day care homes, RP §11-111.1.
Homeowners association, RP §11B-111.1.

Deadly agent.
Catastrophic health emergency disease
surveillance and response program, HG
§18-901.
Governor's health emergency powers, PS
§14-3A-01.

Deaf, 30 §31.

Deaf and hard of hearing individuals.
Office of the deaf and hard of hearing, SG
§9-2401.

Deaf child.
Education, ED §8-301.

Deaf, dumb or blind, 30 §31.

Dealer.
Automotive warranty enforcement, CL §14-1501.
Boats and boating, NR §8-701.
Equipment dealer contracts, CL §19-101.
Explosives licenses, PS §11-101.
Firearms, PS §5-101.
Gasohol and gasoline products marketing, CL
§11-301.
Merchandise delivery, CL §14-1801.
Motor fuel, BR §10-301.

DEFINED TERMS —Cont'd
Dealer —Cont'd
Motor fuel tax, TG §9-301.
Motor vehicle leasing contracts, CL §14-2001.
Motor vehicles, TR §§11-111, 15-101.
Pawnbrokers, BR §12-101.
Turf grass, AG §9-101.
Dealer processing charge.
Motor vehicles, TR §15-311.1.
Dealer's license.
Firearms, PS §5-101.
Death benefits.
Estates and trusts, ET §11-105.
Death taxes, TG §7-101.
Debilitation or debilitated.
Standby guardians, ET §13-901.
Debt.
Debt collection.
Fraudulent conveyances, CL §15-201.
Income tax refunds, TG §13-912.
Debt adjusting, CL §14-1316.
Debt cancellation agreement.
Credit grantor closed end credit, CL §12-1001.
Retail installment sales, CL §12-601.
Debt collection activities.
Criminal injuries compensation, CP §11-809.
Debt instrument.
Commercial banks, FI §3-101.
Debt management counselor.
Debt management services, FI §12-901.
Debt management services, FI §12-901.
Debt management services agreement, FI §12-901.
Debt management services provider, FI §12-901.
Debtor.
Credit life, health and unemployment insurance, IN §13-101.
Debt collection, CL §15-101.
Income tax refunds, TG §13-912.
Secured transactions, CL §9-102.
Debtor in bankruptcy.
Partnerships, revised act, CA §9A-101.
Debtor's correct name.
Secured transactions, financing statements, CL §9-506.
Debt service.
Highway user revenues, TR §8-401.
Transportation, TR §3-101.
Decedent.
Cremation, HG §5-508.
Rules of interpretation, 1 §6.
Deception.
Exploitation of vulnerable adult, CR §8-801.
Theft, CR §7-101.
Declarant.
Discretionary trusts, ET §14-401.
Health care decisions, HG §5-601.
Homeowners association, RP §11B-101.
Declaration.
Homeowners association, RP §11B-101.
Declaration of loss.
Negotiable instruments, CL §3-312.
Decree, CJ §2-101.
Deed, RP §1-101.
Deed of trust, RP §1-101.
Deemed status.
Accreditation of health care facilities, HG §19-2301.
Deep mining.
Coal, EN §15-501.

DEFINED TERMS —Cont'd
Deep mining —Cont'd
Control, EN §15-601.
Deep trough.
Chesapeake Bay and tributaries, EN §5-1101.
Deepwater port.
Siting, NR §3-602.
De facto cancellation.
Distributorships, CL §11-1301.
Default.
Self-service storage, CL §18-501.
Defective alarm system, CR §9-610.
Defendant.
Battered spouse syndrome.
Evidence, CJ §10-916.
Civil infractions.
Code counties, 25B §13C.
Crime victims' restitution, CP §11-601.
Default judgments, CivProCir Rule 2-613.
Landlord and tenant, RP §8-301.
Not criminally responsible determination, notification of victim, CP §3-123.
Notoriety of crimes contracts, CP §11-621.
Uniform commercial code, CL §1-201.
Defense contractors.
Maryland economic adjustment fund, 83A §6-501.
Defense related activity, CR §9-701.
Highways, TR §8-627.
Deficiency.
Distributorships, CL §11-1301.
Nursing homes, HG §19-1401.
Deficits.
School budget and management, ED §5-114.
Defined parking area.
Automated teller machines, FI §1-401.
Defoliant.
Pesticide registration and labeling, AG §5-101.
Degree.
Strip mining, EN §15-501.
Degreed recipient.
McAuliffe teacher education award, ED §18-703.
Degree program in human services.
Developmental disabilities, mental health, child welfare and juvenile services workforce tuition assistance program, ED §18-2101.
Delegate.
Consumer cooperatives, CA §5-5A-02.
Delegated medical acts.
Physician assistants, HO §15-101.
Delegated pharmacy act.
Pharmacists and pharmacies, HO §12-101.
Delinquency petition.
Expungement of criminal charge transferred to juvenile court, CP §10-106.
Delinquency proceeding.
Continuing care contracts, 70B §7.
Insurer liquidation, rehabilitation, etc., IN §9-201.
Delinquent act.
Juvenile causes, CJ §3-8A-01.
Victims of crime, CP §11-101.
Delinquent child, CJ §3-8A-01.
Delinquent juvenile.
Interstate compact on juveniles, 83C §3-103.
Delinquent tenant.
Public housing authorities, 88A §17C.
Deliver.
Controlled dangerous substances, CR §5-101.
Unauthorized recording of sounds or images, CR §7-308.
Delivered for final consumption.
Public service company tax, TG §8-401.

DEFINED TERMS —Cont'd
Delivery.
Computer information transactions, CL §22-102.
Investment securities, CL §§8-102, 8-301.
Uniform commercial code, CL §1-201.
Delivery order.
Documents of title, CL §7-102.
Demand deposit.
Commercial banks.
Reserves, FI §3-607.
Demolition.
Historic area zoning, 66B §8.01.
Near underground facilities, PUC §12-101.
Demonstration.
Possession of firearm at public demonstration, CR
§4-208.
Demonstration site.
Child support enforcement privatization pilot
program, FL §10-119.2.
Family investment program, 88A §55.
Demonstrator.
Motorized wheelchair warranty enforcement, CL
§14-2701.
De novo.
Rules of interpretation, 1 §32.
De novo branch.
Banks, FI §5-1001.
Dental appliance, HO §4-101.
Dental hygienist, HO §4-101.
Dental hygienist rehabilitation committee, HO
§4-508.
Dental laboratory, HO §4-101.
Dental laboratory work, HO §4-101.
Dental managed care organization.
Medical assistance, HG §15-101.
Dental plan, IN §14-401.
Dental plan organization, IN §14-401.
Dental point-of-service option, IN §15-114.
Dental radiation technologist, HO §4-505.
Dental rehabilitation committee, HO §4-501.1.
Dental review committee, HO §4-501.
Dental school.
University of Maryland medical system, ED
§13-301.
Dental service.
Dental plan organizations, IN §14-401.
Medical assistance, HG §15-101.
Dental technician.
Dental laboratories, HO §4-401.
Dentist.
Health occupations, HO §4-101.
Deoxyribonucleic acid.
Evidence, CJ §10-915.
Departmental inspection area.
Milk products, HG §21-401.
Department head.
Counties and municipal corporations, 24 §1-107.
Department of juvenile services employee,
COR §8-201.
Dependent.
Criminal injuries compensation fund, CP §11-801.
Dependent child.
Health insurance, IN §§15-407, 15-408.
Deposit.
Bank holding companies, FI §5-901.
Continuing care contracts, 70B §7.
Custom home protection, RP §10-501.
Savings and loan associations.
Interstate acquisitions, FI §9-1001.
Deposit account.
Credit unions, FI §6-101.

DEFINED TERMS —Cont'd
Deposit account —Cont'd
Secured transactions, CL §9-102.
Depositary.
Fiduciaries, ET §15-101.
Depositary bank.
Bank deposits and collections, CL §§4-104, 4-105.
Deposit association.
Savings and loan associations, FI §9-101.
Deposited or exchanged.
Fiduciaries, ET §15-101.
Deposit in lieu of surety bond.
Money transmission, FI §12-401.
Deposit insurance.
State treasury, SF §6-201.
Depositor.
Deposit of unexpended or surplus money by local
government, 95 §22O.
Depository.
Homeowners association, RP §11B-101.
Depository institution.
Financial institutions, FI §§1-204, 1-205, 1-210.
Depository library.
State publications, ED §23-301.
Deposit-taking office.
Savings and loan associations.
Interstate acquisitions, FI §9-1001.
Depreciation.
Principal and income, ET §15-525.
Depressant or stimulant drug.
Controlled dangerous substances, CR §5-101.
Deprive.
Exploitation of vulnerable adult, CR §8-801.
Robbery, CR §3-401.
Theft, CR §7-101.
Derivative.
Principal and income, ET §15-521.
Derivative instrument.
Investments of life insurers, IN §5-511.
Derivative transaction.
Investments of life insurers, IN §5-511.
Desiccant.
Pesticide registration and labeling, AG §5-101.
Designated anonymous HIV test site.
HIV/AIDS case reports, HG §18-207.
Designated assessment services provider.
Child in need of services pilot program, CJ
§3-8A-10.1.
Designated beneficiary.
Legislative pension plan, SG Title 2 Subtitle 3
(note).
Pensions, SPP §20-101.
Designated company.
State retirement and pension system, SPP
§30-101.
Designated household.
Assisted housing preservation, HS §7-101.
Condominiums, RP §11-137.
Cooperative housing corporation, CA §5-6B-07.
Designated law enforcement agency.
Firearms, PS §5-101.
Designated name.
Real estate brokers and sales persons, BOP
§17-527.2.
Designated neighborhood.
Neighborhood business development program, HS
§6-301.
Designated pharmacy.
Physician assistants, HO §15-101.
Designated procurement unit.
Small business reserve program, SF §14-501.

DEFINED TERMS —Cont'd
Designated requestor.
Anatomical donations, HG §19-310.
Designated state official.
Qualifications of educational personnel, ED §6-604.
Designatee of the commissioner.
Health insurance complaint process, IN §15-10A-01.
Designation.
Community action agencies, HS §8-101.
Design coordination.
Architects, BOP §3-101.
Certified interior designers, BOP §8-101.
Engineers, BOP §14-101.
Landscape architects, BOP §9-101.
Land surveyors, BOP §15-101.
Designee.
Alimony, FL §11-109.
Substance abuse prevention and treatment, HG §8-901.
Destitute adult child, FL §13-101.
Destitute parent, FL §13-101.
Destructive device, CR §4-501.
Detention.
Juvenile causes, CJ §3-8A-01.
Determination.
Property tax.
Appeal procedures, TP §14-506.
Determination date.
Business combinations.
Corporations, CA §3-603.
Detoxification facility, HG §8-101.
Developed land area.
Cemeteries, BR §5-602.
Developer.
Chesapeake Bay critical area and Atlantic coastal bays critical area protection programs, NR §8-1802.
Condominiums, RP §11-101.
Cooperative housing corporation, CA §5-6B-01.
Time-sharing, RP §11A-101.
Developer control board.
Time-sharing, RP §11A-101.
Development.
Chesapeake Bay critical area and Atlantic coastal bays critical area protection programs, NR §8-1802.
Homeowners association, RP §11B-101.
Land use, 66B §1.00.
Maryland food center, 41 §13-104.
Sewerage bonds, EN §9-801.
State finance.
Information technology, SF §3-402.
Washington suburban sanitary district.
Construction of subdivision lines, 29 §3-101.1.
Youghiogheny river, NR §8-409.
Zoning and planning, 66B §1.00.
Developmental disability, HG §7-101.
Children in need of assistance, CJ §3-801.
Courts, CJ §3-1001.
Juvenile cases, CJ §3-8A-01.
Developmentally disabled individual.
State funded corporation serving, SF §7-405.
Development costs.
Community development administration, HS §4-201.
Maryland housing fund, HS §3-205.
Neighborhood business development program, HS §6-301.
Rental housing production program, HS §4-1501.

DEFINED TERMS —Cont'd
Development permit, SG §11-101.
Development project.
Permits, SG §11-101.
Development rights.
Transfer taxes.
Agricultural land, TP §13-306.
Washington county, TP §13-501.
Development rights and responsibilities agreement.
Land use, 66B §1.00.
Montgomery county, 28 §7-121.
Zoning and planning, 66B §1.00.
Device.
Food and drugs, HG §21-101.
Pesticide applicators, AG §5-201.
Pharmacists and pharmacies, HO §12-101.
Devisee.
Transfer-on-death security registration, ET §16-101.
Diagnostically certified optometrist, HO §11-101.
Diagnostic services.
Health insurance, IN §15-121.
Diameter.
Pine tree reforestation, NR §5-501.
Diesel vehicles, TR §23-401.
Dietetic rehabilitation committee, HO §5-314.
Dietitian-nutritionist, HO §5-101.
Die without issue, ET §4-410.
Dining area.
Alcoholic beverages.
Montgomery county, 2B §6-101.
Restaurants and hotels, 2B §6-101.
Direct access.
National crime prevention and privacy compact, CP §10-239.
Direct care expenses.
Health insurance, behavioral health care services, IN §15-127.
Direct care staff.
Developmental disabilities, HG §7-205.
Direct damages.
Computer information transactions, CL §22-102.
Direct grant fund.
Family day care homes, FL §5-550.
Direct grants.
Community colleges.
State and county aid, ED §16-305.
Direct incentive grant.
Child care quality incentive grant program, FL §5-594.
Direct labor hours.
Products made by blind persons, CL §14-2801.
Direct loan agreement.
Unlawful subleasing of motor vehicle, CR §8-408.
Direct molding process.
Hulls of vessels, CL §11-1001.
Director.
Corporations, CA §§1-101, 2-418.
Transportation compacts, TR §10-204.
Water resources, EN §5-101.
Directory information.
Medical records, HG §4-301.
Directory publisher.
Recycling, EN §9-1709.
Directory stock.
Recycling, EN §9-1709.
Direct payments.
Health insurance, behavioral health care services, IN §15-127.

DEFINED TERMS —Cont'd

Direct rollover.
State retirement and pension system, SPP §21-601.

Direct service employee.
Developmental disabilities, mental health, child welfare and juvenile services workforce tuition assistance program, ED §18-2101.

Direct supervision.
Board of veterinary medical examiners, AG §2-301.
Health occupations, HO §1-301.
Occupational therapists, HO §10-101.
Pharmacists and pharmacies, HO §12-101.

Direct wine seller, 2B §7.5-101.
Alcoholic beverage tax, TG §5-101.

Dirt bikes, TR §25-102.1.

Disability, SG §9-1101.
Children generally, FL §5-101.
Condominiums, RP §11-137.
Employment discrimination, 49B §15.
Housing discrimination, 49B §20.
Judicial disability and sanctionable conduct, CJA Rule 16-803.
Rehabilitation services, ED §21-301.

Disability benefit.
Health insurance, disability and adverse benefit determination, IN §15-1010.

Disabled.
Elections, EL §1-101.
Workers' compensation.
Vocational rehabilitation, LE §9-670.

Disabled person.
Adult protective services, FL §14-101.
Adult residential environment program, 88A §138.
Domestic violence.
Address confidentiality program, FL §4-519.
Estates and trusts, ET §13-101.
Rehabilitation services, HG §20-108.

Disabled public safety employee.
Student financial assistance, ED §18-601.

Disabled veteran.
Property tax credit, TP §9-104.
Property tax exemptions, TP §7-208.

Disablement.
Workers' compensation.
Occupational disease, LE §9-502.

Disadvantaged child.
Education, ED §8-101.

Disbarment.
Discipline of attorneys, CJA Rule 16-701.

Discharge.
Controlled hazardous substances, EN §7-201.
Hazardous substance.
Immunity of persons assisting in controlling, CJ §5-617.
Sanitary facilities, EN §9-101.
Water pollution, EN §4-401.

Discharge check.
Consumer protection.
Return of checks, CL §14-1312.

Discharge permit.
Water pollution, EN §9-301.

Disciplinary action.
Juvenile justice monitoring unit, SG §6-401.

Disclaimant.
Disclaimer of property interests, ET §9-201.

Disclaimed interests.
Disclaimer of property interests, ET §9-201.

Disclaimer.
Disclaimer of property interests, ET §9-201.

DEFINED TERMS —Cont'd

Disclose or disclosure.
Medical records, HG §4-301.

Disclosure statement.
Adult dependent care programs, HG §19-1901.
Charitable organizations, BR §6-101.
Door-to-door solicitation, CL §14-2601.

Discounted present value.
Structured settlements, transfer of payment rights, CJ §5-1101.

Discrimination.
Commercial discrimination, SF §19-103.

Discriminatory boycott, CL §11-102.

Discriminatory housing practice, 49B §20.

Disease.
Honeybees, AG §5-501.

Dishonor.
Letters of credit, CL §5-102.

Disinfector.
Bedding, HG §24-401.

Dislocated worker.
Workforce investment act, LE §11-503.

Disparity amount.
Developmental disabilities, HG §7-307.

Dispense.
Controlled dangerous substances, CR §5-101.
Pharmacists and pharmacies, HO §12-101.

Dispensing.
Pharmacists and pharmacies, HO §12-101.

Displaced homemaker.
Family law, FL §4-601.
Waiver of tuition.
Community colleges, ED §16-106.

Displaced person.
Eminent domain, RP §12-201.

Displacing agency.
Eminent domain, RP §12-201.

Display of license.
Drivers' licenses, TR §16-112.

Disposable wages.
Attachment of wages, CL §15-601.1.

Disposal.
Radioactive waste, EN §7-301.

Disposal system.
Sanitary facilities, EN §9-101.

Disposition hearing.
Children in need of assistance, CJ §3-801.
Juvenile causes, CJ §3-8A-01.

Disqualification.
Motor vehicles, TR §11-111.1.

Disqualified person.
Advance health care directives, HG §5-602.
Professional service corporations, CA §5-101.

Disqualified stockholder.
Professional service corporations, CA §5-114.

Disqualifying crime.
Firearms, PS §5-101.

Disqualifying work.
Maryland historical trust, rehabilitation tax credits, SF §5A-303.

Disseminate.
Criminal justice information system, CP §10-201.

Distilled spirits.
Taxation, TG §5-101.

Distiller.
Property tax, TP §8-112.

Distressed area.
Maryland housing fund, HS §3-202.

Distress for rent, RP §8-301.

Distress sale, CL §11-1101.

DEFINED TERMS —Cont'd
Distributable cash flow.
Income tax, TG §10-102.1.
Distribute.
Commercial feed, AG §6-101.
Commercial fertilizers, AG §6-201.
Controlled dangerous substances, CR §5-101.
Crimes against public health and safety, CR
    §10-101.
Obscene matter, CR §11-201.
    To minors, CR §11-203.
Pharmacists and pharmacies, HO §12-101.
Distribution.
Corporations, CA §2-301.
Partnerships, revised act, CA §9A-101.
Distribution of accessible information.
Disabled persons, SF §3-901.
Distribution organization.
Statewide nutrition assistance program, 88A
    §130A.
Distribution permit.
Pharmacists and pharmacies, HO §12-602.
Distribution territory.
Electric customer choice and competition act, PUC
    §7-501.
Distributor, CL §11-1301.
Agricultural liming materials and gypsum, AG
    §6-301.
Egg law, AG §4-301.
Elections, EL §1-101.
Gasohol and gasoline products marketing, CL
    §11-301.
Motor fuel tax, TG §9-301.
Motor vehicles, TR §§11-112, 15-201.
Pesticide registration and labeling, AG §5-101.
Toxics, EN §9-1901.
District.
BWI zoning district, TR §5-509.
Historic area zoning, 66B §8.01.
Maryland transit administration, TR §7-101.
Potomac water authority, EN §5-401.
Sanitary commissions, EN §9-601.
District account.
Sanitary commissions, EN §9-660.
Diversion.
Susquehanna river basin compact, EN §5-301.
Divided highway, TR §11-113.
Diving apparatus.
Oysters and clams, NR §4-1001.
Division.
Used vehicle inspection, TR §23-101.
Division custody.
Consecutive and concurrent sentences, multiple
    jurisdictions, COR §9-202.
Division of correction, COR §1-101.
Division of parole and probation, COR §1-101.
DNA.
DNA database system, PS §2-501.
DNA technology fund, 41 §4-301.
Postconviction review, CP §8-201.
DNA profile.
Evidence, CJ §10-915.
DNA record.
DNA database system, PS §2-501.
DNA sample.
DNA database system, PS §2-501.
DNA technology equipment.
DNA technology fund, 41 §4-301.
Do construction business.
Business licenses, BR §17-601.
Doctoral degree in psychology, HO §18-101.

DEFINED TERMS —Cont'd
Document.
Administration of courts.
    Form interrogatories, Form 2.
Letters of credit, CL §5-102.
Secured transactions, CL §9-102.
Transfer taxes, TP §13-205.
Documentary draft.
Bank deposits and collections, CL §4-104.
Document ballot, EL §1-101.
Document of title.
Computer information transactions, CL §22-102.
Uniform commercial code, CL §1-201.
**Documents which evidence the merger or
    consolidation of foreign corporations,
    foreign limited liability companies or
    foreign limited partnerships.**
Recordation taxes, TP §12-101.
Transfer taxes, TP §13-101.
Doing public business.
Disclosures by persons doing public business, EL
    §14-101.
Dollar roll transaction.
Investments of life insurers, IN §5-511.
Domain name.
Spam, CR §3-805.1.
Domestic corporation.
Property tax, TP §1-101.
Domestic individual.
Foreign discriminatory boycotts, CL §11-102.
Domestic insurer, IN §1-101.
Risk based capital standards for insurers, IN
    §4-301.
Domestic jurisdiction.
Investments of life insurers, IN §5-511.
**Domestic limited liability company, CA §§3-101,
    4A-101.**
Real estate investment trusts, CA §8-501.1.
Domestic limited partnership, CA §3-101.
Partnerships, revised act, CA §9A-101.
Real estate investment trusts, CA §8-501.1.
Domestic partnership, CA §3-101.
Real estate investment trust, CA §8-501.1.
Domestic violence.
Local domestic violence fatality review teams, FL
    §4-701.
Domestic violence program.
Local domestic violence fatality review teams, FL
    §4-701.
Domicile.
Motor vehicles, TR §11-113.1.
Risk retention groups, IN §25-101.
Domicile of an alien insurer, IN §6-302.
Domiciliary care.
Hospitals, HG §19-301.
Domiciliary state.
Insurer liquidation, rehabilitation, etc., IN §9-201.
Interstate insurance product regulation compact,
    IN §29-101.
Do not resuscitate order, HG §5-601.
Door-to-door sale, CL §14-301.
Door-to-door solicitation, CL §14-2601.
Door-to-door transportation.
Maryland senior ride demonstration program, TR
    §7-1001.
Dormitory.
Sprinkler systems, PS §9-201.
Double-faced.
Outdoor advertising, TR §8-725.
Down payment.
Land installment contracts, RP §10-101.

DEFINED TERMS —Cont'd

Down payment —Cont'd
  Layaway sales, CL §14-1101.
  Retail installment sales, CL §12-601.
Downtown plaza, 2B §9-223.
Draft.
  Bank deposits and collections, CL §4-104.
  Consumer protection, CL §13-318.
  Negotiable instruments, CL §§3-103, 3-104.
  Return of checks to customers, FI §5-513.
  Sales, CL §3-104.
Drafthouse.
  Alcoholic beverages, 2B §§8-701, 8-702.
Drawee.
  Negotiable instruments, CL §3-103.
Drawer.
  Bad checks, CR §8-101.
  Consumer protection, CL §13-318.
  Negotiable instruments, CL §3-103.
Draw schedule.
  Custom home protection, RP §10-501.
Dredge.
  Aquaculture, NR §4-11A-01.
  Oysters and clams, NR §§4-1001, 4-1101.
Dredge boat.
  Oysters and clams, NR §4-1001.
Dredged material.
  Chesapeake Bay and tributaries, EN §5-1101.
  Dredged material disposal alternatives program, 83A §6-801.
Dredged material reuse facility.
  Dredged material disposal alternatives program, 83A §6-801.
Dredging.
  Wetlands and riparian rights, EN §16-101.
Drift.
  Mines and mining, EN §15-101.
Drinking water loan fund.
  Water quality financing, EN §9-1601.
Drive, TR §11-114.
Driveaway operation.
  Brake equipment, TR §22-301.
Driver, TR §11-115.
Driver certificate.
  Controlled hazardous substances, EN §7-201.
Driver education program, TR §16-501.
Driver's license, TR §11-116.
  Anatomical gift act, TR §12-303.
  Elections, EL §1-101.
  Juvenile causes, CJ §3-8A-19.
  Underage drinking, CR §10-119.
Drivers' school, TR §§15-701, 16-501.
Driving instructor, TR §15-801.
DROP.
  Law enforcement officers' pension system, SPP §26-401.1.
  State police retirement system, SPP §24-401.1.
DROP member.
  Law enforcement officers' pension system, SPP §26-401.1.
  State police retirement system, SPP §24-401.1.
Drop-off site.
  Prescription drug repository program, HG §15-601.
Drug, CR §5-101.
  Alcohol and drug abuse, HG §8-101.
  Drug induced conduct, CR §5-624.
  Food and drugs, HG §21-101.
  Food, drugs and cosmetics, HG §21-1113.
  Local department guardianships and adoptions, FL §5-323.

DEFINED TERMS —Cont'd

Drug —Cont'd
  Port administration drug-free workplace, TR §6-102.1.
Drug abuse, HG §8-101.
  Discrimination by health insurers, HG §19-703.1; IN §15-802.
Drug crime.
  Financial transactions involving proceeds of drug crime, CR §5-623.
Drug dependence, HG §8-101.
Drug dependent person, CR §5-101.
Drug kingpin, CR §5-613.
Drug misuse, HG §8-101.
Drug or alcohol screening test.
  Altering results of drug or alcohol screening, CR §10-111.
Drug trafficking crime, CR §5-621.
  Bulletproof body armor, CR §4-106.
Dual agent.
  Real estate brokers, BOP §17-530.
Dual eligibility.
  Medicaid, HG §15-132.
Due process complaint.
  Disabled student placement, ED §8-413.
Duly designated agency.
  Patuxent river watershed, NR §8-1301.
Dumbwaiter.
  Elevator safety, PS §12-801.
Dumping site.
  Dumping site surveillance systems, CR §10-112.
Dump service registration.
  Motor vehicles, TR §13-919.
Dunnaged boat.
  Oysters and clams, NR §4-1001.
Duplicate.
  Evidence, CJ §10-103.
Durable medical equipment.
  Health care assistance, HG §15-129.
Durable power of attorney, ET §13-601.
Duty of support.
  Uniform interstate family support act, FL §10-301.
  URESA, FL §10-301.
Dwelling.
  Arson and burning, CR §6-101.
  Burglary, CR §6-201.
  Historic St. Mary's City commission, ED §24-513.
  Property tax.
    Baltimore City, TP §§9-105, 9-304.
    Credit for spouse of fallen rescue worker, TP §9-210.
    Elderly or disabled renters, TP §9-102.
    Homeowners credit, TP §9-104.
    Homestead credit, TP §9-105.
    Rezoned real property, TP §8-226.
    Unoccupied new or rehabilitated dwellings, TP §§9-207, 9-401.
Dwelling house.
  Property tax exemptions.
    Blind individual, TP §7-207.
    Disabled veteran, TP §7-208.
Dwelling type.
  Charles county, 66B §14.05.
Dwelling unit.
  Energy allocation equipment, PUC §7-304.
  Gas or electric meters, PUC §7-303.
  Sprinkler systems, PS §9-201.
  Submetering, PUC §7-303.
Dyed diesel fuel, BR §10-101.

DEFINED TERMS —Cont'd

Early child care and education enhancement grants.
Judith P. Hoyer early child care and education enhancement program, ED §5-217.

Early termination cost.
Motorized wheelchair warranty enforcement, CL §14-2701.

Early termination savings.
Motorized wheelchair warranty enforcement, CL §14-2701.

Earnable compensation.
Pensions, SPP §20-101.

Earned premium.
Nonprofit health service plans, IN §14-117.

Earnings.
Support, FL §10-101.

Earnings withholding notice.
Support and maintenance, FL §10-120.

Earnings withholding order.
Support and maintenance, FL §10-120.

Easement.
Property tax, TP §8-219.

Easily removed.
Rechargeable batteries, EN §6-1101.

Eastern shore.
Code counties, 25B §2.

E-commerce.
E-commerce, advisory board, SG §9-2201.

Economically depressed or physically deteriorated area.
Housing authorities, HS §12-101.

Economically disadvantaged individuals.
Procurement, minority business enterprises, SF §14-301.
Tax credits, TG §10-702.

Economic damages, CJ §11-109.
Health care malpractice, CJ §3-2A-01.

Economic development project.
Commercial discrimination, SF §19-103.
Property taxes, TP §7-504.3.

Economic impact.
Alcoholic beverages, 2B §16-507.

Economic impact analysis.
Bills of general assembly, SG §§2-1505.1, 2-1505.2.

Economic impact analysis rating.
Bills of general assembly, SG §§2-1505.1, 2-1505.2.

Ecosystem.
Endangered species, NR §§4-2A-01, 10-2A-01.
Natural resources, NR §4-205.1.
Nongame and endangered species conservation, NR §10-2A-01.

Education.
Cancer prevention, education, screening and treatment program, HG §13-1101.

Educational decision making process.
Handicapped children, ED §8-412.

Educational institution.
Public ethics, SG §15-523.
Unemployment insurance, LE §8-101.

Educational personnel.
Qualifications, ED §6-604.

Educational program.
Higher education, ED §10-101.
Respiratory care, HO §14-5A-08.

Educational purpose.
Motor vehicles, TR §11-117.
Public recreation on private and local government lands, NR §5-1101.

DEFINED TERMS —Cont'd

Educational service.
McAuliffe teacher education award, ED §18-703.

Educational service agency.
Unemployment insurance, LE §8-909.

Educational services.
Procurement, unsolicited proposals, SF §13-107.1.

Educator.
Filing charges against, CJ §2-608.

Educator or human service worker.
Child abuse and neglect, FL §5-701.

Effective date.
Correctional officers' retirement system, SPP §31-2B-01.
Law enforcement officers' pension system.
Participation in, SPP §31-2A-01.
Local fire and police pension system, SPP §31-201.
State retirement and pension system, SPP §31-101.

Effective date of legislative authority for the acquisition of the property.
Eminent domain, RP §12-105.

Effective date of selection.
State retirement and pension system, SPP §29-422.

Effective rate of simple interest.
Interest in usury, CL §12-101.

Effluent limitation.
Sanitary facilities, EN §9-101.

Elderly.
Elections, EL §1-101.

Elderly and handicapped person.
Mass transit, TR §7-705.
Transportation, TR §2-103.3.

Elderly citizen.
Senior citizen activities centers capital improvement grants, 70B §26.

Elderly household.
Development finance division, HS §4-101.

Elderly individual.
Health care, HG §14-201.
State funded corporation serving, SF §7-405.

Elderly person.
Home care services, 88A §85.
Landlord and tenant, RP §8-214.

Elderly rental housing project.
Development finance division, HS §4-101.

Elected member.
Garrett county board of education, ED §3-601.
Montgomery county board of education, ED §3-901.

Election, EL §1-101.
Unemployment insurance.
Contributions, LE §8-601.

Election authority.
Petitions, EL §6-101.

Election cycle, EL §1-101.

Electrical installation.
Electrical code, PS §12-601.

Electrical systems.
New home warranties, RP §10-601.

Electric company, PUC §1-101.
Public utility interference, CR §6-303.

Electricity supplier.
Income tax, TG §10-704.1.

Electric or communication facility.
Conversion of overhead facility to underground locations, PUC §12-301.

Electric personal assistive mobility device or EPAMD.
Traffic laws, TR §21-101.

DEFINED TERMS —Cont'd
Electric plant, PUC §1-101.
  Electric cooperatives, CA §5-601.
Electric service.
  Conversion of overhead facilities to underground
    locations, PUC §12-301.
Electrologist, HO §8-6B-01.
Electrology instructor, HO §8-6B-01.
Electronic.
  Computer information transactions, CL §22-102.
  Electronic transactions, CL §21-101.
Electronic agent.
  Computer information transactions, CL §22-102.
  Electronic transactions, CL §21-101.
Electronic chattel paper.
  Secured transactions, CL §9-102.
Electronic communication.
  Evidence, CJ §10-401.
  Pen registers and trap and trace devices, CJ
    §10-4B-01.
Electronic communication service, CJ §10-401.
  Pen registers and trap and trace devices, CJ
    §10-4B-01.
Electronic communications system.
  Evidence, CJ §10-401.
Electronic error.
  Computer information transactions, CL §22-214.
Electronic mail.
  Misuse, CR §3-805.
Electronic mail service provider.
  Spam, CR §3-805.1.
Electronic, mechanical or other device.
  Evidence, CJ §10-401.
Electronic message.
  Computer information transactions, CL §22-102.
Electronic payment.
  Homeowners' associations, RP §11B-114.
  Premium finance companies, IN §23-307.1.
Electronic postmark certificate, CL §21-118.1.
Electronic record.
  Electronic transactions, CL §21-101.
Electronic security system.
  Code grabbing devices, CR §7-301.
Electronic signature.
  Electronic transactions, CL §21-101.
Electronic storage.
  Evidence, CJ §10-401.
Electronic storage format.
  Elections, EL §1-101.
Electronic terminal.
  Banking institutions, FI §5-502.
  Savings and loan associations, FI §9-310.
Electronic toll collection.
  Failure to pay electronic toll, TR §21-1414.
Electronic transactions, SG §6-201.
Electronic transmission.
  Condominiums, RP §11-101.
  Cooperative housing corporation, CA §5-6B-01.
  Corporations, CA §1-101.
  Homeowners' associations, RP §11B-101.
Elementary and secondary education, ED
    §1-101.
Elevated blood level.
  Lead poisoning, EN §6-801.
Elevator.
  Elevator safety, PS §12-801.
Elevator contractor.
  Elevator safety, PS §12-801.
Elevator mechanic.
  Elevator safety, PS §12-801.

DEFINED TERMS —Cont'd
Elevator refinisher.
  Elevator safety, PS §12-801.
Elevator renovator contractor.
  Elevator safety, PS §12-801.
Elevator renovator mechanic.
  Elevator safety, PS §12-801.
Elevator unit.
  Elevator safety, PS §12-801.
Eligibility period.
  Unemployment insurance.
    Extended benefits, LE §8-1101.
Eligibility service.
  Pensions, SPP §20-101.
Eligible applicant.
  Voluntary cleanup program, EN §7-501.
Eligible assessment.
  Property tax.
    Enterprise zones, TP §9-103.
Eligible building.
  Income tax credits, TG §10-722.
Eligible business.
  Energy efficiency and economic development loan
    program, SG §9-20A-01.
  Industrial development financing authority, 83A
    §5-927.
Eligible child.
  Adoption subsidy act, FL §5-401.
  Developmental disabilities, HG §7-701.
Eligible children.
  Fraternal benefit societies, IN §8-428.
Eligible client.
  Legal services corporation, 10 §45C.
Eligible consortium.
  Technology for education, ED §7-901.
Eligible contract.
  Procurement.
    Hiring agreements, SF §13-224.
Eligible costs.
  Bay restoration fund, EN §9-1605.2.
  Water pollution control, AG §8-701.
Eligible county.
  Agricultural land preservation foundation, AG
    §2-508.
Eligible-customer generator.
  Net energy metering, PUC §7-306.
Eligible donor.
  Community colleges.
    Contributions, ED §16-317.
Eligible economic development project.
  One Maryland economic development tax credits,
    83A §5-1501.
Eligible educational institution.
  College investment plan, ED §18-19A-01.
Eligible employee.
  Adult dependent care programs, HG §19-1901.
  Health insurance portability and accountability.
    Dependents in group policies, IN §15-1406.1.
  Small employer health insurance, IN §15-1201.
  State retirement and pension system, SPP
    §30-101.
    Supplemental retirement plans.
      Optional defined contribution system, SPP
        §32-101.
Eligible employment.
  Math/science student core, ED §18-1601.
Eligible field of employment.
  Student financial assistance.
    Repayment program, ED §18-1501.
Eligible for free or reduced price meals.
  Schools, compensatory education grants, ED
    §5-207.

DEFINED TERMS —Cont'd

Eligible governmental unit.
Correctional officers' retirement system, SPP §31-2B-01.
Law enforcement officers' pension system.
Participation in, SPP §31-2A-01.
Local fire and police pension system, SPP §31-201.
State retirement and pension system, SPP §31-101.

Eligible gubernatorial ticket.
Public campaign financing, EL §15-102.

Eligible homebuyer.
Down payment and settlement expense loan program, HS §4-301.

Eligible individuals.
Breast cancer program, HG §20-116.
Children's health program, HG §15-301.1.
Community attendant services and supports program, 41 §6-7A-01.
Community mental health or developmental disabilities services providers, HG §16-201.2.
Developmental disabilities, HG §7-709.
Health insurance portability, IN §15-1301.
Maryland health insurance plan, IN §14-501.
Senior prescription drug assistance program, IN §14-510.

Eligible institution.
Child care provider grant program, ED §18-705.
Community colleges.
Contributions, ED §16-317.
Health manpower shortage incentive grant program, ED §18-803.
Higher education.
Private donation incentive program, ED §17-301.
Maryland HOPE scholarships, ED §18-2301.
Maryland teacher scholarships, ED §18-2201.
McAuliffe teacher education award, ED §18-703.
Mental health professional grant, ED §18-707.
Nursing scholarships, ED §18-706.
Physical and occupational therapists and assistants grant program, ED §18-704.
Physician assistants and nurse practitioners.
Student financial assistance, ED §18-802.
Workforce shortage student tuition grants, ED §18-708.

Eligible institution of higher education.
College savings plan of Maryland, ED §18-1901.

Eligible landowner.
Woodland incentives program, NR §5-301.

Eligible local bus service.
Local bus systems grants, TR §10-207.

Eligible low income taxpayer.
Income tax, TG §10-709.

Eligible obligation.
Credit unions, FI §6-609.

Eligible organization.
Nursing scholarships, ED §18-706.
Physician assistants and nurse practitioners.
Student financial assistance, ED §18-802.

Eligible party.
Approved paid work-based learning programs, ED §21-501.

Eligible person.
Developmental disabilities, HG §7-706.
Patuxent institution, COR §4-101.

Eligible population.
Substance abuse treatment outcomes partnership fund, HG §8-6C-01.

Eligible presiding officer.
Legislative pension plan, SG Title 2 Subtitle 3 (note).

DEFINED TERMS —Cont'd

Eligible private contribution.
Public campaign financing, EL §15-102.

Eligible private donor.
Higher education.
Private donation incentive program, ED §17-301.

Eligible program.
Child care provider grant program, ED §18-705.
Community colleges.
Contributions, ED §16-317.
Higher education.
Private donation incentive program, ED §17-301.
Physical and occupational therapists and assistants grant program, ED §18-704.

Eligible project cost.
One Maryland economic development tax credits, 83A §5-1501.

Eligible property.
Voluntary cleanup program, EN §7-501.

Eligible retirement plan.
State retirement and pension system, SPP §21-601.

Eligible rollover distribution.
State retirement and pension system, SPP §21-601.

Eligible school.
National board certified teacher pilot program, ED §6-118.
Principal fellowship and leadership development program, ED §6-116.

Eligible start-up costs.
One Maryland economic development tax credits, 83A §5-1501.

Eligible subscriber.
Telephone lifeline service, PUC §8-201.

Eligible veteran.
State personnel.
Skilled service and professional service appointments, SPP §7-207.

Elude.
Boats and boating.
Enforcement of subtitle, NR §8-727.

EMaryland marketplace.
Procurement, SF §13-101.

Emergency.
Adult protective services, FL §14-101.
Air quality, EN §2-101.
Arrest process, CP §2-101.
Banking institutions.
Bank holidays, FI §5-707.
Emergency management, governor's powers, PS §14-307.
Estates and trusts, ET §13-101.
Interference with emergency communication, CR §9-601.
Juvenile curfew, 25B §13C-1.
Maryland emergency management agency (MEMA), PS §14-101.
Medical records, HG §4-301.
Pesticide application in schools, AG §5-208.1.
Radiation, EN §8-101.
State police, powers, PS §2-412.
Workers' compensation, LE §9-232.1.

Emergency evaluee.
Emergency mental health evaluations, HG §10-620.

Emergency facility.
Mental health evaluations, HG §10-620.

DEFINED TERMS —Cont'd
Emergency family maintenance.
Domestic violence, FL §4-501.
Emergency management.
Maryland emergency management agency
(MEMA), PS §14-101.
Emergency management and civil defense.
Emergency shelters, CJ §5-602.
Emergency medical condition.
Health insurance coverage, IN §15-126.
Emergency medical dispatcher (EMD), ED
§13-516.
Emergency medical services, ED §13-516.
Emergency medical services provider, ED
§13-516.
Emergency medical technician-basic (EMT-B),
ED §13-516.
**Emergency medical technician-paramedic
(EMT-P),** ED §13-516.
Health occupations, HO §14-305.
Emergency medical treatment.
Child abuse and neglect, FL §5-712.
Emergency road service.
Motor clubs, IN §26-101.
Emergency service.
Fire-rescue education and training, ED §11-501.
Negligent operation of emergency vehicle, TR
§19-103.
Emergency services personnel, CJ §2-608.
Emergency service transporter.
Medicaid, HG §15-114.1.
Emergency vehicle, TR §11-118.
Negligent operation liability, TR §19-103.
Emissions control program, TR §23-201.
Emissions equipment, TR §23-201.
**Emissions equipment and misfueling
inspection,** TR §23-201.
Emissions inspector.
Diesel vehicles, TR §23-401.
Emissions related repair, TR §23-201.
Emissions standard, TR §23-201.
Air quality, EN §2-101.
Diesel vehicles, TR §23-401.
Emissions test.
Diesel vehicles, TR §23-401.
Employee.
Attachment of wages, CL §15-601.
Child care centers, FL §5-586.
Child care facilities, FL §5-560.
Counties and municipal corporations, 24 §1-107.
Drug-free workplace program, TR §6-102.1.
Employment discrimination, 49B §15.
Firefighters and emergency medical personnel.
Judicial review of disciplinary decisions, LE
§4-601.
Franchise health insurance policies, IN §15-1102.
Group health insurance, IN §15-302.
Health care payroll assessment, LE §8.5-101.
Health care worker whistleblower protection, HO
§1-501.
Health program integrity and recovery activities,
HG §2-501.
Labor relations.
Mass transit, TR §7-601.
Local government tort claims act, CJ §5-301.
Negotiable instruments, CL §3-405.
Occupational safety and health, LE §5-101.
Information about dangerous substances, LE
§5-401.
Pawnbrokers, BR §12-101.

DEFINED TERMS —Cont'd
Employee —Cont'd
Public safety officers.
Employment rights, LE §4-501.
Public works contracts, SF §17-201.
Railroad safety and health, LE §5.5-101.
Savings and loan associations, FI §9-101.
State personnel.
Disciplinary actions, SPP §11-101.
State retirement and pension system, SPP
§31-101.
Whistleblower protection for state contractor
employees, SF §11-301.
Employee assistance program.
Private review agents, IN §15-10B-01.
Employee holiday.
State personnel, SPP §9-201.
Employee membership entity.
Elections, EL §13-241.
Employee occupant.
Child care centers, FL §5-586.
Employee organization.
Insurance administrators, IN §8-301.
Labor relations.
Community colleges, ED §16-412.
Prince George's county public employment
relations, ED §16-414.1.
Public safety officers.
Employment rights, LE §4-501.
School employees, ED §6-401.
School personnel, ED §§6-401, 6-501.
State personnel, SPP §3-101.
Employee retirement system.
Income tax, TG §10-209.
Employees' pension system, SPP §20-101.
Employee sponsored plan.
Health insurance portability, IN §15-1301.
Employees' retirement system, SPP §20-101.
Employees' system.
Employee retirement and pension systems, SPP
§21-305.3.
State retirement and pension system, SPP
§§21-305, 31-101.
Employee theft.
Shoplifting and employee theft, CJ §3-1301.
Employer.
Administration of courts.
Domestic relations interrogatories, Form 4.
Adoption leave, LE §3-801.
Agriculture, AG §1-201.
Child care facilities, FL §5-560.
Commercial drivers' licenses, TR §16-803.
Economic stabilization act, LE §11-301.
Employment discrimination, 49B §15.
Grievance procedures, SPP §12-101.
Health care payroll assessment, LE §8.5-101.
Insurance administrators, IN §8-301.
Lie detector tests, LE §3-702.
Municipal corporations, 23A §48.
Nurses, HO §8-504.
Occupational safety and health, LE §5-101.
Information about dangerous substances, LE
§5-401.
Political subdivisions, 24 §1-106.
Public ethics, SG §15-102.
Public safety officers.
Employment rights, LE §4-501.
Sex discrimination.
Wages, LE §3-301.
Support, FL §10-101.
Tax withholding, TG §10-905.

DEFINED TERMS —Cont'd
Employer —Cont'd
Unemployment insurance, LE §8-101.
Wages and hours, LE §3-401.
   Payment and collection, LE §3-501.
Whistleblower protection for state contractor
   employees, SF §11-301.
Workers' compensation, TG §1-204.
   Compliance, LE §1-202.
Employer association.
Unemployment insurance.
   Work sharing, LE §8-1201.
Employer industry category.
Unemployment insurance.
   Contributions, LE §8-609.
Employer pickup contribution.
Pension, SPP §20-101.
Employer school system.
Principal fellowship and leadership development
   program, ED §6-116.
Employer sponsored plan.
Health insurance portability, IN §§15-1301,
   15-1401.
Employing institution.
State retirement and pension system, SPP
   §30-101.
Employing unit.
Unemployment insurance, LE §8-101.
Employment.
Sex offender registration, CP §11-701.
Employment agency, BR §9-101.
Employment discrimination, 49B §15.
Employment purposes.
Consumer credit reporting agencies, CL §14-1201.
EMS.
Public safety officers.
   Employment rights, LE §4-501.
Enable use.
Computer information transactions, CL §22-602.
Enabling Act.
State debt, SF §§8-101, 8-201.
Enclosure.
Stray domestic animals, AG §3-602.
Encumbrance.
Secured transactions, CL §9-102.
Endangered highway, TR §24-204.
Endangered species, NR §10-2A-01.
Fish and fisheries, NR §4-2A-01.
Endangered species act, NR §10-2A-01.
Endorsement.
Commercial drivers' licenses, TR §16-803.
Endorsement contract.
Athlete agents, BR §4-401.
Endowment.
Higher education.
   Private donation incentive program, ED
   §17-301.
Endowment fund.
Management of institutional funds act, ET
   §15-401.
End-stage condition.
Health care decisions, HG §5-601.
Energy allocation system.
Apartments, PUC §7-304.
Energy audit.
Industrial development financing, 83A §5-901.
Energy code.
Energy conservation building standards, PUC
   §7-401.
Energy conservation project.
Community development administration, HS
   §4-201.

DEFINED TERMS —Cont'd
Energy conservation project —Cont'd
Industrial development financing, 83A §5-901.
Maryland housing fund, HS §3-201.
Energy-consumption analysis, SF §4-801.
Energy costs savings.
Community energy loan program, SG §9-2101.
Energy efficiency and economic development loan
   program, SG §9-20A-01.
Energy emergency.
Emergency management, governor's powers, PS
   §14-301.
Energy assistance program act, 41 §6-402.
State standby petroleum fuel set-aside program,
   PS §14-501.
Energy performance contract.
Procurement, SF §11-101.
Energy performance index, SF §4-801.
Energy project.
Industrial development financing, 83A §5-901.
Engage in the business of a dealer.
Motor fuel tax, TG §9-301.
Engage in the business of a distributor.
Motor fuel tax, TG §9-301.
Engage in the business of an out-of-state
   vendor.
Sales tax, TG §11-701.
Engage in the business of a retail vendor.
Sales tax, TG §11-701.
Engage in the business of a special fuel seller.
Motor fuel tax, TG §9-301.
Engage in the business of a turbine fuel seller.
Motor fuel tax, TG §9-301.
Engage in the business of providing electrical
   services.
Electricians, BOP §6-101.
Engage in the operation of a cemetery, BR
   §5-101.
Engagement review.
Accountants.
   Peer review, BOP §2-4A-01.
Engineering services.
Procurement, SF §11-101.
Engineer's analysis.
Waterproofing.
   Consumer protection, CL §14-12A-01.
Enhanced 911 system.
911 emergency telephone system, PS §1-301.
Enhanced nutrient removal.
Water quality financing, EN §9-1601.
Enology.
Winery and grape growers' advisory commission,
   AG §10-1201.
Enrollee.
Dental plan organizations, IN §14-401.
Health insurance, IN §15-121.
Health insurance provider panels, IN §15-112.
Health maintenance organizations.
   Payments to providers not under contract, HG
   §19-710.1.
Insurance, IN §27-910.
Medical assistance, HG §15-101.
Medicare option prescription drug program, HG
   §15-124.3.
Senior prescription drug assistance program, IN
   §14-510.
Enrollment date.
Health insurance portability, IN §§15-1301,
   15-1401.
Enter.
Burglary, CR §6-201.

DEFINED TERMS —Cont'd

Enterprise.
Franchises, 83A §5-1041.

Enterprise zone, 83A §5-401.
Tax credits, TG §10-702.

Entitlement holder.
Investment securities, CL §8-102.

Entitlement order.
Investment securities, CL §8-102.

Entity.
Names, CA §1-501.
Principal and income act, ET §15-508.
Public ethics, SG §15-102.

Entity doing business with the state.
Public ethics, SG §15-102.

Entrance fee.
Continuing care contracts, 70B §7.

Entrusting.
Sales, UCC, CL §2-403.

Entry.
Mines and mining, EN §15-101.

Environmental covenant, EN §1-801.

Environmental effects report, NR §1-301.

Environmental hazards.
Children's environmental health and protection
advisory council, HG §13-1501.

Environmental justice, EN §1-701.

Environmental law.
Estates and trusts, ET §1-101.
Fiduciaries, ET §15-101.

Environmental modifications.
Medicaid, HG §15-132.

Environmental noise standard.
Noise control, EN §3-101.

Environmental response project.
Environmental covenant, EN §1-801.

Environmental service, NR §3-101.

Environmental settings.
Historic area zoning, 66B §8.01.

Environmental surcharges.
Property tax.
Harford county, TP §9-314.
Prince George's county, TP §9-318.

Equal access.
Equal access to public services for persons with
limited English proficiency, SG §10-1102.

Equine dealer and breeding stables, AG §2-701.

Equipment.
Labor and employment.
High voltage lines, LE §6-109.
Secured transactions, CL §9-102.
Used vehicle inspection, TR §23-101.
Vehicle preventive maintenance, TR §23-301.

Equity participation financing.
Franchises, 83A §5-1041.

Equity security.
Corporations, CA §3-601.
Stock insurers, IN §3-119.
Unsolicited takeovers of corporations and real
estate investment trusts, CA §3-801.

Equivalent dwelling unit.
Water quality financing, EN §9-1601.

Equivalent of X dollars per capita.
State police.
Protection fund, 41 §4-403.

Erect.
Outdoor advertising, TR §8-701.

ERISA.
Insurance administrators, IN §8-301.

Escalator.
Elevator safety, PS §12-801.

DEFINED TERMS —Cont'd

Escaped property.
Property tax, TP §8-417.

Escrow account.
Closed-end credit, CL §12-1026.
Interest on, CL §12-109.
Management of, CL §12-109.2.

Escrow act.
Tobacco, escrow act compliance, BR §16-501.

Essential parts.
Motor vehicles, TR §13-104.2.

Essential property insurance.
Joint insurance association, IN §25-401.

Essential service facilities.
Property tax.
Payments in lieu, TP §§7-502, 7-503.

Established catalog price.
Procurement, SF §13-220.

Established name.
Food and drugs, HG §21-201.
Pharmacists and pharmacies, HO §12-505.

Establishment.
Beer and light wine licenses, 2B §§5-101, 5-401.
Beer licenses, 2B §§3-101, 3-201, 3-401.
Juvenile curfew, 25B §13C-1.

Establish or operate.
Airports, TR §5-401.

Estate, ET §13-101.
Estate tax, TG §7-301.

Estate inheritance tax, TG §7-201.

Estimated delivery date.
Merchandise delivery, CL §14-1801.

Estimated general fund revenues.
Revenue stabilization account, SF §7-311.

Ethanol.
Renewable energy credits, AG §10-1501.

Ethnic affairs unit.
State finance, SF §2-701.

Evaluated bid price.
Procurement, SF §13-101.

Evaluation.
Executive branch of government.
Legislative review, SG §8-401.

Evaluation committee.
Executive branch of government.
Legislative review, SG §8-401.

Evaluation date.
Executive branch of government.
Legislative review, SG §8-401.

Evaluation report.
Administrative procedures.
Regulations, SG §10-130.

Evaluation team.
Patuxent institution, COR §4-101.

Event of withdrawal of original partner.
Limited partnerships, CA §10-101.

Evidence of coverage.
Dental plan organizations, IN §14-401.

Examination.
Commissioner of financial regulation, FI §11-101.
Office of legislative audits, SG §2-1219.1.

Examiner.
Banking institutions, FI §5-101.
Credit unions, FI §6-403.

Examining authority.
Mines and mining, EN §15-301.

Excavation.
Near underground facilities, PUC §12-101.

Excavations and workings.
Mines and mining, EN §15-101.

DEFINED TERMS —Cont'd
Exceptional circumstances.
  Trade secrets, CL §11-1202.
Excess first year premium.
  Insurance companies.
    Standard valuation law, IN §5-307.
Excess personal property.
  Procurement, SF §4-501.
Exchange company.
  Time-sharing, RP §11A-101.
Exchange program.
  Time-sharing, RP §11A-101.
Excise tax.
  Electric or hybrid motor vehicles, TR §13-815.
Excluded organization.
  Food establishments, HG §21-301.
Exclusionary time out.
  Student behavior intervention, ED §7-1101.
Exclusive representative.
  Labor relations.
    Community colleges, ED §16-412.
  Prince George's county public employment
      relations, ED §16-414.1.
  Public safety officers.
    Employment rights, LE §4-501.
  State personnel.
    Collective bargaining, SPP §3-101.
Excursion train.
  Maryland transit administration, TR §7-101.
Executed.
  Funds transfers, CL §4A-301.
Execution date.
  Funds transfers, CL §4A-301.
Executive action.
  Public ethics, SG §15-102.
Executive agency.
  Economic development opportunities program, SF
      §7-314.
Executive authority.
  Extradition, CP §9-101.
  Extradition of persons of unsound mind, HG
      §10-1301.
Executive committee.
  Pest control compact, AG §5-702.
Executive director.
  DNA technology fund, 41 §4-301.
  Law enforcement equipment fund, PS §4-301.
  Legislative services department, SG §2-1201.
  Ports, TR §6-101.
  Protective body armor fund, PS §4-101.
  Residential child care capital grant program, 41
      §18-701.
Executive head.
  Driver license compact, TR §16-701.
  Interstate placement of children, FL §5-601.
  Pest control compact, AG §5-716.
Executive officer.
  Banking institutions.
    Loans to directors, officers or employees, FI
        §5-512.
  Emergency management, PS §14-403.
  Money transmission, FI §12-401.
Executive order.
  Governor, SG §3-401.
  National crime prevention and privacy compact,
      CP §10-239.
  Secretary of state, SG §7-201.
Executive service.
  State personnel, SPP §1-101.
Executive unit.
  Public ethics, SG §15-102.

DEFINED TERMS —Cont'd
Exempt commercial policyholder.
  Insurance rate filings, IN §11-206.
Exempt entity.
  Check cashing services, FI §12-101.
Exempt lender.
  Homebuilder registration, BR §4.5-101.
Exert control.
  Theft, CR §7-101.
Exhaust emissions test.
  Motor vehicles, TR §23-201.
Exhibitor.
  Business licenses, BR §17-1801.
Existing building.
  Building rehabilitation code, PS §12-1001.
Existing business.
  Franchises, 83A §5-1041.
Existing electricity generation facility.
  Property tax credits, TP §9-239.
Expanded water appropriation permit.
  Water conservation, EN §5-5B-01.
Expansion.
  Continuing care contracts, 70B §7.
Expected claims.
  Health insurance, stop-loss policies, IN §15-129.
Expedited eligibility.
  Medical assistance, HG §15-101.
Expenditure.
  Elections, EL §1-101.
Expenditures for fire protection.
  Senator William H. Amoss fire, rescue and
      ambulance fund, PS §8-101.
Expenditures for police protection.
  State police, 41 §4-403.
**Expense of an emergency response,
    containment, cleanup and abatement.**
  Emergency response reimbursement, CJ §3-1201.
  Emergency services, CJ §3-1101.
Expenses.
  Corporations, CA §2-418.
  Land patents, RP §13-101.
Experience period.
  Credit life, health and unemployment insurance,
      IN §13-111.
Expert child abuse or neglect care, FL §5-712.
Explanation.
  Secured transactions , disposition of collateral
      after default, CL §9-616.
Exploitation.
  Adult protective services, FL §14-101.
Exploratory activities.
  Geothermal resources, EN §5-601.
Explosive composition.
  Fireworks, PS §10-101.
Explosive material.
  Destructive devices, CR §4-501.
Explosives.
  Explosives licenses, PS §11-101.
  Motor vehicles, TR §11-119.
  Natural resources.
    Gas and oil, EN §14-109.
Explosives for use in firearms.
  Explosives licenses, PS §11-101.
Export-related financing transaction.
  Industrial development financing, 83A §5-901.
Exposure.
  Health care providers, HG §18-338.1.
  HIV testing for health care workers and first
      responders, HG §18-338.3.
  Inmate diseases, HG §18-338.

DEFINED TERMS —Cont'd

Exposure to deadly agent.
  Catastrophic health emergency disease
    surveillance and response program, HG
    §18-901.
  Governor's health emergency powers, PS
    §14-3A-01.
Expressway, TR §8-101.
  Outdoor signs along, TR §8-739.
  Traffic laws, TR §21-101.
Expunge.
  Criminal records, CP §10-101.
Expungement.
  Criminal records, CP §10-101.
  Expungement of records, Crim Rule 4-502.
Ex-ship.
  Sales, UCC, CL §2-322.
Extended benefits.
  Unemployment insurance, LE §8-1101.
Extended warranty.
  Consumer protection, CL §14-1311.
Extension of credit.
  Credit services businesses, CL §14-1901.
Extension of credit for a commercial purpose.
  Closed end credit, CL §12-1001.
  Revolving credit, CL §12-901.
Extensive contract.
  Continuing care contracts, 70B §7.
Exterior surfaces.
  Lead poisoning, EN §6-801.
External provider.
  Health maintenance organizations, HG §19-713.2.
External safety locks.
  Handgun safety devices, PS §5-132.
External support.
  Developmental disabilities, HG §7-101.
Extract.
  Vital records, SG §9-1015.
**Extraordinary economic development
    opportunity.**
  Economic development opportunities program, SF
    §7-314.
Extraordinary majority.
  Housing authorities, HS §12-101.
Extraordinary medical expenses.
  Child support guidelines, FL §12-201.
Extremely hazardous substance.
  Community right-to-know fund, EN §7-601.
Face.
  Mines and mining, EN §15-101.
Facilities.
  Adult day care, HG §24-701.
  Automated external defibrillator program, ED
    §13-517.
  Community health, HG §24-601.
  Community right-to-know fund, EN §7-601.
  Continuing care contracts, 70B §7.
  Environmental service, NR §3-101.
  Gas and oil.
    Coastal facilities review, EN §14-501.
  Grants to assisted living facilities, HG §24-1001.
  Hazardous materials, EN §7-101.
  Hazardous material security, EN §7-701.
  Hazardous waste facilities, EN §7-401.
  Health services cost review commission, HG
    §§19-201, 19-213.
  Hospital residents property, HG §19-346.
  Hospitals, HG §19-308.3.
  Individual rights in hospitals, HG §19-343.
  Industrial development financing, 83A §5-901.
  Juvenile justice monitoring unit, SG §6-401.

DEFINED TERMS —Cont'd

Facilities —Cont'd
  Juvenile residential facilities, ED §22-301.
  Juvenile services.
    Facilities capital program, 83C §4-101.
  Medical assistance, HG §15-101.
  Mental hygiene, HG §10-101.
  Mental retardation, HG §7-803.
  Nursing facility conversion grant program, HG
    §24-1401.
  Property tax exemptions.
    Continuing care for aged, TP §7-206.
  Rights of mentally ill, HG §10-701.
  Stadium authority, FI §13-701.
  Susquehanna river basin compact, EN §5-301.
  Used vehicle inspection, TR §23-101.
  Water quality financing, EN §9-1601.
Facility applicant.
  Industrial development financing, 83A §5-901.
Facility fees.
  Time-sharing, RP §11A-101.
Facility for food consumption.
  Taxation, TG §11-206.
Facility for handicapped individuals.
  State finance, SF §2-501.
Facility permit.
  Controlled hazardous substances, EN §7-201.
Facility user.
  Industrial development financing, 83A §5-901.
Facsimile device.
  Corporations, CA §1-201.
  Unsolicited transmissions, CL §14-1313.
Facsimile signature.
  State finance, SF §2-301.
Fact-finding.
  Labor relations.
    Community colleges, ED §16-412.
  Prince George's county public employment
    relations, ED §16-414.1.
Factory branch.
  Motor vehicles, TR §15-201.
Faculties.
  Physicians, HO §14-101.
Faculty practice plan.
  Health occupations, HO §1-301.
Fair, BR §3-101.
Fair average value.
  Property tax.
    Stock in business, TP §8-110.
Fair Hill.
  Pari-mutuel betting, BR §11-811.
Fair market value.
  Assisted housing preservation.
    Protected actions, right of first purchase, HS
      §7-205.
  Grain dealers, AG §13-201.
  Outdoor advertising removal, 25 §122E.
  Vehicle excise tax, TR §13-809.
Fair value.
  Property tax.
    Distilled spirits, TP §8-112.
    Stock in business, TP §8-110.
Fallen law enforcement officer.
  Property tax credits, TP §9-210.
Fallen rescue worker.
  Property tax credits, TP §9-210.
False alarm.
  Alarm systems, CR §9-607.
  Calvert county, 25 §236D.
  Frederick county, 25 §221A.
  Washington county, 25 §236E.

DEFINED TERMS —Cont'd
Falsely emboss.
    Credit card crimes, CR §8-205.
Falsely make.
    Credit card crimes, CR §8-205.
False representation.
    Medicaid fraud, CR §8-508.
Falsify.
    Vehicle identification number, TR §14-107.
Familial status.
    Housing discrimination, 49B §20.
Family.
    AIDS insurance, HG §15-201.
    Developmental disabilities, HG §7-701.
    Housing discrimination, 49B §20.
Family beer.
    Alcoholic beverages, 2B §1-102.
Family contribution.
    Children's health program, HG §15-301.1.
Family councils.
    Nursing homes, HG §19-1416.
Family day care.
    Child care, FL §5-501.
Family day care home, RP §2-121.
    Child care, FL §5-501.
    Condominiums, RP §11-111.1.
    Homeowners association, RP §11B-111.1.
Family day care provider, FL §5-550.
    Child care provider grant program, ED §18-705.
Family day provider.
    Child care quality incentive grant program, FL
        §5-594.
Family farm.
    Corporations, CA §1-209.
Family farm unit.
    Property tax, TP §8-209.
Family home.
    Divorce, FL §8-201.
Family investment administration.
    Social services, 88A §1A.
Family member.
    Abuse or neglect of vulnerable adult, CR §3-604.
    Child abuse, CR §3-601.
    Child abuse and neglect, FL §5-701.
    Equipment dealer contracts, CL §19-101.
Family of limited income.
    Community development administration, HS
        §4-201.
    Lead hazard reduction grant and loan programs,
        HS §4-701.
    Maryland housing rehabilitation program, HS
        §4-901.
    Self-help homeownership technical assistance
        program, HS §4-1701.
Family of lower income.
    Rental housing production program, HS §4-1501.
Family of low or moderate income.
    Residential mortgage programs for certain
        counties, HS §4-1601.
Family practice.
    Medical scholarships, ED §18-702.
Family support services.
    Developmental disabilities, HG §7-701.
Family use personal property.
    Divorce, FL §8-201.
Family wine.
    Alcoholic beverages, 2B §1-102.
Farm.
    Labor contractors, LE §7-101.
    Unemployment insurance, LE §8-207.
Farm area motor vehicle, TR §13-935.

DEFINED TERMS —Cont'd
Farm cooperative.
    Gasohol and gasoline products marketing, CL
        §11-301.
Farm equipment.
    Motor vehicles, TR §11-120.
Farmer.
    Classified vehicles, TR §13-911.
    Gleaning.
        Limitation of actions, CJ §5-404.
    Workers' compensation, LE §9-210.
Farming operation.
    Secured transactions, CL §9-102.
Farm labor contractor, LE §7-101.
Farm operation.
    Eminent domain, RP §12-201.
Farm products.
    Classified vehicles, TR §13-911.
    Farm products certification, AG §10-601.
    Farm products trademarks, AG §10-501.
    Secured transactions, CL §9-102.
    Taxation, TG §10-207.
Farm tractor, TR §11-121.
Farm trailer or semitrailer.
    Registration, TR §13-930.
Farm truck.
    Registration, TR §13-921.
Farm truck tractor.
    Registration, TR §13-924.
Farm vehicle.
    Classified vehicles, TR §13-911.
F.A.S.
    Sales, UCC, CL §2-319.
Fault.
    Uniform commercial code, CL §1-201.
FBI.
    National crime prevention and privacy compact,
        CP §10-239.
FCC order.
    911 emergency telephone system, PS §1-301.
FDA.
    Health insurance, IN §15-827.
Federal act.
    Career and technology education, ED §21-201.
    Community right-to-know fund, EN §7-601.
    Controlled hazardous substances, EN §7-201.
    Deepwater port siting, NR §3-602.
    Drinking water, EN §9-401.
    Federal highway programs, TR §8-501.
    Rehabilitation services, ED §21-301.
    Savings banks, FI §4-604.
    Voluntary cleanup program, EN §7-501.
    Wages and hours, LE §3-401.
    Workforce investment act, LE §11-503.
Federal agency.
    Drinking water, EN §9-401.
    Rights of mentally ill, HG §10-808.
    Water and sewer authorities, EN §9-901.
Federal-aid primary highway.
    Outdoor advertising, TR §8-725.
Federal approval of the state program.
    Strip mining, EN §15-501.
Federal association.
    Savings and loan associations, FI §9-101.
Federal banking authority, FI §5-101.
Federal certificate.
    Handicapped persons.
        Wages and hours, LE §3-414.
Federal child and dependent care credit.
    Income tax, TG §10-716.

DEFINED TERMS —Cont'd

Federal covered advisor.
Securities regulation, CA §11-101.

Federal covered security.
Securities act, CA §11-101.

Federal credit.
Generation-skipping transfer tax, TG §7-401.

Federal credit estate tax, TG §7-304.

Federal estate tax, TG §7-301.

Federal facility.
Wildlife, NR §10-101.

Federal financial assistance.
Eminent domain, RP §12-201.

Federal flood insurance program.
Flood control and watershed management, EN §5-801.

Federal food, drug and cosmetic act.
Poultry products inspection act, AG §4-201.

Federal generation-skipping transfer tax, TG §7-401.

Federal government.
Abandoned property, CL §17-101.
Potomac water authority, EN §5-401.
Susquehanna river basin compact, EN §5-301.

Federal holiday.
Banking institutions, FI §5-701.

Federal insurance.
Financial institutions.
Deposit insurance, FI §10-101.

Federal law.
Disabled student placement, ED §8-413.

Federal law enforcement officer, CP §2-104.

Federally qualified health center, HG §24-1301.
Cancer prevention, education, screening and treatment program, HG §13-1101.

Federal meat inspection act, AG §4-101.

Federal official.
Federal nontax liabilities.
Withholding of tax refunds and payments, TG §13-930.

Federal performance incentive dollars.
Child support reinvestment fund, FL §10-106.1.

Federal poultry products inspection act, AG §4-201.

Federal prospectus.
Securities, CA §11-503.

Federal registration statement.
Securities, CA §11-503.

Federal regulation on the protection of human subjects.
Human subject research, HG §13-2001.

Federal safe drinking water act.
Water quality financing, EN §9-1601.

Federal stock savings and loan association.
Conversion of national banking association into commercial bank, FI §3-801.

Federal stock savings bank.
Conversion of national banking association into commercial bank, FI §3-801.

Federal water pollution control act.
Water quality financing, EN §9-1601.

Federated cooperative.
Corporations, CA §5-5A-02.

Feed ingredient, AG §6-101.

Feeding site.
Statewide nutrition assistance program, 88A §130A.

Feeding zone.
Waterfowl, NR §10-1001.

Fee-for-service, ADR Rule 17-102.

DEFINED TERMS —Cont'd

Fellow.
Principal fellowship and leadership development program, ED §6-116.

Female breast.
Visual surveillance of individual in private place with prurient intent, CR §3-902.

Female genital mutilation, HG §§20-601 to 20-603.

Fertilizer material, AG §6-201.

Festival.
Montgomery county wine festival license, 2B §8-310.1.

Festival organization.
Montgomery county wine festival license, 2B §8-310.1.

Fetal death.
Vital statistics, HG §4-201.

Fictitious.
Used vehicle inspection certificates, TR §23-109.

Fidelity bond.
Pilot program for long term employment of qualified ex-felons, LE §11-701.

Fiduciary.
Disclaimer of property interests, ET §9-201.
Estates and trusts, ET §15-101.
Fiduciary security transfers, ET §15-301.
Guidelines and standards for investment, ET §15-114.
Income tax, TG §10-101.
Negotiable instruments, CL §3-307.
Pensions, SPP §21-201.
Principal and income act, ET §15-501.
Property tax, TP §1-203.
Safe-deposit companies, FI §12-602.
State retirement and pension system, SPP §35-301.
Uniform fiduciaries act, ET §15-201.

Fiduciary assets.
Guidelines and standards for investments, ET §15-114.

Fiduciary deposit surety bond.
Financial institutions, FI §1-206.

Fiduciary estate tax, TG §7-308.

Fiduciary institution.
Confidential financial records, FI §1-301.

Field.
Natural resources.
Gas and oil, EN §14-102.

Fifth pathway program.
Physicians, HO §14-308.

Fifth wheel travel trailer, TR §11-121.1.

50/50.
Harford county, CR §13-1501.

File.
Consumer credit reporting agencies, CL §14-1201.
Credit services businesses, CL §14-1901.
Denial of credit, CL §14-1701.
Vital statistics, HG §4-201.

File number.
Secured transactions, CL §9-102.

Filing date.
Risk based capital standards for insurers, IN §4-301.

Filing office.
Secured transactions, CL §9-102.

Filing-office rule.
Secured transactions, CL §9-102.

Filling.
Wetlands and riparian rights, EN §16-101.

DEFINED TERMS —Cont'd
Filling material.
Bedding, HG §24-401.
Film production activity.
Film production activity employer wage rebate
program, 83A §5-1801.
Final decision.
Firefighters and emergency medical personnel.
Judicial review of disciplinary decisions, LE
§4-601.
Final disposition.
Drug asset forfeiture, CP §12-101.
Gambling forfeitures, CP §13-101.
Vital statistics, HG §4-201.
Final judgment.
Appeals, CJ §12-101.
Final peace order, CJ §3-1501.
Final project planning phase.
Long range highway programs, TR §8-610.
Final protective order.
Domestic violence, FL §4-501.
Final report.
Nursing homes, Medicaid liability audits and
review, HG §19-14A-01.
Final tax liability.
Property tax.
Homeowners credit, TP §9-104.
Finance charge.
Credit life or disability insurance premiums, IN
§27-901.
Retail credit accounts, CL §12-501.
Retail installment sales, CL §12-601.
Finance lease.
Commercial code, CL §2A-103.
Financial accommodation contract.
Computer information transactions, CL §22-102.
Financial asset.
Computer information transactions, CL §22-102.
Investment securities, CL §8-102.
Financial assistance.
Community legacy program, HS §6-201.
Economic development assistance fund, 83A
§5-1401.
Economic development opportunities program, SF
§7-314.
Housing and community development, HS §1-101.
Industrial development financing, 83A §5-901.
Maryland historical trust, SF §5A-301.
Financial authority.
Gambling forfeitures, CP §13-101.
Financial difficulty.
Continuing care contracts, 70B §7.
Financial exploitation, FI §1-306.
Financial institution, FI §1-101.
Commercial discrimination, SF §19-103.
Credit agreements, CJ §5-408.
Currency transaction reporting, FI §12-802.
Franchise taxes, TG §8-101.
Income tax, TG §10-403.
Retail credit accounts, CL §12-501.
Special registration vehicle plates, TR §13-623.
State debt, SF §8-135.
State treasury, SF §6-201.
Support, FL §10-108.2.
Tax enforcement, TG §13-804.
UTMA, ET §13-301.
Financial institution franchise tax, TG §1-101.
Financial institution holding company.
Income tax, TG §10-403.
Financial interest.
Public ethics, SG §15-102.

DEFINED TERMS —Cont'd
Financially responsible county.
Educational funding.
Children in out-of-county living arrangements,
ED §4-122.
Financial officer.
Political subdivisions, 24 §2-101.
Public debt.
Capital leases, SF §8-407.
State debt, SF §8-211.
Financial organization.
Abandoned property, CL §17-101.
Financial records.
Confidentiality, FI §1-301.
Health and social welfare organizations, SF
§7-403.
Financial services transaction.
Computer information transactions, CL §22-102.
Financial transaction.
Financial transactions involving proceeds of drug
crime, CR §5-623.
Financier.
Computer information transactions, CL §22-102.
Financing.
Maryland housing fund, HS §3-201.
Financing agency.
Sales, UCC, CL §2-104.
Financing agreement, CL §12-125.
Closed end credit, CL §12-1022.
Revolving credit, CL §12-922.
Financing a sale.
Consumer credit contracts, CL §14-1302.
Financing entity.
Viatical settlement contracts, IN §8-601.
Financing lease.
Reporting requirements for public service
companies, PUC §6-201.
Financing party.
Electric customer competition and choice act.
Rate stabilization, PUC §7-520.
Financing statement.
Secured transactions, CL §9-102.
Finders' fees.
Loans, CL §12-801.
Fine, CJ §7-501.
Fine print.
Consumer protection, CL §14-501.
Finishing and assembling building.
Fireworks, PS §10-101.
FIP.
Family investment program, 88A §44A.
Firearm, PS §5-101.
Bulletproof body armor, CR §4-106.
Burglary, CR §6-201.
Child's access to firearm, CR §4-104.
Possession by person convicted of drug crime, CR
§5-622.
Possession of firearm at public demonstration, CR
§4-208.
Firearm applicant, PS §5-101.
Firearm application, PS §5-101.
Firearm silencer.
Drug trafficking crime, CR §5-621.
Fire department official.
Occupational safety and health, LE §5-409.
Firefighter.
Law enforcement officers' pension system, SPP
§31-2A-01.
Local fire and police pension system, SPP §31-201.
Fire investigations.
Disclosure of fire loss investigation reports, PS
§9-601.

DEFINED TERMS —Cont'd

Fire marshal.
Charging by citation, CP §4-101.

Fire official.
Inspections by local fire departments, PS §9-801.
Professional architects immunity, CJ §5-426.
Professional engineers immunity, CJ §5-425.

Fire, rescue or emergency medical services entity.
Mutual aid agreements by fire, rescue or emergency services entities, PS §7-101.

Fire sprinkler contractors.
Licensing, PS §9-901.

Fireworks, PS §10-101.

Fireworks plant.
Fireworks, PS §10-101.

Firm.
Accountants, CJ §9-110.
Private detectives, BOP §13-101.
Security guards, BOP §19-101.
Security systems technicians, BOP §18-101.

Firm member.
Private detectives, BOP §13-101.
Security guards, BOP §19-101.

First eligible period.
Community colleges, ED §16-317.

First purchased dwelling.
Property tax.
Baltimore City, TP §9-304.

First responder, HG §18-213.2.
Emergency medical services, ED §13-516.
HIV testing for health care workers and first responders, HG §18-338.3.

First sale.
Sanitary facilities, EN §9-201.

First-stage manufacturer.
Motor vehicles, TR §13-113.2.

First-time Maryland home buyer.
Division of cost of recordation taxes, RP §14-104.
Transfer taxes, TP §13-203.

First user.
Industrialized buildings and manufactured homes, PS §12-301.

Fish, NR §4-101.

Fishery management, NR §4-215.

Fishery management plan, NR §4-215.

Fishery or fishery resource.
Management plans, NR §4-215.

Fishing activities.
Tidal fish license, NR §4-701.

Fit hearing aids, HO §2-101.

Fixed asset financing.
Industrial development financing authority, 83A §5-927.

Fixed assets.
Credit unions, FI §6-101.

Fixed business address.
Pawnbrokers, BR §12-101.

Fixed charges.
Insurance companies.
Investments, IN §5-608.

Fixed facility.
Emergency response reimbursement, CJ §§3-1101, 3-1201.

Fixed glazed panel immediately adjacent to an entrance or exit door.
Building codes, safety glazing, PS §12-401.

Fixed termini.
Motor vehicles, TR §11-122.

Fixture filing.
Leases, UCC, CL §2A-309.

DEFINED TERMS —Cont'd

Fixture filing —Cont'd
Secured transactions, CL §9-102.

Fixtures.
Secured transactions, CL §9-102.

Flag.
Uniform flag law, CR §10-701.

Flammable liquid.
Motor vehicles, TR §11-123.

Flee.
Extradition of persons of unsound mind, HG §10-1301.

Fleet.
Motor vehicle registration, TR §13-610.

Flight.
Extradition of persons of unsound mind, HG §10-1301.

Flighted mallard ducks, NR §10-101.

Flood hazard area.
Flood control and watershed management, EN §5-801.

Flood insurance coverage.
Real estate loans, CL §12-124.

Flower seed, AG §9-201.

F.O.B.
Sales, UCC, CL §2-319.

Focus area.
Enterprise zones, 83A §5-401.
Tax credits, TG §10-702.

Focus area employee.
Tax credits, TG §10-702.

Food.
County resort taxes, 25B §13H.
Food and drugs, HG §21-101.
Kosher products, CL §14-901.
Maryland food center, 41 §13-104.

Food additive.
Food and drugs, HG §21-101.
Poultry products inspection act, AG §4-201.
Wholesome meat act, AG §4-101.

Food establishment, HG §21-301.

Food instrument.
Food programs, HG §18-108.

Food processing plant, HG §21-301.

Food service facility, HG §21-301.
Egg law, AG §4-301.

Food stores.
Alcoholic beverage licenses, 2B §9-108.
Alcoholic beverages, 2B §9-217.

Food taxation, TG §11-206.

Foot peddler.
Business licenses, BR §17-904.

Footprinting.
Newborn infants, HG §20-401.

Force.
General assembly, SG §2-106.

Forced air system.
Heating and air conditioning, BR §9A-101.

Foreclosure consultant.
Protection of homeowners in foreclosure, RP §7-301.

Foreclosure consulting contract.
Protection of homeowners in foreclosure, RP §7-301.

Foreclosure consulting service.
Protection of homeowners in foreclosure, RP §7-301.

Foreclosure purchaser.
Protection of homeowners in foreclosure, RP §7-301.

DEFINED TERMS —Cont'd
Foreclosure reconveyance.
  Protection of homeowners in foreclosure, RP
    §7-301.
Foreclosure surplus acquisition.
  Protection of homeowners in foreclosure, RP
    §7-301.
Foreclosure surplus purchaser.
  Protection of homeowners in foreclosure, RP
    §7-301.
Foreign association.
  Savings and loan associations, FI §9-801.
Foreign bank, FI §§1-101, 12-201.
Foreign bank holding company, FI §5-901.
Foreign banking corporation, FI §12-201.
Foreign business trust, CA §3-101.
  Real estate investment trusts, CA §8-501.1.
Foreign charitable organization or
    representative, BR §6-202.
Foreign contractor.
  Unemployment insurance.
    Contributions, LE §8-609.
Foreign cooperative, CA §5-5A-02.
Foreign corporation, CA §§1-101, 3-101.
  Property tax, TP §1-101.
Foreign country.
  Insurer liquidation, rehabilitation, etc., IN §9-201.
Foreign currency.
  Investments of life insurers, IN §5-511.
Foreign entity.
  Industrial development financing, 83A §5-901.
Foreign government.
  Foreign discriminatory boycotts, CL §11-102.
Foreign insurer, IN §1-101.
  Risk based capital standards for insurers, IN
    §4-301.
Foreign investment.
  Investments of life insurers, IN §5-511.
Foreign judgment.
  Evidence, CJ §10-701.
  Uniform enforcement of foreign judgments, CJ
    §11-801.
Foreign jurisdiction.
  Investments of life insurers, IN §5-511.
  Product liability.
    Limitation of actions, CJ §5-115.
Foreign limited liability company, CA §4A-101.
  Business trusts, CA §12-101.
  Corporations, CA §3-101.
  Real estate investment trusts, CA §8-501.1.
Foreign limited liability partnership.
  Partnerships, revised act, CA §9A-101.
Foreign limited partnership, CA §§3-101, 10-101.
  Business trusts, CA §12-101.
  Partnerships, revised act, CA §9A-101.
  Real estate investment trusts, CA §8-501.1.
Foreign marriage.
  Family law, FL §2-502.
Foreign medical school.
  Physicians, HO §14-308.
Foreign partnership, CA §3-101.
  Limited partnerships.
    Merger, CA §10-208.
  Real estate investment trust, CA §8-501.1.
Foreign person.
  Foreign discriminatory boycotts, CL §11-102.
  International banking.
    International banking facility, TG §8-205.
Foreign professional corporation, CA §5-101.
Foreign school or college of pharmacy, HO
  §12-302.

DEFINED TERMS —Cont'd
Foreign state.
  Evidence, CJ §10-701.
Foreign trade zone.
  Property taxes, TP §9-231.
Foreign vehicle, TR §11-124.
Forest.
  Conservation of forest, NR §5-1601.
  Reforestation, NR §5-103.
Forest conservation, NR §5-1601.
Forest conservation plan, NR §5-1601.
Forest cover.
  Conservation of forest, NR §5-1601.
Forested slopes.
  Conservation of forest, NR §5-1601.
Forest game birds and mammals, NR §10-101.
Forest mitigation banking, NR §5-1601.
  Reforestation, NR §5-103.
Forestry, BOP §7-101; NR §5-102.1.
Forestry activity.
  Nontidal wetlands, EN §5-901.
Forest stand delineation.
  Conservation of forest, NR §5-1601.
Forfeiting authority.
  Drug asset forfeiture, CP §12-101.
  Drug trafficking crime, CR §5-621.
For-hire driver's license, PUC §10-101.
For hire vehicles, TR §13-913.
Form.
  Governmental procedures.
    Forms management, SG §10-604.
Formal complaint.
  Judicial disability and sanctionable conduct, CJA
    Rule 16-803.
Format.
  Medicare supplement insurance, IN §15-917.
Former commissioner.
  Workers' compensation commission, LE §9-302.
Former judge.
  Courts, CJ §1-302.
Former member.
  Pensions, SPP §20-101.
Former owner.
  Highways, TR §8-309.
Former prisoner of war.
  Angler's license, NR §4-607.
  Hunter's license, NR §10-303.
Former service member.
  Unemployment insurance, LE §8-1501.
Formulary.
  Health insurance, coverage of prescription drugs,
    IN §15-831.
Forward contract.
  Insurance companies, liquidation and
    rehabilitation, IN §9-229.1.
Foster care, FL §5-501.
Foster care recipient.
  Tuition exemption, ED §15-106.1.
Foster parent, FL §5-529.
  Liability insurance and reimbursement, 83C
    §2-131.
Foundation program.
  Educational financing.
    State assistance, ED §5-202.
Foundation seed, AG §9-201.
Foundation sod.
  Turf grass, AG §9-101.
Four-year average annual full-time equivalent
    enrollment.
  Maryland school for the blind.
    Appropriations, ED §8-317.

DEFINED TERMS —Cont'd

Four-year average annual full-time equivalent enrollment —Cont'd

Maryland school for the deaf, ED §8-310.3.

Four-year cohort.

Graduation records.

Collection, maintenance, analysis and report, ED §7-203.2.

Fractional parts of units.

Weights and measures, AG §11-301.

Franchise, BR §14-201.

Beer franchise fair dealing act, 2B §17-101.

Equity participation investment program, 83A §5-1041.

Motor vehicles, TR §11-125.

Franchised establishment.

Alcoholic beverages, 2B §9-211.

Franchisee, BR §14-201.

Beer franchise fair dealing act, 2B §17-101.

Franchise fee, BR §14-201.

Franchisor, BR §14-201.

Beer franchise fair dealing act, 2B §17-101.

Fraternal organization.

Class C, on-sale beer, wine and liquor license in Harford county, 2B §6-301.

Property tax exemptions, TP §7-202.

Fraud.

Health care fraud, HG §15-123.

Health program integrity and recovery activities, HG §2-501.

Public assistance fraud, CR §8-501.

Social services administration.

Reading of statement of conduct constituting fraud, 88A §16.

Fraud division.

Insurance, IN §2-401.

Insurance fraud division, IN §2-401.

Fraudulent indorsement.

Negotiable instruments, CL §3-405.

Fraudulent viatical settlement act.

Viatical settlement contracts, IN §8-601.

Free appropriate public education.

Children with disabilities, ED §8-401.

Free-play console machines.

Amusement devices, 24 §11-201; BR §17-401.

Free-play pinball machines, 24 §11-201; BR §17-401.

Freestanding ambulatory care facility, HG §19-3B-01.

Cancer reports, HG §18-204.

Freestanding birthing center.

Freestanding ambulatory care facilities, HG §19-3B-01.

Freestanding endoscopy facility.

Freestanding ambulatory care facilities, HG §19-3B-01.

Freestanding facility operating major medical equipment.

Freestanding ambulatory care facilities, HG §19-3B-01.

Free-standing medical facility, HG §19-3A-01.

Freeze.

Telephone slamming, PUC §8-401.

Fresh pursuit.

Uniform act on fresh pursuit, CP §2-304.

Fringe benefits.

Administration of courts.

Domestic relations interrogatories, Form 4.

Frozen dessert.

Food products, HG §21-801.

DEFINED TERMS —Cont'd

Fruit.

Container marking, AG §10-701.

Fuel cell.

Income tax credits, TG §10-722.

Fuel economy.

Motor vehicles, TR §13-818.

Fuel vendor.

Energy assistance program act, 41 §6-402.

Fugitive.

Harboring and escape, CR §9-401.

Fugitive from justice.

Firearms, PS §5-101.

Full day.

Judith P. Hoyer early child care and education enhancement program, ED §5-217.

Full funding rate.

State retirement and pension system, SPP §21-304.

Full-time equivalent enrollment.

Educational financing.

State assistance, ED §5-202.

Grants for limited-English proficiency education, ED §5-208.

Grants for school transportation services, ED §5-205.

Schools, compensatory education grants, ED §5-207.

Schools, guaranteed tax base grants, ED §5-210.

Special education grants, ED §5-209.

Full-time equivalent student.

Baltimore City community college, ED §16-502.

Community colleges.

State and county aid, ED §16-305.

Full-time position.

Job creation tax credit, 83A §5-1101.

One Maryland economic development tax credits, 83A §5-1501.

Property taxes.

Job creation, TP §9-230.

Full-time student.

Unemployment insurance, LE §8-220.

Functional behavioral assessment.

Student behavior intervention, ED §7-1101.

Functional need.

Community attendant services and supports program, 41 §6-7A-01.

Fund.

Community health resources commission, HG §19-2201.

Community reinvestment fund, HS §9-101.

Debt management services, FI §12-901.

Down payment and settlement expense loan program, HS §4-301.

Elderly rental housing program, HS §4-401.

Film production activity employer wage rebate program, 83A §5-1801.

Law enforcement equipment fund, PS §4-301.

Lead hazard reduction grant and loan programs, HS §4-701.

Maryland affordable housing trust, HS §10-101.

Maryland cancer fund income tax checkoff, HG §20-117.

Maryland health care provider rate stabilization fund, IN §19-801.

Maryland home financing program, HS §4-801.

Maryland housing fund, HS §3-201.

Maryland medical professional liability insurance rate stabilization fund, IN §19-104.1.

Maryland state Appalachian housing fund, HS §11-101.

DEFINED TERMS —Cont'd
Fund —Cont'd
Mortgage lender-originator fund, FI §11-601.
Neighborhood business development program, HS §6-301.
Neighborhood housing services fund, HS §4-1001.
Partnership rental housing program, HS §4-1201.
Protective body armor fund, PS §4-101.
Rental housing production program, HS §4-1501.
School bus safety enforcement fund, PS §4-201.
Senator William H. Amoss fire, rescue and ambulance fund, PS §8-101.
Special loan programs fund, HS §4-505.
State and local facilities loan fund, SF §8-125.
State board of public accountancy fund, BR §2-106.5.
State personnel.
 Health and welfare benefits, SPP §2-516.
Trauma physician services fund, HG §19-130.
Volunteer company assistance fund, PS §8-201.
Wine and grape promotion fund and council, AG §2-1101.
Funding.
Priority funding areas, SF §5-7B-01.
Funding ratio for the employees' systems.
State retirement and pension system, SPP §21-304.
Funding ratio for the teachers' systems.
State retirement and pension system, SPP §21-304.
Fund plan.
Common trust funds, FI §3-501.
Fund producer.
Insurance, IN §1-101.
Fund-raising council.
Charitable organizations, BR §6-101.
Fundraising organization.
Charles county, CR §13-1101.
Funds.
Bad checks, CR §8-101.
Community energy loan program, SG §9-2101.
Emergency medical system operations, TR §13-955.
Financial institutions.
 Deposit insurance, FI §10-101.
Heritage areas, FI §13-1101.
Home improvement, BR §8-101.
Kidney disease, HG §13-310.1.
Oil cleanups, EN §4-701.
State insurance program, SF §9-101.
Undeliverable checks, SF §7-229.
Unpresented checks, SF §7-230.
Water quality financing, EN §9-1601.
Funds transfer, CL §4A-104.
Computer information transactions, CL §22-102.
Funds-transfer business day, CL §4A-105.
Funds-transfer system, CL §4A-105.
Funds-transfer system rule, CL §4A-501.
Funeral director, HO §7-101.
Funeral establishment, HO §7-101.
Fungi.
Pesticide registration and labeling, AG §5-101.
Fungible.
Uniform commercial code, CL §1-201.
Fungicide.
Pesticide registration and labeling, AG §5-101.
Fur.
Wildlife, NR §10-101.
Fur-bearing mammal, NR §10-101.
Fur dealer.
Hunting restrictions, NR §10-501.

DEFINED TERMS —Cont'd
Furnishings.
Government house trust, SG §9-606.
Future goods.
Sales, UCC, CL §2-105.
Future interest.
Disclaimer of property interests, ET §9-201.
Game and freshwater fish, NR §4-101.
Game birds or mammals, NR §10-101.
Game of entertainment.
Amusement tax, TG §4-101.
Gaming commission.
Washington county, CR §13-2414.
Gaming device, CR §12-101.
Charles county, CR §13-1101.
Garrett county, CR §13-1401.
St. Mary's county, CR §13-2101.
Worcester county, CR §13-2619.
Gaming event, CR §12-101.
Anne Arundel county, CR §13-401.
Baltimore City, CR §13-501.
Baltimore county, CR §13-601.
Calvert county, CR §13-701.
Carroll county, CR §13-901.
Charles county, CR §13-1101.
Frederick county, CR §13-1301.
Garrett county, CR §13-1401.
Harford county, CR §13-1501.
Local gaming provisions, CR §13-201.
St. Mary's county, CR §13-2101.
Gaming permit.
Charles county, CR §13-1101.
Garage.
Abandoned vehicles, TR §25-201.
Business licenses, BR §17-801.
Garage license.
Business licenses, BR §17-801.
Garbage.
Livestock and poultry, AG §3-404.
Garrett county amusement device license.
Business licenses, BR §17-432.
Gas.
Natural resources, EN §14-102.
Plumbers, BOP §12-101.
Underground storage, EN §14-201.
Gas company, PUC §1-101.
Public utility interference, CR §6-304.
Gas master meter operator, PUC §1-101.
Gasoline.
Fuel taxes, TG §8-101.
Gasoline products.
Gasohol and gasoline products marketing, CL §11-301.
Gas plant, PUC §1-101.
Gas storage company.
Underground storage, EN §14-201.
Gas supplier.
Public utility companies, PUC §1-101.
Gassy mine, EN §15-101.
Gate.
Caves, NR §5-1401.
GCEI adjustment.
Educational financing, state assistance, ED §5-202.
Gene product.
Insurance, IN §27-909.
General assets.
Continuing care contracts, 70B §7.
Insurer liquidation, rehabilitation, etc., IN §9-201.
General common elements.
Condominiums, RP §11-101.

DEFINED TERMS —Cont'd
General health condition.
Medical records, HG §4-301.
General hospice care program, HG §19-901.
General intangible.
Secured transactions, CL §9-102.
General license.
Hospice care, HG §19-901.
Radiation, EN §8-101.
General manager.
Maryland correctional enterprises, COR §3-501.
General partner.
Limited partnerships, CA §10-101.
General purchases of easements.
Agricultural land preservation foundation, AG §2-508.
General selection board.
Procurement, SF §13-301.
General supervision.
Dental hygienists, HO §4-308.
Generate.
Radioactive waste, EN §7-301.
Generation-skipping transfer taxation, TG §7-401.
Generator.
Radioactive waste, EN §7-301.
Generator lead route.
Power plant research program, NR §3-301.
Genetic information.
Insurance, IN §27-909.
Genetic services.
Insurance, IN §27-909.
Genetic test.
Insurance, IN §27-909.
Genuine.
Uniform commercial code, CL §1-201.
Genuine crash parts.
Automotive, CL §14-2301.
Geotechnical.
Well drillers, EN §13-101.
Geothermal heat pump.
Geothermal heat pump grant program, SG §9-2008.
Geothermal resources.
Board of public works, SF §10-307.
Geriatric nursing assistant, HO §8-6A-01.
Germination.
Seeds, AG §9-201.
Gift certificate, CL §14-1319.
Gifted and talented student.
Education, ED §8-201.
Gift instrument.
Management of institutional funds act, ET §15-401.
Gifts.
Commercial code, CL §1-201.
Public ethics, SG §15-102.
Rules of interpretation, 1 §22.
State finance, SF §2-201.
Give notice.
Computer information transactions, CL §22-102.
Glean.
Limitation of actions, CJ §5-404.
Gleaning cooperative.
Income tax, TG §10-208.
Taxation, TG §10-207.
Goal.
Managing for results, SF §3-1001.
Good cause.
Equipment dealer contracts, CL §19-101.

DEFINED TERMS —Cont'd
Good faith.
Computer information transactions, CL §22-102.
Funds transfers, CL §4A-105.
Investment securities, CL §8-102.
Letters of credit, CL §5-102.
Motor vehicle manufacturers, distributors and factory branches, TR §15-206.1.
Negotiable instruments, CL §3-103.
Sales, UCC, CL §2-103.
Secured transactions, CL §9-102.
Uniform commercial code, CL §1-201.
Goods.
Bills of lading and warehouse receipts, CL §18-101.
Business licenses, BR §17-101.
Computer information transactions, CL §22-102.
Consignees, CL §11-801.
Convict made, CL §11-903.
Documents of title, CL §7-102.
Retail credit accounts, CL §12-501.
Retail installment sales, CL §12-601.
Consumer goods, CL §12-612.
Sales finance companies, FI §11-401.
Sales, UCC, CL §2-105.
Secured transactions, CL §9-102.
Good standing.
Chiropractors, HO §3-202.
Governing board.
Higher education commission, ED §11-301.
Management of institutional funds act, ET §15-401.
Pest control compact, AG §5-702.
Representative of governor, SG §3-306.
Universities and colleges.
Tuition increases, ED §15-106.5.
Governing body.
Boats and boating, NR §8-701.
Community action agencies, HS §8-101.
Condominiums, RP §11-101.
Continuing care contracts, 70B §7.
Correctional farms, COR §11-401.
Drug asset forfeiture, CP §12-101.
Higher education, ED §10-101.
Homeowners' associations, RP §11B-101.
Homeowners associations, condominiums and cooperative housing, RP §14-118.
Issuance of notes by community colleges, ED §16-302.1.
Local government investment guidelines, 95 §22F.
Mutual aid agreements, CP §2-105.
National capital region mutual aid agreements, PS §14-8A-01.
Property tax, TP §1-101.
Public recreation and parks, 25 §223.
Sanitary commissions, EN §9-601.
Sewerage bonds, EN §9-801.
Water and sewer authorities, EN §9-901.
Governing body of a political subdivision.
Obstructing aviation regulations, TR §5-705.1.
Governing instrument.
Business trusts, CA §12-101.
Governmental activity.
Executive branch of government.
Legislative review, SG §8-401.
Governmental agency.
Electronic transactions, CL §21-101.
Forests and parks.
Open space program, NR §5-901.
Gas and oil.
Coastal facilities review, EN §14-501.

DEFINED TERMS —Cont'd
Governmental agency —Cont'd
Sanitary commissions, EN §9-640.
Workers' compensation.
Hearings, LE §9-724.
Governmental body.
Land patents, RP §13-101.
Governmental charge.
Payment of governmental charges by credit or
debit card, 24 §9-1401.
Governmental entity, 26 §1.
Disclosures by persons doing public business, EL
§14-101.
Procurement, SF §13-110.
Setback line restrictions.
Limitation of actions, CJ §5-114.
Unemployment insurance, LE §8-101.
Governmental plan.
Health insurance portability, IN §§15-1301,
15-1401.
Governmental self-insurance group.
Workers' compensation, LE §9-401.
Governmental unit.
Automated mapping-geographic information
systems, SG §10-901.
Development permits, SG §11-101.
Housing and community development, HS §1-101.
Labor and employment, LE §1-101.
Lottery agency, SG §9-101.
Management and productivity council, SG
§9-1801.
Offender employment coordination, COR §2-301.
Optometrists, HO §11-401.
Public ethics, SG §15-102.
Secured transactions, CL §9-102.
Taxation, TG §13-101.
Government identification document.
Identity fraud, CR §8-303.
Government obligation.
County transportation bonds, TR §3-310.
Washington suburban sanitary district, 29 §4-101.
Government plan.
Health insurance portability, IN §15-1301.
Governor.
Compact for education, ED §25-102.
Legal services corporation, 10 §45C.
URESA, FL §10-301.
Governor-elect, SG §3-201.
Governor's plan.
Workforce investment act, LE §11-503.
Grade.
Commercial fertilizers, AG §6-201.
State police department, PS §2-101.
Grade A distribution station.
Milk products, HG §21-401.
Grade A distributor.
Milk products, HG §21-401.
Grade A milk product, HG §21-401.
Grade A pasteurized milk ordinance, HG
§21-401.
Graduation rate.
Graduation records.
Collection, maintenance, analysis and report,
ED §7-203.2.
Graduation rate formula.
Graduation records.
Collection, maintenance, analysis and report,
ED §7-203.2.
Grain dealer, AG §13-201.
Grant.
Apprenticeship incentive program, ED §18-1801.

DEFINED TERMS —Cont'd
Grant —Cont'd
Health manpower shortage incentive grant
program, ED §18-803.
Real property, RP §1-101.
Water quality financing, EN §9-1601.
Grant agreement.
Rural legacy program, NR §5-9A-02.
Water quality financing, EN §9-1601.
Grant diversion.
Family investment program, 88A §44A.
Grantee.
Legal services corporation, 10 §45C.
Senior citizen activities centers capital
improvement grants, 70B §26.
Water quality financing, EN §9-1601.
Grantee in interest.
Hart-Miller-Pleasure Island chain, NR §5-1202.2.
Grant fund.
Land trust grant fund, NR §3-2A-01.
Grantor.
Distributorships, CL §11-1301.
Grant program.
Lead hazard reduction grant and loan programs,
HS §4-701.
Grant recipient.
Apprenticeship incentive program, ED §18-1801.
Grape grower.
Winery and grape growers' advisory commission,
AG §10-1201.
Gratuity.
Mobile home parks, RP §8A-101.
Green base building.
Income tax credits, TG §10-722.
Green crab, NR §4-801.
Green pelt, NR §10-101.
Green tenant space.
Income tax credits, TG §10-722.
Green whole building.
Income tax credits, TG §10-722.
Grievance.
Employee grievance procedures.
University of Maryland, ED §13-201.
Health insurance.
Complaint process for adverse decisions or
grievances, IN §15-10A-01.
Juvenile justice monitoring unit, SG §6-401.
Labor relations.
Community colleges, ED §16-412.
Morgan State University.
Classified employees grievance procedures, ED
§14-301.
Prince George's county public employment
relations, ED §16-414.1.
Private review agents, IN §15-10B-01.
State personnel.
Procedures, SPP §12-101.
Grievance decision.
Health insurance.
Complaint process, IN §15-10A-01.
Private review agents, IN §15-10B-01.
Gross combination weight rating.
Commercial drivers' licenses, TR §16-803.
Gross income.
Nutrient management consultants, AG §8-803.1.
Property tax.
Elderly or disabled renters, TP §9-102.
Farm or agricultural use land, TP §8-209.
Homeowners credit, TP §9-104.
Gross misconduct.
Unemployment insurance, LE §8-1002.

DEFINED TERMS —Cont'd

Gross receipts.
Public service company tax, TG §8-401.
Gross vehicle weight rating.
Commercial drivers' licenses, TR §16-803.
State standby petroleum fuel set-aside program, PS §14-504.
Gross weight.
Motor vehicles, TR §11-126.
Group care.
Child care, FL §5-501.
Group contract.
Health insurance.
Divorced spouse and dependent children, IN §15-408.
Involuntarily terminated employees, IN §15-409.
Notice to employer of succeeding coverage, IN §15-415.
Surviving spouse and dependent children, IN §15-407.
Group health care.
Nonprofit health service plans, IN §14-120.
Group health insurance, IN §15-301.
Group home.
Developmental disabilities, HG §7-101.
Food establishments, HG §21-323.
Group home financing program, HS §4-601.
Housing discrimination, 49B §21.
Group home sponsor.
Group home financing program, HS §4-601.
Group practice.
Health occupations, HO §1-301.
Growth allocation.
Chesapeake Bay critical area and Atlantic coastal bays critical area protection programs, NR §8-1802.
Growth in the per pupil basic current expense figure.
Maryland school for the blind.
Appropriations, ED §8-317.
Maryland school for the deaf, ED §8-310.3.
Growth-related project.
Priority funding areas, SF §5-7B-01.
Guarantee.
Flammable products, HG §22-401.
Guaranteed.
Securities, CA §11-101.
Guaranteed analysis.
Commercial fertilizers, AG §6-201.
Guaranteed arrest bond certificate.
Traffic citations, TR §26-404.
Guaranteed benefits.
Fraternal benefit societies, IN §8-445.
Guaranteed investment contract.
Insurance advisers, IN §10-202.
Guaranteed ride home.
Tax credits for employer-provided commuter benefits, EN §2-901.
Guaranteed tax base program per pupil amount.
Schools, guaranteed tax base grants, ED §5-210.
Guarantee duration.
Insurance companies.
Standard valuation law, IN §5-306.
Guaranteed wealth per pupil.
Schools, guaranteed tax base grants, ED §5-210.
Guarantee fund.
Real estate brokers, BOP §17-101.
Guarantor.
Extended warranties, CL §14-1311.

DEFINED TERMS —Cont'd

Guarantor —Cont'd
Service contracts and consumer products guaranty, CL §14-401.
Guaranty.
Service contracts and consumer products guaranty, CL §14-401.
Guardian.
Children in need of assistance, CJ §3-801.
Courts, CJ §3-201.
Discretionary trusts, ET §14-401.
Estates and trusts, ET §13-101.
Juvenile curfew, 25B §13C-1.
Guardianship.
Children in need of assistance, CJ §3-801.
Local department guardianships and adoptions, FL §5-301.
Private agency adoptions and guardianships, FL §5-3A-01.
Termination of parental rights, Juv Rule 11-501.
Gubernatorial ticket.
Public campaign financing, EL §15-102.
Guest.
Alcoholic beverages.
Hotels and restaurants, 2B §6-101.
Guidelines.
Illumination in public buildings, guidelines, PS §12-204.
Gun shows.
Applications for purchases, rents or transfers of firearms, PS §5-130.
Gypsum.
Agricultural liming materials and gypsum, AG §6-301.
Commercial fertilizers, AG §6-201.
Habilitation.
Developmental disabilities, HG §7-101.
Habilitative services.
Health insurance.
Required benefits, IN §15-835.
Habitual drunkard.
Firearms, PS §5-101.
Habitual user.
Firearms, PS §5-101.
Hair dye.
Cosmetics, HG §21-230.
Handgun, CR §4-201.
Firearms, PS §5-101.
Handgun permits, PS §5-301.
Handgun roster, PS §5-401.
Handgun safety devices, PS §5-132.
Possession of firearm at public demonstration, CR §4-208.
Handgun roster, PS §5-401.
Handgun roster board.
Handgun safety devices, PS §5-132.
Handicapped child.
Physical and occupational therapists and assistants grant program, ED §18-704.
Handicapped citizen.
Condominium conversions, RP §11-102.1.
Cooperative housing corporation, CA §5-6B-05.
Handicapped individual.
Facilities for handicapped, SF §2-501.
Handle.
Horse racing, BR §11-101.
Handscrape.
Oysters and clams, NR §4-1001.
Harassment or intimidation.
Schools, ED §7-424.

DEFINED TERMS —Cont'd
Harbor.
 Harboring and escape, CR §9-401.
Hard cider, 2B §1-102.
Hard-shell clams, NR §4-1001.
Harford county jukebox license, BR §17-1312.
Harness racing, BR §11-101.
Harvest.
 Oysters and clams, NR §4-1001.
Harvest reserve.
 Oysters and clams, NR §4-1001.
Hauler.
 Fluid dairy products, AG §11-401.
Hauler certificate.
 Controlled hazardous substances, EN §7-201.
Hazardous chemical.
 Community right-to-know fund, EN §7-601.
Hazardous condition.
 Hospital deficiencies, HG §19-361.
Hazardous financial condition.
 Risk retention groups, IN §25-101.
Hazardous life.
 Radioactive waste, EN §7-301.
Hazardous liquid.
 Hazardous liquid pipelines, PUC §11-201.
Hazardous location.
 Building codes, safety glazing, PS §12-401.
Hazardous materials, EN §7-101; HG §22-501.
 Commercial drivers' licenses, TR §16-803.
 Emergency response reimbursement, CJ §§3-1101,
  3-1201.
 Security of hazardous material facilities, EN
  §7-701.
Hazardous materials inspector.
 Motor carrier safety, TR §25-111.
 Vehicle preventive maintenance, TR §23-301.
Hazardous or toxic chemical.
 Public information, EN §6-501.
Hazardous substance.
 Controlled hazardous substances, EN §7-201.
Hazardous waste.
 Hazardous waste facilities, EN §7-401.
Header information.
 Spam, CR §3-805.1.
Health advocacy unit.
 Complaint process for adverse decisions or
  grievances, IN §15-10A-01.
Health and human services referral system,
 HG §24-1201.
Health benefit plan.
 Complaint procedure, IN §15-10A-01.
 Fee assessment by health care commission, HG
  §19-111.
 Health care regulatory fund, IN §2-112.2.
 Health insurance.
  Complaint process for coverage decisions, IN
   §15-10D-01.
 Health insurance portability, IN §15-1301.
 Health insurance provider panels, IN §15-112.
 Portability of health insurance, IN §§15-1301,
  15-1401.
 Small employer health insurance, IN §15-1201.
Health care.
 Medical records, HG §4-301.
Health care entity.
 Health occupations, HO §1-301.
Health care facility.
 Accreditation of health care facilities, HG
  §19-2301.
 Catastrophic health emergency disease
  surveillance and response program, HG
  §18-901.

DEFINED TERMS —Cont'd
Health care facility —Cont'd
 Health care decisions, HG §5-615.
 Health care providers, HG §18-338.1.
 Health planning, HG §19-114.
 Massage therapists, HO §3-5A-01.
 Medical mutual liability insurance society of
  Maryland, IN §24-201.
 Nurses, HG §19-2001.
 Physical rehabilitation, HG §19-1201.
 Pregnant women.
  HIV testing, HG §18-338.2.
 Private review agents, IN §15-10B-01.
Health-care-insurance receivable.
 Secured transactions, CL §9-102.
Health care practitioner, HO §1-208.
 Catastrophic health emergency disease
  surveillance and response program, HG
  §18-901.
 Fee assessment by health care commission, HG
  §19-111.
 Freestanding ambulatory care facilities, HG
  §19-3B-01.
 Health care decisions, HG §5-601; HO §1-301.
 Health insurance, IN §§15-110, 15-113.
 Health insurance claims forms, IN §15-1003.
 Health planning and development, HG §19-114.
 Medical care data collection, HG §19-132.
Health care provider, HG §§4-403, 18-338.1.
 Catastrophic health emergency disease
  surveillance and response program, HG
  §18-901.
 Child fatality review teams, HG §5-701.
 Complaint process for adverse decisions or
  grievances, IN §15-10A-01.
 Destruction of medical records, HG §4-403.
 Disease control, HG §18-328.
 Disease testing, HG §18-336.
 Governor's health emergency powers, PS
  §14-3A-01.
 Health care decisions, HG §5-601.
 Health care malpractice, CJ §3-2A-01.
 Health insurance, IN §§15-116, 15-1008.
  Complaint process for coverage decisions, IN
   §15-10D-01.
  Credentialing of providers, IN §15-112.1.
  Restrictions on transferring contracts, IN
   §15-125.
  Transfer of provider's contract, IN §15-124.
 HIV testing for health care workers and first
  responders, HG §18-338.3.
 Inmate diseases, HG §18-338.
 Maryland health care provider rate stabilization
  fund, IN §19-801.
 Maryland medical professional liability insurance
  rate stabilization fund, IN §19-104.1.
 Medical care data collection, HG §19-132.
 Medical mutual liability insurance society of
  Maryland, IN §24-201.
 Medical records, CJ §10-104; HG §4-301.
 Nonprofit health service plans, IN §14-101.
 People's insurance counsel, SG §6-301.
 Positive disease test results, HG §18-337.
 Pregnant women.
  HIV testing, HG §18-338.2.
 Private review agents, IN §15-10B-01.
Health care service.
 Medicaid fraud, CR §8-508.
Health care service reviewer.
 Private review agents, IN §15-10B-01.

DEFINED TERMS —Cont'd

Health care services.
Certificate of health care need, HG §19-120.
Coinsurance payments, IN §15-118.
Complaint process for adverse decisions or
grievances, IN §15-10A-01.
Health insurance, IN §§15-110, 15-121.
Complaint process for coverage decisions, IN
§15-10D-01.
Health occupations, HO §1-301.
HMOs, HG §19-701.
Medicaid, HG §15-132.
Medical care data collection, HG §19-132.
Nonprofit health service plans, IN §14-101.
Provider-sponsored organizations, HG §19-7A-01.
Health club services.
Consumer protection, CL §14-12B-01.
Health club services agreement.
Consumer protection, CL §14-12B-01.
Health coverage.
Insurance unfair trade practices, IN §27-221.
Health department.
Incompetency and criminal responsibility, CP
§3-101.
Health hazard.
Washington suburban sanitary district.
Construction of subdivision lines, 29 §3-101.1.
Health insurance, IN §1-101.
Health insurance benefits.
Health care payroll assessment, reporting by
Secretary, LE §8.5-106.
Health insurance costs.
Health care payroll assessment, LE §8.5-101.
Health insurance coverage.
Children, IN §15-405.
Child support orders.
Inclusion of child on health insurance, FL
§12-102.
Medical assistance, IN §15-406.
Health insurer.
Insurance regulation assessment, IN §2-501.
Nonprofit health service plans, IN §14-130.
Risk based capital standards for insurers, IN
§4-301.
Health insurer assessment portion.
Insurance regulation assessment, IN §2-501.
Health maintenance organization, HG §19-701.
Health planning, HG §19-121.
Medical directors, IN §15-10C-01.
Health network, IN §27-910.
Health occupation, HO §1-204.
Manpower shortage incentive grant program, ED
§18-803.
Health officer, EN §1-101; HG §1-101.
County health boards, HG §3-101.
Victims of crime, CP §11-107.
Health officer music festivals, BR §17-1401.
Health or social services.
Procurement, unsolicited proposals, SF §13-107.1.
Health or social welfare organization.
State finance, SF §7-403.
Health practitioner.
Adult protective services, FL §14-101.
Child abuse and neglect, FL §5-701.
Self-administration of asthma medication by
pupils, ED §7-421.
Health related services.
Continuing care contracts, 70B §7.
Health service area.
Health planning, HG §19-114.

DEFINED TERMS —Cont'd

Health status-related factor.
Health insurance portability, IN §15-1301.
Insurance unfair trade practices, IN §27-221.
Portability of health insurance, IN §§15-1301,
15-1401.
Small employer health insurance, IN §15-1201.
Hearing.
General assembly.
Investigations, SG §2-1601.
Law enforcement officers' bill of rights, PS §3-101.
Property tax, TP §14-510.
Hearing aid, HO §2-101.
Health insurance coverage, IN §15-838.
Sales, CL §14-2501.
**Hearing aid dispenser rehabilitation
committee,** HO §2-318.2.
Hearing board.
Home improvement, BR §8-101.
Real estate brokers, BOP §17-101.
Hearing impaired individual.
Developmental disabilities, HG §10-908.
Hearing-impaired infant, HG §13-601.
Heating boiler.
Boilers and pressure vessels, PS §12-901.
Heating, cooling and ventilating systems.
New home warranties, RP §10-601.
Heating oil tank.
Water pollution, EN §4-401.
Heating system.
Heating and air conditioning, BR §9A-101.
**Heating, ventilation, air conditioning and
refrigeration contractor,** BR §9A-101.
Hedging transaction.
Investments of life insurers, IN §5-511.
Heirs, ET §13-101.
Transfer-on-death security registration, ET
§16-101.
Hemodialysis drugs and devices.
Pharmacists and pharmacies, HO §12-603.
HEPA-vacuum.
Lead poisoning, EN §6-801.
Herbicide.
Pesticide registration and labeling, AG §5-101.
Herd, AG §3-501.
Hereditary disorder.
Health care, HG §13-101.
Heritage area, FI §13-1101.
Canal place preservation and development
authority, FI §13-1001.
Herring Run watershed, EN §5-1201.
High density residential areas.
Forest conservation, NR §5-1601.
High efficiency particle air vacuum.
Lead poisoning, EN §6-801.
Higher education.
Powers and duties of higher education
commission, ED §11-105.
Higher education loan.
Dent-care program, ED §18-2401.
Math/science student core, ED §18-1601.
Repayment program, ED §18-1501.
High level nuclear waste.
Controlled hazardous substances, EN §7-225.
Nuclear waste, EN §8-401.
High level policy form.
Health insurance portability, IN §15-1301.
High performance building.
Capital projects, SF §3-602.
Property taxes, TP §9-242.

DEFINED TERMS —Cont'd

High pressure, high temperature water boiler.
Boilers and pressure vessels, PS §12-901.

High-rise buildings.
Fires and fire protection, high-rise buildings, PS §9-401.

High voltage line.
Labor and employment, LE §6-101.

Highway, TR §11-127.
Open containers of alcoholic beverages in motor vehicles, CR §10-123.
Setback line restrictions.
Limitation of actions, CJ §5-114.
Transportation, TR §8-101.

Highway authority, TR §8-627.

Highway facility, TR §3-101.

Highway needs inventory.
Long range highway programs, TR §8-610.

Highway user revenues.
County transportation bonds, TR §3-301.
Highways, TR §8-401.

Hippodrome performing arts center facility, FI §13-701.

Hippodrome performing arts center financing fund, FI §13-701.

Hippodrome performing arts center site, FI §13-701.

Hiring agreement.
Procurement, SF §13-224.

Historic dollar value.
Management of institutional funds act, ET §15-401.

Historic motor vehicle, TR §13-936.

Historic property.
Maryland historical trust, SF §5A-301.

Historic provider.
Medical assistance, HG §15-101.

Historic register.
Maryland historical trust, historic funds and capital projects, SF §5A-322.

Historic resources, NR §1-301.

HIV.
Donors, HG §18-334.
Health care providers, HG §18-338.1.
HIV testing for health care workers and first responders, HG §18-338.3.
Pregnant women.
Testing, HG §18-338.2.
Sterile needle and syringe exchange, Baltimore City, HG §24-801.
Sterile needle and syringe exchange, Prince George's county, HG §24-901.
Testing, HG §18-336.

HIV/AIDS case report, HG §18-207.

Hive.
Honeybees, AG §5-501.

Holder.
Abandoned property, CL §17-101.
Credit card number protection, CR §8-213.
Environmental covenant, EN §1-801.
Mortgage releases, RP §3-105.1.
Retail credit accounts, CL §12-501.
Retail installment sales, CL §12-601.
Uniform commercial code, CL §1-201.

Holder in due course.
Negotiable instruments, CL §§3-103, 3-302.

Holder's signature.
Credit card number protection, CR §8-213.

Holding company.
Savings and loan associations, FI §8-101.

DEFINED TERMS —Cont'd

Hold order.
Telephone slamming, PUC §8-401.

Holiday, Rule 1-202.

Holocaust victim.
Holocaust victim insurance, IN §28-101.
Income tax, TG §10-207.
Inheritance tax, TG §7-203.

Home.
Domestic violence, FL §4-501.
Veterans' homes, SG §9-909.

Home and hospital teacher, ED §6-401.

Home appliance.
Consumer protection, CL §13-307.

Home-based hospice care program, HG §19-901.

Home builder.
Homebuilder registration, BR §4.5-101.

Home builder registration number, BR §4.5-101.

Homebuyer education.
Down payment and settlement expense loan program, HS §4-301.

Homebuyer education or housing counseling.
Homeowner equity protection, CL §§12-124.1, 12-311, 12-1029.

Home health agency, HG §19-401.

Home health aid services.
Nursing referral service agencies, HG §19-4B-01.

Home health care, HG §19-401.
Health insurance, IN §15-808.
Residential service agencies, HG §19-4A-01.

Home health care services.
Long-term care insurance, IN §18-110.

Home hemodialysis distribution permit.
Pharmacists and pharmacies, HO §12-603.

Home improvement, BR §8-101.

Home improvement contract, BR §8-101.

Home improvement project.
Community development administration, HS §4-201.

Home inspection.
Home inspectors, BOP §16-101.

Home inspector, BOP §16-101.

Homeless individual.
Shelter, nutrition and services, 88A §132.

Home medical equipment services.
Residential service agencies, HG §19-4A-01.

Home or usual place of abode.
Kidnapping, CR §3-501.

Homeowner.
Airport noise assistance programs, TR §5-1201.
Historic St. Mary's City commission, ED §24-513.
Property tax.
Baltimore City, TP §§9-105, 9-304.
Credits and relief, TP §9-101.
Homeowners credit, TP §9-104.
Homestead credit, TP §9-105.
Rezoned real property, TP §8-226.
Protection of homeowners in foreclosure, RP §7-301.

Homeowner corporation.
Washington suburban sanitary district.
Plan of system repairs, 29 §10-107.

Homeowners association, RP §11B-101.
Personal liability, CJ §5-406.

Homeowners association depository, RP §11B-101.

Homeowners insurance.
Joint insurance association, IN §25-401.

Homeowners insurer.
People's insurance counsel, SG §6-301.

DEFINED TERMS —Cont'd

Home purchaser.
Property tax.
Homeowners credit, TP §9-104.

Home service provider.
911 emergency telephone system, PS §1-301.

Home state.
Branch banking, FI §5-1001.
Driver license compact, TR §16-703.
Insurance producers, IN §10-101.
Interstate wildlife violator compact, NR §10-1201.
Uniform child custody jurisdiction and
    enforcement act, FL §9.5-101.
Uniform interstate family support act, FL
    §10-301.

Home state regulator.
Branch banking, FI §5-1001.

Honey house.
Honeybees, AG §5-501.

Honor.
Letters of credit, CL §5-102.
Uniform commercial code, CL §1-201.

Honorarium.
Public ethics, SG §15-102.

Hoophouses.
Property tax, TP §8-114.

Horse.
Horse industry board, AG §2-701.

Horse riding and rental stables, AG §2-701.

Hospice facility, HG §19-901.

Hospital, HG §19-301.
Health and educational facilities, 43C §3.
Health insurance, IN §15-1003.
Health insurance, provider panels, IN §15-112.
HIV testing for health care workers and first
    responders, HG §18-338.3.
Medical care data collection, HG §19-132.
Physician assistants, HO §15-101.
Physicians, HO §14-101.
Unemployment insurance, LE §8-101.

Hospital or related institution.
Health occupations, HO §1-204.

Hospital services.
Health services cost review commission, HG
    §19-201.

Hospital warrant.
Incompetency and criminal responsibility, CP
    §3-101.

Host county.
State personnel.
Credits in selection tests, SPP §7-207.

Host district.
State personnel.
Credits in selection tests, SPP §7-207.

Host state.
Branch banking, FI §5-1001.
Radioactive waste, EN §7-301.

Hotel.
Alcoholic beverages, 2B §8-218.
Hotel rental tax, 24 §9-301.
Liens by, CL §16-501.
Operating agreements, CL §23-101.
Sprinkler systems, PS §9-201.

Hotel rental tax.
Political subdivisions, 24 §9-301.

Hours of approved training.
Environmental sanitarians, EN §11-101.

Hours of darkness.
Automated teller machines, FI §1-401.

House.
General assembly, SG §2-101.

DEFINED TERMS —Cont'd

Household.
Abuse or neglect of vulnerable adult, CR §3-604.
Child abuse and neglect, FL §5-701.
Condominiums, RP §11-137.
Household hazardous waste, EN §9-1801.

Household goods.
Documents of title, CL §7-209.
Household goods movers enforcing carrier's lien,
    CL §14-3101.
Merchandise delivery, CL §14-1801.

Household goods mover.
Enforcing carrier's lien, CL §14-3101.

Household goods moving services.
Mover enforcing carrier's lien, CL §14-3101.

Household hazardous waste, EN §9-1801.

Household member.
Abuse or neglect of vulnerable adult, CR §3-604.
Child abuse, CR §3-601.
Child abuse and neglect, FL §5-701.
Health occupations, HO §1-101.

Household of limited income.
Maryland home financing program, HS §4-801.

Household of lower income.
Partnership rental housing program, HS §4-1201.

Household substance.
Packaging, HG §22-301.

Housing.
Maryland housing fund, HS §3-201.

Housing agency.
Condominiums, RP §11-101.
Housing assistance fraud, CR §8-523.

Housing assistance.
Housing assistance fraud, CR §8-523.

Housing authority.
Partnership rental housing program, HS §4-1201.

Housing bonds.
Allocation of private activity bond authority, FI
    §13-801.

Housing crisis.
Homeless individual, 88A §132.

Housing for older persons.
Housing discrimination, 49B §20.

Housing manager.
Senior housing managers training, 70B §25.

Housing project.
Baltimore City housing authority, HS §15-101.
Housing authorities, HS §12-101.
Montgomery county housing opportunities
    commission, HS §16-101.
Prince George's county housing authority, HS
    §17-101.
Queen Anne's county housing authority, HS
    §18-101.
Washington county housing authority, HS
    §21-101.

HOV lanes.
Traffic control devices, TR §25-105.

Human cloning.
Maryland stem cell research program, 83A
    §5-2B-01.

Humane method.
Livestock slaughtering, AG §4-123.1.

Humane society.
Crimes relating to animals, CR §10-601.

Human papillomavirus screening test.
Health insurance, IN §15-829.

Human remains.
Maryland historical trust, archaeological property,
    SF §5A-333.

DEFINED TERMS —Cont'd
Human service worker.
Adult protective services, FL §14-101.
Human subject.
Human subject research, HG §13-2001.
Hunt, NR §10-101.
Metropolitan district property, 28 §5-113.1.
Hybrid.
Seeds, AG §9-201.
Hydraulic brake fluid, TR §22-305.
Hydraulic clam dredge, NR §§4-1001, 4-1101.
Hydrocarbon.
Deepwater port siting, NR §3-602.
Hydronic system.
Heating and air conditioning, BR §9A-101.
I.
Insurance companies.
Standard valuation law, IN §5-306.
ICF-MR.
Intermediate care facilities for the mentally
retarded, HG §7-517.
ICF-MR income.
Intermediate care facilities for the mentally
retarded, HG §7-517.
Identification.
Administration of courts.
Form interrogatories, Form 2.
Computer information transactions, CL §22-102.
Sales, UCC, CL §2-501.
Identification badge, CR §9-701.
Identification card, CR §9-701.
Identification mark.
Rental electric storage batteries, CL §11-902.
Identification number.
Criminal offenses.
Motor vehicles, TR §14-107.
Identify.
Administration of courts.
Form interrogatories, Form 2.
Identifying information.
Child abuse and neglect, FL §5-701.
Independent adoptions, FL §5-3B-01.
Local department guardianships and adoptions,
FL §5-301.
Mutual consent voluntary adoption registry, FL
§5-4C-01.
Private agency adoptions and guardianships, FL
§5-3A-01.
Identity.
Administration of courts.
Form interrogatories, Form 2.
Identity fraud, CR §8-305.
Identity theft passport, CR §8-305.
Ignition interlock system, TR §27-107.
III system.
National crime prevention and privacy compact,
CP §10-239.
ILEV vehicles.
Traffic control devices, TR §25-105.
Illicit alcoholic beverages, 2B §1-102.
Illicit sex.
Sale or display of obscene matter to minor, CR
§11-203.
Illuminated exit sign.
Maryland efficiency standards act, SG §9-2006.
Imbedded software.
Property taxes, TP §7-238.
Immediate container.
Poultry products inspection act, AG §4-201.
Immediate family.
Chesapeake Bay critical area and Atlantic coastal
bays critical area protection programs, NR
§8-1808.2.

DEFINED TERMS —Cont'd
Immediate family —Cont'd
Public ethics, SG §15-102.
Savings and loan associations.
Board of commissioners and division, FI §8-101.
State personnel, SPP §9-601.
Immediate family member.
Health occupations, HO §1-301.
Nonprofit health service plans, IN §14-115.
Real estate brokers, BOP §17-511.
Immediate family relative.
Credit unions, FI §6-302.
Immediate follow-up care.
Replacement contact lens prescriptions, HO
§§11-404.4, 14-507.
Immediate threat.
Unsafe food.
State liability, CJ §5-633.
Immigration consultant, CL §14-3301.
Immigration matter, CL §14-3301.
Imminent and substantial endangerment.
Voluntary cleanup program, EN §7-501.
**Imminent danger to the health and safety of
the public.**
Strip mining, EN §15-501.
ImmuNet, HG §18-109.
Impacted land use area.
Noise zones.
Aviation, TR §5-801.
Impaired insurer, IN §9-201.
Life and health insurance guaranty corporation,
IN §9-401.
Impasse.
Labor relations.
Community colleges, ED §16-412.
Prince George's county public employment
relations, ED §16-414.1.
Implement of cockfighting, CR §10-608.
Import.
Alcoholic beverages, 2B §1-102.
Importer.
Alcoholic beverages, 2B §1-102.
**Imprisonment for life without possibility of
parole,** CR §2-101.
Improper means.
Trade secrets, CL §11-1201.
Improve.
Local military installation redevelopment
authorities, 83A §5-1701.
Improvement.
Closed end credit, insurance, CL §12-1007.
Property tax.
Damaged by fire, flood or shifting land, TP
§8-230.
Real estate loans, CL §12-124.
Revolving credit, CL §12-909.
Sanitary commissions, EN §9-601.
Secondary mortgage loans, CL §12-410.
Senior citizen activities centers capital
improvement grants, 70B §26.
Warranties.
Land installment contracts, RP §10-201.
Water and sewer authorities, EN §9-901.
Inactive association.
Public drainage associations, 25 §102.
Public watershed associations, 25 §217.1.
Inbred line.
Seeds, AG §9-201.
Incapable of making an informed decision.
Health care decisions, HG §5-601.

DEFINED TERMS —Cont'd

Incapacity.
Discipline of attorneys, CJA Rule 16-701.

Incapacity or incapacitated.
Standby guardians, ET §13-901.

Incendiary material.
Destructive devices, CR §4-501.

Incidental damages.
Computer information transactions, CL §22-102.

Incidental taking.
Nongame and endangered species, NR §10-2A-01.

Incineration.
Controlled hazardous substances, EN §7-201.

Includes.
Chesapeake Bay critical area and Atlantic coastal bays critical area protection programs, NR §8-1802.

Includes or including, EN §1-101.
Economic development corporation, 83A §5-201.
Education, ED §1-101.
Financial institutions, FI §1-101.
Health occupations, HO §1-101.
Political subdivisions, 24 §1-101.
Property tax, TP §1-101.
Rules of interpretation, 1 §30.
State finance, SF §1-101.
State government, SG §1-101.
Transportation, TR §1-101.
University of Maryland medical system, ED §13-301.

Income.
Child support guidelines, FL §12-201.
Motor vehicle insurance, IN §19-505.
Principal and income act, ET §15-501.
Uniform interstate family support act, FL §10-301.

Income beneficiary.
Principal and income act, ET §15-501.

Income disregard.
Pharmacy assistance program, HG §15-124.

Income interest.
Principal and income act, ET §15-501.

Income tax, TG §1-101.

Income tax checkoff system.
Chesapeake Bay and endangered species fund, NR §1-701.
Maryland cancer fund income tax checkoff, HG §20-117.

Income tax return preparer, TG §13-207.

Income withholding order.
Uniform interstate family support act, FL §10-301.

Incompetent.
Death sentence, COR §3-904.

Incompetent to proceed.
Juvenile cases, CJ §3-8A-01.

Incompetent to stand trial, CP §3-101.

Incomplete credit card.
Credit card crimes, CR §8-208.

Incomplete instrument.
Negotiable instruments, CL §§3-103, 3-115.

Incomplete vehicle, TR §13-113.2.

Increase in a policy premium.
Insurance, IN §11-317.

Increase in premium.
Motor vehicle insurance, IN §27-613.
Motor vehicle insurance, private passenger liability coverage, IN §27-614.

Incremental cost of building-integrated photovoltaic modules.
Income tax credits, TG §10-722.

DEFINED TERMS —Cont'd

Inculpable person.
Voluntary cleanup program, EN §7-501.

Incumbent.
Legislative newsletters, EL §13-406.

Indebtedness.
Credit life, health and unemployment insurance, IN §13-101.

Independent agency.
Heating and air conditioning, BR §9A-101.

Independent casualty actuary.
Insurance, IN §8-105.

Independent contractor.
Mortgage originator, FI §11-601.

Independent evidence of commercial purpose.
Mortgage lending, FI §11-501.

Independent expenditure.
Elections, EL §1-101.

Independent insurance producer, IN §1-101.

Independent jobber.
Gasohol and gasoline products marketing, CL §11-301.

Independent professional advice.
Structured settlements, transfer of payment rights, CJ §5-1101.

Independent system.
Sanitary commissions, EN §9-601.

Independent system operator.
Electric customer choice and competition act, PUC §7-501.

Independent unit.
Governmental procedures.
Forms management, SG §10-604.
Private providers of care, SF §7-404.

Indian.
Indian affairs commission, 41 §6-901.

Indicated.
Child abuse and neglect, FL §5-701.
Child welfare accountability, FL §5-1301.

Indictment.
Law enforcement officers, CJ §2-608.

Individual.
Access to court records, CJA Rule 16-1001.
Life and health insurance guaranty corporation, IN §9-401.

Individual contract.
Insurance unfair trade practices, IN §27-221.

Individual health benefit plan.
Portability of health insurance, IN §15-1301.

Individual income tax, TG §10-101.

Individualized case-management project.
Family investment program, 88A §44A.

Individualized education program.
Deaf and blind children, ED §8-408.

Individual sewerage system, EN §9-501.

Individual support services.
Developmental disabilities, HG §§7-101, 7-706.

Individual water supply system, EN §9-501.

Individual who died in the line of duty.
Property tax exemptions, TP §7-208.

Individual with a disability.
Workforce investment act, LE §11-503.

Individual with disabilities.
Community rehabilitation programs, ED §21-401.

Indorsement.
Investment securities, CL §8-102.
Negotiable instruments, CL §§3-103, 3-204.

Indorser.
Negotiable instruments, CL §§3-103, 3-204.

Industrial.
Equipment dealer contracts, CL §19-101.

DEFINED TERMS —Cont'd
Industrial building.
  Industrial development financing, 83A §5-901.
Industrial development corporation, 45A §3.
Industrial development fund.
  Industrial development financing, 83A §5-901.
Industrial insured.
  Insurance companies.
    Unauthorized insurers, IN §4-201.
Industrialized building.
  Homebuilder registration, BR §4.5-101.
  Industrialized buildings and manufactured homes,
    PS §12-301.
  Model performance code for building construction,
    PS §12-201.
Industrial life insurance, IN §1-101.
Industrial operator.
  Waterworks operators, EN §12-101.
Industrial process.
  Industrial development financing, 83A §5-901.
Industrial process load.
  Renewable energy portfolio standard, PUC §7-701.
Industrial quality eye protective device.
  Public schools, ED §7-407.
Industrial user.
  Sanitary facilities, EN §9-101.
Industrial wastewater works, EN §12-101.
Inert ingredient.
  Pesticide registration and labeling, AG §5-101.
Inert matter.
  Seeds, AG §9-201.
Infamous crime.
  Elections, EL §1-101.
Infant.
  Hearing impaired infants, HG §13-601.
Infectious waste.
  Sewerage systems, EN §9-227.
Informal kinship care.
  Admission of students, ED §7-101.
  Kinship care, consent to medical care for minor,
    HG §20-105.
  School funding, ED §4-122.1.
Information.
  Catastrophic health emergency disease
    surveillance and response program, HG
    §18-904.
  Computer information transactions, CL §22-102.
  Electronic transactions, CL §21-101.
  Law enforcement officers, CJ §2-608.
Informational content.
  Computer information transactions, CL §22-102.
Informational meeting.
  Department of the environment, EN §1-101.
  Natural resources department, NR §1-106.
Informational rights.
  Computer information transactions, CL §22-102.
Information processing system.
  Computer information transactions, CL §22-102.
  Electronic transactions, CL §21-101.
Information technology, SF §3-402.
  Information technology investment program, TR
    §2-111.
  State finance, SF §3-402.
  Streamlined process for information technology
    services, SF §13-401.
Information technology services.
  State finance, SF §3-402.
Information technology system or product.
  Year 2000 litigation, CJ §5-527.
Infrastructure project.
  Community development administration, HS
    §4-201.

DEFINED TERMS —Cont'd
Infrastructure project —Cont'd
  Maryland housing fund, HS §3-201.
Ingredient statement.
  Pesticide registration and labeling, AG §5-101.
Inhabitants.
  Commercial banks, FI §3-101.
Inheritance tax, TG §1-101.
Inherited metabolic disease.
  Health insurance, IN §15-807.
  Health maintenance organizations, HG §19-705.5.
Initial allowance.
  State retirement and pension system, SPP
    §29-401.
Initial assessment.
  Sexual offenses, HG §15-127.
Initial cost.
  Potomac water authority, EN §5-401.
Initial determination.
  Uniform child custody jurisdiction and
    enforcement act, FL §9.5-101.
Initial implementation date.
  Electric customer choice and competition act, PUC
    §7-501.
Initially providing or referring.
  Nurses, HG §19-2001.
Initial project planning phase.
  Long range highway programs, TR §8-610.
Initial purchaser.
  Cooperative housing corporation, CA §5-6B-01.
Initial sale.
  Cooperative housing corporation, CA §5-6B-01.
Initiate.
  Spam, CR §3-805.1.
Initiating state.
  URESA, FL §10-301.
Initiating tribunal.
  Uniform interstate family support act, FL
    §10-301.
Initiative.
  Child abuse and neglect centers of excellence, HG
    §13-2201.
Injunctive relief.
  Labor relations, LE §4-301.
Injured person.
  Contribution among joint tortfeasors, CJ §3-1401.
Inmate, COR §1-101.
  Alcohol abuse and drug abuse treatment, HG
    §8-6A-01.
  Criminal law, CR §1-101.
  Criminal procedure, CP §1-101.
  Death sentence, incompetent inmate, COR §3-904.
  Interstate corrections compact, COR §8-603.
Inmate of a public institution.
  Health assistance, HG §15-113.
Innkeepers.
  Rights and responsibilities, BR §15-201.
Innovative and alternative septic system, EN
    §9-1401.
Innovative idea.
  State personnel.
    Incentive awards, SPP §10-203.
In-office ancillary services.
  Health occupations, HO §1-301.
Insect.
  Pesticide registration and labeling, AG §5-101.
Insecticide, AG §5-101.
Insider.
  Debt collection, CL §15-101.
Insolvency proceedings.
  Uniform commercial code, CL §1-201.

DEFINED TERMS —Cont'd

Insolvent.
Debt collection, CL §15-101.
Uniform commercial code, CL §1-201.
Insolvent insurer.
Life and health insurance guaranty corporation,
IN §9-401.
Property and casualty insurance guaranty
corporation, IN §9-301.
Insolvent self-insurance group, IN §25-301.
Inspected sod.
Turf grass, AG §9-101.
Inspection.
Property tax, TP §2-217.
Inspection certificate.
Used vehicle inspection, TR §23-101.
Inspection service.
Poultry products inspection act, AG §4-201.
Inspection station.
Used vehicle inspection, TR §23-101.
Inspector.
Poultry products inspection act, AG §4-201.
Wholesome meat act, AG §4-101.
Install.
Homebuilder registration, BR §4.5-101.
Industrialized buildings and manufactured homes,
PS §12-301.
Installment contract.
Sales, UCC, CL §2-612.
Installment lease contract, CL §2A-103.
Installment loan.
Closed end credit, CL §12-1001.
Consumer credit, FI §11-302.
Installment sale.
Income tax, TG §10-703.2.
Installment sale agreement.
Retail sales, CL §12-601.
Sales finance companies, FI §11-401.
Unlawful subleasing of motor vehicle, CR §8-408.
Institute.
Emergency medical services.
University of Maryland, ED §13-501.
Payments to providers not under contract, HG
§19-710.1.
University of Maryland medical system, ED
§13-301.
Institutional.
Management of institutional funds act, ET
§15-401.
Institutional control period.
Radioactive waste, EN §7-301.
Institutional development area.
Forest conservation, NR §5-1601.
Institutional facility.
Therapy management contracts, HO §12-6A-01.
Institutional fund.
Management of institutional funds act, ET
§15-401.
Institutional review board.
Human subject research, HG §13-2001.
Maryland stem cell research program, 83A
§5-2B-01.
Institutional user.
Rechargeable batteries, EN §6-1101.
Institution of higher education, ED §10-101.
Health and educational facilities, 43C §3.
Student loan repayment pilot program, SPP
§10-501.
Unemployment insurance, LE §8-101.
Institution of postsecondary education, ED
§10-101.

DEFINED TERMS —Cont'd

Institutions.
Community attendant services and supports
program, 41 §6-7A-01.
Disease prevention, HG §18-202.
Donors, HG §18-334.
Interstate corrections compact, COR §8-603.
Mental health compact, HG §11-103.
National guard, tuition assistance, PS §13-405.
Newborn infants, HG §20-401.
University system of Maryland, ED §12-101.
Vital statistics, HG §4-201.
Waiver of tuition for senior citizens.
Morgan State University, ED §14-107.
St. Mary's College, ED §14-406.
University of Maryland, ED §13-701.
Instruction.
Investment securities, CL §8-102.
Instructional programming.
Technology for education, ED §7-901.
Instrument.
Adoptees, inclusion in real property grants, RP
§2-123.
Commercial code.
Secured transactions, CL §9-102.
Computer information transactions, CL §22-102.
Negotiable instruments, CL §§3-103, 3-104.
Tax credits for employer-provided commuter
benefits, EN §2-901.
Instrument of payment.
State finance, SF §2-301.
Instrument of writing.
Recordation taxes, TP §12-101.
Transfer taxes, TP §13-101.
Insurance, IN §1-101.
Long-term care insurance, IN §18-102.
Risk retention groups, IN §25-101.
Insurance business, IN §1-101.
Liquidation, rehabilitation, etc., of insurer, IN
§9-201.
Insurance company.
Traffic citations, TR §26-404.
Insurance consumers.
People's insurance counsel, SG §6-301.
Insurance contract, IN §1-101.
Insurance corporation.
Abandoned property, CL §17-101.
Insurance fraud, IN §§2-401, 27-801.
Insurance fund.
Pest control compact, AG §5-702.
Insurance holding company.
Insurance acquisitions disclosure and control, IN
§7-101.
Insurance holding company system.
Insurance acquisitions disclosure and control, IN
§7-101.
Insurance policies.
Holocaust victim insurance, IN §28-101.
Insurance producer, IN §1-101.
Insurance services transaction.
Computer information transactions, CL §22-102.
Insured.
Health insurance.
Divorced spouses and dependent children, IN
§15-408.
Involuntarily terminated employees, IN
§15-409.
Surviving spouses and dependent children, IN
§15-407.
Insurance companies.
Unauthorized insurers, IN §4-210.

DEFINED TERMS —Cont'd
Insured —Cont'd
Preferred provider organizations, IN §14-201.
Insured depository institution.
Bank holding companies, FI §5-901.
Branch banking, FI §5-1001.
Insured individual.
Health insurance, IN §15-412.
Insured institution.
Financial institutions.
Deposit insurance, FI §10-101.
Insured payroll.
Workers' compensation commission.
Tax, LE §9-316.
Insurer, IN §1-101.
Child support orders.
Inclusion of child on health insurance, FL
§12-102.
Competitive rating, IN §11-342.
Disclosure of fire loss investigation reports, PS
§9-601.
Homeowner's insurance policies, IN §19-201.
Insurance regulation assessment, IN §2-501.
Interstate insurance product regulation compact,
IN §29-101.
People's insurance counsel, SG §6-301.
Risk based capital standards for insurers, IN
§4-301.
Workers' compensation commission.
Tax, LE §9-316.
Insuring parent.
Health insurance, IN §15-405.
Intake officer.
Juvenile causes, CJ §3-8A-01.
Intangible transition charges.
Electric customer choice and competition act, PUC
§7-501.
Intangible transition property.
Electric customer choice and competition act, PUC
§7-501.
Integrated mechanical safety device.
Handgun safety devices, PS §5-132.
Integrated pest management.
Pesticide application in schools, AG §5-208.1.
Intellectual property.
Trademark counterfeiting, CR §8-611.
Intensive care policy.
Health insurance, IN §15-104.
Health maintenance organizations, HG §19-713.1.
Interactive computer service provider.
Commercial electronic mail.
Unauthorized, false or misleading information,
CL §14-3001.
Social security number privacy, CL §14-3401.
Interactive computer system.
Theft, CR §7-101.
Interagency committee on aging services, 70B
§1.
Intercept.
Evidence, CJ §10-401.
Intercollegiate sport.
Athlete agents, BR §4-401.
Intercounty connector.
Transportation authority, TR §4-321.
Interest.
Interest in usury, CL §12-101.
Limited liability companies, CA §4A-101.
Public ethics, SG §15-102.
Interested party.
Fiduciaries, ET §15-1A-04.
Property taxes, TP §14-847.

DEFINED TERMS —Cont'd
Interested party —Cont'd
Structured settlements, transfer of payment
rights, CJ §5-1101.
Interested person.
Estates and trusts, ET §§1-101, 13-101.
Interested shares, CA §3-701.
Interested stockholder, CA §3-601.
Interest in a business.
Real estate brokers, BOP §17-511.
Interest in land.
Corporations, CA §3-101.
Interest in real property.
Mortgage lending, FI §11-501.
**Intergovernmental cooperative purchasing
agreement,** SF §13-110.
Interim peace order, CJ §3-1501.
Interim protective order.
Domestic violence, FL §4-501.
Interior design services, BOP §8-101.
Interior space.
Asbestos removal, EN §6-401.
Intermediary bank.
Bank deposits and collections, CL §§4-104, 4-105.
Funds transfers, CL §4A-104.
**Intermediate care facility for the mentally
retarded (ICF-MR),** HG §7-517.
Intermediate level of care.
Medicaid, HG §15-132.
Intermediate sanction.
Hospital deficiencies, HG §19-361.
Interment, BR §5-101.
Intermittent stream.
Forest conservation, NR §5-1601.
Internal revenue code, TG §1-101.
General assembly.
Private activity bonds, SG §2-1010.
Legal services corporation, 10 §45C.
Property tax, TP §1-101.
International building code.
Building codes, PS §12-501.
International commercial arbitration.
Courts, CJ §3-2B-01.
International commission.
Holocaust victim insurance, IN §28-101.
International organization.
Foreign discriminatory boycotts, CL §11-102.
International trade agreement, SG §3-308.
Internet.
Spam, CR §3-805.1.
Internet protocol address.
Spam, CR §3-805.1.
Interrogating officer.
Law enforcement officers and personnel, PS
§3-104.
Interstate association.
Savings and loan associations.
Interstate acquisitions, FI §9-1001.
Interstate commerce.
Agriculture, AG §1-101.
Interstate commission.
Adult offender supervision, COR §6-203.
Interstate highway, TR §8-101.
Interstate identification index system.
National crime prevention and privacy compact,
CP §10-239.
Interstate pipeline.
Hazardous liquid pipelines, PUC §11-201.
Intertrack betting, BR §11-101.
**In the business of selling or renting a
dwelling.**
Housing discrimination, 49B §20.

DEFINED TERMS —Cont'd
In the public interest.
　Pharmacists and pharmacies, HO §12-102.
In this state.
　Alcoholic beverages, 2B §1-102.
Intra-company agent.
　Real estate brokers, BOP §17-530.
Intrastate pipeline.
　Hazardous liquid pipelines, PUC §11-201.
Introduction.
　Nonnative oysters, NR §4-1008.
Invasive disease.
　Laboratory examination reports, HG §18-205.
Inventory.
　Equipment dealer contracts, CL §19-101.
　Secured transactions, CL §9-102.
Investigating committee.
　General assembly, SG §2-1601.
Investigating officer.
　Law enforcement officers and personnel, PS
　　§3-104.
Investigative consumer report.
　Consumer credit reporting agencies, CL §14-1201.
　Credit services businesses, CL §14-1901.
Investigative or law enforcement officer.
　Evidence, CJ §10-401.
Investment.
　Income tax credit for biotechnology companies, TG
　　§10-725.
Investment account.
　College investment plan, ED §18-19A-01.
Investment advisor, CA §11-101.
　Fiduciaries, ET §15-114.
Investment advisor representative, CA §11-101.
Investment company.
　Shares hailed in fiduciary capacity for benefit of
　　other class of shares, CA §2-310.2.
Investment company security.
　Investment securities, CL §§8-102, 8-103.
Investment fund.
　Principal and income, ET §15-508.
Investment manager.
　Local government investment guidelines, 95 §22F.
Investment property.
　Computer information transactions, CL §22-102.
　Secured transactions, CL §9-102.
Invitation for bids.
　Procurement, SF §11-101.
Invoice.
　Procurement, SF §15-101.
Involuntary admission.
　Mental hygiene, HG §10-613.
Involuntary unemployment benefit insurance.
　Consumer loans, CL §12-312.
　Secondary mortgage loans, CL §12-410.
Island vehicle, TR §13-935.
Isolated nontidal wetland, EN §5-901.
Issue.
　Bad checks, CR §8-101.
　Negotiable instruments, CL §§3-103, 3-105.
Issuer.
　Allocation of private activity bond authority, FI
　　§13-801.
　Credit card crimes, CR §8-201.
　Documents of title, CL §7-102.
　Investment securities, CL §§8-102, 8-201.
　Letters of credit, CL §5-102.
　Negotiable instruments, CL §§3-103, 3-105.
　Securities, CA §11-101.
Issuer's jurisdiction.
　Investment securities, CL §8-110.

DEFINED TERMS —Cont'd
Issue year basis.
　Insurance companies.
　　Standard valuation law, IN §5-306.
Issuing authority.
　Alcoholic beverages, 2B §10-401.
Issuing court.
　Uniform child custody jurisdiction and
　　enforcement act, FL §9.5-101.
Issuing state.
　Interstate wildlife violator compact, NR §10-1201.
　Uniform child custody jurisdiction and
　　enforcement act, FL §9.5-101.
　Uniform interstate family support act, FL
　　§10-301.
Issuing tribunal.
　Uniform interstate family support act, FL
　　§10-301.
Item.
　Bank deposits and collections, CL §4-104.
　Computer information transactions, CL §22-102.
　Sale or display of obscene matter to minor, CR
　　§11-203.
Job access project.
　Transportation department, TR §2-103.6.
Job applicant.
　Medical laboratories, HG §17-214.
Job-related.
　Medical laboratories, HG §17-214.
Jockey fund, BR §11-901.
Johns Hopkins institutions.
　Cancer prevention, education, screening and
　　treatment program, HG §13-1101.
Joint account.
　Financial institutions, FI §1-204.
Joint hearing.
　Development permits, SG §11-501.
Jointly held property.
　Disclaimer of property interests, ET §9-201.
Joint tortfeasors, CJ §3-1401.
Joint venture.
　Reporting requirements for public service
　　companies, PUC §6-201.
Journeyman license.
　Heating and air conditioning, BR §9A-101.
Journeyman natural gas fitter, BOP §12-101.
Journeyman restricted license.
　Heating and air conditioning, BR §9A-101.
Journey plumber, BOP §12-101.
Judge, CJ §§1-101, 2-101.
　Judicial disability and sanctionable conduct, CJA
　　Rule 16-803.
　Judicial leave, CJA Rule 16-104.
　Marriage, FL §2-406.
　Tax court, TG §3-101.
Judges' retirement system, SPP §20-101.
Judgment.
　Motor vehicles, TR §17-201.
Judgment of restitution.
　Crime victims' restitution, CP §11-601.
Judicial agency.
　Access to court records, CJA Rule 16-1001.
Judicial function.
　Governmental procedures.
　　Meetings, SG §10-502.
Judicial lien.
　Debt collection, CL §15-101.
Judy center.
　Judith P. Hoyer early child care and education
　　enhancement program, ED §5-217.

DEFINED TERMS —Cont'd
Judy center grant.
Judith P. Hoyer early child care and education
enhancement program, ED §5-217.
Junk.
Business licenses, BR §17-1001.
Junkyards, TR §8-801.
Junk dealer.
Business licenses, BR §17-1001.
Junk dealer or scrap metal processor license.
Business licenses, BR §17-1005.
Junkyard, EN §5-10A-01.
Transportation, TR §8-801.
Jurisdiction.
Emergency management assistance compact, PS
§14-802.
Interjurisdictional sewage disposal rates, PUC
§4-304.
Motor vehicles, TR §12-401.
Zoning and planning, 66B §1.00.
Jurisdictional emergency medical services
operational program.
Automated external defibrillator program, ED
§13-517.
Jurisdiction of organization.
Secured transactions, CL §9-102.
Jurisdictions.
Maryland emergency management assistance
compact, PS §14-801.
Jury commissioner, CJ §8-101.
Jury plan, CJ §8-101.
Just and reasonable rate.
Public service companies, PUC §4-101.
Juvenile court.
Family law, FL §1-101.
Juvenile justice monitor.
Juvenile justice monitoring unit, SG §6-401.
Juvenile program.
Facilities capital program, 83C §4-101.
Juvenile services, 83C §2-115.
Keg.
Beer keg registration, 2B §21-106.
Keg licensee.
Beer keg registration, 2B §21-106.
Key shareholder.
Money transmission, FI §12-401.
Kidney dialysis center.
Freestanding ambulatory care facilities, HG
§19-3B-01.
Kind.
Seeds, AG §9-201.
Turf grass, AG §9-101.
Kinship care.
Child care, FL §5-501.
Child welfare accountability, FL §5-1301.
Kinship parent.
Kinship care program, FL §5-534.
Knowingly.
Obscene matter, CR §11-201.
Sale of alcohol to habitual drunkards, 2B §12-110.
Theft, CR §7-102.
Unemployment compensation.
Transfers for purpose of lowering contribution
rates, LE §8-614.
Knowledge.
Commercial code, CL §1-201.
Computer information transactions, CL §22-102.
Kosher.
Consumer protection, CL §14-901.
Label.
Commercial feed, AG §6-101.

DEFINED TERMS —Cont'd
Label —Cont'd
Commercial fertilizers, AG §6-201.
Food and drugs, HG §21-101.
Pesticide applicators, AG §5-201.
Pesticide registration and labeling, AG §5-101.
Poultry products inspection act, AG §4-201.
Recycling, EN §9-1710.
Wholesome meat act, AG §4-101.
Labeling.
Commercial fertilizers, AG §6-201.
Food and drugs, HG §21-101.
Pesticide applicators, AG §5-201.
Pesticide registration and labeling, AG §5-101.
Poultry products inspection act, AG §4-201.
Seeds, AG §9-201.
Turf grass, AG §9-101.
Wholesome meat act, AG §4-101.
Labor, agricultural or horticultural
organization.
Charitable organization volunteer personal
liability, CJ §5-407.
Employment discrimination, 49B §15.
Laboratory.
Donors, HG §18-334.
Medical laboratories, HG §17-214.
Laboratory instructor.
Driver education, TR §16-501.
Labor dispute.
Injunctions, LE §4-301.
Mass transit, TR §7-602.
Land.
Abandoned mine drainage control, EN §15-701.
Abandoned mine reclamation, EN §15-1101.
Highways, TR §8-301.
Judgment liens, CJ §11-402.
Land patents, RP §13-101.
Mechanics' liens, RP §9-101.
Public recreation on private and local government
lands, NR §5-1101.
State development plan, SF §5-601.
Strip mining, EN §15-501.
Surface mining, EN §15-801.
Land affected.
Strip mining, EN §15-501.
Landbanking.
Community legacy program, HS §6-201.
Land classification.
Chesapeake Bay critical area and Atlantic coastal
bays critical area protection programs, NR
§8-1802.
Land conservation program.
Natural resources, NR §1-404.
Land eligible for remining.
Strip mining, EN §15-501.
Land installment contract.
Real property, RP §10-101.
Landlord, RP §8-214.
Real property, RP §1-101.
Security deposits, RP §8-203.
Landowners.
Forest conservancy districts, NR §5-601.
Pine tree reforestation, NR §5-501.
Public watershed associations, 25 §169.
Strip mining, EN §15-501.
Surface mining, EN §15-801.
Landscape architect, BOP §9-101.
Land surveyor, BOP §15-101.
Land trust.
Forests and parks.
Open space program, NR §5-901.

DEFINED TERMS —Cont'd
Land trust —Cont'd
Grant fund, NR §3-2A-01.
Property tax.
Conservation lands, TP §9-220.
Recordation tax exemptions, TP §12-108.
Rural legacy program, NR §5-9A-02.
Landward boundary of wetlands, EN §16-101.
Lapse.
Vehicle insurance, TR §17-101.
Large packaged air-conditioning equipment.
Maryland efficiency standards act, SG §9-2006.
Large private group home.
Mental hygiene, HG §10-514.
Last known address.
Self-service storage, CL §18-501.
Late enrollee.
Health insurance portability, IN §15-1401.
Small employer health insurance, IN §15-1201.
Late fee, CL §14-1315.
Latent defects.
Tax credits, RP §10-702.
Lateral system construction costs.
Water and sewerage systems, SF §2-401.
Launch service, PUC §1-101.
Law.
Fraternal benefit societies, IN §8-401.
Property tax, TP §1-101.
Uniform interstate family support act, FL §10-301.
URESA, FL §10-301.
Water and sewer authorities, EN §9-901.
Law enforcement agency.
Adult protective services, FL §14-101.
Arrest of pupils for reportable offenses, ED §7-303.
Child abuse and neglect, FL §5-701.
Expungement of records, Crim Rule 4-502.
Hospital residents, HG §19-347.
Missing children, FL §9-401.
Nurses, HO §8-509.
Police training commission, PS §3-201.
Post conviction review, CP §8-201.
Refusal to register motor vehicles, TR §13-406.1.
Reports on traffic stops, TR §25-113.
School bus safety enforcement fund, PS §4-201.
Security systems, CL §14-1314.
State police department, PS §2-101.
Suspension, revocation or refusal of drivers' license, TR §16-204.
Law enforcement equipment.
Law enforcement equipment fund, PS §4-301.
Law enforcement officer, HG §18-213.2.
Assault, CR §3-201.
Courts, CJ §2-608.
Death benefits, public safety officers and personnel, PS §1-202.
Death penalty, sentencing procedure, CR §2-303.
Disarming law enforcement officer, CR §4-103.
Disease reports, HG §18-213.
Handguns, CR §4-201.
Law enforcement officers' bill of rights, PS §3-101.
Law enforcement officers' pension system.
Participation in, SPP §31-2A-01.
Local fire and police pension system, SPP §31-201.
Possession of firearm at public demonstration, CR §4-208.
Reports on traffic stops, TR §25-113.
Law enforcement officers' pension system, SPP §20-101.

DEFINED TERMS —Cont'd
Law enforcement official.
Professional engineers immunity, CJ §5-425.
Law enforcement unit.
Alarm systems, CR §9-607.
Criminal injuries compensation board, CP §11-807.
Criminal justice information system, CP §10-216.
Expungement of criminal records, CP §10-101.
Law firm.
Insurance agents and brokers, IN §10-125.
Lawful custodian.
Child abduction, FL §9-301.
Lawyer, BOP §10-101.
Legal mutual liability insurance society of Maryland, IN §24-101.
Lawyer counseling committee, BOP §10-502.
Layaway agreement, CL §14-1101.
Layaway price, CL §14-1101.
Lead agency.
Children, youth and families services, 49D §1-101.
Eminent domain, RP §12-201.
Lead-based paint, EN §6-801.
Lead containing substance.
Lead paint, EN §6-1001.
Lead-contaminated dust, EN §6-801.
Lead-free, EN §6-801.
Lead hazard reduction activity.
Lead hazard reduction grant and loan programs, HS §4-701.
Lead-safe housing, EN §6-801.
Leaf tobacco market, AG §7-101.
Lease.
Commercial code, CL §2A-103.
Motor vehicle leasing contracts, CL §14-2001.
Motor vehicles, TR §12-107.
Real property, RP §1-101.
Lease agreement.
Commercial code, CL §2A-103.
Lease contract.
Commercial code, CL §2A-103.
Unlawful subleasing of motor vehicle, CR §8-408.
Leased oyster bottom, NR §4-1101.
Aquaculture, NR §4-11A-01.
Leased space.
Self-service storage, CL §18-501.
Leasehold interest.
Commercial code, CL §2A-103.
Leasehold property.
Estates and trusts, ET §5-503.
Lease intended as security.
Motor vehicles, TR §11-127.1.
Lease option agreement.
Landlord and tenant, RP §8-202.
Leave.
Work release and home detention programs, Baltimore County, COR §11-705.
Leave bank.
State employees' leave bank, SPP §9-601.
Leave donation program.
State personnel, SPP §9-601.
Leave of absence.
Health assistance, HG §15-117.
Legacy, ET §1-101.
Legal assistance.
Legal services corporation, 10 §45C.
Legal assistance organization.
Consumer protection, CL §13-206.
Legal authority.
Elections.
Petitions, EL §6-101.

DEFINED TERMS —Cont'd
Legal holiday.
 Political subdivisions, 24 §1-104.
 Property tax, TP §1-303.
 Rules of interpretation, 1 §27.
 Taxation, TG §1-201.
Legal interest.
 Property tax.
  Homeowners credit, TP §9-104.
  Homestead credit, TP §9-105.
  Rezoned real property, TP §8-226.
Legal proceeding.
 Support, FL §10-115.
Legal representative.
 Discretionary trusts, ET §14-401.
 UTMA, ET §13-301.
Legal services.
 Immigration consultants, CL §14-3301.
Legatee.
 Estates and trusts, ET §1-101.
Legislation.
 Municipal corporations, 23A §2B.
Legislative action.
 Public ethics, SG §15-102.
Legislative body.
 Housing authorities, HS §12-101.
 State retirement and pension system, SPP
  §31-101.
Legislative delegation.
 Study commission.
  Washington county, 24 §12-201.
Legislative function.
 Governmental procedures.
  Meetings, SG §10-502.
Legislative newsletter, EL §13-406.
Legislative pension plan.
 Pensions, SPP §20-101.
Legislative unit.
 Public ethics, SG §15-102.
Lender.
 Closed and credit, CL §12-1022.
 Consumer loans, CL §12-301.
 Controlled hazardous substances, EN §7-201.
 Denial of credit, CL §14-1701.
 Financing agreements, CL §12-125.
 Finder's fees, CL §12-801.
 Industrial development financing authority, 83A
  §5-927.
 Interest in usury, CL §12-101.
 Management of escrow accounts, CL §12-109.2.
 Mortgages and deeds of trust.
  Subordination of lender's interest, RP §4-111.
 Revolving credit, CL §12-922.
 Secondary mortgage loans, CL §12-401.
 Water pollution, EN §4-401.
 Water quality financing.
  Linked deposit loans, EN §9-1606.1.
Lender's inspection fee.
 Closed and credit, CL §12-1027.
 Real estate loans, CL §12-121.
Lending institution.
 Agricultural and resource-based industry
  development corporation, 41 §13-501.
 Closed and credit, CL §12-1026.
 Interest on escrow accounts, CL §12-109.
LEP.
 Grants for limited-English proficiency education,
  ED §5-208.
LEP enrollment count.
 Grants for limited-English proficiency education,
  ED §5-208.

DEFINED TERMS —Cont'd
LEP per pupil amount.
 Grants for limited-English proficiency education,
  ED §5-208.
Lessee.
 Commercial code, CL §2A-103.
 Motor vehicle leasing contracts, CL §14-2001.
 Rental motor vehicles.
  Collision damage waivers, CL §14-2101.
Lessee in ordinary course of business.
 Commercial code, CL §2A-103.
Lessor.
 Abandoned vehicles, TR §25-201.
 Commercial code, CL §2A-103.
 Motor vehicle leasing contracts, CL §14-2001.
 Rental motor vehicles.
  Collision damage waivers, CL §14-2101.
 Rental-purchase agreements, CL §12-1101.
 Unlawful subleasing of motor vehicle, CR §8-408.
Lessor's residual interest.
 Commercial code, CL §2A-103.
Less than absolute interest.
 Inheritance tax, TG §7-201.
Letter of compliance.
 Child care centers, FL §5-570.
Letter of credit, CL §5-102.
 Computer information transactions, CL §22-102.
 Sales, UCC, CL §2-325.
Letter-of-credit right.
 Secured transactions, CL §9-102.
Letters.
 Estates and trusts, ET §1-101.
Liability.
 Health club services, CL §14-12B-02.
 International tax liability, TG §8-205.
 Risk retention groups, IN §25-101.
Liability reserve.
 Income tax, TG §10-102.1.
Liable parent.
 Crime victims' restitution, CP §11-601.
Library agreement.
 Interstate library compact, ED §25-303.
License.
 Accountants, BOP §2-101.
 Acupuncturists, HO §1A-101.
 Administrative procedures.
  Contested cases, SG §§10-202, 10-226.
 Ambulance services, ED §13-515.
 Architects, BOP §3-101.
 Asbestos removal, EN §6-401.
 Athlete agents, BR §4-401.
 Automotive dismantler and recyclers, TR §15-501.
 Bail bondsmen, IN §10-301.
 Barbers, BOP §4-101.
 Bedding, HG §24-401.
 Board of veterinary medical examiners, AG
  §2-301.
 Boxing, BR §4-301.
 Business licenses, BR §§17-201, 17-301.
 Business license violations, BR §17-2101.
 Check cashing services, FI §12-101.
 Child care, FL §5-501.
 Child care centers, FL §5-570.
 Chiropractors, HO §3-101.
 Cigarette licenses, BR §16-201.
 Clinical professional counselors, HO §17-3A-01.
 Collection agencies, BR §7-101.
 Computer information transactions, CL §22-102.
 Consumer loans, FI §11-201.
 Cosmetologists, BOP §5-101.
 Dentistry, HO §4-101.

DEFINED TERMS —Cont'd
License —Cont'd
Dietitians and nutritionists, HO §5-101.
Drivers' schools, TR §15-701.
Driving instructors, TR §15-801.
Electricians, BOP §6-101.
Electrologists, HO §8-6B-01.
Elevator safety, PS §12-801.
Engineers, BOP §14-101.
Environmental sanitarians, EN §11-101.
Farm labor contractors, LE §7-101.
Food establishments, HG §21-301.
Foresters, BOP §7-101.
Freestanding ambulatory care facilities, HG §19-3B-01.
Frozen desserts, HG §21-801.
Hearing aid dispensers and audiologists, HO §2-101.
Heating and air conditioning, BR §9A-101.
Home inspectors, BOP §16-101.
Hospitals, HG §19-301.
Insurance adjusters, IN §10-401.
Insurance advisers, IN §10-201.
Insurance producers, IN §10-101.
Interstate wildlife violator compact, NR §10-1201.
Landscape architects, BOP §9-101.
Land surveyors, BOP §15-101.
Laundries and dry cleaners, BR §17-1101.
Lottery agency, SG §9-101.
Marriage, FL §2-101.
Mental hygiene, HG §10-501.
Money transmission, FI §12-401.
Montgomery county alcoholic beverage licenses, 2B §9-102.1.
Mortgage lending, FI §11-501.
Mortgage originator, FI §11-601.
Morticians, HO §7-101.
Motor clubs, IN §26-101.
Motor fuel tax, TG §9-301.
Motor vehicle dealers, TR §15-301.
Motor vehicles, TR §§11-128, 15-201.
Nurses, HO §8-101.
Nursing home administrators, HO §9-101.
Nursing referral service agencies, HG §19-4B-01.
Occupational therapists, HO §10-101.
Optometrists, HO §11-101.
Pharmacists and pharmacies, HO §12-101.
Physical therapists, HO §13-101.
Physicians, HO §14-101.
Pilots, BOP §11-101.
Plumbers, BOP §12-101.
Podiatrists, HO §16-101.
Polysomnographic technologists, HO §13-5C-01.
Private detectives, BOP §13-101.
Private home detention monitoring, BOP §20-101.
Private mental health group homes, HG §10-514.
Professional service corporations, CA §5-101.
Proration of certain license fees, BOP §1-207.
Provider-sponsored organizations, HG §19-7A-01.
Psychologists, HO §18-101.
Real estate brokers, BOP §17-101.
Reinsurance intermediaries, IN §8-501.
Respiratory care, HO §14-5A-01.
Sales finance companies, FI §11-401.
Security guards, BOP §19-101.
Security systems technicians, BOP §18-101.
Social workers, HO §19-101.
State licensing, BR §2-110.
Stationary engineers, BOP §6.5-101.
Storage warehouse licenses, BR §17-1201.
Support, FL §10-119.3.

DEFINED TERMS —Cont'd
License —Cont'd
Trading stamps, BR §17-2001.
Vehicle salesmen, TR §15-401.
Well drillers, EN §13-101.
Licensed agent.
Lottery agency, SG §9-101.
Licensed apprentice.
Heating and air conditioning, BR §9A-101.
Morticians, HO §7-101.
Licensed architect, BOP §3-101.
Licensed area.
Waterfowl, NR §10-1001.
Licensed associate real estate broker, BOP §17-101.
Licensed associate social worker, HO §19-101.
Licensed audiologist, HO §2-101.
Licensed certified public accountant, BOP §2-101.
Licensed certified social worker, HO §19-101.
Privileged communications.
Courts, CJ §9-121.
Licensed certified social worker-clinical, HO §19-101.
Licensed chiropractor, HO §3-101.
Motor vehicle registration plates for individuals with disabilities, TR §13-616.
Licensed clinical professional counselor.
Mental hygiene admissions, HG §10-601.
Licensed collection agency, BR §7-101.
Licensed contractor.
Heating and air conditioning, BR §9A-101.
Home improvement, BR §8-101.
Licensed cosmetologist, BOP §5-101.
Licensed dealer.
Motor vehicles, TR §11-129.
Licensed dental hygienist, HO §4-101.
Licensed dentist, HO §4-101.
Licensed distributor.
Motor vehicles, TR §11-129.
License dealer.
Motor fuel tax, TG §9-301.
Licensed electrologist, HO §8-6B-01.
Licensed electrology instructor, HO §8-6B-01.
Licensed factory branch.
Motor vehicles, TR §11-129.
Licensed farm labor contractor, LE §7-101.
Licensed forester, BOP §7-101.
Licensed funeral director, HO §7-101.
Licensed graduate alcohol and drug counselor, HO §17-3A-01.
Licensed graduate marriage and family therapist, HO §17-3A-01.
Licensed graduate professional counselor, HO §17-3A-01.
Licensed graduate social worker, HO §19-101.
Licensed health care professional.
Assisted suicide, CR §3-101.
Licensed health professionals.
Nursing referral service agencies, HG §19-4B-01.
Licensed hearing aid dispenser, HO §2-101.
Licensed home inspector, BOP §16-101.
Licensed horse racing, BR §11-101.
Licensed hospital.
Anatomical gift act, ET §4-501.
Licensed insurance producer, IN §1-101.
License distributor.
Motor fuel tax, TG §9-301.
Licensed landscape architect, BOP §9-101.
Licensed manufacturer.
Cigarette licenses, BR §16-201.

DEFINED TERMS —Cont'd

Licensed manufacturer —Cont'd
Motor vehicles, TR §11-129.
Licensed master electrician, BOP §6-101.
Licensed master plumber, BOP §12-302.
Licensed morticians, HO §7-101.
Licensed nursing home administrator, HO §9-101.
Licensed occupational therapist, HO §10-101.
Licensed occupational therapy assistant, HO §10-101.
Licensed optometrist, HO §11-101.
Motor vehicle registration plates for individuals with disabilities, TR §13-616.
Licensed pawnbrokers, BR §12-101.
Licensed pharmacist, HO §12-101.
Licensed physical therapist, HO §13-101.
Licensed physical therapist assistant, HO §13-101.
Licensed physician, HO §14-101.
Motor vehicle registration plates for individuals with disabilities, TR §13-616.
Therapy management contracts, HO §12-6A-01.
Licensed pilot, BOP §11-101.
Licensed podiatrist, HO §16-101.
Motor vehicle registration plates for individuals with disabilities, TR §13-616.
Licensed polysomnographic technologist, HO §13-5C-01.
Licensed practical nurse, HO §8-101.
Licensed private detective agency, BOP §13-101.
Licensed private home detention monitoring agency, BOP §20-101.
Licensed professional.
Professional malpractice, CJ §3-2C-01.
Licensed property line surveyor, BOP §15-101.
Licensed psychologist, HO §18-101.
Licensed real estate appraiser, BOP §16-101.
Licensed real estate broker, BOP §17-101.
Licensed real estate salesperson, BOP §17-101.
Licensed respiratory care practitioner, HO §14-5A-01.
Licensed retailer.
Cigarette licenses, BR §16-201.
Licensed security guard agency, BOP §19-101.
Licensed senior cosmetologist, BOP §5-101.
Licensed special fuel seller.
Motor fuel tax, TG §9-301.
Licensed speech-language pathologist, HO §2-101.
Licensed storage warehouse.
Cigarette licenses, BR §16-201.
Licensed subwholesaler.
Cigarette licenses, BR §16-201.
Licensed trader.
Business licenses, BR §17-1801.
Licensed tree expert, NR §5-415.
Licensed turbine fuel seller.
Motor fuel tax, TG §9-301.
Licensed vending machine operator.
Cigarette licenses, BR §16-201.
Licensed wholesaler.
Cigarette licenses, BR §16-201.
Tobacco, escrow act compliance, BR §16-501.
Tobacco tax, TG §12-301.
Licensee.
Alcoholic beverages, 2B §1-102.
Check cashing services, FI §12-101.
Commissioner of financial regulation, FI §11-101.
Computer information transactions, CL §22-102.

DEFINED TERMS —Cont'd

Licensee —Cont'd
Consumer loans, CL §12-301.
Debt management services, FI §12-901.
Firearms, PS §5-101.
Horse racing, BR §11-101.
Mental retardation facilities, HG §7-909.
Mortgage lending, FI §11-501.
Mortgage originator, FI §11-601.
Morticians, HO §7-101.
Motor clubs, IN §26-101.
Motor vehicles, TR §12-201.
Real estate brokers, BOP §17-101.
Residential centers, HG §7-1001.
Secondary mortgage loans, CL §12-401.
Surface mining, EN §15-801.
Licensee in ordinary course of business.
Secured transactions , priority of security interests, CL §9-321.
License fee.
Accountants, BOP §2-101.
Architects, BOP §3-101.
Engineers, BOP §14-101.
Landscape architects, BOP §9-101.
Land surveyors, BOP §15-101.
License holder.
Alcoholic beverages, 2B §1-102.
Licensing agency.
Children, youth and families services.
Operators of residential child care programs, 49D §6-101.
Licensing authority.
Driver license compact, TR §16-701.
Interstate wildlife violator compact, NR §10-1201.
Support, FL §10-119.3.
Licensing unit.
Professional service corporations, CA §5-101.
Licensor.
Computer information transactions, CL §22-102.
Lien.
Commercial code, CL §2A-103.
Contract liens, RP §14-201.
Drug asset forfeiture, CP §12-101.
Lien creditor.
Secured transactions, CL §9-102.
Lienholder.
Boats and boating, NR §8-701.
Drug asset forfeiture, CP §12-101.
Lien on real property.
Secondary mortgage loans, CL §12-401.
Lien property.
Commercial real estate broker's lien, RP §14-301.
Life-cycle costs.
Energy, SF §4-801.
Life expectancy.
Trusts, ET §14-107.
Life insurance, IN §1-101.
Life insurer, IN §1-101.
Insurance regulation assessment, IN §2-501.
Risk based capital standards for insurers, IN §4-301.
Life insurer assessment portion.
Insurance regulation assessment, IN §2-501.
Life of the building.
Energy, SF §4-801.
Life-sustaining procedure.
Disabled persons, ET §13-711.
Health care decisions, HG §5-601.
Light rail transit.
Maryland transit administration, TR §7-101.
Light wine, 2B §4-101.

DEFINED TERMS —Cont'd
Liming materials, AG §6-301.
Limited benefit plan.
Small employer health insurance, IN §15-1201.
Limited dividend corporation.
Community development administration, HS
§4-201.
Limited English proficiency.
Equal access to public services, SG §10-1102.
Grants for limited-English proficiency education,
ED §5-208.
Limited hospice care program, HG §19-901.
Limited income household.
Community reinvestment fund, HS §9-101.
Limited laboratory examinations.
Medical laboratories, HG §17-205.
Limited liability company, CA §§3-101, 4A-101.
Criminal process, CP §4-203.
Limited partnerships.
Merger, CA §10-208.
Limited liability partnership, CA §9A-101.
Limited license.
Cosmetologists, BOP §5-101.
Engineers, BOP §14-101.
Hearing aid dispensers and audiologists, HO
§2-101.
Heating and air conditioning, BR §9A-101.
Hospice care, HG §19-901.
Pilots, BOP §11-101.
Plumbers, BOP §12-101.
**Limited license to practice speech-language
pathology,** HO §2-101.
**Limited license to provide hearing aid
services,** HO §2-101.
Limited line credit insurance.
Insurance producers, IN §10-101.
Limited line credit insurance producer, IN
§10-101.
Limited occupational therapy, HO §10-101.
Limited occupational therapy practice, HO
§10-101.
Limited partner, CA §10-101.
Limited partnership, CA §§3-101, 9A-101, 10-101,
10-1105.
Limited liability companies, CA §4A-101.
Partnerships, revised act, CA §9A-101.
Limited peripheral development.
Priority funding areas, SF §5-7B-01.
Limited service hospital, HG §19-301.
Certificates of need, HG §19-120.
Limit for cumulative noise exposure.
Noise zones.
Aviation, TR §5-801.
Limousine, TR §11-129.1.
Open containers of alcoholic beverages in motor
vehicles, CR §10-123.
Limousine service.
For-hire driving services, PUC §10-101.
Linear project.
Forest conservation, NR §5-1601.
Linked deposit.
Industrial development financing authority, 83A
§5-927.
Water quality financing, EN §9-1606.1.
Linked deposit loan.
Water quality financing, EN §9-1606.1.
Linked deposit program.
Industrial development financing, 83A §5-901.
Water quality financing, EN §9-1606.1.
Liquefied natural gas, PUC §11-101.
Liquefied natural gas facility, PUC §11-101.

DEFINED TERMS —Cont'd
Liquefied petroleum gas.
Containers, CL §11-601.
Liquid assets.
Kidney disease, HG §13-302.
Liquidating asset.
Principal and income, ET §15-517.
Liquid waste.
Environmental service, NR §3-101.
Liquor, 2B §16-414.
Liquor control board, 2B §15-201.
Listed facility.
Radiation, EN §8-305.
Litter.
Litter control law, CR §10-110.
Sewerage systems, EN §9-501.
Live independently.
Developmental disabilities, HG §7-101.
Live poultry market.
Avian influenza, regulation of poultry to control,
AG §3-801.
Livery vessel owner, NR §8-712.3.
Livestock, AG §§1-101, 3-301.
Livestock slaughtering, AG §4-123.1.
Livestock dealer, AG §3-301.
Livestock market, AG §3-301.
Lloyds underwriters, IN §4-102.
Load-bearing portions of the home.
New home warranties, RP §10-601.
Loading zone.
School vehicles, TR §22-228.
Loan.
Closed end credit, CL §12-1001.
Commercial banks.
Maximum liabilities of person, FI §3-601.
Consumer credit, FI §11-201.
Consumer loans, CL §12-301.
Mortgage releases, RP §3-105.1.
Revolving credit, CL §12-901.
Secondary mortgage loans, CL §12-401.
Water quality financing, EN §9-1601.
Loan agreement.
Water quality financing, EN §9-1601.
Loan application.
Closed end credit, CL §12-1022.
Financing agreements, CL §12-125.
Mortgage lending, FI §11-501.
Mortgage originator, FI §11-601.
Revolving credit, CL §12-922.
Loan documents.
Small business development financing authority,
83A §5-1001.
Loan obligation.
Water quality financing, EN §9-1601.
Loan program.
Lead hazard reduction grant and loan programs,
HS §4-701.
Loan review committee.
Financial institutions, FI §1-205.
Lobbying.
Public ethics, SG §15-102.
Lobbyists.
Campaign finance, EL §13-210.
Local agency.
Food programs, HG §18-108.
Local area.
Summer youth connection program, LE §11-602.
Local association of employees.
Charitable organization volunteer personal
liability, CJ §5-407.

DEFINED TERMS —Cont'd
Local authority.
  Motor vehicles, TR §11-130.
Local bar association, BOP §10-502.
Local board.
  Elections, EL §1-101.
  Foster care, FL §5-501.
Local code violation.
  Nuisance actions by community associations, RP
    §§14-123 to 14-125.1.
Local community.
  Water and sewerage services.
    Code counties, 25B §13E-1.
Local contribution rate.
  Educational financing.
    State assistance, ED §5-202.
Local coordinating council.
  Children, youth and families services, 49D §1-101.
Local correctional facility, COR §1-101.
  Criminal law, CR §1-101.
  Criminal procedure, CP §1-101.
Local current expense per student.
  Children in out-of-county living arrangements, ED
    §4-122.
  School funding, ED §4-122.1.
  Schools near boundary of two counties, ED §4-121.
Local department.
  Adult protective services, FL §14-101.
  Child abuse and neglect, 88A §6A; FL §§5-701,
    5-705.1.
  Children in need of assistance, CJ §3-801.
  Child welfare accountability, FL §5-1301.
  Domestic violence, FL §4-501.
  Family investment program, 88A §44A.
  Family law, FL §1-101.
  Juvenile causes, CJ §3-8A-01.
  Procurement.
    Hiring agreements, SF §13-224.
Local detention center officer.
  Correctional officers' retirement system, SPP
    §31-2B-01.
Local development agency.
  Community development administration, HS
    §4-201.
Local development entity.
  Community development administration, HS
    §4-201.
Local domestic violence fatality review team.
  Immunity of members, CJ §5-637.1.
Local economic development fund.
  Economic development assistance fund, 83A
    §5-1401.
Local economic development opportunity.
  Economic development assistance fund, 83A
    §5-1401.
Local emergency planning commission.
  Community right-to-know fund, EN §7-601.
Local enforcement agency.
  Industrialized buildings and manufactured homes,
    PS §12-301.
Local entity.
  Employee political activities, 24 §13-101.
Local executive.
  Land use, 66B §1.00.
  Zoning and planning, 66B §1.00.
Local family trade.
  Crabs, NR §4-807.
Local financial authority.
  Drug asset forfeiture, CP §12-101.
Local fire and police system.
  Pensions, SPP §20-101.

DEFINED TERMS —Cont'd
Local fire department.
  Fires and fire protection, high-rise buildings, PS
    §9-401.
Local forest conservation program, NR §5-1601.
Local governing authority.
  Social services administration, 88A §4.
Local governing bodies.
  Emergency management, PS §14-401.
  Forests and parks.
    Open space program, NR §5-901.
  Long range highway programs, TR §8-610.
Local government.
  Deposit of unexpended or surplus money by local
    government, 95 §22O.
  Development permits, SG §11-101.
  Economic development assistance fund, 83A
    §5-1401.
  Insurance pools, IN §19-603.
  Lead risk reduction in rental housing, regulation
    of landlords, 24 §19-101.
  Local government investment pool, 95 §22G.
  Local government tort claims act, CJ §5-301.
  Setback line restrictions.
    Limitation of actions, CJ §5-114.
  Water quality financing, EN §9-1601.
  Year 2000 litigation, CJ §5-527.
Local government unit.
  Administrative procedure, SG §10-101.
  Investment guidelines, 95 §22F.
Local health officer.
  Cancer prevention, education, screening and
    treatment program, HG §13-1101.
  Tobacco use prevention and cessation program,
    HG §13-1001.
Local health official.
  Sanitary facilities, EN §9-201.
Local health planning agency, HG §§1-101,
  19-114.
Local historic district.
  Maryland historical trust, rehabilitation tax
    credits, SF §5A-303.
Local issuer.
  Allocation of private activity bond authority, FI
    §13-801.
Locality.
  Public works contracts, SF §17-201.
Local jurisdiction.
  Building codes, PS §12-501.
  Building rehabilitation code, PS §12-1001.
  Canal place preservation and development
    authority, FI §13-1001.
  Chesapeake Bay critical area and Atlantic coastal
    bays critical area protection programs, NR
    §8-1802.
  Community energy loan program, SG §9-2101.
  Land use, 66B §1.00.
  Local pension systems, SPP §40-101.
  New home warranties, RP §10-601.
Local law enforcement agency.
  DNA technology fund, 41 §4-301.
  Law enforcement equipment fund, PS §4-301.
  Protective body armor fund, PS §4-101.
Local law enforcement unit.
  Pawnbrokers, BR §12-101.
  Sex offender registration, CP §11-701.
Local legislative body.
  Land use, 66B §1.00.
  Zoning and planning, 66B §§1.00, 7.02.
Local legislative delegation.
  Long range highway programs, TR §8-610.

DEFINED TERMS —Cont'd
Local license.
 Electricians, BOP §6-101.
Local licensing authority.
 Explosives licenses, PS §11-101.
Local licensing board.
 Alcoholic beverages, 2B §1-102.
Locally designated growth area.
 Priority funding areas, SF §5-7B-01.
Locally grown food.
 Procurement, SF §14-407.
Local management board.
 Children, youth and families services, 49D §1-101.
 Judith P. Hoyer early child care and education
 enhancement program, ED §5-217.
Local obligation.
 Community development administration, HS
 §4-201.
Local official.
 Public ethics, SG §15-102.
 Withholding tax refund due to local government
 debts, TG §13-925.
**Local organization for emergency
 management.**
 Maryland emergency management agency
 (MEMA), PS §14-101.
Local pension system.
 Correctional officers' retirement system, SPP
 §31-2B-01.
 Law enforcement officers' pension system.
 Participation in, SPP §31-2A-01.
 Local fire and police pension system, SPP §31-201.
 State retirement and pension system, SPP
 §31-101.
Local performance standards.
 Schools, comprehensive master plans, ED §5-401.
Local petition.
 Elections, EL §6-101.
Local plan.
 Heritage areas, FI §13-1101.
 Workforce investment act, LE §11-503.
Local police department.
 Speed restrictions on motor vehicles, Montgomery
 county, TR §21-809.
Local projects.
 Forests and parks.
 Open space program, NR §5-901.
Local public health cancer grant.
 Cancer prevention, education, screening and
 treatment program, HG §13-1101.
Local public health component.
 Cancer prevention, education, screening and
 treatment program, HG §13-1101.
 Tobacco use prevention and cessation program,
 HG §13-1001.
Local public health tobacco grant.
 Tobacco use prevention and cessation program,
 HG §13-1001.
Local redevelopment authority, 83A §5-1701.
Local rehabilitation program.
 Maryland housing rehabilitation program, HS
 §4-901.
Local school superintendent.
 Handicapped children, ED §8-412.
Local school system.
 Arrest of pupils for reportable offenses, ED
 §7-303.
Local share of the foundation program.
 Educational financing.
 State assistance, ED §5-202.

DEFINED TERMS —Cont'd
Local state's attorney.
 Adult protective services, FL §14-101.
 Child abuse and neglect, FL §5-701.
Local superintendent.
 Arrest of pupils for reportable offenses, ED
 §7-303.
Local support enforcement office, FL §10-101.
Local team.
 Local domestic violence fatality review teams, FL
 §4-701.
Local units.
 Public assistance programs, 88A §64.
Local wealth per pupil.
 Grants for limited-English proficiency education,
 ED §5-208.
 Schools, compensatory education grants, ED
 §5-207.
 Schools, guaranteed tax base grants, ED §5-210.
 Special education grants, ED §5-209.
Lockout.
 State personnel.
 Collective bargaining, SPP §3-304.
Lodge.
 Fraternal benefit societies, IN §8-401.
Lodging establishments.
 Rights and responsibilities of innkeepers, BR
 §15-201.
Lodging or rooming house.
 Sprinkler systems, PS §9-201.
Long distance telecommunications service.
 Public service company tax, TG §8-401.
Loose material.
 Securing loads on vehicles, TR §24-106.1.
Loss ratio.
 Credit life, health and unemployment insurance,
 IN §13-111.
 Health insurance, IN §15-109.
 Long-term care insurance, IN §18-101.
 Medicare supplement insurance, IN §15-911.
Lot.
 Commercial fertilizers, AG §6-201.
 Homeowners association, RP §11B-101.
 Sales, UCC, CL §2-105.
 Seeds, AG §9-201.
 Sewerage systems, EN §9-501.
 Turf grass, AG §9-101.
Lot consolidation.
 Maryland home financing program, HS §4-801.
 Rental housing production program, HS §4-1503.
Lottery device, CR §12-201.
Low-dose mammography.
 Medicare supplement insurance, IN §15-907.
Lower grade investment.
 Investments of life insurers, IN §5-511.
Low income.
 Summer youth connection program, LE §11-602.
Low-income individual.
 Workforce investment act, LE §11-503.
Low-income to moderate-income.
 Maryland senior ride demonstration program, TR
 §7-1001.
Low-income worker.
 Transportation department.
 Job access program, TR §2-103.6.
Low-level nuclear waste.
 Controlled hazardous substances, EN §7-201.
 Hazardous waste facilities, EN §7-401.
 Nuclear waste, EN §8-401.
Low-level nuclear waste facility.
 Controlled hazardous substances, EN §7-201.

DEFINED TERMS —Cont'd

Low-level nuclear waste facility permit.
Controlled hazardous substances, EN §7-201.

Low level policy form.
Health insurance portability, IN §15-1301.

Low-level waste.
Radioactive waste, EN §7-301.

Low protein modified food product, IN §15-807.
Health maintenance organizations, HG §19-705.5.

Low speed vehicle, TR §11-130.1.

Low-voltage dry-type distribution transformer.
Maryland efficiency standards act, SG §9-2006.

Lump sum appropriation.
State finance, SF §7-207.

Machine gun, CR §4-401.

Machinery and equipment of a new electricity generation facility.
Property tax credits, TP §9-239.

Machinery and equipment of an existing electricity generation facility.
Property tax credits, TP §9-239.

Magazine seller license, BR §17-915.

Mail.
Corporations, CA §1-101.
Financial institutions, FI §1-101.
Land patents, RP §13-101.
Motor vehicles, TR §11-131.

Maintenance.
Highways, TR §8-101.

Maintenance drug.
Health insurance, IN §15-824.

Maintenance fee.
Debt management services, FI §12-901.

Maintenance work.
Occupational safety and health.
Work in confined spaces, LE §5-602.

Main traveled way.
Highways, TR §8-701.
Junkyards, TR §8-801.

Major adverse reaction.
Disease control, HG §18-328.

Major association.
Financial institutions.
Deposit insurance, FI §10-101.

Major capital project.
Department of transportation, SF §7-238.
Transportation, TR §2-103.1.

Major component part.
Motor vehicle repair facilities, TR §15-113.1.

Major information technology development project.
State finance, SF §3-402.

Major insurer.
Homeowner's insurance, geographic distribution of premiums, IN §11-321.
Motor vehicle insurer, IN §11-321.

Majority in interest of the limited partners.
Limited partnerships, CA §10-208.

Majority party.
Elections, EL §1-101.

Major medical equipment.
Freestanding ambulatory care facilities, HG §19-3B-01.

Make.
Bedding, HG §24-401.

Maker.
Negotiable instruments, CL §3-103.

Making available either medical and nursing services or other health related services.
Continuing care contracts, 70B §7.

DEFINED TERMS —Cont'd

Maliciously.
Arson and burning, CR §6-101.

Mammogram, HG §20-115.
Breast cancer program, HG §20-116.
Health insurance, IN §15-814.

Managed behavioral health care organizations.
Health insurance, behavioral health care services, IN §15-127.

Managed care organization.
Medical assistance, HG §15-101.

Managed care system.
Discrimination by health insurers, HG §19-703.1; IN §15-802.
Health insurance, required benefits, IN §15-835.

Management.
Banking institutions.
Affiliates and bank service corporations, FI §5-401.
Controlled hazardous substances, EN §7-201.
Radioactive waste, EN §7-301.
Water pollution, EN §4-401.

Management personnel.
Labor unions.
Schools, ED §6-501.

Management plan.
Heritage areas, FI §13-1101.

Management service.
State personnel, SPP §1-101.

Managerial employee.
Day of rest, LE §3-704.

Managing agent.
Trusts and trustees.
Construction industry, RP §9-201.

Managing entity.
Time-sharing, RP §11A-101.

Managing for results, SF §3-1001.

Managing general agent.
Insurance, IN §8-201.

Managing official.
Contraband at place of confinement, CR §9-410.
Correctional services, COR §1-101.
Criminal procedure, CP §1-101.

Mandate.
Administrative procedures, SG §10-101.
General assembly, SG §2-1501.

Mandated health insurance service, IN §15-1501.
Medical care data collection, HG §19-132.

Mandatory income interest.
Principal and income act, ET §15-501.

Mandatory set-asides.
Minority business enterprise program.
County public libraries, ED §23-402.
Prince George's community college, ED §16-312.
Prince George's county board of education, ED §4-125.

Mandatory subcontracting.
Minority business enterprise program.
County public libraries, ED §23-402.
Prince George's community college, ED §16-312.
Prince George's county board of education, ED §4-125.

Mandatory supervision, COR §§6-101, 7-101.

Manufacture.
Commercial feed, AG §6-101.
Controlled dangerous substances, CR §5-101.
CVISN transponders, TR §25-112.
Telecommunications theft, CR §7-313.

Manufactured home.
Industrialized buildings and manufactured homes, PS §12-301.

DEFINED TERMS —Cont'd

Manufactured home —Cont'd
Secured transactions, CL §9-102.
Manufactured home construction and safety standards act.
Industrialized buildings and manufactured homes, PS §12-301.
Manufactured-home transaction.
Secured transactions, CL §9-102.
Manufacturer.
Alcoholic beverages, 2B §1-102.
Alcoholic beverage tax, TG §5-101.
Bedding, HG §24-401.
Boats and boating, NR §8-701.
Cigarette licenses, BR §16-201.
Explosives licenses, PS §11-101.
Extended warranties, CL §14-1311.
Handgun identification requirements, PS §5-131.
Ignition interlock system, TR §16-404.1.
Mercury fever thermometers, EN §6-905.
Motor fuel, BR §10-301.
Motorized wheelchair warranty enforcement, CL §14-2701.
Motor vehicles, TR §11-132.
Product liability, CJ §5-405.
Limitation of actions, CJ §5-115.
Property tax.
Payments in lieu, TP §7-508.
Recycling, EN §9-1701.
Toxics, EN §9-1901.
Manufacturer, factory branch or distributor.
Automotive warranty enforcement, CL §14-1501.
Motor vehicle leasing contracts, CL §14-2001.
Motor vehicles, TR §15-201.
Manufacturer of a tobacco product.
Medicaid subrogation claims, HG §15-120.
Manufacturer's warranty period.
Automotive warranty enforcement, CL §14-1501.
Manufacturing.
Property tax, TP §1-101.
Marijuana, CR §5-101.
Marina.
Motor fuel tax, TG §9-301.
Marine environment.
Deepwater port siting, NR §3-602.
Marine facility.
Drug-free workplace, TR §6-102.1.
Marine insurance, IN §1-101.
Marine protection and indemnity insurance, IN §1-101.
Marine repair contractor, NR §8-701.
Marine sanitation device.
Sewage, NR §8-741.
Marital property, FL §8-201.
Marital status.
Housing discrimination, 49B §20.
Mark.
Liquefied petroleum gas containers, CL §11-601.
Trademarks, BR §1-401.
Marked container.
Liquefied petroleum gas containers, CL §11-601.
Marked crosswalk, TR §21-101.
Market.
Insurance rate making, IN §11-301.
Marketable oyster, NR §§4-1001, 4-1101.
Marketer.
Mercury fever thermometers, EN §6-905.
Rechargeable batteries, EN §6-1101.
Marketing agreement.
Gasohol and gasoline products marketing, CL §11-301.

DEFINED TERMS —Cont'd

Market-rate rental housing project.
Property tax.
Baltimore City, TP §9-304.
Market value.
Corporations, CA §3-601.
Market value of program assets.
College savings plan of Maryland, ED §18-1901.
Marriage and family therapy, HO §17-101.
Maryland adolescent survey.
Tobacco use prevention and cessation program, HG §13-1001.
Maryland association.
Savings and loan associations.
Interstate acquisitions, FI §9-1001.
Maryland bank.
Bank holding companies, FI §5-901.
Maryland bank holding company, FI §5-901.
Savings and loan associations.
Emergency interstate acquisitions, FI §5-1101.
Maryland base amount.
Income tax credits, TG §10-721.
Maryland cancer registry.
Cancer prevention, education, screening and treatment program, HG §13-1101.
Maryland consumer loan law, FI §11-201.
Maryland coordinate system, RP §14-401.
Maryland corporation, CA §1-101.
Maryland defense force.
Militia, PS §13-101.
Maryland estate tax, TG §§1-101, 7-301.
Maryland firm.
Resident business preference, 24 §8-102.
Maryland generation skipping transfer tax, TG §1-101.
Maryland gross receipts.
Income tax credits, TG §10-721.
Maryland institute for emergency medical services systems.
Biological agent registry program, HG §17-601.
Confidentiality of records, CJ §5-601.
Maryland justice analysis center.
Reports on traffic stops, TR §25-113.
Maryland qualified research and development.
Income tax credits, TG §10-721.
Maryland qualified research and development expenses.
Income tax credits, TG §10-721.
Maryland railroad company, PUC §9-301.
Maryland real estate investment trust.
Corporations, CA §8-501.1.
Maryland Rx program.
State personnel.
Health and welfare benefits, SPP §2-502.1.
Maryland savings and loan holding company.
Interstate acquisitions, FI §9-1001.
Maryland school performance program, ED §§5-204, 5-211.
Maryland science, engineering and technology development corporation.
Cancer prevention, education, screening and treatment program, HG §13-1101.
Maryland state ceiling.
Allocation of private activity bond authority, FI §13-801.
Maryland taxable income, TG §10-101.
Maryland technology development corporation.
Cancer prevention, education, screening and treatment program, HG §13-1101.
Maryland transportation plan, TR §1-101.

DEFINED TERMS —Cont'd
Maryland trauma specialty referral centers.
  Trauma physician services fund, HG §19-130.
Massage therapy, HO §3-5A-01.
Massage therapy advisory committee, HO
  §3-5A-01.
Mass-market license.
  Computer information transactions, CL §22-102.
Mass-produced device.
  Weights and measures, AG §11-204.
Mastectomy.
  Breast cancer program, HG §20-116.
  Health insurance, IN §15-815.
  Health insurance, mastectomy coverage, IN
    §15-832.
Master barber, BOP §4-101.
Master electrician, BOP §6-101.
Master license.
  Heating and air conditioning, BR §9A-101.
Master natural gas fitter, BOP §12-101.
Master plan.
  Senior citizen activities centers capital
    improvement grants, 70B §26.
Master plumber, BOP §12-101.
Master restricted license.
  Heating and air conditioning, BR §9A-101.
Master settlement agreement.
  Tobacco, escrow act compliance, BR §16-501.
  Tobacco use prevention and cessation program,
    HG §13-1001.
Matching purchases of easements.
  Agricultural land preservation foundation, AG
    §2-508.
Material.
  Savings and loan associations.
    False statements, FI §9-913.
Material litigation.
  Money transmission, FI §12-401.
Materially falsified.
  Spam, CR §3-805.1.
Material transaction.
  Insurance acquisitions disclosure and control, IN
    §7-703.
Matter.
  Obscene matter, CR §11-201.
Mature cantaloupe.
  Cantaloupes, AG §10-901.
Maturity date.
  Financial institutions, FI §1-210.
Maxi-cube vehicle.
  Vehicle length and loads, TR §24-104.1.
Maximum annual debt service.
  Transportation, TR §3-104.
Maximum available power.
  Electric or hybrid motor vehicles, TR §13-815.
May not.
  Rules of interpretation, 1 §26.
MBRC.
  Building rehabilitation code, PS §12-1001.
MCHP premium plan.
  Children's health program, HG §15-301.1.
Measurement.
  Public schools.
    Evaluation of students, ED §7-204.
Meat.
  Kosher products, CL §14-901.
  Wholesome meat act, AG §4-101.
Meat broker, AG §4-101.
Meat by-product, AG §4-101.
Mechanical breakdown insurance.
  Service contracts and consumer products
    guaranty, CL §14-401.

DEFINED TERMS —Cont'd
Mechanical repair contract.
  Closed end credit, CL §12-1001.
  Retail installment sales, CL §12-601.
Mechanical restraint.
  Student behavior intervention, ED §7-1101.
MEDCO.
  Bainbridge development corporation, 83A §5-1601.
  Local military installation redevelopment
    authorities, 83A §5-1701.
  Penmar development corporations, 83A §5-1201.
Median annual family income.
  Maryland home financing program, HS §4-801.
Mediation, ADR Rule 17-102.
  Health care malpractice, alternative dispute
    resolution, CJ §3-2A-06C.
  Labor relations.
    Community colleges, ED §16-412.
  Prince George's county public employment
    relations, ED §16-414.1.
Mediation communication, ADR Rule 17-102.
Mediator.
  Agricultural mediation program, AG §1-1A-01.
  Health care malpractice, alternative dispute
    resolution, CJ §3-2A-06C.
Medicaid, HG §15-132.
  Medicare supplement insurance, IN §15-901.
Medical assistance program account.
  Maryland medical professional liability insurance
    rate stabilization fund, IN §19-104.1.
Medical board, SPP §21-126.
  Legislative pension plan, SG Title 2 Subtitle 3
    (note).
  Pensions, SPP §20-101.
Medical care facility, HG §18-213.2.
Medical device.
  Dietitians and nutritionists, HO §5-101.
Medical direction.
  Emergency medical services, ED §13-516.
Medical director.
  Health maintenance organizations, IN
    §15-10C-01.
Medical education center.
  Student financial assistance.
    Physician assistants and nurse practitioners,
      ED §18-802.
Medical equipment.
  Residential service agencies, HG §19-4A-01.
Medical examinations.
  Hearing aid dispensers and audiologists, HO
    §2-314.1.
Medical examiner, HG §1-101.
Medical examiner's case.
  Postmortem examiners, HG §5-301.
**Medical expenses recovery under subrogation
    provision.**
  Contract not to contain provision allowing, HG
    §19-713.1.
Medical facility.
  Interference with access to and egress from
    medical facility, CR §10-204.
Medical food, IN §15-807.
  Health maintenance organizations, HG §19-705.5.
Medical information.
  Consumer credit reporting agencies, CL §14-1201.
Medical injury.
  Health care malpractice, CJ §3-2A-01.
  Maryland health care provider rate stabilization
    fund, IN §19-801.
  Maryland medical professional liability insurance
    rate stabilization fund, IN §19-104.1.

DEFINED TERMS —Cont'd
Medical injury —Cont'd
People's insurance counsel, SG §6-301.
Medical laboratory, HG §17-201.
Medical literature.
Health insurance, IN §15-804.
Medically and functionally impaired.
Medicaid, HG §15-132.
Medically handicapped adult, HG §14-301.
Medically ineffective treatment.
Health care decisions, HG §5-601.
Medically uninsurable individual.
Maryland health insurance plan, IN §14-501.
Medical nutrition.
Dietitians and nutritionists, HO §5-101.
Medical professional liability insurance, IN
§10-133.
Medical professional liability insurer.
Maryland health care provider rate stabilization
fund, IN §19-801.
Maryland medical professional liability insurance
rate stabilization fund, IN §19-104.1.
People's insurance counsel, SG §6-301.
Medical record, HG §§4-301, 4-304.
Medical report.
Child abuse and neglect, 88A §6A.
Medical review committee, HO §1-01.
Medical review officer.
Medical laboratories, HG §17-214.
Medical service.
Certificate of health care need, HG §19-120.
Medical study program.
Anatomy board, HG §5-401.
Medical support notice.
Child support orders.
Inclusion of child on health insurance, FL
§12-102.
Health insurance, IN §15-405.
Medical system.
University of Maryland medical system, ED
§13-301.
Medical system assets.
University of Maryland medical system, ED
§13-301.
Medical system corporation.
University of Maryland medical system, ED
§13-301.
Medical system corporation employees.
University of Maryland medical system, ED
§13-301.
Medical system liabilities.
University of Maryland medical system, ED
§13-301.
Medical system personnel.
University of Maryland medical system, ED
§13-301.
Medical system university personnel.
University of Maryland medical system, ED
§13-301.
Medicare benefit period.
Supplemental insurance, IN §15-901.
Medicare eligible expense.
Supplement insurance, IN §15-901.
Medicare modernization act.
Medicare option prescription drug program, HG
§15-124.3.
Medicare part D prescription drug benefit.
Medicare option prescription drug program, HG
§15-124.3.
Medicare supplement insurance, IN §15-901.
Medicare supplement policy, IN §15-901.

DEFINED TERMS —Cont'd
Medication.
Self-administration of asthma medication by
pupils, ED §7-421.
Medigap policy, IN §15-901.
Medium density residential areas.
Forest conservation, NR §5-1601.
Medium grade investment.
Investments of life insurers, IN §5-511.
Meet.
Governmental procedures, SG §10-502.
Meeting.
Child fatality review teams, HG §5-701.
St. Mary's county open meetings, 24 §4-202.
MEMA.
Maryland emergency management agency
(MEMA), PS §14-101.
Member.
Adult offender supervision, COR §6-203.
Agricultural cooperatives.
Corporations, CA §5-501.
Board of veterinary medical examiners, AG
§2-301.
Charitable organizations, BR §6-102.
Community reinvestment fund, HS §9-101.
Consumer cooperative, CA §5-5A-02.
Cooperative housing corporation, CA §5-6B-01.
Electric cooperatives, CA §5-601.
Health insurance, IN §15-827.
Behavioral health care services, IN §15-127.
Complaint process for adverse decisions or
grievances, IN §15-10A-01.
Complaint process for coverage decisions, IN
§15-10D-01.
Coverage of prescription drugs, IN §15-831.
Referrals to specialists, IN §15-830.
HMO's, HG §19-701.
Income tax, TG §10-102.1.
Interstate insurance product regulation compact,
IN §29-101.
Legislative pension plan, SG Title 2 Subtitle 3
(note).
Limited liability companies, CA §4A-101.
Motor clubs, IN §26-101.
National guard, tuition assistance, PS §13-405.
Pensions, SPP §20-101.
Savings and loan associations.
Organization, FI §9-301.
Tobacco, AG §7-101.
Video clubs, CL §14-1602.1.
Member association.
Financial institutions.
Deposit insurance, FI §10-101.
Member contribution.
Legislative pension plan, SG Title 2 Subtitle 3
(note).
Pensions, SPP §20-101.
Member county.
Sanitary commissions, EN §9-601.
Member in good standing.
Credit unions, FI §6-101.
Member insurer.
Life and health insurance guaranty corporation,
IN §9-401.
Property and casualty insurance guaranty
corporation, IN §9-301.
Member of household.
Public ethics, SG §15-102.
Member of minor's family.
UTMA, ET §13-301.

DEFINED TERMS —Cont'd

Member of the adoptive family.
Adoption search, contact and reunion services, FL §5-4B-01.

Member of the beneficiary's family.
Discretionary trusts, ET §14-401.

Membership.
Video clubs, CL §14-1602.1.

Membership capital.
Consumer cooperatives, CA §5-5A-02.

Membership certificate.
Cooperative housing corporation, CA §5-6B-01.

Members-only bingo.
Harford county, CR §13-1501.

Mental abuse.
Rights of mentally ill, HG §10-701.

Mental deficiency.
Mental health compact, HG §11-103.

Mental disorder.
Children in need of assistance, CJ §3-801.
Emergency evaluations, HG §10-620.
Incompetency and criminal responsibility, CP §3-101.
Juvenile cases, CJ §3-8A-01.
Mental hygiene, HG §10-101.

Mental facility.
Estates and trusts, ET §13-101.

Mental health care provider.
Personal liability, CJ §5-609.

Mental health director.
Mental health records, HG §4-307.

Mental health expense ratio.
Health insurance, behavioral health care services, IN §15-127.

Mental health facility.
Mental health professional grant, ED §18-707.

Mental health services.
Medical records, HG §4-301.

Mental illness.
Mental health compact, HG §11-103.

Mental injury.
Child abuse and neglect, FL §5-701.
Children in need of assistance, CJ §3-801.

Mentally defective individual.
Sexual crimes, CR §3-301.

Mentally handicapped child.
Juvenile causes, CJ §3-8A-01.

Mentally incapacitated individual.
Sexual crimes, CR §3-301.

Mentally retarded.
Criminal law, CR §2-202.

Mental retardation, HG §7-101.
Juvenile cases, CJ §3-8A-01.

Mercantile establishment.
Shoplifting and employee theft, CJ §3-1301.

Merchandise.
Consumer protection, CL §§13-101, 14-1301.
Shoplifting and employee theft.
Courts, CJ §3-1301.

Merchant.
Computer information transactions, CL §22-102.
Consumer protection, CL §13-101.
Internet sales contracts, CL §14-1321.
Sales, UCC, CL §2-104.
Shoplifting and employee theft, CJ §3-1301.
Telephone solicitation, CL §14-2201.

Merchant lessee.
Commercial code, CL §2A-103.

Mercury-added fluorescent lamp, EN §6-905.3.

Mercury-added product, EN §6-905.

DEFINED TERMS —Cont'd

Merging credit union.
Credit unions, FI §6-803.

Metal tire, TR §11-133.

Mezuzah.
Kosher products, CL §14-901.

MHT grant fund.
Maryland historical trust, MHT grant program, SF §5A-328.

MHT grant program.
Maryland historical trust, MHT grant program, SF §5A-328.

MHT loan fund.
Maryland historical trust, MHT loan program, SF §5A-327.

MHT loan program.
Maryland historical trust, MHT loan program, SF §5A-327.

Microenterprise.
Neighborhood business development program, HS §6-301.

Midnight deadline.
Bank deposits and collections, CL §4-104.

Migrant agricultural worker, LE §7-101.

Migrant farm worker.
Workers' compensation, LE §9-210.

Migratory game bird, NR §10-101.

Mile thoroughbred racing, BR §11-101.

Military personnel.
Housing authorities, HS §12-101.

Military retirement income.
Income tax, TG §10-207.

Military service.
Income tax, TG §10-207.

Militia.
Emergency management, governor's powers, PS §14-306.

Milk, HG §21-401.
Northeast interstate dairy compact, AG §2-801.

Milk fat, HG §21-401.

Milk or other fluid dairy products, AG §11-401.

Milk plant, HG §21-401.

Milk producer, HG §21-401.

Milk tank truck, HG §21-401.

Milk transportation company, HG §21-401.

Mine, EN §15-101.
Workers' compensation, LE §9-216.

Mine opening sealing.
Deep mine control, EN §15-601.

Mineral.
Surface mining, EN §15-801.
Workers' compensation, LE §9-216.

Minimum livability code.
Maryland housing rehabilitation program, HS §4-901.

Minimum mandatory standards.
Standards for correctional facilities, COR §8-101.

Mining.
Interstate mining compact, EN §15-901.

Mining and reclamation plan.
Surface mining, EN §15-801.

Ministerial act.
Real estate brokers, BOP §17-528.

Minor.
Criminal law, CR §1-101.
Employment of, LE §3-201.
Estates and trusts, ET §13-101.
Recovery in tort, ET §13-401.
Rules of interpretation, 1 §24.
UTMA, ET §13-301.

Minor capital project, TR §2-103.1.

DEFINED TERMS —Cont'd
Minor finishing operations.
  Motor vehicles, TR §13-113.2.
Minority business enterprise.
  Allocation of private activity bond authority, FI §13-801.
  Board of public works, SF §10-308.
  Community colleges.
    Contract bidding, ED §16-311.
  County public libraries, ED §23-402.
  Economic development opportunities program, SF §7-314.
  Educational financing.
    Contract bidding, ED §5-112.
  Prince George's community college, ED §16-312.
  Prince George's county board of education, ED §4-125.
  Procurement, SF §14-301.
Minority individual.
  Cancer prevention, education, screening and treatment program, HG §13-1101.
  Tobacco use prevention and cessation program, HG §13-1001.
Minority person.
  Office of minority affairs, SG §9-301.
  Office of minority health and health disparities, HG §20-1001.
Minor traffic violation.
  Expungement of criminal records, CP §10-101.
Misappropriation.
  Trade secrets, CL §11-1201.
Misbranded.
  Commercial feed, AG §6-101.
  Commercial fertilizers, AG §6-201.
  Pesticide registration and labeling, AG §5-101.
  Poultry products inspection act, AG §4-201.
  Wholesome meat act, AG §4-101.
Misbranded milk product, HG §21-401.
Miscellaneous fees.
  Motor vehicles, TR §12-120.
Miscellaneous organization or club.
  Class C, on-sale beer, wine and liquor license in Harford county, 2B §6-301.
Misfueling.
  Motor vehicles, TR §23-201.
Missing child, FL §9-401.
Mission.
  Managing for results, SF §3-1001.
Mitigation banking.
  Nontidal wetlands, EN §5-901.
Mixed fertilizer, AG §6-201.
Mixed-to-order.
  Commercial fertilizers, AG §6-201.
Mixed use development.
  Forest conservation, NR §5-1601.
Mixing building.
  Fireworks, PS §10-101.
Mixture.
  Turf grass, AG §9-101.
Mobile food service facility, HG §21-309.
Mobile home, TR §11-134.
  Charles county tax, 24 §9-402.
  Homebuilder registration, BR §4.5-101.
  Liens on, CL §16-201.
  Mobile home parks, RP §8A-101.
  Property tax, TP §8-234.
Mobile seafood vendor, TR §24-301.
Mobile telecommunications sourcing act.
  Sales and use tax on telecommunications service.
    Prince George's county, 24 §9-606.

DEFINED TERMS —Cont'd
Mobile training center.
  Motorcycle safety, TR §16-601.
Mobile unit.
  Check cashing services, FI §12-101.
Modal administration.
  Department of transportation, SF §7-238.
  Transportation, TR §1-101.
Model steam boiler.
  Boilers and pressure vessels, PS §12-901.
Model type.
  Motor vehicles, TR §13-818.
Model year.
  Motor vehicles, TR §13-818.
Moderate income.
  Property tax.
    Deferral of payment, TP §10-203.
Moderate priced dwelling units.
  Montgomery county housing opportunities commission, HS §16-110.
Modification.
  Building rehabilitation code, PS §12-1001.
  Power plants, PUC §7-205.
  Uniform child custody jurisdiction and enforcement act, FL §9.5-101.
Modified contract.
  Continuing care contracts, 70B §7.
Modified Maryland adjusted gross income.
  Taxation, TG §10-207.
Modular building.
  Sales and use tax, TG §11-104.
Mold.
  Hulls of vessels, CL §11-1001.
Monetary instrument.
  Financial transactions involving proceeds of drug crime, CR §5-623.
Monetary value.
  Money transmission, FI §12-401.
Money.
  Uniform commercial code, CL §1-201.
Money judgment.
  Judgment liens, CJ §11-401.
Money transmission, FI §12-401.
Money transmission fund, FI §12-404.
Monitoring data.
  Controlled hazardous substances, EN §7-239.1.
Montebello assets, ED §13-401.
Montebello liabilities, ED §13-401.
Montebello site, ED §13-401.
Montebello University employee, ED §13-401.
Montgomery county conference center facilities.
  Stadium authority, FI §13-701.
Montgomery county fire and explosive investigator, CP §2-208.1.
Moody's corporate bond yield average.
  Insurance companies.
    Standard valuation law, IN §5-306.
  Life and health insurance guaranty corporation, IN §9-401.
Moped, TR §11-134.1.
Morbid obesity.
  Health insurance coverage for treatment, IN §15-839.
Morgan State University.
  Classified employees separation and grievance procedures, ED §14-301.
Mortgage.
  Consumer protection, CL §13-316.
  Eminent domain, RP §12-201.
  Financial institutions, FI §1-101.

DEFINED TERMS —Cont'd
Mortgage —Cont'd
  Management of escrow accounts, CL §12-109.2.
  Maryland housing fund, HS §3-201.
  Real property, RP §1-101.
  Secured transactions, CL §9-102.
Mortgage broker.
  Loans.
    Finder's fees, CL §12-801.
Mortgagee.
  Condominiums, RP §11-101.
Mortgage lender, FI §11-501.
  Mortgage originator, FI §11-601.
Mortgage lending business.
  Mortgage originator, FI §11-601.
Mortgage loans.
  Closed end credit, insurance, CL §12-1007.
  Consumer loans, insurance, CL §12-312.
  Financing community development projects, HS
    §4-235.
  Lenders, FI §11-501.
  Mortgage originator, FI §11-601.
  Secondary mortgage loans, CL §12-410.
Mortgage or deed of trust.
  Release of certain commercial loans, RP §3-105.1.
Mortgage originator, FI §11-601.
Mortician, HO §7-101.
  Vital statistics, HG §4-201.
Mortician rehabilitation committee, HO §7-408.
Motorboat, NR §8-701.
Motor carrier, TR §11-134.2.
  Emergency response reimbursement, CJ §§3-1101,
    3-1201.
  Taxation, TG §9-201.
Motor carrier tax, TG §1-101.
Motor club, IN §26-101.
  Traffic citation, TR §26-404.
Motor club service, IN §26-101.
Motorcycle, TR §11-136.
Motorcycle safety courses, TR §16-601.
Motorcycle safety training center, TR §16-601.
Motorcyclist organization.
  Motor vehicle registration, TR §13-619.
Motor fuel, BR §10-101.
  Fuel taxes, TG §8-101.
Motor fuel tax, TG §1-101.
Motor home, TR §11-134.3.
  Motor vehicle manufacturers, distributors and
    factory branches, TR §15-212.
  Open containers of alcoholic beverages in motor
    vehicles, CR §10-123.
Motorized wheelchair.
  Warranty enforcement, CL §14-2701.
Motorized wheelchair dealer.
  Warranty enforcement, CL §14-2701.
Motorized wheelchair lessor.
  Warranty enforcement, CL §14-2701.
Motor scooter, TR §11-134.5.
Motor vehicle, TR §11-135.
  Automotive crash parts, CL §14-2301.
  Carjacking, CR §3-405.
  Consumer protection.
    Automotive repair facilities, CL §14-1001.
  Fuel taxes, TG §8-101.
  Insurance, IN §19-501.
  Leasing contracts, CL §14-2001.
  Liens on, CL §16-201.
  Motor fuel, BR §10-101.
  Open containers of alcoholic beverages in motor
    vehicles, CR §10-123.
  Registration surcharge, TR §13-954.

DEFINED TERMS —Cont'd
Motor vehicle —Cont'd
  Retail installment sales, CL §12-601.
  Seat belts, TR §22-412.
  Theft, CR §7-101.
  Unlawful subleasing of motor vehicle, CR §8-408.
  Warranty enforcement, CL §14-1501.
Motor vehicle accident.
  Insurance, IN §19-501.
Motor vehicle agreement.
  Unlawful subleasing of motor vehicle, CR §8-408.
Motor vehicle liability insurance.
  Automobile insurance fund, IN §20-101.
Motor vehicle peddler.
  Business licenses, BR §17-904.
Motor vehicle physical damage insurance.
  Automobile insurance fund, IN §20-101.
Motor vehicle rental company.
  Insurance, IN §10-601.
Movie theater.
  Beer, wine and liquor licenses, 2B §8-216.1.
Moving expenses.
  Condominiums, RP §11-101.
  Cooperative housing corporation, CA §5-6B-01.
Moving vessels.
  Injury reports, HG §20-702.
Moving violation.
  Expungement of driving records, TR §16-117.1.
  Motor vehicles, TR §11-136.1.
  Open containers of alcoholic beverages in motor
    vehicles, CR §10-123.
Moving walk.
  Elevator safety, PS §12-801.
Multicraft construction site.
  Approved paid work-based learning programs, ED
    §21-501.
Multidisciplinary team.
  Child abuse and neglect centers of excellence, HG
    §13-2201.
  Child abuse or neglect care, FL §5-712.
Multi-drawing raffle.
  Carroll county, CR §13-904.
Multifamily rental dwelling.
  Lead poisoning, EN §6-801.
Multifamily residential dwelling.
  Sprinkler systems, PS §9-201.
Multijurisdictional electric company.
  Income tax, TG §10-713.
Multilevel distribution company, BR §14-301.
Multiple.
  Spam, CR §3-805.1.
Multiple gaming device permit.
  Worcester county, CR §13-2619.
Multiple mutual pool.
  Horse racing, BR §11-101.
Multiple-party account.
  Financial institutions, FI §1-204.
Multiple project assurance contract.
  Health insurance, IN §15-827.
Multiple risk factors.
  Health insurance, IN §15-829.
Multipurpose passenger vehicle, TR §11-136.2.
Multi-user contract.
  Procurement, SF §13-217.
Multiuse sewerage system, EN §9-501.
Multiuse water supply system, EN §9-501.
Municipal area.
  Corporations, CA §1-101.
  Financial institutions, FI §1-101.
Municipal authority.
  Municipal bonds, EN §9-701.

DEFINED TERMS —Cont'd
Municipal charter.
Home rule, 23A §9.
Municipal corporation.
Forests and parks.
Open space program, NR §5-901.
Home rule, 23A §9.
Property tax, TP §1-101.
State police, powers, PS §2-412.
Municipal corporation property tax, TP §1-101.
Municipal infraction.
Municipal corporations, 23A §3.
Municipality.
Allocation of private activity bond authority, FI
§13-801.
Community energy loan program, SG §9-2101.
Environmental service, NR §3-101.
Highways, TR §8-507.
Highway user revenues, TR §8-401.
Industrial development financing, 83A §5-901.
Sewerage bonds, EN §9-801.
State police.
Protection fund, 41 §4-403.
Municipal system.
Sanitary commissions, EN §9-601.
Mutilated.
Drivers' licenses, TR §16-114.
Mutual aid agreement.
Correctional mutual aid agreements, COR §2-401.
Mutual aid agreements by fire, rescue or
emergency services entities, PS §7-101.
Mutual association.
Savings and loan associations, FI §§9-101, 9-1101.
Mutual holding company.
Savings banks, FI §4-101.
Mutual insurance holding company.
Conversion of mutual insurer to stock insurer, IN
§3-121.1.
Mutual insurer, IN §1-101.
Name.
Motor vehicles, TR §11-137.
Named insured.
Motor vehicle insurance, IN §19-501.
Narcotic drug, CR §5-101.
National accreditation.
Universities and colleges, ED §11-208.
National banking association.
Branch banking, FI §5-1001.
Financial institutions, FI §1-101.
State treasury, SF §6-201.
National capital region.
National capital region mutual aid agreements,
PS §14-8A-01.
National certifying board.
Respiratory care, HO §14-5A-01.
National certifying examination.
Physician assistants, HO §15-101.
National defense.
Property tax exemptions, TP §7-211.2.
National fingerprint file.
National crime prevention and privacy compact,
CP §10-239.
National guard.
Militia, PS §13-101.
National guard students.
Universities and colleges, special provisions, ED
§15-106.3.
National identification index.
National crime prevention and privacy compact,
CP §10-239.

DEFINED TERMS —Cont'd
National indices.
National crime prevention and privacy compact,
CP §10-239.
National instructional materials access center.
Individualized education programs to insure
ability to communicate effectively, ED §8-408.
**National pollutant discharge elimination
system.**
Sanitary facilities, EN §9-101.
National primary drinking water regulations.
Drinking water, EN §9-401.
National public education fund.
Tobacco use prevention and cessation program,
HG §13-1001.
National registry.
Emergency medical services, ED §13-516.
Native.
Natural resources, NR §4-205.1.
Native American.
Maryland historical trust, archaeological property,
SF §5A-333.
Natural clam bar, NR §4-1101.
Aquaculture, NR §4-11A-01.
Natural father.
Mutual consent voluntary adoption registry, FL
§5-4C-01.
Natural gas vehicles, PUC §7-308.
Natural open character.
Property tax.
Land subject to easement, TP §8-219.
Natural oyster bar, NR §§4-1001, 4-1101.
Aquaculture, NR §4-11A-01.
Natural regeneration.
Forest conservation, NR §5-1601.
Natural resources.
Forest conservancy districts, NR §5-601.
Natural sibling.
Mutual consent voluntary adoption registry, FL
§5-4C-01.
Natural wood waste.
Recycling, EN §9-1701.
Natural wood waste recycling facility, EN
§9-1701.
Navigational aid.
Acquisition of land by United States, SG §14-105.
Nazi Germany.
Holocaust victim insurance, IN §28-101.
Income tax, TG §10-207.
Inheritance tax, TG §7-203.
NBCOT.
Occupational therapists, HO §10-101.
NBC teacher.
National board certified teacher pilot program, ED
§6-118.
Negative trend.
Risk based capital standards for insurers, IN
§4-301.
Neglect.
Abuse or neglect of vulnerable adult, CR §3-604.
Adult protective services, FL §14-101.
Child abuse and neglect, FL §5-701.
Children in need of assistance, CJ §3-801.
Child welfare accountability, FL §5-1301.
Negotiable instrument, CL §§3-103, 3-104.
Negotiate.
Insurance, IN §1-101.
Labor unions.
Public school employees, ED §§6-408, 6-510.
Negotiation.
Negotiable instruments, CL §§3-103, 3-201.

DEFINED TERMS —Cont'd
Neighborhood corporation.
  Neighborhood housing services fund, HS §4-1001.
Neighboring.
  Surface mining, EN §15-801.
Nematicide.
  Pesticide registration and labeling, AG §5-101.
Nematode.
  Pesticide registration and labeling, AG §5-101.
NERB.
  Dentists, HO §4-306.
Net annual income.
  Trusts, ET §14-107.
Net branch office.
  Mortgage originator, FI §11-601.
Net costs.
  Equipment dealer contracts, CL §19-101.
Net direct written premiums.
  Industry automobile insurance association, IN
    §20-405.
  Property and casualty insurance guaranty
    corporation, IN §9-301.
Net earnings available for fixed charges.
  Insurance companies.
    Investments, IN §5-608.
Net energy metering, PUC §7-306.
Net estate.
  Elective share of decedent's estate, ET §3-203.
  Estates and trusts, ET §1-101.
Net income.
  Principal and income act, ET §15-501.
Net landed weights.
  Sales, UCC, CL §2-321.
Net operating expenses.
  Old aged assistance, 70B §11B.
Net proceeds.
  Income tax withholding, TG §10-912.
  Secondary mortgage loans, CL §12-401.
Net project construction cost.
  Shore erosion control, NR §8-1001.
Net project costs.
  Mass transit, TR §7-102.1.
Net savings.
  Consumer cooperatives, CA §5-5A-02.
Net state contribution.
  Health cost reviews, HG §19-213.
Net sum.
  Recovery by minor in tort, ET §13-401.
Net taxable income.
  County public libraries, ED §23-501.
  Educational financing.
    State assistance, ED §5-202.
  State police.
    Protection fund, 41 §4-403.
Netting agreement.
  Insurance companies, liquidation and
    rehabilitation, IN §9-229.1.
Net tract area.
  Forest conservation, NR §5-1601.
Net worth.
  Property tax.
    Elderly or disabled renters, TP §9-102.
    Homeowners credit, TP §9-104.
  Savings and loan associations, FI §9-324.
Net worth certificate.
  Savings and loan associations, FI §9-101.
Neutral case evaluation, ADR Rule 17-102.
  Health care malpractice, alternative dispute
    resolution, CJ §3-2A-06C.
Neutral experts.
  Alternative dispute resolution, ADR Rule
    17-105.1.

DEFINED TERMS —Cont'd
Neutral fact-finding.
  Alternative dispute resolution, ADR Rule 17-102.
  Health care malpractice, alternative dispute
    resolution, CJ §3-2A-06C.
Neutral provider.
  Health care malpractice, alternative dispute
    resolution, CJ §3-2A-06C.
New.
  Bedding, HG §24-401.
Newborn.
  Hearing-impaired infants, HG §13-601.
New credit union, FI §6-803.
New debtor.
  Secured transactions, CL §9-102.
New drug, HG §21-201.
New electricity generation facility.
  Property tax credits, TP §9-239.
New employer.
  Unemployment insurance.
    Contributions, LE §8-609.
New home.
  Homebuilder registration, BR §4.5-101.
  Warranties, RP §10-601.
New home warranty, RP §10-601.
New home warranty security plan, RP §10-601.
Newly constructed.
  Property tax.
    Baltimore City, TP §9-304.
Newly constructed dwelling.
  Property tax.
    Baltimore City, TP §9-304.
New or expanded premises.
  Property taxes.
    Job creation, TP §9-230.
New permanent full-time position.
  Property taxes.
    Job creation, TP §9-230.
New residential development.
  Charles county, 66B §14.05.
New school capacity construction bonds.
  Charles county, 66B §14.05.
News media.
  Privileged communications.
    Courts, CJ §9-112.
**Newspaper devoted to the dissemination of
  general news,** 1 §28.
Newspaper in general circulation, 1 §28.
Newsprint.
  Recycling, EN §9-1707.
New statewide value.
  Property tax.
    Assessment of real property, TP §8-103.
New system.
  State retirement and pension system, SPP
    §37-101.
New value.
  Secured transactions, CL §9-102.
New vehicles, TR §11-138.
Next of kin.
  Anatomical gift act, ET §4-501.
NFPA 70.
  Building codes, emergency power and lighting
    systems, PS §12-702.
NFPA 101.
  Building codes, emergency power and lighting
    systems, PS §12-702.
Nicotine replacement therapy.
  Health insurance coverage for smoking cessation
    treatment, IN §15-841.

DEFINED TERMS —Cont'd
Nighttime.
  Waterfowl hunting, NR §10-602.
  Wildlife, NR §10-101.
NIH.
  Health insurance, IN §15-827.
NIMAS.
  Individualized education programs to insure
    ability to communicate effectively, ED §8-408.
911 accessible service.
  911 emergency telephone system, PS §1-301.
911 fee.
  911 emergency telephone system, PS §1-301.
911 service carrier.
  911 emergency telephone system, PS §1-301.
911 system, PS §1-301.
  Minors, use of wireless communications device
    while driving, TR §21-1124.
911 trust fund.
  911 emergency telephone system, PS §1-301.
No arrival, no sale.
  Sales, UCC, CL §2-324.
No-impact home-based business.
  Cooperative housing corporation, CA §5-6B-01.
  Family day care homes, RP §11-111.1.
  Homeowners' associations, RP §11B-111.1.
Noise.
  Noise control, EN §3-101.
Noise zone.
  Airport noise assistance programs, TR §5-1201.
  Aviation generally, TR §5-801.
Nolle prosequi, CP §1-101.
Nolo contendere, CP §1-101.
Nominated person.
  Letters of credit, CL §5-102.
Nonaccredited hospital, HG §19-301.
Nonaccredited residential treatment center,
    HG §19-301.
Noncash proceeds.
  Secured transactions, CL §9-102.
Noncertificated employee.
  Labor unions.
    Schools, ED §6-501.
Noncollegiate educational institution, ED
    §§2-206, 2-304.
  Education of children in state-supervised care, ED
    §8-501.
Noncommissioned rank.
  State police department, PS §2-101.
Noncommunity water system, EN §9-401.
Noncompacting state.
  Adult offender supervision, COR §6-203.
  Interstate insurance product regulation compact,
    IN §29-101.
Nonconformity.
  Motorized wheelchair warranty enforcement, CL
    §14-2701.
Noncontributory system.
  State retirement and pension system, SPP
    §37-101.
Noncontrolled substance, CR §5-101.
Noncriminal justice purposes.
  National crime prevention and privacy compact,
    CP §10-239.
Nondegreed recipient.
  McAuliffe teacher education award, ED §18-703.
Non-division custody.
  Consecutive and concurrent sentences, multiple
    jurisdictions, COR §9-202.
Noneconomic damages.
  Health care malpractice, CJ §3-2A-01.

DEFINED TERMS —Cont'd
Noneconomic damages —Cont'd
  Judgments, CJ §11-108.
Nonenclosed shopping center.
  Transient or temporary vendors licenses, 24
    §11-301.
Nonexclusive license.
  Computer information transactions, CL §22-102.
Nonexpendable item.
  Procurement, SF §4-501.
Nongame birds and mammals, NR §10-101.
Nongame species, NR §10-2A-01.
Nonissuer distribution or transaction.
  Securities, CA §11-101.
Non-Maryland user.
  Potomac water authority, EN §5-401.
Nonnative.
  Natural resources, NR §4-205.1.
  Nonnative oysters, NR §4-1008.
Nonparticipating manufacturer.
  Tobacco, escrow act compliance, BR §16-501.
Nonparty state.
  National crime prevention and privacy compact,
    CP §10-239.
Nonpreferred provider.
  Preferred provider organizations, IN §14-201.
Nonprescription drug.
  Food, drugs and cosmetics, HG §21-1113.
  Pharmacists and pharmacies, HO §12-101.
Nonprofit entity.
  Substance abuse prevention and treatment, HG
    §8-901.
Nonprofit health entity.
  Acquisition, SG §6.5-101.
Nonprofit health maintenance organization.
  Insurance premium tax, IN §6-121.
Nonprofit health service plan.
  Acquisition of nonprofit health entities, SG
    §6.5-101.
Nonprofit organization.
  Administrative procedures.
    Litigation expenses, SG §10-224.
  Adult day care, HG §24-701.
  Community energy loan program, SG §9-2101.
  Community health, HG §24-601.
  Family investment program, 88A §44A.
  Federally qualified health centers grant program,
    HG §24-1301.
  Grants to assisted living facilities, HG §24-1001.
  Housing and community development, HS §1-101.
  Juvenile services.
    Facilities capital program, 83C §4-101.
  Neighborhood and community assistance program,
    HS §6-401.
  Nursing facility conversion grant program, HG
    §24-1401.
  Residential child care capital grant program, 41
    §18-701.
Nonprofit sponsor.
  Development finance division, HS §4-101.
  Maryland housing rehabilitation program, HS
    §4-901.
Nonpublic general education school, ED §8-417.
Nonpublic institution of higher education.
  Universities and colleges, establishment of new
    programs, ED §11-206.1.
Nonpublic school.
  Student behavior intervention, ED §7-1101.
  Transportation of students, ED §7-801.
Nonremovable.
  Rechargeable batteries, EN §6-1101.

DEFINED TERMS —Cont'd

Nonresident.
Motor vehicles, TR §11-139.
Tax tables, TG §2-106.

Nonresident commercial real estate brokers, BOP §17-536.

Nonresident commercial real estate salesperson, BOP §17-536.

Nonresident contractor.
Taxation, TG §13-803.

Nonresident dealer.
Alcoholic beverage tax, TG §5-101.

Nonresident entity.
Income tax, TG §10-102.1.
Income tax withholding, TG §10-912.

Nonresident firm.
Resident business preference, 24 §8-102.

Nonresidential child care program.
Nonpublic general education schools, ED §8-417.

Nonresident income tax, TG §10-101.

Nonresident itinerant magazine seller.
Business licenses, BR §17-915.

Nonresident junk dealer.
Business licenses, BR §17-1005.

Nonresident pharmacy.
Pharmacists and pharmacies, HO §12-101.

Nonresident scrap metal processor.
Business licenses, BR §17-1005.

Nonresident's privilege to drive, TR §11-140.

Nonresident taxable income.
Income tax, TG §10-102.1.

Nontax liability due the state.
Withholding of tax refunds and payments, TG §13-930.

Nontidal water.
Fish and fisheries, NR §4-101.

Nontidal wetland, EN §5-901.
Forest conservation, NR §5-1601.

Nontransient noncommunity water system, EN §9-401.

Nonvisual access.
State finance, SF §3-402.

Normal repairs and maintenance.
Property tax, TP §8-235.

Normal retirement age.
Pensions, SPP §20-101.

Normal weekly work hours.
Unemployment insurance.
Work sharing, LE §8-1201.

Notation credit.
Letters of credit, CL §5-108.

Not criminally responsible, CP §3-109.

Notes.
Environmental service, NR §3-101.
Issuance of notes by community colleges, ED §16-302.1.
Negotiable instruments, CL §§3-103, 3-104.

Not for profit organization.
Unemployment insurance, LE §8-101.

Notice.
Closed end credit, CL §12-1018.
Commercial code, CL §1-201.
Computer information transactions, CL §22-102.
Education of children in state-supervised care, ED §8-501.
Expungement of records, Crim Rule 4-502.
Revolving credit, CL §12-918.

Notice of arrearage.
Support, FL §10-107.

Notice of intent.
Assisted housing preservation, HS §7-101.

DEFINED TERMS —Cont'd

Notice record.
Access to court records, CJA Rule 16-1001.

Notification.
Commercial code, CL §1-201.

Notification date.
Property taxes.
Job creation, TP §9-230.
Secured transactions , disposition of collateral after default, CL §9-611.

Notify.
Commercial code, CL §1-201.
Computer information transactions, CL §22-102.

Notoriety of crimes contracts.
Crime victims' compensation, CP §11-621.

Noxious weeds.
Turf grass, AG §9-101.

Noxious weed seed, AG §9-201.

Nuisance, HG §§20-101, 20-301.
Actions, RP §14-120.
Community association actions, RP §§14-123 to 14-125.1.
Control, EN §10-305; HG §20-313.

Nuisance birds, AG §5-801.

Nuisance organism.
Natural resources, NR §4-205.1.

Nunchaku, CR §4-101.

Nurse anesthetist, HO §8-503.
Health insurance, IN §15-708.
Medical assistance, HG §15-103.

Nurse midwife, HO §8-503.
Health insurance, IN §15-709.

Nurse practitioner, HO §8-508.
Student financial assistance, ED §18-802.

Nursery stock.
Plant disease control, AG §5-301.

Nurses.
Overtime, LE §3-421.

Nursing care.
Hospitals, HG §19-301.

Nursing facility.
Home or community-based waiver programs, HG §15-135.
Medicaid, HG §15-132.
Medical care data collection, HG §19-132.

Nursing home, HG §19-1401.
Administrators, HO §9-101.
Death of resident, 70B §5A.
Fee assessment by health care commission, HG §19-111.
Nursing homes, Medicaid liability audits and review, HG §19-14A-01.

Nursing home administrator.
Health occupations, HO §9-101.

Nursing home administrator rehabilitation committee, HO §9-317.

Nursing home transition grants.
Community attendant services and supports program, 41 §6-7A-01.

Nursing personnel.
Nurses, HG §19-2001.

Nursing referral service agencies, HG §19-4B-01.

Nursing shortage area.
Physician assistants and nurse practitioners.
Student financial assistance, ED §18-802.
Scholarships, ED §18-706.

Nursing staff agency.
Nurses, HG §19-2001.

Nursing student.
Physician assistants and nurse practitioners.
Student financial assistance, ED §18-802.

DEFINED TERMS —Cont'd

Nursing student —Cont'd
Scholarships, ED §18-706.
Nutrient management plan.
Soil conservation districts, AG §8-801.
Oaths.
Business regulation, BR §1-201.
Rules of interpretation, 1 §9.
Object.
Interference with commercial athletic event, CR §10-203.
Objective.
Managing for results, SF §3-1001.
Objective measurable criteria.
Procurement, SF §13-101.
Obligated bank.
Negotiable instruments, CL §§3-312, 3-411.
Obligation.
Insurance companies.
Investments, IN §5-608.
Workers' compensation, IN §25-306.
Obligations secured by goods.
Commercial banks.
Maximum liabilities of person, FI §3-601.
Obligee.
Housing authorities, HS §12-101.
Support, FL §10-101.
Uniform interstate family support act, FL §10-301.
URESA, FL §10-301.
Obligor.
Income tax liens, TG §13-812.
Secured transactions, CL §9-102.
Support, FL §10-101.
Tax enforcement, TG §13-804.
Uniform interstate family support act, FL §10-301.
URESA, FL §10-301.
Obscene.
Sale or display of obscene matter to minor, CR §11-203.
Obsolete rank.
State police department, promotions, PS §2-404.
Obtain.
Bad checks, CR §8-101.
Exploitation of vulnerable adult, CR §8-801.
Robbery, CR §3-401.
Theft, CR §7-101.
Occasional use.
Maryland youth camp, HG §14-401.
Occupancy expenses.
Time-sharing, RP §11A-101.
Occupancy rent.
Property tax.
Elderly or disabled renters, TP §9-102.
Occupant.
Condominiums, RP §11-101.
Self-service storage, CL §18-501.
Occupational disease.
Limitation of actions, CJ §5-113.
Workers' compensation, LE §9-101.
Wrongful death, CJ §3-904.
Occupational safety and health standard, LE §5-101.
Occupational therapist.
Grant program, ED §18-704.
Health occupations, HO §10-101.
Occupational therapist rehabilitation committee, HO §10-319.
Occupational therapy, HO §10-101.

DEFINED TERMS —Cont'd

Occupational therapy assistant, HO §10-101.
Grant program, ED §18-704.
Occupational therapy practice, HO §10-101.
Occupational therapy principles, HO §10-101.
Occupational therapy procedures, HO §10-101.
Occupying agency.
Child care centers, FL §5-586.
Occurrence.
Administration of courts.
Motor vehicle tort interrogatories, Form 6.
Ocean City convention center facilities.
Stadium authority, FI §13-701.
Ocean City convention center fund, FI §13-701.
Ocean City convention center site.
Stadium authority, FI §13-701.
OctaBDE, EN §6-1201.
Ocular practitioner.
Optometrists, HO §11-401.
Off-duty hours.
Overtime compensation.
Law enforcement employees, SPP §8-308.
Offender.
Adult offender supervision, COR §6-203.
Community service providers.
Liability, CJ §5-805.
Offender employment coordination, COR §2-301.
Parole and probation, COR §6-101.
Sex offender registration, CP §11-701.
Offense.
Additional cost in criminal cases, CJ §7-409.
Law enforcement officers, CJ §2-608.
Moving violations, TR §16-213.
Offer, CA §11-102.
Securities, CA §11-101.
Offeror.
Lead poisoning, EN §6-826.
Offer to sell, CA §11-102.
Office.
Continuing care contracts, 70B §7.
Energy assistance program act, 41 §6-402.
Incompetency and criminal responsibility, CP §3-101.
Legislative services department.
Legislative information systems, SG §2-1228.
Office of policy analysis, SG §2-1234.
Recycling, EN §9-1701.
Office building.
Gas or electric meters, PUC §7-303.
Submetering, PUC §7-303.
Office facility.
Medical care data collection, HG §19-132.
Office for the practice of law.
Discipline of attorneys, CJA Rule 16-701.
Office or other commercial space conversion.
Rental housing production program, HS §4-1501.
Officer.
College of southern Maryland, ED §16-602.
Credit unions, FI §6-101.
Nonprofit health service plans, IN §14-115.1.
Parking violations, TR §26-301.
Official.
Credit unions, FI §6-101.
Death sentence, custody, COR §3-903.
National racing compact, BR §11-1301.
State finance, SF §2-106.
Official action.
St. Mary's county open meetings, 24 §4-202.
Official capacity.
Corporations, CA §2-418.

DEFINED TERMS —Cont'd
Official certificate.
   Poultry products inspection act, AG §4-201.
   Wholesome meat act, AG §4-101.
Official compendium.
   Food and drugs, HG §21-101.
Official custodian.
   Access to public records, SG §10-611.
Official device.
   Poultry products inspection act, AG §4-201.
   Wholesome meat act, AG §4-101.
Official establishment.
   Poultry products inspection act, AG §4-201.
   Wholesome meat act, AG §4-101.
Official inspection legend.
   Poultry products inspection act, AG §4-201.
Official legend.
   Wholesome meat act, AG §4-101.
Officially recognized.
   Seeds, AG §9-201.
   Turf grass, AG §9-101.
Official mark.
   Poultry products inspection act, AG §4-201.
   Wholesome meat act, AG §4-101.
Official of a governmental entity, 26 §1.
Official proceeding.
   Influencing or intimidating victim or witness, CR §9-301.
Official rating.
   Video sales and rentals, CL §14-1601.
Official sample.
   Commercial feed, AG §6-101.
   Commercial fertilizers, AG §6-201.
Off-label use.
   Health insurance, IN §15-804.
Off-road vehicle.
   Hunting restrictions, NR §10-410.
Off-sale.
   Alcoholic beverage licenses, 2B §9-108.
   Alcoholic beverages, 2B §9-217.
Offset.
   Debt collection, CL §15-701.
Offshore.
   Waterfowl hunting, NR §10-601.
Offshore blind site.
   Waterfowl hunting, NR §10-601.
Offshore stationary blind.
   Waterfowl hunting, NR §10-601.
Off-the-road motorcycle, TR §25-102.1.
Of legal age.
   Rules of interpretation, 1 §24.
Oil.
   Natural resources, EN §14-102.
   Oil cleanups, EN §4-701.
   Water pollution, EN §4-401.
Oil pipeline corporation.
   Power to condemn, PUC §5-404.
Oil storage facility.
   Water pollution, EN §4-401.
Old growth timber.
   Renewable energy portfolio standard, PUC §7-701.
Old vital record.
   Archives, SG §9-1015.
Ombudsmen program.
   Medical assistance, HG §15-101.
On consignment.
   Works of fine art, CL §11-8A-01.
On duty.
   Workers' compensation.
      Volunteer fire or rescue company, LE §9-234.

DEFINED TERMS —Cont'd
1.3 G fireworks.
   Fireworks, PS §10-101.
1.4 G fireworks.
   Fireworks, PS §10-101.
One-call system.
   Excavation or demolition near underground facilities, PUC §12-101.
One horse peddler.
   Business licenses, BR §17-904.
100-year flood event.
   Flood control and watershed management, EN §5-801.
One hundred year floodplain.
   Forest conservation, NR §5-1601.
One-stop center.
   Pilot program for long term employment of qualified ex-felons, LE §11-701.
On-farm food service facility, HG §21-309.
On-farm home processing facility, HG §21-308.
Ongoing pattern.
   Nursing homes, HG §19-1401.
On premise outdoor sign.
   Highways, TR §8-701.
On-sale.
   Alcoholic beverage licenses, 2B §9-108.
   Alcoholic beverages, 2B §9-217.
On-site generated electricity.
   Special use tax, TG §11-1A-01.
On-site supervision.
   Occupational therapists, HO §10-101.
On time.
   Graduation records.
      Collection, maintenance, analysis and report, ED §7-203.2.
Oocyte.
   Maryland stem cell research program, 83A §5-2B-01.
Open area.
   Forests and parks, NR §5-1201.
   Property tax, TP §9-208.
   Strip mining.
      Bonds, EN §15-507.
Open-area limit.
   Strip mining bonds, EN §15-507.
Open container.
   Open containers of alcoholic beverages in motor vehicles, CR §10-123.
Open end account.
   Retail credit accounts, CL §12-501.
Opening.
   Deep mine control, EN §15-601.
Opening air burning.
   Forest fire prevention, NR §5-720.
Open-pit mining.
   Coal, EN §15-501.
Open purse.
   Horse racing, BR §11-518.
Open season.
   Fish and fisheries, NR §4-101.
   Wildlife, NR §10-101.
Open space.
   Forests and parks, NR §5-1201.
   Property tax, TP §9-208.
Operate.
   Boats and boating, NR §8-701.
   Maryland youth camp, HG §14-401.
   Motor vehicles, TR §11-141.
Operate aircraft, TR §5-101.
Operate a motor vehicle for hire.
   For-hire driving services, PUC §10-101.

DEFINED TERMS —Cont'd

Operating agreement.
Hotels and retirement communities, CL §23-101.
Limited liability companies, CA §4A-101.

Operating budget.
Neighborhood housing services fund, HS §4-1001.

Operating costs.
Rental housing production program, HS §4-1501.

Operating deficit.
Local bus systems grants, TR §10-207.

Operating expenditure.
Department of transportation, SF §7-110.

Operating procedures.
Interstate insurance product regulation compact,
IN §29-101.

Operating property.
Property tax, TP §1-101.

Operating ratio.
Common carriers, regulation of rates, PUC
§4-302.

Operating support.
Historical and cultural museum assistance
program, SF §5A-349.

Operating unit.
Property tax, TP §1-101.

Operation.
Farm nuisance suits, CJ §5-403.
Surface mining, EN §15-801.

Operator.
Automated teller machines, FI §1-401.
Boats and boating, NR §8-701.
Deep mine control, EN §15-601.
Mines and mining, EN §15-101.
Motor vehicles, TR §11-142.
Nuisance actions, RP §14-120.
Pine tree reforestation, NR §5-501.
Radioactive waste, EN §7-301.
Residential boarding education programs for
at-risk youth, ED §8-701.
Self-service storage, CL §18-501.
Strip mining, EN §15-501.
Waterworks operators, EN §12-101.

Opiate, CR §5-101.

Opinion.
Insurance companies, IN §5-201.

Optimum carrying capacity.
Fish and fisheries.
Endangered species, NR §4-2A-01.
Nongame and endangered species conservation,
NR §10-2A-01.

Optional bank holiday, FI §5-701.

Optometrist.
Health occupations, HO §11-101.

Optometrist rehabilitation committee, HO
§11-405.

Oral communication.
Evidence, CJ §10-401.

Oral competency.
Health occupations, HO §1-101.

Oral language services.
Equal access to public services for persons with
limited English proficiency, SG §10-1102.

Order.
Health insurance, IN §15-405.
Independent adoptions, FL §5-3B-04.
Local department adoptions and guardianships,
FL §5-305.
Negotiable instruments, CL §3-103.

Order for money or goods.
Counterfeiting, CR §8-609.

DEFINED TERMS —Cont'd

Order of relief.
Debt collection, CL §15-101.

Ordinance.
Municipal corporations, 23A §17D.

Ordinary and necessary expenses.
Child support guidelines, FL §12-201.

Ordinary care.
Negotiable instruments, CL §3-103.

Organization.
Alcoholic beverages, 2B §7-101.
Commercial code, CL §1-201.
Credit unions, FI §6-301.
Debt management services, FI §12-901.
Door-to-door solicitation, CL §14-2601.
Gaming, CR §12-101.
Organizational insignia, BR §19-201.

Organized crime.
Corporations, CA §1-405.

Organized militia.
Workers' compensation, LE §9-215.

Organized police agency.
Private detectives.
Experience, BOP §13-303.
Security guard agency licensure, BOP §19-303.

Organizing committee.
Incorporation of municipal corporation, 23A §20.

Organizing community.
Incorporation of municipal corporation, 23A §20.

Origin.
Turf grass, AG §9-101.

Original.
Evidence, CJ §10-103.

Original articles of incorporation, CA §3-601.

Original debtor.
Secured transactions, CL §9-102.

Original licenses.
Montgomery county alcoholic beverage licenses,
2B §9-102.1.

Original mortgagor.
Recordation taxes.
Exemptions, TP §12-108.

**Original transfer or generation-skipping
transfer tax,** TG §7-401.

Originating state.
Qualifications of educational personnel, ED
§6-604.

Originator.
Funds transfers, CL §4A-104.

Originator's bank.
Funds transfers, CL §4A-104.

Orphaned land.
Strip mining, EN §15-501.

Orphaned land reclamation project.
Strip mining, EN §15-501.

Orthopedic brace.
Health insurance, IN §15-820.

Osteoporosis, HG §13-1901.

Other business entity.
Business trusts, CA §12-101.

Other information.
Witness immunity.
Courts, CJ §9-123.

Other service options.
Community attendant services and supports
program, 41 §6-7A-01.

Other-state bank, FI §1-101.
Branch banking, FI §5-1001.

Other taxing agency.
Property tax.
Collection, TP §14-801.

DEFINED TERMS —Cont'd

Other tobacco product.
Tobacco tax, TG §12-101.

Other valid coverage.
Health insurance, IN §§15-222, 15-223.

Outdoor advertising sign.
Compensation for removal, 25 §122E.

Outdoor music festival.
Business licenses, BR §17-1401.

Outdoor sign.
Highways, TR §8-701.

Out-of-home placement.
Child care, FL §5-501.
Child welfare accountability, FL §5-1301.
Integration of child welfare and substance abuse
treatment act, FL §5-1201.

Out-of-service order.
Commercial motor vehicles, TR §16-812.

Out-of-state association.
Savings and loan associations.
Interstate acquisitions, FI §9-1001.

Out-of-state bank.
Branch banking, FI §5-1001.

Out-of-state bank holding company, FI §5-901.
Savings and loan associations.
Emergency interstate acquisitions, FI §5-1101.

Out-of-state credit union.
Credit unions, FI §6-101.

Out-of-state employer group contract.
Long-term care insurance, IN §18-101.

**Out-of-state savings and loan holding
company.**
Interstate acquisitions, FI §9-1001.

Outreach efforts.
Cancer prevention, education, screening and
treatment program, HG §13-1101.

Outstanding and unpaid.
Revenue facilities, TR §4-101.
Transportation, TR §3-101.

Outstanding balance.
Retail installment sales, CL §12-601.

Outstanding liabilities.
Health club services, CL §14-12B-02.

Outstanding payment instrument.
Money transmission, FI §12-401.

Outstanding unpaid indebtedness.
Revolving credit, CL §12-901.

Outstanding warrant.
Refusal to register motor vehicles, TR §13-406.1.
Suspension, revocation or refusal of drivers'
license, TR §16-204.

Overburden.
Strip mining, EN §15-501.
Surface mining, EN §15-801.

Overhead costs of the system.
Automated mapping-geographic information
systems, SG §10-901.

Overissue.
Investment securities, CL §§8-102, 8-210.

Overseas.
Sale of goods, CL §2-323.
Sales, UCC, CL §2-323.

Overserved district.
Alcoholic beverages, 2B §9-203.

Own.
Public utility companies, PUC §1-101.

Owner.
Abandoned property, CL §17-101.
Assisted housing preservation, HS §7-101.
Boats and boating, NR §8-701.
Caves, NR §5-1401.

DEFINED TERMS —Cont'd

Owner —Cont'd
Commercial real estate broker's lien, RP §14-301.
Drug asset forfeiture, CP §12-101.
Dumping site surveillance systems, CR §10-112.
Excavation or demolition near underground
facilities, PUC §12-101.
Homebuilder registration, BR §4.5-101.
Home improvement, BR §8-101.
Lead hazard insurance for rental property, IN
§19-701.
Lead poisoning, EN §6-801.
Liens on personal property, CL §16-101.
Liquefied petroleum gas containers, CL §11-601.
Mechanics' liens, RP §9-101.
Motor vehicles, TR §11-143.
Motor vehicle theft, CR §7-105.
Natural resources.
Gas and oil, EN §14-102.
New home warranties, RP §10-601.
Nuisance actions, RP §14-120.
Public recreation on private and local government
lands, NR §5-1101.
Sale of tobacco products through vending
machine, BR §16-3A-01.
Special use tax on certain electricity, TG
§11-1A-01.
Speed restrictions on motor vehicles, Montgomery
county, TR §21-809.
Theft, CR §7-101.
Traffic control devices, TR §21-202.1.
Well drilling, EN §9-1301.
Woodrow Wilson bridge and tunnel compact, TR
§10-303.

Owner-builder.
Self-help homeownership technical assistance
program, HS §4-1701.

**Owner-contractor information exchange
system.**
Excavation or demolition near underground
facilities, PUC §12-101.

Owner-member.
Excavation or demolition near underground
facilities, PUC §12-101.

Owner-occupied residential property.
Property taxes.
Semiannual payment schedule, TP §10-204.3.

Owner of land.
Public watershed associations, 25 §169.

Owner's cash contribution.
Strip mining, EN §15-501.

Owner's offer.
Assisted housing preservation, HS §7-101.

Owner's real property.
Dangerous dogs, CR §10-619.

Package.
Childproof packaging, HG §22-301.
Consumer protection.
Gold and silver, CL §14-601.
Food and drugs, HG §21-101.
Toxics, EN §9-1901.
Weights and measures, AG §11-101.

Packaged air-conditioning equipment.
Maryland efficiency standards act, SG §9-2006.

Packaged bee.
Honeybees, AG §5-501.

Packaged food product.
Kosher products, CL §14-904.

Packaging component.
Toxics, EN §9-1901.

DEFINED TERMS —Cont'd
Packer.
   Egg law, AG §4-301.
   Livestock slaughtering, AG §4-123.1.
   Oysters and clams, NR §4-1001.
Page.
   Elections.
      Petition, EL §6-101.
   Real property, RP §3-601.
Paleontology.
   Geological survey, NR §2-101.
Panel.
   Historical and cultural museum assistance
         program, SF §5A-349.
   Mines and mining, EN §15-101.
Paper.
   Rules of interpretation, 1 §28.
Paper gaming, CR §13-302.
   Garrett county, CR §13-1404.
Parasailing, NR §8-701.
Pardon, COR §7-101.
Parent.
   Children in need of assistance, CJ §3-801.
   Disabled student placement, ED §8-413.
   Handicapped children.
      Education, ED §8-412.
   Immunization of minors, HG §18-4A-01.
   Independent adoptions, FL §5-3B-01.
   Local department guardianships and adoptions,
         FL §5-301.
   Private agency adoptions and guardianships, FL
         §5-3A-01.
   Reporting requirements for public service
         companies, PUC §6-201.
   Wrongful death, CJ §3-901.
Parent surrogate.
   Handicapped children.
      Education, ED §8-412.
Pari-mutuel betting.
   Horse racing, BR §11-101.
Park.
   Mobile home parks, RP §8A-101.
   Motor vehicles, TR §11-144.
Park and planning commission.
   Horse racing, BR §11-526.
Park corridor.
   Canal place preservation and development
         authority, FI §13-1001.
Parker Heights corridor.
   Pimlico community development authority, BR
         §11-1201.
Park fee.
   Mobile home parks, RP §8A-101.
Parking lot.
   Towing of vehicles, TR §21-10A-01.
Parking subsidy.
   Tax credits for employer-provided commuter
         benefits, EN §2-901.
Park owner.
   Liens on mobile homes, CL §16-201.
   Mobile home parks, RP §8A-101.
Parole, COR §7-101.
Parolee, COR §§6-101, 7-101.
Partial hospitalization.
   Discrimination by health insurers, HG §19-703.1;
         IN §15-802.
Partially nude figure.
   Sale or display of obscene matter to minor, CR
         §11-203.
Partially regulated plant.
   Northeast interstate dairy compact, AG §2-801.

DEFINED TERMS —Cont'd
Partial pardon, COR §7-101.
Participant.
   Anne Arundel county correctional facility, COR
         §11-703.
   Food programs, HG §18-108.
   Ignition interlock system, TR §16-404.1.
   Legislative pension plan, SG Title 2 Subtitle 3
         (note).
   Pensions, SPP §20-101.
   Sterile needle and syringe exchange, Baltimore
         City, HG §24-801.
   Sterile needle and syringe exchange, Prince
         George's county, HG §24-901.
   Voluntary cleanup program, EN §7-501.
   Workforce investment act, LE §11-503.
   Work release and home detention programs,
         Baltimore County, COR §11-705.
Participants in live racing.
   National racing compact, BR §11-1301.
Participating agencies.
   Acid rain, NR §3-3A-01.
   Community service programs, COR §8-701.
Participating agencies and programs.
   Judith P. Hoyer early child care and education
         enhancement program, ED §5-217.
Participating credit union.
   Credit unions, share guaranty corporations, FI
         §7-201.
Participating employee.
   State retirement and pension system, SPP
         §30-101.
      Supplemental retirement plans.
         Optional defined contribution system, SPP
               §32-101.
Participating employer.
   Pensions, SPP §20-101.
Participating governmental unit.
   Pensions, SPP §20-101.
   State retirement and pension system, SPP
         §21-309.
Participating hospital.
   Health and educational facilities, 43C §3.
Participating institution for higher education.
   Health and educational facilities, 43C §3.
Participating investors.
   Venture capital trust, 83A §5-301.
Participating manufacturer.
   Tobacco, escrow act compliance, BR §16-501.
Participating provider.
   Health assistance, HG §15-122.1.
Participating state.
   Interstate wildlife violator compact, NR §10-1201.
   Northeast interstate dairy compact, AG §2-801.
Participating unit.
   Student loan repayment pilot program, SPP
         §10-501.
Part I crimes.
   State aid for police protection, 41 §4-403.
Parties in interest.
   Trustee powers, ET §14-109.
Partisan organization.
   Elections, EL §1-101.
Partner.
   Limited partnerships, CA §10-101.
Partnership, CA §3-101.
   Limited liability company, CA §4A-101.
   Limited partnerships, CA §10-101.
   Real estate investment trust, CA §8-501.1.
   Uniform partnership act, revised act, CA §9A-101.

DEFINED TERMS —Cont'd
Partnership agreement.
Limited partnerships, CA §10-101.
Uniform partnership act, revised act, CA §9A-101.
Partnership at will.
Uniform partnership act, revised act, CA §9A-101.
Partnership funding.
Substance abuse treatment outcomes partnership fund, HG §8-6C-01.
Partnership interest.
Limited partnerships, CA §10-101.
Uniform partnership act, revised act, CA §9A-101.
Partnership project.
Partnership rental housing program, HS §4-1201.
Partnership rental housing.
Partnership rental housing program, HS §4-1201.
Partner's interest.
Uniform partnership act, revised act, CA §9A-101.
Part of body.
Anatomical gift act, ET §4-501.
Part-time employee.
Day of rest, LE §3-704.
State personnel, SPP §7-701.
Part-time student.
Financial assistance, ED §18-1401.
Party.
Children in need of assistance, CJ §3-801.
Child support.
Affidavit of support, FL §10-1A-01.
Commercial code, CL §1-201.
Commercial discrimination, SF §19-103.
Computer information transactions, CL §22-102.
Contract liens, RP §14-201.
Corporations, CA §2-418.
Financial institutions, FI §1-204.
Juvenile causes, CJ §3-8A-01.
Local department guardianships and adoptions, FL §5-301.
Party state.
National crime prevention and privacy compact, CP §10-239.
National racing compact, BR §11-1301.
Radioactive waste, EN §7-301.
Pass.
Bad checks, CR §8-101.
Passed a regional board.
Dentists, HO §4-306.
Passenger.
Crimes involving railroads, CR §6-503.
Passenger area.
Drinking while driving, TR §21-903.
Open containers of alcoholic beverages in motor vehicles, CR §10-123.
Passenger car, TR §11-144.1.
Fuel efficiency, TR §13-818.
Motor vehicle insurance, IN §19-512.
Rental motor vehicles.
Collision damage waiver, CL §14-2101.
Pass-through cabinet.
Maryland efficiency standards act, SG §9-2006.
Pass-through entity.
Income tax, TG §10-102.1.
Pasteurized.
Milk products, HG §21-401.
Patent.
Land patents, RP §13-101.
Patent tongs.
Oysters and clams, NR §§4-1001, 4-1101.
Paternity docket.
Paternity proceedings, FL §5-1047.

DEFINED TERMS —Cont'd
Patient.
Medical records, HG §4-301.
Mental health compact, HG §11-103.
Patient care personnel.
Hospitals, HG §19-308.1.
Patient cost.
Health insurance, IN §15-827.
Patuxent programs.
Patuxent institution, COR §4-101.
Patuxent river watershed.
Water management, EN §4-301.
Paved highway.
Rules of the road, TR §21-404.
Pawnbroker, BR §12-101.
Pawn transaction.
Pawnbrokers, BR §12-101.
Pay.
Failure to pay electronic toll, TR §21-1414.
Payable at a definite time.
Negotiable instruments, CL §§3-103, 3-108.
Payable on demand.
Negotiable instruments, CL §§3-103, 3-108.
Payable to bearer.
Negotiable instruments, CL §§3-103, 3-109.
Payable to order.
Negotiable instruments, CL §§3-103, 3-109.
Payee.
Structured settlements, transfer of payment rights, CJ §5-1101.
Paymaster.
Tax liens, TG §13-811.
Payment.
Negotiable instruments, CL §§3-103, 3-602.
Principal and income, ET §15-516.
Payment by beneficiary's bank to beneficiary.
Funds transfers, CL §4A-405.
Payment by originator to beneficiary.
Funds transfers, CL §4A-406.
Payment by sender to receiving bank.
Funds transfers, CL §4A-403.
Payment date.
Funds transfers, CL §4A-401.
Payment device number.
Credit card number protection, CR §8-213.
Identity fraud, CR §8-301.
Printing on electronic receipts, CL §14-1318.
Payment instrument.
Check cashing services, FI §12-101.
Money transmission, FI §12-401.
Payment intangible.
Secured transactions, CL §9-102.
Payment order.
Commercial code, CL §4A-103.
Computer information transactions, CL §22-102.
Funds transfers, CL §4A-103.
Payment period.
Closed end credit, CL §12-1009.
Prepayment of outstanding unpaid indebtedness, CL §12-126.
Secondary mortgage loans, CL §12-401.
Payment security.
Little Miller Act, SF §17-101.
Procurement, SF §13-225.
Payment subject to withholding.
Tax withholding, TG §10-905.
Payor.
Fee assessment by health care commission, HG §19-111.
Freestanding ambulatory care facilities, HG §19-3B-01.

DEFINED TERMS —Cont'd

Payor —Cont'd
Medical care data collection, HG §19-132.
Tax withholding, TG §10-905.

Payor bank.
Bank deposits and collections, CL §§4-104, 4-105.

Payor institution.
Banking institutions.
Deposits, FI §5-309.
Savings and loan associations, FI §9-909.

Pay period.
Unemployment insurance.
Partial insured employment, LE §8-204.

Peace officer.
Criminal rules, Crim Rule 4-102.
Emergency mental health evaluations, HG §10-620.

Peace order proceeding.
Juvenile causes, CJ §3-8A-01.

Peace order request.
Juvenile causes, CJ §3-8A-01.

Peddler.
Business licenses, BR §17-901.

Peddler's license.
Business licenses, BR §17-901.

Pedestrian, TR §11-145.

Peeler.
Crabs, NR §4-801.

Peer review.
Accountants, BOP §2-4A-01.

Pelt.
Wildlife, NR §10-101.

Penalty.
Courts, CJ §2-101.
Secondhand watches, CL §14-701.

Pen register.
Pen registers and trap and trace devices, CJ §10-4B-01.

Pension, SPP §20-101.

Pension reserve, SPP §20-101.

Pension system.
State retirement and pension system, SPP §30-101.

PentaBDE, EN §6-1201.

Pepper mace, CR §4-101.

Percentage interests.
Condominiums, RP §11-101.

Percentage points.
Minority business enterprise program.
County public libraries, ED §23-402.
Prince George's community college, ED §16-312.
Prince George's county board of education, ED §4-125.

Percentage preference.
Procurement, SF §14-206.

Percentage price preference.
Procurement, SF §14-407.

Percent; percentage, AG §6-101.
Commercial fertilizers, AG §6-201.

Per diem.
Jury, CJ §8-425.

Perennial stream.
Forest conservation, NR §5-1601.

Perfected.
Security interest.
Motor vehicles, TR §13-201.

Perform acupuncture.
Physicians, HO §14-101.

Perform a farm labor contracting service, LE §7-101.

DEFINED TERMS —Cont'd

Performance.
Unauthorized recording of sounds or images, CR §7-308.

Performance audit.
School funding, ED §5-110.

Performance measure.
Managing for results, SF §3-1001.

Performance of duties.
Death benefits, public safety officers and personnel, PS §1-202.

Performance requirement.
Economic development opportunities program, SF §7-314.

Performance security.
Little Miller Act, SF §17-101.
Procurement, SF §13-225.
Washington suburban sanitary district.
Construction of subdivision lines, 29 §3-101.1.

Performance standards.
Workforce investment act, LE §11-503.

Performing arts theater.
Beer, wine and liquor licenses, 2B §8-216.1.

Performing rights society.
Copyright royalties, CL §11-1401.

Periodic supervision.
Occupational therapists, HO §10-101.

Permanent appointment.
Appointment of police officers, supervisors and administrators, PS §3-215.
Correctional training commission, COR §8-201.

Permanent cemetery.
Crimes relating to human remains, CR §10-401.

Permanent partial disability.
Sundry claims board, COR §10-301.

Permanent part-time legislative employee.
General assembly, SG §2-103.

Permanent total disability.
Sundry claims board, COR §10-301.

Permissible investment.
Money transmission, FI §12-401.

Permit.
Accountants, BOP §2-101.
Architects, BOP §3-101.
Cholesterol testing, HG §17-501.
Development, SG §11-101.
Handgun permits, PS §5-301.
Horse racing, BR §11-815.
Kent county, CR §13-1701.
Landscape architects, BOP §9-101.
Land surveyors, BOP §15-101.
Medical laboratory, HG §17-201.
Milk products, HG §21-401.
Queen Anne's county, gaming, CR §13-2001.
Strip mining, EN §15-501.
Tissue banks, HG §17-301.

Permit fee.
Accountants, BOP §2-101.
Architects, BOP §3-101.
Landscape architects, BOP §9-101.
Land surveyors, BOP §15-101.

Permit holder.
Food, drugs and cosmetics, HG §21-1113.

Permittee.
Surface mining, EN §15-801.

Permit year.
Direct wine seller's permit, 2B §7.5-101.

Per pupil basic current expense figure.
Maryland school for the blind.
Appropriations, ED §8-317.
Maryland school for the deaf, ED §8-310.3.

DEFINED TERMS —Cont'd
Per se.
  Homicide by motor vehicle or vessel while under
    the influence, CR §2-503.
Persistent vegetative state.
  Health care decisions, HG §5-601.
Person, EN §1-101.
  Abandoned property, CL §17-101.
  Access to court records, CJA Rule 16-1001.
  Administration of courts.
    Form interrogatories, Form 2.
  Adult offender supervision, COR §6-203.
  Agricultural and resource-based industry
    development corporation, 41 §13-501.
  Agricultural land drainage, AG §8-603.
  Agriculture, AG §1-101.
  Air quality, EN §2-101.
  Alcoholic beverages, 2B §§1-102, 6-201.
  Alcoholic beverage tax, TG §5-101.
  Amusement tax, TG §4-101.
  Anatomical gift act, ET §4-501.
  Antitrust, CL §11-201.
  Assignment of wages, CL §15-301.
  Athlete agents, BR §4-401.
  Automobile insurance fund, IN §20-101.
  Bainbridge development corporation, 83A §5-1601.
  Beer franchise fair dealing act, 2B §17-101.
  Bills of lading and warehouse receipts, CL
    §18-101.
  Biological agent registry program, HG §17-601.
  Business occupations and professions, BOP
    §1-101.
  Business regulation, BR §1-101.
  Business trusts, CA §12-101.
  Caves, NR §5-1401.
  Charles county, CR §13-1101.
  Commercial code, CL §1-201.
  Commissioner of financial regulation, FI §11-101.
  Computer information transactions, CL §22-102.
  Consignees, CL §11-801.
  Consumer cooperatives, CA §5-5A-02.
  Consumer credit reporting agencies, CL §14-1201.
  Consumer debt collection, CL §14-201.
  Consumer loans, CL §12-301; FI §11-201.
  Consumer protection, CL §§13-101, 14-1301.
    Automotive repair facilities, CL §14-1001.
    Consumer credit contracts, CL §14-1302.
    Consumer credit reporting agencies, CL
      §14-1201.
    Fine print, CL §14-501.
    Gold and silver, CL §14-601.
    Kosher products, CL §14-901.
    Secondhand watches, CL §14-701.
    Unit pricing, CL §14-101.
    Used radio and television sets, CL §14-801.
  Continuing care contracts, 70B §7.
  Controlled hazardous substances, EN §7-201.
  Corporations, CA §1-101.
  Correctional services, COR §1-101.
  Credit card number protection, CR §8-213.
  Credit services businesses, CL §14-1901.
  Criminal law, CR §1-101.
  Criminal procedure, CP §1-101.
  Currency transaction reporting, FI §12-802.
  Custom home protection, RP §10-501.
  Debt collection, CL §15-102.
  Declaratory judgments, CJ §3-401.
  Disclaimer of property interests, ET §9-201.
  Discretionary trusts, ET §14-401.
  Distress sales, CL §11-1101.
  Door-to-door sales, CL §14-301.

DEFINED TERMS —Cont'd
Person —Cont'd
  Drinking water, EN §9-401.
  Economic development corporation, 83A §5-201.
  Education, ED §1-101.
  Electric cooperatives, CA §5-601.
  Electronic transactions, CL §21-101.
  Eminent domain, RP §12-201.
  Employment discrimination, 49B §15.
  Environmental covenant, EN §1-801.
  Environmental service, NR §3-101.
  Equal credit opportunity, CL §12-701.
  Estate tax, TG §7-308.
  Excavation or demolition near underground
    facilities, PUC §12-101.
  False advertising and related crimes, CL
    §§11-701, 14-2901.
  Family law, FL §1-101.
  Fiduciaries, ET §15-101.
  Fiduciary security transfers, ET §15-301.
  Financial institutions, FI §§1-101, 1-205.
  Fish and fisheries, NR §4-101.
  Food and drugs, HG §21-101.
  Foreign discriminatory boycotts, CL §11-102.
  Forest conservation, NR §5-1601.
  Forests and parks, NR §5-101.
  For-hire driving services, PUC §10-101.
  Gas and oil.
    Coastal facilities review, EN §14-501.
  Gasohol and gasoline products marketing, CL
    §11-301.
  Geothermal resources, EN §5-601.
  Health, HG §1-101.
  Health care fraud, HG §15-123.
  Health occupations, HO §1-101.
  Hospitals, HG §19-301.
  Housing and community development, HS §1-101.
  Housing authorities, HS §12-101.
  Housing discrimination, 49B §20.
  Insurance, IN §1-101.
  Interest in usury, CL §12-101.
  Juvenile services, 83C §1-101.
  Kosher products, CL §14-901.
  Labor and employment, LE §1-101.
  Lead paint, EN §6-1001.
  Liens on personal property, CL §16-101.
  Limited partnerships, CA §10-101.
  Liquefied petroleum gas containers, CL §11-601.
  Loans.
    Finder's fees, CL §12-801.
  Local military installation redevelopment
    authorities, 83A §5-1701.
  Mortgage lending, FI §11-501.
  Natural resources.
    Gas and oil, EN §14-102.
  Northeast Maryland waste disposal authority, NR
    §3-904.
  Occupational safety and health, LE §5-101.
  Operating agreements.
    Hotels and retirement communities, CL
      §23-101.
  Penmar development corporations, 83A §5-1201.
  Pensions, SPP §20-101.
  Pine tree reforestation, NR §5-501.
  Political subdivisions, 24 §1-101.
  Principal and income act, ET §15-501.
  Procurement, SF §§11-101, 13-301.
  Products made by blind persons, CL §14-2801.
  Property tax, TP §1-101.
  Public safety, PS §1-101.

DEFINED TERMS —Cont'd
Person —Cont'd
Public service company.
Reporting requirements, PUC §6-201.
Public utility companies, PUC §1-101.
Radiation, EN §8-101.
Radioactive waste, EN §7-301.
Real property, RP §1-101.
Regulation of animals, 24 §11-507.
Retail credit accounts, CL §12-501.
Retail installment sales, CL §12-601.
Sales below cost, CL §11-401.
Cigarettes, CL §11-501.
Sales finance companies, FI §11-401.
Sales tax, TG §11-101.
Sanitary facilities, EN §9-201.
Secondary mortgage loans, CL §12-401.
Securities, CA §11-101.
Service contracts and consumer products
guaranty, CL §14-401.
Settlement of decedents' estates, Estates Rule
6-105.
Social security number privacy, CL §14-3401.
Standing to sue.
Environmental matters, NR §1-501.
State government, SG §1-101.
State personnel, SPP §1-101.
State standby petroleum fuel set-aside program,
PS §14-501.
Strip mining, EN §15-501.
Surface mining, EN §15-801.
Susquehanna river basin compact, EN §5-301.
Taxation, TG §1-101.
Trademarks, BR §1-401.
Trade regulation, CL §11-901.
Trade secrets, CL §11-1201.
Transportation, TR §1-101.
Unemployment compensation.
Transfers for purpose of lowering contribution
rates, LE §8-614.
Uniform child custody jurisdiction and
enforcement act, FL §9.5-101.
Uniform commercial code, CL §1-201.
Uniform fiduciaries act, ET §15-201.
UTMA, ET §13-301.
Video sales and rentals, CL §14-1601.
Water and water resources, NR §8-101.
Water management, EN §4-101.1.
Water pollution, EN §9-301.
Water pollution control, AG §8-701.
Water quality financing, EN §9-1601.
Water quality laboratories, EN §9-1001.
Water resources, EN §5-101.
Well drillers, EN §13-101.
Wetlands and riparian rights, EN §16-101.
Wildlife, NR §10-101.
Wrongful death, CJ §3-901.
Person acting as parent.
Uniform child custody jurisdiction and
enforcement act, FL §9.5-101.
Personal assistant.
Community attendant services and supports
program, 41 §6-7A-01.
Personal care.
Hospitals, HG §19-301.
Personal care services.
Medicaid, HG §15-132.
Personal consumer.
Direct wine seller's permit, 2B §7.5-101.
Personal flotation device.
Child flotation devices, NR §8-743.

DEFINED TERMS —Cont'd
Personal identifying information.
Identity fraud, CR §8-301.
Personal information.
Access to public records, SG §10-611.
Motor vehicle administration, TR §12-112.
Personal injury protection policy.
Organization recovering payments made to
subscriber under.
Contract not to contain provision allowing, HG
§19-713.1.
Personal insurance.
Cancellation or nonrenewal of insurance, IN
§27-601.
Personalized handgun.
Handgun safety devices, PS §5-132.
Personally prepare and dispense.
Nurses, HO §8-508.
Pharmacists and pharmacies, HO §12-102.
Personal net worth.
Procurement, minority business enterprises, SF
§14-301.
Personal note.
Disclosure of mental health records, HG §4-307.
Personal property.
Abandoned property, CL §17-101.
Educational financing.
State assistance, ED §5-202.
Self-service storage, CL §18-501.
Personal recognizance.
Interstate wildlife violator compact, NR §10-1201.
Personal record.
Access to public records, SG §10-624.
Personal representative.
Courts, CJ §3-201.
Discretionary trusts, ET §14-401.
Estates and trusts, ET §1-101.
Transfer-on-death security registration, ET
§16-101.
UTMA, ET §13-301.
Personal watercraft.
Boats and boating, NR §8-701.
Person at risk.
Lead poisoning, EN §6-801.
Person eligible for relief.
Domestic violence, FL §4-501.
Person engaged in a trade or business.
Corporations, BR §1-502.
Person entitled to enforce.
Negotiable instruments, CL §§3-103, 3-301.
Person entitled under the document.
Documents of title, CL §7-102.
Person guaranteed.
Service contracts and consumer products
guaranty, CL §14-401.
Person in a position of authority.
Sexual offense in the fourth degree, CR §3-308.
Person in control.
Emergency response reimbursement, CJ §3-1101.
Person in emergency management service.
Civil relief during emergency periods, PS §14-201.
Person in interest.
Access to public records, SG §10-611.
Burial sites, RP §14-121.
Children, youth and families services.
Disclosure of information to public agencies,
49D §3-101.
Medical records, HG §4-301.
Recording military discharge papers, CJ §2-207.
Person in position of seller.
Sale of goods, CL §2-707.

DEFINED TERMS —Cont'd

Person interested in the estate.
Estate tax, TG §7-308.

Person in the position of a seller.
Sales, UCC, CL §2-707.

Personnel merit system.
Court personnel, CJ §2-5A-01.

Person of lower income.
Group home financing program, HS §4-601.

Person participating or interested in a labor dispute.
Injunctions, LE §4-301.

Person related to, individual.
Secured transactions, CL §9-102.

Person related to, organization.
Secured transactions, CL §9-102.

Person responsible for discharge.
Economic development assistance fund, 83A §5-1401.
Water pollution, EN §4-401.

Persons of eligible income.
Baltimore City housing authority, HS §15-101.
Housing authorities, HS §12-101.
Montgomery county housing opportunities commission, HS §16-108.
Prince George's county housing authority, HS §17-101.
Queen Anne's county housing authority, HS §18-101.
Washington county housing authority, HS §21-101.

Person suffering injury or damage.
Civil relief during emergency periods, PS §14-201.

Pertussis vaccine, HG §18-328.

Pest control.
Pesticide applicators, AG §5-201.

Pest control applicator.
Pesticide applicators, AG §5-201.

Pest control consultant.
Pesticide applicators, AG §5-201.

Pesticide.
Application of pesticides in schools, AG §5-208.1.
Registration and labeling, AG §5-101.

Pesticide business license.
Pesticide applicators, AG §5-201.

Pesticide chemical.
Poultry products inspection act, AG §4-201.
Wholesome meat act, AG §4-101.

Pests.
Pest control compact, AG §5-702.
Pesticide applicators, AG §5-201.

Pet.
Damages for injury, CJ §11-110.

Petition.
Debt collection, CL §15-101.
Elections, EL §6-101.
Expungement of records, Crim Rule 4-502.
Juvenile causes, CJ §3-8A-01.
Labor relations.
Consent elections, LE §4-206.
Settlement of decedents' estates, Estates Rule 6-105.

Petitioner.
Domestic violence, FL §4-501.
Patient care, HG §19-370.
Peace orders, CJ §3-1501.
Uniform child custody jurisdiction and enforcement act, FL §9.5-301.

Petition for disciplinary or remedial action.
Discipline of attorneys, CJA Rule 16-701.

DEFINED TERMS —Cont'd

Petition for review.
Property taxes, TP §14-501.

Petroleum transporter.
Motor fuel, BR §10-101.

Pharmaceutical care.
Pharmacists and pharmacies, HO §12-101.

Pharmaceutical product.
Health insurance, IN §15-805.

Pharmacist.
Health occupations, HO §12-101.

Pharmacist rehabilitation committee, HO §12-317.

Pharmacy, HO §12-101.

Pharmacy permit, HO §12-101.

Pharmacy review committee, HO §12-318.

Pharmacy student, HO §12-101.

Pharmacy technician trainee, HO §12-101.

Phased in value.
Property tax.
Assessment of real property, TP §8-103.

Photographs.
Evidence, CJ §10-103.

Photovoltaic property, TG §10-719.
Solar energy grant program, SG §9-2007.

Physical custody.
Uniform child custody jurisdiction and enforcement act, FL §9.5-101.

Physical injury.
Assault, CR §3-203.

Physically helpless individual.
Sexual crimes, CR §3-301.

Physical restraint.
Student behavior intervention, ED §7-1101.

Physical therapist.
Grant program, ED §18-704.
Health occupations, HO §13-101.

Physical therapist assistant, HO §13-101.
Grant program, ED §18-704.

Physical therapist rehabilitation committee, HO §13-319.

Physician, EN §1-101.
Abortion restrictions, HG §20-207.
Anatomical gift act, ET §4-501.
Charitable health care services.
Civil liability, CJ §5-606.
Donors, HG §18-334.
Health, HG §1-101.
Health care decisions, HG §5-601.
Health occupations, HO §§1-101, 14-101.
Medical mutual liability insurance society of Maryland, IN §24-201.
Mental hygiene admissions, HG §10-601.
Volunteer sports program physicians, CJ §5-607.

Physician assistant.
Health occupations, HO §15-101.
Student financial assistance, ED §18-802.

Physician performing a postmortem examination, HG §18-213.2.

Physician-pharmacist agreement.
Therapy management contracts, HO §12-6A-01.

Physician rehabilitation committee, HO §14-101.

Picking plant.
Food establishments, HG §21-301.

Pier.
Chesapeake Bay critical area and Atlantic coastal bays area protection programs.
Prince George's county, NR §8-1808.4.
Wetlands and riparian rights, EN §16-101.

Pilot, BOP §11-101.

DEFINED TERMS —Cont'd
Pilot community.
Child in need of services pilot program, CJ §3-8A-10.1.
Pilot-in-training, BOP §11-101.
Pilot program.
Autism spectrum disorder screening practices in schools, ED §8-601.
Child care centers, FL §5-589.
Educational technology pilot program, ED §7-10A-01.
Employment of qualified ex-felons, LE §11-701.
Health and human services referral system, HG §24-1201.
Pinball machine license.
Business licenses, BR §17-405.
Pine.
Reforestation, NR §5-501.
Pipeline facility.
Hazardous liquid pipelines, PUC §11-201.
Pipeline operator.
Hazardous liquid pipelines, PUC §11-201.
Pit.
Surface mining, EN §15-801.
PJM region.
Healthy air act, EN §2-1001.
Renewable energy portfolio standard, PUC §7-701.
Placement.
Interstate placement of children, FL §5-603.
Placement agency.
Education of children in state-supervised care, ED §8-501.
Place of business.
Alcoholic beverages, 2B §8-216.
Door-to-door sales, CL §14-301.
Pesticide applicators, AG §5-201.
Secured transactions, debtor's location, CL §9-307.
Place of confinement.
Contraband at place of confinement, CR §9-410.
Harboring and escape, contraband, CR §9-401.
Place of employment.
Occupational safety and health, LE §5-101.
Place of public accommodation.
Discrimination, 49B §5.
Place of public entertainment.
Sanitary fixtures, HG §24-211.
Plaintiff.
Default judgments, CivProCir Rule 2-613.
Plan.
Children, youth and family services.
Contracts for residential child care programs, 49D §7-101.
College savings plan of Maryland, ED §18-1901.
Governmental procedures.
Forms management, SG §10-604.
Insurance administrators, IN §8-301.
Land use, 66B §1.00.
Maryland health insurance plan, IN §14-501.
Patuxent river policy plan, SF §5-801.
Religious corporations, CA §5-301.
Schools, comprehensive master plans, ED §5-401.
Southern Maryland tri-county council, 20 §1-102.
State development plan, SF §5-601.
Western Maryland tri-county council, 20A §1-102.
Zoning and planning, 66B §1.00.
Planned unit development.
Chesapeake Bay critical area and Atlantic coastal bays critical area protection programs, NR §8-1813.1.
Forest conservation, NR §5-1601.

DEFINED TERMS —Cont'd
Planning and service area.
Aging, 70B §1.
Plan of operation.
Maryland health insurance plan, IN §14-501.
Plan of operation or feasibility study.
Risk retention groups, IN §25-101.
Plan of reorganization.
Fiduciaries, ET §15-101.
Plan review.
Fire marshal, fees, PS §6-308.
Plan sponsor.
Insurance administrators, IN §8-301.
Plant.
Nongame and endangered species conservation, NR §10-2A-01.
Public utility companies, PUC §1-101.
Plant regulator.
Pesticide registration and labeling, AG §5-101.
Plan type A.
Insurance companies.
Standard valuation law, IN §5-306.
Plan type B.
Insurance companies.
Standard valuation law, IN §5-306.
Plan type C.
Insurance companies.
Standard valuation law, IN §5-306.
Plastic bottle.
Recycling, EN §9-1710.
Plat.
Highways, TR §8-301.
Real property, RP §3-108.1.
Plate.
Consumer protection.
Fine print, CL §14-501.
Play vehicle.
Traffic laws, TR §21-101.
Plug.
Hulls of vessels, CL §11-1001.
Plumber's license, BR §17-1501.
Plumbing systems.
New home warranties, RP §10-601.
P.O.D. account.
Financial institutions, FI §1-204.
Podiatrist.
Health occupations, HO §16-101.
Podiatrist rehabilitation committee, HO §16-403.
P.O.D. payee.
Financial institutions, FI §1-204.
Point.
Interest in usury, CL §12-101.
Point-of-service option.
Health maintenance organizations, HG §19-710.2.
Pole trailer.
Motor vehicles, TR §11-146.
Police administrator.
Appointment of police officers, supervisors and administrators, PS §3-215.
Police department.
Abandoned vehicles, TR §25-201.
Vehicle impoundment, TR §27-111.
Police employee.
State police department, PS §2-101.
Police officer.
Adult protective services, FL §14-101.
Arrest process, CP §2-101.
Aviation, TR §5-101.
Boats and boating, NR §8-727.
Charging by citation, CP §4-101.

DEFINED TERMS —Cont'd
Police officer —Cont'd
Child abuse and neglect, FL §5-701.
Diesel vehicle emissions control program, TR §23-401.
Impersonating a police officer, PS §3-502.
Motor carrier safety inspections, TR §25-111.
Motor carrier tax, TG §9-222.
Motor fuel inspection.
Petroleum transporters, BR §10-412.
Motor vehicle equipment, TR §22-106.
Motor vehicles, TR §11-147.
Police training commission, PS §3-201.
Resisting or interfering with arrest, CR §9-408.
Used vehicle inspection, TR §23-101.
Weighing and measuring vehicles, TR §24-111.
Police record.
Expungement of criminal records, CP §10-101.
Expungement of records, Crim Rule 4-502.
Police supervisor.
Appointment of police officers, supervisors and administrators, PS §3-215.
Police training commission.
Reports on traffic stops, TR §25-113.
Policy.
Insurance, IN §1-101.
Medicare supplement insurance, IN §15-901.
Viatical settlement contracts, IN §8-601.
Policy form.
Medicare supplement insurance, IN §15-901.
Policyholder.
Injured workers' insurance fund, LE §10-101.
Political action committee, EL §1-101.
Political committee, EL §1-101.
Gaming, CR §12-101.
Political contribution.
Public ethics, SG §15-102.
Political party, EL §1-101.
Political subdivision, 24 §§2-101, 14-101.
Air quality, EN §2-101.
Bribery, CR §9-201.
Counties and municipal corporations, 24 §1-108.
Economic development corporation, 83A §5-201.
Economic development opportunities program, SF §7-314.
Energy conservation building standards, PUC §7-401.
Enterprise zones, 83A §5-401.
Extortion by government officer or employee, CR §3-702.
Financial institutions, FI §1-101.
Highways, TR §8-627.
Housing and community development, HS §1-101.
Housing authorities, HS §12-101.
Maryland emergency management agency (MEMA), PS §14-101.
Municipal bonds, EN §9-720.
Noise control, EN §3-101.
Off-road vehicle used on public property, CR §6-405.
Records, SG §10-601.
Returning veterans reemployment, 24 §10-101.
Standing to sue.
Environmental matters, NR §1-501.
Transportation, TR §1-101.
Water and sewer authorities, EN §9-901.
Pollutant.
Sanitary facilities, EN §9-101.
Pollution.
Sanitary facilities, EN §9-101.
Water and water resources, NR §8-101.

DEFINED TERMS —Cont'd
Pollution —Cont'd
Water management, EN §4-101.1.
Water resources, EN §5-101; NR §8-101.
Pomace brandy.
Limited winery license, 2B §2-205.
Pool.
Natural resources.
Gas and oil, EN §14-102.
Pooling agreement.
Water pollution control, AG §8-701.
Pool plant.
Northeast interstate dairy compact, AG §2-801.
Population.
Community colleges.
State and county aid, ED §16-305.
County public libraries, ED §23-501.
Population ratio quota.
Alcoholic beverages, 2B §9-222.
Port facility.
Transportation, TR §§3-101, 6-101.
Position.
State personnel, SPP §1-101.
Positive behavioral interventions and support program.
Schools, ED §7-304.1.
Positive identification.
National crime prevention and privacy compact, CP §10-239.
Possess.
Controlled dangerous substances, CR §5-101.
Possession.
Administration of courts.
Motor vehicle tort interrogatories, Form 6.
Possessory document.
Consignees, CL §11-801.
Possessory liens.
Secured transactions , priority of security interests, CL §9-333.
Postal authority.
Electronic postmarks, CL §21-118.1.
Potential for more than minimal harm deficiency.
Nursing homes, HG §19-1401.
Potential income.
Child support guidelines, FL §12-201.
Potomac river.
Potomac water authority, EN §5-401.
Poultry.
Agriculture, AG §1-101.
Avian influenza, regulation of poultry to control, AG §3-801.
Poultry dealer.
Avian influenza, regulation of poultry to control, AG §3-801.
Poultry litter.
Renewable energy portfolio standard, PUC §7-701.
Poultry or livestock manure spreading equipment.
Income tax, TG §10-208.
Poultry product.
Poultry products inspection act, AG §4-201.
Poultry products broker.
Poultry products inspection act, AG §4-201.
Pouring license.
Alcoholic beverages, 2B §8-222.
Poverty income standard.
Income tax, TG §10-709.
Power boiler.
Boilers and pressure vessels, PS §12-901.

DEFINED TERMS —Cont'd
Power booster system.
Motor vehicle engines, TR §22-404.5.
Power equipment.
Occupational safety and health.
Training of operators, LE §5-501.
Power of attorney.
Financial institutions, FI §1-204.
POW/MIA flag, SG §13-205.
Pozzolan.
Mines and mining, EN §15-407.
Practice acupuncture, HO §1A-101.
Practice alcohol and drug counseling, HO §17-101.
Practice architecture, BOP §3-101.
Practice as an environmental sanitarian, EN §11-101.
Practice as a physician assistant, HO §15-101.
Practice associate social work, HO §19-101.
Practice audiology, HO §2-101.
Practice barbering, BOP §4-101.
Practice certified public accountancy.
Out-of-state licensed accountants, BOP §2-321.
Practice certified social work, HO §19-101.
Practice chiropractic, HO §3-101.
Practice clinical social work, HO §19-101.
Practice cosmetology, BOP §5-101.
Practice dental hygiene, HO §4-101.
Practice dental radiation technology, HO §4-505.
Practice dentistry, HO §4-101.
Practice dietetics, HO §5-101.
Practice electrology, HO §8-6B-01.
Practice engineering, BOP §14-101.
Practice graduate alcohol and drug counseling, HO §17-3A-01.
Practice graduate marriage and family therapy, HO §17-3A-01.
Practice graduate professional counseling, HO §17-3A-01.
Practice graduate social work, HO §19-101.
Practice landscape architecture, BOP §9-101.
Practice land surveying, BOP §15-101.
Nurses, HO §8-101.
Practice law.
Legal mutual liability insurance society of Maryland, IN §24-101.
Practice limited physical therapy, HO §13-101.
Practice marriage and family therapy, HO §17-101.
Practice massage therapy, HO §3-5A-01.
Practice medical radiation technology, HO §14-5B-01.
Practice medicine, HO §14-101.
Medical mutual liability insurance society of Maryland, IN §24-201.
Practice mortuary science, HO §7-101.
Practice non-therapeutic massage, HO §3-5A-01.
Practice nuclear medicine technology, HO §14-5B-01.
Practice nurse midwifery, HO §8-601.
Practice of clinical alcohol and drug abuse counseling, HO §17-3A-01.
Practice of clinical marriage and family therapy, HO §17-3A-01.
Practice of clinical professional counseling, HO §17-3A-01.
Practice of veterinary medicine.
Board of veterinary medical examiners, AG §2-301.

DEFINED TERMS —Cont'd
Practice optometry, HO §11-101.
Practice osteopathy.
Physicians, HO §14-321.
Practice patent law, BOP §10-206.
Practice pharmacy, HO §12-101.
Practice physical therapy.
Chiropractors, HO §3-101.
Physical therapists, HO §13-101.
Practice podiatry, HO §16-101.
Practice polysomnography, HO §13-5C-01.
Practice professional counseling, HO §17-101.
Practice profile.
Health maintenance organizations, HG §19-710.
Practice property line surveying, BOP §15-101.
Practice psychology, HO §18-101.
Practice radiation oncology/therapy technology, HO §14-5B-01.
Practice registered nursing, HO §8-101.
Practice respiratory care, HO §14-5A-01.
Practice social work, HO §19-101.
Practice speech-language pathology, HO §2-101.
Practice well drilling, EN §13-101.
Practitioner.
Cremation, HG §5-508.
Precinct.
Elections, EL §1-101.
Precinct register.
Elections, EL §1-101.
Precious metal object.
Precious metal dealers, BR §12-101.
Precomputed interest charge.
Closed end credit, CL §12-1009.
Prepayment of outstanding unpaid indebtedness, CL §12-126.
Predecessor employer.
Unemployment insurance.
Contributions, LE §8-601.
Predetermined parole release agreement, COR §7-101.
Preexisting authority.
Housing authorities, HS §12-101.
Preexisting condition.
Health insurance portability, IN §§15-1301, 15-1401.
Long-term care insurance, IN §18-101.
Small employer health insurance, IN §15-1201.
Preexisting condition provision.
Small employer health insurance, IN §15-1201.
Preference.
Procurement, SF §§14-401, 14-406.
Preferential basis.
Preferred provider organizations, IN §14-201.
Preferred claim.
Continuing care contracts, 70B §20R.
Liquidation, rehabilitation, etc., of insurers, IN §9-227.
Preferred dividends requirements.
Insurance companies.
Investments, IN §5-608.
Preferred interest rate.
Maryland home financing program, HS §4-801.
Preferred provider, IN §14-201.
Preferred provider insurance policy, IN §14-201.
Preferred ship mortgage.
Liens on boats, CL §16-205.
Prefile.
Legislation, SG §2-1502.
Pre-law surface mine, EN §15-801.

DEFINED TERMS —Cont'd
Preliminary evaluation.
Executive branch of government.
Legislative review, SG §8-401.
Preliminary screening procedure.
Medical laboratories, HG §17-214.
Premises.
Alcoholic beverages, 2B §§6-201, 12-201, 12-213.
Animals in care of veterinarians or boarding
kennels.
Supervision, CL §11-905.
Beer and light wine licenses, 2B §5-101.
County resort taxes, 25B §13H.
Taxation, TG §11-206.
Premium finance agreement, IN §23-101.
Premium finance company, IN §23-101.
Premium increase.
Motor vehicle insurance, IN §27-613.
Motor vehicle insurance, private passenger
liability coverage, IN §27-614.
Premiums.
Closed end credit, insurance, CL §12-1007.
Consumer loans, insurance, CL §12-312.
Fraternal benefit societies, IN §8-401.
Health care regulatory fund, IN §2-112.2.
Insurance, IN §1-101.
Insurance regulation assessment, IN §2-501.
Life and health insurance guaranty corporation,
IN §9-401.
People's insurance counsel, SG §6-301.
Secondary mortgage loans, CL §12-410.
Premiums written.
Joint insurance association, IN §25-401.
Premium tax exemption value.
Insurance premium tax, IN §6-121.
Prenatal care.
Pregnant women.
HIV testing, HG §18-338.2.
Preneed burial contract, BR §5-701.
Preneed contract.
Cremation, HG §5-508.
Morticians, HO §7-101.
Preneed goods.
Cemeteries, BR §5-101.
Preneed services.
Burial contracts, BR §5-701.
Prepaid contract.
College savings plan of Maryland, ED §18-1901.
Preparation costs.
Maryland historical trust, historic funds and
capital projects, SF §5A-322.
Prepared.
Wholesome meat act, AG §4-101.
Prescription.
Counterfeiting, CR §8-610.
Prescription drug, CR §5-101.
Food and drugs, HG §21-201.
Food, drugs and cosmetics, HG §21-1113.
Pharmacists and pharmacies, HO §12-602.
Prescription drug plan.
Medicare option prescription drug program, HG
§15-124.3.
Prescriptive authority.
Physician assistants, HO §15-101.
Presentation.
Letters of credit, CL §5-102.
Presenter.
Letters of credit, CL §5-102.
Presenting bank.
Bank deposits and collections, CL §§4-104, 4-105.

DEFINED TERMS —Cont'd
Presentment.
Negotiable instruments, CL §§3-103, 3-501.
Present sale.
Sale of goods, CL §2-106.
Sales, UCC, CL §2-106.
Present value.
Uniform commercial code, CL §1-201.
Preservation.
Maryland historical trust, SF §5A-301.
Preservation district.
Canal place preservation and development
authority, FI §13-1001.
President.
General assembly, SG §2-101.
State personnel, SPP §3-101.
Presiding officer.
Administrative procedures.
Contested cases, SG §10-202.
Legislative pension plan, SG Title 2 Subtitle 3
(note).
Press building.
Fireworks, PS §10-101.
Pressure vessel.
Boilers and pressure vessels, PS §12-901.
Presumed.
Commercial code, CL §1-201.
Presumption.
Commercial code, CL §1-201.
Prevailing party.
County discrimination laws, 49B §41.
Housing discrimination, 49B §20.
Prevailing wage rate.
Public works contracts, SF §17-201.
Prevention.
Cancer prevention, education, screening and
treatment program, HG §13-1101.
Previous system.
State retirement and pension system, SPP
§37-101.
Price amendment.
Securities, CA §11-503.
Primary care.
Student financial assistance.
Physician assistants and nurse practitioners,
ED §18-802.
Primary cause.
Workers' compensation, LE §9-507.
Primary claimant.
Limitation on noneconomic damages in personal
injury actions, CJ §11-108.
Primary development.
Homeowners association, RP §11B-101.
Primary drinking water regulation.
Drinking water, EN §9-401.
Primary highway.
Highways, TR §8-101.
Junkyards, TR §8-801.
Primary housing expenses.
Foreclosure purchaser obligations, RP §7-311.
Primary law-enforcement officer.
Refusal to register motor vehicles, TR §13-406.1.
Service of arrest warrants, CP §2-103.
Suspension, revocation or refusal of drivers'
license, TR §16-204.
Primary law enforcement unit.
Pawnbrokers, BR §12-101.
Primary mental health services.
Medical assistance, HG §15-101.
Primary procurement units, SF §11-101.

DEFINED TERMS —Cont'd

Primary provider of mental health services.
Medical records, HG §4-301.

Primary source verification.
Physicians, HO §14-501.

Primary standards.
Weights and measures, AG §11-101.

Prime suppliers.
State standby petroleum fuel set-aside program,
PS §14-501.

Prince George authority.
Prince George's county housing authority, HS
§17-101.

Principal.
Homebuilder registration, BR §4.5-101.
Principal and income act, ET §15-501.
Small business surety bond program, 83A
§5-1032.
Uniform fiduciaries act, ET §15-201.
Wholesale sales representatives.
Payment of commission, LE §3-601.

Principal balance.
Retail installment sales, CL §12-601.

Principal business.
Collection agencies, BR §7-102.

Principal minority party.
Elections, EL §1-101.

Principal office.
Corporations, CA §1-101.

Principal office of a domestic corporation.
Property tax, TP §1-101.

**Principal office of a foreign corporation in the
state.**
Property tax, TP §1-101.

Principal owner.
Strip mining, EN §15-501.

Principal place of business.
Bank holding companies, FI §5-901.
Savings and loan associations.
Interstate acquisitions, FI §9-1001.

Principal political parties, EL §1-101.

Principal political party.
Public ethics, SG §15-102.

Principal residence.
Historic St. Mary's City commission, ED §24-513.

Principal unit.
State personnel, SPP §1-101.
Incentive awards, SPP §10-201.

Print.
Consumer protection.
Fine print, CL §14-501.

Printed statement.
Adult dependent care programs, HG §19-1901.

Print instructional materials.
Individualized education programs to insure
ability to communicate effectively, ED §8-408.

Priority funding area.
Community legacy program, HS §6-201.
Neighborhood and community assistance program,
HS §6-401.
Rural legacy program, NR §5-9A-02.

Prisoner.
Prisoner litigation, CJ §5-1001.

Private activity bond.
General assembly, SG §2-1010.

Private agency.
Adult dependent care programs, HG §19-1901.
Eminent domain, RP §12-201.
Nursing referral service agencies, HG §19-4B-01.

Private applicator, AG §5-201.

DEFINED TERMS —Cont'd

Private area of an individual.
Visual surveillance of individual in private place
with prurient intent, CR §3-902.

Private career school.
Higher education, ED §10-101.

Private carriers.
Maryland transit administration, TR §7-101.
Transportation compacts, TR §10-204.

Private corporation.
Foreign trade zones, 23 §466.

Private detective, BOP §13-101.

Private detective agency, BOP §13-101.

Private foundation.
Corporations, CA §5-401.

Private group home.
Developmental disabilities, HG §7-602.
Mental hygiene, HG §10-514.

Private home detention monitor, BOP §20-101.

Private home detention monitoring agency,
BOP §20-101.

Private library agency.
Interstate library compact, ED §25-303.

Privately owned residential community.
Municipal corporations, 23A §49.

Private passenger automobile.
Energy absorption system, TR §22-416.

Private passenger premium.
Motor vehicle insurance, IN §11-321.

Private place.
Visual surveillance of individual in private place,
CR §3-901.
With prurient intent, CR §3-902.

Private residential rehabilitative institution.
Educational programs in private residential
institutions, 83C §2-137.

Private review agent, IN §15-10B-01.

Private road or driveway.
Traffic laws, TR §21-101.

Private sector enterprise.
Economic development opportunities program, SF
§7-314.

Private sector entity.
Construction apprenticeship assistance program,
LE §11-601.

Private therapeutic group home.
Mental health programs, HG §10-920.

Private transit companies.
Transportation compacts, TR §10-204.

Private wetlands.
Wetlands and riparian rights, EN §16-101.

Probable cause.
Juvenile services.
Interstate compact on juveniles, 83C §3-103.

Probationary employee.
Washington suburban sanitary district, 29
§11.5-101.

Probation before judgment.
Expungement of records, Crim Rule 4-502.

Proceedings.
Alimony, FL §11-110.
Corporations, CA §2-418.
Courts, CJ §6-402.
Public utility companies, PUC §1-101.

Proceeds.
Community services trust fund, HG §24-1101.
Drug asset forfeiture, CP §12-101.
Financial transactions involving proceeds of drug
crime, CR §5-623.
Holocaust victim insurance, IN §28-101.

DEFINED TERMS —Cont'd
Proceeds —Cont'd
  Public debt.
    Capital leases, SF §8-407.
  Secured transactions, CL §9-102.
  State debt, SF §§8-131.1, 8-211.
  Transportation, TR §3-103.
Proceeds of a letter of credit, CL §5-114.
Process.
  Poultry products inspection act, AG §4-201.
Processing fee.
  Continuing care contracts, 70B §7.
Process of posting.
  Bank deposits and collections, CL §4-109.
Procurement, SF §11-101.
Procurement contract, SF §11-101.
  Public ethics, SG §15-102.
Procurement officer, SF §11-101.
Produce.
  Controlled dangerous substances, CR §5-101.
Producer.
  Fluid dairy products, AG §11-401.
  Motor fuel, BR §10-101.
  Natural resources.
    Gas and oil, EN §14-102.
Producer register.
  Insurance producers, IN §10-118.
Product.
  Flammable products, HG §22-401.
  Interstate insurance product regulation compact,
    IN §29-101.
  Natural resources.
    Gas and oil, EN §14-102.
  Product liability, CJ §5-405.
    Limitation of actions, CJ §5-115.
Production activity.
  Sales tax, TG §11-101.
Production facility.
  Avian influenza, regulation of poultry to control,
    AG §3-801.
Production machinery or equipment.
  Sales tax, TG §11-101.
Production-money crops.
  Secured transactions, CL §9-102.
Production-money obligation.
  Secured transactions, CL §9-102.
Production of crops.
  Secured transactions, CL §9-102.
Product liability.
  Risk retention groups, IN §25-101.
Product made by the blind, CL §14-2801.
Professional association.
  Group life insurance, IN §17-204.
Professional corporation.
  Professional service corporations, CA §5-101.
Professional counselor.
  Psychiatric-mental health nursing specialist, CJ
    §9-109.1.
**Professional counselor rehabilitation
  committee,** HO §17-317.
Professional employee.
  Day of rest, LE §3-704.
  Education, ED §2-205.
  Labor relations.
    Community colleges, ED §16-412.
Professional engineer, BOP §14-101.
Professional land surveyor, BOP §15-101.
Professional misconduct.
  Discipline of attorneys, CJA Rule 16-701.
Professional service.
  Professional service corporations, CA §5-101.

DEFINED TERMS —Cont'd
Professional service —Cont'd
  State personnel, SPP §1-101.
Professional solicitor.
  Charitable organizations, BR §6-101.
Professional-sports-services contract.
  Athlete agents, BR §4-401.
Professional sports team.
  Maryland stadium authority, FI §13-724.
Program.
  Agricultural land link program, AG §2-1201.
  AIDS insurance, HG §15-201.
  Alternative teaching opportunity program, ED
    §6-120.
  Anne Arundel county correctional facility, COR
    §11-703.
  Appropriation act, SF §7-201.
  Biological agent registry program, HG §17-601.
  Breast cancer program, HG §20-116.
  Cecil county volunteer fire departments, length of
    service awards, PS §7-209.
  Charitable giving information program, BR
    §6-201.
  College readiness outreach program, ED
    §18-303.1.
  College savings plan of Maryland, ED §18-1901.
  Community attendant services and supports
    program, 41 §6-7A-01.
  Community energy loan program, SG §9-2101.
  Community legacy program, HS §6-201.
  Developmental disabilities, HG §§7-701, 7-706,
    7-709.
  Developmental disabilities, mental health, child
    welfare and juvenile services workforce
    tuition assistance program, ED §18-2101.
  Distribution of accessible information for disabled
    persons, SF §3-901.
  Domestic violence.
    Address confidentiality program, FL §4-519.
  Down payment and settlement expense loan
    program, HS §4-301.
  Elderly rental housing program, HS §4-401.
  Employment in recovery pilot program, HG
    §8-6B-01.
  Energy efficiency and economic development loan
    program, SG §9-20A-01.
  Food programs, HG §18-108.
  Governmental procedures.
    Records management, SG §10-631.
  Group home financing program, HS §4-601.
  Health program integrity and recovery activities,
    HG §2-501.
  Hearing impaired individuals, HG §10-908.
  Hearing impaired infants, HG §13-601.
  Higher education, ED §10-101.
  Historical and cultural museum assistance
    program, SF §5A-349.
  Home detention program, COR §3-401.
  Insect sting emergency treatment program, HG
    §13-702.
  Insurance consumer education and advocacy
    program, IN §2-301.
  Juvenile residential facilities, ED §22-301.
  Kidney disease, HG §13-302.
  Long-term care, HG §15-401.
  Maryland home financing program, HS §4-801.
  Maryland housing rehabilitation program, HS
    §4-901.
  Maryland public art initiative, 83A §4-6A-02.
  Medical assistance, HG §15-101.

DEFINED TERMS —Cont'd

Program —Cont'd

Medicare option prescription drug program, HG
§15-124.3.

National board certified teacher pilot program, ED
§6-118.

Neighborhood business development program, HS
§6-301.

Neighborhood housing services fund, HS §4-1001.

Nurses, HO §8-208.

Partnership rental housing program, HS §4-1201.

Port administration drug-free workplace, TR
§6-102.1.

Power plant research program, NR §3-301.

Prescription drug repository program, HG
§15-601.

Principal fellowship and leadership development
program, ED §6-116.

Radium pilot grant program, HS §4-1301.

Rental allowance program, HS §4-1401.

Rental housing production program, HS §4-1501.

Residential boarding education programs for
at-risk youth, ED §8-701.

Residential mortgage programs for certain
counties, HS §4-1601.

Rural legacy program, NR §5-9A-02.

Self-help homeownership technical assistance
program, HS §4-1701.

Senior prescription drug assistance program, IN
§14-510.

Septic systems, EN §9-1401.

State insurance program, SF §9-101.

State personnel.

Health and welfare benefits, SPP §2-501.

State retirement and pension system, SPP
§30-101.

Sterile needle and syringe exchange, Baltimore
City, HG §24-801.

Sterile needle and syringe exchange, Prince
George's county, HG §24-901.

Student loan repayment pilot program, SPP
§10-501.

Veterans outreach and advocacy program, SG
§9-940.

Voluntary cleanup program, EN §7-501.

Program amendment.

Chesapeake Bay critical area and Atlantic coastal
bays critical area protection programs, NR
§8-1802.

Program applicant.

Maryland senior ride demonstration program, TR
§7-1001.

Program fee.

Drinking driver monitor program supervision fees,
COR §6-115.

Program loan.

Down payment and settlement expense loan
program, HS §4-301.

Group home financing program, HS §4-601.

Maryland housing rehabilitation program, HS
§4-901.

Rental housing production program, HS §4-1501.

Program of compensatory education.

Disadvantaged children, ED §8-101.

Program participant.

Distribution of accessible information for disabled
persons, SF §3-901.

Domestic violence.

Address confidentiality program, FL §4-519.

Maryland senior ride demonstration program, TR
§7-1001.

DEFINED TERMS —Cont'd

Program provider.

Educational technology pilot program, ED
§7-10A-01.

Program recipient.

Medical assistance, HG §15-101.

Program refinement.

Chesapeake Bay critical area and Atlantic coastal
bays critical area protection programs, NR
§8-1802.

Prohibited exposure.

Victims of crime, CP §11-107.

Prohibited noxious weed.

Turf grass, AG §9-101.

Prohibited noxious weed seed.

Seeds, AG §9-201.

Prohibited referral.

Health insurance, IN §15-110.

Project.

Agricultural and resource-based industry
development corporation, 41 §13-501.

Bainbridge development corporation, 83A §5-1601.

Baltimore City schools, ED §4-301.

Community energy loan program, SG §9-2101.

Economic development corporation, 83A §5-201.

Energy efficiency and economic development loan
program, SG §9-20A-01.

Environmental service, NR §3-101.

Health and educational facilities, 43C §3.

Higher education.

Auxiliary and academic facilities bond
authority, ED §19-101.

Highways, TR §8-101.

Issuance of notes by community colleges, ED
§16-302.1.

Local military installation redevelopment
authorities, 83A §5-1701.

Maryland food center, 41 §13-104.

Natural resources, NR §1-404.

Neighborhood business development program, HS
§6-301.

Northeast Maryland waste disposal authority, NR
§3-904.

Penmar development corporations, 83A §5-1201.

Ports, TR §6-101.

Potomac water authority, EN §5-401.

Rental housing production program, HS §4-1501.

Sanitary commissions, EN §9-601.

Self-help homeownership technical assistance
program, HS §4-1701.

Senior citizen activities centers capital
improvement grants, 70B §26.

Strip mining, EN §15-501.

Susquehanna river basin compact, EN §5-301.

Time-sharing, RP §11A-101.

Water and sewer authorities, EN §9-901.

Water pollution control, AG §8-701.

Woodrow Wilson bridge and tunnel compact, TR
§10-303.

Project approval.

Chesapeake Bay critical area and Atlantic coastal
bays critical area protection programs, NR
§8-1802.

Project-based section 8 rental assistance.

Assisted housing preservation, HS §7-101.

Project development phase.

Transportation, TR §2-103.1.

Projectile.

Handgun identification requirements, PS §5-131.

Project instrument.

Time-sharing, RP §11A-101.

DEFINED TERMS —Cont'd
Project planning phase.
Long range highway programs, TR §8-610.
Promise.
Labor relations.
Promises restricting union membership, LE §4-304.
Negotiable instruments, CL §3-103.
Promissory note.
Secured transactions, CL §9-102.
Promote.
Pyramid promotional schemes, CR §8-404.
Promoter.
Business licenses, BR §17-1801.
Outdoor musical festivals, BR §17-1401.
Promoter license.
Outdoor musical festivals, BR §17-1401.
Proof of fare payment.
Maryland transit administration, TR §7-101.
Property.
Administration of courts.
Domestic relations interrogatories, Form 4.
Bad checks, CR §8-101.
Condominiums, RP §11-101.
Drug asset forfeiture, CP §12-101.
Education, ED §1-101.
Estates and trusts, ET §§1-101, 13-101.
Exploitation of vulnerable adult, CR §8-801.
False advertising and related crimes, CL §14-2901.
Governmental procedures.
Reorganizations, SG §10-702.
Industrial development financing, 83A §5-901.
Land installment contracts, RP §10-101.
Liens on aircraft, boats, mobile homes and motor vehicles, CL §16-201.
Nuisance actions, RP §14-120.
Oil pipeline corporation, power to condemn, PUC §5-404.
Partnerships, revised act, CA §9A-101.
Property tax, TP §1-101.
Real property, RP §1-101.
Robbery, CR §3-401.
Taxation, TG §1-101.
Theft, CR §7-101.
Transfer-on-death security registration, ET §16-101.
Transportation, TR §1-101.
Washington suburban sanitary district, 29 §1-202.
Property and casualty insurer.
Insurance regulation assessment, IN §2-501.
Risk based capital standards for insurers, IN §4-301.
Property and casualty insurer assessment portion.
Insurance regulation assessment, IN §2-501.
Property bondsmen, CP §5-209.
Property construction cost.
Shore erosion control, NR §8-1001.
Property insurance, IN §1-101.
Property insurance coverage.
Closed end credit, CL §12-1007.
Consumer loans, CL §12-312.
Real estate loans, CL §12-124.
Revolving credit, CL §12-909.
Secondary mortgage loans, CL §12-410.
Property line.
Setback line restrictions.
Limitation of actions, CJ §5-114.
Property line surveyor, BOP §15-101.

DEFINED TERMS —Cont'd
Property of another.
Theft, CR §7-101.
Property owner's cash contribution.
Shore erosion control, NR §8-1001.
Property payable.
Bank deposits and collections, CL §4-104.
Property tax attributable to an increase in an assessment.
Brownfields taxation, TP §9-229.
Property tax credit.
Duties of governing body, TP §9-201.
Property taxes, TP §1-101.
Payment, TP §10-101.
Property that passes from a decedent.
Inheritance tax, TG §7-201.
Proposal.
Procurement, SF §11-101.
Secured transactions, CL §9-102.
Substance abuse treatment outcomes partnership fund, HG §8-6C-01.
Proposed budget.
State operating budget, SF §7-101.
Proposed county plan.
Sewerage systems, EN §9-501.
Proposed state action.
Environmental policy, NR §1-301.
Proprietary lease.
Cooperative housing corporation, CA §5-6B-01.
Proprietor.
Copyright royalties, CL §11-1401.
Propulsion tank.
Motor fuel, BR §10-101.
Prosecuting attorney.
Victims of crime, CP §11-101.
Prosecutor.
Witness immunity.
Courts, CJ §9-123.
Prospect.
Strip mining, EN §15-501.
Prospective adoptee.
Independent adoptions, FL §5-3B-01.
Prospective juror, CJ §8-101.
Prosthetic device.
Health insurance, IN §15-820.
Prostitution, CR §11-301.
Protected action.
Assisted housing preservation, HS §7-101.
Protected birds.
Wildlife, NR §10-101.
Protected building.
Carroll county micro-brewery licenses, 2B §9-207.
Protected computer.
Spam, CR §3-805.1.
Protected individual.
Unlawful publication by video tape distributor, CR §3-907.
Protected land.
Natural resources, NR §1-404.
Protected purchaser.
Investment securities, CL §§8-102, 8-303.
Protection and advocacy services.
Developmental disabilities.
Courts, CJ §3-1001.
Protective body armor.
Protective body armor fund, PS §4-101.
Protective proceeding.
Estates and trusts, ET §13-101.
Protest.
Negotiable instruments, CL §3-505.
Procurement, SF §15-215.

DEFINED TERMS —Cont'd

Protocol.

Physician assistants, HO §15-101.

Therapy management contracts, HO §12-6A-01.

Prove.

Funds transfers, CL §4A-105.

Negotiable instruments, CL §3-103.

Provide bail bondsman services, IN §10-301.

Provide burial goods, BR §5-101.

Provide check cashing services, FI §12-101.

Provide electrical services.

Electricians, BOP §6-101.

Provide esthetic services.

Cosmetologists, BOP §5-101.

Provide hearing aid services.

Hearing aid dispensers and audiologists, HO §2-101.

Provide heating, ventilation, air conditioning or refrigeration services, BR §9A-101.

Provide home inspection services, BOP §16-101.

Provide lead paint abatement services, EN §6-1001.

Provide makeup artist services.

Cosmetologists, BOP §5-101.

Provide manicuring services.

Cosmetologists, BOP §5-101.

Provide natural gas services, BOP §12-101.

Provide passenger-for-hire services.

For-hire driving services, PUC §10-101.

Provide pilotage, BOP §11-101.

Provide plumbing services, BOP §12-101.

Provide private detective services, BOP §13-101.

Provide propane services.

Plumbers, BOP §12-101.

Provider.

Administrative service provider contracts, HG §19-713.2.

Child abuse or neglect care, FL §5-712.

Children, youth and family services.

Contracts for residential child care programs, 49D §7-101.

Coinsurance payments for health care services, IN §15-118.

Community services reimbursement rate commission, HG §13-801.

Concealment of medical records, HG §4-401.

Continuing care contracts, 70B §7.

Health insurance, IN §15-121.

Behavioral health care services, IN §15-127.

Health insurance provider panels, IN §15-112.

Health program integrity and recovery activities, HG §2-501.

HMO's, HG §19-701.

Medicaid, HG §15-105.

Preferred provider organizations, IN §14-201.

Provider-sponsored organizations, HG §19-7A-01.

Service contracts and consumer products guaranty, CL §14-401.

Provide real estate appraisal services, BOP §16-101.

Provide real estate brokerage services, BOP §17-101.

Provider of dental care.

Dentistry, HO §4-501.

Provider panel.

Dental plans, IN §15-114.

Health insurance, IN §15-112.

Credentialing of providers, IN §15-112.1.

Referrals to specialists, IN §15-830.

Health maintenance organizations, HG §19-710.2.

DEFINED TERMS —Cont'd

Provider review panel.

Emergency medical services, ED §13-516.

Provider service contract.

Preferred provider organizations, IN §14-201.

Provider-sponsored organization, HG §19-7A-01.

Provide stationary engineer services, BOP §6.5-101.

Provide taxicab services, PUC §10-101.

Providing security systems services.

Security systems technicians, BOP §18-101.

Provisional ballot, EL §1-101.

Provision for claim payments.

Workers' compensation insurance, IN §11-330.

Proximate cause.

Occupational disease.

Limitation of actions, CJ §5-113.

Psychiatric-mental health nursing specialist.

Privileged communications.

Courts, CJ §9-109.1.

Psychological methods, HO §18-101.

Psychological principles, HO §18-101.

Psychological procedures, HO §18-101.

Psychologist.

Health occupations, HO §18-101.

Mental hygiene admissions, HG §10-601.

Psychologist rehabilitation committee, HO §18-318.

Psychotherapy.

Social workers, HO §19-101.

Public adjuster.

Insurance, IN §10-401.

Public agency.

Children, youth and families services, 49D §1-101.

Conversion on overhead electric or communication facilities to underground locations, PUC §12-301.

Disabled student placement, ED §8-413.

Eminent domain, RP §12-201.

Handicapped children.

Education, ED §8-412.

St. Mary's county, 24 §4-202.

Sanitary commissions, EN §9-1103.

Public agency applicator.

Pesticide applicators, AG §5-201.

Public and commercial building.

Asbestos removal, EN §6-401.

Public area.

Tobacco smoking, HG §24-501.

Public assets.

Nonprofit health entities.

Acquisition, SG §6.5-101.

Publication expense.

Legislative newsletter, EL §13-406.

Public bicycle area.

Rules of the road, TR §21-101.

Public body.

Gas and oil.

Underground storage, EN §14-201.

Governmental procedures.

Meetings, SG §10-502.

Industrial development financing, 83A §5-901.

Occupational safety and health, LE §5-101.

Procurement, SF §16-101.

Public works contracts, SF §17-201.

State finance, SF §2-106.

Steel procurement, SF §17-301.

Public body obligation.

Closed or delicensed hospitals, 43C §16A.

DEFINED TERMS —Cont'd
Public buildings.
Facilities for handicapped, SF §2-501.
Illumination in public buildings, guidelines, PS §12-204.
Public business.
St. Mary's county open meetings, 24 §4-202.
Public charter school, ED §9-102.
Public communication.
Written policies, SG §10-801.
Public contribution.
Public campaign financing, EL §15-102.
Public conveyance.
Disturbing the peace, disorderly conduct, CR §10-201.
Public corporation.
Foreign trade zones, 23 §466.
Public debt.
Public schools financing, 31 §33.
Public drinking water system.
Water quality laboratories, EN §9-1001.
Public emergency.
Emergency management, governor's powers, PS §14-301.
Public employee.
Bribery, CR §9-201.
Labor relations.
Community colleges, ED §16-412.
Prince George's county public employment relations, ED §16-414.1.
Public employees association.
Group life insurance, IN §17-205.
Public employer.
Group life insurance, IN §17-205.
Labor relations.
Community colleges, ED §16-412.
Prince George's county public employment relations, ED §16-414.1.
Public employment office.
Unemployment insurance, LE §8-303.
Public entity.
Insurance pools, IN §19-602.
Life insurance, IN §16-116.
Public exigency.
Transportation, TR §2-109.
Public facilities.
Washington county, 66B §14.08.
Public-finance transaction.
Secured transactions, CL §9-102.
Public funds.
Local government investment guidelines, 95 §22F.
Public group home.
Developmental disabilities, HG §7-602.
Public health facility.
Physician assistants, HO §15-101.
Public health veterinarian.
Rabies, HG §18-312.
Public hearing, EN §1-101.
Executive branch of government, SG §8-306.
Natural resources department, NR §1-106.
Public housing.
Delinquent payments to public housing authorities, 88A §17C.
Public housing authority.
Delinquent payments, 88A §17C.
Public improvements.
State finance, SF §4-401.
Public institution of higher education.
Universities and colleges, establishment of new programs, ED §11-206.1.

DEFINED TERMS —Cont'd
Public library agency.
Interstate library compact, ED §25-303.
Public local laws.
Code counties home rule, 25B §1.
Publicly owned treatment works.
Sanitary facilities, EN §9-101.
Publicly owned utility.
Highways, TR §8-506.
Publicly post or display.
Social security number privacy, CL §14-3401.
Public notice.
Wetlands and riparian rights, EN §16-101.
Public officer.
Anatomy board, HG §5-401.
Forest fire prevention, NR §5-720.
Public official.
Designation of individuals, SG §15-103.
Professional architects immunity, CJ §5-426.
Professional engineers immunity, CJ §5-425.
Public ethics, SG §§15-102, 15-103.
Public or private property.
Alcoholic beverages, 2B §19-204.
Litter control law, CR §10-110.
Public place.
Alcoholic beverages, 2B §19-104.
Disturbing the peace, disorderly conduct, CR §10-201.
Juvenile curfew, 25B §13C-1.
Possession of firearm at public demonstration, CR §4-208.
Public port.
Industrial development financing, 83A §5-901.
Public provider.
Community service providers.
Liability, CJ §5-805.
Public purpose program.
Electric customer choice and competition act, PUC §7-501.
Public purpose project.
Community development administration, HS §4-201.
Maryland housing fund, HS §3-201.
Public record.
Access, SG §10-611.
Service of subpoena for public records, CJ §6-410.
Public restroom, HG §24-211.
Public roads.
Inmate work force, COR §9-501.
Public safety agency.
911 emergency telephone system, PS §1-301.
Public safety answering point.
911 emergency telephone system, PS §1-301.
Public safety contribution.
Charitable contributions, BR §6-101.
Public safety employee.
Workers' compensation.
Compensation for less than 75 weeks, LE §9-628.
Public safety official.
Professional architects immunity, CJ §5-426.
Professional engineers immunity, CJ §5-425.
Public safety organization.
Charitable contributions, BR §6-101.
Public safety personnel.
Emergency medical services, ED §13-516.
Public safety solicitor.
Charitable contributions, BR §6-101.
Public safety worker.
HIV testing for health care workers and first responders, HG §18-338.3.

DEFINED TERMS —Cont'd

Public school.
Education, ED §1-101.
McAuliffe teacher education award, ED §18-703.
Public school bus.
Transportation of students, ED §7-801.
Public school employee, ED §6-401.
Labor unions, ED §§6-401, 6-501.
Public school employer, ED §6-401.
Labor unions, ED §§6-401, 6-501.
Public school facility.
Baltimore City schools, ED §4-301.
Charles county, 66B §14.05.
Public security.
State finance, SF §2-301.
Public senior higher education institution, ED §10-101.
Property tax exemptions, TP §7-211.
Public service commission inspector.
Motor carrier safety, TR §25-111.
Vehicle preventive maintenance, TR §23-301.
Public service company, PUC §1-101.
Reporting requirements, PUC §6-201.
Special use tax on certain electricity, TG §11-1A-01.
Taxation, TG §8-401.
Public service company franchise tax, TG §1-101.
Public unit.
Asbestos removal, EN §6-401.
Public use.
Certified interior designers, BOP §8-101.
Land patents, RP §13-101.
Public use airport.
Aviation, TR §5-301.
Development easements, TR §5-4A-01.
Public utility.
Conversion of overhead electric or communication facilities to underground locations, PUC §12-301.
Highways, TR §8-627.
Public water system.
Drinking water, EN §9-401.
Sprinkler systems, PS §9-201.
Water conservation, EN §5-5B-01.
Public way.
Fires and fire protection, high-rise buildings, PS §9-401.
Sanitary commissions, EN §9-637.
Public work.
Public works contracts, SF §17-201.
Public work contract.
Procurement, SF §17-201.
Publish.
Telephone credit card number or code, CR §8-210.
Unlawful publication by video tape distributor, CR §3-907.
Published informational content.
Computer information transactions, CL §22-102.
Pupil generation rate.
Charles county, 66B §14.05.
Purchase.
Commercial code, CL §1-201.
Revolving credit, CL §12-901.
Purchase money.
Time-sharing, RP §11A-116.
Purchase-money collateral.
Secured transactions, CL §9-103.
Purchase money deed of trust.
Recordation taxes.
Exemptions, TP §12-108.

DEFINED TERMS —Cont'd

Purchase money loan.
Consumer credit contracts, CL §14-1302.
Purchase money mortgage.
Recordation taxes.
Exemptions, TP §12-108.
Purchase-money obligation.
Secured transactions, CL §9-103.
Purchase price.
Door-to-door sales, CL §14-301.
Purchaser.
Commercial code, CL §1-201.
Fluid dairy products, AG §11-401.
Land installment contracts, RP §10-101.
Real property, RP §1-101.
Time-sharing, RP §11A-101.
Vacation club membership, CL §14-2401.
Warranties.
Land installment contracts, RP §10-201.
Purchasing group.
Risk retention, IN §25-101.
Pure seed, AG §9-201.
Purse horse racing, BR §11-101.
Pursuant to commitment.
Secured transactions, CL §9-102.
Pyramid promotional scheme, CR §8-404.
Pyrotechnic composition.
Fireworks, PS §10-101.
Qualified actuary.
Insurance companies.
Reserves, IN §5-201.
Qualified addictions specialist.
Integration of child welfare and substance abuse treatment act, FL §5-1201.
Qualified beneficiary.
College savings plan of Maryland, ED §18-1901.
Principal and income act, ET §15-502.3.
Qualified Brownfields site.
Economic development assistance fund, 83A §5-1401.
Property taxes, TP §9-229.
Abatement, TP §14-902.
Qualified business entity.
Job creation tax credit, 83A §5-1101.
One Maryland economic development tax credits, 83A §5-1501.
Qualified candidate.
Alternative teaching opportunity program, ED §6-120.
Qualified child care expenses.
Aid to families with dependent children.
Tax credits for qualified employment opportunity employees, 88A §54.
Family investment program, 88A §54.
Qualified child care or transportation expenses.
Rehabilitation services, ED §21-309.
Qualified county.
Noise control, EN §3-403.
Qualified designated beneficiary.
College investment plan, ED §18-19A-01.
Qualified developmental disability professional, HG §7-1002.
Qualified distressed county.
Economic development assistance authority, 83A §5-1401.
Industrial development financing, 83A §5-901.
One Maryland economic development tax credits, 83A §5-1501.
Senior citizen activities center operating fund, 70B §33.

DEFINED TERMS —Cont'd
Qualified distressed county project.
Economic development assistance authority, 83A §5-1401.
Qualified electric vehicle.
Electric or hybrid motor vehicles, TR §13-815.
Qualified elevator inspector.
Elevator safety, PS §12-801.
Qualified employee.
Job creation tax credit, 83A §5-1101.
One Maryland economic development tax credits, 83A §5-1501.
Tax credits, TG §10-702.
Qualified employee wages.
Film production activity employer wage rebate program, 83A §5-1801.
Qualified employee with a disability.
Rehabilitation services, ED §21-309.
Qualified employment opportunity employee.
Aid to families with dependent children.
Tax credits for wages and child care expenses, 88A §54.
Family investment program, 88A §54.
Qualified energy resources.
Income tax, TG §10-720.
Qualified entity.
Distribution of accessible information for disabled persons, SF §3-901.
Qualified escrow fund.
Tobacco, escrow act compliance, BR §16-501.
Qualified ex-felon employee.
Pilot program for long term employment of qualified ex-felons, LE §11-701.
Qualified expert.
Juvenile cases, CJ §3-8A-01.
Professional malpractice, CJ §3-2C-01.
Qualified film production employer.
Film production activity employer wage rebate program, 83A §5-1801.
Qualified financial contract.
Insurance companies, liquidation and rehabilitation, IN §9-229.1.
Qualified financial institution.
Reinsurance intermediaries, IN §8-501.
Qualified guarantor.
Investments of life insurers, IN §5-511.
Qualified higher education expenses.
College investment plan, ED §18-19A-01.
College savings plan of Maryland, ED §18-1901.
Qualified hybrid vehicle.
Electric or hybrid motor vehicles, TR §13-815.
Motor vehicle emissions inspection, TR §23-206.3.
Qualified individual.
Health insurance, IN §15-823.
Qualified investor.
Income tax credit for biotechnology companies, TG §10-725.
Qualified juror, CJ §8-101.
Qualified Maryland biotechnology company.
Income tax credit for biotechnology companies, TG §10-725.
Qualified Maryland facility.
Income tax, TG §10-720.
Qualified Maryland venture capital firm.
Income tax credit for biotechnology companies, TG §10-725.
Qualified medical person.
Evidence, CJ §10-304.
Qualified medical support order.
Health insurance, IN §15-405.

DEFINED TERMS —Cont'd
Qualified member.
Anne Arundel county, gaming events, CR §13-403.
Qualified minor's trust.
Transfers to minors act, ET §13-301.
Qualified organization.
Gaming, Montgomery county, CR §13-1801.
Local gaming provisions, CR §13-201.
Prince George's county, CR §13-1901.
St. Mary's county, CR §13-2101.
Qualified owner.
Motor vehicle registration, TR §13-610.
Qualified person.
Automobile insurance fund, IN §20-601.
Evidence, CJ §10-304.
Professional service corporations, CA §5-101.
Qualified plan.
Insurance companies.
Life insurance and annuities, IN §5-512.
Life insurance and annuities.
Investments of life insurers, IN §5-512.
Qualified position.
Job creation tax credit, 83A §5-1101.
One Maryland economic development tax credits, 83A §5-1501.
Qualified primary credit source.
Investments of life insurers, IN §5-511.
Qualified prison facility.
State personnel.
Credits in selection tests, SPP §7-207.
Qualified property.
Property tax.
Enterprise zones, TP §9-103.
Qualified rate order.
Electric customer choice and competition act, PUC §7-501.
Electric customer competition and choice act.
Rate stabilization, PUC §7-520.
Qualified rate stabilization charge.
Electric customer competition and choice act.
Rate stabilization, PUC §7-520.
Qualified rehabilitation expenditure.
Maryland historical trust, rehabilitation tax credits, SF §5A-303.
Qualified resident.
Mobile home parks, RP §8A-202.
Qualified secondary beneficiary.
Health insurance.
Divorced spouses and dependent children, IN §15-408.
Surviving spouses and dependent children, IN §15-407.
Qualified security.
Franchises, 83A §5-1041.
Qualified state tuition program.
College investment plan, ED §18-19A-01.
College savings plan of Maryland, ED §18-1901.
Qualified surplus lines broker, IN §3-301.
Qualified to vote.
Home rule.
Municipal corporations, 23A §9.
Qualifying alternate energy sources.
Income tax credits, TG §10-722.
Qualifying biomass.
Renewable energy portfolio standard, PUC §7-701.
Qualifying borrower.
Assistive technology guaranteed loan fund, 41 §14-901.
Qualifying business.
Property tax.
Washington county, TP §9-323.

DEFINED TERMS —Cont'd
Qualifying corporate headquarters.
  Income tax.
    Multijurisdictional electric companies, TG §10-713.
Qualifying individual.
  Income tax.
    Child and dependent care credit, TG §10-716.
Qualifying municipality.
  State police.
    Protection fund, 41 §4-403.
Qualifying not-for-profit organizations.
  State personnel.
    Health and welfare benefits, SPP §2-512.
Qualifying relative.
  Public ethics, SG §15-102.
Qualifying residing artist.
  Arts and entertainment districts, 83A §4-701.
Quality review.
  Accountants.
    Courts, CJ §9-110.
Quarter.
  Taxation, TG §2-101.
Quarterly date of finality.
  Property tax, TP §1-101.
Quasi-governmental entity.
  Substance abuse prevention and treatment, HG §8-901.
Quasi-judicial function.
  Governmental procedures.
    Meetings, SG §10-502.
Quasi-legislative function.
  Governmental procedures.
    Meetings, SG §10-502.
Queen Anne's authority.
  Queen Anne's county housing authority, HS §18-101.
Quorum.
  Governmental procedures.
    Meetings, SG §10-502.
  St. Mary's county open meetings, 24 §4-202.
R.
  Insurance companies.
    Standard valuation law, IN §5-306.
R1.
  Insurance companies.
    Standard valuation law, IN §5-306.
R2.
  Insurance companies.
    Standard valuation law, IN §5-306.
Race meeting.
  Horse racing, BR §11-101.
Race-neutral measure.
  Procurement, minority business enterprises, SF §14-301.
Racquet club.
  Class C, on-sale beer, wine and liquor license in Harford county, 2B §6-301.
Radiation, EN §8-101.
Radiation fallout shelter.
  Property tax, TP §8-236.
Radiation machine.
  Radiation, EN §8-304.
Radon testing device.
  Radiation, EN §8-305.
Raffle.
  Baltimore City, CR §13-501.
  Carroll county, CR §13-904.
  Kent county, CR §13-1701.
  Queen Anne's county, CR §13-2001.
  Worcester county, CR §13-2619.

DEFINED TERMS —Cont'd
Railroad, PUC §1-101.
  Crimes involving railroads, CR §§6-503, 6-505.
  Railroad safety and health, LE §5.5-101.
Railroad carrier.
  Crimes involving railroads, CR §6-503.
Railroad company.
  Maryland transit administration, TR §7-101.
  Railroad police, PS §3-401.
  Railroad safety and health, LE §5.5-101.
Railroad corridor property, TR §7-901.
Railroad facility.
  Maryland transit administration, TR §7-101.
  Transportation, TR §3-101.
Railroad grade separation.
  Highways, TR §8-101.
Railroad police officer, PS §3-401.
Railroad property.
  Crimes involving railroads, CR §6-503.
Railroad safety and health, LE §5.5-115.
Railroad service.
  Maryland transit administration, TR §7-101.
Railroad sign.
  Traffic laws, TR §21-101.
Railroad signal.
  Traffic laws, TR §21-101.
Railroad train.
  Traffic laws, TR §21-101.
Railroad vehicle.
  Crimes involving railroads, CR §6-501.
Rank.
  State police department, PS §2-101.
Rates.
  Community services reimbursement rate commission, HG §13-801.
  Developmental disabilities, HG §7-307.
  Insurance rates, IN §11-101.
  Public utility companies, PUC §1-101.
  Subrogation provision included in contract, HG §19-713.
Rate stabilization account.
  Maryland medical professional liability insurance rate stabilization fund, IN §19-104.1.
Rate stabilization bond.
  Electric customer competition and choice act.
    Rate stabilization, PUC §7-520.
Rate stabilization cost.
  Electric customer competition and choice act.
    Rate stabilization, PUC §7-520.
Rate stabilization plan.
  Electric customer competition and choice act.
    Rate stabilization, PUC §7-520.
Rate stabilization property.
  Electric customer competition and choice act.
    Rate stabilization, PUC §7-520.
Rating organization.
  Insurance, IN §11-101.
Rating year.
  Unemployment compensation, LE §8-606.
Raw agricultural commodity.
  Poultry products inspection act, AG §4-201.
  Wholesome meat act, AG §4-101.
Raw milk.
  Milk products, HG §21-401.
RBC instructions.
  Risk based capital standards for insurers, IN §4-301.
RBC level.
  Risk based capital standards for insurers, IN §4-301.

DEFINED TERMS —Cont'd

RBC plan.
Risk based capital standards for insurers, IN §4-301.

RBC report.
Risk based capital standards for insurers, IN §4-301.

Reach-in cabinet.
Maryland efficiency standards act, SG §9-2006.

Reacquisition.
Negotiable instruments, CL §§3-103, 3-207.

Readily accessible to the general public.
Evidence, CJ §10-401.

Readily attachable components.
Motor vehicles, TR §13-113.2.

Real estate.
Brokers, BOP §17-101.
Real estate appraisers, BOP §16-101.

Real estate appraiser trainee, BOP §16-101.

Real estate broker, BOP §17-101.

Real estate investment trust.
Corporations, CA §8-101.

Real estate salesperson.
Real estate brokers, BOP §17-101.

Real or personal property.
Board of public works, SF §10-301.
County public libraries, ED §23-501.
Drug asset forfeiture, CP §12-101.
Financial institutions, FI §1-101.
Property tax, TP §1-101.

Real property.
Housing authorities, HS §12-101.

Realty.
Warranties.
Land installment contracts, RP §10-201.

Reasonable accommodation.
Public accommodations discrimination, 49B §5.

Reasonable and necessary expenses.
Alimony, FL §11-110.
Divorce, FL §§7-107, 8-214.

Reasonable and necessary maintenance.
Service contracts and consumer products guaranty, CL §14-401.

Reasonable attempt to repair.
Motorized wheelchair warranty enforcement, CL §14-2701.

Reasonable fee.
Access to public records, SG §10-621.

Reasonable time.
Commercial code, CL §1-204.

Reasonably predictable.
Uniform commercial code, CL §1-201.

Receipt.
Computer information transactions, CL §22-102.
Sales, UCC, CL §2-103.

Receipt of services.
Health care collections, HG §16-101.

Receive.
Computer information transactions, CL §22-102.

Receiver.
Continuing care contracts, 70B §7.
Insurer liquidation, rehabilitation, etc., IN §9-201.

Receiving agency.
School funding, ED §4-122.1.

Receiving bank.
Funds transfers, CL §4A-103.

Receiving county.
Schools near boundary of two counties, ED §4-121.

Receiving school.
Education of children in state-supervised care, ED §8-501.

DEFINED TERMS —Cont'd

Receiving school —Cont'd
Principal fellowship and leadership development program, ED §6-116.

Receiving school system.
Principal fellowship and leadership development program, ED §6-116.

Receiving state.
Interstate agreement on detainers, COR §8-404.
Interstate corrections compact, COR §8-603.
Interstate placement of children, FL §5-603.
Juvenile services.
Interstate compact on juveniles, 83C §3-105.
Mental health compact, HG §11-103.
Qualifications of educational personnel, ED §6-604.

Receiving station.
Milk products, HG §21-401.

Receiving track.
Horse racing, BR §11-101.

Recent birth, marriage or divorce record.
Archives, SG §9-1015.

Recent death record.
Archives, SG §9-1015.

Recent vital record.
Archives, SG §9-1015.

Reception center.
Hospitals and reception centers, 25 §252.

Rechargeable battery, EN §6-1101.

Rechargeable product.
Batteries, EN §6-1101.

Recipient.
AIDS insurance, HG §15-201.
Child care provider grant program, ED §18-705.
Family investment program, 88A §44A.
Health program integrity and recovery activities, HG §2-501.
Kidney disease, HG §13-302.
Medical records, HG §4-301.
Mental health professional grant, ED §18-707.
Physical and occupational therapists and assistance grant program, ED §18-704.
Public assistance programs, 88A §64.

Recipient of individual support services.
Facility licensing, HG §7-901.

Recipient school.
School performance program standards improvement awards, ED §5-211.

Reciprocal basis.
Savings and loan associations.
Interstate acquisitions, FI §9-1001.

Reciprocal insurance, IN §1-101.

Reciprocal insurer, IN §1-101.

Reciprocal license.
Electricians, BOP §6-501.
Real estate brokers, BOP §17-3A-01.

Reciprocal state.
Insurer liquidation, rehabilitation, etc., IN §9-201.

Reciprocating state.
Insurance companies, IN §3-128.

Reclaimed water, EN §9-301.

Reclamation.
Surface mining, EN §15-801.

Reclamation facility.
Mercury-added products, EN §6-905.

Recognized heritage area, FI §13-1101.

Recognized profession.
Psychologists, HO §18-102.

Reconstructed vehicle, TR §13-104.2.

Reconstruction.
Building rehabilitation code, PS §12-1001.

DEFINED TERMS —Cont'd
Reconstructive breast surgery.
Health insurance, IN §15-815.
Recordation tax, TP §12-101.
Record book.
Religious corporations, CA §5-301.
Recorded article.
Unauthorized recording of sounds or images, CR
§7-308.
Recorded covenants and restrictions.
Homeowners association, RP §11B-101.
Recorded images.
Access to public records, SG §10-616.
Speed restrictions on motor vehicles, Montgomery
county, TR §21-809.
Traffic control devices, TR §21-202.1.
Records.
Archives, SG §9-1015.
Athlete agents, BR §4-401.
Child abuse and neglect, FL §5-701.
Computer information transactions, CL §22-102.
Continuing care contracts, 70B §7.
Electronic transactions, CL §21-101.
Environmental covenant, EN §1-801.
Expungement of records, Crim Rule 4-502.
Letters of credit, CL §5-102.
Physicians, HO §14-411.
Public utility companies, PUC §1-101.
Secured transactions, CL §9-102.
Seeds, AG §9-201.
Turf grass, AG §9-101.
Uniform child custody jurisdiction and
enforcement act, FL §9.5-109.
Recovery.
Health program integrity and recovery activities,
HG §2-501.
Recreational purpose.
Public recreation on private and local government
lands, NR §5-1101.
Recreational vehicle.
Mobile home and trailer park taxes, 24 §9-401.
Recyclable materials, EN §9-1701.
University of Maryland, ED §13-703.
Recycled.
Used oil, EN §5-1001.
Recycled materials.
Procurement, SF §14-405.
Recycled paper.
Procurement, SF §14-402.
Recycling, EN §9-1701.
Recycling services, EN §9-1701.
Redeposit.
Chesapeake Bay and tributaries, EN §5-1101.
Hart-Miller-Pleasure Island chain, NR §5-1202.2.
Redevelopment assistance.
Neighborhood and community assistance program,
HS §6-401.
Reduction in operations.
Economic stabilization act, LE §11-301.
Refer.
Optometrists, HO §11-404.2.
Referral.
Health occupations, HO §1-301.
Refine.
Motor fuel tax, TG §9-301.
Refiner.
Motor fuel, BR §10-101.
Reforestation, NR §5-219.
Forest conservation, NR §5-1601.
Refrigeration system.
Heating and air conditioning, BR §9A-101.

DEFINED TERMS —Cont'd
Refund.
Withholding income tax refunds, TG §13-920.
Withholding tax refund due to local government
debts, TG §13-925.
Refunding.
Revenue facilities, TR §4-101.
Transportation, TR §3-101.
Refuse.
Surface mining, EN §15-801.
Region.
Community colleges.
State and county aid, ED §16-305.
Maryland home financing program, HS §4-801.
Mid-shore regional council, 20C §1-101.
Northeast interstate dairy compact, AG §2-801.
Radioactive waste, EN §7-301.
Savings and loan associations.
Interstate acquisitions, FI §9-1001.
Southern Maryland tri-county council, 20 §1-102.
Tri-county council for lower eastern shore of
Maryland, 20B §1-101.
Upper shore regional council, 20D §1-101.
Western Maryland tri-county council, 20A §1-102.
Regional administrator.
Automated external defibrillator program, ED
§13-517.
Regional agency.
Counties and municipal corporations, 24 §1-107.
Regional board.
Dentists, HO §4-306.
Regional council.
Automated external defibrillator program, ED
§13-517.
Rural Maryland prosperity investment fund, SF
§2-207.
Regional council AED committee.
Automated external defibrillator program, ED
§13-517.
Regional facility.
Radioactive waste, EN §7-301.
Regional higher education center, ED §10-101.
Register.
Death taxes, TG §7-101.
Estates and trusts, ET §2-201.
Income tax, TG §13-906.
Sale of insurance company securities, IN §3-127.
Transfer-on-death security registration, ET
§16-101.
Uniform interstate family support act, FL
§10-301.
URESA, FL §10-301.
Registered cemeterian, BR §5-101.
Registered dietitian, HO §5-101.
Registered employee.
Pesticide applicators, AG §5-201.
Registered environmental sanitarian, EN
§11-101.
Registered form.
Investment securities, CL §8-102.
Registered mail.
Rules of interpretation, 1 §20.
Registered massage practitioner, HO §3-5A-01.
Registered nurse.
Health occupations, HO §8-101.
Registered organization.
Secured transactions, CL §9-102.
Registered pharmacy technician, HO §12-101.
Registered polysomnographic technologist, HO
§13-5C-01.
Registered seed, AG §9-201.

DEFINED TERMS —Cont'd
Registered seller.
  Burial goods, BR §5-101.
Registered sod.
  Turf grass, AG §9-101.
Registered voter.
  Code counties home rule, 25B §1.
Registering court.
  URESA, FL §10-301.
Registering entity.
  Transfer-on-death security registration, ET
    §16-101.
Registering tribunal.
  Uniform interstate family support act, FL
    §10-301.
Registrant.
  Advance directive registry, HG §5-619.
  Agricultural liming materials and gypsum, AG
    §6-301.
  Commercial fertilizers, AG §6-201.
  Controlled dangerous substances, CR §5-101.
  Homebuilder registration, BR §4.5-101.
  Pesticide registration and labeling, AG §5-101.
Registration.
  Cemeteries, BR §5-101.
  Massage therapists, HO §3-5A-01.
  Pharmacists and pharmacies, HO §12-101.
  Rehabilitation practitioners, LE §9-6A-01.
  Vital statistics, HG §4-201.
Registration fund.
  Homebuilder registration, BR §4.5-101.
Registration plate.
  Alter or forge.
    Motor vehicles, TR §14-110.
Registration plate cover.
  Motor vehicle registration, TR §13-411.1.
Registry.
  Advance directive registry, HG §5-619.
  Mutual consent voluntary adoption registry, FL
    §5-4C-01.
Regular benefits.
  Unemployment compensation.
    Self-employment assistance, LE §8-1601.
  Unemployment insurance, LE §8-1101.
Regular interest.
  Legislative pension plan, SG Title 2 Subtitle 3
    (note).
  Pensions, SPP §20-101.
Regular mutuel pool.
  Horse racing, BR §11-101.
Regular or periodic tidal action.
  Wetlands and riparian rights, EN §16-101.
Regular place of business.
  Taxation, TG §13-803.
Regular schedule.
  Motor vehicles, TR §11-148.
Regular undergraduate program.
  Maryland HOPE scholarships, ED §18-2301.
  Science and technology scholarships, ED
    §18-2001.
Regulated activity.
  Nontidal wetlands, EN §5-901.
Regulated area.
  Northeast interstate dairy compact, AG §2-801.
Regulated emissions.
  Air quality, EN §2-101.
Regulated firearm.
  Firearms, PS §5-101.
Regulated lobbyist.
  Public ethics, SG §15-102.

DEFINED TERMS —Cont'd
Regulating entity.
  Nonprofit health entities.
    Acquisition, SG §6.5-101.
Regulations.
  Administrative procedures, SG §10-101.
  Land use, 66B §1.00.
  Political subdivisions, 24 §3-101.
  Secretary of state, SG §7-201.
  Zoning and planning, 66B §1.00.
Regulatory plan.
  Development rights and responsibilities
    agreement.
    Montgomery county, 28 §7-121.
Rehabilitation.
  Rehabilitation services, ED §21-301.
Rehabilitation project.
  Building rehabilitation code, PS §12-1001.
  Maryland housing rehabilitation program, HS
    §4-901.
Reimbursement.
  Health insurance.
    Retroactive denial of reimbursement, IN
      §15-1008.
Reimbursement payment.
  Unemployment insurance.
    Contributions, LE §8-601.
Reinstatement.
  Discipline of attorneys, CJA Rule 16-701.
Reinsurance, IN §1-101.
Reinsurance broker, IN §8-501.
Reinsurance intermediary, IN §8-501.
Reinsurance manager, IN §8-501.
Reinsurer, IN §8-501.
  Insurance companies.
    Reinsurance, IN §5-901.
Reinsuring carrier.
  Small employer health insurance, IN §15-1201.
Related development.
  Homeowners association, RP §11B-101.
Related entity.
  Savings and loan associations.
    Board of commissioners and division, FI §8-101.
Related institution.
  Health assistance, HG §15-114.
  Health services cost review commission, HG
    §19-201.
  Hospitals, HG §19-301.
Related party.
  Lead poisoning, EN §6-801.
Related provider trust.
  Viatical settlement contracts, IN §8-601.
Related services.
  Children with disabilities, ED §8-401.
Relative.
  Admission of students, ED §7-101.
  Child abduction, FL §9-301.
  Child in need of assistance, CJ §3-801.
  General assembly, SG §2-107.
  Kinship care, consent to medical care for minor,
    HG §20-105.
  Public service commission.
    Ethics generally, PUC §2-301.
  School funding, ED §4-122.1.
Release.
  Computer information transactions, CL §22-102.
  Controlled hazardous substances, EN §7-201.
  Developmental disabilities, HG §7-101.
  Rights of mentally ill, HG §10-801.
  Sex offender registration, CP §11-701.

DEFINED TERMS —Cont'd

Release from confinement.
Victims of crime, CP §11-508.

Religion.
Employment discrimination, 49B §15.

Relocate.
Publicly owned utility facilities, TR §8-506.

Relocation expenses.
Assisted housing preservation, HS §7-101.
Lead poisoning, EN §6-801.

Remain.
Juvenile curfew, 25B §13C-1.

Remainder beneficiary.
Principal and income act, ET §15-501.

Remaining loan balance.
Credit grantor closed end credit, CL §12-1001.

Remediation.
Patuxent institution, COR §4-101.

Remedy.
Commercial code, CL §1-201.

Remitter.
Negotiable instruments, CL §3-103.

Remitting bank.
Bank deposits and collections, CL §4-105.

Remote access.
Access to court records, CJA Rule 16-1001.

Removable data storage device.
Elections, EL §11-101.

Removal costs.
Water pollution, EN §4-401.

Remove.
Vehicle identification number, TR §14-107.

Remuneration.
For-hire driving services, PUC §10-101.

Renderer.
Poultry products inspection act, AG §4-201.
Wholesome meat act, AG §4-101.

Rendering state.
URESA, FL §10-301.

Renewable energy credit.
Renewable energy portfolio standard, PUC §7-701.

Renewable energy portfolio standard, PUC §7-701.

Renewable on-site generator.
Renewable energy portfolio standard, PUC §7-701.

Renovate.
Bedding, HG §24-401.

Renovation.
Building rehabilitation code, PS §12-1001.
Continuing care contracts, 70B §7.

Renovator.
Bedding, HG §24-401.

Rent.
Firearms, PS §5-101.
Mobile home parks, RP §8A-101.
Motor vehicles, TR §18-101.

Rental agreement.
Mobile home parks, RP §8A-101.
Motor vehicle rental company insurance, IN §10-601.
Motor vehicles.
Collision damage waiver, CL §14-2101.
Self-service storage, CL §18-501.

Rental dwelling unit.
Lead hazard insurance for rental property, IN §19-701.
Lead poisoning, EN §6-801.
Lead risk reduction in rental housing, regulation of landlords, 24 §19-101.

Rental facility.
Condominiums, RP §§11-101, 11-137, 11-138.

DEFINED TERMS —Cont'd

Rental housing emergency.
Cooperative housing corporation, CA §5-6B-10.

Rental motor vehicle.
Collision damage waiver, CL §14-2101.

Rental property.
Rental-purchase agreements, CL §12-1101.

Rental-purchase agreement, CL §12-1101.

Rental vehicle, TR §11-148.1.
Parking, TR §26-301.

Rental vehicle company, TR §18-108.

Renter.
Motor vehicle rental company insurance, IN §10-601.
Property tax.
Elderly or disabled renters, TP §9-102.

Rent subsidy.
Lead poisoning, EN §6-801.

Reorganization agreement.
Fiduciaries, ET §15-101.

Reorganized employer.
Unemployment insurance.
Contributions, LE §8-613.

Reorganized stock insurer.
Conversion of mutual insurer to stock insurer, IN §3-121.1.

Repair.
Building rehabilitation code, PS §12-1001.

Repair company.
Consumer protection, CL §13-307.

Repair order certification.
Used vehicle inspection, TR §23-101.

Repeal law.
Property tax.
Credits and relief, TP §9-101.

Replace.
Service contracts and consumer products guaranty, CL §14-401.

Replacement contact lens prescription, HO §§11-404.4, 14-507.

Replacement cost.
Cigarettes, CL §11-501.
Closed end credit, insurance, CL §12-1007.
Real estate loans, CL §12-124.
Revolving credit, CL §12-909.
Sales below cost, CL §11-401.

Replication transaction.
Investments of life insurers, IN §5-511.

Report.
Child abuse and neglect, FL §5-701.
Financial exploitation, FI §1-306.
HIV/AIDS case reports, HG §18-207.

Reportable condition.
Rehabilitation services, HG §20-108.

Reportable event.
Criminal justice information system, CP §10-201.

Reportable offense.
Arrest of student, ED §7-303.

Report review.
Accountants.
Peer review, BOP §2-4A-01.

Repository.
Prescription drug repository program, HG §15-601.

Representation.
Medicaid fraud, CR §8-508.

Representative.
Commercial code, CL §1-201.
Community attendant services and supports program, 41 §6-7A-01.
Motor clubs, IN §26-101.

DEFINED TERMS —Cont'd
Representative —Cont'd
Pretrial procedures, CP §11-302.
Representative drawer.
Bad checks, CR §8-101.
Charles county, CR §13-1101.
Representative member.
Private detectives, BOP §13-101.
Security guards, BOP §19-101.
Security systems technicians, BOP §18-101.
Represented county.
Potomac water authority, EN §5-401.
Represented person.
Negotiable instruments, CL §3-307.
Reproduction.
Business regulation, BR §1-305.
Repurchase agreement.
Insurance companies, liquidation and
rehabilitation, IN §9-229.1.
Repurchase transaction.
Investments of life insurers, IN §5-511.
Request.
Secured transactions, disposition of collateral
after default, CL §9-616.
Secured transactions, information as to collateral,
CL §9-210.
Request for an accounting.
Secured transactions, CL §9-210.
Request for partnership funding.
Substance abuse treatment outcomes partnership
fund, HG §8-6C-01.
Request for proposals.
Procurement, SF §11-101.
Requesting state.
Pest control compact, AG §5-702.
Request regarding a list of collateral.
Secured transactions, CL §9-210.
Request regarding a statement of account.
Secured transactions, CL §9-210.
Require.
Motor vehicle dealers, TR §15-207.
Required security.
Vehicle insurance, TR §17-101.
Resale.
Foreclosure purchaser obligations, RP §7-311.
Resale price.
Foreclosure purchaser obligations, RP §7-311.
Rescission.
Sales, UCC, CL §2-720.
Research.
Human subject research, HG §13-2001.
Research and development.
Taxation, TG §11-217.
Reseller.
Telephone slamming, PUC §8-401.
Residence.
Domestic violence, FL §4-501.
Juvenile services.
Interstate compact on juveniles, 83C §3-103.
Peace orders, CJ §3-1501.
Residence in foreclosure.
Protection of homeowners in foreclosure, RP
§7-301.
Residence state.
Interstate compact on adoption and medical
assistance, FL §5-4A-01.
Resident.
Alcoholic beverages, 2B §8-219.
Angler's license, NR §4-604.
Home or community-based waiver programs, HG
§15-135.

DEFINED TERMS —Cont'd
Resident —Cont'd
Liens on aircraft, boats, mobile homes and motor
vehicles, CL §16-201.
Life and health insurance guaranty corporation,
IN §9-401.
Mobile home parks, RP §8A-101.
Motor vehicles, TR §11-149.
Property and casualty insurance guaranty
corporation, IN §9-301.
Sex offender registration, CP §11-705.
Tax tables, TG §2-106.
Unauthorized insurers false advertising process
act, IN §27-701.
Wildlife, NR §10-101.
Resident agent.
Corporations, CA §1-101.
Debt management services, FI §12-901.
Resident bidder.
Procurement, SF §14-401.
Resident campus.
College of southern Maryland, ED §16-602.
Resident entity.
Income tax withholding, TG §10-912.
Residential and noncommercial users.
People's counsel, PUC §2-201.
Residential building.
Community development administration, HS
§4-201.
Residential camp.
Maryland youth camp, HG §14-401.
Residential child care program, HO §20-101.
Children, youth and families services, 49D §7-101.
Operators of residential child care programs,
49D §6-101.
Nonpublic general education schools, ED §8-417.
Residential child care capital grant program, 41
§18-701.
School enrollment, duties of facility, ED §7-309.
Residential crisis services.
Health insurance, IN §15-840.
Residential district.
Traffic laws, TR §21-101.
Residential dwelling.
Barbeque grills, restrictions on use, PS §9-1001.
Water quality financing, EN §9-1601.
Residential educational facility.
Child care, FL §5-501.
Residential energy audit.
Community development administration, HS
§4-201.
Residential facility.
Juvenile residential facilities, ED §22-301.
Residential facility for children.
Child welfare services, FL §5-533.
Residential mortgage loan.
Community development administration, HS
§4-201.
Residential placement.
Children, youth and families services, 49D §1-101.
Residential property.
Lead risk reduction in rental housing, regulation
of landlords, 24 §19-101.
Residential real estate related transaction.
Housing discrimination, 49B §20.
Residential real property.
Closed end credit, CL §12-1001.
Homeowner equity protection, CL §§12-311,
12-409.1.
Homeowner's ability to repay loan, CL §12-127.
Mortgage lending, FI §11-501.

DEFINED TERMS —Cont'd
Residential real property —Cont'd
Revolving credit, CL §12-901.
Residential rental facility.
Cooperative housing corporation, CA §5-6B-01.
Residential service agency.
Home health care, HG §19-4A-01.
Residential street service.
Municipal corporations, 23A §49.
Residential treatment care.
Child care, FL §5-501.
Residential treatment center, HG §19-301.
Resident income tax, TG §10-101.
Resident offeror.
Procurement, SF §14-401.
Resident of the state.
Property tax, TP §1-101.
Residue.
Sterile needle and syringe exchange, Baltimore
City, HG §24-801.
Sterile needle and syringe exchange, Prince
George's county, HG §24-901.
Resolution.
Higher education.
Auxiliary and academic facilities bond
authority, ED §19-101.
Legislative pension plan, SG Title 2 Subtitle 3
(note).
Revenue facilities, TR §4-101.
Sewerage bonds, EN §9-801.
State debt, SF §8-201.
Resolution of participation.
Northeast Maryland waste disposal authority, NR
§3-904.
Resolution session.
Disabled student placement, ED §8-413.
Resort area.
County resort taxes, 25B §13H.
Resource recovery facility.
Recycling, EN §9-1701.
Resource sharing.
State finance, SF §3-402.
Respite care.
Developmentally and functionally disabled
persons, 88A §128.
Mental retardation, HG §7-509.
Respite care services.
Medicaid, HG §15-132.
Respondent.
Domestic violence, FL §4-501.
Housing discrimination, 49B §20.
Juvenile causes, CJ §3-8A-01.
Peace orders, CJ §3-1501.
Public ethics, SG §15-102.
Uniform child custody jurisdiction and
enforcement act, FL §9.5-301.
Responding state.
Pest control compact, AG §5-702.
Uniform interstate family support act, FL
§10-301.
URESA, FL §10-301.
Responding tribunal.
Uniform interstate family support act, FL
§10-301.
Response time.
Security systems, CL §14-1314.
Responsibility.
Negotiable instruments, CL §3-405.
Responsible administrative authority.
Structured settlements, transfer of payment
rights, CJ §5-1101.

DEFINED TERMS —Cont'd
Responsible bidder or offeror.
Procurement, SF §11-101.
Responsible charge.
Engineers, BOP §14-101.
Landscape architects, BOP §9-101.
Land surveyors, BOP §15-101.
Waterworks operators, EN §12-101.
Responsible entity.
Rechargeable batteries, EN §6-1101.
Responsible member.
Architects, BOP §3-401.
Landscape architects, BOP §9-401.
Responsible officers.
Elections, EL §1-101.
Responsible official.
Rights of mentally ill, HG §10-806.
Responsible party.
Nurses, HG §19-2001.
Responsible person.
Community right-to-know fund, EN §7-601.
Controlled hazardous substances, EN §7-201.
Economic development assistance fund, 83A
§5-1401.
Mortgage releases, RP §3-105.1.
Shoplifting and employee theft.
Courts, CJ §3-1301.
Water management, EN §4-104.
Responsible relative.
Health care collections, HG §16-101.
Responsive bid.
Procurement, SF §11-101.
Restaurant.
Alcoholic beverages.
Allegany county, 2B §11-501.
Queen Anne's county, 2B §8-218.
Washington county, 2B §9-222.
Restaurant license, BR §17-1601.
Restitution.
Premium finance companies, IN §23-208.
Restitution obligor.
Crime victims' restitution, CP §11-601.
Restricted license.
Physicians, HO §14-321.
Well drillers, EN §13-101.
Restricted noxious weed.
Turf grass, AG §9-101.
Restricted noxious weed seed, AG §9-201.
Restricted use pesticide.
Pesticide applicators, AG §5-201.
Restrictive bidding.
Minority business enterprise program.
County public libraries, ED §23-402.
Prince George's community college, ED §16-312.
Prince George's county board of education, ED
§4-125.
Restrictive covenants.
Housing discrimination, 49B §20.
Restrictive price quotations.
Minority business enterprise program.
County public libraries, ED §23-402.
Prince George's community college, ED §16-312.
Prince George's county board of education, ED
§4-125.
Retail credit account, CL §12-501.
Credit life or disability insurance premiums, IN
§27-901.
Retail dealer.
Alcoholic beverages, 2B §1-102.
Alcoholic beverage tax, TG §5-101.

DEFINED TERMS —Cont'd

Retailer.
Cigarette licenses, BR §16-201.
Egg law, AG §4-301.
Less than 20 cigarettes per package, CL §11-5A-01.
Maryland efficiency standards act, SG §9-2006.
Sales below cost, CL §11-401.
Cigarettes, CL §11-501.
Retail establishment.
Industrial development financing, 83A §5-901.
Retail gas customer.
Public utility companies, PUC §1-101.
Retail sale.
Gasohol and gasoline products marketing, CL §11-301.
Installment sales, CL §12-601.
Layaway sales, CL §14-1101.
Sales below cost, CL §11-401.
Sales finance companies, FI §11-401.
Sales tax, TG §11-101.
Retail sale of cigarettes.
Sales below cost, CL §11-501.
Retail seedsman.
Seeds, AG §9-201.
Retail service station dealer.
Motor fuel, BR §10-101.
Motor fuel tax, TG §9-301.
Retail store.
Tobacco smoking, HG §24-501.
Retail value.
Trademark counterfeiting, CR §8-611.
Retaliate.
Commercial discrimination, SF §19-103.
Retaliatory evictions.
Landlord and tenant, RP §§8-206, 8-208.1.
Mobile home parks, RP §8A-1301.
Retention.
Forest conservation, NR §5-1601.
Retirees.
Legislative pension plan, SG Title 2 Subtitle 3 (note).
Pensions, SPP §20-101.
State personnel.
Health and welfare benefits, SPP §2-508.
Retirement.
Pensions, SPP §20-101.
Retirement allowance.
Legislative pension plan, SG Title 2 Subtitle 3 (note).
Pensions, SPP §20-101.
Retirement community.
Operating agreements, CL §23-101.
Retirement payment.
Unemployment insurance, LE §8-1008.
Retirement system.
State retirement and pension system, SPP §30-101.
Return.
Bail and recognizance, CP §5-208.
Computer information transactions, CL §22-102.
Limited partnerships.
Return of contribution, CA §10-608.
Sales, UCC, CL §2-326.
Returnable container, BR §19-301.
Returnable textile, BR §19-301.
Return card.
Elections, EL §3-502.
Returning veteran.
State personnel.
Reinstatements, SPP §2-701.

DEFINED TERMS —Cont'd

Reunderwrite.
Insurance unfair trade practices, IN §27-221.
Reuse.
Dredged material disposal alternatives program, 83A §6-801.
Revenue.
Agricultural and resource-based industry development corporation, 41 §13-501.
Revenue bonds.
Health and educational facilities, 43C §3.
Revenue bonds of prior issues.
Revenue facilities, TR §4-101.
Revenues.
Bainbridge development corporation, 83A §5-1601.
Economic development corporation, 83A §5-201.
Local military installation redevelopment authorities, 83A §5-1701.
Northeast Maryland waste disposal authority, NR §3-904.
Penmar development corporations, 83A §5-1201.
Sewerage bonds, EN §9-801.
Taxation, TG §2-101.
Reverse equity mortgage loan.
Financing community development projects, HS §4-235.
Reverse repurchase agreement.
Insurance companies, liquidation and rehabilitation, IN §9-229.1.
Reverse repurchase transaction.
Investments of life insurers, IN §5-511.
Reverse stock split.
Corporations, CA §2-309.
Reverse waiver juvenile.
Educational programs in private residential institutions, 83C §2-137.
Review.
Accountants.
Peer review, BOP §2-4A-01.
Review board.
Adult protective services, FL §14-101.
Review panel.
Sentence review, CP §8-101.
Revised RBC plan.
Risk based capital standards for insurers, IN §4-301.
Revitalization area.
Job creation tax credit, 83A §5-1101.
Revitalization district.
Property tax.
Deferral of payment, TP §10-202.1.
Revoke.
Motor vehicles, TR §11-150.
Revolving credit plan, CL §12-901.
Rezoned real property.
Property tax, TP §8-226.
Ridesharing, TR §11-150.1.
Workers' compensation.
Vanpool operator or passenger, LE §9-230.
Rifles, CR §4-201; PS §5-201.
Right-of-way.
Crimes involving railroads, CR §6-503.
Mobile seafood vendors, TR §24-301.
Traffic laws, TR §21-101.
Rights.
Commercial code, CL §1-201.
Rigid plastic container, EN §9-1710.
Risk assets.
Credit unions, FI §6-703.
Risk-assuming carrier.
Small employer health insurance, IN §15-1201.

DEFINED TERMS —Cont'd

Risk factor.
Hearing impaired infants, HG §13-601.
Risk reduction standard.
Lead poisoning, EN §6-801.
Risk retention group.
Insurance, IN §25-101.
Ritual slaughter.
Livestock slaughtering, AG §4-123.1.
Road.
Highways, TR §8-101.
Roadside tree, NR §5-401.
Roadway, TR §11-151.
Municipal corporations, 23A §49.
Robbery, CR §3-401.
Rodenticide.
Pesticide registration and labeling, AG §5-101.
Rollback.
Motor vehicles, TR §11-151.1.
Roll-in cabinet.
Maryland efficiency standards act, SG §9-2006.
Roll-through cabinet.
Maryland efficiency standards act, SG §9-2006.
Route.
Power plant research program, NR §3-301.
Routine activity.
Maryland youth camp, HG §14-401.
Routine conveyance.
Spam, CR §3-805.1.
Routine maintenance.
Historic area zoning, 66B §8.01.
Royalty or royalties.
Copyright royalties, CL §11-1401.
Rule.
Interstate insurance product regulation compact, IN §29-101.
State police department, PS §2-101.
Ruled out.
Child abuse and neglect, FL §5-701.
Child welfare accountability, FL §5-1301.
Rules and regulations.
Adult offender supervision, COR §6-203.
Fraternal benefit societies, IN §8-401.
Long-term care insurance, IN §18-102.
Mobile home parks, RP §8A-101.
Rural area.
Rural Maryland prosperity investment fund, SF §2-207.
Rural legacy area, NR §§1-404, 5-9A-02.
Rural legacy plan, NR §5-9A-02.
Rural village.
Priority funding areas, SF §5-7B-01.
Saddle-mount and full-mount combinations.
Vehicle length and loads, TR §24-104.1.
Sadomasochistic abuse.
Adult sexual displays, CR §11-101.
Obscene matter, CR §11-201.
Safe-deposit box.
Rental companies, FI §12-601.
Safe-deposit company, FI §12-601.
Safety code.
Elevator safety, PS §12-801.
Safety glass.
Motor vehicles, TR §22-406.
Safety glazing material.
Building codes, safety glazing, PS §12-401.
Safety-sensitive employee.
Port administration drug-free workplace, TR §6-102.1.
Safety violation.
Civil liability of public service companies, PUC §13-202.

DEFINED TERMS —Cont'd

Safety zone.
Traffic laws, TR §21-101.
Said to contain.
Documents of title, CL §7-301.
Sale.
Business licenses, BR §17-101.
Cigarette licenses, BR §16-101.
Computer information transactions, CL §22-102.
Consumer protection, CL §§13-101, 14-1301.
Door-to-door sales, CL §14-301.
Sale of goods, CL §2-106.
Sales tax, TG §11-101.
Sales, UCC, CL §§2-106, 2-326.
Securities, CA §§11-101, 11-102.
Turf grass, AG §9-101.
Sale for use.
Sales tax, TG §11-101.
Sale in bulk.
Weights and measures, AG §11-101.
Sale of cigarettes at retail.
Cigarette licenses, BR §16-101.
Sale on approval.
Sales, UCC, CL §2-326.
Sales agent.
Vacation club membership, CL §14-2401.
Sales and use tax, TG §1-101.
Sales barns.
Horse industry board, AG §2-701.
Sales contract.
Time-sharing, RP §11A-101.
Sales finance company, FI §11-401.
Retail installment sales, CL §12-601.
Sales floor buyer.
Tobacco, AG §7-101.
Sales floor buyer's agent.
Tobacco, AG §7-101.
Sales floor seller.
Tobacco, AG §7-101.
Salesperson.
Home improvement, BR §8-101.
License.
Home improvement, BR §8-101.
Sales representatives.
Payment of commission, LE §3-601.
Sales territory.
Beer franchise fair dealing act, 2B §17-101.
Salvage.
Motor vehicles, TR §11-152.
Sample.
Fluid dairy products, AG §11-401.
Sample ballot, EL §1-101.
Sanctionable conduct.
Judges, CJA Rule 16-803.
Sanitarian in training.
Environmental sanitarian, EN §11-101.
Sanitarian in training program.
Environmental sanitarians, EN §11-101.
Sanitary commission, EN §9-601.
Sanitary fixture, HG §24-211.
Satellite organization.
State personnel.
Health and welfare benefits, SPP §2-501.
Satellite simulcast betting.
Horse racing, BR §11-815.
Savings accounts.
Financial institutions.
Deposit insurance, FI §10-101.
Savings and loan associations, FI §9-101.
Emergency interstate acquisitions, FI §5-1101.

DEFINED TERMS —Cont'd
Savings and loan association, FI §9-101.
  Approval of sale, transfer or pledge of assets, FI §9-712.
  Board of commissioners and division, FI §8-101.
  Conversions to capital stock associations, FI §§9-611, 9-612.
  Emergency interstate acquisitions, FI §5-1101.
  Franchise taxes, TG §8-101.
  Interstate acquisitions, FI §9-1001.
  Mutual holding companies, FI §4-801.
  Property tax exemption.
    Property used in processing deposits or loans, TP §7-221.1.
  Records, FI §9-501.
Savings and loan association franchise tax, TG §1-101.
Savings and loan holding company.
  Interstate acquisitions, FI §9-1001.
Savings bank, FI §§4-101, 5-101.
  Franchise taxes, TG §8-101.
Savings deposit account.
  Savings and loan associations, FI §9-101.
Savings liability.
  Savings and loan associations, FI §9-101.
Savings return.
  Consumer cooperatives, CA §5-5A-02.
Savings share account.
  Savings and loan associations, FI §9-101.
SAV protection zone, NR §4-1006.1.
Scenic corridor.
  Youghiogheny river, NR §8-408.
Scenic river.
  Deer creek study, NR §8-402.
Schedule I.
  Controlled dangerous substances, CR §5-101.
Schedule II.
  Controlled dangerous substances, CR §5-101.
Schedule III.
  Controlled dangerous substances, CR §5-101.
Schedule IV.
  Controlled dangerous substances, CR §5-101.
Schedule V.
  Controlled dangerous substances, CR §5-101.
School-based employee.
  Teachers, ED §6-306.
School bus, TR §11-153.
School of medicine.
  Scholarships, ED §18-702.
  University of Maryland medical system, ED §13-301.
School resource officer, ED §26-102.
Schools.
  Airport noise assistance programs, TR §5-1201.
  Alcoholic beverages, 2B §9-223.
  Asbestos removal, EN §6-401.
  Fire-rescue education and training, ED §11-501.
  Higher education commission.
    Solicitation of students, ED §11-402.
  Pesticide application in schools, AG §5-208.1.
  Reciprocal scholarship agreements, ED §18-308.
School system.
  Public ethics, SG §15-102.
School vehicle, TR §11-154.
  Length of use of school buses, ED §7-804.
  School bus safety enforcement fund, PS §4-201.
Scientific identification evidence.
  Postconviction review, CP §8-201.
Scooter, TR §11-154.1.
Scope.
  Computer information transactions, CL §22-102.

DEFINED TERMS —Cont'd
S corporation.
  Income tax, TG §10-101.
Scrap metal.
  Business licenses, BR §17-1001.
Scrap metal processing facility, EN §5-10A-01.
  Junkyards, TR §8-801.
Scrap metal processor.
  Business licenses, BR §17-1001.
Scrap processor.
  Motor vehicles, TR §15-501.
Scrap tire.
  Sanitary facilities, EN §9-201.
Scrap tire collection facility.
  Sanitary facilities, EN §9-201.
Scrap tire hauler.
  Sanitary facilities, EN §9-201.
Scrap tire recycler.
  Sanitary facilities, EN §9-201.
Screening.
  Cancer prevention, education, screening and treatment program, HG §13-1101.
Seafood.
  Maryland food center, 41 §13-104.
  Mobile vendors, TR §24-301.
Sealed container.
  Product liability, CJ §5-405.
Sealed record information.
  National crime prevention and privacy compact, CP §10-239.
Search, contact and reunion services, FL §5-4B-01.
Seasonable.
  Commercial code, CL §1-204.
  Computer information transactions, CL §22-102.
Seasonably.
  Uniform commercial code, CL §1-204.
Seatbelt.
  Motor vehicle child safety seats, TR §22-412.2.
  Motor vehicles, TR §22-412.
Seaworthy condition, NR §8-712.3.
Seclusion.
  Student behavior intervention, ED §7-1101.
Secondary claimant.
  Limitation on noneconomic damages in personal injury actions, CJ §11-108.
Secondary highway.
  Highways, TR §8-101.
Secondary mortgage loan, CL §12-401.
Secondary obligor.
  Secured transactions, CL §9-102.
Secondary sale.
  Firearms, PS §5-101.
Secondary standards.
  Weights and measures, AG §11-101.
Second eligible period.
  Community colleges.
    Contributions, ED §16-317.
Secondhand.
  Bedding, HG §24-401.
Secondhand watch.
  Consumer protection, CL §14-701.
Second-stage manufacturer, TR §15-201.
  Motor vehicles, TR §13-113.2.
Secretarial services.
  Immigration consultants, CL §14-3301.
Secretary.
  Agricultural land drainage, AG §8-603.
  Agriculture, AG §1-101.
  Corporations, BR §1-502.
  Criminal procedure, CP §1-101.

DEFINED TERMS —Cont'd

Secretary —Cont'd

Governor's health emergency powers, PS §14-3A-01.

Motor vehicle emissions, TR §23-201.

Secretary's reserve.

Allocation or private activity bond authority, FI §13-801.

Secured claim.

Continuing care contracts, 70B §7.

Insurer liquidation, rehabilitation, etc., IN §9-201.

Secured party.

Motor vehicles, TR §11-155.

Secured transactions, CL §9-102.

Unlawful subleasing of motor vehicle, CR §8-408.

Securities contract.

Insurance companies, liquidation and rehabilitation, IN §9-229.1.

Securities intermediary.

Investment securities, CL §8-102.

Securities lending transaction.

Investments of life insurers, IN §5-511.

Security.

Corporations, CA §11-101.

Fiduciaries, ET §15-101.

Fiduciary security transfers, ET §15-301.

Insurance companies, liquidation and rehabilitation, IN §9-229.1.

Investment securities, CL §8-102.

Transfer-on-death registration, ET §16-101.

Security account.

Investment securities, CL §8-501.

Transfer-on-death security registration, ET §16-101.

Security agreement.

Motor vehicles, TR §11-156.

Recordation taxes, TP §12-101.

Secured transactions, CL §9-102.

Unlawful subleasing of motor vehicle, CR §8-408.

Security certificate.

Investment securities, CL §8-102.

Security deposit.

Landlord and tenant, RP §8-203.

Mobile home parks, RP §8A-101.

Security entitlement.

Investment securities, CL §8-102.

Security guard, BOP §19-101.

Security guard agency, BOP §19-101.

Security guard services, BOP §19-101.

Security interest.

Boats and boating, NR §8-701.

Commercial code, CL §1-201.

Motor vehicles, TR §11-157.

Recordation taxes, TP §12-101.

Retail installment sales, CL §12-601.

Sales finance companies, FI §11-401.

Uniform commercial code, CL §1-201.

Unlawful subleasing of motor vehicle, CR §8-408.

Security officer.

Nuclear power plant facilities, CR §9-706.1.

Security procedure.

Electronic transactions, CL §21-101.

Funds transfers, CL §4A-201.

Security system, CL §14-1314.

Security systems technician, BOP §18-101.

Sedan service.

For-hire driving services, PUC §10-101.

Seed, AG §9-201.

Seed capital financing.

Venture capital trust, 83A §5-301.

DEFINED TERMS —Cont'd

Seedlings.

Forest conservation, NR §5-1601.

Pine tree reforestation, NR §5-501.

Seed money.

Public campaign financing, EL §15-102.

Seismic operations.

Natural resources.

Gas and oil, EN §14-109.

Seismic section.

Natural resources.

Gas and oil, EN §14-109.

Seizing authority.

Drug asset forfeiture, CP §12-101.

Selection A (Additional member contributions).

Employees' and teachers' retirement systems, SPP §22-101.

State retirement and pension system, SPP §29-401.

Selection B (Limited cost-of-living adjustment).

Employees' and teachers' retirement systems, SPP §22-101.

State retirement and pension system, SPP §29-401.

Selection board.

Procurement, SF §13-301.

Selection C (Combination formula).

Employees' and teachers' retirement systems, SPP §22-101.

State retirement and pension system, SPP §29-401.

Selective clearing.

Forest conservation, NR §5-1601.

Self-administer.

Self-administration of asthma medication by pupils, ED §7-421.

Self-contained appliance.

Heating and air conditioning, BR §9A-101.

Self-dealing.

Trusts, ET §14-303.

Self-employed provider.

Medicaid, HG §15-132.1.

Self-employment assistance activities.

Unemployment compensation, LE §8-1601.

Self-employment assistance allowance.

Unemployment compensation, LE §8-1601.

Self-employment assistance program.

Unemployment compensation, LE §8-1601.

Self-help rehabilitator.

Self-help homeownership technical assistance program, HS §4-1701.

Self-insurance agreement.

Workers' compensation, IN §25-301.

Self-insurance group.

Workers' compensation, IN §25-301.

Self-neglect.

Adult protective services, FL §14-101.

Self-service storage facility, CL §18-501.

Sell.

Business licenses, BR §17-101.

Cigarette sales below cost, CL §11-501.

Consumer protection.

Gold and silver, CL §14-601.

Secondhand watches, CL §14-701.

Container marking, AG §10-701.

CVISN transponders, TR §25-112.

Insurance, IN §1-101.

Less than 20 cigarettes per package, CL §11-5A-01.

Rechargeable batteries, EN §6-1101.

Tobacco tax, TG §12-101.

DEFINED TERMS —Cont'd
Sell —Cont'd
Weights and measures, AG §11-101.
Sell a home improvement, BR §8-101.
Seller.
Business opportunities, BR §14-101.
Consumer credit contracts, CL §14-1302.
Door-to-door sales, CL §14-301.
Layaway sales, CL §14-1101.
Preneed burial contracts, BR §5-701.
Preneed contracts.
Morticians, HO §7-405.
Product liability, CJ §5-405.
Limitation of actions, CJ §5-115.
Retail credit accounts, CL §12-501.
Retail installment sales, CL §12-601.
Sale of goods, CL §2-103.
Sales finance companies, FI §11-401.
Sales, UCC, CL §2-103.
Security systems, CL §14-1314.
Unlawful subleasing of motor vehicle, CR §8-408.
Waterproofing, CL §14-12A-01.
Seller's analysis.
Waterproofing.
Consumer protection, CL §14-12A-01.
Semiannual date of finality.
Property tax, TP §1-101.
Semitrailer, TR §11-158.
Senate.
General assembly, SG §2-101.
Send.
Commercial code, CL §1-201.
Computer information transactions, CL §22-102.
Secured transactions, CL §9-102.
Sender.
Funds transfers, CL §4A-103.
Sending agency.
Interstate placement of children, FL §5-603.
School funding, ED §4-122.1.
Sending county.
Schools near boundary of two counties, ED §4-121.
Sending school.
Education of children in state-supervised care, ED §8-501.
Sending state.
Interstate agreement on detainers, COR §8-404.
Interstate corrections compact, COR §8-603.
Juvenile services.
Interstate compact on juveniles, 83C §3-105.
Mental health compact, HG §11-103.
Sending track.
Horse racing, BR §11-101.
Senior.
Maryland senior ride demonstration program, TR §7-1001.
Senior citizen.
Condominium conversions, RP §11-102.1.
Condominiums, RP §11-137.
Cooperative housing corporation, CA §5-6B-05.
Waiver of tuition.
Morgan State University, ED §14-107.
St. Mary's college, ED §14-406.
University of Maryland, ED §13-701.
Senior citizen activities center.
Capital improvement grants, 70B §26.
Senior citizen activities center operating fund, 70B §33.
Senior elected official.
Emergency management assistance compact, PS §14-802.

DEFINED TERMS —Cont'd
Senior elected official —Cont'd
Maryland emergency management assistance compact, PS §14-801.
Senior housing.
Aging.
Managers training, 70B §25.
Sensitive areas.
Land use, 66B §1.00.
Sentencing court.
Sentence review, CP §8-101.
Sentencing judge.
Sentence review, CP §8-101.
Serious and immediate threat.
Nursing homes, HG §19-1401.
Serious bodily injury.
Leaving scene of accident, TR §27-113.
Serious crime.
Discipline of attorneys, CJA Rule 16-701.
Serious family hardship.
Admission of students, ED §7-101.
Kinship care, consent to medical care for minor, HG §20-105.
School funding, ED §4-122.1.
Serious injury.
Medicaid fraud, CR §8-508.
Serious physical injury.
Abuse or neglect of vulnerable adult, CR §3-604.
Criminal law, CR §3-201.
Local domestic violence fatality review teams, FL §4-701.
Serious traffic violation.
Commercial drivers' licenses, TR §16-803.
Service.
Antitrust, CL §11-201.
Bad checks, CR §8-101.
Commercial discrimination, SF §19-103.
Consumer protection, CL §§13-101, 14-1301.
Developmental disabilities, HG §7-101.
Expungement of records, Crim Rule 4-502.
Hazardous waste facilities, EN §7-401.
Procurement, SF §11-101.
Retail credit accounts, CL §12-501.
Robbery, CR §3-401.
Sanitary facilities, EN §9-201.
Service contracts and consumer products guaranty, CL §14-401.
State personnel.
Service contracts, SPP §13-401.
Theft, CR §7-101.
Service address.
Sales and use tax on telecommunications service.
Prince George's county, 24 §9-606.
Service area.
Sanitary commissions, EN §9-601.
Service charge.
Abandoned property, CL §17-101.
Service company.
Workers' compensation, IN §25-303.
Service contract.
Extension for appliance, CL §14-1306.
Service contracts and consumer products guaranty, CL §14-401.
State personnel, SPP §13-401.
Service contractor.
Extension of appliance service contract, CL §14-1306.
Service deficit.
Local bus systems grants, TR §10-207.
Service-disabled veteran.
Military reservists and service-related no-interest loan program, 83A §6-901.

DEFINED TERMS —Cont'd

Service district.
Environmental service, NR §3-101.
Service facilities.
Property tax.
Payments in lieu, TP §7-506.
Service obligation.
Child care provider grant program, ED §18-705.
Maryland HOPE scholarships, ED §18-2301.
Maryland teacher scholarships, ED §18-2201.
McAuliffe teacher education award, ED §18-703.
Medical scholarships, ED §18-702.
Mental health professional grant, ED §18-707.
Nursing scholarships, ED §18-706.
Physical and occupational therapists and assistants grant program, ED §18-704.
Science and technology scholarships, ED §18-2001.
William Donald Schaefer scholarship program, ED §18-2701.
Service provider.
Motor vehicle registration, TR §13-610.
Service providing local education agency.
Children in out-of-county living arrangements, ED §4-122.
Servicer.
Consumer protection.
Mortgages, CL §13-316.
Services coordination.
Developmental disabilities, HG §7-101.
Services to persons with mental illness.
Mental health, HG §10-1201.
Service vehicles.
Vehicle equipment, TR §22-201.
Session.
Courts, CJ §6-402.
Setback line.
Setback line restrictions.
Limitation of actions, CJ §5-114.
Setback line restrictions.
Limitation of actions, CJ §5-114.
Settle.
Bank deposits and collections, CL §4-104.
Settlement.
Foreclosure purchaser obligations, RP §7-311.
Purchase money mortgages, RP §7-109.
Settlement conference.
Alternative dispute resolution, ADR Rule 17-102.
Health care malpractice, alternative dispute resolution, CJ §3-2A-06C.
Settlement expenses.
Down payment and settlement expense loan program, HS §4-301.
Setups.
Alcoholic beverages.
Howard county, 2B §20-106.
Prince George's county, 2B §20-108.1.
Several systems, SPP §21-102.
Pensions.
Fiduciary responsibilities, SPP §21-201.
Severe injury.
Dangerous dogs, CR §10-619.
Severe physical injury.
Child abuse, CR §3-601.
Severn river watershed.
Water management, EN §4-301.
Sewage.
Marine sewage, NR §8-741.
Sanitary commissions, EN §9-601.
Sanitary facilities, EN §9-201.
Sewerage systems, EN §9-501.

DEFINED TERMS —Cont'd

Sewage —Cont'd
Vessels and boats.
Marine sanitation devices, NR §8-741.
Water and sewer authorities, EN §9-901.
Water pollution, EN §9-301.
Sewage disposal company, PUC §1-101.
Sewage sludge.
Chesapeake Bay and tributaries, EN §5-1101.
Sanitary facilities, EN §9-201.
Sewage sludge generator.
Sanitary facilities, EN §9-201.
Sewage sludge utilization permit.
Sanitary facilities, EN §9-201.
Sewage sludge utilizer.
Sanitary facilities, EN §9-201.
Sewage treatment plant, EN §9-342.1.
Sewerage facility.
Sewerage bonds, EN §9-801.
Sewerage system, EN §9-501.
Sanitary commissions, EN §9-601.
Sanitary facilities, EN §9-201.
Water and sewer authorities, EN §9-901.
Water pollution, EN §9-301.
Sexual abuse.
Abuse or neglect of vulnerable adult, CR §3-604.
Child abuse, CR §3-602; FL §5-701.
Children in need of assistance, CJ §3-801.
Sexual act.
Prostitution and related crimes, CR §11-301.
Sexual crimes, CR §3-301.
Sexual conduct.
Adult sexual displays, CR §11-101.
Obscene matter, CR §11-201.
Sexual contact.
Prostitution and related crimes, CR §11-301.
Sexual crimes, CR §3-301.
Sexual excitement.
Adult sexual displays, CR §11-101.
Obscene matter, CR §11-201.
Sexually violent offender.
Sex offender registration, CP §11-701.
Sexually violent offense.
Sex offender registration, CP §11-701.
Sexually violent predator.
Sex offender registration, CP §11-701.
Sexual misconduct.
Health occupations, HO §1-212.
Sexual offense.
Consecutive sentences, COR §9-201.
Sexual orientation.
Employment discrimination, 49B §16.
Hate crimes, CR §10-301.
Housing discrimination, 49B §20.
Shaft.
Mines and mining, EN §15-101.
Shallow land burial.
Radioactive waste, EN §7-301.
Share.
Credit unions, FI §6-101.
Real estate investment trusts, CA §8-101.
Share account.
Credit unions, FI §6-101.
Shared facility.
Sanitary commissions, EN §9-672.
Shared physical custody.
Child support guidelines, FL §12-201.
Share exchange.
Corporations, CA §1-101.
Shell business entity.
Investments of life insurers, IN §5-511.

DEFINED TERMS —Cont'd

Shell casing.
Handgun identification requirements, PS §5-131.

Shell eggs.
Egg law, AG §4-301.

Shellfish.
Weights and measures, AG §11-101.

Shelter care.
Children in need of assistance, CJ §3-801.
Juvenile causes, CJ §3-8A-01.

Shelter care hearing.
Children in need of assistance, CJ §3-801.

Sheltered workshop.
Pharmacy assistance program, HG §15-124.
Procurement, SF §14-101.

Shelter, nutrition and service program.
Homeless individual, 88A §132.

Sheriff.
Harford county, CR §13-1501.
St. Mary's county, CR §13-2101.

Shinnecock rake.
Oysters and clams, NR §§4-1001, 4-1101.

Ship lifeboat, NR §8-701.

Shipper.
Documents of title, CL §7-102.

Shipper's weight, load and count.
Documents of title, CL §7-301.

Shipping container.
Poultry products inspection act, AG §4-201.

Ship-to-shore communication device.
Vessels and boats, NR §8-740.1.

Shooting blind or shooting stand.
Waterfowl, NR §10-1001.

Shoplift.
Shoplifting and employee theft.
Courts, CJ §3-1301.

Shopping center.
Gas or electric meters, PUC §7-303.
Mobile seafood vendors, TR §24-301.
Submetering, PUC §7-303.

Shopping mall.
Telecommunications for disabled individuals, SF §3-902.

Shore erosion control project, NR §8-1001.
Short-barreled rifle, CR §4-201; PS §5-201.
Short-barreled shotgun, CR §4-201; PS §5-201.
Short term car or truck rental.
Taxation, TG §11-104.

Short-term debt.
Reporting requirements for public service companies, PUC §6-201.

Short-term loan.
Maryland home financing program, HS §4-801.
Shotgun, CR §4-201; PS §5-201.
Shoulder.
Traffic laws, TR §21-101.

Show.
Business licenses, BR §17-1801.

Shuttle.
Motor vehicles, TR §13-626.

Shuttle permit.
Motor vehicles, TR §13-626.

Siblings.
Adoption search, contact and reunion services, FL §5-4B-01.

SIC code and short title.
Reporting requirements for public service companies, PUC §6-201.

Sidewalk.
Traffic laws, TR §21-101.

DEFINED TERMS —Cont'd

Sign.
Documents of title, CL §7-102.

Signal.
Alarm systems, CR §9-607.

Signatory.
Transportation compacts, TR §10-204.

Signatory party.
Susquehanna river basin compact, EN §5-301.

Signed.
Commercial code, CL §1-201.

Signed print.
Consumer protection.
Fine print, CL §14-501.

Significant beneficial interest.
Private review agents, IN §15-10B-01.

Significant change.
Transportation, TR §2-103.1.

Significant strategic economic development opportunity.
Economic development assistance fund, 83A §5-1401.

Significant violation.
Sewage treatment, EN §9-342.1.

Signs.
Micro-breweries, 2B §12-104.

Simple interest.
Interest in usury, CL §12-101.

Single axle weight.
Vehicle weight, TR §24-109.

Single-drawing raffle.
Carroll county, CR §13-904.

Single parent services, FL §6-101.

Single point of entry.
Children, youth and families services.
Residential child care programs, 49D §7-101.

Single premium coverage.
Closed end credit, insurance, CL §12-1007.
Consumer loans, insurance, CL §12-312.
Homeowner equity protection, CL §§12-124.1, 12-1007.
Secondary mortgage loans, CL §12-410.

Single-service device.
Weights and measures, AG §11-204.

Single site.
Water quality financing, EN §9-1601.

Single-use test device.
Medical laboratories, HG §17-214.

Sinkhole.
Caves, NR §5-1401.

Site.
Hazardous waste facilities, EN §7-401.
Historic area zoning, 66B §8.01.
Industrialized buildings and manufactured homes, PS §12-301.
Power plant and generator lead routes, NR §3-305.

Site rehabilitation.
Oil cleanups, EN §4-701.

Skilled nursing assistant training, HO §8-6A-01.
Skilled service.
State personnel, SPP §1-101.

SLAPP suit, CJ §5-807.
Slate.
Elections, EL §1-101.

Slaughterer.
Livestock slaughtering, AG §4-123.1.

Slope.
Mines and mining, EN §15-101.

Slot machine, CR §12-301.

DEFINED TERMS —Cont'd

Slug.
Theft, CR §7-101.

Small business.
Bills of general assembly, SG §§2-1505.1, 2-1505.2.
Inheritance tax, TG §7-218.
Neighborhood business development program, HS §6-301.
Procurement, SF §14-201.
Small business pollution compliance loan fund, EN §2-801.
Small business reserve program, SF §14-501.

Small business employer.
Military reservists and service-related no-interest loan program, 83A §6-901.

Small business preference.
Procurement, SF §14-201.

Small business reserve, SF §14-501.

Small claim action.
District Court, CJ §4-405.

Small community college.
State and county aid, ED §16-305.

Small denomination bonds.
State debt, SF §8-123.2.

Small employer.
Health insurance, IN §§15-1201, 15-1203.

Small grains.
Renewable energy credits, AG §10-1501.

Small private group home.
Mental hygiene, HG §10-514.

Small procurement, SF §13-109.

Small rural electric cooperative, PUC §1-101.

Smoke.
Mufflers, TR §22-402.

Smokeless tobacco.
Medicaid subrogation claims, HG §15-120.

Smoke screen.
Alcoholic beverages, 2B §16-413.

Smoking.
Tobacco smoking, HG §24-501.

Snack food.
Sales and use tax, TG §11-206.

Snare trap.
Hunting restrictions, NR §10-410.

Snow tires.
Snow emergency routes, TR §21-1119.

Socially and economically disadvantaged individuals.
Procurement, minority business enterprises, SF §14-301.

Socially disadvantaged individuals.
Procurement, minority business enterprises, SF §14-301.

Social organization.
State aid, SF §7-402.

Social security integration level.
Pensions, SPP §20-101.

Social worker rehabilitation committee, HO §19-315.

Society.
Fraternal benefit societies, IN §8-401.

Sod.
Turf grass, AG §9-101.

Soda fountain license.
Business licenses, BR §17-1701.

Soft drink.
Food establishments, HG §21-301.

Soft drink registration.
Food establishments, HG §21-301.

Soft-shell clams, NR §4-1001.

DEFINED TERMS —Cont'd

Software.
Secured transactions, CL §9-102.

Soil conditioner.
Commercial fertilizers, AG §6-201.

Soil conservation, AG §8-101.

Soil conservation and water quality plan.
Nontidal wetlands, EN §5-901.

Soil injection/pressure pumping.
Waterproofing.
Consumer protection, CL §14-12A-01.

Solar energy project.
Community development administration, HS §4-201.
Industrial development financing, 83A §5-901.
Maryland housing fund, HS §3-201.

Solar energy property, TG §10-719.
Solar energy grant program, SG §9-2007.

Solar water heating property, TG §10-719.
Solar energy grant program, SG §9-2007.

Solicit.
Criminal gang offenses, CR §9-801.
Insurance, IN §1-101.
Prostitution and related crimes, CR §11-301.
Sexual solicitation of minor, CR §3-324.

Solicitor.
Door-to-door solicitation, CL §14-2601.
Higher education commission.
Solicitation of students, ED §11-402.

Solid waste.
Controlled hazardous substances, EN §7-201.
Environmental service, NR §3-101.
Sanitary facilities, EN §9-101.

Solid waste acceptance facility.
Sanitary commissions, EN §9-601.
Sewerage systems, EN §9-501.

Solid waste disposal project.
Environmental service, NR §3-101.

Solid waste disposal system.
Sanitary commissions, EN §9-601.
Sewerage systems, EN §9-501.

Solid waste stream.
Recycling, EN §9-1701.

Sound amplification system.
Motor vehicles, TR §21-1122.

Sound level limit.
Noise control, EN §3-101.

Source.
Air quality, EN §2-101.
Noise control, EN §3-101.

Source pool.
Juries, CJ §8-101.

Southern Maryland.
Code counties, 25B §2.
College of southern Maryland, ED §16-602.

Space spraying.
Pesticide application in schools, AG §5-208.1.

Sparkling wine, 2B §1-102.

Speaker.
General assembly, SG §2-101.

Speargun.
Fish and fisheries, NR §4-510.

Special accrued liability.
Employee retirement and pension systems, SPP §21-305.3.
Fire and police pension system, SPP §21-306.
Law enforcement officers' pension system, SPP §21-306.1.

Special administrator.
Estates and trusts, ET §1-101.

DEFINED TERMS —Cont'd
Special deposit claim.
 Continuing care contracts, 70B §7.
 Insurer liquidation, rehabilitation, etc., IN §9-201.
Special education.
 Children with disabilities, ED §8-401.
Special education per pupil amount.
 Special education grants, ED §5-209.
Special education student.
 Special education grants, ED §5-209.
· **Special enrollment period.**
 Health insurance portability, IN §15-1401.
 Small employer health insurance, IN §15-1201.
Special exception.
 Land use, 66B §1.00.
 Zoning and planning, 66B §1.00.
Special fuel.
 Fuel taxes, TG §8-101.
 Motor fuel, BR §10-101.
Special fuel seller.
 Motor fuel tax, TG §9-301.
Special housing facility.
 Community development administration, HS §4-201.
Special indorsement.
 Negotiable instruments, CL §§3-103, 3-205.
Specialists.
 Health insurance, referrals to specialists, IN §15-830.
Specialized appraisal services, BOP §16-402.
Specialized customer premises equipment.
 Distribution of accessible information for disabled persons, SF §3-901.
Specialized economic development opportunity.
 Economic development assistance fund, 83A §5-1401.
Specialized formats.
 Individualized education programs to insure ability to communicate effectively, ED §8-408.
Specialized rehabilitation program, HG §19-1201.
Special loan program.
 Maryland housing rehabilitation program, HS §4-901.
Specially constructed vehicle, TR §13-104.2.
Special mobile equipment.
 Motor vehicles, TR §11-159.
Special order transaction.
 Layaway sales, CL §14-1101.
Special police officers, PS §3-301.
Special retirement or pension system.
 Counties, SPP §39-101.
Special secretary.
 Juvenile justice monitoring unit, SG §6-401.
Special Sunday license.
 Alcoholic beverages, 2B §8-202.
Special thoroughbred racing.
 Horse racing, BR §11-101.
Specialty fertilizer.
 Commercial fertilizers, AG §6-201.
Specialty mental health services.
 Medical assistance, HG §15-101.
Species.
 Fish and fisheries.
  Endangered species, NR §4-2A-01.
 Nongame and endangered species conservation, NR §10-2A-01.
Specific attachment point.
 Health insurance, stop-loss policies, IN §15-129.

DEFINED TERMS —Cont'd
Specific funds.
 Preneed burial contracts, BR §5-701.
Specific license.
 Radiation, EN §8-101.
Specified disease policy, HG §19-713.1.
 Health insurance, IN §§15-104, 15-109.
Specimen.
 Medical laboratories, HG §17-214.
Specimen ballot, EL §1-101.
Specimen of blood.
 Implied consent law, TR §16-205.1.
Speech-language pathologists.
 Health occupations, HO §2-101.
Speech-language pathologists rehabilitation committee.
 Speech pathologists, HO §2-318.1.
Speed monitoring system.
 Speed restrictions on motor vehicles, Montgomery county, TR §21-809.
Speed monitoring system operator.
 Speed restrictions on motor vehicles, Montgomery county, TR §21-809.
Speleogen.
 Caves, NR §5-1401.
Speleothem.
 Caves, NR §5-1401.
Spoil.
 Hart-Miller-Pleasure Island chain, NR §5-1202.2.
Spoil pile.
 Strip mining, EN §15-501.
 Surface mining, EN §15-801.
Sponsor.
 Community energy loan program, SG §9-2101.
 Elections.
  Petitions, EL §6-101.
 Local land preservation programs, NR §5-9B-01.
 Maryland housing rehabilitation program, HS §4-901.
 Rental housing production program, HS §4-1501.
 Rural legacy program, NR §5-9A-02.
Sponsoring organization.
 Child passenger safety technicians, CJ §5-640.
Sponsoring physician.
 Automated external defibrillator program, ED §13-517.
Sports facility.
 Stadium authority, FI §13-701.
Sport shooting range, CJ §5-403.1.
Sports program.
 Volunteer physicians.
  Civil liability, CJ §5-607.
Spousal support order.
 Uniform interstate family support act, FL §10-301.
Sprinkler systems, PS §9-201.
Stadium authority.
 Amusement tax, TG §4-101.
Staff meeting.
 St. Mary's county open meetings, 24 §4-202.
Staff member.
 Pesticide application in schools, AG §5-208.1.
Stakeholder.
 Administrative procedure.
  Regulations, SG §10-130.
Stalking, CR §3-802.
Stamped.
 Consumer protection.
  Gold and silver, CL §14-601.
Stamped cigarettes.
 Cigarette licenses, BR §16-201.

DEFINED TERMS —Cont'd

Stand.
Motor vehicles, TR §11-160.
Standard deduction.
Taxation, TG §10-217.
Standard form.
Computer information transactions, CL §22-102.
Standardized test.
Public schools, ED §7-204.
Standard license.
Real estate brokers, BOP §17-3A-01.
Standard offer service.
Electric customer choice and competition act, PUC §7-501.
Standard plan.
Small employer health insurance, IN §15-1201.
Standard rate.
Unemployment compensation.
Contributions, LE §8-608.
Standard reference compendia.
Health insurance, IN §15-804.
Standards.
Building codes, PS §12-501.
Standby guardian, ET §13-901.
Standing committee.
General assembly, SG §2-101.
Star knife, CR §4-101.
Starter dosage.
Nurses, HO §8-508.
State.
Adult offender supervision, COR §6-203.
Athlete agents, BR §4-401.
Bank holding companies, FI §5-901.
Business and economic development, 83A §1-101.
Business occupations and professions, BOP §1-101.
Certification of questions of law, CJ §12-601.
Compact for education, ED §25-102.
Computer information transactions, CL §22-102.
Correctional services, COR §1-101.
Criminal law, CR §1-101.
Criminal procedure, CP §1-101.
Discipline of attorneys, CJA Rule 16-701.
Discretionary trusts, ET §14-401.
Driver license compact, TR §16-703.
Educational personnel.
Qualifications, ED §6-604.
Electronic transactions, CL §21-101.
Environmental covenant, EN §1-801.
Extradition, CP §9-101.
Extradition of persons of unsound mind, HG §10-1301.
Family law, FL §1-101.
Health occupations, HO §1-101.
Higher education.
Auxiliary and academic facilities bond authority, ED §19-101.
Insurance, IN §1-101.
Insurer liquidation, rehabilitation, etc., IN §9-201.
Interstate agreement on detainers, COR §8-404.
Interstate corrections compact, COR §8-603.
Interstate insurance product regulation compact, IN §29-101.
Interstate mining compact, EN §15-901.
Interstate wildlife violator compact, NR §10-1201.
Juvenile services, 83C §1-101.
Labor and employment, LE §1-101.
Limited liability companies, CA §4A-101.
Limited partnerships, CA §10-101.
Mortgage lending, FI §11-501.
Motor vehicles, TR §11-161.

DEFINED TERMS —Cont'd

State —Cont'd
National crime prevention and privacy compact, CP §10-239.
National racing compact, BR §11-1301.
Partnerships, revised act, CA §9A-101.
Political subdivisions, 24 §1-101.
Procurement, SF §11-101.
Property tax, TP §1-101.
Public safety, PS §1-101.
Public utility companies, PUC §1-101.
Risk retention groups, IN §25-101.
Secured transactions, CL §9-102.
Securities, CA §11-101.
State finance, SF §§1-101, 2-301.
State government, SG §1-101.
State personnel, SPP §1-101.
Transportation compacts, TR §10-204.
Unemployment insurance, LE §8-101.
Uniform act on fresh pursuit, CP §2-304.
Uniform child custody jurisdiction and enforcement act, FL §9.5-101.
Uniform interstate family support act, FL §10-301.
URESA, FL §10-301.
Year 2000 litigation, CJ §5-527.
State active duty.
Militia, PS §13-101.
State administrator.
Elections, EL §1-101.
State adopted federal regulation.
Packaging, HG §22-301.
State adopted federal rule or regulation.
Food and drugs, HG §21-201.
State advisory council.
Mental hygiene, HG §10-101.
Physical fitness, HG §13-401.
State agencies.
Environmental policy, NR §1-301.
Income tax refunds, TG §13-912.
State publications depository and distribution, ED §23-301.
State aid.
Social organizations, SF §7-402.
State airway.
Aviation, TR §5-207.
State appropriation.
Baltimore City community college, ED §16-502.
State bank, FI §3-101.
State board.
Elections, EL §1-101.
Foster care, FL §5-501.
State bond.
State debt, SF §8-101.
State complex.
Child care centers, FL §5-586.
State comprehensive plan.
Managing for results, SF §3-1001.
State contributory employee' pension system, SPP §37-101.
State contributory law enforcement officers' pension system, SPP §37-101.
State contributory teachers' pension system, SPP §37-101.
State correctional facilities, COR §1-101.
Consecutive sentences for sexual offenses, COR §9-201.
Construction of facilities, COR §10-101.
Criminal law, CR §1-101.
Criminal procedure, CP §1-101.
Procurement, SF §11-101.

DEFINED TERMS —Cont'd
State council.
Adult offender supervision, COR §6-203.
State dairy regulation.
Northeast interstate dairy compact, AG §2-801.
State debt.
Finance and procurement, SF §8-101.
Stated rate of interest.
Interest in usury, CL §12-101.
State employees' leave bank, SPP §9-601.
State facility.
Executive branch of government, SG §8-306.
Mental hygiene, HG §10-101.
Sale and transfer of state owned cemeteries, SF §10-309.
State fair society.
Horse racing, BR §11-523.
State finance, SF §1-101.
State financial institution.
Deposit of unexpended or surplus money by local government, 95 §22O.
State-funded stem cell research.
Maryland stem cell research program, 83A §5-2B-01.
State health plan, HG §19-114.
Medicaid fraud, CR §8-508.
State highway, TR §8-101.
Mobile seafood vendors, TR §24-301.
State highway system, TR §8-101.
State historic preservation officer.
Maryland historical trust, SF §5A-301.
State income tax, TG §§2-601, 10-101.
State issuer.
Allocation of private activity bond authority, FI §13-801.
General assembly.
Private activity bonds, SG §2-1010.
State jukebox license.
Business licenses, BR §17-1301.
State junk license.
Business licenses, BR §17-1005.
State license.
Electricians, BOP §6-101.
State lottery, SG §9-101.
State member.
State retirement and pension system, SPP §21-304.
Statement.
Child crime victims, CP §11-304.
Partnerships, revised act, CA §9A-101.
Statement of charges.
Discipline of attorneys, CJA Rule 16-701.
Law enforcement officers, CJ §2-608.
Statement of lien.
Contract liens, RP §14-201.
State money.
State treasury, SF §6-201.
State-occupied building.
Child care centers, FL §5-586.
State official.
Public ethics, SG §15-102.
State of Maryland.
Foreign discriminatory boycotts, CL §11-102.
State of nuisance.
Natural resources, NR §4-205.1.
State of principal use.
Boats and boating, NR §8-701.
State or local public safety employee.
Student financial assistance, ED §18-601.
State or local retirement or pension system, SPP §37-101.

DEFINED TERMS —Cont'd
State performance standards.
Schools, comprehensive master plans, ED §5-401.
State personnel.
Immunity and liability, SG §12-101.
Payment of settlements and judgments, SG §12-401.
State pest control compact, AG §5-702.
State plan.
Developmental disabilities, HG §7-301.
State plan for higher education, ED §10-101.
State plumbing code, BOP §12-101.
State police officer.
Vehicle preventive maintenance, TR §23-301.
State police retirement system.
Pensions, SPP §20-101.
State postconviction review process.
Warrant of execution, COR §3-902.
State priority funding area.
Job creation tax credits, 83A §5-1101.
State property tax, TP §1-101.
State publication.
Depository and distribution, ED §23-301.
State public body.
Housing authorities, HS §12-101.
State report on transportation.
Transportation, TR §1-101.
State residential center.
Developmental disabilities, HG §7-101.
State room.
Government house trust, SG §9-606.
State's attorney.
Legal officials, 10 §39A.
State service.
State personnel, SPP §2-508.
State set-aside product.
State standby petroleum fuel set-aside program, PS §14-501.
State set-aside program.
State standby petroleum fuel set-aside program, PS §14-501.
State set-aside volume.
State standby petroleum fuel set-aside program, PS §14-501.
State share.
Community colleges.
State and county aid, ED §16-305.
State share of compensatory education funding, ED §5-207.
State share of LEP funding.
Grants for limited-English proficiency education, ED §5-208.
State share of special education funding.
Special education grants, ED §5-209.
State share of the foundation program.
Educational financing.
State assistance, ED §5-202.
State sources.
Residential boarding education programs for at-risk youth, ED §8-709.
State subcontractor.
Commercial discrimination, SF §19-103.
State superintendent.
Child care centers, FL §§5-570, 5-586.
Early childhood development advisory council, FL §5-590.
Family day care homes, FL §5-550.
State supplemental plan.
State retirement and pension system.
Optional defined contribution system, SPP §32-101.

DEFINED TERMS —Cont'd
State system.
Legislative pension plan, SG Title 2 Subtitle 3 (note).
Pensions, SPP §20-101.
State tax.
Taxation, TG §13-504.
State unit.
Development permits, SG §11-101.
Maryland historical trust, SF §5A-301.
State veterans' cemetery, SG §9-906.
State wetlands.
Wetlands and riparian rights, EN §16-101.
Statewide academic health center.
Cancer prevention, education, screening and treatment program, HG §13-1101.
Statewide academic health center cancer research grant.
Cancer prevention, education, screening and treatment program, HG §13-1101.
Statewide academic health center component.
Cancer prevention, education, screening and treatment program, HG §13-1101.
Statewide academic health center network grant.
Cancer prevention, education, screening and treatment program, HG §13-1101.
Statewide academic health center tobacco-related diseases research grant.
Cancer prevention, education, screening and treatment program, HG §13-1101.
Statewide DNA database system, PS §2-501.
Statewide DNA repository, PS §2-501.
Statewide public health component.
Tobacco use prevention and cessation program, HG §13-1001.
Statewide wealth per pupil.
Grants for limited-English proficiency education, ED §5-208.
Schools, compensatory education grants, ED §5-207.
Schools, guaranteed tax base grants, ED §5-210.
Special education grants, ED §5-209.
State wildlands.
Forests and parks, NR §5-1201.
Stationary engineer, BOP §6.5-101.
Statutory merger.
Savings and loan associations, FI §9-101.
Statutory pension plan.
Legislative pension plan, SG Title 2 Subtitle 3 (note).
Stem cell.
Maryland stem cell research program, 83A §5-2B-01.
Stepchild.
Death benefits, public safety officers and personnel, PS §1-202.
Death benefits, survivors of state employees, SPP §10-404.
Estates and trusts, ET §3-104.
Step-down aftercare, 83C §2-127.1.
Step-down aftercare plan, 83C §2-127.1.
Stinger-steered automobile transporter.
Vehicle length and loads, TR §24-104.1.
Stock acquisition.
Commercial banks, FI §3-314.
Stockholder.
Corporations, CA §1-101.
Unsolicited takeovers of corporations and real estate investment trusts, CA §3-801.

DEFINED TERMS —Cont'd
Stockholder rights plan.
Corporations, CA §1-101.
Stock in business.
Property tax, TP §8-110.
Stock insurer, IN §1-101.
Stockyard.
Livestock slaughtering, AG §4-123.1.
Stop.
Motor vehicles, TR §11-162.
Stop-loss insurance.
Health insurance, stop-loss policies, IN §15-129.
Stop-sale.
Seeds, AG §9-201.
Storage building.
Fireworks, PS §10-101.
Storage warehouse.
Cigarette licenses, BR §16-201.
Stored value device.
Money transmission, FI §12-401.
Storehouse.
Burglary, CR §6-201.
Store scrap tires.
Sanitary facilities, EN §9-201.
Strategic plan.
Managing for results, SF §3-1001.
Straw purchase.
Firearms, PS §5-101.
Stream buffer.
Forest conservation, NR §5-1601.
Street, TR §11-163.
Highways, TR §8-101.
Street railroad, PUC §1-101.
Street rod.
Motor vehicles, TR §13-937.1.
Strike.
Labor relations.
Community colleges, ED §16-412.
Montgomery county housing opportunities commission, collective bargaining, HS §16-317.
Prince George's county public employment relations, ED §16-414.1.
State personnel.
Collective bargaining, SPP §3-303.
Strip mining.
Coal, EN §15-501.
Structural defect.
New home warranties, RP §10-601.
Structure.
Arson and burning, CR §6-101.
Aviation, TR §5-101.
Building codes, PS §12-501.
Historic area zoning, 66B §8.01.
Riots, PS §14-1001.
Structured settlement.
Tort claims act, SG §12-107.
Transfer of payment rights, CJ §5-1101.
Structured settlement agreement.
Transfer of payment rights, CJ §5-1101.
Structured settlement obligor.
Transfer of payment rights, CJ §5-1101.
Structured settlement payment rights.
Transfer, CJ §5-1101.
Student.
Approved paid work-based learning programs, ED §21-501.
Polysomnographic technologists, HO §13-5C-01.
Technology for education, ED §7-901.
Student-athlete.
Athlete agents, BR §4-401.

DEFINED TERMS —Cont'd
Student credit hours.
Baltimore City community college, ED §16-502.
Community colleges.
State and county aid, ED §16-305.
Student loan.
Credit unions, FI §6-609.
Judgments, CJ §11-106.
Student loan repayment pilot program, SPP §10-501.
Studies.
Abandoned mine drainage control, EN §15-701.
Study Center.
Emergency medical services.
University of Maryland, ED §13-501.
Subagent.
Real estate brokers, BOP §17-528.
Subcontracted work authorization.
Dental laboratory, HO §4-401.
Subcontractor.
Home improvement, BR §8-101.
Mechanics' liens, RP §9-101.
Subcontractor's license.
Home improvement, BR §8-101.
Subdivision.
Flood control and watershed management, EN §5-801.
Forest conservation, NR §5-1601.
Forests and parks.
Open space program, NR §5-901.
Hazardous waste facilities, EN §7-401.
Land use, 66B §1.00.
Northeast Maryland waste disposal authority, NR §3-904.
Sewerage systems, EN §9-501.
State police.
Protection fund, 41 §4-403.
Zoning and planning, 66B §1.00.
Subdivision approval, RP §3-108.1.
Subdivision lines.
Washington suburban sanitary district, 29 §3-101.1.
Subdivision of the state.
Heating and air conditioning, BR §9A-101.
Subfranchisor, BR §14-201.
Subject of insurance.
Insurance companies.
Limitation of risk, IN §5-1001.
Sublease.
Commercial code, CL §2A-103.
Submerged.
Maryland historical trust, SF §5A-301.
Submerged aquatic vegetation, NR §4-213.
Submerged archaeological historic property.
Maryland historical trust, archaeological property, SF §5A-333.
Submetering.
Electric and gas meters, PUC §7-303.
Gas or electric meters, PUC §7-303.
Submission date.
Enterprise zones, 83A §5-401.
Subordination agreement.
Mortgages and deeds of trust.
Subordination of lender's interest, RP §4-111.
Subpoena.
Financial institutions.
Confidential records, FI §1-304.
Subrogation.
Provision included in contract, HG §19-713.1.
Adjusted rate methodology reflecting provision, HG §19-713.

DEFINED TERMS —Cont'd
Subscriber.
Consumer cooperatives, CA §5-5A-02.
Continuing care contracts, 70B §7.
HMOS, HG §19-701.
Insurance, IN §3-201.
Preferred provider organizations, IN §14-201.
Subsequent interest.
Inheritance tax, TG §7-201.
Subsequent proceedings.
Post-conviction proceedings, CP §11-503.
Subsidence.
Deep mine control, EN §15-601.
Subsidiary.
Corporations, CA §3-601.
Homeowner's insurance, geographic distribution of premiums, IN §11-321.
Insurance acquisitions disclosure and control, IN §7-101.
Motor vehicle insurance, IN §11-321.
Nonprofit health service plans, IN §14-133.
Savings and loan associations.
Board of commissioners and division, FI §8-101.
Interstate acquisitions, FI §9-1001.
Unsolicited takeovers of corporations and real estate investment trusts, CA §3-801.
Subsidiary corporation.
Recordation taxes, TP §12-101.
Transfer taxes, TP §13-101.
Subsidiary savings bank, FI §4-101.
Subsidy.
Adoption subsidy act, FL §5-401.
Subsidy factor.
Maryland health care provider rate stabilization fund, IN §19-801.
Substance abuse testing.
Integration of child welfare and substance abuse treatment act, FL §5-1201.
Substance abuse treatment.
Integration of child welfare and substance abuse treatment act, FL §5-1201.
Substance abuse treatment personnel.
Integration of child welfare and substance abuse treatment act, FL §5-1201.
Substantial financial interest.
Health occupations, HO §1-101.
Substantial grocery or market business.
County resort taxes, 25B §13H.
Sales and use tax, TG §11-206.
Substantial labor surplus area.
Steel procurement, SF §17-304.
Substantially alter.
Airport zoning, TR §§5-501, 5-601.
Noise zones.
Aviation, TR §5-801.
Substantial rehabilitation.
Maryland historical trust, rehabilitation tax credits, SF §5A-303.
Substantively, EN §1-101.
Administrative procedures, SG §10-101.
Substituted judgment.
Disabled persons, ET §13-711.
Subwholesaler.
Cigarette licenses, BR §16-201.
Succeeding insurer.
Health insurance, IN §15-415.
Succeeding policy.
Health insurance, IN §15-415.
Successor.
Commercial banks.
Consolidations, mergers and transfers of assets, FI §3-701.

DEFINED TERMS —Cont'd
Successor —Cont'd
Corporations, CA §§1-101, 3-201.
Recordation taxes, TP §12-101.
Transfer taxes, TP §13-101.
Successor employer.
Unemployment insurance.
Contributions, LE §8-613.
Successor fiduciary.
Trusts, ET §15-1A-01.
Successor of a beneficiary.
Letters of credit, CL §5-102.
Suicide.
Assisted suicide, CR §3-101.
Suit.
Charitable organization.
Volunteer liability, CJ §5-407.
Personal liability of agents of certain associations
or organizations, CJ §5-406.
Volunteers and physicians.
Charitable health care services, CJ §5-606.
Suitable gainful employment.
Workers' compensation.
Vocational rehabilitation, LE §9-675.
Suitable work.
Unemployment insurance.
Extended benefits, LE §8-1104.
Summer.
Summer youth connection program, LE §11-602.
Summons.
Courts, CJ §9-301.
Family law, FL §1-101.
Superintendent.
Mines and mining, EN §15-101.
Waterworks operators, EN §12-101.
Superseded part.
Equipment dealer contracts, CL §19-101.
Supervisee.
Drinking driver monitor program supervision fees,
COR §6-115.
Probation, CP §6-226.
Supervising appraiser.
Real estate appraiser trainees, BOP §16-101.
Supervising authority.
Sex offender registration, CP §11-701.
Supervising law enforcement officer.
Hostage and barricade situations, CJ §10-413.
Supervising physician.
Physician assistants, HO §15-101.
Supervision.
Acupuncture, HO §1A-101.
Dentistry, HO §4-101.
Dietitians and nutritionists, HO §5-101.
Occupational therapists, HO §10-101.
Pesticide applicators, AG §5-201.
Pharmacists and pharmacies, HO §12-101.
Physician assistants, HO §15-101.
Polysomnographic technologists, HO §13-5C-01.
Radiation oncology/therapy, medical radiation, and
nuclear medicine technologists, HO
§14-5B-01.
Real estate appraiser trainees, BOP §16-101.
Respiratory care, HO §14-5A-01.
Social workers, HO §19-101.
Supervision fee.
Drinking driver monitor program supervision fees,
COR §6-115.
Supervisor.
Health care worker whistleblower protection, HO
§1-501.
Property tax, TP §1-101.

DEFINED TERMS —Cont'd
Supervisor —Cont'd
Tobacco smoking, HG §24-501.
Supervisory agency.
Financial institutions.
Confidential records, FI §1-301.
Supervisory employee.
Labor relations.
Community colleges, ED §16-412.
Labor unions.
Schools, ED §6-501.
Prince George's county public employment
relations, ED §16-414.1.
Supervisory official.
Evidence, CJ §10-4A-06.
Supplement.
Judges' retirement system, SPP §27-407.
Supplemental board.
State retirement and pension system.
Optional defined contribution system, SPP
§32-101.
Supplemental contract.
Life and health insurance guaranty corporation,
IN §9-401.
Supplemental foods, HG §18-108.
Supplemental instrument of writing.
Recordation taxes, TP §12-101.
Supplemental plan.
State retirement and pension system, SPP
§21-601.
Supplemental retirement plans, SPP §35-101.
State retirement and pension system, SPP
§30-101.
Supplementary rate information.
Insurance, IN §11-101.
Supplementary services.
Public assistance programs, 88A §64.
Supplementation.
Judicial compensation, CJ §1-705.
Supplier.
Commercial code, CL §2A-103.
Equipment dealer contracts, CL §19-101.
Injury to person or property.
Limitation of actions, CJ §5-108.
Little Miller Act, SF §17-101.
State standby petroleum fuel set-aside program,
PS §14-501.
Supplier of water, EN §9-401.
Supplies.
Procurement, SF §§4-301, 11-101.
Supply contract.
Commercial code, CL §2A-103.
Supply dealer.
Bedding, HG §24-401.
Support, FL §§1-101, 10-101, 10-120.
Support and maintenance, FL §10-120.
Support enforcement agency, FL §10-101.
Uniform interstate family support act, FL
§10-301.
Supporting obligation.
Secured transactions, CL §9-102.
Supportive housing arrangement.
Adult residential environment program, 88A §138.
Supportive services.
Workforce investment act, LE §11-503.
Support order.
Uniform interstate family support act, FL
§10-301.
URESA, FL §10-301.
Support services.
Developmental disabilities, HG §7-709.

DEFINED TERMS —Cont'd

Surcharge.
Continuing care contracts, 70B §7.
Surety.
Bail bondsmen, IN §10-301.
Commercial code, CL §1-201.
Retail installment sales, CL §12-601.
Sales finance companies, FI §11-401.
Uniform commercial code, CL §1-201.
Surety bond.
Property and casualty insurance guaranty corporation, IN §9-301.
Surety company.
Traffic citation, TR §26-404.
Surety device.
Money transmission, FI §12-401.
Surety insurance, IN §1-101.
Surety insurer.
Bail bondsmen, IN §10-301.
Surface coal mining, EN §15-501.
Surface mining, EN §15-801.
Surgeon.
Anatomical gift act, ET §4-501.
Surgical services.
Freestanding ambulatory care facilities, HG §19-3B-01.
Surimi.
Food establishments, HG §21-301.
Surplus.
Nonprofit health service plans, IN §14-117.
Surplus lines insurance, IN §1-101.
Surplus personal property.
Procurement, SF §4-501.
Surplus to policyholders.
Insurance companies.
Limitation of risk, IN §5-1001.
Surveillance and evaluation component.
Cancer prevention, education, screening and treatment program, HG §13-1101.
Tobacco use prevention and cessation program, HG §13-1001.
Surveillance image.
Access to public records, SG §10-616.
Dumping site surveillance systems, CR §10-112.
Survey.
Geological survey, NR §2-101.
Land patents, RP §13-101.
Surveyor.
Land patents, RP §13-101.
Surviving credit union, FI §6-803.
Surviving spouse.
Morticians, HO §7-101.
Property tax credits.
Fallen rescue workers, TP §9-210.
Property tax exemptions.
Blind individual, TP §7-207.
Disabled veteran, TP §7-208.
Student financial assistance, ED §18-601.
Survivor allowance.
Legislative pension plan, SG Title 2 Subtitle 3 (note).
Suspend.
Motor vehicles, TR §11-164.
Suspends payments.
Bank deposits and collections, CL §4-104.
Suspension.
Discipline of attorneys, CJA Rule 16-701.
Interstate wildlife violator compact, NR §10-1201.
Sustained compliance.
Nursing homes, HG §19-1401.

DEFINED TERMS —Cont'd

Swap agreement.
Insurance companies, liquidation and rehabilitation, IN §9-229.1.
Sworn officer.
State police.
Protection fund, 41 §4-403.
Synthetic investment contract.
Insurance advisers, IN §10-202.
System.
Automated mapping-geographic information, SG §10-901.
Distribution of accessible information for disabled persons, SF §3-901.
Higher education.
Auxiliary and academic facilities bond authority, ED §19-101.
Municipal bonds, EN §9-701.
State police department, interagency law enforcement system, PS §2-305.
System institution.
State personnel, SPP §3-101.
System products.
Automated mapping-geographic information systems, SG §10-901.
System repair.
Washington suburban sanitary district, 29 §10-107.
System review.
Accountants.
Peer review, BOP §2-4A-01.
Systems development life cycle plan.
State finance.
Information technology, SF §3-402.
System services.
Automated mapping-geographic information systems, SG §10-901.
Tag.
Consumer protection.
Gold and silver, CL §14-601.
Take.
Fish and fisheries.
Endangered species, NR §4-2A-01.
Nongame and endangered species conservation, NR §10-2A-01.
Takeout.
Horse racing, BR §11-101.
Taking under the power of eminent domain.
Condominiums, RP §11-112.
Tamper.
Drinking water, EN §9-401.
Tandem axles.
Load limits, TR §24-108.
Tandem axle weight.
Vehicle weight, TR §24-109.
Tangible chattel paper.
Secured transactions, CL §9-102.
Tangible personal property.
Sales tax, TG §11-101.
Tangible personal property used in a manufacturing process.
Sales and use tax, TG §11-107.
Tank vehicle.
Commercial drivers' licenses, TR §16-803.
Targeted area.
Forests and parks.
Open space program, NR §5-901.
Targeted cancer.
Cancer prevention, education, screening and treatment program, HG §13-1101.

DEFINED TERMS —Cont'd
Targeted minority population.
  Tobacco use prevention and cessation program,
    HG §13-1001.
Target per pupil foundation amount.
  Educational financing.
    State assistance, ED §5-202.
Task force report.
  Cancer prevention, education, screening and
    treatment program, HG §13-1101.
  Tobacco use prevention and cessation program,
    HG §13-1001.
Taxable assessment.
  Property tax.
    Homestead credit, TP §9-105.
Taxable expenditures.
  Trusts, ET §14-303.
Taxable income.
  Health care charges, HG §16-405.
Taxable net earnings.
  Franchise taxes, TG §8-201.
Taxable price.
  County resort taxes, 25B §13H.
  Sales tax, TG §11-101.
Taxable service.
  Sales tax, TG §11-101.
Taxable wage base.
  Pension, SPP §20-101.
  Unemployment insurance.
    Contributions, LE §8-601.
Taxable year.
  Property tax, TP §1-101.
Taxable year income tax, TG §10-101.
Tax collector, TG §13-101.
  Political subdivisions, 24 §1-101.
Tax court, TG §§3-101, 13-501.
Tax determining agency, TG §13-501.
Tax district.
  Emergency management, PS §14-404.
Taxes.
  Eminent domain, RP §12-110.
  Estate tax, TG §7-308.
  Property tax.
    Collection, TP §14-801.
    Reciprocity, TP §1-302.
Taxicab, PUC §1-101; TR §11-165.
  Open containers of alcoholic beverages in motor
    vehicles, CR §10-123.
Taxicab driver's license, PUC §10-101.
Taxicab license.
  Criminal history records checks, CP §10-234.
Tax information, TG §13-201.
  Political subdivisions, 24 §9-702.
  Property tax, TP §1-301.
Taxing authority.
  Property tax.
    Constant yield tax rate, TP §§2-205, 6-308.
Taxing jurisdiction.
  Property taxes, TP §9-229.
Taxing official, TG §13-203.
  Property tax, TP §2-207.
  Withholding income tax refunds, TG §13-920.
Tax on commissions, TG §1-101.
Taxpayer.
  Alcoholic beverages.
    Prince George's and St. Mary's counties, 2B
      §1-102.
Taxpayer identity information, TG §13-205.
Tax preference items, TG §10-222.
Tax roll.
  Property tax, TP §1-101.

DEFINED TERMS —Cont'd
Tax setoff.
  County tax rate in certain municipal corporations,
    TP §6-305.
Tax stamp.
  Alcoholic beverage tax, TG §5-101.
  Tobacco tax, TG §12-101.
Tax supported debt.
  State debt, SF §8-104.
Teach.
  McAuliffe teacher education award, ED §18-703.
Teacher.
  McAuliffe teacher education award, ED §18-703.
Teacher recipient.
  McAuliffe teacher education award, ED §18-703.
Teachers' pension system, SPP §20-101.
Teachers' retirement system.
  Pensions, SPP §20-101.
Technical assistance.
  After-school opportunity fund program, ED
    §7-1201.
  Priority funding areas, SF §5-7B-01.
Technical assistance grant.
  Self-help homeownership technical assistance
    program, HS §4-1701.
Technology.
  Community colleges, ED §16-318.
    Contributions, ED §16-317.
  Morgan State University, ED §14-109.
  Technology for education, ED §7-901.
Technology-based business.
  Franchises, 83A §5-1041.
Tefillin.
  Kosher products, CL §14-901.
Telecast.
  Boxing tax, TG §6-101.
Telecommunications.
  Procurement, SF §3-701.
  State finance, SF §3-402.
Telecommunications device or access code.
  Telecommunications theft, CR §7-313.
Telecommunication service provider.
  Telecommunications theft, CR §7-313.
Telecommunication services.
  Telecommunications theft, CR §7-313.
  Telephone slamming, PUC §8-401.
Telegram.
  Uniform commercial code, CL §1-201.
Telegraph company, PUC §1-101.
  Private communication, divulging or failing to
    deliver, CR §3-906.
Telegraph lines, PUC §1-101.
  Private communication, divulging or failing to
    deliver, CR §3-906.
Telephone.
  Records, obtaining without authorization, CR
    §7-304.
Telephone company, PUC §1-101.
  Private communication, divulging or failing to
    deliver, CR §3-906.
  Records, obtaining without authorization, CR
    §7-304.
Telephone directory.
  Recycling, EN §9-1709.
Telephone lifeline service, PUC §8-201.
Telephone lines, PUC §1-101.
  Private communication, divulging or failing to
    deliver, CR §3-906.
Telephone records, CR §7-304.
Telephone solicitation, CL §14-2201.
  Access to public records, SG §10-611.

DEFINED TERMS —Cont'd
Telephone solicitation —Cont'd
Caller identification blocking, PUC §8-205.
Motor vehicle administration, TR §12-112.
Teller's check.
Negotiable instruments, CL §§3-103, 3-104.
Temporary cash assistance.
Family investment program, 88A §44A.
Temporary employee.
State personnel, SPP §1-101.
Temporary food service facility, HG §21-309.
Temporary license.
Occupational therapists, HO §10-101.
Respiratory care, HO §14-5A-01.
Temporary peace order, CJ §3-1501.
Peace orders, CJ §3-1501.
Temporary protective order.
Domestic violence, FL §4-501.
Tenant.
Nuisance actions, RP §14-120.
Real property, RP §1-101.
Security deposits, RP §8-203.
Tenant improvements.
Income tax credits, TG §10-722.
Tenant protection assistance.
Assisted housing preservation, HS §7-101.
Tenant space.
Income tax credits, TG §10-722.
Term.
Computer information transactions, CL §22-102.
Uniform commercial code, CL §1-201.
Terminal condition.
Health care decisions, HG §5-601.
Terminally ill.
Viatical settlement contracts, IN §8-601.
Terminal rental adjustment clauses, TR §13-211.
Terminate.
Condominiums, RP §11-102.2.
Termination.
Computer information transactions, CL §22-102.
Equipment dealer contracts, CL §19-101.
Sales, UCC, CL §2-106.
Vehicle insurance, TR §17-101.
Termination of service.
Gas or electric service terminated to low income
customers, PUC §7-307.
Judges' retirement system, SPP §27-101.
Termination statement.
Health insurance, IN §15-408.
Secured transactions, CL §9-102.
Term of confinement.
Diminution credits, COR §3-701.
Revocation of mandatory supervision, COR
§7-504.
Terms of a trust.
Principal and income act, ET §15-501.
Terms of structured settlement.
Transfer of payment rights, CJ §5-1101.
Terms of the citation.
Interstate wildlife violator compact, NR §10-1201.
Terrestrial.
Maryland historical trust, SF §5A-301.
Test.
Fluid dairy products, AG §11-401.
Implied consent law, TR §16-205.1.
Public schools, ED §7-204.
Test objectivity.
Public schools, ED §7-204.
Test reliability.
Public schools, ED §7-204.

DEFINED TERMS —Cont'd
Test validity.
Public schools, ED §7-204.
The arts.
Arts council, 83A §4-608.
The case.
Debt collection, CL §15-101.
The court.
Debt collection, CL §15-101.
The estate.
Debt collection, CL §15-101.
Theft, CR §7-101.
**The person responsible for the payment of the
money.**
Recovery by minor in tort, ET §13-401.
Therapeutically certified optometrist, HO
§11-101.
Therapeutic services.
Health insurance, IN §15-121.
Therapy management contract, HO §12-6A-01.
Thermostat.
Mercury, EN §6-905.
Third party.
Dentistry, HO §4-101.
Nursing homes, Medicaid liability audits and
review, HG §19-14A-01.
Third party claim.
Oil cleanups, EN §4-701.
Third-party filer.
Interstate insurance product regulation compact,
IN §29-101.
Third party liability audit.
Nursing homes, Medicaid liability audits and
review, HG §19-14A-01.
Third party liability review.
Nursing homes, Medicaid liability audits and
review, HG §19-14A-01.
Third party payee.
Family investment programs, 88A §44A.
Third party payor, HO §1-208.
**36-month Moody's corporate bond yield
average.**
Insurance companies.
Standard valuation law, IN §5-306.
Threatened species.
Fish and fisheries, NR §4-2A-01.
Nongame and endangered species conservation,
NR §10-2A-01.
3-D livestock, AG §3-301.
Three-year cycle.
Property tax.
Assessment of real property, TP §8-103.
Through highway.
Traffic laws, TR §21-101.
Tidal fish license, NR §4-101.
Tidal water.
Fish and fisheries, NR §4-101.
Tier 1 renewable source.
Renewable energy portfolio standard, PUC §7-701.
Tier 2 renewable source.
Renewable energy portfolio standard, PUC §7-701.
Tier I LEP funding.
Grants for limited-English proficiency education,
ED §5-208.
Tier II LEP funding.
Grants for limited-English proficiency education,
ED §5-208.
Tier II LEP per pupil amount.
Grants for limited-English proficiency education,
ED §5-208.

DEFINED TERMS —Cont'd

Tier I special education funding.
Special education grants, ED §5-209.
Tier II special education funding.
Special education grants, ED §5-209.
Tier II special education per pupil amount.
Special education grants, ED §5-209.
Timber.
Pine tree reforestation, NR §5-501.
Timber stand improvement, NR §5-219.
Time balance.
Retail installment sales, CL §12-601.
Time deposit.
Commercial banks, FI §3-607.
Timely.
Real estate brokers, BOP §17-528.
Time of distribution.
Disclaimer of property interests, ET §9-201.
Time sale price.
Retail credit accounts, CL §12-501.
Time-share, RP §11A-101.
Time-share estate, RP §11A-101.
Time-share estate project, RP §11A-101.
Time-share expenses, RP §11A-101.
Time-share instrument, RP §11A-101.
Time-share license, RP §11A-101.
Time-share plan, RP §11A-101.
Time-share project, RP §11A-101.
Time-share unit, RP §11A-101.
Tip.
Unemployment insurance, LE §8-101.
Tip jar.
Washington county, CR §13-2414.
Tip jar license.
Washington county, CR §13-2414.
Tip jar packet.
Washington county, CR §13-2414.
Tire dealer.
Sanitary facilities, EN §9-201.
Tire wholesaler.
Sanitary facilities, EN §9-201.
Tissue bank, HG §17-301.
Donors, HG §18-334.
Title agency.
Insurance agents and brokers, IN §10-125.
Title insurance, IN §1-101.
Title insurance producer, IN §10-101.
Title insurance producer independent contractor.
Insurance producers, IN §10-101.
Title plant.
Insurance companies.
Admitted assets, IN §5-104.
Title service agent.
Motor vehicles, TR §15-601.
Title tax.
Boats and boating, NR §8-701.
Tobacco product.
Carroll county and Garrett county, sale of tobacco products, 24 §15-102.
Crimes against public health and safety, CR §10-101.
Health insurance coverage for smoking cessation treatment, IN §15-841.
Medicaid subrogation claims, HG §15-120.
Sale of tobacco products through vending machine, BR §16-3A-01.
Tobacco use prevention and cessation program, HG §13-1001.
Tobacco product manufacturer.
Tobacco, escrow act compliance, BR §16-501.

DEFINED TERMS —Cont'd

Tobacco-related diseases.
Cancer prevention, education, screening and treatment program, HG §13-1101.
Tobacco tax, TG §1-101.
Token.
Gaming, CR §12-101.
Tolerance.
Turf grass, AG §9-101.
Toll bridge.
Public utility companies, PUC §1-101.
Ton.
Commercial feed, AG §6-101.
Commercial fertilizers, AG §6-201.
Tong.
Aquaculture, NR §4-11A-01.
Oysters and clams, NR §§4-1001, 4-1101.
Tong boat.
Oysters and clams, NR §4-1001.
Topiary garden.
Class C, on-sale beer, wine and liquor license in Harford county, 2B §6-301.
Torchiere lighting fixture.
Maryland efficiency standards act, SG §9-2006.
To rent.
Housing discrimination, 49B §20.
Tort claim.
Montgomery county, tort claims act, SG §12-103.2.
Torture.
Children in need of assistance, CJ §3-812.
Total adjusted capital.
Risk based capital standards for insurers, IN §4-301.
Total amount to be allotted.
Agricultural land preservation foundation, AG §2-508.
Total daily receipts.
Alcoholic beverages, 2B §1-102.
Total direct costs of a film production activity.
Film production activity employer wage rebate program, 83A §5-1801.
Total income.
Condominium conversions, RP §11-102.1.
Cooperative housing corporation, CA §5-6B-05.
Total par value of a class of capital stock.
Corporations, CA §1-204.
Total payment.
Income tax withholding, TG §10-912.
Total project cost.
Forests and parks.
Open space program, NR §5-901.
Total project funding.
Capital projects, SF §3-602.
Total purchase price.
Vehicle excise tax, TR §13-809.
Total real property tax.
Homeowners credit, TP §9-104.
Total state operating fund.
Community colleges.
State and county aid, ED §16-305.
Total state service.
State personnel.
Annual leave, SPP §9-302.
Total tax liability on property, TP §14-101.
Total value.
Transfer taxes.
Agricultural land, TP §13-301.
Towaway operation.
Brake equipment, TR §22-301.
Town house.
Sprinkler systems, PS §9-201.

DEFINED TERMS —Cont'd
Tow truck, TR §13-920.
Toxic material.
  Destructive devices, CR §4-501.
TPR proceeding.
  Children in need of assistance, CJ §3-801.
Track.
  Horse racing, BR §11-101.
Tract.
  Forest conservation, NR §5-1601.
  Surface mining, EN §15-801.
Trade or business.
  Unemployment compensation.
    Transfers for purpose of lowering contribution
      rates, LE §8-614.
Trade or commerce.
  Antitrust, CL §11-201.
Trader.
  Business licenses, BR §17-101.
Trader's license, BR §17-101.
Trade secret, CL §11-1201.
  Occupational safety and health, LE §5-217.
Trading stamp.
  Business licenses, BR §17-2001.
  Trading stamp companies, BR §13-101.
Trading stamp company, BR §13-101.
Trading stamp issuer, BR §17-2001.
Traffic, TR §11-166.
Traffic control device, TR §11-167.
Traffic control signal, TR §11-168.
Traffic control signal monitoring system, TR
  §21-202.1.
Traffic signal.
  Maryland efficiency standards act, SG §9-2006.
Traffic signal module.
  Maryland efficiency standards act, SG §9-2006.
Traffic stop.
  Reports by law enforcement officers, TR §25-113.
Trailer, TR §11-169.
  Vehicle excise tax, TR §13-809.
Transaction.
  Currency transaction reporting, FI §12-802.
  Electronic transactions, CL §21-101.
  Industrial development financing, 83A §5-901.
Transfer.
  Computer information transactions, CL §22-102.
  Continuing care contracts, 70B §7.
  Elections, EL §1-101.
  Expungement of records, Crim Rule 4-502.
  Fiduciary security transfers, ET §15-301.
  Hazardous materials, EN §7-101.
  Insurer liquidation, rehabilitation, etc., IN §9-201.
  Oil spills, EN §4-411.
  Partnerships, revised act, CA §9A-101.
  Stock restrictions.
    Close corporations, CA §4-503.
  Structured settlements, transfer of payment
      rights, CJ §5-1101.
Transferability.
  Sales, UCC, CL §2-105.
Transferable record.
  Electronic transactions, CL §21-115.
Transfer agent.
  Fiduciary security transfers, ET §15-301.
Transfer agreement.
  Structured settlements, transfer of payment
      rights, CJ §5-1101.
Transfer assets.
  Commercial banks, FI §3-701.
  Corporations, CA §1-101.
  Savings banks, FI §4-701.

DEFINED TERMS —Cont'd
Transfer buyer.
  Tobacco, AG §7-101.
Transfer date.
  Montebello Center, ED §13-401.
  University of Maryland medical system, ED
    §13-301.
Transferee.
  Nonprofit health entities.
    Acquisition, SG §6.5-101.
Transfer of instrument.
  Negotiable instruments, CL §§3-103, 3-203.
Transferor.
  Nonprofit health entities.
    Acquisition, SG §6.5-101.
  UTMA, ET §13-301.
Transfer or discretionary trusts, ET §14-401.
Transfer out.
  Graduation records.
    Collection, maintenance, analysis and report,
      ED §7-203.2.
Transfer statement.
  Secured transactions, title transfers upon default,
    CL §9-619.
Transfer station.
  Milk products, HG §21-401.
Transfer tax, TP §13-201.
Transformer.
  Maryland efficiency standards act, SG §9-2006.
Transgenic.
  Aquaculture, NR §4-11A-01.
Transient.
  Sex offender registration, CP §11-701.
Transient charge.
  Hotel rental tax, 24 §9-301.
Transient or temporary vendors.
  Issuance of licenses, 24 §11-302.
  Political subdivisions, 24 §11-301.
Transient vendor.
  Business licenses, BR §17-20A-01.
Transit facility.
  Bicycle and pedestrian access, TR §2-601.
  Maryland transit administration, TR §7-101.
  Transportation, TR §3-101.
  Transportation compacts, TR §10-204.
Transitional assistance.
  Family investment program, 88A §44A.
Transition bond.
  Electric customer choice and competition act, PUC
    §7-501.
Transition cost.
  Electric customer choice and competition act, PUC
    §7-501.
Transitioning student.
  Rehabilitation services, ED §21-305.
Transition services.
  Transitioning students with disabilities, ED
    §21-305.
Transit service.
  Maryland transit administration, TR §7-101.
  Transportation compacts, TR §10-204.
Transit vehicle.
  Maryland transit administration, TR §7-101.
Transit zone.
  Transportation compacts, TR §10-204.
Transmitting utility.
  Secured transactions, CL §9-102.
Transport.
  Horses, AG §3-901.
Transportation emergency, TR §25-111.

DEFINED TERMS —Cont'd

Transportation expenses.
Family investment program, 88A §54.
Transportation facilities project, TR §2-103.1.
Revenue facilities, TR §4-101.
Transportation facility, TR §§2-103.1, 3-101.
Bicycle and pedestrian access, TR §2-601.
Revenue facilities, TR §4-101.
Transportation of persons for hire, PUC §1-101.
Transportation provider.
Job access program, TR §2-103.6.
Transportation selection board.
Procurement, SF §13-301.
Transportation service, TR §2-103.3.
Transportation ticket policy.
Health insurance, IN §15-1103.
Transportation unit.
Procurement, SF §§13-301, 15-108.
Transporter.
Special registration vehicle plates, TR §13-625.
Transuranic waste.
Controlled hazardous substances, EN §7-201.
Nuclear waste, EN §8-401.
Radioactive waste, EN §7-301.
Transverse dimension.
Possession of undersized hard-shell clam, NR §4-1031.
Trap and trace device.
Pen registers and trap and trace devices, CJ §10-4B-01.
Trauma center.
Payments to providers not under contract, HG §19-710.1.
Trauma physician services fund, HG §19-130.
Trauma patient.
Payments to providers not under contract, HG §19-710.1.
Trauma physician.
Payments to providers not under contract, HG §19-710.1.
Trauma physician services fund, HG §19-130.
Travel camp.
Maryland youth camp, HG §14-401.
Traveler's check, CL §§3-103, 3-104.
Travel trailer, TR §11-170.
Vehicle excise tax, TR §13-809.
Treasurer.
Elections, EL §1-101.
Public campaign financing, EL §15-102.
Treated.
Seeds, AG §9-201.
Treated egg.
Egg law, AG §4-301.
Treatment.
Cancer prevention, education, screening and treatment program, HG §13-1101.
Controlled hazardous substances, EN §7-201.
Developmental disabilities, HG §7-101.
Employment in recovery pilot program, HG §8-6B-01.
Mental hygiene, HG §10-101.
Treatment service plan.
Juvenile causes, CJ §3-8A-20.1.
Tree.
Forest conservation, NR §5-1601.
Pine tree reforestation, NR §5-501.
Tree and shrub seed, AG §9-201.
Tree expert, NR §5-415.
Tribe.
Certification of questions of law, CJ §12-601.

DEFINED TERMS —Cont'd

Tribe —Cont'd
Uniform child custody jurisdiction and enforcement act, FL §9.5-101.
Uniform interstate family support act, FL §10-301.
Tribunal.
Child support orders.
Affidavit of support, FL §10-1A-01.
Inclusion of child on health insurance, FL §12-102.
Support and maintenance, FL §10-120.
Uniform interstate family support act, FL §10-301.
Tributyltin compound.
Antifouling paints, AG §5-901.
Trip camp.
Maryland youth camp, HG §14-401.
Truck, TR §11-171.
State standby petroleum fuel set-aside program, PS §14-504.
Truck component part.
Motor vehicles, TR §15-101.
Trucker or hauler.
Livestock and poultry, AG §3-301.
Truck tractor, TR §11-172.
Truncated account.
Return of checks to customers, FI §5-513.
Trust.
College savings plan of Maryland, ED §18-1901.
Disclaimer of property interests, ET §9-201.
Discretionary trusts, ET §14-401.
Land trust grant fund, NR §3-2A-01.
Maryland affordable housing trust, HS §10-101.
Maryland historical trust, SF §5A-301.
Real property grants by deed, RP §2-122.
Trust account.
Debt management services, FI §12-901.
Financial institutions, FI §1-204.
Preneed burial contracts, BR §5-701.
Trust company.
Banking institutions, FI §5-101.
Commercial banks, FI §3-101.
Common trust funds, FI §3-501.
Estates and trusts, ET §1-101.
Trusts, ET §15-1A-01.
UTMA, ET §13-301.
Trusteed assets.
Insurance companies, IN §5-801.
Trustees.
Business trusts, CA §12-101.
Debt collection, CL §15-101.
Discretionary trusts, ET §14-401.
Maryland affordable housing trust, HS §10-101.
Maryland historical trust, board of trustees, SF §5A-309.
Pre-need burial contracts, HO §7-405.
Principal and income act, ET §15-501.
Religious corporations, CA §5-301.
Trust fund.
Community services trust fund, HG §24-1101.
Trust money.
Attorney trust accounts, BOP §10-301.
Real estate brokers.
Trust accounts, BOP §17-501.
Title insurance, IN §22-103.
Trust property.
Discretionary trusts, ET §14-401.
Tuition.
College savings plan of Maryland, ED §18-1901.
Foster care recipient's exemption, ED §15-106.1.

DEFINED TERMS —Cont'd
Tuition —Cont'd
Income tax, TG §10-207.
National guard, tuition assistance, PS §13-405.
Universities and colleges.
Tuition increases, ED §15-106.5.
Waiver for senior citizens.
Community colleges, ED §16-106.
Morgan State University, ED §14-107.
St. Mary's College, ED §14-406.
University of Maryland, ED §13-701.
Tuition assistance.
Child care provider grant program, ED §18-705.
McAuliffe teacher education award, ED §18-703.
Physical and occupational therapists and
assistance grant program, ED §18-704.
Tunnel.
Toll facilities, TR §21-1401.
Turbine fuel.
Fuel taxes, TG §8-101.
Turbine fuel seller.
Motor fuel tax, TG §9-301.
Turf.
Turf grass, AG §9-101.
Turf grass.
Advertisement, AG §9-101.
Turf plug, AG §9-101.
Turf sod, AG §9-101.
Turf sprig, AG §9-101.
**12-month Moody's corporate bond yield
average.**
Insurance companies.
Standard valuation law, IN §5-306.
Two horse peddler.
Business licenses, BR §17-904.
Two-stage vehicle.
Motor vehicles, TR §§13-113.2, 15-101.
Type I school vehicle, TR §11-173.
Type II school vehicle, TR §11-174.
UCX benefits.
Unemployment insurance.
X-service members, LE §8-1501.
Ultimate user.
Controlled dangerous substances, CR §5-101.
Umbrella corporation.
Neighborhood housing services fund, HS §4-1001.
Unaccompanied homeless child.
Handicapped children.
Education, ED §8-412.
Unaffiliated declarant.
Homeowners association, RP §11B-101.
Unanimous stockholders' agreement.
Close corporations, CA §4-101.
Unappropriated surplus.
Joseph fund, SF §7-327.
Unattended transit vehicle or facility.
Mass transit, TR §7-704.1.
Unauthorized insurer, IN §1-101.
Unauthorized signature.
Uniform commercial code, CL §1-201.
Unavailable.
Handicapped children.
Education, ED §8-412.
Health care decisions, HG §5-605.
Uncertificated security.
Investment securities, CL §8-102.
Unclaimed deceased nursing home resident,
70B §5A.
Unclaimed funds.
Abandoned property, CL §17-302.

DEFINED TERMS —Cont'd
Unclassified service of the state.
Employees' and teachers' pension systems, SPP
§23-404.
Employees' and teachers' retirement systems, SPP
§22-404.
Uncompensated care.
Trauma physician services fund, HG §19-130.
Under common control with.
Corporations, CA §3-601.
Insurance acquisitions disclosure and control, IN
§7-101.
Underground facility.
Excavation or demolition near, PUC §12-101.
Underground oil storage tank.
Oil cleanups, EN §4-701.
Water pollution, EN §4-401.
Underground storage.
Natural resources.
Gas and oil, EN §14-102.
Underground storage of gas, EN §14-201.
Underground storage reservoir.
Gas and oil, EN §14-201.
Natural resources.
Gas and oil, EN §14-102.
Underground water.
Well drilling, EN §9-1301.
Underserved district.
Alcoholic beverages, 2B §9-203.
Undertaking.
Maryland historical trust, SF §5A-301.
Under the influence, CJ §10-307.
Under the influence of alcohol per se.
Criminal law, CR §3-211.
Motor vehicles, TR §11-174.1.
**Under the supervision of an approved alcohol
and drug supervisor,** HO §17-301.
Undisputed amount.
Construction contracts.
Prompt payment of subcontractors, SF §15-226.
Undistributed income.
Principal and income act, ET §15-507.
Undivided interest.
Time-sharing, RP §11A-101.
Undue influence.
Exploitation of vulnerable adult, CR §8-801.
Uneconomic remnant.
Eminent domain, RP §12-201.
Unexpected child death.
Child fatality review teams, HG §5-701.
Unfair and deceptive act or practice.
Insurance, IN §27-201.
Unfair method of competition.
Insurance, IN §27-201.
Unfair or deceptive trade practices.
Consumer protection, CL §§13-101, 13-301.
Uniform accounting standards.
Health and social welfare organizations, SF
§7-403.
Uniform application.
Insurance producers, IN §10-101.
Uniform business entity application.
Insurance producers, IN §10-101.
Uniform claims form.
Health occupations, HO §1-208.
Uniform credentialing form.
Health insurance, credentialing of providers, IN
§15-112.1.
Uniform standard.
Interstate insurance product regulation compact,
IN §29-101.

DEFINED TERMS —Cont'd
Unimpaired surplus.
  Commercial banks.
    Maximum liabilities of person, FI §3-601.
Uninsured employer.
  Workers' compensation, LE §9-1001.
Uninsured individual.
  Cancer prevention, education, screening and
    treatment program, HG §13-1101.
  Tobacco use prevention and cessation program,
    HG §13-1001.
Uninsured motor vehicle, IN §19-509.
  Automobile insurance fund, IN §20-101.
Unit.
  Appropriations, reversion, SF §7-302.
  Condominiums, RP §11-101.
  Contested cases.
    Declaratory rulings, SG §10-301.
    Licenses, SG §10-226.
    Regulations, SG §10-101.
      Review and evaluation, SG §10-130.
  Cooperative housing corporation, CA §5-6B-01.
  Equal employment opportunity.
    State personnel, SPP §5-201.
  Governmental procedures.
    Civil penalties, SG §10-1001.
  Juvenile justice monitoring unit, SG §6-401.
  Maryland youth camp, HG §14-401.
  Noise control, EN §3-501.
  Office of legislative audits, SG §2-1220.
  Political subdivisions, 24 §14-101.
  Principal and income, ET §15-508.
  Procurement, SF §11-101.
  Public communications.
    Written policies, SG §10-801.
  Rechargeable batteries, EN §6-1101.
  Secretary of state, SG §7-201.
  State personnel.
    Service contracts, SPP §13-401.
  Time-sharing, RP §11A-101.
Unit counsel.
  Administrative procedures, SG §10-107.
United States.
  Commercial drivers' licenses, TR §16-803.
Unit heater.
  Maryland efficiency standards act, SG §9-2006.
Unit management program.
  Rechargeable batteries, EN §6-1101.
Unit of state government.
  Services to persons with disabilities, SG §9-1101.
Unit owner.
  Condominiums, RP §11-101.
Unit price.
  Consumer protection, CL §14-101.
Unitrust.
  Principal and income act, ET §15-501.
Units sold.
  Tobacco, escrow act compliance, BR §16-501.
Universal notification.
  Pesticide application in schools, AG §5-208.1.
Universal registration.
  Voter registration, EL §3-401.
Universal service programs.
  Electric customer choice and competition act, PUC
    §7-501.
University.
  Finance and procurement, SF §11-203.
  University system of Maryland, ED §12-101.
University of Maryland, ED §12-101.
  Rules of interpretation, 1 §31.

DEFINED TERMS —Cont'd
University of Maryland group.
  Cancer prevention, education, screening and
    treatment program, HG §13-1101.
University of Maryland system, ED §12-101.
Unknown.
  Handicapped children.
    Education, ED §8-412.
Unlawful access device.
  Telecommunications theft, CR §7-313.
**Unlawful telecommunication device or access
  code.**
  Telecommunications theft, CR §7-313.
Unlimited common elements.
  Condominiums, RP §11-101.
Unofficial returns.
  Elections, EL §11-101.
Unpaid work-based learning experience.
  Schools, ED §7-114.
Unprotected bird, NR §10-101.
Unprotected mammal, NR §10-101.
Unreclaimed.
  Surface mining, EN §15-801.
Unregistered family daycare home, FL §5-501.
Unreimbursed medical expenses.
  Condominiums, RP §11-137.
Unrelated individual.
  Hospitals, HG §19-301.
Unsecured days funds.
  Savings and loan associations, FI §9-101.
Unsound or unsafe business practice.
  Nonprofit health service plans, IN §14-116.
Unstamped cigarettes.
  Cigarette licenses, BR §16-201.
  Tobacco tax, TG §12-101.
Unsubstantiated.
  Child abuse and neglect, FL §5-701.
  Child welfare accountability, FL §5-1301.
Unused sick leave.
  Pensions, SPP §20-206.
Upholstered furniture, HG §24-401.
Upland game birds and mammals, NR §10-101.
Urban and community forestry, NR §5-424.
Urban area.
  Highways, TR §8-507.
Urban district.
  Traffic laws, TR §21-101.
Urban highway, TR §8-630.
Urban renewal area.
  Property tax.
    Payments in lieu, TP §7-506.
Usage of trade.
  Commercial code, CL §1-205.
  Computer information transactions, CL §22-102.
Use.
  Boats and boating, NR §8-701.
  Sales tax, TG §11-101.
Used major component part.
  Motor vehicle repair facilities, TR §15-113.1.
Used oil.
  Recycling, EN §5-1001.
Used radio and television sets.
  Consumer protection, CL §14-801.
Used vehicle, TR §11-175.
User.
  Potomac water authority, EN §5-401.
Using agency.
  Procurement, SF §4-301.
U.S. No. 1 Irish potato, AG §9-301.
Usury, CL §12-101.

DEFINED TERMS —Cont'd
Utility.
Abandoned property, CL §17-101.
Equipment dealer contracts, CL §19-101.
Utility emergency, TR §25-111.
Utility providers.
Waivers of consumer liability, IN §1-203.1.
Utility service.
Mobile home parks, RP §8A-101.
Utility vendor.
Energy assistance program act, 41 §6-402.
Utilization review.
Private review agents, IN §15-10B-01.
Alcoholism, drug abuse or mental illness
treatment services, IN §15-10B-03.
Utilization review plan.
Private review agents, IN §15-10B-01.
Utilize sewage sludge.
Sanitary facilities, EN §9-201.
Vacant dwelling.
Property tax.
Baltimore City, TP §9-304.
Vacant land.
Land patents, RP §13-101.
Vacation accommodation.
Vacation club membership, CL §14-2401.
Vacation club membership, CL §14-2401.
Vacation club membership plan, CL §14-2401.
Hotels, BR §15-101.
Vaccine.
Statewide advisory commission on immunization,
HG §18-214.
Vaginal intercourse.
Prostitution and related crimes, CR §11-301.
Sexual crimes, CR §3-301.
Valid loss-of-time coverage.
Health insurance, IN §15-224.
Valuable consideration.
Maryland stem cell research program, 83A
§5-2B-01.
Valuation.
Property tax, TP §1-101.
Valuation date.
Business combinations.
Corporations, CA §3-603.
Common trust funds, FI §3-501.
Value.
Bad checks, CR §8-101.
Commercial code, CL §1-201.
Exploitation of vulnerable adult, CR §8-801.
Judgment liens.
Execution, CJ §11-504.
Negotiable instruments, CL §§3-103, 3-303.
Property tax, TP §1-101.
Secured transactions, third party assignees, CL
§9-403.
Theft, CR §7-103.
Uniform commercial code, CL §1-201.
Vanpool operation, TR §11-175.1.
Workers' compensation, LE §9-230.
Variance.
Land use, 66B §1.00.
Zoning and planning, 66B §1.00.
Variety.
Seeds, AG §9-201.
Turf grass, AG §9-101.
Vegetable.
Container marking, AG §10-701.
Vegetable or herb seed.
Seeds, AG §9-201.

DEFINED TERMS —Cont'd
Vehicle, TR §11-176.
Administration of courts.
Motor vehicle tort interrogatories, Form 6.
Dismantlers, recyclers and scrap processors, TR
§15-501.
Handguns, CR §4-201.
Manslaughter by vehicle or vessel, CR §2-209.
Motor fuel, BR §10-101.
Motor vehicle rental company insurance, IN
§10-601.
Preventive maintenance, TR §23-301.
Seat belts in emergency vehicles, TR §22-412.4.
Trespass, CR §6-401.
Used vehicle inspection, TR §23-101.
Vehicle certificate.
Controlled hazardous substances, EN §7-201.
Vehicle identification number, TR §11-177.
Vehicle parking facility.
Revenue facilities, TR §4-101.
Vehicle salesman, TR §15-101.
Vehicles supplying emergency service.
Use of endangered highways, TR §24-204.
Vehicle storage facility.
Motor vehicle repair facilities, TR §15-113.1.
Vehicular crossing.
Toll facilities, TR §21-1401.
Vending facility.
Business enterprise program for the blind, SF
§14-109.
Vending machine.
Business enterprise program for the blind, SF
§14-109.
Sale of tobacco products through vending
machine, BR §16-3A-01.
Theft, CR §7-101.
Vending machine income.
Business enterprise program for the blind, SF
§14-109.
Vending machine license, BR §17-1901.
Vending machine operator.
Cigarette licenses, BR §16-201.
Cigarette sales below cost, CL §11-501.
Less than 20 cigarettes per package, CL
§11-5A-01.
Vendor.
Land installment contracts, RP §10-101.
Real property, RP §1-101.
Sales tax, TG §11-101.
Warranties.
Land installment contracts, RP §10-201.
Vendor payment.
Withholding of tax refunds and payments for
federal nontax liabilities, TG §13-930.
Withholding tax refund due to local government
debts, TG §13-925.
Venereal disease.
Crimes against public health and safety, CR
§10-101.
Ventilation system.
Heating and air conditioning, BR §9A-101.
Venture capital fund, 83A §5-301.
Verification.
Correctional services, COR §1-201.
Verify.
Land patents, RP §13-101.
Vessel.
Criminal law, CR §§2-101, 3-211.
Vessels and boats, NR §8-701.
Antifouling paints, AG §5-901.
Child flotation devices, NR §8-743.

DEFINED TERMS —Cont'd
Vessels and boats —Cont'd
  Hulls of vessels, CL §11-1001.
  Marine sewage devices, NR §8-741.
  Unemployment insurance.
    Location of employment, LE §8-202.
Vested allowance.
  Pensions, SPP §20-101.
Veteran, SG §9-901.
  Respiratory care, HO §14-5A-08.
  Rules of interpretation, 1 §29.
  State veterans' cemeteries, SG §9-906.
Veterans' memorials and monuments, SG §9-908.
Veterans' program.
  Respiratory care, HO §14-5A-08.
Veterinarian, AG §2-301.
Veterinary hospital, AG §2-304.1.
Veterinary inspector.
  Wholesome meat act, AG §4-108.
Veterinary practitioner, AG §2-301.
Veterinary review committee, AG §2-302.1.
Veterinary technician, AG §2-301.
Viable.
  Murder or manslaughter of viable fetus, CR §2-103.
Viatical settlement broker.
  Viatical settlement contracts, IN §8-601.
Viatical settlement contract.
  Viatical settlement contracts, IN §8-601.
Viatical settlement provider.
  Viatical settlement contracts, IN §8-601.
Viaticated policy.
  Viatical settlement contracts, IN §8-601.
Viator.
  Viatical settlement contracts, IN §8-601.
Victim.
  Commutation, pardon or remission of sentence, notice, COR §7-805.
  Crime victims' restitution, CP §11-601.
  Crime victims' services, CP §11-910.
  Criminal injuries compensation fund, CP §11-801.
  Domestic violence, FL §4-501.
  HIV testing, CP §11-107.
  Influencing or intimidating victim or witness, CR §9-301.
  Juvenile causes, CJ §3-8A-01.
  Not criminally responsible determination, notification, CP §3-123.
  Notoriety of crimes contracts, CP §11-621.
  Parole release hearing, victim's rights, COR §7-801.
  Patuxent institution, COR §4-101.
  Post-conviction proceedings, CP §11-501.
  Pretrial procedures, CP §11-302.
  Pretrial rights, CP §11-202.
  Victims of crime, CP §11-104.
Victim of domestic violence, FL §4-513.
  Insurance discrimination, IN §27-504.
Victim of September 11, 2001 terrorist attacks.
  Scholarships, ED §18-601.
Victim's representative.
  HIV testing, CP §11-107.
  Not criminally responsible determination, notification, CP §3-123.
  Notoriety of crimes contracts, CP §11-621.
  Post-conviction proceedings, CP §11-501.
  Sentencing, CP §11-401.
  Victims of crime, CP §11-104.
Video.
  Membership contracts in video clubs, CL §14-1602.1.

DEFINED TERMS —Cont'd
Video club.
  Membership contracts, CL §14-1602.1.
Video equipment.
  Membership contracts in video clubs, CL §14-1602.1.
Video-monitoring system.
  Failure to pay electronic toll, TR §21-1414.
Video movie.
  Sales and rentals, CL §14-1601.
Video tape distributor.
  Unlawful publication by video tape distributor, CR §3-907.
Vintage registration plate.
  Motor vehicles, TR §13-936.1.
Violates or attempts to violate.
  Unemployment compensation.
    Transfers for purpose of lowering contribution rates, LE §8-614.
Violation.
  Fish and fisheries.
    Expungement of records, NR §4-1208.
  Juvenile causes, CJ §3-8A-01.
  Minors possession tobacco products, CR §10-108.
  Traffic laws, TR §21-1126.
Violence prevention program, ED §24-401.
Violent crime.
  Parole and mandatory release, COR §7-101.
  Victims of crime, CP §11-103.
Visible.
  Outdoor advertising, TR §8-701.
Visible from the traveled way.
  Outdoor advertising removal, 25 §122D.
Visual or audible signal.
  Boats and boating.
    Enforcement of subtitle, NR §8-727.
  Fleeing police, TR §21-904.
Visual surveillance.
  Visual surveillance of individual in private place, CR §3-901.
  With prurient intent, CR §3-902.
Vital documents.
  Equal access to public services for persons with limited English proficiency, SG §10-1102.
Vital record.
  Archives, SG §9-1015.
  Health statistics, HG §4-201.
Viticulture.
  Winery and grape growers' advisory commission, AG §10-1201.
Vocational assessment.
  Workers' compensation.
    Vocational rehabilitation, LE §9-675.
Vocational rehabilitation services.
  Rehabilitation practitioners, LE §9-6A-01.
  Workers' compensation, LE §9-675.
Vocational services.
  Developmental disabilities, HG §7-101.
Voluntary placement.
  Children in need of assistance, CJ §3-801.
Voluntary placement agreement.
  Child care, FL §5-501.
Voluntary placement hearing.
  Children in need of assistance, CJ §3-801.
Volunteer.
  Charitable organizations.
    Civil liability, CJ §5-606.
  Community recreation program.
    Personal liability, CJ §5-802.
  Personal liability.
    Charitable organization, CJ §5-407.

DEFINED TERMS —Cont'd
Volunteer —Cont'd
Personal liability of agents of certain associations
    or organizations, CJ §5-406.
Sovereign immunity, CJ §5-518.
Volunteer company.
Volunteer company assistance fund, PS §8-201.
Workers' compensation, LE §9-234.
Volunteer fire company.
Emergency response reimbursement, CJ §3-1101.
Vote.
Elections, EL §1-101.
Voter.
Agricultural commodity promotion, AG §10-101.
Voter information material.
Distributing or depositing in Montgomery county,
    EL §1-303.
Voter registry, EL §3-401.
Vote tabulation.
Elections, EL §11-101.
Vote tallying.
Elections, EL §11-101.
Voting machine, EL §1-101.
Voting machine ballot, EL §1-101.
Voting stock, CA §3-601.
Voting system, EL §1-101.
Vulnerable adult.
Abuse or neglect of vulnerable adult, CR §3-604.
Adult protective services, FL §14-101.
Domestic violence, FL §4-501.
Exploitation of vulnerable adult, CR §8-801.
W.
Insurance companies.
    Standard valuation law, IN §5-306.
Wagering.
Income tax withholding, TG §10-905.
Wages.
Administration of courts.
    Domestic relations interrogatories, Form 4.
Aid to families with dependent children.
    Tax credits for qualified employment
        opportunity employees, 88A §54.
Assignment of, CL §15-301.
Attachment of, CL §15-601.
Consumer loans, CL §12-301.
Debt collection, CL §15-102.
Family investment program, 88A §54.
Health care payroll assessment, LE §8.5-101.
Income tax, TG §10-101.
Income tax withholding, TG §10-905.
Injured workers' insurance fund, LE §10-101.
Interest in usury, CL §12-101.
Minimum, LE §3-401.
Payment and collection, LE §3-501.
Pilot program for long term employment of
    qualified ex-felons, LE §11-701.
Rehabilitation services, ED §21-309.
Retail installment sales, CL §12-601.
Secondary mortgage loan, CL §12-401.
Sex discrimination, LE §3-301.
Tax tables, TG §2-106.
Unemployment insurance, LE §8-101.
Waiting period.
Health insurance portability, IN §§15-1301,
    15-1401.
Waiver.
Medicaid, HG §15-132.
Waiver services.
Medicaid, HG §15-132.
Waivers of consumer liability.
Utility providers, IN §1-203.1.

DEFINED TERMS —Cont'd
Walk-around services.
Elections, EL §13-245.
Wanton.
Trespass, CR §6-401.
Warden.
Dorchester County department of corrections,
    COR §11-711.
Kent County detention center, COR §11-716.
Ward of the state.
Handicapped children.
    Education, ED §8-412.
Warehouse.
Documents of title, CL §7-102.
Warehouseman.
Bills of lading and warehouse receipts, CL
    §18-101.
Warehouser.
Property tax.
    Payments in lieu, TP §7-509.
Warehouse receipt, CL §18-101.
Uniform commercial code, CL §1-201.
Warning.
Discipline of attorneys, CJA Rule 16-701.
Warrant.
Disbursements, SF §7-201.
Uniform child custody jurisdiction and
    enforcement act, FL §9.5-101.
Warrant of execution, COR §3-902.
Warranty.
Automotive warranty enforcement, CL §14-1501.
Motor vehicle leasing contracts, CL §14-2001.
Warranty date.
New home warranties, RP §10-601.
Warranty period.
Motor vehicle leasing contracts, CL §14-2001.
War veterans organization.
Class C, on-sale beer, wine and liquor license in
    Harford county, 2B §6-301.
Washington authority.
Washington county housing authority, HS
    §21-101.
Wastes.
Northeast Maryland waste disposal authority, NR
    §3-904.
Wastewater facility.
Water quality financing, EN §9-1601.
Wastewater purification project.
Environmental service, NR §3-101.
Wastewater works.
Waterworks operators, EN §12-101.
Water company, PUC §1-101.
Water conservation, EN §5-5B-01.
Waterfowl processing operation, NR §10-101.
Waterfowl safety zone.
Waterfowl hunting, NR §10-601.
Water plant, PUC §1-101.
Waterproofing technique.
Consumer protection, CL §14-12A-01.
Water quality fund, EN §9-1601.
Water quality laboratory, EN §9-1001.
Water quality standard.
Sanitary facilities, EN §9-101.
Water resources.
Susquehanna river basin compact, EN §5-301.
Waters.
Susquehanna river basin compact, EN §5-301.
Watershed.
Herring run, EN §5-1201.
Patuxent river, NR §8-1301.
Reforestation, NR §5-103.

DEFINED TERMS —Cont'd
Watershed —Cont'd
Water management, EN §4-301.
Watershed association.
County commissioners, 25 §169.
Waters of the state, NR §8-101.
Boats and boating, NR §8-701.
Sanitary facilities, EN §9-101.
Water management, EN §4-101.1.
Water resources, EN §5-101.
Water supply.
Well drillers, EN §13-101.
Water supply facility, EN §9-420.
Water supply project.
Environmental service, NR §3-101.
Water supply system, EN §9-501.
Sanitary facilities, EN §9-201.
Water quality financing, EN §9-1601.
Water system.
Sanitary commissions, EN §9-601.
Water and sewer authorities, EN §9-901.
Waterworks.
Waterworks operators, EN §12-101.
Wealth.
Community colleges.
State and county aid, ED §16-305.
County public libraries, ED §23-501.
Educational financing.
State assistance, ED §5-202.
Grants for limited-English proficiency education,
ED §5-208.
Schools, compensatory education grants, ED
§5-207.
Schools, guaranteed tax base grants, ED §5-210.
Special education grants, ED §5-209.
Wealth assessment.
State aid for police protection, 41 §4-403.
Wealth base.
State police.
Protection fund, 41 §4-403.
Weapon.
Contraband at place of confinement, CR §9-410.
Dangerous weapons, CR §4-101.
Weapons in correctional facilities, COR §8-801.
Weed.
Pesticide registration and labeling, AG §5-101.
Turf grass, AG §9-101.
Weed seed.
Seeds, AG §9-201.
Week.
Unemployment insurance, LE §8-101.
Weekend inmate, COR §11-801.
Weight.
Weights and measures, AG §11-101.
Weighted average.
Health insurance portability, IN §15-1301.
Weighted enrollment growth.
Maryland school for the blind.
Appropriations, ED §8-317.
Maryland school for the deaf, ED §8-310.3.
Well.
Geothermal resources, EN §5-601.
Well drillers, EN §13-101.
Well drilling, EN §9-1301.
Well driller, EN §9-1301.
Well driller's license, EN §13-101.
Well system equipment.
Well drillers, EN §13-101.
Western Maryland.
Code counties, 25B §2.
Regional tourism bureau, 20A §4-101.

DEFINED TERMS —Cont'd
Wetland game birds, NR §10-101.
Wet marine and transportation insurance, IN
§1-101.
When he deems himself insecure.
Commercial code, CL §1-208.
Whip.
Forest conservation, NR §5-1601.
White goods.
Recycling, EN §9-1701.
Wholesale farm machinery dealer's license.
Business licenses, BR §17-701.
Wholesale life insurance, IN §1-101.
Wholesale market value.
Income tax, TG §10-208.
Taxation, TG §10-207.
Wholesale price.
Tobacco tax, TG §12-101.
Wholesale purchaser-reseller.
State standby petroleum fuel set-aside program,
PS §14-501.
Wholesaler.
Alcoholic beverage tax, TG §5-101.
Bedding, HG §24-401.
Cigarette licenses, BR §16-201.
Less than 20 cigarettes per package, CL
§11-5A-01.
Sales below cost, CL §11-401.
Cigarettes, CL §11-501.
Tobacco tax, TG §12-101.
Wholesaler's license.
Washington county, CR §13-2414.
Wholesale sale.
Sales below cost, CL §11-401.
Wholesale sale of cigarettes.
Sales below cost, CL §11-501.
Wholesale seedsman, AG §9-201.
Wholly owned.
Community health, HG §24-601.
Federally qualified health centers grant program,
HG §24-1301.
Grants to assisted living facilities, HG §24-1001.
Juvenile services.
Facilities capital program, 83C §4-101.
Nursing facility conversion grant program, HG
§24-1401.
Residential child care capital grant program, 41
§18-701.
Senior citizen activities centers capital
improvement grants, 70B §26.
Wicomico county pinball machine license.
Business licenses, BR §17-420.
Widely available in Maryland.
Maryland efficiency standards act, SG §9-2006.
Wild birds, NR §10-101.
Wildlands.
Forests and parks, NR §5-1201.
Wildlife, NR §10-101.
Interstate wildlife violator compact, NR §10-1201.
Wildlife law.
Interstate wildlife violator compact, NR §10-1201.
Wildlife violation.
Interstate wildlife violator compact, NR §10-1201.
Wild mammal, NR §10-101.
Wild quadruped, NR §10-101.
Wild river.
Deer creek study, NR §8-402.
Wild waterfowl, NR §10-101.
Will.
Adoptees, ET §4-414.
Estates and trusts, ET §1-101.

DEFINED TERMS —Cont'd

Willfully.
Arson and burning, CR §6-101.

Wine.
Alcoholic beverages, 2B §1-102.
Taxation, TG §5-101.
Winery and grape growers' advisory commission, AG §10-1201.

Wine industries.
Business licenses, BR §17-1801.

Winery.
Winery and grape growers' advisory commission, AG §10-1201.

Wire communication.
Evidence, CJ §10-401.
Pen registers and trap and trace devices, CJ §10-4B-01.

Wireless communication device.
Minors, use of wireless communications device while driving, TR §21-1124.

Wireless enhanced 911 service.
911 emergency telephone system, PS §1-301.

Withdrawal.
Susquehanna river basin compact, EN §5-301.

Withdrawal date.
State retirement and pension system, SPP §31-301.

Withdrawal liability.
Local fire and police pension system, SPP §21-306.

Withhold.
Tax withholding, TG §10-905.

Within this state.
Alcoholic beverages, 2B §1-102.

Without charge.
Service contracts and consumer products guaranty, CL §14-401.

Witness.
Courts, CJ §9-301.
Influencing or intimidating victim or witness, CR §9-301.
Juvenile causes, CJ §3-8A-01.
Victims of crime, CP §11-508.

WMATC.
Transportation compacts, TR §10-204.

Woman of childbearing age.
Folic acid supplement distribution program, HG §13-2301.

Woodlands or forest lands.
Forest conservancy districts, NR §5-601.

Work activity.
Family investment program, 88A §44A.

Work authorization.
Dental laboratory, HO §4-401.

Workday.
Amusement attractions, BR §3-406.

Worker.
Public works contracts, SF §17-201.

Workforce investment area.
Pilot program for long term employment of qualified ex-felons, LE §11-701.
Workforce investment act, LE §11-503.

Workforce investment area board, LE §11-503.

Working capital.
Economic development assistance fund, 83A §5-1401.
Maryland economic adjustment fund, 83A §6-501.
Small business development financing authority, 83A §5-1001.

Working day.
Insurance rates, IN §11-101.
Railroad safety and health, LE §5.5-101.

DEFINED TERMS —Cont'd

Working place.
Mines and mining, EN §15-101.

Work of fine art.
Consignment of, CL §11-8A-01.

Workplace.
Economic stabilization act, LE §11-301.
State substance abuse policy, SPP §2-306.

Work plan.
Administrative procedures.
Regulations, SG §10-130.

Work sharing benefit.
Unemployment insurance, LE §8-1201.

Work sharing employer.
Unemployment insurance, LE §8-1201.

Work sharing plan.
Unemployment insurance, LE §8-1201.

Wraparound services.
Handicapped children, placement in nonpublic educational programs, ED §8-406.

Writ, CJ §2-101.

Write-in candidate, EL §1-101.

Write-in vote, EL §1-101.

Writing.
Evidence, CJ §10-103.
Uniform commercial code, CL §1-201.

Written.
Uniform commercial code, CL §1-201.

Written agreement.
Continuing care contracts, 70B §7.

Wrongful act.
Wrongful death, CJ §3-901.

Wrongful breach of a guaranty.
Service contracts and consumer products guaranty, CL §14-401.

Wrongful breach of a service contract.
Service contracts and consumer products guaranty, CL §14-401.

Wrongful detainer, RP §8-402.4.

Yacht or boat club.
Class C, on-sale beer, wine and liquor license in Harford county, 2B §6-301.

Yard.
Crimes involving railroads, CR §6-503.

Yard waste.
Recycling, EN §9-1701.

Year 2000-ready, CJ §5-527.

Year of service.
Legislative pension plan, SG Title 2 Subtitle 3 (note).

Youth.
Maryland conservation corps, NR §5-218.

Youth camp, HG §14-401.

Youth overnight program.
Maryland youth camp, HG §14-401.

Youth program.
Patuxent institution, COR §4-401.

Youth services bureau, 83C §2-122.
Suicide prevention, ED §7-502.

Youth tobacco survey.
Tobacco use prevention and cessation program, HG §13-1001.

Y2K date data problem.
Year 2000 litigation, CJ §5-527.

Y valve.
Marine sewage, NR §8-741.

Zone.
Transportation compacts, TR §10-204.

Zoning official, 66B §7.02.

DELAWARE.

Southern regional education compact.
Admission of Delaware state, ED §25-204.

DELEGATES.
House of delegates.
See GENERAL ASSEMBLY.

DELEGATE SCHOLARSHIPS, ED §§18-501 to 18-507.

DELINQUENTS.
Juvenile causes.
General provisions.
See JUVENILE CAUSES.
Minors.
See MINORS.

DELIVERY.
Bills of lading.
Generally.
See BILLS OF LADING.
Sales.
See SALES.

DELIVERY BY MISTAKE.
Credit card crimes.
Receiving card known to have been misdelivered, CR §8-204.
Theft.
Control over property lost, mislaid or delivered by mistake, CR §7-104.

DELMARVA ADVISORY COUNCIL.
Appointment, 32B §1-102.
Appropriations, 32B §1-111.
Bylaws.
Adoption, 32B §1-107.
Chairman, 32B §1-103.
Compensation, 32B §1-104.
Creation, 32B §1-101.
Duties, 32B §1-108.
Funding, 32B §1-111.
Gifts.
Acceptance, 32B §1-109.
Grants.
Acceptance, 32B §1-109.
Meetings, 32B §1-105.
Public attendance, 32B §1-106.
Membership, 32B §1-102.
Officers, 32B §1-103.
Reimbursement for expenses, 32B §1-104.
Responsibilities, 32B §1-108.
Rules and regulations.
Adoption, 32B §1-107.
Staff, 32B §1-110.

DEMAND DEPOSITS.
Bank deposits and collections.
Generally, CL §§4-101 to 4-504.
See BANK DEPOSITS AND COLLECTIONS.

DEMAND FOR JURY TRIAL.
Circuit courts, CivProCir Rule 2-325.
Certain transfers from District Court, CivProCir Rule 2-326; CivProDist Rule 3-325.
Criminal procedure, Crim Rule 4-301.
District Court, CivProDist Rule 3-325; CJ §§4-302, 4-402.

DEMOLITION.
Near underground utility facilities.
Generally, PUC §§12-101 to 12-113.
See UNDERGROUND UTILITY FACILITIES.
Montgomery county, PUC §§12-201 to 12-203.

DEMONSTRATIONS.
Firearm possessed at public demonstration, CR §4-208.

DEMURRERS.
Pleading.
See PLEADINGS.

DENIALS.
Answers.
Circuit courts, CivProCir Rule 2-323.

DENSITY ZONING, 66B §4.01.
Baltimore City.
Grant of power, 66B §2.01.
Park and planning commission.
District councils for regional districts, 28 §8-101.

DENTAL ACRYLICS.
Sale of methyl methacrylate liquid monomer in salon prohibited, HG §24-303.

DENTAL HYGIENISTS.
General provisions.
See DENTISTS.

DENTAL INSURANCE, IN §15-114.
Dental care coverage under general health insurance policies.
Procedures requiring general anesthesia, IN §15-828.
Self-funded group insurance plans, IN §15-702.
Small employer health insurance, IN §15-1204.

DENTAL PLAN ORGANIZATIONS, IN §§14-401 to 14-418.
Applicability of provisions, IN §14-402.
Bond, IN §14-404.
Carriers.
Credentialing of providers, IN §15-112.1.
Cease and desist orders, IN §14-416.
Certificates of authority.
Disapproval, IN §14-407.
Generally, IN §§14-405 to 14-409.
Issuance, IN §14-407.
Required, IN §14-403.
Claims.
Reimbursement for preauthorized care, IN §15-1009.
Retroactive denial of reimbursement, IN §15-1008.
Communication of information by health care providers, IN §15-116.
Compensation of health care practitioners, IN §15-113.
Complaint process for adverse decisions or grievances.
Generally, IN §§15-10A-01 to 15-10A-09.
Complaints.
Coverage decisions, IN §§15-10D-01 to 15-10D-04.
Complaint system, IN §14-412.
Contributing to impairment, IN §9-231.
Court's authority, IN §14-417.
Credentialing intermediaries.
Credentialing of providers, IN §15-112.1.
Definitions, IN §14-401.
Disclosures required in sales materials, IN §15-121.
Emerging medical and surgical treatments, IN §15-123.
Evidence of coverage, IN §14-410.
Defined, IN §14-401.
Expenditure limitations, IN §14-414.
Grievances.
Complaint process for adverse decisions or grievances.
Generally, IN §§15-10A-01 to 15-10A-09.
Complaint process for coverage decisions, IN §§15-10D-01 to 15-10D-04.

DENTAL PLAN ORGANIZATIONS —Cont'd
Health care decisions.
Disbursement of advance directive information
sheet by carrier, IN §15-122.1.
Health insurance generally.
See HEALTH INSURANCE.
Injunctions, IN §14-417.
Insolvency, IN §14-417.
Investigations and examinations, IN §14-411.
Misrepresentations, IN §14-415.
Notice of impairment, IN §9-231.
Point-of-service option required, IN §15-114.
Primary care physicians.
Referrals to specialists, IN §15-830.
Prohibited terms and conditions.
Provider panels, IN §§15-112, 27-222.
Provider panels, IN §15-112.
Providers.
Credentialing, IN §15-112.1.
Records, IN §14-418.
Complaints by enrollees, IN §14-412.
Preservation of records, IN §14-411.
Referrals to specialists, IN §15-830.
Renewal of coverage.
Notice of renewal, IN §15-122.
Reports, IN §14-413.
Public documents, IN §14-418.
**Restrictions on assigning, transferring or
subcontracting,** IN §15-125.
Retroactive denial of reimbursement, IN
§15-1008.
Specialists.
Referrals to specialists, IN §15-830.
Surplus requirements, IN §14-404.
Transfer of health care provider's contract, IN
§15-124.
Restrictions on assigning, transferring or
subcontracting, IN §15-125.

DENT-CARE PROGRAM, ED §§18-2401 to
18-2408.
Definitions, ED §18-2401.
Established, purpose, ED §18-2402.
Funding, ED §18-2408.
Higher education assistance grant, ED
§18-2404.
Duration, ED §18-2406.
Number awarded, amount, ED §18-2405.
Office of oral health.
Administration of program, duties, ED §18-2403.
Rules and regulations, ED §18-2407.

DENTISTS.
Actions.
Board of dental examiners.
Suits by and against board, HO §4-208.
Licenses.
Injunctive actions, HO §4-320.
Acupuncturists.
Performance of acupuncture not limited, HO
§1A-102.
Advertising.
Penalties for violations, HO §4-606.
Requirements generally, HO §4-503.
Alcoholic beverages.
Providing professional services while under the
influence of alcohol or controlled dangerous
substances.
Denials, reprimands, probations, suspensions or
revocations of licenses, HO §4-315.
Appeals.
Disciplinary proceedings.
Administrative and judicial review, HO §4-319.

DENTISTS —Cont'd
Applicability of provisions, HO §4-102.
Automobile accident injury report.
Certain counties, HG §20-701.
Board of dental examiners.
Administrative and judicial review, HO §4-319.
Appointment of members, HO §4-202.
Compensation of members, HO §4-204.
Composition, HO §4-202.
Consumer members, HO §4-202.
Defined, HO §4-101.
Dental hygienist members, HO §4-202.
Dentist members, HO §4-202.
Elections, HO §4-203.
Established, HO §4-201.
Expenses.
Reimbursement, HO §4-204.
Fees.
Establishment of fees by board, HO §4-207.
Funds.
Disposition, HO §4-207.
Inspections.
Office of dentist, HO §4-205.
Liability.
Good faith exemption from civil liability for acts
within scope of jurisdiction of board, CJ
§5-705.
Persons giving information to board.
Immunity, HO §4-209.
Licensing. See within this heading, "Licenses."
Meetings, HO §§4-202, 4-204.
Membership, HO §4-202.
Oaths, HO §4-202.
Officers, HO §4-203.
Powers and duties.
Generally, HO §4-205.
Program evaluation act, SG §8-403.
Qualifications of members, HO §4-202.
Removal of members, HO §4-202.
Rules and regulations.
Adoption by board, HO §§4-205, 4-206.
Expansion of practice of dental hygiene, HO
§4-206.
Permitting additional intraoral functions, HO
§4-206.
Secretary of board, HO §4-203.
Staff, HO §4-204.
State board of dental examiners fund, HO §4-207.
Suits by and against board, HO §4-208.
Tenure, HO §4-202.
Terms of office, HO §4-203.
Vacancies, HO §4-202.
Boating accident injury reports, HG §20-702.
Citation of act, HO §4-701.
Complaints.
Licenses.
Commencement of proceedings, HO §4-316.
Mediation, HO §4-316.
Conflict of laws.
Dental review bodies and peer review activities.
Law governing recoveries, HO §4-502.
Contempt.
Licenses.
Subpoenas.
Enforcement by contempt, HO §4-318.
Continuing education, HO §4-205.
Controlled dangerous substances.
Providing professional services while under the
influence of alcohol or controlled substances.
Denials, reprimands, probations, suspensions
and revocations of licenses, HO §4-315.

DENTISTS —Cont'd
Crimes and offenses.
Advertising dental appliance, HO §4-606.
Dental hygienists.
Unauthorized practice, HO §4-606.
Dental laboratory work offense, HO §4-606.
Unauthorized practice, HO §4-606.
Definitions, HO §4-101.
Dental hygienist rehabilitation committee, HO §4-508.
Dental laboratory work, HO §4-401.
Dental review committee, HO §4-501.
General supervision, HO §4-308.
Dental appliance.
Defined, HO §4-101.
Dental hygienists.
Continuing education, HO §4-205.
Defined, HO §4-101.
Dental hygienist rehabilitation committees.
Defined, HO §4-508.
Discovery.
Proceedings, records and files, HO §4-508.
Evidence.
Admissibility of proceedings, records and files, HO §4-508.
Liability.
Good faith exemption from civil liability, HO §4-508.
Scope of authority, HO §4-508.
General supervision by dentist, HO §4-308.
Independent practice of dental hygiene, HO §4-308.
Licenses, HO §4-308.
Denial, HO §4-315.
Examinations.
Licensees in other states, HO §4-306.
General license to practice dental hygiene, HO §4-308.
Reciprocal recognition, examination requirement, HO §4-306.
Temporary license to practice dental hygiene, HO §4-312.
Unauthorized practice of dental hygiene.
Misdemeanor, HO §4-606.
Misdemeanors.
Unauthorized practice of dental hygiene, HO §4-606.
Practice dental hygiene.
Defined, HO §4-101.
Ownership or operation of dental or dental hygiene practice, HO §4-605.
Scheduling recall appointment, HO §4-308.
Dental laboratories.
Defined, HO §4-101.
Dental laboratory work.
Authorization for work, HO §4-403.
Definitions.
Generally, HO §4-401.
Distribution of forms, HO §4-404.
Forms.
Distribution, HO §4-404.
Inspections, HO §4-407.
Misdemeanors.
Violations of subtitle, HO §4-606.
Prohibitions.
Specific prohibitions, HO §4-406.
Records, HO §4-404.
Requirements for performing.
Exceptions to requirements, HO §4-402.
Generally, HO §4-402.
Specific prohibitions, HO §4-406.

DENTISTS —Cont'd
Dental laboratory work —Cont'd
Work authorization, HO §4-403.
Exceptions to requirements, HO §4-405.
Requirements generally.
Exceptions to requirements, HO §4-405.
Dental radiation technologists. See within this heading, "Radiation."
Dental rehabilitation committee, HO §4-501.1.
Funding, HO §4-207.
Dental review committee.
Conflict of laws.
Recoveries against dental review bodies, HO §4-502.
Definitions, HO §4-501.
Dent-care program, ED §§18-2401 to 18-2408.
Definitions, ED §18-2401.
Established, purpose, ED §18-2402.
Funding, ED §18-2408.
Higher education assistance grant, ED §18-2404.
Duration, ED §18-2406.
Number awarded, amount, ED §18-2405.
Office of oral health.
Administration of program, duties, ED §18-2403.
Rules and regulations, ED §18-2407.
Discovery.
Dental hygienist.
Dental hygienist rehabilitation committees.
Proceedings, records and files, HO §4-508.
Education.
Licenses.
Continuing education requirements.
Adoption of regulations, HO §4-205.
Evidence.
Dental hygienist.
Dental hygienist rehabilitation committees.
Admissibility of proceedings, records and files, HO §4-508.
Examinations, HO §§4-305, 4-306, 4-310.
Executors and administrators.
Notice of disposition of medical records, ET §7-401.
Fees.
Board of dental examiners.
Establishment of fees by board, HO §4-207.
Examinations, HO §4-305.
Licenses.
Applications, HO §4-304.
Reinstatement of expired licenses, HO §4-311.
Replacement of lost or destroyed licenses, HO §4-307.
Funds.
Board of dental examiners.
Disposition, HO §4-207.
Gunshot injuries, reporting, HG §20-703.
Health insurance coverage.
Procedures requiring general anesthesia, IN §15-828.
Hearings.
Licenses.
Right to hearing in disciplinary matters, HO §4-318.
Higher education loan assistance grant.
Dent-care program, ED §§18-2401 to 18-2408.
Hospitals.
Assessment of medical risk of procedures, HO §4-507.
Hospital admission history and physical examination.
Completion by dentist, HO §4-507.

DENTISTS —Cont'd
Hospitals —Cont'd
Use of facilities and staff privileges for qualified
dentists, HG §19-351.
Hygienists. See within this heading, "Dental
hygienists."
Immunity.
Board of dental examiners.
Good faith exemption from civil liability for acts
within scope of jurisdiction of board, CJ
§5-705.
Persons giving information to board, HO §4-209.
Dental hygienists.
Dental hygienist rehabilitation committees.
Good faith exemption from civil liability, HO
§4-508.
Injunctions.
Disciplinary actions, HO §4-320.
Injury reports.
Accidents involving moving vessels, HG §20-702.
Certain counties, HG §20-701.
Gunshot causing injury, HG §20-703.
Inspections.
Dental laboratory work.
Evidence of violations, HO §4-407.
Liability.
Board of dental examiners.
Good faith exemption from civil liability for acts
within scope of jurisdiction of board, CJ
§5-705.
Immunity of persons giving information to
board, HO §4-209.
Dental hygienist.
Dental hygienist rehabilitation committees.
Good faith exemption from civil liability, HO
§4-508.
Licenses.
Administrative review, HO §4-319.
Advertising, HO §4-503.
Aiding or abetting unauthorized practice of dental
hygiene, HO §4-601.
Appeals.
Administrative and judicial review, HO §4-319.
Applicants.
Qualifications, HO §4-302.
Waiver, HO §4-303.
Applications.
Generally, HO §4-304.
Renewal of licenses, HO §4-309.
Change of address, HO §4-313.
Complaints.
Commencement of proceedings, HO §4-316.
Contents, HO §4-307.
Continuing education requirements.
Adoption of regulations, HO §4-205.
Crimes involving moral turpitude.
Reports by clerks of court, HO §4-604.
Defined, HO §4-101.
Denials.
Commencement of proceedings, HO §4-316.
Grounds, HO §4-315.
Dental hygienists, HO §4-308.
Denial, HO §4-315.
General license to practice dental hygiene, HO
§4-308.
Temporary license to practice dental hygiene,
HO §4-312.
Depositions, HO §4-318.
Display of licenses, HO §4-313.
Examinations, HO §§4-305, 4-306, 4-310.
Reciprocal recognition of licensee, HO §4-306.

DENTISTS —Cont'd
Licenses —Cont'd
Exceptions to requirements, HO §4-301.
Ex parte hearings, HO §4-318.
Expired licenses.
Reinstatement, HO §4-311.
Fees.
Applications, HO §4-304.
Reinstatement of expired licenses, HO §4-311.
Replacement of lost or destroyed licenses, HO
§4-307.
Felonies.
Reports by clerks of court, HO §4-604.
Fraud.
Misrepresentation, HO §4-602.
Penalties, HO §4-606.
Practicing without license, HO §4-601.
General license to practice dental hygiene, HO
§4-308.
General license to practice dentistry, HO §4-308.
Hearings.
Application of administrative procedure act, HO
§4-318.
Right to hearing, HO §4-318.
Inactive status, HO §4-310.
Renewal of inactive status, HO §4-310.
Waiver of examinations, HO §4-310.
Injunctive actions, HO §4-320.
Issuance, HO §4-307.
Judicial review, HO §4-319.
Limitations on practice, HO §4-603.
Limited license to practice dentistry, HO §4-308.
Application, HO §4-304.
Expiration, HO §4-309.
Qualifications of applicants, HO §4-302.
Waiver of education requirements, HO §4-303.1.
Location of licenses, HO §4-313.
Lost or destroyed licenses.
Replacement, HO §4-307.
Misrepresentation, HO §4-602.
Notice.
Change of address, HO §4-313.
Oaths, HO §4-318.
Penalties.
Instead of or in addition to suspension,
revocation or reprimand, HO §4-317.
Suspension or revocation of licenses, HO
§§4-316, 4-317.
Penalty instead of or in addition to, HO
§4-317.
Unauthorized practice, HO §4-606.
Practice limitations, HO §4-603.
Practicing without license, HO §4-601.
Probation.
Commencement of proceedings, HO §4-316.
Grounds, HO §4-315.
Qualifications of applicants, HO §4-302.
Waiver, HO §4-303.
Reciprocity, examination requirement, HO §4-306.
Reinstatement of expired licenses, HO §4-311.
Renewal of licenses, HO §4-309.
Inactive status, HO §4-310.
Issuance, HO §4-309.
Replacement of lost licenses, HO §4-307.
Reprimands.
Commencement of proceedings, HO §4-316.
Grounds, HO §4-315.
Penalty instead of or in addition to, HO §4-317.
Requirements generally, HO §4-301.
Exceptions, HO §4-301.

DENTISTS —Cont'd
Licenses —Cont'd
Revocations.
Commencement of proceedings, HO §4-316.
Grounds, HO §4-315.
Penalty instead of or in addition to, HO §4-317.
Scope of licenses, HO §4-308.
Specialization.
Guidelines generally, HO §4-504.
Subpoenas, HO §4-318.
Contempt to enforce, HO §4-318.
Surrender, HO §4-314.
Suspensions.
Commencement of proceedings, HO §4-315.
Grounds, HO §4-315.
Penalty instead of or in addition to, HO §4-317.
Teacher's license to practice dentistry and dental
hygiene, HO §4-308.
Waiver for, HO §4-303.
Temporary license to practice dental hygiene.
Authority to issue, HO §4-312.
Scope of provisions, HO §4-312.
Surrender, HO §4-314.
Term, HO §4-312.
Terms of licenses, HO §4-309.
Unauthorized practice, HO §4-601.
Penalties, HO §4-606.
Volunteer dentists and dental hygienists, HO
§4-302.
Waiver of education requirements, HO §4-303.1.
Waiver of qualifications for license to practice
dentistry, HO §4-303.
Witness fees and expenses, HO §4-318.
Maryland dent-care program, ED §§18-2401 to
18-2408.
Medicaid.
Managed care organizations, HG §15-103.2.
Medical records.
Personal medical records generally, HG §§4-401 to
4-403.
Misdemeanors, HO §4-606.
Nitrous oxide.
Exceptions to certain powers of board as to use of,
HO §4-205.
Notices.
Center for disease control's guidelines on
universal precautions.
Display, HO §4-313.
Examinations, HO §4-305.
Licenses.
Change of address, HO §4-313.
**Ownership or operation of dental or dental
hygiene practice.**
Prohibited by dental hygienists, HO §4-605.
Penalties.
Licenses, HO §§4-316, 4-317.
Practice dental hygiene.
Defined, HO §4-101.
Ownership or operation of dental or dental
hygiene practice.
Prohibited by dental hygienists, HO §4-605.
Practice dentistry.
Defined, HO §4-101.
Ownership or operation of dental or dental
hygiene practice.
Prohibited by dental hygienists, HO §4-605.
Prescriptions.
Impoundment of drugs or records, HG §21-1113.
Property tax credit.
Dentistry practice in underserved area of state.
Credit on personal property used in practice, TP
§9-237.

DENTISTS —Cont'd
Radiation.
Dental radiation technologists, HO §4-505.
Definitions, HO §4-505.
Rules and regulations, HO §4-505.
Fees, EN §8-301.
Patient protection during use of radiation, HO
§4-506.
Rules and regulations.
Dental office or facility, EN §8-301.
Records.
Evidence.
Admissibility of dental records, CJ §10-104.
Impoundment of drugs or records, HG §21-1113.
Personal medical records generally, HG §§4-401 to
4-403.
Reports.
Injury reports.
Accidents involving moving vessels, HG
§20-702.
Certain counties, HG §20-701.
Gunshot causing injury, HG §20-703.
Rules and regulations.
Board of dental examiners.
Expansion of practice of dental hygiene, HO
§4-206.
Radiation sources.
Dental office or facility, EN §8-301.
Scholarships.
Dental scholarships.
Authority of counties and Baltimore City to
grant, ED §18-801.
Terms and conditions, ED §18-801.
Scope of title, HO §4-102.
Sexual misconduct.
Disciplinary action, HO §1-212.
Short title, HO §4-701.
Specialization.
Guidelines, HO §4-504.
Termination of title, HO §4-702.
Third party.
Defined, HO §4-101.
Title.
Scope of title, HO §4-102.
Short title, HO §4-701.
Termination, HO §4-702.
Volunteer dentists and dental hygienists.
Licenses, HO §4-302.
Retired, application for license, HO §4-304.
Waiver.
Education requirements, limited license to
practice dentistry, HO §4-303.1.
Examination requirements, HO §4-306.
Inactive status, HO §4-310.
License requirements, HO §4-303.
Weapons.
Injury caused by, report.
Certain counties, HG §20-701.
X rays.
Patient protection during use of radiation, HO
§4-506.

DEPARTMENT OF AGING.
General provisions.
See AGED.

DEPARTMENT OF DISABILITIES.
See HANDICAPPED PERSONS.

**DEPARTMENT OF HEALTH AND MENTAL
HYGIENE,** HG §§2-101 to 2-305.
See HEALTH AND MENTAL HYGIENE
DEPARTMENT.

DEPARTMENT OF JUVENILE SERVICES.
See JUVENILE SERVICES DEPARTMENT.

DEPARTMENT OF LEGISLATIVE SERVICES.
General provisions.
　See LEGISLATIVE SERVICES DEPARTMENT.

DEPARTMENT OF PLANNING.
Generally, SF §§5-201 to 5-615.
See PLANNING DEPARTMENT.

**DEPARTMENT OF PUBLIC SAFETY AND
　CORRECTIONAL SERVICES.**
Another state operating facility in state, COR
　§10-601.
Baltimore City detention center, COR §§5-401 to
　5-406.
Case records.
　Inmates in custody of division of correction, COR
　　§§3-601 to 3-609.
　See CORRECTION, DIVISION OF.
Commission on correctional standards, COR
　§§8-106 to 8-117.
　See PRISONS AND PRISONERS.
Community adult rehabilitation centers, COR
　§§11-301 to 11-320.
　See COMMUNITY ADULT REHABILITATION
　　CENTERS.
Construction of state correctional facilities,
　COR §§10-101 to 10-107.
　See PRISONS AND PRISONERS.
Correctional training commission, COR §§8-201
　to 2-210.
　See CORRECTIONAL TRAINING COMMISSION.
Death penalty.
　Procedures for carrying out death penalty
　　generally, COR §§3-901 to 3-909.
　See DEATH PENALTY.
Diminution credits.
　Inmates committed to custody of commissioner of
　　correction, COR §§3-701 to 3-711.
　See DIMINUTION OF INMATE'S TERM OF
　　CONFINEMENT.
Division of correction.
　Generally, COR §§3-101 to 3-222.
　　See CORRECTION, DIVISION OF.
　Prerelease unit for women, COR §§3-301 to 3-305.
Division of parole and probation, COR §§6-101
　to 6-116.
　See PAROLE AND PROBATION.
Division of pretrial detention and services,
　COR §§5-101 to 5-203.
Generally, COR §§2-101 to 2-201.
　See PUBLIC SAFETY AND CORRECTIONAL
　　SERVICES DEPARTMENT.
Grievances.
　Inmate grievance office, COR §§10-201 to 10-210.
　See PRISONS AND PRISONERS.
Home detention program.
　Inmates in custody of commissioner of correction,
　　COR §§3-401 to 3-415.
　See HOME DETENTION PROGRAM.
Inmates sentenced to jurisdiction of division
　of correction.
　Generally.
　　See PRISONS AND PRISONERS.
Internal investigative unit, COR §10-701.
Interstate corrections compact, COR §§8-601 to
　8-611.
　See PRISONS AND PRISONERS.
Law-enforcement and correctional training
　fund, COR §§8-301 to 8-305.

**DEPARTMENT OF PUBLIC SAFETY AND
　CORRECTIONAL SERVICES** —Cont'd
Leave of inmate from confinement.
　Work release program.
　　Inmate sentenced to jurisdiction of division of
　　　correction, COR §§3-801 to 3-807.
　　See WORK RELEASE PROGRAMS.
Maryland correctional enterprises, COR §§3-501
　to 3-528.
　See MARYLAND CORRECTIONAL
　　ENTERPRISES.
Parole commission, COR §§7-201 to 7-208.
　See PAROLE AND PROBATION.
Parole, release on mandatory supervision, COR
　§§7-101 to 7-805.
　See PAROLE AND PROBATION.
Patuxent institution, COR §§4-101 to 4-401.
　See PATUXENT INSTITUTION.
Pretrial release services program, COR §§5-301,
　5-302.
Standards for correctional services, COR
　§§8-101 to 8-117.
　See PRISONS AND PRISONERS.
State reimbursement of local correctional
　facilities, COR §§9-401 to 9-405.
Sundry claims board, COR §§10-301 to 10-310.
　See PRISONS AND PRISONERS.
Transfer of inmates.
　Generally, COR §§9-301 to 9-308.
　See PRISONS AND PRISONERS.
Work release program.
　Inmate sentence jurisdiction of division of
　　correction, COR §§3-801 to 3-807.
　See WORK RELEASE PROGRAMS.

DEPARTMENT OF STATE POLICE, PS §§2-101
　to 2-801.
See STATE POLICE DEPARTMENT.

DEPOSIT INSURANCE.
State treasury.
　Definitions, SF §6-201.
　Depositaries, SF §6-209.

DEPOSIT INSURANCE FUND CORPORATION.
Accrual of certain rights, claims and liabilities
　of fund to successor, FI §10-120.
Applicability of state insurance laws, FI
　§10-115.
Appropriations.
　Policy of state, FI §10-116.
Board of directors, FI §§10-103, 10-103.1.
Conflicts of interest.
　Fund director, FI §10-108.
Defenses.
　Immunity, FI §10-121.
Definitions, FI §10-101.
Department of labor, licensing and regulation.
　Accrual of certain rights, claims and liabilities of
　　fund, FI §10-120.
Deposit insurance fund, FI §§10-110, 10-110.2,
　10-112.
Employees, FI §10-104.
Established, FI §10-102.
Exchange of information, FI §10-114.
Fund director.
　Appointment, FI §10-103.
　Conflicts of interest, FI §§10-103, 10-108.
　Devoting full time to duties, FI §10-107.
　Exchange of information, FI §10-114.
　Exercise of corporate powers, FI §10-103.
　Prohibited activities, FI §10-109.

DEPOSIT INSURANCE FUND CORPORATION
—Cont'd

Fund director —Cont'd

Term of office, FI §10-103.

Immunity.

Defense, FI §10-121.

Defense of sovereign immunity, CJ §5-520.

Insurable loss.

Determination.

Duty of fund director, FI §10-110.1.

Limitations, FI §10-110.1.

Subrogation, FI §10-110.1.

Insurance laws.

Applicability of state insurance laws, FI §10-115.

Liability.

General provisions, CJ §5-520.

Membership.

Application, FI §10-111.

Certification by division director, FI §10-111.

Effective upon approval, FI §10-112.

Eligibility.

Major associations, FI §10-117.

Other associations, FI §10-118.

Withdrawal, FI §10-112.

Penalties.

Submitting false information, FI §10-119.

Rules and regulations.

Adoption, FI §10-113.

Salaries.

Employees, FI §10-104.

Seal, FI §10-106.

Secretary of licensing and regulation.

Authority, FI §10-105.

Staff, FI §10-104.

State insurance laws.

Applicability, FI §10-115.

Submitting false information.

Penalties, FI §10-119.

Successor agencies.

Accrual of certain rights, claims and liabilities of fund, FI §10-120.

Withdrawal from fund, FI §10-113.

DEPOSITIONS.

Actions.

Deposition taken in another action.

Use of depositions.

Circuit courts, CivProCir Rule 2-419.

Arbitration and award.

Authority of arbitrators, CJ §3-218.

Associations.

Designation of person to testify for organization.

Notice.

Circuit courts, CivProCir Rule 2-412.

Attachment.

Body attachment of material witness.

Deposition of witness in custody, Crim Rule 4-267.

Audiotape.

Generally.

Circuit courts, CivProCir Rule 2-416.

Notice.

Circuit courts, CivProCir Rule 2-412.

Body attachment.

Material witnesses.

Deposition of witness in custody, Crim Rule 4-267.

Certification.

Circuit courts, CivProCir Rule 2-415.

Tape recordings.

Videotape and audiotape depositions, CivProCir Rule 2-416.

DEPOSITIONS —Cont'd

Changes.

Circuit courts, CivProCir Rule 2-415.

Child custody proceedings.

Uniform child custody jurisdiction and enforcement act.

Obtaining testimony of witness located in another state, FL §9.5-110.

Circuit courts, Crim Rule 4-261.

Conflicts of interest.

Officers before whom depositions taken.

Circuit courts, CivProCir Rule 2-414.

Contradiction.

Use of depositions.

Circuit courts, CivProCir Rule 2-419.

Copies.

Furnishing copies.

Circuit courts, CivProCir Rule 2-415.

Corporations.

Designation of person to testify for organization.

Notice.

Circuit courts, CivProCir Rule 2-412.

Correction.

Circuit courts, CivProCir Rule 2-415.

Criminal rules, Crim Rule 4-261.

Cross-examination.

Circuit courts, CivProCir Rule 2-415.

Defendants.

Presence of defendant.

Criminal rules, Crim Rule 4-261.

Designation of person to testify for organization.

Notice.

Circuit courts, CivProCir Rule 2-412.

District Court.

Criminal rules, Crim Rule 4-261.

General provisions governing discovery, CivProDist Rule 3-401.

Perpetuation of testimony, CivProDist Rule 3-431.

Documents.

Production of documents and tangible things.

Circuit courts, CivProCir Rule 2-415.

Generally.

Circuit courts, CivProCir Rule 2-422.

Notice, CivProCir Rule 2-412.

Effect of deposition.

Circuit courts, CivProCir Rule 2-419.

Evidence.

Admissibility.

Objection to admissibility.

Circuit courts, CivProCir Rule 2-419.

Criminal rules, Crim Rule 4-261.

Use for substantive evidence.

Criminal rules, Crim Rule 4-261.

Examinations.

Circuit courts, CivProCir Rule 2-415.

Written questions.

Circuit courts, CivProCir Rule 2-417.

Expenses for failure to pursue deposition.

Circuit courts, CivProCir Rule 2-434.

Expert witnesses.

Use of depositions.

Circuit courts, CivProCir Rule 2-419.

Videotape deposition of expert.

Use of depositions.

Circuit courts, CivProCir Rule 2-419.

Foreign countries.

Officers before whom depositions taken.

Circuit courts, CivProCir Rule 2-414.

Uniform foreign depositions act.

Authority to act, CJ §9-401.

DEPOSITIONS —Cont'd
Foreign countries —Cont'd
Uniform foreign depositions act —Cont'd
Citation.
Short title, CJ §9-403.
Interpretation.
Uniformity, CJ §9-402.
Uniformity of interpretation, CJ §9-402.
General assembly.
Joint committee on administrative, executive and legislative review.
Power to take depositions of witnesses, SG §2-507.
Joint committee on the management of public funds, SG §2-807.
Legislative policy committee.
Power to cause depositions, SG §2-408.
Standing committees, SG §2-1104.
How taken.
Criminal rules, Crim Rule 4-261.
Impeachment.
Criminal rules, Crim Rule 4-261.
Use of depositions.
Circuit courts, CivProCir Rule 2-419.
Joinder.
Defendants.
Criminal rules, Crim Rule 4-261.
Judgments.
Discovery in aid of enforcement.
Circuit courts, CivProCir Rule 2-633.
Limitations on right to take.
Circuit courts, CivProCir Rule 2-411.
Methods of discovery.
Circuit courts, CivProCir Rule 2-401.
Motions.
Motion to suppress.
Circuit courts, CivProCir Rule 2-415.
Nonparties.
Place for depositions.
In state.
Circuit courts, CivProCir Rule 2-413.
Out of state.
Circuit courts, CivProCir Rule 2-413.
Nonresidents.
Uniform foreign depositions act. See within this heading, "Foreign countries."
Notice.
Failure of party giving notice to attend.
Expenses for failure to pursue deposition, CivProCir Rule 2-434.
Generally.
Circuit courts, Crim Rule 4-212.
Written questions.
Circuit courts, CivProCir Rule 2-417.
Oaths.
Officer before whom deposition taken.
In state, CivProCir Rule 2-414.
Procedure.
Circuit courts, CivProCir Rule 2-415.
Objections.
Admissibility of deposition.
Circuit courts, CivProCir Rule 2-419.
Criminal rules, Crim Rule 4-261.
Notice.
Circuit courts, CivProCir Rule 2-412.
Officers before whom depositions taken.
Circuit courts, CivProCir Rule 2-414.
Recording with testimony.
Circuit courts, CivProCir Rule 2-415.
Tape recordings.
Videotape and audiotape depositions.
Circuit courts, CivProCir Rule 2-416.

DEPOSITIONS —Cont'd
Objections —Cont'd
Written questions.
Objection to form.
Circuit courts, CivProCir Rule 2-417.
Officers before whom depositions taken, CivProCir Rule 2-414.
Orders.
Criminal rules, Crim Rule 4-261.
Partial use.
Circuit courts, CivProCir Rule 2-419.
Criminal rules, Crim Rule 4-261.
Parties.
Adverse parties.
Use of depositions.
Circuit courts, CivProCir Rule 2-419.
Failure of party giving notice to attend.
Expenses for failure to pursue deposition.
Circuit courts, CivProCir Rule 2-434.
Place for depositions.
Circuit courts, CivProCir Rule 2-413.
Partnerships.
Designation of person to testify for organization.
Notice.
Circuit courts, CivProCir Rule 2-412.
Perpetuation of testimony.
District Court, CivProDist Rule 3-431.
Physicians.
Disciplinary actions.
Rules governing taking, adoption by board, HO §14-405.
Place for depositions.
Circuit courts, CivProCir Rule 2-413.
Poultry products inspection.
Deposition of witnesses, AG §4-222.
Presence of defendant.
Criminal rules, Crim Rule 4-261.
Prisons and prisoners.
Right to take.
Circuit courts, CivProCir Rule 2-411.
Procedure for depositions.
Circuit courts, CivProCir Rule 2-415.
Production of documents and tangible things.
Discovery generally.
Circuit courts, CivProCir Rule 2-422.
Materials produced.
Circuit courts, CivProCir Rule 2-415.
Notice.
Circuit courts, CivProCir Rule 2-412.
Real estate brokers.
Real estate commission.
Taking depositions in connection with disciplinary proceedings, BOP §17-209.
Records.
Testimony.
Circuit courts, CivProCir Rule 2-415.
Refusal to answer.
Circuit courts, CivProCir Rule 2-415.
Right to take.
Circuit courts, CivProCir Rule 2-411.
Limitations.
Circuit courts, CivProCir Rule 2-411.
Sequence and timing of discovery.
Circuit courts, CivProCir Rule 2-401.
Signatures.
Correction and signature.
Circuit courts, CivProCir Rule 2-415.
State departments and agencies.
Designation of person to testify for organization.
Notice.
Circuit courts, CivProCir Rule 2-412.

DEPOSITIONS —Cont'd
Stipulations.
Stipulations regarding discovery procedure.
Circuit courts, CivProCir Rule 2-401.
Subpoenas.
Criminal rules, Crim Rule 4-261.
Failure to subpoena witnesses.
Expenses for failure to pursue deposition.
Circuit courts, CivProCir Rule 2-434.
Objections to subpoena for deposition.
Circuit courts, CivProCir Rule 2-510.
District Court, CivProDist Rule 3-510.
Substitution of party.
Circuit courts, CivProCir Rule 2-401.
Suppression.
Motion to suppress.
Circuit courts, CivProCir Rule 2-415.
Tape recordings.
Videotape and audiotape depositions.
Circuit courts, CivProCir Rules 2-412, 2-416, 2-419.
Tax court.
Appeals to tax court, TG §13-521.
Telephones.
Deposition by telephone.
Circuit courts, CivProCir Rule 2-418.
Testimony.
Oath and record of testimony.
Circuit courts, CivProCir Rule 2-415.
Time.
Sequence and timing of discovery.
Circuit courts, CivProCir Rule 2-401.
Uniform foreign depositions act.
General provisions. See within this heading, "Foreign countries."
Use of depositions.
Circuit courts, CivProCir Rule 2-419.
Videotape.
Expert witnesses.
Use of depositions.
Circuit courts, CivProCir Rule 2-419.
Generally.
Circuit courts, CivProCir Rule 2-416.
Notice.
Circuit courts, CivProCir Rule 2-412.
Witnesses.
Expert witnesses.
Use of depositions.
Circuit courts, CivProCir Rule 2-419.
Failure to subpoena witness.
Expenses for failure to pursue deposition.
Circuit courts, CivProCir Rule 2-434.
Impeachment.
Use of depositions.
Circuit courts, CivProCir Rule 2-419.
Poultry products inspection, AG §4-222.
Unavailability of witness or other exceptional circumstances.
Use of depositions.
Circuit courts, CivProCir Rule 2-419.
Workers' compensation.
Claims procedure.
Limited to perpetuation of testimony, LE §9-719.
State workers' compensation commission.
Investigative and enforcement powers, LE §9-309.
Written questions.
Examinations.
Circuit courts, CivProCir Rule 2-417.

DEPOSITIONS —Cont'd
Written questions —Cont'd
Notice.
Circuit courts, CivProCir Rule 2-417.
Objection.
Objection to form.
Circuit courts, CivProCir Rule 2-417.

DEPOSITORIES.
Bonds, surety.
Security approved by governor, MD Const Art VI §3.
Environmental service.
Securities, NR §3-126.
Federal deposit insurance corporation.
Security for deposit exceeding, 31 §7.
General depository law, SF §§6-205 to 6-210.
See STATE TREASURY.
Governor.
Security approved by governor, MD Const Art VI §3.
Municipal corporations.
Designation, 23A §2.
Safe deposit companies.
See SAFE-DEPOSIT COMPANIES.
Sinking funds.
Security for deposits, 31 §7.
Uninvested funds, 31 §7.
State publications depository and distribution program, ED §§23-301 to 23-304.
State treasurer.
Designation of financial institutions as depositaries, SF §6-205.
Approval by governor, SF §6-206.
Higher education loans to be considered, SF §6-207.
Selection by treasurer.
Approval by governor, MD Const Art VI §3.
State treasury, SF §§6-205 to 6-210.
See STATE TREASURY.

DEPOSITS.
Abandoned property disposition, CL §§17-101 to 17-326.
See ABANDONED PROPERTY DISPOSITION.
Air conditioning and heating contractors.
Board.
Disposition of money, BR §9A-207.
Amusements and recreation.
Pinball machines.
License fees, BR §17-410.
Wicomico County.
Disposition of money, BR §17-424.
Athletic commission.
Disposition of money, BR §4-206.
Attorneys at law.
Trust accounts, BOP §10-304.
General provisions, CJA Rules 16-601 to 16-612.
See ATTORNEYS AT LAW.
Baltimore City community college.
Disposition of funds, ED §16-507.
Bank deposits and collections, CL §§4-101 to 4-504.
See BANK DEPOSITS AND COLLECTIONS.
Banks and trust companies.
See BANKS AND TRUST COMPANIES.
Calvert County.
Hawkers and peddlers.
Disposition of money, BR §17-918.
Cemeteries.
Deposit from sales.
Perpetual care of cemeteries, BR §5-602.

DEPOSITS —Cont'd
Charities.
  Secretary of state.
    Disposition of money, BR §6-207.
  Solicitations, BR §6-505.
Collection agencies.
  Disposition of money, BR §7-206.
Condominium.
  Purchasers of new units, RP §11-121.
Consignment.
  Consignee, CL §11-805.
Cooperative housing corporations.
  Sales of cooperative interests.
    Held in escrow, CA §5-6B-11.
Costs.
  General provisions.
    See COSTS.
Counties.
  Deposit of unexpended or surplus money without
    security, 95 §22O.
Credit unions.
  See CREDIT UNIONS.
Day-care centers.
  Adult day care centers.
    State's right of recovery.
      Deposit of funds recovered, HG §24-706.
Dwellings.
  Deposits on new homes, RP §§10-301 to 10-306.
  See HOUSING.
Employment agencies.
  Commissioner.
    Disposition of money, BR §9-202.
Fiduciaries.
  Assets of estate.
    Agreement of fiduciary and surety for deposit of
      assets, ET §15-105.
    Withdrawal of deposit, ET §15-105.
  Banks and trust companies.
    Securities.
      Fiduciary authorized to deposit securities
        with clearing corporation.
      Bank or trust company as custodian or
        agent for fiduciary, ET §15-104.
  General provisions.
    See FIDUCIARIES.
  Name of fiduciary.
    In name of fiduciary as such, ET §15-206.
  Personal accounts.
    Fiduciary personal account, ET §15-208.
  Principal.
    In name of principal, ET §15-207.
  Securities.
    Fiduciary authorized to deposit securities with
      clearing corporation, ET §15-104.
Fines.
  Deposits on new homes.
    Failure of vendor to maintain escrow account or
      surety bond, RP §10-305.
General services department.
  Excess and surplus property.
    Auction or sale.
      Proceeds, SF §4-505.
Hawkers and peddlers.
  Calvert County.
    Disposition of money, BR §17-918.
Home improvements.
  Commission.
    Disposition of money, BR §8-213.
Horse racing.
  Harness racing.
    Maryland standardbred race fund, BR §11-629.

DEPOSITS —Cont'd
Horse racing —Cont'd
  Thoroughbred racing.
    Maryland-bred race fund, BR §11-535.
Housing.
  Deposits on new homes, RP §§10-301 to 10-306.
  See HOUSING.
Insurance companies, IN §§5-701 to 5-709.
  Liquidation, rehabilitation, etc., of insurers.
    Deposit of monies collected in delinquency
      proceedings, IN §9-222.
Juvenile services facilities capital program.
  Recovery of funds by state.
    Deposit of funds recovered, 83C §4-106.
Land installment contracts.
  Deposits on new homes, RP §§10-301 to 10-306.
  See HOUSING.
Landlord and tenant.
  Security deposits.
    See LANDLORD AND TENANT.
  Tenants' deposits.
    See LANDLORD AND TENANT.
Maryland food center authority.
  Bonds eligible for deposit, 41 §13-114.
Mental hygiene law.
  Community mental health facilities.
    State's right of recovery.
      Deposit of funds recovered, HG §24-606.
Mining.
  Strip mining.
    Bond or deposit.
      Forfeiture.
        Deposit of funds, EN §15-514.
Mobile homes.
  Security deposits.
    See MOBILE HOMES.
Motorcycles.
  Safety program.
    Authorization for deposits, TR §16-605.
Municipal corporations.
  Deposit of unexpended or surplus money without
    security, 95 §22O.
Precious metals and gem dealers.
  Disposition of money, BR §12-104.
Preneed burial contracts.
  Failure to deposit money, BR §5-712.
Real estate brokers.
  Trust accounts.
    See REAL ESTATE BROKERS.
Real property.
  Deposits on new homes, RP §§10-301 to 10-306.
  See HOUSING.
Savings and loan associations.
  See SAVINGS AND LOAN ASSOCIATIONS.
Securities.
  State treasurer.
    Deposit of physical securities, SF §2-602.
    Storage of securities not in physical form, SF
      §2-602.1.
Security deposits.
  See LANDLORD AND TENANT.
Senior citizen activities centers.
  Capital improvement grants program.
    Defaults.
      Deposit of funds recovered, 70B §31.
Sentence and punishment.
  Deposits on new homes.
    Failure of vendor to maintain escrow account or
      surety bond, RP §10-305.
State lottery.
  Agents.
    Licensed agents.
      Required deposits, SG §9-119.

DEPOSITS —Cont'd
State treasury.
Depositaries, SF §§6-205 to 6-210.
See STATE TREASURY.
Investments.
Deposits in financial institutions, SF §6-223.
Subdivisions.
Deposits on new homes, RP §§10-301 to 10-306.
See HOUSING.
Tenants' deposits.
General provisions.
See LANDLORD AND TENANT.
Vendor and vendee.
Deposits on new homes, RP §§10-301 to 10-306.
See HOUSING.

DEPRESSANTS.
Controlled dangerous substances.
Generally, CR §§5-101 to 5-1101.
See CONTROLLED DANGEROUS
SUBSTANCES.
Depressant drug defined, CR §5-101.
Names of controlled substances, CR §5-401.
Schedule I, CR §5-402.
Schedule II, CR §5-403.
Schedule III, CR §5-404.
Schedule IV, CR §5-405.

DEPUTIES.
Sheriffs.
General provisions.
See SHERIFFS.

DERELICT BOATS.
Acquiring title to abandoned vessels, NR
§8-722.
Removal and disposal of abandoned vessels,
NR §8-721.

DERIVATIVE ACTIONS.
Limited liability companies, CA §§4A-801 to
4A-804.
Limited partnerships, CA §§10-1001 to 10-1004.

DES.
Health insurance upon exposure to DES, IN
§15-503.

DESCENT AND DISTRIBUTION.
Absentee property act.
See ABSENT PERSONS.
Aliens.
Right to own and dispose of property, RP §14-101.
Bastards.
Child not to include illegitimate child, 1 §16.
Children.
Determining relationship.
General provisions, ET §§1-201 to 1-210.
See DECEDENTS' ESTATES.
Illegitimate child.
Word "child" not to include illegitimate child, 1
§16.
Courts.
Distribution by court. See within this heading,
"Order of distribution."
Custodian.
Appointment for distribution to minor, ET §9-109.
Death.
Absence as evidence of death and absentee
property act.
See ABSENT PERSONS.
Simultaneous death act.
Uniform law.
See DEATH.

DESCENT AND DISTRIBUTION —Cont'd
Death by wrongful act.
General provisions.
See DEATH BY WRONGFUL ACT.
Decedents' estates.
General provisions, ET §§1-101 to 12-103.
See DECEDENTS' ESTATES.
Deeds.
Distribution in kind.
Evidence of title, ET §9-105.
Determining relationship.
General provisions, ET §§1-201 to 1-210.
See DECEDENTS' ESTATES.
Devises and bequests.
See WILLS.
Disclaimer of property interests act.
Uniform disclaimer of property interests act. See
within this heading, "Uniform disclaimer of
property interests act."
Distribution by court.
Generally. See within this heading, "Order of
distribution."
Equity.
Distribution under jurisdiction of court, ET
§15-108.
Escheat.
Legatee not found or residing outside United
States.
Payment to county board of education, ET
§9-108.
Evidence.
Distribution in kind.
Title, ET §9-105.
Excise tax.
Deed for distribution in kind.
Exemption from excise tax, ET §9-105.
Fiduciaries.
Decree or order of court.
Protection when distribution made in
conformity therewith, ET §15-108.
General legacy.
Order of abatement, ET §9-103.
Guardian and ward.
Appointment for distribution to minor, ET §9-109.
Heirs.
Closing estates.
Liability of heirs to creditor, ET §10-102.
Determining relationship.
General provisions, ET §§1-201 to 1-210.
See DECEDENTS' ESTATES.
Improper distribution.
General provisions, ET §9-106.
In kind distribution.
General provisions. See within this heading,
"Order of distribution."
Insurance.
Death of insured.
Passing of property insurance, IN §12-303.
Interested persons.
Distribution by court.
Meeting of interested persons, ET §9-112.
Procedure when interested person not known,
ET §9-112.
Intestate succession.
General provisions, ET §§3-101 to 3-112.
See DECEDENTS' ESTATES.
Legatee.
Wills.
See WILLS.
Liability.
Distributee, ET §9-106.

DESCENT AND DISTRIBUTION —Cont'd
**Maryland uniform disclaimer of property
     interests act,** ET §§9-201 to 9-216. See within
     this heading, "Uniform disclaimer of property
     interests act."
Meeting of distributees, Estates Rule 6-443.
Minors.
  Custodian, ET §9-109.
  Guardian, ET §9-109.
  Money.
    General provisions, ET §9-109.
  Personal property.
    Tangible personal property, ET §9-109.
Motor vehicles.
  Registration.
    Passage of title to legatee or distributee, TR
       §13-504.
  Transfer by operation of law.
    Transferred to legatee or distributee, TR
       §13-114.
Nonresidents.
  Outside United States and not found.
    Payment of share to county board of education,
       ET §9-108.
Nontestamentary transfers, ET §1-401.
Order of distribution.
  Contingent claim, ET §8-112.
  Debts and claims.
    Order in which assets appropriated, ET §9-103.
  Distribution by court, Estates Rule 6-443.
    Procedure, ET §9-112.
    Sale of property, ET §9-112.
    Tangible personal property.
      Disagreement concerning distribution, ET
         §9-112.
  Improper distribution, ET §9-106.
  In kind.
    Application of provisions, ET §9-104.
    Effect of distribution, ET §9-106.
    Evidence of title.
      Execution and delivery of evidence of title, ET
         §9-105.
    Generally, ET §9-104.
    Objection.
      Right to object, ET §9-104.
    Residuary estate, ET §9-104.
    Specific legacy, ET §9-104.
    Title.
      Evidence of title.
        Execution and delivery, ET §9-105.
    Valuation, ET §9-104.
      Using federal estate tax values, ET §11-107.
  Legatee not found or residing outside United
     States.
    Payment to county board of education, ET
       §9-108.
    Refund from board of education, ET §9-108.
  Liability of distributee, ET §9-106.
  Meeting of distributees, Estates Rule 6-443.
  Minors.
    Custodian, ET §9-109.
    Guardian, ET §9-109.
    Money.
      General provisions, ET §9-109.
    Personal property.
      Tangible personal property, ET §9-109.
  Partition.
    For purpose of distribution, Estates Rule 6-444;
       ET §9-107.
  Proposal for distribution of property, Estates Rule
     6-442.

DESCENT AND DISTRIBUTION —Cont'd
Order of distribution —Cont'd
  Purchasers from distributees protected, ET
     §9-106.
  Release.
    From heir or legatee, ET §9-111.
  Title of distributees, ET §9-106.
Partition.
  For purpose of distribution, Estates Rule 6-444;
     ET §9-107.
Per stirpes.
  Representation.
    Intestate succession, ET §1-210.
Procedure.
  Distribution by court, ET §9-112.
Property interests act.
  Uniform disclaimer of property interests act. See
     within this heading, "Uniform disclaimer of
     property interests act."
Proposal for distribution of property, Estates
     Rule 6-442.
Releases.
  Personal representative may obtain verified
     release from heir or legatee, ET §9-111.
Renunciation.
  By testamentary trustee, ET §9-102.
  Disclaimer of property interests, ET §§9-201 to
     9-216. See within this heading, "Uniform
     disclaimer of property interests act."
Residuary estate.
  Conversion into cash, ET §9-104.
  Distribution in kind, ET §9-104.
Sales.
  Distribution by court.
    Sale of property, ET §9-112.
  Partition for purpose of distribution.
    Property sold which cannot be partitioned, ET
       §9-107.
  Protection of purchasers, ET §9-106.
Simultaneous death act.
  Uniform law.
    See DEATH.
Small estates.
  General provisions, ET §§5-601 to 5-607.
    See EXECUTORS AND ADMINISTRATORS.
Specific legacy.
  Distribution in kind, ET §9-104.
  Order of abatement, ET §9-103.
Surviving spouse.
  Divorce or annulment, ET §1-202.
  Share, ET §3-102.
  Statutory share.
    General provisions, ET §§3-203 to 3-208.
      See DECEDENTS' ESTATES.
Time for distribution, ET §7-101.
Title.
  Distributee, ET §9-106.
  Distribution in kind.
    Evidence of title.
      Execution and delivery, ET §9-105.
  Personal property.
    Determination of title by court, ET §1-301.
  Personal representative holds title for
     administration and distribution, ET §1-301.
Trusts and trustees.
  Final distribution.
    Commissions, ET §14-103.
  Testamentary trustee.
    Renunciation by, ET §9-102.
Uniform disclaimer of property interests act,
     ET §§9-201 to 9-216.
  Bars to disclaimer, ET §9-210.

DESCENT AND DISTRIBUTION —Cont'd
Uniform disclaimer of property interests act
—Cont'd
Citation of act, ET §9-216.
Conflict of laws.
Rights under other statutes not affected, ET
§9-215.
Definitions, ET §9-201.
Delivery of disclaimer, ET §9-209.
Disclaimer generally, ET §9-202.
Effect of disclaimer, ET §9-203.
Federal laws and regulations.
Effect, ET §9-211.
Fiduciaries.
Disclaimer by, ET §9-202.
Other fiduciaries, effectiveness as to, ET
§9-208.
Time of taking effect, ET §9-208.
Trustees, ET §9-205.
Filing of disclaimer, ET §9-212.
Fees, ET §2-206.
Irrevocability of disclaimer, ET §9-202.
Joint holders, ET §9-204.
Partial disclaimer, ET §9-202.
Powers of appointment.
Disclaimer by appointee of power, ET §9-207.
Delivery of disclaimer, ET §9-209.
Holder disclaiming non-fiduciary power, ET
§9-206.
Recordation of disclaimer, ET §9-212.
Registration of disclaimer, ET §9-212.
Rights under other statutes not affected, ET
§9-215.
Severability of provisions, ET §9-214.
Time disclaimer takes effect, ET §9-203.
Disclaimer by fiduciaries, ET §9-208.
Joint holders, ET §9-204.
Title of act, ET §9-216.
Trustees.
Disclaimer by, ET §9-205.
Unexercised disclaimers under former provisions,
ET §9-213.
Waiver of right to disclaim.
Disclaimer barred by, ET §9-210.
Wills.
General provisions, ET §§4-101 to 4-512.
See WILLS.

DESERTION AND NONSUPPORT.
See SUPPORT AND MAINTENANCE.

DESSERTS.
Frozen desserts, HG §§21-801 to 21-821.
See FROZEN DESSERTS.

DESTRUCTION OF PROPERTY.
Cemeteries.
Funerary objects or foliage, CR §10-404.
Hate crimes, CR §§10-301 to 10-308.
Malicious destruction of property, CR §6-301.
Public utility interference, CR §§6-303 to 6-305.
Throwing object at vehicle, CR §6-302.

DESTRUCTIVE DEVICES, CR §§4-501 to 4-503.
Arrest without a warrant.
Fire marshal's authority.
Specified violations, CP §2-208.
**Burglary with explosives or destructive
device,** CR §6-207.
Definitions, CR §4-501.
Exceptions to subtitle, CR §4-502.
Manufacture or possession prohibited, CR
§4-503.

DESTRUCTIVE DEVICES —Cont'd
Representation of destructive device.
Manufacturing, possessing or transporting, CR
§9-505.
Restitution ordered for violation, CR §4-503.
Scope of subtitle, CR §4-502.
Warrantless arrest.
Fire marshal's authority.
Specified violations, CP §2-208.

DETACHABLE MAGAZINES.
Prohibited, CR §4-305.

DETAINERS.
Detainee entitled to true copy, COR §9-611.
District Court.
Jurisdiction, CJ §4-401.
General provisions.
See FORCIBLE ENTRY AND DETAINER.
Interstate agreement on detainers, COR §§8-401
to 8-417.
See INTERSTATE AGREEMENT ON
DETAINERS.
Intrastate detainers, COR §§8-501 to 8-503.
Dismissal of indictment.
Inmate not informed that detainer lodged,
failure to bring to trial, COR §8-503.
Legislative findings, COR §8-501.
Notice to inmate that detainer lodged and right to
request final disposition, COR §8-503.
Notice upon receipt of untried indictment,
information, warrant or complaint, COR
§8-503.
Policy of state, purposes, COR §8-501.
Request for final disposition, COR §8-502.
Notice to inmate of right to make, COR §8-503.
Statement from managing official having
supervision over inmate.
Request for final disposition to be accompanied
by, COR §8-502.
Time for trial after inmate's request for final
disposition, COR §8-502.
Continuance, authority of court to grant, COR
§8-502.
Dismissal of indictment for failure to bring to
trial, COR §8-503.
Transportation of inmate, COR §8-503.
Mental hygiene law.
Emergency evaluations.
Arrested individuals, HG §10-626.

DETECTIVES.
Private detectives, BOP §§13-101 to 13-801.
See PRIVATE DETECTIVES.

DETINUE, PropAct Rule 12-602.
Judgments and decrees.
Enforcement of judgment in the alternative, CJ
§11-104.
Replevin.
See REPLEVIN.
Sale of goods, UCC.
Buyer's right to detinue of goods, CL §2-716.
Venue.
Additional venue permitted, CJ §6-202.

DETOXIFICATION CENTERS.
See DRUG OR ALCOHOL ABUSE.

DEVELOPMENT.
**Business and economic development
department.**
See BUSINESS AND ECONOMIC
DEVELOPMENT DEPARTMENT.

DEVELOPMENT —Cont'd

Canal place preservation and development authority, FI §§13-1001 to 13-1031.
See CANAL PLACE PRESERVATION AND DEVELOPMENT AUTHORITY.

Charles county.
New school capacity financing mechanism, 66B §14.05.

Chesapeake Bay critical area and Atlantic coastal bays critical areas programs.
Generally, NR §§8-1801 to 8-1817.
See CHESAPEAKE BAY CRITICAL AREA AND ATLANTIC COASTAL BAYS CRITICAL AREA PROTECTION PROGRAMS.

Counties.
Tax increment financing act.
Financing development of industrial, commercial or residential areas generally, 41 §§14-201 to 14-214.
See TAX INCREMENT FINANCING ACT.

Film production activity employer wage rebate program, 83A §§5-1801 to 5-1807.
See FILM PRODUCTION ACTIVITY EMPLOYER WAGE REBATE PROGRAM.

Housing and community development department.
General provisions.
See HOUSING AND COMMUNITY DEVELOPMENT DEPARTMENT.

Local military installation redevelopment authorities, 83A §§5-1701 to 5-1711.
See LOCAL MILITARY INSTALLATION REDEVELOPMENT AUTHORITIES.

Municipal corporations.
Tax increment financing act.
Financing development of industrial, commercial, or residential areas generally, 41 §§14-201 to 14-214.
See TAX INCREMENT FINANCING ACT.

Rural legacy program, NR §§5-9A-01 to 5-9A-09.
See RURAL LEGACY PROGRAM.

Tri-county council for southern Maryland.
See TRI-COUNTY COUNCIL FOR SOUTHERN MARYLAND.

Tri-county council for western Maryland.
See TRI-COUNTY COUNCIL FOR WESTERN MARYLAND.

DEVELOPMENTAL DISABILITIES.

Ability-to-pay schedule.
Prenatal and infant care services.
Local health agency.
Assessment, HG §16-201.1.

Abuse or neglect of vulnerable adult, CR §§3-604 to 3-606.
Exploitation of vulnerable adult, CR §8-801.

Administration.
Community services advisory commission, HG §7-204.
Creation, HG §7-201.
Defined, HG §7-101.
Director. See within this heading, "Director."
Established, HG §7-201.

Admissions.
Notice.
Provisions of title, HG §16-402.

Admission to state residential centers, HG §7-502.
Defined, HG §7-101.
Habeas corpus.
Individuals admitted, HG §7-506.

DEVELOPMENTAL DISABILITIES —Cont'd

Admission to state residential centers —Cont'd
Hearing, HG §7-503.
Determination of hearing officer.
Finality, HG §7-504.
Findings supporting admission, HG §7-503.
Notice of admission, HG §7-503.
Reevaluation of individual admitted, HG §7-505.

Advocacy services, CJ §3-1001.

Alternative living units.
Authorized, HG §7-601.
Defined, HG §7-101.
Emergency management plans, PS §14-110.1.
Single-family dwellings.
Deemed conclusively to be, HG §7-603.

Appeals.
Decisions of secretary of health and mental hygiene, HG §7-407.
State residential centers.
Release.
Petition for release, HG §7-507.

Assessments.
Intermediate care facilities, HG §7-517.

Audits.
Services co-ordination.
Funding distribution system for private community-based services, HG §7-306.1.

Chargeable persons.
Liability.
Applicability of subtitle, HG §16-403.
General rule, HG §16-404.
Schedules of charges, HG §16-405.

Charges for services.
Alternative requirements, HG §16-205.
Collections, HG §16-204.
Alternative requirements, HG §16-205.
Enforcement.
Uniformity of enforcement, HG §16-208.
Establishment of charges, HG §16-201.
Financial ability to pay.
Determination of financial ability to pay, HG §16-202.
Liability for payments, HG §16-203.
Liability of chargeable persons, HG §16-403.
General rule, HG §16-404.
Schedules of charges, HG §16-405.

Citation of law.
Short title, HG §7-1201.

Collections.
Applicability of other subtitles, HG §16-401.
Charges for services, HG §16-204.

Community-based residential programs.
Alternative living units. See within this heading, "Alternative living units."
Authorized, HG §7-601.
Group homes. See within this heading, "Group homes."

Community-based services for individuals.
Funding system for distribution to private contract providers, HG §7-306.1.
Penalty, failure to comply with reporting requirements, HG §7-910.

Community developmental disabilities services providers.
Reimbursement for approved services, HG §16-201.2.

Community services advisory commission.
Composition, HG §7-204.
Creation, HG §7-204.
Planning.
Five-year plan, HG §7-204.
Updating, HG §7-204.

DEVELOPMENTAL DISABILITIES —Cont'd
Community services advisory commission
—Cont'd
Reports, HG §7-204.
**Community supported living arrangements
services program.**
Community advocacy organizations.
Involvement in development of state plan, HG
§7-713.
Definitions, HG §7-709.
Findings of legislature, HG §7-710.
Funding.
Distribution of available funds, HG §7-713.
Individual support plan.
Services to be provided in accordance with, HG
§7-711.
Legislative declaration, HG §7-710.
Licensing of providers of services, HG §7-711.
Services for which license required, HG §7-903.
Policy of state, HG §7-710.
Provider organizations.
Involvement in development of state plan, HG
§7-713.
Quality assurance program, HG §7-712.
Rules and regulations, HG §7-714.
Licensing of providers of services, HG §7-711.
State plan.
Amendment.
Review of amendments affecting program, HG
§7-712.
Contents, HG §7-303.
Development, HG §7-713.
Comprehensive evaluation.
Notice.
Provisions of title, HG §16-402.
Confidentiality of information.
Rights of individuals, HG §7-1003.
Construction and interpretation.
Individual support services program, HG §7-707.
**Contract providers of community-based
services to individuals.**
Funding system for distribution to, HG §7-306.1.
Penalty, failure to comply with reporting
requirements, HG §7-910.
Cost of care.
Alternative requirements, HG §16-205.
Definitions, HG §16-101.
Enforcement.
Uniformity of enforcement, HG §16-208.
Financial ability to pay.
Determination of financial ability to pay, HG
§16-202.
Liability for payments, HG §16-203.
Responsibility for cost, HG §16-102.
Counties.
Family support services program.
Grants.
Amount of grant to county, HG §7-703.
Group homes.
Public group homes.
Acquisition of site.
Notice required prior to acquisition, HG
§7-606.
Courts.
Costs of court ordered examinations, HG §16-406.
Day habilitation services.
Licenses.
Services for which license required, HG §7-903.
Death.
Disposition of property on death of mentally
retarded individual, HG §16-407.

DEVELOPMENTAL DISABILITIES —Cont'd
Death —Cont'd
Individuals in service or program, HG §7-207.
Mortality and quality review committee, HG
§§5-801 to 5-810.
Death sentence.
Defined, not imposed on mentally retarded, CR
§2-202.
Definitions, HG §7-101.
Board, HG §7-510.
Community-based residential programs, HG
§7-602.
Community supported living arrangements
services program, HG §7-709.
Cost of care, HG §16-101.
Facilities, HG §7-803.
Family support services program, HG §7-701.
Generally, HG §7-101.
Individual support services program, HG §7-706.
In-service training program, HG §7-205.
Licensee, HG §§7-909, 7-1001.
Recipient of individual support services, HG
§7-901.
Respite care, 88A §128; HG §7-509.
Rights of individuals, HG §§7-1001, 7-1002.
Abuse, HG §7-1005.
State plan, HG §7-301.
Department of human resources.
Respite care.
Development of programs, 88A §129.
Director.
Appointment, HG §7-202.
Assistant directors, HG §7-202.
Defined, HG §7-101.
Deputy directors, HG §7-202.
Head of administration, HG §7-202.
Transfers.
Authority of director, HG §7-801.
Elections.
Rights of individuals.
Infringement of right to vote, HG §7-1004.
Evaluation.
Comprehensive evaluation.
Notice.
Provisions of title, HG §16-402.
Examinations.
Costs of court ordered examinations, HG §16-406.
Exploitation of vulnerable adult, CR §8-801.
External support.
Defined, HG §7-101.
Facilities.
Community mental health facilities, HG §§24-601
to 24-607.
See MENTAL HEALTH FACILITIES.
Defined, HG §7-803.
Transferring residents of facilities, HG §7-803.
Family support services program.
Budgetary support.
Certain projects in Baltimore and Anne Arundel
counties, HG §7-704.
Operation of program.
General requirements, HG §7-704.
Requests for, HG §7-704.
Creation of program, HG §7-703.
Definitions, HG §7-701.
Eligible child.
Defined, HG §7-701.
Existing programs.
Coordinating services available under, HG
§7-703.

DEVELOPMENTAL DISABILITIES —Cont'd
Family support services program —Cont'd
Funding.
　Requests for budgetary support, HG §7-704.
Legislative declaration, HG §7-702.
Licenses.
　Services for which license required, HG §7-903.
Policy of state, HG §7-702.
Reimbursement.
　Sliding payment scale for, HG §7-703.
Secretary of health and mental hygiene.
　Budgetary support.
　　Assumption of financial responsibility, HG
　　　§7-704.
　　Certain projects in Baltimore and Anne
　　　Arundel counties.
　　　Assumption of financial responsibility, HG
　　　　§7-704.
Funding system.
Distribution to private contract providers of
　community-based services to individuals, HG
　§7-306.1.
Penalty, failure to comply with reporting
　requirements, HG §7-910.
General assembly.
Group homes.
　Public group homes.
　　Acquisition of site.
　　　Notice required to members of the district
　　　　affected prior to acquisition, HG §7-606.
Group homes.
Authorized, HG §7-601.
Defined, HG §7-101.
Emergency management plans, PS §14-110.1.
Private group homes.
　Certificates of approval.
　　Application, HG §7-610.
　　　Approval or denial, HG §7-612.
　　　Contents, HG §7-610.
　　　Hearing on, HG §7-611.
　　　Investigation of applicant, HG §7-611.
　　Investigation of applicant, HG §7-611.
　　Issuance, HG §7-612.
　　Obtaining, HG §7-608.
　　Qualifications, HG §7-609.
　　Required, HG §7-608.
　　Rules and regulations, HG §7-607.
　Defined, HG §7-602.
　Hearings.
　　Application for certificate of approval, HG
　　　§7-611.
　Investigations.
　　Application for certificate of approval, HG
　　　§7-611.
　Notice.
　　Hearing on application for certificate of
　　　approval, HG §7-611.
　Qualifications for certificate of approval, HG
　　§7-609.
　Rules and regulations.
　　Certificates of approval, HG §7-607.
Public group homes.
　Acquisition of sites, HG §7-606.
　　Notice, HG §7-606.
　Defined, HG §7-602.
　Need.
　　Determination of need, HG §7-604.
　Operation, HG §7-606.
　Secretary of health and mental hygiene.
　　Determination of need, HG §7-604.

DEVELOPMENTAL DISABILITIES —Cont'd
Group homes —Cont'd
Public group homes —Cont'd
　Secretary of health and mental hygiene
　　—Cont'd
　　Sites.
　　　Choosing, HG §7-605.
　　Sites, HG §7-605.
　　　Acquisition, HG §7-606.
　Single-family dwellings.
　　Deemed conclusively to be, HG §7-603.
Habeas corpus.
State residential centers.
　Individuals admitted, HG §7-506.
Habilitation.
Defined, HG §7-101.
Funding.
　Use of local funds for day habilitation, HG
　　§7-705.
Licenses.
　Generally, HG §§7-901 to 7-910. See within this
　　heading, "Licenses."
Rights of individuals.
　Plan of habilitation, HG §7-1006.
　　Approval, HG §7-1006.
Hearings.
Group homes.
　Private group homes.
　　Application for certificate of approval, HG
　　　§7-611.
Licenses.
　Denial, suspension or revocation, HG §7-910.
Procedure, HG §7-406.
Request for informal hearing, HG §7-406.
State residential centers.
　Admission, HG §§7-503, 7-504.
Transfers.
　Mental health program.
　　Transfer to, HG §7-802.
Husband and wife.
Rights of individuals.
　Right of spouses to share rooms, HG §7-1003.
Immunity.
Rights of individuals.
　Abuse, HG §7-1005.
　　Reports.
　　　Immunity from civil liability, CJ §5-625.
Improvement of quality of care.
Mortality and quality review committee, HG
　§§5-801 to 5-810.
Individual support services.
Construction and interpretation, HG §7-707.
Defined, HG §§7-101, 7-706.
Eligibility, HG §7-403.
Eligible persons selected for services.
　Notice.
　　Required, HG §7-708.
Establishment of program, HG §7-708.
Licenses.
　Services for which license required, HG §7-903.
Policy of chapter, HG §7-707.
Purpose of chapter, HG §7-707.
Recipient of individual support services.
　Defined, HG §7-901.
In-service training program.
Generally, HG §7-205.
Participation.
　Requirement, HG §7-205.
Standards.
　Establishment, HG §7-205.

DEVELOPMENTAL DISABILITIES —Cont'd
Inspections.
Licenses, HG §7-909.
Report of inspection, HG §7-909.
Insurance.
Charges for services.
Liability of chargeable persons.
Collection of insurance proceeds, HG §16-404.
Intermediate care facilities, HG §7-517.
Interpretation and construction, HG §7-103.
Investigations.
Group homes.
Private group homes.
Application for certificate of approval, HG §7-611.
Licenses.
Applicants, HG §7-906.
Jury.
State residential centers.
Release.
Petition for release.
Jury trial, HG §7-507.
Juvenile cases.
Competency or incompetency to proceed.
Evaluation of child's mental and developmental levels, CJ §§3-8A-17.1 to 3-8A-17.12.
Juvenile services.
Providing services to juveniles, HG §16-206.
Laboratories.
Public health and clinical laboratory services, HG §16-207.
Law enforcement personnel.
State residential centers.
Employees.
Appointment as law enforcement officers, HG §7-516.
Legislative declaration, HG §7-102.
Family support services program, HG §7-702.
Liability.
Chargeable persons, HG §16-403.
General rules, HG §16-404.
Schedules of charges, HG §16-405.
Charges for services.
Liability for payments, HG §16-203.
Cost of care.
Liability for payments, HG §16-203.
Licenses.
Applicability of provisions.
Services for which license required, HG §7-903.
Applications, HG §7-905.
False statements.
Penalty, HG §7-910.
Information to accompany, HG §7-905.
Investigation of applicants, HG §7-906.
Authority of licensee, HG §7-908.
Community supported living arrangements services.
Services for which licenses required, HG §7-903.
Day habilitation services.
Services for which license required, HG §7-903.
Denial, HG §§7-907, 7-910.
Family support services.
Services for which license required, HG §7-903.
Health occupations.
Practice not limited, HG §7-902.
Hearings.
Denial, suspension or revocation, HG §7-910.
Individual support services.
Services for which license required, HG §7-903.
Inspections, HG §7-909.
Reports, HG §7-909.

DEVELOPMENTAL DISABILITIES —Cont'd
Licenses —Cont'd
Investigation of applicants, HG §7-906.
Issuance, HG §7-907.
Licensees.
Authority, HG §7-908.
Defined, HG §§7-909, 7-1001.
Rights of individuals. See within this heading, "Rights of individuals."
Practice of health occupation.
Not limited by provision, HG §7-902.
Reports.
Inspections, HG §7-909.
Requirement.
Services for which license required, HG §7-903.
Waiver, HG §7-903.
Residential services.
Services for which license required, HG §7-903.
Rules and regulations, HG §7-904.
Services coordination.
Services for which license required, HG §7-903.
Services for which license required, HG §7-903.
Waiver, HG §7-903.
Suspension or revocation, HG §7-910.
Vocational services.
Services for which license required, HG §7-903.
Waiver.
Services for which license required, HG §7-903.
Living independently.
Defined, HG §7-101.
Mental hygiene administration.
Referrals to, HG §7-403.
Mental retardation defined, HG §7-101.
Minors.
Juvenile cases.
Competency or incompetency to proceed.
Evaluation of child's mental and developmental levels, CJ §§3-8A-17.1 to 3-8A-17.12.
Misdemeanors.
Compensation.
Receiving unauthorized compensation, HG §7-1104.
Licenses.
Applications.
False statements, HG §7-910.
Nonbudgeted funds.
Accepting, HG §7-1104.
Providing services unlawfully, HG §7-1101.
Rights of individuals.
Interference with, HG §7-1102.
Mortality and quality review committee, HG §§5-801 to 5-810.
Access to information and records.
Death being review, HG §5-806.
Aggregate incident data.
Defined, HG §5-801.
Office of health care quality to provide and review, HG §5-806.1.
Chairperson, HG §5-804.
Closed meetings, HG §5-810.
Confidentiality of records, HG §5-809.
Consultants, HG §5-806.1.
Death reports, review by committee, HG §5-805.
Definitions, HG §5-801.
Disclosure by involved persons, HG §5-809.
Duties, HG §5-803.
Established, HG §5-802.
Expenses, reimbursement, HG §5-804.
Immunity of members, HG §5-807.
Improving quality of care, purpose, HG §5-802.

DEVELOPMENTAL DISABILITIES —Cont'd
Mortality and quality review committee
—Cont'd
Investigation after reviewing death report, HG
§5-805.
Maintenance of records, HG §5-809.
Meetings, quorum, HG §5-804.
Closed meetings, HG §5-810.
Membership, terms, HG §5-804.
Persons to provide information on review of death,
HG §5-806.
Preliminary findings or recommendation, issuing,
HG §5-808.
Preventing avoidable deaths, purpose, HG §5-802.
Questioning involved person in civil or criminal
proceeding, HG §5-809.
Recordkeeping, HG §5-809.
Removal of member, HG §5-804.
Report for public distribution, preparation
annually, HG §5-808.
Report to committee by office of health care
quality, HG §5-805.
Review of deaths of service recipients.
Office of health care quality, HG §5-805.
Staff, HG §5-804.
Municipal corporations.
Group homes.
Public group homes.
Acquisition of site.
Notice required prior to acquisition, HG
§7-606.
Murder in the first degree.
Death sentence.
Defined, not imposed on mentally retarded, CR
§2-202.
Nonresidential programs.
Community supported living arrangements
services program, HG §§7-709 to 7-714. See
within this heading, "Community supported
living arrangements services program."
Family support services program, HG §§7-701 to
7-704. See within this heading, "Family
support services program."
Notices.
Admissions to facilities.
Provisions of title, HG §16-402.
Comprehensive evaluation.
Provisions of title, HG §16-402.
Group homes.
Private group homes.
Hearing on application for certificate of
approval, HG §7-611.
Public group homes.
Acquisition of site.
Notice to be given prior to acquisition, HG
§7-606.
Individual support services program.
Eligible persons selected.
Notice required, HG §7-708.
Rights of individuals.
Records.
Change.
Notice of refusal to change record, HG
§7-1011.
State residential centers.
Admission, HG §7-503.
Penalties.
Compensation.
Receiving unauthorized compensation, HG
§7-1104.

DEVELOPMENTAL DISABILITIES —Cont'd
Penalties —Cont'd
Licenses.
Applications.
False statements, HG §7-910.
Nonbudgeted funds.
Accepting, HG §7-1104.
Providing services unlawfully, HG §7-1101.
Rights of individuals.
Interference with, HG §7-1102.
Petitions.
State residential centers.
Release, HG §7-507.
Planning.
Community services advisory commission.
Five-year plan, HG §7-204.
State plan.
Community supported living arrangements
services program. See within this heading,
"Community supported living arrangements
services program."
Contents, HG §7-303.
Defined, HG §7-301.
Implementation, HG §7-306.
Purpose, HG §7-302.
Revision, HG §7-303.
Policy of state, HG §§7-102, 7-204.
Family support services program, HG §7-702.
Posting and copies of policy, HG §7-1002.
Procedures for carrying out policy, HG §7-1003.
Rights of individuals, HG §7-1002.
Prenatal and infant care services.
Services and ability-to-pay schedule.
Local health agency.
Assessment, HG §16-201.1.
Prevention of avoidable deaths.
Mortality and quality review committee, HG
§§5-801 to 5-810.
**Private providers of community-based services
to individuals.**
Funding system for distribution to, HG §7-306.1.
Penalty, failure to comply with reporting
requirements, HG §7-910.
Prohibited acts.
Compensation.
Unauthorized compensation, HG §7-1104.
Providing services unlawfully, HG §7-1101.
Records.
Disclosure by custodians, HG §7-1103.
Rights of individuals.
Interference with, HG §7-1102.
Property.
Rights of individuals.
Infringement of right to receive, hold and
dispose of property, HG §7-1004.
Rape in second degree.
Victim mentally defective or incapacitated, CR
§3-304.
Records.
Rights of individuals.
Availability for inspection, HG §7-1008.
Change, HG §7-1011.
Contents, HG §7-1008.
Director.
Access to records.
Licensee required to give director access,
HG §7-1007.
Disclosure of records, HG §§7-1009, 7-1011,
7-1103. See within this heading, "Rights of
individuals."
Required, HG §7-1008.

DEVELOPMENTAL DISABILITIES —Cont'd
Records —Cont'd
  Rights of individuals —Cont'd
    Security, HG §7-1008.
  State residential centers.
    Release.
      Petition for release, HG §7-507.
    Transfers, HG §7-801.
Referrals, HG §§7-403, 7-405.
Reimbursement for services.
  Applicability of other subtitles, HG §16-401.
  Community service providers, HG §7-307.
Release.
  Defined, HG §7-101.
  Disposition of property on release of individual,
    HG §16-407.
  Property.
    Disposition of property on release of individual,
      HG §16-407.
  State residential centers, HG §7-508.
    Conditional release, HG §7-508.
    Petition for release, HG §7-507.
Reports.
  Community services advisory commission, HG
    §7-204.
  Death of individual in service or program, HG
    §7-207.
  Licenses.
    Inspections, HG §7-909.
  Rights of individuals.
    Abuse, HG §7-1005.
      Immunity from liability, CJ §5-625; HG
        §7-1005.
    Violations of provisions, HG §7-1003.
  State residential centers.
    Citizens' advisory boards, HG §7-515.
Residential services.
  Licenses.
    Services for which license required, HG §7-903.
Resource coordinator.
  Habilitation plan, duties, HG §7-1006.
Respite care.
  Agreements for services, 88A §129.
  Defined, 88A §128.
  Department of human resources.
    Development of programs, 88A §129.
  Limits on individual respite care, 88A §128.
  Rules and regulations.
    Promulgation by department of human
      resources, 88A §129.
Rights of individuals.
  Abuse.
    Defined, HG §7-1005.
    Law enforcement agencies.
      Duties, HG §7-1005.
    Reports, HG §7-1005.
      Immunity from liability, CJ §5-625; HG
        §7-1005.
  Clothing and personal effects, HG §7-1003.
  Confidentiality of information, HG §7-1003.
  Definitions, HG §§7-1001, 7-1002.
    Abuse, HG §7-1005.
  Grievances, HG §7-1003.
  Habilitation.
    Plan of habilitation, HG §7-1006.
  Information.
    Licensee required to give director certain
      information, HG §7-1007.
  Interference with rights, HG §7-1102.
  Licensees.
    Defined, HG §7-1001.

DEVELOPMENTAL DISABILITIES —Cont'd
Rights of individuals —Cont'd
  Licensees —Cont'd
    Duties, HG §7-1003.
      Posting and copies of policy of state, HG
        §7-1002.
    Information.
      Required to give director certain information,
        HG §7-1007.
  Misdemeanors.
    Interference with rights, HG §7-1102.
  Penalties.
    Interference with rights, HG §7-1102.
  Policy of state, HG §7-1002.
    Posting and copies of policy, HG §7-1002.
    Procedures for carrying out policy, HG §7-1003.
  Property.
    Infringement of right to receive, hold and
      dispose of property, HG §7-1004.
  Records.
    Availability for inspection, HG §7-1008.
    Change.
      Request to change record, HG §7-1011.
        Notice of refusal, HG §7-1011.
    Contents, HG §7-1008.
    Contest, HG §7-1011.
    Director.
      Access to records.
        Licensee required to give director access,
          HG §7-1007.
    Disclosure, HG §7-1009.
      Consent, HG §7-1010.
      Contest, HG §7-1011.
      Copies.
        Fees allowed, HG §7-1010.
      Custodian.
        Defined, HG §7-1103.
        Liability for unlawful disclosure, HG
          §7-1103.
      Liability of custodian for unlawful disclosure,
        HG §7-1103.
      List of disclosures, HG §7-1010.
      Punitive damages.
        Liability of custodian for unlawful
          disclosure, HG §7-1103.
      Refusal of licensee to disclose, HG §7-1010.
      Unlawful disclosure.
        Liability of custodian, HG §7-1103.
      When permitted, HG §7-1010.
      When required, HG §7-1010.
    Required, HG §7-1008.
    Security, HG §7-1008.
  Reports.
    Abuse, HG §7-1005.
      Immunity from liability, HG §7-1005.
    Violations of provisions, HG §7-1003.
  Rules and regulations.
    Enforcement of rights, HG §7-1002.
  Spouses.
    Right to share rooms, HG §7-1003.
  Telephones.
    Access to, HG §7-1003.
  Treatment.
    Information regarding treatment of individuals,
      HG §7-1003.
    Participation of individuals in treatment, HG
      §7-1003.
  Violations of provisions.
    Reports, HG §7-1003.
  Visitation, HG §7-1003.

DEVELOPMENTAL DISABILITIES —Cont'd
Rights of individuals —Cont'd
Voting.
Infringement of right to vote, HG §7-1004.
Work assignments, HG §7-1003.
Rules and regulations.
Community supported living arrangements services program, HG §7-714.
Licensing of providers of services, HG §7-711.
Prioritization of incidents, HG §7-909.
Respite care.
Promulgation by department of human resources, 88A §129.
Rights of individuals.
Enforcement of rights, HG §7-1002.
Secretary of health and mental hygiene, HG §7-401.
Group homes.
Private group homes.
Certificates of approval, HG §7-607.
Licenses, HG §7-904.
Secretary of health and mental hygiene.
Appeals from decisions of secretary, HG §7-407.
Community-based services.
Funding distribution system, HG §7-306.1.
Delegation of authority, powers and duties, HG §7-203.
Director.
Appointment, HG §7-202.
Duties, HG §§7-305, 7-306.
Delegation, HG §7-203.
Family support services program.
Budgetary support.
Assumption of financial responsibility, HG §7-704.
Certain projects in Baltimore and Anne Arundel counties.
Assumption of financial responsibility, HG §7-704.
Powers.
Delegation, HG §7-203.
Rules and regulations, HG §7-401.
Group homes.
Private group homes.
Certificates of approval, HG §7-607.
Licenses, HG §7-904.
State residential centers.
Admissions.
Approval by secretary, HG §7-502.
Serious reportable incidents.
Prioritization regulations and protocol, HG §7-909.
Services.
Application for services, HG §7-402.
Action on, HG §7-403.
Contents, HG §7-403.
Evaluations, HG §7-404.
Defined, HG §7-101.
Duties of secretary of health and mental hygiene as to, HG §7-305.
Eligibility, HG §§7-403, 7-405.
Evaluation of applicants, HG §7-404.
Family support services program, HG §§7-701 to 7-704. See within this heading, "Family support services program."
Individual support services. See within this heading, "Individual support services."
Licenses, HG §§7-901 to 7-910. See within this heading, "Licenses."
Providing services unlawfully, HG §7-1101.

DEVELOPMENTAL DISABILITIES —Cont'd
Services —Cont'd
Vocational services. See within this heading, "Vocational services."
Services coordination.
Community-based services.
Funding distribution system, HG §7-306.1.
Defined, HG §7-101.
Duties of secretary of health and mental hygiene, HG §7-305.
Licenses.
Generally, HG §§7-901 to 7-910. See within this heading, "Licenses."
Sexual abuse of vulnerable adult, CR §§3-604, 3-606.
Sexual offense in the second degree.
Victim mentally defective or incapacitated, CR §3-306.
Sexual offense in the third degree.
Victim mentally defective or incapacitated, CR §3-307.
Short title of law, HG §7-1201.
State residential centers.
Administrative head.
Appointment, HG §7-501.
Admission, HG §7-502.
Habeas corpus.
Individuals admitted, HG §7-506.
Hearing, HG §7-503.
Determination of hearing officer.
Finality, HG §7-504.
Findings supporting admission, HG §7-503.
Notice of admission, HG §7-503.
Reevaluation of individual admitted, HG §7-505.
Citizens' advisory boards.
Advisory capacity, HG §7-515.
Appointment of members, HG §7-512.
Composition, HG §§7-501, 7-512.
Creation, HG §7-511.
Definition of "board," HG §7-510.
Election of officers, HG §7-513.
Established, HG §7-511.
Expenses of members.
Reimbursement, HG §7-514.
Meetings, HG §7-514.
Regulations for conduct of meetings, HG §7-515.
Number of members, HG §7-512.
Officers.
Election, HG §7-513.
Qualifications of members, HG §7-512.
Residence requirement for membership, HG §7-512.
Terms of members, HG §7-512.
Creation, HG §7-501.
Defined, HG §7-101.
Emergency management plans, PS §14-110.1.
Habeas corpus.
Individuals admitted, HG §7-506.
Intermediate care facilities, HG §7-517.
Law enforcement officers.
Appointment of employees as, HG §7-516.
Least restrictive service.
Providing, HG §7-502.
Reevaluations, HG §7-505.
Release, HG §§7-507, 7-508.
Reports.
Citizens' advisory boards, HG §7-515.
Respite care, HG §7-509.
Secretary of health and mental hygiene.
Admissions.
Approval by secretary, HG §7-502.

DEVELOPMENTAL DISABILITIES —Cont'd
Title of law.
　Short title, HG §7-1201.
Transfers.
　Director.
　　Authority of director, HG §7-801.
　Facilities.
　　Residents of facilities, HG §7-803.
　Findings.
　　Written findings required, HG §7-801.
　Mental health program.
　　Transfer to, HG §7-802.
　Records, HG §7-801.
Treatment.
　Defined, HG §7-101.
　Rights of individuals.
　　Information regarding treatment of individuals, HG §7-1003.
　　Participation of individuals in treatment, HG §7-1003.
Visitation.
　Rights of individuals, HG §7-1003.
Vocational services.
　Defined, HG §7-101.
　Funding.
　　Use of local funds, HG §7-705.
　Licenses.
　　Generally, HG §§7-901 to 7-910. See within this heading, "Licenses."
Waiting list equity fund.
　Community-based services, HG §7-206.
Waiver.
　Licenses.
　　Services for which license required, HG §7-903.
Zoning.
　Community-based residential programs.
　　Not subject to certain zoning provisions, HG §7-603.

DEVELOPMENTAL DISABILITIES, MENTAL HEALTH, CHILD WELFARE AND JUVENILE SERVICES WORKFORCE TUITION ASSISTANCE PROGRAM, ED §§18-2101 to 18-2108.
Amount of assistance, ED §18-2104.
Community-based employment requirement, ED §18-2106.
Definitions, ED §18-2101.
Duration of assistance, ED §18-2105.
Established, ED §18-2102.
Funding, ED §18-2108.
Noncompliance with requirements.
　Repayment of funds, ED §18-2107.
Repayment of funds upon noncompliance with requirements, ED §18-2107.
Rules and regulations, ED §18-2102.
Use of awards, ED §18-2103.

DEVELOPMENT CREDIT CORPORATION.
Industrial development corporations.
　General provisions, 45A §§1 to 3.
　　See INDUSTRIAL DEVELOPMENT CORPORATIONS.
Securities.
　Exempt securities, CA §11-601.

DEVELOPMENT FINANCE DIVISION, HS §§4-101 to 4-1813.
Community development administration.
　Generally, HS §§4-201 to 4-255.
　　See COMMUNITY DEVELOPMENT ADMINISTRATION.

DEVELOPMENT FINANCE DIVISION —Cont'd
Community development administration —Cont'd
　Units in division, HS §4-103.
Counties.
　Residential mortgage programs for certain counties, HS §§4-1601 to 4-1610.
Defined terms, HS §4-101.
Down payment and settlement expense loan program.
　Generally, HS §§4-301 to 4-309.
　　See DOWN PAYMENT AND SETTLEMENT EXPENSE LOAN PROGRAM.
　Units in division, HS §4-103.
Elderly rental housing program, HS §§4-401 to 4-409.
　Units in division, HS §4-103.
Established, HS §4-102.
Federal and state weatherization program.
　Units in division, HS §4-103.
Funds, HS §§4-501 to 4-505.
　Appropriations, HS §4-501.
　Homeownership programs fund, HS §4-502.
　Investments, HS §4-501.
　Partnership rental housing fund, HS §4-503.
　Rental housing programs fund, HS §4-504.
　Special loan programs fund, HS §4-505.
　Status of funds, HS §4-501.
Governmental units of department, HS §2-201.
Grants.
　Workforce housing grant program, HS §§4-1801 to 4-1813.
Group home financing program, HS §§4-601 to 4-612.
　Units in division, HS §4-103.
Homeownership programs fund, HS §4-502.
Infrastructure development.
　Local government infrastructure program.
　　Units in division, HS §4-103.
Lead hazard reduction grant and loan programs, HS §§4-701 to 4-712.
　Units in division, HS §4-103.
Maryland home financing program, HS §§4-801 to 4-816.
　Units in division, HS §4-103.
Maryland housing rehabilitation program, HS §§4-901 to 4-933.
　Units in division, HS §4-103.
Neighborhood housing services fund, HS §§4-1001 to 4-1005.
　Units in division, HS §4-103.
Operating assistance grants demonstration projects, HS §§4-1101 to 4-1105.
　Administration.
　　Regulations, HS §4-1105.
　Amount of grants, HS §4-1104.
　Authorized uses of grants, HS §4-1103.
　Eligibility, HS §4-1101.
　　Limited income housing, HS §4-1102.
　Limited income housing, HS §4-1102.
　Purpose of grants, HS §4-1101.
　Regulations, HS §4-1105.
　Source of grants, HS §4-1104.
　Terms of grants, HS §4-1101.
　Units in division, HS §4-103.
　Uses of grants, HS §4-1103.
Partnership rental housing fund, HS §4-503.
Partnership rental housing program, HS §§4-1201 to 4-1209.
　Units in division, HS §4-103.

DEVELOPMENT FINANCE DIVISION —Cont'd
Radium pilot grant program.
  Units in division, HS §4-103.
Rental allowance program, HS §§4-1401 to
    4-1408.
  Administration of program, HS §4-1404.
  Amount of award, HS §4-1408.
  Authorized uses, HS §4-1407.
  Award of grant, HS §4-1408.
  Eligibility, HS §4-1406.
  Established, HS §4-1402.
  Income limits, HS §4-1405.
  Limitations on eligibility, HS §4-1406.
  Maximum allowances, HS §4-1405.
  Percentage retained by department, HS §4-1408.
  Program defined, HS §4-1401.
  Purposes, HS §4-1403.
  Secretary.
    Duties, HS §4-1405.
  Units in division, HS §4-103.
  Use of payments, HS §4-1407.
Rental housing production program, HS
    §§4-1501 to 4-1511.
  Units in division, HS §4-103.
Rental housing programs fund, HS §4-504.
**Self-help homeownership technical assistance
    program,** HS §§4-1701 to 4-1710.
  Units in division, HS §4-103.
Special loan programs fund, HS §4-505.
Units in division, HS §4-103.
Workforce housing grant program, HS §§4-1801
    to 4-1813.
  Appropriations, distribution, HS §4-1805.
  Established, HS §4-1802.
  Funding, HS §4-1802.
    Matching funds, HS §4-1804.
    Use of funds, HS §4-1808.
  Matching funds, HS §4-1804.
  Participation, requirements, HS §4-1803.
  Purpose, HS §4-1802.
  Qualifying local governments.
    Drawing down program funds, requirements,
      HS §4-1806.
    Income eligibility limits, extension, HS §4-1809.
    Per unit maximum amount, HS §4-1810.
    Redistribution of available funds, HS §4-1807.
  Reports, HS §4-1812.
  Regulations, HS §4-1813.
  Rental units to remain affordable, time limits, HS
    §4-1811.
  Transfer of units by initial buyer.
    Requirements, HS §4-1811.

DEVELOPMENT IMPACT FEES.
Carroll county.
  Powers, 25 §9F.
Charles county.
  Schools.
    Additional school sites required by development.
      Compensation of county by landowner, 66B
      §5.08.
Code counties.
  Powers, 25B §13D.
Garrett county.
  Powers, 25 §9H.
Municipal corporations.
  Assistance to county in collecting, 23A §8C.
Prince George's county.
  Contracts for sale of real property.
    Imposition, RP §14-117.

DEVELOPMENT PERMITS.
Consolidated procedures, SG §§11-101 to 11-523.
  See PERMITS.

DEVELOPMENT RIGHTS.
Local land preservation programs.
  Purchasing, NR §§5-9B-01 to 5-9B-06.

**DEVELOPMENT RIGHTS AND
    RESPONSIBILITIES AGREEMENTS.**
Generally, 66B §13.01.
Montgomery county, 28 §7-121.
Prince George's county, 28 §7-121.1.

DEVISEES.
See WILLS.

DEWATERING SERVICE.
Temporary dewatering service.
  Installing to facilitate installation of underground
    facilities, EN §§9-1306, 13-301.

DIABETES.
Health insurance coverage for treatment, IN
    §15-822.
Identification bracelet, tag or card.
  Persons with condition wearing, CP §2-107.

DIAMONDBACK TERRAPIN.
Catching and conservation, NR §4-903.
Licenses, NR §4-902.
State reptile, SG §13-313.
University of Maryland.
  Mascot of Flagship University at College Park, SG
    §13-313.

DICE GAMES.
Carroll county.
  Prohibition, CR §13-906.
Howard county.
  Prohibited, CR §§13-1603, 13-1604.

DIESEL FUEL.
Inspections.
  General provisions, BR §§10-101 to 10-502.
  See MOTOR FUEL INSPECTION.
Motor fuel tax.
  General provisions, TG §§9-301 to 9-337.
  See MOTOR FUEL TAX.
Possession of destructive device, CR §§4-501 to
    4-503.

**DIESEL VEHICLE EMISSIONS CONTROL
    PROGRAM,** TR §§23-401 to 23-404.

DIETHYLSTILBESTROL (DES).
Cancer.
  See CANCER.
Health insurance upon exposure to DES, IN
    §15-503.

DIETITIANS.
Administrative procedure.
  Administrative appeals, HO §5-313.
Appeals.
  Final decision of board, HO §5-313.
Applicability of title, HO §5-103.
Board of dietetic practice.
  Compensation, HO §5-204.
  Composition, HO §5-202.
  Creation, HO §5-201.
  Duties.
    Generally, HO §5-205.
  Fund.
    State board of dietetic practice fund, HO §5-206.
  Meetings, HO §5-204.
  Members, HO §5-202.

DIETITIANS —Cont'd
Board of dietetic practice —Cont'd
Officers, HO §5-203.
Powers and duties.
Generally, HO §5-205.
Qualifications of members, HO §5-202.
Quorum, HO §5-204.
Removal of members, HO §5-202.
Staff, HO §5-204.
Terms of members, HO §5-202.
Citation of title, HO §5-501.
Contempt.
Board of dietetic practice.
Enforcement of subpoenas, etc., HO §5-312.
Continuing education, HO §5-308.
Definitions, HO §5-101.
Dietetic rehabilitation committees, HO §5-314.
Discovery.
Proceedings, records and files, HO §5-314.
Evidence.
Dietetic rehabilitation committees.
Admissibility of proceedings, records and files,
HO §5-314.
Examinations.
Passing score, HO §5-304.
Required, HO §5-302.
Waiver, HO §5-305.
Fees.
Licenses, HO §§5-206, 5-303.
Renewal, HO §5-308.
Funds.
Payment of funds collected into general fund, HO
§5-206.
Immunity.
Dietetic rehabilitation committees.
Good faith exemption from civil liability, HO
§5-314.
Insurance coverage for services, IN §15-706.
Licenses.
Applications, HO §5-303.
Authority of license, HO §5-307.
Change of address.
Notice, HO §5-310.
Contents, HO §5-306.
Continuing education, HO §5-308.
Denial.
Appeals, HO §5-313.
Grounds, HO §5-311.
Hearings, HO §5-312.
Examinations, HO §5-302.
Passing score, HO §5-304.
Waiver, HO §5-305.
Expiration, HO §5-308.
Fees, HO §§5-206, 5-303.
Renewal, HO §5-308.
Inactive status, HO §5-309.
Issuance, HO §5-306.
Lapse of license pending investigation or charges,
HO §5-310.1.
Notice.
Issuance, HO §5-306.
Production upon request, HO §5-310.
Qualifications of licensees, HO §5-302.
Reactivation of license placed on inactive status,
HO §5-309.
Reinstatement.
Dietitian-nutritionist failing to renew, HO
§5-309.
Renewal.
Fees, HO §§5-206, 5-308.
Notice, HO §5-308.

DIETITIANS —Cont'd
Licenses —Cont'd
Renewal —Cont'd
Reinstatement of dietitian-nutritionist failing to
renew, HO §5-309.
Required, HO §5-301.
Exceptions, HO §5-301.
Revocation or suspension.
Appeals, HO §5-313.
Grounds, HO §5-311.
Hearings, HO §5-312.
Penalties, HO §5-311.1.
Surrender of license pending investigation or
charges, HO §5-310.1.
Unauthorized practice, HO §5-401.
Violation of provisions.
Penalties, HO §5-403.
Medical records.
Destruction, HG §4-403.
Misrepresentation of title, HO §5-402.
Names.
Misrepresentation of title, HO §5-402.
Penalties.
Violations by licensee, HO §5-311.1.
Purpose of title, HO §5-102.
Records.
Destruction of patient's medical records, HG
§4-403.
Sexual misconduct.
Disciplinary action, HO §1-212.
Short title, HO §5-501.
State board of dietetic practice.
Program evaluation act.
2004 deadline, SG §8-403.
Termination of title, HO §5-502.
Unauthorized practice, HO §5-401.
Violations of provisions.
Penalties, HO §5-403.

DIGITAL LIBRARY, ED §§11-801 to 11-804.

DIGITAL SIGNATURES.
Motor vehicle administration records, TR
§12-111.

DILATORY TACTICS.
Pleadings.
Effect of signing pleadings and other papers, Rule
1-311.

**DIMINUTION OF INMATE'S TERM OF
CONFINEMENT.**
**Inmates committed to custody of commissioner
of correction,** COR §§3-701 to 3-711.
Admittance to mental health facility, credit
allowed, COR §3-710.
Assigned work task credit, COR §3-705.
Calculation of credit.
Education credit, COR §3-706.
Good conduct, COR §3-704.
Special projects credit, COR §3-707.
Concurrent state sentence served in foreign
jurisdiction.
Allowance of credit, COR §3-703.
Controlled substance offense.
Good conduct credit, calculating, COR §3-704.
Crime of violence.
Good conduct credit, calculating, COR §3-704.
Discipline violation, revocation of credit, COR
§3-709.
Educational and training courses credit, COR
§3-706.
Entitlement, COR §3-702.

DIMINUTION OF INMATE'S TERM OF CONFINEMENT —Cont'd
Inmates committed to custody of commissioner of correction —Cont'd
Exempt periods.
Good conduct credit, COR §3-704.
Good conduct credit, COR §3-704.
Limitation on number of days for calendar month deducted, COR §3-708.
Mental health facility admittance, credit allowed, COR §3-710.
Parole violation resulting in revocation of parole.
Credits awarded before inmate's release not applied toward inmate's term, COR §3-711.
Restoration of revoked credit, COR §3-709.
Revocation of credits for discipline violation, COR §3-709.
Special selected work projects or other special programs credit, COR §3-707.
Term of confinement defined, COR §3-701.
Vocational courses credit, COR §3-706.
Work task credit, COR §3-705.
Inmates imprisoned at local correctional facilities, COR §§11-501 to 11-509.
Baltimore City detention center, subtitle applicable to, COR §11-501.
Committment of inmate to custody of commissioner of correction.
Forwarding of credits, COR §11-508.
Discipline rules violations, revocation of credits, COR §11-507.
Employment of inmate, COR §11-605.
Good conduct.
Postsentence confinement, COR §11-504.
Presentence confinement, COR §11-503.
Industrial, agricultural or administrative tasks, performance, COR §11-505.
Postsentence confinement, deductions allowed, COR §11-502.
Postsentence, deductions allowed.
Good conduct, COR §11-504.
Presentence confinement, deductions allowed, COR §11-502.
Good conduct, COR §11-503.
Industrial, agricultural or administrative tasks, performance, COR §11-505.
Revocation credits, discipline rules violations, COR §11-507.
Scope of provisions, COR §11-501.
Special programs, COR §11-506.
Transfer to another local facility.
Credits forwarded, COR §11-508.
Transfer to hospital or mental institution.
Credits not denied, COR §11-509.
Violation of rules discipline, COR §11-507.
Vocational or other educational or training courses, COR §11-505.
Work projects or other special programs, COR §11-506.
Mandatory supervision.
Revocation.
Credits awarded prior to release.
Not applied to term upon revocation of release, COR §7-502.
Credits revoked, new credits not awarded, COR §7-504.
Patuxent institution inmates, COR §§4-213, 4-308.

DIPHTHERIA.
Exposure to virus.
Medical and law enforcement personnel.
Notification of exposure, HG §§18-213 to 18-213.2.
DIPLOMATIC IMMUNITY DRIVERS' LICENSES, TR §§16-901 to 16-905.
DIPLOMATIC OFFICERS.
Ambassadors.
See AMBASSADORS AND CONSULS.
DIRECT DEPOSIT.
State personnel wages paid by, SPP §2-405.
DIRECTED VERDICTS.
Motion for judgment.
Circuit courts, CivProCir Rule 2-519.
DIRECTORY ASSISTANCE CHARGES.
Telephone companies, PUC §8-202.
DIRECT WINE SELLER'S PERMIT, 2B §§7.5-101 to 7.5-110.
See ALCOHOLIC BEVERAGES.
DIRK.
Carry concealed or with intent to injure, CR §4-101.
Minor carrying, hours prohibited, CR §4-101.
DISABILITY.
Absentee voting.
Generally, EL §§9-301 to 9-312.
See ELECTIONS.
Attendant care program.
Community attendant services and supports program, 41 §§6-7A-01 to 6-7A-06.
General provisions, 41 §§18-601 to 18-604.
See ATTENDANT CARE PROGRAM.
Blind persons.
See BLIND PERSONS.
Building codes.
Accessibility code, PS §12-202.
Certified adult residential environment program.
Social services.
Housing, 88A §§138 to 143.
See SOCIAL SERVICES.
Community attendant services and supports program, 41 §§6-7A-01 to 6-7A-06.
Community colleges.
Supplemental services and support for students with disabilities, ED §16-319.
Deaf and hearing impaired.
See DEAF AND HEARING IMPAIRED.
Decedents' estates.
Notice to disabled person, ET §1-103.
Developmental disabilities generally.
See DEVELOPMENTAL DISABILITIES.
Elections.
Absentee voting.
Generally, EL §§9-301 to 9-312.
See ELECTIONS.
Executors and administrators.
Effect.
Judicial determination of disability, ET §6-304.
Personal representative or guardian of deceased or disabled personal representative.
Duties, ET §6-304.
Termination.
See EXECUTORS AND ADMINISTRATORS.
Family caregiver assistance program.
Grants to caregivers.
Assistance in caring for individual with long-term care needs, 50B §45.

DISABILITY —Cont'd
Guardian and ward.
General provisions, ET §§13-101 to 13-222.
See GUARDIAN AND WARD.
Guardian of the person of a disabled person, ET §§13-704 to 13-713.
See GUARDIAN AND WARD.
Handicapped persons.
General provisions.
See HANDICAPPED PERSONS.
Housing.
Certified adult residential environment program, 88A §§138 to 143.
See SOCIAL SERVICES.
Infants.
Minors.
See MINORS.
Legal disabilities.
See LEGAL DISABILITIES.
Limitation of actions.
Computation of time.
Person under disability, CJ §5-201.
Mentally ill.
See MENTALLY ILL.
Minors.
See MINORS.
Paternity proceedings.
Party under legal disability, FL §5-1013.
Power of attorney.
Effect of acts performed for an incapacitated principal, ET §13-601.
Not revoked without actual knowledge of disability, ET §13-602.
When power of attorney not affected by disability of principal, ET §13-601.
Protection of property, ET §§13-201 to 13-222.
See GUARDIAN AND WARD.
Rehabilitation services, ED §§21-301 to 21-309.
See REHABILITATION SERVICES.
Schools.
Handicapped children generally.
See SCHOOLS.

DISABILITY BENEFITS.
Health insurance.
Disability and adverse benefit determination, IN §15-1010.
Inmates at correctional facilities.
Permanent partial or permanent total disability while working for wage.
Sundry claims board, COR §§10-301 to 10-310.
See PRISONS AND PRISONERS.

DISABILITY INSURANCE.
Consent requirement, IN §27-901.
Finance charge computation considerations, IN §27-901.

DISAPPEARANCE.
See ABSENT PERSONS.

DISARMING A LAW ENFORCEMENT OFFICER, CR §4-103.

DISASTERS.
Arrest without a warrant.
Authorized during state of emergency, CP §2-206.
Emergency management, PS §§14-101 to 14-1004.
See EMERGENCY MANAGEMENT.
Farmer disaster loan program, AG §§2-601 to 2-605.
Mining.
Inspection, EN §15-405.

DISASTERS —Cont'd
Mining —Cont'd
Notice, EN §15-405.
Nursing license exception.
Red cross assigning nurses to disaster situation in state, HO §8-301.
Service leave.
State employees, SPP §9-1102.
Warrantless arrest.
Authorized during state of emergency, CP §2-206.

DISASTER SERVICE LEAVE.
State personnel, SPP §9-1102.

DISBARMENT.
Attorneys at law.
See ATTORNEYS AT LAW.
Discrimination.
Commercial discrimination.
Contested case hearings, SF §19-110.
False or frivolous allegations, SF §19-111.

DISBURSEMENTS AND EXPENDITURES.
Appropriations.
General provisions.
See APPROPRIATIONS.
Checks.
Appropriations, SF §§7-227, 7-227.1, 7-229, 7-230.
See APPROPRIATIONS.
State treasurer.
Authority for disbursements in accordance with warrants, SF §7-226.
Unspent balances of appropriations, SF §§7-301 to 7-308.
See APPROPRIATIONS.
Warrants for payment of money.
Appropriations.
Warrants for disbursements of appropriations, SF §§7-216 to 7-223.
See APPROPRIATIONS.

DISCHARGE.
Defined, EN §9-101.
Disposal systems.
Defined, EN §9-101.
Hazardous materials and substances, EN §7-229.
Solid waste disposal.
Incinerators, EN §2-406.

DISCHARGE OF FIREARM.
From motor vehicle.
Reckless endangerment, CR §3-204.
Local regulation allowed, CR §4-209.

DISCIPLINE AND INACTIVE STATUS OF ATTORNEYS.
General provisions, CJA Rules 16-701 to 16-781.
See ATTORNEYS AT LAW.

DISCLAIMER.
Executors and administrators.
Settlement of decedents' estates, Estates Rule 6-412.
Property and casualty insurance, IN §19-110.
Uniform disclaimer of property interests act, ET §§9-201 to 9-216.
See DESCENT AND DISTRIBUTION.

DISCLOSURES BY PERSONS DOING PUBLIC BUSINESS.
Contributions to candidates for public office, EL §§14-101 to 14-108.
See CAMPAIGN FINANCE.

DISCOVERY.
Actions.
Perpetuation of evidence.
Before action instituted, CivProCir Rule 2-404.
Admission of facts and genuineness of documents.
Circuit courts, CivProCir Rule 2-424.
Alibis.
Witnesses.
Discovery by state.
Criminal rules, Crim Rule 4-263.
Appeals.
Perpetuation of evidence.
Pending appeal, CivProCir Rule 2-404.
Circuit courts, CivProCir Rule 2-404.
Attorneys at law.
Disbarment or suspension.
Petition for disciplinary or remedial action, CJA Rule 16-756.
Lawyer counseling committees.
Matters not discoverable, BOP §10-502.
Trial preparation.
Scope of discovery.
Circuit courts, CivProCir Rule 2-402.
Audiologists, hearing aid dealers and speech-language pathologists.
Hearing aid dealer rehabilitation committees, HO §2-318.2.
Speech-language pathologist rehabilitation committee.
Proceedings, records and files, HO §2-318.1.
Certificate requirement.
Dispute pertaining to discovery.
Circuit courts, CivProCir Rule 2-431.
Child fatality review teams.
Information, documents and records not subject to discovery, HG §5-709.
Chiropractors.
Chiropractor rehabilitation committees.
Proceedings, records and files, HO §3-406.
Circuit courts.
Criminal rules, Crim Rule 4-263.
Class actions.
Circuit courts, CivProCir Rule 2-231.
Codefendants.
Statements of codefendants.
Disclosure upon request.
Criminal rules, Crim Rule 4-263.
Compelling discovery.
Motion to compel discovery.
Criminal rules, Crim Rule 4-263.
Order compelling discovery, CivProCir Rule 2-432.
Sanctions.
Failure to comply with order compelling discovery.
Circuit courts, CivProCir Rule 2-433.
Continuances.
Discovery not completed.
Circuit courts, CivProCir Rule 2-508.
District Court, CivProDist Rule 3-508.
Continuing duty to disclose.
Criminal rules, Crim Rule 4-263.
Criminal rules.
Circuit courts, Crim Rule 4-263.
District Court, Crim Rule 4-262.
Defendants.
Matters not subject to discovery by defendant.
Criminal rules, Crim Rule 4-263.
Property of defendant.
Disclosure upon request.
Criminal rules, Crim Rule 4-263.

DISCOVERY —Cont'd
Defendants —Cont'd
Statements of codefendants.
Disclosure upon request.
Criminal rules, Crim Rule 4-263.
Statements of defendant.
Disclosure upon request.
Criminal rules, Crim Rule 4-263.
Dental hygienist rehabilitation committees.
Proceedings, records and files, HO §4-508.
Depositions.
See DEPOSITIONS.
Dietitians.
Proceedings, records and files, HO §5-314.
Disclosure upon request.
Criminal rules.
Circuit courts, Crim Rule 4-263.
Disclosure without request.
Criminal rules.
Circuit courts, Crim Rule 4-263.
Dispute pertaining to discovery.
Certificate requirement.
Circuit courts, CivProCir Rule 2-431.
District Court.
Civil procedure, CivProDist Rules 3-401 to 3-431.
Criminal rules, Crim Rule 4-262.
Generally, CivProDist Rule 3-401.
Documents and property.
Circuit courts, CivProCir Rule 2-424.
Domestic violence.
Local domestic violence fatality review teams.
Information available in judicial proceedings, FL §4-707.
Eminent domain, PropAct Rule 12-206.
Examinations.
Mental or physical examination of persons.
Circuit courts, CivProCir Rule 2-423.
Expert witnesses.
Reports or statements of experts.
Criminal rules, Crim Rule 4-263.
Trial preparation.
Scope of discovery.
Circuit courts, CivProCir Rule 2-402.
Failure to provide discovery.
Order compelling discovery.
Circuit courts, CivProCir Rule 2-432.
Production of statement.
Motion by nonparty to compel production of statement.
Circuit courts, CivProCir Rule 2-432.
Sanctions.
Award of expenses.
Circuit courts, CivProCir Rule 2-433.
Immediate sanctions for certain failures of discovery, CivProCir Rule 2-432.
Noncompliance with order compelling discovery.
Circuit courts, CivProCir Rule 2-433.
Type of sanctions, CivProCir Rule 2-433.
Time for filing motion upon failure, CivProCir Rule 2-432.
Fees.
Trial preparation.
Experts.
Scope of discovery.
Circuit courts, CivProCir Rule 2-402.
Filing.
Perpetuation of evidence.
Notice, request or motion to be filed.
Circuit courts, CivProCir Rule 2-404.
Fires and fire prevention.
Center for the study of the health effects of fire.
Information collected not discoverable, HG §18-705.

DISCOVERY —Cont'd
Health.
Center for the study of the health effects of fire.
Information collected not discoverable, HG
§18-705.
Hospitals.
Hazardous conditions.
Intermediate sanction.
Appeals.
Prehearing discovery, HG §19-364.
Identification.
Discovery by the state.
Criminal rules, Crim Rule 4-263.
Insurance.
Scope of discovery.
Insurance agreements.
Circuit courts, CivProCir Rule 2-402.
Interrogatories.
See INTERROGATORIES.
Judgments.
Discovery in aid of enforcement.
Circuit courts, CivProCir Rule 2-633.
District Court, CivProDist Rule 3-633.
Judicial disabilities and sanctionable conduct.
Proceedings before commission, CJA Rule 16-808.
Juvenile causes, Juv Rule 11-109.
Landlord-tenant and grantee actions.
Applicable procedure.
District Court, CivProDist Rule 3-711.
Material.
Circuit courts, CivProCir Rule 2-401.
District Court, CivProDist Rule 3-401.
Matters not subject to discovery by defendant.
Criminal rules, Crim Rule 4-263.
Mediation.
Privileged communications, ADR Rule 17-109.
Methods.
Circuit courts, CivProCir Rule 2-401.
District Court, CivProDist Rule 3-401.
Mortician rehabilitation committee.
Proceedings, records and files, HO §7-408.
Motions.
Compelling discovery.
Criminal rules, Crim Rule 4-263.
Failure to provide discovery.
Circuit courts, CivProCir Rule 2-432.
Perpetuation of evidence.
Before action instituted.
Circuit courts, CivProCir Rule 2-404.
Protective orders.
Circuit courts, CivProCir Rule 2-403.
Notice.
Perpetuation of evidence.
Before action instituted.
Circuit courts, CivProCir Rule 2-404.
Nursing home administrator rehabilitation committee.
Proceedings, records and files, HO §9-317.
Obligations of state's attorney.
Criminal rules, Crim Rule 4-263.
District Court, Crim Rule 4-262.
Occupational therapists rehabilitation committees.
Proceedings, records and files, HO §10-319.
Optometrist rehabilitation committees.
Proceedings, records and files, HO §11-405.
Orders.
Compelling discovery.
Circuit courts, CivProCir Rule 2-432.
Sanction for failure to comply.
Circuit courts, CivProCir Rule 2-433.

DISCOVERY —Cont'd
Orders —Cont'd
Perpetuation of evidence.
Before action instituted.
Court order.
Circuit courts, CivProCir Rule 2-404.
Protective orders.
Circuit courts, CivProCir Rule 2-403.
Criminal rules, Crim Rule 4-263.
Parties.
Substitution of party.
Circuit courts, CivProCir Rule 2-401.
Perpetuation of evidence.
Before action instituted.
Circuit courts, CivProCir Rule 2-404.
District Court, CivProDist Rule 3-431.
Physicians.
Board.
Discoverability or admissibility in evidence of
board documents, HO §14-410.
Disciplinary actions.
Rules governing, adoption by board, HO
§14-405.
Plan, CivProCir Rule 2-401.
Trial preparation.
Scope of discovery.
Circuit courts, CivProCir Rule 2-402.
Podiatrist rehabilitation committees.
Proceedings, records and files, HO §16-403.
Preparation for trial.
Scope of discovery.
Circuit courts, CivProCir Rule 2-402.
Procurement.
Contracts.
Bids and proposals, SF §13-210.
Dispute resolution.
Appeals board.
Appeals to board, SF §15-221.
Production of documents and tangible things.
See PRODUCTION OF DOCUMENTS AND
TANGIBLE THINGS.
Professional counselor rehabilitation committees.
Proceedings, records and files, HO §17-317.
Property.
Defendant's property.
Disclosure upon request.
Criminal rules, Crim Rule 4-263.
Protective orders.
Criminal rules, Crim Rule 4-263.
Psychologist rehabilitation committees.
Proceedings, records and files, HO §18-318.
Receivers and assignees or trustees for creditors.
When authorized, Receivers Rule 13-103.
Sanctions.
Failure to provide discovery.
Circuit courts, CivProCir Rules 2-432, 2-433.
Scope.
Circuit courts, CivProCir Rule 2-401.
Criminal rules.
District Court, Crim Rule 4-262.
Matters not subject to discovery by defendant.
Criminal rules, Crim Rule 4-263.
Trial preparation, CivProCir Rule 2-402.
Service of process.
Perpetuation of evidence.
Before action instituted.
Service of notice, request or motion.
Circuit courts, CivProCir Rule 2-404.

DISCOVERY —Cont'd
Small claim actions.
　Nonavailability of discovery.
　　District Court, CivProDist Rule 3-701.
Social worker rehabilitation committees.
　Proceedings, records and files, HO §19-315.
State of Maryland.
　Discovery by state.
　　Criminal rules, Crim Rule 4-263.
State's attorney.
　Criminal rules.
　　District Court, Crim Rule 4-262.
　　Obligation of state's attorney, Crim Rule 4-263.
Stipulations.
　Stipulations regarding discovery procedure,
　　CivProCir Rule 2-401.
Subpoenas.
　Perpetuation of evidence.
　　Before action instituted.
　　　Circuit courts, CivProCir Rule 2-404.
Supplementation of responses.
　Circuit courts, CivProCir Rule 2-401.
Testimony.
　Perpetuation of testimony.
　　District Court, CivProDist Rule 3-431.
Time.
　Criminal rules, Crim Rule 4-263.
　Sequence and time of discovery.
　　Circuit courts, CivProCir Rule 2-401.
Trade secrets.
　Confidentiality during discovery.
　　How confidentiality preserved, CL §11-1205.
Trial.
　Continuances.
　　Discovery not completed.
　　　Circuit courts, CivProCir Rule 2-508.
Trial preparation.
　Experts.
　　Scope of discovery.
　　　Circuit courts, CivProCir Rule 2-402.
　Materials.
　　Scope of discovery.
　　　Circuit courts, CivProCir Rule 2-402.
　Party's or witness' own statement.
　　Scope of discovery.
　　　Circuit courts, CivProCir Rule 2-402.
Witnesses.
　Alibi witnesses.
　　Discovery by state.
　　　Criminal rules, Crim Rule 4-263.
　Disclosure upon request.
　　Criminal rules, Crim Rule 4-263.
　Trial preparation.
　　Experts.
　　　Scope of discovery.
　　　　Circuit courts, CivProCir Rule 2-402.
　　Scope of discovery.
　　　Circuit courts, CivProCir Rule 2-402.

DISCRETIONARY TRUSTS, ET §§14-401 to
　14-408.
See TRUSTS AND TRUSTEES.

DISCRIMINATION.
Actions.
　Commercial discrimination.
　　Limitation of actions.
　　　Complaint for discrimination, SF §19-101.
　　Pending actions, effect of, SF §19-118.
　Public accommodations.
　　Right to bring civil actions not denied, 49B §12.

DISCRIMINATION —Cont'd
Agricultural marketing associations, AG
　§§10-201 to 10-204.
Alcoholic beverage tax.
　Imposition of discriminatory tax or charge by
　　other jurisdiction, TG §5-102.
　Rate of retaliatory tax, TG §5-105.
　Public accommodations.
　　Premises selling alcoholic beverages.
　　　Private clubs.
　　　　Exception, 49B §5.
Aviation.
　Airports.
　　Monitoring of employment practices in state
　　　airports, TR §5-408.
Baltimore county.
　Civil actions for discriminatory acts, 49B §43.
Boards and commissions.
　Public accommodations.
　　Cases involving state agencies, 49B §7.
Cease and desist orders, 49B §11.
Commercial discrimination, SF §§19-101 to
　19-120.
　Actions.
　　Limitation of actions.
　　　Complaint for discrimination, SF §19-101.
　　Pending actions, effect of, SF §19-118.
　Administrative complaints, SF §§19-106 to 19-108.
　　Initial findings and recommendations.
　　　Factors for consideration, SF §19-108.
　　Investigations.
　　　Discrimination and retaliation complaints, SF
　　　　§19-107.
　　　Factors for consideration, SF §19-108.
　Appeals.
　　Final administrative decision.
　　　Judicial review, SF §19-113.
　　Judicial review of commission action.
　　　Construction of act, SF §19-105.
　Applicability of policy, SF §§19-101, 19-104.
　Citation of title and regulations.
　　Commercial nondiscrimination policy, SF
　　　§19-120.
　Commission.
　　Defined, SF §19-103.
　　Reporting requirements, SF §19-119.
　　Rulemaking authority, SF §19-119.
　Construction of act, SF §§19-104, 19-105.
　　Citation of title and regulations, SF §19-120.
　　Public policy, SF §§19-101, 19-102.
　　Remedies additional to other remedies, SF
　　　§19-117.
　Contested case hearings.
　　Failure to properly request hearing.
　　　Effect of, SF §19-109.
　　Mediation, SF §19-110.
　　Notice requirements, SF §19-109.
　　Office of administrative hearings.
　　　Delegation of matter to office, SF §19-109.
　　Remedy when allegation sustained, SF §19-110.
　　Request for hearing, SF §19-109.
　Contracts provisions.
　　Nondiscrimination clause.
　　　Condition of entering into contract, SF
　　　　§19-114.
　　　Form, SF §19-114.
　　Request for bids or proposals.
　　　Certification of compliance required, SF
　　　　§19-115.
　　State contracts.
　　　Required language in all state contracts, SF
　　　　§19-116.

DISCRIMINATION —Cont'd
Commercial discrimination —Cont'd
Criminal prosecution.
Contested case hearings.
Remedy when allegation sustained, SF §19-110.
Definitions, SF §19-103.
Disbarment.
Contested case hearings.
Remedy when allegation sustained, SF §19-110.
Economic development projects.
Conditions of participation, SF §19-104.
Contracts to contain nondiscrimination clauses, SF §19-104.
False or frivolous allegations.
Hearing and penalty, SF §19-109.
Remedy for filing, SF §19-111.
Final administrative decision.
Issuance of order, SF §19-112.
Judicial review, SF §19-113.
When hearing not required, SF §19-112.
Judicial review of commission action.
Construction of provisions, SF §19-105.
Mediation.
Contested case hearings.
Remedy when allegation sustained, SF §19-110.
Office of administrative hearings.
Contested case hearings.
Delegation of matter to office, SF §19-109.
Public policy, SF §§19-101, 19-102.
Remedies under title.
Additional to other remedies, SF §19-117.
Request for bids or proposals.
Certification of compliance required, SF §19-115.
Retaliation complaints.
Investigation, SF §19-107.
Title of act.
Commercial nondiscrimination policy, SF §19-120.
Commission.
Agreement for elimination of discrimination, 49B §10.
Applicability of subtitle, 49B §9.
Complaints to be filed with commission, 49B §9A.
Findings, 49B §10.
Investigations, 49B §10.
Meetings of commission, 49B §9A.
Common carriers discriminating against other common carriers in transferring, receiving or forwarding passengers, PUC §9-101.
Constitution of Maryland.
Sex discrimination.
Equality of rights not abridged because of sex, MD Const DofR Art 46.
Consumer loans.
Prohibited, CL §12-305.
Contracts.
Public accommodations.
Elimination of discrimination, 49B §10.
Contract state employees.
Recruitment and selection, SPP §13-203.
Cooperatives.
Agricultural marketing associations.
General provisions, AG §§10-201 to 10-204.
See AGRICULTURAL COOPERATIVES.
General provisions.
See COOPERATIVES.

DISCRIMINATION —Cont'd
Country clubs.
Tax status.
Effect, TP §§8-214, 8-215.
Definitions.
Commercial discrimination, SF §19-103.
Housing, 49B §20.
Housing discrimination, 49B §19.
Public accommodations, 49B §5.
Department of labor, licensing and regulation.
Discrimination by persons, businesses, etc., licensed or regulated by department.
Penalties.
Civil penalties, 49B §8.
Prohibited, 49B §8.
Drug or alcohol abuse.
Facilities and services, HG §8-402.
Health insurers, HG §19-703.1; IN §15-802.
Prohibited, HG §8-703.
Equal credit opportunity, CL §§12-701 to 12-708.
See EQUAL CREDIT OPPORTUNITY.
Fines.
Public accommodations.
Generally, 49B §12.
Receiving remuneration for participation in racial demonstration, 49B §6.
Foreign discriminatory boycotts, CL §§11-101 to 11-115.
See FOREIGN DISCRIMINATORY BOYCOTTS.
Fraternal benefit societies, IN §8-467.
Freestanding ambulatory care facilities.
Discrimination against patients prohibited, HG §19-3B-03.
Gender.
Constitution of Maryland.
Equality of rights not abridged because of sex, MD Const DofR Art 46.
Grievance procedures.
Right to bring grievance free of discrimination, SPP §12-103.
Handicapped persons.
Life insurance, health insurance or annuity contracts, IN §§27-208, 27-210.
Teachers.
Discrimination against handicapped teachers prohibited, ED §6-104.
Health maintenance organizations.
Lack of discrimination, HG §19-710.
Provider panels, IN §15-112.
Rates, HG §19-713.
Holocaust victims insurance act, IN §§28-101 to 28-110.
See HOLOCAUST VICTIMS INSURANCE.
Home health agencies.
Prohibited, HG §19-408.
Homeowners' associations.
Recorded covenant or restriction based on race, religion or national origin.
Deletion, RP §11B-113.3.
Hospitals.
General prohibition, HG §19-355.
Housing.
Access for disabled, 49B §22.
Administration of subtitle, 49B §19.
Administrative proceedings, 49B §32.
Agreements.
Conciliation agreements, 49B §28.
Applicability of subtitle, 49B §21.
Children, tenants with, 49B §22.
Coercion, 49B §24.

DISCRIMINATION —Cont'd
Housing —Cont'd
Commission.
Duties, 49B §26.
Complaints.
Certification, 49B §30.
Civil actions by aggrieved person, 49B §33.
Civil actions by commission, 49B §32.
Action on its own initiative, 49B §34.
Dismissal, 49B §30.
Filing, 49B §27.
Investigation, 49B §27.
Conciliation agreements, 49B §28.
Cooperation with local agencies, 49B §36.
Definitions, 49B §20.
Discovery, 49B §31.
Exemptions from subtitle, 49B §21.
Hearings, 49B §32.
Intimidation.
Force or threat of force, 49B §37.
Local agencies.
Cooperation with, 49B §36.
Multiple listing services.
Access to, 49B §23.
Ordinances.
Enactment of ordinances on subjects covered by
subtitle, 49B §38.
Penalties.
Civil penalties, 49B §32.
Policy.
Declaration of policy, 49B §19.
Preliminary relief, 49B §29.
Real estate brokers.
Discrimination generally. See within this
heading, "Real estate brokers."
Real estate brokers' organizations.
Access to, 49B §23.
Residential real estate transactions.
Availability of, 49B §23.
Review of findings, 49B §32.
Rules and regulations.
Adoption, 49B §35.
Severability, 49B §39.
State agency, officer or employee.
Discrimination cases involving, 49B §7.
State departments and agencies.
Duties, 49B §25.
Subpoenas, 49B §31.
Temporary relief, 49B §29.
Threats, 49B §24.
Injury, intimidation, etc., by threat or force, 49B
§37.
Unlawful practices, 49B §22.
Howard county.
Civil actions for discriminatory acts, 49B §42.
Human relations commission.
General provisions.
See HUMAN RELATIONS COMMISSION.
Hearings, 49B §11.
Housing discrimination.
Duties, 49B §26.
Public accommodations.
Enforcement powers, 49B §§9 to 13.
Insurance, IN §27-212.
Appeals, IN §27-505.
Domestic violence based discrimination, IN
§27-504.
Health insurance, IN §§27-208, 27-210.
Treatment of mental illnesses, emotional
disorders and drug and alcohol abuse, IN
§15-802.

DISCRIMINATION —Cont'd
Insurance —Cont'd
Health insurance provider panels, IN §15-112.
Health networks, IN §27-910.
Insurance producers, IN §27-503.
Life insurance and annuities, IN §§27-208,
27-210.
Motor vehicle insurance, IN §27-501.
Nonprofit health service plans, IN §14-136.
Orders to accept risk or business after violation,
IN §27-505.
Rate making, IN §11-205.
Title insurance, IN §11-402.
Surety insurance, IN §27-502.
Third party administrators, IN §8-318.
Underwriting, IN §27-501.
Underwriting and rate-setting practices, IN
§2-202.
Interest.
Prohibited, CL §12-113.
Investigations.
Public accommodations.
Human relations commission, 49B §10.
Jury.
Prohibited grounds for exclusion from jury service,
CJ §8-102.
Labor and employment relations.
Discrimination in employment, 49B §§14 to 18.
See LABOR AND EMPLOYMENT
RELATIONS.
Leases.
Leasing of property for commercial usage.
Discrimination prohibited, 49B §8A.
Limitation of actions.
County governments, 49B §§42, 43.
Loans, CL §12-113.
Mobile homes.
Discrimination in mobile home parks prohibited,
RP §8A-801.
Montgomery county.
Civil actions for discriminatory acts, 49B §42.
Mortgages and deeds of trust, CL §12-113.
Secondary mortgage loans.
Age discrimination, CL §12-403.1.
Occupational safety and health.
Retaliatory action prohibited, LE §5-604.
Ordinances.
Housing discrimination.
Enactment of ordinances on subjects covered by
subtitle, 49B §38.
Prince George's county.
Civil actions for discriminatory acts, 49B §42.
Privileged communications.
Public accommodations.
Human relations commission.
Investigations and findings by commission.
Exception as to disclosures, 49B §10.
Procurement.
Contracts.
Nondiscrimination clause required, SF §13-219.
Public accommodations.
Actions.
Right to bring civil actions not denied, 49B §12.
Agreements.
Elimination of discrimination, 49B §10.
Alcoholic beverages.
Premises selling alcoholic beverages.
Private clubs.
Exception, 49B §5.
Applicability of subtitle, 49B §9.

DISCRIMINATION —Cont'd
Public accommodations —Cont'd
  Boards and commissions.
    Cases involving state agencies, 49B §7.
  Complaint.
    Filed with commission, 49B §9A.
    Issuance.
      By commission, 49B §9A.
      Maliciously made, 49B §12.
  Definitions.
    Public accommodations, 49B §5.
  Departments.
    Cases involving state agencies, 49B §7.
  Disclosures of publicity, 49B §10.
  Enforcement.
    Commission's orders, 49B §12.
  Fines.
    Generally, 49B §12.
    Receiving remuneration for participation in
      racial demonstration, 49B §6.
  Human relations commission.
    Powers.
      Enforcement powers, 49B §§9 to 13.
  Investigations.
    Human relations commission, 49B §10.
  Officers.
    Cases involving state officer or employee, 49B
      §7.
  Penalties.
    Civil penalties, 49B §5.
  Privileged communications.
    Investigation and findings by commission.
      Exceptions as to disclosures, 49B §10.
  Prohibited, 49B §5.
  Racial demonstration.
    Receiving remuneration for participation.
      Penalty, 49B §6.
  Real estate brokers.
    Discrimination generally. See within this
      heading, "Real estate brokers."
  Violations of article.
    Aiding or abetting violations, 49B §12A.
Public utilities, rate discrimination, PUC
  §4-503.
Racial demonstration.
  Receiving remuneration for participation, 49B §6.
**Railroads supplying cars to meet demand to
  transport freight.**
  Prohibition, PUC §9-401.
Rate discrimination.
  Public utilities, PUC §4-503.
Real estate brokers.
  Baltimore City.
    Discriminatory real estate practices, BOP
      §17-525.
      Penalties, BOP §17-613.
      Reports of convictions, BOP §17-614.
      Solicitation of listings, BOP §17-527.
  Montgomery county.
    Discriminatory real estate practices, BOP
      §17-526.
      Penalties, BOP §17-613.
      Reports of convictions, BOP §17-614.
  Penalties for violations generally, BOP §17-613.
  Prohibited acts.
    "Blockbusting," BOP §17-608.
    Solicitation of residential listings, BOP §17-609.
  Reports of certain convictions, BOP §17-614.
**Remuneration for participation in racial
  demonstration.**
  Public accommodations, 49B §6.

DISCRIMINATION —Cont'd
Retail credit accounts law.
  General provisions, CL §12-503.
Sales.
  Installment sales.
    General provisions, CL §12-603.
Schools.
  Teachers.
    Discrimination on account of race, religion,
      color, national origin, handicap or sex
      unlawful, ED §6-104.
Secondary mortgage loan law.
  Age discrimination, CL §12-403.1.
Sex discrimination.
  Constitution of Maryland.
    Equality of rights not abridged because of sex,
      MD Const DofR Art 46.
  Equal credit opportunity, CL §§12-701 to 12-708.
    See EQUAL CREDIT OPPORTUNITY.
  Health insurance, IN §27-208.
  Insurance, IN §27-212.
  Labor and employment relations.
    Equal pay for equal work, LE §§3-301 to 3-309.
      See LABOR AND EMPLOYMENT
        RELATIONS.
State agencies, officer and employees.
  Discriminatory practices prohibited, 49B §7.
  Housing discrimination case involving, 49B §7.
State personnel.
  Employee grievance procedures, SPP §§12-101 to
    12-405.
    See GRIEVANCE PROCEDURES.
  Prohibited, SPP §2-302.
Statute of limitations.
  County governments, 49B §§42, 43.
Transportation department employees.
  Grievance rights, TR §2-103.4.
University of Maryland.
  Medical system.
    Prohibition on discrimination, ED §13-303.
Unlawful practices.
  Housing discrimination.
    Access for disabled, 49B §22.
    Sale or rental of dwellings, 49B §22.
  Public accommodations, 49B §5.
Wage discrimination.
  Equal pay for equal work, LE §§3-301 to 3-309.
    See LABOR AND EMPLOYMENT
      RELATIONS.
Washington suburban sanitary district.
  Prohibited, 29 §1-107.
  Water and sewer systems, 29 §3-102.

DISCS.
Unauthorized recording of sounds or images,
  CR §§7-306 to 7-310.

DISEASES.
Acquired immune deficiency syndrome (AIDS).
  General provisions.
    See ACQUIRED IMMUNE DEFICIENCY
      SYNDROME (AIDS).
Alzheimer's disease.
  Health insurance coverage, IN §15-801.
Arthritis prevention and control program, HG
  §§13-501 to 13-512.
  See ARTHRITIS AND RELATED DISEASES.
Asthma control program, HG §§13-1701 to
  13-1706.
Biological products.
  Products usable for treatment or prevention of
    disease transmissible to humans.
    Possession prohibited, AG §3-201.1.

DISEASES —Cont'd
Cancer.
General provisions.
See CANCER.
Cancer prevention, education, screening and treatment program, HG §§13-1101 to 13-1119.
See CANCER PREVENTION, EDUCATION, SCREENING AND TREATMENT PROGRAM.
Catastrophic health emergency.
Disease surveillance and response program, HG §§18-901 to 18-908.
See CATASTROPHIC HEALTH EMERGENCY.
Governor's power to proclaim, PS §§14-3A-01 to 14-3A-08.
See HEALTH EMERGENCIES.
Cholesterol testing, HG §§17-501 to 17-511.
See CHOLESTEROL TESTING.
Chronic disease centers, HG §§19-501 to 19-513.
See HOSPITALS.
Communicable diseases.
General provisions.
See CONTAGIOUS DISEASES.
Contagious diseases.
General provisions.
See CONTAGIOUS DISEASES.
Livestock.
See LIVESTOCK.
Contaminating water supply or food or drink, CR §3-214.
Cosmetologists.
Infectious or contagious diseases.
Careless or negligent practice, BOP §5-607.
Penalties, BOP §5-609.
Restrictions on certain personnel, BOP §5-607.
Food, drugs and cosmetics.
Employees with communicable diseases, HG §21-328.
Health insurance.
Specified disease policy minimum loss ratios, IN §15-109.
Hepatitis.
Medical and law enforcement personnel.
Notification of exposure, HG §§18-213 to 18-213.2.
Human immunodeficiency virus.
General provisions.
See HUMAN IMMUNODEFICIENCY VIRUS.
Human subject research.
Generally, HG §§13-2001 to 13-2004.
Immunization.
See IMMUNIZATION.
Infectious diseases.
General provisions.
See CONTAGIOUS DISEASES.
Investigation by secretary.
Suspected disease endangering public health, HG §18-102.
Life insurance.
Prohibited policy provisions, IN §16-216.
Livestock.
Contagious and infectious diseases.
See LIVESTOCK.
Meningitis.
College or university student residing in on-campus housing.
Vaccination, HG §18-102.
Fire fighters, emergency medical technicians, rescue squadmen, law enforcement officers and correctional officers.
Notification of exposure to, HG §18-213.

DISEASES —Cont'd
Metabolic diseases.
Health insurance.
Screening, required child wellness coverage, IN §15-817.
Health maintenance organizations.
Coverage for prescribed food products, HG §19-705.5.
Milk and milk products.
Handling milk by individuals with diseases, HG §21-435.
Notifying secretary, HG §21-435.
Mononucleosis.
Fire fighters, emergency medical technicians, rescue squadmen, law enforcement officers and correctional officers.
Notification of exposure to, HG §18-213.
Osteoporosis.
Prevention and education task force, HG §§13-1901 to 13-1906.
Pertussis, HG §§18-328 to 18-332.
See PERTUSSIS.
Plague.
Medical and law enforcement personnel.
Notification of exposure, HG §§18-213 to 18-213.2.
Plant disease control.
General provisions, AG §§5-301 to 5-314.
See PLANT DISEASE CONTROL.
Quarantine.
General provisions.
See QUARANTINE.
Rabies, HG §§18-312 to 18-320.
See RABIES.
Sickle cell anemia, HG §§18-501 to 18-505.
See SICKLE CELL ANEMIA.
Syphilis.
Blood test required, HG §18-307.
Scope of section, HG §18-307.
Tobacco-related diseases.
Cancer prevention, education, screening and treatment program.
Generally, HG §§13-1101 to 13-1119.
See CANCER PREVENTION, EDUCATION, SCREENING AND TREATMENT PROGRAM.
Tuberculosis.
General provisions, HG §§18-322 to 18-325.
See TUBERCULOSIS.
Vaccination.
See VACCINATION.
Venereal diseases.
Chlamydia screening tests.
Health insurance, required coverage, IN §15-829.
Consent by minor to treatment, HG §20-102.
Cures or remedies.
Advertising cure.
Prohibition, penalty, CR §10-102.
Defined, CR §10-101.
Prescription requirements, CR §10-103.
Selling or dispensing remedies.
Prohibition, penalties, CR §10-103.

DISHONOR.
Bank deposits and collections.
Documentary drafts, CL §§4-501, 4-503, 4-504.
Payor banks, CL §4-301.
Liability of payor bank for wrongful dishonor, CL §4-402.

DISHONOR —Cont'd
Negotiable instruments.
Certificate of dishonor, CL §3-505.
Form, CL §3-503.
Notice, CL §§3-503, 3-504.
Presentment, CL §3-501.
Presumption, CL §3-505.
Protest defined, CL §3-505.
Special provisions, CL §3-502.

DISHONORED CHECKS.
Bad checks, CR §§8-101 to 8-108.
Collection of dishonored checks and other instruments.
Criminal penalties.
Location on notice, CL §15-803.
Damages.
Time for seeking after dishonor, when prohibited, CL §15-802.
Defenses, CL §15-802.
Definitions, CL §15-801.
Exceptions to provisions, CL §15-804.
Liability.
Location on notice, CL §15-803.
Notice of dishonor, CL §15-802.
Form, CL §15-803.
District Court jurisdiction, CJ §4-401.
Transfer of case to circuit court, CJ §4-402.

DISINFECTION OF BEDDING AND UPHOLSTERED FURNITURE.
See BEDDING AND UPHOLSTERED FURNITURE.

DISINTERMENT.
Ascertaining cause of death.
Removal of human remains from burial site, CR §10-402.

DISMANTLERS, RECYCLERS AND SCRAP PROCESSORS.
Motor vehicles.
See MOTOR VEHICLE DISMANTLERS, RECYCLERS AND SCRAP PROCESSORS.

DISMISSAL OF ACTIONS.
Adoption.
Local department adoptions.
Adoption without prior termination of parental rights.
Contested petition, dismissal of, FL §5-340.
Assault charge, CR §3-207.
Class actions.
Circuit courts, CivProCir Rule 2-231.
Criminal charges.
Assault, CR §3-207.
Defendant incompetent to stand trial, CP §3-107.
Engineers.
Complaints against licensees, BOP §14-318.
Expungement of records.
Notice to defendant of right to file for, CP §6-232.
Right to file for, CP §10-105.
Judicial disabilities and sanctionable conduct.
Complaints against judge, CJA Rule 16-807.
Lack of jurisdiction or prosecution.
Deferral of dismissal.
Circuit courts, CivProCir Rule 2-507.
District Court, CivProDist Rule 3-507.
Entry of dismissal.
Circuit courts, CivProCir Rule 2-507.
District Court, CivProDist Rule 3-507.
Notice of contemplated dismissal.
Circuit courts, CivProCir Rule 2-507.

DISMISSAL OF ACTIONS —Cont'd
Lack of jurisdiction or prosecution —Cont'd
Notice of contemplated dismissal —Cont'd
District Court, CivProDist Rule 3-507.
Scope.
Circuit courts, CivProCir Rule 2-507.
District Court, CivProDist Rule 3-507.
Motions.
Circuit courts.
Defenses which may be made by motion to dismiss, CivProCir Rule 2-322.
Prisoner litigation, CJ §5-1004.
Real estate brokers.
Guaranty fund.
Claims against fund, BOP §17-407.
SLAPP suits.
Remedies of defendant, CJ §5-807.
Surveys and surveyors.
Licenses.
Denial, revocation or suspension or reprimand of licensee, BOP §15-318.
Trial.
Lack of jurisdiction or prosecution.
Circuit courts, CivProCir Rule 2-507.
District Court, CivProDist Rule 3-507.
Voluntary dismissal.
Circuit courts, CivProCir Rule 2-506.
District Court, CivProDist Rule 3-506.

DISORDERLY CONDUCT, CR §10-201.
Citation.
Police officer authorized to charge by, CP §4-101.
Disorderly intoxication, 2B §§19-101 to 19-104.
In cemeteries, CR §10-404.
Schools.
Athletic contests.
Possession of intoxicating liquors, ED §26-103.

DISORDERLY HOUSES.
Prostitution generally.
See PROSTITUTION.

DISPENSERS OF CONTROLLED DANGEROUS SUBSTANCES.
Registration, CR §§5-301 to 5-310.

DISPLACED HOMEMAKERS.
Community colleges.
Definition of displaced homemaker, ED §16-106.
Waiver of tuition for senior citizens, ED §16-106.
Defined, FL §4-601.
Intent of provisions, FL §4-602.
Legislative declaration, FL §4-602.
Multipurpose service center.
Establishment, FL §4-605.
Evaluation.
Duties of secretary of human resources, FL §4-612.
Functions, FL §4-606.
Job training programs, FL §4-607.
Location, FL §4-605.
Programs, FL §4-607.
Rules and regulations, FL §4-611.
Secretary of human resources.
Definition of "secretary," FL §4-101.
Delegation of authority, FL §4-613.
Duties.
Cooperation with government agencies, FL §4-610.
Establishment of center, FL §4-605.
Evaluation, FL §4-612.
Funds and contributions, FL §4-610.

DISPLACED HOMEMAKERS —Cont'd
Multipurpose service center —Cont'd
Secretary of human resources —Cont'd
Duties —Cont'd
Rules and regulations.
Adoption, FL §4-611.
Establishment of center, FL §4-605.
Powers, FL §4-613.
Rules and regulations, FL §4-611.
Staff, FL §4-608.
Duties, FL §4-609.
Training, FL §4-608.
Rules and regulations.
Multipurpose service center, FL §4-611.

DISPOSITION OF ABANDONED PROPERTY.
General provisions, CL §§17-101 to 17-326.
See ABANDONED PROPERTY DISPOSITION.

DISPUTE RESOLUTION.
Administrative procedure.
Procurement, SF §15-216.
Arbitration.
See ARBITRATION AND AWARD.
Counties.
Construction contracts, 25 §1A; 25A §1A; 25B
§13A.
Heritage areas authority, FI §13-1108.
Appeals, FI §13-1124.
Mediation.
Collective bargaining generally, LE §§4-101 to
4-405.
See COLLECTIVE BARGAINING.
Labor dispute arbitration or mediation, LE
§§4-101 to 4-111.
See COLLECTIVE BARGAINING.
Procurement.
Appeals board.
See PROCUREMENT.
Architectural and engineering services.
Exception to dispute resolution provisions, SF
§15-202.
Schools.
Children in state-supervised care, ED §8-505.
**State center for alternative dispute resolution
and violence prevention,** ED §24-401.

DISRUPTIVE STUDENTS.
Special programs, ED §7-304.

DISSOCIATION OF PARTNER.
See PARTNERSHIPS, REVISED ACT.

DISSOLUTION.
Banks and trust companies.
See BANKS AND TRUST COMPANIES.
Business trusts, CA §12-202.
Corporations.
General provisions.
See CORPORATIONS.
Credit unions.
See CREDIT UNIONS.
Electric cooperatives, CA §§5-630 to 5-632, 5-636.
Insurance companies.
Foreign risk retention groups.
Voluntary dissolution or delinquency
proceedings, IN §25-103.
Risk retention groups.
Insurance insolvency guaranty funds, IN
§25-104.
Limited partnerships, CA §§10-801 to 10-805.
See LIMITED PARTNERSHIPS.
Partnerships.
Limited partnerships, CA §§10-801 to 10-805.
See LIMITED PARTNERSHIPS.

DISSOLUTION —Cont'd
Partnerships, revised act, CA §§9A-801 to
9A-807.
See PARTNERSHIPS, REVISED ACT.
Savings and loan associations.
See SAVINGS AND LOAN ASSOCIATIONS.

DISTRESS FOR RENT.
Accidents.
Termination of tenancy for unavoidable accident,
RP §8-112.
Action at law, RP §8-302.
Amendments.
Levy and inventory, RP §8-305.
Petition or other pleadings, RP §8-327.
Appeals.
Jury trial, RP §8-332.
Right to appeal, RP §8-332.
Stay.
Appeal bond, RP §8-332.
Order of court, RP §8-332.
Time for taking, RP §8-332.
Trial de novo, RP §8-332.
Assignments.
Liability of assignee of lease, RP §§8-325, 8-329.
Attorneys at law.
Exemptions from levy, RP §8-307.
Auctions.
Manner of sale, RP §8-319.
Bonds, surety.
Removal of levied goods, RP §8-310.
Affixed to property, RP §8-313.
Return of levied goods, RP §8-316.
Security for cost of sale, RP §8-321.
Stay of appeal, RP §8-332.
Complaint.
Repossession.
Landlord complaint procedure.
See LANDLORD AND TENANT.
Corporations.
Corporate tenant ceasing to exist, RP §8-328.
Costs, RP §8-322.
Removing goods for sale, RP §8-319.
Restitution of possession of premises, RP §8-324.
Security for cost of sale, RP §8-321.
Court.
Defined, RP §8-301.
Crops.
Lien on crops.
Advances in certain counties, RP §8-115.
Reserved as rent, RP §8-115.
Damages.
Rights of third party when goods sold under
distress, RP §8-323.
Death.
Effect of death of tenant, RP §8-328.
Recovery of rent on death of landlord who is life
tenant, RP §8-106.
Defendant.
Answer, RP §8-314.
Defined, RP §8-301.
Definitions, RP §8-301.
**Disposition of unsold goods or surplus
proceeds,** RP §8-320.
Distress.
Defined, RP §8-301.
District Court.
Jurisdiction, RP §8-302.
Emergency management.
Civil relief during emergency periods, PS §14-213.
Illegal distraint of property, PS §14-218.

DISTRESS FOR RENT —Cont'd
Executions.
   Stay, RP §8-332.
Executors and administrators.
   Notice to personal representative of deceased
      defendant, RP §8-328.
Exemptions.
   Disposition of unsold goods or surplus proceeds of
      sale, RP §8-320.
   Enforcement of deficiency judgment, RP §8-325.
   Exclusions from levy, RP §8-306.
   Generally, RP §8-307.
Fires and fire protection.
   Termination of tenancy for fire, RP §8-112.
Fixtures.
   Liability for removal of goods affixed to realty, RP
      §8-313.
Forms.
   Petition, RP §8-303.
Goods.
   Defined, RP §8-301.
   Husband and wife.
      Levy, RP §8-326.
   In custody of court, RP §8-308.
   Subject to levy, RP §8-306.
      Assignment of leases, RP §8-329.
   Subject to security interest, RP §8-307.
Hearings.
   Appeals, RP §8-332.
   Defendant's answer, RP §8-314.
   Deficiency judgment, RP §8-325.
Husband and wife.
   Levy on goods of husband and wife, RP §8-326.
Inventory.
   Amendment, RP §8-305.
   Generally, RP §8-305.
Judgments and decrees.
   Deficiency judgment, RP §8-325.
Jurisdiction.
   Appeals, RP §8-332.
   Generally, RP §8-302.
   Goods removed to another jurisdiction, RP §8-315.
   Third-party claim, RP §8-323.
Jury.
   Right to jury trial.
      Appeals, RP §8-332.
Leases.
   Assignment of lease.
      Liability of assignee, RP §§8-325, 8-329.
   Renewal of lease.
      Back rent on renewal of lease, RP §8-111.
   Termination of leases, RP §8-324.
Levy.
   Amended levy, RP §8-305.
   Bonds, surety.
      Indemnity for goods removed from property, RP
         §8-313.
      Removal of levied goods, RP §8-310.
      Return of levied goods, RP §8-316.
   Entry under levy, RP §8-309.
   Exclusions from levy, RP §8-306.
      Removal of goods of third person, RP §8-311.
   Exemptions from levy.
      Generally, RP §8-307.
   Finality of levy, RP §8-311.
   Forcible entry.
      Order to follow removed goods, RP §8-315.
      Order to make, RP §8-317.
      When order required, RP §8-309.
   Goods.
      Assignee of lease, RP §8-329.

DISTRESS FOR RENT —Cont'd
Levy —Cont'd
   Goods —Cont'd
      In custody of court, RP §8-308.
      Risk of loss or destruction, RP §8-312.
      Subject to levy, RP §8-306.
   Husband and wife.
      Goods of husband and wife, RP §8-326.
   Lien.
      Continuation until sale, RP §8-312.
   Order of levy, RP §8-305.
      Forcible entry, RP §8-309.
   Removal of levied goods, RP §8-310.
      Expenses, RP §8-313.
      Goods of third persons, RP §8-311.
      Liability for removal of goods affixed to
         property, RP §8-313.
   Return, RP §8-305.
   Risk of loss or destruction of goods, RP §8-312.
   Service of order, RP §8-305.
   Third-party claims, RP §8-311.
      Rights when goods sold, RP §8-323.
   Time of levy, RP §8-309.
   Title.
      Effect on title to goods, RP §8-312.
Liens.
   Crops reserved as rent, RP §8-115.
      Lien not divested by sale, insolvency or process
         of law, RP §8-115.
   Effect of levy, RP §8-312.
Limitation of actions.
   General provisions, RP §8-107.
   Third-party claims, RP §8-311.
Mail.
   Service of process, RP §8-330.
   Stay when notice not received, RP §8-331.
Merger.
   Remedy upon covenants in case of merger, RP
      §8-102.
Nonresidents.
   Petition.
      Service on nonresident, RP §8-303.
Notices.
   Hearing on defendant's answer, RP §8-314.
   Sales, RP §8-318.
      Contents of notice, RP §8-318.
      Posting on courthouse, RP §8-318.
      Publication by newspaper, RP §8-318.
   Service of process by mail, RP §8-330.
   Stay when notice not received, RP §8-331.
   Tenant dying or ceasing to exist.
      Notice to personal representative or officers, RP
         §8-328.
Oaths.
   Petition.
      Oath or affirmation, RP §8-303.
Orders of court.
   Disposition of unsold goods or surplus proceeds,
      RP §8-320.
   Excluding goods of third persons, RP §8-311.
   Final order of sale, RP §8-314.
   Following removed goods, RP §8-315.
   Forcible entry, RP §8-309.
   Levy, RP §8-305.
   Making forcible entry after levy on goods, RP
      §8-317.
   Release of levied goods, RP §8-316.
   Restitution of premises, RP §8-324.
   Show cause order, RP §8-304.
      Failure of defendant to appear, RP §8-304.

DISTRESS FOR RENT —Cont'd
Orders of court —Cont'd
Stay, RP §8-332.
Notice not received, RP §8-331.
Tenant dying or ceasing to exist.
Requiring posting of petition, RP §8-328.
Termination of lease, RP §8-324.
Parties, RP §8-303.
Tenant dying or ceasing to exist, RP §8-328.
Petition.
Amendment of petition or other pleading, RP §8-327.
Contents, RP §8-303.
Existence of perfected security interest, RP §8-307.
Deficiency judgment, RP §8-325.
Form, RP §8-303.
For order directing forcible entry, RP §8-309.
Goods removed to another jurisdiction, RP §8-315.
Nonresident.
Service on nonresident, RP §8-303.
Oath or affirmation, RP §8-303.
Posting.
Tenant dying or ceasing to exist, RP §8-328.
Release of levied goods, RP §8-316.
Removal of levied goods, RP §8-310.
Requesting inclusion of additional goods, RP §8-305.
Service, RP §8-305.
Nonresident or defendant not amenable to service, RP §8-303.
Third-party claims, RP §8-311.
Verification, RP §8-303.
Physicians and surgeons.
Exemptions from levy, RP §8-307.
Pleading.
Amendments, RP §8-327.
Answer of defendant, RP §8-314.
Restitution to plaintiff, RP §8-324.
Possession of premises.
Repossession procedure.
General provisions.
See LANDLORD AND TENANT.
Publication.
Notice of sale, RP §8-318.
Remainders, reversions and executory interests.
Remedies of and against transferee of reversion, RP §8-101.
Sale of reversion when rent is in arrears.
Rights of purchaser, RP §14-103.
Repossession.
Landlord complaint procedure.
See LANDLORD AND TENANT.
Right of entry.
Entry under levy, RP §8-309.
Forcible entry.
Order to make entry after levy on goods, RP §8-317.
When order required, RP §8-309.
Order to follow removed goods, RP §8-315.
Sales.
Bonds, surety.
Security for cost of sale, RP §8-321.
Costs.
Amount of cost, RP §8-322.
Removing goods for sale, RP §8-319.
Security for cost of sale, RP §8-321.
Date of sale, RP §8-314.
Deficiency judgment, RP §8-325.
Disposition of unsold goods, RP §8-320.

DISTRESS FOR RENT —Cont'd
Sales —Cont'd
Manner of sale, RP §8-319.
Notices, RP §8-318.
Contents, RP §8-318.
Posting on courthouse, RP §8-318.
Publication by newspaper, RP §8-318.
Order in which goods to be sold, RP §8-320.
Order of court, RP §8-314.
Place of sale, RP §8-319.
Public auction, RP §8-319.
Removal for sale, RP §8-319.
Removal of levied goods pending sale, RP §8-310.
Surplus proceeds.
Disposition, RP §8-320.
Payment of judgment or claim out of surplus, RP §8-320.
Third parties.
Rights when goods sold under distress, RP §8-323.
Unsold goods.
Disposition, RP §8-320.
Payment of judgment or claim out of, RP §8-320.
Service of process.
By mail, RP §8-330.
Stay when notice not received, RP §8-331.
Nisi order of termination of lease, RP §8-324.
Order of levy, RP §8-305.
Third-party claims, RP §8-311.
Petition, RP §8-305.
Service on nonresident or defendant not amenable to service, RP §8-303.
Sundays and holidays.
Service prohibited on Sundays, CivProCir Rule 2-125; CivProDist Rule 3-125; CJ §6-302.
Tenant dying or ceasing to exist, RP §8-328.
Stay.
Appeals, RP §8-332.
When notice not received, RP §8-331.
Sundays and holidays.
Service of writ prohibited, CivProCir Rule 2-125; CivProDist Rule 3-125; CJ §6-302.
Third-party claims.
Levy on goods of third persons, RP §8-311.
Rights of third party when goods sold, RP §8-323.
Title.
Effect of levy on title to goods, RP §8-312.
Venue.
Generally, RP §8-302.
Verification.
Petition, RP §8-303.
Warrants.
Restitution of possession of premises, RP §8-324.

DISTRESS SALES.
Advertising.
Compliance with provisions of subtitle required, CL §11-1102.
Conducted on provisions of subtitle required, CL §11-1101.
Counties.
Minimum standards, CL §11-1105.
Definitions, CL §11-1101.
Enforcement of subtitle, CL §11-1105.
Inventory, CL §11-1104.
Municipal corporations.
Minimum standards, CL §11-1105.
Prohibited activities, CL §11-1103.
Violation of article, CL §11-1106.

DISTRIBUTING CONTROLLED DANGEROUS SUBSTANCE, CR §§5-602, 5-607 to 5-609.
Counterfeit substances, CR §§5-604, 5-607.
Drug kingpins, CR §5-613.
Faked controlled substances, CR §5-617.
Firearm possessed, used, worn, carried or transported.
Separate offense, enhanced sentence, forfeiture, CR §5-621.
Minors used, CR §5-628.
Registrants.
Unauthorized distribution, CR §5-902.
Schools.
Manufacturing, distributing, dispensing or possessing near, CR §5-627.
Unlawful distribution by registrants, CR §5-904.

DISTRIBUTION.
Descent.
See DESCENT AND DISTRIBUTION.
Maryland fair distributorship act, CL §§11-1301 to 11-1306.
See FAIR DISTRIBUTORSHIP ACT.
Multilevel distribution companies.
General provisions, BR §§14-301 to 14-305.
See MULTILEVEL DISTRIBUTION COMPANIES.

DISTRIBUTORS OF CONTROLLED DANGEROUS SUBSTANCES.
Registration, CR §§5-301 to 5-310.

DISTRICT COURT.
Administration of courts, CJA Rules 16-101 to 16-824.
See ADMINISTRATION OF COURTS.
Administrative memorandum of court.
Effective date of judicial documents, SG §7-222.
Administrative orders.
Effective date, SG §7-222.
Administrative regulations.
Chief judge.
Promulgation, CJ §1-605.
Alcoholic beverages.
Committing individuals for detoxification.
Authority of court, CJ §4-202.
Alcoholism.
Treatment of alcoholism.
Authority of court, CJ §4-202.
Amendments to constitution.
Implementing, MD Const Art IV §41-I.
Appeals.
General provisions, CJ §§12-401 to 12-404.
See APPEALS FROM DISTRICT COURT.
Appearances.
Initial appearance of defendant.
Criminal cases, Crim Rule 4-213.
Applicability of rules, Rule 1-101.
Arbitration and award.
Uniform arbitration act.
General provisions, CJ §§3-201 to 3-234.
See ARBITRATION AND AWARD.
Arrest warrants.
Authority of judges to issue, CJ §1-609.
Assignments.
Wages.
Entry upon docket, CL §15-302.
Proof of service on employer, CL §15-303.
Attachment.
Original process.
Jurisdiction, CJ §4-401.

DISTRICT COURT —Cont'd
Attorneys at law.
Continuance.
Appearance of attorney.
When continuance may be granted, CJ §6-409.
Auditors.
Supervising auditors, CJ §2-601.
Appointment, CJ §2-602.
Automotive warranty enforcement act.
Civil jurisdiction, CJ §4-401.
Bad check actions.
Transfer of action from District Court to circuit court, CivProDist Rule 3-326.
Bail and recognizance, CP §5-205.
Bonds, surety.
Premiums.
Trial magistrates, clerks, etc.
Paid by county, 25 §33.
Budgets.
Organization of costs, CJ §1-608.
Charging documents.
Use, Crim Rule 4-201.
Chief judge. See within this heading, "Judges."
Circuit courts.
Transfer of action to District Court, CivProCir Rule 2-327.
Warrants.
Issuance, Crim Rule 4-212.
Civil jurisdiction.
Concurrent jurisdiction, CJ §4-402.
Domestic violence.
Protection from, CJ §4-404.
Exceptions, CJ §4-402.
Exclusive original jurisdiction, CJ §4-401.
Jury trial, CJ §4-402.
Small claims actions, CJ §4-405.
Civil procedure.
Actions.
Commencement of action, CivProDist Rule 3-101.
Form of action, CivProDist Rule 3-301.
Process.
Requirements preliminary to summons, CivProDist Rule 3-111.
Appearances, CivProDist Rule 3-331.
Attorneys at law, CivProDist Rule 3-131.
Attachment.
Prejudgment attachment, CivProDist Rule 3-115.
Attorneys at law.
Appearances, CivProDist Rule 3-131.
Continuances, CivProDist Rule 3-508.
Discovery, CivProDist Rules 3-401 to 3-431.
See DISCOVERY.
Execution, CivProDist Rules 3-641, 3-642.
Garnishment, CivProDist Rules 3-645, 3-646.
Interrogatories, CivProDist Rule 3-421.
Intervention, CivProDist Rule 3-214.
Joinder.
General provisions.
See JOINDER.
Judgments and decrees.
Attachment before judgment, CivProDist Rule 3-115.
General provisions, CivProDist Rules 3-601 to 3-649.
See JUDGMENTS AND DECREES.
Prejudgment attachment, CivProDist Rule 3-115.

DISTRICT COURT —Cont'd
Civil procedure —Cont'd
　Jury trial.
　　Certain transfers from District Court, CivProCir
　　　Rule 2-326.
　Liens.
　　Judgment liens, CivProDist Rule 3-621.
　Motions.
　　General provisions.
　　　See MOTIONS.
　Parties, CivProDist Rules 3-201 to 3-241.
　　See PARTIES.
　Pleading, CivProDist Rules 3-301 to 3-342.
　　See PLEADINGS.
　Pretrial conference, CivProDist Rule 3-504.
　Service of process, CivProDist Rules 3-121 to
　　3-126.
　　See SERVICE OF PROCESS.
　Small claim actions, CivProDist Rule 3-701.
　Subpoenas, CivProDist Rule 3-510.
　Substitution of parties, CivProDist Rule 3-241.
　Summons.
　　Content, CivProDist Rule 3-114.
　　Duration, dormancy and renewal, CivProDist
　　　Rule 3-113.
　　Issuance of summons, CivProDist Rule 3-112.
　　Requirements preliminary to summons,
　　　CivProDist Rule 3-111.
　Third-party practice, CivProDist Rule 3-332.
　Trial, CivProDist Rule 3-533.
　　Date and time, CivProDist Rule 3-102.
　　General provisions, CivProDist Rules 3-503 to
　　　3-536.
　　　See TRIAL.
Class actions.
　Jurisdiction.
　　Civil jurisdiction.
　　　Concurrent jurisdiction.
　　　　Separate claims may be aggregated to meet
　　　　　minimum amount in controversy
　　　　　requirement, CJ §4-402.
Clerks of court.
　Assistant chief clerks, CJ §2-601.
　　Appointment, CJ §2-602.
　　Term of employment, CJ §2-602.
　Chief administrative clerk, CJ §2-601; MD Const
　　Art IV §41F.
　　Appointment, CJ §2-602.
　　　Power of chief judge, CJ §1-605.
　　Duties.
　　　Generally, CJ §2-603.
　　General provisions, CJ §2-601.
　　Term of employment, CJ §2-602.
　Chief clerk.
　　Appointment, CJ §§1-605, 2-602.
　　Duties, CJ §2-603.
　　General provisions, MD Const Art IV §41F.
　　Office, CJ §1-606.
　　Term of employment, CJ §2-602.
　Deputies, MD Const Art IV §41F.
　Duties, CJ §2-603.
　In each county, MD Const Art IV §41F.
Commissioners, MD Const Art IV §41G.
　Appointment, CJ §2-607.
　　Approval by chief judge, CJ §1-605.
　Authority, CJ §2-607.
　Code of conduct for masters, examiners, auditors,
　　referees and District Court commissioners.
　　Adoption, CJA Rule 16-814.
　Compensation, CJ §2-607.

DISTRICT COURT —Cont'd
Commissioners —Cont'd
　Coordinator of commissioner activities, CJ
　　§§2-601, 2-602.
　Duties.
　　Generally, CJ §2-607.
　General provisions, CJ §2-607.
　Multicounty district.
　　Performance of duties in multicounty districts,
　　　CJ §2-607.
　Number, CJ §2-607.
　Persons arrested in another county.
　　Authorization of commissioners to perform
　　　duties regarding, CJ §2-607.
　Qualifications, CJ §2-607.
　Salaries, CJ §2-607.
　Temporary service in contiguous county, CJ
　　§2-607.
　Tenure, CJ §2-607.
Composition, CJ §1-603.
Consolidation of cases, CivProDist Rule 3-503.
Constables.
　Appointment, CJ §2-604.
　Classified service.
　　Full-time constables, CJ §2-604.
　Duties.
　　Generally, CJ §2-606.
　Levy of executions, CJ §2-606.
　Public transportation, CJ §2-604.
　Service of process, CJ §§2-605, 2-606.
　Terms of employment, CJ §2-604.
Contracts.
　Jurisdiction, CJ §4-401.
Coordinator of commissioner activity, CJ
　§§2-601, 2-602.
Coram nobis.
　Writs of error coram nobis.
　　Authority of judges to issue, CJ §1-609.
Corporations.
　Appearances in civil matters.
　　Attorney requirement, CivProDist Rule 3-131.
　　Exceptions to attorney requirements, BOP
　　　§10-206.
Costs.
　Bad checks.
　　Additional costs, CJ §7-301.
　　Service charge, CJ §7-208.
　Civil cases, CJ §7-301.
　Collection, CJ §7-302.
　Criminal cases, CJ §7-301.
　　Additional costs imposed on defendant, CJ
　　　§7-409.
　　Criminal injuries compensation.
　　　Waiver of costs, CJ §7-405.
　Criminal injuries compensation fund.
　　Payment into, CJ §7-301.
　Disposition, CJ §7-302.
　Indigent persons.
　　Waiver of prepayment in cases of indigency, CJ
　　　§7-301.
　Law enforcement and correctional training fund.
　　Payment into, CJ §7-301.
　Maintenance, operation and administration costs,
　　CJ §1-608.
　Schedule, CJ §7-301.
　State helicopter replacement fund.
　　Surcharge for in traffic cases, CJ §7-301.
　Traffic cases, CJ §7-301.
　Victim and witness protection and relocation
　　program.
　　Payment into, CJ §7-301.

DISTRICT COURT —Cont'd
Costs —Cont'd
Waiver of prepayment in cases of indigency, CJ §7-301.
Courts of record, MD Const Art IV §1.
Credit cards.
Offenses.
Jurisdiction.
Violation of credit card laws, CJ §4-301.
Crime victims' compensation.
Restitution judgment.
Recording and indexing, CP §11-610.
Criminal procedure.
Insane persons.
Authority of court as to competency or sanity of criminal defendants, CJ §4-202.
Jurisdiction.
Concurrent jurisdiction, CJ §4-302.
School attendance cases, CJ §4-302.
Exceptions, CJ §4-302.
Exclusive original jurisdiction, CJ §4-301.
Juvenile causes, CJ §§4-302, 4-303.
Preliminary hearings, CJ §4-304.
Preliminary hearings, CJ §4-304.
Process.
Criminal process, CJ §2-605.
Criminal rules.
Applicability of rules, Rule 1-101.
Motions.
Content, Crim Rule 4-251.
Determination, Crim Rule 4-251.
Effect of determination before trial, Crim Rule 4-251.
Reassignment in District Court, Crim Rule 4-254.
Trial.
Beginning trial in District Court, Crim Rule 4-301.
Date.
Change in District Court, Crim Rule 4-271.
Video conferencing, Crim Rule 4-231.
Definitions, CJ §4-101.
Collection, CJ §1-605.
Depositions.
Criminal rules, Crim Rule 4-261.
General provisions governing discovery, CivProDist Rule 3-401.
Perpetuation of testimony, CivProDist Rule 3-431.
Discovery.
Civil procedure, CivProDist Rules 3-401 to 3-431.
See DISCOVERY.
Criminal rules, Crim Rule 4-262.
Generally, CivProDist Rule 3-401.
Jurisdiction, RP §8-302.
Districts.
Division of state, MD Const Art IV §41B.
Enumerated, CJ §1-602.
State divided into districts, CJ §1-602.
Divisions.
Functional divisions, CJ §1-607.
Domestic violence.
Protection from.
Jurisdiction.
Concurrent jurisdiction with circuit courts, CJ §4-404.
Transfer of actions from circuit court to District Court, CivProCir Rule 2-327.
Transfer of actions from District Court to circuit court, CivProDist Rule 3-326.
Drug abuse control and rehabilitation.
Authority to commit individuals for treatment, CJ §4-202.

DISTRICT COURT —Cont'd
Dumping site surveillance systems.
Election to stand trial for violations, CJ §7-302.
Effective date of judicial documents, SG §7-222.
Ejectment.
Appeals.
When grantor remains in possession after delivery of deed and in violation of agreement, RP §14-109.
Jurisdiction.
When grantor remains in possession after delivery of deed and in violation of agreement, RP §14-109.
Electronic filing of pleadings and papers, CJA Rule 16-506.
Employees.
Appointment, CJ §2-601.
Power of chief judge, CJ §1-605.
Employee theft.
Civil penalties.
Exclusive original civil jurisdiction, CJ §3-1308.
Equity jurisdiction.
Exceptions, CJ §4-402.
Established, CJ §1-601.
Execution.
Civil procedure, CivProDist Rules 3-641, 3-642.
Extradition.
Habeas corpus ad prosequendum.
Authority of judges to issue writ, CJ §1-609.
Fees.
Accounts and returns.
Exception, MD Const Art XV §1.
Felonies.
Jurisdiction, CJ §§4-301, 4-302.
Filing.
Electronic filing of pleadings and papers, CJA Rule 16-506.
Financial institutions article violations.
Jurisdiction, CJ §4-301.
Fines.
See FINES.
Forcible entry and detainer.
Jurisdiction, CJ §4-401.
Garnishment.
Civil procedure, CivProDist Rules 3-645, 3-646.
General assembly.
Confirmation of appointment of judges, MD Const Art IV §41D.
Eligibility for legislature, MD Const Art III §11.
Governor.
Appointment of judges, MD Const Art IV §41D.
Grantee suit.
Jurisdiction, CJ §4-401.
Habeas corpus.
Writs of habeas corpus ad testificandum or ad prosequendum.
Authority of judges to issue, CJ §1-609.
Health.
Authority of court provided in health-general article, CJ §4-202.
Hearings.
Preliminary hearings.
Felony cases, CJ §4-304.
Injunctions.
Petition.
Jurisdiction, CJ §4-401.
Interrogatories.
Civil procedure, CivProDist Rule 3-421.
General provisions governing discovery, CivProDist Rule 3-401.

DISTRICT COURT —Cont'd
Intervention.
Civil procedure, CivProDist Rule 3-214.
Joinder.
Civil procedure.
General provisions.
See JOINDER.
Judges.
Administrative judge.
Appointment, CJ §1-607.
Appointment, MD Const Art IV §41D.
Assignment.
From other districts, CJ §1-605.
Associate judges.
Number, CJ §1-603.
Baltimore county.
Places of sitting, CJ §1-603.
Chief judge, MD Const Art IV §41E.
Administrative judge.
Appointment, CJ §1-607.
Administrative officer, CJ §1-605.
Administrative regulations, CJ §1-605.
Assignment of judges, CJ §1-605.
Duties.
Generally, CJ §1-605.
Effective date of administrative regulations, SG §7-222.
Employee hiring, CJ §2-601.
General provisions, CJ §1-603.
Office, CJ §1-606.
Personnel hiring, CJ §2-601.
Powers.
Generally, CJ §1-605.
Salary, CJ §1-702.
Traffic cases.
Adoption of trial procedures, TR §26-304.
Duties, MD Const Art IV §41C.
Expenses.
Reimbursable expenses, CJ §1-706.
Group health or group hospitalization plan.
Benefits for certain judges of District Court, CJ §1-707.
Habeas corpus.
Writ of habeas corpus ad testificandum or ad prosequendum.
Authority of judges to issue, CJ §1-609.
Health or hospitalization benefits.
Certain judges of District Court, CJ §1-707.
Number, MD Const Art IV §41B.
Associate judges, CJ §1-603.
Increasing or decreasing, MD Const Art IV §41C.
In each district, CJ §1-603.
Personnel hiring, CJ §2-601.
Places of sitting, CJ §1-603.
Qualifications, MD Const Art IV §41C.
Residence requirement, MD Const Art IV §41B.
Resident judge.
In each county, CJ §1-603.
Salaries.
General provisions, CJ §§1-701 to 1-708.
See JUDGES.
Not to be reduced, MD Const Art IV §41H.
Terms of office, MD Const Art IV §41D.
Warrants, authority to issue, CJ §1-609.
Writs.
Authority to issue, CJ §1-609.
Judgments and decrees.
Civil procedure.
General provisions, CivProDist Rules 3-601 to 3-649.
See JUDGMENTS AND DECREES.

DISTRICT COURT —Cont'd
Judgments and decrees —Cont'd
Civil procedure —Cont'd
Prejudgment attachment, CivProDist Rule 3-115.
Jurisdiction, MD Const Art IV §41A.
Alcoholism.
Authority to commit individuals for treatment, CJ §4-202.
Civil jurisdiction. See within this heading, "Civil jurisdiction."
Court of limited jurisdiction, CJ §1-601.
Criminal jurisdiction. See within this heading, "Criminal procedure."
Detoxification.
Authority to commit individuals for detoxification, CJ §4-202.
Domestic violence.
Protection from.
Concurrent jurisdiction with circuit court, CJ §4-404.
Drug abuse control and rehabilitation.
Authority to commit individuals for treatment of drug abuse, CJ §4-202.
Extent, CJ §4-201.
Health.
Authority of court provided in health-general article, CJ §4-202.
Juvenile causes.
Criminal jurisdiction, CJ §§4-302, 4-303.
Mental disorders.
Authority of court to order emergency evaluation, CJ §4-202.
Minors purchasing or consuming alcohol, 2B §12-108.
Sanity or competency of criminal defendants, CJ §4-202.
Small claim actions, CJ §4-405.
Jury.
Appeals.
Criminal appeal tried de novo.
Right to jury trial, CJ §12-401.
Demand for jury trial.
Certain transfers from District Court, CivProCir Rule 2-326.
Depriving court of civil jurisdiction, CJ §4-402.
Depriving court of criminal jurisdiction, CJ §4-302.
General provisions, CJ §§8-101 to 8-507.
See JURY.
Transferred actions from District Court.
New demand not required, CivProCir Rule 2-325.
Justices of the peace.
When statutory references to justices deemed to refer to District Court, MD Const Art IV §41-I.
Juvenile causes.
Jurisdiction.
Criminal jurisdiction, CJ §§4-302, 4-303.
Landlord and tenant.
Jurisdiction, CJ §4-401.
Landlord complaint procedure.
General provisions.
See DISTRESS FOR RENT.
Tenants holding over.
General provisions.
See LANDLORD AND TENANT.
Law enforcement personnel.
Charging documents against law enforcement officers.
Application filed in District Court, CJ §2-608.

DISTRICT COURT —Cont'd

Liens.
Civil procedure.
Judgment liens, CivProDist Rule 3-621.

Maintenance and operation.
Costs, CJ §1-608.

Mental hygiene.
Authority to order emergency evaluations for
mental disorders, CJ §4-202.

Misdemeanors.
Jurisdiction over violations, CJ §4-301.

Motions.
Civil procedure.
General provisions.
See MOTIONS.
Criminal rules, Crim Rule 4-251.
Content, Crim Rule 4-251.
Determination, Crim Rule 4-251.
Effect of determination before trial, Crim Rule
4-251.

Motor vehicles.
Appearance.
Notice to appear required in traffic citation, TR
§26-201.
Bonds, surety.
Reimbursement of forfeited bond or collateral,
TR §27-104.
Failure to comply with traffic citation.
Action by District Court, TR §26-204.
Parking.
Adoption of trial procedures by chief judge, TR
§26-304.
Report of convictions.
For violation of motor vehicle laws, CJ §1-605.
Traffic cases. See within this heading, "Traffic
cases."

Municipal infractions.
Jurisdiction, CJ §4-401.

Official character.
Authentication, MD Const Art IV §1.

Orders of court.
Effective date of judicial documents, SG §7-222.

Parties.
Civil procedure, CivProDist Rules 3-201 to 3-241.
See PARTIES.

Penalties.
Fines.
See FINES.

People's courts.
Statutory references to people's courts deemed to
refer to District Court, MD Const Art IV
§41-I.

Pleading.
Amount of controversy is one thousand dollars or
less.
No formal pleadings, CJ §6-403.
Civil procedure, CivProDist Rules 3-301 to 3-342.
Complied with Maryland district rules, CJ §6-403.
Destruction of pleadings, papers and files, CJ
§1-605.
Electronic filing of pleadings and papers, CJA
Rule 16-506.
Size of claims.
Formality of pleading, CJ §6-403.

Pleas.
Time, Crim Rule 4-242.

Powers.
Vested in, MD Const Art IV §1.

Preliminary hearings in District Court.
Criminal rules, Crim Rule 4-221.

DISTRICT COURT —Cont'd

Pretrial conference.
Civil procedure, CivProDist Rule 3-504.

Probation.
Powers of court as to, CP §§6-222, 6-223.
Violation of conditions.
Sentencing in District Court, CP §6-224.

Process.
Authentication, MD Const Art IV §1.

Public defender.
General provisions, 27A §§1 to 14.
See PUBLIC DEFENDER.

Reassignment in District Court.
Criminal cases, Crim Rule 4-254.

Records.
Destruction of pleadings, papers and files, CJ
§1-605.
Procedures for keeping, CJ §1-605.

Replevin.
Jurisdiction, CJ §4-401.
Jury trial demanded.
Action transmitted to appropriate court after
writ returned, CJ §4-402.

Rules of court.
Applicability.
Size of claim, CJ §6-403.
Chief judge.
Promulgation, CJ §1-605.
Effective date of judicial documents, SG §7-222.

Salaries.
Judges.
General provisions, CJ §§1-701 to 1-708.
See JUDGES.
Officers of courts, MD Const Art IV §41F.

Search warrants.
Authority of judges to issue, CJ §1-609.

Sentence and punishment.
Generally, COR §§9-101 to 9-202.
See SENTENCE AND PUNISHMENT.

Service of process, CivProDist Rules 3-121 to
3-126; CJ §2-605.

Shoplifting.
Civil penalties.
Jurisdiction.
Exclusive original civil jurisdiction, CJ
§3-1308.

Small claim actions, CJ §4-405.
Civil procedure, CivProDist Rule 3-701.
Jurisdictional amount, CJ §4-405.
No formal pleadings, CJ §6-403.

Subpoenas.
Civil procedure, CivProDist Rule 3-510.

Substitution of parties.
Civil procedure, CivProDist Rule 3-241.

Summons and process.
Authentication, MD Const Art IV §1.
Civil procedure.
Content, CivProDist Rule 3-114.
Duration, dormancy and renewal, CivProDist
Rule 3-113.
Issuance, CivProDist Rule 3-112.
Requirements preliminary to summons,
CivProDist Rule 3-111.

Third-party practice.
Civil procedure, CivProDist Rule 3-332.

Torts.
Jurisdiction, CJ §4-401.

Traffic cases.
Adoption of trial procedures by chief judge, TR
§26-304.
Costs, CJ §7-301.

DISTRICT COURT —Cont'd
Traffic cases —Cont'd
Election to stand trial for parking violations, CJ
§7-302.
Failure to comply with citation, TR §26-201.
Jurisdiction.
Violations of vehicle laws, CJ §4-301.
Notice to appear in citation, TR §26-201.
Parking fines, CJ §7-302.
Reimbursement for forfeited bond as collateral,
TR §27-104.
Report of convictions, CJ §1-605.
Traffic control signal monitoring systems.
Citations issued as result of, CJ §7-302.
**Transfers from District Court on demand for
jury trial.**
Circuit courts, CivProCir Rule 2-326.
Action not within exclusive original jurisdiction
of District Court.
Governing procedure, CivProCir Rule 2-326.
Exclusive original jurisdiction of District Court.
Governing procedure, CivProCir Rule 2-326.
Notice, CivProCir Rule 2-326.
Transfers to District Court from circuit court,
CivProCir Rule 2-327.
Trial.
Civil procedure.
Date and time, CivProDist Rule 3-102.
General provisions, CivProDist Rules 3-503 to
3-536.
See TRIAL.
Criminal rules.
Beginning trial in District Court, Crim Rule
4-301.
Date.
Change in District Court, Crim Rule 4-271.
Venue.
Appeals from District Court.
Circuit court of county in which judgment
entered.
Appeal taken to, CJ §12-403.
Transfer of domestic violence actions from District
Court to circuit court, CivProDist Rule 3-326.
Vessels and boats.
Jurisdiction.
Violations of state boat act, CJ §4-301.
Volunteer company assistance fund.
Surcharge for in traffic cases, CJ §7-301.
Warrants.
Authority of judges to issue, CJ §1-609.
Washington county.
Health code violation.
Failure to pay fine or elect trial, 25 §236F.
Witnesses.
Prisoners as witnesses.
Writ of habeas corpus ad testificandum.
Authority of judges to issue, CJ §1-609.

DISTRICT COURT COMMISSIONERS.
Adoption, CJA Rule 16-814.

DISTRICT OF COLUMBIA.
Compacts.
Washington metropolitan area transit authority.
General provisions, TR §10-204.
Washington metropolitan area transit authority
compact.
General provisions, TR §§10-201 to 10-207.
See WASHINGTON METROPOLITAN AREA
TRANSIT AUTHORITY COMPACT.
Constitutional provisions, US Const Art I §8;
Amd 23.

DISTRICT OF COLUMBIA —Cont'd
Elections.
Electors of president and vice-president, US Const
Amd 23.
**Maryland-national capital park and planning
commission.**
See MARYLAND-NATIONAL CAPITAL PARK
AND PLANNING COMMISSION.
Maryland-Washington metropolitan district.
See MARYLAND-WASHINGTON
METROPOLITAN DISTRICT.
Maryland-Washington regional district.
See MARYLAND-WASHINGTON REGIONAL
DISTRICT.
Motor vehicles.
Registration.
Exemption from registration fees, TR §13-903.
State.
Defined, SG §1-101.

DISTRICTS.
Agricultural cooperatives.
Directors.
Election by districts, CA §5-514.
Arts and entertainment districts, 83A §§4-701 to
4-703.
Beach erosion control districts.
General provisions.
See SHORE EROSION CONTROL.
Community action agencies.
Housing and community development, HS §§8-101
to 8-109.
Conflict between general and local laws.
Public local laws shall prevail, 1 §13.
Consumer cooperatives.
Directors.
Election by districts, CA §5-5A-14.
Drainage districts.
General provisions, 25 §§52 to 121H.
See DRAINING LANDS.
Environmental service districts.
General provisions.
See ENVIRONMENTAL SERVICE.
Felonies.
Preliminary hearings, CJ §4-304.
Forest conservancy districts.
General provisions, NR §§5-601 to 5-610.
See FORESTS AND PARKS.
General assembly.
Legislative districting plan of 1992, SG §§2-201 to
2-205.
See GENERAL ASSEMBLY.
Historic area zoning.
General provisions.
See ZONING.
Housing and community development.
Community action agencies, HS §§8-101 to 8-109.
Legislative districting plan of 1992, SG §§2-201
to 2-205.
See GENERAL ASSEMBLY.
Maryland Transit Administration.
General provisions.
See MARYLAND TRANSIT
ADMINISTRATION.
Maryland-Washington metropolitan district.
See MARYLAND-WASHINGTON
METROPOLITAN DISTRICT.
Maryland-Washington regional district.
See MARYLAND-WASHINGTON REGIONAL
DISTRICT.

DISTRICTS —Cont'd
Mental hygiene law.
Division of state into districts, HG §10-204.
Municipal corporations.
Infrastructure improvements.
Financing new infrastructure improvements.
Special taxing districts, 23A §44A.
Northeast Maryland waste disposal authority.
Service districts, NR §3-903.
Sanitary districts.
See SANITARY COMMISSIONS.
Shore erosion control.
Beach erosion control districts.
See SHORE EROSION CONTROL.
Soil conservation districts.
General provisions.
See SOIL CONSERVATION.
Special taxing districts.
See TAXATION.
Tax districts.
See TAXATION.
Washington suburban sanitary district.
See WASHINGTON SUBURBAN SANITARY
DISTRICT.
Waters of the state.
Waterway improvement districts.
See VESSELS AND BOATS.
Waterway improvement districts.
See VESSELS AND BOATS.
Zoning.
Historic area zoning.
Power to establish, etc., 66B §8.02.

DISTURBANCE OF THE PEACE.
Citation.
Police officer authorized to charge by, CP §4-101.
Conduct constituting, CR §10-201.
Schools.
Prohibited, ED §26-101.
Secured transactions.
Default.
Agreements as to rights and duties inapplicable
to breach of the peace, CL §9-603.
Repossession.
No sanctioning of breach of the peace, CL
§9-609.
Universities and colleges.
Prohibited, ED §26-101.

DIVIDENDS.
Banks and trust companies.
See BANKS AND TRUST COMPANIES.
Corporations.
See CORPORATIONS.
Credit unions.
Directors, FI §§6-306, 6-328.
General provisions, FI §6-502.
Horse racing.
Fair Hill.
Salary or dividends for officers prohibited, BR
§11-702.
Thoroughbred racing.
Park and planning commission, BR §11-526.
Income tax.
Corporations.
Maryland modified income.
Subtractions from federal taxable income, TG
§10-307.
Insurance companies.
Mutual insurers, IN §3-115.
Life insurance and annuities, IN §16-206.
Adjustable policy loan interest rates, IN §16-208.

DIVIDENDS —Cont'd
Life insurance and annuities —Cont'd
Annuity and pure endowment contracts, IN
§16-406.
**Receivers and assignees or trustees for
creditors.**
Partial distribution, Receivers Rule 13-502.
Unclaimed money or dividends.
Payment into court, Receivers Rule 13-503.
Savings and loan associations.
See SAVINGS AND LOAN ASSOCIATIONS.

DIVISION OF CORRECTION.
Case records, COR §§3-601 to 3-609.
See CORRECTION, DIVISION OF.
Community adult rehabilitation centers, COR
§§11-301 to 11-320.
See COMMUNITY ADULT REHABILITATION
CENTERS.
Death penalty.
Procedures for carrying out death penalty
generally, COR §§3-901 to 3-909.
See DEATH PENALTY.
Diminution credits.
Inmates committed to custody of commissioner of
correction, COR §§3-701 to 3-711.
See DIMINUTION OF INMATE'S TERM OF
CONFINEMENT.
Generally, COR §§3-101 to 3-222.
See CORRECTION, DIVISION OF.
Home detention program.
Inmates in custody of commissioner of correction,
COR §§3-401 to 3-415.
See HOME DETENTION PROGRAM.
Inmates sentenced to jurisdiction of division.
Generally.
See PRISONS AND PRISONERS.
Leave of inmate from confinement.
Work release program.
Inmate sentenced to jurisdiction of division of
correction, COR §§3-801 to 3-807.
See WORK RELEASE PROGRAMS.
Maryland correctional enterprises, COR §§3-501
to 3-528.
See MARYLAND CORRECTIONAL
ENTERPRISES.
Patuxent institution, COR §§4-101 to 4-401.
See PATUXENT INSTITUTION.
Prerelease unit for women, COR §§3-301 to
3-305.
Sentencing to correctional facility, COR §§9-101
to 9-202.
See SENTENCE AND PUNISHMENT.
**State reimbursement of local correctional
facilities,** COR §§9-401 to 9-405.
Transfer of inmates.
Generally, COR §§9-301 to 9-308.
See PRISONS AND PRISONERS.
Work release program.
Inmate sentenced to the jurisdiction of division of
correction, COR §§3-801 to 3-807.
See WORK RELEASE PROGRAMS.

DIVISION OF PAROLE AND PROBATION, COR
§§6-101 to 6-116.
See PAROLE AND PROBATION.

**DIVISION OF PRETRIAL DETENTION AND
SERVICES,** COR §§5-101 to 5-203.
Pretrial release services program, COR §§5-301,
5-302.

DIVISION OF STATE DOCUMENTS.
General provisions, SG §§7-201 to 7-222.
  See DOCUMENTS.

DIVORCE.
Absolute divorce, FL §7-103.
  Condonation.
    Not absolute bar, FL §7-103.
  Decrees, FL §7-103.
  Grounds, FL §7-103.
  Limited divorce.
    Application for absolute divorce.
      Effect of limited divorce, FL §7-103.
    Decree of limited divorce on prayer for absolute
      divorce, FL §7-102.
  Name.
    Restoration of former name, FL §7-105.
  Recrimination.
    Not bar, FL §7-103.
Adultery.
  Grounds for absolute divorce, FL §7-103.
Agreement in settlement.
  Property.
    Exemptions from county transfer tax, TP
      §13-403.
Alimony.
  Appeals.
    Contempt of court, CJ §12-304.
  General provisions, FL §§11-101 to 11-112.
  See ALIMONY.
  Imprisonment for delinquent payment.
    Not imprisonment for debt, MD Const Art III
      §38.
  Jurisdiction.
    Nonresident defendant in civil action involving
      child support or alimony, CJ §6-103.1.
A mensa.
  Supplemental bill.
    Bill for divorce a vinculo following a mensa,
      FamLaw Rule 9-202.
Annulment of marriage.
  General provisions.
    See ANNULMENT OF MARRIAGE.
Appeals.
  Alimony.
    Contempt of court, CJ §12-304.
  Property disposition, FL §8-213.
Attorneys' fees.
  Award of reasonable and necessary expenses, FL
    §§7-107, 8-214.
A vinculo.
  Supplemental bills.
    Bill for divorce a vinculo following a mensa,
      FamLaw Rule 9-202.
Child custody.
  General provisions, FL §§9-101 to 9-307.
    See CHILD CUSTODY.
  Uniform child custody jurisdiction and
    enforcement act, FL §§9.5-101 to 9.5-318.
    See CHILD CUSTODY.
Circuit courts.
  Family law actions, FamLaw Rules 9-201 to
    9-210.
Clerks of court.
  Record of divorce decrees, FL §7-106.
  Reports, FL §2-503.
Complaints.
  Pleadings, FamLaw Rule 9-202.
Condonation.
  Absolute divorce.
    Not absolute bar, FL §7-103.

DIVORCE —Cont'd
Contempt.
  Deeds, agreements and settlements between
    spouses.
    Powers of courts to enforce provisions by, FL
      §8-105.
Corroboration of testimony.
  Deeds, agreements and settlements between
    spouses.
    Voluntary separation agreement as, FL §8-104.
  Required, FL §7-101.
Cruelty.
  Grounds for limited divorce, FL §7-102.
Custody of children.
  General provisions.
    See CHILD CUSTODY.
Decedents' estates.
  Waiver of rights in decedent's estate, ET §3-205.
Declaratory judgments.
  Excluded from subtitle, CJ §3-409.
Decrees.
  Absolute divorce, FL §7-103.
  Limited divorce, FL §7-102.
    Revocation of decree, FL §7-102.
  Property disposition. See within this heading,
    "Property disposition."
  Record of divorce decrees, FL §7-106.
Deeds, agreements and settlements between
  spouses.
  Contempt.
    Powers of courts to enforce provisions by, FL
      §8-105.
  Corroboration of testimony.
    Voluntary separation agreement as, FL §8-104.
  Modification, FL §8-103.
    Authority of court, FL §8-105.
  Not bar to divorce, FL §8-102.
  Property.
    Exemption from county transfer tax, TP
      §13-403.
  Provisions merged in divorce decree.
    Contempt.
      Powers of courts to enforce provisions by, FL
        §8-105.
  Provisions not merged in decree.
    Contempt.
      Powers of courts to enforce provisions by, FL
        §8-105.
  Validity, FL §8-101.
Default of defendant.
  Order of default, FamLaw Rule 9-204.
  Testimony.
    Over thirty days old, FamLaw Rule 9-209.
Definitions.
  Property disposition, FL §8-201.
Desertion and nonsupport.
  Grounds for divorce.
    Absolute divorce, FL §7-103.
    Limited divorce, FL §7-102.
Displaced homemakers, FL §§4-601 to 4-613.
  See DISPLACED HOMEMAKERS.
Domestic violence.
  Orders of court.
    Protection from abuse.
      Inadmissible evidence in divorce proceedings,
        FL §7-103.1.
Educational seminars, FamLaw Rule 9-204.
  Child support, custody or visitation, FL §7-103.2.
Evidence.
  Domestic violence.
    Orders of court.
      Protective orders inadmissible, FL §7-103.1.

DIVORCE —Cont'd
Evidence —Cont'd
Testimony.
Generally, FamLaw Rule 9-209.
Expenses.
Award of reasonable and necessary expenses, FL
§§7-107, 8-214.
Family home.
Property disposition. See within this heading,
"Property disposition."
Family use personal property.
Property disposition. See within this heading,
"Property disposition."
Fees.
Record of divorce decrees.
Clerk of circuit court, FL §7-106.
Filing pleadings.
Financial statements to be filed, FamLaw Rule
9-202.
Form of financial statements, FamLaw Rule
9-203.
Financial statements.
Form, FamLaw Rule 9-203.
Required, FamLaw Rule 9-202.
Forms.
Financial statements, FamLaw Rule 9-203.
Property.
Joint statements of marital and non-marital
property, FamLaw Rule 9-207.
General assembly.
Not to be granted by legislature, MD Const Art III
§33.
Grounds.
Absolute divorce, FL §7-103.
Limited divorce, FL §7-102.
Health insurance.
Conversion rights of ex-spouse, IN §15-414.
Injunctions.
Issuance in action for divorce, FL §1-203.
Insanity.
Grounds for absolute divorce, FL §7-103.
Insurance.
Health insurance.
Continuation of coverage, IN §15-408.
Enrollment of child under coverage of insuring
parent, IN §15-405.
**Joint statement of marital and nonmarital
property,** FamLaw Rule 9-207.
Jurisdiction.
Equity courts, FL §1-201.
Limited divorce, FL §7-102.
Absolute divorce.
Application for absolute divorce.
Effect of limited divorce, FL §7-103.
Decree of limited divorce on prayer for absolute
divorce, FL §7-102.
Decrees, FL §7-102.
Revocation of decree, FL §7-102.
Grounds, FL §7-102.
Reconciliation.
Attempts at reconciliation, FL §7-102.
Lis pendens.
Divorce not to constitute lis pendens with respect
to property of party, FL §1-203.
Marital property.
Property disposition. See within this heading,
"Property disposition."
Masters.
Referral of matters to masters, FamLaw Rule
9-208.

DIVORCE —Cont'd
Mediation.
Property disposition, ADR Rule 17-104.
Military pension.
Consideration in determination of marital
property, FL §8-203.
Minors.
Custody.
Pleadings, FamLaw Rule 9-202.
Misdemeanors.
Record of divorce decrees.
Failure or refusal by clerk to make record, FL
§7-106.
Monetary award.
Marital property, FL §8-205.
Pensions, retirement, profit sharing or deferred
compensation plans.
Transfer of rights and interests, FL §8-205.
Names.
Absolute divorce.
Restoration of former name, FL §7-105.
Orders of court.
Default of defendant, FamLaw Rule 9-204.
Medical support orders, IN §15-405.
Property.
Joint statements of marital and non-marital
property.
Failure to comply with requirement.
Sanctions, orders court may enter, FamLaw
Rule 9-207.
Ownership of personal and real property.
Decree and order, FL §8-202.
Determination, FL §8-202.
Penalties.
Record of divorce decrees.
Failure or refusal of clerk to make record, FL
§7-106.
Pleadings.
Child custody, FamLaw Rule 9-202.
Filing of financial statements, FamLaw Rule
9-202.
Form, FamLaw Rule 9-203.
Signing, FamLaw Rule 9-202.
Supplemental bill, FamLaw Rule 9-202.
Procedure, FamLaw Rules 9-201 to 9-210.
Property.
Joint statements of marital and non-marital
property, FamLaw Rule 9-207.
Settlement.
Exemption from county transfer tax, TP
§13-403.
Mediation, ADR Rule 17-104.
Property disposition.
Appeals, FL §8-213.
Decree or order.
Enforcement, FL §8-213.
Family home and family use personal property.
Award of possession and use, FL §8-208.
Constructive desertion.
Order or decree not evidence of constructive
desertion, FL §8-211.
Determination, FL §8-207.
Power of court over order or decree, FL
§8-209.
Termination, FL §8-210.
Ownership of personal and real property, FL
§8-202.
Definitions, FL §8-201.
Expenses.
Award of reasonable and necessary expenses,
FL §8-214.

DIVORCE —Cont'd
Property disposition —Cont'd
 Family home.
  Award of possession and use, FL §8-208.
  Constructive desertion.
   Not evidence of, FL §8-211.
  Decree or order, FL §8-207.
   Award of possession and use, FL §8-208.
   Constructive desertion.
    Decree or order not evidence of, FL §8-211.
   Determination, FL §8-207.
   Power of court over, FL §8-209.
   Termination, FL §8-210.
  Defined, FL §8-201.
  Determination, FL §8-207.
  Financial responsibility.
   Allocation, FL §8-208.
  Legislative policy, FL §8-206.
  Remarriage of party with possession or use of
    property, FL §8-210.
 Family use personal property.
  Award of possession and use, FL §8-208.
  Constructive desertion.
   Not evidence of constructive desertion, FL
     §8-211.
  Decree or order, FL §8-207.
   Award of possession and use, FL §8-208.
   Constructive desertion.
    Decree or order not evidence of constructive
      desertion, FL §8-211.
   Determination, FL §8-207.
   Power of court over, FL §8-209.
   Termination, FL §8-210.
  Defined, FL §8-201.
  Determination, FL §8-207.
  Legislative policy, FL §8-206.
  Remarriage of party with possession or use of
    property, FL §8-210.
 Foreign divorce or annulment.
  Exercise of powers by court after, FL §8-212.
 Marital property.
  Defined, FL §8-201.
  Determination, FL §8-203.
  Monetary award, FL §8-205.
  Pension, retirement, profit sharing or deferred
    compensation plans.
   Transfer of rights and interests, FL §8-205.
  Valuation, FL §8-204.
 Mediation, ADR Rule 17-104.
Rape or sexual offense.
 Separation or limited divorce.
  Prosecution for crime against spouse, CR
    §3-318.
Reconciliation.
 Limited divorce.
  Attempts at reconciliation, FL §7-102.
 Offer or attempt, FL §7-104.
 Refusal or rejection, FL §7-104.
Records.
 Decrees, FL §7-106.
 Vital records.
  See VITAL RECORDS.
Recrimination.
 Absolute divorce.
  Not bar, FL §7-103.
Reports.
 Clerks of court, FL §2-503.
Residence.
 Requirement, FL §7-101.
Settlement.
 Property.
  Exemption from county transfer tax, TP
    §13-403.

DIVORCE —Cont'd
Signatures.
 Pleadings, FamLaw Rule 9-202.
Stale testimony, FamLaw Rule 9-209.
Supplemental bill.
 A mensa.
  Bill for divorce a vinculo following a mensa,
    FamLaw Rule 9-202.
 A vinculo.
  Bill for divorce a vinculo following a mensa,
    FamLaw Rule 9-202.
 Generally, FamLaw Rule 9-202.
Surviving spouse.
 Divorce in another state, ET §1-202.
 Marriage to third party, ET §1-202.
 Valid divorce, ET §1-202.
Testimony.
 Generally, FamLaw Rule 9-209.
 Stale testimony, FamLaw Rule 9-209.
Venue.
 Additional venue permitted, CJ §6-202.
Voluntary separation.
 Grounds for divorce.
  Absolute divorce, FL §7-103.
  Limited divorce, FL §7-102.
Wills.
 Effect, ET §4-105.

DNA.
Blood tests generally.
 See BLOOD TESTS.
DNA technology fund, 41 §4-301.
Missing persons.
 Unidentified human remains.
  Office of chief medical examiners to maintain
    files of samples, PS §3-603.
New trial, Crim Rule 4-331.
Paternity proceedings.
 Genetic tests, FL §5-1029.
Post conviction procedure.
 DNA testing, Crim Rule 4-401.
Profiles.
 Criminal procedure.
  Admissibility of evidence, CJ §10-915.
  Postconviction review, CP §8-201.
  Preservation of scientific identification evidence,
    time period, CP §8-201.
 Definitions, CJ §10-915.
 Evidence.
  Admissibility, CJ §10-915.
  Postconviction review, CP §8-201.
Sex offender registration.
 Provision of DNA sample, CP §11-708.
Statewide DNA database system, PS §§2-501 to
 2-512.
 See DNA DATABASE SYSTEM.

DNA DATABASE SYSTEM, PS §§2-501 to 2-512.
Collection.
 Authorized collectors, PS §2-504.
Crime laboratories.
 Contracts with, PS §2-502.
 Defined, PS §2-501.
 Duties, PS §2-502.
 Proficiency testing, PS §2-507.
 Record retention, PS §2-502.
Criminal law and procedure.
 Prohibited acts, PS §2-512.
Defined terms, PS §2-501.
Director.
 Defined, PS §2-501.
 Duties, PS §2-502.

DNA DATABASE SYSTEM —Cont'd
Director —Cont'd
Rules and regulations.
Required regulations, PS §2-503.
DNA profile.
Availability, PS §2-508.
DNA samples.
Collection, PS §2-504.
Defined, PS §2-501.
Population database, PS §2-509.
Storage, PS §2-506.
Testing, PS §2-505.
Established, PS §2-502.
Evidence.
Use of match as evidence, PS §2-510.
Expungement of DNA information, PS §2-511.
Failure to provide DNA sample, PS §2-504.
Fines.
Prohibited acts, PS §2-512.
Misdemeanors.
Prohibited acts, PS §2-512.
Population database.
DNA samples, PS §2-509.
Probable cause.
Use of match as evidence, PS §2-510.
Proficiency testing.
Crime laboratories, PS §2-507.
Prohibited acts, PS §2-512.
Purpose of chapter, PS §2-502.
Purpose of testing DNA samples, PS §2-505.
Quality assurance guidelines.
Required regulations, PS §2-503.
Records.
DNA profile.
Availability, PS §2-508.
Expungement of records, PS §2-511.
Limitations, PS §2-505.
Population database, PS §2-509.
Storage, PS §2-506.
Rules and regulations.
Required regulations, PS §2-503.
Second DNA sample, PS §2-504.
Sex offender registration.
Provision of DNA sample, CP §11-708.
Testing of DNA samples, PS §2-505.
Typing results.
DNA profile.
Availability, PS §2-508.
Storage, PS §2-506.

DNA TECHNOLOGY FUND, 41 §4-301.

DOCKETS.
Administration of courts, CJA Rule 16-305.
Asbestos cases, CJA Rule 16-203.
Filing and removal of papers, CJA Rule 16-306.
Information system.
Report of docketing and disposition of cases,
CJA Rule 16-308.
Adoption.
Clerk to keep, FamLaw Rule 9-112.
Appeals.
Appeals from District Court.
Maintaining, AppRevCir Rule 7-110.
Record on appeal.
Contents of record, AppRevCir Rule 7-109.
Separate appeals on same record, AppRevCir
Rule 7-110.
Dismissal of appeals.
Reconsideration of dismissal.
Reinstatement on docket, AppRev Rule 8-602.
Docketing of appeals, AppRev Rule 8-421.

DOCKETS —Cont'd
Charging documents.
Citations.
Docket in place of citation, Crim Rule 4-201.
Estate docket.
Registers of wills.
Fee, ET §2-206.
Expungement of records.
Bound volume.
Procedures for expungement, Crim Rule 4-511.
Case file jacket.
Procedures for expungement, Crim Rule 4-511.
Microfilmed dockets, indices and case files.
Procedures for expungement, Crim Rule 4-511.
Juvenile causes.
Separate docket.
Duties of clerk, Juv Rule 11-104.
Land patents.
Application for patent.
Entry on docket, RP §13-305.
Maintaining, RP §13-204.
Mechanics' liens.
Claims, RP §9-105.
Paternity docket, FL §5-1047.
Registers of wills.
See REGISTERS OF WILLS.

DOCKING FEES, 24 §9-605.
Licensed docking masters' fees, PUC §4-303.1.

DOCTORS.
Physicians generally.
See PHYSICIANS.

DOCUMENTARY DRAFTS.
Bank deposits and collections.
Dishonor.
Duty to notify customer, CL §4-501.
Privilege of presenting bank to deal with goods,
CL §4-504.
Reporting reasons for dishonor, CL §4-503.
Presentment.
Duty to send for presentment, CL §4-501.
On arrival drafts, CL §4-502.

DOCUMENTS.
**Admission of facts and genuineness of
documents.**
Request for admission.
Effect of admission.
Circuit courts, CivProCir Rule 2-424.
Expenses of failure to admit.
Circuit courts, CivProCir Rule 2-424.
Generally.
Circuit courts, CivProCir Rule 2-424.
Response.
Circuit courts, CivProCir Rule 2-424.
Determination of sufficiency of response.
Circuit courts, CivProCir Rule 2-424.
Anatomical gift act.
General provisions.
See ANATOMICAL GIFT ACT.
Ancient documents.
Requirements of identification or authentication,
Evid Rule 5-901.
Authentication.
Requirement of authentication, Evid Rule 5-901.
Self authentication, Evid Rule 5-902.
Charging documents.
See CHARGING DOCUMENTS.
Code of Maryland regulations. See within this
heading, "State documents."

DOCUMENTS —Cont'd
Commercial code.
Prima facie evidence by third-party documents, CL §1-202.
Condominiums.
Delivery to council of unit owners by developer, RP §11-132.
Contents.
Admissibility of other evidence and contents, Evid Rule 5-1004.
Contracts.
State documents.
Printing contracts, SG §7-211.
Court of appeals.
Submission of copies by clerk, SG §7-213.
Court papers.
Form of court papers, Rule 1-301.
Discovery.
Admission of facts and genuineness of documents.
Circuit courts, CivProCir Rule 2-424.
Circuit courts, CivProCir Rule 2-422.
Production of documents and tangible things.
Circuit courts, CivProCir Rule 2-415.
Generally.
Circuit courts, CivProCir Rule 2-422.
Notice, CivProCir Rule 2-412.
Division of state documents. See within this heading, "State documents."
Duplicates.
Admissibility, Evid Rule 5-1003.
Forms.
Court papers, Rule 1-301.
Interrogatories.
Parties.
Scope of discovery.
District Court, CivProDist Rule 3-421.
Judicial documents.
Submission by clerk of court of appeals, SG §7-213.
Notice.
State documents, SG §7-214.
Constructive notice, SG §7-219.
Original.
Requirement of original, Evid Rule 5-1002.
Presumptions.
State documents, SG §7-220.
Publications.
State documents. See within this heading, "State documents."
Public information.
General provisions.
See PUBLIC INFORMATION.
Records.
General provisions.
See RECORDS.
Public information.
General provisions.
See PUBLIC INFORMATION.
Release of public records.
Legislative services department, SG §2-1249.
Self authentication, Evid Rule 5-902.
State documents.
Administrator. See within this subheading, "Division."
Annotations.
Authorized, SG §7-208.
Preparation, SG §7-208.
Changes in documents.
Units required to reimburse division, SG §7-215.

DOCUMENTS —Cont'd
State documents —Cont'd
Code of Maryland regulations.
Certification, SG §7-205.
Compilation, SG §7-204.
Date of issuance, SG §7-205.
Defined, SG §7-201.
Distribution, SG §7-216.
Editing, SG §7-204.
Editorial standards, SG §7-212.
Effective date of judicial documents, SG §7-222.
Generally, SG §7-205.
Permanent supplements, SG §7-205.
Publication.
Duty of division and administrator, SG §7-204.
Reimbursement of unit, SG §7-205.
Reprinting text from other specified publications.
Restrictions, SG §7-207.
Severability, SG §7-221.
Supplements.
Permanent supplements, SG §7-205.
Committee.
Defined, SG §7-201.
Computer data bases.
Availability to public, SG §7-206.2.
Copies.
Submission of copies to administrator, SG §7-213.
Corrections of publication errors, SG §7-218.
Definitions, SG §7-201.
Discrepancies between official text and other text.
Official text only valid and enforceable text, SG §7-217.
Distribution.
Free distribution, SG §7-216.
Guidelines for price, SG §7-216.
Division.
Administrator.
Appointment, SG §7-203.
Authority to include annotations in register, SG §7-208.
Compilation and editing of Maryland regulations, SG §7-204.
Defined, SG §7-201.
General responsibilities, SG §7-204.
Position, SG §7-203.
Preparation of annotations, SG §7-208.
Publication.
Duty to publish code of Maryland regulations, SG §7-204.
Secretary of state.
Authority, SG §7-203.
Tenure, SG §7-203.
Defined, SG §7-201.
Established, SG §7-202.
In office of secretary of state, SG §7-202.
Special fund in division of state documents.
Established, purposes, nature, composition, investment, expenditures, SG §7-216.1.
Electronic filing, SG §7-213.
Errors in publication.
General corrections, SG §7-218.
Legal effect of errors, SG §7-218.
Executive orders.
Defined, SG §7-201.
Judicial documents.
Effective date, SG §7-222.
Submission of judicial documents to administrator, SG §7-213.

DOCUMENTS —Cont'd
State documents —Cont'd
Notice.
Constructive notice, SG §7-219.
Effect on other requirements, SG §7-214.
Requirements for full compliance, SG §7-214.
Time for submission, SG §7-214.
Obsolete regulations.
Deletion, SG §7-209.
Official text, SG §7-217.
Presumptions.
Publication of document creates certain
presumptions, SG §7-220.
Printing.
Contracts, SG §7-211.
Prohibited commercial purposes, SG §7-206.2.
Prohibited documents, SG §7-207.
Prohibited texts, SG §7-207.
Publication.
Changes in documents.
Reimbursement for costs, SG §7-215.
Errors, SG §7-218.
Frequency of publication, SG §7-210.
Index to register, SG §7-210.
Notice.
Constructive notice, SG §7-219.
Presumptions, SG §7-220.
Prohibited texts, SG §7-207.
Restrictions on publication, SG §7-207.
Register.
Certification, SG §7-206.
Contents, SG §7-206.
Defined, SG §7-201.
Editorial standards, SG §7-212.
Effective date of judicial documents, SG §7-222.
Frequency of publication, SG §7-210.
Generally, SG §7-206.
Index.
Frequency of publication, SG §7-210.
Reimbursement, SG §7-206.
Regulations.
Defined, SG §7-201.
Deletion of obsolete regulations, SG §7-209.
Reprints.
Printing contracts, SG §7-211.
Severability of provisions, SG §7-221.
Special fund in division of state documents.
Established, purposes, nature, composition,
investment, expenditures, SG §7-216.1.
Units.
Defined, SG §7-201.
Subscribing witness' testimony unnecessary,
Evid Rule 5-903.

DOCUMENTS OF TITLE, CL §§7-101 to 7-603.
Agriculture.
Warehouse receipts.
Storage of commodities under government bond,
CL §7-201.
Alcoholic beverages.
Warehouse receipts.
Storage under government bond, CL §7-201.
Alteration.
Bills of lading, CL §7-306.
Warehouse receipts, CL §7-208.
Attachment of goods.
Goods covered by negotiable document, CL §7-602.
Bailments.
Law not modified or repealed, CL §7-103.
Bills of lading.
Altered bills, CL §7-306.

DOCUMENTS OF TITLE —Cont'd
Bills of lading —Cont'd
Care owing from carrier, CL §7-309.
Consignments.
Reconsignment, CL §7-303.
Contractual limitation of carrier's liability, CL
§7-309.
Delivery of goods, CL §7-303.
Description of goods.
"Said to contain," CL §7-301.
"Shipper's weight, load and count," CL §7-301.
Destination bills, CL §7-305.
Diversion of goods, CL §7-303.
Generally, CL §§7-301 to 7-309.
Handling of goods.
Improper handling, CL §7-301.
Instructions.
Change, CL §7-303.
Liability.
Contractual limitation of carrier's liability, CL
§7-309.
Nonreceipt or misdescription of goods, CL
§7-301.
Lien of carrier, CL §7-307.
Enforcement, CL §7-308.
Naming person to be notified of arrival of goods.
Negotiability not limited, CL §7-501.
Negotiability, CL §7-104.
Receipt of goods.
Liability for nonreceipt, CL §7-301.
Sale of goods.
Enforcement of carrier's lien, CL §7-308.
Set of parts.
Tangible bill issued in, CL §7-304.
Third-party documents.
Prima facie evidence, CL §1-202.
Through bills and similar documents, CL §7-302.
Citation of article.
Short title, CL §7-101.
Claims.
Conflicting claims.
Interpleader, CL §7-603.
Commercial code's general provisions, CL
§§1-101 to 1-208.
See COMMERCIAL CODE.
Consignor and consignee.
Bills of lading.
Reconsignment, CL §7-303.
Construction and interpretation.
Relationship of article to treaty, statute, tariff,
classification or regulation, CL §7-103.
Contracts.
Bills of lading.
Limitation of carrier's liability, CL §7-309.
Sale, lease or conditions of letter of credit.
Document adequate to fulfill obligations, CL
§7-509.
Warehouse receipts.
Limitation of liability, CL §7-204.
Crops.
Warehouse receipts.
Storage under government bond, CL §7-201.
Definitions, CL §7-102.
General commercial code definitions, CL §1-201.
Course of dealing, CL §1-205.
Reasonable time and seasonably, CL §1-204.
Usage of trade, CL §1-205.
Index of definitions, CL §7-102.
Delivery of goods.
Bills of lading, CL §7-303.
Excuses, CL §7-403.

DOCUMENTS OF TITLE —Cont'd
Warehouse receipts —Cont'd
Government bond.
Storage under, CL §7-201.
Household goods.
Warehouse's lien, CL §7-209.
Liability.
Contractual limitation of liability, CL §7-204.
Lien of warehouse, CL §7-209.
Enforcement, CL §7-210.
Removal of goods from warehouse.
Warehouse requiring, CL §7-206.
Sale of goods by warehouse, CL §7-206.
Enforcement of warehouse lien, CL §7-210.
Security interest.
Warehouse reserving against bailor, CL §7-209.
Separation of goods, CL §7-207.
Termination of storage by warehouse, CL §7-206.
Terms, CL §7-202.
Title defeated in certain cases, CL §7-205.
Who may issue, CL §7-201.
Warranties.
Negotiation and transfer, CL §7-507.
Collecting bank's warranties as to documents, CL §7-508.

DOGFIGHTS.
Arranging, conducting or using dog in, CR §10-607.
Attending, CR §10-605.

DOGS.
Abandoning domestic animal, CR §10-612.
Birds and game.
General provisions.
See BIRDS AND GAME.
Blind persons.
Guide dogs.
Blind pedestrians, TR §21-511.
Damages.
Liability of blind or visually handicapped person for damages done to premises or facilities by dog, 30 §33.
Right of blind person to be accompanied by guide dog, 30 §33.
Rights of blind or visually handicapped person not using guide dog, 30 §33.
Trainers' rights, 30 §33.
Dangerous dogs, CR §10-619.
Deaf or mute persons.
Guide dogs.
Damages.
Liability of blind or visually handicapped persons for damages done to premises or facilities by dog, 30 §33.
Right of deaf or mute person to be accompanied by guide dog, 30 §33.
Rights of deaf or mute persons not using guide dog, 30 §33.
Trainers' rights, 30 §33.
Dogfights.
Arranging, conducting or using dog in, CR §10-607.
Attending, CR §10-605.
Fees.
Licenses.
"Dog guide" exempt from fees, 24 §11-502.
Females in heat.
Running at large.
Prohibited in certain counties, 24 §11-512-11-514.

DOGS —Cont'd
Field trials.
General provisions, NR §§10-701 to 10-703.
See BIRDS AND GAME.
Handicapped persons.
Dog guides for mobility impaired.
Use, 30 §33.
Kennel inspections, CR §10-616.
Killing.
Destroying game birds and animals.
Natural resources police officer, NR §10-413.
Prohibited means, CR §10-611.
Licenses, 24 §§11-501, 11-503.
"Dog guides" exempt from fees, 24 §11-502.
Police dogs.
State police department, PS §2-313.
Misdemeanors.
Misdemeanor for violations, 24 §11-509.
Motor vehicles.
Blind pedestrians, TR §21-511.
Standing or parked vehicle.
Dogs left in, TR §21-1004.1.
Personal property.
Unlicensed dogs.
Deemed personalty when ownership can be proved, 24 §11-506.
Poisoning, CR §10-618.
Police dogs.
Licenses.
State police department, PS §2-313.
Puppies.
Selling less than eight week old puppy, CR §10-613.
Rabies.
General provisions, HG §§18-312 to 18-320.
See RABIES.
Rules and regulations, 24 §11-511.
Running at large, NR §10-413.
Calvert county, 24 §11-510.
Females in heat.
Prohibited in certain counties, 24 §§11-512 to 11-514.
Special dog training areas.
General provisions, NR §§10-701 to 10-703.
See BIRDS AND GAME.
State dog.
Chesapeake Bay retriever designated as state dog, SG §13-303.
Strays.
When animal deemed, CR §10-615.
Tags, 24 §§11-501, 11-503.
Dog guides exempt from fees, 24 §11-502.
Special provisions as to Anne Arundel and Calvert counties, 24 §11-503.
Training dogs, NR §10-413.
Special dog training areas.
General provisions, NR §§10-701 to 10-703.
See BIRDS AND GAME.
Vaccinations.
Proof of vaccination, HG §18-318.
Records.
Use of records, HG §18-319.
Required vaccination, HG §18-318.
Responsibilities of veterinarian, HG §18-319.
Vicious dogs.
Attacking livestock, etc., 24 §11-505.
Compensation payable, 24 §11-508.
Killing of dog, 24 §11-508.
Payment of damages for claims, 24 §11-507.
Payment of damages for claims, 24 §11-507.
Regulation, 24 §11-504.

DOMESTIC RELATIONS.
Adoption.
General provisions, FL §§5-301 to 5-415.
See ADOPTION.
Mutual consent voluntary adoption registry, FL
§§5-4C-01 to 5-4C-07.
Adult protective services generally.
See ADULT PROTECTIVE SERVICES.
Alienation of affections, FL §§3-101 to 3-104.
Alimony, FL §§11-101 to 11-112.
See ALIMONY.
Annulment of marriage.
See ANNULMENT OF MARRIAGE.
Attorneys at law.
Appointment of counsel for minor, FL §1-202.
Breach of promise to marry, FL §§3-101 to 3-104.
Child abuse and neglect.
General provisions, FL §§5-701 to 5-714.
See CHILD ABUSE AND NEGLECT.
Child custody, FL §§9-101 to 9-307.
See CHILD CUSTODY.
Child placement.
Interstate compact on the placement of children,
FL §§5-601 to 5-611.
See CHILD PLACEMENT.
Child support.
General provisions, FL §§12-101 to 12-105.
See SUPPORT AND MAINTENANCE.
Child visitation.
See CHILD VISITATION.
Displaced homemakers, FL §§4-601 to 4-613.
See DISPLACED HOMEMAKERS.
Divorce.
Alimony, FL §§11-101 to 11-112.
See ALIMONY.
Child custody, FL §§9-101 to 9-307.
See CHILD CUSTODY.
Deeds, agreements and settlements between
spouses, FL §§8-101 to 8-105.
See DIVORCE.
General provisions, FL §§7-101 to 7-107.
See DIVORCE.
Property disposition, FL §§8-201 to 8-214.
See DIVORCE.
Domestic violence.
Generally, FL §§4-501 to 4-516.
See DOMESTIC VIOLENCE.
Local domestic violence fatality review teams, FL
§§4-701 to 4-707.
See DOMESTIC VIOLENCE.
Foster care, FL §§5-525 to 5-547.
See FOSTER CARE.
Guidelines, FL §§12-201 to 12-204.
See SUPPORT AND MAINTENANCE.
Husband and wife.
See HUSBAND AND WIFE.
Interrogatories.
Administration of courts, Interrogatories Forms 4,
5.
Jurisdiction.
Equity courts, FL §1-201.
Marriage.
Annulment of marriage.
See ANNULMENT OF MARRIAGE.
Divorce, FL §§7-101 to 7-107.
See DIVORCE.
General provisions, FL §§2-101 to 2-503.
See MARRIAGE.
Neglected children, FL §§5-701 to 5-714.
See CHILD ABUSE AND NEGLECT.

DOMESTIC RELATIONS —Cont'd
Paternity proceedings, FL §§5-1001 to 5-1048.
See PATERNITY PROCEEDINGS.
Relatives.
See RELATIVES.
Services to families with children, FL §§4-401 to
4-403.
See SERVICES TO FAMILIES WITH
CHILDREN.
Single parents, FL §§6-101 to 6-103.
Support and maintenance.
Alimony, FL §§11-101 to 11-112.
See ALIMONY.
Child support.
General provisions, FL §§12-101 to 12-105.
See SUPPORT AND MAINTENANCE.
Guidelines, FL §§12-201 to 12-204.
See SUPPORT AND MAINTENANCE.
Parents and adult children, FL §§13-101 to
13-109.
See SUPPORT AND MAINTENANCE.
Unattended children.
Confinement in dwelling, building or enclosure,
FL §5-801.
**Uniform child custody jurisdiction and
enforcement act,** FL §§9.5-101 to 9.5-318.
See CHILD CUSTODY.
Victims of domestic violence, FL §§4-513 to
4-516.
See DOMESTIC VIOLENCE.

DOMESTIC VIOLENCE, FL §§4-501 to 4-516.
Abuse.
Petition for relief from abuse, FL §4-504.
Address confidentiality program, FL §§4-519 to
4-530.
Actual address of program participant.
Confidentiality of record of, FL §4-528.
Election-related purposes, use for, FL §4-527.
Obtaining prohibited, FL §4-529.
Applications to participate, FL §4-522.
False attestation or information, FL §4-523.
Cancellation of participation, FL §4-525.
Change of name, address or telephone number.
Notification by program participant, FL §4-524.
Failure to notify as grounds for cancellation of
participation, FL §4-525.
Definitions, FL §4-519.
Elections.
Use of actual address for election-related
purposes, FL §4-527.
Establishment of program, FL §4-521.
Legislative declaration.
Purpose of program, FL §4-520.
Obtaining actual address or telephone number
prohibited, FL §4-529.
Public records.
Actual address of program participant not
public record, FL §4-528.
Purpose of program, FL §4-520.
Regulations, FL §4-530.
Secretary of state.
Establishment of program, FL §4-521.
Regulations, FL §4-530.
Substitute address.
Request for state or local agency to use, FL
§4-526.
Who may apply to participate, FL §4-522.
Appeals.
Orders of court.
Protection from abuse, FL §4-507.

DOMESTIC VIOLENCE —Cont'd
Arrest.
Warrantless arrest, CP §2-204.
Costs.
Petition for relief from abuse.
Waiver or deferral of cost of petition, FL §4-504.
Definitions, FL §4-501.
Address confidentiality program, FL §4-519.
Victim of domestic violence, FL §4-513.
Evidence of battered spouse syndrome, CJ §10-916.
District Court commissioner.
Interim protective order issued by commissioner, FL §4-504.1.
Authority to order, CJ §2-607.
Criminal penalties for violating, FL §4-509.
Interim protective order defined, FL §4-501.
Petition filed with, FL §4-504.1.
Divorce.
Orders of court.
Protection from abuse.
Inadmissible evidence in divorce proceedings, FL §7-103.1.
Evidence.
Battered spouse syndrome.
Admissibility of evidence, CJ §10-916.
Orders of court.
Protection from abuse.
Inadmissible evidence in divorce proceedings, FL §7-103.1.
Fatality review teams, FL §§4-701 to 4-707. See within this heading, "Local domestic violence fatality review teams."
Firearms.
Protective orders.
Restrictions on possession, PS §5-133.
Restrictions on sale, rental or transfer, PS §5-134.
Removing firearms from scene, FL §4-511.
Fund for domestic violence unit pilot program, FL §4-503.2.
Insurance discrimination against victims, IN §27-504.
Interim protective order.
Authority of commissioner to order, CJ §2-607.
Criminal penalties for violating, FL §4-509.
Defined, FL §4-501.
Order issued by commissioner, FL §4-504.1.
Law enforcement officer.
Assisting victims of spousal assault, CJ §5-610.
Duty to help victims, FL §4-502.
Notice to victim of rights, FL §4-503.
Report of abuse, copies provided, FL §4-503.1.
Local domestic violence fatality review teams, FL §§4-701 to 4-707.
Access to information, FL §4-705.
Authorization for county to establish, FL §4-702.
Case review.
Number and type of cases, FL §4-704.
Chair, FL §4-703.
Closed meetings, FL §4-706.
Confidentiality of information, FL §4-707.
Meetings, FL §4-706.
Definitions, FL §4-701.
Immunity.
Local team members and persons cooperating with, CJ §5-637.1.
Information available to public, FL §4-707.
Members, FL §4-703.
Open meetings, FL §4-706.
Protocols, FL §4-704.

DOMESTIC VIOLENCE —Cont'd
Local domestic violence fatality review teams —Cont'd
Purpose, FL §4-704.
Representatives to be designated, FL §4-703.
Who may organize, FL §4-702.
Misdemeanors.
Violations of orders, FL §4-509.
Mutual battery.
Self defense considered in determining whether to arrest, CP §2-204.
Penalties.
Violations of orders, FL §4-509.
Petitions.
Filed with commissioner.
Clerk's office not open, FL §4-504.1.
Relief from abuse, FL §4-504.
Probable cause.
Warrantless arrest, CP §2-204.
Protection from.
Jurisdiction, CJ §4-404.
Protective orders, FL §4-506.
Appeals, FL §4-507.
Arrest.
Probable cause person in violation of order, FL §4-509.
Contempt.
Violations of orders, FL §4-508.
Contents, FL §4-506.
Divorce proceedings.
Protective orders inadmissible evidence, FL §7-103.1.
Duration of final order, FL §4-506.
Final protective order.
Defined, FL §4-501.
Entry of order, FL §4-506.
Hearing substituted for temporary order hearing, FL §4-505.
Service, FL §4-506.
Firearms.
Restrictions on possession, PS §5-133.
Restrictions on sale, rental or transfer, PS §5-134.
Firearms possessed by respondent.
Ordering surrender, FL §4-506.
Hearings on, FL §4-506.
Interagency law enforcement system.
State police department, PS §2-305.
Interim protective orders.
Authority of commissioner to order, CJ §2-607.
Criminal penalties for violating, FL §4-509.
Defined, FL §4-501.
Issuance by commissioner, FL §4-504.1.
Modification, FL §4-507.
Mutual protective order.
Both parties filing petition, FL §4-506.
Other remedies not precluded, FL §4-510.
Out-of-state protective orders, FL §4-508.1.
Immunity of law enforcement officer enforcing, CJ §5-610.1.
Penalties.
Violations of orders, FL §4-509.
Petition for relief from abuse, FL §4-504.
Protection from abuse, FL §4-508.1.
Relief authorized in final order, FL §4-506.
Rescission, FL §4-507.
Sanction for violating.
Stated in order, FL §4-508.
Service of final protective order, FL §4-506.
Service of temporary ex parte orders, FL §4-505.

DOMESTIC VIOLENCE —Cont'd
Protective orders —Cont'd
State police department.
Interagency law enforcement system, PS §2-305.
Temporary ex parte order, FL §4-505.
Criminal penalties for violating, FL §4-509.
Defined, FL §4-501.
Notice to respondent included, FL §4-506.
Protective order hearing.
Date and time to be stated, FL §4-506.
Service, FL §4-505.
Tribal orders for protection, FL §4-508.1.
Vacation of home by respondent.
Factors in ordering, FL §4-506.
Violations of orders.
Penalties, FL §4-509.
Pretrial release not authorized, CP §5-202.
Sanctions, FL §4-508.
Reports.
Battered spouse program.
Annual report on, FL §4-516.
Police incident report, copies provided, FL §4-503.1.
Self-defense.
Considered when determining whether to arrest.
Mutual battery occurring, CP §2-204.
Service of process.
Final protective order, FL §4-506.
Transfer of actions from circuit court to District Court, CivProCir Rule 2-327.
Transfer of actions from District Court to circuit court, CivProDist Rule 3-326.
Victim of domestic violence.
Address confidentiality program, FL §§4-519 to 4-530. See within this heading, "Address confidentiality program."
Administration of program, FL §4-516.
Definitions, CJ §10-916; FL §4-513.
Establishment of program, FL §4-515.
Evidence of battered spouse syndrome.
Admissibility, CJ §10-916.
Definitions, CJ §10-916.
Expansion of program, FL §4-515.
Funding of program, FL §4-516.
Insurance discrimination against victims, IN §27-504.
Legislative declaration, FL §4-514.
Notice of rights to be delivered, FL §4-503.
Reports.
Annual report on program, FL §4-516.
Shelters.
Authorized, FL §4-515.
Conditions, FL §4-515.
Warrantless arrest, CP §2-204.
Weapons.
Firearms.
Removing from scene, FL §4-511.

DOMICILE.
Alcoholic beverages.
Permits.
Change of domicile permit, 2B §2-101.
Compromise of death taxes.
See INHERITANCE TAX.
Husband and wife.
Determination of domicile, FL §4-201.
Independent domicile, FL §4-201.
Minors, FL §5-204.
Residence.
See RESIDENCE.

DONATIONS.
Coercing or intimidating another to contribute or donate, CR §3-707.
Food donations under federal programs.
Unauthorized disposition or conversion, CR §8-505.
Fraudulent fundraising.
Campaigns to benefit police, fire departments or public safety officers, CR §8-520.

DO NOT RESUSCITATE ORDERS.
Authorization to follow emergency medical services order in outpatient setting, HG §5-608.
Emergency medical services do not resuscitate orders.
Authorization to follow, HG §5-608.
Guardians for disabled persons.
Medical treatment decisions, ET §§13-708, 13-711 to 13-713.
Health care decisions act, HG §§5-601 to 5-618.
See HEALTH CARE DECISIONS.
Immunity of emergency medical services providers.
Following emergency medical services do not resuscitate orders, HG §5-608.

DOOR-TO-DOOR SALES.
Home solicitation sales, CL §§14-301 to 14-306.
See HOME SOLICITATION SALES.
Maryland door-to-door solicitations act, CL §§14-2601 to 14-2603.
Transient vendors.
Licensing requirements, BR §§17-20A-01 to 17-20A-06.
See TRANSIENT VENDORS.

DORCHESTER COUNTY.
Agricultural land subject to nutrient management plan.
Property tax credits, TP §9-311.
Alcoholic beverages.
Beer and light wine licenses.
Class A, off-sale, 2B §5-101.
Class C, on-sale, 2B §5-301.
Class D, on-sale, 2B §5-401.
Class E, on-sale.
Restaurants, 2B §5-201.
Hours and days for sale, 2B §11-510.
Beer and wine festival, 2B §8-307.
Beer licenses.
Class A, off-sale, 2B §3-101.
License fee, 2B §3-101.
Class B, on-sale.
Hotels and restaurants, 2B §3-201.
License fee, 2B §3-201.
Class C, on-sale.
Clubs, 2B §3-301.
Class D, on-sale, 2B §3-401.
Hours and days for sale, 2B §11-510.
Beer, wine and liquor licenses.
Bar and counter sales.
Sundays, 2B §11-403.
Bottle clubs, 2B §20-105.1.
Class A, off-sale, 2B §6-101.
Class B, on-sale.
Hotels and restaurants, 2B §6-201.
Class C, on-sale.
Clubs, 2B §6-301.
Hours and days for sale, 2B §11-510.
Board of license commissioners.
Powers, 2B §15-112.

DORCHESTER COUNTY —Cont'd
Alcoholic beverages —Cont'd
Bottle clubs, 2B §20-105.1.
Consumption of beverages, 2B §16-202.
Regulations, 2B §16-202.
Criminal history records checks.
License applicants, 2B §10-103.
Dispensaries.
Continuation of dispensary system, 2B §18-201.
Elections.
Exercise of privileges of licensee on election day,
2B §11-401.
Fines and forfeitures, 2B §§16-502, 16-507.
Loitering around place of business, 2B §12-210.
Unlawful consumption, 2B §16-202.
Hours and days for sale, 2B §11-510.
Election day, 2B §11-401.
New Year's day, 2B §11-402.
License commissioners.
County commissioners ex officio, 2B §15-105.
Salaries, 2B §15-109.
Licenses.
Applications.
Criminal history check of applicants, 2B
§10-103.
Exceptions, 2B §10-104.
Notice on premises, 2B §10-202.
Churches and schools.
Prohibited in Hurlock near church or public
school, 2B §9-210.
Criminal history records checks.
License applicants, 2B §10-103.
Death of licensee.
Procedure, 2B §10-506.
Dispensary system continuation, 2B §18-201.
Fees.
Collection and disposition, 2B §10-204.
More than one license for same person or
premises, 2B §9-102.
Residency requirement, 2B §10-103.
Revocation and suspension.
Nudity and sexual displays on licensee's
premises, 2B §10-405.
Special and temporary licenses, 2B §7-101.
Substitution of corporate or club officer's name
on license, 2B §10-301.
Transfer, 2B §10-503.
Wine tasting licenses, 2B §8-405.1.
Light wine licenses.
Class A, off-sale, 2B §4-201.
Loitering around place of business prohibited, 2B
§12-210.
Micro-brewery licenses, 2B §2-208.
Minors.
Employment of minors by retail dealers, 2B
§12-302.
Nudity and sexual displays on licensee's premises.
Revocation of license, 2B §10-405.
Penalties.
Local penalties, 2B §16-507.
Sales.
Beer for cash, 2B §12-112.
Election day, 2B §11-401.
Hours and days of sale, 2B §11-510.
Sundays.
General restrictions, 2B §11-403.
Appeals.
Shared facilities.
Appeal following denial of petition, EN §9-676.
Appearance fees in circuit courts.
Distribution, CJ §7-204.

DORCHESTER COUNTY —Cont'd
Aquaculture.
Oysters and clams.
Private oyster culture.
Leases.
Restrictions, NR §4-11A-05.
Assessments.
Benefit assessments.
Shared facilities. See within this heading,
"Sanitary commissions."
Uniform benefit assessments.
Bonnie Brook service area, EN §9-657.
Bailiff.
Compensation, CJ §2-507.
Beer and wine festivals.
Licenses, 2B §8-307.
Billing code.
Provisions for, 25 §3.
Bingo, CR §13-1203.
Daily bingo license fee, CR §13-1207.
License fee, CR §13-1207.
License required, CR §13-1203.
Minors not allowed to play, conduct or operate
game, CR §13-1204.
Qualified organizations, CR §13-1203.
Birds and game.
Spotlighting, NR §10-410.
Boats.
Regulation of docking, mooring and abandonment.
Power of county commissioners, 25 §11C.
Bottle clubs.
Alcoholic beverages, 2B §20-105.1.
Bridges.
Construction or repair, 25 §37B.
Building code.
Agricultural buildings.
Exemption for buildings used for agritourism,
PS §12-508.
Building excise tax, 24 §9-1002.
Cambridge Little League, Inc.
Property tax credits, TP §9-311.
Cambridge Skeet and Gun Club, Inc.
Property tax credits, TP §9-311.
Cedar Meadows Rod and Gun Club, Inc.
Property tax credits, TP §9-311.
Chesapeake Audubon Society, Inc.
Property tax credits, TP §9-311.
**Chesapeake Bay critical area and Atlantic
coastal bays critical area protection
programs.**
Critical areas commission.
Members on commission, NR §8-1804.
Growth allocation, location in resource
conservation area, NR §8-1808.1.
Churches.
Alcoholic beverages.
Licenses.
Prohibited near church, 2B §9-210.
Circuit courts.
Appearance fees.
Distribution, CJ §7-204.
Judicial circuit, MD Const Art IV §19.
Number of judges, CJ §1-503.
Clerks of court.
Recording and indexing.
Ordinances, resolutions and regulations, 25 §4.
Codes.
Building, electrical and plumbing codes.
Adoption, 25 §3.
Commissioners.
Alcoholic beverages.
License commissioners.
County commissioners ex officio, 2B §15-105.

DORCHESTER COUNTY —Cont'd
Commissioners —Cont'd
Harbor facilities.
Authority to regulate, 25 §11C-1.
Labor camps.
Permits required, 25 §27A.
Mooring.
Power to regulate, 25 §11C.
Piers.
Power to regulate, 25 §11C-1.
Powers.
Enumerated, 25 §3.
Real property, 25 §9.
Public docks.
Power to regulate, 25 §11C-1.
Community services program.
Person sentenced to confinement in department of corrections, COR §11-711.
Compassionate leave for individuals confined in department of corrections, COR §11-711.
Cooperative activities.
Powers of commissioners, 25 §3.
County board of elections.
Confirmation of member by house of delegates, EL §2-201.
County boards generally, EL §§2-201 to 2-303.
See ELECTIONS.
Crabs.
Use of crab pots in Chesapeake Bay waters, NR §4-812.
Crimes and offenses.
Alcoholic beverages.
Regulation of consumption, 2B §16-202.
Dog licenses, 24 §11-504.
Licensing of free-play machines and other musical devices, 24 §11-201.
Deeds.
Straw deeds.
Recordation, RP §3-104.
Definitions.
Shared facilities, EN §9-672.
Shared facility areas, EN §9-672.
Department of corrections.
Community service, authorized program, COR §11-711.
Compassionate leave for individuals confined in department, COR §11-711.
Home detention, authorized program, COR §11-711.
Pretrial release, authorized program, COR §11-711.
Work release, authorized program, COR §11-711.
Docks, piers and harbor facilities.
Power of commissioners to adopt regulations concerning, 25 §11C-1.
Dog and cat regulations, 24 §11-504.
Dogs running at large.
Females in heat, 24 §11-512.
Economic development fund, 83A §5-216.
Elections.
County boards of education generally, EL §§8-801 to 8-806.
Employees' pension system.
Contributions, SPP §21-307.
Employees' retirement system.
Contributions, SPP §21-307.
Erosion prevention works.
Annual benefit assessment, 25 §165.
Family YMCA, Inc.
Sale of parcel of real property located at 201 Talbot Avenue, Cambridge, Maryland, 25 §9.

DORCHESTER COUNTY —Cont'd
Federal and state aid.
Powers of commissioners, 25 §3.
Fines.
Alcoholic beverages.
Loitering around place of business, 2B §12-210.
Unlawful consumption, 2B §16-202.
Violations, 2B §16-502.
Fire department.
Volunteer fire departments.
County contributions, PS §8-302.
Fish and fisheries.
Regulation of fishing, docking and mooring.
Power of county commissioners, 25 §11C.
Restrictions in county waters, NR §4-719.
Riparian rights.
Exceptions, NR §4-712.
Seafood harvesting and seafood industry, local regulation authorized, 25 §232.
Forest land subject to forest management plan.
Property tax credit, TP §9-311.
Gaming, bazaar, carnival and raffles, CR §§13-201 to 13-205, 13-1201 to 13-1207.
Coin or slot machines not authorized, CR §13-1205.
Conducting event for benefit of qualified organization.
Allowed, CR §13-203.
Definitions, CR §§13-201, 13-1201.
Enforcement, CR §13-1206.
Gaming event defined, CR §§13-201, 13-1201.
Individual benefit prohibited, CR §13-203.
License fee, CR §13-1207.
Management through organizations members, CR §13-205.
Prizes and gaming devices allowed, CR §13-204.
Provisions applicable to county, CR §§13-202, 13-301, 13-1202.
Qualified organization defined, CR §13-201.
Sunday gaming prohibited, CR §13-1204.
Garbage and trash.
Collection and disposal.
Licensing of collectors, 25 §3.
Health.
Powers of commissioners, 25 §3.
Hearings.
Proposed ordinances or resolutions.
Special provisions as to certain counties, 25 §3.
Home detention program.
Person sentenced to confinement in department of corrections, COR §11-711.
Housing code.
Provisions for, 25 §3.
Indexes.
Ordinances, resolutions and regulations, 25 §4.
Investments.
Uniform benefit assessments.
Dorchester county service area number 1, EN §9-657.
Judges.
Pensions.
General provisions, ET §2-108.
Labor camps.
Nuisance.
Abatement as nuisance, 25 §27A.
Permits required from board of county commissioners, 25 §27A.
Penalty for violation, 25 §27A.
Licenses.
Alcoholic beverages. See within this heading, "Alcoholic beverages."

DORCHESTER COUNTY —Cont'd
Licenses —Cont'd
  Beer and wine festival license, 2B §8-307.
  Garbage and trash.
    Collectors, 25 §5.
  Powers of commissioners, 25 §3.
Liens.
  Shared facilities.
    Lien for unpaid benefit assessments, EN §9-679.
Merit system.
  Application, 25 §3.
  Special provisions, 25 §3.
Minors.
  Alcoholic beverages.
    Employment of minors by retail dealers, 2B
      §12-302.
Misdemeanors.
  Alcoholic beverages.
    Regulation of consumption, 2B §16-202.
  Dog licenses, 24 §11-504.
  Licensing of free-play machines and other musical
    devices, 24 §11-201.
Municipal corporations.
  Appropriations to incorporated municipalities, 25
    §3.
Nuisances.
  Abatement of labor camp violation, 25 §27A.
  Powers of commissioners, 25 §3.
Ordinances.
  Recording and indexing, 25 §4.
Orphans' court.
  Judges.
    Compensation, ET §2-108.
Oysters and clams.
  Dredging in county waters, NR §4-1012.
  Hydraulic clam dredge.
    Where use prohibited, NR §§4-1037, 4-1038.
  Patent tonging in Chesapeake Bay adjacent to
    county, NR §4-1011.
  Private oyster culture.
    Leases.
      Restrictions, NR §4-11A-05.
  Tonging.
    Patent tonging prohibited, NR §4-1011.
Personal property.
  Purchase or lease of.
    Powers, 25 §9D.
Petitions.
  Shared facilities. See within this heading,
    "Sanitary commissions."
Piers.
  Regulation of public docks, piers and harbor
    facilities, 25 §11C-1.
Pretrial release program.
  Person sentenced to confinement in department of
    corrections, COR §11-711.
Real property.
  Commissioners.
    Powers, 25 §9.
Recordation.
  Deeds, RP §3-104.
  Ordinances, resolutions and regulations, 25 §4.
  Payment of taxes prior to transfer on assessment
    books or records, RP §3-104.
  Plats of subdivisions.
    Size of plat, RP §3-108.
  Taxation.
    Payment of taxes prior to transfer on
      assessment books or records, RP §3-104.
Rules and regulations.
  Sanitary commissions.
    Shared facilities, EN §9-677.

DORCHESTER COUNTY —Cont'd
Sales.
  Alcoholic beverages. See within this heading,
    "Alcoholic beverages."
Sanitary commissions.
  Assessments.
    Benefit assessments, EN §9-656.
    Levy, EN §9-658.
  Shared facilities.
    Advances by county, EN §9-678.
    Appeals.
      Denial of petition, EN §9-676.
    Applicability of subtitle, EN §9-673.
    Assessments, EN §9-679.
    Classification and assessment of property.
      Rules and regulations, EN §9-677.
    Definitions, EN §9-672.
    Denial.
      Appeals, EN §9-676.
    District.
      Powers of district, EN §9-674.
    Liens, EN §9-679.
    Limitations on service by shared facility, EN
      §9-674.
    Notices.
      Classification and assessment, EN §9-679.
    Permitted locations, EN §9-674.
    Petitions.
      Action on petition, EN §9-676.
      Applicable standards, EN §9-676.
      Approval, EN §9-676.
      Contents, EN §9-675.
      Expenses, EN §9-675.
      Filing with commission, EN §9-675.
      When decision required, EN §9-676.
    Powers of commission, EN §9-674.
    Records.
      Liens, EN §9-679.
    Repayment, EN §9-678.
    Rules and regulations.
      Adoption, EN §9-677.
      Classification and assessment of property, EN
        §9-677.
    Scope of part, EN §9-673.
    Shared facility area, EN §9-672.
Sanitary districts.
  Dorchester county service area number 1.
    Assessments, EN §9-657.
Schools.
  Alcoholic beverages.
    Licenses.
      Prohibited near school, 2B §9-210.
  County board of education.
    Compensation, ED §3-5A-04.
    Election generally, EL §§8-801 to 8-806.
    Expenses, ED §4-107.
    Meetings, ED §3-5A-05.
    Members, ED §3-5A-01.
    Officers, ED §3-5A-03.
    Persons subject to authority of board.
      Ineligibility to serve as member, ED §3-114.
    Removal of member, ED §3-5A-02.
    Terms, ED §3-5A-01.
    Vacancies, ED §3-5A-01.
  Educational technology pilot program.
    Implementation plan.
      School systems in which implemented, ED
        §7-10A-04.
  Holidays, ED §7-103.
**Seafood harvesting and seafood industry, local
  regulation authorized,** 25 §232.

DORCHESTER COUNTY —Cont'd
Shared facilities, EN §§9-672 to 9-679. See within
    this heading, "Sanitary commissions."
Sheriff, CJ §2-309.
    Second in command, CJ §2-310.
Ships.
    Regulation of docking, mooring and abandonment.
        Power of county commissioners, 25 §11C.
Slot machines.
    Ownership and operation by eligible organization,
        CR §12-304.
State's attorney, 10 §40.
Subdivisions.
    Plats of subdivisions.
        Size of plat, RP §3-108.
Sundays and holidays.
    Alcoholic beverages.
        Hours and days of sale, 2B §§11-403, 11-510.
Taxation.
    Building excise tax, 24 §9-1002.
    Credits.
        Property tax credits.
            Cambridge Little League, Inc., TP §9-311.
            Cambridge Skeet and Gun Club, Inc., TP
                §9-311.
            Cedar Meadows Rod and Gun Club, Inc., TP
                §9-311.
            Chesapeake Audubon Society, Inc., TP §9-311.
            Women's Auxiliary of the Dorchester
                Memorial Hospital, TP §9-311.
    Delinquent taxes.
        Interest, TP §14-603.
    Exemptions.
        Personal property.
            Reduction or elimination of percentage of
                assessment, TP §7-513.
    Recordation.
        Payment of taxes prior to transfer on
            assessment books or records, RP §3-104.
        Exception as to, RP §3-104.
    Redemption.
        Rate of redemption, TP §14-820.
    Sales.
        Expenses of sales.
            Auctioneer's fee, TP §14-813.
Treasurer.
    Salary, 25 §51.
Truancy reduction pilot program, CJ §§3-8C-01
    to 3-8C-10.
    See TRUANCY REDUCTION PILOT PROGRAM.
Vessels and boats.
    Regulation of docking, mooring and abandonment.
        Power of county commissioners, 25 §11C.
Volunteer fire departments.
    County contributions, PS §8-302.
Water and sewer authorities.
    Bond issues.
        Special provisions, EN §9-934.
Water and sewer systems.
    Shared facilities. See within this heading,
        "Sanitary commissions."
Wine festivals.
    Licenses, 2B §8-307.
Wine tasting licenses, 2B §8-405.1.
Witnesses.
    Compensation, CJ §9-202.
    Mileage, CJ §9-202.
Women's Auxiliary of the Dorchester Memorial
    Hospital.
    Property tax credits, TP §9-311.

DORCHESTER COUNTY —Cont'd
Work release program.
    Person sentenced to confinement in department of
        corrections, COR §11-711.

DORCHESTER COUNTY ECONOMIC
    DEVELOPMENT FUND, 83A §5-216.

DORMITORIES.
Barbeque grills.
    Restrictions on use, PS §9-1001.
Building codes.
    Emergency power and lighting systems, PS
        §12-702.

DOUBLE-DIPPING.
Employees' and teachers' retirement systems.
    Suspension of early retirement benefits, SPP
        §22-404.

DOUBLE JEOPARDY.
See JEOPARDY.

DOWER.
Abolished, ET §3-202.
Surviving spouse.
    Elective share.
        General provisions, ET §§3-102, 3-203 to 3-208.
        See DECEDENTS' ESTATES.

DOWN PAYMENT AND SETTLEMENT
    EXPENSE LOAN PROGRAM, HS §§4-301 to
    4-309.
Applications for loans.
    Review, HS §4-307.
Default on loan, HS §4-307.
Defined terms, HS §4-301.
Development finance division.
    Units in division, HS §4-103.
Eligible homebuyers.
    Qualifications, HS §4-305.
Established, HS §4-302.
False statements or reports, HS §4-309.
Fees.
    Powers and duties of department, HS §4-304.
Financing of program, HS §4-306.
Fines.
    False statements or reports, HS §4-309.
Homebuyer education, HS §4-308.
Operation of program, HS §4-306.
Powers and duties of department, HS §4-304.
Purchase of loans.
    Powers and duties of department, HS §4-304.
Purpose, HS §4-303.
Sale or transfer of property, HS §4-307.
Security for loans, HS §4-307.
Uses of loans, HS §4-307.

DOWNTOWN MANAGEMENT DISTRICTS.
Property tax exemptions, TP §7-504.2.

DOWRY INSURANCE.
Holocaust victims insurance act, IN §§28-101 to
    28-110.
    See HOLOCAUST VICTIMS INSURANCE.

DRAFTHOUSES.
Alcoholic beverages.
    Drafthouse licenses.
        Frederick county, 2B §8-701.

DRAFTS.
Bank deposits and collections.
    General provisions, CL §§4-101 to 4-504.
    See BANK DEPOSITS AND COLLECTIONS.

DRAFTS —Cont'd

Banks and trust companies.

Acceptance, FI §§3-206, 3-604.

What drafts may be accepted, FI §3-604.

Certification.

Prohibited when there are not sufficient funds on deposit, FI §3-606.

Valid against bank or trust company, FI §3-606.

Return of cancelled checks, FI §5-513.

Termination of provisions, FI §2-401.

Contracts.

Sale of goods.

Documents against which draft is drawn.

When deliverable, CL §2-514.

Counterfeiting private instrument or document, CR §8-601.

Issuing counterfeited instrument or document, CR §8-602.

Documentary drafts.

Bank deposits and collections.

Dishonor.

Duty to notify customer, CL §4-501.

Privilege of presenting bank to deal with goods, CL §4-504.

Reporting reasons, CL §4-503.

Generally, CL §§4-101 to 4-504.

See BANK DEPOSITS AND COLLECTIONS.

Presentment.

Duty to send, CL §4-501.

On arrival drafts, CL §4-502.

Failure to deliver documents for merchandise, CR §7-116.

Letters of credit.

General provisions, CL §§5-101 to 5-118.

See LETTERS OF CREDIT.

Money orders and travelers checks.

See MONEY TRANSMISSION.

Negotiable instruments generally, CL §§3-101 to 3-605.

See NEGOTIABLE INSTRUMENTS.

Savings and loan associations.

Month and year account opened to appear on drafts, FI §9-412.1.

DRAINING LANDS.

Accounts and accounting.

Board of managers, 25 §92.

Actions.

Public drainage associations or public watershed associations.

Officers or directors.

Immunity from liability, 25 §60.

Agriculture.

Drainage of agricultural land.

Agricultural drainage projects financed or managed by public drainage associations, AG §8-603.

Cost sharing in maintenance of drainage outlet systems, AG §8-602.

Powers and duties of secretary, AG §8-601.

Appeals.

Circuit court, 25 §80.

Classification and assessment, 25 §117.

County commissioners.

Order of review, 25 §79.

Appropriations.

Drainage districts.

By state, 25 §121H.

Assessments.

Against persons who will benefit, 25 §73.

DRAINING LANDS —Cont'd

Assessments —Cont'd

County commissioners.

Authority to contribute or allocate funds, 25 §73.

Ditches or drains.

Already constructed, 25 §74.

Drainage districts.

By drainage commissioners, 25 §118.

Taxation. See within this heading, "Taxation."

Associations. See within this heading, "Public drainage associations."

Board of managers.

Accounts and accounting, 25 §92.

Appointment.

By county commissioners.

When appointed, 25 §58.

Bond issues.

Power to issue, 25 §90.

Chairman.

General provisions, 25 §60A.

Classification of land.

Woodland or cropland, 25 §§82, 96.

Condemnation.

Powers, 25 §86.

Determining term of office, 25 §61.

Dissolution.

Procedure, 25 §102.

Easements, 25 §88.

Election.

Annual meeting, 25 §64.

General provisions, 25 §58.

Funds.

Alternate plan for raising funds, 25 §90.

Payment of wages and expenses from first funds available, 25 §91.

Improvements.

Borrowing money, 25 §92.

Plan for improvements.

Procedure to carry out, 25 §90.

Repairs, 25 §96.

Meeting of landowners, 25 §63.

Business transacted at annual meeting, 25 §64.

Watershed work plans.

Adoption, 25 §68.

Meeting of taxables.

Organization meeting, 25 §60A.

Petitions.

Delivered to board by county commissioners, 25 §62.

Report of viewers.

Annual report, 25 §64.

Delivered to board by county commissioners, 25 §62.

Right of way, 25 §88.

Secretary.

General provisions, 25 §60A.

Tax roll.

Proceedings, 25 §87.

Term of office, 25 §66.

Determination of which managers serve until first annual meeting and for years thereafter, 25 §61.

Vacancy.

Filling by county commissioners, 25 §65.

Watershed work plans.

Adoption, 25 §68.

Development of plan, 25 §67.

Filing, 25 §69.

Right of entry, 25 §67.

DRAINING LANDS —Cont'd
Board of viewers.
Acceptance in writing, 25 §70.
Appeals.
County commissioners.
Appointment of other viewers, 25 §79.
Appointment, 25 §70.
Assessment against persons who will benefit, 25 §73.
Ditches or drains.
Already constructed, 25 §74.
Compensation, 25 §101.
Damages.
Consideration, 25 §72.
Drainage districts. See within this heading, "Drainage districts."
Duties.
Generally, 25 §71.
Engineers.
Appointment, 25 §71.
Examination, 25 §105.
Expenses.
Payment, 25 §91.
Notice of proceedings, 25 §70A.
Number, 25 §70.
Qualifications, 25 §70.
Report and map.
Filed with county commissioners, 25 §105.
Report to county commissioners.
Action of county commissioners on report, 25 §84.
Copy delivered to board of managers and state soil conservation committee, 25 §62.
Expenses when report rejected, 25 §81.
In triplicate, 25 §82A.
Rejection.
Expenses when report rejected, 25 §81.
Requirements, 25 §82A.
Subsequent board of viewers, 25 §82.
Surveys, 25 §105.
Two or more counties, 25 §§55, 70.
Vacancies, 25 §70.
Bond issues, 25 §90.
Drainage districts, 25 §§121B, 121C.
Bonds, surety.
Drainage districts.
Contractor's bond, 25 §121D.
Formation of drainage districts, 25 §104.
Superintendent of construction, 25 §116.
Bridges.
Cost of construction, 25 §99.
Costs.
Amendment of petition, 25 §78.
Counties.
Chartered counties.
Powers of county, 25A §5.
County commissioners.
Advancement of funds on request of board of managers, 25 §91.
Board of managers.
Appointment, 25 §58.
Vacancy.
Filling, 25 §66.
Clerk.
Drainage file, 25 §75.
Dissolution of public drainage associations, 25 §102.
Drainage commissioners.
Appointment by county commissioners, 25 §115.
Drainage districts. See within this heading, "Drainage districts."

DRAINING LANDS —Cont'd
County commissioners —Cont'd
Establishment of association, 25 §52.
Hearing, 25 §85.
Public hearing on report, 25 §84.
Report from viewers.
Action of commissioners on receipt of report, 25 §84.
Contents, 25 §82A.
Copy delivered to board of managers and state soil conservation committee, 25 §62.
Expenses when report rejected, 25 §81.
Levy of tax to pay expenses, 25 §81.
Tax roll.
Certification by commissioners, 25 §87.
County treasurers.
Compensation, 25 §89.
Record.
Public drainage associations, 25 §91.
Report and distribution of taxes, 25 §90.
Retention of percentage for compensation, 25 §89.
Two or more counties.
Tax procedure, 25 §93.
Damages.
Consideration of damage by board of viewers, 25 §72.
Ditches across land of another, 25 §97.
Payment from first funds available, 25 §91.
Definitions.
Agricultural drainage projects financed or managed by public drainage associations, AG §8-603.
Inactive association, 25 §102.
Ditches and drains.
Across land of another, 25 §97.
Already constructed.
Adopting improvements already constructed, 25 §90.
Assessments, 25 §74.
Obstruction of free flow of water.
Penalty, 25 §98.
Prohibited, 25 §98.
Drainage districts.
Appropriations, 25 §121H.
Assessments.
By drainage commissioners, 25 §118.
Authority to establish, 25 §103.
Board of viewers.
Appointment.
By county commissioners, 25 §104.
Classification of land benefited by improvement, 25 §109.
Compensation, 25 §121F.
Damages.
Assessment, 25 §108.
Duties.
Generally, 25 §107.
Expenses.
Payment, 25 §121H.
General provisions. See within this heading, "Board of viewers."
Powers.
Generally, 25 §107.
Records and report.
Expenses of survey, 25 §110.
Survey.
Records and report of expenses, 25 §110.
Bond issues.
Issuance.
For cost of improvement, 25 §121B.
Generally, 25 §121C.

DRAINING LANDS —Cont'd
Drainage districts —Cont'd
Bond issues —Cont'd
Issuance —Cont'd
Notice, 25 §121B.
Sale, 25 §121C.
Bonds, surety.
Contractor's bond, 25 §121D.
Bridge.
Obstruction, 25 §121E.
Commissioners.
Drainage commissioners.
Assessments, 25 §118.
Certification of costs to county commissioners, 25 §117.
General provisions, 25 §115.
Condemnation.
Right of way or outlet over and through lands, 25 §121.
Construction.
Bids, 25 §121D.
Bonds, surety.
Contractor's bond, 25 §121D.
Construction of law, 25 §121H.
Costs.
Ascertainment of cost of improvement including damages, 25 §117.
Certification of costs to county commissioners, 25 §117.
County commissioners.
Board of viewers.
Approval or rejection, 25 §106.
Hearing.
Final hearing, 25 §113.
Notice, 25 §111.
Report.
Action on final report of commissioners, 25 §111.
Summoning defendant landowners who have not signed petition, 25 §112.
Easement record, 25 §114.
Engineer.
Classification of land benefited by improvement, 25 §109.
Compensation, 25 §121F.
Damages.
Assessment, 25 §108.
Duties.
Generally, 25 §107.
Expenses.
Payment, 25 §121H.
Powers.
Generally, 25 §107.
Survey.
Records and report of expenses, 25 §110.
Establishment.
Authority to establish, 25 §103.
Petition.
Procedure, 25 §104.
Hearing.
Final hearing, 25 §113.
Highways.
Benefits, 25 §119.
Immunity.
Officers and directors, CJ §5-508.
Improvements.
Repairs, 25 §121E.
Laborers.
Compensation, 25 §121F.
Land not affected or benefited, 25 §120.

DRAINING LANDS —Cont'd
Drainage districts —Cont'd
Lateral drains.
Outlets, 25 §121A.
Liens.
Assessments, 25 §118.
Loans from state, 25 §121H.
Maps.
Official copies, 25 §114.
Obstruction.
Injury or obstruction of bridge, fence or floodgate, 25 §121E.
Outlets for lateral drains, 25 §121A.
Petition.
Procedure upon petition, 25 §104.
Profiles.
Copies by official, 25 §114.
Public property.
Benefits, 25 §119.
Railroads.
Benefits, 25 §119.
Record book, 25 §114.
Repairs.
General provisions, 25 §121E.
Report and map to be filed.
Approval or rejection by county commissioners, 25 §106.
Right of way.
Condemnation, 25 §121.
Surveys.
Payment, 25 §121H.
Two or more counties, 25 §104.
Unaffected or unbenefited land, 25 §120.
United States.
Cooperation with, 25 §121G.
Easements.
Board of managers, 25 §88.
Elections.
Board of managers, 25 §58.
Eminent domain.
Drainage districts.
Right of way or outlet over and through lands, 25 §121.
Power of board of managers, 25 §86.
Engineer.
Appointment.
Board of managers.
Watershed work plans, 25 §67.
By board of viewers, 25 §71.
Compensation, 25 §101.
Drainage districts. See within this heading, "Drainage districts."
Right of entry.
Watershed work plans, 25 §67.
Wages and expenses.
Payment, 25 §91.
Expenses.
Payment.
First funds available, 25 §91.
Fines.
Obstructing free flow of water, 25 §98.
Funds.
Drainage district fund, 25 §121H.
First funds available.
Payment of wages and expenses, 25 §91.
Inclusion in state budget, AG §8-602.
Health.
General provisions as to health and sanitation, 25 §52.
Hearings.
Before county commissioners, 25 §85.

DRAINING LANDS —Cont'd
Hearings —Cont'd
Dissolution.
Public drainage associations, 25 §102.
Drainage districts.
County commissioners, 25 §§111, 113.
Public drainage associations.
Petitions to establish, 25 §§54, 57.
Public hearing by commissioner on report, 25 §84.
Highways.
Drainage districts.
Benefits of highway, 25 §119.
Improvement crossing intersection of highway
with watercourse.
Cost of construction of bridges, 25 §99.
Immunity.
Public drainage associations or public watershed
associations.
Officers or directors, 25 §60.
Improvements.
Highways.
Crossing highway at intersection of highway
with watercourse, 25 §99.
Obstructing free flow of water.
Penalty, 25 §98.
Plan.
By board of managers, 25 §92.
Railroads.
Crossing railroad at intersection of watercourse,
25 §100.
Repairs.
Keeping in good repair, 25 §96.
Subdivision of property.
Proration of tax, 25 §94.
Injunctions.
Agricultural drainage projects financed or
managed by public drainage associations.
Failure to obtain or comply with approved
plans, AG §8-603.
Interpretation and construction.
Construction of law, 25 §121H.
Jury.
Appeals to circuit court, 25 §80.
Liability.
Drainage districts.
Officers or directors.
Immunity from liability, CJ §5-508.
Public drainage associations or public watershed
associations.
Officers or directors.
Immunity from liability, 25 §60.
Liens.
Assessments.
Drainage districts, 25 §118.
Managers. See within this heading, "Board of
managers."
Maps.
Drainage districts, 25 §114.
Mechanics' liens.
Attachment of lien, RP §9-102.
Mills and milldams.
Effect on, 25 §95.
Mining.
Abandoned mine drainage control.
General provisions, EN §§15-701 to 15-706.
See MINING.
Misdemeanors.
Watershed work plans.
Preventing right of entry, 25 §67.
Nonresidents.
Notice to, 25 §76.

DRAINING LANDS —Cont'd
Notices.
Bond issues, 25 §90.
Drainage districts.
Hearing by county commissioners, 25 §111.
Nonresidents.
Proceedings of county commissioners, 25 §76.
Proceedings of board of viewers, 25 §70A.
Public drainage associations.
Dissolution, 25 §102.
Petition for establishment, 25 §54.
Watershed work plans.
Adoption, 25 §68.
Officers and employees.
Immunity from liability, 25 §60.
Wages.
Payment.
First funds available, 25 §91.
Petitions.
Amendments.
Proceedings, 25 §78.
Copy delivered to board of managers and state
soil conservation committee, 25 §62.
Public drainage associations.
Petitions to establish.
Review of petitions, 25 §54.
Proxies.
Election.
Voting at meeting of taxables to elect board of
managers, 25 §58.
Publication.
Board of viewers.
Notice of proceedings, 25 §70A.
Public benefit, 25 §52.
Public drainage associations.
Authority, 25 §59.
Costs.
Assessment, 25 §73.
Dissolution.
Inactive associations, 25 §102.
Procedure, 25 §102.
Established.
Authority, 25 §52.
Notice to secretary of agriculture and soil
conservation committee, 25 §52.
Petitions and accompanying reports, 25 §53.
Expenses.
Payment, 25 §91.
Immunity from liability.
Officers or directors, 25 §60.
Inactive associations.
Dissolution, 25 §102.
Jurisdiction.
Two or more counties, 25 §§52, 55.
Officers or directors.
Immunity from liability, 25 §60.
Petition.
Amendment, 25 §78.
Dissolution, 25 §102.
Establishment of association, 25 §53.
Access to petition, 25 §54.
Accompanying report from local soil
conservation districts, 25 §53.
Notice, 25 §54.
Public hearing, 25 §§54, 57.
Review of petition, 25 §54.
Tax on signers when report rejected, 25 §81.
Records.
Kept by county treasurer, 25 §89.
Rights, 25 §59.

DRAINING LANDS —Cont'd
Public property.
  Benefits of public property, 25 §119.
Public watershed associations.
  Immunity from liability.
    Officers or directors, 25 §60.
Quorum.
  Board of managers.
    Taxables in proceedings for election, 25 §58.
Railroads.
  Benefits of railroad, 25 §119.
  Crossing at intersection of watercourse.
    Cost of bridges, 25 §100.
    Damages to railroads, 25 §100.
Reports.
  Board of managers.
    Annual report, 25 §64.
  Board of viewers to county commissioners, 25
    §82A.
  Rejection of report.
    Expenses when report rejected, 25 §81.
  County treasurer.
    Distribution of taxes, 25 §90.
  Drainage districts, 25 §§110, 111.
Right of entry.
  Board of managers.
    Watershed work plans, 25 §67.
Rights of way.
  Board of managers, 25 §88.
Sales.
  Drainage districts.
    Failure to pay assessments, 25 §118.
Secretary of agriculture.
  Drainage of agricultural land.
    Cost sharing in maintenance of drainage outlet
      systems, AG §8-602.
    Powers and duties, AG §8-601.
Soil conservation committee.
  State soil conservation committee.
    Copy of viewers map and report for two, 25 §62.
State.
  Aid.
    Drainage districts.
      Loans from state, 25 §121H.
Subdivisions.
  Taxation.
    Proration of tax, 25 §94.
Summons and process.
  Drainage districts.
    Defendant landowners who have not signed
      petition, 25 §112.
Superintendent of construction.
  Appointment by drainage commissioners, 25 §116.
  Bond, surety, 25 §116.
  General provisions, 25 §116.
Taxation.
  Against land benefited, 25 §94.
  Assessments, 25 §90.
    Against owners benefited, 25 §§73, 74.
    Drainage districts, 25 §118.
  Disbursements.
    By county treasurer, 25 §89.
  Drainage tax roll, 25 §87.
  Expenses when report rejected.
    Levy of tax by commissioners to pay expenses,
      25 §81.
  How drainage taxes disbursed, 25 §89.
  Maintenance.
    Levy for maintenance, 25 §96.
  Report of county treasurer to board of managers.
    Collection of taxes, 25 §90.

DRAINING LANDS —Cont'd
Taxation —Cont'd
  Subdivision of property.
    Effect, 25 §94.
  Taxables.
    Meeting of taxables, 25 §60A.
  Two or more counties.
    Procedure, 25 §93.
Two or more counties.
  Drainage districts, 25 §104.
  General provisions, 25 §55.
  Taxation.
    Procedure, 25 §93.
United States.
  Drainage districts.
    Cooperation with United States, 25 §121G.
Venue.
  Two or more counties, 25 §55.
Viewers. See within this heading, "Board of
    viewers."
Watershed work plans.
  Adoption, 25 §68.
  Boards of drainage viewers.
    Appointment after approval of plan, 25 §70.
  Contents, 25 §69.
  Development of plan, 25 §67.
  Filing, 25 §69.
  Misdemeanors.
    Preventing right of entry, 25 §67.
  Right of entry.
    Development of plan, 25 §67.
  Statement of board of managers, 25 §69.
Waters of the state.
  Effect on water rights, 25 §95.

DRAINS.
Counties.
  Chartered counties.
    Storm drainage.
      Powers of county, 25A §5.
  Roads, 25 §138.
Insurance.
  Homeowner's insurance coverage for water
    backing up through drains, IN §19-202.

DRAWBACKS.
**Rate discrimination by public service
    company,** PUC §4-503.

**DREDGED MATERIAL DISPOSAL
    ALTERNATIVES PROGRAM,** 83A §§6-801,
    6-802.

DREDGING.
Oysters and clams.
  See OYSTERS AND CLAMS.
Submerged aquatic vegetation zones, NR
    §4-1006.1.
Waterway improvement fund, NR §§8-707 to
    8-709.

DRESSING ROOMS.
Surveillance of individual in private place, CR
    §3-901.
  With prurient intent, CR §3-902.

DRILLING.
Well drilling, EN §§9-1301 to 9-1311.
  See WELL DRILLING.

DRINKING DRIVER MONITOR PROGRAM.
Division of parole and probation.
  Administration and funding of program, COR
    §6-104.

DRINKING DRIVER MONITOR PROGRAM
  —Cont'd
Fees for supervision, COR §6-115.
Fund, COR §6-116.

DRINKING WATER.
Administrator.
  Defined, EN §9-401.
  Records and reports, EN §9-407.
Analysis, HG §21-336.
Artesian water.
  Collecting, bottling or delivering, HG §21-336.
Bottled water, HG §21-336.1.
Community water supply systems.
  Defined, EN §9-401.
  Prerequisites to commencement of operation, EN
    §9-417.
Conservation of water.
  Public water systems, EN §§5-5B-01 to 5-5B-05.
Contaminant.
  Dangerous contaminant, EN §9-405.
  Defined, EN §9-401.
Contaminant level.
  Notice by water suppliers.
    Failure to comply with maximum levels, EN
      §9-410.
Contamination, CR §3-214.
  Family day care homes.
    Notice to family day care homes, FL §5-551.
      Water suppliers to provide notice, EN §9-410.
  Noncollegiate educational institutions.
    Notices required, ED §2-206.
      Water suppliers to provide notice, EN §9-410.
  Prevention and recall, HG §21-336.
  Public schools.
    Notices required, ED §7-422.
      Water suppliers to provide notice, EN §9-410.
Contempt.
  Hearings on violations.
    Failure to obey orders of department in
      connection with, EN §9-415.
Dangerous contaminant.
  Action by secretary to prevent contamination, EN
    §9-405.
  Defined, EN §9-405.
Definitions, EN §9-401.
  Administrator, EN §9-401.
  Collecting, bottling or delivering, HG §21-336.
  Contaminant, EN §9-401.
  Dangerous contaminant, EN §9-405.
  Federal act, EN §9-401.
  Federal agency, EN §9-401.
  National primary drinking water regulations, EN
    §9-401.
  Person, EN §9-401.
  Primary drinking water regulations, EN §9-401.
  Public water system, EN §9-401.
  Supplier of water, EN §9-401.
  Water supply facility, EN §9-420.
Department of the environment.
  Powers supplemental, EN §9-403.
Effect of subtitle on other powers, EN §9-403.
Emergencies.
  Safe drinking water emergencies.
    Adoption of plan, EN §9-406.
  Secretary.
    Power to act in emergencies, EN §9-406.
Family day care homes.
  Contamination.
    Notice to family day care homes, FL §5-551.
      Water suppliers to provide notice, EN §9-410.

DRINKING WATER —Cont'd
Federal act.
  Defined, EN §9-401.
Federal agency.
  Defined, EN §9-401.
**Financial assistance for water supply
    facilities.**
  Authority to make awards, EN §9-420.
  County water and sewer plans.
    Inclusion of project in.
      Required, EN §9-426.
  Eligible costs, EN §9-425.
    Limitation on state assistance, EN §9-421.
  Establishment of program, EN §9-420.
  Grants, EN §9-421.
    Conditions, EN §9-422.
    Federal grants.
      Effect, EN §9-421.
  Limitations on state assistance.
    Amount of loan guarantees, EN §9-424.
    Amount of loans, EN §9-422.
  Loan guarantees, EN §9-424.
  Loans, EN §9-421.
    Amount.
      Limitations, EN §9-422.
    Interest, EN §9-422.
    Terms and conditions, EN §9-422.
  Planning.
    County water and sewer plans.
      Inclusion of project in.
        Required, EN §9-426.
  Project priorities systems, EN §9-423.
  Rules and regulations, EN §9-423.
Injunctions.
  Secretary may bring action.
    Injunction, EN §9-411.
  Violators of rules or regulations.
    Action for injunction against, EN §9-416.
Inspections, HG §21-336.
  Right of entry.
    Representatives of secretary, EN §9-261.
Interest.
  Financial assistance for water supply facilities.
    Loans, EN §9-422.
Labels, HG §21-336.
Laboratories.
  Water quality laboratories, EN §§9-1001 to
    9-1027.
  See WATER QUALITY LABORATORIES.
Legislative policy, EN §9-402.
Licenses.
  Collecting, bottling or delivering, HG §21-336.
    Suspension or revocation, HG §21-336.
Loans.
  Financial assistance for water supply facilities.
    See within this heading, "Financial assistance
      for water supply facilities."
Mineral water.
  Collecting, bottling or delivering, HG §21-336.
National primary drinking water regulations.
  Defined, EN §9-401.
Natural water.
  Collecting, bottling or delivering, HG §21-336.
**Nontransient noncommunity water supply
    systems.**
  Defined, EN §9-401.
  Prerequisites to commencement of operation, EN
    §9-417.
Notices.
  Public water systems, EN §9-410.

DRINKING WATER —Cont'd
Penalties.
Civil penalty, EN §§9-412.1, 9-413, 9-628.
Collecting, bottling or delivering.
Violations of provisions, HG §21-336.
Criminal penalties, EN §9-314.
Permits.
Revocation, change and expiration, EN §9-262.
Person.
Defined, EN §9-401.
Primary drinking water regulations. See within
this heading, "State primary drinking water
regulations."
Prohibited acts, EN §§9-412, 9-412.1.
Penalties, EN §9-314.
Public water system.
Action by secretary to prevent contamination, EN
§9-405.
Defined, EN §9-401.
Notice given, EN §9-410.
Purified water.
Collecting, bottling or delivering, HG §21-336.
Purpose of subtitle, EN §9-402.
Records.
Required records, EN §9-261.
Registration.
Required to sell water shipped from outside state,
HG §21-336.
Right of entry.
Representatives of secretary, EN §9-261.
Rules and regulations.
Collecting, bottling or delivering, HG §21-336.
Financial assistance for water supply facilities,
EN §9-423.
State primary drinking water regulations, EN
§§9-407 to 9-409.
**Schools, family day care homes and child care
centers.**
Contamination.
Noncollegiate educational institutions.
Notices required, ED §2-206.
Notice to family day care homes, FL §5-551.
Public schools.
Notices required, ED §7-422.
Water supplier notices, EN §9-410.
Secretary.
Action to prevent public water system
contamination, EN §9-405.
Emergencies.
Power to act in emergencies, EN §9-406.
Failure to comply with order.
Civil penalty, EN §§9-268, 9-413.
Injunctions, EN §9-411.
Power to act, EN §9-405.
Safe drinking water emergency.
Secretary to adopt plan, EN §9-406.
Spring water.
Collecting, bottling or delivering, HG §21-336.
State primary drinking water regulations.
Adoption by secretary, EN §9-407.
Application, EN §9-408.
Definition, EN §9-401.
Exceptions, EN §9-408.
Scope of enforcement procedures, EN §9-407.
Variances, EN §9-409.
Subpoenas.
Hearings on violations, EN §9-415.
Suppliers of water.
Defined, EN §9-401.
Prohibited acts, EN §9-412.

DRINKING WATER —Cont'd
Tampering with public water system.
Civil penalty, EN §9-412.1.
Definition of "tamper," EN §9-401.
Prohibited, EN §9-412.1.
Testing bottled water, HG §21-336.
Testing procedures.
Notice by water suppliers.
Failure to comply, EN §9-410.
Tests of water and wastewater, EN §9-255.
Treatment techniques.
Notice by water suppliers.
Failure to comply, EN §9-410.
Violations.
Civil penalty, EN §§9-412.1, 9-413, 9-628.
Criminal penalties, EN §9-413.
Injunctions.
Action for, EN §9-416.
Order or notice.
Hearings on, EN §9-415.
Order or notice by department, EN §9-414.
Water conservation.
Public water systems, EN §§5-5B-01 to 5-5B-05.
Water quality laboratories, EN §§9-1001 to
9-1027.
See WATER QUALITY LABORATORIES.
Water supply facilities.
Defined, EN §9-420.
Financial assistance, EN §§9-420 to 9-426. See
within this heading, "Financial assistance for
water supply facilities."
Well drilling, EN §§9-1301 to 9-1311.
See WELL DRILLING.
Well water.
Collecting, bottling or delivering, HG §21-336.

DRINKING WATER REVOLVING LOAN FUND,
EN §9-1605.1.

DRINKS.
Alcoholic beverages.
See ALCOHOLIC BEVERAGES.
Soft drinks.
See SOFT DRINKS.

DRIVER EDUCATION PROGRAM, TR §§16-501
to 16-507.
Certificates.
Refusal, suspension or revocation of certificate, TR
§16-506.
**County boards of education may offer
instruction,** ED §7-414.
Credit.
Determined by state board of education, ED
§7-414.
Definitions, TR §16-501.
Drivers' schools, TR §§15-101 to 15-113, 15-701 to
15-710.
See DRIVERS' SCHOOLS.
Elective or required course.
Determined by county boards of education, ED
§7-414.
Eligibility, TR §16-503.
Established, TR §16-502.
Hearings.
Refusal, suspension or revocation of certificate, TR
§16-506.
Identification of motor vehicles, ED §7-414.
Instructors.
Definitions, TR §16-501.
Driving instructors generally, TR §§15-101 to
15-113, 15-801 to 15-807.
See DRIVING INSTRUCTORS.

DRIVER EDUCATION PROGRAM —Cont'd
Instructors —Cont'd
Qualifications and certification, TR §16-504.
Refusal, suspension or revocation of certificate, TR §16-506.
Purpose, TR §16-502.
Regulations, TR §16-505.
Short title, TR §16-507.
Students.
Driving by, TR §16-105.1.

DRIVER IMPROVEMENT PROGRAM, TR §16-212.

DRIVER LICENSE COMPACT, TR §§16-701 to 16-708.
Administrator, TR §16-703.
Alternate compact administrator.
Designation, TR §16-704.
Compensation, TR §16-706.
Designation.
Motor vehicle administrator designated as compact administrator, TR §16-704.
Expenses.
Reimbursement, TR §16-706.
Interchange of information, TR §§16-703, 16-705.
Powers, TR §16-703.
Appeals.
Judicial review, TR §16-708.
Applicability of other laws, TR §16-703.
Applications for new licenses, TR §16-703.
Conviction.
Effect, TR §§16-703, 16-707.
Reports, TR §16-703.
Declaration of policy, TR §16-703.
Definitions, TR §§16-701, 16-703.
Effective date, TR §16-703.
Enacted and entered into with other jurisdictions, TR §16-702.
Findings, TR §16-703.
Foreign jurisdictions.
Compact enacted and entered into with other jurisdictions, TR §16-702.
Interchange of information.
Administration to furnish information or documents to other states, TR §16-705.
Interpretation and construction, TR §16-703.
Judicial review, TR §16-708.
New licenses.
Applications, TR §16-703.
Point system.
Suspension, revocation or refusal of license.
Assessment of points upon notice of conviction of certain offenses by a party state, TR §16-402.1.
Reports.
Convictions, TR §16-703.
Severability of provisions, TR §16-703.
Suspension, revocation or refusal of license.
Point system.
Assessment of points upon notice of conviction of certain offenses by a party state, TR §16-402.1.
Text of compact, TR §16-703.

DRIVERS' LICENSES, TR §§16-101 to 16-904.
Address.
Notice of change of address, TR §16-116.
Advance directives, TR §12-303.1.
Age.
Requirements, TR §16-103.

DRIVERS' LICENSES —Cont'd
Alcoholic beverages.
See DRIVING UNDER THE INFLUENCE.
Aliens.
Exemption of nonresidents of United States, TR §16-102.
Anatomical gift act.
Notation that licensee is donor, TR §§12-303, 12-303.1.
Appeals.
Suspension, revocation or refusal of license.
Child support arrearages, FL §10-119; TR §16-203.
Application, TR §16-106.
Anatomical gift act.
Notation that licensee is donor, TR §§12-303, 12-303.1.
Authority to approve or reject, TR §12-106.
Examination, TR §16-110.
Time for taking examination for driver's license, TR §16-105.
Fraudulently using false or fictitious name, TR §16-301.
Minors.
Signing by parent or guardian or other responsible person, TR §16-107.
Suspension of minor's license on request of cosigner, TR §16-108.
Vision requirements of applicant, TR §16-110.1.
Bioptic telescopic lenses, TR §16-110.2.
Daylight driving only and outside mirrors each side restricted licenses, TR §16-110.3.
Armed forces and dependents.
Exemption, TR §16-102.
Suspension and revocation of license.
Point system, TR §16-403.
Blind persons.
Public assistance for blindness.
Administration to obtain names of persons receiving, TR §16-120.
Vision requirements, TR §16-110.1.
Boat trailers.
Noncommercial licenses.
Authority to tow boat trailers, TR §16-104.1.
Burden of proof.
Driving while privilege suspended, refused or revoked, TR §13-705.1.
Camping trailers.
Noncommercial licenses.
Authority to tow camping trailers, TR §16-104.1.
Cancelled license.
Authority of administration, TR §16-201.
"Cancel" defined, TR §11-107.
Driving while privilege is cancelled, TR §16-303.
Surrender to administration, TR §16-201.
Carried with driver, TR §16-112.
Child support.
Suspension or restriction for arrearages, FL §10-119; TR §16-203.
Classes, TR §16-104.
Age requirements, TR §16-103.
Driving vehicle not authorized by license, TR §16-104.
Number of points assessed, TR §16-402.
Indicated on license, TR §16-111.
Noncommercial licenses, TR §16-104.1.
Commercial drivers' licenses, TR §§16-801 to 16-820.
See COMMERCIAL DRIVERS' LICENSES.

DRIVERS' LICENSES —Cont'd
Compact, TR §§16-701 to 16-708.
  See DRIVER LICENSE COMPACT.
Congress.
  Nonresidents.
    Persons exempt from license, TR §16-102.
Contents, TR §16-111.
Corrected licenses, TR §16-114.1.
Definitions, TR §11-116.
  "Cancel," TR §11-107.
  Commercial drivers' licenses, TR §11-109.
  Conviction, TR §11-110.
  License to drive, TR §11-128.
  Revocation, TR §11-150.
  Suspension, TR §11-164.
  Underage drinking, CR §10-119.
Diplomatic immunity licensees.
  Applicability of provisions, TR §16-901.
  Copies of documents to be sent to State
    Department, TR §16-904.
  Duties of administration, TR §16-903.
  Duties of police officer, TR §16-902.
Disabled persons.
  Examinations, TR §16-119.
Disclosure of personal information, TR §12-112.
Display to uniformed officer, TR §16-112.
Driving test, TR §16-110.
Drugs.
  Conviction.
    Persons convicted of certain offenses involving
      drugs, TR §16-205.
Drunkenness.
  See DRIVING UNDER THE INFLUENCE.
Duplicate license, TR §16-114.
  Fees, TR §16-111.2.
Duplication, TR §16-302.
Examination, TR §16-110.
  Commercial drivers' licenses.
    Issued upon passing examination, TR §16-110.
  Disabled persons, TR §16-119.
  Driving test, TR §16-110.
  Reexamination, TR §16-207.
  Time for taking examination for driver's license,
    TR §16-105.
  Vision tests.
    Test prerequisite for renewal of license, TR
      §16-115.
    Waiver prohibited, TR §16-110.
Exceptions.
  What persons are exempt from license, TR
    §16-102.
Expiration, TR §16-115.
Expungement of certain driving records, TR
  §16-117.1.
Eyes.
  Bioptic telescopic lenses, TR §16-110.2.
  Vision tests, TR §16-110.1.
    Daylight driving only and outside mirrors each
      side restricted licenses, TR §16-110.3.
    Renewal of license, TR §16-115.
    Waiver prohibited, TR §16-110.
False name.
  Giving to officer, TR §16-112.
Fees, TR §§16-111.1, 16-111.2.
  Corrected licenses, TR §16-114.1.
  Restoring revoked driving privilege, TR §16-209.
For-hire drivers' licenses generally, PUC
  §§10-101 to 10-112.
  See FOR-HIRE DRIVING SERVICES.
Form, TR §16-111.

DRIVERS' LICENSES —Cont'd
Hearings.
  Suspension, revocation or refusal of license.
    Child support arrearages, TR §16-203.
Identification cards.
  Special identification cards, TR §§12-301, 16-302.
Identity fraud, CR §§8-301 to 8-305.
Ignition interlock system program, TR
  §16-404.1.
Immunity.
  Diplomatic officers, TR §§16-901 to 16-905.
Issuance, TR §16-111.1.
  When applicant entitled to receive license, TR
    §16-111.
  Without learner's permit, TR §16-105.
Learner's permit, TR §16-105.
  Age requirement, TR §16-103.
  Fee, TR §16-111.2.
Medical advisory board, TR §16-118.
Minors.
  Causing or permitting unauthorized minor to
    drive, TR §16-304.
    Number of points assessed, TR §16-402.
  Destructive devices, manufacture or possession.
    Suspension of driving privilege, CR §4-503.
  False statement concerning destructive device or
    toxic material.
    Suspension of driving privilege, CR §9-504.
  Signing by parent of application of minor, TR
    §16-107.
  Suspension of minor's license on request of
    cosigner, TR §16-108.
Mopeds, TR §16-104.2.
Motorcycles.
  Class M license, TR §16-104.1.
Motor voter registration.
  Application procedures, EL §3-203.
  Authorized method of registering, EL §3-201.
Moving violations.
  Sanctions, TR §16-213.
Name.
  Application.
    Name change, TR §16-106.
    Notice of change of name, TR §16-116.
New residents.
  Exempt, TR §16-102.
Noncommercial license.
  Classes, TR §16-104.1.
  Fees, TR §16-111.2.
Nonresidents.
  Copy of driver's record from another jurisdiction,
    TR §16-106.
  Issuance without learner's permit, TR §16-105.
  No driving under refused, suspended or revoked
    foreign license in this state, TR §16-211.
  Surrender of out-of-state license, TR §16-111.
Notice.
  Change of address or name, TR §16-116.
  Expiration, TR §16-115.
  Suspension, revocation or refusal of license.
    Child support arrearages, FL §10-119; TR
      §16-203.
Not to be licensed.
  What persons shall not be licensed, TR §16-103.1.
Number, TR §16-111.
One license per person, TR §16-111.
Penalties, TR §27-101.
  Persons exempt from license requirements, TR
    §16-102.
  Surcharges, TR §27-101.2.

DRIVERS' LICENSES —Cont'd
Point system, TR §§16-401 to 16-407.
Accumulated points.
Effect, TR §16-404.
Administration.
Action by, TR §16-404.
Maintenance of system, TR §16-401.
Applicability of point system, TR §16-303.
Assessment of points, TR §16-402.
Conviction of certain offenses by party state to driver license compact, TR §16-402.1.
Certain violations not to be recorded against employee of vehicle's owner, TR §16-406.
Conviction.
Multiple charges, TR §16-402.
Duration of points, TR §16-407.
Duration of suspension, TR §16-404.
Employment of licensee.
Adverse effects, TR §16-405.
Enumeration of points, TR §16-402.
Extension of license revocation, TR §16-402.
Initial points, TR §16-402.
Maintenance by administration, TR §16-401.
Military personnel, TR §16-403.
Notice.
Administration to issue notice, TR §16-404.
Prohibited.
What persons shall not be licensed, TR §16-103.1.
Provisional drivers' licenses.
Age requirement, TR §16-103.
Minors.
Provisional license holders transporting, TR §21-1123.
Wireless communications devices, use while driving, TR §21-1124.
Seat belt restriction, TR §16-113.
Qualifications.
Determined by administration, TR §16-110.
Records.
Expungement of certain driving records, TR §16-117.1.
Forwarding driver's record to another jurisdiction, TR §16-106.
Kept by administration, TR §16-117.
Reinstatement.
Suspension or restriction child support arrearages, FL §10-119; TR §16-203.
Removal to another state.
Forwarding driver's record, TR §16-106.
Renewal, TR §16-115.
Fees, TR §16-111.2.
Renting vehicles to another, TR §18-103.
Reproduction, TR §16-302.
Required, TR §16-101.
Restricted licenses, TR §§16-110.1, 16-113.
Rules and regulations.
Suspension or restriction for child support arrearages, FL §10-119; TR §16-203.
Selective service administration registration.
Information of male applications provided by administration, TR §12-304.
Signature, TR §16-111.
In presence of officer.
Officer determining whether driver licensee, TR §16-112.
Social security number.
Use as identifying number, TR §16-111.
Students.
Nonresidents.
Persons exempt from license, TR §16-102.

DRIVERS' LICENSES —Cont'd
Surrender and return.
Suspension, cancellation or revocation of license, TR §16-210.
Suspension, revocation or refusal of license.
Accidents.
Reports.
Failure to make report, TR §20-109.
Authority of administration, TR §16-206.
Automobile insurance fund.
Cancellation, rejection or nonrenewal of coverage, IN §§20-516, 20-518.
Continuation of coverage for family members, IN §20-519.
Child subject to suspension under, CJ §3-8A-19; TR §16-206.
Child support arrearages, FL §10-119; TR §16-203.
Suspension of driving privileges for, FL §10-119.
Commercial drivers' licenses.
See COMMERCIAL DRIVERS' LICENSES.
Definitions.
"Cancel," TR §11-107.
Conviction, TR §11-110.
Revocation of driver's license, TR §11-150.
Suspension of driver's license, TR §11-164.
Display of such license, TR §16-301.
Driving while privilege is suspended, refused or revoked, TR §16-303.
Burden of proof, TR §13-705.1.
Impoundment or immobilization or vehicle, TR §27-111.
Penalties, TR §27-101.
Suspension of registration, TR §13-705.1.
Examination.
Reexamination, TR §16-207.
Fees.
Restoring revoked driving privilege, TR §16-209.
Fines.
Suspension for nonpayment, TR §27-103.
Foreign license.
No driving under refused, suspended or revoked foreign license in this state, TR §16-211.
Grounds.
Generally, TR §16-206.
Hearing, TR §16-206.
Intoxication, TR §16-205.1.
Minors.
Provisional license holders transporting, TR §21-1123.
Wireless communications devices used while driving, TR §21-1124.
Motor fuel, failure to pay after dispensing, TR §16-206.1.
Nonpayment of fine, TR §27-103.
Nonresidents.
Authority of administration, TR §16-202.
Conviction.
Reporting, TR §16-202.
Drunkenness.
Suspension of driving privileges, TR §16-205.1.
Implied consent to chemical tests, TR §16-205.1.
Notice.
General provisions, TR §16-206.
Notice of suspension to nonresident's state of residence, TR §16-202.
Outstanding warrants, TR §16-204.
Owner of vehicle.
Certain violations not to be recorded against employee of vehicle's owner, TR §16-406.

DRIVERS' LICENSES —Cont'd
Suspension, revocation or refusal of license
     —Cont'd
  Period of suspension, TR §16-208.
  Persons subject to suspension, TR §16-206.
  Point system, TR §§16-401 to 16-407. See within
     this heading, "Point system."
  Police.
     Stopping, etc., driver suspected of being under
        influence of drugs or intoxicants.
        Duty of police, TR §16-205.1.
  Possession of such license, TR §16-301.
  Registration suspension for driving when license
     suspended or revoked, TR §13-705.1.
  Reinstatement of revoked license, TR §16-208.
     Fee, TR §16-209.
  Required security.
     Failure to furnish evidence, TR §17-105.
  Return of license, TR §16-210.
  Surrender of license, TR §16-210.
  Unsatisfied judgments, TR §§17-201 to 17-209.
     See MOTOR VEHICLE REGISTRATION.
Taxicabs.
  Fee, PUC §2-111.
  For-hire drivers' licenses generally, PUC §§10-101
     to 10-112.
     See FOR-HIRE DRIVING SERVICES.
Temporary drivers' licenses.
  General provisions, TR §16-116.
Towing.
  Noncommercial licenses.
     Towing activities authorized, TR §16-104.1.
Trailers.
  Noncommercial licenses.
     Towing activities authorized, TR §16-104.1.
Travel trailers.
  Noncommercial licenses.
     Authority to tow travel trailers, TR §16-104.1.
Unauthorized person.
  Causing or permitting vehicle to be driven by, TR
     §16-305.
     Number of points assessed, TR §16-402.
     Unauthorized minor, TR §16-304.
Unauthorized use.
  General provisions, TR §16-301.
Violations.
  Certain violations not to be recorded against
     employee of vehicle's owner, TR §16-406.
  General provisions, TR §§16-301 to 16-305.
Vision tests, TR §16-110.1.
  Daylight driving only and outside mirrors each
     side restricted licenses, TR §16-110.3.
  Prerequisite for renewal of license, TR §16-115.
  Restricted licenses, TR §16-110.1.
  Waiver prohibited, TR §16-110.
Voter registration.
  Application procedures, EL §3-203.
  Authorized method of registering, EL §3-201.

DRIVERS' SCHOOLS, TR §§15-101 to 15-113,
     15-701 to 15-710.
Applications for license, TR §15-102.
  Fee, TR §§15-102, 15-703.
  Information required.
     Licensees to report changed information, TR
        §15-106.
Bonds, surety, TR §§15-103, 15-705.
  Proof, TR §15-706.
Condition of vehicles.
  Requirements, TR §15-708.
Definitions, TR §15-701.

DRIVERS' SCHOOLS —Cont'd
Display of license.
  Required, TR §15-707.
Duplicate license, TR §15-107.
Duty of licensee to keep record, TR §15-105.
Fees, TR §15-704.
  License application fee, TR §§15-102, 15-703.
Hearings.
  Refusal, suspension or revocation of license, TR
     §15-110.
Inspection of records, TR §15-105.
Instructors.
  General provisions, TR §§15-101 to 15-113, 15-801
     to 15-807.
     See DRIVING INSTRUCTORS.
  Use of licensed instructors, TR §15-709.
Issuance of license, TR §15-104.
Location requirements, TR §15-105.
Refusal of license.
  Grounds, TR §§15-109, 15-710.
  Hearing, TR §15-110.
Renewal of license, TR §15-107.
  Suspension or revocation following, TR §15-710.
Requirement of license, TR §15-702.
Revocation or suspension of license.
  Conciliatory conferences, TR §15-110.1.
  Grounds, TR §§15-109, 15-710.
  Hearing, TR §15-110.
  Renewal.
     Suspension or revocation after renewal, TR
        §15-710.
  Return of license, TR §15-111.
Scope of license, TR §15-707.

DRIVE-THRU DELIVERIES, IN §15-812.

DRIVE-THRU PURCHASE FACILITIES.
Alcoholic beverage licenses, 2B §§9-211.1, 9-214,
     10-503.
  Carroll county, 2B §12-207.
  Cecil county, 2B §10-503.
  Frederick, 2B §§9-211.1, 10-503.
  Harford county, 2B §§9-213, 10-503.
  Howard county, 2B §§9-214, 10-503.
  St. Mary's county, 2B §§9-219, 10-503.
  Worcester county, 2B §§9-224, 10-503.

DRIVING INSTRUCTORS, TR §§15-101 to
     15-113, 15-801 to 15-807.
Applications for license, TR §15-102.
  Additional information required, TR §15-804.
     Licensees to report changed information, TR
        §15-106.
Bonds, surety, TR §15-103.
Definitions, TR §15-801.
Driver education program, TR §§16-501 to
     16-507.
     See DRIVER EDUCATION PROGRAM.
Drivers' schools.
  Use of licensed instructors, TR §15-709.
Duplicate licenses, TR §15-107.
Duty of licensee to keep record, TR §15-105.
Fees, TR §15-805.
  License application fee, TR §15-102.
Hearings.
  Refusal, suspension or revocation of license, TR
     §15-110.
Inspection of records, TR §15-105.
Issuance of license, TR §15-104.
Location requirements, TR §15-105.
Penalties.
  Suspension, revocation, or refusal to renew
     license.
     Fine instead of, or in addition to, TR §15-807.

DRIVING INSTRUCTORS —Cont'd
Qualifications, TR §15-803.
Refusal of license.
  Grounds, TR §§15-109, 15-807.
  Hearing, TR §15-110.
Requirement of license, TR §15-802.
Revocation or suspension of license.
  Conciliatory conferences, TR §15-110.1.
  Grounds, TR §§15-109, 15-807.
  Hearing, TR §15-110.
  Return of license, TR §15-111.
Scope of license, TR §15-806.

DRIVING UNDER THE INFLUENCE.
Ability impaired by consumption of alcohol.
  Lesser included offenses, TR §26-405.
  Scope of subtitle, TR §21-901.
Alcohol and drug abuse education, TR §§16-212,
    16-212.1.
  Probation, conditions, CP §§6-219, 6-220.
Analysis of alcohol on breath or in blood.
  Evidence, presumption of impairment, CJ
    §10-307.
Arrest for serious offenses, TR §26-201.
Breath tests, TR §16-205.2.
  Alcohol concentration limitation, TR §21-902.
Chemical tests.
  Administration, CJ §10-304; TR §16-205.1.
  Admissibility by analysis.
    Extent of limits on admissibility, CJ §10-309.
    Lack of presence or testimony of technician, CJ
      §10-306.
  Analysis, CJ §10-307.
  Breath tests, TR §16-205.2.
  Circumstances under which chemical tests
    required, TR §16-205.1.
  Controlled dangerous substances in blood.
    Results of tests, evidence, CJ §10-308.
  Definitions, CJ §10-301.1.
  Evidence of alcohol on breath or in blood, CJ
    §10-307.
  Evidence of controlled dangerous substances in
    blood.
    Results of tests, CJ §10-308.
  Introduction of other evidence, CJ §10-308.
  Persons administering tests, CJ §10-304.
  Police.
    Officer arresting individuals may not administer
      chemical test of breath, CJ §10-304.
  Preliminary breath test, TR §16-205.2.
  Presumptions, CJ §10-307.
  Prima facie evidence of impairment or alcohol in
    blood, CJ §10-307.
  Procedure where individual incapable of refusal,
    CJ §10-305; TR §16-205.1.
  Purpose, CJ §10-302.
  Refusal to submit to test, CJ §10-309.
  Request by accused, CJ §10-304.
  Specimens, CJ §10-303.
  Subpoena for toxicologists, CJ §10-304.
  Time limitations, CJ §10-303.
  Types, CJ §10-305.
Commercial drivers' licenses.
  Disqualification, TR §§16-205.1, 16-812.
**Consumption of alcoholic beverages while
    driving,** TR §21-903.
Definitions.
  Under the influence, CJ §10-307.
  Under the influence of alcohol per se, CR §2-501;
    TR §11-174.1.

DRIVING UNDER THE INFLUENCE —Cont'd
Drinking driver monitor program.
  Division of parole and probation.
    Administration and funding of program, COR
      §6-104.
  Fees for supervision, COR §6-115.
  Fund, COR §6-116.
Drivers' licenses.
  Commercial drivers' licenses, TR §§16-205.1,
    16-812.
  Drugs, TR §§16-103.1, 16-205.
  Habitual drunkards.
    What persons shall not be licensed, TR
      §16-103.1.
  Suspension of license on refusal to submit to
    chemical tests, TR §§16-205, 16-205.1.
Driving after arrest, TR §§21-902.1, 27-101.
Evidence.
  Analysis of alcohol on breath or in blood, CJ
    §10-307.
  Drugs or controlled dangerous substances in
    blood.
    Results of tests, CJ §10-308.
  Other evidence, CJ §10-308.
  Prima facie evidence.
    Impairment or alcohol in blood, CJ §10-307.
  Refusal to submit to test, CJ §10-309.
General prohibition, TR §21-902.
**Homicide by vehicle or vessel while impaired
    or under the influence.**
  Alcohol concentration measurement, determining,
    CR §2-502.
  Indictment, information or charging document,
    sufficiency, CR §2-507.
  Notice of conviction to motor vehicle
    administration, CR §2-508.
  Presumptions and evidentiary rules, CR §2-502.
  Under the influence of alcohol or under the
    influence of alcohol per se, CR §2-503.
  Under the influence the influence of alcohol or
    under the influence of alcohol per se.
    Under the influence of alcohol per se defined,
      CR §2-501.
  While impaired by alcohol, CR §2-504.
  While impaired by controlled dangerous
    substance, CR §2-506.
    Entitlement to use of controlled dangerous
      substance, exception, CR §2-506.
  While impaired by drugs, CR §2-505.
    Entitlement to use of drugs, defense, CR §2-505.
Ignition interlock system, TR §§27-107, 27-108.
  Probation before judgment, conditions of, CP
    §6-220.
Ignition interlock system program, TR
    §16-404.1.
Impairment of ability.
  Consumption of alcohol and/or drugs, TR §21-902.
  Penalties, TR §27-101.
Implied consent law, TR §16-205.1.
Impoundment of immobilization of vehicle, TR
    §27-111.
**Life threatening injury by motor vehicle of
    vessel while impaired or under the
    influence.**
  Charging documents, CR §3-212.
  Definitions, CR §3-211.
  Impaired by alcohol, CR §3-211.
  Impaired by controlled dangerous substance, CR
    §3-211.
  Impaired by drugs, CR §3-211.

DRIVING UNDER THE INFLUENCE —Cont'd
Life threatening injury by motor vehicle of vessel while impaired or under the influence —Cont'd
Under the influence of alcohol or alcohol per se, CR §3-211.
Life threatening injury by motor vehicle or vessel while impaired or under the influence.
Alcohol concentration.
Determining, presumptions, evidentiary rules, CR §3-211.
Minors as passengers.
Prohibitions while transporting, TR §21-902.
Penalties, TR §27-101.
Ignition interlock system, TR §§27-107, 27-108.
Surcharge, TR §27-101.2.
Percentage of alcohol in blood, CJ §10-307.
Legal limit, TR §21-902.
Point system.
Assessment of points, TR §16-402.
Police.
Breath tests.
Officer arresting individual may not administer chemical test of breath, CJ §10-304.
Duty of police on stopping or detaining suspected person, TR §16-205.1.
Preliminary breath tests, TR §16-205.2.
Prima facie evidence.
Impairment or alcohol in blood, CJ §10-307.
Refusal to submit to test, CJ §10-309.
Rental of vehicles to persons under influence of alcohol or drugs, TR §18-105.
Transportation of minors.
Penalties, TR §27-101.
Twelve-hour prohibition on driving after arrest, TR §§21-902.1, 27-101.
Under the influence defined, CJ §10-307.
Unlicensed persons.
Chemical test refusal.
Suspension of driving privileges, TR §16-205.1.

DROP.
Law enforcement officers' pension system.
Deferred retirement option program, SPP §26-401.1.

DROUGHT.
Emergency management, PS §§14-101 to 14-1004.
See EMERGENCY MANAGEMENT.

DRUG ASSET FORFEITURE, CP §§12-101 to 12-505.
Definitions, CP §12-101.
Disposition of forfeited property, CP §§12-401 to 12-404.
Options for governing body, CP §12-403.
Posthearing orders, CP §12-402.
Powers of court, CP §12-401.
Terms of sale, CP §12-404.
Forfeiture proceedings, CP §§12-301 to 12-311.
Answer to complaint, CP §12-307.
Application for forfeiture of money, CP §12-302.
Complaint process, CP §§12-303 to 12-308.
Contents and distribution of complaint, CP §12-305.
Contents of complaint, CP §12-305.
Deadline for filing complaint, CP §12-304.
Distribution of complaint, CP §12-305.
Filing of complaint, CP §12-303.
Generally, CP §12-301.
Hearing on claim, CP §12-308.

DRUG ASSET FORFEITURE —Cont'd
Forfeiture proceedings —Cont'd
Notice of proceedings, CP §12-306.
Real property, CP §§12-309 to 12-312.
Rebuttable presumption property subject to forfeiture, CP §12-312.
Lienholders.
Effect of title, CP §12-505.
Laws governing sale of collateral securing an obligation, CP §12-502.
Proceeds of sale, CP §12-503.
Redemption of interest or repossession of property, CP §12-504.
Sale of seized property, CP §12-501.
Money and weapons.
Property subject to forfeiture, CP §12-102.
Motor vehicles.
Seizure of property, CP §12-203.
No consent or privity to violation.
Conditions for excluding property from forfeiture, CP §12-103.
No knowledge of violation.
Conditions for excluding property from forfeiture, CP §12-103.
Notice.
Forfeiture proceedings.
Real estate forfeitures, CP §12-310.
Lienholder sale of seized property, CP §12-501.
Owner obtaining possession of seized property, CP §12-208.
Redemption of interest or repossession of property, CP §12-504.
Principal family residence.
Property excluded from forfeiture, CP §12-103.
Property used as principal family residence exempted, CP §12-312.
Stay of forfeiture of principal family residence, CP §12-311.
Property excluded from forfeiture, CP §12-103.
Property subject to forfeiture, CP §12-102.
Real property forfeiture proceedings, CP §§12-309 to 12-312.
Criteria for forfeiture, CP §12-309.
Generally, CP §12-309.
Notice of pending litigation, CP §12-310.
Property used as principal family residence exempted, CP §12-312.
Stay of forfeiture of principal family residence, CP §12-311.
Venue, CP §12-310.
Seizure of motor vehicles, CP §§12-204 to 12-208.
Bond in lieu of seizure, CP §12-208.
Excepted motor vehicles, CP §12-205.
Owner obtaining possession of seized property, CP §12-208.
Recommendation by seizing authority, CP §12-206.
Return to owner after seizure, CP §12-207.
Standards applicable, CP §12-204.
Seizure of property generally, CP §§12-201 to 12-211.
Motor vehicles, CP §§12-204 to 12-208.
Property not repleviable, CP §12-203.
Removal of seized property, CP §12-203.
Seizure with and without warrant, CP §12-202.
Sequestering, CP §12-203.
Seizure of real property, CP §§12-209 to 12-211.
Prohibited acts, CP §12-211.

DRUG DEALER LIABILITY ACT.
Death caused by use of controlled dangerous substances, CJ §§3-1601 to 3-1607.
Actual cause of death, standard of liability, CJ §3-1604.
Assumption of risk inapplicable, CJ §3-1607.
Contributory negligence inapplicable, CJ §3-1607.
Controlled dangerous substance defined, CJ §3-1601.
Damages recoverable, CJ §3-1606.
Defenses not applicable, CJ §3-1607.
Economic damages, CJ §3-1606.
Law enforcement officer furthering official investigation.
Exempt from liability, CJ §3-1605.
Liability of dealers, CJ §3-1602.
Noneconomic damages, CJ §3-1606.
Persons acting in cooperation with law enforcement.
Exempt from liability, CJ §3-1605.
Persons who may bring action, CJ §3-1603.
Proximate cause of death, standard for liability, CJ §3-1604.
Right of action, CJ §3-1603.

DRUG-FREE SCHOOL ZONES.
Signs.
County boards of education.
Board may designate areas and adopt regulations, ED §4-124.
Hotline number.
Baltimore City, ED §4-124.

DRUG-FREE WORKPLACE.
Port administration, TR §6-102.1.

DRUG INDUCED CONDUCT.
Administering controlled dangerous substance without person knowledge, CR §5-624.

DRUG KINGPINS, CR §5-613.
Conspiracy to manufacture, distribute, dispense or transport into state, CR §5-613.
Defined, CR §5-613.
Enhanced penalty allowed, CR §5-613.
Merger of conviction with other crimes, prohibition, CR §5-613.
Pretrial release.
Restrictions on, CP §5-202.
Probation, prohibition, CR §5-613.
Prosecution for other crime allowed, CR §5-613.

DRUG OR ALCOHOL ABUSE.
Administration.
Commitment of criminal defendants for treatment.
Obligations of administration, HG §8-507.
Defined, HG §8-101.
Director.
Appointment, HG §8-202.
Defined, HG §8-101.
Duties.
Generally, HG §8-204.
Subject to authority of secretary, HG §8-203.
Powers.
Generally, HG §8-204.
Subject to authority of secretary, HG §8-203.
Qualifications, HG §8-202.
Reports to deputy secretary, HG §8-203.
Salary, HG §8-202.
Tenure, HG §8-202.
Established, HG §8-201.
Facilities and services.
Powers and duties, HG §8-402.

DRUG OR ALCOHOL ABUSE —Cont'd
Administration —Cont'd
Funds.
Special funds.
Acceptance and use, HG §8-206.
Programs.
Powers and duties generally, HG §8-401.
Admissions.
Facilities and services.
Alcohol abusers.
Detoxification facilities. See within this heading, "Detoxification facilities."
Private and public hospitals, HG §8-509.
Alcohol abuse.
Defined, HG §8-101.
State substance abuse policy, SPP §2-306.
Alcohol dependence.
Defined, HG §8-101.
Alcohol misuse.
Defined, HG §8-101.
Arrest.
Intoxicated persons.
Disposition, HG §8-502.
Authorized personnel.
Responsibility, HG §8-504.
Childbirth.
Fetal alcohol syndrome.
Public awareness campaign, HG §18-309.
Citation of title, HG §8-801.
Clinical alcohol and drug abuse counselors.
Licensing, HO §§17-3A-01 to 17-3A-13.
See PROFESSIONAL COUNSELORS AND THERAPISTS.
Commitments.
Alcohol abusers.
Privileged information.
Evidence and results of proceedings, HG §8-601.
Drug abusers.
Privileged information.
Evidence and results of proceedings, HG §8-601.
Evaluation.
Admissions to facilities, HG §8-506.
Duration, HG §8-506.
Leaving facility without authorization.
Notice to court that committed individual, HG §8-506.
Notice.
Leaving facility without authorization, HG §8-506.
Release, HG §8-506.
Prerequisites, HG §8-506.
Release, HG §8-506.
Services required, HG §8-506.
Termination, HG §8-506.
Transportation to facilities, HG §8-506.
Minors.
Admission to inpatient facilities, HG §8-502.1.
Contracts.
Facilities and services.
Authority of administration to enter contracts, HG §8-402.
Correctional institutions.
Administration facilities not correctional institutions, HG §8-402.
Programs in, HG §8-401.
Counties.
Local drug and alcohol abuse councils, HG §8-1001.
Creation, HG §8-201.

DRUG OR ALCOHOL ABUSE —Cont'd

Criminal defendants.
Commitment for evaluation, HG §8-506.
Commitment for treatment, HG §8-507.
Evaluation.
Generally, HG §8-505.
Treatment.
Commitment for, HG §8-507.

Criminal procedure.
Commitment of defendants for evaluation, HG §8-506.
Commitment of defendants for treatment, HG §8-507.
Evaluation of criminal defendants before or during trial, HG §8-505.

Custodial examinations.
Evaluation of criminal defendants, HG §8-505.

Definitions, HG §8-101.
Alcohol abuse and drug abuse treatment programs, HG §8-403.
Job-related alcohol and controlled dangerous substances testing, HG §17-214.

Detention facilities.
Evaluation of criminal defendants.
Custodial examinations, HG §8-505.

Detoxification facilities.
Admissions.
Generally, HG §8-502.
Publicly intoxicated individuals, HG §8-501.
Voluntary admissions.
Outpatient treatment programs, HG §8-508.
Arrested individuals.
Disposition, HG §8-503.
Defined, HG §8-101.
Detention.
Length of, HG §8-502.
Determinations.
Outpatient treatment programs.
Admissions, HG §8-508.
Intermediate care facility, alcoholic (type C or type D), HG §8-403.
Length of detention, HG §8-502.
Notice.
Right to leave, HG §8-502.
Outpatient treatment programs, HG §8-508.
Privileged information.
Evidence and results of proceedings, HG §8-601.
Publicly intoxicated individuals.
Admittance, HG §8-501.
Disposition generally, HG §8-501.
Right to leave.
Notice, HG §8-502.
Treatment.
Outpatients, HG §8-508.
Voluntary admissions.
Outpatient treatment programs, HG §8-508.

Director.
Generally. See within this heading, "Administration."

Discrimination.
Facilities and services, HG §8-402.
Health insurers, HG §19-703.1; IN §15-802.
Prohibited, HG §8-703.

District Court.
Authority to commit individuals for treatment, CJ §4-202.

Drug.
Defined, HG §8-101.

Drug abuse.
Defined, HG §8-101.
State substance abuse policy, SPP §2-306.

DRUG OR ALCOHOL ABUSE —Cont'd

Drug dependence.
Defined, HG §8-101.

Drug misuse.
Defined, HG §8-101.

Employers and employees.
Job-related alcohol and controlled dangerous substances testing, HG §17-214.
State substance abuse policy, SPP §2-306.

Evaluation.
Commitment for, HG §8-506.
Criminal defendants, HG §8-505.
Nolle prosequi or stet with requirement of drug or alcohol abuse treatment, CP §6-229.

Facilities and services.
Administration.
Powers and duties, HG §8-402.
Admissions.
Alcohol abusers.
Detoxification facilities. See within this heading, "Detoxification facilities."
Private and public hospitals, HG §8-509.
Commitments generally. See within this heading, "Commitments."
Community mental health facilities, HG §§24-601 to 24-607.
See MENTAL HEALTH FACILITIES.
Contracts.
Authority of administration to enter, HG §8-402.
Correctional institutions.
Administration facilities not correctional institutions, HG §8-402.
Detoxification facilities. See within this heading, "Detoxification facilities."
Discrimination prohibited, HG §8-402.
Generally, HG §8-402.
Identification, HG §8-402.
Intermediate care facility, alcoholic (type C or type D), HG §8-403.
Minors.
Admission to inpatient facilities, HG §8-502.1.
Operation, HG §8-402.
Programs.
Administration.
Powers and duties generally, HG §8-401.
Treatment programs. See within this heading, "Treatment programs."

Fetal alcohol syndrome.
Public awareness campaign, HG §18-309.

Fines.
Adjudication as drug or alcohol abuser or dependent.
Unlawful or improper adjudication, HG §8-701.
Treatment programs.
Operation in violation of title, HG §8-702.

Firearms.
Habitual drunkards or users.
Restrictions on sale, rental or transfer, PS §5-134.
Handgun permits.
Carrying, wearing or transporting handgun while under the influence, PS §5-314.
Disqualification, PS §5-306.
Restrictions on possession, PS §5-133.
Visibly intoxicated persons.
Restrictions on sale, rental or transfer, PS §5-134.

Fireworks plants.
Personnel safety standards, PS §10-209.

DRUG OR ALCOHOL ABUSE —Cont'd
Funds.
Maryland drug and alcohol grants program fund,
CR §5-1002.
Maryland substance abuse fund, HG §8-6A-01.
Special funds.
Acceptance and use by administration, HG
§8-206.
Gifts.
Acceptance and use by administration, HG §8-206.
Guardian and ward.
Admission of minor to inpatient facilities.
Application by guardian, HG §8-502.1.
Habeas corpus.
Commitment of criminal defendants for
treatment.
Questioning legality, HG §8-507.
Evaluation of criminal defendants.
Detention for examination.
Questioning legality of detention, HG §8-505.
Handgun permits.
Carrying, wearing or transporting handgun while
under the influence, PS §5-314.
Disqualification, PS §5-306.
Health insurance.
Managed behavioral health care organizations.
Responsibilities of carriers, IN §15-127.
Private review agents.
Review of services for treatment of drug abuse,
IN §15-10B-03.
Health insurers.
Discrimination, HG §19-703.1; IN §15-802.
Health officers.
Defined, HG §8-101.
Hospitals.
Chronic alcoholics.
Admission to private and public hospitals, HG
§8-509.
Intoxicated persons.
Admission to private and public hospitals, HG
§8-509.
Insurance.
Long-term care insurance limitations and
exclusions, IN §18-109.
Insurance coverage for treatment, IN §15-802.
**Integration of child welfare and substance
abuse services,** FL §§5-1201 to 5-1209.
See CHILD WELFARE AND SUBSTANCE
ABUSE SERVICES, INTEGRATION.
**Intermediate care facility, alcoholic (type C or
type D),** HG §8-403.
Intoxicated persons.
Arrested individuals.
Disposition, HG §8-503.
Authorized personnel.
Responsibility, HG §8-504.
Detoxification facilities. See within this heading,
"Detoxification facilities."
Facilities and services.
Disposition of arrested individuals, HG §8-503.
Disposition of publicly intoxicated persons
generally, HG §8-501.
Hospitals.
Admission to private and public hospitals, HG
§8-509.
Police responsibility, HG §8-504.
Publicly intoxicated persons.
Authorized personnel, HG §8-501.
Responsibility, HG §8-504.
Disposition.
Generally, HG §8-501.

DRUG OR ALCOHOL ABUSE —Cont'd
Intoxicated persons —Cont'd
Publicly intoxicated persons —Cont'd
Records.
Disposition of person, HG §8-501.
Rules and regulations.
Authorized personnel, HG §8-501.
Jails.
Treatment programs for inmates, HG §§8-6A-01,
8-6A-02.
**Job-related alcohol and controlled dangerous
substances testing,** HG §17-214.
Juvenile services.
Special programs, 83C §2-118.
Local drug and alcohol abuse councils, HG
§8-1001.
**Long-term care insurance limitations and
exclusions,** IN §18-109.
Managed behavioral health care organizations.
Responsibilities of carriers, IN §15-127.
Maryland substance abuse fund, HG §8-6A-01.
Minors.
Admission to inpatient facilities, HG §8-502.1.
Capacity to consent to treatment, HG §20-102.
Misdemeanors.
Adjudication as drug or alcohol abuser or
dependent.
Unlawful or improper adjudication, HG §8-701.
Treatment programs.
Operation in violation of title, HG §8-702.
Violations of title, HG §8-404.
Nolle prosequi with treatment requirement, CP
§6-229.
**Nonprofit or quasi-governmental
organizations.**
Designation to receive funds for prevention and
treatment programs, HG §§8-901, 8-902.
Notice.
Commitment.
Evaluation.
Leaving facility without authorization.
Notice to court committing, HG §8-506.
Release, HG §8-506.
Treatment.
Leaving facilities without authorization.
Notification of court committing individuals,
HG §8-507.
Detoxification facilities.
Right to leave.
Notice of, HG §8-502.
Job-related alcohol and controlled dangerous
substances testing.
Notification of positive test results, HG §17-214.
Treatment programs.
Certification.
Filing of application, HG §8-405.
Outpatient examination.
Evaluation of criminal defendants, HG §8-505.
Parent and child.
Admission of minor to inpatient facilities.
Application by parent, HG §8-502.1.
Penalties.
Adjudication as drug or alcohol abuser or
dependent.
Unlawful or improper adjudication, HG §8-701.
Treatment programs.
Operation in violation of title, HG §8-702.
Violations of title, HG §8-404.
Pilot programs.
Generally, HG §8-401.

DRUG OR ALCOHOL ABUSE —Cont'd
Police.
Intoxicated persons.
Duties generally, HG §8-504.
Pregnant or postpartum women.
Treatment programs, HG §8-403.1.
Youth camps, HG §15-103.
Prisons and prisoners.
Treatment programs for inmates, HG §§8-6A-01,
8-6A-02.
Privileged communications.
Commitments.
Drug abusers.
Evidence and results of proceedings, HG
§8-601.
Generally, HG §8-601.
Job-related alcohol and controlled dangerous
substances testing.
Confidential information, HG §17-214.
Professional counselors and therapists.
General provisions.
See PROFESSIONAL COUNSELORS AND
THERAPISTS.
Programs.
Administration.
Powers and duties generally, HG §8-401.
Generally, HG §8-401.
Treatment programs. See within this heading,
"Treatment programs."
Prohibited acts, HG §§8-701 to 8-703.
Records.
Intoxicated persons.
Publicly intoxicated persons.
Disposition, HG §8-501.
Privileged matter, HG §8-601.
Release of information, HG §8-205.
Reports.
Acquired reports, HG §8-205.
Administration.
Director.
Reports to deputy secretary, HG §8-203.
Treatment programs for inmates, HG §8-6A-02.
Annual reports, HG §8-405.
Research programs.
Generally, HG §8-401.
Rules and regulations.
Publicly intoxicated persons.
Disposition.
Authorized personnel, HG §8-501.
Treatment programs, HG §8-404.
Salaries.
Administration.
Director, HG §8-202.
Schools.
Preservation of rights of student seeking to
overcome drug abuse, ED §7-412.
Program of drug education, ED §7-411.
Secretary for public health services.
Powers and duties.
Generally, HG §8-203.
Sentence and punishment.
Commitment of criminal defendants for
treatment.
Credit against sentence, HG §8-507.
Criminal defendants.
Evaluation prior to sentencing, HG §8-505.
Short title, HG §8-801.
State employees.
State substance abuse policy, SPP §2-306.
Stet with treatment requirement, CP §6-229.
Substance abuse fund, HG §8-6A-01.

DRUG OR ALCOHOL ABUSE —Cont'd
**Substance abuse treatment outcome
partnership fund,** HG §§8-6C-01 to 8-6C-04.
Award of funding, HG §8-6C-04.
Definitions, HG §8-6C-01.
Established, HG §8-6C-02.
Evaluation of request for funding, HG §8-6C-04.
Funding and administration, HG §8-6C-02.
Partnership funding defined, HG §8-6C-01.
Regulations, adoption, HG §8-6C-03.
Report annually, HG §8-6C-03.
Request for partnership funding, HG §8-6C-04.
Tests.
Altering results of drug or alcohol screening, CR
§10-111.
Job-related alcohol and controlled dangerous
substances testing, HG §17-214.
Treatment programs.
Certification.
Application, HG §8-404.
Denial, HG §8-404.
Notice of filing, HG §8-405.
Issuance of certificate, HG §8-404.
Regulations.
Adoption, HG §8-404.
Requirements generally, HG §8-404.
Exemptions, HG §8-403.
Defined, HG §8-403.
Generally, HG §8-403.
Local correctional facilities.
Calvert county, COR §11-706.
Minors.
Admission to inpatient facilities, HG §8-502.1.
Neighborhood crime, drug and alcohol abuse
prevention and education programs, CR
§5-1001.
Maryland drug and alcohol grants program
fund, CR §5-1002.
Nolle prosequi with treatment requirement, CP
§6-229.
Penalties.
Operation of program in violation of title, HG
§8-702.
Violations, HG §8-404.
Pregnant or postpartum women, HG §8-403.1.
Youth camps, HG §15-103.
Prohibited acts.
Operation of program in violation of title, HG
§8-702.
Reports.
Annual reports, HG §8-405.
Rules and regulations.
Adoption, HG §8-404.
Stet with treatment requirement, CP §6-229.
Vessels and boats.
Operating vessel while intoxicated or while under
the influence of alcohol or drugs, NR §8-738.
Weapons.
Regulated firearms.
Habitual users of controlled dangerous
substances.
See WEAPONS.
Youth services bureaus.
Assessment and referral services.
Bureaus to provide, 83C §2-122.

DRUG PARAPHERNALIA, CR §5-619.
Advertising, CR §5-619.
Authorized providers, prohibited acts, CR
§5-902.

DRUG PARAPHERNALIA —Cont'd
Controlled paraphernalia, CR §5-620.
　Defined, CR §5-101.
Defined, CR §5-101.
Delivery or sale, CR §5-619.
Drug asset forfeiture.
　Property subject to forfeiture, CP §12-102.
Factors considered to determine, CR §5-619.
Immunity from criminal liability.
　Public officials and employees engaged in
　　enforcement or prosecution of laws, CR
　　§5-808.
Innocence of owner.
　Not dispositive of finding intention or design, CR
　　§5-619.
Use or possession with intent to use, CR §5-619.

DRUGS.
Abuse.
　General provisions.
　　See DRUG OR ALCOHOL ABUSE.
Acquired immune deficiency syndrome (AIDS).
　Educational program for violators of controlled
　　dangerous substances act, HG §18-339.
Alcoholic beverages.
　Beer, wine and liquor licenses.
　　Class A, off-sale.
　　　Regulations as to drugstores, 2B §6-101.
　Prescriptions.
　　Sale, 2B §2-101.
Animals.
　Sodium pentobarbital.
　　Destruction of animals.
　　　Permit authorizing use, AG §2-305.
Aviation.
　Aircraft.
　　Operation under influence, TR §5-1006.
Commercial drivers' licenses.
　Disqualification of license, TR §16-812.
Controlled dangerous substances.
　Drug asset forfeiture, CP §§12-101 to 12-505.
　　See DRUG ASSET FORFEITURE.
　Maryland controlled dangerous substances act, CR
　　§§5-101 to 5-1101.
　　See CONTROLLED DANGEROUS
　　　SUBSTANCES.
Crimes.
　Controlled dangerous substances, CR §§5-601 to
　　5-628.
　　See CONTROLLED DANGEROUS
　　　SUBSTANCES.
**Dealer's liability for death caused by use of
　controlled dangerous substances,** CJ
　§§3-1601 to 3-1607.
　See DRUG DEALER LIABILITY ACT.
**Death caused by use of controlled dangerous
　substances.**
　Drug dealer liability, CJ §§3-1601 to 3-1607.
　　See DRUG DEALER LIABILITY ACT.
Food, drugs and cosmetics.
　General provisions, HG §§21-101 to 21-1215.
　　See FOOD, DRUGS AND COSMETICS.
Generic drugs.
　Medicaid.
　　Use and list of interchangeable drugs, HG
　　　§15-118.
Handgun permit holder under the influence.
　Carrying, wearing or transporting handgun, CR
　　§4-206.
Health insurance.
　Choice of pharmacy, IN §15-806.

DRUGS —Cont'd
Health insurance —Cont'd
　Electronic reimbursement of pharmacy, IN
　　§15-131.
　Health insurance benefit card, prescription benefit
　　card, or other technology, IN §15-130.
　Maintenance drugs, IN §15-824.
　Off-label use of drugs, IN §15-804.
　Reimbursement for pharmaceutical products, IN
　　§15-805.
**Homicide by motor vehicle or vessel while
　impaired or under the influence,** CR
　§§2-501 to 2-508.
Human immunodeficiency virus.
　Violators of controlled dangerous substances act.
　　Education program for, HG §18-339.
Impaired by drugs.
　Driving under the influence.
　　Generally.
　　　See DRIVING UNDER THE INFLUENCE.
Insecticides and fungicides.
　General provisions.
　　See PESTICIDES.
Job testing for drugs, HG §17-214.
Labor and industry.
　Job-related alcohol and drug testing, HG §17-214.
Liability.
　Administering drugs lawfully.
　　Immunity, CJ §5-629.
　Administering drugs unlawfully, HG §18-401.
Licensing person convicted of drug crimes.
　Persons convicted of drug crimes.
　　Commercial drivers' licenses, 41 §1-506.
　　Definitions, 41 §1-501.
　　Determining whether defendant holds license,
　　　Crim Rule 4-340.
　　Disclosure of convictions, 41 §1-502.
　　Issuance of license, 41 §1-502.
　　Probation.
　　　Conditions, 41 §1-504.
　　　Imposition, 41 §1-503.
　　　Violations, 41 §1-504.
　　Procedures, 41 §1-505.
　　Rules and regulations, 41 §1-507.
　　Suspension or revocation.
　　　Completion of contracts, 41 §1-501.
　　　Considerations, 41 §1-505.
　　　Imposition, 41 §1-503.
**Life threatening injury by motor vehicle or
　vessel while impaired or under the
　influence,** CR §§3-211, 3-212.
Maryland controlled dangerous substances act,
　CR §§5-101 to 5-1101.
　See CONTROLLED DANGEROUS
　　SUBSTANCES.
Maryland pharmacy assistance program, HG
　§15-124.
Medicaid.
　Atypical anti psychotic medications.
　　Exemption from prior authorization
　　　requirement, HG §15-119.
　Form for prescribing drugs, HG §15-118.
　Interchangeable drugs.
　　List and reimbursement, HG §15-118.
　Use of generic drugs, HG §15-118.
Methyl alcohol.
　Putting in medicine, CR §8-902.
Misuse of drugs.
　General provisions.
　　See DRUG OR ALCOHOL ABUSE.

DRUGS —Cont'd
Motor vehicles.
Alcohol and drug abuse education, TR §16-212.1.
Commercial drivers' licenses.
Driving while under influence of.
Grounds for disqualification, TR §16-812.
Manufacturing, distributing or dispensing controlled dangerous substances.
Duration of disqualification, TR §16-812.
Drivers' licenses.
Suspension or revocation of licenses.
Conviction of certain offenses involving drugs, TR §16-205.
What persons shall not be licensed, TR §16-103.1.
Driving while under the influence of drugs, TR §21-902.
Lesser included offenses, TR §26-405.
Homicide by motor vehicle or vessel while impaired or under the influence, CR §§2-501 to 2-508.
Life threatening injury by motor vehicle or vessel while impaired or under the influence, CR §§3-211, 3-212.
Rental of vehicles to persons under influence of drugs prohibited, TR §18-105.
New drugs.
General provisions.
See FOOD, DRUGS AND COSMETICS.
Optometrists.
Administration of drugs or medicine, HO §11-404.
Permits.
Sodium pentobarbital.
Destruction of animals.
Permit authorizing use, AG §2-305.
Pesticides.
General provisions.
See PESTICIDES.
Pharmacists and pharmacies.
See PHARMACISTS AND PHARMACIES.
Pharmacy assistance program, HG §15-124.
Poor.
Medicaid.
Form for prescribing drugs, HG §15-118.
Use of generic drugs, HG §15-118.
Prescription drug repository program, HG §§15-601 to 15-609.
Prescriptions and prescription drugs.
Generally.
See PRESCRIPTIONS AND PRESCRIPTION DRUGS.
Registration of manufacturers, distributors and dispensers.
Controlled dangerous substances, CR §§5-301 to 5-310.
Scholarships.
Pledge to remain drug free, ED §18-111.
Schools.
Drug free school zones.
County boards of education.
Signs.
Board may designate areas and adopt regulations, ED §4-124.
Sodium pentobarbital.
Animals.
Destruction of animals.
Permit authorizing use, AG §2-305.
Urinalysis.
Job-related testing, HG §17-214.
Vessels and boats.
Homicide by motor vehicle or vessel while impaired or under the influence, CR §§2-501 to 2-508.

DRUGS —Cont'd
Vessels and boats —Cont'd
Life threatening injury by motor vehicle or vessel while impaired or under the influence, CR §§3-211, 3-212.
Operating vessel while intoxicated or under influence of alcohol or drugs, NR §8-738.
Weapons.
Handguns.
See WEAPONS.

DRUG SCREENING AS CONDITION OF EMPLOYMENT, HG §17-214.

DRUG TRAFFICKING, CR §§5-602, 5-607 to 5-609.
Counterfeit substances, CR §§5-604, 5-607.
Drug kingpins, CR §5-613.
Faked controlled substances, CR §5-617.
Firearm possessed, used, worn, carried or transported.
Separate offense, enhanced sentence, forfeiture, CR §5-621.
Minors used, CR §5-628.
Schools.
Manufacturing, distributing, dispensing or possessing near, CR §5-627.

DRUNKENNESS.
Alcoholic beverages.
Knowingly.
Defined, 2B §12-110.
Sales to habitual drunkards prohibited, 2B §12-110.
Sales to intoxicated persons prohibited, 2B §12-108.
Alcoholism generally.
See DRUG OR ALCOHOL ABUSE.
Athletics.
Possession of intoxicating beverages at school athletic contests, ED §26-103.
Crimes and offenses.
Disorderly intoxication, 2B §19-102.
Definitions.
Disorderly intoxication.
Public property, 2B §19-201.
Disorderly intoxication.
Counties.
Prohibited ordinances or resolutions, 2B §19-101.
Excepted counties, 2B §19-103.
Municipal corporations.
Prohibited ordinances or resolutions, 2B §19-101.
Penalty, 2B §19-102.
Prohibited acts, 2B §19-101.
Public property.
Defined, 2B §19-201.
Escape.
Intoxication not defense, CR §9-406.
Evidence.
Motor vehicles.
Operation under influence.
Test for intoxication.
Presumptions, CJ §10-307.
Firearms.
Carrying, wearing or transporting handgun while under the influence, PS §5-314.
Visibly intoxicated persons.
Restrictions on sale, rental or transfer, PS §5-134.

DRUNKENNESS —Cont'd
Handgun permits.
 Carrying, wearing or transporting handgun while
  under the influence, PS §5-314.
Misdemeanors.
 Disorderly intoxication, 2B §19-102.
Motor vehicles.
 See DRIVING UNDER THE INFLUENCE.
Penalties.
 Disorderly intoxication, 2B §19-102.
Presumptions.
 Motor vehicles.
  Operation under influence.
   Test for intoxication, CJ §10-307.
Public property.
 Authorization of consumption.
  Adoption of standards, 2B §19-203.
 Defined, 2B §19-201.
 Drinking prohibited, 2B §19-202.
  Penalty, 2B §19-204.
Schools.
 Athletic contests.
  Possession of intoxicating beverages, ED
   §26-103.

DRY CLEANERS.
Containers used to transport goods to.
 Returnable containers and textiles.
  Registration, prohibited acts, BR §§19-301 to
   19-307.
Licenses, BR §§17-1101 to 17-1103.
 Defined, BR §17-1101.
 Fees, BR §17-1103.
 Required, BR §17-1102.

DUCKLINGS.
Selling or coloring, CR §10-614.

DUCKS.
Waterfowl and migratory birds.
 General provisions.
  See BIRDS AND GAME.

DUE PROCESS OF LAW.
Check cashing services.
 Discipline for violations, FI §12-123.
Constitutional provisions, MD Const DofR Art
 23; US Const Amd 5.
Injunctions.
 Prior notice and opportunity for hearing, SpecPro
  Rule 15-505.

DUI.
See DRIVING UNDER THE INFLUENCE.

DUMBWAITERS.
Defined.
 Elevator safety, PS §12-801.
Elevator safety generally, PS §§12-801 to 12-842.
 See ELEVATORS.

DUMPING SITE SURVEILLANCE SYSTEMS,
 CR §10-112.
Citations, procedure, CJ §7-302.

DUMPS.
Counties.
 Regulation of public or private dumps, 25 §122A.
Garbage and refuse.
 See GARBAGE AND REFUSE.
Junkyards.
 Calvert county, BR §§17-1015 to 17-1024.
  See CALVERT COUNTY.
 General provisions, BR §§17-1001 to 17-1013; TR
  §§8-801 to 8-812.
  See JUNK DEALERS.

DUMPS —Cont'd
Landfills.
 See LANDFILLS.

DURABLE POWER OF ATTORNEY.
Heath care decisions.
 See HEALTH CARE DECISIONS.

DURESS.
Commercial code.
 Applicability of general principles, CL §1-103.
Negotiable instruments.
 Defenses to recoupment, CL §3-305.
 Rescission of negotiation, CL §3-202.
Operating agreements.
 Hotels and retirement communities.
  Defense of fraud not limited, CL §23-106.
Physician assistants.
 Coercion to enter delegation agreement with
  physician, HO §15-302.

DUTY OF CARE.
**Excavation or demolition near underground
 facilities.**
 Persons performing excavation or demolition, PUC
  §12-108.
Partnerships, revised act.
 Partner's duty, CA §9A-404.
Warehouse's liability, CL §7-204.

DUTY OF LOYALTY.
Partnerships, revised act.
 Partner's duty, CA §9A-404.

DWELLINGS.
Arson and burning, CR §§6-101 to 6-111.
Blind persons.
 Tax exemption, TP §7-207.
Bonds, surety.
 Deposits on new homes, RP §§10-301 to 10-306.
  See HOUSING.
Burglary in the first degree, CR §6-202.
 Dwelling defined, CR §6-202.
Burglary in the third degree.
 Breaking and entering with intent to commit
  crime, CR §6-204.
Custom home protection.
 General provisions, RP §§10-501 to 10-509.
  See CUSTOM HOME PROTECTION.
Deposits.
 New homes, RP §§10-301 to 10-306.
  See HOUSING.
Eminent domain.
 Relocation assistance.
  Additional payment to owner-occupant, RP
   §§12-202, 12-203.
  Election to accept moving expense allowance,
   RP §12-205.
Housing generally.
 See HOUSING.
New home warranties, RP §§10-601 to 10-610.
 See WARRANTY.
Surveillance by camera of private residence,
 CR §3-903.
Taxation.
 Credits.
  Cemetery property, TP §9-202.
  Repaired or reconstructed dwellings, TP §9-109.
  Unsold or unrented newly constructed or
   rehabilitated dwellings.
   Statewide tax credit, TP §9-207.
 Exemptions.
  Blind persons, TP §7-207.

DWELLINGS —Cont'd
Taxation —Cont'd
Exemptions —Cont'd
Repaired or reconstructed dwellings, TP §7-307.
Veterans, TP §7-208.
Unlawful picketing and assembly, CR §3-904.
Veterans.
Tax exemption.
Dwelling house of disabled veterans, TP §7-208.
Warranties.
New home warranties, RP §§10-601 to 10-610.
See WARRANTY.
Wetlands.
Construction on piers, EN §16-104.

DWI.
See DRIVING UNDER THE INFLUENCE.

DYED DIESEL FUEL.
Defined, BR §10-101.
Notice stating dyed diesel fuel, nontaxable.
Provided by terminal operator or distributor, BR §10-323.2.
Operation of vehicle with fuel or propulsion tanks containing.
Restrictions, penalty, BR §10-323.2.
Sale or delivery from retail pump.
Restrictions, penalty for violations, BR §10-323.2.

DYEING ESTABLISHMENTS.
Containers used to transport goods to.
Returnable containers and textiles.
Registration, prohibited acts, BR §§19-301 to 19-307.

DYEING OR BLEACHING.
See CLEANERS, DYERS AND PRESSERS.

DYNAMITE.
General provisions.
See EXPLOSIONS AND EXPLOSIVES.
Possession of destructive device, CR §§4-501 to 4-503.

E

EARLY CHILD CARE AND EDUCATION PROGRAMS.
Judith P. Hoyer early child care and education enhancement program, ED §5-217.

EARLY CHILDHOOD MENTAL HEALTH SERVICES PILOT PROGRAM, HG §§10-1501 to 10-1503.

EARNED INCOME TAX CREDIT, TG §10-704.

EARPHONES.
Bicycles.
Wearing earphones, headsets, etc., prohibited, TR §21-1210.
Electronic personal assistive mobility device.
Wearing earphones, headsets, etc., prohibited, TR §21-1210.
Motor vehicles.
Wearing earphones, headsets, etc., prohibited, TR §21-1120.

EARPLUGS.
Bicycles.
Wearing earplugs, headsets, etc., prohibited, TR §21-1210.
Electronic personal assistive mobility device.
Wearing earphones, headsets, etc., prohibited, TR §21-1210.

EARPLUGS —Cont'd
Motor vehicles.
Wearing earplugs, headsets, etc., prohibited, TR §21-1120.

EARTHQUAKES.
Emergency management, PS §§14-101 to 14-1004.
See EMERGENCY MANAGEMENT.

EASEMENTS.
Advertising.
Conservation easements.
Restricting advertising, RP §2-118.
Public utilities.
Chartered counties.
Granted without advertisement, 25A §5.
Agricultural land preservation foundation.
See AGRICULTURE.
Airport development, reservation of rights, TR §5-4A-01.
Airport noise assistance programs.
Avigation easement.
Defined, TR §5-1201.
Homeowners assistance pilot program.
Grant of avigation easement, TR §5-1204.
Annapolis.
Architectural easements.
Board of public works, Maryland historical trust, SF §5A-305.
Architectural easements.
Annapolis.
Board of public works, Maryland historical trust, SF §5A-305.
Cemeteries, state owned.
Transfer or sale of easement, SF §10-309.
Condominiums.
Council of unit owners.
Authority to grant specific easements, RP §11-125.
Conservation easements.
Advertising.
Restricting, RP §2-118.
Creation, RP §2-118.
Environmental trust, NR §3-203.1.
Heritage conservation fund.
Acquisition.
Approval by board of public works.
Required, NR §5-1506.
Authority, NR §5-1503.
Counties.
Consultation with, NR §5-1503.
Criteria.
Establishment, NR §5-1503.
Income tax credits.
Easements conveyed for certain purposes, TG §10-723.
Incorporeal property interest created, RP §2-118.
Purposes, RP §2-118.
Trustee donating, ET §14-111.
Counties.
Chartered counties.
Public utilities.
Granted without advertisement, 25A §5.
Creation.
Words of inheritance not necessary to create, RP §4-105.
Departments.
Recordation, RP §3-104.
Draining lands.
Board of managers, 25 §88.
Environmental service.
Acquisition, NR §3-104.

EASEMENTS —Cont'd
Environmental trust.
Conservation easements, NR §3-203.1.
Income tax credits.
Easements conveyed for certain purposes, TG §10-723.
Forests and parks.
Hart-Miller-Pleasure Island chain.
State to grant easement, NR §5-1202.2.
Garrett county.
Forests and parks.
Authority to purchase land in Garrett county, NR §5-207.
Hart-Miller-Pleasure Island chain.
State to grant easement, NR §5-1202.2.
Heritage conservation fund.
Conservation easements.
Acquisition.
Approval by board of public works.
Required, NR §5-1506.
Authority, NR §5-1503.
Criteria.
Establishment, NR §5-1503.
Income tax.
Credits.
Easements conveyed for certain purposes, TG §10-723.
Inheritance.
Words of inheritance not necessary to create, RP §4-105.
Land trust grant fund.
Conditions of grants.
Dedication of conservation easement may be required, NR §3-2A-08.
Local land preservation programs.
Purchasing, NR §§5-9B-01 to 5-9B-06.
Maryland environmental trust.
Grants, etc., to trust, RP §2-118.
Maryland historical trust.
Grants, etc., to trust, RP §2-118.
Notice.
Conservation easements, NR §3-203.1.
Perpetuities.
Grant or reservation construed to pass or reserve in perpetuity, RP §4-105.
Public utilities.
Chartered counties.
Granted without advertisement, 25A §5.
Deeds.
Requirements for deeds conveying easements to public utility, RP §3-104.
Recordation.
For public utilities or governmental agencies, RP §3-104.
Rural legacy program.
Nature and scope, NR §5-9A-05.
Purchase of development rights as part of easement, NR §5-9A-05.
Solar energy.
Conservation easements.
Preservation or exposure of devices, RP §2-118.
Taxation.
Foreclosure of right of redemption.
Effect of final order, TP §14-844.
Telegraph or telephone company facilities, PUC §8-106.
Watershed associations.
Acquiring, 25 §200.
Channel improvements, 25 §200B.
Record, 25 §200.

EASEMENTS —Cont'd
Zoning.
Architectural easements.
Historic area zoning.
Purchase in connection with structures in or adjacent to district, 66B §8.04.

EASTER.
Schools.
Legal holiday, ED §7-103.

EASTERN SHORE EARLY CHILDHOOD MENTAL HEALTH SERVICES PILOT PROGRAM, HG §§10-1501 to 10-1503.

EASTERN SHORE HOSPITAL CENTER.
Laundry contracts, HG §10-409.

EATING PLACES.
General provisions.
See FOOD AND FOOD ESTABLISHMENTS.

EAVESDROPPING.
Interception of wire or oral communications, Crim Rule 4-611.
Mandatory motions in circuit courts.
Criminal rules, Crim Rule 4-252.
State personnel monitoring or recording telephone conversation, CR §9-602.
Wiretapping generally, CJ §§10-401 to 10-414.
See WIRETAPPING.

EBOLA VIRUS.
Catastrophic health emergency.
Governor's power to proclaim, PS §§14-3A-01 to 14-3A-08.
See HEALTH EMERGENCIES.
Hemorrhagic fevers generally.
Medical and law enforcement personnel.
Notification of exposure, HG §§18-213 to 18-213.2.

E-COMMERCE ADVISORY BOARD, SG §§9-2201 to 9-2204.

ECONOMICALLY DISADVANTAGED.
Indigent persons generally.
See INDIGENT PERSONS.

ECONOMIC DAMAGES.
Drug dealer liability act, CJ §3-1606.

ECONOMIC DEVELOPMENT.
Housing and community development, HS §§1-101 to 11-106.
See HOUSING AND COMMUNITY DEVELOPMENT.

ECONOMIC DEVELOPMENT ASSISTANCE AUTHORITY, 83A §5-1403.

ECONOMIC DEVELOPMENT ASSISTANCE FUND, 83A §§5-1401 to 5-1412.
Acquisition or construction of buildings or real estate.
Uses of fund to finance, 83A §5-1405.
Amount of financial assistance, 83A §5-1405.
Authorized assistance from former funds and acts, 83A §5-1412.
Brownfields revitalization incentive program.
Participation by local government, 83A §5-1408.
Brownfields sites redevelopment.
Uses of fund to finance, 83A §5-1405.
Child care special loans, 83A §5-1409.
Definitions, 83A §5-1401.
Economic development assistance authority, 83A §5-1403.

ECONOMIC DEVELOPMENT ASSISTANCE FUND —Cont'd

Eligibility for financial assistance, 83A §5-1405.

Eligible industry sectors, 83A §5-1410.

Established, 83A §5-1404.

Financial assistance provided under former funds, authorized, 83A §5-1412.

Form of assistance provided local government, 83A §5-1406.

Generally, 83A §5-1404.

Grant from fund to local economic development fund.

Application by local government, 83A §5-1407.

Loans.

Generally, 83A §5-1405.

Local economic development opportunity.

Financial assistance for, 83A §5-1406.

Local government feasibility studies, costs.

Uses of fund to finance, 83A §5-1405.

Purpose, 83A §5-1402.

Resolution of local government.

Required for financial assistance to local government, 83A §5-1405.

Specialized economic development opportunity.

Financial assistance, 83A §5-1406.

Strategic economic development opportunity.

Loans from fund, 83A §5-1406.

Use, 83A §5-1405.

Voluntary cleanup program.

Grant for site assessment, 83A §5-1408.

Working capital.

Uses of fund to finance, 83A §5-1405.

ECONOMIC DEVELOPMENT COMMISSION, 83A §§1-201 to 1-204.

See BUSINESS AND ECONOMIC DEVELOPMENT DEPARTMENT.

ECONOMIC DEVELOPMENT CORPORATION.

Accounts and accounting, 83A §5-212.

Appropriations.

Initial appropriation, 83A §5-211.

Audits, 83A §5-212.

Board of directors, 83A §5-203.

Composition, 83A §5-203.

Consultant.

Employment, 83A §5-204.

Executive director.

Appointment, 83A §5-204.

Officers, 83A §5-203.

Staff.

Appointment, 83A §5-204.

Terms of members, 83A §5-203.

Bond issues.

Definition of "bonds," 83A §5-201.

Generally, 83A §5-206.

Investments.

Eligibility, 83A §5-209.

Power to issue bonds, 83A §§5-205, 5-206.

Refunding bonds, 83A §5-206.

Rights of bondholders.

Enforcement, 83A §5-208.

State not obligated, 83A §5-206.

Tax exemption, 83A §5-210.

Trust indenture, 83A §5-206.

Construction and interpretation.

Liberal construction of provisions, 83A §5-217.

Definitions, 83A §5-201.

Dorchester county economic development fund, 83A §5-216.

Established, 83A §5-203.

ECONOMIC DEVELOPMENT CORPORATION —Cont'd

Executive director, 83A §5-204.

Fiscal year, 83A §5-212.

Funds, 83A §5-212.

Investments.

Bonds of corporation.

Eligibility, 83A §5-209.

Money of corporation, 83A §5-212.

Legislative declaration, 83A §5-202.

Conclusiveness of finding as to legislative intent in suit or action, 83A §5-215.

Other laws.

Applicability, 83A §5-214.

Powers, 83A §5-205.

Public purpose.

Conclusiveness of finding as to in suit or action, 83A §5-215.

Rates.

Powers as to rates and charges, 83A §5-207.

Real property, 83A §5-213.

Reports.

Annual report, 83A §5-212.

Staff, 83A §5-204.

Status, 83A §5-214.

Taxation.

Exemption, 83A §5-210.

ECONOMIC DEVELOPMENT REVENUE BOND ACT.

Acquisition.

Defined, 41 §14-101.

Authority.

Defined, 41 §14-101.

Benefit of net earnings of authority, 41 §14-103.

Changes in or termination of authority, 41 §14-103.

Chief executive officer.

Defined, 41 §14-101.

Construction of subtitle, 41 §14-102.

Contracts.

Security for revenue bond.

Applicability and prerequisites, 41 §14-108.

Counties.

Defined, 41 §14-101.

Implementation of authority to issue bond by county, 41 §14-104.

Powers and discretion, 41 §14-103.

Declaration of purpose, 41 §14-102.

Definitions, 41 §14-101.

Facilities.

Defined, 41 §14-101.

Facility applicants.

Defined, 41 §14-101.

Facility users.

Defined, 41 §14-101.

Finance board.

Defined, 41 §14-101.

Industrial development authority, 41 §14-103.

Leases.

Applicability and prerequisites for lease as security for revenue bond, 41 §14-108.

Defined, 41 §14-101.

Legislative findings, 41 §14-102.

Loan agreements.

Defined, 41 §14-101.

Municipal corporations.

Defined, 41 §14-101.

Implementation of authority to issue bond, 41 §14-104.

Powers and discretion, 41 §14-103.

**ECONOMIC DEVELOPMENT REVENUE BOND
    ACT** —Cont'd
Permitted exercise of powers, 41 §14-102.
Public bodies.
    Defined, 41 §14-101.
Public ports.
    Defined, 41 §14-101.
Receivers.
    Appointment, 41 §14-106.
Revenue bonds.
    Definition of "bonds," 41 §14-101.
    Execution, 41 §14-106.
    Exemption from taxation, 41 §14-105.
    Form, 41 §14-106.
    Issuance, 41 §14-104.
    Maturity, 41 §14-106.
    Receivers.
        Appointment, 41 §14-106.
    Sale, 41 §14-104.
    Security, 41 §14-106.
        Leases or contracts, 41 §14-108.
Sale agreements.
    Defined, 41 §14-101.
Short title, 41 §14-109.
Taxation.
    Exemption of bonds, 41 §14-105.
Title.
    Short title, 41 §14-109.

ECONOMIC LOSS PROTECTION LAW.
Motor vehicle insurance.
    Primary coverage, IN §§19-501 to 19-516.
        See MOTOR VEHICLE INSURANCE.

ECONOMIC OPPORTUNITY OFFICE.
Energy assistance program act.
    See ENERGY ASSISTANCE PROGRAM ACT.

ECONOMIC STABILIZATION ACT.
Applicability of provisions.
    Limitations, LE §11-302.
Definitions, LE §11-301.
Department of labor, licensing and regulation.
    Powers and duties, LE §11-304.
Establishment of program, LE §11-303.
Rules and regulations, LE §11-304.

EDUCATION.
Accountants.
    Licenses, BOP §2-303.
        Continuing education, BOP §2-312.
        Qualifications of applicants, BOP §§2-302,
            2-303.
Acquired immune deficiency syndrome (AIDS).
    Bawdy houses and houses of ill fame, prostitution,
        etc.
        Educational program for violators, HG §18-339.
    Controlled dangerous substances.
        Educational program for violators of act, HG
            §18-339.
After-school opportunity fund program, ED
    §§7-1201 to 7-1207.
    See AFTER-SCHOOL OPPORTUNITY FUND
        PROGRAM.
Air conditioning and heating contractors.
    Inspectors.
        Continuing education requirement, BR §9A-403.
Alcoholism.
    Program of health education dealing with alcohol
        abuse, ED §7-413.
Alternative dispute resolution.
    State center for alternative dispute resolution and
        violence prevention, ED §24-401.

EDUCATION —Cont'd
Architects.
    Licenses.
        Continuing education requirement, BOP
            §3-309.1.
        Qualifications of applicants, BOP §3-303.
Arts council.
    General provisions, 83A §§4-601 to 4-609.
        See ARTS COUNCIL.
Athletics.
    Athlete agents, BR §§4-401 to 4-421.
        See ATHLETE AGENTS.
At-risk youth.
    Residential boarding education programs for
        at-risk youth, ED §§8-701 to 8-710.
Attorneys at law.
    Admission to the bar. See within this heading,
        "Bar admissions."
Authorities.
    Health and higher educational facilities authority.
        General provisions, 43C §§1 to 24.
            See HEALTH AND HIGHER EDUCATIONAL
                FACILITIES AUTHORITY.
Aviation.
    Air schools.
        See AVIATION.
Bar admissions.
    Certification by law school, BarAdm Rule 6.
    Law students.
        Legal assistance by law students, BarAdm Rule
            16.
        Registration, BarAdm Rule 2.
    Pre-legal education, BarAdm Rule 3.
    Qualification of applicants, BOP §10-207.
    Recognition of law schools, BarAdm Rule 4.
    Required course on professionalism, BarAdm Rule
        11.
        Out-of-state attorneys, BarAdm Rule 13.
Birds and game.
    Collection of wildlife, nests, or eggs for scientific
        or educational purposes.
        Permits, NR §10-909.
Cardiovascular disease prevention programs.
    Advisory council.
        Programs to educate the public, HG §13-205.
Career and technology education.
    Apprenticeship standards and on-the-job training
        activities, LE §§11-401 to 11-408.
        See LABOR AND EMPLOYMENT
            RELATIONS.
    General provisions, ED §§21-201 to 21-203.
        See CAREER AND TECHNOLOGY
            EDUCATION.
Children in state-supervised care, ED §§8-501 to
    8-506.
    See SCHOOLS.
Child support, custody or visitation.
    Educational seminars applicable to divorce, FL
        §7-103.2.
Chiropractors.
    Board approval of schools of chiropractic, HO
        §3-402.
Citation of article, 1 §25.
Compacts.
    Compact for education, ED §§25-101 to 25-104.
        See SCHOOLS.
    Interstate agreement on qualification of
        educational personnel, ED §§6-601 to 6-604.
        See SCHOOLS.
    Southern regional education compact, ED
        §§25-201 to 25-205.
        See SCHOOLS.

EDUCATION —Cont'd
Confidentiality of student records.
Denial of access, SG §10-616.
Consumer protection.
Funds and media.
Education of public and study of consumer
problems, CL §13-203.
Controlled dangerous substances.
Manufacturing, distributing, dispensing or
possessing near school, CR §5-627.
Deadly weapons on school property, CR §4-102.
Handguns, sentencing, CR §4-203.
Dentists.
Continuing education requirements.
Adoption of regulations, HO §4-205.
Renewal of license.
Satisfactory evidence of compliance, HO
§4-309.
Department of education.
See SCHOOLS.
Education coordinating committee.
Composition, ED §24-102.
Duties, ED §24-104.
Established, ED §24-101.
Meetings, ED §24-103.
Officers, ED §24-103.
Powers, ED §24-104.
Staff, ED §24-105.
Electrologists, education program.
Approval, HO §8-6B-16.
Instruments and procedures, HO §8-6B-24.
Misrepresentation, HO §8-6B-23.
Periodic review, HO §8-6B-16.
Withdrawal of approval, HO §8-6B-17.
Engineers.
Licenses.
Qualifications of applicants, BOP §§14-304,
14-305.
Firearms.
Deadly weapons on school property, CR §4-102.
Handguns, sentencing, CR §4-203.
Fund-raising campaigns.
Sales and use tax exemptions, TG §11-204.
Handguns.
Deadly weapons on school property, CR §4-102.
Sentencing, CR §4-203.
Hazing, CR §3-607.
Health pilot program.
See SCHOOLS.
Human immunodeficiency virus.
Bawdy houses and houses of ill fame, prostitution,
etc.
Educational program for violators, HG §18-339.
Controlled dangerous substances.
Educational program for violators, HG §18-339.
Insurance agents and brokers.
Continuing education, IN §10-116.
Interior designers' certificates.
Qualifications of applicants, BOP §8-302.
Job training.
Career and technology education generally, ED
§§21-201 to 21-203.
See CAREER AND TECHNOLOGY
EDUCATION.
Juvenile care facilities.
Educational programs in private residential
institutions, 83C §2-137.
Kidney diseases commission.
Miscellaneous powers and duties, HG §13-307.
Knives.
Deadly weapons on school property, CR §4-102.

EDUCATION —Cont'd
Landscape architects.
Licenses.
Qualifications of applicants, BOP §§9-302,
9-303.
Lida Lee Tall learning resources center, ED
§24-106.
Medicaid.
Programs for handicapped children, HG §15-126.
Medical and dental education.
Maryland statewide medical education and
training system, ED §13-102.
Mercury.
Public education, outreach and assistance
program, EN §6-907.
Use of elemental or chemical mercury in schools,
EN §6-906.
Morticians.
Licenses.
Qualifications, HO §7-303.
Mortuary science school, HO §7-403.
Motor vehicles.
Alcohol and drug abuse education, TR §16-212.1.
Driver education program, TR §§16-501 to 16-507.
See DRIVER EDUCATION PROGRAM.
Drivers' schools.
See DRIVERS' SCHOOLS.
Nursing education programs.
Initial approval.
Requirements, HO §8-402.
Powers and duties of board generally, HO §8-401.
Qualifications of licensed applicants, HO §8-302.
Removal from approved list, HO §8-404.
Nutrient management consultants, AG §8-803.3.
Occupational therapists.
Licenses.
Continuing competency, HO §10-311.
Optometrists.
Topical ocular diagnostic pharmaceutical agents.
Certification as qualified to administer.
Requirements, HO §11-404.
Physicians.
Licenses.
Foreign medical school graduates, HO §14-308.
Limited license for postgraduate teaching, HO
§14-318.
Maryland statewide medical education and
training system, ED §13-102.
Physician assistant-nurse practitioner training
program, ED §18-802.
Podiatrists.
Licenses.
Qualifications, HO §16-302.
**Public recreation on private and local
government lands.**
General provisions, NR §§5-1101 to 5-1109.
See RECREATIONAL TRESPASS.
Real estate brokers.
Licenses.
Qualifications of applicants, BOP §17-305.
Real estate salesperson license, BOP §17-303.
Records.
Student records.
Denial of inspection, SG §10-616.
**Residential boarding education programs for
at-risk youth,** ED §§8-701 to 8-710.
Residential child care program administrators.
Certification.
Continuing education.
Renewal of certificate, HO §20-310.
Qualifications, HO §20-302.

EDUCATION —Cont'd
Scholarships.
General provisions.
See SCHOLARSHIPS.
Schools.
See SCHOOLS.
Sex offender registration.
Change of address.
Notice to schools and education authorities, CP §11-709.
Employment at schools prohibited, CP §11-722.
Entry onto school property prohibited, CP §11-722.
Sports agents, BR §§4-401 to 4-421.
See ATHLETE AGENTS.
Stationary engineers.
Licenses.
Qualifications of applicants, BOP §6.5-303.
Surveys and surveyors.
Licenses.
Qualifications of applicants, BOP §§15-304, 15-305.
Taxation.
Exemption of real and personal property, TP §7-202.
Teachers.
See SCHOOLS.
Technology education.
Apprenticeship standards and on-the-job training activities, LE §§11-401 to 11-408.
See LABOR AND EMPLOYMENT RELATIONS.
Generally, ED §§21-201 to 21-203.
See CAREER AND TECHNOLOGY EDUCATION.
Universities and colleges.
See UNIVERSITIES AND COLLEGES.
Vessels and boats.
Boating safety education.
Generally, NR §8-712.2.
Ordering completion of education course upon certain violations, NR §8-740.
Violence prevention.
State center for alternative dispute resolution and violence prevention, ED §24-401.
Vocational education.
Apprenticeship standards and on-the-job training activities, LE §§11-401 to 11-408.
See LABOR AND EMPLOYMENT RELATIONS.
Career and technology education generally, ED §§21-201 to 21-203.
See CAREER AND TECHNOLOGY EDUCATION.
Weapons.
Deadly weapons on school property, CR §4-102.
Handguns, sentencing, CR §4-203.
Well drillers.
Licenses.
Educational experience, EN §13-306.

EDUCATIONAL CREDIT ON TERM OF CONFINEMENT.
Inmates committed to custody of commissioner of correction, COR §3-706.

EDUCATIONAL ORGANIZATIONS.
Annuity agreements with donors, IN §16-114.
Benefit performances.
Prince George's county, CR §§13-1901 to 13-1907.
Bingo.
Baltimore City, CR §§13-507 to 13-509.

EDUCATIONAL ORGANIZATIONS —Cont'd
Bingo —Cont'd
Benefit performances.
Prince George's county, CR §§13-1901 to 13-1907.
Frederick county, CR §13-1306.
Howard county, CR §§13-1602, 13-1603.
Gaming, bazaar, carnival and raffles.
Frederick county, CR §§13-1301 to 13-1307.
Kent county, CR §§13-1701 to 13-1706.
Prince George's county, CR §§13-1901 to 13-1912.
Queen Anne's county, CR §§13-2001 to 13-2006.
Raffles generally, statewide provisions, CR §12-106.
Worcester county, CR §§13-2619 to 13-2628.
Tip jars and punch board.
Frederick county, CR §13-1305.
Unemployment compensation.
When not covered employment, LE §8-208.

EDUCATIONAL TECHNOLOGY PILOT PROGRAM, ED §§7-10A-01 to 7-10A-08.
Definitions, ED §7-10A-01.
Established, ED §7-10A-02.
Funding, ED §7-10A-07.
Grant, ED §7-10A-06.
Implementation plan.
Development, ED §7-10A-04.
Requirements, ED §7-10A-05.
Purpose, ED §7-10A-03.
Reports, ED §7-10A-08.

EDUCATIONAL TELEVISION.
See SCHOOLS.

EDUCATION INSURANCE.
Holocaust victims insurance act, IN §§28-101 to 28-110.
See HOLOCAUST VICTIMS INSURANCE.

EDUCATION PARTNERSHIP FUND, ED §2-207.

EELS.
Fish and fisheries.
See FISH AND FISHERIES.

EFFICIENCY 2000 COMMISSION.
See MANAGEMENT AND PRODUCTIVITY COUNCIL.

EGGS.
Adulterated eggs, AG §4-311.
Consumer.
Defined, AG §4-301.
Definitions, AG §4-301.
Distributors.
Defined, AG §4-301.
Inspection fee, AG §4-311.6.
Records, AG §4-311.7.
Registration, AG §§4-311.1 to 4-311.4. See within this heading, "Registration of packers and distributors."
Reports, AG §4-311.6.
Egg law fund, AG §4-311.5.
Fees.
Packer or distributor inspection fee, AG §4-311.6.
Food service facility.
Defined, AG §4-301.
Packers.
Defined, AG §4-301.
Inspection fees, AG §4-311.6.
Records, AG §4-311.7.
Registration, AG §§4-311.1 to 4-311.4. See within this heading, "Registration of packers and distributors."

EGGS —Cont'd
Packers —Cont'd
Reports, AG §4-311.6.
Penalties.
Civil penalties under subtitle, AG §4-311.8.
General provisions, AG §§12-101 to 12-104.
Records.
Packers or distributors, AG §4-311.7.
Registration of packers and distributors, AG
§§4-311.1 to 4-311.4.
Applications, AG §4-311.2.
Denial, suspension or revocation, AG §4-311.4.
Display, AG §4-311.3.
Expiration, AG §4-311.3.
Fees, AG §4-311.2.
Relocation of business, notification to secretary,
AG §4-311.3.
Renewal, AG §4-311.3.
Required, AG §4-311.1.
Reports.
False reports, AG §4-309.
Packers or distributors, AG §4-311.6.
Retailer.
Defined, AG §4-301.
Right of entry.
Secretary of agriculture, AG §4-310.
Rules and regulations.
Penalties.
Civil penalties under subtitle, AG §4-311.8.
Shell eggs, AG §4-304.
Eggs exceeding required standards, AG §4-306.
Sales.
Stop-sale order.
Secretary of agriculture, AG §4-310.
Shell eggs.
Advertising.
Use of terms, AG §4-303.
Classification.
Size or weight, AG §4-304.
Defined, AG §4-301.
Delivery.
Invoice delivery ticket, AG §4-308.
Grades.
Special grades.
Establishment, AG §4-306.
Rules and regulations.
Adoption by secretary, AG §4-306.
Invoice delivery ticket, AG §4-308.
Quality.
Designation, AG §4-307.
Presumption when not designated U.S.D.A.
grade B, AG §4-307.
Standards, AG §4-305.
Eggs exceeding required standards, AG
§4-306.
Refrigeration, AG §4-305.1.
Registration of packers and distributors, AG
§§4-311.1 to 4-311.4. See within this heading,
"Registration of packers and distributors."
Reports.
Failure or refusal to make, AG §4-309.
Rules and regulations.
Adoption by secretary, AG §4-304.
Special grades superior to U.S.D.A. grade A,
AG §4-306.
Secretary of agriculture.
Right of entry, AG §4-310.
Rules and regulations, AG §4-304.
Special grades superior to U.S.D.A. grade A,
AG §4-306.

EGGS —Cont'd
Shell eggs —Cont'd
Secretary of agriculture —Cont'd
Sales.
Stop-sale order, AG §4-310.
Size.
Classification, AG §4-304.
Designation, AG §4-307.
Eggs exceeding required standards, AG §4-306.
Standards.
Compliance with subtitle, AG §4-302.
Quality standards, AG §4-305.
Refrigeration, AG §4-305.1.
Weight.
Classification, AG §4-304.
Short title, AG §4-312.
Standards.
Compliance with subtitle, AG §4-302.
Title.
Short title, AG §4-312.
Trademarks.
Farm products, AG §§10-501 to 10-504.
Treated eggs.
Defined, AG §4-301.
Unfit eggs, AG §4-311.

800 NUMBERS.
Copyright royalties, CL §11-1402.

EJECTMENT.
Appeals.
When grantor remains in possession after delivery
of deed and in violation of agreement, RP
§14-109.
Attorneys at law.
Certain persons representing tenants in summary
ejectment proceedings.
Bar admission requirement exception, BOP
§10-206.
Bonds, surety.
Appeals.
When grantor remains in possession after
delivery of deed and in violation of
agreement, RP §14-109.
Costs.
Warrant of resurvey.
Deposit of costs, PropAct Rule 12-101.
District Court.
When grantor remains in possession after delivery
of deed and in violation of agreement.
Jurisdiction of appeal, RP §14-109.
Execution.
Warrant of resurvey, PropAct Rule 12-101.
Filing.
Warrant of resurvey.
Plat to be filed, PropAct Rule 12-101.
Ground rent.
Costs and expenses recoverable, RP §8-402.3.
Six months arrearage as grounds for action, RP
§8-402.2.
Judgments and decrees.
Landlord and tenant.
Notice of judgment, RP §8-402.2.
When grantor remains in possession after delivery
of deed and in violation of agreement, RP
§14-109.
Landlord and tenant.
Costs and expenses recoverable, RP §8-402.3.
Notice of judgment, RP §8-402.2.
Tenants holding over, RP §8-204.

EJECTMENT —Cont'd
Notices.
Appeals.
When grantor remains in possession after
delivery of deed and in violation of
agreement, RP §14-109.
Landlord and tenant.
Notice of judgment, RP §8-402.2.
Plats.
Warrant of resurvey.
Filing plat, PropAct Rule 12-101.
Summary ejectment.
Attorneys at law.
Admission to the bar, exceptions.
Certain persons representing tenants in
summary ejectment proceedings, BOP
§10-206.
District Court, CivProDist Rule 3-711.
Summary proceedings.
Tenants holding over.
General provisions.
See LANDLORD AND TENANT.
Summons and process.
When grantor remains in possession after delivery
of deed and in violation of agreement, RP
§14-109.
Surveyors.
Warrant of resurvey, PropAct Rule 12-101.
Vendor and vendee.
When grantor remains in possession after delivery
of deed and in violation of agreement, RP
§14-109.
Venue.
Additional venue permitted, CJ §6-202.
Warrant of resurvey, PropAct Rule 12-101.
Warrants.
When grantor remains in possession after delivery
of deed and in violation of agreement, RP
§14-109.

ELDERLY PERSONS.
Day-care for the elderly, HG §§14-201 to 14-206.
See DAY-CARE FOR THE ELDERLY.
General provisions.
See AGED.
Innovations in aging services program, 70B
§36.
Long-term care insurance, IN §§18-101 to
18-120.
See LONG-TERM CARE INSURANCE.
Maryland senior ride demonstration program,
TR §§7-1001 to 7-1005.
Property taxes.
See PROPERTY TAXES.
Senior citizen activities center operating fund,
70B §§33 to 35.
Senior citizen activities centers.
Capital improvement grants program, 70B §§26 to
32.
See SENIOR CITIZEN ACTIVITIES CENTERS.

ELDERLY RENTAL HOUSING PROGRAM, HS
§§4-401 to 4-409.
Defined terms, HS §4-401.
Development finance division.
Units in division, HS §4-103.
Established, HS §4-402.
Fund.
Additional or replaced money, HS §4-405.
Loans.
Applications, HS §4-408.
Deferred payment loans, HS §4-409.

ELDERLY RENTAL HOUSING PROGRAM
—Cont'd
Powers and duties of department, HS §4-404.
Projects.
Qualifications, HS §4-407.
Purpose, HS §4-403.
Regulations, HS §4-406.

ELECTION CONTESTS.
Judicial review of election, EL §§12-201 to
12-204.
Recounts, EL §§12-101 to 12-107.

ELECTION JUDGES, EL §§10-201 to 10-207.

ELECTION OF RIGHTS AND REMEDIES.
Appeals.
Court of special appeals, AppRev Rule 8-207.
Decedents' estates.
Surviving spouse elective share.
General provisions, ET §§3-203 to 3-208.
See DECEDENTS' ESTATES.
Eminent domain.
Abandonment of condemnation proceedings, RP
§12-109.
Trial by court, PropAct Rule 12-207.
Executions.
Release of property from levy.
Election of exemption by judgment debtor.
Circuit courts, CivProCir Rule 2-643.
District Court, CivProDist Rule 3-643.
Forms.
Surviving spouse.
Rights in decedent's estate, ET §3-207.
Health care malpractice claims.
Waiver of arbitration, CJ §§3-2A-06A, 3-2A-06B.
Judgments and decrees.
Foreign judgments.
Action by creditor to enforce judgment rather
than proceeding under enforcement of
foreign judgment provisions authorized, CJ
§11-805.
Jury trial.
Circuit courts, CivProCir Rule 2-325.
Levies.
Release of property from levy.
Election of exemption by judgment debtor.
Circuit courts, CivProCir Rule 2-643.
District Court, CivProDist Rule 3-643.
Surviving spouse.
Elective share.
General provisions, ET §§3-203 to 3-208.
See DECEDENTS' ESTATES.
Wills.
Effect of election upon will, ET §3-208.
No benefits under will, ET §3-208.
Surviving spouse.
Form of election, ET §3-207.
Intestate share.
Contribution to payment, ET §3-208.

ELECTIONS, EL §§1-101 to 16-1001.
Absentee voting, EL §§9-310 to 9-312.
Administration by local boards.
Guidelines to be established by state board, EL
§9-303.
Affidavit.
Agent used in absentee voting, EL §9-307.
Agent.
Use to pick up and deliver ballot, EL §9-307.
Applicability of provision, EL §9-301.
Application for ballot, EL §9-305.
Rejection, notice, EL §9-306.

ELECTIONS —Cont'd
Absentee voting —Cont'd
Application for ballot —Cont'd
Review, EL §9-306.
Assistance in marking ballot, EL §9-308.
Canvassing of ballots, EL §11-302.
Appeal of rejection of ballot, EL §11-304.
Compensation to local board members.
Extra compensation for duties performed under
subtitle, EL §9-311.
Content and arrangement of ballot, EL §9-204.
Content of ballot.
Identical to ballot used in polling place, EL
§9-213.
Criminal penalty for offenses relating to, EL
§9-312.
Disabled persons, MD Const Art I §3.
Disabled voters.
Assigned polling place inaccessible, EL §10-102.
Assistance in marking ballot, EL §9-308.
Documentation of absentee voting in county.
Local board to maintain records, EL §9-302.
Elderly voters.
Assigned polling place inaccessible, EL §10-102.
Envelopes, EL §9-310.
Federal preemption, EL §9-304.
Forms prescribed by state board, EL §9-301.
Guidelines for administration by local boards, EL
§9-303.
Illiterate voters.
Assistance in marking ballot, EL §9-308.
Ill persons, MD Const Art I §3.
Instructions to accompany ballot, EL §9-309.
Lost, destroyed or spoiled ballots, EL §9-306.
Municipal corporations.
Right to vote by absentee ballot, 23A §47.
One ballot issued to voter, EL §9-306.
Permissible, EL §9-304.
Polling place inaccessible to elderly or disabled,
EL §10-102.
Qualifications to vote absentee.
Review, EL §9-306.
Record of absentee voting in county.
Local board to maintain, EL §9-302.
Rejection of application.
Notice, appeal to local board, EL §9-306.
Rejection of ballot by board of canvassers, EL
§11-302.
Appeal of rejection of ballot, EL §11-304.
Review of application, EL §9-306.
Special application for ballot, EL §9-305.
Time for receipt of application, EL §9-305.
Voting systems for absentee voting.
Selection, certification and decertification, EL
§§9-101 to 9-105.
Access to voting room, EL §10-308.
Advertising.
Campaign finance entities.
Campaign materials, EL §§13-401 to 13-403.
Affidavits.
Dwelling principal residence, TP §2-218.
Age.
Right to vote.
Not to be abridged on account of age, US Const
Amd 26.
Voters.
Requirements, MD Const Art I §1.
Voting age, EL §3-102.
Alcoholic beverages.
Providing voters on election day, CR §9-203.

ELECTIONS —Cont'd
Alcoholic beverages —Cont'd
Sale and use prohibited on election day, 2B
§11-401.
Use at polling place, EL §16-207.
Assistance in marking ballot.
Absentee voting, EL §9-308.
Choosing individual to assist, EL §10-310.
Provisional ballot voting, EL §9-406.
Attorney general, MD Const Art V §1.
Contributions to political campaigns during
general assembly sessions.
Prohibition, exceptions, EL §13-235.
Determining election.
By governor, MD Const Art V §2.
Filing fee, EL §5-401.
Returns to governor, MD Const Art V §2.
Tie vote.
Governor determining, MD Const Art V §2.
Ballot questions, EL §§7-101 to 7-105.
Act of general assembly.
Qualifying as question, EL §7-102.
Alphabetical identifier.
Assigned county questions, EL §7-103.
Arrangement of questions on ballot, EL §9-211.
Bond referendums.
Qualifying as question, EL §7-102.
Complete text of questions.
Posting or making available for public
inspection, EL §7-105.
Constitutional conventions, amendments or new
or altered constitution.
Qualifying as question, EL §7-102.
Contributions and expenditures, signed
statement.
Question under Article XI-A of Maryland
Constitution, EL §7-104.
County charters, adoption or amendment.
Qualifying as question, EL §7-102.
Filing petitions.
Election of charter board or question under
Article XI-A of Maryland Constitution, EL
§7-104.
Home rule county government, creation.
Qualifying as question, EL §7-102.
Incorporation of municipality.
Qualifying as question, EL §7-102.
Information required on ballot, EL §7-103.
Certification, EL §7-103.
Notice, EL §7-105.
Numerical identifier.
Assigned statewide questions or question
relating to general assembly enactment, EL
§7-103.
Petition.
Requirements generally, EL §§6-101 to 6-211.
Publication or dissemination by mass
communication.
Method of providing notice, EL §7-105.
Qualification as ballot question, EL §7-102.
Recount.
Petition, EL §12-103.
Counterpetition, EL §12-104.
Regulation regarding notice.
State board to adopt, EL §7-105.
Specimen ballot.
Method of providing notice, EL §7-105.
Types of questions.
Applicability of provisions, EL §7-101.
Ballots, EL §§9-201 to 9-217.
Absentee voting, EL §§9-301 to 9-312.

ELECTIONS —Cont'd

Ballots —Cont'd

Accountability for ballots, EL §9-216.

All voting by ballot, EL §9-201.

At large election contest.

Arrangement on ballots, EL §9-210.

Baltimore City, offices voted on.

Arrangement on ballot, EL §9-210.

Change after ballots printed, EL §9-208.

Compliance with subdivision required, EL §9-201.

Content and arrangement.

Absentee ballot or provisional ballot, EL §9-213.

Arrangement for use in county.

Duty of local board to prepare, EL §9-207.

Candidates and offices, EL §9-210.

Certification, placement of candidates, questions, EL §9-202.

Absentee ballots, EL §9-204.

Delivery to local board of copy, EL §9-207.

Establishing later date, petition to court of appeals, EL §9-207.

Time for, EL §9-207.

Heading, EL §9-206.

Judicial review by registered voter, EL §9-209.

Modification, time limitation, EL §9-207.

Offices and candidates, EL §9-210.

Questions on ballot, EL §9-211.

Requirements, EL §9-205.

Correction.

Error or change after ballots printed, EL §9-208.

Judicial review to correct error, EL §9-209.

County offices to be voted on.

Arrangement on ballot, EL §9-210.

Delaying delivery, EL §16-206.

Destroying or defacing, EL §16-206.

Distinguishing mark placed on ballot, EL §16-206.

Error.

Change in ballot after printing, EL §9-208.

Judicial review to correct error, EL §9-209.

Governor and lieutenant governor.

Joint listing of names, MD Const Art II §1B.

Heading of ballot.

Requirements, EL §9-206.

House of delegates candidates.

Identified by county in which candidate resides, EL §9-210.

Instructions to voters.

Candidates or questions appearing on reverse side, EL §9-212.

Judicial offices to be voted on.

Arrangement on ballot, EL §9-210.

Judicial review.

Content and arrangement or correction of error, EL §9-209.

Misrepresenting persons ability to vote, EL §16-206.

Names of candidates authorized to appear on ballot.

Ballot to contain, EL §9-210.

Number of printed ballots required at polling place, EL §9-215.

Offenses as to ballots and balloting, EL §16-206.

Offices to be vote on.

Arrangement on ballot, EL §9-210.

Party affiliation.

Indicated on ballot, EL §9-210.

Petition.

Review of content and arrangement or correction of error, EL §9-209.

ELECTIONS —Cont'd

Ballots —Cont'd

Possessing official ballot before election day, EL §16-206.

Presidential or vice presidential candidates.

Identified by state in which candidate resides, EL §9-210.

Primaries.

Arrangement of candidates on ballot, EL §9-210.

Printing, EL §9-215.

Local boards, time for, EL §9-207.

Reprinting, error or change, EL §9-208.

Prohibited practices, EL §9-217.

Provisional ballots, EL §§9-401 to 9-408. See within this heading, "Provisional ballots."

Questions on ballot.

Arrangement of ballot, EL §9-211.

Removal from building in which voting occurs, EL §16-206.

Reprinting ballots.

Error or change, EL §9-208.

Vacancy in candidacy properly filled, EL §5-1204.

Required, MD Const Art I §1.

Requirements for each ballot, EL §9-203.

Content, EL §9-205.

Heading of ballot, EL §9-206.

Reverse side of ballot.

Candidates or questions appearing, instructions, EL §9-212.

Specimen ballots, EL §9-214.

Posting at polling place, EL §10-306.

Statewide offices to be voted on.

Arrangement on ballot, EL §9-210.

Substituting, altering, adding or removing voted ballot, EL §16-304.

Supply of printed ballots at polling place.

Number required, EL §9-215.

Unauthorized distribution, printing, possession or reproduction, EL §9-217.

Uniformity, EL §9-204.

Use for unauthorized purposes, EL §9-201.

Vacancy in candidacy properly filled.

Reprinting ballots, EL §5-1204.

Voting machine ballot.

Arrangement on ballots, EL §9-210.

Voting systems for voting in polling places.

Selection, certification and decertification, EL §§9-101 to 9-105.

Write-in votes.

Voter afforded opportunity to cast in general election, EL §9-210.

Boards of canvassers.

Local boards, EL §11-301.

State board, EL §11-502.

Breach of peace, EL §16-204.

Bribery of voter, CR §9-203.

Campaign financing.

Disclosures by persons doing public business.

Contributions to candidates, EL §§14-101 to 14-108.

See CAMPAIGN FINANCE.

Generally, EL §§13-101 to 13-605.

See CAMPAIGN FINANCE.

Public campaign financing, EL §§15-101 to 15-111.

See CAMPAIGN FINANCE.

Campaign managers.

Appointment by individual, EL §13-212.

Campaign materials, EL §§13-401 to 13-403.

Advertising or press agency used.

Rates charged by newspaper or periodical, EL §13-402.

ELECTIONS —Cont'd
Campaign materials —Cont'd
Advertising rates charged by newspapers or
periodical, EL §13-402.
Authority line, EL §13-401.
Copies retain by finance entity, EL §13-403.
Legislative newsletters, EL §§13-406 to 13-409.
Material not authorized by candidate.
Statement required, EL §13-401.
Montgomery county.
Multiresidential structures, distributing or
depositing, EL §1-303.
Candidates, EL §§5-101 to 5-1303.
Advertising by campaign finance entities.
Campaign materials generally, EL §§13-401 to
13-403.
Certificate of candidacy, EL §§5-301 to 5-304.
Board to determine whether candidate meets
requirements, EL §5-301.
Campaign finance entity statement to
accompany certificate, EL §5-304.
Certified mail, messenger service or delivery
service.
Filing by, EL §5-304.
Democratic national convention candidates.
Time for filing, EL §5-303.
Facsimile service or other electronic
transmission.
Filing by prohibited, EL §5-304.
Fee to accompany certificate, EL §5-304.
Filing, EL §5-301.
Manner of filing, EL §5-304.
Oath, appropriate board, EL §5-302.
Time, EL §5-303.
Filing fees.
Candidates for various offices, EL §5-401.
County governing body, transfer to, EL
§5-403.
Distribution, EL §5-403.
Local boards, distribution to, EL §5-403.
Return to candidate, EL §5-402.
Waiver, petition for, EL §5-401.
Information specified on certificate, EL §5-304.
Judge of court of appeals standing for
continuance in office, EL §5-301.
Judge of court of special appeals standing for
continuance in office, EL §5-301.
Local board, filing with, EL §5-302.
Making, defacing or destroying, EL §16-901.
Name to appear on ballot.
Candidate to indicate on certificate, EL
§5-301.
Nomination by party not required to nominate
by party primary, EL §5-703.1.
Nomination by petition.
Candidates required to file, time, EL §5-703.
Oath, filing under, EL §5-302.
Presidential or vice presidential candidates.
Not required to file, EL §5-301.
Required to be candidate, EL §5-301.
Special election candidates.
Time for filing, EL §5-303.
State board, filing with, EL §5-302.
Suppressing certificate duly filed, EL §16-901.
Vacancy in candidacy, individual designated to
fill.
Filing required, EL §5-1202.
Withdrawal, EL §5-502.
Write-in candidate.
Filing, EL §§5-301, 5-704.
Time for filing, EL §5-303.

ELECTIONS —Cont'd
Candidates —Cont'd
Certificate of declination, filing, EL §5-801.
Certificate of withdrawal, EL §§5-501 to 5-504.
Authorized to withdraw by filing, EL §§5-501,
5-502.
Effect of filing, EL §5-504.
Filing, EL §5-503.
Special election to fill representative vacancy in
congress, EL §§5-502, 5-503.
Compliance with subtitle.
Required to become candidate, EL §5-101.
Contributions and expenses of campaign.
Disclosures by persons doing public business.
Contributions to candidates for political office,
EL §§14-101 to 14-108.
See CAMPAIGN FINANCE.
Generally, EL §§13-101 to 13-605.
See CAMPAIGN FINANCE.
Public campaign financing, EL §§15-101 to
15-111.
See CAMPAIGN FINANCE.
Conviction.
Ineligibility to be elected or appointed to office,
time period, EL §16-1001.
Court of appeals judges.
Notice to state board of name of judge to be
placed on ballot, EL §5-301.
Court of special appeals judges.
Notice to state board of name of judge to placed
on ballot, EL §5-301.
Death.
Vacancy, filling, EL §§5-901 to 5-1303.
Declination of nomination, EL §5-801.
Vacancy, filling, EL §§5-901 to 5-1303.
Disqualification.
Failure to file campaign finance reports, EL
§13-332.
Vacancy, filling, EL §§5-901 to 5-1303.
Failure to file campaign finance reports.
Disqualification, EL §13-332.
Filing fees, EL §§5-401 to 5-403.
Vacancy in candidacy, individual designated to
fill.
Payment required, EL §5-1202.
Financing campaign.
Disclosures by persons doing public business.
Contributions to candidates for political office,
EL §§14-101 to 14-108.
See CAMPAIGN FINANCE.
Generally, EL §§13-101 to 13-605.
See CAMPAIGN FINANCE.
Public campaign financing, EL §§15-101 to
15-111.
See CAMPAIGN FINANCE.
For more than one political party office.
Prohibited, EL §5-204.
Governor and lieutenant governor.
Candidate for governor to designate candidate
for lieutenant governor, MD Const Art II
§1B.
Considered unit for nomination and voting
purposes, EL §5-205.
Death of candidate, declination of nomination or
disqualification of nominee, EL §5-1201.
Designation of candidate for lieutenant
governor.
Candidate for governor to designate, EL
§5-205.
Joint listing of names on ballot, MD Const Art
II §1B.

ELECTIONS —Cont'd
Candidates —Cont'd
Governor and lieutenant governor —Cont'd
Vacancy in candidacy for petition candidates, EL §5-1101.
Vacancy in unit occurring before primary, EL §§5-902 to 5-905.
Nomination.
By petition, EL §5-703.
Petition requirements generally, EL §§6-101 to 6-211.
Vacancy in candidacy for petition candidates, EL §5-1101.
Certificate of declination, filing, EL §5-801.
Certificate of election.
Issued after primary results certified, EL §5-705.
Certificate of nomination, EL §5-705.
Making, defacing or destroying, EL §16-901.
Suppressing certificate duly filed, EL §16-901.
Declination of nomination, EL §5-801.
Certificate of declination, filing, EL §5-801.
Defeated candidates name not to appear on general election ballot, EL §5-706.
Governor and lieutenant.
Death of candidate, declination of nomination or disqualification of nominee, EL §5-1201.
Methods of nominating candidate, EL §5-701.
Names of nominees submitted to voters, EL §5-1203.
Requirements, EL §5-702.
Vacancy.
After primary election, EL §§5-1001 to 5-1005.
In candidacy for petition candidates, EL §5-1101.
In candidacy occurring before primary, EL §§5-901 to 5-905.
Miscellaneous provisions, EL §§5-1201 to 5-1204.
Withdrawal of candidacy.
Governor and lieutenant governor unit.
Vacancy before primary, EL §§5-902 to 5-905.
Vacancy in candidacy for petition candidates, EL §5-1101.
Write-in candidates, EL §5-704.
Nomination by party not required to nominate by party primary, EL §5-703.1.
Nomination by petition, EL §§5-701, 5-703.
Certificate of candidacy, filing, EL §5-703.
Declaration of intent, filing, EL §5-703.
Petition requirements generally, EL §§6-101 to 6-211.
Signatures required on petition, EL §5-703.
Vacancy in candidacy for petition candidates.
Governor and lieutenant governor unit, EL §5-1101.
Political affiliation.
Required to be candidate for political party, EL §5-203.
Primary election ballot.
Qualifications, EL §5-601.
Primary elections generally, EL §§8-201 to 8-205.
Process by which individual becomes candidate.
Subtitle governs, EL §5-101.
Qualifications.
Political affiliation.
Required to be candidate for political party, EL §5-203.

ELECTIONS —Cont'd
Candidates —Cont'd
Qualifications —Cont'd
Primary election ballot, EL §5-601.
Registered voter, EL §5-202.
Residence requirement imposed by law, EL §5-202.
Petition to challenge residency of certain candidates, EL §5-305.
Satisfaction of qualifications required, EL §5-201.
Raffles, CR §12-106.
Registered voter.
Required to qualify, EL §5-202.
Residence requirement imposed by law, EL §5-202.
Petition to challenge residency of certain candidates, EL §5-305.
Simultaneously candidate for political party office and public office, EL §5-204.
Unopposed candidates.
Primary elections.
Word placed by candidate's name on ballot, EL §8-204.
Vacancy in candidacy.
After primary election, EL §§5-1001 to 5-1005.
Certificate of designation or candidacy received to fill vacancy, EL §5-1001.
Change in nomination.
Certificate of designation or candidacy received to fill vacancy, EL §5-1001.
Congress, state senator or member of house of delegates, EL §5-1003.
County office, EL §5-1004.
Governor and lieutenant governor unit, EL §5-1005.
Statewide office except governor or lieutenant governor, EL §5-1002.
Successor nominee, certification, EL §5-1001.
Certificate of candidacy and filing fees.
Filing and payment required by individual designated to fill, EL §5-1202.
For petition candidates.
Governor and lieutenant governor unit, EL §5-1101.
Late vacancy before general election.
Applicability of provisions, EL §5-1301.
Certificate of designation, filing time limit, EL §5-1302.
Nominee receiving enough votes to be elected, EL §5-1302.
Occurring after primary but before certificate of election issued, EL §5-1303.
Occurring before primary, EL §§5-901 to 5-905.
Central committee or governing body of political party.
Filling, EL §5-901.
Governor and lieutenant governor unit, EL §§5-902 to 5-905.
Reprinting ballots.
Candidacy properly filled and certified, EL §5-1204.
Withdrawal of candidacy.
After filing but before primary.
Certificate of withdrawal, EL §§5-501 to 5-504.
Governor and lieutenant governor unit.
Vacancy before primary, EL §§5-902 to 5-905.
Vacancy in candidacy, filling, EL §§5-901 to 5-1303.

ELECTIONS —Cont'd
Candidates —Cont'd
Write-in candidates.
Certificate of candidacy.
Filing, EL §§5-301, 5-704.
Time for filing, EL §5-303.
Canvass, EL §§11-101 to 11-605.
Absentee ballots, EL §11-302.
Appeal of rejection of ballot, EL §11-304.
Board of state canvassers, EL §11-502.
Canvass by, EL §§11-501, 11-503.
Certification of election results.
After verification of vote count, EL §11-308.
Board of state canvassers, EL §11-603.
By local board of canvassers, EL §11-308.
Congress members.
Effect of issuance of certificate to, EL §11-604.
False reports, EL §16-601.
Presidential and congressional elections.
Governor's determination and proclamation, EL §11-601.
Referendum held by county, municipal corporation or political subdivision, EL §11-605.
Commission of election.
Issuance by governor, EL §11-602.
Congress members.
Effect of issuance of certificate of results to, EL §11-604.
Correction of errors in documents or records, EL §11-307.
Custody of documents and records.
Security, EL §11-306.
Definitions, EL §11-101.
Dissent or concern by board of canvassers member.
Filing, EL §11-308.
Documents and records.
Custody and security, EL §11-306.
Errors in documents, EL §11-307.
Election judges.
Procedures for vote counting, EL §11-202.
Errors in documents or records, EL §11-307.
Governor's determination and proclamation.
Presidential and congressional elections, EL §11-601.
Local boards of canvassers, EL §11-301.
Presidential and congressional elections.
Governor's determination and proclamation, EL §11-601.
Procedures for vote counting by election judges, EL §11-202.
Provisional ballots, EL §11-303.
Referendum held by county, municipal corporation or political subdivision.
Reporting results, EL §11-605.
Regulations, state board to adopt, EL §11-201.
Rejection of ballot by board of canvassers.
Absentee ballots, EL §11-302.
Appeal of rejection of ballot, EL §11-304.
Provisional ballots, EL §11-303.
Appeal of rejection of ballot, EL §11-305.
Statement of results by precinct, EL §11-402.
False reports, EL §16-601.
Statewide elections, EL §§11-501, 11-503.
Time.
Verification of vote count after election, EL §11-308.
Transmittal of results, EL §11-401.
Verification of vote count, EL §11-308.

ELECTIONS —Cont'd
Canvass —Cont'd
Voting systems.
Security and inspection following verification of vote, EL §11-403.
Write-in votes.
Statement of returns of votes cast, EL §11-401.
Central committee.
Filling vacancy in office of senator or delegate.
Power of committee, MD Const Art III §13.
Procedure, MD Const Art III §13.
Certificate of candidacy, EL §§5-301 to 5-304.
Board to determine whether candidate meets requirements, EL §5-301.
Campaign finance entity statement to accompany certificate, EL §5-304.
Certified mail, messenger service or delivery service.
Filing by, EL §5-304.
Democratic national convention candidates.
Time for filing, EL §5-303.
Facsimile service or other electronic transmission.
Filing by prohibited, EL §5-304.
Fee to accompany certificate, EL §5-304.
Filing, EL §5-301.
Manner of filing, EL §5-304.
Oath, appropriate board, EL §5-302.
Time, EL §5-303.
Filing fees.
Candidates for various offices, EL §5-401.
County governing body, transfer to, EL §5-403.
Distribution, EL §5-403.
Local boards, distribution to, EL §5-403.
Return to candidate, EL §5-402.
Waiver, petition for, EL §5-401.
Information specified on certificate, EL §5-304.
Judge of court of appeals standing for continuance in office, EL §5-301.
Judge of court of special appeals standing for continuance in office, EL §5-301.
Local board, filing with, EL §5-302.
Making, defacing or destroying, EL §16-901.
Name to appear on ballot.
Candidate to indicate on certificate, EL §5-301.
Nomination by party not required to nominate by party primary, EL §5-703.1.
Nomination by petition.
Candidates required to file, time, EL §5-703.
Oath, filing under, EL §5-302.
Presidential or vice presidential candidates.
Not required to file, EL §5-301.
Required to be candidate, EL §5-301.
Special election candidates.
Time for filing, EL §5-303.
State board, filing with, EL §5-302.
Suppressing certificate duly filed, EL §16-901.
Vacancy in candidacy, individual designated to fill.
Filing required, EL §5-1202.
Write-in candidate.
Filing, EL §§5-301, 5-704.
Time for filing, EL §5-303.
Certificate of declination, EL §5-801.
Certificate of election.
Issued after primary, EL §5-705.
Certificate of nomination, EL §5-705.
Making, defacing or destroying, EL §16-901.
Suppressing certificate duly filed, EL §16-901.
Certificate of withdrawal, EL §§5-501 to 5-504.
Authorized to withdraw by filing, EL §§5-501, 5-502.
Effect of filing, EL §5-504.

ELECTIONS —Cont'd
Certificate of withdrawal —Cont'd
Filing, EL §5-503.
Special election to fill representative vacancy in
    congress, EL §§5-502, 5-503.
**Certification and decertification of voting
    systems,** EL §§9-101 to 9-105.
Certification of election results.
After verification of vote count, EL §11-308.
Board of state canvassers, EL §11-603.
By local board of canvassers, EL §11-308.
Congress members.
    Effect of issuance of certificate to, EL §11-604.
False reports, EL §16-601.
Presidential and congressional elections.
    Governor's determination and proclamation, EL
        §11-601.
Referendum held by county, municipal corporation
    or political subdivision, EL §11-605.
Challenge of individual's right to vote, EL
    §10-312.
Challengers, EL §10-311.
Admitting before polling place opens, EL §10-303.
    Time for, EL §10-309.
Designating.
    Persons or entities with right to designate, EL
        §10-311.
Evidence of right, certificate, EL §10-311.
Leaving polling place before opening.
    Election judge may require, EL §10-303.
Nonaccredited challengers.
    Right to enter polling place, EL §10-311.
Positioning, EL §10-311.
Protection by election judge, EL §10-303.
Reasonable time to examine polling lists.
    Election judge may designate, EL §10-303.
Restrictions and prohibitions, EL §10-311.
Rights, EL §10-311.
Citation of article, 1 §25.
Clerks of court.
Contested elections.
    Decided by house of delegates, MD Const Art IV
        §12.
Closing polls, EL §§10-314, 11-202.
Collective bargaining.
Choice of bargaining representative.
    Consent elections, LE §§4-206 to 4-217.
        See COLLECTIVE BARGAINING.
State personnel.
    Exclusive representative.
        See STATE PERSONNEL.
Commission of election.
Issuance by governor, EL §11-602; MD Const Art
    IV §§11 to 13.
Comptroller, MD Const Art VI §1.
Contributions to political campaigns during
    general assembly sessions.
    Prohibition, exceptions, EL §13-235.
Filing fee, EL §5-401.
Computer equipment at polling places.
Record of registered voters, EL §10-302.
Computing time for performing any act, EL
    §1-301.
Congress.
Certificate of results issued to member.
    Effect, EL §11-604.
Filing fee.
    Senator or representative, EL §5-401.
Governor's determination of votes cast and
    proclamation of results, EL §11-601.

ELECTIONS —Cont'd
Congress —Cont'd
House of representatives, US Const Art I §4.
    Congressional districts.
        First congressional district, EL §8-702.
        Second congressional district, EL §8-703.
        Third congressional district, EL §8-704.
        Fourth congressional district, EL §8-705.
        Fifth congressional district, EL §8-706.
        Sixth congressional district, EL §8-707.
        Seventh congressional district, EL §8-707.
        Eighth congressional district, EL §8-709.
        Eight districts, state divided into, EL §8-701.
        References to districts, wards, precincts, etc.,
            EL §8-701.
    Vacancy for representative.
        Special election to fill, EL §8-710.
            Nomination by petition, filing petition, EL
                §5-703.
            Withdrawal of candidacy, EL §§5-502,
                5-503.
        Special primary, EL §§8-710, 8-711.
        Vacancy in nomination after primary election,
            EL §5-1003.
    Senate.
        Vacancy in office.
            Appointment by governor of eligible
                individual, EL §8-602.
            Special primary and special general election,
                EL §8-602.
            When election held, EL §8-601.
Congressional elections.
Representatives.
    Vacancies in office.
        Special election. See within this heading,
            "Special elections."
Constitution of Maryland.
Amendments, MD Const Art XIV §1.
Bribery.
Buying and selling votes, MD Const Art I §6.
Contested elections.
General assembly.
    Each house to judge own elections, MD Const
        Art III §19.
House of delegates.
    Decided by house of delegates, MD Const Art IV
        §12.
Judicial review of election, EL §§12-201 to 12-204.
    Appeal directly to court of appeals, EL §12-203.
    Applicability of subtitle, EL §12-201.
    Assignment to three judge panel, EL §12-203.
    Challenge by registered voter for act or
        omission, EL §12-202.
    Judgment, EL §12-204.
    Procedure, EL §12-203.
    Time, challenge by register voter, EL §12-202.
Legal expenses relating to contested results.
    Volunteering to pay, EL §13-233.
Legislature to make provisions for, MD Const Art
    I §8.
Recounts, EL §§12-101 to 12-107.
Contributions and expenses of campaign.
Disclosures by persons doing public business.
    Contributions to candidates for political office,
        EL §§14-101 to 14-108.
    See CAMPAIGN FINANCE.
Generally, EL §§13-101 to 13-605.
    See CAMPAIGN FINANCE.
**Corrupt or fraudulent acts in performance of
    official duties,** EL §16-301.

ELECTIONS —Cont'd
Counting votes.
Canvass, EL §§11-101 to 11-605.
County boards of education, ED §§3-114, 3-1301;
EL §§8-801 to 8-806.
Death, disqualification or declining nomination,
EL §8-805.
Nonpartisan basis, elected on, EL §8-802.
Primaries.
Any voter may vote, EL §8-802.
Nomination by, EL §8-804.
Provisions govern nomination and election, EL
§8-801.
Qualification of candidates, EL §8-803.
Requirements to be candidate, EL §8-802.
Responsibilities on election day, EL §10-307.
Voting for, EL §8-806.
County boards of elections.
Absentee voting.
Duties and responsibilities generally, EL
§§9-301 to 9-312.
Extra compensation for performing duties, EL
§9-311.
Accountable to state board, EL §2-201.
Alteration of precinct boundaries, procedures, EL
§2-202.1.
Appeal to board, EL §2-206.
Appointment, EL §2-201.
Appropriation by counties of funds for operation,
EL §2-203.
Availability of members on election day and
during canvass, EL §2-302.
Availability on election day, EL §10-307.
Board in each county of state, EL §2-201.
Certificate of candidacy.
Filing with local board, EL §5-302.
Classified employees, EL §2-207.
Conduct of election, EL §8-101.
Conviction, disqualification, EL §16-1001.
Counsel.
Appointing or retaining, compensation, EL
§2-205.
Death, resignation or removal of regular member,
EL §2-201.
Employees.
Appointment or removal, EL §2-207.
Expense reimbursement to regular members, EL
§2-204.
Hours of business, EL §2-302.
Instructional meeting for local board members, EL
§2-104.
Required attendance, time and place,
reimbursement, EL §2-104.
State board to conduct, EL §2-104.
Judicial proceeding to which local board party.
Copy of initiating pleading provided state
boards, EL §2-105.
Right of state board to join as party, EL §2-105.
Notice of elections.
Providing, EL §8-102.
Number of members, EL §2-201.
Oath, EL §2-201.
Political activities, restrictions, EL §2-301.
Political parties.
Division of membership, EL §2-201.
Powers and duties, EL §2-202.
Precincts and precinct boundaries, powers, EL
§2-303.
President, EL §2-201.
Qualifications, EL §2-201.

ELECTIONS —Cont'd
County boards of elections —Cont'd
Records management, EL §2-106.
Certified copies as evidence, EL §2-106.
Regulations, EL §2-202.1.
Removal, EL §2-201.
Salary of regular members, EL §2-204.
Skilled or professional service employees, EL
§2-207.
Substitute members.
Absence or vacancy of regular member.
Exercise of powers and duties, EL §2-201.
Compensation, EL §2-204.
Death, resignation or removal of regular
member, EL §2-201.
Number, EL §2-201.
Term, EL §2-201.
Court of appeals judges.
Notice to state board of name of judge to be placed
on ballot, EL §5-301.
Court of special appeals judges.
Notice to state board of name of judge to placed
on ballot, EL §5-301.
Credit unions.
Election of directors and officers, FI §§6-329,
6-330.
Criminal offenses and penalties, EL §§16-101 to
16-1001.
Absentee voting, EL §9-312.
Adding or deleting votes, EL §16-304.
Alcoholic beverage use at polling place, EL
§16-207.
Ballots and balloting, EL §16-206.
Campaign finance generally, EL §§13-602, 13-603.
Contributions by persons doing public business.
Disclosure violations, EL §14-107.
Public campaign financing, EL §15-110.
Campaign finance reports.
Failure to file, EL §13-335.
False or misleading statements, EL §13-601.
Canvassing.
Certification or statement of results.
False reports, EL §16-601.
Certificates of candidacy or nomination, EL
§16-901.
Corrupt or fraudulent acts in performance of
official duties, EL §16-301.
Defacing or removing election records, EL
§16-701.
Disobeying lawful command of election official, EL
§16-203.
Disturbing peace, EL §16-204.
Election officials, individuals attired or equipped
as prohibited, EL §16-903.
Violations, penalty, EL §16-1002.
False oath or affirmation, EL §16-501.
General penalty provision, EL §16-1001.
Interfering with election officials, EL §16-205.
Operation of polling place, EL §16-303.
Petitions, EL §16-401.
Provisional ballot voting, EL §9-408.
Public campaign financing, EL §15-110.
Removal of equipment or supplies placed in
polling place, EL §16-803.
Tampering with election records, EL §16-302.
Voter registration, EL §16-601.
Copy of voter registration list used for
commercial solicitation, EL §3-506.
Voting, EL §16-201.
Person convicted of infamous crime, EL §16-202.

ELECTIONS —Cont'd
Criminal offenses and penalties —Cont'd
Voting equipment.
Concealing, damaging, destroying or removing
from official's custody, EL §16-801.
Tampering with or attempting to damage, EL
§16-802.
Voting systems.
Tampering with electronic system, EL §16-804.
Wagering on elections, EL §16-902.
Date of elections.
General election, MD Const Art XV §7.
Death of candidate.
Vacancy, filling, EL §§5-901 to 5-1303.
Declination of nomination, EL §5-801.
Vacancy, filling, EL §§5-901 to 5-1303.
Defacing or removing election records, EL
§16-701.
Definitions, EL §1-101.
Canvass, EL §11-101.
Democratic national convention.
Candidates for delegates.
Certificate of candidacy.
Time for filing, EL §5-303.
Developmental disabilities.
Rights of individuals.
Infringement of right to vote, HG §7-1004.
Disabled voters.
Absentee voting, MD Const Art I §3.
**Disobeying lawful command of election
official,** EL §16-203.
Disqualification of candidate.
Vacancy, filling, EL §§5-901 to 5-1303.
Disqualification of voters, EL §3-102.
District of Columbia.
Electors for president and vice-president, US
Const Amd 23.
Districts.
Residence.
Requirements, MD Const Art I §1.
Voting in more than one district.
Penalty, MD Const Art I §5.
Disturbing peace, EL §16-204.
Domestic violence.
Address confidentiality program.
Use of actual address for election-related
purposes, FL §4-527.
Early voting, EL §10-301.1.
Elderly voters.
Polling place inaccessible.
Assignment of alternative, issuance of absentee
ballot, EL §10-102.
Election directors.
Appeal of decision to local board, EL §2-206.
Appointment by county board, EL §2-202.
Political activities, restrictions, EL §2-301.
Powers and duties, EL §2-206.
Election judges, EL §§10-201 to 10-207.
Admitting challenger or watcher before polls open.
Time restrictions, EL §10-309.
Appointment, EL §10-203.
Substitute.
Vacancy during voting hours, EL §10-305.
Assistance to voters in marking ballots, EL
§10-310.
Authority and duties, EL §10-303.
Badge, wearing on election day, EL §10-303.
Challenged voters.
Procedures, EL §10-312.
Chief judge.
Designation, supervision of staff, EL §10-203.

ELECTIONS —Cont'd
Election judges —Cont'd
Closing polls, EL §§10-314, 11-202.
Compensation, EL §10-205.
Conviction, disqualification, EL §16-1001.
Corrupt or fraudulent acts, EL §16-301.
Disobeying lawful command of official, EL
§16-203.
Equal number for political parties, EL §10-201.
Failure to challenge voter not entitled to vote, EL
§16-303.
Guidelines for determining qualification.
Adoption by local board, EL §10-202.
Instructing voters prior to voting, EL §10-310.
Instruction for, EL §10-206.
Interfering with election officials, EL §16-205.
Interfering with person lawfully casting vote, EL
§16-303.
Keeping the peace.
Authority, duty, EL §10-303.
Minors as judges, EL §10-201.
Exception to maximum work hours, LE §3-210.
Neglect of official duties, EL §16-301.
Number provided to staff polling place, EL
§10-201.
Oath, EL §10-204.
Obstructing view of person lawfully at polling
place, EL §16-303.
Partisan or political activity, restrictions, EL
§10-202.
Permitting ballot to be placed in ballot box prior
to time for voting, EL §16-304.
Placing ballot in ballot box, EL §16-304.
Political activities, restrictions, EL §2-301.
Protection of challengers or watchers, EL §10-303.
Qualifications, EL §10-202.
Qualifying voters, EL §10-310.
Refusal to follow instructions, EL §16-303.
Removal, EL §10-207.
Responsibilities on election day.
Before polls open, EL §10-309.
During voting hours, EL §10-310.
Setting up polling place.
Responsibility before polls open, EL §10-309.
State employees, EL §10-202.
Substitute, appointment.
Vacancy during voting hours, EL §10-305.
Term, EL §10-203.
Training, EL §10-206.
Unfit or incompetent.
Removal, EL §10-207.
Vacancy, filling, EL §10-203.
During voting hours, EL §10-305.
Vote counting, procedures for, EL §11-202.
Election officials.
Individuals attired or equipped as prohibited, EL
§16-903.
Violations, penalty, EL §16-1002.
Electors.
Congress, US Const Art I §2; Amds 14, 17.
District of Columbia, US Const Amd 23.
Electoral college, US Const Art II §1; Amds 12, 14.
House of representatives, US Const Art I §2; Amd
12.
Senate, US Const Amds 14, 17.
Vice-president, US Const Art II §1; Amds 12, 14.
Electronic filing of documents.
Facsimile transmittal, EL §1-302.
Electronic format of election results, EL
§11-402.

ELECTIONS —Cont'd
Emergency circumstances interfering with electoral process, EL §8-103.
Equipment and supplies.
Delivery to polling place, EL §10-302.
Evidence.
Certified copies of records maintained by boards of elections, EL §2-106.
Facsimile transmittal.
Electronic filing of documents, EL §1-302.
Fair campaign financing act.
Preservation of purity of elections.
Laws to be passed for, MD Const Art I §7.
False name, voting under, EL §16-201.
False oath or affirmation, EL §16-501.
Fax.
Electronic filing of documents, EL §1-302.
Fees.
Campaign finance reports.
Late filing fee, EL §§13-321, 13-331.
Administrative waiver, EL §13-337.
Distributions, EL §13-340.
Filing fees.
Candidates, EL §§5-401 to 5-403.
Vacancy in candidacy, individual designated to fill.
Payment required, EL §5-1202.
Financing campaigns.
Disclosures by persons doing public business.
Contributions to candidates for political office, EL §§14-101 to 14-108.
See CAMPAIGN FINANCE.
Generally, EL §§13-101 to 13-605.
See CAMPAIGN FINANCE.
Public campaign financing, EL §§15-101 to 15-111.
See CAMPAIGN FINANCE.
Fines.
Buying and selling votes, MD Const Art I §6.
Illegal voting, MD Const Art I §5.
Firearms.
Bringing to polling places, prohibited, EL §16-903.
Violations, penalty, EL §16-1002.
Force, threats, menace, intimidation, bribery, reward.
Breach of peace by threat or violence, EL §16-204.
Influencing voter's decision by, EL §16-201.
Franchise, MD Const Art I §§1 to 12.
Fraternal benefit societies.
Officers, IN §8-420.
Free and frequent, MD Const DofR Art 7.
Funds.
Election modernization fund, EL §2-107.
General assembly.
Contributions to political campaigns during sessions.
Prohibition, exceptions, EL §13-235.
County in which candidate resides.
Identification on ballot, EL §9-210.
Filing fee, EL §5-401.
Legislative newsletters, EL §§13-406 to 13-409.
Power to regulate or prohibit right to vote, MD Const Art I §4.
Vacancy in nomination after primary election, EL §5-1003.
General election.
Certification of content and arrangement of ballot, EL §9-207.
Statewide general election.
When held, EL §8-301.
Time for holding, MD Const Art XV §7.

ELECTIONS —Cont'd
Governor and lieutenant governor.
Ballots.
Joint listing of names of candidates for governor and lieutenant governor, MD Const Art II §1B.
Commission of election.
Issuance by governor, EL §11-602.
Considered unit for nomination and voting purposes, EL §5-205.
Contributions to political campaigns during general assembly sessions.
Prohibition, exceptions, EL §13-235.
Death, withdrawal or disqualification of candidate, EL §5-1201.
Before primary, EL §§5-902 to 5-905.
Designation of candidate for lieutenant governor.
Candidate for governor to designate, EL §5-205.
Filing fee, EL §5-401.
Manner of holding, MD Const Art II §2.
Petition candidates.
Vacancy in candidacy, EL §5-1101.
Place of holding, MD Const Art II §2.
Presidential and congressional elections.
Determination of votes cast and proclamation of results, EL §11-601.
Public campaign financing.
Eligible gubernatorial ticket generally, EL §§15-101 to 15-111.
See CAMPAIGN FINANCE.
Qualifications of voters, MD Const Art II §2.
Questions relating to election determined by house of delegates, MD Const Art II §4.
Results.
Ascertaining, MD Const Art II §3.
Returns, MD Const Art II §2.
Tie election.
How decided, MD Const Art II §4.
Time of holding, MD Const Art II §2.
Vacancy in candidacy before primary.
Candidate for governor, EL §§5-904, 5-905.
Candidate for lieutenant governor, EL §5-903.
Designation of successor.
Remaining candidate, EL §5-902.
Successor unit formed after withdrawal, EL §5-902.
Withdrawal of remaining candidate, EL §5-902.
Vacancy in candidacy of petition candidates, EL §5-1101.
Vacancy in nomination after primary election, EL §5-1005.
Handicapped voters.
Assistance in marking ballot.
Absentee voting, EL §9-308.
Choosing individual to assist, EL §10-310.
Provisional ballot voting, EL §9-406.
Polling place inaccessible.
Assignment of alternative, issuance of absentee ballot, EL §10-102.
Holiday.
Statewide general election day as legal holiday, 1 §27.
Hours for voting, EL §10-301.
Early voting, EL §10-301.1.
Identification.
Proof of identity, EL §10-312.
Illiterate voters.
Assistance in marking ballot.
Choosing individual to assist, EL §10-310.
Provisional ballot voting, EL §9-406.

ELECTIONS —Cont'd

Impersonating another in order to vote, EL §16-201.

Infamous crime, voting by person convicted of, EL §16-202.

Information for voters at polling places, EL §10-306.

Insane persons, MD Const Art I §4.

Instructional meeting for local board members and election officials, EL §2-104.

Required attendance, time and place, reimbursement, EL §2-104.

State board to conduct, EL §2-104.

Intent of article, EL §1-201.

Interfering with election officials, EL §16-205.

Judges of courts.

General provisions.

See JUDGES.

Judicial appointees.

Code of conduct for judicial appointees.

Appointee who is a candidate, CJA Rule 16-814 Canon 5.

Discipline for campaign conduct, CJA Rule 16-814 Canon 5.

Judicial review of election, EL §§12-201 to 12-204.

Appeal directly to court of appeals, EL §12-203.

Applicability of subtitle, EL §12-201.

Assignment to three judge panel, EL §12-203.

Challenge by registered voter for act or omission, EL §12-202.

Judgment, EL §12-204.

Procedure, EL §12-203.

Time, challenge by register voter, EL §12-202.

Legal holiday.

Defined, 1 §27.

Legislative newsletters, EL §§13-406 to 13-409.

Libel and slander.

Liability of broadcasting stations for statements.

Statements as to opponents, CJ §3-503.

Statements as to persons other than opponents, CJ §3-504.

Limitation of actions.

Prosecution of certain misdemeanors under election code, CJ §5-106.

Local boards of canvassers, EL §11-301.

Local boards of elections.

County boards generally, EL §§2-201 to 2-303.

Mentally ill individuals in facilities.

Depriving individuals of right to vote, HG §10-704.

Modernization fund, EL §2-107.

Montgomery county housing opportunities commission.

Collective bargaining.

Exclusive representatives, HS §16-306.

Eligibility to vote, HS §16-307.

Municipal corporations.

Absentee ballots.

Right to vote by absentee ballot, 23A §47.

Annexation, 23A §19.

Property qualifications.

Not to be imposed as requirement to vote, 23A §46.

Referendum election.

Merger of corporations, 23A §19A.

Special elections, 23A §2.

National presidential nomination conventions.

Delegates and alternates.

Selection and certification by political parties, EL §8-501.

ELECTIONS —Cont'd

Neglect of duties.

Officials of elections or political parties, EL §16-301.

Nomination by party not required to nominate by party primary, EL §5-703.1.

Nomination by petition, EL §§5-701, 5-703.

Certificate of candidacy, filing, EL §5-703.

Declaration of intent, filing, EL §5-703.

Petition requirements generally, EL §§6-101 to 6-211.

Signatures required on petition, EL §5-703.

Vacancy in candidacy for petition candidates.

Governor and lieutenant governor unit, EL §5-1101.

Nominations.

By petition, EL §5-703.

Petition requirements generally, EL §§6-101 to 6-211.

Vacancy in candidacy for petition candidates, EL §5-1101.

Certificate of declination, EL §5-801.

Certificate of election.

Issued after primary results certified, EL §5-705.

Certificate of nomination, EL §5-705.

Making, defacing or destroying, EL §16-901.

Suppressing certificate duly filed, EL §16-901.

Death of nominee.

Vacancy, filling, EL §§5-901 to 5-1303.

Declination, EL §5-801.

Vacancy, filling, EL §§5-901 to 5-1303.

Defeated candidates name not to appear on general election ballot, EL §5-706.

Disqualification.

Vacancy, filling, EL §§5-901 to 5-1303.

Governor and lieutenant.

Death of candidate, declination of nomination or disqualification of nominee, EL §5-1201.

Methods of nominating candidate, EL §5-701.

Names of nominees submitted to voters, EL §5-1203.

Primary elections generally, EL §§8-201 to 8-205.

Requirements, EL §5-702.

Vacancy.

After primary election, EL §§5-1001 to 5-1005.

Certificate of candidacy and filing fees.

Filing and payment required by individual designated to fill, EL §5-1202.

Late vacancy before general election, EL §§5-1301 to 5-1303.

Occurring before primary, EL §§5-901 to 5-905.

Petition candidates.

Governor and lieutenant governor unit, EL §5-1101.

Reprinting ballots.

Candidacy properly filled and certified, EL §5-1204.

Withdrawal of candidacy.

Governor and lieutenant governor unit.

Vacancy before primary, EL §§5-902 to 5-905.

Vacancy in candidacy, filling, EL §§5-901 to 5-1303.

Write-in candidates, EL §5-704.

Notice, EL §8-102.

Alteration of precinct boundaries.

Local board procedures, EL §2-202.1.

Ballot questions, EL §7-105.

Campaign finance entity.

Service on responsible officers, EL §13-214.

ELECTIONS —Cont'd
Notice —Cont'd
Campaign finance reports.
Failure to file.
Show cause notice, EL §13-335.
Overdue reports.
Local board to provide state board notice, EL §13-328.
Requirement to file, EL §13-321.
Local boards to provide, EL §8-102.
Oaths.
Officers.
Forms, MD Const Art I §9.
Officers.
Buying and selling votes.
Penalties, MD Const Art I §6.
Orphans' court.
Judges, MD Const Art IV §40.
Petitions, EL §§6-101 to 6-211.
Advance determination of sufficiency.
Request, EL §6-210.
Affidavit by individual witnessing signatures, EL §6-204.
Altering petition after filed, EL §16-401.
Applicability of provisions, EL §6-102.
Ballot content and arrangement or error.
Judicial review, EL §9-209.
Certification that process completed, EL §6-208.
Time for, EL §6-210.
Conflicts with state constitution.
Not interpreted to conflict with, EL §6-102.
Contents, EL §6-201.
Declaratory relief pursuant to uniform declaratory judgments act, EL §6-209.
Deficiency, EL §6-206.
Definitions, EL §6-101.
Falsifying signature, EL §16-401.
Filing, EL §6-205.
Format.
Submission for sufficiency determination, EL §6-202.
Advance determination, request, EL §6-210.
Fraud, duress or force, obtaining signature, EL §16-401.
Guidelines and instructions.
Preparation by state board, EL §6-103.
Inducing person to sign or not sign, EL §16-401.
Information page.
Content requirements, EL §6-201.
Judicial review of determination, EL §6-209.
Time for, EL §6-210.
Misrepresenting fact, EL §16-401.
Nomination by petition, EL §§5-701, 5-703.
Notice of determination, EL §6-210.
Offenses and penalties, EL §§6-211, 16-401.
Random signature samples.
Optional verification of signatures, EL §6-207.
Recount, EL §12-101.
Ballot question, EL §12-103.
Counterpetition, EL §12-102.
Ballot question, EL §12-104.
Regulations.
Adoption by state board, EL §6-103.
Removal of signature, EL §6-203.
Review after filing, EL §6-206.
Satisfaction of requirements established by law.
Determination, EL §6-208.
Signature page.
Affidavit by individual witnessing signatures, EL §6-204.
Content requirements, EL §6-201.

ELECTIONS —Cont'd
Petitions —Cont'd
Signing, EL §6-203.
Offenses relating to signing petition, EL §16-401.
Sufficiency determination, EL §6-206.
Summary of proposal on signature page.
Full text to be available, EL §6-201.
Validated and counted signature, EL §6-203.
Verification and counting of signatures, EL §6-207.
Time for, EL §6-210.
Political activities, restrictions.
Boards of elections and election officials, EL §2-301.
Montgomery county charter restrictions.
Article not to preempt, EL §1-304.
Political committees.
Financing campaign.
Generally, EL §§13-101 to 13-605.
See CAMPAIGN FINANCE.
Political parties.
Financing campaign.
Generally, EL §§13-101 to 13-605.
See CAMPAIGN FINANCE.
Generally.
See POLITICAL PARTIES.
Polling places.
Alcoholic beverage license held by owner or occupant on building.
Use of building as polling place, EL §10-101.
Alcoholic beverage use at polling place, EL §16-207.
Alternative places.
Elderly or disabled individuals, EL §10-102.
Canvassing, electioneering or posting campaign materials.
In polling place or beyond line established, EL §16-206.
Closing polls, EL §§10-314, 11-202.
Delivery of equipment and supplies to, EL §10-302.
Designating location.
Local board's powers, EL §§2-303, 10-101.
Elderly or disabled individuals.
Alternative places, EL §10-102.
Election judges, EL §§10-201 to 10-207.
Number provided to staff polling place, EL §10-201.
Hours for voting, EL §10-301.
Information for voters, EL §10-306.
Line prohibiting electioneering beyond.
Establishing, EL §16-206.
Offenses relating to operation, EL §16-303.
Police officers on duty at.
Duties, EL §10-304.
Posting informational material, EL §10-306.
Requirements, EL §10-101.
Setting up before polls open.
Duty of election judges, EL §10-309.
Staffing.
Election judges, EL §§10-201 to 10-207.
Local board to provide, EL §10-307.
Vacancy in staff during election hours, EL §10-305.
Vacancy in staff during election hours, EL §10-305.
Volunteer fire company or rescue squad building used.
Payment for use of building, EL §10-101.

ELECTIONS —Cont'd
Polling places —Cont'd
Voting room.
Access to, EL §10-308.
Poll tax.
Failure to pay poll tax or other tax.
Denial or abridgement of right to vote by reason of failure prohibited, US Const Amd 24.
Potomac Highlands airport authority.
Power of authority to elect, TR §10-103.
Precincts.
Alteration of precinct boundaries.
Local board procedures, EL §2-202.1.
Boundaries.
Creating or changing.
Local boards, EL §2-303.
College campus precincts, EL §2-303.
Establishing, combining or abolishing.
Local board's powers, EL §2-303.
Preservation of purity.
Laws to be passed for, MD Const Art I §7.
Presidential elections, EL §§8-501 to 8-505.
Certificate of candidacy.
Presidential or vice presidential candidates need not file, EL §5-301.
Delegates and alternates to national nominating convention.
Selection and certification, EL §8-501.
Governor's determination of votes cast and proclamation of results, EL §11-601.
Presidential electors.
Election, EL §8-504.
Meeting, casting votes, EL §8-505.
Nomination, EL §8-503.
Primaries.
Placement of names of candidates on ballots, EL §8-502.
State in which candidate resides.
Identified on ballot by, EL §9-210.
Presidential electors.
Election, EL §8-504.
Meeting, casting votes, EL §8-505.
Nomination, EL §8-503.
Primaries.
Arrangement of candidates on ballot, EL §9-210.
Certificate of election.
Issued after primary, EL §5-705.
Certification of content and arrangement of ballot, EL §9-207.
Certification of names of candidates on ballot in county, EL §8-203.
County boards of education.
Any voter may vote, EL §8-802.
Nomination by, EL §8-804.
Date for holding, EL §8-201.
Defeated candidate.
Name not permitted on next general election ballot, EL §5-706.
Electing members of local central committees of political parties.
Purposes for holding primary election, EL §8-202.
Governor and lieutenant governor unit.
Vacancy in candidacy occurring before primary, EL §§5-902 to 5-905.
Method of nominating candidate, EL §5-701.
Nomination of candidates.
Purposes for holding primary election, EL §8-202.
Presidential elections.
Placement of names of candidates on ballots, EL §8-502.

ELECTIONS —Cont'd
Primaries —Cont'd
Purposes, EL §8-202.
Qualification of candidate for ballot, EL §§5-601, 8-204.
Statewide primary, EL §8-201.
Unopposed candidates.
Word placed by candidates name on ballot, EL §8-204.
Vacancy in candidacy occurring before primary, EL §§5-901 to 5-905.
Central committee or governing body of political party filling, EL §5-901.
Governor and lieutenant governor unit, EL §§5-902 to 5-905.
Voting system configured for, EL §9-204.
When held, EL §8-201.
Write-in votes.
Prohibited, EL §8-205.
Prisoners, MD Const Art I §4.
Buying and selling votes.
Penalty on conviction, MD Const Art I §6.
Procurement contracts.
Political contributions reporting requirements.
Contract clause covering compliance obligation, SF §17-402.
Definition of "contribution," SF §17-401.
Proof of identity, EL §10-312.
Provisional ballots, EL §§9-401 to 9-408.
Administration of voting.
Guidelines established by state board, EL §9-403.
Applicability of subtitle, EL §9-401.
Assistance in casting ballot, EL §9-406.
Budget to include funding, EL §9-401.
Canvassing, EL §11-303.
Completion, EL §9-405.
Content identical to ballot used in polling place, EL §9-213.
Criminal penalties for violation, EL §9-408.
Disabled voters.
Assistance in casting ballot, EL §9-406.
Documentation of voting.
Local board to maintain for each voter, EL §9-402.
Eligibility to cast, EL §9-404.
Envelopes, EL §9-407.
Forms prescribed by state board, EL §9-401.
Guidelines established by state board, EL §9-403.
Illiterate voters.
Assistance in casting ballot, EL §9-406.
Instructions, EL §9-407.
Record of voting.
Local board to maintain for each voter, EL §9-402.
Rejection of ballot by board of canvassers, EL §11-303.
Violations, EL §16-304.
Publication.
Ballot questions.
Notice, EL §7-105.
Notice of election by, EL §8-102.
Public campaign financing, EL §§15-101 to 15-111.
See CAMPAIGN FINANCE.
Public confidence and trust.
Ensuring, intention of article, EL §1-201.
Public contracts.
Contributions to candidates for political office.
Disclosures by persons doing public business, EL §§14-101 to 14-108.
See CAMPAIGN FINANCE.

ELECTIONS —Cont'd
Quadrennial elections.
Board of supervisors.
Terms.
Commencement, MD Const Art XVII §6.
Exceptions to provisions, MD Const Art XVII §7.
Provisions inconsistent with article.
Repealed or abrogated, MD Const Art XVII §9.
Purpose of article, MD Const Art XVII §1.
State and county officers, MD Const Art XVII §3.
Definition of officers, MD Const Art XVII §1.
Exceptions, MD Const Art XVII §3.
Terms.
Appointed by governor and county
commissioners, MD Const Art XVII §5.
Elected by voters, MD Const Art XVII §3.
When elections to be held, MD Const Art XVII
§2.
Qualifications to vote, EL §3-102.
Qualifying voters.
Election judges, EL §10-310.
Questions on ballot, EL §§7-101 to 7-105.
Petition.
Requirements generally, EL §§6-101 to 6-211.
Recount.
Petition and counterpetition, EL §§12-103,
12-104.
Records.
Certified copies, evidence, EL §2-106.
Defacing or removing, EL §16-701.
State and local boards of elections.
Certified copies, evidence, EL §2-106.
Records management, EL §2-106.
Recounts, EL §§12-101 to 12-107.
Bond filed with petition or counterpetition, EL
§12-105.
Costs, liability for, EL §12-107.
Counterpetition, EL §12-102.
Ballot question, EL §12-104.
Duties of boards of elections, EL §12-106.
Local boards' duties, EL §12-106.
Notice to boards of elections.
Petition filed, EL §12-101.
Petition for recount, EL §12-101.
Ballot question, EL §12-103.
Counterpetition, EL §12-102.
Ballot question, EL §12-104.
Question on ballot.
Petition, EL §12-103.
Counterpetition, EL §12-104.
State board's duties, EL §12-106.
Time.
Filing counterpetition for recount, EL §12-102.
Ballot question, EL §12-104.
Filing petition for recount, EL §12-101.
Ballot question, EL §12-103.
Referendum, MD Const Art XVI §§1 to 6.
Generally.
See REFERENDUM.
Registers of wills.
General provisions, MD Const Art IV §41.
Registration of voters, EL §§3-101 to 3-602.
See VOTER REGISTRATION.
Regulation of elections.
Power of legislature, MD Const Art III §49.
Reports.
Election directors, EL §2-206.
Residence.
Verification that dwelling is principal residence,
TP §2-218.

ELECTIONS —Cont'd
Residence —Cont'd
Voters.
Change of residence for purpose of voting, MD
Const Art I §5.
Requirements, MD Const Art I §1.
Results, transmittal, EL §11-401.
Rules and regulations.
Power of legislature to regulate, MD Const Art III
§49.
Schools.
Employee organizations, ED §§6-405, 6-406.
Noncertificated public school employees, ED
§§6-506, 6-507.
Legal holidays.
Primary and general election days, ED §7-103.
Special provisions as to Worcester county, ED
§7-103.
Use of property for other than school purposes.
General provisions, ED §7-108.
Security guards.
Individuals attired or equipped as prohibited, EL
§16-903.
Violations, penalty, EL §16-1002.
**Selection, certification and decertification of
voting systems,** EL §§9-101 to 9-105.
Sheriffs, MD Const Art IV §44.
Slates.
Campaign finance.
Two or more candidates with separate finance
entities, EL §13-209.
Special elections.
Certificate of candidacy.
Time for filing, EL §5-303.
Filling vacancies in congressional office or county
council.
Purposes for holding, EL §8-401.
Vacancy in office of representative, EL §§8-710,
8-711.
Vacancy in office of United States senator, EL
§8-602.
Specimen ballots, EL §9-214.
Method of providing notice, EL §8-102.
Ballot questions, EL §7-105.
Posting at polling place, EL §10-306.
State administrator of elections.
Appointment, EL §§2-102, 2-103.
Chief state election official, EL §2-103.
Duties, EL §2-103.
Injunctive or judicial relief, powers as to, EL
§2-103.
Oath, EL §2-103.
Political activities, restrictions, EL §2-301.
Removal, EL §2-103.
Statewide voter registration list, duties, EL
§3-101.
State board of elections.
Appointment, EL §2-101.
Availability of members on election day and
during canvass, EL §2-302.
Certificate of candidacy.
Filing with state board, EL §5-302.
Chairman.
Election, EL §2-101.
Consecutive terms, EL §2-101.
Conviction, disqualification, EL §16-1001.
Expense reimbursement, EL §2-101.
Hours open for business, EL §2-302.
Instructional meeting for local boards members
and election officials.
Conducting, EL §2-104.

ELECTIONS —Cont'd
State board of elections —Cont'd
Judicial proceeding in which local board party.
Copy of initiating pleading provided state board, EL §2-105.
Joinder as party, authority, EL §2-105.
Majority vote requirement, EL §2-102.
Management and supervision of elections.
Responsibility, EL §2-102.
Number of members, EL §2-101.
Oath, EL §2-101.
Per diem compensation, EL §2-101.
Political activities, restrictions, EL §2-301.
Powers, EL §2-102.
Principal political party membership.
Required, EL §2-101.
Qualifications, EL §2-101.
Records management, EL §2-106.
Certified copies as evidence, EL §2-106.
Removal for cause, EL §2-101.
Term, EL §2-101.
Vacancies, EL §2-101.
Statement of election results by precinct, EL §11-402.
State of emergency declared by governor.
Interference with electoral process, EL §8-103.
State personnel.
Collective bargaining.
Exclusive representative.
See STATE PERSONNEL.
Political activities, SPP §2-304.
State's attorneys, MD Const Art V §§7, 8.
Determining election, MD Const Art V §8.
Statewide general election.
When held, EL §8-301.
Suffrage.
Constitutional provisions, US Const Amds 15, 19.
Tampering with election records, EL §16-302.
Taxation.
Denial or abridgement of right to vote.
Failure to pay poll tax or any other tax, US Const Amd 24.
Voting systems.
Exemptions, TP §7-232.
Tied elections.
Attorney general.
Governor determining, MD Const Art V §2.
General elections, MD Const Art XV §7.
Governor.
Decided by general assembly, MD Const Art II §4.
New election ordered by governor, MD Const Art XVII §8.
Execution, MD Const Art XVII §8.
State's attorneys, MD Const Art V §8.
Time.
Ballot questions.
Certification of information on ballot, EL §7-103.
Constitutional conventions.
Automatic qualification of question on holding, EL §7-102.
Filing petition for election of charter board, EL §7-104.
Notice, EL §7-105.
Campaign finance reports.
Deadlines and reporting periods, EL §§13-309 to 13-313.
Certificate of candidacy.
Filing, EL §5-303.
Nomination by petition, filing, EL §5-703.

ELECTIONS —Cont'd
Time —Cont'd
Certificate of declination, filing, EL §5-801.
Computing time for performing any act, EL §1-301.
Judicial review of election.
Challenge by register voter for act or omission, EL §12-202.
Petition for nomination, ballot question or new political party, EL §6-210.
Primary elections.
Holding, EL §8-201.
Recounts.
Filing counterpetition for recount, EL §12-102.
Ballot question, EL §12-104.
Filing petition for recount, EL §12-101.
Ballot question, EL §12-103.
Statewide general election.
When held, EL §8-301.
Verification of vote count after election, EL §11-308.
Time off for employees to vote, EL §10-315.
Treasurers of political election campaigns.
Campaign finance generally, EL §§13-101 to 13-605.
See CAMPAIGN FINANCE.
Tri-county council for southern Maryland.
Chairman of council, 20 §2-401.
Uniform process for all elections, EL §8-101.
University of Maryland.
Campaign fund-raising by members of board of regents.
Restrictions, ED §12-115.
Unopposed candidates.
Primary elections.
Word placed by candidates name on ballot, EL §8-204.
Vacancy in candidacy.
After primary election, EL §§5-1001 to 5-1005.
For petition candidates, EL §5-1101.
Late vacancy before general election, EL §§5-1301 to 5-1303.
Miscellaneous, EL §§5-1201 to 5-1204.
Occurring before primary, EL §§5-901 to 5-905.
Voter information material.
Montgomery county.
Multiresidential structures, distributing or depositing, EL §1-303.
Voter registration, EL §§3-101 to 3-602.
See VOTER REGISTRATION.
Voters.
Absentee voting, MD Const Art I §3. See within this heading, "Absentee voting."
Age, MD Const Art I §1.
Persons eighteen years of age, US Const Amd 26.
Right to vote not to be abridged on account of age, US Const Amd 26.
Alcoholic beverages provided on election day, CR §9-203.
Bribery, CR §9-203.
Buying and selling votes, MD Const Art I §6.
Constitutional provisions, US Const Amd 15.
Disabled voters.
Absentee voting, MD Const Art I §3.
Insane persons.
Prohibited from voting, MD Const Art I §4.
Qualifications, MD Const Art I §§1, 4.
Governor's election, MD Const Art II §2.
Persons eighteen years of age, US Const Amd 26.

ELECTIONS —Cont'd

Voters —Cont'd

Removal from voter roll.
Effect, MD Const Art I §1.
Residence.
Change of residence for purpose of voting, MD
Const Art I §5.
Requirements, MD Const Art I §1.

Vote tally, tabulation and certification.
Canvass, EL §§11-101 to 11-605.

Voting.
Absentee voting, EL §§9-301 to 9-312.
Access to voting room, EL §10-308.
Assistance in marking ballot.
Absentee voting, EL §9-308.
Choosing individual to assist, EL §10-310.
Provisional ballot voting, EL §9-406.
Ballot offenses, EL §16-206.
Buying and selling votes.
Penalty, MD Const Art I §6.
Casting vote by other than qualified voter, EL
§16-304.
Challenge of individual's right to vote, EL
§10-312.
Early voting, EL §10-301.1.
Hours for voting, EL §10-301.
Illegal voting, MD Const Art I §5.
Inducing voter to mark ballot in certain way, EL
§16-206.
Instructing voters prior to voting, EL §10-310.
Interfering with voter in polling place, EL
§16-206.
Misrepresenting persons ability to vote, EL
§16-206.
More than once, EL §16-201.
More than one district, MD Const Art I §5.
Offenses relating to, EL §16-201.
Person convicted of infamous crime, EL §16-202.
Persons eighteen years of age, US Const Amd 26.
Proof of identity, EL §10-312.
Provisional ballots, EL §§9-401 to 9-408.
Qualifying voters prior to voting, EL §10-310.
Registration required, MD Const Art I §2.
Substituting, altering, adding or removing voted
ballot, EL §16-304.
Taxation.
Exemption, TP §7-232.
Time off for employees to vote, EL §10-315.
Write-in voting, EL §10-313.
Written or printed material.
Taking into polling place, EL §10-310.

Voting age, EL §3-102.

Voting equipment.
Concealing, damaging, destroying or removing
from official's custody, EL §16-801.
Keys, unauthorized possession, EL §16-802.
Preventing correct operation, EL §16-802.
Removal or destruction, EL §16-803.
Tampering with or attempting to damage, EL
§16-802.

Voting machines.
Arrangement of candidates on ballot, EL §9-210.

Voting room.
Access to, EL §10-308.

Voting systems.
Acquisition of selected and certified system, EL
§9-101.
By purchase, lease or rental, EL §9-105.
Alternative systems.
Review and evaluation by state board, EL
§9-102.

ELECTIONS —Cont'd

Voting systems —Cont'd

Bonds to finance costs of system.
County may issue, EL §9-104.
Considerations in making certification
determination, EL §9-102.
Decertification of system, EL §9-103.
Instructing voters prior to voting, EL §10-310.
Primary elections.
Configured for, EL §9-204.
Purchase, lease or rental.
Acquisition of system by, EL §9-105.
Regulations as to requirements for systems, EL
§9-102.
Regulations for review, certification and
decertification.
State board to adopt, EL §9-102.
Requirements for certification, EL §9-102.
Security and inspection following verification of
vote, EL §11-403.
Selection and certification by state board, EL
§9-101.
Tampering with electronic system, EL §16-804.
Unlocking device without authority, EL §16-206.
Use in all counties.
Selected and certified system, EL §9-101.

Wagering on elections, EL §16-902.

Washington suburban sanitary district.
Collective bargaining.
Exclusive representative, 29 §11.5-106.

Watchers, EL §10-311.
Admitting before polling place opens, EL §10-303.
Time for, EL §10-309.
Designating.
Persons or entities with right to designate, EL
§10-311.
Election results produced at polling place.
Admission of watcher to hear, EL §10-314.
Evidence of right, certificate, EL §10-311.
Leaving polling place before opening.
Election judge may require, EL §10-303.
Positioning, EL §10-311.
Protection by election judge, EL §10-303.
Reasonable time to examine polling lists.
Election judge may designate, EL §10-303.
Restrictions and prohibitions, EL §10-311.
Rights, EL §10-311.

Withdrawal of candidacy.
After filing but before primary.
Certificate of withdrawal, EL §§5-501 to 5-504.
Governor and lieutenant governor unit.
Vacancy before primary, EL §§5-902 to 5-905.
Vacancy in candidacy.
Filling, EL §§5-901 to 5-1303.

Woman suffrage, US Const Amd 19.

Write-in candidates.
Certificate of candidacy.
Filing, EL §§5-301, 5-704.
Time for filing, EL §5-303.

Write-in votes, EL §10-313.
Primary, prohibition, EL §8-205.
Statement of returns of votes cast, EL §11-401.
Voter afforded opportunity to cast in general
election, EL §9-210.

ELECTRIC ALARM BELLS.
Railroads placing at crossing.
County determination that crossing needs
protection, PUC §9-311.

ELECTRICAL CONSUMER PRODUCTS.
Unfair or deceptive trade practices.
Testing laboratory symbol, CL §13-308.

ELECTRICAL EXTENSION CORDS.
Unfair or deceptive trade practices.
Designation of maximum number of amperes, CL
§13-309.

ELECTRIC COMPANIES.
**Acquisition by affiliate of power to exercise
influence over policies and actions of
companies.**
Prior authorization from commission.
Required, application for authorization, review,
PUC §6-105.
Additional charge over net total costs.
Commission authorizing, PUC §7-305.
Affiliates.
Acquisition of power to exercise influence over
policies and actions of companies.
Prior authorization from commission.
Required, application for authorization,
review, PUC §6-105.
Annual reports by public service companies,
PUC §§6-201 to 6-210.
Billing customers, PUC §7-305.
**Biomass, solar or wind electric generating
facility.**
Net energy metering.
Customer owning or leasing and operating, PUC
§7-306.
Central heating or cooling systems.
Providing services for residential multiple
occupancy buildings or new shopping centers,
PUC §7-301.
**Certificate of public convenience and
necessity.**
Constructing generating station or overhead
transmission lines, PUC §7-207.
Joint construction, PUC §7-208.
Classification of companies, PUC §6-202.
Clean air act modifications, PUC §7-206.
Competition, customer choice.
Electric customer choice and competition act.
Generally, PUC §§7-501 to 7-517.
See ELECTRIC CUSTOMER CHOICE AND
COMPETITION ACT.
Rate stabilization, PUC §§7-520 to 7-549.
See ELECTRIC CUSTOMER CHOICE AND
COMPETITION ACT.
**Connection with electrical conductor to use
electricity.**
Prohibition, penalty, CR §6-303.
**Construction of generating station and
overhead transmission lines.**
Examination of alternatives to construction of new
transmission line, PUC §7-209.
**Conversion of overhead facilities to
underground locations,** PUC §§12-301 to
12-317.
See UNDERGROUND UTILITY FACILITIES.
**Costs and expenses of public service
commission, payment,** PUC §2-110.
Defined, PUC §1-101.
Electric customer choice and competition act.
Generally, PUC §§7-501 to 7-517.
See ELECTRIC CUSTOMER CHOICE AND
COMPETITION ACT.
Rate stabilization, PUC §§7-520 to 7-549.
See ELECTRIC CUSTOMER CHOICE AND
COMPETITION ACT.
Electric plant.
Defined, PUC §1-101.

ELECTRIC COMPANIES —Cont'd
Energy conservation building standards.
Certification by builder that building meets latest
edition of energy code.
Copies of certificate or statement of waiver
furnished public by company, PUC §7-405.
Electric company knowingly providing service in
violation of provisions, PUC §7-407.
Electric service not furnished to building unless
builder files certificate of statement of
waiver, PUC §7-405.
Filing certificate with electric company, PUC
§7-403.
Immunity of electric company for supplying
service to noncomplying building, PUC
§7-405.
Waiver of certification requirements, filing
electric company, PUC §7-404.
Inclusion in long-range plan, PUC §2-118.
Energy efficiency programs, promotion, PUC
§7-211.
**Environmental surcharge, adding to
customers' bills,** PUC §7-203.
Equipment, material or facilities.
Interference with or tampering with, CR §6-303.
**Excavation or demolition near underground
facilities.**
Generally, PUC §§12-101 to 12-113.
See UNDERGROUND UTILITY FACILITIES.
Montgomery county, PUC §§12-201 to 12-203.
Fuel rate adjustment, PUC §§4-401, 4-402.
Generating stations.
Certificate of public convenience and necessity
required to construct, PUC §7-207.
Healthy air act, EN §§2-1001 to 2-1005.
On-site generated electricity.
Approval process, PUC §7-207.1.
**Generation of electrician by eligible
customer-generator and fed back to
company.**
Net energy metering, PUC §7-306.
Healthy air act, EN §§2-1001 to 2-1005.
**Heating season, termination of service to low
income customers,** PUC §7-307.
Income tax.
Credits.
Multijurisdictional electric companies.
Wages paid at corporate headquarters, TG
§10-713.
Maryland modified income of corporations, TG
§10-309.
Independent audit opinion, PUC §4-208.
**Influence over policies and actions of
companies.**
Acquisition by affiliate of power to exercise.
Prior authorization from commission.
Required, application for authorization,
review, PUC §6-105.
**Inspection of plant by public service
commission,** PUC §2-114.
Interference with electrical equipment, CR
§6-303.
Prima facie evidence of violation, CR §6-303.
**Joint construction of generating station and
associated overhead transmission lines,**
PUC §7-208.
Jurisdiction of public service commission, PUC
§7-101.
Laying of power lines, PUC §7-103.
Alternatives to construction of new transmission
line, examination, PUC §7-209.

ELECTRIC COMPANIES —Cont'd
Laying of power lines —Cont'd
Certificate of public convenience and necessity
required.
Overhead transmission lines, PUC §7-207.
Joint construction of generating station and
overhead transmission lines, PUC §7-208.
Notice to property owners, PUC §7-204.
Long-range plans, PUC §7-201.
Low income residential customers,
termination of service to, PUC §7-307.
Make whole rate proceedings, PUC §4-207.
Manufacturing, selling and furnishing electric
power, PUC §7-103.
Meters.
Commission authorization to furnish or put into
use, PUC §7-301.
Incorrect meters, replacement, PUC §7-302.
Individual metering for residential occupancy
buildings or shopping centers, PUC §7-301.
Inspection by consumer, request, PUC §7-302.
Net energy metering, PUC §7-306.
Submetering, PUC §7-303.
Tampering with, penalty, CR §6-303.
Testing for accuracy, PUC §7-301.
Modification to power plants, PUC §7-205.
Clean air act modifications, PUC §7-206.
Municipal electric plants, PUC §7-210.
Net energy metering for eligible
customer-generators, PUC §7-306.
Notice of intent to run line or similar
transmission device over, on or under
land, PUC §7-204.
Notice of public hearing on constructing
generating station and overhead
transmission lines, PUC §§7-207, 7-208.
Overhead transmission lines.
Certificate of public convenience and necessity
required to construct, PUC §7-207.
People's counsel.
Generally, PUC §§2-201 to 2-206.
See PUBLIC SERVICE COMMISSION.
Pollution control equipment.
Installation in order to comply with clean air act.
Prior approval of commission.
Required, expedited review and approval,
PUC §7-206.
Power lines, laying, PUC §7-103.
Powers, PUC §7-103.
Prices.
Matters requiring commission investigation, PUC
§3-102.
Procedure before public service commission.
Generally, PUC §§3-101 to 3-114.
See PUBLIC SERVICE COMMISSION.
Public convenience and necessity.
Constructing generating station or overhead
transmission lines, PUC §7-207.
Joint construction, PUC §7-208.
Public hearing on constructing generating
station and overhead transmission lines,
PUC §§7-207, 7-208.
Public service commission.
Generally, PUC §§2-101 to 5-106.
See PUBLIC SERVICE COMMISSION.
Public service company franchise tax.
Companies to which tax applicable, TG §8-402.1.
Credits against tax, TG §8-417.
Public utilities generally.
See PUBLIC UTILITIES.

ELECTRIC COMPANIES —Cont'd
Purchase of power plant sites by state, PUC
§7-202.
Rate regulation and proceedings.
Billing customers under applicable rate filed for
service, PUC §7-305.
Fuel rate adjustment, PUC §4-402.
Generally, PUC §§4-101 to 4-503.
See PUBLIC SERVICE COMMISSION.
Just and reasonable rate defined, PUC §4-101.
Net energy metering, PUC §7-306.
Rate stabilization.
Companies obligated to provide standard offer
service, PUC §§7-520 to 7-549.
See ELECTRIC CUSTOMER CHOICE AND
COMPETITION ACT.
Reliability of electric power supply.
Matters requiring investigation by commission,
PUC §3-102.
Renewable energy portfolio standard.
General provisions, PUC §§7-701 to 7-713.
See RENEWABLE ENERGY PORTFOLIO
STANDARD.
Safety violations, penalties, PUC §13-202.
Security deposits.
Exemption of dwelling units of elderly subscribers
from cash deposit requirement, PUC §5-105.
Sliding scale to adjust costs of fuel or
purchased power, PUC §4-401.
State purchase of power plant sites, PUC
§7-202.
Termination of service to low income
residential customers, PUC §7-307.

ELECTRIC COOPERATIVES, CA §§5-601 to
5-642.
Acknowledgments.
Disqualification from taking acknowledgments
prohibited, CA §5-639.
Articles of consolidation, CA §5-627.
Filing, CA §5-636.
Articles of conversion, CA §5-630.
Filing, CA §5-630.
Articles of dissolution, CA §§5-630 to 5-632.
Filing, CA §5-636.
Articles of incorporation, CA §5-608.
Amendment, CA §5-609.
Filing, CA §5-636.
Articles of merger, CA §5-628.
Filing, CA §5-636.
Board of directors.
Bylaw provisions, CA §5-622.
Election of directors, CA §5-623.
Generally, CA §5-622.
Initial directors, CA §5-623.
Officers, CA §5-624.
Terms of office, CA §5-623.
Vacancies, CA §5-623.
Bylaws, CA §5-611.
Board of directors.
Provisions as to, CA §5-622.
Districts.
Provision for, CA §5-612.
Citation of act, CA §5-642.
Cold storage services.
Power to furnish, CA §5-607.
Consolidation, CA §5-627.
Articles of consolidation, CA §5-627.
Filing, CA §5-636.
Effect, CA §5-629.
Construction and interpretation, CA §5-602.

ELECTRIC COOPERATIVES —Cont'd
Conversion of corporation to cooperative, CA
§5-630.
Articles of conversion, CA §5-630.
Filing, CA §5-636.
Definitions, CA §5-601.
Dissolution, CA §§5-630 to 5-632.
Articles of dissolution, CA §§5-630 to 5-632.
Filing, CA §5-636.
Districts, CA §5-612.
Encumbrances on property, CA §5-640.
Fees, CA §5-637.
Filing of documents, CA §5-636.
Fees, CA §5-637.
Formation.
Articles of incorporation, CA §5-608.
Amendment, CA §5-609.
Filing, CA §5-636.
Authorized, CA §5-606.
Number of organizers, CA §5-606.
Purpose, CA §5-605.
Governing law, PUC §7-104.
Interpretation and construction, CA §5-602.
Liens, CA §5-641.
Consolidation or merger.
Effect, CA §5-629.
Encumbrances on property generally, CA §5-640.
Meetings of members.
Dissolution of cooperative that has begun doing
business.
Approval, CA §5-632.
Generally, CA §5-616.
Notice, CA §5-617.
Property dispositions.
Approval, CA §5-640.
Quorum, CA §5-618.
Voting, CA §5-619.
Members.
Dissolution of cooperative that has begun doing
business.
Approval, CA §5-632.
Eligibility for membership, CA §5-615.
Excess revenues.
Allocation to members and other persons, CA
§5-638.
Generally, CA §5-615.
Meetings of members, CA §§5-616 to 5-619.
Property dispositions.
Approval, CA §5-640.
Quorum for meetings, CA §5-618.
Termination of membership, CA §5-615.
Voting, CA §5-619.
Merger, CA §5-628.
Articles of merger, CA §5-628.
Filing, CA §5-636.
Effect, CA §5-629.
Names, CA §5-610.
Officers, CA §5-624.
Powers, CA §5-607.
Principal office.
Articles of incorporation to include address, CA
§5-608.
Change, CA §5-635.
Processing plant services.
Power to furnish, CA §5-607.
Property dispositions, CA §5-640.
Purpose of organization, CA §5-605.
Resident agent.
Articles of incorporation to include name and
address, CA §5-608.
Change, CA §5-635.

ELECTRIC COOPERATIVES —Cont'd
Revenues, CA §5-638.
Small rural electric cooperatives.
Defined, PUC §1-101.
Exemptions from electric customer choice and
competition act, PUC §7-502.
Taxation.
Exemption from excise and income taxes, CA
§5-637.
Title of act, CA §5-642.
ELECTRIC CUSTOMER CHOICE AND
COMPETITION ACT, PUC §§7-501 to 7-517.
Affiliates.
Transfer of assets, PUC §7-508.
Air quality surcharge or other mechanism to
protect environment.
Establishment, commission study, PUC 7-516.
Alternative forms of regulations, PUC §7-505.
Antitrust principles.
Investigation of anticompetitive conduct, PUC
§7-514.
Assessment of utility supply, PUC §7-505.
Billing practices.
Competitive billing, PUC §7-511.
Cease and desist orders, PUC §7-507.
Citation of act, PUC §7-517.
Competitive billing and metering, PUC §7-511.
Competitive transition charge, PUC §7-513.
Construction of act.
Supplementary nature of rights and remedies,
PUC §7-514.
Consumer complaints.
Consumer, defined, PUC §7-501.
Investigation of, PUC §7-507.
Consumer education programs, PUC §7-505.
Consumer, defined, PUC §7-501.
Consumer protection regulations, PUC §7-507.
Counties.
Acting as aggregator, PUC §7-510.
Customer choice.
Defined, PUC §7-501.
Effective date, PUC §7-509.
Initial implementation date, defined, PUC §7-501.
Phased implementation, PUC §7-510.
Definitions, PUC §7-501.
Rate stabilization, PUC §7-520.
Disciplinary action against licensees, PUC
§§7-507, 7-511.
Distribution services, PUC §7-506.
Distribution territory, defined, PUC §7-501.
Effective date.
Consumer choice, PUC §7-509.
Transfer of assets, PUC §7-508.
Electric bills.
Rate stabilization.
Required statements, PUC §7-541.
Electric companies.
Authority regulate, PUC §7-509.
Investor-owned electric companies.
Transition procedures, PUC §7-516.
Obligations of electric company, PUC §7-510.
Previously unregulated companies, PUC §7-512.
Transfer of assets, PUC §7-508.
Transition costs, PUC §7-513.
Transition to a restructured electric company,
PUC §7-505.
Valuation of assets, PUC §7-508.
Electricity purchased under existing
contracts.
Transition procedures, PUC §7-516.

ELECTRIC CUSTOMER CHOICE AND
COMPETITION ACT —Cont'd
Environmental laws.
Compliance with state and federal law, PUC
§7-507.
Transition procedures, PUC §7-516.
Exemptions.
Small rural electric cooperatives, PUC §7-502.
Intangible transition charge, PUC §7-513.
Internet services, PUC §7-507.
Interstate competition, PUC §7-515.
Investor-owned electric companies.
Transition procedures, PUC §7-516.
Legislative intent, PUC §7-504.
Licenses to supply electricity, PUC §7-507.
Applications, PUC §7-507.
Low-income customers.
Consumer, defined, PUC §7-501.
Services to customers, PUC §7-505.
Universal service program, PUC §7-512.1.
Defined, PUC §7-501.
Metering.
Competitive metering, PUC §7-511.
Municipal corporations.
Acting as aggregator, PUC §7-510.
People's counsel.
Authority of, PUC §7-507.
Phased implementation of customer choice,
PUC §7-510.
Public policy, PUC §§7-504, 7-505.
Public service programs.
Previously unregulated companies.
Recovering costs, PUC §7-512.
Qualified rate order.
Rate stabilization.
Defined, PUC §7-520.
Generally, PUC §§7-520 to 7-549.
Recovery of transition costs, PUC §7-513.
Rate caps, PUC §7-505.
Rate stabilization.
Inapplicability to companies subject to cap
during rate stabilization plan period, PUC
§7-521.
Rate stabilization, PUC §§7-520 to 7-549.
Appeals.
Qualified rate order.
Review by, PUC §7-528.
Applicability of provisions, PUC §7-521.
Investor-owned electric companies.
Special provisions, PUC §7-547.
Assignment of rate stabilization property, PUC
§7-542.
Assignee not public service company or electric
supplier, PUC §7-544.
Bankruptcy of company.
Qualified rate order not effected, PUC §7-540.
Circuit court of Baltimore City.
Qualified rate order.
Review by appeal, PUC §7-528.
Companies obligated to provide standard offer
services.
Applicability of provisions, PUC §7-521.
Court of appeals.
Qualified rate order.
Review by appeal, PUC §7-528.
Deferral of expenses.
Actual cost of carrying.
Recovery as additional rate stabilization
costs, PUC §7-525.
Rate stabilization plan.
Permissible deferrals, PUC §7-522.

ELECTRIC CUSTOMER CHOICE AND
COMPETITION ACT —Cont'd
Rate stabilization —Cont'd
Deferral of expenses —Cont'd
Rate stabilization plan —Cont'd
Secured through rate stabilization bonds,
PUC §7-523.
Voluntary or mandatory.
Commission may require, PUC §7-523.
Definitions, PUC §7-520.
Electric bills.
Required statements, PUC §7-541.
Financing parties.
Not public service company or electric supplier,
PUC §7-544.
Investor-owned electric companies.
Actual costs of carrying costs and expenses.
Recovery, PUC §7-549.
Applicability of special provisions to, PUC
§7-547.
Rate stabilization plan, PUC §7-548.
Lien and security interest in rate stabilization
property, PUC §7-542.
Qualified rate order.
Additional orders, issuance, PUC §7-534.
Adoption by commission.
Funds required, PUC §7-526.
Application, PUC §7-526.
As part of stabilization plan, PUC §7-524.
Bankruptcy of company.
Order not effected, PUC §7-540.
Costs to be recovered.
Order to include, PUC §7-527.
Defined, PUC §7-520.
Effective date, PUC §7-528.
Electric bills.
Required statements, PUC §7-541.
Final decision by commission.
Time limit after filing request, PUC §7-529.
Imposition and collection of charges
nonbypassable.
Provision included in order, PUC §7-530.
Irrevocability after order becomes effective, PUC
§7-528.
Modification, PUC §7-534.
Permissible provisions, PUC §7-536.
Rehearing by commission, subject to, PUC
§7-528.
Retiring and refunding rate stabilization bonds.
Order providing for, PUC §7-533.
Review by appeal.
Venue, time for taking, PUC §7-528.
Successors to electric company.
Obligations and rights under, PUC §7-543.
Termination and expiration.
Time, extension, PUC §7-532.
Time period for cost recovery.
Order to include, time limit, PUC §7-527.
Rate stabilization bonds.
Deferred expenses secured through, PUC
§7-523.
Defined, PUC §7-520.
Electric bills.
Required statements, PUC §7-541.
Issuance of additional bonds.
Additional order authorizing, PUC §7-534.
New bonds.
Additional order authorizing, status, PUC
§7-534.
Not debt, liability or pledge of state or other
governmental unit, PUC §7-535.

ELECTRIC CUSTOMER CHOICE AND COMPETITION ACT —Cont'd
Rate stabilization —Cont'd
Rate stabilization bonds —Cont'd
Notice on face of bonds.
Not obligation of state or other governmental unit, PUC §7-535.
Not obligation of state or other governmental unit, PUC §7-535.
Retiring and refunding.
Order may provide, adjustment of charges, PUC §7-533.
Rights and remedies of bondholders and assignees.
Orders may state and protect, PUC §7-536.
Rate stabilization charges.
Adjustment.
Retiring and refunding rate stabilization bonds, PUC §7-533.
Defined, PUC §7-520.
Exemption from taxes and other charges.
Transactions involving receipt, PUC §7-538.
Imposition and collection of charges nonbypassable.
Provision included in order, PUC §7-530.
Overcollections and undercollections.
Correction, procedure and time frames, commission to establish, PUC §7-531.
Proceeds of rate stabilization property.
Revenues and collections from charges, PUC §7-537.
Review and adjustment.
Procedure and time frames, commission to establish, PUC §7-531.
Rate stabilization costs.
Actual cost of carrying deferred expenses.
Recovery as additional costs, PUC §7-525.
Defined, PUC §7-520.
Financing and recovery, PUC §7-526.
Investor-owned electric companies.
Actual costs of carrying costs and expenses, recovery, PUC §7-549.
Reduction by funds contributed from other sources, PUC §7-526.
Rate stabilization plan.
Deferral of expenses.
Permissible deferrals, PUC §7-522.
Secured through rate stabilization bonds, PUC §7-523.
Voluntary or mandatory.
Commission may require, PUC §7-523.
Defined, PUC §7-520.
Filing, PUC §7-522.
Investor-owned electric companies.
Special provisions, PUC §7-548.
Tariffs implementing, PUC §7-524.
Rate stabilization property.
Account or general intangible under commercial law.
Property not deemed, PUC §7-542.
Defined, PUC §7-520.
Exemption from taxes and other charges.
Transactions involving transfer and ownership, PUC §7-538.
Lien or assignment, PUC §7-542.
Present property right, PUC §7-537.
Proceeds of property.
Revenues and collections from charges, PUC §7-537.
Rights and interests of electric companies, PUC §7-537.

ELECTRIC CUSTOMER CHOICE AND COMPETITION ACT —Cont'd
Rate stabilization —Cont'd
Rate stabilization property —Cont'd
Sale or other absolute transfer.
Transfer agreement stating, PUC §7-539.
Setoff, counterclaim, surcharge or defense.
Assignee's or pledgee's interest not subject to, PUC §7-540.
State pledge not to impair value, PUC §7-535.
Status, PUC §§7-537, 7-542.
True sale.
Agreement stating transfer sale or absolute transfer, PUC §7-539.
Status as true sale, PUC §7-539.
Scope of part, PUC §7-547.
Setoff, counterclaim, surcharge or defense.
Assignee's or pledgee's interest in rate stabilization property not subject to, PUC §7-540.
Successors to electric company.
Obligation, performance and satisfaction, PUC §7-543.
Tariffs implementing plan, PUC §7-524.
Recovery of transition costs, PUC §7-513.
Renewable portfolio standards.
Transition procedures, PUC §7-516.
Rulemaking authority.
Competitive billing and metering, PUC §7-511.
Consultation requirements, PUC §7-507.
Implementation of customer choice, PUC §7-510.
Rural electric cooperatives.
Exemptions for small cooperatives, PUC §7-502.
Service charges, PUC §7-507.
Short title of act, PUC §7-517.
Standard offer service, PUC §7-506.
Defined, PUC §7-501.
Rate stabilization.
Applicability to companies obligated to provide, PUC §7-521.
Generally, PUC §§7-520 to 7-549.
Termination of universal service.
Limitations, PUC §7-512.1.
Title of act, PUC §7-517.
Transitions costs, PUC §7-513.
Unfair discriminatory practices, PUC §7-507.
Investigation of anticompetitive conduct, PUC §7-514.
Universal service program fund, PUC §7-512.1.
Universal service programs, PUC §7-512.1.
Telephone lifeline service.
Eligible subscribers, PUC §8-201.

ELECTRIC FUEL RATE ADJUSTMENT, PUC §4-402.

ELECTRIC GENERATION FACILITY PLANNING.
Environmental surcharge, PUC §7-203.
Modification of power plant, PUC §7-205.
Notice to property owner of intent to run line or transmission device, PUC §7-204.
On-site generated electricity.
Approval process, PUC §7-207.1.
State purchase of power plant sites, PUC §7-202.
Ten-year plan, PUC §7-201.

ELECTRICIANS.
Appeals.
Disciplinary actions.
Judicial review of board, BOP §6-318.

ELECTRICIANS —Cont'd
Board.
State board of master electricians, BOP §§6-201 to
6-208. See within this heading, "State board
of master electricians."
Bonds, surety.
Local licenses.
Satisfaction of bond requirement by proof of
insurance, BOP §6-604.
Building codes.
Electrical code, PS §§12-601 to 12-607.
Model performance code for building construction,
PS §12-201.
Citation of act.
Short title, BOP §6-701.
Conflicts of interest.
Electrical inspectors, BOP §6-313.
Definitions, BOP §§6-101, 6-501.
Employers and employees.
Authorized individuals, BOP §6-605.
Evidence.
Disciplinary actions.
Evidence of intent to violate provisions, BOP
§6-316.
Fees.
Disposition of money collected, BOP §6-207.
Licenses.
Assignment of local licenses.
Change of status of licensee, BOP §6-402.
State licenses, BOP §6-309.
Examination fee, BOP §6-305.
Inactive status, BOP §6-311.
Electrical inspectors, BOP §6-313.
Reinstatement of expired licenses, BOP
§6-312.
Renewal fee, BOP §6-310.
Inactive status, BOP §6-311.
Hearings.
Disciplinary actions, BOP §6-317.
Injunctions.
State board of master electricians.
Actions for injunctions, BOP §6-206.
Insurance.
General liability and property insurance.
Requirements, BOP §6-604.
Legislative declaration, BOP §6-102.
Licenses.
Assignment of local licenses.
Change of status of licensee, BOP §6-402.
Defined, BOP §6-101.
Fees.
Change of status of licensee, BOP §6-402.
Generally, BOP §6-401.
Notices.
Change of status of licensee, BOP §6-402.
Restrictions, BOP §6-401.
Contents, BOP §6-309.
Defined, BOP §6-101.
Expiration, BOP §6-310.
Fees. See within this heading, "Fees."
Issuance.
Notice to qualified applicant, BOP §6-309.
Local licenses, BOP §6-601.
Assignment, BOP §§6-401, 6-402.
Bonds, surety.
Satisfaction of bond requirement by proof of
insurance, BOP §6-604.
Defined, BOP §6-101.
Duties of local governments, BOP §6-301.
Examinations.
Waiver of requirement, BOP §6-602.

ELECTRICIANS —Cont'd
Licenses —Cont'd
Local licenses —Cont'd
Required, BOP §6-601.
Waiver of examination requirement, BOP
§6-602.
Notice. See within this heading, "Notice."
Reciprocal licenses.
Assignment, BOP §6-506.
Defined, BOP §6-501.
Reciprocal action.
Local jurisdictions, BOP §6-502.
Reciprocal action between local
jurisdictions, BOP §6-504.
Reciprocal action between state board and
local jurisdictions, BOP §6-503.
Reinstatement.
Prohibited, BOP §6-505.
Renewal, BOP §6-505.
Transfer.
Prohibited, BOP §6-505.
Renewal, BOP §6-310.
Reciprocal licenses, BOP §6-505.
State licenses.
Applications, BOP §6-305.
Qualifications of applicants, BOP §6-304.
Change of name, address or employment.
Notice to board, BOP §6-314.
Credit for experience, BOP §6-308.
Defined, BOP §6-101.
Denial.
Disciplinary actions generally, BOP §§6-315
to 6-321.
Disciplinary actions.
Effect, BOP §6-319.
Evidence of intent to violate provisions, BOP
§6-316.
Grounds, BOP §6-316.
Hearings, BOP §6-317.
Judicial review, BOP §6-318.
Lapse of license.
Effect, BOP §6-315.
Reinstatement of revoked license, BOP
§6-319.
Notice, BOP §6-320.
Voluntary surrender of license.
Effect, BOP §6-315.
Effect, BOP §6-302.
Examinations, BOP §6-306.
Notices, BOP §6-306.
Testing service.
Used to administer examinations, BOP
§6-306.1.
Waiver of examination requirements, BOP
§6-307.
Reciprocal waiver, BOP §6-308.
Exceptions to requirement, BOP §6-303.
Expiration.
Inactive status, BOP §6-311.
Reinstatement, BOP §6-312.
Fees.
Examination fee, BOP §6-305.
Inactive status, BOP §6-311.
Electrical inspectors, BOP §6-313.
Reinstatement of expired licenses, BOP
§6-312.
Renewal fee, BOP §6-310.
Inactive status, BOP §6-311.
Inactive status, BOP §6-311.
Electrical inspectors, BOP §6-313.

ELECTRICIANS —Cont'd
Licenses —Cont'd
State licenses —Cont'd
Insurance.
General liability and property insurance.
Requirements, BOP §6-604.
Issuance, BOP §6-309.
Local governments to require, BOP §6-301.
Notices.
Change of name, address or employment,
BOP §6-314.
Disciplinary actions.
Revocation, suspension or reinstatement of
license, BOP §6-320.
Examinations, BOP §6-306.
Public utility companies.
Exceptions to requirement of license, BOP
§6-303.
Qualifications of applicants, BOP §6-304.
Reinstatement of expired licenses, BOP §6-312.
Renewal.
Inactive status, BOP §6-311.
Reprimand of licensee.
Disciplinary actions generally, BOP §§6-315
to 6-321.
Revocation or suspension.
Disciplinary actions generally, BOP §§6-315
to 6-321.
Scope, BOP §6-302.
Testing service.
Used to administer examinations, BOP
§6-306.1.
Waiver of examination requirements, BOP
§6-307.
Reciprocal waiver, BOP §6-308.
Statewide electrical licensing board.
Program evaluation act, SG §8-403.
Term, BOP §6-310.
Master electricians.
Board.
State board of master electricians. See within
this heading, "State board of master
electricians."
Defined, BOP §6-101.
Disciplinary actions.
Notice and report, BOP §6-321.
Statewide electrical licensing board.
Program evaluation act, SG §8-403.
Notice.
Disciplinary actions against master electricians.
State board and local licensing entity, BOP
§6-321.
Insurance.
Cancellation of required insurance.
Notice to state board, BOP §6-604.
Licenses.
Assignment of local licenses.
Change in status of license, BOP §6-402.
State licenses.
Change of name, address or employment,
BOP §6-314.
Disciplinary actions.
Revocation, suspension or reinstatement of
license, BOP §6-320.
Examinations, BOP §6-306.
Issuance.
Notice to qualified applicant, BOP §6-309.
Renewal notice, BOP §6-310.
Permits.
Notice of electrical requirements, BOP §6-603.

ELECTRICIANS —Cont'd
Oaths.
State board of master electricians.
Oath of office of members, BOP §6-202.
Ordinances.
Local regulations or ordinances, BOP §6-103.
Permits, BOP §6-603.
Policy of state, BOP §6-102.
Reciprocity.
Licenses.
Reciprocal licenses, BOP §§6-501 to 6-506. See
within this heading, "Licenses."
State licenses.
Waiver of examination requirements, BOP
§6-308.
Reports.
Disciplinary actions against master electricians.
Local licensing jurisdiction to report to state
board, BOP §6-321.
Rules and regulations.
Local regulations, BOP §6-103.
Termination of regulations adopted under
provisions, BOP §6-702.
Scope of provisions, BOP §6-103.
**Secretary of labor, licensing and regulation
department.**
State board of master electricians.
Authority of secretary, BOP §6-208.
Revenues of board.
Responsibilities as to, BOP §6-606.
Security systems technicians.
General provisions, BOP §§18-101 to 18-701.
See SECURITY SYSTEMS TECHNICIANS.
Licensed electricians.
Inapplicability of title, BOP §18-102.
Seminars.
State board of master electricians.
Duty to hold seminars, BOP §6-205.
Short title of act, BOP §6-701.
State board of master electricians.
Appointment of members, BOP §6-202.
Compensation of members, BOP §6-204.
Composition, BOP §6-202.
Creation, BOP §6-201.
Definition of "state board," BOP §6-101.
Disposition of money collected, BOP §6-207.
Enforcement powers, BOP §6-206.
Established, BOP §6-201.
Expenses of members.
Reimbursement, BOP §6-204.
Meetings, BOP §6-204.
Number of members, BOP §6-202.
Oaths.
Oath of office of members, BOP §6-202.
Officers.
Election, BOP §6-203.
Qualifications of members, BOP §6-202.
Quorum, BOP §6-204.
Removal of members, BOP §6-202.
Secretary of labor, licensing and regulation
department.
Authority of secretary, BOP §6-208.
Revenues of board.
Responsibilities as to, BOP §6-606.
Seminars.
Duty to hold seminars, BOP §6-205.
Staff, BOP §6-204.
Terms of members, BOP §6-202.
Vacancies, BOP §6-202.
Subpoenas.
State board of master electricians.
Powers, BOP §6-206.

ELECTRICIANS —Cont'd
Termination of provisions, BOP §6-702.
Title of act.
Short title, BOP §6-701.

ELECTRICITY.
Air quality control.
Electric company operating permit for generating station, EN §2-405.
Installation of pollution control equipment or changes in method of operation.
Consolidation of procedures, EN §2-405.
Assisted living programs.
Emergency electrical power generator, HG §19-1812.
Batteries.
Fraud as to storage batteries, CL §11-902.
Board of statewide electrical licensing.
Program evaluation act, SG §8-403.
Building codes.
Electrical code, PS §§12-601 to 12-607.
Emergency power and lighting systems, PS §12-702.
Model performance code for building construction, PS §12-201.
Code, PS §§12-601 to 12-607.
Consumer protection.
Appliance service contracts, CL §14-1306.
Extension cords.
Labeling, CL §13-309.
Labeling electrical consumer product with symbol of testing laboratory.
Required, CL §13-308.
Ladders.
Capable of conducting electricity, CL §14-1307.
Waivers of consumer liability not considered insurance, IN §1-203.1.
Cooperatives.
General provisions, CA §§5-601 to 5-642.
See ELECTRIC COOPERATIVES.
Governing law, PUC §7-104.
Counties.
County codes.
Electrical code, 25 §3.
Districts.
Electric lighting districts, 25 §2B.
Somerset county.
Special provisions, 25 §2B.
Electric customer choice and competition act.
Generally, PUC §§7-501 to 7-517.
See ELECTRIC CUSTOMER CHOICE AND COMPETITION ACT.
Rate stabilization, PUC §§7-520 to 7-549.
See ELECTRIC CUSTOMER CHOICE AND COMPETITION ACT.
Energy allocation equipment and procedures used by apartment owners, operators or managers.
Determining amount of electricity used by individual dwelling unit, PUC §7-304.
Environmental surcharge for electricity generated within state, PUC §7-203.
Extension cords.
Designation of maximum number of amperes, CL §13-309.
Fish and fisheries.
Electronic and electrical devices.
Regulations, NR §4-509.
Fraud and deceit.
Storage batteries, CL §11-902.

ELECTRICITY —Cont'd
Generating stations.
Healthy air act, EN §§2-1001 to 2-1005.
On-site generated electricity.
Approval process, PUC §7-207.1.
Operating permit for generating station, EN §2-405.
High voltage lines.
General provisions, LE §§6-101 to 6-110.
See HIGH VOLTAGE LINES.
Hydroelectric power.
Susquehanna river basin commission, EN §5-301.
Income tax credits.
Qualified energy resources, TG §10-720.
Ladders capable of conducting electricity, CL §14-1307.
Lines.
High voltage lines.
General provisions, LE §§6-101 to 6-110.
See HIGH VOLTAGE LINES.
Mining.
General provisions.
See MINING.
Municipal corporations.
Power in general, 23 §182.
Ratification by people, 23 §183.
Permits.
Consolidated procedures for development permits.
Applicability of title to electrical projects, SG §11-103.
Operating permit for generating station, EN §2-405.
Pollution control equipment.
Electric company operating permit for generating station.
Installation of equipment or changes in method of operation.
Consolidation of procedures, EN §2-405.
Power plants.
Certificate of public convenience and necessity.
Applications.
Review and recommendations concerning construction, NR §3-306.
Same as appropriation or use permit application, EN §5-502.
Research program.
Acid deposition.
Responsibilities of program director, NR §3-3A-02.
Acquisition.
General provisions, NR §3-305.
Definitions, NR §3-301.
Director.
Acid deposition.
Responsibilities, NR §3-3A-02.
Environmental research program.
General provisions, NR §3-303.
Implementation, NR §3-303.
Environmental trust fund, NR §3-302.
Evaluation.
Long-range power plant site evaluation, NR §3-304.
Generator lead routes.
Defined, NR §3-301.
Designation, NR §3-305.
Judicial review, NR §3-307.
Local zoning rules, etc.
Use of sites in inventory without regard to local zoning rules, etc., NR §3-306.1.
Long-range power plant site evaluation, NR §3-304.

ELECTRICITY —Cont'd
Power plants —Cont'd
Research program —Cont'd
Program.
Defined, NR §3-301.
Review of decisions, NR §3-307.
Site acquisition, NR §3-305.
Site evaluation.
Long-range power plant site evaluation, NR §3-304.
Property taxes.
Credits.
Electricity generation facilities.
Effect of personal property tax credits on state aid for machinery and equipment, TP §9-239.
Exemptions.
Machinery used to generate electricity, TP §7-237.
Property used to heat, cool or generate electricity for state, TP §7-211.1.
Sales and use tax.
Special use tax on certain electricity, TG §§11-1A-01 to 11-1A-06.
School buildings.
Solar energy pilot program, ED §5-301.1.
Statewide electrical licensing board.
Program evaluation act, SG §8-403.
Waivers of consumer liability.
Not considered insurance, IN §1-203.1.

ELECTRIC METERS.
Accuracy, testing, PUC §7-301.
Apartments.
Submetering, PUC §7-303.
Fees for meter test services.
Commissioned to set uniform fees, PUC §7-302.
Furnishing or putting into use for billing purposes, authorization by commission, PUC §7-301.
Incorrect meters, replacement, PUC §7-302.
Individual metering for residential multiple occupancy buildings and shopping centers, PUC §7-301.
Inspection by consumer, request, PUC §7-302.
Submetering, PUC §7-303.
Testing of meters accuracy, PUC §7-301.

ELECTRIC OPERATED RAILROADS.
Power to condemn, PUC §5-409.

ELECTROLOGISTS, HO §§8-6B-01 to 8-6B-29.
Advertising, HO §8-6B-23.
Advisory letters.
Issuance, HO §8-6B-19.
Board of electrologists.
Liability.
Good faith exemption from civil liability for acts within scope of jurisdiction of board, CJ §5-706.
Licensing. See within this heading, "Licenses."
Program evaluation act, SG §8-403.
Continuing education, HO §8-6B-14.
Criminal history records checks.
License applicants, HO §§8-6B-08, 8-6B-09.
Renewal of license, HO §8-6B-14.
Definitions, HO §8-6B-01.
Display of health precautions notice, HO §8-6B-26.
Education program.
Approval, HO §8-6B-16.
Instruments and procedures, HO §8-6B-24.

ELECTROLOGISTS —Cont'd
Education program —Cont'd
Misrepresentation, HO §8-6B-23.
Periodic review, HO §8-6B-16.
Withdrawal of approval, HO §8-6B-17.
Fees.
Establishment and distribution, HO §8-6B-04.
Immunity.
Board of electrologists.
Good faith exemption from civil liability for acts within scope of jurisdiction of board, CJ §5-706.
Instructors.
Approval of education program, HO §8-6B-16.
Instruments and procedures, HO §8-6B-24.
Licenses, HO §8-6B-13.
Misrepresentation, HO §8-6B-23.
Liability.
Board of electrologists.
Good faith exemption from civil liability for acts within scope of jurisdiction of board, CJ §5-706.
Licenses.
Advisory letters, HO §8-6B-19.
Applications, HO §8-6B-09.
Contents, HO §8-6B-12.
Criminal history records checks, HO §§8-6B-08, 8-6B-09.
Renewal of license, HO §8-6B-14.
Disciplinary action, HO §8-6B-18.
Appeal of decision, HO §8-6B-21.
Hearings, HO §8-6B-19.
Penalties, HO §8-6B-20.
Reinstatement, HO §8-6B-22.
Duration, HO §8-6B-14.
Examination.
Conduct, HO §8-6B-10.
Required, HO §8-6B-08.
Waiver, HO §8-6B-11.
Exceptions, HO §8-6B-07.
Inactive status, HO §8-6B-14.
Instructors, HO §8-6B-13.
Issuance, HO §§8-6B-09, 8-6B-12.
Qualifications, HO §8-6B-08.
Reciprocity, HO §8-6B-11.
Reinstatement, HO §8-6B-14.
After suspension or revocation, HO §8-6B-22.
Renewal, HO §8-6B-14.
Requirement, HO §8-6B-07.
Scope, HO §8-6B-13.
Surrender, HO §8-6B-15.
Suspension or revocation, HO §8-6B-18.
Appeal of decision, HO §8-6B-21.
Hearings, HO §8-6B-19.
Penalty in lieu of, HO §8-6B-20.
Reinstatement, HO §8-6B-22.
Medical records.
Destruction, HG §4-403.
Notice from centers for disease control.
Health precautions notice, display, HO §8-6B-26.
Practice committee.
Created, HO §8-6B-05.
Members, HO §8-6B-05.
Powers and duties, HO §8-6B-06.
Term of membership, HO §8-6B-05.
Qualifications for license, HO §8-6B-08.
Records.
Destruction of patient's medical records, HG §4-403.
Regulations, adoption, HO §8-6B-03.

ELECTROLOGISTS —Cont'd
Reports.
Education program, periodic review, HO §8-6B-16.
Scope of provisions, HO §8-6B-02.
Sexual misconduct.
Disciplinary action, HO §1-212.
Termination of provisions, HO §8-6B-29.
Title of provisions, HO §8-6B-28.
Violations of subtitle, HO §8-6B-27.
Waiver of examination, HO §8-6B-11.

ELECTRONIC AUDIO AND AUDIO-VIDEO.
Circuit courts.
Recording of proceedings, CJA Rule 16-405.
Access to recordings, CJA Rule 16-406.

ELECTRONIC CHATTEL PAPER.
Secured transactions.
Control, CL §9-105.
Perfection by control, CL §9-314.
Defined, CL §9-102.

ELECTRONIC FILINGS.
Administration of courts, CJA Rule 16-804.
District Court, CJA Rule 16-506.
Elections.
Facsimile transmittal, EL §1-302.
Pleadings and papers, CJA Rule 16-307.
State documents, SG §7-213.

ELECTRONIC FUNDS TRANSFERS.
Commercial code, CL §§4A-101 to 4A-507.
See FUNDS TRANSFERS.
Credit card crimes, CR §§8-201 to 8-217.
See CREDIT CARDS.

ELECTRONIC HOME SUPERVISION.
Home detention program.
Inmates in correctional facilities in division of
correction.
Method of supervision, COR §3-403.

ELECTRONIC MAIL.
See EMAIL.

**ELECTRONIC PERSONAL ASSISTIVE
MOBILITY DEVICE (EPAMD).**
Due care of drivers, TR §21-1209.
Earphones.
Wearing prohibited, TR §21-1210.
Earplugs.
Wearing prohibited, TR §21-1210.
Headsets.
Wearing prohibited, TR §21-1210.
Highways.
Riding on roadways or highways.
Regulations, TR §21-1205.1.
Interfering with view or balance, TR §21-1206.
Operation.
Parent knowingly permitting minor or ward to
violate provisions of subtitle, TR §21-1201.
Securing to certain objects, TR §21-1208.
Speed limits, TR §21-1205.1.
Subject to traffic regulations, TR §21-501.1.
Tampering with, TR §21-1206.
Throwing object at, TR §21-1209.
Transporting articles, TR §21-1206.

ELECTRONIC POSTMARKS, CL §21-118.1.

ELECTRONIC SECURITY SYSTEMS.
Code grabbing devices.
Manufacturing, selling or possessing, CR §7-301.
Deactivation tool or device.
Possessing, using, CR §7-301.

ELECTRONIC SECURITY SYSTEMS —Cont'd
**Devices shielding merchandise from system
detection.**
Possessing, CR §7-301.
Removal of system or device, CR §7-301.

ELECTRONIC SIGNATURES.
Electronic transactions generally, CL §§21-101
to 21-120.
See ELECTRONIC TRANSACTIONS.

**ELECTRONIC SIGNATURES IN GLOBAL AND
NATIONAL COMMERCE ACT.**
Environmental covenants.
Modified and limited by act, exceptions, EN
§1-812.

ELECTRONIC SURVEILLANCE.
Interception of communications, CJ §§10-401 to
10-414.
See WIRETAPPING.
**Visual surveillance of individual in private
place,** CR §3-901.
With prurient intent, CR §3-902.

ELECTRONIC TERMINALS.
Banks and trust companies.
See BANKS AND TRUST COMPANIES.
Savings and loan associations.
See SAVINGS AND LOAN ASSOCIATIONS.

ELECTRONIC TOLL COLLECTION.
Penalty for failure to pay, TR §27-110.

**ELECTRONIC TRANSACTION EDUCATION,
ADVOCACY AND MEDIATION UNIT.**
Office of the Attorney General, SG §§6-201 to
6-203.

ELECTRONIC TRANSACTIONS, CL §§21-101 to
21-120.
**Acceptance and distribution of electronic
records.**
Governmental agencies, CL §21-117.
Acknowledgment, CL §21-110.
Admissibility in evidence, CL §21-112.
Agreements, CL §21-104.
Application of provisions, CL §§21-102, 21-103.
Construction, CL §21-105.
Attorney General.
Electronic transaction education, advocacy and
mediation unit, SG §§6-201 to 6-203.
Attributable to specific person, CL §21-108.
Authoritative copy.
Transfer of records, CL §21-115.
Automated transactions, CL §21-113.
Changes, CL §21-109.
Computer information transactions generally,
CL §§22-101 to 22-816.
See COMPUTER INFORMATION
TRANSACTIONS.
Construction of provisions, CL §21-105.
Severability, CL §21-119.
Conversion of records, CL §21-116.
Corporations.
Electronic transmissions.
Defined, CA §1-101.
Notice of stockholders' meetings, CA §2-504.
Definitions, CL §21-101; SG §6-201.
Effect, CL §21-108.
Electronic postmarks, CL §21-118.1.
Enforceability, CL §21-106.
Errors, CL §21-109.
Evidence, CL §21-112.

ELECTRONIC TRANSACTIONS —Cont'd
Formation of contract by automated transactions, CL §21-113.
Governmental agencies.
  Acceptance and distribution of electronic records, CL §21-117.
  Conversion of written records, CL §21-116.
  Defined, CL §21-101.
  Interoperability, CL §21-118.
Legal recognition of electronic transactions, CL §21-106.
Notarization, CL §21-110.
Original records, CL §21-111.
Place of sending, CL §21-114.
Postmarks.
  Use of electronic postmarks, CL §21-118.1.
Presentation of records, CL §21-107.
Procurement.
  Authorized, SF §13-226.
Receipt of record, CL §21-114.
Retention of records, CL §§21-111, 21-116.
Scope, CL §§21-102, 21-103.
Severability, CL §21-119.
Short title, CL §21-120.
Standards, CL §21-118.
Time of sending, CL §21-114.
Title, CL §21-120.
Transferability, CL §21-115.
Variation by agreements, CL §21-104.
Writing, conversion by governmental agencies, CL §21-116.
Writing, necessity of having information in, CL §21-107.

ELEVATOR RECEIPTS.
Misuse of document of title, CR §8-406.
Party receiving, accepting or taking document in trust.
  Failure to fulfill terms and conditions of trust, CR §8-406.

ELEVATORS, PS §§12-801 to 12-842.
Certificates.
  Defined, PS §12-801.
  Issuance, PS §12-811.
  Periodic inspection, PS §12-812.
  Required, PS §12-807.
  Term, PS §12-812.
Commissioner.
  Defined, PS §12-801.
  Registration and inspection.
    Administration and enforcement, PS §12-805.
    Registration with commissioner, PS §12-808.
Contractors.
  Defined, PS §12-801.
  Licenses.
    Required, PS §12-826.
    Scope of license, PS §12-832.
  Qualifications, PS §12-827.
Defined terms, PS §12-801.
Elevator safety review board.
  See ELEVATOR SAFETY REVIEW BOARD.
Emergency elevator mechanic licenses, PS §12-835.
Fees.
  Elevator safety review board.
    Authority to establish, PS §12-824.
  Inspections, PS §12-809.
  Licenses.
    Applications, PS §12-828.
    Emergency mechanics, PS §12-835.
    Examinations, PS §12-829.

ELEVATORS —Cont'd
Fees —Cont'd
  Licenses —Cont'd
    Renewal, PS §12-833.
Fines.
  Licenses.
    Criminal penalties, PS §12-840.
    Denial, refusal to renew, suspension or revocation.
      Civil penalty, PS §12-837.
Fires and fire protection.
  Warning signs in case of fire, PS §12-815.
Inspections, PS §§12-804 to 12-816.
  Administration, PS §12-805.
  Applicability, PS §12-804.
  Cancellation, PS §12-813.
  Certificates.
    Issuance, PS §12-811.
    Required, PS §12-807.
    Term, PS §12-812.
  Enforcement, PS §12-805.
  Final acceptance inspection, PS §12-810.
  Generally, PS §12-809.
  Penalties.
    Unsafe conditions, PS §12-814.
  Periodic inspection, PS §12-812.
  Records, PS §12-813.
  Registration with commissioner, PS §12-808.
  Rules and regulations, PS §12-805.
  Safety standards, PS §12-806.
  Scope of part, PS §12-804.
  Signs.
    Warning signs in case of fire, PS §12-815.
  Unsafe conditions.
    Penalties, PS §12-814.
    Prohibition against use of unsafe elevator, PS §12-814.1.
Inspectors.
  Chief elevator inspector.
    Appointment, LE §2-104.
Insurance.
  Licenses.
    Insurance requirements, PS §12-836.
Licenses, PS §§12-826 to 12-842.
  Applications, PS §12-828.
  Continuing education, PS §12-833.
  Denial, refusal to renew, suspension or revocation, PS §12-837.
    Appeals, PS §12-838.
  Disciplinary proceedings, PS §12-837.
    Prohibited acts, PS §12-839.
  Emergency elevator mechanic licenses, PS §12-835.
  Examinations, PS §12-829.
    Reciprocal waiver of requirements, PS §12-830.
  Exceptions, PS §12-826.
  Fees.
    Applications, PS §12-828.
    Examinations, PS §12-829.
    Renewal, PS §12-833.
  Insurance requirements, PS §12-836.
  Issuance, PS §12-831.
  Notice of qualification, PS §12-831.
  Prohibited acts, PS §12-839.
    Penalties, PS §12-840.
  Qualifications, PS §12-827.
  Renewal, PS §12-833.
  Required, PS §12-826.
  Scope of license, PS §12-832.
  Temporary elevator mechanic licenses, PS §12-834.

ELEVATORS —Cont'd
Licenses —Cont'd
  Term of license, PS §12-833.
  Types, PS §12-826.
Mechanics.
  Defined, PS §12-801.
  Licenses.
    Emergency elevator mechanic licenses, PS §12-835.
    Required, PS §12-826.
    Scope of license, PS §12-832.
    Temporary elevator mechanic licenses, PS §12-834.
  Qualifications, PS §12-827.
  Temporary elevator mechanic licenses, PS §12-834.
New buildings.
  Elevators to accommodate rescue litters, PS §12-816.
Notice.
  Inspections.
    Requested inspections, PS §12-809.
  Licenses.
    Notice of qualification, PS §12-831.
  Prohibition against use of unsafe elevator, PS §12-814.1.
Penalties.
  Licenses.
    Prohibited acts, PS §12-840.
  Unsafe conditions, PS §12-814.
Prohibited acts.
  Licenses, PS §12-839.
    Penalties, PS §12-840.
  Use of unsafe elevator, PS §12-814.1.
Reciprocity.
  License examinations.
    Reciprocal waiver of requirements, PS §12-830.
Records.
  Required, PS §12-813.
Registration and inspection, PS §§12-804 to 12-816.
  Administration, PS §12-805.
  Applicability, PS §12-804.
  Certificates.
    Issuance, PS §12-811.
    Required, PS §12-807.
    Term, PS §12-812.
  Enforcement, PS §12-805.
  Inspections.
    Cancellation, PS §12-813.
    Final acceptance inspection, PS §12-810.
    Generally, PS §12-809.
    Periodic inspection, PS §12-812.
  Records, PS §12-813.
  Registration with commissioner, PS §12-808.
  Rules and regulations, PS §12-805.
  Safety standards, PS §12-806.
  Scope of part, PS §12-804.
Rescue equipment.
  New elevators to accommodate rescue litters, PS §12-816.
Rules and regulations.
  Registration and inspection, PS §12-805.
Safety review board, PS §§12-819 to 12-842.
Safety standards, PS §12-806.
  New buildings.
    Elevators to accommodate rescue litters, PS §12-816.
Secretary.
  Defined, PS §12-801.

ELEVATORS —Cont'd
Signs.
  Warning signs in case of fire, PS §12-815.
Stretchers.
  New elevators to accommodate rescue litters, PS §12-816.
Temporary elevator mechanic licenses, PS §12-834.
Unsafe conditions.
  Penalties, PS §12-814.
  Prohibition against use of unsafe elevator, PS §12-814.1.

ELEVATOR SAFETY REVIEW BOARD, PS §§12-819 to 12-842.
Board defined, PS §12-801.
Chairman, PS §12-821.
Composition, PS §12-820.
Established, PS §12-819.
Fees.
  Authority to establish, PS §12-824.
  Licenses.
    Applications, PS §12-828.
    Examinations, PS §12-829.
    Renewal, PS §12-833.
Fines.
  Licenses.
    Criminal penalties, PS §12-840.
    Denial, refusal to renew, suspension or revocation.
      Civil penalties, PS §12-837.
Licenses, PS §§12-826 to 12-842.
  Applications, PS §12-828.
  Denial, refusal to renew, suspension or revocation, PS §12-837.
    Appeals, PS §12-838.
  Disciplinary proceedings, PS §12-837.
  Examinations, PS §12-829.
  Exceptions, PS §12-826.
  Insurance requirements, PS §12-836.
  Issuance, PS §12-831.
  Mechanic licenses.
    Emergency, PS §12-835.
    Temporary, PS §12-834.
  Penalties, PS §12-841.
  Prohibited acts, PS §12-839.
  Qualifications, PS §12-827.
  Reciprocity, PS §12-830.
  Renewal, PS §12-833.
  Required, PS §12-826.
  Scope, PS §12-832.
Meetings, PS §12-822.
Members, PS §12-820.
  Compensation and reimbursement for travel expenses, PS §12-822.
Notice.
  Qualification for license, PS §12-831.
Powers, PS §12-823.
  Authority of secretary, PS §12-825.
Secretary.
  Authority, PS §12-825.
Sunset law, SG §8-403.
Termination of title, PS §12-842.

ELISORS.
Service of process.
  By whom served, CivProCir Rule 2-123.
    District Court, CivProDist Rule 3-123.

ELUDING A POLICE OFFICER, TR §21-904.
Vessels and boats, NR §8-727.

EMAIL.
Child pornography, CR §11-207.
  Removal of child pornography from Internet, CR
      §11-208.1.
Cigarette sales.
  Direct sales and shipping by computer network or
      other electronic network, BR §16-223.
Cooperative housing corporations.
  Electronic transmission defined, CA §5-6B-01.
  Notice of meetings and other information, CA
      §5-6B-18.3.
  Voting, CA §5-6B-18.4.
Corporations.
  Consent to actions by stockholders, CA §2-505.
  Electronic transmissions defined, CA §1-101.
  Notice of stockholders' meetings, CA §2-504.
Misuse, CR §3-805.
Sex offender registration.
  Email notice of release of offender into
      community, CP §11-717.
Spam, CR §3-805.1.
Unauthorized access to computers, CR §7-302.
Unauthorized, false or misleading information.
  Commercial electronic mail, CL §§14-3001 to
      14-3003.
    Blocking, CL §14-3002.
    Damages, CL §14-3002.
    Definitions, CL §14-3001.
    Presumption, recipient resident of state, CL
        §14-3002.
Wine sales.
  Direct wine seller's permit, 2B §§7.5-101 to
      7.5-110.
    See ALCOHOLIC BEVERAGES.

EMANCIPATION OF MINORS.
Age of majority, 1 §24.
Special education.
  Age of majority, transfer or rights, ED §8-412.1.

EMARYLAND.
E-commerce, advisory board, SG §§9-2201 to
    9-2204.
EMaryland marketplace.
  Defined, SF §13-101.
  User fees, SF §13-102.1.
University of Maryland.
  EMaryland ASP consortium, SG §9-2204.

EMBALMERS.
Morticians.
  See MORTICIANS.

EMBEZZLEMENT, CR §7-113.
Charging documents.
  Crimes involving instruments, CP §4-108.
Continuing care contracts.
  Liquidation, conservation or rehabilitation of
      providers, 70B §20G.
Intent to defraud.
  Proving, CR §1-401.
Theft.
  Generally, CR §§7-101 to 7-110.
  See THEFT.
**Wills, codicils, deeds, land patents, writs of
    estate,** CR §§8-701, 8-702.

EMBLEMS.
See INSIGNIA AND EMBLEMS.

EMERGENCIES.
Adoption.
  Independent adoptions.
    Access to adoption records.
      Emergency medical information, FL §5-3B-28.

EMERGENCIES —Cont'd
Adoption —Cont'd
  Local department adoptions.
    Access to adoption records.
      Emergency medical information, FL §5-358.
  Private agency adoptions.
    Access to adoption records.
      Emergency medical information, FL §5-3A-41.
Air quality control.
  Air pollution emergency.
    Secretary to advise governor, EN §2-105.
  Conditions not violations, EN §2-613.
  Defined, EN §2-101.
Arrest without warrant.
  During state of emergency, CP §2-206.
Banks and trust companies, FI §5-707.
Bee stings, HG §§13-701 to 13-709.
  See INSECT STING EMERGENCY TREATMENT
      PROGRAM.
Building codes.
  Emergency power and lighting systems, PS
      §12-702.
Catastrophic health emergency.
  Disease surveillance and response program, HG
      §§18-901 to 18-908.
    See CATASTROPHIC HEALTH EMERGENCY.
  Governor's power to proclaim, PS §§14-3A-01 to
      14-3A-08.
    See HEALTH EMERGENCIES.
Communications.
  Interference with, CR §9-601.
  Prerecorded emergency message, transmitting, CR
      §9-603.
Condominiums.
  Rental housing emergency, RP §11-140.
Cooperative housing corporations.
  Rental housing emergencies.
    Actions by local governments to protect
        consumers from displacement, CA §5-6B-10.
Disaster service leave.
  State personnel, SPP §9-1102.
Drinking water.
  Safe drinking water emergencies.
    Adoption of plan, EN §9-406.
Elections.
  Interference with electoral process, EL §8-103.
Elevator mechanics.
  Emergency elevator mechanic licenses, PS
      §12-835.
Emergency management, PS §§14-101 to 14-1004.
  See EMERGENCY MANAGEMENT.
**Excavation or demolition near underground
    facilities,** PUC §12-105.
False alarms, CR §9-604.
General services department.
  State leasing of real property.
    Exceptions to provisions, SF §4-318.
Governor.
  Emergency powers and duties of governor, SG
      §3-304.
Guardianships.
  Local department guardianships.
    Emergency review hearings, FL §5-326.
Harness racing.
  Transfer of racing days due to emergency, BR
      §11-612.
Hazardous materials and substances.
  Power of department to sue for immediate
      injunction, EN §7-263.
Health maintenance organizations.
  Emergency services, HG §19-705.6.

EMERGENCIES —Cont'd
Health maintenance organizations —Cont'd
Reimbursement for hospital emergency facility and provider, HG §19-712.5.
Housing and community development.
Assisted housing preservation.
Rental housing emergencies, HS §7-220.
Insect sting emergency treatment program, HG §§13-701 to 13-709.
See INSECT STING EMERGENCY TREATMENT PROGRAM.
Interference with emergency communication, CR §9-601.
Juvenile causes.
Emergency detention.
See JUVENILE CAUSES.
Maryland energy administration.
Energy emergencies, SG §9-2005.
Medical care and service.
Emergency medical technician-paramedic, HO §14-305.
Good Samaritans, CJ §5-603.
Institute for emergency medical services.
See UNIVERSITY OF MARYLAND.
Minors.
Consent to emergency care, HG §20-102.
Rescue squads.
General provisions.
See RESCUE SQUADS.
Mental health facilities.
Emergency evaluation.
See MENTAL HEALTH FACILITIES.
Milk emergencies, HG §21-430.
Minors.
Medical treatment.
Capacity to consent to emergency medical treatment, HG §20-102.
911 emergency telephone system, PS §§1-301 to 1-312.
See 911 EMERGENCY TELEPHONE SYSTEM.
Noise control.
Conditions not violations, EN §3-408.
Pharmacists and pharmacies.
Prescription refills.
State of emergency, HO §12-506.
Prerecorded emergency message. transmitting, CR §9-603.
Procurement, SF §§13-102, 13-108.
Public utilities.
Duties of utility company, TR §25-111.
Radiation.
Action by secretary, EN §8-105.
Defined, EN §8-101.
Impounding radiation sources, EN §8-302.
Injunctions, EN §8-507.
Railroads.
Unauthorized access to railroad vehicle.
Exceptions, CR §6-503.
Rental housing emergencies.
Actions by local governments to protect consumers from displacement, CA §5-6B-10.
Safe drinking water emergencies, EN §9-406.
State emergency management, PS §§14-801 to 14-803.
See EMERGENCY MANAGEMENT.
State of emergency.
See EMERGENCY MANAGEMENT.
State personnel.
Disaster service leave, SPP §9-1102.
State police.
Police powers, authority to exercise, PS §2-412.

EMERGENCIES —Cont'd
Thoroughbred racing.
Transfer of racing days due to emergency, BR §11-513.
Transient vendors.
Stop sale order or seizure.
Emergency action, BR §17-20A-04.
University of Maryland.
Institute for emergency medical services.
See UNIVERSITY OF MARYLAND.
Vessels and boats.
Flashing red and yellow lights or signal devices.
Use, NR §8-727.1.
Veterinarians.
Veterinarians rendering aid in emergency not liable for civil damages, CJ §5-614.
Warrantless arrest.
During state of emergency, CP §2-206.
Water pollution.
Injunctions, EN §9-339.

EMERGENCY COMMUNICATIONS.
False alarms, CR §9-604.
Interference with, CR §9-601.
Prerecorded emergency message.
Transmitting, CR §9-603.

EMERGENCY MANAGEMENT, PS §§14-101 to 14-1004.
Actions.
Owners permitting use of property for civil defense.
Prohibited actions, CJ §5-602.
Agency, PS §§14-101 to 14-115. See within this heading, "Maryland emergency management agency (MEMA)."
Appeals.
State standby petroleum fuel set-aside program.
Prime suppliers, PS §14-507.
Assisted living facilities.
Emergency plans, PS §14-110.1.
Catastrophic health emergency.
Disease surveillance and response program, HG §§18-901 to 18-908.
See CATASTROPHIC HEALTH EMERGENCY.
Governor's power to proclaim, PS §§14-3A-01 to 14-3A-08.
See HEALTH EMERGENCIES.
Civil defense volunteers.
Workers' compensation.
Covered employees and employers, LE §§9-232, 9-232.1.
Civil relief during emergency periods, PS §§14-201 to 14-218.
Administrative remedies, PS §14-206.
Affidavits.
False affidavits prohibited, PS §14-218.
Applicability, PS §14-203.
Civil rights.
Attempts to delay enforcement, PS §14-206.
Contracts.
Fines or penalties for nonperformance, PS §14-209.
Installment contracts, PS §14-213.
Defined terms, PS §14-201.
Distress for rent, PS §14-213.
Illegal distraint of property, PS §14-218.
Effects of subtitle, PS §14-202.
Enforcement, PS §14-204.
Evictions, PS §14-212.
Illegal evictions, PS §14-218.

EMERGENCY MANAGEMENT —Cont'd
Civil relief during emergency periods —Cont'd
Failure to appear.
Emergency management service workers or
persons suffering injury or damage, PS
§14-208.
Income taxes, PS §14-217.
Installment contracts, PS §14-213.
Legislative policy, PS §14-202.
Limitation of actions, PS §14-207.
Missing persons.
Presumption when person reported missing, PS
§14-207.
Mortgages and deeds of trust, PS §14-214.
Motion where no proceeding pending, PS §14-204.
Motor vehicle sales or repossessions, PS §14-215.
Illegal repossessions, PS §14-218.
Penalties, PS §14-218.
Period of applicability, PS §14-203.
Prohibited acts, PS §14-218.
Purpose, PS §14-202.
Real property taxes, PS §14-216.
Scope, PS §14-203.
Stays, postponements or suspensions of
enforcement, PS §14-210.
Effect on sureties, guarantors and endorsers, PS
§14-205.
Failure to appear.
Emergency management service workers or
persons suffering injury or damage, PS
§14-208.
Period and terms of stay, PS §14-211.
Compacts.
Emergency management assistance compact
(interstate), PS §§14-701, 14-702.
Interstate emergency management and civil
defense compact, PS §§14-601 to 14-605.
Maryland emergency management assistance
compact (intrastate), PS §§14-801 to 14-803.
Compulsory work during state of war, PS
§§14-901 to 14-908.
Applicability, PS §14-901.
Appointment of assistants, PS §14-902.
Assignment to work, PS §14-904.
Assistants.
Appointment, PS §14-902.
Circuit court clerk.
Registration for work, duties, PS §14-903.
Compensation, PS §14-906.
Duration and nature of work, PS §14-904.
Failure to register for work, PS §14-907.
Failure to work, PS §14-908.
Law enforcement officers.
Failure to register, enforcement duties, PS
§14-907.
Qualifications for assignments, PS §14-904.
Registration for work, PS §14-903.
Rules and regulations, PS §14-905.
Scope of subtitle, PS §14-901.
Damages.
Liability for damages.
Real estate or premises used without charge.
Prohibited action, CJ §5-602.
Use of shelters, CJ §5-602.
Disaster service leave.
State personnel, SPP §9-1102.
**Effective period of laws, ordinances
resolutions and regulations.**
Military or warlike catastrophe, PS §14-406.
Emergency management agency, PS §§14-101 to
14-115. See within this heading, "Maryland
emergency management agency (MEMA)."

EMERGENCY MANAGEMENT —Cont'd
Emergency management assistance compact,
PS §§14-701, 14-702.
Contents, PS §14-702.
Participation of other jurisdictions, PS §14-701.
Emergency response plans.
Access to public records.
Denial of inspection, SG §10-618.
Energy emergencies, PS §14-304.
Standby petroleum fuel set-aside program, PS
§§14-501 to 14-511.
Enforcement.
Maryland emergency management agency
(MEMA), PS §14-113.
Finance and funding.
Emergency expenditures, PS §14-112.
Federal funding, PS §14-112.
Governor's powers, PS §§14-3A-01 to 14-3A-08,
14-301 to 14-309.
Closing of businesses, PS §14-307.
Construction and interpretation, PS §14-302.
Defined terms, PS §14-301.
Executive officer killed, sick or unavailable, PS
§14-403.
Interstate emergency management and civil
defense compact.
Authority to enter into and execute, PS §14-603.
Law enforcement agencies.
Cooperation among state and local agencies, PS
§14-305.
Legislative intent, PS §14-302.
Maryland emergency management agency
(MEMA), PS §14-106.
State of emergency, authority to declare, PS
§14-107.
Militia, PS §14-306.
Penalties, PS §14-309.
Prohibited acts, PS §14-309.
Repairing damaged property.
Duty of state, PS §14-308.
State of emergency.
Authority to declare, PS §14-107.
Energy emergencies, PS §14-304.
Notice, PS §14-304.
Orders, rules and regulations, PS §14-304.
Proclamation, PS §14-303.
Violations, PS §14-309.
Hazardous materials and substances.
Local emergency plans, PS §14-110.
Hospitals.
Emergency plans, PS §14-110.1.
Human services facilities.
Emergency plans for, PS §14-110.1.
**Interstate emergency management and civil
defense compact,** PS §§14-601 to 14-605.
Contents, PS §14-602.
Copies of compact, transmittal, PS §14-604.
Governor.
Authority to enter into and execute, PS §14-603.
Preamble, PS §14-601.
Ratification, PS §14-603.
Severability of provisions, PS §14-605.
Labor and employment relations.
Compulsory work during state of war, PS
§§14-901 to 14-908.
Law enforcement agencies.
Cooperation among state and local agencies, PS
§14-305.
Law enforcement officers and personnel.
Compulsory work during state of war.
Failure to register, enforcement duties, PS
§14-907.

EMERGENCY MANAGEMENT —Cont'd
Law enforcement officers and personnel
   —Cont'd
Enforcement, PS §14-113.
Liability for damages.
Real estate or premises used without charge.
   Prohibited actions, CJ §5-602.
Limitation of actions.
Civil relief during emergency periods, PS §14-207.
Real estate or premises used without charge.
   Prohibited actions, CJ §5-602.
Riots, PS §14-1003.
Local emergency plans, PS §14-110.
Local governing bodies.
Defined, PS §14-401.
Executive officer killed, sick or unavailable, PS
   §14-403.
Majority killed, sick or unavailable, PS §14-402.
Powers during military or warlike catastrophe, PS
   §14-405.
Tax district official killed, sick or unavailable, PS
   §14-404.
Maryland emergency management agency
   (MEMA), PS §§14-101 to 14-115.
Citation of subtitle, PS §14-115.
Defined terms, PS §14-101.
Director, PS §14-104.
   Defined, PS §14-101.
Emergency expenditures, PS §14-112.
Emergency management advisory council, PS
   §14-105.
Enforcement, PS §14-113.
Established, PS §14-103.
Federal funding, PS §14-112.
Governor.
   Powers, PS §14-106.
   State of emergency, PS §14-107.
Hazardous materials and substances.
   Local emergency plans, PS §14-110.
Legislative policy, PS §14-102.
Local emergency plans, PS §14-110.
Local organizations for emergency management,
   PS §14-109.
   Defined, PS §14-101.
Local state of emergency, PS §14-111.
Penalties, PS §14-114.
Prohibited acts, PS §14-114.
Purpose, PS §14-102.
Radiological emergency response plan.
   Local emergency plans, PS §14-110.
Salaries.
   Director, PS §14-104.
   Emergency management advisory council, PS
      §14-105.
Short title, PS §14-115.
State of emergency.
   Declaration by another state, PS §14-108.
   Declaration by governor, PS §14-107.
   Local state of emergency, PS §14-111.
Maryland emergency management assistance
   compact, PS §§14-801 to 14-803.
Contents, PS §14-803.
Defined terms, PS §14-801.
Entered into with other jurisdictions, PS §14-803.
Entry into, PS §14-802.
Participation with other jurisdictions, PS §14-802.
Purpose, PS §14-803.
Maryland-national capital park and planning
   commission.
Activities of members and staff, 28 §2-117.

EMERGENCY MANAGEMENT —Cont'd
Military or warlike catastrophe.
Effective period of laws, ordinances resolutions
   and regulations, PS §14-406.
Local governing bodies.
   Powers during military or warlike catastrophe,
      PS §14-405.
Militia.
Governor's powers, PS §14-306.
Missing persons.
Civil relief during emergency periods.
   Presumption when person reported missing, PS
      §14-207.
Nursing homes.
Emergency plans, PS §14-110.1.
Penalties.
Civil relief during emergency periods, PS §14-218.
Compulsory work during state of war.
   Failure to register for work, PS §14-907.
   Failure to work, PS §14-908.
Governor's powers, PS §14-309.
Maryland emergency management agency
   (MEMA), PS §14-114.
State standby petroleum fuel set-aside program,
   PS §14-511.
Prohibited acts.
Civil relief during emergency periods, PS §14-218.
Compulsory work during state of war.
   Failure to register for work, PS §14-907.
   Failure to work, PS §14-908.
Governor's powers, PS §14-309.
Maryland emergency management agency
   (MEMA), PS §14-114.
State standby petroleum fuel set-aside program,
   PS §14-511.
Radiological emergency response plan.
Local emergency plans, PS §14-110.
Real property.
Use without charge.
   Damages.
      Prohibited actions, CJ §5-602.
Repairing damaged property.
Duty of state, PS §14-308.
Reports.
Prime suppliers.
   State standby petroleum fuel set-aside program,
      PS §14-505.
State standby petroleum fuel set-aside program,
   PS §14-510.
Riots.
Liability of county or municipality for damages,
   PS §§14-1001 to 14-1004.
   Conditions of liability, PS §14-1002.
   Generally, PS §14-1001.
   Limitation of actions, PS §14-1003.
   Notice and ability to prevent damage, effect, PS
      §14-1002.
   Pleadings, PS §14-1004.
   Reasonable diligence, effect, PS §14-1002.
Rules and regulations.
Compulsory work during state of war, PS §14-905.
Salaries.
Compulsory work during state of war, PS §14-906.
Maryland emergency management agency
   (MEMA).
   Director, PS §14-104.
   Emergency management advisory council, PS
      §14-105.
Shelters.
Use without charge.
   Actions for damages prohibited, CJ §5-602.

EMERGENCY MANAGEMENT —Cont'd
State of emergency.
　Arrest without a warrant, CP §2-206.
　Declaration by another state, PS §14-108.
　Electoral process interfered with, EL §8-103.
　Governor's powers.
　　Authority to declare, PS §14-107.
　　Energy emergencies, PS §14-304.
　　Notice, PS §14-304.
　　Orders, rules and regulations, PS §14-304.
　　Proclamation, PS §14-303.
　　Violations, PS §14-309.
　Local state of emergency, PS §14-111.
　Warrantless arrest, CP §2-206.
State personnel.
　Disaster service leave, SPP §9-1102.
**State standby petroleum fuel set-aside
　program,** PS §§14-501 to 14-511.
　Accumulation of state set-aside volumes.
　　Prohibited, PS §14-509.
　Administration, PS §14-502.
　Appeals.
　　Prime suppliers, PS §14-507.
　Applicability, PS §14-503.
　Applications for assignments, PS §14-506.
　Assignments, PS §14-506.
　Defined terms, PS §14-501.
　　Use during energy emergencies, PS §14-504.
　Director.
　　Administration and enforcement, PS §14-502.
　Enforcement, PS §14-502.
　Established, PS §14-502.
　Penalties, PS §14-511.
　Percentage levels, PS §14-503.
　Prime suppliers.
　　Appeals, PS §14-507.
　　Assignments, PS §14-506.
　　Defined, PS §14-501.
　　Release of state set-aside volume, PS §14-508.
　　Reports, PS §14-505.
　Prohibited acts, PS §14-511.
　Replacing set-aside products, PS §14-506.
　Reports, PS §14-510.
　　Prime suppliers, PS §14-505.
　State set-aside volumes.
　　Accumulation prohibited, PS §14-509.
　　Release, PS §14-508.
　Use during energy emergencies, PS §14-504.
Storage.
　Use of shelter for stocking of food, water, etc.
　　Liability for damages, CJ §5-602.
Succession planning.
　Executive officer killed, sick or unavailable, PS
　　§14-403.
　Local governing bodies.
　　Defined, PS §14-401.
　　Executive officer killed, sick or unavailable, PS
　　　§14-403.
　　Majority killed, sick or unavailable, PS §14-402.
　　Tax district official killed, sick or unavailable,
　　　PS §14-404.
War.
　Compulsory work during state of war, PS
　　§§14-901 to 14-908.
Workers' compensation.
　Covered employees and employers.
　　Civil defense volunteers, LE §§9-232, 9-232.1.

**EMERGENCY MANAGEMENT ADVISORY
　COUNCIL.**
**Maryland emergency management agency
　(MEMA),** PS §14-105.

**EMERGENCY MANAGEMENT AGENCY
　(MEMA),** PS §§14-101 to 14-115.
See EMERGENCY MANAGEMENT.

**EMERGENCY MANAGEMENT ASSISTANCE
　COMPACT,** PS §§14-701, 14-702.
**Maryland emergency management assistance
　compact (intrastate),** PS §§14-801 to 14-803.

**EMERGENCY MEDICAL CARE AND
　SERVICES.**
AIDS.
　HIV testing for health care workers and first
　　responders, HG §§18-336 to 18-338.3.
　Notification of emergency medical technicians of
　　exposure to virus, HG §18-213.
Ambulance services.
　Generally.
　　See AMBULANCES.
　Licensing, regulating, ED §13-515.
Appeals.
　Discipline of employees.
　　Judicial review of final decisions, LE §§4-601 to
　　　4-603.
Automated external defibrillator program, ED
　§13-517.
　County boards of education to develop and
　　implement programs, ED §7-425.
Board of nursing.
　Referral of complaints by EMS board to, ED
　　§13-516.
Board of regents of University of Maryland.
　Powers, ED §13-512.
Cardiac rescue technicians.
　Performance of specified medical procedures, ED
　　§13-516.
**Charles McC. Mathias, Jr. national study
　center for trauma and emergency medical
　systems,** ED §13-513.
Collective bargaining, LE §§4-501 to 4-505.
See COLLECTIVE BARGAINING.
Contagious diseases.
　Notification of emergency medical technicians of
　　exposure to contagious disease, HG §18-213.
Coordination of medical services.
　Institute for emergency medical services systems.
　　Administrative agency responsible for, ED
　　　§13-504.
Criminal law and procedure.
　Impersonating firefighters or emergency services
　　personnel, PS §7-402.
　Interference with or obstruction of emergency
　　assistance, PS §7-402.
Death in the line of duty.
　Death benefits, PS §1-202.
　Reward for information regarding person who
　　causes death, PS §1-201.
Definitions, ED §§13-501, 13-516.
　Discipline of employees.
　　Judicial review, LE §4-601.
Diphtheria.
　Notification of exposure, HG §§18-213 to 18-213.2.
Discipline of employees.
　Judicial review of final decisions.
　　Collective bargaining agreement, LE §4-603.
　　Definitions, LE §4-601.
　　Generally, LE §4-602.
**Disciplining emergency medical services
　providers,** ED §13-516.
Do not resuscitate orders.
　Authorization to follow in the outpatient setting.
　　Health care decisions, HG §5-608.

EMERGENCY MEDICAL CARE AND SERVICES —Cont'd

Emergency medical care technician-paramedic.

Contagious diseases.

Notification of exposure to contagious disease, HG §18-213.

Generally, HO §14-305.

Emergency medical dispatchers.

Performance of specified medical procedures, ED §13-516.

Emergency medical services advisory council.

Established, ED §13-511.

Membership, chairperson, functions, staff, ED §13-511.

Emergency medical services field operations.

Institute for emergency medical services systems.

Included in institute, ED §13-504.

Emergency medical system plan, ED §13-509.

Emergency medical technicians.

Performance of specified medical procedures, ED §13-516.

Emergency telephone systems.

Health and human services referral system, HG §§24-1201 to 24-1205.

911 emergency telephone system, PS §§1-301 to 1-312.

EMS board.

Automated external defibrillator program.

Administration, powers, ED §13-517.

Chairperson and vice chairperson, ED §13-505.

Disciplining emergency medical services providers, ED §13-516.

Emergency medical system plan.

Adoption, ED §13-509.

Executive director.

Appointment, duties and functions, ED §13-506.

Responsibilities, ED §13-510.

Foundations created subject to audit, ED §13-506.

Helicopter transporting patients.

Regulations, adoption, ED §13-509.

Institute for emergency medical services systems.

Governed by board, ED §13-503.

Licensing or certification of persons providing emergency medical services, ED §13-516.

Majority approval required for actions, ED §13-507.

Meetings, ED §13-507.

Membership, qualifications, terms, ED §13-505.

Powers and duties, ED §13-508.

Provider review panel, ED §13-516.

Quorum for transaction of business, ED §13-507.

Rules or procedures, adoption, ED §13-507.

Travel expenses, ED §13-507.

EMS board provider fund, ED §13-516.

False impersonations.

Impersonating firefighters or emergency services personnel, PS §7-402.

Funds.

Maryland emergency medical service system fund, SF §7-313.

Good Samaritan law.

Immunity for special personnel, CJ §5-603.

Health and human services referral board, HG §24-1203.

Health and human services referral system, HG §§24-1201 to 24-1205.

Appropriations, HG §24-1205.

Board, HG §24-1203.

Defined terms, HG §24-1201.

Duties, HG §24-1204.

EMERGENCY MEDICAL CARE AND SERVICES —Cont'd

Health and human services referral system —Cont'd

Funding, HG §24-1205.

Legislative intent, HG §24-1202.

Purposes, HG §24-1202.

Reports, HG §24-1204.

Heart attack.

Death benefits.

Death as result of personal injury in performance of duties.

Presumption, PS §1-202.

Helicopter transporting patients.

Regulations, adoption by EMS board, ED §13-509.

Hemorrhagic fevers.

Notification of exposure, HG §§18-213 to 18-213.2.

Hepatitis.

Exposure to.

Notification, HG §§18-213 to 18-213.2.

Human immunodeficiency virus.

HIV testing for health care workers and first responders, HG §§18-336 to 18-338.3.

Notification of emergency medical technicians of exposure to virus, HG §18-213.

Institute for emergency medical services.

See UNIVERSITY OF MARYLAND.

Institute for emergency medical services systems.

Coordination of medical services.

Administrative agency responsible for, ED §13-504.

Emergency medical services field operations.

Included in institute, ED §13-504.

Established, ED §13-503.

Funding, ED §13-503.

Governed by emergency medical services board, ED §13-503.

Located at University of Maryland, Baltimore, ED §13-503.

Staff and funds as provided by budget, ED §13-504.

Insurance.

Blanket health insurance authorized for volunteer groups, IN §15-305.

Interference with or obstruction of emergency assistance, PS §7-402.

Legislative findings, ED §13-502.

Licensing or certification of persons providing emergency medical services, ED §13-516.

Medicaid.

Reimbursement for emergency service transporters, HG §15-114.1.

Meningitis.

Exposure to.

Notification of emergency medical technicians, HG §18-213.

Minors.

Consent to emergency treatment, HG §20-102.

Mononucleosis.

Exposure to.

Notification of emergency medical technicians, HG §18-213.

Mutual aid agreements, PS §§7-101 to 7-107.

Construction and interpretation, PS §7-102.

Defined terms, PS §7-101.

Expenditures, PS §7-107.

Federal government, PS §7-104.

Other states and entities of other states, PS §7-103.

**EMERGENCY MEDICAL CARE AND
  SERVICES** —Cont'd
Mutual aid agreements —Cont'd
Training.
  Emergency response measures, PS §7-105.
Workers' compensation benefits.
  Line of duty, PS §7-106.
Rabies.
Notification of exposure, HG §§18-213 to 18-213.2.
R. Adams Cowley shock trauma center, ED
  §13-514.
Reports.
Health and human services referral system, HG
  §24-1204.
Rescue squads.
General provisions.
  See RESCUE SQUADS.
Rewards.
Death in the line of duty.
  Reward for information regarding person who
    causes death, PS §1-201.
Scholarships.
Charles W. Riley fire and emergency medical
    services tuition reimbursement program, ED
    §18-603.
Stroke.
Death benefits.
  Death as result of personal injury in
    performance of duties.
    Presumption, PS §1-202.
Training.
Emergency response measures.
  Mutual aid agreements, PS §7-105.
Tuberculosis.
Exposure to tuberculosis.
  Notification of emergency medical technicians,
    HG §18-213.
University of Maryland.
Board of regents.
  Powers, ED §13-512.
**Unlicensed or uncertified persons providing
    emergency medical services.**
Criminal penalties, ED §13-516.
Workers' compensation.
Mutual aid agreements.
  Line of duty, PS §7-106.

EMERGENCY MEDICAL DISPATCHERS.
Performance of specified medical procedures,
  ED §13-516.

EMERGENCY MEDICAL TECHNICIANS.
Death in the line of duty.
Death benefits, PS §1-202.
  Reward for information regarding person who
    causes death, PS §1-201.
**HIV testing for health care workers and first
    responders,** HG §§18-336 to 18-338.3.
Performance of specified medical procedures,
  ED §13-516.
Reward.
Death in the line of duty.
  Reward for information regarding person who
    causes death, PS §1-201.

EMERGENCY NUMBER SYSTEMS BOARD, PS
  §1-305.

EMERGENCY TELEPHONE SYSTEMS.
Health and human services referral system,
  HG §§24-1201 to 24-1205.
911 emergency telephone system.
See 911 EMERGENCY TELEPHONE SYSTEM.

EMERGENCY VEHICLES.
Ambulances.
General provisions.
  See AMBULANCES.
Defined, TR §§11-118, 22-412.4.
Drivers.
Liability, CJ §5-639; TR §§19-103, 21-106.
Drivers' licenses, exemptions, TR §16-102.
Flashing red lamps, TR §22-218.
Judgments and decrees.
Effect of judgment against owner or lessee, CJ
    §5-639; TR §19-103.
**Liability for negligent operation of emergency
    vehicle,** CJ §5-639; TR §§19-103, 21-106.
Passing emergency vehicles, TR §21-1009.
Pedestrians to yield right-of-way, TR §21-510.
Police vehicles, TR §22-218.
State police.
  Off-duty use, PS §2-407.
Visual signals not required, TR §21-106.
Privileges, TR §21-106.
Right of way.
Operation of vehicles on approach of authorized
    emergency vehicles, TR §21-405.
Pedestrians yield to authorized emergency
    vehicles, TR §21-510.
Seat belts or restraining devices, TR §22-412.4.
Signals.
Audible and visual signals.
  Use required, TR §21-106.
Sirens, whistles and bells, TR §22-218.
Authorized, TR §22-401.
Sound level limits for operation of vehicles.
Exemption of authorized emergency vehicles, TR
    §22-604.
**Spot lamps, fog lamps and auxiliary driving
    lamps.**
Section not applicable, TR §22-217.
Toll bridges and tunnels.
Turning regulated, TR §21-1408.

EMINENT DOMAIN.
Abandonment.
Costs.
  Recovery of expenses, PropAct Rule 12-211.
Effect of filing election to abandon, RP §12-109.
Effect on records, PropAct Rule 12-211.
Limitation on abandonment, RP §12-109.
Method of abandoning proceeding for
    condemnation, PropAct Rule 12-211.
Recovery of fees by defendant, RP §12-109.
When allowed, PropAct Rule 12-211.
Admissibility of relevant evidence, Evid Rule
  5-402.
Appeals.
Attorneys' fees, PropAct Rule 12-209; RP §12-107.
Costs, PropAct Rule 12-209; RP §12-107.
Possession of property pending appeal, RP
    §12-107.
Right to appeal, PropAct Rule 12-209; RP §12-107.
Application of title, RP §12-101.
Appraisals.
Real estate appraisers, RP §12-111.
Relocation assistance.
  Definition of "appraisal," RP §12-201.
Right of entry, RP §12-111.
Attorneys at law.
Abandonment of condemnation proceedings.
  Recovery of fees by defendant, RP §12-109.
Appeals.
  Fees, RP §12-107.

EMINENT DOMAIN —Cont'd
Attorneys at law —Cont'd
Judgment for defendant.
Fees, RP §12-106.
Aviation.
State airports and facilities.
Administration power as to condemnation of
property, TR §5-405.
Award.
Allowance for removal of personal property, dead
body, grave marker or monument, RP
§12-112.
Board of property review, PropAct Rule 12-213.
Damages. See within this heading, "Damages."
Interest on award, RP §12-106.
Payment, PropAct Rule 12-210.
Right of award, MD Const Art III §40.
Baltimore City.
Applicable provisions, RP §12-101.
General provisions.
See BALTIMORE CITY.
Land development and redevelopment, MD Const
Art XI-B §1.
Specific provisions, MD Const Art III §40A.
Baltimore county.
Specific provisions, MD Const Art III §40A.
Board of property review, PropAct Rule 12-213.
Bonds, surety.
Taking possession of property pending appeal, RP
§12-107.
Borings and soil tests.
Right of entry to make, RP §12-111.
Bridge and canal companies.
Condemnation in event of failure to agree or
disability to contract, 23 §141.
Burial grounds.
Acquisition of cemetery, PropAct Rule 12-204.
**Canal place preservation and development
authority.**
Acquisition of property interests, FI §13-1009.
Cecil county.
Specific provisions, MD Const Art III §40A.
Cemeteries.
Acquisition of cemetery, PropAct Rule 12-204.
Dead bodies.
Allowance for removal, RP §12-112.
Grave markers or monuments.
Allowance for removal, RP §12-112.
Publication, PropAct Rule 12-204.
Chesapeake Bay.
Public access to Chesapeake Bay and tributaries.
Big Blackwater River and Little Blackwater
River, NR §8-204.
Clerks.
Board of property review.
Certification to board, PropAct Rule 12-213.
Community development administration, HS
§4-214.
Comparable replacement dwellings.
Definition, RP §12-201.
Compensation.
Right of award, MD Const Art III §40.
Complaints, PropAct Rule 12-205.
Condominiums, RP §11-112.
Construction and interpretation.
Scope of provisions, PropAct Rule 12-201.
Costs.
Abandonment of condemnation proceedings.
Recovery of fees or expenses by defendant, RP
§12-109.
Appeals, PropAct Rule 12-209; RP §12-107.

EMINENT DOMAIN —Cont'd
Costs —Cont'd
Payment of judgment and costs by plaintiff,
PropAct Rule 12-210.
Effect, RP §12-108.
When property deemed to have been taken, RP
§12-102.
Trial court, RP §12-106.
Counties.
Acquisition of property for public purposes, 25
§11A.
Applicable provisions, RP §12-101.
Erosion districts, 25 §162.
Roads, 25 §138.
County boards of elections.
Report of condemned buildings to local board for
voter registration purposes, EL §3-504.
Damages, PropAct Rule 12-208.
Adjustment of taxes not paid, RP §12-110.
Allowance for removal of personal property, dead
body, grave marker or monument, RP
§12-112.
Civil engineers, land surveyors and real estate
appraisers.
Liabilities, RP §12-111.
Easements.
Land over which easement donated to Maryland
historical trust, RP §12-104.
Fair market value, RP §§12-104, 12-105.
Ocean beach replenishment fund, NR §8-1104.
Improvements taken.
Parks, RP §12-104.
Interest on award, RP §12-106.
Maryland environmental trust.
Land over which easement donated to, RP
§12-104.
Maryland historical trust.
Land over which easement donated to Maryland
historical trust, RP §12-104.
Moving and relocation expenses, RP §12-205.
Ocean beach replenishment fund.
Land being acquired to implement.
Factors in determining fair market value, NR
§8-1104.
Part of land taken, RP §12-104.
Relocation assistance. See within this heading,
"Relocation assistance."
Severance damages, RP §12-104.
Shore erosion control.
Ocean beach replenishment fund.
Factors in determining fair market value, NR
§8-1104.
Taking entire land, RP §12-104.
Taxes paid by condemnee, RP §12-110.
Valuation of tenants' interest, RP §12-104.
Dead bodies.
Allowance for removal, RP §12-112.
Definitions.
Relocation assistance, RP §12-201.
Discovery, PropAct Rule 12-206.
Displacing agencies.
Relocation assistance.
Definition of "displacing agency," RP §12-201.
Draining lands.
Drainage districts.
Right of way or outlet over and through lands,
25 §121.
Power of board of managers, 25 §86.
Dwellings.
Relocation assistance.
Additional payment to owner-occupant, RP
§§12-202, 12-203.

EMINENT DOMAIN —Cont'd
Dwellings —Cont'd
Relocation assistance —Cont'd
Election to accept moving expense allowance,
RP §12-205.
Election of rights and remedies.
Abandonment of condemnation proceedings, RP
§12-109.
Trial by court, PropAct Rule 12-207.
Environmental service.
Powers generally, NR §3-104.
Environmental trust.
Easements.
Land over which easement donated to Maryland
environmental trust, RP §12-104.
Evidence.
Assessed value of property.
As determined by department of assessments
and taxation, RP §12-105.
Farmers.
Relocation assistance.
Election to accept fixed payment, RP §12-205.
Farm operation.
Defined, RP §12-201.
Federal aid.
Allowance for removal of personal property.
Effect of payment or reimbursement out of
federal funds, RP §12-112.
Relocation assistance.
Federal financial assistance.
Defined, RP §12-201.
Fees.
Attorneys' fees.
Judgment for defendant, RP §12-106.
On appeal, RP §12-107.
Filing.
Board of property review.
Certification to board, PropAct Rule 12-213.
Fines.
Stakes or markers.
Obliterating, damaging or removing, RP
§12-111.
Forests and parks, NR §5-208.
Underground storage.
Prince George's county.
See PRINCE GEORGE'S COUNTY.
Gas companies.
Power to condemn, PUC §5-403.
General assembly.
Regulations, MD Const Art III §40.
Harford county.
Specific provisions, MD Const Art III §40A.
Hazardous materials and substances.
Controlled hazardous substances.
Condemnation by department, EN §7-228.
Hearings.
Board of property review, PropAct Rule 12-213.
Highways.
Administration.
Entry by state highway administration
employees to conduct environmental and
engineering studies, RP §12-111.
Quick-take act.
General provisions, TR §§8-318 to 8-339.
See HIGHWAYS.
State roads commission.
Applicable provisions, RP §12-101.
Taxation.
Special tax districts.
Acquisition by state roads commission of
property.
Subject to assessment by special tax
district, TR §8-307.

EMINENT DOMAIN —Cont'd
Income tax.
Relocation assistance.
Payment not to be considered as income, RP
§12-211.
Inquisition.
Judgment on inquisition, PropAct Rule 12-209.
Recordation, PropAct Rule 12-212.
Notation if judgment set aside, PropAct Rule
12-212.
Other county, PropAct Rule 12-212.
Verdict, PropAct Rule 12-208.
Interest.
On award, RP §12-106.
Judgments and decrees.
Inquisition, PropAct Rule 12-209.
No right to condemn, PropAct Rule 12-209.
Payment of judgment and costs by plaintiff.
Effect, RP §12-108.
When property deemed to have been taken, RP
§12-102.
Junk dealers.
Removal or screening of junkyards, TR §8-809.
Jurisdiction.
Generally, PropAct Rule 12-202.
Jury.
Highways.
Payment of further sum subsequently awarded
by jury, MD Const Art III §40B.
Method of jury trial, PropAct Rule 12-207.
Opening statement, PropAct Rule 12-207.
Right of award by, MD Const Art III §40.
Verdicts, PropAct Rule 12-208.
View, PropAct Rule 12-207.
Land in more than one county, PropAct Rule
12-212.
Landlord and tenant.
Improvement or installation.
Right of tenant to remove, RP §12-104.
Relocation assistance.
Additional payment to tenants and certain
occupants, RP §12-204.
Removal of personal property from leased
premises.
Adjustment of allowance for removal, RP
§12-112.
Valuation of tenant's interest, RP §12-104.
Limitation of actions.
Abandonment of condemnation proceedings, RP
§12-109.
Removal of personal property, dead body, grave
marker or monument, RP §12-112.
Maryland Transit Administration.
Power of authority, TR §7-401.
Maryland-Washington metropolitan district.
Acquisition of property by condemnation, 28
§5-105.
Relocation assistance, 28 §5-105.1.
Militia.
Acquisition of property.
Air national guard, PS §13-216.
Montgomery county.
Specific provisions, MD Const Art III §40A.
Mortgages and deeds of trust.
Relocation assistance.
Mortgage, defined, RP §12-201.
Mosquito control.
Acquisition of property, AG §5-401.
Municipal corporations.
Applicable provisions, RP §12-101.

EMINENT DOMAIN —Cont'd
Notice.
Board of property review.
Hearing, PropAct Rule 12-213.
Cemeteries.
Publication.
Acquisition of cemetery, PropAct Rule 12-204.
Land in more than one county.
Constructive notice of proceeding, PropAct Rule 12-212.
Removal of personal property.
Notice prior to removal, RP §12-112.
Ocean Beach replenishment fund.
Land being acquired to implement.
Fair market value.
Factors in determining, NR §8-1104.
Oil pipeline corporations.
Power to condemn, PUC §5-404.
Outdoor advertising.
Removal of preexisting, nonconforming signs, TR §8-743.
Parks.
Awarding damages, RP §12-104.
Parties.
Board of property review.
Rights of parties, PropAct Rule 12-213.
Defendants, PropAct Rule 12-203.
Personal property.
Allowance for removal of personal property, RP §12-112.
Petitions.
Allowance for removal of personal property.
Limitation on time for filing petition, RP §12-112.
Plats.
Board of property review, PropAct Rule 12-213.
Policy.
Real property acquisition policies, RP §§12-207 to 12-212. See within this heading, "Real property acquisition policies."
Port authority.
General provisions, TR §§6-301 to 6-309.
See PORT AUTHORITY.
Possession.
Pending appeal, RP §12-107.
When property deemed to have been taken, RP §12-102.
Prince George's county.
Gas and oil.
Underground storage.
See PRINCE GEORGE'S COUNTY.
Water, sewerage and drainage systems of the Washington suburban sanitary commission, MD Const Art III §40C.
Public agencies.
Relocation assistance.
Public agency defined, RP §12-201.
Publication.
Cemeteries.
Acquisition, PropAct Rule 12-204.
Public recreation and parks.
Acquisition by condemnation, 25 §224.
Public service companies.
Condemnation generally, PUC §§5-401 to 5-411.
Public works.
Board.
Condemnation of property, SF §10-202.
Quick-take act, TR §§8-318 to 8-339.
See HIGHWAYS.
Railroads, PUC §§5-405 to 5-409.
Cable operated railroads, PUC §5-409.

EMINENT DOMAIN —Cont'd
Railroads —Cont'd
Electric operated railroads, PUC §5-409.
Railroad corridor property.
Acquisition by condemnation, TR §7-901.
Real property acquisition policies.
Acquisition leaving only uneconomic remnant, RP §12-207.
Appraisal, RP §12-207.
Buildings, structures and improvements on acquired realty, RP §12-208.
Compensation.
Payment.
Before surrender of possession, RP §12-207.
Not to be considered as income, RP §12-211.
Compliance with other provisions of code, RP §12-210.
Damages.
No new element of damage created, RP §12-212.
Deposit.
Before surrender of possession, RP §12-207.
Expenses.
Reimbursement of owner for expenses incidental to transfer to public agency, RP §12-209.
Income tax.
Payments not to be considered as income, RP §12-211.
Legal proceedings.
Responsibility for instituting, RP §12-207.
Negotiation, RP §12-207.
Notice.
Prior to requiring owner to move, RP §12-207.
Occupancy of acquired land.
On rental basis, RP §12-207.
Payment.
Before surrender of possession, RP §12-207.
Not to be considered as income, RP §12-211.
Procedures, RP §12-210.
Public assistance.
Payments not to be considered as income, RP §12-211.
Rules and regulations, RP §12-210.
Transfer of land.
Reimbursement of owner for expenses incidental to transfer to public agency, RP §12-209.
Valuation.
No new element of value created, RP §12-212.
Recordation.
Inquisition, PropAct Rule 12-212.
Recording inquisition in other county, PropAct Rule 12-212.
Records.
Abandonment.
Effect on records, PropAct Rule 12-211.
Religion.
Churches.
Awarding damages, RP §12-104.
Relocation assistance.
Advisory services.
General provisions, RP §12-206.
Appraisals.
Defined, RP §12-201.
Business.
Defined, RP §12-201.
Election to accept fixed payment, RP §12-205.
Comparable replacement dwellings.
Defined, RP §12-201.
Compliance with other provisions, RP §12-210.
Condemning authority, RP §12-210.

EMINENT DOMAIN —Cont'd
Relocation assistance —Cont'd
Damages.
No new element of damage created, RP §12-212.
Displaced persons.
Defined, RP §12-201.
Moving and relocation expenses, RP §12-205.
Owner-occupant.
Additional payment required under certain circumstances, RP §12-202.
Limitation of payment, RP §12-203.
Tenants and certain other occupants, RP §12-204.
Displacing agency.
Defined, RP §12-201.
Dwellings.
Displaced persons.
Election to accept fixed payment, RP §12-205.
Expenses.
Moving and relocation expenses, RP §12-205.
Farm operation.
Defined, RP §12-201.
Election to accept fixed payment, RP §12-205.
Federal financial assistance.
Defined, RP §12-201.
Federal statute.
Carrying out by condemning authority, RP §12-210.
Income tax.
Payments not to be considered as income, RP §12-211.
Lead agency.
Defined, RP §12-201.
Maryland-Washington metropolitan district, 28 §5-105.1.
Mortgage.
Defined, RP §12-201.
Owner-occupant.
Additional payment, RP §§12-202, 12-203.
Payments.
Not to be considered as income, RP §12-211.
Person.
Defined, RP §12-201.
Private agency.
Defined, RP §12-201.
Procedures, RP §12-210.
Public agency.
Defined, RP §12-201.
Public assistance.
Payments not to be considered as income, RP §12-211.
Rules and regulations, RP §12-210.
Tenants and certain other occupants.
Additional payment, RP §12-204.
Uneconomic remnant.
Defined, RP §12-201.
Value.
No new element of value created, RP §12-212.
Right of entry.
Engineers, land surveyors and real estate appraisers, RP §12-111.
Rules and regulations.
Relocation assistance, RP §12-210.
St. Mary's College of Maryland.
Acquisition and disposition of property, ED §14-405.
Sanitary commissions.
Acquisition of existing systems, EN §9-665.
Acquisition of land by districts, EN §9-633.
Cemeteries.
Condemnation of cemeteries, EN §9-668.

EMINENT DOMAIN —Cont'd
Sanitary commissions —Cont'd
Property rights.
Purchase or condemnation, EN §9-668.
Schools.
County boards of education.
Powers, ED §4-119.
Scope of provisions, PropAct Rule 12-201.
Severn river watershed.
Riparian rights.
Use of water for agriculture not lost when land taken by condemnation, EN §4-311.
Shore erosion control.
Ocean Beach replenishment fund.
Factors in determining fair market value of land acquired, NR §8-1104.
Signatures.
Verdicts, PropAct Rule 12-208.
State.
Applicable provisions, RP §12-101.
State roads commission.
General provisions.
See HIGHWAYS.
Surveys and surveyors.
Abandonment of condemnation proceedings.
Recovery of fees by defendant, RP §12-109.
Damages to or destruction of property, RP §12-111.
Judgment for defendant.
Allowance for engineering fees, RP §12-106.
Right of entry, RP §12-111.
Stakes and markers.
Obliterating, damaging or removing, RP §12-111.
Susquehanna river basin authority, EN §5-301.
Taxation.
Adjustment of taxes not paid, RP §12-110.
Assessed value.
Evidence of value when greater than appraised value, RP §12-105.
Benefit charges assessed by special taxing district.
Payment and adjustment, RP §12-110.
Condemnee.
Payment of taxes by condemnee, RP §12-110.
Property qualifying for tax credit.
Acquisition of exempt property by eminent domain, RP §12-105.
Removal of property from tax rolls, RP §12-106.
State roads commission.
Payment of proportionate share of taxes on property acquired, TR §8-306.
Tax increment financing act.
Acquisition of property by eminent domain, 41 §14-213.
Telegraph companies, PUC §5-410.
Telephone companies, PUC §5-410.
Time.
Board of property review.
Dissatisfaction with award, PropAct Rule 12-213.
Cemeteries.
Publication, PropAct Rule 12-204.
Inquisition.
Recordation, PropAct Rule 12-212.
Title.
When property deemed to have been taken, RP §§12-102, 12-108.
Trial.
Election of trial by court, PropAct Rule 12-207.
Generally, PropAct Rule 12-207.
Opening statement, PropAct Rule 12-207.

EMINENT DOMAIN —Cont'd
Trial —Cont'd
Removal.
No right of removal, PropAct Rule 12-207.
Verdicts, PropAct Rule 12-208.
Uneconomic remnants.
Defined, RP §12-201.
United States.
Condemnation proceedings, SG §14-104.
Relocation assistance.
Carrying out provisions of federal statute, RP
§12-210.
Value.
Assessed value.
Acquisition of exempt property by eminent
domain, RP §12-105.
Damages. See within this heading, "Damages."
Determined.
Time as of which value determined, RP §12-103.
Fair market value, RP §12-105.
Allowance for removal of personal property not
to exceed fair market value, RP §12-112.
Verdicts.
Generally, PropAct Rule 12-208.
Inquisition, PropAct Rule 12-208.
Incorporation of inquisition in judgment,
PropAct Rule 12-209.
Washington suburban sanitary commission.
Benefit charges.
Payment and adjustment, RP §12-110.
Prince George's county.
Water, sewerage and drainage systems, MD
Const Art III §40C.
Water and sewer systems.
Municipal corporations.
Acquisition of property by municipal authority,
EN §9-706.
Takeover of privately owned system, EN §9-707.
Water companies, PUC §5-411.
Watershed associations.
Procedure, 25 §201.
Waters of the state.
Wild and scenic rivers.
Limitation on acquisition of land by eminent
domain, NR §8-411.
When property deemed to have been taken, RP
§12-102.
Payment of judgment and costs, RP §12-108.
Witnesses.
Board of property review, PropAct Rule 12-213.
Youghiogheny river.
Scenic corridor.
Limitations on acquisition of land by eminent
domain, NR §8-411.

EMISSION CERTIFICATION PROGRAM.
Motor vehicles.
See AIR QUALITY CONTROL.

**EMISSIONS FROM ELECTRIC GENERATING
FACILITIES.**
Healthy air act, EN §2-1002.

EMISSIONS INSPECTION.
Motor vehicles, TR §§23-201 to 23-209, 23-401 to
23-404.
See MOTOR VEHICLE EMISSIONS
INSPECTION.

EMOTIONAL DISORDERS.
Managed behavioral health care organizations.
Responsibilities of carriers, IN §15-127.

EMOTIONAL DISORDERS —Cont'd
Medicaid coverage.
Seriously emotionally disturbed individuals, HG
§15-130.

EMOTIONAL DISTRESS.
Consumer debt collection, CL §14-203.
Intentional infliction.
Statute of limitations, CJ §§5-101, 5-105.

**EMPLOYED PERSONS WITH DISABILITIES
PROGRAM.**
Medicaid, HG §15-138.

**EMPLOYEE ALCOHOL AND CONTROLLED
DANGEROUS SUBSTANCE TESTING,** HG
§17-214.

**EMPLOYEES AND RETIREES HEALTH AND
WELFARE BENEFITS FUND,** SPP §2-516.

EMPLOYEES' PENSION SYSTEM, SPP §§23-101
to 23-409.
Administration.
State retirement and pension system.
General provisions, SPP §§21-101 to 21-604.
See STATE RETIREMENT AND PENSION
SYSTEM.
Alternative contributory pension selection,
SPP §§23-221, 23-222.
Normal service retirement, SPP §23-401.
Purchase of service credits, SPP §23-307.5.
Benefits, SPP §§23-401 to 23-409.
Additional contributions, SPP §23-405.
Continuation, SPP §23-501.
Early service retirement, SPP §23-402.
Employment of retiree by participating employer,
SPP §23-407.
Normal service retirement, SPP §23-401.
Other benefits, SPP §23-409.
Reduction of allowance.
Unpaid accumulated contributions, SPP
§23-406.
Retirement after termination of membership, SPP
§23-403.
Special early retirement, SPP §23-404.
Contributions.
Accumulated contributions, SPP §§29-501, 29-502.
Employer contributions, SPP §21-307.
Accrued liability contribution, SPP §21-305.2.
Normal contributions, SPP §21-305.1.
Partial withdrawal from system, SPP §21-305.6.
Required contributions, SPP §21-305.4.
Special accrued liability contributions, SPP
§21-305.3.
Withdrawal liability contribution, SPP
§21-305.5.
Contributory pension benefit, SPP §§23-217,
23-218, 23-307.1.
Service credit eligibility, SPP §23-303.1.
Racing commission employee or agent, SPP
§§23-306.2, 23-306.3.
Transfer of service credit between systems, SPP
§37-203.1.
Cost-of-living adjustments.
General provisions, SPP §§29-401 to 29-427.
See STATE RETIREMENT AND PENSION
SYSTEM.
Three percent limited adjustment, SPP §§29-404
to 29-407.
Death benefits.
Election of allowance by surviving spouse, SPP
§29-206.

EMPLOYEES' PENSION SYSTEM —Cont'd
Deferred vested benefits.
  Generally, SPP §§29-301 to 29-305.
Definitions.
  Appointed official, SPP §23-404.
  Break in service, SPP §23-303.
Disability benefits.
  General provisions, SPP §§29-101 to 29-118.
    See STATE RETIREMENT AND PENSION
      SYSTEM.
Inheritance tax.
  Exemption of payments received under plan, TG
    §7-203.
Long-term employees of state.
  Purchase of service credit, SPP §23-307.3.
Membership, SPP §§23-201 to 23-217.
  Alternative contributory pension selection, SPP
    §§23-221, 23-222.
    Normal service retirement, SPP §23-401.
    Purchase of service credits, SPP §23-307.5.
  Application, SPP §23-201.
  Condition of employment, SPP §23-203.
  Contribution by members, SPP §23-212.
  Determination of eligibility, SPP §23-205.
  Election, SPP §23-204.
  Eligibility determination, SPP §23-205.
  Exceptions to application, SPP §23-201.
  Interest on member contributions, SPP §23-213.
  Optional membership, SPP §23-204.
  Termination of membership, SPP §23-214.
Military service credits, SPP §§38-101 to 38-105.
Scope of title, SPP §23-101.
Service credits, SPP §§23-301 to 23-310.
  Approved leaves of absence, SPP §23-306.
  Break in service rules, SPP §23-303.
  Contributory pension benefit.
    Eligibility of members subject to, SPP
      §23-303.1.
      Racing commission employee or agent, SPP
        §§23-306.2, 23-306.3.
  Creditable service, SPP §23-309.
  Eligibility, SPP §23-301.
  Frederick county members, SPP §23-307.2.
  Frostburg city employee, SPP §31-111.3.
  Military service credits, SPP §§38-101 to 38-105.
    Eligibility service, SPP §23-305.
  Purchases, SPP §23-307.
    Alternative contributory pension selection, SPP
      §23-307.5.
    Former employees of private vendors of child
      support enforcement services in Baltimore
      City, SPP §23-307.4.
    Long-term employees of state, SPP §23-307.3.
    Separation of member from employment, SPP
      §23-304.1.
    Racing commission employee or agent, SPP
      §23-306.1.
  Rules for computation, SPP §23-302.
  Sick leave.
    Treatment of unused sick leave as creditable
      service, SPP §23-310.
  Supportive service employee of board of education
    of Kent county, SPP §31-111.1.
  Transferred service credit, SPP §23-304.
Sick leave.
  Unused sick leave.
    Treatment as creditable service, SPP §23-310.
Social security benefits, SPP §§36-101, 36-102.
State retirement and pension system.
  General provisions, SPP §§21-101 to 21-604.
    See STATE RETIREMENT AND PENSION
      SYSTEM.

EMPLOYEES' RETIREMENT SYSTEM, SPP
  §§22-101 to 22-408.
Administration.
  State retirement and pension system.
    General provisions, SPP §§21-101 to 21-604.
      See STATE RETIREMENT AND PENSION
        SYSTEM.
Alternate retirement selections.
  Selection A (Additional member contributions),
    SPP §22-219.
  Selection B (Limited cost-of-living adjustment),
    SPP §22-220.
  Selection C (Combination formula), SPP §22-221.
Benefits, SPP §§22-401 to 22-408.
  Early service retirement, SPP §22-402.
  Effect of employment of retiree, SPP §22-406.
    Restoration of membership in retirement
      system, SPP §22-406.1.
    Temporary or contractual employee, SPP
      §22-406.
  Governor and surviving spouse, SPP §22-405.
  Normal service retirement, SPP §22-401.
  Other benefits, SPP §22-408.
  Retirement after termination of membership, SPP
    §22-403.
  Special early retirement, SPP §22-404.
Contributions.
  Accumulated contributions, SPP §§29-501, 29-502.
  Employer contributions, SPP §21-307.
    Accrued liability contribution, SPP §21-305.2.
    Normal contributions, SPP §21-305.1.
    Partial withdrawal from system, SPP §21-305.6.
    Required contributions, SPP §21-305.4.
    Special accrued liability contributions, SPP
      §21-305.3.
    Withdrawal liability contribution, SPP
      §21-305.5.
Cost-of-living adjustments.
  Combination adjustment, SPP §§29-421, 29-422.
  Five percent limited adjustment, SPP §§29-416 to
    29-418.
  General provisions, SPP §§29-401 to 29-427.
    See STATE RETIREMENT AND PENSION
      SYSTEM.
  Unlimited adjustment, SPP §§29-410 to 29-413.
Death benefits.
  Generally, SPP §§29-201 to 29-207.
Deferred vested benefits.
  Generally, SPP §§29-301 to 29-305.
Definitions, SPP §22-101.
  Appointed official, SPP §22-404.
Disability benefits.
  General provisions, SPP §§29-101 to 29-118.
    See STATE RETIREMENT AND PENSION
      SYSTEM.
Maryland Transit Administration.
  Establishment and maintenance, TR §7-206.
Membership, SPP §§22-201 to 22-217.
  Application, SPP §22-201.
  Conditions, SPP §22-202.
  Continuation of membership, SPP §§22-209 to
    22-211.
    Former officials, SPP §22-211.
    Officials, SPP §22-210.
    Rights generally, SPP §22-209.
  Contributions by members, SPP §22-214.
  Election, SPP §22-203.
  Eligibility determination, SPP §22-204.
  Exceptions to application requirements, SPP
    §22-201.
  Interest on member contributions, SPP §22-215.

EMPLOYEES' RETIREMENT SYSTEM —Cont'd
Membership —Cont'd
  Limitations on continuation of membership, SPP
    §22-209.
  Optional membership, SPP §22-203.
  Restrictions, SPP §22-202.
  Right to continue membership, SPP §22-209.
  Termination of membership, SPP §22-217.
  Transfer of membership, SPP §22-212.
  Transfer of vested rights, SPP §22-213.
Military service credits, SPP §§38-101 to 38-105.
Scope of title, SPP §22-102.
Service credits, SPP §§22-301 to 22-308.
  Creditable service, SPP §22-308.
  Elected or appointed officials, SPP §22-306.
  Eligibility, SPP §22-301.
  Military service credits, SPP §§38-101 to 38-105.
  Purchases.
    Former employees of private vendors of child
      support enforcement services in Baltimore
      City, SPP §22-305.1.
    Former official, SPP §22-307.
    Member's cost, SPP §22-304.
    Payment of full cost, SPP §22-305.
    Separation of member from employment, SPP
      §22-303.1.
    Rules for computation, SPP §22-302.
    Types of service credit, SPP §22-303.
Social security benefits, SPP §§36-101, 36-102.
State retirement and pension system.
  General provisions, SPP §§21-101 to 21-604.
  See STATE RETIREMENT AND PENSION
    SYSTEM.

EMPLOYEE STOCK OWNERSHIP PLANS.
Public service companies using them.
  Public service commission may not discourage in
    setting rates, PUC §4-103.

EMPLOYERS AND EMPLOYEES.
**Access to information about hazardous and
  toxic substances.**
  General provisions, LE §§5-401 to 5-410.
  See OCCUPATIONAL SAFETY AND HEALTH.
**Catastrophic health emergency disease
  surveillance and response program.**
  Quarantine directive issued by secretary.
    Discharge from employment prohibited, HG
      §18-906.
Child care.
  Criminal background investigations for employees,
    etc., of facilities, FL §§5-560 to 5-568.
  See CHILD CARE.
Child labor.
  General provisions, LE §§3-201 to 3-216.
  See CHILD LABOR.
Child support enforcement administration.
  Payments sent to support enforcement agency, FL
    §10-108.7.
Collective bargaining.
  General provisions, LE §§4-101 to 4-405.
  See COLLECTIVE BARGAINING.
  Prince George's county.
    Public employment relations, ED §16-414.1.
Community colleges.
  Employees.
    See COMMUNITY COLLEGES.
  Prince George's county.
    Public employment relations, ED §16-414.1.
Correctional facility inmates.
  Permanent partial or permanent total disability
    while working for wage.
    Sundry claims board, COR §§10-301 to 10-310.
    See PRISONS AND PRISONERS.

EMPLOYERS AND EMPLOYEES —Cont'd
Correctional facility inmates —Cont'd
  Work force, COR §§9-501 to 9-520.
    See PRISONS AND PRISONERS.
  Work release programs.
    Local correctional facilities.
      Employment of inmate as alternative to
        confinement, COR §§11-601 to 11-607.
Credit unions.
  General provisions.
  See CREDIT UNIONS.
Criminal history records checks.
  Generally, CP §§10-231 to 10-250.
    See CRIMINAL HISTORY RECORDS
      CHECKS.
  Prince George's county.
    Prospective employees, CP §10-236.
  Washington county.
    Prospective employees, CP §10-235.
Disabled persons.
  Sheltered workshop employment.
    General provisions.
    See HANDICAPPED PERSONS.
Displaced homemakers.
  Employment to aid displaced homemakers.
  See SOCIAL SERVICES.
Drug testing, HG §17-214.
Employee theft.
  Generally, CJ §§3-1301 to 3-1308.
    See LABOR AND EMPLOYMENT
      RELATIONS.
Employment agencies, BR §§9-101 to 9-501.
  See EMPLOYMENT AGENCIES.
Equal employment opportunity, SPP §§5-201 to
  5-215.
  See EQUAL EMPLOYMENT OPPORTUNITY.
Equal pay for equal work.
  General provisions, LE §§3-301 to 3-309.
    See LABOR AND EMPLOYMENT
      RELATIONS.
Ex-felons.
  Long-term employment of qualified ex-felons.
    Pilot program, LE §§11-701 to 11-705.
Farm labor contractors.
  General provisions, LE §§7-101 to 7-507.
  See MIGRANT LABOR.
General provisions, LE §§1-101 to 11-508.
  See LABOR AND EMPLOYMENT RELATIONS.
Group life insurance, IN §17-201.
  Readjustment, reduction, etc., of rates not
    prohibited, IN §27-210.
  Trustee of fund as policyholder, IN §17-203.
Handicapped persons.
  Sheltered workshop employment.
    General provisions.
    See HANDICAPPED PERSONS.
Hazardous substance information access.
  General provisions, LE §§5-401 to 5-410.
    See OCCUPATIONAL SAFETY AND HEALTH.
Health care payroll assessment, LE §§8.5-101 to
  8.5-107.
High voltage lines.
  General provisions, LE §§6-101 to 6-110.
    See LABOR AND EMPLOYMENT
      RELATIONS.
Home detention program.
  Inmates in correctional facilities in division of
    correction.
    Restrictions on movement, COR §3-406.
Industrial development corporations.
  General provisions, 45A §§1 to 3.
    See INDUSTRIAL DEVELOPMENT
      CORPORATIONS.

EMPLOYERS AND EMPLOYEES —Cont'd
Inmates at correctional facilities.
Permanent partial or permanent total disability
while working for wage.
Sundry claims board, COR §§10-301 to 10-310.
See PRISONS AND PRISONERS.
Work release programs.
Local correctional facilities.
Employment of inmate as alternative to
confinement, COR §§11-601 to 11-607.
Inmate work force, COR §§9-501 to 9-520.
See PRISONS AND PRISONERS.
Insurance.
County employees and officers, 25 §3.
Group life insurance, IN §17-201.
Trustee of fund as policyholder, IN §17-203.
Health insurance.
Child support.
Medical support orders, IN §15-405.
Continued coverage of health insurance upon
termination, IN §15-409.
Group and blanket health insurance, IN
§§15-301 to 15-310.
Conversion from group to individual policy,
IN §§15-412 to 15-414.
Notice to parents of impeding loss of child's
coverage, IN §15-416.
Part-time students with disabilities, coverage,
IN §15-417.
Portability and accountability, IN §§15-1401
to 15-1409.
Reimbursement for services under self-funded
plans, IN §15-702.
Succeeding policy notices, IN §15-415.
Health care payroll assessment, LE §§8.5-101 to
8.5-107.
Open enrollment of terminated spouse losing
coverage, IN §15-411.
Small employers, IN §§15-1201 to 15-1225.
Key employee insurance.
Insurable interest requirement, IN §12-201.
Life insurance liability limitations for hazardous
occupations, IN §16-215.
Maryland health insurance plan, IN §§14-501 to
14-515.
See MARYLAND HEALTH INSURANCE
PLAN.
Reduction, readjustment, etc., of rates not
prohibited, IN §27-210.
Small employer health insurance, IN §§15-1201 to
15-1225.
See SMALL EMPLOYER HEALTH
INSURANCE.
Job training.
Workforce investment act, LE §§11-501 to 11-508.
See WORKFORCE INVESTMENT ACT.
Large employers.
Health care payroll assessment, LE §§8.5-101 to
8.5-107.
Maryland wage and hour law.
General provisions, LE §§3-401 to 3-431.
See MINIMUM WAGE.
Maryland wage payment and collection law.
General provisions, LE §§3-501 to 3-509.
See LABOR AND EMPLOYMENT
RELATIONS.
Maryland workforce investment act, LE
§§11-501 to 11-508.
See WORKFORCE INVESTMENT ACT.
Maternity leave, 49B §17.

EMPLOYERS AND EMPLOYEES —Cont'd
Migrant labor.
General provisions, LE §§7-101 to 7-507.
See MIGRANT LABOR.
Minimum wage.
General provisions, LE §§3-401 to 3-431.
See MINIMUM WAGE.
Occupational safety and health.
Labor and employment relations.
General provisions, LE §§5-101 to 5-901.
See OCCUPATIONAL SAFETY AND
HEALTH.
Railroad employees, LE §§5.5-101 to 5.5-123.
See RAILROAD SAFETY AND HEALTH.
Overtime.
See OVERTIME.
Payroll deductions.
See INCOME WITHHOLDING.
Plant closings, LE §§11-301 to 11-304.
Prince George's county.
Community college.
Public employment relations, ED §16-414.1.
Criminal history record checks.
Prospective employees, CP §10-236.
Prisoners at correctional facilities.
Permanent partial or permanent total disability
while working for wage.
Sundry claims board, COR §§10-301 to 10-310.
See PRISONS AND PRISONERS.
Work release programs.
Local correctional facilities.
Employment of inmate as alternative to
confinement, COR §§11-601 to 11-607.
Prisoner work force, COR §§9-501 to 9-520.
See PRISONS AND PRISONERS.
Private home detention monitoring agencies.
Responsibility for acts of employees, BOP §20-501.
Railroad employees.
Occupational safety and health, LE §§5.5-101 to
5.5-123.
See RAILROAD SAFETY AND HEALTH.
References from former employers.
Liability of employer.
Adult dependent care programs, HG §19-1911.
Retaliatory discharges, 49B §16.
Occupational safety and health, LE §5-604.
Unemployment compensation, LE §§8-1002,
8-1003.
Workers' compensation, LE §9-1105.
Schools.
Employees.
See SCHOOLS.
Sex discrimination.
Equal pay for equal work, LE §§3-301 to 3-309.
See LABOR AND EMPLOYMENT
RELATIONS.
Small farm employers.
Group workers' compensation policies, IN
§§25-201 to 25-204.
State personnel.
General provisions, SPP §§1-101 to 15-201.
See STATE PERSONNEL.
Sundays, working on, LE §3-704.
Support and maintenance.
Administrative contests of withholding, FL
§12-102.3.
Earnings withholding.
Deductions from obligors' earnings.
Employers' liability for willfully violating
subsection, FL §10-129.

EMPLOYERS AND EMPLOYEES —Cont'd
Support and maintenance —Cont'd
Earnings withholding —Cont'd
Present and future employers.
Order binding on, FL §10-128.
Service of order.
Copy served on employer, FL §10-123.
Order served on employer, FL §10-124.
Toxic substance information access.
General provisions, LE §§5-401 to 5-410.
See OCCUPATIONAL SAFETY AND HEALTH.
Unemployment compensation.
General provisions, LE §§8-101 to 8-1608.
See UNEMPLOYMENT COMPENSATION.
Universities and colleges.
Employees.
See UNIVERSITIES AND COLLEGES.
Wage discrimination.
Equal pay for equal work, LE §§3-301 to 3-309.
See LABOR AND EMPLOYMENT
RELATIONS.
Wages.
Assignments.
See WAGES.
Minimum wage.
General provisions, LE §§3-401 to 3-431.
See MINIMUM WAGE.
Washington county.
Criminal history record checks.
Prospective employees, CP §10-235.
Wholesale sales representatives.
Generally, LE §§3-601 to 3-607.
See LABOR AND EMPLOYMENT
RELATIONS.
Workers' compensation.
General provisions, LE §§9-101 to 10-320.
See WORKERS' COMPENSATION.
Workforce investment act, LE §§11-501 to 11-508.
See WORKFORCE INVESTMENT ACT.
Work release programs.
Local correctional facilities.
Employment of inmate as alternative to
confinement, COR §§11-601 to 11-607.
See JAILS.
Youth apprenticeship program, ED §§18-1801 to
18-1809.
See YOUTH APPRENTICESHIP PROGRAM.

EMPLOYMENT AGENCIES.
Advertising.
Requirements, BR §9-304.
Advisory board.
Program evaluation act, SG §8-403.
Applicability of title, BR §9-102.
Bonds, surety.
Licenses, BR §9-301.
Citation of title, BR §9-501.
Clients.
Defined, BR §9-101.
Documents provided to clients, BR §9-309.
Reimbursement, BR §9-308.
Temporary placement fees.
Fault of client, BR §9-306.
Commissioner.
Defined, BR §9-101.
Disposition of money, BR §9-202.
Powers and duties.
Delegation, BR §9-201.
Contracts.
Required language, BR §9-305.

EMPLOYMENT AGENCIES —Cont'd
Definitions, BR §9-101.
Acceptance of position by applicant, BR §9-305.
Discrimination in employment.
General provisions, 49B §§14 to 18.
See LABOR AND EMPLOYMENT
RELATIONS.
Fees.
Collection of placement fee.
Restrictions, BR §9-307.
Placement fees.
Contracts, BR §9-305.
Reimbursement of client, BR §9-308.
Temporary placement fees, BR §9-306.
Forms.
Agency recordkeeping, BR §9-303.
Licenses.
Applications.
Contents, BR §9-301.
Procedure, BR §9-301.
Surety bond, BR §9-301.
Commissioner delegation of power, BR §9-201.
Disciplinary actions.
Grounds, BR §9-302.
Doing business without license, BR §9-401.
Reprimands.
Grounds, BR §9-302.
Penalties.
Licenses.
Doing business without license, BR §9-401.
Placement fees.
Collection restrictions, BR §9-307.
Contracts, BR §9-305.
Temporary placement fees, BR §9-306.
Records.
Advertisements, BR §9-304.
Form, BR §9-303.
Scope of title, BR §9-102.
Title of act.
Short title, BR §9-501.

EMPLOYMENT AND SOCIAL SERVICES.
General provisions.
See SOCIAL SERVICES.

**EMPLOYMENT OF INMATE AT LOCAL
CORRECTIONAL FACILITIES.**
Alternative to confinement, COR §§11-601 to
11-607.
See JAILS.

EMPLOYMENT SECURITY.
Department of human resources.
General provisions.
See SOCIAL SERVICES.
General provisions, LE §§8-101 to 8-1608.
See UNEMPLOYMENT COMPENSATION.
Health care payroll assessment, LE §§8.5-101 to
8.5-107.

EN BANC REVIEW.
Generally.
Circuit courts, CivProCir Rule 2-551.
Sentencing, Crim Rule 4-352.

ENCUMBRANCES.
Deeds.
Covenant that grantor has not encumbered land,
RP §2-110.
Further assurances.
Effect of covenant, RP §2-112.
General covenant against encumbrances, RP
§2-111.

ENCUMBRANCES —Cont'd
Land patents.
Existing encumbrances not affected, RP §13-503.
Liens.
See LIENS.

ENDANGERED SPECIES.
Fish.
Endangered species of fish conservation act, NR
§§4-2A-01 to 4-2A-09.
See FISH AND FISHERIES.
Funds.
Chesapeake Bay and endangered species fund, NR
§§1-701 to 1-706.
See CHESAPEAKE BAY AND ENDANGERED
SPECIES FUND.
**Nongame and endangered species
conservation act,** NR §§10-2A-01 to 10-2A-09.
See BIRDS AND GAME.

ENDORSEMENTS.
Commercial code.
See INDORSEMENTS.
Emergency management.
Civil relief during emergency periods.
Stays, postponements or suspensions of
enforcement.
Effect on sureties, guarantors and endorsers,
PS §14-205.

ENDOSCOPY FACILITIES.
Ambulatory care facilities.
Generally, HG §§19-3B-01 to 19-3B-09.
See FREESTANDING AMBULATORY CARE
FACILITIES.

ENEMY ATTACK.
Emergency management, PS §§14-101 to 14-1004.
See EMERGENCY MANAGEMENT.

ENERGY ALLOCATION EQUIPMENT.
**Apartment owners, operators or managers
using to determine amount of gas or
electricity to be used in individual units,**
PUC §7-304.

ENERGY ASSISTANCE PROGRAM ACT, 41
§§6-401 to 6-406.
Citation of title, 41 §6-401.
Definitions, 41 §6-402.
Development of programs, 41 §6-406.
Energy emergency.
Defined, 41 §6-402.
Fuel vendor.
Defined, 41 §6-402.
Liaison with fuel vendors.
Office of home energy programs, 41 §6-405.
Implementation of programs, 41 §6-406.
Liaison with agencies and fuel vendors, 41
§6-405.
Office of home energy programs.
Community services administration, office as part
of, 41 §6-404.
Created, 41 §6-403.
Defined, 41 §6-402.
Development of programs, 41 §6-406.
Employees, 41 §6-405.
Fuel vendors.
Liaison, 41 §6-405.
Implementation of programs, 41 §6-406.
Information.
Collection and dissemination, 41 §6-405.
Liaison.
Other agencies and fuel vendors, 41 §6-405.

ENERGY ASSISTANCE PROGRAM ACT
—Cont'd
Secretary of human resources.
Authority, 41 §6-404.
Short title, 41 §6-401.
Telephone lifeline service.
Eligible subscribers.
Persons receiving assistance under act, PUC
§8-201.
Utility vendor.
Defined, 41 §6-402.

**ENERGY CONSERVATION BUILDING
STANDARDS.**
**Certificate by builder to electric company that
building meets latest edition of energy
code.**
Contents of certificate, PUC §7-403.
Copies of certificate or statement of waiver
furnished public by electric company, PUC
§7-405.
Duty of builder, PUC §7-403.
Electric company knowingly providing service in
violation of provisions, PUC §7-407.
Electric service not provided to builder.
Failure to file certificate or statement of waiver,
PUC §§7-405, 7-407.
False certificate or statement of waiver, PUC
§7-407.
Filing certificate with electric company, PUC
§7-403.
Filing statement of waiver with electric company,
PUC §7-404.
Immunity of electric company for furnishing
electricity to noncomplying building, PUC
§7-405.
Liability of builder to purchaser for failing to
comply with certificate requirements, PUC
§7-406.
Purchaser of building furnished copy of certificate
or statement of waiver by builder, PUC
§7-406.
Waiver of certification requirements, PUC §7-404.
Definitions, PUC §7-401.
**Electric companies to include in long-range
service plans,** PUC §2-118.
Energy code adopted by political subdivision.
Inapplicability of provisions, PUC §7-402.
Energy conservation building standards act.
Subtitle cited as, PUC §7-408.
**Gas company and electric company to promote
energy efficiency,** PUC §7-211.
Report by public service commission, PUC
§2-122.
Scope of subtitle, PUC §7-402.

ENERGY EFFICIENCY.
Energy conservation building standards, PUC
§§7-401 to 7-408.
See ENERGY CONSERVATION BUILDING
STANDARDS.
**Energy efficiency and economic development
loan program,** SG §§9-20A-01 to 9-20A-09.
See MARYLAND ENERGY ADMINISTRATION.
Income tax.
Green buildings credits, TG §10-722.
Maryland efficiency standards act, SG §9-2006.
Maryland housing fund, HS §§3-201 to 3-208.
**Promotions by gas companies and electric
companies,** PUC §7-211.
Renewable energy credits, AG §§10-1501 to
10-1507.
See RENEWABLE ENERGY CREDITS.

ENERGY EFFICIENCY —Cont'd
Renewable energy portfolio standard.
General provisions, PUC §§7-701 to 7-713.
See RENEWABLE ENERGY PORTFOLIO
STANDARD.

ENERGY FINANCING ADMINISTRATION.
Industrial development financing authority.
Powers and duties of authority, 83A §5-911.

**ENERGY OVERCHARGE RESTITUTION
FUND,** SF §7-315.

ENERGY PERFORMANCE CONTRACTS.
Consultation with energy administration, SF
§12-301.
Energy administration.
Monitoring responsibilities, SF §12-302.
Modification of contract requirements, SF
§12-303.
Terms of contract, SF §12-301.
Waiver of contract requirements, SF §12-303.

ENERGY RESOURCES.
Community energy loan program.
Generally, SG §§9-2101 to 9-2109.
Maryland energy administration generally, SG
§§9-2001 to 9-2007.
Emergency management.
Energy emergencies, PS §14-304.
Standby petroleum fuel set-aside program, PS
§§14-501 to 14-511.
General services department, SF §§4-801 to
4-808.
See GENERAL SERVICES DEPARTMENT.
Geothermal resources, EN §§5-601 to 5-609.
See GEOTHERMAL RESOURCES.
Maryland energy administration, SG §§9-2001
to 9-2007.
Community energy loan program, SG §§9-2101 to
9-2109.
Public buildings and grounds.
General services department, SF §§4-801 to 4-808.
See GENERAL SERVICES DEPARTMENT.
Renewable energy portfolio standard.
General provisions, PUC §§7-701 to 7-713.
See RENEWABLE ENERGY PORTFOLIO
STANDARD.
**State standby petroleum fuel set-aside
program.**
Energy emergencies, PS §§14-501 to 14-511.

ENGINEERS.
Appeals.
State board for professional engineers.
Judicial review of actions, BOP §14-210.
Board, BOP §§14-201 to 14-211. See within this
heading, "State board for professional
engineers."
Bounding lands.
Appointment to assist court, RP §14-111.
Markers.
Penalty for damage or removal of markers set
in property by civil engineer, RP §14-111.
Citation of act.
Short title, BOP §14-601.
Civil engineers.
General provisions.
See SURVEYS AND SURVEYORS.
Civil penalties for violations, BOP §14-508.
Corporations.
Practice of engineering.
Licenses.
Exception to requirement, BOP §14-302.

ENGINEERS —Cont'd
Corporations —Cont'd
Practice of engineering —Cont'd
Practice through corporation, BOP §14-401.
Definitions, BOP §14-101.
Design coordination.
Defined, BOP §14-101.
Performing, BOP §14-101.
Dismissal of actions.
Complaints against licensees, BOP §14-318.
Education.
Qualifications of applicants for licenses, BOP
§§14-304, 14-305.
Endorsement of documents, BOP §14-403.
Prohibited acts, BOP §14-504.
Ethics.
Code of ethics.
Adoption and distribution by board, BOP
§14-205.
Examinations.
Licenses. See within this heading, "Licenses."
Fees.
Disposition of money collected, BOP §14-209.
Establishment of fees, BOP §14-209.
Licenses, BOP §14-312.
Applications, BOP §14-306.
Certification concerning licensee, BOP §14-207.
Examinations.
Early administration of fundamentals
examination.
Certification fee, BOP §14-310.
Limited licenses.
Application fee, BOP §14-316.
Reinstatement of expired licenses, BOP §14-315.
Reinstatement of revoked license, BOP §14-320.
Renewal fee, BOP §14-314.
Replacement of license certificate, BOP §14-312.
Proceedings to establish boundary lines, RP
§14-111.
Fines, BOP §14-508.
Fraud.
Denial, revocation, suspension, or reprimand of
licensee, BOP §14-317.
Hearings.
Licenses.
Denial, revocation, suspension, or reprimand of
licensee, BOP §§14-318, 14-319.
Highways.
Counties.
Engineering advice to counties, TR §8-635.
Employment by commission, TR §8-204.
Immunity.
Professional engineers, CJ §5-425.
Impersonating professional engineer.
Prohibited, BOP §14-503.
Injunctions.
State board for professional engineers.
Actions for injunctions, BOP §14-206.
Legislative declaration, BOP §14-102.
Licenses.
Applications.
Contents, BOP §14-306.
Fees, BOP §14-306.
Qualifications of applicant, BOP §§14-304,
14-305.
Certification concerning licensee, BOP §14-207.
Defined, BOP §14-101.
Denial.
Grounds, BOP §14-317.
Hearings, BOP §§14-318, 14-319.

ENGINEERS —Cont'd
Licenses —Cont'd
Effect, BOP §14-313.
Limited licenses, BOP §14-316.
Examinations, BOP §14-307.
Early administration of fundamentals
examination, BOP §14-310.
Failure to pass, BOP §14-308.
Reexamination, BOP §14-309.
Notice, BOP §14-307.
Failure to pass, BOP §14-308.
Qualifications of applicants, BOP §§14-304,
14-305.
Reexamination, BOP §14-309.
Testing service.
Used to administer examinations, BOP
§14-307.1.
Waiver of examination requirements, BOP
§14-311.
Exceptions to requirement, BOP §14-301.
Corporate officers and employees, BOP §14-302.
Employees and other subordinates, BOP
§14-303.
Expiration, BOP §14-314.
Endorsement of documents while license
expired.
Prohibited, BOP §14-504.
Limited licenses, BOP §14-316.
Reinstatement, BOP §14-315.
False information.
Giving to board to obtain license.
Prohibited, BOP §14-505.
Fees, BOP §14-312.
Applications, BOP §14-306.
Certification concerning licensee, BOP §14-207.
Examinations.
Early administration of fundamentals
examination.
Certification fee, BOP §14-310.
Limited licenses.
Application fee, BOP §14-316.
Reinstatement of expired licenses, BOP §14-315.
Reinstatement of revoked license, BOP §14-320.
Renewal fee, BOP §14-314.
Replacement of license certificate, BOP §14-312.
Issuance, BOP §14-312.
Limited licenses, BOP §14-316.
Defined, BOP §14-101.
Maintenance of list of licensees and certificate
holders, BOP §14-208.1.
Notices.
Denial, revocation or suspension or reprimand
of licensee.
Hearings, BOP §14-319.
Examinations, BOP §14-307.
Failure to pass, BOP §14-308.
Issuance.
Notice to qualified applicant, BOP §14-312.
Renewal notice, BOP §14-314.
Practicing without license.
Prohibited, BOP §14-501.
Qualifications of applicants, BOP §§14-304,
14-305.
Reinstatement of expired licenses, BOP §14-315.
Reinstatement of revoked license, BOP §14-320.
Renewal, BOP §14-314.
Designation of mailing address, BOP §14-208.1.
Replacement of license certificate, BOP §14-312.
Reprimand of licensee.
Grounds, BOP §14-317.
Hearings, BOP §§14-318, 14-319.

ENGINEERS —Cont'd
Licenses —Cont'd
Required, BOP §14-301.
Corporate officers and employees, BOP §14-302.
Employees and other subordinates, BOP
§14-303.
Revocation or suspension.
Endorsement of documents while license
revoked or suspended.
Prohibited, BOP §14-504.
Grounds, BOP §14-317.
Hearings, BOP §§14-318, 14-319.
Prohibited acts while license suspended or
revoked, BOP §§14-504, 14-506.
Reinstatement of revoked license, BOP §14-320.
Scope, BOP §14-313.
Limited licenses, BOP §14-316.
Term, BOP §14-314.
Limited licenses, BOP §14-316.
Testing service.
Used to administer examinations, BOP
§12-304.1.
Using license of another.
Prohibited, BOP §14-503.
Waiver of examination requirements, BOP
§14-311.
Limitation of actions.
Injuries or damages.
Professional engineer, CJ §5-108.
Malpractice, CJ §§3-2C-01, 3-2C-02.
Misdemeanors.
Violations of provisions, BOP §14-508.
Misrepresentation as authorized practitioner.
Prohibited, BOP §14-502.
Newsletter.
Publication by board, BOP §14-208.1.
Notices.
Denial, revocation or suspension or reprimand of
licensee.
Hearings, BOP §14-319.
Examinations, BOP §14-307.
Failure to pass, BOP §14-308.
Issuance of license.
Notice to qualified applicant, BOP §14-312.
Renewal of license, BOP §14-314.
Oaths.
Denial, revocation or suspension, or reprimand of
licensee.
Administration of oaths in connection with
proceedings, BOP §14-319.
State board for professional engineers.
Oath of office of members, BOP §14-202.
Partnerships.
Practice of engineering.
Practice through partnership, BOP §14-401.
Penalties.
Criminal and civil penalties for violations, BOP
§14-508.
Disciplinary actions for violations, BOP §14-317.
Practice of engineering.
Areas in which individual not competent.
Practice prohibited, BOP §14-507.
Corporations.
Exception to license requirement.
Practice by corporate officers and employees,
BOP §14-302.
Practice through corporation, BOP §14-401.
Defined, BOP §14-101.
Licenses.
General provisions, BOP §§14-301 to 14-320.
See within this heading, "Licenses."

ENGINEERS —Cont'd
Practice of engineering —Cont'd
Misrepresentation as authorized practitioner.
Prohibited, BOP §14-502.
Partnerships.
Practice through partnership, BOP §14-401.
Prohibited acts.
Misrepresentation as authorized to practice,
BOP §14-502.
Practicing in area in which individual not
competent, BOP §14-507.
Practicing while license suspended or revoked,
BOP §14-506.
Practicing without license, BOP §14-501.
Professional engineer.
Defined, BOP §14-101.
Professional malpractice, CJ §§3-2C-01, 3-2C-02.
Prohibited acts.
Practice of engineering. See within this heading,
"Practice of engineering."
Purposes of provisions, BOP §14-102.
Railroad crossings.
Stream or canal.
Application to circuit court by railroad for
approval.
Examination by engineer, PUC §9-304.
Responsible charge.
Defined, BOP §14-101.
Rules and regulations.
Distribution, BOP §14-208.1.
State board for professional engineers, BOP
§14-208.
Termination of regulations adopted under
provisions, BOP §14-602.
Seals and sealed instruments, BOP §14-402.
Endorsement of documents, BOP §14-403.
Prohibited acts, BOP §14-504.
State board for professional engineers.
Adoption of seal required, BOP §14-208.
**Secretary of labor, licensing and regulation
department.**
State board for professional engineers.
Authority of secretary, BOP §14-211.
Short title of act, BOP §14-601.
Signing, sealing and dating documents, BOP
§14-103.
State board for professional engineers.
Annual meeting, BOP §14-204.1.
Appeals.
Judicial review of board actions, BOP §14-210.
Appointment of members, BOP §14-202.
Bylaws.
Adoption, BOP §14-208.
Certification concerning licensee, BOP §14-207.
Code of ethics.
Adoption and distribution, BOP §14-205.
Composition, BOP §14-202.
Creation, BOP §14-201.
Definition of "board," BOP §14-101.
Duties, BOP §14-208.
Established, BOP §14-201.
Expenses of members.
Reimbursement, BOP §14-204.
False information.
Giving false information to board, BOP §14-505.
Injunctions, BOP §14-206.
Judicial review of actions, BOP §14-210.
Maintenance of list of licensees and certificate
holders, BOP §14-208.1.
Meetings, BOP §14-204.
Annual meeting, BOP §14-204.1.

ENGINEERS —Cont'd
State board for professional engineers —Cont'd
Number of members, BOP §14-202.
Oaths.
Oath of office of members, BOP §14-202.
Officers, BOP §14-203.
Powers, BOP §§14-206, 14-208, 14-209.
Program evaluation act, SG §8-403.
Qualifications of members, BOP §14-202.
Quorum, BOP §14-204.
Removal of members, BOP §14-202.
Rules and regulations, BOP §14-208.
Secretary of labor, licensing and regulation
department.
Authority of secretary, BOP §14-211.
Staff, BOP §14-204.
Investigative staff, BOP §14-206.
Subpoena powers, BOP §14-206.
Terms of members, BOP §14-202.
Vacancies, BOP §14-202.
Website.
Publication of newsletter, BOP §14-208.1.
State correctional facilities, construction.
Approval of design and services, COR §10-102.
Procurement of services by state, COR §10-102.
Supervisory responsibility, COR §10-104.
Stationary engineers, BOP §§6.5-101 to 6.5-502.
See STATIONARY ENGINEERS.
Subpoenas.
State board for professional engineers.
Powers of board, BOP §14-206.
Termination of provisions, BOP §14-602.
Title of act.
Short title, BOP §14-601.
Website.
Publication of newsletter, BOP §14-208.1.

ENGLAND.
British common law and statutes.
See BRITISH COMMON LAW AND STATUTES.

ENGLISH LANGUAGE.
Baltimore City community college.
English for Speakers of Other Languages
program.
Student grants, ED §16-508.
Colleges and universities.
English for Speakers of Other Languages
program.
Student grants, ED §16-305.
Equal access to public services.
Persons with limited English proficiency, SG
§§10-1101 to 10-1105.
Fraternal benefit societies.
Documents filed to be in English, IN §8-412.
Minutes of proceedings to be in English, IN
§8-422.
Schools.
Non- and limited-English proficient students.
Grants for limited-English proficiency
education, ED §5-208.
State grants for instruction and services to.
Baltimore City community colleges, ED
§16-508.
Colleges and universities, ED §16-305.

ENJOYMENT, LOSS OF.
Drug dealer liability act.
Noneconomic damages, CJ §3-1606.

ENTERPRISE FUND, 83A §§5-501 to 5-503.

ENTERPRISE ZONES.
**Assessment of effectiveness of tax credits
provided to businesses within,** 83A §5-405.

ENTERPRISE ZONES —Cont'd
Counties.
Application by county on behalf of municipal
    corporation, 83A §5-402.
Joint applications, 83A §5-402.
Definitions, 83A §5-401.
Designation of zones, 83A §5-402.
Requirements, 83A §5-403.
Determination of zone.
Data considered in determining eligibility, 83A
    §5-403.
Discrimination.
State contracts.
    Commercial discrimination, SF §§19-101 to
        19-120.
    See DISCRIMINATION.
Eligibility for incentives, 83A §5-404.
Expansion of existing zone, 83A §5-402.
Federal law.
Designation of enterprise zones, 83A §5-402.
Incentives and initiatives, 83A §5-404.
Assessment of effectiveness of tax credits provided
    to businesses within, 83A §5-405.
Income tax.
Credits.
    Wages paid in enterprise zone, TG §10-702.
    Effect of credit, TG §10-706.
**Location of business predating zone
    designation.**
No incentive or initiative benefit, 83A §5-404.
Political subdivisions.
Application by political subdivision, 83A §5-402.
Request for designation of zone by political
    subdivision, 83A §5-402.
State contracts.
Discrimination.
    Commercial discrimination, SF §§19-101 to
        19-120.
    See DISCRIMINATION.
Taxation.
Income tax credits.
    Effect, TG §10-706.
    Wages paid in zone, TG §10-702.
Tax credits for qualified property in enterprise
    zone, TP §9-103.

ENTERTAINMENT PLACES.
Amusements and recreation generally.
See AMUSEMENTS AND RECREATION.
Public restrooms within.
Distribution of sanitary fixtures, HG §24-211.
Unfair or deceptive trade practices.
Reserved seat tickets, CL §13-310.

ENTIRETIES.
Grant of property held by, RP §4-108.
Tenants by the entirety.
See TENANTS.

ENTRY, RIGHT OF.
See RIGHT OF ENTRY.

ENVIRONMENT.
Abatement of nuisances.
Secretary of environment or local health officers,
    EN §§10-101 to 10-305.
    See NUISANCES.
Actions.
Environmental standing act, NR §§1-501 to 1-508.
    See ENVIRONMENTAL STANDING ACT.
Air quality control, EN §§2-101 to 2-614.
See AIR QUALITY CONTROL.

ENVIRONMENT —Cont'd
**Appalachian states low-level radioactive waste
    compact,** EN §§7-301 to 7-306.
See APPALACHIAN STATES LOW-LEVEL
    RADIOACTIVE WASTE COMPACT.
Asbestos.
General provisions, EN §§6-401 to 6-422.
    See ASBESTOS.
Attorney general.
Legal counsel to department, EN §1-407.
Batteries.
Mercuric oxide batteries.
    Disposal and recycling, EN §§6-901, 6-902.
Budgets.
Secretary.
    Responsibilities, EN §1-404.
Cancers.
Patient-identification information.
    Release to cancer control agencies in other
        states, EN §1-405.
Citation of article, 1 §25.
**Commission on environmental justice and
    sustainable communities,** EN §1-701.
Confidential research records.
Custody, EN §1-502.
Defined, EN §1-501.
Use, EN §1-502.
Violation of subtitle.
    Penalties, EN §1-503.
Conservation of water,
Public water systems, EN §§5-5B-01 to 5-5B-05.
County officials.
Qualifications of officials other than health officer,
    EN §1-301.
Secretary of department.
    Delegation of powers and duties to county
        officials, EN §1-301.
Definitions, EN §1-101.
Confidential research records, EN §1-501.
Employer, EN §1-202.
Department.
Composition, EN §1-406.
Defined, EN §1-101.
Established, EN §1-401.
    Legal counsel, EN §1-407.
Permit issued by department.
    Application, public participation, EN §§1-601 to
        1-607.
Secretary. See within this heading, "Secretary."
Staff, EN §1-403.
Units included in department, EN §1-406.
Deputy secretary, EN §1-403.
Documents.
Verification, EN §1-201.
Drinking water.
General provisions, EN §§9-401 to 9-417.
    See DRINKING WATER.
Enforcement.
Secretary to enforce provisions of article, EN
    §§1-301, 1-404.
Executors and administrators.
Compliance with environmental laws.
    Powers of personal representative, ET §7-401.
**Falsifying or altering permits, licenses or
    certificates,** EN §1-302.
Federal clean air act.
Reports concerning, EN §2-103.1.
Fiduciaries.
Compliance with environmental laws.
    Powers of fiduciaries, ET §15-102.

ENVIRONMENT —Cont'd
Fines.
Confidential research records.
Violation of subtitle, EN §1-503.
Flammable products.
Maryland flammable products act, HG §§22-401 to 22-407.
See FLAMMABLE SUBSTANCES.
Hazardous materials and substances.
General provisions, EN §§7-201 to 7-306; HG §§22-501 to 22-508.
See HAZARDOUS MATERIALS AND SUBSTANCES.
Public access to information on hazardous or toxic chemicals, EN §§6-501 to 6-504.
See HAZARDOUS MATERIALS AND SUBSTANCES.
Transfer of hazardous materials.
Between one mode of transportation and another, EN §§7-101 to 7-114.
See HAZARDOUS MATERIALS AND SUBSTANCES.
Voluntary cleanup program generally, EN §§7-501 to 7-516.
See VOLUNTARY CLEANUP PROGRAM.
Health hazards to children.
Administrative procedure act.
Submission of proposals for impact on children's health, SG §10-110.
Investigations.
Secretary.
Authority, EN §1-405.
Junkyards and related facilities.
Adjoining river, stream or other body of water.
Requirements for preventing dumping into waters, EN §§5-10A-01 to 5-10A-03.
Landfills.
General provisions.
See LANDFILLS.
Lead risk reduction in rental housing.
Generally, EN §§6-801 to 6-852.
See LEAD RISK REDUCTION IN RENTAL HOUSING.
Regulation of landlords, 24 §§19-101 to 19-104.
Licenses.
Permits. See within this heading, "Permits."
Noise control, EN §§3-101 to 3-408.
See NOISE CONTROL.
Nuisances.
Secretary of environment or local health officers, EN §§10-101 to 10-305.
See NUISANCES.
Oaths.
Verification of documents, EN §1-201.
Officers.
Defined, EN §1-101.
Oil contaminated site environmental cleanup fund, EN §§4-701 to 4-708.
See OIL CONTAMINATED SITE ENVIRONMENTAL CLEANUP FUND.
Patuxent river watershed.
Sediment waste control.
General provisions, EN §§4-301 to 4-314.
See PATUXENT RIVER WATERSHED.
Perjury.
Verification of documents.
Declaration made under penalty of perjury, EN §1-201.
Permits.
Falsifying or altering, EN §1-302.

ENVIRONMENT —Cont'd
Permits —Cont'd
Issuance.
Consideration of violations, EN §1-203.
Public participation in department permitting process, EN §§1-601 to 1-607.
Appeal of final determination.
Contested case hearing, EN §1-605.
Applicability of provision, EN §1-601.
Applications for departmental permits, EN §1-603.
Notice of completed applications or reasons for incompleteness, EN §1-607.
Consolidation of public meetings and hearings, EN §1-601.
Contested case hearing, EN §1-605.
Dismissal, EN §1-606.
Opportunity for, EN §1-601.
Determination, EN §1-604.
Appeal of final determination, EN §1-605.
Dismissal of request for adjudication, EN §1-606.
Informational meeting on application, EN §1-603.
Mailing notice.
Informational meetings or public hearings, EN §1-602.
Notice of completed applications or reasons for incompleteness, EN §1-607.
Notice, publication, EN §1-602.
Applications for permits, EN §1-603.
Request for adjudication.
Dismissal of request for adjudication, EN §1-606.
Time for submitting, EN §1-605.
Review times for licensing and permitting programs, EN §1-606.
Tentative determination, EN §1-604.
Zoning and land use requirements or conformity to county plan.
Not challenged at contested case hearing, EN §1-605.
Renewal.
Verification of payment of taxes and unemployment insurance contributions, EN §1-203.
Workers' compensation.
Certificate of compliance with act prior to issuance of permit, EN §1-202.
Physicians.
Defined, EN §1-101.
Pollution.
Water pollution, EN §§4-401 to 4-420.
Radiation.
General provisions, EN §§8-101 to 8-601.
See RADIATION.
Rechargeable batteries disposal generally, EN §§6-1101 to 6-1114.
See BATTERIES.
Records.
Confidential research records, EN §§1-501 to 1-503. See within this heading, "Confidential research records."
Reports.
Enforcement activities, EN §1-301.
Federal clean air act, EN §2-103.1.
Sanitary commissions, EN §§9-601 to 9-699.
See SANITARY COMMISSIONS.
Secretary.
Appointment, EN §1-402.

ENVIRONMENT —Cont'd
Secretary —Cont'd
  Budgets.
    Responsibilities, EN §1-404.
  Cancer.
    Information about certain cancers, EN §1-405.
  Defined, EN §1-101.
  Deputy secretary, EN §1-403.
  Duties.
    Generally, EN §1-402.
  Enforcement of article, EN §§1-301, 1-404.
  Grants-in-aid.
    Apply for, receive and spend, EN §1-405.
  Investigations, EN §1-405.
  Nuisances, EN §§10-101 to 10-305.
    See NUISANCES.
  Powers and duties.
    Delegation to county officials, EN §1-301.
  Public service commission orders and decisions.
    Right to judicial review, PUC §3-202.
  Right of entry, EN §1-404.
  Salary, EN §1-402.
  Staff, EN §1-403.
  Subpoenas.
    Powers, EN §1-404.
  Term of office, EN §1-402.
Sediment control, EN §§4-101 to 4-116.
  See SEDIMENT CONTROL.
Severn river watershed.
  Sediment waste control.
    General provisions, EN §§4-301 to 4-314.
      See SEVERN RIVER WATERSHED.
Sewage sludge.
  Regulation of use, utilization permits.
    See SEWAGE SLUDGE.
Stormwater management, EN §§4-201 to 4-215.
  See STORMWATER MANAGEMENT.
Task force on green building, SF §5-9A-01.
Trusts and trustees.
  Compliance with environmental laws, ET §14-108.
**Underground storage tank upgrade and
    replacement fund,** EN §§4-601 to 4-607.
  See UNDERGROUND STORAGE TANK
    UPGRADE AND REPLACEMENT FUND.
Uniform environmental covenants act, EN
    §§1-801 to 1-815.
  See ENVIRONMENTAL COVENANTS.
Verification of documents.
  Declaration made under oath, EN §1-201.
  Effect of statement, EN §1-201.
  Procedure, EN §1-201.
Voluntary cleanup program, EN §§7-501 to
    7-516.
  See VOLUNTARY CLEANUP PROGRAM.
Water and sewer systems.
  County water and sewage plans, EN §§9-501 to
    9-521.
    See WATER AND SEWER SYSTEMS.
  General provisions.
    See WATER AND SEWER SYSTEMS.
  Sanitary commissions, EN §§9-601 to 9-699.
    See SANITARY COMMISSIONS.
Water conservation.
  Public water systems, EN §§5-5B-01 to 5-5B-05.
Water management.
  Attorney general.
    Responsibility for cases arising under title, EN
      §4-502.
  Fines, EN §4-501.
  Patuxent river watershed, EN §§4-301 to 4-314.
    See PATUXENT RIVER WATERSHED.

ENVIRONMENT —Cont'd
Water management —Cont'd
  Penalties, EN §4-501.
  Sediment control, EN §§4-101 to 4-116.
    See SEDIMENT CONTROL.
  Severn river watershed.
    Sediment waste control.
      General provisions, EN §§4-301 to 4-314.
  Stormwater management, EN §§4-201 to 4-215.
    See STORMWATER MANAGEMENT.
  Violations.
    Penalties.
      General provisions, EN §4-501.
Water pollution.
  General provisions, EN §§4-401 to 4-420.
    See WATER POLLUTION.
  Water pollution control.
    General provisions, EN §§9-301 to 9-351.
      See WATER POLLUTION.
Water resources, EN §§5-101 to 5-1302.
  See WATER RESOURCES.
Waterworks and waste systems operators, EN
    §§12-101 to 12-602.
  See WATERWORKS AND WASTE SYSTEMS
    OPERATORS.
Workers' compensation.
  Compliance with act, EN §1-202.

**ENVIRONMENTAL AND ESTUARINE
    STUDIES.**
General provisions.
  See NATURAL RESOURCES.

ENVIRONMENTAL COVENANTS, EN §§1-801 to
    1-815.
Activity and use limitations.
  Instrument creating restrictions qualifying as.
    Valid and enforceable, EN §1-804.
**Adverse possession, prescription,
    abandonment, waiver, lack of enforcement
    or acquiescence.**
  Extinguished, limited or impaired by, EN §1-808.
Amendment, EN §1-809.
  Recordation, EN §1-807.
**Applied and construed to effectuate purpose of
    act,** EN §1-813.
Assignment, EN §1-809.
Assumption of obligations.
  Agencies, persons signing, EN §1-803.
Changed circumstances doctrine.
  Termination for cause, EN §1-808.
Civil actions, EN §1-810.
Consent.
  Amending or terminating, requirements, EN
    §1-809.
Construction of provisions, EN §1-813.
Copies, distribution, EN §1-806.
Defective distribution of copies.
  Validity not affected, EN §1-806.
Definitions, EN §1-801.
**Electronic signatures in global and national
    commerce act.**
  Modified and limited by act, exceptions, EN
    §1-812.
Extinguished, limited or impaired.
  Legal proceedings, EN §1-808.
Forms.
  Notice of covenant, amendment or termination
    filed in land records, EN §1-811.
Generally, EN §1-802.
Holders, EN §1-803.
  Assignment of interest, EN §1-809.

ENVIRONMENTAL COVENANTS —Cont'd

Holders —Cont'd

Removal and replacement, EN §1-809.

Vacancies in position, EN §1-809.

Information required, EN §1-802.

Injunction or other equitable relied, EN §1-810.

Interest in real property.

Amendment or termination of covenant, no effect, EN §1-809.

Interest of holder, EN §1-803.

Invalidity of provision.

Severability, EN §1-815.

Liability for environmental remediation.

Persons with right to enforce covenant not subject to, EN §1-810.

Nature of covenant, EN §1-804.

Perpetual nature, EN §1-808.

New holders.

Assignment to, EN §1-809.

Notice of covenant, amendment or termination.

Recording in land records in lieu of recording entire covenant, EN §1-811.

Parties who may maintain action.

Injunctive or other equitable relief, EN §1-810.

Perpetual nature, EN §1-808.

Persons to whom copies distributed, EN §1-806.

Persons who may hold, EN §1-803.

Prior interests not invalidated, EN §1-804.

Priority of interest under other law, EN §1-803.

Recordation, EN §1-807.

Notice of covenant, amendment or termination.

Recording in land records in lieu of recording entire covenant, EN §1-811.

Registry containing covenants, amendments and terminations, EN §1-811.

Regulatory authority not limited, EN §1-810.

Replacement holders.

Assignment to, EN §1-809.

Runs with land, EN §1-804.

Severability of provisions, EN §1-815.

Short title, EN §1-814.

Signing.

Persons having interest in real property, EN §1-802.

State laws applicable.

Laws governing recording, priority of interest, EN §1-807.

Subordination agreement in covenant, EN §1-803.

Tax deed.

Extinguished, limited or impaired by, EN §1-808.

Tax lien foreclosure.

Extinguished, limited or impaired by, EN §1-808.

Termination, EN §1-809.

Cause, termination for, EN §1-808.

Recordation, EN §1-807.

Uniform environmental covenants act.

Short title, EN §1-814.

Valid and enforceable, EN §1-804.

Defective distribution of copies, EN §1-806.

Zoning and other laws.

Effect generally, covenant more restrictive, EN §1-805.

ENVIRONMENTAL HEALTH.

Children's environmental health and protection advisory council, HG §§13-1501 to 13-1506.

See CHILDREN'S ENVIRONMENTAL HEALTH AND PROTECTION ADVISORY COUNCIL.

ENVIRONMENTAL JUSTICE COMMISSION, EN §1-701.

ENVIRONMENTAL NOISE STANDARDS, SOUND LEVELS AND NOISE CONTROL RULES AND REGULATIONS, EN §§3-401, 3-402.

ENVIRONMENTAL POLICY ACT, NR §§1-301 to 1-305.

Declaration of policy, NR §1-302.

Definitions, NR §1-301.

Environmental effects reports.

Contents, NR §1-304.

Defined, NR §1-301.

Historic resources.

Defined, NR §1-301.

Policy.

Declaration of policy, NR §1-302.

Proposed state action.

Defined, NR §1-301.

Short title, NR §1-305.

State agencies.

Defined, NR §1-301.

Responsibilities and duties, NR §1-303.

ENVIRONMENTAL SANITARIANS.

Board of environmental sanitarians.

Appeals.

Judicial review of final decisions, EN §11-314.

Appointment, EN §11-202.

Chairman, EN §11-203.

Compensation and reimbursement of members for expenses, EN §11-204.

Composition, EN §11-202.

Consumer member.

Licensure examinations.

Participation by consumer member of board, EN §11-304.

Qualifications, EN §11-202.

Restrictions, EN §11-202.

Defined, EN §11-101.

Duties, EN §11-205.

Elections, EN §11-203.

Established, EN §11-201.

Fees, EN §11-205.

Establishment, EN §11-206.

Funds.

Disposition, EN §11-206.

Immunity.

Board and persons cooperating therewith, CJ §5-702.

Liability.

Good faith exemption from civil liability for acts within scope of jurisdiction of board, CJ §5-702.

Immunity of persons participating in board activities, EN §11-207.

Licenses.

Code of ethics.

Adoption by board, EN §11-312.

Denials, reprimands, suspensions and revocations.

Hearings, EN §11-313.

Requirement of license, EN §11-301.

Meetings, EN §11-204.

Membership, EN §11-202.

Oath of members, EN §11-202.

Officers, EN §11-203.

Powers, EN §11-205.

Quorum, EN §11-204.

Removal of members, EN §11-202.

ENVIRONMENTAL SANITARIANS —Cont'd
Board of environmental sanitarians —Cont'd
Reports, EN §11-205.
Seals, EN §11-205.
Secretary, EN §11-203.
Staff, EN §11-204.
Tenure, EN §11-202.
Vacancies, EN §11-202.
Vice-chairman, EN §11-203.
Citation, EN §11-501.
Definitions, EN §11-101.
Elections.
Board of environmental sanitarians, EN §11-203.
Examinations.
Licenses.
Generally, EN §11-304.
Specific examination requirements for
registered environmental sanitarian
applicants, EN §11-305.
Waiver, EN §11-303.
Reciprocal waiver, EN §11-306.
Fees.
Board of environmental sanitarians, EN §11-205.
Establishment, EN §11-206.
Licenses.
Applications, EN §11-302.
Funds.
Board of environmental sanitarians.
Disposition, EN §11-206.
Hearings.
Licenses.
Denials, reprimands, suspensions and
revocations, EN §11-313.
Hours of approved training.
Defined, EN §11-101.
Immunity.
Board and persons cooperating therewith, CJ
§5-702.
Liability.
Board of environmental sanitarians.
Good faith exemption from civil liability for acts
within scope of jurisdiction of board, CJ
§5-702.
Immunity of persons participating in board
activities, EN §11-207.
Licenses.
Applications, EN §11-302.
Fees, EN §11-302.
Record, EN §11-311.
Board of environmental sanitarians.
Code of ethics.
Adoption by board, EN §11-312.
Denials, reprimands, suspensions and
revocations.
Hearings, EN §11-313.
Requirement of license, EN §11-301.
Charges, EN §11-312.
Code of ethics.
Adoption by board, EN §11-312.
Contents, EN §11-307.
Denials, reprimands, suspensions and revocations.
Generally, EN §11-312.
Hearings, EN §11-313.
Reinstatement of revoked license, EN §11-315.
Examinations.
Generally, EN §11-304.
Waiver.
Reciprocal waiver, EN §11-306.
Expired licenses.
Reinstatement, EN §11-310.

ENVIRONMENTAL SANITARIANS —Cont'd
Licenses —Cont'd
Hearings.
Denials, reprimands, suspensions and
revocations, EN §11-313.
Issuance, EN §11-307.
Lost, destroyed or mutilated license.
Replacement, EN §11-307.
Performance of duties by unlicensed
environmental sanitarian, EN §11-305.
Prohibited acts.
Denials, reprimands, suspensions and
revocations, EN §11-312.
Qualifications of applicants, EN §11-303.
Reexamination, EN §11-304.
Registration. See within this heading,
"Registration."
Reinstatement.
Expired license, EN §11-310.
Revoked license, EN §11-315.
Renewal, EN §11-309.
Replacement, EN §11-307.
Required, EN §11-301.
Scope of licensure, EN §11-308.
Term, EN §11-309.
Unlicensed environmental sanitarian.
Performance of duties by, EN §11-305.
Notices.
Licenses.
Denials, reprimands, suspensions and
revocations.
Hearings, EN §11-313.
Examination, EN §11-304.
Term and renewal.
Registered environmental sanitarians, EN
§11-309.
Oaths.
Board of environmental sanitarians, EN §11-202.
Prohibited acts.
Licenses.
Denials, reprimands, suspensions and
revocations, EN §11-312.
Misrepresentation as registered environmental
sanitarian, EN §11-401.
Penalties, EN §11-402.
Reciprocity.
Examinations.
Reciprocal waiver, EN §11-306.
Records.
Licenses.
Applications, EN §11-311.
Examinations, EN §11-304.
Registration.
Defined, EN §11-101.
Licenses.
Qualifications for registered environmental
sanitarians, EN §11-305.
Scope of licensure, EN §11-308.
Term and renewal of licenses, EN §11-309.
Waiver of requirements for examination, EN
§§11-303, 11-306.
Misrepresentation as registered environmental
sanitarian, EN §11-401.
Regulatory programs.
Termination of title, EN §11-502.
Reports.
Board of environmental sanitarians, EN §11-205.
**Right to practice health occupation not
limited,** EN §11-102.
Seals.
Board of environmental sanitarians.
Official seal, EN §11-205.

ENVIRONMENTAL SANITARIANS —Cont'd
Short title of act, EN §11-501.
Subpoenas.
Licenses.
Denials, reprimands, suspensions and
revocations.
Hearings, EN §11-313.
Termination of title, EN §11-502.
Title of act, EN §11-501.
Waiver.
Examinations, EN §11-303.
Reciprocal waiver, EN §11-306.
Registration.
Licenses.
Examination of qualifications for registered
environmental sanitarians, EN §11-303.

ENVIRONMENTAL SCIENCE.
University of Maryland center for
environmental science, NR §§3-401 to 3-403.

ENVIRONMENTAL SERVICE, NR §§3-101 to
3-130.
Accounts and accounting.
Financial accounting, NR §3-126.
Actions.
Power to sue and be sued, NR §3-104.
Remedies of bondholders and trustees, NR §3-120.
Activities.
Generally, NR §3-105.
Appeals.
Public service commission.
Appeal of decision of commission, NR §3-128.
Arbitration.
Public service commission, NR §3-128.
Assignment of wages.
Not binding on service, NR §3-124.
Attorney general.
Duties generally, NR §3-103.
Audit.
Annual independent audit, NR §3-126.
Bids.
Procurements by service, NR §3-103.
Board of directors.
Definition of "board," NR §3-101.
Generally, NR §3-103.
Bonds or notes.
Additional bond.
General provisions, NR §3-114.
Anticipation notes, NR §3-116.
Bondholders.
Remedies of bondholders and trustees, NR
§3-120.
Borrowing money, NR §3-104.
Debts.
Not to be deemed state or local debt, NR §3-122.
Definition of "bonds," NR §3-101.
Disposition of proceeds.
Sale of bonds under trust agreement, NR
§3-117.
Exemption from certain provisions of law, NR
§3-113.
Exemption from taxation, NR §3-123.
Form, NR §3-113.
General obligation of service, NR §3-114.
Grant anticipation notes, NR §3-116.
Industrial development bonds, NR §3-116.
Interim receipts, NR §3-116.
Investments.
Legal investments, NR §3-121.
Issuance.
Authority to issue revenue bonds, NR §3-112.

ENVIRONMENTAL SERVICE —Cont'd
Bonds or notes —Cont'd
Issuance —Cont'd
Consent of state unit not required, NR §3-113.
Determine matters relating thereto, NR §3-112.
Refunding bonds, NR §3-115.
Renewal notes, NR §3-115.
Negotiable instruments, NR §3-113.
Payment.
Source of payment, NR §3-114.
Pledged fund, NR §3-118.
Power to issue and secure, NR §3-104.
Provisions applicable to all bonds, NR §3-113.
Refunding.
Revenue refunding bonds, NR §3-115.
Registration, NR §3-113.
Replacement, NR §3-113.
Revenue anticipation notes, NR §3-116.
Signatures.
Validity of former officer's signature, NR §3-113.
Sinking fund, NR §3-118.
Source of payment, NR §3-114.
Surety.
Service not required to give bond, NR §3-124.
State or local debt, NR §3-122.
Taxation.
Exemption, NR §3-123.
Temporary bonds, NR §3-116.
Treasurer, NR §3-103.
Trust agreement securing bonds, NR §3-117.
Bylaws.
Adoption, NR §3-104.
Charges.
Authority to fix, alter, etc., NR §3-104.
Generally, NR §3-118.
Project or service charges, NR §3-108.
Unpaid charges.
Lien against property of persons failing to pay,
NR §3-108.
Construction of subtitle, NR §3-102.
Contracts.
Federal, state and municipal governments, NR
§3-104.
Generally, NR §3-104.
Mandatory agreements to provide requested
service, NR §3-107.
Municipalities within districts, NR §3-106.
Waste collection services.
Management and operation, NR §3-107.
Contributions.
Generally, NR §3-104.
Corporations.
Exercise of general corporate powers, NR §3-104.
Costs.
Defined, NR §3-101.
Project or service charges in costs, NR §3-108.
Reduction of costs levied against district by
amount of grants, NR §3-107.
Crimes and offenses.
Violations of subtitle, NR §3-129.
Definitions, NR §3-101.
Department of general services.
Service exempt from subtitle, NR §3-103.
Depositories.
Security, NR §3-126.
Director.
Defined, NR §3-101.
Generally, NR §3-103.
Districts.
Creation, NR §3-106.
Defined, NR §3-101.

ENVIRONMENTAL SERVICE —Cont'd
Districts —Cont'd
  Service districts.
    Defined, NR §3-101.
  Solid waste disposal service districts.
    Responsibilities of service, NR §3-106.
  Wastewater purification service districts.
    Responsibility of service and special provisions,
      NR §3-106.
Easements.
  Acquisition, NR §3-104.
Eminent domain.
  Power.
    Generally, NR §3-104.
Employees, NR §3-103.1.
  Appointment, NR §3-104.
  Exemption from state personnel management
    system, NR §3-103.2.
  Health and welfare benefits program.
    Enrollment and participation, SPP §2-511.
  Pension system contributions by employers, SPP
    §21-307.
  Retirement system contributions by employers,
    SPP §21-307.
Established, NR §3-103.
Exemption.
  Taxation, NR §3-123.
Facilities.
  Defined, NR §3-101.
  Transfer of existing facilities to service, NR
    §3-107.
Fees.
  Authority to fix, alter, etc., NR §3-104.
  Charged by county for final disposal of solid
    wastes, NR §3-108.
  Generally, NR §3-118.
Finance and procurement article.
  Exemption from, NR §3-103.
Financial affairs.
  Generally, NR §3-126.
Fines.
  Violations of subtitle, NR §3-129.
Fiscal year, NR §3-126.
Franchises.
  Acquisition, NR §3-104.
Funds.
  Creation, administration and deposit, NR §3-126.
  Investment of funds, NR §3-126.
  Pledged funds, NR §3-118.
  Reserve fund.
    Creation, NR §3-103.
  Sinking funds, NR §3-118.
  Trust funds, NR §3-119.
Grants.
  Generally, NR §3-104.
  Reduction of cost levied against district by
    amount of grants, NR §3-107.
Hazardous waste facility siting.
  Application for certificate.
    Service may apply to board for certificate, EN
      §7-411.
  Duties, EN §§7-410, 7-411.
  Surveys, EN §7-410.
Hearings.
  Conducting, NR §3-104.
Highways.
  Entry upon and excavation, NR §3-104.
Intent.
  Legislative intent, NR §3-102.
Interpretation and construction.
  General provisions, NR §3-102.

ENVIRONMENTAL SERVICE —Cont'd
Investigations.
  Conducting, NR §3-104.
Investments.
  Bonds as legal investments, NR §3-121.
  Funds, NR §3-126.
Legal advisor.
  Attorney general, NR §3-103.
Legislative intent, NR §3-102.
Liens.
  Notice of liens.
    Creation in favor of service, NR §3-125.
  Service not required to suffer liens, NR §3-124.
  Unpaid charges to be lien against property.
    Person failing to pay for projects, NR §3-108.
Limitation upon powers, NR §3-105.
Liquid waste.
  Defined, NR §3-101.
Misdemeanors.
  Violations of subtitle, NR §3-129.
Municipal corporations.
  Authority to contract with service, NR §3-122.
  Contracts.
    Municipality within districts, NR §3-106.
  Failure to pay for project.
    State funds to be paid to service, NR §3-108.
  Municipality.
    Defined, NR §3-101.
  Permitting to construct, operate, etc., project.
    Service unable to do so, NR §3-104.
  Powers.
    Limitation of powers, NR §3-104.
  Solid waste collection, treatment or disposal.
    Rates and charges, NR §3-123.
  Zoning or land use planning.
    Effect of subtitle, NR §3-102.
Negotiable instruments.
  Bond deemed negotiable instruments, NR §3-113.
Northeast Maryland waste disposal authority.
  Contracts between subdivision and Maryland
    environmental service, NR §3-919.
  Transfer of funds appropriated to Maryland
    environmental service, NR §3-903.
Notes.
  Defined, NR §3-101.
  Generally. See within this heading, "Bonds or
    notes."
Office facilities, NR §3-104.
Officers, NR §3-103.
Organization, NR §3-103.
Person.
  Defined, NR §3-101.
Personal property.
  Acquisition, NR §3-104.
Personnel system, NR §3-103.1.
  Exemption from state personnel management
    system, NR §3-103.2.
Plans.
  Five-year plan.
    Adoption, NR §3-106.
    Biennial revision and readoption, NR §3-106.
  Impact statement to be included in findings, NR
    §3-104.
  Making, NR §3-104.
Pollution abatement projects.
  Control and operation by service, NR §3-110.
  Failure of manufacturing or industrial
    establishment to comply with order, NR
    §3-109.
  Inability to recoup costs, NR §3-110.

ENVIRONMENTAL SERVICE —Cont'd
Pollution abatement projects —Cont'd
Projects for manufacturing or industrial
establishment upon failure to comply with
order, NR §3-109.
Provided upon direction of secretary, NR §3-110.
Power plant siting.
General provisions.
See ELECTRICITY.
Powers.
Generally, NR §3-104.
Limitations upon powers, NR §§3-104, 3-105.
Procurements by service, NR §3-103.
Projects.
Acquisition, etc., of facilities and maintenance in
operation, NR §3-106.
Combining projects, NR §3-104.
Compensation for existing projects, NR §3-107.
Defined, NR §3-101.
Duplicating or using projects similar to
service-provided projects, NR §3-111.
Failure of manufacturing or industrial
establishment to comply with order, NR
§3-109.
Pollution abatement project, NR §3-109.
Powers of service generally, NR §3-104.
Requests, NR §3-107.
Reserve funds, NR §3-103.
Secretary of the environment.
Projects to be provided upon direction of, NR
§3-109.
Solid waste disposal projects. See within this
heading, "Solid wastes."
Transfer of existing projects to service, NR §3-106.
Defined, NR §3-101.
Property.
Acquisition, NR §3-104.
Public service commission.
Appeals of decision, NR §3-128.
Binding arbitration, NR §3-128.
Purchases, NR §3-103.
Purpose of subtitle, NR §3-102.
Rates.
Authority to fix, alter, etc., NR §3-104.
Generally, NR §3-118.
Real property.
Acquisition, NR §3-104.
Records.
Copies, NR §3-103.
Refuse disposal works.
Correction and operation of deficient existing
system, NR §3-109.
Regions.
Definitions, NR §3-101.
Generally, NR §3-106.
Rentals.
Generally, NR §3-118.
Reports.
Annual reports, NR §3-126.
Reserve fund.
Creation, NR §3-103.
Responsibilities.
Generally, NR §3-105.
Right of entry.
Lands, waters and premises for certain purposes,
NR §3-104.
Rights of way.
Acquisition, NR §3-104.
Rules and regulations.
General provisions, NR §3-127.
Promulgation, NR §3-104.

ENVIRONMENTAL SERVICE —Cont'd
Seal.
Adoption of official seal, NR §3-104.
Secretary.
Duties.
Generally, NR §3-103.
Pollution abatement projects provided, NR §3-110.
Projects to be provided upon direction of, NR
§3-109.
Supervision of service, NR §3-103.
Service districts.
Defined, NR §3-101.
Service regions, NR §3-101.
Sewage system.
Correction and operation of deficient existing
system, NR §3-109.
Solid wastes.
Fees.
Disposal of solid wastes, NR §3-108.
Rates and charges, NR §3-123.
Solid waste disposal projects.
Defined, NR §3-101.
Responsibility to service districts, NR §3-106.
Staff. See within this heading, "Employees."
State treasury.
Investments in obligations of environmental
service, SF §6-224.
Streets and alleys.
Entry upon and excavation of municipal streets,
roads and other public ways, NR §3-104.
Surveys.
Hazardous waste facility siting, EN §7-410.
Impact statements to be included in findings, NR
§3-104.
Making, NR §3-104.
Taxation.
Bond issues.
Exemption from taxation, NR §3-123.
Title of act, NR §3-130.
Treasurer.
Generally, NR §3-103.
Trusts and trustees.
Bond issues.
Remedies of bondholders and trustees, NR
§3-120.
Trust agreement securing bonds, NR §3-117.
Trust funds, NR §3-119.
Violations.
Fines, NR §3-129.
Wastes.
Collection services.
Contracts for management and operation, NR
§3-107.
Liquid wastes.
Defined, NR §3-101.
Solid wastes. See within this heading, "Solid
wastes."
Water purification project.
Defined, NR §3-101.
Responsibilities for service districts, NR §3-106.
Wastewater purification projects.
Defined, NR §3-101.
Responsibilities for service districts, NR §3-106.
Water rights.
Acquisition, NR §3-104.
Water supply.
Projects.
Defined, NR §3-101.
Zoning.
Land use planning.
Effect of subtitle, NR §3-102.

ENVIRONMENTAL STANDING ACT, NR §§1-501 to 1-508.
Compromise of action.
　Approval of court required, NR §1-507.
Declaration of policy and intent, NR §1-502.
Declaratory relief, NR §1-503.
Defenses, NR §1-504.
Definitions, NR §1-501.
Discontinuance of action.
　Approval of court required, NR §1-507.
Dismissal of action.
　Approval of court required, NR §1-507.
Equitable relief, NR §1-503.
Existing rights and remedies.
　Not abrogated or altered by subtitle provisions, NR §1-508.
Judgments.
　Declaratory and equitable relief, NR §1-503.
Limitations on right of action, NR §1-504.
Person.
　Defined, NR §1-501.
Pleadings, NR §1-505.
Policy and intent of subtitle provisions, NR §1-502.
Political subdivision.
　Defined, NR §1-501.
Procedure, NR §§1-505, 1-507.
Purpose of subtitle provisions, NR §1-502.
Remedies.
　Declaratory and equitable relief, NR §1-503.
　Existing remedies not abrogated or altered by subtitle provisions, NR §1-508.
　Limitations on right of action, NR §1-504.
Stay of proceedings, NR §1-506.
Venue, NR §1-505.

ENVIRONMENTAL SURCHARGE.
Electricity generated within state, PUC §7-203.

ENVIRONMENTAL TRUST.
Advisory council.
　General provisions, NR §3-204.
Attorney general.
　Legal counsel, NR §3-206.
Committees.
　Governor's committee to keep Maryland beautiful.
　　Functions and activities.
　　　Transfer to trust, NR §3-210.
　Subcommittees.
　　Appointed by political subdivisions of state, NR §3-209.
Construction of subtitle, NR §3-211.
Contracts.
　General provisions, NR §3-208.
Director.
　Appointment, NR §3-205.
　Removal by trustees at will, NR §3-205.
Easements.
　Conservation easements.
　　Donation of perpetual conservation easement, NR §3-203.1.
　　　Notification required, NR §3-203.1.
　Grants, etc., to trust, RP §2-118.
　Income tax credits.
　　Easements conveyed for certain purposes, TG §10-723.
　Land over which easement donated to Maryland environmental trust, RP §12-104.
Eminent domain.
　Easements.
　　Land over which easement donated to Maryland environmental trust, RP §12-104.

ENVIRONMENTAL TRUST —Cont'd
Employees.
　Generally, NR §3-205.
Established, NR §3-201.
Existence.
　Perpetual existence, NR §3-201.
Federal aid.
　Grants from federal government, NR §3-207.
Funds.
　Transfer of money or property to trust, NR §3-207.
Gifts.
　Grants, etc., to trust, RP §2-118.
Governor's committee to keep Maryland beautiful.
　Functions and activities.
　　Transfer to trust, NR §3-210.
Grants, RP §2-118.
　Federal government or political subdivisions of state, NR §3-207.
Interpretation and construction.
　Construction of subtitle, NR §3-211.
Land trust grant fund.
　Administration of fund, NR §3-2A-02.
　Definition of "trust," NR §3-2A-01.
　Reports.
　　Annual reports, NR §3-2A-14.
Legal counsel.
　Attorney general, NR §3-206.
Notice.
　Conservation easements.
　　Donation of perpetual conservation easement, NR §3-203.1.
Perpetual existence, NR §3-201.
Property.
　Grants, etc., to trust, RP §2-118.
　Selling, conveying, leasing, etc., NR §3-208.
　Transfer to trust, NR §3-207.
Purposes.
　Generally, NR §3-201.
Subcommittees.
　Appointed by political subdivisions of state, NR §3-209.
Trustees.
　Chairman.
　　Election, NR §3-204.
　Compensation.
　　Serve without compensation, NR §3-202.
　Duties.
　　Generally, NR §3-203.
　Ex officio trustees, NR §3-202.
　Meetings, NR §3-204.
　Number of trustees, NR §3-202.
　Powers.
　　Generally, NR §3-203.
　Quorum, NR §3-204.
　Selection of trustees, NR §3-202.
　Terms of office, NR §3-202.
　Vacancies.
　　Filling of vacancies, NR §3-202.

EPAMD.
See ELECTRONIC PERSONAL ASSISTIVE MOBILITY DEVICE (EPAMD).

EPIDEMICS.
Contagious diseases generally.
See CONTAGIOUS DISEASES.

EPILEPSY.
Identification bracelet, tag or card.
　Persons with condition wearing, CP §2-107.

EPISCOPAL CHURCH.
Corporations.
See PROTESTANT EPISCOPAL CHURCH.

EQUAL ACCESS FOR HANDICAPPED PERSONS, SF §§2-501 to 2-511.
See HANDICAPPED PERSONS.

EQUAL CREDIT OPPORTUNITY.
Actions.
Civil liability, CL §12-707.
Administration of subtitle, CL §12-706.
Applicability of act.
Federal equal credit opportunity act, CL §12-704.
Applicant.
Defined, CL §12-701.
Banking commissioner.
Jurisdiction, CL §12-703.
Cease and desist orders, CL §12-703.
Citation of subtitle, CL §12-708.
Civil liability, CL §12-707.
Commissioner.
Administration of subtitle, CL §12-706.
Defined, CL §12-701.
Jurisdiction, CL §12-703.
Complaints.
Investigation, CL §12-703.
Compliance.
Creditors, CL §12-704.
Credit.
Defined, CL §12-701.
Creditors.
Civil liability, CL §12-707.
Compliance.
Federal equal credit opportunity act, CL §12-704.
Defined, CL §12-701.
Federal equal credit opportunity act.
Violations, CL §12-704.
Violations.
What constitutes, CL §12-704.
Damages.
Civil liability, CL §12-707.
Definitions, CL §12-701.
Discriminatory practices, CL §12-705.
Discrimination.
Discriminatory practices.
Defined, CL §12-705.
Prohibited, CL §12-704.
Federal equal credit opportunity act.
Applicability of act, CL §12-704.
Findings of general assembly, CL §12-702.
Hearings.
Complaints, CL §12-703.
Limitation of actions.
Civil liability, CL §12-707.
Person.
Defined, CL §12-701.
Protected persons.
Scope of protection, CL §12-704.
Purpose of subtitle, CL §12-702.
Short title, CL §12-708.

EQUAL EMPLOYMENT OPPORTUNITY, SPP §§5-201 to 5-215.
Affirmative action plans.
Duties of units.
"Unit" defined, SPP §5-201.
Appeals.
Decisions, SPP §5-213.
Complaint resolution procedures.
Election to pursue allegation under, SPP §5-203.

EQUAL EMPLOYMENT OPPORTUNITY
—Cont'd
Complaints.
Appeals, SPP §5-210.
Decisions, SPP §5-212.
Filing, SPP §5-211.
Investigations, SPP §5-212.
Representation of complainant, SPP §5-210.
Compliance of units with provisions, SPP §5-205.
"Unit" defined, SPP §5-201.
Confidentiality of information, SPP §5-214.
Coordinator.
Defined, SPP §5-201.
Duties, SPP §5-206.
Coverage of program, SPP §5-202.
Decisions.
Appeals, SPP §5-213.
Issuance, SPP §5-212.
Definitions, SPP §5-201.
Duties of secretary, SPP §5-204.
Executive branch.
Personnel actions, SPP §5-208.
Fair practices officer, SPP §5-207.
Investigations, SPP §5-212.
Management service.
Personnel actions, SPP §§5-208, 5-209.
Maternity leave.
Notice of employee rights and protections, SPP §5-101.
Medical disqualifications.
Notice of employee rights and protections, SPP §5-101.
Morgan State University.
Employees.
Complaint or grievance procedure, election of, SPP §5-209.
Notice of employee rights and protections, SPP §5-101.
Officers, SPP §5-207.
Professional service.
Complaints or grievances, SPP §5-209.
Personnel actions, SPP §5-208.
Program established, SPP §5-202.
"Program" defined, SPP §5-201.
Purpose of program, SPP §5-202.
Reporting requirements.
Duties of units.
"Unit" defined, SPP §5-201.
Reports by units, SPP §5-205.
Representation of complainant, SPP §5-210.
Rulemaking authority, SPP §5-204.
Secretary duties, SPP §5-204.
Sick or maternity leave.
Notice of employee rights and protections, SPP §5-101.
Skilled or professional service.
Complaints or grievances, SPP §5-209.
Personnel actions, SPP §5-208.
State personnel, SPP §2-302.
State personnel management system.
Employees.
Complaint or grievance procedure, election of, SPP §5-209.
"Unit" defined, SPP §5-201.
University of Maryland.
Annual reports, SPP §5-206.
University System of Maryland.
Employees.
Complaint or grievance procedure, election of, SPP §5-209.

EQUAL EMPLOYMENT OPPORTUNITY
—Cont'd
Violation of subtitle.
Disciplinary action, SPP §5-215.

EQUAL PAY COMMISSION, LE §3-309.

EQUAL PAY FOR EQUAL WORK.
Labor and employment relations.
Wage discrimination, LE §§3-301 to 3-309.
See LABOR AND EMPLOYMENT
RELATIONS.

EQUAL RIGHTS FOR WOMEN LAW.
Constitution of Maryland.
Equality of rights not abridged because of sex,
MD Const DofR Art 46.

EQUIPMENT DEALER CONTRACTS.
Certification of shipped parts, CL §19-204.
**Change, cancellation or nonrenewal of
contract.**
Prohibited acts, CL §19-103.
Contract.
Defined, CL §19-101.
Current net price.
Defined, CL §19-101.
Dealer.
Death.
Repurchase of inventory, CL §§19-201, 19-202.
Defined, CL §19-101.
Incompetency.
Repurchase of inventory, CL §19-201.
Death of dealer.
Repurchase of inventory, CL §§19-201, 19-202.
Definitions, CL §19-101.
Good cause.
Defined, CL §19-101.
Required to change contract, CL §19-103.
When existing, CL §19-102.
Industrial.
Defined, CL §19-101.
Inspections.
Inventory.
Terms of repurchase, CL §19-202.
Inventories.
Defined, CL §19-101.
Repurchases, CL §19-201.
Excepted inventory, CL §19-203.
Inspection of inventory, CL §19-202.
Shipment of inventory, CL §19-202.
Net cost.
Defined, CL §19-101.
**Notice of termination, cancellation or
nonrenewal.**
Supplier, notice to, CL §19-103.
Repurchases.
Inventory, CL §19-201.
Excepted inventory, CL §19-203.
Shipment and inspection, CL §19-202.
Payment.
Generally, CL §19-202.
Terms, CL §19-202.
Secured transactions.
Inventory security interests not affected by title,
CL §19-204.
Shipment of inventory.
Terms of repurchase, CL §19-202.
Supplier.
Defined, CL §19-101.
Rights upon repurchase of inventory, CL §19-202.
Termination.
Defined, CL §19-101.

EQUIPMENT DEALER CONTRACTS —Cont'd
Termination —Cont'd
Repurchase of inventory upon termination of
contract, CL §19-201.
Violations by suppliers.
Actions authorized, CL §19-303.
Civil penalties, CL §19-302.
Limitation of actions, CL §19-304.
Prohibited acts, CL §19-301.
Severability of provisions, CL §19-305.
Warranty.
Claims of warranty, CL §19-205.

EQUITY.
Accounts and accounting.
Auditors.
See AUDITORS.
Adoption.
See ADOPTION.
Annulment.
See ANNULMENT OF MARRIAGE.
Arbitration.
Uniform arbitration act.
See ARBITRATION AND AWARD.
Auditors.
Court of equity.
See AUDITORS.
Condominiums.
Declaration.
Amendments or corrections.
Participation of council of unit owners to
circuit court in equity, RP §11-103.
Corporations.
Assets subject to charitable or other restrictions.
Decree as to dissolution, merger, consolidation
or transfer of assets, CA §5-702.
Costs.
Court-ordered sales.
Payment of costs, RP §14-103.
Courts.
Auditors.
See AUDITORS.
Descent and distribution.
Distribution under jurisdiction of court, ET
§15-108.
Divorce.
See DIVORCE.
Environmental standing act.
Actions for equitable relief, NR §1-503.
Executors and administrators.
Distribution under jurisdiction of court, ET
§15-108.
Fiduciaries.
Cases not provided for in subtitle, ET §15-209.
Distribution under jurisdiction of court, ET
§15-108.
Fraudulent conveyances.
Cases not provided for in subtitle, CL §15-211.
Guardian and ward.
Distribution under jurisdiction of court, ET
§15-108.
Judgments and decrees.
Sale, lease or mortgage of property subject to
remainder or vested or contingent interest,
RP §14-110.
Judicial power to extend to cases in, US Const
Art III §2; Amd 11.
Jurisdiction.
Trusts and trustees.
General jurisdiction as to trust, ET §14-101.

EQUITY —Cont'd
Jurisdiction —Cont'd
Wages.
Enjoining enforcement of assignment of wages, CL §15-305.
Land installment contracts.
Right of purchaser to enforce provisions of subtitle, RP §10-108.
Landlord and tenant.
Lease of property subject to remainder or vested or contingent interest, RP §14-110.
Mechanics' liens.
Suits to enforce or contest validity of liens, RP §9-109.
Mortgages and deeds of trust.
Property subject to remainder or vested or contingent interest, RP §14-110.
Natural resources.
Actions for equitable relief, NR §1-503.
Negotiable instruments.
Enforcement of lost, destroyed or stolen instruments, CL §3-309.
Rescission of instruments, CL §3-202.
Parties.
Virtual representation.
Sale, lease or mortgage of property subject to remainder or vested or contingent interest, RP §14-110.
Partition.
General provisions.
See PARTITION.
Perpetuities.
Modification of rule against perpetuities.
Application to legal and equitable interest, ET §11-103.
Quieting title.
General provisions, RP §14-108.
Recordation.
Payment of costs in court-ordered sales, RP §14-103.
Remainders, reversions and executory interests.
Sales.
Property subject to remainder or vested or contingent interest, RP §14-110.
Reversion when rent in arrears, RP §14-103.
Sales.
Payment of costs, RP §14-103.
Remainders, reversions and executory interests.
Property subject to remainder or vested or contingent interest, RP §14-110.
Sale of reversion when rent in arrears, RP §14-103.
Right to legal title, RP §14-103.
Specific performance.
See SPECIFIC PERFORMANCE.
Trusts and trustees.
Distribution under jurisdiction of court, ET §15-108.
Jurisdiction.
Generally, ET §14-101.
Vendor's lien.
Court of equity may decree sale, RP §7-202.
Virtual representation.
Sale, lease or mortgage of property subject to remainder or vested or contingent interest, RP §14-110.
Warranty.
Relief in case of breach of warranty, RP §10-204.

EQUITY COURTS.
Injunctions.
Power of court in alimony, annulment or divorce actions, FL §1-203.
Jurisdiction.
Family law, FL §1-201.

EQUITY PARTICIPATION INVESTMENT PROGRAM, 83A §§5-1041 to 5-1047.
See SMALL BUSINESS DEVELOPMENT FINANCING AUTHORITY.

ERISA.
Insurance.
Third party administrators, IN §§8-301 to 8-322.
See INSURANCE.

EROSION.
Calvert county.
Erosion and sediment control in Calvert county, 25 §10K.
Counties.
General provisions, 25 §§161 to 167.
See COUNTIES.
Sediment control.
General provisions.
See SEDIMENT CONTROL.
Shore erosion control.
Districts, 25 §§167A to 167F.
See SHORE EROSION CONTROL.
General provisions.
See SHORE EROSION CONTROL.
Waterway improvement fund, NR §§8-707 to 8-709.
Soil conservation.
Districts.
Shore erosion control districts, 25 §§167A to 167F.
See SHORE EROSION CONTROL.
Taxation.
Property tax credits.
Erosion control structures or devices, TP §9-217.

ESCALATORS.
Defined.
Elevator safety, PS §12-801.
Elevator safety generally, PS §§12-801 to 12-842.
See ELEVATORS.

ESCAPE.
Abandoned property disposition.
Mental hygiene law, HG §16-303.
Bail and recognizance.
Restrictions on pretrial release.
Escapees, CP §5-202.
Committed person found not criminally responsible, CP §3-113.
Consecutive sentence, CR §9-407.
Contraband in correctional facility to effect escape, COR §8-803; CR §9-413.
Departing from custody without authorization.
Escape in the second degree, CR §9-405.
Escape in the first degree, CR §9-404.
Escape in the second degree, CR §9-405.
Expenses incurred in returning person, CR §9-407.
Harboring escaped inmate, CR §9-403.
Home detention.
Escape in the second degree, CR §9-405.
Inmates in correctional facilities in division of corrections.
Violation of restriction on movement constitutes, COR §3-409.

ESCROW —Cont'd
Recordation.
Instrument designating beneficiary recorded prior
to disposition by trustee, RP §14-112.
Instrument limiting power of person taking title
to property in representative or fiduciary
capacity, RP §14-112.
Sentence and punishment.
Deposits on new homes.
Failure of vendor to maintain escrow account or
surety bond, RP §10-305.
Subdivisions.
Deposits on new homes.
See HOUSING.
Time-sharing.
Purchase money escrow account, RP §11A-116.
Tobacco manufacturers.
Escrow act compliance, BR §§16-501 to 16-508.
See TOBACCO.

ESTATES.
Decedents' estates.
See DECEDENTS' ESTATES.
Frauds, statute of.
Creation.
Certain estates created by parol are estates at
will, RP §5-101.
One-year exception, RP §5-102.
Medical assistance.
Claims against estates, HG §15-121.

ESTATE TAIL.
Deeds.
Tenant of estate tail may grant in fee simple, RP
§2-102.

ESTATE TAX.
Amount of tax, TG §7-304.
Apportionment of tax.
Maryland uniform estate tax apportionment act,
TG §7-308.
Assessments.
Federal adjustments made, TG §13-409.
Death taxes generally, TG §§7-101 to 7-122.
See TAXATION.
Definitions, TG §§1-101, 7-301.
Maryland uniform estate tax apportionment act,
TG §7-308.
Distribution of revenue.
General fund, TG §2-801.
Executors and administrators.
General provisions.
See EXECUTORS AND ADMINISTRATORS.
Exemptions, TG §7-303.
Federal estate tax.
Change in federal estate tax law.
Effect, TG §7-309.
Defined, TG §7-301.
Federal credit, TG §7-304.
General provisions.
See FEDERAL ESTATE TAX.
General fund.
Distribution of revenue, TG §2-801.
Refunds.
Payment from, TG §2-802.
Imposition of tax, TG §7-302.
Interest.
Unpaid tax, TG §13-601.
Interpretation and construction.
Maryland uniform estate tax apportionment act.
Uniformity of construction, TG §7-308.

ESTATE TAX —Cont'd
Liens.
Unpaid tax, TG §13-805.
Limitation of actions.
Refunds.
Filing of claims, TG §13-1104.
Net estate.
Calculation of share of surviving spouse, ET
§3-102.
Nonresidents.
Exemptions, TG §7-303.
Imposition of tax, TG §7-302.
Payment of tax, TG §7-306.
Alternative payment schedule, TG §7-307.
Amended return.
Payment pursuant to, TG §7-306.
Apportionment.
Maryland uniform estate tax apportionment act,
TG §7-308.
Change in federal estate tax law.
Effect, TG §7-309.
Schedule.
Alternative payment schedule, TG §7-307.
Refunds.
Claims for refunds, TG §13-901.
Time for filing, TG §13-1104.
Payment, TG §2-802.
Time for filing claims, TG §13-1104.
Returns, TG §7-305.
Amendment, TG §7-305.
Extension of time for filing, TG §7-305.1.

ESTOPPEL.
Commercial code.
Applicability of general principles, CL §1-103.
Limited liability companies.
Agency of member established through proof or
estoppel, CA §4A-401.

ESTUARINE STUDIES.
**Center for environmental and estuarine
studies.**
General provisions.
See NATURAL RESOURCES.

ETHANOL.
Renewable energy credits, AG §§10-1501 to
10-1507.
See RENEWABLE ENERGY CREDITS.

ETHER.
Inhaling, CR §5-708.

ETHICS.
Agencies.
Enumeration, SG §15-104.
Architects.
Code of ethics.
Adoption by board, BOP §3-205.
Attorneys at law.
Discipline and inactive status.
See ATTORNEYS AT LAW.
Rules of professional conduct.
Adoption, CJA Rule 16-812.
Complaints against state employees.
Procedures, SG §15-404.
Engineers.
Code of ethics.
Adoption and distribution by board, BOP
§14-205.
General assembly.
Conflicts of interest.
See PUBLIC ETHICS.

ETHICS —Cont'd
General assembly —Cont'd
Joint committee on legislative ethics.
General provisions, SG §§2-701 to 2-709.
Lobbying.
See PUBLIC ETHICS.
Rules of legislative ethics.
Joint committee on legislative ethics, SG
§2-707.
Housing authorities.
Applicability of local ethics laws, HS §12-311.
Joint committee on legislative ethics, SG
§§2-701 to 2-709.
Judges.
Code of judicial conduct, CJA Rule 16-813.
See JUDGES.
Financial disclosure statements, CJA Rule 16-815.
Judicial appointees, CJA Rule 16-816.
Judicial ethics committee, CJA Rule 16-812.1.
Judicial appointees.
Code of conduct for judicial appointees, CJA Rule
16-814.
Maryland affordable housing trust.
Board of trustees.
Compliance with ethics laws, HS §10-109.
Maryland economic adjustment fund.
Applicability of public ethics law, 83A §6-504.
Public ethics.
See PUBLIC ETHICS.
Public service commissioners, general counsel,
people's counsel and employees of public
service commission.
Generally, PUC §§2-301 to 2-310.
See PUBLIC SERVICE COMMISSION.
Real estate brokers.
Code of ethics.
Adoption and distribution by commission, BOP
§17-207.
Surveys and surveyors.
Land surveyors.
Code of ethics.
Adoption and distribution by board, BOP
§15-205.
Tree experts.
Promulgation of rules, NR §5-421.
Veterinarians.
Standards of conduct and ethics, AG §§2-304,
2-310.

ETHNIC HERITAGE COMMISSION.
Ethnic affairs units.
Defined, SF §2-701.
Funding, SF §2-702.
Annual fiscal audit, SF §2-702.

ETHNIC ORIGINS.
Equal credit opportunity, CL §§12-701 to 12-708.
See EQUAL CREDIT OPPORTUNITY.

EUTHANASIA.
Disposal of domestic animals, CR §10-617.
Killing dogs or cats.
Prohibited means, CR §10-611.
Prohibited, HG §5-611.

EVACUATION.
Buildings.
Occupants needing evacuation assistance.
See BUILDINGS.
Catastrophic health emergency.
Governor's order, PS §14-3A-03.
Human services facilities.
Emergency management plans to include
procedures for, PS §14-110.1.

EVERGREEN SHRUBS.
Transportation.
General provisions, NR §§5-412 to 5-414.
See CHRISTMAS TREES AND SHRUBS.

EVICTION.
Constructive eviction, RP §§2-117, 8-208.2.
Landlord and tenant.
See LANDLORD AND TENANT.

EVIDENCE.
Absent persons.
General provisions.
See ABSENT PERSONS.
Accident reports.
Public service companies.
Notifying commission of accidents, PUC §5-304.
Accountants.
Privileged communications, CJ §9-110.
Accounts and accounting.
Proof of accounts.
Photography.
Copies of business and public records as
evidence act, CJ §10-102.
Written record, CJ §10-101.
Accused.
Character evidence, Evid Rule 5-404.
Testimony by accused.
Preliminary questions, Evid Rule 5-104.
Adjudicative facts.
Judicial notice, Evid Rule 5-201.
Administrative procedure.
Additional evidence, AppRevCir Rule 7-208.
Admissibility.
Limited admissibility, Evid Rule 5-105.
Preliminary questions, Evid Rule 5-104.
Admission of party.
Writings, recordings or photographs.
Testimony of written admission, Evid Rule
5-1007.
Affirmation.
Witnesses, Evid Rule 5-603.
Agriculture.
Farm products.
Official certificates, AG §10-606.
Alcoholic beverages.
Beverages taken as evidence, 2B §16-405.
Confiscated property.
Destruction of evidence, 2B §1-201.
Motor vehicles.
Operation under influence of intoxicating
liquors. See within this heading, "Motor
vehicles."
Sales at unlicensed premises.
Display or offer for sale of alcoholic beverages,
2B §16-406.
Witnesses.
Power to summon witnesses, 2B §16-410.
Alcoholic beverage tax.
Payment of tax, TG §5-301.
Ancient documents.
Authentication or identification, Evid Rule 5-901.
Hearsay exceptions, Evid Rule 5-803.
Antitrust act.
State judgment as evidence, CL §11-210.
Appeals.
Impeachment by evidence of conviction of crime.
Pendency of appeal, Evid Rule 5-609.
Mandate as evidence of order of court, AppRev
Rule 8-606.
Record on appeal from District Court.
Statement of case in lieu of entire record,
AppRevCir Rule 7-109.

EVIDENCE —Cont'd
Applicability of rules, Evid Rule 5-101; Rule 1-101.
Appeals heard de novo.
Appellate review in circuit court, AppRevCir Rule 7-112.
Controlled dangerous substance cases.
Procedures required after sentencing, Crim Rule 4-340.
Criminal investigation, Crim Rule 4-641.
Executors and administrators.
Settlement of decedents' estates, Estates Rule 6-462.
Holocaust victim insurance, IN §28-104.
Juvenile causes.
Detention or shelter care hearings, Juv Rule 11-112.
Disposition hearing, Juv Rule 11-115.
Waiver of jurisdiction, Juv Rule 11-113.
Post-conviction hearings, Crim Rule 4-406.
Preliminary hearing in District Court, Crim Rule 4-221.
Pre-trial release, Crim Rule 4-216.
Probation revocation, Crim Rule 4-347.
Release after conviction, Crim Rule 4-349.
Search warrant issuance, Crim Rule 4-601.
Small claim actions, CivProDist Rule 3-701.
Summons or warrant.
Issuance, service and execution, Crim Rule 4-212.
Arbitration and award.
Hearings.
Arbitrators not bound by technical rules of evidence, CJ §3-214.
Assault.
Serious physical injury.
Expert testimony admissible, not required, CR §3-208.
Attorneys at law.
Disbarment or suspension.
Perpetuation of evidence and testimony, CJA Rule 16-733.
Lawyer counseling committees.
Matters not discoverable or admissible, BOP §10-502.
Unauthorized practice of law.
Investigation by attorney general.
Powers of attorney general as to, BOP §10-404.
Rights of person under investigation, BOP §10-403.
Audiologists, hearing aid dealers and speech-language pathologists.
Hearing aid dealer rehabilitation committees, HO §2-318.2.
Speech-language pathologist rehabilitation committee.
Proceedings, records and files.
Admissibility, HO §2-318.1.
Authentication or identification.
Illustrations of requirement, Evid Rule 5-901.
Requirement, Evid Rule 5-901.
Self authentication, Evid Rule 5-902.
Certify certificate or certification.
Defined, Evid Rule 5-902.
Subscribing witness testimony unnecessary, Evid Rule 5-903.
Bad checks.
Issuing or passing, CR §8-104.
Banks and trust companies.
Merger, consolidation or transfer.
Certificate of merger as evidence, FI §3-709.

EVIDENCE —Cont'd
Banks and trust companies —Cont'd
Stock and stockholders.
Stock ledger.
Presumptive evidence of fact, FI §3-309.
Baptismal certificates.
Hearsay exceptions, Evid Rule 5-803.
Bar admissions.
Out-of-state attorneys.
Supporting data and exhibits, BarAdm Rule 13.
Registration of law students.
Character.
Proof of character, BarAdm Rule 2.
Battered spouse syndrome.
Admissibility of evidence, CJ §10-916.
Bedding and upholstered furniture.
Presumptions, HG §24-417.
Best evidence rule.
Writings, recordings or photographs, Evid Rule 5-1002.
Bias.
Impeachment of witness, Evid Rule 5-616.
Bills for goods or services.
Admissibility, CJ §10-105.
Birth certificates.
Use as evidence, HG §4-223.
Boundaries.
Hearsay exceptions, Evid Rule 5-803.
Bribery.
Compelling testimony in such cases, MD Const Art III §50.
Business records.
Hearsay exceptions, Evid Rule 5-803.
Photographic copies as evidence, CJ §10-102.
Business regulation and licensure.
Prima facie evidence of sale, BR §17-2105.
Witness refusal to give evidence, BR §1-203.
Cable television service, interference with.
Prima facie evidence of intent, CR §7-303.
Campaign finance reports.
Copies, EL §13-341.
Capacity.
Impeachment of witness, Evid Rule 5-616.
Carriers.
Food, drugs and cosmetics.
Use of evidence against carrier prohibited, HG §21-250.
Case record of inmate sentenced to jurisdiction of division of correction, COR §3-604.
Chain of custody.
Controlled dangerous substances.
Statement of mortician, CJ §10-1004.
Post conviction review of DNA samples, CP §8-201.
Character evidence.
Accused, Evid Rule 5-404.
Conduct.
Admissibility to prove, Evid Rule 5-404.
Specific instances of conduct, Evid Rule 5-405.
Definitions, Evid Rule 5-404.
Methods of proving character, Evid Rule 5-405.
Opinion, Evid Rule 5-405.
Other crimes, wrongs or acts, Evid Rule 5-404.
Reputations, Evid Rule 5-405.
Hearsay exception, Evid Rule 5-803.
Specific instances of conduct, Evid Rule 5-405.
Victims, Evid Rule 5-404.
Witness, Evid Rule 5-404.
Impeachment, Evid Rule 5-608.
Rehabilitations, Evid Rule 5-608.

EVIDENCE —Cont'd
Character evidence —Cont'd
Witness —Cont'd
Truthfulness, Evid Rules 5-608, 5-616.
Child abuse.
Custody or visitation proceedings.
Evidence of abuse against certain individuals,
FL §9-101.1.
Child custody.
See CHILD CUSTODY.
Child pornography, CR §11-207.
Children in need of assistance.
Report of study of child, CJ §3-816.
Rules of evidence, CJ §3-817.
Chiropractors.
Chiropractor rehabilitation committees.
Admissibility of proceedings, records and files,
HO §3-406.
Cigars and cigarettes.
Cigarette sales below cost act.
Prima facie evidence of intent, CL §11-506.
Circuit courts.
Suppression of evidence.
Motions in circuit court in criminal cases, Crim
Rule 4-252.
Circumstantial evidence.
Authentication or identification, Evid Rule 5-901.
Code of Maryland.
Public general law, CJ §10-201.
References to the public general laws, 1 §2A.
Regulations, CJ §10-203.
Collective bargaining.
Temporary restraining orders.
Opportunity to show cause, LE §4-315.
Commercial code.
Prima facie evidence by third-party documents,
CL §1-202.
Usage of trade, CL §1-205.
Commercial fertilizers.
Official analysis.
Prima facie evidence of composition, AG §6-215.
Commissioners.
Take depositions in this state.
General provisions.
See DEPOSITIONS.
Take evidence from other states.
General provisions.
See WITNESSES.
Comparison of specimens.
Authentication or identification, Evid Rule 5-901.
Competency of witness, Evid Rule 5-601.
Judge as witness, Evid Rule 5-605.
Juror as witness, Evid Rule 5-606.
Compromise and offers to compromise, Evid
Rule 5-408.
Computer generated evidence, CivProCir Rule
2-504.3.
Computer information transactions.
Parole or extrinsic, CL §22-301.
Conduct.
Character evidence.
Admissibility to prove, Evid Rule 5-404.
Specific instances of conduct, Evid Rule 5-405.
Habit or routine practice, Evid Rule 5-406.
Witnesses.
Impeachment, Evid Rule 5-616.
Specific instances of conduct, Evid Rule 5-608.
Confusion.
Relevance.
Exclusion of relevant evidence on grounds of
confusion, Evid Rule 5-403.

EVIDENCE —Cont'd
Consignment.
Conversion by consignee.
Prima facie evidence, CL §11-809.
Construction of rules, Evid Rule 5-102.
Contracts.
Sale of goods.
Breaches with respect to accepted goods, CL
§2-607.
Disputed goods.
Preserving evidence, CL §2-515.
Parol or extrinsic evidence, CL §2-202.
Price.
Proof of market price, CL §2-723.
Proof of market price.
Admissibility of market quotations, CL
§2-724.
Sales contracts.
Parol and extrinsic evidence, CL §2-202.
Controlled dangerous substances.
Bail or sentencing hearing.
Hearsay, CR §5-809.
Chain of custody.
Statement establishing chain, CJ §10-1004.
Chemical tests.
Reports, CJ §10-1001.
Near schools.
Map as evidence, CR §5-627.
Nuisances.
Property used for controlled dangerous
substance offenses.
Abatement actions.
Admissible evidence, RP §14-120.
Reports.
Availability to defense counsel, CJ §10-1003.
Conviction of crime.
Impeachment, Evid Rule 5-609.
Effect of plea of nolo contendere, Evid Rule
5-609.
Extrinsic evidence, Evid Rule 5-616.
Witnesses.
Impeachment by evidence of conviction of crime,
Evid Rules 5-609, 5-616.
Copies.
Duplicates. See within this heading, "Duplicates."
Election records maintained by boards of
elections, EL §2-106.
Photographic copies.
Uniform photographic copies of business and
public records as evidence act, CJ §10-102.
Records.
Copies as evidence, CJ §10-204.
Corporations.
Charter.
Acceptance of record.
Conclusive evidence of formation of
corporation, CA §§1-206, 2-102.
Restatement, CA §2-611.
Revival.
Evidentiary effect of acceptance of articles,
CA §3-510.
Fees and taxes.
Acceptance of charter for record.
Conclusive evidence of payment of fees and
taxes, CA §1-206.
Formation of corporation.
Conclusive evidence of formation, CA §§1-206,
2-102.
Payment of fees and taxes.
Conclusive evidence, CA §1-206.

EVIDENCE —Cont'd
Death —Cont'd
Simultaneous death act.
  General provisions, CJ §§10-801 to 10-807.
  See DEATH.
Death by wrongful act.
Slayer's rule.
  Weight given criminal conviction, CJ §10-919.
Death certificates.
Use as evidence, HG §4-223.
Debts.
Foreign debts.
  Foreign money judgments.
    See FOREIGN MONEY JUDGMENTS.
  Generally, CJ §10-601.
Definitions.
Accused.
  Character evidence, Evid Rule 5-404.
Certifies, certificate or certification.
  Self authentication, Evid Rule 5-902.
Crime.
  Character evidence, Evid Rule 5-404.
Declarant.
  Hearsay, Evid Rule 5-801.
Duplicates, CJ §10-103; Evid Rule 5-1001.
Hearsay, Evid Rule 5-801.
Original, Evid Rule 5-1001.
Photographs, Evid Rule 5-1001.
Recordings, Evid Rule 5-1001.
Relevant evidence, Evid Rule 5-401.
Statement.
  Hearsay, Evid Rule 5-801.
Unavailability as a witness.
  Hearsay exceptions, Evid Rule 5-804.
Verdict.
  Competency of juror as witness, Evid Rule
    5-606.
Writings, Evid Rule 5-1001.
Delay.
Relevance.
  Exclusion of relevant evidence on grounds of
    undue delay, Evid Rule 5-403.
Dental hygienist rehabilitation committees.
Admissibility of proceedings, records and files, HO
  §4-508.
Dental records.
Admissibility, CJ §10-104.
Depositions.
Objection to admissibility.
  Circuit courts, CivProCir Rule 2-419.
  Criminal rules, Crim Rule 4-261.
Use for substantive evidence.
  Criminal rules, Crim Rule 4-261.
Descent and distribution.
Distribution in kind.
  Title, ET §9-105.
Diagnosis or treatment.
Hearsay exceptions, Evid Rule 5-803.
Diesel emission standards violations.
Admissibility of test results, CJ §10-312.
Dietetic rehabilitation committees.
Admissibility of proceedings, records and files, HO
  §5-314.
Discovery.
Disclosure upon request of evidence for use at
  trial.
  Criminal rules, Crim Rule 4-263.
Perpetuation of evidence.
  Circuit courts, CivProCir Rule 2-404.
Discrimination.
Commercial discrimination.
  Contested case hearings, SF §19-110.

EVIDENCE —Cont'd
Discrimination —Cont'd
Commercial discrimination —Cont'd
  Discrimination and retaliation complaints, SF
    §19-107.
  Initial findings and recommendations, SF
    §19-108.
Divorce.
Domestic violence.
  Protective orders inadmissible, FL §7-103.1.
Testimony.
  Generally, FamLaw Rule 9-209.
DNA database system.
Use of match as evidence, PS §2-510.
DNA profiles.
Admissibility, CJ §10-915.
New trial, Crim Rule 4-331.
Postconviction review, CP §8-201.
Documents of title.
Bills of lading.
  Third party documents.
    Prima facie evidence, CL §1-202.
Domestic violence.
Battered spouse syndrome.
  Admissibility of evidence, CJ §10-916.
Local domestic violence fatality review teams.
  Information available in judicial proceedings,
    FL §4-707.
Orders of court.
  Protection from abuse.
    Inadmissible evidence in divorce proceedings,
      FL §7-103.1.
Driving under the influence.
Analysis of alcohol on breath or in blood, CJ
  §10-307.
Drugs or controlled dangerous substances in
  blood.
  Results of tests, CJ §10-308.
Other evidence, CJ §10-308.
Prima facie evidence.
  Impairment or alcohol in blood, CJ §10-307.
Refusal to submit to test, CJ §10-309.
Drug asset forfeiture.
Photographs as evidence, CP §12-202.
Drunkenness.
Motor vehicle operation under influence.
  Test for intoxication.
    Presumptions, CJ §10-307.
Duplicates.
Admissibility, CJ §10-103; Evid Rule 5-1003.
Best evidence, Evid Rule 5-1003.
Definitions, CJ §10-103; Evid Rule 5-1001.
Election records maintained by boards of
  elections.
  Certified copies, EL §2-106.
Dying declarations.
Hearsay exceptions, Evid Rule 5-804.
Election records.
Certified copies of records maintained by boards of
  elections, EL §2-106.
Electric company materials, equipment or
  facilities.
Interfering with or tampering with, CR §6-303.
Electricians.
Disciplinary actions.
  Evidence of intent to violate provisions, BOP
    §6-316.
Electronic transactions, CL §21-112.
Eminent domain.
Assessed value of property.
  As determined by department of assessments
    and taxation, RP §12-105.

EVIDENCE —Cont'd
Emotional condition.
Hearsay exceptions, Evid Rule 5-803.
Employee theft.
Civil penalties.
Payment not admissible in criminal prosecution, CJ §3-1306.
Erroneous rulings on evidence.
Effect, Evid Rule 5-103.
Excited utterance.
Hearsay exceptions, Evid Rule 5-803.
Exclusion of witness, Evid Rule 5-615.
Exemptions.
Assignment of claims to nonresidents.
Depriving debtor of rights under exemption laws.
Assignment or transfers prima facie evidence, CL §15-502.
Expert witnesses.
See EXPERT WITNESSES.
Explanation of ruling on evidence, Evid Rule 5-103.
Extrinsic evidence.
Impeachment, Evid Rule 5-616.
Prior conduct, Evid Rule 5-608.
Prior inconsistent statements, Evid Rule 5-613.
Family history.
Hearsay exceptions.
Declarant unavailable, Evid Rule 5-804.
Unavailability of declarant not required, Evid Rule 5-803.
Family records.
Hearsay exceptions, Evid Rule 5-803.
Feedstuffs.
Official analysis.
Prima facie evidence of composition, AG §6-114.
Fetal death certificates.
Use as evidence, HG §4-223.
Fiduciaries.
Transfer of securities, ET §15-304.
Fires and fire prevention.
Center for the study of the health effects of fire.
Inadmissibility of information collected, HG §18-705.
Foreign debts.
Debt of record.
Proof, CJ §10-601.
Method of proof, CJ §10-601.
Money judgment recognition.
General provisions, CJ §§10-701 to 10-709.
See FOREIGN MONEY JUDGMENTS.
Foreign laws.
Judicial notice of foreign laws.
General provisions, CJ §§10-501 to 10-507.
See JUDICIAL NOTICE.
Former testimony.
Hearsay exceptions, Evid Rule 5-804.
Fraternal benefit societies.
Amendment of constitution or laws.
Printed copies as prima facie evidence, IN §8-419.
Appointment of commissioner as attorney for service of process.
Copy of appointment as evidence, IN §8-407.
Benefit certificates.
Certified copies as evidence, IN §8-432.
Certificates of authority.
Prima facie evidence of society's existence, IN §8-417.
Frequency analyzers, CJ §10-911.

EVIDENCE —Cont'd
Functions of court and jury.
Writings, recordings and photographs, Evid Rule 5-1008.
Gas company material, equipment or facilities.
Interference with, CR §6-304.
Guardian and ward.
Life-sustaining procedures.
Withdrawal or withholding, ET §13-712.
Best interest determination, ET §13-713.
Defined, ET §13-711.
Veteran's guardianship.
Necessity for appointment of guardian of minor beneficiary, ET §13-802.
Guilty pleas.
Withdrawn or unaccepted pleas.
Admissibility, Evid Rule 5-410.
Habit, Evid Rule 5-406.
Handwriting.
Authentication or identification.
Nonexpert opinion, Evid Rule 5-901.
Hazardous materials and substances.
Investigations.
Results available as evidence, HG §22-508.
Health.
Center for the study of the health effects of fire.
Information collected inadmissible, HG §18-705.
Health care malpractice claims.
Award, SpecPro Rule 15-403.
Expressions of regret or apology by health care provider.
Admissibility, CJ §10-920.
Health insurance.
Application forms, IN §12-206.
Hearsay.
Controlled dangerous substances bail or sentencing hearing, CR §5-809.
Credibility of declarant.
Attacking and supporting, Evid Rule 5-806.
Criminal cases.
Exceptions.
Declarant unavailable, CJ §10-901.
Definition, Evid Rule 5-801.
Unavailability as witness, Evid Rule 5-804.
Exceptions.
Declarant unavailable, Evid Rule 5-804.
Criminal cases, CJ §10-901.
Prior statements by witnesses, Evid Rule 5-802.1.
Unavailability of declarant not required, Evid Rule 5-803.
General rule, Evid Rule 5-802.
Hearsay within hearsay, Evid Rule 5-805.
Prior statements by witnesses.
Hearsay exceptions, Evid Rule 5-802.1.
History.
Family or personal history.
Hearsay exceptions.
Declarant unavailable, Evid Rule 5-804.
Unavailability of declarant not required, Evid Rule 5-803.
Holocaust victim insurance.
Applicability of rules, IN §28-104.
Hospital expenses.
Payment of expenses.
Admissibility, Evid Rule 5-409.
Hospital records.
Admissibility, CJ §10-104.
Hospitals.
Hazardous conditions.
Intermediate sanction.
Appeals, HG §19-364.

EVIDENCE —Cont'd

Impeachment, Evid Rule 5-616.
Bias, Evid Rule 5-616.
Capacity, Evid Rule 5-616.
Character evidence, Evid Rule 5-608.
Conduct of witnesses, Evid Rules 5-608, 5-616.
Conviction of crime, Evid Rule 5-609.
Extrinsic evidence, Evid Rule 5-616.
Personal knowledge, Evid Rule 5-616.
Prejudice, Evid Rule 5-616.
Prior statements of witnesses, Evid Rules 5-613, 5-616.
Rehabilitation, Evid Rule 5-616.
Religious beliefs or opinions, Evid Rule 5-610.
Who may impeach, Evid Rule 5-607.

Income tax.
Credits.
Evidence of entitlement required, TG §10-705.

Incompetency to stand trial, examination made by health department.
Admissibility of statements made by defendant, CP §§3-105, 3-108.

Inconsistent statements.
Witnesses, Evid Rule 5-613.

Injuries.
Payment of medical, hospital or other similar expenses.
Admissibility to prove liability for injury, Evid Rule 5-409.

Inmate's case records, COR §3-604.

Instructions to the jury.
Reference to evidence, Crim Rule 4-325.
Circuit courts, CivProCir Rule 2-520.

Insurance.
Commissioner's hearing, IN §2-213.
Examination reports, IN §2-209.
Health insurance.
Application forms, IN §12-206.
Liability insurance.
Admissibility, Evid Rule 5-411.
Life insurance and annuities.
Application forms, IN §12-206.
Liquidation, rehabilitation, etc., of insurers.
Claims against insurers.
Judgments as evidence of liability or damages, IN §9-228.
Policy or certificate as prima facie evidence, CL §1-202.

Intercepted communications.
Wiretapping.
Admissibility of evidence, CJ §10-405.

Interrogation of witnesses.
By court, Evid Rule 5-616.
Mode and order, Evid Rule 5-611.
Prior statements, Evid Rule 5-613.

Interstate commerce commission.
Printed copies of I.C.C. schedules, etc.
Admissible and presumed correct, CJ §10-207.

Investment securities.
Rules concerning certificated securities, CL §8-114.

Irrelevant evidence.
Inadmissible, Evid Rule 5-402.

Judges.
Competency as witness, Evid Rule 5-605.
Explanation of ruling on evidence, Evid Rule 5-103.
Function of court and jury.
Writings, recordings or photographs, Evid Rule 5-1008.

EVIDENCE —Cont'd

Judgments and decrees.
Boundaries.
Hearsay exceptions, Evid Rule 5-803.
Foreign money judgments.
General provisions, CJ §§10-701 to 10-709.
See FOREIGN MONEY JUDGMENTS.
General history.
Hearsay exceptions, Evid Rule 5-803.
Personal or family history.
Hearsay exceptions, Evid Rule 5-803.
Revisory power of court.
Newly-discovered evidence.
District Court, CivProDist Rule 3-535.

Judicial notice.
General provisions.
See JUDICIAL NOTICE.
Uniform judicial notice of foreign law act.
General provisions.
See JUDICIAL NOTICE.

Jury trial.
Competency of juror as witness, Evid Rule 5-606.
Exhibits.
Circuit courts, CivProCir Rule 2-516.
Hearing of jury.
Inadmissible evidence suggested to the jury, Evid Rule 5-103.
Preliminary questions, Evid Rule 5-104.
Instructions to jury.
Reference to evidence, Crim Rule 4-325.
Circuit courts, CivProCir Rule 2-520.
Items taken to jury room.
Review of evidence, Crim Rule 4-326.
Circuit courts, CivProCir Rule 2-521.
Judicial notice.
Instructing jury, Evid Rule 5-201.
Jury request to review, Crim Rule 4-326.
Limited admissibility.
Instructing jury, Evid Rule 5-105.
Misleading the jury.
Exclusion of relevant evidence on ground of misleading the jury, Evid Rule 5-403.
Objections to evidence.
Continuing objections to evidence, Crim Rule 4-323.
Method of making, Crim Rule 4-323.
Production of evidence.
When court may require production of evidence.
Circuit courts, CivProCir Rule 2-514.
Review of evidence.
Circuit courts, CivProCir Rule 2-521.
Jury request to review evidence, Crim Rule 4-326.
Writings, recordings or photographs.
Functions of court and jury, Evid Rule 5-1008.

Juvenile cases.
Competency or incompetency to proceed.
Competency hearings, CJ §3-8A-17.4.
Statements by child, expert's report, admissibility, restrictions, CJ §3-8A-17.10.

Juvenile causes.
Adjudicatory hearing.
Presentation of evidence, Juv Rule 11-114.

Law enforcement officers and personnel.
Disciplinary hearings, PS §3-107.

Lay witnesses.
Opinion testimony, Evid Rule 5-701.

Leading questions, Evid Rule 5-611.

Learned treatises.
Hearsay exceptions, Evid Rule 5-803.

EVIDENCE —Cont'd

Leases.
Commercial code.
Extrinsic evidence, CL §2A-202.

Letters.
Duplicates. See within this heading, "Duplicates."

Liability insurance.
Admissibility, Evid Rule 5-411.

Licenses.
Tax payment.
Licenses as evidence, TG §2-105.

Life insurance and annuities.
Application forms, IN §12-206.

Limited admissibility, Evid Rule 5-105.

Liquefied petroleum gas.
Unlawful use of containers.
Presumptive evidence, CL §11-604.

Machine guns, possession.
Presence in room, boat or vehicle, CR §4-402.

Maps.
Limits of counties on navigable waters, 75 §83.

Market reports.
Hearsay exceptions, Evid Rule 5-803.

Market value.
Commercial code, CL §§2-723, 2-724.

Marriage certificates.
Hearsay exceptions, Evid Rule 5-803.

Maryland register, CJ §10-203.

Maryland-Washington regional district.
Building regulations in Prince George's county.
Printed copies deemed prima facie evidence, 28 §8-115.

Medicaid.
Long-term care transaction forms.
Eligibility under program.
Admissibility into evidence, HG §15-109.

Medical diagnosis or treatment.
Hearsay exceptions, Evid Rule 5-803.

Medical expense.
Payment of expenses.
Admissibility, Evid Rule 5-409.

Medical records.
Admissibility, CJ §10-104.

Memory.
Writing or other item used to refresh memory, Evid Rule 5-612.

Mental condition.
Hearsay exceptions, Evid Rule 5-803.

Mental hygiene law.
Private group homes.
Investigation of license applications.
Use as evidence, HG §10-520.

Military affairs.
Federal finding of presumed death, CJ §10-208.
Signature and authority, CJ §10-210.
Federal record of missing individual, CJ §10-209.
Signature and authority, CJ §10-210.
Military discharge papers recorded by clerk.
Admissibility, CJ §2-207.

Minimum wage.
Investigations.
Powers to obtain evidence, LE §3-408.

Mortgages and deeds of trust.
Marking evidence of indebtedness paid or cancelled, RP §3-105.
Mortgage lenders.
Independent evidence of commercial purpose, FI §11-521.
Investigations by commissioner.
Powers of commissioner, FI §11-515.

EVIDENCE —Cont'd

Mortgages and deeds of trust —Cont'd
Recorded release.
Furnishing evidence, RP §7-106.

Morticians.
Chain of custody.
Statement of mortician establishing chain, CJ §10-1004.

Motor vehicles.
Diesel emission standards violations.
Admissibility of test results, CJ §10-312.
Electronic toll collection video monitoring systems.
Admissibility of recorded images by, CJ §10-310.
Emergency vehicles.
Seat belts or restraining devices, failure to use.
Evidence of civil actions, TR §22-412.4.
Operation under influence of intoxicating liquors.
Chemical tests for intoxication.
Administration of test, CJ §10-304.
Admissibility of test results.
Lack of presence or testimony of technician, CJ §10-306.
Analysis obtained under TR section 16-205.1, CJ §10-309.
Chemical analysis, CJ §10-307.
Extent of limits on admissibility of analysis, CJ §10-309.
Introduction of other evidence, CJ §10-308.
Person administering test, CJ §10-304.
Persons incapable of test refusal, CJ §10-305.
Presumptions, CJ §10-307.
Purpose, CJ §10-302.
Refusal to submit to test, CJ §10-309.
Request by accused, CJ §10-304.
Subpoena for toxicologists, CJ §10-304.
Time limitation, CJ §10-303.
Type of test, CJ §10-305.
Prima facie evidence, CJ §10-307.
Seat belts.
Emergency vehicles.
Failure to use.
Evidence in civil actions, TR §22-412.4.
Speed.
Proof of speed by devices employing radio-micro waves, CJ §10-301.

Negotiable instruments.
Notice of dishonor, CL §3-505.
Parol evidence, CL §3-117.

New trial.
Newly discovered evidence.
Criminal rules, Crim Rule 4-331.

Noise.
Measurement.
Sound level meters and frequency analyzers, CJ §10-911.

Nolo contendere.
Impeachment by evidence of conviction of crime.
Effect of plea, Evid Rule 5-609.
Withdrawn or unaccepted pleas.
Admissibility, Evid Rule 5-410.

Notaries public, SG §18-105.
Commissioned officers, SG §19-205.

Not criminally responsible.
Release of committed person found not criminally responsible.
Hearing, CP §3-115.

Notice.
Judicial notice.
See JUDICIAL NOTICE.

EVIDENCE —Cont'd
Nursing home administrators.
Nursing home administrator rehabilitation
    committees.
    Admissibility of proceedings, records and files,
      HO §9-317.
Oath or affirmation, Evid Rule 5-603.
Witnesses, Evid Rule 5-603.
Objections.
Competency of judge as witness, Evid Rule 5-605.
Continuing objections.
    Circuit courts, CivProCir Rule 2-517.
Erroneous rulings on evidence.
    Effect, Evid Rule 5-103.
Method of making.
    Circuit courts, CivProCir Rule 2-517.
Witnesses.
    Calling by court, Evid Rule 5-614.
Occupational therapists.
Occupational therapists rehabilitation committees.
    Admissibility of proceedings, records and files,
      HO §10-319.
Offer of proof.
Erroneous rulings on evidence.
    Effect, Evid Rule 5-103.
Offers to compromise, Evid Rule 5-408.
Opinion testimony.
Chastity of victim, prior sexual conduct.
    Rape or sexual offense prosecutions, CR §3-319.
Expert witnesses generally.
    See EXPERT WITNESSES.
Optometrists.
Optometrist rehabilitation committees.
    Admissibility of proceedings, records and files,
      HO §11-405.
Ordinances.
County ordinances, 25 §4; CJ §10-203.
Municipal ordinances, CJ §10-203.
Regulations, etc., of counties, cities and certain
    commissions, CJ §10-203.
Originals.
Definition, Evid Rule 5-1001.
Other evidence of contents.
    Admissibility, Evid Rule 5-1004.
Oysters and clams.
Dredging.
    Prima facie evidence of dredging, NR §4-1012.
Pardon.
Impeachment by evidence of conviction of crime.
    Effect of pardon, Evid Rule 5-609.
Parol evidence.
Sales contracts.
    Parol and extrinsic evidence, CL §2-202.
Surety matters, CJ §10-907.
Party-opponents.
Statements by.
    Hearsay exceptions, Evid Rule 5-803.
Patented lands.
Proof, CJ §10-909.
Paternity proceedings.
Blood tests, FL §5-1029.
    Failure to submit to tests, FL §5-1029.
Pretrial inquiry by state's attorney, FL §5-1019.
Personal history.
Hearsay exceptions.
    Declarant unavailable, Evid Rule 5-804.
    Unavailability of declarant not required, Evid
      Rule 5-803.
Personal injuries.
Settlement agreement or release of claim by
    injured individual.
    Use as evidence, CJ §5-401.1.

EVIDENCE —Cont'd
Personal knowledge.
Witnesses.
    Requirement, Evid Rule 5-602.
Pesticides.
Applicators.
    Injunctions, AG §5-210.4.
Pharmacists and pharmacies.
Disciplinary action against licensees.
    Refusal to submit to examination, HO §12-320.
Photographs.
Admission of party.
    Testimony or written admission, Evid Rule
      5-1007.
Best evidence rule, Evid Rule 5-1002.
Contents of photographs, Evid Rules 5-1001 to
    5-1008.
Definitions, Evid Rule 5-1001.
Duplicates, Evid Rule 5-1003.
    Defined, CJ §10-103.
Electronic toll collection video monitoring systems.
    Admissibility of photographs by, CJ §10-310.
Function of court and jury, Evid Rule 5-1008.
Other evidence of contents, Evid Rule 5-1004.
Photographic copies of business and public records
    as evidence act, CJ §10-102.
Requirement of original, Evid Rule 5-1002.
Summaries, Evid Rule 5-1006.
Toll collection video monitoring systems.
    Admissibility of photographs by, CJ §10-310.
Physical condition.
Hearsay exception, Evid Rule 5-803.
Physicians.
Board.
    Discoverability or admissibility in evidence of
      board documents, HO §14-410.
Plats.
Proof of plats, CJ §10-908.
Pleas, plea discussions and related statements.
Admissibility, Evid Rule 5-410.
Podiatrists.
Podiatrist rehabilitation committees.
    Admissibility of proceedings, records and files,
      HO §16-403.
Post-conviction procedures.
Hearings, Crim Rule 4-406.
Postmortem examiners.
Medical examiners.
    Taking possession and delivery of evidence, HG
      §5-309.
Prejudice.
Impeachment of witness, Evid Rule 5-616.
Relevance.
    Exclusion of relevant evidence on grounds of
      prejudice, Evid Rule 5-403.
Preliminary questions, Evid Rule 5-104.
Prescriptions, counterfeiting.
Affidavit of authorized provider, CR §5-705.
Present sense impression.
Hearsay exceptions, Evid Rule 5-803.
Presumptions.
Other jurisdictions.
    Applicability, Evid Rule 5-302.
Several actions, Evid Rule 5-301.
Prior statements.
Witnesses, Evid Rule 5-613.
    Hearsay exceptions, Evid Rule 5-802.1.
    Impeachment, Evid Rule 5-616.
Prisoner's case record, COR §3-604.
Privileges.
Existence.
    Preliminary questions, Evid Rule 5-104.

EVIDENCE —Cont'd
Privileges —Cont'd
Self-incrimination.
General provisions.
See WITNESSES.
Process used to produce exhibit or testimony.
Authentication or identification, Evid Rule 5-901.
Production of documents and things.
When court may require production of evidence.
Circuit courts, CivProCir Rule 2-514.
District Court, CivProDist Rule 3-514.
Professional counselors and therapists.
Professional counselor rehabilitation committees.
Admissibility of proceedings, records and files, HO §17-317.
Property interest.
Records or documents affecting.
Hearsay exceptions, Evid Rule 5-803.
Psychologists.
Expert testimony, CJ §9-120.
Psychologist rehabilitation committees.
Admissibility of proceedings, records and files, HO §18-318.
Public local laws of Maryland/compilation of municipal charters, CJ §10-201.1.
Public records. See within this heading, "Records and documents."
Public service commission proceedings.
Commission not bound by rules of evidence or procedure of any court, PUC §3-101.
Judicial review of decisions or orders.
New evidence, limitation on introduction on further evidence, PUC §3-208.
Official record, adding evidence to, copy of record, PUC §3-111.
Public service company accident reports, PUC §5-304.
Published compilations.
Hearsay exceptions, Evid Rule 5-803.
Purpose of rules, Evid Rule 5-102.
Questioning of witnesses.
By court, Evid Rule 5-614.
Mode and order, Evid Rule 5-611.
Prior statements, Evid Rule 5-613.
Radar.
Speed of motor vehicles.
Proof of speed by devices employing radio-micro waves, CJ §10-301.
Rape.
Reputation and opinion evidence as to victim's chastity, CR §3-319; Evid Rule 5-412.
Specific instances of victim's prior sexual conduct, CR §3-319; Evid Rule 5-412.
Rape shield law, CR §3-319; Evid Rule 5-412.
Reckless endangerment.
Serious physical injury.
Expert testimony admissible, not required, CR §3-208.
Recorded recollection.
Hearsay exceptions, Evid Rule 5-803.
Recorded statements.
Remainder of or related recorded statements, Evid Rule 5-106.
Records and documents.
Admission of party.
Testimony or written admission, Evid Rule 5-1007.
Ancient documents.
Hearsay exceptions, Evid Rule 5-803.
Authentication, Evid Rule 5-901.

EVIDENCE —Cont'd
Records and documents —Cont'd
Baptismal certificates.
Hearsay exceptions, Evid Rule 5-803.
Best evidence rule, Evid Rule 5-1002.
Business activity.
Hearsay exceptions, Evid Rule 5-803.
Confidential records.
Inadmissible, CJ §10-205.
Copies as evidence, CJ §10-204.
Definitions.
Recordings, Evid Rule 5-1001.
Dental records and writings.
Admissibility, CJ §10-104.
Duplicates, Evid Rule 5-1003.
Family records.
Hearsay exceptions, Evid Rule 5-803.
Function of court and jury, Evid Rule 5-1008.
Hospital records and writings.
Admissibility, CJ §10-104.
Interest in property.
Documents affecting.
Hearsay exceptions, Evid Rule 5-803.
Marriage certificates.
Hearsay exceptions, Evid Rule 5-803.
Medical records and writings.
Admissibility, CJ §10-104.
Other evidence of contents, Evid Rule 5-1004.
Photographic copies of business and public records as evidence act, CJ §10-102.
Proof of accounts and records, CJ §10-101.
Public records and reports.
Admissibility generally, CJ §10-204.
Exceptions, CJ §10-205.
Authentication or identification, Evid Rule 5-901.
Certified copies, Evid Rule 5-1005.
Hearsay exceptions, Evid Rule 5-803.
Recordings.
Contents, Evid Rules 5-1001 to 5-1008.
Definition, Evid Rule 5-1001.
Religious organizations.
Hearsay exceptions, Evid Rule 5-803.
Replacement of worn and dilapidated records, CJ §10-206.
Requirement of original, Evid Rule 5-1002.
Self authentication, Evid Rule 5-902.
Summaries, Evid Rule 5-1006.
Vital statistics.
Hearsay exceptions, Evid Rule 5-803.
Written records.
Proof of accounts and records, CJ §10-101.
Refreshing memory.
Writing or other item used to refresh memory, Evid Rule 5-612.
Regulations.
Code of Maryland regulations, CJ §10-203.
County and municipal regulations, CJ §10-203.
Rehabilitation.
Impeachment, Evid Rule 5-616.
Relevance.
Accused.
Character, Evid Rule 5-404.
Admissibility.
Relevant evidence generally admissible, Evid Rule 5-402.
Character evidence, Evid Rule 5-404.
Methods of proving character, Evid Rule 5-405.
Compromise and offers to compromise, Evid Rule 5-408.
Definition of relevant evidence, Evid Rule 5-401.

EVIDENCE —Cont'd
Relevance —Cont'd
Exclusion of relevant evidence.
   Prejudice, confusion, etc., Evid Rule 5-403.
Habit, Evid Rule 5-406.
Hospital expenses.
   Payment, Evid Rule 5-409.
Insurance.
   Liability insurance, Evid Rule 5-411.
Liability insurance, Evid Rule 5-411.
Medical expenses.
   Payment, Evid Rule 5-409.
Opinion as to character, Evid Rule 5-405.
Other crimes, wrongs or acts.
   Admissibility to prove character, Evid Rule
      5-404.
Pleas, plea discussions and related statements,
   Evid Rule 5-410.
Preliminary questions.
   Conditioned on fact, Evid Rule 5-104.
Rape shield law, Evid Rule 5-412.
Reputation of character, Evid Rule 5-405.
Routine practice, Evid Rule 5-406.
Settlements, Evid Rule 5-408.
Sex offense cases.
   Victim's past behavior, Evid Rule 5-412.
Specific instances of conduct.
   Admissibility to prove character, Evid Rule
      5-405.
Subsequent remedial measures, Evid Rule 5-407.
Victims.
   Character, Evid Rule 5-404.
   Sex offense cases.
      Past behavior, Evid Rule 5-412.
Witnesses.
   Character, Evid Rule 5-404.
Religion.
Corporations.
   Plan of operation.
      Presumption of record of plan, CA §5-312.
Religious beliefs or opinions.
Witnesses, Evid Rule 5-610.
Religious organizations.
Records.
   Hearsay exceptions, Evid Rule 5-803.
Remedial measures.
Subsequent remedial measures, Evid Rule 5-407.
Reports.
Market reports.
   Hearsay exceptions, Evid Rule 5-803.
Public records and reports.
   Certified copies, Evid Rule 5-1005.
   Hearsay exceptions, Evid Rule 5-803.
Reputation.
Boundaries.
   Hearsay exceptions, Evid Rule 5-803.
Character.
   Hearsay exceptions, Evid Rule 5-803.
   Methods of proving character, Evid Rule 5-405.
   Witnesses, Evid Rule 5-608.
Chastity of victim, prior sexual conduct.
   Rape or sexual offense prosecutions, CR §3-319;
      Evid Rule 5-412.
Family history.
   Hearsay exceptions, Evid Rule 5-803.
History.
   Hearsay exceptions, Evid Rule 5-803.
Personal history.
   Hearsay exceptions, Evid Rule 5-803.
Witnesses.
   Character, Evid Rule 5-608.

EVIDENCE —Cont'd
Returnable containers and textiles.
Registration, BR §19-303.
Robbery.
Proof of intent to withhold property of another,
   CR §3-401.
Routine practice, Evid Rule 5-406.
Rulings on evidence, Evid Rule 5-103.
Sales.
Parol and extrinsic evidence, CL §2-202.
Sales below cost act, CL §11-404.
Scope of rules, Evid Rule 5-101.
Securities.
Securities act.
   Investigations.
      Taking of evidence, CA §11-701.
Self authentication, Evid Rule 5-902.
Certifies, certificate or certification.
   Defined, Evid Rule 5-902.
Self-incrimination.
General provisions.
   See WITNESSES.
Serious physical injury.
Assault or reckless endangerment.
   Expert testimony admissible, not required, CR
      §3-208.
Settlements.
Compromises or offers to settle, Evid Rule 5-408.
Sexual offense.
Reputation or opinion as to victim's chastity, CR
   §3-319; Evid Rule 5-412.
Specific instances of victim's prior sexual conduct,
   CR §3-319; Evid Rule 5-412.
Shoplifting.
Civil penalties.
   Payment.
      Evidence not admissible in criminal
         prosecution, CJ §3-1306.
Simultaneous death act.
General provisions, CJ §§10-801 to 10-807.
   See DEATH.
Social workers.
Social worker rehabilitation committees.
   Admissibility of proceedings, records and files,
      HO §19-315.
Sound level meters, CJ §10-911.
Speed monitoring system.
Recorded images produced by, CJ §10-311.
Statement against interest.
Hearsay exceptions, Evid Rule 5-804.
Statement by party-opponent.
Hearsay exceptions, Evid Rule 5-803.
Statement under belief of impending death.
Hearsay exceptions, Evid Rule 5-804.
State of mind.
Hearsay exceptions, Evid Rule 5-803.
State retirement and pension system.
Board of trustees.
   Applicability of rules of evidence, SPP §21-111.
Statutes, CJ §10-203.
Bond statutes.
   Uniform judicial notice of foreign law act.
      General provisions, CJ §§10-501 to 10-507.
Code of 1957.
   General provisions, CJ §10-201.
Foreign statutes.
   Judicial notice of foreign law.
      General provisions, CJ §§10-501 to 10-507.
      See JUDICIAL NOTICE.
Public general laws.
   General provisions, CJ §10-201.

EVIDENCE —Cont'd
Statutes —Cont'd
References to the public general laws, 1 §2A.
Replacement volumes, CJ §10-201.
Uniform proof of statutes act, CJ §10-202.
Subpoenas.
Perpetuation of evidence.
Before action instituted.
Circuit courts, CivProCir Rule 2-404; Crim
Rule 4-264.
Subsequent remedial measures, Evid Rule 5-407.
Summaries.
Writings, etc., Evid Rule 5-1006.
Support and maintenance.
Criminal nonsupport and desertion.
Baltimore City.
State's attorney, powers, FL §10-213.
Parents and adult children.
Pretrial inquiry.
Powers of state's attorney, FL §13-104.
Uniform reciprocal enforcement of support act.
Husband and wife.
Privilege not to apply, FL §10-320.
Rules of evidence, FL §10-321.
Suretyship.
Parol evidence.
Admissible, CJ §10-907.
Surveys and surveyors.
Plats.
Proof, CJ §10-908.
System used to produce exhibit or testimony.
Authentication or identification, Evid Rule 5-901.
Taxation.
Actions for collection.
Certificate of authority charged with collection.
Prima facie evidence, TP §14-869.
Alcoholic beverage tax.
Payment of tax, TG §5-301.
Certificate of sale, TP §14-823.
Corporations.
Conclusive evidence of payment of taxes, CA
§1-206.
Revival of charter.
Acceptance of articles of revival as evidence of
payment of taxes, CA §3-510.
Income tax credits.
Evidence of entitlement required, TG §10-705.
Licenses.
Evidence of tax payment, TG §2-105.
Property transfer tax.
Payment of tax, TP §13-208.
Tax court.
Appeals to tax court.
See TAX COURT.
Telephone conversations.
Authentication or identification, Evid Rule 5-901.
Telephones and telegraph.
Wiretapping.
See WIRETAPPING.
Testimony.
Accused.
Preliminary questions, Evid Rule 5-104.
Admission of party.
Contents of writings, recordings or photographs,
Evid Rule 5-1007.
Opinion testimony.
See EXPERT WITNESSES.
Theft.
Proof of theft generally, CR §7-109.
Tolls.
Electronic toll collection video monitoring systems.
Admissibility of recorded images by, CJ
§10-310.

EVIDENCE —Cont'd
Traffic control signal monitoring system.
Recorded images produced by, CJ §10-311.
Treatises.
Hearsay exceptions, Evid Rule 5-803.
Trial.
Exhibits.
Circuit courts, CivProCir Rule 2-516.
District Court, CivProDist Rule 3-516.
Objections to evidence.
Continuing objections to evidence.
Circuit courts, CivProCir Rule 2-517.
Criminal rules, Crim Rule 4-323.
District Court, CivProDist Rule 3-517.
Method of making.
Circuit courts, CivProCir Rule 2-517.
Criminal rules, Crim Rule 4-323.
District Court, CivProDist Rule 3-517.
Production of evidence.
District Court, CivProDist Rule 3-514.
When court may require.
Circuit courts, CivProCir Rule 2-514.
Ultimate issue.
Opinion testimony, Evid Rule 5-704.
Unemployment compensation.
Aliens.
Eligibility for benefits.
Standard of proof, LE §8-905.
Uniform laws.
Foreign laws.
Judicial notice.
General provisions, CJ §§10-501 to 10-507.
See JUDICIAL NOTICE.
Foreign money judgments.
General provisions.
See FOREIGN MONEY JUDGMENTS.
Photographic copies of business and public records
as evidence act, CJ §10-102.
Proof of statutes act, CJ §10-202.
Simultaneous death act.
General provisions, CJ §§10-801 to 10-807.
See DEATH.
Verdict.
Definition.
Competency of juror as witness, Evid Rule
5-606.
Vessels and boats.
Intoxication.
Operating vessel while intoxicated or while
under the influence of alcohol or drugs, NR
§8-738.
Veterans.
General provisions.
See VETERANS.
Victims of crime.
Character of victim.
Admissibility to prove conduct, Evid Rule 5-404.
Child victims.
Admissibility of out-of-court statements, CP
§11-304.
HIV testing.
Admissibility of test results, CP §11-114.
Charged person, CP §11-111.
Restitution hearing.
Proof of injuries and damages, CP §11-615.
Sex offense cases.
Past behavior, Evid Rule 5-412.
Videotape.
Electronic toll collection video monitoring systems.
Admissibility of videotapes by, CJ §10-310.

EVIDENCE —Cont'd

Visitation.

Child abuse and neglect.

Evidence of abuse against certain individuals, FL §9-101.1.

Vital records.

Hearsay exceptions, Evid Rule 5-803.

Use of birth, death or fetal death certificates as evidence, HG §4-223.

Voice identification.

Authentication or identification, Evid Rule 5-901.

Wages.

Assignment of wages or salaries.

Proof of service on employer, CL §15-303.

Waste of time.

Relevance.

Exclusion of relevant evidence on grounds of wasting time, Evid Rule 5-403.

Water pollution.

Prima facie evidence.

Finding of department deemed prima facie evidence in injunction proceedings, EN §4-416.

Weight of the evidence.

Preliminary questions, Evid Rule 5-104.

Weights and measures.

Official certificate as prima facie evidence, CL §1-202.

Wiretapping.

Admissibility of evidence, CJ §10-405.

Withdrawn pleas and offers, Evid Rule 5-410.

Witnesses.

Affirmation, Evid Rule 5-603.

Authentication.

Knowledge, Evid Rule 5-901.

Subscribing witness.

Necessity, Evid Rule 5-903.

Bias.

Impeachment, Evid Rule 5-616.

Calling of.

By court, Evid Rule 5-614.

Capacity.

Impeachment, Evid Rule 5-616.

Character evidence, Evid Rule 5-404.

Impeachment, Evid Rule 5-616.

Truthfulness, Evid Rule 5-608.

Competency, Evid Rule 5-601.

Conduct.

Specific instances of conduct, Evid Rule 5-608.

Conviction of crime.

Impeachment by evidence of, Evid Rule 5-609.

Cross-examination.

Character witnesses.

Impeachment, Evid Rule 5-608.

Experts, Evid Rule 5-703.

Scope, Evid Rule 5-611.

Exclusion, Evid Rule 5-615.

General provisions.

See WITNESSES.

Impeachment, Evid Rule 5-616.

Bias, Evid Rule 5-616.

Character, Evid Rules 5-608, 5-616.

Conduct, Evid Rules 5-608, 5-616.

Conviction of crime, Evid Rule 5-609.

Extrinsic evidence, Evid Rule 5-616.

Prejudice, Evid Rule 5-616.

Prior statements, Evid Rules 5-613, 5-616.

Rehabilitation, Evid Rules 5-608, 5-616.

Who may impeach, Evid Rule 5-607.

Inconsistent statements.

Extrinsic evidence of, Evid Rule 5-613.

EVIDENCE —Cont'd

Witnesses —Cont'd

Interrogation.

By court, Evid Rule 5-614.

Mode and order, Evid Rule 5-611.

Prior statements, Evid Rule 5-613.

Judge as witness.

Competency, Evid Rule 5-605.

Juror as witness.

Competency, Evid Rule 5-606.

Objections.

Calling and interrogation of witnesses by court, Evid Rule 5-614.

Personal knowledge.

Impeachment, Evid Rule 5-616.

Requirement, Evid Rule 5-602.

Prejudice.

Impeachment, Evid Rule 5-616.

Presentation.

Hearsay exceptions, Evid Rule 5-802.1.

Mode and order, Evid Rule 5-611.

Prior statements, Evid Rule 5-613.

Qualifications.

Preliminary questions, Evid Rule 5-104.

Questioning.

By court, Evid Rule 5-614.

Mode and order, Evid Rule 5-611.

Prior statements, Evid Rule 5-613.

Refreshing memory.

Writing or other item used to refresh memory, Evid Rule 5-612.

Religious beliefs or opinions, Evid Rule 5-610.

Reputation.

Character for truthfulness, Evid Rule 5-608.

Workers' compensation.

Burden of proof.

Conduct of appeal proceedings, LE §9-745.

Claims processing.

Transcript of investigation.

Acceptance as evidence, LE §9-718.

Illegally employed minor.

Conclusive evidence of legality, LE §9-606.

Investigations.

Conduct of investigations.

Rules of evidence inapplicable, LE §9-715.

Writings.

Admission of party.

Testimony or written admission, Evid Rule 5-1007.

Authentication, Evid Rule 5-901.

Best evidence rule, Evid Rule 5-1002.

Contents, Evid Rules 5-1001 to 5-1008.

Definition, Evid Rule 5-1001.

Duplicates, Evid Rule 5-1003.

Defined, CJ §10-103.

Functions of court and jury, Evid Rule 5-1008.

Other evidence of contents, Evid Rule 5-1004.

Proof of execution, CJ §10-906.

Refreshing memory, Evid Rule 5-612.

Remainder of or related writings, Evid Rule 5-106.

Requirement of original, Evid Rule 5-1002.

Self authentication, Evid Rule 5-902.

Summaries, Evid Rule 5-1006.

EXAMINATIONS.

Accountant licenses, BOP §§2-302, 2-305 to 2-308.

See ACCOUNTANTS.

Acupuncturists.

Submission to examination while under investigation, HO §1A-315.

EXAMINATIONS —Cont'd

Architects.
Licenses, BOP §§3-305 to 3-306.

Audiologists, hearing aid dealers and speech-language pathologists.
See AUDIOLOGISTS AND SPEECH-LANGUAGE PATHOLOGISTS.

Banks and trust companies.
See BANKS AND TRUST COMPANIES.

Bar admissions.
See ATTORNEYS AT LAW.

Barbers.
Licenses.
See BARBERS.

Birds and game.
Taxidermists and fur tanning license required, NR §10-512.

Chiropractors.
See CHIROPRACTORS.

Circuit courts.
Order to complete examination, CivProCir Rule 2-542.

Commissioner of financial regulation.
Expense reimbursements, FI §11-101.

Credit unions.
See CREDIT UNIONS.

Dentists.
See DENTISTS.

Depositions.
Circuit courts, CivProCir Rule 2-415.
Written questions, CivProCir Rule 2-417.

Dietitians.
See DIETITIANS.

Discovery.
Mental or physical examination of persons.
Circuit courts, CivProCir Rule 2-423.

Drivers' licenses.
See DRIVERS' LICENSES.

Electricians.
Licenses.
State licenses, BOP §§6-306 to 6-308.

Electrologists, licenses.
Conduct, HO §8-6B-10.
Required, HO §8-6B-08.
Waiver, HO §8-6B-11.

Engineers.
Licenses.
See ENGINEERS.

Fraternal benefit societies, IN §§8-461 to 8-463.

Health maintenance organizations.
Health care services, HG §19-719.

Insurance.
See INSURANCE.

Interior designers.
Certificates, BOP §8-302.
Waiver of requirement, BOP §8-304.

Judgments.
Discovery in aid of enforcement.
Circuit courts, CivProCir Rule 2-633.
District Court, CivProDist Rule 3-633.

Jury trial.
Jurors.
Circuit courts, CivProCir Rule 2-512.
Criminal rules, Crim Rule 4-312.

Juvenile causes.
Order for physical and mental examination of respondent.
Forms, Form 905-OE.
Physical and mental examination, Juv Rule 11-105.

EXAMINATIONS —Cont'd

Laboratories.
Reports required, HG §18-205.
Penalty for violations of provisions, HG §18-215.

Landscape architects.
Licenses, BOP §§9-302, 9-305, 9-305.1.

Life and health insurance guaranty corporation, IN §9-415.
Examination of member insurer, IN §9-412.

Mental and physical examinations of persons.
Discovery provisions.
Circuit courts, CivProCir Rule 2-423.
Juvenile causes, Juv Rule 11-105.

Mental hygiene law.
Cost of court ordered examinations, HG §16-302.

Mental retardation.
Cost of court-ordered examinations, HG §16-406.

Militia.
Officers, PS §13-603.

Milk and milk products.
Authority of secretary to examine individuals with disease, HG §21-435.

Money transmission, FI §12-424.

Morticians.
See MORTICIANS.

Motor vehicles.
Drivers' licenses.
See DRIVERS' LICENSES.

Nurses.
See NURSES.

Nursing home administrators.
See NURSING HOME ADMINISTRATORS.

Occupational therapists.
See OCCUPATIONAL THERAPISTS.

Optometrists.
See OPTOMETRISTS.

Pharmacists and pharmacies.
See PHARMACISTS AND PHARMACIES.

Physical therapists.
See PHYSICAL THERAPISTS.

Physicians.
See PHYSICIANS.

Plumbers.
Licenses, BOP §§12-302, 12-304.

Podiatrists.
See PODIATRISTS.

Property and casualty insurance guaranty corporation, IN §9-311.

Psychologists.
See PSYCHOLOGISTS.

Real estate appraisers.
See REAL ESTATE APPRAISERS AND HOME INSPECTORS.

Real estate brokers.
Licenses, BOP §§17-305, 17-306.

Records.
Access to public records.
Permissible denials, SG §10-618.

Residential child care program administrators.
Certification.
Applicants, HO §20-305.
Waiver of examination, HO §20-306.

Savings and loan associations.
See SAVINGS AND LOAN ASSOCIATIONS.

Schools.
Physical examinations for children entering public school system, ED §7-402.

Social workers.
See SOCIAL WORKERS.

Surveys and surveyors.
Licenses.
See SURVEYS AND SURVEYORS.

EXAMINATIONS —Cont'd
Tanneries.
Licenses, NR §10-512.
Taxidermists.
Licenses, NR §10-512.
Tree experts, NR §5-420.
Veterinarians.
See VETERINARIANS.
Waterworks and waste systems operators.
See WATERWORKS AND WASTE SYSTEMS OPERATORS.
Well drillers.
See WELL DRILLERS.

EXAMINERS.
Administration of courts.
Adoption of code of conduct, CJA Rule 16-814.
Appointment.
Employees authorized, CJ §2-501.
Special examiners.
Circuit courts, CivProCir Rule 2-542.
Special officers, CJ §2-102.
Standing examiners.
Circuit courts, CivProCir Rule 2-542.
Circuit courts, CivProCir Rule 2-542.
Code of conduct for masters, examiners, auditors, referees and District Court commissioners.
Adoption, CJA Rule 16-814.
Judgments.
Discovery in aid of enforcement.
Examination before judge or examiner.
Circuit courts, CivCircuit Rule 2-633.
District Court, CivProDist Rule 3-633.

EXCAVATIONS.
Mining.
General provisions, EN §§15-101 to 15-1109.
See MINING.
Near underground utility facilities.
Generally, PUC §§12-101 to 12-113.
See UNDERGROUND UTILITY FACILITIES.
Montgomery county, PUC §§12-201 to 12-203.
Occupational safety and health.
Deputies for inspection of excavation work.
Generally, LE §5-203.
Sanitary commissions, EN §9-637.

EXCISE TAXES.
Vessels and boats.
Levied on issuance certificate of title or sale, NR §8-716.

EXECUTION OF INMATE SENTENCED TO DEATH.
Procedures generally, COR §§3-901 to 3-909.
See DEATH PENALTY.

EXECUTIONS.
Appeals from District Court.
Stay of execution, AppRevCir Rule 7-111.
Appraisals.
Sheriffs.
Appraisal of property at time of levy, CJ §11-504.
Attorneys at law.
Lien of attorney, BOP §10-501.
Auctioneer.
Employment for sale, CJ §11-503.
Bankruptcy and insolvency.
Exemptions.
Federal bankruptcy exemptions, CJ §11-504.
Bills of lading.
Lien on goods covered by a negotiable document, CL §7-602.

EXECUTIONS —Cont'd
Bonds, surety.
Release of property from levy.
Posting of bond.
Circuit courts, CivProCir Rule 2-643.
District Court, CivProDist Rule 3-643.
Sheriff's bond.
Circuit courts, CivProCir Rule 2-641.
District Court, CivProDist Rule 3-641.
Bulk transfers.
Limitation of levies, CL §6-111.
Sales excepted from article, CL §6-103.
Business trusts.
Subject to attachment and execution, CA §12-501.
College savings plan of Maryland.
Seizure by attachment, execution, garnishment, etc, ED §18-1913.
Constables.
General provisions.
See CONSTABLES.
Sales.
Seizure and sale of property, CJ §11-501.
Content of writ.
Circuit courts, CivProCir Rule 2-641.
District Court, CivProDist Rule 3-641.
Continuing care contracts.
Prohibited during delinquency proceedings against providers, 70B §§20N, 20O.
Costs.
By state's attorney, 10 §36.
Sales.
Publication of notice of sale, CJ §11-502.
Deeds.
See DEEDS.
Distress for rent.
Stay, RP §8-332.
District Court.
Blank executions.
Issuance prohibited, CJ §11-702.
Ejectment.
Warrant of resurvey, PropAct Rule 12-101.
Election of rights and remedies.
Release of property from levy.
Election of exemption by judgment debtor.
Circuit courts, CivProCir Rule 2-643.
District Court, CivProDist Rule 3-643.
Executors and administrators.
Prohibited against property of estate, ET §8-114.
Exemptions.
Assignment of claims to nonresidents.
Depriving debtor of rights under exemption laws.
General provisions, CL §§15-501 to 15-503.
Bankruptcy.
Federal bankruptcy exemptions, CJ §11-504.
Books.
Exemption from execution, CJ §11-504.
General provisions, CJ §11-504.
Homestead exemptions, CivProCir Rule 2-643; CivProDist Rule 3-643; CJ §11-504.
Distress for rent, RP §§8-306, 8-307.
Medicaid.
Spousal homestead protection, HG §15-122.
Insurance benefits, etc., CJ §11-504.
Levy.
Release of property from levy.
Election of exemption by judgment debtor.
Circuit courts, CivProCir Rule 2-643.
District Court, CivProDist Rule 3-643.
Mechanics' liens.
Exemptions not to impair lien, CJ §11-507.

EXECUTIONS —Cont'd
Exemptions —Cont'd
One thousand dollar exemption.
Generally, CJ §11-504.
Lien.
Exemptions not to impair lien, CJ §11-507.
Waiver of exemption, CJ §11-506.
Protecting property from execution.
Laws to be passed, MD Const Art III §44.
Tools.
Exemption from execution, CJ §11-504.
Vendor's lien.
Exemptions not to impair lien, CJ §11-507.
Wage attachments.
Exemptions not applicable, CJ §11-504.
Waiver, CJ §11-506.
Wearing apparel.
Exemption from execution, CJ §11-504.
Fees.
General provisions.
See FEES.
Sheriffs, CJ §7-402.
Forfeitures.
Recognizance to appear or testify, CJ §11-513.
Fraternal benefit societies.
Benefits exempt from execution, IN §8-431.
Fraud by execution debtor.
Removal of personal property.
Intent to defraud, CR §8-403.
Garnishment.
Amount of levy, CJ §11-602.
Banks and trust companies.
Joint accounts, CJ §11-603.
Property held in trust, CJ §11-603.
Husband and wife.
Spousal property, CJ §11-603.
Plea in bar, CJ §11-601.
Spousal property, CJ §11-603.
Hearings.
Release of property from levy.
Circuit courts, CivProCir Rule 2-643.
District Court, CivProDist Rule 3-643.
Homestead exemptions, CivProCir Rule 2-643;
CivProDist Rule 3-643; CJ §11-504.
Distress for rent, RP §§8-306, 8-307.
Medicaid.
Spousal homestead protection, HG §15-122.
Housing authorities.
Exemptions, HS §12-104.
Injunction.
Sale of personal property under execution, CJ
§11-512.
Insurance.
Life insurance and annuities.
Proceeds exempt from creditors, IN §16-111.
Surety insurance.
Insurers authority to execute bonds, IN
§21-101.
Issuance of writ.
Generally.
Circuit courts, CivProCir Rule 2-641.
District Court, CivProDist Rule 3-641.
Judgments.
Levy, CivProCir Rule 2-642.
District Court, CivProDist Rule 3-642.
Release of property from levy, CivProCir Rule
2-643.
Writ of execution.
Circuit courts, CivProCir Rules 2-641, 2-642.
District Court, CivProDist Rules 3-641, 3-642.

EXECUTIONS —Cont'd
**Laws to be passed protecting property from
execution,** MD Const Art III §44.
Levy.
Circuit courts, CivProCir Rules 2-642 to 2-644.
District Court, CivProDist Rules 3-642 to 3-644.
Liens.
Exemptions not to impair certain lien, CJ §11-507.
Life insurance and annuities.
Proceeds exempt from creditors, IN §16-111.
Mechanics' liens.
Exemptions not to impair, CJ §11-507.
Sale under execution of land against which lien
established, RP §9-108.
Motions.
Release of property from levy.
Judgment debtor's motion.
Circuit courts, CivProCir Rule 2-643.
District Court, CivProDist Rule 3-643.
Nonresidents.
Assignment of claims.
Depriving debtor of rights under exemption
laws.
General provisions, CL §§15-501 to 15-503.
Notice of levy.
Circuit courts, CivProCir Rule 2-642.
District Court, CivProDist Rule 3-642.
Sale of property under levy.
Circuit courts, CivProCir Rule 2-644.
District Court, CivProDist Rule 3-644.
Partnerships, revised act.
Actions by and against partnership and partners,
CA §9A-307.
Charging partners transferable interest to satisfy
judgment, CA §9A-504.
Personal property.
Levy.
Circuit courts, CivProCir Rule 2-642.
District Court, CivProDist Rule 3-642.
Sale of property under levy.
Circuit courts, CivProCir Rule 2-644.
District Court, CivProDist Rule 3-644.
Third person in possession.
Circuit courts, CivProCir Rule 2-642.
District Court, CivProDist Rule 3-642.
Pleadings.
Demand for proof.
District Court, CivProDist Rule 3-308.
Posting.
Release of property from levy.
Bond posted.
Circuit courts, CivProCir Rule 2-643.
District Court, CivProDist Rule 3-643.
Ratification of sheriff's sale, CJ §11-505.
Real property.
Levy.
Circuit courts, CivProCir Rule 2-642.
District Court, CivProDist Rule 3-642.
Sale of property under levy.
Circuit courts, CivProCir Rule 2-644.
District Court, CivProDist Rule 3-644.
Recognizance.
Forfeiture of recognizance to appear or testify, CJ
§11-513.
Recordation.
Sales.
Protection of purchaser against unrecorded
interest, RP §14-103.
**Removal of personal property by execution
debtor.**
Intent to defraud, CR §8-403.

EXECUTIONS —Cont'd
Reports.
Sale of property under levy.
Circuit courts, CivProCir Rule 2-644.
District Court, CivProDist Rule 3-644.
Returns.
Levy.
Circuit courts, CivProCir Rule 2-642.
District Court, CivProDist Rule 3-642.
Sales.
Auctioneer.
Employment, CJ §11-503.
Constables.
Seizure and sale of property, CJ §11-501.
Conveyance to purchaser, CJ §11-509.
Division.
Sale of property which cannot be divided, CJ
§11-508.
Injunction.
Sale of personal property under execution, CJ
§11-512.
Notice by publication.
Costs.
Defendant liable for cost, CJ §11-502.
Sheriff to give notice, CJ §11-502.
Time of publication, CJ §11-502.
Personal property.
Injunction against sale, CJ §11-512.
Proceeds.
Dispute as to proceeds, CJ §11-511.
Property.
Sale of property which cannot be divided, CJ
§11-508.
Sheriff.
Seizure and sale, CJ §11-501.
Ratification of sheriff's sale, CJ §11-505.
Real property.
Purchaser.
Protection against unrecorded interest, RP
§14-103.
Recordation.
Protection of purchaser against unrecorded
interest, RP §14-103.
Sheriff.
Appraisals, CJ §11-504.
Bringing money into court.
Court may order, CJ §11-510.
Conveyance to purchaser, CJ §11-509.
Fees, CJ §7-402.
Notice.
Sheriff to give notice, CJ §11-502.
Seizure and sale of property, CJ §11-501.
Satisfaction of judgment.
Release of property from levy.
Circuit courts, CivProCir Rule 2-643.
District Court, CivProDist Rule 3-643.
Sheriffs.
Appraisals, CJ §11-504.
Bonds, surety.
Circuit courts, CivProCir Rule 2-641.
District Court, CivProDist Rule 3-641.
Bringing money into court.
Court may order, CJ §11-510.
Conveyance to purchaser, CJ §11-509.
Directed to sheriff, CJ §2-302.
Fees, CJ §7-402.
Levy.
Sale of property under levy.
Circuit courts, CivProCir Rule 2-644.
District Court, CivProDist Rule 3-644.

EXECUTIONS —Cont'd
Sheriffs —Cont'd
Notice of sale.
Sheriff to give notice, CJ §11-502.
Return.
Failure to return, CJ §2-304.
Seizure and sale of property, CJ §11-501.
Transmittal of writ to sheriff.
Circuit courts, CivProCir Rule 2-641.
District Court, CivProDist Rule 3-641.
State's attorneys.
Fines and penalties.
Application for, 10 §36.
Third parties.
Levy.
Possession of personal property by third person.
Circuit courts, CivProCir Rule 2-642.
District Court, CivProDist Rule 3-642.
Release of property from levy.
Claim of third person.
Circuit courts, CivProCir Rule 2-643.
District Court, CivProDist Rule 3-643.
Trade names.
Actions by creditors of persons using a trade
name.
Execution on judgment, CJ §6-406.1.
Universities and colleges.
College savings plan of Maryland.
Seizure by attachment, execution, garnishment,
etc., ED §18-1913.
Warehouse receipts.
Lien on goods covered by a negotiable document,
CL §7-602.
Witnesses.
Failure of witness to appear.
Discharge from execution, CJ §9-204.
Workers' compensation.
Payment of award.
Prohibition against execution, LE §9-732.

EXECUTION WARRANT.
Death sentence, COR §3-902.

EXECUTIVE COUNCIL OF GOVERNOR, SG
§§8-101 to 8-105.
See GOVERNOR.

EXECUTIVE DEPARTMENT.
Governor.
General provisions.
See GOVERNOR.
Governor's executive council, SG §§8-101 to
8-105.
See GOVERNOR.
Governor's office on service and volunteerism.
Creation, SG §9-1302.
Definitions, SG §9-1301.
Director, SG §9-1303.
Duties.
Generally, SG §9-1304.
Executive fellows program, SG §9-1306.
Maryland service corps, SG §9-1305.
**Maryland state employees surety bond
committee,** SG §§9-1701 to 9-1707.
Approval and filing, SG §9-1707.
Authority to set type and amounts of bonds, SG
§9-1704.
Cancellation or termination, SG §9-1706.
Commencement of coverage, SG §9-1704.
Committee, defined, SG §9-1701.
Discretionary bonding, SG §9-1705.
Established, SG §9-1702.

EXECUTIVE DEPARTMENT —Cont'd
Maryland state employees surety bond committee —Cont'd
Membership, SG §9-1703.
Purchase of bonds, SG §9-1706.
Records, SG §9-1707.
Office of administrative hearings, SG §§9-1601 to 9-1610.
Administrative law judges.
Generally, SG §9-1605.
Selection, SG §§9-1606, 9-1607.
Advisory council.
Appointment of members, SG §9-1608.
Chairman, SG §9-1609.
Chief administrative law judge.
Meetings and conferences with, SG §9-1604.
Compensation of members, SG §9-1609.
Composition, SG §9-1608.
Establishment, SG §9-1608.
Expenses.
Reimbursement, SG §9-1609.
Meetings, SG §9-1610.
Powers and duties, SG §9-1610.
Terms of members, SG §9-1609.
Applicability of procedural regulations, SG §9-1607.2.
Applicability of provisions, SG §9-1601.
Audits, SG §9-1606.
Chief administrative law judge.
Generally, SG §§9-1603, 9-1604.
Cooperation of state government units, SG §9-1606.
Establishment, SG §9-1602.
Exceptions, SG §9-1601.
Procedural regulations.
Applicability, SG §9-1607.2.
Reports.
Chief administrative law judge's reports, SG §9-1604.
Representation before office by person not licensed to practice law, SG §9-1607.1.
Temporary exemptions, SG §9-1601.
Office of smart growth, SG §§9-1401 to 9-1406.
Definitions, SG §9-1401.
Duties, SG §9-1405.
Established, SG §9-1403.
Findings of legislature, SG §9-1402.
Legislative declaration, SG §9-1402.
Powers, SG §9-1405.
Smart growth subcabinet, SG §9-1406.
Special secretary of smart growth, SG §9-1404.
Penalties.
Civil penalties.
Considerations in setting amount, SG §10-1001.
Surety bond committee.
Maryland state employees surety bond committee, SG §§9-1701 to 9-1707.

EXECUTIVE FELLOWS PROGRAM, SG §9-1306.

EXECUTIVE ORDERS.
Governor.
General provisions, SG §§3-401 to 3-406.
See GOVERNOR.

EXECUTORS AND ADMINISTRATORS.
Absence as evidence of death and absentee property act.
See ABSENT PERSONS.
Accounts and accounting.
Auditors.
See AUDITORS.

EXECUTORS AND ADMINISTRATORS —Cont'd
Accounts and accounting —Cont'd
Duty to account, Estates Rule 6-417; ET §7-301.
Exceptions to accounts, ET §7-501.
Failure to render accounts.
Effect, ET §7-306.
Filing.
Exceptions to accounts, ET §7-501.
Notice to interested persons, Estates Rule 6-417; ET §7-301.
Final account.
Effect of approval of final account, Estates Rule 6-417; ET §10-101.
Inheritance tax.
Payment, ET §7-307.
Certificate of payment, ET §7-307.
Initial account.
Generally, Estates Rule 6-417; ET §7-302.
Notices.
Interested person notified of matters filed in proceedings, Estates Rule 6-417; ET §7-501.
Rendering account.
Failure to render accounts, ET §7-306.
Removal of personal representative, Estates Rule 6-452.
Resignation of personal representative, Estates Rule 6-451.
When to render accounts, ET §7-305.
Resignation of personal representative, Estates Rule 6-451.
Subsequent accounts, Estates Rule 6-417; ET §7-303.
Time.
Extensions, ET §7-305.
When to render accounts, ET §7-305.
Actions.
Against personal representative.
Frauds, statute of, ET §8-109.
Creditor's claim.
Against former personal representative, ET §8-101.
Against person to whom property has been distributed, ET §8-101.
Commencement of suit, ET §8-104.
Where insurance exists, ET §8-104.
Debts and claims.
Against the personal representative, ET §8-107.
Lien not affected, ET §8-103.
Expenses of estate litigation, ET §7-603.
Personal injuries.
Instituted before death, ET §8-103.
Powers of personal representative, ET §7-401.
Property.
Damages to property.
Actions instituted before death, ET §8-103.
Recover possession of property or determine title, ET §7-102.
Administration.
Opening estates. See within this heading, "Opening estates."
Small estates. See within this heading, "Small estates."
Administrative probate.
General provisions, ET §§5-301 to 5-304.
See WILLS.
Administrator.
Includes term executor, 1 §5.
Affidavits.
Mortgages and deeds of trust.
Where mortgagee or party secured by deed of trust.
Consideration true and bona fide, RP §4-106.

EXECUTORS AND ADMINISTRATORS —Cont'd

After-discovered property.

Small estates, Estates Rule 6-212; ET §5-605.

Subsequent administration, Estates Rule 6-422; ET §10-104.

Aged.

Claims.

Order of payment when assets insufficient to pay claims in full, ET §8-105.

Alcoholic beverages.

Death of licensee.

Effect on license, 2B §10-506.

Sales permitted without license or permit, 2B §1-201.

Aliens.

Right to letters.

Exclusion of person not citizen of the United States, ET §5-105.

Appeals.

Commission of personal representative.

Appeal from allowance by court, ET §7-601.

Settlement of decedents' estates.

Orphans' court.

Striking of notice of appeal, Estates Rule 6-464.

Tax on commissions.

Appeals to court of special appeals, Estates Rule 6-463; TG §13-511.

Appearance.

Settlement of decedents' estates.

Attorneys at law, Estates Rule 6-132.

Registers of wills.

Appointment of personal representative.

Presence before register not required, Estates Rule 6-131.

Special appearances abolished, Estates Rule 6-132.

Appointment.

By register of wills, ET §5-302.

Conditions of appointment, ET §6-101.

Expenses of estate litigation, ET §7-603.

Letters of administration. See within this heading, "Letters of administration."

Notice.

Creditors, ET §7-103.1.

Form, ET §7-103.

Personal notice to heirs and legatees, ET §7-104.

Opening estates.

Personal representative.

Consent to appointment.

Form, Estates Rule 6-313.

Register of wills.

Form, Estates Rule 6-321.

Petition for probate.

Notice of appointment, Estates Rules 6-302, 6-311.

Resident agent.

Form, Estates Rule 6-315.

Order of right to letters, ET §5-104.

Personal representative.

Judicial probate, ET §§5-401 to 5-407.

See WILLS.

Presence before register of wills, Estates Rule 6-131.

Reappointment.

After request for judicial probate, ET §6-307.

Resident agent.

Opening estates.

Form, Estates Rule 6-315.

EXECUTORS AND ADMINISTRATORS —Cont'd

Appointment —Cont'd

Resident agent —Cont'd

Small estates.

Form, Estates Rule 6-205.

Several personal representatives, ET §5-106.

Small estates.

Notice of appointment.

Form, Estates Rule 6-209.

Personal representative.

Consent to appointment of personal representative.

Form, Estates Rule 6-203.

Resident agent, Estates Rule 6-205.

Special administrator. See within this heading, "Special administrator."

Substitution of personal representative.

Form, Estates Rule 6-203.

Termination.

By court, Estates Rule 6-421; ET §10-101.

By request, Estates Rule 6-421; ET §10-101.

Confirmatory acts, Estates Rule 6-422; ET §10-105.

Appraisal.

Inventory. See within this heading, "Inventory."

Arbitration and award.

Powers of personal representative, ET §7-401.

Assets.

Actions to recover possession, ET §7-102.

Control of estate, ET §7-102.

Distribution.

Fiduciary responsibility, ET §7-101.

General provisions, ET §§9-102 to 9-112.

See DESCENT AND DISTRIBUTION.

Indemnity for distribution, ET §7-101.

Powers of personal representative, ET §7-401.

Protection of persons dealing with personal representative, ET §7-404.

Time, ET §7-101.

Inheritance tax.

Application to fix inheritance tax on non-probate assets.

Form, Estates Rule 6-405.

Inventory. See within this heading, "Inventory."

Non-probate assets.

Application to fix inheritance tax.

Form, Estates Rule 6-405.

Order in which assets appropriated, ET §9-103.

Possession, ET §7-102.

Powers of personal representative, ET §7-401.

Renunciation.

By testamentary trustee, ET §9-102.

Valuation.

Distribution in kind, using federal estate tax values, ET §11-107.

Attorneys at law.

Settlement of decedents' estates.

Appearance of attorneys, Estates Rule 6-132.

Attorney may act for person, Estates Rule 6-133.

Term "person" defined, Estates Rule 6-105.

Effect of signature by attorney.

Certification by attorney with out-of-state office, Estates Rule 6-135.

Entry of appearance, Estates Rule 6-132.

Personal representative.

Attorney may not sign documents required by law to be filed by personal representative, Estates Rule 6-133.

Petitions.

Requirements, Estates Rule 6-135.

EXECUTORS AND ADMINISTRATORS —Cont'd

Attorneys at law —Cont'd

Settlement of decedents' estates —Cont'd

Petitions —Cont'd

Signing of petitions and other papers.
Requirements, Estates Rules 6-134, 6-135.

Special appearances abolished, Estates Rule 6-132.

Withdrawal of appearance, Estates Rule 6-132.

Attorneys' fees.

Settlement of decedents' estates.

Bad faith-unjustified proceedings, Estates Rule 6-141.

Generally, Estates Rule 6-416; ET §7-602.

Auditors.

Employment.

Powers of personal representative, ET §7-401.

Banks and trust companies.

Bonds, surety.

Not required to give when serving as personal representative, ET §6-102.

Fiduciary capacity.

See BANKS AND TRUST COMPANIES.

Bonds, surety.

Generally, ET §6-102.

Inheritance tax.

Liability for payment, ET §7-307.

Opening estates.

Personal representative, Estates Rule 6-312.

Penalty.

Amount, ET §6-102.

Personal representative's bond, Estates Rule 6-222.

Required for appointment, ET §6-101.

Exceptions, ET §6-102.

Settlement of decedents' estates.

After-discovered property.

Subsequent administration, Estates Rule 6-422; ET §10-104.

Small estates.

Personal representative, ET §5-604.

Special administrator, Estates Rule 6-454; ET §6-402.

Surety.

General provisions, ET §6-102.

Trust company not required to give, ET §6-102.

Waiver, ET §6-102.

Borrowing money.

Powers of personal representative, ET §7-401.

Bulk transfers.

Transfers excepted from article, CL §6-103.

Business.

Continuation of any unincorporated business or venture.

Powers of personal representative, ET §7-401.

Caveat.

Petitions.

Generally, Estates Rule 6-431.

Notice, Estates Rule 6-431.

Register's notice, Estates Rule 6-432.

Order to answer, Estates Rule 6-432.

Subsequent procedure, Estates Rule 6-433.

Certification.

Settlement of decedents' estates.

Foreign personal representatives.

Application to set inheritance tax, Estates Rule 6-501.

Charities.

Satisfaction of charitable pledges of decedent, ET §7-401.

EXECUTORS AND ADMINISTRATORS —Cont'd

Circuit courts.

Settlement of decedents' estates.

Contested issues of fact.

Transmitting issues to circuit court, Estates Rule 6-434.

Orphans' court, Estates Rule 6-463.

Striking of notice of appeal, Estates Rule 6-464.

Claims.

Debts and claims. See within this heading, "Debts and claims."

Clerks of court.

Right to letters.

Exclusion, ET §5-105.

Closing estates.

After-discovered property.

Subsequent administration, Estates Rule 6-422; ET §10-104.

Confirmatory acts.

Personal representative to perform ministerial or confirmatory acts, Estates Rule 6-422; ET §10-105.

Debts and claims.

Liability of distributees, ET §10-102.

Notice, Estates Rule 6-417; ET §10-101.

Recovery against person receiving property or from former personal representative individually, ET §8-101.

Final account.

Effect of final approval of final account, Estates Rule 6-417; ET §10-101.

Personal representative.

Acceptance and consent.

Form, Estates Rule 6-342.

Petition.

Discharge of personal representatives, Estates Rule 6-421; ET §10-101.

Subsequent administration.

After-discovered property, Estates Rule 6-422; ET §10-104.

Termination of appointment, Estates Rule 6-421; ET §10-101.

Commissions.

Generally, ET §7-601.

Payment, ET §7-604.

Order of payment when assets insufficient to pay claims in full, ET §8-105.

Petition for personal representative's commissions, Estates Rule 6-416.

Separate or joint petitions for personal representative's commissions.

Filing, Estates Rule 6-416.

Tax on commissions.

Death taxes generally, TG §§7-101 to 7-122.

See TAXATION.

Orphan's court.

Appeals to court of special appeals from, TG §13-511.

Common law.

Settlement of decedents' estates.

Rules of construction, Estates Rule 6-104.

Compensation.

Termination of appointment of personal representative, ET §6-308.

Compromise and settlement.

Powers of personal representative, ET §7-401.

Confirmatory acts.

Authority to perform, Estates Rule 6-422; ET §10-105.

EXECUTORS AND ADMINISTRATORS —Cont'd
Consent.
  Closing estates.
    Personal representative's acceptance and
        consent.
      Form, Estates Rule 6-342.
  Settlement of decedents' estates.
    Waiver, Estates Rule 6-126.
  Small estates.
    Consent to appointment of personal
        representative.
      Form, Estates Rule 6-203.
Construction of term, 1 §5.
Contempt.
  Settlement of decedents' estates.
    Orphans' court.
      Enforcement, Estates Rule 6-113; ET §2-103.
Contracts.
  Liability.
    Contracts made during the administration, ET
        §8-109.
  Perform decedent's contracts.
    Powers of personal representative, ET §7-401.
Contribution and exoneration.
  Order in which assets appropriated.
    Adjustments and contributions in other
        interests in remaining assets, ET §9-103.
Copersonal representatives. See within this
    heading, "Several personal representatives."
Corporations, ET §7-401.
Corrections, filing, Estates Rule 6-127.
Costs.
  Expenses of estate litigation, ET §7-603.
  Order of payment when assets insufficient, ET
      §8-105.
Counterclaim and cross-claim.
  Deduction of counterclaim, ET §8-113.
Courts.
  Petition by representative for permission to act,
      ET §7-402.
  Powers of personal representative.
    Approval when, ET §7-401.
Creditors.
  Debts. See within this heading, "Debts and
      claims."
  Distribution to creditors.
    Meeting, Estates Rule 6-441; ET §8-109.
    Proposal for distribution, Estates Rule 6-442.
  Liability of heir or legatee to creditor, ET §10-102.
  Limitation of actions.
    Effect of statute of limitations, ET §8-102.
  Meeting for distribution, Estates Rule 6-441; ET
      §8-109.
    Proposal for distribution, Estates Rule 6-442.
  Notice.
    Actual notice, Estates Rule 6-401.
    Appointment, ET §7-103.1.
    Proposed payment to personal representative or
        attorney, Estates Rule 6-414; ET §7-502.
  Opening estates.
    Petition for probate.
      Notice of appointment, Estates Rule 6-311.
  Order of right to letters, ET §5-104.
  Payment.
    Meeting of creditors for distribution.
      Proposal for distribution, Estates Rule 6-442.
  Settlement of decedents' estates.
    Meeting for distribution, Estates Rule 6-441; ET
        §8-109.
  Small estates.
    Notice of appointment, Estates Rule 6-209.

EXECUTORS AND ADMINISTRATORS —Cont'd
Death.
  Absence as evidence of death and absentee
      property act.
    See ABSENT PERSONS.
  Creditors' claims.
    Effect of death, ET §8-102.
  Effect, ET §6-304.
  Personal representative or guardian of deceased
      or disabled personal representative.
    Duties, ET §6-304.
  Termination. See within this heading, "Letters of
      administration."
Death by wrongful act.
  Funeral expenses.
    Limitation on recovery, ET §7-401.
  General provisions, CJ §§3-901 to 3-904.
    See DEATH BY WRONGFUL ACT.
Debts and claims.
  Allowance against personal representative, ET
      §8-107.
    Effect, ET §8-109.
  Allowance of claim, ET §8-107.
  Appointment of personal representative.
    Proceedings after appointment, ET §8-101.
    Required before claim may be revived or
        commenced against estate, ET §8-101.
  Claimant's petition, Estates Rule 6-413.
  Closing estates.
    Liability of distributees, ET §10-102.
    Notice, Estates Rule 6-417; ET §10-101.
    Recovery against person receiving property or
        from former personal representative
        individually, ET §8-101.
  Commencement of suit, ET §8-104.
  Contingent claim.
    Procedure, ET §8-112.
  Counterclaim.
    Deduction of claim, ET §8-113.
  Death.
    Effect of death, ET §8-102.
  Delivery to personal representative, ET §8-104.
  Disallowance.
    Effect, Estates Rule 6-413; ET §8-107.
  Due date.
    Claim not yet due, ET §8-110.
  Execution.
    Prohibited, ET §8-114.
  Filing.
    Claims against nonresident decedents, ET
        §5-503.
    With registers of wills, ET §8-104.
  Funeral expenses, ET §8-106.
  Insurance.
    Action against estate where insurance exists,
        ET §8-104.
  Judgment against personal representative.
    Allowance of claim, ET §8-107.
  Levy.
    Prohibited, ET §8-114.
  Liability of personal representative, ET §8-109.
  Life insurance, annuities and fraternal benefit
      societies.
    Exemption of proceeds, ET §8-115.
  Limitation of actions.
    Effect of statute of limitations, ET §8-102.
  Medical assistance program.
    Actions against recipients, ET §8-103.
  Nonresidents.
    Against nonresident decedents, ET §5-503.

EXECUTORS AND ADMINISTRATORS —Cont'd
Debts and claims —Cont'd
Notice.
  Closing estates, Estates Rule 6-417; ET §10-101.
  Creditor notified of proposed payment to
    personal representative or attorney, Estates
    Rule 6-414; ET §7-502.
  Disallowance of claims, Estates Rule 6-413; ET
    §8-107.
  Presentation of claim.
    Date of notice, ET §8-103.
  Register of suit, Estates Rule 6-413.
Order in which assets appropriated, ET §9-103.
Order of payment of debts.
  Assets insufficient to pay all claims in full, ET
    §8-105.
Payment.
  At any time, ET §8-108.
  Contingent claim, ET §8-112.
  Creditor notified of proposed payment to
    personal representative or attorney, Estates
    Rule 6-414; ET §7-502.
  General provisions, ET §8-108.
  Indemnity, ET §7-101.
  Meeting of creditors for distribution, Estates
    Rule 6-441; ET §8-109.
  Nine months after decedent's death, ET §8-108.
  Order of payment, ET §8-105.
  Powers of personal representative, ET §7-401.
  Prohibition against preference, ET §8-105.
  Proposed payment to personal representative or
    attorney.
    Finality of order, Estates Rule 6-414; ET
      §7-502.
  Protection of persons dealing with personal
    representative, ET §7-404.
  Secured claim, ET §8-111.
    Not yet due.
      Procedure, ET §8-110.
  Security for refund.
    Failure to give, ET §8-108.
  Time for payment, ET §8-108.
  Unsecured claim.
    Not yet due.
      Procedure, ET §8-110.
Preference.
  Prohibition against preference, ET §8-105.
Presentation of claim, Estates Rule 6-413.
  Action.
    Commencement of suit, ET §8-104.
  Conduct of personal representative, ET §8-103.
  Content, Estates Rule 6-413.
  Damages to property.
    Action as to before death, ET §8-103.
  Delivery to personal representative, ET §8-104.
  Filing.
    With register, ET §8-104.
  Form, Estates Rule 6-413; ET §8-104.
  Limitations, ET §8-103.
  Manner of presentation, ET §8-104.
  Notice.
    Date of notice, ET §8-103.
  Personal injuries.
    Action as to before death, ET §8-103.
  Requirement of presentation, ET §8-103.
  Slander, ET §8-103.
  Time, ET §8-103.
Proceeding to enforce claim, ET §8-101.
Proposed payment to personal representative or
  attorney.
  Certificate of counsel not required, Estates Rule
    6-414; ET §7-502.

EXECUTORS AND ADMINISTRATORS —Cont'd
Debts and claims —Cont'd
Prosecute, defend or submit to arbitration.
  Powers of personal representative, ET §7-401.
Registers of wills.
  Presentation of claim.
    Filing with register, ET §8-104.
Secured claim.
  Exhaustion of security.
    Payment of balance, ET §8-111.
  Not yet due.
    Procedure, ET §8-110.
  Payment, ET §8-111.
  Security in whole.
    Amount due creditor, ET §8-111.
Small estates, Estates Rule 6-211.
Unsecured claim.
  Not yet due.
    Procedure, ET §8-110.
Decedents' estates.
General provisions, ET §§1-101 to 12-103.
See DECEDENTS' ESTATES.
Declaratory judgments.
Rights, CJ §3-408.
Deeds.
Execution and delivery of evidence of title, ET
  §9-105.
Indexing, ET §9-105.
Personal representative's deed.
  Forms, RP §4-202.
Recordation.
  Payment of costs of recordation, ET §9-105.
Taxation.
  Exemption from excise taxes, ET §9-105.
Definitions, 1 §5.
Settlement of decedents' estates, Estates Rule
  6-105.
Attorneys at law.
  Signing of petitions and other papers.
    "Office for the practice of law," Estates Rule
      6-135.
Dentists.
Notice and disposition of medical records, ET
  §7-401.
Deposit of assets.
Powers of personal representative, ET §7-401.
Disability.
Judicial determination of disability, ET §6-304.
Personal representative or guardian of deceased
  or disabled personal representative.
  Duties, ET §6-304.
Termination. See within this heading, "Letters of
  administration."
Disclaimer.
Interest in decedent's property, Estates Rule
  6-412.
Uniform disclaimer of property interests act, ET
  §§9-201 to 9-216.
See DESCENT AND DISTRIBUTION.
Distress for rent.
Notice to personal representative of deceased
  defendant, RP §8-328.
Distribution.
General provisions, ET §§9-102 to 9-112.
See DESCENT AND DISTRIBUTION.
Duties.
Fiduciary duty, ET §7-101.
  Breach of fiduciary duty, ET §7-403.
General provisions, ET §7-101.
Personal representative or guardian of deceased
  or disabled personal representative, ET
  §6-304.

EXECUTORS AND ADMINISTRATORS —Cont'd
Duties —Cont'd
Personal representatives of deceased guardian, ET §13-220.
Special administrator, Estates Rule 6-454; ET §6-403.
Successor personal representative, ET §6-202.
Suspension, Estates Rule 6-453; ET §6-301.
Termination. See within this heading, "Letters of administration."
Time of accrual, ET §6-105.
Environmental laws.
Powers of personal representative, ET §7-401.
Equity.
Distribution under jurisdiction of court, ET §15-108.
Evidence.
Applicability of rules.
Settlement of decedents' estates, Estates Rule 6-462.
Executions.
Prohibited against property of estate, ET §8-114.
Exemptions.
Proceeds of life insurance, annuity contracts and benefits of fraternal benefit societies, ET §8-115.
Expenses.
Estate litigation, ET §7-603.
Funeral expenses. See within this heading, "Funeral expenses."
Order of payment, ET §8-105.
Federal estate tax.
Distribution in kind, using federal estate tax values, ET §11-107.
General provisions.
See FEDERAL ESTATE TAX.
Fees.
Appraisal fees, ET §7-202.
Small estates.
Registers of wills, ET §5-606.
Fiduciaries.
General provisions, ET §§15-201 to 15-211.
See FIDUCIARIES.
Successor corporate fiduciaries, ET §§15-1A-01 to 15-1A-05.
See FIDUCIARIES.
Fiduciary duty.
Breach of fiduciary duty, ET §7-403.
Foreclosures.
Mortgages.
Parties, PropSales Rule 14-202.
Foreign personal representatives. See within this heading, "Nonresidents."
Forms.
Bonds, surety, ET §6-102.
Closing estates.
Personal representative.
Acceptance and consent, Estates Rule 6-342.
Creditor's claim.
Manner of presentation, ET §8-104.
Deeds.
Personal representative's deed, RP §4-202.
Letters of administration, ET §6-104.
Notice of appointment, ET §7-103.
Opening estates.
Administrative probate order.
Appointment of personal representative, Estates Rule 6-321.
Consent appointment, Estates Rule 6-313.
Letters of administration, Estates Rule 6-322.
List of interested persons, Estates Rule 6-316.

EXECUTORS AND ADMINISTRATORS —Cont'd
Forms —Cont'd
Opening estates —Cont'd
Notice to interested persons, Estates Rule 6-317.
Personal representative's bond, Estates Rule 6-312.
Petition for probate, Estates Rule 6-301.
Appointment.
Notice of appointment, Estates Rule 6-311.
Modification for form, Estates Rule 6-301.
Notice of judicial probate, Estates Rule 6-302.
Resident agent.
Appointment of resident agent, Estates Rule 6-315.
Settlement of decedents' estates.
Application to fix inheritance tax on non-probate assets, Estates Rule 6-405.
Appraisal of inventory, Estates Rule 6-403.
Attorneys' fees.
Notice of petition for attorneys' fees, Estates Rule 6-416.
Caption of case, Estates Rule 6-121.
Commission of personal representative.
Notice of petition for personal representative's commissions, Estates Rule 6-416.
Debts and claims.
Disallowance of claim, Estates Rule 6-413.
Presentation of claim, Estates Rule 6-413; ET §8-104.
Funeral expenses.
Petition and order for funeral expenses, Estates Rule 6-415.
Information report, Estates Rule 6-404.
Inheritance tax on non-probate assets.
Application to fix inheritance tax, Estates Rule 6-405.
Inventory, Estates Rule 6-402.
Nonresidents.
Foreign personal representatives.
Application to set inheritance tax, Estates Rule 6-501.
Notice of appointment of foreign personal representative, Estates Rule 6-501.
Notices.
Form of waiver, Estates Rule 6-126.
Service of process.
Certificate of service, Estates Rule 6-125.
Waiver.
Notices, Estates Rule 6-126.
Wills.
Proof of execution of will, Estates Rule 6-152.
Small estates.
Appointment.
Notice of appointment, Estates Rule 6-209.
Consent to appointment, Estates Rule 6-203.
Interested persons.
Notice to interested persons, Estates Rule 6-210.
Letters of administration, Estates Rule 6-207.
Petition for administration, Estates Rule 6-201.
List of interested persons, Estates Rule 6-202.
Register's order, Estates Rule 6-208.
Resident agent.
Appointment, Estates Rule 6-205.
Fraternal benefit societies.
Payment of benefits to personal representative of member, IN §8-430.
Payment to personal representative or attorney.
Final and binding unless fraud, ET §7-502.

EXECUTORS AND ADMINISTRATORS —Cont'd
Frauds, statute of.
Actions against personal representative, ET
§8-109.
Funeral expenses.
Allowance, ET §8-106.
Death by wrongful act.
Limitation on recovery, ET §7-401.
Order of payment when assets insufficient, ET
§8-105.
Payment, ET §8-106.
Powers of personal representative, ET §7-401.
Petition of creditor, ET §8-106.
Settlement of decedents' estates.
Petition and order for funeral expenses, Estates
Rule 6-415.
Small estates, ET §5-603.
Guardians.
Personal representatives of deceased guardian.
Powers and duties, ET §13-220.
Hearings.
Removal of personal representative, ET §6-306.
Revision of inventory, ET §7-204.
Settlement of decedents' estates.
Debts and claims.
Claimant's petition, Estates Rule 6-413.
Heirs.
Claims against heirs and legatees.
Limitation of actions, ET §10-103.
Notice.
Closing estates, Estates Rule 6-417; ET §10-101.
Personal notice of appointment, ET §7-104.
Exception, ET §7-104.
Opening estates.
Petition for appointment.
Notice of appointment, Estates Rule 6-311.
Small estates.
Notice of appointment, Estates Rule 6-209.
Unknown heirs.
Petition for probate.
Notice of appointment, Estates Rule 6-311.
Hospitals.
Payment.
Order of payment when assets insufficient to
pay claims in full, ET §8-105.
Income tax.
Return by person on behalf of individual, TG
§10-808.
Indemnity.
Payment of claims or distribution of assets, ET
§7-101.
Inheritance tax.
Foreign personal representatives.
Lien for payment of tax, ET §5-505.
Procedure for fixing tax, ET §5-504.
Gift to surviving spouse in will, qualifying for
estate tax marital deduction, ET §11-106.
Inventory, TG §7-225.
Lien.
Payment of taxes, ET §5-505.
Nonresident decedents.
Procedure for fixing, ET §5-504.
Responsibility for payment of other death taxes,
ET §5-504.
Payment by personal representative.
Certificate of payment, ET §7-307.
General provisions, ET §7-307.
Reports.
Information report, TG §7-224.
Insane persons.
Personal representative.
Judicial determination of disability, ET §6-304.

EXECUTORS AND ADMINISTRATORS —Cont'd
Insane persons —Cont'd
Right to letters.
Exclusion of mentally incompetent, ET §5-105.
Insurance.
Creditor's claim.
Action against estate where insurance exists,
ET §8-104.
Life insurance, annuities, etc.
Exemption of proceeds, ET §8-115.
Payment of proceeds without letters of
administration, IN §16-110.
Powers of personal representative, ET §7-401.
Temporary licenses, IN §10-120.
Interested persons.
Exceptions to an account, ET §7-501.
Notice.
Closing estates, Estates Rule 6-417; ET §10-101.
Small estates, Estates Rule 6-210.
Notified of matters filed in proceedings, ET
§7-501.
Opening estates.
Notice to interested persons.
Form, Estates Rule 6-317.
Right of action against personal representative.
Breach of fiduciary duty, ET §7-403.
Failure to render account, ET §7-306.
Small estates.
List of interested persons.
Form, Estates Rule 6-202.
Notice to interested persons, Estates Rule
6-210.
Petition for administration.
List of interested persons, Estates Rules
6-201, 6-202.
Interpretation and construction.
Construction of term, 1 §5.
Settlement of decedents' estates.
Applicability of rules, Estates Rules 6-101,
6-461.
Repeal of local rules, Estates Rule 6-102.
Method of rule citation, Estates Rule 6-103.
Rules of construction, Estates Rule 6-104.
Intestate succession.
General provisions, ET §§3-101 to 3-112.
See DECEDENTS' ESTATES.
Inventory.
Appraisal.
Appointment of appraisers.
Officially appointed appraisers, ET §7-202.
Basis, Estates Rule 6-403.
Fees.
Allowed as administration expense, ET
§7-202.
General provisions, ET §7-202.
Officially appointed appraisers, ET §7-202.
Personal representative appraisal, ET §7-202.
Reappraisal, ET §7-203.
Required content, Estates Rule 6-403.
Special appraisers, ET §7-202.
Contents, Estates Rule 6-402; ET §7-201.
Filing.
Generally, Estates Rule 6-402; ET §7-201.
Supplemental inventory, ET §7-203.
Form, Estates Rule 6-402.
Methods of appraisal, ET §7-202.
Preparation.
Duty of personal representative to prepare,
Estates Rule 6-402; ET §7-201.
Revision.
Generally, ET §§7-203, 7-204.

EXECUTORS AND ADMINISTRATORS —Cont'd
Inventory —Cont'd
  Supplemental inventory.
    General provisions, ET §7-203.
  Verification.
    Requirement, Estates Rule 6-123; ET §1-102.
Investments.
  Employment of investment advisers.
    Powers of personal representative, ET §7-401.
  General provisions.
    See INVESTMENTS.
  Powers of personal representative, ET §7-401.
Judges.
  Right to letters.
    Exclusions, ET §5-105.
Judgments and decrees.
  Settlement of decedents' estates.
    Entry of judgment, Estates Rule 6-171.
    Orphans' court.
      Enforcement, Estates Rule 6-113; ET §2-103.
Jurisdiction.
  Over persons outside this state.
    General provisions.
      See JURISDICTION.
  Settlement of decedents' estates.
    Orphans' court.
      Effectuation of jurisdiction, Estates Rule
        6-113; ET §2-103.
    Rules of construction, Estates Rule 6-104.
    Written consent to personal jurisdiction, ET
      §6-101.
Landlord and tenant.
  Foreign personal representatives.
    Leasehold property.
      Defined, ET §5-503.
  Powers of personal representative, ET §7-401.
  Rent.
    Payment.
      Order of payment when assets insufficient to
        pay claims in full, ET §8-105.
Leases.
  Foreign personal representatives.
    Transfer of real property, ET §5-502.
  Powers.
    Survival, ET §15-107.
Legatees and devisees.
  Notice.
    Closing estates, Estates Rule 6-417; ET §10-101.
    Personal notice of appointment, ET §7-104.
  Order of right to letters.
    Residuary legatee, ET §5-104.
  Valuation.
    Distribution in kind, using federal estate tax
      values, ET §11-107.
Letters of administration.
  Acts of others.
    Ratification, ET §6-105.
  Administrative probate.
    General provisions, ET §§5-301 to 5-304.
  Conditions of appointment, ET §6-101.
  Contents of letters, ET §6-103.
  Corrections.
    Filing revised and corrected documents, Estates
      Rule 6-127; ET §7-105.
  Definition of letters, ET §1-101.
  Duties.
    Personal representative or guardian of deceased
      or disabled personal representative, ET
      §6-304.
  Time of accrual, ET §6-105.

EXECUTORS AND ADMINISTRATORS —Cont'd
Letters of administration —Cont'd
  Foreign personal representatives.
    Letters in Maryland not required, ET §5-501.
  Form, ET §6-104.
  Granted.
    Classes, ET §5-106.
    Issuance, ET §6-103.
  Judicial probate.
    General provisions, ET §§5-401 to 5-407.
      See WILLS.
  Life insurance and annuities.
    Payment of proceeds without letters of
      administration, IN §16-110.
  Necessity of proceeding, ET §5-102.
  Notice of appointment, ET §§7-103, 7-104.
  Opening estates.
    Form, Estates Rule 6-322.
    Right to letters.
      Renunciation, Estates Rule 6-314.
  Petition for probate.
    Request for grant of letters and order for
      qualification, ET §5-205.
  Powers.
    Interim powers.
      After request for judicial probate, ET §6-307.
    Time of accrual, ET §6-105.
  Prior acts.
    Validity, ET §6-105.
  Ratification of others' acts, ET §6-105.
  Reappointment.
    After request for judicial probate, ET §6-307.
  Renunciation.
    Opening estates, Estates Rule 6-314.
    Small estates, Estates Rule 6-204.
  Revision.
    Filing revised and corrected documents, Estates
      Rule 6-127; ET §7-105.
  Right to letters, ET §5-104.
    Exclusions, ET §5-105.
  Scope of title, ET §5-101.
  Several personal representatives.
    Priority among different letters, ET §6-201.
  Small estates.
    Form, Estates Rule 6-207.
    Petition for administration.
      Proceeding after petition, Estates Rule 6-206.
    Right to letters.
      Renunciation, Estates Rule 6-204.
  Special administrator. See within this heading,
    "Special administrator."
  Suspension.
    Generally, Estates Rule 6-453; ET §6-301.
  Termination.
    Acts prior to termination, ET §6-303.
    Closing estates, Estates Rule 6-421; ET §10-101.
    Compensation.
      Awarded by court, ET §6-308.
    Confirmatory acts, Estates Rule 6-422; ET
      §10-105.
    Death.
      Effect, ET §6-304.
    Disability.
      Effect, ET §6-304.
    Effect, ET §6-303.
    Generally, Estates Rule 6-421; ET §6-302.
    Grounds, Estates Rule 6-421; ET §6-302.
    Judicial probate.
      Request for, ET §6-307.
    Liability, ET §6-303.
    Removal, ET §6-306.

EXECUTORS AND ADMINISTRATORS —Cont'd
Letters of administration —Cont'd
Termination —Cont'd
Request for judicial probate, ET §6-307.
Resignation.
Effective, Estates Rule 6-451; ET §6-305.
Special administrator.
General provisions. See within this heading, "Special administrator."
Levy.
Against property of estate prohibited, ET §8-114.
Liability.
Breach of fiduciary duty, ET §7-403.
Claims against estate, ET §8-109.
Contracts made during administration, ET §8-109.
Creditors' meeting, Estates Rule 6-441; ET §8-109.
Proposal for distribution, Estates Rule 6-442.
Protect and indemnify personal representative, ET §8-109.
Determination of liability, ET §8-109.
Distribution pursuant to direction of court, ET §9-112.
Doubt concerning, ET §8-109.
Failure to render account, ET §7-306.
Financial responsibility, ET §7-101.
General provisions, ET §8-109.
Heir or legatee to creditor, ET §10-102.
Improper payments of claims against estate, ET §8-108.
Indemnity, ET §7-101.
Individual liability to third parties, ET §8-109.
Opening estates.
Bonds, surety.
Liability of surety on bond, Estates Rule 6-312.
Small estates, ET §5-604.
Termination of administration, ET §6-303.
Torts, ET §8-109.
Libel and slander.
Claim for slander barred against estate of decedent, ET §8-103.
Liens.
Foreign personal representatives.
Payment of taxes, ET §5-505.
Limitation on presentation of claim.
Does not affect lien, ET §8-103.
Payment of secured claim, ET §8-111.
Powers of personal representative, ET §7-401.
Limitation of actions.
Closing estates.
Claims against heirs and legatees, ET §10-103.
Proceedings against personal representatives, ET §10-103.
Commissions.
Appeal of allowance to circuit court, ET §7-601.
Creditors' claims.
Effect of statute of limitations, ET §8-102.
Limited liability companies.
Continuation by last remaining member's personal representative, CA §4A-902.
Conversion of sole proprietorship to limited liability company, ET §7-401.
Mail.
Settlement of decedents' estates.
Certified mail.
Defined, Estates Rule 6-105.
Medical care.
Order of payment when assets insufficient to pay claims in full, ET §8-105.

EXECUTORS AND ADMINISTRATORS —Cont'd
Mentally incompetent.
Right to letters denied, ET §5-105.
Minors.
Distribution to minor.
General provisions, ET §9-109.
Right to letters.
Exclusion of person under age of 18 years, ET §5-105.
Mistake.
Payment to personal representative or attorney.
Final or binding unless material mistake, ET §7-502.
Modified administration, Estates Rule 6-455; ET §§5-701 to 5-710.
Extension of time to file final report and make distribution, Estates Rule 6-456.
Final report, Estates Rule 6-455.
Extension of time to file final report and make distribution, Estates Rule 6-456.
Forms, Estates Rule 6-455.
Mortgages and deeds of trust.
Affidavit by mortgagee or party secured by deed of trust.
Consideration true and bona fide, RP §4-106.
Foreign personal representative.
Power to transfer real property, ET §5-502.
Payment of secured claim, ET §8-111.
Powers, ET §7-401.
Survival, ET §15-107.
Morticians.
Licenses.
Personal representative of deceased mortician's estate, HO §7-308.1.
Nonresidents.
Application.
Fixing inheritance tax, ET §5-504.
Application sent by personal representative, Estates Rule 6-501.
Claims against nonresident decedents.
Statement of claim, ET §5-503.
Conveyances.
Power to transfer real property, ET §5-502.
Death taxes.
Responsibility for payment, ET §5-504.
Definitions.
Leasehold property, ET §5-503.
Inheritance tax.
Procedure for fixing, ET §5-504.
Leasehold property.
Defined, ET §5-503.
Order directing transfer of title, ET §5-506.
Power to transfer real property, ET §5-502.
Letters in Maryland.
Not required, ET §5-501.
Lien.
Payment of taxes, ET §5-505.
Mortgages and deeds of trust.
Power to transfer real property, ET §5-502.
Notice by representatives, ET §5-503.
Powers, ET §5-502.
Publication of notice.
By representative, ET §5-503.
Real property.
Order directing transfer of title, ET §5-506.
Power to transfer real property, ET §5-502.
Receipt.
Register's receipt for payment of tax, ET §5-504.
Registers of wills.
Fees in proceedings involving foreign personal representatives, ET §2-206.

EXECUTORS AND ADMINISTRATORS —Cont'd
Nonresidents —Cont'd
Right to letters.
Exclusions, ET §5-105.
Taxes.
Responsibility for payment of other death taxes,
ET §5-504.
Transfers of real property, ET §5-502.
Nontestamentary transfers, ET §1-401.
Notices.
Appointment.
Form, ET §7-103.
Personal notice to heirs and legatees, ET
§7-104.
Exception, ET §7-104.
Publication, ET §7-103.
Closing estates, Estates Rule 6-417; ET §10-101.
Creditors, Estates Rule 6-401; ET §7-103.1.
Debts and claims.
Disallowance of claims, Estates Rule 6-413; ET
§8-107.
Presentation of claim.
Date of notice, ET §8-103.
Register of suit, Estates Rule 6-413.
Foreign personal representatives, ET §5-503.
Interested person notified of matters filed in
proceedings, ET §7-501.
Opening estates.
First personal representative.
Delivery of published notice, Estates Rule
6-331.
Publication of notice of appointment, Estates
Rule 6-331.
Notice to interested persons.
Form, Estates Rule 6-317.
Petition for probate.
Judicial probate, Estates Rule 6-302.
Payment.
Proposed payment to personal representative or
attorney, Estates Rule 6-414; ET §7-502.
Personal notice to heirs and legatees, ET §7-104.
Personal representative not required to give notice
to himself, ET §1-103.
Registers of wills.
Personal notice to heirs and legatees, Estates
Rule 6-210; ET §2-210.
Removal of personal representatives, ET §6-306.
Resignation.
Written notice, Estates Rule 6-451; ET §6-305.
Settlement of decedents' estates.
After-discovered property.
Subsequent administration, Estates Rule
6-422; ET §10-104.
Attorneys at law.
Effect of notice by or to attorney for person,
Estates Rule 6-133.
Term "person" defined, Estates Rule 6-105.
Commission of personal representative.
Form, Estates Rule 6-416.
Creditors.
Meeting of creditors, Estates Rule 6-441.
Debts and claims.
Disallowance of claims, Estates Rule 6-413;
ET §8-107.
Register of suit, Estates Rule 6-413.
Disclaimer.
Interest in decedent's property.
Requirements, Estates Rule 6-412.
Form of waiver, Estates Rule 6-126.
Orders of court, Estates Rule 6-172.
Ex parte orders, Estates Rule 6-173.

EXECUTORS AND ADMINISTRATORS —Cont'd
Notices —Cont'd
Settlement of decedents' estates —Cont'd
Payment.
Proposed payment to personal representative
or attorney, Estates Rule 6-414; ET
§7-502.
Petition for attorneys' fees.
Form, Estates Rule 6-416.
Small estates.
Objection to petition for administration, ET
§5-603.
Waiver.
Generally, Estates Rule 6-126.
Nurses.
Payment.
Order of payment when assets insufficient to
pay claims in full, ET §8-105.
Objections and exceptions.
Small estates.
Objection to proceedings, ET §5-603.
Opening estates.
Administrative probate order.
Appointment of personal representative, Estates
Rule 6-321.
Bonds, surety.
Personal representative's bond.
Form, Estates Rule 6-312.
Conversion to small estate proceedings, Estates
Rule 6-351.
Interested persons.
List of interested persons.
Form, Estates Rule 6-316.
Notice to interested persons.
Form, Estates Rule 6-317.
Letters of administration.
Form, Estates Rule 6-322.
Right to letters.
Renunciation, Estates Rule 6-314.
Personal representative.
Appointment.
Register of wills, Estates Rule 6-321.
Consent to appointment.
Form, Estates Rule 6-313.
Form of bond, Estates Rule 6-312.
Notice of appointment, Estates Rule 6-302.
Petition for probate, Estates Rule 6-301.
Administrative probate.
Additional documents, Estates Rule 6-301.
Appointment.
Notice of appointment, Estates Rules 6-302,
6-311.
Conversion to small estate proceedings, Estates
Rule 6-351.
Hearing, Estates Rule 6-302.
Judicial probate.
Additional documents, Estates Rule 6-301.
Form of notice, Estates Rule 6-302.
Notice, Estates Rule 6-302.
Service of petition, Estates Rule 6-302.
Proceedings for judicial probate.
Generally, Estates Rule 6-302.
Publication.
Generally, Estates Rule 6-331.
Options.
Powers of personal representative, ET §7-401.
Optometrists.
Notice of disposition of medical records, ET
§7-401.

EXECUTORS AND ADMINISTRATORS —Cont'd
Orders of court.
Settlement of decedents' estates.
After-discovered property.
Subsequent administration, Estates Rule 6-422; ET §10-104.
Creditors.
Meeting of creditors, Estates Rule 6-441.
Debts and claims.
Payment.
Proposed payment to personal representative or attorney, finality of order, Estates Rule 6-414; ET §7-502.
Entry of order, Estates Rule 6-171.
Ex parte application or orders.
When allowed, Estates Rule 6-173.
Notice of orders, Estates Rule 6-172.
Show cause orders.
Nonapplicability to issuance, Estates Rule 6-172.
Orphans' court.
Enforcement, Estates Rule 6-113; ET §2-103.
Petitions, Estates Rule 6-122.
Attorneys' fees as commission, Estates Rule 6-416.
Show cause order, Estates Rule 6-124.
Notice of orders.
Nonapplicability to issuance, Estates Rule 6-172.
Orphans' court.
Appeals, stay of proceedings.
Exceptions, CJ §12-701.
Appeals to court of special appeals, Estates Rule 6-463.
Striking of notice of appeal, Estates Rule 6-464.
Opening estates.
Petition for probate.
Hearing, Estates Rule 6-302.
Settlement of decedents' estates.
Attorneys at law.
Appearance of attorney, Estates Rule 6-132.
Bad faith-unjustified proceedings, Estates Rule 6-141.
Contested issues of fact.
Transmittal to circuit court, Estates Rule 6-434.
Court schedule, Estates Rule 6-113.
Enforcement.
Generally, Estates Rule 6-113; ET §2-103.
Extension of time.
Request to court, Estates Rule 6-107.
Filings.
Amendments and corrections, Estates Rule 6-127.
Form of caption of case, Estates Rule 6-121.
Judgments and decrees.
Entry of judgment by court, Estates Rule 6-171.
Legibility and durability of writings, Estates Rule 6-121.
Orders of court.
Entry of order, Estates Rule 6-171.
Ex parte orders.
When allowed, Estates Rule 6-173.
Recording of proceedings, Estates Rule 6-114.
Rules of court.
Application of Maryland rules as to summoning witnesses, depositions and discovery, Estates Rule 6-461; ET §2-104.
Subpoenas.
Witnesses, Estates Rule 6-161.

EXECUTORS AND ADMINISTRATORS —Cont'd
Parent and child.
Order of right to letters, ET §5-104.
Parties.
Real party in interest.
Circuit courts, CivProCir Rule 2-201.
Personal property.
Power to dispose.
Passes to survivor or successor, ET §15-107.
Petitions.
After-discovered property.
Subsequent administration, Estates Rule 6-422; ET §10-104.
Caveat.
Generally, Estates Rule 6-431.
Notice, Estates Rule 6-431.
Register's notice, Estates Rule 6-432.
Order to answer, Estates Rule 6-432.
Subsequent procedure, Estates Rule 6-433.
Closing estates, Estates Rule 6-417; ET §10-101.
Court's permission to act, ET §7-402.
Debts and claims.
Presentation of claim.
Claimant's petition, Estates Rule 6-413.
Defined, Estates Rule 6-105.
Discharging personal representative, Estates Rule 6-421; ET §10-101.
Generally, Estates Rule 6-122.
Opening estates. See within this heading, "Opening estates."
Request for extension of time, Estates Rule 6-107.
Settlement of decedents' estates.
Generally, Estates Rule 6-122.
Request for extension of time, Estates Rule 6-107.
Signing of petitions and other papers.
Requirement, Estates Rule 6-134.
Small estates. See within this heading, "Small estates."
Physicians and surgeons.
Notice of disposition of medical records, ET §7-401.
Order of payment when assets insufficient to pay claims in full, ET §8-105.
Pledge.
Powers of personal representative, ET §7-401.
Podiatrists.
Notice of disposition of medical records, ET §7-401.
Powers.
Copersonal representatives.
Surviving representative, ET §6-204.
Court's permission to act, ET §7-402.
Exercise of powers, ET §7-401.
General powers, ET §7-401.
Improper exercise of power, ET §7-403.
Protection of persons dealing with personal representative, ET §7-404.
Interim powers.
After request for judicial probate, ET §6-307.
Personal representatives of deceased guardian, ET §13-220.
Special administrator, Estates Rule 6-454; ET §6-403.
Successor personal representative, ET §6-202.
Suspension, Estates Rule 6-453; ET §6-301.
Termination. See within this heading, "Letters of administration."
Time of accrual of powers, ET §6-105.
Priorities.
Debts and claims.
Order of payment when assets insufficient to pay claims in full, ET §8-105.

EXECUTORS AND ADMINISTRATORS —Cont'd
Priorities —Cont'd
Letters of administration.
Among different letters, ET §6-201.
Prisoners.
Right to letters.
Exclusion of person convicted of serious crime,
ET §5-105.
Probate.
Administrative probate.
General provisions, ET §§5-301 to 5-304.
See WILLS.
Judicial probate.
General provisions, ET §§5-401 to 5-407.
See WILLS.
Property.
Action for damages to property instituted before
death, ET §8-103.
After-discovered property. See within this
heading, "After-discovered property."
Assets. See within this heading, "Assets."
Disclaimer.
Settlement of decedents' estates, Estates Rule
6-412.
Uniform disclaimer property interests act, ET
§§9-201 to 9-216.
See DESCENT AND DISTRIBUTION.
Distribution of property.
Proposal for distribution, Estates Rule 6-442.
Personal property.
Disposal.
Power to dispose passes to survivor or
successor, ET §15-107.
Real property. See within this heading, "Real
property."
Subject to administration.
Defined, ET §7-601.
Publication.
Claims against nonresident decedents.
Notice by foreign personal representatives, ET
§5-504.
Notice of appointment, ET §7-103.
First personal representative, Estates Rule
6-331.
Notice to creditors, Estates Rule 6-401; ET
§7-103.1.
Opening estates.
Certificate of publication, Estates Rule 6-331.
Small estates.
Appointment.
Certificate of publication, Estates Rule 6-209.
Notice of appointment, Estates Rule 6-209.
Proceedings after publication, Estates Rule
6-211.
Ratification.
Others' acts, ET §6-105.
Real property.
Foreign personal representatives.
Order directing transfer of title, ET §5-506.
Power to dispose of real and personal property.
Passes to survivor or successor, ET §15-107.
Sales.
Commission of personal representative, ET
§7-601.
Payment of commissions, ET §7-604.
Receipts.
Accounts and accounting, Estates Rule 6-417; ET
§§7-302, 7-303.
Registers of wills.
Payment of tax by foreign personal
representatives, ET §5-504.

EXECUTORS AND ADMINISTRATORS —Cont'd
Registers of deeds.
Settlement of decedents' estates.
Debts and claims.
Notice to register of suit, Estates Rule 6-413.
Registers of wills.
Administration proceedings.
Record book kept by register of wills, ET §2-211.
Debts and claims.
Presentation of claim.
Filing with register, ET §8-104.
Defaults.
Past default of personal representative, ET
§2-208.
Fees, ET §2-206.
Filing revised and corrected documents, Estates
Rule 6-127; ET §7-105.
Opening estates.
Appointment of personal representative.
Administrative probate order.
Form, Estates Rule 6-321.
Receipts.
Payment of tax by foreign personal
representatives, ET §5-504.
Right to letters.
Exclusion, ET §5-105.
Settlement of decedents' estates.
Acceptance of papers, Estates Rule 6-108.
Amendment and correction of papers, Estates
Rule 6-127.
Appointment of personal representative.
Presence before register not required, Estates
Rule 6-131.
Disclaimer of interest in decedent's property.
Time for filing with register, Estates Rule
6-412.
Extension of time.
Request to register, Estates Rule 6-107.
Filings.
Acceptance of papers, Estates Rule 6-108.
Amendments and corrections, Estates Rule
6-127.
Form of caption of case, Estates Rule 6-121.
Judgments and decrees.
Entry by register, Estates Rule 6-171.
Legibility and durability of writings, Estates
Rule 6-121.
Orders of court.
Entry by register, Estates Rule 6-171.
Petition to caveat.
Register's notice and service, Estates Rule
6-432.
Small estates.
Appointment.
Publication of notice of appointment, Estates
Rule 6-209.
Form of register's order, Estates Rule 6-208.
Petition for administration.
Proceeding after petition, Estates Rule 6-206.
Releases.
Distribution.
Personal representative may require a verified
release from heir or legatee, ET §9-111.
Powers of personal representative, ET §7-401.
**Remainders, reversions and executory
interests.**
Powers of personal representative, ET §7-401.
Termination. See within this heading, "Letters of
administration."
Removal.
Failure to render account, Estates Rule 6-452; ET
§7-306.

EXECUTORS AND ADMINISTRATORS —Cont'd
Renunciation.
By testamentary trustee, ET §9-102.
Letters of administration.
Right to letters.
Opening estates, Estates Rule 6-314.
Small estates, Estates Rule 6-204.
Uniform disclaimer of property interests act, ET
§§9-201 to 9-216.
See DESCENT AND DISTRIBUTION.
Reporters.
Orphans' court.
Recording of proceedings, Estates Rule 6-114.
Reports.
Settlement of decedents' estates.
Information report, Estates Rule 6-404.
Resident agent.
Opening estates.
Appointment of resident agent, Estates Rule
6-315.
Small estates.
Appointment of resident agent, Estates Rule
6-205.
Resignation.
Co-personal representative, Estates Rule 6-451;
ET §6-305.
Failure to render accounts, Estates Rule 6-451;
ET §7-306.
Termination. See within this heading, "Letters of
administration."
Responsibility.
Fiduciary responsibility, ET §7-101.
Salaries.
Order of payment when assets insufficient to pay
claims in full, ET §8-105.
Sales.
Powers.
Survival, ET §15-107.
Proceeds.
Deposit of funds, ET §7-401.
Protection of person dealing with personal
representative, ET §7-404.
Real property.
Commission of personal representative, ET
§7-601.
Payment of commissions, ET §7-604.
Sanctions.
Attorneys at law.
Bad faith-unjustified proceedings, Estates Rule
6-141.
Petitions.
Signing of petitions and other papers, Estates
Rule 6-134.
Seals.
Opening estates.
Bond of personal representative.
Form, Estates Rule 6-312.
Small estates.
Letters of administration.
Validity, Estates Rule 6-207.
Securities.
Hold security in name of nominee.
Powers of personal representative, ET §7-401.
Service of process.
Opening estates.
Petition for probate.
Service of petition, Estates Rule 6-302.
Settlement of decedents' estates.
Amendments and corrections, Estates Rule
6-127.

EXECUTORS AND ADMINISTRATORS —Cont'd
Service of process —Cont'd
Settlement of decedents' estates —Cont'd
Method of service.
Generally, Estates Rule 6-125.
Written consent to personal jurisdiction, ET
§6-101.
Several personal representatives.
Appointment, ET §5-106.
Co-personal representatives.
Concurrence, ET §6-203.
Joint action.
When required, ET §§6-203, 6-305.
Resignation, Estates Rule 6-451; ET §6-305.
Surviving representative.
Powers, ET §6-204.
Third persons.
Protection of persons dealing with copersonal
representatives, ET §6-203.
Letters.
Priority among different letters, ET §6-201.
Successor personal representative.
Appointment, ET §§6-304 to 6-306.
Inventory, ET §7-205.
Powers and duties, ET §6-202.
Revised and corrected documents.
Filing, Estates Rule 6-127; ET §7-105.
Termination. See within this heading, "Letters
of administration."
Show cause order, Estates Rule 6-124.
Notice of orders.
Nonapplicability to issuance, Estates Rule
6-172.
Small estates.
Administration governed by sections 5-602
through 5-607, ET §5-601.
After-discovered property.
Generally, Estates Rule 6-212; ET §5-605.
Applicability of other provisions of article, ET
§5-607.
Appointment.
Notice of appointment.
Form, Estates Rule 6-209.
Bonds, surety.
Personal representative, ET §5-604.
Compensation.
Personal representative, ET §5-604.
Debts and claims.
Payments and distribution, Estates Rule 6-211.
Duties.
Personal representative, ET §5-604.
Family allowances, ET §5-603.
Fees.
Registers of wills, ET §5-606.
Funeral expenses, ET §5-603.
Interested persons.
List of interested persons.
Form, Estates Rule 6-202.
Notice to interested persons, Estates Rule
6-210.
Petition for administration.
List of interested persons, Estates Rules
6-201, 6-202.
Judicial probate.
Proceedings under judicial probate, Estates
Rule 6-221.
Letters of administration.
Form, Estates Rule 6-207.
Petition for administration.
Proceeding after petition, Estates Rule 6-206.

EXECUTORS AND ADMINISTRATORS —Cont'd
Small estates —Cont'd
  Letters of administration —Cont'd
    Right to letters.
      Renunciation, Estates Rule 6-204.
    Liability, ET §5-604.
    Life insurance and annuities.
      Payment of proceeds without letters of
        administration, IN §16-110.
    Opening estates.
      Conversion to small estate proceedings, Estates
        Rule 6-351.
    Personal representative.
      Consent to appointment, Estates Rule 6-203.
    Petition for administration.
      Additional documents, Estates Rule 6-201.
      Contents, ET §5-602.
      Determinations on petition, ET §5-603.
      Filing.
        By whom, ET §5-602.
      Form of petition, Estates Rule 6-201.
      Information required, ET §5-602.
      Notice.
        Objection to proceedings, ET §5-603.
      Opening estates.
        Conversion to small estate proceedings,
          Estates Rule 6-351.
      Proceeding after petition, Estates Rule 6-206;
        ET §5-603.
    Probate.
      Proceedings under judicial probate, Estates
        Rule 6-221.
    Resident agent.
      Appointment.
        Form, Estates Rule 6-205.
Special administrator.
  Allowance.
    Appeal from allowance by court, ET §7-601.
  Appointment, Estates Rule 6-454; ET §6-404.
    Order of right to letters, ET §5-104.
    Purpose of appointment, Estates Rule 6-454; ET
      §6-401.
    Termination, ET §6-404.
    When appointed, Estates Rule 6-454; ET
      §6-401.
  Bonds, surety, Estates Rule 6-454; ET §6-402.
  Commission.
    Allowance, ET §7-601.
  Compensation, ET §7-601.
  Death or disability of personal representative, ET
    §6-304.
  Defined, ET §1-101.
  Duties, Estates Rule 6-454; ET §6-403.
  Petition.
    Who may file petition, Estates Rule 6-454; ET
      §6-401.
  Powers, Estates Rule 6-454; ET §6-403.
  Qualifications, Estates Rule 6-454; ET §6-401.
  Termination of appointment.
    Grounds, ET §6-404.
Statutes.
  Settlement of decedents' estates.
    Rules of construction, Estates Rule 6-104.
Subpoenas.
  Settlement of decedents' estates.
    Administration proceedings, Estates Rule 6-161.
Subsequent administration.
  After-discovered property.
    Property discovered after estate closed, Estates
      Rule 6-422; ET §10-104.

EXECUTORS AND ADMINISTRATORS —Cont'd
Successor in interest.
  Survival of power to dispose of estate, ET §15-107.
Successor personal representative.
  Appointment, ET §§6-304 to 6-306.
    Order of priority, ET §5-104.
  Inventory, ET §7-205.
  Powers and duties, ET §6-202.
  Revised and corrected documents.
    Filing, Estates Rule 6-127; ET §7-105.
  Termination. See within this heading, "Letters of
    administration."
Taxation.
  Commissions. See within this heading,
    "Commissions."
  Federal estate tax.
    See FEDERAL ESTATE TAX.
  Inheritance tax. See within this heading,
    "Inheritance tax."
  Liability, TP §1-203.
  Payment of taxes and assessments.
    Powers of personal representative, ET §7-401.
    Retaining sums for payment, TP §1-203.
  Residence.
    Place of residence, TP §1-202.
  Settlement of decedents' estates.
    Inheritance tax.
      Foreign personal representatives.
        Application to set inheritance tax, Estates
          Rule 6-501.
        Non-probate assets, Estates Rule 6-405.
  Taxes due by the decedent.
    Order of payment when assets not sufficient to
      pay claims in full, ET §8-105.
Termination.
  Closing estates. See within this heading, "Closing
    estates."
  Letters of administration. See within this
    heading, "Letters of administration."
Time.
  Settlement of decedents' estates.
    Computation of time, Estates Rule 6-106.
    Disclaimer.
      Interest in decedent's property.
        Time for filing with register, Estates Rule
          6-412.
      Extension of time, Estates Rule 6-107.
Title.
  Foreign personal representatives.
    Order directing transfer of title to real or
      leasehold property, ET §5-506.
  Personal representative holds title for
    administration and distribution, ET §1-301.
Torts.
  Action for personal injuries instituted before
    death, ET §8-103.
  Liability of personal representative, ET §8-109.
Trusts and trustees.
  Testamentary trustee.
    Renunciation by, ET §9-102.
Uniform disclaimer of property interests act.
  Descent and distribution, ET §§9-201 to 9-216.
    See DESCENT AND DISTRIBUTION.
Unsatisfied claim and judgment fund.
  Claims against fund.
    Presentation, ET §8-104.
Validation.
  Acts prior to grant of letters, ET §6-105.
  Copersonal representatives.
    When joint action required, ET §6-203.

EXECUTORS AND ADMINISTRATORS —Cont'd
Validation —Cont'd
Several personal representatives.
Acts of personal representatives subsequently
appointed, ET §6-201.
Venue.
Administration, Estates Rule 6-111; ET §5-103.
Settlement of decedents' estates.
Rules of construction, Estates Rule 6-104.
Verification.
Settlement of decedents' estates.
Documents, Estates Rule 6-123.
Wages.
Payment.
Order of payment when assets insufficient to
pay claims in full, ET §8-105.
Waiver.
Bonds, surety, ET §6-102.
Opening estates.
Waiver of bond.
Form, Estates Rule 6-312.
Settlement of decedents' estates.
Notices, Estates Rule 6-126.
Wills.
General provisions, ET §§4-101 to 4-512.
See WILLS.
Petition for probate.
Requests respecting personal representative, ET
§5-205.
Powers.
Incorporation by reference, ET §4-107.
Settlement of decedents' estates.
Filing of will, Estates Rule 6-151.
Proof of execution of will, Estates Rule 6-152.
Witnesses.
Settlement of decedents' estates.
Orphans' court.
Subpoenas, Estates Rule 6-161.

EXECUTORY INTERESTS.
See REMAINDERS, REVERSIONS AND
EXECUTORY INTERESTS.

EXEMPTIONS.
Executions.
See EXECUTIONS.
Homestead exemptions.
Bankruptcy, CJ §11-504.
Distress for rent, RP §§8-306, 8-307.
Executions generally, CivProCir Rule 2-643;
CivProDist Rule 3-643; CJ §11-504.
Medicaid.
Spousal homestead protection, HG §15-122.
Income tax.
See INCOME TAX.
Inheritance tax.
See INHERITANCE TAX.
Life insurance and annuities.
Proceeds exempt from creditors, IN §16-111.
Property taxes.
General provisions, TP §§7-101 to 7-513.
See PROPERTY TAXES.
Taxation.
General provisions.
See TAXATION.

EXERCISE FACILITIES.
Steroids and human growth hormone.
Warning of consequences of illegal use, posting,
CR §5-710.

EXERTING CONTROL OVER PROPERTY.
Theft.
Generally, CR §§7-101 to 7-110.
See THEFT.

EX-FELONS.
Long-term employment of qualified ex-felons.
Pilot program, LE §§11-701 to 11-705.
Application to be designated, LE §11-703.
Created, LE §11-702.
Definitions, LE §11-701.
Designation, LE §11-703.
Duties of department, LE §11-702.
Fidelity bonds provided to business entities, LE
§11-702.
Implementation in workforce investment areas,
LE §11-702.
One-stop center, LE §11-702.
Application to be designated, LE §11-703.
Defined, LE §11-701.
Purpose, LE §11-702.
Qualified ex-felon employee defined, LE §11-701.
Regulation, LE §11-705.
Tax credit for business hiring through program,
LE §11-704.
Termination, LE §11-702.
Tax credit for wages paid, TG §10-704.10.

EXHAUST PIPES, TR §§22-402 to 22-402.2,
22-609.
See MOTOR VEHICLE EQUIPMENT.

EXHIBITORS.
Trader licenses.
General provisions, BR §§17-1801 to 17-1816.
See TRADERS.

EXHIBITS.
Circuit court trials, CivProCir Rule 2-516.
District Court trials, CivProDist Rule 3-516.
Jury trial, Crim Rule 4-322.
Motions, CivProDist Rule 3-311.

EXIT SIGNS.
Illuminated exit signs.
Efficiency standards, SG §9-2006.

EXONERATION.
General provisions.
See CONTRIBUTION AND EXONERATION.

EXOTIC BIRDS, HG §§24-101 to 24-110.
See BIRDS AND GAME.

EXOTIC DANCING.
Baltimore county.
Alcoholic beverages.
Adult entertainment prohibited at places
serving, 2B §12-204.

EXPENDITURES.
See DISBURSEMENTS AND EXPENDITURES.

EXPERT WITNESSES.
Court appointed experts, Evid Rule 5-706.
Depositions.
Use of depositions.
Circuit courts, CivProCir Rule 2-419.
Videotape deposition of expert.
Use of depositions.
Circuit courts, CivProCir Rule 2-419.
Discovery.
Reports of experts.
Disclosure upon request.
Criminal rules, Crim Rule 4-263.
Discovery by state, Crim Rule 4-263.
Trial preparation.
Scope of discovery.
Circuit courts, CivProCir Rule 2-402.

EXPERT WITNESSES —Cont'd
Malpractice.
Health care malpractice claims.
Certificate of qualified expert.
Filing, CJ §3-2A-04.
Supplemental certificate, CJ §3-2A-06D.
Qualifications, requirements, CJ §3-2A-02.
Professional malpractice.
Certificate of qualified expert, CJ §§3-2C-01,
3-2C-02.
Opinion testimony, Evid Rule 5-702.
Bases of opinion testimony by experts, Evid Rule
5-703.
Court appointed experts, Evid Rule 5-706.
Disclosure of facts or data underlying expert
opinion, Evid Rule 5-705.
Ultimate issue, Evid Rule 5-704.
Psychologists, CJ §9-120.

EXPLOSIONS AND EXPLOSIVES, PS §§11-101
to 11-118.
Applicability, PS §11-102.
Blaster's permits.
Applications, PS §11-106.
Criminal history records checks, PS §11-106.
Denial of application, PS §11-107.
Issuance, PS §11-107.
Workers' compensation.
Certificate of compliance, PS §11-107.
Blasting.
Strip mining.
Prerequisites, EN §15-525.
Boilers and pressure vessels.
Inspections, PS §12-909.
Burden of proof, PS §11-118.
**Burglary with explosives or destructive
device,** CR §6-207.
Criminal history records checks.
Licenses and permits, PS §11-106.
Defined terms, PS §11-101; TR §11-119.
Destructive devices, CR §§4-501 to 4-503.
Arrest without a warrant.
Fire marshal's authority, CP §2-208.
Burglary with explosives or destructive device, CR
§6-207.
Definitions, CR §4-501.
Exceptions to subtitle, CR §4-502.
False statement or rumor, CR §9-504.
Manufacture or possession prohibited, CR §4-503.
Representation of destructive device.
Manufacturing, possessing or transporting, CR
§9-505.
Restitution ordered for violation, CR §4-503.
Scope of subtitle, CR §4-502.
Warrantless arrest.
Fire marshal's authority, CP §2-208.
Dynamiting.
Fish and fisheries.
Use prohibited, NR §4-503.
Emergency management, PS §§14-101 to 14-1004.
See EMERGENCY MANAGEMENT.
Fees.
Fire marshal, PS §11-104.
Licenses, PS §11-106.
Fines.
Dynamiting.
Birds and game, NR §4-503.
License or other violations, PS §11-114.
Additional penalties, PS §11-116.
Merger of convictions, PS §11-117.

EXPLOSIONS AND EXPLOSIVES —Cont'd
Firearms.
Explosives for use in firearms.
License to possess, PS §11-105.
Penalties for violations, PS §11-115.
Fire hazards.
Maintenance of fire hazard prohibited, PS §6-317.
Fire marshal.
Powers, PS §11-104.
Revocation of licenses, PS §11-111.
Theft of explosives, PS §11-113.
Fire prevention commission.
Regulations, authority to adopt, PS §11-103.
Fireworks, PS §§10-101 to 10-210.
See FIREWORKS.
Forfeiture of vehicle for violations, CP §13-301.
Gas and oil.
Seismic operations.
Definition of explosives, EN §14-109.
Use of explosives, EN §14-109.
General assembly.
Bringing explosives or incendiary devices into
senate or house chambers, SG §2-1702.
Investigations.
Fire marshal's powers, PS §§6-309, 11-104.
Labor and employment relations.
Employees of businesses that use explosives.
Sale, distribution and use of explosives, PS
§11-110.
Liability insurance.
Licenses.
Proof of, PS §11-106.
Licenses, PS §§11-101 to 11-118.
Applications, PS §11-106.
Denial of application, PS §11-107.
Burden of proof, PS §11-118.
Criminal history records checks, PS §11-106.
Dealer's license, PS §11-105.
Scope of license, PS §11-108.
Defined terms, PS §11-101.
Denial of application, PS §11-107.
Employees of businesses that use explosives.
Sale, distribution and use of explosives, PS
§11-110.
Fees, PS §11-106.
Information required, PS §11-106.
Issuance, PS §11-107.
Liability insurance.
Proof of, PS §11-106.
License to possess, PS §11-105.
Manufacturer's license, PS §11-105.
Notice of issuance, PS §11-107.
Penalty for violations, PS §11-114.
Additional penalties, PS §11-116.
Explosives for use in firearms, PS §11-115.
Merger of convictions, PS §11-117.
Records and reports, PS §11-112.
Theft of explosives, PS §11-113.
Required, PS §11-105.
Revocation, PS §11-111.
Scope of subtitle, PS §11-102.
Term of license, PS §11-109.
Unlicensed practice, PS §11-114.
Workers' compensation.
Certificate of compliance, PS §11-107.
Maryland Transit Administration.
Carrying or possessing on transit vehicles or
facilities, TR §7-705.
Mining.
Strip mining.
Prerequisites for blasting, EN §15-525.

EXPLOSIONS AND EXPLOSIVES —Cont'd
Motor vehicles.
Forfeiture of vehicle for violations, CP §13-301.
Railroad grade crossings.
Vehicles carrying explosives must stop, TR §21-703.
Vehicles transporting.
Carrying flares or other warning devices, TR §22-407.
Warning devices.
Placing of warning signals where disabled vehicle is used in transporting, TR §22-408.
Motor vehicle size, weight, etc.
Transport of explosives and munitions.
Length of semitrailer, TR §24-104.1.
Municipal corporations.
Regulations, 23A §2.
Penalties for violations, PS §11-114.
Additional penalties, PS §11-116.
Explosives for use in firearms, PS §11-115.
Forfeiture of vehicle, CP §13-301.
Merger of convictions, PS §11-117.
Permits.
Blaster's permits.
Applications, PS §11-106.
Criminal history records checks, PS §11-106.
Denial of application, PS §11-107.
Issuance, PS §11-107.
Workers' compensation.
Certificate of compliance, PS §11-107.
Possession.
License to possess, PS §11-105.
Information required, PS §11-106.
Possession without a license, PS §11-114.
Additional penalties, PS §11-116.
Prohibited acts, PS §11-114.
Additional penalties, PS §11-116.
Explosives for use in firearms, PS §11-115.
Merger of convictions, PS §11-117.
Records.
Manufacturers and dealers, PS §11-112.
Reports.
Explosives for use in firearms.
Failure to file, PS §11-115.
Investigations of explosions and fires, PS §11-104.
Manufacturers and dealers, PS §11-112.
Theft of explosives, PS §11-113.
Right of entry.
Fire marshal.
Investigations of explosions and fires, PS §11-104.
Rules and regulations.
Authority to adopt, PS §11-103.
Revocation of licenses, PS §11-111.
Safety signals.
Applicability, PS §11-102.
Sales.
Employees of businesses that use explosives, PS §11-110.
Explosives for use in firearms.
Penalties for violations, PS §11-115.
Sales to unlicensed persons, PS §11-114.
Scope of subtitle, PS §11-102.
Strip mining.
Prerequisites for blasting, EN §15-525.
Theft of explosives.
Reports, PS §11-113.
Transportation, PS §11-102.
Unlicensed sale or possession, PS §11-114.
Workers' compensation.
Licenses.
Certificate of compliance, PS §11-107.

EX POST FACTO LAWS.
Constitution of the United States, US Const Art I §§9, 10.
Prohibited, MD Const DofR Art 17.

EXPOSURE TO DEADLY AGENTS.
Catastrophic health emergency.
Governor's power to proclaim, PS §§14-3A-01 to 14-3A-08.
See HEALTH EMERGENCIES.

EXPRESS POWERS ACT.
Chartered counties, 25A §§1 to 8.
See COUNTIES.

EXPRESS WARRANTIES.
Leases, UCC, CL §2A-210.
Third-party beneficiaries, CL §2A-216.
Sale of goods, UCC, CL §2-313.
Cumulation and conflict, CL §2-314.
Exclusions, CL §§2-316, 2-316.1.
Modification, CL §§2-316, 2-316.1.
Third-party beneficiaries, CL §2-318.

EXPRESSWAYS.
Defined, TR §21-101.
Highways generally.
See HIGHWAYS.
Outdoor advertising, TR §§8-739 to 8-745.

EXPULSION OF STUDENTS, ED §7-305.

EXPUNGEMENT OF RECORDS.
Access to court records.
Denial of inspection, expunged records, CJA Rule 16-1006.
Child abuse and neglect.
Records and reports made in accordance with subtitle, FL §5-707.
Criminal records, CP §§10-101 to 10-109.
Amendments.
Applications, petitions or answers, Crim Rule 4-506.
Appeals.
Expungement of record after charge filed, CP §10-105.
How taken, Crim Rule 4-509.
Stay of order pending appeal, Crim Rule 4-509.
Applicability of provisions, CP §10-102; Crim Rule 4-501.
Applications.
Defined, Crim Rule 4-502.
No charge filed.
Amendment, Crim Rule 4-506.
Answer, Crim Rule 4-505.
Contents, Crim Rule 4-505.
Effect of failure to answer, Crim Rule 4-505.
Contents, Crim Rule 4-503.
Copies for service, Crim Rule 4-503.
Form for application for expungement of police record, Form 4-503.3.
Hearing, Crim Rule 4-507.
Procedure upon filing application, Crim Rule 4-503.
Scope, Crim Rule 4-503.
Time for filing, Crim Rule 4-503.
Venue, Crim Rule 4-503.
Birds, game and inland water fish, NR §4-1208.
Case files.
Procedures for expungement, Crim Rule 4-511.
Certificate of compliance.
Form, Form 4-508.3.

EXPUNGEMENT OF RECORDS —Cont'd
Criminal records —Cont'd
Construction and interpretation.
Applicability of provisions, Crim Rule 4-501.
Copies.
Applications.
No charges filed, Crim Rule 4-503.
Petitions.
Charges filed, Crim Rule 4-504.
Court records.
Defined, Crim Rule 4-502.
Courts.
Defined, Crim Rule 4-502.
Definitions, CP §10-101; Crim Rule 4-502.
Destruction by shredding.
Schedule, Crim Rule 4-512.
Disclosure of expunged records, CP §§10-108, 10-109.
Disposition of expunged records, Crim Rule 4-512.
Dispositions of charges that create right to file, CP §10-105.
Dockets.
Bound volume.
Procedures for expungement, Crim Rule 4-511.
Case file jacket.
Procedures for expungement, Crim Rule 4-511.
Microfilmed dockets, indices and case files.
Procedures for expungement, Crim Rule 4-511.
Drivers' licenses, TR §16-117.1.
Exclusions from provisions, CP §10-102.
Filing.
Applications.
No charges filed, Crim Rule 4-503.
Petitions.
Charges filed, Crim Rule 4-504.
Fish and fisheries, NR §4-1208.
Form.
Order for expungement of records, Forms 4-508.1, 4-508.2.
Forms.
Application for expungement of police record, Form 4-503.3.
Certificate of compliance, Form 4-508.3.
General waiver and release, Form 4-503.2.
Notice of hearing, Form 4-503.4.
Notice of release from detention or confinement without charge.
Request for expungement, Form 4-503.1.
Petition for expungement of records, Form 4-504.1.
Criminal charge transferred to juvenile court, Juv Rule 11-601.
Probation or stet disposition, Form 4-504.2.
Service of order and compliance form, Crim Rule 4-508.
Hearings, Crim Rule 4-507.
Charges filed, CP §10-105.
Notice of hearing.
Form, Form 4-503.4.
Indexes.
Bound volume.
Procedures for expungement, Crim Rule 4-511.
Case file jacket.
Procedures for expungement, Crim Rule 4-511.
Disposition of expunged records, Crim Rule 4-512.

EXPUNGEMENT OF RECORDS —Cont'd
Criminal records —Cont'd
Indexes —Cont'd
Microfilmed dockets, indices and case files.
Procedures for expungement, Crim Rule 4-511.
Judgments.
Finality of order of court for expungement, Crim Rule 4-508.
Juvenile causes, CJ §3-8A-27.
Juvenile causes, CJ §3-8A-27.
Criminal charge transferred to juvenile court, CP §10-106.
Procedure and form, Juv Rule 11-601.
Law enforcement agencies.
Defined, Crim Rule 4-502.
Motor vehicles.
Certain driving records expunged, TR §16-117.1.
Nolle prosequi.
Expungement of records on before service, CP §10-104.
Notice.
Charges filed.
Notice of compliance, CP §10-105.
Defined, Crim Rule 4-502.
Expungement of police record when no charge filed, CP §10-103.
General waivers and releases.
Disposition of expunged records, Crim Rule 4-512.
Hearings.
Form for notice, Form 4-503.4.
Release from detention or confinement without charge.
Forms, Form 4-503.1.
Right to file to have records expunged, CP §6-232.
Opening expunged records, CP §10-108.
Orders.
Compliance with court order for expungement, Crim Rule 4-510.
Content of order for expungement of records, Crim Rule 4-508.
Ex parte order allowing access to expunged record, CP §§10-108, 10-109.
Expungement of police record when no charge filed, CP §10-103.
Finality, Crim Rule 4-508.
Form, Forms 4-508.1, 4-508.2.
Service of order and compliance form, Crim Rule 4-508.
Stay pending appeal, Crim Rule 4-509.
Oysters and clams, NR §4-1208.
Pardons.
Petition for expungement of records.
Form, Form 4-504.3.
Petitions.
Charges filed, CP §10-105.
Amendment, Crim Rule 4-506.
Answer, Crim Rule 4-505.
Contents, Crim Rule 4-505.
Effect of failure to answer, Crim Rule 4-505.
Contents, Crim Rule 4-504.
Copies for service, Crim Rule 4-504.
Hearing, Crim Rule 4-507.
Procedure upon filing petition, Crim Rule 4-504.
Retrieval or reconstruction of case file, Crim Rule 4-504.
Scope, Crim Rule 4-504.

EXPUNGEMENT OF RECORDS —Cont'd
Criminal records —Cont'd
Petitions —Cont'd
Charges filed —Cont'd
Time for filing petition, Crim Rule 4-504.
Venue, Crim Rule 4-504.
Criminal charge transferred to juvenile court,
Juv Rule 11-601.
Defined, Crim Rule 4-502.
Forms, Forms 4-504.1, 4-504.3.
Criminal charge transferred to juvenile court,
Juv Rule 11-601.
Probation or stet disposition, Form 4-504.2.
Police records.
Charge filed, CP §10-105.
Defined, Crim Rule 4-502.
No charge filed, CP §10-103.
Nolle prosequi entered prior to service, CP
§10-104.
Probation.
Petition for expungement of records, Form
4-504.2.
Probation on stay of entry of judgment.
Defined, Crim Rule 4-502.
Procedures for expungement.
Generally, Crim Rule 4-511.
Prohibited acts, CP §§10-108, 10-109.
Records.
Defined, Crim Rule 4-502.
Removal.
Disposition of expunged records, Crim Rule
4-512.
Retention of expunged records.
Minimum period.
Disposition, Crim Rule 4-512.
Same incident, transaction, or set of facts.
Charges arising from, CP §10-107.
Schedule for destruction, Crim Rule 4-512.
Seals.
Expunged records, Crim Rule 4-512.
Unsealing, Crim Rule 4-512.
Service of process.
Applications.
No charges filed.
Copies for service, Crim Rule 4-503.
Defined, Crim Rule 4-502.
Order and compliance form, Crim Rule 4-508.
Petitions.
Charges filed.
Copies for service, Crim Rule 4-504.
Shredding.
Destruction by shredding.
Schedule, Crim Rule 4-512.
Storage in denied access area on premises.
Transfer prohibited, Crim Rule 4-512.
Time.
Applications.
No charges filed.
Time for filing, Crim Rule 4-503.
Petitions.
Charges filed.
Time for filing, Crim Rule 4-504.
Transfer.
Defined, Crim Rule 4-502.
Prohibition on transfer.
Disposition of expunged records, Crim Rule
4-512.
Venue.
Applications.
No charges filed, Crim Rule 4-503.

EXPUNGEMENT OF RECORDS —Cont'd
Criminal records —Cont'd
Venue —Cont'd
Petitions.
Charges filed, Crim Rule 4-504.
Waiver.
General waiver and release.
Disposition of expunged records, Crim Rule
4-512.
Form, Form 4-503.2.
DNA database system, PS §2-511.
Husband and wife.
Criminal procedure.
Refusal to testify on basis that not compelled to
testify against spouse.
Record of assertion, CJ §9-106.
Law enforcement officers and personnel.
Formal complaints, when expunged, PS §3-110.

EXTENSION CORDS.
Labeling electrical products, CL §§13-308,
13-309.

EXTORTION, CR §§3-701 to 3-707.
By false accusation, CR §3-704.
**By state or local government officer or
employee,** CR §3-702.
Inducing another to give up compensation, CR
§3-703.
By verbal threat, CR §3-705.
By written threat, CR §3-706.
Contributions or donations.
Coercing or intimidating another to make, CR
§3-707.
Generally, CR §3-701.
Property of five hundred dollars or more.
Penalty, CR §§3-701, 3-702.
Property of less than five hundred dollars.
Penalty, CR §§3-701, 3-702.
Statute of limitation on prosecution, CR §3-701.
By state or local government officer or employee,
CR §3-702.
Inducing another to give up compensation, CR
§3-703.
Wages, hours or working conditions.
Provisions inapplicable to employees seeking to
obtain, CR §3-701.

EXTRADITION.
Accused held in another state, CP §9-105.
Accused held in this state, CP §9-105.
Appeals.
Denial of habeas corpus, CP §9-110.
Arrest.
Arrest before requisition, CP §9-113.
Arrest without warrant, CP §9-114.
Authority of arresting officer, CP §9-109.
Rights of person arrested, CP §9-110.
Temporary custody of prisoner arrested, CP
§9-112.
Warrant of arrest, CP §9-107.
Arrest before requisition, CP §9-113.
Authority of arresting officer under, CP §9-109.
Execution, CP §9-108.
Recall of warrant, CP §9-121.
Asylum.
No right of asylum, CP §9-126.
Bail and recognizance, CP §9-115.
Bond, CP §9-116.
Discharge, recommitment, or renewal of bail, CP
§9-117.
Forfeiture of bail, CP §9-118.

EXTRADITION —Cont'd
Commitment to await requisition, CP §9-115.
Confinement in correctional facility, CP §9-112.
Constitution of the United States, US Const Art IV §2.
Construction and interpretation.
Uniform criminal extradition act, CP §9-127.
Definitions, CP §9-101.
Detainers.
Interstate agreement on detainers, COR §§8-401 to 8-417.
See INTERSTATE AGREEMENT ON DETAINERS.
Fugitive from justice.
Constitutional provisions, US Const Art IV §2.
Fugitives from another state.
Demand, CP §9-103.
Investigation when demand made, CP §9-104.
Duties of governor, CP §9-102.
Fugitives from this state.
Application for requisition, CP §9-123.
Duties of governor, CP §9-122.
Governor.
Fugitives from another state.
Duties, CP §9-102.
Investigation called for by governor, CP §9-104.
Fugitives from this state.
Duties, CP §9-122.
Warrant of arrest, CP §§9-107 to 9-109.
Recall of warrant, CP §9-121.
Guilt or innocence of accused.
Inquiry into prohibited, CP §9-120.
Habeas corpus.
Application for writ, CP §9-110.
Habeas corpus ad prosequendum.
District Court judges.
Authority of judges to issue writ, CJ §1-609.
Immunity from other criminal prosecutions within state.
No immunity, CP §9-126.
Inquiry into guilt or innocence of accused.
Prohibited, CP §9-120.
Interpretation and construction.
Uniform criminal extradition act, CP §9-127.
Investigation.
Governor may call for investigation, CP §9-104.
Mentally ill, HG §§10-1301 to 10-1306.
Noncompliance with delivery procedures, CP §9-111.
Persons imprisoned or awaiting trial in another state, CP §9-105.
Persons not present in demanding state at time of commission of crime, CP §9-106.
Persons under criminal prosecution in this state at time of requisition, CP §9-119.
Rights of accused person, CP §9-110.
Noncompliance with, CP §9-111.
Temporary custody of prisoner, CP §9-112.
Uniform criminal extradition act.
Construction and interpretation, CP §9-127.
General provisions, CP §§9-101 to 9-128.
Short title, CP §9-128.
Waiver.
Interstate agreement on detainers.
Request for final disposition by prisoner constitutes, COR §8-405.
Waiver of extradition proceedings, CP §9-124.
No waiver by this state, CP §9-125.
Warrant of arrest, CP §9-107.
Arrest before requisition, CP §9-113.
Authority of arresting officer under, CP §9-109.

EXTRADITION —Cont'd
Warrant of arrest —Cont'd
Execution, CP §9-108.
Recall of warrant, CP §9-121.

EXTRADITION OF PERSONS OF UNSOUND MIND, HG §§10-1301 to 10-1306.
Definitions, HG §10-1301.
Interpretation and construction, HG §10-1305.
Limitation of actions, HG §10-1304.
Procedures, HG §10-1303.
Scope, HG §10-1302.
Short title, HG §10-1306.

EXTRAORDINARY REMEDIES.
Habeas corpus.
See HABEAS CORPUS.
Injunctions.
See INJUNCTIONS.
Mandamus.
See MANDAMUS.
Quo warranto.
See QUO WARRANTO.

EXTRINSIC EVIDENCE.
Leases, UCC, CL §2A-202.
Sale of goods, UCC, CL §2-202.

EYEGLASSES.
Safety requirements for eyeglass and sunglass lenses and frames, HG §24-301.

EYES.
Anatomical gift act.
Corneas.
When chief medical examiner or his deputy or assistant may provide cornea for transplant, ET §4-509.1.
Corneas.
When chief medical examiner or his deputy or assistant may provide cornea for transplant, ET §4-509.1.
Motor vehicles.
Drivers' licenses.
Vision requirements, TR §16-110.1.
Bioptic telescopic lenses, TR §16-110.2.
Daylight driving only and outside mirrors each side restricted licenses, TR §16-110.3.
Tests of vision.
Renewal of license, TR §16-115.
Optometrists.
See OPTOMETRISTS.
Schools.
Protective eye devices.
Use in certain courses, ED §7-407.
Vocational education.
Protective eye devices.
Vocational shops or laboratories, ED §7-407.

F

FACSIMILE SIGNATURES AND SEALS.
Authorized officers.
Defined, SF §2-301.
Use of facsimile signatures, SF §2-303.
Citation of act.
Short title, SF §2-306.
Corporations.
Documents filed for record by means of, CA §1-201.
Definitions, SF §2-301.

FACSIMILE SIGNATURES AND SEALS —Cont'd
Effect.
Legal effect.
Facsimile seals, SF §2-304.
Facsimile signatures, SF §2-303.
Felony.
Prohibited acts, SF §2-305.
Instruments of payment.
Defined, SF §2-301.
Interpretation and construction, SF §2-302.
Legal effect.
Facsimile seals, SF §2-304.
Facsimile signatures, SF §2-303.
Partnerships.
Limited partnerships.
Documents filed for record by means of, CA §1-201.
Penalties.
Prohibited acts, SF §2-305.
Prohibited acts, SF §2-305.
Securities.
Public securities.
Defined, SF §2-301.
Short title of act, SF §2-306.
Use.
Facsimile seal, SF §2-304.
Facsimile signatures, SF §2-303.
Prohibited acts, SF §2-305.

FACSIMILE TRANSMISSIONS.
Banks and trust companies.
Return of checks to customer, FI §5-513.
Elections.
Electronic filing of documents, EL §1-302.
Unsolicited transmissions, CL §14-1313.

FACTORS.
Agency.
See AGENCY.
Consignment.
General provisions.
See CONSIGNMENT.

FAILURE TO DELIVER DOCUMENTS FOR MERCHANDISE, CR §7-116.

FAILURE TO RETURN RENTAL VEHICLE, CR §7-205.

FAIR CAMPAIGN FINANCING FUND, EL §15-103.
Public campaign financing generally, EL §§15-101 to 15-111.
See CAMPAIGN FINANCE.

FAIR DISTRIBUTORSHIP ACT, CL §§11-1301 to 11-1306.
Agreement.
Applicability of state law, CL §11-1307.
Defined, CL §11-1301.
Applicability of state law, CL §11-1307.
Applicability of subtitle, CL §11-1302.
Arbitration, CL §11-1306.
Cancel.
Defined, CL §11-1301.
Commercial goods.
Defined, CL §11-1301.
De facto cancellation.
Defined, CL §11-1301.
Definitions, CL §11-1301.
Grantor's notification to distributor, CL §11-1303.
Alteration of terms, CL §11-1303.

FAIR DISTRIBUTORSHIP ACT —Cont'd
Grantor's notification to distributor —Cont'd
Deficiencies in notice, CL §11-1305.
"Deficiency" defined, CL §11-1301.
Failure of grantor to comply, CL §11-1302.1.
Notice and cure provisions.
Applicability, CL §11-1303.
Requirements, CL §11-1303.
When compliance not required, CL §11-1303.
Inapplicability of subtitle, CL §11-1302.
Opportunity to cure or dispute asserted deficiencies.
Grantor's notification to distributor, CL §11-1302.1.
Right of repurchase, CL §11-1304.

FAIR HILL.
Horse racing, BR §§11-701 to 11-704.
See HORSE RACING.
Improvement fund, NR §5-908.

FAIRS.
Agricultural fair board, AG §§10-301 to 10-303.
See AGRICULTURE.
Amusements and recreation.
General provisions, BR §§3-101 to 3-601.
See AMUSEMENTS AND RECREATION.
Prince George's county.
Benefit performance by qualified organization, CR §§13-1901 to 13-1907.

FAIR SHARE HEALTH CARE FUND, HG §15-142.

FAIR TRADE ACT.
Sales below cost act, CL §§11-401 to 11-406.
See SALES.

FAITH HEALING.
Child abuse and neglect.
Nonmedical religious remedial care and treatment recognized by state law.
Abuse and neglect not to include, FL §5-701.

FAKED CONTROLLED SUBSTANCES.
Distributing, CR §5-617.

FAKE ID.
Identity fraud, CR §§8-301 to 8-305.

FALCONS.
Hunting with, NR §10-907.

FALL-OUT SHELTERS.
Home improvement law.
General provisions, BR §§8-101 to 8-702.
See HOME IMPROVEMENTS.

FALSE ACCUSATION.
Extortion by, CR §3-704.

FALSE ADVERTISING.
See ADVERTISING.

FALSE ALARMS, CR §9-604.
Activation of alarm system, CR §9-608.
Defective system, notice to user, use after notice, CR §9-610.
Definitions, CR §9-607.
Multiple false of alarms, CR §9-609.
Nonemergency activation of signal, CR §9-608.
Destructive device or toxic material.
False statement or rumor concerning, CR §9-504.
Frederick county.
Providing civil citations and penalties for, 25 §221A.
Warrantless arrest, CP §2-203.

FALSE IDENTITY.
Alcoholic beverages.
Misrepresentation of age.
    False documentation, CR §10-115.
Horse racing.
Racing horse under false name, CR §8-904.
Identity fraud, CR §§8-301 to 8-305.

FALSE IMPERSONATIONS.
Ambulances.
Impersonating firefighters or emergency services
    personnel, PS §7-402.
Controlled dangerous substances.
Obtaining by falsely assuming title of authorized
    provider or dispenser, CR §5-601.
Emergency medical care and services.
Impersonating firefighters or emergency services
    personnel, PS §7-402.
Engineers.
Impersonating professional engineer prohibited,
    BOP §14-503.
Fire department.
Impersonating firefighters or emergency services
    personnel, PS §7-402.
Fire marshal or employee, PS §6-602.
Fraternal, military or patriotic organization
    member, BR §19-207.
Homebuilder registration, BR §4.5-501.
Insignia and emblems.
Unauthorized wearing.
    See INSIGNIA AND EMBLEMS.
Law enforcement officers and personnel.
Impersonating a police officer, PS §3-502.
Natural resources.
Police force.
    Impersonation of officer, NR §1-207.
Police.
Impersonating a police officer, PS §3-502.
Natural resources police force.
    Impersonation of officer, NR §1-207.
Rescue squads.
Impersonating firefighters or emergency services
    personnel, PS §7-402.
State personnel.
Examination of applicants, SPP §§15-101, 15-201.
Surveys and surveyors.
Impersonating licensee prohibited, BOP §15-605.
Voter registration.
Impersonation in order to register, EL §16-101.
Voting.
Impersonating another in order to vote, EL
    §16-201.
Weights and measures.
Impersonation of officer.
    Prohibited, AG §11-208.
        Civil penalties, AG §11-208.1.

FALSE PRETENSES AND FALSE
    STATEMENTS.
Alcoholic beverages.
Misrepresentation of age, CR §10-113.
    False documentation, CR §10-115.
Athlete agents.
Contracts, BR §4-413.
Business regulation and licensure.
False swearing under oath, BR §1-202.
Charging documents.
Crimes involving instruments, CP §4-108.
Common law criminal defamation.
Repealed, CR §9-507.
Community development administration.
False statements or reports, HS §4-255.

FALSE PRETENSES AND FALSE
    STATEMENTS —Cont'd
Controlled dangerous substances.
Obtaining, CR §5-601.
Credit card crimes.
False statements as to identity to procure, CR
    §8-203.
Generally, CR §§8-201 to 8-217.
    See CREDIT CARDS.
Obtaining property by counterfeiting, theft or
    misrepresentation, CR §8-206.
Credit cards.
General provisions.
    See CREDIT CARDS.
Down payment and settlement expense loan
    program.
False statements or reports, HS §4-309.
Drivers of motor vehicles.
Giving false name to officer, TR §16-112.
False statement or report as to crime or
    hazard, CR §9-503.
False statement or rumor as to destructive
    device or toxic material, CR §9-504.
False statement, report or complaint to law
    enforcement officer, CR §9-501.
When person under arrest, CR §9-502.
Firearms.
Applications for firearm purchase or dealer's
    license, PS §5-139.
Fraternal benefit societies.
Misrepresentation as to condition of society or
    insurance contracts, IN §8-468.
Fraudulent conveyances.
General provisions, CL §§15-201 to 15-214.
    See FRAUDULENT CONVEYANCES.
Group home financing program.
False statements or reports, HS §4-612.
Health insurance.
Misrepresentations in applications, IN §12-207.
Historical and cultural museum assistance
    program.
False statements or reports, SF §5A-359.
Housing and community development.
Assisted housing preservation.
    False statements or reports, HS §7-404.
Neighborhood business development program.
    False statement or reports, HS §6-311.
Housing assistance fraud, CR §8-523.
Indian affairs commission.
False statements or representations, 41 §6-912.
Insurance, IN §§27-202 to 27-205.
Fraudulent claims, statements, etc., IN §§27-403,
    27-406.
Life and health insurance or annuities.
    Misrepresentations in applications, IN §12-207.
Nonprofit health service plans, IN §14-140.
Rate making, IN §11-231.
    Competitive rating, IN §11-343.
    Title insurance, IN §11-408.
Twisting, IN §27-213.
Unauthorized insurers, IN §§27-701 to 27-706.
Intent to defraud.
Proving, CR §1-401.
Lead hazard reduction grant and loan
    programs, HS §4-712.
Life insurance and annuities.
Misrepresentations in applications, IN §12-207.
Maryland higher education commission fund
    application.
False or concealed material fact, CR §9-506.

FALSE PRETENSES AND FALSE STATEMENTS —Cont'd

Maryland historical trust.
Historical and cultural museum assistance program.
False statements or reports, SF §5A-359.

Maryland home financing program.
False statements or reports, HS §4-816.

Maryland housing rehabilitation program.
False statements or reports, HS §4-933.

Medicaid fraud, CR §§8-508 to 8-517.

Minors.
Aid to families with dependent children.
Application.
Statements punishable as perjury, 88A §62.

Motor vehicles.
Accident reports.
False report, TR §20-108.
Certificate of title.
Applications, TR §13-704.
Drivers' licenses.
Unlawful use of license, TR §16-301.
Giving false name to officer.
Drivers, TR §16-112.
Refusing registration.
Grounds, TR §13-406.

Museums.
Historical and cultural museum assistance program.
False statements or reports, SF §5A-359.

Neighborhood revitalization division.
Neighborhood business development program.
False statement or reports, HS §6-311.

Nonprofit health service plans, IN §14-140.

Partnership rental housing program.
False statements or reports, HS §4-1209.

Penalties.
Small business development financing authority.
Guaranty fund.
False statements or reports to authority, 83A §5-1031.

Small business development financing authority.
Guaranty fund, 83A §5-1031.

Social services.
Application for assistance.
Punishable as perjury, 88A §62.
Reading of statement of what constitutes fraud.
Prerequisite to receipt of assistance, 88A §16.

Theft.
Generally, CR §§7-101 to 7-110.
See THEFT.

Trading stamp companies.
Prohibited acts, BR §13-109.

FALSE TESTIMONY.
Inducing victim or witness to give, CR §9-302.
Perjury, CR §§9-101 to 9-103.

FAMILY CAREGIVER ASSISTANCE PROGRAM.
Assistance in caring for individual with long-term care needs.
Adult dependent defined, 70B §45.
Definitions, 70B §45.
Established, 70B §45.
Family caregiver defined, 70B §45.
Funding program, 70B §45.
Grants to eligible family caregivers, 70B §45.
Individual with long term care needs defined, 70B §45.

FAMILY CAREGIVER ASSISTANCE PROGRAM —Cont'd

Assistance in caring for individual with long-term care needs —Cont'd
Purpose of program.
Grants to eligible family caregivers, 70B §45.
Regulations, adoption, 70B §45.

FAMILY DAY CARE HOMES.
Drinking water suppliers.
Contamination.
Notice to family day care homes, EN §9-410; FL §5-551.

General provisions.
See CHILD CARE.

Liability insurance, IN §§19-202, 19-203.
Condominiums, RP §11-111.1.
Homeowners, associations, RP §11-111.1.
Motor vehicle insurers, IN §19-106.

FAMILY DAY CARE PROVIDER DIRECT GRANT FUND, FL §§5-559.1 to 5-559.8.
See CHILD CARE.

FAMILY INVESTMENT PROGRAM, 88A §§44A to 56.

Amount of assistance, 88A §49.

Business entity.
Defined, 88A §54.

Cash assistance, 88A §50.
Adult or minor parent substance abuse treatment, 88A §50A.
Limitations, 88A §51.

Contracting powers of department, 88A §47.

Cooperative living project defined, 88A §44A.

Definitions, 88A §44A.

Demonstration projects, 88A §53.

Duties of secretary, 88A §46.

Eligibility, 88A §48.
Revision of rules by secretary, 88A §49.

FIP defined, 88A §44A.

FIP demonstration site, 88A §55.

Funding for program, 88A §52.

Grant diversion defined, 88A §44A.

Individualized case-management project defined, 88A §44A.

Job skills enhancement program, 88A §53A.

Local department defined, 88A §44A.

Mentoring program for former FIP recipients, 88A §56.

Nonprofit organization defined, 88A §44A.

Periodic recertification, 88A §52.

Proposals for demonstration projects, 88A §53.

Purpose of provisions, 88A §45.

Qualified child care expenses, 88A §54.

Qualified employment opportunity employee, 88A §54.

Recertification, 88A §52.

Recipient defined, 88A §44A.

Religious organization participation, 88A §47.

Requirements for eligibility, 88A §48.
Revision of rules by secretary, 88A §49.

Scope, 88A §49.

Secretary's duties, 88A §46.

Self-sufficiency of families.
Purpose of provisions, 88A §45.

Surplus funds, 88A §52.

Tax credits, 88A §54.

Telephone lifeline service.
Eligible subscribers.
Persons receiving assistance under program, PUC §8-201.

FARMS AND FARMERS —Cont'd
Anne Arundel county.
Right to farm, 24 §18-101.
Boys' and girls' club work, 25 §160.
Cooperation with department of agriculture of the United States, 25 §160.
Cooperative demonstration work.
Authority to make appropriations, 25 §160.
Corporations.
Family farms, cessation.
Filing charter amendments, CA §1-209.
Crops.
See CROPS.
Eminent domain.
Relocation assistance.
Election to accept fixed payment, RP §12-205.
Farm operation.
Defined, RP §12-201.
Farm products.
General provisions.
See AGRICULTURE.
General provisions.
See AGRICULTURE.
Group workers' compensation policies, IN §§25-201 to 25-204.
Home demonstration work, 25 §160.
Maryland agricultural land link program, AG §2-1201.
Ponds.
See PONDS.
Property taxes.
See PROPERTY TAXES.
Right to farm.
Anne Arundel county, 24 §18-101.
Small farms.
Group workers' compensation policies, IN §§25-201 to 25-204.
Taxation.
Property taxes.
See PROPERTY TAXES.

F.A.S.
Sale of goods, UCC, CL §2-319.

FATHERHOOD.
Commission on responsible fatherhood, 41 §§18-401 to 18-408.
Alternates, 41 §18-404.
Commission defined, 41 §18-401.
Composition, 41 §18-403.
Duties, 41 §18-407.
Established, 41 §18-402.
Goals, 41 §18-406.
Limitations, 41 §18-408.
Location within state government, 41 §18-402.
Meetings, 41 §18-404.
Members, 41 §18-403.
Powers, 41 §18-407.
Limitations, 41 §18-408.
Purposes, 41 §18-406.
Quorum, 41 §18-404.
Staff, 41 §18-405.
Staff director, 41 §18-405.
Parent and child generally.
See PARENT AND CHILD.
Paternity proceedings generally.
See PATERNITY PROCEEDINGS.

FAX.
Elections.
Electronic filing of documents, EL §1-302.

FAX —Cont'd
Unsolicited transmissions.
Commercial purposes.
Prohibited, CL §14-1313.

FEDERAL AID.
Adoption.
Interstate compact on adoption and medical assistance.
Applications for federal aid, FL §5-4A-08.
Aviation.
Contracts.
Law governing, TR §5-213.
State airports and facilities.
Administration as agent, TR §§5-407, 5-411.
Baltimore City Community College.
Local educational agent.
Classified as for federal subsidies, grants, etc., ED §16-503.
Birds and game.
Wildlife restoration.
Assent to public law 415, NR §10-208.
Career and technology education.
Acceptance, ED §21-202.
Community services administration.
Acceptance of federal aid, 41 §6-204.
Counties.
Acceptance of federal aid, 25 §3.
Housing.
Participation in federal lower-income housing assistance programs, 24 §6-203.
Notices, 24 §6-301.
Regional council of governments, 25 §26A.
State and federal aid, 25 §26A.
Watershed projects.
Federally assisted watershed projects.
Powers of counties, 25 §3.
Eminent domain.
Allowance for removal of personal property.
Effect of payment or reimbursement out of federal funds, RP §12-112.
Relocation assistance.
Federal financial assistance.
Defined, RP §12-201.
Environmental trust.
Grants, NR §3-207.
Fish and fisheries.
Department of natural resources.
Authority to accept and use, NR §4-205.
Flood control.
Long range program.
Cooperation with federal and local government to develop, EN §5-701.
Food and food establishments.
Schools, food programs, ED §7-602.
Surplus food, SF §2-205.
Food coupons.
General provisions.
See SOCIAL SERVICES.
Forests and parks.
Conservancy districts.
Acceptance and custody of federal appropriations, NR §5-609.
Open spaces and areas.
Program open space.
See FORESTS AND PARKS.
General assembly.
Power to receive, administer and distribute grants from United States, MD Const Art III §46.

FEDERAL AID —Cont'd
Handicapped persons.
Facilities for the handicapped.
Ramps or curb cuts.
Certification to determine eligibility for
federal assistance, SF §2-505.
Health.
Secretary of health and mental hygiene.
Applications for federal funds or aid, HG
§2-104.
Highways.
Acceptance of federal funds, TR §8-502.
Administration.
Power to comply with federal acts, TR §8-503.
Use of federal funds by administration, TR
§8-505.
Authority to comply with conditions and
provisions, TR §8-502.
Beautification of highway.
Acquisition of adjacent land.
Authority of state highway administration,
TR §§8-204, 8-315.
Declared to be in public interest, TR §8-315.
Counties.
Highway construction funds, TR §8-507.
Power of administration and counties to comply
with federal acts, TR §8-503.
Power to raise funds, TR §8-504.
Elimination of highway hazards, TR §8-505.
Federal acts.
Defined, TR §8-501.
Legislative policy, TR §8-502.
Matching funds.
Sources for federal acts, TR §8-504.
Municipal corporations.
Power to comply with federal acts, TR §8-503.
Sources of matching funds for federal acts.
Power of municipalities to raise funds, TR
§8-504.
Outdoor advertising.
Along federal-aid primary highways.
General provisions, TR §§8-725 to 8-737.
Payment to owner of utility relocated, etc.
Result of interstate highway construction, TR
§8-506.
Publicly owned utility.
Payment for relocation, TR §8-506.
Housing.
Lower-income housing assistance.
County and municipal participation in federal
programs, 24 §6-203.
Maryland Transit Administration.
Contributions by federal government, TR
§7-102.1.
Mining.
Abandoned mine drainage control act.
Federal program, EN §15-706.
Municipal corporations.
Notices, 24 §6-301.
Powers to participate in federal projects.
Enumeration of powers, 24 §6-201.
Lower-income housing assistance, 24 §6-203.
Validation of prior acts or contracts, 24 §6-201.
Natural resources.
Secretary.
Authority to apply for, accept, etc., NR §1-103.
Notices.
Instructional and research aid.
Requirements from units of state government,
SF §2-203.
Nuclear compact, 41 §16-103.

FEDERAL AID —Cont'd
Patuxent river.
Planning.
Patuxent river policy plan.
Funds for program, SF §5-807.
Planning.
Patuxent river policy plan.
Funds for program, SF §5-807.
Port administration.
General provisions, TR §6-204.
Grants, TR §6-204.
Public works.
Appalachian regional development act of 1965,
83A §6-701.
Railroads.
Crossings.
Elimination of highway hazards, TR §8-505.
Rehabilitation services.
Acceptance of act of congress, ED §21-302.
Research.
Notices.
Instructional and research aid.
Requirements from units of state government,
SF §2-203.
Rules and regulations.
Information required from units of state
government, SF §2-203.
Schools.
Food programs, ED §7-602.
General provisions, ED §5-214.
Social services.
Department authorized to accept and distribute,
88A §15.
Surplus food, SF §2-205.
Transportation department.
Responsibility of secretary, TR §2-103.

FEDERAL BANKING AUTHORITIES.
Banks and trust companies.
Acceptance of examination or report by, FI §5-204.
Confidential financial records.
Definitions, FI §1-301.
Disclosure prohibited, FI §1-302.
Information obtained in examinations, FI
§5-209.
Penalties, FI §1-305.
Permitted disclosures.
Subpoena, FI §1-304.
Examination of banks by commissioner.
Effect on duties, FI §5-204.
Receiver.
Appointment as receiver for institution in
commissioner's possession, FI §5-605.
Rights as receiver, FI §5-614.
Reserves.
Requirements, FI §3-607.
Savings and loan associations.
Conservatorship.
Insuring agency as receiver or conservator, FI
§9-709.
Insurance.
Required, FI §9-901.
Receivership.
Insuring agency as receiver or conservator, FI
§9-709.

FEDERAL CLEAN AIR ACT.
Modification to power plants, PUC §7-206.
Reports, EN §2-103.1.

FEDERAL CONSTITUTION.
See CONSTITUTION OF THE UNITED STATES.

FEDERAL COURTS.
Supreme court of the United States.
Constitutional provisions.
See CONSTITUTION OF THE UNITED
STATES.
United States courts.
See UNITED STATES COURTS.

**FEDERAL DEPOSIT INSURANCE
CORPORATION.**
Banks and trust companies.
Memberships authorized, FI §5-509.
Depositories.
Security for deposit exceeding, 31 §7.

FEDERAL ESTATE TAX.
Decedents' estates.
Distribution in kind, using federal estate tax
values, ET §11-107.

FEDERAL GOVERNMENT.
See UNITED STATES.

FEDERAL INTERSTATE SYSTEM.
Interstate system.
See HIGHWAYS.

FEDERAL LAW ENFORCEMENT OFFICERS.
Authority, CP §2-104.
Immunity from suit when exercising, CJ §5-611.
Park police officers.
Authority to enforce state laws within park, CP
§2-104.1.
Authority to issue citations, CP §§2-104.1, 4-101.

FEDERAL LIEN INDEX, RP §3-403.
Fee for indexing, RP §3-404.

**FEDERALLY QUALIFIED HEALTH CENTERS
GRANT PROGRAM,** HG §§24-1301 to
24-1308.
See HOSPITALS.

**FEDERAL PHILANTHROPY PROTECTION
ACT OF 1995.**
Securities act.
State laws not preempted by, CA §11-103.

FEDERAL RESERVE SYSTEM.
Banks and trust companies.
Memberships authorized, FI §5-509.
Reserves.
Requirements, FI §3-607.

FEDERAL TAX LIEN.
Revised uniform lien registration act.
General provisions, RP §§3-401 to 3-405.
See UNITED STATES.

FEDERAL TRUTH IN LENDING ACT.
Credit.
Credit grantor closed end credit provisions.
Applicability of disclosure requirements, CL
§12-1014.

FEDERATIONS.
Organizational names and insignia.
Registration, prohibited acts, BR §§19-201 to
19-207.

FEEDSTUFFS.
Administration of subtitle.
Fund for payment of costs, AG §6-103.
State chemist, AG §6-102.
Adulteration.
Defined, AG §6-101.
Distribution of adulterated feed.
Prohibited, AG §6-112.

FEEDSTUFFS —Cont'd
Adulteration —Cont'd
Procedure when inspection and analysis indicate,
AG §6-106.
Analysis.
Generally, AG §6-106.
Official analysis.
Prima facie evidence of composition, AG §6-114.
Brand.
Defined, AG §6-101.
Commercial feed.
Commercial equine feed assessments, AG
§6-107.2.
Defined, AG §6-101.
Condemnation.
Generally, AG §6-113.
Confiscation, AG §6-113.
Contract feed.
Defined, AG §6-101.
Labeling, AG §6-110.
Poultry waste.
Additives to reduce phosphorus in.
Inclusion in contract feed fed to chickens, AG
§6-107.1.
Contract feeder.
Defined, AG §6-101.
Customer-formula feed.
Defined, AG §6-101.
Labeling, AG §6-110.
Definitions, AG §6-101.
Distributor.
Defined, AG §6-101.
Evidence.
Official analysis.
Prima facie evidence of composition, AG §6-114.
Feed ingredient.
Defined, AG §6-101.
Fees.
Registration, AG §6-107.
Disposition, AG §6-103.
Fund for payment of administration expenses,
AG §6-103.
Fund.
Administration expenses.
Fund for payment, AG §6-103.
Information.
Publication.
Secretary of agriculture, AG §6-105.
Injunctions.
Restraining violations, AG §6-116.
Inspection.
Generally, AG §6-106.
Right of entry, AG §6-106.
Labels.
Contents, AG §6-109.
Contract feed, AG §6-110.
Customer-formula feed, AG §6-110.
Defined, AG §6-101.
Deleterious substances, AG §6-111.
Nonnutritive substance, AG §6-111.
Placement, AG §6-109.
Poisonous substances, AG §6-111.
Required, AG §6-109.
Manufacture.
Defined, AG §6-101.
Misbranded.
Defined, AG §6-101.
Distribution of misbranded feed, AG §6-112.
Procedure when inspection and analysis indicate,
AG §6-106.

FEEDSTUFFS —Cont'd
Official sample.
Defined, AG §6-101.
Penalties.
General provisions, AG §§12-101 to 12-104.
Percentage.
Defined, AG §6-101.
Poultry waste.
Additives to reduce phosphorus in poultry waste.
Inclusion in contract feed fed to chickens, AG §6-107.1.
Publication.
Information.
Secretary of agriculture, AG §6-105.
Registration.
Application, AG §6-107.
Approval.
Copy to be furnished, AG §6-107.
Cancellation, AG §6-108.
Changes in guarantee of composition of registered feed, AG §6-108.
Customer-formula feed mixers, AG §6-107.
Exemptions, AG §6-107.
Expiration, AG §6-107.
Fees, AG §6-107.
Disposition, AG §6-103.
Fund for payment of administration expenses, AG §6-103.
Refusal, AG §6-108.
Required, AG §6-107.
Reports.
Violations of subtitle, AG §6-115.
Right of entry.
Inspection by secretary, AG §6-106.
Rules and regulations.
Adoption.
Secretary of agriculture, AG §6-104.
Violations.
Stop-sale orders, AG §6-113.
Samples.
Official sample.
Defined, AG §6-101.
Methods of sampling an analysis, AG §6-106.
Secretary of agriculture.
Information.
Publication of information, AG §6-105.
Injunctions.
Restraining violations, AG §6-116.
Right of entry.
Inspection, AG §6-106.
Rules and regulations.
Adoption, AG §6-104.
Stop-sale orders.
Issuance and enforcement, AG §6-113.
Short title, AG §6-117.
State chemist.
Administration of subtitle, AG §6-102.
Stop-sale orders, AG §6-113.
Testing.
Methods, AG §6-106.
Title.
Short title, AG §6-117.
Ton.
Defined, AG §6-101.
Violations of subtitle.
Injunctions.
Restraining violations, AG §6-116.
Minor violation, AG §6-115.
Report for criminal prosecution, AG §6-115.
Stop-sale orders, AG §6-113.

FEES.
Accountants.
See ACCOUNTANTS.
Accounts and accounting.
Officers whose compensation is derived from fees, MD Const Art XV §1.
Adult protective services.
Schedule, FL §14-204.
Agricultural lime.
Registration fees.
Fund to defray expenses, AG §6-303.
Agriculture.
Farm products.
Certification.
Disposition of money collected, AG §10-604.
Organic agricultural commodities, AG §10-1406.
Air conditioning and heating contractors.
Board.
Establishment, BR §9A-207.
Licenses.
Reexamination, BR §9A-307.
Air quality control.
Permits and registration, EN §2-403.
Alcoholic beverages.
General provisions.
See ALCOHOLIC BEVERAGES.
Alternative dispute resolution.
Schedules of fees, ADR Rule 17-108.
Ambulances.
Licenses.
Ambulance services, ED §13-515.
Amusements and recreation.
Copies of regulations, BR §3-313.
Pinball machines.
License fees, BR §17-410.
Appeals.
Appeals from District Court.
Filing fees, AppRevCir Rule 7-103.
Court of special appeals.
Notice of appeal.
Filing fee, AppRev Rule 8-201.
Aquaculture.
Oysters and clams.
Culture of oysters.
Advertisement, NR §4-11A-06.
Disposition.
Fees, NR §4-11A-08.
Lease, NR §4-11A-06.
Privately owned artificial ponds or lakes.
Permit to establish and operate, NR §4-11A-20.
Arbitration and award.
Expenses and fees for arbitrator, CJ §3-221.
Architects.
See ARCHITECTS.
Archives.
Copies of records, SG §9-1009.
Assumed business name.
Trade names generally, CA §1-406.
Athlete agents.
Fee-splitting prohibited, BR §4-413.
Licenses.
Application, BR §4-404.
Issuance, BR §4-405.
Attachment.
Sheriffs, CJ §7-402.
Attorney general.
Prohibited from receiving, MD Const Art V §3.
Attorneys at law.
Bar admissions. See within this heading, "Bar admissions."

FEES —Cont'd

Attorneys' fees.
See ATTORNEYS' FEES.

Audiologists, hearing aid dealers and speech-language pathologists.
See AUDIOLOGISTS AND SPEECH-LANGUAGE PATHOLOGISTS.

Aviation.
Licenses.
Airports, TR §5-304.
Air schools, TR §5-904.

Bank holding companies.
Acquisitions.
Application for acquisition, FI §5-904.

Banks and trust companies.
Articles of incorporation.
Amendments, FI §§3-213, 4-210.
Filing with commissioner.
Commercial banks, FI §3-203.
Savings banks, FI §4-203.
Branch banking.
Establishment of branch, FI §5-1005.
Supervisory and examination fees, FI §5-1009.
Charter amendments.
Commercial banks, FI §3-213.
Savings banks, FI §4-210.
Commercial banks.
Articles of incorporation, FI §3-203.
Filing fees, FI §3-203.
Commissioner of financial regulation.
Certified copies of records, FI §2-108.
Common trust funds, FI §3-515.
Foreign corporations.
Offices and electronic terminals.
Power of commissioner to set fees for permits, FI §12-211.
Incorporation, FI §§3-203, 4-203.
Savings banks, FI §§4-203, 4-210.
Savings banks.
Filing annual reports, CA §1-203.
Disposition, TP §2-220.
Incorporation, FI §§4-203, 4-210.
Trust companies.
Articles of incorporation, FI §3-203.
Filing fees, FI §3-203.

Bar admissions.
Examination fee, BarAdm Rule 6.
Taking after failure, BarAdm Rule 9.
Out-of-state attorneys.
Filing fee, BarAdm Rule 13.
Prescription by board, BarAdm Rule 18.
Registration of law students.
Filing fee, BarAdm Rule 2.
Taking examination after failure, BarAdm Rule 9.

Barbers.
See BARBERS.

Beer kegs.
Registration fee, 2B §21-106.

Billiard and pool tables.
License fees, BR §17-504.

Birds and game licenses.
See BIRDS AND GAME.

Boards and commissions.
Commissions exempt from fees, RP §3-603.

Boat docking and storage fees, 24 §9-605.

Boilers and pressure vessels.
Inspections, PS §12-909.

Boxing, sparring and wrestling.
Licenses, BR §4-305.

Building and loan associations.
Annual reports.
Filing fees, CA §1-203.
Disposition, TP §2-220.

FEES —Cont'd

Building codes.
Implementation and enforcement of performance standards, PS §12-505.
Industrialized buildings and manufactured homes.
Department's duties, PS §12-304.

Business regulation and licensure.
Dishonor of instrument paying fee.
Suspension of license, BR §1-209.
Late fees.
Failure to get license in timely manner, BR §1-206.
Local licenses, fees and taxes.
Prohibition, BR §1-204.
Proration of certain license fees, BR §1-208.

Business trusts, CA §12-701.

Calvert county.
Hawkers and peddlers.
License fees, BR §17-918.

Campaign finance reports.
Late filing fee, EL §13-331.
Administrative waiver, EL §13-337.
Distributions, EL §13-340.

Certified copies of public records, CJ §10-204.

Chain store licenses, BR §17-1809.

Charities.
Charitable giving information program.
Purchasing and preparing computer data information, BR §6-201.
Noncompliance with title by applicant for registration.
Notice and fee, BR §6-404.
Registration of charitable representatives.
Single fees, BR §6-302.
Schedule of annual fees, BR §6-407.

Check cashing services.
License application, FI §12-108.
License renewal, FI §12-111.
Maximum fees, FI §12-120.
Posting of fee schedule, FI §12-118.

Child care.
Criminal background investigations for employees, etc., of facilities, FL §5-561.

Child support enforcement administration.
Collection of fees, FL §10-110.

Chiropractors.
See CHIROPRACTORS.

Cholesterol testing permits.
Applications, HG §17-506.
Waiver of permit fees for local and county health departments, HG §§17-506, 17-508.

Circuit courts.
See CIRCUIT COURTS.

Clerks of court.
Supplementary proceedings, CJ §7-401.

Collection agencies.
License applications.
Nonrefundable fee, BR §7-302.
Local license fees prohibited, BR §7-104.

Commercial fertilizers.
Administration of subtitle.
Fund for payment of expenses, AG §6-204.
Registration and inspection, AG §6-208.

Community colleges.
See COMMUNITY COLLEGES.

Comptroller.
Officers whose compensation is derived from fees.
Report showing officers who complied with section, MD Const Art XV §1.
Property liens.
Recording and indexing of property liens arising under certain taxes.
Exemption from fees, RP §3-603.

FEES —Cont'd
Computers manufacturer registration fee, EN §9-1728.
Consumer loans.
Applications for licenses, FI §11-206.
Collection, CL §12-307.
Excess fees, CL §12-313.
Contractors.
Construction licenses, BR §17-603.
Cooperatives.
Agricultural cooperatives.
Membership fees.
Payment prior to issuance of certificate, CA §5-509.
Recording fees, CA §1-203.
Copies.
Certified copies, RP §3-602.
Commissions exempt from fees, RP §3-603.
Counties exempt from fees, RP §3-603.
Public records, CJ §10-204.
Reproduced copies, RP §3-602.
Commissions exempt from fees, RP §3-603.
Counties exempt from fees, RP §3-603.
Corporations.
See CORPORATIONS.
Correctional facility inmates.
Visits to health care providers.
Local correctional facility inmates, COR §11-203.
Cosmetologists.
See COSMETOLOGISTS.
Counties.
Code counties.
Restriction on levy, MD Const Art XI-F §9.
Housing and community development.
Residential mortgage programs for certain counties.
Fees from borrowers, HS §4-1605.
Payment by credit or debit card, 24 §9-1401.
Private activity bond issuance fee.
Powers, 25 §3.
Court of appeals.
State court administrator to determine amount, CJ §7-102.
Court of special appeals.
State court administrator to determine amount, CJ §7-102.
Credit grantor closed-end credit provisions.
Attorneys' fees, CL §12-1028.
Lender's inspection fee, CL §12-1027.
Credit unions.
Capital, FI §6-314.
Filing annual report, CA §1-203.
Disposition, TP §2-220.
Filing articles of incorporation and bylaws, FI §6-307.
Organization and capitalization fees, CA §1-204.
Share guaranty corporations.
Certificates of authority.
Application fee, FI §7-206.
Criminal history record checks.
Prince George's county prospective employees, CP §10-236.
Washington county prospective employees, CP §10-235.
Debt management services, FI §12-904.
Additional fees, FI §12-918.
Decedents' estates.
Appraisers, ET §2-301.
Dental plan organizations.
Certificates of authority.
Application fees, IN §14-405.

FEES —Cont'd
Dental plan organizations —Cont'd
Certificates of authority —Cont'd
Renewal fees, IN §14-408.
Dentists.
See DENTISTS.
Development impact fees.
See DEVELOPMENT IMPACT FEES.
Dietitians.
See DIETITIANS.
Discovery.
Trial preparation.
Experts.
Scope of discovery.
Circuit courts, CivProCir Rule 2-402.
Dog licenses, 24 §11-501.
"Dog guides" exempt from fees, 24 §11-502.
Down payment and settlement expense loan program.
Powers and duties of department, HS §4-304.
Drinking driver monitor program.
Supervision fees, COR §6-115.
Dry cleaners.
License fees, BR §17-1203.
Egg packers and distributors.
Inspection fees, AG §4-311.6.
Registration, AG §4-311.2.
Elections.
Campaign finance reports.
Late filing fee, EL §13-331.
Administrative waiver, EL §13-337.
Distributions, EL §13-340.
Candidate filing fee, EL §5-401.
Electric cooperatives, CA §5-637.
Electricians.
See ELECTRICIANS.
Electrologists.
Establishment and distribution, HO §8-6B-04.
Elevators.
Elevator safety review board.
Authority to establish, PS §12-824.
Emergency elevator mechanic licenses, PS §12-835.
Inspections, PS §12-809.
Licenses.
Applications, PS §12-828.
Examinations, PS §12-829.
Renewal, PS §12-833.
Elevator safety review board.
Authority to establish, PS §12-824.
EMaryland marketplace.
User fees, SF §13-102.1.
Eminent domain.
Attorney's fee.
Judgment for defendant, RP §12-106.
On appeal, RP §12-107.
Employment agencies.
Collection of placement fee.
Restrictions, BR §9-307.
Placement fees.
Contracts, BR §9-305.
Reimbursement of client, BR §9-308.
Temporary placement fees, BR §9-306.
Engineers.
General provisions.
See ENGINEERS.
Proceedings to establish boundary lines, RP §14-111.
Environmental service.
Authority to fix, alter, etc., NR §3-104.

FEES —Cont'd
Environmental service —Cont'd
Changed by county for final disposal of solid
    wastes, NR §3-108.
Generally, NR §3-118.
Excavation or demolition near underground
    facilities.
Marking or re-marking fee by political subdivision
    or municipal corporation, PUC §12-111.
Executions.
Sheriffs, CJ §7-402.
Executors and administrators.
See EXECUTORS AND ADMINISTRATORS.
Explosives.
Fire marshal, PS §11-104.
Feedstuffs.
Registration fees, AG §6-107.
    Disposition, AG §6-103.
    Fund for payment of expenses, AG §6-103.
Fictitious business name.
Trade names generally, CA §1-406.
Fiduciaries.
Assessment and waiver, Guardian Rule 10-107.
Financing statements filing fee, RP §3-601.
Firearms.
Applications for purchases, rents or transfers, PS
    §5-118.
    Copies, PS §5-120.
    Secondary transactions, PS §5-124.
Dealers' licenses.
    Applications, PS §5-107.
    Criminal history records checks, PS §5-108.
Handgun permits.
    Applications, PS §5-304.
Fire marshal, PS §6-308.
Explosives, PS §11-104.
Fireworks.
Permits, PS §10-104.
Sparklers.
    Registration of distributors and wholesalers, PS
    §10-113.
Fireworks plants.
License to operate, PS §10-201.
Fish and fisheries.
See FISH AND FISHERIES.
Foresters.
See FORESTERS.
Franchises.
Interpretive opinions, BR §14-209.
Registration.
    Application fee, BR §14-215.
    Application for amendment to registration, BR
    §14-220.
    Claims of exemption, BR §14-214.
    Renewal fee, BR §14-219.
Fraternal benefit societies.
Filing annual statement, IN §8-444.
Freestanding ambulatory care facilities.
Licenses, HG §19-3B-05.
Frozen desserts.
Licenses.
    Applications, HG §21-808.
    Renewal fee, HG §21-812.
Garages.
License fees, BR §17-803.
Garrett county.
Licensing amusement devices, BR §17-435.
Gas and oil.
Coastal facilities review act.
    Permit fees, EN §14-504.

FEES —Cont'd
Gas and oil —Cont'd
Underground storage.
    Use fee.
        Prince George's county, EN §14-207.
General assembly.
Investigating committee.
    Persons subpoenaed to appear at hearings, SG
    §2-1608.
Ginseng.
Disposition, AG §9-606.
Secretary may charge fees, AG §9-605.
Grain.
Licenses, AG §13-203.
Group home financing program.
Authority to establish, HS §4-604.
Guardian and ward.
Assessment and waiver, Guardian Rule 10-107.
Handgun permits.
Applications, PS §5-304.
Hawkers and peddlers.
License fees, BR §17-907.
    Calvert county, BR §17-918.
    St. Mary's county, BR §17-907.
Sale of produce in municipal corporation.
    Local license, fee or tax prohibited, BR §17-912.
Hazardous materials and substances.
Pipelines.
    Inspections of hazardous liquid pipelines, PUC
    §11-206.
Security of hazardous material facilities.
    Analysis, EN §7-702.
Transfer of hazardous materials between one
    mode of transportation and another.
    Facility permit, EN §§7-107, 7-113.
Health.
Cost review commission.
    Closed or delicensed hospitals, HG §19-223.
Secretary of health and mental hygiene, HG
    §2-104.
User fees.
    Definitions, HG §19-213.
Health and higher educational facilities
    authority, 43C §14.
Health maintenance organizations.
Application for certificate, HG §19-709.
Investigation fees, HG §19-709.
Home improvements.
Certification of licensing status, BR §8-210.
Guaranty fund.
    Initial fee, BR §8-404.
Licenses.
    Application fee, BR §8-303.
Records.
    Copy fees, BR §8-209.
Horse racing.
Harness racing.
    Driver's fee deducted from purse, BR §11-619.
    Notice of license and fees, BR §11-608.
Return of fees and award of replacement days, BR
    §11-307.
Housing and community development.
Residential mortgage programs for certain
    counties.
    Fees from borrowers, HS §4-1605.
Hunting licenses, NR §10-301.
Stamps, NR §10-301.
Inmates at correctional facilities.
Health care services, COR §2-118.
Visits to health care providers.
    Local correctional facility inmates, COR
    §11-203.

FEES —Cont'd
Installment loans.
  Licenses.
    Application fee, FI §11-303.
Insurance.
  Adjusters.
    Reinstatement of certificate after expiration, IN
      §10-408.1.
  Adviser reinstatement fees, IN §10-211.1.
  Agents and brokers.
    Examinations, IN §§10-107, 10-108.
    Reinstatement of certificate after expiration, IN
      §10-116.1.
  Commissioner's fees for certain services, IN
    §2-112.
    Insurance regulation assessment in lieu of other
      fees, IN §2-504.
  Dental plan organizations.
    Certificates of authority.
      Application fees, IN §14-405.
      Renewal fees, IN §14-408.
  Disposition of money, IN §2-114.
  Fraud prevention fee, IN §§6-201 to 6-204.
  Legal mutual liability insurance society of
    Maryland.
    Membership fees, IN §24-108.
  Life and health insurance guaranty corporation.
    Exemption from payment of fees, IN §9-416.
  Liquidation, rehabilitation, etc., of insurers.
    Commissioner exempt from fees, IN §9-206.
  Medical mutual liability insurance society of
    Maryland.
    Membership fees, IN §24-208.
  Payment of fees in immediately available funds,
    IN §2-113.
  Premium finance agreements, IN §§23-301 to
    23-310.
    See PREMIUM FINANCE COMPANIES.
  Property and casualty insurance guaranty
    corporation.
    Exemption from payment of fees, IN §9-312.
  Rating organization licenses, IN §11-218.
  Reinsurance intermediaries.
    Application fee, IN §8-506.
    Name additions or deletions on license, IN
      §8-510.
  Retaliation for fees imposed by foreign states, IN
    §§6-301 to 6-305.
  Third party administrators.
    Applications for registration, IN §8-305.
    Reinstatement of registration, IN §8-308.1.
Interest.
  Collected by governmental agency.
    Not considered interest, CL §12-105.
Interior designers.
  Certificates.
    See INTERIOR DESIGNERS.
Judges.
  Receiving fees or prerequisites prohibited, MD
    Const Art IV §6; DofR Art 33.
Juke boxes.
  Harford county license fees, BR §17-1314.
  License fees, BR §17-1305.
Junk dealers.
  Licenses.
    Applications, BR §17-1007.
    Junkyards, TR §8-805.
Kidney disease program.
  Annual fee, HG §13-313.

FEES —Cont'd
Labor and employment relations.
  Commissioner of labor and industry.
    Filing fees.
      Payment not to be required in certain actions,
        CJ §7-403.
Laboratories.
  Medical laboratories.
    Application for license, HG §17-207.
    Establishment of fees, HG §17-204.
  Public laboratories.
    Establishment of fees, HG §17-103.
Lakes.
  Privately owned artificial ponds or lakes.
    Permit to establish and operate, NR §4-11A-20.
Landscape architects.
  See LANDSCAPE ARCHITECTS.
Laundries and dry cleaners.
  License fees, BR §17-1103.
Law enforcement officers and personnel.
  Disciplinary hearings.
    Witness fees, PS §3-107.
  Special police officers.
    Applications for commissions, PS §3-304.
**Lead hazard reduction grant and loan
  programs.**
  Loan fees and charges, HS §4-704.
**Legal mutual liability insurance society of
  Maryland.**
  Membership fees, IN §24-108.
Licenses.
  Fishing guides, NR §4-210.
Liens.
  Federal lien, RP §3-404.
**Life and health insurance guaranty
  corporation.**
  Exemption from payment of fees, IN §9-416.
Lime.
  Inspection fees, AG §6-305.
    Payment, AG §6-306.
  Registration fees, AG §6-305.
    Fund to defray expenses, AG §6-303.
Limited liability companies.
  Filing of documents.
    Payment of fees, CA §4A-207.
  Generally, CA §1-203.
Livestock licenses.
  Sales, AG §3-303.
    Constitute a fund, AG §3-302.
    Disposition of fees, AG §3-302.
Machine guns.
  Registration by purchaser, CR §4-403.
Marriage.
  Judge's or clerk's fee for performing, FL §2-410.
  Licenses, FL §2-404.
Maryland home financing program.
  Application fees, HS §4-805.
Maryland housing rehabilitation program.
  Authority to charge and collect, HS §4-908.
**Maryland-national capital park and planning
  commission.**
  Commissions exempt from fees, RP §3-603.
Maryland-Washington regional district.
  Subdivisions.
    Clerk's fee, 28 §7-115.
    Fees for commission's subdivision work, 28
      §7-115.
Massage therapists.
  Funding of certification program, HO §3-5A-03.
**Medical mutual liability insurance society of
  Maryland.**
  Membership fees, IN §24-208.

FEES —Cont'd
Meridian line.
County clerk, 25 §125.
Mining.
Deep mine control.
See MINING.
Fire-boss.
Certificates, EN §15-308.
Examination fee, EN §15-303.
First-class mine foreman.
Certificates, EN §15-308.
Examination fee, EN §15-303.
Licenses.
Strip mining, EN §15-504.
Lost or destroyed certificates, EN §15-308.
Permits of competence.
Certificate, EN §15-305.
Examination fee, EN §15-308.
Strip mining.
Licenses, EN §15-504.
Permit fee, EN §15-505.
Special reclamation fee, EN §15-505.
Surface mining.
License, EN §15-807.
Permit fees, EN §15-808.
Modification of permit, EN §15-815.
Renewal, EN §15-816.
Transfer of permit, EN §15-819.
Special reclamation fee, EN §15-808.
Mobile home parks.
See MOBILE HOMES.
Money transmissions.
Licenses.
Application, FI §12-407.
Voluntary surrender of license, FI §12-422.
Redemption of unused payment instruments, FI
§12-420.
Morgan State University.
Payment by credit card, ED §15-102.
Mortgage originators.
Investigations of complaints, FI §11-613.
License application, FI §11-606.
Renewal of license, FI §11-609.
Mortgages and deeds of trust.
Finder's fees.
General provisions.
See MORTGAGES AND DEEDS OF TRUST.
Mortgage lenders, FI §§11-507, 11-515.
Surcharges, FI §§11-507, 11-512.
Releases.
Trustee prohibited from charging or demanding
fees not specified in instrument, RP §7-106.
Secondary mortgage loans.
Certain fees permitted by mortgage purchase
agreements, CL §12-404.1.
Finders' fees or points, CL §12-406.
Origination fees, CL §12-405.
Morticians.
See MORTICIANS.
Motor clubs.
Application fees.
Disposition upon denial of license, IN §26-205.
Renewal fee, IN §26-206.
Representatives.
Initial registration fee, IN §26-301.
Motorcycles.
Safety program.
Registration fee, TR §16-603.
Municipal corporations.
Payment by credit or debit card, 24 §9-1401.

FEES —Cont'd
Name.
Fictitious names, CA §1-406.
Trade names, CA §1-406.
911 fee, PS §1-310.
Additional charges, PS §1-311.
Expenditures by counties, PS §1-312.
**Nolle prosequi with requirement of drug or
alcohol treatment.**
Administrative court fee, CP §6-229.
Notaries public, SG §18-112.
Nurses.
Board of nursing, HO §8-206.
Licenses.
Renewal, HO §8-312.
Nursing home administrators.
See NURSING HOME ADMINISTRATORS.
Nutrient management consultants.
Certification and licenses, AG §8-806.
Occupational therapists.
See OCCUPATIONAL THERAPISTS.
Officers.
Compensation derived from fees.
Accounts, MD Const Art XV §1.
Disposition of excess fees, MD Const Art XV §1.
Returns, MD Const Art XV §1.
Oil transfer license, EN §4-411.
Optometrists.
See OPTOMETRISTS.
Outdoor advertising.
License fee, NR §4-1017; TR §8-710.
Parole supervision fee, COR §7-702.
Partnerships.
Limited partnerships, SpecPro Rule 15-403.
Statements filed generally, CA §1-203.
Permits.
Consolidated procedures for development permits.
Collection authority of local governments and
state units, SG §11-103.
Pesticides.
Disposition, AG §§5-103, 5-203.
Registration fees, AG §5-105.
Pharmacists and pharmacies.
See PHARMACISTS AND PHARMACIES.
Physical therapists.
See PHYSICAL THERAPISTS.
Physicians.
See PHYSICIANS.
Pilots.
See PILOTS.
Pipelines.
Hazardous liquid pipelines.
Inspections, PUC §11-206.
Plant disease control.
Plant protection fund, AG §5-302.
Plumbers and gas fitters.
Generally.
See PLUMBERS AND PLUMBING.
License fees, BR §17-1504.
Podiatrists.
See PODIATRISTS.
Postmortem examiners.
Autopsies.
Fee for pathologist.
Chief medical examiner to set fee, HG §5-310.
Medical examiners.
Authority to charge reasonable fees in certain
cases, HG §5-311.
Potatoes.
Inspections.
Authority to require payment, AG §9-302.

FEES —Cont'd
Potatoes —Cont'd
Inspections —Cont'd
Disposition of fees, AG §9-303.
Poultry products inspection.
Witnesses, AG §4-222.
Premium finance companies.
Agreements.
See PREMIUM FINANCE COMPANIES.
Registration.
Application fee, IN §23-203.
Prepayment of filing fees, Rule 1-325.
Prescription drug repository program.
Dispensing by repository, HG §15-605.
Prisoner litigation.
Filing fees, CJ §5-1002.
Prisoners at local correctional facilities.
Visits to health care providers.
Local correctional facility inmates, COR §11-203.
Prisoners at state correctional facilities.
Health care services, COR §2-118.
Private detectives.
See PRIVATE DETECTIVES.
Procurement.
Electronic transactions, SF §13-226.
Professional counselors and therapists.
Certification, HO §17-303.
State board of examiners.
Establishment, HO §17-206.
Professional service corporations.
Name.
Certificate of authorization for corporate name, CA §5-108.
Property and casualty insurance guaranty corporation.
Exemption from payment of fees, IN §9-312.
Psychologists.
See PSYCHOLOGISTS.
Public assistance program.
No fees to be paid, 88A §80.
Public defender.
Denial of public defender representation.
Payment of filing fees by state, Rule 1-325.
Public officers and employees.
General provisions.
See PUBLIC OFFICERS AND EMPLOYEES.
Public records, certified copies, CJ §10-204.
Public safety solicitors.
Application for registration, BR §6-5A-02.
Public service commission, PUC §§2-111, 2-123.
Queen Anne's county.
Subdivisions.
Recordation of plats, RP §3-108.1.
Rabies.
Antirabies clinics, HG §18-315.
Radiation.
Dental radiation, EN §8-301.
Radiation oncology/therapy, medical radiation, and nuclear medicine technologists.
Certification, HO §14-5B-04.
Railroad police.
Applications, PS §3-404.
Real estate appraisers.
Certification.
Application, BOP §16-505.
Examination, BOP §16-506.
Renewal, BOP §16-510.
Examination, BOP §16-304.
Licenses, BOP §16-303.
Reinstatement of lapsed license, BOP §16-310.
See REAL ESTATE APPRAISERS AND HOME INSPECTORS.

FEES —Cont'd
Real estate appraisers —Cont'd
Specialized appraisal services, BOP §16-402.
Trainee appraiser license, BOP §16-5A-01.
Real estate brokers.
See REAL ESTATE BROKERS.
Rebuilder registration, BR §4.5-304.
Renewal, BR §4.5-305.
Receivers and assignees or trustees for creditors.
Compensation and fees, Receivers Rule 13-303.
Recordation.
Corporations, CA §1-203.
Exemption of volunteer fire companies and rescue squads, CA §1-203.1.
Instruments not printed or typed, CA §1-203.
Records.
Access to court records, CJA Rule 16-1002.
Access to public records.
Custodian may charge fee, SG §10-621.
Waiver of fees, SG §10-621.
Automated mapping-geographic information systems, SG §10-904.
Data and records on state fees, SF §2-107.
Public records, certified copies, CJ §10-204.
Recycling solid waste.
Newsprint recycling by newspapers.
Recycling incentive fee, EN §9-1707.
Telephone directories.
Recycling incentive fee, EN §9-1709.
Tire recycling fee, EN §9-228.
Registers of wills.
See REGISTERS OF WILLS.
Reinsurance intermediaries.
Application fee, IN §8-506.
Name additions or deletions on license, IN §8-510.
Religion.
Corporations.
Plan of operation.
Recording with department, CA §1-203.
Rental motor vehicles.
Fees and charges, separately stated by rental vehicle company, TR §18-108.
Reports.
Data and records on state fees.
Biennial report, SF §2-107.
Respiratory care practitioners.
Funding to cover costs, HO §14-5A-04.
Restaurants.
License fees, BR §17-1604.
Retail credit accounts law.
Attorneys' fees, CL §12-508.
Rules of professional conduct, ProfCond Rule 1.5.
Sales.
Finance companies.
Licenses.
Applications, FI §11-404.
Installment sales.
Refund.
Recording and filing fees, CL §12-616.
Livestock.
Licenses, AG §3-303.
Savings and loan associations.
Electronic terminals.
Application, FI §9-310.
Incorporation.
Application to organize, FI §9-205.
Investments.
Expenses charged borrowers, FI §9-424.
Outside officials, FI §9-312.

FEES —Cont'd
Schools.
  Construction or remodeling, ED §4-117.
  Negotiations between employer and employee
      organization.
    Fees charged to employees, ED §6-407.
Secondary mortgage loan law.
  Certain fees permitted by mortgage purchase
      programs, CL §12-404.1.
  Finders' fees or points, CL §12-406.
  Origination fees, CL §12-405.
  Recording and satisfying instrument carrying
      loan, CL §12-405.
Secretary of state.
  Authentication of records, SG §7-106.
Secured transactions.
  Filing office fees, CL §9-525.
  Information requests.
    Response charges, CL §9-210.
Securities.
  Registration of broker-dealers, agents, investment
      advisors and investment advisor
      representatives.
    Filing fees, CA §11-407.
  Registration of securities.
    Filing fees, CA §11-506.
    Indefinite amount of securities, CA §11-510.1.
  Securities act.
    Interpretative opinions of commissioner, CA
        §11-206.
Security guards.
  Certification, BOP §19-402.
    Application fee, BOP §19-402.
    Renewal, BOP §19-404.1.
  Security guard agencies.
    Licenses, BOP §§19-304, 19-308.
Security systems technicians.
  License application fee, BOP §18-303.
    Renewal processing fee, BOP §18-307.
  Registration.
    Renewal, BOP §18-3A-07.
Seeds.
  Permits.
    Wholesale seedsman, AG §9-204.
Service of process.
  Corporations, CA §1-203.
  Private process servers, CJ §7-404.
  Sheriffs, CJ §7-402.
Sheriffs.
  Civil cases, CJ §7-402.
  Paid to treasurer of county or Baltimore City, MD
      Const Art IV §44.
Social services.
  Attorneys' fees.
    Representing local departments, 88A §7.
  Public assistance program.
    No fees to be paid, 88A §80.
Social workers.
  See SOCIAL WORKERS.
Soda fountain license, BR §17-1703.
Soil conservation districts.
  Development of fee system, AG §8-311.
Special police officers.
  Applications for commissions, PS §3-304.
Start-up business ventures.
  Disclosure statement.
    Amendments to documents, BR §14-116.
State lottery.
  Agents.
    Cashing fee, SG §9-117.

FEES —Cont'd
State police department.
  Document search fee, PS §2-308.
  Fingerprinting fees, PS §2-312.
State's attorneys.
  Assisting comptroller and treasurer, 10 §38.
  Disposition of fees, 10 §40.
  Prohibited, MD Const Art V §9.
Stationary engineers.
  Board may set fees for services, BOP §6.5-207.
  Licenses, BOP §6.5-207.
    Reinstatement of expired license, BOP §6.5-313.
**Stet with requirement of drug or alcohol
    treatment.**
  Administrative court fee, CP §6-229.
Storage warehouses.
  License fees, BR §17-1203.
Subdivisions.
  Plats.
    Recordation, RP §3-304.
Surveys and surveyors.
  Certification concerning licensee or permit holder,
      BOP §15-207.
  Disposition of money collected, BOP §15-209.
  Licenses.
    See SURVEYS AND SURVEYORS.
  Permits.
    See SURVEYS AND SURVEYORS.
  Proceedings to establish boundary lines, RP
      §14-111.
Taxation.
  Collection fees, TG §§13-413, 13-832.
    Code counties, TP §14-810.
Terrapins.
  Commercial licenses, NR §4-902.
Time-sharing.
  Facility fees, RP §11A-101.
Tissue banks.
  Establishment of fees, HG §17-304.
  Permits.
    Application for permit, HG §17-307.
Tobacco.
  Licenses, AG §7-209.
  Warehouse sales floor.
    Tobacco sold on, AG §7-412.
Trade names, CA §1-406.
Trader licenses.
  Additional licenses and fees prohibited, BR
      §17-1803.
  Disputing value of stock in trade.
    Payment of license fee, BR §17-1812.
  Schedule of fees, BR §17-1808.
  Transfer fee, BR §17-1813.
Trading stamp insurers.
  License fees, BR §17-2003.
Tree experts.
  Licenses, NR §5-419.
**Underground storage tank upgrade and
    replacement fund,** EN §4-602.
  Termination of imposition, EN §4-607.
Vending machines.
  License fees, BR §17-1904.
Vessels and boats.
  Certificate of title.
    Originals and duplicates, NR §8-716.
  Historical watercraft identification plaque, NR
      §8-737.
  Manufacturer's or dealer's license, NR §8-710.
  Numbering of vessel, NR §8-712.
  Vessel validation sticker, NR §8-712.1.

FEES —Cont'd
Veterinarians.
Examination fee, AG §2-307.
Registration fee, AG §2-308.
Vital records.
Copies, HG §4-217.
Voluntary cleanup program, EN §7-506.1.
Warehouses and warehousemen.
License fees, BR §17-1203.
Washington suburban sanitary commission.
Commissions exempt from fees, RP §3-603.
Water and sewer systems.
Liens, EN §9-949.
Shutting off water for failure to pay for sewage service, EN §9-951.
State to pay certain fees, SF §2-403.
Tire recycling fee, EN §9-228.
Water pollution.
Oil discharge containment, control and cleanup.
Transferring oil.
Licenses, EN §4-411.
Oil spills.
Compensatory fee for oil spillage, EN §4-408.
Water quality laboratories.
Exemption from fees, EN §9-1002.
Waterworks and waste systems operators.
Board of waterworks and waste systems operators.
Certificates.
Issuance and renewal, EN §12-206.
Weapons.
Machine guns.
Registration by purchaser, CR §4-403.
Weights and measures.
Registration, AG §11-204.7.
Testing for conformity with national conference on weights and measures requirements, AG §11-204.1.
Well drillers.
See WELL DRILLERS.
Well drilling.
Permits, EN §§9-1305, 9-1307.
Wholesale farm machinery dealers.
License fee, BR §17-703.
Wicomico county.
Licensing pinball machines, BR §17-424.
Witnesses.
Poultry products inspection, AG §4-222.

FEE SIMPLE.
Deeds.
Form of deed, RP §4-202.
Tenant of estate tail may grant in fee simple, RP §2-102.
Words of inheritance not necessary to create fee simple estate, RP §4-105.
Heritage conservation fund.
Fee simple or other interest.
Acquisition, NR §5-1503.
Limitations on rights of entry or reverter.
General provisions.
See REMAINDERS, REVERSIONS AND EXECUTORY INTERESTS.

FELLATIO.
Sexual offense in first or second degree, CR §§3-305, 3-306, 3-311, 3-312.
Unnatural or perverted sexual practice, CR §3-322.

FELONIES.
Abuse or neglect of vulnerable adult, CR §3-604.
Exploitation of vulnerable adult, CR §8-801.

FELONIES —Cont'd
Aircraft.
Firearms or explosives aboard, TR §5-1008.
Alcoholic beverages.
Out-of-state unlicensed sellers, 2B §16-506.1.
Architectural and engineering services act violations, SF §13-322.
Armed carjacking, CR §3-405.
Arson in the first degree, CR §6-102.
Arson in the second degree, CR §6-103.
Assault in the first degree, CR §3-202.
Assisted living programs.
Unlicensed operation, HG §19-1809.
Assisted suicide, CR §3-104.
Attainder.
No law to attaint for treason or felony, MD Const DofR Art 18.
Attempted poisoning, CR §3-213.
Attempted rape in the first degree, CR §3-309.
Authorized communication interception.
Interference, CJ §10-414.
Bad check.
Value of property or services $500 or more, CR §8-107.
Banks and trust companies.
False records, FI §5-803.
Bigamy, CR §10-502.
Boards and commissions.
Suspension or removal for criminal activities, SG §8-502.
Burglary in first degree, CR §6-202.
Burglary in second degree, CR §6-203.
Burglary in third degree, CR §6-204.
Burglary with explosives or destructive device, CR §6-207.
Carjacking, CR §3-405.
Child abuse, CR §3-601.
Child custody.
Prohibited acts, FL §9-307.
Child kidnapping, CR §3-503.
Child pornography, CR §11-207.
Cockfight, CR §10-608.
Communications interception, CJ §10-402.
Intercepting device manufacture, CJ §10-403.
Computers, unauthorized access, CR §7-302.
Contaminating water supply or food or drink, CR §3-214.
Contraband in correctional facility to effect escape, COR §8-803.
Contraband in place of confinement.
Delivery, concealment or receipt for purposes of aiding, CR §9-413.
Weapons, CR §9-414.
Controlled dangerous substances, CR §§5-607 to 5-609, 5-901.
Drug kingpin, CR §5-613.
Faked controlled substances.
Distributing, CR §5-617.
False registration by manufacturer, distributor, or dispenser, CR §5-903.
Financial transactions involving proceeds of drug crime, CR §5-623.
Importers, CR §5-614.
Minors used distribute, deliver or manufacture, CR §5-628.
Schools.
Manufacturing, distributing, dispensing or possessing near, CR §5-627.
Corporations.
Alcoholic beverage licenses.
Revocation and suspension.
Felony conviction of stockholder, 2B §10-401.

FELONIES —Cont'd
Counterfeiting.
Orders for money or goods, CR §8-609.
Private instrument or documents, CR §8-601.
Issuing, CR §8-602.
Public documents, CR §8-605.
Trademark, CR §8-611.
United States currency.
Intent to defraud, CR §8-604.
Credit card crimes.
Card numbers, access device numbers.
Unauthorized disclosure or use, possession, CR §8-216.
Completing incomplete card, CR §8-206.
Counterfeiting, CR §8-205.
Honoring counterfeited or stolen card.
Value of goods and service $500 or more, CR §8-207.
Machinery, plates or devices to reproduce, possessing, CR §8-206.
Obtaining property with counterfeited, stolen or fraudulent card.
Value of goods and services $500 or more, CR §8-206.
Receiving property by stolen, counterfeit or misrepresented card.
Value or property $500 or more, CR §8-209.
Credit unions.
False statements or records, FI §6-903.
Custom home protection, RP §10-507.
Defense related activity.
Acting with intent to hinder, CR §§9-702, 9-703.
Disarming law enforcement officer, CR §4-103.
Dogfights.
Arranging, conducting or using dog in, CR §10-607.
Drug kingpin, CR §5-613.
Eavesdropping equipment violations, CJ §10-412.
Elections.
Adding or deleting votes, EL §16-304.
Canvassing.
Certification or statement of results.
False reports, EL §16-601.
Defacing or removing election records, EL §16-701.
Tampering with election records, EL §16-302.
Voting by person convicted of infamous crime, EL §16-202.
Voting equipment.
Concealing, damaging, destroying or removing from official's custody, EL §16-801.
Voting systems.
Tampering with electronic system, EL §16-804.
Environment.
Controlled hazardous substance violations generally, EN §7-265.
Escape in the first degree, CR §9-404.
Exploitation of vulnerable adult, CR §8-801.
Explosions and explosives.
Aboard aircraft, TR §5-1008.
License or other violations, PS §11-116.
Merger of convictions, PS §11-117.
Extortion.
By state or local officer or employee.
Inducing another to give up compensation, CR §3-703.
Property value greater than five hundred dollars, CR §3-702.
By verbal threat, CR §3-705.
By written threat, CR §3-706.

FELONIES —Cont'd
Extortion —Cont'd
Property value five hundred dollars or more, CR §3-701.
Facsimile signatures and seals.
Prohibited acts, SF §2-305.
False statement concerning destructive device or toxic material, CR §9-504.
Female genital mutilation, HG §§20-601 to 20-603.
Firearms.
Aboard aircraft, TR §5-1008.
Possession by person convicted of drug crime, CR §5-622.
Restrictions on possession, PS §5-133.
Restrictions on sale, rental or transfer, PS §5-134.
Fraud.
Insurance fraud, IN §27-408.
Hate crimes, CR §10-306.
Hazardous materials and substances.
Knowing violations, EN §7-265.
Hit and run.
Serious bodily harm, TR §27-113.
Homicide by motor vehicle or vessel while impaired by alcohol, CR §2-504.
Homicide by motor vehicle or vessel while impaired by controlled dangerous substance, CR §2-506.
Homicide by motor vehicle or vessel while impaired by drugs, CR §2-505.
Homicide by motor vehicle or vessel while under the influence of alcohol, CR §2-503.
Horse racing.
Interference with race horse, CR §10-620.
Human cloning, 83A §5-2B-13.
Identity fraud, CR §8-301.
Incest, CR §3-323.
Insurance.
Fraud, IN §27-408.
Interference with railroad, CR §5-502.
Jurisdiction.
District Court, CJ §4-302.
Kidnapping, CR §3-501.
Child kidnapping, CR §3-503.
Leaving scene of an accident.
Serious bodily harm, TR §27-113.
Malicious burning of personal property in first degree, CR §5-604.
Manslaughter by vehicle or vessel, CR §2-209.
Manufacture or possession of destructive device, CR §4-503.
Maryland stem cell research program.
Human cloning, 83A §5-2B-13.
Medicaid fraud, CR §8-516.
Minority business participation violations, SF §14-308.
Money transmission.
Knowing and willful violation of subtitle, FI §12-430.
Mortgages and deeds of trust.
Mortgage lenders.
Misappropriation or conversion, FI §11-523.
Mortgage originators.
Willful violations of provisions, FI §11-617.
Motor vehicle theft, CR §7-105.
Procurement.
Architectural and engineering services.
Violations of provisions, SF §13-322.
Falsification, concealment, etc., of material facts in connection with contracts, SF §11-205.1.

FELONIES —Cont'd
Procurement —Cont'd
Minority business participation.
  Prohibited acts, SF §14-308.
Rape in the first degree, CR §3-303.
  Attempted rape in the first degree, CR §3-309.
Rape in the second degree, CR §3-304.
  Attempted rape in second degree, CR §3-310.
Real estate brokers.
  Occurrence of felony on property.
    Failure to disclose certain facts, BOP §17-322.1.
Real property sales.
  New home deposits.
    Surety bond violations, RP §10-305.
Representation of destructive device.
  Manufacturing, possessing or transporting, CR
    §9-505.
Robbery, CR §3-402.
  With dangerous weapon, CR §3-403.
Sabotage.
  Defense related activity.
    Acting with intent to hinder, CR §§9-702, 9-703.
Sex offender registration offenses, CP §11-721.
Sexual abuse of minor, CR §3-602.
Sexual offense in the first degree, CR §3-305.
  Attempted sexual offense in first degree, CR
    §3-311.
Sexual offense in the second degree, CR §3-306.
  Attempted sexual offense in the second degree, CR
    §3-312.
Sexual offense in the third degree, CR §3-307.
Sexual solicitation of minor, CR §3-324.
Sodomy, CR §3-321.
State finance and procurement violations, SF
  §2-305.
Stem cell research.
  Human cloning, 83A §5-2B-13.
Suicide.
  Assisted suicide, CR §3-104.
Telecommunications services theft, CR §7-316.
Theft of services or property.
  Motor vehicle theft, CR §7-105.
  Value $500 or more, CR §7-104.
Tobacco tax.
  Stamps.
    Unstamped cigarettes.
      Willful transportation, TG §13-1015.
Trademark counterfeiting, CR §8-611.
Treason.
  No law to attaint for treason or felony, MD Const
    DofR Art 18.
Voter registration disqualifications, EL §3-102.
  Report of voter status from clerk of court, EL
    §3-504.
Weapons.
  Correctional facility inmates.
    Delivery to or possession with intent to deliver,
      receipt, COR §8-802.
Wiretapping.
  Unlawful acts, CJ §10-402.
Work release program.
  Inmate's failure to return, COR §3-803.

FELONS.
Firearms.
  Restrictions on possession, PS §5-133.
  Restrictions on sale, rental or transfer, PS §5-134.
Handgun permits.
  Disqualification, PS §5-306.
Long-term employment of qualified ex-felons.
  Pilot program, LE §§11-701 to 11-705.

FEMALE GENITAL MUTILATION, HG §§20-601
  to 20-603.

FEMALES.
See WOMEN.

FEME COVERT.
See MARRIED WOMEN.

FEME SOLE.
See WOMEN.

FENCES.
Advertising.
  Placing on trees, fences, buildings, etc., without
    permission, NR §5-407.
Charles county.
  Junkyards.
    Failure to screen or fence, fines, 25 §122B.
Counties.
  Chartered counties, powers, 25A §5.
Drainage districts.
  Injury or obstruction of bridge, fence or floodgate,
    25 §121E.
Fireworks plants, PS §10-204.
Prince George's county.
  Regulation by municipalities, 28 §8-104.

FENDERS, TR §22-413.
Motor vehicle equipment generally.
  See MOTOR VEHICLE EQUIPMENT.

FENTANYL ANALOGUE.
Importers, CR §5-614.

FERRETS.
Hunting with prohibited, NR §10-410.
Quarantine for rabies, HG §18-320.
Vaccinations.
  Required, HG §18-318.
  Responsibilities of veterinarian, HG §18-319.

FERRIES.
Ferry companies.
  Defined as common carrier, PUC §1-101.
Militia.
  Free passage over roads, bridges and ferries while
    traveling to and from duties, PS §13-212.
Somerset county.
  Franchise to ferry company, 25 §3D.

FERTILITY PRACTITIONERS.
Disposition of unused material.
  Information provided persons treated by
    practitioners, 83A §5-2B-10.

FERTILIZERS.
Agricultural lime.
  General provisions, AG §§6-301 to 6-311.
    See LIME.
Commercial fertilizers.
  Administration of subtitle.
    Expenses.
      Fund for payment, AG §6-204.
    State chemist, AG §6-202.
  Adulterated.
    Defined, AG §6-201.
    Distribution of adulterated fertilizers
      prohibited, AG §6-211.
  Ammonium nitrate fertilizer.
    Records of sale or distribution, AG §6-209.1.
  Analysis and testing.
    Evidence.
      Official analysis.
        Prima facie evidence, AG §6-215.
    Generally, AG §6-206.

FERTILIZERS —Cont'd
Commercial fertilizers —Cont'd
Analysis and testing —Cont'd
Guaranteed analysis.
Defined, AG §6-201.
Brand.
Defined, AG §6-201.
Bulk fertilizer.
Defined, AG §6-201.
Statement to accompany delivery, AG §6-210.
Buyer's mixture.
Defined, AG §6-201.
Chesapeake Bay.
Signs required at retail outlets advising
customers about effects of overuse of
fertilizer on waters of state, AG §6-210.1.
Condemnation and confiscation, AG §6-214.
Custom-mix.
Defined, AG §6-201.
Definitions, AG §6-201.
Distribute.
Defined, AG §6-201.
Enforcement.
Secretary of agriculture, AG §6-203.
Evidence.
Official analysis.
Prima facie evidence of composition, AG
§6-215.
Fees.
Fund for payment of administration expenses,
AG §6-204.
Registration and inspection fees, AG §6-208.
Fertilizer material.
Defined, AG §6-201.
Grade.
Defined, AG §6-201.
Guaranteed analysis.
Defined, AG §6-201.
Gypsum.
Defined, AG §6-201.
Information concerning fertilizers.
Publication by secretary, AG §6-205.
Injunctions.
Restraining violations, AG §6-217.
Inspection.
Fees, AG §6-208.
Generally, AG §6-206.
Labels, AG §6-210.
Defined, AG §6-201.
Lot.
Defined, AG §6-201.
Misbranded.
Defined, AG §6-201.
Distribution of misbranded fertilizer or soil
conditioners prohibited, AG §6-211.
Mixed fertilizer.
Defined, AG §6-201.
Mixed-to-order.
Defined, AG §6-201.
Labels, AG §6-210.
Penalties.
Generally, AG §§12-101 to 12-104.
Plant nutrient content.
Deficiency in guaranteed primary plant
nutrient, AG §6-219.
Short weight, AG §6-212.
Percentage.
Defined, AG §6-201.
Plant nutrient content.
Changes in, AG §6-213.

FERTILIZERS —Cont'd
Commercial fertilizers —Cont'd
Plant nutrient content —Cont'd
Deficient plant nutrients.
Determination, AG §6-219.
Penalty, AG §6-219.
Excess plant nutrients, AG §6-219.
Records.
Ammonium nitrate fertilizer, sale or
distribution, AG §6-209.1.
Distributor to keep records, AG §6-209.
Registration, AG §6-207.
Administrative penalties, AG §6-401.
Cancellation, AG §6-218.
Fees, AG §6-208.
Refusal, AG §6-218.
Reports.
Sales to nonregistrants, AG §6-209.
Statement of tonnage sold, AG §6-209.
Violations, AG §6-216.
Right of entry.
Inspections, testing, etc., AG §6-206.
Rules and regulations.
Adoption.
Secretary of agriculture, AG §6-203.
Product standards, AG §6-221.
Violations.
Stop-sale orders, AG §6-214.
Sale.
Reports, AG §6-209.
Signs required at retail outlets, AG §6-210.1.
Statement of tonnage sold, AG §6-209.
Stop-sale orders, AG §6-214.
Samples.
Generally, AG §6-206.
Official sample.
Defined, AG §6-201.
Secretary of agriculture.
Enforcement of subtitle, AG §6-203.
Information concerning fertilizers.
Publication, AG §6-205.
Right of entry.
Inspection, testing, etc., AG §6-206.
Rules and regulations.
Adoption, AG §6-203.
Stop-sale orders.
Issuance and enforcement, AG §6-214.
Short title, AG §6-220.
Short weight, AG §6-212.
Signs required at retail outlets, AG §6-210.1.
Soil conditioners.
Condemnation and confiscation of conditioners
in violation of subtitle, AG §6-214.
Defined, AG §6-201.
Distribution of misbranded soil conditioners.
Prohibited, AG §6-211.
Labels, AG §6-210.
Stop-sale orders, AG §6-214.
Specialty fertilizers.
Defined, AG §6-201.
Labels, AG §6-210.
Standards.
Regulations regarding product standards, AG
§6-221.
State chemist.
Administration of subtitle, AG §6-203.
Statements.
Accompanying delivery, AG §6-210.
Tonnage sold, AG §6-209.
Stop-sale orders, AG §6-214.

FERTILIZERS —Cont'd
Commercial fertilizers —Cont'd
Title.
Short title, AG §6-220.
Ton.
Defined, AG §6-201.
Short weight, AG §6-212.
Statement of tonnage sold, AG §6-209.
Violations.
Administrative penalties, AG §6-401.
Injunctions, AG §6-217.
Minor violations, AG §6-216.
Report for criminal prosecutions, AG §6-216.
Stop-sale orders, AG §6-214.
Counties.
Agricultural lime.
General provisions, AG §§6-301 to 6-311.
See LIME.
Manufacturers.
Regulation, 25 §3.
Lime.
Agricultural lime.
General provisions, AG §§6-301 to 6-311.
See LIME.
Municipal corporations.
Powers as to manufacture, 23A §2.

FESTIVALS.
Beer festivals generally.
See ALCOHOLIC BEVERAGES.
Outdoor music festivals.
Promoter licenses, BR §§17-1401 to 17-1407.
See OUTDOOR CONCERTS.
Wine festivals generally.
See ALCOHOLIC BEVERAGES.

FETAL ALCOHOL SYNDROME.
Public awareness campaign, HG §18-309.

FETAL DEATH.
Vital records.
See VITAL RECORDS.

FETUS.
Murder or manslaughter of viable fetus, CR §2-103.

FEVER THERMOMETERS.
Mercury fever thermometers.
Definitions, EN §6-905.
Selling or providing without prescription prohibited, EN §6-905.1.

FICTITIOUS PAYEES.
Negotiable instruments, CL §3-404.

FIDUCIARIES.
Abandoned property disposition.
Intangible personal property held in fiduciary capacity.
When property presumed abandoned, CL §17-306.
Absent or unknown persons.
Appointment of attorney, Guardian Rule 10-604.
Assumption of jurisdiction, Guardian Rule 10-601.
Distribution of property, Guardian Rule 10-605.
Hearings, Guardian Rule 10-603.
Notice, Guardian Rule 10-602.
Venue.
Petition for assumption of jurisdiction, Guardian Rule 10-601.
Accounts.
Estates including guardianships of property. See within this heading, "Estates including guardianships of property."

FIDUCIARIES —Cont'd
Agents.
Employment.
Powers of fiduciaries, ET §15-102.
Applicability of rules Titles 1 and 2, Guardian Rule 10-102.
Assets.
Power to receive and retain assets, ET §15-102.
Valuation.
Distribution in kind, using federal estate tax values, ET §11-107.
Associations.
Prudent investment rule.
Directors and officers.
Standard of care required for directors, CA §2-405.1.
Attorneys at law.
Appointment of attorney or investigator, Guardian Rule 10-106.
Automobile insurance fund.
Producers as fiduciaries, IN §20-510.
Banks and trust companies.
Agent or custodian for fiduciary.
Authorized to deposit securities with securities clearing corporation, ET §15-104.
Authority to act as, FI §3-207.
Commercial banks.
Exercise of fiduciary powers.
Requirements and standards, FI §3-103.
Defined, ET §15-201.
Deposits. See within this heading, "Deposits."
Institution acting in fiduciary capacity, FI §§3-804, 5-615.
Personal account.
Fiduciary personal account, ET §15-208.
Preferences.
Acting in fiduciary capacity, FI §§3-804, 5-615.
Successor corporate fiduciaries, ET §§15-1A-01 to 15-1A-05. See within this heading, "Successor corporate fiduciaries."
Bond issues.
Transfer.
Uniform act. See within this heading, "Uniform acts."
Bonds, surety.
Agreement of fiduciary and surety for deposit of assets, ET §15-105.
Corporations that act as fiduciaries not liable as sureties, ET §15-115.
Estates including guardianship of property, Guardian Rule 10-702.
Release from liability.
Resignation of fiduciary does not release, ET §15-111.
Bulk transfers.
Transfers excepted from article, CL §6-103.
Charities.
Solicitations, BR §6-508.
Checks.
Deposit in name of fiduciary as such, ET §15-206.
Deposit in name of principal, ET §15-207.
Deposit in personal account of fiduciary, ET §15-208.
Drawn by and payable to fiduciary, ET §15-205.
Drawn by fiduciary to third person, ET §15-204.
Claims.
Payment.
Powers of fiduciaries, ET §15-102.
Commercial code.
Representative defined, CL §1-201.

FIDUCIARIES —Cont'd
Commissions.
General provisions, ET §14-103.
Committee.
Defined, ET §15-101.
Liability, ET §15-103.
Successor corporate fiduciaries, ET §§15-1A-01 to 15-1A-05. See within this heading, "Successor corporate fiduciaries."
Contracts.
Power to perform, ET §15-102.
Corporate fiduciary.
Defined, ET §§14-107, 15-1A-01, 15-101.
Incorporation.
Powers of fiduciaries, ET §15-102.
Investments by corporate fiduciary.
Lawful investments, ET §15-106.
Liability of corporations that act as fiduciaries.
Not liable as sureties, ET §15-115.
Liability of holder of stock in fiduciary capacity, CA §2-215.
Prudent investment rule.
Directors and officers.
Standard of care required of directors, CA §2-405.1.
Stock subscriptions.
Powers of fiduciaries, ET §15-102.
Successor corporate fiduciaries, ET §§15-1A-01 to 15-1A-05. See within this heading, "Successor corporate fiduciaries."
Voting of shares by certain holders, CA §2-508.
Custodian.
Successor corporate fiduciaries, ET §§15-1A-01 to 15-1A-05. See within this heading, "Successor corporate fiduciaries."
Transfers to minors act, ET §§13-301 to 13-324. See MINORS.
Debts.
Compromise.
Power to compromise debt, ET §15-102.
Declaratory judgments.
Rights of fiduciaries, CJ §3-408.
Definitions, ET §§15-101, 15-102, 15-201; Guardian Rule 10-103.
Security transfers.
Uniform act, ET §15-301.
Depositary.
Defined, ET §15-101.
Liability, ET §15-103.
Deposited or exchanged.
Defined, ET §15-101.
Deposits.
Assets of estate, ET §15-105.
Banks and trust companies.
Securities.
Fiduciary authorized to deposit securities with clearing corporation.
Bank or trust company as custodian or agent for fiduciary, ET §15-104.
Name of fiduciary.
In name of fiduciary as such, ET §15-206.
Personal accounts, ET §15-208.
Principal.
In name of principal, ET §15-207.
Securities.
Fiduciary authorized to deposit securities with clearing corporation, ET §15-104.
Disclaimer of property interests by fiduciaries, ET §9-202.
Other fiduciaries, effectiveness as to, ET §9-208.
Time of taking effect, ET §9-208.

FIDUCIARIES —Cont'd
Disclaimer of property interests by fiduciaries —Cont'd
Trustees, ET §9-205.
Distribution.
Commissions.
Final distribution, ET §14-103.
Decree or order of court.
Protection when distribution made under jurisdiction of court, ET §15-108.
Valuation.
Distribution in kind, using federal estate tax values, ET §11-107.
Embezzlement, CR §7-113.
Environmental law.
Compliance.
Powers of fiduciaries, ET §15-102.
Defined, ET §15-101.
Equity.
Cases not provided for in subtitle, ET §15-209.
Distribution under jurisdiction of court, ET §15-108.
Estates including guardianships of property.
Accounting.
Annual fiduciary accounts, Guardian Rule 10-706.
Final distribution, Guardian Rule 10-710.
Removal for cause or other sanctions.
Final accounting and delivery of property, Guardian Rule 10-712.
Report of trust clerk, Guardian Rule 10-708.
Restricted accounts, Guardian Rule 10-705.
Appointment of substitute or successor, Guardian Rule 10-711.
Bonds, surety, Guardian Rule 10-702.
Compromise of claim or dispute, Guardian Rule 10-703.
Final distribution, Guardian Rule 10-710.
Foreign fiduciaries.
Transfer of estate, Guardian Rule 10-709.
Inventory, Guardian Rule 10-707.
Notice.
Removal for cause or other sanctions, Guardian Rule 10-712.
Resignation of fiduciary and appointment of substitute or successor, Guardian Rule 10-711.
Termination of estate, Guardian Rule 10-710.
Transfer of estate to foreign fiduciary, Guardian Rule 10-709.
Notice of compromise, Guardian Rule 10-703.
Removal for cause or other sanctions, Guardian Rule 10-712.
Report of trust clerk, Guardian Rule 10-708.
Resignation of fiduciary, Guardian Rule 10-711.
Restricted accounts, Guardian Rule 10-705.
Scope of rules, Guardian Rule 10-701.
Securities in name of disabled person.
Titling of assets, Guardian Rule 10-704.
Termination of estate, Guardian Rule 10-710.
Titling of assets, Guardian Rule 10-704.
Transfer of estate to foreign fiduciary, Guardian Rule 10-709.
Venue.
Compromise of claim or dispute, Guardian Rule 10-703.
Removal for cause or other sanctions, Guardian Rule 10-712.
Resignation and appointment of substitute or successor, Guardian Rule 10-711.
Termination of estate, Guardian Rule 10-710.

FIDUCIARIES —Cont'd
Estates including guardianships of property
　—Cont'd
Venue —Cont'd
　Transfer of estate to foreign fiduciary, Guardian
　　Rule 10-709.
Estates other than guardianships.
Administration of estate, Guardian Rule 10-504.
Hearings.
　Petition for assumption of jurisdiction,
　　Guardian Rule 10-503.
Jurisdiction.
　Petition for assumption, Guardian Rule 10-501.
　Termination, Guardian Rule 10-505.
Notice.
　Petition for assumption of jurisdiction,
　　Guardian Rule 10-502.
Petition for assumptions of jurisdiction, Guardian
　Rule 10-501.
Termination of jurisdiction, Guardian Rule 10-505.
Venue.
　Petition for assumption of jurisdiction,
　　Guardian Rule 10-501.
Evidence.
Transfer of securities, ET §15-304.
Federal estate tax.
Distribution in kind, using federal estate tax
　values, ET §11-107.
Fees.
Assessment and waiver, Guardian Rule 10-107.
Funds.
Power to deposit, ET §15-102.
Guardians generally.
See GUARDIAN AND WARD.
Immunity from liability.
Uniform act for simplification of fiduciary security
　transfers, ET §15-307.
Income tax.
Defined, TG §10-101.
Individuals.
　Exemptions, TG §10-212.
　Returns, TG §10-813.
Institutional funds.
General provisions, ET §§15-401 to 15-409.
　See INVESTMENTS.
Prudent man rule.
　Standard of conduct, ET §15-406.
Insurance.
Automobile insurance fund.
　Producers as fiduciaries, IN §20-510.
Contract of insurance on life of grantor, ET
　§15-116.
Power to insure property, ET §15-102.
Interpretation and construction.
Uniform acts.
　Uniform act for the simplification of fiduciary
　　security transfers.
　　Uniformity of interpretation, ET §15-310.
　Uniform fiduciaries act.
　　Uniformity of interpretation of subtitle, ET
　　　§15-210.
Investments.
Guidelines and standards, ET §15-114.
Institutional funds.
　General provisions, ET §§15-401 to 15-409.
　See INVESTMENTS.
Lawful investments, ET §15-106.
Judicial proceedings.
Powers of fiduciaries, ET §15-102.
Jurisdiction.
Applicability of rules and scope of jurisdiction,
　Guardian Rule 10-101.

FIDUCIARIES —Cont'd
Jurisdiction —Cont'd
Over persons outside this state.
　General provisions.
　　See JURISDICTION.
Transfer of action, Guardian Rule 10-109.
Uniform act.
　Simplification of fiduciary security transfers, ET
　　§15-308.
Law merchant.
Cases not provided for in subtitle, ET §15-209.
Leases.
Powers.
　Survival, ET §15-107.
Liability.
Committee, depositary or recipient, ET §15-103.
Immunity.
　Uniform act for simplification of fiduciary
　　security transfer, ET §15-307.
Joint and several liability of trust company
　affiliates, ET §15-113.
Uniform act for simplification of fiduciary security
　transfers.
　Immunity from liability, ET §15-307.
Limited liability companies.
Conversion of sole proprietorship to limited
　liability company, ET §15-102.
Money.
Power to borrow money, ET §15-102.
Mortgages and deeds of trust.
Payment.
　Powers of fiduciary, ET §15-102.
Powers, ET §15-102.
　Person taking title to property in representative
　　or fiduciary capacity, RP §14-112.
Survival, ET §15-107.
Release.
　Powers of fiduciary, ET §15-102.
Motor vehicle insurance.
Automobile insurance fund.
　Producers as fiduciaries, IN §20-510.
Negotiable instruments.
Breach of fiduciary duty.
　Notice of, CL §3-307.
Cases not provided for in subtitle, ET §15-209.
Checks.
　Drawn by and payable to fiduciary, ET §15-205.
　Drawn by fiduciary to third person, ET §15-204.
Transfer by fiduciary, ET §15-203.
Notice.
Simplification of fiduciary security transfers.
　Adverse claim, ET §15-305.
Successor corporate fiduciary.
　Delivery.
　　Defined, ET §15-1A-04.
　Interested party.
　　Defined, ET §15-1A-04.
　Substitution, ET §15-1A-04.
Options.
Power of fiduciary to exercise options, ET §15-102.
Order assuming jurisdiction over fiduciary
　estate other than guardianship, Guardian
　Rule 10-108.
Orders of court.
Distribution.
　Protection when distribution made in
　　conformity with decree or order of court, ET
　　　§15-108.
Partnerships.
Powers of fiduciaries, ET §15-102.

FIDUCIARIES —Cont'd
Partnerships, revised act.
Fiduciary duties of partners, CA §9A-404.
Payments.
Application of payments made to fiduciaries, ET §15-202.
Person.
Defined, ET §§15-101, 15-102; SG §1-101.
Personal property.
Power to dispose of personal property.
Passes to survivor or successor, ET §15-107.
Pledge.
Power to satisfy pledges, ET §15-102.
Power of attorney.
Extent of power of person taking title to property in representative or fiduciary capacity, RP §14-112.
Powers.
Estates and trusts generally, ET §15-102.
Person taking title to property in representative or fiduciary capacity, RP §14-112.
Presumptions.
Corporation or transfer agent.
Registering security in name of fiduciary not required to make inquiry, ET §15-302.
Security transfers.
Assumptions.
Generally, ET §15-303.
Principal.
Defined, ET §15-201.
Deposit in name of principal, ET §15-207.
Principal and income act.
Duties, ET §15-502.
Generally, ET §§15-501 to 15-530.
See PRINCIPAL AND INCOME.
Property.
Power of fiduciary, ET §15-102.
Prudent investment rule.
Corporations and associations.
Directors and officers.
Standard of care required of directors, CA §2-405.1.
Guardians.
Degree of care and skill exercised, ET §13-212.
Institutional funds.
Standard of conduct, ET §15-406.
Transfers to minors.
Custodians.
Investment of custodial property, ET §13-312.
Real property.
Power to dispose of real and personal property.
Passes to survivor or successor, ET §15-107.
Receipts.
Power to receive assets, ET §15-102.
Sufficiency of release of fiduciary to whom property transferred by another, ET §15-109.
Receivers.
Bonds, surety, Receivers Rule 13-107.
Successor corporate fiduciaries, ET §§15-1A-01 to 15-1A-05. See within this heading, "Successor corporate fiduciaries."
Recipient.
Liability, ET §15-103.
Releases.
Sufficiency of release of fiduciary to whom property transferred by another, ET §15-109.
Removal.
Applicability.
Section not applicable to personal representatives, ET §15-112.
Failure to give countersecurity, ET §15-110.

FIDUCIARIES —Cont'd
Removal —Cont'd
Grounds.
Discretionary grounds, ET §15-112.
Mandatory grounds, ET §15-112.
Procedures, ET §15-112.
Reorganization.
Agreement.
Defined, ET §15-101.
Securities.
Who may accept and dispose of securities, ET §15-103.
Plan.
Defined, ET §15-101.
Resignation.
Effect, ET §15-111.
Right or title acquired.
Not invalid in consequence of misapplication by fiduciary, ET §15-202.
Sales.
Commissions, ET §14-103.
Powers.
Person taking title to property in representative or fiduciary capacity, RP §14-112.
Survival, ET §15-107.
Securities.
Authority to deposit with securities clearing corporation, ET §15-104.
Bank or trust company holding securities as custodian or agent for fiduciary, ET §15-104.
Certification in writing of account, ET §15-104.
Duty of fiduciary, ET §15-104.
Defined, ET §15-101.
Power to hold securities in name of nominee, ET §15-102.
Power to vote stocks, ET §15-102.
Reorganization agreements.
Who may accept and dispose of securities, ET §15-103.
Transfer.
Uniform act. See within this heading, "Uniform acts."
Show cause orders, Guardian Rule 10-104.
Simplification of fiduciary security transfers, ET §§15-301 to 15-311.
State retirement and pension system.
Board of trustees.
Fiduciary responsibilities, SPP §§21-201 to 21-210.
See STATE RETIREMENT AND PENSION SYSTEM.
Supplemental retirement plans, SPP §§35-301, 35-302.
Substitution.
Successor corporate fiduciaries act, ET §§15-1A-01 to 15-1A-05.
Subtitle.
Cases not provided for in subtitle, ET §15-209.
Citation.
Short title, ET §15-211.
Interpretation.
Uniformity, ET §15-210.
Successor corporate fiduciaries, ET §§15-1A-01 to 15-1A-05.
Adoption of resolution, ET §15-1A-02.
Assets, ET §15-1A-03.
Bank.
Defined, ET §15-1A-01.
Bank holding company.
Defined, ET §15-1A-01.

FIDUCIARIES —Cont'd
Successor corporate fiduciaries —Cont'd
Beneficiary.
Defined, ET §15-1A-01.
Corporate fiduciary.
Defined, ET §15-1A-01.
Definitions, ET §15-1A-01.
Delivery, ET §15-1A-04.
Interested party, ET §15-1A-04.
Fiduciary defined, ET §15-1A-01.
Liability.
Joint and several liability, ET §15-1A-03.
Notice.
Delivery.
Defined, ET §15-1A-04.
Interested party.
Defined, ET §15-1A-04.
Substitution, ET §15-1A-04.
Form and content, ET §15-1A-04.
Requirements of notice, ET §15-1A-04.
Powers, ET §15-1A-02.
Survival, ET §15-107.
Qualifications, ET §15-1A-03.
Removal, ET §15-1A-05.
Rights and obligations, ET §15-1A-02.
Substitution, ET §15-1A-02.
Adoption of resolution, ET §15-1A-02.
How affected, ET §15-1A-02.
Notice, ET §15-1A-04.
Form and content, ET §15-1A-04.
Requirements of notice, ET §15-1A-04.
Removal, ET §15-1A-05.
Written instruments.
When substitution applicable to written
instruments, ET §15-1A-02.
Successor fiduciary.
Defined, ET §15-1A-01.
Trust company.
Defined, ET §15-1A-01.
Suretyship.
Agreement with surety for deposit of assets, ET
§15-105.
Countersecurity, ET §15-110.
Resignation of fiduciary does not release from
liability, ET §15-111.
Taxation.
Gift to surviving spouse in will, qualifying for
estate tax marital deduction, ET §11-106.
Liability, TP §1-203.
Payment.
Powers of fiduciaries, ET §15-102.
Retaining sums for payment, TP §1-203.
Uniform act.
Simplification of fiduciary security transfers.
Act not to affect obligations with respect to
estate taxes, ET §15-309.
Transfer of action, Guardian Rule 10-109.
Transfers to minors.
Prudent man rule.
Custodians.
Investment of custodial property, ET §13-312.
Trustees.
Discretionary trust, ET §14-405.
Joint and several liability of trust company
affiliates, ET §15-113.
Uniform acts.
Simplification of fiduciary security transfers.
Applicability, ET §15-308.
Assignments.
Assumptions generally, ET §15-303.
Defined, ET §15-301.

FIDUCIARIES —Cont'd
Uniform acts —Cont'd
Simplification of fiduciary security transfers
—Cont'd
Citation of subtitle, ET §15-311.
Claims.
Beneficial interest claim adverse to transfer of
security pursuant to assignment by
fiduciary, ET §15-305.
Defined, ET §15-301.
Corporation or transfer agent.
Defined, ET §15-301.
Law governing rights and duties, ET §15-308.
Liability, ET §15-306.
No liability imposed, ET §15-307.
When security registered in name of
fiduciary, ET §15-302.
Registering security in name of fiduciary not
required to make inquiry, ET §15-302.
Definitions, ET §15-301.
Evidence required when fiduciary not registered
owner, ET §15-304.
Immunity, ET §15-307.
Interpretation.
Uniformity of interpretation, ET §15-310.
Jurisdiction.
Corporation or transfer agent.
No liability if action authorized by act, ET
§15-306.
Law governing rights and duties of
corporation, etc., ET §15-308.
Liability.
Absence of actual knowledge of misuse of
proceeds, CJ §5-421.
Immunity from liability, ET §15-307.
Corporations or transfer agents.
Immunity from liability, ET §15-307.
Persons guaranteeing signature of fiduciaries,
CJ §5-421.
Immunity from liability, ET §15-307.
Third persons.
Nonliability, ET §15-307.
Misuse of proceeds.
Absence of actual knowledge.
Immunity from liability, ET §15-307.
Notice.
Claim of beneficial interest adverse to
fiduciary, ET §15-305.
Person.
Defined, ET §15-301.
Presumptions.
Fiduciary relationship, ET §15-302.
Generally, ET §15-303.
Registration.
Corporation or transfer agent.
Registering security in name of fiduciary
not required to make inquiry, ET
§15-302.
Evidence required when fiduciary not
registered owner, ET §15-304.
Security.
Defined, ET §15-301.
Short title, ET §15-311.
Signatures of fiduciaries.
Persons guaranteeing.
Immunity from liability, ET §15-307.
Taxation.
Obligations with respect to estate taxes not
affected, ET §15-309.
Third persons.
Nonliability, ET §15-307.

FIDUCIARIES —Cont'd
Uniform acts —Cont'd
Simplification of fiduciary security transfers
—Cont'd
Transfer.
Assumptions.
Continuation of fiduciary relationship, ET
§15-303.
Defined, ET §15-301.
Evidence required when fiduciary not
registered owner, ET §15-304.
Pursuant to assignment by fiduciary.
Assumptions generally, ET §15-303.
Uniform fiduciaries act, ET §§15-201 to 15-211.
Citation, ET §15-211.
Waiver of notice, Guardian Rule 10-105.
Wills.
Devises and bequests.
Distribution in kind, using federal estate tax
values, ET §11-107.
Executors and administrators.
General provisions.
See EXECUTORS AND ADMINISTRATORS.
Successor corporate fiduciaries, ET §§15-1A-01
to 15-1A-05. See within this heading,
"Successor corporate fiduciaries."
Federal estate tax.
Distribution in kind, using federal estate tax
values, ET §11-107.
Incorporation by reference, ET §4-107.

FIELD TRIALS.
Dogs.
General provisions, NR §§10-701 to 10-703.
See BIRDS AND GAME.

FIFTH WHEEL TRAVEL TRAILERS, TR
§11-121.1.

FILING.
Administration of courts.
Clients' security fund.
Report and audit, CJA Rule 16-811.
Court reporters.
Circuit court reporters.
Maintenance and filing of administrative
records, CJA Rule 16-404.
Electronic filing of pleadings and papers, CJA
Rule 16-307.
Generally, CJA Rule 16-308.
Reports to be filed, CJA Rule 16-105.
Attorneys at law.
Bar admissions.
Defined, BarAdm Rule 1.
Out-of-state attorneys.
Petition, BarAdm Rule 13.
Registration of law students.
Fee for filing, BarAdm Rule 2.
Bonds, surety.
Approval, Rule 1-402.
Clients' security fund.
Report and audit, CJA Rule 16-811.
Counterclaims.
Time for filing.
Circuit courts, CivProCir Rule 2-331.
District Court, CivProDist Rule 3-331.
Criminal rules, Crim Rule 4-211.
Cross-claims.
Time for filing.
Circuit courts, CivProCir Rule 2-331.
District Court, CivProDist Rule 3-331.

FILING —Cont'd
Discovery.
Perpetuation of evidence.
Notice, request or motion to be filed.
Circuit courts, CivProCir Rule 2-404.
Divorce, annulment and alimony.
Pleadings.
Form of financial statements, FamLaw Rule
9-203.
Ejectment.
Warrant of resurvey.
Plat to be filed, PropAct Rule 12-101.
Eminent domain.
Board of property review.
Certification to board.
Filing, PropAct Rule 12-213.
Examiners.
Hearings.
Record.
Circuit courts, CivProCir Rule 2-542.
Expungement of records.
Applications.
No charges filed.
Time for filing, Crim Rule 4-503.
Petitions.
Charges filed, Crim Rule 4-504.
Foreclosures.
Commencement of action, PropSales Rule 14-203.
Health care malpractice claims.
Commencement of action.
Notice, SpecPro Rule 15-403.
Declaration, SpecPro Rule 15-403.
Judgments notwithstanding the verdict.
Time for filing.
Circuit courts, CivProCir Rule 2-532.
Juvenile causes.
Juvenile petition, Juv Rule 11-103.
Waiver of jurisdiction.
Charging documents, Crim Rule 4-222.
Mechanics' liens.
Enforcement of lien.
Petition to enforce.
Time for filing, PropAct Rule 12-305.
New trial.
Motion for new trial.
Time for filing.
Circuit courts, CivProCir Rule 2-533.
District Court, CivProDist Rule 3-533.
Papers, Rule 1-322.
Photocopies or facsimile copies, Rule 1-322.
Pleadings, Rule 1-322.
Answers.
Time for filing.
Circuit courts, CivProCir Rule 2-321.
Counterclaims or cross-claims.
Time for filing.
Circuit courts, CivProCir Rule 2-331.
District Court, CivProDist Rule 3-331.
Demand for jury trial.
District Court, CivProDist Rule 3-325.
Notice of intention to defend.
District Court, CivProDist Rule 3-307.
Effect of failure to file.
District Court, CivProDist Rule 3-307.
Prepayment of filing fees, Rule 1-325.
Waiver, Rule 1-325.
Public defenders.
Denial of public defender representation.
Payment of filing fees by state, Rule 1-325.
**Receivers and assignees or trustees for
creditors.**
Reports, Receivers Rule 13-501.

FILING —Cont'd
Receivers and assignees or trustees for creditors —Cont'd
Schedule of debtor's property and debts.
Preparation and filing by debtor, Receivers Rule 13-203.
Sentencing.
Review of sentence.
Application, Crim Rule 4-344.
Third parties.
Pleadings.
Time for filing.
Circuit courts, CivProCir Rule 2-332.
District Court, CivProDist Rule 3-341.

FILLING STATIONS.
Service stations.
See SERVICE STATIONS.

FILM.
Generally.
See MOTION PICTURES.
Obscenity and pornography.
Adult sexual displays, CR §§11-101 to 11-107.
See OBSCENITY AND PORNOGRAPHY.
Obscene matter generally, CR §§11-201 to 11-211.
See OBSCENITY AND PORNOGRAPHY.

FILMING INDIVIDUAL IN PRIVATE PLACE, CR §3-901.
With prurient intent, CR §3-902.

FILM PRODUCTION ACTIVITY EMPLOYER WAGE REBATE PROGRAM, 83A §§5-1801 to 5-1807.
Amount of rebate, 83A §5-1803.
Applications, 83A §5-1804.
Definitions, 83A §5-1801.
Fund, 83A §5-1805.
Grant agreement, 83A §5-1804.
Legislative intent, 83A §5-1802.
Notice of intent to seek rebate, 83A §5-1804.
Regulations, 83A §5-1806.
Reports, 83A §5-1807.

FILM PRODUCTION ACTIVITY TAX EXEMPTIONS, 83A §4-501.

FINANCE.
Appropriations.
General provisions.
See APPROPRIATIONS.
Budget and management.
General provisions.
See BUDGET AND MANAGEMENT.
Procurement.
General provisions.
See PROCUREMENT.
Public debt.
General provisions.
See PUBLIC DEBT.
Revenues.
General provisions.
See REVENUES.
State treasury.
General provisions.
See STATE TREASURY.
Taxation.
General provisions.
See TAXATION.

FINANCE COMPANIES.
Advertising.
Installment sales.
Regulations, CL §12-602.

FINANCE COMPANIES —Cont'd
Consumer loan licensing provisions.
General provisions.
See CONSUMER LOANS.
Equal credit opportunity, CL §§12-701 to 12-708.
See EQUAL CREDIT OPPORTUNITY.
Industrial development financing authority, 83A §§5-901 to 5-933.
See INDUSTRIAL DEVELOPMENT FINANCING AUTHORITY.
Installment sales.
General provisions, CL §§12-601 to 12-636.
See SALES.
Mortgages and deeds of trust.
Mortgage lender law, FI §§11-501 to 11-524.
See MORTGAGE LENDERS.
Mortgage originators, FI §§11-601 to 11-618.
See MORTGAGE ORIGINATORS.
Motor vehicles.
Registration.
Plates, TR §13-623.
Offsets.
Defined, CL §15-701.
Prohibited, CL §15-702.
Sales finance companies.
See SALES.
Small loans.
Credit provisions.
See SMALL LOANS.
Licensing provisions.
See SMALL LOANS.

FINANCE DEPARTMENT.
Board of public works.
General provisions.
See PUBLIC WORKS.
Composition, MD Const Art VI §1.
Comptroller.
Supervise fiscal affairs of state, MD Const Art VI §2.
Warrants for payment of money.
Comptroller.
See COMPTROLLER.

FINANCE LEASES.
Commercial code leases.
General provisions, CL §§2A-101 to 2A-532.
See LEASES, UCC.

FINANCIAL AID FOR STUDENTS.
Applicability of general provisions subtitle, ED §18-102.
Bonds of scholarship recipients.
Enforcement, ED §18-109.
Control of institution not affected, ED §18-104.
Definitions, ED §18-101.
Delegate scholarships, ED §§18-501 to 18-507.
See SCHOLARSHIPS.
Dent-care program, ED §§18-2401 to 18-2408.
Distinguished scholar program.
Community college students, ED §18-1106.
Generally, ED §§18-1101 to 18-1106.
See SCHOLARSHIPS.
Drug use.
Pledge to remain drug free, ED §18-111.
Economic development grants, ED §§18-701 to 18-708.
See SCHOLARSHIPS.
Educational excellence awards, ED §§18-301 to 18-310.
See SCHOLARSHIPS.
Eligible institutions, ED §18-103.

FINANCIAL AID FOR STUDENTS —Cont'd
Grades.
  Disclosure of grades of scholarship students to sponsor, ED §18-105.
Interest rate, calculation, ED §18-112.
Janet L. Hoffman loan assistance repayment program.
  Universities and colleges.
    Loan assistance repayment program, ED §§18-1501 to 18-1505.
      See UNIVERSITIES AND COLLEGES.
Judith A. Resnik memorial postgraduate fellowship program, ED §18-901.
Loan assistance repayment program, ED §§18-1501 to 18-1505.
  See UNIVERSITIES AND COLLEGES.
Math/science student corps, ED §§18-1601 to 18-1604.
  See UNIVERSITIES AND COLLEGES.
Medical, dental and nursing scholarships, ED §§18-801 to 18-803.
  See SCHOLARSHIPS.
Military personnel.
  Scholarships, ED §§18-601 to 18-604.
    See SCHOLARSHIPS.
Minors.
  Disability of infancy removed for recipients of benefits, ED §18-108.
Multiple scholarships and grants, ED §18-113.
Nurses.
  Nonresidents enrolled in courses.
    Tuition reduction, ED §18-110.
  Nursing scholarships, ED §§18-801 to 18-803.
    See SCHOLARSHIPS.
Part-time grant program, ED §§18-1401 to 18-1404.
  See UNIVERSITIES AND COLLEGES.
Private career school student grant program, ED §§18-1201 to 18-1207.
  See SCHOLARSHIPS.
Public safety personnel.
  Scholarships, ED §§18-601 to 18-604.
    See SCHOLARSHIPS.
Refund where recipient withdraws, ED §18-106.
Religious discrimination, ED §18-104.
Repayment obligations, ED §18-112.
Senatorial scholarships, ED §§18-401 to 18-408.
Source of funds, ED §18-107.
State scholarships.
  See SCHOLARSHIPS.
Student financial assistance office, ED §§18-201 to 18-205.
Universities and colleges.
  Development of financial programs, ED §10-203.
Unused funds, ED §18-107.

FINANCIAL DISCLOSURES.
Motor vehicles.
  Registration.
    Nonpayment of judgments, TR §§17-201 to 17-209.
      See MOTOR VEHICLE REGISTRATION.
Public ethics.
  See PUBLIC ETHICS.

FINANCIAL EXPLOITATION.
Banks and trust companies.
  Disclosure of client financial records, FI §1-306.

FINANCIAL INSTITUTION FRANCHISE TAX.
Abatement, TG §13-908.

FINANCIAL INSTITUTION FRANCHISE TAX —Cont'd
Administration of provisions.
  Department of assessments and taxation, TG §8-211.
Allocation of taxable net earnings, TG §8-206.
Assessments.
  Application for revision or claim for refund, TG §13-508.
  Erroneous assessments, TG §13-509.
  Time for, TG §13-1101.
Business premises credits, TG §8-217.
Checks.
  Payment by dishonored checks.
    Assessment of service charge, TG §13-713.
Child care credits, TG §8-216.
Community and neighborhood assistance credit, TG §8-215.
Commuter benefits, tax credit, TG §8-221.
Computation of taxable net earnings, TG §8-204.
Credits.
  Child care, TG §8-216.
  Commuter benefits, TG §8-221.
  Employees with disabilities, TG §8-216.
  Estimated taxes, TG §8-207.
  Long-term care insurance provided by employer, TG §8-218.
  Maryland project costs and start-up costs, TG §8-220.
  Neighborhood and community assistance, TG §8-215.
  New or expanded business premises, TG §8-217.
  Qualified employment opportunity employees.
    Wages and child care, TG §8-213.
  Student wages under work-study program, TG §8-219.
  Taxes paid to other states, TG §8-208.
  Wage credit, TG §8-214.
    Employees with disabilities, TG §8-216.
Crimes and offenses.
  Returns.
    Willful failure to file return, TG §13-1001.
    Willfully filing false return.
      Perjury, TG §13-1002.
Definitions, TG §§1-101, 8-101, 8-201.
Department of assessments and taxation.
  Administration of provisions, TG §8-211.
Distribution of revenue, TG §2-501.
Employees with disabilities.
  Credits, TG §8-216.
Estimated taxes.
  Credits, TG §8-207.
  Declaration, TG §8-209.
  Payment, TG §8-210.
Imposition of tax, TG §8-201.
  Restrictions, TG §8-202.
Interest.
  Estimated tax.
    Deficiency, TG §13-602.
  Payment of interest by dishonored checks.
    Assessment of service charge, TG §13-713.
International banking facilities.
  Taxable net earnings, TG §8-205.
Limitation of actions.
  Assessments, TG §13-1101.
  Refunds.
    Filing claims for, TG §13-1104.
Long-term care insurance credit, TG §8-218.
Military services.
  Death of members of armed forces.
    Abatement of tax, TG §13-908.

FINANCIAL INSTITUTION FRANCHISE TAX
—Cont'd
Misdemeanors.
Returns.
Willful failure to file, TG §13-1001.
Neighborhood and community assistance credit, TG §8-215.
Offsets, TG §13-909.
Payment of tax, TG §8-210.
Checks.
Dishonored checks.
Assessment of service charge, TG §13-713.
Failure to pay.
Penalty, TG §13-701.
Penalties.
Failure to pay tax, TG §13-701.
Payment by dishonored checks.
Assessment of service charge, TG §13-713.
Returns.
Willful failure to file, TG §13-1001.
Willfully filing false return.
Perjury penalty, TG §13-1002.
Underestimation of tax, TG §13-702.
Perjury.
Willfully filing false return, TG §13-1002.
Qualified employment opportunity employees.
Credit for wages and child care, TG §8-213.
Rate of tax, TG §8-203.
Refunds.
Payment, TG §2-502.
Certifications, TG §8-212.
Time for filing claims, TG §13-1104.
Returns, TG §8-209.
Willful failure to file return, TG §13-1001.
Willfully filing false return.
Perjury, TG §13-1002.
Student work-study wages, credit, TG §8-219.
Taxable net earnings.
Allocation, TG §8-206.
Computation, TG §8-204.
International banking facilities, TG §8-205.
Rate of tax based on, TG §8-203.
Taxes paid to other states.
Credits, TG §8-208.
Wage credit, TG §8-214.
Employees with disabilities, TG §8-216.

FINANCIAL INSTITUTIONS.
Attorneys at law.
Trust accounts.
General provisions, CJA Rules 16-601 to 16-612.
See ATTORNEYS AT LAW.
Automated teller machines, FI §§1-401 to 1-406.
See AUTOMATED TELLER MACHINES.
Bank deposits and collections.
Generally, CL §§4-101 to 4-504.
See BANK DEPOSITS AND COLLECTIONS.
Banks and trust companies.
See BANKS AND TRUST COMPANIES.
Check cashing services, FI §§12-101 to 12-127.
See CHECK CASHING SERVICES.
Child support enforcement.
Attachment and seizure of funds for arrears from financial institution, FL §§10-108.3, 10-108.4.
Reports requested by child support enforcement administration, FL §10-108.2.
Citation of article, 1 §25.
Collateral.
Fiduciary deposit surety bonds, FI §1-206.
Consumer loans.
See CONSUMER LOANS.

FINANCIAL INSTITUTIONS —Cont'd
Credit.
Credit grantor closed end credit provisions.
Applicability of certain provisions of financial institutions article, CL §12-1015.
General provisions, CL §§12-1001 to 12-1029.
See CREDIT.
Credit grantor revolving credit provisions.
Applicability of certain provisions of financial institutions article, CL §12-915.
General provisions, CL §§12-901 to 12-921.
See CREDIT.
Extensions of credit.
State regulation, FI §1-209.
Credit unions.
See CREDIT UNIONS.
Currency transactions.
Definitions, FI §12-802.
Purpose of subtitle, FI §12-801.
Reports.
Transactions in excess of $10,000, FI §12-803.
Access to reports, FI §12-804.
Failure to make.
Civil penalties, FI §12-805.
Information no longer available from federal agency, FI §12-806.
Debt management services, FI §§12-901 to 12-931.
See DEBT MANAGEMENT SERVICES.
Definitions.
Currency transactions, FI §12-802.
Depositaries.
See STATE TREASURY.
Deposit insurance fund corporation, FI §§10-101 to 10-121.
See DEPOSIT INSURANCE FUND CORPORATION.
Development credit corporation.
See DEVELOPMENT CREDIT CORPORATION.
Discrimination.
State contracts.
Commercial discrimination, SF §§19-101 to 19-120.
See DISCRIMINATION.
Documents of title.
General provisions, CL §§7-101 to 7-603.
See DOCUMENTS OF TITLE.
Equal credit opportunity.
See EQUAL CREDIT OPPORTUNITY.
Fiduciary deposit surety bonds.
Authorized collateral, FI §1-206.
Funds transfers.
General provisions, CL §§4A-101 to 4A-507.
See FUNDS TRANSFERS.
Housing and community development department.
Linked deposit program.
Eligible financial institutions, SF §6-211.
Income tax.
Allocation of income from subsidiaries, TG §10-403.
Tax attributes between and among organizations, TG §10-109.
Industrial development financing authority, 83A §§5-901 to 5-933.
See INDUSTRIAL DEVELOPMENT FINANCING AUTHORITY.
Installment loans.
See INSTALLMENT LOANS.
Investments.
See INVESTMENTS.

FINANCIAL INSTITUTIONS —Cont'd
Limitation of actions.
Certificates of deposit.
Action to enforce obligation of depository institution to pay, FI §1-210.
Loans.
Consumer loans.
See CONSUMER LOANS.
Small loans.
See SMALL LOANS.
Money transmission, FI §§12-401 to 12-431.
See MONEY TRANSMISSION.
Mortgages and deeds of trust.
Mortgage lender law, FI §§11-501 to 11-524.
See MORTGAGE LENDERS.
Mortgage originators, FI §§11-601 to 11-618.
See MORTGAGE ORIGINATORS.
Notices.
Automated teller machines.
Fees charged, FI §1-404.
Safety precautions, FI §1-402.
Real estate appraisers.
Policies and procedures governing real estate appraisal, FI §1-208.
Reports.
Currency transactions.
Transactions in excess of $10,000, FI §12-803.
Access to reports, FI §12-804.
Failure to make.
Civil penalties, FI §12-805.
Information no longer available from federal agency, FI §12-806.
Supervision and examination of tax exempt institutions, FI §12-704.
Taxation.
Requests for information to assist enforcement, TG §13-804.
Savings and loan associations.
See SAVINGS AND LOAN ASSOCIATIONS.
Small loans.
See SMALL LOANS.
State treasury.
See STATE TREASURY.
Supervision and examination of tax exempt institutions.
Appeals, FI §12-707.
Application, FI §12-701.
Fees, FI §12-703.
Form, FI §12-703.
Qualifications of applicant, FI §12-702.
Assessments, FI §12-708.
Eligibility for application, FI §12-701.
Hearings.
Termination of power to supervise and examine.
Actions of commissioner, FI §12-706.
Qualifications, FI §12-702.
Regulations.
Adoption, FI §12-709.
Reports.
Requirements, FI §12-704.
Termination of power to supervise and examine.
Commissioner.
Hearings, FI §12-706.
Powers, FI §12-705.
Disciplinary actions, FI §12-705.
Warning, FI §12-705.
Taxation.
Franchise taxes.
Financial institution franchise tax, TG §§2-501, 2-502, 8-201 to 8-221.
See FINANCIAL INSTITUTION FRANCHISE TAX.

FINANCIAL INSTITUTIONS —Cont'd
Taxation —Cont'd
Franchise taxes —Cont'd
Savings and loan association franchise tax, TG §§2-1401, 2-1402, 8-301 to 8-305.
See SAVINGS AND LOAN ASSOCIATION FRANCHISE TAX.
Information or assistance for enforcement purposes, TG §13-804.
FINANCIAL REPORTS.
Counties, municipal corporations and taxing districts, 24 §2-101.
Time for filing, 19 §37.
FINANCING ELECTION CAMPAIGNS.
Disclosures by person doing public business.
Contributions to candidates, EL §§14-101 to 14-108.
See CAMPAIGN FINANCE.
Generally, EL §§13-101 to 13-605.
See CAMPAIGN FINANCE.
Public campaign financing, EL §§15-101 to 15-111.
See CAMPAIGN FINANCE.
FINE ART.
Consignment of works of fine art, CL §§11-8A-01 to 11-8A-04.
See ART.
FINES.
Adoption.
Independent adoptions.
Payment or compensation for services, FL §5-3B-32.
Local department adoptions.
Payment or compensation for services, FL §5-362.
Private agency adoptions.
Payment or compensation for services, FL §5-3A-45.
Adult dependent care programs.
Criminal history records checks.
Failure to disclose conviction or pending charges, HG §19-1909.
Agricultural cooperatives.
Violations, CA §5-532.
Agriculture.
Consignment of agricultural products.
Failure to provide accountings of sales, AG §1-305.
Violation of duties by consignees, AG §1-304.
Violations of article.
First offense, AG §12-101.
Rules and regulations, AG §12-103.
Second or subsequent offense, AG §12-102.
Air conditioning and heating contractors.
Violation of act, BR §9A-505.
Aircraft.
Minimum altitude over sporting arenas, TR §5-1007.
Airport parking violations, TR §5-427.
Airport zoning violations, TR §§5-511, 5-617.
Air schools.
Licensing violations, TR §5-906.
Alcoholic beverages.
See ALCOHOLIC BEVERAGES.
Ambulance service, ED §13-515.
Recyclable materials, ED §13-703.
Amusements and recreation.
Bungee jumping operations, BR §3-503.
False representations and statements, BR §3-501.

FINES —Cont'd
Amusements and recreation —Cont'd
Militia.
Exclusion of members from places of
amusement or recreation, PS §13-904.
Pinball machines, BR §§17-417, 17-438.
Wicomico county, BR §17-429.
Schedule of fines, BR §3-504.
Willful violation causing death, BR §3-502.
Appeals.
District Court.
Commitment for nonpayment, CJ §12-404.
Aquaculture.
Privately owned artificial ponds or lakes.
Operation without permit, NR §4-11A-20.
Architectural license violations, BOP §3-605.
Arrest.
Resisting or interfering with arrest, CR §9-408.
Assisted living programs.
Unlicensed operation, HG §19-1809.
Athlete agents.
Civil penalties, BR §4-416.
Criminal penalties, BR §4-414.
Automated dialing, telephone solicitation, PUC
§8-204.
Automobile insurance fund, IN §20-701.
Aviation administration.
Conflicts of interest, TR §5-217.
Aviation commission.
Conflicts of interest, TR §5-217.
Aviation violations, TR §5-1105.
Bail and recognizance.
Failure to appear in response to citation, CP
§5-212.
Failure to surrender after forfeiture of bail or
recognizance, CP §5-211.
Solicitation of business by a bail bondsmen or
agent, CP §5-210.
Beer keg registration, 2B §21-106.
Billiard and pool tables.
Commercial use of billiard table.
Keeping without license, BR §17-505.
Birds and game.
See BIRDS AND GAME.
Blood tests.
Altering results of drug or alcohol screening, CR
§10-111.
Bodily fluid.
Ingesting.
Causing another to ingest, CR §3-215.
Boilers and pressure vessels.
Civil penalties.
Continued use of prohibited vessel, PS §12-915.
Generally, PS §12-916.
Criminal penalties, PS §12-917.
Bonds, surety.
Deposits on new homes.
Failure of vendor to maintain surety bond or
escrow account, RP §10-305.
Registers of wills.
Compliance failures, ET §2-204.
Boundaries.
State boundary monuments.
Violation of subtitle, NR §2-407.
Boxing, sparring and wrestling.
License disciplinary actions, BR §4-310.
Violations of provisions, BR §4-322.
Building codes.
Electrical code violations, PS §12-607.
Industrialized buildings and manufactured homes.
Knowing and willful violations, PS §12-313.

FINES —Cont'd
Building codes —Cont'd
Safety glazing violations, PS §12-407.
Structural iron or steel.
Beams or girders with studs or reinforcing
shear connectors, PS §12-704.
Burial contracts.
Failure to deposit money, BR §5-712.
Business regulation and licensure.
General business licensing.
Blank licenses, BR §17-203.
General penalty provision, BR §17-2106.
Business trusts.
Transacting business after forfeiture of right to do
so, CA §12-809.
Calvert county.
Hawkers and peddlers.
Acting without license, BR §§17-921, 17-922.
Catastrophic health emergency, PS §14-3A-08.
Cemeteries, BR §5-904.
Druid Hill park.
Burial or funeral procession prohibited, BR
§5-802.
Perpetual care of cemeteries.
Prohibited acts, BR §5-608.
Charities.
Grossly negligent violations, BR §§6-614, 6-619.
Willful violations, BR §§6-613, 6-619.
Check cashing services, FI §§12-125, 12-126.
Checks.
Bad checks.
Paying fines with bad check, CR §8-108.
Children in need of assistance.
Contributing to certain conditions of child, CJ
§3-828.
Chiropractors.
Title violations, HO §3-506.
Cigarette business licenses.
Doing business without license, BR §16-214.
Sealing vending machines, BR §16-221.
Violating comptroller regulations, BR §16-401.
Cigarette sales at retail in counties.
Licensing violations, BR §16-309.
Circuit courts.
Appeal to circuit court.
Disposition upon appeal, CJ §7-206.
Collection.
By sheriff.
See SHERIFFS.
Collection agencies.
Doing business without license, BR §7-401.
Collection of unpaid fines, CJ §7-505.
Collective bargaining.
Injunctions.
Constructive criminal contempt, LE §4-322.
Commissioner of financial regulation.
Enforcement of provisions, FI §2-116.
Community development administration.
False statements or reports, HS §4-255.
Community energy loan program, SG §9-2109.
Consignment of agricultural products.
Failure to provide accountings of sales, AG
§1-305.
Violation of duties by consignees, AG §1-304.
Contact lenses.
Plano and Zero powered lenses.
Dispensing or selling, HG §24-301.1.
Controlled dangerous substances.
See CONTROLLED DANGEROUS
SUBSTANCES.

FINES —Cont'd

Corporations.
See CORPORATIONS.

Counties.
Road signs or fingerboards.
Injuring or destroying, 25 §154.

Courts-martial.
Militia.
Payment and collection, PS §13-814.

Credit services businesses, CL §14-1915.

Credit unions.
Confidential information, FI §6-909.
False statements or records, FI §6-903.
Improper loans, FI §6-904.
Share guaranty corporations.
Enforcement of provisions, FI §7-209.
Violations of subtitle, FI §7-220.
Unauthorized use of name or title, FI §6-901.
Untrue statements, FI §6-902.

Crime victims' compensation.
Priority of payments.
Earnings withholding orders, CP §11-617.

Criminal justice information system.
Prohibited acts concerning inspection of or
challenge to criminal history record
information, CP §10-228.

Debt management services.
Enforcement of provisions generally, FI §12-928.
Reports, failure to file, FI §12-921.
Specific penalty for violations, FI §12-929.

Definitions, CJ §7-501.

Deposits.
Deposits on new homes.
Failure of vendor to maintain escrow account or
surety bond, RP §10-305.

Discrimination.
Commercial discrimination.
False or frivolous allegations, SF §19-111.

Disposition of fines, CJ §7-507.

District Court.
Appeals.
Commitment for nonpayment of fine, CJ
§12-404.
Collection, CJ §1-605.

Division of state documents.
Use of state documents for prohibited commercial
purpose, SG §7-206.2.

DNA database system.
Prohibited acts, PS §2-512.

Domestic violence.
Address confidentiality program.
Applications to participate.
False attestation or information, FL §4-523.
Obtaining actual address or telephone number,
FL §4-529.
Local domestic violence fatality review teams.
Confidential information.
Generally, FL §4-707.
Meetings, FL §4-706.

**Down payment and settlement expense loan
program.**
False statements or reports, HS §4-309.

Drug or alcohol abuse.
Adjudication as drug or alcohol abuser or
dependent.
Unlawful or improper adjudication, HG §8-701.
Treatment programs.
Operation in violation of title, HG §8-702.

Dyed diesel fuel.
Operation of vehicle containing fuel in tanks, BR
§10-323.2.

FINES —Cont'd

Dyed diesel fuel —Cont'd
Sale or delivery from retail pump, BR §10-323.2.

Elections.
Absentee voting violations, EL §9-312.
Buying and selling votes, MD Const Art I §6.
Provisional ballot voting violations, EL §9-408.
Voting.
Illegal voting, MD Const Art I §5.

Electrologists.
Disciplinary action, HO §8-6B-20.
Violations of subtitle, HO §8-6B-27.

Elevators.
Licenses.
Criminal penalties, PS §12-840.
Denial, refusal to renew, suspension or
revocation.
Civil penalty, PS §12-837.

Emergency management.
Civil relief during emergency periods, PS §14-218.
Compulsory work during state of war.
Failure to register for work, PS §14-907.
Failure to work, PS §14-908.
Governor's orders, violations, PS §14-309.
Maryland emergency management agency
(MEMA), PS §14-114.
State standby petroleum fuel set-aside program
violations, PS §14-511.

Eminent domain.
Stakes or markers.
Obliterating, damaging or removing, RP
§12-111.

Employment agencies.
Doing business without a license, BR §9-401.

**Energy efficiency and economic development
loan program.**
False statements, SG §9-20A-09.

Enforcement of money judgments.
Criminal rules, Crim Rule 4-354.

Engineers, BOP §14-508.

Environment.
Confidential research records.
Violation of subtitle, EN §1-503.
Falsifying or altering permits, licenses or
certificates, EN §1-302.
Water management.
General provisions, EN §4-501.

Environmental service.
Violations of subtitle, NR §§3-128, 3-129.

Escrow.
Deposits on new homes.
Failure of vendor to maintain surety bond or
escrow account, RP §10-305.

Excessive.
Expungement of criminal records, CP §§10-108,
10-109.
Prohibited, US Const Amd 8.

Explosives.
Explosives for use in firearms, PS §11-115.
License or other violations, PS §11-114.
Additional penalties, PS §11-116.
Merger of convictions, PS §11-117.

Extortion by false accusation, CR §3-705.

Extortion by written threat, CR §3-706.

Extradition.
Noncompliance with delivery procedures, CP
§9-111.

Female genital mutilation, HG §20-603.

Fertilizers.
Commercial fertilizers, AG §6-401.

FINES —Cont'd
Firearms.
  Handgun permits.
    Failure to return revoked permit, PS §5-313.
  Handguns.
    Carrying, wearing or transporting handgun
        while under the influence, PS §5-314.
    Manufacture or sale of guns not on roster, PS
        §5-406.
    Possession of short-barreled rifles or shotguns, PS
        §5-203.
    Target practice without landowner permission, CR
        §4-108.
Fires and fire protection.
  Inspections by local fire departments.
    Hindering, obstructing or refusing to allow
        inspection, PS §9-805.
  Smoke detector violations, PS §9-109.
  Sprinkler system violations, PS §9-206.
    Fire sprinkler contractor licensing, PS §9-905.
Fireworks.
  Possession, sale or permit violations, PS §10-111.
  Sparklers.
    Registration of distributors and wholesalers, PS
        §10-113.
Fireworks plants, PS §10-210.
Fish and fisheries.
  Collection, NR §4-1202.
  Common carriers transporting fish.
    Exemption, NR §4-1201.
  Dynamiting, NR §4-503.
  Electronic or electrical devices, NR §4-509.
  Nonnative aquatic organisms, NR §4-205.1.
  Nontidal waters.
    Rules and regulations affecting fish in.
      Violations, NR §4-602.
  Rockfish.
    Purchase, sale or transportation, NR §4-731.
  Stake nets.
    Noncompliance with subsection, NR §4-711.
  Violation of title.
    Common carriers transporting fish.
      Exemption, NR §4-1201.
Food and food establishments.
  See FOOD AND FOOD ESTABLISHMENTS.
Food, drugs and cosmetics.
  Vending machine sale of drugs or medicine, HG
      §21-1111.
  Violations of provisions, HG §21-1215.
Foreclosure.
  Protection of homeowners.
    Violation of provisions, RP §7-321.
Foresters.
  License violations, BOP §7-506.
Forests and parks.
  Fires.
    Failure to render aid when summoned, NR
        §5-701.
    Maliciously setting fires, NR §5-704.
  Railroads.
    Failure to maintain safety strips, NR §5-714.
  Violation of title, NR §5-1301.
    Collection of fines, NR §5-1302.
Forfeitures.
  General provisions.
    See FORFEITURES.
For-hire driving services, PUC §13-206.
Franchises.
  Registration.
    Amendment to registration.
      Failure to notify of material change, BR
          §14-232.

FINES —Cont'd
Franchises —Cont'd
  Registration —Cont'd
    Offer or sale of franchise without registration,
        BR §14-228.
Fraternal benefit societies.
  Misrepresentations, IN §8-468.
Fraternal society insignia or name.
  Unauthorized use, BR §19-207.
Freestanding ambulatory care facilities.
  Violation of subtitle, HG §19-3B-09.
Freestanding medical facilities.
  Violation of provisions, HG §19-3A-05.
Frozen desserts.
  Manufacturing on invalid license, HG §21-819.
  Manufacturing without license, HG §21-818.
  Sale of products from unlicensed plant, HG
      §21-820.
**Funerals, obstruction of entry or exit or of
    procession,** CR §10-205.
Gangs.
  Criminal gang offenses, CR §9-802.
    Schools, CR §9-803.
Gas and oil.
  Coastal facilities review act.
    Violations of subtitle, EN §14-510.
  Storage.
    Prince George's county.
      Violation of subtitle, EN §14-308.
  Violations of subtitle, EN §14-120.
Governor.
  Remission, MD Const Art II §20.
Group home financing program.
  False statements or reports, HS §4-612.
Guardian and ward.
  Local department guardianships.
    Payment or compensation for services, FL
        §5-362.
  Private agency guardianships.
    Payment or compensation for services, FL
        §5-3A-45.
Handgun permits.
  Failure to return revoked permit, PS §5-313.
Handguns.
  Carrying, wearing or transporting handgun while
      under the influence, PS §5-314.
  Manufacture or sale of guns not on roster, PS
      §5-406.
Hawkers and peddlers.
  Acting as peddler without license, BR §17-911.
    Calvert county, BR §§17-921, 17-922.
  Sale of produce in municipal corporation, BR
      §17-912.
Hazardous materials and substances.
  Knowing violations, EN §7-265.
  Offenses and penalties, EN §7-265.
Health.
  See HEALTH.
Health insurance.
  Private review agents, IN §15-10B-12.
Highways.
  Closure or restricted access to certain properties.
    Violation of order, TR §8-627.
  Excavations.
    Violation, TR §8-646.
  Railroad grade crossings or separations.
    Administration orders.
      Compliance failures, TR §8-643.
  Removal of dirt, sand, gravel, etc., from side of
      roadway, TR §8-647.

FINES —Cont'd
Highways —Cont'd
Signs, signals or markers.
Destruction or damaging, TR §8-605.
Historical and cultural museum assistance program.
False statements or reports, SF §5A-359.
Hit and run.
Serious bodily harm, TR §27-113.
Holocaust victim insurance, IN §28-107.
Filing false or misleading certification or report, IN §28-105.
Homebuilder registration violations.
Civil penalties, BR §§4.5-308, 4.5-502.
Criminal penalties, BR §§4.5-501, 4.5-504.
Home improvements.
False proof of completion, BR §8-602.
License disciplinary actions.
Penalty in lieu of revocation, BR §8-311.
Licenses.
Acting without license, BR §8-601.
Violations of act, BR §§8-620, 8-623.
Horse industry board, AG §2-718.
Horse racing.
License disciplinary actions, BR §11-308.
Holding race meet without license, BR §11-1001.
Horses.
Transporting horses.
Civil penalties for violations, AG §3-903.
Hospices.
Violation of subtitle, HG §19-911.
Hospitals.
Discharge or transfer of residents.
Violation by facility or resident agent, HG §19-345.3.
Discharge violations, HG §19-308.8.
Reports of unexpected occurrences or incidents, violations, HG §19-304.
Standards and inspections.
Violations by employees, HG §19-308.
Veterinary hospitals.
Supervision of animals in care of veterinarians, CL §11-905.
Housing.
Deposits on new homes.
Failure of vendor to maintain escrow account or surety bond, RP §10-305.
Housing and community development.
Assisted housing preservation.
False statements or reports, HS §7-404.
Neighborhood business development program.
False statement or reports, HS §6-311.
Identity fraud.
Government identification document, CR §8-303.
Immigration consultants, CL §14-3306.
ImmuNet program.
Confidentiality violations, HG §18-109.
Impersonating a police officer, PS §3-502.
Inability to pay, CJ §7-504.
Indian affairs commission.
False statements or representations, 41 §6-912.
Informers.
Payment to informer prohibited, CJ §7-506.
Insurance.
Adjusters.
Unlicensed adjusters, IN §10-403.
Automobile insurance fund.
Filing false notice or document, IN §20-701.
Fraud, IN §27-408.
General criminal penalty, IN §1-301.

FINES —Cont'd
Insurance —Cont'd
Health insurance.
Private review agents, IN §15-10B-17.
Holocaust victim insurance, IN §28-107.
Filing false or misleading certification or report, IN §28-105.
Investigations, examinations or hearings.
Failure to appear, testify, produce evidence or give answer, IN §2-203.
Premium finance companies, IN §23-208.
Criminal fines, IN §23-506.
Risk retention groups.
Regulatory violations, IN §25-110.
Surety insurance discrimination, IN §27-502.
Third party administrators, IN §8-322.
Title insurance agents and brokers, IN §10-132.
Workers' compensation insurance.
Approval of policy forms, IN §19-402.
Setting premium rates, IN §19-403.
Insurance acquisitions disclosure and control, IN §7-807.
Insurers, IN §7-406.
Insurance agents and brokers, IN §§10-126, 10-131.
Insurance companies.
Liquidation, rehabilitation, etc.
Contributing to impairment, IN §9-231.
Obstruction, interference or failure to cooperate with commissioner, IN §9-230.
Receipt of premium after insolvency, IN §9-232.
Penalty in lieu of revocation or suspension of certificate of authority, IN §4-113.
Unauthorized insurers, IN §4-212.
Workers' compensation insurance.
Office and personnel requirements, LE §9-410.
Interior designers.
Certificate violations, BOP §8-502.
Juke boxes.
Keeping without license, BR §17-1309.
Harford county, BR §17-1318.
Junk dealers.
Failure to submit report, BR §17-1022.
General penalty, BR §17-1024.
Historic markers or plaques.
Violations, BR §17-1012.
Licenses, BR §17-1013.
Purchases from minors, BR §17-1023.
Jury.
Employers.
Prohibited acts by, CJ §§8-501, 8-502.
Failure to appear for jury service, CJ §8-504.
Failure to complete jury service, CJ §8-505.
Failure to return completed juror qualification form, CJ §8-503.
Grand jury.
Secrecy violations, CJ §8-507.
Juror qualification form.
Failure to return completed form, CJ §8-503.
Material misrepresentation, CJ §8-506.
Juvenile causes.
Adult.
Contributing to condition which renders child delinquent, etc., CJ §3-8A-30.
Juvenile curfew, 25B §13C-1.
Kennels.
Commercial boarding kennels, CL §11-905.
Lakes.
Privately owned artificial ponds or lakes.
Operation without permit, NR §4-11A-20.

FINES —Cont'd
Landlord and tenant.
  Tobacco.
    Interference with stripping and marketing of
      tobacco, RP §8-116.
Lead-based paint.
  Violations of provisions, EN §6-302.
**Lead hazard reduction grant and loan
    programs.**
  False statements or reports, HS §4-712.
Leaving scene of accident.
  Serious bodily harm, TR §27-113.
Limitation of actions, CJ §5-107.
Limited partnerships.
  Forfeiture of right to do business.
    Transacting business after forfeiture, CA
      §10-217.
Livestock enclosure.
  Opening enclosure of another, AG §3-701.
Livestock slaughtering, AG §4-123.1.
Maryland historical trust.
  Archaeological property, violations, SF §5A-346.
  Historical and cultural museum assistance
    program.
    False statements or reports, SF §5A-359.
Maryland home financing program.
  False statements or reports, HS §4-816.
Maryland housing rehabilitation program.
  False statements or reports, HS §4-933.
Massage therapists, HO §3-5A-11.
Mass transit.
  Fare citations.
    Failure to appear, TR §7-704.1.
  Violations, TR §7-705.
Medicine or patent medicine shows.
  Violation of provision, HG §21-1212.
Meridian line.
  Notice variations from.
    Surveyor not complying, 25 §124.
METRO.
  Fare citations.
    Failure to appear, TR §7-704.1.
Migrant labor, LE §7-506.
Military organization insignia or name.
  Unauthorized use, BR §19-207.
Militia.
  Courts-martial, PS §13-812.
    Payment and collection, PS §13-814.
  Exclusion of members from places of amusement
    or recreation, PS §13-904.
  Misapplication or conversion of property, PS
    §13-903.
  Sale, purchase or improper use of property, PS
    §13-902.
  Unlawful wearing of uniform, PS §13-901.
Milk and milk products.
  Milk cans.
    Fine for violation, HG §21-1202.
  Violation of subtitle, HG §21-1203.
Mining.
  Deep mining control, EN §15-618.
  Strip mining.
    General penalty, EN §15-520.
  Surface mining permit violations, EN §15-808.
  Violation of title, EN §15-1001.
Money.
  Expressed in dollars and cents, CJ §11-101.
Money transmission.
  Administrative procedure, FI §12-428.
  Amount to enforce subtitle, FI §12-426.

FINES —Cont'd
Money transmission —Cont'd
  Change of location or control of business.
    Noncompliance with provisions, FI §12-415.
  Knowing and willful violation of subtitle, FI
    §12-430.
  Surety devices.
    Penalties payable from, FI §12-412.
Mortgage originators.
  Civil violations, FI §11-615.
  Criminal violations, FI §11-617.
Mortgages and deeds of trust.
  Trustee charging or demanding release fees not
    specified in instrument, RP §7-106.
Motor clubs.
  Regulatory violations, IN §26-502.
Motor fuel inspection.
  Refueling service for disabled drivers, BR §10-320.
  Violation of provisions, BR §10-324.
    Petroleum transporters, BR §10-411.
**Motor vehicle insurance appraisers or
    adjusters,** IN §10-504.
Motor vehicles.
  Automobile insurance fund.
    Filing false notice or document, IN §20-701.
  Disabled drivers.
    Refueling service by retail dealer, BR §10-320.
Multilevel distribution companies.
  Violations of provisions, BR §14-305.
Municipal corporations.
  General penalty, 23A §3.
  Power of municipal corporations, 23A §3.
Museums.
  Historical and cultural museum assistance
    program.
    False statements or reports, SF §5A-359.
Natural resources.
  Police force.
    Violation of subtitle, NR §1-209.
  Prepayable fines, NR §1-801.
Neighborhood revitalization division.
  Neighborhood business development program.
    False statement or reports, HS §6-311.
Nudity and sexual displays.
  Violation of municipal ordinances regulating, 23A
    §4A.
Nurses.
  Disciplinary actions regarding licensing, HO
    §8-316.
  Failure to renew license, HO §8-711.
Nursing assistants.
  Failure to renew certificate and practicing during
    expiration of certificate, HO §8-6A-09.
Nursing home administrators.
  Civil fine imposed on licenses, HO §9-314.1.
  Criminal penalty for violations, HO §9-407.
Nursing homes.
  Actual harm deficiency, amount.
    Defined, HG §19-1401.
  Amount, HG §19-1404.
  Appeal, hearing, HG §19-1406.
  Escrow account, deposit on request for appeal, HG
    §19-1406.
  Health care quality account, HG §19-1407.
  Imposition, deficiency existing, HG §19-1402.
  Minimal harm deficiency, amount, HG §19-1404.
    Defined, HG §19-1401.
  Order proposing, HG §19-1403.
  Reduction, waiver of right to hearing, HG
    §19-1406.

FINES —Cont'd

Nursing homes —Cont'd

Serious and immediate threat, amount, HG §19-1404.

Defined, HG §19-1401.

Time limit on issuing order proposing penalty, HG §19-1403.

Occupational safety and health.

See OCCUPATIONAL SAFETY AND HEALTH.

Office of legislative audits, SG §2-1227.

Open containers of alcoholic beverages in motor vehicles' passenger areas, CR §§10-126, 10-127.

Ordinances.

General penalty, 23A §3.

Organizational insignia or name.

Unauthorized use, BR §19-207.

Outdoor advertising, TR §8-749.

Outdoor concerts.

Acting as promoter without license, BR §17-1407.

Oysters and clams, NR §4-1201.

Collection, NR §4-1202.

Nonnative oysters.

Introduction into waters of state.

Violation of requirements, NR §4-1008.

Quarantine, NR §4-743.

Parking in Prince George's county.

Commercial vehicles, TR §21-1010.

Partnership rental housing program.

False statements or reports, HS §4-1209.

Patent medicine shows.

Milk cans.

Prohibited acts, HG §21-1202.

Violations of provisions, HG §21-1212.

Patriotic organization insignia or name.

Unauthorized use, BR §19-207.

Patuxent river watershed.

Violation of subtitle, EN §4-314.

Payment.

Collection of unpaid fines, CJ §7-505.

Default in payment.

Imprisonment for, CJ §7-504.

Inability to pay, CJ §7-504.

Method, CJ §7-503.

Natural resources.

Prepayable fines, NR §1-801.

Time, CJ §7-503.

To whom paid, CJ §7-506.

Pesticides.

Registration.

Noncomplying pesticides, AG §5-107.1.

Pharmacists and pharmacies.

Nonresident pharmacy.

Penalty in lieu of disciplinary action, HO §12-410.

Pilots.

Disciplinary action against licensees, BOP §11-409.

Plumbing violations, BOP §12-607.

Ponds.

Privately owned artificial ponds or lakes.

Operation without permit, NR §4-11A-20.

Port administration.

Conflicts of interest, TR §6-212.

Violations, TR §6-602.

Possession, writ of.

Reentry after eviction, RP §14-114.

Precious metals and gem dealers.

Violations of act, BR §12-502.

Premium finance companies.

Regulatory violations, IN §23-208.

FINES —Cont'd

Private home detention monitoring, BOP §20-701.

Probation.

Fine as condition of sentence to, CJ §7-503.

Procurement.

Falsification, concealment, etc., of material facts in connection with contracts, SF §11-205.1.

Property taxes.

See PROPERTY TAXES.

Psychologists.

License violations, HO §18-313.1.

Public officers and employees.

Debts purchased by sheriffs, constables or collectors of taxes, SG §17-107.

Public safety solicitors.

Unregistered solicitation, BR §6-5A-10.

Willful violations, BR §6-5A-11.

Public service company civil liability generally, PUC §13-201.

Radiation oncology/therapy, medical radiation, and nuclear medicine technologists.

Penalties for violations, HO §14-5B-19.

Railroads.

Failure to maintain safety strips, NR §5-714.

Grade crossings or separations.

Administration orders.

Compliance failures, TR §8-643.

Violation of title, NR §5-1301.

Collection, NR §5-1302.

Railroad safety and health, LE §§5.5-122, 5.5-123.

Civil fines, LE §5.5-123.

Violations causing death, LE §5.5-122.

Real estate appraisers and home inspectors, BOP §16-706.

Real estate settlements.

Consideration for settlement of real estate transactions.

Payment or receipt, RP §14-127.

Registered organizational insignia or name.

Unauthorized use, BR §19-207.

Registers of wills.

Acceptance of fees and gifts, ET §2-203.

Surety bonds.

Compliance failures, ET §2-204.

Remissions, CP §1-207.

By governor, MD Const Art III §20.

Rental housing production program.

False statements or reports, HS §4-1511.

Respiratory care practitioners, HO §14-5A-23.

Retail and wholesale establishments.

Sunday blue laws, BR §18-101.

St. Mary's county.

Bottle clubs.

Circumvention of ABC laws, 2B §20-109.

Schools.

See SCHOOLS.

Securities act.

See SECURITIES.

Security guards, BOP §19-607.

Regulations adopted to include schedule, BOP §19-202.

Security systems technicians.

False statements in applications, BOP §§18-503, 18-504.

Misrepresentation, BOP §§18-502 to 18-504.

Regulations to include schedule, BOP §18-402.

Unlicensed businesses, BOP §§18-501, 18-502.

Sediment control.

Violation of subtitle, EN §4-116.

FINES —Cont'd

Sentence and punishment.
Enforcement of money judgment, Crim Rule 4-354.
Stay of execution, Crim Rule 4-348.

Severn river watershed.
Violation of subtitle, EN §4-314.

Sex offender registration offenses, CP §11-721.
School or day care, entry onto property prohibited, CP §11-722.

Sexual solicitation of minor, CR §3-324.

Sheriffs.
Collection.
General provisions.
See SHERIFFS.

Smoke detectors.
Violations, PS §9-109.

Soft drinks.
Violation of provisions, HG §21-1214.

Sprinkler systems.
Violations, PS §9-206.
Fire sprinkler contractor licensing, PS §9-905.

Start-up business ventures.
Fraud and deceit, BR §14-127.
Violations of act, BR §14-128.

State documents.
Use for prohibited commercial purpose, SG §7-206.2.

State lottery.
Unlawful sale of tickets and shares, SG §9-124.

State's attorneys.
Execution for fines and penalties, 10 §36.

Statutes.
Repeal or revision of statute.
Effect on penalty or liability previously incurred, 1 §3.

Subdivisions.
Deposits on new homes.
Failure of vendor to maintain escrow account or surety bond, RP §10-305.

Sunday Blue laws.
Retail and wholesale establishments, BR §18-101.

Surveys and surveyors.
Noting variations from meridian line.
Surveyor not complying, 25 §124.

Survey stations, violations, BOP §1-304.

Taxation.
See TAXATION.

Taxicabs, PUC §13-206.

Telephone slamming, PUC §8-409.

Telephone solicitation.
Automated dialing, PUC §8-204.
Caller identification blocking, PUC §8-205.

Title insurance.
Agents and brokers, IN §10-132.

Tobacco escrow act compliance.
Criminal penalties, BR §16-507.
Violations, BR §16-507.

Tobacco sales.
Carroll county and Garrett county.
Display of products, 24 §15-102.
Vending machines, products sold through, BR §16-3A-03.

Trade names.
Fraudulent use or imitation of trade names, BR §1-415.

Traders.
Visually handicapped applicants.
Violating license provisions, BR §17-1816.

Trading stamp companies.
Violations of provisions, BR §13-110.

FINES —Cont'd

Traffic control signal monitoring systems, TR §21-202.1.

Transient vendors.
Conducting business without displaying license, BR §17-20A-05.

Trusts and trustees.
Real estate investment trust.
Failure to file reports, CA §8-701.

Unemployment compensation.
Reemployment.
Failure of employing unit to file report, LE §8-626.1.

Vending machines.
Removing or tampering with seal, BR §17-1907.
Selling without license, BR §17-1906.

Veterans' organization insignia or name.
Unauthorized use, BR §19-207.

Veterinarians.
Hospitals.
Supervision of animals in care of veterinarians, CL §11-905.

Viatical settlement contracts.
Disciplinary action against registrants, IN §8-609.

Warehouses and warehousemen.
Storage warehouses.
Buyer's purchase of insurance, BR §17-1204.

Washington county.
Animal control violations, 25 §236A.
Health officers.
Authority to issue for health code violation, 25 §236F.

Washington suburban sanitary district.
Board of ethics.
Violation of regulations, 29 §12-106.

Waste.
After injunction, RP §14-102.

Water pollution.
Violations of subtitle, EN §4-417.

Water resources, EN §5-1301.
Appropriation or use permits.
Violations of subtitle, EN §5-514.
General provisions, NR §8-2001.

Weapons.
Handgun permits.
Failure to return revoked permit, PS §5-313.
Handguns.
Carrying, wearing or transporting handgun while under the influence, PS §5-314.
Manufacture or sale of guns not on roster, PS §5-406.
Possession of short-barreled rifles or shotguns, PS §5-203.
Target practice without landowner permission, CR §4-108.

Weights and measures.
Civil penalties, AG §11-208.1.

Wetlands.
General provisions, EN §16-501.
State wetlands.
Dredging or filling.
Violations, EN §16-202.

Witnesses.
Failure of witness to appear, CJ §9-201.

Woodrow Wilson bridge and tunnel compact.
Provision violations, TR §10-303.

Workers' compensation.
Insurance coverage.
Setting premium rates, IN §19-403.
Medical benefits, LE §9-664.
Self-insurance groups, IN §25-308.

FINES —Cont'd
Workers' compensation —Cont'd
State workers' compensation commission.
  Assessment against insurers, LE §9-313.
Vocational rehabilitation services.
  Failure to submit report, LE §9-675.
Workers' compensation insurance.
Insurance coverage.
  Office and personnel requirements, LE §9-410.
Zoning.
Civil penalties, 66B §7.02.

FINGERPRINTING.
Adult dependent care programs.
Eligible employees, HG §19-1904.
Alcoholic beverages.
License applicants, 2B §10-103.
Check cashing services.
Requirements for license, FI §12-107.
Child care.
Criminal background investigations for employees,
  etc., of facilities, FL §5-562.
Children.
Juvenile brought to Baltimore City juvenile
  services center, CP §10-220.
Voluntary fingerprinting programs, FL §9-403.
Criminal history records checks.
Carroll county current or prospective employees,
  CP §10-232.
Montgomery county taxicab licensees, CP §10-234.
Prince George's county prospective employees, CP
  §10-236.
Washington county prospective employees, CP
  §10-235.
Criminal justice information center.
Juvenile brought to Baltimore City juvenile
  services center, CP §10-220.
Criminal justice information system, CP
  §10-216.
Debt management services.
License application, FI §12-909.
Fees.
State police department, PS §2-312.
Firearms.
Dealers' licenses.
  Applications, PS §5-107.
Fire department.
Criminal history record checks, PS §6-306.
Fire marshal.
Criminal history record checks, PS §6-306.
Horse racing.
Individuals required to provide, BR §11-312.
License applicants, BR §11-1307.
**Inmates sentenced to jurisdiction of division
  of correction,** COR §3-601.
**Juvenile brought to Baltimore City juvenile
  services center,** CP §10-220.
Money transmission.
Licenses.
  Applications.
    Fingerprints of applicant, FI §12-408.
Montgomery county.
Alcoholic beverages licenses, 2B §10-104.
Mortgage lenders.
License applicants, FI §11-506.1.
Mortgage originators.
License applicants, FI §11-606.
Nurses.
License applicants, HO §8-303.
Paramedics.
Criminal history record checks, PS §6-306.

FINGERPRINTING —Cont'd
Precious metals and gem dealers.
License applicants.
  Individuals requiring criminal history records
    checks, BR §12-204.
Private detectives.
Applicant for license to submit, BOP §13-304.
Certification, requirement, BOP §13-403.
  Renewal, BOP §13-404.1.
Real estate appraisers.
Applicant for appraisers license, BOP §16-303.
Rescue squads.
Criminal history record checks, PS §6-306.
Residential child care program administrators.
Certification.
  Applications, HO §20-303.
Security guards.
Certification, BOP §19-402.
Security guard agencies.
  Renewal, BOP §19-308.
  Submission required with application for
    license, BOP §19-304.
Security systems technicians.
Registration, BOP §18-3A-03.
  Renewal, BOP §18-3A-07.
Renewal of license, BOP §18-307.
Sex offender registration.
Supervising authority to obtain fingerprints of
  registrant, CP §11-708.
State police department.
Fees, PS §2-312.

FIP, 88A §§44A to 56.
See FAMILY INVESTMENT PROGRAM.

FIRE ALARMS.
Audible systems.
Equipped to automatically silence, CR §9-611.
Defective system.
Notice to user, use after notice, CR §9-610.
Definitions, CR §9-607.
False alarms, CR §9-608.
Multiple alarms, CR §9-609.

FIREARMS, PS §§5-101 to 5-143.
Affidavits.
Applications for purchases, rents or transfers, PS
  §5-118.
Dealers' licenses.
  Applications, PS §5-107.
Ammunition.
Sale, rental or transfer to minors, PS §5-134.
Antique firearms.
Defined, CR §4-201.
Use in commission of crime, CR §4-204.
Appeals.
Applications for purchases, rents or transfers, PS
  §5-127.
Dealers' licenses.
  Disapproval, PS §5-110.
  Suspension or revocation, PS §5-116.
Applicability of subtitle, PS §5-102.
Effect of subtitle, PS §5-103.
Applications for purchases, rents or transfers,
  PS §§5-117 to 5-130.
Affidavits, PS §5-118.
Appeals, PS §5-127.
Applicability, PS §5-117.
Approved applications.
  Validity, PS §5-125.
Certified firearms safety training course, PS
  §5-118.
Exemption, PS §5-119.

FIREARMS —Cont'd
Applications for purchases, rents or transfers
—Cont'd
Completed transactions, PS §5-123.
Secondary transactions, PS §5-124.
Copies, distribution, PS §5-120.
Corporations, PS §5-118.
Criminal history records checks.
Multiple purchases within thirty days, PS
§5-129.
Criminal law and procedure.
Multiple purchases within thirty days, PS
§5-129.
Disapproval, PS §5-122.
Effect, PS §5-125.
Display.
Temporary transfer permits, gun shows, PS
§5-130.
False statements in applications, PS §5-139.
Fees, PS §5-118.
Copies, PS §5-120.
Secondary transactions, PS §5-124.
Grounds for disapproval, PS §5-122.
Gun shows, PS §5-130.
Hearings.
Actions of secretary, PS §5-126.
Identification.
Information required, PS §5-118.
Incomplete transactions, PS §5-123.
Secondary transactions, PS §5-124.
Information required, PS §5-118.
Investigations, PS §5-121.
Temporary transfer permits, gun shows, PS
§5-130.
Misdemeanors.
Multiple purchases within thirty days, PS
§5-129.
Notice.
Disapproval, PS §5-122.
One purchase limit within thirty days, PS §5-128.
Multiple purchases allowed, PS §5-129.
On hold applications, PS §5-125.
Records.
Retention of copies, PS §5-120.
Required, PS §5-117.
Seven day waiting period, PS §5-123.
Secondary transactions, PS §5-124.
Temporary transfer permits.
Gun shows, PS §5-130.
Thirty day limit.
One purchase limit within thirty days, PS
§5-128.
Multiple purchases allowed, PS §5-129.
Time for completion of transaction, PS §5-123.
Venue.
Hearings on actions of secretary, PS §5-126.
Warning required, PS §5-118.
Temporary transfer permits, gun shows, PS
§5-130.
Armed carjacking, CR §3-405.
Assault pistols, CR §§4-301 to 4-306.
Defined, types and brands enumerated, CR
§4-301.
Persons excepted from provisions, CR §4-302.
Punishment, CR §4-306.
Scope of subtitle, CR §4-302.
Seizure and disposal as contraband, CR §4-304.
Transporting into state, selling or purchasing,
prohibition, CR §4-303.
Use in commission of crime.
Punishment, CR §4-306.

FIREARMS —Cont'd
Assault weapons.
Regulated firearms, PS §5-101.
Assault with firearm.
Assault in first degree, CR §3-202.
Breaking and entering with intent to steal.
Burglary in the second degree, CR §6-203.
Carrying or possessing on school property, CR
§4-102.
Cease fire council, PS §§5-501 to 5-504.
Council defined, PS §5-501.
Duties, PS §5-503.
Established, PS §5-502.
Grants, PS §5-504.
Members, PS §5-502.
Powers, PS §5-503.
Purpose, PS §5-503.
Certified firearms safety training course.
Applications for purchases, rents or transfers, PS
§5-118.
Exemption, PS §5-119.
Sale, rental or transfer.
Exemptions, PS §5-134.
Required, PS §5-134.
Child's access to, CR §4-104.
Concealed weapons.
Warrantless arrest, CP §2-203.
Conflict of laws.
Preemption by state, PS §5-104.
Sale, rental or transfer, PS §5-134.
Contraband in place of confinement, CR §9-414.
Corporations.
Applications for purchases, rents or transfers, PS
§5-118.
Dealers' licenses.
Applications, PS §5-107.
Crime laboratories.
Handgun identification requirements, PS §5-131.
Crimes of violence.
Dealers' licenses.
Suspension or revocation, PS §5-114.
Restrictions on possession, PS §5-133.
Restrictions on sale, rental or transfer, PS §5-134.
Criminal history records checks.
Applications for purchases, rents or transfers.
Multiple purchases within thirty days, PS
§5-129.
Dealers' licenses, PS §5-108.
Criminal law and procedure.
Applications for purchases, rents or transfers.
Multiple purchases within thirty days, PS
§5-129.
Handguns.
Manufacture or sale of guns not on roster, PS
§5-406.
Knowing participation in violation of subtitle, PS
§5-143.
Possession of short-barreled rifles or shotguns, PS
§5-203.
Restrictions on possession, PS §5-133.
Restrictions on sale, rental or transfer, PS §5-134.
Rifles and shotguns.
Possession by person with mental disorder, PS
§5-205.
Straw purchases.
Knowing participation in, PS §5-141.
Dealers' licenses, PS §§5-106 to 5-116.
Affidavits.
Applications, PS §5-107.
Appeals.
Disapproval, PS §5-110.

FIREARMS —Cont'd
Dealers' licenses —Cont'd
Appeals —Cont'd
Suspension or revocation, PS §5-116.
Applications, PS §5-107.
False statements in applications, PS §5-139.
Investigations, PS §5-109.
Corporations.
Applications, PS §5-107.
Crimes of violence.
Suspension or revocation, PS §5-114.
Criminal history records checks, PS §5-108.
Disapproval, PS §5-110.
Display, PS §5-113.
False information.
Disapproval, PS §5-110.
Fees.
Applications, PS §5-107.
Criminal history records checks, PS §5-108.
Fingerprinting.
Applications, PS §5-107.
Fugitives.
Suspension or revocation, PS §5-114.
Gun shows, PS §5-130.
Habitual drunkards or users.
Suspension or revocation, PS §5-114.
Handgun identification requirements, PS §5-131.
Hearings.
Suspension or revocation, PS §5-115.
Identification.
Applications, PS §5-107.
Display of identity and location of place of business, PS §5-113.
Investigations, PS §5-109.
Mentally ill.
Suspension or revocation, PS §5-114.
New place of business.
Nontransferability, PS §5-112.
Nontransferability, PS §5-112.
Notice.
Disapproval, PS §5-110.
Suspension or revocation, PS §5-114.
One license for each place of business, PS §5-106.
Nontransferability, PS §5-112.
Renewal, PS §5-111.
Required, PS §5-106.
Revocation, PS §5-114.
Appeals, PS §5-116.
Hearings, PS §5-115.
Sale, rental or transfer of firearms, PS §§5-134 to 5-143.
Suspension, PS §5-114.
Appeals, PS §5-116.
Hearings, PS §5-115.
Temporary transfer permits.
Gun shows, PS §5-130.
Term, PS §5-111.
Warning on applications, PS §5-107.
Defined terms, PS §5-101.
Rifles and shotguns, PS §5-201.
Detachable magazines.
Prohibited, CR §4-305.
Disarming law enforcement officer, CR §4-103.
Discharge of firearm.
From motor vehicle.
Reckless endangerment, CR §3-204.
Local regulation allowed, CR §4-209.
Domestic violence.
Protective orders.
Restrictions on possession, PS §5-133.

FIREARMS —Cont'd
Domestic violence —Cont'd
Protective orders —Cont'd
Restrictions on sale, rental or transfer, PS §5-134.
Drug crimes.
Possession by person convicted of, CR §5-622.
Possession or use.
Separate offense, enhanced sentence, forfeiture, CR §5-621.
Drug or alcohol abuse.
Habitual drunkards or users.
Restrictions on sale, rental or transfer, PS §5-134.
Restrictions on possession, PS §5-133.
Visibly intoxicated persons.
Restrictions on sale, rental or transfer, PS §5-134.
Effect of subtitle, PS §5-103.
Elections.
Bringing to polling places, prohibited, EL §16-903.
Violations, penalty, EL §16-1002.
Exclusions from subtitle, PS §5-103.
Explosives for use in firearms.
License to possess, PS §11-105.
Penalties for violations, PS §11-115.
External safety locks.
Handgun safety devices, PS §5-132.
False statements.
Applications for firearm purchase or dealer's license, PS §5-139.
Fees.
Applications for purchases, rents or transfers, PS §5-118.
Copies, PS §5-120.
Secondary transactions, PS §5-124.
Dealers' licenses.
Applications, PS §5-107.
Criminal history records checks, PS §5-108.
Felons.
Restrictions on possession, PS §5-133.
Restrictions on sale, rental or transfer, PS §5-134.
Fines.
Handguns.
Manufacture or sale of guns not on roster, PS §5-406.
Possession of short-barreled rifles or shotguns, PS §5-203.
Fingerprinting.
Dealers' licenses.
Applications, PS §5-107.
Forfeitures.
Drug trafficking crimes, CR §5-621.
Handgun forfeitures, CP §§13-201 to 13-206.
Seizure of firearms sold, rented or transferred in violation, PS §5-135.
Fugitives.
Dealers' licenses.
Suspension or revocation, PS §5-114.
Restrictions on possession, PS §5-133.
Restrictions on sale, rental or transfer, PS §5-134.
Gunpowder.
Explosives for use in firearms.
License to possess, PS §11-105.
Gun shows, PS §5-130.
Habitual drunkards or users.
Dealers' licenses.
Suspension or revocation, PS §5-114.
Restrictions on possession, PS §5-133.
Restrictions on sale, rental or transfer, PS §5-134.
Handgun forfeitures, CP §§13-201 to 13-206.

FIREARMS —Cont'd

Handguns, CR §§4-201 to 4-209.
  Assault pistols, CR §§4-301 to 4-306.
    Defined, types and brands enumerated, CR §4-301.
    Persons excepted from provisions, CR §4-302.
    Punishment, CR §4-306.
    Scope of subtitle, CR §4-302.
    Seizure and disposal as contraband, CR §4-304.
    Transporting into state, selling or purchasing, prohibition, CR §4-303.
    Use in commission of crime.
      Punishment, CR §4-306.
  Child's access to firearm, CR §4-104.
  Definitions, CR §4-201.
  Disarming law enforcement officer, CR §4-103.
  Discharge.
    Local regulation, CR §4-209.
  Identification requirements, PS §5-131.
  Law enforcement officers and personnel.
    Disposal of handguns owned by law enforcement agencies, PS §3-501.
      State police, PS §2-415.
    Firearms training courses.
      Certification, PS §3-208.
    State police.
      Disposition upon retirement, PS §2-415.
  Legislative findings, CR §4-202.
  Limited search, seizure and arrest, CR §4-206.
  Permits, PS §§5-301 to 5-314.
  Probation on conviction.
    Limitation, CR §4-205.
  Public demonstration.
    Possession at, CR §4-208.
  Reduction of mandatory minimum sentence by court.
    Limitation, CR §4-205.
  Roster, PS §§5-401 to 5-406.
  Safety devices, PS §5-132.
  School property.
    Carrying or possessing on, CR §4-102.
  State police.
    Disposition upon retirement, PS §2-415.
  State preemption of regulation, CR §4-209.
  Suspension of mandatory minimum sentence by court.
    Limitation, CR §4-205.
  Use in commission of crime, CR §4-204.
  Wearing, carrying or transporting.
    Prohibition, penalty, sentencing, CR §4-203.
Identification.
  Applications for purchases, rents or transfers.
    Information required, PS §5-118.
  Dealers' licenses.
    Applications, PS §5-107.
    Display of identity and location of place of business, PS §5-113.
Identification marks or numbers.
  Removal or alteration, PS §5-142.
Integrated mechanical safety device.
  Handgun safety devices, PS §5-132.
Investigations.
  Applications for purchases, rents or transfers, PS §5-121.
    Temporary transfer permits, gun shows, PS §5-130.
  Dealers' licenses, PS §5-109.
Juvenile causes.
  Delinquency and contributing cases.
    Restrictions on possession, PS §5-133.

FIREARMS —Cont'd

Knowing participation in violation of subtitle, PS §5-143.
Law enforcement officers and personnel.
  Disposal of handguns owned by law enforcement agencies, PS §3-501.
    State police, PS §2-415.
  Firearms training courses.
    Certification, PS §3-208.
  Law enforcement equipment fund, PS §§4-301 to 4-304.
  State police.
    Disposition of handguns upon retirement, PS §2-415.
Licenses.
  Dealers' licenses, PS §§5-106 to 5-116.
Local laws.
  Preemption of local laws by state, PS §5-104.
  Restrictions on possession, PS §5-133.
Machine guns, CR §§4-401 to 4-407.
  Confiscation or destruction of seized machine gun, CR §4-402.
  Definitions, CR §4-401.
  Evidence of possession.
    Presence in room, boat or vehicle, CR §4-402.
  Exceptions to possession prohibition, CR §4-402.
  Fee for registering, CR §4-403.
  Possession, CR §4-402.
  Presumption of aggressive or offensive purposes, CR §4-405.
  Public record exception.
    Registration data, CR §4-403.
  Registration by person acquiring machine gun, CR §4-403.
  Registration of machine guns manufactured or handled by manufacturer, CR §4-403.
  Search warrants to seize illegally possessed machine gun, CR §4-402.
  Statute of limitations for prosecutions.
    Use for aggressive or offensive purposes, CR §4-405.
  Uniformity of interpretation and construction of subtitle, CR §4-406.
  Uniform machine gun act.
    Short title, CR §4-407.
  Use for aggressive or offensive purposes, CR §4-405.
  Use in commission of crime, CR §4-404.
Mandatory sentence for crime of violence.
  Second, third or fourth conviction, CR §14-101.
Manufacturers.
  Handgun identification requirements, PS §5-131.
  Handgun roster, PS §§5-401 to 5-406.
Mentally ill.
  Dealers' licenses.
    Suspension or revocation, PS §5-114.
  Restrictions on possession, PS §5-133.
  Restrictions on sale, rental or transfer, PS §5-134.
  Rifles.
    Possession by person with mental disorder, PS §5-205.
  Shotguns.
    Possession by person with mental disorder, PS §5-205.
Militia.
  Sale of superfluous armories, PS §13-217.
Minors.
  Ammunition.
    Sale, rental or transfer to minors, PS §5-134.
  Restrictions on possession, PS §5-133.
  Restrictions on sale, rental or transfer, PS §5-134.

FIREARMS —Cont'd

Misdemeanors.
Applications for purchases, rents or transfers.
Multiple purchases within thirty days, PS §5-129.
Handguns.
Manufacture or sale of guns not on roster, PS §5-406.
Knowing participation in violation of subtitle, PS §5-143.
Possession of short-barreled rifles or shotguns, PS §5-203.
Rifles and shotguns.
Possession by person with mental disorder, PS §5-205.
Straw purchases.
Knowing participation in, PS §5-141.

Notice.
Applications for purchases, rents or transfers.
Disapproval, PS §5-122.
Dealers' licenses.
Disapproval, PS §5-110.
Suspension or revocation, PS §5-114.

One purchase limit within thirty days.
Applications for purchases, rents or transfers, PS §5-128.
Multiple purchases allowed, PS §5-129.

Out-of-state purchases, PS §5-137.

Permits.
Temporary transfer permits.
Gun shows, PS §5-130.

Personalized handguns.
Handgun safety devices, PS §5-132.

Possession.
Restrictions, PS §5-133.

Preemption of local laws by state, PS §5-104.
Sale, rental or transfer, PS §5-134.

Projectiles.
Handgun identification requirements, PS §5-131.

Public demonstrations.
Possession at, CR §4-208.

Purchases.
Firearms applications, PS §§5-117 to 5-130.
One purchase limit within thirty days, PS §5-128.
Multiple purchases allowed, PS §5-129.

Reckless endangerment.
Discharge from motor vehicle, CR §3-204.

Records.
Applications for purchases, rents or transfers.
Retention of copies, PS §5-120.

Removal or alteration of identification marks or numbers, PS §5-142.

Rent, PS §§5-134 to 5-143.
Firearms applications, PS §§5-117 to 5-130.
Handgun safety devices, PS §5-132.

Reports.
Handgun safety devices, PS §5-132.

Restrictions on possession, PS §5-133.

Rifles, PS §§5-201 to 5-205.
Defined terms, CR §4-201; PS §5-201.
Mentally ill.
Possession by person with mental disorder, PS §5-205.
Purchases in adjacent states, PS §5-204.
Scope of subtitle, PS §5-202.
Short-barreled rifles.
Defined, CR §4-201; PS §5-201.
Possession prohibited, PS §5-203.

Robbery with dangerous weapon, CR §3-403.

Rules and regulations, PS §5-105.

FIREARMS —Cont'd

Safety devices.
Handguns, PS §5-132.

Safety training course.
Applications for purchases, rents or transfers, PS §5-118.
Exemption, PS §5-119.
Sale, rental or transfer.
Exemptions, PS §5-134.
Required, PS §5-134.

Sale, rental or transfer, PS §§5-134 to 5-143.
Certified firearms safety training course.
Exemptions, PS §5-134.
Required, PS §5-134.
False statements in applications, PS §5-139.
Firearms applications, PS §§5-117 to 5-130.
General restrictions, PS §5-134.
Handgun roster, PS §§5-401 to 5-406.
Handgun safety devices, PS §5-132.
Identification marks or numbers.
Removal or alteration, PS §5-142.
Out-of-state purchases, PS §5-137.
Preemption by state, PS §5-134.
Seizure of firearms sold, rented or transferred in violation, PS §5-135.
Stolen firearms, PS §5-138.
Straw purchases.
Knowing participation in, PS §5-141.
Prohibited, PS §5-136.
Transporting for unlawful sale, PS §5-140.

Schools.
Deadly weapons on school property, CR §4-102.
Handguns, sentencing, CR §4-203.
Violations, ED §7-305.

Scope of subtitle, PS §5-102.
Effect of subtitle, PS §5-103.

Secretary.
Applications for purchases, rents or transfers.
Hearings on actions of secretary, PS §5-126.
Investigations, PS §5-121.
Defined, PS §5-101.
Rules and regulations, PS §5-105.

Seven day waiting period.
Applications for purchases, rents or transfers, PS §5-123.
Secondary transactions, PS §5-124.

Shell casings.
Handgun identification requirements, PS §5-131.

Short-barreled rifles.
Defined, CR §4-201; PS §5-201.
Possession prohibited, PS §5-203.

Short-barreled shotguns.
Defined, CR §4-201; PS §5-201.
Possession prohibited, PS §5-203.

Shotguns, PS §§5-201 to 5-205.
Defined, CR §4-201; PS §5-201.
Mentally ill.
Possession by person with mental disorder, PS §5-205.
Purchases in adjacent states, PS §5-204.
Scope of subtitle, PS §5-202.
Short-barreled shotguns.
Defined, CR §4-201; PS §5-201.
Possession prohibited, PS §5-203.

State preemption of local regulation, CR §4-209.

Stolen firearms.
Sale, rental or transfer, PS §5-138.

Straw purchases.
Knowing participation in, PS §5-141.
Prohibited, PS §5-136.
Restrictions on sale, rental or transfer, PS §5-134.

FIREARMS —Cont'd
Strict liability.
Handgun manufacturers.
Handgun roster, PS §5-402.
Substance abuse.
Addicts, restrictions on possession, PS §5-133.
Temporary transfer permits.
Gun shows, PS §5-130.
Thirty day limit.
One purchase limit within thirty days, PS §5-128.
Multiple purchases allowed, PS §5-129.
Transfers, PS §§5-134 to 5-143.
Handgun safety devices, PS §5-132.
Transporting for unlawful sale, PS §5-140.
**Trapshooting, skeetshooting or other target
shooting.**
Environmental sound level limits and noise
control rules and regulations, EN §3-401.
Noise control ordinance, rule or regulation
prohibiting during certain hours.
Power of political subdivisions to adopt, EN
§3-105.
Trigger locks.
Handgun safety devices, PS §5-132.
Venue.
Applications for purchases, rents or transfers.
Hearings on actions of secretary, PS §5-126.
Violation of subtitle.
Knowing participation in, PS §5-143.
Violence reduction.
Cease fire council, PS §§5-501 to 5-504.
Weapons generally.
See WEAPONS.

FIREARMS APPLICATIONS.
Purchases, rents or transfers, PS §§5-117 to
5-130.

FIREARM SILENCER.
Drug trafficking crime.
Use, enhanced sentence, CR §5-621.

FIRE DEPARTMENT.
Acquired immune deficiency syndrome (AIDS).
HIV testing for health care workers and first
responders, HG §§18-336 to 18-338.3.
Notification of fire fighters of exposure to virus,
HG §18-213.
Allegany county.
Firefighters appointed as deputy sheriffs, PS
§§7-301 to 7-303.
Ambulances.
Volunteer firemen and rescue squadmen
generally. See within this heading, "Volunteer
firemen and rescue squadmen."
Appeals.
Discipline of employees.
Judicial review of final decisions, LE §§4-601 to
4-603.
Autopsies.
Toxicological examinations, HG §5-310.
Charitable contributions.
Public safety solicitors, BR §§6-5A-01 to 6-5A-11.
See CHARITIES.
Collective bargaining, LE §§4-501 to 4-505.
See COLLECTIVE BARGAINING.
Contagious diseases.
Notification of fire fighters of exposure to
contagious disease, HG §18-213.
Corporations.
Provision of fire, ambulance and rescue services
by for-profit entities, PS §7-401.

FIRE DEPARTMENT —Cont'd
Counties.
Volunteer fire departments.
Money and loans for, PS §§8-301 to 8-303.
Powers of county commissioners, 25 §3.
Criminal history records checks.
Firefighters, rescue squad members and
paramedics, PS §6-306.
Criminal law and procedure.
Impersonating firefighters or emergency services
personnel, PS §7-402.
Inspections by local fire departments.
Hindering, obstructing or refusing to allow
inspection, PS §9-805.
Interference with or obstruction of emergency
assistance, PS §7-402.
Death in the line of duty.
Autopsies of fire fighters, HG §5-310.
Death benefits, PS §1-202.
Reward for information regarding person who
causes death, PS §1-201.
Diphtheria.
Notification of exposure, HG §§18-213 to 18-213.2.
Discipline of employees.
Judicial review of final decisions.
Collective bargaining agreement, LE §4-603.
Definitions, LE §4-601.
Generally, LE §4-602.
Drivers' licenses.
Exemptions, TR §16-102.
Emergency trust fund.
Volunteer company emergency trust fund. See
within this heading, "Volunteer firemen and
rescue squadmen."
Emergency vehicles.
See EMERGENCY VEHICLES.
False alarms.
Warrantless arrest, CP §2-203.
False impersonations.
Impersonating firefighters or emergency services
personnel, PS §7-402.
Fines.
Inspections by local fire departments.
Hindering, obstructing or refusing to allow
inspection, PS §9-805.
Fingerprinting.
Criminal history record checks, PS §6-306.
Fire marshal.
See FIRE MARSHAL.
Fire service technology.
Tuition.
Reimbursement of firemen and rescue
squadmen for tuition, ED §18-603.
Flag benefit.
Firefighter killed in performance of duty.
Issuance to family, PS §1-202.
For-profit entities.
Provision of fire, ambulance and rescue services
by for-profit entities, PS §7-401.
Funds.
County money and loans for volunteer fire
companies, PS §§8-301 to 8-303.
Senator William H. Amoss fire, rescue and
ambulance fund, PS §§8-101 to 8-106.
Volunteer company assistance fund, PS §§8-201 to
8-206.
**General assembly member may be nonelected
fire worker,** MD Const Art III §11.
Good Samaritan law.
Immunity from civil liability, CJ §5-604.

FIRE DEPARTMENT —Cont'd
Heart attack.
Death benefits.
Death as result of personal injury in
performance of duties.
Presumption, PS §1-202.
Hemorrhagic fevers.
Notification of exposure, HG §§18-213 to 18-213.2.
Hepatitis.
Exposure to.
Notification, HG §§18-213 to 18-213.2.
Holding more than one office of profit.
Membership in fire department or agency.
Not considered office of profit, MD Const DofR
Art 35.
Human immunodeficiency virus.
HIV testing for health care workers and first
responders, HG §§18-336 to 18-338.3.
Notification of fire fighters of exposure to virus,
HG §18-213.
Inspections by local fire departments, PS
§§9-801 to 9-805.
Applicability, PS §9-802.
Defined terms, PS §9-801.
Fire inspections authorized, PS §9-803.
Fire officials.
Defined, PS §9-801.
Powers, PS §9-803.
Hindering, obstructing or refusing to allow
inspection, PS §9-805.
Notice.
Removal of combustible material, PS §9-804.
Rescue squads.
Obstructing prohibited, PS §9-803.
Scope of subtitle, PS §9-802.
Insurance.
Blanket health insurance authorized for volunteer
departments, IN §15-305.
Group life insurance for volunteer fire fighters, IN
§17-208.
Liability insurance for individuals assisting
department, IN §19-105.
**Interference with or obstruction of emergency
assistance,** PS §7-402.
Liability.
Immunity from civil liability for acts or omissions
in course of duties, CJ §5-604.
Life insurance and annuities.
Group life insurance for volunteer fire fighters, IN
§17-208.
Loans.
Volunteer fire departments.
Guarantee of loans, PS §8-303.
Meningitis.
Exposure to.
Notification of fire fighters, HG §18-213.
Minors.
Volunteer firemen and rescue squadmen.
Deceased or disabled.
Education of children, ED §18-602.
Mononucleosis.
Exposure to.
Notification of fire fighters, HG §18-213.
Motor vehicles.
Assistance to other political subdivisions, 23A
§8C.
Drivers' licenses exemptions, TR §16-102.
Fire hose.
Crossing prohibited, TR §21-1110.
Following fire apparatus prohibited, TR §21-1109.
General provisions, 23A §2.

FIRE DEPARTMENT —Cont'd
Motor vehicles —Cont'd
Lights.
Oscillating, blinking, etc., lights on certain
vehicles, TR §22-218.
Seat belts or restraining devices in emergency
vehicles, TR §22-412.4.
Mutual aid agreements, PS §§7-101 to 7-107.
Construction and interpretation, PS §7-102.
Defined terms, PS §7-101.
Expenditures, PS §7-107.
Federal government, PS §7-104.
Other states and entities of other states, PS
§7-103.
Training.
Emergency response measures, PS §7-105.
Workers' compensation benefits.
Line of duty, PS §7-106.
Negligence.
Immunity from civil liability for acts or omissions
performed in course of duties, CJ §5-604.
911 emergency telephone system, PS §§1-301 to
1-312.
See 911 EMERGENCY TELEPHONE SYSTEM.
Notice.
Inspections by local fire departments.
Removal of combustible material, PS §9-804.
Overtime compensation.
Alternative work periods, SPP §8-305.
Plague.
Notification of exposure, HG §§18-213 to 18-213.2.
Private water sources.
Right to enter private property to obtain water,
PS §7-403.
Rabies.
Notification of exposure, HG §§18-213 to 18-213.2.
Rescue squad.
Volunteer firemen and rescue squadmen
generally. See within this heading, "Volunteer
firemen and rescue squadmen."
Retirement and pension systems.
Local fire and police pension system, SPP
§§28-101 to 28-403.
See LOCAL FIRE AND POLICE PENSION
SYSTEM.
Rewards.
Death in the line of duty.
Reward for information regarding person who
causes death, PS §1-201.
Scholarships.
Children of firemen killed in line of duty, ED
§18-602.
Children or surviving spouses of public safety
employees killed in line of duty, ED §18-601.
Service awards.
Volunteer firemen and rescue squadmen, PS
§§7-208 to 7-213.
Sheriffs.
Firefighters appointed as deputy sheriffs, PS
§§7-301 to 7-303.
Commanding officer.
Defined, PS §7-301.
Counties designated, PS §§7-302, 7-303.
Powers, PS §§7-302, 7-303.
Stroke.
Death benefits.
Death as result of personal injury in
performance of duties.
Presumption, PS §1-202.
Taxation.
Exemption.
Nonprofit incorporated fire company.
Property exempt, TP §7-209.

FIRE DEPARTMENT —Cont'd
Taxation —Cont'd
State adjustments for firefighters, TG §10-208.
Training.
Emergency response measures.
Mutual aid agreements, PS §7-105.
Tuberculosis.
Exposure to tuberculosis.
Notification of fire fighters, HG §18-213.
Vessels and boats.
Fire department vessels.
Flashing red and yellow lights or signal devices.
Use, NR §8-727.1.
Misdemeanors.
Violations of section by operators, NR §8-727.1.
Volunteer company assistance fund, PS §§8-201 to 8-206.
Volunteer firemen and rescue squadmen.
Children of disabled or deceased firemen and rescue squadmen.
Care, ED §18-602.
Pensions, ED §18-602.
Corporations.
Recordation fees.
Exemption, CA §1-203.1.
County money and loans for volunteer fire companies, PS §§8-301 to 8-303.
Death in the line of duty.
Death benefits, PS §§1-202, 7-201 to 7-205.
Board defined, PS §7-201.
Eligibility, PS §7-203.
Funding, PS §7-204.
On duty defined, federal act, PS §7-205.
Reward for information regarding person who causes death, PS §1-201.
Disability and death benefits, PS §§7-201 to 7-205.
Board defined, PS §7-201.
Disability benefits, eligibility, PS §7-202.
Eligibility, PS §7-203.
Disability benefits, PS §7-202.
Funding, PS §7-204.
On duty defined, federal act, PS §7-205.
Drivers' licenses exemptions, TR §16-102.
Food service.
Written notice of intent to serve food to the public, HG §21-304.1.
Funds.
Volunteer company assistance fund, PS §§8-201 to 8-206.
Good Samaritan law.
Immunity from liability, CJ §5-603.
Howard county.
Alcoholic beverage licenses.
Luxury restaurant license, 2B §8-214.
Insurance.
Blanket health insurance authorized, IN §15-305.
Length of service awards, PS §§7-208 to 7-213.
Calvert county, PS §7-208.
Cecil county, PS §7-209.
Charles county, PS §7-210.
Frederick county, PS §7-211.
St. Mary's county, PS §7-212.
Washington county, PS §7-213.
Waiver.
Immunity from civil liability.
Waiver of immunity, CJ §5-604.
Workers' compensation.
Mutual aid agreements.
Line of duty, PS §7-106.

FIRE DEPARTMENT —Cont'd
Workers' compensation —Cont'd
Permanent partial disability.
Compensation for less than 75 weeks.
Rate, LE §9-628.

FIRE ESCAPES.
Generally.
See FIRES AND FIRE PROTECTION.

FIRE EXTINGUISHERS.
Fireworks plants, PS §10-207.

FIRE FIGHTERS.
Fire department.
See FIRE DEPARTMENT.
Local fire and police pension system, SPP §§28-101 to 28-403.
See LOCAL FIRE AND POLICE PENSION SYSTEM.

FIRE HAZARDS.
Abatement orders, PS §6-318.
Failure to comply with order, PS §6-320.
Service of process, PS §6-319.
Additional remedies, PS §6-321.
Buildings.
Search warrants.
See FIRE MARSHAL.
Citation for maintaining.
Fire marshal authorized to charge by, CP §4-101.
Maintenance of fire hazard prohibited, PS §6-317.

FIRE INSURANCE.
Antiarson applications, IN §§19-301 to 19-309.
Alternative applications, IN §19-306.
Assignment of policy or contract, IN §19-304.
Defined, IN §19-301.
Designation of geographic areas.
Effect of designation, IN §19-308.
Extension to other types of policies, IN §19-304.
Forms, IN §19-305.
Limitations on insurer, IN §19-308.
Misrepresentation in application, IN §19-307.
Notice of changes, IN §19-307.
Owner-occupied dwellings for one to four families.
Applicability of subsection, IN §19-308.
Part of the policy, IN §19-307.
Purpose of subtitle, IN §19-302.
Regulations, IN §19-303.
Requirement, IN §19-304.
Scope of subtitle, IN §19-302.
Termination of policy or contract, IN §19-309.
Arson.
Insurance.
Fire insurance rates, IN §11-205.
Confidentiality of information.
Disclosure of fire loss investigation reports, PS §9-604.
Immunity from criminal and civil liability, PS §9-605.
Criminal law and procedure.
Disclosure of fire loss investigation reports.
Violations, PS §9-606.
Disclosure of fire loss investigation reports, PS §§9-601 to 9-606.
Confidentiality of information, PS §9-604.
Immunity from criminal and civil liability, PS §9-605.
Cooperation with fire investigator, PS §9-602.
Defined terms, PS §9-601.
Immunity from criminal and civil liability, PS §9-605.

FIRE INSURANCE —Cont'd
Disclosure of fire loss investigation reports
—Cont'd
Insurer's disclosures, PS §9-602.
Loss caused by incendiary means, PS §9-603.
Prohibited acts, PS §9-606.
Violations, PS §9-606.
Holocaust victims insurance act, IN §§28-101 to
28-110.
See HOLOCAUST VICTIMS INSURANCE.
Investigations.
Cooperation with fire investigator, PS §9-602.
Loss caused by incendiary means, PS §9-603.
Disclosure of fire loss investigation reports, PS
§§9-601 to 9-606.
Joint insurance association, IN §§25-401 to
25-410.
See JOINT INSURANCE ASSOCIATION.
Property and casualty insurance.
Generally.
See PROPERTY AND CASUALTY
INSURANCE.
Guaranty corporation, IN §§9-301 to 9-316.
See PROPERTY AND CASUALTY
INSURANCE GUARANTY
CORPORATION.
Rates, IN §11-205.
Reports.
Disclosure of fire loss investigation reports, PS
§§9-601 to 9-606.
Losses by insurers, PS §6-314.

FIRE MARSHAL, PS §§6-301 to 6-322.
Abatement orders, PS §6-318.
Failure to comply with order, PS §6-320.
Service of process, PS §6-319.
Appeals, PS §§6-501 to 6-503.
Judicial review of commission's decision, PS
§6-503.
Procedure, PS §6-502.
Right to file appeal to commission, PS §6-501.
Appointment, PS §6-302.
Arrest.
Authority, PS §6-311.
Arrest without a warrant.
Authority of fire marshal and assistants, CP
§2-208.
Arson.
Arrest without warrant.
Persons committing specified violations, CP
§2-208.
Assistant state fire marshals, PS §6-304.
Baltimore City, PS §§6-401 to 6-403.
Applicability, PS §6-401.
Assistance to chief of Baltimore City fire
department, PS §6-402.
Building codes.
Inspections.
Electrical code, duties, PS §12-605.
Chimney fires.
Reports, PS §6-313.
Citations, charging by, CP §4-101.
Construction law.
Plan review, fees, PS §6-308.
Contagious disease or virus.
Notification of members of fire marshal's office of
exposure to, HG §18-213.1.
Criminal history records checks.
Firefighters, rescue squad members and
paramedics, PS §6-306.

FIRE MARSHAL —Cont'd
Criminal law and procedure.
Impersonation of fire marshal or employee, PS
§6-602.
Interference with or obstruction of emergency
assistance, PS §6-602.
Interference with or obstruction of investigations,
PS §6-602.
Death in the line of duty.
Death benefits, PS §1-202.
Reward for information regarding person who
causes death, PS §1-201.
Defined terms, PS §6-101.
Department.
Defined, PS §6-101.
Deputy state fire marshals, PS §6-303.
Duties, PS §6-305.
Emergencies.
Interference with or obstruction of emergency
assistance, PS §6-602.
Enforcement powers, PS §6-305.
Abatement orders, PS §6-318.
Failure to comply with order, PS §6-320.
Service of process, PS §6-319.
Administrative search warrants.
Inspections, PS §6-316.
Investigations, PS §6-315.
Arrest, PS §6-311.
Authority to take testimony, PS §6-310.
Establishment of office, PS §6-301.
Explosions and explosives.
Investigations, PS §6-309.
Powers, PS §11-104.
Revocation of licenses, PS §11-111.
Theft of explosives, PS §11-113.
Fees, PS §6-308.
Explosives, PS §11-104.
Fingerprinting.
Criminal history record checks, PS §6-306.
Fire hazards.
Abatement orders, PS §6-318.
Failure to comply with order, PS §6-320.
Service of process, PS §6-319.
Additional remedies, PS §6-321.
Maintaining.
Citation, authorized to issue, CP §4-101.
Prohibited, PS §6-317.
Fire insurance.
Losses by insurers, PS §6-314.
Fire prevention commission.
Authority, PS §6-205.
Fire sprinkler contractor licensing.
Duties, PS §9-904.
Fireworks.
Generally.
See FIREWORKS.
Permits.
Authority to grant, PS §10-103.
Fireworks plants.
License to operate, PS §10-201.
Rules and regulations, PS §10-202.
Flag benefit.
Firefighter killed in performance of duty.
Issuance to family, PS §1-202.
Heart attack.
Death benefits.
Death as result of personal injury in
performance of duties.
Presumption, PS §1-202.
Immunities from liability and exemption.
Warrantless arrest power, acting under, CP
§2-208.

FIRE MARSHAL —Cont'd
Impersonation, PS §6-602.
Injunctions.
  Abatement orders, PS §6-318.
    Failure to comply with order, PS §6-320.
    Service of process, PS §6-319.
Inspections.
  Administrative search warrants, PS §6-316.
  Building codes.
    Electrical code, duties, PS §12-605.
  Fees, PS §6-308.
  Public buildings, PS §6-307.
Investigations, PS §6-309.
  Administrative search warrants, PS §6-315.
  Arrest authority, PS §6-311.
  Interference with or obstruction, PS §6-602.
  Reports, PS §6-312.
Law enforcement officers generally, PS §§3-101
  to 3-603.
  See LAW ENFORCEMENT OFFICERS AND
    PERSONNEL.
Notice.
  Exposure of members of fire marshal's office to
    contagious disease or virus, HG §18-213.1.
  Warrantless arrest power, acting under, CP
    §2-208.
Oaths.
  Authority to take testimony, PS §6-310.
Office.
  Established, PS §6-301.
  Staff, PS §6-303.
  State police department, unit of, PS §2-207.
Perjury.
  False testimony, PS §6-310.
Plan review.
  County and municipal fire prevention codes, PS
    §9-702.
  Fees, PS §6-308.
Powers, PS §6-305.
  Secretary, PS §6-322.
Qualifications, PS §6-302.
  Assistant state fire marshals, PS §6-304.
  Deputy state fire marshals, PS §6-303.
  Special assistant state fire marshals, PS §6-304.
Removal, PS §6-302.
  Assistant and special assistant state fire
    marshals, PS §6-304.
Reports.
  Baltimore City fire department, PS §6-403.
  Chimney fire reports, PS §6-313.
  Investigations, PS §6-312.
    Explosions and fires, PS §11-104.
  Losses by insurers, PS §6-314.
Reward.
  Death in the line of duty.
    Reward for information regarding person who
      causes death, PS §1-201.
Right of entry.
  Investigations of explosions and fires, PS §11-104.
Salary, PS §6-302.
Searches and seizures.
  Inspections.
    Administrative search warrants, PS §6-316.
  Investigations.
    Administrative search warrants, PS §6-315.
  Search warrants.
    Directed to fire marshal or authorized assistant,
      CP §1-203.
Secretary.
  Authority of secretary, PS §6-322.
  Defined, PS §6-101.

FIRE MARSHAL —Cont'd
Service of process.
  Abatement orders, PS §6-319.
Smoke detectors.
  Smoke detection installation orders, PS §9-108.
Special assistant state fire marshals, PS §6-304.
Sprinkler systems, PS §§9-201 to 9-206.
  Fire sprinkler contractor licensing.
    Duties, PS §9-904.
Staff, PS §6-303.
Stroke.
  Death benefits.
    Death as result of personal injury in
      performance of duties.
      Presumption, PS §1-202.
Subpoenas.
  Authority to take testimony, PS §6-310.
Term, PS §6-302.
Violations of title, PS §§6-601, 6-602.
Warrantless arrest.
  Authority of fire marshal and assistants, CP
    §2-208.
Witnesses.
  Authority to take testimony, PS §6-310.
Workers' compensation.
  Occupational diseases.
    Statutory presumption, LE §9-503.

FIREPLACES.
Consumer protection.
  Sale, distribution or installation of freestanding
    fireplaces, CL §14-1309.

FIRE PREVENTION COMMISSION, PS §§6-201
  to 6-207.
Appeals, PS §§6-501 to 6-503.
  Judicial review of commission's decision, PS
    §6-503.
  Procedure, PS §6-502.
  Right to file appeal to commission, PS §6-501.
Baltimore City, PS §§6-401 to 6-403.
  Applicability, PS §6-401.
  Assistance to chief of Baltimore City fire
    department, PS §6-402.
Building codes.
  Emergency power and lighting systems, PS
    §12-702.
Chairman, PS §6-203.
Composition, PS §6-202.
Conflict of laws.
  Regulations, PS §6-206.
Created, PS §6-201.
Defined terms, PS §6-101.
Department.
  Defined, PS §6-101.
Duties, PS §6-205.
Education and training.
  Annual seminars, PS §6-205.
Established, PS §6-201.
Explosives generally, PS §§11-101 to 11-118.
  See EXPLOSIONS AND EXPLOSIVES.
Fire marshal.
  Authority, PS §6-205.
  Generally, PS §§6-301 to 6-322.
    See FIRE MARSHAL.
Fireworks.
  Rules and regulations, PS §10-109.
Hearings.
  Adoption of regulation, PS §6-206.
Meetings, PS §6-204.
Members, PS §6-202.
  Compensation and reimbursement for expenses,
    PS §6-204.

FIRE PREVENTION COMMISSION —Cont'd
Officers, PS §6-203.
Powers, PS §6-205.
  Secretary, PS §6-207.
Quorum, PS §6-204.
Reports.
  Annual report, PS §6-205.
  Baltimore City fire department, PS §6-403.
Rules and regulations, PS §6-206.
  Fireworks, PS §10-109.
  Violations, PS §§6-601, 6-602.
Secretary.
  Authority generally, PS §6-207.
  Defined, PS §6-101.
  Rules and regulations, PS §6-206.
Sprinkler systems.
  Fire sprinkler contractor licensing.
    Duties, PS §9-902.
State fire marshal, PS §§6-301 to 6-322.
  See FIRE MARSHAL.
State fire prevention code.
  Copies, PS §6-206.
State police department, unit of, PS §2-207.
  Department defined, PS §6-101.
Vice chairman, PS §6-203.
Violations, PS §§6-601, 6-602.

FIRE SALES, CL §§11-1101 to 11-1106.
See DISTRESS SALES.

FIRES AND FIRE PROTECTION, PS §§9-101 to
  9-1001.
Alarm systems.
  Audible systems.
    Equipped to automatically silence, CR §9-611.
  Defective system.
    Notice to user, use after notice, CR §9-610.
  Definitions, CR §9-607.
  False alarms, CR §9-608.
    Multiple alarms, CR §9-609.
Appeals.
  Orders of compliance.
    High-rise buildings, PS §9-404.
Automatic fire extinguishing systems.
  Specified buildings, PS §9-503.
Automatic sprinkler systems.
  High-rise buildings, PS §§9-401 to 9-404.
Barbeque grills.
  Restrictions on use, PS §9-1001.
**Center for the study of the health effects of
  fire,** HG §§18-701 to 18-711.
  Advisory council.
    Chairperson, HG §18-708.
    Duties, HG §18-710.
    Established, HG §18-706.
    Expenses, reimbursement, HG §18-709.
    Meetings, HG §18-709.
    Members, HG §18-707.
  Confidentiality of information collected, HG
    §18-705.
  Definitions, HG §18-701.
  Director, chief medical examiner, HG §18-703.
  Duties, HG §18-704.
  Established, HG §18-702.
  Inadmissibility of information collected in civil or
    criminal proceeding, HG §18-705.
  Registry of individuals suffering from fire related
    injury or death, HG §18-704.
  Regulations, adoption, HG §18-711.
  Repository for information, HG §18-704.
  Staff, HG §18-703.

FIRES AND FIRE PROTECTION —Cont'd
Chimney fires.
  Fire marshal's report, PS §6-313.
Conflict of laws.
  Evacuation procedures.
    Effect on other fire safety laws, PS §9-501.
  Smoke detectors.
    New residential construction.
      More stringent local laws, PS §9-103.
  Sprinkler systems.
    More stringent local laws, PS §9-202.
    Fast response residential systems, PS §9-301.
Consumer protection.
  Insulation.
    Fire resistant insulating material, CL §13-313.
Counties.
  Assistance to other political subdivisions, 25 §219.
  Authority to adopt fire prevention codes, PS
    §9-701.
  Fire hydrants.
    Powers as to, 25 §2.
  Inspections by fire marshal, PS §9-702.
  Inspections by local fire departments, PS §§9-801
    to 9-805.
  Plan review, PS §9-702.
Criminal law and procedure.
  Evacuation procedure violations, PS §9-506.
  Interference with or obstruction of emergency
    assistance, PS §6-602.
  Smoke detectors.
    Violations, PS §9-109.
  Sprinkler systems.
    Violations, PS §9-206.
    Fire sprinkler contractor licensing, PS §9-905.
Definitions.
  Center for the study of the health effects of fire,
    HG §18-701.
Discovery.
  Center for the study of the health effects of fire.
    Information collected not discoverable, HG
      §18-705.
Distress for rent.
  Termination of tenancy for fire, RP §8-112.
Elevators.
  Warning signs in case of fire, PS §12-815.
Emergencies.
  Interference with or obstruction of emergency
    assistance, PS §6-602.
Emergency management, PS §§14-101 to 14-1004.
  See EMERGENCY MANAGEMENT.
Evacuation procedures, PS §§9-501 to 9-506.
  Automatic fire extinguishing systems.
    Specified buildings, PS §9-503.
  Conflict of laws.
    Effect on other fire safety laws, PS §9-501.
  Hospitals.
    Alternative requirements for acute care
      hospitals, PS §9-505.
  Notice.
    Posting required, PS §9-502.
  Posting required, PS §9-502.
  Scope, PS §9-501.
  Violations, PS §9-506.
Evidence.
  Center for the study of the health effects of fire.
    Inadmissibility of information collected, HG
      §18-705.
False fire alarms, CR §9-604.
  Activating alarm system, CR §§9-607 to 9-609.
Fines.
  Smoke detectors.
    Violations, PS §9-109.

FIRES AND FIRE PROTECTION —Cont'd
Fines —Cont'd
    Sprinkler systems.
        Violations, PS §9-206.
            Fire sprinkler contractor licensing, PS §9-905.
Fire department.
    See FIRE DEPARTMENT.
Fire extinguishers.
    Fireworks plants, PS §10-207.
Fire hazards.
    Maintenance of fire hazard prohibited, PS §6-317.
Fire hydrants.
    Powers of counties, 25 §2.
Fire marshal.
    Generally, PS §§6-301 to 6-322.
        See FIRE MARSHAL.
Fire prevention commission.
    Generally, PS §§6-201 to 6-207.
        See FIRE PREVENTION COMMISSION.
Fire resistant insulating material.
    Fire retardancy standards, CL §13-313.
Forests and parks.
    Fire hazards.
        Generally, NR §§5-701 to 5-706.
            See FORESTS AND PARKS.
        Railroads, NR §§5-707 to 5-714.
            See FORESTS AND PARKS.
    Middle Atlantic interstate forest fire protection
        compact, NR §5-801.
**General assembly member may be nonelected
    fire worker,** MD Const Art III §11.
Health.
    Center for the study of the health effects of fire,
        HG §§18-701 to 18-711.
High-rise buildings, PS §§9-401 to 9-404.
    Appeals.
        Orders of compliance, PS §9-404.
    Defined terms, PS §9-401.
    Legislative findings, PS §9-402.
    Purpose, PS §9-402.
    Sprinkler systems.
        Required, PS §9-403.
Hospitals.
    Evacuation procedures.
        Alternative requirements for acute care
            hospitals, PS §9-505.
Hotels.
    Smoke detectors.
        Installation required, PS §9-102.
Immunity.
    Disclosure of information concerning fire loss
        investigation, CJ §5-409.
Inspections.
    Counties.
        Inspections by fire marshal, PS §9-702.
    Local fire departments, PS §§9-801 to 9-805.
    Municipal corporations.
        Inspections by fire marshal, PS §9-702.
Insulation.
    Consumer protection.
        Fire resistant insulating material, CL §13-313.
Insurance.
    Smoke detectors.
        Failure to comply as defense in property
            insurance claim, PS §9-107.
**Interference with or obstruction of emergency
    assistance,** PS §6-602.
Investigations.
    Disclosure of fire loss investigation reports, PS
        §§9-601 to 9-606.
    Fire marshal, PS §6-309.

FIRES AND FIRE PROTECTION —Cont'd
Investigations —Cont'd
    Loss investigations.
        Disclosure of information concerning fire loss
            investigation.
                Immunity, CJ §5-409.
    Search warrants.
        See FIRE MARSHAL.
Landlord and tenant.
    Effect of covenant to surrender premises in good
        repair, RP §8-113.
    Smoke detectors.
        General requirements, PS §9-104.
        Installation required, PS §9-102.
    Termination of tenancy for fire or unavoidable
        accident, RP §8-112.
Licenses.
    Sprinkler systems.
        Fire sprinkler contractor licensing, PS §§9-901
            to 9-905.
Local fire and police pension system.
    General provisions, SPP §§28-101 to 28-403.
        See LOCAL FIRE AND POLICE PENSION
            SYSTEM.
Loss investigations.
    Disclosure of information concerning fire loss
        investigation.
            Immunity, CJ §5-409.
Maryland fire and rescue institute.
    General provisions.
        See UNIVERSITY OF MARYLAND.
Motels.
    Smoke detectors.
        Installation required, PS §9-102.
Municipal corporations.
    Authority to adopt fire prevention codes, PS
        §9-701.
    Inspections by fire marshal, PS §9-702.
    Inspections by local fire departments, PS §§9-801
        to 9-805.
    Plan review, PS §9-702.
Notice.
    Evacuation procedures.
        Posting required, PS §9-502.
    Inspections by local fire departments.
        Removal of combustible material, PS §9-804.
Occupational safety and health.
    Hazardous and toxic substances.
        Access to information for fire control, LE §5-409.
Privileged communications.
    Center for the study of the health effects of fire.
        Confidentiality of information collected, HG
            §18-705.
Railroads.
    Fire hazards.
        Abatement, NR §§5-707 to 5-714.
            See FORESTS AND PARKS.
    Liability for damages from fire, presumption of
        negligence, PUC §9-309.
Reports.
    Losses by insurers, PS §6-314.
Rescue squads.
    Inspections by local fire departments.
        Obstructing prohibited, PS §9-803.
Rules and regulations.
    Center for the study of the health effects of fire,
        HG §18-711.
Sales.
    Smoke detectors, PS §9-105.

FIRES AND FIRE PROTECTION —Cont'd
Scholarships.
Fire service technology.
  Reimbursement of firemen and rescue
    squadmen for tuition required for courses,
    ED §18-603.
Schools.
Fire drills, ED §7-408.
Fire-rescue education and training commission,
  ED §11-502.
  Definitions, ED §11-501.
  Duties, ED §11-503.
  Staff services, ED §11-503.
Smoke detectors, PS §§9-101 to 9-109.
Battery or electric power, PS §9-103.
  Requirements, PS §9-104.
Conflict of laws.
  New residential construction.
    More stringent local laws, PS §9-103.
Effect of subtitle, PS §9-101.
Fire marshal.
  Smoke detection installation orders, PS §9-108.
General requirements, PS §9-104.
Hotels.
  Installation required, PS §9-102.
Installation, PS §9-105.
  Required, PS §9-102.
Insurance.
  Failure to comply as defense in property
    insurance claim, PS §9-107.
Landlord and tenant.
  General requirements, PS §9-104.
  Installation required, PS §9-102.
Minimum number required.
  New residential units, PS §9-103.
Motels.
  Installation required, PS §9-102.
New residential units, PS §9-103.
Requirements, PS §§9-102, 9-104.
  New residential units, PS §9-103.
Sales, PS §9-105.
Scope of subtitle, PS §9-101.
Smoke detection installation orders, PS §9-108.
Sprinkler systems.
  Installed as alternative, PS §9-106.
Violations, PS §9-109.
Sprinkler systems, PS §§9-201 to 9-206.
Automatic fire extinguishing systems.
  Specified buildings, PS §9-503.
Conflict of laws.
  More stringent local laws, PS §9-202.
    Fast response residential systems, PS §9-301.
Defined terms, PS §9-201.
Effect of subtitle, PS §9-202.
Enforcement, PS §9-203.
  Violations, PS §9-206.
Exceptions.
  Authority to grant, PS §9-205.
Fast response residential systems, PS §§9-301 to
  9-306.
  Conflict of laws.
    More stringent local laws, PS §9-301.
  Enforcement, PS §9-302.
  Installation.
    Costs, PS §9-305.
    Required, PS §9-303.
  Requirements for system, PS §9-304.
  Scope, PS §9-301.
  Violations, PS §9-306.
Fire sprinkler contractor licensing, PS §§9-901 to
  9-905.

FIRES AND FIRE PROTECTION —Cont'd
Sprinkler systems —Cont'd
High-rise buildings.
  Required, PS §9-403.
Installation.
  Required, PS §9-204.
    Fast response residential systems, PS §9-303.
Required, PS §9-204.
  High-rise buildings, PS §9-403.
Smoke detectors.
  Sprinkler systems installed as alternative, PS
    §9-106.
Standards, PS §9-204.
Violations, PS §9-206.
Transportation department.
Contracts.
  Waterborne marine fire protection, TR §2-110.
University of Maryland.
Maryland fire and rescue institute.
  General provisions.
    See UNIVERSITY OF MARYLAND.
Violations.
Evacuation procedures, PS §9-506.
Fire marshal regulations, PS §§6-601, 6-602.
Fire prevention commission regulations, PS
  §§6-601, 6-602.
Volunteer fire department.
See FIRE DEPARTMENT.
Workers' compensation.
Average weekly wage.
  Fire fighters in natural resources department,
    LE §9-602.
  Volunteer fire or rescue company member, LE
    §9-602.
Covered employees and employers.
  Volunteer fire or rescue company, LE §9-234.
Insurance coverage.
  Volunteer fire company or rescue squad.
    Coverage required, LE §9-402.

FIREWORKS, PS §§10-101 to 10-210.
Advertising.
Display or discharge of fireworks, PS §10-108.
Applicability.
Scope of title, PS §10-102.
Bonds, surety.
Permits, PS §10-105.
Citation for discharging without permit.
Fire marshal authorized to charge by, CP §4-101.
Defined terms, PS §10-101.
Explosives generally, PS §§11-101 to 11-118.
See EXPLOSIONS AND EXPLOSIVES.
Fees.
Permits, PS §10-104.
Sparklers.
  Registration of distributors and wholesalers, PS
    §10-113.
Fines.
Possession, sale or permit violations, PS §10-111.
Health insurance.
Permits.
  Accident insurance, PS §10-106.
Inspections.
Permits, PS §10-107.
Insurance.
Permits.
  Accident insurance, PS §10-106.
  Liability insurance, PS §10-105.
  Workers' compensation, PS §10-106.
Investigations.
Permits, PS §10-107.

FIREWORKS —Cont'd
Permits.
Accident insurance, PS §10-106.
Application process, PS §10-104.
Authority to grant, PS §10-103.
Bonds, surety, PS §10-105.
Fees, PS §10-104.
Findings required, PS §10-103.
Inspections, PS §10-107.
Investigations, PS §10-107.
Liability insurance, PS §10-105.
Prohibited acts, PS §10-110.
  Penalties, PS §10-111.
Required, PS §10-104.
Sparklers.
  Registration of distributors and wholesalers, PS §10-113.
Workers' compensation, PS §10-106.
Plants, PS §§10-201 to 10-210.
Prohibited acts, PS §10-110.
Penalties, PS §10-111.
Sparklers, PS §10-112.
Rules and regulations, PS §10-109.
Sales.
Sparklers, PS §10-112.
  Registration of distributors and wholesalers, PS §10-113.
Unlawful sale, PS §10-110.
  Penalties, PS §10-111.
  Sparklers, PS §10-112.
Scope of title, PS §10-102.
Sparklers, PS §10-112.
Registration of distributors and wholesalers, PS §10-113.
Workers' compensation.
Permit requirements, PS §10-106.

FIREWORKS PLANTS, PS §§10-201 to 10-210.
Building construction, PS §10-205.
Location, PS §10-204.
Safety standards, PS §10-207.
Drug or alcohol abuse.
Personnel safety standards, PS §10-209.
Equipment, PS §10-206.
Personnel safety standards, PS §10-209.
Experimental testing, PS §10-208.
Fencing, PS §10-204.
Fines, PS §10-210.
Fire extinguishers, PS §10-207.
Garbage and refuse.
Safety standards, PS §10-207.
Heating equipment, PS §10-206.
Inspections, PS §10-203.
License to operate, PS §10-201.
License to operate, PS §10-201.
Unlicensed operation, PS §10-210.
Manufacture.
Unauthorized manufacture, PS §10-210.
Maximum number of employees, PS §10-209.
Personnel.
Safety standards, PS §10-209.
Plant safety officer, PS §10-209.
Prohibited acts, PS §10-210.
Rules and regulations, PS §10-202.
Safety standards, PS §10-207.
Personnel, PS §10-209.
Sanitation.
Safety standards, PS §10-207.
Security guards.
Safety standards, PS §10-207.

FIREWORKS PLANTS —Cont'd
Storage.
Unauthorized storage, PS §10-210.
Testing fireworks, PS §10-208.
Tobacco use.
Personnel safety standards, PS §10-209.
Unlicensed operation, PS §10-210.
Zoning.
Building location, PS §10-204.

FIRM OFFERS.
Leases, UCC, CL §2A-205.
Sale of goods, UCC, CL §2-205.

FIRST AID TRAINING.
Family day care homes.
Current certification.
  Regulations to provide, FL §5-551.

FISCAL NOTES.
Bills.
See GENERAL ASSEMBLY.

FISCAL RESEARCH BUREAU.
See LEGISLATIVE SERVICES DEPARTMENT.

FISCAL YEAR.
Accounts and accounting.
Use in balancing books and accounts, SF §2-101.
Appropriations.
Use in appropriating money, SF §2-101.
Counties.
General provisions, 19 §35.
Credit unions, FI §6-710.
Date specified, 24 §1-102.
Economic development corporation, 83A §5-212.
Environmental service, NR §3-126.
Municipal corporations.
General provisions, 19 §35.
Records.
Use in keeping records, SF §2-101.
Reports.
Use in making reports, SF §2-101.
State, SF §2-101.

FISH AND FISHERIES.
Advisory commissions, NR §4-204.
Aged.
Licenses.
  Consolidated senior sport fishing licenses, NR §4-216.
Allegany county.
See ALLEGANY COUNTY.
Anchor.
Setting anchor.
  Restrictions on use of stationary fishing gear, setting anchor or mooring buoy, NR §4-710.
Angler's license. See within this heading, "Licenses."
Angling.
Defined, NR §4-601.
Animals.
Transporting.
  Boat containing shellfish, NR §4-741.
Anne Arundel county.
Restrictions in county waters, NR §4-714.
Riparian rights.
  Exceptions, NR §4-712.
Appearances in court.
Immediate suspension of license for failure to appear, NR §4-1209.
Apprenticeship permit.
Issuance to person to gain experience in presence of tidal fish licensee, NR §4-701.1.

FISH AND FISHERIES —Cont'd
Aquaculture.
  General provisions, NR §§4-11A-01 to 4-11A-22.
    See AQUACULTURE.
Armed forces members on leave in state.
  Trout stamps, waiver of requirement, NR §4-614.
Arrest.
  Endangered species of fish conservation act
      violations, NR §4-2A-07.
Atlantic states marine fisheries commission.
  General provisions, NR §§4-301 to 4-307.
Bait fish.
  Use of nets, NR §4-620.
Baltimore county.
  Restrictions in county waters, NR §4-715.
  Riparian rights.
    Exceptions, NR §4-712.
Bass.
  Black bass.
    Method of taking and catching, NR §4-617.
    Restrictions generally, NR §4-735.
  Open season, NR §4-603.
  Size.
    Commercial fish, NR §4-734.
  Striped bass.
    Rockfish. See within this heading, "Rockfish."
Blinds.
  Migratory waterfowl season.
    Fishing near prohibited, NR §4-512.
Bluefish.
  Size.
    Commercial fish, NR §4-734.
Boats. See within this heading, "Vessels and boats."
Boundaries.
  Tidal and nontidal waters.
    Authority to establish, NR §4-205.
Bow and arrow.
  Shooting carp, NR §4-620.
Bush-bobs and bank poles.
  Use, NR §4-617.
Butterfish.
  Size.
    Commercial fish, NR §4-734.
Calvert county.
  Riparian rights.
    Exceptions, NR §4-712.
Caroline county.
  Restrictions in county waters, NR §4-716.
  Riparian rights.
    Exceptions, NR §4-712.
Carp.
  Bow and arrow.
    Shooting with, NR §4-620.
  Catching, NR §4-620.
  Open season, NR §4-603.
  Rigs.
    Use, NR §4-620.
Carroll county.
  See CARROLL COUNTY.
Catch.
  Defined, NR §4-101.
  Taking for management purposes, NR §4-409.
Catfish.
  Open season, NR §4-603.
  Size.
    Commercial fish, NR §4-734.
Cecil county.
  Restrictions in county waters, NR §§4-717, 4-720.
Chain pickerel, NR §4-735.
Channel bass.
  Size.
    Commercial fish, NR §4-734.

FISH AND FISHERIES —Cont'd
Charles county.
  See CHARLES COUNTY.
Charts.
  Restricted waters.
    Availability of chart, NR §4-744.
Chesapeake Bay.
  Charter boat permit, NR §4-210.2.
  Nets and seines.
    Use of nets generally, NR §4-728.
  Restrictions in bay waters, NR §4-728.
  Sport fishing license, NR §4-745.
Choptank river.
  Restrictions in waters, NR §4-729.
Closed seasons. See within this heading, "Open
    and closed seasons."
Closure of state waters for finfishing, NR
    §4-215.1.
**Collection of fish, fish eggs, crustaceans or
    mollusks for scientific purposes.**
  Certificates permitting, NR §4-212.
Commercial fishing equipment.
  Interference with, NR §4-514.
Commercial license.
  Tidal fish license, NR §4-701.
Commission.
  Atlantic states marine fisheries commission, NR
      §§4-301 to 4-307.
Compacts.
  Atlantic states marine fisheries commission, NR
      §§4-301 to 4-307.
    See ATLANTIC STATES MARINE FISHERIES
        COMMISSION.
  Department of natural resources.
    Authority to negotiate, NR §4-205.
  Potomac river compact of 1958.
    Powers of Potomac river fisheries commission,
        NR §4-307.
  Regulations.
    Recording, NR §4-306.
    Terms, NR §4-306.
Compliance with subtitle, NR §4-627.
Conservation.
  Endangered species of fish conservation act.
    General provisions. See within this heading,
        "Endangered species of fish conservation
        act."
Conservation and management measures.
  Fisheries management plans, NR §4-215.
Consolidated senior sport fishing licenses, NR
    §4-216.
Contracts.
  Department of natural resources.
    Research or scientific investigation, NR §4-205.
Counties.
  Chartered counties.
    Powers of county, 25A §5.
  Defined, NR §4-101.
Crabs.
  General provisions, NR §§4-801 to 4-816.
    See CRABS.
Creel limits.
  Chain pickerel, NR §4-735.
  Regulation department, NR §4-616.
Crimes and offenses.
  Dams.
    Fish ladders.
      Violations of section, NR §4-502.
  Dynamite.
    Use in streams, NR §4-503.
  Electronic and electrical devices, NR §4-509.

FISH AND FISHERIES —Cont'd
Crimes and offenses —Cont'd
Interference with lawful taking of fish, NR §4-506.1.
Nets and seines.
Pound or stake nets, NR §4-711.
Vessels and boats passing through nets, NR §4-508.
Nonnative aquatic organisms, NR §4-205.1.
Nontidal waters.
Violation of rules and regulations affecting fish in, NR §4-602.
Prohibitions and restrictions on method of fishing, NR §4-710.
Rockfish.
Purchase, sale or transportation, NR §4-731.
Violation of title, NR §4-1201.
Croakers.
Size, NR §4-734.
Dams.
Fish ladders.
Required, NR §4-502.
Fish pots, NR §4-620.
Obstruction to passage of fish, NR §4-501.
Dealing in fish caught in tidal waters.
Tidal fish license, NR §4-701.
Deep Creek lake.
Police.
Effect of section, NR §4-625.
Wharf, pier or dock.
Permission of department required, NR §4-625.
Definitions.
Angler's license.
Resident, NR §4-604.
Angling, NR §4-601.
Catch, NR §4-101.
Complimentary licenses.
Former prisoner of war, NR §4-607.
Endangered species of fish conservation act, NR §4-2A-01.
Fishery management plans, NR §4-215.
Game and freshwater fish, NR §4-101.
Speargun, NR §4-510.
Submerged aquatic vegetation, NR §4-213.
Department of natural resources.
Duties generally, NR §4-205.
Fishery management plans.
Annual report, NR §4-215.
Closure of state waters for finfishing, NR §4-215.1.
Preparation of plan, NR §4-215.
Secretary.
Adoption of plan, NR §4-215.
Species of fish, NR §4-215.
Powers generally, NR §4-205.
Responsibilities generally, NR §4-205.
Secretary.
Fishery management plans.
Adoption, NR §4-215.
Responsibilities, NR §4-202.
Taking of fish for management purposes, NR §4-409.
Transfer of functions to, NR §4-203.
Department of tidewater fisheries.
State boat act.
See VESSELS AND BOATS.
Disability license exemption.
One-day license exemption.
Nonprofit organizations taking individuals with disabilities fishing, NR §4-217.

FISH AND FISHERIES —Cont'd
Dorchester county.
See DORCHESTER COUNTY.
Dynamite.
Use in streams prohibited, NR §4-503.
Eels.
Catching, NR §4-620.
Slat baskets.
Use for catching, NR §4-617.
Catch report, NR §4-736.
Licensing requirements, NR §4-736.
Open season, NR §4-603.
Use of slat baskets for catching, NR §4-617.
Electronic and electrical devices, NR §4-509.
Endangered species of fish conservation act.
Arrests.
Violation of article, NR §4-2A-07.
Citation of subtitle, NR §4-2A-09.
Conservation of fish resources.
Generally, NR §4-2A-03.
Construction of subtitle, NR §4-2A-08.
Definitions, NR §4-2A-01.
Ecosystem.
Defined, NR §4-2A-01.
Endangered and threatened species determination, NR §4-2A-04.
Exceptions, NR §4-2A-02.
Forfeitures.
Equipment, merchandise, fish or records seized under provisions of act, NR §4-2A-07.
Governor.
Duties, NR §4-2A-06.
Investigation of fish resources.
Generally, NR §4-2A-03.
Legislative findings, NR §4-2A-02.
Lists.
Endangered and threatened species, NR §4-2A-04.
Review of listed or unlisted species, NR §4-2A-05.
Optimum carrying capacity.
Defined, NR §4-2A-01.
Penalties.
Generally, NR §4-2A-07.
Permits.
Prohibited acts, NR §4-2A-05.
Scientific research, NR §4-2A-05.
Police.
Searches and seizures by police, NR §4-2A-07.
Prohibited acts.
Enumerated, NR §4-2A-05.
Generally, NR §4-2A-03.
Permits for prohibited acts, NR §4-2A-05.
Reports.
Annual status reports, NR §4-2A-04.
Rockfish.
Catching hybrid striped bass in freshwater impoundments, NR §4-2A-08.1.
Construction of subtitle, NR §4-2A-08.
Removal of moratoriums on taking, possession, sale and transportation, NR §4-2A-05.1.
Searches and seizures, NR §4-2A-07.
Species.
Defined, NR §4-2A-01.
Review of listed or unlisted species, NR §4-2A-05.
State departments and agencies.
Duties, NR §4-2A-06.
Striped bass.
Catching hybrid striped bass in freshwater impoundments, NR §4-2A-08.1.

FISH AND FISHERIES —Cont'd
Endangered species of fish conservation act
—Cont'd
Striped bass —Cont'd
Construction of subtitle, NR §4-2A-08.
Removal of moratoriums on taking, possession,
sale and transportation, NR §4-2A-05.1.
Threatened species.
Conservation, NR §4-2A-05.
Programs for, NR §4-2A-06.
Defined, NR §4-2A-01.
Determination and listing, NR §4-2A-04.
Review of listed or unlisted species, NR
§4-2A-05.
Unlawful taking, possession, transportation, etc.,
of fish deemed in need of conservation, NR
§4-2A-03.
Violations generally, NR §4-2A-07.
Extension service.
Department of natural resources.
Seafood production, NR §4-205.
Failure to appear in court.
Immediate suspension of license, NR §4-1209.
Federal aid.
Department of natural resources.
Authority to accept and use, NR §4-205.
Federal law.
Public law 681, 81st congress.
Acceptance, NR §4-207.
Fees for licenses.
Angler's license, NR §4-604.
Chesapeake Bay sport fishing license, NR §4-745.
Fishing guides, NR §4-210.
Taxidermist, NR §4-211.
Tidal fish license, NR §4-701.
Trout.
Special trout stamp, NR §4-614.
Fines.
Collection, NR §4-1202.
Common carriers transporting fish.
Exemption, NR §4-1201.
Dynamite.
Use in streams, NR §4-503.
Electronic or electrical devices, NR §4-509.
Nontidal waters.
Rules and regulations affecting fish in.
Violations, NR §4-602.
Rockfish.
Purchase, sale or transportation, NR §4-731.
Stake nets.
Noncompliance with subsection, NR §4-711.
Violation of title, NR §4-1201.
Finfish.
Application, NR §4-704.
Closure of state waters for finfishing, NR
§4-215.1.
Licenses.
Required, NR §§4-702, 4-704.
Pound nets.
Restrictions on licenses for pound nets, NR
§4-704.
Fish and wildlife administration.
Transfer of functions to department, NR §4-203.
Fish eggs.
Certificates permitting collection for scientific
purposes, NR §4-212.
Fishery management plans, NR §4-215.
Closure of state waters for finfishing, NR
§4-215.1.
Fishing guides.
Chesapeake Bay charter boat permit, NR
§4-210.2.

FISH AND FISHERIES —Cont'd
Fishing guides —Cont'd
Licenses, NR §4-210.
Freshwater fishing guides, NR §4-210.1.
Tidal fish license, NR §4-701.
Fishing privileges.
Allocation and assignment among groups.
Fisheries management plans, NR §4-215.
Fish ladders.
Required, NR §4-502.
Fish packers and dealers.
Department's authority, NR §4-206.
Reporting requirements, NR §4-206.
Flounder.
Summer flounder.
Size.
Commercial fish, NR §4-734.
Free fishing days, NR §4-214.
Angler's license.
Exemption from requirement, NR §4-604.
Chesapeake Bay sport fishing license.
Exemption from requirement, NR §4-745.
Freshwater fish.
Rules and regulations affecting fish in nontidal
waters, NR §4-602.
Funds.
Fisheries management and protection fund, NR
§4-208.
Angler's license.
Fees credited to fund, NR §4-608.
Fisheries research and development fund, NR
§4-209.
Game and freshwater fish.
Defined, NR §4-101.
Game and inland water fish department.
Transfer of functions to department of natural
resources, NR §4-203.
General assembly.
Endangered species of fish conservation act.
Legislative findings, NR §4-2A-02.
Gifts.
Department of natural resources.
Authority to accept and use, NR §4-205.
Governor.
Endangered species of fish conservation act.
Duties of governor, NR §4-2A-06.
Guides, NR §4-210.
Freshwater fishing guides, NR §4-210.1.
Tidal fish licenses, NR §4-701.
Hardheads.
Size.
Commercial fish, NR §4-734.
Harford County.
Gunpowder River.
Jewish holiday exception to restrictions on
fishing, NR §4-715.
Restrictions in county waters, NR §§4-720, 4-721.
Hatcheries. See within this heading, "Refuges and
hatcheries."
Haul seines. See within this heading, "Nets and
seines."
Herring.
Open season, NR §4-603.
Taking, NR §4-617.
Hooks.
Number permitted per line, NR §4-617.
Restrictions on certain hooks, NR §4-710.
Snagging with hooks prohibited, NR §4-620.
Ice fishing.
Regulation and control, NR §4-617.

FISH AND FISHERIES —Cont'd
Injunctions.
　Fish ladders.
　　Enforcement of section, NR §4-502.
Inspections.
　Department of natural resources.
　　Authority, NR §4-205.
　Nonnative aquatic organisms, NR §4-205.1.
**Interference with commercial fishing
　equipment,** NR §4-514.
**Interfering with lawful taking of fish or
　marine life,** NR §4-506.1.
Jurisdiction.
　Department of game and inland water fish.
　　Transfer to department of natural resources,
　　　NR §4-203.
　Fish and wildlife administration.
　　Transfer to department of natural resources,
　　　NR §4-203.
Kent county.
　Restrictions in county waters, NR §4-722.
　Riparian rights.
　　Exceptions, NR §4-712.
　Threshing streams, NR §4-504.
Legal size of certain fish, NR §4-734.
Licenses.
　Aged persons.
　　Consolidated senior sport fishing licenses, NR
　　　§4-216.
　Angler's license.
　　Application, NR §4-604.
　　Complimentary licenses, NR §4-607.
　　Confiscation, NR §4-613.
　　Display, NR §4-610.
　　　Inadvertent violation, NR §4-612.
　　Duration, NR §4-604.
　　Exemptions, NR §4-604.
　　Fees, NR §4-604.
　　　Accounting to state treasurer, NR §4-608.
　　　Disposition, NR §4-608.
　　General provisions, NR §4-604.
　　Intent of provisions, NR §4-604.
　　Issuance, NR §4-604.
　　Lost license, NR §4-609.
　　Nontransferable, NR §4-604.
　　Possession, NR §4-610.
　　　Inadvertent violation, NR §4-612.
　　Private property.
　　　Fishing on without permission, NR §4-604.
　　Reciprocal license, NR §4-606.
　　Required, NR §4-604.
　　Resident.
　　　Defined, NR §4-604.
　　Sale.
　　　Person engaged in retail business, NR §4-611.
　Breeding, propagating and selling, NR §4-11A-21.
　Chesapeake Bay charter boat permit, NR
　　§4-210.2.
　Chesapeake Bay sport fishing licenses, NR §4-745.
　　Agents to sell, NR §4-745.
　　Charter boats.
　　　Special license valid for all individuals on
　　　　boat, NR §4-745.
　　Exemption from requirement, NR §4-745.
　　Fees, NR §4-745.
　　Required to fish for finfish in bay and
　　　tributaries, NR §4-745.
　　Special licenses, complementary licenses, NR
　　　§4-745.
　　Suspension, NR §4-745.
　　Use of revenue collected from sale, NR §4-745.

FISH AND FISHERIES —Cont'd
Licenses —Cont'd
　Commercial license.
　　Tidal fish license, NR §4-701.
　Consolidated senior sport fishing licenses, NR
　　§4-216.
　Disability exemption.
　　One-day license exemption.
　　　Nonprofit organizations taking individuals
　　　　with disabilities fishing, NR §4-217.
　Endangered species of fish conservation act.
　　Permits for prohibited acts, NR §4-2A-05.
　Fishing guides, NR §4-210.
　　Freshwater fishing guides, NR §4-210.1.
　　Limited fishing guides, NR §4-210.
　　Master fishing guide license, NR §4-210.
　Free fishing days, NR §4-214.
　　Angler's license.
　　　Exemption from requirement, NR §4-604.
　　Chesapeake Bay sport fishing license.
　　　Exemption from requirement, NR §4-745.
　Issuance.
　　When license forfeited, NR §4-205.
　Live bait dealers.
　　Certain counties, NR §4-11A-19.
　Master fishing guide license, NR §4-701.
　Nets and seines.
　　License to operate. See within this heading,
　　　"Nets and seines."
　Nonresidents.
　　Licenses to fish in Atlantic ocean, NR §4-710.
　Prisoners of war.
　　Complimentary licenses, NR §4-607.
　Privately owned artificial ponds or lakes.
　　Establishment and operation, NR §4-11A-20.
　Social security numbers in application, NR §4-205.
　Striped bass.
　　Required to catch, NR §4-704.1.
　Suspension and revocation.
　　Failure to appear in court, NR §4-1209.
　　Immediate suspension of license, NR §4-1209.
　　Second conviction of rule or regulation, NR
　　　§4-626.
　　Violation of title, NR §4-1207.
　Taxidermist, NR §4-211.
　Tidal fish license, NR §4-701.
　　Activities authorized, NR §4-701.
　　Apprenticeship permit, NR §4-701.1.
　　Authorization, NR §4-701.
　　Conversion of authorization, NR §4-701.
　　Defined, NR §4-101.
　　Fees, NR §4-701.
　　Finfish, NR §4-704.
　　Guides and persons dealing in fish caught in
　　　tidal waters.
　　　Applicability of provisions to, license required,
　　　　NR §4-701.
　　Identification number assigned, NR §4-701.
　　Inspection by police, NR §4-701.
　　Issuance when licenses forfeited, NR §4-205.
　　Master fishing guide license, NR §4-701.
　　Nonresidents.
　　　Surcharge, NR §4-701.
　　Number of authorizations, NR §4-701.
　　Oysters, catching for sale.
　　　Surcharge, NR §4-701.
　　Possession required when engaged in activity,
　　　NR §4-701.
　　Relinquishment of authorization, NR §4-701.
　　Renewal, NR §4-701.

FISH AND FISHERIES —Cont'd
Licenses —Cont'd
Tidal fish license —Cont'd
Stripped bass, catching for sale.
Surcharge, NR §4-701.
Surcharge, NR §4-701.
Suspension or revocation, NR §4-701.
Synopsis of laws to accompany, NR §4-744.
Term, NR §4-701.
Transfer of license or authorization to family members, NR §4-701.
Transfer of license or authorization to family members.
Tidal fish license, NR §4-701.
Trespass upon private property.
Suspension, NR §4-1207.
Trout.
Special trout stamp, NR §4-614.
Veterans.
Complimentary licenses, NR §4-607.
Live bait dealers.
Licenses.
Certain counties, NR §4-11A-19.
Regulations, NR §4-11A-19.
Lobsters.
Harvest.
Rules and regulations, NR §4-901.
Methods of fishing.
Prohibited methods generally, NR §4-710.
Misdemeanors.
Dams.
Fish ladders.
Violations of section, NR §4-502.
Dynamite.
Use in streams, NR §4-503.
Electronic and electrical devices, NR §4-509.
Nets and seines.
Pound or stake nets, NR §4-711.
Vessels and boats passing through nets, NR §4-508.
Prohibited methods generally, NR §4-710.
Rockfish.
Purchase, sale or transportation, NR §4-731.
Violation of title, NR §4-1201.
Mollusks.
Certificates permitting collection for scientific purposes, NR §4-212.
Mooring buoy.
Restrictions on use, NR §4-710.
Nets and seines.
Armed forces service or war emergency.
License renewal or expiration, NR §4-705.
Bait fish nets, NR §4-620.
Carroll county.
Prohibited, NR §4-620.
Cast nets.
Monofilament cast nets, NR §4-710.
Chesapeake Bay.
Use of nets generally, NR §4-728.
Dip nets, NR §4-617.
Fyke or hoop nets.
Use, NR §4-710.
Gill nets.
Anchored gill nets, NR §4-710.
Chesapeake Bay.
Use in, NR §4-728.
Monofilament webbing.
Prohibited, NR §4-710.
Haul seines.
Interference with, NR §4-507.
Limit on use, NR §4-710.

FISH AND FISHERIES —Cont'd
Nets and seines —Cont'd
Hedging or lead, NR §4-710.
Hoop net.
Use, NR §4-710.
Interference with prohibited, NR §4-506.
Haul seines, NR §4-507.
License to operate, NR §4-705.
Pound nets.
Restrictions on licenses, NR §4-704.
Revocation or suspension.
Operation of net when license suspended or revoked, NR §4-708.
Mesh of nets.
Sizes, NR §4-710.
Monofilament nets.
Cast nets or throw nets, NR §4-710.
Nonresident.
Prohibited from using, NR §4-618.
Pound nets.
Chesapeake Bay.
Use in headwaters, NR §4-728.
Licenses, NR §4-704.
Regulations, NR §4-711.
Removal of nets or gear without permission, NR §4-505.
Riparian owners.
Rights to nets or haul seines, NR §4-712.
Stake nets, NR §4-711.
Chesapeake Bay.
Use in headwaters, NR §4-728.
Regulations, NR §4-711.
Throw nets.
Monofilament throw nets, NR §4-710.
Vessels and boats.
Passing through nets prohibited, NR §4-508.
Night fishing.
Trout streams, NR §4-615.
Nonnative aquatic organisms.
Authority over, NR §4-205.1.
Nonresidents.
License to fish in the Atlantic ocean, NR §4-710.
Use of nets, NR §4-618.
Nontidal waters.
Boundaries.
Authority to establish, NR §4-205.
Defined, NR §4-101.
Rules and regulations affecting fish in, NR §4-602.
Notice.
Dams.
Fish ladders.
Violations of section, NR §4-502.
Obstruction to fishery, NR §4-507.
Obstruction to passage of fish, NR §4-501.
Open and closed seasons.
Black bass, NR §4-735.
Chain pickerel, NR §4-735.
Defined, NR §4-101.
Freshwater fish, NR §4-603.
Game fish, NR §4-603.
Shad, NR §4-737.
Otter or beam trawl.
Use permitted in Atlantic ocean, NR §4-710.
Oysters and clams.
General provisions.
See OYSTERS AND CLAMS.
Patuxent river.
Restrictions in waters, NR §4-730.
Penalties.
Endangered species of fish conservation act.
Violations of article, NR §4-2A-07.

FISH AND FISHERIES —Cont'd
Penalties —Cont'd
Nontidal waters.
Rules and regulations affecting fish in.
Violations, NR §4-602.
Pennsylvania.
Angler's license.
Reciprocal license, NR §4-606.
Perch.
Size.
Commercial fish, NR §4-734.
Person.
Defined, NR §4-101.
Petitions.
Rules and regulations affecting fish in nontidal
waters.
Petition by residents proposing rule or
regulation, NR §4-602.
Pike.
Open season, NR §4-603.
Transportation, NR §4-740.
Wall-eyed pike.
Closed season, NR §4-740.
Commercial fish, NR §4-734.
Restrictions, NR §4-740.
Size.
Commercial fish, NR §4-734.
Pollution.
Shellfish.
Inspections, testing and restrictions on taking,
NR §4-742.
Ponds.
Trespass to fish in private pond, NR §4-11A-22.
Potomac river fisheries commission.
General provisions.
See POTOMAC RIVER FISHERIES
COMMISSION.
Pots, NR §4-620.
Pound nets. See within this heading, "Nets and
seines."
Prisoners of war.
Complimentary licenses, NR §10-303.
Propagation.
Hatcheries. See within this heading, "Refuges and
hatcheries."
Private propagation of game fish, NR §4-11A-21.
Property taxes.
Exemptions.
Game and Fish Protective Association, property
owned by, TP §7-306.
Public hearings.
Fisheries management plans.
Rules and regulations, NR §4-215.
Public law 681, 81st congress.
Assent to, NR §4-207.
**Public recreation on private and local
government lands.**
General provisions, NR §§5-1101 to 5-1109.
See RECREATIONAL TRESPASS.
Quarantine.
Shellfish, NR §4-743.
Queen Anne's county.
Riparian rights.
Exceptions, NR §4-712.
Threshing streams, NR §4-504.
Records.
Expungement of records, NR §4-1208.
Taxidermists, NR §4-211.
Red drum.
Size.
Commercial fish, NR §4-734.

FISH AND FISHERIES —Cont'd
Refuges and hatcheries.
Acquisition, NR §4-401.
Allegany county.
Acquisition of land, NR §4-401.
Control of land or water, NR §4-402.
Deeds, NR §4-403.
Erection and maintenance of hatchery, NR §4-408.
Exchanges.
Area of water or land, NR §4-403.
Garrett county.
Acquisition of land, NR §4-401.
Leased lands and waters, NR §4-406.
Owner.
Application of owner for refuge, NR §4-406.
Parks.
Use of state park, NR §4-403.
Rules and regulations.
Promulgation, NR §4-407.
Sale.
Area of land or water, NR §4-403.
Effect of sale of property upon which no charge
made, NR §4-406.
State fish refuges, NR §4-405.
Title to land or water, NR §4-402.
Trespassing.
Prohibited, NR §4-410.
Use of land or water, NR §4-404.
Reports.
Eel catch reports, NR §4-736.
Fishery management plans.
Annual report by department of natural
resources, NR §4-215.
Closure of state waters for finfishing, NR
§4-215.1.
Fishing guides.
Monthly reports, NR §4-210.
Research.
Contracts.
Issuance by department, NR §4-205.
Fisheries research and development fund, NR
§4-209.
Resource management programs.
Separate programs for certain waters, NR §4-205.
Restricted waters.
Chart.
Availability, NR §4-744.
Rigs.
Carp, NR §4-620.
Use of certain rigs prohibited, NR §4-619.
Riparian rights.
In certain counties, NR §4-712.
Rockfish.
Annual survey, NR §4-746.
Designation as state fish, SG §13-304.
Endangered species of fish conservation act.
Construction of subtitle, NR §4-2A-08.
Hybrid striped bass.
Catching in freshwater impoundments, NR
§4-2A-08.1.
Legal size of fish, NR §4-734.
Open season, NR §4-603.
Penalty.
Violations, NR §§4-731, 4-1201.
Purchase.
Regulations, NR §4-731.
Removal of moratoriums on taking, possession,
sale and transporting, NR §4-2A-05.1.
Sale, NR §4-731.
Spawning season.
Authority to prohibit fishing during spawning
season, NR §4-732.

FISH AND FISHERIES —Cont'd
Rockfish —Cont'd
Survey.
Annual survey, NR §4-746.
Tidal fish license, surcharge, NR §4-701.
Transportation.
Regulations, NR §4-731.
Young-of-the-year striped bass index, NR §4-734.
Rods.
Number permitted, NR §4-617.
Rules and regulations.
Collection of fish, fish eggs, crustaceans or
mollusks for scientific purposes, NR §4-212.
Compliance with, NR §4-627.
Free fishing days.
Establishment by regulation, NR §4-214.
Licenses.
Suspension for violation, NR §4-626.
Nontidal waters.
Rules and regulations affecting fish in, NR
§4-602.
Refuges and hatcheries.
Promulgation, NR §4-407.
Size.
Department to regulate, NR §4-616.
Sturgeon, NR §4-739.
St. Mary's county.
Restrictions in county waters, NR §4-723.
Riparian rights.
Exceptions, NR §4-712.
Sales.
Angler's license.
Person engaged in retail business, NR §4-611.
Applicability of law, NR §4-102.
Sales and use tax.
Exemptions.
Seafood harvesting purposes, TG §11-218.
Searches and seizures.
Endangered species of fish conservation act.
When searches allowed, NR §4-2A-07.
Fish unlawfully caught, sold, etc., NR §4-1205.
Nonnative aquatic organisms, NR §4-205.1.
Unlawful devices, equipment or property, NR
§4-1206.
Warrants.
Search warrants, NR §4-1203.
Warrantless search, NR §4-1204.
Secretary.
Fishery management plans.
Adoption of plan, NR §4-215.
Responsibility, NR §4-202.
Seines. See within this heading, "Nets and seines."
Shad.
Open season, NR §§4-603, 4-737.
Possession or sale, NR §4-737.
Taking, NR §4-617.
Virginia.
Coincide with season in Virginia, NR §4-737.
Shellfish.
Animals.
Carrying domestic animals on boat with
shellfish, NR §4-741.
Oysters and clams.
General provisions.
See OYSTERS AND CLAMS.
Pollution.
Restriction of waters for taking, etc., of shellfish
because of pollution, NR §4-742.
Quarantine, NR §4-743.
Size and weight.
Applicability of law, NR §4-102.

FISH AND FISHERIES —Cont'd
Size and weight —Cont'd
Determination.
Possession of fish in such condition that size or
weight cannot be determined, NR §4-733.
Legal size of certain fish, NR §4-734.
Regulation by department, NR §4-616.
Snagging.
Taking or catching certain fish by hooks, NR
§4-710.
Somerset county.
See SOMERSET COUNTY.
Speargun.
Defined, NR §4-510.
Use restricted, NR §4-510.
**Species for which management plans
prepared,** NR §4-215.
Sport fisheries.
Advisory commission, NR §4-204.
Chesapeake Bay sport fishing licenses, NR §4-745.
Spotted sea trout.
Size.
Commercial fish, NR §4-734.
Stake nets.
Chesapeake Bay.
Use in headwaters, NR §4-728.
Regulations, NR §4-711.
Stamps.
Trout, NR §4-614.
State fish.
Striped bass or rockfish designated state fish, SG
§13-304.
Stationary fishing gear.
Restrictions on use, NR §4-710.
Striped bass.
Designation as state fish, SG §13-304.
Licenses.
Required to catch, NR §4-704.1.
Rockfish generally. See within this heading,
"Rockfish."
Tidal fish license, surcharge, NR §4-701.
Sturgeon.
Rules and regulations, NR §4-739.
Size.
Commercial fish, NR §4-734.
Submerged aquatic vegetation.
Harvesting, cutting, removing or eradicating, NR
§4-213.
Suckers.
Open season, NR §4-603.
Sunfish.
Open season, NR §4-603.
Surveys.
Striped bass.
Annual survey, NR §4-746.
Susquehanna salmon.
Wall-eyed pike.
Commercial fish, NR §4-734.
Restrictions, NR §4-740.
Synopsis of laws.
Department to issue, NR §4-744.
Talbot county.
Restrictions in county waters, NR §4-725.
Taxidermist.
Licenses, NR §4-211.
Taylor.
Size.
Commercial fish, NR §4-734.
Terrapins.
General provisions, NR §§4-902, 4-903.
See TERRAPINS.

FISH AND FISHERIES —Cont'd
Threshing streams.
  Kent and Queen Anne's counties.
    Exceptions, NR §4-504.
  Prohibited, NR §4-504.
Tidal fisheries.
  Advisory commission, NR §4-204.
Tidal fish license. See within this heading,
  "Licenses."
Tidal waters.
  Boundaries.
    Authority to establish, NR §4-205.
  Defined, NR §4-101.
  Submerged aquatic vegetation.
    Harvesting, cutting, removing or eradicating,
      NR §4-213.
Trawl.
  Use of otter trawl or beam trawl in certain
      waters.
    Regulations, NR §4-710.
Trespass.
  Fishing in private ponds, NR §4-11A-22.
  Fish refuges, NR §4-410.
  Hatcheries, NR §4-410.
  Ponds.
    Fishing in private ponds, NR §4-11A-22.
  Suspension of fishing license, NR §4-1207.
Trout.
  Night fishing in streams stocked with trout, NR
      §4-615.
  Open season, NR §4-603.
  Size.
  Commercial fish, NR §4-734.
  Special trout stamp, NR §4-614.
Turtles.
  Snapping turtles.
    Fishing restrictions, NR §4-738.
  Turtle pots.
    Areas where use may not be prohibited, NR
      §4-738.
Vessels and boats.
  Chesapeake Bay charter boat permit, NR
      §4-210.2.
  Department.
    Acquisition and maintenance, NR §4-205.
  Fishing guides.
    Operation of vessels carrying passengers for
        hire.
      Licensing requirement, NR §4-210.
  Nets and seines.
    Passing through nets prohibited, NR §4-508.
    Tying or anchoring boat to, NR §4-506.
  Passing through nets prohibited, NR §4-508.
Veterans.
  Complimentary licenses, NR §4-607.
Virginia.
  Angler's license.
    Reciprocal license, NR §4-606.
  Shad.
    Coincide with season in Virginia, NR §4-737.
Waiver.
  Licenses.
    Tidal fish license.
      Fees may be waived, NR §4-701.
Walleye.
  Open season, NR §4-603.
War.
  Nets and seines.
    License renewal or expiration during war
        emergency, NR §4-705.

FISH AND FISHERIES —Cont'd
Warrants.
  Search warrants, NR §4-1203.
    Searching without warrants, NR §4-1204.
Washington county.
  See WASHINGTON COUNTY.
Weakfish.
  Size.
    Commercial fish, NR §4-734.
Weight. See within this heading, "Size and weight."
West Virginia.
  Angler's license.
    Reciprocal license, NR §4-606.
Worcester county.
  Restrictions in county waters, NR §4-727.

FISH AND WILDLIFE ADMINISTRATION.
Transfer of functions.
  Department of natural resources, NR §4-203.

FISHERY MANAGEMENT PLANS, NR §§4-215,
  4-215.1.

FISHING GUIDES.
Licenses, NR §4-210.
  Freshwater fishing guides, NR §4-210.1.
  Tidal fish license, NR §4-701.

FISH LADDERS, NR §4-502.

FITNESS CLUBS.
Health club services generally, CL §§14-12B-01
  to 14-12B-08.
  See HEALTH CLUB SERVICES.

FITNESS FACILITIES.
Steroids and human growth hormone.
  Warning of consequences of illegal use, posting,
    CR §5-710.

FIXTURES.
Distress for rent.
  Liability for removal of goods affixed to realty, RP
    §8-313.
Landlord and tenant.
  Erected by tenant.
    Right to remove not impaired by new lease, RP
        §8-114.
Leases, UCC.
  Defined, CL §§2A-103, 2A-309.
  Lessors' and lessees' rights when goods become
      fixtures, CL §2A-309.
Plumbers.
  Installation of unapproved fixtures, BOP §12-605.
  Required fixtures and devices in buildings and
      structures, BOP §12-606.
Secured transactions.
  Defaults.
    Procedure when fixtures involved, CL §9-604.
    Removal of fixtures, CL §9-604.
      Injury from removal, CL §9-604.
  Priority of security interests in, CL §9-334.
    Consent, disclaimer, or right to remove fixture.
      Effect on priority, CL §9-334.
    Construction mortgage, CL §9-334.
    Continuation of interest, CL §9-334.
    Purchase money priority, CL §9-334.
    Real property, interests in, CL §9-334.
    Real property law security interests, CL §9-334.
    Subordination, CL §9-334.

FLAG BURNING, CR §10-704.

FLAGMEN.
Railroad crossings.
  County determination that crossing needs
      protection, PUC §9-311.

FLAGS.
Death in the line of duty.
Flag benefits, PS §1-202.
Firefighter, police officer or member of state fire marshal's office.
Death in performance of duty.
State flag issued to family, PS §1-202.
Highways.
Rest areas, welcome centers and exhibit centers, TR §8-652.
Homeowners.
Display of United States flag, RP §14-128.
POW/MIA flag.
State house grounds, flying over, days, SG §13-205.
Public safety.
Death in the line of duty.
Flag benefits, PS §1-202.
Sales and use tax.
Exemptions, TG §11-205.
Schools.
Display of flags, ED §7-105.
State flag.
Adoption, SG §13-201.
Arrangement, SG §13-204.
Description, SG §13-202.
Display on state house, SG §13-204.
Flagstaff.
Ornament, SG §13-203.
Tenants.
Display of United States flag, RP §14-128.
Uniform flag law, CR §§10-701 to 10-706.
Construed to carry out general purpose, CR §10-705.
Display of flag with word, figure, mark, picture, design or advertisement, CR §10-703.
Flag defined, CR §10-701.
Mutilating, defacing, destroying, burning or trampling flag, CR §10-704.
Placing word, figure, mark, picture, design or advertisement on flag, CR §10-703.
Scope of law, CR §10-702.
Selling, manufacturing or possessing merchandise marked with flag, CR §10-703.
Short title, CR §10-706.

FLAK JACKETS.
Bulletproof body armor.
Defined, CR §4-106.
Permit to use, possess or purchase, CR §4-107.
Wearing in crime of violence or drug trafficking crime.
Prohibition, CR §4-106.
Law enforcement equipment fund, PS §§4-301 to 4-304.
Protective body armor fund, PS §§4-101 to 4-107.

FLAME RETARDANTS.
Octabde and pentabde.
Manufacturing, processing, selling or distributing product containing.
Prohibition, EN §§6-1201 to 6-1205.

FLAMETHROWER.
Possession of destructive device, CR §§4-501 to 4-503.

FLAMMABLE SUBSTANCES.
Carcinogenic fire retardants, HG §22-404.
Definitions.
Flammable products act, HG §22-401.

FLAMMABLE SUBSTANCES —Cont'd
Injunctions.
Flammable products act, HG §22-405.
Maryland flammable products act.
Carcinogenic chemicals.
Determination of department, HG §22-404.
Definitions, HG §22-401.
Fire retardants.
Carcinogenic chemicals, HG §22-404.
Guaranty.
Defined, HG §22-401.
False guaranty, HG §22-406.
Scope of guaranty, HG §22-406.
Injunctions.
Products sold in violation of subtitle, HG §22-405.
Inspections.
Right of entry, HG §22-403.
Samples, HG §22-403.
Nonconforming products.
Manufacture or sale, HG §22-406.
Penalties.
Violations, HG §22-407.
Products.
Defined, HG §22-401.
Prohibited acts.
Scope of guaranty, HG §22-406.
Right of entry, HG §22-403.
Rules and regulations.
Adoption, HG §22-402.
Samples.
Right of entry to take sample, HG §22-403.
Violations.
Penalties, HG §22-407.
Misdemeanors.
Violations of provisions, HG §22-407.
Penalties.
Flammable products act.
Violations of subtitle, HG §22-407.
Repair or demolition of fire hazards.
See FIRE MARSHAL.
Right of entry.
Flammable products act.
Inspections, HG §22-403.
Rules and regulations.
Flammable products act, HG §22-402.

FLATS.
Susquehanna Flats.
General provisions.
See BIRDS AND GAME.

FLAVORING EXTRACTS.
Alcoholic beverages.
Manufacturers' use permit, 2B §2-101.

FLEEING A POLICE OFFICER, TR §21-904.

FLEEING TO AVOID ARREST.
Fresh pursuit, CP §2-301.
Authority of officers in another state to arrest in this state.
Uniform act on fresh pursuit, CP §§2-304 to 2-309.

FLOATING ZONES.
Ordinances providing for or requiring encouraged, 66B §10.01.

FLOOD CONTROL.
Attorney general.
Enforcement of subtitle, EN §5-805.
Citation of subtitle, EN §5-809.
Coordination of activities, EN §5-803.

FLOOD CONTROL —Cont'd
Definitions, EN §5-801.
Department of the environment.
  Assistance to local governments and other state
      agencies, EN §5-701.
    Administration, EN §5-703.
  Delegation of responsibilities, EN §5-806.
  Duties, EN §5-804.
  Federal aid.
    Long range program.
      Cooperation with federal and local
          government to develop, EN §5-701.
  Responsibilities, EN §5-701.
Division of state into watersheds, EN §5-803.
  Tax credit for flood-damaged residential property,
      TP §9-211.
Emergency management, PS §§14-101 to 14-1004.
  See EMERGENCY MANAGEMENT.
Enforcement of subtitle, EN §5-805.
Financial assistance.
  Department of the environment, EN §5-701.
    Administration, EN §5-703.
  Funding, EN §5-808.
Flood hazard management act of 1976, EN
    §§5-801 to 5-809.
Funding, EN §5-808.
Generally, EN §§5-701 to 5-809.
Grants, EN §5-803.
Herring Run public watershed association, EN
    §§5-1201 to 5-1206.
  See HERRING RUN PUBLIC WATERSHED
      ASSOCIATION.
Jones Falls.
  Flood management plan, EN §5-803.
Jurisdiction.
  Interjurisdictional watersheds for safety and flood
      control, EN §5-503.
Legislative finding and declaration, EN §5-802.
Maps.
  Flood hazard area maps, EN §5-803.
Maryland-Washington metropolitan district.
  Other uses of lands acquired for flood control, 28
      §5-118.
  Powers of commission, 28 §5-118.
Other provisions.
  Subtitle additional to other provisions, EN §5-807.
Patuxent river watershed.
  General provisions.
    See PATUXENT RIVER WATERSHED.
Plans.
  Flood management plans generally, EN §5-803.
Policy of subtitle, EN §5-802.
Program.
  Comprehensive flood management program, EN
      §5-803.
Projects.
  Gas contributions, NR §8-1005.
Purposes of subtitle, EN §5-802.
Requirements generally, EN §5-803.
Reservoirs, dams or waterways.
  Federally constructed reservoirs, EN §5-702.
Rules and regulations.
  Governing uses within flood hazards areas, EN
      §5-803.
State construction projects.
  Duties of department, EN §5-804.
Subdivisions.
  Duties, EN §5-805.
  Failure to enforce divisions of subtitle.
    Actions by attorney general, EN §5-805.

FLOOD CONTROL —Cont'd
Subtitle additional to other provisions, EN
    §5-807.
Susquehanna river basin commission, EN
    §5-301.
Taxation.
  Flood-damaged residential property.
    Tax credit, TP §9-211.
Violations.
  Restraining violation, EN §5-805.
Warning systems.
  Required, EN §5-803.
Washington suburban sanitary commission.
  General provisions.
    See WASHINGTON SUBURBAN SANITARY
        DISTRICT.
Watershed associations, 25 §§169 to 218.
  See WATERSHED ASSOCIATIONS.
Watersheds.
  Division of state into watersheds, EN §5-803.
  Nontidal wetlands.
    Watershed management plans, EN §5-908.
Wetlands.
  Nontidal wetlands.
    Statewide program established, EN §5-903.
    Watershed management plans, EN §5-908.

FLOOD INSURANCE.
First mortgages and first deeds of trust.
  Lender requiring of borrower, limitation, CL
      §12-124.
Homeowner's insurance.
  Information and advice concerning, insurer to
      provide, IN §19-206.

FLOWERS.
Black-eyed Susan designated state flower, SG
    §13-305.
Plant disease control.
  General provisions, AG §§5-301 to 5-314.
  See PLANT DISEASE CONTROL.
Promotion of use and sale.
  General provisions.
    See AGRICULTURAL PRODUCTS.
Roses.
  Multiflora rose management, AG §§9-701 to 9-705.
  See MULTIFLORA ROSE MANAGEMENT.
Seeds.
  General provisions, AG §§9-201 to 9-214.
  See SEEDS.

FLUORINATED HYDROCARBON.
Inhaling, CR §5-708.

FLU VACCINATIONS.
Emergency medical technicians administering,
    ED §13-516.
Residents or employees in nursing facilities,
    HG §18-404.

F.O.B.
Sale of goods, UCC, CL §2-319.
  Bill of lading required in overseas shipments, CL
      §2-323.

FOG LAMPS.
Motor vehicle equipment, TR §22-217.

FOLIC ACID SUPPLEMENT DISTRIBUTION
    PROGRAM.
Funding, HG §13-2303.
Generally, HG §13-2302.
Woman of childbearing age.
  Defined, HG §13-2301.

FOLK DANCING.
Official state folk dance, SG §13-314.

FOLLOWING ANOTHER.
Harassment, CR §3-803.
Stalking, CR §3-802.

FOOD AND FOOD ESTABLISHMENTS.
Adulteration or misbranding of food and
drink.
See FOOD, DRUGS AND COSMETICS.
Advertising.
Kosher food.
See KOSHER FOOD.
Alcoholic beverages.
Free food prohibited, 2B §12-106.
Retail sales in supermarkets or food stores.
Floor space, 2B §9-108.
Blind persons.
Right of blind person to public facilities, 30 §33.
Closed food container in food store.
Opening, HG §21-259.1.
Contaminating food, CR §3-214.
Contamination.
See FOOD, DRUGS AND COSMETICS.
Crab meat.
General provisions, HG §§21-339 to 21-343.
See CRAB MEAT.
Deaf or mute persons.
Right of deaf or mute persons to public facilities,
30 §33.
Definitions.
Restaurant, 2B §1-102.
Discrimination in public accommodations.
General provisions, 49B §§5 to 8A.
See DISCRIMINATION.
Donated food under program of federal
government.
Unauthorized disposition or conversion, CR
§8-505.
Drugs.
Food, drug and cosmetic act.
See FOOD, DRUGS AND COSMETICS.
Eggs.
Maryland egg law.
General provisions, AG §§4-301 to 4-312.
See EGGS.
Federal aid.
Surplus food, SF §2-205.
Federal food coupons.
General provisions.
See SOCIAL SERVICES.
Food, drug and cosmetic act.
See FOOD, DRUGS AND COSMETICS.
Food stamps, 88A §88.
Frozen desserts.
General provisions, HG §§21-801 to 21-821.
See FROZEN DESSERTS.
Frozen food.
See FROZEN FOOD.
Handicapped persons.
Unobstructed entrances, TR §21-1007.
Heimlich maneuver, HG §21-326.
Highways.
Conduct of restaurants on acquired property
prohibited, TR §8-313.
Insurance coverage for medical foods, IN
§15-807.
Jurisdiction.
Over persons outside this state.
General provisions.
See JURISDICTION.

FOOD AND FOOD ESTABLISHMENTS —Cont'd
Kosher food.
See KOSHER FOOD.
Licenses.
Food, drug and cosmetic act.
Food establishments.
See FOOD, DRUGS AND COSMETICS.
Juke boxes.
General provisions, BR §§17-1301 to 17-1309.
See JUKE BOXES.
Harford county, BR §§17-1312 to 17-1318.
See HARFORD COUNTY.
Restaurant license, BR §§17-1601 to 17-1604.
Soda fountain license, BR §§17-1701 to 17-1703.
See within this heading, "Soda fountain
license."
Vending machine license, BR §§17-1901 to
17-1907.
See VENDING MACHINES.
Lifesaving charts.
Posting required, HG §21-326.
Maryland food center authority.
Baltimore food market authority.
See MARYLAND FOOD CENTER
AUTHORITY.
Negligence.
Removing object lodged in throat of another.
Liability, HG §21-326.
Opening closed food container in food store,
HG §21-259.1.
Poultry products inspection.
General provisions.
See POULTRY PRODUCTS INSPECTION.
Restaurant license, BR §§17-1601 to 17-1604.
Restaurants.
Alcoholic beverages.
General provisions.
See ALCOHOLIC BEVERAGES.
Definitions, 2B §§1-102, 8-218.
Taverns.
See TAVERNS.
Sales.
Implied warranty of merchantability, CL §2-314.
Sales and use tax.
Exemptions, TG §11-206.
Seafood.
Surimi products.
Labeling requirements, HG §21-329.
Shellfish generally.
See SHELLFISH.
Snack tax, TG §11-206.
Soda fountain license, BR §§17-1701 to 17-1703.
Defined, BR §17-1701.
Fees, BR §17-1703.
Required, BR §17-1702.
Stamps.
Food stamps.
Federal food coupons.
General provisions.
See SOCIAL SERVICES.
Surimi products.
Labeling requirements, HG §21-329.
Taverns.
See TAVERNS.
Vending machine license, BR §§17-1901 to
17-1907.
See VENDING MACHINES.
Warranties.
Implied warranty of merchantability, CL §2-314.
Wholesome meat act.
General provisions, AG §§4-101 to 4-131.
See WHOLESOME MEAT ACT.

FOOD AT CORRECTIONAL FACILITIES.
Standards for correctional facilities generally,
    COR §§8-101 to 8-117.
    See PRISONS AND PRISONERS.
FOOD DONATIONS.
Federal programs.
    Unauthorized disposition or conversion, CR
    §8-505.
FOOD, DRUGS AND COSMETICS, HG §§21-201
    to 21-263.
Abatement.
    Abatement orders, HG §21-261.
    Hearings, HG §21-261.
Actions.
    Detainment and destruction of articles, HG
    §21-253.
    Immediate threat.
    Actions against food posing immediate threat,
        HG §21-254.
Administrative procedure.
    Compliance with act in adoption of rule or
        regulation, HG §21-234.
    Hearings.
    Application of act to hearing, HG §21-236.
Adopted federal rule or regulation.
    Defined, HG §21-201.
Adulterated cosmetics, HG §21-230.
Adulterated drugs and devices, HG §21-216.
    Defined, HG §21-101.
    Grounds for action, HG §21-253.
Adulterated food.
    Application of sections, HG §21-207.
    Confectionery products, HG §21-209.
    Food components, HG §21-208.
    Grounds for action, HG §21-253.
    When food considered adulterated, HG §21-207.
Advertisements.
    Defined, HG §21-101.
    False advertising, HG §21-247.
    Particular representations regarding drugs and
        devices considered false advertisements,
        HG §21-248.
    Liability of persons in business of disseminating
        advertisements, HG §21-260.
    Misleading labeling and advertising, HG §21-102.
    Surimi products.
    Food service establishments.
        Notice requirements, HG §21-329.
Agency.
    Employees.
    Imputation of act or omission, HG §21-205.
Analysis of samples, HG §21-251.
Antibiotic drug.
    Additional grounds of drug misbranding, HG
    §21-218.
    Defined, HG §21-218.
Antiseptics.
    Construction of representations that drug is
        antiseptic, HG §21-204.
Artesian water.
    Collecting, bottling or delivering, HG §21-336.
Artificial coloring.
    Authorization for use for food additives and color
        additives, HG §21-239.
    Exemption to misbranding statute, HG §21-210.
Auctions, HG §21-1110.
Bed and breakfast establishments, HG
    §21-323.1.
Beverages.
    Alcoholic beverages.
    See ALCOHOLIC BEVERAGES.

FOOD, DRUGS AND COSMETICS —Cont'd
Beverages —Cont'd
    Soft drinks.
    General provisions.
        See SOFT DRINKS.
Bottled water.
    Cleaning containers, HG §21-334.
    Collecting, bottling or delivering, HG §21-336.
Burden of proof.
    Defenses to charges, HG §21-260.
Carriers.
    Evidence.
    Use of evidence against carrier prohibited, HG
        §21-250.
    Records.
    Inspection of records, HG §21-250.
Color additives.
    Authorization for use, HG §21-239.
    Defined, HG §21-101.
    Misbranded food.
    Statutory exemption, HG §21-210.
Confectioneries.
    Products containing alcohol, HG §21-209.
    Rules and regulations.
    Adulteration, HG §21-209.
Consumer commodities.
    Defined, HG §21-101.
    Violation of label and packaging requirements,
        HG §21-257.
Containers.
    Maryland food, drug and cosmetic act.
    Application of label requirements to outside
        container or wrapper, HG §21-203.
Contaminated food.
    Control of food subject to contamination with
        microorganisms, HG §21-211.
Copies of statutes.
    Duty of secretary, HG §21-244.
Cosmetics.
    Adulterated cosmetics, HG §21-230.
    Defined, HG §21-101.
Counterfeit drugs.
    Defined, HG §21-201.
Crab meat.
    General provisions, HG §§21-339 to 21-343.
    See CRAB MEAT.
Criminal violations.
    Reporting, HG §21-255.
Defenses.
    Lack of direct dealing and overcharge actions, HG
        §21-1114.
    Violations, HG §21-260.
Definitions, HG §21-101.
    Advertisement, HG §21-101.
    Antibiotic drug, HG §21-218.
    Color additives, HG §21-101.
    Consumer commodities, HG §21-101.
    Cosmetics, HG §21-101.
    Counterfeit drug, HG §21-201.
    Devices, HG §21-101.
    Drugs, HG §21-101.
    Federal act, HG §21-101.
    Food, HG §21-101.
    Food additive, HG §21-101.
    Food establishments, HG §21-301.
    Hair dye, HG §21-230.
    Immediate threat, HG §21-254.
    Labeling, HG §21-101.
    Labels, HG §21-101.
    Maryland food, drug and cosmetic act, HG
        §21-201.

FOOD, DRUGS AND COSMETICS —Cont'd
Definitions —Cont'd
Official compendium, HG §21-101.
Packages, HG §21-101.
Secretary, HG §21-101.
Detainment and destruction of articles, HG §21-253.
Devices.
Adulterated drugs and devices, HG §21-216.
Grounds for action, HG §21-253.
Defined, HG §21-101.
Diseases.
Employees with communicable diseases, HG §21-328.
Donated food.
Exemption of certain food donors from liability, CJ §5-634; HG §21-322.
Inspection and handling, HG §21-322.
Drinking water.
Collecting, bottling or delivering, HG §21-336.
Drinks.
Alcoholic beverages.
See ALCOHOLIC BEVERAGES.
Soft drinks.
See SOFT DRINKS.
Drugs.
Adulterated drugs and devices, HG §21-216.
Grounds for action, HG §21-253.
Defined, HG §21-101.
Misbranded drugs. See within this heading, "Misbranded drugs and devices."
Standards of quality, purity, strength, etc., HG §21-237.
Employees.
Imputation of act or omission, HG §21-205.
Established name, HG §21-201.
False advertisements, HG §21-247.
Particular representation regarding drugs and devices considered false advertisements, HG §21-248.
False reports, HG §21-259.
Federal act.
Defined, HG §21-101.
Labeling requirements for food subject to additional processing, labeling or packing.
Application of exemptions adopted under act, HG §21-212.
Permits.
Temporary permits issued under federal act, HG §21-238.
Rules and regulations.
Conformance to federal act, HG §21-235.
Special dietary use.
Rules and regulations.
Automatic adoption of federal rules and regulations, HG §21-213.
Fines.
Vending machine sale of drugs or medicine, HG §21-1111.
Violations of provisions, HG §21-1215.
Food.
Adulterated food. See within this heading, "Adulterated food."
Contaminated food, HG §21-211.
Defined, HG §21-101.
Exemptions from labeling requirements, HG §21-212.
Misbranded food, HG §21-210.
Grounds for action, HG §21-253.
Special dietary use.
Rules and regulations.
Automatic adoption of federal rules, HG §21-213.

FOOD, DRUGS AND COSMETICS —Cont'd
Food additives.
Defined, HG §21-101.
Food establishments.
Bed and breakfast establishments, HG §21-323.1.
Construction, remodeling or alteration, HG §21-321.
Crab meat.
General provisions, HG §§21-339 to 21-343.
See CRAB MEAT.
Definitions, HG §21-301.
Diseases.
Employees with communicable diseases, HG §21-328.
Employees.
Communicable diseases, HG §21-328.
Exemptions from subtitle, HG §21-302.
Hearings.
Denial, suspension or revocation of license, HG §21-316.
Heimlich maneuver, HG §21-326.
Inspections, HG §21-313.
Licenses.
Advertisement information, HG §21-312.1.
Application, HG §21-306.
Catering services contracts.
Licensing information, HG §21-312.1.
County licenses, HG §21-305.
Denial, HG §21-311.
Hearings, HG §§21-311, 21-316.
Judicial review, HG §§21-311, 21-317.
Display, HG §21-312.
Expiration, HG §21-309.
Fees, HG §21-308.
Inspections.
Prerequisite to issuance, HG §21-307.
Issuance, HG §21-310.
Mobile food service facility.
Defined, HG §21-309.
Nontransferable, HG §21-305.
Qualifications of applicant, HG §21-307.
Renewal, HG §21-309.
Required, HG §21-305.
Scope, HG §21-310.
Suspension or revocation.
Grounds, HG §21-315.
Hearings, HG §21-316.
Judicial review, HG §21-317.
Temporary food service facility, HG §21-309.
Term, HG §21-309.
Vending machines, HG §21-305.
Lifesaving charts.
Posting required, HG §21-326.
Low-calorie frozen desserts.
Pasteurization and requirements after rehydration, HG §21-330.
Negligence,
Removing object lodged in throat of another.
Liability, HG §21-326.
Notice.
Violation of subtitle, unsanitary conditions, etc., HG §21-314.
Purpose of subtitle, HG §21-303.
Restrooms.
Required in certain places, HG §21-325.
Rules and regulations.
Adoption, HG §21-304.
Violations.
Order to abate, HG §21-318.
Scope of subtitle, HG §21-302.

FOOD, DRUGS AND COSMETICS —Cont'd
Food establishments —Cont'd
Seafood.
  Surimi products.
    Menus and advertising.
      Labeling and notice requirements, HG
        §21-329.
Shellfish.
  See OYSTERS AND CLAMS.
Sleeping prohibited on certain premises, HG
  §21-327.
Small residential group homes for children.
  Applicability of rules and regulations, HG
    §21-323.
Soft drinks.
  See SOFT DRINKS.
Surimi products.
  Menus and advertising.
    Labeling and notice requirements, HG
      §21-329.
Unsanitary conditions.
  Notice, HG §21-314.
Violation of subtitle.
  Notice, HG §21-314.
  Order to abate, HG §21-318.
Volunteer fire companies.
  Written notice of intent to serve food to the
    public, HG §21-304.1.
Frozen desserts, HG §§21-801 to 21-821.
  See FROZEN DESSERTS.
Group homes for children.
Applicability of rules and regulations, HG
  §21-323.
Hair dye.
Defined, HG §21-230.
Hearings.
Abatement orders, HG §21-261.
Administrative procedure.
  Application of act of hearings, HG §21-236.
Food establishments.
  Denial, suspension or revocation of license, HG
    §21-316.
Protests, HG §21-242.
Immediate threat.
Actions against food posing immediate threat, HG
  §21-254.
Defined, HG §21-254.
Exclusion from personal liability, CJ §5-633.
Sovereign immunity.
  Limited waiver, CJ §5-633.
Immunity.
Actions against food posing immediate threat.
  Immunity from liability of secretary, HG
    §21-254.
Food donors.
  Immunity from liability, CJ §5-634; HG
    §21-322.
Immediate threat.
  Limited waiver of sovereign immunity, CJ
    §5-633.
Impoundment of drugs or records, HG §21-1113.
Injunctions.
Actions for injunction, HG §21-252.
Inspections.
Bed and breakfast establishments, HG §21-323.1.
Carriers.
  Records, HG §21-250.
Contaminated food, HG §21-211.
Donated food, HG §21-322.
Food establishments, HG §21-313.
General powers to inspect, HG §21-249.

FOOD, DRUGS AND COSMETICS —Cont'd
Inspections —Cont'd
Prescription drugs.
  Extended inspections, HG §21-249.
  Reports, HG §21-249.
Small group homes for children, HG §21-323.
Insurance coverage for medical foods, IN
  §15-807.
Investigations.
New drugs.
  Exemption when intended for investigational
    use only, HG §21-224.
Judicial actions, HG §21-253.
Labeling.
Caution statements, HG §21-220.
Consumer commodities.
  Violation of label and packaging requirements,
    HG §21-257.
Defined, HG §21-101.
Drugs and devices subject to additional
  processing, labeling or packing.
Exemptions from labeling and packaging
  requirements, HG §21-219.
Foods subject to additional processing, labeling or
  packing, HG §21-212.
Maryland food, drug and cosmetic act.
  Application of label requirements to outside
    container or wrapper, HG §21-203.
Misbranded cosmetics.
  When cosmetic deemed misbranded, HG
    §21-231.
Misbranded drugs and devices. See within this
  heading, "Misbranded drugs and devices."
Misbranded food, HG §21-210.
  Grounds for action, HG §21-253.
Misleading labeling, HG §21-102.
Prescriptions.
  Caution statements, HG §21-220.
  Label requirements for prescription drugs, HG
    §21-221.
Seafood.
  Surimi products.
    Requirements, HG §21-329.
Lack of direct dealing as defense to action, HG
  §21-1114.
Liability.
Immunity generally. See within this heading,
  "Immunity."
Licenses.
Contaminated food, HG §21-211.
Drinking water.
  Collecting, bottling or delivering, HG §21-336.
Federal permits, HG §21-238.
Food establishments. See within this heading,
  "Food establishments."
State permits, HG §21-238.
Low-calorie frozen desserts.
Pasteurization and requirements after
  rehydration, HG §21-330.
Maryland food, drug and cosmetic act.
Antiseptics.
  Construction of representations that drug is
    antiseptic, HG §21-204.
Construction of subtitle.
  Imputation of act or omission, HG §21-205.
Counterfeit drug.
  Defined, HG §21-201.
Definitions, HG §21-201.
Established name.
  Defined, HG §21-201.

FOOD, DRUGS AND COSMETICS —Cont'd
Maryland food, drug and cosmetic act —Cont'd
Fine and imprisonment for violation, HG
§21-1215.
Imputation of act or omission, HG §21-205.
Labels.
Application of label requirements to outside
container or wrapper, HG §21-203.
New drug.
Defined, HG §21-201.
Outside container or wrapper.
Application of label requirements, HG §21-203.
Prescription drug.
Defined, HG §21-201.
Scope of subtitle, HG §21-202.
State adopted federal rule or regulation.
Defined, HG §21-201.
Title of act.
Short title, HG §21-263.
Medicine or patent medicine shows, HG
§21-1112.
Milk and milk products.
General provisions.
See MILK AND MILK PRODUCTS.
Mineral water.
Collecting, bottling or delivering, HG §21-336.
Minors.
Small residential group homes for children, HG
§21-323.
Minor violations, HG §21-255.
Misbranded cosmetics, HG §21-231.
Misbranded drugs and devices.
Additional grounds of drug misbranding, HG
§21-218.
Application of sections, HG §21-217.
Drugs recognized in official compendium.
Application of requirements, HG §21-218.
Exemptions from labeling requirements, HG
§21-217.
Grounds for action, HG §21-253.
Prescriptions.
Improperly dispensed drug considered
misbranded, HG §21-220.
Rules and regulations, HG §21-218.
When drug or device misbranded, HG §21-217.
Misbranded food, HG §21-210.
Grounds for action, HG §21-253.
Misdemeanors.
Vending machine violations, HG §21-1204.
Violations of provisions, HG §21-1215.
Misuse of information, HG §21-259.
Motor vehicles.
Cleanliness of certain vehicles, HG §21-324.
Natural water.
Collecting, bottling or delivering, HG §21-336.
New drugs, HG §21-201.
Applications.
Filing with secretary, HG §21-223.
Approval, HG §21-223.
Construction of section, HG §21-226.
Defined, HG §21-201.
Disapproval, HG §21-223.
Inspections.
Records, HG §21-225.
Investigations.
Exemption when intended for investigational
use only, HG §21-224.
Orders.
Records and reports, HG §21-223.
Printed information for use of practitioners, HG
§21-226.

FOOD, DRUGS AND COSMETICS —Cont'd
New drugs —Cont'd
Prohibition, HG §21-223.
Records, HG §21-223.
Inspections, HG §21-225.
Reports, HG §21-223.
Rules and regulations, HG §21-224.
Records and reports, HG §21-223.
Scope of section, HG §21-223.
Secretary.
Filing application with secretary, HG §21-223.
Provision of information on request, HG
§21-227.
Notice.
Auction sale of drugs, medicine or cosmetics, HG
§21-1110.
Food establishments.
Licenses.
Renewal notice, HG §21-309.
Violation of subtitle, unsanitary conditions, etc.,
HG §21-314.
Food service.
Volunteer fire companies.
Written notice of intent to serve food to the
public, HG §21-304.1.
Surimi products.
Labeling requirements, HG §21-329.
Official compendium.
Adulterated drugs and devices.
Testing drugs recognized in official compendium,
HG §21-216.
Defined, HG §21-101.
Misbranded drugs and devices.
Application of requirements for drugs
recognized in official compendium, HG
§21-218.
Opening closed food container in food store,
HG §21-259.1.
Overcharge actions.
Avoidance of duplicative liability, HG §21-1114.
Packages.
Defined, HG §21-101.
Penalties, HG §21-1215.
Surimi products.
Labeling requirements.
Violations of section, HG §21-329.
Physicians.
Impoundment of drugs or records, HG §21-1113.
New drugs.
Printed information for use of practitioners, HG
§21-226.
Poisons.
Authorization for the use of added poisonous or
otherwise deleterious substances, etc., HG
§21-239.
Prescription drugs.
See PRESCRIPTIONS AND PRESCRIPTION
DRUGS.
Prohibited acts, HG §21-256.
Abatement orders, HG §21-261.
Drugs and devices, HG §21-258.
False reports, HG §21-259.
Label and packaging requirements for consumer
commodities, HG §21-257.
Opening closed food container in food store, HG
§21-259.1.
Penalties, HG §21-1215.
Vending machine sales, HG §21-1111.
Protests.
Effect, HG §21-241.
Hearings, HG §21-242.

FOOD, DRUGS AND COSMETICS —Cont'd
Protests —Cont'd
  Orders after hearing, HG §21-243.
  Persons adversely affected by rules or regulations,
      HG §21-240.
  State adopted federal rules and regulations, HG
      §21-241.
Purified water.
  Collecting, bottling or delivering, HG §21-336.
Records.
  Carriers.
    Inspection of records, HG §21-250.
  New drugs, HG §21-223.
    Inspection of records, HG §21-225.
Reports.
  Criminal violations, HG §21-255.
  False reports, HG §21-259.
  Inspections, HG §21-249.
  New drugs, HG §21-223.
Restrooms.
  Required in certain places, HG §21-325.
Right of entry.
  Contaminated food, HG §21-211.
Rules and regulations.
  Administrative procedure act.
    Compliance with act in adoption of rule or
        regulation, HG §21-234.
  Confectionery products.
    Adulteration, HG §21-209.
  Conformance of state rules and regulations, HG
      §21-235.
  Contaminated food.
    Permits, HG §21-211.
  Definitions and standards of identity and quality,
      HG §21-237.
  Drugs and devices subject to additional
      processing, labeling or packing, HG §21-219.
  Effective date, HG §21-230.
  Federal act.
    Conformance to federal act, HG §21-235.
  Food establishments, HG §21-304.
    Violations.
      Order to abate, HG §21-318.
  Food or color additives.
    Automatic adoption of federal rules and
        regulations, HG §21-239.
  Labeling requirements for food subject to
      additional processing, labeling or packing.
    Adoption by secretary, HG §21-212.
  Misbranded drugs, HG §21-218.
  Misbranded food.
    Exemptions by rules and regulations, HG
        §21-210.
  New drugs, HG §21-223.
    Adoption, HG §21-224.
    Federal rules and regulations.
      Automatic adoption, HG §21-224.
    Inconsistent rules and regulations, HG §21-224.
    Records and reports, HG §21-223.
  Prescriptions.
    Exemptions by rule or regulation, HG §21-220.
  Protests, HG §21-240.
    Hearings on protest, HG §21-242.
    Orders after hearing, HG §21-243.
  Secretary.
    Adoption by secretary, HG §21-234.
  Special dietary use.
    Rules and regulations.
      Automatic adoption of federal rules, HG
          §21-213.

FOOD, DRUGS AND COSMETICS —Cont'd
Rules and regulations —Cont'd
  State adopted federal rule or regulation.
    Defined, HG §21-201.
    Effective date, HG §21-241.
    Protests, HG §21-241.
  United States department of agriculture.
    Conformance to rules and regulations of
        department, HG §21-235.
Sales.
  Application of provisions relating to sale, HG
      §21-102.
  Vending machine sales of drugs or medicine, HG
      §21-1111.
    Fine for violations, HG §21-1204.
Samples.
  Analysis, HG §21-251.
  Examination by samples considered sufficient test
      for violation, HG §21-260.
  Power to take samples, HG §21-249.
Sanitation.
  Cleanliness of certain premises and vehicles, HG
      §21-324.
  When unclean or unsanitary conditions exist, HG
      §21-324.
Scope of title, HG §21-102.
Seafood.
  Surimi products.
    Labeling requirements, HG §21-329.
Secretary.
  Collecting and disseminating information, HG
      §21-244.
  Copies of statutes, HG §21-244.
  Defined, HG §21-101.
  Injunctive actions, HG §21-252.
  New drugs.
    Powers and duties, HG §21-223.
    Provision of information on request of secretary,
        HG §21-227.
  Rules and regulations.
    Adoption, HG §21-234.
Shellfish generally.
  See SHELLFISH.
Short title.
  Maryland food, drug and cosmetic act, HG
      §21-263.
Sleep-inducing drugs.
  Barbital and other sleep inducing drugs.
    See CONTROLLED DANGEROUS
        SUBSTANCES.
Sleeping.
  Food establishments.
    Prohibited in certain premises, HG §21-327.
Soft drinks.
  General provisions.
    See SOFT DRINKS.
Sovereign immunity.
  Immediate threat.
    Limited waiver of sovereign immunity, CJ
        §5-633.
Special dietary use.
  Rules and regulations.
    Automatic adoption of federal rules, HG
        §21-213.
Spices.
  Misbranding, HG §21-210.
Spring water.
  Collecting, bottling or delivering, HG §21-336.
State's attorneys.
  Criminal violations.
    Reporting, HG §21-255.

FOOD, DRUGS AND COSMETICS —Cont'd
Surimi products.
Labeling requirements, HG §21-329.
Tests.
Analysis of samples, HG §21-251.
Drugs purported to be recognized in official
compendium, HG §21-216.
Taking samples, HG §21-249.
Violations.
Examination by samples considered sufficient
test, HG §21-260.
Toilets.
Restrooms required in certain places, HG §21-325.
Transportation.
Cleanliness of vehicles used to transport food, HG
§21-324.
United States department of agriculture.
Conformance to rules and regulations, HG
§21-235.
Vending machines.
Vending machine sale of drugs or medicine, HG
§21-1111.
Fine for violations, HG §21-1204.
Violations.
Abatement orders, HG §21-261.
Continuing violations, HG §21-1215.
Criminal violations.
Opportunity for alleged violator to present view,
HG §21-255.
Reports, HG §21-255.
Defenses to alleged violations, HG §21-260.
Drugs and devices, HG §21-258.
False reports, HG §21-259.
Label and packaging requirements for consumer
commodities, HG §21-257.
Minor violations, HG §21-255.
Misuse of information, HG §21-259.
Penalties, HG §21-1215.
Prohibited acts, HG §21-256.
Samples.
Examination by samples considered sufficient
test, HG §21-260.
Vending machine sale of drugs or medicine.
Fine, HG §21-1204.
Volunteer fire companies.
Food service.
Written notice of intent to serve food to the
public, HG §21-304.1.
Well water.
Collecting, bottling or delivering, HG §21-336.

FOOD STAMPS.
Controlled substance felony.
Custodial parent with prior conviction, 88A §65A.
Federal food coupons, 88A §88.
Public assistance fraud, CR §§8-501 to 8-505.

FOOT RACING EVENTS, TR §21-1211.1.

FORCE.
Extortion and other threats, CR §§3-701 to
3-708.
Law enforcement officers and personnel.
Excessive force allegations.
Statute of limitations for administrative
charges, waiver, PS §3-106.
Voting.
Influencing voter's decision by use of, EL §16-201.

FORCIBLE ENTRY AND DETAINER.
Detainers.
See DETAINERS.

FORCIBLE ENTRY AND DETAINER —Cont'd
Wrongful detainer generally.
See WRONGFUL DETAINER.

FORECLOSURES.
Assignments.
Mortgages.
Release and assignment, PropSales Rule
14-209.
Audits.
Mortgage sales, PropSales Rule 14-206.
Bankruptcy and insolvency.
Effect of petition, PropSales Rule 14-209.
Bonds, surety.
Mortgage sales, PropSales Rule 14-206.
Commencement of action, PropSales Rule 14-203.
Methods of commencing, PropSales Rule 14-204.
Conveyances.
Mortgage sales, PropSales Rule 14-206.
Decrees.
Assent to a decree.
Defined, PropSales Rule 14-201.
Mortgages.
Person authorized to sell under assent to a
decree, PropSales Rule 14-206.
Who may institute action, PropSales Rule
14-202.
Mortgages.
Order directing sale before final decree in
exceptional case, PropSales Rule 14-205.
Sale.
Deficiency of proceeds, PropSales Rule 14-208.
Definitions, PropSales Rule 14-201.
Emergency management.
Civil relief during emergency periods, PS §14-214.
Filing.
Commencement of action, PropSales Rule 14-203.
Homeowners protection, RP §§7-301 to 7-321.
See within this heading, "Protection of
homeowners."
Injunctions, PropSales Rule 14-209.
Insolvency.
Effect of petition, PropSales Rule 14-209.
Judicial sales.
Generally, PropSales Rules 14-301 to 14-306.
See JUDICIAL SALES.
Jurisdiction.
Commencement of action.
Docketing.
Jurisdiction attaches upon docketing,
PropSales Rule 14-203.
Land installment contracts, PropSales Rule
14-203.
Location of public sale, PropSales Rule 14-101.
Mail.
Mortgage sales.
Notice by certified mail, PropSales Rule 14-206.
Maryland economic adjustment fund.
Loan documents, 83A §6-509.
Mortgages.
Commencement of action.
Method of commencing action where mortgage
contains both power of sale and assent to
decree, PropSales Rule 14-203.
Procedures, PropSales Rule 14-204.
Conveyances.
Sale, PropSales Rule 14-206.
Crops.
Effect of foreclosure on annual crops, RP §7-105.
Decrees.
Order directing sale before final decree in
exceptional case, PropSales Rule 14-205.

FORECLOSURES —Cont'd
Mortgages —Cont'd
Decrees —Cont'd
Sale.
Deficiency of proceeds, PropSales Rule 14-208.
Generally, PropSales Rule 14-205.
Order directing sale, PropSales Rule 14-205.
Parties, PropSales Rule 14-202.
Power of sale.
Bonds, surety, PropSales Rule 14-206; RP §14-103.
Person authorized to sell, PropSales Rule 14-207.
Release and assignment, PropSales Rule 14-209.
Sale, PropSales Rule 14-207.
Bonds, surety, PropSales Rule 14-206; RP §14-103.
Deficiency decree, PropSales Rule 14-208.
Order directing sale, PropSales Rule 14-205.
Proceeds, PropSales Rule 14-208.
Protection of purchaser against unrecorded instrument, PropSales Rule 14-206; RP §14-103.
Taxation.
Foreclosure of rights of redemption.
General provisions.
See PROPERTY TAXES.
Motions.
Mortgage sales.
Deficiency, PropSales Rule 14-208.
Notice.
Record owner of residential property.
Notice of commencement of action, PropSales Rule 14-204.
Notice of order directing sale of property, PropSales Rule 14-205.
Orders.
Mortgages.
Order of court directing sale, PropSales Rule 14-205.
Release or assignment, PropSales Rule 14-209.
Parties.
Mortgages, PropSales Rule 14-202.
Partnerships, revised act.
Charging partners transferable interest to satisfy judgment.
Foreclosure of interest subject to charging order, CA §9A-504.
Petitions.
Deeds of trust.
Release.
Removal of trustee, PropSales Rule 14-210.
Insolvency.
Effect of petition, PropSales Rule 14-209.
Power of sale.
Conveyance to purchaser where vendor and purchaser are the same, PropSales Rule 14-206.
Defined, PropSales Rule 14-201.
Mortgages.
Bonds, surety, PropSales Rule 14-206; RP §14-103.
Person authorized to sell under power of sale, PropSales Rule 14-206.
Who may institute action, PropSales Rule 14-202.
Procedure following sale, PropSales Rule 14-207.
Property.
Defined, PropSales Rule 14-201.
Protection of homeowners, RP §§7-301 to 7-321.
Action for damages by homeowner, RP §7-320.
Applicability of provisions, RP §7-302.

FORECLOSURES —Cont'd
Protection of homeowners —Cont'd
Criminal penalties, RP §7-321.
Definitions, RP §7-301.
Foreclosure consultants.
Contracts for consulting, RP §7-306.
Prohibited activities, RP §7-307.
Prohibited activities.
Foreclosure consultant, RP §7-307.
Waiver of rights, RP §7-318.
Purchaser obligations, RP §7-311.
Reconveyance of foreclosure, RP §7-310.
Rescission, RP §7-305.
Surplus purchaser contracts, RP §7-315.
Surplus acquisition, RP §7-314.
Violations, RP §7-319.
Action for damages by homeowner, RP §7-320.
Criminal penalties, RP §7-321.
Foreclosure consultant prohibited activities, RP §7-307.
Waiver of rights, RP §7-318.
Waiver of rights, RP §7-318.
Publication.
Mortgage sales.
Notice, PropSales Rule 14-206.
Sales.
Defined, PropSales Rule 14-201.
Judgment awarding possession, PropSales Rule 14-102.
Judicial sales, PropSales Rules 14-301 to 14-306.
See JUDICIAL SALES.
Location of public sale, PropSales Rule 14-101.
Mortgages, PropSales Rule 14-206.
Order of court directing sale.
Conditions, PropSales Rule 14-205.
Procedure following sale, PropSales Rule 14-207.
Proceeds.
Deficiency, PropSales Rule 14-208.
When conveyance to creditor not fraudulent, CL §15-210.1.
Scope of provisions, PropSales Rule 14-201.
Secured transactions.
Defaults.
Enforcement after default, CL §9-601.
Execution sale forecloses security interest, CL §9-601.
Senior citizen activities centers.
Capital improvement grants program.
Defaults.
Enforcement and foreclosure of judgment liens, 70B §31.
Stays.
Injunction to stay foreclosure, PropSales Rule 14-209.
Taxation.
Mortgages.
Foreclosure of rights of redemption.
See PROPERTY TAXES.
Venue.
Commencement of actions, PropSales Rule 14-203.

FOREIGN.
Acknowledgments.
Outside United States, SG §19-104.
Aliens.
See ALIENS.
Banks and trust companies.
See BANKS AND TRUST COMPANIES.
Constitutional provisions, US Const Art I §§8, 10; Amd 11.

FOREIGN —Cont'd
Corporations.
  See FOREIGN CORPORATIONS.
Courts.
  Judicial notice.
    Uniform foreign law act, CJ §§10-501 to 10-507.
      See JUDICIAL NOTICE.
Debts.
  Foreign debts and other instruments.
  Proof.
    See EVIDENCE.
  Money judgment recognition, CJ §§10-701 to
    10-709.
    See FOREIGN MONEY JUDGMENTS.
Depositions.
  Officers before whom depositions taken.
    Circuit courts, CivProCir Rule 2-414.
  Uniform foreign depositions act.
    See DEPOSITIONS.
Discriminatory boycotts.
  See FOREIGN DISCRIMINATORY BOYCOTTS.
Executors and administrators.
  General provisions, ET §§5-501 to 5-506.
    See EXECUTORS AND ADMINISTRATORS.
Guardian and ward.
  Powers of foreign fiduciaries, ET §13-222.
Judgments and decrees.
  Foreign money judgments, CJ §§10-701 to 10-709.
    See FOREIGN MONEY JUDGMENTS.
Judicial notice.
  Uniform foreign law act, CJ §§10-501 to 10-507.
    See JUDICIAL NOTICE.
Laws.
  Uniform foreign law act, CJ §§10-501 to 10-507.
    See JUDICIAL NOTICE.
Officers.
  Foreign powers.
    Presents to officers from prohibited, MD Const
      DofR Art 35.
Personal representatives, ET §§5-501 to 5-506.
  See EXECUTORS AND ADMINISTRATORS.
Savings and loan associations.
  Foreign associations.
    See SAVINGS AND LOAN ASSOCIATIONS.
Statutes.
  Judicial notice.
    Uniform foreign law act, CJ §§10-501 to 10-507.
      See JUDICIAL NOTICE.
Trade zones.
  See FOREIGN TRADE ZONES.
Vessels and boats.
  Manufacturers or dealers.
    Boat shows.
      Exemption from licensing requirement, NR
        §8-710.

**FOREIGN CHILD CUSTODY
  DETERMINATIONS.**
**Uniform child custody jurisdiction and
  enforcement act.**
  Generally, FL §§9.5-101 to 9.5-318.
    See CHILD CUSTODY.

FOREIGN CORPORATIONS.
Actions.
  Compliance with subtitle not consent to suit, CA
    §7-210.
  Revocation of permit for conduct connected with
    organized crime, CA §1-405.
  When suit may be maintained by corporation, CA
    §7-301.

FOREIGN CORPORATIONS —Cont'd
Agents.
  Resident agent.
    Certification, CA §7-205.
    Change of resident agent or principal office, CA
      §7-205.
    Index of names and addresses.
      Kept by department, CA §7-209.
    Required, CA §7-205.
    Resignation, CA §7-205.
    Service of process, CA §1-401.
Business.
  Activities not considered intrastate, interstate or
    foreign business, CA §§7-103, 7-104.
  Must be permitted by laws of Maryland, CA
    §7-102.
Charter.
  Amendments.
    Filing certified copies of amendments.
      Penalty for failure to file, CA §7-303.
  Intrastate business.
    Filing copies of charter before doing, CA §7-203.
  Qualifications.
    Termination, CA §7-208.
  Registration.
    Termination, CA §7-208.
Compliance with subtitle.
  Not consent to suit, CA §7-210.
Conflict of laws.
  Consolidation, merger and other transfers of
    property, CA §3-117.
**Consolidation, merger and other transfers of
  property.**
  Application of laws of foreign jurisdictions, CA
    §3-117.
  Approval of articles, CA §3-106.
  Certificate of consolidation or merger.
    Prepared and filed by department, CA §3-117.
  Certificates of successor to be filed with
    department, CA §3-117.
  Conflict of laws, CA §3-117.
  Defined, CA §3-101.
  Effect, CA §3-102.
  Ownership of land in state.
    Statement of certain actions filed with
      department, CA §7-206.
  Statement of certain actions filed with
    department, CA §7-206.
  Successor corporation, CA §3-117.
  Time articles effective, CA §3-113.
Contracts.
  Failure to comply with subtitle 2 not to affect
    contracts, CA §7-305.
Definitions, CA §1-101.
Dissolution.
  Statement of certain actions filed with
    department, CA §7-206.
Doing business in this state.
  Activities not considered intrastate, interstate or
    foreign business, CA §§7-103, 7-104.
Fees.
  Recording and filing fees, CA §1-203.
Fines.
  Doing business without qualifying or registering,
    CA §7-302.
Foreclosing mortgages and deeds of trust, CA
    §7-104.
Forfeiture of rights to do intrastate business.
  Failure to pay late filing penalties, CA §7-304.
Insurance companies.
  Deposit of securities, IN §4-106.

FOREIGN CORPORATIONS —Cont'd
Insurance companies —Cont'd
Investments, IN §5-602.
Risk based capital standards, IN §4-312.
Trusteed assets of alien insurers, IN §§5-801 to
5-807.
Interstate and foreign business.
Registration, CA §7-202.
Application of sections, CA §7-202.1.
When deemed registered, CA §7-202.
Intrastate business.
Activities not considered intrastate, interstate or
foreign business, CA §§7-103, 7-104.
Forfeiture of rights to do intrastate business.
Failure to file required reports, CA §7-304.
Qualification.
When qualified, CA §7-203.
Limitation of actions.
Denial of defense of limitations, CJ §5-204.
Limitation on business, CA §7-102.
Names, CA §2-106.
Registration, CA §7-101.
Foreign entities generally, CA §1-506.
Notices.
Service, CA §1-401.
Officers and agents.
Fines for doing business without qualifying or
registering, CA §7-302.
Resident agents. See within this heading,
"Agents."
Offices.
Principal office in this state.
Certificate to show address, CA §7-205.
Index.
Department to keep index of names and
addresses, CA §7-209.
Qualifications.
Effect of failure to qualify, CA §§7-301, 7-302.
Exceptions, CA §7-201.
Termination, CA §7-208.
Recording, CA §1-203.
Registration, CA §7-201.
Certificate of registration, CA §7-204.
Effect of failure to register, CA §§7-301, 7-302.
Exceptions, CA §7-201.
General provisions, CA §7-201.
Interstate and foreign business, CA §7-202.
Intrastate business.
Filing copies of charter before doing, CA §7-203.
Termination, CA §7-208.
Reports.
Failure to file.
Effect, CA §7-304.
Filing fees, CA §1-203.
Disposition, TP §2-220.
Resident agents. See within this heading,
"Agents."
**Revocation of permit for conduct connected
with organized crime,** CA §1-405.
Service of process.
Notice, CA §1-401.
Resident agent, CA §1-401.
State law.
Assent to, CA §7-105.
Statement of actions.
Filing with department, CA §7-206.
Merger or consolidation, CA §7-206.
Taxation.
Revenues of foreign corporations, MD Const Art
III §58.

FOREIGN DISCRIMINATORY BOYCOTTS.
Actions.
Civil actions, CL §11-109.
Administration of subtitle, CL §11-101.
Admissions.
Assurance of discontinuance of prohibited act not
considered admission, CL §11-106.
Antitrust laws.
Applicability, CL §11-114.
Attorney general.
Administration of subtitle, CL §11-101.
Assurance of discontinuance of prohibited act.
Attorney general may accept, CL §11-106.
Civil actions.
Proceedings by attorney general, CL §11-109.
Criminal proceedings, CL §11-107.
Investigations, CL §11-107.
Production of documents for inspection by, CL
§11-105.
Prosecutions, CL §11-107.
Rules and regulations.
Promulgation, CL §11-113.
Violations.
Report to attorney general, CL §11-104.
Citation of subtitle, CL §11-115.
Contracts.
Voiding of contract provisions, CL §11-112.
**Cooperation with federal government and
other states,** CL §11-108.
Criminal procedure, CL §11-107.
Damages.
Action for damages, CL §11-109.
Definitions, CL §11-102.
Injunctions.
Actions for injunction, CL §11-109.
Inspections.
Documents.
Production for inspection by attorney general,
CL §11-105.
Interpretation and construction.
Liberal construction of subtitle, CL §11-101.
Investigations, CL §11-107.
Limitation of actions.
Civil actions, CL §11-109.
Criminal proceedings, CL §11-107.
Participation in boycott.
Unlawful, CL §11-103.
Penalties.
Violations of subtitle, CL §11-111.
Policy.
Declaration, CL §11-101.
Prohibited acts, CL §11-103.
Assurance of discontinuance, CL §11-106.
Penalties, CL §11-111.
Remedies.
Cumulative remedies, CL §11-110.
Reports.
Responsibility to report violations, CL §11-104.
Rules and regulations.
Promulgation, CL §11-113.
Short title of subtitles, CL §11-115.
State's attorneys.
Investigations, CL §11-107.
Prosecution, CL §11-107.
United States.
Cooperation with federal government, CL §11-108.
Violations.
Penalties, CL §11-111.
Prohibited acts, CL §11-103.
Responsibility to report, CL §11-104.

FOREIGN HEALTH MAINTENANCE ORGANIZATIONS.
Transferring domicile to Maryland, HG §19-735.

FOREIGN LIMITED LIABILITY COMPANIES.
See LIMITED LIABILITY COMPANIES.

FOREIGN LIMITED LIABILITY PARTNERSHIPS, REVISED ACT, CA §§9A-1101 to 9A-1111.
See LIMITED LIABILITY PARTNERSHIPS, REVISED ACT.

FOREIGN MONEY JUDGMENTS.
Appeals.
Stay pending appeals, CJ §10-706.
Applicability of subtitle, CJ §10-702.
Citations.
Short title, CJ §10-709.
Definitions, CJ §10-701.
Enforcement, CJ §10-703.
Grounds for nonrecognition, CJ §10-704.
Interpretation and construction.
Uniformity of interpretation, CJ §10-708.
Jurisdiction.
Personal jurisdiction, CJ §10-705.
Nonrecognition.
Grounds, CJ §10-704.
Recognition, CJ §10-703.
Nonrecognition.
Grounds, CJ §10-704.
Situations not covered by subtitle, CJ §10-707.
Stay.
Pending appeals, CJ §10-706.
Uniform enforcement of foreign judgments act.
General provisions, CJ §§11-801 to 11-807.
See JUDGMENTS AND DECREES.

FOREIGN TRADE ZONES.
Application.
Approval of governor in Maryland port administration, 23 §467.
Conditions and restrictions, 23 §468.
Private corporation defined, 23 §466.
Property tax credit, TP §9-231.
Public corporation defined, 23 §466.
Supplemental authority granted to Maryland port administration, 23 §469.

FOREST AND PARK CONCESSION ACCOUNT, NR §5-212.1.

FOREST CONSERVATION.
General provisions, NR §§5-1601 to 5-1613.
See FORESTS AND PARKS.

FORESTERS.
Appeals.
Disciplinary actions on licenses, BOP §7-312.
Board, BOP §§7-201 to 7-208. See within this heading, "State board of foresters."
Bonds, surety.
State board of foresters.
Secretary of board, BOP §7-203.
Citation of act.
Short title, BOP §7-601.
Conservancy districts.
Duties of forester, NR §5-607.
Definitions, BOP §7-101.
Endorsement of documents, BOP §7-402.
Prohibited acts, BOP §7-504.
Fees.
Disposition of money collected, BOP §7-207.
Licenses, BOP §7-306.
Application fee, BOP §7-305.

FORESTERS —Cont'd
Fees —Cont'd
Licenses —Cont'd
Reinstatement of revoked license, BOP §7-313.
Renewal fee, BOP §7-308.
Replacement of license, BOP §7-306.
Fines.
License violations, BOP §7-506.
Fraud.
Disciplinary actions on licenses.
Grounds, BOP §7-309.
Hearings.
Disciplinary actions on licenses, BOP §§7-310, 7-311.
Legislative declaration, BOP §7-102.
Licenses.
Applications, BOP §7-305.
Fee, BOP §7-305.
Qualifications of applicants, BOP §7-304.
Criminal penalty, BOP §7-506.
Defined, BOP §7-101.
Denial, BOP §7-306.
Disciplinary action generally, BOP §§7-309 to 7-313.
Disciplinary action.
Complaints.
Commencement of proceedings, BOP §7-310.
Grounds, BOP §7-309.
Hearings, BOP §§7-310, 7-311.
Judicial review, BOP §7-312.
Reinstatement of revoked license, BOP §7-313.
Effect, BOP §7-307.
Expiration, BOP §7-308.
Endorsement of documents while license expired, BOP §7-504.
False information.
Giving to board in attempt to obtain license. Prohibited, BOP §7-505.
Fees, BOP §7-306.
Application fee, BOP §7-305.
Reinstatement of revoked license, BOP §7-313.
Renewal fee, BOP §7-308.
Replacement of license, BOP §7-306.
Fines, BOP §7-506.
Issuance, BOP §7-306.
Nonresident foresters.
Practice without license, BOP §7-303.
Notices.
Disciplinary action.
Hearing, BOP §7-311.
Issuance.
Notice to qualified applicant, BOP §7-306.
Renewal notice, BOP §7-308.
Prohibited acts and penalties, BOP §§7-501 to 7-506.
Qualifications of applicants, BOP §7-304.
Reinstatement of revoked license, BOP §7-313.
Renewal, BOP §7-308.
Replacement of lost, mutilated or destroyed certificate, BOP §7-306.
Reprimand of licensee.
Disciplinary action generally, BOP §§7-309 to 7-313.
Required, BOP §7-301.
Exceptions, BOP §§7-302, 7-303.
Revocation or suspension.
Disciplinary action generally, BOP §§7-309 to 7-313.
Endorsement of documents while license revoked or suspended, BOP §7-504.
Roster of licensees, BOP §7-206.

FORESTERS —Cont'd
Licenses —Cont'd
Scope, BOP §7-307.
Term, BOP §7-308.
Unlicensed practice.
Prohibited, BOP §7-501.
Using license of another.
Prohibited, BOP §7-503.
Maps.
Endorsement of documents generally, BOP §7-402.
Prohibited acts, BOP §7-504.
Misdemeanors.
Violations of provisions, BOP §7-506.
Misrepresentation as authorized practitioner, BOP §7-502.
Nonresidents.
Practice without license, BOP §7-303.
Notices.
Licenses.
Disciplinary action.
Hearings, BOP §7-311.
Issuance.
Notice to qualified applicant, BOP §7-306.
Renewal notice, BOP §7-308.
Oaths.
State board of foresters.
Administration of oaths, BOP §7-205.
Penalties.
Violations of provisions, BOP §7-506.
Policy of state, BOP §7-102.
Practice of forestry.
Licenses.
Generally, BOP §§7-301 to 7-313. See within this heading, "Licenses."
Required, BOP §7-301.
Exceptions, BOP §§7-302, 7-303.
Unlicensed practice prohibited, BOP §7-501.
Misrepresentation as authorized practitioner, BOP §7-502.
Nonresident foresters.
Practice without license, BOP §7-303.
Supervised practice, BOP §7-302.
Records.
State board of foresters, BOP §7-206.
Responsible charge.
Supervised practice, BOP §7-302.
Rules and regulations.
Termination of regulations adopted under provisions, BOP §7-602.
Seals and sealed instruments, BOP §7-401.
Short title of act, BOP §7-601.
State board of foresters.
Appointment of members, BOP §7-202.
Authority of secretary, BOP §7-208.
Bonds, surety.
Secretary of board, BOP §7-203.
Composition, BOP §7-202.
Creation, BOP §7-201.
Definition of "board," BOP §7-101.
Disposition of money, BOP §7-207.
Duties, BOP §7-206.
Established, BOP §7-201.
Expenses of members.
Reimbursement, BOP §7-204.
False information.
Giving to board.
Prohibited acts, BOP §7-505.
Meetings, BOP §7-204.
Number of members, BOP §7-202.

FORESTERS —Cont'd
State board of foresters —Cont'd
Oaths.
Power to administer oaths, BOP §7-205.
Officers, BOP §7-203.
Powers, BOP §§7-205, 7-206.
Program evaluation act, SG §8-403.
Qualifications of members, BOP §7-202.
Quorum, BOP §7-204.
Records, BOP §7-206.
Removal of members, BOP §7-202.
Staff, BOP §7-204.
Investigative staff, BOP §7-205.
Terms of members, BOP §7-202.
Vacancies, BOP §7-202.
Subpoenas.
State board of foresters.
Subpoena power, BOP §7-205.
Termination of provisions, BOP §7-602.
Title of act.
Short title, BOP §7-601.
Titles.
Use of certain titles by unlicensed persons, BOP §7-502.

FOREST MITIGATION BANKS, NR §§5-1601, 5-1610.1.

FORESTS AND PARKS.
Abandonment.
Lost or abandoned property within state forests, park or wildlife management area.
Disposition, NR §5-213.
Admission.
Aged persons.
Persons possessing Maryland golden age pass, NR §5-1009.
Boy Scouts and Camp Fire Girls.
Free admission to state parks, NR §5-1008.
Advertising.
Roadside trees.
Placing on trees, fences, buildings, etc., without permission, NR §5-407.
Advisory commissions.
Established, NR §5-204.
Aged persons.
Admission.
Persons possessing Maryland golden age pass, NR §5-1009.
Allegany county.
Acquisition projects, NR §5-910.
Appalachian trail, NR §5-1001.
Appropriations.
Conservancy districts.
Acceptance and custody of federal appropriations, NR §5-609.
Tree planting and care, NR §5-411.
Wildlife areas.
Limitations upon, NR §5-1204.
Arrest.
Roadside trees.
Protection of trees by warden, NR §5-404.
Auxiliary state forest reserves, NR §5-1007.
Big Salvage mountain wildlands.
Description, NR §5-1203.
Boards.
District forestry board, NR §§5-605, 5-606.
Boy Scouts.
Free admission to state parks, NR §5-1008.
Camp Fire Girls.
Free admission to state parks, NR §5-1008.

FORESTS AND PARKS —Cont'd
Christmas trees and evergreen shrubs.
Transportation.
General provisions, NR §§5-412 to 5-414.
See CHRISTMAS TREES AND SHRUBS.
Community forestry, NR §§5-424 to 5-427.
See URBAN AND COMMUNITY FORESTRY.
Concession account, NR §5-212.1.
Conservancy districts.
Appropriations, NR §5-609.
Definitions, NR §5-601.
Department of natural resources.
Powers and duties, NR §5-603.
District forestry board.
Defined, NR §5-601.
Powers and duties, NR §5-606.
Exemptions, NR §5-610.
Forester.
Duties of forester, NR §5-607.
Landowners.
Defined, NR §5-601.
Licenses, NR §5-608.
Natural resources.
Defined, NR §5-601.
Department duties, NR §5-603.
Organization, NR §5-605.
Policy of state, NR §5-602.
Rules and regulations, NR §5-604.
Woodlands or forest lands.
Defined, NR §5-601.
Conservation.
Forest conservation.
Generally, NR §§5-1601 to 5-1613. See within
this heading, "Forest conservation."
Counties.
Defined, NR §5-101.
Plans.
Assistance of secretary, NR §5-210.
Urban and community forestry, NR §§5-424 to
5-427.
See URBAN AND COMMUNITY FORESTRY.
Crimes and offenses.
Fires.
Maliciously setting fires, NR §5-704.
Railroads.
Engines to be provided with appliances to
prevent fires, NR §5-711.
Violations of title, NR §5-1301.
Damages.
Cutting and burning.
Liability to aggrieved parties, NR §5-409.
Declaration of policy, NR §5-102.
Deep Creek lake.
General provisions.
See DEEP CREEK LAKE.
Definitions, NR §5-101.
Conservancy districts, NR §5-601.
Forest conservation, NR §5-1601.
Forest fire prevention, NR §5-720.
Forestry, NR §5-102.1.
Open space or open areas, NR §5-1201.
Pine tree reforestation, NR §5-501.
Program open space, NR §5-901.
Reforestation, NR §5-103.
Reforestation and timber stand improvements, NR
§5-219.
Roadside trees, NR §5-401.
Timber stand improvements.
Reforestation and timber stand improvements,
NR §5-219.
Wildland areas, NR §5-1201.

FORESTS AND PARKS —Cont'd
Definitions —Cont'd
Woodland incentives program, NR §5-301.
Department of natural resources.
Maryland conservation corps, NR §5-218.
Patuxent river watershed.
General provisions.
See PATUXENT RIVER WATERSHED.
Pine tree reforestation.
Defined, NR §5-501.
Enforcement, NR §5-508.
Rules and regulations, NR §5-503.
Printing and distribution.
Material relating to forests and parks, NR
§5-211.
Purchases.
Authority to purchase land in Garrett county.
Limitations, NR §5-207.
Reforestation.
Land clearing, etc.
Consultation with department, NR §5-103.
Reforestation fund.
Management of fund, NR §5-103.
Role of department, NR §5-201.
Scenic rivers.
General provisions.
See WATERS OF THE STATE.
Transfer of jurisdiction.
Department of forests and parks, NR §5-201.
Districts.
Forest conservancy districts. See within this
heading, "Conservancy districts."
Easements.
Authority to purchase land in Garrett county.
Limitations, NR §5-207.
Hart-Miller-Pleasure Island chain.
State to grant easement, NR §5-1202.2.
Eminent domain, NR §5-208.
Evergreen shrubs.
Transportation.
General provisions, NR §§5-412 to 5-414.
See CHRISTMAS TREES AND SHRUBS.
Experts.
Tree experts.
General provisions, NR §§5-415 to 5-423.
See TREE EXPERTS.
Fair Hill improvement fund, NR §5-908.
Federal aid.
Conservancy districts.
Acceptance and custody of federal
appropriations, NR §5-609.
Renewable forest resources plan.
Acceptance of federal funds, NR §5-214.
Fines.
Fires.
Failure to render aid when summoned, NR
§5-701.
Maliciously setting fires, NR §5-704.
Railroads.
Failure to maintain safety strips, NR §5-714.
Violation of title, NR §5-1301.
Collection, NR §5-1302.
Fires.
Extinguishing.
Defined.
Failure to render help, NR §5-701.
Duty to extinguish, NR §5-704.
Expenses.
Accounts of warden, NR §5-701.
Distribution, NR §5-702.

FORESTS AND PARKS —Cont'd
Fires —Cont'd
Extinguishing —Cont'd
Expenses —Cont'd
Incurred in fighting or extinguishing, NR §5-702.
Summoning relief.
Penalty for failure to respond, NR §5-701.
Wardens.
Accounting for expenses, NR §5-701.
Powers, NR §5-701.
Junior forest fire fighters.
Warden may summon, NR §5-701.
Liability for causing, NR §5-705.
Aggrieved party for burning, NR §5-409.
Maliciously setting fires, NR §5-704.
Civil liability, NR §5-705.
Penalties, NR §5-704.
Middle Atlantic interstate forest fire protection compact.
General provisions, NR §5-801.
Negligently setting fires, NR §5-704.
Civil liability, NR §5-705.
Notices as to forest fire laws.
Posting, NR §5-703.
Open air burning, NR §5-720.
Penalties.
Extinguishing.
Failure to respond, NR §5-701.
Maliciously setting fires, NR §5-704.
Railroads.
Abatement of hazards, NR §5-707.
Report.
Duty to report fire, NR §5-704.
State's attorney.
Enforcement of subtitle, NR §5-706.
Wildland areas.
Control, NR §5-1213.
Measures to protect nearby private land, NR §5-1213.1.
Fish and fisheries.
Refuges and hatcheries.
Use of state parks, NR §4-403.
Forest advisory commission, NR §5-204.
Forest conservation, NR §§5-1601 to 5-1613.
Afforestation, NR §5-1606.
Forest mitigation banks, NR §5-1610.1.
Priority, NR §5-1607.
Applicability of subtitle, NR §5-1602.
Definitions, NR §5-1601.
Exceptions to provisions of subtitle, NR §5-1602.
Forest conservation threshold, NR §5-1606.
Forest mitigation banks, NR §5-1610.1.
Forest resource inventory.
Statewide inventory, NR §5-1609.
Forest stand delineation, NR §5-1604.
Guidance manuals.
Development, NR §5-1609.
Inventory.
Statewide forest resource inventory, NR §5-1609.
Land use categories, NR §5-1606.
Local programs, NR §5-1603.
Provisions developed by local government, NR §5-1607.
Mitigation banks, NR §5-1610.1.
Notice.
Forest conservation plan.
Completeness, NR §5-1605.
Forest stand delineation.
Completeness and correctness, NR §5-1604.

FORESTS AND PARKS —Cont'd
Forest conservation —Cont'd
Penalties.
Noncompliance with subtitle, NR §5-1608.
Placement of land forested, afforested or reforested under subtitle, NR §5-1607.
Plan, NR §5-1605.
Approval.
Final subdivision plan or grading or sediment control, NR §5-1608.
Review.
Concurrent review, NR §5-1608.
Preferred sequence.
Afforestation and reforestation, NR §5-1607.
Priority, NR §5-1607.
Reforestation.
Forest mitigation banks, NR §5-1610.1.
Reforestation ratio, NR §5-1606.
Preferred sequence for reforestation, NR §5-1607.
Regulations.
Adoption, NR §5-1609.
Retention and protection of forest.
Priority, NR §5-1607.
Standards and options for meeting afforestation or reforestation requirements, NR §5-1607.
Violations of subtitle.
Penalties, NR §5-1608.
Forest conservation fund.
Afforestation.
Time period, NR §5-1610.
Contributions, NR §5-1610.
Deposits, NR §5-1610.
Enforcement, NR §5-1612.
Established, NR §5-1610.
Funds.
Disposition, NR §5-1610.
Local forest conservation fund, NR §5-1610.
Management, NR §5-1610.
Injunctions, NR §5-1612.
Local programs.
Fund, NR §5-1610.
Penalties.
Violations of subtitle, NR §5-1612.
Plan.
Revocation, NR §5-1612.
Reforestation ratio.
Time period, NR §5-1610.
Reports.
Annual report, NR §5-1613.
Stop work orders.
Violations.
Issuance for, NR §5-1612.
Variances, NR §5-1611.
Violations of subtitle, NR §5-1612.
Foresters.
General provisions, BOP §§7-101 to 7-602.
See FORESTERS.
Rangers, NR §5-206.
Forest mitigation banks, NR §5-1610.1.
Forest, park and wildlife service.
Established, NR §5-202.
Forestry.
Defined, NR §5-102.1.
Funds.
Fair Hill improvement fund, NR §5-908.
Forest conservation fund, NR §5-1610.
Heritage conservation fund, NR §§5-1501 to 5-1506.
See HERITAGE CONSERVATION FUND.

FORESTS AND PARKS —Cont'd
Funds —Cont'd
  Open spaces and areas. See within this heading,
    "Open spaces and areas."
  Reforestation, NR §5-103.
  Renewable forest resources plan, NR §5-214.
  Reserve fund, NR §5-212.
Gifts.
  Authority to accept, NR §5-207.
  Wildland areas.
    Acceptance of gifts of land or wetlands, NR
    §5-1217.
Girl Scouts.
  Free admission to state parks, NR §5-1008.
Governor.
  Advisory commissions.
    Appointment of members, NR §5-204.
Hart-Miller-Pleasure Island chain.
  Declared open area, NR §5-1202.1.
  Easements to be granted by state, NR §5-1202.2.
Hearings.
  Trails.
    Development of abandoned railroad corridor
    property, NR §5-1010.
  Wildlife areas, NR §§5-1208, 5-1209.
Heritage conservation fund, NR §§5-1501 to
  5-1506.
  See HERITAGE CONSERVATION FUND.
**Highway construction by unit of state or local
  government.**
  Cutting or clearing restrictions, NR §5-103.
Income tax.
  Reforestation and timber stand improvements.
    Rules and regulations relating to income tax
    modifications, NR §5-219.
Injunctions.
  Eminent domain, NR §5-208.
  Forest conservation.
    Violations of subtitle, NR §5-1612.
  Pine tree reforestation.
    Enjoining violations, NR §5-508.
Jurisdiction.
  Transfer to department of natural resources.
    Department of forests and parks, NR §5-201.
  Wildlife areas.
    Jurisdiction of units continued, NR §5-1204.
Land clearing for construction of highways.
  Cutting or clearing restrictions, reforestation, NR
    §5-103.
Liability.
  Cutting, burning or injuring merchantable trees
    or timber, NR §5-409.
  Fires.
    Civil liability for causing fires, NR §5-705.
Licenses.
  Conservancy districts.
    Forest products business, NR §5-608.
  Foresters.
    See FORESTERS.
Local land preservation programs, NR
  §§5-9B-01 to 5-9B-06.
Lost or abandoned property.
  Disposition, NR §5-213.
Maryland conservation corps.
  Established, NR §5-218.
**Maryland-national capital park and planning
  commission.**
  See MARYLAND-NATIONAL CAPITAL PARK
    AND PLANNING COMMISSION.
Matthew Henson state park, NR §5-1004.

FORESTS AND PARKS —Cont'd
Mining.
  Wildland areas.
    Mineral and property rights, NR §5-1203.
Misdemeanors.
  Fires.
    Maliciously setting fires, NR §5-704.
  Railroads.
    Engines to be provided with appliances to
      prevent fire, NR §5-711.
  Violation of title, NR §5-1301.
Motorcycles, NR §5-209.
Municipal corporations.
  Plans.
    Assistance of secretary, NR §5-210.
  Urban and community forestry, NR §§5-424 to
    5-427.
  See URBAN AND COMMUNITY FORESTRY.
Nature conservancy.
  Wildland and open areas.
    Agreements by secretary with nature
      conservancy, NR §5-1222.
    Proposal by nature conservancy, NR §5-1220.
      Action by secretary on proposal, NR §5-1221.
North Point state park, NR §5-1005.
Notices.
  Forest conservation.
    Forest conservation plan.
      Completeness, NR §5-1605.
    Forest stand delineation.
      Correctness and completeness, NR §5-1604.
  Forest fire and trespass law, NR §5-703.
  Open spaces and areas.
    Acquisition projects.
      Annual list of state acquisition projects.
        Notice to be given to legislators prior to
          submission, NR §5-904.
  Railroads.
    Maintenance of safety strip.
      Notice to property owner, NR §5-707.
  Wildlife areas.
    Designation, NR §5-1208.
Nurseries.
  State forest nursery.
    Acquisition of land for establishment, NR
      §5-410.
    Establishment, NR §5-402.
Off-road vehicles, NR §5-209.
Old Fort Frederick reforestation program, NR
  §5-1006.
Open air burning, NR §5-720.
Open spaces and areas.
  Acquisition of interests in real property for
    preservation, NR §5-1202.
  Acquisition projects.
    Annual list of state acquisition projects, NR
      §5-904.
    By local governing body.
      Appropriations to assist, NR §5-903.
    Land in Allegany county, NR §5-910.
    Legislative limitations.
      State parks, NR §5-907.
  Annual list of state acquisition projects.
    Notice to be given to legislators prior to
      submission, NR §5-904.
  Definitions, NR §5-1201.
  Funds.
    Annual report to general assembly.
      Submission by office of planning, NR §5-903.
    Available funds.
      Advance option and purchase fund, NR
        §5-904.

FORESTS AND PARKS —Cont'd
Open spaces and areas —Cont'd
Funds —Cont'd
Available funds —Cont'd
Apportionment.
Committee to prepare and adopt
apportionment formula, NR §5-903.
Baltimore City.
Additional grants, NR §5-903.
Bay access areas fund, NR §5-904.
Expenditure, NR §5-904.
Local governing bodies.
Appropriations to assist, NR §5-903.
State agencies.
Use of half of fund, NR §5-903.
Fair Hill improvement fund, NR §5-908.
Natural resources property maintenance fund,
NR §5-909.
Program open space contingency fund, NR
§5-903.1.
General assembly.
Approval of revisions to plan, NR §5-907.
Hart-Miller-Pleasure Island chain, NR §5-1202.1.
Easement granted by state, NR §5-1202.2.
State to grant easement, NR §5-1202.2.
Intent of legislature, NR §5-902.
Legislative declaration, NR §5-902.
Local governing body.
Appropriations to assist, NR §5-903.
Local projects, NR §5-906.
Nature conservancy.
Agreements by secretary with nature
conservancy, NR §5-1222.
Proposal by nature conservancy.
Action by secretary, NR §5-1221.
Plans.
Legislative limitations, NR §5-907.
Revisions, NR §5-907.
Program open space.
Advance option and purchase fund.
Established, NR §5-904.
Apportionment of funds, NR §5-903.
Capital improvements.
Use of funds for, NR §5-903.
Definitions, NR §5-901.
Designation of program, NR §5-902.
Funds.
Advance option and purchase fund, NR
§5-904.
Allocation, NR §5-903.
Apportionment of funds, NR §5-903.
Bay access areas fund, NR §5-904.
Contingency fund, NR §5-903.1.
Establishment of funding program, NR
§5-902.
Expenditure, NR §5-904.
Governmental agency.
Defined, NR §5-901.
Land trust.
Defined, NR §5-901.
Grants or agreements with, NR §5-903.
Lists.
Preparation of annual list, NR §5-904.
Local projects, NR §5-906.
Compliance with state comprehensive outdoor
recreation and land preservation plan
required, NR §5-906.
Defined, NR §5-901.
Methods of program, NR §5-902.
Municipal corporations.
Defined, NR §5-901.

FORESTS AND PARKS —Cont'd
Open spaces and areas —Cont'd
Program open space —Cont'd
State acquisition projects.
Annual list, NR §5-904.
Notice to be given to legislators prior to
submission, NR §5-903.
Subdivisions.
Defined, NR §5-901.
Targeted areas.
Defined, NR §5-901.
Total project cost.
Defined, NR §5-901.
Program open space contingency fund, NR
§5-903.1.
State comprehensive outdoor recreation and land
preservation plan.
Generally, NR §5-906.
Tax credits, TP §9-208.
Wildland areas. See within this heading,
"Wildland areas."
Park advisory commission, NR §5-204.
Parks and recreation.
General provisions.
See PARKS AND RECREATION.
Patapsco River.
State park.
Between Brooklyn Mud Flats and Liberty
reservoir, NR §5-1003.
Penalties.
Collection, NR §5-1302.
Fires.
Failure to render aid when summoned, NR
§5-701.
Forest conservation.
Noncompliance with subtitle, NR §5-1608.
Violations of subtitle, NR §5-1612.
Violation of title, NR §5-1301.
Forest conservation subtitle, NR §5-1612.
Person.
Defined, NR §5-101.
Pine tree reforestation.
Cutting operation.
Cutting reserved tree in area in which cutting
operation conducted, NR §5-506.
Defined, NR §5-501.
Prerequisites, NR §5-505.
Reserved tree.
Cutting in area in which cutting operation
conducted, NR §5-506.
Definitions, NR §5-501.
Enforcement, NR §5-508.
Exemptions, NR §5-507.
General assembly.
Declaration of policy, NR §5-502.
Injunctions.
Violations, NR §5-508.
Intent of subtitle, NR §5-502.
Person.
Defined, NR §5-501.
Reseeding.
Trees to be left for purposes of reseeding, NR
§5-504.
Rules and regulations, NR §5-503.
Subtitle 13 not applicable, NR §5-509.
Trees to be left for purposes of reseeding, NR
§5-504.
Violations.
Enjoining violations, NR §5-508.
Plan.
Renewable forest resources plan, NR §5-214.

FORESTS AND PARKS —Cont'd

Policy.

Declaration of policy, NR §5-102.

Publication.

Materials relating to forests and parks, NR §5-211.

Public recreation and parks.

General provisions, 25 §§222 to 230.
See PUBLIC RECREATION AND PARKS.

Public recreation on private and local government lands.

General provisions, NR §§5-1101 to 5-1109.
See RECREATIONAL TRESPASS.

Purchases.

Authority to purchase land, NR §5-207.

Railroads.

Boilers.
Appliances to prevent fire, NR §5-711.
Engines to be provided with appliances to prevent fire, NR §5-711.
Fire hazards.
Abatement of hazards, NR §5-707.
Maintenance of safety strips.
Abutting owners.
Duties of persons owning property abutting tracks, NR §5-710.
Clearing parts of right of way, NR §5-707.
Compliance not bar to recovery for damages, NR §5-712.
Damage to property owner.
Prohibited, NR §5-707.
Duty to maintain, NR §5-709.
Failure to maintain safety strips.
Penalty, NR §5-714.
Inconsistent laws repealed, NR §5-713.
Owners of property, NR §5-707.
Right of entry, NR §5-708.
Safety strips.
Maintenance. See within this subheading, "Maintenance of safety strips."
Trails.
Abandoned railroad corridor property as, NR §5-1010.

Rangers.

Foresters, BOP §§7-101 to 7-602.
See FORESTERS.
Forest, park and wildlife rangers, NR §5-206.

Reforestation, NR §5-219.

Forest conservation.
Forest mitigation banks, NR §5-1610.1.
Preferred sequence and priorities, NR §5-1607.
Reforestation ratio, NR §5-1606.
Highway construction by state or local government, NR §5-103.
Old Fort Frederick, NR §5-1006.

Renewable forest resources plan, NR §5-214.

Reports.

Forest conservation.
Annual report, NR §5-1613.
Forest fires, NR §5-704.
Reforestation.
Annual report, NR §5-103.

Reserve fund, NR §5-212.

Reserves.

Auxiliary state forest reserves, NR §5-1007.
Use of trees for planting, NR §5-408.

Right of entry.

Railroads.
Maintenance of safety strips.
Department to have right of entry, NR §5-708.

FORESTS AND PARKS —Cont'd

Roadside trees.

Appropriations.
Tree planting and care, NR §5-411.
Arrest without warrant.
Protection of trees, NR §5-404.
Cutting down.
Permit required, NR §5-406.
Defined, NR §5-401.
Department.
Powers, NR §5-402.
Examinations.
Payment for making examinations, NR §5-405.
Injuring.
Arrest, NR §5-404.
Prohibited, NR §5-406.
Levies.
Tree planting and care, NR §5-411.
Mutilating.
Prohibited, NR §5-406.
Nurseries.
State forest nursery.
Acquisition of land, NR §5-410.
Establishment, NR §5-402.
Permits.
Cutting down or trimming trees, NR §5-406.
Plans for planting or care, NR §5-403.
Wardens.
Examination of planting.
Payment for examination, NR §5-405.
Planting.
Plans, NR §5-403.
Rules and regulations.
Promulgation, NR §5-402.
Signs.
Affixing to trees without permission, NR §5-407.
State forest reserve.
Use of trees for planting, NR §5-408.
Trimming, NR §5-406.
Wardens.
Payment for making examinations, NR §5-405.
Police powers, NR §5-404.

Rules and regulations.

Conservancy districts.
Promulgation, NR §5-604.
Enforcement, NR §5-209.
Forest conservation.
Adoption, NR §5-1609.
Off-road vehicles, NR §5-209.
Pine tree reforestation, NR §5-503.
Posting, NR §5-209.
Promulgation.
Department of natural resources, NR §5-209.
Reforestation and timber stand improvements, NR §5-219.
Roadside trees, NR §5-402.
Woodland incentives program.
Adoption of regulations, NR §5-303.

Rural legacy program, NR §§5-9A-01 to 5-9A-09.
See RURAL LEGACY PROGRAM.

Sewers and sewage.

Disposal of raw sludge sewage on certain state land, NR §5-217.

Signs.

Roadside trees.
Placing on without permission, NR §5-407.

Snowmobiles, NR §5-209.

South Mountain battlefield.

Civil War state battlefield, NR §5-1801.

State board of foresters.

See FORESTERS.

FORESTS AND PARKS —Cont'd
State's attorneys.
  Fires.
    Enforcement of subtitle, NR §5-706.
Taxation.
  Income tax, NR §5-219.
  Open space or open area.
    Tax credit on land determined to be, TP §9-208.
  Woodland areas.
    Assessments, TP §8-211.
Timber stand improvements, NR §5-219.
Trails.
  Abandoned railroad corridor property as, NR
    §5-1010.
  Appalachian trail, NR §5-1001.
Transportation.
  Christmas trees and evergreen shrubs.
    General provisions, NR §§5-412 to 5-414.
      See CHRISTMAS TREES AND SHRUBS.
Tree experts.
  General provisions, NR §§5-415 to 5-423.
    See TREE EXPERTS.
Trespass.
  Notice as to trespass law, NR §5-703.
Urban and community forestry, NR §§5-424 to
  5-427.
    See URBAN AND COMMUNITY FORESTRY.
Violation of title.
  Fines, NR §5-1301.
    Collection, NR §5-1302.
Wardens.
  Appointment, NR §5-206.
  Duties.
    Generally, NR §5-206.
  Forest, parks and wildlife rangers.
    Commissioned as, NR §5-206.
    Powers and duties as, NR §5-206.
  Powers.
    Generally, NR §5-206.
    Issuance of citations to minors for alcoholic
      beverages violations, CR §10-119.
  Roadside trees.
    Arrest for injury, NR §5-404.
  State boundary monuments.
    Enforcement of subtitle, NR §2-405.
  Terms of office, NR §5-206.
Wildland areas.
  Acquiring privately owned property.
    Not without consent of owner, NR §5-1218.
    Within perimeter of designated areas, NR
      §5-1216.
  Adjustment of boundaries, NR §5-1209.
  Administration.
    Responsibility of unit, NR §5-1211.
  Appropriations.
    Limitation upon, NR §5-1204.
  Bear Pen wildland.
    Description, NR §5-1203.
  Belt Woods wildland, NR §5-1203.
  Big Savage/Little Savage wildland.
    Description, NR §5-1203.
  Big Savage mountain wildland.
    Description, NR §5-1203.
  Black Marsh wildland.
    Description, NR §5-1203.
  Boundaries.
    Adjustment, NR §5-1209.
  Boundary roadways.
    Maintenance and improvement, NR §5-1203.
  Calvert Cliffs wildland.
    Description, NR §5-1203.

FORESTS AND PARKS —Cont'd
Wildland areas —Cont'd
  Cedar Island wildland.
    Description, NR §5-1203.
  Cunningham Falls state park wildlands, NR
    §5-1203.
  Cypress Swamp wildland.
    Description, NR §5-1203.
  Declaration of policy, NR §5-1203.
  Deep Run wildland.
    Description, NR §5-1203.
  Definitions, NR §5-1201.
  Designation.
    Certain state owned roadless areas and islands.
      Wildlife refuges and public hunting areas, NR
        §5-1206.
    Generally, NR §5-1205.
    Hearings, NR §5-1208.
    Notice, NR §5-1208.
  Development of resources and facilities, NR
    §5-1214.
  Devoted to public purposes, NR §5-1211.
  Facilities.
    Development, NR §5-1214.
  Fire.
    Control, NR §5-1213.
      Measures to protect nearby private land, NR
        §5-1213.1.
  Gifts.
    Acceptance of land or wetlands, NR §5-1217.
  Gunpowder Falls wildland.
    Description, NR §5-1203.
  Idylwild wildland, NR §5-1203.
  Insects and diseases.
    Control, NR §5-1213.
      Measures to protect nearby private land, NR
        §5-1213.1.
  Islands of the Potomac Wildland, NR §5-1203.
  Jurisdiction of units continued, NR §5-1204.
  Maple Run wildland.
    Description, NR §5-1203.
  Mattawoman wildland.
    Description, NR §5-1203.
  Middle Fork wildland.
    Description, NR §5-1203.
  Mineral and property rights, NR §5-1203.
  Mingo Branch/Bush Cabin Run Wildland, NR
    §5-1203.
  Morgan Run wildland.
    Description, NR §5-1203.
  Motorboats.
    When permitted, NR §5-1213.
  Nature conservancy.
    Agreements with nature conservancy by
      secretary, NR §5-1222.
    Proposal by nature conservancy, NR §5-1220.
      Action by secretary, NR §5-1221.
  Nearby private land.
    Measures to protect, NR §5-1213.1.
  Open spaces and areas.
    General provisions. See within this heading,
      "Open spaces and areas."
  Panther Branch wildland.
    Description, NR §5-1203.
  Patuxent river wildland.
    Description, NR §5-1203.
  Pocomoke river wildland.
    Description, NR §5-1203.
  Policy.
    Declaration, NR §5-1203.
  Potomac Bends wildland, NR §5-1203.

FORESTS AND PARKS —Cont'd
Wildland areas —Cont'd
Property rights, NR §5-1203.
Resources.
    Development, NR §5-1214.
Responsibility of units for administering areas,
    NR §5-1211.
Restriction on certain uses, NR §5-1212.
    Areas open to activities prior to wildlands
        designation, NR §5-1212.1.
Rocky Gap wildland.
    Restriction, NR §5-1203.
St. Mary's river wildland.
    Description, NR §5-1203.
Savage Ravines wildland, NR §5-1203.
Secretary of natural resources.
    Action by secretary, NR §5-1221.
    Agreements by secretary, NR §5-1222.
Sideling hill wildland.
    Description, NR §5-1203.
Soldiers' Delight wildland.
    Description, NR §5-1203.
South Savage wildland, NR §5-1203.
State forest.
    Effect upon, NR §5-1210.
State parks and wildlife refuge system.
    Effect upon, NR §5-1210.
State wildlands preservation system.
    Establishment, NR §5-1203.
Surrounded areas.
    Access rights of owners, NR §5-1215.
    Acquisition of privately owned lands, NR
        §5-1216.
Sweathouse Branch wildland.
    Description, NR §5-1203.
Woodland incentives program.
Approved practice.
    Defined, NR §5-301.
Cost-share assistance.
    Agreement, NR §5-306.
    Amount, NR §5-305.
    Applicants.
        Requirements, NR §5-304.
    Defined, NR §5-301.
    Limitations, NR §5-305.
    Requirement of applicants, NR §5-304.
Declaration.
    Legislative declaration, NR §5-302.
Definitions, NR §5-301.
Findings.
    Legislative findings, NR §5-302.
Funds.
    Woodland incentives fund, NR §5-307.
        Defined, NR §5-301.
Landowners.
    Eligible landowners.
        Cost-share assistance.
            Agreement required, NR §5-306.
        Defined, NR §5-301.
        Incentives to, NR §5-302.
Legislative declaration and findings, NR §5-302.
Programs.
    Development of programs.
        Duty, NR §5-303.
Regulations, NR §5-303.
Youth groups.
Free admission to state parks for certain groups,
    NR §5-1008.

FORFEITURES.
Bail bonds, Crim Rule 4-217.
Beneficial owners' interests.
    Failure to contribute, CA §12-301.

FORFEITURES —Cont'd
Business trusts.
Forfeiture of right to do business, CA §§12-801 to
    12-810.
Cable television service, interference with.
Devices used, CR §7-303.
Campaign finance reports.
Failure to file report, salary forfeited, EL §13-334.
Controlled dangerous substances.
Generally, CP §§12-101 to 12-505.
    See DRUG ASSET FORFEITURE.
Manufacturers, dispensers or distributors.
    Suspension or revocation of registration, CR
        §5-309.
Criminal forfeiture.
Cable television service, interference with.
    Devices used, CR §7-303.
Drug trafficking crimes.
    Firearms, CR §5-621.
    Generally, CP §§12-101 to 12-505.
        See DRUG ASSET FORFEITURE.
Interference with emergency communication.
    Two way radio and related equipment used in
        violation, CR §9-601.
Recorded devices.
    Unauthorized recording of sounds or images, CR
        §7-309.
Remission, CP §1-207.
Telecommunications services theft.
    Unlawful devices, CR §7-316.
Drug trafficking crimes.
Firearms, CR §5-621.
Generally, CP §§12-101 to 12-505.
    See DRUG ASSET FORFEITURE.
Enforcement of money judgments.
Criminal rules, Crim Rule 4-354.
Explosions and explosives.
Forfeiture of vehicle for violations, CP §13-301.
Fines.
General provisions.
    See FINES.
Firearms.
Drug trafficking crimes, CR §5-621.
Handgun forfeitures, CP §§13-201 to 13-206.
Seizure of firearms sold, rented or transferred in
    violation, PS §5-135.
Fireworks.
Possession, sale or permit violations, PS §10-111.
Gambling forfeitures, CP §§13-101 to 13-109.
See GAMBLING FORFEITURES.
Governor.
Remission.
    Powers of governor, MD Const Art II §20.
Handgun forfeitures, CP §§13-201 to 13-206.
Interference with emergency communication.
Two way radio and related equipment used in
    violation, CR §9-601.
Money.
Expressed in dollars and cents, CJ §11-101.
Nonprofit health service plans.
Violations by officers, directors or employees, IN
    §14-139.
Paint.
Antifouling paints, AG §5-905.
Penalties.
See PENALTIES.
Public service commission.
Action to recover, PUC §2-117.
Receivers.
Compensation forfeited upon removal of receiver,
    Receivers Rule 13-703.

FORFEITURES —Cont'd
Receivers and assignees or trustees for creditors.
  Conflicts of interest.
    Failure to disclose required information.
      Compensation may be forfeited, Receivers Rule 13-302.
  Reports.
    Failure to file.
      Forfeiture of commission, Receivers Rule 13-501.
Recorded devices.
  Unauthorized recording of sounds or images, CR §7-309.
Remission of forfeiture, CP §1-207.
Sentencing.
  Enforcement of money judgments, Crim Rule 4-354.
Spam, CR §3-805.1.
Telecommunications services theft.
  Unlawful devices, CR §7-316.
Tobacco manufacturers.
  Escrow act compliance.
    Violations, BR §§16-507, 16-508.
Vessels and boats.
  Antifouling paints, AG §5-905.
  Concealed number, name or home port designation.
    Operating vessel with, NR §8-713.1.
Weapons.
  Drug trafficking crimes.
    Firearms, CR §5-621.
Wiretapping.
  Devices for interception, CJ §10-404.

FORGERY, CR §§8-601 to 8-613.
See COUNTERFEITING AND FORGERY.

FOR-HIRE DRIVING SERVICES, PUC §§10-101 to 10-112.
Baltimore City.
  Driver's license.
    Required course, PUC §10-104.
County or municipal corporations power to license taxicab drivers, PUC §10-103.
Definitions, PUC §10-101.
Driver's license.
  Application, PUC §10-104.
  Baltimore City.
    Required course, PUC §10-104.
  County or municipal corporation power to license, PUC §10-103.
  Criminal record and driving record check, PUC §10-104.
  Defacing, removing or obliterating official entry, PUC §10-108.
  Defined, PUC §10-101.
  Denial, PUC §§10-104, 10-105.
  Hearing on denial, PUC §10-105.
  Issuance, PUC §10-104.
  Judicial review when license suspended or revoked, PUC §10-110.
  License hearing officer, PUC §10-110.
  Operating without license, PUC §§10-401, 10-402.
  Possession whenever operating vehicle for hire, PUC §10-108.
  Rehearing when suspended or revoked or civil penalty imposed, PUC §10-110.
  Renewal, PUC §10-106.
  Required to operate motor vehicle for hire in state, PUC §10-103.
  Temporary license and badge, PUC §10-107.

FOR-HIRE DRIVING SERVICES —Cont'd
Driver's license —Cont'd
  Term of license, PUC §10-106.
Enforcement fund, PUC §10-112.
Fines for violations, PUC §13-206.
Funding of provisions, PUC §10-111.
Hearings involving violations.
  License hearing officer, PUC §10-110.
Judicial review when license or permit suspended or revoked or civil penalty imposed, PUC §10-110.
License hearing officer, PUC §10-110.
Misdemeanors.
  Fines for violations, PUC §13-206.
Motor vehicles subject to provisions, PUC §10-102.
Operating without license, PUC §§10-401, 10-402.
Permits.
  Assessments.
    Enforcement fund, PUC §10-112.
Political subdivisions.
  Power to adopt reasonable traffic regulations, PUC §10-102.
Public service commission.
  Generally, PUC §§2-101 to 5-106.
  See PUBLIC SERVICE COMMISSION.
Rehearing when license or permit suspended or revoked, PUC §10-110.
Scope of provisions, PUC §10-102.
Staffing employed to implement responsibilities, PUC §10-111.
Supplementation of other laws relating to operation and licensing of motor vehicles, PUC §10-102.
Temporary license and badge, PUC §10-107.
Toll highways or bridges.
  Passengers electing to use route, assessment of charges to passenger, PUC §10-109.
Transportation of person for hire.
  Defined, PUC §1-101.

FORMER JEOPARDY, US Const Amd 5.
See JEOPARDY.

FORMS.
Acknowledgments, RP §4-204.
Administration of courts.
  Interrogatories.
    Domestic relations definitions, Interrogatories Form 4.
    Domestic relations interrogatories, Interrogatories Form 5.
    General definitions, Interrogatories Form 2.
    General interrogatories, Interrogatories Form 3.
    Instructions, Interrogatories Form 1.
    Motor vehicle tort definitions, Interrogatories Form 6.
    Motor vehicle tort interrogatories, Interrogatories Form 7.
    Personal injury interrogatories, Interrogatories Form 8.
    Products liability, Interrogatories Forms 9, 10.
Administrative procedure act.
  Forms management, SG §§10-604 to 10-608.
  See ADMINISTRATIVE PROCEDURE.
Adoption.
  Consent of parent to adoption, FamLaw Rule 9-102.
Affidavits, Rule 1-304.
Anatomical gift act.
  Gift by living donor, ET §4-505.

FORMS —Cont'd

Appeals.
Court papers, AppRev Rule 8-112.
Order for appeal, Form 22.

Appendix of forms.
Discretionary nature, Rule 1-302.

Arrest.
Design by district court judges, CJ §1-605.

Attorneys at law.
Court papers.
Designation, Rule 1-301.

Bail bonds, Crim Rule 4-217.
Conditions of bond, Form 4-217.2.
Declaration of trust of real estate to secure
performance of bail bond, Form 4-217.1.

Bank holding companies.
Applications, notices and reports, FI §5-904.

Bicycles.
Certificates of title, TR §13-107.

Caption.
Court papers, Rule 1-301.

Clerks of court.
Recordation.
Typed or printed, RP §3-104.

Collective bargaining.
Petition for consent election, LE §4-207.

Condominiums.
Notices.
Conversion to condominium, RP §11-102.1.

Consent to medical care for minor.
Relative providing kinship care, HG §20-105.

Constitution of Maryland.
Public commissions, grants, writs, process and
indictments, MD Const Art IV §13.

Cooperative housing corporations.
Residential rental facility.
Facility acquired or owned by cooperative
housing corporation.
Notice to tenants, CA §5-6B-05.

Court papers generally, Rule 1-301.

Credit services businesses.
Consumer contracts.
Cancellation of contracts.
Notice, CL §14-1906.

Death penalty.
Findings and sentencing determinations, Crim
Rule 4-343.

Decedents' estates.
Surviving spouse.
Elective share, ET §3-207.
Extension of time for making election, Estates
Rule 6-411.
Form of election, Estates Rule 6-411.
Verification, Estates Rule 6-123; ET §1-102.

Deed of trust, RP §4-202.

Deeds, RP §4-202.
Assignment.
Mortgage, RP §4-203.
Covenants.
Limitations and restrictions.
Conditions, RP §4-201.
Release of mortgage or deed of trust, RP §4-203.
Sufficient for purpose intended, RP §4-201.

**Discretionary nature of forms contained in
appendix,** Rule 1-302.

Dishonored checks and other instruments.
Notice of dishonored check, CL §15-803.

Distress for rent.
Petition, RP §8-303.

Divorce.
Joint statements of marital and non-marital
property, FamLaw Rule 9-207.

FORMS —Cont'd

Documents of title.
Warehouse receipts, CL §7-202.

Election of rights and remedies.
Surviving spouse.
Rights in decedent's estate, ET §3-207.

Employment agencies.
Agency recordkeeping, BR §9-303.

Environmental covenants.
Notice of covenant, amendment or termination
filed in land records, EN §1-811.

Executors and administrators.
Bonds, surety, ET §6-102.
Closing estates.
Personal representative.
Acceptance and consent, Estates Rule 6-342.
Creditor's claim.
Manner of presentation, ET §8-104.
Deeds.
Personal representative's deed, RP §4-202.
Letters of administration, ET §6-104.
Notice of appointment, ET §7-103.
Opening estates.
Appointment of personal representative.
Administrative probate order, Estates Rule
6-321.
Letters of administration, Estates Rule 6-322.
List of interested persons, Estates Rule 6-316.
Notice to interested persons, Estates Rule
6-317.
Personal representative.
Bond, Estates Rule 6-312.
Consent to appointment of personal
representative, Estates Rule 6-313.
Petition for probate, Estates Rule 6-301.
Modification, Estates Rule 6-301.
Notice of appointment, Estates Rule 6-311.
Notice of judicial probate, Estates Rule 6-302.
Resident agent.
Appointment of resident agent, Estates Rule
6-315.
Settlement of decedents' estates.
Application to fix inheritance tax on
non-probate assets, Estates Rule 6-405.
Appraisal of inventory, Estates Rule 6-403.
Attorneys' fees.
Notice of petition for attorneys' fees, Estates
Rule 6-416.
Caption of case, Estates Rule 6-121.
Commission of personal representative.
Notice of petition for personal representative's
commissions, Estates Rule 6-416.
Debts and claims.
Disallowance of claim, Estates Rule 6-413.
Presentation of claim, Estates Rule 6-413; ET
§8-104.
Funeral expenses.
Petition and order for funeral expenses,
Estates Rule 6-415.
Information report, Estates Rule 6-404.
Inheritance tax on non-probate assets.
Application to fix inheritance tax, Estates
Rule 6-405.
Inventory, Estates Rule 6-402.
Nonresidents.
Foreign personal representatives.
Application to set inheritance tax, Estates
Rule 6-501.
Notice of appointment of foreign personal
representative, Estates Rule 6-501.

FORMS —Cont'd
Executors and administrators —Cont'd
Settlement of decedents' estates —Cont'd
Notices.
Form of waiver, Estates Rule 6-126.
Service of process.
Certificate of service, Estates Rule 6-125.
Proof of service, Estates Rule 6-125.
Waiver.
Notices, Estates Rule 6-126.
Wills.
Proof of execution of will, Estates Rule 6-152.
Small estates.
Appointment.
Notice of appointment, Estates Rule 6-209.
Interested persons.
Notice to interested persons, Estates Rule
6-210.
Letters of administration, Estates Rule 6-207.
Personal representative.
Consent to appointment of personal
representative, Estates Rule 6-203.
Substitution of personal representative.
Consent to appointment of personal
representative, Estates Rule 6-203.
Petition for administration, Estates Rule 6-201.
List of interested persons, Estates Rule 6-202.
Register's order, Estates Rule 6-208.
Resident agent.
Appointment, Estates Rule 6-205.
Expungement of records.
Application for expungement of police record,
Form 4-503.3.
Certificate of compliance, Form 4-508.3.
Criminal charge transferred to juvenile court, Juv
Rule 11-601.
General waiver and release, Form 4-503.2.
Notice.
Hearing, Form 4-503.4.
Release from detention or confinement without
charge.
Request for expungement, Form 4-503.1.
Order for expungement of records, Forms 4-508.1,
4-508.2.
Petition for expungement of records, Form
4-504.1.
Probation or stet disposition, Form 4-504.2.
Service of order and compliance form, Crim Rule
4-508.
Fee simple deeds, RP §4-202.
Fire insurance antiarson applications, IN
§19-305.
Forms management.
Administrative procedure act, SG §§10-604 to
10-608.
See ADMINISTRATIVE PROCEDURE.
Grants, RP §4-202.
Grievance procedures, SPP §12-108.
Health care decisions.
Advance directive, HG §5-603.
Information sheet, HG §5-615.
Patient's plan of care, HG §5-608.1.
Health maintenance organizations.
Uniform claims forms, HO §1-208.
Uniform consultation referral form, HG §19-713.5.
Home solicitation sales.
Door-to-door solicitations act.
Pledge form, CL §14-2603.
Hospitals.
Notice of discharge or transfer of resident, HG
§19-345.1.

FORMS —Cont'd
Husband and wife.
Acknowledgments, RP §4-204.
Income tax.
Similarity of state and federal forms, TG §2-104.
Insurance.
Adjuster license applications, IN §10-405.
Adviser agreements, IN §10-215.
Fire insurance antiarson applications, IN §19-305.
Health insurance.
Claim forms, IN §15-212.
Uniform claims forms, HO §1-208.
Copies to be available to enrollees, IN §15-127.
Preparation fees, IN §15-127.
Referral forms, IN §§15-119, 15-120.
Uniform claims forms, IN §§15-1002 to 15-1004.
Premium finance companies.
Registration form, IN §23-209.
Juvenile causes.
Adjudication.
Order of adjudication, Form 914-O/A.
Attachment.
Writ of attachment, Form 904-WA.
Commitment.
Order, Form 915-O/CJ.
Order rescinding commitment and for aftercare
supervision, Form 916-O/RCAS.
Petition for revocation of probation and
commitment of delinquent child, Form
916-P/RPC.
Petition for revocation of protective supervision
and for commitment, Form 916-P/RPSC.
Delinquent child.
Order, Form 915-O/PDC.
Termination of probation or protective
supervision, Form 916-O/TPPS.
Petition for revocation of probation and
commitment of delinquent child, Form
916-P/RPC.
Emergency detention or shelter care.
Authorization, Form 912-A.
Continued detention or shelter care.
Order, Form 912-O/CDSC.
Notice, Form 912-N.
Judgments.
Restitution.
Order for judgment of restitution, Form
918-O/JR.
Petitions, Form 903-P/C.
Adults, Form 903-P/A.
Physical and mental examination of respondent.
Order, Form 905-OE.
Probation.
Adult.
Order, Form 915-O/PA.
Protective supervision.
Order, Form 915-O/PS.
Order terminating probation or protective
supervision, Form 916-O/TPPS.
Petition for revocation of protective supervision
and for commitment, Form 916-P/RPSC.
Recognizance of parent, guardian or custodian,
Form 904-R.
Restitution.
Order for judgment of restitution, Form
918-O/JR.
Show cause order, Form 916-SCO.
Subpoenas.
Request for witness subpoena, Form 904-R/WS.
Summons, Form 904-S.

FORMS —Cont'd
Juvenile causes —Cont'd
  Supervision.
    Order rescinding commitment and for aftercare
      supervision, Form 916-O/RCAS.
  Support.
    Order for support, Form 918-O/S.
  Termination of proceedings.
    Final order, Form 920-FOT.
  Waiver of juvenile jurisdiction.
    Order, Form 913-O/W.
    Petition, Form 913-P/W.
Land installment contracts.
  General provisions, RP §10-102.
Landlord and tenant.
  Lease, RP §4-202.
Life estate deeds, RP §4-202.
Marriage.
  License and certificates, FL §2-403.
Migrant labor.
  License applications.
    Availability of forms, LE §7-302.
  Responsibilities of farm labor contractors.
    Disclosures to migrant agricultural workers, LE
      §7-401.
Mortgages and deeds of trust.
  Assignment of mortgage, RP §4-203.
  Certificate of partial satisfaction or partial
    release, RP §4-203.
  Certificate of satisfaction, RP §4-203.
  Deed of trust to secure debts for other purposes,
    RP §4-202.
  Mortgage of property, RP §4-202.
  Release, RP §4-203.
    Affidavit of release, RP §4-203.
    Certificate of partial satisfaction or partial
      release, RP §4-203.
  Secondary mortgage loans.
    Commissioner to develop form, CL §12-407.1.
    Required explanation of forfeiture of rights, CL
      §12-407.1.
Motor clubs.
  Licenses.
    Approval of applicant or licensee forms, IN
      §26-103.
Motor vehicles.
  Accident report forms, TR §20-113.
  Administration.
    Preparing and providing, TR §12-105.
  Continuation, TR §12-119.
  Exclusion or modification of implied warranties,
    TR §13-119.
  Security interests.
    Prepared and provided by administration, TR
      §12-105.
New trial.
  Motion for new trial, Crim Rule 4-331.
Oaths, Rule 1-303.
Officers.
  Oath of office, 1 §10; MD Const Art I §9.
Order for appeal, Form 22.
Parties.
  Court papers, Rule 1-301.
Partition.
  Commissioner's deed, RP §4-202.
Peace orders.
  District Court form, CivProDist Rule 3-731.
Permits.
  Consolidated procedures for development permits.
    State master application form.
      Appendices to form, SG §11-404.

FORMS —Cont'd
Permits —Cont'd
  Consolidated procedures for development permits
    —Cont'd
    State master application form —Cont'd
      Development and use, SG §11-402.
      Specifications for form, SG §11-403.
Petition for peace order.
  District Court form, CivProDist Rule 3-731.
Pleadings.
  Circuit courts, CivProCir Rule 2-303.
  District Court, CivProDist Rule 3-303.
Premium finance company.
  Registration form, IN §23-203.
Preneed burial contracts.
  Trust accounts, BR §5-706.
Products liability.
  Interrogatories, Interrogatories Forms 9, 10.
Release of mortgage or deed of trust, RP §4-203.
Rental-purchase agreements, CL §12-1111.
Secondary mortgage loan law, CL §12-407.1.
Secured transactions.
  Defaults.
    Disposition of collateral after.
      Consumer goods transactions.
        Notification, CL §9-614.
      Notification, CL §9-613.
  Financing statements.
    Amendment form, CL §9-521.
    Initial financing statement form, CL §9-521.
Securities.
  Transfer-on-death registration, ET §16-110.
Sentence and punishment.
  Death penalty.
    Written findings and determination, Crim Rule
      4-343.
Sentencing.
  Review of sentence.
    Application, Crim Rule 4-344.
Sheriffs.
  Deeds, RP §4-202.
Small claim actions.
  District Court, CivProDist Rule 3-701.
State contracts.
  Commercial discrimination.
    Nondiscrimination clause in public contracts,
      SF §19-114.
    Required language in all state contracts, SF
      §19-116.
Subpoenas.
  Circuit courts, CivProCir Rule 2-510.
  Criminal rules, Crim Rule 4-266.
  District Court, CivProDist Rule 3-510.
Summary judgment.
  Affidavits.
    Circuit courts, CivProCir Rule 2-501.
Taxation, TG §2-104.
  Clubs.
    Country clubs, TP §8-218.
  Redemption.
    Foreclosure of right of redemption.
      Order of publication, TP §14-840.
  Tax sale.
    Certificate of sale, TP §14-820.
    Notice, TP §14-812.
Titling.
  Court papers, Rule 1-301.
Trial.
  Subpoenas.
    Circuit courts, CivProCir Rule 2-510.

FORMS —Cont'd
Trusts and trustees.
  Discretionary trusts.
    Creation, ET §14-407.
  Trustee's deed under decree, RP §4-202.
Viatical settlement contracts.
  Disclosure statement, IN §8-606.
Warehouse receipts, CL §7-202.
Warrants.
  Robbery, CR §3-404.
Warranty.
  Motor vehicles.
    Form for exclusion or modification of implied
      warranties, TR §13-119.
  New home warranties.
    Notice to purchaser of home covered by
      warranty, RP §10-605.
Wills.
  Notice or request for judicial probate, ET §5-403.
  Petition for probate, ET §5-206.
Workers' compensation.
  Certificate of compliance.
    Application forms, LE §9-105.
  Claims procedure, LE §9-703.
  Injured workers' insurance fund.
    Insurance program.
      Schedule of premium rates, LE §10-130.
Writs and process, MD Const Art IV §13.

FORMS MANAGEMENT.
Administrative procedure act, SG §§10-604 to
  10-608.
See ADMINISTRATIVE PROCEDURE.

FORT RITCHIE.
Development.
  Penmar development corporation, 83A §§5-1201 to
    5-1210.
    See PENMAR DEVELOPMENT
      CORPORATION.

FORTUNE-TELLERS.
Licenses.
  Calvert county, 24 §11-403.

FORUM FOR RURAL MARYLAND, 41 §§15-101
  to 15-110.
See RURAL MARYLAND COUNCIL.

FOSTER CARE.
Administrative review, FL §5-525.
Adoption, FL §5-525.1.
  Support by department, FL §5-530.
Criminal background investigations for
  employees.
  Foster care family homes or group facilities.
    Facilities requiring investigation, FL §5-561.
Damages.
  Reimbursement for damages, 83C §2-131.
Defined, 83C §2-131; FL §5-501.
Developmentally disabled child.
  Voluntary placement, FL §5-525.
Duties of local department, FL §5-525.
Educational programs in private residential
  institutions, 83C §2-137.
Foster care family homes.
  Criminal background investigations for employees.
    Facilities requiring investigation, FL §5-561.
Funeral expenses.
  Payment, FL §5-531.
Group homes and institutions.
  Criminal background investigations for employees.
    Facilities requiring investigation, FL §5-561.

FOSTER CARE —Cont'd
Group homes and institutions —Cont'd
  Provision of services through, FL §5-526.
Hearings.
  Contesting of placement with adoptive family, FL
    §5-525.
Insurance.
  Liability insurance, 83C §2-131; FL §5-529.
Juvenile services.
  Liability insurance, 83C §2-131.
  Reimbursement for injury or property damage,
    83C §2-131.
Local review boards, FL §§5-540 to 5-545.
Medical costs.
  Reimbursement, FL §5-528.
Mentally ill child.
  Voluntary placement, FL §5-525.
Out-of-home placement, FL §5-525.
  Defined, FL §5-501.
  Establishment of program, FL §5-525.
  Local boards of review for minor children in
    out-of-home placement, FL §§5-540 to 5-545.
Permanency plan, FL §5-525.
Rates, FL §5-527.
Reimbursement for costs, 83C §2-131.
Reimbursement for loss to foster parents, FL
  §5-529.
Reimbursement for medical costs, FL §5-528.
Review boards.
  Local review boards, FL §§5-540 to 5-545.
Rights of foster parents, FL §5-504.
Rules and regulations, FL §5-532.
State review board, FL §§5-534 to 5-539.
Tuition at public institution of higher
  education.
  Recipient exempt from paying, ED §15-106.1.
Visitation.
  Sibling visitation rights, FL §5-525.2.
Voluntary placement.
  Custody of child with developmental disability or
    mental illness, FL §5-525.

FOUNDATIONS.
Organizational names and insignia.
  Registration, prohibited acts, BR §§19-201 to
    19-207.
Private foundations.
  Administration of trusts, ET §§14-303 to 14-307.
    See TRUSTS AND TRUSTEES.
  General provisions.
    See PRIVATE FOUNDATIONS.

FOWL.
Birds and game.
  General provisions.
    See BIRDS AND GAME.

FOXES.
Bounties.
  Killing.
    Counties, 25 §2.
Damaging or destroying property.
  Hunting or trapping permitted, NR §10-406.
Dangerous animals.
  Importing, selling, or trading in, CR §10-621.
Dorchester county.
  Open season all year, NR §10-406.
Sundays and holidays.
  Chasing on Sundays, NR §10-410.

FOXHUNTING.
Exception to hunting license requirement, NR
  §10-301.

FRANCHISES.
Advertising.
  Franchise offerings, BR §14-225.
Alcoholic beverages.
  Beer distributors, 2B §§17-101 to 17-107.
    See ALCOHOLIC BEVERAGES.
Applicability of act, BR §14-203.
Attorney general.
  Notified when unconstitutionality of franchise
    alleged, CJ §3-405.
Bonds, surety.
  Registration.
    Escrow requirements, BR §14-217.
Business opportunities.
  General provisions, BR §§14-101 to 14-129.
    See START-UP BUSINESS VENTURES.
Citation of title, BR §14-233.
Commissioner.
  Cease and desist orders, BR §14-210.
  Criminal proceedings authorized, BR §14-211.
  Defined, BR §14-201.
  Delegation of powers and duties, BR §14-205.
  Enforcement powers.
    Delegation, BR §14-205.
  Interpretive opinions, BR §14-209.
  Investigations, BR §14-208.
    Enforcement powers, BR §14-212.
  Publication of information, BR §14-207.
  Registration generally. See within this heading,
    "Registration."
  Rulemaking authority, BR §14-206.
Conflict of laws.
  Act in addition to other law, BR §14-204.
Contracts and documents.
  Action to recover damages, BR §14-227.
  Copies to franchisees, BR §14-223.
  Failure to notify of material change, BR §14-232.
  Omissions of material fact, BR §14-229.
    Applications, notices or reports, BR §14-231.
    Prospectus offering or amendment, BR §14-230.
  Release from liability as condition of sale, BR
    §14-226.
  Remedies for violation, BR §14-227.
  Untrue statements, BR §14-229.
    Applications, notices or reports, BR §14-231.
    Prospectus offering or amendment, BR §14-230.
Corporations.
  Franchise tax.
    See TAXATION.
Counties.
  Chartered counties, 25A §5.
    Power to displace or limit competition, 25A §5A.
  Code counties.
    Power to displace or limit competition, 25B
      §13B.
  Community antenna television systems, 25 §3C.
  Powers of county commissioners, 25 §§3, 3D.
Declaratory judgments.
  Construction or validity, CJ §3-406.
Definitions, BR §14-201.
Election franchise, MD Const Art I §§1 to 12.
Environmental service.
  Acquisition, NR §3-104.
Fees, registration.
  Application fee, BR §14-215.
  Application for amendment to registration, BR
    §14-220.
  Claims of exemption, BR §14-214.
  Interpretive opinions, BR §14-209.
  Renewal fee, BR §14-219.

FRANCHISES —Cont'd
Financial statements.
  Prospectus offerings, BR §14-216.
Fraud or deceit, BR §14-229.
Insurance for employees, IN §15-1102.
Legislative policy, BR §14-202.
Multilevel distribution companies.
  General provisions, BR §§14-301 to 14-305.
    See MULTILEVEL DISTRIBUTION
      COMPANIES.
Municipal corporations.
  General provisions, 23A §§2, 2A.
  Restrictions imposed on transfer or sale, CA
    §3-102.
Penalties.
  Fraud or deceit, BR §14-229.
    Applications, notices or reports, BR §14-231.
    Prospectus offering or amendment, BR §14-230.
  Registration.
    Failure to notify of material change, BR
      §14-232.
    Offer or sale of franchise without registration,
      BR §14-228.
Prospectus offerings.
  Contents, BR §14-216.
  Copies to franchisees, BR §14-223.
  False or misleading statement, BR §14-230.
Public policy, BR §14-202.
Public service companies.
  Abandoning or discontinuing franchise, right or
    permit, PUC §5-103.
  Commission authorization required, PUC
    §5-202.
  Authority to exercise, documents required, PUC
    §5-201.
  Capitalization, PUC §6-103.
  Continuation of service granted under franchise,
    right or permit.
    Public service commission ordering company,
      PUC §5-103.
  Taxation.
    Public service company franchise tax, TG
      §§2-1201, 8-401 to 8-417.
      See PUBLIC SERVICE COMPANY
        FRANCHISE TAX.
Records.
  Requirements, BR §14-224.
Registration.
  Amendments to registration, BR §14-220.
    Failure to notify of material change, BR
      §14-232.
  Applications.
    Alternative application, BR §14-215.
    Amendments to registration, BR §14-220.
    Prospectus, BR §14-216.
    Renewal, BR §14-219.
    Signature and verification required, BR
      §14-215.
    Untrue statements or omissions of material
      fact, BR §14-231.
  Claims of exemption, BR §14-214.
  Effective date, BR §14-218.
  Escrow requirements, BR §14-217.
  Exemptions from requirement, BR §14-214.
  Fees. See within this heading, "Fees, registration."
  Issuance, BR §14-218.
    Renewal, BR §14-219.
    Stop orders, BR §14-221.
  Offer or sale without registration, BR §14-228.
  Prospectus, BR §14-216.
  Renewal, BR §14-219.

FRANCHISES —Cont'd
Registration —Cont'd
Required, BR §14-214.
Stop orders, BR §14-222.
Grounds for issuance, BR §14-221.
Surety bonds, BR §14-217.
Term of registration, BR §14-219.
Releases.
Condition of sale, BR §14-226.
Savings and loan associations.
Taxation.
Savings and loan association franchise tax, TG
§§2-1401, 2-1402, 8-301 to 8-305.
See SAVINGS AND LOAN ASSOCIATION
FRANCHISE TAX.
Scope of act, BR §14-203.
Signatures.
Registration applications, BR §14-215.
**Small business development financing
authority.**
Equity participation investment program, 83A
§§5-1041 to 5-1047.
See SMALL BUSINESS DEVELOPMENT
FINANCING AUTHORITY.
Taxation.
Definitions, TG §8-101.
Financial institution franchise tax, TG §§1-101,
8-101, 8-201.
Public service company franchise tax, TG
§§1-101, 8-101, 8-401.
Financial institution franchise tax, TG §§2-501,
2-502, 8-201 to 8-221.
See FINANCIAL INSTITUTION FRANCHISE
TAX.
Franchise tax.
Corporations.
See TAXATION.
General provisions.
See TAXATION.
Imposed, TG §8-102.
Public service company franchise tax, TG
§§2-1201, 8-401 to 8-417.
See PUBLIC SERVICE COMPANY
FRANCHISE TAX.
Savings and loan association franchise tax, TG
§§2-1401, 2-1402, 8-301 to 8-305.
See SAVINGS AND LOAN ASSOCIATION
FRANCHISE TAX.
Title of act.
Short title, BR §14-233.
Unconstitutionality alleged.
Notice to attorney general, CJ §3-405.

FRATERNAL BENEFIT SOCIETIES.
Accident benefit societies.
Application of subtitle, IN §8-404.
Additional benefits, IN §8-427.
**Amendments to articles of incorporation,
constitution or laws,** IN §8-419.
Foreign or alien societies, IN §8-424.
**Appeal from decision or finding of
commissioner,** IN §8-465.
Applicability of other provisions of article, IN
§1-202.
**Application of subtitle and other insurance
laws,** IN §§8-403, 8-404.
Articles of incorporation.
Amendments, IN §8-419.
Benefit certificate's effect, IN §8-432.
Foreign or alien societies, IN §8-424.
Contents, IN §8-411.

FRATERNAL BENEFIT SOCIETIES —Cont'd
Articles of incorporation —Cont'd
Execution, IN §8-411.
Filing, IN §8-412.
Assets, IN §8-442.
Consolidations and mergers, IN §8-439.
Attachment.
Benefits exempt from, IN §8-431.
Beneficiaries, IN §8-430.
Benefits on lives of children, IN §8-428.
Benefits, IN §§8-427 to 8-433.
Life benefit certificates, IN §8-433.
Valuation of certificates, IN §8-445.
Bonds, surety.
Conditioned upon return of applicants' fees, IN
§8-412.
Capital.
Minimum capital, IN §8-413.
Cash surrender values, IN §8-429.
Certificate loans, IN §8-429.
Certificates of authority.
Evidentiary effect, IN §8-417.
Examination and additional information, IN
§8-417.
Expiration, IN §8-423.
Foreign or alien societies, IN §8-424.
Issuance, IN §8-417.
Preliminary certificate, IN §8-414.
Duration, IN §8-416.
Recording, IN §8-417.
Renewal, IN §8-423.
Certificates of benefits, IN §§8-432 to 8-433.
Charitable institutions.
Creation and operation authorized, IN §8-437.
Taxation exemption, IN §8-405.
Compensation for obtaining new members, IN
§8-404.
Complaint procedure, IN §8-422.
Completing organization of society, IN §§8-415,
8-416.
Consideration for insurance.
Prohibited consideration, IN §8-467.
Consolidations.
Effect, IN §8-439.
Procedure, IN §8-438.
Constitution and laws, IN §8-418.
Amendment, IN §8-419.
Benefit certificate's effect, IN §8-432.
Foreign or alien societies, IN §8-424.
Filing, IN §8-412.
Impairment of reserves, IN §8-446.
Conversion to mutual life insurer, IN §8-440.
Definitions, IN §8-401.
Eligible children, IN §8-428.
Guaranteed benefits, IN §8-445.
Discrimination prohibited, IN §8-467.
Educational institutions.
Creation and operation authorized, IN §8-437.
English language requirement.
Filed documents, IN §8-412.
Minutes of proceedings, IN §8-422.
Examinations.
Domestic societies, IN §8-461.
Foreign and alien societies, IN §8-462.
Execution of judgments.
Benefits exempt from, IN §8-431.
Exemptions, IN §8-404.
Existing incorporated societies.
Retention of powers, IN §8-406.
Expenses.
Examination of societies, IN §§8-461, 8-462.

FRATERNAL BENEFIT SOCIETIES —Cont'd
Expenses —Cont'd
  Payments available for expenses, IN §8-422.
Filing requirements, IN §8-412.
  Foreign or alien societies, IN §8-424.
Foreign or alien societies, IN §8-424.
  Examinations, IN §8-462.
Formation.
  General provisions, IN §§8-410 to 8-424.
Funeral expenses, IN §8-430.
Funeral homes, IN §8-437.
Garnishment.
  Benefits exempt from, IN §8-431.
Grievance or complaint procedure, IN §8-422.
Group coverage prohibited, IN §8-427.
Impairment of reserves, IN §8-446.
Impersonating member, BR §19-207.
Incomplete comparison of insurance contracts, IN §8-468.
Incorporated societies.
  Retention of powers by existing societies, IN §8-406.
Incorporation.
  Articles of incorporation. See within this heading, "Articles of incorporation."
  Incorporators, IN §8-410.
Injunctions, IN §8-464.
Insurance laws.
  Applicability, IN §§8-403, 8-404.
Insurance producers.
  Certificates of qualification, IN §8-449.
Investments, IN §8-443.
Laws of society. See within this heading, "Constitution and laws."
Life benefit certificates, IN §8-433.
Liquidation, IN §8-464.
Lives insurable, IN §8-427.
  Children's lives, IN §8-428.
Loans.
  Certificate loans and other options, IN §8-429.
Lodge system.
  Societies deemed operating on system, IN §8-402.
Meetings.
  Place of meeting, IN §8-422.
Members, IN §8-421.
  Compensation for obtaining new members, IN §8-404.
  Impersonating, BR §19-207.
  Solicitation of members, IN §8-415.
    Part-time solicitation exception to insurance producer certification requirements, IN §8-449.
  Statements by member.
    Not warranties, IN §8-432.
Mergers.
  Effect, IN §8-439.
  Procedure, IN §8-438.
Minimum capital, IN §8-413.
Minors.
  Benefits on lives of children, IN §8-428.
Minutes to be in English, IN §8-422.
Misdemeanors.
  Misrepresentations, IN §8-468.
Mutual life insurers.
  Conversions to, IN §8-440.
Name, IN §8-411.
Names and insignia.
  Registration, prohibited acts, BR §§19-201 to 19-207.
  Unauthorized use, BR §19-207.
Nonforfeiture benefits, IN §8-429.

FRATERNAL BENEFIT SOCIETIES —Cont'd
Office location, IN §8-422.
Officers, IN §8-420.
Options authorized and required, IN §8-429.
Organization, IN §§8-410 to 8-424.
  Articles of incorporation. See within this heading, "Articles of incorporation."
Organizational names and insignia.
  Registration, prohibited acts, BR §§19-201 to 19-207.
  Unauthorized use, BR §19-207.
Personal representatives.
  Payment of benefits to, IN §8-430.
Powers, IN §8-418.
  Limitation on powers, IN §8-411.
Preliminary certificate of authority, IN §8-414.
  Duration, IN §8-416.
Premiums.
  Advance premiums held in trust, IN §8-415.
Presumption in determining incompleteness of comparison, IN §8-468.
Purposes.
  Limitation on purpose, IN §8-411.
Rebates prohibited, IN §8-467.
Reinsurance, IN §8-441.
Reports.
  Annual statement, IN §8-444.
  Examination of societies, IN §§8-461, 8-463.
  Valuation of certificates, IN §8-445.
Representative form of government.
  Societies deemed to have, IN §8-402.
Reserves, IN §8-445.
  Impairment of reserves, IN §8-446.
Service of process.
  Commissioner as agent for service of process, IN §8-407.
Societies deemed fraternal benefit society, IN §8-402.
Solicitation of members, IN §8-415.
  Part-time solicitation exception to insurance producer certification requirements, IN §8-449.
Special funds, IN §8-442.
Taxation, IN §8-405.
Time for completing organization, IN §8-416.
Trusts.
  Advance premiums held in trust, IN §8-415.
Unincorporated societies.
  Transaction of business prohibited, IN §8-466.
Valuation of certificates, IN §8-445.
Valuation of options, IN §8-429.
Waiver of constitution and laws, IN §8-418.

FRATERNAL ORGANIZATIONS.
Alcoholic beverages.
  Beer, wine and liquor licenses.
    Class C, on-sale, 2B §6-301.
    Class D, on-sale, 2B §7-101.
Benefit performances.
  Prince George's county, CR §§13-1901 to 13-1907.
Bingo.
  Anne Arundel county, CR §13-407.
  Baltimore City, CR §§13-507 to 13-509.
  Calvert county, CR §§13-705 to 13-709.
    Exemption from license requirement, CR §13-706.
  Carroll county, CR §§13-907, 13-908.
  Cecil county, CR §§13-1001 to 13-1005.
  Charles county, CR §§13-1109 to 13-1115.
  Frederick county, CR §13-1306.
  Howard county, CR §§13-1602, 13-1603.

FRATERNAL ORGANIZATIONS —Cont'd
Bingo —Cont'd
Kent county, CR §13-1705.
Montgomery county, CR §§13-1801 to 13-1815.
Prince George's county.
Benefit performances, CR §§13-1901 to 13-1907.
Queen Anne's county, CR §13-2005.
St. Mary's county, CR §§13-2101 to 13-2110.
Somerset county, CR §13-2202.
Wicomico county, CR §§13-2501 to 13-2508.
Casino.
Baltimore county, CR §13-604.
Credit unions.
General provisions.
See CREDIT UNIONS.
Gaming, bazaar, carnival and raffles.
Anne Arundel county, CR §§13-401 to 13-408.
Baltimore City, CR §§13-501 to 13-510.
Baltimore county, CR §§13-601 to 13-607.
Calvert county, CR §§13-701 to 13-704.
Carroll county, CR §§13-901 to 13-909.
Cecil county, CR §§13-1001 to 13-1005.
Charles county, CR §§13-1101 to 13-1115.
Frederick county, CR §§13-1301 to 13-1307.
Local gaming events generally, CR §§13-201 to 13-205.
Montgomery county.
Raffles generally, CR §§13-1801 to 13-1815.
Prince George's county, CR §§13-1901 to 13-1912.
Queen Anne's county.
Raffles and other gaming devices, CR §§13-2001 to 13-2006.
Raffles generally, statewide provision, CR §12-106.
St. Mary's county, CR §§13-2111 to 13-2115.
Wicomico county, CR §§13-2501 to 13-2508.
Worcester county, CR §§13-2619 to 13-2628.
Slot machines.
Ownership and operation in certain counties, CR §12-304.
Taxation.
Exemption from taxation, TP §7-202.
Tip jars and punch board.
Frederick county, CR §13-1305.
Washington county.
Tip jars generally, CR §§13-2414 to 13-2439.

FRATERNITIES.
Hazing, CR §3-607.
Sprinkler systems, PS §§9-201 to 9-206.

FRAUD.
Accountants.
Licenses.
Denial, suspension or revocation or reprimand of licensee.
Grounds, BOP §2-315.
Permits.
Denial, suspension or revocation or reprimand of permit holder.
Grounds, BOP §2-410.
Advertising.
False advertisements generally.
See ADVERTISING.
Aged, assistance for.
Fraudulent acts, 88A §62.
Alcoholic beverages.
False statements, 2B §16-501.
Prevention by comptroller, 2B §12-113.
Amusements and recreation.
False representations and statements, BR §3-501.

FRAUD —Cont'd
Architects.
Licenses.
Denial, revocation or suspension or reprimand of licensee.
Grounds, BOP §3-311.
Attachment.
Against whom available, CJ §3-303.
Attorneys at law.
Admission to the bar.
Revocation of admission fraudulently obtained, BOP §10-214.
Legal services corporation.
Fraudulently obtaining legal assistance, 10 §45M.
Audiologists, hearing aid dealers and speech-language pathologists.
Licenses.
See AUDIOLOGISTS AND SPEECH-LANGUAGE PATHOLOGISTS.
Bad checks, CR §§8-101 to 8-108.
Banks and trust companies.
Derogatory statements prohibited, FI §5-805.
Unauthorized representation as bank prohibited, FI §5-806.
Barbers.
Licenses.
Denial, revocation or suspension or reprimand of licensee.
Grounds, BOP §4-314.
Permits.
Denial, revocation or suspension or reprimand of permit holder.
Grounds, BOP §4-513.
Registration.
Students and apprentice barbers.
Denial, revocation or suspension.
Grounds, BOP §4-407.
Batteries, CL §11-902.
Bicycles.
Certificates of title.
Grounds for refusal, TR §13-110.
Bills of lading.
Carriers.
Inducing carrier to issue bill when goods not received, CL §18-204.
Duplicate bills.
Issue of bills not so marked, CL §18-202.
False statement.
Issue of bill containing, CL §18-206.
Goods not in carrier's possession.
Negotiation of bill when goods not in carrier's possession, CL §18-203.
Issuance of bill for goods not received, CL §18-201.
Mortgaged goods.
Negotiation of bill for mortgaged goods, CL §18-207.
Non-negotiable bill.
Issuance when not so marked, CL §18-205.
Blind persons.
False representation of manufacturer, CL §14-2803.
Burning with intent to defraud, CR §6-106.
Cable television service, interference with, CR §7-303.
Carriers.
Bills of lading.
Inducing carrier to issue bill when goods not received, CL §18-204.
Chiropractors.
Licenses.
See CHIROPRACTORS.

FRAUD —Cont'd

Collection agencies.
Licenses, BR §7-308.

Commercial code.
Applicability of general principles, CL §1-103.

Community energy loan program, SG §9-2109.

Computer information transactions, CL §22-806.

Condominiums.
Disclosure requirements, RP §11-126.

Consigned goods.
Purchasing from transporter.
Prohibition, liability, CL §14-1317.

Consumer credit reporting agencies.
Obtaining information under false pretenses, CL §14-1215.

Continuing care contracts.
Liquidation, conservation or rehabilitation of providers, 70B §20G.

Contracts.
Interparty agreements, CL §20-103.
Sale of goods.
Remedies for fraud, CL §2-721.

Controlled dangerous substance.
Obtaining by, CR §5-601.

Conversion.
Consignment.
General provisions.
See CONSIGNMENT.

Corporate officers and agents.
Misrepresentation with intent to defraud, CR §8-402.

Corporations.
Sale or disposition of stock for services at less than par, CA §2-216.

Cosmetologists.
Licenses.
Denial, revocation or suspension or reprimand of licensee.
Grounds, BOP §5-314.

Counterfeiting and forgery, CR §§8-601 to 8-613.

Credit.
Credit grantor closed end credit provisions.
False or misleading financing statements, CL §12-1023.1.
Credit grantor revolving credit provisions.
Consumer borrowers.
False or misleading financing statement, CL §12-923.1.

Credit card crimes, CR §§8-201 to 8-217.
See CREDIT CARDS.

Credit cards.
General provisions.
See CREDIT CARDS.

Credit unions.
Unauthorized use of word "credit union," FI §6-901.

Dentists.
Licenses.
See DENTISTS.

Documents of title, misuse, CR §8-406.

Election officials.
Corrupt or fraudulent acts, EL §16-301.

Electricity.
Storage batteries, CL §11-902.

Electrologists.
License suspension or revocation, HO §8-6B-18.
Misrepresentation, HO §8-6B-23.

Embezzlement, CR §7-113.

FRAUD —Cont'd

Engineers.
Licenses.
Denial, revocation or suspension or reprimand of licensee.
Grounds, BOP §14-317.

Environmental permits, licenses or certificates.
Falsifying or altering, EN §1-302.

Executors and administrators.
Payment to personal representative or attorney.
Final and binding unless fraud, ET §7-502.

Foresters.
Licenses.
Disciplinary action.
Grounds, BOP §7-309.

Franchises, BR §14-229.
Applications, notices or reports, BR §14-231.
Prospectus offering or amendment, BR §14-230.

Fraudulent conveyances.
General provisions, CL §§15-201 to 15-214.
See FRAUDULENT CONVEYANCES.

Fundraising for police, fire departments or public safety officers, CR §8-520.

Gold.
Merchandise, CL §§14-601 to 14-608.
See GOLD.

Homebuilders.
Revocation of registration, BR §4.5-308.

Home improvements.
Advertising, BR §8-610.
Deceptive acts, BR §8-608.

Housing assistance fraud, CR §8-523.

Identity fraud, CR §§8-301 to 8-305.

Insurance.
Agents, brokers, etc.
Doing business with unlicensed persons, IN §27-404.
Antifraud plans, IN §§27-803, 27-804.
Applicability of provisions, IN §27-402.
Attorneys soliciting motor vehicle accident victims, IN §27-407.
Definitions.
Claim, IN §27-401.
Division of insurance fraud, IN §2-401.
Insurance fraud, IN §27-801.
Division of insurance fraud, IN §§2-401 to 2-408.
Deposits into fund, IN §2-114.
Excess premiums, IN §27-403.
Failure to return premiums, IN §27-403.
False or misleading claims, statements, etc., IN §§27-403, 27-406.
Investigation of fraudulent claims, IN §2-201.
Misappropriation of funds or benefits, IN §27-403.
Nonprofit health service plans.
Recovery of cost and expenses, IN §14-105.
Penalties, IN §§27-408, 27-804.
Physicians soliciting motor vehicle accident victims, IN §27-407.
Premium finance companies.
Grounds for disciplinary action, IN §23-208.
Inducement to obtain multiple initial service fees, IN §23-503.
Prevention fee, IN §§6-201 to 6-204.
Reporting suspected fraud, IN §§27-802 to 27-805.
Risk retention groups.
Foreign groups, IN §25-103.
Unlicensed insurance producers, IN §27-405.

Intent to defraud.
Proving, CR §1-401.

FRAUD —Cont'd
Interior designers.
Disciplinary proceedings.
Grounds, BOP §8-310.
Judgments.
Revisory power of court.
Circuit courts, CivProCir Rule 2-535.
District Court, CivProDist Rule 3-535.
Landscape architects.
Licenses.
Giving false information to obtain, BOP §9-604.1.
Leased or rented goods, conversion, CR §8-407.
Leases, UCC.
Effect of fraud on rights and remedies, CL §2A-505.
Legal services corporation.
Fraudulent obtaining of legal assistance, 10 §45M.
Letters of credit, CL §5-109.
Limitation of actions.
Ignorance of cause of action induced by fraud, CJ §5-203.
Knowledge of cause of action kept from party induced by fraud, CJ §5-203.
Maryland economic adjustment fund.
False statement or report, 83A §6-511.
Medicaid fraud, CR §§8-508 to 8-517.
Medical records.
Fraudulent obtaining of records, HG §4-309.
Midwives.
Special licensed nurse midwives.
See NURSES.
Mining.
Abstracting minerals from plaintiff's land.
Measure of damages, CJ §11-202.
Misrepresentation generally.
See MISREPRESENTATION.
Money transmission.
Authorized delegates, FI §12-414.
Enforcement of subtitle, FI §12-426.
Mortgages and deeds of trust.
Secondary mortgage loans.
False or misleading advertising matter, CL §12-403.
Motor clubs.
Grounds for disciplinary action, IN §26-208.
Action against representative, IN §26-307.
Motor fuel inspection.
Commingling gasoline with intent to defraud, BR §10-322.
Motor fuel tax.
Refunds.
Penalties for fraudulent claims for refunds, TG §13-1030.
Motor vehicles.
Accident reports.
False report, TR §20-108.
Applications for certificate of title or registration of vehicle, TR §13-704.
Disabled persons.
Special registration plates, TR §13-616.
Drivers' licenses.
Application, TR §16-301.
Unlawful use, TR §16-301.
Handicapped persons.
Permits for reserved parking spaces, TR §21-1005.
Special registration plates, TR §13-616.
Identification cards.
Special identification cards, TR §12-301.

FRAUD —Cont'd
Motor vehicles —Cont'd
Refusing registration.
Grounds, TR §13-406.
Negotiable instruments.
Employee's fraudulent indorsement, CL §3-405.
Fictitious payees, CL §3-404.
Forged signature or alteration of instruments, CL §3-406.
Impostors, CL §3-404.
Unauthorized signatures, CL §3-403.
Nurses.
See NURSES.
Nursing home administrators.
Licenses.
See NURSING HOME ADMINISTRATORS.
Occupational safety and health.
False representations and statements.
Prohibition, LE §5-804.
Occupational therapists.
Licenses.
See OCCUPATIONAL THERAPISTS.
Operating agreements.
Hotels and retirement communities.
Defense of fraud not limited, CL §23-106.
Optometrists.
Licenses.
See OPTOMETRISTS.
Pari-mutuel betting tickets.
Counterfeit or altered betting tickets, CR §8-905.
Partnership assets.
Fraudulent conversion, CR §8-401.
Penalties.
Legal services corporation.
Fraudulent obtaining of legal assistance, 10 §45M.
Personal property.
Removal with intent to defraud, CR §8-403.
Pharmacists and pharmacies.
Licenses.
See PHARMACISTS AND PHARMACIES.
Physical therapists.
Licenses.
See PHYSICAL THERAPISTS.
Physicians.
Licenses.
See PHYSICIANS.
Pilots.
Licenses.
Denial, revocation or suspension or reprimand of licensee.
Grounds, BOP §11-409.
Plumbers.
Licenses.
Denial, revocation or suspension or reprimand of licensee.
Ground, BOP §12-312.
Podiatrists.
Licenses.
See PODIATRISTS.
Poor.
Medicaid.
See MEDICAID.
Premium finance companies.
Grounds for disciplinary action, IN §23-208.
Inducement to obtain multiple initial service fees, IN §23-503.
Private detectives.
Certification.
Disciplinary action.
Grounds, BOP §13-409.

FRAUD —Cont'd
Private detectives —Cont'd
Licenses.
Disciplinary action.
Grounds, BOP §13-313.
Private home detention monitoring.
Grounds for disciplinary action, BOP §20-314.
Procurement.
Collusion for purpose of defrauding state, SF §11-205.
Minority business participation.
Prohibited acts, SF §14-308.
Psychologists.
Licenses.
See PSYCHOLOGISTS.
Public assistance fraud, CR §§8-501 to 8-505.
Medicaid fraud, CR §§8-508 to 8-517.
Public defender representation.
Obtaining by fraud, CR §8-521.
Pyramid promotional schemes, CR §8-404.
Radio and television.
Used, reconditioned, etc., television or radio sets.
Sale and advertisement, CL §14-802.
Definitions, CL §14-801.
Penalties, CL §14-803.
Railroad safety and health.
False statements, LE §5.5-122.
Real estate brokers.
Licenses.
Denial, revocation or suspension or reprimand of licensee.
Grounds, BOP §17-322.
Receipts.
Issuance prior to receipt of goods, CL §18-201.
Registered rehabilitation practitioners.
Registration, LE §9-6A-15.
Removal of personal property.
Intent to defraud, CR §8-403.
Residential child care program administrators.
Certification.
Fraudulent certificates, HO §20-403.
Secondary mortgage loan law.
Advertising.
False or misleading advertising matter, CL §12-403.
Securities act.
General provisions, CA §§11-101 to 11-805.
See SECURITIES.
Security systems technicians.
False statements in applications, BOP §§18-503, 18-504.
Grounds for disciplinary action against licensee, BOP §18-309.
Silver.
Merchandise, CL §§14-601 to 14-608.
See SILVER.
Simulation of document to induce payment, CR §8-522.
Social services.
Medicaid.
See MEDICAID.
Obtaining public assistance by fraud.
Statement of what constitutes fraud.
Reading, 88A §16.
Social workers.
Licenses.
See SOCIAL WORKERS.
Start-up business ventures.
Sale of business opportunities, BR §14-121.
Criminal penalty, BR §14-127.

FRAUD —Cont'd
State personnel.
Deception by applicant, SPP §§15-104, 15-201.
Falsifying examination grade, result or standing, SPP §§15-103, 15-201.
Interference with examination rights of others, SPP §§15-102, 15-201.
Statute of frauds.
General provisions.
See FRAUDS, STATUTE OF.
Subleasing motor vehicle, CR §8-408.
Surveys and surveyors.
Licenses.
Denial, revocation or suspension or reprimand of licensee.
Grounds, BOP §15-318.
Taxation.
Penalties.
Fraudulent failure to file return, TG §13-704.
Motor fuel tax.
Fraudulent claim for refund, TG §13-1030.
Theft.
Generally, CR §§7-101 to 7-110.
See THEFT.
Trademarks and service marks.
Fraudulent registration, BR §1-413.
Trading stamp companies, BR §13-109.
Unemployment compensation.
Administration of claims.
Recovery of benefits.
False statements or misrepresentation, LE §8-809.
Fraudulently obtaining or increasing benefit, LE §8-1301.
Uniform fraudulent conveyance act.
General provisions, CL §§15-201 to 15-214.
See FRAUDULENT CONVEYANCES.
Vessel cargo, wrongful disposal, CR §8-405.
Vessels and boats.
Abandoned vessels.
Obtaining title through fraudulent means, NR §8-722.
Viatical settlement contracts.
Disciplinary action against registrants, IN §8-608.
Misappropriation of funds or benefits, IN §27-403.
Warehouse receipts.
Duplicate receipts.
Issuance of receipts not so marked, CL §18-302.
False statement.
Issuance of receipt containing false statement, CL §18-303.
Issuance of receipts for goods not received, CL §18-301.
Receipts which do not state that goods belong to warehouseman.
Issuance prohibited, CL §18-304.
Watches.
Secondhand watches, CL §§14-701 to 14-706.
See WATCHES.
Water quality laboratories.
Certification.
Fraudulently or unlawfully obtained certification, EN §9-1023.
Grounds for reprimands, suspensions or revocations, EN §9-1016.
Welfare.
Limitation of actions, CJ §5-106.
Well drillers.
Licenses.
See WELL DRILLERS.

FRAUD —Cont'd
Wills.
Administrative probate.
Grounds for setting aside, Estates Rule 6-431;
ET §5-304.
Embezzle, steal, destroy, impair or alter, CR
§§8-701, 8-702.
Wills, codicils, deeds, land patents, writs of estate.
Embezzle, steal, destroy, impair, alter, CR
§§8-701, 8-702.
Witnesses.
Testifying in supplementary proceeding.
Immunity, CJ §9-119.
Workers' compensation.
Accidental injury.
Claim application, LE §9-709.
Death from accidental injury, LE §9-710.
Claims procedure.
Accidental injury, LE §9-709.
Readjustment of rate of compensation, LE
§9-736.
Entitlement to compensation.
Compensation prohibited, LE §9-502.
Injured workers' insurance fund.
Misrepresentation of payroll, LE §10-141.
Insurance fraud division.
Referral of certain fraud cases to, LE §9-310.2.
Modification of award.
Failure to file application, time limit for filing,
LE §9-736.

FRAUDS, STATUTE OF.
Assignments.
Beneficial interest in trust, RP §5-106.
General provisions, RP §5-103.
Wages.
Required to be in writing, CL §15-302.
Cemeteries.
Perpetual care of cemeteries.
Trust agreement, BR §5-604.
Charities.
Solicitation agreements, BR §6-501.
Commercial code.
Modification, CL §2-209.
Personal property.
Kinds of personalty not otherwise covered, CL
§1-206.
Consumer credit.
Credit agreements.
Enforceability, CJ §5-408.
Contracts.
Executory contracts, CJ §5-901; RP §5-104.
Credit agreements.
Enforceability, CJ §5-408.
Estates.
Creation.
Certain estates created by parol are estates at
will, RP §5-101.
One-year exception, RP §5-102.
Executors and administrators.
Actions against personal representative, ET
§8-109.
Executory contracts, CJ §5-901; RP §5-104.
Grants.
General provisions, RP §5-103.
Not applicable to resulting or constructive trust or
to trust transferred or extinguished by
operation of law, RP §5-107.
Other requirements of article not repealed, RP
§5-108.

FRAUDS, STATUTE OF —Cont'd
Insurance adviser agreements, IN §10-215.
Investment securities.
Inapplicable, CL §8-113.
Landlord and tenant.
Estates created by parol are estates at will, RP
§5-101.
Exceptions as to lease term of one year, RP
§5-102.
Leases, UCC, CL §2A-201.
Personal property.
Commercial code.
Kinds of personalty not otherwise covered, CL
§1-206.
Surrender of interest in property, RP §5-103.
Trusts and trustees.
Beneficial interest in trust.
Assignment, RP §5-106.
Not applicable to resulting or constructive trust
or to trust transferred or extinguished by
operation of law, RP §5-107.
Declarations of trust.
Requirements, RP §5-105.
Resulting or constructive trusts.
Not applicable to, RP §5-107.

**FRAUDULENT CONVERSION OF LEASED OR
RENTED GOODS,** CR §8-407.

**FRAUDULENT CONVERSION OF
PARTNERSHIP ASSETS,** CR §8-401.

FRAUDULENT CONVEYANCES.
Assets.
Defined, CL §15-201.
Bankruptcy and insolvency, CL §§15-101,
15-202, 15-204.
Bulk transfers, CL §§6-101 to 6-111.
See BULK TRANSFERS.
Business conveyances, CL §15-205.
Citation.
Uniform fraudulent conveyance act, CL §15-214.
Consideration.
Fair consideration, CL §15-203.
Conveyance without fair consideration, CL
§15-205.
"Conveyance" defined, CL §15-201.
Corporations.
Involuntary dissolution.
Fraudulent preferences, payments and
transfers, CA §3-418.
Creditors.
Defined, CL §15-201.
Rights of creditors.
Whose claims have matured, CL §15-209.
Whose claims have not matured, CL §15-210.
Sales.
When conveyance to creditor not fraudulent, CL
§15-210.1.
Debtor.
Person about to incur debts, CL §15-206.
Debts.
Conveyance by person about to incur debts, CL
§15-206.
Defined, CL §15-201.
Definitions, CL §15-201.
Equity.
Cases not provided for in subtitle, CL §15-211.
Garnishment, CL §15-209.
Injunctions.
Rights of creditors whose claims have not
matured, CL §15-210.

FRAUDULENT CONVEYANCES —Cont'd

Insolvency.

Conveyance by insolvent, CL §15-204.

Defined, CL §15-202.

General provisions, CL §15-202.

Partnerships, CL §15-202.

Void, CL §15-101.

Intent to defraud, CL §15-207.

Interpretation and construction.

Subtitle construed, CL §15-212.

Judicial sales.

When conveyance to creditor not fraudulent, CL §15-210.1.

Levy of property, CL §15-209.

Liens.

Sale of property under levy.

When conveyance to creditor not fraudulent, CL §15-210.1.

Sale to enforce a statutory lien.

When conveyance to creditor not fraudulent, CL §15-210.1.

Limited liability company property, CL §15-208.

Partnerships.

Conveyance of partnership property, CL §15-208.

Insolvency, CL §15-202.

Receivers.

Rights of creditors whose claims have not matured.

Appointment of receiver, CL §15-210.

Repeal of inconsistent legislation.

Certain statutes not repealed, CL §15-213.

Security.

Retention of property as security, CL §15-209.

Setting aside, CL §15-209.

Right of creditors whose claims have not matured, CL §15-210.

Uniform fraudulent conveyance act, CL §§15-201 to 15-214.

Cases not provided in, CL §15-211.

Construction, CL §15-212.

Name of subtitle, CL §15-214.

Without fair consideration, CL §15-205.

FRAUDULENT MISREPRESENTATION BY CORPORATE OFFICERS OR AGENTS, CR §8-402.

FREDERICK CITY.

Alcoholic beverages.

Disorderly intoxication.

Regulation of possession or consumption.

Authority of mayor and aldermen, 2B §19-103.

Road work by offenders, assignment, COR §9-518.

FREDERICK COUNTY.

Administrative assistant.

Clerk of board of commissioners known as, 25 §1.

Agricultural preservation land.

Property tax credits, TP §9-312.

Alarm system contractors or alarm users, registering, 25 §221A.

Alcoholic beverages.

Appeals.

Powers of court.

Remand to local board, 2B §16-101.

Beer and light wine licenses.

Class A, off-sale, 2B §5-101.

Class B, on-sale.

Hotels and restaurants, 2B §5-201.

Number of licenses issued, 2B §9-211.

FREDERICK COUNTY —Cont'd

Alcoholic beverages —Cont'd

Beer and light wine licenses —Cont'd

Class C, on-sale.

Clubs, 2B §5-301.

Hours for sale.

Sundays, 2B §11-302.

Restrictions, 2B §8-211.

Beer festival license, 2B §8-803.

Beer licenses.

Class A, off-sale, 2B §3-101.

Number of licenses issued, 2B §9-211.

Class B, on-sale, 2B §3-201.

Number of licenses issued, 2B §9-211.

Class C, on-sale.

Clubs, 2B §3-301.

Hours of sale.

Sundays, 2B §11-301.

Restrictions, 2B §8-211.

Stadium beer on-sale license, 2B §8-211.1.

Beer, wine and liquor licenses.

Class A, off-sale, 2B §6-101.

Number of licenses issued, 2B §9-211.

Class B-B.F., on-sale.

Hotels and restaurants, 2B §6-201.

Class B-DT, on-sale.

Hotels and restaurants, 2B §6-201.

Class B, on-sale.

Bed and breakfasts, 2B §6-201.

Hotels and restaurants, 2B §6-201.

Class C (golf and country club), 2B §8-211.

Class C, on-sale.

Clubs, 2B §6-301.

Special class C, 2B §7-101.

Hours and days for sale.

Sunday sales, 2B §11-303.

Restrictions, 2B §8-211.

Special class C, 2B §7-101.

Special licenses, 2B §6-301.

Board of license commissioners, 2B §15-103.

Clerical assistants, 2B §15-112.

Salaries, 2B §15-109.

Caterers, 2B §6-703.1.

Class A license not to be issued to certain establishments, 2B §9-211.

Consumption.

Restrictions, 2B §11-304.

Criminal history records checks.

License applicants, 2B §10-103.

Disorderly intoxication.

Ordinances or resolutions authorized, 2B §19-103.

Drafthouse licenses.

Class B-DH license, 2B §8-701.

Drive-through purchase facilities.

Licenses.

Prohibition on licensing, 2B §9-211.1.

Elections.

Exercise of privileges of licensee on election day, 2B §11-401.

Hours and days for sale.

Beer, wine and liquor licenses.

Sunday sales, 2B §11-303.

Election days, 2B §11-401.

Manufacturers' licenses, 2B §11-101.

Inspection, 2B §15-103.

Employment, 2B §15-112.

License commissioners.

Board of license commissioners. See within this subheading, "Board of license commissioners."

FREDERICK COUNTY —Cont'd
Alcoholic beverages —Cont'd
Licenses.
Applications.
Police records of applicants, 2B §10-103.
Beer festival, 2B §8-803.
Class A license not to be issued to certain
establishments, 2B §9-211.
Criminal history records checks.
License applicants, 2B §10-103.
Drive-thru purchase facilities.
Prohibition on licensing, 2B §9-211.1.
Fees.
Disposition, 2B §10-204.
Light wine licenses.
Baseball stadiums, 2B §8-211.1.
Class A, off-sale, 2B §4-201.
Manufacturers.
Hours and days for sale, 2B §11-101.
Micro-brewery license, 2B §2-208.
Partnerships, 2B §9-101.
Quota.
Where licenses exceed quota, 2B §9-211.
Revocation and suspension.
Nudity and sexual displays on licensee's
premises, 2B §10-405.
Stadiums, 2B §8-211.1.
Transfer, 2B §10-503.
Violations.
Civil citations, 2B §16-408.
Where prohibited or restricted, 2B §8-211.
Wine tasting license, 2B §8-406.
Light wine licenses.
Baseball stadiums, 2B §8-211.1.
Manufacturers.
Licenses.
Hours and days for sale, 2B §11-101.
Micro-brewery licenses, 2B §2-208.
Minors.
Citation for violations, CR §10-119.
Possession prohibited, 2B §12-108.
Nudity and sexual displays on licensee's premises.
Revocation of license, 2B §10-405.
Penalties.
Local penalties, 2B §16-507.
Sales.
Beer for cash, 2B §12-112.
Election days, 2B §11-401.
Summons and process, 2B §16-410.
Wine tasting license, 2B §8-406.
Amusement parks.
Permits required, 25 §27.
Appearance fees in circuit courts.
Distribution, CJ §7-204.
Aquaculture.
Live bait dealers, NR §4-11A-19.
Audubon Society of Central Maryland, Inc.
Property tax credits, TP §9-312.
Bailiff.
Compensation, CJ §2-507.
Bingo, CR §13-1306.
Permit required, CR §13-1306.
Prizes, CR §13-1306.
Qualified organizations which may conduct, CR
§13-1306.
Unqualified persons, CR §13-1306.
Birds and game.
Spotlighting, NR §10-410.
Bond issues.
Bond rating enhancement reserve, 25 §221B.

FREDERICK COUNTY —Cont'd
Boxing and wrestling arenas.
Permits required, 25 §27.
Building code.
Agricultural buildings.
Exemption for buildings used for agritourism,
PS §12-508.
Provisions for, 25 §3.
Caterers.
Beer, wine and liquor licenses, 2B §6-703.1.
Cemeteries.
Real property.
Exceptions to limits on land held, BR §5-501.
Circuit courts.
Appearance fees.
Distribution, CJ §7-204.
Judicial circuit, MD Const Art IV §19.
Number of judges, CJ §1-503.
Codes.
Plumbing, building and housing codes.
Adoption, 25 §3.
Commissioners.
Administrative assistant.
Clerk of board to be known as, 25 §1.
Clerk of board.
Known as administrative assistant, 25 §1.
Development impact fees.
Power to fix, impose, etc., 25 §§9I, 9J.
Pensions.
Teachers, 25 §13.
Powers.
Development impact fees, 25 §9I.
Power to fix, impose, etc., 25 §9J.
Enumerated, 25 §3.
Community college.
Board of community college trustees, ED §16-407.
County board of elections.
Compensation, EL §2-204.
County boards generally, EL §§2-201 to 2-303.
See ELECTIONS.
County working contracts.
Competitive bidding in bonds, 25 §3.
Courts.
Circuit court. See within this heading, "Circuit
courts."
Crimes and offenses.
Alcoholic beverages.
Board of licensed commissioners.
Conflicts of interest, 2B §15-103.
Licensing of transient or temporary vendors, 24
§11-302.
Dance halls.
Permits required, 25 §27.
Deeds.
Deputy tax collector.
Execution of tax deed when copy of judgment
served on him, TP §14-847.
Recordation.
Prepayment of taxes prior to transfer on
assessment books.
Subdivisions, RP §3-104.
Straw deeds, RP §3-104.
Deputies. See within this heading, "Sheriff."
Development impact fees.
Power to fix, impose, etc., 25 §§9I, 9J.
Dog and kennel licenses, 24 §11-501.
Rules and regulations, 24 §11-504.
Dogs.
Regulation, 24 §11-511.
Dogs running at large.
Females in heat, 24 §11-512.

FREDERICK COUNTY —Cont'd
Domestic animals.
Regulation, 24 §11-511.
Drive-thru purchase facilities.
Alcoholic beverages.
Licenses.
Prohibition on licensing, 2B §9-211.1.
Drunkenness.
Disorderly intoxication.
Ordinances or resolutions regulating allowed, 2B §19-103.
Emmitsburg Civic Association, Inc.
Property tax credits, TP §9-312.
Environmental noise control and sound level limits rules or regulations.
No power in department to adopt in county, EN §3-401.
False alarms, providing civil citations and penalties for, 25 §221A.
Fines.
Alcoholic beverages.
Minors.
Possession, 2B §12-108.
Fires and fire protection.
Authority to adopt fire prevention codes, PS §9-701.
Firefighters appointed as deputy sheriffs, PS §§7-301 to 7-303.
Volunteer fire departments.
Length of service awards, PS §7-211.
Fish and fisheries.
Live bait dealers.
Inspection of bait boxes, NR §4-11A-19.
Licenses, NR §4-11A-19.
Seines or nets regulated, NR §4-617.
Transportation and sale outside of county, NR §4-11A-19.
Forest, park and wildlife rangers, NR §5-206.
Frederick Optimist Boy's Foundation, Inc.
Property tax credits, TP §9-312.
Gaming, bazaar, carnival and raffles, CR §§13-201 to 13-205, 13-1301 to 13-1307.
Conducting event for benefit of qualified organization.
Allowed, CR §13-203.
Definitions, CR §§13-201, 13-1301.
Gaming event defined, CR §§13-201, 13-1301.
Individual benefit prohibited, CR §13-203.
Limitations on conducting event, CR §13-1304.
Management through organizations members, CR §13-205.
Paddle wheel and wheel or fortune.
Provision applicable to, CR §13-1303.
Permit for gaming event required, CR §13-1304.
Prizes and gaming devices allowed, CR §§13-204, 13-1304.
Provisions applicable to county, CR §§13-202, 13-301, 13-1302, 13-1303.
Qualified organization defined, CR §§13-201, 13-1303.
Additional qualified organization, CR §13-1303.
Qualified organizations which may conduct, listed, CR §§13-1303, 13-1304.
Regulations, adoption by commissioners, CR §13-1304.
Tip jar and punchboard.
Accounting by beneficiary, CR §13-1305.
Included in definition of gaming event, CR §13-1301.
Provision applicable to, CR §13-1303.

FREDERICK COUNTY —Cont'd
Gaming, bazaar, carnival and raffles —Cont'd
Tip jar and punchboard —Cont'd
Purchase from licensed distributors, CR §13-1305.
Qualified beneficiaries, CR §13-1305.
Qualified operators, CR §13-1305.
Records, inspection and copying, CR §13-1305.
Violations, penalty, CR §13-1307.
Hearings.
Proposed ordinances or resolutions.
Special provisions as to certain counties, 25 §3.
Historic area zoning.
General provisions.
See ZONING.
Historic districts.
Real property on which improvements are made to existing structures within historic districts.
Property tax credits, TP §9-312.
Hotel rental tax.
Exemptions, 24 §9-305.
Hotels and restaurants.
Beer licenses.
Class B, on-sale, 2B §3-201.
Hunting nongame birds and mammals.
License required, NR §10-301.
Improvements.
Development impact fees.
Power to fix, impose, etc., 25 §9I.
Licenses.
Alcoholic beverages. See within this heading, "Alcoholic beverages."
Live bait dealers, NR §4-11A-19.
Mining.
Surface mining.
Dewatering in karst terrain, EN §§15-812, 15-813.
Minors.
Alcoholic beverages.
Possession prohibited, 2B §12-108.
Misdemeanors.
Alcoholic beverages.
Board of licensed commissioners.
Conflicts of interest, 2B §15-103.
Licensing of transient or temporary vendors, 24 §11-302.
Monocacy river.
Speed limit on certain areas, NR §8-725.6.
Mortgages and deeds of trust.
Interest.
Payable after sale, RP §7-105.
Motor vehicles.
Size and weight.
Power of county commissioners to regulate, 25 §25.
Tires.
Studs, cleats, etc.
Sale regulated, TR §22-405.2.
Use allowed during certain months, TR §22-405.2.
Nonprofit community or civic association or corporation.
Property tax credits, TP §9-312.
Nonprofit schools.
Property tax credits, TP §9-312.
Ordinances.
Filed with clerk of court.
Exception as to Frederick county, 25 §4.
Orphans' court.
Judges.
Compensation, ET §2-108.

FREDERICK COUNTY —Cont'd
Parks and recreation.
Establishment of recreation and park board or commission, 25 §226.
Penalties.
Alcoholic beverages.
Local penalties, 2B §16-507.
Pensions.
Contributory pension benefit, additional liabilities, SPP §21-307.
Eligibility service for service credit, SPP §23-307.2.
Teachers' pensions, 25 §13.
Permits.
Dance halls and other places of amusement, tourist camps, etc., 25 §27.
Plumbing and zoning permits, 25 §3.
Personal property.
Purchase or lease of.
Powers, 25 §9D.
Planning commission.
County commissioners overruling action, 66B §14.06.
Plats.
Rights of way.
Recordation, RP §3-109.1.
Plumbing.
Code.
Provisions for, 25 §3.
Permits, 25 §3.
Potomac water authority.
General provisions.
See POTOMAC WATER AUTHORITY.
Public works.
Development impact fees.
Power to fix, impose, etc., 25 §9I.
Real property.
Sale.
Authority to sell certain property, 25 §11A.
Sales.
Notice in contract of sale of property subject to certain taxes or fees, RP §10-704.
Recordation.
Deeds.
Exceptions as to Frederick county, RP §3-104.
Rights of way.
Recordation of plats, RP §3-109.1.
Records of alarm system contractors, monitoring services and manufacturer of security system, 25 §221A.
Region of state.
Designation, 25 §221.
Rent control.
Power of commissioners, 25 §10H.
Residential mortgage programs for certain counties, HS §§4-1601 to 4-1610.
Roads.
Presumed closed, 25 §137A.
Ruritan clubs.
Property tax credits, TP §9-312.
Schools.
County board of education.
Closed sessions, ED §3-5B-05.
Compensation, ED §§3-5B-04, 4-107.
Election, ED §§3-5B-01, 3-114.
Generally, EL §§8-801 to 8-806.
Expenses, ED §4-107.
Health insurance, ED §3-5B-04.
Persons subject to authority of board.
Ineligibility to serve as member, ED §3-114.

FREDERICK COUNTY —Cont'd
Schools —Cont'd
County board of education —Cont'd
President.
Annual election, ED §3-5B-03.
Compensation, ED §3-5B-04.
Public sessions, ED §3-5B-05.
Qualifications of members, ED §3-5B-01.
Removal of members, ED §3-5B-01.
Sessions, ED §3-5B-05.
Spouses.
Exclusion from board, ED §3-5B-02.
Terms of members, ED §3-5B-01.
Vacancies, ED §3-5B-01.
Employee organizations.
Designation required, ED §6-505.
Pensions.
Teachers, 25 §13.
Property tax credits.
Certain property owned by nonprofit schools, TP §9-312.
Leased property used exclusively for public school education purposes, TP §9-312.
Sheriff.
Deputies, CJ §2-309.
Firefighters appointed as deputy sheriffs, PS §§7-301 to 7-303.
Jail wardens.
Salaries, CJ §2-309.
Salary, CJ §2-309.
Second in command, CJ §2-310.
Smoking.
Regulation of smoking in public buildings, 25 §3.
State's attorney, 10 §40.
Subdivisions.
Deeds.
Prepayment of taxes prior to transfer on assessment books, RP §3-104.
Sundays and holidays.
Alcoholic beverages.
Hours and days for sale, 2B §11-511.
Taxation.
Credits.
Property tax credits, TP §9-312.
Deeds.
Deputy collector.
Execution of tax deed when copy of decree served on him, TP §14-847.
Hotel rental tax.
Exemptions, 24 §9-305.
Interest.
Overdue taxes, TP §14-603.
Redemption.
Rate of redemption, TP §14-820.
Sales to collect.
Notice, TP §14-813.
Transportation.
Levy of tax for public transportation services, TR §7-801.
Tip jar and punchboard.
Accounting by beneficiary, CR §13-1305.
Included in definition of gaming event, CR §13-1301.
Provision applicable to, CR §13-1303.
Purchase from licensed distributors, CR §13-1305.
Qualified beneficiaries, CR §13-1305.
Qualified operators, CR §13-1305.
Records, inspection and copying, CR §13-1305.
Tourist camps.
Permits required, 25 §27.

FREDERICK COUNTY —Cont'd
Transient or temporary vendors.
Licenses, 24 §11-302.
Transportation tax, TR §7-801.
Trapshooting or other target shooting on property approved by department of planning and zoning.
Environmental sound level limits and noise control rules and regulations, restrictions on adopting, EN §3-401.
Volunteer fire departments.
Length of service awards, PS §7-211.
Water and sewer authorities.
Bond issues.
Special provisions for Middletown, EN §9-934.
Water and sewer systems.
Failure of county to comply with provisions, EN §9-708.
Weather modification.
Powers of county commissioners as to, 25 §3.
Wine tasting license, 2B §8-406.
Witnesses.
Itinerant allowances, CJ §9-202.
Mileage, CJ §9-202.
Workers' compensation.
Volunteer police officer.
Covered employees and employers, LE §9-233.
Zoning.
Board of appeals, 66B §14.06.
Commercial or industrial zoned property.
Plat approved and recorded before transfer of property, 66B §14.06.
Historic area zoning.
General provisions.
See ZONING.
Subdivision.
Lots.
Sale or transfer in approved subdivisions, 66B §5.05.

FREEDOM.
Arts council.
Interference with freedom of expression or arts programs, 83A §4-609.
Aviation.
Right to free transit through state air space, TR §5-1001.
Press, MD Const DofR Art 40; US Const Amd 1.
Religion.
Religious freedom, MD Const DofR Arts 36, 37; US Const Amd 1.
Speech, MD Const DofR Art 40; US Const Amd 1.
Congress.
Members of congress, US Const Art I §6.
General assembly.
Speech, debate and proceedings in legislature, MD Const DofR Art 10.

FREEDOM OF INFORMATION.
Meetings.
Administrative procedure.
Open sessions, SG §§10-501 to 10-512.
See ADMINISTRATIVE PROCEDURE.
Open meetings.
Public bodies, 41 §1-205.
Records.
Access to public records, SG §§10-611 to 10-628.
See RECORDS.

FREE EXERCISE OF RELIGIOUS BELIEFS,
MD Const DofR Arts 36, 37; US Const Amd 1.
Hate crime.
Obstructing, CR §10-303.

FREESTANDING AMBULATORY CARE FACILITIES, HG §§19-3B-01 to 19-3B-03.
Accreditation.
Health care facilities generally, HG §§19-2301, 19-2302.
Reports, HG §19-3B-03.
Ambulatory surgical facilities.
Defined, HG §19-3B-01.
Medicare certification, HG §19-3B-03.
Birthing center.
Defined, HG §19-3B-01.
Certificates of need.
License application, HG §19-3B-04.
Certified mail.
Notice of hearing.
License revocation, suspension, restriction or denial, HG §19-3B-08.
Complaint investigations, HG §19-3B-07.
Inspection of facilities, HG §19-3B-03.
Credentials.
Establishment of procedures, HG §19-3B-03.
Crimes and offenses.
Violation of provisions, HG §19-3B-09.
Defined, HG §19-3B-01.
Discharge procedures, HG §19-3B-03.
Discrimination against patients prohibited, HG §19-3B-03.
Emergency procedure establishment, HG §19-3B-03.
Endoscopy facility.
Defined, HG §19-3B-01.
Fees.
Licenses, HG §19-3B-05.
Fines, HG §19-3B-09.
Health care practitioners.
Complaint investigations.
Referral to licensing board, HG §19-3B-07.
Defined, HG §19-3B-01.
Joint ventures, HG §19-3B-06.
Qualifications, standards for, HG §19-3B-03.
Hearings.
Licenses.
Revocation, suspension, restriction or denial, HG §19-3B-08.
Inspections, HG §19-3B-03.
Joint ventures, HG §19-3B-06.
Kidney dialysis centers.
Defined, HG §19-3B-01.
Inspection, HG §19-3B-03.
Medicare certification, HG §19-3B-03.
Licenses.
Accreditation report.
Satisfaction of licensing requirements, HG §19-3B-03.
Application, HG §19-3B-04.
Defined, HG §19-3B-01.
Expiration, HG §19-3B-05.
Fees, HG §19-3B-05.
Issuance, HG §19-3B-02.
Denial, HG §19-3B-08.
Renewal, HG §19-3B-05.
Required, HG §19-3B-02.
Restriction, HG §19-3B-08.
Review and approval of rates and services.
No exemptions, HG §19-3B-05.
Revocation, HG §19-3B-08.
Suspension, HG §19-3B-08.
Transfer prohibited, HG §19-3B-02.
Major medical equipment.
Defined, HG §19-3B-01.

FREESTANDING AMBULATORY CARE FACILITIES —Cont'd
Major medical equipment —Cont'd
Freestanding facility operating major medical equipment.
Defined, HG §19-3B-01.
Misdemeanors, HG §19-3B-09.
Notices.
Hearings.
License revocation, suspension, restriction or denial, HG §19-3B-08.
Peer review.
Establishment of procedures, HG §19-3B-03.
Penalties, HG §19-3B-09.
Postoperative recovery procedures, HG §19-3B-03.
Quality control procedures.
Biomedical equipment, HG §19-3B-03.
Reports.
Accreditation report, HG §19-3B-03.
Investigation of facilities, HG §19-3B-03.
Review and approval of rates and services.
License no exemption, HG §19-3B-05.
Rules and regulations.
Administrative penalty for violations, HG §19-3B-09.
Establishment of standards and procedures for operation of facilities, HG §19-3B-03.
Service of process.
Notice of hearing.
License revocation, suspension, restriction or denial, HG §19-3B-08.
Standards, establishment.
Regulations for implementation of subtitle, HG §19-3B-03.
Surgical services.
Defined, HG §19-3B-01.

FREESTANDING BIRTHING CENTERS.
Ambulatory care.
Generally, HG §§19-3B-01 to 19-3B-09.
See FREESTANDING AMBULATORY CARE FACILITIES.

FREESTANDING MEDICAL FACILITIES.
Ambulatory care.
Generally, HG §§19-3B-01 to 19-3B-09.
See FREESTANDING AMBULATORY CARE FACILITIES.
Centers for disease control.
Guidelines on universal precautions.
Compliance with and notice explaining, HG §19-3A-02.
Counties.
Rules and regulations.
Adoption, HG §19-3A-04.
Definitions, HG §19-3A-01.
Establishment of review and approval process, HG §19-131.
Injunctions.
Violations of provisions, HG §19-3A-06.
Licensing.
Emergency facilities, HG §19-3A-03.
Issuance of certificate, HG §19-3A-03.
Pilot project, HG §19-3A-07.
Regulations.
Adoption, HG §19-3A-02.
Standards, HG §19-3A-02.
Suspension for violation of provisions, HG §19-3A-05.
Notices.
Centers for disease controls guidelines on universal precautions.
Compliance with and explaining, HG §19-3A-02.

FREESTANDING MEDICAL FACILITIES —Cont'd
Penalties.
Violation of provisions, HG §19-3A-05.
Pilot project, HG §19-3A-07.
Rules and regulations.
Counties.
Adoption, HG §19-3A-04.
Emergency regulations to establish review and approval process, HG §19-131.
Licensing, HG §19-3A-02.
Violation of provisions.
Injunctions, HG §19-3A-06.
Penalties, HG §19-3A-05.

FREEWAYS.
General provisions, TR §§8-619 to 8-622.
See HIGHWAYS.

FREEZER CABINETS.
Abandonment, CR §10-109.

FREIGHT.
Carriers.
See CARRIERS.
Railroads.
See RAILROADS.
Rates.
See PUBLIC SERVICE COMMISSION.
Vessels and boats.
See VESSELS AND BOATS.

FRESH PURSUIT.
Militia.
Maryland defense force, PS §13-506.
Pursuit by forces from other states, PS §13-507.
Officers in state.
Elements, conditions for, authority of officers engaged in, CP §2-301.
Officers of other states, CP §§2-304 to 2-309.
Arrest in this state, authority of officers, CP §2-305.
Definitions, CP §2-304.
Discharge of arrested person, arrest unlawful, CP §2-306.
Fresh pursuit defined, CP §2-304.
Hearing to determine lawfulness of arrest, CP §2-306.
Notice to other states of passage of act, CP §2-307.
Uniform act on fresh pursuit.
Short title, CP §2-309.
Validity of part, CP §2-308.
State police.
Municipal corporations, authority to act within, PS §2-412.

FRIEND OF THE COURT.
Appellate procedure, AppRev Rule 8-511.
Costs, AppRev Rule 8-607.

FRISKING OF PERSON.
Handguns.
Limited search, seizure and arrest, CR §4-206.

FRONTING AGREEMENTS.
Credit life, health and unemployment insurance, IN §13-116.

FROSTBURG, CITY OF.
Employees' retirement system service credit.
Frostburg city employee, SPP §31-111.3.

FROZEN DESSERTS.
Administrative procedure.
Denial, suspension or revocation of licenses.
Appeals, HG §21-815.

FROZEN DESSERTS —Cont'd
Administrative procedure —Cont'd
Hearings.
Application of act, HG §21-814.
Appeals.
Denial, suspension or revocation of licenses.
Right to appeal, HG §21-815.
Construction of subtitle, HG §21-802.
Copies of statutes.
Secretary to provide, HG §21-803.
Definitions, HG §21-801.
Employees.
Imputation of act or omission, HG §21-802.
Federal act.
Conformance to federal act, HG §21-804.
Fees.
Licenses.
Applications, HG §21-808.
Renewal fee, HG §21-812.
Fines.
Manufacturing on invalid license, HG §21-1205.
Manufacturing without license, HG §21-1206.
Sale of products from unlicensed plant, HG §21-820.
Hearings.
Right to hearing, HG §21-814.
Ice cream.
Weights and measures.
Sale, AG §11-312.
Ice milk.
Weights and measures.
Sale, AG §11-312.
Imputation of act or omission, HG §21-802.
Injunctions.
Repeated offenses, HG §21-819.
Inspections.
License applicants, HG §21-809.
Labels.
Application of requirements to outside container or wrapper, HG §21-802.
Licenses.
Appeals.
Suspensions and revocations, HG §21-815.
Applications, HG §21-808.
Defined, HG §21-801.
Fees.
Application fee, HG §21-808.
Renewal fee, HG §21-812.
Inspections, HG §21-809.
Invalid licenses.
Manufacturing on invalid license, HG §21-819.
Fine, HG §21-1205.
Issuance, HG §21-810.
Manufacturing without license, HG §21-818.
Fine for violation, HG §21-1206.
Nontransferability, HG §21-812.
Qualifications for plants outside state, HG §21-809.
Renewal, HG §21-812.
Required, HG §21-807.
Sale of products from unlicensed plant, HG §21-820.
Scope of license, HG §21-811.
Separate license for each manufacturing plant, HG §21-807.
Suspensions and revocations, HG §21-813.
Appeal, HG §21-815.
Hearings, HG §21-814.
Term of license, HG §21-812.
Low-calorie frozen desserts.
Pasteurization and requirements after rehydration, HG §21-330.

FROZEN DESSERTS —Cont'd
Manufacturing plants.
Licenses.
Separate license for each plant, HG §21-807.
Qualifications for plants outside state, HG §21-809.
Misdemeanors.
Manufacturing on invalid license, HG §21-1205.
Manufacturing without license, HG §21-1206.
Notices.
Licenses.
Renewal notice, HG §21-812.
Violations, HG §21-813.
Outside container or wrapper.
Application of label requirements, HG §21-802.
Prohibited acts.
Injunctions.
Repeated offenses, HG §21-819.
Licenses.
Manufacturing on invalid license, HG §21-819.
Manufacturing without license, HG §21-818.
Sale of products from unlicensed plants, HG §21-820.
Repeated offenses.
Injunctions, HG §21-819.
Sale of products from unlicensed plant.
Fine, HG §21-820.
Rules and regulations.
Adoption, HG §21-804.
Sales.
Products for which standards not set, HG §21-821.
Products from unlicensed plants, HG §21-820.
Secretary.
Collecting and disseminating information, HG §21-803.
Copies of statutes, HG §21-803.
Rules and regulations.
Adoption by secretary, HG §21-804.
Violations.
Injunctions.
Repeated offenses, HG §21-819.
Licenses.
Manufacturing on invalid license, HG §21-819.
Fine, HG §21-1205.
Manufacturing without license, HG §21-818.
Sale of products from unlicensed plants, HG §21-820.
Notice of violations, HG §21-813.
Repeated offenses.
Injunctions, HG §21-819.
Weights and measures.
Ice milk or ice cream.
Sale, AG §11-312.

FROZEN FOOD.
Frozen desserts.
General provisions, HG §§21-801 to 21-821.
See FROZEN DESSERTS.

FRUITS AND VEGETABLES.
Apple grade law.
General provisions, AG §§10-801 to 10-807.
See APPLES.
Cantaloupes.
General provisions, AG §§10-901 to 10-909.
See CANTALOUPES.
Containers.
Marking, AG §10-703.
Noncomplying containers, AG §10-704.
Definitions, AG §10-701.
Examination.
Samples, etc., AG §10-705.

FRUITS AND VEGETABLES —Cont'd
Farm products.
Generally.
See AGRICULTURE.
Grades. See within this heading, "Standards and grades."
Inspections.
Department or United States department of agriculture.
No prosecution when inspection by, AG §10-707.
Marking.
Containers, AG §10-703.
Noncomplying containers, AG §10-704.
Migrant labor.
General provisions, LE §§7-101 to 7-507.
See MIGRANT LABOR.
Packing.
Not liable when not party to, AG §10-706.
Penalties.
Generally, AG §§12-101 to 12-104.
Potatoes.
Seed potato inspections.
General provisions, AG §§9-301 to 9-307.
See POTATOES.
Promotion of use or sale.
General provisions, AG §§10-101 to 10-116.
See AGRICULTURAL PRODUCTS.
Prosecution.
Inspection by department or United States department of agriculture, AG §10-707.
State's attorney, AG §10-708.
Right of entry.
Examination purposes, AG §10-705.
Rules and regulations.
Adoption and enforcement, AG §10-702.
Sales.
Defined, AG §10-701.
Effect on right to sell, AG §10-704.
Secretary of agriculture.
Rules and regulations.
Adoption and enforcement, AG §10-702.
Seeds.
General provisions, AG §§9-201 to 9-214.
See SEEDS.
Standards and grades.
Containers.
Marking, AG §10-703.
Effective date, AG §10-703.
Establishment, AG §10-703.
Grading and packing.
Liability, AG §10-706.
Sale.
Effect on right to sell, AG §10-704.
State's attorney.
Prosecution of violations, AG §10-708.
Trademarks.
Farm products.
General provisions, AG §§10-501 to 10-504.
See AGRICULTURE.
Violations.
Prosecution, AG §10-708.
Weights and measures.
Sale.
Berries and small fruits, AG §11-314.

FUEL.
Emergency management.
State standby petroleum fuel set-aside program, PS §§14-501 to 14-511.

FUEL —Cont'd
Fuel taxes.
Definitions generally, TG §9-101.
Motor carrier tax, TG §§2-1001, 2-1002, 9-201 to 9-222.
See MOTOR CARRIER TAX.
Motor fuel tax, TG §§2-1101 to 2-1104, 9-301 to 9-337.
See MOTOR FUEL TAX.
Gas and oil development.
General provisions, EN §§14-101 to 14-511.
See GAS AND OIL.
Mining.
General provisions, EN §§15-101 to 15-1109.
See MINING.
Motor fuel tax.
General provisions, TG §§2-1101 to 2-1104, 9-301 to 9-337.
See MOTOR FUEL TAX.
Sales and use tax.
Exemptions, TG §11-207.

FUEL OIL.
Possession of destructive device, CR §§4-501 to 4-503.

FUEL RATE ADJUSTMENTS, PUC §§4-401, 4-402.

FUGITIVES FROM JUSTICE.
Extradition.
General provisions, CP §§9-101 to 9-128.
See EXTRADITION.
Firearms.
Dealers' licenses.
Suspension or revocation, PS §5-114.
Restrictions on possession, PS §5-133.
Restrictions on sale, rental or transfer, PS §5-134.
Fresh pursuit, CP §2-301.
Authority of officers in another state to arrest in this state.
Uniform act on fresh pursuit, CP §§2-304 to 2-309.
Harboring, CR §9-402.

FULL FAITH AND CREDIT.
Child custody proceedings.
Uniform child custody jurisdiction and enforcement act.
Out-of-state orders, FL §9.5-313.
County transportation revenue bonds.
Pledge, TR §3-513.
Judgments and decrees.
Foreign judgments.
Enforcement of foreign judgments, CJ §§11-801 to 11-807.
See JUDGMENTS AND DECREES.
Recognition of foreign money judgments, CJ §§10-701 to 10-709.
See FOREIGN MONEY JUDGMENTS.
Public acts.
Judicial proceedings, etc., of a state, US Const Art IV §1.
Transportation.
Bond issues.
Full faith and credit not pledged, TR §4-319.
Consolidated transportation bonds, TR §3-213.

FUNDING AGREEMENTS.
Life insurance and annuities, IN §16-113.

FUNDRAISING.
Election campaign finance.
Disclosures by person doing public business.
Contributions to candidates, EL §§14-101 to
14-108.
See CAMPAIGN FINANCE.
Generally, EL §§13-101 to 13-605.
See CAMPAIGN FINANCE.
Public campaign financing, EL §§15-101 to 15-111.
See CAMPAIGN FINANCE.
Fraud.
Campaigns to benefit police, fire departments or
public safety officers, CR §8-520.
Gaming events and devices by qualified
organization.
Anne Arundel county, CR §§13-401 to 13-408.
Baltimore City, CR §§13-501 to 13-510.
Calvert county, CR §§13-701 to 13-709.
Carroll county, CR §§13-901 to 13-909.
Cecil county, CR §§13-1001 to 13-1005.
Charles county, CR §§13-1101 to 13-1115.
Dorchester county, CR §§13-1201 to 13-1207.
Frederick county, CR §§13-1301 to 13-1307.
Generally, CR §§13-101 to 13-205.
Harford county, CR §§13-1501 to 13-1512.
Howard county, CR §§13-1601 to 13-1604.
Kent county, CR §§13-1701 to 13-1706.
Montgomery county, CR §§13-1801 to 13-1815.
Prince George's county, CR §§13-1901 to 13-1912.
Queen Anne's county, CR §§13-2001 to 13-2006.
St. Mary's county, CR §§13-2101 to 13-2115.
Somerset county, CR §§13-2201, 13-2202.
Talbot county, CR §13-2301.
Washington county, CR §§13-2401 to 13-2438.
Wicomico county, CR §§13-2501 to 13-2508.
Worcester county, CR §§13-2601 to 13-2628.
Political fundraisers.
Anne Arundel county.
Paddle wheel or wheel of fortune, CR §13-406.
Baltimore City.
Paddle wheel or wheel of fortune, CR §13-506.
Baltimore county.
Paddle wheel or wheel of fortune, CR §13-605.

FUND-RAISING ORGANIZATIONS.
Charitable corporations.
Perpetuities, ET §11-102.
Property holding, CA §§5-701, 5-702.
Charitable trusts.
See TRUSTS AND TRUSTEES.
Charities.
Generally.
See CHARITIES.

FUNDS.
Accountants.
State board of public accountancy fund, BR
§2-106.5.
Acupuncture board fund, HO §1A-206.
After-school opportunity fund program, ED
§§7-1201 to 7-1207.
See AFTER-SCHOOL OPPORTUNITY FUND
PROGRAM.
Agricultural education and rural development
assistance fund, SF §2-206.
Agricultural land preservation fund, AG §2-505.
See AGRICULTURE.
Air quality control.
Maryland clean air fund, EN §2-107.
Ambulances.
Senator William H. Amoss fire, rescue and
ambulance fund, PS §§8-101 to 8-106.

FUNDS —Cont'd
Ambulances —Cont'd
Volunteer company assistance fund, PS §§8-201 to
8-206.
Animal health fund.
Livestock diseases, AG §3-117.
Archives fund, SG §9-1013.
Assistive technology guaranteed loan fund, 41
§§14-901 to 14-914.
See ASSISTIVE TECHNOLOGY GUARANTEED
LOAN FUND.
Attorneys at law.
Clients' protection fund, BOP §§10-310 to 10-313.
See ATTORNEYS AT LAW.
Disbarment or suspension.
Attorney grievance commission.
Disciplinary fund, CJA Rule 16-714.
Audiologists, hearing aid dealers and
speech-language pathologists.
Board of examiners' fund, HO §2-206.
Automobile insurance fund.
General provisions, IN §§20-101 to 20-701.
See AUTOMOBILE INSURANCE FUND.
Baltimore City police death relief fund, 24
§§16-101 to 16-106.
See BALTIMORE CITY.
Baltimore convention center financing fund, FI
§13-716.
Barn preservation fund, SF §5A-403.
Bay restoration fund, EN §9-1605.2.
Beach replenishment fund, NR §§8-1103, 8-1104.
See SHORE EROSION CONTROL.
Birds and game.
Chesapeake Bay and endangered species fund, NR
§§1-701 to 1-706.
See CHESAPEAKE BAY AND ENDANGERED
SPECIES FUND.
Nongame and endangered species conservation
act.
Birdwatcher's fund, NR §10-2A-06.1.
State wildlife management and protection fund,
NR §10-209.
Upland wildlife habitat fund, NR §10-301.
Bituminous coal open-pit mining reclamation
fund, EN §15-515.
Black bear damage reimbursement, NR
§10-423.1.
Canal place preservation and development
authority.
Financing fund, FI §13-1017.
Cancer.
Maryland cancer fund.
Income tax checkoff, HG §20-117.
Cemeteries.
Oversight fund, BR §5-205.
Trust fund required.
Perpetual care of cemeteries, BR §5-602.
Chesapeake Bay and endangered species fund,
NR §§1-701 to 1-706.
See CHESAPEAKE BAY AND ENDANGERED
SPECIES FUND.
Children' cabinet fund.
Children, youth and families services, 49D
§§5-101 to 5-104.
Children's trust fund, HG §13-2207.
Child support reinvestment fund, FL §10-106.1.
Cigarette restitution fund, SF §7-317.
Clients' security fund, CJA Rule 16-811.
Commercial ambulance service fund, ED
§13-515.

FUNDS —Cont'd

Community energy loan program fund, SG
§9-2107.
Community health resources commission fund,
HG §19-2201.
Community reinvestment fund, HS §§9-101 to
9-501.
Community right-to-know fund.
Hazardous materials and substances, EN §§7-601
to 7-605.
Community services trust fund, HG §§24-1101 to
24-1105.
Contingent fund.
Governor, MD Const Art III §32.
Credit unions, FI §6-306.
Reserve fund, FI §§6-306, 6-703.
Criminal injuries compensation fund.
Minors to pay costs.
Alcoholic beverages convictions, CR §10-119.
Debt management services fund, FI §12-905.
Deep Creek Lake.
Recreation maintenance and management fund,
NR §5-215.
Deposit insurance fund corporation.
See DEPOSIT INSURANCE FUND
CORPORATION.
Dietitians.
Board of dietetic practice fund, HO §5-206.
DNA technology fund, 41 §4-301.
Dog license fund, 24 §11-507.
Domestic violence unit pilot program, FL
§4-503.2.
Draining lands.
Drainage district fund, 25 §121H.
Drinking driver monitor program fund, COR
§6-116.
Drinking water revolving loan fund, EN
§9-1605.1.
Drug or alcohol abuse.
Maryland drug and alcohol grants program fund,
CR §5-1002.
Maryland substance abuse fund, HG §8-6A-01.
Economic development assistance fund, 83A
§§5-1401 to 5-1412.
Educational excellence fund, ED §18-310.
Education partnership fund, ED §2-207.
Egg law fund, AG §4-311.5.
Elderly rental housing fund.
See HOUSING AND COMMUNITY
DEVELOPMENT DEPARTMENT.
Election modernization fund, EL §2-107.
Electric companies.
Universal service program fund, PUC §7-512.1.
Electricity.
Environmental trust fund.
Power plants research program, NR §3-302.
Emergency medical service system fund, SF
§7-313.
**Employees and retirees health and welfare
benefits fund,** SPP §2-516.
EMS board provider fund, ED §13-516.
Endangered species.
Chesapeake Bay and endangered species fund, NR
§§1-701 to 1-706.
See CHESAPEAKE BAY AND ENDANGERED
SPECIES FUND.
**Energy efficiency and economic development
loan program fund,** SG §9-20A-07.
Energy overcharge restitution fund, SF §7-315.
Escrow funds.
See ESCROW.

FUNDS —Cont'd

Fair campaign financing fund, EL §15-103.
Fair Hill improvement fund, NR §5-908.
Fair share health care fund, HG §15-142.
Family daycare provider direct grant fund, FL
§§5-559.1 to 5-559.8.
See CHILD CARE.
Film production employer wage rebate fund,
83A §5-1805.
Fire department.
Senator William H. Amoss fire, rescue and
ambulance fund, PS §§8-101 to 8-106.
Volunteer company assistance fund, PS §§8-201 to
8-206.
Fish and fisheries.
Fisheries research and development fund, NR
§4-209.
State fisheries management and protection fund,
NR §4-208.
Anglers' licenses.
Fees credited to fund, NR §4-608.
Forests and parks.
Forest conservation fund, NR §5-1610.
General provisions.
See FORESTS AND PARKS.
Reforestation.
Reforestation fund, NR §5-103.
Woodland incentives fund, NR §5-307.
Governor.
Contingent fund, MD Const Art III §32.
Grain.
Administrative fund, AG §§13-202, 13-205.
Hazardous materials and substances.
Community right-to-know fund, EN §§7-601 to
7-605.
State hazardous substance control fund, EN
§§7-218 to 7-221.
See HAZARDOUS MATERIALS AND
SUBSTANCES.
Health care commission fund.
Deposits into fund, IN §15-111.
Health care regulatory fund, IN §§2-112.2,
2-112.3.
Healthchoice performance incentive fund, HG
§15-103.3.
Health club services.
Health club administration fund, CL §14-12B-03.
Health services cost review commission fund,
HG §19-213.
Heritage areas authority financing fund, FI
§13-1114.
Heritage conservation fund, NR §§5-1501 to
5-1506.
See HERITAGE CONSERVATION FUND.
**Hippodrome performing arts center financing
fund,** FI §13-717.2.
Historic marker program fund, SF §5A-329.
Historic St. Mary's City fund, ED §24-511.
Homebuilder registration, BR §4.5-203.
Home improvements.
Guaranty fund, BR §§8-401 to 8-411.
See HOME IMPROVEMENTS.
Horse industry fund, AG §2-708.2.
Commercial equine feed assessments, AG
§6-107.2.
Horse racing.
Maryland backstretch employees pension fund.
Administration, BR §11-319.
Maryland-bred racing fund.
General provisions, BR §§11-529 to 11-541.
See THOROUGHBRED RACING.

FUNDS —Cont'd

Horse racing —Cont'd

Maryland harness track employees pension fund.
Administration, BR §11-319.

Maryland horsemen's assistance fund.
Disposition of money, BR §11-909.

Maryland jockey injury compensation fund.
General provisions, BR §§11-901 to 11-906.
See HORSE RACING.

Maryland race track employees pension fund.
Administration, BR §11-319.

Maryland standardbred race fund.
General provisions, BR §§11-623 to 11-636.
See HARNESS RACING.

Special fund, BR §§11-401 to 11-406.
See HORSE RACING.

Hospital employees retraining fund, LE §11-201.

Housing.

Home improvement guaranty fund, BR §§8-401 to 8-411.
See HOME IMPROVEMENTS.

Housing and community development.

Community legacy financial assistance fund, HS §6-213.

Community reinvestment fund, HS §§9-101 to 9-501.

Neighborhood business development fund, HS §6-310.

Industrial development fund, 83A §5-914.

Information technology.

Major information technology development fund, SF §3-410.2.

Inmate welfare funds, COR §§10-501 to 10-504.

Insurance regulation fund, IN §2-505.

Joint committee on the management of public funds, SG §§2-801 to 2-807.

Kidney disease fund, HG §13-310.1.

Land trust grant fund, NR §§3-2A-01 to 3-2A-14.
See LAND TRUST GRANT FUND.

Law-enforcement and correctional training fund, COR §§8-301 to 8-305.

Law enforcement equipment fund, PS §§4-301 to 4-304.

Law enforcement officers and personnel.

Law enforcement equipment fund, PS §§4-301 to 4-304.

Protective body armor fund, PS §§4-101 to 4-107.

School bus safety enforcement fund, PS §§4-201 to 4-204.

Lead accreditation fund, EN §6-1004.

Lead poisoning prevention fund, EN §§6-843 to 6-845.

Legal mutual liability insurance society of Maryland.

Rate stabilization reserve fund, IN §24-107.

Libraries.
See LIBRARIES.

Libraries, county.
See LIBRARIES, COUNTY.

Licensing testing fund, BR §2-106.

Lottery.

State lottery fund, SG §9-118.

Maryland affordable housing trust fund.

Established, HS §10-201.

Investments, HS §10-206.

Purposes, HS §10-202.

Source of revenue, HS §10-204.
Solicitation of funds by board, HS §10-205.

Status, HS §10-203.

FUNDS —Cont'd

Maryland after-school opportunity fund program, ED §§7-1201 to 7-1207.
See AFTER-SCHOOL OPPORTUNITY FUND PROGRAM.

Maryland agricultural education and rural development assistance fund, SF §2-206.

Maryland automobile insurance fund, IN §§20-101 to 20-701.
See AUTOMOBILE INSURANCE FUND.

Maryland cancer fund.

Income tax checkoff, HG §20-117.

Maryland economic adjustment fund, 83A §§6-501 to 6-512.
See BUSINESS AND ECONOMIC DEVELOPMENT DEPARTMENT.

Maryland economic development assistance fund, 83A §§5-1401 to 5-1412.

Maryland election modernization fund, EL §2-107.

Maryland health care commission fund, HG §19-111.

Maryland health care provider rate stabilization fund, IN §§19-801 to 19-808.
See MARYLAND HEALTH CARE PROVIDER RATE STABILIZATION FUND.

Maryland health insurance plan.

Established, IN §14-504.

Fund financial report, IN §14-503.

Senior prescription drug assistance program, IN §§14-504, 14-513.
Advertising and promotional materials, IN §14-515.

Maryland historical trust.

Historic marker program fund, SF §5A-329.

MHT grant fund, SF §5A-328.

MHT loan fund, SF §5A-327.

Maryland horse industry fund, AG §2-708.2.

Commercial equine feed assessments, AG §6-107.2.

Maryland legal services corporation fund, CJ §7-408.

Maryland medical professional liability insurance rate stabilization fund, IN §19-104.1.

Maryland public art fund, 83A §4-6A-03.

Maryland renewable energy fund, PUC §7-707.

Maryland stadium authority.

Baltimore convention center financing fund, FI §13-716.

Financing fund, FI §13-715.
Payments by Baltimore City, FI §13-715.1.

Hippodrome performing arts center financing fund, FI §13-717.2.

Lotteries benefiting the authority, SG §9-120.1.

Montgomery county conference center financing fund, FI §13-717.1.

Ocean City convention center financing fund, FI §13-717.

Public school construction fund.
Payments, FI §13-715.2.

Maryland stadium facilities fund, SF §7-312.

Distribution of state lottery fund, SG §9-120.

Maryland state Appalachian housing fund, HS §§11-101 to 11-106.

Definition of fund, HS §11-101.

Establishment, HS §11-102.

Investments, HS §11-106.

Purpose, HS §11-103.

Source of revenue, HS §11-105.

Status, HS §11-104.

FUNDS —Cont'd

Maryland trauma physician services fund, HG §19-130.

Maryland virtual learning opportunities fund, ED §7-1002.

Maryland-Washington regional district.
Land acquisition revolving fund, 28 §7-106.

Mental hygiene community-based services fund, HG §10-208.

MHT grant fund, SF §5A-328.

MHT loan fund, SF §5A-327.

Mining.
Abandoned mine drainage capital fund, EN §15-704.

Water supply replacement reserve fund, EN §15-524.

Money transmission fund, FI §12-404.

Montgomery county conference center financing fund, FI §13-717.1.

Mortgage lender-originator fund, FI §11-610.

Motor vehicles.
Emergency medical system operations fund, TR §§13-954, 13-955.

Maryland automobile insurance fund, IN §§20-101 to 20-701.
See AUTOMOBILE INSURANCE FUND.

Security interests.
Assurance fund, TR §13-209.

Natural resources property maintenance fund, NR §5-909.

Neighborhood business development fund, HS §6-310.

Neighborhood housing services fund, HS §§4-1001 to 4-1005.
Development finance division.
Units in division, HS §4-103.

Occupational therapy practice fund, HO §10-206.

Ocean beach replenishment fund, NR §§8-1103, 8-1104.
See SHORE EROSION CONTROL.

Ocean City convention center financing fund, FI §13-717.

Oil contaminated site environmental cleanup fund.
General provisions, EN §§4-701 to 4-708.
See ENVIRONMENT.

Organ and tissue donation awareness fund, HG §13-901.

Partnership for workforce quality fund, 83A §3-702.1.
Use, 83A §3-703.

People's insurance counsel fund, SG §6-305.

Pest control compact.
Insurance fund.
See PESTS.

Physical therapy examiners fund, HO §13-207.

Physicians.
Board of physicians fund, HO §14-207.
Maryland trauma physician services fund, HG §19-130.

Pilots.
Maintenance and replacement fund, BOP §11-506.

Planning.
Capital program.
General construction project contingency fund, SF §3-609.
Revolving preliminary planning fund, SF §3-608.

Postretirement health benefits trust fund, SPP §34-101.
Commission to study retiree health care funding options, SPP §34-201.

FUNDS —Cont'd

Prince George's county and Montgomery county historic property grant program, 28 §5-306.

Professional counselors and therapists.
State board of professional counselors and therapists fund, HO §17-206.

Protective body armor fund, PS §§4-101 to 4-107.

Public school construction fund, SF §7-326.
Payments by Maryland stadium authority, FI §13-715.2.

Public utility regulation fund, PUC §2-110.1.

Radiation.
State radiation control fund, EN §8-306.

Real estate brokers.
Guaranty fund, BOP §§17-401 to 17-412.
See REAL ESTATE BROKERS.

Real estate commission fund, BR §2-106.2.

Recycling solid waste.
Newsprint recycling by newspapers.
State recycling trust fund, EN §9-1707.
Used tires.
State used tire cleanup and recycling fund, EN §§9-273 to 9-278.
See TIRES.

Rehabilitation services.
Employment program fund, ED §21-303.

Renewable energy fund, PUC §7-707.

Rescue squads.
Senator William H. Amoss fire, rescue and ambulance fund, PS §§8-101 to 8-106.
Volunteer company assistance fund, PS §§8-201 to 8-206.

Rural broadband assistance fund, 83A §§5-1901, 5-1902.

Rural Maryland prosperity investment fund, SF §2-207.

Savings and loan associations.
Expense fund.
Incorporators, FI §9-220.

Savings banks.
Guaranty fund.
See BANKS AND TRUST COMPANIES.

Scholarships.
See SCHOLARSHIPS.

School bus safety enforcement fund, PS §§4-201 to 4-204.

Schools.
See SCHOOLS.

Schools for success fund, ED §5-204.

Seafood.
Seafood marketing fund, AG §10-1002.

Senator William H. Amoss fire, rescue and ambulance fund, PS §§8-101 to 8-106.

Senior citizen activities center operating fund, 70B §§33 to 35.

Sewage sludge.
Sewage sludge utilization fund, EN §9-244.

Shore erosion control.
Construction loan fund, NR §8-1005.
Ocean beach replenishment fund, NR §§8-1103, 8-1104.

Small business development center network fund.
University of Maryland, ED §13-104.

Small business development financing authority.
See SMALL BUSINESS DEVELOPMENT FINANCING AUTHORITY.

FUNDS —Cont'd

Small business pollution compliance loan fund, EN §§2-801 to 2-806.

Somers Cove Marina improvement fund, NR §5-908.1.

Spinal cord injury research trust fund, HG §13-1406.

State and local facilities loan fund.
State bonds, SF §8-125.

State board of veterinary medical examiners fund, AG §2-303.

State employees' leave bank, SPP §§9-601 to 9-608.

State occupational and professional licensing design board's fund, BR §2-106.1.

State police helicopter replacement fund, PS §2-801.
Motor vehicle violation surcharge, deposit, TR §27-101.2.

State reserve fund, SF §7-309.

State school fund, ED §5-201.

Stem cell research fund, 83A §5-2B-03.

Strip mining.
Bituminous coal open-pit mining reclamation fund, EN §15-515.

Substance abuse treatment outcome partnership fund, HG §§8-6C-01 to 8-6C-04.

Tax increment financing act.
Special fund.
Agreements to pay revenue from taxes or on tax increments into special fund, 41 §14-209.
Resolution creating, 41 §14-207.
Uses of special fund, 41 §14-208.

Tires.
State used tire cleanup and recycling fund, EN §§9-273 to 9-278.
See TIRES.

Transportation department.
See TRANSPORTATION DEPARTMENT.

Transportation trust fund.
See TRANSPORTATION TRUST FUND.

Trauma physician services fund, HG §19-130.

Underground storage tank upgrade and replacement fund, EN §§4-601 to 4-607.
See UNDERGROUND STORAGE TANK UPGRADE AND REPLACEMENT FUND.

Unemployment compensation.
See UNEMPLOYMENT COMPENSATION.

University of Maryland.
Medical system.
Operating reserve fund, ED §13-309.

Used tires.
State used tire cleanup and recycling fund, EN §§9-273 to 9-278.
See TIRES.

Vehicle theft prevention fund, PS §2-703.
Defined terms, PS §2-701.

Virtual learning opportunities fund, ED §7-1002.

Voluntary cleanup fund, EN §7-504.

Volunteer company assistance fund, PS §§8-201 to 8-206.
Motor vehicle violation surcharge, deposit, TR §27-101.2.

Waiting list equity fund.
Developmental disabilities.
Community based services, HG §7-206.

Water and sewer systems.
On-site and small community waste water disposal fund.
Carroll county, EN §9-1105.

FUNDS —Cont'd

Water and sewer systems —Cont'd
Sanitary facilities fund, EN §9-218.
Tires.
Used tires.
State used tire cleanup and recycling fund, EN §§9-273 to 9-278.

Water pollution.
Maryland clean water fund, EN §9-320.
Maryland oil disaster containment, cleanup and contingency fund, EN §4-411.
Water pollution control fund, EN §§9-345 to 9-351.
See WATER POLLUTION CONTROL FUND.

Water quality revolving loan fund, EN §§9-1605, 9-1605.1.

Waterway improvement fund, NR §§8-707 to 8-709.

Weights and measures fund, AG §11-204.6.

Wetlands.
Nontidal wetland compensation fund, EN §5-909.
Wetlands compensation fund, EN §16-205.

William Donald Schaefer scholarship fund, ED §18-2706.

Wine and grape promotion fund, AG §2-1102.

Woodland incentives program.
Woodland incentives fund, NR §5-307.

Workers' compensation.
Injured workers' insurance fund, LE §§10-101 to 10-141.
Self-insurers' guaranty fund, IN §25-305.
Subsequent injury fund, LE §§10-201 to 10-219.
Uninsured employers fund, LE §§10-301 to 10-320.

Workers' compensation fund, LE §9-319.

Workforce shortage student assistance grant fund, ED §18-708.

FUNDS TRANSFERS, CL §§4A-101 to 4A-507.

Account of customer.
Debit of account.
Preclusion of objection, CL §4A-505.

Account of sender.
Order of charges and withdrawals, CL §4A-504.

Applicability of article, CL §4A-102.

Bank deposits and collections.
General provisions, CL §§4-101 to 4-504.
See BANK DEPOSITS AND COLLECTIONS.

Citation of article.
Short title, CL §4A-101.

Commercial code's general provisions, CL §§1-101 to 1-208.
See COMMERCIAL CODE.

Conflict of laws, CL §4A-507.
Federal electronic fund transfer act of 1978, CL §4A-107.
Federal reserve regulations and operating circulars, CL §4A-107.

Creditor process served on receiving bank, CL §4A-502.

Definitions, CL §§4A-103 to 4A-105.
Creditor process, CL §4A-502.
Execution and execution date, CL §4A-301.
Funds-transfer system rule, CL §4A-501.
Payment date, CL §4A-401.
Security procedure, CL §4A-201.

Discharge of underlying obligation.
Payment of payment order by originator to beneficiary, CL §4A-406.

Federal electronic fund transfer act of 1978.
Applicability of article, CL §4A-108.

FUNDS TRANSFERS —Cont'd
Federal reserve regulations and operating circulars.
Effect on article, CL §4A-107.
Funds-transfer system rule, CL §4A-501.
Injunctions, CL §4A-503.
Interpretation and construction.
Commercial code's general provisions, CL §§1-101 to 1-208.
See COMMERCIAL CODE.
Payment orders.
Acceptance, CL §4A-209.
Amendment, CL §4A-211.
Authorized orders, CL §4A-202.
Beneficiary bank's description.
Misdescription, CL §4A-208.
Beneficiary's description.
Misdescription, CL §4A-207.
Cancellation, CL §4A-211.
Charging to account, CL §4A-504.
Defined, CL §4A-103.
Erroneous orders, CL §4A-205.
Execution, CL §4A-301.
Erroneous execution, CL §4A-303.
Duty of sender to report, CL §4A-304.
Improper execution.
Liability, CL §4A-305.
Obligations of receiving bank, CL §4A-302.
Execution date, CL §4A-301.
Instruction to make more than one payment to beneficiary.
Effect as separate payment order with respect to each payment, CL §4A-103.
Interest, CL §4A-506.
Intermediary bank's description.
Misdescription, CL §4A-208.
Issuance.
When sent, CL §4A-103.
Payment.
Instructions.
More than one payment to beneficiary, CL §4A-103.
Obligation of beneficiary's bank to pay, CL §4A-404.
Obligation of sender to pay receiving bank, CL §4A-402.
Payment by beneficiary's bank to beneficiary, CL §4A-405.
Payment by originator to beneficiary, CL §4A-406.
Payment by sender to receiving bank, CL §4A-403.
Payment date, CL §4A-401.
Refund of payment.
Unauthorized orders, CL §4A-204.
Rejection, CL §4A-210.
Liability and duty of receiving bank, CL §4A-212.
Security procedure, CL §4A-201.
Time received, CL §4A-106.
Transmission, CL §4A-206.
Unauthorized orders, CL §4A-204.
Verified orders, CL §4A-202.
Unenforceability of certain orders, CL §4A-203.
Restraining orders, CL §4A-503.
Security procedure, CL §4A-201.
Setoff by beneficiary's bank, CL §4A-502.
Short title, CL §4A-101.
Variation of article by agreement, CL §4A-501.

FUNERAL DIRECTORS.
See MORTICIANS.

FUNERALS.
Burial insurance, IN §27-218.
Business of burial insurance subject to provisions concerning life insurers, IN §16-115.
Preneed burial contracts not insurance, BR §5-702.
Child care.
Foster care.
Payment of funeral expenses, FL §5-531.
Compassionate leave from confinement.
Inmates sentenced to jurisdiction of division of correction, COR §3-808.
Death by wrongful act.
Petition and order for funeral expenses.
Form, Estates Rule 6-415.
Executors and administrators.
Settlement of decedents' estates.
Funeral expenses.
Petition and order for funeral expenses.
Form, Estates Rule 6-415.
Expenses.
Aid to families with dependent children.
Payment of funeral expenses by local unit, 88A §62A.
Burial insurance, IN §27-218.
Business of burial insurance subject to provisions concerning life insurers, IN §16-115.
Preneed burial contracts not insurance, BR §5-702.
Child care.
Foster care.
Payment of funeral expenses, FL §5-531.
Counties.
Provided for paupers, 25 §20.
Executors and administrators.
Allowance, ET §8-106.
Death by wrongful act.
Limitation on recovery, ET §7-401.
Payment, ET §8-106.
Order of payment when assets insufficient, ET §8-105.
Powers of personal representative, ET §7-401.
Petition and order for funeral expenses.
Form, Estates Rule 6-415.
Petition of creditor, ET §8-106.
Foster care program.
Payment of funeral expenses by local unit, 88A §62A.
General public assistance.
Payment of funeral expenses by local unit, 88A §62A.
Indigent inmates at state correctional facility, payment, COR §9-604.
Petition and order for funeral expenses.
Form, Estates Rule 6-415.
Fraternal benefit societies.
Funeral benefits, IN §8-430.
Ownership of funeral home prohibited, IN §8-437.
Inmates sentenced to jurisdiction of division of correction.
Compassionate leave from confinement, COR §3-808.
Militia.
Vietnam veterans.
Honor guard at burial service, PS §13-215.
Morticians.
See MORTICIANS.
Nursing homes.
Unclaimed deceased resident.
Director to set guidelines for funeral and burial arrangements, 70B §5A.

FUNERALS —Cont'd
Obstruction of entry or exit or of procession, CR §10-205.
Pre-need burial contracts.
Definitions, HO §7-101.
Funding by life insurance policy or annuity, HO §7-405.
Morticians.
Powers and duties under, HO §7-405.
Processions.
Motor vehicles.
Following too closely.
Exception as to funeral processions, TR §21-310.
Headlights required to be turned on, TR §21-207.
Regulations, TR §21-207.
Vietnam veterans.
Militia.
Honor guard at burial service, PS §13-215.

FUNERARY OBJECTS.
Defined, CR §10-401.
Destroying, CR §10-404.
Selling unlawfully removed objects, CR §10-403.

FUNGIBLE GOODS.
Buyer in the ordinary course of business.
Delivery by warehouse, CL §7-205.
Duplicate receipt or bill.
Rights conferred, CL §7-402.
Warehouseman.
Duty to keep goods separate, CL §7-207.
Liability for commingling goods, CL §7-207.

FUNGICIDES.
Pesticides generally.
See PESTICIDES.

FUTURE ADVANCES.
Secured transactions.
Priority of security interests.
Buyers of goods, ordinary course of business, CL §9-323.
Commitment, advances pursuant to, CL §9-323.
Buyers of receivables holding interest, CL §9-323.
Lessees of goods, CL §9-323.
Commitment, advances pursuant to, CL §9-323.
Lien creditors, CL §9-323.
Time of advance basis, CL §9-323.
Security interest in, CL §9-204.

G

GALENA.
Alcoholic beverages.
Profits and reserves.
Accounted, 2B §15-207.

GAMBLING.
Gaming.
See GAMING.
Lotteries, CR §§12-201 to 12-212.
See LOTTERIES.
Maryland horse racing act.
General provisions, BR §§11-101 to 11-1205.
See HORSE RACING.
Harness racing, BR §§11-601 to 11-636.
See HARNESS RACING.

GAMBLING —Cont'd
Maryland horse racing act —Cont'd
Pari-mutuel betting, BR §§11-801 to 11-832.
See PARI-MUTUEL BETTING.
Thoroughbred racing, BR §§11-501 to 11-541.
See THOROUGHBRED RACING.
Slot machines, CR §§12-301 to 12-307.
See SLOT MACHINES.

GAMBLING FORFEITURES, CP §§13-101 to 13-109.
Complaint for forfeiture.
Application process, CP §13-105.
Notice requirement, CP §13-108.
Prima facie evidence money is contraband, CP §13-107.
Complaint for return of money.
Deadline for filing, CP §13-106.
Generally, CP §13-106.
Prima facie evidence money not contraband, CP §13-107.
Definitions, CP §13-101.
Judicial discretion.
Effect of subtitle, CP §13-109.
Money presumed contraband, CP §13-102.
Deposit and investment of seized money, CP §13-104.
Photographing the money, CP §13-103.
Recording the sum quantity of each denomination, CP §13-103.

GAMBLING LOSS.
Competent witness to prove loss, CR §12-110.
Recovery as common debt, CR §12-110.

GAME LAWS.
General provisions.
See BIRDS AND GAME.

GAME WARDENS.
Natural resources police force, NR §§1-201 to 1-210.
See NATURAL RESOURCES.

GAMING, CR §§12-101 to 12-113.
Betting, wagering or gambling prohibited, CR §12-102.
Bill of particulars.
Charging document, CR §12-111.
Book or pool.
Making or selling prohibited, CR §12-102.
Caroline county.
Alcoholic beverages.
Class A beer, wine or liquor licenses.
Persons under age 18 engaging in games of chance or skill, 2B §12-206.
Certain games prohibited, CR §12-103.
Charging document, CR §12-111.
Charitable organization.
Raffles, CR §12-106.
Citations.
Baltimore City, CR §12-102.
Compulsive gamblers.
Defined, HG §19-801.
Grants and aid, HG §19-804.
Legislative findings, HG §19-802.
Pilot center.
Established, HG §19-803.
Providers, HG §19-804.
Construction and interpretation of criminal provisions, CR §12-113.
Craps, playing prohibited, CR §12-103.
Cruise ships, TR §6-209.

GAMING —Cont'd
Definitions, CR §12-101.
Elections.
　Wagering on elections, EL §16-902.
Fixing horse race results, CR §12-109.
Gambling forfeitures, CP §§13-101 to 13-109.
　See GAMBLING FORFEITURES.
Gaming device.
　Conducting or keeping on or over the waters of
　　the state, CR §12-105.
　Defined, CR §12-101.
　Keeping, dealing, managing or having interest in,
　　CR §12-104.
　Law enforcement officer's duty.
　　Suspicion that gaming device kept unlawfully,
　　　CR §12-111.
　Recovery of money lost.
　　Common debt, competent witness as to loss, CR
　　　§12-110.
Gaming events.
　Accepting credit to allow person to play, CR
　　§12-108.
　Defined, CR §12-101.
　Local provisions.
　　Anne Arundel county, CR §§13-401 to 13-408.
　　Baltimore City, CR §§13-501 to 13-510.
　　Baltimore county, CR §§13-601 to 13-607.
　　Calvert county, CR §§13-701 to 13-709.
　　Carroll county, CR §§13-901 to 13-909.
　　Cecil county, CR §§13-1001 to 13-1005.
　　Charles county, CR §§13-1101 to 13-1115.
　　Dorchester county, CR §§13-1201 to 13-1207.
　　Frederick county, CR §§13-1301 to 13-1307.
　　Garrett county, CR §§13-1401 to 13-1406.
　　Harford county, CR §§13-1501 to 13-1512.
　　Howard county, CR §§13-1601 to 13-1604.
　　Kent county, CR §§13-1701 to 13-1706.
　　Montgomery county, CR §§13-1801 to 13-1815.
　　Prince George's county, CR §§13-1901 to
　　　13-1912.
　　Queen Anne's county, CR §§13-2001 to 13-2006.
　　St. Mary's county, CR §§13-2101 to 13-2115.
　　Scope of provisions, CR §13-101.
　　Somerset county, CR §§13-2201, 13-2202.
　　Talbot county, CR §13-2301.
　　Washington county, CR §§13-2401 to 13-2438.
　　Wicomico county, CR §§13-2501 to 13-2508.
　　Worcester county, CR §§13-2601 to 13-2628.
　Tokens, use allowed, CR §12-108.
Income tax.
　Estimated tax.
　　Income from wagering.
　　　Declaration, TG §10-820.
　　　Payment of estimated tax, TG §10-902.
Keeping place for purposes of betting,
　wagering or gambling, CR §§12-102, 12-104.
　For gaming device, CR §12-105.
Law enforcement officer's duty.
　Suspicion that gaming device kept unlawfully, CR
　　§12-111.
Liberal construction of provisions, CR §12-111.
Little joker, playing prohibited, CR §12-103.
Lotteries, CR §§12-201 to 12-212.
　See LOTTERIES.
Maryland horse racing act.
　General provisions, BR §§11-101 to 11-1205.
　　See HORSE RACING.
　Harness racing, BR §§11-601 to 11-636.
　　See HARNESS RACING.
　Pari-mutuel betting, BR §§11-801 to 11-832.
　　See PARI-MUTUEL BETTING.

GAMING —Cont'd
Maryland horse racing act —Cont'd
　Thoroughbred racing, BR §§11-501 to 11-541.
　　See THOROUGHBRED RACING.
Militia.
　Commanding officers.
　　Powers to regulate or prohibit, PS §13-208.
Passenger cruise vessels, TR §6-209.
Political committee or candidate.
　Raffles, CR §12-106.
Prearrangement or predetermination of horse
　race results, CR §12-109.
Raffles.
　See RAFFLES.
Receiving or becoming depository of money,
　CR §12-102.
Recovery of money lost.
　Common debt, competent witness as to loss, CR
　　§12-110.
Slot machines, CR §§12-301 to 12-307.
　See SLOT MACHINES.
Thimbles, playing prohibited, CR §12-103.
Vessels and boats.
　Keeping vessel or structure for gaming device, CR
　　§12-105.
　Passenger cruise vessels, TR §6-209.

GANGS.
Criminal gang offenses, CR §§9-801 to 9-803.
　Definitions, CR §9-801.
　Generally, CR §9-802.
　Penalties, CR §9-802.
　　Schools, CR §9-803.
　Schools, CR §9-803.

GARAGE DOOR OPENERS.
Code grabbing devices.
　Manufacturing, selling or possessing, CR §7-301.
Deactivation tool or device.
　Possessing, using, CR §7-301.
Removal of system or device, CR §7-301.

GARAGES.
Citation for recordkeeping violations, TR
　§§13-113.1 to 15-116.
Home improvement law.
　General provisions, BR §§8-101 to 8-702.
　　See HOME IMPROVEMENTS.
Licenses, BR §§17-801 to 17-803.
Mechanics' liens.
　General provisions, CL §§16-201 to 16-209.
　　See MECHANICS' LIENS.
Motor vehicle repairs, CL §§14-1001 to 14-1009.
　See MOTOR VEHICLE REPAIR FACILITIES.

GARBAGE AND REFUSE.
Counties.
　Chartered counties.
　　Powers as to waste disposal, 25A §5.
　Collection and disposal.
　　Household hazardous waste.
　　　Definitions, EN §9-1801.
　　　Feasibility study, EN §9-1802.
　　　　Assistance by secretary, EN §9-1803.
　　Powers of county commissioners, 25 §3.
　Disposal facilities.
　　Powers of county commissioners, 25 §14A.
　Household hazardous waste.
　　Collection and acceptance from residents.
　　　Definitions, EN §9-1801.
　　　Feasibility study, EN §9-1802.
　　　　Assistance by secretary, EN §9-1803.

GARBAGE AND REFUSE —Cont'd
Counties —Cont'd
Municipal corporations.
Contracts with county for disposal of refuse.
Power of county commissioners, 25 §14A.
Definitions.
Household hazardous waste, EN §9-1801.
Dumping site surveillance systems, CR §10-112.
Citations, procedure, CJ §7-302.
Fireworks plants.
Safety standards, PS §10-207.
Highways.
Putting glass, injurious substances or refuse on
highways prohibited, TR §21-1111.
Household hazardous waste.
Collection and acceptance by residents of counties.
Definitions, EN §9-1801.
Feasibility study, EN §9-1802.
Assistance by secretary, EN §9-1803.
Litter control law, CR §10-110.
Dumping site surveillance systems, CR §10-112.
Citations, procedure, CJ §7-302.
Maryland food center authority.
Disposition of refuse, 41 §13-109.
Municipal corporations.
Disposal facilities.
Contract with county for purpose of disposing of
refuse, 25 §14A.
Powers as to, 23A §2.
Recycling solid waste.
General provisions, EN §§9-1701 to 9-1706.
See RECYCLING SOLID WASTE.
Swine.
Feeding garbage to swine, AG §3-404.
Vessels and boats.
Depositing refuse upon waters of the state.
Prohibited, NR §8-726.
Waters of the state.
Depositing refuse in waters prohibited, NR
§8-726.
Throwing or dumping into prohibited, NR §8-726.

GARNISHMENT.
Answers.
Circuit courts, CivProCir Rules 2-645, 2-646.
District Court, CivProDist Rules 3-645, 3-646.
Attachment.
Prejudgment attachment.
Retention of garnished property.
Circuit courts, CivProCir Rule 2-115.
District Court, CivProDist Rule 3-115.
Wages.
General provisions, CivProCir Rule 2-646;
CivProDist Rule 3-646; CL §§15-601 to
15-607.
See ATTACHMENT.
Banks and trust companies.
Adverse claim to money, etc., in hands of bank, FI
§5-306.
Joint accounts, CJ §11-603.
Property held in trust, CJ §11-603.
Bulk transfers.
Limitation of levies, CL §6-111.
Campaign finance reports.
Failure to file.
Withholding salary, EL §13-334.
Child support, FL §§5-1032, 5-1033.
Circuit court civil rules, CivProCir Rules 2-645,
2-646.
College savings plan of Maryland.
Seizure by attachment, execution, garnishment,
etc, ED §18-1913.

GARNISHMENT —Cont'd
Continuing care contracts.
Prohibited during delinquency proceedings against
providers, 70B §§20N, 20O.
District Court civil rules, CivProDist Rules
3-645, 3-646.
Emergency management.
Civil relief during emergency periods, PS §14-210.
Stays, postponements or suspensions of
enforcement.
Period and terms of stay, PS §14-211.
Fraternal benefit societies.
Benefits exempt from garnishment, IN §8-431.
Fraudulent conveyances, CL §15-209.
Funds transfers.
Creditor process served on receiving bank, CL
§4A-502.
Husband and wife.
Spousal property, CJ §11-603.
Insurance companies.
Liquidation, rehabilitation, etc.
Garnishment of assets, IN §9-220.
Interrogatories.
Circuit courts, CivProCir Rule 2-645.
District Court, CivProDist Rule 3-645.
Levy of execution.
Amount, CJ §11-602.
Paternity proceedings, FL §§5-1032, 5-1033.
Plea in bar.
Garnishee against defendant, CJ §11-601.
Property.
Circuit courts, CivProCir Rule 2-645.
District Court, CivProDist Rule 3-645.
Satisfaction by garnishee.
Circuit court, CivProCir Rule 2-645.
District Court, CivProDist Rule 3-645.
Service of process.
Circuit courts, CivProCir Rule 2-645.
District Court, CivProDist Rule 3-645.
Spousal property, CJ §11-603.
Third parties.
Property.
Claim by third person.
Circuit courts, CivProCir Rule 2-645.
District Court, CivProDist Rule 3-645.
Universities and colleges.
College savings plan of Maryland.
Seizure by attachment, execution, garnishment,
etc., ED §18-1913.
Wages.
Circuit courts, CivProCir Rule 2-646.
District Court, CivProDist Rule 3-646.

GARRETT COUNTY.
**Agricultural land located in agricultural land
preservation district,** TP §9-313.
Agricultural land preservation foundation.
Natural gas rights owners or lessees.
Subordination of interest to foundation,
exception, AG §2-509.
Alcoholic beverages.
Additional bar or serving counter.
Approval of liquor control board, 2B §9-102.
Beer and light wine licenses.
Class A, off-sale, 2B §5-101.
Class D, on-sale, 2B §5-401.
Beer licenses.
Beer and wine tasting, 2B §8-406.1.
Class A, off-sale.
Fee, 2B §3-101.
Class D, on-sale, 2B §3-401.

GARRETT COUNTY —Cont'd
Alcoholic beverages —Cont'd
Beer, wine and liquor licenses.
Class B, on-sale.
Hotels and restaurants, 2B §6-201.
Class C, on-sale.
Clubs, 2B §6-301.
Class D, on-sale, 2B §6-401.
Off-sale consumptions.
Regulations, 2B §9-212.
Special class C, 2B §7-101.
Bonds, surety.
Retailers, 2B §14-101.
Caterers, 2B §6-703.2.
Disorderly intoxication.
Ordinances or resolutions, 2B §19-103.
Dispensaries.
General provisions, 2B §15-203.
Elections.
Exercise of privilege of licensee on election day, 2B §11-401.
Fines and forfeitures, 2B §16-507.
Hours and days for sale, 2B §11-512.
Election days, 2B §11-401.
New Year's Eve day and New Year's day, 2B §§11-402, 11-512.
License commissioners.
Administrative, clerical and accounting services, 2B §15-205.
Clerk.
Abolition of office, 2B §15-205.
County commissioners ex officio, 2B §15-105.
Salaries, 2B §15-109.
Licenses.
Beer tasting, 2B §8-406.1.
Bonds, surety.
Retailers, 2B §14-101.
Criminal records check and fingerprints of applicant, 2B §10-103.
Disqualification of licensee, 2B §10-404.
Fees.
Disposition, 2B §10-204.
Light wine licenses.
Class A2, on-sale and off-sale, 2B §4-203.
Proration, 2B §10-301.
Regulations and restrictions, 2B §9-212.
Renewal, 2B §10-301.
Restrictions on licensee, 2B §12-212.
Issuance, 2B §9-212.
Revocation and suspension.
Bonds, surety, 2B §14-101.
Grounds, 2B §10-401.
Nudity and sexual displays on licensee's premises, 2B §10-405.
Special class C licenses, 2B §7-101.
Transfer, 2B §10-503.
Wine festival, 2B §8-308.1.
Wine tasting licenses, 2B §8-406.1.
Light wine licenses.
Class A, off-sale, 2B §4-201.
Liquor control board, 2B §§15-201 to 15-210.
Administration of article, 2B §15-108.
Rules and regulations.
Off-sale consumption, 2B §9-212.
Micro-brewery licenses, 2B §2-208.
Minors.
Employment of minors by retail dealers, 2B §12-302.
Sales to prohibited, 2B §12-108.
Nudity and sexual displays on licensee's premises.
Revocation of license, 2B §10-405.

GARRETT COUNTY —Cont'd
Alcoholic beverages —Cont'd
Open containers.
Possession in certain places.
Applicability of provisions, 2B §19-303.
Retailers.
Bonds, surety.
Required, 2B §14-101.
Sales.
Beer for cash, 2B §12-112.
Election days, 2B §11-401.
New Year's Eve day and New Year's day, 2B §11-402.
Prohibited to minors and intoxicated persons, 2B §12-108.
Sundays.
General restrictions, 2B §11-403.
Taxation.
County taxes on beer, 2B §8-212.
Wine festival.
License, 2B §8-308.1.
Amusement devices.
Licensing, BR §§17-432 to 17-438.
Appearance fees in circuit courts.
Distribution, CJ §7-204.
Bailiff.
Compensation, CJ §2-507.
Birds and game.
Spotlighting, NR §10-410.
Wildlife management areas.
Acquisition of land or water by state, NR §10-801.
Bittinger Community Center.
Property tax credits, TP §9-313.
Board of education. See within this heading, "Schools."
Bond issues.
Special taxing districts, 24 §9-1301.
Bowling.
Mechanical bowling games.
Licensing of amusement devices, BR §§17-432 to 17-438.
Carey Run Sanctuary.
Property tax credits, TP §9-313.
Caterers.
Beer, wine and liquor licenses, 2B §6-703.2.
Circuit courts.
Appearance fees.
Distribution, CJ §7-204.
Number of judges, CJ §1-503.
Claw machines.
Licensing of amusement devices, BR §§17-432 to 17-438.
Coal tax.
Authorization, 24 §9-501.
County treasurer.
Adoption of regulations, 24 §9-508.
Deposit of tax revenue, 24 §9-504.
Exemptions, 24 §9-503.
Liens, 24 §9-505.
Municipal corporation share, 24 §9-506.
Rate, 24 §9-502.
Commissioner districts.
County board of elections.
Evaluation and recommendation of adjustment following census, EL §2-202.
County board of elections.
Commissioner districts.
Evaluation and recommendation of adjustment following census, EL §2-202.
Compensation, EL §2-204.

GARRETT COUNTY —Cont'd
County board of elections —Cont'd
County boards generally, EL §§2-201 to 2-303.
See ELECTIONS.
Substitute members.
Compensation, EL §2-204.
Courts.
Circuit court.
Judicial circuit, MD Const Art IV §19.
Number of judges, CJ §1-503.
Crellin Community Center.
Property tax credits, TP §9-313.
Crimes and offenses.
Alcoholic beverages.
Special license to sell draft beer, 2B §8-212.
Development impact fees.
Powers, 25 §9H.
Dog and cat regulations, 24 §11-504.
Kennel licenses.
Fees, 24 §11-501.
Dog wardens and pounds, 24 §11-504.
Easements.
Forests and parks.
Authority to purchase land in Garrett county.
Limitations, NR §5-207.
Emergency snow routes, 25 §3.
Eminent domain, 25 §139.
Fees.
Licensing amusement devices, BR §17-435.
Fish and fisheries.
Refuges and hatcheries.
Acquisition of land, NR §4-401.
Forest, park and wildlife rangers, NR §5-206.
Forests and parks.
Purchases.
Authority to purchase land in Garrett county.
Limitation, NR §5-207.
Gaming, bazaar, carnival and raffles, CR §§13-201 to 13-205.
Conducting event for benefit of qualified organization.
Allowed, CR §13-203.
Definitions, CR §13-201.
Gaming event defined, CR §§13-201, 13-1401.
Individual benefit prohibited, CR §13-203.
Management through organizations members, CR §13-205.
Permits for gaming events, CR §§13-1401 to 13-1406.
Applicability of provisions, CR §13-1402.
Bingo, CR §13-1405.
Definitions, CR §13-1401.
Paper gaming, CR §13-1404.
Duration, CR §13-1403.
Fees, CR §13-1403.
Nontransferable, CR §13-1403.
Paper gaming, CR §13-1404.
Prizes, CR §13-1403.
Qualifying organizations, CR §13-1403.
Regulations, CR §13-1406.
Required, CR §13-1403.
Terms and conditions, CR §13-1403.
Prizes and gaming devices allowed, CR §13-204.
Restrictions on prizes, CR §13-1403.
Provisions applicable to county, CR §§13-202, 13-301, 13-1401.
Qualified organization defined, CR §13-201.
Permits, qualifying organizations, CR §13-1403.
Garbage and trash.
Collection and disposal regulations, 25 §3.

GARRETT COUNTY —Cont'd
Garrett County Agricultural Fair Association, Inc.
Property tax credits, TP §9-313.
Grantsville volunteer fire department.
Property tax credits, TP §9-313.
Hawkers and peddlers.
License fees, BR §17-907.
Highways.
Eminent domain.
Procedure, 25 §139.
Snow removal, TR §8-602.
Home detention program, COR §11-713.
Inspections.
Septic tanks, EN §9-1101.
Insurance.
Group health and hospital insurance.
Officers and employees, 25 §3.
Libraries.
Public library system known as Ruth Enlow Library of Garrett County, ED §23-402.
Licenses.
Alcoholic beverages. See within this heading, "Alcoholic beverages."
Amusement devices, BR §§17-432 to 17-438.
Certificate.
Issuance and display, BR §17-436.
Definitions, BR §17-432.
Fees, BR §17-435.
Penalties for violations, BR §17-438.
Requirement of license, BR §17-434.
Scope of provisions, BR §17-433.
Transferability of license, BR §17-437.
Garbage and refuse collection, 25 §3.
Marriage licenses, fees, FL §2-404.
Pinball machines, BR §§17-432 to 17-438.
Marriage.
Clerk's fee for performing ceremony.
Disposition, FL §2-410.
Marriage licenses, fees, FL §2-404.
Merit system.
Application, 25 §3.
Minors.
Alcoholic beverages.
Employment of minors by retail dealers, 2B §12-302.
Misdemeanors.
Alcoholic beverages.
Special license to sell draft beer, 2B §8-212.
Motor vehicles.
Size and weight.
Power of county commissioners to regulate, 25 §25.
Tires.
Studs, cleats, etc.
Sale regulated, TR §22-405.2.
Use allowed during certain months, TR §22-405.2.
Trucks, load limit of axles, TR §24-108.
Noise control.
Trapshooting, skeet shooting, etc.
Limitations on authority, EN §§3-105, 3-401.
Officers and employees.
Group health and hospital insurance, 25 §3.
Pension and retirement benefit plans, 25 §3.
Orphans' court.
Judges.
Compensation, ET §2-108.
Penalties.
Licensing of amusement devices, BR §17-438.
Septic tanks, EN §9-1101.

GARRETT COUNTY —Cont'd
Pensions.
Providing pension benefit plans for officers and
employees, 25 §3.
Permits.
Septic tanks, EN §9-1101.
Personal property.
Purchase or lease of.
Powers, 25 §9D.
Pinball machines, BR §§17-432 to 17-438.
Poolrooms or bowling alleys.
Alcoholic beverages.
Licenses prohibited, 2B §9-212.
Potomac water authority.
General provisions.
See POTOMAC WATER AUTHORITY.
Procurement.
Purchase of goods and services, 25 §3.
Property taxes.
Manufacturing property exempt from taxation,
inapplicability, TP §7-225.
**Public recreation on private and local
government lands,** NR §5-1109.
Purchase of goods and services, 25 §3.
Recordation.
Plats of subdivisions.
Size of plats, RP §3-108.
Retirement.
Providing retirement benefit plans for officers and
employees, 25 §3.
Roads.
Eminent domain.
Procedure, 25 §139.
Snow removal, TR §8-602.
Sanitary commissions, EN §9-629.
Schools.
County board of education, ED §3-114.
Compensation and expenses, ED §§3-603, 4-107.
Composition, ED §3-601.
Elected member defined, ED §3-601.
Elections, ED §§3-114, 3-601.
Generally, EL §§8-801 to 8-806.
Executive sessions, ED §3-604.
Expenses, ED §3-603.
Meetings, ED §3-604.
Election of president and vice-president, ED
§3-602.
Members, ED §3-601.
Persons subject to authority of board.
Ineligibility to serve as member, ED §3-114.
President and vice-president, ED §3-602.
Employee organizations.
Designation required in Garrett county, ED
§6-505.
Employees.
Public school employees.
Defined, ED §6-401.
Negotiations between employer and employee.
Representation in Garrett county.
Fees charged for nonmembers, ED §6-407.
Septic tanks, EN §9-1101.
Sewerage service.
Unpaid bills, EN §9-662.
Sheriff, CJ §2-309.
Second in command, CJ §2-310.
Shuffleboard games.
Licensing of amusement devices, BR §§17-432 to
17-438.
Skiing.
Cross country skiing.
Public recreation on private and local
government lands, NR §5-1109.

GARRETT COUNTY —Cont'd
Snow.
Emergency snow routes, 25 §3.
Snowmobiles.
Operation on controlled access highways, TR
§21-104.1.
Public recreation on private and local government
lands, NR §5-1109.
Special taxing districts, 24 §9-1301.
State's attorney.
Accounts for services and expenses.
County excepted from section, 10 §39.
Assistants, 10 §40.
Salaries and expenses, 10 §40.
Subdivisions.
Size of plats, RP §3-108.
Sundays and holidays.
Alcoholic beverages.
Hours and days for sale, 2B §§11-403, 11-512.
Surplus real property sales.
Means of sale authorized, 25 §11A.
Private sales if no bids taken, 25 §11A.
Swanton Community Center.
Property tax credits, TP §9-313.
Taxation.
Credits.
Property tax credits, TP §9-313.
Exemptions.
Personal property.
Reduction or elimination of percentage of
assessment, TP §7-511.
Hotel rental tax, 24 §§9-301 to 9-326.
See COUNTIES.
Interest.
Overdue taxes, TP §14-603.
Municipal corporations.
Sale of property on which taxes are delinquent,
TP §14-809.
Proration of personal property taxes, TP §10-305.
Redemption.
Foreclosure of right of redemption.
Form of order of publication, TP §14-840.
Sales.
Certificate of sale, TP §14-820.
Date and time to be set by resolution, TP
§14-808.
Form of advertising, TP §14-813.
Notice, TP §14-813.
Special taxing districts.
Authorized, 24 §9-1301.
Transportation services, public, TR §7-801.
Tobacco product sales, 24 §§15-101 to 15-104.
Transportation services tax, TR §7-801.
**Trapshooting, skeetshooting or other target
shooting.**
Environmental sound level limits and noise
control rules and regulations, EN §3-401.
Noise control ordinances, rules or regulations
prohibiting, EN §3-105.
Treasurer, 25 §51.
Tri-county council for western Maryland.
See TRI-COUNTY COUNCIL FOR WESTERN
MARYLAND.
United Methodist Church.
Assets of certain churches in Garrett county, CA
§5-328.
Water and sewer systems.
Charges for discontinuing and restoring water
service, 25 §9L.
Multiple bedroom facilities.
Minimum health requirements for lots and
parcels of ground used, EN §9-260.

GARRETT COUNTY —Cont'd
Watersheds.
Reports, EN §15-203.
Weather modification.
Powers of county commissioners as to, 25 §3.
Wine.
Wine tasting licenses, 2B §8-406.1.
Wine festival.
Licenses, 2B §8-308.1.
Witnesses.
Itinerant allowances, CJ §9-202.
Mileage, CJ §9-202.

GAS AND OIL.
Actions.
Petitions of interested persons, EN §14-114.
Advertising.
Used oil recycling act.
Informing general public of prohibitions, EN §5-1001.
Appeals.
Coastal facilities review act.
Permit for construction of facilities.
Judicial review of action on application, EN §14-509.
Decision of department, EN §14-117.
Attorney general.
Coastal facilities review act.
Injunctions against violations, EN §14-510.
Bonds, surety.
Drilling wells.
Performance bonds, EN §14-111.
Permits, EN §14-108.
Chesapeake Bay critical area.
Drilling wells.
Prohibited, EN §14-107.
Chesapeake Bay critical area and Atlantic coastal bays critical area protection programs.
Production or exploration under Chesapeake Bay critical area, NR §8-1817.
Coalbed methane wells.
Definition, EN §14-102.
Inspection of production, EN §14-121.
Location, EN §14-112.
Coastal facilities review act.
Appeals.
Judicial review of action on application for permit, EN §14-509.
Attorney general.
Injunctions against violations, EN §14-510.
Citation of subtitle, EN §14-502.
Coastal area.
Defined, EN §14-501.
Construction.
Defined, EN §14-501.
Permits for construction. See within this subheading, "Permits."
Cooperation of state units and departments, EN §14-504.
Counties.
Permits for construction of facilities.
County action prerequisite to processing application, EN §14-506.
Definitions, EN §14-501.
Facility.
Defined, EN §14-501.
Hearings.
Permits, EN §14-507.
Impact statements required, EN §14-506.
Injunctions, EN §14-510.

GAS AND OIL —Cont'd
Coastal facilities review act —Cont'd
Inspections, EN §14-508.
Legislative findings, EN §14-502.
Notices.
Hearings on permits, EN §14-507.
Penalties.
Construction of subtitle, EN §14-511.
Violations of subtitle, EN §14-510.
Permits.
Appeals, EN §14-509.
Application, EN §14-504.
County action prerequisite to processing, EN §14-506.
Effect of application, EN §14-505.
Denials, EN §14-508.
Exemptions, EN §14-503.
Fees, EN §14-504.
Grant or denial, conditional, EN §14-508.
Hearings, EN §14-507.
Impact statement required, EN §14-506.
Information to accompany application, EN §14-504.
Information to be made available to public, EN §14-507.
Inspections, EN §14-508.
Judicial review of action on application, EN §14-509.
Prerequisites to further action by secretary, EN §14-507.
Required, EN §14-503.
Rules and regulations, EN §14-508.
Rules and regulations.
Adoption, EN §14-503.
Permits, EN §14-508.
Violations.
Injunctions, EN §14-510.
Compact.
Interstate compact, EN §§14-401 to 14-404. See within this heading, "Interstate oil and gas compact."
Contempt.
Enforcement of subpoena, EN §14-115.
Contracts.
Applicability of sales chapter of commercial code, CL §2-107.
Counties.
Coastal facilities review act.
Permits for construction of facilities.
County action prerequisite to processing application for permit, EN §14-506.
Crimes and offenses.
Multiple violations of provisions and subtitle, EN §14-120.
Used oil recycling act violations, EN §5-1001.
Definitions, EN §14-102.
Coastal facilities review act, EN §14-501.
Discharge containment, control and cleanup, EN §4-411.
Seismic operations, EN §14-109.
Used oil recycling act, EN §5-1001.
Department of the environment.
Authority generally, EN §14-103.
Developmental resources.
Bifurcation of process, EN §14-106.
Definitions, EN §14-102.
Legislative findings, EN §14-101.
Drilling wells.
Bifurcation of process, EN §14-106.
Environmental assessments, EN §14-104.

GAS AND OIL —Cont'd
Drilling wells —Cont'd
Exploration and production.
Bifurcation of process, EN §14-106.
Hearings.
Permits, EN §14-105.
Liability.
Drilling on lands or in waters of state.
Strict liability, NR §5-1703.
Location of wells, EN §14-112.
Notices.
Permits, EN §14-105.
Permits.
Applications generally, EN §14-105.
Bonds, surety, EN §14-108.
Performance bond, EN §14-111.
Conditions, EN §14-110.
Denial, EN §14-108.
Duties of permittees, EN §14-111.
Hearings, EN §14-105.
Liability insurance coverage, EN §14-111.
Required, EN §14-104.
Royalties.
Payment.
Leased land, EN §14-113.
State lands or waters of state.
Strict liability of persons drilling, NR §5-1703.
Violations of permits, EN §14-110.
Emergency management.
State standby petroleum fuel set-aside program,
PS §§14-501 to 14-511.
**Energy allocation equipment and procedures
used by apartment owners, operators or
managers.**
Determination of amount of gas used by
individual dwelling unit, PUC §7-304.
**Environmental, fiscal and economic impact
statements.**
Drilling wells.
Environmental assessments, EN §14-104.
Leasing of state oil and gas resources, NR
§5-1702.
Fees.
Coastal facilities review act.
Permit fees, EN §14-504.
Fines.
Coastal facilities review act.
Violations of subtitle, EN §14-510.
Violations of subtitle, EN §14-120.
Gas fitters.
License, BR §§17-1501 to 17-1504.
Gasohol.
See GASOHOL.
Gas stations.
See SERVICE STATIONS.
Hearings.
Coastal facilities review act.
Permits for construction of facilities, EN
§14-507.
Drilling wells.
Permits, EN §14-105.
Rehearings, EN §14-116.
Rules, regulations and orders, EN §14-114.
Subpoenas, EN §14-115.
Heating oil tanks.
Abandonment of use of heating oil as fuel.
Removal of heating oil tanks, EN §4-420.
Impact statements.
Coastal facilities review act.
Permits for construction of facilities.
Impact statement required, EN §14-506.

GAS AND OIL —Cont'd
Injunctions.
Coastal facilities review act, EN §14-510.
Restraining violations or attempted violations, EN
§14-118.
Inspections.
Coastal facilities review act.
Compliance with terms of permit, EN §14-508.
Gas meters, EN §14-119.
General provisions, BR §§10-101 to 10-502.
See MOTOR FUEL INSPECTION.
Insurance.
Drilling wells.
Permits.
Liability insurance coverage, EN §14-111.
Interstate oil and gas compact.
Commission.
Department of natural resources.
Membership unit of, NR §1-102.
Contents, EN §14-404.
Extensions.
Authorized, EN §14-402.
Governor.
Assistant representative.
Power to appoint, EN §14-403.
Directed to join, EN §14-401.
Official representative, EN §14-403.
Joining.
Governor directed to join, EN §14-401.
Representatives, EN §14-403.
Terms, EN §14-404.
Withdrawal, EN §14-402.
Leasing of state oil and gas resources.
Areas for possible leasing.
Regulations for nomination of, NR §5-1701.
Board of public works.
Environmental, fiscal and economic impact
statement.
Preparation, NR §5-1702.
Rules and regulations, NR §5-1701.
Costs.
Environmental, fiscal and economic impact
statement.
Recovery, NR §5-1702.
Drilling on lands or in waters of state.
Strict liability, NR §5-1703.
Environmental, fiscal and economic impact
statement, NR §5-1702.
Inspections.
Environmental, fiscal and economic impact
statement.
Availability to public, NR §5-1702.
Lease required for production, NR §5-1701.
Liability.
Strict liability.
Persons drilling for oil or gas on lands or in
waters of state, NR §5-1703.
Nomination of areas for possible leasing.
Regulations, NR §5-1701.
Procedures for award, NR §5-1701.
Restrictions, NR §5-1701.
Rules and regulations, NR §5-1701.
Standards for award, NR §5-1701.
Liability.
Leasing of state oil and gas resources.
Persons drilling on state lands or waters of
state.
Strict liability, NR §5-1703.
Liquefied natural gas facilities, PUC §11-101.
Liquefied petroleum gas.
Unlawful use, CL §§11-601 to 11-606.
See LIQUEFIED PETROLEUM GAS.

GAS AND OIL —Cont'd
Maryland energy administration, SG §§9-2001 to 9-2007.
Meters.
Gas to be metered, EN §14-119.
Mining.
General provisions, EN §§15-101 to 15-1109.
See MINING.
Misdemeanors.
Used oil recycling act.
Violations, EN §5-1001.
Willful violations of provisions of subtitle, EN §14-120.
Municipal corporations.
Disposal of gas plant.
Ratification by people, 23 §183.
Notices.
Coastal facilities review act.
Hearings on permits, EN §14-507.
Rules, regulations and orders, EN §14-114.
Oil contaminated site environmental cleanup fund, EN §§4-701 to 4-708.
Permits.
Coastal facilities review act. See within this heading, "Coastal facilities review act."
Drilling wells. See within this heading, "Drilling wells."
Gas fitters licensing, BR §§17-1501 to 17-1504.
Seismic operations.
Application for permit, EN §14-109.
Petroleum divestment law, BR §10-311.
Prince George's county.
Storage.
General provisions.
See PRINCE GEORGE'S COUNTY.
Propane gas.
Landlord and tenant.
Ownership of containers on leased land, RP §8-117.
Rates and charges.
General provisions.
See PUBLIC SERVICE COMMISSION.
Recycling used oil, EN §5-1001.
Resources.
Development.
Bifurcation of process, EN §14-106.
Legislative findings, EN §14-101.
Royalties.
Payment.
When leased land included under unit agreement, EN §14-113.
Rules and regulations.
Adoption and enforcement, EN §14-103.
Coastal facilities review act, EN §§14-503, 14-508.
Hearings, EN §14-114.
Leasing of state oil and gas resources, NR §5-1701.
Notices, EN §14-114.
Seismic operations.
Application for permit, EN §14-109.
Service stations.
See SERVICE STATIONS.
State.
Leasing of state oil and gas resources, NR §§5-1701 to 5-1703. See within this heading, "Leasing of state oil and gas resources."
State standby petroleum fuel set-aside program.
Energy emergencies, PS §§14-501 to 14-511.
Storage.
Prince George's county, EN §§14-301 to 14-308.
See PRINCE GEORGE'S COUNTY.

GAS AND OIL —Cont'd
Storage —Cont'd
Underground storage. See within this heading, "Underground storage."
Summons and process.
Power of department, EN §14-115.
Underground storage.
Defined, EN §14-102.
Environmental assessments, EN §14-104.
Permits.
Required to drill well, EN §14-104.
Prince George's county, EN §§14-201 to 14-209.
See PRINCE GEORGE'S COUNTY.
Wells for underground storage.
Environmental assessments, EN §14-104.
Location, EN §14-112.
Permits required, EN §14-104.
Used oil recycling act, EN §5-1001.
Violations of subtitle.
Defined, EN §14-120.
Water pollution.
Damages.
Liability for damages caused by oil spillage, EN §4-409.
Emergency oil spilling.
Development of program to respond to, EN §4-406.
Fees.
Compensatory fee for oil spillage, EN §4-408.
Heating oil.
Abandonment of use as fuel.
Removal of heating oil tanks, EN §4-420.
Maryland oil disaster containment cleanup and contingency fund, EN §4-411.
Spillages.
Liability for damages, EN §4-409.
Program to respond to emergency spillages, EN §4-406.
Property taxes.
Exemption of property of nonprofit organization engaged in containment of coastal and tidal oil spills, TP §7-240.
Terminal facilities.
Procedure upon violations of subtitle, EN §4-412.
Transfer, storage, etc., of oil.
Regulations, EN §4-405.
Vessels discharging.
Bonds, surety.
Required of vessels entering to discharge or receive oil cargo, EN §4-407.
General provisions, EN §4-410.
Wells.
Drilling wells. See within this heading, "Drilling wells."

GAS COMPANIES.
Additional charge over net total costs.
Commission authorizing, PUC §7-305.
Affiliates.
Policies and actions of companies, influence over.
Prior authorization from commission required, PUC §6-105.
Annual reports by public service companies, PUC §§6-201 to 6-210.
Billing customers, PUC §7-305.
Central heating or cooling systems.
Providing service for residential multiple occupancy buildings or shopping centers, PUC §7-301.
Classification of companies, PUC §6-202.

GAS COMPANIES —Cont'd
Condemnation, power, PUC §5-403.
Consumer protection.
Suppliers and supply, PUC §§7-601 to 7-607.
Applicability, PUC §7-605.
Commission.
Adoption of regulations or orders in public
interest, PUC §7-606.
Consumer protection orders or regulations, PUC
§7-604.
Dispute resolution, PUC §7-605.
Licensing, PUC §7-603.
Purpose, legislative findings, PUC §7-602.
Short title, PUC §7-607.
**Costs and expenses of public service
commission, payment,** PUC §2-110.
Damaging or defrauding, penalty, CR §6-304.
Defined, PUC §1-101.
Eminent domain.
Power to condemn, PUC §5-403.
Energy efficiency programs, promotion, PUC
§7-211.
**Excavation or demolition near underground
facilities.**
Generally, PUC §§12-101 to 12-113.
See UNDERGROUND UTILITY FACILITIES.
Montgomery county, PUC §§12-201 to 12-203.
Gas plant.
Defined, PUC §1-101.
Hazardous liquid pipelines, PUC §§11-201 to
11-208.
**Heating seasons, termination of service to low
income customers,** PUC §7-307.
Income tax.
Maryland modified income of corporations, TG
§10-309.
Independent audit opinion, PUC §4-208.
**Influence over policies and actions of
companies.**
Affiliates.
Prior authorization from commission required,
PUC §6-105.
**Inspection of plant by public service
commission,** PUC §2-114.
**Interfering with materials, equipment or
facilities,** CR §6-304.
Prima facie evidence of violation, CR §6-304.
Jurisdiction of commission, PUC §7-101.
Licenses.
Suppliers. See within this heading, "Consumer
protection."
**Low income customers, termination of service
to,** PUC §7-307.
Make whole rate proceedings, PUC §4-207.
Manufacture, sale and distribution of gas, PUC
§7-102.
Meters.
Furnishing or putting into use, commission
authorization, PUC §7-301.
Incorrect meters, replacement, PUC §7-302.
Individual metering for residential occupancy
buildings or shopping centers, PUC §7-301.
Inspection by consumer, request, PUC §7-302.
Submetering, PUC §7-303.
Testing for accuracy, PUC §7-301.
Municipal plants supplying gas or electricity,
PUC §7-210.
People's counsel.
Consumer protection.
Dispute resolution, PUC §7-605.

GAS COMPANIES —Cont'd
People's counsel —Cont'd
Generally, PUC §§2-201 to 2-206.
See PUBLIC SERVICE COMMISSION.
Pipelines.
Hazardous liquid pipelines, PUC §§11-201 to
11-208.
Laying under roads or other public ways, PUC
§7-102.
Powers, PUC §7-102.
Prices.
Matters requiring commission investigation, PUC
§3-102.
Procedure before public service commission.
Generally, PUC §§3-101 to 3-114.
See PUBLIC SERVICE COMMISSION.
Public service commission.
Generally, PUC §§2-101 to 5-106.
See PUBLIC SERVICE COMMISSION.
Public service company franchise tax.
Companies to which tax applicable, TG §8-402.1.
Credits against tax, TG §8-417.
Public utilities generally.
See PUBLIC UTILITIES.
Rate regulation and proceedings.
Billing customers under applicable rate filed for
service, PUC §7-305.
Generally, PUC §§4-101 to 4-503.
See PUBLIC SERVICE COMMISSION.
Just and reasonable rate defined, PUC §4-101.
Reliability of gas power supply.
Matters requiring investigation by commission,
PUC §3-102.
Safe service requirement, violations, PUC
§13-203.
Safety violations, penalties, PUC §13-202.
Security deposits.
Exemption of dwelling units of elderly subscribers
from cash deposit requirement, PUC §5-105.
**Sliding scale to adjust costs of fuel or
purchased gas,** PUC §4-401.
Suppliers.
Licensing and consumer protection. See within
this heading, "Consumer protection."
**Tampering with materials, equipment or
facilities,** CR §6-304.
**Termination of service to low income
residential customers,** PUC §7-307.
**Transmission of gas, consent of commission
required,** PUC §7-102.

GAS MASTER METER OPERATORS.
**Actions by public service commission to
enforce article,** PUC §2-117.
Defined, PUC §1-101.
**Power of public service commission to
regulate services,** PUC §5-101.
Public service commission.
Generally.
See PUBLIC SERVICE COMMISSION.
Safe service requirement, violations, PUC
§13-203.

GAS METERS.
Apartments.
Submetering, PUC §7-303.
Fee for meter test services, PUC §7-302.
**Furnishing or putting into use for revenue
building purposes.**
Authorization by commission required, PUC
§7-301.
Incorrect meters, replacement, PUC §7-302.

GAS METERS —Cont'd
Individual metering, PUC §7-301.
Inspection by consumer, PUC §7-302.
Residential multiple occupancy buildings.
Individual meter to service or submetering, PUC §7-301.
Shopping centers.
Individual meter service or submetering, PUC §7-301.
Submetering, PUC §7-303.
Testing accuracy, PUC §7-301.

GASOHOL.
Marketing agreements.
General provisions.
See GASOLINE.
Testing program, 41 §18-202.

GASOLINE.
Failure to pay after dispensing, CR §7-104.
Drivers' license suspension, TR §16-206.1.
Gas and oil generally.
See GAS AND OIL.
Gasohol.
See GASOHOL.
Inspections.
General provisions, BR §§10-101 to 10-502.
See MOTOR FUEL INSPECTION.
Marketing agreement, CL §§11-301 to 11-308.
See GASOLINE MARKETING AGREEMENTS.
Maryland energy administration, SG §§9-2001 to 9-2007.
Motor fuel tax, TG §§9-301 to 9-337.
See MOTOR FUEL TAX.
Possession of destructive device, CR §§4-501 to 4-503.

GASOLINE MARKETING AGREEMENTS.
Cancellation.
Dealer's right to cancel, CL §11-304.
Defenses to actions based on cancellation, CL §11-305.
Liability for wrongful cancellation, CL §11-307.
Notice of intent, CL §11-306.
Controlled outlet.
Defined, CL §11-301.
Credit care use.
Defined, CL §11-301.
Damages.
Wrongful termination or cancellation, CL §11-307.
Dealer.
Defined, CL §11-301.
Definitions, CL §11-301.
Distributor.
Defined, CL §11-301.
Farm cooperative.
Defined, CL §11-301.
Franchises.
Devolving, CL §11-304.
Gasohol.
Included in term "gasoline products," CL §11-301.
Gasoline products.
Defined, CL §11-301.
Hours of business, CL §11-304.
Independent jobber.
Defined, CL §11-301.
Information given by distributor to prospective dealer, CL §11-303.
Leases.
Rental based on volume of sales, CL §11-304.
Legislative finding and declaration, CL §11-302.
Liability for wrongful termination, CL §11-307.

GASOLINE MARKETING AGREEMENTS
—Cont'd
Notice.
Intent not to renew, CL §11-304.
Reasons for nonrenewal set forth in notice, CL §11-304.
Intent to terminate or cancel, CL §11-306.
Person.
Defined, CL §11-301.
Policy.
Public policy statement, CL §11-302.
Price setting, CL §11-304.
Promotions, CL §11-304.
Prospective dealer.
Information given by distributor, CL §11-303.
Provisions to which subject, CL §11-304.
Remedies for violations, CL §11-307.
Rent.
Based on monthly volume of sales, CL §11-304.
Retail sale.
Defined, CL §11-301.
Short title, CL §11-308.
Termination, CL §11-304.
Defenses to actions based on termination, CL §11-305.
Liability for wrongful termination, CL §11-307.
Notice of intent, CL §11-306.
Trial marketing agreement, CL §11-304.
Violations.
Remedies, CL §11-307.
Wholesale price of gasoline to noncontrolled outlets, CL §11-304.

GAS STATIONS.
General provisions.
See SERVICE STATIONS.
Motor fuel inspection, BR §§10-101 to 10-502.
See MOTOR FUEL INSPECTION.

GASTRIC BYPASS SURGERY.
Morbid obesity.
Health insurance coverage for treatment, IN §15-839.

GATHLAND PARK.
Development.
Purposes of public education and recreation, NR §5-1002.

G.E.D.
High school certificate or diploma, ED §7-206.

GEMS.
Secondhand precious metals and gem dealers, BR §§12-101 to 12-601.
See PRECIOUS METALS AND GEM DEALERS.

GENDER.
Annuity contracts.
Misstatement of sex, IN §16-405.
Constitution of Maryland.
Equality of rights not abridged because of sex, MD Const DofR Art 46.
Definitions.
One gender includes the other gender, 1 §7.
Discrimination.
Equal credit opportunity, CL §§12-701 to 12-708.
See EQUAL CREDIT OPPORTUNITY.
General provisions.
See SEX DISCRIMINATION.
Pure endowment contracts.
Misstatement of sex, IN §16-405.

GENERAL ASSEMBLY.
Absence.
Compelling attendance of members, MD Const Art
III §20.
Accounts and accounting.
House of delegates.
Powers as grand inquest of state, MD Const Art
III §24.
Acts of assembly.
Bills. See within this heading, "Bills."
Adjournment.
Consent of both houses required, MD Const Art
III §25.
Powers of smaller number than quorum, MD
Const Art III §20.
Administrative, executive and legislative
review.
Joint committee, SG §§2-501 to 2-507.
Advisory commission on federal-state-local
relations.
Joint committee on federal relations, SG §§2-901
to 2-906.
Advisory committee on naming state facilities,
roads and bridges, SG §2-10A-09.
Affordability.
Spending affordability committee, SG §§2-1001 to
2-1010.
Age.
Senators and delegates, MD Const Art III §9.
Agency.
Compensation.
Extra compensation to public officer, agent or
contractor, MD Const Art III §35.
Legislative agents.
See PUBLIC ETHICS.
Agriculture.
What legislature should encourage, MD Const
DofR Art 43.
Amendments to bills.
Inconsistent amendments to same code section or
subsection, 1 §17.
Annapolis.
Meeting place, MD Const DofR Art 11.
Change place of meeting of legislature, MD
Const Art II §16.
Annotated code of Maryland distribution.
Legislative services department, SG §2-1247.
Appointments.
Replacement of officers, MD Const Art XV §5.
Apportionment.
Legislative districting and apportionment plan of
1992, SG §§2-201 to 2-205.
Appropriations, MD Const Art III §32.
Appropriation act.
Defined, SF §7-201.
State operating budget.
See BUDGET AND MANAGEMENT.
Bills, MD Const Art III §§32, 52.
Disapproval of items by governor, MD Const Art
II §17.
Restriction as to referendum, MD Const Art XVI
§2.
Disbursements and expenditures.
Amendment of appropriation for legislative
branch program, SF §7-208.
Statement of receipts and expenditures, MD Const
Art III §32.
Archaeological work, costs of state projects.
Inclusion in budget bill for project, SF §7-114.1.
Attendance.
Compelling attendance of members, MD Const Art
III §20.

GENERAL ASSEMBLY —Cont'd
Attorney general.
Authorization of additional counsel, MD Const Art
V §3.
Written opinions to assembly, MD Const Art V §3.
Attorneys at law.
Continuances because of legislative duties.
Members attorneys of record in proceedings, CJ
§6-402.
Investigating committee.
Counsel for persons testifying before committee,
SG §2-1609.
Joint committee on legislative ethics.
Counsel to committee, SG §2-709.
Audits.
House of delegates.
Powers as grand inquest of state, MD Const Art
III §24.
Joint audit committee, SG §§2-601 to 2-605.
Office of legislative audits, SG §§2-1217 to 2-1227.
See LEGISLATIVE SERVICES DEPARTMENT.
Baltimore City.
Charter.
Powers and restrictions, MD Const Art XI-A
§§2, 4, 6.
Control over city, MD Const Art XI §9.
General provisions.
See BALTIMORE CITY.
Banks and trust companies.
Books, papers and accounts.
Inspection, MD Const Art III §39.
Benefits for members, SG Title 2 Subtitle 3 (note).
Bills.
Actuarial analysis.
Request for or waiver of, SG §2-1505.
Amendments.
Inconsistent amendments to same code section
or subsection, 1 §17.
Appropriations, MD Const Art III §§32, 52.
Disapproval of items in bills by governor, MD
Const Art II §17.
Restrictions as to referendum, MD Const Art
XVII §2.
Approval or disapproval by governor, MD Const
Art II §17.
Archaeological projects.
Inclusion of costs in budget bill for project, SF
§7-114.1.
Authority to prefile, SG §2-1502.
Bond and revenue bills, submission by Governor,
SF §7-106.
Budget bill, MD Const Art III §52.
Certified, MD Const Art III §30.
Chapter numbers.
Assignment, SG §2-1511.
Record, SG §2-1512.
Committee sponsorship, SG §2-1503.
Consent calendar, MD Const Art III §27.
Passage of bills, MD Const Art III §28.
Dates for prefiling, SG §2-1502.
Defined, SG §2-1508.
Directives.
Requirements, SG §2-1502.
Disposition of bills, SG §2-1513.
Economic impact analysis, SG §2-1505.1.
Agency regulations, SG §2-1505.2.
Effective date, MD Const Art III §31; Art XVI §2.
Embrace but one subject, MD Const Art III §29.
Emergency law, MD Const Art XVI §2.
Fiscal notes, SG §2-1505.

GENERAL ASSEMBLY —Cont'd
Bills —Cont'd
  Governor.
    Presented to governor for approval, MD Const
      Art III §30.
    Introduction.
      Limit on time of introduction, MD Const Art III
        §27.
      When and where originated, MD Const Art III
        §27.
  Joint resolutions.
    Bill includes joint resolution, SG §2-1501.
    Notice of action under joint resolution, SG
      §2-1514.
  Legislative services.
    Synopsis of bill, SG §2-1504.
  Listing of and access to prefiled bills, SG §2-1502.
  Local laws, MD Const Art III §33.
    Cannot enact local laws on subjects covered by
      express powers, MD Const Art XI-A §4.
  Mandate on local government unit, SG §2-1504.
    Definition of "mandate," SG §2-1501.
    Report of legislation imposing, SG §2-1505.
  Notice.
    Action under joint resolutions, SG §2-1514.
  Origination, MD Const Art III §27.
  Passage, MD Const Art III §28.
    Return to originating house upon passage, SG
      §2-1506.
  Prefiling, SG §2-1502.
  Presentment to governor, SG §2-1509.
    Designee for presentment, SG §2-1510.
  Publication.
    General provisions, MD Const Art III §30.
      See STATUTES.
    Statement of receipts and expenditures, MD
      Const Art III §32.
  Reading.
    Consent calendar, MD Const Art III §27.
    Three readings, MD Const Art III §27.
  Recordation.
    Court of appeals, MD Const Art III §30.
  Return to originating house, SG §2-1506.
  Revival, MD Const Art III §29.
  Secretary of state.
    Chapter numbers.
      Assignment by secretary, SG §2-1511.
    Delivery of bills to clerk of court of appeals, SG
      §2-1513.
    Delivery to office of secretary, SG §2-1511.
    Entry of bills becoming law, SG §2-1512.
    Vetoed bills, SG §§2-1512, 2-1513.
  Special acts.
    Enumeration of cases prohibited, MD Const Art
      III §33.
    Municipal purposes in corporations, MD Const
      Art III §48.
    Prohibited when, MD Const Art III §33.
  Standing committees.
    Copies of proposed bills, SG §2-1103.
    Sponsorship, SG §2-1503.
    Waiver of actuarial analysis, SG §2-1505.
  Style, MD Const Art III §29.
  Synopsis, SG §2-1504.
  Time.
    Prefiling dates, SG §2-1502.
  Titles, MD Const Art III §29.
  Vetoed bills, MD Const Art II §17.
    Delivery by secretary of state, SG §2-1513.
    Reconsideration by legislature, MD Const Art II
      §17.

GENERAL ASSEMBLY —Cont'd
Bills —Cont'd
  Vetoed bills —Cont'd
    Record of vetoed bills, SG §2-1512.
    Veto power of governor, MD Const Art II §17.
      Item veto, MD Const Art III §52.
  Yeas and nays.
    Recorded, MD Const Art III §28.
Boards and commissions.
  Advisory commission on federal-state-local
    relations.
    Joint committee on federal relations, SG
      §§2-901 to 2-906.
Bond issues.
  Spending affordability committee.
    Private activity bonds, SG §2-1010.
Books.
  Purchase of books, etc., for use of general
    assembly, MD Const Art III §16.
Branches.
  Consists of two branches, MD Const Art III §1.
Bribery, CR §9-201.
  Member or officer, MD Const Art III §50.
Briefs.
  Continuance to prepare, CJ §6-402.
Budget and management.
  Balanced budget required, MD Const Art III §52.
  Bills, MD Const Art III §52.
  Inquiries to secretary from general assembly, SF
    §3-205.
  Made how, MD Const Art III §52.
  State operating budget.
    Budget bill, SF §§7-108 to 7-114.1.
    Budget books.
      Distribution of copies to general assembly
        members, SF §7-115.
Campaign finance.
  Contributions to political campaigns during
    sessions.
    Prohibition, exceptions, EL §13-235.
Chesapeake Bay critical areas committee, SG
  §2-10A-01.
Citizenship.
  Senators and delegates, MD Const Art III §9.
Civil immunity.
  Privileges for members, SG §2-1801.
Clerks of court.
  Fees and charges system, MD Const Art III §45.
Code of fair procedures.
  Investigating committee.
    Establishment by subtitle, SG §2-1602.
Code of Maryland.
  Amendments, MD Const Art III §29.
    Inconsistent amendments to same code section
      or subsection, 1 §17.
Collectors.
  Failure to account for public money, MD Const
    Art III §12.
Commissions.
  Judicial disabilities commission.
    See JUDICIAL DISABILITIES COMMISSION.
Committees.
  Advisory committee on naming state facilities,
    roads and bridges, SG §2-10A-09.
  Bills.
    Committee sponsorship, SG §2-1503.
    Requirements for committee action.
      Fiscal notes and waivers, SG §2-1505.
  Chesapeake Bay critical areas committee, SG
    §2-10A-01.

GENERAL ASSEMBLY —Cont'd
Committees —Cont'd
Continuance because of legislative duties, CJ §6-402.
Disrupting or interfering with committees, SG §2-1702.
Duties of presiding officers, SG §2-1101.
Health care delivery and financing, SG §2-10A-02.
House of delegates.
Committee of the whole.
Doors kept open, MD Const Art III §21.
Joint audit committee, SG §§2-601 to 2-605.
Joint standing committee of senate and house, MD Const Art III §24.
Investigating committee, SG §§2-1601 to 2-1609.
Joint committee on administrative, executive and legislative review, SG §§2-501 to 2-507.
Joint committee on children, youth and families, SG §2-10A-06.
Joint committee on federal relations, SG §§2-901 to 2-906.
Joint committee on legislative ethics, SG §§2-701 to 2-709.
Joint committee on the management of public funds, SG §§2-801 to 2-807.
Joint committee on the port of Baltimore, SG §2-10A-07.
Joint oversight committee on Department of Juvenile Services, SG §2-10A-10.
Legislative policy committee, SG §§2-401 to 2-410.
Mental health.
Joint committee on access to mental health services, SG §2-10A-05.
Naming state facilities, roads and bridges, advisory committee, SG §2-10A-09.
Port of Baltimore, SG §2-10A-07.
Presiding officers.
Duties, SG §2-1101.
Senate.
Committee of the whole.
Doors kept open, MD Const Art III §21.
Joint audit committee, SG §§2-601 to 2-605.
Joint standing committee of senate and house, MD Const Art III §24.
Spending affordability committee, SG §§2-1001 to 2-1010.
Standing committees.
Bills.
Committee sponsorship, SG §2-1503.
Copies of proposed bills, SG §2-1103.
Waiver of actuarial analysis, SG §2-1505.
Continuation, SG §2-1102.
Defined, SG §2-101.
Depositions, SG §2-1104.
Miscellaneous powers and duties, SG §2-1103.
Oaths, SG §2-1104.
Perjury, SG §2-1104.
Reports.
Copies of proposed bills and joint resolutions, SG §2-1103.
Studies by governmental units, SG §2-1105.
Subpoenas, SG §2-1104.
Waiver of actuarial analysis for certain bills, SG §2-1505.
Comptroller.
Inspection of records or accounts by members, SG §4-107.
Report of comptroller to legislature, MD Const Art VI §2.
Conflicts of interest.
Joint committee on legislative ethics, SG §§2-701 to 2-709.

GENERAL ASSEMBLY —Cont'd
Conflicts of interest —Cont'd
Public ethics generally.
See PUBLIC ETHICS.
Congress.
Persons holding office under United States not eligible as senators or delegates, MD Const Art III §10.
Consent calendar, MD Const Art III §27.
Passage of bills, MD Const Art III §28.
Construction and interpretation.
Legislative districting plan of 1992.
Severability of subtitle, SG §2-205.
Contempt.
Investigating committee, SG §2-1608.
Joint committee on administrative, executive and legislative review.
Subpoenas.
Contempt to enforce, SG §2-507.
Joint committee on the management of public funds.
Subpoenas.
Enforcement by contempt, SG §2-807.
Legislative policy committee.
Subpoenas.
Enforcement, SG §2-408.
Standing committees.
Subpoenas.
Enforcement by contempt, SG §2-1104.
Continuance.
Because of legislative duties, CJ §6-402.
Contractors.
Compensation to contractors, MD Const Art III §35.
Contract state employees.
Transfer of contractual employees to budgeted positions, SPP §§13-301 to 13-305.
See CONTRACT STATE EMPLOYEES.
Contributions to political campaigns during sessions.
Prohibition, exceptions, EL §13-235.
Corporations.
Charter.
Powers over, MD Const Art III §48.
Foreign corporations.
Taxation of revenues, MD Const Art III §58.
Regulations, MD Const Art III §48.
Taxation.
Revenues of foreign corporations, MD Const Art III §58.
Counties.
Charter.
Powers and restrictions, MD Const Art XI-A §§2, 4, 6.
Code counties.
Power to elect public local laws affecting code county, MD Const Art XI-F §4.
Debts, MD Const Art III §54.
Formation, MD Const Art XIII §§1, 2.
Home rule for code counties.
Limitations on property tax rate and indebtedness.
Authority of general assembly, 25B §22.
Internal improvements.
Restrictions on, MD Const Art III §54.
Subsidizing members in maintenance of space, services or equipment prohibited, SG §2-102.
Courts.
Officers.
Compensation, MD Const Art IV §9.

GENERAL ASSEMBLY —Cont'd

Credit.

Restrictions on extension of state credit, MD
Const Art III §34.

Criminal procedure.

Debate.

Members not liable for criminal prosecution for
words spoken in debate, MD Const Art III
§18.

Debate.

Freedom of speech, MD Const DofR Art 10.

Not liable for words spoken in debate, MD Const
Art III §18.

Debts.

Imprisonment for debt prohibited, MD Const Art
III §38.

Restrictions on loans and extension of credit, MD
Const Art III §34.

Defamation.

Immunity of members, CJ §5-526.

Definitions, SG §2-101.

Bills, SG §§2-1501, 2-1508.

Prefiling, SG §2-1502.

Committees.

Joint committee on administrative, executive
and legislative review, SG §2-501.

Joint committee on federal relations, SG §2-901.

Joint committee on legislative ethics, SG
§2-701.

Joint committee on the management of public
funds, SG §2-801.

Legislative policy committee, SG §2-401.

Spending affordability committee, SG §2-1001.

Private activity bonds, SG §2-1010.

Continuance because of legislative duties, CJ
§6-402.

Federal relations, SG §2-901.

House, SG §2-101.

Investigations, SG §2-1601.

Permanent part-time legislative employee, SG
§2-103.

President, SG §2-101.

Private activity bonds, SG §2-1010.

Senate, SG §2-101.

Speaker, SG §2-101.

Spending affordability committee, SG §2-1001.

Standing committee, SG §2-101.

Delegates.

House of delegates. See within this heading,
"House of delegates."

Delegate scholarships, ED §§18-501 to 18-507.

See SCHOLARSHIPS.

Department of Juvenile Services.

Joint oversight committee, SG §2-10A-10.

Department of legislative services.

General provisions.

See LEGISLATIVE SERVICES DEPARTMENT.

Depositions.

Joint committee on administrative, executive and
legislative review.

Power to take depositions of witnesses, SG
§2-507.

Joint committee on the management of public
funds, SG §2-807.

Legislative policy committee.

Power to cause depositions, SG §2-408.

Standing committees, SG §2-1104.

Developmental disabilities.

Public group homes.

Acquisition of site.

Notice required to members of the district
affected prior to acquisition, HG §7-606.

GENERAL ASSEMBLY —Cont'd

Disruption of legislative process, SG §2-1702.

Distribution of annotated code, SG §2-1247.

Distribution of session laws and journals.

Legislative services department, SG §2-1244.

District Court.

Confirmation of appointment of judges, MD Const
Art IV §41D.

Districts, MD Const Art III §3.

House of delegates. See within this heading,
"House of delegates."

Legislative districting plan of 1992, SG §§2-201 to
2-205.

Requirements, MD Const Art III §4.

Senate. See within this heading, "Senate."

Divorce.

Not to be granted by legislature, MD Const Art III
§33.

Documents.

Destroying, defacing or altering official
documents, SG §2-1702.

Doors kept open, MD Const Art III §21.

Elections, MD Const Art III §§2, 6, 7.

Contested elections.

Legislature to make provisions for, MD Const
Art I §8.

Contributions to political campaigns during
sessions.

Prohibition, exceptions, EL §13-235.

County in which candidate resides.

Identification on ballot, EL §9-210.

Each house judge of elections of its members, MD
Const Art III §19.

Electrical voting machines.

Use by nonmembers, SG §2-1701.

Filing fee, EL §5-401.

House of delegates. See within this heading,
"House of delegates."

Legislative newsletters, EL §§13-406 to 13-409.

Preservation of purity of elections, MD Const Art I
§7.

Regulation of elections.

Power of legislature, MD Const Art III §49.

Senate. See within this heading, "Senate."

Time, MD Const Art III §7.

Vacancy in nomination after primary election, EL
§5-1003.

Emergency law.

Bills, MD Const Art XVI §2.

Eminent domain.

Regulations, MD Const Art III §40.

Highways, MD Const Art III §40B.

Employees.

Administration of section, SG §2-103.

Credits, SG §2-104.

Interference with members and staff prohibited,
SG §2-1702.

Leaves of absence, SG §2-105.

Permanent part-time legislative employees, SG
§2-103.

Relatives.

Restrictions on employment, SG §2-107.

Rights, privileges and benefits, SG §2-103.

Time records, SG §2-103.

Transfer, SG §2-104.

Employees' retirement system.

What legislature should encourage, MD Const
DofR Art 43.

Equipment.

Duty of state to provide, SG §2-102.

GENERAL ASSEMBLY —Cont'd
Equipment —Cont'd
Limitations on political subdivisions subsidizing
members, SG §2-102.
Ethics.
Conflicts of interest.
See PUBLIC ETHICS.
Joint committee on legislative ethics, SG §§2-701
to 2-709.
Lobbying.
See PUBLIC ETHICS.
Rules of legislative ethics.
Joint committee on legislative ethics, SG
§2-707.
Evaluation of programs.
Maryland program evaluation act, SG §§8-401 to
8-413.
See PROGRAM EVALUATION ACT.
Executions.
Laws to be passed protecting property from
execution, MD Const Art III §44.
Expenses of members, SG Title 2 Subtitle 3
(note); MD Const Art III §15.
Explosions and explosives.
Bringing explosives or incendiary devices into
senate or house chambers, SG §2-1702.
Federal aid.
Receipt, administration and distribution, MD
Const Art III §46.
Federal relations.
Joint committee on federal relations, SG §§2-901
to 2-906.
Fees.
Consent of legislature required for levy, MD Const
DofR Art 14.
Investigating committee.
Persons subpoenaed to appear at hearings, SG
§2-1608.
Firearms.
Bringing firearms into chambers, SG §2-1702.
Fiscal notes, SG §2-1505.
Funds.
Joint committee on the management of public
funds, SG §§2-801 to 2-807.
Governor.
Bills.
Approval or disapproval by governor, MD Const
Art II §17.
Bond and revenue bills, submission to General
Assembly, SF §7-106.
Delivery to office of secretary of state, SG
§2-1511.
Presentment to governor, SG §2-1509.
Vetoed bills.
Record, SG §2-1512.
Convening by governor, MD Const Art II §16.
Designee for presentment of bills, SG §2-1510.
Extraordinary occasions.
Convening legislature by governor, MD Const
Art II §16.
Legislative policy committee.
Communication with committee, SG §3-305.
Meetings.
Changing place of meeting of legislature, MD
Const Art II §16.
Extending session of general assembly for
passage of budget bill, MD Const Art III
§52.
Proclamation convening extraordinary session.
Upon petition of members, MD Const Art III
§14.

GENERAL ASSEMBLY —Cont'd
Governor —Cont'd
Pardons.
Report to general assembly, MD Const Art II
§20.
Recommendations to assembly by governor, MD
Const Art II §19.
Vacancy in legislature.
Filling by governor, MD Const Art III §13.
Vacancy in office of governor.
Filling by general assembly, MD Const Art II
§6.
Habeas corpus.
Legislature not to suspend writ, MD Const Art III
§55.
Health care delivery and financing committee,
SG §2-10A-02.
Hearings.
Investigating committee, SG §§2-1601 to 2-1609.
Highways.
Eminent domain.
Board of property review.
Members of general assembly not to be
members of board, TR §8-327.
Regulations, MD Const Art III §40B.
Holding other office.
Civil office in state prohibited, MD Const Art III
§11.
Persons holding office under United States not
eligible, MD Const Art III §10.
Home rule.
Powers and restrictions, MD Const Art XI-A §§2,
4, 6.
House.
Defined, SG §2-101.
House of delegates.
Accounts.
Failure to account for public money, MD Const
Art III §12.
Adjournment.
Consent of both houses required, MD Const Art
III §25.
Age, MD Const Art III §9.
Bills.
General provisions. See within this heading,
"Bills."
Chief clerk.
Bill signed in presence of, MD Const Art III §30.
State seal.
Use by chief clerk, SG §13-105.
Committees.
Committee of the whole.
Doors kept open, MD Const Art III §21.
Joint audit committee, SG §§2-601 to 2-605.
Joint standing committee of senate and house,
MD Const Art III §24.
Compensation, SG Title 2 Subtitle 3 (note); MD
Const Art III §15.
Debate.
Not liable for words spoken in debate, MD
Const Art III §18.
Definition of "house," SG §2-101.
Delegate scholarships, ED §§18-501 to 18-507.
See SCHOLARSHIPS.
Disruption or interference prohibited, SG §2-1702.
Distribution of house journal.
Legislative services department, SG §2-1244.
Districts, MD Const Art III §§3 to 5.
Composition of legislative districts, SG §2-202.
Requirements, MD Const Art III §4.
Subdivision of districts, MD Const Art III §3.

GENERAL ASSEMBLY —Cont'd
House of delegates —Cont'd
Doors kept open, MD Const Art III §21.
Elections, MD Const Art III §6.
  Districts. See within this subheading,
    "Districts."
  Each house judge of elections, MD Const Art III
    §19.
  Governor.
    Deciding question of election, MD Const Art II
      §4.
  Judges, clerks and registers of wills.
    Tied and contested elections, MD Const Art
      IV §12.
  Time of holding, MD Const Art III §7.
Established, MD Const Art III §1.
Expulsion and punishment of members, MD Const
  Art III §19.
Grand inquest of state.
  Powers of house, MD Const Art III §24.
Hall of records commission.
  Member of house appointed to commission, SG
    §9-1003.
Holding other office.
  Civil office in state prohibited, MD Const Art III
    §11.
  United States office prohibited, MD Const Art
    III §10.
Impeachments.
  Power in house of delegates, MD Const Art III
    §26.
Journals, MD Const Art III §22.
  Votes entered in, MD Const Art III §17.
Legislative policy committee, SG §§2-401 to 2-410.
Liability.
  Not liable for words spoken in debate, MD
    Const Art III §18.
Mileage, SG Title 2 Subtitle 3 (note); MD Const
  Art III §15.
Number of members, MD Const Art III §2.
Oaths.
  Official oath, SG §16-103.
Office created during own term.
  Not eligible, MD Const Art III §17.
Officers.
  Appointment of own officers, MD Const Art III
    §19.
Picketing restricted, SG §2-1702.
Presiding officer. See within this subheading,
  "Speaker."
Punishment and expulsion of members, MD Const
  Art III §19.
Qualifications, MD Const Art III §9.
  Each house judge of qualifications, MD Const
    Art III §19.
Quorum, MD Const Art III §20.
  Powers of smaller number than quorum, MD
    Const Art III §20.
Residence, MD Const Art III §9.
Rules and regulations.
  Making, MD Const Art III §19.
Scholarships.
  Delegate scholarships, ED §§18-501 to 18-507.
  See SCHOLARSHIPS.
Sentence and punishment, MD Const Art III §23.
Speaker.
  Bill signed in presence of, MD Const Art III §30.
  Committees.
    Responsibility of speaker, SG §2-1101.
  Compensation, SG Title 2 Subtitle 3 (note); MD
    Const Art III §15.

GENERAL ASSEMBLY —Cont'd
House of delegates —Cont'd
  Speaker —Cont'd
    Discharge duties of governor during vacancy,
      MD Const Art II §7.
    Governor.
      Open election returns for governor, MD Const
        Art II §§2, 3.
    Joint committee on legislative ethics.
      Referrals authorized, SG §2-708.
    Legislative policy committee.
      Cochairmen of committee, SG §2-404.
      Speaker member of committee, SG §2-403.
  Terms of office, MD Const Art III §6.
Husband and wife.
Property of wife protected from debts of husband,
  MD Const Art III §43.
Immunity.
Civil immunity privilege, SG §2-1801.
Constituent service.
  Member providing, CJ §5-525.
Defamation, CJ §5-526.
Impeachments, MD Const Art III §26.
Inconsistent laws.
Legislative districting plan of 1992.
  Repeal of inconsistent laws, SG §2-204.
Indexes.
Compilation, indexing and printing of session
  laws.
  Legislative services department, SG §2-1243.
Information systems.
Legislative information systems generally, SG
  §§2-1228 to 2-1233.
  See LEGISLATIVE SERVICES DEPARTMENT.
Interest.
Legal rate of interest, MD Const Art III §57.
Interference with legislative process, SG
  §2-1702.
Interference with members and staff, SG
  §2-1702.
Intermediate courts of appeal.
Judges.
  Eligibility of members of general assembly, MD
    Const Art IV §14B.
Investigations.
Code of fair procedures.
  Establishment, SG §2-1602.
Committee, SG §§2-1601 to 2-1609.
Definitions, SG §2-1601.
Effect of subtitle on other powers, SG §2-1602.
Hearings, SG §2-1609.
  Defined, SG §2-1601.
Powers of house of delegates as grand inquest of
  state, MD Const Art III §24.
Scope of subtitle, SG §2-1602.
Jeopardy.
No member expelled a second time for same
  offense, MD Const Art III §19.
Joint audit committee, SG §§2-601 to 2-605.
Committee, defined, SG §2-601.
Established, SG §2-602.
Membership, SG §2-603.
Officers, SG §2-604.
Powers and duties, SG §2-605.
**Joint committee on access to mental health
services,** SG §2-10A-05.
**Joint committee on administrative, executive
and legislative review,** SG §§2-501 to 2-507.
**Joint committee on Chesapeake Bay critical
areas,** SG §2-10A-01.

GENERAL ASSEMBLY —Cont'd

Joint committee on children, youth and families, SG §2-10A-06.

Joint committee on federal relations, SG §§2-901 to 2-906.

Joint committee on health care delivery and financing, SG §2-10A-02.

Joint committee on legislative ethics, SG §§2-701 to 2-709.

Joint committee on the management of public funds, SG §§2-801 to 2-807.

Joint committee on the port of Baltimore, SG §2-10A-07.

Joint committee on welfare reform, SG §2-10A-04.

Joint committee on workers' compensation benefit and insurance oversight, SG §2-10A-03.

Joint oversight committee on Department of Juvenile Services, SG §2-10A-10.

Joint resolutions.
Bills include joint resolutions, SG §2-1501.
Certain bills not to include joint resolution, SG §2-1508.
Notice of action under joint resolution, SG §2-1514.

Journals, MD Const Art III §22.
Veto passage entered in, MD Const Art II §17.
Votes entered in, MD Const Art II §17.

Judges.
Eligibility of members to be judge, MD Const Art IV §21.
Removal, MD Const Art IV §4.

Judicial disabilities commission.
General provisions.
See JUDICIAL DISABILITIES COMMISSION.

Jurisdiction.
United States.
Legislative intent, CJ §6-101.

Laws.
Bills. See within this heading, "Bills."
Suspension, MD Const DofR Art 9.

Leaves of absence.
Members or employees, SG §2-105.

Legal analysis.
Office of policy analysis, SG §2-1238.

Legislation.
Bills. See within this heading, "Bills."

Legislative districting plan of 1992.
Boundaries.
Constitutional amendment, MD Const Art III §5.
Descriptions are to geographical boundaries existing on April 1, 1990, SG §2-201.
Composition of districts, SG §2-202.
Constitutionality of provisions.
Severability of subtitle, SG §2-205.
Construction and interpretation.
Severability of subtitle, SG §2-205.
Division of state into districts, SG §2-201.
Enumeration of districts, SG §2-201.
General provisions, SG §2-201.
Inconsistent laws.
Repeal, SG §2-204.
Number of districts, SG §2-201.
Number of senators and delegates from each district, SG §2-201.
Repeal of inconsistent laws, SG §2-204.
Residence of delegates.
Districts containing more than two counties, SG §2-201.

GENERAL ASSEMBLY —Cont'd

Legislative districting plan of 1992 —Cont'd
Severability of subtitle, SG §2-205.
Subdivision of district, SG §2-201.

Legislative information systems, SG §§2-1228 to 2-1233.
See LEGISLATIVE SERVICES DEPARTMENT.

Legislative newsletters, EL §§13-406 to 13-409.
Campaign account of campaign finance entity.
Payment from, EL §13-408.
Definitions, EL §13-406.
Late filing fee for overdue campaign finance report, EL §13-409.
Paid for with public funds, prohibition, EL §13-408.
Personal funds of incumbent.
Payment from, EL §13-408.
Use of funds appropriated in state budget not restricted, EL §13-407.

Legislative policy committee, SG §§2-401 to 2-410.
Governor.
Communications with committee, SG §3-305.
Notice of action under joint resolution, SG §2-1514.

Legislative security force, SG §2-106.

Legislative services department.
See LEGISLATIVE SERVICES DEPARTMENT.

Libel and slander.
Members not liable for words spoken in debate, MD Const Art III §18.

Libraries.
Legislative services department.
Duties of department, SG §2-1241.
Maryland manual.
Distribution, SG §9-1027.

Lobbying.
Affidavit that appropriation has not been obtained by paid lobbyists.
Extra compensation to public officer, agent or contractor, MD Const Art III §35.
Public ethics.
General provisions.
See PUBLIC ETHICS.

Local laws.
Not to enact local laws on subjects covered by express powers, MD Const Art XI-A §4.
Prohibited when, MD Const Art III §33.

Lotteries.
Grants, MD Const Art III §36.

Management of public funds.
Joint committee on the management of public funds, SG §§2-801 to 2-807.

Maryland food center authority.
Legislative intent, 41 §13-102.

Maryland manual.
Distribution to former general assembly members, SG §9-1027.

Meetings.
Annapolis.
Place of meeting, MD Const DofR Art 11.
Convened by secretary of state to fill vacancy in office of governor, MD Const Art II §7.
Convening frequently, MD Const DofR Art 12.
Duration of sessions, MD Const Art III §15.
Extended session.
Passage of budget bill, MD Const Art III §52.
Extraordinary sessions.
Upon petition of members, MD Const Art III §14.

GENERAL ASSEMBLY —Cont'd
Meetings —Cont'd
Special sessions.
Budget amendment not to affect, MD Const Art III §52.
Duration of sessions, MD Const Art III §15.
Proclamation for special session, MD Const Art III §14.
Time of meeting, MD Const Art III §14.
Mental health services.
Joint committee on access to mental health services, SG §2-10A-05.
Mental hygiene law.
Private group homes.
Application for license.
Notice to be given to members from the district where the private group home is to be located, HG §10-520.
Mileage.
General provisions, SG Title 2 Subtitle 3 (note); MD Const Art III §15.
Military service.
Aiding or compensating members of armed forces in time of war, MD Const Art III §34.
Militia.
Consent to governor to command in person, MD Const Art II §8.
Provision for, MD Const Art IX §§1, 2.
Misdemeanors.
Electrical voting machines.
Use by nonmembers, SG §2-1701.
Interfering with or disrupting activities of general assembly, SG §2-1702.
Mortgages and deeds of trust.
Taxation, MD Const Art III §51.
Municipal corporations.
Special acts, MD Const Art III §48.
Subsidizing members of general assembly in maintenance of space, services or equipment prohibited, SG §2-102.
Naming state facilities, roads and bridges, advisory committee, SG §2-10A-09.
Nepotism.
Employment of relatives restricted, SG §2-107.
Noise control.
State government duties and authority, EN §§3-501 to 3-506.
See NOISE CONTROL.
Notice.
Investigating committee.
Notice of hearing, SG §2-1609.
Joint resolutions.
Notice to legislative policy committee of action under joint resolution, SG §2-1514.
Oaths.
Investigating committee.
Persons testifying before committee, SG §2-1609.
Joint committee on administrative, executive and legislative review.
Administration of oaths, SG §2-507.
Legislative policy committee.
Authority to administer oaths, SG §2-408.
Oath to support constitution of the United States, US Const Art VI; Amd 14.
Official oaths, SG §16-103.
Standing committees.
Power to administer oaths, SG §2-1104.
Office of legislative audits, SG §§2-1217 to 2-1227.
See LEGISLATIVE SERVICES DEPARTMENT.

GENERAL ASSEMBLY —Cont'd
Officers.
Bribery.
General provisions, MD Const Art III §50.
Civil officers under state not eligible as senators or delegates, MD Const Art III §11.
Compensation.
Extra compensation to public officers, MD Const Art III §35.
Income tax.
Not exempted from income tax, MD Const Art III §35A.
Increasing or diminishing during term of office prohibited, MD Const Art III §35.
Imprisonment.
Limit on, MD Const Art III §23.
Senators or delegates.
Not eligible to office created, etc., during his term, MD Const Art III §17.
Offices.
Duty of state to provide office space, SG §2-102.
Limitation on political subdivisions subsidizing members, SG §2-102.
Pardons.
Governor's pardons reported to assembly, MD Const Art II §20.
Parole.
Convicts, MD Const Art III §60.
Penalties.
Electrical voting machines.
Use by nonmembers, SG §2-1701.
Firearms.
Bringing firearms into chambers, SG §2-1702.
Interfering with or disrupting activities of general assembly, SG §2-1702.
Pensions, SG Title 2 Subtitle 3 (note).
Bills affecting funding of state pension system actuarial analysis, SG §2-1505.
General pension system prohibited, MD Const Art III §59.
Perjury.
Legislative policy committee.
False swearing by witness before committee, SG §2-408.
Standing committees.
False swearing before standing committee, SG §2-1104.
Petitions.
Right to petition for redress of grievances, MD Const DofR Art 13.
Picketing.
Restriction on picketing, SG §2-1702.
Police.
Legislative security force, SG §2-106.
Policy analysis.
Office of policy analysis generally, SG §§2-1234 to 2-1241.
See LEGISLATIVE SERVICES DEPARTMENT.
Policy committee, SG §§2-401 to 2-410.
Port development.
Baltimore City, MD Const Art XI-D §§1, 2.
Powers.
Legislature may pass laws for carrying into execution powers vested by constitution, MD Const Art III §56.
Separation of powers, MD Const DofR Art 8.
President.
Defined, SG §2-101.
Printing, compilation and indexing of session laws.
Legislative services department, SG §2-1243.

GENERAL ASSEMBLY —Cont'd
Prisoners.
Imprisonment of members.
Limit on, MD Const Art III §23.
Private activity bonds.
Spending affordability committee.
Definitions, SG §2-1010.
Reports of state issuer, SG §2-1010.
Privileges for members, SG §2-1801.
Proceedings.
Not to be impeached in any court, MD Const DofR
Art 10.
Program evaluation act, SG §§8-401 to 8-413.
See PROGRAM EVALUATION ACT.
Publication.
Bills.
Fiscal notes.
Publication not required, SG §2-1505.
Statement of receipts and expenditures, MD Const
Art III §32.
Publications distributed or submitted to.
Legislative services department, SG §2-1246.
Public debt.
General obligation debt.
Enabling acts, SF §§8-117, 8-126 to 8-128.
See PUBLIC DEBT.
Restrictions on loans and extension of credit, MD
Const Art III §34.
Public ethics.
General provisions.
See PUBLIC ETHICS.
Joint committee on legislative ethics, SG §§2-701
to 2-709.
Public local law compilations.
Legislative services department, SG §2-1245.
Public records.
Access to public records.
Right of members to acquire certain
information, SG §10-612.
Public resources, use of, SG §2-108.
Qualifications.
Disqualification.
Failure to account for public money, MD Const
Art III §12.
Quorum.
General provisions, MD Const Art III §20.
Investigating committee, SG §2-1606.
Joint committee on administrative, executive and
legislative review, SG §2-505.
Joint committee on the management of public
funds, SG §2-805.
Legislative policy committee, SG §2-406.
Receivers.
Failure to account for public money.
Disqualification, MD Const Art III §12.
**Recommendations to general assembly by
governor,** MD Const Art II §19.
Records.
Access to public records.
Right of members to acquire certain
information, SG §10-612.
Employees.
Time records, SG §2-103.
Referendum.
Soldiers' bonus, MD Const Art III §34.
Registers of wills.
Fees and charges.
Provision for system, MD Const Art III §45.
Registration.
Legislative agents. See within this heading,
"Lobbying."

GENERAL ASSEMBLY —Cont'd
Repeal of inconsistent laws.
Legislative districting plan of 1992, SG §2-204.
Reports.
Joint committee on administrative, executive and
legislative review, SG §2-506.
Joint committee on federal relations, SG §2-906.
Joint committee on the management of public
funds, SG §2-806.
Legislative policy committee, SG §2-409.
Spending affordability committee, SG §2-1005.
Private activity bonds.
State issuer's reports, SG §2-1010.
Residence.
Senators and delegates, MD Const Art III §9.
Resolutions.
Bills. See within this heading, "Bills."
Joint resolutions. See within this heading, "Joint
resolutions."
Passage, MD Const Art III §28.
Retirement of members, SG Title 2 Subtitle 3
(note).
Right to petition for redress of grievances, MD
Const DofR Art 13.
Rules and regulations.
Investigating committee.
Adoption of rules, SG §2-1607.
Joint committee on administrative, executive and
legislative review.
Failure to comment on regulations, SG §2-506.
Joint committee on legislative ethics, SG §2-707.
Salaries.
Compensation and allowances of members, SG
Title 2 Subtitle 3 (note); MD Const Art III
§15.
Compensation commission, MD Const Art III §15.
Members and presiding officers, MD Const Art III
§15.
Senators or delegates.
Not eligible to office in which salaries increased
during his term, MD Const Art III §17.
Scholarships.
Delegate scholarships, ED §§18-501 to 18-507.
See SCHOLARSHIPS.
Senatorial scholarships, ED §§18-401 to 18-408.
See SCHOLARSHIPS.
Seal.
Great seal affixed thereto, MD Const Art III §30.
Secretaries.
Duty of state to provide secretarial services, SG
§2-102.
Secretary of state.
Bills.
Assignment of chapter numbers, SG §2-1511.
Delivery to clerk of court of appeals, SG
§2-1513.
Delivery to office of secretary, SG §2-1511.
Entry of bills becoming law, SG §2-1512.
Vetoed bills.
Delivery, SG §§2-1511, 2-1513.
Record for vetoed bills, SG §2-1512.
Convening general assembly to fill vacancy in
office of governor, MD Const Art II §7.
Records inspected by general assembly, MD Const
Art II §23.
Vetoed bills.
Delivery, SG §§2-1511, 2-1513.
Record for vetoed bills, SG §2-1512.
Security.
Legislative security force, SG §2-106.

GENERAL ASSEMBLY —Cont'd
Senate.
Accounts.
Failure to account for public money, MD Const
Art III §12.
Adjournment.
Consent of both houses required, MD Const Art
III §25.
Age, MD Const Art III §9.
Bills.
General provisions. See within this heading,
"Bills."
Budget bill sent to, MD Const Art III §52.
Committees.
Committee of the whole.
Doors kept open, MD Const Art III §21.
Joint audit committee, SG §§2-601 to 2-605.
Joint standing committee of senate and house,
MD Const Art III §24.
Compensation, SG Title 2 Subtitle 3 (note); MD
Const Art III §15.
Convening by governor, MD Const Art II §16.
Debate.
Not liable for words spoken in debate, MD
Const Art III §18.
Defined, SG §2-101.
Disruption or interference prohibited, SG §2-1702.
Distribution of senate journal.
Legislative services department, SG §2-1244.
Districts, MD Const Art III §§2, 3.
Requirements, MD Const Art III §4.
Doors kept open, MD Const Art III §21.
Elections, MD Const Art III §§2, 6.
Districts. See within this subheading,
"Districts."
Time of holding, MD Const Art III §7.
Established, MD Const Art III §1.
Governor.
Appointment of state officers.
Approval of senate, MD Const Art II §11.
Effect of rejection by senate of person
nominated by governor, MD Const Art II
§12.
Convening senate alone, MD Const Art II §16.
When civil officers to be nominated to senate,
MD Const Art II §13.
Hall of records commission.
Member of commission, SG §9-1003.
Holding other office.
Civil offices under state prohibited, MD Const
Art III §11.
Impeachment.
Tried by, MD Const Art III §26.
Legislative policy committee, SG §§2-401 to 2-410.
Liability.
Not liable for words spoken in debate, MD
Const Art III §18.
Mileage, SG Title 2 Subtitle 3 (note); MD Const
Art III §15.
Number of members, MD Const Art III §2.
Oaths.
Official oath, SG §16-103.
Office created during own term.
Not eligible, MD Const Art III §17.
Officers.
Appointment of own officers, MD Const Art III
§19.
Picketing restricted, SG §2-1702.
President.
Bill signed in presence of, MD Const Art III §30.
Budget bill sent to, MD Const Art III §52.

GENERAL ASSEMBLY —Cont'd
Senate —Cont'd
President —Cont'd
Committees.
Responsibilities of president as to committees,
SG §2-1101.
Compensation, SG Title 2 Subtitle 3 (note); MD
Const Art III §15.
Defined, SG §2-101.
Discharge duties of governor during vacancy in
office, MD Const Art II §7.
Joint committee on legislative ethics.
Referrals authorized, SG §2-708.
Legislative policy committee.
Cochairmen of committee, SG §2-404.
President member of committee, SG §2-403.
Qualifications for senator, MD Const Art III §§9 to
12.
Each house to be judge of qualifications, MD
Const Art III §19.
Quorum, MD Const Art III §20.
Powers of smaller number than quorum, MD
Const Art III §20.
Residence, MD Const Art III §9.
Rules and regulations.
Making own rules, MD Const Art III §19.
Secretary.
Bill signed in presence of, MD Const Art III §30.
Sentence and punishment, MD Const Art III §23.
Terms of office, MD Const Art III §6.
Vacancy in office.
Filling by governor, MD Const Art III §13.
Sentence and punishment.
House of delegates.
Powers as grand inquest of state, MD Const Art
III §24.
Indeterminate sentences, MD Const Art III §60.
Members and officers, MD Const Art III §23.
Punishment and expulsion of members, MD Const
Art III §19.
Suspension, MD Const Art III §60.
Soldiers' bonus.
Referendum, MD Const Art III §34.
Speaker of the house. See within this heading,
"House of delegates."
Special laws.
Prohibited when, MD Const Art III §33.
Special sessions.
Meetings. See within this heading, "Meetings."
Proclamation of governor, MD Const Art III §14.
Spending affordability committee, SG §§2-1001,
2-1010.
Standing committees.
Bills.
Committee sponsorship, SG §2-1503.
Waiver of actuarial analysis, SG §2-1505.
Continuation, SG §2-1102.
Copies of proposed bills, SG §2-1103.
Defined, SG §2-101.
Depositions, SG §2-1104.
Miscellaneous powers and duties, SG §2-1103.
Oaths, SG §2-1104.
Perjury, SG §2-1104.
Reports.
Copies of proposed bills and joint resolutions,
SG §2-1103.
Studies by governmental units, SG §2-1105.
Subpoenas.
Authority as to subpoenas, SG §2-1104.
Waiver of actuarial analysis for certain bills, SG
§2-1505.

GENERAL ASSEMBLY —Cont'd
State code distribution.
  Legislative services department, SG §2-1247.
State flag.
  Display on state house, SG §13-204.
State library.
  Contracts.
    Investigations.
      House of delegates.
        Powers as grand inquest of state, MD Const
          Art III §24.
State lottery.
  Legislative audits, SG §9-121.
State pension commissioner.
  Office prohibited, MD Const Art III §59.
State treasurer.
  Accounts.
    Copies submitted to legislature, MD Const Art
      VI §4.
    Selection of treasurer by legislature, MD Const
      Art VI §1.
Statutes.
  See STATUTES.
Styled general assembly of Maryland, MD Const
  Art III §1.
Style manual for statutory laws.
  Office of policy analysis, SG §2-1238.
Subpoenas.
  Investigating committee, SG §2-1608.
  Joint committee on administrative, executive and
    legislative review, SG §2-507.
  Joint committee on the management of public
    funds, SG §2-807.
  Legislative policy committee, SG §2-408.
  Standing committees, SG §2-1104.
  Witnesses.
    Members in civil or administrative actions, CJ
      §9-122.
Suspension of writ.
  Legislature not to suspend writ, MD Const Art III
    §55.
Synopsis of bills, SG §2-1504.
Taxation.
  Consent of legislature required for levy, MD Const
    DofR Art 14.
  Mortgages and deeds of trust.
    Taxed where, MD Const Art III §51.
  Personal property.
    Where taxed, MD Const Art III §51.
Time.
  Bills.
    Prefiling dates, SG §2-1502.
Trustees of public, MD Const DofR Art 6.
United States.
  Federal relations.
    Joint committee on federal relations, SG
      §§2-901 to 2-906.
  Power to receive grants from United States,
    administer and distribute same, MD Const
    Art III §46.
  Senators and delegates.
    Holding federal office prohibited, MD Const Art
      III §10.
Vacancies.
  Acceptance of federal office, MD Const Art III §10.
  Filling by governor, MD Const Art III §13.
  Grounds, MD Const Art III §13.
  Replacement of officers, MD Const Art XV §5.
Voting machines.
  Use of electrical voting machines by nonmembers,
    SG §2-1701.

GENERAL ASSEMBLY —Cont'd
Waiver.
  Bills.
    Fiscal notes and waivers.
      Request for waiver of actuarial analysis, SG
        §2-1505.
Weapons.
  Use of firearms and other devices, SG §2-1702.
Welfare reform committee, SG §2-10A-04.
Witnesses.
  House of delegates.
    Powers as grand inquest of state, MD Const Art
      III §24.
  Investigating committee, SG §2-1609.
  Joint committee on administrative, executive and
    legislative review.
    Power to compel attendance, SG §2-507.
  Joint committee on the management of public
    funds.
    Authority to compel attendance, SG §2-807.
  Legislative policy committee.
    Compelling attendance of witnesses, SG §2-408.
  Privileges from testifying, SG §2-1801.
  Subpoena of members in civil or administrative
    actions, CJ §9-122.
**Workers' compensation benefit and insurance
  oversight committee,** SG §2-10A-03.
Yeas and nays.
  Recorded, MD Const Art III §28.

**GENERAL COUNSEL TO PUBLIC SERVICE
  COMMISSION,** PUC §2-106.
**Ethics, commissioners, general counsel,
  people's counsel and officers and
  employees of commission.**
  Generally, PUC §§2-301 to 2-310.
  See PUBLIC SERVICE COMMISSION.
**Procedure before public service commission
  generally,** PUC §§3-101 to 3-114.
  See PUBLIC SERVICE COMMISSION.

GENERAL SERVICES DEPARTMENT.
Advertising.
  State leasing of real property.
    Need to rent building space, SF §4-320.
Advisory units.
  Secretary.
    Creation, SF §4-204.
Annapolis.
  Public buildings and grounds.
    Maintenance, operation and protection.
      Appropriation for services provided by city of
        Annapolis, SF §4-608.
Appraisals.
  Public improvements.
    Duties of department as to appraisals, SF
      §4-406.
Appropriations.
  Public buildings and grounds.
    Maintenance, operation and protection.
      Appropriation for services provided by city of
        Annapolis, SF §4-608.
Architectural and engineering services.
  See PROCUREMENT.
Architectural review.
  Board of architectural review, SF §§4-701 to
    4-704.
  Unit of department, SF §4-206.
Artistic property commission.
  General provisions.
    See ARTISTIC PROPERTY COMMISSION.

GENERAL SERVICES DEPARTMENT —Cont'd
Attorney general.
Assistant attorneys general.
Assignment to department, SF §4-205.
Legal adviser to department, SF §4-205.
Auctions.
Excess and surplus property.
Disposal of property, SF §4-504.
Proceeds of auction or sale, SF §4-505.
Audits.
Procurement.
Inventory, SF §4-306.
Baltimore City.
Purchases through purchasing bureau, 41 §18-201.
Baltimore county.
Metropolitan district.
Public improvements made by district.
Exceptions to provisions, SF §4-402.
Bids and bidding.
Procurement.
Conflicts of interest, SF §4-304.
Definition of "bids," SF §4-301.
Public improvements.
Duties of department as to bids, SF §4-406.
Board of architectural review, SF §§4-701 to 4-704.
Consultation with board.
Duty of state agencies, SF §4-704.
Definition of "board," SF §4-701.
Established, SF §4-702.
Membership, SF §4-703.
Board of public works.
Functions assigned to department by board, SF §4-207.
Powers necessary and proper to accomplish functions, SF §4-208.
Boards and commissions.
Architectural review board, SF §§4-701 to 4-704.
Professional services selection board.
See PROCUREMENT.
Budget and management.
Secretary.
Responsibility for budgets of units of department, SF §4-204.
Buildings.
Energy.
Generally, SF §§4-801 to 4-808. See within this heading, "Energy."
Enforcement of state building code.
Duty of department, SF §4-403.
Public buildings and grounds. See within this heading, "Public buildings and grounds."
Conflicts of interest.
Procurement, SF §4-304.
Contracts.
Architectural and engineering services.
See CONTRACTS.
Land acquisition division.
Review and approval of contracts for acquisition of land, SF §4-415.
Printing for state, SF §4-305.
Counsel to department, SF §4-205.
Counties.
Public improvements.
Exceptions to provisions.
Improvements made by counties or units thereof, SF §4-402.
Purchases through purchasing bureau, 41 §18-201.
Chartered counties, 25A §5.

GENERAL SERVICES DEPARTMENT —Cont'd
Counties —Cont'd
Purchases through purchasing bureau —Cont'd
Powers of commissioners, 25 §3A.
Definitions, SF §4-101.
Architectural review.
Board of architectural review.
Definition of "board," SF §4-701.
Energy, SF §4-801.
Excess and surplus property, SF §4-501.
Land acquisition division, SF §4-401.
Procurement, SF §4-301.
Public improvements, SF §4-401.
Deposits.
Excess and surplus property.
Auction or sale.
Proceeds, SF §4-505.
Divisions.
Land acquisition, SF §§4-411 to 4-416.
Emergencies.
State leasing of real property.
Exceptions to provisions, SF §4-318.
Energy.
Buildings.
Defined, SF §4-801.
Evaluations required, SF §4-803.
Life of the building.
Defined, SF §4-801.
Adoption of definition, SF §4-808.
Definitions, SF §4-801.
Efficiency.
Standards and procedures to evaluate, SF §4-807.
Energy consuming equipment replacement or supplementation, SF §4-804.
Energy-consumption analysis.
Defined, SF §4-801.
Energy performance indices, SF §4-806.
Defined, SF §4-801.
Evaluations required, SF §4-803.
Legislative policy, SF §4-802.
Life-cycle costs.
Defined, SF §4-801.
Projection, SF §4-808.
Life of the building.
Defined, SF §4-801.
Policy of state, SF §4-802.
Standards.
Energy performance indices, SF §4-806.
Evaluation of efficiency, SF §4-807.
Established, SF §4-201.
Excess and surplus property.
Auction or sale, SF §4-504.
Proceeds, SF §4-505.
Central location.
Moving to central location, SF §4-503.
Declaration of excess personal property and surplus personal property, SF §4-502.
Definitions, SF §4-501.
Disposal of property, SF §4-504.
Duties of department, SF §4-506.
List of excess personal property.
Distribution, SF §4-506.
Moving of property, SF §4-503.
Nonexpendable items.
Defined, SF §4-501.
Replacement, SF §4-508.
Rules and regulations, SF §4-506.
Trade-in, SF §4-504.
Proceeds, SF §4-507.

GENERAL SERVICES DEPARTMENT —Cont'd
Excess and surplus property —Cont'd
Use by department.
Excess personal property, SF §4-506.
Food.
Procurement.
Percentage price preference for locally grown
foods, SF §14-407.
Functions, SF §4-207.
Government house trust.
Inventory by department, SG §9-606.
Handicapped persons.
Facilities for the handicapped.
Enforcement of provisions, SF §2-510.
Housing authorities.
Public improvements.
Exceptions to provisions, SF §4-402.
Improvements.
Public improvements. See within this heading,
"Public improvements."
Inspections.
Junior or community colleges and regional
community colleges, SF §4-409.
Public improvements.
Duty of department, SF §4-406.
Inventories.
Procurement, SF §4-306.
Invoices.
Procurement of supplies.
Approval of invoices by secretary, SF §4-311.
Payment of certain unapproved invoices
prohibited, SF §4-315.
Jurisdiction.
Public buildings and grounds.
Maintenance, operation and protection, SF
§4-601.
Keys used in locks on property owned by state.
Regulations for use and distributions, adoption,
CR §7-204.
Land acquisition division, SF §§4-411 to 4-416.
Acquisition in name of acquiring entity, SF
§4-412.
Appraisal of real property acquired.
Independent appraisals, SF §4-416.
Board of public works.
Supervision of expenditures for acquisition of
land, SF §4-415.
Chief, SF §4-413.
Defined, SF §4-401.
Powers and duties, SF §4-414.
Contracts for acquisition of land.
Review and approval, SF §4-415.
Definition of "division," SF §4-401.
Development of acquired land.
Division not responsible, SF §4-412.
Duties, SF §4-412.
Established, SF §4-411.
Independent appraisals of real property, SF
§4-416.
Local projects.
Division not responsible for acquiring land for,
SF §4-412.
Notice of potential acquisition, SF §4-415.
Leases.
State leasing of real property.
See PROCUREMENT.
Legal counsel to department, SF §4-205.
**Maryland-national capital park and planning
commission.**
Public improvements.
Exceptions to provisions.
Improvements made by commission, SF
§4-402.

GENERAL SERVICES DEPARTMENT —Cont'd
Misdemeanors.
Procurement.
Conflicts of interest, SF §4-304.
Public buildings and grounds.
Maintenance, operation and protection.
Violations of regulations, SF §4-607.
Missing children.
Display of photograph, SF §4-209.
Morgan State University.
Powers and duties relating to public
improvements, SF §4-406.
Motor vehicles.
Public buildings and grounds.
Parking and motor vehicle laws.
Enforcement authority, SF §4-606.
Powers and duties of department, SF §4-604.
Municipal corporations.
Public improvements.
Exceptions to provisions.
Improvements made by municipal
corporations, SF §4-402.
Purchases through purchasing bureau, 41
§18-201.
Newspapers.
State leasing of real property.
Advertising of need to rent building space, SF
§4-320.
Notices.
Land acquisition division.
Potential acquisitions, SF §4-415.
State leasing of real property, SF §4-319.
Oaths.
Secretary.
Oath of office, SF §4-202.
Organization.
Units in department, SF §4-206.
Paper.
Procurement of recycled paper.
Percentage price preferences, SF §14-405.
Preference, SF §14-402.
Penalties.
Procurement.
Conflicts of interest, SF §4-304.
Public buildings and grounds.
Maintenance, operation and protection.
Violations of regulations, SF §4-607.
Personal property.
Excess and surplus property, SF §§4-501 to 4-508.
Police force.
Law enforcement officers generally, PS §§3-101 to
3-603.
See LAW ENFORCEMENT OFFICERS AND
PERSONNEL.
Police training commission, PS §§3-201 to 3-218.
See POLICE TRAINING COMMISSION.
Powers.
Necessary and proper powers, SF §4-208.
Printing.
Contracts for printing for state, SF §4-305.
Prisons and prisoners.
State correctional facilities.
Powers and duties relating to public
improvements, SF §4-406.
Procurement.
Bids.
Conflicts of interest, SF §4-304.
Defined, SF §4-301.
Conflicts of interest, SF §4-304.
Definitions, SF §4-301.

GENERAL SERVICES DEPARTMENT —Cont'd
Procurement —Cont'd
Electrical equipment consistent with nonvisual access technology.
    Secretary to set standards, SF §4-312.
Establishment of purchasing bureau, SF §4-302.
Food.
    Percentage price preference for locally grown foods, SF §14-407.
Inventory, SF §4-306.
Invoices for supplies.
    Approval of invoices by secretary, SF §4-311.
    Payment of certain unapproved invoices prohibited, SF §4-315.
Misdemeanors.
    Conflicts of interest, SF §4-304.
Paper.
    Recycled paper.
        Percentage price preferences, SF §14-405.
        Preference, SF §14-402.
Penalties.
    Conflicts of interest, SF §4-304.
Printing.
    Contracts for printing for state, SF §4-305.
Purchasing bureau.
    Delegation of authority to chief of bureau, SF §4-303.
    Established, SF §4-302.
    Unit of department, SF §4-206.
Real property.
    State leasing of real property.
        See PROCUREMENT.
Secretary.
    Conflicts of interest, SF §4-304.
    Delegation of authority to chief of purchasing bureau, SF §4-303.
    Supplies.
        Approval of invoices, SF §4-311.
        Approval of purchases, SF §4-310.
        Procurement by secretary, SF §4-313.
Standards.
    Secretary to set, SF §4-312.
Supplies.
    Amount.
        Estimates of amount or quality, SF §4-314.
    Approval of invoices by secretary, SF §4-311.
    Approval of purchases by secretary, SF §4-310.
    Awards for supplies.
        Copies to using agency, SF §4-307.
    Defined, SF §4-301.
    Estimates of amount or quality, SF §4-314.
    Invoices.
        Approval by secretary, SF §4-311.
        Payment of certain unapproved invoices prohibited, SF §4-315.
    Purchase, SF §4-310.
    Quality.
        Estimates of amount or quality, SF §4-314.
    Secretary.
        Approval of invoices, SF §4-311.
        Approval of purchases, SF §4-310.
        Procurement by secretary, SF §4-313.
    Standards set by secretary, SF §4-312.
Using agency.
    Awards for supplies.
        Copies to using agency, SF §4-307.
    Defined, SF §4-301.
Public buildings and grounds.
Architectural review.
    Board of architectural review, SF §§4-701 to 4-704.

GENERAL SERVICES DEPARTMENT —Cont'd
Public buildings and grounds —Cont'd
Architectural review —Cont'd
    Energy, SF §§4-801 to 4-808.
Maintenance, operation and protection.
    Annapolis.
        Appropriation for services provided by city of Annapolis, SF §4-608.
    Divisions.
        Secretary may establish, SF §4-603.
    Duties of department, SF §4-604.
    Jurisdiction of department, SF §4-601.
    Misdemeanors.
        Violations of regulations, SF §4-607.
    Motor vehicle laws.
        Concurrent enforcement authority, SF §4-606.
        Control of pedestrian and vehicular traffic.
            Powers and duties of department, SF §4-604.
    Offices.
        Secretary may establish, SF §4-603.
    Parking and motor vehicle laws.
        Concurrent enforcement authority, SF §4-606.
        Control of pedestrian and vehicular traffic.
            Powers and duties of department, SF §4-604.
    Penalties.
        Violations of regulations, SF §4-607.
    Powers of department, SF §4-604.
    Regulations, SF §4-607.
    Security force, SF §4-605.
    Superintendents, SF §4-602.
Motor vehicles.
    Parking and motor vehicle laws.
        Concurrent enforcement authority, SF §4-606.
        Control of pedestrian and vehicular traffic.
            Powers and duties of department, SF §4-604.
Operation and protection.
    Generally, SF §§4-601 to 4-608. See within this subheading, "Maintenance, operation and protection."
Rules and regulations.
    Maintenance, operation and protection, SF §4-607.
Superintendents, SF §4-602.
Public improvements.
Appraisals.
    Duty of department, SF §4-406.
Assistance and advice to other units of state government, SF §4-403.
Bids.
    Duties of department as to, SF §4-406.
Defined, SF §4-401.
Duties of department, SF §§4-403, 4-406.
    Maintenance and repair, SF §4-407.
Exceptions to provisions, SF §4-402.
Inspection.
    Duty of department, SF §4-406.
Maintenance and repair, SF §4-407.
    Policies and standards.
        Establishment, SF §4-407.
    Recommendations, SF §4-408.
    Reports, SF §4-408.
Maintenance, operation and protection of improvements and grounds.
    Generally, SF §§4-601 to 4-608. See within this heading, "Public buildings and grounds."
Plans and specifications.
    Approval by department, SF §4-406.
Records, SF §4-406.

GENERAL SERVICES DEPARTMENT —Cont'd
Public improvements —Cont'd
Reports.
    Maintenance and repair, SF §4-408.
Scope of provisions.
    Exceptions, SF §4-402.
Purchases.
Counties, municipalities and Baltimore City.
    Purchases through purchasing bureau, 41
        §18-201.
Purchasing bureau, SF §§4-302, 4-303.
Real property.
Land acquisition division, SF §§4-411 to 4-416.
State leasing of real property.
    See PROCUREMENT.
Records.
Public improvements, SF §4-406.
Religious materials.
Purchase on behalf of private schools, prohibition,
    41 §18-201.
Reports.
Public improvements.
    Maintenance and repair, SF §4-408.
Secretary.
    Annual report, SF §4-204.
Rules and regulations.
Excess and surplus property, SF §4-506.
Public buildings and grounds.
    Maintenance, operation and protection, SF
        §4-607.
Secretary, SF §4-204.
Salaries.
Secretary, SF §4-202.
Seal.
Secretary, SF §4-204.
Secretary.
Administration of department, SF §4-202.
Advisory units.
    Creation, SF §4-204.
Appointment, SF §4-202.
Budgets.
    Responsibility as to, SF §4-204.
Defined, SF §4-101.
Deputy secretary, SF §4-203.
Oath of office, SF §4-202.
Planning.
    Responsibility as to, SF §4-204.
Powers, SF §4-204.
Printing.
    Contracts for printing for state.
        Made through or with approval of secretary,
            SF §4-305.
Procurement.
    Conflicts of interest, SF §4-304.
    Delegation of authority to chief of purchasing
        bureau, SF §4-303.
    Supplies.
        Approval of invoices, SF §4-311.
        Approval of purchase, SF §4-310.
        Procurement by secretary, SF §4-313.
Reports.
    Annual report to governor, SF §4-204.
Responsibility to governor, SF §4-202.
Rules and regulations, SF §4-204.
Salary, SF §4-202.
Seal, SF §4-204.
Staff, SF §4-203.
Units in department to report to secretary, SF
    §4-206.
Security force.
Arrest without a warrant.
    Generally, CP §§2-201 to 2-210.
    See WARRANTLESS ARREST.

GENERAL SERVICES DEPARTMENT —Cont'd
Security force —Cont'd
Authority granted police officers generally, CP
    §2-102.
Definitions.
    Police officer, CP §2-101.
Fresh pursuit, CP §2-301.
Law enforcement procedures generally, CP
    §§2-101 to 2-107.
    See POLICE.
Powers.
    Granted to police officers generally, CP §2-102.
Warrantless arrest.
    Generally, CP §§2-201 to 2-210.
    See WARRANTLESS ARREST.
Status.
Principal department of state government, SF
    §4-201.
Supplies.
Procurement, SF §§4-310 to 4-315.
Surplus property, SF §§4-501 to 4-508.
Units in department, SF §4-206.
Universities and colleges.
Inspections.
    Junior or community colleges and regional
        community colleges, SF §4-409.
Nonpublic institutions.
    Purchases through department, ED §17-106.
War memorial commission.
Unit of department, SF §4-206.
Washington suburban sanitary district.
Public improvements.
    Exceptions to provisions.
        Improvements made by Washington suburban
            sanitary commission, SF §4-402.

GENERAL STATE SCHOOL FUND, ED §5-201.

GENERATION-SKIPPING TRANSFER TAX.
Amount of tax, TG §7-403.
Assessments.
Federal adjustments made, TG §13-409.
Death taxes generally, TG §§7-101 to 7-122.
    See TAXATION.
Definitions, TG §§1-101, 7-401.
Determination of value of property, TG §7-404.
Distribution of revenue.
General fund, TG §2-901.
Exemptions, TG §7-402.
Federal credit.
Amount of tax, TG §7-403.
Defined, TG §7-401.
General fund.
Distribution of revenue, TG §2-901.
Refunds.
    Payment from fund, TG §2-902.
Imposition of tax, TG §7-402.
Interest.
Unpaid tax, TG §13-601.
Liens.
Unpaid tax, TG §13-805.
Limitation of actions.
Refunds.
    Filing of claims, TG §13-1104.
Payment of tax, TG §7-406.
Refunds.
Claims for refunds, TG §13-901.
    Time for filing, TG §13-1104.
Payment, TG §2-902.
Time for filing claims, TG §13-1104.
Returns, TG §7-405.
Value of property, TG §7-404.

GENERATORS.
Building codes.
Emergency power and lighting systems, PS §12-702.

GENETICS.
Blood testing generally.
See BLOOD TESTS.
DNA testing.
See DNA.
Hereditary and congenital disorders programs, HG §§13-101 to 13-110.
See HEREDITARY AND CONGENITAL DISORDERS PROGRAMS.

GEOLOGY.
Maryland geological survey, NR §§2-101 to 2-407.
See MARYLAND GEOLOGICAL SURVEY.

GEORGE WASHINGTON MEMORIAL PARKWAY.
Reversion of title to state, SG §14-201.

GEORGE WASHINGTON'S BIRTHDAY.
See WASHINGTON'S BIRTHDAY.

GEOTHERMAL HEAT PUMP GRANT PROGRAM, SG §9-2008.

GEOTHERMAL RESOURCES.
Appeals.
Judicial review of action on application for permit, EN §5-607.
Appropriation or use permits, EN §5-605.
Bond required, EN §5-606.
Judicial review of action on application, EN §5-607.
Bonds, surety.
Applicants for permits, EN §5-606.
Construction of subtitle, EN §5-609.
Definitions, EN §5-601.
Department of the environment, EN §5-603.
Exploratory permits, EN §5-604.
Bond required, EN §5-606.
Judicial review of action on application, EN §5-607.
Findings, EN §5-602.
Injunctions, EN §5-608.
Intent, EN §5-602.
Penalties, EN §5-608.
Permits.
Appropriation or use of geothermal resources, EN §5-605.
Bond required, EN §5-606.
Exploratory permits, EN §5-604.
Judicial review of action on application, EN §5-607.
Public works.
Board.
Transfer of geothermal resources on state-owned property, SF §10-307.
Tax credits, TP §9-203.
Violations, EN §5-608.

GHOSTS IN THE ATTIC.
Real property sales disclosures, RP §2-120.

GIFT CARDS.
Terms and conditions, CL §14-1320.

GIFT CERTIFICATES.
Terms and conditions, CL §14-1319.

GIFT ENTERPRISE.
Barter, sale or trade, CR §12-212.

GIFTS.
Anatomical gift act, ET §§4-501 to 4-512.
See ANATOMICAL GIFT ACT.
Artistic property commission.
Acceptance, SG §9-1020.
Boxing, sparring and wrestling.
Accepting money or gifts for favors, BR §4-321.
Coercing or intimidating another to contribute or donate, CR §3-707.
Consumer protection.
Certificate when gift or other inducement not available to customer, CL §13-306.
Unconditional gift.
Unsolicited sending of merchandise, CL §14-1304.
Corporations.
Power to make, CA §2-103.
Defined, SF §2-201.
Delmarva advisory council.
Acceptance, 32B §1-109.
Division of correction employees or officers prohibited from accepting from inmates, COR §3-218.
Drug or alcohol abuse.
Acceptance and use by administration, HG §8-206.
Ethics.
Public ethics.
See PUBLIC ETHICS.
Fish and fisheries.
Department of natural resources.
Authority to accept and use, NR §4-205.
Foreign presents to United States officials, US Const Art I §9.
Forests and parks.
Authority to accept, NR §5-207.
Wildland areas.
Acceptance of land or wetlands, NR §5-1217.
Fraudulent fundraising.
Campaigns to benefit police, fire departments or public safety officers, CR §8-520.
Governor.
Acceptance of gifts by officer or unit of state.
Assent by governor, SF §2-201.
Historic St. Mary's City commission.
Property, ED §24-512.
Home improvements.
Gifts as inducements, BR §8-503.
Inspections.
Denial of inspection of gifts, SG §10-616.
Judges.
Code of judicial conduct, CJA Rule 16-813.
Judicial appointees.
Code of conduct for judicial appointees.
Compensation, CJA Rule 16-814 Canon 4.
Maryland environmental trust.
Grants, etc., to trust, RP §2-118.
Maryland historical trust.
Grants, etc., to trust, RP §2-118.
Minors.
Transfers to minors act, ET §§13-301 to 13-324.
See MINORS.
Mosquito control.
Acceptance of gifts or loans from federal government, AG §5-402.
Multiflora rose management.
Acceptance and use of aid, gift or grants, AG §9-705.
Officers.
Assent by governor to acceptance, SF §2-201.
Persons in public trust not to receive presents from other states, etc., MD Const DofR Art 35.

GIFTS —Cont'd
Phragmites management and control.
Wildlife habitat areas.
Authority of secretary to accept gifts, NR §8-2104.
Physical fitness.
Acceptance and use of aid, HG §13-410.
Promotional sales.
Certificate in lieu of gift, CL §13-306.
Public ethics.
See PUBLIC ETHICS.
Public parks and recreation.
Acceptance of gifts, 25 §228.
Public service commissioners, people's counsel, general counsel or officers and employees of commission.
Accepting gifts from public service company, PUC §2-307.
Public service company offering gifts to, PUC §2-308.
Registers of wills.
Receipt prohibited, ET §2-203.
Sanitary commissions.
Acceptance, EN §9-638.
Schools.
Commissioners to have power to receive in trust gifts, 25 §158.
State's attorneys' duty to see that trust carried into effect, 25 §159.
County boards of education.
Powers as to donations, ED §4-118.
State lottery.
Giving lottery ticket or share as gift not prohibited, SG §9-124.
United States.
Foreign presents to United States officials, US Const Art I §9.
Unsolicited sending of merchandise, CL §14-1304.
Veterans.
Homes for veterans.
Authority to accept gifts and grants, SG §9-912.
Wildlife habitat areas.
Phragmites management and control.
Authority of secretary to accept gifts, NR §8-2104.

GINSENG.
Dealers.
Fees, AG §9-605.
Registration, AG §9-602.
Definitions, AG §9-601.
Fees, AG §9-605.
Disposition, AG §9-606.
Permits.
Collection permit, AG §9-602.
Fees, AG §9-605.
Records, AG §9-604.
Registration.
Dealers, AG §9-602.
Fees, AG §9-605.
Secretary.
Authority, AG §9-603.

GIRL SCOUTS OF AMERICA.
Forests and parks.
Free admission to state parks, NR §5-1008.
Taxation.
Exemptions, TP §7-233.

GIVING FALSE NAME TO OFFICER.
Drivers, TR §16-112.

GLASS.
Building codes.
Safety glazing, PS §§12-401 to 12-407.
Motor vehicle equipment, TR §22-406.

GLASS DOORS.
Transparent glass doors.
Duty of department, HG §24-207.

GLAUCOMA.
Eyes generally.
See EYES.
Optometrists generally.
See OPTOMETRISTS.
Quality assurance program.
Joint treatment of patients, HO §11-404.3.
Therapeutically certified optometrists.
Treatment procedures, HO §11-404.2.

GLENN DALE HOSPITAL.
Maryland-Washington regional district.
Acquisition of title upon sale of, 28 §8-127.

GLUE SNIFFING.
Inhaling listed substances, CR §5-708.

GOAT'S MILK.
Frozen desserts.
General provisions.
See FROZEN DESSERTS.
Goat's milk products.
Included within definition of frozen dessert, HG §21-801.

GOD.
Religion.
Belief in existence of required for certain offices, MD Const DofR Arts 36, 37.

GOGGLES.
Schools, ED §7-407.

GOING OUT OF BUSINESS SALES, CL §§11-1101 to 11-1106.
See DISTRESS SALES.

GOLD.
Fines, CL §14-608.
Merchandise made of gold.
Definitions, CL §14-601.
Gold plate and similar gold content merchandise, CL §14-603.
Karat requirements, CL §14-602.
Marks, CL §14-602.
Requirements generally, CL §14-602.
Standard, CL §14-602.
Secondhand precious metals and gem dealers, BR §§12-101 to 12-601.
See PRECIOUS METALS AND GEM DEALERS.

GOLF CARTS.
Low speed vehicles.
See LOW SPEED VEHICLES.
Registration.
Smith Island.
Exemption, TR §13-402.

GOLF COURSES.
Beer, wine and liquor licenses, 2B §§8-501 to 8-507.
Caroline county.
Class GC beer, wine and liquor license, 2B §8-507.1.
Montgomery county.
Alcoholic beverage licenses, 2B §9-102.2.
Property taxes.
Assessments.
Agreements, TP §8-213.

GOLF COURSES —Cont'd
Property taxes —Cont'd
Assessments —Cont'd
Discrimination, TP §8-214.
Determination of discrimination and consent agreements, TP §8-215.
Qualifications, TP §8-212.
Forms, TP §8-218.
Generally, TP §8-216.
Regulations, TP §8-218.
Transfer of agreements, TP §8-217.
Reclaimed water.
Use for irrigation purposes, EN §9-303.1.

GONOCOCCAL OPHTHALMIA NEONATORUM, HG §18-308.

GONORRHEA.
Venereal disease cures or remedies.
Advertising cure.
Prohibition, penalty, CR §10-102.
Defined, CR §10-101.
Prescription requirements, CR §10-103.
Selling or dispensing remedies.
Prohibition, penalties, CR §10-103.

GOOD BEHAVIOR CREDITS FOR INMATES.
Public work, COR §9-506.
Road work, COR §9-513.

GOOD CONDUCT CREDIT.
Inmates committed to custody of commissioner of division of correction, COR §3-704.
Inmates confinement at local correctional facilities, COR §§11-503, 11-504.

GOOD DRIVER DISCOUNT FOR MOTOR VEHICLE INSURANCE, IN §27-907.

GOOD FAITH.
Commercial code.
Definitions, CL §2-103.
Generally, CL §1-201.
Exercising option to accelerate, CL §1-208.
Knowledge.
Defined, CL §1-201.
Obligation of good faith, CL §1-203.
Sales, CL §2-103.
Health care worker whistleblower protection.
Requirements for protection, HO §1-503.
Hotels and retirement communities.
Operating agreements.
Implied covenant of good faith and fair dealing, CL §23-105.
Motor vehicle manufacturers, distributors and factory branches, TR §15-206.1.
Negotiable instruments.
Defined, CL §3-103.
Partnerships, revised act.
Obligation of partner, CA §9A-404.
State personnel.
Collective bargaining.
Requirement, SPP §3-501.

GOOD FRIDAY.
Legal holiday, 1 §27.

GOOD SAMARITAN PROVISIONS.
Fire department.
Immunity from civil liability, CJ §5-604.
Hospitals.
Support for emergency medical system, CJ §5-607.
Immunity for special personnel, CJ §§5-603, 5-604.
Physicians for school sports programs, CJ §5-607.

GOOD SAMARITAN PROVISIONS —Cont'd
Physicians.
School sports programs.
Voluntary and uncompensated service as physician for, CJ §5-607.
Rescue squads.
Immunity for rescue squad personnel, CJ §5-604.
Sports.
Physicians for school sports programs, CJ §5-607.
Support for emergency medical system, CJ §5-608.

GOODS AND CHATTELS.
Personal property.
See PERSONAL PROPERTY.
Retail credit accounts law, CL §§12-501 to 12-515.
See RETAIL CREDIT ACCOUNTS LAW.

GOVERNMENT.
Compact theory of government, MD Const DofR Art 1.
Exclusive right of people to regulate, MD Const DofR Art 4.
Federal government.
See UNITED STATES.
Origin, MD Const DofR Art 1.
Powers of the people, MD Const DofR Art 4.
Reformation.
Establishment of new government, MD Const DofR Art 6.
Republican form.
Guaranteed, US Const Art IV §4.
Right to alter, MD Const DofR Arts 1, 6.

GOVERNMENTAL IMMUNITY.
Sovereign immunity.
See IMMUNITY.

GOVERNMENT HOUSE.
Wanton trespass, CR §6-410.

GOVERNMENT HOUSE TRUST.
Advisory nonvoting members, SG §9-603.
Bylaws, SG §9-605.
Chairman, SG §9-604.
Committees.
Appointment, SG §9-605.
Compensation of members, SG §9-605.
Composition, SG §9-603.
Created, SG §9-602.
Definitions.
Furnishings, SG §9-606.
State room, SG §9-606.
Trust, SG §9-601.
Duties generally, SG §9-606.
Established, SG §9-602.
Expenses of members.
Reimbursement, SG §9-605.
Furnishings.
Defined, SG §9-606.
State room.
Limitation on changes, SG §9-606.
General services department.
Inventory by department, SG §9-606.
Historical societies.
Consultation with Maryland historical society.
Renovation, furnishing and decoration of state room, SG §9-606.
Inventories.
Department of general services, SG §9-606.
Limitations.
Decorative changes of state room, SG §9-606.

GOVERNMENT HOUSE TRUST —Cont'd
Meetings, SG §9-605.
Members generally, SG §9-603.
Powers generally, SG §9-606.
State room.
　Limitation on changes, SG §9-606.
Voting members, SG §9-603.

GOVERNOR.
Abandoned property disposition.
　Abandoned property in federal custody.
　　Certification of agreement with federal
　　　government, CL §17-204.
Acting governor, MD Const Art II §6.
Age, MD Const Art II §5.
Air quality control.
　Air pollution emergencies.
　　Executive orders, EN §2-105.
Alcoholic beverages.
　License commissioners.
　　Appointment by governor and senate, 2B
　　　§15-101.
　　Removals by governor, 2B §15-110.
Amusements and recreation.
　State amusement ride safety advisory board.
　　Appointment of chairman, BR §3-305.
Annapolis.
　Reside at seat of government, MD Const Art II
　　§21.
Appointments by.
　Aging commission, 70B §3.
　Agricultural commission, AG §2-203.
　Agricultural land preservation foundation.
　　Board of trustees, AG §2-503.
　Agriculture.
　　Board of review, AG §2-402.
　　　Removal of members, AG §2-403.
　　Secretary, AG §2-102.
　Alcoholic beverages.
　　Licensed commissioners, 2B §15-101.
　Amusements and recreation.
　　State amusement ride safety advisory board
　　　chairman, BR §3-305.
　Arts council, 83A §4-604.
　Assessments and taxation department director,
　　TP §2-102.
　Baltimore City community college.
　　Board of trustees, ED §16-504.
　Baltimore county board of community college
　　trustees, ED §16-402.
　Banking board, FI §2-202.
　Blind persons.
　　Trading in employment center trustees, 30 §5.
　Chesapeake college board of trustees, ED §16-406.
　Commission on the aging, 70B §3.
　Community services administration.
　　Executive director, 41 §6-202.
　District Court judges, MD Const Art IV §41D.
　Executive departments.
　　Secretaries, SG §8-203.
　Fair board, AG §10-301.
　Forests and parks advisory commission, NR
　　§5-204.
　Frederick county board of community college
　　trustees, ED §16-407.
　Harford county board of community college
　　trustees, ED §16-408.
　Health and higher education facilities authority,
　　43C §4.
　Home improvements commission chairman, BR
　　§8-203.

GOVERNOR —Cont'd
Appointments by —Cont'd
　Howard county board of community college
　　trustees, ED §16-410.
　Human relations commission.
　　Chairman, 49B §1.
　　Executive director, 49B §2.
　Industrial development financing authority, 83A
　　§5-905.
　Judges.
　　Appointment to fill vacancy, MD Const Art IV
　　　§5.
　　District Court judges, MD Const Art IV §41D.
　　Judicial disabilities commission, MD Const Art IV
　　　§4A.
　List of appointees.
　　Legislative services department, SG §2-1248.
　Maryland food center authority, 41 §13-103.
　Maryland geological survey director, NR §2-201.
　Maryland school-based health policy advisory
　　council, ED §7-4A-03.
　Montgomery county board of community college
　　trustees, ED §16-411.
　Natural resources secretary, NR §1-101.
　Officers, MD Const Art II §10.
　　Between primary election and inauguration of
　　　next governor, MD Const Art II §10A.
　Potomac water authority.
　　Chairman, EN §5-403.
　Prince George's county board of community college
　　trustees, ED §16-414.
　Public broadcasting commission, ED §24-202.
　Public defenders.
　　Board of trustees, 27A §9.
　Recess of senate, MD Const Art II §11.
　Rejection by senate or person nominated by
　　governor.
　　Effect, MD Const Art II §12.
　St. Mary's college of Maryland board of trustees,
　　ED §14-402.
　Schools.
　　County boards of education, ED §3-108.
　　Public broadcasting commission, ED §24-202.
　Secretary of agriculture, AG §2-102.
　Secretary of natural resources, NR §1-101.
　Secretary of state, MD Const Art II §22.
　Sheriffs.
　　Filling vacancy, MD Const Art IV §44.
　Taxation.
　　Director of department of assessments and
　　　taxation, TP §2-102.
　Term of office.
　　Appointed officers, MD Const Art II §13; Art
　　　XVII §5.
　Tobacco authority, AG §7-202.
　Vacancies.
　　During session of senate, MD Const Art II §14.
　　Power of governor to fill, MD Const Art II §11.
　Veterinary medical examiners board, AG §2-302.
　Washington county board of trustees, ED §16-419.
　When civil officers to be nominated to senate, MD
　　Const Art II §13.
Appropriations.
　Bills.
　　Disapproval of items by governor, MD Const Art
　　　II §17.
　　Submitted to general assembly, MD Const Art
　　　III §52.
　Disbursements and expenditures.
　　Programs.
　　　Amendment of appropriation for executive
　　　　branch program, SF §7-209.

GOVERNOR —Cont'd

Appropriations —Cont'd

Disbursements and expenditures —Cont'd

Reductions, SF §7-213.

Reduction of appropriations, SF §7-213.

Archives.

State archives established in office of governor, SG §9-1002.

Arts council.

Appointment by governor, 83A §4-604.

Asian lunar new year day.

Annual proclamation, SG §13-405.

Attorney at law.

Governor not to employ additional counsel unless approved by general assembly, MD Const Art V §3.

Attorney general.

Discharging duties of office of governor during vacancy, MD Const Art II §7.

Election.

Determining election and qualification by governor, MD Const Art V §2.

Oaths.

Administration, MD Const Art V §2.

Vacancy in office of attorney general.

Filling by governor, MD Const Art V §5.

Baltimore City.

Mayor.

Removal of mayor by governor, MD Const Art XI §6.

Baltimore City Community College.

Board of trustees.

Appointment of members, ED §16-504.

Baltimore county board of community college trustees.

Appointment of members, ED §16-402.

Banks and trust companies.

Banking board.

Appointment, FI §2-202.

Emergencies, FI §5-707.

Bills, bond and revenue.

Submission to General Assembly, SF §7-106.

Blind persons.

Training and employment centers.

Trustees.

Appointment by governor, 30 §5.

White cane safety day.

Proclamation by governor, 30 §33.

Boards.

General provisions.

See BOARDS AND COMMISSIONS.

Bond and revenue bills, submission to General Assembly, SF §7-106.

Budget and management.

Generally, MD Const Art III §52.

Campaign finance.

Contributions to political campaigns during general assembly sessions.

Prohibition, exceptions, EL §13-235.

Chesapeake college.

Board of trustees.

Appointment of members, ED §16-406.

Citizenship.

Requirements, MD Const Art II §5.

Commission on aging.

Appointment, 70B §3.

Commissions.

Commission on uniform state laws, SG §§9-201 to 9-206.

See UNIFORM LAWS.

GOVERNOR —Cont'd

Commissions —Cont'd

General provisions.

See BOARDS AND COMMISSIONS.

Secretary of state to maintain records of commissions issued by governor to civil officers, SG §7-105.

Community services administration.

Appointment of executive director, 41 §6-202.

Commutation of sentence.

Power of governor, COR §7-601.

Compensation, MD Const Art II §21.

Complaints against civil or military officers.

Powers and duties as to, SG §3-307.

Comptroller.

Discharging duties of office of governor during vacancy, MD Const Art II §7.

Examination by governor, MD Const Art II §18.

Inspection of records, SG §4-107.

Removal.

Hearing of charges, MD Const Art VI §6.

Constitutional office.

Creation of position, SG §3-101.

Contributions to political campaigns during general assembly sessions.

Prohibition, exceptions, EL §13-235.

Councils.

Governor's executive council, SG §§8-101 to 8-105.

Counties.

Commissioners.

Filling vacancy in office of county commissioners, 25 §16.

Creation of position, SG §3-101.

Crime control and prevention office.

Law enforcement equipment fund, PS §§4-301 to 4-304.

Death sentence.

Power to commute or change into confinement, COR §7-601.

Stay of warrant of execution, COR §3-902.

Deepwater port siting.

Duties generally, NR §3-605.

Definitions.

Executive orders, SG §3-401.

Governor's executive council, SG §8-101.

Depositories.

Security approved by governor, MD Const Art VI §3.

Disability, MD Const Art II §6.

District Court.

Appointment of judges, MD Const Art IV §41D.

Division of state documents.

Executive orders.

Distribution to administrator, SG §3-405.

Economic development revenue bond act, 41 §§14-101 to 14-109.

See ECONOMIC DEVELOPMENT REVENUE BOND ACT.

Elections.

Ballots.

Joint listing of names of candidates for governor and lieutenant governor, MD Const Art II §1B.

Candidates.

Joint listing of names of candidates for governor and lieutenant governor on ballot, MD Const Art II §1B.

Commission of election.

Issuance by governor, EL §11-602.

Contributions to political campaigns during general assembly sessions.

Prohibition, exceptions, EL §13-235.

GOVERNOR —Cont'd
Elections —Cont'd
Governor and lieutenant governor unit.
Considered unit for nomination and voting
purposes, EL §5-205.
Death, withdrawal or disqualification of
candidate, EL §5-1201.
Before primary, EL §§5-902 to 5-905.
Petition candidates, EL §5-1101.
Designation of candidate for lieutenant
governor.
Candidate for governor to designate, EL
§5-205.
Petition candidates.
Vacancy in candidacy, EL §5-1101.
Vacancy in candidacy for petition candidates,
EL §5-1101.
Vacancy in candidacy unit before primary.
Candidate for governor, EL §§5-904, 5-905.
Candidate for lieutenant governor, EL §5-903.
Designation of successor.
Remaining candidate, EL §5-902.
Successor unit formed after withdrawal, EL
§5-902.
Withdrawal of remaining candidate, EL
§5-902.
Vacancy in nomination after primary election,
EL §5-1005.
Manner of holding, MD Const Art II §2.
Place of holding, MD Const Art II §2.
Presidential and congressional elections.
Determination of votes cast and proclamation of
results, EL §11-601.
Public campaign financing.
Eligible gubernatorial ticket generally, EL
§§15-101 to 15-111.
See CAMPAIGN FINANCE.
Qualifications of voters, MD Const Art II §2.
Questions relating to election determined by
house of delegates, MD Const Art II §4.
Results.
Ascertaining, MD Const Art II §§2, 3.
Returns, MD Const Art II §2.
Tied elections.
Decided how, MD Const Art II §4.
New election ordered by governor, MD Const
Art XVII §8.
Time of holding, MD Const Art II §2.
Emergencies.
Emergency powers and duties of governor, SG
§3-304.
Emergency management, powers, PS §§14-3A-01
to 14-3A-08, 14-301 to 14-309.
Closing of businesses, PS §14-307.
Construction and interpretation, PS §14-302.
Defined terms, PS §14-301.
Energy emergencies, PS §14-304.
Health emergency powers, PS §§14-3A-01 to
14-3A-08.
See HEALTH EMERGENCIES.
Interstate emergency management and civil
defense compact.
Authority to enter into and execute, PS §14-603.
Law enforcement agencies.
Cooperation among state and local agencies, PS
§14-305.
Legislative intent, PS §14-302.
Maryland emergency management agency
(MEMA), PS §14-106.
State of emergency, authority to declare, PS
§14-107.

GOVERNOR —Cont'd
Emergency management, powers —Cont'd
Militia, PS §14-306.
Repairing damaged property, PS §14-308.
State of emergency.
Authority to declare, PS §14-107.
Energy emergencies, PS §14-304.
Notice, PS §14-304.
Orders, rules and regulations, PS §14-304.
Proclamation, PS §14-303.
Violations, PS §14-309.
Employees' and teachers' retirement systems.
Allowance for governor, SPP §22-405.
Executive branch.
Head of executive branch, SG §3-302.
Names.
Restrictions on name changes, SG §8-303.
Principal departments. See within this heading,
"Executive departments."
Executive council.
Composition, SG §8-103.
Council defined, SG §8-101.
Established, SG §8-102.
Executive secretary, SG §8-105.
Purposes, SG §8-104.
State superintendent of schools.
Member, ED §2-303.
Executive departments.
Coordination among departments, SG §8-204.
Economic development revenue bond act, 41
§§14-101 to 14-109.
See ECONOMIC DEVELOPMENT REVENUE
BOND ACT.
Enumeration of principal departments, SG §8-201.
Established, SG §8-201.
Meetings of boards, etc.
Open to public, 41 §1-205.
Officers, SG §8-202.
Organizational chart, SG §8-305.
Recommendations for new programs or new units
within appropriate department, SG §8-301.
Reorganization, MD Const Art II §24.
Responsibilities of governor, SG §8-301.
Secretaries.
Appointment, SG §8-203.
Coordination among departments, SG §8-204.
Qualifications, SG §8-203.
Recommendations to governor, SG §8-302.
Representation of intergovernmental unit, SG
§8-203.
Responsibilities, SG §8-302.
Units in executive departments, SG §8-202.
Executive orders.
Air pollution emergencies, EN §2-105.
Amendments.
Form of amendment, SG §3-402.
Assignment of chapter numbers, SG §2-1511.
Codification, SG §3-406.
Controlled hazardous waste facility permits, EN
§7-234.
Defined, SG §3-401.
Delivery to secretary of state, SG §3-404.
Department of legislative services.
Distribution to director, SG §3-405.
Publication by director, SG §3-406.
Disposition, SG §3-404.
Distribution, SG §3-405.
Division of state documents.
Distribution to administrator, SG §3-405.
Effective date, SG §3-403.
Form of amendment, SG §3-402.

GOVERNOR —Cont'd
Executive orders —Cont'd
  Indexing, SG §3-404.
  Low-level nuclear waste disposal.
    Storage or disposal capacity.
      Suspension of requirements by executive
        order, EN §8-406.
  Publication, SG §3-406.
  Secretary of state.
    Delivery, SG §3-404.
  Time.
    Effective date of order, SG §3-403.
Executive power vested in, MD Const Art II §1.
Extradition.
  See EXTRADITION.
Federal programs.
  Designation of units, SG §8-304.
Fines.
  Remission, CP §1-207; MD Const Art II §20.
  Power of governor, MD Const Art II §20.
Fish and fisheries.
  Endangered species of fish.
    Duties of governor, NR §4-2A-06.
Forests and parks.
  Advisory commissions.
    Appointment of members, NR §5-204.
  Middle Atlantic interstate forest fire protection
    compact.
    Authority, NR §5-801.
Forfeitures.
  Remission, CP §1-207.
    Powers of governor, MD Const Art II §20.
**Frederick county board of community college
  trustees.**
  Appointment of members, ED §16-407.
Funds.
  Contingent fund, MD Const Art III §32.
Gas and oil.
  Interstate oil and gas compact.
    Directed to join, EN §14-401.
    Official representative, EN §14-403.
General assembly.
  Approval or disapproval of bills, MD Const Art II
    §17.
  Bills.
    Appropriation bill.
      Disapproval of items in bill by governor, MD
        Const Art II §17; Art III §52.
    Approval or disapproval by governor, MD Const
      Art II §17; Art III §52.
    Bond and revenue bills, submission of, SF
      §7-106.
    Budget bill.
      Procedure, MD Const Art III §52.
    Delivery to office of secretary of state, SG
      §2-1511.
    Presented to governor for approval and signing,
      SG §2-1509; MD Const Art III §30.
    Vetoed bills record, SG §2-1512.
  Convening legislature on extraordinary occasions,
    MD Const Art II §16.
  Proclamation for special session, MD Const Art
    III §14.
  Designee for presentment of bills, SG §2-1510.
  Extraordinary occasions.
    Convening legislature by governor, MD Const
      Art II §16.
  House of delegates.
    Speaker.
      Opening election returns for governor, MD
        Const Art II §3.

GOVERNOR —Cont'd
General assembly —Cont'd
  Legislative policy committee.
    Communication with committee, SG §3-305.
  Meetings.
    Changing place of meeting of legislature, MD
      Const Art II §16.
    Extending session of general assembly for
      passage of budget bill, MD Const Art III
      §52.
    Proclamation convening extraordinary session,
      MD Const Art III §14.
  Pardons.
    Reported to general assembly, MD Const Art II
      §20.
  Recommendations to assembly by governor, MD
    Const Art II §19.
  Vacancy in legislature, MD Const Art III §13.
  Vacancy in office of governor, MD Const Art II §6.
Gifts.
  Acceptance of gifts by officer or unit of state.
    Assent by governor, SF §2-201.
Governor-elect.
  Gubernatorial transition, SG §§3-201 to 3-209.
    See within this heading, "Gubernatorial
    transition."
Gubernatorial transition.
  Applicability of subtitle, SG §3-203.
  Appropriations, SG §3-208.
  Budget responsibilities, SG §3-205.
  Citation of subtitle, SG §3-209.
  Consultants, SG §3-207.
  Duty of governor, SG §3-204.
  Findings of legislature, SG §3-202.
  Governor-elect.
    Applicability of subtitle, SG §3-203.
    Authority to obtain information, SG §3-204.
    Defined, SG §3-201.
    Scope of inquiry, SG §3-204.
  Legislative policy, SG §3-202.
  Office space, supplies and furnishings, SG §3-207.
  Purpose of subtitle, SG §3-202.
  Scope of subtitle, SG §3-203.
  Services and facilities, authorized, SG §3-207.
  Short title of subtitle, SG §3-209.
  Staff, SG §3-206.
Handicapped persons.
  Office for handicapped individuals.
    See HANDICAPPED PERSONS.
**Harford county board of community college
  trustees.**
  Appointment of members, ED §16-408.
Hazardous materials and substances.
  Controlled hazardous substances facilities permit.
    Executive order, EN §7-234.
Head of executive branch, SG §3-302.
Health.
  Emergency powers, PS §§14-3A-01 to 14-3A-08.
    See HEALTH EMERGENCIES.
  Local health services inclusion in state budget,
    HG §2-301.
**Health and higher educational facilities
  authority.**
  Appointment, 43C §4.
Hearings.
  Budget bill, MD Const Art III §52.
Highways.
  State highway projects.
    Report to governor on status of projects, TR
      §8-616.

GOVERNOR —Cont'd
Home improvements commission.
Appointment of chairman, BR §8-203.
House.
Artistic property commission.
Duties generally, SG §§9-1021, 9-1022.
Trust, SG §§9-601 to 9-606.
See GOVERNMENT HOUSE TRUST.
Howard county board of community college trustees.
Appointment of members, ED §16-410.
Human relations commission.
Chairman.
Designation by governor, 49B §1.
Executive director.
Appointment by governor, 49B §2.
Impeachment.
Powers of legislature, MD Const Art II §7.
Indexes.
Executive orders, SG §3-404.
Industrial development financing authority.
Membership.
Appointment or approval of governor, 83A §5-905.
International trade agreements.
Binding agreements by governor or state officials, SG §3-308.
Interstate emergency management and civil defense compact.
Authority to enter into and execute, PS §14-603.
John Hanson's birthday.
Annual proclamation, SG §13-401.
Judges.
Commissions of office.
Issuance, MD Const Art IV §11.
Removal of judges, MD Const Art IV §4.
Retirement, MD Const Art IV §§3, 3B.
Vacancies.
Appointment to fill vacancy, MD Const Art IV §5.
Judicial disabilities commission.
Appointment of members, MD Const Art IV §4A.
Labor, licensing and regulation secretary.
Responsibility to governor, BR §2-102.
Law day.
Annual proclamation by governor, SG §13-402.
Laws.
Enforcement, MD Const Art II §9.
Legislative policy committee.
Communications with committee, SG §3-305.
Legislative services.
Executive orders.
Distribution to director, SG §3-405.
Publication by director, SG §3-406.
Lieutenant governor.
General provisions.
See LIEUTENANT GOVERNOR.
Livestock quarantine.
Declaration, AG §3-102.
Lotteries.
State lottery agency, SG §§9-101 to 9-125.
See STATE LOTTERY.
Low-level nuclear waste.
Interstate compact.
Authority of governor to negotiate, EN §7-227.
Maryland defense force.
Governor's duties, PS §13-505.
Maryland food center authority.
Appointment of members, 41 §13-103.
Military services.
Commander-in-chief.
Land and naval forces of state, MD Const Art II §8.

GOVERNOR —Cont'd
Military services —Cont'd
Officers.
Suspension and removal of military officers, MD Const Art II §15.
Militia.
Commander-in-chief, SG §3-303; MD Const Art II §8.
Complaints against civil or military officers. See within this heading, "Complaints against civil or military officers."
General powers as to militia, SG §3-303.
Land militia.
General powers as to, SG §3-303.
Maryland defense force.
Governor's duties, PS §13-505.
Naval militia.
General powers as to, SG §3-303.
Officers.
Brevet commissions, PS §13-605.
Suspension and removal of officers, MD Const Art II §15.
Minorities.
Office of minority affairs, SG §§9-301 to 9-306.
See OFFICE OF MINORITY AFFAIRS.
Montgomery county board of community college trustees.
Appointment of members, ED §16-411.
Motor vehicles.
Display of state seal on vehicle, TR §22-404.2.
Registration.
Reciprocal agreements with other jurisdictions. Approval of governor, TR §12-412.
Name.
Executive branch of government.
Restrictions on name changes, SG §8-303.
National guard.
Governor's powers, PS §13-401.
Natural resources department.
Removal of appointees.
Approval of governor, NR §1-101.
Natural resources secretary.
Appointment, NR §1-101.
Nuclear compact.
Directed to execute compact, 41 §16-101.
Oaths, US Const Art VI; Amd 14.
Official oath, SG §16-101.
Office of minority affairs, SG §§9-301 to 9-306.
See OFFICE OF MINORITY AFFAIRS.
Officers.
Complaints against civil officers. See within this heading, "Complaints against civil or military officers."
Nominations to senate, MD Const Art II §13.
Qualifying before, MD Const Art I §10.
Removal, MD Const Art II §15.
Suspension, MD Const Art II §15.
Terms of office, MD Const Art II §13.
Vacancies, MD Const Art II §11.
Declared for officers whose compensation is from fees.
Failure to file reports, MD Const Art XV §1.
Order of succession, MD Const Art II §7.
Orders.
Executive orders, SG §§3-401 to 3-406. See within this heading, "Executive orders."
Organizational chart.
Principal department secretary, SG §8-305.
Organizational chart of executive departments, SG §8-305.

GOVERNOR —Cont'd
Orphans' court.
  Judges.
    Filling vacancies, MD Const Art IV §40.
Pardons, MD Const Art II §20.
  Impeachment.
    Governor has no power to pardon or reprieve,
      MD Const Art II §20.
  Power of governor, COR §7-601; MD Const Art II
    §20.
  Sole judge as to violations, COR §7-602.
Penalties.
  Remission, MD Const Art II §20.
Pest control compact.
  General provisions.
    See PESTS.
Poet laureate.
  Designation, SG §13-306.
Poetry day.
  Annual proclamation, SG §13-403.
Powers of governor.
  Additional powers, SG §3-301.
  Complaints against civil or military officers, SG
    §3-307.
  Emergency powers, SG §3-304.
  Executive departments, SG §8-301.
  Generally, SG §3-301.
  Head of executive branch, SG §3-302.
  Militia.
    General powers as to militia, SG §3-303.
  Separation, MD Const DofR Art 8.
**Prince George's county board of community
    college trustees.**
  Appointment of members, ED §16-414.
Principal departments. See within this heading,
    "Executive departments."
Proclamations.
  Budget bill.
    Extension of session of general assembly for
      passage, MD Const Art III §52.
  Constitutional amendments, MD Const Art XIV
    §1.
  Extension of session of general assembly for
    passage of budget bill, MD Const Art III §52.
  Extraordinary session of general assembly, MD
    Const Art III §14.
  Referendum.
    Results, MD Const Art XVI §5.
  Special session of general assembly, MD Const Art
    III §14.
Publication.
  Executive orders, SG §3-406.
Public debt.
  General obligation debt management program.
    Consolidated loan budget.
      Submission, SF §8-114.
    Preliminary determination, SF §8-113.
Public defender.
  Appointment of board of trustees, 27A §9.
Public service commission.
  Appointment and removal of commissioners, PUC
    §2-102.
  Appointment of chairman, PUC §2-103.
Public works.
  Member of board of public works, MD Const Art
    XII §1.
Qualifications, MD Const Art II §5.
  Eligibility determined by house of delegates, MD
    Const Art II §4.
  Time, MD Const Art II §3.

GOVERNOR —Cont'd
Quarantine.
  Livestock.
    Declaration, AG §3-102.
Radiation.
  Low-level nuclear waste disposal.
    Storage or disposal capacity.
      Suspension of requirements by executive
        order, EN §8-406.
Referendum.
  Election.
    Proclamation of results, MD Const Art XVI §5.
Remission of fine or forfeiture, CP §1-207.
Remit part of sentence subject to conditions.
  Power of governor, COR §7-601.
Reorganization of executive department, MD
    Const Art II §24.
Reports.
  Contingent fund.
    Report to general assembly, MD Const Art III
      §32.
Representative of governor.
  Meetings of governing boards of corporations or
    institutions, SG §3-306.
Reprieves.
  General provisions, MD Const Art II §20.
  Power of governor to grant, MD Const Art II §20.
Residence.
  General provisions, MD Const Art II §21.
  Requirements, MD Const Art II §5.
St. Mary's college of Maryland.
  Board of trustees.
    Appointment, ED §14-402.
Salaries.
  General provisions, SG §3-102; MD Const Art II
    §21.
Savings and loan associations.
  Director of division, FI §8-302.
Scholarships.
  Merit scholastic awards, ED §7-207.
Schools.
  County boards of education.
    Appointment by governor, ED §3-108.
  Early childhood development and education.
    Interagency advisory committee.
      Designation of chairman, ED §24-302.
  Public broadcasting commission.
    Appointment, ED §24-202.
Seals.
  State seal.
    Use by governor, SG §13-104.
Secretaries of principal departments, SG
    §§8-205, 8-206.
Secretary of agriculture.
  Appointment, AG §2-102.
Secretary of state.
  Clerical duties, MD Const Art II §23.
  Commissions.
    Secretary to maintain records of commissions
      issued by governor, SG §7-105.
  Executive orders.
    Delivery to secretary, SG §3-404.
**Small business development financing
    authority,** 83A §§5-1004, 5-1011.
Southern regional education compact.
  Authorized and directed to sign, ED §25-201.
Special police officers.
  Governor to appoint, PS §3-302.
State house trust, SG §§9-501 to 9-506.
  See STATE HOUSE TRUST.

GOVERNOR —Cont'd
State lottery agency, SG §§9-101 to 9-125.
  See STATE LOTTERY.
State prosecutor.
  Selection and disabilities commission, SG §9-1211.
State seal.
  Use by governor, SG §13-104.
State treasurer.
  Depositaries.
    Approval by governor, MD Const Art VI §3.
    Examination by governor, MD Const Art II §18.
  Publication of accounts.
    Directed by governor, MD Const Art VI §4.
  Removal.
    Hearing of charges, MD Const Art VI §6.
  Vacancy of treasurer.
    Filling vacancy, MD Const Art VI §1.
State treasury.
  Depositaries.
    Designation of financial institutions as
      depositaries.
      Approval by governor, SF §6-206.
Stay of warrant of execution, COR §3-902.
Succession to office, MD Const Art II §6.
  Ineligible to succeed self after two terms, MD
    Const Art II §1.
  Order of succession, MD Const Art II §7.
Task forces.
  Establishment by governor, SG §8-301.
Taxation.
  Director of department of assessments and
    taxation.
    Appointment of director, TP §2-102.
Term of office, MD Const Art II §1.
Time.
  Executive orders.
    Effect of date, SG §3-403.
Trusts and trustees.
  Government house trust, SG §§9-601 to 9-606.
    See GOVERNMENT HOUSE TRUST.
  State house trust, SG §§9-501 to 9-506.
    See STATE HOUSE TRUST.
Uniform laws.
  Commission on uniform state laws, SG §§9-201 to
    9-206.
    See UNIFORM LAWS.
Universities and colleges.
  Charter for higher education.
    Duties of governor, ED §10-206.
University of Maryland.
  Funds for satisfaction of award, ED §13-207.
Vacancies.
  During session of senate, MD Const Art II §14.
  Filling.
    By general assembly, MD Const Art II §§6, 7.
  Officers.
    Approval of governor's appointment by state
      senate, MD Const Art II §11.
      Effect of rejection, MD Const Art II §12.
  Vacancy not provided for in constitution, MD
    Const Art II §7.
Veto.
  Item veto, MD Const Art III §52.
  Power of governor, MD Const Art II §17.
  Procedure, MD Const Art II §17.
Warrant of execution, stay, COR §3-902.
Washington metropolitan area transit
    authority compact.
  Execution of compact, TR §10-202.

**GOVERNOR'S OFFICE OF CRIME CONTROL
    AND PREVENTION.**
Law enforcement equipment fund, PS §§4-301
  to 4-304.
**GOVERNOR'S WORKFORCE INVESTMENT
    BOARD,** LE §11-505.
GOVERNOR WELLMOBILE PROGRAM, HG
  §§13-1301 to 13-1303.
Advisory board, HG §13-1302.
**Established within University of Maryland
    school of nursing,** HG §13-1301.
Funded from state budget, HG §13-1301.
Geographic areas served, HG §13-1303.
**Nonprofit corporation for accepting of grants
    and donations.**
  Establishment authorized, HG §13-1303.
**Operated, managed and administered by
    University of Maryland school of nursing,**
    HG §13-1301.
Partnerships, development, HG §13-1303.
Purpose, HG §13-1301.
Report, HG §13-1303.

**GOVERNOR WILLIAM DONALD SCHAEFER
    INTERNATIONAL TERMINAL,** TR §5-413.

GRADE CROSSINGS.
Railroads.
  Crossings, TR §§8-639 to 8-643.
  See RAILROADS.

GRADING PERMITS.
Power of counties and municipalities to issue,
  EN §4-103.

GRAFFITI.
Malicious destruction of property, CR §6-301.
Restitution, CR §6-301.
  Determination.
    Crime victim's compensation, CP §11-603.

GRAIN.
Air quality control.
  Grain drying operations.
    Rules and regulations, EN §2-301.
Appeals.
  Licensing of grain dealers.
    Suspension or revocation, AG §13-209.
Bonds, surety.
  Licensing of grain dealers.
    Bond required prior to issuance of license, AG
      §13-212.
Buyers.
  Licenses generally. See within this heading,
    "Licenses."
Crimes and offenses.
  Dealer licensing violations, AG §13-214.
Dealers.
  Directory, AG §13-206.
  Licenses. See within this heading, "Licenses."
  Records.
    Business records.
      Refusal to make available upon request, AG
        §13-204.
    Required records, AG §13-204.
Definitions.
  Grain dealers licensing, AG §13-201.
Directory of grain dealers, AG §13-206.
Failure to deliver documents for merchandise,
  CR §7-116.
Fees.
  Licenses, AG §13-203.

GRAIN —Cont'd
Financial statement.
  Licensing of grain dealers.
    Required as prerequisite to issuance of license,
      AG §13-212.
Fraud.
  Licensing of grain dealers.
    Fraudulent or deceptive statements on
      application, AG §13-208.
Funds.
  Administrative fund, AG §13-202.
  Disposition of funds, AG §13-205.
Grain drying operations.
  Rules and regulations, EN §2-301.
Guaranty.
  Licensing of grain dealers.
    Cash guaranty required prior to issuance of
      license, AG §13-212.
Injunctions.
  Licensing of grain dealers.
    Enjoining violations of provisions, AG §13-215.
Insurance.
  Licenses, AG §13-211.
    Failure to maintain adequate insurance.
      Grounds for refusal, suspension or revocation,
        AG §13-208.
    Issuance.
      Proof of adequate insurance required, AG
        §13-203.
    Proof of insurance required prior to issuance of
      license, AG §13-212.
    Required, AG §13-211.
Licenses.
  Administrative fund, AG §13-202.
  Disposition of funds, AG §13-205.
  Appeals.
    Suspension or revocation, AG §13-209.
  Applications.
    Fraudulent or deceptive statements on.
      Ground for refusal, suspension or revocation,
        AG §13-208.
  Bond, surety.
    Required as prerequisite to issuance, AG
      §13-212.
  Cash guaranty.
    Prerequisite to issuance, AG §13-212.
  Change and status as to the type of license, AG
    §13-203.
  Dealer.
    Defined, AG §13-201.
  Definitions, AG §13-201.
  Determination of type of license, AG §13-203.
  Directory of grain dealers, AG §13-206.
  Expiration, AG §13-203.
  Fee, AG §13-203.
  Financial statement.
    Required as prerequisite to issuance, AG
      §13-212.
  Fraudulent or deceptive statements on
    applications.
    Grounds for refusal, suspension or revocation,
      AG §13-208.
  Injunctions.
    Enjoining violations of provisions, AG §13-215.
  Insurance.
    Failure to maintain adequate insurance.
      Grounds for refusal, suspension or revocation,
        AG §13-208.
    Prerequisite to issuance of license, AG §13-203.
    Proof of insurance coverage required prior to
      issuance of license, AG §13-212.

GRAIN —Cont'd
Licenses —Cont'd
  Insurance —Cont'd
    Required, AG §13-211.
  Issuance.
    Oath.
      Required prior to issuance, AG §13-203.
  Letter of credit.
    Irrevocable letter of credit prerequisite to
      issuance, AG §13-212.
  Notice.
    Suspension or revocation, AG §13-209.
  Penalties.
    Violations of provisions, AG §13-214.
  Posting, AG §13-210.
  Refusal.
    Grounds, AG §13-208.
  Renewal, AG §13-203.
  Required, AG §13-203.
  Rules and regulations.
    Adoption, AG §13-213.
    Violations.
      Grounds for refusal, suspension or revocation,
        AG §13-208.
  Suspension or revocation.
    Grounds, AG §13-208.
    Notice, AG §13-209.
    Review, AG §13-209.
  Type of license.
    Requirements as to, AG §13-212.
  Violations of provisions.
    Grounds for refusal, suspension or revocation,
      AG §13-208.
Misdemeanors.
  Dealer licensing violations, AG §13-214.
Notice.
  Licenses.
    Change and status as to the type of license.
      Requirements, AG §13-203.
    Suspension or revocation, AG §13-209.
Penalties.
  Civil penalty, AG §13-216.
Records.
  Dealers.
    Refusal to make available upon request, AG
      §13-204.
    Required records, AG §13-204.
Rules and regulations.
  Licensing of grain dealers, AG §13-213.
  Regulatory violations, AG §13-208.
Violations of provisions.
  Licensing of grain dealers.
    Grounds for refusal, suspension or revocation,
      AG §13-208.

GRAND JURY.
Additional grand juries, CJ §8-413.
Attendees, CJ §8-414.
Bailiff.
  Oath, CJ §8-415.
Baltimore City.
  Investigations, CJ §8-417.
  Reports, CJ §8-417.
  State's attorney for Baltimore City.
    Attendance, CJ §8-414.
Clerk.
  Oath, CJ §8-415.
Constitution of the United States, US Const
  Amd 5.
Court reporters.
  Attendance, CJ §8-414.

GRAND JURY —Cont'd
Court reporters —Cont'd
Duties, CJ §8-416.
Taking and transcribing testimony, CJ §§2-503, 8-415.
Failure of juror to serve for entire period of service.
Grand jury not invalidated, CJ §8-412.
Foreperson.
Jury plan.
Required provisions, CJ §8-211.
Immunity.
Compelling testimony or documents on condition of immunity, Crim Rule 4-631.
Interpreters.
Attendance, CJ §8-414.
Oath, CJ §8-415.
Investigations.
State correctional facilities, COR §9-607.
Subpoenas to appear before grand jury, Crim Rule 4-643.
Multiple service, CJ §8-403.
Number of jurors, CJ §8-412.
Oaths, CJ §8-415.
Paid leave for service, SPP §§9-1101, 9-1104.
Photographing court proceedings.
Prohibition, exception, violation contempt, CP §1-201.
Radio.
Broadcasting criminal proceeding.
Prohibition, exception, violation contempt, CP §1-201.
Recording or broadcasting criminal proceeding.
Prohibition, exception, violation contempt, CP §1-201.
Records, CJ §8-416.
Secrecy violations, CJ §8-507.
State personnel.
Paid leave for service, SPP §§9-1101, 9-1104.
State's attorney for Baltimore City.
Attendance, CJ §8-414.
Television.
Broadcasting criminal proceeding.
Prohibition, exception, violation contempt, CP §1-201.
Visitation of local correctional facility, COR §9-608.
Witnesses.
Person testifying before, CJ §9-118.

GRANDPARENTS.
Child custody.
Visitation.
Petition by grandparents, FL §9-102.
Child support obligation.
Parent of child unemancipated minor, FL §5-203.
Health insurance for grandchildren, IN §15-403.
Newly born or adopted children, IN §15-401.
Unmarried dependent incapacitated children, IN §15-402.

GRANTEE ACTIONS.
District Court, CivProDist Rule 3-711.

GRANTS.
Agricultural mediation program, AG §1-1A-03.
Assisted living facilities, HG §§24-1001 to 24-1007.
See ASSISTED LIVING PROGRAMS.

GRANTS —Cont'd
Baltimore City Community College.
Board of trustees.
Powers, ED §16-505.
Block grants, SF §2-202.
Buses.
Local bus systems, TR §10-207.
Chesapeake Bay and endangered species fund, NR §1-704.
Child care quality incentive grant program, FL §§5-594 to 5-594.8.
Code of Maryland.
Rights under charter or grant from state, 1 §4.
Community colleges.
English for Speakers of Other Languages (ESOL) program.
Student grants, ED §§16-305, 16-508.
Community development administration.
Limitation on grants, HS §4-206.
Community health resources commission.
Fund, use of grants, HG §19-2201.
Condominiums, RP §§11-101 to 11-143.
See CONDOMINIUMS.
Counties.
Local bus systems, TR §10-207.
Paratransit service, TR §2-103.5.
County library capital project grant program, ED §23-510.
Crime victims' services.
State board of victim services, CP §11-919.
Day-care centers.
Adult day care centers, HG §§24-702 to 24-705.
See DAY-CARE CENTERS.
Defective grants.
Validation, RP §4-109.
Definitions, RP §1-101.
Block grants, SF §2-202.
Construed to pass whole interest, RP §2-101.
Delmarva advisory council.
Acceptance, 32B §1-109.
Drug or alcohol abuse.
Acceptance and use by administration, HG §8-206.
Neighborhood crime, drug and alcohol abuse prevention and education programs, CR §5-1001.
Environmental service.
Generally, NR §3-104.
Reduction of costs levied against district by amount of grants, NR §3-107.
Family caregiver assistance program, 70B §45.
Federally qualified health centers grant program, HG §§24-1301 to 24-1308.
See HOSPITALS.
Flood control, EN §5-803.
Forms, RP §4-202.
Frauds, statute of.
General provisions, RP §5-103.
Not applicable to resulting or constructive trust or to trust transferred or extinguished by operation of law, RP §5-107.
Other requirements of article not repealed, RP §5-108.
Geothermal heat pump grant program, SG §9-2008.
Grant anticipation notes.
Public debt.
State units, SF §§8-213 to 8-221.
See PUBLIC DEBT.
Health manpower shortage incentive grant program, ED §18-803.
Heritage areas, FI §13-1113.

GRANTS —Cont'd

Historic preservation.
Maryland advisory committee on historic agricultural structure preservation.
Barn preservation fund, SF §5A-403.

Horizontal property act, RP §§11-101 to 11-143.
See CONDOMINIUMS.

Housing and community development department.
Lead hazard reduction grant and loan programs, HS §§4-701 to 4-712.

Judith P. Hoyer early child care and education enhancement program, ED §5-217.

Land patents.
General provisions, RP §§13-101 to 13-504.
See LAND PATENTS.

Land trust grant fund.
General provisions, NR §§3-2A-01 to 3-2A-14.
See LAND TRUST GRANT FUND.

Lead hazard reduction grant and loan programs, HS §§4-701 to 4-712.

Maryland environmental trust, RP §2-118.
Federal government or political subdivisions of state, NR §3-207.

Maryland historical trust, RP §2-118.
MHT grant program, SF §5A-328.

Maryland stem cell research programs, 83A §5-2B-08.

Mental health professional grant, ED §18-707.

Mental hygiene law.
Administration by director, HG §10-204.
Community mental health facilities, HG §§24-602 to 24-605.

MHT grant program, SF §5A-328.

Multiflora rose management.
Acceptance and use, AG §9-705.

Nonpossessory corporeal estates.
Grantor, RP §8-104.

Nursing facility conversion grant program, HG §§24-1401 to 24-1407.
See NURSING HOMES.

Paratransit service provided by local governments, TR §2-103.5.

Patuxent river watershed.
Program open space.
Application by counties, NR §8-1314.

Pesticides.
Applicators.
Administration of subtitle.
Receipt or issuance of grant, AG §5-202.

Phragmites management and control.
Wildlife habitat areas.
Authority of secretary to accept grants, NR §8-2104.

Physical fitness.
Acceptance and use of aid, HG §13-410.

Public debt.
State units.
Grant anticipation notes, SF §§8-213 to 8-221.
See PUBLIC DEBT.

Radium pilot grant program, HS §§4-1301 to 4-1308.
See RADIUM PILOT GRANT PROGRAM.

Real property.
Power of attorney.
Selling or granting real estate, RP §4-107.

Remainders, reversions and executory interests.
Alienability of possibilities to revert, RP §6-104.

GRANTS —Cont'd

Right of entry.
Alienability of rights of entry, RP §6-104.

Rural legacy program.
Agreements generally, NR §5-9A-07.
Sponsor of designated area, NR §5-9A-06.

Rural Maryland prosperity investment fund, SF §2-207.

Senior citizen activities centers.
Capital improvement grants program, 70B §§26 to 32.
See SENIOR CITIZEN ACTIVITIES CENTERS.

Solar energy grant program, SG §9-2007.

State.
Rights not affected by adoption of code of Maryland, 1 §4.

Stem cell research.
State funded research, 83A §5-2B-08.

Student assistance.
Economic development student assistance grants program, ED §§18-701 to 18-708.
See SCHOLARSHIPS.
Math/science student corps program, ED §§18-1601 to 18-1604.
See UNIVERSITIES AND COLLEGES.
Part-time students grant program, ED §§18-1401 to 18-1404.
See UNIVERSITIES AND COLLEGES.
Private career school student grant program, ED §§18-1201 to 18-1207.
See SCHOLARSHIPS.
Student financial assistance.
See STUDENT FINANCIAL ASSISTANCE.

Tires.
State used tire cleanup and recycling fund.
Financial assistance, EN §9-278.

Validation.
Defective grants.
General provisions, RP §4-109.

Warranty.
General provisions, RP §§10-201 to 10-205.
See WARRANTY.

Wildlife habitat areas.
Phragmites management and control.
Authority of secretary to accept grants, NR §8-2104.

Workforce shortage student tuition grants, ED §18-708.

GRAPE GROWERS.

Wine and grape promotion.
Council, AG §2-1103.
Definitions, AG §2-1101.
Fund, AG §2-1102.

Winery and grape growers' advisory commission, AG §§10-1201 to 10-1206.
See ALCOHOLIC BEVERAGES.

GRAPHIC ART.

Consignment of works of fine art.
General provisions, CL §§11-8A-01 to 11-8A-04.
See ART.

GRASS.

Maryland turf grass law, AG §§9-101 to 9-110.
See TURF GRASS LAW.

Phragmites.
Wildlife habitat areas.
Management and control of phragmites, NR §§8-2101 to 8-2107.
See PHRAGMITES.

GRATUITIES.
Public service commissioners, people's counsel, general counsel or officers and employees of commission.
Accepting gifts from public service company, PUC §2-307.
Public service company offering gifts to, PUC §2-308.

GRAVEYARDS.
Generally.
See CEMETERIES.

GREAT SEAL OF MARYLAND.
State seal generally, SG §§13-101 to 13-105.
See SEALS.

GREENBELT, CITY OF.
Alcoholic beverages.
Beer and wine licenses.
Class B-DH (on-sale only) drafthouses, 2B §8-702.

GREENBELT LAW.
Real property tax.
Assessments.
Farm or agricultural use, TP §8-209.
Credits for conservation lands, TP §9-220.

GREENHOUSE GASES.
Healthy air act.
Electric generating facilities, EN §§2-1001 to 2-1005.

GRENADES.
Possession of destructive device, CR §§4-501 to 4-503.

GRIEVANCE PROCEDURES, SPP §§12-101 to 12-405.
Appeals, SPP §§12-204, 12-205.
Effect of failure to appeal, SPP §12-106.
Records, SPP §12-403.
Applicability of title, SPP §12-102.
Back pay awards, SPP §12-402.
Coercion.
Right to bring grievance free of coercion, SPP §12-103.
Conference.
Appeal to administrative head, SPP §12-204.
Expenses, SPP §12-405.
Initiation of grievance proceeding, SPP §12-203.
Consolidation of grievances, SPP §12-404.
Construction of title, SPP §12-102.
Decisions.
Appeal to administrative head, SPP §12-204.
Appeal to secretary, SPP §12-205.
Duties of decision maker, SPP §12-401.
Extension of time, SPP §12-107.
Failure to decide, SPP §12-106.
Initiation of grievance proceeding, SPP §12-203.
Peer review panel, SPP §12-303.
Definitions, SPP §12-101.
Departmental employees.
Separate grievance procedures, SPP §12-104.
Discrimination.
Right to bring grievance free of discrimination, SPP §12-103.
Exclusive remedy, SPP §12-103.
Failure to appeal or decide.
Effect, SPP §12-106.
Forms, SPP §12-108.
"Grievance" defined, SPP §12-101.
Hearing.
Appeal to secretary, SPP §12-205.

GRIEVANCE PROCEDURES —Cont'd
Hearing —Cont'd
Expenses, SPP §12-405.
Inapplicability of title, SPP §12-102.
Informal discussion, SPP §12-202.
Initiation of grievance proceeding.
Consolidation of grievances, SPP §12-404.
Filing written grievance, SPP §12-203.
Informal discussion, SPP §12-202.
Records, SPP §12-403.
Representation, SPP §12-105.
Interference.
Right to bring grievance free of interference, SPP §12-103.
Office of administrative hearings.
Appeals to, SPP §12-205.
Disposition of case or conduct of hearing, SPP §4-401.
Peer review panel.
Decision, SPP §12-303.
Duties, SPP §12-302.
Election to use, SPP §12-301.
Personnel department.
Separate grievance procedures, SPP §12-104.
Reclassification grievance.
Appeal to secretary, SPP §12-205.
Back pay awards, SPP §12-402.
Records, SPP §12-403.
Remedies available, SPP §12-402.
Representation, SPP §12-105.
Grievance representative.
Release time and expense reimbursement, SPP §12-405.
Reprisal or restraint.
Right to bring grievance free of, SPP §12-103.
Resolution encouraged, SPP §12-109.
Right to bring grievance, SPP §12-103.
Scope of title, SPP §12-102.
Steps in grievance procedure, SPP §12-201.
Time.
Extension of period for decision, SPP §12-107.
Waiver of limitations, SPP §12-107.
Waiver of time limitations, SPP §12-107.
Whistleblower protection.
Effect on grievance procedures, SPP §5-302.
Morgan State University employees.
Election of complaint or grievance procedure, SPP §5-307.
State personnel management system employees.
Election of complaint or grievance procedure, SPP §5-307.
University system of Maryland employees.
Election of complaint or grievance procedure, SPP §5-307.
Witnesses.
Release time and expense reimbursement, SPP §12-405.

GRIEVANCES BY INMATES AT STATE CORRECTIONAL FACILITY.
Inmate grievance office, COR §§10-201 to 10-210.
See PRISONS AND PRISONERS.

GROCERY CARTS.
Theft, CR §7-201.

GROCERY STORES.
Food establishments.
See FOOD AND FOOD ESTABLISHMENTS.

GROUND RENT, PropAct Rule 12-501.
Advertising sale without disclosing, CL §14-2902.

GROUND RENT —Cont'd
Costs.
Actions to recover, RP §8-402.3.
Ejectment.
Costs and expenses recoverable, RP §8-402.3.
Six months arrearage as grounds for action, RP §8-402.2.
Fee for application for redemption or extinguishment, CA §1-203.
Improvements.
Notice of transfer of improvements on property subject to ground rents, RP §14-116.
Notice.
Transfer of improvements on property subject to ground rent, RP §14-116.
Recordation.
Redemption certificates, RP §3-102.
Tax, TP §12-105.
Redemption of certain reversions, RP §8-110.
Fund for payments to former owners, CA §1-203.3.
Sale of property subject to ground rent.
Contract disclosure, RP §14-117.
Taxation.
Foreclosure of right of redemption.
Effect of final order, TP §14-844.
Leases creating ground rent, TP §12-105.
Property transfer tax, TP §13-205.
Sale of property subject to ground rent, TP §14-816.

GROUNDWATER CONTAMINATION.
Notification by department, EN §4-411.2.

GROUP DAY-CARE CENTERS.
Schools.
Use of school property.
Priority, ED §7-109.

GROUP HOME FINANCING PROGRAM, HS §§4-601 to 4-612.
Administration of program, HS §4-605.
Criminal law and procedure.
False statements or reports, HS §4-612.
Defined terms, HS §4-601.
Department of housing and community development.
Duties of department, HS §4-605.
Powers of department, HS §4-604.
Regulations, adoption, HS §4-606.
Development finance division.
Units in division, HS §4-103.
Eligibility standards, HS §4-604.
Established, HS §4-602.
False statements or reports, HS §4-612.
Fees and charges.
Authority to establish, HS §4-604.
Goals of program, HS §4-603.
Group home sponsors.
Defined, HS §4-601.
Qualifications, HS §4-607.
Loan applications.
Process, HS §4-610.
Review process, HS §4-609.
Terms of loans, HS §4-610.
Maximum loans.
Authority to establish, HS §4-604.
Nonresidential uses of group homes, HS §4-611.
Operation of program, HS §4-608.
Program established, HS §4-602.
Purpose of program, HS §4-603.
Qualifications of sponsors, HS §4-607.
Regulations, adoption, HS §4-606.

GROUP HOME FINANCING PROGRAM —Cont'd
Review of loan applications, HS §4-609.
Selection of homes to be financed, HS §4-604.
Special loan programs fund.
Operation of program, HS §4-608.
Terms of loans, HS §4-610.
Use of homes.
Nonresidential uses of group homes, HS §4-611.

GROUP HOMES.
Developmental disabilities.
Location, residential zones, HG §7-603.
Emergency management plan, PS §14-110.1.
Financing program, HS §§4-601 to 4-612.

GROUP INSURANCE.
Blanket insurance, IN §§15-305 to 15-310.
County offices and employees, 25 §3.
Credit life, health and unemployment insurance, IN §§13-101 to 13-117.
See CREDIT LIFE, HEALTH AND UNEMPLOYMENT INSURANCE.
Fictitious groups, IN §27-217.
Health insurance, IN §§15-301 to 15-310.
Conversion from group to individual policy, IN §§15-412 to 15-414.
Expense-incurred policies.
Extension of coverage after termination, IN §15-833.
Notice to parents of impeding loss of child's coverage, IN §15-416.
Part-time students with disabilities, coverage, IN §15-417.
Portability and accountability, IN §§15-1401 to 15-1409.
Reimbursements for services under self-funded plans, IN §15-702.
Self-funded plans.
Reimbursement of dentists, physicians and podiatrists, IN §15-702.
Succeeding policy notices, IN §15-415.
Life insurance, IN §§17-101 to 17-311.
See LIFE INSURANCE AND ANNUITIES.
Long-term care insurance, IN §§18-101 to 18-120.
See LONG-TERM CARE INSURANCE.
Maryland health insurance plan, IN §§14-501 to 14-515.
See MARYLAND HEALTH INSURANCE PLAN.
Preferred rates, IN §27-217.
Premium reduction, readjustment, etc., IN §27-210.
Workers' compensation.
Agricultural group policies, IN §§25-201 to 25-204.

GUARANTY.
Emergency management.
Civil relief during emergency periods.
Stays, postponements or suspensions of enforcement.
Effect on sureties, guarantors and endorsers, PS §14-205.
Grain.
Licensing of grain dealers.
Cash guaranty required prior to issuance of license, AG §13-212.
Service contracts and consumer products guaranty.
General provisions, CL §§14-401 to 14-410.
See SERVICE CONTRACTS AND CONSUMER PRODUCTS GUARANTY.

GUARANTY —Cont'd
Vendors' liens.
  Acceptance of guarantee or collateral does not
    waive liens, RP §7-205.
GUARANTY CORPORATIONS.
Life and health insurance guaranty
    corporation, IN §§9-401 to 9-419.
  See LIFE AND HEALTH INSURANCE
    GUARANTY CORPORATION.
Property and casualty insurance guaranty
    corporation, IN §§9-301 to 9-316.
  See PROPERTY AND CASUALTY INSURANCE
    GUARANTY CORPORATION.
GUARDIAN AD LITEM.
Notices.
  Waiver, ET §1-103.
Paternity proceedings.
  Party under legal disability.
    Guardian ad litem not required, FL §5-1013.
GUARDIAN AND WARD.
Accounts and accounting.
  Guardian of the person of a minor.
    Accounting not required, ET §13-703.
  Protection of property, ET §13-209.
  Veteran's guardianship, ET §13-804.
Adoption.
  Consent, FamLaw Rule 9-102.
    Notice to consenting persons, FamLaw Rule
      9-104.
  Foreign jurisdictions, FamLaw Rule 9-103.
  Hearings, FamLaw Rule 9-109.
  Judgment of adoption or guardianship, FamLaw
    Rule 9-111.
  Local department adoptions.
    Adoption after termination of parental rights,
      FL §§5-345 to 5-353.
      See ADOPTION.
    Adoption without prior termination of parental
      rights, FL §§5-331 to 5-342.
      See ADOPTION.
  Medical history of child, FamLaw Rule 9-113.
  Notice.
    Additional notice of guardianship proceedings,
      FamLaw Rule 9-105.
    Petitions for guardianship, FamLaw Rule 9-103;
      Juv Rule 11-501.
  Private agency adoptions, FL §§5-3A-29 to
    5-3A-37.
    See ADOPTION.
Advice of rights.
  Person, guardian of, Guardian Rule 10-204.
Appeals from proceedings from guardianship,
    AppRev Rule 8-122.
  Depriving natural guardian of custody of child, CJ
    §12-303.
  Record on appeal.
    Access to record, AppRev Rule 8-122.
Applicability of rules titles 1 and 2, Guardian
    Rule 10-102.
Applicability of title.
  Standby guardians, ET §13-902.
Appointment.
  Person, guardian of.
    Petition for appointment, Guardian Rules
      10-201 to 10-203.
  Protection of property. See within this heading,
    "Protection of property."
Attorneys at law.
  Appointment of attorney or investigator, Guardian
    Rule 10-106.

GUARDIAN AND WARD —Cont'd
Attorneys at law —Cont'd
  Appointment of counsel.
    Disabled parties, FamLaw Rule 9-105.
  Protection of property.
    Appointment of counsel, ET §13-211.
Banks and trust companies.
  Fiduciary capacity.
    See BANKS AND TRUST COMPANIES.
Best interest of a disabled person.
  Defined, ET §13-711.
  Life-sustaining procedures.
    Withholding or withdrawal, ET §13-713; HG
      §5-605.
Bicycles.
  Operation of bicycles and play vehicles.
    Parent knowingly permitting minor or ward to
      violate provisions of subtitle, TR §21-1201.
Bonds, surety.
  Guardian of the person of a minor.
    Bond not required, ET §13-703.
  Protection of property.
    General provisions, ET §13-208.
    Qualification of guardian, ET §13-206.
  Standby guardians, ET §13-908.
  Veteran's guardianship, ET §13-803.
Capacity of person.
  Adjudication to have no bearing on issue, ET
    §13-205.
Children in need of assistance.
  Granting custody and guardianship, CJ §3-819.2.
  Venue of action for guardianship, CJ §6-203.
Circuit courts.
  Jurisdiction, ET §13-105.
Classification of abode, ET §13-101.
Combination of guardianship petitions,
    Guardian Rule 10-110.
Compensation.
  Amount, ET §13-218.
  Guardian of the person of a minor, ET §13-703.
  Veteran's guardianship.
    Limitation upon compensation, ET §13-806.
Consolidation of proceedings, Juv Rule 11-501.
Court.
  Defined, ET §13-101.
Dead bodies.
  Consent for postmortem examination, HG §5-501.
Death.
  Protection of property.
    Effect of death of guardian, ET §13-220.
Declaratory judgments.
  Rights of, CJ §3-408.
Definitions, ET §13-101; Guardian Rule 10-103;
    Rule 1-202.
  Guardian of the person, ET §13-711.
  Standby guardians, ET §13-901.
Descent and distribution.
  Appointment for distribution to minor, ET §9-109.
Director.
  Defined, ET §13-101.
Disabled persons.
  Advice of rights, Guardian Rule 10-204.
  Appointment of guardian, ET §§13-705 to 13-707.
  Capacity.
    Adjudication to have no bearing on issue, ET
      §13-205.
  Commitment to mental institution.
    Adjudication of disability not basis for
      commitment, ET §13-706.
  Court's authority, ET §13-704.
  Defined, ET §13-101.

GUARDIAN AND WARD —Cont'd
Disabled persons —Cont'd
  Determination of disability of party, FamLaw
    Rule 9-105.
  Duties of guardian, ET §13-708.
  Emergency protective services, ET §13-709;
    Guardian Rules 10-201 to 10-213.
  Immunity from liability, ET §13-710.
  Jurisdiction, ET §13-105.
  Medical consent, ET §§13-708, 13-711 to 13-713.
  Physicians' certificates, Guardian Rule 10-202.
  Powers of guardians, ET §13-708.
  Protection of property. See within this heading,
    "Protection of property."
  Reports, Guardian Rule 10-206.
    Temporary guardian for protective services,
      Guardian Rule 10-213.
  Rights of guardians, ET §13-708.
  Services provided directly to disable person, ET
    §13-708.
Drug or alcohol abuse.
  Admission of minor to inpatient facilities.
    Application by guardian, HG §8-502.1.
Duties.
  Breach of fiduciary duty, ET §13-216.
  Guardian of the person of a disabled person, ET
    §13-708.
Emergencies.
  Defined, ET §13-101.
  Emergency protective services, ET §13-709;
    Guardian Rules 10-201 to 10-213.
  Guardian of the person of a disabled person.
    Emergency protective services, ET §13-709.
Equity.
  Distribution under jurisdiction of court, ET
    §15-108.
Estate.
  Defined, ET §13-101.
Evidence.
  Veteran's guardianship.
    Necessity for appointment of guardian of minor
      beneficiary, ET §13-802.
Expenses.
  Reimbursement, ET §13-218.
Fees.
  Assessment and waiver, Guardian Rule 10-107.
Fiduciaries.
  General provisions, ET §§15-201 to 15-211.
    See FIDUCIARIES.
  Successor corporate fiduciaries, ET §§15-1A-01 to
    15-1A-05.
    See FIDUCIARIES.
Foreign.
  Powers of foreign fiduciaries, ET §13-222.
Guardian.
  Defined, ET §13-101.
Guardian of property.
  Administration of guardianship, Guardian Rule
    10-305.
  Advice of rights, Guardian Rule 10-303.
  Fiduciary estates including guardianships of
    property, Guardian Rules 10-701 to 10-712.
  Hearing, Guardian Rule 10-304.
  Notice.
    Petition for appointment, Guardian Rule
      10-302.
  Petition for appointment, Guardian Rule 10-301.
    Service, Guardian Rule 10-302.
  Service of process.
    Petition for appointment, Guardian Rule
      10-302.

GUARDIAN AND WARD —Cont'd
Guardian of property —Cont'd
  Venue.
    Petition for appointment, Guardian Rule
      10-301.
Hearings.
  Court appointment of guardian of disabled person,
    ET §13-705.
  Judge to conduct hearings, Juv Rule 11-501.
  Person, guardian of, Guardian Rule 10-205.
Heirs.
  Defined, ET §13-101.
Hospitals.
  Guardian of the person of a disabled person.
    Emergency protective services, ET §13-709.
Immunity.
  Guardian of the person of a disabled person.
    Immunity from civil liability or criminal
      penalty, ET §13-710.
Insurance.
  Authority to insure minor's property, IN §12-302.
  Health insurance, IN §15-403.1.
    Newly born or newly adopted wards, IN
      §15-401.
    Unmarried dependent incapacitated individuals
      under guardianship, IN §15-402.
  Life insurance and annuities.
    Payment of proceeds to minor without
      appointment of legal guardian, IN §16-110.
  Minors.
    Consent of guardian, ET §13-503.
Interested person.
  Defined, ET §13-101.
  Protection of property.
    Petition for orders granting relief, ET §13-210.
    Petition to terminate proceedings, ET §13-221.
    Right to invoke jurisdiction of court, ET
      §13-203.
Interpretation and construction.
  Title, ET §13-102.
Inventory.
  Protection of property, ET §13-209.
Investments.
  Veteran's guardianship, ET §13-805.
Jurisdiction.
  Applicability of rules and scope of jurisdiction,
    Guardian Rule 10-101.
  Disabled persons, ET §13-105.
  Minors, ET §13-105.
    Equity court jurisdiction, FL §1-201.
  Protection of property.
    Transfer of property to other jurisdiction, ET
      §13-222.
  Transfer of action, Guardian Rule 10-109.
Juvenile causes.
  Appointment of guardian, Juv Rule 11-117.
  General provisions, CJ §§3-8A-01 to 3-8A-34.
    See JUVENILE CAUSES.
  Recognizance of parent, guardian or custodian,
    Form 904-R.
Letters of guardianship, Guardian Rule 10-108.
  Protection of property.
    Recordation, ET §13-217.
Liability.
  Breach of fiduciary duty, ET §13-216.
  Guardian of the person of a disabled person.
    Immunity from civil liability or criminal
      penalty, ET §13-710.
Life insurance and annuities.
  Payment of proceeds to minor without
    appointment of legal guardian, IN §16-110.

GUARDIAN AND WARD —Cont'd
Life-sustaining procedures, ET §§13-711 to
      13-713.
   Defined, ET §13-711.
   Withholding or withdrawal, ET §13-712.
      Best interest determination, ET §13-713.
         Defined, ET §13-711.
         Surrogate decision making under health care
            decision act, HG §5-605.
Local department guardianships.
   Addresses of parents, clerk to keep, FL §5-314.
   Adoption after termination of parental rights, FL
      §§5-345 to 5-353.
      See ADOPTION.
   Adoption without prior termination of parental
      rights, FL §§5-331 to 5-342.
      See ADOPTION.
   Appeal, right to, FL §5-310.
   Applicability of subtitle, FL §5-302.
   Appointment of attorney for parent and/or child,
      FL §5-307.
   Authority of court to grant, FL §5-320.
   Conditional consent or acquiescence, FL §5-320.
      Non-fulfillment of condition, FL §5-327.
   Consents, requirements, FL §5-321.
   Contents of petition, FL §5-313.
   Costs and fees, FL §5-309.
   Definitions, FL §5-301.
   Effort to locate parents, FL §5-316.
   Foreign orders, FL §5-305.
   Hearing on petition for consensual guardianship,
      FL §5-318.
   Investigatory powers of court, FL §5-317.
   Legislative findings and purpose, FL §5-303.
   Nonconsensual guardianship, FL §5-323.
   Notice of filing of petition, FL §5-315.
      Website for posting notices, 88A §18.
   Order denying or granting.
      Consensual guardianship, entry of order, FL
         §5-322.
      Contents, FL §5-324.
      Effect of order, FL §5-325.
   Paternity determination, FL §5-306.
   Post-adoption contact, agreements, FL §5-308.
   Prohibition on payment or compensation for
      services, FL §5-362.
   Relation to other provisions, FL §5-304.
   Review hearings, FL §5-326.
   Show cause order, FL §5-316.
   Termination, FL §5-328.
   Time limits for actions by court, FL §5-319.
   Waiver of local department's obligation.
      Nonconsensual guardianship, FL §5-323.
Maryland rules.
   Defined, ET §13-101.
Medical procedures for disabled persons, ET
      §§13-708, 13-711 to 13-713.
   Surrogate decision making under health care
      decision act, HG §5-605.
Mental facility.
   Defined, ET §13-101.
Mental health facilities.
   Guardian of the person of a disabled person.
      Emergency protective services, ET §13-709.
Mental hygiene law.
   Voluntary admissions.
      Application by guardian, HG §10-610.
Mentally ill.
   Disabled persons. See within this heading,
      "Disabled persons."

GUARDIAN AND WARD —Cont'd
Minors.
   Accounting by guardian, ET §13-703.
   Bond of guardian, ET §13-703.
   Compensation of guardian, ET §13-703.
   Court appointment of guardian, ET §13-702.
   Defined, ET §13-101.
   Exemption of certain guardianship proceedings
      from scope of provisions, FL §5-201.
   Insurance.
      Consent of guardian, ET §13-503.
   Jurisdiction, ET §13-105.
      Equity court jurisdiction, FL §1-201.
   Life insurance and annuities.
      Payment of proceeds to minor without
         appointment of legal guardian, IN §16-110.
   Protection of property. See within this heading,
      "Protection of property."
   Recoveries in tort.
      Appointment of guardian, ET §13-403.
      Payment by check to guardian, ET §13-403.
   Standby guardians, ET §§13-901 to 13-908. See
      within this heading, "Standby guardians."
   Testamentary appointment of guardian, ET
      §13-701.
Motor vehicle insurance.
   Guardian authorized to insure minor's property,
      IN §12-302.
Motor vehicles.
   Drivers' licenses.
      Signing of application by guardian, TR §16-107.
      Suspension of minor's license on request of
         cosigner, TR §16-108.
Negligence.
   Custodian's negligence.
      Not imputed to infant, CJ §10-910.
Nonresidents.
   Court appointment of guardian of the person of a
      disabled person.
      Nonresident not disqualified, ET §13-707.
   Protection of property.
      Nonresident not disqualified for appointment as
         guardian, ET §13-207.
   Powers of foreign fiduciaries, ET §13-222.
Notice.
   Local department guardianships.
      Entry of order for consensual guardianship, FL
         §5-322.
      Filing of guardianship petition, FL §5-315.
         Website for posting notices, 88A §18.
      Hearing on petition for consensual
         guardianship, FL §5-318.
      Non-fulfillment of condition of consent, FL
         §5-327.
      Paternity claim, FL §5-306.
   Private agency guardianships.
      Entry of order, FL §5-3A-20.
      Notice of filing of petition, FL §5-3A-14.
         Website for posting notices, 88A §18.
      Notice of status report, FL §5-3A-23.
      Paternity claim, FL §5-3A-06.
   Protection of property.
      Appointment of guardian, ET §13-201.
   Standby guardians.
      Determination of incapacity or debilitation, ET
         §13-906.
   Sufficient notice, ET §13-104.
   Waiver, ET §1-103; Guardian Rule 10-105.
Order appointing guardian, Guardian Rule
      10-108.

GUARDIAN AND WARD —Cont'd
Orphans' court.
General provisions, ET §13-106.
Jurisdiction, ET §§13-105, 13-106.
Powers.
Generally, ET §13-106.
Parties.
Real party in interest.
Circuit courts, CivProCir Rule 2-201.
Person.
Defined, SG §1-101.
Guardian of the person generally, ET §§13-701 to
13-713; Guardian Rules 10-201 to 10-213.
Petitions.
Combination of petitions, Guardian Rule 10-110.
Judicial appointment.
Following determination of incapacity,
debilitation or parental consent, ET
§13-904.
Person, guardian of.
Appointment, petition for, Guardian Rules
10-201 to 10-203.
Emergency protective services.
Assumption of jurisdiction, Guardian Rule
10-210.
Notice of petition, Guardian Rule 10-211.
Notice of petition, Guardian Rule 10-203.
Property, guardian of.
Appointment, petition for, Guardian Rule
10-301.
Standby guardians.
Additional methods for filing for appointment,
ET §13-905.
Judicial appointment, ET §13-903; Guardian
Rule 10-402.
Following parental designation, ET §13-904;
Guardian Rule 10-403.
Termination of parental rights cases, Juv Rule
11-501.
Power of attorney.
Appointment of guardian for principal.
Power of guardian, ET §13-601.
Powers.
Guardian of the person of a disabled person, ET
§13-708.
Inter vivos powers.
Exercise by guardian, ET §15-102.
Protection of property. See within this heading,
"Protection of property."
Priorities.
Court appointment of guardian of the person of a
disabled person.
Persons entitled to appointment, ET §13-707.
Private agency guardianships.
Appeal, right to, FL §5-3A-10.
Applicability of subtitle, FL §5-3A-02.
Appointment of attorney for parent and/or child,
FL §5-3A-07.
Consent.
Failed conditional consent, FL §5-3A-24.
Revocation, FL §5-3A-19.
When required, FL §5-3A-18.
Written consents, contents, FL §5-3A-19.
Contents of petition, FL §5-3A-13.
Costs and fees, FL §5-3A-09.
Definitions, FL §5-3A-01.
Foreign orders, FL §5-3A-05.
Investigatory powers of court, FL §5-3A-16.
Legislative findings and purpose, FL §5-3A-03.
Notice of filing of petition, FL §5-3A-14.
Website for posting notices, 88A §18.

GUARDIAN AND WARD —Cont'd
Private agency guardianships —Cont'd
Order of guardianship.
Authority to enter, FL §5-3A-20.
Contents, FL §5-3A-21.
Effect of order, FL §5-3A-22.
Paternity determination, FL §5-3A-06.
Post-adoption contact, agreements, FL §5-3A-08.
Prohibition on payment or compensation for
services, FL §5-3A-45.
Relation to other provisions, FL §5-3A-04.
Reports and reviews, FL §5-3A-23.
Show cause orders, FL §5-3A-15.
Termination, FL §5-3A-25.
Time limit for ruling and entry of order, FL
§5-3A-17.
Property.
Defined, ET §13-101.
Protection of property.
Accounts and accounting, ET §13-209.
Adjudication.
No bearing on issue of capacity, ET §13-205.
Administration.
Guardian in administration.
Degree of care and skill, ET §13-212.
Powers.
Generally, ET §13-213.
Agent.
Statutory agent of minor or disabled person, ET
§13-206.
Application of property, ET §13-203.
Appointment of counsel, ET §13-211.
Appointment of guardian.
Certain officials and employees disqualified, ET
§13-207.
Disabled persons, ET §13-201.
General provisions, ET §13-206.
Minors, ET §13-201.
Nonresidents.
Not disqualified, ET §13-207.
Notice, ET §13-201.
Persons entitled to appointment, ET §13-207.
Petition, ET §13-201.
Preservation and application of property.
Power of court, ET §13-203.
Selection by court, ET §13-207.
Successor, ET §13-220.
Termination, ET §13-220.
Waiver and substitution, ET §13-207.
Attorney at law.
Appointment of counsel, ET §13-211.
Authorization of specific transaction without
appointment of guardian, ET §13-204.
Bonds, surety, ET §13-208.
Qualification of guardian, ET §13-206.
Capacity.
Adjudication to have no bearing on issue of
capacity, ET §13-205.
Death or disability of guardian, ET §13-220.
Distribution.
Guardian in distribution, ET §13-214.
Duties.
Fiduciary duty.
Breach, ET §13-216.
Guardian in distribution, ET §13-214.
Foreign fiduciaries.
Powers, ET §13-222.
Inventory, ET §13-209.
Jurisdiction.
Transfer of property to other jurisdiction, ET
§13-222.

GUARDIAN AND WARD —Cont'd
Protection of property —Cont'd
  Letters.
    Recording, ET §13-217.
  Liability.
    Breach of fiduciary duty, ET §13-216.
  Nonresidents.
    Not disqualified for appointment as guardian,
      ET §13-207.
    Powers of foreign fiduciaries, ET §13-222.
  Notice.
    Appointment of guardian, ET §13-201.
  Orders of court.
    Issuance of order, ET §13-210.
    Petition for orders granting relief, ET §13-210.
    Recording, ET §13-217.
  Person dealing with guardian.
    Protection, ET §13-219.
  Petition.
    Orders granting relief, ET §13-210.
    Terminate guardianship, ET §13-221.
  Powers.
    Fiduciaries, ET §15-102.
    Foreign fiduciaries, ET §13-222.
    Guardian in administration, ET §13-212.
      General provisions, ET §13-213.
    Guardian in distribution, ET §13-214.
    Limitation on powers imposed by will or court,
      ET §13-215.
  Preservation of property, ET §13-203.
  Priority.
    Persons entitled to appointment as guardian,
      ET §13-207.
  Procedure.
    Protective proceedings, ET §13-211.
  Purchasers.
    Rights of purchasers, ET §13-216.
  Qualification of guardian, ET §13-206.
  Recordation.
    Letters and orders, ET §13-217.
  Removal of guardian, ET §13-220.
  Resignation of guardian, ET §13-220.
  Selection of guardian by court, ET §13-207.
  Successor.
    Appointment, ET §13-220.
  Termination, ET §13-220.
    Petition to terminate, ET §13-221.
  Title.
    General provisions, ET §13-206.
  Venue, ET §13-202.
  Without appointment of guardian.
    Authorization of specific transaction, ET
      §13-204.
Protective proceeding.
  Defined, ET §13-101.
  General provisions, ET §§13-201 to 13-222.
Prudent man rule.
  Degree of care and skill of guardian, ET §13-212.
Purchasers.
  Rights of purchasers dealing with guardian, ET
    §§13-216, 13-219.
Purposes of title, ET §13-102.
Recordation.
  Protection of property.
    Letters and orders, ET §13-217.
Registers of wills.
  Appointment of guardian.
    Entering fees, ET §2-206.
  Powers and duties.
    Generally, ET §13-107.

GUARDIAN AND WARD —Cont'd
Removal.
  Person, guardian of, Guardian Rule 10-208.
  Protection of property, ET §13-220.
Resignation.
  Person, guardian of, Guardian Rule 10-207.
  Protection of property, ET §13-220.
Service of process.
  Local department guardianships.
    Consents, requirements, FL §5-321.
    Show cause order, FL §5-316.
  Person, guardian of.
    Notice, Guardian Rules 10-203, 10-204.
  Private agency guardianships.
    Show cause order, FL §5-3A-15.
  Property, guardian of.
    Petition for appointment, Guardian Rule
      10-302.
Show cause orders, Guardian Rule 10-104.
  Local department guardianships, FL §5-316.
  Private agency guardianships, FL §5-3A-15.
Standby guardians, ET §§13-904 to 13-908;
  Guardian Rules 10-401 to 10-409.
  Accounting, Guardian Rule 10-406.
  Applicability of title, ET §13-902.
  Appointment.
    Additional methods, ET §13-905.
    Judicial appointment, ET §13-903.
      Following determination of incapacity,
        debilitation or parental consent, ET
        §13-904.
    Parental designation, ET §13-904.
    Renunciation, ET §13-903.
  Bonds, ET §13-908; Guardian Rule 10-409.
  Commencement of authority, ET §§13-903, 13-904.
  Debilitation.
    Defined, ET §13-901.
    Determination of, ET §13-906.
  Decree of court, ET §13-903.
  Definitions, ET §13-901; Guardian Rule 10-401.
  Determination of incapacity or debilitation, ET
    §13-906.
  Findings of court.
    Parental designation, ET §13-904.
  Form.
    Written parental designation, ET §13-904.
  Hearing, Guardian Rule 10-404.
  Incapacity.
    Determination of, ET §13-906.
  Judicial appointment, ET §13-903.
    Following determination of incapacity,
      debilitation or parental consent, ET
      §13-904.
  Limitation on authority, ET §13-907.
  Notice.
    Determination of incapacity or debilitation, ET
      §13-906.
  Order, Guardian Rule 10-405.
  Parental designation, ET §13-904.
  Parental rights, ET §13-907.
  Petition, Guardian Rules 10-402, 10-403.
    Additional methods for filing for appointment,
      ET §13-905.
    Judicial appointment, ET §13-903.
      Following determination of incapacity,
        debilitation or parental consent, ET
        §13-904.
  Renunciation of appointment, ET §§13-903,
    13-904.
  Revocation.
    By petitioner, ET §13-903.

GUARDIAN AND WARD —Cont'd
Standby guardians —Cont'd
Revocation by parent, ET §13-904.
Revocation, renunciation, and resignation,
Guardian Rule 10-408.
Sanctions, Guardian Rule 10-407.
Written designation.
Parental designation, ET §13-904.
Substitute or successor guardians.
Person, guardian of, Guardian Rule 10-207.
Taxation.
Liability, TP §1-203.
Payment.
Retaining sums for payment, TP §1-203.
Residence.
Place of residence, TP §1-202.
Termination.
Person, guardian of, Guardian Rule 10-209.
Protection of property. See within this heading,
"Protection of property."
Title.
Construction, ET §13-102.
Transfer of actions, Guardian Rule 10-109.
Transfers to minors act, ET §§13-301 to 13-324.
See MINORS.
Trust companies.
Defined, ET §13-101.
Venue.
Action for guardianship, CJ §6-203.
Court appointment of guardian of the person of a
minor, ET §13-702.
Disabled persons.
Court appointment of guardian, ET §13-705.
Protection of property, ET §13-202.
Verification.
Sufficient verification, ET §13-103.
Veterans' guardianship act.
General provisions, ET §§13-801 to 13-806.
See VETERANS.
Waiver of notice, Guardian Rule 10-105.
Wills.
Guardian of the person.
Testamentary appointment of guardian of a
minor, ET §13-701.

GUARDIAN OF THE PERSON, ET §§13-701 to
13-713; Guardian Rules 10-201 to 10-213.
Guardian and ward generally.
See GUARDIAN AND WARD.

GUARDS.
Security guards, BOP §§19-101 to 19-701.
See SECURITY GUARDS.

GUBERNATORIAL TRANSITION ACT, SG
§§3-201 to 3-209.
See GOVERNOR.

GUIDE ANIMALS.
Blind pedestrians, TR §21-511.
Damages.
Liability of blind or visually handicapped person
for damages, 30 §33.
**Right of blind person to be accompanied by
guide dog,** 30 §33.
**Rights of trainer to be accompanied by service
dog,** 30 §33.

GUIDED TOURS OF WINERIES.
**Number of ounces of wine served at no charge
to persons on tour,** 2B §§2-204, 2-205.

GUIDES.
Fishing guides.
Chesapeake Bay charter boat permit, NR
§4-210.2.

GUIDES —Cont'd
Fishing guides —Cont'd
Licensing requirement, NR §4-210.
Freshwater fishing guides, NR §4-210.1.
Tidal fish license, NR §4-701.
Hunting guides.
Waterfowl hunting guide license, NR §10-309.

GUILTY PLEAS.
Criminal rules.
See CRIMINAL RULES.
**Disclosure of notice of additional or
mandatory penalties,** Crim Rule 4-245.
Insanity defense.
Defense of not criminally responsible by reason of
insanity.
Plea of guilty entered with plea of not
criminally responsible.
Trial of issue of criminal responsibility, Crim
Rule 4-314.
Method of pleading, Crim Rule 4-242.
Offer to plead guilty, Evid Rule 5-410.
Permitted pleas, Crim Rule 4-242.
Pleas to other offenses, Crim Rule 4-244.
Plea to a degree, Crim Rule 4-242.
Requirements for court to accept, Crim Rule
4-242.
Subsequent offenders.
Disclosure of notice of additional or mandatory
penalties, Crim Rule 4-245.
Withdrawn plea of guilty, Evid Rule 5-410.

GUNPOWDER.
Explosives generally, PS §§11-101 to 11-118.
See EXPLOSIONS AND EXPLOSIVES.

GUNPOWDER VALLEY CONSERVANCY, INC.
Property taxes.
Credit for certain property owned by conservancy,
TP §9-305.

GUNPOWDER YOUTH CAMPS.
Taxation.
Exemptions, TP §7-212.

GUNS.
Firearms generally.
See FIREARMS.
Weapons generally.
See WEAPONS.

GUNSHOT INJURY REPORT.
Physicians, pharmacists, dentists or nurses,
HG §20-703.

GUN SHOWS.
**Applications for purchases, rents or transfers
of firearms,** PS §5-130.

GYMS.
Health club services, CL §§14-12B-01 to
14-12B-08.
See HEALTH CLUB SERVICES.
Steroids and human growth hormone.
Warning of consequences of illegal use, posting,
CR §5-710.

GYNECOLOGISTS.
Health insurance coverage, IN §15-816.
Primary care classification, HG §19-706.

GYPSUM.
Agricultural lime.
General provisions, AG §§6-301 to 6-311.
See LIME.

H

HABEAS CORPUS.
Absence of judge.
Return to another court or judge, SpecPro Rule 15-307.
Alternative remedies.
Post conviction procedure, SpecPro Rule 15-304.
Appeals.
Bail.
Application for leave to appeal, CJ §3-707.
Discharge on ground on unconstitutionality.
Review by court of special appeals, SpecPro Rule 15-312.
Applicability of rules, SpecPro Rule 15-301.
Application.
Who may apply, CJ §3-702.
Appropriate remedy, SpecPro Rule 15-310.
Bail and recognizance.
Application for leave to appeal, CJ §3-707.
General provisions, CJ §3-704.
Issuance of writ, SpecPro Rule 15-306.
Procedure on petition, SpecPro Rule 15-303.
Commitment.
Corrections of errors on face, SpecPro Rule 15-310.
Competency to stand trial determination.
Legality of confinement of defendant awaiting examination, CP §3-105.
Constitutional law.
Discharge for unconstitutionality of law.
Court of special appeals review, CJ §3-706; SpecPro Rule 15-312.
Habeas corpus not to be suspended, US Const Art I §9.
Court of special appeals.
Discharge on ground of unconstitutionality, SpecPro Rule 15-312.
Review by court of special appeals, CJ §3-706.
Developmental disabilities.
State residential centers.
Individuals admitted, HG §7-506.
Discharge, CJ §3-704.
Imprisoned for same offense prohibited, CJ §3-705.
Unconstitutionality of law, CJ §3-706.
District Court judges.
Writ of habeas corpus ad testificandum or ad prosequendum.
Authority of judges to issue, CJ §1-609.
Drug or alcohol abuse.
Commitment of criminal defendants for treatment.
Challenge to legality, HG §8-507.
Evaluation of criminal defendants.
Detention for examination.
Challenge to legality, HG §8-505.
Errors on face of commitment.
Correction, SpecPro Rule 15-310.
Evasion of writ, SpecPro Rule 15-306.
Extradition.
Application for writ, CP §9-110.
General assembly.
Suspension of writ.
Legislature not to suspend writ, MD Const Art III §55.
Granting.
Authority, CJ §3-701.
Procedure upon receiving petition, CJ §3-702.
Hearings, CJ §3-704; SpecPro Rule 15-309.

HABEAS CORPUS —Cont'd
Imprisonment for same offense prohibited, CJ §3-705.
Incompetency to stand trial determination.
Legality of confinement of defendant awaiting examination, CP §3-105.
Inquiry into the character of the detention, CJ §3-704.
Issuance of writ, SpecPro Rule 15-306.
Judges.
Absence of judge, SpecPro Rule 15-307.
Authority to grant, CJ §3-701.
Discharge for unconstitutionality of law.
Opinion of court of special appeals, CJ §3-706; SpecPro Rule 15-312.
Discretion of judge when prior writ has been refused, CJ §3-703.
Memorandum by judge, SpecPro Rule 15-311.
Jurisdiction, CJ §3-701.
Mental hygiene law.
Right of individuals, HG §10-804.
Mental retardation.
Rights on admission, HG §7-704.
Notice.
Response to show cause order, SpecPro Rule 15-303.
State's attorney to be notified, SpecPro Rule 15-301.
Orders.
Evasion of writ, SpecPro Rule 15-306.
Petitions, CJ §3-702; SpecPro Rule 15-302.
Procedure on petition, SpecPro Rule 15-303.
Post conviction procedure.
Alternative remedy to writ, SpecPro Rule 15-304.
General provisions.
See POST CONVICTION PROCEDURE.
Referral of petition, SpecPro Rule 15-303.
Refusal of prior writ.
Discretion of judge, CJ §3-703.
Remanded to custody, CJ §3-704.
Returns.
Absence of judge.
Return to another court or judge, SpecPro Rule 15-307.
Before whom returnable, SpecPro Rule 15-305.
Service of process.
Procedure following issuance of writ, SpecPro Rule 15-306.
Show cause order, SpecPro Rule 15-303.
Sheriffs.
Evasion of writ.
Immediate execution by sheriff, SpecPro Rule 15-306.
Failure to bring person into court, CJ §2-305.
Show cause order, SpecPro Rule 15-303.
State's attorney.
Notice to state's attorney, SpecPro Rule 15-308.
Suspension.
Legislature not to suspend writ, MD Const Art III §55.
To whom writ directed, SpecPro Rule 15-305.

HABIT EVIDENCE, Evid Rule 5-406.

HABITUAL OFFENDERS.
Alcohol offenses.
Drivers' licenses.
Persons not to be licensed, TR §16-103.1.
Firearms.
Habitual drunkards or users.
Restrictions on possession, PS §5-133.

HABITUAL OFFENDERS —Cont'd
Firearms —Cont'd
Habitual drunkards or users —Cont'd
Restrictions on sale, rental or transfer, PS §5-134.
Firearms dealers' licenses.
Habitual drunkards or users.
Suspension or revocation, PS §5-114.
Generally, Crim Rule 4-245.
Railroad safety and health.
Violations causing death, LE §5.5-122.

HACKERS.
Unauthorized computer access, CJ §5-106.

HACKING.
Unauthorized access to computers, CR §7-302.

HAGERSTOWN.
Taxicabs.
Permit to operate taxicab business in or from point in city generally, PUC §§10-202 to 10-207.
See TAXICABS.

HAGUE CONVENTION.
Child custody orders made under convention.
Uniform child custody jurisdiction and enforcement act.
Enforcement of orders, FL §9.5-302.

HAIR PROSTHESIS.
Health insurance benefits, IN §15-836.

HAIR REMOVAL.
Electrologists, HO §§8-6B-01 to 8-6B-29.
See ELECTROLOGISTS.

HALFWAY HOUSES.
Fires and fire protection.
Automatic fire extinguishing systems.
Specified buildings, PS §9-503.

HALL OF RECORDS.
Administration of courts.
Disposition of records, CJA Rule 16-818.
Archives.
State archives, SG §§9-1001 to 9-1015.
See ARCHIVES.
Commission.
Compensation of members, SG §9-1004.
Defined, RP §13-101; SG §9-1001.
Established, SG §9-1002.
Function of commission, SG §9-1004.
Meetings, SG §9-1004.
Membership, SG §9-1003.
Staff services, SG §9-1004.
Definitions, SG §9-1001.
General responsibilities for records, SG §9-1009.
Preservation and use of records, SG §9-1009.

HALLUCINOGENS.
Controlled dangerous substances.
Generally, CR §§5-101 to 5-1101.
See CONTROLLED DANGEROUS SUBSTANCES.
Schedule I, CR §5-402.

HANDBILLS.
Advertising.
See ADVERTISING.

HAND-FIRED HEATING STOVES.
Kerosene heaters.
Venting, CL §14-1310.
Sale, distribution or installation, CL §14-1309.

HANDGUN FORFEITURES, CP §§13-201 to 13-206.
Disposition of forfeited property, CP §13-206.
Post-seizure procedures, CP §13-203.
Property subject of forfeiture, CP §13-201.
Seized handgun criminal cases, CP §13-205.
Determining owner's knowledge, CP §13-204.
Disposition of forfeited property, CP §13-206.
Seizure of property, CP §13-202.

HANDGUN PERMITS, PS §§5-301 to 5-314.
Appeals.
Informal review of secretary's actions, PS §5-311.
Review by board, PS §5-312.
Applications, PS §5-304.
Board.
Appeals.
Review by board, PS §5-312.
Compensation, PS §5-302.
Defined, PS §5-301.
Established, PS §5-302.
Members, PS §5-302.
Carrying handgun.
Possession required, PS §5-308.
Criminal history records checks, PS §5-305.
Criminal law and procedure.
Carrying, wearing or transporting handgun while under the influence, PS §5-314.
Disqualification, PS §5-306.
Failure to return revoked permit, PS §5-313.
Defined terms, PS §5-301.
Drug or alcohol abuse.
Carrying, wearing or transporting handgun while under the influence, PS §5-314.
Disqualification, PS §5-306.
Fees.
Applications, PS §5-304.
Felons.
Disqualification, PS §5-306.
Fines.
Carrying, wearing or transporting handgun while under the influence, PS §5-314.
Failure to return revoked permit, PS §5-313.
Investigations.
Qualifications, PS §5-306.
Limitations, PS §5-307.
Minors.
Prohibited, PS §5-306.
Possession required, PS §5-308.
Qualifications, PS §5-306.
Renewal, PS §5-309.
Required, PS §5-303.
Return of permit.
Revocations, PS §5-310.
Failure to return revoked permit, PS §5-313.
Revocations, PS §5-310.
Failure to return revoked permit, PS §5-313.
Scope of permit, PS §5-307.
Secretary.
Appeals.
Informal review of secretary's actions, PS §5-311.
Defined, PS §5-301.
Term, PS §5-309.
When required, PS §5-303.

HANDGUN ROSTER, PS §§5-401 to 5-406.
Appeals.
Placement on roster, PS §5-405.
Applicability of subtitle, PS §5-402.
Board.
Composition, PS §5-404.

HANDGUN ROSTER —Cont'd
Board —Cont'd
Defined, PS §5-401.
Duties, PS §5-405.
Established, PS §5-404.
Meetings, PS §5-404.
Procedures, PS §5-405.
Compilation.
Duties of board, PS §5-405.
Criteria for placement on roster, PS §5-405.
Defined terms, PS §5-401.
Injunctions.
Manufacture or sale of guns not on roster, PS §5-406.
Manufacture or sale.
Prohibitions, PS §5-406.
Petition to place on roster, PS §5-405.
Placement process, PS §5-405.
Publication.
Duties of board, PS §5-405.
Rules and regulations, PS §5-403.
Secretary.
Defined, PS §5-401.
Strict liability, PS §5-402.

HANDGUNS, CR §§4-201 to 4-209.
Assault pistols, CR §§4-301 to 4-306.
Defined, types and brands enumerated, CR §4-301.
Persons excepted from provisions, CR §4-302.
Punishment, CR §4-306.
Scope of subtitle, CR §4-302.
Seizure and disposal as contraband, CR §4-304.
Transporting into state, selling or purchasing, prohibition, CR §4-303.
Use in commission of crime.
Punishment, CR §4-306.
Child's access to firearm, CR §4-104.
Crime laboratories.
Handgun identification requirements, PS §5-131.
Criminal law and procedure.
Manufacture or sale of guns not on roster, PS §5-406.
Definitions, CR §4-201.
Disarming law enforcement officer, CR §4-103.
Discharge.
Local regulation, CR §4-209.
External safety locks, PS §5-132.
Firearms generally, PS §§5-101 to 5-143.
See FIREARMS.
Forfeitures, CP §§13-201 to 13-206.
Identification requirements, PS §5-131.
Injunctions.
Manufacture or sale of guns not on roster, PS §5-406.
Integrated mechanical safety device, PS §5-132.
Law enforcement officers and personnel.
Disposal of handguns owned by law enforcement agencies.
State police, PS §2-415.
Firearms training courses.
Certification, PS §3-208.
Law enforcement equipment fund, PS §§4-301 to 4-304.
State police.
Disposition upon retirement, PS §2-415.
Legislative findings, CR §4-202.
Limited search, seizure and arrest, CR §4-206.
Mandatory sentence for crime of violence.
Second, third or fourth conviction, CR §14-101.

HANDGUNS —Cont'd
Manufacture and sale.
Handgun roster, PS §§5-401 to 5-406.
Prohibitions, PS §5-406.
Permits, PS §§5-301 to 5-314.
Personalized handguns.
Safety devices, PS §5-132.
Probation on conviction.
Limitation, CR §4-205.
Public demonstration.
Possession at, CR §4-208.
Reduction of mandatory minimum sentence by court.
Limitation, CR §4-205.
Reports.
Handgun safety devices, PS §5-132.
Roster, PS §§5-401 to 5-406.
Safety devices, PS §5-132.
Sales.
Handgun roster, PS §§5-401 to 5-406.
School property.
Carrying or possessing on, CR §4-102.
State police.
Disposition upon retirement, PS §2-415.
State preemption of regulation, CR §4-209.
Suspension of mandatory minimum sentence by court.
Limitation, CR §4-205.
Trigger locks.
Safety devices, PS §5-132.
Use in commission of crime, CR §4-204.
Weapons generally.
See WEAPONS.
Wearing, carrying or transporting.
Prohibition, penalty, sentencing, CR §4-203.

HANDICAPPED PERSONS.
Absentee voting.
Assistance in marking ballot, EL §9-308.
Generally, EL §§9-301 to 9-312.
See ELECTIONS.
Abuse or neglect of vulnerable adult, CR §§3-604 to 3-606.
Exploitation of vulnerable adult, CR §8-801.
Accessibility.
Building codes.
Accessibility code, PS §12-202.
Facilities for the handicapped.
Citation of act.
Short title, SF §2-511.
Curb cuts.
Required, SF §2-505.
Definitions, SF §2-501.
Department of general services.
Enforcement of provisions, SF §2-510.
Drinking fountains.
Symbols required on certain facilities, SF §2-508.
Enforcement of provisions, SF §2-510.
Federal aid.
Ramps or curb cuts.
Certification to determine eligibility for federal assistance, SF §2-505.
Floors or levels.
Braille or raised print numbers required, SF §2-506.
Legislative findings, SF §2-502.
Plans and specifications for buildings.
Provision for facilities, SF §2-504.
Political subdivisions.
Enforcement by governing bodies, SF §2-510.

HANDICAPPED PERSONS —Cont'd
Accessibility —Cont'd
Facilities for the handicapped —Cont'd
Public buildings.
Defined, SF §2-501.
Floors or levels.
Braille or raised print numbers required,
SF §2-506.
Legislative findings, SF §2-502.
Plans and specifications to provide for
facilities, SF §2-504.
Scope of provisions, SF §2-503.
Ramps.
Required, SF §2-505.
Scope of provisions, SF §2-503.
Short title of act, SF §2-511.
Standards, SF §2-509.
Symbols required on certain facilities, SF
§2-508.
Telephones.
Teletypewriters.
Requirements, SF §2-507.
Teletypewriters, SF §2-507.
Title of act.
Short title, SF §2-511.
Toilets.
Symbols required on certain facilities, SF
§2-508.
Food and food establishments.
Unobstructed entrances, TR §21-1007.
Specialized customer premises equipment, SF
§§3-901 to 3-906.
Access to audio news and information service,
SF §3-906.
Board.
Defined, SF §3-901.
Duties, SF §3-903.
Contracts for distribution of information, SF
§3-906.
Definitions, SF §3-901.
Department of general services.
Definition of "department," SF §3-901.
Financial assistance, SF §3-904.
Governor's office.
Duties, SF §3-903.
Program.
Administration, SF §3-902.
Defined, SF §3-901.
Established, SF §3-902.
Regulations, SF §3-905.
**Advisory council for services to individuals
with disabilities.** See within this heading,
"Services to individuals with disabilities."
Aid to permanently and totally disabled.
Application, 88A §62.
Misuse of public assistance lists and records, 88A
§6.
Records, 88A §6.
Americans with disabilities act.
Attorneys at law.
Bar examinations, accommodations,
BarAdmBoard Rule 3.
Attendant care program.
Community attendant services and supports
program, 41 §§6-7A-01 to 6-7A-06.
General provisions, 41 §§18-601 to 18-604.
See ATTENDANT CARE PROGRAM.
Attorneys at law.
Admission to the bar.
Examinations, accommodations, BarAdmBoard
Rule 3.

HANDICAPPED PERSONS —Cont'd
Blind persons.
See BLIND PERSONS.
Building codes.
Accessibility code, PS §12-202.
Specialized customer premises equipment, SF
§§3-901 to 3-906.
Children.
Schools.
Handicapped children.
See SCHOOLS.
Services to handicapped children.
Medical assistance.
Program for crippled children, HG §15-125.
Sign language.
Academic credit, ED §4-111.
Commission on disabilities.
Chairman, SG §9-1110.
Creation, SG §9-1109.
Duties, SG §9-1112.
Members, SG §9-1110.
Travel expense reimbursement, SG §9-1111.
Staff, SG §9-1111.
Subcommittees, SG §9-1112.
**Community attendant services and supports
program,** 41 §§6-7A-01 to 6-7A-06.
Community rehabilitation programs, ED
§§21-401 to 21-404.
Court appearances.
Notice of need for accommodation, Form 1-332;
Rule 1-332.
Crippled children.
Medical assistance.
Program for crippled children, HG §15-125.
Deaf and hearing impaired.
See DEAF AND HEARING IMPAIRED.
Definitions.
Attendant care program, 41 §18-601.
Community rehabilitation programs, ED §21-401.
Facilities for the handicapped, SF §2-501.
Rehabilitation services for disabled individuals,
HG §20-108.
Telecommunications for disabled individuals, SF
§§3-801, 3-901.
Department of disabilities.
Assistive technology guaranteed loan program.
Oversight and administrative duties, SG
§9-1118.
Attorney general.
Duties, SG §9-1105.
Constituent services and ombudsmen program.
Oversight and administrative duties, SG
§9-1118.
Definition of department, SG §9-1101.
Duties, SG §9-1106.
Program oversight, SG §9-1118.
Established, SG §9-1102.
Functions, SG §9-1106.
Information to be provided by units of state
government, SG §9-1107.
Office of personal assistance services.
Oversight and administrative duties, SG
§9-1118.
Personal assistance services advisory
committee, SG §9-1119.
Personal assistance services advisory committee,
SG §9-1119.
Secretary, SG §9-1102.
Deputy secretary, SG §9-1103.
Duties, SG §9-1104.
State disabilities plan, SG §9-1117.

HANDICAPPED PERSONS —Cont'd
Department of disabilities —Cont'd
Staff, SG §9-1103.
Developmentally disabled persons.
See DEVELOPMENTAL DISABILITIES.
Discrimination.
Handicapped teachers, ED §6-104.
Insurance, IN §§27-208, 27-210, 27-212.
Drivers' licenses.
Reports of certain disorders by physicians, etc.,
TR §16-119.
What persons shall not be licensed, TR §16-103.1.
Elections.
Absentee voting.
Assistance in marking ballot, EL §9-308.
Generally, EL §§9-301 to 9-312.
See ELECTIONS.
Assistance in marking ballot.
Absentee voting, EL §9-308.
Choosing individual to assist, EL §10-310.
Provisional ballot voting, EL §9-406.
Polling place inaccessible.
Assignment of alternative, issuance of absentee
ballot, EL §10-102.
Provisional ballot voting.
Assistance in marking ballot, EL §9-406.
Employed persons with disabilities program.
Medicaid, HG §15-138.
Exploitation of vulnerable adult, CR §8-801.
Facilities for the handicapped.
Building codes.
Accessibility code, PS §12-202.
Citation of act.
Short title, SF §2-511.
Curb cuts.
Required, SF §2-505.
Definitions, SF §2-501.
Department of general services.
Enforcement of provisions, SF §2-510.
Drinking fountains.
Symbols required on certain facilities, SF
§2-508.
Enforcement of provisions, SF §2-510.
Federal aid.
Ramps or curb cuts.
Certification to determine eligibility for
federal assistance, SF §2-505.
Floors or levels.
Braille or raised print numbers required, SF
§2-506.
Legislative findings, SF §2-502.
Plans and specifications for buildings.
Provision for facilities, SF §2-504.
Political subdivisions.
Enforcement by governing bodies, SF §2-510.
Public buildings.
Defined, SF §2-501.
Floors or levels.
Braille or raised print numbers required, SF
§2-506.
Legislative findings, SF §2-502.
Plans and specifications to provide for facilities,
SF §2-504.
Scope of provisions, SF §2-503.
Ramps.
Required, SF §2-505.
Scope of provisions, SF §2-503.
Short title of act, SF §2-511.
Specialized customer premises equipment, SF
§§3-901 to 3-906.
Standards, SF §2-509.

HANDICAPPED PERSONS —Cont'd
Facilities for the handicapped —Cont'd
Symbols required on certain facilities, SF §2-508.
Telephones.
Teletypewriters.
Requirements, SF §2-507.
Teletypewriters, SF §2-507.
Title of act.
Short title, SF §2-511.
Toilets.
Symbols required on certain facilities, SF
§2-508.
Family caregiver assistance program.
Grants to caregivers.
Assistance in caring for individual with
long-term care needs, 50B §45.
Federal aid.
Facilities for the handicapped.
Ramps or curb cuts.
Certification to determine eligibility for
federal assistance, SF §2-505.
Financial institution franchise tax.
Credits, TG §8-216.
Fishing licenses.
Disability license exemption.
One-day license exemption.
Nonprofit organizations taking individuals
with disabilities fishing, NR §4-217.
Food and food establishments.
Unobstructed entrances, TR §21-1007.
General services department.
Facilities for the handicapped.
Enforcement of provisions, SF §2-510.
Governor.
Office for services to individuals with disabilities.
See within this heading, "Services to
individuals with disabilities."
Income tax.
Credits for employees with disabilities, TG
§10-704.7.
State adjustments, TG §10-205.
Insurance.
Discrimination, IN §§27-208, 27-210, 27-212.
Motor vehicle insurance.
Cancellation, nonrenewal or premium increase
due to handicap, IN §27-902.
Interagency disabilities board.
Chairman.
Duties, SG §9-1115.
Duties, SG §9-1115.
Established, SG §9-1113.
Members, SG §9-1114.
Purpose, SG §9-1113.
Staff, SG §9-1114.
Maryland Transit Administration.
Free transportation, TR §7-505.
Medicaid.
Employed persons with disabilities program, HG
§15-138.
Minimum wage.
Authority to waive minimum wage, LE §3-414.
Required wages, LE §3-414.
Motor fuel inspection.
Retail service station dealers.
Refueling service for disabled drivers, BR
§10-320.
Motor vehicle emissions inspection.
Exemptions from mandatory inspection, TR
§23-206.2.
Motor vehicle insurance.
Primary coverage.
Rental of specially equipped vehicles, IN
§19-516.

HANDICAPPED PERSONS —Cont'd
Motor vehicle registration.
Special plates, TR §13-616.
Office for services to individuals with disabilities. See within this heading, "Services to individuals with disabilities."
Office of minority affairs.
General provisions, SG §§9-301 to 9-306.
See OFFICE OF MINORITY AFFAIRS.
Office of personal assistance services.
Department, oversight and administrative duties, SG §9-1118.
Personal assistance services advisory committee, SG §9-1119.
Paratransit service grants, TR §2-103.5.
Parking.
Fines posted on signs, TR §21-1004.
Permits, TR §13-616.1.
Temporary permits, TR §13-616.2.
Privileges, TR §13-616.
Prohibition against parking in space for use of handicapped persons, TR §21-1003.
Fraud and deceit relating to permits, TR §21-1005.
Parking lots, TR §21-1006.
Persons confined to wheelchair, TR §21-1005.
Parks and recreation.
Facilities for the handicapped.
General provisions, SF §§2-501 to 2-511. See within this heading, "Facilities for the handicapped."
Personal assistance services advisory committee, SG §9-1119.
Poisons.
Packaging for handicapped individuals, HG §22-310.
Property taxes.
Deferred payments, TP §10-204.
Property tax credits.
Homeowners, TP §9-101.
Rental dwellings providing reduced rents for disabled tenants, TP §9-219.
Renters, TP §9-102.
Public buildings and grounds.
Facilities for the handicapped.
General provisions, SF §§2-501 to 2-511. See within this heading, "Facilities for the handicapped."
Public service company franchise tax.
Employees with disabilities, TG §8-413.
Rape in second degree.
Victim physically helpless, CR §3-304.
Rehabilitation services.
General provisions, ED §§21-301 to 21-309.
See REHABILITATION SERVICES.
School buses.
Transportation of handicapped children.
Drivers' regulations, TR §21-1118.
Schools.
Blind persons.
Maryland school for the blind.
See SCHOOLS.
Deaf and hearing impaired.
See SCHOOLS.
Facilities for the handicapped.
General provisions, SF §§2-501 to 2-511. See within this heading, "Facilities for the handicapped."
Handicapped children.
General provisions.
See SCHOOLS.

HANDICAPPED PERSONS —Cont'd
Services to individuals with disabilities.
Children.
Services to handicapped children. See within this heading, "Children."
Commission on disabilities, SG §§9-1109 to 9-1112.
Definitions, SG §9-1101.
Department of disabilities. See within this heading, "Department of disabilities."
Interagency disabilities board, SG §§9-1113 to 9-1115.
Office.
Program evaluation act, SG §8-403.
State disabilities plan, SG §9-1116.
Duties of secretary, SG §9-1117.
Units of state government.
Information to be provided by, SG §9-1107.
Plans, SG §9-1108.
Sexual abuse of vulnerable adult, CR §§3-604, 3-606.
Sexual offense in the second degree.
Victim physically helpless, CR §3-306.
Sexual offense in the third degree.
Victim physically helpless, CR §3-307.
Sign language.
Academic credit, ED §4-111.
Specialized customer premises equipment. See within this heading, "Telecommunications for disabled individuals."
Supermarkets.
Unobstructed entrances, TR §21-1007.
Taxation.
Property taxes.
Deferred payments, TP §10-204.
Homeowners tax credit, TP §9-101.
Rental dwelling tax credits, TP §§9-102, 9-219.
Teachers.
Discrimination against handicapped teachers prohibited, ED §6-104.
Telecommunications for disabled individuals, SF §§3-801 to 3-807.
Board.
Compensation, SF §3-804.
Composition, SF §3-804.
Created, SF §3-802.
Defined, SF §3-801.
Department of general services.
Duties in consultation with board, SF §3-805.
Reports, SF §3-804.
Definitions, SF §3-801.
Specialized customer premises equipment, SF §3-901.
Department of general services.
Duties in consultation with board, SF §3-805.
Dual party telephone message relay program.
Defined, SF §3-801.
Established, SF §3-803.
Rules and regulations.
Adoption, SF §3-806.
Specialized customer premises equipment, SF §3-806.
Specialized customer premises equipment, SF §§3-901 to 3-906.
Access to audio news and information service, SF §3-906.
Board.
Defined, SF §3-901.
Duties, SF §3-903.
Contracts for distribution of information, SF §3-906.

HANDICAPPED PERSONS —Cont'd
Telecommunications for disabled individuals
—Cont'd
Specialized customer premises equipment
—Cont'd
Definitions, SF §3-901.
Department defined, SF §3-901.
Financial assistance, SF §3-904.
Governor's office.
Duties, SF §3-903.
Program.
Administration, SF §3-902.
Defined, SF §3-901.
Established, SF §3-902.
Regulations, SF §3-905.
Universal service trust fund.
Generally, SF §3-807.
Telephone directory assistance calls.
Exemption from charges if disability precludes use
of telephone directory, PUC §8-202.
Teletypewriters, SF §2-507.
Toilets.
Facilities for the handicapped.
Symbols required on certain facilities, SF
§2-508.
Traffic laws.
Special vehicles.
Driving on sidewalk, TR §21-1103.
Transportation department.
Funding of services for, TR §2-103.3.
Paratransit service grants, TR §2-103.5.
Veterans, disabled.
Birds and game.
Complimentary licenses, NR §10-303.
Dwellings.
Tax exemption, TP §7-208.
Fish and fisheries.
Complimentary licenses, NR §4-607.
Military reservists and service-related no-interest
loan program.
Assistance to service-disabled veterans, 83A
§6-901.
Voter registration agencies.
Offices providing services to the disabled, EL
§3-204.
Voting.
Assistance in marking ballot.
Absentee voting, EL §9-308.
Choosing individual to assist, EL §10-310.
Provisional ballot voting, EL §9-406.
Polling place inaccessible to disabled voters.
Alternative assigned, issuance of absentee
ballot, EL §10-102.
Workers' compensation.
Average weekly wage.
Handicapped student, LE §9-602.
Covered employees and employers.
Handicapped students, LE §9-228.

HANDWRITING.
Requirement of authentication or
identification, Evid Rule 5-901.
Writing.
See WRITING.

HARASSMENT, CR §3-803.
Course of conduct defined, CR §3-801.
Hate crime, CR §10-304.
Jurisdiction.
Equity courts.
Injunction to protect party from, FL §1-201.
Misuse of electronic mail, CR §3-805.

HARASSMENT —Cont'd
Misuse of laser pointer, CR §3-806.
Misuse of telephone facilities and equipment,
CR §3-804.
Schools.
Harassment or intimidation.
Reporting incidents against students, ED
§7-424.
Stalking.
See STALKING.
State personnel.
Prohibited, SPP §2-302.
Transportation department employee
grievance rights, TR §2-103.4.
Unlawful picketing and assembly, CR §3-904.

HARBORING.
Escaped inmate, CR §9-403.
Fugitive, CR §9-402.

HARBORS.
Bond issues.
Public debt.
General provisions, 31 §§1 to 12.
See PUBLIC DEBT.
Deepwater ports siting.
Applications, NR §3-605.
Defined, NR §3-602.
Restriction on state applicants, NR §3-603.
Definitions, NR §3-602.
Governor's duties, NR §3-605.
Purpose of act, NR §3-601.
Secretary of natural resources.
Duties, NR §3-604.
Port administration.
General provisions, TR §§6-101 to 6-602.
See PORT ADMINISTRATION.
Waterway improvement fund, NR §§8-707 to
8-709.

HARD CIDER.
Home consumption.
Manufacture without license, 2B §1-201.

HARFORD COUNTY.
Advertising.
Outdoor advertising restrictions, 25 §122D.
Agriculture.
Property tax credits, TP §9-314.
Alcohol awareness programs.
Special provisions, 2B §13-101.
Alcoholic beverages.
Appeals, 2B §16-102.
Beer and light wine licenses.
Class A, off-sale, 2B §5-101.
Class B, on-sale, 2B §5-201.
Class C, on-sale.
Clubs, 2B §5-301.
Special and temporary licenses, 2B §7-101.
Licenses generally. See within this subheading,
"Licenses."
Premises.
Defined, 2B §5-101.
Wine and fermented beverages.
Alcoholic content, 2B §5-101.
Beer tasting license, 2B §8-407.
Beer, wine and liquor licenses.
Caterers in Harford county, 2B §6-704.
Class A, off-sale, 2B §6-101.
Hotels and restaurants, 2B §6-201.
Class B-3 restaurant/hotel license, 2B §6-201.
Class BDR, on-sale, 2B §6-201.

HARFORD COUNTY —Cont'd
Alcoholic beverages —Cont'd
 Beer, wine and liquor licenses —Cont'd
  Class BNR, on-sale.
   Hotels and restaurants, 2B §6-201.
  Class B, on-sale.
   Hotels and restaurants.
    Class B-3 restaurant-hotel license, 2B
     §6-201.
  Class C, on-sale.
   Clubs, 2B §6-301.
   Special and temporary licenses, 2B §7-101.
  Class CWBT, 2B §8-407.
  Class D, on-sale, 2B §6-401.
  Class F.
   Passenger trains, 2B §§8-213, 8-407.
  Class WBT, 2B §8-407.
  Licenses generally. See within this subheading,
   "Licenses."
  Special class C, 2B §7-101.
  Wine festival, 2B §8-309.
 Bonds, surety.
  Liquor control department, 2B §15-201.
  Retailers.
   Cash bond deposit in lieu of bond, 2B
    §14-101.
 Clubs.
  Beer, wine and liquor licenses.
   Class C, on-sale, 2B §6-301.
 Consumption.
  Prohibited acts, 2B §11-304.
 Criminal history records checks.
  License applicants, 2B §10-103.
 Drive-through purchase facilities.
  Licenses.
   Prohibition on issuance or transfer, 2B
    §9-213.
   Transfer prohibited, 2B §10-503.
 Elections.
  Exercise of privileges of licensee on election day,
   2B §11-401.
 Hours and days for sale, 2B §11-513.
  Election days, 2B §11-401.
  New Year's day, 2B §11-402.
 Licenses.
  Applications.
   Exceptions, 2B §10-104.
   Notice on premises, 2B §10-202.
   Publication of decision, 2B §10-202.
   Qualifications of applicant, 2B §10-203.
   Statement as to whether applicant adjudged
    guilty of offense against laws of state or
    United States, 2B §10-103.
  Beer and light wine licenses. See within this
   subheading, "Beer and light wine licenses."
  Beer, wine and liquor licenses. See within this
   subheading, "Beer, wine and liquor
   licenses."
  Books, accounts and records of licensees, 2B
   §12-213.
  Bowling alleys, 2B §9-213.
  Caterers, 2B §§6-704, 9-213.
  Chain stores, supermarkets, discount houses,
   etc., 2B §9-213.
  Churches and schools.
   Sale within certain distances prohibited, 2B
    §9-213.
  Class BDR (deluxe restaurant) licenses (on-sale
   only), 2B §9-213.
  Class GC (golf course) beer, wine and liquor
   license, 2B §8-503.

HARFORD COUNTY —Cont'd
Alcoholic beverages —Cont'd
 Licenses —Cont'd
  Clubs, 2B §9-213.
  Corporations, 2B §9-101.
  Criminal history records checks.
   License applicants, 2B §10-103.
  Drive-through purchase facility.
   Prohibition on issuance or transfer, 2B
    §10-503.
  Employees.
   Minimum age of employees, 2B §12-213.
  Exemption from execution and distraint, 2B
   §10-501.
  Fees.
   Disposition, 2B §10-204.
   Proration, 2B §10-205.
   Refund, 2B §10-205.
  Interest in more than one license, 2B §9-213.
  Issuance.
   Liquor control board, 2B §10-203.
  Limited liability companies, 2B §9-101.
  Manufacturers.
   Hours and days for sale, 2B §11-101.
  Minimum age of employees, 2B §12-213.
  New licenses.
   Restrictions as to new licenses, 2B §9-213.
  Premises.
   Defined, 2B §12-213.
  Renewal.
   Procedure, 2B §10-301.
  Reports to liquor board by licensee, 2B §12-213.
  Restrictions on licensees, 2B §12-213.
   New licensees, 2B §9-213.
  Revocation and suspension, 2B §12-213.
   Grounds, 2B §10-401.
   Nudity and sexual displays on licensee's
    premises, 2B §10-405.
  Stadium on-sale license, limitations, 2B
   §8-213.1.
  Transfer, 2B §10-503.
   Limitation, 2B §9-213.
  Violations.
   Civil citations, 2B §16-408.
  Wine festival, 2B §8-309.
 Light wine licenses.
  Class A, off-sale, 2B §4-201.
 Liquor control department.
  Appeals.
   Procedure, 2B §16-102.
  Applicability of provisions, 2B §15-210.
  Appointment.
   By county executive, 2B §15-201.
   Time, 2B §15-201.
  Bonds, surety, 2B §15-201.
   Fidelity bond of employees, 2B §15-205.
  Compensation, 2B §15-201.
  Duties and rights, 2B §15-201.
  Employees.
   Supervision, 2B §15-205.
  General manager, 2B §15-205.
  Hearings.
   Alterations of rules and regulations, 2B
    §15-205.
  Inspectors.
   Additional inspectors, 2B §15-112.
   General provisions, 2B §15-205.
  Investigation of complaints, 2B §16-403.
  Licenses.
   Appeals, 2B §16-102.
   Investigations, 2B §10-203.

HARFORD COUNTY —Cont'd
Alcoholic beverages —Cont'd
Liquor control department —Cont'd
Licenses —Cont'd
Issuance, 2B §10-203.
Loans.
Limit on, 2B §15-202.
Meetings, 2B §15-201.
Officers or inspectors, 2B §15-205.
Powers.
Borrowing power, 2B §15-202.
Generally, 2B §15-205.
Qualifications, 2B §15-201.
Rules and regulations, 2B §15-205.
Salaries, 2B §15-205.
Term of office, 2B §15-201.
Vacancies, 2B §15-201.
Manufacturers.
Licenses.
Hours and days for sale, 2B §11-101.
Micro-brewery licenses, 2B §2-208.
Minors.
Citation for violations, CR §10-119.
Sales to prohibited, 2B §12-108.
Nudity and sexual displays on licensee's premises.
Revocation of license, 2B §10-405.
Open containers.
Restriction on possession, 2B §19-303.
Penalties, 2B §16-507.
Possession not deemed unlawful, 2B §12-213.
Pub-brewery licenses, 2B §2-207.
Restaurants.
Beer and light wine licenses.
Class B, on-sale, 2B §5-201.
Class BDR (deluxe restaurant) licenses
(on-sale), 2B §9-213.
Defined, 2B §1-102.
Requirements, 2B §1-102.
Retailers.
Surety bonds required, 2B §14-101.
Sales.
Beer for cash, 2B §12-112.
Election days, 2B §11-401.
New Year's day, 2B §11-402.
Prohibited to drunkards and mentally deficient
persons, 2B §12-110.
Prohibited to minors and intoxicated persons,
2B §12-108.
Sampling and tasting licenses, 2B §8-407.
Schools.
Licenses.
Sale within 1,000 feet prohibited.
Exceptions, 2B §9-213.
Seasonal operation of premises.
Authorized closings, 2B §10-504.
Stadium on-sale license, limitations, 2B §8-213.1.
Sundays.
General restrictions, 2B §11-403.
Hours and days of sale, 2B §11-513.
Wine festival.
License, 2B §8-309.
Wine tasting license, 2B §8-407.
Appearance fees in circuit courts.
Distribution, CJ §7-204.
Bailiff.
Compensation, CJ §2-507.
Baseball games.
Alcoholic beverages.
Stadium on-sale license, limitations, 2B
§8-213.1.

HARFORD COUNTY —Cont'd
**Bingo, members only instant bingo, paddle
wheels and raffles,** CR §§13-1501 to 13-1512.
Bingo defined, CR §13-1501.
Bingo, generally, prizes, minors prohibited, CR
§13-1504.
Definitions, CR §13-1501.
Disqualification from licensure, CR §13-1511.
Enforcement, CR §13-1512.
Fees for licenses, CR §13-1503.
50/50.
Defined, CR §13-1501.
License not required, locations, prizes, CR
§13-1508.
Gaming event defined, CR §13-1501.
Instant bingo locations, limitation, CR §13-1504.
License required for gaming event, CR §13-1503.
Members only instant bingo.
Defined, CR §13-1501.
License, limitation, prizes, location, CR
§13-1505.
Paddle wheel license.
Authorization to conduct bingo, CR §13-1504.
Limitations, prizes, CR §13-1507.
Professional involvement prohibited, CR §13-1503.
Provision applicable only to county, CR §13-1502.
Qualified organizations that may obtain license,
CR §13-1503.
Raffles.
Limitations, prizes, bond, CR §13-1506.
Reports required, CR §13-1509.
Slot machines and coin machines not authorized,
CR §13-1502.
Unlicensed operation, CR §13-1510.
Violations, penalty, CR §13-1510.
Birds and game.
Trapping.
Snare trapping, NR §10-410.
Bonds, surety.
Competitive bidding, 25 §3.
Bowling alleys.
Alcoholic beverage licenses, 2B §9-213.
Building code.
Agricultural buildings.
Exemption for buildings used for agritourism,
PS §12-508.
Provisions for, 25 §3.
Bush River fishing restrictions, NR §4-721.
Caterers.
Beer, wine and liquor licenses, 2B §§6-704, 9-213.
**Chesapeake Bay critical area and Atlantic
coastal bays critical area protection
programs.**
Critical areas commission.
Members on commission, NR §8-1804.
Churches.
Alcoholic beverages.
Sale within three hundred feet prohibited, 2B
§9-213.
Circuit courts.
Fees.
Distribution of appearance fees, CJ §7-204.
Judicial circuit, MD Const Art IV §19.
Clerks of court.
Fees.
Administering public money, CJ §2-213.
Clubs.
Alcoholic beverage licenses, 2B §9-213.
Commissioners.
Adoption of plumbing, building and housing codes,
25 §3.

HARFORD COUNTY —Cont'd
Commissioners —Cont'd
Powers.
Enumerated, 25 §3.
Zoning certificates or permits.
Fees, 25 §3.
Community associations.
Property tax credits, TP §9-314.
Community college.
Board of community college trustees, ED §16-408.
Merger of Harford Community College
Foundation, Inc., with Harford educational
foundation, ED §16-409.
Correctional facility.
Home detention program, COR §11-714.
Work release, rehabilitation and education of
prisoners, COR §11-714.
County work and awarding of contracts.
Competitive bidding, 25 §3.
Crimes and offenses.
Dog regulations, 24 §11-504.
Fish and fisheries.
Restrictions in county waters, NR §4-720.
Dangerous weapons.
Minors carrying, prohibited hours, CR §4-101.
Deeds.
Recordation.
Prepayment of taxes prior to transfer on
assessment books, RP §3-104.
Straw deeds, RP §3-104.
Deposit of funds.
Collateral for deposit, 24 §7-101.
Development impact fee.
School construction financing, 24 §9-10A-01.
Dogs.
Female dogs in heat.
Running at large, 24 §11-513.
Licenses, 24 §11-501.
Regulations, 24 §11-504.
**Drive-thru alcoholic beverage purchase
facilities.**
Licenses.
Prohibition on issuance or transfer, 2B §9-213.
Transfer prohibited, 2B §10-503.
Elections.
County board of elections.
Compensation, EL §2-204.
County boards generally, EL §§2-201 to 2-303.
See ELECTIONS.
County boards of education generally, EL §§8-801
to 8-806.
Election judges.
Compensation, EL §10-205.
Eminent domain.
Specific provisions, MD Const Art III §40A.
Execution sales.
Employment of auctioneer, CJ §11-503.
Fines.
Alcoholic beverages.
Violations, 2B §16-507.
Fire department.
Firefighters appointed as deputy sheriffs, PS
§§7-301 to 7-303.
Fish and fisheries.
Restrictions in county waters, NR §§4-720, 4-721.
Jewish holiday exception on Gunpowder River,
NR §4-715.
Funds.
Collateral for deposit of funds, 24 §7-101.
Golf courses.
Beer, wine and liquor licenses.
Class GC (golf course) beer, wine and liquor
license, 2B §8-503.

HARFORD COUNTY —Cont'd
Gunpowder River fishing restrictions, NR
§4-721.
Jewish holiday exception, NR §4-715.
Habonim Camp Association Company, Inc.
Property tax credits, TP §9-314.
Havre De Grace Little League, Inc.
Property tax credits, TP §9-314.
Hawkers and peddlers.
Display of tag or stamp, BR §17-910.
License fees, BR §17-907.
Scope of license, BR §17-905.
**Home detention program, individuals
sentenced to correctional facility,** COR
§11-714.
Housing code.
Provision for, 25 §3.
Hunting.
Boats, hunting from, NR §10-605.
Anchored boat, NR §10-606.
Waters, hunting while standing in, NR §10-604.
Injury reports.
Automobile accident or lethal weapon causing
injury.
Physicians, pharmacists, dentists or nurses, HG
§20-701.
John F. Kennedy memorial highway.
Elimination of ramp tolls, TR §4-312.1.
Judges.
Former judges.
Recall for temporary assignment.
Maximum period of assignment, CJ §1-302.
Juke box licensing.
Approval, BR §17-1315.
Assignment, BR §17-1316.
Display, BR §17-1317.
Fees, BR §17-1314.
Harford county juke box license defined, BR
§17-1312.
Issuance, BR §17-1315.
Keeping without license, BR §17-1318.
Posting, BR §17-1317.
Required, BR §17-1313.
Transferability, BR §17-1316.
Ladew Topiary Gardens.
Property tax credits, TP §9-314.
Libraries.
Authority of county commissioners to borrow for
capital construction costs, 25 §233.
Licenses.
Alcoholic beverages. See within this heading,
"Alcoholic beverages."
Juke boxes, BR §§17-1312 to 17-1318. See within
this heading, "Juke box licensing."
Limited liability companies.
Alcoholic beverages.
Licenses, 2B §9-101.
Marriage.
Clerk's fee for performing ceremony.
Disposition, FL §2-410.
Marriage license fees, FL §2-404.
Maryland food center authority.
General provisions, 41 §§13-101 to 13-123.
See MARYLAND FOOD CENTER
AUTHORITY.
Maryland Ornithological Society, Inc.
Property tax credits, TP §9-314.
Minors.
Alcoholic beverages.
Sales to prohibited, 2B §12-108.

HARFORD COUNTY —Cont'd
Minors —Cont'd
Dangerous weapons, carrying.
Prohibited hours, CR §4-101.
Misdemeanors.
Dog regulations, 24 §11-504.
Fish and fisheries.
Restrictions in county waters, NR §4-720.
Motor vehicles.
Size and weight.
Power of county commissioners, 25 §25.
Northeast Maryland waste disposal authority.
Participating county, NR §3-903.
North Harford Game and Fish Association, Inc.
Property tax credits, TP §9-314.
Oil pipeline corporation acquiring property under power to condemn, PUC §5-404.
Orphans' court.
Judges.
Chief judge, ET §2-107.
Compensation.
Exception in Harford county, ET §2-108.
Judges of circuit court.
Sit on orphans' court in county, MD Const Art IV §20.
Sessions, ET §2-106.
Pedestrians.
Soliciting donations from roadway or median, TR §21-507.
Penalties.
Alcoholic beverages.
Sales to minors and intoxicated persons, 2B §12-108.
Juke box licensing.
Keeping juke box without license, BR §17-1318.
Permits.
Plumbing permits, 25 §3.
Plumbing.
Permits, 25 §3.
Purchases and supplies.
Competitive bidding.
Minimum purchase price, 25 §3.
Railroads.
Alcoholic beverages.
Beer, wine and liquor licenses.
Class F, 2B §8-213.
Recordation.
Deeds.
Prepayment of taxes prior to transfer on assessment books, RP §3-104.
Straw deeds, RP §3-104.
Plats of subdivisions.
Inapplicability of section, RP §3-108.
Rural legacy program.
Property tax credit, TP §9-314.
Salaries.
County treasurer, 25 §51.
School construction financing.
Development impact fee, 24 §9-10A-01.
Schools.
Alcoholic beverage licenses.
Sale within 1,000 feet prohibited.
Exceptions, 2B §9-213.
County board of education.
Board of community college trustees.
Appointment of members, ED §16-408.
County superintendent.
Evaluation of professional performance, ED §4-201.
Notice of candidacy for reappointment, ED §4-201.

HARFORD COUNTY —Cont'd
Schools —Cont'd
County board of education —Cont'd
Election generally, EL §§8-801 to 8-806.
Expenses.
Reimbursement for travel and other expenses, ED §3-112.
Reimbursement for travel and other expenses, ED §3-112.
Shared space council, ED §3-111.
Sheriff.
Compensation, CJ §2-309.
Firefighters appointed as deputy sheriffs, PS §§7-301 to 7-303.
Inmates.
Plan for use of inmates for certain tasks, CJ §2-309.
Rank of employees, CJ §2-309.
Second in command, CJ §2-310.
Special deputies, CJ §2-309.
Termination of employees.
Just cause required, CJ §2-309.
Stadiums.
Alcoholic beverages.
Stadium on-sale license, limitations, 2B §8-213.1.
State's attorney.
General provisions, 10 §§34 to 41.
See STATE'S ATTORNEYS.
Subdivision plats.
Recordation.
Inapplicability of section, RP §3-108.
Sundays and holidays.
Alcoholic beverages.
Hours and days for sale, 2B §§11-403, 11-513.
New Year's day, 2B §11-402.
Susquehanna River.
Pound, stake or gill net restrictions, NR §4-721.
Swan Creek.
Haul seine or stake net restrictions, NR §4-721.
Taxation.
Development impact fee, school construction financing, 24 §9-10A-01.
Property tax credits, TP §9-314.
Recordation.
Deposit of revenues, TP §12-113.
Redemption.
Rate of redemption, TP §14-820.
Trapping.
Snare traps, NR §10-410.
Treasurer.
Deputy treasurer, 25 §51.
Volunteer fire companies and ambulance companies.
Property tax credits, TP §9-314.
Water and sewer systems.
County plans.
Exceptions to county plan, EN §9-514.
Wine festival.
License, 2B §8-309.
Work release program, individuals sentenced to correctional facility, COR §11-714.
Zoning and planning.
Certificates or permits.
Issuance, 25 §3.

HARNESS RACING, BR §§11-601 to 11-636.
Applicability of title, BR §11-602.
Average handle.
$125,000 or less.
Pension fund exemption, BR §11-618.

HARNESS RACING —Cont'd
Average handle —Cont'd
$600,000 and over.
  Allocation of licensee's takeout share, BR
    §11-615.
  General takeout allocation, BR §11-614.
$600,000 or less.
  Allocation of licensee's takeout share, BR
    §11-617.
  General takeout allocation, BR §11-616.
Defined, BR §11-601.
Pension fund exemption, BR §11-618.
Commission.
State racing commission.
  General provisions, BR §§11-201 to 11-214.
    See HORSE RACING.
Definitions, BR §11-101.
Maryland standardbred race fund, BR §11-623.
Emergencies.
Transfer of racing days due to emergency, BR
  §11-612.
Foaled stakes program.
Running of Fund races.
  Eligibility requirements, BR §11-632.
Judges.
Three harness, judges required, BR §11-604.
Licenses.
Applications.
  Notice requirements, BR §11-608.
Daily fee, BR §11-608.
Driver's fee.
  Deduction from purse, BR §11-619.
Estimated taxes, BR §11-620.
Limited to standardbred horses, BR §11-603.
Number of license, BR §11-609.
Racing days.
  Emergencies.
    Transfer of racing days due to emergency, BR
      §11-612.
    Hearing for increased or transferred days, BR
      §11-612.
Restrictions, BR §11-609.
Takeout and winnings.
  Average handle, BR §§11-614 to 11-618. See
    within this heading, "Average handle."
  Breakage, BR §11-613.
Transfer of race meetings, BR §11-611.
Maryland standardbred race fund.
Administration of fund, BR §11-629.
Advisory committee.
  Chairman.
    Designation, BR §11-627.
  Compensation, BR §11-628.
  Composition, BR §11-626.
  Defined, BR §11-623.
  Designation of chairman, BR §11-627.
  Establishment, BR §11-625.
  Meetings, BR §11-628.
  Membership, BR §11-626.
Creation, BR §11-624.
  Advisory committee, BR §11-625.
Definitions, BR §11-623.
Establishment, BR §11-624.
  Advisory committee, BR §11-625.
Running of Fund races, BR §§11-631 to 11-636.
  Cancellation of Fund race, BR §11-636.
  Conditions, BR §11-634.
  Eligibility requirements.
    Foaled stakes program, BR §11-632.
    Sires stakes program, BR §11-633.
  Provision, BR §11-631.

HARNESS RACING —Cont'd
Maryland standardbred race fund —Cont'd
Running of Fund races —Cont'd
  Purses, BR §11-635.
  Regulations and conditions, BR §11-634.
Undisbursed money, BR §11-629.
Officiating.
Three harness judges required, BR §11-604.
Pari-mutuel betting.
General provisions, BR §§11-801 to 11-832.
  See PARI-MUTUEL BETTING.
Race meetings.
Holding without license prohibited, BR §11-1001.
Racing days, BR §11-610.
Sunday racing authorized, BR §11-605.
Racing times.
Restriction, BR §11-606.
Running of Fund Races, BR §§11-631 to 11-636.
  See within this heading, "Maryland
    standardbred race fund."
Scope of title, BR §11-602.
Short title, BR §11-1101.
Sires stakes program.
Running of Fund races.
  Eligibility requirements, BR §11-633.
Standardbred horses.
Racing limitation, BR §11-603.
Sunday racing.
Commission approval required, BR §11-605.
Sunset law, BR §11-1102.
Takeout and winnings.
Average handle of $125,000 or less.
  Pension fund exemption, BR §11-618.
Average handle of $600,000 or less.
  Allocation of licensee's takeout share, BR
    §11-617.
  General takeout allocation, BR §11-616.
Average handle over $600,000.
  Allocation of licensee's takeout share, BR
    §11-615.
  General takeout allocation, BR §11-614.
Breakage, BR §11-613.
Driver's fee.
  Deduction from purse, BR §11-619.
Running of Fund races.
  Purses excluded from other prize money, BR
    §11-635.
Three harness judges required, BR §11-604.
Winnings. See within this heading, "Takeout and
  winnings."

HART-MILLER-PLEASURE ISLAND CHAIN.
Chesapeake Bay.
Redeposit of spoil, EN §5-1103.
  Citizens oversight committee, EN §5-1104.
Declared open area, NR §5-1202.1.
Easements.
State to grant easement, NR §5-1202.2.

HATCHERIES.
Fish hatcheries.
General provisions, NR §§4-401 to 4-410.
  See FISH AND FISHERIES.

HATE CRIMES, CR §§10-301 to 10-308.
**Damage to property because of race, color,
  religious beliefs, national origin or sexual
  orientation,** CR §10-304.
Associated building, damaging, CR §10-305.
Religious entity, property of, CR §10-302.
First amendment rights protected, CR §10-308.

HATE CRIMES —Cont'd
**Harassment because of race, color, religious
    beliefs, national origin or sexual
    orientation,** CR §10-304.
Penalty, CR §10-306.
Prosecution for other crimes not precluded,
    CR §10-307.
Religion.
  Harassment, CR §10-304.
  Obstructing exercise of religious belief, CR
    §10-303.
  Property damage motivated by religious belief, CR
    §10-304.
  Property damage to property of religious entity,
    CR §10-302.
Sexual orientation.
  Defined, CR §10-301.
State police department.
  Statistics, PS §2-307.

HAULING.
Carriers.
  See CARRIERS.

HAUNTED HOUSES.
Real property sales.
  Disclosure, RP §2-120.

HAVRE DE GRACE.
Alcoholic beverages.
  Dispensaries, 2B §15-203.
    Profits and reserves.
      Accounted, 2B §15-207.
  Liquor control department.
    Distribution of net proceeds, 2B §15-207.

HAWKERS AND PEDDLERS.
Calvert county.
  Peddler licensing, BR §§17-915 to 17-922.
    See CALVERT COUNTY.
Counties.
  Licenses.
    Powers of county commissioners, 25 §3.
Licenses.
  Acting without license, BR §17-911.
  Applicability of title, BR §17-905.
  Applications.
    Fees, BR §17-907.
      St. Mary's county, BR §17-913.
  Calvert county.
    General provisions, BR §§17-915 to 17-922.
      See CALVERT COUNTY.
  Definitions, BR §§17-901, 17-904.
  Failure to have or show license, BR §17-911.
  Issuance.
    Tag or stamp, BR §17-908.
  Mandatory license requirement, BR §17-906.
  Required, BR §17-906.
  Sale of produce in municipal corporation, BR
    §17-912.
  Scope of license, BR §17-909.
  Scope of title, BR §17-905.
  Tag or stamp.
    Display of, BR §17-910.
    Issuance, BR §17-908.
    Sale of produce in municipal corporation.
      Identification cards or tags authorized, BR
        §17-912.
Penalties.
  Licenses, BR §17-911.
Taxation.
  Sale of produce in municipal corporation.
    Local license, fee or tax prohibited, BR §17-912.

HAWKINS POINT LANDFILL.
Hazardous materials and substances.
  Disposal of controlled hazardous substances.
    Applicability, EN §7-205.

HAWKS.
Bounties.
  Counties, 25 §2.
Hunting with.
  Permits, NR §10-907.

HAZARDOUS LIQUID PIPELINES, PUC
    §§11-201 to 11-208.
Authority.
  Scope of commission's authority, PUC §11-202.
Best practices.
  Development and introduction, PUC §11-203.
Certifications, PUC §11-202.
Definitions, PUC §11-201.
Federal law, implementation of, PUC §11-202.
Injunctive relief, PUC §11-207.
Inspections, PUC §11-203.
  Fees, PUC §11-206.
  Notification to national response center.
    Duties of commission, PUC §11-204.
Jurisdiction of commission, PUC §11-202.
**Notification to national response center,
    commission.**
  Significant errors or information, PUC §11-204.
Penalties, PUC §11-208.
Regulation assistance.
  Staff engineer.
    Public service commission, PUC §2-108.
Reports.
  Commission, PUC §§11-202, 11-204.
  Operator of pipeline, PUC §11-205.
Safety standards and practices, PUC §11-203.
Violations, PUC §11-208.

HAZARDOUS MATERIALS AND SUBSTANCES,
    EN §§7-101 to 7-306; HG §§22-501 to 22-508.
Administrative procedure.
  Hearings.
    Application of act, EN §7-261.
    Immediate ban where imminent hazard exists.
      Hearings in accordance with act, HG §22-504.
Advisory council.
  Controlled hazardous substance advisory council.
    See within this heading, "Controlled
      hazardous substances."
**Appalachian states low-level radioactive waste
    compact,** EN §§7-301 to 7-306.
  See APPALACHIAN STATES LOW-LEVEL
    RADIOACTIVE WASTE COMPACT.
Appeals.
  Final decisions of department, EN §7-264.
  Persons adversely affected by rules or regulations,
    HG §22-505.
Attorney general.
  Controlled hazardous substances control fund.
    Actions for costs, EN §7-221.
  Responsibility for cases arising under subtitle, EN
    §7-268.
Bonds, surety.
  Transfer of hazardous materials between one
    mode of transportation and another.
    Facility permit, EN §7-111.
Clerks of court.
  Judicial review of rules or regulations.
    Duties of clerk, HG §22-505.

HAZARDOUS MATERIALS AND SUBSTANCES
—Cont'd

Community right-to-know.

Collection of required information from owners or operators.

Community right-to-know fund.

Establish, use, EN §7-604.

Definitions, EN §7-601.

Exception from paying annual fee, EN §7-604.

False information submitted, prohibition, EN §7-603.

Fee for facilities required to report, EN §7-604.

Information required to be provided, EN §7-602.

Regulations, EN §7-602.

Repository for information.

Department to serve as, EN §7-602.

Violations, enforcement and penalties, EN §7-605.

Community right-to-know fund, EN §§7-601 to 7-605.

Public access to information on hazardous or toxic chemicals.

Duties of department, EN §6-503.

"Hazardous or toxic chemical" defined, EN §6-501.

Notice of request for information, EN §6-503.

Persons allowed access, EN §6-503.

Purpose of subtitle, EN §6-502.

Rules and regulations, EN §6-504.

Compacts.

Appalachian states low-level radioactive waste compact, EN §§7-301 to 7-306.

See APPALACHIAN STATES LOW-LEVEL RADIOACTIVE WASTE COMPACT.

Interstate compact on low-level nuclear waste. See within this heading, "Controlled hazardous substances."

Complaints.

Hearings, EN §7-261.

Issuance, EN §7-258.

Notice.

Issuance, EN §7-259.

Orders.

Issuance, EN §7-259.

Service, EN §7-260.

Subpoenas, EN §7-261.

Contempt.

Hearings on complaint.

Enforcement of subpoenas, EN §7-261.

Contribution and exoneration.

Controlled hazardous substances control fund.

Uniform contribution among tortfeasors act, EN §7-221.

Controlled hazardous substances, EN §§7-201 to 7-268.

Chemical warfare materials, EN §§7-239.1 to 7-239.4.

Compliance with requirements of subtitle, EN §7-239.2.

Legislative findings, EN §7-239.2.

Operation of facility, EN §7-239.4.

Permits, EN §7-239.3.

Renewal or modification of permits, EN §7-239.4.

Complaints.

Hearings, EN §7-261.

Issuance, EN §7-258.

Notice.

Issuance, EN §7-259.

Order.

Issuance, EN §7-259.

HAZARDOUS MATERIALS AND SUBSTANCES
—Cont'd

Controlled hazardous substances —Cont'd

Complaints —Cont'd

Service, EN §7-260.

Subpoenas, EN §7-261.

Condemnation by department, EN §7-228.

Construction of subtitle, EN §7-204.

Control fund, EN §§7-218 to 7-221.

Accounts, EN §7-220.

Action for costs, EN §7-221.

Contribution among tortfeasors, EN §7-221.

Established, EN §7-218.

Financing, EN §7-219.

Recovery of cost, EN §7-221.

Reimbursements, EN §7-221.

Use of fund, EN §7-220.

Controlled hazardous substance facility.

Defined, EN §7-201.

Controlled hazardous substance hauler.

Defined, EN §7-201.

Controlled hazardous substance vehicle drivers.

Defined, EN §7-201.

Controlled hazardous substance vehicles.

Defined, EN §7-201.

Council, EN §§7-211 to 7-215.

Advising and assisting department, EN §7-215.

Compensation, EN §7-214.

Composition, EN §7-212.

Defined, EN §7-201.

Duties, EN §7-215.

Established, EN §7-211.

Expenses.

Reimbursement, EN §7-214.

Meetings, EN §7-214.

Officers, EN §7-213.

Qualifications of public members, EN §7-212.

Tenure, EN §7-212.

Vacancies, EN §7-212.

Definitions, EN §7-201.

Department.

Powers and duties.

Generally, EN §7-207.

Discharge.

Defined, EN §7-201.

Disposal, EN §7-205.

Driver's certificate.

Defined, EN §7-201.

Enforcement, EN §§7-256 to 7-268.

Facility permits, EN §§7-232 to 7-246.

Application, EN §7-235.

Denial, EN §7-240.

Conditions prerequisite to issuance, EN §7-236.

Defined, EN §7-201.

Denial of application.

Grounds, EN §7-240.

Equivalent permit, EN §7-232.

Executive orders, EN §7-234.

Fees, EN §7-237.

Issuance, EN §§7-232, 7-239.

Conditions prerequisite to issuance, EN §7-236.

Low-level nuclear waste facilities.

Additional requirements, EN §7-242.

Defined, EN §7-201.

Issuance, EN §7-233.

Nontransferability, EN §7-241.

Notification of radiation escape required, EN §7-243.

Maintenance.

Required standards for maintaining permit, EN §7-242.

HAZARDOUS MATERIALS AND SUBSTANCES
—Cont'd
Controlled hazardous substances —Cont'd
Facility permits —Cont'd
Nontransferability, EN §7-241.
Public participation permitting process, EN
§§1-601 to 1-607.
Appeal of final determination.
Contested case hearing, EN §1-605.
Applicability of provision, EN §1-601.
Applications for departmental permits, EN
§1-603.
Notice of completed applications or reasons
for incompleteness, EN §1-607.
Consolidation of public meetings and
hearings, EN §1-601.
Contested case hearing, EN §1-605.
Dismissal, EN §1-606.
Opportunity for, EN §1-601.
Determination, EN §1-604.
Appeal of final determination, EN §1-605.
Dismissal of request for adjudication, EN
§1-606.
Informational meeting on application, EN
§1-603.
Mailing notice.
Informational meetings or public hearings,
EN §1-602.
Notice of completed applications or reasons
for incompleteness, EN §1-607.
Notice, publication, EN §1-602.
Applications for permits, EN §1-603.
Publication of notice, EN §1-602.
Request for adjudication.
Dismissal of request for adjudication, EN
§1-606.
Time for submitting, EN §1-605.
Review times for licensing and permitting
programs, EN §1-606.
Tentative determination, EN §1-604.
Zoning and land use requirements or
conformity to county plan.
Not challenged at contested case hearing,
EN §1-605.
Radiation escape.
Permit holders to notify department, EN
§7-243.
Required, EN §7-232.
Separate permit for each facility, EN §7-232.
Suspension and revocation, EN §7-257.
Term and renewal of permits, EN §7-238.
False statements and documents, EN §7-267.
Federal act.
Defined, EN §7-201.
Generators.
Disposal of controlled hazardous substances.
Prerequisites, EN §7-205.
Requirements, EN §7-209.
Rules and regulations.
Applicability of certain rules and regulations,
EN §7-209.
Shipment of hazardous substances off premises.
Manifest required, EN §7-209.
Hauler certificate.
Defined, EN §7-201.
Hawkins Point landfill.
Disposal provisions.
Applicability to Hawkins Point landfill, EN
§7-205.
Hazardous substance response plan, EN §7-223.

HAZARDOUS MATERIALS AND SUBSTANCES
—Cont'd
Controlled hazardous substances —Cont'd
High-level nuclear waste.
Defined, EN §7-225.
Facility.
Prohibited, EN §7-225.
Incineration.
Defined, EN §7-201.
Injunctions.
Power of department to bring action, EN
§7-263.
Inspection of facilities, EN §7-245.
Municipal inspections, EN §7-256.
Power of health officers to inspect facilities, EN
§7-246.
Right of entry for inspection of facilities, EN
§7-256.
Legislative policy, EN §7-203.
Limitation of actions, CJ §5-106.
Listing of hazardous waste sites, EN §7-223.
Low-level nuclear waste.
Compact, EN §7-227.
Defined, EN §7-201.
Disposal.
See RADIATION.
Facility. See within this subheading, "Low-level
nuclear waste facility."
Reports, EN §7-244.
Rules and regulations, EN §7-208.
Separate considerations by secretary, EN
§7-206.
Low-level nuclear waste facility.
Additional requirements, EN §7-242.
Defined, EN §7-201.
Notification of radiation escape.
Required, EN §7-243.
Permits.
Defined, EN §7-201.
Issuance, EN §§7-233, 7-239.
Nontransferability, EN §7-241.
Renewal, EN §7-238.
Reports, EN §7-244.
Nuisances.
Suppression by subtitle, EN §7-204.
Offenses.
Specific offenses and penalties, EN §7-265.
Orders, EN §7-262.
Penalties.
Civil penalties, EN §7-266.
Criminal penalties, EN §7-267.
Punitive damages, EN §7-266.1.
Person.
Defined, EN §7-201.
Pollution.
Subtitle not to abate, EN §7-204.
Prohibited acts.
Generally, EN §7-224.
High-level nuclear waste facility prohibited, EN
§7-225.
Low-level nuclear waste, EN §7-224.
Storage, discharge or disposal not in accordance
with article, EN §7-224.
Purpose of subtitle, EN §7-203.
Records.
Inspections of facilities, EN §7-245.
Release.
Defined, EN §7-201.
Reports.
Low-level nuclear waste reports, EN §7-244.
Notification report, EN §7-226.

HAZARDOUS MATERIALS AND SUBSTANCES
—Cont'd
Controlled hazardous substances —Cont'd
Right of entry.
Inspection of facilities, EN §7-256.
Riparian owners.
Title not to take rights, EN §7-204.
Rules and regulations, EN §7-208.
Applicability, EN §7-209.
Scope of subtitle, EN §7-202.
Secretary.
Supervision and control, EN §7-206.
Separate considerations of low-level nuclear
waste, EN §7-206.
Service of process, EN §7-260.
Transportation, EN §§7-249 to 7-253.
Generators.
Transportation standards, EN §7-253.
Hauler certificates.
Low-level nuclear waste, EN §7-250.
Required, EN §7-249.
Scope, EN §7-251.
Standards, EN §7-252.
Suspension and revocation, EN §7-257.
Transportation not requiring, EN §7-249.
Low-level nuclear waste hauler certificate.
Issuance, EN §7-250.
Restrictions on transportation, EN §7-249.
Transuranic waste.
Defined, EN §7-201.
Treatment.
Defined, EN §7-201.
Vehicle certificate.
Defined, EN §7-201.
Violations.
Injunctions, EN §7-263.
Suspension and revocation of permits or
certificates, EN §7-257.
Witnesses.
Power of department to subpoena, EN §7-261.
Crimes and offenses.
Toxics in packaging, EN §9-1906.
Definitions.
Chemical warfare material, EN §7-239.1.
Controlled hazardous substance facility, EN
§7-201.
Controlled hazardous substance hauler, EN
§7-201.
Controlled hazardous substances, EN §7-201.
Controlled hazardous substance vehicle, EN
§7-201.
Controlled hazardous substance vehicle driver,
EN §7-201.
Council, EN §7-201.
Driver certificate, EN §7-201.
Emergency response, containment, clean-up and
abatement.
Paid fire companies and rescue squads.
Reimbursement for cost, CJ §3-1201.
Volunteer fire companies, rescue squads or
ambulance companies, CJ §3-1101.
Facility permits, EN §7-201.
Federal act, EN §7-201.
Hauler certificate, EN §7-201.
Hazardous material, HG §22-501.
Hazardous substance, EN §7-201.
High-level nuclear waste, EN §7-225.
Incineration, EN §7-201.
Low-level nuclear waste, EN §7-201.
Low-level nuclear waste facility, EN §7-201.

HAZARDOUS MATERIALS AND SUBSTANCES
—Cont'd
Definitions —Cont'd
Low-level nuclear waste facility permit, EN
§7-201.
Monitoring data, EN §7-239.1.
Person, EN §7-201.
Release, EN §7-201.
Responsible person, EN §7-201.
Security of hazardous material facilities, EN
§7-701.
Solid waste, EN §7-201.
Toxics in packaging, EN §9-1901.
Transfer of hazardous materials, EN §7-101.
Transuranic waste, EN §7-201.
Treatment, EN §7-201.
Vehicle certificate, EN §7-201.
Discharge.
Defined, EN §7-229.
Immunity of persons providing assistance in
connection with, CJ §5-617; EN §7-229.
Emergency management.
Local emergency plans, PS §14-110.
**Emergency response, containment, cleanup
and abatement.**
Cost responsibility for those at fault, CJ
§§3-1102.1, 3-1202.1.
Paid fire companies and rescue squads.
Assistance to paid fire company, CJ §3-1207.
Injunctions.
Power of department to sue for immediate
injunction, EN §7-263.
Reimbursement for cost.
Assistance to paid fire company, CJ §3-1207.
Definitions, CJ §3-1201.
Farm vehicles.
Exemptions, CJ §3-1205.
Liability or immunity of paid fire company,
rescue squad or personnel, CJ §3-1204.
Negotiations and actions for reimbursement,
CJ §3-1203.
Responsibility of motor carrier, CJ §3-1202.
Responsibility of person at fault, CJ
§3-1202.1.
Scope of subtitle, CJ §3-1206.
Responsibility of person at fault, CJ §§3-1102.1,
3-1202.1.
Volunteer fire companies, rescue squads or
ambulance companies.
Assistance to volunteer fire company, CJ
§3-1108.
Reimbursement for cost.
Actions for reimbursement, CJ §3-1103.
Assistance to volunteer fire company, CJ
§3-1108.
Definitions, CJ §3-1101.
Farm vehicles.
Exemptions, CJ §3-1106.
Liability or immunity of volunteer fire
company or rescue squad or personnel,
CJ §3-1105.
Motor carrier's responsibility, CJ §3-1102.
Negotiations, CJ §3-1103.
Purchase of personal protective equipment or
chemicals, CJ §3-1104.
Responsibility of motor carrier, CJ §3-1102.
Responsibility of person at fault, CJ
§3-1102.1.
Scope of subtitle, CJ §3-1107.
Eminent domain.
Controlled hazardous substances.
Condemnation by department, EN §7-228.

HAZARDOUS MATERIALS AND SUBSTANCES
  —Cont'd
Evidence.
  Investigations.
    Results available as evidence, HG §22-508.
Excluded material, HG §22-501.
Facility permit. See within this heading,
  "Controlled hazardous substances."
False statements and documents, EN §7-267.
Federal act.
  Release.
    Removal or remedial actions.
      Duplicate actions under federal act, EN
        §7-222.
Fees.
  Hazardous liquid pipelines.
    Inspections, PUC §11-206.
  Transfer of hazardous materials between one
    mode of transportation and another.
    Facility permit, EN §§7-107, 7-113.
Felonies.
  Knowing violations, EN §7-265.
Fines, EN §7-265.
Fire hazards.
  Abatement orders, PS §6-318.
    Failure to comply with order, PS §6-320.
    Service of process, PS §6-319.
  Additional remedies, PS §6-321.
  Maintenance of fire hazard prohibited, PS §6-317.
Funds.
  Community right-to-know fund, EN §§7-601 to
    7-605.
  State hazardous substance control fund, EN
    §§7-218 to 7-221. See within this heading,
    "Controlled hazardous substances."
Governor.
  Controlled hazardous substances facilities permit.
    Executive order, EN §7-234.
Hawkins Point landfill.
  Disposal of controlled hazardous substances, EN
    §7-205.
Hearings, EN §7-261.
  Complaints.
    Application of administrative procedure act, EN
      §7-261.
  Immediate ban where imminent hazard exists,
    HG §22-504.
  Subpoenas, EN §7-261.
High-level nuclear waste, EN §7-225.
Immediate ban where imminent hazard exists,
  HG §22-504.
Immunity.
  Discharge.
    Persons providing assistance in connection with,
      CJ §5-617; EN §7-229.
Information or documents.
  Duty to provide to department, EN §7-221.
Injunctions.
  Hazardous liquid pipelines, PUC §11-207.
  Power of department to bring action for
    injunction, EN §7-263.
  Release into environment.
    Removal or remedial actions.
      Denial of entry, EN §7-222.
  Toxics in packaging, EN §§9-1905, 9-1906.
Inspections.
  Collecting and reporting hazardous material
    investigations, HG §22-507.
  Conditions for entry, HG §22-506.
  Controlled hazardous substance facilities, EN
    §7-245.
    Health officers.
      Power to inspect, EN §7-246.

HAZARDOUS MATERIALS AND SUBSTANCES
  —Cont'd
Inspections —Cont'd
  Controlled hazardous substance facilities —Cont'd
    Municipal inspections, EN §7-256.
      Right of entry for inspection of facilities, EN
        §7-256.
  Entry for purpose of inspection, HG §22-506.
  Pipelines.
    Hazardous liquid pipelines, PUC §11-203.
      Fees, PUC §11-206.
  Scope of inspection, HG §22-506.
Investigations.
  Collecting and reporting hazardous material in
    investigations, HG §22-507.
  Results available as evidence, HG §22-508.
Joinder.
  Controlled hazardous substances control fund.
    Action for costs, EN §7-221.
Labels.
  Rules and regulations.
    Exemption from labeling requirements, HG
      §22-502.
Landfills.
  Permits for landfills by hazardous waste, EN
    §9-226.
Liability.
  Discharge.
    Persons providing assistance in connection with.
      Immunity from liability, CJ §5-617; EN
        §7-229.
Limitation of actions.
  Controlled hazardous substances, CJ §5-106.
Loading or unloading hazardous materials.
  Generally, EN §§7-101 to 7-114. See within this
    heading, "Transfer of hazardous materials
    between one mode of transportation and
    another."
Low-level nuclear waste. See within this heading,
  "Controlled hazardous substances."
Low-level radioactive waste.
  Appalachian states low-level radioactive waste
    compact, EN §§7-301 to 7-306.
  See APPALACHIAN STATES LOW-LEVEL
    RADIOACTIVE WASTE COMPACT.
Misbranded hazardous materials.
  When materials considered misbranded, HG
    §22-503.
Misdemeanors.
  Toxics in packaging, EN §9-1906.
Motor vehicles.
  Transportation of controlled hazardous
    substances. See within this heading,
    "Controlled hazardous substances."
Municipal corporations.
  Inspections of hazardous substance facilities.
    Municipal agencies, EN §7-256.
Notices.
  Radiation escape.
    Controlled hazardous substances facility permit
      holders to notify department, EN §7-243.
  Transfer of hazardous materials between one
    mode of transportation and another.
    Facility permit, EN §7-109.
Nuclear waste.
  High-level nuclear waste. See within this heading,
    "Controlled hazardous substances."
  Low-level nuclear waste.
    General provisions. See within this heading,
      "Controlled hazardous substances."

HAZARDOUS MATERIALS AND SUBSTANCES
—Cont'd
Nuclear waste —Cont'd
Low-level nuclear waste —Cont'd
Radiation act, EN §§8-101 to 8-601.
See RADIATION.
Offenses.
Specific offenses and penalties, EN §7-265.
Orders.
Appeals, EN §7-264.
Duty of department to enforce, EN §7-262.
Final corrective orders, EN §7-262.
Penalties.
Attorney general.
Responsibility for recovery of penalty, EN
§7-268.
Civil penalties, EN §7-266.
Criminal penalties, EN §7-267.
Knowing violations, EN §7-265.
Hazardous liquid pipelines, PUC §11-208.
Punitive damages, EN §7-266.1.
Security of hazardous material facilities.
Civil penalty, EN §7-708.
Transfer of hazardous materials between one
mode of transportation and another, EN
§§7-112, 7-113.
Permits.
Controlled hazardous substances facility permits.
See within this heading, "Controlled
hazardous substances."
Public participation permitting process, EN
§§1-601 to 1-607.
Appeal of final determination.
Contested case hearing, EN §1-605.
Applicability of provision, EN §1-601.
Applications for departmental permits, EN
§1-603.
Notice of completed applications or reasons
for incompleteness, EN §1-607.
Consolidation of public meetings and hearings,
EN §1-601.
Contested case hearing, EN §1-605.
Dismissal, EN §1-606.
Opportunity for, EN §1-601.
Determination, EN §1-604.
Appeal of final determination, EN §1-605.
Dismissal of request for adjudication, EN
§1-606.
Informational meeting on application, EN
§1-603.
Mailing notice.
Informational meetings or public hearings,
EN §1-602.
Notice of completed applications or reasons for
incompleteness, EN §1-607.
Notice, publication, EN §1-602.
Applications for permits, EN §1-603.
Publication of notice, EN §1-602.
Request for adjudication.
Dismissal of request for adjudication, EN
§1-606.
Time for submitting, EN §1-605.
Review times for licensing and permitting
programs, EN §1-606.
Tentative determination, EN §1-604.
Zoning and land use requirements or conformity
to county plan.
Not challenged at contested case hearing, EN
§1-605.
Transfer of hazardous materials between one
mode of transportation and another.
Facility permit.
Application, EN §7-105.

HAZARDOUS MATERIALS AND SUBSTANCES
—Cont'd
Permits —Cont'd
Transfer of hazardous materials between one
mode of transportation and another —Cont'd
Facility permit —Cont'd
Denial, EN §7-110.
Exemptions, EN §7-103.
Fees, EN §7-107.
Disposition, EN §7-113.
Notice, EN §7-109.
Prerequisites for issuance, EN §7-106.
Regulations, EN §7-104.
Required, EN §7-103.
Requirements for issuance, EN §7-111.
Separate permit for each facility, EN §7-103.
Term, EN §7-108.
Petitions.
Rules and regulations.
Persons seeking judicial review.
Time for filing petition, HG §22-505.
Pipelines.
Hazardous liquid pipelines, PUC §§11-201 to
11-208.
Planning.
Revised state hazardous substance response plan,
EN §7-208.
Prohibited acts.
Controlled hazardous substances. See within this
heading, "Controlled hazardous substances."
**Public access to information on hazardous or
toxic chemicals.**
Collection of required information from owners or
operators.
Community right-to-know fund.
Establish, use, EN §7-604.
Definitions, EN §7-601.
Exception from paying annual fee, EN §7-604.
False information submitted, prohibition, EN
§7-603.
Fee for facilities required to report, EN §7-604.
Information required to be provided, EN §7-602.
Regulations, EN §7-602.
Repository for information.
Department to serve as, EN §7-602.
Violations, enforcement and penalties, EN
§7-605.
Community right-to-know fund, EN §§7-601 to
7-605.
Duties of department, EN §6-503.
"Hazardous or toxic chemical" defined, EN §6-501.
Notice of request for information, EN §6-503.
Persons allowed access, EN §6-503.
Purpose of subtitle, EN §6-502.
Rules and regulations, EN §6-504.
Publication.
Information concerning hazardous material, HG
§22-507.
Radiation escape.
Notification required, EN §7-243.
Radioactive waste.
Appalachian states low-level radioactive waste
compact, EN §§7-301 to 7-306.
See APPALACHIAN STATES LOW-LEVEL
RADIOACTIVE WASTE COMPACT.
Generally.
See RADIATION.
Records.
Controlled hazardous substances facilities.
Inspections, EN §7-245.

HAZARDOUS MATERIALS AND SUBSTANCES
—Cont'd

Releases, EN §7-222.
  Immunity of persons providing assistance in connection with, EN §7-229.
Reports.
  Controlled hazardous substance notification report, EN §7-226.
  Low-level nuclear waste reports, EN §7-244.
Right of entry.
  Conditions for entry, HG §22-506.
  Controlled hazardous substances.
    Inspection of facilities, EN §7-256.
  Entry for purpose of inspection, HG §22-506.
  Release into environment.
    Removal or remedial actions, EN §7-222.
Rules and regulations, HG §22-502.
  Controlled hazardous substances.
    Adoption of rules and regulations by department, EN §7-208.
    Applicability of certain rules and regulations, EN §7-209.
    Scope of rules and regulations, EN §7-208.
  Judicial review, HG §22-505.
  Labeling requirements.
    Exemptions, HG §22-502.
  Public access to information on hazardous or toxic chemicals, EN §6-504.
  Security of hazardous material facilities, EN §7-705.
  Time for filing petition, HG §22-505.
  Toxics in packaging, EN §9-1907.
  Transfer of hazardous materials between one mode of transportation and another.
    Facility permits, EN §7-104.
Samples.
  Entry and inspection of samples, HG §22-506.
Searches and seizures.
  Administrative search warrants, EN §7-256.1.
  Release into environment.
    Removal or remedial actions.
      Obtaining search warrants where entry denied, EN §7-222.
Secretary.
  Rules and regulations.
    Judicial review.
      Duties of secretary, HG §22-505.
Security of hazardous material facilities, EN §§7-701 to 7-709.
  Analysis, EN §7-702.
    Audit to verify, EN §7-704.
  Applicability of provisions, EN §7-702.
  Community right-to-know fund.
    Use of funds, EN §7-706.
  Definitions, EN §7-701.
  False information.
    Submission prohibited, EN §7-707.
  Other requirements unaffected, EN §7-709.
  Penalties.
    Civil penalty, EN §7-708.
  Regulations, EN §7-705.
  Standards, EN §7-703.
Service of process.
  Complaints.
    Orders, notices, etc., EN §7-260.
Statutes of limitation.
  Controlled hazardous substances, CJ §5-106.
Subpoenas.
  Power of department, EN §7-261.
Tests.
  Entry and inspection for samples, HG §22-506.

HAZARDOUS MATERIALS AND SUBSTANCES
—Cont'd

Toxics in packaging, EN §§9-1901 to 9-1907.
  Applicability of provisions, EN §9-1903.
  Concentration levels, EN §9-1902.
  Conditional exemptions, EN §9-1904.
    Certification, EN §9-1905.
  Criminal penalties, EN §9-1906.
  Definitions, EN §9-1901.
  Effective date, EN §9-1903.
  Enforcement, EN §9-1905.
  Injunctions, EN §§9-1905, 9-1906.
  Penalties, EN §9-1906.
  Prohibited acts, EN §9-1902.
  Regulations, EN §9-1907.
  Tin plated steel, EN §9-1902.
Transfer of hazardous materials between one mode of transportation and another, EN §§7-101 to 7-114.
  Compliance with title required, EN §7-102.
  Definitions, EN §7-101.
  Enforcement of provisions, EN §7-112.
  Facility permit.
    Application, EN §7-105.
    Bond or other security, EN §7-111.
    Denial, EN §7-110.
    Exemptions, EN §7-103.
    Facility defined, EN §7-101.
    Fees, EN §7-107.
      Disposition, EN §7-113.
    Issuance.
      Requirements for, EN §7-111.
    Notice, EN §7-109.
    Prerequisites for issuance, EN §7-106.
    Regulations, EN §7-104.
    Required, EN §7-103.
    Requirements for issuance, EN §7-111.
    Separate permit for each facility, EN §7-103.
    Term, EN §7-108.
  False information.
    Submitted to department, EN §7-114.
  Hazardous material.
    Defined, EN §7-101.
  Information submitted to department, EN §7-114.
  Penalties for violations, EN §7-112.
    Disposition of penalties, EN §7-113.
  Prohibited acts, EN §7-102.
Transportation of controlled hazardous substances. See within this heading, "Controlled hazardous substances."
Transportation of hazardous materials, TR §22-409.
Violations.
  Controlled hazardous substances. See within this heading, "Controlled hazardous substances."
  Injunctions, EN §7-263.
  Knowing violations.
    Penalties, EN §7-265.
  Separate offense for each day, EN §7-265.
Voluntary cleanup program, EN §§7-501 to 7-516.
  See VOLUNTARY CLEANUP PROGRAM.
Warrants.
  Administrative search warrants, EN §7-256.1.
Witnesses.
  Power of department to subpoena, EN §7-261.

HAZARDOUS WASTE FACILITY SITING.
Appeals.
  Decisions of board, EN §7-412.

HAZARDOUS WASTE FACILITY SITING
—Cont'd
Board, EN §7-403.
Appeal from decision of board, EN §7-412.
Certificates of public necessity.
Issuance.
Generally. See within this heading,
"Certificates of public necessity."
Data and information furnished from department,
EN §7-409.
Defined, EN §7-401.
Department.
Board to be unit of department, EN §7-409.
Informational services, EN §7-409.
Powers, EN §7-409.
Records, EN §7-406.
Rules and regulations, EN §7-404.
Statewide solid waste management plan.
Inclusion of data, EN §7-409.
Ten year hazardous waste management plan.
Preparation of plan, EN §7-409.
Certificates of public necessity.
Advice and comments sought by board, EN
§7-406.
Applicability of other requirements, EN §7-407.
Applications, EN §§7-406, 7-411.
Applicant's report, EN §7-406.
Contents, EN §7-405.
Copies.
Distribution, EN §7-406.
Exemptions, EN §7-405.
Failure to commence construction or operation,
EN §7-408.
Issuance, EN §§7-405, 7-406.
Factors to be considered, EN §7-405.
Hearings, EN §7-406.
Rules of procedure for obtaining, EN §7-406.
Scope, EN §7-405.
Sites applied for by Maryland environmental
service, EN §7-406.
Considerations, EN §7-402.
Damages.
Liability of subdivisions, EN §7-413.
Definitions, EN §7-401.
Environmental service.
Department of the environment.
Furnishing copies of relevant information and
data, EN §7-409.
Duties, EN §§7-410, 7-411.
Sites applied by Maryland environmental service,
EN §7-406.
Hazardous waste.
Defined, EN §7-401.
Inventory of potential sites, EN §7-410.
Duties of environmental service as to inventoried
sites, EN §7-411.
Filing copies of inventories, EN §7-410.
Potential sites.
Inventory of potential sites, EN §7-410.
Duties of environmental service, EN §7-411.
Filing copies required, EN §7-410.
Purpose of provisions, EN §7-402.
Rules and regulations.
Board, EN §7-404.
Taxation.
Payments by environmental service in lieu of local
taxes, EN §7-411.

HAZING, CR §3-607.

HEADINGS.
Construction and interpretation, Rule 1-201.

HEAD INJURIES.
Health insurance.
Diagnostic and surgical procedures for bones of
the head, IN §15-821.
Respite care, 88A §§128, 129.

HEADLIGHTS.
Lights generally, TR §§22-201 to 22-232.
See MOTOR VEHICLE EQUIPMENT.

HEADSETS.
Bicycles.
Wearing earplugs, headsets, etc., prohibited, TR
§21-1210.
Electronic personal assistive mobility device.
Wearing earphones, headsets, etc., prohibited, TR
§21-1210.
Motor vehicles.
Wearing earphones, headsets, etc., prohibited, TR
§21-1120.

HEAD START.
**Judith P. Hoyer early child care and education
enhancement program,** ED §5-217.

HEALTH.
Abatement of nuisances.
Secretary of health and mental hygiene or local
health officers, HG §§20-310 to 20-314.
See NUISANCES.
Accounts and accounting.
Cost review commission.
Accounting principles for rate determinations,
HG §19-221.
Uniform accounting and financial reporting
system, HG §19-215.
Accreditation of health care facilities, HG
§§19-2301, 19-2302.
Acquired immune deficiency syndrome (AIDS).
Department of health and mental hygiene.
Insurance assistance pilot program, HG
§§15-201 to 15-205.
See ACQUIRED IMMUNE DEFICIENCY
SYNDROME (AIDS).
Research and information program, HG §18-333.
Administrative procedure.
Planning and development.
Appeal of administrative decisions, HG §19-128.
Aged.
Day-care for the elderly, HG §§14-201 to 14-206.
See DAY-CARE FOR THE ELDERLY.
AIDS.
See ACQUIRED IMMUNE DEFICIENCY
SYNDROME (AIDS).
Air quality control, EN §§2-101 to 2-614.
See AIR QUALITY CONTROL.
Alcoholism.
General provisions.
See DRUG OR ALCOHOL ABUSE.
Ambient air quality control, EN §§2-101 to
2-614.
See AIR QUALITY CONTROL.
Ambulatory care facilities.
Freestanding facilities.
Generally, HG §§19-3B-01 to 19-3B-09.
See FREESTANDING AMBULATORY CARE
FACILITIES.
Planning and development.
Certificates of need, HG §19-125.
Anatomical gift act, ET §§4-501 to 4-512.
See ANATOMICAL GIFT ACT.
Animal control.
General provisions, HG §§18-217 to 18-222.
See ANIMAL CONTROL.

HEALTH —Cont'd
Animals dangerous to human health.
 Prohibition on selling, purchasing, raising,
  keeping, HG §18-219.
Appeals.
 Board of review, HG §§2-206, 2-207.
 Cost review commission.
  Right to appeal, HG §19-227.
 Planning and development.
  Administrative decisions, HG §19-128.
Arthritis prevention and control program, HG
 §§13-501 to 13-512.
 See ARTHRITIS AND RELATED DISEASES.
Asbestos removal, EN §§6-401 to 6-422.
 See ASBESTOS.
Assisted living programs, HG §§19-1801 to
 19-1812.
 See ASSISTED LIVING PROGRAMS.
Asthma control program, HG §§13-1701 to
 13-1706.
Attorney general.
 Department of health and mental hygiene.
  Counsel to department, HG §2-107.
Authorities.
 Health and higher educational facilities authority,
  43C §§1 to 24.
  See HEALTH AND HIGHER EDUCATIONAL
   FACILITIES AUTHORITY.
Bedding and upholstered furniture.
 General provisions, HG §§24-401 to 24-435.
  See BEDDING AND UPHOLSTERED
   FURNITURE.
Beverages.
 Soft drinks.
  See SOFT DRINKS.
Biological agents registry, HG §§17-601 to
 17-605.
Blood pressure.
 High blood pressure and related cardiovascular
  risk factors commission, HG §§13-201 to
  13-206.
  See HEART DISEASE AND STROKE
   PREVENTION PROGRAMS.
Boards.
 Counties. See within this heading, "County boards
  of health."
Breast cancer.
 Alternative methods of treatment, HG §20-113.
 Health insurance.
  Mastectomy coverage, IN §15-832.
  Prosthesis coverage, IN §15-834.
 Mammography testing, HG §20-115.
  Insurance coverage, IN §15-814.
   Medicare supplement insurance, IN §15-907.
  Low-income underinsured and uninsured
   women, HG §20-116.
 Mastectomy, HG §20-116.
 Program, HG §20-116.
 Reconstructive surgery.
  Insurance coverage, IN §15-815.
Breast implantation.
 Duty of physician to inform as to risks,
  advantages, HG §20-114.
 Health insurance, IN §§15-105, 15-504.
 Statute of limitations on actions for damages, CJ
  §5-116.
Budget and management.
 Secretary of health and mental hygiene.
  General authority and duties of secretary, HG
   §2-104.

HEALTH —Cont'd
Budget and management —Cont'd
 Special supplemental food program for women,
  infants and children.
  Funds included in annual budget, HG §18-108.
Cancer.
 General provisions.
  See CANCER.
 Secretary of health and mental hygiene.
  General responsibilities of secretary for disease
   prevention, HG §18-104.
Candy or cakes.
 Deleterious.
  See FOOD AND FOOD ESTABLISHMENTS.
Cardiovascular disease prevention programs,
 HG §§13-201 to 13-206.
 See HEART DISEASE AND STROKE
  PREVENTION PROGRAMS.
Catastrophic health emergency.
 Disease surveillance and response program, HG
  §§18-901 to 18-908.
  See CATASTROPHIC HEALTH EMERGENCY.
 Governor's power to proclaim, PS §§14-3A-01 to
  14-3A-08.
  See HEALTH EMERGENCIES.
Centers for disease control.
 Notice.
  Guidelines on universal precautions, HO §1-207.
Centers for disease control system survey.
 Schools.
  Administration and parental information, ED
   §7-420.
Certificates of need.
 Planning and development.
  Ambulatory care facilities, HG §19-125.
  Applications.
   Action on applications, HG §19-126.
  Health care facilities, HG §19-120.
  Health maintenance organizations, HG §19-121.
  Issuance.
   Action on applications, HG §19-126.
   Notice of filing of application, HG §19-126.
Cholesterol testing, HG §§17-501 to 17-511.
 See CHOLESTEROL TESTING.
Citation of article, 1 §25.
Commissions.
 Commission on planning. See within this heading,
  "Planning and development."
 Cost review commission. See within this heading,
  "Cost review commission."
 High blood pressure and related cardiovascular
  risk factors commission, HG §§13-201 to
  13-206.
  See HEART DISEASE AND STROKE
   PREVENTION PROGRAMS.
Communicable diseases.
 General provisions.
  See CONTAGIOUS DISEASES.
 Secretary of health and mental hygiene.
  General responsibilities of secretary for disease
   prevention, HG §18-103.
Community health resources commission.
 See COMMUNITY HEALTH RESOURCES
  COMMISSION.
Community mental health services, HG
 §§10-901 to 10-905.
 See COMMUNITY MENTAL HEALTH
  SERVICES.
**Community services reimbursement rate
 commission,** HG §§13-801 to 13-810.
 See COMMUNITY SERVICES
  REIMBURSEMENT RATE COMMISSION.

HEALTH —Cont'd

Community services trust fund, HG §§24-1101 to 24-1105.

Comprehensive health planning. See within this heading, "Planning and development."

Comprehensive physical rehabilitation facilities.
General provisions, HG §§19-1201 to 19-1208.
See COMPREHENSIVE PHYSICAL REHABILITATION FACILITIES.

Condoms.
Sale by vending machines or other devices, HG §18-335.

Confidential records.
Defined, HG §4-101.
Penalty, HG §4-103.
Protected, HG §4-102.

Conflicts of interest.
Secretary of health and mental hygiene and staff, HG §2-103.

Consent provisions, HG §§20-101 to 20-117.

Contagious diseases.
General provisions.
See CONTAGIOUS DISEASES.
Secretary of health and mental hygiene.
General responsibilities of secretary for disease prevention, HG §18-102.

Contracts.
Cost review commission, HG §19-217.

Cosmetics.
Food, drugs and cosmetics, HG §§21-101 to 21-1215.
See FOOD, DRUGS AND COSMETICS.

Cost review commission, HG §§19-201 to 19-227.
Accounts and accounting.
Uniform accounting and financial reporting system, HG §19-215.
Additional information, HG §19-218.
Adjustment of rates, HG §19-219.
Appeals, HG §19-227.
Appointment of members, HG §19-203.
Audits.
Generally, HG §19-226.
Compensation, HG §19-206.
Composition, HG §19-203.
Contracts, HG §19-207.
Notification of certain contracts, HG §19-217.
Definitions, HG §19-201.
Regulated rates, HG §19-220.
Determination and collection of funds, HG §19-219.
Diversity of membership, HG §19-203.
Duties.
Generally, HG §19-207.
Established, HG §19-202.
Executive director, HG §19-205.
Executive sessions, HG §19-220.
Facilities.
Additional information, HG §19-218.
Defined, HG §19-201.
Reports, HG §19-216.
Fees.
Closed or delicensed hospitals, HG §19-223.
Financial status, HG §19-212.
Fund, HG §19-213.
Hearings.
Change of rate structures or charges, HG §19-222.
Generally, HG §19-225.
Hospital uncompensated care.
Causes and development of alternatives, HG §19-214.

HEALTH —Cont'd

Cost review commission —Cont'd
Investigations.
Further investigations authorized, HG §19-226.
Generally, HG §19-225.
Jurisdiction of commission, HG §19-211.
Meetings, HG §19-206.
Membership, HG §19-203.
Merger or consolidation.
Incentives for, HG §19-222.
Notice.
Certain financial transactions, contracts or agreements, HG §19-217.
Change of rate structures or charges, HG §19-222.
Oaths.
Hearings and investigations, HG §19-225.
Officers, HG §19-204.
Powers and duties.
Generally, HG §19-207.
Procedures for rate review and approval, HG §19-220.
Qualifications of members, HG §19-203.
Quorum, HG §19-206.
Rates.
Accounting principles for rate determinations, HG §19-221.
Alternate rate setting methods, HG §19-219.
Change of rate structure or charges, HG §19-222.
Compilation of rate structures, HG §19-220.
Financial status, HG §19-212.
Procedures for review and approval, HG §19-220.
Rate setting restricted, HG §19-211.
Reasonableness of rates, HG §19-220.
Review and approval of rates and costs, HG §19-219.
Records, HG §19-207.
Reduced-cost or free care to low-income patients without health insurance.
Policies for hospitals, HG §19-214.1.
Reimbursement for expenses, HG §19-206.
Related institutions.
Defined, HG §19-201.
Reports.
Additional information, HG §19-218.
Annual reports, HG §19-207.
Required reports of facilities, HG §19-216.
Transactions with nonprofit facilities, HG §19-224.
Uniform accounting and financial reporting system, HG §19-215.
Review and approval of rates and costs, HG §19-219.
Secretary of health.
Limitations on secretary, HG §19-208.
Staff, HG §19-206.
Tenure, HG §19-203.
Uncompensated care.
Causes and development of alternatives to hospital uncompensated care, HG §19-214.
Uniform accounting and financial reporting system, HG §19-215.
User fees, HG §19-213.
Vacancies, HG §19-203.

Counties.
Assistance to other political subdivisions, 25 §219.
Boards. See within this heading, "County boards of health."

HEALTH —Cont'd
Counties —Cont'd
Chartered counties.
Powers of county, 25A §5.
Officers. See within this heading, "Health officers."
Provisions provided by county commissioners, 25 §3.
County boards of health, HG §§3-101 to 3-310.
Appointment, HG §3-201.
Authority, HG §§3-201, 3-202.
Code or charter county, HG §3-201.
Definitions, HG §3-101.
Disease, HG §3-202.
Fees.
Rules and regulations, HG §3-202.
Governing body of county is ex officio board of health for county, HG §3-201.
Health officers, HG §§3-301 to 3-310.
Annual evaluation, HG §3-305.
Appointment or rejection of nominees, HG §3-302.
Assignments.
Temporary assignment, HG §3-308.
Compensation, HG §3-304.
Conferences, HG §3-309.
Defined, HG §3-101.
Duties.
Generally, HG §3-306.
Evaluation procedures, HG §3-305.
Food and drug samples.
Obtaining, HG §3-306.
Holding multiple offices, HG §3-301.
Nomination procedures, HG §3-302.
Notification of officer in Howard county, HG §3-306.1.
Oaths, HG §3-302.
Offices established, HG §3-301.
Powers and duties.
Generally, HG §3-306.
Qualifications, HG §3-302.
Removal, HG §3-302.
Responsibility to county governing body and secretary, HG §3-302.
Restrictions upon employment, HG §3-303.
Right of entry, HG §3-307.
Secretary.
Delegation of duties, powers and functions to, HG §3-306.
Special appointment status, HG §3-304.
Temporary assignment, HG §3-308.
Inspections.
Health officers, HG §3-307.
Miscellaneous powers and duties, HG §3-202.
Montgomery county, HG §3-310.
Nuisances, HG §3-202.
Powers and duties, HG §3-202.
Right of entry.
Health officers, HG §3-307.
Rules and regulations.
Fees and charges, HG §3-202.
Scope of authority, HG §3-202.
Crab meat.
General provisions, HG §§21-339 to 21-343.
See CRAB MEAT.
Crimes and offenses.
Crimes against public health and safety, CR §§10-101 to 10-111.
ImmuNet program.
Confidentiality violations, HG §18-109.
Crisis response system, HG §§10-1401 to 10-1405.
See MENTAL HEALTH CRISIS RESPONSE SYSTEM.

HEALTH —Cont'd
Cultural competency pilot program, HG §20-1201.
Day-care centers.
Medically handicapped adults, HG §§14-301 to 14-304.
See DAY-CARE CENTERS.
Day-care for the elderly.
General provisions, HG §§14-201 to 14-206.
See DAY-CARE FOR THE ELDERLY.
Deficiencies in services and facilities.
Secretary of health.
Powers, HG §2-108.
Definitions.
Center for the study of the health effects of fire, HG §18-701.
Chronic disease centers, HG §19-501.
Comprehensive physical rehabilitation facilities, HG §19-1201.
Cost review commission, HG §19-201.
Regulated rates, HG §19-220.
County, HG §1-101.
County boards of health, HG §3-101.
Department of health and mental hygiene, HG §1-101.
Board of review, HG §2-201.
Health occupations, HO §1-101.
Discharge, EN §7-201.
Generally, HG §1-101.
Health officer, HG §1-101.
Health planning and development, HG §19-114.
Home health agencies, HG §19-401.
Hospitals, HG §19-301.
ImmuNet program, HG §18-109.
Medical care data collection, HG §19-132.
Medical examiner, HG §1-101.
Officers, EN §1-101.
Person, HG §1-101.
Physician, HG §1-101.
Planning and development.
Aggrieved party, HG §19-128.
Certificates of need, HG §19-120.
Health maintenance organizations, HG §19-121.
Rates.
Regulated rates, HG §19-220.
Receivership of nursing facilities and community residential programs, HG §19-333.
Secretary, HG §1-101.
Special supplemental food program for women, infants and children, HG §18-108.
State, HG §1-101.
User fees, HG §19-213.
Department of health and mental hygiene, HG §§2-101 to 2-305.
See HEALTH AND MENTAL HYGIENE DEPARTMENT.
Department of the environment.
Air quality control, EN §§2-101 to 2-614.
See AIR QUALITY CONTROL.
Drinking water, EN §§9-401 to 9-426.
See DRINKING WATER.
Hazardous substances, EN §§7-101 to 7-306; HG §§22-501 to 22-508.
See HAZARDOUS MATERIALS AND SUBSTANCES.
Noise control, EN §§3-101 to 3-408.
See NOISE CONTROL.
Sanitary commissions, EN §§9-601 to 9-699.
See SANITARY COMMISSIONS.

HEALTH —Cont'd
Department of the environment —Cont'd
  Water and sewer systems.
    See WATER AND SEWER SYSTEMS.
  Water pollution.
    See WATER POLLUTION.
Developmental disabilities, HG §§7-101 to
    7-1201.
  See DEVELOPMENTAL DISABILITIES.
Discovery.
  Center for the study of the health effects of fire.
    Information collected not discoverable, HG
      §18-705.
Diseases.
  County boards of health, HG §3-202.
  General provisions.
    See DISEASES.
District Court.
  Authority of Court provided in health-general
    article, CJ §4-202.
Districts.
  Sanitary districts.
    Commissions, EN §§9-601 to 9-699.
      See SANITARY COMMISSIONS.
    Washington suburban sanitary district.
      See WASHINGTON SUBURBAN SANITARY
        DISTRICT.
Doctors.
  See PHYSICIANS.
Documents.
  Verification, HG §1-201.
Draining lands.
  General provisions as to health and sanitation, 25
    §52.
Drinking water, EN §§9-401 to 9-426.
  See DRINKING WATER.
Drug abuse.
  See DRUG OR ALCOHOL ABUSE.
Drugs.
  Food, drugs and cosmetics, HG §§21-101 to
    21-1215.
    See FOOD, DRUGS AND COSMETICS.
  Generally.
    See DRUGS.
  Hemodialysis drug distribution permits, HO
    §12-603.
**Early childhood mental health services pilot
    program,** HG §§10-1501 to 10-1503.
Elderly persons.
  Day-care for the elderly, HG §§14-201 to 14-206.
    See DAY-CARE FOR THE ELDERLY.
Environmental service, NR §§3-101 to 3-130.
  See ENVIRONMENTAL SERVICE.
Evidence.
  Center for the study of the health effects of fire.
    Information collected inadmissible, HG §18-705.
Exotic birds, HG §§24-101 to 24-110.
  See BIRDS AND GAME.
Federal aid.
  Secretary of health and mental hygiene.
    Applications for federal funds or aid, HG
      §2-104.
Fees.
  Cost review commission.
    Closed or delicensed hospitals, HG §19-223.
  County boards of health.
    Rules and regulations, HG §3-202.
  Secretary of health and mental hygiene, HG
    §2-104.
  User fees.
    Cost review commission.
      Assessment and collection authorized, HG
        §19-213.

HEALTH —Cont'd
Fees —Cont'd
  User fees —Cont'd
    Definitions, HG §19-213.
    Interest penalties, HG §19-213.
Fires and fire prevention.
  Center for the study of the health effects of fire,
    HG §§18-701 to 18-711.
  See FIRES AND FIRE PROTECTION.
Flammable products.
  Maryland flammable products act, HG §§22-401 to
    22-407.
  See FLAMMABLE SUBSTANCES.
Food, drugs and cosmetics, HG §§21-101 to
    21-1215.
  See FOOD, DRUGS AND COSMETICS.
Freestanding ambulatory care facilities, HG
    §§19-3B-01 to 19-3B-09.
  See FREESTANDING AMBULATORY CARE
    FACILITIES.
Freestanding medical facilities, HG §§19-3A-01
    to 19-3A-07.
  See FREESTANDING MEDICAL FACILITIES.
Frozen desserts, HG §§21-801 to 21-821.
  See FROZEN DESSERTS.
Funds.
  Community services trust fund, HG §§24-1101 to
    24-1105.
  Secretary of health and mental hygiene, duties,
    HG §2-104.
Gambling.
  Compulsive gamblers, HG §§19-801 to 19-804.
    See GAMING.
Genetics.
  Hereditary and congenital disorders programs,
    HG §§13-101 to 13-110.
  See HEREDITARY AND CONGENITAL
    DISORDERS PROGRAMS.
Hazardous materials and substances, EN
    §§7-101 to 7-306; HG §§22-501 to 22-508.
  See HAZARDOUS MATERIALS AND
    SUBSTANCES.
Health care facilities.
  Freestanding ambulatory care facilities, HG
    §§19-3B-01 to 19-3B-09.
    See FREESTANDING AMBULATORY CARE
      FACILITIES.
  Hospitals generally.
    See HOSPITALS.
  Planning and development.
    Certificates of need, HG §19-120.
Health maintenance organizations, HG §§19-701
    to 19-735.
  See HEALTH MAINTENANCE
    ORGANIZATIONS.
**Health manpower shortage incentive grant
    program,** ED §18-803.
Health officers, HG §§3-301 to 3-310.
  Contagious diseases.
    Control of diseases.
      General duties, HG §18-208.
    Records to be kept, HG §18-212.
  County boards of health.
    Annual evaluation, HG §3-305.
    Appointment or rejection of nominees, HG
      §3-302.
    Assignments.
      Temporary assignment, HG §3-308.
    Compensation, HG §3-304.
    Conferences, HG §3-309.
    Defined, HG §3-101.

HEALTH —Cont'd
Health officers —Cont'd
County boards of health —Cont'd
Duties.
Generally, HG §3-306.
Evaluation procedures, HG §3-305.
Food and drug samples.
Obtaining, HG §3-306.
Holding multiple offices, HG §3-301.
Nomination procedures, HG §3-302.
Notification of officer in Howard county, HG §3-306.1.
Oaths, HG §3-302.
Offices established, HG §3-301.
Powers and duties.
Generally, HG §3-306.
Qualifications, HG §3-302.
Removal, HG §3-302.
Responsibility to county governing body and secretary, HG §3-302.
Restrictions upon employment, HG §3-303.
Right of entry, HG §3-307.
Secretary.
Delegation of duties, powers and functions to, HG §3-306.
Special appointment status, HG §3-304.
Temporary assignment, HG §3-308.
Dead bodies.
Control of body by health officer, HG §5-506.
Duties.
Contagious diseases.
General duties, HG §18-208.
Mental health services act.
Social workers generally, HO §§19-101 to 19-502.
See SOCIAL WORKERS.
Montgomery county, HG §3-310.
Tuberculosis, HG §§18-322 to 18-325.
Instructions and supplies furnished to health officer, HG §18-323.
Health services cost review commission, HG §§19-201 to 19-227. See within this heading, "Cost review commission."
Hearings.
Cost review commission.
Generally, HG §19-225.
Rates.
Change of rate structures or charges, HG §19-222.
Review and approval of rates and costs, HG §19-219.
Hereditary and congenital disorders programs, HG §§13-101 to 13-110.
See HEREDITARY AND CONGENITAL DISORDERS PROGRAMS.
Home health agencies, HG §§19-401 to 19-410.
See HOME HEALTH AGENCIES.
Hospices, HG §§19-901 to 19-913.
See HOSPICES.
Hospitals.
See HOSPITALS.
Human subject research.
Generally, HG §§13-2001 to 13-2004.
ImmuNet program, HG §18-109.
Immunization.
See IMMUNIZATION.
Indigent persons.
Breast cancer program, HG §20-116.
Medicaid, HG §§15-101 to 15-141.
See MEDICAID.

HEALTH —Cont'd
Injunctions.
Planning and development.
Developments or operation in violation of title, HG §19-127.
Injury reports.
Physicians, pharmacists, dentists and nurses, HG §§20-701 to 20-703.
Insect sting emergency treatment program, HG §§13-701 to 13-709.
See INSECT STING EMERGENCY TREATMENT PROGRAM.
Inspections.
Accreditation of health care facilities, HG §19-2302.
Comprehensive physical rehabilitation facilities, HG §19-1205.
County boards of health.
Health officers, HG §3-307.
Secretary of health and mental hygiene.
Right of entry, HG §2-104.
Insurance.
Credit life, health and unemployment insurance, IN §§13-101 to 13-117.
See CREDIT LIFE, HEALTH AND UNEMPLOYMENT INSURANCE.
Dental plan organizations, IN §§14-401 to 14-418.
See DENTAL PLAN ORGANIZATIONS.
Generally.
See HEALTH INSURANCE.
Long-term care insurance, IN §§18-101 to 18-120.
See LONG-TERM CARE INSURANCE.
Managed care organizations, HG §§15-102.2 to 15-103.
Impairment of provider participation, IN §15-115.
Reports, plans, etc., IN §15-605.
Nonprofit health service plans, IN §§14-101 to 14-140.
See NONPROFIT HEALTH SERVICE PLANS.
Small employer health insurance, IN §§15-1201 to 15-1225.
Investigations.
Cost review commission.
Further investigations.
Authorized, HG §19-226.
Generally, HG §19-225.
Department of health and mental hygiene.
Board of review.
Complaints, HG §2-207.
Disease prevention.
General responsibilities of secretary, HG §18-101.
Jurisdiction.
Cost review commission, HG §19-211.
Kidney diseases.
General provisions, HG §§13-301 to 13-316.
See KIDNEY DISEASES.
Laboratories.
Medical laboratories, HG §§17-201 to 17-217.
See LABORATORIES.
Public laboratories, HG §§17-101 to 17-103.
See LABORATORIES.
Tissue banks, HG §§17-301 to 17-314.
See TISSUE BANKS.
Water quality laboratories, EN §§9-1001 to 9-1027.
See WATER QUALITY LABORATORIES.
Licenses.
Comprehensive physical rehabilitation facilities, HG §§19-1201 to 19-1208.
See COMPREHENSIVE PHYSICAL REHABILITATION FACILITIES.

HEALTH —Cont'd
Licenses —Cont'd
Hospitals.
See HOSPITALS.
Livestock.
Avian influenza, regulation to control, AG §§3-801 to 3-805.
Contagious and infectious diseases, AG §§3-101 to 3-117.
See LIVESTOCK.
Local boards.
Chartered counties, 25A §5.
Local health services funding, HG §2-301.
Adjustments in funding, HG §2-302.
Amount, HG §2-302.
Funds transfers prohibited, HG §2-305.
Local matching funds, HG §2-303.
Matching funds, HG §2-303.
Programs, HG §2-304.
Services to be provided, HG §2-304.
Transfer of funds prohibited, HG §2-305.
Malpractice, CJ §§3-2A-01 to 3-2A-10; SpecPro Rules 15-401 to 15-403.
See MALPRACTICE.
Maryland commission for men's health, HG §§13-2401 to 13-2408.
Maryland mental health crisis response system, HG §§10-1401 to 10-1405.
See MENTAL HEALTH CRISIS RESPONSE SYSTEM.
Maryland trauma physician services fund, HG §19-130.
Medicaid, HG §§15-101 to 15-141.
See MEDICAID.
Medically handicapped adults.
Day-care centers, HG §§14-301 to 14-304.
See DAY-CARE CENTERS.
Medical malpractice, CJ §§3-2A-01 to 3-2A-10; SpecPro Rules 15-401 to 15-403.
See MALPRACTICE.
Men's health.
Maryland commission for men's health, HG §§13-2401 to 13-2408.
Mental health crisis response system, HG §§10-1401 to 10-1405.
See MENTAL HEALTH CRISIS RESPONSE SYSTEM.
Mental health facilities.
See MENTAL HEALTH FACILITIES.
Mental health services.
Community mental health services, HG §§10-901 to 10-905.
See COMMUNITY MENTAL HEALTH SERVICES.
Mental hygiene law, HG §§10-101 to 10-1203.
Mentally ill.
See MENTALLY ILL.
Mental retardation.
Developmental disabilities.
See DEVELOPMENTAL DISABILITIES.
Milk and milk products, HG §§21-401 to 21-436.
See MILK AND MILK PRODUCTS.
Mining, EN §§15-101 to 15-1109.
See MINING.
Minorities.
Office of minority health and health disparities, HG §§20-1001 to 20-1007.
Minors.
Administrative procedure act.
Submission of proposed regulations for impact on children's environmental health, SG §10-110.

HEALTH —Cont'd
Minors —Cont'd
Diseases.
Secretary of health and mental hygiene.
General responsibilities of secretary for disease prevention, HG §18-107.
Special supplemental food program for women, infants and children, HG §18-108.
Misdemeanors.
Chronic disease centers.
Alcoholic beverage violations, HG §19-513.
Comprehensive physical rehabilitation facilities, HG §19-1208.
Cost review commission.
Report of transactions with nonprofit facilities.
Willful failure to file, HG §19-224.
Freestanding medical facilities, HG §19-3A-01.
Home health agencies.
Operating without license, HG §19-409.
Residential service agencies.
Operating in violation of regulations, HG §19-4A-09.
Operating without license, HG §19-4A-08.
Mosquito control, AG §§5-401 to 5-405.
See MOSQUITO CONTROL.
Municipal corporations.
Assistance to other political subdivisions authorized, 23A §8C.
Department of health and mental hygiene.
Powers as to, 23A §2.
Home rule.
Powers as to, 23A §31.
Regulations.
Powers as to, 23A §2.
Noise control, EN §§3-101 to 3-408.
See NOISE CONTROL.
Nonprofit health service plans, IN §§14-101 to 14-140.
See NONPROFIT HEALTH SERVICE PLANS.
Notice.
Centers for disease control.
Explanation of guidelines on universal precautions, HO §1-207.
Cost review commission.
Change of rate structures or charges, HG §19-222.
Department of health and mental hygiene.
Appeals from board of review, HG §2-207.
Notification of certain financial transactions, contracts or agreements, HG §19-217.
Nuisances.
County boards of health, HG §3-202.
Secretary of health and mental hygiene or local health officers, HG §§20-310 to 20-314.
See NUISANCES.
Nursing referral service agencies, HG §§19-4B-01 to 19-4B-06.
Oaths.
Cost review commission.
Hearings and investigations, HG §19-225.
County boards of health.
Officers, HG §3-302.
Department of health and mental hygiene.
Board of review, HG §2-207.
Secretary of health and mental hygiene, HG §2-104.
Administration of oaths, HG §2-104.
Occupational deafness, LE §§9-649 to 9-652.
See WORKERS' COMPENSATION.
Occupational diseases.
See WORKERS' COMPENSATION.

HEALTH —Cont'd
Occupational safety and health.
General provisions, LE §§5-101 to 5-901.
See OCCUPATIONAL SAFETY AND HEALTH.
Railroad employees, LE §§5.5-101 to 5.5-123.
See RAILROAD SAFETY AND HEALTH.
Office of minority health and health
disparities, HG §§20-1001 to 20-1007.
Osteoporosis.
Prevention and education task force, HG
§§13-1901 to 13-1906.
Parties.
Cost review commission appeals, HG §19-227.
Patient referrals, HO §§1-301 to 1-306.
Beneficial interest disclosure.
Form and content, HO §1-303.
Required, HO §1-303.
Third party payors.
Failure to comply, HO §1-304.
Definitions, HO §1-301.
Financial interest disclosure.
Third party payors, HO §1-304.
Health care practitioners, HO §1-306.
Prohibited referrals, HO §1-305; IN §15-110.
Disclosures, HO §1-302.
HMO claims resulting from prohibited referral,
HG §19-712.4.
Uniform consultation referral forms, IN §§15-119,
15-120.
Penalties.
Confidential records, HG §4-103.
User fees.
Interest penalties, HG §19-213.
Perjury.
Verification of documents, HG §1-201.
Pertussis, HG §§18-328 to 18-332.
See PERTUSSIS.
Pesticides.
Registration and labeling law, AG §§5-101 to
5-114.
See PESTICIDES.
Physical fitness, HG §§13-401 to 13-410.
See PHYSICAL FITNESS.
Physicians.
See PHYSICIANS.
Planning and development.
Administrative decisions.
Appeals, HG §19-128.
Ambulatory care facilities.
Certificates of need, HG §19-125.
Ambulatory surgical facility.
Defined, HG §19-114.
Appeals.
Administrative decisions, HG §19-128.
Certificates of need.
Ambulatory care facilities, HG §19-125.
Applications.
Action on applications, HG §19-126.
Defined, HG §19-114.
Health care facilities, HG §19-120.
Health maintenance organizations, HG §19-121.
Issuance.
Action on applications, HG §19-126.
Notice of filing of application, HG §19-126.
Commission.
Program evaluation act, SG §8-403.
Consolidation of hospitals, HG §19-129.
Continuing care community.
Comprehensive care nursing bed, admission
into, HG §19-124.

HEALTH —Cont'd
Planning and development —Cont'd
Continuing care community —Cont'd
Exemption from certificate of need requirement,
loss, HG §19-123.
Deficiencies in services and facilities.
Secretary of health.
Powers, HG §2-108.
Definitions, HG §19-114.
Aggrieved party, HG §19-128.
Certificates of need, HG §19-120.
Health maintenance organizations, HG
§19-121.
Domiciliary care projects.
Certificates of need.
Not required, HG §19-122.
Governor.
Health service areas.
Designation, HG §19-117.
Health care commission.
Appeal of administrative decisions, HG §19-128.
Certificates of need.
Action on applications, HG §19-126.
Duties, HG §§19-115, 19-116.
Institution-specific plan, HG §19-119.
State health plan, HG §19-118.
Health care facilities.
Certificates of need, HG §19-120.
Defined, HG §19-114.
Health maintenance organizations.
Certificates of need, HG §19-121.
Health service areas.
Defined, HG §19-114.
Designation, HG §19-117.
Injunctions.
Developments or operations in violation of title,
HG §19-127.
Institution-specific plan.
Contents, HG §19-119.
Duty of commission, HG §19-119.
Priorities, HG §19-119.
Use of plan, HG §19-119.
Local health planning agencies.
Defined, HG §19-114.
Establishment, HG §19-120.
Powers and duties, HG §19-120.
Proposed program and budgetary proprietaries,
HG §19-119.
Maryland trauma physician services fund, HG
§19-130.
Merger or consolidation of hospitals, HG §19-129.
Secretary of health and mental hygiene.
Systems capacity in health services.
Studies, HG §19-116.
State health plan, HG §19-118.
Defined, HG §19-114.
Systems capacity in health services.
Studies, HG §19-116.
Trauma physician services fund, HG §19-130.
Plant disease control, AG §§5-301 to 5-314.
See PLANT DISEASE CONTROL.
Poor.
Breast cancer program, HG §20-116.
Medicaid, HG §§15-101 to 15-141.
See MEDICAID.
Poultry.
Avian influenza, regulation to control, AG §§3-801
to 3-805.
Contagious and infectious diseases, AG §§3-101 to
3-117.
See LIVESTOCK.

HEALTH —Cont'd
Poultry products inspection, AG §§4-201 to 4-230.1.
  See POULTRY PRODUCTS INSPECTION.
Pregnancy.
  Generally.
    See PREGNANCY.
Primary adult care network.
  Medicaid, HG §15-140.
Primary drinking water regulations, EN §§9-401 to 9-426.
  See DRINKING WATER.
Privileged communications.
  Center for the study of the health effects of fire.
    Information collection confidential, HG §18-705.
Procurement.
  Local health departments, SF §12-109.
Prophylactics.
  Sale of condoms by vending machines or other devices, HG §18-335.
Quality care at the end of life.
  State advisory council, HG §§13-1601 to 13-1604.
Quarantine.
  General provisions.
    See QUARANTINE.
Rabies, HG §§18-312 to 18-320.
  See RABIES.
Radiation.
  General provisions, EN §§8-101 to 8-601.
    See RADIATION.
  Hazardous materials and substances, EN §§7-101 to 7-306; HG §§22-501 to 22-508.
    See HAZARDOUS MATERIALS AND SUBSTANCES.
Railroad employees.
  Occupational safety and safety, LE §§5.5-101 to 5.5-123.
    See RAILROAD SAFETY AND HEALTH.
Rates.
  Cost review commission.
    Accounting principles for rate determinations, HG §19-221.
    Alternate rate setting methods, HG §19-219.
    Change of rate structures or charges, HG §19-222.
    Compilation of rate structures, HG §19-220.
    Financial status, HG §19-212.
    Procedures for review and approval, HG §19-220.
    Rate setting restricted, HG §19-211.
    Reasonableness of rates, HG §19-220.
    Review and approval of rates and costs, HG §19-219.
Records.
  Confidential records.
    Defined, HG §4-101.
    Penalties, HG §4-103.
    Protection, HG §4-102.
    Use and custody restricted, HG §4-102.
  Cost review commission, HG §19-207.
  Department of health and mental hygiene.
    Archives.
      Vital records, SG §9-1015.
  Verification of documents, HG §1-201.
Reports.
  Cost review commission.
    Additional information, HG §19-218.
    Annual report, HG §19-207.
    Required reports of facilities, HG §19-216.
    Transactions with nonprofit facilities, HG §19-224.

HEALTH —Cont'd
Reports —Cont'd
  Cost review commission —Cont'd
    Uniform accounting and financial reporting system, HG §19-215.
  Department of health and mental hygiene.
    Board of review.
      Annual report, HG §2-206.
    Hepatitis C virus, HG §18-1002.
  Injury reports.
    Physicians, pharmacists, dentists and nurses, HG §§20-701 to 20-703.
  Secretary of health and mental hygiene.
    Units in department, HG §2-104.
  Sickle cell anemia.
    Adult sickle cell anemia, HG §20-1101.
  Verification of documents, HG §1-201.
Residential service agencies, HG §§19-4A-01 to 19-4A-10.
  See RESIDENTIAL SERVICE AGENCIES.
Right of entry.
  County boards of health.
    Health officers, HG §3-307.
  Secretary of health and mental hygiene, HG §2-104.
  Inspections, HG §2-104.
Sales and use tax.
  Exemptions.
    Health and physical aids, TG §11-211.
Sanitary commissions.
  Department of the environment.
    Powers not limited, EN §9-604.
Schools.
  Alcohol abuse.
    Program of health education, ED §7-413.
  Centers for disease control system survey.
    Administration and parental information, ED §7-420.
  Development of public standards and guidelines, ED §7-401.
  Duty of county boards, ED §7-401.
  Hearing and vision screening tests, ED §7-404.
  School health program, ED §7-415.
  School health services program coordinator, ED §7-401.
  Vaccination of pupils, ED §7-403.
Seals.
  Secretary of health and mental hygiene, HG §2-104.
Secretary of the environment.
  Air pollution emergencies.
    Secretary to advise governor, EN §2-105.
  Disease prevention.
    Occupational diseases, EN §6-701.
  Drainage.
    Rules and regulations, EN §10-103.
  Drinking water, EN §§9-401 to 9-426.
    See DRINKING WATER.
  Hazardous materials and substances, EN §§7-101 to 7-306; HG §§22-501 to 22-508.
    See HAZARDOUS MATERIALS AND SUBSTANCES.
  Occupational diseases.
    General responsibilities of secretary for disease prevention, EN §6-701.
  Plumbing.
    Rules and regulations, EN §10-103.
  Right of entry, EN §10-104.
  Sanitary interests of state, EN §10-101.
  Streets.
    Rules and regulations, EN §10-103.

HEALTH —Cont'd
Secretary of the environment —Cont'd
Water supply.
Rules and regulations, EN §10-103.
Septic systems, EN §§9-1401 to 9-1406.
See SEPTIC SYSTEMS.
Services cost review commission. See within
this heading, "Cost review commission."
Sewer systems.
See WATER AND SEWER SYSTEMS.
Sickle cell anemia, HG §§18-501 to 18-505.
See SICKLE CELL ANEMIA.
**Special supplemental food program for
women, infants and children,** HG §18-108.
Stem cell research program, 83A §§5-2B-01 to
5-2B-13.
See STEM CELL RESEARCH.
Subpoenas.
Secretary of health and mental hygiene, HG
§2-104.
Summons and process.
Secretary of health and mental hygiene, HG
§2-104.
Testimony.
Secretary of health and mental hygiene, HG
§2-104.
Tests.
Cholesterol testing, HG §§17-501 to 17-511.
See CHOLESTEROL TESTING.
Tissue banks, HG §§17-301 to 17-314.
See TISSUE BANKS.
Trauma physician services fund, HG §19-130.
Tuberculosis, HG §§18-322 to 18-325.
See TUBERCULOSIS.
Vaccination.
See VACCINATION.
Verification of documents, HG §1-201.
Veterinarians.
See VETERINARIANS.
Water and sewer systems.
See WATER AND SEWER SYSTEMS.
Water pollution.
See WATER POLLUTION.
Water quality laboratories, EN §§9-1001 to
9-1027.
See WATER QUALITY LABORATORIES.
Well drilling, EN §§9-1301 to 9-1311.
See WELL DRILLING.
Wholesome meat act, AG §§4-101 to 4-131.
See WHOLESOME MEAT ACT.
Witnesses.
Department of health and mental hygiene.
Board of review, HG §2-207.
Subpoenas, oaths and testimony, HG §2-104.
Women.
Pregnancy.
Secretary of health and mental hygiene.
General responsibilities of secretary for
disease prevention, HG §18-107.
Special supplemental food program for women,
infants and children, HG §18-108.
Workers' compensation.
Compliance with workers' compensation act, HG
§1-202.
General provisions, LE §§9-101 to 10-320.
See WORKERS' COMPENSATION.
Occupational diseases.
Secretary of health and mental hygiene.
General responsibilities of secretary for
disease prevention, EN §6-701.

**HEALTH AND HIGHER EDUCATIONAL
FACILITIES AUTHORITY,** 43C §§1 to 24.
Acquisition of property, 43C §7.
Appointment, 43C §4.
Attorneys at law, 43C §4.
Audit.
Annual audit, 43C §20.
Authority.
Defined, 43C §3.
Bond issues.
Bond anticipation notes, 43C §11.
Bondholders.
Enforcement of rights and duties, 43C §16.
Defined, 43C §3.
General provisions, 43C §11.
Investments.
Declared legal investments, 43C §19.
Issuance of notes, 43C §10.
Not debt or liability of state or political
subdivision, 43C §13.
Payment, 43C §13.
Program for closed or delicensed hospitals, 43C
§16A.
Refunding bonds, 43C §18.
Sinking fund, 43C §14.
Tax exemption, 43C §17.
Trust agreement securing bonds, 43C §12.
Use of bond proceeds and revenues, 43C §15.
Bonds, surety.
Each member of authority, 43C §4.
Chairman, 43C §4.
Charges, 43C §14.
Citation.
Short title, 43C §1.
Collateral.
Release of collateral, 43C §9.
Compensation, 43C §4.
Composition, 43C §4.
Construction.
Defined, 43C §3.
Construction and interpretation, 43C §23.
Cost.
Defined, 43C §3.
Creation, 43C §4.
Definitions, 43C §3.
Director, 43C §4.
Enforcement of rights and duties, 43C §16.
Executive director, 43C §4.
Existence.
Termination of existence of authority, 43C §21.
Expenses, 43C §4.
Payment, 43C §6.
Fees, 43C §14.
General counsel, 43C §4.
Governor.
Appointment, 43C §4.
Hospitals.
Defined, 43C §3.
Program for closed or delicensed hospitals, 43C
§16A.
Institution for higher education.
Defined, 43C §3.
Interpretation and construction, 43C §23.
Investments.
Bonds declared legal investments, 43C §19.
Oaths, 43C §4.
Officers, 43C §4.
Participating hospital.
Defined, 43C §3.
**Participating institutions for higher
education.**
Defined, 43C §3.

HEALTH AND HIGHER EDUCATIONAL FACILITIES AUTHORITY —Cont'd

Policy.

Declaration of policy, 43C §2.

Powers.

Additional and supplemental, 43C §22.

General provisions, 43C §5.

Projects.

Conveyance of title to projects to participating institutions or hospitals, 43C §8.

Defined, 43C §3.

Quorum, 43C §4.

Rates.

General provisions, 43C §14.

Records.

Inspection, 43C §4.

Rents.

General provisions, 43C §14.

Reports.

Annual report to governor, 43C §20.

Resolutions, 43C §4.

Scope of article, 43C §22.

Severability, 43C §24.

Sinking fund, 43C §14.

Surety bonds, 43C §4.

Tax exemption, 43C §17.

Termination of existence, 43C §21.

Terms of office, 43C §4.

Trusts and trustees.

Agreement securing bonds, 43C §12.

Vacancies, 43C §4.

HEALTH AND HUMAN SERVICES REFERRAL SYSTEM, HG §§24-1201 to 24-1205.

HEALTH AND MENTAL HYGIENE DEPARTMENT, HG §§2-101 to 2-305.

Abatement of nuisances.

Secretary of health and mental hygiene or local health officers, HG §§20-310 to 20-314.

See NUISANCES.

Acquired immune deficiency syndrome (AIDS).

Insurance assistance pilot program, HG §§15-201 to 15-205.

See ACQUIRED IMMUNE DEFICIENCY SYNDROME (AIDS).

Appeals.

Board of review. See within this heading, "Board of review."

Investigation of complaint, HG §2-207.

Notice of appeal to department, HG §2-207.

Procedures for review, HG §2-207.

Archives.

Vital records, SG §9-1015.

Assisted living programs.

Duties, HG §§19-1804, 19-1805.

Grants to facilities, HG §§24-1001 to 24-1007.

License renewal, acceptance of reports from accredited organization, HG §19-1805.

Regulations, HG §19-1805.

Supervision and monitoring, HG §19-1802.

Attorney general as legal adviser, HG §2-107.

Board of review, HG §§2-201 to 2-207.

Annual report, HG §2-206.

Appeals to be heard and determined by board, HG §§2-206, 2-207.

Appointments, HG §2-203.

Chairman, HG §2-204.

Compensation, HG §2-205.

Composition, HG §2-203.

Defined, HG §2-201.

Disqualification of member, HG §2-206.

HEALTH AND MENTAL HYGIENE DEPARTMENT —Cont'd

Board of review —Cont'd

Duties.

Generally, HG §2-206.

Established, HG §2-202.

Meetings, HG §2-205.

Membership, HG §2-203.

Oaths, HG §2-207.

Powers and duties.

Generally, HG §2-206.

Procedures for review, HG §2-207.

Removal of members, HG §2-203.

Right of appeal, HG §2-207.

Staff, HG §2-205.

Tenure, HG §2-203.

Terms, HG §2-203.

Vacancies, HG §2-203.

Witnesses, HG §2-207.

Board of spinal injury research, HG §§13-1401 to 13-1407.

See SPINAL INJURY RESEARCH.

Breast cancer.

Alternative methods of treatment.

Duties of department, HG §20-113.

Cancer prevention, education, screening and treatment program, HG §§13-1101 to 13-1119.

See CANCER PREVENTION, EDUCATION, SCREENING AND TREATMENT PROGRAM.

Children's environmental health and protection advisory council, HG §§13-1501 to 13-1506.

See CHILDREN'S ENVIRONMENTAL HEALTH AND PROTECTION ADVISORY COUNCIL.

Community services reimbursement rate commission.

Community services rate commission, HG §§13-801 to 13-810.

See COMMUNITY SERVICES REIMBURSEMENT RATE COMMISSION.

Controlled dangerous substances.

Generally, CR §§5-101 to 5-1101.

See CONTROLLED DANGEROUS SUBSTANCES.

Powers and responsibilities, CR §§5-201 to 5-204.

Registration of manufacturers, dispensers and distributors, CR §§5-301 to 5-310.

Counsel to department, HG §2-107.

Created, HG §2-101.

Criminal proceedings.

Incompetency or not criminally responsible proceedings.

Adoption of rules relating to department, CP §3-102.

Incompetency to stand trial.

Examination of defendant, duties, report, CP §3-105.

Generally, CP §§3-101 to 3-108.

Report by health department on person ordered committed, CP §3-108.

Not criminally responsible.

Commitment of person not criminally responsible to department, CP §3-112.

Conditional release of committed person, application by department, CP §3-120.

Examination of defendant, duties, report, CP §3-111.

Generally, CP §§3-109 to 3-123.

Day-care centers.

Medically handicapped adults, HG §14-304.

Funds.

Use of appropriated funds, HG §14-205.

HEALTH AND MENTAL HYGIENE DEPARTMENT —Cont'd
Day-care centers —Cont'd
Medically handicapped adults —Cont'd
Responsibilities.
General responsibilities, HG §14-204.
Decedents' estates.
Escheat, ET §3-105.
Defined, HG §1-101.
Escheat in intestate successions, ET §3-105.
Established, HG §2-101.
Folic acid supplement distribution program, HG §§13-2301 to 13-2303.
Health insurance.
Reimbursement of department for services paid, IN §15-603.
Health program integrity and recovery activities, HG §§2-501 to 2-505.
Actions by employees, HG §2-505.
Definitions, HG §2-501.
Duties of providers, HG §2-505.
Immunity from civil liability, HG §2-505.
Inspector general, HG §§2-502 to 2-504.
Prohibited acts by providers, HG §2-505.
Hepatitis C virus.
Duties regarding, HG §§18-1001, 18-1002.
Home health agencies, HG §§19-401 to 19-410.
See HOME HEALTH AGENCIES.
Hospitals.
See HOSPITALS.
Incompetency or not criminally responsible proceedings.
Adoption of rules relating to department, CP §3-102.
Incompetency to stand trial.
Examination by department, duties, report, CP §3-105.
Generally, CP §§3-101 to 3-108.
See INCOMPETENCY TO STAND TRIAL.
Report by health department on person ordered committed, CP §3-108.
Not criminally responsible.
Commitment of person not criminally responsible to department, CP §3-112.
Conditional release of committed person, application by department, CP §3-120.
Examination of defendant, duties, report, CP §3-111.
Generally, CP §§3-109 to 3-123.
See NOT CRIMINALLY RESPONSIBLE.
Insect sting emergency treatment program, HG §§13-701 to 13-709.
See INSECT STING EMERGENCY TREATMENT PROGRAM.
Inspector general, HG §§2-502 to 2-504.
Duties, HG §§2-503, 2-504.
Office established, HG §2-502.
Integration of child welfare and substance abuse services, FL §§5-1201 to 5-1209.
See CHILD WELFARE AND SUBSTANCE ABUSE SERVICES, INTEGRATION.
Judicial review, HG §2-207.
Juvenile causes.
Committing child to custody of department for inpatient care and treatment, CJ §3-8A-19.
Maryland commission for men's health, HG §§13-2401 to 13-2408.
Mentally ill.
See MENTALLY ILL.
Minorities.
Office of minority health and health disparities, HG §§20-1001 to 20-1007.

HEALTH AND MENTAL HYGIENE DEPARTMENT —Cont'd
Nuisances.
Secretary of health and mental hygiene or local health officers, HG §§20-310 to 20-314.
See NUISANCES.
Nursing homes.
Quality assurance, HG §§19-1401 to 19-1417.
See NURSING HOMES.
Office of health care quality.
Nursing staff agencies, HG §19-2002.
Office of minority health and health disparities, HG §§20-1001 to 20-1007.
Oral health program.
Prevention and detection of oral cancer, HG §§18-801 to 18-803.
Police force.
Law enforcement officers generally, PS §§3-101 to 3-603.
See LAW ENFORCEMENT OFFICERS AND PERSONNEL.
Postmortem examiners.
See POSTMORTEM EXAMINERS.
Schools.
Hearing and vision screenings.
Rules and regulations, ED §7-404.
Units in department, HG §2-106.
Vaccination of pupils, ED §7-403.
Secretary of health and mental hygiene.
Additional staff, HG §2-103.
Administration of department, HG §2-102.
Advisory board, HG §2-104.
Advisory councils, HG §2-104.
Agricultural ombudsman, HG §2-104.
Appointment, HG §2-102.
Budgets.
General authority and duties of secretary, HG §2-104.
Cancer.
General responsibilities of secretary for disease prevention, HG §18-104.
Childhood diseases.
General responsibilities of secretary, HG §18-107.
Communicable diseases.
General responsibilities of secretary, HG §18-103.
Community services reimbursement rate commission.
Authority of secretary, HG §13-808.
Consultants, HG §2-103.
Contagious diseases.
General responsibilities of secretary, HG §18-102.
Cost review commission.
Limitation on secretary, HG §19-208.
County boards of health.
Delegation of duties, powers and functions to health officers, HG §3-306.
Deficiencies in services and facilities.
Powers of secretary, HG §2-108.
Defined, HG §1-101.
Deputy secretaries, HG §2-103.
Determination of staff to resident ratio, HG §2-103.
Developmental disabilities.
See DEVELOPMENTAL DISABILITIES.
Disease prevention, HG §§18-101 to 18-109.
Cancer, HG §18-104.
Childhood diseases, HG §18-107.
Communicable diseases, HG §18-103.

HEALTH AND MENTAL HYGIENE
  DEPARTMENT —Cont'd
Secretary of health and mental hygiene
  —Cont'd
Disease prevention —Cont'd
  Contagious diseases, HG §18-102.
  Infectious diseases, HG §18-102.
  Investigation into causes of disease and
    mortality, HG §18-101.
  Lead poisoning screening program, HG §18-106.
  Pregnancy and childhood diseases, HG §18-107.
  Toxic substances, HG §18-105.
Disposition of funds, HG §2-104.
Drainage rules and regulations, HG §20-303.
Duties.
  Establishment of general policy, HG §2-105.
  Generally, HG §2-104.
  Potomac river.
    Recreational use, NR §1-605.
Enforcement of provisions, HG §2-104.
Establishment of general policy, HG §2-105.
Exotic birds, HG §§24-101 to 24-110.
  See BIRDS AND GAME.
Federal funds, HG §2-104.
Fish and fisheries.
  Collection of fish, fish eggs, crustaceans or
    mollusks for scientific purposes.
    Effect of subtitle on authority of secretary,
      NR §4-212.
Funds, HG §2-104.
General authority and duties of secretary, HG
  §2-104.
Health planning and development.
  Systems capacity in health services.
    Studies, HG §19-116.
Infectious diseases.
  General responsibilities of secretary, HG
    §18-102.
Inspections.
  Right of entry, HG §2-104.
    Infectious and contagious diseases, HG
      §18-102.
Investigations.
  Causes of disease and mortality, HG §18-101.
Lead poisoning screening program, HG §18-106.
Mental hygiene law.
  Authority, HG §10-203.
  Community residential mental health programs
    for children and adolescents.
    Rules and regulations, HG §10-922.
Nuisances.
  Secretary of health and mental hygiene or local
    health officers, HG §§20-310 to 20-314.
  See NUISANCES.
Oaths, HG §2-104.
Planning and development.
  Plans, proposals and projects, HG §2-104.
  Staff, functions and funds, HG §2-104.
Plumbing.
  Rules and regulations.
    Adoption by secretary, HG §20-303.
Policies.
  Establishment of general policy, HG §2-105.
Position, HG §2-102.
Potomac river, recreational use.
  Powers and duties, NR §1-605.
Powers.
  Acquired immune deficiency syndrome (AIDS).
    Research and information program, HG
      §18-333.
  Authority over units in department, HG §2-106.

HEALTH AND MENTAL HYGIENE
  DEPARTMENT —Cont'd
Secretary of health and mental hygiene
  —Cont'd
Powers —Cont'd
  Establishment of general policy, HG §2-105.
  Generally, HG §2-104.
Pregnancy and childhood diseases.
  General responsibilities of secretary, HG
    §18-107.
Rabies.
  General provisions, HG §§18-312 to 18-320.
    See RABIES.
  Statewide system provided by secretary, HG
    §18-313.
Reports.
  Units in department, HG §2-104.
Responsibility to governor, HG §2-102.
Right of entry.
  Authority to enter and inspect private property,
    HG §20-304.
  Inspections, HG §2-104.
    Infectious and contagious diseases, HG
      §18-102.
Rules and regulations.
  Adoption and promulgation, HG §2-104.
Salary, HG §2-102.
Schools.
  Vaccination of pupils.
    Powers of secretary, ED §7-403.
Seal, HG §2-104.
Staff, HG §2-103.
  Personnel at grade 18 and above.
    Conflict of interest prohibited, HG §2-103.
    Disclosure of other employment and
      compensation required, HG §2-103.
Streets.
  Rules and regulations, HG §20-303.
Subpoenas, HG §2-104.
Testimony, HG §2-104.
Toxic substances.
  General responsibilities of secretary for disease
    prevention, HG §18-105.
Transfer of functions, staff or funds, HG §2-104.
Units in department.
  Secretary's authority over units, HG §2-106.
Water supply.
  Rules and regulations.
    Adoption by secretary, HG §20-303.
Witnesses.
  Subpoenas, oaths and testimony, HG §2-104.
Spinal cord injury research.
State board, HG §§13-1401 to 13-1407.
  See SPINAL INJURY RESEARCH.
State board of spinal injury research, HG
  §§13-1401 to 13-1407.
See SPINAL INJURY RESEARCH.
Stem cell research program, 83A §§5-2B-01 to
  5-2B-13.
See STEM CELL RESEARCH.
Tobacco-related diseases.
Cancer prevention, education, screening and
  treatment program.
  Generally, HG §§13-1101 to 13-1119.
    See CANCER PREVENTION, EDUCATION,
      SCREENING AND TREATMENT
      PROGRAM.
Tobacco use prevention and cessation
  program, HG §§13-1001 to 13-1015.
See TOBACCO USE PREVENTION AND
  CESSATION PROGRAM.

HEALTH AND MENTAL HYGIENE DEPARTMENT —Cont'd
Units in department, HG §2-106.
Vital records.
  Archives, SG §9-1015.
Voter registration information.
  Individuals reported deceased within state.
    Report of names to state board of elections, EL §3-504.

HEALTH CARE COMMISSION, HG §§19-101 to 19-111.
See MARYLAND HEALTH CARE COMMISSION.

HEALTH CARE DECISIONS.
Absence of directive.
  No presumption as to consent to or refusal of life-sustaining procedures, HG §5-602.
Actions by health care providers, HG §5-612.
Advance directive.
  Anatomical gifts, HG §5-604.1.
  Directive executed before effective date, HG §5-616.
  Effect of making directive on life insurance, HG §5-614.
  Form, HG §5-603.
  Medicaid.
    Plan for dissemination of advance directive information, HG §15-109.1.
  Mental health services, HG §5-602.1.
  Patient who refuses to comply with transfer by health care provider, HG §5-613.
  Procedure for making, HG §5-602.
  Revocation, HG §5-604.
  Transfer, patient's plan of care, HG §5-602.
  Willful destruction, concealment, etc., HG §5-610.
Advance directive registry, HG §§5-619 to 5-626.
  Administration, HG §5-622.
  Amendment or revocation of advance directive.
    Notification, HG §5-623.
  Database, HG §5-624.
  Definitions, HG §5-619.
  Established, HG §5-620.
  Fees, HG §5-622.
  Immunity of health care providers from liability, HG §5-626.
  Registration, HG §5-623.
  Regulations, HG §5-621.
  Requirements of advance directive, HG §5-625.
Anatomical gifts.
  Advance directives, HG §5-604.1.
Burden of proof, HG §5-609.
Certification of condition, HG §5-606.
Certification of incapacity, HG §5-606.
Certification that patient incapable of making informed decision.
  Directive becomes effective on, HG §5-602.
Citation of subtitle.
  Short title, HG §5-618.
Construction and interpretation, HG §5-611.
Declarations made prior to effective date of act, HG §5-614.
Definitions, HG §5-601.
  Advance directive registry, HG §5-619.
  Health care facility.
    Provision of information, HG §5-615.
  Surrogate decision making, HG §5-605.
Dental plan organizations.
  Disbursement of advance directive information sheet by carrier, IN §15-122.1.
Do not resuscitate orders.
  Authorization to follow in outpatient setting, HG §5-608.

HEALTH CARE DECISIONS —Cont'd
Ethically inappropriate treatment, HG §5-611.
Euthanasia.
  Prohibited, HG §5-611.
Existence of directive, notice to physician, HG §5-602.
Forms.
  Advance directive, HG §5-603.
  Information sheet, HG §5-615.
  Patient's plan of care, HG §5-608.1.
Guardian and ward.
  Defined, ET §13-711.
  Withholding or withdrawal, ET §13-712; HG §5-605.
    Best interest determination, ET §13-713.
    Defined, ET §13-711.
Immunity, HG §5-609.
  Advance directive registry.
    Immunity of health care providers from liability, HG §5-626.
Information sheet.
  Forms, HG §5-615.
Information to be provided to individuals on admittance to facility, HG §5-615.
Insurance.
  Effect of making advance directive on life insurance, HG §5-614.
  Malpractice insurance, IN §19-104.
Life-sustaining procedures.
  Disabled persons, ET §§13-711 to 13-713.
Malpractice insurance, IN §19-104.
Medicaid.
  Plan for dissemination of advance directive information, HG §15-109.1.
Medically ineffective treatment, HG §5-611.
Medical treatment without consent, HG §5-607.
Mercy killing.
  Prohibited, HG §5-611.
Nonprofit health service plans.
  Disbursement of advance directive information sheet by carrier, IN §15-122.1.
Notice to health care agent.
  Person named as agent in directive, HG §5-602.
Notice to physicians, HG §5-602.
Oral advance directive.
  Procedure for making, HG §5-602.
Owner, operator or employee of health care facility.
  Serving as health care agent, HG §5-602.
Patient's plan of care.
  Form, HG §5-608.1.
  Medicaid.
    Plan for dissemination of advance directive information, HG §15-109.1.
  Transfer of patient, HG §5-602.
Patient who refuses to comply with advance directive or treatment decision.
  Transfer of patient by health care provider, HG §5-613.
Petitions by health care providers, HG §5-612.
Preservation of existing rights, HG §5-616.
Presumptions, HG §5-609.
Reciprocities, HG §5-617.
Revocation of directive, HG §5-604.
Short title, HG §5-618.
Suicide.
  Withholding or withdrawing life sustaining procedures, HG §5-614.
Surrogate decision making, HG §5-605.
  Guardians for disabled persons, ET §§13-708, 13-711 to 13-713.

HEALTH CARE DECISIONS —Cont'd
Transfer of patient.
Patient's plan of care, HG §5-602.
Form, HG §5-608.1.
Treatment without consent, HG §5-607.
Witnesses to written directive, HG §5-602.
Written advance directive.
Directive executed before effective date, HG §5-616.
Effect of making directive on life insurance, HG §5-614.
Patient who refuses to comply with.
Transfer of patient by health care provider, HG §5-613.
Procedure for making, HG §5-602.
Revocation, HG §5-604.
Willful destruction, concealment, damage, etc., HG §5-610.

HEALTH CARE DURABLE POWER OF ATTORNEY.
See HEALTH CARE DECISIONS.

HEALTH CARE FACILITIES.
Accreditation.
Definitions, HG §19-2301.
Generally, HG §19-2302.
Aged persons.
Day-care for the elderly.
General provisions, HG §§14-201 to 14-206.
See DAY-CARE FOR THE ELDERLY.
Ambulatory care, HG §§19-3B-01 to 19-3B-09.
See FREESTANDING AMBULATORY CARE FACILITIES.
Authorities.
Health and higher educational facilities authority, 43C §§1 to 24.
See HEALTH AND HIGHER EDUCATIONAL FACILITIES AUTHORITY.
Centers for disease control.
Occupational safety and health.
Reporting noncompliance with guidelines on universal precautions, LE §5-205.
Comprehensive physical rehabilitation facilities, HG §§19-1201 to 19-1208.
See COMPREHENSIVE PHYSICAL REHABILITATION FACILITIES.
Elderly persons.
Day-care for the elderly, HG §§14-201 to 14-206.
See DAY-CARE FOR THE ELDERLY.
Freestanding birthing centers.
Ambulatory care facilities, HG §§19-3B-01 to 19-3B-09.
See FREESTANDING AMBULATORY CARE FACILITIES.
Freestanding medical facilities.
Ambulatory care facilities, HG §§19-3B-01 to 19-3B-09.
See FREESTANDING AMBULATORY CARE FACILITIES.
General provisions, HG §§19-3A-01 to 19-3A-07.
See FREESTANDING MEDICAL FACILITIES.
General provisions.
See HOSPITALS.
Handicapped persons.
Day-care centers.
Medically handicapped adults, HG §§14-301 to 14-304.
See DAY-CARE CENTERS.
Health maintenance organizations, HG §§19-701 to 19-735.
See HEALTH MAINTENANCE ORGANIZATIONS.

HEALTH CARE FACILITIES —Cont'd
Home health agencies, HG §§19-401 to 19-410.
See HOME HEALTH AGENCIES.
Hospices, HG §§19-901 to 19-913.
See HOSPICES.
Insane persons.
Maryland psychiatric research center, HG §§10-401 to 10-429.
Interference with access to or egress from medical facility, CR §10-204.
Long-term care insurance, IN §§18-101 to 18-120.
See LONG-TERM CARE INSURANCE.
Medical laboratories, HG §§17-201 to 17-217.
See LABORATORIES.
Mental health facilities.
Community residential mental health programs for children and adolescents, HG §§10-920 to 10-926.
See MENTAL HEALTH FACILITIES.
Maryland psychiatric research center.
See MENTAL HEALTH FACILITIES.
Mental retardation.
State residential centers.
See DEVELOPMENTAL DISABILITIES.
Nursing facilities.
General provisions.
See HOSPITALS.
Nursing homes.
See NURSING HOMES.
Nursing referral service agencies, HG §§19-4B-01 to 19-4B-06.
Occupational safety and health.
Centers for disease control.
Reporting noncompliance with guidelines on universal precautions, LE §5-205.
Private review agents.
General provisions, IN §§15-10B-01 to 15-10B-20.
See HEALTH INSURANCE.
Residential service agencies, HG §§19-4A-01 to 19-4A-10.
See RESIDENTIAL SERVICE AGENCIES.
University of Maryland.
Medical system, ED §§13-301 to 13-313.
See UNIVERSITY OF MARYLAND.

HEALTH CARE FINANCING ADMINISTRATION.
Medicare supplement insurers information to administration, IN §15-926.

HEALTH CARE MALPRACTICE CLAIMS, CJ §§3-2A-01 to 3-2A-10; SpecPro Rules 15-401 to 15-403.
See MALPRACTICE.

HEALTH CARE PAYROLL ASSESSMENT, LE §§8.5-101 to 8.5-107.
Computation, LE §8.5-104.
Deductions from wages prohibited, LE §8.5-104.
Defined terms, LE §8.5-101.
Health insurance benefits.
Reporting by Secretary, LE §8.5-106.
Duties of Secretary, LE §8.5-107.
Failure to report or make payments, LE §8.5-105.
Nonprofit organizations, LE §8.5-104.
Reports.
Annual report of payroll information and exemptions, LE §8.5-103.
Failure to report or make payments, LE §8.5-105.
Secretary, reports by, LE §8.5-106.

HEALTH CARE PAYROLL ASSESSMENT
—Cont'd
Scope of provisions, LE §8.5-102.
Secretary.
Duties, LE §8.5-107.
Reports by, LE §8.5-106.

HEALTH CARE REGULATORY FUND, IN
§§2-112.2, 2-112.3.

HEALTH CARE WORKER WHISTLEBLOWER
PROTECTION, HO §§1-501 to 1-506.
Applicability of protection, HO §1-503.
Civil actions for violations, HO §§1-504 to 1-506.
Defenses, HO §1-506.
Definitions, HO §1-501.
Limitation of actions, HO §1-504.
Prohibited acts, HO §1-502.
Remedies, HO §1-505.

HEALTHCHOICE PERFORMANCE
INCENTIVE FUND, HG §15-103.3.

HEALTH CLUBS.
Steroids and human growth hormone.
Warning of consequences of illegal use, posting,
CR §5-710.

HEALTH CLUB SERVICES, CL §§14-12B-01 to
14-12B-08.
Agreement.
Automatic renewal clauses, CL §14-12B-06.
Cancellation, CL §14-12B-06.
Right to cancel where facility fails to open for
business by date specified, CL §14-12B-05.
Defined, CL §14-12B-01.
Automatic renewal clauses, CL §14-12B-06.
Bankruptcy.
Information required by seller upon, CL
§14-12B-07.
Bonds, surety, CL §14-12B-02.
Cease and desist orders, CL §14-12B-08.
Closed facility, CL §14-12B-04.
Information required by seller upon permanent
closing or bankruptcy, CL §14-12B-07.
Deceptive trade practices, CL §14-12B-08.
Definitions, CL §14-12B-01.
Disability of buyer, CL §14-12B-04.
Division.
Defined, CL §14-12B-01.
Inspections, CL §14-12B-02.
Failure to open for business by date specified.
Cancellation of agreement, CL §14-12B-05.
Fund.
Health club administration fund, CL §14-12B-03.
Inspections.
Duty of division to make inspection, CL
§14-12B-02.
Mandamus.
Authority of division to bring action for
mandamus for failure to register, CL
§14-12B-02.
Massage therapists generally, HO §§3-5A-01 to
3-5A-14.
See MASSAGE THERAPISTS.
Notice.
Agreement.
Cancellation of agreement, CL §14-12B-06.
Records.
Inspection of records, CL §14-12B-02.
Refunds.
Cancellation right where facility fails to open for
business by date specified, CL §14-12B-05.

HEALTH CLUB SERVICES —Cont'd
Registration, CL §14-12B-02.
Remedies of injured buyers, CL §14-12B-02.
Resident agent, CL §14-12B-02.
Service of process.
Resident agent for purposes of service, CL
§14-12B-02.
Unfair trade practices.
Failure to comply with subtitle, CL §14-12B-08.

HEALTH EMERGENCIES.
Catastrophic health emergency.
Definitions, PS §14-3A-01.
Disease surveillance and response program, HG
§§18-901 to 18-908.
See CATASTROPHIC HEALTH EMERGENCY.
Effect upon other laws, PS §14-3A-07.
Governor's orders, PS §14-3A-03.
Governor's proclamation, PS §14-3A-02.
Health care providers, immunity of, PS §14-3A-06.
Penalties, PS §14-3A-08.
Prohibited activities, PS §14-3A-08.
Quarantine.
Directive issued by secretary, PS §14-3A-05.
Refusal to be tested or treated, PS §14-3A-04.
Emergency management, PS §§14-101 to 14-1004.
See EMERGENCY MANAGEMENT.

HEALTH INSURANCE.
Affiliates.
Offer of plan by affiliate of nonrenewing carrier.
Individual health benefit plans, IN §15-1308.
Age of insured, IN §§15-204, 15-220.
Agreements to issue other policies or amend
applications, IN §12-202.
Alcohol abuse, IN §15-802.
Alzheimer's disease, IN §15-801.
Anesthetist's services.
Nurse anesthetists, IN §15-708.
Applicability of title, IN §15-101.
Application forms, IN §§12-205 to 12-207.
Application or consent requirement, IN
§12-202.
Assessment of fees on insurers, etc., IN §15-111.
Beneficiaries.
Change of beneficiary, IN §15-218.
Blanket insurance, IN §§15-305 to 15-310.
Eligible persons and organizations, IN §15-305.
Expense-incurred policies.
Extension of coverage after termination, IN
§15-833.
Individual applications and certificates, IN
§15-308.
Issuance of policies, IN §15-306.
Out-of-state policies, IN §15-310.
Payment of benefits, IN §15-309.
Policies, required provisions, IN §15-307.
Blood products, IN §15-803.
Breast cancer.
Mastectomy coverage, IN §15-832.
Prosthesis coverage, IN §15-834.
Breast implants.
Coverage information to commissioner, IN
§15-105.
Effect of implants on coverage, IN §15-504.
Breast reconstructive surgery.
Coverage, IN §15-815.
Calvert county.
County board of education.
Elected members, ED §3-303.
Cancellation.
Line of business canceled, IN §27-606.

HEALTH INSURANCE —Cont'd
Cancellation —Cont'd
Notice of cancellation option and refund, IN §15-201.
Portability, IN §§15-1309, 15-1409.
Capacity of insured, IN §12-202.
Carriers.
Credentialing of providers, IN §15-112.1.
Catastrophic health insurance policies, IN §15-1101.
Changes to policy, IN §15-207.
Child birth, IN §§15-811 to 15-813.
Marital status of women, IN §15-506.
Child support.
Condition allowing inclusion of child in parent's coverage, FL §12-102.
Deduction of premiums from employee's earnings, FL §12-102.
Elimination of coverage by employer, FL §12-102.
Employer's duties on receipt of notice order child's coverage, FL §12-102.
Enrollment of child under coverage of insuring parent, IN §15-405.
Foreign court order requiring coverage of child, FL §12-102.2.
Inclusion of child on health insurance policy, FL §§12-102, 12-102.1.
Medical support notice.
Issuance, format, content, force and effect, FL §12-102.1.
Notice to employer of order requiring coverage of child, FL §12-102.
Notice to employer.
Order requiring coverage of child, FL §12-102.
Prohibited acts against employee, FL §12-102.
Termination or lapse of coverage, notice, FL §12-102.
Willful violation of order requiring child's coverage, FL §12-102.
Withholdings orders, FL §12-102.
Order requiring child's coverage issued sperate from or in conjunction with, FL §12-102.
Child wellness services, IN §15-817.
Chiropractic services, IN §15-705.
Chlamydia screening tests.
Required coverage, IN §15-829.
Choice of providers.
Blanket insurance, IN §15-309.
Group insurance, IN §15-304.
Pharmacies, IN §15-806.
Claims.
Additional information required, IN §§15-1004, 15-1005.
Adverse claims.
Congenital or genetic birth defect, IN §15-835.
Disability and adverse benefit determination, IN §15-1010.
Forms, IN §15-212.
Uniform claims forms, IN §§15-1002 to 15-1004.
Notice of claim, IN §15-211.
Notice of reason for denial, IN §15-1006.
Payment of claims, IN §§15-214, 15-215.
Blanket policies, IN §15-309.
Deduction of premium owed, IN §15-225.
Prompt payment required, IN §15-1005.
Penalties for violations, IN §15-1005.
Reimbursement for preauthorized care, IN §15-1009.
Summary explanation of benefits, IN §15-1007.
Time limits for submission of claims, IN §15-1005.
Cleft lip or palate, IN §15-818.

HEALTH INSURANCE —Cont'd
Clinical trials.
Coverage, IN §15-827.
Coinsurance payments, IN §15-118.
Child birth, IN §15-812.
Diabetes treatment, IN §15-822.
HMO's, HG §19-706.
Mental illness, emotional disorders and drug and alcohol abuse treatment, IN §15-802.
Unfair trade practices.
Similar benefits required for all diseases, IN §27-913.
Colorectal cancer screening.
Coverage for, IN §15-837.
Community health resources, reimbursement to, IN §15-715.
Compensation of health care practitioners, IN §15-113.
Complaint process for adverse decisions or grievances, IN §§15-10A-01 to 15-10A-09.
Applicability, IN §15-10A-01.1.
Burden of proof.
Review of grievance decision by commissioner, IN §15-10A-03.
Coverage, IN §15-10A-01.1.
Definitions, IN §15-10A-01.
Establishment by carriers.
Required, IN §15-10A-02.
Independent professional judgment, IN §15-10A-05.
Issuance of decisions by commissioner, IN §15-10A-04.
Medical experts, IN §15-10A-05.
Notification of commissioner's final decision, IN §15-10A-04.
Regulations, IN §15-10A-09.
Reports by carriers to commissioner, IN §15-10A-06.
Reports by health advocacy unit, IN §§15-10A-07, 15-10A-08.
Requirements, IN §15-10A-02.
Review of grievance decisions by commissioner, IN §15-10A-03.
Complaints.
Coverage decisions, IN §§15-10D-01 to 15-10D-04.
Appeals, IN §15-10D-02.
Carrier's obligations, IN §15-10D-03.
Definitions, IN §15-10D-01.
Regulations.
Commissioner may adopt, IN §15-10D-04.
Conflict of laws.
Prohibited provisions in policy or contract, IN §12-209.
Congenital or genetic birth defect.
Defined, IN §15-835.
Consent requirements, IN §12-202.
Continuation coverage generally, IN §§15-407 to 15-410.
Conversion from group to individual policy, IN §§15-412 to 15-414.
Coordination of coverage.
Policy provisions permitted, IN §15-104.
Copayments.
Unfair trade practices.
Similar benefits required for all diseases, IN §27-913.
Costs.
Annual determination of costs, IN §15-1501.
Counseling services, IN §15-704.
Coverage decisions.
Complaint process. See within this heading, "Complaints."

HEALTH INSURANCE —Cont'd
Credentialing intermediaries.
  Credentialing of providers, IN §15-112.1.
**Credit life, health and unemployment
    insurance,** IN §§13-101 to 13-117.
  See CREDIT LIFE, HEALTH AND
      UNEMPLOYMENT INSURANCE.
Death certificates.
  Notice regarding group insurance included with
      copy of certificates, HG §4-217.
Death of insured.
  Autopsies, IN §15-216.
  Continuation coverage for surviving spouse and
      dependent children, IN §§15-407, 15-410.
  Conversion rights of surviving spouse, IN §15-414.
  Payment of claims, IN §15-215.
Deductibles.
  Unfair trade practices.
    Similar benefits required for all diseases, IN
        §27-913.
**Dental care coverage, general anesthesia
    required,** IN §15-828.
Dental plan organizations, IN §§14-401 to
    14-418.
  See DENTAL PLAN ORGANIZATIONS.
Dental plans, IN §15-114.
  Self-funded group plans, IN §15-702.
Department of health and mental hygiene.
  Reimbursement for services paid, IN §15-603.
Diabetes treatment, IN §15-822.
Diethylstilbestrol (DES) exposure, IN §15-503.
Dietitian's services, IN §15-706.
Direct payments to hospital or provider.
  Blanket insurance, IN §15-309.
  Group insurance, IN §15-304.
Disability benefits.
  Consent requirement, IN §27-901.
  Conversion from group to individual policy, IN
      §15-413.
  Exclusion of payments for leaving home
      confinement, IN §15-505.
  Finance charge computation, IN §27-901.
  Increase in social security payments, IN §15-501.
  Pregnancy or child birth, IN §15-813.
Disapproval of forms, IN §12-205.
Discharge of insurer upon payment, IN §12-208.
Disclosures in sales materials, IN §15-121.
Discrimination, IN §§27-208, 27-210.
  Health networks, IN §27-910.
  Mental illness, emotional disorders or substance
      abuse, HG §19-703.1; IN §15-802.
Divorce.
  Child support, FL §§12-102, 12-102.1.
    Enrollment of child under coverage of insuring
        parent, IN §15-405.
  Continuation of coverage, FL §11-111; IN §15-408.
  Conversion rights of ex-spouse, IN §15-414.
  Displaced homemakers, FL §§4-601 to 4-613.
    See DISPLACED HOMEMAKERS.
Drive thru deliveries, IN §15-812.
Drug abuse, IN §15-802.
Drug or alcohol abuse.
  Managed behavioral health care organizations.
    Responsibilities of carriers, IN §15-127.
Elderly care, IN §15-801.
Emergency 911 systems.
  Right to access, IN §15-126.
Emerging medical and surgical treatments, IN
    §15-123.
Emotional disorders, IN §15-802.
  Managed behavioral health care organizations.
    Responsibilities of carriers, IN §15-127.

HEALTH INSURANCE —Cont'd
Employment termination.
  Continuation coverage, IN §15-409.
  Conversion from group to individual policy, IN
      §§15-412 to 15-414.
  Open enrollment of terminated spouse losing
      coverage, IN §15-411.
"Entire contract" provision, IN §15-207.
Evaluation of services.
  Mandated health insurance services evaluation,
      IN §§15-1501, 15-1502.
Expense-incurred policies.
  Extension of coverage after termination, IN
      §15-833.
Explanation of benefits, IN §15-1007.
**Fee assessed payors by health care
    commission,** HG §19-111.
Fireworks permits.
  Accident insurance, PS §10-106.
Food, IN §15-807.
Forms.
  Approval by commissioner, IN §§12-203 to 12-205.
    Blanket health insurance, IN §15-306.
  Claim forms, IN §15-212.
    Uniform claims forms, IN §§15-1002 to 15-1004.
  Copies to be available to enrollees, IN §15-127.
  Filing period, IN §12-203.
  Preparation fees, IN §15-127.
  Referral forms, IN §§15-119, 15-120.
Franchise health insurance policies, IN
    §15-1102.
Frederick county.
  County board of education, ED §3-5B-04.
Funeral directors.
  Continuation of group health benefits.
    Duty of licensed funeral directors to provide
        notice of, HO §7-407.
Genetic test use, IN §27-909.
Grace period for premium payments, IN
    §15-209.
  Extension by commissioner, IN §12-210.
Grandchildren, IN §15-403.
  Newly born or adopted grandchildren, IN §15-401.
  Unmarried dependent incapacitated
      grandchildren, IN §15-402.
Grievances.
  Complaint process for adverse decisions or
      grievances, IN §§15-10A-01 to 15-10A-09. See
      within this heading, "Complaint process for
      adverse decisions or grievances."
  Complaint process for coverage decisions, IN
      §§15-10D-01 to 15-10D-04.
  Coverage decisions. See within this heading,
      "Complaints."
Group insurance, IN §§15-301 to 15-310.
  Continuation coverage upon death, IN §15-410.
  Conversion from group to individual policy, IN
      §§15-412, 15-413.
  County officers and employees, 25 §3.
  Definitions, IN §15-301.
  Direct payment to hospital or health care
      provider, IN §15-304.
  Eligibility for group insurance, IN §15-302.
  Expense-incurred policies.
    Extension of coverage after termination, IN
        §15-833.
  Maryland health insurance plan, IN §§14-501 to
      14-515.
  Notice to parents of impeding loss of child's
      coverage, IN §15-416.
  Out-of-state policies, IN §15-310.

HEALTH INSURANCE —Cont'd
Group insurance —Cont'd
Part-time students with disabilities, coverage, IN §15-417.
Portability and accountability, IN §§15-1401 to 15-1409.
Readjustment of premium rate not prohibited, IN §27-210.
Self-funded plans.
Reimbursement of dentists, physicians and podiatrists, IN §15-702.
Succeeding policy notices, IN §15-415.
Guaranty corporation, IN §§9-401 to 9-419.
See LIFE AND HEALTH INSURANCE GUARANTY CORPORATION.
Guardianship, IN §15-403.1.
Newly born or adopted wards, IN §15-401.
Gynecological care, IN §15-816.
Habilitative services.
Defined, IN §15-835.
Hair prosthesis, IN §15-836.
Head or facial bones.
Diagnostic and surgical procedures, IN §15-821.
Health care payroll assessment, LE §§8.5-101 to 8.5-107.
Health care regulatory fund, IN §§2-112.2, 2-112.3.
Hearing aids.
Coverage for minor child, IN §15-838.
Holocaust victims insurance act, IN §§28-101 to 28-110.
See HOLOCAUST VICTIMS INSURANCE.
Home confinement.
Exclusion of payments for leaving home confinement, IN §15-505.
Home health care, IN §15-808.
Home medical equipment, IN §15-106.
Hospice care, IN §15-809.
Hospital reimbursement, IN §§15-601, 15-602.
Rates, IN §15-604.
Small employer health insurance, IN §15-1214.
Uniform claims forms, IN §§15-1003, 15-1004.
Incontestability clause, IN §15-208.
Indemnification of insurers, IN §15-117.
Insurable interest, IN §12-201.
Insurance regulation assessment.
Generally, IN §§2-501 to 2-507.
Interest.
Late payment of claim, IN §15-1005.
Premiums for health insurance of borrower not considered interest, CL §12-105.
In vitro fertilization, IN §15-810.
Key employee insurance.
Insurable interest, IN §12-201.
Kickbacks, IN §§27-209, 27-210.
Life and health insurance guaranty corporation, IN §§9-401 to 9-419.
See LIFE AND HEALTH INSURANCE GUARANTY CORPORATION.
Limitation of actions, IN §15-217.
Defenses of insurer, IN §15-208.
Policies may not shorten limitations period, IN §12-209.
Limits, maximum.
Unfair trade practices.
Similar benefits required for all diseases, IN §27-913.
Long-term care insurance, IN §§18-101 to 18-120.
See LONG-TERM CARE INSURANCE.

HEALTH INSURANCE —Cont'd
Loss-of-time benefits.
Notice of claims, IN §15-211.
Relation of earnings to insurance, IN §15-224.
Low-cost hospitals, IN §15-601.
Mammograms, IN §15-814.
Medicare supplement insurance, IN §15-907.
Managed behavioral health care organizations.
Responsibilities of carriers, IN §15-127.
Managed care organizations, HG §§15-102.2 to 15-103.
Appeals of adjustment of capitation rates, IN §15-605.
Impairment of provider participation, IN §15-115.
Prescription drugs.
Electronic reimbursement of pharmacy, IN §15-131.
Health insurance benefit card, prescription benefit card, or other technology, IN §15-130.
Reports, plans, etc., IN §15-605.
Managed care system.
Defined, IN §15-835.
Mandated health insurance services evaluation, IN §§15-1501, 15-1502.
Maryland health care provider rate stabilization fund, IN §§19-801 to 19-808.
See MARYLAND HEALTH CARE PROVIDER RATE STABILIZATION FUND.
Maryland health insurance plan, IN §§14-501 to 14-515.
Maryland health insurance reform act, IN §§15-1201 to 15-1225.
See SMALL EMPLOYER HEALTH INSURANCE.
Massage therapists.
Reimbursement, HO §3-5A-13.
Mastectomies.
Coverage for reconstructive breast surgery, IN §15-815.
Prosthesis coverage, IN §15-834.
Required coverage, IN §15-832.
Maternity and newborn care.
Private review agents.
Determinations, IN §15-10B-09.
Medicaid.
Business plans from managed care organizations, IN §15-605.
Coverage for recipients, IN §§15-406, 15-502.
Rates for payments to hospitals, IN §15-604.
Medical malpractice insurance, IN §19-104.
Consumer education and advocacy program.
Medical professional liability insurance premiums, comparison guide, IN §2-303.2.
Deductibles in medical malpractice policies, IN §19-114.
Exclusive appointment agreements prohibited, IN §10-133.
Maryland medical professional liability insurance rate stabilization fund, IN §19-104.1.
Medical mutual liability insurance society of Maryland, IN §§24-201 to 24-214.
Reporting requirements.
Financial disclosures, IN §4-405.
Malpractice claims or actions, IN §4-401.
Immunity from liability, CJ §5-701.
Medical records.
Disclosure by insurer, IN §4-403.
Inspection of medical files, IN §4-402.
Medicare supplement insurance, IN §§15-901 to 15-928.
See MEDICARE SUPPLEMENT INSURANCE.

HEALTH INSURANCE —Cont'd
Mental illness, IN §15-802.
Managed behavioral health care organizations.
Responsibilities of carriers, IN §15-127.
Residential crisis services, IN §15-840.
Methadone maintenance.
Maximum copayment allowed, HG §19-703.1; IN
§15-802.
Midwife's services, IN §15-709.
Minors.
Addition of children after death of spouse, IN
§15-404.
Application for insurance on minor, IN §12-202.
Child birth, IN §§15-811 to 15-813.
Child support, FL §§12-102, 12-102.1.
Enrollment of child under coverage of insuring
parent, IN §15-405.
Child wellness services, IN §15-817.
Grandchildren generally, IN §15-403.
Hearing aids.
Coverage, IN §15-838.
Newly born or adopted children, IN §15-401.
Orders creating right to receive benefits under
parent's insurance, IN §15-405.
Unmarried dependent incapacitated children, IN
§15-402.
Misrepresentations in applications, IN §12-207.
Time limit on defense, IN §15-208.
Neck bone diagnostic or surgical procedures,
IN §15-821.
911 systems.
Right to access, IN §15-126.
Nonduplication provisions, IN §15-104.
Nonprofit health entities.
Acquisition, SG §§6.5-101 to 6.5-401.
See NONPROFIT HEALTH ENTITIES.
Nonprofit health service plans, IN §§14-101 to
14-140.
See NONPROFIT HEALTH SERVICE PLANS.
Nonresident insureds.
Conformity of policy with statutes of residence, IN
§15-226.
Nursing home care, IN §15-801.
Medicare supplement insurance.
Statements to prospective buyers, IN §15-919.
Nursing services.
Certified nurse practitioners, IN §15-703.
Elderly care, IN §15-801.
Midwives, IN §15-709.
Nurse anesthetists, IN §15-708.
Nutritionist's services, IN §15-706.
Obesity.
Coverage for treatment of morbid obesity, IN
§15-839.
Obstetrical care, IN §15-816.
Obstetricians.
Referrals to specialists.
Standing referrals for pregnancy, IN §15-830.
Occupational changes, IN §15-219.
Optometrist's services, IN §15-710.
Orthopedic braces, IN §15-820.
Osteoporosis, IN §15-823.
"Other insurance" clauses, IN §§15-221 to
15-223.
Outpatient services, IN §15-819.
Diabetes treatment, IN §15-822.
Payment of proceeds and release, IN §12-208.
Persons covered, IN §15-201.
Pharmaceutical benefits, IN §15-805.
Choice of pharmacy, IN §15-806.
Maintenance drugs, IN §15-824.

HEALTH INSURANCE —Cont'd
Pharmaceutical benefits —Cont'd
Notice of change in benefits, IN §15-107.
Off-label use of drugs, IN §15-804.
Physical examination of insured, IN §15-216.
Physical therapy, IN §15-711.
Physician assistant's services, IN §15-712.
Physicians and surgeons.
Choice of providers.
Blanket insurance, IN §15-309.
Group insurance, IN §15-304.
Communication of information by health care
providers, IN §15-116.
Compensation of health care practitioners, IN
§15-113.
Provider panels, IN §15-112.
Reimbursement for health care services generally,
IN §§15-701 to 15-715.
Retroactive denial of reimbursements, IN
§15-1008.
Reporting medical malpractice claims and actions,
IN §4-401.
Immunity, CJ §5-701.
Podiatrist's services, IN §15-713.
Self-funded group plans, IN §15-702.
Policies generally.
Blanket insurance.
Out-of-state policies, IN §15-310.
Changes to policy, IN §15-207.
Domestic insurers' policies in other states, IN
§15-205.
Foreign or alien insurers' policies, IN §15-205.
Form and content of policies, IN §§15-201, 15-202.
Nonduplication and coordination provisions, IN
§15-104.
Simplified language, IN §15-103.
Stop-loss insurance policies, IN §15-129.
Variance from requirements, IN §15-206.
Portability and accountability, IN §§15-1301 to
15-1409.
Actuarial value of benefits under individual policy,
IN §15-1307.
Applicability of provisions.
Group policies, IN §15-1402.
Individual policies, IN §15-1302.
Cancellation.
Group policies, IN §15-1409.
Individual policies, IN §15-1309.
Carrier's requirements.
Individual policies, IN §15-1303.
Certification of creditable coverage.
Group policies, IN §15-1403.
Individual policies, IN §15-1310.
Definitions.
Group policies, IN §15-1401.
Individual policies, IN §15-1301.
Dependents.
Group policies, IN §15-1406.1.
Eligibility for group policy, IN §15-1406.
Group policies generally, IN §§15-1401 to 15-1409.
Individual policies generally, IN §§15-1301 to
15-1313.
Issuance of individual plans, IN §15-1308.
Period of creditable coverage.
Group policies, IN §§15-1404, 15-1405.
Individual policies, IN §15-1311.
Policy forms.
Individual policies, IN §§15-1305, 15-1306.
Preexisting conditions.
Group policies, IN §15-1404.
Individual policies, IN §§15-1305, 15-1308.

HEALTH INSURANCE —Cont'd
Portability and accountability —Cont'd
Premium or contribution rates.
Group rates, IN §15-1407.
Individual policies, IN §15-1312.
List of carriers of individual health benefit
plans, IN §15-1313.
Renewal.
Group policies, IN §§15-1408, 15-1409.
Individual policies, IN §§15-1308, 15-1309.
Small employer health insurance, IN §§15-1202,
15-1403.
Preexisting conditions, IN §§15-507, 15-508.
Breast implants, IN §15-504.
Disapproval of forms, IN §12-205.
Long-term care insurance, IN §§18-109, 18-113.
Medicare supplement insurance, IN §§15-909,
15-919.
Portability and accountability.
Group policies, IN §15-1404.
Individual policies, IN §§15-1305, 15-1308.
Restrictions on application forms, IN §12-205.
Small employer health insurance, IN §15-1208.
Time limit on defenses, IN §15-208.
Preferred provider organizations, IN §§14-201
to 14-206.
Pregnancy.
Child birth, IN §15-811.
Disability caused by pregnancy or child birth, IN
§15-813.
Home visits, IN §§15-812, 15-817.
In vitro fertilization, IN §15-810.
Length of inpatient hospitalization care, IN
§15-812.
Marital status of woman, IN §15-506.
Referrals to specialists.
Standing referrals for pregnancy, IN §15-830.
Premiums.
Grace period for payments, IN §§15-209, 15-210.
Nonpayment.
Deduction of amount owed from payment of
claim, IN §15-225.
Subsequent acceptance of premium by insurer,
IN §15-210.
Reduction, readjustment, etc., not prohibited, IN
§27-210.
Prescription drugs.
Coverage, IN §15-831.
Health insurance benefit card, prescription benefit
card, or other technology, IN §15-130.
Senior prescription drug assistance program.
Maryland health insurance plan, IN §§14-501 to
14-515.
Primary care physicians.
Referrals to specialists, IN §15-830.
Private review agents, IN §§15-10B-01 to
15-10B-20.
Adverse decisions.
Appeal, IN §15-10B-07.
Defined, IN §15-10B-01.
Alcoholism.
Review of services for treatment, IN
§15-10B-03.
Appeals.
Adverse decision, IN §15-10B-07.
Review of services for treatment of alcoholism,
drug abuse or mental illness, IN
§15-10B-03.
Appeals and hearings.
Orders of commissioner, IN §15-10B-13.

HEALTH INSURANCE —Cont'd
Private review agents —Cont'd
Certificates.
Applications, IN §15-10B-04.
Fees, IN §§15-10B-04, 15-10B-05.
Information to accompany, IN §15-10B-05.
Defined, IN §15-10B-01.
Expiration, IN §15-10B-10.
Issuance, IN §15-10B-03.
List of agents issued certificates, IN §15-10B-15.
Qualifications, IN §15-10B-03.
Renewal, IN §15-10B-10.
Required, IN §15-10B-03.
Submission, IN §15-10B-18.
Transfer, IN §15-10B-03.
Withdrawal, IN §15-10B-18.
Definitions, IN §15-10B-01.
Determinations by, IN §15-10B-06.
Maternity and newborn care, IN §15-10B-09.
Time frame, IN §15-10B-06.
Drug abuse.
Review of services for treatment, IN
§15-10B-03.
Examinations by commissioner, IN §15-10B-19.
Grievance decisions.
Requirements of, IN §15-10B-09.1.
Grievance process, internal.
Established, IN §15-10B-08.
Grievance decisions.
Requirements of, IN §15-10B-09.1.
List of agents issued certificates, IN §15-10B-15.
Maternity and newborn care.
Determinations, IN §15-10B-09.
Mental illness.
Review of services for treatment, IN
§15-10B-03.
Orders of commissioner.
Hearings and appeals, IN §15-10B-13.
Penalties for violations, IN §§15-10B-12,
15-10B-17.
Pharmacy benefit managers, IN §15-10B-20.
Purpose of provisions, IN §15-10B-02.
Reconsiderations of determinations, IN
§15-10B-06.
Referrals, IN §15-10B-17.
Regulations, IN §15-10B-03.
Reports, IN §15-10B-16.
Certificate requirements, meeting, IN
§15-10B-03.
Utilization review programs, IN §15-10B-16.
Social security act.
Utilization review of patients eligible for
hospital services under Title XVIII.
Waiver of requirements, IN §15-10B-14.
Utilization review of patients eligible for hospital
services under Title XVIII.
Waiver of requirements, IN §15-10B-14.
Violations, IN §15-10B-11.
Penalties, IN §15-10B-12.
Prohibited conditions.
Provider panels, IN §§15-112, 27-222.
Prohibited provisions in policy or contract, IN
§12-209.
Proof of loss, IN §15-213.
Prostate cancer, IN §15-825.
Prosthetic devices, IN §15-820.
Provider panels, IN §15-112.
Providers.
Credentialing, IN §15-112.1.
Psychologist's services, IN §15-714.
Rates for health plans, IN §15-605.

HEALTH INSURANCE —Cont'd
Rebates, IN §§27-209, 27-210.
Recordkeeping procedures, IN §15-108.
Referrals.
  Prohibited referrals, IN §15-110.
  Uniform referral forms, IN §§15-119, 15-120.
Referrals to specialists, IN §15-830.
Reimbursement of providers, IN §§15-601 to
    15-606.
  Small employer health insurance, IN §15-1214.
  Uniform claims forms, IN §§15-1003, 15-1004.
Reinstatement of policy, IN §15-210.
Release upon payment of proceeds, IN §12-208.
Religious organizations.
  Exclusion of religious organizations, IN §15-826.
Renewal of coverage.
  Notice of renewal, IN §§15-122, 15-201.
  Right to refuse renewal, IN §15-203.
Rented medical equipment, IN §15-106.
**Restrictions on assigning, transferring or
    subcontracting,** IN §15-125.
Risk based capital standards for insurers, IN
    §§4-301 to 4-314.
  See INSURANCE COMPANIES.
Sales.
  Disclosures in sales materials, IN §15-121.
Scope of title, IN §15-101.
Second opinions, IN §15-819.
Secured transactions.
  Health-care-insurance receivables.
    Defined, CL §9-102.
    Third party assignments.
      Claims and defenses against assignee, taking
        subject to.
        Inapplicability of provisions, CL §9-404.
      Modification of assigned contract, CL §9-405.
      Restrictions on assignments, CL §§9-406,
        9-408.
Self-funded group insurance.
  Reimbursement of dentists, physicians and
    podiatrists, IN §15-702.
Sexually transmitted diseases.
  Chlamydia screening tests.
    Required coverage, IN §15-829.
Simplified language requirement, IN §15-103.
Small employers, IN §§15-1201 to 15-1225.
  See SMALL EMPLOYER HEALTH INSURANCE.
Smoking cessation treatment, coverage, IN
    §15-841.
Social security.
  Reduction of disability payments upon increase in
    social security payments, IN §15-501.
Social worker's services, IN §15-707.
Specialists.
  Referrals to specialists, IN §15-830.
Specified disease policies.
  Minimum loss ratio, IN §15-109.
Spouse authorized to insure other spouse, IN
    §12-202.
Statute of limitations, IN §15-217.
  Defenses of insurer, IN §15-208.
  Policies may not shorten limitations period, IN
    §12-209.
Stop-loss insurance policies, IN §15-129.
Substitute provisions, IN §15-202.
Succeeding policy notices, IN §15-415.
Third-party ownership of policies, IN §15-102.
Transfer of health care provider's contract, IN
    §15-124.
  Restrictions on assigning, transferring or
    subcontracting, IN §15-125.

HEALTH INSURANCE —Cont'd
Transportation ticket policies, IN §15-1103.
Unfair trade practices.
  Copayment, coinsurance, deductibles, and limits.
    Similar benefits required for all diseases, IN
      §27-913.
**Unmarried dependent incapacitated
    individuals under guardianship,** IN §15-402.
Utilization review, IN §15-1001.
  Private review agents, IN §§15-10B-01 to
    15-10B-20. See within this heading, "Private
    review agents."

HEALTH INSURANCE ADVISORY COUNCIL,
    SPP §§2-505, 2-506.

HEALTH MAINTENANCE ORGANIZATIONS,
    HG §§19-701 to 19-735.
Accreditation of health care facilities, HG
    §§19-2301, 19-2302.
Acquiring interest or control, HG §19-711.3.
Action by provider not under contract.
  Failure to pay for services rendered enrollee, HG
    §19-910.1.
Acts prohibited, HG §19-729.
Actuarial soundness and net worth, HG
    §19-710.
Administrative service contracting providers.
  Registration before entering contract with, HG
    §19-713.3.
Advertising.
  Prohibited advertising, HG §19-724.
  Solicitation of members, HG §19-724.
Advocating patient interest by provider, IN
    §15-112.
Agents and brokers.
  Limited lines licenses, IN §10-124.
Amendment of contracts, HG §19-713.
Appeals.
  Decisions of commissioner or orders of secretary,
    HG §19-732.
Appropriate health care plan, HG §19-710.
Assessment of fees on HMO, IN §15-111.
Audits.
  Periodic audits, HG §19-710.
Authority.
  Generally, HG §19-712.
Bankruptcy and insolvency.
  Insolvency plans.
    Continuation of benefits to subscribers and
      enrollees, HG §19-710.
Basic requirements for operation, HG §19-710.
Benefit packages, HG §19-703.
  Defined, HG §19-701.
Blood products.
  Payments for, IN §15-803.
    Applicability to health maintenance
      organizations, HG §19-706.
Breast cancer.
  Mastectomy coverage, IN §15-832.
  Prosthesis coverage, IN §15-834.
Breast reconstructive surgery.
  Coverage, IN §15-815.
Cancellation of enrollment, HG §19-725.
Carrier.
  Credentialing of providers, IN §15-112.1.
  Defined.
    Point-of-service option, HG §19-710.2.
**Centers for disease control guidelines on
    universal precautions.**
  Compliance with and notice explaining, HG
    §19-705.3.

HEALTH MAINTENANCE ORGANIZATIONS
—Cont'd
Certificate of authority.
Applications, HG §19-708.
Commissioner to issue, HG §19-711.
Contacting potential members, HG §19-707.
Continuing authority to operate, HG §19-721.
Expiration, HG §19-721.
Fees.
Application fee, HG §19-709.
Issuance, HG §19-706.
Renewal, HG §19-721.
Refusal to renew, HG §19-722.
Required, HG §19-707.
Suspension or revocation, HG §19-706.
Changes in pharmaceutical benefits.
Notice to pharmacies, HG §19-712.2.
Childbirth.
Hospitalization benefits for newborns, HG §19-703.
Choice of pharmacy, HG §19-706.
Citation of act, HG §19-734.
Claims.
Adverse claims.
Congenital or genetic birth defect, IN §15-835.
Disability and adverse benefit determination, IN §15-1010.
Prompt payment of claims required, IN §15-1005.
Penalties for violations, IN §15-1005.
Providers not under contract rendering services to enrollee.
Failure to pay, HG §19-910.1.
Rehabilitation or liquidation of health maintenance organizations, HG §19-706.1.
Reimbursement for preauthorized care, IN §15-1009.
Reimbursement to community health resources, HG §19-712.7.
Report of pattern, HG §19-712.4.
Retroactive denial of reimbursement, IN §15-1008.
Uniform claims forms, HO §1-208.
Cleft lip or palate.
Benefits for treatment, IN §15-818.
Coinsurance payments for health care services.
Applicability to health maintenance organizations, HG §19-706.
Colorectal cancer screening.
Coverage for, IN §15-837.
Commissioner.
Appeals from decision, HG §19-732.
Certificate of authority.
Issuance, suspension or revocation by commissioner, HG §19-706.
Defined, HG §19-701.
Rehabilitation or liquidation of organizations.
Authority of commissioner as rehabilitator or liquidator, HG §19-706.1.
Responsibilities, HG §19-728.
Supervision of organizations, HG §19-723.
Community health resources, reimbursement to, HG §19-712.7; IN §15-715.
Compensation of health care practitioners, IN §15-113.
Complaint process for adverse decisions or grievances.
Generally, IN §§15-10A-01 to 15-10A-09.
Complaints.
Coverage decisions, IN §§15-10D-01 to 15-10D-04.
Members and subscribers, HG §19-705.2.

HEALTH MAINTENANCE ORGANIZATIONS
—Cont'd
Congenital or genetic birth defect.
Defined, IN §15-835.
Consolidation, HG §§19-711, 19-711.3.
Continuing care facilities.
Subscriber or enrollee as resident of facility, HG §19-712.6.
Contracts.
Administrative service provider contracts, HG §§19-712, 19-713.2.
Plan requirements, HG §19-713.2.
Amendments, HG §19-713.
Disapproval of filings, HG §19-713.
Effective date of filings, HG §19-713.
Filing, HG §19-713.
Hold harmless clause, HG §19-710.
Nonduplication or coordination of coverage provisions, HG §19-713.1.
Rehabilitation or liquidation.
Authority of commissioner as rehabilitator or liquidator, HG §19-706.1.
Standards of quality and care, HG §19-710.
Terms of contracts, HG §19-710.
Contributing to impairment, IN §9-231.
Corporate practice of medicine, HG §19-704.
Cost review commission, HG §19-720.
Covered services.
Food products prescribed for metabolic diseases, HG §19-705.5.
Liability of enrollees and subscribers, HG §19-710.
Point-of-service option, HG §19-710.2.
Credentialing intermediaries.
Credentialing of providers, IN §15-112.1.
Declaration of intent and policy, HG §19-702.
Definitions, HG §19-701.
Administrative service contracting providers, HG §19-713.3.
Administrative service provider contracts, HG §19-713.2.
Conformance with definition, HG §19-710.
Centers for disease control guidelines on universal precautions, HG §19-705.3.
Congenital or genetic birth defect, IN §15-835.
Habilitative services, IN §15-835.
Inherited metabolic disease, HG §19-705.5.
Intensive care policies, HG §19-713.1.
Low protein modified food product, HG §19-705.5.
Managed care system, IN §15-835.
Medical directors, IN §15-10C-01.
Medical food, HG §19-705.5.
Payments to providers not under contract, HG §19-710.1.
Planning and development.
Certificate of need, HG §19-121.
Practice profile, HG §19-710.
Dental plans, IN §15-114.
Department.
Quality assurance unit, HG §19-705.8.
Responsibilities, HG §19-728.
Supervision of organizations, HG §19-723.
Disclosures in enrollment sales materials, HG §19-706; IN §15-121.
Discrimination.
Lack of discrimination, HG §19-710.
Mental illness, emotional disorders or substance abuse, HG §19-703.1; IN §15-802.
Provider panels, IN §15-112.
Rates, HG §19-713.
Drug or alcohol abuse.
Discrimination, HG §19-703.1; IN §15-802.

HEALTH MAINTENANCE ORGANIZATIONS
  —Cont'd
Emergency 911 systems.
  Right to access, IN §15-126.
Emergency services, HG §19-705.6.
  Reimbursement for hospital emergency facility
    and provider, HG §19-712.5.
Emerging medical and surgical treatments, IN
  §15-123.
Enrollment.
  Application or offer of enrollment, HG §19-715.
  Cancellation, HG §19-725.
  Liability of enrollees or subscribers for covered
    services, HG §19-710.
Examination by commissioner, HG §19-706.
Examinations.
  Health care services, HG §19-719.
Expense-incurred policies.
  Extension of coverage after termination, IN
    §15-833.
**Fee assessed payors by health care
  commission,** HG §19-111.
Fees.
  Application for certificate, HG §19-709.
  Investigation fees, HG §19-709.
Financially hazardous condition, IN §§9-101 to
  9-104.
Foreign health maintenance organizations.
  Transferring domicile to Maryland, HG §19-735.
Forms.
  Uniform claims forms, HO §1-208.
  Uniform consultation referral form, HG §19-713.5.
Fraud prevention fee, IN §§6-201 to 6-204.
  Applicability to health maintenance organizations,
    HG §19-706.
Fraudulent insurance acts.
  Applicability of provision, HG §19-706.
Genetic test use, IN §27-909.
Geographical accessibility.
  Primary care classification, HG §19-706.
  Standards for quality of care, HG §19-705.1.
Grievances.
  Complaint process for adverse decisions or
    grievances.
    Generally, IN §§15-10A-01 to 15-10A-09.
  Complaint process for coverage decisions, IN
    §§15-10D-01 to 15-10D-04.
Habilitative services.
  Defined, IN §15-835.
Hair prosthesis, IN §15-836.
Health care plans.
  Appropriate health care plan, HG §19-710.
Health care practitioners.
  Provider panels, IN §15-112.
Health care services, HG §19-719.
  Cost review commission, HG §19-720.
  Covered services. See within this heading,
    "Covered services."
  Defined, HG §19-701.
  Examinations, HG §19-719.
Hearing aids.
  Coverage for minor child, IN §15-838.
Hospices.
  Benefits for hospice services, HG §19-703.
Hospitalization services.
  Scope of subtitle, HG §19-703.
Hospitals.
  Emergency facilities.
    Reimbursement for, HG §19-712.5.
  Uniform claims forms.
    Use when submitting claim or bill for
      reimbursement to, HG §19-350.1.

HEALTH MAINTENANCE ORGANIZATIONS
  —Cont'd
Indemnity.
  Requiring provider to indemnify or hold harmless
    health maintenance organization.
    Prohibited, HG §19-710.
Indigent persons.
  Limited benefits through county programs, HG
    §19-703.
Information.
  Availability to members and general public, HG
    §19-716.
Inherited metabolic diseases, HG §19-705.5.
  Coverage for prescribed food products, HG
    §19-705.5.
Insurance.
  Adequate insurance required, HG §19-710.
  Applicability of certain insurance laws, HG
    §19-706.
  Enforcement.
    Examinations of insurers, etc., by commissioner,
      IN §2-205.
  Examinations of insurers, etc., by commissioner.
    Conduct of examinations, IN §2-207.
    Expense of examinations, IN §2-208.
    Reports of examinations and investigations, IN
      §2-209.
  Health insurance generally.
    See HEALTH INSURANCE.
  Medicare supplement and specified disease act.
    Applicability of law to, HG §19-706.
  Prohibited use of certain insurance industry
    names, HG §19-726.
Insurers.
  Continuation of benefits to subscribers and
    enrollees, HG §19-710.
Intensive care policies, HG §19-713.1.
Interest.
  Late payment of claims, IN §15-1005.
Internal grievance systems, HG §19-710.
Internal peer review, HG §19-710.
Interpretation and construction.
  Applicability of other laws, HG §19-706.
Investigations.
  Complaints of members and subscribers, HG
    §19-705.2.
  Fees, HG §19-709.
In vitro fertilization, coverage, HG §19-706.
Late payment of claims.
  Interest, IN §15-1005.
Liability.
  Covered services.
    Liability of enrollees and subscribers, HG
      §19-710.
Limitations on covered services and visits, HG
  §19-705.4.
Line of business.
  Cancellation or nonrenewal, HG §19-706.
Liquidation.
  Rehabilitation or liquidation of organizations, HG
    §19-706.1.
List of providers, IN §15-112.
Long-term care insurance, IN §§18-101 to
  18-120.
  See LONG-TERM CARE INSURANCE.
Low protein modified food product.
  Defined.
    Inherited metabolic diseases, HG §19-705.5.
Managed behavioral health care organizations.
  Responsibilities of carriers, IN §15-127.

HEALTH MAINTENANCE ORGANIZATIONS
—Cont'd

Managed care organizations, HG §§15-102.2 to
15-103.
Appeals of adjustment of capitation rates, IN
§15-605.
Impairment of provider participation, IN §15-115.
Reports, plans, etc., IN §15-605.
Managed care system.
Defined, IN §15-835.
Marketing documents, HG §19-714.
**Maryland health maintenance organization
act.**
Citation of act, HG §19-734.
Massage therapists.
Reimbursement, HO §3-5A-13.
Mastectomies.
Coverage, IN §15-832.
Prosthesis coverage, IN §15-834.
Medical directors, IN §§15-10C-01 to 15-10C-04.
Certificates.
Applications, IN §15-10C-03.
Qualifications, IN §15-10C-03.
Regulations for certification, IN §15-10C-02.
Suspension or revocation, IN §15-10C-04.
Definitions, IN §15-10C-01.
Delegation of responsibilities, IN §15-10C-03.
Regulations, IN §15-10C-02.
Medical food.
Defined.
Inherited metabolic diseases, HG §19-705.5.
Medical records.
Maintenance of system, HG §19-710.
Medicare skilled nursing facility.
Subscriber or enrollee as resident of facility, HG
§19-712.6.
Members.
Complaints, HG §19-705.2.
Defined, HG §19-701.
Participation by members, HG §19-710.
Reimbursement to organization.
Payments to providers not under contract, HG
§19-710.1.
Mental illness.
Managed behavioral health care organizations.
Responsibilities of carriers, IN §15-127.
Residential crisis services, IN §15-840.
Mental illness coverage, HG §19-703.
Merger, HG §§19-711, 19-711.3.
Metabolic diseases.
Coverage for prescribed food products, HG
§19-705.5.
Methadone maintenance.
Maximum copayment allowed, HG §19-703.1; IN
§15-802.
Needy persons.
Limited benefits through county program, HG
§19-703.
Negligence.
Requiring provider to indemnify or hold harmless
health maintenance organization.
Prohibited, HG §19-710.
Newborns.
Hospitalization benefits for, HG §19-703.
911 systems.
Right to access, IN §15-126.
Nonprofit health entities.
Acquisition, SG §§6.5-101 to 6.5-401.
See NONPROFIT HEALTH ENTITIES.
Nonprofit health service and other plans, HG
§19-706.

HEALTH MAINTENANCE ORGANIZATIONS
—Cont'd

Notices.
Centers for disease control guidelines on universal
precautions.
Compliance with and notice explaining, HG
§19-705.3.
Changes in pharmaceutical benefits.
Notice to pharmacies, HG §19-712.2.
Congenital or genetic birth defect.
Required coverage, IN §15-835.
Disapproval of filed rates and contracts, HG
§19-713.
Establishment of complaint system, HG §19-705.2.
Impairment of insurance companies, IN §9-231.
Penalties.
Procedure before imposition of penalty, HG
§§19-730, 19-731.
Unsound fiscal operation, HG §19-728.
Nurse practitioner as primary care provider,
HG §19-705.1.
Obesity.
Coverage for treatment of morbid obesity, IN
§15-839.
Obstetrician and gynecological care.
Primary care classification, HG §19-706.
Offers of enrollment, HG §19-715.
Operation.
Basic requirements, HG §19-710.
Participation by members, HG §19-710.
**Payment to providers not under written
contract,** HG §19-710.1.
Penalties.
Centers for disease control guidelines on universal
precautions.
Failure to comply with requirements, HG
§19-705.3.
Claims.
Prompt payment requirement violations, IN
§15-1005.
Failure to pay provider not under contract.
Provider rendering to services to enrollee, HG
§19-910.1.
Notice, HG §§19-730, 19-731.
Violations, HG §§19-730, 19-731.
Pharmaceutical services, HG §19-713.4.
Changes in pharmaceutical benefits.
Notice to pharmacies, HG §19-712.2.
Pharmacy, choice for filling prescriptions, HG
§19-706.
Planning and development.
Certificate of need, HG §19-121.
Point-of-service option, HG §19-710.2.
Policies.
Violations, HG §19-725.
Policy of state, HG §19-702.
Powers generally, HG §19-712.
Practice profiles, HG §19-710.
Premiums.
Rehabilitation or liquidation of organizations.
Authority of commissioner as rehabilitator or
liquidator, HG §19-706.1.
Prescription drugs.
Electronic reimbursement of pharmacy, IN
§15-131.
Health insurance benefit card, prescription benefit
card, or other technology, IN §15-130.
Primary care physicians.
Referrals to specialists, IN §15-830.
Priority of claims.
Rehabilitation or liquidation of organizations, HG
§19-706.1.

HEALTH MAINTENANCE ORGANIZATIONS
—Cont'd
Privileged communications.
Administrative service provider contracts.
Plan and supporting documentation
confidential, HG §19-713.2.
Prohibited acts, HG §19-729.
Prohibited conditions.
Provider panels, IN §§15-112, 27-222.
Prompt payment of claims required, IN
§15-1005.
Provider panels, IN §15-112.
Defined.
Point-of-service option, HG §19-710.2.
Providers.
Administrative service contracting providers.
Registration before entering contract with, HG
§19-713.3.
Credentialing, IN §15-112.1.
Defined, HG §19-701.
Point-of-service option.
Treatment outside of provider panel, HG
§19-710.2.
Providers not under contract.
Payment, HG §19-710.1.
Quality assurance unit, HG §19-705.8.
Quality of care.
Standards, HG §§19-705.1, 19-710.
Rates.
Disapproval of filings, HG §19-713.
Discriminatory rates, HG §19-713.
Effective date of filings, HG §19-713.
Filings, HG §19-713.
Receivers.
Rehabilitation or liquidation of organizations.
Claims and expenses incurred in receivership,
HG §19-706.1.
Records.
Medical records system, HG §19-710.
Referrals to health care practitioners.
Prohibited referrals, HG §19-712.4.
Uniform consultation referral form, HG §19-713.5.
Referrals to specialists, IN §15-830.
**Registration of administrative service
contracting provider.**
Required before entering contract with, HG
§19-713.3.
Regulation, HG §19-706.
Rehabilitation or liquidation of organizations,
HG §19-706.1.
Reports.
Annual reports, HG §19-717.
Pattern of claims, HG §19-712.4.
**Restrictions on assigning, transferring or
subcontracting,** IN §15-125.
Retroactive denial of reimbursement, IN
§15-1008.
Risk based capital standards, HG §19-710.
Rules and regulations.
Adoption by secretary, HG §19-705.
Quality of care standards, HG §19-705.1.
Medical directors, IN §15-10C-02.
Scope of subtitle, HG §19-703.
Service and visit limitations, HG §19-705.4.
Short title of act, HG §19-734.
Smoking cessation treatment, coverage, IN
§15-841.
Solicitation.
Organizations may solicit members, HG §19-724.
Specialists.
Referrals to specialists, IN §15-830.

HEALTH MAINTENANCE ORGANIZATIONS
—Cont'd
Statement of intent, HG §19-702.
Subscribers.
Complaints, HG §19-705.2.
Defined, HG §19-701.
Liability for covered services, HG §19-710.
Supervision.
Commissioner and department to supervise, HG
§19-723.
Surviving spouses.
Coverage for, HG §19-703.
Taxation.
Applicability of tax laws, HG §19-727.
Insurance premium tax, IN §§6-101 to 6-121.
Transfers from nonprofit organizations to
medical assistance program account, IN
§6-121.
Telephones.
Toll-free telephone access, HG §19-705.7.
Terms.
Prohibited use of certain terms, HG §19-726.
Time limits for submission of claims, IN
§15-1005.
Title of act, HG §19-734.
Transfer of health care provider's contract, IN
§15-124.
Restrictions on assigning, transferring or
subcontracting, IN §15-125.
Treatment outside provider panel.
Point-of-service option, HG §19-710.2.
Unfair claim settlement practices.
Applicability, HG §19-706.
Uniform claims forms.
Use when submitting claim or bill for
reimbursement to, HG §19-350.1.
Uniform consultation referral form, HG
§19-713.5.
Universal precautions.
Centers for disease control guidelines.
Compliance with and notice explaining, HG
§19-705.3.
Violations.
Penalties, HG §§19-730, 19-731.
Policies, HG §19-725.
Prohibited acts, HG §19-729.
Remedies, HG §19-729.
Widows and widowers.
Coverage for surviving spouses, HG §19-703.

HEALTH NETWORKS.
Discrimination, IN §27-910.

HEALTH OCCUPATIONS, HO §§1-101 to 1-208.
Alcohol and drug counselors, HO §§17-101 to
17-502.
See PROFESSIONAL COUNSELORS AND
THERAPISTS.
Areas of shortage.
Employment vacancy rates, HO §1-204.
Audiologists, HO §§2-101 to 2-502.
See AUDIOLOGISTS AND SPEECH-LANGUAGE
PATHOLOGISTS.
Board of review.
Defined, HO §1-101.
Fees.
Establishment of fees, HO §1-205.
Chiropractors, HO §§3-101 to 3-602.
See CHIROPRACTORS.
Clinical resource management system.
Developed to control costs, HG §19-135.

HEALTH OCCUPATIONS —Cont'd
Counselors, HO §§17-101 to 17-502.
  See PROFESSIONAL COUNSELORS AND
    THERAPISTS.
County.
  Defined, HO §1-101.
Definitions, HO §1-101.
Dentists, HO §§4-101 to 4-702.
  See DENTISTS.
Department of health and mental hygiene.
  Defined, HO §1-101.
Dietitians, HO §§5-101 to 5-502.
  See DIETITIANS.
Electrologists, HO §§8-6B-01 to 8-6B-29.
  See ELECTROLOGISTS.
Employer.
  Defined, HO §1-202.
Employment vacancy rates.
  Areas of shortage, HO §1-204.
Fee assessed by health care commission, HG
  §19-111.
Health care commission.
  Fee assessed health care practitioners, HG
    §19-111.
  License applications.
    Fees, HO §1-209.
  List of persons licensed or certified, HO §1-210.
Hearing aid dealers, HO §§2-101 to 2-502.
  See AUDIOLOGISTS AND SPEECH-LANGUAGE
    PATHOLOGISTS.
Household member.
  Defined, HO §1-101.
Includes or including.
  Defined, HO §1-101.
Insurance.
  Reimbursement for health care services generally,
    IN §§15-701 to 15-715.
    Retroactive denial of reimbursement, IN
      §15-1008.
Licenses.
  Fees.
    Establishment of fees, HO §1-205.
    Health care commission, HO §1-209.
  Renewal, HO §1-213.
  Unemployment insurance contributions, required,
    HO §1-213.
  Workers' compensation act.
    Compliance before issuing, HO §1-202.
Marriage and family therapists, HO §§17-101 to
  17-502.
  See PROFESSIONAL COUNSELORS AND
    THERAPISTS.
Massage therapists, HO §§3-5A-01 to 3-5A-14.
Medical radiation technologists, HO §§14-5B-01
  to 14-5B-21.
  See RADIATION ONCOLOGY/THERAPY,
    MEDICAL RADIATION, AND NUCLEAR
    MEDICINE TECHNOLOGISTS.
Morticians, HO §§7-101 to 7-602.
  See MORTICIANS.
Nuclear medicine technologists, HO §§14-5B-01
  to 14-5B-21.
  See RADIATION ONCOLOGY/THERAPY,
    MEDICAL RADIATION, AND NUCLEAR
    MEDICINE TECHNOLOGISTS.
Nurses, HO §§8-101 to 8-802.
  See NURSES.
Nursing assistants, HO §§8-6A-01 to 8-6A-16.
  See NURSING ASSISTANTS.
Nursing home administrators, HO §§9-101 to
  9-502.
  See NURSING HOME ADMINISTRATORS.

HEALTH OCCUPATIONS —Cont'd
Oaths.
  Verification of documents, HO §1-201.
Occupational therapists, HO §§10-101 to 10-502.
  See OCCUPATIONAL THERAPISTS.
Optometrists, HO §§11-101 to 11-602.
  See OPTOMETRISTS.
Perjury.
  Verification of documents, HO §1-201.
Permits.
  Unemployment insurance contributions, required,
    HO §1-213.
  Workers' compensation act.
    Compliance before issuing, HO §1-202.
Person.
  Defined, HO §1-101.
Pharmacists and pharmacies, HO §§12-101 to
  12-802.
  See PHARMACISTS AND PHARMACIES.
Physical therapists, HO §§13-101 to 13-502.
  See PHYSICAL THERAPISTS.
Physician assistants, HO §§15-101 to 15-502.
  See PHYSICIANS.
Physicians.
  Generally, HO §§14-101 to 14-702.
    See PHYSICIANS.
  Persons giving information concerning.
    Liability, CJ §5-638.
Podiatrists, HO §§16-101 to 16-602.
  See PODIATRISTS.
Polysomnographic technologists, HO §§13-5C-01
  to 13-5C-25.
Professional counselors and therapists, HO
  §§17-101 to 17-502.
  See PROFESSIONAL COUNSELORS AND
    THERAPISTS.
Psychologists, HO §§18-101 to 18-502.
  See PSYCHOLOGISTS.
Radiation oncology/therapy, medical radiation,
  and nuclear medicine technologists, HO
  §§14-5B-01 to 14-5B-21.
  See RADIATION ONCOLOGY/THERAPY,
    MEDICAL RADIATION, AND NUCLEAR
    MEDICINE TECHNOLOGISTS.
Records.
  Verification of documents, HO §1-201.
Referrals, HO §§1-301 to 1-306.
  Health insurance.
    Prohibited referrals, IN §15-110.
    Uniform consultation referral forms, IN
      §§15-119, 15-120.
  HMO claims resulting from prohibited referral,
    HG §19-712.4.
Respiratory care practitioners, HO §§14-5A-01
  to 14-5A-25.
  See RESPIRATORY CARE PRACTITIONERS.
Secretary of health and mental hygiene.
  Defined, HO §1-101.
  Powers and duties, HO §1-203.
Sexual exploitation.
  Disciplinary action against licensee or certificate
    holder, HO §1-212.
Social workers, HO §§19-101 to 19-502.
  See SOCIAL WORKERS.
Speech-language pathologists, HO §§2-101 to
  2-502.
  See AUDIOLOGISTS AND SPEECH-LANGUAGE
    PATHOLOGISTS.
State.
  Defined, HO §1-101.

HEALTH OCCUPATIONS —Cont'd
Statewide commission on the shortage in the health care workforce, HO §1-601.
Substantial financial interest.
Defined, HO §1-101.
Surgeons.
Physicians generally, HO §§14-101 to 14-702.
See PHYSICIANS.
Therapy management contracts, HO §§12-6A-01 to 12-6A-10.
Unemployment compensation.
Prerequisites to license renewal, HO §1-213.
Verification of documents, HO §1-201.
Waterworks and waste systems operators, EN §§12-101 to 12-602.
See WATERWORKS AND WASTE SYSTEMS OPERATORS.
Well drillers, EN §§13-101 to 13-602.
See WELL DRILLERS.
Workers' compensation.
Compliance with act, HO §1-202.

HEALTH OFFICERS, HG §§3-301 to 3-310.
See HEALTH.

HEALTH SERVICES COST REVIEW COMMISSION, HG §§19-201 to 19-227.
See HEALTH.

HEALTH SPAS.
Health club services generally, CL §§14-12B-01 to 14-12B-08.
See HEALTH CLUB SERVICES.

HEALTHY AIR ACT.
Electric generating facilities, EN §§2-1001 to 2-1005.
Definitions, EN §2-1001.
Emission standards, EN §2-1002.
Exception from compliance, EN §2-1003.
Mercury standards, EN §2-1002.
Penalties for violations, EN §2-1005.
Regional greenhouse gas initiative participation, EN §2-1002.
Regulations of department, EN §2-1004.
Report on emissions compliance, EN §2-1003.

HEALTHY FAMILY SITES.
Judith P. Hoyer early child care and education enhancement program, ED §5-217.

HEARING AID DEALERS.
Audiologists and speech-language pathologists, HO §§2-101 to 2-502.
See AUDIOLOGISTS AND SPEECH-LANGUAGE PATHOLOGISTS.
Hearing aid sales, CL §§14-2501 to 14-2506.
See HEARING AID SALES.

HEARING AID SALES, CL §§14-2501 to 14-2506.
Billing for diagnostic tests to be separate, CL §14-2502.1.
Cancellation of purchase, CL §14-2503.
Deceptive trade practices, CL §14-2504.
Seller violations, CL §14-2505.
Construction of act, CL §14-2502.
Contracts.
Cancellation of purchase, CL §14-2503.
Deceptive trade practices, CL §14-2504.
"Hearing aid" defined, CL §14-2501.
Notice requirements.
Cancellation of purchase, CL §14-2503.
Refunds.
Cancellation of purchase, CL §14-2503.

HEARING AID SALES —Cont'd
Refunds —Cont'd
Failure to pay refunds, CL §14-2505.
Returned goods.
Cancellation of purchase.
Condition of returned goods, CL §14-2503.
Surrender of right.
Cancellation of purchase, CL §14-2503.
Violations of act.
Deceptive trade practices, CL §§14-2504, 14-2506.
Failure to pay refunds, CL §14-2505.
Penalties, CL §14-2506.
Waiver of right.
Cancellation of purchase, CL §14-2503.

HEARING IMPAIRED.
See DEAF AND HEARING IMPAIRED.

HEARINGS.
Abandoned property disposition.
Claim to property or proceeds of sale.
Consideration of claim by administrator, CL §17-319.
Accountants.
Licenses.
Denial, suspension or revocation of license or reprimand of licensee, BOP §2-317.
Permits.
Denial, revocation or suspension of license or reprimand of permit holder, BOP §2-412.
Administration of courts.
Motion day.
Assignment when hearing required, CJA Rule 16-201.
Administrative hearings, office of, SG §§9-1601 to 9-1610.
See EXECUTIVE DEPARTMENT.
Adoption, FamLaw Rule 9-109; Juv Rule 11-501.
Independent adoptions, FL §5-3B-17.
Local department adoptions.
Adoption after termination of parental rights.
Hearing on petition, FL §5-347.
Adoption without prior termination of parental rights.
Hearing on petition, FL §5-335.
Private agency adoptions.
Hearing on petition, FL §5-3A-32.
Air quality control.
Action after hearing, EN §2-606.
Ambient air quality control permits.
Issuance, EN §2-404.
Corrective orders, EN §2-604.
Electric company operating permit for generating station.
Installation of pollution control equipment or changes in method of operation, EN §2-405.
Rules and regulations.
Adoption, EN §2-303.
Temporary fuel variances, EN §2-503.
Alimony.
Scope of alimony hearing and determination, FL §1-203.
Ambulances, ED §13-515.
Amusements and recreation.
Citations.
Hearing examiner, BR §3-406.
Appeals.
Dismissal of appeals.
Motion to dismiss, AppRev Rule 8-603.
Motions, AppRev Rule 8-431.
Dismissal of appeal, AppRev Rule 8-603.

HEARINGS —Cont'd

Appeals from District Court.
De novo hearings.
Procedure, AppRevCir Rule 7-112.
Arbitration and award.
Uniform arbitration act, CJ §§3-201 to 3-234.
See ARBITRATION AND AWARD.
Architects.
Licenses.
Denial, revocation or suspension of license or
reprimand of licensee, BOP §3-313.
Arrest in state by officers of another state.
Fresh pursuit, lawfulness of arrest, CP §2-306.
Asbestos.
Removal or encapsulation.
Notices, EN §6-414.1.
Signs, EN §6-414.1.
Revocation and suspension of license, EN §6-416.
Athlete agents.
License suspension or revocation, BR §4-407.
**Audiologists, hearing aid dealers and
speech-language pathologists.**
See AUDIOLOGISTS AND SPEECH-LANGUAGE
PATHOLOGISTS.
Auditors.
Circuit courts, CivProCir Rule 2-543.
Automobile insurance fund.
Actions against producers, IN §20-514.
Aviation.
Administration.
Powers generally, TR §5-209.
Airports.
Approval of site, TR §5-303.
Issuance of license, TR §5-304.
Federal-state joint hearings, TR §5-206.
Notice and opportunity, TR §5-210.
Banks and trust companies.
Removal of officers or directors, FI §5-801.
Unfair trade practices.
Cease and desist orders, FI §5-808.
Bar admissions.
Character committees, BarAdm Rule 5.
Out-of-state attorneys, BarAdm Rule 13.
Barbers.
Licenses.
Denial, suspension or revocation, or reprimand
of licensee, BOP §4-315.
Permits.
Denial, revocation or suspension, or reprimand
of permit holder, BOP §4-514.
Registration.
Student and apprentice barbers.
Denial, revocation or suspension, BOP §4-408.
Boxing, sparring and wrestling.
Licensure disciplinary hearings.
Application of contested case provisions, BR
§4-311.
Failure to appear, BR §4-311.
Grounds, BR §4-310.
Judicial review, BR §4-312.
Right to hearing, BR §4-311.
Calvert county.
Real property.
Sales at public or private sale, 25 §11A.
Storm water management districts, 25 §155B.
**Catastrophic health emergency disease
surveillance and response program.**
Quarantine.
Directive issued by secretary, HG §18-906.
Cecil county.
Real property.
Transfers by commissioners, 25 §8.

HEARINGS —Cont'd

Charities.
Registration.
Noncompliance with title by applicant, BR
§6-404.
Charles county.
Real property.
Transfer or sale of real property no longer
needed, 25 §11A.
Child care.
Foster care.
Contest of placement with adoptive family, FL
§5-525.
Child custody.
Change of custody.
Petition by child to change custody.
Hearing required, FL §9-103.
Children in need of assistance.
See CHILDREN IN NEED OF ASSISTANCE.
Child support arrearages.
Driver's license suspension or restriction, TR
§16-203.
Chiropractors.
See CHIROPRACTORS.
Cholesterol testing.
Permits.
Denial, suspension or revocation, HG §17-509.
Closed hearings.
Rape or sexual offense prosecutions.
Reputation for chastity, prior sexual conduct,
CR §3-319.
Collective bargaining.
Consent elections.
Report on investigations.
Consideration of exception to report, LE
§4-216.
Montgomery County housing opportunities
commission.
Dispute resolution, HS §16-309.
Consumer loans, FI §11-217.
Consumer protection.
Adoption of rules and regulations, CL §13-205.
Division of consumer protection.
Public hearings to determine violations, CL
§13-403.
Waiver of right to hearings in replevin action, CL
§14-1303.
Contempt.
Constructive contempt, SpecPro Rule 15-207.
Controlled dangerous substances.
Registered manufacturers, dispensers or
distributors.
Suspension or revocation of registration, CR
§5-308.
**Conversion of overhead electric or
communication facilities to underground
locations.**
Resolution of intent to order conversion, PUC
§12-309.
Cosmetologists.
Licenses.
Denial, revocation or suspension, or reprimand
of licensee, BOP §5-315.
Permits.
Denial, revocation or suspension, or reprimand
of permittee, BOP §5-523.
Registration.
Students and apprentices.
Denial, revocation or suspension, or
reprimand of registrant, BOP §5-408.

HEARINGS —Cont'd
Counties.
Adoption of code form of home rule.
Public hearings by board of county
commissioners, 25B §5.
Erosion prevention works.
By county commissioners, 25 §164.
Home rule for code counties.
Resort taxes, 25B §13H.
Ordinances or resolutions, 25 §3.
Credit services businesses, CL §14-1911.
Dams.
Permit applications, EN §5-506.
Death sentence.
Inmate incompetent, COR §3-904.
Declaratory judgments.
Advancing on court calendar, CJ §3-409.
Speedy hearings, CJ §3-409.
Dentists.
See DENTISTS.
Developmental disabilities.
Group homes.
Private group homes.
Application for certificate of approval, HG
§7-611.
Licenses.
Denial, suspension or revocation, HG §7-910.
Procedure, HG §7-406.
Request for informal hearing, HG §7-406.
State residential centers.
Admission, HG §§7-503, 7-504.
Transfers.
Mental health program, HG §7-802.
Discrimination.
Human relations commission, 49B §11.
Distress for rent.
Appeals, RP §8-332.
Deficiency judgment, RP §8-325.
On defendant's answer, RP §8-314.
Dorchester county.
Proposed ordinances or resolutions.
Special provisions as to certain counties, 25 §3.
Draining lands.
Before county commissioners, 25 §85.
Dissolution.
Public drainage associations, 25 §102.
Drainage districts.
County commissioners, 25 §§111, 113.
Public drainage associations.
Petitions to establish, 25 §§54, 57.
Public hearing by commissioner on report, 25 §84.
Driver education program.
Refusal, suspension or revocation of certificate, TR
§16-506.
**Electric companies constructing generating
stations or transmission lines.**
Certification procedure, PUC §7-207.
Joint construction, PUC §7-208.
Electricians.
Disciplinary actions, BOP §6-317.
Electrologists.
License suspension or revocation, HO §8-6B-19.
Eminent domain.
Board of property review, PropAct Rule 12-213.
En banc review.
Circuit courts, CivProCir Rule 2-551.
Engineers.
Licenses.
Denial, revocation or suspension of license or
reprimand of licensee, BOP §§14-318,
14-319.

HEARINGS —Cont'd
Environmental sanitarians.
Licenses.
Denials, reprimands, suspensions and
revocations, EN §11-312.
Environmental service.
Conducting, NR §3-104.
Equal credit opportunity.
Complaints, CL §12-705.
Examiners.
Circuit courts, CivProCir Rule 2-542.
Executions.
Levy.
Release of property from levy.
Circuit courts, CivProCir Rule 2-643.
District Court, CivProDist Rule 3-643.
Executive agencies.
Office of administrative hearings, SG §§9-1601 to
9-1610.
See EXECUTIVE DEPARTMENT.
Executors and administrators.
Removal of personal representative, ET §6-306.
Revision of inventory, ET §7-204.
Settlement of decedents' estates.
Debts and claims.
Claimant's petition, Estates Rule 6-413.
Expungement of records, Crim Rule 4-507.
Notice of hearing.
Form for notice of hearing, Form 4-503.4.
Fiduciaries for absent or unknown persons,
Guardian Rule 10-603.
**Fiduciary estates including guardianships of
property.**
Removal for cause or other sanctions, Guardian
Rule 10-712.
Fiduciary estates other than guardianships.
Petition for assumption of jurisdiction, Guardian
Rule 10-503.
Fisheries management plans.
Public hearings.
Rules and regulations, NR §4-215.
Food, drugs and cosmetics.
Abatement orders, HG §21-261.
Administrative procedure.
Application of act of hearings, HG §21-236.
Food establishments.
Denial, suspension or revocation of license, HG
§21-316.
Protests, HG §21-242.
Foresters.
Licenses.
Disciplinary action, BOP §§7-310, 7-311.
Forests and parks.
Trails.
Abandoned railroad corridor property.
Development as, NR §5-1010.
Wildland areas, NR §§5-1208, 5-1209.
Foster care.
Sibling placement and visitation rights, FL
§5-525.2.
Fraternal benefit societies.
Injunctions, IN §8-464.
Frederick county.
Proposed ordinances or resolutions.
Special provisions as to certain counties, 25 §3.
Freestanding ambulatory care facilities.
License revocation, suspension, restriction or
denial, HG §19-3B-08.
**Fresh pursuit by police officers from another
state.**
Lawfulness of arrest in state, CP §2-306.

HEARINGS —Cont'd
Frozen desserts.
Right to hearing, HG §21-814.
Gas and oil.
Coastal facilities review act.
Permits for construction of facilities, EN §14-507.
Drilling wells.
Permits, EN §14-105.
Rehearings, EN §14-116.
Rules, regulations and orders, EN §14-114.
Subpoenas, EN §14-115.
Governor.
Budget bill, MD Const Art III §52.
Grievances by inmates at state correctional facilities.
Referral of complaint by inmate grievance office to office of administrative hearing, COR §10-208.
Guardian of person, Guardian Rule 10-205; Juv Rule 11-501.
Emergency protective services, Guardian Rule 10-212.
Guardian of property, Guardian Rule 10-304.
Guardianships.
Local department guardianships.
Hearing on petition for consensual guardianship, FL §5-318.
Review hearings, FL §5-326.
Habeas corpus, CJ §3-704; SpecPro Rule 15-309.
Hazardous materials and substances, EN §7-261.
Complaints.
Application of administrative procedure act, EN §7-261.
Immediate ban where imminent hazards exists, HG §22-504.
Subpoenas, EN §7-261.
Health.
Cost review commission.
Generally, HG §19-225.
Rates.
Change of rate structures or charges, HG §19-222.
Review and approval of rates and costs, HG §19-219.
Health insurance.
Private review agents, IN §15-10B-13.
Heritage areas.
Certified area designation, FI §13-1111.
Highways.
Eminent domain.
Board of property review, TR §8-328.
Horse racing.
Licenses.
Disciplinary actions.
Right to hearing, BR §11-309.
Hearing committee, BR §11-310.
Hospitals.
Community programs.
Receiverships.
Procedural requirements, HG §19-335.
Discharge of resident, HG §19-345.1.
Licenses.
Denials or revocations, HG §19-327.
Nursing facilities.
Receiverships.
Procedural requirements, HG §19-335.
Transfer of resident, HG §19-345.1.
Human relations commission, 49B §11.
Income tax.
Withholding refunds due to state agency debt, TG §13-917.

HEARINGS —Cont'd
Injunctions.
Prior notice and opportunity for hearing, SpecPro Rule 15-505.
Insurance.
Acquisitions disclosure and control, IN §7-107.
Automobile insurance fund.
Actions against producers, IN §20-514.
Commissioner, IN §§2-203, 2-210 to 2-215.
Financially hazardous condition.
Regulation of entities in financially hazardous condition, IN §9-104.
Liquidation, rehabilitation, etc., of insurers.
Claims against the insurer, IN §9-226.
Seizure order review, IN §9-215.
Motor vehicle insurance.
Cancellation, nonrenewal, premium increase or reduction in coverage, IN §27-613.
Nonprofit health service plans, IN §14-124.
Ratemaking, IN §§11-501, 11-502.
Disapproval of rates, IN §11-208.
Title insurance, IN §11-404.
Risk based capital standards for insurers.
Challenges by insurer, IN §4-309.
Surety insurance discrimination, IN §27-502.
Interpreters.
Administrative procedure, SG §10-507.1.
Investigations.
Secrecy, Crim Rule 4-642.
Joint and consolidated hearings on permits, SG §§11-501 to 11-523.
See PERMITS.
Judicial disabilities commission, CJA Rule 16-808; MD Const Art IV §4B.
Juvenile causes.
Adjudicatory hearing, Juv Rule 11-114.
Children in need of assistance.
See CHILDREN IN NEED OF ASSISTANCE.
Competency or incompetency to proceed.
Competency hearings.
Time for holding, evidence, findings, burden of proof, CJ §3-8A-17.4.
Hearings on other matters before adjudication under subtitle, CJ §3-8A-17.10.
Controlling conduct of person before court, Juv Rule 11-110.
Detention granted.
Adjudicatory or waiver hearing, CJ §3-8A-15.
Disposition hearing, Juv Rule 11-115.
Emergency detention or shelter care, Juv Rule 11-112.
General provisions.
See JUVENILE CAUSES.
Liability of parents, Juv Rule 11-118.
Modification or vacation of order.
When hearing required, Juv Rule 11-116.
Notice, Juv Rule 11-110.
Petitions.
Multiple petitions, Juv Rule 11-110.
Place, Juv Rule 11-110.
Recording proceedings, Juv Rule 11-110.
Scheduling of hearing.
Duties of clerk, Juv Rule 11-104.
Shelter care granted.
Adjudicatory or waiver hearing, CJ §3-8A-15.
Waiver of jurisdiction, Juv Rule 11-113.
Pretrial release hearing, Crim Rule 4-222.
Landfills.
Request for permit for landfill refuse disposal system, EN §9-209.

HEARINGS —Cont'd
Landlord and tenant.
Failure to pay rent.
Escrow account in certain landlord-tenant
actions, RP §8-118.
Landscape architects.
Disciplinary action against licensees, BOP §9-312.
Judicial review, BOP §9-207.1.
State board of examiners.
Power to hold hearings, BOP §9-205.
Levy.
Release of property from levy.
District Court, CivProDist Rule 3-643.
Libraries.
Personnel.
Dismissal, ED §23-406.
Mandamus.
Objection to answer sustained.
When hearing not required, SpecPro Rule
15-701.
Maryland Transit Administration.
General provisions, TR §§7-206, 7-506.
Maryland-Washington regional district.
Board of zoning appeals of Prince George's county,
28 §8-111.
Commencement.
When to commence, 28 §8-108.1.
Continuances, 28 §8-108.1.
Prince George's county.
See MARYLAND-WASHINGTON REGIONAL
DISTRICT.
Subdivision regulations, 28 §7-116.
Masters.
Circuit courts, CivProCir Rule 2-541.
Mechanics' liens, PropAct Rule 12-304.
Mental hygiene law.
Private group homes.
Application for license, HG §10-520.
Migrant labor.
See OCCUPATIONAL SAFETY AND HEALTH.
Milk and milk products.
Suspension or revocation of permits, HG §21-419.
Mining.
Deep mine control, EN §§15-610, 15-611.
Abandonment.
Permit to abandoned mine.
Notice of opportunity to request hearing
required, EN §15-606.
Open-pit mining.
Permits.
Notice of opportunity to request hearing
required, EN §15-505.
Strip mining.
Oaths, subpoenas and records of hearing, EN
§15-526.
Open-pit mining.
Adjudicatory hearings.
Requests for, EN §15-508.
Revocation of permit.
Adjudicatory hearings, EN §15-508.
Permits.
Application for.
Notice of opportunity to request hearing
required, EN §15-505.
Reclamation plans.
Approval or rejection by land reclamation
committee, EN §15-205.
Revocation of permits, EN §15-514.
Surface mining.
Dewatering in karst terrain.
Contested case hearings, EN §15-813.

HEARINGS —Cont'd
Mining —Cont'd
Surface mining —Cont'd
Permits, EN §15-810.
Public informational hearing, EN §15-809.
Suspension or revocation, EN §15-821.
Morgan State University.
Employees.
Classified employees separation procedures.
See MORGAN STATE UNIVERSITY.
Mortgage originators.
Right to hearing prior to sanctions, FI §11-616.
Mortgages and deeds of trust.
Mortgage lenders.
Cease and desist orders, FI §11-518.
Morticians.
See MORTICIANS.
Motions.
Circuit courts, CivProCir Rule 2-311.
District Court, CivProDist Rule 3-311.
Motor vehicle insurance.
Automobile insurance fund.
Actions against producers, IN §20-514.
Motor vehicles.
Administration hearings, TR §§12-201 to 12-209.
Determinations, TR §12-208.
Judicial review, TR §12-209.
Failure to appear, TR §12-208.
"Licensee" defined, TR §12-201.
Notice.
Adverse decision, TR §12-208.
Required hearings, TR §12-202.
Right to request hearing, TR §12-203.
Scheduled hearing.
Contents of notice, TR §12-204.
Place, TR §12-205.
Procedure, TR §12-206.
Required hearings.
Notice, TR §12-202.
Right to request, TR §12-203.
Scheduled hearings.
Notice.
Contents, TR §12-204.
Security interests.
Hearing for damages from administration, TR
§13-210.
Time, TR §12-205.
Transcript, TR §12-207.
Commercial drivers' licenses.
Drunkenness.
Disqualification on refusal to submit to
chemical test for intoxication, TR
§16-205.1.
Dealers.
Refusal, suspension or revocation of license, TR
§15-110.
Dismantlers, recyclers and scrap processors.
Refusal, suspension or revocation of license, TR
§15-110.
Driver education program.
Refusal, suspension or revocation of certificate,
TR §16-506.
Drivers' licenses.
Suspension of license on refusal to submit to
chemical tests for intoxication, TR
§16-205.1.
Suspension or restriction for child support
arrearages, TR §16-203.
Drivers' schools.
Refusal, suspension or revocation of license, TR
§15-110.

HEARINGS —Cont'd
Motor vehicles —Cont'd
Driving instructors.
Refusal, suspension or revocation of licenses, TR §15-110.
Equipment.
Hearing on question of compliance of approved device, TR §22-102.
Manufacturers, distributors and factory branches.
Refusal, suspension or revocation of license, TR §15-110.
Noise abatement program.
Adoption and publication of sound level limits, TR §22-601.
Salesmen.
Refusal, suspension or revocation of license, TR §15-110.
Title service agents.
Refusal, suspension or revocation of licenses, TR §15-110.
Wreckers and scrap processors.
Refusal, suspension or revocation of license, TR §15-110.
Municipal corporations.
Financing new infrastructure improvements, 23A §44A.
Noise control.
Environmental noise standards.
Adoption, EN §3-402.
Nonprofit health service plans, IN §14-124.
Not criminally responsible.
Release of committed person found not criminally responsible, CP §3-115.
Court review of hearing office report, CP §3-117.
Revocation of conditional release, CP §3-121.
Nurses.
See NURSES.
Nursing home administrators.
See NURSING HOME ADMINISTRATORS.
Occupational therapists.
See OCCUPATIONAL THERAPISTS.
Optometrists.
See OPTOMETRISTS.
Parole release hearings.
Closing of hearings, COR §7-304.
Denying admission or continued attendance at hearing to individual, COR §7-304.
Frequency of hearings at correctional facilities, COR §7-302.
Hearing conducted by commission panel, COR §7-307.
Hearing conducted by hearing examiner, COR §7-306.
Notice to inmate, COR §7-303.
Open to public on victim's request, COR §7-304.
Restricting number of individuals allowed to attend, COR §7-304.
Video conference or other electronic transmission means.
Holding hearings through, COR §7-304.
Vote of commissioner available to public, COR §7-304.
Paternity proceedings.
Hearing on complaint, FL §§5-1024 to 5-1029.
See PATERNITY PROCEEDINGS.
Patuxent river policy plan.
Amendment, SF §5-805.
Patuxent river watershed.
Sewage disposal plan, EN §4-304.
Peace orders, CJ §3-1505.

HEARINGS —Cont'd
Permits.
Joint and consolidated hearings on permits, SG §§11-501 to 11-523.
See PERMITS.
Pharmacists and pharmacies.
See PHARMACISTS AND PHARMACIES.
Physical therapists.
See PHYSICAL THERAPISTS.
Physicians.
See PHYSICIANS.
Pilots.
Licenses.
Denial, revocation or suspension of license or reprimand of licensee, BOP §11-410.
Planning.
Patuxent river policy plan.
Amendment of plan, SF §5-805.
Plumbers.
Licenses.
Denial, revocation or suspension of license or reprimand of licensee, BOP §12-313.
Podiatrists.
See PODIATRISTS.
Polysomnographic technologists.
Disciplinary action.
Hearings, HO §13-5C-17.
Post conviction procedure.
Evidence, Crim Rule 4-406.
Judge, Crim Rule 4-406.
Presence of petitioner, Crim Rule 4-406.
When required, Crim Rule 4-406.
Postmortem examiners.
Autopsies by medical examiners.
Refusal to correct findings and conclusions, HG §5-310.
Power plant sites.
Purchase by state, PUC §7-202.
Private detectives.
Certification.
Disciplinary action, BOP §13-411.
Licenses.
Disciplinary action, BOP §13-315.
Probation.
Violation of conditions, Crim Rule 4-347.
Procurement.
Contractors.
Debarment, SF §§16-301 to 16-312.
See PROCUREMENT.
Program evaluation act.
Evaluation committees.
Public hearings, SG §8-409.
Psychologists.
See PSYCHOLOGISTS.
Public ethics.
Complaints, SG §15-404.
Findings, SG §15-405.
Public service commission.
Cease and desist orders, PUC §13-208.
Conduct of proceedings generally, PUC §3-104.
Disputes as to bill for costs and expenses of public service commission, PUC §2-110.
Proceedings before commission generally, PUC §§3-101 to 3-114.
Rehearings, PUC §3-114.
Denial, judicial review, PUC §3-204.
Right of person subject to complaint to hearing, PUC §3-102.
Public works.
Board.
Conveyance of title to lands owned by state due to their relationship to state waters.
Public hearing required, SF §10-402.

HEARINGS —Cont'd
Public works contracts.
Wages.
Prevailing wage rates.
Review of determination, SF §17-211.
Violations of provisions, SF §17-221.
Quarantine.
Catastrophic health emergencies.
Directive issued by secretary, HG §18-906.
Hearing to contest isolation or quarantine, PS §14-3A-05.
Radiation.
See RADIATION.
Rape or sexual offense prosecutions.
Closed hearings.
Reputation for chastity, prior sexual conduct, CR §3-319.
Real estate appraisers.
See REAL ESTATE APPRAISERS AND HOME INSPECTORS.
Real estate brokers.
Guaranty fund.
Claims against fund, BOP §§17-407 to 17-409.
Hearing board.
See REAL ESTATE BROKERS.
Licenses.
Denial, revocation or suspension, or reprimand of licensee, BOP §17-324.
Summary revocation based on actions of other agencies, BOP §17-327.
Summary suspension for trust fund violations, BOP §17-328.
Power of commission to hold hearings, BOP §17-209.
Receivers and assignees or trustees for creditors.
Claims.
Exceptions to claims, Receivers Rule 13-402.
Registered rehabilitation practitioners.
Licensing, LE §9-6A-16.
Reorganization of government.
Hearings pending before abolished or superseded units, SG §10-704.
Reservoirs.
Permit applications, EN §5-506.
Respiratory care practitioners.
Licensed disciplinary actions, HO §14-5A-17.
Risk based capital standards for insurers.
Challenges by insurer, IN §4-309.
St. Mary's county.
Proposed ordinances or resolutions.
Special provisions as to certain counties, 25 §3.
Real property.
Sales at public or private sale, 25 §11A.
Sales.
Finance companies, FI §11-415.
Sales and use tax.
Licenses.
Denial, suspension or revocation of license or reprimand of licensee, TG §11-711.
Sanitary commissions.
Claims, EN §9-665.
Schools.
Building site selection, ED §4-116.
Expulsion of pupils, ED §7-305.
Firearm violations on school property, ED §7-305.
Handicapped children.
Suspension or expulsion, ED §7-305.
Noncollegiate educational institutions.
Deficiencies, ED §2-206.
Suspension of pupils, ED §7-305.

HEARINGS —Cont'd
Securities.
Securities act.
Public hearings, CA §11-204.
Registration of broker-dealers, agents, investment advisors and investment advisor representatives.
Denial, revocation, suspension or cancellation.
Prerequisites to order, CA §11-416.
Fines for violations of title, CA §11-417.
Summary cease and desist orders.
Violations of title, CA §11-701.1.
Security systems technicians.
Disciplinary action against licensees, BOP §18-310.
Registration.
Actions against applicant, BOP §18-3A-10.
Sediment control.
Enforcement of subtitle, EN §4-112.
Notice, EN §4-109.
Sentence and punishment.
Revisory power of court, Crim Rule 4-345.
Severn river watershed.
Sewage disposal plan, EN §4-304.
Sewage sludge.
Penalties for violations, EN §9-269.
Utilization.
Permits, EN §9-234.
Prior to issuance, amendment or renewal, EN §§9-234.1, 9-238.
Social workers.
See SOCIAL WORKERS.
Special taxing districts in certain counties.
Public hearing, 24 §9-1301.
State retirement and pension system.
Board of trustees.
Compliance and enforcement, SPP §21-111.
Stormwater management.
Adoption of rules and regulations by department, EN §4-202.
Violations, EN §4-211.
Final corrective orders, EN §4-212.
Subpoenas.
Preparation by clerk.
Criminal rules, Crim Rule 4-265.
Preparation by parties.
Criminal rules, Crim Rule 4-265.
Support and maintenance.
Withholding earnings.
Contempt or other proceedings, FL §10-138.
Stay of order, FL §10-133.
Surveys and surveyors.
Licenses.
Denial, revocation or suspension of license or reprimand of licensee, BOP §§15-318, 15-319.
Talbot county board of education.
Removal of members, ED §3-12A-02.
Taxation.
Assessments.
Appeals, TP §14-502.
Personal property, TP §8-413.
Dates, TP §8-412.
Presence of supervisor at hearings before property tax assessment appeal board, TP §2-214.
Real property, TP §8-406.
Dates, TP §8-405.
Death taxes.
Interstate arbitration of death taxes, TG §7-105.

HEARINGS —Cont'd
Taxation —Cont'd
Sales and use tax.
Licenses.
Denial, suspension or revocation of license, or reprimand of licensee, TG §11-711.
Taxicab or for-hire driving services.
Denial of for-hire driver's license, PUC §10-105.
Time-sharing.
Certificates of registration.
Revocation, RP §11A-121.
Trademarks and service marks.
Contested case.
Application of contested case provisions, BR §1-406.
Denial of registration of mark not to constitute, BR §1-407.
Opportunity for hearing, BR §1-407.
Transient vendors.
Disciplinary actions against licensees.
Opportunity for hearing, BR §17-20A-03.
Tri-County Council for Southern Maryland.
General development plan, 20 §3-102.
Tri-County Council for Western Maryland.
General development plan, 20A §3-102.
Unemployment compensation.
See UNEMPLOYMENT COMPENSATION.
Visitation.
Foster care.
Sibling visitation rights, FL §5-525.2.
Washington county.
Railroad lines.
Acquisition and construction, 25 §236C.
Washington suburban sanitary district.
Collective bargaining.
Unfair labor practices, 29 §11.5-113.
Commission.
Pretreatment program, 29 §18-104.3.
Water and sewer systems.
Permits.
Landfill refuse disposal systems, EN §9-209.
Rates and charges.
Proposed rates, EN §9-727.
Water pollution.
Adoption of rules and regulations, EN §9-316.
Complaints, EN §9-337.
Effluent limitations violations by sewage treatment facility.
Significant violations, EN §9-342.1.
Water quality laboratories.
Reprimands, suspensions and revocations of certification.
Right to hearing, EN §9-1017.
Water resources.
Permits.
Applications, EN §5-506.
Watershed associations.
Report of watershed viewers, 25 §193.
Waterworks and waste systems operators.
See WATERWORKS AND WASTE SYSTEMS OPERATORS.
Well drillers.
See WELL DRILLERS.
Wetlands.
Nontidal wetlands.
Permits, EN §5-906.
Violations.
Request for hearing.
General provisions, EN §16-503.
Wills.
Judicial probate, ET §5-404.

HEARINGS —Cont'd
Workers' compensation.
See WORKERS' COMPENSATION.
Youth camps.
Certificates.
Denial, suspension or revocation, HG §14-409.
Zoning.
General provisions.
See ZONING.
Notice, publication, 66B §4.04.

HEARSAY.
Child crime victims.
Admissibility of out-of-court statements, CP §11-304.
Controlled dangerous substances.
Admissibility at bail or sentencing hearing, CR §5-809.
Credibility of declarant.
Attacking and supporting, Evid Rule 5-806.
Criminal cases.
Exceptions.
Declarant unavailable, CJ §10-901.
Definitions, Evid Rule 5-801.
Exceptions.
Availability of declarant immaterial, Evid Rule 5-803.
Declarant unavailable, Evid Rule 5-804.
Criminal cases, CJ §10-901.
Generally, Evid Rule 5-802.
Hearsay within hearsay, Evid Rule 5-805.
Rule, Evid Rule 5-802.

HEART ATTACK.
Automated external defibrillator program, ED §13-517.
County boards of education to develop and implement programs, ED §7-425.
Law enforcement officers, correctional officers, firefighters, rescue squad members, members of the state fire marshal's office.
Death benefits.
Death as result of personal injury in performance of duties.
Presumption, PS §1-202.

HEART-BALM ACT.
Action for alienation of affections, FL §3-103.
Actions for breach of promise to marry, FL §3-102.
Construction of title, FL §3-101.
Contracts for settlement of and abolished or prohibited claim, FL §3-104.

HEART CONDITION.
Identification bracelet, tag or card.
Persons with condition wearing, CP §2-107.

HEART DISEASE AND STROKE PREVENTION PROGRAMS.
Advisory council.
Compensation, HG §13-204.
Composition, HG §13-203.
Created, HG §13-202.
Defined, HG §13-201.
Educational programs, HG §13-205.
Evaluation of programs, HG §13-206.
Tenure, HG §13-203.
Counties.
Guidelines for programs, HG §13-206.
Definitions.
Advisory council, HG §13-201.
Education.
Advisory council.
Programs to educate the public, HG §13-205.

HEART DISEASE AND STROKE PREVENTION PROGRAMS —Cont'd
Evaluation of programs.
Duty of commission, HG §13-206.

HEART MONITOR AND DEFIBRILLATOR.
Automated external defibrillator program, ED §13-517.
County boards of education to develop and implement programs, ED §7-425.

HEATING AND AIR CONDITIONING.
Air conditioner efficiency standards, SG §9-2006.
Air conditioning and heating contractors, BR §§9A-101 to 9A-602.
See AIR CONDITIONING AND HEATING CONTRACTORS.
Boilers and pressure vessels, PS §§12-901 to 12-919.
See BOILERS AND PRESSURE VESSELS.
Environmental sound level limits and noise control rules and regulations for air conditioners, EN §3-401.
Fireworks plants.
Heating equipment, PS §10-206.
Geothermal resources, EN §§5-601 to 5-609.
See GEOTHERMAL RESOURCES.
Kerosene-fired heaters, CL §14-1310.
Lighting.
Illumination in public buildings, guidelines, PS §12-204.
Low-income customers.
Termination of service, PUC §7-307.
Motor vehicles air conditioners, TR §22-410.
Unit heaters.
Efficiency standards, SG §9-2006.

HEATING OIL TANKS.
Abandonment of use of heating oil as fuel.
Removal of heating oil tanks, EN §4-420.
Owners.
Reimbursement from oil contaminated site environmental cleanup fund.
Costs of site rehabilitation, EN §§4-701 to 4-708.

HEAT PUMPS.
Environmental sound level limits and noise control rules and regulations, EN §3-401.
Geothermal heat pump grant program, SG §9-2008.

HEIRS.
Aliens.
Right to own and dispose of property, RP §14-101.
Criminal proceedings.
Charging documents speaking of.
Naming one and speaking of named partner and another or others, CP §4-105.
Decedents' estates.
General provisions, ET §§1-101 to 12-103.
See DECEDENTS' ESTATES.
Definitions, ET §1-101.
Descent and distribution.
See DESCENT AND DISTRIBUTION.
Determining relationship.
General provisions, ET §§1-201 to 1-210.
See DECEDENTS' ESTATES.
Executors and administrators.
Claims against heirs and legatees.
Limitation of actions, ET §10-103.
Notice.
Closing estates, Estates Rule 6-417; ET §10-101.

HEIRS —Cont'd
Executors and administrators —Cont'd
Notice —Cont'd
Personal notice of appointment, ET §7-104.
Opening estates.
Petition for appointment.
Notice of appointment, Estates Rule 6-311.
Small estates.
Notice of appointment, Estates Rule 6-209.
Legatees and devisees.
General provisions.
See WILLS.
Registers of wills.
Personal notice to heirs and legatees, Estates Rule 6-210; ET §2-210.
Unknown heirs.
Opening estates.
Petition for probate.
Notice of appointment, Estates Rule 6-311.
Water resources.
Reservoirs, dams or waterways.
Construction or repair permits.
Binding of heirs, successors or assigns, EN §5-508.
Wills.
Legatees and devisees.
See WILLS.

HELICOPTERS.
Emergency medical services.
Regulations for transporting patients.
EMS board to adopt, ED §13-509.
State police helicopter replacement fund, PS §2-801.
Motor vehicle violation surcharge, deposit, TR §27-101.2.

HELMETS.
Bicycles.
Requirements, TR §21-1207.1.
Motor scooters.
Requirements, TR §21-1207.2.

HEMODIALYSIS.
Pharmacists and pharmacies.
Hemodialysis distribution permits, HO §12-603.

HEMOGLOBIN C TRAIT.
Life insurance discrimination, IN §§27-208, 27-210.

HEMORRHAGIC FEVERS.
Notices.
Medical and law enforcement personnel.
Notice of exposure, HG §§18-213 to 18-213.2.

HEPATITIS.
Boxers and kick boxers.
Blood tests.
License applicants, BR §4-304.1.
Contagious diseases generally.
See CONTAGIOUS DISEASES.
Notices.
Firefighters, medical and law enforcement personnel.
Exposure, HG §§18-213 to 18-213.2.

HEPATITIS B.
Vaccinations.
Emergency medical technicians administering, ED §13-516.

HEPATITIS C VIRUS.
Department of health and mental hygiene.
Duties, HG §§18-1001, 18-1002.

HERBICIDES.
Pesticides generally.
See PESTICIDES.

HEREDITARY AND CONGENITAL DISORDERS.
Health insurance.
Required coverage, IN §15-835.

HEREDITARY AND CONGENITAL DISORDERS PROGRAMS, HG §§13-101 to 13-110.
Advisory council on hereditary and congenital disorders.
Appointment of members, HG §13-104.
Chairman, HG §13-105.
Compensation, HG §13-106.
Composition, HG §13-104.
Creation, HG §13-103.
Established, HG §13-103.
Expenses.
Compensation and reimbursement for expenses, HG §13-106.
Meetings, HG §13-106.
Membership, HG §13-104.
Officers, HG §13-105.
Powers and duties.
Establishment of subcommittees, HG §13-107.
Specific powers as to hereditary disorders, HG §13-108.
Qualifications of members, HG §13-104.
Quorum, HG §13-106.
Reports.
Annual report, HG §13-107.
Staff, HG §13-106.
Subcommittees, HG §13-107.
Tenure, HG §13-104.
Vacancies in office, HG §13-104.
Vice chairman, HG §13-105.
Legislative findings, HG §13-102.
Reports.
Advisory council on hereditary and congenital disorders.
Annual report, HG §13-107.
Rules and regulations, HG §13-109.
Enforcement by secretary of health and mental hygiene, HG §13-110.
Secretary of health and mental hygiene.
Duties of secretary, HG §13-110.
Standards, HG §13-109.
Subcommittees.
Advisory council on hereditary and congenital disorders.
Miscellaneous powers and duties, HG §13-107.

HERITAGE AREAS, FI §§13-1101 to 13-1124.
Appeals.
Decisions of authority, FI §13-1124.
Authority.
Administrative staff, FI §13-1106.
Appeal of decisions of authority, FI §13-1124.
Bond payment, FI §13-1116.
Duties generally, FI §13-1108.
Established, FI §13-1103.
Financing fund, FI §13-1114.
Meetings, FI §13-1105.
Membership, FI §13-1104.
Powers generally, FI §13-1107.
Terms of members, FI §13-1104.
Voting, FI §13-1105.
Bond issues.
Approval by board of public works, FI §13-1115.

HERITAGE AREAS —Cont'd
Bond issues —Cont'd
Authorization, FI §13-1115.
Conditions, FI §13-1117.
Investments, FI §13-1122.
Liability, FI §13-1120.
Marketability enhancement, FI §13-1122.
Payment, FI §13-1116.
Pledge of revenue, FI §13-1119.
Refunding bonds, FI §13-1121.
Resolutions, FI §13-1118.
Tax exemption, FI §13-1123.
Terms, FI §13-1117.
Trust agreements, FI §13-1118.
Boundaries.
Recognized areas, FI §13-1110.
Canal place historic preservation district.
Certified area, FI §13-1111.
Certified areas.
Designation, FI §13-1111.
Program statement, FI §13-1112.
System, FI §13-1109.
Construction of subtitle, FI §13-1102.
Definitions, FI §13-1101.
Funding, FI §13-1113.
Authority financing fund, FI §13-1114.
Grants, FI §13-1113.
Hearings.
Certified area designation, FI §13-1111.
Investments.
Bond issues, FI §13-1122.
Management plan for recognized area.
Designation of certified areas, FI §13-1111.
Proposals.
Certified areas, FI §13-1111.
Recognized areas, FI §13-1110.
Recognized areas.
Designation, FI §13-1110.
System, FI §13-1109.
Reports.
Duties of authority, FI §13-1108.
Tax exemption for bonds, FI §13-1123.

HERITAGE CONSERVATION FUND, NR §§5-1501 to 5-1506.
Appropriations.
Sources, NR §5-1505.
Board of public works.
Approval of acquisition required, NR §5-1506.
Conservation easements, NR §5-1503.
Approval by board of public works required, NR §5-1506.
Established, NR §5-1501.
Fee simple or other interest acquisitions, NR §5-1503.
Approval by board of public works required, NR §5-1506.
Management of land or interest in land acquired, NR §5-1504.
Purposes, NR §5-1502.
Recreational opportunities.
Management of land or interest in land acquired, NR §5-1504.

HEROIN.
Controlled dangerous substances.
Generally, CR §§5-101 to 5-1101.
See CONTROLLED DANGEROUS SUBSTANCES.
Schedule I, CR §5-402.

HERRING.
Fish and fisheries generally, NR §§4-101 to 4-1209.
See FISH AND FISHERIES.

HERRING RUN PUBLIC WATERSHED ASSOCIATION, EN §§5-1201 to 5-1206.
Commission.
Advisory committee.
Appointment, EN §5-1203.
Chairman, EN §5-1204.
Composition, EN §5-1203.
Duties, EN §5-1205.
Established, EN §5-1203.
Funding, EN §5-1206.
Meetings, EN §5-1204.
Quorum, EN §5-1204.
Staff, EN §5-1206.
Voting, EN §5-1204.
Composition, EN §5-1202.
Definitions, EN §5-1201.
Establishment, EN §5-1202.

HEXAVALENT CHROMIUM.
Toxics in packaging, EN §§9-1901 to 9-1907.
See TOXICS IN PACKAGING.

HIGH BLOOD PRESSURE.
Cardiovascular disease prevention programs, HG §§13-201 to 13-206.
See HEART DISEASE AND STROKE PREVENTION PROGRAMS.

HIGHER EDUCATION/BUSINESS PARTNERSHIPS PROGRAM, ED §10-213.
Promotion of economic interests, ED §15-107.

HIGHER EDUCATION COMMISSION.
See UNIVERSITIES AND COLLEGES.

HIGHER EDUCATION INVESTMENT PROGRAM.
College savings plan of Maryland board, ED §§18-1904, 18-1905.
Income tax state adjustments.
Refunds received under program, TG §10-205.

HIGHER EDUCATION LOAN PROGRAM.
Corporation.
State treasury.
Investment in obligations of higher education loan corporation, SF §6-225.
Interest.
Statement furnished by lender to borrower.
Exemption as to Maryland higher education loan corporation, CL §12-106.
State treasury.
Depositaries.
Designation of financial institutions as depositaries.
Higher education loans to be considered, SF §6-207.
Obligations of higher education loan corporation.
Investment in, SF §6-225.
Usury.
Statement furnished by lender to borrower.
Exemption as to Maryland higher education loan corporation, CL §12-106.

HIGH-LEVEL NUCLEAR WASTE.
Defined, EN §7-225.
Facilities prohibited, EN §7-225.
Hazardous materials and substances generally, EN §§7-101 to 7-306; HG §§22-501 to 22-508.
See HAZARDOUS MATERIALS AND SUBSTANCES.

HIGH-LEVEL NUCLEAR WASTE —Cont'd
Radiation, EN §§8-101 to 8-601.
See RADIATION.

HIGH SCHOOLS.
General provisions.
See SCHOOLS.

HIGH VOLTAGE LINES.
Administration of title, LE §6-104.
Administrative search warrant, LE §6-105.
Defined, LE §6-101.
Enforcement of title, LE §6-104.
Misdemeanors.
Violations of title, LE §6-110.
Penalties.
Violations of title, LE §6-110.
Presumptions, LE §6-103.
Restrictions on activity within 10 feet of high voltage line, LE §6-106.
Duty of owner, lessee or user of equipment, LE §6-109.
Duty of owner or operator of high voltage line, LE §6-108.
Duty of person performing activity, LE §6-107.
Scope of title, LE §6-102.

HIGHWAY ADMINISTRATION.
Accounts, TR §8-206.
Acquisition of real property.
Powers.
Generally, TR §8-302.
Administrator, TR §8-202.
Alternatives to proposed project, TR §8-102.
Bicycle routes, project resulting in severance or destruction of, TR §8-601.1.
Books and records, TR §8-205.
Bridges.
See BRIDGES.
Counties.
State highways.
Administration generally responsible only for state highways, TR §8-633.
Eminent domain.
Applicable provisions, RP §12-101.
Entry by state highway administration employees to conduct environmental and engineering studies, RP §12-111.
Employees, TR §8-204.
Equipment and materials, TR §8-204.
Established, TR §8-201.
Federal aid.
Power to comply with federal acts, TR §8-503.
Use of federal funds by administration, TR §8-505.
Footpaths, bicycle trails and bridle paths.
Establishment and maintenance, TR §8-409.
Funds.
Distribution of highway funds, TR §§8-403 to 8-408.
Interstate Route 95.
Expenditures for construction through Prince George's county, TR §8-601.
Maryland historical trust.
Construction and interpretation of subtitle, SF §5A-306.
Offices.
Lease of offices, TR §8-204.
Plats.
Property or rights of way acquired or granted by administration, RP §3-109.

HIGHWAY ADMINISTRATION —Cont'd
Powers.
Generally, TR §§8-203, 8-204.
Public use areas.
Control, TR §8-204.
Railroads.
Construction and maintenance of crossings by railroad and administration, TR §8-640.
Crossings.
Elimination of crossings, TR §8-640.
Records, TR §8-205.
Rules and regulations.
Adoption, TR §8-204.
Sidewalks.
Construction by developers of industrial, commercial or apartment areas adjoining roads, TR §8-629.
State roads commission.
Part of, TR §8-210.
References to commission mean administration, TR §8-207.
Transportation department.
Included within department, TR §2-107.
Part of transportation department, TR §8-201.

HIGHWAYS.
Abandonment.
County roads, 25 §§135 to 143.
See COUNTIES.
Sale of land no longer needed, TR §8-309.
Abutting property owners.
Freeways.
No right of ingress and egress, TR §8-619.
Parkways.
Right of abutting owners to ingress and egress, TR §8-619.
Accidents.
Reports, TR §§20-101 to 20-113.
See MOTOR VEHICLE ACCIDENTS.
Accounts and accounting.
Gasoline and motor vehicle account.
Highway user revenues, TR §8-402.
Acquisition of real property.
Definitions, TR §8-301.
Duties of administration, TR §8-305.
Freeways, TR §8-619.
Interest which may be acquired, TR §8-313.
Land adjacent to federal aid highways, TR §8-314.
Other than for highway purposes, TR §8-315.
Private use of acquired land, TR §8-308.
Protection of highways, TR §8-313.
Motels, restaurants, service stations, etc., prohibited, TR §8-313.
Purpose, TR §8-313.
Quick-take act, TR §§8-318 to 8-339. See within this heading, "Quick-take act."
Right of transferor to continue use, TR §8-308.
Scope of part, TR §8-312.
State highway administration.
Powers, TR §8-302.
Taxation.
Payment of proportionate share of taxes on property acquired, TR §8-306.
Special tax districts.
Acquisition by state roads commission of property.
Subject to assessment by special tax district, TR §8-307.
Subject to assessment by special tax district, TR §8-307.

HIGHWAYS —Cont'd
Administration.
State highway administration.
See HIGHWAY ADMINISTRATION.
Advertising.
Acquisition of signs by state highway administration, TR §8-743.
Outdoor advertising, TR §§8-701 to 8-749.
See OUTDOOR ADVERTISING.
Prohibited within 660 feet of expressway, TR §8-740.
Alternatives to proposed projects, TR §8-102.
Animals.
Accidents.
Duty on striking domestic animals, TR §20-106.
Lamps on animal-drawn vehicles, TR §22-216.
Livestock crossing signs, TR §21-708.
Persons riding animals or driving animal-drawn vehicles, TR §21-104.
Removal of carcasses of animals from highways, TR §8-602.
Appeals.
Board of property review.
Appeal from award of board, TR §8-329.
State highway access valuation board, TR §8-310.
Appraisals.
Sale of land no longer needed, TR §8-309.
Attorneys at law.
Employment by commission, TR §8-204.
Auctions.
Sale of land no longer needed, TR §8-309.
Baltimore City.
Funds.
Allocation of highway user revenues, TR §8-403.
Distribution of funds, TR §8-406.
General provisions.
See BALTIMORE CITY.
Municipal urban area highway construction fund, TR §8-507.
Baltimore county.
General provisions.
See BALTIMORE COUNTY.
Beautification of highways.
Acquisition of property, TR §8-315.
Bicycles.
Bike lanes, TR §21-1205.1.
Establishment and maintenance of bicycle trails, TR §8-409.
Pathways, TR §8-630.
Prohibited on certain highways, TR §21-1205.1.
Riding on roadways or on highway.
Regulations, TR §21-1205.
Birds and game.
Shooting on, from or across prohibited, NR §10-410.
Board of property review.
Eminent domain. See within this heading, "Eminent domain."
Quick-take act. See within this heading, "Quick-take act."
Bond issues.
County transportation bonds, TR §§3-301 to 3-310.
See COUNTIES.
Debt service.
Defined, TR §8-401.
Distribution and use of revenues.
Highway user revenues.
Security of highway construction bonds not affected, TR §§3-216, 8-402.

HIGHWAYS —Cont'd
Bond issues —Cont'd
Public debt.
General provisions, 31 §§1 to 12.
See PUBLIC DEBT.
State highway construction bonds.
Highway user revenues.
Modification as to distribution and use.
Security not affected, TR §§3-216, 8-402.
Bridges.
See BRIDGES.
Bridle paths.
Establishment and maintenance, TR §8-409.
Brush removal, TR §8-602.
Buffer and setback requirements.
Reclaimed water used for irrigation purposes, EN §9-303.1.
Cattle.
Driving on improved highway, AG §§3-501 to 3-504.
See LIVESTOCK.
Livestock crossing signs, TR §21-708.
Cemeteries.
Roads through.
Consent of owner required to pass through, 25 §144.
Closing.
County roads, 25 §§135 to 155A.
See COUNTIES.
Commission.
State roads commission. See within this heading, "State roads commission."
Compacts.
Transit authority compact, TR §§10-201 to 10-207.
Transit regulation compact.
See WASHINGTON METROPOLITAN AREA TRANSIT AUTHORITY COMPACT.
Condemnation. See within this heading, "Eminent domain."
Conflicts of interest, TR §8-217.
Construction and repair.
Administration.
Responsibility of administration generally, TR §8-601.
Responsible only for state highways, TR §8-633.
Alternatives to proposed projects, TR §8-102.
Bicycle trails.
Establishment and maintenance, TR §8-409.
Bids.
General provisions, TR §8-614.
Bridle paths.
Establishment and maintenance, TR §8-409.
Brush removal, TR §8-602.
Construction program, TR §8-613.
Contracts for construction or reconstruction.
General provisions, TR §8-614.
Convict labor, TR §8-607.
Counties.
Approval required for construction or reconstruction by county, TR §8-410.
Dirt, sand, gravel and other material.
Removal prohibited, TR §8-647.
Driving or walking on road before opened prohibited, TR §21-1114.
Footpaths, TR §8-409.
Fund.
Accounts as to construction fund, TR §8-206.
Landscaping highways.
Responsibility of administration, TR §8-603.
Location.
Changes in, TR §8-204.

HIGHWAYS —Cont'd
Construction and repair —Cont'd
Location —Cont'd
Termini of highway to be constructed or reconstructed, TR §8-319.
Maintenance.
Agreement to change status of county and state roads, TR §8-304.
Defined, TR §8-101.
Parkways, TR §8-619.
Municipal corporations.
Approval required for construction or reconstruction by municipality, TR §8-410.
Persons working on highways.
Regulations, TR §21-105.
Phragmite control, TR §8-609.
Alternative management and control methods, TR §8-609.1.
Plats or maps.
Preparation showing proposed construction, TR §8-320.
Preservation. See within this heading, "Preservation."
Prince George's county.
I-95 in Prince George's county, TR §8-601.
Prisoners.
Convict labor, TR §8-607.
Project planning program, TR §8-612.
Responsibility of administration, TR §8-601.
Secondary highway construction and reconstruction programs, TR §8-611.
Utility sleeves, TR §8-608.
Valuation.
Estimate of value of property taken and damage to remainder, TR §8-320.
Contracts.
Commissioners and employees not to be interested in contracts, TR §8-217.
Construction and repair.
General provisions, TR §8-614.
Controlled-access highways.
Defined, TR §21-101.
Motor vehicles.
Leaving vehicle on prohibited, TR §21-509.
Riding animals or driving animal-drawn vehicles.
Regulations, TR §21-104.
Convict road force.
Labor, TR §8-607.
Persons working on highways.
Regulations, TR §21-105.
Correctional facility inmates.
Road work by inmates at correctional facilities, COR §§9-501 to 9-520.
See PRISONS AND PRISONERS.
Counties.
Administration.
Notice of receipts and disbursements, TR §8-412.
Report of expenditures allocated for each county, TR §8-412.
Allocation of highway user revenues, TR §§8-403, 8-404.
Bond issues.
County transportation bonds, TR §§3-301 to 3-310.
See COUNTIES.
Chartered counties.
Powers of county, 25A §5.
County highway construction fund.
Transfer to and from construction fund, TR §8-507.

HIGHWAYS —Cont'd
Counties —Cont'd
County roads.
Defined, TR §8-101.
Federal aid.
Power to comply with federal acts, TR §8-503.
Power to raise funds, TR §8-504.
Grants to local bus systems, TR §10-207.
Highway user revenues. See within this heading, "Highway user revenues."
Levy.
Relief from county levy, TR §8-406.
Municipal corporations.
Payment of cost of highway projects within municipalities, 25 §2A.
Reports by counties, TR §8-636.
State roads commission.
Engineering advice to counties, TR §8-635.
Transfer of jurisdiction to state, TR §8-303.
Utility sleeves.
General provisions, TR §8-608.
Crimes and offenses.
Fines. See within this heading, "Fines."
Crossings.
Industrial crossings, TR §8-626.
Railroads, TR §§8-639 to 8-643.
See RAILROADS.
Crossover.
Defined, TR §21-101.
Crosswalks.
Defined, TR §21-101.
Damages.
County roads.
Assessments for opening or altering public roads, 25 §§146 to 149.
Operation of vehicles causing damage to roads prohibited, TR §24-202.
Debt service.
Defined, TR §8-401.
Deeds.
Acquisition of property to protect highways, TR §8-313.
Defense-related activities.
Closure or restricted access to certain properties, TR §8-627.
Definitions, TR §8-101.
Acquisition of real property, TR §8-301.
Controlled-access highway, TR §21-101.
Crosswalks, TR §21-101.
Expressways, TR §21-101.
Highway preservation, TR §24-201.
Highway user revenues, TR §8-401.
Long range highway programs, TR §8-610.
Municipality in urban area, TR §8-507.
Publicly owned utility, TR §8-506.
Roadway, TR §11-151.
Through highway, TR §21-101.
Urban area, TR §8-507.
Directions.
Signs, TR §8-605.
Director of highways.
Administrator of highways.
See HIGHWAY ADMINISTRATION.
Chairman of state roads commission. See within this heading, "State roads commission."
Continuation and change of resolutions, rules, forms, orders and directives, TR §8-207.
Distances.
Signs, TR §8-605.
Distribution and use of special funds.
Highway user revenues. See within this heading, "Highway user revenues."

HIGHWAYS —Cont'd
Divided highways.
Definitions, TR §11-113.
Draining lands.
Drainage districts.
Benefits of highway, 25 §9.
Dual lane highways.
Riding animals or driving animal-drawn vehicles, TR §21-104.
Electronic personal assistive mobility devices.
Prohibited on certain roadways and highways, TR §21-1205.1.
Eminent domain.
Applicable provisions, RP §12-101.
County roads, 25 §138.
General provisions, RP §§12-101 to 12-212.
See EMINENT DOMAIN.
Quick-take act. See within this heading, "Quick-take act."
Regulations, MD Const Art III §40B.
State highway administration.
Entry by employees to conduct environmental and engineering studies, RP §12-111.
Engineers.
Counties.
Engineering advice to counties, TR §8-635.
Employment by administration, TR §8-204.
Environmental service.
Entry upon and excavation, NR §3-104.
Excavations.
By side of roadway.
Removal of sand, gravel, etc., regulated, TR §8-647.
Permits for digging up highways.
General provisions, TR §8-646.
Grades.
Conformity to grades in cities, TR §8-606.
Expressways.
Acquisition of signs by state highway administration, TR §8-743.
Defined, TR §§8-101, 8-739, 21-101.
Designation of existing highway, TR §8-620.
Outdoor advertising.
General provisions, TR §§8-739 to 8-745.
See OUTDOOR ADVERTISING.
Federal aid, TR §§8-501 to 8-507.
Acceptance of federal funds, TR §8-503.
Administration.
Power to comply with federal acts, TR §8-503.
Use of federal funds by administration, TR §8-505.
Authority to comply with conditions and provisions, TR §8-503.
Authority to raise funds, TR §8-504.
Beautification of highway.
Acquisition of adjacent land.
Authority of state highway administration, TR §§8-204, 8-315.
Declared to be in public interest, TR §8-315.
Counties.
County highway construction funds, TR §8-507.
Power of administration and counties to comply with federal acts, TR §8-503.
Power to raise funds, TR §8-504.
Elimination of highway hazards, TR §8-505.
Expenditure of funds prior to federal matching funds, TR §8-743.
Federal acts.
Defined, TR §8-501.
Legislative policy, TR §8-502.

HIGHWAYS —Cont'd
Federal aid —Cont'd
Matching funds.
Sources for federal acts, TR §8-504.
Municipal corporations.
Power to comply with federal acts, TR §8-503.
Sources of matching funds for federal acts.
Power of municipalities to raise funds, TR §8-504.
Outdoor advertising.
Along federal-aid primary highways.
General provisions, TR §§8-725 to 8-737.
Publicly owned utility.
Payment for relocation, TR §8-506.
Fines.
Excavations.
Violation, TR §8-646.
Removal of dirt, sand, gravel, etc., from side of roadway, TR §8-647.
Signs, signals or markers.
Destruction or damaging, TR §8-605.
Flags.
Rest areas, welcome centers and exhibit centers, TR §8-652.
Food and food establishments.
Conduct of restaurants on acquired property prohibited, TR §8-313.
Footpaths.
Establishment and maintenance, TR §8-409.
Foot racing events, TR §21-1211.1.
Forests and parks.
Land clearing by state or local government.
Cutting or clearing restrictions, reforestation, NR §5-103.
Roadside trees, NR §§5-401 to 5-411.
See FORESTS AND PARKS.
Freeways.
Acquisition of real property, TR §8-619.
Construction.
Authority, TR §8-619.
Establishment.
Authority, TR §8-619.
Ingress and egress.
No right of abutting owners, TR §8-619.
Regulation, TR §8-621.
Right of access.
When property held under one ownership, TR §8-622.
Use, TR §8-621.
Funds.
Federal matching funds.
Expenditure of funds prior to federal matching funds, TR §8-743.
Highway user revenues. See within this heading, "Highway user revenues."
Transportation trust fund.
See TRANSPORTATION TRUST FUND.
General assembly.
Eminent domain.
Board of property review.
Members of general assembly not to be members of board, TR §8-327.
Governor.
State highway projects.
Report to governor on status of projects, TR §8-616.
Grade crossings.
General provisions, TR §§8-639 to 8-643.
See RAILROADS.
Grades.
Municipal corporations.
Conformity to grades in cities, TR §8-606.

HIGHWAYS —Cont'd
Hazards.
Elimination, TR §8-505.
Hearings.
Eminent domain.
Board of property review, TR §8-327.
Highway safety program, TR §§2-401 to 2-403.
See TRANSPORTATION DEPARTMENT.
Highway user revenues.
Administration.
Information to be furnished, TR §8-411.
Reports to counties and Baltimore City, TR §8-413.
Allocation to counties, TR §8-404.
Amount.
Computation of amount, TR §8-404.
Counties, TR §8-404.
Municipalities, TR §8-405.
Baltimore City.
Account of expenditures of highway user revenues by Baltimore City, TR §8-412.
Permitted uses, TR §8-408.
Reports of administration to Baltimore City, TR §8-413.
Basis of distribution, TR §8-404.
Bicycle trails.
Establishment and maintenance, TR §8-409.
Counties.
Allocation to counties, TR §§8-403, 8-404.
Approval required for construction or reconstruction by county, TR §8-410.
Defined, TR §8-401.
Disbursement of funds.
Manner of disbursement, TR §8-407.
Permitted uses, TR §8-408.
Relief from county levy for roads, TR §8-406.
Reports of administration to counties, TR §8-413.
Debt service.
Defined, TR §8-401.
Definitions, TR §8-401.
Disbursement of revenues, TR §8-407.
Conditions on distribution, TR §8-406.
Levy and certification required before distribution, TR §8-406.
Footpaths, bridle paths, horse trails and bicycle trails.
Establishment and maintenance, TR §8-409.
Gasoline and motor vehicle revenue account, TR §8-402.
Information.
Furnishing information to administration, TR §8-411.
Kent county.
Permitted uses, TR §8-408.
Mileage.
Reports as to mileage, TR §8-411.
Municipal corporations.
Approval required for construction or reconstruction, TR §8-410.
Computation of amount, TR §8-405.
Disbursement of funds.
Manner of disbursement, TR §8-407.
Permitted uses of highway user revenues, TR §8-408.
Prince George's county.
Special improvement districts, TR §8-405.
Reports.
Administration reports to counties and Baltimore City, TR §8-413.
Mileage, TR §8-411.

HIGHWAYS —Cont'd
Highway user revenues —Cont'd
Reversion of funds, TR §8-406.
Horses.
Persons riding animals or driving animal-drawn
vehicles, TR §21-104.
Improvement of transportation system.
Alternatives to proposed projects, TR §8-102.
Industrial corporations.
Access to highway.
Calculation of traffic volume, TR §8-625.
Crossings, TR §8-626.
Permit required, TR §8-625.
Width and locations, TR §8-625.
Informational signs, TR §8-605.
Power to erect, TR §4-405.
Rules and regulations.
Conformity, TR §4-405.
Ingress and egress.
Commercial property, TR §§8-625, 8-626.
Expressways.
Rights of abutting property owner, TR §8-620.
Freeways.
No right of abutting owner, TR §8-619.
Locations, TR §8-625.
Parkways, TR §8-619.
Right of access.
When property held under one ownership, TR
§8-622.
Traffic safety.
Determination of commission, TR §8-625.
Width, TR §8-625.
Inmates at correctional facilities, COR §§9-501
to 9-520.
See PRISONS AND PRISONERS.
Intersections.
Right-of-way, TR §21-401.
Entering stop or yield intersection, TR §21-403.
"T" intersection without traffic control device,
TR §21-401.1.
Speed.
Reduction of speed in certain circumstances, TR
§21-801.
Stop intersections.
Authority to designate, TR §25-109.
Entering.
Right-of-way, TR §21-403.
Yield intersections.
Authority to designate, TR §25-109.
Right-of-way, TR §21-403.
Interstate highway.
Defined, TR §8-101.
Interstate system.
Construction.
Expenditures for construction of I-95 through
Prince George's county, TR §8-601.
Informational signs, TR §§4-405, 8-605.
Publicly owned utility.
Definition, TR §8-506.
Payment to owner of utility relocated, etc.
Result of interstate highway construction, TR
§8-506.
Signs, displays and devices.
Informational signs, TR §§4-405, 8-605.
Regulations, TR §8-605.
John F. Kennedy Memorial Highway.
Elimination of ramp tolls in Harford and Cecil
counties, TR §4-312.1.
Outdoor advertising.
General provisions, TR §§8-701 to 8-749.
See OUTDOOR ADVERTISING.

HIGHWAYS —Cont'd
John F. Kennedy Memorial Highway —Cont'd
Railroad tracks on highway prohibited, TR §4-403.
Service facilities on highway, TR §4-404.
Jurisdiction.
Transfer to state by county, municipality or other
political subdivision, TR §8-303.
Korean war veterans memorial highway, TR
§8-651.
Land binding thereon.
Conveyance of title, RP §2-114.
Landscaping highways.
Administration to provide landscaping, TR §8-603.
Lights or guards.
Nighttime illumination of urban highways, TR
§8-630.
Removal or moving prohibited, TR §21-1115.
Livestock.
Crossing signs, TR §21-708.
Driving on improved highways, AG §§3-501 to
3-504.
See LIVESTOCK.
Long range highway programs.
Annual status report, TR §8-613.1.
Construction program, TR §8-613.
Definitions, TR §8-610.
Inventory.
Primary and secondary highway needs
inventory, TR §8-611.
Primary and secondary highway needs inventory,
TR §8-611.
Project planning program, TR §8-612.
Reports.
Annual status report, TR §8-613.1.
Markers.
Signs, signals and markers. See within this
heading, "Signs, signals and markers."
Maryland-Washington metropolitan district.
Construction near Rock creek, 28 §5-101.
Maryland-Washington regional district.
Acquisition of land for highways, 28 §7-106.
Master plan of highways.
Mandatory referral and approval of public
roads, parks, buildings, etc., after adoption,
28 §7-112.
Subdivisions.
Street dedication, 28 §7-115.
Motels.
Conduct of motel, etc., on acquired property
prohibited, TR §8-313.
Motorcycles.
Operating motorcycles on roadways laned for
traffic, TR §21-1303.
Motor scooters.
Prohibited on certain roadways and highways, TR
§21-1205.1.
Riding on roadway or highway, TR §21-1205.
Motor vehicles.
Accident reports.
General provisions, TR §§20-101 to 20-113.
See MOTOR VEHICLE ACCIDENTS.
Construction.
Use of road before opened prohibited, TR
§21-1114.
Controlled-access highway.
Bicycles.
Prohibited, TR §21-1205.1.
Defined, TR §21-101.
Entering, TR §21-312.
Leaving, TR §21-312.
Leaving vehicle on prohibited, TR §21-509.

HIGHWAYS —Cont'd
Motor vehicles —Cont'd
Controlled-access highway —Cont'd
Restrictions on use, TR §21-313.
Crossover.
Defined, TR §21-101.
Entering highway from crossover.
Right-of-way, TR §21-404.1.
Damages to highway.
Liability for damage to highway or structure,
TR §24-208.
Prohibited, TR §21-1114.
Defined, TR §11-127.
Divided highways.
Defined, TR §11-113.
Driving on, TR §21-311.
General provisions.
See MOTOR VEHICLES.
Laned for traffic, TR §21-1303.
Direction-control signals, TR §21-204.1.
Driving on roadways laned for traffic, TR
§21-309.
One-way roadways.
Designated by state highway administration,
TR §21-308.
Parking, TR §21-1004.
Operation of vehicles causing damage to highways
prohibited, TR §24-202.
Parking strip.
Driving on, TR §21-1114.
Persons riding animals or driving animal-drawn
vehicles.
Regulations, TR §21-104.
Persons working on highways.
Regulations, TR §21-105.
Placing along highway causing traffic hazard, TR
§21-1113.
Provisions refer to vehicles upon highways, TR
§21-101.1.
Racing or speed contest.
Prohibited, TR §21-1116.
Restrictions.
On right to use highways.
Authority of state roads commission or local
authorities, TR §24-204.
Powers of local authorities, TR §25-102.
Right-of-way, TR §21-101.
Roadblocks, TR §19-102.
Roadway.
Bicycles, TR §21-1205.1.
Speed limits.
See SPEED RESTRICTIONS FOR MOTOR
VEHICLES.
Through highways.
Authority to designate, TR §25-109.
Defined, TR §21-101.
Right-of-way on entering, TR §21-403.
Trucks.
Testing of trucks on state highways, TR
§24-207.
Use of road before opened prohibited, TR
§21-1114.
Municipal corporations.
Counties.
Payment of cost of highway projects within
municipalities, 25 §2A.
Defined, TR §8-401.
Federal aid.
Power to comply with federal acts, TR §8-503.
Sources of matching funds for federal acts.
Power of municipalities to raise funds, TR
§8-504.

HIGHWAYS —Cont'd
Municipal corporations —Cont'd
Grades.
Conformity to grades in cities and towns, TR
§8-606.
Land clearing on construction of highway by local
government.
Cutting and clearing restrictions, reforestation,
NR §5-103.
Municipality-urban area highway construction
fund, TR §8-507.
Transfer of jurisdiction to state, TR §8-303.
Names, TR §8-604.
Advisory committee on naming state facilities,
roads and bridges, SG §2-10A-09.
Nighttime illumination of urban highways, TR
§8-630.
Notices.
Administration.
County allotments.
Receipts, disbursements and balance, TR
§8-412.
Sale of land no longer needed, TR §8-309.
Oaths.
State roads commission, TR §8-212.
Obstructions.
Permits.
Digging up highways, TR §8-646.
Open containers.
Alcoholic beverages.
Possession in motor vehicles' passenger areas,
CR §§10-123 to 10-127.
Outdoor advertising.
Along federal-aid primary highways, TR §§8-701
to 8-749.
See OUTDOOR ADVERTISING.
Overpasses.
Signs.
Erection of signs denoting height, TR §21-208.
Owner.
Damages for opening, etc., public roads.
Ascertainment of damages, 25 §146.
Parkways.
Abutting owners.
Right of abutting owners to ingress and egress,
TR §8-619.
Acquisition of real property, TR §8-619.
Construction, TR §8-619.
Regulation of use, TR §8-621.
Patapsco tunnel.
Toll bridges and tunnels.
Operation of motor vehicles.
See TRAFFIC LAWS.
Payment into court.
Quick-take act, TR §8-323.
Rights of commission, TR §8-324.
Pedestrians.
Controlled-access highway.
Walking on prohibited, TR §21-509.
Crossing at other than crosswalks, TR §21-503.
Footpaths and bridle paths.
Establishment and maintenance of footpaths,
TR §8-409.
General provisions.
See PEDESTRIANS.
Permits.
Bond of nongovernment applicant, TR §8-646.
Digging up highways.
General provisions, TR §8-646.
Entrances to commercial or industrial properties,
TR §8-625.

HIGHWAYS —Cont'd
Permits —Cont'd
Excavations.
General provisions, TR §8-646.
Phragmite control.
Alternative management and control methods, TR §8-609.1.
Generally, TR §8-609.
Plats.
Property or rights of way acquired or granted by state highway administration, RP §3-109.
Quick-take act. See within this heading, "Quick-take act."
Recordation, 25 §§138, 142.
Preservation.
Administration.
Authority to preserve highways, TR §24-203.
Restricting use of endangered highways, TR §24-204.
Authority to preserve, TR §24-203.
Damage of highways.
Prohibited, TR §24-202.
Definitions, TR §24-201.
Liability for damage to highways or structure, TR §24-208.
Restricting use of endangered highways.
Authority of local authorities and state highway administration, TR §24-204.
Primary highway.
Defined, TR §8-101.
Primary systems.
Defined, TR §8-801.
Prince George's county.
Construction and repair.
I-95 in Prince George's county, TR §8-601.
Traffic hazards.
Selling or displaying produce or merchandise on highways, TR §21-1113.
Prisoners working on roads.
Generally, COR §§9-501 to 9-520.
See PRISONS AND PRISONERS.
Regulations, TR §21-105.
Road work by prisoners, TR §8-607.
Programs for highway construction.
Long range highway programs. See within this heading, "Long range highway programs."
Projects.
Alternatives to proposed project, TR §8-102.
Defined, TR §8-101.
Property.
Interest which may be acquired, TR §8-313.
Public accountants.
Employment by state roads commission, TR §8-204.
Public utilities.
Closure or restricted access to certain properties, TR §8-627.
Definition of publicly owned utility, TR §8-506.
Eminent domain.
Installation of utility facilities, TR §8-324.
Publicly owned utility facilities.
Payment for relocation, TR §8-506.
Quick-take act, TR §§8-318 to 8-339.
Accelerated procedure.
Entry on property.
Commission may take possession of property, TR §8-336.
Estimates.
Payment, TR §8-335.
Final award, TR §8-339.

HIGHWAYS —Cont'd
Quick-take act —Cont'd
Accelerated procedure —Cont'd
General condemnation law applicability, TR §8-334.
Payment.
Effect of payment, TR §8-338.
Withdrawal of funds paid into court, TR §8-337.
Petition for condemnation, TR §8-335.
Possession of property.
Commission may take possession, TR §8-336.
Withdrawal of funds paid into court, TR §8-337.
Appeals.
Appeal from award of board, TR §8-329.
Board of property review.
Additional boards, TR §8-327.
Appeals from board, TR §8-329.
Appointment by circuit court, TR §8-327.
Certification to board, TR §8-326.
Chairman, TR §8-327.
Compensation, TR §8-327.
Composition, TR §8-327.
Condemnation cases.
Cases which shall be filed as condemnation cases, TR §8-326.
Created, TR §8-327.
Duties, TR §8-328.
Established, TR §8-327.
General assembly.
Members not to be members of board, TR §8-327.
Hearings, TR §8-328.
Meetings, TR §8-327.
Members, TR §8-327.
Officers of court, TR §8-327.
Powers, TR §8-328.
Qualifications, TR §8-327.
Rules, TR §8-327.
Term of office, TR §8-327.
Vacancies, TR §8-327.
Value.
When date of value determined, TR §8-328.
Compensation.
Estimate of value of property taken and damage to remainder, TR §8-320.
Negotiation with property owners, TR §8-325.
Payment of final award, TR §8-331.
Payment to property owners or into court, TR §8-323.
Construction plans, TR §8-320.
Damages.
Estimates, TR §8-320.
Delay.
Effect of commission's delay in acquiring title or filing suit, TR §8-330.
Entry on property, TR §8-324.
Estimates.
Approval of commission required, TR §8-321.
Payment, TR §8-323.
Permanent record of commission, TR §8-322.
Property values and damages, TR §8-320.
Recording, TR §8-321.
Signing, TR §8-321.
Filing of cases in court, TR §8-326.
Final award.
Payment, TR §8-331.
General condemnation law.
Applicability, TR §8-318.
Limitation on manner of acquisition, TR §8-313.
Negotiation with property owners, TR §8-325.

HIGHWAYS —Cont'd
Quick-take act —Cont'd
Other than highway purposes, TR §8-315.
Owner of property.
Payments to property owner, TR §8-323.
Payment to owners or into court, TR §8-323.
Rights of commission, TR §8-324.
Petition for condemnation, TR §8-323.
Plats.
Approval of commission required, TR §8-321.
Contents, TR §8-320.
Permanent record of commission, TR §8-322.
Preparation showing proposed construction, TR §8-320.
Recording, TR §8-321.
Signing, TR §8-321.
Possession of property.
Commission may take possession of property, TR §8-324.
Payment to owner or into court, TR §8-323.
Right to take possession by commission, TR §8-324.
Procedure.
Available procedures, TR §8-318.
Property values.
Estimates, TR §8-320.
Public utilities.
Installation of facilities on land acquired, TR §8-324.
State roads commission.
Records, TR §8-322.
Termini.
Location of termini of highway to be constructed or reconstructed, TR §8-319.
Valuation date, TR §§8-325, 8-328.
Alternate date, TR §8-330.
Value.
Board of property review.
As of what date value of property determined, TR §8-328.
Date as of which value to be determined, TR §§8-325, 8-328.
Alternate date of valuation, TR §8-330.
Effect of commissions delay in acquiring title or filing suit, TR §8-330.
Quorum.
State roads commission, TR §8-213.
Railroads.
Crossings, PUC §9-306.
Protection generally, PUC §9-311.
Warning signs, PUC §9-313.
Using or occupying road, street, alley or other public way, PUC §5-407.
Real property.
Conveyance of surplus land to promote economic development, TR §8-309.
Land binding thereon.
Grant of title, RP §2-114.
State highway administration.
Sale of land no longer needed, TR §8-309.
Reclaimed water used for irrigation purposes.
Buffer and setback requirements, EN §9-303.1.
Records.
State roads commission, TR §8-216.
Reforestation.
Construction of highways by state or local government, NR §5-103.
Reports.
Administration.
Funds allotted to counties, TR §8-413.
Counties, TR §8-636.

HIGHWAYS —Cont'd
Reports —Cont'd
Highway user revenues.
Report of administration to counties and Baltimore City, TR §8-413.
Long range highway programs.
Annual status report, TR §8-613.1.
State highway projects.
Report to governor, TR §8-616.
Revenue.
Highway user revenues. See within this heading, "Highway user revenues."
Rights-of-way.
Annual status report, TR §8-613.1.
Broadband communication infrastructure, installation by nonprofit telecommunications services, TR §8-654.
Fund.
Construction funds.
Accounting, TR §8-206.
Phragmite control, TR §8-609.
Alternative management and control methods, TR §8-609.1.
Plats.
Recorded and indexed, RP §3-109.
Reports.
Annual status report, TR §8-613.1.
Road force, TR §§8-607, 21-105.
Roads.
County roads.
See COUNTIES.
Defined, TR §8-101.
State highway administration. See within this heading, "State highway administration."
Roadside trees.
General provisions.
See FORESTS AND PARKS.
Roadway.
Defined, TR §11-151.
Route 2.
Trucks.
Semitrailer and trailer operated in combination with truck tractor.
Restrictions, TR §24-104.1.
Rules and regulations.
Freeways, TR §8-621.
Informational signs, TR §4-405.
Outdoor advertising.
See OUTDOOR ADVERTISING.
Preservation and use of roads, TR §24-203.
Safety program.
See TRANSPORTATION DEPARTMENT.
Sales.
Land no longer needed.
Authority and procedure of state highway administration, TR §8-309.
Secondary highways.
Defined, TR §8-101.
Service stations.
Conduct of gasoline and automobile service stations on acquired property prohibited, TR §8-313.
Severn river watershed.
Approval of plans for construction, etc., for public roads, EN §4-308.
Sidewalks.
Construction by developers of industrial, commercial or apartment areas adjoining roads, TR §8-629.
Urban highways.
Adjacent to certain urban-type highways, TR §8-630.

HIGHWAYS —Cont'd
Signs, signals and markers.
Bridges.
Weight and speed of vehicles passing over
bridges, TR §24-206.
Conformity with administration manual, TR
§§25-104, 25-106.1.
Damaging or removing.
Penalty, TR §8-605.
Distances and directions, TR §8-605.
Informational signs, TR §8-605.
Power to erect, TR §4-405.
Rules and regulations.
Conformity required, TR §4-405.
Interstate systems.
Regulations for signs, displays and devices, TR
§8-605.
Livestock crossings.
Obedience required, TR §21-708.
Posting, TR §21-708.
Maintenance, TR §8-605.
Outdoor advertising.
General provisions, TR §§8-701 to 8-749.
See OUTDOOR ADVERTISING.
Overpasses.
Erection of signs denoting height of overpasses,
TR §21-208.
Oversize and overweight vehicles.
Restriction of use of highways, TR §24-204.
Traffic-control devices generally.
See TRAFFIC CONTROL DEVICES.
Snow and ice.
Clearing highways.
Garrett county, TR §8-602.
General rule, TR §8-602.
Snow emergency routes, TR §21-1119.
Snowmobiles.
Operation of snowmobiles on designated
highways, TR §21-104.1.
Speed.
See SPEED RESTRICTIONS FOR MOTOR
VEHICLES.
State archives.
Maps and plats showing construction.
Recordation, TR §8-321.
State highway access valuation board, TR
§8-310.
State highway administration.
Applicable provisions, RP §12-101.
Bond issues.
General provisions. See within this heading,
"Bond issues."
Eminent domain.
Entry by state highway administration
employees to conduct environmental and
engineering studies, RP §12-111.
General provisions.
See HIGHWAY ADMINISTRATION.
Transportation department.
General provisions.
See TRANSPORTATION DEPARTMENT.
State highway system.
Agreement to change status of county and state
roads, TR §8-304.
Defined, TR §8-101.
State highway administration.
Powers, TR §8-204.
State police.
Industrial crossings.
Power to close, TR §8-626.

HIGHWAYS —Cont'd
State roads commission.
Acquisition of real property.
General power to acquire private property, TR
§8-302.
Appointment.
By governor, TR §8-211.
By secretary of transportation, TR §8-211.
Bylaws, TR §8-213.
Chairman.
Administrator is chairman of commission, TR
§8-211.
Powers.
Generally, TR §8-218.
Code.
Reference in code to commission means
transportation department, TR §3-102.
Composition, TR §8-211.
Condemnation by commission, TR §8-302.
Conflicts of interest.
Financial interests in contracts, TR §8-217.
Continuation and change of resolutions, rules,
forms, orders and directives, TR §8-207.
Contracts.
Not to have personal interest in, TR §8-217.
Director of highways.
Certain references to the director of highways
means the administrator, TR §8-207.
Duties.
Generally, TR §8-218.
Vested in, TR §8-218.
Established, TR §8-210.
Forms.
Transportation department.
Forms to remain in effect until changed by
department, TR §3-102.
Journal, TR §8-216.
Maryland Transit Administration.
General provisions, TR §§7-101 to 7-707.
Meetings.
Generally, TR §8-213.
Oath of office, TR §8-211.
Orders.
Transportation department.
Orders to remain in effect until changed by
department, TR §3-102.
Powers.
Generally, TR §8-218.
Transfer of certain powers, duties, etc., to
transportation authority, TR §§3-102,
4-209.
Vested in, TR §8-218.
Purchase of property.
Quick-take condemnation, TR §8-218.
Qualifications, TR §8-211.
Quick-take condemnation, TR §8-218.
Quorum, TR §8-213.
Records.
Generally, TR §8-216.
Open to public, TR §8-216.
References to state roads commission, TR §8-207.
Resolutions.
Transportation department.
Resolutions to remain in effect until changed
by department, TR §3-102.
Rules and regulations.
Transportation department.
Rules and regulations to remain in effect until
changed by department, TR §3-102.
Salaries, TR §8-212.

HIGHWAYS —Cont'd
State roads commission —Cont'd
Secretary, TR §8-214. ·
Assistant secretaries, TR §8-215.
Taxation.
Acquisition of property.
Payment of proportionate share of taxes on
property acquired, TR §8-306.
Terms of office, TR §8-212.
Transportation department.
General provisions.
See TRANSPORTATION DEPARTMENT.
Included within department, TR §2-107.
Reference to commission means department, TR
§3-102.
Rules and regulations to remain in effect until
changed by department, TR §3-102.
Vacancies, TR §8-212.
Storm drain covers, TR §8-648.
Storm water management facilities.
Included within definition of highway, TR §8-101.
Street.
Defined, TR §8-101.
Taxation.
Special tax districts.
Acquisition by state roads commission.
Property subject to assessment by special tax
district, TR §8-307.
State roads commission.
Payment of proportionate share of taxes
acquired, TR §8-306.
Termini.
Location of termini of highway to be constructed
or reconstructed, TR §8-319.
Through highway.
Defined, TR §21-101.
Title.
Land binding on highway or street.
Granting, RP §2-114.
Land purchased for public roads, 25 §138.
Tolls.
Toll bridges and tunnels.
See TRAFFIC LAWS.
Traffic control devices.
See TRAFFIC CONTROL DEVICES.
Traffic hazards.
Placing along highway prohibited, TR §21-1113.
Transportation department.
Bond issues.
County transportation bonds, TR §§3-301 to
3-310.
See COUNTIES.
General provisions.
See TRANSPORTATION DEPARTMENT.
Transportation trust fund.
See TRANSPORTATION TRUST FUND.
Trees and timber.
Roadside trees.
See FORESTS AND PARKS.
Trucks.
Route 2.
Semitrailer and trailer operated in combination
with truck tractor.
Restrictions, TR §24-104.1.
**Twelve-year construction and reconstruction
program.**
State highway construction bonds, second issue,
TR §§3-216, 8-402.
United States.
Federal-aid highways.
Outdoor advertising, TR §§8-725 to 8-737.

HIGHWAYS —Cont'd
United States —Cont'd
Interstate systems.
Signs, displays and devices.
Regulations, TR §8-605.
State highway administration.
Powers of administration, TR §8-204.
Urban highways, TR §8-630.
Veterans of foreign wars memorial highway,
TR §8-653.
Vietnam veterans memorial highway, TR
§8-650.
Washington suburban sanitary commission, 29
§§10-101 to 10-108.
See WASHINGTON SUBURBAN SANITARY
DISTRICT.
Watershed associations.
Bridges.
Constructing and maintaining.
Where improvement crosses public highway,
25 §215.
Yards.
Public roads not to be opened through without
consent of owner, 25 §144.

HIGHWAY SAFETY PROGRAM, TR §§2-401 to
2-403.
Administration of program, TR §2-403.
Authority of governor, TR §2-401.
**Coordination with federal government
programs,** TR §2-402.

HIPPODROME PERFORMING ARTS CENTER,
FI §§13-701, 13-709, 13-711.
Subject to property taxes, payment in lieu of,
TP §7-504.4.

**HIPPODROME PERFORMING ARTS CENTER
FINANCING FUND,** FI §13-717.2.

HIRED DRIVERS.
For-hire driving services generally, PUC
§§10-101 to 10-112.
See FOR-HIRE DRIVING SERVICES.

HISPANICS.
**Health care disparities in minority
populations.**
Office of minority health and health disparities,
HG §§20-1001 to 20-1007.
Minorities generally.
See MINORITIES.

**HISTORICAL AND CULTURAL MUSEUM
ASSISTANCE PROGRAM,** SF §§5A-349 to
5A-359.
Defined terms, SF §5A-349.
Duties of trust, SF §5A-355.
Eligibility of museums, SF §5A-356.
Established, SF §5A-352.
False statements or reports, SF §5A-359.
Findings, SF §5A-351.
Museum assistance review panel, SF §5A-354.
Purposes, SF §5A-353.
Regulations, SF §5A-358.
Reserve money, amount allowed, SF §5A-357.
Scope of part, SF §5A-350.

**HISTORICAL AND CULTURAL PROGRAMS
DIVISION,** SF §§5A-101 to 5A-359.
**African American history and culture
commission.**
Generally, SF §§5A-201 to 5A-208.
See AFRICAN AMERICAN HISTORY AND
CULTURE COMMISSION.

HISTORICAL AND CULTURAL PROGRAMS DIVISION —Cont'd
African American history and culture commission —Cont'd
Units in division, SF §5A-102.
Established, SF §5A-101.
Historical and cultural museum assistance program.
Generally, SF §§5A-349 to 5A-359.
See HISTORICAL AND CULTURAL MUSEUM ASSISTANCE PROGRAM.
Indian affairs commission.
Generally, 41 §§6-901 to 6-912.
See INDIAN AFFAIRS COMMISSION.
Maryland historical trust.
Generally, SF §§5A-301 to 5A-359.
See MARYLAND HISTORICAL TRUST.
Units in division, SF §5A-102.
Units in division, SF §5A-102.

HISTORICAL SOCIETIES.
Government house trust.
Consultation with Maryland historical society.
Renovation, furnishing and decoration of state room, SG §9-606.
Organizational names and insignia.
Registration, prohibited acts, BR §§19-201 to 19-207.
Tax exemptions, TP §7-214.

HISTORICAL TRUST, SF §§5A-301 to 5A-359.
See MARYLAND HISTORICAL TRUST.

HISTORICAL WATERCRAFT IDENTIFICATION PLAQUE, NR §8-737.

HISTORIC AREA ZONING, 66B §§8.01 to 8.17.
See ZONING.

HISTORIC DISTRICT COMMISSION.
Historic area zoning.
See ZONING.

HISTORIC DISTRICTS.
Rehabilitation tax credits.
Insurance companies, IN §6-105.2.

HISTORIC LANDMARKS.
Acquisition.
Board of public works, Maryland historical trust, SF §5A-304.
Baltimore City.
Zoning and preservation, 66B §2.12.
Tax credits, TP §§9-204, 9-204.1.

HISTORIC MARKER PROGRAM FUND, SF §5A-329.

HISTORIC MOTOR VEHICLES.
Display of registration plates and tags, TR §13-411.
Registration and equipment, TR §13-936.
Vintage registration plates, TR §13-936.1.

HISTORIC PRESERVATION.
Maryland advisory committee on historic agricultural structure preservation, SF §§5A-401 to 5A-406.
Barn preservation fund.
Applications for grants, SF §5A-403.
Establishment, SF §5A-403.
Fund, defined, SF §5A-401.
Grants from fund, SF §5A-403.
Committee, defined, SF §5A-401.
Establishment, SF §5A-402.

HISTORIC PRESERVATION —Cont'd
Maryland advisory committee on historic agricultural structure preservation —Cont'd
Loss of historic status.
Repayment of grant, SF §5A-405.
Membership, SF §5A-402.
Recordation of grant awards, SF §5A-406.
Repayment of grant on loss of historic status, SF §5A-405.
Rulemaking authority, SF §5A-404.
Maryland historical trust, SF §§5A-301 to 5A-359.
See MARYLAND HISTORICAL TRUST.

HISTORIC PRESERVATION ADVISORY COUNCIL.
Maryland historical trust, SF §5A-324.

HISTORIC PROPERTY GRANTS.
Prince George's and Montgomery counties.
Historic property grant program, 28 §§5-301 to 5-307.
See PRINCE GEORGE'S COUNTY.

HISTORIC ST. MARY'S CITY COMMISSION, ED §§24-501 to 24-525.
Claims against, ED §24-509.
Collaboration, ED §24-508.
Construction of subtitle, ED §24-525.
Declarations and findings, ED §24-502.
Employees, ED §24-510.
Established, ED §24-501.
Executive committee, ED §24-506.
Executive director, ED §24-510.
Fund, ED §24-511.
Gifts and donations, ED §24-512.
Joint programs, ED §24-508.
Legislative intent, ED §24-502.
Liability insurance, ED §24-509.
Membership, ED §24-505.
Mission, ED §24-503.
Name of commission, ED §24-504.
Officers, ED §24-506.
Particular purposes, ED §24-503.
Powers and duties.
Generally, ED §§24-504, 24-507.
Procurement, ED §24-512.
Real property.
Acquisition.
Dwellings, ED §24-513.
Preservation land trusts and foundations, ED §24-514.
Transfer of state property, ED §24-515.
Transfer or disposal, ED §24-512.
Revenue bonds.
Authority to issue, ED §24-516.
Enhancing marketability, ED §24-523.
Investments, ED §24-523.
Liability, ED §24-521.
Payment, ED §24-517.
When payable, ED §24-518.
Pledge of revenues as security, ED §24-520.
Proceeds, ED §24-516.
Proposed issuance, ED §24-516.
Refunding bonds, ED §24-522.
Resolution or trust agreements, ED §24-519.
Rights of bondholder, ED §24-521.
Tax exemptions, ED §24-524.

HIT AND RUN.
Information to be provided, TR §§20-104 to 20-105.1.

HIT AND RUN —Cont'd
Misdemeanor, TR §27-101.
Render assistance, TR §20-104.
Serious bodily injury caused.
Penalties, TR §27-113.
Stay at scene, TR §§20-102, 20-103.

HITCHHIKING.
Prohibited, TR §§21-313, 21-507.
Toll bridges and tunnels, TR §21-1406.

HIV.
Human immunodeficiency virus.
See HUMAN IMMUNODEFICIENCY VIRUS.
Sterile needle and syringe exchange.
Baltimore City, HG §§24-801 to 24-809.
See STERILE NEEDLE AND SYRINGE
EXCHANGE.
Prince George's county, HG §§24-901 to 24-909.
See STERILE NEEDLE AND SYRINGE
EXCHANGE.
Viatical settlement contracts, IN §§8-601 to
8-611.
See VIATICAL SETTLEMENT CONTRACTS.

HMO.
Health maintenance organizations.
See HEALTH MAINTENANCE
ORGANIZATIONS.

HOGS.
Swine.
General provisions.
See LIVESTOCK.

HOLDERS IN DUE COURSE.
Bank deposits and collections.
Collection of items by depositary and collecting
banks.
When bank gives value, CL §4-211.
Negotiable instruments.
Generally, CL §§3-101 to 3-605.
See NEGOTIABLE INSTRUMENTS.

HOLDING COMPANIES.
Bank holding companies.
Emergency interstate acquisitions.
General provisions, FI §§5-1101 to 5-1107.
See BANKS AND TRUST COMPANIES.
General provisions, FI §§5-901 to 5-910.
See BANK HOLDING COMPANIES.
Out-of-state bank holding companies.
Savings and loan associations.
Emergency interstate acquisitions, FI §§5-1101
to 5-1107.
See BANKS AND TRUST COMPANIES.

HOLDING OTHER OFFICE.
Baltimore City.
Mayor and councilmen not to hold other office,
etc., MD Const Art XI §5.
Congress.
Members of general assembly not eligible, MD
Const Art III §10.
General assembly.
Civil office in state prohibited, MD Const Art III
§11.
Persons holding office under United States not
eligible, MD Const Art III §10.
Judges.
Prohibited, MD Const DofR Art 33.
Notaries public.
Office of notary not within meaning of article, MD
Const DofR Art 35.

HOLDING OTHER OFFICE —Cont'd
Officers.
Office of profit.
Prohibited, MD Const DofR Art 35.

HOLIDAYS.
Alcoholic beverages.
Anne Arundel county, 2B §8-202.
Asian lunar new year day, SG §13-405.
Banks and trust companies, FI §§5-701, 5-705.
Court sessions, CJA Rule 16-106.
Defined, Rule 1-202.
Elections.
Statewide general election day as legal holiday, 1
§27.
Interpretation and construction, 1 §27.
John Hanson's birthday, SG §13-401.
Law day, SG §13-402.
Legal holidays.
Enumerated, 1 §27.
Poetry day, SG §13-403.
Schools.
Required school days and holidays, ED §7-103.
Service of process, CivProCir Rule 2-125;
CivProDist Rule 3-125; CJ §6-302.
State personnel, SPP §§9-201 to 9-205.
See STATE PERSONNEL.
Taxation.
Legal holiday.
Defined, TG §1-201.
Due dates falling on, TG §1-201.

HOLOCAUST VICTIMS INSURANCE, IN
§§28-101 to 28-110.
Applicability, IN §28-101.
Citation of act, IN §28-110.
Civil procedure.
Applicability of rules, IN §28-104.
Commissioner.
Toll-free telephone number.
Duty to establish, IN §28-102.
Commission investigations, IN §28-103.
Compliance, effect on other laws, IN §28-108.
Conflict of laws.
Compliance, effect on other laws, IN §28-108.
Defined terms, IN §28-101.
Evidence.
Applicability of rules, IN §28-104.
Fines, IN §28-107.
Filing false or misleading certification or report,
IN §28-105.
Insurers.
Duties, IN §28-103.
Investigations.
Commission investigations, IN §28-103.
Laches, IN §28-104.
Penalties, IN §28-107.
Filing false or misleading certification or report,
IN §28-105.
Records of policies held by Holocaust victims,
IN §28-105.
Regulations, IN §28-109.
Reports.
Commission, IN §28-106.
Insurers, IN §28-105.
Rules of civil procedure, applicability, IN
§28-104.
Rules of evidence, applicability, IN §28-104.
Statute of limitations, IN §28-104.
Title of act, IN §28-110.
Toll-free telephone number.
Duty to establish, IN §28-102.

HOLOCAUST VICTIMS INSURANCE —Cont'd
Unfair and deceptive insurance practices, IN
§28-103.

HOLOCAUST VICTIMS, TAX EXEMPTIONS.
Income tax.
Subtractions from federal adjusted gross income,
TG §10-207.
Inheritance tax.
Exemptions, TG §7-203.

HOLOGRAPHIC WILLS.
General provisions, ET §4-103.

HOME APPLIANCES.
Unfair or deceptive trade practices.
Bill of costs of repairing, CL §13-307.

HOMEBUILDER REGISTRATION, BR §§4.5-101
to 4.5-701.
Application, BR §4.5-303.
Authority under registration, BR §4.5-304.
Building code violations, notice, BR §4.5-602.
Building development law violations.
Discipline of registrants, BR §4.5-308.
Change of information, BR §4.5-306.
Contract for new home, information required,
BR §4.5-603.
Contract with unregistered builder,
enforceability, BR §4.5-605.
Definitions, BR §4.5-101.
Disciplinary action, BR §4.5-308.
Display of registration number, BR §4.5-307.
Dispute resolution, BR §4.5-401.
Environmental protection law violations.
Discipline of registrants, BR §4.5-308.
Expiration of registration, BR §4.5-305.
Fee, BR §4.5-304.
Renewal, BR §4.5-305.
Fraud, deception or misrepresentation.
Discipline of registrants, BR §4.5-308.
Fund, BR §4.5-203.
Industrial buildings for residential use, BR
§4.5-604.
Issuance, BR §4.5-304.
Liability insurance, BR §4.5-302.
Mobile homes, BR §4.5-604.
Permit to build, requirements for issuance, BR
§4.5-601.
Prohibited acts, BR §4.5-501.
Advertising without registration number, BR
§4.5-503.
Civil action against violators, BR §4.5-502.
Criminal penalty, BR §4.5-504.
Registration required, BR §4.5-301.
Reinstatement after revocation, bond, BR
§4.5-302.
Remedies of owner or buyer, BR §4.5-401.
Renewal, BR §4.5-305.
Revocation or suspension, BR §4.5-308.
Bond posting for re-registration, BR §4.5-302.
Title of provisions, BR §4.5-701.
Transferring, assigning or pledging
registration.
Prohibition, BR §4.5-304.
Unit within division, BR §4.5-201.
Powers and duties, BR §4.5-202.
Zoning law violations.
Discipline of registrants, BR §4.5-308.

HOME BUSINESSES.
Unfair or deceptive trade practices.
Work-at-home advertisements, CL §13-314.

HOME BUYER ASSISTANCE PROGRAM.
Live near your work.
Community development administration, HS
§§4-215, 4-217.

HOME BUYING WARRANTIES.
Implied warranties.
Fitness for particular purpose, CL §2-315.
Merchantability, CL §2-314.
Usage of trade, CL §2-314.

HOME DEMONSTRATION WORK.
Counties.
Farmers' cooperative demonstration work, 25
§160.

HOME DETENTION MONITORING DEVICES.
Code grabbing devices.
Manufacturing, selling or possessing, CR §7-301.
Deactivation tool or device.
Possessing, using, CR §7-301.
Removal of system or device, CR §7-301.

HOME DETENTION PROGRAM, COR §§3-401 to
3-415.
Arrests.
Power of correctional employees to make, COR
§3-412.
Warrantless arrest, CP §2-207.
Authorization, COR §3-402.
Child abuse, persons convicted of ineligible,
COR §3-404.
Commissioner of by inmate constitutes
violation of conditions, COR §3-409.
Conditions of placement, COR §3-405.
Violations, COR §3-409.
Correctional employees monitoring and
providing security.
Employment by commissioner, powers,
qualifications, COR §3-412.
Crimes of violence, persons committing
ineligible, COR §3-404.
Diminution credits not affected by
participation in program, COR §3-411.
Direct contact by employees of division,
method of supervision, COR §3-403.
Division of parole and probation program,
COR §6-108.
Search of dwelling, COR §6-109.
Division of pretrial detention and services,
COR §5-202.
Electronic devices, method of supervision, COR
§3-403.
Electronic supervision, method of supervision.
Fees for costs, division to establish, COR §3-408.
Eligibility for program, COR §3-404.
Employment, restrictions on movement, COR
§3-406.
Escape.
Violation of restriction on movement constitutes,
COR §3-409.
Escape in the second degree, CR §9-405.
Escape, persons convicted of ineligible, COR
§3-404.
Fees for cost of electronic supervision,
division to establish, COR §3-408.
Food, clothing, shelter and utilities, expenses
inmate responsibility, COR §3-407.
Inmates not agent or employee of division,
COR §3-410.
Life sentence, persons serving ineligible, COR
§3-404.

HOME DETENTION PROGRAM —Cont'd
Living expenses, inmate responsibility, COR §3-407.
Local correctional facilities.
　Allegany county, COR §11-702.
　Escape, violation of restriction on movement, COR §11-726.
　Individual county provisions.
　　Anne Arundel County, COR §11-703.
　　Baltimore County, COR §11-705.
　　Carroll County, COR §11-708.
　　Cecil County, COR §11-709.
　　Dorchester County, COR §11-711.
　　Frederick County, COR §11-712.
　　Garrett County, COR §11-713.
　　Harford County, COR §11-714.
　　Kent County, COR §11-716.
　　Washington County, COR §11-723.
　　Wicomico county, authorized program, COR §11-724.
　Misdemeanor, violation of condition, COR §11-726.
　Violation of restriction on movement or other condition, COR §11-726.
Medical or mental-health treatment, restrictions on movement, COR §3-406.
Methods of supervision, COR §3-403.
Parole eligibility not affected by participation, COR §3-411.
Parole, modification of conditions, COR §7-402.
Placement, conditions, COR §3-405.
　Violations, COR §3-409.
Program defined, COR §3-401.
Regulations to be adopted by commissioner, COR §3-414.
Removal of inmate from program, COR §3-413.
Restitution, satisfaction by inmate in program, COR §3-408.
Restrictions on movement, COR §3-406.
　Violation constitutes escape, COR §3-409.
St. Mary's county.
　Home detention and work release programs, COR §11-720.
Search warrants.
　Application, scope, execution and return, COR §3-415.
　Power of correctional employees to obtain and execute, COR §3-412.
Support payments for dependents, condition of participation, COR §3-407.
Violations of conditions of placement, COR §3-409.
Warrantless arrest.
　Authority of employees monitoring or supervising inmates, CP §2-207.

HOME HEALTH AGENCIES, HG §§19-401 to 19-410.
Accreditation of health care facilities, HG §§19-2301, 19-2302.
Applicability of subtitle, HG §19-403.
Applications.
　Qualifications of applicants, HG §19-406.
Criminal history records checks of employees, HG §§19-1901 to 19-1912.
　See ADULT DEPENDENT CARE PROGRAMS.
Definitions.
　Generally, HG §19-401.
Discrimination.
　Prohibited, HG §19-408.
Inspections.
　Authority of department of health, HG §19-407.

HOME HEALTH AGENCIES —Cont'd
Insurance coverage for services, IN §15-808.
Legislative declaration, HG §19-402.
Licenses.
　Issuance, HG §19-407.
　Operating without a license, HG §19-409.
　Practicing without license, HG §19-408.
　Prohibited acts, HG §19-408.
　Qualifications of applicants, HG §19-406.
　Requirements generally, HG §19-405.
　Revocation.
　　Grounds, HG §19-407.
　Rules and regulations as to, HG §19-404.
Operation without license, HG §19-409.
Physical rehabilitation services, HG §19-410.
Purpose of subtitle, HG §19-402.
Rehabilitation.
　Physical rehabilitation services, HG §19-410.
Rules and regulations.
　Adoption, HG §19-404.
Scope of subtitle, HG §19-403.
Statement of purpose, HG §19-402.

HOME HEALTH CARE.
Insurance coverage, IN §15-808.
Life insurance policies, IN §16-214.
Long-term care insurance.
　Limitations and exclusions of benefits, IN §18-110.

HOME IMPROVEMENTS, BR §§8-101 to 8-702.
Advertising.
　False, deceptive or misleading advertising, BR §8-610.
　Inducements.
　　Tangible items for advertising, BR §8-503.
　License number requirement, BR §8-615.
Attachment.
　Actions against persons arising out of home improvement transactions, CJ §3-303.
Bonds, surety.
　Commission.
　　Executive director, BR §8-205.
Building code violations.
　Notification requirements, BR §8-505.
Building permits.
　License number requirement, BR §8-504.
Commission, BR §§8-201 to 8-214.
　Administration of act, BR §8-208.
　Authority of secretary, BR §8-214.
　Certification of licensing status, BR §8-210.
　Chairman.
　　Appointment, BR §8-203.
　Compensation, BR §8-204.
　　Executive director, BR §8-205.
　Complaints.
　　Staff investigation, BR §8-206.
　Composition, BR §8-202.
　Contract list.
　　County receipt, BR §8-211.
　Contractual experts, BR §8-206.
　Creation, BR §8-201.
　Defined, BR §8-101.
　Disposition of money, BR §8-213.
　Duties, BR §8-212.
　　Administration of act, BR §8-208.
　　Authority of secretary, BR §8-214.
　　Certification of licensing status, BR §8-210.
　　Records, BR §8-209.
　　Regulations, BR §8-207.
　Enforcement of act, BR §8-208.
　Establishment, BR §8-201.
　Executive director, BR §8-205.

HOME IMPROVEMENTS —Cont'd
Commission —Cont'd
  Failure to comply with order or requirements, BR §8-616.
  Investigative staff, BR §8-206.
  Licenses generally. See within this heading, "Licenses."
  Meetings, BR §8-204.
  Membership, BR §8-202.
  Noncompliance with order or requirements, BR §8-616.
  Office, BR §8-204.
  Powers, BR §8-212.
    Administration of act, BR §8-208.
    Authority of secretary, BR §8-214.
    Certification of licensing status, BR §8-210.
    Records, BR §8-209.
    Regulations, BR §8-207.
  Program evaluation act, SG §8-403.
  Qualifications, BR §8-202.
  Quorum, BR §8-204.
  Recordkeeping requirements, BR §8-209.
    Copies of regulations, BR §8-207.
    Copy fees, BR §8-209.
  Removal, BR §8-202.
  Rulemaking authority, BR §8-207.
  Staff, BR §8-206.
Completion certificate or proof.
  False proof of completion, BR §8-602.
Construction licenses, BR §8-317.
Contractor.
  Acting without license, BR §8-601.
  Construction license requirement, BR §8-317.
  Defined, BR §8-101.
  Licensing. See within this heading, "Licenses."
  Relationship of salespersons and contractors, BR §8-310.
    Change of contractual relationship, BR §8-613.
Contractor list.
  Supplied to counties, BR §8-211.
Contracts.
  Abandonment of contract, BR §8-605.
  Changes, BR §8-501.
  Contents, BR §8-501.
  Debt limitation, BR §8-609.
  Deposit limited, BR §8-617.
  Doing business with unlicensed person, BR §8-612.
  Failure of performance, BR §8-605.
  Form, BR §8-501.
  Fraud, BR §8-608.
  Gifts as inducements, BR §8-503.
  "Home improvement contract" defined, BR §8-101.
  Inducements, BR §8-503.
  Misrepresentation, BR §8-607.
  Mortgage or lien created by contract.
    Notice, BR §8-501.
      Failure to give notice as misrepresentation, BR §8-607.
  Payment before signing contract, BR §8-617.
  Waiver of title provisions prohibited, BR §8-103.
Definitions, BR §8-101.
  Actual loss, BR §8-401.
  Building code, BR §8-505.
Fraud.
  Advertising, BR §8-610.
  Deceptive acts, BR §8-608.
Fund, BR §§8-401 to 8-411.
  "Actual loss" defined, BR §8-401.
  Administration, BR §8-403.
  Applicability of subtitle, BR §8-402.

HOME IMPROVEMENTS —Cont'd
Fund —Cont'd
  Assessments, BR §8-404.
  Claims against fund.
    Action on claim by commission, BR §8-407.
    Acts of subcontractors, salespersons and employees, BR §8-405.
    Administrative proceedings, BR §8-408.
    Arbitration agreements, BR §8-405.
    Bankruptcy proceedings, BR §8-410.
    Denial of claim, BR §8-405.
    Excluded claimants, BR §8-405.
    Hearings, BR §8-407.
    Insufficient balance, BR §8-409.
    Joinder of proceedings, BR §8-408.
    Legal proceedings, BR §8-408.
    Limitation on recovery, BR §8-405.
    Limitations period, BR §8-405.
    Order of payment, BR §8-409.
    Payments, BR §8-409.
    Procedure for submitting claims, BR §8-406.
    Reimbursements, BR §8-410.
    Review and investigation of claim, BR §8-407.
    Submitting claims.
      Procedure, BR §8-406.
    Subrogation, BR §8-410.
    Withholding of tax refund, BR §8-410.
  Defined, BR §8-401.
  Disciplinary proceedings, BR §8-411.
    Failure to pay assessment, BR §8-411.
  Disposition of money, BR §8-403.
  Establishment, BR §8-403.
  Fees.
    Initial fee, BR §8-404.
  Investments, BR §8-403.
  Proceedings on proposed order, BR §8-407.
  Scope of subtitle, BR §8-402.
Gifts as inducements, BR §8-503.
Governmental transactions.
  Scope of title, BR §8-102.
Guaranty fund, BR §§8-401 to 8-411. See within this heading, "Fund."
Hearing board.
  Defined, BR §8-101.
  Generally, BR §8-313.
Injunctions.
  Commission.
    Enforcement power, BR §8-208.
Liability insurance.
  Required of applicants for license and licensed contractors, BR §8-302.1.
Licenses, BR §§8-301 to 8-317.
  Acting without license, BR §8-601.
  Applications, BR §8-303.
    Inactive status, BR §8-308.1.
    Misrepresentation, BR §8-607.
    Qualifications of applicants, BR §8-302.2.
    Reapplication for license, BR §8-316.
    Renewal of license, BR §8-308.
  Change of information, BR §8-309.
  Construction license, BR §8-317.
  Contractor license.
    Application fee, BR §8-303.
    Construction license requirement, BR §8-317.
    Credit report, BR §§8-303, 8-308.
    Defined, BR §8-101.
    Inactive status certificate, BR §8-308.1.
    Issuance, BR §8-306.
    Liability insurance required, BR §8-302.1.
      Prerequisite to license issuance, BR §8-306.
    Renewal, BR §8-308.

HOME IMPROVEMENTS —Cont'd
Licenses —Cont'd
  Contractor license —Cont'd
    Required, BR §8-301.
    Scope of license, BR §8-307.
  Credit report requirement.
    Contractor licenses, BR §§8-303, 8-308.
  Defined, BR §8-101.
  Denials.
    Grounds, BR §8-311.
    Hearing requirement, BR §8-305.
    Notification, BR §8-305.
  Disciplinary actions.
    Claims against fund, BR §8-411.
    Effect of loss of license, BR §8-315.
    Failure to pay assessment, BR §8-404.
    Grounds, BR §8-311.
    Hearings, BR §8-312.
    Judicial review, BR §8-314.
    Reinstatement of suspended or revoked license,
      BR §8-316.
  Disclosure requirements.
    Relationship of salespersons and contractors,
      BR §8-310.
  Doing business with unlicensed person, BR
    §8-612.
  Educational qualifications of applicants, BR
    §8-302.1.
  Examinations, BR §8-302.
  Exceptions to requirement, BR §8-301.
  Experience qualifications of applicants, BR
    §8-302.2.
  Expiration, BR §8-308.
    Effect of loss of license, BR §8-315.
  Hearing board, BR §8-313.
    Defined, BR §8-101.
    Judicial review of final decision, BR §8-314.
    Referral of cases, BR §8-314.
  Issuance, BR §8-306.
    Inactive status certificate, BR §8-308.1.
  Liability insurance.
    Required, BR §8-302.1.
  License number on permits, BR §8-504.
  Notice of approval or denial, BR §8-305.
  Payment of compensation, BR §8-315.
  Reapplication for license, BR §8-316.
  Reinstatement of license, BR §8-316.
  Relationship of salespersons and contractors, BR
    §8-310.
  Reprimands.
    Grounds, BR §8-311.
  Required, BR §8-101.
  Salesperson license.
    Application fee, BR §8-303.
    Defined, BR §8-101.
    Inactive status certificate, BR §8-308.1.
    Issuance, BR §8-306.
    Renewal, BR §8-308.
    Required, BR §8-301.
  Scope of license, BR §8-307.
  Staggered terms authorized, BR §8-308.
  Subcontractor license.
    Application fee, BR §8-303.
    Construction license requirement, BR §8-317.
    Defined, BR §8-101.
    Inactive status certificate, BR §8-308.1.
    Issuance, BR §8-306.
    Renewal, BR §8-308.
    Required, BR §8-301.
    Scope of license, BR §8-307.
  Term and renewal, BR §8-308.

HOME IMPROVEMENTS —Cont'd
Licenses —Cont'd
  Violation of state laws, BR §8-611.
Maryland home improvement commission, BR
  §§8-201 to 8-214. See within this heading,
  "Commission."
Misrepresentation.
  Deceptive acts, BR §8-607.
Names.
  Conducting business under another name, BR
    §8-614.
Notices.
  Mortgage or lien created by contract, BR §8-501.
    Failure to give notice as misrepresentation, BR
      §8-607.
Penalties.
  Civil penalties, BR §8-620.
  Criminal penalties, BR §8-623.
  False proof of completion, BR §8-602.
  License disciplinary actions.
    Fine in lieu of revocation, BR §8-311.
  Licenses.
    Acting without license, BR §8-601.
Permits, BR §8-504.
Prohibited acts generally, BR §§8-601 to 8-623.
Records, BR §8-209.
Restitution.
  Commission.
    Enforcement power, BR §8-208.
Salespersons.
  Acting without license, BR §8-601.
  Compensation, BR §8-502.
  Defined, BR §8-101.
  Failure to account for or remit payment, BR
    §8-606.
  Licensing. See within this heading, "Licenses."
  Relationship of salespersons and contractors, BR
    §8-310.
    Notice of change of contractual relationship, BR
      §8-613.
Scope of title, BR §8-102.
**Service contracts and consumer products
  guaranty.**
  Inapplicability of article to licensed contractors,
    CL §14-409.
Subcontractor.
  Acting without license, BR §8-601.
  Construction license requirement, BR §8-317.
  Defined, BR §8-101.
  Licensing. See within this heading, "Licenses."
Sunset law, BR §8-702.
Termination of title, BR §8-702.
Title of act, BR §8-701.
Waiver of title provisions prohibited, BR
  §8-103.
Waterproofing, CL §§14-12A-01 to 14-12A-04.
  See WATERPROOFING.

HOME INSPECTORS.
Generally, BOP §§16-101 to 16-802.
  See REAL ESTATE APPRAISERS AND HOME
    INSPECTORS.

HOMELESS PERSONS.
Social services.
  Certified adult residential environment program,
    88A §§138 to 143.
    See SOCIAL SERVICES.
  Shelter, nutrition and service program for
    homeless individuals, 88A §§131 to 137.
    See SOCIAL SERVICES.

HOME OR COMMUNITY-BASED WAIVER PROGRAMS.
Nursing facility residents, HG §15-135.
Denial of access prohibited, HG §15-137.

HOMEOWNERS' ASSOCIATIONS.
Actions against governing body, RP §14-118.
Advertising for political candidates, RP §11B-111.2.
Agents.
Personal liability, CJ §5-406.
Annual charge, RP §11B-113.4.
Applicability of provisions, RP §11B-102.
Candidate signs, RP §11B-111.2.
Citation of act, RP §11B-115.
Clerks of court.
Depository.
Duties, RP §11B-113.
Common areas.
Defined, RP §11B-101.
Improvements.
Warranties, RP §11B-110.
Use for meetings, RP §11B-111.4.
Contracts.
Sale of lots. See within this heading, "Sale of lots."
Covenants.
Recorded covenants and restrictions.
Defined, RP §11B-101.
Damages.
Actions against governing body, RP §14-118.
Sale of lots.
Untrue statements or omissions by vendor, RP §11B-109.
Declarants.
Defined, RP §11B-101.
Declaration.
Defined, RP §11B-101.
Definitions, RP §11B-101.
Actions against governing body.
Governing body, RP §14-118.
Annual charge, RP §11B-113.4.
Family day care homes, RP §11B-111.1.
Delinquent assessments or installments.
Late charges, RP §11B-112.1.
Depositories, RP §11B-113.
Defined, RP §11B-101.
Development.
Defined, RP §11B-101.
Discrimination.
Recorded covenant or restriction based on race, religion or national origin.
Deletion, RP §11B-113.3.
Door-to-door distributions.
Association information, RP §11B-111.3.
Electronic payment fees, RP §11B-114.
Electronic transmission.
Defined, RP §11B-101.
Notice, RP §11B-113.1.
Votes or proxies, RP §11B-113.2.
Exceptions to provisions, RP §11B-102.
Family day care homes, RP §11B-111.1.
Flag of the United States.
Rules and regulations regarding display, RP §14-128.
Governing body.
Action against governing body, RP §14-118.
Personal liability of directors or officers, CJ §5-422.
Defined, RP §11B-101.
Meetings, RP §11B-111.

HOMEOWNERS' ASSOCIATIONS —Cont'd
Howard county.
Columbia association.
Annexation of certain parcels of land, RP §11B-113.5.
Immunity.
Governing body, CJ §5-422; RP §14-118.
Improvements to common areas.
Implied and express warranties to association, RP §11B-110.
Insurance.
Family day care homes.
Liability insurance, RP §11B-111.1.
Pooling to purchase casualty or property insurance, IN §19-601.
Late charges, RP §11B-112.1.
Liability.
Actions against governing body.
Directors or officers.
Immunity, RP §14-118.
Personal liability, CJ §5-422.
Personal liability of agents, CJ §5-406.
Sale of lots.
Untrue statements or omissions by vendor, RP §11B-109.
Limitation of actions.
Sale of lots.
Untrue statements or omissions by vendor.
Actions for damages, RP §11B-109.
Local laws.
Restrictions on local laws, ordinances and regulations, RP §11B-104.
Lots.
Sale of lots generally. See within this heading, "Sale of lots."
Meetings, RP §11B-111.
Common areas used for, RP §11B-111.4.
Notices.
Common areas.
Warranties as to improvements.
Notice of defect, RP §11B-110.
Family day care homes.
Opening, RP §11B-111.1.
Holders of subordinate interest.
Sales, RP §7-105.
Meetings, RP §11B-111.
Electronic transmission of notice, RP §11B-113.1.
Sale of lots.
Resale.
Developments containing twelve or fewer lots, RP §11B-106.
Ordinances, RP §11B-104.
Political candidates, signs for, RP §11B-111.2.
Powers of attorney.
Evasion of provisions prohibited, RP §11B-103.
Primary development.
Defined, RP §11B-101.
Property and casualty insurance.
Joint insurance association, IN §§25-401 to 25-410.
See JOINT INSURANCE ASSOCIATION.
Recordation.
Depository.
Material contained in depository not viewed as recordation, RP §11B-113.
Records.
Charge for review or copying, RP §11B-112.
Depository.
Document filed separate from land records, RP §11B-113.

HOMEOWNERS' ASSOCIATIONS —Cont'd
Records —Cont'd
  Examination, RP §11B-112.
  Withholding from public inspection, RP §11B-112.
Related development.
  Defined, RP §11B-101.
Restrictions.
  Recorded covenants and restrictions.
    Defined, RP §11B-101.
Rules and regulations.
  Family day care homes, RP §11B-111.1.
Sale of lots.
  Contracts.
    Cancellation, RP §11B-108.
    Initial sale.
      Developments containing more than twelve
        lots, RP §11B-105.
      Developments containing twelve or fewer lots,
        RP §11B-106.
      Lot not intended to be occupied or rented for
        residential purposes, RP §11B-107.
    Resale, RP §11B-106.
  Developments containing more than twelve lots,
    RP §11B-105.
  Developments containing twelve or fewer lots, RP
    §11B-106.
  Foreclosure sales, RP §§11B-105 to 11B-109.
  Information to be supplied by vendor.
    Initial sale.
      Developments containing more than twelve
        lots, RP §11B-105.
      Developments containing twelve or fewer lots,
        RP §11B-106.
      Lot not intended to be occupied or rented for
        residential purposes, RP §11B-107.
    Resale, RP §11B-106.
    Untrue statements or omissions by vendor.
      Liability for damages, RP §11B-109.
  Lot not intended to be occupied or rented for
    residential purposes, RP §11B-107.
  Resale.
    Developments containing twelve or fewer lots,
      RP §11B-106.
  Waiver or termination of purchasers' rights under
    section prohibited, RP §11B-108.
Short title of act, RP §11B-115.
Unaffiliated declarants.
  Defined, RP §11B-101.
Variance of provisions.
  Prohibited, RP §11B-103.
Waiver.
  Waiver of rights prohibited, RP §11B-103.
Warranty.
  Common area improvements, RP §11B-110.
Zoning.
  Laws, ordinances and regulations to be given full
    force and effect, RP §11B-104.

HOMEOWNERSHIP PROGRAMS FUND, HS
  §4-502.

HOMEOWNER'S INSURANCE, IN §§19-201 to
  19-207.
Annual summary statements, IN §19-205.
Definitions, IN §19-201.
Family day care providers, IN §§19-202, 19-203.
Flood insurance.
  Information and advice concerning, insurer to
    provide, IN §19-206.
**Geographic distribution of residential
  property premium,** IN §§11-321 to 11-326.
  Confidentiality of information, IN §11-326.

HOMEOWNER'S INSURANCE —Cont'd
**Geographic distribution of residential
  property premium** —Cont'd
  Defined terms, IN §11-321.
  Filing of data, IN §11-323.
  Scope of part, IN §11-322.
Holocaust victims insurance act, IN §§28-101 to
  28-110.
  See HOLOCAUST VICTIMS INSURANCE.
Joint insurance association.
  General provisions, IN §§25-401 to 25-410.
  See JOINT INSURANCE ASSOCIATION.
Lead hazard coverage for rental property, IN
  §§19-701 to 19-706.
Medical expense payments, IN §§19-203, 19-204.
Optional coverage.
  Statement of optional coverage available, IN
    §19-207.
People's insurance counsel division.
  Annual assessment.
    Collection from homeowners insurers, SG
      §6-304.
  Evaluation of matters pending before
    commissioner, SG §6-306.
  Generally, SG §§6-301 to 6-308.
    See PEOPLE'S INSURANCE COUNSEL
      DIVISION.
**Summary statement of coverages and
  exclusions.**
  Annual summary statement, IN §19-205.
Underwriting standards, IN §27-501.
Water damage, IN §19-202.

HOME RULE.
Baltimore City, MD Const Art XI-A §§1 to 7.
  See BALTIMORE CITY.
Counties, MD Const Art XI-A §§1 to 7.
  Code counties.
    General provisions, 25B §§1 to 22; MD Const
      Art XI-F §§1 to 10.
    See COUNTIES.
Municipal corporations.
  See MUNICIPAL CORPORATIONS.

HOME SECURITY SYSTEMS.
Code grabbing devices.
  Manufacturing, selling or possessing, CR §7-301.
Deactivation tool or device.
  Possessing, using, CR §7-301.
Removal of system or device, CR §7-301.

HOME SOLICITATION SALES, CL §§14-301 to
  14-306, 14-2601 to 14-2603.
Cancellation.
  Notice of cancellation, CL §14-302.
    Violation of notice requirement, CL §14-303.
Citation.
  Short title, CL §14-306.
Damages.
  Violations of subtitle, CL §14-304.
Definitions, CL §14-301.
  Maryland door-to-door solicitations act, CL
    §14-2601.
Door-to-door sales.
  Defined, CL §14-301.
Door-to-door solicitations act, CL §§14-2601 to
  14-2603.
  Acceptance of money, check, etc., CL §14-2603.
  Compliance required, CL §14-2602.
  Definitions, CL §14-2601.
  Pledge form.
    Contents, CL §14-2603.

HOME SOLICITATION SALES —Cont'd
Door-to-door solicitations act —Cont'd
Unfair and deceptive trade practices, CL
§14-2602.
Violations.
Payments, pledges or promises voidable, CL
§14-2602.
Forms.
Door-to-door solicitations act.
Pledge form, CL §14-2603.
Maryland door-to-door solicitations act, CL
§§14-2601 to 14-2603.
Notice of cancellation.
General provisions, CL §14-302.
Payments, pledges or promises.
Door-to-door solicitations act, CL §14-2602.
Penalties, CL §14-305.
Door-to-door solicitations act, CL §14-2602.
Unlawful practices.
Cancellation of door-to-door sales, CL §14-303.
Door-to-door solicitations act.
Noncompliance with act, CL §14-2602.
Enumerated, CL §14-302.
Violations.
Door-to-door solicitations act, CL §14-2602.
Liability for damages, CL §14-304.
Penalty, CL §14-305.

HOMESTEAD ASSOCIATIONS.
Savings and loan associations.
See SAVINGS AND LOAN ASSOCIATIONS.

HOMESTEAD EXEMPTIONS.
Bankruptcy, CJ §11-504.
Distress for rent, RP §§8-306, 8-307.
Executions, CivProCir Rule 2-643; CivProDist Rule
3-643; CJ §11-504.
Generally.
See EXECUTIONS.
Exemptions generally.
See EXEMPTIONS.
Medicaid.
Spousal homestead protection, HG §15-122.

HOME WARRANTIES.
New home warranties, RP §§10-601 to 10-610.
See WARRANTY.

HOMICIDE.
**By vehicle or vessel while impaired or under
the influence.**
Alcohol concentration measurement, determining,
CR §2-502.
Indictment, information or charging document,
sufficiency, CR §2-507.
Notice of conviction to motor vehicle
administration, CR §2-508.
Presumptions and evidentiary rules, CR §2-502.
Under the influence of alcohol or under the
influence of alcohol per se, CR §2-503.
Under the influence of alcohol per se defined,
CR §2-501.
While impaired by alcohol, CR §2-504.
While impaired by controlled dangerous
substance, CR §2-506.
Entitlement to use of controlled dangerous
substance, exception, CR §2-506.
While impaired by drugs, CR §2-505.
Entitlement to use of drugs, defense, CR §2-505.
Child custody.
Parent convicted of murder of certain persons, FL
§9-101.2.
Definitions, CR §2-101.

HOMICIDE —Cont'd
Fetus.
Murder or manslaughter of viable fetus, CR
§2-103.
Landlord and tenant.
Disclosures concerning real property offered for
lease.
Occurrence of homicide not to constitute
material fact or latent defect, RP §2-120.
Mandatory sentence for crime of violence.
Second, third or fourth conviction, CR §14-101.
Manslaughter.
By vehicle or vessel, CR §2-209.
Indictment, sufficiency, CR §2-209.
Vehicle defined, CR §2-209.
Vessel defined, CR §2-101.
Fetus.
Murder or manslaughter of viable fetus, CR
§2-103.
Indictment, sufficiency, CR §2-208.
By vehicle or vessel, CR §2-209.
Motor vehicles. See within this heading, "Motor
vehicles."
Punishment, CR §2-207.
Spousal adultery not mitigating factor, CR §2-207.
Motor vehicles.
Limitation of prosecutions, CJ §5-106.
Refusal of bail to person charged with crime while
free on bail.
Limitation of prosecutions, CJ §5-106.
Murder.
Child custody.
Parent convicted of murder of certain persons,
FL §9-101.2.
Fetus.
Murder or manslaughter of viable fetus, CR
§2-103.
Murder in the first degree, CR §2-201.
Attempt to commit.
Punishment, CR §2-205.
Death sentence, CR §§2-201, 2-202.
Automatic review by court of appeals, CR
§2-401.
Notice of intent to seek or withdrawal of intent.
Filing with clerk of court of appeals, CR
§2-301.
Procedure, CR §2-303.
Rules governing sentencing proceedings,
adoption, CR §2-305.
Indictment, sufficiency, CR §2-208.
Life imprisonment, CR §2-201.
Life imprisonment without possibility of parole,
CR §§2-201, 2-203.
Defined, CR §2-101.
Procedure, CR §2-304.
Rules governing sentencing proceedings,
adoption, CR §2-305.
Verdict.
Jury to state degree of murder found, CR
§2-302.
Murder in the second degree, CR §2-204.
Attempt.
Punishment, CR §2-206.
Indictment, sufficiency, CR §2-208.
Verdict.
Jury to state degree of murder found, CR
§2-302.
Prisons and prisoners.
Investigation of death of inmates, COR §9-602.1.
Real estate brokers.
Occurrence of homicide on property.
Failure to disclose certain facts, BOP §17-322.1.

HOMICIDE —Cont'd
Real property.
Disclosures concerning real property offered for
sale or lease.
Occurrence of homicide on property not to
constitute material fact or latent defect, RP
§2-120.
Sentence and punishment.
Murder.
First degree. See within this heading, "Murder
in the first degree."
Vehicular homicide.
Limitation of prosecutions, CJ §5-106.
Vital records.
Death certificates.
Notice to medical examiner, HG §4-212.
Year and a day rule eliminated, CR §2-102.

**HOMICIDE BY VEHICLE OR VESSEL WHILE
IMPAIRED OR UNDER THE INFLUENCE.**
**Alcohol concentration measurement,
determining,** CR §2-502.
**Indictment, information or charging
document, sufficiency,** CR §2-507.
**Notice of conviction to motor vehicle
administration,** CR §2-508.
Presumptions and evidentiary rules, CR §2-502.
**Under the influence of alcohol or under the
influence of alcohol per se,** CR §2-503.
Under the influence of alcohol per se defined, CR
§2-501.
While impaired by alcohol, CR §2-504.
**While impaired by controlled dangerous
substance,** CR §2-506.
Entitlement to use of controlled dangerous
substance, exception, CR §2-506.
While impaired by drugs, CR §2-505.
Entitlement to use of drugs, defense, CR §2-505.

HOMING PIGEONS.
General provisions.
See PIGEONS.

HONEY.
Bees.
General provisions, AG §§5-501 to 5-507.
See BEEKEEPING INDUSTRY.

HONORARIUM.
Public ethics.
Acceptance or solicitation, SG §15-505.

HOPE FOR NONTRADITIONAL STUDENTS.
**Community college transfer scholarship
program,** ED §§18-2501 to 18-2507.

HORIZONTAL PROPERTY ACT.
General provisions, RP §§11-101 to 11-143.
See CONDOMINIUMS.

HORNS.
Warning devices.
See MOTOR VEHICLE EQUIPMENT.

HORSE INDUSTRY BOARD, AG §§2-701 to
2-719.
Chairman, AG §2-705.
Composition, AG §2-704.
Created, AG §§2-702, 2-703.
Crimes and offenses.
Violations of provisions, AG §2-718.
Definitions, AG §2-701.
Duties, AG §2-708.1.
Exemptions, AG §2-702.
Expenses, AG §2-706.

HORSE INDUSTRY BOARD —Cont'd
Fees.
Inspection fee, AG §2-711.
Funds.
Disposition of funds collected, AG §2-708.
Maryland horse industry fund, AG §2-708.2.
Commercial equine feed assessments, AG
§6-107.2.
Impounding horses, AG §2-716.
Injunctions, AG §2-717.
Inspections.
Duties of board, AG §2-708.1.
Fees, AG §2-711.
Required, AG §2-713.
Inspectors, AG §2-709.
Licenses.
Application, AG §2-711.
Creation of classes, AG §2-713.
Display, AG §2-714.
Expiration and renewal, AG §2-712.
Property of state, AG §2-714.
Renewal, AG §2-712.
Required, AG §2-710.
Suspension or revocation, AG §2-715.
Transfer, AG §2-714.
Meetings, AG §2-706.
Misdemeanors, AG §2-718.
Oaths, AG §2-704.
Officers, AG §2-705.
Penalties, AG §2-718.
Removal of members, AG §2-704.
Rules and regulations, AG §2-707.
Termination, AG §2-719.
Secretary of agriculture.
Authority, AG §2-707.
Staff, AG §2-706.
**Termination of subtitle provisions and
regulations,** AG §2-719.
Terms, AG §2-704.

HORSE RACING.
Audits.
Licenses.
Financial disclosure by licensees, BR §11-313.
Betting.
Pari-mutuel betting, BR §§11-801 to 11-832.
See PARI-MUTUEL BETTING.
Cape Pine Farm in Church Hill.
Queen Anne's county.
Scope of title, BR §11-103.
Cecil County Breeders' Fair, Inc.
Racing at Fair Hill.
Scope of title, BR §11-701.
Citation of title, BR §11-1101.
Commission, BR §§11-201 to 11-214.
Authority of commission.
Hearing committee, BR §11-310.
Authority of secretary, BR §11-214.
Chairman.
Election, BR §11-203.
Compensation, BR §11-204.
Executive director, BR §11-205.
Staff, BR §11-206.
Cooperation by law enforcement officers.
Required, BR §11-208.
Creation, BR §11-201.
Criminal history records checks.
Individuals subjected to, BR §11-312.
Defined, BR §11-101.
Establishment, BR §11-201.

HORSE RACING —Cont'd
Commission —Cont'd
Executive director.
Duties, BR §11-205.
Fingerprints.
Required to provide, BR §11-312.
Licensing. See within this heading, "Licenses."
Meetings, BR §11-204.
Membership, BR §11-202.
Pensions.
Contributions by employers, SPP §21-307.
Pension system service credits.
Contributory pension benefit, eligibility of
members subject to, SPP §§23-306.2,
23-306.3.
Employees or teachers, SPP §23-306.1.
Personnel hiring, BR §11-207.
Fingerprinting, BR §§11-206, 11-207.
Staff, BR §11-206.
Powers.
Authority of secretary, BR §11-214.
Enforcement authority, BR §11-209.
Investigative power, BR §11-211.
Regulatory power, BR §11-210.
Removal power, BR §11-211.
Scope, BR §11-209.
Program evaluation act, SG §8-403.
Prohibited regulations, BR §11-210.
Qualifications, BR §11-202.
Quorum, BR §11-204.
Removal, BR §11-202.
Reporting requirements, BR §11-213.
Retired state personnel.
Health and welfare benefit subsidy, SPP §2-508.
Staff, BR §11-206.
Tenure, BR §11-202.
Chairman, BR §11-203.
Executive director, BR §11-205.
Testing laboratory.
Maintenance authorized, BR §11-212.
Conflict of laws.
Contrary local laws invalid, BR §11-102.
Conflicts of interest.
Commission.
Members, BR §11-202.
Staff, BR §11-206.
Licenses.
Financial disclosure by licensees, BR §§11-313,
11-315.
Contracts.
Approval required, BR §11-318.
Counties.
Special fund.
Failure to submit timely reports, BR §11-405.
Crimes and offenses.
Licenses.
Holding race meet without license, BR
§11-1001.
Criminal history records checks.
Individuals subjected to, BR §11-312.
Prospective buyers of licensees, BR §11-316.
Definitions, BR §11-101.
Beneficial ownership, BR §11-301.
Jockey fund, BR §11-901.
Dividends.
Fair Hill.
Salary or dividends for officers prohibited, BR
§11-702.
Elkridge-Harford Point to Point.
Scope of title, BR §11-103.

HORSE RACING —Cont'd
Employees.
Citizenship and residency requirements, BR
§11-320.
Commission.
Criminal history records checks.
Individuals subjected to, BR §11-312.
Executive director, BR §11-205.
Fingerprints.
Required to provide, BR §11-312.
Staff, BR §11-206.
Track employees, BR §11-207.
Criminal history records checks.
Individuals subjected to, BR §11-312.
Fingerprints.
Required to provide, BR §11-312.
Executive director.
Criminal history records checks.
Individuals subjected to, BR §11-312.
Fingerprints.
Required to provide, BR §11-312.
Fair Hill.
Quarter horse racing, BR §11-703.
Scope of title, BR §11-701.
Steeplechase, hurdle and flat racing.
License authorized, BR §11-702.
Takeout and winnings, BR §11-704.
Financial background review.
Prospective buyers of licensees, BR §11-316.
Fines.
Licenses.
Disciplinary actions, BR §11-308.
Holding race meet without license, BR
§11-1001.
Fingerprints.
Individuals required to provide, BR §11-312.
Fixing results, CR §12-109.
Grand National.
Scope of title, BR §11-103.
Harness racing.
General provisions, BR §§11-601 to 11-636.
See HARNESS RACING.
Hearings.
Licenses.
Disciplinary actions.
Right to hearing, BR §11-309.
Hearing committee, BR §11-310.
Horse breeder's association.
Running of Fund races, BR §§11-536 to 11-541.
See THOROUGHBRED RACING.
Hunt-type race.
Scope of title, BR §11-103.
Interference with race horse, CR §10-620.
Jockey injury compensation fund, BR §§11-901
to 11-906.
Law enforcement officers.
Commission.
Cooperation by officers, BR §11-208.
Licenses, BR §§11-301 to 11-320.
Administration of pension funds, BR §11-319.
Applications, BR §11-303.
Approval required.
Agreements and improvements, BR §11-318.
Assessments for jockey fund, BR §11-906.
Beneficial owner.
Defined, BR §11-301.
Beneficial ownership.
Affidavits required, BR §11-314.
Disclosure required, BR §11-314.
Statements to be signed under oath, BR
§11-315.

HORSE RACING —Cont'd
Licenses —Cont'd
Citizenship of employees, BR §11-320.
Contents, BR §11-304.
Controls on licensees, BR §11-305.
Criminal history records checks.
Individuals subjected to, BR §11-312.
Denials.
Grounds, BR §11-308.
Hearings, BR §11-309.
Disciplinary actions.
Grounds, BR §11-308.
Hearings.
Application of contested case provisions, BR §11-309.
Judicial review, BR §11-311.
Fees.
Return of fees of replacement days, BR §11-307.
Financial disclosure, BR §11-313.
Statements to be signed under oath, BR §11-315.
Fingerprints.
Individuals required to provide, BR §11-312.
Hearing committee, BR §11-310.
Holding race meet without license, BR §11-1001.
Issuance, BR §11-304.
Prospective buyers.
Background review required, BR §11-316.
Racing day.
No right of ownership in, BR §11-306.
Transferability, BR §11-317.
Recordkeeping requirements.
Power of commission to require of licensees, BR §11-211.
Replacement days.
Return of fees and award of, BR §11-307.
Reprimands.
Grounds, BR §11-308.
Hearings, BR §11-309.
Required, BR §11-302.
Requirements for issuance, BR §11-304.
Residency requirements for employees, BR §11-320.
Transferability, BR §11-317.
When required, BR §11-302.
Marlboro trials.
Scope of title, BR §11-103.
Maryland backstretch employees pension fund.
Administration, BR §11-319.
Maryland-bred race fund.
General provisions, BR §§11-529 to 11-541.
See THOROUGHBRED RACING.
Maryland harness track employees pension fund.
Administration, BR §11-319.
Maryland Horsemen's Assistance Fund, Inc., BR §11-909.
Maryland hunt cup.
Scope of title, BR §11-103.
Maryland jockey injury compensation fund, BR §§11-901 to 11-906.
Assessments for jockey fund, BR §11-906.
Board of directors, BR §11-904.
Defined as "jockey fund," BR §11-901.
Establishment, BR §11-902.
Incorporation, BR §11-902.
Purpose, BR §11-903.
Workers' compensation insurance.
Administration of program for jockeys, BR §11-905.

HORSE RACING —Cont'd
Maryland jockey injury compensation fund —Cont'd
Workers' compensation insurance —Cont'd
Covered employees under labor and employment article, BR §11-903.
Liability, BR §11-905.
Maryland race track employees pension fund.
Administration, BR §11-319.
Maryland Standardbred Horsemen's Assistance Fund, Inc., BR §11-909.
Maryland standardbred race fund, BR §§11-623 to 11-636.
See HARNESS RACING.
National racing compact, BR §§11-1301 to 11-1312.
See NATIONAL RACING COMPACT.
Pari-mutuel betting, BR §§11-801 to 11-832.
See PARI-MUTUEL BETTING.
Penalties.
Holding racing meet without license, BR §11-1001.
License disciplinary actions, BR §11-308.
Personal and financial background review.
Prospective buyers of licensees, BR §11-316.
Potomac trials.
Scope of title, BR §11-103.
Prearrangement or predetermination of results, CR §12-109.
Prospective buyers of licensees.
Personal and financial prior to purchase, BR §11-316.
Quarter horse racing.
Racing at Fair Hill, BR §11-703.
Queen Anne's county.
Cape Pine Farm in Church Hill.
Scope of title, BR §11-103.
Racing day.
No right of ownership, BR §11-306.
Racing horse under false name, CR §8-904.
Racing schedule.
Fair Hill, BR §11-702.
Scope of title, BR §11-103.
Short title, BR §11-1101.
Simulcast betting, BR §§11-815 to 11-832.
See PARI-MUTUEL BETTING.
Special fund, BR §§11-401 to 11-406.
Composition, BR §11-402.
Creation, BR §11-401.
Disposition of money, BR §11-402.
Establishment, BR §11-401.
Grants.
Allocation after deductions, BR §§11-404.1, 11-406.
Minimum payments.
Grants in half-yearly installments, BR §11-404.
Schedule, BR §11-403.
Use of annual grants, BR §11-403.
Grants in half-yearly installments, BR §11-404.
Reporting requirements, BR §11-405.
State racing commission.
Generally, BR §§11-201 to 11-214. See within this heading, "Commission."
Steeplechase race.
Scope of title, BR §11-103.
Sunset law, BR §11-1101.
Taxation.
Payment to subdivision.
Discontinuance, 19 §§38, 39.
Termination of title, BR §11-1101.

HORSE RACING —Cont'd
Testing laboratory.
Maintenance by commission, BR §11-212.
Thoroughbred racing.
General provisions, BR §§11-501 to 11-541.
See THOROUGHBRED RACING.
Title of act, BR §11-1101.
Track improvements.
Approval required, BR §11-318.
Tracks.
Alcoholic beverages.
Hours and days of sale.
Anne Arundel county, 2B §11-502.
Licenses.
Anne Arundel county, 2B §8-202.
Baltimore county, 2B §8-601.
Howard county, 2B §8-602.
Worcester county, 2B §8-603.
Trespass in stable area of track, CR §6-407.
Workers' compensation.
Insurance coverage.
Coverage required, LE §9-402.
Jockeys.
Average weekly wage, LE §9-602.
Claims procedure.
Maryland Jockey Injury Compensation Fund,
Inc., LE §9-1015.
Covered employees and employers, LE §9-212.
Race horse owners and trainers, LE §9-212.
Insurance coverage required, LE §9-402.

HORSES.
Bridle paths.
Establishment and maintenance, TR §8-409.
Commercial equine feed assessments, AG
§6-107.2.
Highways.
Persons riding animals or driving animal-drawn
vehicles.
Regulations, TR §21-104.
Lamps on animal-drawn vehicles, TR §22-216.
Livestock slaughtering, AG §4-123.1.
Maryland horse industry board, AG §§2-701 to
2-719.
See HORSE INDUSTRY BOARD.
Racing.
General provisions, BR §§11-101 to 11-1205.
See HORSE RACING.
Harness racing, BR §§11-601 to 11-636.
See HARNESS RACING.
Pari-mutuel betting, BR §§11-801 to 11-832.
See PARI-MUTUEL BETTING.
Thoroughbred racing, BR §§11-501 to 11-541.
See THOROUGHBRED RACING.
Stray domestic animals, AG §§3-601 to 3-603.
Transporting horses.
Civil penalties for violations, AG §3-903.
Definition of "transport," AG §3-901.
Requirements, AG §3-902.
Wholesome meat act.
Equine carcasses.
Separate establishments, AG §4-114.

HOSPICES, HG §§19-901 to 19-913.
Admissions.
Restriction on admissions, HG §19-913.
Construction and safety standards, HG §19-904.
Criminal history records checks of employees,
HG §§19-1901 to 19-1912.
See ADULT DEPENDENT CARE PROGRAMS.
Definitions, HG §19-901.

HOSPICES —Cont'd
Director.
Qualifications, HG §19-906.
Fines.
Violation of subtitle, HG §19-911.
Health insurance coverage for services, IN
§15-809.
Health maintenance organizations.
Benefits for hospice services, HG §19-703.
Home-based hospice services.
Licenses, HG §19-906.
Licenses.
Applicants, HG §19-906.
Applications, HG §19-907.
Denials, HG §19-911.
Fees.
Application fee may not be refunded, HG
§19-907.
Home-based hospice services, HG §19-906.
Issuance, HG §19-908.
Operating without license, HG §19-912.
Qualifications, HG §19-906.
Renewal, HG §19-910.
Required, HG §19-905.
Revocation, HG §19-911.
Scope of license, HG §19-909.
Term of license, HG §19-910.
Life expectancy of patients.
Admission restriction, HG §19-913.
Medical assistance program.
Reimbursement for services provided, HG
§15-128.
Penalties.
Violation of subtitle, HG §19-911.
Prohibited classification, HG §19-904.
Rules and regulations, HG §19-903.
Safety.
Standards for safety, HG §19-904.
Standards for construction and safety, HG
§19-904.
Statement of purpose, HG §19-902.
Violations of subtitle, HG §19-911.

HOSPITALS, HG §§19-301 to 19-374.
Abortion.
Permitting abortions in hospitals, HG §20-214.
Abuse of patients. See within this heading,
"Rights of individuals."
Accidents.
Lien against claim of patients. See within this
heading, "Liens."
Accounts and accounting.
Rights to individuals, HG §19-346.
Accreditation of health care facilities, HG
§§19-2301, 19-2302.
Accredited hospital.
Defined, HG §19-301.
Qualifications for license, HG §19-319.
Surveys.
Availability of survey findings, HG §19-308.
Utilization review program, HG §19-319.
Acquired immune deficiency syndrome (AIDS).
Testing of inmates of correctional institutions.
Liability for breach of patient confidentiality,
HG §18-338.
Positive test results.
Liability, HG §18-337.
Administrative procedure.
Licenses.
Appeals, HG §19-330.

HOSPITALS —Cont'd
Admissions.
Chronic disease centers, HG §19-505.
Restrictions by Montgomery and Prince George's counties, HG §19-329.
Restrictions by secretary, HG §19-328.
Rights of individuals.
Application or contract for admission, HG §19-344.
Agency.
Rights of individuals.
Applicant's agent, HG §19-344.
Alzheimer's disease.
In-service education program as to, HG §19-319.1.
Anatomical gift act.
Consent procedures generally, HG §19-310.
Eligible donees, ET §4-504.
Licensed hospital.
Defined, ET §4-501.
Procurement of organs and tissues.
Protocol for, HG §19-319.
Annuity agreements with donors, IN §16-114.
Apartment units.
Defined, HG §19-301.
Appeals.
Discharge or transfer of residents.
Civil damages for violations of provisions, HG §19-345.3.
Discharge violations.
Appeal of fines imposed, HG §19-308.8.
Hazardous conditions.
Intermediate sanction, HG §§19-364, 19-367.
Licenses.
Administrative and judicial review, HG §19-330.
Applicability of provisions, HG §19-302.
Artificial insemination.
Permitting artificial insemination in hospitals, HG §20-214.
Bed capacity.
Licensed bed capacity, HG §19-307.2.
Bedding and upholstered furniture.
Selling hospital bedding, HG §24-432.
Bingo.
Carroll county.
Conducting, CR §§13-907, 13-908.
Frederick county, CR §13-1306.
Births.
Universal newborn hearing screening program, HG §19-308.5.
Blood banks.
Public cord blood banks.
Umbilical cord blood donations, hospitals to arrange, HG §19-308.7.
Blood tests.
Liability for taking blood without consent, HG §20-110.
Boards.
Chronic disease centers.
Advisory boards. See within this heading, "Chronic disease centers."
Citizens' nursing home boards.
See NURSING HOMES.
Bond issues.
Program for closed or delicensed hospitals.
General provisions, 43C §16A.
Building codes.
Emergency power and lighting systems, PS §12-702.
Centers for disease control and prevention.
Occupational safety and health.
Compliance with and notice explaining, HG §19-319.

HOSPITALS —Cont'd
Centers for disease control and prevention —Cont'd
Occupational safety and health —Cont'd
Reporting noncompliance with guidelines on universal precautions, LE §5-205.
Cervical cancer.
Examinations, HG §19-348.
Chronic disease centers, HG §§19-501 to 19-513.
Admissions generally, HG §19-505.
Advisory boards.
Compensation of members, HG §19-511.
Composition, HG §19-509.
Defined, HG §19-501.
Duties, HG §19-512.
Election, HG §19-510.
Established, HG §19-508.
Meetings, HG §19-511.
Membership, HG §19-509.
Officers, HG §19-510.
Powers and duties, HG §19-512.
Prohibited acts, HG §19-513.
Term of office, HG §19-510.
Vacancies, HG §19-509.
Definitions, HG §19-501.
Discharges.
Failure to leave, HG §19-506.
Requirements, HG §19-506.
Location, HG §19-502.
Programs.
Establishment, HG §19-504.
Prohibited acts, HG §19-513.
Purpose, HG §19-502.
Rules and regulations.
Adoption by secretary of health, HG §19-503.
Secretary of health.
Rules and regulations.
Adoption, HG §19-503.
Transfers, HG §19-507.
Classifications of hospitals and related institutions, HG §19-307.
Closing.
Alternative building or site uses, HG §19-326.
Training displaced workers.
Fees, HG §19-326.1.
Commissions.
Department of health and mental hygiene.
See HEALTH AND MENTAL HYGIENE DEPARTMENT.
Health services cost review commission, HG §§19-201 to 19-227.
See HEALTH.
Community needs assessment.
Nonprofit hospitals, HG §19-303.
Community programs.
Receivership.
General provisions, HG §§19-333 to 19-339.
See NURSING HOMES.
Complaints.
Inspections to investigate complaints, HG §19-309.
Comprehensive care facilities.
Applications or contracts for admission, HG §19-308.1.
Comprehensive physical rehabilitation facilities, HG §§19-1201 to 19-1208.
See COMPREHENSIVE PHYSICAL REHABILITATION FACILITIES.
Compulsive gamblers, HG §§19-801 to 19-804.
See GAMING.

HOSPITALS —Cont'd
Confidentiality of information.
Patient care advisory committees.
Proceedings, HG §19-374.
Rights of individuals, HG §19-344.
Conflicts of interest.
Pharmaceutical suppliers.
Penalty for violation, HG §19-357.
Consent.
Written consent to discharge or transfer, HG §19-345.2.
Violations by facility or resident's agent, HG §19-345.3.
Construction, conversion or other changes.
Approval.
Applications, HG §19-313.
Action on applications, HG §19-314.
Qualifications for approval, HG §19-312.
Required, HG §19-311.
Financing and refinancing.
Assistance, HG §19-315.
Contagious diseases.
Institution reports, HG §18-202.
Contracts.
Community programs.
Receivership, HG §19-337.
Comprehensive care facilities.
Contracts for admission, HG §19-308.3.
Extended care facilities.
Contracts for admission, HG §19-308.3.
Nursing facilities.
Receivership, HG §19-337.
Rights of individuals.
Contracts for admission, HG §19-344.
Counties.
Authority to establish hospital or reception center, 25 §252.
Chartered counties.
Establishment, 25A §5.
Credentialing process for physicians.
Establishment as condition of licensure, HG §19-319.
Uniform standard credentialing form, use, HG §19-319.
Credit cards.
Acceptance as payment for bills, 25 §253.
Death of patient.
Reports of unexpected occurrences or incidents, HG §19-304.
Deficiencies.
Correction, HG §19-360.
Requirements for corrective action, HG §19-360.
Definitions.
Chronic disease centers, HG §19-501.
Community programs.
Receivership, HG §19-333.
Comprehensive physical rehabilitation facilities, HG §19-1201.
Generally, HG §19-301.
Hazardous conditions.
Intermediate sanction, HG §19-361.
Home health agencies, HG §19-401.
Nursing facilities.
Receivership, HG §19-333.
Patient care advisory committees, HG §19-370.
Patient care personnel, HG §19-308.1.
Receivership of nursing facilities and community programs, HG §19-333.
Rights of individuals, HG §19-343.
Abuse, HG §19-347.
Property of residents, HG §19-346.

HOSPITALS —Cont'd
Definitions —Cont'd
Rights of individuals —Cont'd
Uniform claims forms, HG §19-350.1.
Dentists.
Assessment of medical risk of procedures, HO §4-507.
Hospital admission history and physical examination.
Completion by dentist, HO §4-507.
Use of facilities and staff privileges for qualified dentists, HG §19-351.
Disability of patient.
Reports of unexpected occurrences or incidents, HG §19-304.
Discharges.
Chronic disease centers, HG §19-506.
Policy generally, HG §19-308.8.
Discovery.
Hazardous conditions.
Intermediate sanction appeals, HG §19-364.
Discrimination.
General prohibition, HG §19-355.
Distribution of funds.
Applicant's agent.
Payment for care of individual, HG §19-344.
Domiciliary care.
Defined, HG §19-301.
Drug or alcohol abuse.
Chronic alcoholics.
Admission to private and public hospitals, HG §8-509.
Intoxicated persons.
Admission to private and public hospitals, HG §8-509.
Emergency management plans, PS §14-110.1.
Emergency rooms.
Collection of payment from health care services subscriber, HG §19-710.
Emergency security codes, HG §19-308.6.
Evidence.
Hazardous conditions.
Intermediate sanction appeals, HG §19-364.
Examinations.
Cervical cancer, HG §19-348.
Executors and administrators.
Payment.
Order of payment when assets insufficient to pay claims in full, ET §8-105.
Expenses.
Recovering expenses, 25 §252.
Extended care facilities.
Applications or contracts for admission, HG §19-308.1.
Federally qualified health centers grant program, HG §§24-1301 to 24-1308.
Allocations, HG §24-1305.
Applications, HG §24-1303.
Approval for grant, HG §24-1302.
Conditions on use of funds, HG §24-1304.
Definitions, HG §24-1301.
Determination of amount, HG §24-1304.
Eligible applicants, HG §24-1303.
Establishment, HG §24-1302.
Recovery of funds expended, HG §24-1306.
Regulations.
Board of public works regulations, HG §24-1305.
Department regulations, HG §§24-1307, 24-1308.
Use of funds, HG §24-1304.

HOSPITALS —Cont'd
Federally qualified health centers grant program —Cont'd
Waiver of right of recovery, HG §24-1306.
Fee assessed by health care commission, HG §19-111.
Financial assistance policy of care for low-income uninsured patients, HG §19-214.1.
Financial statements.
Nursing facilities.
Itemized financial statements, HG §19-350.
Fines.
Discharge or transfer of residents.
Violation by facility or resident agent, HG §19-345.3.
Discharge violations, HG §19-308.8.
Reports of unexpected occurrences or incidents, violations, HG §19-304.
Standards and inspections.
Violations by employees, HG §19-308.
Fires and fire protection.
Evacuation procedures.
Alternative requirements for acute care hospitals, PS §9-505.
Forms.
Notice of discharge or transfer of resident, HG §19-345.1.
Freestanding ambulatory care facilities, HG §§19-3B-01 to 19-3B-09.
See FREESTANDING AMBULATORY CARE FACILITIES.
Freestanding medical facilities, HG §§19-3A-01 to 19-3A-07.
See FREESTANDING MEDICAL FACILITIES.
Gaming, bazaar, carnival and raffles.
Carroll county.
Conducting gaming events generally, CR §§13-901 to 13-909.
Frederick county, CR §§13-1301 to 13-1307.
Glen Dale hospital.
Maryland-Washington regional district.
Acquisition of title upon sale of hospital, 28 §8-127.
Good Samaritan law.
Support for emergency medical system, CJ §5-608.
Grievances.
Rights of individuals, HG §19-344.
Reports, HG §19-344.
Hazardous conditions.
Defined, HG §19-361.
Intermediate sanction.
Appeals, HG §19-364.
Decision of hearings office, HG §19-367.
Definitions, HG §19-361.
Escrow account, HG §19-363.
Amount, HG §19-363.
Establishment, HG §19-363.
Failure to establish, HG §19-366.
Release of escrowed funds, HG §19-365.
Termination of escrow and return of balance, HG §19-365.
Failure to establish escrow account or correct hazardous condition, HG §19-366.
Further sanctions.
Imposition, HG §19-366.
Hearings.
Appeals, HG §19-364.
Imposition, HG §19-362.
Plan of correction, HG §19-362.
Submission, HG §19-362.

HOSPITALS —Cont'd
Hazardous conditions —Cont'd
Intermediate sanction —Cont'd
Release of escrowed funds, HG §19-365.
Sanction order, HG §19-362.
Health and higher educational facilities authority.
General provisions, 43C §§1 to 24.
See HEALTH AND HIGHER EDUCATIONAL FACILITIES AUTHORITY.
Health maintenance organizations, HG §§19-701 to 19-735.
See HEALTH MAINTENANCE ORGANIZATIONS.
Health services cost review commission, HG §§19-201 to 19-227.
See HEALTH.
Hearings.
Community programs.
Receiverships.
Procedural requirements, HG §19-335.
Discharge of resident, HG §19-345.1.
Licenses.
Denials or revocations, HG §19-327.
Nursing facilities.
Receiverships.
Procedural requirements, HG §19-335.
Transfer of resident, HG §19-345.1.
Home health agencies, HG §§19-401 to 19-410.
See HOME HEALTH AGENCIES.
Hospices, HG §§19-901 to 19-913.
See HOSPICES.
Human immunodeficiency virus.
Blood tests.
Inmates of correctional institutions.
Liability, HG §18-338.
Positive test results.
Liability of hospitals or other health care providers, HG §18-337.
Husband and wife.
Rights of individuals.
Spouses sharing rooms, HG §19-344.
Visitation rights, HG §19-344.
Identification.
Personnel required to wear identification tags, HG §19-308.4.
Immunity.
Abuse of patients.
Reports, HG §19-347.
Liability in tort.
Generally, CJ §5-632.
Reports.
Abuse of patients, HG §19-347.
Rights of individuals.
Abuse.
Immunity for filing reports, CJ §5-631.
Injunctions.
Discharge or transfer of residents.
Violation of requirements, HG §19-345.3.
Inspections.
Comprehensive physical rehabilitation facilities, HG §19-1205.
Investigation of complaints, HG §19-309.
Reports, HG §19-308.
Rules and regulations.
Adoption, HG §19-308.
Veterinary hospitals.
Board of veterinary medical examiners, AG §2-304.
Insurance.
Health insurance generally.
See HEALTH INSURANCE.

HOSPITALS —Cont'd
Insurance —Cont'd
Liquidation, rehabilitation, etc., of insurers.
  Priority of claims against insurers.
    Current financing moneys of hospitals, IN
      §9-227.
Nonprofit health service plans, IN §§14-101 to
    14-140.
  See NONPROFIT HEALTH SERVICE PLANS.
Uniform claims forms.
  Use when submitting claim or bill for
    reimbursement to third-party payors, HG
    §19-350.1.
**Interference with access to or egress from
  medical facility,** CR §10-204.
Investigations.
Abuse of patients, HG §19-347.
Non-life threatening deficiencies.
  Inspections to investigate, HG §19-309.
Rights of individuals.
  Abuse of patients, HG §19-347.
Involuntary discharge.
Requirements, HG §19-345.2.
Violations by facility or resident's agent, HG
    §19-345.3.
Liability in tort.
Generally, CJ §5-632; HG §19-354.
Licenses.
Administrative procedure.
  Appeals, HG §19-330.
Admission restrictions by secretary, HG §19-328.
Appeals, HG §19-330.
Applications.
  Contents, HG §19-320.
  Fees, HG §19-320.
  Form, HG §19-320.
  Generally, HG §19-320.
  Refunds.
    Prohibited, HG §19-320.
  Renewal, HG §19-323.
Comprehensive physical rehabilitation facilities.
  See COMPREHENSIVE PHYSICAL
    REHABILITATION FACILITIES.
Contents, HG §19-321.
Credentialing process for physicians.
  Establishment as condition of license, HG
    §19-319.
Defined, HG §19-301.
Delicensure.
  Alternative building or site uses, HG §19-326.
  Appeals, HG §19-325.
  Order of secretary, HG §19-325.
  Parties, HG §19-325.
  Petition, HG §19-325.
  Training displaced workers.
    Fees, HG §19-326.1.
Denial.
  Authority of secretary, HG §19-327.
  Grounds, HG §19-327.
  Hearings, HG §19-327.
  Montgomery and Prince George's counties, HG
    §19-329.
Hearings.
  Denials or revocations, HG §19-327.
Home health agencies, HG §§19-401 to 19-410.
  See HOME HEALTH AGENCIES.
Issuance, HG §19-321.
  Renewal, HG §19-323.
Nursing facilities.
  Term, HG §19-323.

HOSPITALS —Cont'd
Licenses —Cont'd
Operation without license.
  Prohibited, HG §19-358.
Qualifications.
  Generally, HG §19-319.
Refunds.
  Prohibited, HG §19-320.
Renewal, HG §19-323.
  Applications, HG §19-323.
  Issuance, HG §19-323.
Requirements generally, HG §19-318.
Revocation.
  Authority of secretary, HG §19-327.
  Bond program for closed or delicensed hospitals.
    General provisions, 43C §16A.
  Grounds, HG §19-327.
  Hearings, HG §19-327.
  Montgomery and Prince George's counties, HG
    §19-329.
Risk management program.
  Establishment of program as condition of
    licensure, HG §19-319.
Scope, HG §19-322.
Secretary of health.
  Denials and revocations, HG §19-327.
Term, HG §19-323.
Transferability, HG §19-324.
Universal precautions.
  Compliance with centers for disease controls
    guidelines on, HG §19-319.
Utilization review programs, HG §19-319.
Liens.
Claim.
  Fifty percent of patient's claim against third
    person, CL §16-601.
    Subordinate only to attorney's lien, CL
      §16-601.
  Filing in clerk's office, CL §16-602.
    Fee, CL §16-605.
  Insurer notified, CL §16-602.
  Liability of persons making payments.
    After notice of hospital's claim, CL §16-603.
  Notice, CL §16-602.
    Liability of persons making payments to
      patient after notice, CL §16-603.
    Mailed by registered or certified mail, CL
      §16-602.
    To whom given, CL §16-602.
Community programs.
  State funds as lien on program, HG §19-338.
Docket.
  Hospital lien docket, CL §16-605.
Estimation of lien, CL §16-604.
Examination of hospital records.
  Ascertain charges and estimate lien, CL
    §16-604.
Fees.
  Clerks of court.
    Hospital lien docket, CL §16-605.
  Fifty percent of patient's claim against third
    person, CL §16-601.
  Subordinate only to attorney's lien, CL §16-601.
Release.
  Clerk's fee, CL §16-605.
  Hospital lien docket, CL §16-605.
Workers' compensation.
  Effect, CL §16-601.
Limitation of actions.
Actions against health care providers, CJ §5-109.
  Actions by claimants under eleven years old, CJ
    §5-109.

HOSPITALS —Cont'd
Limitation of actions —Cont'd
Actions against health care providers —Cont'd
Age limitations in certain actions.
Effect of other provisions, CJ §5-109.
Tolling statute, CJ §5-109.
Claims.
Effect of filing claim, CJ §5-109.
Limited service hospitals.
Defined, HG §19-301.
Regulations, HG §19-307.1.
Mail.
Lien of hospital against third parties for
accidents.
Notice mailed to insurance carrier, CL §16-602.
Malpractice.
Health care malpractice claims.
See MALPRACTICE.
Mammograms.
Mammography educational materials, HG
§19-348.
Medicaid.
Acute general and chronic care hospitals.
Reimbursement authorized, HG §15-110.
Rights of individuals.
Notice of discharge or transfer, HG §19-345.1.
Recipients of benefits, HG §19-345.
Medical assistance program.
Eligibility for participation.
Revocation for various violations or offenses,
HG §19-357.
Medical utilization review.
Health insurance requirements, IN §15-1001.
Mental health facilities.
See MENTAL HEALTH FACILITIES.
Mentally ill.
See MENTALLY ILL.
Mental retardation.
State residential centers.
See DEVELOPMENTAL DISABILITIES.
Mergers.
Alternative building or site uses, HG §19-326.
Training of displaced workers.
Fees, HG §19-326.1.
Misdemeanors.
Individuals rights.
Misuse of fund, HG §19-336.
Medical referral services, HG §19-356.
Operating in violation of regulations, HG §19-359.
Operating without a license, HG §19-358.
Pharmaceutical suppliers.
Rebates, commissions, etc., HG §19-357.
Standards and inspections.
Violations by employees, HG §19-308.
Municipal corporations.
Authority to establish hospital or reception center,
25 §252.
Name tags.
Personnel required to wear identification tags, HG
§19-308.4.
Newborn hearing screening program.
Universal program, HG §19-308.5.
Nonaccredited hospitals.
Defined, HG §19-301.
Nonprofit health entities.
Acquisition, SG §§6.5-101 to 6.5-401.
See NONPROFIT HEALTH ENTITIES.
Nonprofit hospitals, HG §19-303.
Notices.
Centers for disease control guidelines on universal
precautions.
Compliance with, HG §19-319.

HOSPITALS —Cont'd
Notices —Cont'd
Discharge of resident, HG §19-345.1.
Violations by facility or resident's agent, HG
§19-345.3.
Lien for fifty percent of patient's claim against
third person.
To whom given, CL §16-602.
Rates.
Increase in charges, HG §19-349.
Transfer of resident, HG §19-345.1.
Violations by facility or resident's agent, HG
§19-345.3.
Nursing care.
Defined, HG §19-301.
Nursing referral service agencies, HG
§§19-4B-01 to 19-4B-06.
Occupational safety and health.
Centers for disease control.
Reporting noncompliance with guidelines on
universal precautions, LE §5-205.
Organ donations.
Procedure, HG §19-310.
Pain assessment management and treatment.
Statement of right to receive, HG §19-353.
Patient care advisory committees, HG §§19-370
to 19-374.
Composition, HG §19-372.
Confidentiality of proceedings, HG §19-374.
Definitions, HG §19-370.
Duties of committee, HG §19-373.
Duties of hospitals, HG §19-371.
Establishment.
Duties of hospitals, HG §19-371.
Liability for advice given, HG §19-374.
Life-threatening conditions.
Advice as to options for individuals with, HG
§19-374.
Advice in cases involving, HG §19-373.
Number of members, HG §19-372.
Petitioner.
Defined, HG §19-370.
Persons accompanying petitioner, HG §19-372.
Rights of individuals.
Notification of individual's rights, HG §19-374.
Patient care personnel.
Defined, HG §19-308.1.
Qualifications.
Rules and regulations, HG §19-308.1.
Patients.
Recovery of expenses, 25 §252.
Rights of individuals. See within this heading,
"Rights of individuals."
Transfer of patients between hospitals, HG
§19-308.2.
Patient's bill of rights.
Copy provided patient, statement of expectations,
HG §19-342.
Payment for bills.
Acceptance of credit cards, 25 §253.
Recovering expenses, 25 §252.
Penalties.
Chronic disease centers.
Prohibited acts, HG §19-513.
Licenses.
Operation without license, HG §19-358.
Pharmaceutical suppliers, HG §19-357.
Referral services, HG §19-356.

HOSPITALS —Cont'd
Penalties —Cont'd
Rights of individuals.
Psychiatric facilities.
Policies and procedures regarding patients'
rights.
Failure to adopt and implement, HG
§19-319.2.
Report of alleged abuse.
Civil penalty for failure to make required
report, HG §19-347.
Rules and regulations, HG §19-359.
Transfer of patients between hospitals, HG
§19-308.2.
Personal care.
Defined, HG §19-301.
Personal identification tags.
Staff required to wear, HG §19-308.4.
Persons.
Defined, HG §19-301.
Pharmaceutical suppliers.
Penalties for offenses, HG §19-357.
Physicians.
Credential process for physicians, HG §19-319.
Employment by or having privileges with
hospitals.
Required report on physicians to board, HO
§14-413.
Podiatrists.
Procedures required to be performed in licensed
hospital, HO §16-103.
Use of facilities and staff privileges, HG §19-351.
Privacy.
Rights of individuals, HG §19-344.
Private review agents.
General provisions, IN §§15-10B-01 to 15-10B-20.
See HEALTH INSURANCE.
Provider-sponsored organizations, HG
§§19-7A-01 to 19-7A-04.
Psychiatric research center.
Maryland psychiatric research center.
See MENTAL HEALTH FACILITIES.
Psychologists.
Use of facilities and staff privileges for licensed
psychologists, HG §19-351.
Rates.
Itemized financial statements, HG §19-350.
Notice.
Increase in charges, HG §19-349.
Rights of individuals. See within this heading,
"Rights of individuals."
Receivership of nursing facilities.
See NURSING HOMES.
Reception centers.
Authority to establish, 25 §252.
Defined, 25 §252.
Records.
Denial of inspection, SG §10-616.
Evidence.
Admissibility of hospital records, CJ §10-104.
Lien of hospital.
Estimation of lien and examination of hospital
records, CL §16-604.
Medical records generally.
See MEDICAL RECORDS.
Subpoenas.
Circuit courts, CivProCir Rule 2-510.
District Court, CivProDist Rule 3-510.
**Reduced-cost or free care to low-income
patients without health insurance.**
Policies to be established, HG §19-214.1.

HOSPITALS —Cont'd
Referral services.
Discounts and split fees, HG §19-356.
Related institutions.
Defined, HG §19-301.
Reports.
Abuse of patients, HG §19-347.
Community programs.
Receivership, HG §19-337.
Contagious diseases.
Institutions, HG §18-202.
Inspections, HG §19-308.
Nursing facilities.
Receivership, HG §19-337.
Physicians employed by or having privileges with.
Required to report to board, HO §14-413.
Reduced-cost or free care to low-income patients
without health insurance.
Policies to be established, HG §19-214.1.
Rights of individuals.
Abuse of patients, HG §19-347.
Grievances, HG §19-344.
Unexpected occurrences or incidents, HG §19-304.
Residential service agencies, HG §§19-4A-01 to
19-4A-10.
See RESIDENTIAL SERVICE AGENCIES.
Rights of individuals.
Abuse.
Report of alleged abuse, HG §19-347.
Immunity from civil liability, CJ §5-631; HG
§19-347.
Accounts and accounting, HG §19-346.
Admissions.
Application or contract for admission, HG
§19-344.
Applicant's agent, HG §19-344.
Cervical cancer.
Examinations, HG §19-348.
Communications, HG §19-344.
Compliance.
Procedures generally, HG §19-344.
Confidential information, HG §19-344.
Contracts for admission, HG §19-344.
Definitions, HG §19-343.
Abuse, HG §19-347.
Property of residents, HG §19-346.
Uniform claims forms, HG §19-350.1.
Developmental disabilities.
See DEVELOPMENTAL DISABILITIES.
Discharge of resident, HG §19-345.
Notice of discharge, HG §19-345.1.
Violation by facility or resident's agent, HG
§19-345.3.
Discrimination prohibited, HG §19-355.
Duties of facilities.
Generally, HG §19-343.
Examinations.
Cervical cancer, HG §19-348.
Exercise of rights, HG §19-344.
Facility.
Defined, HG §19-343.
Financial statements, HG §19-350.
Financial transactions.
Control over, HG §19-346.
Funds.
Surrender, HG §19-346.
Grievances, HG §19-344.
Hearings.
Notice of discharge or transfer, HG §19-345.1.
Hospitals generally, HG §19-342.
Information on treatment, HG §19-344.

HOSPITALS —Cont'd
Rights of individuals —Cont'd
Interest on accounts, HG §19-346.
Involuntary discharge, HG §19-345.2.
Violations by facility or resident's agent, HG
§19-345.3.
Legislative declaration, HG §19-343.
Mammography educational materials, HG
§19-348.
Medicaid.
Recipients of benefits, HG §19-345.
Notice of increase in charges, HG §19-349.
Nursing facilities, HG §19-343.
Pain assessment management and treatment.
Statement of right to receive, HG §19-353.
Participation in planning treatment, HG §19-344.
Patient care advisory committees.
Notification of individual's rights, HG §19-374.
Patient liability, HG §19-346.
Patient's bill of rights.
Copy provided patient, statement of
expectations, HG §19-342.
Personal effects, HG §19-344.
Policy generally, HG §19-343.
Privacy, HG §19-344.
Procedures for compliance.
Generally, HG §19-344.
Prohibited service, HG §19-344.
Property of residents, HG §19-346.
Psychiatric facilities.
Policies and procedures regarding patients'
rights, HG §19-319.2.
Rates.
Notice of increase in charges, HG §19-349.
Statement of services and charges, HG §19-344.
Statements after payment of charges, HG
§19-350.
Related institutions, HG §19-343.
Reports.
Abuse, HG §19-347.
Grievances, HG §19-344.
Responses to requests, HG §19-344.
Responsibility for carrying out provisions, HG
§19-344.
Spouses.
Sharing rooms, HG §19-344.
Visitors, HG §19-344.
Staff.
Applicability of subtitle, HG §19-351.
Statement of services and charges, HG §19-344.
Third-party payors.
Uniform claims forms.
Use when submitting claim or bill for
reimbursement to, HG §19-350.1.
Tort liability of hospital, HG §19-354.
Transfer of resident, HG §19-345.
Notice of transfer, HG §19-345.1.
Violations by facility or resident's agent, HG
§19-345.3.
Treatment.
Information on treatment, HG §19-344.
Visitors, HG §19-344.
Withdrawals from accounts, HG §19-346.
Written statement included in document of rights,
HG §19-344.
Risk management program, HG §19-319.
Root cause analysis.
Reports of unexpected occurrences or incidents,
HG §19-304.
Rules and regulations.
Chronic disease centers, HG §19-503.

HOSPITALS —Cont'd
Rules and regulations —Cont'd
Comprehensive care facilities.
Applications or contracts for admission, HG
§19-308.3.
Extended care facilities.
Applications or contracts for admission, HG
§19-308.3.
Limited service hospitals, HG §19-307.1.
Patient care personnel.
Qualifications, HG §19-308.1.
Penalty for violation, HG §19-359.
Reports of unexpected occurrences or incidents,
HG §19-304.
Standards and inspections, HG §19-308.
Scope of subtitle, HG §19-302.
Secretary of health and mental hygiene.
Admission restrictions, HG §19-328.
Chronic disease centers.
Adoption of rules and regulations, HG §19-503.
Inspections.
Adoption of rules and regulations, HG §19-308.
Licenses.
Denials and revocations, HG §19-327.
Standards.
Adoption of rules and regulations, HG §19-308.
Security codes.
Emergency security codes, HG §19-308.6.
Smoking in hospitals, HG §24-205.
Special rehabilitation hospitals.
Classification of hospitals as, HG §§19-318,
19-358.
Staff.
Dentists.
Use of facilities and staff privileges for qualified
dentists, HG §19-351.
Psychologists.
Use of facilities and staff privileges for licensed
psychologists, HG §19-351.
Rights of individuals.
Applicability of subtitle, HG §19-351.
Standards.
Adoption, HG §19-308.
State-aided institutions.
Charges against.
By state administration, 88A §3.
State hospitals.
Educational programs.
Director, ED §22-201.
Funds, ED §22-202.
Other agencies.
Jurisdiction not affected, ED §22-203.
Statement of services and charges.
Rights of individuals, HG §19-344.
Sterilization.
Permitting sterilization, HG §20-214.
Subpoenas.
Hazardous conditions.
Intermediate sanction.
Appeals, HG §19-364.
Subtitle.
Scope, HG §19-302.
Third-party payors.
Uniform claims forms.
Use when submitting claim or bill for
reimbursement to, HG §19-350.1.
Tip jars and punch board.
Frederick county, CR §13-1305.
Tort liability, CJ §5-632; HG §19-354.
Transfers.
Chronic disease centers.
Generally, HG §19-507.

HOSPITALS —Cont'd
Transfers —Cont'd
Transfer of patients between hospitals, HG §19-308.2.
Unemployed hospital employees.
Division of employment and training.
Retraining and placement of unemployed hospital employees, LE §11-201.
Unemployment compensation.
Defined, LE §8-101.
General provisions, LE §§8-101 to 8-1608.
See UNEMPLOYMENT COMPENSATION.
Interns, patients and student nurses.
Not covered employment, LE §8-218.
Unexpected occurrences or incidents.
Reports, HG §19-304.
United States.
Construction of hospitals, 25 §255.
Universal precautions.
Compliance with and notice explaining centers for disease control guidelines, HG §19-319.
Unrelated individuals.
Defined, HG §19-301.
Utilization review program, HG §19-319.
Health insurance requirements for utilization review, IN §15-1001.
Private review agents.
General provisions, IN §§15-10B-01 to 15-10B-20.
See HEALTH INSURANCE.
Veterinarians.
Inspection.
Board of veterinary medical examiners, AG §2-304.
Supervision of animals in care of veterinarians, CL §11-905.
Unlicensed person not to operate, AG §2-313.
Violations.
Corrective action, HG §19-360.
Visitors.
Rights of individuals, HG §19-344.
Water and sewer systems.
Permit for landfills near hospitals, EN §9-225.
Workers' compensation.
Effect as to hospital lien, CL §16-601.

HOSTAGE AND BARRICADE COMMUNICATIONS SPECIALISTS, CJ §10-413.

HOTCHPOT.
Advancement.
Generally, ET §3-106.

HOTELS.
Alcoholic beverages.
Beer and light wine licenses.
Class B, on-sale, 2B §5-201.
Beer, wine and liquor licenses.
Class B, 2B §3-201, 6-201.
Definition of hotel, 2B §1-102.
Hours of sale.
Beer licenses, 2B §11-301.
Beer, wine and liquor licenses, 2B §11-303.
Lien on baggage. See within this heading, "Liens."
Bad checks.
Obtaining services by issuing or passing, CR §§8-101 to 8-108.
Baggage rooms.
Loss of property, BR §15-106.
Barbeque grills.
Restrictions on use, PS §9-1001.

HOTELS —Cont'd
Blind persons.
Rights of blind persons to public facilities, 30 §33.
Boardinghouses.
Blind, deaf or mute persons.
Rights to public facilities, 30 §33.
Discrimination in public accommodations, 49B §§5 to 8A.
See DISCRIMINATION.
Liens.
Personal effects, goods or furniture of boarder or lodger, CL §16-503.
Building codes.
Emergency power and lighting systems, PS §12-702.
Checkrooms.
Loss of property, BR §15-105.
Counties.
Hotel rental tax, 24 §§9-301 to 9-326.
See COUNTIES.
Deaf or mute persons.
Rights to public facilities, 30 §33.
Definitions, 2B §§1-102, 8-218; CL §16-501.
Alcoholic beverages, 2B §1-102.
Valuable, BR §15-101.
Discrimination in public accommodations, 49B §§5 to 8A.
See DISCRIMINATION.
Disturbing the peace, disorderly conduct, CR §10-201.
Fires and fire protection.
Evacuation procedures, PS §§9-501 to 9-506.
Property loss, BR §15-107.
Smoke detectors.
Installation required, PS §9-102.
Guest rooms.
Loss of property, BR §15-104.
Hotel rental tax, 24 §§9-301 to 9-326.
See COUNTIES.
Jewelry.
Hotel liability for valuables, BR §§15-101 to 15-107.
Liens.
Baggage and other property of guests, CL §16-502.
Boardinghouses.
Personal effects, goods or furniture of boarder, CL §16-503.
Definitions, CL §16-501.
Procedure to obtain, CL §16-502.
Sale of property.
Procedure, CL §16-502.
Money.
Hotel liability for valuables, BR §§15-101 to 15-107.
Montgomery county.
Beer, wine and liquor licenses, 2B §9-102.1.
Negligence.
Fire property loss, BR §15-107.
Operating agreements, CL §§23-101 to 23-106.
Breach, remedies, CL §23-102.
Conflicts between agreement and law governing principal and agent relationship.
Terms of agreement to govern, CL §23-102.
Continuation of agreement for period of time or happening of event.
Enforceability until expiration of period or happening of event, CL §23-104.
Definitions, CL §23-101.
Duties and obligations enforceable against party.
Express covenant or other agreement provision creating, CL §23-103.

HOTELS —Cont'd
Operating agreements —Cont'd
Duties and obligations enforceable against party
—Cont'd
No duties implied, CL §23-105.
Fraud, duress or illegality.
Defenses not limited, CL §23-106.
Good faith and fair dealing.
Covenant implied, CL §23-105.
Specific performance.
Remedy for breach or termination of agreement,
CL §23-102.
Third party claims not affected, CL §23-106.
Property loss, BR §§15-101 to 15-107.
Applicability of title, BR §15-102.
Baggage rooms, BR §15-106.
Checkrooms, BR §15-105.
Fire losses, BR §15-107.
General liability for loss of valuables, BR §15-103.
Guest rooms, BR §15-104.
Maximum liability, BR §15-103.
Notice of provisions displayed in guest rooms.
Applicability of provisions to hotels displaying,
BR §15-102.
Scope of title, BR §15-102.
"Valuable" defined, BR §15-101.
Valuables deposited with hotel, BR §15-103.
Valuables not deposited with hotel, BR §15-103.
Resort taxes, 25B §13H.
Rights and responsibilities of innkeepers, BR
§§15-201 to 15-206.
Advance damage deposit.
Innkeeper may require when guest is minor,
refund, BR §15-205.
Definitions, BR §15-201.
Demonstration of ability to pay.
Innkeeper may require, BR §15-204.
Discrimination by innkeeper or lodging
establishment.
Subtitles not construed to alter prohibition, BR
§15-202.
Grounds for refusing lodging or removal from
establishment, BR §15-203.
Innkeeper defined, BR §15-201.
Minors as guests, BR §15-205.
Parent's or guardian's acceptance of liability.
Innkeeper may require when guest is minor, BR
§15-205.
Posting copy of subtitle and rules of
establishment, BR §15-206.
Refusal to provide lodging, BR §15-203.
Registration and production of identification.
Innkeeper may require, BR §15-204.
Removal from establishment, BR §15-203.
Securities.
Hotel liability for valuables, BR §§15-101 to
15-107.
Smoke detectors.
Installation required, PS §9-102.
Sprinkler systems, PS §§9-201 to 9-206.
Taxation.
Admissions and amusement tax.
See ADMISSIONS AND AMUSEMENT TAX.
Hotel rental tax, 24 §§9-301 to 9-326.
See COUNTIES.
Resort taxes, 25B §13H.
**Theft of services available only for
compensation,** CR §7-104.

HOT PURSUIT.
Conflicts of law.
Natural resources police force.
Pursuit of offenders across Maryland-Virginia
water boundary, NR §1-210.
Fleeing or eluding a police officer, TR §21-904.
State police.
Municipal corporations, authority to act within,
PS §2-412.

HOUSEBREAKING.
See BURGLARY.

HOUSEHOLD APPLIANCES.
Unfair or deceptive trade practices.
Electrical consumer products.
Symbol of testing laboratory, CL §13-308.

**HOUSEHOLD ELECTRICAL EXTENSION
CORDS.**
Unfair or deceptive trade practices.
Designation of maximum number of amperes, CL
§13-309.

HOUSEHOLD FURNISHINGS.
Movers.
Washington metropolitan area transit authority
compact.
See WASHINGTON METROPOLITAN AREA
TRANSIT AUTHORITY COMPACT.

HOUSEHOLD GOODS MOVERS.
Carriers generally.
See CARRIERS.
**Enforcing carrier's lien or refusing to deliver
during intrastate move.**
Prohibition, CL §14-3102.
Definitions, CL §14-3101.
Unfair or deceptive trade practice, penalty, CL
§14-3103.
Short title, CL §14-3104.
Receipt on completion of intrastate move, CL
§14-3102.1.

HOUSEHOLD HAZARDOUS WASTE.
**Collection and acceptance from residents of
counties.**
Feasibility study, EN §9-1802.
Assistance by secretary, EN §9-1803.
Definitions, EN §9-1801.

HOUSE OF DELEGATES.
See GENERAL ASSEMBLY.

HOUSE OF PROSTITUTION, CR §11-306.

HOUSE OF REFORMATION.
Minors.
See CHELTENHAM YOUTH FACILITY.

HOUSE OF REPRESENTATIVES.
See CONGRESS.

HOUSING.
Affordable housing.
Zoning.
Inclusionary zoning, 66B §12.01.
Baltimore City.
Taxation.
Limited distribution housing in Baltimore City.
Exemption, TP §7-504.
Newly constructed dwellings, TP §9-304.
Property tax credits, TP §9-304.
Blind persons, 30 §33.
Bonds, surety.
Deposits on new homes. See within this heading,
"Deposits on new homes."

HOUSING —Cont'd
Building codes generally, PS §§12-101 to
   12-1007.
  See BUILDING CODES.
Certified adult residential environment
   program, 88A §§138 to 143.
  See SOCIAL SERVICES.
Cooperative housing corporations.
  See COOPERATIVE HOUSING
    CORPORATIONS.
Corporations.
  Cooperative housing corporations.
   See COOPERATIVE HOUSING
    CORPORATIONS.
Custom home protection.
  General provisions, RP §§10-501 to 10-509.
  See CUSTOM HOME PROTECTION.
Deaf or mute persons, 30 §33.
Definitions.
  Housing and community development department.
  See HOUSING AND COMMUNITY
    DEVELOPMENT DEPARTMENT.
Deposits on new homes, RP §§10-301 to 10-306.
  Bonds, surety.
   Blanket bond, RP §10-302.
   Failure to maintain.
    Penalty, RP §10-305.
   Form, RP §10-302.
   How long maintained, RP §10-301.
   Maintained by vendor receiving deposit, RP
    §10-301.
    Penalty for failure to maintain, RP §10-305.
   Payable to state, RP §10-302.
   Rules and regulations.
    Adoption, RP §10-303.1.
   When required, RP §10-301.
  Charitable purposes.
   Programs for generation of interest, RP
    §10-301.1.
  Commingling.
   Interest on commingled accounts paid to
    corporation quarterly, RP §10-301.1.
  Disclosure forms, RP §10-306.
  Escrow account.
   Failure to maintain.
    Penalty, RP §10-305.
   How long maintained, RP §10-301.
   Maintained by vendor receiving deposit, RP
    §10-301.
    Penalty for failure to maintain, RP §10-305.
   When required, RP §10-301.
  Exemptions.
   Sales exempt from subtitle, RP §10-304.
  Fines.
   Failure to maintain escrow account or surety
    bond, RP §10-305.
  Forms for disclosure, RP §10-306.
  Interest.
   Programs for generation of interest for
    charitable purposes.
    Optional, RP §10-301.1.
  Investments.
   Investment of trust moneys and other
    investment vehicles, RP §10-301.1.
  Letters of credit.
   Irrevocable letters.
    Amount, RP §10-303.
    Blanket letters, RP §10-303.
    Form, RP §10-303.
    Generally, RP §10-301.

HOUSING —Cont'd
Deposits on new homes —Cont'd
  Letters of credit —Cont'd
   Irrevocable letters —Cont'd
    Maintained by vendor receiving deposit, RP
     §10-301.
     Penalty for failure to maintain, RP §10-305.
    Regulations.
     Adoption, RP §10-303.1.
     Requirements, RP §10-303.
  Real estate brokers.
   Exemptions from subtitle, RP §10-304.
  Sentence and punishment.
   Failure to maintain escrow account or surety
    bond, RP §10-305.
  Trust money.
   Commingling.
    Pooling or commingling small amounts held
     for a short time, RP §10-301.1.
  Unfair or deceptive trade practices, RP §10-305.
Disability.
  Certified adult residential environment program,
   88A §§138 to 143.
  See SOCIAL SERVICES.
Discrimination in housing.
  General provisions, 49B §§19 to 39.
  See DISCRIMINATION.
  Real estate brokers.
   Discrimination generally.
    See REAL ESTATE BROKERS.
Escrow.
  Deposits on new homes. See within this heading,
   "Deposits on new homes."
Federal aid.
  Lower-income housing assistance.
   County and municipal participation in federal
    programs, 24 §6-203.
Fines.
  Deposits on new homes.
   Failure of vendor to maintain escrow account or
    surety bond, RP §10-305.
Fires and fire protection.
  Automatic fire extinguishing systems.
   Specified buildings, PS §9-503.
Home improvement law.
  General provisions, BR §§8-101 to 8-702.
  See HOME IMPROVEMENTS.
Housing and community development, HS
   §§1-101 to 11-106.
  See HOUSING AND COMMUNITY
    DEVELOPMENT.
Housing assistance fraud, CR §8-523.
Loans.
  Housing and community development department.
  See HOUSING AND COMMUNITY
    DEVELOPMENT DEPARTMENT.
Migrant labor.
  Responsibilities of farm labor contractors.
   Disclosures to migrant agricultural workers, LE
    §7-401.
Mortgages and deeds of trust.
  General provisions.
   See MORTGAGES AND DEEDS OF TRUST.
New home warranties, RP §§10-601 to 10-610.
  See WARRANTY.
Property taxes.
  Baltimore City.
   Limited distribution housing in Baltimore City.
    Exemption from taxation, TP §7-504.
   Property tax credits, TP §9-304.

HOUSING —Cont'd
Property taxes —Cont'd
  Charles county.
    Fair share school construction excise tax on new
      residential dwellings, 66B §14.05.
  Flood-damaged residential property.
    Tax credit, TP §9-211.
  Governmentally subsidized rental housing.
    Exemptions, TP §§7-505 to 7-506.1.
  Housing authority property.
    Exemptions, TP §7-215.
  Low income families.
    Exemptions, TP §§7-503, 7-506.2.
    Payments in lieu of taxes, TP §7-503.
  Newly constructed dwellings, TP §9-304.
  Senior citizens.
    Exemptions, TP §7-502.
    Payments in lieu of tax, TP §7-502.
  Subsidized housing, TP §7-506.1.
Real estate brokers.
  General provisions, BOP §§17-101 to 17-702.
  See REAL ESTATE BROKERS.
Rules and regulations.
  Deposits on new homes, RP §10-303.1.
Sentence and punishment.
  Deposits on new homes.
    Failure of vendor to maintain surety bond or
      escrow account, RP §10-305.
Vendor and vendee.
  Deposits on new homes. See within this heading,
    "Deposits on new homes."
Warranties.
  New home warranties, RP §§10-601 to 10-610.
  See WARRANTY.
Zoning.
  Affordable housing.
    Inclusionary zoning, 66B §12.01.

**HOUSING AND COMMUNITY
  DEVELOPMENT,** HS §§1-101 to 11-106.
**Accessory, shared and sheltered housing
  program.**
  Maryland housing rehabilitation program.
    Units in program, HS §4-905.
Affordable housing trust, HS §§10-101 to 10-301.
Appalachian housing fund, HS §§11-101 to
  11-106.
  See MARYLAND STATE APPALACHIAN
    HOUSING FUND.
Assisted housing preservation, HS §§7-101 to
  7-501.
  Applicability.
    Scope of title, HS §7-102.
  Assisted households.
    Defined, HS §7-101.
    Limits on gross annual income, HS §7-104.
  Assisted projects, HS §7-105.
    Defined, HS §7-101.
  Authorized enforcement entities, HS §7-401.
  Citation of title, HS §7-501.
  Conflict of laws.
    Effect of title, HS §7-106.
  Consumer protection division.
    Enforcement, HS §7-403.
  Covenants as to use of property.
    Protected actions, HS §7-208.
  Defined terms, HS §7-101.
    Fair market value.
      Protected actions, right of first purchase, HS
        §7-205.

HOUSING AND COMMUNITY DEVELOPMENT
  —Cont'd
Assisted housing preservation —Cont'd
  Designated households.
    Protected actions, HS §7-213.
      Additional notice, HS §7-217.
      Application to assisted households, HS
        §7-216.
      Extended leases, HS §7-214.
      Sale or conveyance of assisted project, HS
        §7-215.
      Termination of extended lease, HS §7-218.
  Duties of owners, HS §7-306.
    Sworn statement of compliance, HS §7-307.
  Duties of tenants, HS §7-301.
  Effect of title, HS §7-106.
  Eligibility.
    Assisted projects, HS §7-105.
    Limits on gross annual income, HS §7-104.
  Enforcement, HS §§7-401 to 7-404.
    Authorized enforcement entities, HS §7-401.
    Consumer protection division, HS §7-403.
    False statements or reports, HS §7-404.
    Injunctions, HS §7-402.
    Regulations, HS §7-103.
  False statements or reports, HS §7-404.
  Injunctions, HS §7-402.
  Notice of intent.
    Applicability to new tenants, HS §7-303.
    Contents, HS §7-202.
    Defined, HS §7-101.
    Required, HS §7-201.
  Owners duties, HS §7-306.
    Sworn statement of compliance, HS §7-307.
  Plans of action.
    Right of first purchase.
      Applicability, HS §7-211.
  Protected actions, HS §§7-201 to 7-220.
    Covenants as to use of property, HS §7-208.
    Defined, HS §7-101.
    Designated households, HS §7-213.
      Additional notice, HS §7-217.
      Application to assisted households, HS
        §7-216.
      Extended leases, HS §7-214.
      Sale or conveyance of assisted project, HS
        §7-215.
      Termination of extended lease, HS §7-218.
    Duties of owners, HS §7-306.
    Notice.
      Additional required notices, HS §7-207.
    Notice of intent.
      Applicability to new tenants, HS §7-303.
      Contents, HS §7-202.
      Defined, HS §7-101.
      Required, HS §7-201.
    Prerequisites to taking, HS §7-203.
    Relocation during rehabilitation, HS §7-219.
    Rental housing emergencies, HS §7-220.
    Right of first purchase.
      Assignment, HS §7-209.
      Offer, HS §7-204.
      Plans of actions, applicability, HS §7-211.
      Political subdivisions and housing authorities,
        HS §7-210.
      Prerequisites to taking action, HS §7-203.
      Terms, appraisal and price adjustments, HS
        §7-205.
    Sale or conveyance if owner's offer not accepted,
      HS §7-206.

HOUSING AND COMMUNITY DEVELOPMENT
—Cont'd

Assisted housing preservation —Cont'd

Protected actions —Cont'd

Tenant protection assistance, HS §7-212.

Defined, HS §7-101.

Regulations, HS §7-103.

Relocation during rehabilitation, HS §7-219.

Rental housing emergencies, HS §7-220.

Right of first purchase.

Assignment, HS §7-209.

Offer, HS §7-204.

Plans of actions, applicability, HS §7-211.

Political subdivisions and housing authorities, HS §7-210.

Prerequisites to taking action, HS §7-203.

Terms, appraisal and price adjustments, HS §7-205.

Rights of tenants.

Excess rent as grounds for termination of lease, HS §7-305.

Notice of intent, applicability to new tenants, HS §7-303.

Relinquishment prohibited, HS §7-302.

Termination of lease without cause, HS §7-304.

Sale or conveyance.

Owner's offer not accepted, HS §7-206.

Scope of title, HS §7-102.

Short title, HS §7-501.

Tenant protection assistance, HS §7-212.

Tenants.

Duties of tenants, HS §7-301.

Rights of tenants.

Excess rent as grounds for termination of lease, HS §7-305.

Notice of intent, applicability to new tenants, HS §7-303.

Relinquishment prohibited, HS §7-302.

Termination of lease without cause, HS §7-304.

Termination of lease.

Designated households, protected actions.

Termination of extended lease, HS §7-218.

Excess rent as grounds for termination of lease, HS §7-305.

Without cause, rights of tenants, HS §7-304.

Bond issues.

Community development administration, HS §§4-244 to 4-253.

Infrastructure projects, local financing, HS §§4-229 to 4-233.

Enabling resolution or ordinance.

Adoption, HS §4-232.

Contents, HS §4-231.

Issuing procedures, HS §4-230.

Local obligations, HS §4-229.

Pledges of faith and credit securing, HS §4-233.

Citation of article, 1 §25.

Commercial and mixed-use revitalization programs, HS §6-103.

Administration of programs, HS §6-102.

Community action agencies, HS §§8-101 to 8-109.

Administration, HS §8-106.

Adoption of regulations, HS §8-109.

Community action boards, HS §8-105.

Community projects, HS §8-107.

Defined terms, HS §8-101.

Designation.

Making, changing or revoking, HS §8-104.

Distribution of money, HS §8-108.

HOUSING AND COMMUNITY DEVELOPMENT
—Cont'd

Community action agencies —Cont'd

Duties, HS §8-107.

Financial assistance, HS §8-108.

Findings, HS §8-102.

Goals, HS §8-103.

Legislative findings, HS §8-102.

Making, changing or revoking designation, HS §8-104.

Policy determinations, HS §8-106.

Powers, HS §8-106.

Program plan, HS §8-107.

Purposes, HS §8-103.

Regulations, HS §8-109.

Community development projects, HS §§4-217 to 4-222.

Energy conservation projects, HS §4-218.

Financing, HS §§4-225 to 4-241.

Generally, HS §4-217.

Home improvement projects, HS §4-219.

Housing and facilities requirements, HS §4-217.

Infrastructure projects, HS §4-220.

Public purpose projects, HS §4-221.

Sale or lease of project property, HS §4-213.

Solar energy projects, HS §4-222.

Community legacy program, HS §§6-201 to 6-213.

Administration of program.

Department powers, HS §6-209.

Advisory committee, HS §6-212.

Board, HS §6-203.

Community development organization, HS §6-204.

Defined, HS §6-201.

Community development plans or projects.

Applications, HS §6-205.

Action on applications, HS §6-207.

Community legacy agreements, HS §6-208.

Community legacy area, designation, HS §6-206.

Community legacy financial assistance fund, HS §6-213.

Defined terms, HS §6-201.

Established, HS §6-202.

Neighborhood intervention projects, HS §6-210.

Purposes, HS §6-202.

Reports, HS §6-211.

Community reinvestment fund, HS §§9-101 to 9-501.

Administration, HS §9-204.

Community reinvestment board, HS §§9-201 to 9-204.

Established, HS §9-201.

Meetings, HS §9-203.

Membership, HS §9-202.

Operation, powers and duties, HS §9-204.

Conflict of laws.

Application of other laws, HS §9-304.

Defined terms, HS §9-101.

Department.

Duties of department, HS §9-306.

Powers of department, HS §9-307.

Established, HS §9-301.

Exemptions, HS §9-302.

Findings, HS §9-102.

Household income limits.

Reinvestment assistance, HS §9-401.

Loan committee, HS §9-204.

Organization, HS §9-303.

Purpose of fund, HS §9-301.

Records, HS §9-204.

HOUSING AND COMMUNITY DEVELOPMENT
—Cont'd
Community reinvestment fund —Cont'd
Reinvestment assistance, HS §§9-401 to 9-404.
  Applications for assistance, HS §9-403.
  Community reinvestment projects,
    requirements, HS §9-402.
  Household income limits, HS §9-401.
  Methods of providing, HS §9-404.
Short title, HS §9-501.
Standards and guidelines, HS §9-204.
Status of fund, HS §9-302.
Use of fund money, HS §9-305.
Conflict of laws.
Assisted housing preservation.
  Effect of title, HS §7-106.
Community reinvestment fund.
  Application of other laws, HS §9-304.
Consumer protection division.
Assisted housing preservation.
  Enforcement, HS §7-403.
Counties.
Residential mortgage programs for certain
  counties, HS §§4-1601 to 4-1610.
Defined terms, HS §1-101.
Department, HS §§2-101 to 2-202.
See HOUSING AND COMMUNITY
  DEVELOPMENT DEPARTMENT.
Discrimination.
State contracts.
  Commercial discrimination, SF §§19-101 to
    19-120.
  See DISCRIMINATION.
**Down payment and settlement expense loan
  program,** HS §§4-301 to 4-309.
See DOWN PAYMENT AND SETTLEMENT
  EXPENSE LOAN PROGRAM.
Economic development assistance authority,
  83A §5-1403.
Economic development assistance fund, 83A
  §§5-1401 to 5-1412.
Economic development commission, 83A
  §§1-201 to 1-204.
See BUSINESS AND ECONOMIC
  DEVELOPMENT DEPARTMENT.
Economic development corporation.
See ECONOMIC DEVELOPMENT
  CORPORATION.
Economic development revenue bond act.
See ECONOMIC DEVELOPMENT REVENUE
  BOND ACT.
Elderly households.
Reverse equity mortgage loans and other
  mortgage loans.
  Financing community development projects, HS
    §4-235.
Energy conservation.
Maryland housing fund, HS §§3-201 to 3-208.
Energy conservation projects, HS §4-218.
Financing, HS §4-227.
Families of limited income.
Community development projects.
  Housing and facilities requirements, exception,
    HS §4-217.
  Determination, HS §4-212.
Financing community development projects,
  HS §§4-225 to 4-241.
Energy conservation projects, HS §4-227.
Infrastructure projects, HS §4-228.
  Enabling resolution or ordinance.
    Adoption, HS §4-232.

HOUSING AND COMMUNITY DEVELOPMENT
—Cont'd
Financing community development projects
—Cont'd
Infrastructure projects —Cont'd
  Enabling resolution or ordinance —Cont'd
    Contents, HS §4-231.
  Issuing procedures, HS §4-230.
  Local obligations, HS §4-229.
  Pledges of faith and credit securing, HS §4-233.
Mortgage lenders.
  Certificate, HS §4-240.
  Limitations, HS §4-236.
  Loans to eligible mortgage lenders, HS §4-239.
Mortgage loans.
  Assignment and assumption, residential, HS
    §4-241.
  Commitment to purchase, HS §4-238.
  Guarantee by GNMA, HS §4-234.
  Purchases and loans.
    Powers of administration, HS §4-237.
  Requirement of mortgage, HS §4-225.
  Reverse equity mortgage loans and other
    mortgage loans, HS §4-235.
Powers of administration, HS §4-226.
Procedures generally, HS §4-225.
Recipients, HS §4-225.
Reverse equity mortgage loans, HS §4-235.
Solar energy projects, HS §4-227.
Sources of money, HS §4-225.
Fines.
Assisted housing preservation.
  False statements or reports, HS §7-404.
Funds.
Community reinvestment fund, HS §§9-101 to
  9-501.
Homeownership programs fund, HS §4-502.
Partnership rental housing fund, HS §4-503.
Rental housing programs fund, HS §4-504.
Special loan programs fund, HS §4-505.
Home improvement projects, HS §4-219.
Homeownership programs fund, HS §4-502.
Indoor plumbing program.
Maryland housing rehabilitation program.
  Units in program, HS §4-905.
Infrastructure development and projects, HS
  §4-220.
Financing, HS §4-228.
  Local obligations, HS §§4-229 to 4-233.
    Enabling resolution or ordinance, adoption,
      HS §4-232.
    Enabling resolution or ordinance, contents,
      HS §4-231.
    Issuing procedures, HS §4-230.
    Pledges of faith and credit securing, HS
      §4-233.
Local government infrastructure program.
  Development finance division.
    Units in division, HS §4-103.
Maryland housing fund, HS §§3-201 to 3-208.
Injunctions.
Assisted housing preservation, HS §7-402.
Liens.
Powers of administration, HS §4-226.
Maryland affordable housing trust, HS §§10-101
  to 10-301.
Maryland housing fund, HS §§3-201 to 3-208.
Maryland state Appalachian housing fund, HS
  §§11-101 to 11-106.
See MARYLAND STATE APPALACHIAN
  HOUSING FUND.

HOUSING AND COMMUNITY DEVELOPMENT
—Cont'd

Mortgages and deeds of trust.
Financing community development projects.
Mortgage lenders.
Certificate, HS §4-240.
Limitations, HS §4-236.
Loans to eligible, HS §4-239.
Mortgage loans.
Assignment and assumption, residential, HS §4-241.
Commitment to purchase, HS §4-238.
Guarantee by GNMA, HS §4-234.
Purchases and loans.
Powers of administration, HS §4-237.
Requirement of mortgage, HS §4-225.
Reverse equity mortgage loans and other mortgage loans, HS §4-235.
Reverse equity mortgage loans, HS §4-235.
Maryland housing fund, HS §§3-201 to 3-208.

Neighborhood and community assistance program, HS §§6-401 to 6-406.
Defined terms, HS §6-401.
Established, HS §6-402.
Proposals for projects in priority funding areas, HS §6-405.
Purposes, HS §6-403.
Regulations, HS §6-406.
Tax credits, HS §6-404.

Neighborhood business development program, HS §§6-301 to 6-311.
Business development program, HS §6-304.
Administration, HS §6-308.
Designation of neighborhoods, HS §6-305.
Financial assistance for small businesses, HS §6-306.
Project development costs, financial assistance, HS §6-307.
Capital access program, HS §6-309.
Defined terms, HS §6-301.
Established, HS §6-303.
False statement or reports, HS §6-311.
Neighborhood business development fund, HS §6-310.
Purposes, HS §6-303.
Small businesses.
Defined, HS §6-301.
Financial assistance for small businesses, HS §6-306.
Qualifications, HS §6-302.

Neighborhood intervention projects.
Community legacy program, HS §6-210.

Notice.
Assisted housing preservation.
Designated households, protected actions.
Additional notice, HS §7-217.
Assisted housing preservation, protected actions.
Additional required notices, HS §7-207.
Notice of intent.
Applicability to new tenants, HS §7-303.
Contents, HS §7-202.
Defined, HS §7-101.
Required, HS §7-201.

Partnership rental housing fund, HS §4-503.
Public purpose projects, HS §4-221.
Rental housing.
Partnership rental housing fund, HS §4-503.
Rental allowance program, HS §§4-1401 to 4-1408.
Development finance division.
Units in division, HS §4-103.

HOUSING AND COMMUNITY DEVELOPMENT
—Cont'd

Rental housing —Cont'd
Rental housing production program, HS §§4-1501 to 4-1511.
Development finance division.
Units in division, HS §4-103.
Rental housing programs fund, HS §4-504.

Rental housing programs fund, HS §4-504.

Reports.
Community legacy program, HS §6-211.

Self-help homeownership technical assistance program, HS §§4-1701 to 4-1710.
Administration of program, HS §4-1705.
Construction grants, HS §4-1708.
Defined terms, HS §4-1701.
Department of housing and community development.
Duties, HS §4-1705.
Eligibility.
Family eligibility, HS §4-1706.
Guidelines, HS §4-1705.
Standards, HS §4-1707.
Established, HS §4-1703.
Family eligibility, HS §4-1706.
Findings, HS §4-1702.
Information and technical assistance grants, HS §4-1709.
Legislative findings, HS §4-1702.
Purpose, HS §4-1704.
Regulations, HS §4-1705.
Standards for eligibility, HS §4-1707.
Technical assistance grants.
Construction, HS §4-1708.
Information and technical assistance, HS §4-1709.
Terms and conditions, HS §4-1710.
Terms and conditions of grants, HS §4-1710.

Solar energy projects, HS §4-222.
Financing, HS §4-227.

Special loan programs fund, HS §4-505.

Tax credits.
Neighborhood and community assistance program, HS §6-404.

Weatherization.
Community development administration.
Weatherization program.
Authority to develop and implement, HS §4-211.
Federal and state weatherization program.
Development finance division.
Units in division, HS §4-103.

HOUSING AND COMMUNITY DEVELOPMENT DEPARTMENT, HS §§2-101 to 2-202.
Administration of department, HS §2-104.
Advisory councils, boards and committees, HS §2-202.
African American history and culture commission.
Generally, SF §§5A-201 to 5A-208.
See AFRICAN AMERICAN HISTORY AND CULTURE COMMISSION.
Historical and cultural programs division.
Units in division, SF §5A-102.
Appropriations.
Workforce housing grant program.
Distribution of appropriations, HS §4-1805.
Assisted housing preservation act, HS §§7-101 to 7-501.

HOUSING AND COMMUNITY DEVELOPMENT DEPARTMENT —Cont'd
Attorney General.
Legal advisor, HS §2-116.
Budget.
Secretary's duties, HS §2-112.
Building codes generally, PS §§12-101 to 12-1007.
See BUILDING CODES.
Building construction.
Safety glazing.
See GLASS.
Community development administration.
Development finance division.
Units in division, HS §4-103.
Generally, HS §§4-201 to 4-255.
See COMMUNITY DEVELOPMENT ADMINISTRATION.
Governmental units of department, HS §2-201.
Community legacy board.
Advisory committee.
Governmental units of department, HS §2-201.
Governmental units of department, HS §2-201.
Community legacy program.
Governmental units of department, HS §2-201.
Community reinvestment fund.
Duties of department, HS §9-306.
Powers of department, HS §9-307.
Counties.
Residential mortgage programs for certain counties, HS §§4-1601 to 4-1610.
Credit assurance division, HS §§3-101 to 3-208.
Administration authority, HS §3-104.
Division defined, HS §3-101.
Elements, HS §3-103.
Established, HS §3-102.
Governmental units of department, HS §2-201.
Maryland housing fund, HS §§3-201 to 3-208.
Deputy secretary, HS §2-106.
Development finance division.
Defined terms, HS §4-101.
Established, HS §4-102.
Generally, HS §§4-101 to 4-1813.
See DEVELOPMENT FINANCE DIVISION.
Governmental units of department, HS §2-201.
Units in division, HS §4-103.
Down payment and settlement expense loan program, HS §§4-301 to 4-309.
Applications for loans.
Review, HS §4-307.
Default on loan, HS §4-307.
Defined terms, HS §4-301.
Development finance division.
Units in division, HS §4-103.
Eligible homebuyers.
Qualifications, HS §4-305.
Established, HS §4-302.
False statements or reports, HS §4-309.
Fees.
Powers and duties of department, HS §4-304.
Financing of program, HS §4-306.
Fines.
False statements or reports, HS §4-309.
Homebuyer education, HS §4-308.
Operation of program, HS §4-306.
Powers and duties of department, HS §4-304.
Purchase of loans.
Powers and duties of department, HS §4-304.
Purpose, HS §4-303.
Sale or transfer of property, HS §4-307.
Security for loans, HS §4-307.

HOUSING AND COMMUNITY DEVELOPMENT DEPARTMENT —Cont'd
Down payment and settlement expense loan program —Cont'd
Uses of loans, HS §4-307.
Duties, HS §2-102.
Elderly rental housing program, HS §§4-401 to 4-409.
Defined terms, HS §4-401.
Development finance division.
Units in division, HS §4-103.
Established, HS §4-402.
Fires and fire protection.
Automatic fire extinguishing systems.
Specified buildings, PS §9-503.
Fund.
Additional or replaced money, HS §4-405.
Loans.
Applications, HS §4-408.
Deferred payment loans, HS §4-409.
Powers and duties of department, HS §4-404.
Projects.
Qualifications, HS §4-407.
Purpose, HS §4-403.
Regulations, HS §4-406.
Established, HS §2-101.
Federal and state weatherization program.
Development finance division.
Units in division, HS §4-103.
Functions, HS §2-102.
Governmental units, HS §2-201.
Advisory councils, boards and committees, HS §2-202.
Grants.
Workforce housing grant program, HS §§4-1801 to 4-1813.
Group home financing program, HS §§4-601 to 4-612.
Development finance division.
Units in division, HS §4-103.
Duties of department, HS §4-605.
Powers of department, HS §4-604.
Historical and cultural programs division, SF §§5A-101 to 5A-359.
Established, SF §5A-101.
Units in division, SF §5A-102.
Housing finance review committee, HS §4-208.
Governmental units of department, HS §2-201.
Indian affairs commission.
Generally, 41 §§6-901 to 6-912.
See INDIAN AFFAIRS COMMISSION.
Indians.
Commission on Indian affairs.
Ethnic affairs unit, SF §§2-701, 2-702.
Infrastructure development.
Local government infrastructure program.
Development finance division.
Units in division, HS §4-103.
Lead hazard advisory committee, HS §4-711.
Governmental units of department, HS §2-201.
Lead hazard reduction grant and loan programs, HS §§4-701 to 4-712.
Development finance division.
Units in division, HS §4-103.
Duties of department, HS §4-705.
Powers of department, HS §4-704.
Legal advisor, HS §2-116.
Linked deposit program.
Duties of department, SF §6-211.
Establishment, SF §6-211.

HOUSING AND COMMUNITY DEVELOPMENT DEPARTMENT —Cont'd

Maryland historical trust, SF §§5A-301 to 5A-359.
  Historical and cultural programs division.
    Units in division, SF §5A-102.
Maryland home financing program, HS §§4-801 to 4-816.
  Development finance division.
    Units in division, HS §4-103.
  Duties of department, HS §4-806.
  Policies, HS §4-806.
  Powers of department, HS §4-805.
Maryland housing fund, HS §§3-201 to 3-208.
  Administration of fund, HS §3-203.
  Composition, HS §3-203.
  Construction and interpretation, HS §3-208.
  Defined terms, HS §3-201.
  Established, HS §3-203.
  Findings, HS §3-202.
  Governmental units of department, HS §2-201.
  Insurance, guarantees or other credit
      enhancements.
    Effect, HS §3-204.
    Eligibility, HS §3-206.
  Powers of department, HS §3-205.
  Purpose, HS §3-203.
  Regulations.
    Authority to adopt, HS §3-207.
  Reports, HS §3-207.
Maryland housing rehabilitation program, HS §§4-901 to 4-933.
  Development finance division.
    Units in division, HS §4-103.
  Powers of department, HS §4-908.
  Program loans secured by mortgages, HS §4-909.
  Regulations, HS §4-910.
Meetings.
  Special meetings.
    Calling, secretary's powers, HS §2-114.
Mobile homes.
  General provisions.
    See MOBILE HOMES.
Native Americans.
  Commission on Indian affairs.
    See INDIANS.
Neighborhood business development program.
  Governmental units of department, HS §2-201.
Neighborhood housing services fund, HS §§4-1001 to 4-1005.
  Development finance division.
    Units in division, HS §4-103.
Neighborhood revitalization division.
  Generally, HS §§6-101 to 6-406.
    See NEIGHBORHOOD REVITALIZATION DIVISION.
  Governmental units of department, HS §2-201.
Office of the secretary, HS §2-107.
  Appointment and removal of staff, HS §2-108.
    Removal of appointees, HS §2-110.
  Regulations, authority to adopt, HS §2-111.
  Reporting authority, HS §2-109.
Operating assistance grants demonstration projects, HS §§4-1101 to 4-1105.
  Development finance division.
    Units in division, HS §4-103.
Partnership rental housing program, HS §§4-1201 to 4-1209.
  Development finance division.
    Units in division, HS §4-103.

HOUSING AND COMMUNITY DEVELOPMENT DEPARTMENT —Cont'd

Planning initiatives.
  Secretary's duties, HS §2-113.
Radium pilot grant program.
  Development finance division.
    Units in division, HS §4-103.
Regulations.
  Authority to adopt, HS §2-111.
Rental allowance program, HS §§4-1401 to 4-1408.
  Development finance division.
    Units in division, HS §4-103.
Rental housing production program, HS §§4-1501 to 4-1511.
  Development finance division.
    Units in division, HS §4-103.
  Powers and duties, HS §4-1506.
  Regulations, HS §4-1507.
Reports.
  Maryland housing fund, HS §3-207.
  Workforce housing grant program.
    Qualifying local governments, HS §4-1812.
Seal, HS §2-105.
Secretary, HS §2-103.
  Administration of department, HS §2-104.
  Appointment, HS §2-103.
  Appointment and removal of staff, HS §2-108.
    Removal of appointees, HS §2-110.
  Assumption of functions and responsibilities.
    Powers, HS §2-115.
  Budget.
    Duties, HS §2-112.
  Compensation, HS §2-103.
  Delegation of authority, HS §2-108.
  Deputy secretary, HS §2-106.
  Duties.
    Budget, HS §2-112.
    Planning initiatives, HS §2-113.
  Oath, HS §2-103.
  Office of the secretary, HS §2-107.
    Appointment and removal of staff, HS §2-108.
      Removal of appointees, HS §2-110.
    Reporting authority, HS §2-109.
  Planning initiatives.
    Duties, HS §2-113.
  Powers.
    Assumption of functions and responsibilities, HS §2-115.
    Special meetings, calling, HS §2-114.
    Regulations, authority to adopt, HS §2-111.
  Seal, HS §2-105.
  Staff, HS §2-107.
    Appointment and removal of staff, HS §2-108.
      Removal of appointees, HS §2-110.
    Reporting authority, HS §2-109.
Self-help homeownership technical assistance program, HS §§4-1701 to 4-1710.
  Development finance division.
    Units in division, HS §4-103.
  Duties of department, HS §4-1705.
Workforce housing grant program, HS §§4-1801 to 4-1813.
  Appropriations, distribution, HS §4-1805.
  Established, HS §4-1802.
  Funding, HS §4-1802.
    Use of funds, HS §4-1808.
  Matching funds, HS §4-1804.
  Participation, requirements, HS §4-1803.
  Purpose, HS §4-1802.

HOUSING AND COMMUNITY DEVELOPMENT DEPARTMENT —Cont'd
Workforce housing grant program —Cont'd
Qualifying local governments.
Drawing down program funds, requirements, HS §4-1806.
Income eligibility limits, extension, HS §4-1809.
Per unit maximum amount, HS §4-1810.
Redistribution of available funds, HS §4-1807.
Reports, HS §4-1812.
Regulations, HS §4-1813.
Rental units to remain affordable, time limits, HS §4-1811.
Transfer of units by initial buyer.
Requirements, HS §4-1811.

HOUSING AUTHORITIES.
Annapolis, HS §§13-101 to 13-111.
See ANNAPOLIS.
Anne Arundel county, HS §§14-101 to 14-103.
Applicability of housing authorities law, HS §14-101.
Commissioners, HS §14-103.
Established, HS §14-102.
Applicability of title.
Annapolis, HS §13-102.
Anne Arundel county, HS §14-101.
Baltimore City, HS §15-102.
Indian housing authorities, HS §22-101.
Montgomery county.
Housing opportunities commission, HS §16-102.
Prince George's county, HS §17-102.
Queen Anne's county, HS §18-102.
Somerset county, HS §20-101.
Washington county, HS §21-103.
Appropriations, HS §12-312.
Areas of operation, HS §12-105.
Powers within, HS §12-503.
Articles of organization.
Adoption.
Prerequisites, HS §12-205.
Amendment, HS §12-207.
Approvals, HS §12-203.
Effect, HS §12-203.
Authorities governed by Titles 2 through 10, HS §12-204.
Contents, HS §§12-203, 12-205.
Custodian of records, duties, HS §12-205.
Optional terms, HS §12-205.
Powers authorized by, HS §12-503.
Preexisting authorities, HS §12-206.
Prohibited terms, HS §12-205.
Records, HS §12-205.
Required terms, HS §12-205.
Restatement, HS §12-207.
Audits, HS §12-404.
Annapolis housing authority, HS §13-111.
Baltimore City.
General provisions, HS §§15-101 to 15-109.
See BALTIMORE CITY.
Legal investments, ET §15-106.
Bond issues.
Conditions, HS §12-703.
Investments, ET §15-106.
Authorized, HS §12-702.
Military housing, HS §12-604.
Issuance, HS §12-701.
Liability, HS §12-702.
Military housing.
Legal investments, HS §12-604.
Negotiability, HS §12-702.

HOUSING AUTHORITIES —Cont'd
Bond issues —Cont'd
Payment, HS §12-702.
Pledges, HS §12-704.
Purposes, HS §12-703.
Rights of obligees, HS §12-705.
Sale, HS §12-703.
Security, HS §12-704.
Signatures, HS §12-703.
Taxation.
Exemptions, HS §12-702.
Terms, HS §12-703.
Budget, HS §12-404.
Annapolis, HS §13-110.
Certificate of approval.
Issuance, HS §12-205.
Certificate of organization.
Effect, HS §12-205.
Citation of article, HS §23-101.
Code authorities, HS §12-203.
Commissioners.
Agents and employees, HS §12-308.
Appointment, HS §§12-205, 12-302.
Certificate of appointment, HS §12-302.
Chairman, HS §12-305.
Compensation, HS §12-307.
Conflicts of interest, HS §12-310.
Eligibility, HS §12-303.
Ethics.
Applicability of local ethics laws, HS §12-311.
Expenses, HS §12-307.
Immunity, HS §12-309.
Legal services, HS §12-308.
Liability, HS §12-309.
Number, HS §12-301.
Preexisting authorities, HS §12-206.
Quorum, HS §12-306.
Removal from office, HS §12-311.
Staff, HS §12-308.
Suspension from office, HS §12-311.
Terms of office, HS §12-304.
Vacancies in office, HS §12-304.
Vesting of power of authority, HS §12-306.
Vice chair, HS §12-305.
Conflict of laws, HS §12-107.
Conflicts of interest.
Annapolis, HS §13-105.
Interest of commissioner or employee in housing projects, etc., HS §12-310.
Custodian of records.
Articles of organization, duties, HS §12-205.
Preexisting authorities, HS §12-206.
Defense housing.
Property taxes.
Exemptions, TP §§7-211, 7-211.2.
Definitions, HS §12-101.
Division II, purpose, HS §12-103.
Donations, HS §12-312.
Economic competition.
Displacement or limitation of, HS §12-504.
Enabling legislation, HS §12-202.
Establishment of authorities, HS §12-201.
Code authorities, HS §12-203.
Ethics.
Applicability of local ethics laws, HS §12-311.
Exemptions from levy and execution, HS §12-104.
Federal housing projects taken over by state body, HS §12-507.
Findings of legislature, HS §12-102.

HOUSING AUTHORITIES —Cont'd
General services department.
Public improvements.
Exceptions to provisions, SF §4-402.
Housing projects.
Applicability of local laws, ordinances, codes, etc.,
HS §12-403.
Building codes.
Applicability, HS §12-403.
Cooperation between authorities, HS §12-506.
Federal housing projects taken over by state body,
HS §12-507.
Powers.
Generally, HS §12-506.
Zoning regulations.
Applicability, HS §12-403.
Immunity.
Commissioners, HS §12-309.
Indian housing authorities, HS §§22-101 to
22-103.
Applicability of housing authorities law, HS
§22-101.
Department or local housing authority acting on
behalf of Indians, HS §22-103.
Established, HS §22-102.
Participation in state or federal programs, HS
§22-103.
Powers, HS §22-103.
Interpretation and construction.
Conflict of laws, HS §12-107.
Investments.
Bonds or other obligations, ET §15-106.
Authorized, HS §12-702.
Military housing, HS §12-604.
Legislature.
Findings and declarations, HS §12-102.
Liability.
Commissioners, HS §12-309.
Loans, HS §12-312.
Meetings.
Annapolis, HS §13-107.
Military housing.
Authorization.
Undertaking projects, HS §12-605.
Bonds or other obligations.
Legal investments, HS §12-604.
Cooperation by public bodies, HS §12-603.
Limitations and restrictions, HS §12-605.
Powers.
Additional and supplemental powers, HS
§12-607.
Generally, HS §12-605.
Territorial extent, HS §12-606.
Purposes, HS §12-601.
Rights, powers, privileges and immunities, HS
§12-601.
United States.
Agent of federal government, HS §12-602.
Montgomery county.
Housing opportunities commission, HS §§16-101
to 16-319.
See MONTGOMERY COUNTY.
Obligees of the authority.
Rights, HS §12-405.
Operations, areas, HS §12-105.
Persons of eligible income.
Defined, HS §12-101.
Determination of qualifying income level, HS
§12-106.
Qualifications, HS §12-106.
Policy of state, HS §12-102.

HOUSING AUTHORITIES —Cont'd
Powers.
Area of operation, powers within, HS §12-503.
Articles of organization, powers authorized by, HS
§12-503.
Enumeration, HS §12-502.
Housing projects, HS §12-506.
Housing projects taken over by state body from
federal government, HS §12-507.
Preexisting authorities, HS §12-204.
Status of authorities generally, HS §12-501.
Vesting rights in obligees, HS §12-405.
Preexisting authorities, HS §12-204.
Articles of organization, HS §12-206.
Commissioners, HS §12-206.
Custodian of records.
Articles of organization, duties, HS §12-206.
Prince George's county, HS §§17-101 to 17-107.
See PRINCE GEORGE'S COUNTY.
Property.
Applicability of state laws regarding property, HS
§12-505.
Purpose of Division II, HS §12-103.
Qualifications.
Persons of eligible income, HS §12-106.
Queen Anne's county, HS §§18-101 to 18-105.
Rentals.
Eligibility, HS §12-402.
Public policy, HS §12-401.
Rates, HS §12-401.
Reports, HS §12-404.
St. Mary's County.
Applicability of article, HS §19-101.
Composition, HS §19-102.
Established, HS §19-102.
Secretary of State.
Records, HS §12-205.
Slum clearance.
Authority granted to municipal corporations and
counties, MD Const Art III §61.
Social services.
Delinquent payments to public housing
authorities.
Deductions from FIP assistance grant, 88A
§17C.
Somerset county.
Applicability of title, HS §20-101.
Membership, HS §20-102.
Status of authorities generally, HS §12-501.
Taxation.
Exemptions, HS §12-104.
Bond issues, HS §12-702.
Tenants.
Selection, HS §12-402.
Title of article.
Short title, HS §23-101.
Torts.
Local government tort claims act.
Applicability, HS §12-309.
United States.
Military housing.
Agent of federal government, HS §12-602.
Washington county, HS §§21-101 to 21-106.

HOUSING FINANCE REVIEW COMMITTEE,
HS §4-208.

HOUSING OF INMATES.
Standards for correctional facilities generally,
COR §§8-101 to 8-117.
See PRISONS AND PRISONERS.

HOWARD COUNTY.
Alcohol awareness programs.
Special provisions, 2B §13-101.
Alcoholic beverage hearing board, 2B §15-107.1.
Alcoholic beverages.
Beer and light wine licenses.
Class A, off-sale, 2B §5-101.
Class B, on-sale.
Restaurants.
Fee, 2B §5-201.
Class C, on-sale.
Clubs, 2B §5-301.
Class D, on-sale, 2B §5-401.
Beer licenses.
Class A, off-sale, 2B §3-101.
Class B, on-sale.
Fee, 2B §3-201.
Class C, on-sale.
Clubs, 2B §3-301.
Class D, on-sale, 2B §3-401.
Beer, wine and liquor licenses.
Class A-1 license, 2B §6-101.
Class A-2.
Fee, 2B §6-101.
Class A, off-sale, 2B §6-101.
Class B, on-sale.
Hotels and restaurants.
Fee, 2B §6-201.
Class C, on-sale.
Clubs, 2B §6-301.
Class D, on-sale.
Taverns, etc., 2B §6-401.
Class GC, golf courses, 2B §8-504.
Luxury restaurant licenses, 2B §9-102.
Wine festival license, 2B §8-309.
Bottle clubs.
Places of public entertainment generally, 2B §20-106.
Clubs.
Beer, wine and liquor licenses.
Class C, on-sale, 2B §6-301.
Conflicts of interest.
Direct or indirect interest in more than one license, 2B §9-301.
Consumption.
Restrictions, 2B §11-304.
Drive-thru purchase facilities.
Licenses.
Prohibition, 2B §9-214.
Elections.
Exercise of privileges of licensee on election day, 2B §11-401.
Fines and forfeitures, 2B §16-507.
Disposition of fines, 2B §16-507.
Hearing board, 2B §15-107.1.
Hours and days for sale, 2B §11-514.
Election days, 2B §11-401.
Manufacturers' licenses, 2B §11-101.
New Year's day, 2B §11-402.
License commissioners.
Appeals.
General provisions, 2B §16-101.
County council ex officio to constitute on permanent basis, 2B §15-107.1.
Licenses.
Application.
Exceptions, 2B §§10-103, 10-104.
New license, 2B §10-202.
Assignment or transfer, 2B §10-503.
Commissioners, 2B §§15-107.1, 16-101.
Corporations, 2B §9-101.

HOWARD COUNTY —Cont'd
Alcoholic beverages —Cont'd
Licenses —Cont'd
Criminal history records checks.
License applicants, 2B §10-103.
Drive-thru purchase facilities not to be licensed, 2B §9-214.
Exemption from execution and distraint, 2B §10-501.
Fees.
Collection and disposition, 2B §10-204.
Issuance.
Refusal.
Reapplication, 2B §10-208.
Limited liability companies, 2B §9-101.
Manufacturers.
Hours and days for sale, 2B §11-101.
Near public schools, 2B §9-214.
Race tracks, 2B §8-602.
Regulations and restrictions, 2B §9-214.
Retailers.
Consumption of beverages not sold by retailer on premises of retailer, 2B §12-107.
Revocation and suspension.
Grounds, 2B §10-401.
Wine festival license, 2B §8-310.
Wine tasting (WT) alcoholic beverages license, 2B §8-408.1.
Manufacturers.
Licenses.
Hours and days for sale, 2B §11-101.
Micro-brewery licenses, 2B §2-208.
Minors.
Restrictions for being on premises of on-sale licensee, 2B §12-214.
Sales to prohibited.
Probation of licensees for violating section.
Proceedings against licensee not barred, 2B §12-108.
New Year's day.
Sales, 2B §11-402.
Open containers.
Possession in certain places.
Applicability of provisions, 2B §19-303.
Penalties.
Local penalties, 2B §16-507.
Places of public entertainment.
Alcohol awareness training, 2B §20-106.
Days and hours of operation, 2B §20-106.
Defined, 2B §20-106.
Persons dispensing or serving food, beverages or setups in, responsibilities, 2B §20-106.
Persons supervising or managing, responsibilities, 2B §20-106.
Refusal to facilitate continued consumption of inebriated person, 2B §20-106.
Setups defined, 2B §20-106.
Race tracks.
Licenses, 2B §8-602.
Restaurants.
Beer and light wine licenses.
Class B, on-sale.
Fee, 2B §5-201.
Beer, wine and liquor licenses.
Luxury restaurant license, 2B §9-102.
Luxury restaurant license, 2B §8-214.
Beer, wine and liquor licenses, 2B §9-102.
Retailers.
Deliveries, 2B §12-301.
Sales.
Election days, 2B §11-401.

HOWARD COUNTY —Cont'd
Alcoholic beverages —Cont'd
Sales —Cont'd
Sundays and holidays, 2B §11-514.
Seven day licenses, 2B §11-514.
Summons.
Records and papers, 2B §16-410.
Sundays and holidays.
Sales, 2B §11-514.
Wine festival.
Licenses, 2B §8-310.
Wine sampling license, 2B §8-408.
Amusement parks.
Permits required, 25 §27.
Appearance fees in circuit courts.
Distribution, CJ §7-204.
Aquaculture.
Oysters and clams.
Exclusive right of riparian or wharf owners to
cultivate shellfish, NR §4-11A-16.
Bailiff.
Compensation, CJ §2-507.
Baltimore City.
Port authority.
Article not applicable in, MD Const Art XI-D §3.
Billiards and pool tables.
Alcoholic beverages.
Minors.
Restrictions of on-sale premise licensee, 2B
§12-214.
Bingo, CR §§13-1602, 13-1603.
Bond issues.
Special taxing districts, 24 §9-1301.
Bottle clubs.
Places of public entertainment generally, alcoholic
beverage regulation, 2B §20-106.
Boxing and wrestling arenas.
Permits required, 25 §27.
Card games, dice games or roulette.
Prohibited in county, CR §§13-1603, 13-1604.
Chance book, CR §13-1603.
Circuit courts.
Fees.
Appearance fees.
Distribution, CJ §7-204.
Judicial circuit, MD Const Art IV §19.
Number of judges, CJ §1-503.
Columbia association.
Annexation of certain parcels of land, RP
§11B-113.5.
Commissioners.
Alcoholic beverages.
License commissioners. See within this heading,
"Alcoholic beverages."
Powers.
Exceptions, 25 §3.
Community associations.
Property tax credits, TP §9-315.
Community college.
Board of community college trustees, ED §16-410.
Conflicts of interest.
Alcoholic beverages.
Direct or indirect interest in more than one
license, 2B §9-301.
Conservation areas.
Exception from section, 23A §7.
Courts.
Circuit courts. See within this heading, "Circuit
courts."

HOWARD COUNTY —Cont'd
Crimes and offenses.
Alcoholic beverages.
Minors.
Prescriptions on presence in on-sale premises,
2B §12-214.
Criminal history records checks.
Prospective employees, CP §10-233.
Dance halls.
Permits required, 25 §27.
Deeds.
Straw deeds.
Recordation, RP §3-104.
Detention center.
Work release program, individuals sentenced to
center, COR §11-715.
Discrimination.
Applicability of subtitle, 49B §40.
Civil actions for discriminatory acts, 49B §42.
Prevailing party.
Defined, 49B §41.
Dog licenses.
Administration and enforcement agency, 24
§11-504.
Fees, 24 §11-501.
Dogs running at large.
Female dogs in heat, 24 §11-514.
Drive-thru purchase facilities.
Alcoholic beverages.
Licenses.
Prohibition, 2B §9-214.
Elections.
Contributions to county executive, county council
member or candidate for offices.
Applicability of state government article, part
VII, EL §13-503.
County board of elections.
Compensation, EL §2-204.
County boards generally, EL §§2-201 to 2-303.
See ELECTIONS.
County boards of education generally, EL §§8-801
to 8-806.
Fines.
Alcoholic beverages.
Minors.
On premises, 2B §12-214.
Gaming, bazaar, carnival and raffles, CR
§§13-201 to 13-205, 13-1601 to 13-1604.
Conducting event for benefit of qualified
organization.
Allowed, CR §13-203.
Definitions, CR §13-201.
Gaming event defined, CR §13-201.
Individual benefit prohibited, CR §13-203.
Management through organizations members, CR
§13-205.
Prizes and gaming devices allowed, CR §13-204.
Provisions applicable to county, CR §§13-202,
13-301, 13-1601.
Qualified organization defined, CR §13-201.
Golf courses.
Beer, wine and liquor licenses, 2B §8-504.
Health officers.
County boards of health.
Notification of officer in Howard county, HG
§3-306.1.
Historic area zoning.
General provisions.
See ZONING.
Hotels and restaurants.
Beer licenses.
Class B, on-sale.
Fee, 2B §3-201.

HOWARD COUNTY —Cont'd
Judges.
Pensions.
General provisions, ET §2-108.
Licenses.
Alcoholic beverages. See within this heading,
"Alcoholic beverages."
Limited liability companies.
Alcoholic beverages.
Licenses, 2B §9-101.
Marriage licenses.
Fees, FL §2-404.
Maryland food center authority.
General provisions, 41 §§13-101 to 13-123.
See MARYLAND FOOD CENTER
AUTHORITY.
Mental hygiene law.
Quasi-public authority, HG §10-1202.1.
Minors.
Alcoholic beverages.
Regulations for being on premises of on-sale
licensee, 2B §12-214.
Sales to prohibited.
Probation of licensees for violating section.
Proceedings against licensee not barred, 2B
§12-108.
Misdemeanors.
Alcoholic beverages.
Minors.
Restrictions on being in on-sale premises, 2B
§12-214.
Motor vehicles.
Size and weight.
Power of county commissioners, 25 §25.
Noise control.
Trapshooting, skeet shooting, etc.
Limitations on authority, EN §§3-105, 3-401.
Northeast Maryland waste disposal authority.
Participating county, NR §3-903.
Obscene performances.
Prohibition, CR §11-204.
**Oil pipeline corporation acquiring property
under power to condemn,** PUC §5-404.
Orphans' court.
Judges.
Compensation, ET §2-108.
Oysters and clams.
Exclusive right of riparian or wharf owners to
cultivate shellfish, NR §4-11A-16.
Paddle wheel or wheel of fortune, CR §13-1603.
Patuxent river watershed.
General provisions.
See PATUXENT RIVER WATERSHED.
Penalties.
Alcoholic beverages.
Local penalties, 2B §16-507.
Minors.
On-sales premises violations, 2B §12-214.
Permits.
Dance halls and other places of amusement,
tourist camps, etc., 25 §27.
Pinball or console machines.
Alcoholic beverages.
Minors.
Restrictions for being on premises of on-sale
licensee, 2B §12-214.
Port authority.
Article not applicable in county, MD Const Art
XI-D §3.
Precious metals and gem dealers.
Copies of records to law enforcement, BR §12-304.

HOWARD COUNTY —Cont'd
Public ethics.
See PUBLIC ETHICS.
Recordation.
Straw deeds, RP §3-104.
**Residential mortgage programs for certain
counties,** HS §§4-1601 to 4-1610.
Sales.
Alcoholic beverages. See within this heading,
"Alcoholic beverages."
Schools.
County board of education.
Chairman, ED §3-702.
Compensation, ED §3-703.
Composition, ED §3-701.
Elections.
Chairman, ED §3-702.
Generally, EL §§8-801 to 8-806.
Members, ED §§3-114, 3-701.
Expenses, ED §3-703.
Meetings.
Closed session, ED §3-704.
Public meetings, ED §3-704.
Persons subject to authority of board.
Ineligibility to serve as member, ED §3-114.
Qualifications, ED §3-701.
Records.
Public records, ED §3-704.
Removal, ED §3-701.
Term of office, ED §3-701.
Vacancy, ED §3-701.
Year-round schools.
Pilot programs, ED §7-103.
Seafood.
Mobile seafood vendors generally.
See SEAFOOD.
Sheriff, CJ §2-309.
Second in command, CJ §2-310.
Special taxing districts, 24 §9-1301.
Bond issues, 24 §9-1301.
State correctional facilities in Jessup area.
Limitation on construction, COR §10-107.
State's attorney.
Private practice of law prohibited, 10 §40.
Statute of limitations.
Discrimination.
Civil actions for discriminatory acts, 49B §42.
Sundays and holidays.
Alcoholic beverages.
Hours and days for sale, 2B §11-514.
Taxation.
Credits.
Property tax credits.
Agricultural land preservation program, TP
§9-315.
Community associations, TP §9-315.
Grants in lieu of property tax credits.
Elderly or disabled renters, TP §9-402.
Deferred property tax payments, TP §10-201.
Municipal corporations.
Double taxation of municipalities, TP §6-307.
Redemption.
Rate of redemption, TP §14-820.
Special taxing districts, 24 §9-1301.
Transportation.
Levy of tax for public transportation services,
TR §7-801.
Therapeutic riding facility.
Property tax credit, TP §9-315.
Tourist camps.
Permits required, 25 §27.

HOWARD COUNTY —Cont'd

Trader licenses.

Approval of zoning authorities, BR §17-1807.

Transportation.

Public transportation services.

Taxation for, TR §7-801.

Trapshooting, skeetshooting or other target shooting.

Environmental sound level limits and noise control rules and regulations, EN §3-401.

Noise control ordinances, rules or regulations prohibiting, EN §3-105.

Treasurer.

Salary, 25 §51.

Washington suburban sanitary commission.

Agreements.

Authorized, 29 §15-102.

Contracts.

Authorized, 29 §15-102.

Water and sewer systems.

Authority of commission, 29 §15-101.

Connections, 29 §15-104.

Maintenance and operation, 29 §15-103.

Contracts.

Authorized, 29 §15-103.

Patuxent river area.

Disposition of sewage, 29 §15-106.

Tampering with or obstructing.

Prohibited, 29 §15-105.

Water.

Restrictions on use, 25 §168.

Ordinances and resolutions, 25 §168.

Water and sewer systems.

Washington suburban sanitary commission, 29 §§15-101 to 15-106.

Wine festival.

License, 2B §8-310.

Wine tastings.

License, 2B §8-408.1.

Work release program.

Individuals sentenced to detention center, COR §11-715.

Zoning.

Historic area zoning.

General provisions.

See ZONING.

HPV.

Health insurance coverage for screening test, IN §15-829.

HUMAN CLONING.

Defined, 83A §5-2B-01.

Prohibited, criminal penalty, 83A §5-2B-13.

State-funded stem sell research.

Research leading to prohibited by person conducting, 83A §5-2B-02.

HUMANE SOCIETY.

Arrests by officers, CR §10-609.

Disposal of domestic animals, CR §10-617.

Giving kitten or puppy unaccompanied by dam, CR §10-613.

Kennel inspections, CR §10-616.

HUMAN GROWTH HORMONE.

Defined, CR §5-710.

Warning of consequences of illegal use, CR §5-710.

HUMAN IMMUNODEFICIENCY VIRUS, HG §§18-333 to 18-339.

AIDS.

Insurance assistance pilot program, HG §§15-201 to 15-205.

See ACQUIRED IMMUNE DEFICIENCY SYNDROME (AIDS).

Blood tests.

Boxers and kickboxers.

License requirement, BR §4-304.1.

Confidentiality of results, BR §4-304.1; HG §18-338.1.

Consent.

Form for consent document, HG §18-336.

Informed consent, HG §18-338.1.

Costs, HG §18-338.1.

Counseling.

Required, HG §18-336.

Definitions, HG §18-336.

Inmates of correctional institutions, HG §18-338.

Positive test results, HG §18-337.

Pregnant women, HG §18-338.2.

First responders, HG §18-338.3.

Generally, HG §18-336.

Health care workers, HG §18-338.3.

Hospitals.

Inmates of correctional institutions.

Liability, HG §18-338.

Identifying numbers, patients, HG §18-336.

Inmates of correctional institutions, HG §18-338.

Notice.

Inmates of correctional institutions.

Notification to correctional employees, HG §18-338.

Positive test results.

Notice to individual from whom blood sample obtained, HG §18-336.

Notice to sexual or needle-sharing partners, HG §18-337.

Results, HG §18-338.1.

Patient identifying numbers, HG §18-336.

Physicians.

Breach of patient confidentiality.

Inmates of correctional institutions.

Physicians not liable, HG §18-338.

Liability, HG §18-337.

Positive test results.

Generally, HG §18-337.

Inmates of correctional institutions, HG §18-338.

Notice.

Individuals from whom blood samples obtained, HG §18-336.

Sexual and needle-sharing partners, HG §18-337.

Physicians' duties, HG §18-336.

Referrals to appropriate services, HG §18-337.

Pregnant women, HG §18-338.2.

Prisoners, HG §18-338.

Results.

Inmates of correctional institutions.

Notice of results to correctional employees, HG §18-338.

Positive test results.

Generally, HG §18-337.

Inmates of correctional institutions, HG §18-338.

HUMAN IMMUNODEFICIENCY VIRUS
—Cont'd
Blood tests —Cont'd
Results —Cont'd
Positive test results —Cont'd
Physicians' duties, HG §18-336.
Charged person.
HIV testing, CP §11-110.
Hearing required, CP §11-111.
Condoms.
Sale by vending machines or other devices, HG §18-335.
Confidentiality of information.
Pregnant women.
Test results, HG §18-338.2.
Consent.
Blood tests.
Form for consent document, HG §18-336.
Informed consent, HG §18-338.1.
Refusal, HG §18-336.
Substitute consent, HG §18-336.
Written informed consent.
Required, HG §18-336.
Controlled dangerous substances.
Education program for violators, HG §18-339.
Conviction of charged person.
HIV testing, CP §11-112.
Notification of health officer, CP §11-113.
Correctional institutions.
Testing of inmates, HG §18-338.
Correctional officers.
Notification of exposure to virus, HG §18-213.
Crimes and offenses.
Knowingly transferring or attempting to transfer virus to another individual, HG §18-601.1.
Definitions.
Blood tests, HG §18-336.
Inmates of correctional institutions, HG §18-338.
Positive test results, HG §18-337.
Pregnant women, HG §18-338.2.
Donors of semen, blood or tissue, HG §18-334.
Drugs.
Violators of controlled dangerous substances act.
Educational program for, HG §18-339.
Educational programs.
Controlled dangerous substances act, HG §18-339.
Prostitution, HG §18-339.
Emergency medical care and services.
Notification of emergency medical technicians of exposure to virus, HG §18-213.
Exposure of infected individuals.
Knowingly transferring or attempting to transfer virus to another individual, HG §18-601.1.
Fire department.
Notification of fire fighters of exposure to virus, HG §18-213.
First responders.
Testing, HG §18-338.3.
Health care workers.
Testing, HG §18-338.3.
Hospitals.
Blood tests.
Inmates of correctional institutions.
Liability, HG §18-338.
Positive test results.
Liability of hospitals or other health care providers, HG §18-337.
Identification.
Blood tests.
Patient identifying numbers, HG §18-336.

HUMAN IMMUNODEFICIENCY VIRUS
—Cont'd
Immunity.
Blood tests.
Inmates of correctional institutions.
Health care providers, HG §18-338.
Positive test results.
Physicians, hospitals or other health care providers, HG §18-337.
Pregnant women.
Health care providers, HG §18-338.2.
Real property.
Failure of owner or seller to disclose certain facts, RP §2-120.
Inmates of correctional institutions.
Testing, HG §18-338.
Jails.
Testing of inmates of correctional institutions, HG §18-338.
Landlord and tenant.
Disclosures concerning real property offered for lease.
Certain matters not to constitute material fact or latent defect, RP §2-120.
Law enforcement personnel.
Notification of exposure to virus, HG §18-213.
Leases.
Disclosures concerning real property offered for lease.
Certain matters not to constitute material fact or latent defect, RP §2-120.
Liability.
Blood tests.
Inmates of correctional institutions.
Health care providers, HG §18-338.
Positive test results, HG §18-337.
Life insurance.
Viatical settlement contracts, IN §§8-601 to 8-611.
See VIATICAL SETTLEMENT CONTRACTS.
Voiding policy because insured has had a disease or ailment, IN §16-216.
Notices.
Blood tests.
Inmates of correctional institutions.
Notice of results to correctional employees, HG §18-338.
Notification of results, HG §18-338.1.
Positive test results.
Notification to individual from whom blood sample obtained, HG §18-336.
Notification to sexual or needle-sharing partners, HG §18-337.
Donors of semen, blood or tissue.
Positive HIV antibody test result, HG §18-334.
Fire fighters, emergency medical technicians, rescue squadmen, law enforcement officers and correctional officers.
Exposure to virus, HG §18-213.
Physicians.
Blood tests.
Inmates of correctional institutions, HG §18-338.
Positive test results.
Liability of physicians, HG §18-337.
Notification to individual from whom blood sample obtained, HG §18-336.
Pregnant women.
Testing, HG §18-338.2.
Prisoners.
Testing of inmates of correctional institutions, HG §18-338.

HUMAN IMMUNODEFICIENCY VIRUS
—Cont'd
Privileged communications.
Blood tests.
Confidentiality of records, HG §18-338.1.
Boxer and kickboxer licensing, BR §4-304.1.
Inmates of correctional institutions.
Notification in accordance with section, HG
§18-338.
Positive test results.
Notification in accordance with section, HG
§18-337.
Donors of semen, blood or tissue.
Positive HIV antibody test results, HG §18-334.
Fire fighters, emergency medical technicians,
rescue squadmen, law enforcement officers
and correctional officers.
Notification of exposure to virus.
Breach of patient confidentiality, HG §18-213.
Reports, HG §18-207.
Prostitution.
Educational program for violators, HG §18-339.
Real estate brokers.
Owner or occupant of property infected with
human immunodeficiency virus.
Failure to disclose certain facts, BOP §17-322.1.
Real property.
Disclosures concerning real property offered for
sale or lease.
Certain matters not to constitute material fact
or latent defect, RP §2-120.
Reports.
Case reports, HG §18-207.
Donors of semen, blood or tissue.
Positive HIV antibody test result, HG §18-334.
Research and information program, HG §18-333.
Rescue squads.
Notification of rescue squadmen of exposure to
virus, HG §18-213.
Research and information program, HG
§18-333.
Transferring virus to another individual, HG
§18-601.1.

**HUMAN PAPILLOMAVIRUS SCREENING
TEST.**
Health insurance coverage, IN §15-829.

HUMAN RELATIONS COMMISSION.
Actions.
Injunctions, 49B §4.
Venue, 49B §4.
Right to bring civil actions not denied, 49B §12.
Age discrimination.
Public accommodations.
Prohibited, 49B §5.
Agreement for elimination of discrimination,
49B §10.
Airports.
Investigation of discriminatory employment
practices.
Administration to refer investigations to
commission, TR §5-408.
Appeals.
Decisions of hearing examiners, 49B §3.
Denial of request for reconsideration of finding of
no probable cause, 49B §10.
Appointment.
By governor, 49B §1.
Attorney at law.
Hearing.
Duty of commissions counsel, 49B §11.

HUMAN RELATIONS COMMISSION —Cont'd
Attorney at law —Cont'd
Represent commission, 49B §2.
Chairman.
Designation, 49B §1.
Hearing.
Duties, 49B §11.
Complaints.
Amendment of complaint, 49B §11.
Applicability of subtitle, 49B §9.
Enforcement powers of commission, 49B §9A.
Executive director.
Consider complaint, 49B §10.
Filed with commission, 49B §9A.
Issuance.
By commission, 49B §9A.
Malicious complaint, 49B §12.
Order dismissing complaint, 49B §11.
Composition, 49B §1.
Contempt hearings.
Enforcement of subpoenas, 49B §11.
Declaration of policy, 49B §14.
Department of labor, licensing and regulation.
Discrimination by persons, businesses, etc.,
licensed or regulated by, 49B §8.
Director.
Complaint.
Consider complaint, 49B §10.
Deputy director, 49B §2.
Executive director, 49B §2.
Disclosures or publicity.
General provisions, 49B §10.
Discrimination.
Agreement for elimination of discrimination, 49B
§10.
Employment, 49B §§14 to 18.
See LABOR AND EMPLOYMENT
RELATIONS.
Housing.
See DISCRIMINATION.
Insurance.
Underwriting and rate-setting practices, IN
§2-202.
Persons, businesses, etc., licensed by department
of labor, licensing and regulation, 49B §8.
Public accommodations, 49B §§5 to 13.
See DISCRIMINATION.
State agency, officer or employee.
Cases involving, 49B §7.
State contracts.
Commercial discrimination, SF §§19-101 to
19-120.
See DISCRIMINATION.
Duties.
Generally, 49B §3.
Housing discrimination, 49B §26.
Expenses of members, 49B §1.
Fines.
Confidential information violations, 49B §13.
Malicious complaint, 49B §12.
General counsel, 49B §2.
Governor.
Appointment, 49B §1.
Director.
Executive director.
Appointment by governor, 49B §2.
Handicapped persons.
Public accommodations.
Discrimination prohibited, 49B §5.
Hearing examiners.
Appeals from decisions, 49B §3.

HUMAN RELATIONS COMMISSION —Cont'd
Hearing examiners —Cont'd
Appointment, 49B §2.
Cease and desist orders, 49B §11.
Compensation, 49B §2.
Duties, 49B §2.
Hearings.
General provisions. See within this heading, "Hearings."
Order dismissing complaint, 49B §11.
Qualifications, 49B §2.
Hearings.
General provisions, 49B §3.
Place of hearing, 49B §3.
Powers of commission, 49B §11.
Procedure, 49B §11.
Purpose, 49B §3.
Relief, 49B §11.
Housing.
Discrimination.
See DISCRIMINATION.
Injunctions, 49B §4.
Insurance.
Discrimination in underwriting and rate-setting practices, IN §2-202.
Investigations, 49B §10.
Confidential investigations, 49B §13.
Discrimination in public accommodations, 49B §10.
Findings, 49B §10.
General provisions, 49B §10.
Labor and employment relations.
Discrimination in employment, 49B §§14 to 18.
See LABOR AND EMPLOYMENT RELATIONS.
Legal assistance, 49B §2.
Legislation.
Recommendations, 49B §3.
Meetings, 49B §9A.
Number of members, 49B §1.
Orders.
Enforcement of commission's orders, 49B §12.
Per diem allowance, 49B §1.
Powers.
Enforcement powers of commission.
Complaint, 49B §9A.
Generally, 49B §3.
Privileged communications.
Investigations.
Confidential character of information relating to investigation, 49B §13.
Public accommodations.
Discrimination prohibited, 49B §5.
General provisions.
See DISCRIMINATION.
Racial demonstrations.
Receiving remuneration for participation prohibited, 49B §6.
Reports.
Annual report to governor and general assembly, 49B §3.
Sentence and punishment.
Confidential information violations, 49B §13.
Malicious complaint, 49B §12.
Sex discrimination.
Public accommodations.
Prohibited, 49B §5.
State agencies, officers and employees.
Discriminatory practices prohibited, 49B §7.
Surveys and studies, 49B §3.
Terms of office, 49B §1.

HUMAN RELATIONS COMMISSION —Cont'd
Travel expenses, 49B §1.
Vacancy.
Filling, 49B §1.
Violations of article.
Aiding or abetting violations, 49B §12A.

HUMAN REMAINS.
Dead bodies generally.
See DEAD BODIES.

HUMAN RESOURCES DEPARTMENT.
Commission on responsible fatherhood, 41 §§18-401 to 18-408.
Social services generally.
See SOCIAL SERVICES.

HUMAN SUBJECT RESEARCH, HG §§13-2001 to 13-2004.
Applicability to all research, HG §13-2002.
Definitions, HG §13-2001.
Federal regulations.
Compliance with, HG §13-2002.
Defined, HG §13-2001.
Injunctive or other relief for violations, HG §13-2004.
Institution review board minutes.
Inspection, not public records, HG §13-2003.
Institutional review board defined, HG §13-2001.

HUMAN TISSUE, ORGANS OR BONES.
Anatomical gift act.
See ANATOMICAL GIFT ACT.
Liability.
Obtaining, possessing, etc., for transplantation, HG §18-402.

HUMAN TRANSPORTER.
Operation.
Parent knowingly permitting minor or ward to violate provisions of subtitle, TR §21-1201.
Subject to traffic regulations, TR §21-501.1.

HUNTING.
Birds and game.
See BIRDS AND GAME.
Licenses.
General provisions.
See BIRDS AND GAME.

HUNTING HERITAGE PROTECTION.
Maintenance of open lands for hunting, NR §10-212.

HUNTING ORGANIZATIONS.
Casino.
Baltimore county, CR §13-604.
Gaming, bazaar, carnival and raffles.
Baltimore county, CR §§13-601 to 13-607.

HURLOCK.
Alcoholic beverage licenses.
Prohibited near church or public school, 2B §9-210.

HURRICANES.
Emergency management, PS §§14-101 to 14-1004.
See EMERGENCY MANAGEMENT.

HUSBAND AND WIFE.
Acknowledgments.
Forms, RP §4-204.
Actions.
Death by wrongful act.
See DEATH BY WRONGFUL ACT.
Surviving spouse.
Action to recover in right of deceased spouse.
Necessary allegations, FL §4-202.

HUSBAND AND WIFE —Cont'd

Alienation of affection.

Prohibited actions, FL §3-103.

General provisions.

See ACTIONS.

Alimony, FL §§11-101 to 11-112.

See ALIMONY.

Annulment of marriage.

General provisions.

See ANNULMENT OF MARRIAGE.

Property disposition in annulment and divorce.

General provisions, FL §§8-201 to 8-214.

See DIVORCE.

Assault and battery.

Spousal assault.

Assistance to victim.

Immunity of law enforcement officer, CJ §5-610.

Assignments.

Wages.

Requirement, CL §15-302.

Automobile insurance fund.

Continuation of coverage for spouse upon cancellation, IN §20-519.

Contempt.

Deeds, agreements and settlements between spouses.

Powers of courts to enforce provisions by, FL §8-105.

Contracts.

Liability.

Husband not liable for wife's contracts, FL §4-301.

Conveyances from.

See HUSBAND AND WIFE.

Credit life, health and unemployment insurance, IN §13-115.

Dead bodies.

Consent for postmortem examination, HG §5-501.

Death.

Simultaneous death act.

Uniform law.

See DEATH.

Death by wrongful act.

Damages.

Death of spouse, CJ §3-904.

Decedents' estates.

Surviving spouse.

See DECEDENTS' ESTATES.

Deeds, agreements and settlements.

Contempt.

Powers of courts to enforce provisions by, FL §8-105.

Corroboration of testimony.

Voluntary separation agreement as, FL §8-104.

Divorce.

Contempt.

Powers of courts to enforce provisions by, FL §8-105.

Corroboration of testimony.

Voluntary separation agreement as, FL §8-104.

Deed or agreement not bar to divorce, FL §8-102.

Modification.

Authority of court, FL §8-105.

Provisions merged in divorce decree.

Contempt.

Powers of courts to enforce provisions by, FL §8-105.

HUSBAND AND WIFE —Cont'd

Deeds, agreements and settlements —Cont'd

Divorce —Cont'd

Provisions not merged in divorce decree.

Contempt.

Powers of courts to enforce provisions by, FL §8-105.

Entireties.

Granting of property held by the entireties, RP §4-108.

Minors.

Conveyances of certain property by married minors, ET §13-503.

Modification, FL §8-103.

Validity, FL §8-101.

Definitions.

"Secretary," FL §4-101.

Desertion and nonsupport.

General provisions.

See SUPPORT AND MAINTENANCE.

Uniform reciprocal enforcement of support act.

See SUPPORT AND MAINTENANCE.

Developmental disabilities.

Rights of individuals.

Right of spouses to share rooms, HG §7-1003.

Displaced homemakers.

General provisions, FL §§4-601 to 4-613.

See DISPLACED HOMEMAKERS.

Job aid for displaced homemakers.

See SOCIAL SERVICES.

Distress for rent.

Levy on goods of husband and wife, RP §8-326.

Divorce.

Alimony, FL §§11-101 to 11-112.

See ALIMONY.

Deeds, agreements and settlements. See within this heading, "Deeds, agreements and settlements."

General provisions, FL §§7-101 to 7-107.

See DIVORCE.

Domestic violence.

General provisions, FL §§4-501 to 4-516.

See DOMESTIC VIOLENCE.

Local domestic violence fatality review teams, FL §§4-701 to 4-707.

See DOMESTIC VIOLENCE.

Domicile.

Determination of domicile, FL §4-201.

Independent domicile, FL §4-201.

Dower.

General provisions.

See DOWER.

Entireties.

Granting of property held by the entireties, RP §4-108.

Equal credit opportunity, CL §§12-701 to 12-708.

See EQUAL CREDIT OPPORTUNITY.

Equity.

Annulment.

See ANNULMENT OF MARRIAGE.

Executors and administrators.

Surviving spouse.

Order of right to letters, ET §5-104.

Expungement of records.

Criminal procedure.

Refusal to testify on basis that not compelled to testify against spouse.

Record of assertion, CJ §9-106.

Forms.

Acknowledgments, RP §4-204.

HUSBAND AND WIFE —Cont'd
Fraudulent conveyances.
General provisions, CL §§15-201 to 15-214.
See FRAUDULENT CONVEYANCES.
Frederick county.
Schools.
County board of education.
Exclusions from board, ED §3-5B-02.
Garnishment.
Spousal property, CJ §11-603.
Homemakers.
Job aid for displaced homemakers.
See SOCIAL SERVICES.
Hospitals.
Rights of individuals.
Spouses sharing rooms, HG §19-344.
Visitation rights, HG §19-344.
Income tax.
Joint returns, TG §10-807.
Rates, TG §10-105.
Insurance.
Automobile insurance fund.
Continuation of coverage for spouse following
cancellation, IN §20-519.
Credit life, health and unemployment insurance,
IN §13-115.
Health insurance.
Spouse authorized to insure other spouse, IN
§12-202.
Life insurance and annuities.
Group life insurance.
Spouse or child of employee or member, IN
§17-209.
Spouse authorized to insure other spouse, IN
§12-202.
Joint tenants and tenants in common.
Granting of property held by the entireties, RP
§4-108.
Judgments.
Liability.
Husband not liable for judgment or decree
against wife, FL §4-301.
Landlord and tenant.
Right of landlord to deal with married woman as
if unmarried, FL §4-205.
Liability.
Contracts.
Husband not liable for wife's contract, FL
§4-301.
Debts of husband.
Wife's property not liable for, FL §4-301.
Judgments and decrees.
Husband not liable for judgment or decree
against wife, FL §4-301.
Obligations incurred before marriage.
No liability for, FL §4-301.
Protection from liability for spouse's obligations,
FL §4-301.
Torts.
Husband not liable for wife's torts, FL §4-301.
Libel and slander.
Slander of female.
Action by husband, CJ §3-502.
Married women.
General provisions.
See MARRIED WOMEN.
Medical assistance for the poor.
Responsibility of spouse, HG §15-122.
Minors.
Conveyance by married minor, ET §13-503.

HUSBAND AND WIFE —Cont'd
Minors —Cont'd
Veterans.
Disability of infancy removed after certain
conveyances, notes, etc., ET §13-503.
Motor vehicle insurance.
Automobile insurance fund.
Continuation of coverage for spouse upon
cancellation, IN §20-519.
Motor vehicles.
Registration.
Transfers between spouses, TR §13-503.1.
Nonsupport.
See SUPPORT AND MAINTENANCE.
Prohibited actions.
Alienation of affection.
General provisions.
See ACTIONS.
Property.
Divorce.
Property disposition, FL §§8-201 to 8-214.
See DIVORCE.
Married women.
See MARRIED WOMEN.
Right of married woman to hold, use and dispose
of property, FL §4-203.
Third parties.
Effect of property transfer from husband to
wife, FL §4-206.
Transfer of property from husband to wife.
Effect on third person, FL §4-206.
Wife's property.
Protected from debts of husband, MD Const Art
III §43.
Rape or sexual offense.
Spousal defense, CR §3-318.
Records.
Criminal procedure.
Refusal to testify on basis that not compelled to
testify against spouse, CJ §9-106.
Rights of married women.
Dealing as if unmarried, FL §4-204.
Property.
Right to hold, use and dispose of, FL §4-203.
**Right to deal with married woman as if
unmarried,** FL §4-205.
Services to families with children, FL §§4-401 to
4-403.
See SERVICES TO FAMILIES WITH
CHILDREN.
Simultaneous death act.
General provisions.
See DEATH.
Slander of females.
General provisions.
See LIBEL AND SLANDER.
Spousal assault.
Assistance to victim.
Immunity of law enforcement officer, CJ §5-610.
Spousal privilege.
Record of assertion, Crim Rule 4-632.
Third parties.
Property transfer from husband to wife.
Effect on third person, FL §4-206.
Right to deal with married woman as if
unmarried, FL §4-205.
Torts.
Liability.
Husband not liable for wife's tort, FL §4-301.
Unemployment compensation.
Employment of spouse.
When not covered employment, LE §8-215.

HUSBAND AND WIFE —Cont'd
Victims of domestic violence, FL §§4-513 to
    4-516.
    See DOMESTIC VIOLENCE.
Widows and widowers.
    General provisions.
        See WIDOWS AND WIDOWERS.
Witnesses.
    Competency as witness.
        Disclosure of confidential information, CJ
            §9-105.
        Generally, CJ §9-101.
    Confidential communications, CJ §9-105.
        Child custody proceedings, uniform child
            custody jurisdiction and enforcement act.
        Spousal privilege prohibited, FL §9.5-310.
    Criminal procedure.
        Not compelled to testify against spouse, CJ
            §9-106.
        Exceptions, CJ §9-106.
    Presumptions.
        Coercion of husband, CJ §10-902.

HUSBAND AND WIFE —Cont'd
Workers' compensation.
    Death benefits.
        General provisions, LE §§9-678 to 9-686.
            See WORKERS' COMPENSATION.
        Surviving spouse.
            When compensation prohibited, LE §9-680.
    Hernias.
        Survival of compensation, LE §9-646.
    Permanent partial disability.
        Survival of compensation, LE §9-632.
    Permanent total disability.
        Survival of compensation, LE §9-640.

HYATTSVILLE.
Alcoholic beverages.
    Licenses.
        General provisions, 2B §8-217.

HYPODERMIC SYRINGES AND NEEDLES.
Drug paraphernalia, CR §5-619.